THE PHILOSOPHER'S INDEX

1993 CUMULATIVE EDITION

VOLUME 27

RELATED PRODUCTS

Retrospective Editions:

The Philosopher's Index: A Retrospective Index to U.S. Publications from 1940 indexes approximately 15,000 philosophy articles from U.S. journals published from 1940–1966, and approximately 5,000 philosophy books published from 1940–1976. Supported by NEH Grant RT-23984-76-375.

Published in April 1978. 1,619 pages. Hardbound in three volumes. $295 (Individuals: $130). ISBN 0-912632-09-7.

The Philosopher's Index: A Retrospective Index to Non-U.S. English Language Publications from 1940 indexes approximately 12,000 philosophy articles published from 1940–1966, and approximately 5,000 philosophy books published from 1940–1978. Supported by NEH Grant RT-27265-77-1360.

Published in April 1980. 1,265 pages. Hardbound in three volumes. $280 (Individuals: $120). ISBN 0-912632-12-7.

CD-ROM and ON-LINE:

The Philosopher's Index is now available on CD-ROM from DIALOG OnDisc.© It contains information from 1940 to the present including over 150,000 articles, books, and contributions to anthologies.

The *Index* is also available on-line from DIALOG, File 57, and from KNOWLEDGE INDEX, which is available through CompuServe.

For additional information on these services, please call DIALOG at (800) 3-DIALOG, or write to: Dialog Information Services, Inc., Marketing Department, 3460 Hillview Avenue, Palo Alto, CA 94304, USA.

Search Aids:

The Philosopher's Index Thesaurus, Second Edition is more comprehensive and designed to assist users in searching the Philosopher's Index Database. This Edition adds many new subject descriptors and cross-references. A summary of indexing policies is also included.

Published in May 1992. 90 pages. $19. ISBN 0-912632-20-8.

***Searching the Philosopher's Index Database on* DIALOG** is a tutorial manual that explains the commands needed to do most searches through DIALOG or KNOWLEDGE INDEX. This manual describes the information contained in the Philosopher's Index Database and includes examples of basic and advanced searches.

Published in 1988. 63 pages. $15. ISBN 0-912632-50-X.

For additional information on products and services, please call the Philosophy Documentation Center at:
(800) 444-2419 *or* **(419) 372-2419 Fax: (419) 372-6987**

The Philosopher's Index

An International Index
To Philosophical Periodicals and Books

1993 CUMULATIVE EDITON
VOLUME 27

Bowling Green State University, Bowling Green, OH 43403-0189, U.S.A.

PHILOSOPHY DOCUMENTATION CENTER

Mission Statement: The mission of the Philosophy Documentation Center is to serve philosophers, students, and others by providing them with reliable information, quality products and needed services.

The Center strives to fulfill its mission by 1) publishing and distributing philosophy indexes, directories, bibliographies, and scholarly journals; 2) providing a computer-searchable philosophy database; 3) publishing philosophy software; 4) offering typesetting and subscription fulfillment services; 5) renting mailing lists; and 6) providing convention exhibit services for philosophy journals and books.

Director

Richard H. Lineback

THE PHILOSOPHER'S INDEX

Editor

Richard H. Lineback

Editorial Staff

Donald Callen, Assistant Editor
Bowling Green State University
Mark Christensen, Assistant Editor
Lourdes College
Douglas D. Daye, Assistant Editor
Bowling Green State University
Robert Goodwin, Assistant Editor
Bowling Green State University
Fred Miller, Assistant Editor
Bowling Green State University

Frederick Rickey, Assistant Editor
Bowling Green State University
René Ruiz, Assistant Editor
Bowling Green State University
Kartik Seshadri, Assistant Editor
Silver Spring, MD
James E. Taylor, Assistant Editor
Bowling Green State University
Robert Wolf, Assistant Editor
Southern Illinois University

Table of Contents

The Philosopher's Index

The Philosopher's Index, ISSN 0031-7993, a publication of the Philosophy Documentation Center, is a subject and author index with abstracts. Philosophy books and journals in English, French, German, Spanish, and Italian are indexed, along with selected books and journals in other languages and related interdisciplinary publications. This periodical is published quarterly and cumulated annually as a service to the philosophical community. Suggestions for improving this service are solicited and should be sent to the Editor.

Policies: Each quarterly issue of the *Index* includes the articles of journals and books that are received in the months prior to its publication. The dates on the journals indexed vary due to dissimilar publishing schedules and to delays encountered in overseas mailing.

The following factors are weighed in selecting journals to be indexed: 1) the purpose of the journal, 2) its circulation, and 3) recommendations from members of the philosophic community. Articles in interdisciplinary journals are indexed only if they are related to philosophy.

Most of the journal articles and books cited in *The Philosopher's Index* can be obtained from the Bowling Green State University Library, through the Inter-Library Loan Department. The library, though, requests that you first try to locate the articles and books through your local or regional library facilities.

Subscriptions should be mailed to *The Philosopher's Index*, Bowling Green State University, Bowling Green, Ohio 43403-0189. The 1994 subscription price (4 numbers) is $165 (Individuals $49). The price of single numbers, including back issues, is $45 (Individuals $15). An annual Cumulative Edition of *The Philosopher's Index* is published in the spring following the volume year. The 1993 Cumulative Edition is $172 (Individuals $59).

Abbreviations of Periodicals Indexed

(*Journal is no longer indexed and/or published. However, the abbreviation is included here for use in conjunction with DIALOG.)

Abraxas*	Abraxas
Acta Phil Fennica	Acta Philosophica Fennica
Aesthetics	Aesthetics
Agora*	Agora
Agora (Spain)	Agora
Agr Human Values	Agriculture and Human Values
Aitia	Aitia
Ajatus*	Ajatus
Aletheia*	Aletheia
Alg Log*	Algebra and Logic
Alg Ned Tijdschr Wijs	Algemeen Nederlands Tijdschrift voor Wijsbegeerte
Amer Cath Phil Quart	American Catholic Philosophical Quarterly (formerly The New Scholasticism)
Amer J Philo	American Journal of Philology
Amer J Theol Phil	American Journal of Theology & Philosophy
Amer Phil Quart	American Philosophical Quarterly
An Cated Suarez*	Anales de la Catedra Francisco Suarez
An Seminar Metaf	Anales del Seminario de Metafisica
Analisis Filosof	Analisis Filosofico
Analysis	Analysis
Ancient Phil	Ancient Philosophy
Ann Esth*	Annales D'Esthétique
Ann Fac Lett Filosof	Annali della Facolta di Lettere e Filosofia
Ann Univ Mariae Curie-Phil	Annales Universitatis Mariae Curie-Skłodowska, Sectio I/Philosophia-Sociologia
Annals Math Log	Annals of Mathematical Logic (see Annals Pure Applied Log)
Annals Pure Applied Log	Annals of Pure and Applied Logic (formerly Annals of Mathematical Logic)
Antioch Rev	Antioch Review
Anu Filosof	Anuario Filosofico
Apeiron	Apeiron
Applied Phil	Applied Philosophy (see Int J Applied Phil)
Aquinas	Aquinas
Arch Begriff*	Archiv für Begriffsgeschichte
Arch Filosof*	Archivio di Filosofia
Arch Gesch Phil	Archiv für Geschichte der Philosophie
Arch Math Log*	Archiv für Mathematische Logik und Grundlagen Forschung
Arch Phil	Archives de Philosophie
Arch Rechts Soz	Archiv für Rechts und Sozialphilosophie
Arch Stor Cult	Archivio di Storia della Cultura
Argumentation	Argumentation
Arion	Arion: A Journal of Humanities and the Classics
Aris Soc	The Aristotelian Society: Supplementary Volume
Asian J Phil	The Asian Journal of Philosophy
Asian Phil	Asian Philosophy
Augustin Stud	Augustinian Studies
Augustinus	Augustinus
Auslegung	Auslegung
Austl J Phil	Australasian Journal of Philosophy
Behavior Phil	Behavior and Philosophy (formerly Behaviorism)
Behaviorism	Behaviorism (see Behavior Phil)
Berkeley News	Berkeley Newsletter
Between Species	Between the Species
Bigaku	Bigaku
Bijdragen	Bijdragen, Tijdschrift voor Filosofie en Theologie
Bioethics	Bioethics
Bioethics Quart	Bioethics Quarterly (see J Med Human)
Biol Phil	Biology & Philosophy
Boll Centro Stud Vichiani	Bollettino del Centro di Studi Vichiani
Boston Col Stud Phil*	Boston College Studies in Philosophy
Brahmavadin*	Brahmavadin
Bridges	Bridges: An Interdisciplinary Journal of Theology, Philosophy, History, and Science
Brit J Aes	The British Journal of Aesthetics
Brit J Phil Sci	British Journal for the Philosophy of Science
Bull Hegel Soc Gt Brit	Bulletin of the Hegel Society of Great Britain
Bull Santayana Soc	Bulletin of the Santayana Society
Bull Sect Log	Bulletin of the Section of Logic
Bull Soc Fr Phil	Bulletin de la Société Française de Philosophie
Bus Ethics Quart	Business Ethics Quarterly
Bus Prof Ethics J	Business & Professional Ethics Journal
Cad Hist Filosof Cie	Cadernos de História e Filosofia da Ciéncia
Can J Phil	Canadian Journal of Philosophy
Can J Theol*	Canadian Journal of Theology
Chin Stud Hist Phil	Chinese Studies in History and Philosophy (see Chin Stud Phil)
Chin Stud Phil	Chinese Studies in Philosophy (formerly Chinese Studies in History and Philosophy)

Cirpho* . . . . Cirpho Review
Cl Quart* . . . . The Classical Quarterly
Clio . . . . Clio
Club Voltaire* . . . . Club Voltaire
Cogito* . . . . Cogito
Cognition . . . . Cognition
Commun Cog . . . . Communication and Cognition
Conceptus . . . . Conceptus
Cont Phil . . . . Contemporary Philosophy
Convivium* . . . . Convivium
Crim Just Ethics . . . . Criminal Justice Ethics
Crit Inquiry . . . . Critical Inquiry
Crit Rev . . . . Critical Review
Crit Texts . . . . Critical Texts
Critica . . . . Crítica
Cuad Etica . . . . Cuadernos de Etica
Cuad Filosof . . . . Cuadernos de Filosofía
Cult Herm . . . . Cultural Hermeneutics (see Phil Soc Crit)
Dalhousie Rev* . . . . Dalhousie Review
Dan Yrbk Phil . . . . Danish Yearbook of Philosophy
Darshan-Manjari . . . . Darshan-Manjari
Darshana Int . . . . Darshana International
De Phil . . . . De Philosophia
Deut Vier Lit* . . . . Deutsche Vierteljahresschrift für Literaturwissenschaft und Geistes Geschichte
Deut Z Phil . . . . Deutsche Zeitschrift für Philosophie
Dialec Hum . . . . Dialectics and Humanism
Dialectica . . . . Dialectica
Dialogo Filosof . . . . Dialogo Filosofico
Dialogos . . . . Diálogos
Dialogue (Canada) . . . . Dialogue: Canadian Philosophical Review
Dialogue (PST) . . . . Dialogue
Dialoog* . . . . Dialoog
Dianoia . . . . Diánoia
Diogenes . . . . Diogenes
Dionysius . . . . Dionysius
Diotima . . . . Diotima
Discurso . . . . Discurso
Doctor Communis* . . . . Doctor Communis
Econ Phil . . . . Economics and Philosophy
Educ Filosof . . . . Educação e Filosofia
Educ Phil Theor . . . . Educational Philosophy and Theory
Educ Stud . . . . Educational Studies
Educ Theor . . . . Educational Theory
Eidos . . . . Eidos
El Basilisco . . . . El Basilisco: Revista de Filosofia, Ciencias Humanas, Teoria de la Ciencia y de la Cultura
Ensay Estud* . . . . Ensayos y Estudios
Environ Ethics . . . . Environmental Ethics
Epistemologia . . . . Epistemologia
Erkenntnis . . . . Erkenntnis
Espiritu . . . . Espíritu
Estetika . . . . Estetika
Estud Filosof* . . . . Estudios Filosóficos
Ethics . . . . Ethics
Ethics Animals* . . . . Ethics and Animals
Ethics Behavior . . . . Ethics and Behavior
Ethics Med . . . . Ethics and Medicine: A Christian Perspective on Issues in Bioethics
Ethos* . . . . Ethos
Etud Phil* . . . . Les Etudes Philosophiques
Etudes* . . . . Etudes
Etyka . . . . Etyka
Euthanasia Rev* . . . . The Euthanasia Review
Exer Pat* . . . . Exercices de la Patience
Exist Psychiat* . . . . Existential Psychiatry
Explor Knowl . . . . Explorations in Knowledge
Faith Phil . . . . Faith and Philosophy
Fem Stud . . . . Feminist Studies
Filosofia . . . . Filosofia
Filozof Cas . . . . Filozoficky Casopis CSAV
Filozof Istraz . . . . Filozofska Istrsazivanja
Filozofia . . . . Filozofia
Found Lang . . . . Foundations of Language (see Ling Phil)
Fran Stud . . . . Franciscan Studies
Franciscanum . . . . Franciscanums: Revista de las Ciencias del Espiritu
Free Inq . . . . Free Inquiry
Frei Z Phil Theol . . . . Freiburger Zeitschrift für Philosophie und Theologie
Futurum* . . . . Futurum
G Crit Filosof Ital . . . . Giornale Critico della Filosofia Italiana

Key to Abbreviations

List of Periodicals Indexed

Acta Philosophica Fennica. ISSN 0355-1792. (irr) Academic Bookstore, Keskuskatu 1, 00100 Helsinki, Finland

Aesthetics. ISSN 0289-0895. (bi-enn) Japanese Society for Aesthetics, c/o Institute of Aesthetics, Faculty of Letters, University of Tokyo, Hongo 7-3-1, Bunkyo-ku, Tokyo 113, Japan

Agora. ISSN 0211-6642. (semi-ann) Servicio de Publicaciones, Universidad de Santiago de Compostela, Santiago de Compostela 15701, Spain

Agriculture and Human Values. ISSN 0889-048X. (q) Managing Editor, 370 ASB, University of Florida, Gainesville, FL 32611, USA

Aitia: Philosophy-Humanities Magazine. ISSN 0731-5880. (3 times a yr) Knapp Hall 15, SUNY at Farmingdale, Farmingdale, NY 11735, USA

Algemeen Nederlands Tijdschrift voor Wijsbegeerte. ISSN 0002-5275. (q) Van Gorcum, Postbus 43, 9400 AA Assen, The Netherlands

American Catholic Philosophical Quarterly. ISSN 1051-3558. (q) American Catholic Philosophical Association, The Catholic University of America, Washington, DC 20064, USA

American Journal of Philology. ISSN 0002-9475. (q) The Johns Hopkins University Press, 701 West 40th Street, Suite 275, Baltimore, MD 21211, USA

American Journal of Theology & Philosophy. ISSN 0194-3448. (3 times a yr) W. Creighton Peden, Editor, Department of Philosophy, Augusta College, Augusta, GA 30910, USA

American Philosophical Quarterly. ISSN 0003-0481. (q) Philosophy Documentation Center, Bowling Green State University, Bowling Green, OH 43403-0189, USA

Anales del Seminario de Metafísica. ISSN 0580-8650. (ann) Editor, Universidad Complutense, Noviciado 3, 28015 Madrid, Spain

Analisis Filosofico. ISSN 0326-1301. (semi-ann) Bulnes 642, 1176 Buenos Aires, Argentina

Analysis. ISSN 0003-2638. (q) Basil Blackwell, 108 Cowley Road, Oxford OX41JF, England (or 3 Cambridge Center, Cambridge, MA 02142, USA)

Ancient Philosophy. ISSN 0740-2007. (semi-ann) Prof. Ronald Polansky, Duquesne University, Pittsburgh, PA 15282, USA

Annales Universitatis Mariae Curie-Skłodowskiej, Sectio 1/Philosophia-Sociologia. ISSN 0137-2025. (ann) Biuro Wydawnictw, Uniwersytet Marii Curie-Skłodowskiej, Pl. Marii Curie-Skłodowskiej 5, 20-031 Lublin, Poland

Annali della Facolta di Lettere e Filosofia. Pubblicazioni dell'Università di Studi di Bari, Palazzo Ateneo, 70100 Bari, Italy

Annals of Pure and Applied Logic. ISSN 0168-0072. Elsevier Science Publishers, Box 211, 1000 AE Amsterdam, The Netherlands

Antioch Review. ISSN 0003-5769. (q) P.O. Box 148, Yellow Springs, OH 45387, USA

Anuario Filosofico. ISSN 0066-5215. Service de Publicaciones de la Universidad de Navarra, S.A. Edificio Bibliotecas, Campus Universitario, 31080 Pamplona, Spain

Apeiron: A Journal of Ancient Philosophy and Science. ISSN 0003-6390. (q) Academic Printing and Publishing, P.O. Box 4834, Edmonton, Alberta, Canada T6E 5G7

Aquinas. ISSN 0003-7362. (3 times a yr) Pontificia Universita Lateranense, Piazza S. Giovanni in Laterano 4, 00120 Città del Vaticano, Vatican City State

Archiv für Geschichte der Philosophie. ISSN 0003-9101. (3 times a yr) Walter de Gruyter, Genthiner Str. 13, 1000 Berlin 30, Germany

Archiv für Rechts und Sozialphilosophie. ISSN 0001-2343. (q) Franz Steiner Verlag Wiesbaden GmbH, P.O.B. 101526, 7000 Stuttgart, Germany

Archives de Philosophie. ISSN 0003-9632. 72 rue des Saints-Pères, 75007 Paris, France

Archivio di Storia della Cultura. (ann) Morano Editore S.P.A., Vico S. Domenico Maggiore, 9-80134 Naples, Italy

Argumentation. ISSN 0920-427X. (q) Kluwer Academic Publishers, P.O. Box 358, Accord-Station, Hingham, MA 02018-0358, USA

Arion: A Journal of Humanities and the Classics. ISSN 0095-5809. (3 times a yr) 745 Commonwealth Avenue #435, Boston, MA 02215, USA

The Aristotelian Society: Supplementary Volume. ISSN 0309-7013. (ann) Members: The Aristotelian Society, Department of Philosophy, Birkbeck College, University of London, Malet Street, London WC1E 7HX, England. Non-members: Basil Blackwell, 108 Cowley Road, Oxford OX4 1JF, England (or 3 Cambridge Center, Cambridge, MA 02142, USA)

The Asian Journal of Philosophy. (semi-ann) Prof. Tran Van Doan, Department of Philosophy, National Taiwan University, Roosevelt Road, Sec. 4, 10764 Taipei, Taiwan, Republic of China

Asian Philosophy. (semi-ann) Carfax Publishing Company, P.O. Box 25, Abingdon, Oxfordshire OX14 3UE, United Kingdom

Augustinian Studies. ISSN 0094-5323. (ann) Tolentine Hall, P.O. Box 98, Villanova University, Villanova, PA 19085, USA

Augustinus. ISSN 0004-802X. (q) P. José Oroz Reta, General Dávila 5, Madrid 28003, Spain

Auslegung: A Journal of Philosophy. ISSN 0733-4311. (semi-ann) Editors, Department of Philosophy, University of Kansas, Lawrence, KS 66045, USA

Australasian Journal of Philosophy. ISSN 0004-8402. (q) Robert Young, Editor, Department of Philosophy, La Trobe University, Bundoora, Victoria 3083, Australia

Behavior and Philosophy. (semi-ann) Boyd Printing, 49 Sheridan Avenue, Albany, NY 12210, USA

Berkeley Newsletter. ISSN 0332-026X. (ann) The Editor, Department of Philosophy, Trinity College, Dublin 2, Ireland

Between the Species: A Journal of Ethics. (q) Schweitzer Center, San Francisco Bay Institute, P.O. Box 254, Berkeley, CA 94701, USA

Bigaku. ISSN 0520-0962. (q) The Japanese Society for Aesthetics, c/o Faculty of Letters, University of Tokyo, Bunkyo-Ku, Tokyo, Japan

Bijdragen, Tijdschrift voor Filosofie en Theologie. ISSN 0006-2278. (q) Administratie Bijdragen, Krips Repro B.V., Postbus 106, 7940 AC Meppel, The Netherlands

Bioethics. ISSN 0269-9702. (q) Basil Blackwell, 108 Cowley Road, Oxford OX4 1JF, United Kingdom (or 3 Cambridge Center, Cambridge, MA 02142, USA)

Biology & Philosophy. ISSN 0169-3867. (q) Kluwer Academic Publishers, 101 Philip Drive, Norwell, MA 02061, USA

Bollettino del Centro di Studi Vichiani. ISSN 0392-7334. (ann) Bibliopolis, Edizioni di Filosofia e Scienze, SpA, Via Arangio Ruiz 83, 80122 Naples, Italy

Bridges: An Interdisciplinary Journal of Theology, Philosophy, History, and Science. ISSN 1042-2234. (semi-ann) Robert S. Frey, Editor, 5702 Yellow Rose Court, Columbia, MD 21045, USA

The British Journal of Aesthetics. ISSN 0007-0904. (q) Oxford University Press, Pinkhill House, Southfield Road, Eynsham, Oxford OX8 1JJ, England

British Journal for the Philosophy of Science. ISSN 0007-0882. (q) Oxford University Press, Pinkhill House, Southfield Road, Eynsham, Oxford OX8 1JJ, England

Bulletin de la Société Française de Philosophie. ISSN 0037-9352. (q) 12 rue Colbert, 75002 Paris, France

Bulletin of the Hegel Society of Great Britain. ISSN 0263-5232. (bi-ann) H. Williams, Department of International Politics, University College of Wales, Penglais Aberystwyth, Dyfed SY23 3DB, Great Britain

Bulletin of the Section of Logic.(q) Managing Editor, Grzegorz Malinowski, 8 Marca 8, 90-365 LAdź, Poland

Bulletin of the Santayana Society. (ann) Santayana Edition, Department of Philosophy, Texas A & M University, College Station, TX 77843-4237, USA

Business Ethics Quarterly. ISSN 1052-150X. (q) Philosophy Documentation Center, Bowling Green State University, Bowling Green, OH 43403-0189, USA

Business & Professional Ethics Journal. ISSN 0277-2027. (q) Center for Applied Philosophy, 243 Dauer Hall, University of Florida, Gainesville, FL 32611, USA

Cadernos de História e Filosofia da Ciéncia. ISSN 0101-3424. (semi-ann) Editor, Centro de Lógica-Unicamp, C.P. 6133, 13.081 Campinas, São Paulo, Brazil

Canadian Journal of Philosophy. ISSN 0045-5091. (q) University of Calgary Press, 2500 University Drive NW, Calgary, Alberta, Canada T2N 1N4

Canadian Philosophical Reviews. ISSN 0228-491X. (m) Academic Printing and Publishing, Box 4834, Edmonton, Alberta, Canada T6E 5G7

Chinese Studies in Philosophy. ISSN 0023-8627. (q) M.E. Sharpe, 80 Business Park Drive, Armonk, NY 10504, USA

Clio. ISSN 0884-2043. (q) Indiana University-Purdue University, Fort Wayne, IN 46805, USA

Cognition: International Journal of Cognitive Science. ISSN 0010-0277. (m) Elsevier Science Publishers, P.O. Box 211, 1000 AE Amsterdam, The Netherlands

Communication and Cognition. ISSN 0378-0880. (q) Blandijnberg 2, B-9000 Gent, Belgium

Conceptus: Zeitschrift für Philosophie. ISSN 0010-5155. (3 times a yr) Verband der Wissenschaftlichen Gesellschaften, Oesterreichs, Lindengasse 37, A-1070 Vienna, Austria

Contemporary Philosophy. (bi-m) P.O. Box 1373, Boulder, CO 80306, USA

Criminal Justice Ethics. ISSN 0731-129X. (semi-ann) The Institute for Criminal Justice Ethics, CUNY, John Jay College of Criminal Justice, 899 Tenth Avenue, New York, NY 10019, USA

Crítica: Revista Hispanoamericana de Filosofía. ISSN 0011-1503. (3 times a yr) Apartado 70-447, 04510 Mexico, DF, Mexico

Critical Inquiry. ISSN 0093-1896. (q) The University of Chicago, Wieboldt Hall 202, 1050 East 59th Street, Chicago, IL 60637, USA

Critical Review: An Interdisciplinary Journal. ISSN 0891-3811. (q) P.O. Box 14528, Dept. 26A, Chicago, IL 60614, USA

Critical Texts: A Review of Theory and Criticism. ISSN 0730-2304. (3 times a yr) Department of English and Comparative Literature, 602 Philosophy Hall, Columbia University, New York, NY 10027, USA

Cuadernos de Etica. ISSN 0326-9523. (semi-ann) Asociación Argentina de Investigacione Etica, Tte. Gral. J. D. Perón 2395-3° "G", 1040 Buenos Aires, Argentina

Cuadernos de Filosofía. ISSN 0590-1901. (semi-ann) Prof. Margarita Costa, Editor, Instituto de Filosofia, 25 de Mayo 217, 1002 Buenos Aires, Argentina

Danish Yearbook of Philosophy. ISSN 0070-2749. (ann) Museum Tusculanum Press, Njalsgade 94, DK 2300 Copenhagen S, Denmark

Darshan-Manjari: The Burdwan University Journal of Philosophy. (ann) Aminul Haque, Gopal Ch. Khan, Editors, Department of Philosophy, The University of Burdwan, Golabag, Burdwan 713104, India

De Philosophia. ISSN 0228-412X. Editor, Department of Philosophy, University of Ottawa, Ottawa, Ontario, Canada K1N 6N5

Deutsche Zeitschrift für Philosophie. ISSN 0012-1045. (m) VEB Deutscher Verlag der Wissenschaften, 1080 Berlin, Germany

Dialectica: Revue Internationale de Philosophie de la Connaissance. ISSN 0012-2017. (q) P.O. Box 1081, CH-2501 Bienne, Switzerland

Dialectics and Humanism. ISSN 0324-8275. (q) Foreign Trade Enterprise, Ars Polona, Krakowskie Przedmiescie 7, 00-068 Warsaw, Poland

Dialogo Filosofico. ISSN 0213-1196. (3 times a yr) Apartado 121, 28770 Colmenar Viejo, Madrid, Spain

Diálogos. ISSN 0012-2122. (semi-ann) Box 21572, UPR Station, Río Piedras, PR 00931, USA

Dialogue. ISSN 0012-2246. (semi-ann) Phi Sigma Tau, Department of Philosophy, Marquette University, Milwaukee, WI 53233, USA

Dialogue: Canadian Philosophical Review-Revue Canadienne de Philosophie. ISSN 0012-2173. (q) Prof. Steven Davis, Editor, Department of Philosophy, Simon Fraser University, Burnaby, British Columbia, Canada V5A 1S6

Diánoia. ISSN 0185-2450. (ann) Instituto de Investigaciones Filosóficas, Dirección del Anuario de Filosofía, Circuito Mtro. Mario de la Cueva, Ciudad de la Investigación en Humanidades, Coyoacán 04510, Mexico, DF, Mexico

Diogenes. ISSN 0392-1921. (q) Berg Publishers Ltd., 150 Cowley Road, Oxford OX4 1JJ, United Kingdom

Dionysius. ISSN 0705-1085. (ann) Department of Classics, Dalhousie University, Halifax, Nova Scotia, Canada B3H 3J5

Diotima. (ann) Hellenic Society for Philosophical Studies, 40 Hypsilantou Street, Athens 11521, Greece

Discurso. ISSN 0103-328X. (ann) Departamento de Filosofia-FFLCH, Universidade de Sao Paulo, 05508 Sao Paulo, Brazil

Economics and Philosophy. ISSN 0266-2671. (semi-ann) Cambridge University Press, 40 West 20th Street, New York, NY 10011, USA (or The Edinburgh Building, Shaftesbury Road, Cambridge CB2 2RU, England)

Educação e Filosofia. ISSN 0102-6801. (semi-ann) Revista "Educação e Filosofia", Universidade Federal de Uberlândia, Av. Universitaria, 155 C.P. 593, Campus Santa Monica, 38.400 Uberlândia MG, Brazil

Educational Philosophy and Theory. ISSN 0013-1857. (semi-ann) D.N. Aspin, Editor, Faculty of Education, Monash University, Clayton, Victoria 3168, Australia

Educational Studies. ISSN 0013-1946. (q) Richard LaBrecque, Editor, 131 Taylor Education Building, University of Kentucky, Lexington, KY 40506-0001, USA

Educational Theory. ISSN 0013-2004. (q) Education Building, University of Illinois, 1310 South 6th Street, Champaign, IL 61820, USA

Eidos: The Canadian Graduate Journal of Philosophy. ISSN 0707-2287. (semi-ann) Editors, Department of Philosophy, University of Waterloo, Waterloo, Ontario, Canada N2L 3G1

El Basilisco: Revista de Filosofía, Ciencias Humanas, Teoria de la Ciencia y de la Cultura. ISSN 0210-0088. (q) Apartado 360, 33080 Oviedo, Spain

Environmental Ethics: An Interdisciplinary Journal Dedicated to the Philosophical Aspects of Environmental Problems. ISSN 0163-4275. (q) Department of Philosophy, The University of North Texas, P.O. Box 13496, Denton, TX 76203-3496, USA

Epistemologia: An Italian Journal for the Philosophy of Science. (semi-ann) Tilgher-Genova s.a.s., via Assarotti 52, 16122 Genova, Italy

Erkenntnis: An International Journal of Analytic Philosophy. ISSN 0165-0106. Kluwer Academic Publishers, 101 Philip Drive, Norwell, MA 02061, USA

Espíritu. ISSN 0014-0716. (ann) Durán y Bas Nr 9, Apartado 1382, 08080 Barcelona, Spain

Estetika. ISSN 0014-1291. (q) Kubon & Sagner GmbH, Hess-Str 39/41, Postfach 34 01 08, 8 München 34, Germany

Ethics: An International Journal of Social, Political, and Legal Philosophy. ISSN 0014-1704. (q) University of Chicago Press, P.O. Box 37005, Chicago, IL 60637, USA

Ethics and Behavior. (q) Journal Subscription Department, LEA, 365 Broadway, Hillsdale, NJ 07642, USA

Ethics and Medicine: A Christian Perspective on Issues in Bioethics. (3 times a yr) Rutherford House Periodicals, 127 Woodland Road, Wyncot, PA 19095, USA

Etyka. (semi-ann) Zaklad Etyki, Instytut Filozofii UW, Krakowskie Przedmescie 3, 00-326, Warsaw 64, Poland

Explorations in Knowledge. ISSN 0261-1376. (semi-ann) David Lamb, Sombourne Press, 294 Leigh Road, Chandlers Ford, Eastleigh, Hants S05 3AU, Great Britain

Faith and Philosophy. ISSN 0739-7046. (q) Michael Peterson, Managing Editor, Asbury College, Wilmore, KY 40390, USA

Feminist Studies. ISSN 0046-3663. (3 times a yr) Claire G. Moses, Women's Studies Program, University of Maryland, College Park, MD 20742, USA

Filosofia. ISSN 0015-1823. (q) Piazzo Statuto 26, 10144 Turin, Italy

Filozofia. ISSN 0046-358X. (bi-m) SLOVART Ltd., nám.Slobody 6, 817 64 Bratislava, Czechoslovakia

Filozoficky Casopis CSAV. ISSN 0015-1831. (bi-m) Kubon & Sagner GmbH, Hess-Str 39/41, Postfach 34 01 08, 8 München 34, Germany

Filozofska Istraživanja. ISSN 0351-4706. Editor, Filozofski Fakultet, D. Salaja 3, p.p. 171, 41000 Zagreb, Yugoslavia

Franciscan Studies. ISSN 0080-5459. (ann) St. Bonaventure University, St. Bonaventure, NY 14778, USA

Franciscanum: Revista de las Ciencias del Espiritu. ISSN 0120-1468. (3 times a yr) Universidad de San Buenaventura, Calle 73 No. 10-45, Apartado Aéreo No. 52312, Bogota, Colombia

Free Inquiry. ISSN 0272-0701. (q) Paul Kurtz, Editor, Box 5, Central Park Station, Buffalo, NY 14215, USA

Freiburger Zeitschrift für Philosophie und Theologie. ISSN 0016-0725. (semi-ann) Editions St.-Paul, Perolles 42, CH-1700 Fribourg, Switzerland

Giornale Critico della Filosofia Italiana. ISSN 0017-0089. (q) LICOSA, SpA, Subscription Department, Via B. Fortini 120/10, 50125 Florence, Italy

Giornale di Metafisica. (3 times a yr) Tilgher-Genova s.a.s., via Assarotti 52, 16122 Genova, Italy

Gnosis: A Journal of Philosophic Interest. ISSN 0316-618X. (ann) Editor, Department of Philosophy, Concordia University, 1455 de Maisonneuve Boulevard West, Montreal, Quebec, Canada H3G 1M8

Graduate Faculty Philosophy Journal. ISSN 0093-4240. (semi-ann) Editor, Department of Philosophy, New School for Social Research, 65 Fifth Avenue, New York, NY 10003, USA

Grazer Philosophische Studien. ISSN 0165-9227. (ann) Humanities Press International, Atlantic Highlands, NJ 07716, USA

Gregorianum. ISSN 0017-4114. (q) 4 Piazza della Pilotta, 1-00187 Rome, Italy

The Harvard Review of Philosophy. ISSN 1062-6239. (ann) Department of Philosophy, Harvard University, Emerson Hall, Cambridge, MA 02138, USA

Hastings Center Report. ISSN 0093-0334. (bi-m) The Hastings Center, 255 Elm Road, Briarcliff Manor, NY 10510, USA

Heidegger Studies. (ann) Duncker & Humblot GmbH, Postfach 41 03 29, 1000 Berlin 41, Germany

Hermathena: A Dublin University Review. ISSN 0018-0750. (semi-ann) The Editor, Trinity College, Dublin 2, Ireland

The Heythrop Journal. ISSN 0018-1196. (q) The Manager, 11 Cavendish Square, London W1M 0AN, England

History and Philosophy of Logic. ISSN 0144-5340. (semi-ann) Taylor & Francis, 4 John Street, London WC1N 2ET, England

History and Philosophy of the Life Sciences. ISSN 0391-9114. (semi-ann) Taylor & Francis, 1900 Frost Road, Suite 101, Bristol, PA 19007, USA (or Rankine Road, Basingstoke, Hants RG24 0PR, England)

History and Theory: Studies in the Philosophy of History. ISSN 0018-2656. (q) Julia Perkins, History and Theory, Wesleyan Station, Middletown, CT 06457, USA

History of European Ideas. ISSN 0191-6599. (bi-m) Pergamon Press, Headington Hill Hall, Oxford OX3 0BW, England

History of Philosophy Quarterly. ISSN 0740-0675. (q) Philosophy Documentation Center, Bowling Green State University, Bowling Green, OH 43403-0189, USA

History of Political Thought. ISSN 0143-781X. (q) Imprint Academic, 32 Haldon Road, Exeter EX4 4DZ, England

Hobbes Studies. (ann) Van Gorcum, P.O. Box 43, 9400 AA Assen, The Netherlands

Horizons Philosophiques. ISSN 0709-4469. (semi-ann) Service de l'Edition, College Edouard-Montpetit, 945 chemin Chambly, Longueuil, Quebec, Canada J4H 3M6

Human Studies: A Journal for Philosophy and the Social Sciences. ISSN 0163-8548. (q) Martinus Nijhoff Publishers, P.O. Box 322, 3300 AH Dordrecht, The Netherlands

The Humanist. ISSN 0018-7399. (bi-m) Rick Szykowny and Gerry O'Sullivan, Editors, American Humanist Assocation, 7 Harwood Drive, P.O. Box 146, Amherst, NY 14226-0146, USA

Hume Studies. ISSN 0319-7336. (semi-ann) Editor, Department of Philosophy, University of Western Ontario, London, Ontario, Canada N6A 3K7

Husserl Studies. ISSN 0167-9848. (q) Kluwer Academic Publishers, P.O. Box 322, 3300 AA Dordrecht, The Netherlands (or 101 Philip Drive, Norwell, MA 02061, USA)

Hypatia: A Journal of Feminist Philosophy. ISSN 0887-5367. (3 times a yr) Linda Lopez McAlister, Editor, University of South Florida, SOC 107, Tampa, FL 33620-8100, USA

Idealistic Studies: An International Philosophical Journal. ISSN 0046-8541. (3 times a yr) Walter Wright, Editor, Department of Philosophy, Clark University, Worcester, MA 01610, USA

Il Protagora. (semi-ann) via A. Gidiuli 19, 73100 Lecce, Italy

The Independent Journal of Philosophy. ISSN 0378-4789. (irr) George Elliott Tucker, Editor, 47 Van Winkle Street, Boston, MA 02124, USA

Indian Philosophical Quarterly. ISSN 0376-415X. The Editor, Department of Philosophy, University of Poona, Pune 411 007, India

Informal Logic. ISSN 0824-2577. (3 times a yr) Assistant to the Editors, Department of Philosophy, University of Windsor, Windsor, Ontario, Canada N9B 3P4

Inquiry: An Interdisciplinary Journal of Philosophy. ISSN 0020-174X. (q) Universitetsforlaget, P.O. Box 2959, Tøyen, 0608 Oslo 6, Norway

International Journal for Philosophy of Religion. ISSN 0020-7047. (q) Kluwer Academic Publishers, Distribution Centre, P.O. Box 322, 3300 AH Dordrecht, The Netherlands

International Journal of Applied Philosophy. ISSN 0739-098X. (semi-ann) Indian River Community College, Fort Pierce, FL 34981-5599, USA

International Journal of Moral and Social Studies. ISSN 0267-9655. (3 times a yr) Journals, One Harewood Row, London NW1 6SE, United Kingdom

International Journal of Philosophical Studies. ISSN 0967-2559. Professor Dermot Moran, Editor, Department of Philosophy, University College Dublin, Dublin 4, Ireland

International Logic Review. (semi-ann) Editor, via Belmeloro 3, 40126 Bologna, Italy

International Philosophical Quarterly. ISSN 0019-0365. (q) Vincent Potter, S.J., Fordham University, Bronx, NY 10458, USA

International Studies in Philosophy. ISSN 0270-5664. (3 times a yr) Scholars Press, P.O. Box 15288, Atlanta, GA 30333, USA

International Studies in the Philosophy of Science. ISSN 0269-8595. (3 times a yr) Carfax Publishing Company, P.O. Box 25, Abingdon, Oxfordshire OX14 3UE, England

Interpretation: A Journal of Political Philosophy. ISSN 0020-9635. (3 times a yr) Hilail Gildin, Editor-in-Chief, King Hall 101, Queens College, Flushing, NY 11367-0904, USA

Irish Philosophical Journal. ISSN 0266-9080. (semi-ann) Dr. Bernard Cullen, Editor, Department of Scholastic Philosophy, Queen's University, Belfast BT7 1NN, Northern Ireland

Isegoria: Revista de Filosofia Moral y Politica. ISSN 1130-2097. (q) Editorial Anthropos, Apartado 387, 08190 Sant Cugat del Valles, Spain

Iyyun: The Jerusalem Philosophical Quarterly. ISSN 0021-3306. (q) Manager, S.H. Bergman Centre for Philosophical Studies, Hebrew University of Jerusalem, Jerusalem 91905, Israel

Journal for the Theory of Social Behavior. ISSN 0021-8308. (q) Basil Blackwell, 108 Cowley Road, Oxford OX4 1JF, England (or 3 Cambridge Center, Cambridge, MA 02142, USA)

The Journal of Aesthetic Education. ISSN 0021-8510. (q) University of Illinois Press, 54 East Gregory Drive, Champaign, IL 61820, USA

The Journal of Aesthetics and Art Criticism. ISSN 0021-8529. (q) Philip A. Alperson, Editor, University of Louisville, Louisville, KY 40292, USA

Journal of Agricultural Ethics. ISSN 0893-4282. (bi-ann) Room 039, MacKinnon Building, University of Guelph, Guelph, Ontario, Canada N1G 2W1

Journal of Applied Philosophy. ISSN 0264-3758. (bi-ann) Carfax Publishing Company, P.O. Box 25, Abingdon, Oxfordshire OX14 3UE, England

Journal of Business Ethics. ISSN 0167-4544. Kluwer Academic Publishers, 101 Philip Drive, Norwell, MA 02061, USA

Journal of Chinese Philosophy. ISSN 0301-8121. (q) Dialogue Publishing Company, P.O. Box 11071, Honolulu, HI 96828, USA

The Journal of Clinical Ethics. ISSN 1406-7690. (q) 107 East Church Street, Frederick, MD 21701, USA

The Journal of Critical Analysis. ISSN 0022-0213. (q) The National Council for Critical Analysis, Shirley Schievella, P.O. Box 137, Port Jefferson, NY 11777, USA

Journal of Dharma. ISSN 0253-7222. (q) Center for the Study of World Religions, Dharmaram College, Bangalore 560029, India

The Journal of Hellenic Studies. ISSN 0075-4269. (ann) Secretary, The Hellenic Society, 31-34 Gordon Square, London WC1H 0PP, England

Journal of Indian Council of Philosophical Research. ISSN 0970-7794. (3 times a yr) Subscription Department, Motilal Banarsidass, Bungalow Road, Jawahar Nagar, Delhi 110007, India

Journal of Indian Philosophy. ISSN 0022-1791. Kluwer Academic Publishers, 101 Philip Drive, Norwell, MA 02061, USA

The Journal of Libertarian Studies. ISSN 0363-2873. (q) Center for Libertarian Studies, P.O. Box 4091, Burlingame, CA 94011, USA

Journal of Medical Ethics: The Journal of the Institute of Medical Ethics. ISSN 0306-6800. (q) Subscription Manager, Professional and Scientific Publications (JME), Tavistock House East, Tavistock Square, London WC1H 9JR, England (or Professional and Scientific Publications, 1172 Commonwealth Avenue, Boston, MA 02134, USA)

The Journal of Medical Humanities. ISSN 1041-3545. (q) Human Sciences Press, 233 Spring Street, New York, NY 10013, USA

The Journal of Medicine and Philosophy. ISSN 0360-5310. Kluwer Academic Publishers, 101 Philip Drive, Norwell, MA 02061, USA

The Journal of Mind and Behavior. ISSN 0271-0137. (q) Circulation Department, P.O. Box 522, Village Station, New York, NY 10014, USA

Journal of Moral Education. ISSN 0305-7240. (3 times a yr) Carfax Publishing Company, P.O. Box 25, Abingdon, Oxfordshire OX14 3UE, England

The Journal of Non-Classical Logic. (bi-ann) Centro de Lógica-Unicamp, C.P. 6133, 13.081 Campinas, São Paulo, Brazil

Journal of Philosophical Logic. ISSN 0022-3611. Kluwer Academic Publishers, 101 Philip Drive, Norwell, MA 02061, USA

Journal of Philosophical Research. ISSN 1053-8364. (ann) Philosophy Documentation Center, Bowling Green State University, Bowling Green, OH 43403-0189, USA

The Journal of Philosophy. ISSN 0022-362X. (m) 709 Philosophy Hall, Columbia University, New York, NY 10027, USA

Journal of Philosophy of Education. ISSN 0309-8249. (semi-ann) Carfax Publishing Company, P.O. Box 25, Abingdon, Oxfordshire OX14 3UE, England

Journal of Pragmatics. ISSN 0378-2166. (bi-m) Elsevier Science Publishers, P.O. Box 211, 1000 AE Amsterdam, The Netherlands

The Journal of Religious Ethics. ISSN 0384-9694. (semi-ann) Scholars Press, P.O. Box 15288, Atlanta, GA 30333, USA

Journal of Semantics. ISSN 0167-5133. (q) Oxford University Press, Pinkhill House, Southfield Road, Eynsham, Oxford OX8 1JJ, England

Journal of Social and Biological Structures. ISSN 1040-1750. (q) JAI Press, Inc., 55 Old Post Road-No. 2, Greenwich, CT 06836, USA (For England, Europe, Africa, and Asia: 118 Pentonville, Road, London N1 9JN, United Kingdom)

Journal of Social Philosophy. ISSN 0047-2786. (3 times a yr) Dr. Peter French, Editor, Trinity University, San Antonio, TX 78212, USA

The Journal of Speculative Philosophy. ISSN 0891-625X. (q) Pennsylvania State University Press, Suite C, 820 North University Drive, University Park, PA 16802, USA

The Journal of Symbolic Logic. ISSN 0022-4812. Association for Symbolic Logic, Department of Mathematics, University of Illinois, 1409 West Green Street, Urbana, IL 61801, USA

The Journal of the British Society for Phenomenology. ISSN 007-1773. (3 times a yr) Haigh & Hochland, JBSP Department, Precinct Centre, Manchester M13 9QA, England

Journal of the History of Ideas. ISSN 0022-5037. (q) Donald R. Kelley, Executive Editor, 442 Rush Rhees Library, University of Rochester, Rochester, NY 14627, USA

Journal of the History of Philosophy. ISSN 0022-5053. (q) Business Office, Department of Philosophy, Washington University, St. Louis, MO 63130, USA

Journal of the Philosophy of Sport. ISSN 0094-8705. (ann) Human Kinetics Publishers, Box 5076, Champaign, IL 61820-9971, USA

Journal of Thought. ISSN 0022-5231. (q) Dr. Robert M. Lang, Editor, College of Education, Leadership, and Educational Policy Studies, Northern Illinois University, Dekalb, IL 60115, USA

The Journal of Value Inquiry. ISSN 0022-5363. (q) Kluwer Academic Publishers, Spuiboulevard 50, 3300 AA Dordrecht, The Netherlands

Kant-Studien: Philosophische Zeitschrift der Kant-Gesellschaft. ISSN 0022-8877. (q) Walter de Gruyter, Genthiner Str. 13, 1000 Berlin 30, Germany

Kennedy Institute of Ethics Journal. ISSN 1054-6863. (q) The Johns Hopkins University Press, Journals Publishing Division, 701 West 40th Street, Suite 275, Baltimore, MD 21211-2190, USA

Kennis en Methode: Tijdschrift voor Wetenschapsfilosofie en Methodologie. ISSN 0165-1773. (q) Boompers, Box 58, 7940 AB Meppel, The Netherlands

Kinesis: Graduate Journal in Philosophy. ISSN 0023-1568. (semi-ann) Department of Philosophy, Southern Illinois University, Carbondale, IL 62901, USA

Kriterion: Revista de Filosofia. (bi-ann) Faculdade de Filosofia e Ciências Humanas, da UFMG, Av Antonio Carlos, C.P. 6627, Belo Horizonte, MG, Brazil

Laval Théologique et Philosophique. ISSN 0023-9054. (3 times a yr) Service de Revues, Les Presses de l'Université Laval, C.P. 2447, Quebec, Canada G1K 7R4

Law and Philosophy: An International Journal for Jurisprudence and Legal Philosophy. ISSN 0167-5249. Kluwer Academic Publishers, 101 Philip Drive, Norwell, MA 02061, USA

Lekton. ISSN 1180-2308. (q) Presses de l'Université du Québec, C.P. 250 Sillery, Québec G1T 2R1, Canada

Linguistics and Philosophy. ISSN 0165-0157. Kluwer Academic Publishers, 101 Philip Drive, Norwell, MA 02061, USA

Listening: Journal of Religion and Culture. ISSN 0024-4414. (3 times a yr) P.O. Box 1108, Route 53, Romeoville, IL 60441-2298, USA

Logique et Analyse. ISSN 0024-5836. (q) Professor Jean Paul Van Bendegem, Editor, U. G. Rozier 44, B-9000 Gent, Belgium

Logos: Revista de Filosofía. ISSN 0185-6375. (3 times a yr) Apartado Postal 18-907, Colonia Tacubaya, Delegación Miguel Hidalgo, C.P. 11800, Mexico, DF, Mexico

Lyceum. (semi-ann) Saint Anselm College, Box 1698, 87 Saint Anselm Drive, Manchester, NH 03102-1310, USA

Magyar Filozófiai Szemle. ISSN 0025-0090. (bi-m) Kultura, P.O. Box 149, H-1389 Budapest 62, Hungary

Man and Nature/L'homme et la Nature. (ann) Academic Printing and Publishing, P.O. Box 4834, South Edmonton, Alberta, Canada T6E 5G7

Man and World: An International Philosophical Review. ISSN 0025-1534. Martinus Nijhoff Publishers, P.O. Box 322, 3300 AH Dordrecht, The Netherlands

Manuscrito: Revista Internacional de Filosofia. ISSN 0100-6045. (bi-ann) Circulation Department, Centro de Lógica, Unicamp C.P. 6133, 13.081 Campinas, São Paulo, Brazil

Mediaeval Studies. ISSN 0076-5872. (ann) Dr. Ron B. Thomson, Director of Publications, Pontifical Institute of Mediaeval Studies, 59 Queen's Park Crescent East, Toronto, Ontario, Canada M5S 2C4

Medical Humanities Review. ISSN 0892-2772. (bi-ann) Institute for the Medical Humanities, University of Texas Medical Branch, Galveston, TX 77550, USA

Metaphilosophy. ISSN 0026-1068. Basil Blackwell, 108 Cowley Road, Oxford OX4 1JF, England (or 3 Cambridge Center, Cambridge, MA 02142, USA)

Method: Journal of Lonergan Studies. ISSN 0736-7392. (semi-ann) The Lonergan Institute, Boston College, Chestnut Hill, MA 02167, USA

Methodology and Science. ISSN 0543-6095. (q) Dr. P.H. Esser, Secretary and Editor, Beelslaan 20, 2012 PK Haarlem, The Netherlands

Midwest Studies in Philosophy. (ann) Dr. Theodore E. Uehling, Jr., Editor, Division of the Humanities, University of Minnesota, 112 Humanities Building, Morris, MN 56267, USA

Mind: A Quarterly Review of Philosophy. ISSN 0026-4423. (q) Oxford University Press, Pinkhill House, Southfield Road, Eynsham, Oxford OX8 1JJ, England

Mind & Language. ISSN 0268-1064. (q) Basil Blackwell, 108 Cowley Road, Oxford OX4 1JF, England (or 3 Cambridge Center, Cambridge, MA 02142, USA)

Minds and Machines: Journal for Artificial Intelligence, Philosophy, and Cognitive Science. ISSN 0924-6495. (q) Kluwer Academic Publishers, P.O. Box 358, Accord Station, Hingham, MA 02018, USA

The Modern Schoolman: A Quarterly Journal of Philosophy. ISSN 0026-8402. (q) William C. Charron, Editor, Department of Philosophy, St. Louis University, St. Louis, MO 63103, USA

Modern Theology. ISSN 0266-7177. (q) Basil Blackwell, 108 Cowley Road, Oxford OX4 1JF, United Kingdom (or 3 Cambridge Center, Cambridge, MA 02142, USA)

The Monist: An International Quarterly Journal of General Philosophic Inquiry. ISSN 0026-9662. (q) The Hegler Institute, P.O. Box 600, La Salle, IL 61301, USA

NAO Revista de la Cultura del Mediterráneo. (3 times a yr) Mansilla 3344, 1° C, 1425 Capital Federal, Argentina

National Forum: Phi Kappa Phi Journal. ISSN 0162-1831. (q) Subscription Department, 129 Quad Center, Auburn University, Auburn University, AL 36849, USA

Nature, Society, and Thought. ISSN 0890-6130. (q) University of Minnesota, 116 Church Street, S.E., Minneapolis, MN 55455, USA

Neue Hefte für Philosophie. ISSN H085-3917. (irr/ann) Vandenhoeck & Ruprecht, Postfach 3753, 3400 Göttingen, Germany

New Vico Studies. ISSN 0733-9542. (ann) Institute for Vico Studies, 69 Fifth Avenue, New York, NY 10003, USA (or Humanities Press International, 171 First Avenue, Atlantic Highlands, NJ 07716, USA)

Nietzsche-Studien: Internationales Jahrbuch fur die Nietzsche-Forschung.(ann) Walter de Gruyter, Genthiner Str. 13, 1000 Berlin 30, Germany

Nomos: Yearbook of the American Society for Political and Legal Philosophy. (ann) Order Department, New York University Press, 70 Washington Square South, New York, NY 10012, USA

Notre Dame Journal of Formal Logic. ISSN 0029-4527. (q) Business Manager, University of Notre Dame, Box 5, Notre Dame, IN 46556, USA

Notre Dame Journal of Law, Ethics & Public Policy. (semi-ann) Zigad I. Naccasha, Managing Editor, University of Notre Dame, Notre Dame, IN 46556, USA

Noûs. ISSN 0029-4624. (q) Department of Philosophy, 126 Sycamore Hall, Indiana University, Bloomington, IN 47405, USA

Nouvelles de la République des Lettres. ISSN 0392-2332. (bi-ann) C.C. 1794767/01, Banca Commerciale Italiana, AG3 Naples, Italy

The Owl of Minerva. ISSN 0030-7580. (semi-ann) Department of Philosophy, Villanova University, Villanova, PA 19085, USA

Pacific Philosophical Quarterly. ISSN 0279-0750. (q) Expediters of the Printed Word, 515 Madison Avenue, New York, NY 10022, USA

Patristica et Mediaevalia. ISSN 0235-2280. (ann) Editor, Miembros del Centro de Estudios de Filosofía Medieval, 25 de Mayo 217, 2° Piso, 1002 Buenos Aires, Argentina

Pensamiento. ISSN 0031-4749. (q) Administración, Pablo Aranda 3, 28006 Madrid, Spain

The Personalist Forum. ISSN 0889-065X. Editor, Department of Philosophy, Furman University, Greenville, SC 29613, USA

Philosophia. ISSN 0031-8000. (ann) Editorial Office-Distribution, Research Center for Greek Philosophy, Academy of Athens, 14 Anagnostopoulou Street, Athens 106 73, Greece

Philosophia: Philosophical Quarterly of Israel. ISSN 0048-3893. (q) Bar-Ilan University, Subscriptions, Department of Philosophy, Ramat-Gan 52100, Israel

Philosophia Mathematica. ISSN 0031-8019. (semi-ann) Journals Division, University of Toronto Press, 5201 Dufferin Street, Downsville, Ontario, Canada, M3H 5T8

Philosophia Naturalis. ISSN 0031-8027. (bi-ann) Vittorio Klostermann GmbH, Postfach 90 06 01, Frauenlobstrasse 22, 6000 Frankfurt AM Main 90, Germany

Philosophia Reformata. ISSN 0031-8035. (q) Centrum voor Reformatorische Wijsbegeerte, P.O. Box 368, 3500 AJ Utrecht, The Netherlands

Philosophic Exchange: Annual Proceedings. ISSN 0193-5046. (ann) Center for Philosophic Exchange, SUNY at Brockport, Brockport, NY 14420, USA

Philosophica. ISSN 0379-8402. (semi-ann) Rozier 44, B-9000 Gent, Belgium

Philosophica. (q) 38A/10 Belgachia Road, Calcutta 700037, India

Philosophica: Zborník Univerzity Komenského. (ann) Dr. Miroslav Marcelli, Editor-in-Chief, Študijné a informačné stredisko Spoločenskovedných pracovísk Univerzity Komenského, Šafarikovo nám estie 6, 808 01 Bratislava, Czechoslovakia

Philosophical Books. ISSN 0031-8051. (q) Basil Blackwell, 108 Cowley Road, Oxford OX4 1JF, England (or 3 Cambridge Center, Cambridge, MA 02142, USA)

The Philosophical Forum. ISSN 0031-806X. (q) CUNY, Baruch College, Box 239, 17 Lexington Avenue, New York, NY 10010, USA

Philosophical Inquiry: An International Quarterly. (a) Prof. D.Z. Andriopoulos, Editor, School of Philosophy, Aristotelian University of Thessaloniki, P.O. Box 84, Thessaloniki, Greece (or P.O. Box 61116, Maroussi, Athens, Greece)

Philosophical Investigations. ISSN 0190-0536. (q) Basil Blackwell, 108 Cowley Road, Oxford OX4 1JF, England (or 3 Cambridge Center, Cambridge, MA 02142, USA)

Philosophical Papers. ISSN 0556-8641. (3 times a yr) Department of Philosophy, Rhodes University, P.O. Box 94, Grahamstown 6140, South Africa

Philosophical Psychology. ISSN 0951-5089. (3 times a yr) Carfax Publishing Company, P.O. Box 25, Abingdon, Oxfordshire OX14 3UE, United Kingdom

Philosophical Quarterly. ISSN 0031-8094. (q) Basil Blackwell, 108 Cowley Road, Oxford OX4 1JF, England (or 3 Cambridge Center, Cambridge, MA 02142, USA)

Philosophical Review. (ann) Editor-in-Chief, Department of Philosophy, National Taiwan University, Taipei 10764, Taiwan, Republic of China

The Philosophical Review. ISSN 0031-8103. (q) 327 Goldwin Smith Hall, Cornell University, Ithaca, NY 14853, USA

Philosophical Studies: An International Journal for Philosophy in the Analytic Tradition. ISSN 0031-8116. Kluwer Academic Publishers, 101 Philip Drive, Norwell, MA 02061, USA

Philosophical Studies in Education: Proceedings of the Annual Meeting of the Ohio Valley Philosophy of Education Society. ISSN 0160-7561. (ann) Terence O'Connor, Indiana State University, Terre Haute, IN 47809, USA

Philosophical Topics. ISSN 0276-2080. (semi-ann) Christopher S. Hill, Editor, Department of Philosophy, University of Arkansas, Fayetteville, AR 72701, USA

Philosophie et Logique. ISSN 0035-4031. (q) Editura Academiei Republicii Socialiste Romania, Str. Gutenberg 3 bis, Sector 6, Bucaresti, Romania

Philosophique. ISSN 0980-0891. (ann) Faculte des Lettres et Sciences Humaines, Université de Franche-Comté, 30 rue Megevand, 25000 Besançon Cédex, France

Philosophiques. ISSN 0316-2923. (semi-ann) Les Editions Bellarmin, 165 rue Deslauriers, Saint-Laurent, Quebec, Canada H4N 2S4

Philosophische Rundschau: Zeitschrift für Philosophische Kritik. ISSN 0031-8159. (q) J.C.B. Mohr (Paul Siebeck), Postfach 2040, 7400 Tübingen, Germany

Philosophy. ISSN 0031-8191. (q plus 2 supps). Cambridge University Press, Edinburgh Building, Shaftesbury Road, Cambridge, CB2 2RU, England, (or 40 West 20th Street, New York, NY 10011, USA)

Philosophy and Literature. ISSN 0190-0013. (semi-ann) The Johns Hopkins University Press, 701 West 40th Street, Suite 275, Baltimore, MD 21211-2190, USA

Philosophy and Phenomenological Research. ISSN 0031-8205. (q) Brown University, Box 1947, Providence, RI 02912, USA

Philosophy and Public Affairs. ISSN 0048-3915. (q) The Johns Hopkins University Press, 701 West 40th Street, Suite 275, Baltimore, MD 21211-2190, USA

Philosophy and Rhetoric. ISSN 0031-8213. (q) Department of Philosophy, The Pennsylvania State University, University Park, PA 16802, USA

Philosophy and Social Action. ISSN 0377-2772. (q) Business Editor, M-120 Greater Kailash-I, New Delhi 110048, India

Philosophy and Social Criticism. ISSN 0191-4537. (q) David M. Rasmussen, Editor, P.O. Box 368, Lawrence, KS 66044, USA

Philosophy and Theology: Marquette University Quarterly. ISSN 0-87462-559-9. (q) A. Tallon, Department of Philosophy and Theology, Marquette University, Milwaukee, WI 53233, USA

Philosophy East and West. ISSN 0031-8221. (q) The University of Hawaii Press, 2840 Kolowalu Street, Honolulu, HI 96822, USA

Philosophy in Science. ISSN 0277-2434. (ann) Pachart Publishing House, 1130 San Lucas Circle, Tucson, AZ 85704, USA

Philosophy of Education: Proceedings of the Philosophy of Education Society. ISSN 8756-6575. (ann) Dr. Thomas W. Nelson, Managing Editor, Illinois State University, Normal, IL 61761, USA

Philosophy of Science. ISSN 0031-8248. (q) Executive Secretary, Philosophy of Science Association, Department of Philosophy, 114 Morrill Hall, Michigan State University, East Lansing, MI 48824-1036, USA

Philosophy of the Social Sciences. ISSN 0048-3931. (q) Sage Publications, 2455 Teller Road, Newbury Park, CA 91320, USA

Philosophy Today. ISSN 0031-8256. (q) DePaul University, 802 West Belden Avenue, Chicago, IL 60614, USA

Phoenix. ISSN 0031-8299. (q) J. Schutz, Editorial Assistant, Trinity College, Larkin 339, University of Toronto, Toronto, Ontario, Canada M5S 1H8

Phronesis: A Journal for Ancient Philosophy. ISSN 0031-8868. (3 times a yr) Van Gorcum, P.O. Box 43, 9400 AA Assen, The Netherlands

Polis. (semi-ann) P. P. Nicholson, Department of Politics, University of York, York YO1 5DD, United Kingdom (or Prof. Kent F. Moors, Department of Political Science, Duquesne University, Pittsburgh, PA 15282-0001, USA)

Political Theory. ISSN 0090-5917. (q) Sage Publications, 2455 Teller Road, Newbury Park, CA 91320, USA

Proceedings and Addresses of the American Philosophical Association. ISSN 0065-972X. (7 times a yr) The American Philosophical Association, University of Delaware, Newark, DE 19716, USA

Proceedings of the American Catholic Philosophical Association. ISSN 0065-7638. (ann) Treasurer, The American Catholic Philosophical Association, Catholic University of America, Washington, DC 20064, USA

Proceedings of the Aristotelian Society. ISSN 0066-7374. Basil Blackwell, 108 Cowley Road, Oxford OX4 1JF, England (distributes to institutions). The Aristotelian Society, Department of Philosophy, Birkbeck College, London WC1E 7HX, United Kingdom

Proceedings of the Biennial Meetings of the Philosophy of Science Association. ISSN 0270-8647. (ann) Philosophy of Science Association, 18 Morrill Hall, Michigan State University, East Lansing, MI 48824-1036, USA

Proceedings of the Boston Area Colloquium in Ancient Philosophy. (ann) Co-publishing Program, University Press of America, 4720 Boston Way, Lanham, MD 20706, USA

Proceedings of the South Atlantic Philosophy of Education Society. (ann) Warren Strandberg, School of Education, Virginia Commonwealth University, Richmond, VA 23284-2020, USA

Process Studies. ISSN 0360-6503. (q) Center for Process Studies, 1325 North College Avenue, Claremont, CA 91711, USA

Public Affairs Quarterly. ISSN 0887-0373. (q) Philosophy Documentation Center, Bowling Green State University, Bowling Green, OH 43403-0189, USA

Quaderns de Filosofia i Ciència. ISSN 0213-5965. (irr) Societat de Filosofia del País Valencià, Facultat de Filosofia i Ciències de l'Educació, Universitat de València, Av. Blasco Ibáñez, 21-46010 València, Spain

Quest: Philosophical Discussions. ISSN 1011-226X. (bi-ann) Circulation Manager, P.O. Box 9114, 9703 LC Groningen, The Netherlands

Radical Philosophy. (3 times a yr) Howard Feather, Thurrock Technical College, Woodview, Grays, Essex RM16 4YR, England

Ratio. ISSN 0034-0066. (semi-ann) Basil Blackwell, 108 Cowley Road, Oxford OX4 1JF, England (or 3 Cambridge Center, Cambridge, MA 02142, USA)

Ratio Juris: An International Journal of Jurisprudence and Philosophy of Law. ISSN 0952-1919. (3 times a year) Basil Blackwell, 3 Cambridge Center, Cambridge, MA 02142 USA

Reason Papers: A Journal of Interdisciplinary Normative Studies. ISSN 0363-1893. (ann) Department of Philosophy, Auburn University, Auburn University, AL 36849, USA

Religious Humanism. ISSN 0034-4095. (q) Fellowship of Religious Humanists, P.O. Box 278, Yellow Springs, OH 45387, USA

Religious Studies. ISSN 0034-4125. (q) Cambridge University Press, Edinburgh Building, Shaftesbury Road, Cambridge, CB2 2RU, United Kingdom (or 40 West 20th Street, New York, NY 10011, USA)

Reports on Mathematical Logic. ISSN 0137-2904. (ann) Centrala Handlu Zagranicznego "Ars Polona," ul. Krakowskie Przedmiescie 7, 00-068 Warsaw, Poland

Reports on Philosophy. ISSN 0324-8712. Elzbieta Paczkowska-Lagowska, Editor-in-Chief, Instytut Filozofii, ul. Grodzka 52, 31-044 Krakow, Poland

Research in Phenomenology. ISSN 0085-5553. (ann) Humanities Press International, Atlantic Highlands, NJ 07716, USA

Research in Philosophy and Technology. (ann) JAI Press, Inc., 55 Old Post Road-No. 2, Greenwich, CT 06836, USA

The Review of Metaphysics. ISSN 0034-6632. (q) Catholic University of America, Washington, DC 20064, USA

Revista de Filosofía. ISSN 0185-3481. (3 times a yr) Universidad Iberoamericana, Prolongaciuon Paseo de la Reforma No. 880, Lomas de Santa Fe, 01210 Mexico, DF, Mexico

Revista de Filosofía. (semi-ann) Centro de Estidios Filosóficos, Edificio Viyaluz piso 8, Apartado 526, Maracaibo, Venezuela

Revista de Filosofia (Daimon). ISSN 1130-0507. (bi-ann) Secretario de Daimon, Departamento de Filosofía y Lógica, Universidad de Murcia, E-30071 Espinardo-Murcia, Spain

Revista de Filosofía: Publicatión de la Asociatión de Estudios Filosóficos. ISSN 0326-8160. (semi-ann) Marcelo Diego Boeri, ADEF C.C. 3758 Correo Central, 1000 Capital Federal, Argentina

Revista de Filosofía de la Universidad de Costa Rica. ISSN 0034-8252. (semi-ann) Editor, Universidad de Costa Rica, Apartado 75-2060, San José, Costa Rica

Revista de Filosofie. ISSN 0034-8260. (bi-m) Rompresfilatelia, Calea Victoriei 125, 79717 Bucharest, Romania

Revista Latinoamericana de Filosofía. ISSN 0325-0725. (3 times a yr) Box 1192, Birmingham, AL 35201, USA (or Casilla de Correo 5379, Correo Central, 1000 Buenos Aires, Argentina)

Revista Portuguesa de Filosofia. ISSN 0035-0400. (q) Faculdade de Filosofia, UCP, 4719 Braga , Portugal

Revista Venezolana de Filosofía. (semi-ann) Departamento de Filosofía, Apartado 80659, Caracas, Venezuela

Revue de Métaphysique et de Morale. ISSN 0035-1571. (q) 156 Avenue Parmentier, 75010 Paris, France

Revue de Théologie et de Philosophie. ISSN 0035-1784. (q) 7 ch. des Cèdres, CH-1004 Lausanne, Switzerland

Revue des Sciences Philosophiques et Théologiques. ISSN 0035-2209. (q) J. Vrin, 6 Place de la Sorbonne, 75005 Paris, France

Revue Internationale de Philosophie. ISSN 0048-8143. 2.000 FB. (q) Imprimérie Universa, rue Hoender 24, B-9230 Wetteren, Belgium

Revue Philosophique de la France et de L'etranger. ISSN 0035-3833. (q) Redaction de la Revue Philosophique, 12 rue Jean-de-Beauvais, 75005 Paris, France

Revue Philosophique de Louvain. ISSN 0035-3841. (q) Editions Peeters, B.P. 41, B-3000 Leuven, Belgium

Revue Thomiste: Revue Doctrinale de Théologie et de Philosophie. ISSN 0035-4295. (q) Ecole de Théologie, Avenue Lacordaire, Cedex, 31078 Toulouse, France

Rivista di Filosofia. ISSN 0035-6239. (q) Societa Editrice Il Mulino, Strada Maggiore 37, 40125 Bologna, Italy

Rivista di Filosofia Neo-Scolastica. ISSN 0035-6247. (q) Pubblicazioni dell'Universita Cattolica del Sacro Cuore, Vita e Pensiero, Largo A. Gemelli, 20123 Milan, Italy

Rivista di Studi Crociani. ISSN 0035-659X. (q) Presso la Societa di Storia Partia, Piazza Municipio, Maschio Angiolino, 80133 Naples, Italy

Rivista Internazionale di Filosofia del Diritto. (q) Casa Editrice Dott. A. Giuffre, via Busto Arsizio 40, 20151 Milan, Italy

Russell: Journal of the Bertrand Russell Archives. ISSN 0036-0163. (q) McMaster University Library Press, McMaster University, Hamilton, Ontario, Canada L8S 4L6

Russian Studies in Philosophy. ISSN 0038-5883. (q) M.E. Sharpe, 80 Business Park Drive, Armonk, NY 10504, USA

S'vara: A Journal of Philosophy, Law, and Judaism. ISSN 1044-0011. (bi-ann) Business Manager, AFSHI, 280 Grand Avenue, Englewood, NJ 07631, USA

Sapientia. ISSN 0036-4703. (q) Bartolome Mitre 1869, 1039 Buenos Aires, Argentina

Sapienza. ISSN 0036-4711. (q) Vicoletto S. Pietro a Maiella, 4-80134 Naples, Italy

Schopenhauer-Jahrbuch. ISSN 0080-6935. (ann) Verlag Kramer, Bornheimer Landwehr 57a, Postfach 600445, 6000 Frankfurt 60, Germany

Science, Technology, and Human Values. ISSN 0162-2439. (q) Sage Publications, 2455 Teller Road, Newbury Park, CA 91320, USA

Scientia: An International Review of Scientific Synthesis. ISSN 0036-8687. (3 times a yr) via F. Ili Bronzetti 20, 20129 Milan, Italy

Social Epistemology: A Journal of Knowledge, Culture, and Policy. ISSN 0269-1728. (q) Taylor and Francis, 1900 Frost Road, Suite 101, Bristol, PA 19007, USA (or Rankine Road, Basingstoke, Hants RG24 OPR, United Kingdom)

Social Indicators Research: An International and Interdisciplinary Journal for Quality-of-Life Measurement. ISSN 0303-8300. Kluwer Academic Publishers, 101 Philip Drive, Norwell, MA 02061, USA

Social Philosophy and Policy. ISSN 0265-0525. (semi-ann) Basil Blackwell, 108 Cowley Road, Oxford OX4 1JF, England (or 3 Cambridge Center, Cambridge, MA 02142, USA)

Social Theory and Practice. ISSN 0037-802X. (3 times a yr) Department of Philosophy R-36C, 203 Dodd Hall, The Florida State University, Tallahassee, FL 32306-1054, USA

Sophia. ISSN 0038-1527. (3 times a yr) School of Humanities, Deakin University, Victoria 3217, Australia

South African Journal of Philosophy. ISSN 0258-0136. (q) Bureau for Scientific Publications, P.O. Box 1758, Pretoria 0001, South Africa

The Southern Journal of Philosophy. ISSN 0038-4283. (q) Editor, Department of Philosophy, Memphis State University, Memphis, TN 38152, USA

Southwest Philosophical Studies. ISSN 0885-9310. (3 times a yr) Jack Weir, Co-Editor, Department of Philosophy, Hardin-Simmons University, Abilene, TX 79698, USA (or Joseph D. Stamey, Co-Editor, Department of Philosophy, McMurry University, Abilene, TX 79697, USA)

Southwest Philosophy Review. ISSN 0897-2346. (semi-ann) Department of Philosophy, University of Central Arkansas, Conway, AR 72302, USA

Stromata. ISSN 0049-2353. (q) Universidad del Salvador, C.C. 10, 1663 San Miguel, Argentina

Studia Leibnitiana. ISSN 0039-3185. (semi-ann) Franz Steiner Verlag Wiesbaden GmbH, Postfach 101526, 7000 Stuttgart, Germany

Studia Logica. ISSN 0039-3215. Kluwer Academic Publishers, 101 Philip Drive, Norwell, MA 02061, USA

Studia Philosophiae Christiane. ISSN 0585-5470. (semi-ann) ATK, ul. Dewajtis 5, 01-653 Warsaw, Poland

Studia Philosophica. (ann) Helmut Holzhey and Jean-Pierre Leyvraz, Editors, Verlag Paul Haupt, Falkenplatz 11/14, CH-3001 Berne, Switzerland

Studia Spinozana. ISSN 0179-3896. (ann) Douglas J. Den Uyl, Bellarmine College, Newburg Road, Louisville, KY 40205, USA

Studies in East European Thought. ISSN 0925-9392. Kluwer Academic Publishers, 101 Philip Drive, Norwell, MA 02061, USA

Studies in History and Philosophy of Science. ISSN 0039-3681. (q) Pergamon Press, Maxwell House, Fairview Park, Elmsford, NY 10523, USA

Studies in Philosophy and Education. ISSN 0039-3746. (q) Kluwer Academic Publishers, P.O. Box 358, Accord Station, Hingham, MA 02018-0358, USA

Studies in Philosophy and the History of Philosophy. (irr) Catholic University of America Press, Washington, DC 20064, USA

Synthese: An International Journal for Epistemology, Methodology, and Philosophy of Science. ISSN 0039-7857. Kluwer Academic Publishers, 101 Philip Drive, Norwell, MA 02061, USA

Teaching Philosophy. ISSN 0145-5788. (q) Philosophy Documentation Center, Bowling Green State University, Bowling Green, OH 43403-0189, USA

Teoria: Rivista di Filosofia. (bi-ann) E.T.S., C.C.P. 12157566, Piazza Torricelli 4, 56100 Pisa, Italy

Thémata Revista de Filosofia. ISSN 0210-8365. (ann) Servicio de Publicaciones de la Universidad de Sevilla, C. San Fernando 4, E-41004, Sevilla C, Spain

Theologie und Philosophie. ISSN 0040-5655. (q) Vierteljahresschrift, 6 Frankfurt 70 den, Offenbacher Lendstr 224, Germany

Theoretical Medicine: An International Journal for the Philosophy and Methodology of Medical Research and Practice. ISSN 0167-9902. Kluwer Academic Publishers, 101 Philip Drive, Norwell, MA 02061, USA

Theoria. ISSN 0495-4548. (3 times a yr) Plaza de Pio XII, 1, 6°, 1ª, Apartado 1.594, 20.080 San Sebastian, Spain

Theoria: A Swedish Journal of Philosophy. ISSN 0040-5825. (3 times a yr) Filosofiska Institution, Kungshuset i Lundagard, S-223 50 Lund, Sweden

Theory and Decision: An International Journal for Philosophy and Methodology of the Social Sciences. ISSN 0040-5833. Kluwer Academic Publishers, 101 Philip Drive, Norwell, MA 02061, USA

Thinking: The Journal of Philosophy for Children. ISSN 0190-3330. (q) The Institute for the Advancement of Philosophy for Children, Montclair State College, Upper Montclair, NJ 07043, USA

The Thomist. ISSN 0040-6325. (q) The Thomist Press, 487 Michigan Avenue NE, Washington, DC 20017, USA

Tijdschrift voor de Studie van de Verlichting en van Het Vrije Denken. ISSN 0774-1847. (q) Centrum voor de Studie van de Verlichting en van Het Vrije Denken, Vrije Universiteit Brussel, Pleinlaan 2-B416, 1050 Brussels, Belgium

Tijdschrift voor Filosofie. ISSN 0040-750X. (q) Kardinaal Mercierplein 2, B-3000 Leuven, Belgium

Topicos: Revista de Filosofía. ISSN 0188-6649. (ann) Dr. Hector Zagal, Editor, Facultad de Filosofía, Universidad Panamericana, A Rodin #498, Plaza de Mixcoac, 03910 Mexico, DF, Mexico

Topoi: An International Review of Philosophy. ISSN 0167-7411. Kluwer Academic Publishers, 101 Philip Drive, Norwell, MA 02061, USA

Tradition and Discovery: The Polanyi Society Periodical. ISSN 1057-1027. (irr) Dr. Richard Gelwick, University of New England, Biddeford, ME 04005, USA

Trans/Form/Ação. ISSN 0101-3173. (ann) Biblioteca Central da UNESP, Av. Vicente Ferreira, 1278 C.P. 603, 17500 Marilia, SP, Brazil

Transactions of the Charles S. Peirce Society: A Quarterly Journal in American Philosophy. ISSN 0009-1774. (q) Editor, Department of Philosophy, Baldy Hall, SUNY at Buffalo, Buffalo, NY 14260, USA

Tulane Studies in Philosophy. ISSN 0082-6776. (ann) Department of Philosophy, Tulane University, New Orleans, LA 70118, USA

Ultimate Reality and Meaning: Interdisciplinary Studies in the Philosophy of Understanding. ISSN 0709-549X. (q) University of Toronto Press, 5201 Dufferin Street, Downsview, Ontario, Canada M3H 5T8

Universitas Philosophica. (semi-ann) Facultad de Filosofía, Univeridad Javeriana, Carrera 7, No. 39-08, Bogota D.E. 2, Colombia

Utilitas: A Journal of Utilitarian Studies. (semi-ann) Oxford University Press, Pinkhill House, Southfield Road, Eynsham, Oxford OX8 1JJ, England

Vera Lex. (semi-ann) Prof. Virginia Black, Editor, Department of Philosophy and Religious Studies, Pace University, Pleasantville, NY 10570, USA

Vivarium: An International Journal for the Philosophy and Intellectual Life of the Middle Ages and Renaissance. ISSN 0042-7543. (semi-ann) E.J. Brill, Plantijnstr. 2, Postbus 9000, 2300 PA Leiden, The Netherlands

Zeitschrift für Mathematische Logik und Grundlagen der Mathematik. ISSN 0044-3050. (bi-m) Deutscher Verlag der Wissenschaften GmbH, Johannes-Dieckmann-Str 10, 1080 Berlin, Germany

Zeitschrift für Philosophische Forschung. ISSN 0044-3301. (q) Vittorio Klostermann GmbH, Postfach 90 06 01, 6000 Frankfurt AM Main 90, Germany

Zygon: Journal of Religion and Science. ISSN 0591-2385. (q) Karl E. Peters, Editor, Rollins College, Winter Park, FL 32789, USA

Guidance on the Use of the Subject Index

The Subject Index lists in alphabetical order the significant subject descriptors and proper names that describe the content of the articles and books indexed. Since titles are frequently misleading, the editors read each article and book to determine which subject headings accurately describe it. Each entry under a subject heading includes the complete title of the book or article and the author's name.

Subject entries fall into the following classes:

1) proper names, such as Quine, Kant, and Hegel;
2) nationalities, such as American and German;
3) historical periods, which are: ancient, medieval, renaissance, modern, nineteenth-century, and twentieth century;
4) major fields of philosophy, which are: aesthetics, axiology, education, epistemology, ethics, history, language, logic, metaphysics, philosophical anthropology, philosophy, political philosophy, religion, science, and social philosophy;
5) subdivisions of the major fields of philosophy, such as: utilitarianism, induction, realism, and nominalism;
6) other specific topics, such as grue, pain, paradox, and Turing-machine;
7) bibliographies, which are listed under "bibliographies," the person or subject, and the appropriate historical period.

The Subject Index is used like the index found in the back of a textbook. Scan the alphabetical listing of significant words until the desired subject is found. If the title confirms your interest, then locate the author's name, which occurs after the title, in the section entitled "Author Index with Abstracts." The title, in addition to suggesting the content of the article or book, indicates the language in which the document is written.

Although every effort is made to standardize subject headings, complete uniformity is impossible. Hence, check for various spellings of subject headings, particularly of proper names. Due consideration should be given to subject headings that sometimes are written with a space, a hyphen, or an umlaut. The following example illustrates some possibilities:

DE MORGAN
DE-MORGAN
DEMORGAN

Not only does the computer treat the above subject headings as different, but it may file other subject headings between them.

Generally, only the last names of famous philosophers are used as subject headings. Last names and first initials usually are used for other philosophers. The following list indicates who of two or more philosophers with the same last name is designated by last name only.

Alexander (Samuel)	James (William)
Austin (J L)	Jung (Carl G)
Bacon (Francis)	Lewis (C I)
Bradley (Francis H)	Mill (John Stuart)
Brown (Thomas)	Moore (G E)
Butler (Joseph)	Niebuhr (Reinhold)
Collins (Anthony)	Paul (Saint)
Darwin (Charles)	Price (Richard)
Eckhart (Meister)	Russell (Bertrand)
Edwards (Jonathan)	Schiller (Friedrich)
Green (Thomas H)	Toynbee (Arnold)
Hartmann (Edward von)	Wolff (Christian)
Huxley (T H)	

ACADEMIA

Moral Pluralism, Intellectual Virtue, and Academic Culture in Moral Education and the Liberal Arts, Mitias, Michael H (ed). Gouinlock, James.

Philosophizing as a Public Good in Frontiers in American Philosophy, Volume I, Burch, Robert W (ed). Durbin, Paul T.

Response—From Priest to Tourist: The Phiosopher of Education in a Post-Philosophic Moment. Collins, Clint.

Splitting the Self: Thoughts on Rortyian Education. Beatham, Mark.

ACADEMY

Platon l'École de Tübingen et Giovanni Reale. Rizzerio, Laura.

Societies, Circles, Academies, and Organizations in Revolution and Continuity, Barker, Peter (ed). Lux, David.

ACCEPTANCE

An Essay on Belief and Acceptance. Cohen, L Jonathan.

On Keith Lehrer's Belief in Acceptance. Piller, Christian.

On the Roles of Trustworthiness and Acceptance. David, Marian.

Reply to Christian Piller's "On Keith Lehrer's Belief in Acceptance". Lehrer, Keith.

Reply to Marian David's "On the Roles of Trustworthiness and Acceptance". Lehrer, Keith.

ACCOUNTABILITY

Pacifying Politics: Resistance, Violence, and Accountability in Seventeenth-Century Contract THeory. Baumgold, Deborah.

ACCOUNTING

On the Gearing Adjustment: An Axiomatic Approach. Gutiérrez, J M.

ACCURACY

Accuracy, Essentiality and Idealization in Idealization III, Brzezinski, Jerzy (ed). Paprzycki, Marcin and Paprzycka, Katarzyna.

ACKERMAN, B

Self-Defeating Civic Republicanism. Christodoulidis, Emilios A.

ACT

see also Conduct, Mental Act, Speech Act

Critical Theoretical Inquiry on the Notion of Act in the Metaphysics of Aristotle and Saint Thomas Aquinas. Lu, Matthias.

Communicative Skills in the Constitution of Illocutionary Acts. Simpson, David.

Response to Alexander's "Voluntary Acts: The Child/Davidson Trilemma". Child, James.

The Suberogatory. Driver, Julia.

Voluntary Acts: The Child/Davidson Trilemma. Alexander, Larry.

ACTING

How To Do Things On Stage. Saltz, David Z.

Tolstoy, Stanislavski, and the Art of Acting. Hughes, R I G.

ACTION

see also Voluntary Action

Action and Agency. Kevelson, Roberta (ed).

Agency in Action: The Practical Rational Agency Machine. Coval, Samuel C and Campbell, P G.

Aquinas on Human Action: A Theory of Practice. McInerny, Ralph.

Aufgeklärtes Eigeninteresse: Eine Theorie theoretischer und praktischer Rationalität. Gosepath, Stefan.

Epistemic Virtue and Doxastic Responsibility. Montmarquet, James.

Hobbes and Human Nature. Green, Arnold W.

Morality and the Emotions. Oakley, Justin.

Philosophie de l'action. Neuberg, Marc.

Scepticism. Hookway, Christopher.

The Dilemma of Narcissus. Gairdner, W T (trans) and Lavelle, Louis.

The Moral Self. Noam, Gil G (ed) and Wren, Thomas (ed).

Understanding Action: An Essay on Reasons. Schick, Frederic.

A Coherence Theory of Autonomy. Ekstrom, Laura Waddell.

A Methodological Note on Ethics, Economics, and the Justification of Action. Weikard, Hans-Peter.

A Reconstruction of Hegel's Account of Freedom of the Will. Moellendorf, Darrel F.

A Riddle Regarding Omissions. Haji, Ishtiyaque.

Act, Content and the Duck-Rabbit in Wittgenstein's Intentions, Canfield, J V (ed). Chisholm, Roderick M.

Acting for Reasons and Acting Intentionally. Mele, Alfred.

Actions, Reasons and Mental Causes (in French). Engel, Pascal.

Agency and Causal Explanation in Mental Causation, Heil, John (ed). Hornsby, Jennifer.

Anchoring Conceptual Content: Scenarios and Perception in Cognition, Semantics and Philosophy, Ezquerro, Jesús (ed). Peacocke, Christopher.

Apparent Circularity in Aristotle's Account of Right Action in the Nicomachean Ethics. Peterson, Sandra.

Audi on Practical Reasoning. Foley, Richard.

Audi's Theory of Practical Reasoning. Barker, John A.

Caesar's Wife: On the Moral SIgnificance of Appearing Good. Driver, Julia.

Can Intelligence Be Artificial?. Dretske, Fred.

Causal Facts as Logical Entailments of Action Statements. Lauer, Henle.

Comments on "Can Intelligence Be Artificial?". McNamara, Paul.

Consapevolezza e riferimento oggettivo: Un problema in Descartes, nell'idealismo e nella filosofia contemporanea. Varnier, Giuseppe.

Davidson and Wittgenstein on Human Action (in Dutch). Cuypers, Stefaan E.

Deontology and Agency. McNaughton, David and Rawling, Piers.

Discourse or Moral Action? A Critique of Postmodernism. Beyer, Landon E and Liston, Daniel P.

Does Intention Define Action? (in French). Neuberg, Marc.

Eternity, Awareness, and Action. Stump, Eleonore and Kretzmann, Norman.

Externalism and Mental Causality (in French). Jacob, Pierre.

Filosofia della mente ed etica in Stuart Hampshire. Reichlin, M.

Habermas: An Unstable Compromise. Meynell, Hugo.

How Many Logically Constant Actions are There?. Segerberg, Krister.

Hume's Theory of Motivation—Part 2. Shaw, Daniel.

Il pensare è spontaneo?. Rosen, Stanley H.

Indeterminism and Free Agency: Three Recent Views. O'Connor, Timothy.

Institutional Theory of Action and Its Significance for Jurisprudence. Weinberger, Ota.

Intention, Intentionality and Causality (in French). Moya, Carlos.

Intentional Action and Unconscious Reasons. Vollmer, Fred.

Intentionality and Madness in Hegel's Psychology of Action. Berthold-Bond, Daniel.

Intentionality and the Phenomenology of Action in John Searle and His Critics, Lepore, Ernest (ed). Wakefield, Jerome and Dreyfus, Hubert.

Joint Action. Miller, Seumas.

Kant on Action and Knowledge. Saugstad, Jens.

Kausalität und Freiheit: Ein Beispiel für den Zusammenhang von Metaphysik und Lebenspraxis. Krüger, Lorenz.

La forma e il limite. Gallino, Guglielmo.

Los sentidos del acto en Aristóteles. Yepes, Ricardo.

Love and Impartiality. Adams, Don.

Meaning and Action in Criss-Crossing A Philosophical Landscape, Schulte, Joachim (ed). Egidi, Rosaria.

On Conventions. Miller, Seumas.

On Logical Form of Action Sentences. Goswami, Chinmoy.

On Some Criticisms of Consent Theory. Boxill, Bernard R.

On the Possibility of Rational Dilemmas: An Axiomatic Approach. Cubitt, Robin P.

Paradigm Intention. Simester, A P.

Philosophical Implications of Chaos Theory: Toward a Meta-Critique of Action. Krieglstein, Werner.

Practical Unreason. Pettit, Philip and Smith, Michael.

Quinn on Doing and Allowing. Fischer, John M.

Rationality, Eudaimonia and Kakodaimonia in Aristotle. Heinaman, Robert.

Recenti studi fichtiani. Rotta, Graziella.

Response: The Background of Intentionality and Action in John Searle and His Critics, Lepore, Ernest (ed). Searle, John R.

Searle on Illocutionary Acts in John Searle and His Critics, LePore, Ernest (ed). Alston, W P.

Searle's Theory of Action in John Searle and His Critics, Lepore, Ernest (ed). O'Shaughnessy, Brian.

Situating Hannah Arendt on Action and Politics. Isaac, Jeffrey C.

Substitution and the Explanation of Action. Bryans, Joan.

Technopraxiology and Development. Tobar-Arbulu, José Felix.

The Body in Action: the Relationship between Action, Intention and Corporal Movement (in French). Dokic, Jérôme.

The Concept of Kartrtva in the Nyaya-Vaisesika Philosophy. Sen, Brinda.

The Constantive-Performance Distinction in a Justificatory Perspective. Lenka, Laxminarayan.

The Diversity and Unity of Action and Perception in The Contents of Experience, Crane, Tim (ed). O'Shaughnessy, Brian.

The Egoist's Objection. Gewirth, Alan.

The Inevitable. Fischer, John M and Ravizza, Mark.

The Nature of Thought. Dretske, Fred.

The Politics of Agonism. Honig, Bonnie.

The Problem of Persons. Janusz, Sharon and Webster, Glenn.

The Relation of Moral Worth to the Good Will in Kant's Ethics. Schaller, Walter E.

Together Bound: A New Look at God's Discrete Actions in History. Kirkpatrick, Frank G.

Transcendence and Judgment in Arendt's Phenomenology of Action. Gendre, Michael.

Trouble with Leprechauns in The Impulse to Philosophise, Griffiths, A Phillips (ed). Hollis, Martin.

Try, Succeed and Fail: A Critique of Empirical Theories of Action (in French). Buekens, Filip.

Trying Without Willing. Cleveland, Timothy.

Two All-or-Nothing Theories of Freedom in Logical Foundations, Mahalingam, Indira (ed). Watkins, John.

Undoubted Truth. McCarty, David Charles.

What Happens When Someone Acts?. Velleman, J David.

Wittgenstein + Heidegger on the Stream of Life. Schatzki, Theodore R.

Yet Another Look at Cognitive Reason and Moral Action in Hume's Ethical System. Johnson, Clarence Sholé.

ACTION THEORY

Intenzionalità e filosofia dell'azione. Marrone, Pierpaolo.

Kazimierz Twardowski filosofo e fondatore. Olejnik, Roman M.

ACTIVISM

Environmental Ethics and Environmental Activism. Durbin, Paul T.

Environmental Philosophizing and Environmental Activism. Allan, George.

Foucault and the Problem of Agency in Ethics and Danger, Dallery, Arleen B (ed). Moussa, Mario.

Reply to George Allan's "Environmental Philosophizing and Environmental Activism". Durbin, Paul T.

ACTIVITY

Agency and Alienation: A Theory of Human Presence. Segal, Jerome M.

Shared Cooperative Activity. Bratman, Michael.

AESTHETICS

Romanticism and Revolution. Cranston, Maurice.

S T Coleridge: El papel de la imaginación en el acto creador. Fonseca, Clotilde.

Santayana's Unbearable Lightness of Being: Aesthetics as a Prelude to Ontology. Alexander, Thomas M.

Scandinavian Aesthetics. Hermerén, Göran.

Schiller über das Erhabene. Petrus, Klaus.

Scruton and Reasons for Looking at Photographs. King, William L.

Seeing Aspects and Art: Tilghman and Wittgenstein. Cebik, L B.

Seeing Blake's Illuminated Texts. Bigwood, Carol.

Seeing, Imaginarily, at the Movies. Levinson, Jerrold.

Shakespeare's Demonic Prince. Mindle, Grant B.

Simone Weil on Beauty in Simone Weil's Philosophy of Culture, Bell, Richard (ed). Sherry, Patrick.

Siting Order at the Limits of Construction: Deconstructing Architectural Place. Risser, James C.

Six Theories in the Bedroom of *The Dead*. Garrett, Roland.

Some Questions about E H Gombrich on Perspective. Turner, Norman.

Something I've Always Wanted to Know About Hanslick. Kivy, Peter.

Sound and Epistemology in Film. Branigan, Edward.

Speaking about the Unspeakable: Plato's Use of Imagery. Tecusan, Manuela.

Still Looking for Proof: A Critique of Smith's Relativism. Bearn, Gordon C F.

Still More in Defense of Colorization. Young, James O.

Still Unconverted: A Reply to Neill. Yanal, Robert J.

Storytelling and Moral Agency. Tirrell, M Lynne.

Supervenience and the 'Science of the Beautiful'. Wicks, Robert.

Talbot's Technologies: Photographic Depiction, Detection, and Reproduction. Maynard, Patrick L.

Taste, Sublimity, and Genius in The Cambridge Companion to Kant, Guyer, Paul (ed). Schaper, Eva.

The "Fundamental Concepts" of Pictures. Elkins, James.

The Aesthetic Dimensions of Religious Experience in Logic, God and Metaphysics, Harris, James F (ed). Hartshorne, Charles.

The Aesthetic Essence of Art. Lind, Richard W.

The Aesthetics of Confucius (in Czechoslovakian). Paik, Ki-soo.

The Apostle, the Genius and the Monkey in Kierkegaard on Art and Communication, Pattison, George (ed). Pyper, Hugh S.

The Appreciation and Perception of Easel Paintings. Wilsmore, S J.

The Arts of Music. Alperson, Philip A.

The Birth of Postmodern Philosophy from the Spirit of Modern Art. Welsch, Wolfgang.

The Canon of Poetry and the Wisdom of Poetry. Cook, Albert.

The Chinese Notion of "Blandness" As a Virtue: A Preliminary Outline. Parkes, Graham R (trans) and Julien, François.

The Concept of Self and Postmodern Painting: Constructing a Post-Cartesian Viewer. Dunning, William V.

The Concept of Whole in the Structuralist Theory of Art (in Czechoslovakian). Grygar, Mojmir.

The Contingency of Cuteness: A Reply to Sanders. Morreall, John.

The Dislocation of the Architectural Self. Goldblatt, David A.

The Embodiment and Durations of Artworks. Krukowski, Lucian.

The Formal Syntax of Modernism: Carnap and Le Corbusier. Bearn, Gordon C F.

The Future of Dance Aesthetics. Sparshott, Francis.

The Hermeneutic of Art as Being-in-the-World (in Czechoslovakian). Calek, Oldrich.

The Idea of Abstraction in German Theories of the Ornament from Kant to Kandinsky. Morgan, David.

The Image of Women in Film: A Defense of a Paradigm. Carroll, Noël.

The Importance of Plato and Aristotle for Aesthetics. Halliwell, Stephen.

The Incoherence of the Aesthetic Response. Slater, Hartley.

The Institutionalization of a Discipline: A Retrospective of The Journal of Aesthetics and Art Criticism and the Amer Soc for Aesthetics, 1939-1992. Goehr, Lydia.

The Integrity of Aesthetics. Novitz, David.

The Inter-Relationship of Moral and Aesthetic Excellence. Bontekoe, Ron and Crooks, Jamie.

The Janus Aesthetic of Duchamp. McMahon, Cliff G.

The Journal of Aesthetics and Danto's Philosophical Criticism. Herwitz, Daniel A.

The Language of Musical Instruction. Barten, Sybil S.

The Logic of Representation. Ujlaki, Gabriella.

The Long Goodbye: The Imaginary Language of Film. Currie, Gregory.

The Moral Imagination and the Aesthetics of Human Existence in Moral Education and the Liberal Arts, Mitias, Michael H (ed). Alexander, Thomas M.

The Nature and Limits of Analytic Aesthetics. Ahlberg, Lars-Olof.

The Philosopher-Artist: A Note on Lyotard's Reading of Kant. Piché, Claude.

The Place of Real Emotion in Response to Fiction. Levinson, Jerrold.

The Politics of Art: The Domination of Style and the Crisis in Contemporary Art. Wartofsky, Marx.

The Preservation of Homeric Tradition: Heroic Re-Performance in the *Republic* and the *Odyssey*. Klonoski, Richard.

The Prisoner and the Prison in 2: Song of Macha's May (in Czechoslovakian). Otruba, Mojmir.

The Process/Product Dichotomy and Its Implications for Creative Dance. Bergmann, Sheryle.

The Purity of Aesthetic Value. Lorand, Ruth.

The Question of the End of Art and the Poetic Character of the World (in Czechoslovakian). Axelos, K.

The Rationale of Restoration. Savile, Anthony.

The Real or the real? Chardin or Rothko?. O'Hear, Anthony.

The Rhetoric of Philosophical "Writing": Emphatic Metaphors in Derrida and Rorty. Trembath, Paul.

The Road from Nice to Necessary: Broudy's Rationale for Art Education. DiBlasio, Margaret Klempay.

The Role of Aesthetic Emotion in R G Collingwood's Conception of Creative Activity. Anderson, Douglas R and Hausman, Carl R.

The Role of Feminist Aesthetics in Feminist Theory. Hein, Hilde.

The Role of Metaphor in Dance. Whittock, Trevor.

The Social Significance of Autonomous Art: Adorno and Bürger. Zuidervaart, Lambert.

The Socratic Quest in Art and Philosophy. Leddy, Thomas W.

The Sounds of Music: First Movement. Kimmel, Larry D.

The Sources of Morality: Function, Conformity and Aesthetics. O'Connell, James.

The Story of Art is the Test of Time. Silvers, Anita.

The Story of the Moral: The Function of Thematizing in Literary Criticism. Seamon, Roger.

The Styles of Art History: Entities or Processes?. MacDonald, Ray A.

The Theory of Jazz Music "It Don't Mean a Thing...". Brown, Lee B.

The Third Man. Davidson, Donald.

The Transcendental Aesthetic in The Cambridge Companion to Kant, Guyer, Paul (ed). Parsons, Charles.

The Value of Music. Goldman, Alan H.

The Work of Art as Psychoanalytical Object: Wollheim on Manet. Herwitz, Daniel A.

The Work of John Duns Scotus in the Light of Textual Criticism (Part I) (in Czechoslovakian). Richter, V.

Theorizing about Art. Leddy, Thomas W.

Thomas Nagel and the Problem of Aesthetics. Tollefsen, Christopher.

Thomson's Problems with Kant: A Comment on Kant's Problems with Ugliness. Guyer, Paul.

Thoughts on Duncan's Dancing Masters. Whittock, Trevor.

Time Out of Joint: Reflections on Anachronism. Barnes, Annette and Barnes, Jonathan.

Tolstoy, Stanislavski, and the Art of Acting. Hughes, R I G.

Toward a Theory of Profundity in Music. White, David A.

Tradition and the Indian Writer. Parthasarathy, R.

Tradition, Innovation, and Aesthetic Experience. Jauss, Hans Robert.

Tragedy as Subclause: George Steiner's Dialogue with Donald MacKinnon. Ward, Graham.

Transcendentality of Beauty in the Middle Ages (in Czechoslovakian). Aertsen, Jan A.

Transforming Images: Photographs of Representations. Savedoff, Barbara.

Tribal Art and Artifact. Dutton, Denis.

Two Women by Giovanni Bellini. Wiseman, Mary Bittner.

Unifying the *Protagoras*. Rutherford, Richard.

Unkantian Notions of Disinterest. Zangwill, Nick.

Using Science's Aesthetic Dimension in Teaching Science. Flannery, Maura.

Ventriloquism: Ecstatic Exchange and the History of the Artwork. Goldblatt, David A.

Violins or Viols?—A Reason to Fret. Davies, Stephen.

Vollenhoven's Legacy for Art Historiography. Seerveld, Calvin S.

What is Abstract About the Art of Music?. Walton, Kendall L.

When Composers Have To Be Performers. Alperson, Philip A.

Whitehead and Japanese Aesthetics. Mayada, Arlene M.

Why Art History Has a History. Carrier, David.

Why Philosophy of Art in Cross-Cultural Perspectives?. Moravcsik, Julius.

Why Spinoza Had No Aesthetics. Morrison, J C.

Will Aesthetics Be the Last Stronghold of Marxism. Khanin, Dmitry.

Wittgenstein, Art and Rule-Following. Oinam, Bhagat.

Wordsworth and the Recovery of Hope. Fischer, Michael.

Writing with Davidson: Some Afterthoughts after Doing *Blind Time IV: Drawing with Davidson*. Morris, Robert.

Yanal and Others on Hume and Tragedy. Neill, Alex.

Zen and the Art of John Dewey. Earls, C Anthony.

Zur Probleme um Auslegung der kantischen "Kritik der Urteilskraft" von R Oderbrecht (in Japanese). Ohkuma, Haruo.

'Fantastic' Images in Aesthetic Illusion, Burwick, Frederick (ed). Stafford, Barbara Maria.

'I Hard a Plaintive Melody' in Wittgenstein Centenary Essays, Griffiths, A Phillips (ed). Hanfling, Oswald.

'Too Low!': Frank Cioffi on Wittgenstein's *Lectures on Aesthetics*. Schroeder, Severin.

AETIUS

Physikai doxai et *problemata physica* d'Aristote à Aétius (et au-delà). Mansfeld, Jaap.

AFFECTION

La dimensión ontológica de la conciencia afectiva según Ferdinand Alquié — Segunda parte. Sodor, A.

AFFIRMATION

El oráculo de Narciso. Lomba, Joaquin.

La reflexión sobre la negación o afirmación de la vida en Schopenhauer, Feuerbach, Wagner y Nietzsche. Cabada Castro, M.

AFFIRMATIVE ACTION

A Liberal's Brief Against *Meyer* and *Pierce*. Wenz, Peter S.

Affirmative Action and Philosophy Instruction. English, Parker.

Compensation and Rights in the Liberal Conception of Justice. Barnett, Randy E.

Racism and Affirmative Action. Corlett, J Angelo.

The Limits of Compensatory Justice. Sunstein, Cass R.

The Moral Status of Affirmative Action. Pojman, Louis.

ALBERT, H

Zur Kritik des kritischen Rationalismus. Bader, Erwin.

ALCMAEON

Alcmeon's and Hippocrates's Concept of 'Aetia' in Greek Studies in the Philosophy and History of Science, Nicolacopoulos, Pantelis (ed). Andriopoulos, D Z.

ALEXANDER

A N Whitehead, R G Collingwood and the Status of Metaphysics (in Dutch). Vanheeswijck, Guido.

A Sometime Companion. McDermott, John J.

Alexander on *Phantasia*: A Hopeless Muddle or a Better Account?. Modrak, D K W.

Alexander's Sea Battle: A Discussion of Alexander of Aphrodisias *De Fato 10*. Gaskin, Richard.

Messages, Motives, and Hate Crimes. Schauer, Frederick.

Response to Alexander's "Voluntary Acts: The Child/Davidson Trilemma". Child, James.

Whitehead and Alexander. Emmet, Dorothy.

ALEXANDER, R

A Response to Ronald G Alexander's 'Personal Identity and Self-Constitution' and Michael Goodman's 'A Sufficient Condition for Personhood'. Montes, Maria J.

ALEXY, R

Application Discourse and the Special Case-Thesis. Dwars, Ingrid.

Critical Remarks on Robert Alexy's "Special-Case Thesis". Günther, Klaus.

ALFONSO OF CASTILE

Did King Alfonso of Castile Really Want to Advise God Against the Ptolemaic System? The Legend in History. Franssen, Maarten.

ALGEBRA

see also Boolean Algebra

EIS for Nilpotent Shifts of Varieties. Graczynska, Ewa.

A Certain Conception of the Calculus of Rough Sets. Bonikowski, Zbigniew.

A Decision Algorithm for Linear Sentences on a PFM. Li, L, Li, H and Liu, Y.

A Deduction Theorem Schema for Deductive Systems of Propositional Logics. Czelakowski, J and Dziobiak, W.

A Diophantine Definition of Rational Integers over Some Rings of Algebraic Numbers. Shlapentokh, Alexandra.

A Modal Analog for Glivenko's Theorem and Its Applications. Rybakov, V V.

A Note on the Diagonzalizable Algebras of PA and ZF. Shavrukov, Y.

A Note on the Extension Principle for Relatively Congruence-Distributive Quasivarieties. Czelakowski, Janusz.

A Word Problem for Normal and Regular Equations. Graczynska, Ewa.

Algebraic Logic for Classical Conjunction and Disjunction. Font, J M and Verdú, V.

Algebraizations of Quantifier Logics, An Introductory Overview. Németi, I.

Amalgamation and Interpolation in Normal Modal Logics. Maksimova, L.

An Algebraic Treatment of the Barwise Compactness Theory. Fleischer, Isidore and Scott, Philip.

Approximations and Logic. Marquis, Jean-Pierre.

Axiomatizing Logics Closely Related to Varieties. Rautenberg, W.

Complete and Atomic Algebras of the Infinite Valued Lukasiewicz Logic. Cignoli, R.

Complexity of Equational Theory of Relational Algebras with Projection Elements. Mikulás, Szabolcs, Sain, Ildikó and Simon, András.

Dynamic Algebras: Examples, Constructions, Applications. Pratt, V.

Loeb Extensions and Ultrapowers of Measures on Fragments. Ng, Siu-Ah.

Logical Atoms and Combinatorial Possibility. Skyrms, Brian.

On Decision Procedures for Sentential Logics. Skura, Tomasz.

On Two Relatives of the Classical Logic. Nowak, Marek.

Projective Geometries of Algebraically Closed Fields of Characteristic Zero. Holland, Kitty L.

Ramsey Sets, the Ramsey Ideal, and Other Classes Over R. Corazza, Paul.

Refutation Calculi for Certain Intermediate Propositional Logics. Skura, Tomasz.

Regular Modal Logics. Swirdowicz, Kazimierz.

Relation Algebras of Every Dimension. Maddux, Roger D.

Remarks on Elementary Duality. Prest, Mike.

Rings, Holes and Substantivalism: On the Program of Leibniz Algebras. Rynasiewicz, Robert.

Stability Among R.E. Quotient Algebras. Love, John.

The Axioms and Algebra of Ambiguity. Fishburn, Peter C.

The Lindenbaum Fixed Point Algebra is Undecidable. Shavrukov, V Y.

The Origin of Relation Algebras in the Development and Axiomatization of the Calculus of Relations. Maddux, R D.

The Problem of Elimination in the Algebra of Logic in Perspectives on the History of Mathematical Logic, Drucker, Thomas (ed). Green, Judy.

Théories syllogistiques et déontiques analysées comme structures algébriques: de Leibniz à Lukasiewicz et Von Wright. Sánchez-Mazas, Miguel.

Triviality, NDOP and Stable Varieties. Hart, B, Pillay, A and Starchenko, S.

Two Sequents of Locally Tabular Superintuitionistic Logic. Mardaev, S I.

Variable-Free Semantics for Anaphora. Böttner, Michael.

ALGORITHM

A Decision Algorithm for Linear Sentences on a PFM. Li, L, Li, H and Liu, Y.

Algorithmic Justice in Deconstruction and the Possibility of Justice, Cornell, Durcilla (ed). Wolfe, Alan.

Natural Heuristics for Proof Construction: Part I—Classical Propositional Logic. Batens, Diderik.

Sequential Voting by Veto: Making the Mueller-Moulin Algorithm More Versatile. Felsenthal, Dan S and Machover, Moshé.

ALIENATION

Agency and Alienation: A Theory of Human Presence. Segal, Jerome M.

Ideology and False Consciousness: Marx and his Historical Progenitors. Pines, Christopher.

Spinoza's Ethics: The View from Within. Schipper, Lewis.

Alienation and Moral Imperatives: A Reply to Kanungo. Sweet, Robert T.

Alienation, Cultural Differences, and Moral Judgment. McLane, Janice.

Isolation, Loneliness and the Falsification of Reality. Art, Brad.

Kant and the Autonomy of Art. Haskins, Casey.

Marx's Deficient Promise. Ormell, Christopher.

Marx, Housework, and Alienation. Kain, Philip J.

Note sul concetto di alienazione in Hegel. Alfano, G.

Virtue and Self-Alienation. Zeis, John.

ALLAN, D

'Eudemian' Ethical Method in Essays in Ancient Greek Philosophy, IV, Anton, John P (ed). Jost, Lawrence J.

ALLEGORY

Myth, Allegory and Argument in Plato. McCabe, Mary Margaret.

Teaching the Allegory of the Cave. Robinson, Jim.

ALLEN, E

Rational Infidels: The American Deists. Walters, Kerry S.

ALLEN, J

Jeffner Allen: A Lesbian Portrait. Zita, Jacquelyn N.

ALLOCATION

Liberalism and Health Care Allocation. Satre, Thomas W.

The Exchange and Allocation of Decision Power. Philipson, Tomas.

ALLUSION

Limits of Allusion. Leddy, Michael.

ALPERSON, P

Do Composers Have To Be Performers Too?. Spade, Paul Vincent.

ALQUIE, F

La dimensión ontológica de la conciencia afectiva según Ferdinand Alquié — Segunda parte. Sodor, A.

ALSTON, W

Emoción. Lyons, William.

Religious Pluralism and the Rationality of Religious Belief. Hick, John.

Response: Meaning, Intentionality, and Speech Acts in John Searle and His Critics, LePore, Ernest (ed). Searle, John R.

ALTERITY

Difference Without the Flux: Pragmatic versus Romantic Conceptions of Alterity. Nevo, Isaac.

Hannah Arendt, Feminism, and the Politics of Alterity: "What Will We Lose If We Win?". Cutting-Gray, Joanne.

The Problem of Evil in Paul Ricoeur: An Aporetic Exploration. Mongin, Olivier.

ALTERNATIVE

Alternative Possibilities, Moral Obligation, and Moral Responsibility. Haji, Ishtiyaque.

The Intuitionistic Alternative Set Theory. Lano, K.

ALTRUISM

Altruism. Paul, Ellen Frankel (ed), Miller, Fred D (ed) and Paul, Jeffrey (ed).

The Structure of Value. Allen, R T.

Abortion, Abandonment, and Positive Rights in Altruism, Paul, Ellen Frankel (ed). Long, Roderick T.

Abortion, Abandonment, and Positive Rights: The Limits of Compulsory Altruism. Long, Roderick T.

Altruism and Christian Love. Browning, Don.

Altruism and Physician Assisted Death. Gunderson, Martin and Mayo, David J.

Altruism and the Argument from Offsetting Transfers. Cowen, Tyler.

Altruism and the Argument from Offsetting Transfers in Altruism, Paul, Ellen Frankel (ed). Cowen, Tyler.

Altruism versus Egoism: A Pseudo-Problem, A Cognitive-Emotive Analysis. Shibles, Warren.

Altruism Versus Self-Interest: Sometimes a False Dichotomy. Badhwar, Neera Kapur.

Altruism Versus Self-Interest: Sometimes a False Dichotomy in Altruism, Paul, Ellen Frankel (ed). Badhwar, Neera Kapur.

Altruistic Surrogacy and Informed Consent. Oakley, Justin.

Beneficence and Self-Love: A Kantian Perspective. Hill Jr, Thomas E.

Cosmopolitan Altruism. Galston, William.

Cosmopolitan Altruism in Altruism, Paul, Ellen Frankel (ed). Galston, William.

Ethics and Evolution: The Biological Basis of Morality. Bradie, Michael.

Evolution, Altruism, and the Prisoner's Dilemma. Haji, Ishtiyaque.

Evolutionary Individualism. Franzwa, Gregg E.

Liberal Philanthropy. Riley, Jonathan.

On Some Alleged Limitations to Moral Endeavor. Wilson, Catherine.

Rational Altruism or the Secession of Successful?: A Paradox of Social Choice. Nelson, Julianne.

Reasons for Altruism. Schmidtz, David.

Reasons for Altruism in Altruism, Paul, Ellen Frankel (ed). Schmidtz, David.

Selflessness and the Loss of Self. Hampton, Jean.

Selflessness and the Loss of Self in Altruism, Paul, Ellen Frankel (ed). Hampton, Jean.

The Evolution of Altruism: Correlation, Cost, and Benefit. Sober, Elliott.

The Evolution of Human Altruism. Kitcher, Philip.

The Interplay between Science and Theology in Uncovering the Matrix of Human Morality. Schwarz, Hans.

The Reasons We Can Share: An Attack on the Distinction between Agent-Relative and Agent-Neutral Values. Korsgaard, Christine.

The Right to Welfare and the Virtue of Charity. Den Uyl, Douglas.

The Right to Welfare and the Virtue of Charity in Altruism, Paul, Ellen Frankel (ed). Den Uyl, Douglas.

Thinking as a Team in Altruism, Paul, Ellen Frankel (ed). Sugden, Robert.

ALTRUISM

Thinking as a Team: Towards an Explanation of Nonselfish Behavior. Sugden, Robert.

'Eth Nic 9.8: Beyond Egoism and Altruism? in Essays in Ancient Greek Philosophy, IV, Anton, John P (ed). Madigan, Arthur R.

'Fitness' and 'Altruism': Traps for the Unwary, Bystander and Biologist Alike. Settle, Tom.

AMALGAMATION

Amalgamation and Interpolation in Normal Modal Logics. Maksimova, L.

AMBIGUITY

Coping With Ambiguity and Uncertainty in Patient- Physician Relationships: II — *Traditio Argumentum Respectus*. Rodning, Charles B.

The Axioms and Algebra of Ambiguity. Fishburn, Peter C.

AMERICAN

see also Latin American, South American

"Yes, But...": Principles and Caveats in American Racial Attitudes. Hochschild, Jennifer L and Herk, Monica.

America's Philosophical Vision—John E Smith. Colapietro, Vincent.

Between Slavery and Freedom: Philosophy and American Slavery. McGary, Howard and Lawson, Bill E.

Bioethics Yearbook, Volume 2—Regional Developments in Bioethics: 1989-1991. Lustig, B Andrew (& other eds).

British Empiricism and American Pragmatism: New Directions and Neglected Arguments. Roth, Robert.

Charles Sanders Peirce: A Life. Brent, Joseph.

Contemporary Political Culture. Gibbins, John R (ed).

Drawing the Line: Life, Death, and Ethical Choices in an American Hospital. Gorovitz, Samuel.

Frontiers in American Philosophy, Volume I. Burch, Robert W (ed) and Saatkamp, Herman J Jr (ed).

In Search of the Ethical: Moral Theory in Twentieth Century America. Edel, Abraham.

Interpreting Tocqueville's "Democracy in America". Masugi, Ken (ed).

John Dewey and American Democracy. Westbrook, Robert B.

Just War and the Gulf War. Johnson, James Turner and Weigel, George.

Keeping Faith: Philosophy and Race in America. West, Cornell.

Liberty/Liberté: The American and French Experiences. Klaits, Joseph (ed) and Haltzel, Michael (ed).

Philosophy of the Social Sciences III: Groundwork for Social Dynamics. Wisdom, J O.

Rational Infidels: The American Deists. Walters, Kerry S.

Semiotics in the United States. Sebeok, Thomas A.

T S Eliot and American Philosophy: The Harvard Years. Jain, Manju.

The Challenge of Pluralism: Education, Politics, and Values. Power, F Clark (ed) and Lapsley, Daniel K (ed).

The Chicago Pragmatists and American Progressivism. Feffer, Andrew.

The Corporation, Ethics, and the Environment. Hoffman, W Michael (ed), Frederick, Robert (ed) and Petry, Edward S (ed).

William James: Pragmatism in Focus. Olin, Doris (ed).

A Reply to Westbrook, Brodsky, and Simpson. West, Cornel.

A Right to Health Care. McCarrick, Pat Milmoe.

Agency Theory: The Dilemma of Thomas C Upham. Adams, Todd.

American Democracy and the Majority Rule. Riley, Jonathan.

American Loss in Cavell's Emerson. Anderson, Douglas R.

American Naturalism from a Non-American Perspective. Karimsky, Anyur M.

American Philosophy Today. Rescher, Nicholas.

American Pragmatism and Ultimate Reality and Meaning as Seen in Religion. Roth, Robert.

An American History Lesson in Theorizing American Literature, Cowan, Bainard (ed). Sussman, Henry.

Anglo-American Aesthetics and Contemporary Criticism: Intention and the Hermeneutics of Suspicion. Carroll, Noël.

Artistic Formalism: Its Achievements and Weaknesses. Dziemidok, Bohdan.

Can You Read? Philosophical Reflections on Labour, Leisure and Literacy. Hunter, Graeme.

Caves, Canons, and the Ironic Teacher in Richard Rorty's Philosophy of Education. Van Hook, Jay M.

Charles S Peirce: American Backwoodsman in Frontiers in American Philosophy, Volume I, Burch, Robert W (ed). Houser, Nathan.

Charles Sanders Peirce and America's Dominant Theory of Law in Peirce and Law, Kevelson, Roberta. Summers, Robert S.

Conceptual Relativism and Philosophy in the Americas in Cultural Relativism and Philosophy, Dascal, Marcelo (ed). Olivé, León.

Conflicting Values in American Higher Education: Development of the Concept of Academic Freedom. Tandy, Charles.

Confucius and Country Music. Sartwell, Crispin.

Contradictions in American Culture in Frontiers in American Philosophy, Volume I, Burch, Robert W (ed). Ryder, John J.

De la "conquista" a la "colonización" del mundo de la vida (Lebenswelt). Dussel, Enrique.

De la "invención" al "descubrimiento" del Nuevo Mundo. Dussel, Enrique.

Defending the Liberal Community. Bellamy, Richard.

Democractic Evasions: Cornel West and the Politics of Pragmatism. Westbrook, Robert B.

Do Engineers have Social Responsibilities?. Johnson, Deborah G.

Early European Feminism and American Women in Women's Rights and the Rights of Man, Arnaud, A J. Goldstein, Leslie Friedman.

Ethics in America: A Report from the Trenches. Conway, Daniel W and Young, Phillips E.

Feminism and Pragmatism. Miller, Marjorie C.

Feminist Ethics: Projects, Problems, Prospects (in Czechoslovakian). Jaggar, Alison M.

Hannah Arendt and the American Republic. Watson, David.

In Search of a Calling. Buford, Thomas O.

Introduction to the Methodology of Paraphronesis, With Example: Religion and Education in Postmodern America. Tandy, Charles.

Japanese American Relocation: Who Is Responsible?. Barton, Mary.

Kennedy and West Virginia in Sartre Alive, Aronson, Ronald (ed). Sartre, Jean-Paul and Bowman, Elizabeth A (trans).

Listening for the Call: Response to Professor Buford. Carbone Jr, Peter F.

Modern Times: Stein, Bergson, and the Ellipses of 'American' Writing in The Crisis in Modernism, Burwick, Frederick (ed). Riddel, Joseph N.

Nuclear Cities: The Bastille Analogy in Sartre Alive, Aronson, Ronald (ed). Stone, Robert.

On American and British Aesthetics. Diffey, T J.

Organ Transplants, Foreign Nationals, and the Free Rider Problem. Davis, Dena S.

Philosophical Biography: The American Scene. Madden, Edward H and Madden, Marian C.

Philosophy of Education in Canada. Hare, William F.

Pluralism and the Problem of God in God, Values, and Empiricism, Peden, Creighton W (ed). Dean, William.

Postmodernism and American Pragmatism. Lavine, Thelma Z.

Postmodernism: Old and New. Stuhr, John.

Pragmatism and the Normative Sciences in Frontiers in American Philosophy, Volume I, Burch, Robert W (ed). Lieb, Irwin C.

Purpose, Power, and Agency. Colapietro, Vincent.

Recent Work on the American Professional Military Ethic: An Introduction and Survey. McGrath, James and Anderson III, Gustaf E.

Romancing the Stone in Theorizing American Literature, Cowan, Bainard (ed). Rowe, John Carlos.

Selves, People, Persons: An Essay in American Personalism in Selves, People, and Persons, Rouner, Leroy S (ed). Kohak, Erazim.

Sobre la legitimidad de la conquista de América: Las Casas y Sepúlveda. Muller, Alfredo Gómez.

Teaching Ethics in Higher Education: Goals, and the Implications of the Empirical Research on Moral Development. Annis, David B.

The Difference of Virtue and the Difference It Makes: Courage Exemplified. Hauerwas, Stanley.

The Incorporation of American Indian Philosophy into Undergraduate Philosophy Courses. Holly, Marilyn.

The Institutionalization of a Discipline: A Retrospective of The Journal of Aesthetics and Art Criticism and the Amer Soc for Aesthetics, 1939-1992. Goehr, Lydia.

The Legacy of Bowne's Empiricism. Anderson, Douglas R.

The Moral Legitimacy of Intellectual Property Claims: American Business and Developing Country Perspectives. Steidlmeier, Paul.

The Nothing That Is in Theorizing American Literature, Cowan, Bainard (ed). Butler, Judith.

The Rise and Fall of Evolutionary Thinking Among American Philosophers. Auxier, Randall.

The Use and Abuse of Modernity: Postmodenrism and the American Philosophic Tradition. Ryder, John J.

Three Types of American Neo-Pragmatism. Avery, Jon.

Thresholds of the Sign in Theorizing American Literature, Cowan, Bainard (ed). Riddel, Joseph N.

Understanding Conflicts between North and South in Cultural Relativism and Philosophy, Dascal, Marcelo (ed). Lacey, Hugh M.

Unger's Advocates: Assessing the Possibilities for Law Practice as a Transformative Vocation. Shelledy, David and Wintgens, Luc J.

West's Evasion of Pragmatism. Brodsky, G M.

AMERICAN INDIANS

Cultural Relativism and Philosophy. Dascal, Marcelo (ed).

Philosophy and Feminist Criticism. Cole, Eve Browning.

AMNESIA

Problems in Personal Identity. Baillie, James.

ANACHRONISM

Time Out of Joint: Reflections on Anachronism. Barnes, Annette and Barnes, Jonathan.

ANALOGY

A Woman and a Man as Prime Analogical Beings. Allen, Prudence.

Ahnlichkeit, Analogie und Homonymie bei Aristoteles. Rapp, Christof.

Analogia storica ed esperienza trascendentale: La "metaistorica" di Max Müller. Volonté, Paolo.

Analogical Concepts: The Fourteenth-Century Background to Cajetan. Ashworth, E J.

Analogical Reasoning: A Logical Inquiry About "Archaic Thought". Van Dormael, Jan.

Analogy as a Guide to Philosophical Thinking. Fethe, Charles.

L'analogia come chiave di lettura della creazione. Melchiorre, Virgilio.

What is an Anlogical Imagination?. Conradie, Ernst.

ANALYSIS

"'Thinking', A Widely Ramified Concept'. Hanfling, Oswald.

Argument and Analysis: An Introduction to Philosophy. Curd, Martin.

Context for Meaning and Analysis. Callaway, H G.

The Human Being as a Logical Thinker. Balzer, Noel.

ANCIENT

Commentary on McPherran's *Ataraxia* and *Eudaimonia* in Ancient Pyrrhonism. Ryan, George E.

Commentary on Reesor's "The Stoic Wise Man". Haase, Wolfgang.

Commentary on Vlastos' "Socratic Piety". Lefkowitz, Mary R.

Connaissance et réminiscence dans le *Ménon*. Brown, L.

Container Metaphysics According to Aristotle's Greek Commentators. Matthews, Gareth.

Copernicus, Apollo, and Herakles in The Uses of Antiquity, Gaukroger, Stephen (ed). Hutchison, Keith.

Critique de l'*anamnésis*. Brague, R.

De l'ontologie à la théologie: Lecture du livre Z de la "Métaphysique" d'Aristote. Gérard, Gilbert.

Diagnosis as Narrative in Ancient Literature. Pearcy, Lee T.

Dottrina non scritta e limiti della comunicabilità filosofica in Platone. Roggerone, Giuseppe A.

El "Nuevo" Platon (Continuación). Juárez, Agustín Uña.

El legado categorial de la ciencia griega presocrática. Céspedes, Guillermo Coronado.

Eleatic Monism in Zeno and Melissus. Curd, Patricia.

Enseigner la vertu?. Barnes, Jonathan.

Fate and Futurity in the Greco-Roman World. Martin, Luther H.

Galien et le stoïcisme. Manuli, Paola.

Giustizia e "carità" nel pensiero greco-romano (I). Pizzorni, R.

Gregory Vlastos. Burnyeat, M F.

Hermeias on Plato *Phaedrus* 238d and Synesius *Dion* 14.2. Dickie, Mathew W.

Ideology and "the Status of Women" in Ancient Greece. Katz, Marilyn.

Il *Filebo* come una 'summa' del pensiero metafisico platonico. Bonagura, P.

Ineffability of Truth in Plato's Philosophy. Przelecki, Marian.

Inherence and Primary Substance in Aristotle's *Categories*. Devereux, Daniel T.

Inside and Outside the *Republic*. Lear, Jonathan.

L'"akrasia" nell'Etica Nicomachea. Mauri Alvarez, M.

L'*Epinomide* o della religione ricondotta entro i limiti della ragione. Pesce, Domenico.

L'actualité de la dialectique de Platon a la lumière de Hegel. Vieillard-Baron, J L.

L'argument par "affinité" dans le "phédon". Rowe, Christopher.

L'utopie législative de Platon. Laks, André.

La signification du *prôton philon* dans le *Lysis*. Samb, Djibril.

La stylométrie et la question de "Métaphysique" K. Rutten, Christian.

La théorie platonicienne de la motivation humaine. Cooper, John.

Le concept de philosophie première chez Aristote: Note complémentaire. Follon, Jacques.

Le concept de philosophie première dans la "Métaphysique" d'Aristote. Follon, Jacques.

Le corps de la terre. Laurent, Jérôme.

Le degré zéro de la philosophie platonicienne: Platon dans l'*Historia critica philosophiae* de J J Brucker (1742). Neschke, Ada.

Le paradoxe de Ménon et l'Ecole d'Oxford. O'Brien, D.

Le paradoxe du *Ménon* et la connaissance définitionnelle. Canto-Sperber, M.

Le status de l'Un dans la "Métaphysique". Coloubaritsis, Lambros.

Le système impossible: remarques sur l'inachèvement des dialectiques platoniciennes. Lavaud, Claudie.

Les multiples lectures du Poème de Parménide. Lafrance, Yvon.

Les principes d'Eduard Zeller concernant l'histoire de la philosophie. Steindler, Larry.

Making Discourse Ethical: The Lessons of Aristotle's *Rhetoric*. Garver, Eugene.

Metafisica e dialettica nel *Commento* di Giacomo Zabarella agli *Analitici posteriori*. Berti, Enrico.

Minds Ancient and Modern. Taylor, C C W.

Nussbaum on Transcendence in Plato and Aristotle. Dorter, Kenneth N.

O Método de Análise da Geometria Grega. De Souza, Roberta Lima.

On the Sense of the Socratic Reply to Meno's Paradox. Jenks, Rod.

Os Sólidos Regulares na Antigüidade. Fossa, John A and Erickson, Glenn W.

Parmenides and Empedocles in Porphyry's *History of Philosophy*. Kohlschitter, Silke.

Parted Bodies, Departed Souls: The Body in Ancient Medicine and Anatomy in The Body in Medical Thought and Practice, Leder, Drew (ed). Zaner, Richard M.

Partendo da Parmenide. Frerari, V.

Participation et prédication chez Platon. Brisson, Luc.

Phaedrus' Cosmology in the *Symposium*. Salman, Charles E.

Philosophical Remarks on Thucydides' Melian Dialogue. Gómez-Lobo, Alfonso.

Plato and Aristotle: A New Look at Their Relationship — The Historical Place of Aristotelian Metaphysics (in Czechoslovakian). Krämer, Hans-Joachim.

Plato and the Computer. Robinson, T M.

Plato and the New Rhapsody. Baltzly, Dirk.

Plato's *Theages*. Cobb, William S.

Plato's Later Political Thought in The Cambridge Companion to Plato, Kraut, Richard (ed). Saunders, Trevor J.

Platon et la "ΔεinothΣ" Tragique. Bres, Yvon.

Platon et Plotin sur la doctrine des parties de l'autre. O'Brien, Denis.

Platon l'École de Tübingen et Giovanni Reale. Rizzerio, Laura.

Politics and the Polis: How to Study Greek Moral and Political Philosophy. Euben, J Peter.

Pouvoir enseigner la vertu?. Brunschwig, J.

Precisazioni metodologiche sulle implicanze e sulle dimensioni storiche del nuovo paradigma ermeneutico nell'interpretazione di Platone. Reale, Giovanni.

Remarks On the Creation of the World (in Czechoslovakian). Patkos, Judit.

Remarques sur Platon et la *technè*. Cambiano, Giuseppe.

Reply to Papers. Nussbaum, Martha C.

Robert Hooke, Physico-Mythology, Knowledge of the World of the Ancients and Knowledge ... in The Uses of Antiquity, Gaukroger, Stephen (ed). Birkett, Kirsten and Oldroyd, David.

Sailing through the Sea Battle. Bäck, Allan.

Socrate prend-il au sérieux le paradoxe de Ménon?. Scott, D.

Socrate: Il demone e il risveglio—Sul senso dell'etica socratica. De Bernardi, P.

Socrates and Plato. Graham, Daniel W.

Socratic Piety. Vlastos, Gregory.

Some Problems in Aristotle's Mathematical Ontology. Halper, Edward.

Some Thoughts on Explanation in Ancient Philosophy in Greek Studies in the Philosophy and History of Science, Nicolacopoulos, Pantelis (ed). Anagnostopoulos, Georgios.

Soul as Attunement: An Analogy or a Model? in Greek Studies in the Philosophy and History of Science, Nicolacopoulos, Pantelis (ed). Scaltsas, Theodore.

Speculation and Judgment. Taminiaux, Jacques M.

Teleology and Myth in the *Phaedo*. Sedley, David.

Tensions and 'Anamalous' Passages: Aristotle's *Metaphysics* and Science, Method and Practice, Deslauriers, Marguerite.

The *Meno* and the Mysteries of Mathematics. Lloyd, G E R.

The Ancient Legal Sources of Seventeenth-Century Probability in The Uses of Antiquity, Gaukroger, Stephen (ed). Franklin, James.

The Aristotelian *Politeia* and the Athenian Society (in Czechoslovakian). Bartfai, Edit.

The Conclusion of the *Meno*. Snider, Eric W.

The Discovery of the Self in Antiquity. Gerson, Lloyd P.

The Fragility of Fortune. Bellamy, Richard.

The Freedom of the One. O'Meara, Dominic.

The Images of Enslavement and Incommensurability in Plato's *Meno*. Turner, Jeffrey S.

The Notion of Paideia in Aristotle's *De Partibus Animalium*. George, Marie I.

The Relation of Philosophy to Sōphrosynē: Zalmoxian Medicine in Plato's *Charmides*. Coolidge, Jr, Francis P.

The Stoic Wise Man. Reesor, Margaret E.

The Theory of Odd and Even in the Ninth Book of Euclid's Elements. Becker, Heribert and Oliver, Charles (trans).

Theaetetus in Bad Company. Williams, C J F.

Tyranny: Ancient and Modern. Bradshaw, Leah.

Un'ipotesi sul concerto aristotelico di astrazione. Cattanei, E.

Una nuova edizione italiana del Trattato aristotelico sulle *Categorie*. Mangiagalli, M.

Unity and *Logos*: A Reading of *Theaetetus* 201c-210a. Miller, Mitchell.

Vlastos on Elenchus and Mathematics. Seeskin, Kenneth.

Vlastos's Socrates. Kahn, Charles.

Voices of Silence: On Gregory Vlastos' Socrates. Nehamas, Alexander.

What Did Socrates Teach and To Whom Did He Teach It?. Nehamas, Alexander.

Why is Annihiliation a Great Gain for Socrates? The Argument of *Apology* 40c3-e2. Calef, Scott.

Why Parmenides Wrote in Verse. Floyd, Edwin D.

Women Philosophers in Antiquity. Leuven, Lienke.

'Place' in Context in Theophrastus, Fortenbaugh, W W (ed). Algra, Keimpe.

'Pretty, Witty and Wise': Courtesans in Athenaeus' *Deipnosophistai* Book 13. Hawley, R.

ANDERSON, A

Exhaustively Axiomatizing RMO with an Appropriate Extension of Anderson and Belnap's "Strong and Natural List of Valid Entailments". Méndez, José M.

ANDERSON, D

A Response to Daniel Holbrook's 'Descartes on Persons' and Doug Anderson's 'The Legacy of Bowne's Empiricism'. Littlejohn, Ronnie L.

Reply to Anderson: Interpreting the Guess of a Physicist. Colapietro, Vincent.

ANDERSON, T

Free-market versus Libertarian Environmentalism. Sagoff, Mark.

ANDERSON, W

Ethical Aspects of Germline Gene Therapy. De Wachter, Maurice.

ANDREAS-SALOME, L

Woman and Modernity: The (Life)styles of Lou Andreas-Salomé. Martin, Biddy.

ANDROGYNY

A Critique of Androgeny. Fouché, Fidéla.

ANELLIS, I

A Note Concerning Irving H Anellis's "Distortions and Discontinuties of Mathematical Progress". Ernest, Paul.

ANGEL

Ein Grinsen ohne Katze: Von der Vergleichbarkeit zwischen 'künstlicher Intelligenz' und 'getrennten Intelligenzen'. Capurro, Rafael.

Where Have All the Angels Gone?. Clark, Stephen R L.

ANGELL, M

Double Agency and the Ethics of Rationing Health Care: A Response to Marcia Angell. Menzel, Paul T.

ANGER

Anger and Hate. Ben-Ze'ev, Aaron.

ANIMAL

Philosophy of Mind: An Introduction. Graham, George.

Practical Ethics (Second Edition). Singer, Peter.

Taking Sides: Clashing Views on Controversial Bioethical Issues (Fifth Edition). Levine, Carol.

The Animals Issue: Moral Theory in Practice. Carruthers, Peter.

The Ethical Dimensions of the Biological Sciences. Bulger, Ruth Ellen (ed), Heitman, Elizabeth (ed) and Reiser, Stanley Joel (ed).

ANTHROPOLOGY
Respuesta a lo ajeno: Sobre la relación entre la cultura propia y la cultura ajena. Waldenfels, Bernhard.
Some Philosophical Problems Concerning Culture and Rationality. Bhattacharyya, Sibajiban.
The "Sovereign Ingratitude" of Spirit toward Nature: Logical Qualities, Corporeity, Animal Magnetism, and Madness in Hegel's "Anthropology". Lucas, Hans-Christian.
The Face in the Sand in Philosophical Interventions in the Unfinished Project of Enlightenment, Honneth, Axel (& other eds). Schnädelbach, Herbert.
The System and Its Fractures: Gilles Deleuze on Otherness. May, Todd G.
Zur Notwendigkeit von Religion aus der Sicht Durkheims und seiner Erben. Steunebrink, Gerrit A J.

ANTHROPOMORPHISM
Anthropomorphism. Stebbins, Sarah.
Comments on "Anthropomorphism". Hilbert, David.
Nature and Morality. Paden, Roger.

ANTI-SEMITISM
A Reply to Crude and Reckless Distortions. Edwards, Paul.
Hannah Arendt and the American Republic. Watson, David.
Understanding Fascism? in Isaiah Berlin: A Celebration, Margalit, Edna (ed). Ignatieff, Michael.

ANTIFOUNDATIONALISM
Anti-Foundationalism: Old and New. Singer, Beth (ed) and Rockmore, Tom (ed).

ANTIGONE
Simone Weil and Antigone: Innocence and Affliction in Simone Weil's Philosophy of Culture, Bell, Richard (ed). Loades, Ann.

ANTINOMINIANISM
Giovanni: Der Ethiker Nicolai Hartmann und die Religion. Hürlimann, Kaspar.

ANTINOMY
A Note on Kant's First Antinomy. Moore, A W.

ANTIQUITY
see also Ancient
The Uses of Antiquity. Gaukroger, Stephen (ed).

ANTIREALISM
Can an Anti-Realist Be Revisionary About Deductive Inference?. Weiss, Bernhard.
How Not to Refute Realism. George, Alexander.
Semántica anti-realista: Intuicionismo matemático y concepto de verdad. González, Wenceslao J.
The Metaphysics of Anti-Realism. Young, James O.

ANZALDUA, G
On Borderlands/La Frontera: An Interpretive Essay. Lugones, María.

APARTHEID
Art and Culture in a Changing World. Degenaar, J J.
Politics beyond Humanism in Working Through Derrida, Madison, Gary B (ed). Bernasconi, Robert.

APEL, K
Die Krise der Gegenwart und die Verantwortung der Philosophie (Vittorio Hösle). Kesserling, Thomas.
Die Zerstückelung des Fu-Tschu-Li. Kohler, Georg.
Response: Meaning, Intentionality, and Speech Acts in John Searle and His Critics, LePore, Ernest (ed). Searle, John R.
Wahre performative Selbstwidersprüche. Steinhoff, Uwe.
Wittgenstein y Apel sobre la crítica del sentido: de la lógica a la antropología?. Conill, J.

APHORISM
Aphorisms—Georg Christoph Lichtenberg. Lichtenberg, Georg Christoph.
On Why Philosophers Redefine their Subject in The Impulse to Philosophise, Griffiths, A Phillips (ed). Brown, Stuart.

APOLLONIUS OF TYANA
The Rhetoric of a "Divine Man": Apollonius of Tyana as Critic of Oratory and as Orator According to Philostratus. Billault, Alain.

APPEARANCE
Caesar's Wife: On the Moral Significance of Appearing Good. Driver, Julia.

APPEL, S
Freud, Drives, and the 'Social'. Fluxman, Tony.

APPLIED ETHICS
The DC-10 Case: A Study in Applied Ethics, Technology, and Society. Fielder, John H and Birsch, Douglas.
Do the Poor Really Pay for the Higher Education of the Rich?. George, Rolf.
L'éthique de l'ingénierie: vers un nouveau paradigme. Racine, Louis.
La transformation des pratiques professionnelles: quelques conséquences pour l'éthique. Bourgeault, Guy.
The Gedankenexperiment Method of Ethics. Jackson, M W.
The Theory and Practice of Applied Ethics. Hoffmaster, C Barry.

APPLIED PHILOSOPHY
Back to Basics: Problems and Prospects for Applied Philosophy. Warren, Bill.
La suggestione delle filosofie di moda e il richiamo al senso comune: Tra Vico e Pareyson. Russo, F.
Some Complaints About and Some Defenses of Applied Philosophy. Kasachkoff, Tziporah.

APPRECIATION
Paintings as an Art in Psychoanalysis, Mind and Art, Hopkins, Jim (ed). Nehamas, Alexander.
The Appreciation and Perception of Easel Paintings. Wilsmore, S J.

APPROXIMATION
Idealization III. Brzezinski, Jerzy (ed) and Nowak, Leszek (ed).
A Certain Conception of the Calculus of Rough Sets. Bonikowski, Zbigniew.
Accuracy, Essentiality and Idealization in Idealization III, Brzezinski, Jerzy (ed). Paprzycki, Marcin and Paprzycka, Katarzyna.
Approximations and Logic. Marquis, Jean-Pierre.
Convergent Realism and Approximate Truth. Resnik, David B.
Towards an Expanded Epistemology for Approximations. Ramsey, Jeffry L.
Truth Approximation by Concretization in Idealization III, Brzenzinski, Jerzy (ed). Kuipers, T A F.

APULEIUS
Apuleius and the Concept of Philosophical Rhetoric. O'Brien, Maeve.

AQUINAS
"Doctor humanitatis": Implicazioni e sviluppi dell'antropologia tomistica alla luce degli Atti del IX Congresso Tomistico Internazionale. Turco, G.
"He spak to [T]hem that wolde lyve parfitly:" Thomas Aquinas, the Wife of Bath and the Two Senses of Religion. Sommers, Mary C.
Ad Litteram: Authoritative Texts and Their Medieval Readers. Jordan, Mark D (ed) and Emery, Jr, Kent (ed).
Aquinas on Human Action: A Theory of Practice. McInerny, Ralph.
Aquinas on Mind. Kenny, Anthony.
Aquinas: An Introduction to the Life and Work of the Great Medieval Thinker. Copleston, F C.
Consent: The Means to an Active Faith According to St Thomas Aquinas. Barad, Judith.
Critical Theoretical Inquiry on the Notion of Act in the Metaphysics of Aristotle and Saint Thomas Aquinas. Lu, Matthias.
Goodness and Rightness in Thomas Aquinas's "Summa Theologiae". Keenan, James F.
Person and Being. Clarke, W Norris.
The Perfection of the Universe According to Aquinas: A Teleological Cosmology. Blanchette, Oliva.
The Trinity: An Analysis of St Thomas Aquinas' 'Expositio' of the 'De Trinitate' of Boethius. Hall, Douglas.
What is God? The Selected Essays of Richard R La Croix. Lucey, Kenneth (ed).
A Contradiction in Saint Thomas's Teaching on Creation. Kondoleon, Theodore J.
A Note on Barth and Aquinas. Roy, Louis.
A Note on Contraries and the Incorruptibility of the Human Soul in St Thomas Aquinas. Wilhelmsen, Frederick.
Advice from a Thomist. Synan, Edward A.
An Analysis of the Use of Rights Language in Pre-Modern Catholic Social Thought. Brady, Bernard V.
Analogical Concepts: The Fourteenth-Century Background to Cajetan. Ashworth, E J.
Aquinas and Natural Human Fulfillment: Inconsistencies. Hayden, R Mary.
Aquinas and the Moral Status of Animals. Drum, Peter.
Aquinas on Disordered Pleasures and Conditions. Daly, Anthony C.
Aquinas on the Active Intellect. Haldane, John.
Aquinas on the Foundations of Knowledge. Stump, Eleonore.
Aquinas on the Resurrection of the Body. Brown, Montague.
Aquinas on the Sufferings of Job in Reasoned Faith, Stump, Eleonore (ed). Stump, Eleonore.
Aquinas on Theological Predication: A Look Backward and a Look Forward in Reasoned Faith, Stump, Eleonore (ed). Alston, W P.
Aquinas's Arguments for Spirit. Foster, David R.
Aquinas's Changing Evaluation of Platon on Creation. Johnson, Mark.
Aquinas's Concept of the Body and Out of Body Situations. Quinn, Patrick.
Aristotle and Aquinas on Cognition. Owens, Joseph.
Augustine and Aquinas on Original Sin and the Function of Political Authority. Weithman, Paul.
Bruce Marshall's Reading of Aquinas. Roy, Louis.
Conocimiento y concepto. Mayol, Víctor Velarde.
Consciousness and Self-Knowledge in Aquinas's Critique of Averroe's Psychology. Black, Deborah.
Der Übergang von der Physik zur Metaphysik im thomistischen Gottesbeweis. Kluxen, Wolfgang.
Distinguishing Charity as Goodness and Prudence as Rightness: A Key to Thomas's Secunda Pars. Keenan, James F.
Does Natural Philosophy Prove the Immaterial? A Rejoinder. Johnson, Mark.
Edith Stein: La dottrina degli Angeli. Tilliette, X.
El hombre entre dos hermenéuticas. Izquierdo Labeaga, José Antonio.
El Index Thomisticus y la semántica lingüística. De Gandolfi, M C Donadío M.
El poema de Parménides y la analogía según Santo Tomás de Aquino. Casaubón, Juan A.
Estetica, teologia e antropologia nel pensiero di Tommaso d'Aquino. Simi Varanelli, E.
Il posto della metafisica nel sapere umano: Il pensiero di Maimonide e eil suo influsso su S Tommaso d'Aquino. Pangallo, Mario.
Incommensurability and Aquinas's Metaphysics. Knasas, John F X.
Individuo y sociedad: En Duns Scot y en Tomás de Aquino. De Gandolfi, M C Donadío M.
Infallibility, Error, and Ignorance. Kretzmann, Norman.
Jephthah's Plight: Moral Dilemmas and Theism in Philosophical Perspectives, 5: Philosophy of Religion, 1991, Tomberlin, James E (ed). Mann, William E.
Kann Gott reale Beziehungen zu den Geschöpfen haben? Logisch-theologische Betrachtungen im Anschluss an Thomas von Aquin. Liske, Michael-Thomas.
L'analogia come chiave di lettura della creazione. Melchiorre, Virgilio.

ART

Oh Boy! You Too! Aesthetic Emotivism Reexamined in The Philosophy of A J Ayer, Hahn, Lewis Edwin (ed). Kivy, Peter.

On American and British Aesthetics. Diffey, T J.

On Defining Art Historically. Oppy, Graham.

On Functional Definitions of Art: A Response to Rowe. Oppy, Graham.

On Kitsch and Sentimentality. Solomon, Robert C.

On Looking at a Picture in Psychoanalysis, Mind and Art, Hopkins, Jim (ed). Budd, Malcolm.

On the Cognitive Triviality of Art. Stolnitz, Jerome.

On the Relationship of Art and World View in the Work of Jan Mukarovsky (in Czechoslovakian). Zouhar, J.

On the Suspicion of an Art Forgery. Cebik, L B.

On 'Free and Dependent Beauty'—A Rejoinder. Lorand, Ruth.

Oppressive Texts, Resisting Readers and the Gendered Spectator: The *New* Aesthetics. Devereaux, Mary.

Or What Should Not Be Said About Representation. Goodman, Nelson.

Original Representation and Anselm Kiefer's Postmodernism. Gilmour, John C.

Painting, Beholder and the Self in Psychoanalysis, Mind and Art, Hopkins, Jim (ed). Savile, Anthony.

Painting, Parapraxes, and Unconscious Intentions. Geller, Jeffery.

Paintings as an Art in Psychoanalysis, Mind and Art, Hopkins, Jim (ed). Nehamas, Alexander.

Philosophy, Aesthetics, and Theology: A Review of Hans Urs von Balthasar's *The Glory of the Lord*. Wood, Robert.

Physiology as Art: Nietzsche on Form. Rampley, Matthew.

Pictorial Ambiguity. Scheffler, Israel.

Plato and Performance. Gould, John.

Plato's Expression Theory of Art. Stecker, Robert A.

Pleasure: Reflections on Aesthetics and Feminism. Korsmeyer, Carolyn.

Postmodern Theory and Feminist Art Practice in Postmodernism and Society, Boyne, Roy (ed). Wolff, Janet.

Postmodernism and the Construct of the Divisible Self[. Dunning, William V.

Postmodernism and the Crisis in Criticism. Negrin, Llewellyn.

Prerogatives Without Restrictions in Philosophical Perspectives, 6: Ethics, 1992, Tomberlin, James E (ed). Scheffler, Samuel.

Process and Product: A Theory of Art. Sartwell, Crispin.

Prolegomena to Any Aesthetics of Rock Music. Baugh, Bruce.

Protected Space: Politics, Censorship, and the Arts. Devereaux, Mary.

Pure Historicism and the Heritage of Hero(in)es: Who Grows in Phillis Wheatley's Garden?. Silvers, Anita.

Realism about Aesthetic Properties. Goldman, Alan H.

Reconciling Analytic and Feminist Philosophy and Aesthetics. Margolis, Joseph.

Reference and Play. Scheffler, Israel.

Refining Art Historically. Levinson, Jerrold.

Refining Not Defining Art Historically. Haines, Victor.

Reflections on Time. Dunning, William V.

Reinterpreting Interpretation. Margolis, Joseph.

Remembrance of the Last "Nestor" of Czech Aesthetics (in Czechoslovakian). Sus, Oleg.

Renaturalizing Aesthetics. Dempster, Douglas.

Reply to Ryckman's "Dickie on Artifactuality". Dickie, George.

Representation and Make-Believe (Kendall L Walton, *Mimesis as Make-Believe*). Goldman, Alan H.

Response to Stecker's "Goldman on Interpreting Art and Literature". Goldman, Alan H.

Rethinking the Particular Forms of Art: Prolegomena to a Rational Reconstruction of Hegel's Theory of the Artforms. Winfield, Richard Dien.

Romanticism and Revolution. Cranston, Maurice.

S T Coleridge: El papel de la imaginación en el acto creador. Fonseca, Clotilde.

Santayana's Unbearable Lightness of Being: Aesthetics as a Prelude to Ontology. Alexander, Thomas M.

Sartre and the Poetics of History in The Cambridge Companion to Sartre, Howells, Christina (ed). Flynn, Thomas R.

Scandinavian Aesthetics. Hermerén, Göran.

Scruton and Reasons for Looking at Photographs. King, William L.

Seeing Aspects and Art: Tilghman and Wittgenstein. Cebik, L B.

Serious Watching in The Interpretive Turn, Hiley, David R (ed). Nehamas, Alexander.

Simone Weil on Beauty in Simone Weil's Philosophy of Culture, Bell, Richard (ed). Sherry, Patrick.

Six Theories in the Bedroom of *The Dead*. Garrett, Roland.

Some Reconceptions in Educational Theory: Irony and the Art of Comedy. Van Der Bogert, Frans.

Something I've Always Wanted to Know About Hanslick. Kivy, Peter.

Supervenience and the 'Science of the Beautiful'. Wicks, Robert.

Taste, Sublimity, and Genius in The Cambridge Companion to Kant, Guyer, Paul (ed). Schaper, Eva.

The "Dutch's Problem" and Leibniz's Point of View on the "Analytic Art". Gatto, Romano and Palladino, Franco.

The "Fundamental Concepts" of Pictures. Elkins, James.

The Aesthetic Essence of Art. Lind, Richard W.

The Aesthetics of Confucius (in Czechoslovakian). Paik, Ki-soo.

The Appreciation and Perception of Easel Paintings. Wilsmore, S J.

The Arts of Music. Alperson, Philip A.

The Birth of Postmodern Philosophy from the Spirit of Modern Art. Welsch, Wolfgang.

The Concept of Self and Postmodern Painting: Constructing a Post-Cartesian Viewer. Dunning, William V.

The Concept of Whole in the Structuralist Theory of Art (in Czechoslovakian). Grygar, Mojmir.

The Dislocation of the Architectural Self. Goldblatt, David A.

The Embodiment and Durations of Artworks. Krukowski, Lucian.

The Grotesque: Illusion versus Delusion in Aesthetic Illusion, Burwick, Frederick (ed). Burwick, Frederick.

The Hermeneutic of Art as Being-in-the-World (in Czechoslovakian). Calek, Oldrich.

The Idea of Abstraction in German Theories of the Ornament from Kant to Kandinsky. Morgan, David.

The Illusion of 'Illusion' in Aesthetic Illusion, Burwick, Frederick (ed). Watzlawick, Paul.

The Importance of Plato and Aristotle for Aesthetics. Halliwell, Stephen.

The Incoherence of the Aesthetic Response. Slater, Hartley.

The Institutionalization of a Discipline: A Retrospective of The Journal of Aesthetics and Art Criticism and the Amer Soc for Aesthetics, 1939-1992. Goehr, Lydia.

The Integrity of Aesthetics. Novitz, David.

The Inter-Relationship of Moral and Aesthetic Excellence. Bontekoe, Ron and Crooks, Jamie.

The Janus Aesthetic of Duchamp. McMahon, Cliff G.

The Journal of Aesthetics and Danto's Philosophical Criticism. Herwitz, Daniel A.

The Logic of Representation. Ujlaki, Gabriella.

The Origin of 'The Origin of the Work of Art' in Reading Heidegger: Commemorations, Sallis, John (ed). Taminiaux, Jacques M.

The Philosopher-Artist: A Note on Lyotard's Reading of Kant. Piché, Claude.

The Politics of Art: The Domination of Style and the Crisis in Contemporary Art. Wartofsky, Marx.

The Prisoner and the Prison in 2: Song of Macha's May (in Czechoslovakian). Otruba, Mojmir.

The Process/Product Dichotomy and Its Implications for Creative Dance. Bergmann, Sheryle.

The Purity of Aesthetic Value. Lorand, Ruth.

The Question of the End of Art and the Poetic Character of the World (in Czechoslovakian). Axelos, K.

The Rationale of Restoration. Savile, Anthony.

The Real or the Real? Chardin or Rothko? in Philosophy, Religion and the Spiritual Life, McGhee, Michael (ed). O'Hear, Anthony.

The Road from Nice to Necessary: Broudy's Rationale for Art Education. DiBlasio, Margaret Klempay.

The Role of Aesthetic Emotion in R G Collingwood's Conception of Creative Activity. Anderson, Douglas R and Hausman, Carl R.

The Role of Feminist Aesthetics in Feminist Theory. Hein, Hilde.

The Social Significance of Autonomous Art: Adorno and Bürger. Zuidervaart, Lambert.

The Socratic Quest in Art and Philosophy. Leddy, Thomas W.

The Sounds of Music: First Movement. Kimmel, Larry D.

The Story of Art is the Test of Time. Silvers, Anita.

The Third Man. Davidson, Donald.

The Tibetan *Tshogs Zhing* (Field of Assembly): General Notes on its Function, Structure and Contents. Jackson, Roger R.

The Work of Art as Psychoanalytical Object: Wollheim on Manet. Herwitz, Daniel A.

Theorizing about Art. Leddy, Thomas W.

Thomson's Problems with Kant: A Comment on Kant's Problems with Ugliness. Guyer, Paul.

Tradition, Innovation, and Aesthetic Experience. Jauss, Hans Robert.

Transforming Images: Photographs of Representations. Savedoff, Barbara.

Tribal Art and Artifact. Dutton, Denis.

Truth, Rightness, and Permanent Acceptability. Künne, Wolfgang.

Understanding: Art and Science. Elgin, Catherine Z.

Unkantian Notions of Disinterest. Zangwill, Nick.

Values of Art and Values of Community in On Community, Rouner, Leroy S (ed). Hepburn, R W.

Ventriloquism: Ecstatic Exchange and the History of the Artwork. Goldblatt, David A.

Vollenhoven's Legacy for Art Historiography. Seerveld, Calvin S.

What is Abstract About the Art of Music?. Walton, Kendall L.

Whitehead and Japanese Aesthetics. Mayada, Arlene M.

Why Art History Has a History. Carrier, David.

Why Philosophy of Art in Cross-Cultural Perspectives?. Moravcsik, Julius.

Why Spinoza Had No Aesthetics. Morrison, J C.

Wittgenstein, Art and Rule-Following. Oinam, Bhagat.

Works, Works Better. Schwartz, Robert.

Writing with Davidson: Some Afterthoughts after Doing *Blind Time IV: Drawing with Davidson*. Morris, Robert.

Zen and the Art of John Dewey. Earls, C Anthony.

'I Hard a Plaintive Melody' in Wittgenstein Centenary Essays, Griffiths, A Phillips (ed). Hanfling, Oswald.

'Too Low!': Frank Cioffi on Wittgenstein's *Lectures on Aesthetics*. Schroeder, Severin.

ART CRITICISM

Keeping Faith: Philosophy and Race in America. West, Cornell.

Figurative Language in Art History in The Language of Art History, Kemal, Salim (ed). Hausman, Carl R.

On Clement Greenberg's Formalistic Criticism (in Japanese). Kawata, Tokiko.

The Language of Art Criticism in The Language of Art History, Kemal, Salim (ed). Baxandall, Michael.

ART HISTORY

The Language of Art History. Kemal, Salim (ed) and Gaskell, Ivan (ed).

Erwin Panofsky and Karl Mannheim: A Dialogue on Interpretation. Hart, Joan.

Figurative Language in Art History in The Language of Art History, Kemal, Salim (ed). Hausman, Carl R.

The Styles of Art History: Entities or Processes?. MacDonald, Ray A.

ARTHUR, C
C J Arthur on Marx and Hegel on Alienation. Duquette, David A.

ARTIFACT
An Essay In Post-Romantic Literary Theory: Art, Artifact, and the Innocent Eye. Fleming, Bruce.

Artifact and Artistic Object (in Czechoslovakian). Chvatik, Kvetoslav.

Authors and Artifacts. Hilpinen, Risto.

Dickie on Artifactuality. Ryckman, Thomas C.

Further Fire: Reply to Haines. Levinson, Jerrold.

Reply to Ryckman's "Dickie on Artifactuality". Dickie, George.

Tribal Art and Artifact. Dutton, Denis.

ARTIFICIAL INTELLIGENCE
"Who Sees with Equal Eye,... Atoms or Systems into Ruin Hurl'd?". DeVries, Willem A.

Agency in Action: The Practical Rational Agency Machine. Coval, Samuel C and Campbell, P G.

Artificial Morality: Virtuous Robots for Virtual Games. Danielson, Peter.

Metaphor and Cognition. Indurkhya, Bipin.

Philosophy and Artificial Intelligence. Moody, Todd C.

Renewing Philosophy. Putnam, Hilary.

What Computers "Still" Can't Do: A Critique of Artificial Reason (Rev Ed). Dreyfus, Hubert L.

What Is Cognitive Science?. Von Eckardt, Barbara.

Artificial Decision-Making and Artificial Ethics: A Management Concern. Khalil, Omar E.

Because Mere Calculating Isn't Thinking: Comments on Hauser's "Why Isn't My Pocket Calculator a Thinking Thing?". Rapaport, William J.

Can Intelligence Be Artificial?. Dretske, Fred.

Comments on "Can Intelligence Be Artificial?". McNamara, Paul.

Comments on Bechtel's "The Case for Connectionism". Christie, Drew.

Confirmation and the Computational Paradigm (Or: Why Do You Think They Call It Artificial Intelligence?). Buller, David J.

Ein Grinsen ohne Katze: Von der Vergleichbarkeit zwischen 'künstlicher Intelligenz' und 'getrennten Intelligenzen'. Capurro, Rafael.

Expert Networks: Paradigmatic Conflict, Technological Rapprochement. Lacher, R C.

Friedman's Permanent Income Hypothesis as an Example of Diagnostic Reasoning. Janssen, Maarten C W and Tan, Yao-Hua.

Heidegger and Artificial Intelligence. Preston, Beth.

How to Build a Person: A Prolegomenon. Schiffer, Stephen.

Implications of Creation. Hiebeler, David E.

On Psychomimesis. Rosen, Robert.

On Thinking. Rotenstreich, Nathan.

Reaping the Whirlwind: Reply to Harnad's Other Bodies, Other Minds. Hauser, Larry.

Searle, Strong AI, and Two Ways of Sorting Cucumbers. Pfeifer, Karl.

Semantik und Handlungskausalität: Zur Diskussion über die 'künstliche Intelligenz'. Hörl, Christoph.

Societies of Minds: Science as Distributed Computing. Thagard, Paul.

The Case for Connectionism. Bechtel, William.

The Cognitive Revolution?. Casti, John L.

The Connectionism/Classical Battle to Win Souls. McLaughlin, Andrew C.

The Curious Case of the Chinese Gym. Copeland, B J.

The Education of Searle's Demon. Bombardi, Ronald J.

The Sense of 'Thinking'. Hauser, Larry.

Who's Afraid of the Turing Test?. Jacquette, Dale.

Why Isn't My Pocket Calculator a Thinking Thing?. Hauser, Larry.

ARTIST
The Rationality of Feeling: Understanding the Arts in Education. Best, David.

The Theory-Death of the Avant-Garde. Mann, Paul.

ARTISTIC
Fondazione, creazione e creazione artistica in Sartre. Gonzi, Andrea.

ARTS
see also Visual Art

Culture and Democracy: Social and Ethical Issues in Public Support for the Arts and Humanities. Buchwalter, Andrew.

Philosophy and Knowledge: A Commentary on Plato's "Theaetetus". Polansky, Ronald.

Aesthetics and Anti-Aesthetics in the Visual Arts. Mattick, Paul.

Aristotle's Peri hermeneias in Medieval Latin and Arabic Philosophy: Logic and the Linguistic Arts. Black, Deborah.

Correspondence, Projective Properties, and Expression in the Arts in The Language of Art History, Kemal, Salim (ed). Wollheim, Richard.

Subjectivity and the Arts: How Hepburn Could Be an Objectivist. Reddiford, Gordon.

The Nature and Limits of Analytic Aesthetics. Ahlberg, Lars-Olof.

ASCETICISM
Ascetic Figures Before and In Early Buddhism: The Emergence of Gautama as the Buddha. Wiltshire, Martin G.

Asceticism/Askesis in Ethics and Danger, Dallery, Arleen B (ed). McWhorter, Ladelle.

Nietzsche and the Suffering of the Indian Ascetic in Nietzsche and Asian Thought, Parkes, Graham R (ed). Parkes, Graham R (trans) and Hulin, Michel.

Shifting Sands: Foucault, Brown and the Framework of Christian Asceticism. Behr, John.

ASCRIPTION
Realism and Folk Psychology in the Ascription of Concepts. Franks, Bradley.

ASIAN
see also Oriental

East Asian Philosophy: With Historical Background and Present Influence. Ho, John E.

Nietzsche and Asian Thought. Parkes, Graham R (ed).

Self as Body in Asian Theory and Practice. Kasulis, Thomas P (ed).

Sinn und Ursprung. Gahlings, Ute.

Can Western Philosophers Understand Asian Philosophies? in Revisioning Philosophy, Ogilvy, James (ed). Walsh, Roger.

Inherent Limitations of the Confucian Tradition in Contemporary East Asian Business Enterprises. Oh, Tai K.

Nietzsche's Early Encounters with Asian Thought in Nietzsche and Asian Thought, Parkes, Graham R (ed). Parkes, Graham R (trans) and Figl, Johann.

Nietzsche's Trans-European Eye in Nietzsche and Asian Thought, Parkes, Graham R (ed). Sprung, G M C.

The Positive Contribution of Confucianism to the Modernization of East Asian Business Enterprises. Han, Cheong K.

The Problem of the Body in Nietzsche and Dōgen in Nietzsche and Asian Thought, Parkes, Graham (ed). Parkes, Graham R (trans) and Kōgaku, Arifuku.

ASSERTION
Probability and Assertion. Dudman, V H.

The Supplement of the Copula. Deely, John N.

ASSESSMENT
Calibrating Assessors of Technological and Environmental Risk. Shrader-Frechette, Kristin.

Evaluations as Assessments, Part I: Properties and Their Signifiers. Magnell, Thomas.

ASSOCIATION
Associations and Democracy. Cohen, Joshua and Rogers, Joel.

The American Marketing Association Code of Ethics: Instructions for Marketers. O'Boyle, Edward J and Dawson Jr, Lyndon E.

ASSUMPTION
Pre-Theoretical Assumptions in Evolutionary Explanations of Female Sexuality. Lloyd, Elisabeth.

ASTRONOMY
Ptolemy's Universe: The Natural Philosophical and Ethical Foundations of Ptolemy's Astronomy. Taub, Liba.

Revolution and Continuity. Barker, Peter (ed) and Ariew, Roger (ed).

Anaximander on the Stability of the Earth. Bodnár, István M.

Astronomy and Antirealism. Shapere, Dudley.

Criteria Concerning the Birth of a New Science in Greek Studies in the Philosophy and History of Science, Nicolacopoulos, Pantelis (ed). Kalfas, Vassilis.

Galileo, Aristotelian Science, and the Rotation of the Earth. Reitan, Eric A.

Innovation and Continuity in the History of Astronomy in Revolution and Continuity, Barker, Peter (ed). Gabbey, Alan.

The Blasphemy of Alfonso X in Revolution and Continuity, Barker, Peter (ed). Goldstein, Bernard.

The Heavens and Earth in Revolution and Continuity, Barker, Peter (ed). Pitt, Joseph C.

Transcendental Background to the Anthropic Reasoning in Cosmology. Balashov, Yuri V.

ASYMMETRY
Agency and Causal Asymmetry. Price, Huw.

Asymmetry and Non-Existence. Belshaw, Christopher.

Asymmetry and Self-Sacrifice. Sider, Theodore R.

Explanatory Unifcation and the Problem of Asymmetry. Barnes, Eric.

Linking Causal and Explanatory Asymmetry. Hausman, Daniel M.

Process Causality and Asymmetry. Dowe, Phil.

ATHEISM
see also Theism

"La Nature, la raison, l'expérience..." ou la réfutation du matérialisme dans l'apologétique chrétienne des Lumières. Boulad-Ayoub, Josiane.

"Nietzsche im christlichen Denken—am Beispiel Bernhard Weltes". Kienzler, Klaus.

Contemporary Perspectives on Religious Epistemology. Geivert, R Douglas (ed) and Sweetman, Brendan (ed).

George Berkeley: Alciphron in Focus. Berman, David (ed).

Homo Metaphisicus. Pezzimenti, Rocco.

The Portable Nietzsche. Kaufmann, Walter (ed).

Creation Stories, Religious and Atheistic. Leslie, John.

Inference to the Best Explanation and the New Teological Argument. Johnson, Jeffery L.

Introduction to the Methodology of Paraphronesis, With Example: Religion and Education in Postmodern America. Tandy, Charles.

Misologia ed irenismo: A proposito di un dialogo dottrinale e di ateismo in K Marx. Gnemmi, Angelo.

Non-Organic Theories of Value and Pointless Evil. O'Leary-Hawthorne, John.

Platon et la "ΔeinothΣ" Tragique. Bres, Yvon.

Quale liberazione per l'uomo dopo il marxismo?. Fidelibus, G.

Sartre's Adolescent Rejection of God. Santoni, Ronald E.

Simone de Beauvoir's Adieux: A Funeral Rite and a Literary Challenge in Sartre Alive, Aronson, Ronald (ed). Idt, Geneviève.

The Birth of God in God, Values, and Empiricism, Peden, Creighton (ed). Sontag, Frederick.

The Possibility of a Christian Ethic in the Philosophy of Nietzsche. Newcomer Scalo, Maria.

Was Hume an Atheist?. Andre, Shane.

AXIOMATIZABILITY

Three-Element Nonfinitely Axiomatizable Matrices. Palasinska, Katarzyna.

AXIOMATIZATION

A Note on the Interpretability Logic of Finitely Axiomatized Theories. De Rijke, Maarten.

A Variable-Free Logic for Mass Terms. Purdy, William C.

Axiomatizing Logics Closely Related to Varieties. Rautenberg, W.

The First Axiomatization of Relevant Logic. Dosen, Kosta.

Two Sequents of Locally Tabular Superintuitionistic Logic. Mardaev, S I.

AYER

A J Ayer Memorial Essays. Griffiths, A Phillips (ed).

The Philosophy of A J Ayer. Hahn, Lewis E (ed).

A J Ayer's Philosophical Method in The Philosophy of A J Ayer, Hahn, Lewis E (ed). Eames, Elizabeth R.

An Interview with A J Ayer. Price, Thomas, Russell, Robert and Kennett, Stephen.

An Interview with A J Ayer in A J Ayer Memorial Essays, Griffiths, A Phillips (ed). Honderich, Ted.

Ayer and Ontology in The Philosophy of A J Ayer, Hahn, Lewis Edwin (ed). Quinton, Lord.

Ayer and Pragmatism in The Philosophy of A J Ayer, Hahn, Lewis E (ed). Campbell, James.

Ayer and the Vienna Circle in The Philosophy of A J Ayer, Hahn, Lewis Edwin (ed). Hung, Tscha.

Ayer and World Views in A J Ayer Memorial Essays, Griffiths, A Phillips (ed). Copleston, F C.

Ayer on Free Will and Determinism in The Philosophy of A J Ayer, Hahn, Lewis Edwin (ed). O'Connor, D J.

Ayer on Metaphysics, a Critical Commentary by a Kind of Metaphysician in The Philosophy of A J Ayer, Hahn, Lewis Edwin (ed). Naess, Arne.

Ayer on Morality and Feeling: From Subjectivism to Emotivism and Back? in The Philosophy of A J Ayer, Hahn, Lewis Edwin (ed). Wiggins, David.

Ayer on Other Minds in The Philosophy of A J Ayer, Hahn, Lewis Edwin (ed). Sprigge, T L S.

Ayer on Perception and Reality in The Philosophy of A J Ayer, Hahn, Lewis Edwin (ed). Sosa, Ernest.

Ayer's Attack on Metaphysics in A J Ayer Memorial Essays, Griffiths, A Phillips (ed). MacKinnon, D M.

Ayer's Ethical Theory in A J Ayer Memorial Essays, Griffiths, A Phillips (ed). Wiggins, David.

Ayer's Hume in The Philosophy of A J Ayer, Hahn, Lewis Edwin (ed). Stroud, Barry G.

Ayer's Philosophy of Logic and Mathematics in The Philosophy of A J Ayer, Hahn, Lewis Edwin (ed). Quesada, Francisco M.

Ayer's Place in the History of Philosophy in A J Ayer Memorial Essays, Griffiths, A Phillips (ed). Quinton, Anthony.

Ayer's Treatment of Russell in The Philosophy of A J Ayer, Hahn, Lewis Edwin (ed). Riverso, Emanuele.

Ayer's Views on Meaning-Rules in The Philosophy of A J Ayer, Hahn, Lewis Edwin (ed). Pears, David.

Ayer: The Man, the Philosopher, the Teacher in A J Ayer Memorial Essays, Griffiths, A Phillips (ed). Wollheim, Richard.

Ayerian 'Qualia' and the Empiricist Heritage in The Philosophy of A J Ayer, Hahn, Lewis Edwin (ed). Park, Désirée.

My Mental Development in The Philosophy of A J Ayer, Hahn, Lewis E (ed). Ayer, A J.

On Sir Alfred Ayer's Theory of Truth in The Philosophy of A J Ayer, Hahn, Lewis E (ed). Gochet, Pual.

Remarks on Logical Empiricism and Some of Ayer's Achievements in The Philosophy of A J Ayer, Hahn, Lewis Edwin (ed). Polikarov, Azarya and Ginev, Dimitri.

Still More of My Life in The Philosophy of A J Ayer, Hahn, Lewis E (ed). Ayer, A J.

BABY

Scenes from a Newborn Life (in Dutch). Hendriks, Ruud.

BACCARINI, E

Reply to Elvio Baccarini's "Rational Consensus and Coherence Methods in Ethics". Lehrer, Keith.

BACHELARD

Emile Meyerson, philosophe oublié. Largeault, Jean.

BACHRACH, J

Literature and Representation: A Note. Pollard, D E B.

BACON

Nietzsche and Modern Times. Lampert, Laurence.

The Essays—Francis Bacon. Bacon, Francis and Pitcher, John (ed).

Bacon's Project: Should It Be Given Up?. Schäfer, Lothar.

Baconian Science in Post-Bellum America: Charles Peirce's "Neglected Argument for the Reality of God". Nadelman, Healther L.

Bentham, Bacon and the Movement for the Reform of English Law Reporting. Munday, Roderick.

The Empire of Progress: Bacon's Improvement Upon Machiavelli. Faulkner, Robert K.

BACTERIA

The Development of a Scientific Specialty: The Case of Microbial Genetics—A Review of *The Emergence of Bacterial Genetics* by Thomas D Brock. Fantini, Bernardino.

BAD

A Change in Plato's Conception of the Good. Robinson, Jim.

The Suberogatory. Driver, Julia.

Toward an Ontology of Virtue Ethics. Savarino, Mary Ella.

BAIER, A

Critical Notice of Annette Baier's *A Progress of Sentiments*. Russell, Paul.

BAKHTIN, M

The Dialogics of Critique. Gardiner, Michael.

Bakhtin's Ethical Vision. Lynch, Richard A.

Hermeneutics and Genre: Bakhtin and the Problem of Communicative Interaction in The Interpretive Turn, Hiley, David R (ed). Kent, Thomas.

BAKHURST, D

Re-Reading Soviet Philosophy: Bakhurst on Ilyenkov. Larvor, Brendan.

BALANCE

Community Ecology, Scale, and the Instability of the Stability Concept. McCoy, E D and Shrader-Frechette, Kristin.

BALDWIN, T

More on Moore. Welbourne, Michael.

BALLARD, D

The Connectionism/Classical Battle to Win Souls. McLaughlin, Andrew C.

BALLET

Thoughts on Duncan's Dancing Masters. Whittock, Trevor.

BALZER, W

La noción de modelo en los análisis de la concepción estructuralista. Falguera, José Luis.

BANNET, E

Tomb of the Sacred Prostitute: 'The Symposium' in Shadow of Spirit, Berry, Philippa (ed). Bell, Shannon.

BARFIELD, O

The "Other" Postmodern Theorist: Owen Barfield's Concept of the Evolution of Consciousness. Hocks, Richard A.

BARGAINING

Second Thoughts About Bluffing. Carson, Thomas.

BARINDUCTION

Proof-Theoretic Investigations on Kruskal's Theorem. Rathjen, Michael and Weiermann, Andreas.

BARKER, J

The Nature and Assessment of Practical Reasoning: A Reply to John A Barker and Richard Foley. Audi, Robert.

BARNAVE, J

J Barnave: Philosopher of a Revolution. Webster, Alison.

BARNES, B

Barnes, Bloor, and the Sociology of Knowledge. Keita, Lansana.

Emergence of a Radical Sociology of Scientific Knowledge. Zibakalam, Saeid.

BARNES, J

A Note on Barnes's Parmenides. Ketchum, Richard J.

BARNETT, R

The Nature of University Education Reconsidered (A Response to Ronald Barnett's *The Idea of Higher Education*). Aviram, Aharon.

BAROQUE

The Crisis of the Subject: From Baroque to Postmodern. Van Reijen, Willem.

BARRESI, J

The Absent Ontology of Society: Response to Juckes and Barresi. Manicas, Peter T.

BARRETT, W

How Sexist is Sartre?. Burstow, Bonnie.

BARTH

A Note on Barth and Aquinas. Roy, Louis.

Aus dem Dunklen ins Helle: Wissenschaft und Theologie im Denken von Heinrich Scholz. Molendijk, A L.

The Revelation of the Holy Other as the Wholly Other: Between Barth's Theology of the Word and Levinas's Philosophy of Saying. Ward, Graham.

BARTHES, R

In Praise of True Pluralism. Harris, Wendell V.

L'Esprit Objectif as a Theory of Language. Martinot, Steve.

Leituras de Barthes: II—Compromiso discreto, luita contínua. Soto, Luis García.

BARTHOLOMEW, B

Locations of Inner Self. Karandikar, A G.

BARTKY, S

Bartky, Domination, and the Subject. Kellner, Douglas.

Bribery and Intimidation: A Discussion of Sandra Lee Bartky's *Femininity and Domination*. Kotzin, Rhoda Hadassa.

Comments on Sandra Lee Bartky's *Femininity and Domination*. Mickett, Carole A.

In Defense of Femininity: Commentary on Sandra Bartky's *Femininity and Domination*. Schweickart, Patrocinio P.

Reading Bartky: Identity, Identification, and Critical Self Reflection. Bar On, Bat-Ami.

BARTLEY, W

Unfathomed Knowledge, Unmeasured Worth and Growth?. Hauptli, Bruce.

BARWISE, J

Anti-Foundation and Self-Reference. McLarty, Colin.

Twenty-Five Basic Theorems in Situation and World Theory. Zalta, Edward N.

BASINGER, D

How Good/Bad is Middle Knowledge? A Reply to Basinger. Hasker, William.

Religious Pluralism and the Rationality of Religious Belief. Hick, John.

BASSON, A

Language and Philosophy in Logical Foundations, Mahalingam, Indira (ed). Burbidge, John W.

BASTIAT, F

Economics as Ethics: Bastiat's Nineteenth Century Interpretation. O'Donnell, M G.

BEING

Truth, Adequacy and Being in Spinoza's *Ethics*. Richey, Lance B.

Where Deathless Horses Weep in Reading Heidegger: Commemorations, Sallis, John (ed). Krell, David Farrell.

Why Heidegger's Godot Might not be Worth the Wait. Bruin, John.

Wild Being, the Prepredicative and Expression: How Merleau-Ponty Uses Phenomenology to Develop an Ontology. Godway, Eleanor M.

'Being and Time' and 'The Basic Problems of Phenomenology' in Reading Heidegger: Commemorations, Sallis, John (ed). Von Herrmann, Friedrich-Wilhelm.

BEKKER, B

Balthasar Bekker and the Crisis of Cartesianism. Fix, Andrew.

BELIEF

see also Faith

"The Will to Believe": James's Defense of Religious Intolerance. Gordon, Jeffrey.

"'Thinking', A Widely Ramified Concept'. Hanfling, Oswald.

A Spinozistic Account of Self-Deception: NASS Monograph #1 (1993). Ablondi, Frederick R.

An Essay on Belief and Acceptance. Cohen, L Jonathan.

Aufgeklärtes Eigeninteresse: Eine Theorie theoretischer und praktischer Rationalität. Gosepath, Stefan.

Balance and Refinement: Beyond Coherence Methods of Moral Inquiry. DePaul, Michael.

Belief Base Dynamics. Hansson, Sven Ove.

Contemporary Perspectives on Religious Epistemology. Geivert, R Douglas (ed) and Sweetman, Brendan (ed).

Contemporary Readings in Epistemology. Goodman, Michael and Snyder, Robert A.

Direct Reference: From Language to Thought. Rashed, Roshdi.

Epistemic Virtue and Doxastic Responsibility. Montmarquet, James.

Hegel on Logic and Religion: The Reasonableness of Christianity. Burbidge, John W.

Knowledge and Belief. Schmitt, Frederick.

Modalities: Philosophical Essays. Marcus, Ruth Barcan.

Morality and the Emotions. Oakley, Justin.

On Feeling, Knowing, and Valuing: Selected Writings—Max Scheler. Scheler, Max.

Paradigms and Barriers: How Habits of Mind Govern Scientific Beliefs. Margolis, Howard.

Reasoning: A Practical Guide. Pinto, Robert C and Blair, John Anthony.

Renewing Philosophy. Putnam, Hilary.

Status y verificación de la creencia religiosa. Tomasini Bassols, Alejandro.

Talk About Beliefs. Crimmins, Mark.

The Life of Irony and the Ethics of Belief. Wisdo, David.

The Nyaya Theory of Linguistic Performance: A New Interpretation of Tattvacintamani. Mukhopadhyay, P K.

Transition to Modernity: Essays on Power, Wealth and Belief. Hall, John A (ed) and Jarvie, I C (ed).

Working Without a Net: A Study of Egocentric Epistemology. Foley, Richard.

A Coherence Theory of Autonomy. Ekstrom, Laura Waddell.

A Mistake about Foundationalism. Rappaport, Steven.

Against Coherence. Fritzman, J M.

Another Day for an Old Dogma. Levy, Robert.

Are Convenient Fictions Harmful to Your Health?. Garner, Richard T.

Audi on Practical Reasoning. Foley, Richard.

Backward-Induction Arguments: A Paradox Regained. Sobel, Jordan Howard.

Being Knowingly Incoherent. Foley, Richard.

Belief Contraction Without Recovery. Hansson, Sven Ove.

Belief vs Commitment, Validity vs Value: A Response to Ward Goodenough. Brink, T L.

Belief, Confidence and the Method of Science. Hookway, Christopher.

Belief-In and Belief In God. Williams, John N.

Believer Versus Unbeliever: Reflections on the Wittgensteinian Perspective. Chaturvedi, Vibha.

Can Religion Give Science a Heart?. Kozhamthadam, Job.

Certainty Made Simple in Certainty and Surface in Epistemology and Philosophical Method, Martinich, A P (ed). Matson, Wallace I.

Changing Beliefs Rationally: Some Puzzles in Cognition, Semantics and Philosophy, Ezquerro, Jesús (ed). Edgington, Dorothy.

Children are Not Meant to be Studied.... Hart, W A.

Coercion and the Hiddenness of God. Murray, Michael J.

Cognitive Spontaneity, Coherence, and Internalism in the Justification of Empirical Belief. Silvers, Stuart.

Conceptual Analysis and the Essence of Knowledge. Taylor, James E.

Confirmational Holism and Bayesian Epistemology. Christensen, David.

Credere e sapere. Iwand, Hans Joachim.

Daniel C Dennett's *The Intentional Stance*. Lumsden, David.

Deception and Belief in Parmenides' *Doxa*. Curd, Patricia Kenig.

Diagnosis of Ailing Belief Sysems. Titiev, Robert.

Direct and Indirect Belief. Brown, Curtis.

Does an Inferential Role Semantics Rest Upon a Mistake?. Boghossian, Paul.

Doubt, Scepticism, and a Serious Justification Game. Schramm, Alfred.

Emergence of a Radical Sociology of Scientific Knowledge. Zibakalam, Saeid.

Empiricism, Fideism and The Nature of Religious Belief. Sweet, William and O'Connell, Colin.

Envy and Pity. Ben-Ze'ev, Aaron.

Epistemic Virtue and Doxastic Responsibility. Montmarquet, James.

Epistemologies in Religious Healing. Hufford, David J.

Externalism (in Chinese). Huang, Yih-mei.

Faith, Belief, and Rationality in Philosophical Perspectives, 5: Philosophy of Religion, 1991, Tomberlin, James E (ed). Audi, Robert.

Fallibilism and Rational Belief. Weintraub, Ruth.

Fear Without Belief. Morreall, John.

Fiction and the Emotions. Neill, Alex.

From Cognitive Science to Folk Psychology: Computation, Mental Representation, and Belief. Horgan, Terence.

Furthering Stich's Fragmentation. Hetherington, Stephen Cade.

Genova, Davidson and Content-Scepticism. Brueckner, Anthony.

Gilson tra Roma e Lovanio. Mangiagalli, M.

Group Membership and Political Obligation. Gilbert, Margaret.

How To Do Things On Stage. Saltz, David Z.

Hume on Natural Belief and Original Principles. Gorman, Michael M.

Hume's Theory of Belief. Gorman, Michael M.

I Falsely Believe that *P*. Crimmins, Mark.

If There Be a God, From Whence Proceed So Many Evils?. Chakraborty, Nirmalya N.

Impressions and Ideas: Vivacity as Verisimilitude. Waxman, Wayne.

Induction and the Gettier Problem. Creath, Richard.

Integrity or "He Who Steals My Purse". Witmer, Judith T.

Intention in Wittgenstein. Bhat, P R.

Intentionality and Teleological Error. Pietroski, Paul.

Interaction with the Reader in Kant's Transcendental Theory of Method. Wilson, Catherine.

Internalistic Foundationalism and the Justification of Memory Belief. Senor, Thomas D.

Is Conceivability a Guide to Possibility?. Yablo, Stephen.

Is It Possible that Belief Isn't Necessary?. Macpherson, Brian.

Is Knowledge Merely True Belief?. Skidmore, Arthur.

Is the Best Good Enough?. Lipton, Peter.

Jump with Common Spirits: Is An *Ad Populum* Argument Fallacious?. Wreen, Michael J.

Justified False Belief. Rajotte, Mark J.

Knowledge and Belief in Plato's 'Republic' in Greek Studies in the Philosophy and History of Science, Nicolacopoulos, Pantelis (ed). Santas, Gerasimos.

Malcolm and Searle on 'Intentional Mental States'. Hacker, P M S.

Modes of Presentation?. Yagisawa, Takashi.

More on Moore. Welbourne, Michael.

Mutual Beliefs and Social Characteristics in Advances in Scientific Philosophy, Schurz, Gerhard (ed). Tuomela, Raimo.

Natural Theology and Positive Predication: Might Maimonides Be a Guide? in Prospects for Natural Theology, Long, Eugene Thomas (ed). Ferré, Frederick.

Nostalgia and the Nostalgic. Reeves, Robert A.

Obstinacy in Religious Belief. Groothuis, Douglas.

On a Pragmatic Argument Against Pragmatism in Ethics. Mercer, Mark Douglas.

On Being One's Own Worst Enemy. Champlin, T S.

On Keith Lehrer's Belief in Acceptance. Piller, Christian.

On the Coherence of Instrumentalism. Kukla, Andre.

On the Ethics of Belief. Nathan, Nicholas.

On the Parallelism between Theoretical and Practical Reasoning in Psychoanalysis, Mind and Art, Hopkins, Jim (ed). Pears, David.

On the Roles of Trustworthiness and Acceptance. David, Marian.

On Why Philosophers Redefine their Subject in The Impulse to Philosophise, Griffiths, A Phillips (ed). Brown, Stuart.

Paradigms of Belief, Theory and Metatheory. Sperry, Roger W.

Perception, Concepts, and Memory. Martin, M G F.

Perry on Indexical Semantics and Belief States. Roberts, Lawrence D.

Philosophy and *Weltanschauung*. Nielsen, Kai.

Pictures of Socrates. Thompson, Caleb.

Positional Objectivity. Sen, Amartya.

Possible Logics for Belief. Van Der Hoek, W and Meyer, J J C.

Rationalising Belief. Leon, Mark.

Rationality and Epistemic Paradox. Kroon, Frederick.

Rejoinder to Bruce Marshall. Crosson, Frederick.

Religious Belief in Wittgenstein's Intentions, Canfield, J V (ed). Cook, John W.

Religious Pluralism and the Rationality of Religious Belief. Hick, John.

Reply to Alfred Schramm's "Doubt, Scepticism, and a Serious Justification Game". Lehrer, Keith.

Reply to Christian Piller's "On Keith Lehrer's Belief in Acceptance". Lehrer, Keith.

Reply to Fred Dretske's "Two Conceptions of Knowledge: Rational versus Reliable Belief". Lehrer, Keith.

Reply to Marian David's "On the Roles of Trustworthiness and Acceptance". Lehrer, Keith.

Reply to Shope's "You Know What You Falsely Believe". Pollock, John.

Representation *versus* Mirroring: A Cognitivist Response to Rorty. Shashidharan, Suryaprabha and Gupta, Amitabha.

Resolving Epistemic Dilemmas. Odegard, Douglas.

Sartre's Adolescent Rejection of God. Santoni, Ronald E.

Schiffer on Modes of Presentation. Adams, Fred, Stecker, Robert and Fuller, Gary.

Sense, Necessity and Belief. Richard, Mark E.

Similarity Semantics and Minimal Changes of Belief. Hansson, Sven Ove.

Simple Attentive Miscalculation. Ruben, David-Hillel.

Social Atmosphere. Gupta, R K.

St Thomas, James Ross, and Exemplarism: A Reply. Dewan, Lawrence.

Substitution and the Explanation of Action. Bryans, Joan.

Suspicion in Wittgenstein's Intentions, Canfield, J V (ed). White, Alan.

BELIEF

Tacit Belief and Other Doxastic Attitudes. Manfredi, Pat A.

Tacitness and Virtual Beliefs. Crimmins, Mark.

Technology and Change in Religious Belief. Sweet, William.

Ten Questions for Psychoanalysis. Phillips, D Z.

The Birth of God in God, Values, and Empiricism, Peden, Creighton (ed). Sontag, Frederick.

The Case against Value-Free Belief in Advances in Scientific Philosophy, Schurz, Gerhard (ed). Klevakina, Elena.

The Epistemology of Belief and the Epistemology of Degrees of Belief. Foley, Richard.

The Examined Life. Dalton, Peter C.

The Floyd Puzzle: Reply to Yagisawa. Adams, Fred, Stecker, Robert and Fuller, Gary.

The Laws of Thought. Kornblith, Hilary.

The Miracle of Minimal Foundationalism: Religious Experience and Justified Belief. Bagger, Matthew C.

The Objective Dimension of Believing *De Re*. Kvart, Igal.

The Place of Experience in the Grounds of Religious Belief in Our Knowledge of God, Clark, Kelly James (ed). Alston, William.

The Practice of Education and the Courtship of Youthful Sensibility. Hogan, Pádrig.

The Principle of the Topical Localization of Symbols and the Meaning of the 'Ultimate Meaning'. Dhooghe, Paul F and Peeters, Guido.

The Proofs of Natural Theology and the Unbeliever. Sparrow, M F.

The Rational Imperative to Believe. Gordon, Jeffrey.

The Rational Role of Experience. Martin, Michael.

The Rationality of Religious Belief. Rowe, William.

The Relation between Belief and Knowledge in Spinoza's Hermeneutical Theory (in Dutch). Vedder, Ben.

The Sentiment of Pragmatism: From the Pragmatism Maxim to a Pragmatic Faith. Ochs, Peter.

The Two Faces of Quine's Naturalism. Haack, Susan.

The Unnamed Fifth: *Republic* 369d. Page, Carl.

Theantropic Foundations of Religious Beliefs. Woznicki, Andrew N.

Thoughts Without Objects. Adams, Fred, Fuller, Gary and Stecker, Robert.

Trust and Testimony: Nine Arguments on Testimonial Knowledge. Govier, T.

Twin Earth Revisited. Stalnaker, Robert.

Two Conceptions of Knowledge: Rational versus Reliable Belief. Dretske, Fred.

Two Routes to Narrow Content: Both Dead Ends. Manfredi, Pat A.

Understanding Synonyms Without Knowing that They are Synonymous. Rieber, Steven.

Undoubted Truth. McCarty, David Charles.

Was William James a Closet Nihilist: A Further Contribution to URAM William James Studies (*URAM* 2:40-58, 73-78). Crosby, Donald A.

Why Believe What People Say?. Stevenson, Leslie.

Why Is There a Discussion of False Belief in the *Theaetetus*?. Benson, Hugh H.

Why We Need Proper Function. Plantinga, Alvin.

William James and the Logic of Faith. Pappas, Gregory.

William James's Theory of Truth. Chisholm, Roderick M.

Wittgenstein on Believing in 'Philosophical Investigations' Part II in Wittgenstein's Philosophical Investigations, Arrington, Robert T (ed). Hunter, J F M.

Wittgenstein on Religious Belief in On Community, Rouner, Leroy S (ed). Putnam, Hilary.

Wittgenstein, Solipsism, and Religious Belief. Huff, Douglas.

You Know What You Falsely Believe (Or: Pollock, Know Theyself!). Shope, Robert K.

'Hume's Theorem' Concerning Miracles. Millican, Peter.

BELIEVING

Humanism's Thorn: The Case of the Bright Believers. Pasquarello, Tony.

What's the Good of Trying?. Lee, Richard T.

BELL'S THEOREM

Bell's Theorem and Determinism. Shanks, Niall.

BELL, C

Sir Charles Bell and the Vitalist Controversy in the Early Nineteenth Century in The Crisis in Modernism, Burwick, Frederick (ed). Burwick, Frederick.

BELL, D

Husserl. Mohanty, J N.

Religion and Postmodernism in Postmodernism/ Jameson/ Critique, Kellner, Douglas M (ed). O'Neill, John.

BELL, J

Bell's Inequality, Information Transmission, and Prism Models. Maudlin, Tim.

Mach's Razor, Duhem's Holism, and Bell's Theorem. Rohatyn, Dennis A and Labson, Sam.

BELLINI, G

Renaissance Madonnas and the Fantasies of Freud. Wiseman, Mary.

Two Women by Giovanni Bellini. Wiseman, Mary Bittner.

BELNAP, N

Exhaustively Axiomatizing RMO with an Appropriate Extension of Anderson and Belnap's "Strong and Natural List of Valid Entailments". Méndez, José M.

Questions and Quantifiers. Brown, Mark.

BELSEY, C

F R Leavis: Intuitionist?. Haynes, Anthony.

BELSHAW, C

The Asymmetry of Early Death and Late Birth. Brueckner, Anthony and Fischer, John Martin.

BELZER, B

Response: Applications of the Theory in John Searle and His Critics, Lepore, Ernest (ed). Searle, John R.

BEN-ZEEV, A

A Note on Schadenfreude and Proverbs 17:5. Harvey, Warren Z.

BENARDETE, J

Metaphysics: The Logical Approach, by José Benardete. Cleveland, Timothy.

BENARDETE, S

Socrates' Second Sailing. Tejera, Victorino.

Sailing Through the *Republic*. Stalley, R F.

BENDER, J

Chronotypes: The Construction of Time by John Bender and David E Wellbery. O'Malley, Michael.

BENEFICENCE

Beneficence and Self-Love: A Kantian Perspective. Hill Jr, Thomas E.

BENEVOLENCE

Bertrand Russell's Characterization of Benevolent Love. Kohl, Marvin.

Revolutionary Writing, Moral Philosophy, and Universal Benevolence in the Eighteenth Century. Radcliffe, Evan.

BENJAMIN, W

Melancholy Dialectics. Pensky, Max.

Framing Redemption in Ethics and Danger, Dallery, Arleen B (ed). Comay, Rebecca.

L'entrelacs du temps. Proust, Françoise.

BENNETT, J

Events, Counterfactuals, and Speed. Lombard, Lawrence Brian.

Response: Meaning, Intentionality, and Speech Acts in John Searle and His Critics, LePore, Ernest (ed). Searle, John R.

BENNETT, W

Teaching Ethics in Higher Education: Goals, and the Implications of the Empirical Research on Moral Development. Annis, David B.

BENTHAM

Bentham and the Nineteenth-Century Revolution in Government in Victorian Liberalism, Bellamy, Richard (ed). Conway, Stephen.

Bentham on Spanish Protectionism. Schwartz, Pedro and Braun, Carlos Rodriguez.

Bentham, Bacon and the Movement for the Reform of English Law Reporting. Munday, Roderick.

Corrugated Subjects: The Three Axes of Personhood. Clifford, Michael.

Foucault and Bentham: A Defence of Panopticism. Semple, Janet.

Hume, Bentham, and the Social Contract. Wolff, Jonathan.

Jeremy Bentham and the Real Property Commission of 1828. Sokol, Mary.

The Origin of Liberal Utilitarianism in Victorian Liberalism, Bellamy, Richard (ed). Rosen, Frederick.

BENTON, T

The Call of Nature: A Reply to Ted Benton and Tim Hayward. Reid, Michael.

BERCIANO, M

El preguntar heideggeriano sobre el ser: Comentario a un libro de Modesto Berciano. Soto, M Jesús.

BERDYAEV

The Desire To Be God: Freedom and the Other in Sartre and Berdyaev. McLachlan, James Morse.

Existential, Literary or Machine Persons?: Analysis of McLachlan, Adams and Steinbeck. Hart, Richard E.

Nicolas Berdyaev's Existentialist Personalism. McLachlan, James M.

The Path to Truth—Ibn-'Arabī and Nikolai Berdiaev (Two Types of Mystical Philosophizing). Smirnov, Andrei.

The Social Philosophy of N Berdiaev in Light of *Perestroika*. Adiushkin, V N.

BERGMANN, G

New Foundations of Ontology. Heald, William (ed), Bergmann, Gustav and Allaire, Edwin B.

On the Need for a Metaphysics of Justification. Bradshaw, D E.

BERGMANN, H

La foi messianique de Hugo Bermann. Kluback, William.

BERGSON

Bergson and Sartre: The Rise of French Existentialism in The Crisis in Modernism, Burwick, Frederick (ed). Gunter, P A Y.

Bergson and the Discourse of the Moderns in The Crisis in Modernism, Burwick, Frederick (ed). Lehan, Richard.

Bergson and the Politics of Vitalism in The Crisis in Modernism, Burwick, Frederick (ed). Schwartz, Sanford.

Bergson's Concept of Order. Lorand, Ruth.

Bergson's Vitalism in the Light of Modern Biology in The Crisis in Modernism, Burwick, Frederick (ed). Wolsky, Maria de Issekutz and Wolsky, Alexander A.

Deleuze's Bergson: Bergson Redux in The Crisis in Modernism, Burwick, Frederick (ed). Douglass, Paul.

El cuerpo como educador del espíritu en la Filosofía de Bergson. Sánchez Rey, María del Carmen.

Henri Bergson in Founders of Constructive Postmodern Philosophy, Griffin, David Ray (& others). Gunter, Pete A Y.

Microphysical Indeterminacy and Freedom: Bergson and Peirce in The Crisis in Modernism, Burwick, Frederick (ed). Capek, Milic.

Modern Times: Stein, Bergson, and the Ellipses of 'American' Writing in The Crisis in Modernism, Burwick, Frederick (ed). Riddel, Joseph N.

Samuel Taylor Coleridge and the Romantic Background to Bergson in The Crisis in Modernism, Burwick, Frederick (ed). Haeger, Jack H.

Some Under- and Over-Rated Great Philosophers. Hartshorne, Charles.

Unmasking Bergson's Idealism. Howe, Lawrence W.

BERKELEY
"Magic Buffalo" and Berkeley's *Theory of Vision*: Learning in Society. Levy, David M.
Berkeley's Philosophy of Mathematics. Jesseph, Douglas M.
George Berkeley: Alciphron in Focus. Berman, David (ed).
A Response to M A Stewart's 'Berkeley's Introduction Draft'. Belfrage, Bertil.
Berkeley and Scepticism: A Fatal Dalliance. Imlay, Robert A.
Berkeley: How to Make a Mistake. Levine, Michael.
Bishop Berkeley Exorcises the Infinite: Fuzzy Consequences of Strict Finitism. Levy, David M.
Descartes, Leibniz and Berkeley on Whether We Can Dream Marks on the Waking State. Wahl, Russell and Westphal, Jonathan.
Kant and Dogmatic Idealism: A Defense of Kant's Refutation of Berkeley. Morgan, Vance.
The Nature of Mind. Lucash, Frank S.
The Neoplatonic Conception of Nature in More, Cudworth, and Berkeley in The Uses of Antiquity, Gaukroger, Stephen (ed). Jacob, Alexander.

BERLEANT, A
Aesthetics and Engagement. Carlson, Allen.

BERLIN, I
Isaiah Berlin: A Celebration. Margalit, Edna (ed) and Margalit, Avishai (ed).
Towards a Postmodern Ethics: Sir Isaiah Berlin and John Caputo. McKinney, Ronald H.

BERNAT, J
Commentary on "How Much of the Brain Must Die in Brain Death". Dagi, Teo Forcht.

BERNHARDT, W
A God of Power or a God of Value in God, Values, and Empiricism, Peden, Creighton (ed). Templin, J Alton.
Bernhardt's Analysis of the Function of Religion in God, Values, and Empiricism, Peden, Creighton (ed). Tremmel, William C.
Bernhardt's Philosophy and the Study of World Religions in God, Values, and Empiricism, Peden, Creighton (ed). Kirk, James.
William Bernhardt's Theory of Religious Values in God, Values, and Empiricism, Peden, Creighton (ed). Milligan, Charles S.
William H Bernhardt's Value Hypothesis: A Systematic Approach in God, Values, and Empiricism, Peden, Creighton W (ed). Brush, Francis.

BERNSTEIN, E
Historical Materialism and Ethics: Eduard Bernstein's Revisionist Perspectives. Steger, Manfred.

BERNSTEIN, R
Incommensurability and Aquinas's Metaphysics. Knasas, John F X.
Review: Bernstein, McCarthy and the Evolution of Critical Theory. Couture, Tony.

BERRY, W
The Political Economy of Community. Farr, Richard.

BERTOCCI, P
Personhood: F R Tennant and Peter Bertocci in the Light of Contemporary Physics. Knott, T Garland.

BERULLE, P
L'image de l'homme chez Descartes et chez le cardinal de Bérulle. Vieillard-Baron, J L.

BETTER
A Logic of *Better*. Goble, Lou.

BHAGAVAD GITA
On 'the Meaning of Life' and the *Bhagavad Gita*. Gelblum, Tuvia.

BHARTRHARI
Intention and Convention in Communications- Reunderstanding Bhartrhari. Patnaik, Tandra.

BHASKAR, R
Reflections Upon Roy Bhaskar's 'Critical Realism'. Suchting, Wal.
Structural Inquiry, Human Agency and the Contribution of Harré and Bhaskar: A Case Study of Wright's "Classes". Adkins, Barbara.

BHAVAVIVEKA
Bhāvaviveka's *Prajnapradipa* (A Translation of Chapter One: "Examination of Causal Conditions"). Ames, William L.

BIAS
Art, Ethics and the Law: Where Should the Law End?. Carroll, Mary Ann and Van Der Bogert, Frans.
Point of View, Bias, and Insight. Garver, Eugene.

BIBLE
see also Old Testament
"New Creation"—the Christian Symbol of Universalism and Our Steps Towards Its Realization. Hummel, Gert.
Catalyst for Controversy: Paul Carus of Open Court. Henderson, Harold.
Hermeneutics Ancient and Modern. Bruns, Gerald L.
Nietzsche's Philosophical and Narrative Styles. Pettey, John Carson.
Philosophy and Biblical Interpretation: A Study in Nineteenth-Century Conflict. Addinall, Peter.
The Beginning of the Gospel According to Saint John: Philosophical Reflections. Mensch, James Richard.
The Love Commandments: Essays in Christian Ethics and Moral Philosophy. Santurri, Edmund N (ed) and Werpehowski, William (ed).
A Study of Part I, Chapters 1-7 of Maimonides' *The Guide of the Perplexed*. Kleven, Terence.
Aquinas on the Sufferings of Job in Reasoned Faith, Stump, Eleonore (ed). Stump, Eleonore.

Authenticating Biblical Reports of Miracles. Wiebe, Phillip H.
Evolution and Special Creation. McMullin, Ernan.
L'analogia come chiave di lettura della creazione. Melchiorre, Virgilio.
Language, Interpretation and Worship—I in Religion and Philosophy, Warner, Marin (ed). Warner, Martin.
Language, Interpretation and Worship—II in Religion and Philosophy, Warner, Marin (ed). Lamarque, Peter.
Loving My Neighbour, Loving Myself. Hanfling, Oswald.
Ordeal and Repetition in Kierkegaard's Treatment of Abraham and Job in Foundations of Kierkegaard's Vision of Community, Connell, George B (ed). Taylor, Mark Lloyd.
Philosophy and the Bible: The Areopagus Speech. Adams, Marilyn McCord.
Regarding Future Neighbours: Thomas Aquinas and Concern for Posterity. George, William P.

BIBLIOGRAPHY
A Locke Dictionary. Yolton, John W.
Augustine's "De Civitate Dei": An Annotated Bibliography of Modern Criticism, 1960-1990. Donnelly, Dorothy F and Sherman, Mark A.
Bibliographia Missionalia Augustiniana: America Latina (1533-1993). Lazcano, Rafael.
Bibliography of Bioethics, V18. Walters, LeRoy (ed) and Kahn, Tamar Joy (ed).
Descrying the Ideal: The Philosophy of John William Miller. Tyman, Stephen.
Friedrich Nietzsche—H L Mencken. Flathman, Richard (ed) and Mencken, H L.
Jacques Derrida: An Annotated Primary and Secondary Bibliography. Schultz, William R and Fried, Lewis L B.
Panorama Bibliográfico de Xavier Zubiri. Lazcano, Rafael.
R G Collingwood: A Bibliographic Checklist. Dreisbach, Christopher.
Royce's Mature Ethics. Oppenheim, Frank.
The Presocratic Philosophers: An Annotated Bibliography. Navia, Luis E.
A Bibliography of the Works of Jacques Derrida in Derrida: A Critical Reader, Wood, David (ed). Keenan, Thomas and Leventure, Albert.
A Bibliography of Works by and on Anton Marty in Mind, Meaning and Metaphysics, Mulligan, Kevin (ed). Bokhove, Niels W and Raynaud, Savina.
Bibliographie P Josef de Vries S J (1898-1989). Scheit, Herbert.
Bibliography of Feminist Epistemologies in Feminist Epistemologies, Alcoff, Linda (ed). Alcoff, Linda (ed).
Bibliography of Paul Weingartner's Publications 1961-1991 in Advances in Scientific Philosophy, Schurz, Gerhard (ed). Stieringer, Eva.
Environmental Ethics: A Select Annotated Bibliography II, 1987-1990. Katz, Eric.
Kant's Aesthetics Between 1980 and 1990: A Bibliography in Kant's Aesthetics, Meerbote, Ralf (ed). Cicovacki, Predrag.
Le point sur les recherches schellingiennes. Tilliette, Xavier.
Notabilia I: Hinweise auf wichtige Neuerscheinungen aus dem Bereich der mittelalterlichen Philosophie. Imbach, Ruedi.
Recent Work on Death and the Meaning of Life. Fischer, John M.
Una nuova edizione italiana di Platone. Bausola, Adriano.
Virtue: A Brief Bibliography. Galston, William A.
Works by Renato Treves. Velicogna, Nella Gridelli and Segre, Vera.

BIBO, I
The Realism of Moralism: The Political Philosophy of Istvan Bibo. Berki, R N.

BICHAT, M
Ensayo de axiomatización de la teoría tisular y su reducción a la teoría celular. De Asúa, Miguel and Klimovsky, Gregorio.

BICKHARD, M
Cognitivism between Computation and Pragmatics: A Peer Review of 'Some Foundational Questions Concerning Language Studies' by Bickhard and Campbell. Leinfellner, Elisabeth.
Comment on M H Bickhard and R L Campbell, 'Some Foundational Questions Concerning Language Studies'. Schneider, Hans Julius.
Criteria of Acceptance: Comments on Bickhard and Campbell, 'Some Foundational Questions Concerning Language Studies'. Yngve, V H.
Dual Textuality and the Phenomenology of Events: On Some Conceptual Problems in the Article by M H Bickhard and R L Campbell. Kirkeby, O F.
Epistemological Fundamentals: Knowledge by Acquaintance and Spontaneous Communication. Buck, Ross W.
Is the Switch 'On'?. Tyler, Stephen A.
Language and Reality. Meseguer, Alvaro G.
More Foundational Questions Concerning Language Studies. Stamenov, Maxim I.
Pragmatics and Foundationalism. Dascal, Marcelo.
Regress is Anathema, Yes. Boguslawski, Andrzej.
Remarks on Interactive Representations and Praguian Linguistic Tradition. Sgall, Petr.
Some Foundational Rejoinders Concerning Language Studies: With a Focus on Pragmatics. Kashar, Asa.
Some Reflections on Foundational Questions. Janney, Richard W.
What is the Role of Model Theory in the Study of Meaning?. Robering, Klaus.
'Some Foundational Questions Concerning Language Studies': Commentary. Hertzberg, Lars.

BIG BANG THEORY
Philosophers and Popular Cosmology. Clark, Stephen R L.
Science and Creation: Big Bang Cosmology and Thomas Aquinas. Carroll, William E.
The Concept of a Cause of the Universe. Smith, Quentin.

BIGELOW, J
Dispositions or Etiologies? A Comment on Bigelow and Pargetter. Mitchell, Sandra.
Reply to Bigelow's 'Sets Are Haecceities' in Ontology, Causality and Mind: Essays in Honour of D M Armstrong, Bacon, John (ed). Armstrong, D M.

BILL OF RIGHTS

The Philosophy of Freedom: Ideological Origins of the Bill of Rights. Rudolph, Samuel B (ed).

BINSWANGER, L

The Problem of the Unconscious in the Later Thought of L Binswanger in *Analecta Husserliana, XXXI*, Tymieniecka, Anna-Teresa (ed). Mishara, Aaron L.

BIOCHEMISTRY

Aims and Achievements of the Reductionist Approach in Biochemistry/Molecular Biology/Cell Biology: A Response to Kincaid. Robinson, Joseph D.

BIOETHICS

see also Medical Ethics

African-American Perspectives on Biomedical Ethics. Flack, Harley E (ed) and Pellegrino, Edmund D (ed).

Bibliography of Bioethics, V18. Walters, LeRoy (ed) and Kahn, Tamar Joy (ed).

Bioethics Yearbook, Volume 2—Regional Developments in Bioethics: 1989-1991. Lustig, B Andrew (& other eds).

Biomedical Ethics (Third Edition). Mappes, Thomas A and Zembaty, Jane S.

Biomedical Ethics Reviews 1992. Humber, James M (ed) and Almeder, Robert F (ed).

Cases in Bioethics: Selections from the Hastings Center Report (Second Edition). Crigger, Bette-Jane (ed).

Contemporary Issues in Paediatric Ethics. Burgess, Michael M (ed) and Woodrow, Brian E (ed).

Ethics in an Aging Society. Moody, Harry R.

Holistic Health and Biomedical Medicine: A Countersystem Analysis. Lyng, Stephen.

Life and Death: Philosophical Essays in Biomedical Ethics. Brock, Dan W.

Taking Sides: Clashing Views on Controversial Bioethical Issues (Fifth Edition). Levine, Carol.

Terra es animata: On Having a Life. Meilaender, Gilbert C.

A Libertarian Critique of H Tristram Engelhardt, Jr's "The Foundations of Bioethics". Fry-Revere, Sigrid.

A Response to a Purported Ethical Difficulty with Randomized Clinical Trials Involving Cancer Patients. Freedman, Benjamin.

African-American Perspectives, Cultural Relativism and Normative Issues in *African-American Perspectives on Biomedical Ethics*, Flack, Harley E (ed). Garcia, Jorge L A.

Against Caring. Nelson, Hilde L.

Altruistic Surrogacy and Informed Consent. Oakley, Justin.

Autonomy Under Duress in *African-American Perspectives on Biomedical Ethics*, Flack, Harley E (ed). Harris, Leonard.

Bioethics and Culture: An African Perspective. Gbadegesin, Segun.

Bioethics and Ethics of Nature. Kemp, Peter.

Bioethics and Paediatrics in *Contemporary Issues in Paediatric Ethics*, Burgess, Michael M (ed). Ost, David.

Bioethics Education: Expanding the Circle of Participants. Thornton, Barbara C, Callahan, Daniel and Nelson, James Lindemann.

Bioethics in a Low Key: A Report from Germany. Leist, Anton.

Brain Death and Slippery Slopes. Veatch, Robert M.

Brain Death: A Durable Consensus?. Wikler, Daniel.

Caring: From Philosophical Concerns to Practice. Vezeau, Toni M.

Compassion, Consensus, and Conflict: Should Caregivers' Needs Influence the Ethical Dialectic?. Dagi, Teo Forcht.

Economic Perspectives on Bioethics. Baden, John A.

Ethics and Evidence. Botkin, Jeffrey R.

Is There an African-American Perspective on Biomedical Ethics? in *African-American Perspectives on Biomedical Ethics*, Flack, Harley E (ed). Banner, William A.

Justice and Care: The Implications of the Kohlberg-Gilligan Debate for Medical Ethics. Sharpe, Virginia A.

Learning to Do No Harm. Gillet, Grant R.

Moral Philosophy and Public Policy: The Case of the New Reproductive Technologies. Kymlicka, Will.

Moving Forward in Bioethical Theory: Theories, Cases, and Specified Principlism. Degrazia, David.

Philosophy of Medicine—From a Medical Perspective. Wulff, Henrik R.

Response to Kwasi Wiredu in *African-American Perspectives on Biomedical Ethics*, Flack, Harley E (ed). Veatch, Robert M.

Scientific Phenomenology and Bioethics in *Analecta Husserliana, XXXI*, Tymieniecka, Anna-Teresa (ed). Tonini, Valerio.

Teaching Bioethics as a New Paradigm for Health Professionals. Tealdi, Juan Carlos.

Teaching Bioethics to Future Health Professionals: A Case-Based Clinical Model. Macklin, Ruth.

Techno-Thanatology: Moral Consequences of Introducing Brain Criteria for Death. Bayertz, Kurt.

The Intellectual Basis of Bioethics in Southern European Countries. Gracia, Diego.

The Jaina Ethic of Voluntary Death. Bilimoria, Purushottama.

The Method of 'Principlism': A Critique of the Critique. Lustig, B Andrew.

The Slippery-Slope Argument Reconstructed: Response to Van Der Burg. Freedman, Benjamin.

The Social Individual in Clinical Ethics. Moreno, Jonathan D.

Transplantation through a Glass Darkly. Nelson, James Lindemann.

What Bioethics Has to Offer the Developing Countires. Qiu, Ren-Zong.

Yes, There Are African-American Perspectives on Bioethics in *African-American Perspectives on Biomedical Ethics*, Flack, Harley E (ed). Dula, Annette.

BIOGRAPHY

Bolzano-Forschung: 1989-1991. Berg, Jan and Morscher, Edgar.

Charles Sanders Peirce: A Life. Brent, Joseph.

Encounters and Dialogues with Martin Heidegger: 1929-1976 — Heinrich Wiegand Petzet. Emad, Parvis (trans), Wiegand Petzet, Heinrich and Maly, Kenneth (trans).

Paul Ricoeur. Clark, Stephen.

Royce's Mature Ethics. Oppenheim, Frank.

Simone Weil: Portrait of a Self-Exiled Jew. Nevin, Thomas R.

The Life of Isaac Newton. Westfall, Richard S.

William James Durant: An Intellectual Biography. Frey, R G.

A N Prior's Rediscovery of Tense Logic. Ohrstrom, Peter and Hasle, Per.

A Response to M A Stewart's 'Berkeley's Introduction Draft'. Belfrage, Bertil.

Ayer: The Man, the Philosopher, the Teacher in *A J Ayer Memorial Essays*, Griffiths, A Phillips (ed). Wollheim, Richard.

Der Familienname von Edmund Husserl. Wagner, Norbert.

Discernment and the Imagination in Simone Weil's Philosophy of Culture, Bell, Richard H (ed). Andic, Martin.

DuBois and James. Campbell, James.

Edmund Wilson and the Problem of Marx: History, Biography, and *To The Finland Station*. Corkin, Stanley.

Existentialism, Feminism and Simone de Beauvoir. Mahon, Joseph.

Harry Broudy and Education for a Democratic Society. Vandenberg, Donald.

Hegel's Intellectual Development to 1807 in *The Cambridge Companion to Hegel*, Beiser, Frederick (ed). Harris, H S.

Kant's Intellectual Development: 1746-1781 in *The Cambridge Companion to Kant*, Guyer, Paul (ed). Beiser, Frederick.

Leibniz Finds a Niche. Rescher, Nicholas.

Memories of Michael Polanyi in Manchester. Calvin, Michael.

Norman Malcolm: A Memoir. Serafini, Anthony.

Paul Weingartner: Philosophy at Work in *Advances in Scientific Philosophy*, Schurz, Gerhard (ed). Zecha, Gerhard.

Phenomenology in Russia: The Contribution of Gustav Shpet. Scanlan, James P.

Philosophical Biography: The American Scene. Madden, Edward H and Madden, Marian C.

Philosophical Self-Portrait in Kotarbinski: Logic, Semantics and Ontology, Wolenski, Jan (ed). Kotarbinski, Tadeusz.

Reflections on the Life and Works of Scotus. Wolter, Allan B.

BIOLOGY

see also Darwinism, Evolution, Life, Vitalism

A Hylomorphic Theory of Mind. Cooney, Brian.

Daimon Life: Heidegger and Life-Philosophy. Krell, David Farrell.

Nurturing Evolution: The Family as a Social Womb. Carter, Richard B.

Search for a Naturalistic World View: Volume I. Shimony, Abner.

The Disorder of Things: Metaphysical Foundations of the Disunity of Science. Duprè, John.

The Ethical Dimensions of the Biological Sciences. Bulger, Ruth Ellen (ed), Heitman, Elizabeth (ed) and Reiser, Stanley Joel (ed).

The Philosophy of Science. Boyd, Richard (ed), Gasper, Philip (ed) and Trout, J D (ed).

White Queen Psychology and Other Essays for Alice. Millikan, Ruth Garrett.

A Kernel of Truth? On the Reality of the Genetic Program. Moss, Lenny.

A Teoria Aristotélica da Respiraçao. Martins, Roberto D A.

Additional Notes on Integration. Van Der Steen, Wim J.

Aims and Achievements of the Reductionist Approach in Biochemistry/Molecular Biology/Cell Biology: A Response to Kincaid. Robinson, Joseph D.

Aristóteles e a Geraçao Espontânea. Pereira Martins, Lilian A C.

Bergson's Vitalism in the Light of Modern Biology in *The Crisis in Modernism*, Burwick, Frederick (ed). Wolsky, Maria de Issekutz and Wolsky, Alexander A.

Biological Perspectives on Fall and Original Sin. Hefner, Philip.

De deconstructie van het kleine verschil. Everts, Saskia I.

Eliminative Pluralism. Ereshefsky, Marc.

Ensayo de axiomatización de la teoría tisular y su reducción a la teoría celular. De Asúa, Miguel and Klimovsky, Gregorio.

Ethics and Evolution: The Biological Basis of Morality. Bradie, Michael.

Evolution, Teleology and Theology. Soontiëns, Frans.

Evolutionary Epistemology: What Phenotype is Selected and Which Genotype Evolves?. Falk, Raphael.

Evolutionary Synthesis: A Search for the Strategy. Tuomi, Juha.

Experimental Ecology on the Pacific Coast: Victor Shelford and His Search for Appropriate Methods. Benson, Keith R.

Explanation in Biopsychology in *Mental Causation*, Heil, John (ed). Millikan, Ruth Garrett.

Formation of Theories and Policy of Difference of the Sexes (in Czechoslovakian). List, Elisabeth.

Freiheit und Evolution. Titze, Hans.

How to Make Oneself Nature's Spokesman? A Latourian Account of Classification in Eighteenth- and Early Nineteenth-Century Natural History?. Stemerding, Dirk.

Inquiry Into the Spatio-Temporal Contingency of Cellular Communication Systems. Allaerts, Wilfried.

Integrating Sciences by Creating New Disciplines: The Case of Cell Biology. Bechtel, William.

J Monod, S Spiegelman et l'adaptation enzymatique: Programmes de recherche, cultures locals et traditions disciplinaires. Gaudillières, Jean-Paul.

La natura della vita: Una indagine filosofica. Crescini, Angelo.

Le concept de vie dans la Grèce ancienne et le serment d'Hippocrate. Angeletti, Luciana Rita.

BODY

Computers and the Mind-Body Problem: On Ontological and Epistemological Dualism. Drozdek, Adam.

Corps et culture. Csepregi, Gabor.

Das Leib-Seele-Pentagon und die Kombinatorik attraktiver Vorstellungen—Ein folgenreiches Konzept der Leibnizschen Frühphilosophie. Busche, Hubertus.

Descartes and Malebranche on Mind and Mind-Body Union. Schmaltz, Tad M.

Descartes on Mind-Body Interaction. Holbrook, Daniel.

Descartes on Mind-Body Interaction and the Conservation of Motion. McLaughlin, Peter.

Discontinuing Becomings: Deleuze on the Becoming-Woman of Philosophy. Braidotti, Rosi.

Eating Disorders: The Feminist Challenge to the Concept of Pathology in The Body in Medical Thought and Practice, Leder, Drew (ed). Bordo, Susan R.

El cuerpo como educador del espíritu en la Filosofía de Bergson. Sánchez Rey, María del Carmen.

Foucault's Political Body in Medical Praxis in The Body in Medical Thought and Practice, Leder, Drew (ed). Spitzack, Carole.

God, Greed, and Flesh: Saint Paul, Thomas Hobbes, and the Nature/Nurture Debate. Kramer, Matthew H.

Goods of the Mind, Goods of the Body and External Goods. Gobetti, Daniela.

How Are Souls Related to Bodies? A Study of John Buridan. Zupko, Jack.

Human Embodiment: Indian Perspectives in Self as Body in Asian Theory and Practice, Kasulis, Thomas P (ed). Koller, John M.

Il concetto cartesiano del pensare e il problema delle altre intelligenze. Messeri, Marco.

Indian Bodies in Self as Body in Asian Theory and Practice, Kasulis, Thomas P (ed). Staal, Frits.

Is the Mind-Body Interface Microscopic?. Rössler, Otto E and Rössler, Reimara.

James Giles on Personal Identity. Flew, Antony.

Kein Platz für phänomenale Qualitäten und Leib- Umwelt- Interaktion?. Pohlenz, Gerd.

Knowledge, Bodies, and Values: Reproductive Technologies and their Scientific Context. Longino, Helen E.

L'immagine della donna secondo Ortega y Gasset. Savignano, Armando.

La ceguera según Aristóteles. Quevedo, Amalia.

La noción de 'spiritus' y de 'spiritualis substantia' en la cuestión disputada De spiritualibus creaturis de Santo Tomás de Aquino. Taubenschlag, C A.

Lacanian Castration in Crises in Continental Philosophy, Dallery, Arleen B (ed). Boothby, Richard.

Le relation mente-corpore in le filosofia e in le scientia contemporanee. Blandino, Giovanni.

Leibanwesenheit und primitive Gegenwart. Kühn, Rolf.

Making Mistakes in Science: Eduard Pflüger, His Scientific and Professional Concept of Physiology, and His Unsuccessful Theory of Diabetes (1903-1910). Schlich, Thomas.

Mind-Body Causation and Explanatory Practice in Mental Causation, Heil, John (ed). Burge, Tyler.

Mind/Brain Science in John Searle and His Critics, LePore, Ernest (ed). Freeman, Walter J and Skarda, Christine A.

Obesity, Objectification, and Identity in The Body in Medical Thought and Practice, Leder, Drew (ed). Moss, Donald.

On Psychomimesis. Rosen, Robert.

On the Body in Medical Self-Care and Holistic Medicine in The Body in Medical Thought and Practice, Leder, Drew (ed). Weston, Anthony.

Parted Bodies, Departed Souls: The Body in Ancient Medicine and Anatomy in The Body in Medical Thought and Practice, Leder, Drew (ed). Zaner, Richard M.

Personal Identity in Reflections on Philosophy, McHenry, Leemon (ed). Fuller, Gary.

Psychosomatics, the Lived Body, and Anthropological Medicine in The Body in Medical Thought and Practice, Leder, Drew (ed). Wiggins, Osborne, Northoff, Georg and Schwartz, Michael Alan.

Public Bodies, Private Selves in Applied Philosophy, Almond, Brenda (ed). Marshall, Sandra E.

Reaping the Whirlwind: Reply to Harnad's Other Bodies, Other Minds. Hauser, Larry.

Residual Asymmetrical Dualism: A Theory of Mind-Body Relations. Efron, Arthur.

Response: The Mind-Body Problem in John Searle and His Critics, LePore, Ernest (ed). Searle, John R.

Reversibility as a Radical Ground for an Ontology of the Body in Medicine. Brannigan, Michael.

Searles Auffassung des Verhältnisses von Geist und Körper und ihre Beziehung zur Ideantitätstheorie. Schröder, Jürgen.

Self and Body in Theravada Buddhism in Self as Body in Asian Theory and Practice, Kasulis, Thomas P (ed). Dissanayake, Wimal.

Spinoza's Argument for the Identity Theory. Della-Rocca, Michael.

Strawson and the Argument for Other Minds. Maclachlan, D L C.

Survival of Bodily Death: A Qeustion of Values. Martin, Raymond.

The Body in Action: the Relationship between Action, Intention and Corporal Movement (in French). Dokic, Jérôme.

The Body in Multiple Sclerosis: A Patient's Perspective in The Body in Medical Thought and Practice, Leder, Drew (ed). Toombs, S Kay.

The Body in the City. Swensen, Cole.

The Body of the Future in The Body in Medical Thought and Practice, Leder, Drew (ed). Cassell, Eric J.

The Body with AIDS: A Post-Structuralist Approach in The Body in Medical Thought and Practice, Leder, Drew (ed). Murphy, Julien S.

The Body—Japanese Style in Self as Body in Asian Theory and Practice, Kasulis, Thomas P (ed). Kasulis, Thomas P.

The Concept of the Body in Self as Body in Asian Theory and Practice, Kasulis, Thomas P (ed). Deutsch, Eliot.

The Human Body as a Microcosmic Source of Macrocosmic Values in Calligraphy in Self as Body in Asian Theory and Practice, Kasulis, Thomas P (ed). Hay, John.

The Market for Bodily Parts in Applied Philosophy, Almond, Brenda (ed). Chadwick, Ruth F.

The Mind-Body Relationship in Pāli Buddhism: A Philosophical Investigation. Harvey, Peter.

The Nature of Mind. Lucash, Frank S.

The Possibility of an Unbodily Self: In Response to Richard Combes. Gough, Martin.

The Problem of the Body in Nietzsche and Dōgen in Nietzsche and Asian Thought, Parkes, Graham (ed). Parkes, Graham R (trans) and Kōgaku, Arifuku.

The Relation of Philosophy to Sōphrosynē: Zalmoxian Medicine in Plato's Charmides. Coolidge, Jr, Francis P.

These New Components of the Spectacle in Postmodernism and Society, Boyne, Roy (ed). Wilson, Elizabeth.

Two Contemporary Japanese Views of the Body: Ichikawa Hiroshi and Yuasa Yasuo in Self as Body in Asian Theory and Practice, Kasulis, Thomas P (ed). Nagatomo, Shigenori.

Viewpoints: Body, Spirit, and Democracy in Revisioning Philosophy, Ogilvy, James (ed). Johnson, Don Hanlon.

Whose Body Is It, Anyway? in Philosophical Perspectives, 6: Ethics, 1992, Tomberlin, James E (ed). Smith, Holly M.

Why Aren't More Doctors Phenomenologists? in The Body in Medical Thought and Practice, Leder, Drew (ed). Baron, Richard J.

William H Poteat: A Laudatio. Scott, R Taylor.

Wittgenstein: Mind, Body, and Society. Schatzki, Theodore R.

'The Best Set of Tools'? Dennett's Metaphors and the Mind-Body Problem. Kirk, Robert.

BOETHIUS

The Trinity: An Analysis of St Thomas Aquinas' 'Expositio' of the 'De Trinitate' of Boethius. Hall, Douglas.

De Consolatione Philosophiae. Haldane, John.

De Consolatione Philosophiae in Philosophy, Religion and the Spiritual Life, McGhee, Michael (ed). Haldane, John.

Heilung im Denken: Zur Sache der philosophischen Tröstung bei Boethius. Schumacher, Thomas.

Presciencia divina y libre arbitrio: Boecio de Consolatione V, 3 y Seneca epistulae ad lucilium II, 16. Tursi, Antonio D.

BOGHOSSIAN, P

Boghossian on Externalism and Inference in Rationality in Epistemology, Villanueva, Enrique (ed). Schiffer, Stephen.

Reply to Block and Boghossian. Fodor, Jerry and LePore, Ernie.

BOHM, D

Holomovement Metaphysics and Theology. Sharpe, Kevin J.

BOHR, N

Bohr's Quantum Philosophy: On the Shoulders of a Giant?. Kragh, Helge.

Quana of Life: Atomic Physics and the Reincarnation of Phage. Kay, Lily E.

Zur Rekonstruktion des Bohrschen Forschungsprogramms I. Zoubek, G and Lauth, B.

Zur Rekonstruktion des Bohrschen Forschungsprogramms II. Zoubek, G and Lauth, B.

BOILEAU, N

The Sublime as a Source of Light in the Works of Nicolas Boileau in Analecta Husserliana, XXXVIII, Tymieniecka, Anna-Teresa (ed). Litman, Theodore.

BOLZANO

Bolzano-Forschung: 1989-1991. Berg, Jan and Morscher, Edgar.

Ontology Without Ultrafilters and Possible Worlds: An Examination of Bolzano's Ontology. Berg, Jan.

BONAVENTURE

Notabilia II: Hinweise auf wichtige Neuerscheinungen aus dem Bereich der mittelalterlichen Philosophie. Imbach, Ruedi.

BONHOEFFER, D

Bonhoeffer on Heidegger and Togetherness. Marsh, Charles.

BONJOUR, B

Cognitive Spontaneity, Coherence, and Internalism in the Justification of Empirical Belief. Silvers, Stuart.

BONNOT DE MABLY, G

Conversations with Phocion: The Political Thought of Mably. Wright, J K.

BONTADINI, G

Gustavo Bontadini: Pensieri e ricordi. Cristaldi, Rosario Vittorio.

BOOK

De Productie, Distributie en Consumptie Van Cultuur. Kloek, J J and Mijnhardt, W W.

Teaching Without Books. Irvine, William B.

The Secret of Books (in Czechoslovakian). Ajvaz, Michal.

BOOKCHIN, M

Social Ecology, Deep Ecology, and Liberalism. Dizerega, Gus.

BOOLEAN ALGEBRA

A Construction of Boolean Algebras from First-Order Structures. Koppelberg, Sabine.

Actualisation, développement et perfectionnement des calculs logiques arithmético-intensionnels de Leibniz. Sánchez-Mazas, Miguel.

An Algebraic Treatment of the Barwise Compactness Theory. Fleischer, Isidore and Scott, Philip.

BRITISH

Bettering Our Condition: Work, Workers and Ethics in British and German Economic Thought. Chmielewski, Philip J.

British Empiricism and American Pragmatism: New Directions and Neglected Arguments. Roth, Robert.

Contemporary Political Culture. Gibbins, John R (ed).

Eighteenth-Century Hermeneutics: Philosophy of Interpretation in England from Locke to Burke. Weinsheimer, Joel C.

Essays on Henry Sidgwick. Schultz, Bart (ed).

La Théorie qui n'en est pas une, or, *Why Clio Doesn't Care.* Steedman, Carolyn.

Philosophy of the Social Sciences III: Groundwork for Social Dynamics. Wisdom, J O.

Bentham, Bacon and the Movement for the Reform of English Law Reporting. Munday, Roderick.

From Liberal-Radicalism to Conservative Corporatism in Victorian Liberalism, Bellamy, Richard (ed). Hooper, Alan.

Henry Sigwick Today in Essays on Henry Sidgwick, Schultz, Bart (ed). Schultz, Bart.

Liberal Political Theory and Working-Class Radicalism in Nineteenth-Century England. Ashcraft, Richard.

Lockean Ideas and 18th Century British Philosophy. Loptson, Peter J.

On American and British Aesthetics. Diffey, T J.

The Concept of Quackery in Early Nineteenth Century British Medical Periodicals. Carter, K Codell.

Whigs and Liberals in Victorian Liberalism, Bellamy, Richard (ed). Fontana, Bianca.

William Temple and the Bombing of Germany: An Exploration in Just War Tradition. Lammers, Stephen.

'Institutional Exploitation' and Workers' Co-operatives—Or How the British Left Persist in Getting Their Concepts Wrong. Carter, Alan.

BROCK, D

Commentator on 'Quality of Life Measures in Health Care and Medical Ethics' in The Quality of Life, Nussbaum, Martha C (ed). Griffin, James.

BROCK, T

The Development of a Scientific Specialty: The Case of Microbial Genetics—A Review of *The Emergence of Bacterial Genetics* by Thomas D Brock. Fantini, Bernardino.

BRODKEY, L

Presence of Mind, Presence of Body: Embodying Positionality in the Classroom. Ardis, Ann.

BRODRIBB, S

A Response to Zerilli and Brodribb. Pocock, J G A.

BRODSKY, G

A Reply to Westbrook, Brodsky, and Simpson. West, Cornel.

BROOK, R

Is It Less Wrong to Harm the Vulnerable than the Secure?. Howard-Snyder, Frances.

BROOME, J

The Connection Between Prudential and Moral Goodness. Vallentyne, Peter.

Weighing Risk. McClennen, Edward and Found, Peter G.

BROUDY, H

Goodness and Greatness: Broudy on Music Education. Colwell, Richard.

Harry Broudy and Discipline-Based Art Education (DBAE). Greer, W Dwaine.

Harry Broudy and Education for a Democratic Society. Vandenberg, Donald.

Research on Broudy's Theory of the Uses of Schooling. Schmitz, John G.

The Road from Nice to Necessary: Broudy's Rationale for Art Education. DiBlasio, Margaret Klempay.

BROUWER, L

Brève note sur l'intuitionnisme de Brouwer. Largeault, Jean.

Intuition et intuitionisme. Largeault, Jean.

L'intuitionisme des mathématiciens avant Brouwer. Largeault, Jean.

Spreads or Choice Sequences?. DeSwart, H C M.

BROWN

Critical Notice of James Robert Brown's *The Rational and the Social.* Matheson, Carl.

Shifting Sands: Foucault, Brown and the Framework of Christian Asceticism. Behr, John.

BROWNSON, O

Orestes Brownson and Christian Philosophy. Maurer, Armand A.

BRUECKNER, A

The Indeterminacy of Identity: A Reply to Brueckner. Parfit, Derek.

BRUMBAUGH, R

Back to Basics: Problems and Prospects for Applied Philosophy. Warren, Bill.

BRUNO

"Averroe quantumque arabo et ignorante di lingua greca...": Note sull'averrosimo di Giordano Bruno. Sturlese, Rita.

La scoperta di nuovi documenti sulla vita di Bruno: Su *Giordano Bruno and the Embassy Affair* di John Bossy. Mancini, Sandro.

BRYSEN, M

"Engendering Equity...". Morgan, K P.

BUBER

On Intersubjectivity and Cultural Creativity—Martin Buber. Eisenstadt, S N (ed) and Buber, Martin.

Martin Buber—Critic of Karl Marx. Yassour, Avraham.

Social Ethic of Mahatma Gandhi and Martin Buber. Henry, Sarojini.

The "Living Center" of Martin Buber's Political Theory. Avnon, Dan.

The Role of Technology in Environmental Questions: Martin Buber and Deep Ecology as Answers to Technological Consciousness. Light, Andrew R F.

BUCHLER, J

Reconstructing Judgment: Emotion and Moral Judgment. Wallace, Kathleen.

Systematic Nonfoundationalism: The Philosophy of Justus Buchler. Singer, Beth.

BUCHMANN, M

"Teacher Thinking, Teacher Change, and the 'Capricious Seamstress'"—A Response. Greene, Maxine.

Conversation as a Romance of Reason: A Response to Buchmann. Garrison, James W.

BUDDHISM

see also Karma, Mahayana, Reincarnation, Zen Buddhism

A History of Buddhist Philosophy. Kalupahana, David J.

Antologia della filosofia cinese. Arena, Leonardo Vittorio.

Ascetic Figures Before and In Early Buddhism: The Emergence of Gautama as the Buddha. Wiltshire, Martin G.

Buddhism, Sexuality, and Gender. Cabezón, José I (ed).

Discovering Philosophy. White, Thomas I.

Disputed Questions in Theology and the Philosophy of Religion. Hick, John.

Ethics of Environment and Development: Global Challenge, International Response. Engel, J Ronald (ed) and Engel, Joan Gibb (ed).

Storia del Buddhismo Ch'an. Arena, Leonardo Vittorio.

A Comparison of the Chinese Buddhist and Indian Buddhist Modes of Thought. Litian, Fang.

An Inquiry into Gender Considerations and Gender Conscious Reflectivity in Early Buddhism. Rajapakse, Vijitha.

Appearance and Reality in Buddhist Metaphysics from a European Philosophical Point of View. Chung, Bongkil.

Are Convenient Fictions Harmful to Your Health?. Garner, Richard T.

Bhāvaviveka's *Prajnapradipa* (A Translation of Chapter One: "Examination of Causal Conditions"). Ames, William L.

Chinese Bhiksunis in the Ch'an Tradition (in Chinese). Shih, Heng-ching.

Derrida and Madhyamika Buddhism: From Linguistic Deconstruction to Criticism of Onto-Theologies. Zong-qi, Cai.

Derrida and Seng-Zhao: Linguistic and Philosophical Deconstructions. Zongqi, Cai.

Duhkha: An Analysis of Buddhist Clue to Understand Human Nature. Chinchore, Mangala R.

Ethics-Based Society of Buddhism. Kochumuttom, Thomas.

Explaining Strange Parallels: The Case of Quantum Mechanics and Mādhyamika Buddhism. Balasubramaniam, Arun.

Heidegger, Buddhism, and Deep Ecology in The Cambridge Companion to Heidegger, Guignon, Charles (ed). Zimmerman, Michael E.

Indra's Postmodern Net. Loy, David.

Is *Prasanga* a form of Deconstruction?. Matilal, Bimal Krishna.

Italian Studies on Far Eastern Thought in Comparative Philosophy. Santangelo, Paolo.

Jabir, the Buddhist Yogi. Walter, Michael.

Mein philosophischer Ausgangspunkt. Nishitani, Keiji.

Nāgārjuna und die Mengenlehre. Blau, U.

Non-Conceptuality, Critical Reasoning and Religious Experience: Some Tibetan Buddhist Discussions. Williams, Paul.

Philosophical Studies (Sinology and Indology) in St Petersburg (Leningrad), 1985-1990. Torchinov, E A.

Reductionist and Nonreductionist Theories of Persons in Indian Buddhist Philosophy. Duerlinger, James.

Religious Concepts of 'World': Comparative Metaphysical. Pratt, Douglas.

Schopenhauer and Buddhism. Abelsen, Peter.

Self and Body in Theravada Buddhism in Self as Body in Asian Theory and Practice, Kasulis, Thomas P (ed). Dissanayake, Wimal.

Soft Natural Theology in Prospects for Natural Theology, Long, Eugene Thomas (ed). Smart, Ninian.

The Deconstruction of Buddhism in Derrida and Negative Theology, Coward, Harold (ed). Loy, David.

The Eloquent Silence of Zarathustra in Nietzsche and Asian Thought, Parkes, Graham (ed). Parkes, Graham R (trans), Aihara, Setsuko (trans) and Muneto, Sonoda.

The Karmic A Priori in Indian Philosophy. Potter, Karl H.

The Mind-Body Relationship in Pāli Buddhism: A Philosophical Investigation. Harvey, Peter.

The No-Self Theory: Hume, Buddhism, and Personal Identity. Giles, James.

The Tibetan *Tshogs Zhing* (Field of Assembly): General Notes on its Function, Structure and Contents. Jackson, Roger R.

The Trouble with Truth: Heidegger on Aletheia, Buddhist Thinkers on Satya. Kapstein, Matthew.

The Uses of Neo-Confucianism: A Response to Professor Tillman. De Bary, W T.

Trying to Become Real: A Buddhist Critique of Some Secular Heresies. Loy, David.

Two Contemporary Japanese Views of the Body: Ichikawa Hiroshi and Yuasa Yasuo in Self as Body in Asian Theory and Practice, Kasulis, Thomas P (ed). Nagatomo, Shigenori.

Vasubandhu's Idealism: An Encounter Between Philosophy and Religion. Rotem, Ornan.

BUFORD, T

Listening for the Call: Response to Professor Buford. Carbone Jr, Peter F.

BULLER, D

A Short Defence of Transcience. Schlesinger, George.

BUNDLE THEORY

Hume's Theory of Moral Responsibility: Some Unresolved Matters. Johnson, Clarence.

BUNGE, M
Les quatre causes: de Bunge à Aristote. Espinoza, Miguel.

BUNTING, J
Another Go at 'Equal Educational Opportunity'. Moulder, James.

BURBULES, N
Tragic Absolutism in Education. Arcilla, René Vincente.

BURCKHARDT
Jacob Burckhardt's Liberal-Conservatism. Sigurdson, Richard.

BUREAUCRACY
Banalité du mal et sens du devoir chez les administrateurs de l'extermination. Joos, Jean-Ernest.

BURGE, T
Burge on Content. Elugardo, Reinaldo.
On Some Difficulties Concerning Intuition and Intuitive Knowledge. Parsons, Charles.
Rationality and Epistemic Paradox. Kroon, Frederick.

BURGER, P
The Social Significance of Autonomous Art: Adorno and Bürger. Zuidervaart, Lambert.

BURGESS-JACKSON, K
Thinking Morality Interpersonally: A Reply to Burgess-Jackson. Walker, Margaret Urban.

BURIAN, D
Additional Notes on Integration. Van Der Steen, Wim J.

BURIDAN
A Buridanian Discussion of Desire, Murder and Democracy. Goldstein, Laurence.
A Theory of Truth Based on a Medieval Solution to the Liar Paradox. Epstein, R L.
Buridan and Skepticism. Zupko, Jack.
How Are Souls Related to Bodies? A Study of John Buridan. Zupko, Jack.
John Buridan and Donald Davidson on *Akrasia*. Saarinen, Risto.
Syllogistique buridanienne. Karger, Élizabeth.

BURKE
Eighteenth-Century Hermeneutics: Philosophy of Interpretation in England from Locke to Burke. Weinsheimer, Joel C.
The Metaphysics of Edmund Burke. Pappin III, Joseph L.
Burke on Politics, Aesthetics, and the Dangers of Modernity. White, Stephen K.
E Burke and the Natural Law: About the Foundations of Conservatisim (in Dutch). Van De Putte, A.
Literal and Symbolic Representations: Burke, Paine and the French Revolution. Whale, John C.

BURTON, S
Thick Concepts Revisited: A Reply to Burton. Garrard, Eve.

BURWOOD, L
Equality Revisited. Wilson, John.

BUSINESS
Business, Ethics, and the Environment: The Public Policy Debate. Hoffman, W Michael (ed), Frederick, Robert (ed) and Pentry, Edward S (ed).
Case Studies in Business Ethics (Third Edition). Donaldson, Thomas and Gini, Al.
Case Studies in Business, Society, and Ethics (Third Edition). Beauchamp, Tom L.
The Corporation as Anomaly. Schrader, David.
The Corporation, Ethics, and the Environment. Hoffman, W Michael (ed), Frederick, Robert (ed) and Petry, Edward S (ed).
A Pragmatic Health Care Policy Tradition: Dewey, Franklin and Social Reconstruction. Miller, Irwin.
A Reply to Robert Allan Cooke's "And the Blind Shall Lead the Blind". Wolfe, Art.
Aristotle: A Pre-Modern Post-Modern? Implications for Business Ethics. Duska, Ronald F.
Business and Games. Heckman, Peter.
Business and Postmodernism: A Dangerous Dalliance. Walton, Clarence C.
Business Ethics and Postmodernism: A Response. Rasmussen, David M.
Business Ethics as a Postmodern Phenomenon. Green, Ronald M.
Conceptions of the Corporation and Ethical Decision Making in Business. Nesteruk, Jeffrey and Risser, David T.
Development of Ethical Awareness: A Model for a Community Business Ethics Forum. Cleary, Claudia M and Kendree, Jack M.
Does Business Ethics Make Economic Sense?. Sen, Amartya.
Does Loyalty in the Workplace Have a Future?. Haughey, John C.
Enterprise and Liberal Education. Bridges, David.
Enterprise and Liberal Education: Some Reservations. Bailey, Charles.
Ethics and the Praise of Diversity: Review of *Workforce America*. Weber, Leonard J.
Ethics in Business and Administration: An International and Historical Perspective. Small, Michael W.
Friedman's Theory of Corporate Social Responsibility. Carson, Thomas.
Inherent Limitations of the Confucian Tradition in Contemporary East Asian Business Enterprises. Oh, Tai K.
Machiavelli's Prince as CEO. D'Andrade, Kendall.
Postmodern Interviews in Business Ethics: A Reply to Ronald Green. Schmidt, David P.
Second Thoughts About Bluffing. Carson, Thomas.
The Positive Contribution of Confucianism to the Modernization of East Asian Business Enterprises. Han, Cheong K.
The Work Ethic and the Work Ethos: The Importance of Ethical Arguments for the Politics of Transition to the Market. Büscher, M.
Understanding the Real "Character Issue:" A Review of the Latest Work of Clarence Walton (*The Moral Manager*, and *Corporate Encounters*). Cooke, Robert.

Varieties of Postmodernism as Moments in Ethics Action Learning. Nielsen, Richard P.
Why Business is Talking About Ethics: Reflections on Foreign Conversations in Revisioning Philosophy, Ogilvy, James (ed). Ciulla, Joanne B.

BUSINESS ETHICS
Ethical Issues in Business: A Philosophical Approach (Fourth Edition). Donaldson, Thomas J and Werhane, Patricia H.
Ethical Theory and Business (Fourth Edition). Beauchamp, Tom L and Bowie, Norman E.
Ethics and the Conduct of Business. Boatright, John R.
The Great Gatsby as a Business Ethics Inquiry. McAdams, Tony.
A Critical Evaluation of Etzioni's Socioeconomic Theory: Implications for the Field of Business Ethics. Swanson, Diane.
Business Ethics and the Liberal Arts in Moral Education and the Liberal Arts, Mitias, Michael H (ed). De George, Richard.
Ethical Issues in Corporate Speechwriting. Seeger, Matthew W.
Fairness in Hierarchical and Entrepreneurial Firms. Green, Michael K.

BUSS, L
Leo Buss's *The Evolution of Individuality*. Resnik, David B.

BUTLER
Reply to Brinton's '"Following Nature" in Butler's Sermons'. Millar, Alan.
Tom Regan, G E Moore, and Bishop Butler's Maxim: A Revisitation. Perkins Jr, Raymond K.

BUYTENDIJK, F
Helmuth Plessner als Philosophischer Wegweiser für F J J Buytendijk. Boudier, Henk Struyker.
The Difference Between Man and Animal: Letters of Max Scheler on F J J Buytendijk (in Dutch). Boudier, Henk Struyker.

BYRNE, P
Reply: A Further Defence of Christian Revelation. Swinburne, Richard.

BYWATER, W
Hermeneutics of Suspicion. Fisher, Linda.

BYZANTINE
Christology and its Philosophical Complexities in the Thought of Leontius of Byzantium. Moutafakis, Nicholas J.

CADY, D
Are Active Pacifists Really Just-Warists in Disguise?. Smithka, Paula J.

CAGE, J
John Cage's 4'33": Using Aesthetic Theory to Understand a Musical Notion. Campbell, Mark Robin.

CAJETAN
Analogical Concepts: The Fourteenth-Century Background to Cajetan. Ashworth, E J.

CALCULATION
Renormalization and the Effective Field Theory Programme. Robinson, Don.
Simple Attentive Miscalculation. Ruben, David-Hillel.

CALCULUS
Cavalieri's Indivisibles and Euclid's Canons in Revolution and Continuity, Barker, Peter (ed). De Gandt, François.
Symbolische Erkenntnis bei Leibniz. Krämer, Sybille.
The Foundations of the Calculus and the Conceptual Analysis of Motion: The Case of the Early Leibniz (1670-1676). White, Michael J.

CALLAHAN, D
Age Rationing, the Virtues, and Wanting More Life. Purviance, Susan M.
Justice, Community Dialogue, and Health Care. Post, Stephen G.

CALLAHAN, R
Education as Hospitality: The Reclamation of Cultural Metaphor and Narrative. Losito, William F.

CALLICLES
Callicles' Hedonism. Rudebusch, George H.

CALLICOTT, J
A Defense of Environmental Ethics: A Reply to Janna Thompson. Nelson, Michael P.
Alternate Foundations for the Land Ethic: Biologism, Cognitivism, and Pragmatism. Wenz, Peter S.
Callicott and the Metaphysical Basis of Ecocentric Morality. Fieser, James.
From Triangles to Tripods: Polycentrism in Environmental Ethics. Rabb, J Douglas.
Minimal, Moderate, and Extreme Moral Pluralism. Wenz, Peter.

CALLIGRAPHY
The Human Body as a Microcosmic Source of Macrocosmic Values in Calligraphy in Self as Body in Asian Theory and Practice, Kasulis, Thomas P (ed). Hay, John.

CALVINISM
Elementen uit de ontstaansgeschiedenis der Reformatorische Wijsbegeerte. Stellingwerff, J.

CAM, P
Searle, Strong AI, and Two Ways of Sorting Cucumbers. Pfeifer, Karl.

CAMPAIGN
Negative Campaigning. Wright, William A.

CAMPBELL, C
'Ahkam al-Bughat': Irregular Warfare and the Law of Rebellion in Islam in Cross, Crescent and Sword, Johnson, James Turner (ed). Abou El Fadl, Khaled.

CAMPBELL, K
Reply to Campbell's 'David Armstrong and Realism about Colour' in Ontology, Causality and Mind: Essays in Honour of D M Armstrong, Bacon, John (ed). Armstrong, D M.

CAMPBELL, R

Cognitivism between Computation and Pragmatics: A Peer Review of 'Some Foundational Questions Concerning Language Studies' by Bickhard and Campbell. Leinfellner, Elisabeth.

Comment on M H Bickhard and R L Campbell, 'Some Foundational Questions Concerning Language Studies'. Schneider, Hans Julius.

Criteria of Acceptance: Comments on Bickhard and Campbell, 'Some Foundational Questions Concerning Language Studies'. Yngve, V H.

Dual Textuality and the Phenomenology of Events: On Some Conceptual Problems in the Article by M H Bickhard and R L Campbell. Kirkeby, O F.

Epistemological Fundamentals: Knowledge by Acquaintance and Spontaneous Communication. Buck, Ross W.

Is the Switch 'On'?. Tyler, Stephen A.

Language and Reality. Meseguer, Alvaro G.

More Foundational Questions Concerning Language Studies. Stamenov, Maxim I.

Pragmatics and Foundationalism. Dascal, Marcelo.

Regress is Anathema, Yes. Boguslawski, Andrzej.

Remarks on Interactive Representations and Praguian Linguistic Tradition. Sgall, Petr.

Some Foundational Rejoinders Concerning Language Studies: With a Focus on Pragmatics. Kashar, Asa.

Some Reflections on Foundational Questions. Janney, Richard W.

What is the Role of Model Theory in the Study of Meaning?. Robering, Klaus.

'Some Foundational Questions Concerning Language Studies': Commentary. Hertzberg, Lars.

CAMUS

Religion from Tolstoy to Camus. Kaufmann, Walter (ed).

CANADIAN

Bioethics Yearbook, Volume 2—Regional Developments in Bioethics: 1989-1991. Lustig, B Andrew (& other eds).

Changing To National Health Care: Ethical and Policy Issues. Huefner, Robert P (ed) and Battin, Margaret P (ed).

Ethical Issues: Perspectives for Canadians. Soifer, Eldon (ed).

Dialectique et désepoir dans "La fatigue culturelle du Canada français". Reid, Jeffrey.

Hume Studies in Canada. Wilson, F F.

L'assassin d'Ulysse. Leroux, François.

L'homme exorbité: Réflexion sur la notion de fatigue culturelle chez Hubert Aquin. Jacques, Daniel.

Le "déprimé explosif". Morin, Michel.

Le chemin de l'immanence. Couture, Yves.

Philosophy of Education in Canada. Hare, William F.

CANALS, F

Francisco Canals y la Escuela tomista de Barcelona. Ayuso Torres, M.

CANCER

A Response to a Purported Ethical Difficulty with Randomized Clinical Trials Involving Cancer Patients. Freedman, Benjamin.

CANTOR

Cantor and the Scholastics. Small, Robin.

Cantor's Power-Set Theorem Versus Frege's Double-Correlation Thesis. Cocchiarella, N B.

CAPITAL PUNISHMENT

see Death Penalty

CAPITALISM

Beyond Liberation Theology. Belli, Humberto and Nash, Ronald.

Democracy. Harrison, Ross.

Dialectical Investigations. Ollman, Bertell.

From Marx to Mises. Steele, David Ramsay.

Hegel: Three Studies. Adorno, Theodor W and Nicholsen, Shierry Weber (trans).

Ideology and False Consciousness: Marx and his Historical Progenitors. Pines, Christopher.

Ideology: An Introduction. Eagleton, Terry.

International Justice and the Third World. Attfield, Robin (ed) and Wilkins, Barry (ed).

Interpreting Tocqueville's "Democracy in America". Masugi, Ken (ed).

Marxism Recycled. Van Parijs, Philippe.

Materialist Feminism and the Politics of Discourse. Hennessy, Rosemary.

Pianificazione e teoria critica. Campani, Carlos.

Post-Liberalism: Studies in Political Thought. Gray, John.

Subject to History: Ideology, Class, Gender. Simpson, David (ed).

The Cult of the Avant-Garde Artist. Kuspit, Donald.

The Deleuze Reader. Boundas, Constantin V (ed).

The Logic of Marx's "Capital": Replies to Hegelian Criticisms. Smith, Tony.

Transition to Modernity: Essays on Power, Wealth and Belief. Hall, John A (ed) and Jarvie, I C (ed).

A Political and Economic Case for the Democratic Enterprise. Bowles, Samuel and Gintis, Herbert.

A Reply to Robert Allan Cooke's "And the Blind Shall Lead the Blind". Wolfe, Art.

Adam Smith and the Ethics of Contemporary Capitalism. Bassiry, G R and Jones, Marc.

After Libertarianism: Rejoinder to Narveson, McCloskey, Flew, and Machan. Friedman, Jeffrey.

Afterword—Marxism and Postmodernism (Including Bibliography) in Postmodernism/ Jameson/ Critique, Kellner, Douglas (ed). Jameson, Fredric.

Alienation and Moral Imperatives: A Reply to Kanungo. Sweet, Robert T.

Asymmetrical Reciprocity in Market Exchange: Implications for Economies in Transition. Buchanan, James M.

Basic Questions about Metaphysics of Technology: Spangler, Heidegger, Günther. Bammé, Arno, Kotzmann, Ernst and Oberheber, Ulrike.

Beyond Selfishness: Adam Smith and the Limits of the Market. Solomon, Robert C.

Business Ethics as a Postmodern Phenomenon. Green, Ronald M.

Charles Sanders Peirce's Sociology of Knowledge and Critique of Capitalism in Frontiers in American Philosophy, Volume I, Burch, Robert W (ed). Stikkers, Kenneth W.

Elster's Marxism. Nielsen, Kai.

Endgame. McCarney, Joseph.

Friedman's Theory of Corporate Social Responsibility. Carson, Thomas.

From Post-Communism to Civil Society: The Reemergence of History and the Decline of the Western Model. Gray, John.

Global Justice, Capitalism and the Third World in International Justice and the Third World, Attfield, Robin (ed). Nielsen, Kai.

Jameson, Marxism, and Postmodernism in Postmodernism/ Jameson/ Critique, Kellner, Douglas M (ed). Kellner, Douglas M.

Lenin's Reformulation of Marxism: The Colonial Question as a National Question. Seth, Sanjay.

Liberalism: Political and Economic. Hardin, Russell.

Libertarianism, Postlibertarianism, and the Welfare State: Reply to Friedman. Narveson, Jan.

Locke on Government in Logical Foundations, Mahalingam, Indira (ed). Atkinson, R F.

Marx's Embryology of Society. Wouters, Arno.

Marx, Cohen and Brenner in Marx's Theory of History, Wetherly, Paul. Carling, Alan.

Marx—From the Abolition of Labour to the Abolition of the Abolition of Labour. Cohen, Avner.

Marxism and Resistance in Postmodernism/ Jameson/ Critique, Kellner, Douglas M (ed). Gross, David.

Marxism and Russian Philosophy. Zamaleev, A F.

Neo-idealism and Finance Capitalism. Herkless, John L.

On the Relation of J L Fischer to Marxist Philosophy (Reply to L Valenta's Polemic Study) (in Czechoslovakian). Tosenovsky, L.

Pagans, Perverts or Primitives? in Judging Lyotard, Benjamin, Andrew (ed). Readings, Bill.

Postmodernism, Cultural Change, and Social Practice in Postmodernism/ Jameson/ Critique, Kellner, Douglas M (ed). Featherstone, Mike.

Power and Wealth in a Competitive Capitalist Economy. Bowles, Samuel and Gintis, Herbert.

Reactionary Postmodernism? in Postmodernism and Society, Boyne, Roy (ed). Callinicos, Alex.

Realism, Modernism, and the Empty Chair in Postmodernism/ Jameson/ Critique, Kellner, Douglas M (ed). Zuidervaart, Lambert.

Reports on International Research in Social Epistemology. Kasavin, Ilya.

Russia's Movement Toward a Market Civilization and the Russian National Character. Smirnov, P I.

Some Rules of Constitutional Design. Ordeshook, Peter C.

Structural Inquiry, Human Agency and the Contribution of Harré and Bhaskar: A Case Study of Wright's "Classes". Adkins, Barbara.

Sustainability and the Right to Development in International Justice and the Third World, Attfield, Robin (ed). Dower, Nigel.

Tactics of Appropriation and the Politics of Recognition in Late Modern Democracies. Coombe, Rosemary J.

The Early Marx on Needs. Chitty, Andrew.

The Factory Acts in Marx's Theory of History, Wetherly, Paul. Wetherly, Paul.

The Future of a Disillusion in Psychoanalysis, Mind and Art, Hopkins, Jim (ed). Cohen, G A.

The Power and Poverty of Libertarian Thought. Cornuelle, Richard.

The Road Out of Serfdom. Cepl, Vojtech.

The Social Market Economy. Barry, Norman.

The Social Philosophy of N Berdiaev in Light of Perestroika. Adiushkin, V N.

The Tagore-Gandhi Controversy Revisited, II. Singh, Ajai and Singh, Shakuntala.

The Work Ethic and the Work Ethos: The Importance of Ethical Arguments for the Politics of Transition to the Market. Büscher, M.

Totalitarianism and the Problems of a Work Ethic. Davydov, I N.

Walrasian Marxism Once Again: A Reply to Joe Roemer. Devine, James and Dymski, Gary.

What are Intellectuals For: A Foucaultian Model of Intellectual Responsibility. Blacker, David.

What Walrasian Marxism Can and Cannot Do. Roemer, John.

Why Liberty is Devoured by Reason in History: Re-Reading Merleau-Ponty During the Days of the Soviet Revolution. Feher, Fererr.

CAPLAN, A

Moral Sensibilities and Moral Standing: Caplan on Xenograft "Donors". Nelson, James Lindemann.

CAPUTO, J

Of Spirit and the Daimon in Ethics and Danger, Dallery, Arleen B (ed). Krell, David Farrell.

The Place of Phronesis in Postmodern Hermeneutics. Gallagher, Shaun.

The Tragic and the Religious: Openness to the Mystery in Caputo's Radical Hermeneutics. Krantz, Susan F L.

Towards a Postmodern Ethics: Sir Isaiah Berlin and John Caputo. McKinney, Ronald H.

CARD, C

Recent Work in Feminist Philosophy. Mendus, Susan.

CAUSALITY

Counterfactuals. Kvart, Igal.
Crime Rates by Race and Causal Relevance: A Reply to Levin. Adler, Jonathan.
Descartes' Problematic Causal Principle of Ideas. O'Toole, Frederick J.
Drawing the Boundary between Subject and Object: Comments on the Mind-Brain Problem. Rosen, Robert.
Duhkha: An Analysis of Buddhist Clue to Understand Human Nature. Chinchore, Mangala R.
Empirical Theology in the Light of Science. Peters, Karl E.
Externalism and Mental Causality (in French). Jacob, Pierre.
Fodor, Adams and Causal Properties. Russow, Lilly-Marlene.
Fodorian Semantics, Pathologies, and "Block's Problem". Adams, Fred and Aizawa, Kenneth.
Fondazione, creazione e creazione artistica in Sartre. Gonzi, Andrea.
Freiheit und Determinismus (Teil I). Seebass, Gottfried.
Gesetz, Befehle und Theorien der Kausalität. Hampe, Michael.
Heritability and Causality. Sesardic, Neven.
How Not to Explain the Errors of the Immune System. Melander, Peter.
In Defence of 'This Worldly' Causality: Comments on Van Fraassen's Laws and Symmetry. Cartwright, Nancy.
Intention, Intentionality and Causality (in French). Moya, Carlos.
Intentionality, Perception, and Causality in John Searle and His Critics, Lepore, Ernest (ed). Armstrong, D M.
Interpretation as Explanation in The Interpretive Turn, Hiley, David R (ed). Roth, Paul A.
Just Like Quarks? in Ontology, Causality and Mind: Essays in Honour of D M Armstrong, Bacon, John (ed). Forrest, Peter.
Kants Wahrnehmungsurteile als Erbe Humes?. Lohmar, Dieter.
Kausalität als Leitbegriff ärztlichen Denkens und Handelns. Hartmann, Fritz.
Kausalität und Freiheit: Ein Beispiel für den Zusammenhang von Metaphysik und Lebenspraxis. Krüger, Lorenz.
Kausalität: Eine Problemübersicht. Heidelberger, Michael.
Knowledge of the Past and Future. Feinberg, Gerald.
La causalité adéquate chez Spinoza. Rice, Lee C.
Logical Atomism and Its Ontological Refinement: A Defense in Language, Truth and Ontology, Mulligan, Kevin (ed). Simons, Peter.
Meeting Hume's Skeptical Challenge. Schlagel, Richard H.
Models of Explanation: An Evaluation of Their Fruitfulness. Weber, Erik.
Objectivism Without Objective Probabilities. Weintraub, Ruth.
On the Acausality of Time, Space, and Space-Time. Le Poidevin, Robin.
On the Reduction of Process Causality to Statistical Relations. Dowe, Phil.
On the Strength of a Causal Chain. Bessie, Joseph D.
Plotin, Descartes et la notion de causa sui. Narbonne, Jean-Marc.
Probabilistic Causality Reexamined. Ray, Greg.
Process Causality and Asymmetry. Dowe, Phil.
Reply to Forrest's 'Just Like Quarks?' in Ontology, Causality and Mind: Essays in Honour of D M Armstrong, Bacon, John (ed). Armstrong, D M.
Reply to Russow's "Fodor, Adams and Causal Properties". Adams, Frederick.
Robustness and Integrative Survival in Significance Testing: The World's Contribution to Rationality. Trout, J D.
Semantic Emphasis in Causal Sentences. Stern, Cindy D.
Semantik und Handlungskausalität: Zur Diskussion über die 'künstliche Intelligenz'. Hörl, Christoph.
Simpson's Paradox and the Fisher-Newcomb Problem. Wagner, Carl G.
Spinoza's Argument for the Identity Theory. Della-Rocca, Michael.
St Thomas Aquinas and Charles Hartshorne's Process Philosophy. Baldner, Steven.
The Causal Theory of Perception. Hyman, John.
The Concept of a Cause of the Universe. Smith, Quentin.
The Deconstruction of Buddhism in Derrida and Negative Theology, Coward, Harold (ed). Loy, David.
The New Problem of Genetics: A Response to Gifford. Smith, Kelly C.
The Occasionalist Proselytizer in Philosophical Perspectives, 5: Philosophy of Religion, 1991, Tomberlin, James E (ed). McCann, Hugh J and Kvanvig, Jonathan L.
The Social Construction of Homosexuality. Thorp, John.
Things Change. Heller, Mark.
Thresholds, Transitivity, Overdetermination, and Events. Hausman, Daniel.
Trying Out Epiphenomenalism. Bieri, Peter.
Two Routes to Narrow Content: Both Dead Ends. Manfredi, Pat A.
Vision and Experience: the Causal Theory and the Disjunctive Conception. Child, William.
Warum-Fragen: Schwierigkeiten mit einem Modell für kausale Erklärungen. Ströker, Elisabeth.
Wesley Salmon's Process Theory of Causality and the Conserved Quantity Theory. Dowe, Phil.

CAUSATION

"Influxus Physicus" in Causation in Early Modern Philosophy, Nadler, Steven (ed). O'Neill, Eileen.
Agency and Alienation: A Theory of Human Presence. Segal, Jerome M.
British Empiricism and American Pragmatism: New Directions and Neglected Arguments. Roth, Robert.
Causation in Early Modern Philosophy. Nadler, Steven (ed).
Descrying the Ideal: The Philosophy of John William Miller. Tyman, Stephen.
Hart's Legal Philosophy: An Examination. Bayles, Michael D.
Mental Causation. Heil, John (ed) and Mele, Alfred (ed).
Moral Personhood: An Essay in the Philosophy of Moral Psychology. Scott, G E.

The Cambridge Companion to Kant. Guyer, Paul (ed).
The Nature of True Minds. Heil, John.
The Philosophy of Mind: Classical Problems/Contemporary Issues. Beakley, Brian (ed) and Ludlow, Peter (ed).
A Debate on Dispositions, Their Nature and Their Role in Causation—Part I—The Armstrong-Place Debate. Armstrong, David M and Place, Ullin T.
A Spinozistic Vision of God. Leslie, John.
Actions, Reasons and Mental Causes (in French). Engel, Pascal.
Adding Potential to a Physical Theory of Causation. Zangari, Mark.
Agency and Causal Explanation in Mental Causation, Heil, John (ed). Hornsby, Jennifer.
An Aristotelian Approach to Case Study Analysis. Malloy, David C and Lang, Donald L.
Animadversions on the Causal Theory of Perception. Vision, Gerald.
Anscombe on Coming Into Existence and Causation. Gordon, David.
Are Causal Laws Contingent/ in Ontology, Causality and Mind: Essays in Honour of D M Armstrong, Bacon, John (ed). Fales, Evan.
Authors and Artifacts. Hilpinen, Risto.
Because Mere Calculating Isn't Thinking: Comments on Hauser's "Why Isn't My Pocket Calculator a Thinking Thing?". Rapaport, William J.
Before Environmental Ethics. Weston, Anthony.
Can Supervenience and 'Non-Strict Laws' Save Anomalous Monism? in Mental Causation, Heil, John (ed). Kim, Jaegwon.
Causal Facts as Logical Entailments of Action Statements. Lauer, Henle.
Causal Knowledge: What Can Psychology Teach Philosophers?. Fales, Evan and Wasserman, Edward A.
Causal Laws and the Foundations of Natural Science in The Cambridge Companion to Kant, Guyer, Paul (ed). Friedman, Michael.
Causation and Preestablished Harmony in the Early Development of Leibniz's Philosophy in Causation in Early Modern Philosophy, Nadler, Steven (ed). Kulstad, Mark.
Causation as a Natural and as a Philosophical Relation. Kukla, Rebecca.
Causation as a Secondary Quality. Menzies, Peter and Price, Huw.
Causation, Extrinsic Relations, and Hume's Second Thoughts about Personal Identity. Loeb, Louis E.
Causation, Liability and Toxic Risk Exposure. Simon, Michael Arthur.
Causation, Probability, and the Monarchy. Rosenberg, Alexander.
Causation, Robustness, and EPR. Healey, Richard A.
Causation: One Thing Just Happens After Another in The Philosophy of A J Ayer, Hahn, Lewis Edwin (ed). Honderich, Ted.
Cause and Essence. Yablo, Stephen.
Compossibility and Law in Causation in Early Modern Philosophy, Nadler, Steven (ed). Wilson, Margaret.
Conjunctive Forks and Temporally Asymmetric Inference. Sober, Elliott and Barrett, Martin.
Constancy, Emergence, and Illusions: Obstacles to a Naturalistic Theory of Vision in Causation in Early Modern Philosophy, Nadler, Steven (ed). Wilson, Catherine.
Content, Causation, and Psychophysical Supervene. Owens, Joseph.
Counterfactuals and Event Causation. Cross, Charles B.
Davidson's Thinking Causes in Mental Causation, Heil, John (ed). Sosa, Ernest.
Defending Backwards Causation. Brown, Bryson.
Descartes and Occasionalism in Causation in Early Modern Philosophy, Nadler, Steven (ed). Garber, Daniel.
Experience and Causal Explanation in Medical Empiricism in Greek Studies in the Philosophy and History of Science, Nicolacopoulos, Pantelis (ed). Pentzopoulou-Valalas, Theresa.
Experimental Ecology on the Pacific Coast: Victor Shelford and His Search for Appropriate Methods. Benson, Keith R.
Explanation in Biopsychology in Mental Causation, Heil, John (ed). Millikan, Ruth Garrett.
Externalism and Mental Causation. Jacob, Pierre.
Externalism and the Explanatory Relevance of Broad Content. Jacob, Pierre.
Fodor's Modal Argument. Adams, Frederick.
General Causal Propensities, Classical and Quantum Probabilities. Sapire, David.
God and Process in Logic, God and Metaphysics, Harris, James F (ed). Edwards, Rem B.
God's General Concurrence with Secondary Causes in Philosophical Perspectives, 5: Philosophy of Religion, 1991, Tomberlin, James E (ed). Freddoso, Alfred.
Graham Oppy on the Kalam Cosmological Argument. Craig, William Lane.
Incompatibilism, Nondeterministic Causation, and the Real Problem of Free Will. Francken, Patrick.
Linking Causal and Explanatory Asymmetry. Hausman, Daniel M.
Malebranche, Models, and Causation in Causation in Early Modern Philosophy, Nadler, Steven (ed). Watson, Richard A.
Mechanism as a Silly Mouse in Causation in Early Modern Philosophy, Nadler, Steven (ed). Lennon, Thomas M.
Mental Causation. Yablo, Stephen.
Mental Causation and Mental Reality. Crane, Tim.
Mental Causation in Mental Causation, Heil, John (ed). Audi, Robert.
Mental Events Again—Or What Is Wrong with Anomalous Monism?. Heckmann, Heinz-Dieter.
Mental Events as Structuring Causes of Behavior in Mental Causation, Heil, John (ed). Dretske, Fred.
Metaphysics and Mental Causation in Mental Causation, Heil, John (ed). Baker, Lynne Rudder.
Mice, Shrews, and Misrepresentation. Clark, Austen G.
Mind-Body Causation and Explanatory Practice in Mental Causation, Heil, John (ed). Burge, Tyler.

CAUSATION

Miracles, Laws of Nature and Causation—I. Hughes, Christopher.

Miracles, Laws of Nature and Causation—II. Adams, Robert Merrihew.

Natural Kinds and Ecological Niches—Response to Johnson's Paper. Hogan, Melinda.

Nomic Dependence and Causation. Clendinnen, F John.

Objects as Causes of Emotions (in Hebrew). Eylon, Yuval.

Occasionalism and General Will in Malebranche. Nadler, Steven.

On Being Wrong: Kripke's Causal Theory of Reference. Powers, John.

On Davidson's Response to the Charge of Epiphenomenalism in Mental Causation, Heil, John (ed). McLaughlin, Brian.

Peirce, a Philosopher for the 21st Century: Part II. Hookway, Christopher.

Perspectives on Decisions263-. Segerberg, Krister.

Rationalising Belief. Leon, Mark.

Realism and the Principle of the Common Cause. Stone, Mark A.

Reaping the Whirlwind: Reply to Harnad's Other Bodies, Other Minds. Hauser, Larry.

Reply to Fales's 'Are Causal Laws Contingent?' in Ontology, Causality and Mind: Essays in Honour of D M Armstrong, Bacon, John (ed). Armstrong, D M.

Response: Perception and the Satisfactions of Intentionality in John Searle and His Critics, Lepore, Ernest (ed). Searle, John R.

Social Causation and Cognitive Neuroscience. Gillett, Grant R.

Some of the Difference in the World: Crane on Intentional Causation. Seymour, Daniel.

States, State Types, and the Causation of Behavior. Beckermann, Ansgar.

Sunburn: Independence Conditions on Causal Relevance. Dardis, Anthony B.

The Metaphysical Aspect of Tenses in Proclus. Plass, Paul.

The Nature of Naturalism—I. Macdonald, Graham.

The Nature of Naturalism—II. Pettit, Philip.

The Non-Reductivist's Troubles with Mental Causation in Mental Causation, Heil, John (ed). Kim, Jaegwon.

The Problem of Psychophysical Causation. Lowe, E J.

The Radical Agent: A Deweyan Theory of Causation. Reuter, Robert.

The Sense of 'Thinking'. Hauser, Larry.

The Unanimity Theory and Probabilistic Sufficiency. Carroll, John W.

The Value of Harmony in Causation in Early Modern Philosophy, Nadler, Steven (ed). Frankel, Lois.

Thinking Causes in Mental Causation, Heil, John (ed). Davidson, Donald.

Three Bad Arguments for Intentional Property Epiphenomenalism. Van Gulick, Robert.

Transitivity, Torts and Kingdom Loss. Gibson, Kevin.

Vision, Causation and Occlusion. Hyman, John.

What Impressions of Necessity?. Flew, Antony.

What Isn't Wrong with Folk Psychology. Dretske, Frederick.

Who's in Charge Here? And Who's Doing All the Work? in Mental Causation, Heil, John (ed). Van Gulick, Robert.

Why Don't Effects Explain Their Causes?. Hausman, Daniel.

Why Isn't My Pocket Calculator a Thinking Thing?. Hauser, Larry.

Why We Believe in Induction: Standards of Taste and Hume's Two Definitions of Causation. Helm, Bennet W.

'I Believe that *P*' in John Searle and His Critics, Lepore, Ernest (ed). Malcolm, Norman.

CAUSE

see also Efficient Cause, First Cause

"Averroe quantumque arabo et ignorante di lingua greca...": Note sull'averrosimo di Giordano Bruno. Sturlese, Rita.

How Should We Explain Remote Correlations?. Forge, John.

Intenzionalità e filosofia dell'azione. Marrone, Pierpaolo.

John Bishop's Natural Agency. Marshall, Graeme.

La scoperta di nuovi documenti sulla vita di Bruno: Su *Giordano Bruno and the Embassy Affair* di John Bossy. Mancini, Sandro.

Le concept de philosophie première dans la "Métaphysique" d'Aristote. Follon, Jacques.

Les quatre causes: de Bunge à Aristote. Espinoza, Miguel.

Making a Difference. Lipton, Peter.

Names, Contents, and Causes. Adams, Fred and Fuller, Gary.

CAVELL, S

Language, Music, and Mind. Raffman, Diana.

American Loss in Cavell's Emerson. Anderson, Douglas R.

Emerson's Words, Nietzsche's Writing. Gould, Timothy.

CEKIC

Cekic and Lukács über die Ontologie des gesellschaftlichen Seins: 'Die Prioritätsfrage' in Analecta Husserliana, XXXI, Tymieniecka, Anna-Teresa (ed). Nikolic, Zivojin.

CELL

Ensayo de axiomatización de la teoría tisular y su reducción a la teoría celular. De Asúa, Miguel and Klimovsky, Gregorio.

Inquiry Into the Spatio-Temporal Contingency of Cellular Communication Systems. Allaerts, Wilfried.

Integrating Sciences by Creating New Disciplines: The Case of Cell Biology. Bechtel, William.

Leo Buss's *The Evolution of Individuality*. Resnik, David B.

CENSORSHIP

Speech, Crime, and the Uses of Language. Greenawalt, Kent.

Art, Ethics and the Law: Where Should the Law End?. Carroll, Mary Ann and Van Der Bogert, Frans.

If Pornography Is the Theory, Is Inequality the Practice?. McCormack, Thelma.

Protected Space: Politics, Censorship, and the Arts. Devereaux, Mary.

CERTAINTY

Certainty and Surface in Epistemology and Philosophical Method. Martinich, A P (ed) and White, Michael J (ed).

De Re Certainty. McGowan, Neale.

Certainty and Authority in Wittgenstein Centenary Essays, Griffiths, A Phillips (ed). Winch, Peter G.

Certainty Made Simple in Certainty and Surface in Epistemology and Philosophical Method, Martinich, A P (ed). Matson, Wallace I.

Defensa de la revelación divina contra las objeciones del librepensador. Arana, Juan (trans) and Euler, L.

Fallibilism and Rational Belief. Weintraub, Ruth.

The Quest for Certainty in Feminist Thought. Clark, Ann.

CERVANTES

"Unreasons' Reason": Cervantes at the Frontiers of Difference. Wilson, Diana de Armas.

CEZANNE

Cézanne's Physicality: The Politics of Touch in The Language of Art History, Kemal, Salim (ed). Shiff, Richard.

CH'ENG

Master Chu's Self-Realization: The Role of *Ch'eng*. Berthrong, John.

CHADWICK, R

Subject to History: Ideology, Class, Gender. Simpson, David (ed).

CHAKRABARTI, K

Reply to Chakrabarti: Some Comments on Contraposition in European and Indian Logic. Dravid, N S.

CHANCE

see also Probability

Der Zufall—eine Chimäre?. Seifen, Johannes.

Imagination and Chance: The Difference Between the Thought of Ricoeur and Derrida. Lawlor, Leonard.

Peirce on Tychism and Determinism. Cosculluela, Victor.

CHANGE

see also Motion

Paradigms and Barriers: How Habits of Mind Govern Scientific Beliefs. Margolis, Howard.

Changing the Past. Ni, Peimin.

Classical Physical Abstraction. Adams, Ernest W.

Giles of Rome on the Instant of Change. Trifogli, Cecilia.

Models of Change in Greek Studies in the Philosophy and History of Science, Nicolacopoulos, Pantelis (ed). Sfendoni-Mentzou, Demetra.

On Time. Priest, Graham.

Realism and Methodological Change. Leplin, Jarrett.

Space, Time, Discreteness. Kilmister, C W.

The Dilemma Facing Contemporary Research in the *Yijing*. Zheng, Liu.

Things Change. Heller, Mark.

Time and Change. Teichmann, Roger.

Time and Change in Kant and McTaggart. Waxman, Wayne.

Transformations of Hegelianism, 1805-1846 in The Cambridge Companion to Hegel, Beiser, Frederick C (ed). Toews, John.

Variation in Analecta Husserliana, XXXIV, Tymieniecka, Anna-Teresa (ed). Olesen, Soren Gosvig.

'Demographic' Factors in Revolutionary Science: The Wave Model. D'Agostino, Fred.

CHAOS

Aspects of Chaos Research Related to Teaching. Pritscher, Conrad P.

Caos, frattali ed altro. Del Vecchio, D.

Defensible Anarchy?. Harriott, Howard.

Defining Chaos. Batterman, Robert W.

Ex Post Facto Explanations. Hobbs, Jesse.

On the Incompleteness of Axiomatized Models for the Empirical Sciences. Da Costa, N C A and Doria, Francisco Antonio.

The Face of Chaos. Stenger, Victor J.

CHARACTER

Character Development in Schools and Beyond (Second Edition). Ryan, Kevin (ed) and Lickona, Thomas (ed).

Chinese Foundations for Moral Education and Character Development. Van Doan, Tran (ed), Shen, Vincent (ed) and McLean, George F (ed).

Morality and the Emotions. Oakley, Justin.

Philosophical Foundations for Moral Education and Character Development: Act and Agent (Second Edition). McLean, George F and Ellrod, Frederick E.

Psychological Foundations of Moral Education and Character Development: An Integrated Theory of Moral Development (Second Edition). McLean, George F (ed) and Knowles, Richard T (ed).

Abortion and Moral Character: A Critique of Smith. Gass, Michael.

Character and Community in the *Defensor Pacis*: Marsiglio of Padua's Adaptation of Aristotelian Moral Psychology. Nederman, Cary J.

Character Development in the Liberal Arts Students in Moral Education and the Liberal Arts, Mitias, Michael H (ed). Giventer, Edwin B.

Fanning the Embers of Civic Virtue: Toward a (Chastened) Politics of Character. Budziszewski, J.

Impersonality, Character, and Moral Expressivism. Moran, Richard A.

Judgments of Character. O'Brien, Wendell.

The *Education of Cyrus* as Xenophon's "Statesman". Ray, John.

The Incompatibility of the Virtues. Walker, A D M.

Understanding the Real "Character Issue:" A Review of the Latest Work of Clarence Walton (*The Moral Manager*, and *Corporate Encounters*). Cooke, Robert.

CHARACTERISTICS

Characteristica Universalis in Language, Truth and Ontology, Mulligan, Kevin (ed). Smith, Barry C.

CHARDIN, PIERRE TEILHARD DE

see Teilhard

CHARISMA

The Representation of Society and the Privatization of Charisma. Seligman, Adam B.

CHARITY

Altruism. Paul, Ellen Frankel (ed), Miller, Fred D (ed) and Paul, Jeffrey (ed).

Liberal Rights: Collected Papers 1981-1991. Waldron, Jeremy.

The Love Commandments: Essays in Christian Ethics and Moral Philosophy. Santurri, Edmund N (ed) and Werpehowski, William (ed).

A Moral Basis for Corporate Philanthropy. Shaw, Bill and Post, Frederick R.

Altruism and the Argument from Offsetting Transfers. Cowen, Tyler.

Distinguishing Charity as Goodness and Prudence as Rightness: A Key to Thomas's *Secunda Pars*. Keenan, James F.

Giustizia e "carità" nel pensiero greco-romano (I). Pizzorni, R.

Global Distributive Justice and the Corporate Duty to Aid. Jackson, Kevin T.

Liberal Philanthropy. Riley, Jonathan.

The Disconsolation of Theology: Irony, Cruelty, and Putting Charity First. Jackson, Timothy P.

The Right to Welfare and the Virtue of Charity. Den Uyl, Douglas.

The Right to Welfare and the Virtue of Charity in Altruism, Paul, Ellen Frankel (ed). Den Uyl, Douglas.

CHARRON, P

René Descartes et Pierre Charron. Adam, M.

CHASTITY

Chastity and the (Male) Philosophers. McGhee, Michael.

CHATER, N

Is Logicist Cognitive Science Possible?. Garnham, Alan.

CHAUVINISM

How Sexist is Sartre?. Burstow, Bonnie.

CHEMISTRY

see also Biochemistry

Greek Studies in the Philosophy and History of Science. Nicolacopoulos, Pantelis (ed).

Condillac, Lavoisier, and the Instrumentalization of Science. Roberts, Lissa.

Darcy's Law and Structural Explanation in Hydrology. Hofmann, James R and Hofmann, Paul A.

On the Evolution of Natural Laws. Balashov, Yury V.

The Value of the Inexact. Polanyi, Michael.

CHENEY, J

Cheney and the Myth of Postmodernism. Smith, Mick.

CHESS

Chess as an Art Form. Humble, P N.

CHIHARA, C

Penelope Maddy's *Realism in Mathematics* and Charles Chihara's *Constructibility and Mathematical Existence*. McCarty, David Charles.

CHILD ABUSE

Rights, Moral Values and Natural Facts: A Reply to Mary Midgley on the Problem of Child-Abuse. Archard, David.

CHILDHOOD

The Moral Self. Noam, Gil G (ed) and Wren, Thomas (ed).

Knowing and Wanting in Cultural-Political Interventions in the Unfinished Project of Enlightenment, Honneth, Axel (& other eds). Nunner-Winkler, Gertrud.

CHILDREN

see also Infant

"At Risk": Development of Personhood. Nowell, Linda.

Contemporary Issues in Paediatric Ethics. Burgess, Michael M (ed) and Woodrow, Brian E (ed).

The Ethics of Reproductive Technology. Alpern, Kenneth D (ed).

Video Icons and Values. Olson, Alan M (ed), Parr, Christopher (ed) and Parr, Debra (ed).

Are Children's Rights Wrong Rights?. Houston, Barbara.

Beetle Crushers Lift the Lid on Mindless Behavior. Murris, Karin.

Between Parents and Children. Machan, Tibor R.

Bioethics and Paediatrics in Contemporary Issues in Paediatric Ethics, Burgess, Michael M (ed). Ost, David.

Bridging the Gap. Katz, Claire Elise.

Child Liberationism and Legitimate Interference. Lipson, Morrice and Vallentyne, Peter.

Children are Not Meant to be Studied.... Hart, W A.

Children's Philosophy in Europe. De Bruijn, Jan.

Excellence as a Guide to Educational Conversation. Noddings, Nel.

For All Its Children. Noddings, Nel.

Good Intentions and a Great Divide: Having Babies by Intending Them. Roberts, Melinda.

Husserl, Child Education, and Creativity in Analecta Husserliana, XXXI, Tymieniecka, Anna-Teresa (ed). Morselli, Graziella.

Immodest Proposals II: Give Children the Vote. Wallace, Vita.

Innovative Lifesaving Treatments in Contemporary Issues in Paediatric Ethics, Burgess, Michael M (ed). Ackerman, Terrence F.

Mature Minors in Contemporary Issues in Paediatric Ethics, Burgess, Michael M (ed). Burgess, Michael.

New Problems in Child-Centered Pedagogy. Margonis, Frank.

Non-Treatment and Non-Compliance as Neglect in Contemporary Issues in Paediatric Ethics, Burgess, Michael M (ed). Sherwin, Susan.

On Children's Rights: A Response to Barbara Houston. Glass, Ronald.

On Constructing a European Cultural Identity by Doing Philosophy with Children. Moriyon, Felix Garcia.

On What We Really Care About in Child-Centeredness. Smeyers, Paul.

Parental Rights in Applied Philosophy, Almond, Brenda (ed). Page, Edgar.

Paternalismus. Wolf, Jean-Claude.

Philosophizing and Learning to Think: Some Proposals for a Qualitative Evaluation. Santi, Marina.

Philosophy for Children and Mathematics Education. English, Lyn.

Philosophy for Children Comes to Africa. Atkinson, Norman.

Philosophy for Children: A Note of Warning. Wilson, John.

Philosophy for Children: Curriculum and Practice. Morehouse, Mort.

Reflections on Personhood: Developing a Sense of Self through Community of Inquiry. Glaser, Jen.

Repression in *The Child's Conception of the World*: A Phenomenological Reading of Piaget. Sipiora, Michael P.

Response to Alexander's "Voluntary Acts: The Child/Davidson Trilemma". Child, James.

Rights, Moral Values and Natural Facts: A Reply to Mary Midgley on the Problem of Child-Abuse. Archard, David.

Rousseau as Progressive Instrumentalist. Darling, John.

Should We Teach Children to be Open-Minded? Or is the Pope Open-Minded about the Existence of God?. Gardner, Peter.

Skills-Grouping as a Teaching Approach to the "Philosophy for Children" Program. Woolcock, Peter G.

Spreading Thoughts. Cresswell, Roger.

Synthesis: The Larger Perspective in Contemporary Issues in Paediatric Ethics, Burgess, Michael M (ed). O'Driscoll, Herbert.

The Contingency of Cuteness: A Reply to Sanders. Morreall, John.

The Necessity for Particularity in Education and Child-Rearing: the Moral Issue. Smeyers, Paul.

The Philosopher's Child. Hughes, Judith.

The Roots of Philosophy. White, John.

The Roots of Philosophy in The Impulse to Philosophise, Griffiths, A Phillips (ed). White, John.

The Young Philosophers. Liverani, Mary Rose.

Voluntary Acts: The Child/Davidson Trilemma. Alexander, Larry.

Why Can't a Baby Pretend to Smile? in Wittgenstein's Intentions, Canfield, J V (ed). Von Savigny, Eike.

Why Philosophy for Children Now?. Kennedy, David.

Withholding/Withdrawing Life-Sustaining Treatment in Contemporary Issues in Paediatric Ethics, Burgess, Michael M (ed). Bartholome, William.

Young Kids Search for the Philosophers' Stone. Neave, Phillippa.

CHILDRESS, J

The Method of 'Principlism': A Critique of the Critique. Lustig, B Andrew.

CHINESE

see also Buddhism, Confucianism, Taoism

Antologia della filosofia cinese. Arena, Leonardo Vittorio.

Chinese Foundations for Moral Education and Character Development. Van Doan, Tran (ed), Shen, Vincent (ed) and McLean, George F (ed).

Confucianism, Buddhism, Daoism, Christianity and Chinese Culture. McLean, George F (ed) and Yi-Jie, Tang.

East Asian Philosophy: With Historical Background and Present Influence. Ho, John E.

Il "Peccato" in Cina: Bene e male nel Neoconfucianesimo dalla metà del XIX secolo, by Paolo Santangelo. Elvin, Mark.

Jurisculture: China. Dorsey, Gray L.

Nietzsche and Asian Thought. Parkes, Graham R (ed).

On Community. Rouner, Leroy S (ed).

Storia del Buddhismo Ch'an. Arena, Leonardo Vittorio.

Tao Teh King By Lao Tzu: Interpreted as Nature and Intelligence. Bahm, Archie.

Tao Teh King—Lao Tzu. Tzu, Lao and Bahm, Archie J (trans).

Taoist Mystical Philosophy: The Scripture of Western Ascension, by Livia Kohn. Chan, Alan K L.

The Butterfly as Companion: Meditations on the First Three Chapters of the Chuang Tzu: Review. Kjellberg, Paul.

Unreason Within Reason: Essays on the Outskirts of Rationality. Graham, A C.

A "Just", A Human Society: A Christian- Marxist- Confucian Dialogue. Swindler, Leonard.

A Comparison of the Chinese Buddhist and Indian Buddhist Modes of Thought. Litian, Fang.

A New Direction in Confucian Scholarship: Approaches to Examining the Differences between Neo-Confucianism and *Tao-hsüeh*. Tillman, Hoyt Cleveland.

A Set Theory Analysis of the Logic of the *I Ching*. Fleming, Jesse.

An Exploration of the Concept of *Zhong* in the Teachings of Confucianism. Rongjie, Chen and Chan, Wing-Tsit.

Appearance and Reality in Buddhist Metaphysics from a European Philosophical Point of View. Chung, Bongkil.

Between Individuality and Universality: An Explication of Chuang Tzu's Theses of Chien-tu and Ch'i-wu. Hara, Wing-Han.

China After Tiananmen Square: Rawls and Justice. Lehman, Glen.

Chinese Bhiksunis in the Ch'an Tradition (in Chinese). Shih, Heng-ching.

Chinese Culture and the Concept of Community in On Community, Rouner, Leroy S (ed). Schwartz, Benjamin.

CHINESE

Chinese Rationality: An Oxymoron?. Ames, Roger T.

Classical Taoism, the *I Ching* and Our Need for Guidance. Dixon, Paul W.

Creativity as Synthesis of Contrasting Wisdoms: An Interpretation of Chinese Philosophy in Taiwan since 1949. Shen, Vincent.

Cultural China: Some Definitional Issues. Cohen, Paul A.

Developments in Chinese Philosophy Over the Last Ten Years. Yanping, Shi and Ruzhuang, Xu (trans).

Discourse and Disclosure in the *I Ching*. Stevenson, Frank W.

Heidegger and Taoism in Reading Heidegger: Commemorations, Sallis, John (ed). Zhang, Shi-Ying.

Higher Moral Education in Taiwan in Chinese Foundations for Moral Education and Character Development, Van Doan, Tran (ed). Sprenger, Arnold.

Husserl's Intentionality and "Mind" in Chinese Philosophy. Zhang, Xian.

Imaging the Imageless: Symbol and Perception in Early Chinese Thought. Doeringer, Franklin M.

Limit and Exhaustibility in the Questions of T'ang. Stevenson, Frank W.

Metaphysical Foundations of Traditional Chinese Moral Educ in Chinese Foundations for Moral Education and Character Development, Van Doan, Tran (ed). Woo, Peter Kun-Yu.

Modern Chinese Thought: A Retrospective View and a Look into the Future. Lai, Chen.

Moral Choice in the Analects: A Way without a Crossroads?. Ruskola, Teemu H.

Nietzsche's 'Will to Power' and Chinese 'Virtuality' (De) in Nietzsche and Asian Thought, Parkes, Graham R (ed). Ames, Roger T.

Object Language and Meta-Language in the Gongsun-long-zi. Vierheller, Ernstjoachim.

On the Deification of Confucius. Gier, Nicholas.

On the Interpretation Circle of Philosophy. Guiquan, Zhang.

On the Problem of Value Reconstruction in Chinese Philosophy under the Impact from European Thought. Liu, Shu-Hsien.

On the Three Major Characteristics of Ethical Thought in Traditional China. Gujia, Chen.

Reports on International Research in Social Epistemology in the People's Republic of China. Kang, Ouyang.

Russell on Chinese Civilization. Dong, Yu.

Selfhood and Spontaneity in Ancient Chinese Thought in Selves, People, and Persons, Rouner, Leroy S (ed). Kohn, Livia.

The "C" Theory: A Chinese Philosophical Approach to Management and Decision-Making. Cheng, Chung-Ying.

The Chinese Notion of "Blandness" As a Virtue: A Preliminary Outline. Parkes, Graham R (trans) and Julien, François.

The Concept of *Ch'i* in the Thought of Wang Ch'ung. Rainey, Lee.

The Continuity of Chinese Humanism in the Shang-Chou Period. Wong, Yeu-Guang.

The Cultural Dilemma of Contemporary China: A Discussion of My Own Views on Culture and Response to Mou Zhongjian. Kejian, Huang.

The Dilemma Facing Contemporary Research in the *Yijing*. Zheng, Liu.

The Euclidean Egg, the Three Legged Chinese Chicken: "Contextual versus Formal Approaches to Reason and Logics". Benesch, Walter.

The Evolution of Three Schools of Latter-Day Zhuang Zi Philosophy. Xiaogan, Liu.

The Highest Chinadom in Nietzsche and Asian Thought, Parkes, Graham R (ed). Kelly, David A.

The Huai-nan Tzu Alteration. Alt, Wayne.

The Human Body as a Microcosmic Source of Macrocosmic Values in Calligraphy in Self as Body in Asian Theory and Practice, Kasulis, Thomas P (ed). Hay, John.

The Impact of the Thought of the School of Confucianism and the School of Daoism on the Culture of China. Dainian, Zhang.

The Mind and the "Shen-ming" in Xunzi. Machle, Edward.

The Uses of Neo-Confucianism: A Response to Professor Tillman. De Bary, W T.

Theodicy in the Book of Job (in Hebrew). Schweid, Eliezer.

Tradition, Modernity, and Confucianism. Dallmayr, Fred.

Was There a Concept of Rights in Confucian Virtue-Based Morality?. Lee, Seung-Hwan.

Yan Fu's Philosophy of Evolution and the Thought of Lao Zi and Zhuang Zi. Dayong, Yang.

CHISHOLM, R

Was sind Ereignisse? Eine Studie zur Analytischen Ontologie. Stoecker, Ralf.

Chisholm on Persons as *Entia Successiva* and the Brain-Microparticle Hypothesis. Jacquette, Dale.

Chisholm, Persons and Identity. Noonan, Harold W.

Persoonlijke identiteit in de analytische wijsbegeerte. Cuypers, Stefaan E.

Possibilità e stati di fatto in Chisholm. Negro, Matteo.

Professor Chisholm and the Problem of the Speckled Hen. Kennedy, Ralph.

Some Problems with Chisholm and Potter's Solution to the Paradox of Analysis. Thomason, Neil.

CHOICE

see also Decision, Free Choice

Contractarian Liberal Ethics and the Theory of Rational Choice. Park, Jung Soon.

Erotic Welfare: Sexual Theory and Politics in the Age of Epidemic. Singer, Linda.

The Moral Dimensions of Public Policy Choice: Beyond the Market Paradigm. Gillroy, John Martin (ed) and Wade, Maurice (ed).

Truth's Debt to Value. Weissman, David.

Abortion and "Choice". Gallagher, Kenneth.

Abortion, Moral Responsibility, and Self-Defense. Huffman, Tom L.

Altruism and the Argument from Offsetting Transfers in Altruism, Paul, Ellen Frankel (ed). Cowen, Tyler.

Choice and Utility in The Utilitarian Response, Allison, Lincoln (ed). Brittan, Samuel.

Crime and Punishment: Abortion as Murder?. Mathieu, Deborah.

Definitions of Personhood: Implications for the Care of PVS Patients. Gormally, Luke.

Democratic Theory and the Democratic Agent. Meyers, Diana.

Freedom of Choice and the Tyranny of Desire. Greif, Gary F.

Individual Choice and the Retreat from Utilitarianism in The Utilitarian Response, Allison, Lincoln (ed). Reeve, Andrew.

On a Problem About Probability and Decision. Cargile, James Thomas.

Physician Assisted Death and Hard Choices. Mayo, David J and Gunderson, Martin.

Public Choice Versus Democracy. Hardin, Russell.

Public Choice Versus Democracy in The Idea of Democracy, Copp, David (ed). Hardin, Russell.

Rational Altruism or the Secession of Successful?: A Paradox of Social Choice. Nelson, Julianne.

Rational Consensus and Coherence Methods in Ethics. Baccarini, Elvio.

Rationality and Principles: A Criticism of the Ethic of Care. Foulk, Gary J and Keffer, M Jan.

Reply to Elvio Baccarini's "Rational Consensus and Coherence Methods in Ethics". Lehrer, Keith.

Respect for Autonomy in the Practice of Rehabilitation. Howie, John.

Satisficing and Virtue. Swanton, Christine.

Self-Interest and Survival. Martin, Raymond.

Social Choice and Democracy in The Idea of Democracy, Copp, David (ed). Christiano, Thomas.

Social Choice Theory: Formalism Infatuation and Policy Making Realities. Iannone, A Pablo.

The Morally Beautiful in African-American Perspectives on Biomedical Ethics, Flack, Harley E (ed). Thomas, Laurence.

Wat is rationaliteit en wat is er zo goed aan?. Derksen, Ton.

Weighing Risk. McClennen, Edward and Found, Peter G.

CHOICE SEQUENCES

Spreads or Choice Sequences?. DeSwart, H C M.

CHOMSKY, N

Chomsky for Philosophers (and Linguists) (in Dutch). Jaspers, D.

Chomsky Versus Quine on the Analytic-Synthetic Distinction. Horwich, Paul.

Some Reflections on Noam Chomsky. Mitra, Kumar.

CHOPIN, F

A Narrative Grammar of Chopin's G Minor Ballade. Tarasti, Eero.

CHRIST

Pacifism: A Philosophical Exploration. Filice, Carlo.

Pacifism: A Reply to Professor Narveson. Filice, Carlo.

Professor Filice's Defense of Pacifism: A Comment. Narveson, Jan.

Seeing (Just) Is Believing: Faith and Imagination. Ferreira, M Jamie.

The Temptation of God Incarnate. Werther, David.

CHRISTIAN

Altruism and Christian Love. Browning, Don.

Congetture e confutazioni. Milano, A.

Humanism's Thorn: The Case of the Bright Believers. Pasquarello, Tony.

Mysticism and Ethics in Western Mystical Traditions. Katz, Steven T.

On the Possibility and Impossibility of Christian Existentialism. Toeplitz, Karol.

Pragmatic Conditions for Jewish-Christian Theological Dialogue. Ochs, Peter.

When Christians Become Naturalists. Robbins, J Wesley.

CHRISTIANITY

see also Catholicism, Protestantism

"Es ist uns aber bestimmt, von Überzeugungen, die wir aus innerer Notwendigkeit denken, zu leben". Kern, Udo.

"New Creation"—the Christian Symbol of Universalism and Our Steps Towards Its Realization. Hummel, Gert.

"Nietzsche im christlichen Denken—am Beispiel Bernhard Weltes". Kienzler, Klaus.

Aquinas: An Introduction to the Life and Work of the Great Medieval Thinker. Copleston, F C.

Aristotle Transformed: The Ancient Commentators and Their Influence. Sorabji, Richard (ed).

Athens and Jerusalem: The Role of Philosophy in Theology. Bonsor, Jack A.

Augustine's "De Civitate Dei": An Annotated Bibliography of Modern Criticism, 1960-1990. Donnelly, Dorothy F and Sherman, Mark A.

Beyond Liberation Theology. Belli, Humberto and Nash, Ronald.

Catalyst for Controversy: Paul Carus of Open Court. Henderson, Harold.

Christian Philosophy. Flint, Thomas P (ed).

Consent: The Means to an Active Faith According to St Thomas Aquinas. Barad, Judith.

Death and Personal Survival: The Evidence for Life After Death. Almeder, Robert F.

Disputed Questions in Theology and the Philosophy of Religion. Hick, John.

Éléments d'une Philosophie Politique. Trigeaud, Jean-Marc.

Empirical Theology: A Handbook. Miller, Randolph Crump (ed).

Ethical Essays, Volume II. Harrison, Jonathan.

Fides Quaerens Intellectum: St Anselm's Method in Philosophical Theology. Adams, Marilyn McCord.

God, Creation, and Revelation: A Neo-Evangelical Theology. Jewett, Paul K.

Goodness and Rightness in Thomas Aquinas's "Summa Theologiae". Keenan, James F.

Hegel on Logic and Religion: The Reasonableness of Christianity. Burbidge, John W.

Hell: The Logic of Damnation. Walls, Jerry.

CHRISTIANITY

La historia entre el nihilismo y la afirmación del sentido. Illanes, José Luis.

Language, Interpretation and Worship—I in Religion and Philosophy, Warner, Marin (ed). Warner, Martin.

Language, Interpretation and Worship—II in Religion and Philosophy, Warner, Marin (ed). Lamarque, Peter.

Las raíces del machismo en la ideología judeo-cristiana de la mujer. Caponi, Orietta.

Light and Metpahor in Plotinus and St Thomas Aquinas. Corrigan, Kevin.

Love and Absolutes in Christian Ethics in Christian Philosophy, Flint, Thomas P (ed). Garcia, Jorge L A.

Ludwig Feuerbach and the Political Theology of Restoration. Breckman, Warren.

MacIntyre's Postmodern Thomism. Hibbs, Thomas.

Mainmise. Lyotard, Jean-François and Constable, Elizabeth (trans).

Médiation ou immédiation et philosophie chrétienne. Floucat, Y.

Monica's Grin of Tension. Benso, Silvia.

Mystik und Philosophie. Margreiter, Reinhard.

Natural Religion, Morality and Lessing's Ditch. Schmitz, K L.

Naturalism and Existentialist Interpretation in God, Values, and Empiricism, Peden, Creighton W (ed). Hardwick, Charley D.

New and Old Histories: The Case of Hölderlin and Württemberg Pietism. Hayden-Roy, Priscilla.

Nicolas Berdyaev's Existentialist Personalism. McLachlan, James M.

Nietzsche et l'égalité des droits: De l'usage juridique d'un concept religieux chrétien. Ledure, Yves.

Nietzsche on Pity and *Ressentiment*. Green, Michael.

Not Exactly Politics or Power?. Lash, Nicholas.

Obstinacy in Religious Belief. Groothuis, Douglas.

Omnipotence: Must God Be Infinite? in God, Values, and Empiricism, Peden, Creighton (ed). Hudson, Yeager.

On Behalf of Classical Trinitarianism: A Critique on Rahner on the Trinity. Cary, Phillip.

On Christian Philosophy: *Una Vera Philosophia?*. Ross, James F.

On Not Being Ashamed of the Gospel: Particularity, Pluralism, and Validation. Yoder, John Howard.

On the Issues Dividing Contemporary Christian Philosophers and Theologians. Keller, James A.

Orestes Brownson and Christian Philosophy. Maurer, Armand A.

Philosophy and the Bible: The Areopagus Speech. Adams, Marilyn McCord.

Philosophy of Religion Today. Jordan, Jeff.

Pigs and Piety: A Theocentric Perspective on Food Animals. Comstock, Gary L.

Plantinga and the Two Problems of Evil. Monasterio, Xavier O.

Prospects for Natural Theology. Smith, John E.

Providence and the Problem of Evil in Christian Philosophy, Flint, Thomas P (ed). Stump, Eleonore.

Punishment, Forgiveness, and Divine Justice. Talbott, Thomas.

Questioning One's 'Own' from the Perspective of the Foreign in Nietzsche and Asian Thought, Parkes, Graham R (ed). Parkes, Graham R (trans) and Scheiffele, Eberhard.

Reason and Faith—II in Religion and Philosophy, Warner, Marin (ed). Trigg, Roger.

Relational *Esse* and the Person. Connor, Robert A.

Religion and Civic Virtue. Budziszewski, J.

Religion and Ethics—I in Religion and Philosophy, Warner, Marin (ed). Sutherland, Stewart.

Religion and Ethics—II in Religion and Philosophy, Warner, Marin (ed). Griffiths, A Phillips.

Religion and Self-Interest. Drum, Peter.

Religion and the Quest for Community in On Community, Rouner, Leroy S (ed). Hill, Patrick.

Religion, Secularization and Modernity. Graham, Gordon.

Religious Concepts of 'World': Comparative Metaphysical. Pratt, Douglas.

Religious Pluralism and the Rationality of Religious Belief. Hick, John.

Reparation and Atonement. McNaughton, David.

Reply: A Further Defence of Christian Revelation. Swinburne, Richard.

Rescuing Girard's Argument?. Kerr, Fergus.

Resentment and Apophasis: The Trace of the Other in Levinas, Derrida and Gans in Shadow of Spirit, Berry, Philippa (ed). Foshay, Toby.

Revealing the Scapegoat Mechanism in Philosophy, Religion and the Spiritual Life, McGhee, Michael (ed). Kerr, Fergus.

Revealing the Scapegoat Mechanism: Christianity after Girard. Kerr, Fergus.

Ricoeur and Hick on Evil: Post-Kantian Myth?. Anderson, Pamela.

Saint Anselm the Student. Fortin, John.

Scotus and the Moral Order. Ingham, Mary Elizabeth.

Shifting Sands: Foucault, Brown and the Framework of Christian Asceticism. Behr, John.

Shinto and Christianity: Dialogue for the Twenty-First Century. Kadowaki, Kakichi.

Simultaneity and God's Timelessness. Oddie, Graham and Perrett, Roy W.

Socialism and the Good Life in Socialism and Morality, McLellan, David (ed). Inglis, Fred.

Soft Natural Theology in Prospects for Natural Theology, Long, Eugene Thomas (ed). Smart, Ninian.

Some Reflections on Michael Polanyi and Catholic Thought. Kroger, Joseph.

Standing Alone Together: Silence, Solitude, and Radical Conversion. Staab, Janice.

Stump, Kretzmann, and Historical Blindness. Griffiths, Paul J.

Subjectivity and Worlds in *Works of Love* in Foundations of Kierkegaard's Vision of Community, Connell, George B (ed). Keeley, Louise Carroll.

Taking St Paul Seriously in Christian Philosophy, Flint, Thomas P (ed). Westphal, Merold.

Technology and Mother Earth: The Rousseauian Roots of the Debate. Malcolmson, Patrick and Myers, Richard.

Temporal Wholes and the Problem of Evil. Nelson, Mark T.

Temptation. Day, J P.

The Christian Theodicist's Appeal to Love. Howard-Snyder, Daniel and Howard-Snyder, Frances.

The Critical Appropriation of Our Intellectual Tradition: Toward a Dialogue Between Polanyi and Lonergan. Colapietro, Vincent.

The Difference of Virtue and the Difference It Makes: Courage Exemplified. Hauerwas, Stanley.

The Dimensions of Faith and the Demands of Reason in Reasoned Faith, Stump, Eleonore (ed). Audi, Robert.

The Empire of Progress: Bacon's Improvement Upon Machiavelli. Faulkner, Robert K.

The End of History. Schroeder, Steven.

The Ethics of Santeria. Canizares, Raul J.

The Existence of God and the Creation of the Universe. Carloye, Jack C.

The Freedom of the One. O'Meara, Dominic.

The Freedom of the Truth: Marxist Salt for Christian Earth. Zademach, Wieland.

The God of Love. Schmitz, Kenneth L.

The Golden Rule as the Core Value in Confucianism and Christianity: Ethical Similarities and Differences. Allinson, Robert E.

The Incarnation and the Natural Law. McMahon, Kevin.

The Logic of Mysticism—I in Religion and Philosophy, Warner, Marin (ed). McCabe, Herbert.

The Logic of Mysticism—II in Religion and Philosophy, Warner, Marin (ed). Barrett, Cyril.

The Love Which *Love's Knowledge* Knows Not: Nussbaum's Evasion of Christianity. Jones, L Gregory.

The Meaning of 'God'—I in Religion and Philosophy, Warner, Marin (ed). Durrant, Michael.

The Meaning of 'God'—II in Religion and Philosophy, Warner, Marin (ed). Geach, Peter.

The Nature of God's Love and Forgiveness. Drabkin, Douglas.

The Philosophy of N F Fedorov. Kogan, L A.

The Possibility of a Christian Ethic in the Philosophy of Nietzsche. Newcomer Scalo, Maria.

The Primacy of God's Will in Christian Ethics in Philosophical Perspectives, 6: Ethics, 1992, Tomberlin, James E (ed). Quinn, Philip.

The Problem and Prospects of a Christian Philosophy—Then and Now. Veatch, Henry B.

The Problem of Hell: A Problem of Evil for Christians in Reasoned Faith, Stump, Eleonore (ed). Adams, Marilyn McCord.

The Problem of Service to Unjust Regimes in Augustine's *City of God*. Burnell, Peter.

The Remembrance of Things (Not) Past in Christian Philosophy, Flint, Thomas P (ed). Wolterstorff, Nicholas.

The Return of Adam: Freud's Myth of the Fall. Humbert, David.

The Roots of Culture. Hodgkin, Robin A.

The Status of Politics in St Augustine's *City of God*. Burnell, Peter J.

The Teaching of *Centesimus Annus*. Schall, James V.

The Workmanship Ideal: A Theologico-Political Chimera?. Murphy, James Bernard.

Thomas, Thomisms and Truth. Marshall, Bruce D.

Toward a Kierkegaardian Understanding of Hitler, Stalin, and the Cold War in Foundations of Kierkegaard's Vision of Community, Connell, George B (ed). Bellinger, Charles.

Tracy in Dialogue: Mystical Retrieval and Prophetic Suspicion. Barnes, Michael.

Transitions to and from Nature in Hegel and Plato. Browning, Gary K.

Truth and Subjectivity in Reasoned Faith, Stump, Eleonore (ed). Adams, Robert Merrihew.

Two Key Elements in Francis J McConnell's Social Ethics. Burrow Jr, Rufus.

Universal and Particular in Atonement Theology. Gunton, Colin.

Virtue Ethics: Making a Case as it Comes of Age. Keenan, James F.

Visions of the Self in Late Medieval Christianity in Philosophy, Religion and the Spiritual Life, McGhee, Michael (ed). Coakley, Sarah.

Visions of the Self in Late Medieval Christianity: Some Cross-Disciplinary Reflections. Coakley, Sarah.

Weeping at the Death of Dido: Sorrow, Virtue, and Augustine's *Confessions*. Werpehowski, William.

West's Evasion of Pragmatism. Brodsky, G M.

What Is the Role of Science in the Dialogue Proposed by William Klink?. Gilbert, Thomas L.

Who Is Nietzsche's Epicurus?. Lampert, Laurence A.

Who Sets the Task? in Foundations of Kierkegaard's Vision of Community, Connell, George B (ed). Dunning, Stephen N.

Why Five Ways?. Johnson, Mark.

Why God is Not a Consequentialist. Chappell, T D J.

Why Heidegger's Godot Might not be Worth the Wait. Bruin, John.

William James on Victorian Agnosticism in God, Values, and Empiricism, Peden, Creighton (ed). Woelfel, James.

Workmanship Revisited: Reply to Professor Murphy. Shapiro, Ian.

Zur Kritik des kritischen Rationalismus. Bader, Erwin.

'Keeping Silent through Speaking' in Kierkegaard on Art and Communication, Pattison, George (ed). Rogan, Jan.

CHRISTMAN, J

History and Personal Autonomy. Mele, Alfred.

CHRONOLOGY

Stylometry and Chronology in The Cambridge Companion to Plato, Kraut, Richard H (ed). Brandwood, Leonard.

Time Out of Joint: Reflections on Anachronism. Barnes, Annette and Barnes, Jonathan.

CLASSIFICATION

Hume's Classification of the Passions and Its Precursors. Fieser, James.

The Human Being as a Logical Thinker. Balzer, Noel.

CLIMACUS, J

Existence and Comedy: An Interpretation of the Concluding Unscientific Postscript. Swindle, Stuart.

CLINICAL ETHICS

Quelques réflexions générales sur la normativité; l'éthique et le droit dans le cadre clinique. Baudouin, Jean-Louis.

CLOSURE

A Note on the Normal Form of Closed Formulas of Interpretability Logic. Hájek, Petr and Svejdar, Vitezslav.

Counting Functions. Johnson, Fred.

COASE, R

The Problem of Social Cost: Coase's Economics Versus Ethics. Hanly, Ken.

COBB, J

For the Common Good?. Heyne, Paul.

CODE

A Kantian Approach to Codes of Ethics. L'Etang, Jacquie.

CODE, L

Feminism and Epistemology: A Response to Code. Basinger, David.

Feminist Epistemology: Rethinking the Dualisms of Atomic Knowledge. Sells, Laura.

Recent Work in Feminist Philosophy. Mendus, Susan.

COERCION

Coerced Birth Control, Individual Rights, and Discrimination in Biomedical Ethics Reviews 1992, Humber, James M (ed). Kuo, Lenore.

Devlin, Hart, and the Proper Limits of Legal Coercion. Nattrass, Mark S.

Founding a Family in Biomedical Ethics Reviews 1992, Humber, James M (ed). Jecker, Nancy S.

Morality and Coercion-By-Violence in Terrorism, Justice and Social Values, Peden, Creighton (ed). Kucheman, Clark A.

Virtue Ethics and Mandatory Birth Control in Biomedical Ethics Reviews 1992, Humber, James M (ed). Vitek, William.

COGITO

"Ego Sum, Ego Existo": Descartes au point d'hérésie. Balibar, M Étienne.

L'expérience métaphysique et le transcendantal. Vieillard-Baron, J L.

Metafisica e soggettività: Alle origini della filosofia moderna—Descartes, Pascal, Spinoza. Deregibus, Arturo.

COGNITION

see also Knowing, Thinking

A Study of Concepts. Peacocke, Christopher.

An Essay on Belief and Acceptance. Cohen, L Jonathan.

An Introduction to Husserlian Phenomenology. Bernet, Rudolf, Kern, Iso and Marbach, Eduard.

Cognition, Semantics and Philosophy. Ezquerro, Jesús (ed) and Larrazabal, Jesús (ed).

Cognition: An Epistemological Inquiry. Owens, Joseph.

Consciousness: Psychological and Philosophical Essays. Davies, Martin (ed) and Humphreys, Glyn W (ed).

Glossary of Cognitive Science. Dunlop, Charles E M and Fetzer, James H.

Languages of the Mind: Essays on Mental Representation. Jackendoff, Ray.

Lectures on Logic—Immanuel Kant. Young, Michael J (ed & trans).

Machinations: Computational Studies of Logic, Language, and Cognition. Spencer-Smith, Richard (ed) and Torrance, Steve (ed).

Metaphor and Cognition. Indurkhya, Bipin.

Metaphysics of Consciousness. Seager, William.

Music and Mind: Philosophical Essays on the Cognition and Meaning of Music. Fiske, Harold E.

Psychology and Nihilism: A Genealogical Critique of the Computational Model of Mind. Evans, Fred.

Reason and Tradition in Indian Thought: An Essay on the Nature of Indian Philosophical Thinking. Mohanty, Jitendra N.

Representation, Meaning, and Thought. Gillett, Grant.

Selected Philosophical and Methodological Papers. Meehl, Paul, Anderson, C Anthony (ed) and Gunderson, Keith (ed).

Talk About Beliefs. Crimmins, Mark.

The Nature of True Minds. Heil, John.

The Perceptual System: A Philosophical and Psychological Perspective. Ben-Ze'ev, Aaron.

The Philosophy of Mind: Classical Problems/Contemporary Issues. Beakley, Brian (ed) and Ludlow, Peter (ed).

The Rediscovery of the Mind. Searle, John R.

Tradition and Individuality: Essays. Nyíri, J C.

What Is Cognitive Science?. Von Eckardt, Barbara.

White Queen Psychology and Other Essays for Alice. Millikan, Ruth Garrett.

A Few Notes on the Relation of Philosophy and Ecology (in Czechoslovakian). Kolarsky, R.

A Matemática como Paradigma da Construçao Filosófica de Descartes: Do Discurso do Método e da Tematizaçao do Cogito. Spinelli, Miguel.

An Evolutionary Context for the Cognitive Unconscious. Reber, Arthur S.

Anchoring Conceptual Content: Scenarios and Perception in Cognition, Semantics and Philosophy, Ezquerro, Jesús (ed). Peacocke, Christopher.

Aquinas on the Active Intellect. Haldane, John.

Are Most of Our Concepts Innate?. Kaye, Lawrence J.

Aristotle and Aquinas on Cognition. Owens, Joseph.

Aunty's Own Argument for the Language of Thought in Cognition, Semantics and Philosophy, Ezquerro, Jesús (ed). Davies, Martin.

Basic Principles of Differentiating of Conception of God (in Polish). Gogacz, Mieczyslaw.

Burge on Content. Elugardo, Reinaldo.

Categories and Realities. Carr, Brian.

Changing Beliefs Rationally: Some Puzzles in Cognition, Semantics and Philosophy, Ezquerro, Jesús (ed). Edgington, Dorothy.

Classical and Connectionist Models: Levels of Description. Corbí, Josep E.

Cognitive Science in Reflections on Philosophy, McHenry, Leemon (ed). Aizawa, Kenneth.

Consciousness, Cognition and the Phenomenol—I. Falk, Barrie.

Consciousness, Cognition and the Phenomenol—II. Mulhall, Stephen.

Control, Connectionism and Cognition: Towards a New Regulatory Paradigm. Hooker, C A, Penfold, H B and Evans, R J.

Currents in Connectionism. Bechtel, William.

Delightful, Delovely and Externalist. Duran, Jane.

Evidence in Testimony and Tradition. Bilimoria, Purusottama.

Existe-t-il une théorie de la simulation et la simulation est-elle une théorie? (in Polish). Latawiec, Anna.

Explanation in Biopsychology in Mental Causation, Heil, John (ed). Millikan, Ruth Garrett.

Hegel and the Search for Epistemological Criteria. Ward, Andrew.

Heidegger and Artificial Intelligence. Preston, Beth.

Hume and Reid on Common Sense. Rysiew, Patrick.

Infinite Intellect and Human Cognition in Spinoza (in Dutch). Bartuschat, W.

Interruptibility as a Constraint on Hybrid Systems. Cooper, Richard and Franks, Bradley.

Les compas cartésiens. Serfati, Michel.

Logical Cognition: Husserl's *Prolegomena* and the Truth in Psychologism. Hanna, Robert.

Making it Concrete: Before, During and After Breakdowns in Revisioning Philosophy, Ogilvy, James (ed). Varela, Francisco.

Mice in Mirrored Mazes and the Mind. Garson, James W.

Modelling the Kinematics of Meaning. Van Benthem, Johan.

Modularity in Cognition: The Case of Phonetic and Semantic Interpretation of Empty Elements. Mascaró, Joan and Rigau, Gemma.

Muddy Waters. Radford, Colin.

Nietzschean Philosophers. Schroeder, William R.

On the Study of Linguistic Performance in Cognition, Semantics and Philosophy, Ezquerro, Jesús (ed). Sànchez de Zavala, Victor.

Question-Begging Psychological Explanations. Ward, Andrew.

Reports on International Research in Social Epistemology in the People's Republic of China. Kang, Ouyang.

Reward Event Systems: Reconceptualizing the Explanatory Roles of Motivation, Desire and Pleasure. Morillo, Carolyn R.

Robustness and Integrative Survival in Significance Testing: The World's Contribution to Rationality. Trout, J D.

Ronald Giere's "Explaining Science: A Cognitive Approach". Resnik, David B.

Schlick's Epistemology and Its Contrib to Modern Empiricism in Greek Studies in the Philosophy and History of Science, Nicolacopoulos, Pantelis (ed). Avgelis, Nikolaos.

Scotus's Doctrine of Intuitive Cognition. Langston, Douglas C.

Social Causation and Cognitive Neuroscience. Gillett, Grant R.

Societies of Minds: Science as Distributed Computing. Thagard, Paul.

Tacit Scientific Knowledge (A Typological Analysis). Geroimenko, Wladimir A.

Tacitness and Virtual Beliefs. Crimmins, Mark.

Taking Mathematical Fictions Seriously. Liston, Michael.

The Canon of Poetry and the Wisdom of Poetry. Cook, Albert.

The Defeat of the Computational Model of the Mind. Margolis, Joseph.

The Justification of Lonergan's Cognitional and Volitional Process. Arndt, Stephen W.

The Labrynth of Attitude Reports in Cognition, Semantics and Philosophy, Ezquerro, Jesús (ed). Quesada, Daniel.

The Organizing Principle of the Cognitive Process or the Mode of Existence in Analecta Husserliana, XXXIV, Tymieniecka, Anna-Teresa (ed). Dawidziak, Piotr.

The Pragmatic Psyche. Bogdan, Radu J.

The Roles of Moral Dispositions in the Cognitional Theories of Newman and Lonergan. Miller, Edward Jeremy.

The Structure-Nominative Reconstruction and the Intelligibility of Cognition. Burgin, Mark and Kuznetsov, Vladimir.

The Theory of Tone Semantics: Concept, Foundation, and Application. Leman, Marc.

Theory and Form in Descartes' *Meditations*. Glouberman, Mark.

Unpacking the Black Box of Cognition. Gillett, Grant.

Van Brakel and the Not-So-Naked Emperor. Hardin, C L.

What is Wrong with the Appendage Theory of Consciousness. Natsoulas, Thomas.

What's a Theory to Do...with Seeing? or Some Empirical Considerations for Observation and Theory. Gilman, Daniel.

Who's Afraid of the Turing Test?. Jacquette, Dale.

COGNITIVE

Cognitive Relativism and Social Science. Raven, Diederick (ed), Van Vucht Tijssen, Lieteke (ed) and De Wolf, Jan (ed).

Contemporary Philosophy of Art. Bender, John and Blocker, Gene H.

Contemporary Readings in Epistemology. Goodman, Michael and Snyder, Robert A.

Semiotics in the United States. Sebeok, Thomas A.

COGNITIVE

The Emancipative Theory of Jürgen Habermas and Metaphysics. McLean, George F (ed) and Badillo, Robert Peter.
The Fate of Art: Aesthetic Alienation from Kant to Derrida and Adorno. Bernstein, J M.
The Structure of Value. Allen, R T.
Alexander on *Phantasia*: A Hopeless Muddle or a Better Account?. Modrak, D K W.
Altruism versus Egoism: A Pseudo-Problem, A Cognitive-Emotive Analysis. Shibles, Warren.
Assisted Performance. Duran, Jane.
Between Similarity and Sameness. Sovran, Tamar.
Clarifying the "Adequate Evidence Condition" in Educational Issues and Research: A Lakoffian View. Miller, Steven I and Fredericks, Janet.
Cognitive Psychology and the Rejection of Brentano. Macnamara, John.
Consciousness and Concepts—I. Kirk, Robert.
Consciousness and Concepts—II. Carruthers, Peter.
Content, Embodiment and Objectivity: The Theory of Cognitive Trails. Cussins, Adrian.
Darwin and Disjunction: Foraging Theory and Univocal Assignments of Content. Shapiro, Lawrence A.
Evolutionary Anthropology and the Non-Cognitive Foundation of Moral Validity. Geiger, Gebhard.
In Defense of Truth and Rationality. Jacobson, Stephen.
Is the Switch 'On'?. Tyler, Stephen A.
Mental Anomaly and the New Mind-Brain Reductionism. Bickle, John.
Mind, Consciousness, and Cognition: Phenomenology versus Cognitive Science. Chokr, Nader N.
On Cognitive Illusions and Rationality in Probability and Rationality, Eells, Ellery (ed). Gigerenzer, Gerd.
On Content. Salmon, Nathan.
Ontology and the Construction of Systems. Küng, Guido.
Socializing Naturalized Philosophy of Science. Downes, Stephen M.
The Illusion of 'Illusion' in Aesthetic Illusion, Burwick, Frederick (ed). Watzlawick, Paul.
The Intentionalist Controversy and Cognitive Science. Gibbs Jr, Raymond W.
The Virtues of Illusion. Hardin, C L.
William James's Concrete Analysis of Experience. Seigfried, Charlene Haddock.
Yet Another Look at Cognitive Reason and Moral Action in Hume's Ethical System. Johnson, Clarence Sholé.

COGNITIVE PSYCHOLOGY

A Stichwork Quilt: Or How I Learned to Stop Worrying and Love Cognitive Relativism. Silvers, Stuart.

COGNITIVE SCIENCE

Belief and Cognitive Architecture. Ramsey, William.
Cognitive Science and Semantic Representations. Le Ny, Jean-François.
Is Logicist Cognitive Science Possible?. Garnham, Alan.
Kant's Theory of Musical Sound: An Early Exercise in Cognitive Science. Butts, Robert E.
Logicism, Mental Models and Everyday Reasoning: Reply to Garnham. Chater, Nick and Oaksford, Mike.
Mental Content. Allen, Colin.
Revisionary Physicalism. Bickle, John.

COGNITIVISM

see also Noncognitivism
The Natural and the Normative: Theories of Spatial Perception from Kant to Helmholtz. Hatfield, Gary.
Thinking Things Through: An Introduction to Philosophical Issues and Achievements. Glymour, Clark.
Are Connectionist Models Cognitive?. Shanon, Benny.
Cognitive Models and Representation. Kukla, Rebecca.
Cognitive Spontaneity, Coherence, and Internalism in the Justification of Empirical Belief. Silvers, Stuart.
Cognitivism between Computation and Pragmatics: A Peer Review of 'Some Foundational Questions Concerning Language Studies' by Bickhard and Campbell. Leinfellner, Elisabeth.
Emotions and Music: A Reply to the Cognitivists. Radford, Colin.
Gibbard's Theory of Norms. Horwich, Paul.
Individualism, Computation and Perceptual Content. Egan, Frances.
Moral Realism and Objective Theories of the Right. Sherline, Edward.
On the Cognitive Triviality of Art. Stolnitz, Jerome.
On Thinking Clearly and Distinctly. Lahav, Ran.
Representation *versus* Mirroring: A Cognitivist Response to Rorty. Shashidharan, Suryaprabha and Gupta, Amitabha.
Scientific Rationality and Human Reasoning. Solomon, Miriam.
The Cognitive Revolution?. Casti, John L.
The Last Stand of Mechanism. McDonough, Richard.
'Philosophical Investigations' Section 128: in Wittgenstein's Philosophical Investigations, Arrington, Robert L (ed). Glock, Hans-Johann.

COHEN, G

A Critique of the Technological Interpretation of Historical Materialism. Duquette, David A.
A Refutation of Historical Materialism? in Marx's Theory of History, Wetherly, Paul. Halfpenny, Peter.
An Analytical Outline of Historical Materialism in Marx's Theory of History, Wetherly, Paul. Wetherly, Paul.
Bread and Butter Ethics in Marx's Theory of History, Wetherly, Paul. Carling, Alan.
Commentators on Cohen and Sen in The Quality of Life, Nussbaum, Martha C (ed). Korsgaard, Christine.

Functional Explanation and Metaphysical Individualism. Schwartz, Justin.
Functional Explanation and the State in Marx's Theory of History, Wetherly, Paul. Carter, Alan.
Marx, Cohen and Brenner in Marx's Theory of History, Wetherly, Paul. Carling, Alan.
Mechanisms, Methodological Individualism and Marxism: A Response to Elster in Marx's Theory of History, Wetherly, Paul. Wetherly, Paul.
Minimalist Historical Materialism in On the Track of Reason, Beehler, Rodger (ed). Cohen, Joshua.
Pre-History: The Debate Before Cohen in Marx's Theory of History, Wetherly, Paul. Cowling, Mark and Manners, Jon.
The Factory Acts in Marx's Theory of History, Wetherly, Paul. Wetherly, Paul.

COHEN, H

Die Entwicklung der Lehre von Grundsätzen—Hermann Cohens Ästhetik (in Japanese). Akiba, Fuminori.
Universalismo e particolarismo nell'etica contemporanea. Guariglia, Osvaldo.

COHEN, J

Probability and Rationality. Eells, Ellery (ed) and Maruszewski, Tomasz (ed).
An Optimist's Pessimism: Conversation and Conjunction in Probability and Rationality, Eells, Ellery (ed). Adler, Jonathan.
Induction and Intuition in the Normative Study of Reasoning in Probability and Rationality, Eells, Ellery (ed). Finocchiaro, Maurice A.
Jonathan Cohen and Thomas Bayes on the Analysis of Chains of Reasoning in Probability and Rationality, Eells, Ellery (ed). Schum, David A.
The Method of Relevant Variables and Idealization in Probability and Rationality, Eells, Ellery (ed). Nowak, Leszek.

COHEN, M

The Faith of a Liberal—Morris Raphael Cohen. Cohen, Morris R.

COHEN, T

Kant's Aesthetics Between 1980 and 1990: A Bibliography in Kant's Aesthetics, Meerbote, Ralf (ed). Cicovacki, Predrag.

COHERENCE

Balance and Refinement: Beyond Coherence Methods of Moral Inquiry. DePaul, Michael.
Against Coherence. Fritzman, J M.
Being Knowingly Incoherent. Foley, Richard.
Can One Get Beyond Foundationalism and the Coherence Theory?: A Critique of Kornblith's Epistemic Account. Donovan, Heather Catherine.
Coherence in Category Theory and the Church-Rosser Property. Jay, C Barry.
Davidson on the Idea of a Conceptual Scheme. Noh, Yang-jin.
Inconsistency: The Coherence Theorist's Nemesis?. Engel, Mylan.
Is Higher Order Vagueness Coherent?. Wright, Crispin.
Is Reflective Equilibrium a Coherentist Model?. Ebertz, Roger.
Justified False Belief. Rajotte, Mark J.
Knowing about Virtue. Sher, George.
Rational Consensus and Coherence Methods in Ethics. Baccarini, Elvio.
Reflective Coherence and Newcomb Problems: A Simple Solution. Malinas, Gary.
Reply to Elvio Baccarini's "Rational Consensus and Coherence Methods in Ethics". Lehrer, Keith.
Reply to Mylan Engel's "Inconsistency: The Coherence Theorist's Nemesis?". Lehrer, Keith.
Unification and Coherence as Methodological Objectives in the Biological Sciences. Burian, Richard M.
Unreckoned Misleading Truths and Lehrer's Theory of Undefeated Justification. Bender, John W.

COINCIDENCE

Causes and Coincidences. Owens, David.

COLE, D

The Irreversibility of Death: Reply to Cole. Tomlinson, Thomas.

COLERIDGE

S T Coleridge: El papel de la imaginación en el acto creador. Fonseca, Clotilde.
Samuel Taylor Coleridge and the Romantic Background to Bergson in The Crisis in Modernism, Burwick, Frederick (ed). Haeger, Jack H.

COLLECTIVE CONSCIOUSNESS

Responsabilidad colectiva y reduccionismo. Welch, John R.

COLLECTIVISM

Philosophy of the Social Sciences III: Groundwork for Social Dynamics. Wisdom, J O.
Beyond Individualism and Collectivism in Revisioning Philosophy, Ogilvy, James (ed). Ogilvy, James.
Cooperating with Cooperators. Rabinowicz, Wlodek.
Disarticulating Voices: Feminism and Philomela. Marder, Elissa.
Popper and Prescriptive Methodology. Tilley, Nicholas.

COLLEGE

see University

COLLI, G

Origen y decadencia del logos. Tusell, Narcís Aragay.

COLLIER, J

Conceiving One's Envatment While Denying Metaphysical Realism. Brueckner, Anthony.

COLLINGWOOD

R G Collingwood: A Bibliographic Checklist. Dreisbach, Christopher.
A N Whitehead, R G Collingwood and the Status of Metaphysics (in Dutch). Vanheeswijck, Guido.
Artistic Control in Collingwood's Theory of Art. Anderson, Douglas R.

COMMUNITY

Peirce and Community in Peirce and Law, Kevelson, Roberta. Kevelson, Roberta.

Persoon, substantie en gemeenschap: Over de innerlijke samenhang tussen de positie van de *liberals* en de *communitarians*. Cobben, Paul.

Possibility of World Community. Mitias, Michael H.

Rationality and Culture: Behavior within the Family as a Case Study. Gupta, Chhanda.

Rawls's Communitarianism. Alejandro, Roberto.

Recalling a Community at Loose Ends in Community at Loose Ends, Miami Theory Collect, (ed). Singer, Linda.

Recreating Classroom Relationships: Mutual Mentoring Joins Critical Hermeneutics and Composition Theory. Abscal-Hildebrand, Mary and Mullins, Joan.

Reflections on Personhood: Developing a Sense of Self through Community of Inquiry. Glaser, Jen.

Refusing to Draw the Circle Around 'the Self': The Quest for Community in the Work of Basehart and Berenson. Downing, Fred.

Religion and the Quest for Community in On Community, Rouner, Leroy S (ed). Hill, Patrick.

Response to "Disavowing Community". Stout, Maureen.

Rousseau and the Problem of Community: Nationalism, Civic Virtue, Totalitarianism. Simon-Ingram, Julia.

Solidarity and Moral Community. Hostetler, Karl.

Speaking to Trees (in Czechoslovakian). Kohak, E.

State and Nation. Cauchy, Venant.

Sustainability and the Moral Community. George, Kathryn Paxton.

The "Living Center" of Martin Buber's Political Theory. Avnon, Dan.

The Apocalypse of Community in On Community, Rouner, Leroy S (ed). Keller, Catherine.

The Community's Absence in Lyotard, Nancy, and Lacoue-Labarthe. May, Todd G.

The Context of Community. Alexander, Thomas M.

The Dignity and Indignity of Service: The Role of the Self in Hindu 'Bhakti' in Selves, People, and Persons, Rouner, Leroy S (ed). Carman, John B.

The Problem of Community. Crocker, Nancy.

Thinking for Tomorrow: Reflections on Avner de-Shalit. Marshall, Peter.

Toward Democracy for the World Community. Glossop, Ronald J.

Values of Art and Values of Community in On Community, Rouner, Leroy S (ed). Hepburn, R W.

COMPACTNESS

A Δ2/2 Well-Order of the Reals and Incompactness of *L*(QMM). Abraham, Uri and Shelah, Saharon.

An Algebraic Treatment of the Barwise Compactness Theory. Fleischer, Isidore and Scott, Philip.

Compacidad *via* eliminación de cuantificadores. Naishtat, Francisco.

Compactness and Normality in Abstract Logics. Caicedo, Xavier.

The Compactness of First-Order Logic: From Gödel to Lindström. Dawson Jr, John W.

The McKinsey Axiom is Not Compact. Wang, Xiaoping.

COMPARATIVE

A Logic of *Better*. Goble, Lou.

Comparative Oughts and Comparative Evils. Anderson, Robert.

Counterparts and Comparatives. Milne, Peter.

Formalizing the Logic of Positive, Comparative, and Superlative. Adams, Ernest.

COMPARATIVE RELIGION

Deep Structure and the Comparative Philosophy of Religion. Levine, Michael.

COMPARATIVISM

Modal Metaphysics and Comparatives. Milne, Peter.

COMPARISON

Contexte des rapports intellectuels entre Hobbes et Locke. Rogers, John.

COMPASSION

Duhkha: An Analysis of Buddhist Clue to Understand Human Nature. Chinchore, Mangala R.

Pigs and Piety: A Theocentric Perspective on Food Animals. Comstock, Gary L.

COMPATIBILISM

Compatibilism and the Free Will Defence. Bishop, John.

Contractualist Impartiality and Personal Commitments. Powers, G Madison.

Divine Foreknowledge and the Libertarian Conception of Human Freedom. Linville, Mark D.

Evaluative Compatibilism and the Principle of Alternate Possibilities. Lamb, James W.

How Determinism Refutes Compatibilism. Settle, Thomas W.

Incompatibilism, Nondeterministic Causation, and the Real Problem of Free Will. Francken, Patrick.

Leibniz and the Compatibilist of Free Will. Borst, Clive.

Middle Actions. Howsepian, A A.

The Principle of Rational Explanation Defended. Double, Richard.

Toward a Compatibility Theory for Internalist and Externalist Epistemologies. Sennett, James F.

Zagzebski on Power Entailment. Hasker, William.

COMPENSATION

Beyond Compensatory Justice?. Johnston, David.

Compensation and Government Takings of Private Property. Munzer, Stephen R.

Compensation and Redistribution. Goodin, Robert E.

Compensation and Rights in the Liberal Conception of Justice. Barnett, Randy E.

Compensation and the Bounds of Rights. Lomasky, Loren.

Compensation Within the Limits of Reliance Alone. Anderson, Elizabeth.

Diagnosing the Takings Problem. Radin, Margaret Jane.

Does Compensation Restore Equality?. Gaus, Gerald.

Justice between Generations: Compensation, Identity, and Group Membership. Fishkin, James S.

On Compensation and Distribution. Levmore, Saul.

Organization Ethics from a Perspective of Praxis. Nielsen, Richard P.

Property as Wealth, Property as Propriety. Rose, Carol M.

Set-Asides, Reparations, and Compensatory Justice. Paul, Ellen Frankel.

The Limits of Compensatory Justice. Sunstein, Cass R.

COMPETENCE

Competence, Knowledge and Education. Hyland, Terry.

Competency, Mastery and the Destruction of Meaning. Strandberg, Warren.

Response to Competency, Mastery and the Destruction of Meaning. Blount, Jackie.

COMPLEMENTARITY

L'immagine della donna secondo Ortega y Gasset. Savignano, Armando.

Le status de l'Un dans la "Métaphysique". Coloubaritsis, Lambros.

COMPLETENESS

see also Incompleteness, Structural-Completeness

A Note on the Interpretability Logic of Finitely Axiomatized Theories. De Rijke, Maarten.

A Sequent- or Tableau-Style System for Lewis's Counterfactual Logic VC. Gent, Ian Philip.

A Structurally Complete Fragment of Relevant Logic. Slaney, John K and Meyer, Robert K.

An Arithmetical Completeness Theorem for Pre-permutations. Tuttas, Friedemann.

Compacidad *via* eliminación de cuantificadores. Naishtat, Francisco.

Complete and Atomic Algebras of the Infinite Valued Lukasiewicz Logic. Cignoli, R.

Cut-Free Systems for Three-Valued Modal Logics. Takano, Mitio.

Le jugement de recognition fregéen et la supposition de détermination complète. Schwartz, Elisabeth.

Nominal Tense Logic. Blackburn, Patrick.

On Boolean Algebras and Integrally Closed Commutative Regular Rings. Nagayama, Misao.

On the Proofs of Arithmetical Completeness for Interpretability Logic. Zambella, Domenico.

Rosser Orderings and Free Variables. De Jongh, Dick and Montagna, Franco.

Rudimentary Kripke Models for the Intuitionistic Propositional Calculus. Dosen, Kosta.

The Analytical Completeness of Dzhaparidze's Polymodal Logics. Boolos, George.

The Completeness of the Lambek Calculus with Respect to Relational Semantics. Mikulás, Szabolcs.

The Gentzen-Kripke Construction of the Intermediate Logic LQ. Akama, Seiki.

The Minimal System *L'o*. Wang, Xuegang.

The Semantics of R4. Mares, Edwin and Meyer, Robert K.

Two Formal Systems for Situation Semantics. Escriba, Juan Barba.

Unary Interpretability Logic. De Rijke, Maarten.

COMPLEXITY

see also Computational Complexity

On the Existence of Very Difficult Satisfiability Problems. Da Costa, N C A and Doria, F A.

COMPOSITE

"Doctor humanitatis": Implicazioni e sviluppi dell'antropologia tomistica alla luce degli Atti del IX Congresso Tomistico Internazionale. Turco, G.

COMPOSITION

Treatise on Style—Louis Aragon. Aragon, Louis and Waters, Alyson (trans).

An Outline of Some Problems in the Philosophy of Music Composition. Trivedi, Saam.

Compositional Supervenience Theories and Compositional Meaning Theories. Schiffer, Stephen.

Counting Functions. Johnson, Fred.

Do Composers Have To Be Performers Too?. Spade, Paul Vincent.

History and the Ontology of the Musical Work. Treitler, Leo.

Polanyian Perspectives on the Teaching of Literature and Composition. Wallace, M Elizabeth (& others).

Recreating Classroom Relationships: Mutual Mentoring Joins Critical Hermeneutics and Composition Theory. Abscal-Hildebrand, Mary and Mullins, Joan.

Semantic Compositionality: Still the Only Game in Town. Kaye, Lawrence J.

Toward a Theory of Profundity in Music. White, David A.

When Composers Have To Be Performers. Alperson, Philip A.

COMPOSSIBILITY

Compossibility and Law in Causation in Early Modern Philosophy, Nadler, Steven (ed). Wilson, Margaret.

COMPROMISE

Judgment and the Art of Compromise. Benjamin, Martin.

COMPUTABILITY

On Compatibility of Theories and Equivalent Translations. Inoué, Takao.

On the Interpretation of Church's Thesis. Cotogno, Paolo.

COMPUTATION

Confirmation and the Computational Paradigm (Or: Why Do You Think They Call It *Artificial* Intelligence?). Buller, David J.

On the Existence of Very Difficult Satisfiability Problems. Da Costa, N C A and Doria, F A.

The Chinese Room Argument in Logical Foundations, Mahalingam, Indira (ed). Narayanan, Ajit.

The Failure of Dennett's Representationalism: A Wittgensteinian Resolution. Ward, Andrew.

COMPUTATIONAL COMPLEXITY

On the Computational Complexity of Integral Equations. Ko, Ker-I.

COMPUTATIONAL MODEL
Endogenous Constraints on Inductive Reasoning. Kukla, Andre.

COMPUTER
see also Machine
Agency in Action: The Practical Rational Agency Machine. Coval, Samuel C and Campbell, P G.
Cyberspace: First Steps. Benedikt, Michael (ed).
Forms of Concrescence: Alfred North Whitehead's Philosophy and Computer Programming Structures. Henry, Granville C.
Machinations: Computational Studies of Logic, Language, and Cognition. Spencer-Smith, Richard (ed) and Torrance, Steve (ed).
Philosophy and Artificial Intelligence. Moody, Todd C.
The Mechanism and Freedom of Logic. Henry, Granville C.
Tradition and Individuality: Essays. Nyíri, J C.
What Computers "Still" Can't Do: A Critique of Artificial Reason (Rev Ed). Dreyfus, Hubert L.
A Reply to "Should Computer Programs Be Ownable?". Johnson, Deborah.
A Reply to Johnson's Reply to "Should Computer Programs Be Ownable?". Carey, David.
Computers and the Mind-Body Problem: On Ontological and Epistemological Dualism. Drozdek, Adam.
How to Build a Person: A Prolegomenon. Schiffer, Stephen.
Introductory Logic Through Multiple Modes of Presentation. Scherer, Donald and Stuart, James.
Mice in Mirrored Mazes and the Mind. Garson, James W.
On the Nonexistence of Computer Ethics in Terrorism, Justice and Social Values, Peden, Creighton (ed). Jason, Gary.
Semantik und Handlungskausalität: Zur Diskussion über die 'künstliche Intelligenz'. Hörl, Christoph.
Should Computer Programs Be Ownable?. Carey, David.
The Case for Connectionism. Bechtel, William.
The Computer as Component: Heidegger and McLuhan. Heim, Michael.
The Connectionism/Classical Battle to Win Souls. McLaughlin, Andrew C.
The Electronic Self in Advances in Scientific Philosophy, Schurz, Gerhard (ed). Bencivenga, Ermanno.
The Essence of VR. Heim, Michael.
Turing Machines and Semantics Symbol Processing: Why Real Computers Don't Mind Chinese Emperors. Yee, Richard Wing.

COMSTOCK, G
Response: Of Pigs and Primitive Notions. Detmer, David J.

COMTE
Emile Meyerson, philosophe oublié. Largeault, Jean.

CONCEIVABILITY
Is Conceivability a Guide to Possibility?. Yablo, Stephen.
Leibniz on Creation, Contingency and Per-Se Modality. McNamara, Paul.

CONCEPT
see also Idea
A Study of Concepts. Peacocke, Christopher.
Ancient Concepts of Philosophy. Jordan, William.
Philosophie de l'action. Neuberg, Marc.
Statement and Referent: An Inquiry into the Foundations of Our Conceptual Order. Shwayder, David S.
Thinking Logically: Basic Concepts for Reasoning (Second Edition). Freeman, James.
A Reconception of Meaning. Heydrich, Wolfgang.
Basic Law (V)—I: Whence the Contradiction?. Boolos, George.
Basic Law (V)—II: Sets and Indefinitely Extensible Concepts and Classes. Clark, Peter.
Causal Powers and Conceptual Connections. Christensen, David.
Challenging the Obvious: The Logic of Colour Concepts. Harvey, J.
Conocimiento y concepto. Mayol, Víctor Velarde.
Darwin and Disjunction: Foraging Theory and Univocal Assignments of Content. Shapiro, Lawrence A.
Geo Siegwarts Szenario: Eine katastrophentheoretische Untersuchung: Zugleich ein Versuch, enttäuschte Kenner wieder aufzurichten. Thiel, Christian.
How to Speak of the Colors. Johnston, Mark.
Impressions and Ideas: Vivacity as Verisimilitude. Waxman, Wayne.
Is the Paradigm Concept Compatible with the Human Sciences? (in Dutch). Antonites, A J.
Ist die konstruktive Abstraktionstheorie inkonsistent?. Hartmann, Dirk.
Les concepts vagues sont-ils sans frontières?. Engel, Pascal.
Logical Renovations: Restoring Frege's Functions. Green, Karen.
Makin's Ontological Argument Again. Oppy, Graham.
Once Again on the Meaning of Physical Concepts in Greek Studies in the Philosophy and History of Science, Nicolacopoulos, Pantelis (ed). Baltas, Aristides.
Perception, Concepts, and Memory. Martin, M G F.
Realism and Folk Psychology in the Ascription of Concepts. Franks, Bradley.
Response-Dependence and Infallibility. Holton, Richard.
The Basic Ontological Categories in Language, Truth and Ontology, Mulligan, Kevin (ed). Chisholm, Roderick M.
The Revolution in the Concept of Politics. Viroli, Maurizio.
The Skeleton in Frege's Cupboard: The Standard Versus Nonstandard Distinction. Hintikka, Jaakko and Sandu, Gabriel.
Truth: Its Definition and Criteria. Jadacki, Jacek J.
Two Problems Concerning Frege's Distinction Between Concepts and Objects. Horsten, Leon.
Zur Inkonsistenz der konstruktivistischen Abstraktionslehre. Siegwart, Geo.

'Person' as an Essentially Contested Concept in the Commonwealth of Discourse. Merrill, S A.

CONCEPTION
Multiple Biological Mothers: The Case for Gestation. Feldman, Susan.

CONCORDANCE
Una voz por la paz en el siglo XV: La noción humanística de concordia. Magnavacca, Silvia.

CONCRETENESS
Soggettività e metafisica. Chiereghin, Franco.

CONDILLAC
Condillac, Lavoisier, and the Instrumentalization of Science. Roberts, Lissa.

CONDITION
see also Necessary Condition, Sufficient Condition, Truth Condition
Aquinas on Disordered Pleasures and Conditions. Daly, Anthony C.
Changing Beliefs Rationally: Some Puzzles in Cognition, Semantics and Philosophy, Ezquerro, Jesús (ed). Edgington, Dorothy.
Conditional Will and Conditional Norms in Medieval Thought. Knuuttila, Simo and Holopainen, Taina.
Epistemic Desiderata. Alston, W P.
Manipulation under Majority Decision-Making When No Majority Suffers and Preferences Are Strict. MacIntyre, I D A.
Objects of Intention. Vermazen, Bruce.
On the Nature of *Inus* Conditionality. Denise, Theodore C.
The Ontological Pre-conditions of Understanding and the Formation of Meaning in Analecta Husserliana, XXXIV, Tymienicka, Anna-Teresa (ed). Kule, Maija.
Zalta's Intensional Logic. Anderson, C Anthony.

CONDITIONAL
see also Implication
A Philosophical Companion to First-Order Logic. Hughes, R I G (ed).
Foundations of Philosophy of Science: Recent Developments. Fetzer, James.
Logical Foundations. Mahalingam, Indira (ed) and Carr, Brian (ed).
On the Logic of Ordinary Conditionals. McLaughlin, Robert N.
A Problem for Anti-Realism. Rogerson, Kenneth.
A Weak Paraconsistent Conditional Logic. Qingyu, Zhang.
Blending Semantics for *If* As a One-Place Nonassertive with Semantics for the Conditional. Sylvan, Richard.
Conditional Logic. Slater, B H.
Conditionals of Freedom and Middle Knowledge. Gaskin, R.
Deontic Tense Logic in Advances in Scientific Philosophy, Schurz, Gerhard (ed). Aqvist, Lennart.
Generalized Probability Kinematics. Wagner, Carl G.
How to Believe a Conditional. Mellor, D H.
Kings and Prisoners (and Aces). Sobel, Jordan Howard.
One Logic or Many Logics? (Epstein's Set-Assignment Semantics for Logical Calculi). Krajewski, Stanislaw.
Probabilities and Conditionals: Distinctions By Example. Butterfield, Jeremy.
Probability and Assertion. Dudman, V H.
Species-Specific Properties and More Narrow Reductive Strategies. Endicott, Ronald P.
Suppose, Suppose. Morton, Adam.
The Logic of the *Nominales*, or, The Rise and Fall of Impossible *Positio*. Martin, Christopher J.
The Meaning of 'If' in Conditional Propositions. Hunter, Geoffrey.
The Paradoxes of Indicative Conditionals in Logical Foundations, Mahalingam, Indira (ed). Carr, Brian.

CONDITIONING
Point of View, Bias, and Insight. Garver, Eugene.

CONDUCT
see also Act
In Search of the Ethical: Moral Theory in Twentieth Century America. Edel, Abraham.
Adam Smith's Aesthetic of Conduct. Lyons, D.
Common Ground in Aristotle's and Dewey's Theories of Conduct. Chambliss, J J.
Vico, Imagination and Education. Iheoma, Eugene O.

CONEE, E
Rationality and Epistemic Paradox. Kroon, Frederick.
Resolving Epistemic Dilemmas. Odegard, Douglas.

CONFESSION
Studies in Augustine and Eriugena. O'Meara, John J and Halton, Thomas (ed).
Augustine's Radiant Confessional—Theatre of Prophecy. Duval, R Shannon.
Presumption and Confession: Augustine, Freud, and Paths to Knowledge. Holley, David M.
Standing Alone Together: Silence, Solitude, and Radical Conversion. Staab, Janice.
Thus Spoke Augustine. Frosolono, Anne-Marie.

CONFIDENCE
Belief, Confidence and the Method of Science. Hookway, Christopher.

CONFIRMATION
see also Verification
Confirmational Holism and Bayesian Epistemology. Christensen, David.
How Scientists Confirm Universal Propositions. Gottlob, Rainer.
On Novel Confirmation. Kahn, James A, Landsburg, Steven E and Stockman, Alan C.

CONFLICT
Philosophy and Biblical Interpretation: A Study in Nineteenth-Century Conflict. Addinall, Peter.

CONFLICT

Conflict of Values in Adjudication in *Ethical Dimensions of Legal Theory*, Sadurski, Wojciech (ed). Gizbert-Studnicki, Tomasz.

Hobbes's Shortsightedness Account of Conflict. Murphy, Mark C.

Understanding Conflicts between North and South in *Cultural Relativism and Philosophy*, Dascal, Marcelo (ed). Lacey, Hugh M.

CONFUCIANISM

Confucian Discourse and Chu Hsi's Ascendancy. Tillman, Hoyt Cleveland.

Confucianism, Buddhism, Daoism, Christianity and Chinese Culture. McLean, George F (ed) and Yi-Jie, Tang.

East Asian Philosophy: With Historical Background and Present Influence. Ho, John E.

Jurisculture: China. Dorsey, Gray L.

Voices of the Past: The Status of Language in Eighteenth-Century Japanese Discourse. Sakai, Naoki.

Way, Learning, and Politics: Essays on the Confucian Intellectual. Wei-ming, Tu.

A "Just", A Human Society: A Christian- Marxist- Confucian Dialogue. Swindler, Leonard.

A Confucian Perspective on Embodiment in *The Body in Medical Thought and Practice*, Leder, Drew (ed). Wei-ming, Tu.

A New Direction in Confucian Scholarship: Approaches to Examining the Differences between Neo-Confucianism and *Tao-hsüeh*. Tillman, Hoyt Cleveland.

An Exploration of the Concept of *Zhong* in the Teachings of Confucianism. Rongjie, Chen and Chan, Wing-Tsit.

Character Consequentialism and Early Confucianism. Ivanhoe, Philip.

Communication and Hermeneutics: A Confucian Postmodern Point of View. In-Sing Leung, Thomas.

Confucianism as Political Philosophy: A Postmodern Perspective. Jung, Hwa Yol.

Creativity as Synthesis of Contrasting Wisdoms: An Interpretation of Chinese Philosophy in Taiwan since 1949. Shen, Vincent.

Cultural Patterns and the Way of Mother and Son: An Early Qing Case. Birdwhistell, Anne D.

Die Renaissance und ihr Bild vom Konfuzianismus. Kodera, Sergius.

Heavenly Order, Sagehood and Tao-t'ung—Some Discussions on the Neo-Confucian View of Values (in Chinese). Chang, Jun-chun.

Hsin-Techniques and Hsin-Leadership in Chinese *Foundations for Moral Education and Character Development*, Van Doan, Tran (ed). T'ui-chieh, Hang Thaddeus.

Inherent Limitations of the Confucian Tradition in Contemporary East Asian Business Enterprises. Oh, Tai K.

May Fourth, the New Confucianism, and the Modernization of Humanity. Shilian, Shan.

Modern Chinese Thought: A Retrospective View and a Look into the Future. Lai, Chen.

On the Relation between Existence and Value (in Chinese). Fu, Pei-jung.

Ritual, Cosmology, and Ontology: Chang Tsai's Moral Philosophy and Neo-Confucian Ethics. Chow, Kai-wing.

Some Thoughts on Confucianism and Modernization. Ihara, Craig K.

Taking Graham Seriously on Taking Chinese Thought Seriously. McCurdy, William James.

The Concept of *Ch'i* in the Thought of Wang Ch'ung. Rainey, Lee.

The Fate of Confucianism and of the New Confucianism: A Philosophical Reflection on the Debate on Culture Since "May Fourth". Jiadong, Zheng.

The Golden Rule as the Core Value in Confucianism and Christianity: Ethical Similarities and Differences. Allinson, Robert E.

The Idea of Confucian Tradition. Cua, A S.

The Impact of the Thought of the School of Confucianism and the School of Daoism on the Culture of China. Dainian, Zhang.

The Mind and the "Shen-ming" in Xunzi. Machle, Edward.

The Positive Contribution of Confucianism to the Modernization of East Asian Business Enterprises. Han, Cheong K.

The Social Self in Japanese Philosophy and American Pragmatism: A Comparative Study of Watsuji Tetsurō and George Herbert Mead. Odin, Steve.

Tradition, Modernity, and Confucianism. Dallmayr, Fred.

CONFUCIUS

Jen and *Li* in the *Analects*. Shun, Kwong-Loi.

Way, Learning, and Politics: Essays on the Confucian Intellectual. Wei-ming, Tu.

Confucius and Country Music. Sartwell, Crispin.

Confucius, The First 'Teacher' of Humanism?. Rogers, Gerald F.

Moral Choice in the Analects: A Way without a Crossroads?. Ruskola, Teemu H.

On the Deification of Confucius. Gier, Nicholas.

The Aesthetics of Confucius (in Czechoslovakian). Paik, Ki-soo.

The Uses of Neo-Confucianism: A Response to Professor Tillman. De Bary, W T.

Was There a Concept of Rights in Confucian Virtue-Based Morality?. Lee, Seung-Hwan.

CONJUNCTION

Algebraic Logic for Classical Conjunction and Disjunction. Font, J M and Verdú, V.

CONNECTION

Causal Powers and Conceptual Connections. Christensen, David.

CONNECTIONISM

"Who Sees with Equal Eye,... Atoms or Systems into Ruin Hurl'd?". DeVries, Willem A.

Belief and Cognitive Architecture. Ramsey, William.

Classical and Connectionist Models: Levels of Description. Corbí, Josep E.

Comments on Bechtel's "The Case for Connectionism". Christie, Drew.

Connectionism, Explicit Rules, and Symbolic Manipulation. Hadley, Robert F.

Connectionisme, plasticiteit en de hoop op betere tijden. Meijsing, Monica.

Control, Connectionism and Cognition: Towards a New Regulatory Paradigm. Hooker, C A, Penfold, H B and Evans, R J.

Currents in Connectionism. Bechtel, William.

Derrida and Connectionism: Différance in Neural Nets. Globus, Gordon G.

Eliminative Connectionism: Its Implications for a Return to an Empiricist/Behaviorist Linguistics. Place, Ullin T.

Eliminativisme gereduceerd tot pragmatisme. Van Brakel, J.

Expert Networks: Paradigmatic Conflict, Technological Rapprochement. Lacher, R C.

Interruptibility as a Constraint on Hybrid Systems. Cooper, Richard and Franks, Bradley.

Neuraal vernunft en gedachteloze kennis: Het moderne pleidooi voor een niet-propositioneel kennismodel. Meijering, T C.

Neurale netwerken en het wetenschappelijk realisme van de waarheid. De Regt, Herman C D G.

On Clark on Systematicity and Connectionism. Butler, Keith.

Paul Churchland: filosofie en conneciltonisme. Derksen, A A.

The Case for Connectionism. Bechtel, William.

The Connectionism/Classical Battle to Win Souls. McLaughlin, Andrew C.

CONNECTIVE

Zero-Place Operations and Functional Completeness, and the Definition of New Connectives. Humberstone, I L.

CONRAD, T

Ein Zeitzeuge über die Anfänge der phänomenologischen Bewegung: Theodor Conrads Bericht aus dem Jahre 1954. Avé-Lallemant, Eberhard and Schuhmann, Karl.

CONRAD-MARTIUS, H

H Conrad-Martius und E Stein Husserls Schülerinen und aristotelisch-thomistische Philosophie (in Polish). Machnacz, J.

CONSCIENCE

To the Other: An Introduction to the Philosophy of Emmanuel Levinas. Peperzak, Adriaan.

Ancora sull'idea d'Europa: Il Medioevo como matrice di una coscienza europea. Baldassarre, M R.

Autocoscienza e conoscenza nel 'primo Rosmini'. De Lucia, Paolo.

Call and Conscience in Tauler and Heidegger. Sikka, Sonya.

Caveats Regarding Slippery Slopes and Physicians' Moral Conscience. Howe, Edmund G.

Conscience and Norm. Rotenstreich, Nathan.

Conscience et Culture. Lalèyê, Issiaka-Prosper.

Considerazioni sul problema della conoscenza. Baccari, Luciano.

L'Origine de la Responsabilité ou De la "Voix de la Conscience" à la Pensée de la "Promesse". Guest, Gérard.

La dimensión ontológica de la conciencia afectiva según Ferdinand Alquié — Segunda parte. Sodor, A.

Psicologia e Crítica Sartreana do Cogito Cartesiano. Simon, Paul Albert.

Slippery Slopes and Moral Reasoning. Devettere, Raymond.

The Call of Conscience and the Call of Language in *Crises in Continental Philosophy*, Dallery, Arleen B (ed). Rodeheffer, Jane Kelley.

The Dialectic of Conscience and the Necessity of Morality in Hegel's *Philosophy of Right*. Dahlstrom, Daniel O.

The Slippery-Slope Argument. Van Der Burg, Wibren.

The Slippery-Slope Argument Reconstructed: Response to Van Der Burg. Freedman, Benjamin.

CONSCIOUS

Mind's Crisis: On Anaxagoras' *Nous*. Laks, André.

CONSCIOUSNESS

see also Awareness, Self-Consciousness

An Introduction to Husserlian Phenomenology. Bernet, Rudolf, Kern, Iso and Marbach, Eduard.

Analecta Husserliana, XXXVIII. Tymieniecka, Anna-Teresa (ed).

Back to the Rough Ground. Dunne, Joseph.

Consciousness Reconsidered. Flanagan, Owen.

Consciousness, Brain and the Physical World: A Reply to Velmans. Rentoul, Robert.

Consciousness: Psychological and Philosophical Essays. Davies, Martin (ed) and Humphreys, Glyn W (ed).

Creativity and Consciousness: Philosophical and Psychological Dimensions. Brzezinski, Jerzy (& other eds).

Dialogue and the Human Image: Beyond Humanistic Psychology. Friedman, Maurice S.

Everything You Always Wanted to Know About Lacan. Zizek, Slavoj (ed).

G E Moore. Baldwin, Thomas and Honderich, Ted (ed).

Husserl's Transcendental Phenomenology—Elisabeth Ströker. Hardy, Lee (trans) and Ströker, Elisabeth.

Identity, Consciousness and Value. Unger, Peter.

Ideology and False Consciousness: Marx and his Historical Progenitors. Pines, Christopher.

Language, Music, and Mind. Raffman, Diana.

Metaphysics of Consciousness. Seager, William.

Mind, Meaning and Metaphysics. Mulligan, Kevin (ed).

Philosophy of Mind: An Introduction. Graham, George.

Reason and Tradition in Indian Thought: An Essay on the Nature of Indian Philosophical Thinking. Mohanty, Jitendra N.

Standing In Your Own Way: Talks On the Nature of Ego. Damiani, Anthony.

CONSCIOUSNESS

CONSCIOUSNESS

What is Wrong with the Appendage Theory of Consciousness. Natsoulas, Thomas.
What Neuropsychology Tells Us about Consciousness. Lahav, Ran.
Yoga Sūtras. Chennakesavan, Sarasvati.
You Can't Get There from Here in The Cambridge Companion to Hegel, Beiser, Frederick (ed). Pippin, Robert B.
'I Believe that *P*' in John Searle and His Critics, Lepore, Ernest (ed). Malcolm, Norman.
'The Best Set of Tools'? Dennett's Metaphors and the Mind-Body Problem. Kirk, Robert.

CONSENSUS

A Disagreement over Agreement and Consensus in Constructionist Sociology. Button, Graham and Sharrock, Wes.
Escaping Hegel. Fritzman, J M.
Hermeneutical Terror and the Myth of Interpretive Consensus. Kent, Thomas.
On Consensus and Stability in Science. Baigrie, Brian S and Hattiangadi, J N.
The Domain of the Political and Overlapping Consensus in The Idea of Democracy, Copp, David (ed). Rawls, John.

CONSENT

Consent: The Means to an Active Faith According to St Thomas Aquinas. Barad, Judith.
Regulating Death, Carlos F Gomez. Cantor, Norman L.
Consent and Nuclear Waste Disposal. Shrader-Frechette, Kristin.
Consent, Ethics, and Community. Loewy, Erich H.
Contract, Consent and Exploitation in Essays on Kant's Political Philosophy, Williams, Howard (ed). Scruton, Roger.
Getting Consent from the Troops? in Biomedical Ethics Reviews 1992, Humber, James M (ed). Fotion, Nicholas.
Mature Minors in Contemporary Issues in Paediatric Ethics, Burgess, Michael M (ed). Burgess, Michael.
Obtaining Consent from the Family: A Horizon for Clinical Ethics. Spinsanti, Sandro.
On Some Criticisms of Consent Theory. Boxill, Bernard R.
Surrogate Consent. Richards, Norvin W.
The Limits of Consent: A Note on Dr Kevorkian. Kleinig, John.
The Physician, the Family, and the Truth. Cattorini, Paolo and Reichlin, Massimo.

CONSEQUENCE

A Note on Unary Rules and a Complete Syntactic Characterization of Propositional Calculi. Zuber, R.
Consequences of Consequentialism. Sosa, David.
Functions and Goal Directedness. Enç, Berent and Adams, Fred.
Nonmonotonic Consequence Based on Intuitionistic Logic. Servi, G F.
On Structural Completeness of Implicational Logics. Wojtylak, Piotr.
Relevant Consequence and Empirical Inquiry. Osherson, Daniel N and Weinstein, Scott.
The Grounds for the Model-Theoretic Account of the Logical Properties. Sánchez-Miguel, Manuel G-C.
The Inevitable. Fischer, John M and Ravizza, Mark.

CONSEQUENTIALISM

Value in Ethics and Economics. Anderson, Elizabeth.
A Consequentialist Case for Rejecting the Right. Howard-Snyder, Frances and Norcross, Alastair.
Act and Maxim: Value-Discrepancy and Two Theories of Power. Oddie, Graham.
After Libertarianism: Rejoinder to Narveson, McCloskey, Flew, and Machan. Friedman, Jeffrey.
Allowing Educational Technologies to Reveal: A Deweyan Perspective. Blacker, David.
Altruism versus Egoism: A Pseudo-Problem, A Cognitive-Emotive Analysis. Shibles, Warren.
An Argument for Consequentialism in Philosophical Perspectives, 6: Ethics, 1992, Tomberlin, James E (ed). Sinnott-Armstrong, Walter.
Character Consequentialism and Early Confucianism. Ivanhoe, Philip.
Consequences of Consequentialism. Sosa, David.
Consequentialism, Incoherence and Choice. Simpson, Peter and McKim, Robert.
Corporate Attorney Whistle-Blowing: Devising a Proper Standard. Dunfee, Thomas W and Maurer, Virginia G.
Deontology and Agency. McNaughton, David and Rawling, Piers.
Die konsequenzialistische Begründung des Lebensschutzes. Pöltner, Günther.
Dissent from "The New Consensus": Reply to Friedman. Flew, Antony.
Elbow-Room for Consequentialists. Howard-Snyder, Frances.
Is It Less Wrong to Harm the Vulnerable than the Secure?. Howard-Snyder, Frances.
Libertarianism, Postlibertarianism, and the Welfare State: Reply to Friedman. Narveson, Jan.
Minimal Statism and Metamodernism: Reply to Friedman. McCloskey, Donald N.
Non-consequentialism, the Person as an End-in-Itself, and the Significance of Status. Kamm, F M.
Normative Ethics: Bad News for the Sensible Compromise?. Farr, Richard.
Of Transplants and Trolleys. Mack, Eric.
On Applying Moral Theories. Upton, Hugh.
On the Ethics of Belief. Nathan, Nicholas.
Pacifism: A Philosophical Exploration. Filice, Carlo.
Prerogatives Without Restrictions in Philosophical Perspectives, 6: Ethics, 1992, Tomberlin, James E (ed). Scheffler, Samuel.
Rule Consequentialism is a Rubber Duck. Howard-Snyder, Frances.
The Hidden Consequentialist Assumption. Hurley, Paul E.
The New Critique of Anti-Consequentialist Moral Theory. Garcia, Jorge L A.
Transplants and Trolleys. Gert, Bernard.

Utilitarianism on Environmental Issues Reexamined. Holbrook, Daniel.
Valuing Lives. Perrett, Roy W.
Why God is Not a Consequentialist. Chappell, T D J.

CONSERVATION

Ecology, Economics, Ethics: The Broken Circle. Bormann, Herbert F (ed) and Kellert, Stephen R (ed).
The Doctrine of Conservation and Free-Will Defence. Jordan, Jeffrey.
The Very Idea of Sustainability. Blatz, Charlie V.

CONSERVATISM

Drug Legalization: For and Against. Evans, Rod L (ed) and Berent, Irwin M (ed).
A Contribution to the End-Extension Problem and the Π1 Conservativeness Problem. Adamowicz, Zofia.
Conservatism Not Much Reconsidered. Honderich, Ted.
Conservatism, Ideology, Rationale, and a Red Light. Honderich, Ted.
Conservatism: A Defence. Tännsjö, Torbjörn.
Conservatism: A Reply to Ted Honderich. O'Sullivan, Noel.
E Burke and the Natural Law: About the Foundations of Conservatisim (in Dutch). Van De Putte, A.
Jacob Burckhardt's Liberal-Conservatism. Sigurdson, Richard.
Keynesian Economic Theory and the Revival of Classical Theory in Terrorism, Justice and Social Values, Peden, Creighton W (ed). Walter, Edward F.
Misunderstanding the Democratic 'We': Richard Rorty's Liberalism and the Radical Urge for a Philosophical Foundation. Moussa, Mario.
Ruling Memory. Norton, Anne.
Socialism and the Good Life in Socialism and Morality, McLellan, David (ed). Inglis, Fred.
The Conservative Misinterpretation of the Educational Ecological Crisis. Bowers, C A.
The Politics of Equilibrium. Grant, Robert A D.
Utilitarianism, Conservatism and Social Policy in The Utilitarian Response, Allison, Lincoln (ed). Gibbins, John R.
Why Business is Talking About Ethics: Reflections on Foreign Conversations in Revisioning Philosophy, Ogilvy, James (ed). Ciulla, Joanne B.

CONSIDERANT, V

Early French Socialism and Politics: The Case of Victor Considérant. Lovell, David W.

CONSISTENCY

see also Inconsistency
Do We Tolerate Inconsistencies?. Havas, K G.
On *NFU*. Crabbé, Marcel.
Reply to Mylan Engel's "Inconsistency: The Coherence Theorist's Nemesis?". Lehrer, Keith.
Unifying Some Modifications of the Henkin Construction. Weaver, George E.
Why Rational Egoism is Not Consistent. Marshall Jr, John.

CONSOLATION

Heilung im Denken: Zur Sache der philosophischen Tröstung bei Boethius. Schumacher, Thomas.

CONSTANT

How Many Logically Constant Actions are There?. Segerberg, Krister.
The Naturalness of the Cosmological Constant in the General Theory of Relativity: A Response to Ray. Curry, Charles.

CONSTITUTION

The Philosophy of Freedom: Ideological Origins of the Bill of Rights. Rudolph, Samuel B (ed).
A propos de la liberté chez les juristes. Rossinelli, Michel.
Constituting Democracy in The Idea of Democracy, Copp, David (ed). Gauthier, David.
Constitution and Ontology: Some Remarks on Husserl's Ontological Position in the *Logical Investigations*. Zahavi, D.
Constitution is Identity. Noonan, Harold W.
Constitutional Hermeneutics in The Interpretive Turn, Hiley, David R (ed). Valauri, John T.
Locke, Taxation and Reform: A Reply to Wood. Hughes, Martin.
Natural Law and Judicial Review. Canavan, Francis.
On Contractarian Constitutional Democracy in The Idea of Democracy, Copp, David (ed). Morris, Christopher.
Patterns of Differences, Sameness and Unity in Some Kantian Principles. Patellis, Ioli.
Pragmatism and Constitutional Interpretation: Deconstruction Without Nihilism. McNicollis, C F.
Some Rules of Constitutional Design. Ordeshook, Peter C.
The Constitution and the Nature of Law. Robison, Wade.
Zijn wij ooit modern geweest?. Pels, D.

CONSTRUCTION

Arithmetized Set Theory. Strauss, Paul.
Construction of Monadic Three-Valued Lukasiewicz Algebras. Monteiro, L, Savini, S and Sewald, J.
Mathematical Construction, Symbolic Cognition and the Infinite Intellect: Reflections on Maimon and Maimonides. Lachterman, David.
Unifying Some Modifications of the Henkin Construction. Weaver, George E.

CONSTRUCTIVE

Constructive Mathematics and Quantum Mechanics: Unbounded Operators and the Spectral Theorem. Hellman, Geoffrey.

CONSTRUCTIVISM

A Problem With Constructivist Epistemology. Matthews, Michael R.
Constructive Ultraproducts and Isomorphisms of Recursively Saturated Ultrapowers. Nelson, G C.

CULTURE

Ricordo di Pietro Piovani. Tessitore, Fulvio.
Rootedness: Culture and Value in Simone Weil's Philosophy of Culture, Bell, Richard H (ed). Springsted, Eric.
Rousseau on the Foundation of National Cultures. Kelly, Christopher.
Russell on Chinese Civilization. Dong, Yu.
Santayana's Whitman Revisited. Tejera, V.
Secession: The Caes of Quebec. Nielsen, Kai.
Sense and Sensibility: Wittgenstein on the *Golden Bough*. Margalit, Avishai.
Sequel to History: Postmodernism and the Crisis of Historical Time. Carr, David.
Shifting Subjects Shifting Ground: The Names and Spaces of the Post-Colonial. Ray, Sangeeta.
Some Disquiet about "Difference". Sypnowich, C A.
Some Philosophical Problems Concerning Culture and Rationality. Bhattacharyya, Sibajiban.
Specific Cultures and the Coexistence of Alternative Rationalities: A Case Study of the Contact of Indian and Greco-European Cultures. Shekhawat, V.
Technology and Culture and the Problem of the Homeless. Lovekin, David.
That Which Resists, After All. Lyotard, Jean-François and Larochelle, Gilbert.
The Aesthetics of Confucius (in Czechoslovakian). Paik, Ki-soo.
The Body in the City. Swensen, Cole.
The Continuity of Chinese Humanism in the Shang-Chou Period. Wong, Yeu-Guang.
The Cultural Dilemma of Contemporary China: A Discussion of My Own Views on Culture and Response to Mou Zhongjian. Kejian, Huang.
The Debate On African Philosophy: A Critical Survey. Oladipo, Olusegun.
The Defeat of Vision: Five Reflections on the Culture of Speech. Ryklin, Mikhail.
The Ecology of Cultural Space in Cultural Relativism and Philosophy, Dascal, Marcelo (ed). Dascal, Marcelo.
The Entelechy and Authenticity of Objective Spirit: Reflections on Husserliana XXVII. Hart, J G.
The European Cultural Tradition and the Limits of Growth. Klíma, Ivan.
The Fate of Confucianism and of the New Confucianism: A Philosophical Reflection on the Debate on Culture Since "May Fourth". Jiadong, Zheng.
The Impact of the Thought of the School of Confucianism and the School of Daoism on the Culture of China. Dainian, Zhang.
The Moral Significance of the Material Culture. Borgmann, Albert.
The New Problem of Curriculum. Martin, Jane Roland.
The Rationality of Culture and the Culture of Rationality: Some Husserlian Proposals. Hart, James G.
The Role of the Hospital in the Evolution of Elite Cultures of Medicine. Dixon, Kathleen.
The Roots of Culture. Hodgkin, Robin A.
Time, Truth, and Culture in Husserl and Hegel in Analecta Husserliana, XXXI, Tymieniecka, Anna-Teresa (ed). Molchanov, Victor.
Towards a Creative Synthesis of Cultures. Gopalan, S.
Translation and Foreign Cultures. Collin, Finn.
Troeltsch's Treatment of the Thomist Synthesis. Dietrich, Wendell S.
Truth, Authenticity, and Culture in Analecta Husserliana, XXXI, Tymieniecka, Anna-Teresa (ed). Alvarez-Calderón, Luz Maria.
Une nouvelle approche de la philosophie d'Ernst Cassirer. Lofts, Steve.
Viewpoints: Body, Spirit, and Democracy in Revisioning Philosophy, Ogilvy, James (ed). Johnson, Don Hanlon.
What is an Anlogical Imagination?. Conradie, Ernst.
Where Ethics Come From and What to Do About It. Elliott, Carl.
Why Philosophy of Art in Cross-Cultural Perspectives?. Moravcsik, Julius.
World Interpretation/Mutual Understanding in Cultural-Political Interventions in the Unfinished Project of Enlightenment, Honneth, Axel (& other eds). Arnason, Johann P.
Wounded Attachments. Brown, Wendy.
Yes, There Are African-American Perspectives on Bioethics in African-American Perspectives on Biomedical Ethics, Flack, Harley E (ed). Dula, Annette.
'Some Foundational Questions Concerning Language Studies': Commentary. Hertzberg, Lars.

CUMMINS, R

Abstraction, Covariance, and Representation. Losonsky, Michael.
Cognitive Models and Representation. Kukla, Rebecca.
Functional Analysis and Etiology. McClamrock, Ron.

CUOMO, M

Political Rhetoric as Political Theory in Terrorism, Justice and Social Values, Peden, Creighton W (ed). Geise, Jack P.

CUPITT, D

All This, and God Too? Postmodern Alternatives to Don Cupitt. Cowdell, Scott.

CURRICULUM

An Intervention Curriculum for Moral Development. Ries, Steven I.
Modernity and the Problem of Cultural Pluralism. Blake, Nigel.
Moral Vocationalism. Hyland, Terry.
Philosophy for Children: Curriculum and Practice. Morehouse, Mort.
Two Rhetorics of Cynicism in Curriculum Deliberation, or Two Riders in a Barren Land. St Maurice, Henry.

CURRIE, G

On Walton's and Currie's Analyses of Literary Fiction. Pettersson, Anders.

CURRY, C

Fundamental Laws and *Ad Hoc* Decisions: A Reply to Curry. Ray, Christopher.

CUSANUS, N

Cusanus's Concept of God and Man in the Light of His Reflections on Time. Fischer, Norbert.

CUSTOM

Solitary Rule-Following. Champlin, T S.

CUT ELIMINATION

2-Sequent Calculus: A Proof Theory of Modalities. Masini, Andrea.
Classical Logic, Intuitionistic Logic, and the Peirce Rule. Africk, Henry.
Cut Elimination for the Unified Logic. Vauzeilles, Jacqueline.

CUTENESS

On 'Cuteness'. Sanders, John T.
The Contingency of Cuteness: A Reply to Sanders. Morreall, John.

CYBERNETICS

Philosophy of the Social Sciences III: Groundwork for Social Dynamics. Wisdom, J O.
Lacan and Maturana: Constructivist Origins for a Third-Order Cybernetics. Kenny, V and Boxer, P.

CYBERSPACE

Cyberspace: First Steps. Benedikt, Michael (ed).

CYNICISM

Truth and Eros: Foucault, Lacan, and the Question of Ethics. Rajchman, John.
Skeptics, Cynics, Pessimists, and Other Malcontents. Godlovitch, Stan.
Two Rhetorics of Cynicism in Curriculum Deliberation, or Two Riders in a Barren Land. St Maurice, Henry.

CZECHOSLOVAKIAN

Essais hérétiques sur la philosophie de l'histoire by Jan Patocka. Tucker, Aviezer.
A Debate Between a Philosopher and a Historian on the Women's Question in Bohemia (in Czechoslovakian). Peskova, Jaroslava and Horska, Pavla.
A Talk on Democracy and Truth (in Czechoslovakian). Mokrejs, A.
Feminist Ethics: Projects, Problems, Prospects (in Czechoslovakian). Jaggar, Alison M.
Havel and the Foundaiton of Political Responsibility. Lawler, Peter Augustine.
On "Philosophy" of Women's Double Role (in Czechoslovakian). Vodakova, Alena.
Remembrance of the Last "Nestor" of Czech Aesthetics (in Czechoslovakian). Sus, Oleg.
Skrach's Trace in the History of Czech Thought (in Czechoslovakian). Karola, J E.
The Road Out of Serfdom. Cepl, Vojtech.
What Is Feminist Philosophy? (in Czechoslovakian). Nagl-Docekalova, Herta.
Who Is Afraid of Feminist Philosophy? (in Czechoslovakian). Havelkova, Hana.

D'COSTA, G

The Intolerance of Religious Pluralism. Donovan, Peter.

DALY, H

For the Common Good?. Heyne, Paul.

DALY, M

Surviving to Speak New Language: Mary Daly and Adrienne Rich. Hedley, Jane.

DAMNATION

The Problem of Hell. Kvanvig, Jonathan L.
Radical Freedom, Radical Evil and the Possibility of Eternal Damnation. Pestana, Mark Stephen.

DANCE

see also Ballet
La simulation du point de vue de la thérie des jeux (in Polish). Latawiec, A.
The Future of Dance Aesthetics. Sparshott, Francis.
The Process/Product Dichotomy and Its Implications for Creative Dance. Bergmann, Sheryle.
The Role of Metaphor in Dance. Whittock, Trevor.
Thoughts on Duncan's Dancing Masters. Whittock, Trevor.

DANCY, J

Internalism in Epistemology and the Internalist Regress. Jacobson, Stephen.

DANGER

Ethics and Danger. Dallery, Arleen B (ed), Scott, Charles E (ed) and Roberts, P Holley (ed).
Ethical Aspects of Germline Gene Therapy. De Wachter, Maurice.
Of Spirit and the Daimon in Ethics and Danger, Dallery, Arleen B (ed). Krell, David Farrell.
Spirit and Danger in Ethics and Danger, Dallery, Arleen B (ed). Caputo, John D.

DANIELS, C

Reincarnation, Closest Continuers, and the Three Card Trick: A Reply to Noonan and Daniels. MacIntosh, J J.

DANISH

The Correspondence of Ernst Mach with a Young Danish Philosopher. Koch, C H.

DANTE

"Liebe, die im Geist mir redet...": Dantes Dame Philosophie. Splett, Jörg.
Word and Spirit: A Kierkegaardian Critique of the Modern Age. Hall, Ronald L.
Dante and Machiavelli: A Last Word. Peterman, Larry.
Das gemeinsame Ziel des Menschengeschlechts in Dantes "Monarchia" und des Averroes Lehre von der Einheit des separaten Intellekts. Ogor, Robert.

DANTO, A

Postmodernism in the Visual Arts in Postmodernism and Society, Boyne, Roy (ed). Crowther, Paul.
The Journal of Aesthetics and Danto's Philosophical Criticism. Herwitz, Daniel A.

DARCY, H

Darcy's Law and Structural Explanation in Hydrology. Hofmann, James R and Hofmann, Paul A.

DARKNESS

Analecta Husserliana, XXXVIII. Tymieniecka, Anna-Teresa (ed).

DEATH

see also Dying

Birth, Suffering, and Death: Catholic Perspectives at the Edges of Life. Wildes, Kevin W (ed), Abel, Francesc (ed) and Harvey, John C (ed).

Daimon Life: Heidegger and Life-Philosophy. Krell, David Farrell.

Death and Personal Survival: The Evidence for Life After Death. Almeder, Robert F.

Disputed Questions in Theology and the Philosophy of Religion. Hick, John.

Drawing the Line: Life, Death, and Ethical Choices in an American Hospital. Gorovitz, Samuel.

Life and Death: Philosophical Essays in Biomedical Ethics. Brock, Dan W.

Regulating Death, Carlos F Gomez. Cantor, Norman L.

Sinn und Ursprung. Gahlings, Ute.

The Metaphysics of Death. Fischer, John Martin (ed).

A Note on Heidegger's Death Analytic: The Tolstoyian Correlative in Analecta Husserliana, XXXVIII, Tymieniecka, Anna-Teresa (ed). Pratt, Alan.

A Polemic on Principles: Reflections on the Pittsburgh Protocol. Weisbard, Alan J.

Altruism and Physician Assisted Death. Gunderson, Martin and Mayo, David J.

Area Bombing, Terrorism and the Death of Innocents in Applied Philosophy, Almond, Brenda (ed). Wallace, Gerry.

Averroes, Aristotle, and the Qur'an on Immortality. Mohammed, Ovey N.

Being a Burden on Others. Jecker, Nancy S.

Brain Death: A Survey of the Debate and the Position in 1991. Jeffery, Peter.

Causing, Intending, and Assisting Death. Brody, Howard.

Criteria for Death: Self-Determination and Public Policy. Sass, Hans-Martin.

D Z Phillips, Self-Renunciation and the Finality of Death. Thomas, Emyr Vaughan.

Death's Badness. Brueckner, Anthony and Fischer, John Martin.

Death, and the Stories We Don't Have. Amato, Joseph.

Death, Time, History in The Cambridge Companion to Heidegger, Guignon, Charles B (ed). Hoffman, Piotr.

Death: The Final Frontier in New Horizons in the Philosophy of Science, Lamb, David (ed). Lamb, David.

Decision Making in an Incapacitated Patient. Freer, Jack P.

Defining Death in Applied Philosophy, Almond, Brenda (ed). Browne, Alister.

Definitions of Personhood: Implications for the Care of PVS Patients. Gormally, Luke.

Epicureanism and Death. Glannon, Walter.

Es la Muerte un acontecimiento de la vida?. Arregui, Jorge Vicente.

Last Words. Kastenbaum, Robert.

Mementos, Death and Nostalgia (in Dutch). Breeur, R.

My Own Death. Benn, Piers.

Non-Heart-Beating Donors of Organs: Are the Distinctions Between Direct and Indirect Effects and Between Killing and Lettie Die Relevant and Helpful?. Childress, James F.

Organ Transplants, Death, and Policies for Procurement. Lamb, David.

Persons and Death: What's Metaphysically Wrong with Our Current Statutory Definition of Death?. Lizza, John.

Physician Assisted Death and Hard Choices. Mayo, David J and Gunderson, Martin.

Problems with Laws, Defining Death and a New Uniform Proposal. Tierney, Travis S.

Quality of Life and the Death of "Baby M". Kuhse, Helga.

Recent Work on Death and the Meaning of Life. Fischer, John M.

Statutory Definitions of Death and the Management of Terminally Ill Patients Who May Become Organ Donors after Death. Cole, David.

Survival of Bodily Death: A Qeustion of Values. Martin, Raymond.

Techno-Thanatology: Moral Consequences of Introducing Brain Criteria for Death. Bayertz, Kurt.

That to Philosophise is to Learn How to Die. Lyas, Colin.

The Asymmetry of Early Death and Late Birth. Brueckner, Anthony and Fischer, John Martin.

The Case for Letting Vegetative Patients Die. Jennett, Bryan.

The Dead Donor Rule: Should We Stretch It, Bend It, or Abandon It?. Arnold, Robert M and Youngner, Stuart J.

The Enigma of Death. Feldman, Fred.

The Impending Collapse of the Whole-Brain Definition of Death. Veatch, Robert M.

The Irreversibility of Death: Reply to Cole. Tomlinson, Thomas.

The Jaina Ethic of Voluntary Death. Bilimoria, Purushottama.

The Limits of Consent: A Note on Dr Kevorkian. Kleinig, John.

The Medicalization of Dying. Burgess, Michael M.

The Patient in a Persistent Vegetative State: An Ethical Re-Appraisal. Schotsmans, P.

The Problem of Proxies with Interests of Their Own: Toward a Better Theory of Proxy Decisions. Hardwig, John.

The Search for the New Pineal Gland: Brain Life and Personhood. Moussa, Mario and Shannon, Thomas A.

The Thought-Experiment: Shewmon on Brain Death. Tardiff, Andrew.

Tropics of Desire: Freud and Derrida. Willett, Cynthia.

When Self-Determination Runs Amok. Callahan, Daniel.

Why is Annihiliation a Great Gain for Socrates? The Argument of *Apology* 40c3-e2. Calef, Scott.

DEATH PENALTY

Aggravated Murder and Capital Punishment. Sorell, Tom.

Healing and Killing, Harming and Not Harming: Physician Participation in Euthanasia and Capital Punishment. Loewy, Erich H.

Locke on Punishment and the Death Penalty. Calvert, Brian.

Retribution, Arbitrariness and the Death Penalty. Calvert, Brian.

Why the Deterrence Argument for Capital Punishment Fails. Reitan, Eric.

DEBATE

Our Longest Lie: Irrelgious Thoughts on the Relation Between Metaphysics and Politics. Kramer, Matthew H.

DEBT

Debt and Underdevelopment: The Case for Cancelling Third World Debate in International Justice and the Third World, Attfield, Robin (ed). Wilkins, Barry.

DECADENCE

Aspects of the Fin-de-Siècle Decadent Paradox. Marvick, Louis W.

Nietzsche, Decadence, and Regeneration in France, 1891-95. Forth, Christopher E.

DECENCY

Decency and Education for Citizenship. White, Patricia.

DECEPTION

see also Self-Deception

A Spinozistic Account of Self-Deception: NASS Monograph #1 (1993). Ablondi, Frederick R.

Frames of Deceit: A Study of the Loss and Recovery of Public and Private Trust. Johnson, Peter.

Irrationality: An Essay on 'Akrasia', Self-Deception, and Self-Control. Mele, Alfred.

Deception and Belief in Parmenides' *Doxa*. Curd, Patricia Kenig.

On Deceiving Others. Barnes, Annette.

Religious Experience as Self Transcendence and Self-Deception. Westphal, Merold.

The Unbearable Slyness of Deconstruction. Nuyen, A T.

DECIDABILITY

Hilbert's Tenth Problem for Weak Theories of Arithmetic. Kaye, Richard.

Nominal Tense Logic. Blackburn, Patrick.

The Contraction Rule and Decision Problems for Logics Without Structural Rules. Ono, Hiroakira.

DECISION

Changing Values in Medical and Health Care Decision Making. Jensen, Uffe Juul (ed) and Mooney, Gavin (ed).

A Decision Algorithm for Linear Sentences on a PFM. Li, L, Li, H and Liu, Y.

Artificial Decision-Making and Artificial Ethics: A Management Concern. Khalil, Omar E.

Audi on Practical Reasoning. Foley, Richard.

Conceptions of the Corporation and Ethical Decision Making in Business. Nesteruk, Jeffrey and Risser, David T.

Decision Making in an Incapacitated Patient. Freer, Jack P.

Doing What the Patient Orders: Maintaining Integrity in the Doctor-Patient Relationship. Blustein, Jeffrey.

Hardwig on Proxy Decision Making. Brody, Baruch A.

How Can an Expert System Help in Choosing the Optimal Decision?. Coletti, G and Regoli, G.

Justice within Intimate Spheres. Carse, Alisa.

Moral Reasoning and Evidence in Legal Decision-Making in Ethical Dimensions of Legal Theory, Sadurski, Wojciech (ed). Klami, Hannu Tapani.

On a Problem About Probability and Decision. Cargile, James Thomas.

On the Possibility of Rational Dilemmas: An Axiomatic Approach. Cubitt, Robin P.

One-Shot Decisions under Linear Partial Information. Kofler, Edward and Zweifel, Peter.

Patients Should Not Always Come First in Treatment Decisions. Strong, Carson.

Personhood, Potentiality, and the Temporarily Comatose Patient. Rogers, Katherin A.

Rationality and Perspective. Foley, Richard.

Risk and Public Decision-Making: Constructivism and the Postpositivist Challenge. Valverde Jr, L James.

Surrogate Consent. Richards, Norvin W.

Taking Family Seriously. Nelson, James Lindemann.

Teaching Ethical Decision-Making. Pfeiffer, Raymond S.

The "C" Theory: A Chinese Philosophical Approach to Management and Decision-Making. Cheng, Chung-Ying.

The Exchange and Allocation of Decision Power. Philipson, Tomas.

The Family in Medical Decisionmaking. Blustein, Jeffrey.

The PSDA and the Depressed Elderly: "Intermittent Competency" Revisited. Shamoo, Adil E and Irving, Dianne N.

Withholding/Withdrawing Life-Sustaining Treatment in Contemporary Issues in Paediatric Ethics, Burgess, Michael M (ed). Bartholome, William.

DECISION PROCEDURE

On Decision Procedures for Sentential Logics. Skura, Tomasz.

DECISION THEORY

Betting on Theories: Cambridge Studies in Probability, Induction, and Decision Theory. Maher, Patrick.

Invariance and Structural Dependence. Odelstad, Jan.

Akrasia, Self-Control, and Second-Order Desires. Mele, Alfred.

Choice and Conditional Expected Utility. Rawling, Piers.

How a Formal Theory of Rationality Can Be Normative. Loui, R P.

J M Keynes's Theoretical Approach to Decision-Making Under Conditions of Risk and Uncertainty. Brady, Michael Emmett.

Local Utility Functions. Bardsley, Peter.

Manipulation under Majority Decision-Making When No Majority Suffers and Preferences Are Strict. MacIntyre, I D A.

Mean Variance Preferences and the Heat Equation. Bardsley, Peter.

Newcomb's Problem as a Thought Experiment in Thought Experiments in Science and Philosophy, Horowitz, Tamara (ed). Horowitz, Tamara.

Perspectives on Decisions263-. Segerberg, Krister.

Revealed Preference and Linear Utility. Clark, Stephen A.

Three Pseudo-Paradoxes in 'Quantum' Decision Theory: Apparent Effects of Observation on Probability and Utility. Marinoff, Louis.

Über Wünsche, Lust und Rationalität—Eine Auseinandersetzung mit der Gleichgewichtstheorie von Anna Kusser. Piller, Christian.

DECONSTRUCTION

DEDEKIND

DEDUCTION

see also Transcendental Deduction

DEDUCTION THEOREM

DEDUCTIVE-NOMOLOGICAL MODEL

DEMOCRACY

From Social Subject to the 'person': *The Belated Tranformation in Latter-Day Soviet Philosophy*. Swiderski, Edward M.

Green on Dictators and Democracies. Gordon, David.

Groundless Democracy in Shadow of Spirit, Berry, Philippa (ed). Horowitz, Gad.

Harry Broudy and Education for a Democratic Society. Vandenberg, Donald.

Has History Refuted Marxism?. Hudelson, Richard.

Hegel, Modernity, and Civic Republicanism. Buchwalter, Andrew.

Heidegger and Politics in Ethics and Danger, Dallery, Arleen B (ed). IJsseling, Samuel.

Independence in Democratic Theory: A Virtue? A Necessity? Both? Neither?. Goodin, Robert E.

John Dewey, Spiritual Democracy, and the Human Future in Revisioning Philosophy, Ogilvy, James (ed). Rockefeller, Steven C.

Judicial Virtue and Democratic Politics. Pinkard, Terry P.

Justified to Whom? in The Idea of Democracy, Copp, David (ed). Sugden, Robert.

Justifying Democracy. Fisk, Milton.

Keaney's *Composition of Aristotle's Athenaion Politeia*. Rhodes, P J.

Kennedy and West Virginia in Sartre Alive, Aronson, Ronald (ed). Sartre, Jean-Paul and Bowman, Elizabeth A (trans).

Liberalism and Democracy. Graham, Gordon.

Locke against Democracy: Consent, Representation and Suffrage in the *Two Treatises*. Wood, E M.

Making Truth Safe for Democracy in The Idea of Democracy, Copp, David (ed). Estlund, David.

Mass Media, Ethical Paradox, and Democratic Freedom: Jacques Ellul's Ethic of the Word. Fasching, Darrell J.

Minima Moralia: The Gulf War in Fragments. Kellner, Douglas M.

Moral Pluralism and Democracy. Galvin, Richard F.

Moral Pluralism and Political Consensus in The Idea of Democracy, Copp, David (ed). Cohen, Joshua.

Must Preferences Be Respected in a Democracy? in The Idea of Democracy, Copp, David (ed). Ferejohn, John.

Nationalism and Nations (in Dutch). Van De Putte, A.

Natural Science, Social Science, and Democratic Practice: Some Political Implications of the Distinction Between the Natural and the Human Sciences. Stauch, Marvin.

Necesidad de una renovación ética. López Quintás, Alfonso.

Neumann versus Habermas: The Frankfurt School and the Case of the Rule of Law. Scheuerman, Bill.

Nietzsche et l'égalité des droits: De l'usage juridique d'un concept religieux chrétien. Ledure, Yves.

On Contractarian Constitutional Democracy in The Idea of Democracy, Copp, David (ed). Morris, Christopher.

One World? One Law? One Culture. Tay, Alice Erh-Soon.

Participating in the Tension. Laird, Frank.

Pluralism and Equality: The Status of Minority Values in a Democracy. Simon, Robert L.

Political Equality. Christiano, Thomas.

Political Theory and Political Education. Esquith, Stephen L.

Postmetaphysics and Democracy. Dallmayr, Fred.

Power and Wealth in a Competitive Capitalist Economy. Bowles, Samuel and Gintis, Herbert.

Power Rivalry-Motivated Democracy: A Response to Stephen Krasner. Gilbert, Alan.

Public Choice Versus Democracy. Hardin, Russell.

Public Choice Versus Democracy in The Idea of Democracy, Copp, David (ed). Hardin, Russell.

Rationality and Democracy: A Critical Appreciation of Israel Scheffler's Philosophy of Education. Arnstine, Donald and Arnstine, Barbara.

Reports on International Research in Social Epistemology. Kasavin, Ilya.

République et Régicide chez Kant. Beyssade, M Jean-Marie.

Resolving the Tension in Graham and Laird. Guston, David.

Responsible and Irresponsible Liberalism: Dostoevsky's Stavrogin. Neumann, Harry.

Review Article of Ann Ferguson's *Sexual Democracy: Women, Oppression, and Revolution*. Soble, Alan.

Rights, Modernity, Democracy in Deconstruction and the Possibility of Justice, Cornell, Durcilla (ed). Heller, Agnes.

S Stur's "Treatise on Life" (in Czechoslovakian). Uher, J.

Science, Democracy, and Public Policy. Shrader-Frechette, Kristin.

Slote on Self-Sufficiency. Hursthouse, Rosalind.

Sobre las bases éticas de la democracia. Ferrari, María Aparecida.

Social Choice and Democracy in The Idea of Democracy, Copp, David (ed). Christiano, Thomas.

Socialism as the Extension of Democracy. Arneson, Richard J.

Socialism, Utopianism and the 'Utopian Socialists'. Lovell, David W.

Some Remarks on Science, Method and Nationalism in John Locke. Heyd, Thomas.

Some Rules of Constitutional Design. Ordeshook, Peter C.

Subversive Rationalization: Technology, Power, and Democracy. Feenberg, Andrew.

Tactics of Appropriation and the Politics of Recognition in Late Modern Democracies. Coombe, Rosemary J.

Technology and the Civil Epistemology of Democracy. Ezrahi, Yaron.

The Democratic Solution to Ethnic Pluralism. Singer, Beth.

The Domain of the Political and Overlapping Consensus in The Idea of Democracy, Copp, David (ed). Rawls, John.

The Early Phase in Spengler's Political Philosophy. Farrenkopf, John.

The Essential Tension in Science and Democracy. Guston, David.

The Future of Democracy in Nigeria in Terrorism, Justice and Social Values, Peden, Creighton W (ed). Nwodo, C S.

The Jeffersonian Option. Dawidoff, Robert.

The Limits and Possibilities of Communicative Ethics for Democratic Theory. Ingram, David.

The Modern Democratic Revolution in Judging Lyotard, Benjamin, Andrew (ed). Keane, John.

The Necessity of the Tension. Graham Jr, George J.

The New Problem of Curriculum. Martin, Jane Roland.

The Possibility of Market Socialism in The Idea of Democracy, Copp, David (ed). Roemer, John E.

The Radical Dimensions of Locke's Political Thought: A Dialogic Essay on the Problems of Interpretation. Ashcraft, Richard.

The Unity of Plato's Political Thought. Shiell, Timothy C.

The Wisdom of the Many: An Analysis of the Arguments of Books III and IV of Aristotle's *Politics*. Bookman, J T.

Thinking about Democracy and Exclusion: Jurgen Habermas' *Theory of Communicative Action* and Contemporary Politics. Hanks, Craig.

Three Fallacies Concerning Majorities, Minorities, and Democratic Politics. Shapiro, Ian.

Tocqueville and Democracy in The Idea of Democracy, Copp, David (ed). Holmes, Stephen.

Tocqueville, Commerce, and Democracy in The Idea of Democracy, Copp, David (ed). Satz, Debra M.

Totalitarianism "with a Human Face": A Methodological Essay. Poliakov, Leonid.

Toward Democracy for the World Community. Glossop, Ronald J.

Two Hundred Years of Error? The Politics of Democracy. Howard, Dick.

Utilitarian Ethics and Democratic Government in The Utilitarian Response, Allison, Lincoln (ed). Riley, Jonathan.

Virtue Ethics and Democratic Values. Slote, Michael.

DEMOCRITUS

Die Rolle der Physiologie in der Philosophie Epikurs. Manolidis, Georgios.

The Presocratic Philosophers: An Annotated Bibliography. Navia, Luis E.

DEMONSTRATION

Demonstrating with Descriptions. Reimer, Marga.

Demonstrative Modes of Presentation. Bezuidenhout, Anne L.

Demonstrative Reference and Unintended Demonstrata. Hand, Michael.

Demonstratives and Intentions, Ten Years Later. Bertolet, Rod.

Intentions and Demonstrations. Bach, Kent.

DENNETT, D

A Sufficient Condition for Personhood. Goodman, Michael.

Daniel C Dennett's *The Intentional Stance*. Lumsden, David.

Dennett's Mind. Lockwood, Michael.

Dennett's Rejection of Dualism. Foster, John.

Is Dennett a Disillusioned Zimbo?. Sprigge, T L S.

Living on the Edge. Dennett, Daniel C.

Mental Content. Allen, Colin.

Minds, Memes, and Rhetoric. Clark, Stephen R L.

Responsibility and the Self-made Self. Waller, Bruce N.

Some Content is Narrow in Mental Causation, Heil, John (ed). Jackson, Frank and Pettit, Philip.

The Failure of Dennett's Representationalism: A Wittgensteinian Resolution. Ward, Andrew.

The Tiger and His Stripes. Lyons, William.

Verificationism, Scepticism, and Consciousness. Seager, William.

'Intuition Pumps' and Contemporary Philosophy. MacLean-Tollefsen, Laurie.

'The Best Set of Tools'? Dennett's Metaphors and the Mind-Body Problem. Kirk, Robert.

DENOTATION

A New Angle on Russell's "Inextricable Tangle" Over Meaning and Denotation. Rodriguez-Consuegra, Francisco A.

DENOTING

Russell's Theory of Meaning and Denotation and "On Denoting". Wahl, Russell.

DENSITY

Leibniz on Density and Sequential or Cauchy Completeness in Greek Studies in the Philosophy and History of Science, Nicolacopoulos, Pantelis (ed). Anapolitanos, D A.

DEONTIC

La Charpente Modale du Sens. Brandt, Per Aage.

DEONTIC LOGIC

Deontic Problems with Prohibition Dilemmas. Almeida, Michael J.

Paul of Venice on Obligations. Sinkler, Georgette.

The Paradoxes of Feldman's Neo-Utilitarianism. Almeida, Michael J.

Théories syllogistiques et déontiques analysées comme structures algébriques: de Leibniz à Lukasiewicz et Von Wright. Sánchez-Mazas, Miguel.

DEONTOLOGY

"The Will to Believe" and James's "Deontological Streak". O'Connell, Robert.

Moral Philosophy: A Reader. Pojman, Louis (ed).

The Practice of Moral Judgment. Herman, Barbara.

Clinical Ethics and Happiness. Devettere, Raymond J.

Deontologism and Moral Weakness. Peterson, John.

Deontology and Agency. McNaughton, David and Rawling, Piers.

Deontology and Economics. Broome, John.

Deontology, Incommensurability and the Arbitrary. Ellis, Anthony.

Ease and Difficulty: A Modal Logic with Deontic Applications. Denyer, Nicholas.

Is It Less Wrong to Harm the Vulnerable than the Secure?. Howard-Snyder, Frances.

Justice and Care: The Implications of the Kohlberg-Gilligan Debate for Medical Ethics. Sharpe, Virginia A.

DEONTOLOGY

Justice, Scheffler and Cicero. Simpson, Peter.
L Hejdanek's Meontology: An Attempt of a Critical Explanation (in Czechoslovakian). Sousedik, S.
Proportionalists, Deontologists and the Human Good. Hoose, Bernard.
Rule Consequentialism is a Rubber Duck. Howard-Snyder, Frances.
Sidgwick and Nineteenth-Century British Ethical Thought in Essays on Henry Sidgwick, Schultz, Bart (ed). Singer, Marcus G.

DEPENDENCY

Invariance and Structural Dependence. Odelstad, Jan.
Degrees of Convex Dependence in Recursively Enumerable Vector Spaces. Nevins, Thomas A.
In Defense of Global Supervenience. Paull, R Cranston and Sider, Theodore R.
Nomic Dependence and Causation. Clendinnen, F John.
One Logic or Many Logics? (Epstein's Set-Assignment Semantics for Logical Calculi). Krajewski, Stanislaw.
Response-Dependence and Infallibility. Holton, Richard.

DERIVATION

A Normal Form for Logical Derivations Implying One for Arithmetic Derivations. Mints, G.

DERRIDA, J

Derrida and Negative Theology. Coward, Harold (ed) and Foshay, Toby (ed).
Derrida: A Critical Reader. Wood, David (ed).
Given Time: I. Counterfeit Money—Jacques Derrida. Derrida, Jacques and Kamuf, Peggy (trans).
Imagination and Chance: The Difference Between the Thought of Ricoeur and Derrida. Lawlor, Leonard.
Jacques Derrida: An Annotated Primary and Secondary Bibliography. Schultz, William R and Fried, Lewis L B.
Matrix and Line: Derrida and the Possibilities of Postmodern Social Theory. Martin, Bill.
Of Derrida, Heidegger, and Spirit. Wood, David (ed).
System and Writing in the Philosophy of Jacques Derrida. Johnson, Christopher.
The Ethics of Deconstruction: Derrida and Levinas. Critchley, Simon.
The Fate of Art: Aesthetic Alienation from Kant to Derrida and Adorno. Bernstein, J M.
The Understanding of Difference in Heidegger and Derrida. Donkel, Douglas L.
Theology and Difference: The Wound of Reason. Lowe, Walter.
Truth in Philosophy. Allen, Barry G.
Truth's Debt to Value. Weissman, David.
Working Through Derrida. Madison, Gary B (ed).
A Bibliography of the Works of Jacques Derrida in Derrida: A Critical Reader, Wood, David (ed). Keenan, Thomas and Leventure, Albert.
A Final Word (Eight Famous Ones) in Modernity and Its Discontents, Marsh, James L (ed). Caputo, John D.
An Allegory of Modernity/Postmodernity in Working Through Derrida, Madison, Gary B (ed). Bernstein, Richard J.
Analytic Phenomenological Deconstruction in Certainty and Surface in Epistemology and Philosophical Method, Martinich, A P (ed). Martinich, A P.
Commentary on "Hegel, Derrida and Bataille's Laughter" in Hegel and His Critics, Desmond, William (ed). Butler, Judith.
De-Divinization and the Vindication of Everyday-Life: Reply to Rorty. Bernstein, J M.
Deconstructing Derrida: Below the Surface of *Differance*. Jones, W T.
Deconstruction and the Teaching Historian. Anderson, Mary R.
Deconstruction, Postmodernism and Philosophy: Habermas on Derrida in Derrida: A Critical Reader, Wood, David (ed). Norris, Christopher.
Derrida and Connectionism: Différance in Neural Nets. Globus, Gordon G.
Derrida and Habermas on the Subject of Political Philosophy in Crises in Continental Philosophy, Dallery, Arleen B (ed). Thorp, Thomas R.
Derrida and Heidegger in Heidegger: A Critical Reader, Dreyfus, Hubert (ed). Spinosa, Charles.
Derrida and Madhyamika Buddhism: From Linguistic Deconstruction to Criticism of Onto-Theologies. Zong-qi, Cai.
Derrida and Seng-Zhao: Linguistic and Philosophical Deconstructions. Zongqi, Cai.
Derrida and the Ethics of Dialogue. Kearney, Richard.
Derrida and the Issues of Exemplarity in Derrida: A Critical Reader, Wood, David (ed). Harvey, Irene E.
Derrida and the Philosophy of Deconstruction. Panneerselvam, S.
Derrida's Ethical Re-Turn in Working Through Derrida, Madison, Gary B (ed). Kearney, Richard.
Early American Antigone in Theorizing American Literature, Cowan, Bainard (ed). Breitwieser, Mitchell.
Elements of a Derridean Social Theory in Ethics and Danger, Dallery, Arleen B (ed). Martin, Bill.
Elliptical Sense in Derrida: A Critical Reader, Wood, David (ed). Nancy, Jean-Luc and Connor, Peter (trans).
Flight of Spirit in Of Derrida, Heidegger, and Spirit, Wood, David (ed). Sallis, John.
Hegel and the Dialects of American Literary Historiography in Theorizing American Literature, Cowan, Bainard (ed). Jay, Gregory S.
Hegel, Derrida and Bataille's Laughter in Hegel and His Critics, Desmond, William (ed). Flay, Joseph C.
Hegel, Heidegger, Derrida in Ethics and Danger, Dallery, Arleen B (ed). Flay, Joseph C.
Illusion and Imagination in Aesthetic Illusion, Burwick, Frederick (ed). Shaffer, Elinor S.
Implications: The 'A' of *Différance*. Tirone, Nicholas D.
Is *Prasanga* a form of Deconstruction?. Matilal, Bimal Krishna.

Is Derrida a Transcendental Philosopher? in Derrida: A Critical Reader, Wood, David (ed). Rorty, Richard.
Is Derrida a Transcendental Philosopher? in Working Through Derrida, Madison, Gary B (ed). Rorty, Richard.
Is Self-Consciousness a Case of 'Présence à Soi? in Derrida: A Critical Reader, Wood, David (ed). Frank, Manfred and Bowie, Andrew (trans).
Levinas on Desire, Dialogue and the Other. Jopling, David.
Light and Metpahor in Plotinus and St Thomas Aquinas. Corrigan, Kevin.
Mosaic Fragment: If Derrida were an Egyptian... in Derrida: A Critical Reader, Wood, David (ed). Bennington, Geoffrey.
No More Stories, Good or Bad: de Man's Criticisms of Derrida on Rousseau in Derrida: A Critical Reader, Wood, David (ed). Bernasconi, Robert.
Of Derrida's Spirit in Of Derrida, Heidegger, and Spirit, Wood, David (ed). Rose, Gillian.
Of Spirit and the Daimon in Ethics and Danger, Dallery, Arleen B (ed). Krell, David Farrell.
On Not Circumventing the Quasi-Transcendental in Working Through Derrida, Madison, Gary B (ed). Caputo, John D.
On the Limits of Classical Reason: Derrida and Aristotle. White, David A.
Patterns of Dissonance: Women and/In Philosophy. Braidotti, Rosi.
Politics beyond Humanism in Working Through Derrida, Madison, Gary B (ed). Bernasconi, Robert.
Predication as Originary Violence in Working Through Derrida, Madison, Gary B (ed). Willard, Dallas.
Resentment and Apophasis: The Trace of the Other in Levinas, Derrida and Gans in Shadow of Spirit, Berry, Philippa (ed). Foshay, Toby.
Responsibility with Indecidability in Derrida: A Critical Reader, Wood, David (ed). Llewelyn, John.
Rorty on Derrida in Ethics and Danger, Dallery, Arleen B (ed). Bell, Roger.
Sartre and the Deconstruction of the Subject in The Cambridge Companion to Sartre, Howells, Christina (ed). Howells, Christina.
Spirit and Danger in Ethics and Danger, Dallery, Arleen B (ed). Caputo, John D.
Spirit's Living Hand in Of Derrida, Heidegger, and Spirit, Wood, David (ed). McNeill, Will.
Spirit's Spirit Spirits Spirit in Of Derrida, Heidegger, and Spirit, Wood, David (ed). Bennington, Geoffrey.
Spiriting Heidegger in Of Derrida, Heidegger, and Spirit, Wood, David (ed). Krell, David Farrell.
The Actualization of Philosophy and the Logic of 'Geist' in Of Derrida, Heidegger, and Spirit, Wood, David (ed). Wood, David.
The Economy of Exteriority in Derrida's *Speech and Phenomena*. Protevi, John.
The Gentle and Rigorous Cogency of Communicative Rationality in Modernity and Its Discontents, Marsh, James L (ed). Marsh, James L.
The Instant and the Living Present: Ricoeur and Derrida Reading Husserl. Bourgeois, Patrick.
The Metaphysics of Presence in Working Through Derrida, Madison, Gary B (ed). Dillon, Martin C.
The Play of Nietzsche in Derrida in Derrida: A Critical Reader, Wood, David (ed). Haar, Michel and McNeill, Will (trans).
The Problem of Closure in Derrida (Part Two). Critchley, Simon.
The Question of Derrida's Women. Thomas, Jennifer.
The Question of the Question: An Ethico-Political Response to a Note in Derrida's 'De l'esprit' in Of Derrida, Heidegger, and Spirit, Wood, David (ed). Critchley, Simon.
The Rhetoric of Jacques Derrida I: Plato's Pharmacy. Rinon, Yoav.
The Rhetoric of Jacques Derrida II: *Phaedrus*. Rinon, Yoav.
The Rhetoric of Philosophical "Writing": Emphatic Metaphors in Derrida and Rorty. Trembath, Paul.
The Sign Over the Barber Shop: Annotations on the Problems of Interpretation. Schmitz, Heinz-Gerd.
The Theater of Personal Identity: From Hume to Derrida. Gallagher, Shaun.
The Unbearable Lightness of Deconstruction. Verges, Frank G.
The Voice that Keeps Reading: Evan's *Strategies of Deconstruction*. Kates, Joshua.
Three Questions to Jacques Derrida in Ethics and Danger, Dallery, Arleen B (ed). Dastur, Françoise.
Tomb of the Sacred Prostitute: 'The Symposium' in Shadow of Spirit, Berry, Philippa (ed). Bell, Shannon.
Tropics of Desire: Freud and Derrida. Willett, Cynthia.
What Does "To Avoid" Mean? On Derrida's *De l'Esprit*. David, Pascal.
What Price Deconstruction? Derrida on Heidegger and the Question of Nazims: A Critical Study. Nevo, Isaac.
Why Bother? Defending Derrida and the Significance of Writing. Ferrell, Robyn.
Wittgenstein and Derrida on Meaning. Rowlands, Mark.

DESCARTES

see also Cartesianism
"Ego Sum, Ego Existo": Descartes au point d'hérésie. Balibar, M Étienne.
Central Readings in the History of Modern Philosophy: Descartes to Kant. Cummins, Robert (ed) and Owen, David (ed).
Descartes on Seeing: Epistemology and Visual Perception. Wolf-Devine, Celia.
Nietzsche and Modern Times. Lampert, Laurence.
Scepticism. Hookway, Christopher.
A Matemática como Paradigma da Construçao Filosófica de Descartes: Do Discurso do Método e da Tematizaçao do Cogito. Spinelli, Miguel.
A Response to Daniel Holbrook's 'Descartes on Persons' and Doug Anderson's 'The Legacy of Bowne's Empiricism'. Littlejohn, Ronnie L.
Alguns Aspectos da Obra Matemática de Descartes. Wanderley, Augusto J M.
Cogito Ergo Sum. Stone, Jim.

DIFFERENCE

Language and Difference: The Problem of Abstraction in Eighteenth-Century Language Study. Paxman, David B.

Poststructuralism, Difference, and Marxism. Fisk, Milton T.

Sexual Differences: The Contingent and the Necessary. Wilson, John.

Social Exclusion, Moral Reflection, and Rights. Meyers, Diana Tietjens.

Some Disquiet about "Difference". Sypnowich, John.

The Economy of Exteriority in Derrida's *Speech and Phenomena*. Protevi, John.

The Theater of Personal Identity: From Hume to Derrida. Gallagher, Shaun.

DIFFUSION

The Development of Freudian Theory in Greek Studies in the Philosophy and History of Science, Nicolacopoulos, Pantelis (ed). Tzavaras, Athanase and Papagounos, G.

DIGNITY

Dignity in Difference in On Community, Rouner, Leroy S (ed). Smith, Huston.

DILEMMA

A New Argument for Genuine Moral Dilemmas?. Statman, Daniel.

Deontic Problems with Prohibition Dilemmas. Almeida, Michael J.

Dilemmas and Incommensurateness. McConnell, Terrance.

Stove on Gene Worship. Levin, Michael E.

Surviving Souls. Moser, Paul K and Vander Nat, Arnold.

DILLER, A

Radicalizing Pluralism. Thompson, Audrey.

DILTHEY

"Historismus" e mondo moderno: Dilthey e Troeltsch. Cacciatore, Giuseppe.

Erlebte und erschlossene Realität. Lenk, Hans.

Husserl vs Dilthey—A Controversy over the Concept of Reason in Analecta Husserliana, XXXIV, Tymieniecka, Anna-Teresa (ed). Walczewska, Slawomira.

Phenomenological Research as *Destruktion*: The Early Heidegger's Reading of Dilthey. Bambach, Charles.

DIMENSION

Relation Algebras of Every Dimension. Maddux, Roger D.

DIMONDSTEIN, G

The Process/Product Dichotomy and Its Implications for Creative Dance. Bergmann, Sheryle.

DINOIA, J

MacIntyre's Postmodern Thomism. Hibbs, Thomas.

DIODORUS CRONUS

Chrysippus's Response to Diodorus's Master Argument. Ide, H A.

DIOGENES LAERTIUS

Doxographie, historiographie philosophique et historiographie historique de la philosophie. Frede, Michael.

DIONYSIUS

From Dionysius to Eriugena: A Bridge for Voluntarism or "Divine Freedom"?. King-Farlow, John.

DIOPHANTINE EQUATION

A Diophantine Definition of Rational Integers over Some Rings of Algebraic Numbers. Shlapentokh, Alexandra.

End Extensions of Models of Arithmetic. Schmerl, James H.

DISABILITY

Disability, Handicap, and the Environment. Amundson, Ron.

DISARMAMENT

Unilateral Nuclear Disarmament and Bilateral Nuclear Sieges. Barry, Robert.

DISCOURSE

Bodies that Matter: On the Discursive Limits of 'Sex'. Butler, Judith.

Burdens of Proof in Modern Discourse. Gaskins, Richard H.

Contemplating Music: Source Readings in the Aesthetics of Music, Volume IV— Community of Discourse. Katz, Ruth (ed) and Dahlhaus, Carl (ed).

El discurso filosófico: Análisis desde la obra de Paul Ricoeur. Villaverde, Marcelino Agís.

Materialist Feminism and the Politics of Discourse. Hennessy, Rosemary.

Merleau-Ponty Vivant. Dillon, M C (ed).

Michel Foucault, Philosopher. Armstrong, Timothy J (trans) and Foucault, Michel.

Moral Aspects of Legal Theory. Lyons, David.

Norms of Rhetorical Culture. Farrell, Thomas B.

On Paul Ricoeur: Narrative and Interpretation. Wood, David (ed).

Paradigms and Barriers: How Habits of Mind Govern Scientific Beliefs. Margolis, Howard.

Philosophy—A Myth?. Verster, Ulrich.

Semiotics in the United States. Sebeok, Thomas A.

System and Writing in the Philosophy of Jacques Derrida. Johnson, Christopher.

The Company of Words: Hegel, Language, and Systematic Philosophy. McCumber, John.

The Emancipative Theory of Jürgen Habermas and Metaphysics. McLean, George F (ed) and Badillo, Robert Peter.

The Nature and Process of Law: An Introduction to Legal Philosophy. Smith, Patricia (ed).

The Truth about Postmodernism. Norris, Christopher.

Theory and Cultural Value. Connor, Steven.

Voices of the Past: The Status of Language in Eighteenth-Century Japanese Discourse. Sakai, Naoki.

A Discourse-Theoretical Conception of Practical Reason. Alexy, Robert.

A Natural Deduction System for Discourse Representation Theory. Saurer, Werner.

Ambiguity and Originality in the Context of Discursive Relations in Objectivity, Method and Point of View, Van Der Dussen, W J (ed). Boucher, David.

Antilogia. Incardona, Nunzio.

Argumentation and Interpretation in Law. MacCormick, Neil.

At the Limits of Discourse: Tracing the Maternal Body with Kristeva. Ziarek, Ewa.

Being, Time, and Politics: The Strauss-Kojève Debate. Pippin, Robert B.

Between Church and State: Nietzsche, Deleuze and the Genealogy of Psychoanalysis. Schrift, Alan D.

Christian Religious Discourse. Sokolowski, Robert.

Commentary on Garver's "Making Discourse Ethical". Griswold, Charles L.

Communicative Ethics and the Morality of Discourse. Aragaki, Hiro.

Condensation Symbols: Their Variety and Rhetorical Function in Political Discourse. Kaufer, David S and Carley, Kathleen M.

Conflicting Views on Practical Reason: Against Pseudo-Arguments in Practical Philosophy. Weinberger, Ota.

Derrida and the Issues of Exemplarity in Derrida: A Critical Reader, Wood, David (ed). Harvey, Irene E.

Descartes' Discourse. Rudolph, Katherine.

Discourse and Disclosure in the *I Ching*. Stevenson, Frank W.

Discourse Competence; or, How to Theorize Strong Women Speakers. Mills, Sara.

Discourses as the Reflective Educator. Walsh, Paddy.

Dislocating the Everyday: David Lynch's *Wild at Heart* as Cinema of the Grotesque. Olivier, Bert.

Epistemological Perspectives in Legal Theory. Van Hoecke, Mark and Ost, François.

Law-Making and Legal Interpretation. Frosini, Vittorio.

Le discours mental selon Hobbes. Pécharman, Martine.

Learning to Stop: A Critique of General Rhetoric in The Critical Turn, Angus, Ian (ed). Angus, Ian.

Making Discourse Ethical: The Lessons of Aristotle's *Rhetoric*. Garver, Eugene.

Marxism and the Logic of Futural Discourse: A Brief Reflection. O'Connell, Colin.

Must We Say What "We" Means? The Politics of Postmodernism. Cutrofello, Andrew.

Negotiating with Our Tradition: Reflecting Again (Without Apologies) on the Feminization of Rhetoric. Biesecker, Barbara.

On Argumentation in Legal Contexts. Holmstrom-Hintikka, Ghita.

On the Autonomy of Legal Reasoning. Raz, Joseph.

Self-Defeating Civic Republicanism. Christodoulidis, Emilios A.

Some Remarks on the Notions of Legal Order and Legal System. Moreso, José Juan and Navarro, Pablo Eugenio.

Some Ways that Technology and Terminology Distort the Euthanasia Issue. Herrera, Christopher.

Speculative Logic, Deconstruction, and Discourse Ethics. Cutrofello, Andrew.

The Algebra of History in The Critical Turn, Angus, Ian (ed). Lanigan, Richard L.

The Long Goodbye: The Imaginary Language of Film. Currie, Gregory.

The Name of the Game: An Analysis of the Grünbaum Debate. Bos, Jaap and Maier, Robert.

The Third Man. Davidson, Donald.

What's "I" Got To Do With It?. Bernstein, Susan David.

Writing with Davidson: Some Afterthoughts after Doing *Blind Time IV: Drawing with Davidson*. Morris, Robert.

'Epistemological' and 'Narrativist' Philosophies of History in Objectivity, Method and Point of View, Van Der Dussen, W J (ed). Fell, Albert P.

DISCOVERY

The Logic of Scientific Discovery. Popper, Karl R.

De la "invención" al "descubrimiento" del Nuevo Mundo. Dussel, Enrique.

Discoveries as the Origin of Modern Economic Values. Janowski, W K.

La scoperta dell'America: Tra la realtà e l'utopia di un "nuovo mondo". Bonilla, Alcira B.

DISCRIMINATION

Biomedical Ethics Reviews 1992. Humber, James M (ed) and Almeder, Robert F (ed).

Moral Controversies: Race, Class, and Gender in Applied Ethics. Gold, Steven Jay.

Moral Matters. Narveson, Jan.

Sharing Responsibility. May, Larry.

Transformations: Recollective Imagination and Sexual Difference. Cornell, Drucilla.

Beyond Compensatory Justice?. Johnston, David.

Coerced Birth Control, Individual Rights, and Discrimination in Biomedical Ethics Reviews 1992, Humber, James M (ed). Kuo, Lenore.

Compensation and Rights in the Liberal Conception of Justice. Barnett, Randy E.

Discrimination and Disadvantage in Feminist Legal Theory: A Review of Deborah Rhode's *Justice and Gender*. Smith, Patricia G.

From Justified Discrimination to Responsive Hiring. Hall, Pamela.

Racial Discrimination is Distinct, If Not "Special". Herrera, Christopher.

Racism and Affirmative Action. Corlett, J Angelo.

Racism: Flew's Three Concepts of Racism. Skillen, Anthony.

The Moral Status of Affirmative Action. Pojman, Louis.

Unlawful Discrimination in Ethical Dimensions of Legal Theory, Sadurski, Wojciech (ed). Campbell, Tom D.

DISEASE

A Sociological Perspective on Disease in New Horizons in the Philosophy of Science, Lamb, David (ed). White, Kevin.

Can We Talk? Contexts of Meaning for Interpreting Illness. Mount Jr, Eric.

Challenge of Ill Health in New Horizons in the Philosophy of Science, Lamb, David (ed). Ledermann, E K.

DISEASE

Do We Need a Concept of Disease?. Hesslow, Germund.

Doentes, Doença, Médicos e Medicina em Luciano de Samósata. Brandao, Jacynthos Lins.

Historique des recherches sur la différenciation des Hépatites A & B. Meyer, Jean-Luc.

Horen, zien en lezen. Pasveer, Bernike.

Kausalität als Leitbegriff ärztlichen Denkens und Handelns. Hartmann, Fritz.

Leibniz's Vorstellungen über den Zusammenhang von Meteorologie und Anthropologie: "physica specialis cum medicina provisionalis". Obst, Godehard.

Making Mistakes in Science: Eduard Pflüger, His Scientific and Professional Concept of Physiology, and His Unsuccessful Theory of Diabetes (1903-1910). Schlich, Thomas.

On the Relevance and Importance of the Notion of Disease. Nordenfelt, Lennart.

The Body in Multiple Sclerosis: A Patient's Perspective in The Body in Medical Thought and Practice, Leder, Drew (ed). Toombs, S Kay.

DISJUNCTION

Algebraic Logic for Classical Conjunction and Disjunction. Font, J M and Verdú, V.

An Alternative Rule of Disjunction in Modal Logic. Williamson, Timothy.

On Negative and Disjunctive Properties in Language, Truth and Ontology, Mulligan, Kevin (ed). Meixner, Uwe.

The Disjunction Property of Intermediate Propositional Logic. Chagrov, Alexander and Zakharyashchev, Michael.

The Disjunction Property of the Logics with Axioms of Only One Variable. Sasaki, Katsumi.

DISOBEDIENCE

see also Civil Disobedience, Obedience

Disorder Is Possible in Cultural-Political Interventions in the Unfinished Project of Enlightenment, Honneth, Axel (& other eds). Frankenberg, Günter.

DISORDER

Problems in Personal Identity. Baillie, James.

Bergson's Concept of Order. Lorand, Ruth.

Disorder Is Possible in Cultural-Political Interventions in the Unfinished Project of Enlightenment, Honneth, Axel (& other eds). Frankenberg, Günter.

DISPOSITION

Found: the Missing Explanation. Menzies, Peter and Philip, Pettit.

Secondary Qualities and Representation. Brooks, D H M.

DISPROPORTIONALITY

Heidegger's Logic of Disproportionality. Schalow, Frank.

DISPUTE

Heidegger's *Sache*: A Family Portrait. Van Buren, E John.

The Enthymeme Buster: A Heuristic Procedure for Position Exploration in Dialogic Dispute. Gilbert, Michael A.

DISTINCTION

Response. Rescher, Nicholas.

The Dialectic of Second-Order Distinctions: The Structure of Arguments about Fallacies. Goodwin, David.

DISTRIBUTION

Ethical Issues: Perspectives for Canadians. Soifer, Eldon (ed).

Justice: Interdisciplinary Perspectives. Scherer, Klaus R (ed).

Compensation and Redistribution. Goodin, Robert E.

Critical Notice: Thomas Nagel's *Equality and Partiality*. Hooker, Bradford.

Distributing Health in The Quality of Life, Nussbaum, Martha C (ed). Roemer, John E.

Distribution in Lukasiewicz Logics. Beavers, Gordon.

On Compensation and Distribution. Levmore, Saul.

Peirce and the Law of Distribution in Perspectives on the History of Mathematical Logic, Drucker, Thomas (ed). Houser, Nathan.

Why the Distributive Law is Sometimes False. Gibbins, P F.

DISTRIBUTIVE JUSTICE

A Proposed Diagram in Aristotle *EN* V3, 1131a24-b20 for Distributive Justice in Proportion. Keyser, Paul.

DIVERSITY

The Diversity of Religions: A Christian Perspective. DiNoia, J A.

Citizenship, Diversity and Education: A Philosophical Perspective. McLaughlin, T H.

Ethics and the Praise of Diversity: Review of *Workforce America*. Weber, Leonard J.

The Diversity Criterion in Public Administration. Stever, James A.

DIVINE

Homo Religiosus ou L'Homme Vertical. Rostenne, Paul.

San Tommaso e Hegel per una teodicea cristologica. Mangiagalli, Maurizio.

The Anselmian 'Single-Divine-Attribute Doctrine'. Hestevold, H Scott.

The Status and Function of Divine Simpleness in *Summa Theologia* 1a, 2-13. Burns, Peter.

Transcending the Natural: Duns Scotus on the Two Affections of the Will. Boler, John F.

DIVINE IMPERATIVE

Arbitrariness, Divine Commands, and Morality. Sullivan, Stephen J.

DIVINE LAW

An Italian View of the Debate on Virtue. Kennedy, Terence.

DIVINITY

Aquinas on Human Action: A Theory of Practice. McInerny, Ralph.

Comprensione e creatività: La filosofia di Whitehead. Arena, Leonardo Vittorio.

Daimon Life: Heidegger and Life-Philosophy. Krell, David Farrell.

Divine Hiddenness and Human Reason. Schellenberg, J L.

Divine Infinity in Greek and Medieval Thought. Sweeney, Leo.

Empirical Theology: A Handbook. Miller, Randolph Crump (ed).

God and Existence (in Hungarian). Joós, Ernó.

Hell: The Logic of Damnation. Walls, Jerry.

On Intersubjectivity and Cultural Creativity—Martin Buber. Eisenstadt, S N (ed) and Buber, Martin.

Person and Being. Clarke, W Norris.

Person and Religion: An Introduction to the Philosophy of Religion. Sandok, Theresa (trans) and Zdybicka, Zofia J.

Santayana, Pragmatism, and the Spiritual Life. Levinson, Henry Samuel.

Simone Weil's Philosophy of Culture. Bell, Richard H (ed).

The Trinity: An Analysis of St Thomas Aquinas' 'Expositio' of the 'De Trinitate' of Boethius. Hall, Douglas.

Trinity and Process: A Critical Evaluation and Reconstruction of Hartshorne's Di-Polar Theism Towards a Trinitarian Metaphysics. Boyd, Gregory.

What is God? The Selected Essays of Richard R La Croix. Lucey, Kenneth (ed).

William of Ockham: A Short Discourse on Tyrannical Government. McGrade, Arthur Stephen (ed) and Kilcullen, John (trans).

A Latter-Day Look at the Foreknowledge Problem. Pike, Nelson.

An Answer on Behalf of Guanilo. Landau, Iddo.

An Anti-Molinist Argument in Philosophical Perspectives, 5: Philosophy of Religion, 1991, Tomberlin, James E (ed). Adams, Robert Merrihew.

Aquinas's Arguments for Spirit. Foster, David R.

Commentary on Gómez-Lobo's "Philosophical Remarks on Thucydides' Melian Dialogue". Pouncy, Peter R.

Consciousness and the Trinity. Lonergan, Bernard J F and Croken, Robert C (ed).

Divine Foreknowledge and the Libertarian Conception of Human Freedom. Linville, Mark D.

Divine Intervention and the Origin of Life. Chandler, Hugh S.

Divine Reservations in Derrida and Negative Theology, Coward, Harold (ed). Joy, Morny.

Divine Simplicity in Our Knowledge of God, Clark, Kelly James (ed). Wolterstorff, Nicholas.

Divine Simplicity in Philosophical Perspectives, 5: Philosophy of Religion, 1991, Tomberlin, James E (ed). Wolterstorff, Nicholas.

Divine Simplicity: A New Defense. Vallicella, William F.

Divine Temporality and Creation Ex Nihilo. Senor, Thomas D.

Emanation *Ex Deus*: A Defense. Oakes, Robert.

Experience of the Holy in the Technological Age. Ott, Heinrich.

God and Evil: Polarities of a Problem. Adams, Marilyn McCord.

God and Process in Logic, God and Metaphysics, Harris, James F (ed). Edwards, Rem B.

Hegel's Philosophy of God in the Light of Kierkegaard's Criticisms in Hegel and His Critics, Desmond, William J (ed). Cullen, Bernard.

Hold Not Thy Peace At My Tears: Methodological Reflections on Divine Impassibility in Our Knowledge of God, Clark, Kelly James (ed). Clark, Kelly James.

In Defence of Divine Forgiveness: A Response to David Londey. Geuras, Dean.

James Ross on the Divine Ideas: A Reply. Maurer, Armand A.

Leibniz and the Compatibilist of Free Will. Borst, Clive.

Monica's Grin of Tension. Benso, Silvia.

On Divine Perfection in Logic, God and Metaphysics, Harris, James F (ed). Power, William L.

Philosophical Remarks on Thucydides' Melian Dialogue. Gómez-Lobo, Alfonso.

Punishment, Forgiveness, and Divine Justice. Talbott, Thomas.

Response to Maurer and Dewan. Ross, James F.

Scotus on the Divine Origin of Possibility. Wolter, Allan B.

Snapshot Ockhamism in Philosophical Perspectives, 5: Philosophy of Religion, 1991, Tomberlin, James E (ed). Fischer, John M.

Social Evil: A Response to Adams. Quinn, Philip.

St Thomas, James Ross, and Exemplarism: A Reply. Dewan, Lawrence.

Temporal Actualism and Singular Foreknowledge in Philosophical Perspectives, 5: Philosophy of Religion, 1991, Tomberlin, James E (ed). Menzel, Christopher.

Temporality and Divinity: An Analytic Hurdle. Oakes, Robert.

The Problem of Divine Perfection and Freedom in Reasoned Faith, Stump, Eleonore (ed). Rowe, William.

The Use of Sophiology. Martz, Erin.

Theantropic Foundations of Religious Beliefs. Woznicki, Andrew N.

Three Types of Divine Power. Gier, Nicholas F.

Transcendence, Instantiation and Incarnation—An Exploration. Durrant, Michael.

DIVISIBILITY

La Curiosa Doctrina de Ockham en Torno a la Divisibilidad del Continuo. Larre, Olga L and Bolzan, J E.

DIVORCE

The State, Marriage and Divorce. Trainor, Brian T.

DNA

Knowledge, Bodies, and Values: Reproductive Technologies and their Scientific Context. Longino, Helen E.

DOCTOR-PATIENT RELATIONSHIP

Doing What the Patient Orders: Maintaining Integrity in the Doctor-Patient Relationship. Blustein, Jeffrey.

The Concept of Medically Indicated Treatment. Miller, Franklin G.

DOCTRINE

Doctrines and the Virtues of Doctrine: The Problematic of Religious Plurality. Griffiths, Paul J.

Dottrina non scritta e limiti della comunicabilità filosofica in Platone. Roggerone, Giuseppe A.

Duns Scotus, Demonstration, and Doctrine. Mann, William E.

DOGEN

The Problem of the Body in Nietzsche and Dōgen in Nietzsche and Asian Thought, Parkes, Graham (ed). Parkes, Graham R (trans) and Kōgaku, Arifuku.

DOGMA

Fools and Heretics in Wittgenstein Centenary Essays, Griffiths, A Phillips (ed). Bambrough, Renford.

Six Dogmas of Relativism in Cultural Relativism and Philosophy, Dascal, Marcelo (ed). Goodman, Lenn E.

DOGMATISM

Ataraxia and *Eudaimonia* in Ancient Pyrrhonism: Is the Skeptic Really Happy?. McPherran, Mark L.

The Banalization of Nihilism. Carr, Karen L.

Commentary on McPherran's *Ataraxia* and *Eudaimonia* in Ancient Pyrrhonism. Ryan, George E.

Fallibilism and Rational Belief. Weintraub, Ruth.

False Prophecy Versus True Quest: A Most Challenge to Contemporary Relativists. Agassi, Joseph.

Fichte's Anti-Dogmatism. Martin, Wayne M.

Hegel and Skepticism. Williams, Robert.

Hume: Between Leibniz and Kant (The Role of Pre-Established Harmony in Hume's Philosophy). Vasilyev, Vadim.

DOING

see Acting

DOMAIN

Three-membered Domains for Aristotele's Syllogistic. Johnson, Fred.

Total Sets and Objects in Domain Theory. Berger, Ulrich.

DOMINATION

Between Slavery and Freedom: Philosophy and American Slavery. McGary, Howard and Lawson, Bill E.

Disciplining Foucault: Feminism, Power, and the Body. Sawicki, Jana.

Materialist Feminism and the Politics of Discourse. Hennessy, Rosemary.

Transforming Power: Domination, Empowerment, and Education. Kreisberg, Seth.

Bartky, Domination, and the Subject. Kellner, Douglas.

Bribery and Intimidation: A Discussion of Sandra Lee Bartky's *Femininity and Domination*. Kotzin, Rhoda Hadassa.

Comments on Sandra Lee Bartky's *Femininity and Domination*. Mickett, Carole A.

Difference and Domination: Reflections on the Relation Between Pluralism and Equality. Carens, Joseph H.

Domination or Emancipation? in Cultural-Political Interventions in the Unfinished Project of Enlightenment, Honneth, Axel (& other eds). Dubiel, Helmut.

Ethnicity and the Problem of Equality. Blanchard Jr, Kenneth C.

Hegel on Slavery and Domination. Smith, Steven B.

Not Lesbian Philosophy. Trebilcot, Joyce.

Possibilities for a Nondominated Female Subjectivity. McLaren, Margaret.

The Call of the Wild. Katz, Eric.

DONAHUE, T

Why Be Moral? A Reply to Donahue and Tierno. Hull, Richard T.

DONALDSON, T

Can We Afford International Human Rights?. Brenkert, George G.

Global Distributive Justice and the Corporate Duty to Aid. Jackson, Kevin T.

Rethinking the Responsibility of International Corporations: A Response to Donaldson. Koehn, Daryl.

DONNELLAN, K

Donnellan's Distinction: Semantics Versus Pragmatics. McKie, John R.

DONOR

Moral Sensibilities and Moral Standing: Caplan on Xenograft "Donors". Nelson, James Lindemann.

DOPPELT, G

Are Methodological Rules Hypothetical Imperatives?. Resnik, David B.

DOUBT

Ancient Concepts of Philosophy. Jordan, William.

Doubt, Scepticism, and a Serious Justification Game. Schramm, Alfred.

Doute pratique et doute spéculatif chez Montaigne et Descartes. Rodis-Lewis, G.

Reply to Alfred Schramm's "Doubt, Scepticism, and a Serious Justification Game". Lehrer, Keith.

Spinoza, Method, and Doubt. Steinberg, Diane.

DOXASTIC LOGIC

Is It Possible that Belief Isn't Necessary?. Macpherson, Brian.

Possible Logics for Belief. Van Der Hoek, W and Meyer, J J C.

DOXOGRAPHY

Doxographie, historiographie philosophique et historiographie historique de la philosophie. Frede, Michael.

DRAMA

Jean-Paul Sartre: Freedom and Commitment. Hill, Charles G.

Comic Illusion and Illusion in Comedy in Aesthetic Illusion, Burwick, Frederick (ed). Pape, Walter.

Dialectical Drama: The Case of Plato's *Symposium*. Warner, Martin.

Expression and the Mask: The Dissolution of Personality in Noh. Lamarque, Peter.

How To Do Things On Stage. Saltz, David Z.

Pity, Fear, and Catharsis in Aristotle's Poetics. Daniels, Charles B and Scully, Sam.

Reading in (Dramatic) Texts in Pre-Hellenistic Greece (in Czechoslovakian). Hlobil, Tomas.

Representation in Words and in Drama in Aesthetic Illusion, Burwick, Frederick (ed). Krieger, Murray.

The Preservation of Homeric Tradition: Heroic Re-Performance in the *Republic* and the *Odyssey*. Klonoski, Richard.

The Prisoner and the Prison in 2: Song of Macha's May (in Czechoslovakian). Otruba, Mojmir.

DRAWING

Instruments of the Eye: Shortcuts to Perspectives. Korsmeyer, Carolyn.

DRAY, W

Objectivity, Method and Point of View. Van Der Dussen, W J (ed) and Rubinoff, Lionel.

W H Dray and the Critique of Historical Thinking in Objectivity, Method and Point of View, Van Der Dussen, W J (ed). Rubinoff, M Lionel.

DREAM

A Refutation of the Dream Argument. Shirley, Edward S.

Aristotle on Sleep and Dreams. Woods, Michael.

Creative Imagination and Dream in Analecta Husserliana, XXXVIII, Tymieniecka, Anna-Teresa (ed). Balzer, Carmen.

Descartes and Dream Skepticsm Revisited. Hanna, Robert.

Wissen, Glauben, Nicht-Wissen: Freuds Vexierspiel für die epistemische Logik. Stephan, Achim.

DREAMING

Aristotle on Sleep and Dreams. Gallop, David.

Descartes, Leibniz and Berkeley on Whether We Can Dream Marks on the Waking State. Wahl, Russell and Westphal, Jonathan.

Imaginary Evil: A Sceptic's Wager. Taliaferro, Charles.

DRETSKE, F

"From Natural Function to Indeterminate Content". Sullivan, Sonja R.

Armstrong and Dretske on the Explanatory Power of Regularities. Lange, Marc.

Comments on "Can Intelligence Be Artificial?". McNamara, Paul.

Reply to Fred Dretske's "Two Conceptions of Knowledge: Rational versus Reliable Belief". Lehrer, Keith.

DREW, E

A Dilemma for Causal Reliabilist Theories of Knowledge. Lipson, Morris and Savitt, Steven.

DREWERMANN, E

Eugen Drewermann: Una lettura in prospettiva filosofica. Giustiniani, P.

DREYFUS, H

Response: The Background of Intentionality and Action in John Searle and His Critics, Lepore, Ernest (ed). Searle, John R.

DRUG

Drug Legalization: For and Against. Evans, Rod L (ed) and Berent, Irwin M (ed).

Forcing Pregnant Drug Addicts to Abort: Rights-Based and Utilitarian Justifications. Schedler, George.

DUALISM

see also Body, Minds

"Ens per accidens": le origini della 'querelle' di Utrecht. Verbeek, Theo.

"Unreasons' Reason": Cervantes at the Frontiers of Difference. Wilson, Diana de Armas.

A Hylomorphic Theory of Mind. Cooney, Brian.

Mind, Brain, Behavior: The Mind-Body Problem and the Philosophy of Psychology. Carrier, Martin and Mittelstrass, Jürgen.

Tat tvam asi as Advaitic Metaphor. Myers, Michael.

The Dilemma of Narcissus. Gairdner, W T (trans) and Lavelle, Louis.

The Human Person: Animal and Spirit. Braine, David.

The Nature of True Minds. Heil, John.

Wittgenstein's Philosophy of Psychology. Budd, Malcolm.

An Embarrassing Question about Reproduction. Haldane, John.

Anomalous Monism and the Mind-Body Problem. Salami, Yunusa Kehinde.

Anomaly and Folk Psychology. Connolly, John M.

Aristotle and the Ideal Life. Lawrence, Gavin.

Aristotle and the Overcoming of the Subject-Object Dichotomy. Mensch, James.

Balthasar Bekker and the Crisis of Cartesianism. Fix, Andrew.

Charles Hartshorne in Founders of Constructive Postmodern Philosophy, Griffin, David Ray (& others). Griffin, David Ray.

Cogito Ergo Sum. Stone, Jim.

Comments on " The Development of Advaita Vedanta as a School of Philosophy". Sharma, R M.

Comments on "The Development of Advaita Vedanta as a School of Philosophy". Venkatachalam, V.

Computers and the Mind-Body Problem: On Ontological and Epistemological Dualism. Drozdek, Adam.

Consciousness and Cosmology: Hyperdualism Ventilated in Consciousness: Psychological and Philosophical Essays, Davies, Martin (ed). McGinn, Colin.

Content and Cause in the Aristotelian Mind. Wedin, Michael V.

Corps et culture. Csepregi, Gabor.

Criticism and Survival: An Interpretation of Popper's Theory of Evolution. Tangwa, Godfrey B.

Deep Dualism. Leal, Fernando and Shipley, Patricia.

Dennett's Rejection of Dualism. Foster, John.

Descartes on Mind-Body Interaction. Holbrook, Daniel.

Descartes on Mind-Body Interaction and the Conservation of Motion. McLaughlin, Peter.

Descartes' Discourse. Rudolph, Katherine.

El cogito también sueña. Zamora, Alvaro.

Evil and the Love of God. McCullagh, C Behan.

God and Evil: Polarities of a Problem. Adams, Marilyn McCord.

DUTY

Is "Adhikāra" Good Enough for 'Rights'?. Bilimoria, Purushottama.

Is There a Duty to Accept Punishment?. Michael, Mark.

Jameson's Strategies of Containment in Postmodernism/ Jameson/ Critique, Kellner, Douglas (ed). Horne, Haynes.

Kant on the State, Law, and Obedience to Authority in the Alleged 'Anti-Revolutionary' Writings. Westphal, Kenneth.

Kant's Concepts of Duty and Happiness. Wahidur Rahman, A N M.

Kantian Duties and Immoral Agents. Harris, N G E.

Medical Ethics in Times of War and Insurrection: Rights and Duties. Benatar, S R.

Owing Loyalty to One's Employer. Pfeiffer, Raymond S.

Rights, Duties and Responsibilities in Health Care. Emson, H E.

Rights, Law, and the Right. Sparrow, Edward G.

Special Ties and Natural Duties. Waldron, Jeremy.

The Correlativity of Duties and Rights. Fieser, James.

The Eloquent Silence of Zarathustra in Nietzsche and Asian Thought, Parkes, Graham (ed). Parkes, Graham R (trans), Aihara, Setsuko (trans) and Muneto, Sonoda.

The Relation of Moral Worth to the Good Will in Kant's Ethics. Schaller, Walter E.

What is Wrong with Kant's Four Examples. Potter, Nelson.

DVAITA

Ramanuja's Theory of Karman. Sawai, Yoshitsugu.

DWORKIN, R

Aesthetics and Adjudication: Intersubjective Requirements and Juridical Judgment. Purviance, Susan.

Dworkin and Hart on The Law. Peak Jr, Ira H.

Empire-Building. Baker, Brenda M.

Equality, Inequality and the Market. Nalezinski, Alix.

DYING

see also Death

Is 'Brain Death' Actually Death?. Siefert, Josef.

My Own Death. Benn, Piers.

DYMASKI, G

What Walrasian Marxism Can and Cannot Do. Roemer, John.

DYNAMIC LOGIC

Dynamic Algebras: Examples, Constructions, Applications. Pratt, V.

How Many Logically Constant Actions are There?. Segerberg, Krister.

DYNAMICS

Defining Chaos. Batterman, Robert W.

EARMAN, J

Armstrong, Cartwright, and Earman on *Laws and Symmetry*. Van Fraassen, Bas.

EARTH

A Few Notes on the Relation of Philosophy and Ecology (in Czechoslovakian). Kolarsky, R.

Anaximander on the Stability of the Earth. Bodnár, István M.

Christianity and Responsibility for the Earth (in Czechoslovakian). Trpak, P.

Ethics of the Earth (Commentary: R Kolarsky) (in Czechoslovakian). Leopold, A.

Galileo, Aristotelian Science, and the Rotation of the Earth. Reitan, Eric A.

Le corps de la terre. Laurent, Jérôme.

Nature—Landscape—Man (in Czechoslovakian). Svobodova, H.

Technology and Mother Earth: The Rousseauian Roots of the Debate. Malcolmson, Patrick and Myers, Richard.

The Ecological Issue and the Crisis of Metaphysical Reason (in Czechoslovakian). Kamaryt, J.

The Heavens and Earth in Revolution and Continuity, Barker, Peter (ed). Pitt, Joseph C.

EAST EUROPEAN

How to Understand Eastern European Developments?. Machan, Tibor R.

Marxism and Actually Existing Socialism in Socialism and Morality, McLellan, David (ed). Sayers, Sean.

EASTERN

see Oriental

Ethics and Mysticism in Eastern Mystical Traditions. Katz, Steven T.

ECHENBERG, R

Compassion, Consensus, and Conflict: Should Caregivers' Needs Influence the Ethical Dialectic?. Dagi, Teo Forcht.

ECKHARDT, W

Doom and Probabilities. Leslie, John.

ECKHART

"Saisir Dieu en son vestiaire": L'articulation theologique du sens chez Maître Eckhart. Malherbe, Jean-François.

Meister Eckhart e la condanna del 1329. Siena, R M.

Mistica o filosofia? A proposito della dottrina dell'immagine di Meister Eckhart. Sturlese, Loris.

Mystik und Philosophie. Margreiter, Reinhard.

ECLECTICISM

Sobre el furor divino y otros textos. Ficino, Marsilio.

Galien et le stoïcisme. Manuli, Paola.

ECO, U

Interpretation and Overinterpretation: Umberto Eco. Collini, Stefan (ed).

ECOLOGY

Ecology, Economics, Ethics: The Broken Circle. Bormann, Herbert F (ed) and Kellert, Stephen R (ed).

Environmental Philosophy: From Animal Rights to Radical Ecology. Zimmerman, Michael (& other eds).

Ethics of Environment and Development: Global Challenge, International Response. Engel, J Ronald (ed) and Engel, Joan Gibb (ed).

Philosophy and Feminist Criticism. Cole, Eve Browning.

The Corporation, Ethics, and the Environment. Hoffman, W Michael (ed), Frederick, Robert (ed) and Petry, Edward S (ed).

The Disorder of Things: Metaphysical Foundations of the Disunity of Science. Duprè, John.

The Ecological Self. Mathews, Freya.

The Morality Maze: An Introduction To Moral Ecology. Daniels, Neil M.

A Critique of Deep Ecology in Applied Philosophy, Almond, Brenda (ed). Grey, William.

A Critique of Deep Ecology? Response to William Grey in Applied Philosophy, Almond, Brenda (ed). Drengson, Alan R.

A Few Notes on the Relation of Philosophy and Ecology (in Czechoslovakian). Kolarsky, R.

American Pragmatism Reconsidered: William James' Ecological Ethic. Fuller, Robert C.

Avons-nous vraiment besoin d'une éthique de l'environnement?. Nguyen, Vinh-De.

Bacon's Project: Should It Be Given Up?. Schäfer, Lothar.

Before Environmental Ethics. Weston, Anthony.

Callicott and the Metaphysical Basis of Ecocentric Morality. Fieser, James.

Character Development in the Liberal Arts Students in Moral Education and the Liberal Arts, Mitias, Michael H (ed). Giventer, Edwin B.

Christianity and Responsibility for the Earth (in Czechoslovakian). Trpak, P.

Community Ecology, Scale, and the Instability of the Stability Concept. McCoy, E D and Shrader-Frechette, Kristin.

Eco-Sophia. Schirmacher, Wolfgang.

Ecocentric Ethics. Lawler, James.

Ecologia categoria etica. Salmona, B.

Ecological Peril, Modern Technology and the Postmodern Sublime in Shadow of Spirit, Berry, Philippa (ed). Bordo, Jonathan.

Ecological Restoration and Environmental Ethics. Cowell, Mark.

Ecology and Ethics: Notes About Technology and Economic Consequences. Lenk, Hans and Maring, Matthias.

Ecology and Human Emancipation. Hayward, Tim.

Ecosystem Ecology and Metaphysical Ecology: A Case Study. Warren, Karen J and Cheney, Jim.

Environmentalism Humanized. Machan, Tibor R.

Ethics, Ecology and Development: Styles of Ethics and Styles of Agriculture. Blatz, Charles V.

Experimental Ecology on the Pacific Coast: Victor Shelford and His Search for Appropriate Methods. Benson, Keith R.

Heidegger, Language, and Ecology in Heidegger: A Critical Reader, Dreyfus, Hubert (ed). Taylor, Charles.

Home on the Range: Planning and Totality. Kolb, David.

Is the Biosphere a Luxury?. Midgley, Mary.

Methodology Revitalized?. Sloep, Peter B.

Moral and Nonmoral Innate Constraints. George, Kathryn Paxton.

Natural Kinds and Ecological Niches—Response to Johnson's Paper. Hogan, Melinda.

Nature and Silence. Manes, Christopher.

Nature, Technology, and Theology. Klink, William H.

Nature—Landscape—Man (in Czechoslovakian). Svobodova, H.

Objektiver Idealismus und ökosoziale Marktwirtschaft. Melle, Ulrich.

On Obligations to Future Generations. Reichenbach, Bruce R.

Pierre Teilhard de Chardin und die ökologische Frage. Modler, Peter.

Place de l'homme dans la nature. Maldamé, J M.

Rethinking the Heidegger-Deep Ecology Relationship. Zimmerman, Michael E.

Social Ecology, Deep Ecology, and Liberalism. Dizerega, Gus.

Speaking to Trees. Kohák, Erazim.

Talking about Talking about Nature: Nurturing Ecological Consciousness. Michael, Mike and Grove-White, Robin.

The Apories of Ethics of the Human Environment (in Czechoslovakian). Hubik, S.

The Conservative Misinterpretation of the Educational Ecological Crisis. Bowers, C A.

The Ecofeminism/Deep Ecology Debate. Salleh, Ariel.

The Ecological Issue and the Crisis of Metaphysical Reason (in Czechoslovakian). Kamaryt, J.

The Relation of Man and Nature in Modern Philosophy (in Czechoslovakian). Znoj, M, Sobotka, M and Major, L.

The Role of Technology in Environmental Questions: Martin Buber and Deep Ecology as Answers to Technological Consciousness. Light, Andrew R F.

Toward the Moral Considerability of Species and Ecosystems. Johnson, Lawrence E.

ECONOMETRICS

Commentary on the Scientific Status of Econometrics. Goldman, Alvin and Shaked, Moshe.

ECONOMICS

"An Essay on the Principle of Population"—T R Malthus. Winch, Donald (ed) and Malthus, T R.

A Companion to Contemporary Political Philosophy. Goodin, Robert E (ed) and Pettit, Philip (ed).

An Inquiry Into the Nature and Causes of the Wealth of Nations—Adam Smith. Smith, Adam.

Axiology: The Science of Values. Bahm, Archie.

Bettering Our Condition: Work, Workers and Ethics in British and German Economic Thought. Chmielewski, Philip J.

ECONOMICS

Dialectical Investigations. Ollman, Bertell.

Die Wirtschaftspolitik des Philosophen Jacobi. Hammacher, Klaus and Hirsch, Hans.

Ecology, Economics, Ethics: The Broken Circle. Bormann, Herbert F (ed) and Kellert, Stephen R (ed).

Essays on Philosophy and Economic Methodology. Hausman, Daniel M.

From Marx to Mises. Steele, David Ramsay.

Philosophie de l'action. Neuberg, Marc.

Philosophy of Economics: On the Scope of Reason in Economic Inquiry. Roy, Subroto.

Praxiologies and the Philosophy of Economics: The International Annual of Practical Philosophy and Methodology. Auspitz, J Lee (ed), Gasparski, Wojciech W (ed) and Mlicki, Marek K (ed).

Soviet Marxism and Analytical Philosophies of History—Eero Loone. Pearce, Brian (trans) and Loone, Eero.

The Corporation as Anomaly. Schrader, David.

The Grounds and Limits of Political Obligation. Capriotti, Emile.

The Idea of Democracy. Copp, David (ed), Hampton, Jean (ed) and Roemer, John E (ed).

The Moral Economy of Labor: Aristotelian Themes in Economic Theory. Murphy, James Bernard.

Value in Ethics and Economics. Anderson, Elizabeth.

A Case Study of Normal Research in Theoretical Economics. Lind, Hans.

A Critical Evaluation of Etzioni's Socioeconomic Theory: Implications for the Field of Business Ethics. Swanson, Diane.

A Methodological Note on Ethics, Economics, and the Justification of Action. Weikard, Hans-Peter.

A Political and Economic Case for the Democratic Enterprise. Bowles, Samuel and Gintis, Herbert.

A Political and Economic Case for the Democratic Enterprise in The Idea of Democracy, Copp, David (ed). Bowles, Samuel and Gintis, Herbert.

A Reply to Professor Weintraub's "But Doctor Salanti, Bumblebees Really Do Fly". Salanti, Andrea.

A Set of Axioms for Neoclassical Economics and the Methodological Status of the Equilibrium Concept. Vilks, Arnis.

Altruism and the Argument from Offsetting Transfers in Altruism, Paul, Ellen Frankel (ed). Cowen, Tyler.

But Doctor Salanti, Bumblebees Really Do Fly. Weintraub, E Roy.

C J Arthur on Marx and Hegel on Alienation. Duquette, David A.

Commentator on 'Life-Style and the Standard of Living' in The Quality of Life, Nussbaum, Martha C (ed). Sen, Amartya.

Commentator on 'Pluralism and the Standard of Living' in The Quality of Life, Nussbaum, Martha C (ed). Parfit, Derek.

Commentator on 'The Relativity of the Welfare Concept' in The Quality of Life, Nussbaum, Martha C (ed). Osmani, Siddiq.

Contemporary Aristotelianism. Wallach, John R.

Cooperation and Contracts. Schick, Frederic.

Deontology and Economics. Broome, John.

Discoveries as the Origin of Modern Economic Values. Janowski, W K.

Ecology and Ethics: Notes About Technology and Economic Consequences. Lenk, Hans and Maring, Matthias.

Economic Ends and Educational Means at the White House: A Case for Citizenship and Casuistry. Sullivan, B Todd.

Economic Perspectives on Bioethics. Baden, John A.

Economic, Retributive and Contractarian Conceptions of Punishment. Avio, K L.

Economics as Ethics: Bastiat's Nineteenth Century Interpretation. O'Donnell, M G.

Economics of Production in Crises in Continental Philosophy, Dallery, Arleen B (ed). Schmidt, Dennis J.

Economics, Ethics, and Long-Term Environmental Damages. Spash, Clive L.

Equity as an Economic Objective in Applied Philosophy, Almond, Brenda (ed). Le Grand, Julian.

Ernest Belfort Bax: Marxist, Idealist, and Positivist. Bevir, Mark.

For the Common Good?. Heyne, Paul.

Free-market versus Libertarian Environmentalism. Sagoff, Mark.

Functioning and Capability: The Foundations of Sen's and Nussbaum's Development Ethic. Crocker, David A.

Game Theory and the History of Ideas about Rationality: An Introductory Survey. Cudd, Ann.

Gender, Metaphor, and the Definition of Economics. Nelson, Julie A.

Government in the Economy: Outlines of a Reformational Rethink. Beukes, E P and Fourie, F C V N.

Hacia un replanteamiento epistemológico del problema del paro en España. Parra Luna, Francisco.

Idealization in the Practice and Methodology of Classical Economics in Idealization III, Brzezinski, Jerzy (ed). Hamminga, Bert.

J M Keynes's Theoretical Approach to Decision-Making Under Conditions of Risk and Uncertainty. Brady, Michael Emmett.

Keynes's Theory of Probability and Its Relevance to His Economics: Three Theses. Cottrell, Allin.

Keynesian Economic Theory and the Revival of Classical Theory in Terrorism, Justice and Social Values, Peden, Creighton W (ed). Walter, Edward F.

Kuhn's Paradigms and Neoclassical Economics. Argyrous, George.

Law and Economics in Greek Studies in the Philosophy and History of Science, Nicolacopoulos, Pantelis (ed). Gemtos, Petros.

Law as a Public Good: The Economics of Anarchy. Cowen, Tyler.

Liberalism, Welfare Economics, and Freedom. Hausman, Daniel.

Liberalism: Political and Economic. Hardin, Russell.

Life-Style and the Standard of Living in The Quality of Life, Nussbaum, Martha C (ed). Bliss, Christopher.

Local Utility Functions. Bardsley, Peter.

Metaphysics, Economics and Progress: A Comment on Glass and Johnson. Hands, D Wade.

Neo-Classical Economics and Evolutionary Theory: Strange Bedfellows?. Rosenberg, Alex.

Objektiver Idealismus und ökosoziale Marktwirtschaft. Melle, Ulrich.

On the Foundations of Hysteresis in Economic Systems. Cross, Rod.

On the Possibility of Rational Dilemmas: An Axiomatic Approach. Cubitt, Robin P.

Pluralism and the Standard of Living in The Quality of Life, Nussbaum, Martha C (ed). Seabright, Paul.

Population Ethics: On Parfit's Views Concerning Future Generations. Pulvertaft, W Robert.

Rationality in Action. Hollis, Martin and Sugden, Robert.

Significación lógica del cambio de estructura de *El Capital* entre 1857 y 1866. Delgado, Manuel.

Sociology in the Economic Mode. Janssen, Maarten C W.

Some Rules of Constitutional Design. Ordeshook, Peter C.

Statistical Stigmata in Deconstruction and the Possibility of Justice, Cornell, Durcilla (ed). Gates, Henry Louis.

The Concept, and Conceptions, of Justice in Applied Philosophy, Almond, Brenda (ed). Flew, Antony.

The Courtship of the Paying Patient. Braithwaite, Susan S.

The Futility of Multiple Utility. Brennan, Timothy J.

The Legacy of Adam Smith in Victorian Liberalism, Bellamy, Richard (ed). Robertson, John E.

The Morality of Law and Economics. Hardin, Russell.

The Problem of Social Cost: Coase's Economics Versus Ethics. Hanly, Ken.

The Relativity of the Welfare Concept in The Quality of Life, Nussbaum, Martha C (ed). Van Praag, B M S.

The Utility of Multiple Utility: A Comment on Brennan. Lutz, Mark A.

The Value of Economics: A Response to Robert Charles Graham. McNulty, T Michael.

Thinking as a Team in Altruism, Paul, Ellen Frankel (ed). Sugden, Robert.

Toward the Sexual and Economic Emancipation of Women: The Philosophy of Grete Meisel-Hess. Melander, Ellinor.

Walrasian Marxism Once Again: A Reply to Joe Roemer. Devine, James and Dymski, Gary.

What Walrasian Marxism Can and Cannot Do. Roemer, John.

ECONOMY

A New Contractarian View of Tax and Regulatory Policy in the Emerging Market Economies. Frank, Robert H.

Adam Smith and the Ethics of Contemporary Capitalism. Bassiry, G R and Jones, Marc.

Asymmetrical Reciprocity in Market Exchange: Implications for Economies in Transition. Buchanan, James M.

China After Tiananmen Square: Rawls and Justice. Lehman, Glen.

Institutions, Nationalism, and the Transition Process in Eastern Europe. Pejovich, Svetozar.

Modern Immaterialism. Luüf, Reginald and Tijmes, Pieter.

The Social Market Economy. Barry, Norman.

ECOSYSTEM

Ecological Restoration and Environmental Ethics. Cowell, Mark.

Economics, Ethics, and Long-Term Environmental Damages. Spash, Clive L.

Ecosystem Ecology and Metaphysical Ecology: A Case Study. Warren, Karen J and Cheney, Jim.

La nature comme sujet de droit? Réflexions sur deux approches du problème. Bégin, Luc.

La Nature est morte, vive la nature!. Callicott, John B.

The Call of the Wild. Katz, Eric.

Toward the Moral Considerability of Species and Ecosystems. Johnson, Lawrence E.

EDER, K

Sociocultural Evolution or the Social Evolution of Practical Reason: Eder's Critique of Habermas. Strydom, Piet.

EDUCATION

see also Adult Education, Higher Education, Liberal Education, Moral Education

"At Risk": Development of Personhood. Nowell, Linda.

"Engendering Equity...". Morgan, K P.

"Is The Personal Political?" Take Two: "Being One's Self Is Always An Acquired Taste". Leach, Mary S.

"Teacher Thinking, Teacher Change, and the 'Capricious Seamstress'"—A Response. Greene, Maxine.

Character Development in Schools and Beyond (Second Edition). Ryan, Kevin (ed) and Lickona, Thomas (ed).

Chinese Foundations for Moral Education and Character Development. Van Doan, Tran (ed), Shen, Vincent (ed) and McLean, George F (ed).

Collected Works of Bernard Lonergan, V10. Doran, Robert M (ed) and Crowe, Frederick E (ed).

Creativity and Consciousness: Philosophical and Psychological Dimensions. Brzezinski, Jerzy (& other eds).

Critical Thinking: A Functional Approach. Zechmeister, Eugene B and Johnson, James E.

Culture and Democracy: Social and Ethical Issues in Public Support for the Arts and Humanities. Buchwalter, Andrew.

EDUCATION

EDUCATION

EPISTEMOLOGY

Consciousness and Concepts—I. Kirk, Robert.

Consciousness and Concepts—II. Carruthers, Peter.

Constituting the Political Subject, Using Foucault. Seitz, Brian.

Constructing Science, Forging Technology and Manufacturing Society. Bowker, Geoffrey C.

Constructivism Liberalized. Velleman, Daniel.

Content, Causation, and Psychophysical Supervience. Owens, Joseph.

Contextualism and Knowledge Attributions. De Rose, Keith.

Contingency, A Prioricity and Acquaintance. Ryckman, Thomas C.

Continuing Empiricist Epistemology: Holistic Aspects in James's Pragmatism. Nevo, Isaac.

Continuity and Discontinuity in Visual Experience. Biggs, Michael A R.

Continuity, Consciousness, and Identity in Hume's Philosophy. Yandell, Keith E.

Contra la Condenación Universal de los Argumentos Ad Hominem. Cabrera, Julio.

Contradiction. Jacquette, Dale.

Cooperating with Cooperators. Rabinowicz, Wlodek.

Corporality, Ethics, Experimentation: Lyotard in the Eighties. Lindsay, Cecile.

Corrugated Subjects: The Three Axes of Personhood. Clifford, Michael.

Cosmic Doing and Undoing Without End: Chauncey Wright's Idea of Ultimate Reality and Meaning. Madden, Edward H.

Counterfactuals and the Law. Beck, Simon.

Counting the Formulas of the Categorical Imperative: One Plus Three Makes Four. Nuyen, A T.

Creativity and the Extensive Continuum as the Ultimate Ground in Alfred North Whitehead's Philosophy of Becoming. Bracken, Joseph A.

Credere e sapere. Iwand, Hans Joachim.

Critical Notice of D M Armstrong, *A Combinatorial Theory of Possibility*. Lewis, David.

Critical Notice of F J Pelletier's *Parmenides, Plato, and the Semantics of Not-Being*. Thom, Paul.

Critical Notice of W V Quine's *Pursuit of Truth*. Woods, John.

Critical Notice: Paul Horwich's *Truth*. Field, Hartry.

Criticism and Survival: An Interpretation of Popper's Theory of Evolution. Tangwa, Godfrey B.

Culture, Textuality and Truth. Lewandowski, Joseph D.

Curing Folk Psychology of 'Arthritis'. McKinsey, Michael.

Das Verschwinden des Originals—Apropos neuerer Forschungen zum sogenannten 'ältesten Systemprogramm' des deutschen Idealismus. Gawoll, Hans-Jürgen.

David Bloor's *Knowledge and Social Imagery*, (Second Edition). Fuller, Steve.

Davidson and Wittgenstein on Human Action (in Dutch). Cuypers, Stefaan E.

Davidson on the Idea of a Conceptual Scheme. Noh, Yang-jin.

De postmoderniteit en haar geschiedenis: Kanttekeningen bij Stephen Toulmins *Kosmopolis*. Tollebeek, Jo.

Deception and Belief in Parmenides' *Doxa*. Curd, Patricia Kenig.

Deconstructing Derrida: Below the Surface of *Differance*. Jones, W T.

Defending Backwards Causation. Brown, Bryson.

Defending Normative Naturalism: A Reply to Ellen Klein. McCauley, Robert N.

Defensa de la revelación divina contra las objeciones del librepensador. Arana, Juan (trans) and Euler, L.

Delightful, Delovely and Externalist. Duran, Jane.

Democractic Evasions: Cornel West and the Politics of Pragmatism. Westbrook, Robert B.

Democracy. Nathan, N M L.

Dennett's Mind. Lockwood, Michael.

Dennett's Rejection of Dualism. Foster, John.

Deontology and Agency. McNaughton, David and Rawling, Piers.

Derrida and Seng-Zhao: Linguistic and Philosophical Deconstructions. Zongqi, Cai.

Derrida and the Ethics of Dialogue. Kearney, Richard.

Descartes and Dream Skepticsm Revisited. Hanna, Robert.

Descartes on Persons. Holbrook, Daniel.

Descartes on the Material Falsity of Ideas. Field, Richard.

Descartes y la fe en la razón. Zurcher, Joyce M.

Descartes' Discourse. Rudolph, Katherine.

Descartes' Problematic Causal Principle of Ideas. O'Toole, Frederick J.

Descartes's Three Hypothetical Doubts. Flage, Daniel.

Descartes, Contradiction, and Time. Kirby, Brian S.

Descartes, Epistemic Principles, Epistemic Circularity, and *Scientia*. De Rose, Keith.

Descartes, Leibniz and Berkeley on Whether We Can Dream Marks on the Waking State. Wahl, Russell and Westphal, Jonathan.

Determining the Primary Problem of Visual Perception: A Gibsonian Response to the 'Correlation' Objection. Glotzbach, Philip A.

Developmental Hypotheses and Perspicuous Representations: Wittgenstein on Frazer's *Golden Bough*. Hacker, P M S.

Deviant Logic and the Paradoxes of Self Reference. Restall, Greg.

Dewey and Feminism: The Affective and Relationships in Dewey's Ethics. Pappas, Gregory Fernando.

Di due diverse filosofie scettiche. Bottani, L.

Diagnosis of Ailing Belief Sysems. Titiev, Robert.

Diagrams: Socrates and Meno's Slave. Giaquinto, Marcus.

Dialectic: The Science of Humanism. Anderson, Albert A.

Dialektik als Letzbegründung bei Hegel. Pleines, Jürgen-Eckardt.

Dialettica di fantasia e logos nella nozione di mito secondo Aristotele. Prisco, Di.

Die akroamatische Dimension der Hermeneutik. Fricke, Christel.

Die Überwindung des Marburger Neukantianismus in der Spätphilosophie Natorps. Wetz, Franz Josef.

Differend and Agonistics: A Transcendental Argument?. Ruthrof, Horst.

Discontinuing Becomings: Deleuze on the Becoming-Woman of Philosophy. Braidotti, Rosi.

Discourse and Disclosure in the *I Ching*. Stevenson, Frank W.

Discussion: Massey and Kirk on the Indeterminacy of Translation. Hitchcock, Christopher R.

Dismissing Skeptical Possibilities. Vogel, Jonathan.

Dispositions or Etiologies? A Comment on Bigelow and Pargetter. Mitchell, Sandra.

Dispute and Conversation: Probability and the Rhetoric of Natural Philosophy in Locke's *Essay*. Walmsley, Peter.

Do We Need a Concept of Disease?. Hesslow, Germund.

Does Intention Define Action? (in French). Neuberg, Marc.

Does Language Determine Our Scientific Ideas?. Callaway, H G.

Does Philosophy Only State What Everyone Admits? A Discussion of the Method of Wittgenstein's *Philosophical Investigations*. Ackerman, Felicia.

Does the Actual World Actually Exist?. McNamara, Paul.

Does Transcendental Subjectivity Meet Transcendental Grammar?. Kanthamani, A.

Double Vision Idealism. Römpp, Georg.

Double-Aspect Foundherentism: A New Theory of Empirical Justification. Haack, Susan.

Doublings in Derrida: A Critical Reader, Wood, David (ed). Sallis, John.

Doubt, Scepticism, and a Serious Justification Game. Schramm, Alfred.

Dream Objects, Reference and Naturalized Epistemology. Mujumdar, Rinita.

Dreams and Reality: The Sankarite Critique of Vijnanavada. Prasad, Chakravarthi Ram.

Duction, Or the Archaeology of Rape. Rendall, Steven.

Duhem et l'atomisme. Maiocchi, Roberto.

Duns Scotus, Demonstration, and Doctrine. Mann, William E.

Edith Stein: Essential Differences. McAlister, Linda L.

El estatuto epistemológico de la fe: Un diálogo con Kant. Odero, José Miguel.

Emanzipation und Befreiung: Lateinamerikas problemat—Verhältnis zur Moderne. Vetter, Ulrich Ben.

Emile Meyerson, philosophe oublié. Largeault, Jean.

Emotivism and Truth Conditions. Stoljar, Daniel.

Empirical Consequences of the 'Double Hermeneutic'. Harbers, Hans and De Vries, Gerard.

Empiricism Versus Pragmatism: Truth Versus Results. Bewaji, J A I.

Empiricism, Difference, and Common Life. Fosl, Peter S.

Endogenous Constraints on Inductive Reasoning. Kukla, Andre.

Enrico De Negri interprete di Hegel '65-85. Angelica.

Epiphenomenalism, Laws and Properties. Robinson, Denis.

Epistéme e Techne: Sobre a Determinaçao da Competência Epistêmica Grega. Spinelli, Miguel.

Epistemic Desiderata. Alston, W P.

Epistemic Logic Without Logical Omniscience in Advances in Scientific Philosophy, Schurz, Gerhard (ed). Dalla Chiara, Maria Luisa.

Epistemic Normativity. Kornblith, Hilary.

Epistemic Parity and Religious Argument in Philosophical Perspectives, 5: Philosophy of Religion, 1991, Tomberlin, James E (ed). Quinn, Philip.

Epistemic Probability and Evil in Our Knowledge of God, Clark, Kelly James (ed). Plantinga, Alvin.

Epistemically-Qualified Judgment: A Nonquantitative Approach. Backman, Wayne.

Epistemological Communities in Feminist Epistemologies, Alcoff, Linda (ed). Nelson, Lynn Hankinson.

Epistemological Foundations of the Evolution of Science According to Carl F Von Weizäcker (in Polish). Maczka, Janusz.

Epistemological Perspectives in Legal Theory. Van Hoecke, Mark and Ost, François.

Epistemologies in Religious Healing. Hufford, David J.

Epistemology and Realism. Grayling, A C.

Epistemology and the Autodevaluation of Morality: Towards an Atheoretical Nietzsche. Hull, Robert.

Epistemology and the Extinction of Species in Revisioning Philosophy, Ogilvy, James (ed). Cashman, Tyrone.

Epistemology in Reflections on Philosophy, McHenry, Leemon (ed). Adams, Frederick.

Epistemology in the *Aufbau*. Friedman, Michael.

Epistemology's Psychological Turn. Hetherington, Stephen Cade.

Ernest Belfort Bax: Marxist, Idealist, and Positivist. Bevir, Mark.

Esperanza y desesperanza de la razón en Kant. Grimaldi, Nicolás.

Ethics and Evolution: The Biological Basis of Morality. Bradie, Michael.

Evading Theory and Tragedy?: Reading Cornel West. Simpson, Lorenzo.

Evaluative Compatibilism and the Principle of Alternate Possibilities. Lamb, James W.

Evidence Against Empiricist Accounts of the Origins of Numerical Knowledge. Wynn, Karen.

Evidence in Testimony and Tradition. Bilimoria, Purusottama.

Evolutionary Epistemology as an Overlapping, Interlevel Theory. Gray Hardcastle, Valerie.

Evolutionary Epistemology on Universals as Innate in Greek Studies in the Philosophy and History of Science, Nicolacopoulos, Pantelis (ed). Krimbas, Costas B.

Ex Post Facto Explanations. Hobbs, Jesse.

Exclusion and Essentialism in Feminist Theory: The Problem of Mothering. DiQuinzio, Patrice.

Existe-t-il une théorie de la simulation et la simulation est-elle une théorie? (in Polish). Latawiec, Anna.

Existential, Literary or Machine Persons?: Analysis of McLachlan, Adams and Steinbeck. Hart, Richard E.

Experiencia y conocimiento en David Hume. Valls, Francisco Rodríguez.

Experimental Inquiry and Democracy: 'Working Union' of Ideal and Real. De Armey, Michael H.

EPISTEMOLOGY

EPISTEMOLOGY

EPISTEMOLOGY

Moore's Argument and Scepticism. Raff, Charles.

Moore-Sätze, Regelfolgen und antiskeptische Strategien in Wittgensteins, Über Gewissheit'. Lauterbach, Hanna.

Moral Incapacity. Shields, Christopher.

Moral Realism and Objective Theories of the Right. Sherline, Edward.

Moral Reflection: Beyond Impartial Reason. Meyers, Diana Tietjens.

Moral Values as Religious Absolutes. Mackey, James P.

More on Empirical Significance. Pokriefka, M L.

Multiple Personality and Personal Identity Revisited. Lizza, John.

Multiples: On the Contemporary Politics of Subjectivity. Flax, Jane.

Must a Metaphysical Relativist Be a Truth Relativist?. Rappaport, Steven.

Mutual Beliefs and Social Characteristics in Advances in Scientific Philosophy, Schurz, Gerhard (ed). Tuomela, Raimo.

Nāgārjuna und die Mengenlehre. Blau, U.

Naming, Reference, and Sense: Theoretical and Practical Attitudes at Odds. Norman, Andrew P.

Narrating the Self in Analecta Husserliana, XXXI, Tymieniecka, Anna-Teresa (ed). Dolis, John.

Natural Kinds and Theories of Reference. Van Brakel, J.

Naturaleza de las ideas innatas cartesianas. Corazón, Rafael.

Naturalismo y argumentos "a priori" en la epistemología de W V Quine. Iranzo Garcia, V.

Necessary Propositions and the Square of Opposition. Roberts, Mark S.

Necessitas moralis ad optimum (III). Knebel, Sven K.

Negotiating with Our Tradition: Reflecting Again (Without Apologies) on the Feminization of Rhetoric. Biesecker, Barbara.

Neo-Classical Economics and Evolutionary Theory: Strange Bedfellows?. Rosenberg, Alex.

Neurath vs Carnap: Naturalism vs Rational Reconstructionism Before Quine. Uebel, Thomas.

Neuraths Protokollsätze als Antwort auf Kritik seines Fallibilismus. Uebel, Thomas E.

Nietzsche and Aestheticism. Leiter, Brian.

Nietzsche, Decadence, and Regeneration in France, 1891-95. Forth, Christopher E.

NO nOt nO in Derrida and Negative Theology, Coward, Harold (ed). Taylor, Mark C.

Nomads and Revolutionaries. Plant, Sadie.

Non-Marxist Historiography of Today: The Evolution of Its Theoretical and Methodological Principles. Mogilnitsky, B G.

Nonfallacious Arguments from Ignorance. Walton, Douglas N.

Normative Ethics: Bad News for the Sensible Compromise?. Farr, Richard.

Normative Naturalism Undefended: A Response to McCauley's Reply. Klein, Ellen R.

Nota sobre el concepto de realismo epistemológico. Cassini, Alejandro.

Novel Colours. Thompson, Evan.

Nyaya Inference: Deductive or Inductive. Pal, Jagat.

O Método de Análise da Geometria Grega. De Souza, Roberta Lima.

Oakeshott and the Practice of Politics. Katzoff, Charlotte.

Object Language and Meta-Language in the Gongsun-long-zi. Vierheller, Ernstjoachim.

Objectivity and Meaning in Historical Studies: Toward a Post-Analytic View (Review Essay of *Objectivity, Method and Point of View*. Martin, Raymond.

Objectivity and Rationality in Epistemology and Education: Scheffler's Middle Road. Neiman, Alven and Siegel, Harvey.

Objectivity in History: Peter Novick and R G Collingwood. Levine, Joseph M.

Objects and Structures in the Formal Sciences. Grosholz, Emily R.

Objects as Causes of Emotions (in Hebrew). Eylon, Yuval.

Objects of Intention. Vermazen, Bruce.

Of Tennis, Persons and Politics. Springsted, Eric O.

Of Transplants and Trolleys. Mack, Eric.

On an Argument Against Omniscience. Simmons, Keith.

On Argumentation in Legal Contexts. Holmstrom-Hintikka, Ghita.

On Being *Nemesetikos* as a Mean. Coker, John C.

On Being One's Own Worst Enemy. Champlin, T S.

On Clark on Systematicity and Connectionism. Butler, Keith.

On Deafness in the Mind's Ear: John Dewey and Michael Polanyi. Tiles, James E.

On Deceiving Others. Barnes, Annette.

On Friedman's Look. Flage, Daniel.

On History, Charm, and Grief. Petricek Jr, Miroslav.

On Interpreting Kant's Architectonic in Terms of the Hermeneutic Model. Nuyen, A T.

On Keith Lehrer's Belief in Acceptance. Piller, Christian.

On Knowing by Being Told. Chakrabarti, Arindam.

On Kripke's and Goodman's Uses of 'Grue'. Hacking, Ian.

On Negative and Disjunctive Properties in Language, Truth and Ontology, Mulligan, Kevin (ed). Meixner, Uwe.

On Peirce's Philosophical Logic: Propositions and Their Objects. Hilpinen, Risto.

On Peirce's Theory of Propositions: A Response to Hilpinen. Houser, Nathan.

On Professor Weingartner's Contribution to Epistemic Logic in Advances in Scientific Philosophy, Schurz, Gerhard (ed). Gochet, Paul and Gillet, Eric.

On Some Difficulties Concerning Intuition and Intuitive Knowledge. Parsons, Charles.

On Some Worldly Worries. Goodman, Nelson.

On the Autonomy of Legal Reasoning. Raz, Joseph.

On the Consistency of Act- and Motive- Utilitarianism: A Reply to Robert Adams. Feldman, Fred.

On the Ethics of Belief. Nathan, Nicholas.

On the Improvement of Our Moral Portrait: Moral Realism, History of Subjectivity, and Expressivist Language. Thiebaut, Carlos.

On the Interpretation Circle of Philosophy. Guiquan, Zhang.

On the Lexical Ordering of Social States According to Rawls' Principles of Justice. Moldau, Juan Hersztajn.

On the Limits of Classical Reason: Derrida and Aristotle. White, David A.

On the Necessity of an Archetypal Concept in Morphology: With Special Reference to the Concepts of "Structure" and "Homology". Young, Bruce A.

On the Need for a Metaphysics of Justification. Bradshaw, D E.

On the Paradox Kripke Finds in Wittgenstein. Collins, Arthur W.

On the Parallelism between Theoretical and Practical Reasoning in Psychoanalysis, Mind and Art, Hopkins, Jim (ed). Pears, David.

On the Possibility of Rational Dilemmas: An Axiomatic Approach. Cubitt, Robin P.

On the Relationship of Art and World View in the Work of Jan Mukarovsky (in Czechoslovakian). Zouhar, J.

On the Relevance and Importance of the Notion of Disease. Nordenfelt, Lennart.

On the Roles of Trustworthiness and Acceptance. David, Marian.

On There Being Philosophical Knowledge. Nielsen, Kai.

On Two Arguments for the Indeterminacy of Personal Identity. Cartwright, Helen Morris.

On Understanding Disaster. Simissen, Herman.

On Values in Science: Is the Epistemic/Non-Epistemic Distinction Useful?. Rooney, Phyllis A.

On Walton's and Currie's Analyses of Literary Fiction. Pettersson, Anders.

On What There Isn't. Horgan, Terence.

Once More on Relative Truth: A Reply to Skillen. Sayers, Sean.

One More Failed Transcendental Argument. Brueckner, Anthony.

One-Shot Decisions under Linear Partial Information. Kofler, Edward and Zweifel, Peter.

Ontología del cambio. Dufour, Adrian.

Ontological Priority and John Duns Scotus. Gorman, Michael M.

Ontology and the Construction of Systems. Küng, Guido.

Ophir's *Plato's Invisible Cities*. Dent, N J H.

Orwell and the Anti-Realists. Clark, Stephen R L.

Outstanding Problems: Replies to ZiF Critics. Elgin, Catherine Z.

Panoptican: A World Order through Education or Education's Encounter with the Other/Difference. Kazmi, Yedullah.

Paradigms for an Open Philosophy. Polis, Dennis F.

Parfit on Persons. Cassam, Quassim.

Parfit on What Matters in Survival. Brueckner, Anthony.

Peirce on "Substance" and "Foundations". Potter, Vincent.

Peirce's Antifoundationalism. Olshewsky, Thomas M.

Peirce's New Way of Signs. Meyers, Robert G.

Penelope's Web: Reconstruction of Philosophy and the Relevance of Reason. Rockmore, Tom.

Perception as Cooperation of Schematization and Figurative Synthesis (in Dutch). Lohmar, D.

Perception of the Self. Pappas, George S.

Perception, Concepts, and Memory. Martin, M G F.

Perceptual Consciousness and Perceptual Evidence. Baergen, Ralph.

Person as Locus of Permanence: Towards Albert Shalom's Metaphysics. Boltuc, Piotr.

Personal Identity and Self-Constitution. Alexander, Ronald G.

Personalism and Persons: A Response to Gendreau and Haddox. Springsted, Eric.

Personhood: F R Tennant and Peter Bertocci in the Light of Contemporary Physics. Knott, T Garland.

Persons and Perspectives: A Personalist Response to Nagel. Sayre, Patricia.

Persons and the Satisfaction of Preferences: Problems in the Rational Kinematics of Values. MacIntosh, Duncan.

Persons and Values. Garrett, Brian.

Persons, Plants and Insects: On Surviving Reincarnation. Laine, Joy E.

Perspectives on Decisions263-. Segerberg, Krister.

Persuasion. Winch, Peter G.

Peter of Capua as a Nominalist. Courtenay, William J.

Peter Van Inwagen's *Material Beings*. Hirsch, Eli.

Phenomenological Research as *Destruktion*: The Early Heidegger's Reading of Dilthey. Bambach, Charles.

Phenomenology and Metaphysics: Husserl, Heidegger, and Merleau-Ponty in Merleau-Ponty Vivant, Dillon, M C (ed). Margolis, Joseph.

Phenomenology, Possible Worlds and Negation. Krysztofiak, Wojciech.

Philosophers and Popular Cosmology. Clark, Stephen R L.

Philosophical Specialization and General Philosophy. O'Connor, David.

Philosophy and *Weltanschauung*. Nielsen, Kai.

Philosophy and Experience. Deely, John N.

Philosophy and Fiction. Anderson, Susan Leigh.

Philosophy and the Outlandishness of Reason. Page, Carl.

Philosophy, Literature, and Intellectual Responsibility. Rockmore, Tom.

Philosophy/Philosophy, an Untenable Dualism. Haack, Susan.

Physicalism, Consciousness and the Antipathetic Fallacy. Papineau, David.

Pictorial Quotation. Bailey, George W S.

Pictures of Socrates. Thompson, Caleb.

Pippin on Hegel's Critique of Kant. Sedgwick, Sally S.

Plantinga, Epistemic Permissiveness, and Metaphysical Pluralism. Christian, Rose Ann.

Plato and Personhood. Hall, Robert W.

Plato and the Sightlovers of the *Republic*. Stokes, Michael C.

Plato's Analysis of Knowledge: An Appraisal. Nair, Sreekala M.

Plato's Metaphysical Epistemology in The Cambridge Companion to Plato, Kraut, Richard H (ed). White, Nicholas P.

Poesia e verità: Lettere a Clotilde Marghieri. Scaravelli, Luigi.

Poetics, Theory, and the Defense of History: Philippe Carrard, *Poetics of the New History*. Carroll, David.

EPISTEMOLOGY

EPISTEMOLOGY

Umbrellas, Laundry Bills, and Resistance: The Place of Foucault's Interviews in his *Corpus*. Cook, Deborah.

Un'ipotesi sul concerto aristotelico di astrazione. Cattanei, E.

Una nuova edizione italiana di Platone. Bausola, Adriano.

Understanding Synonyms Without Knowing that They are Synonymous. Rieber, Steven.

Understanding: Art and Science. Elgin, Catherine Z.

Unequal Property and Subjective Personality in Liberal Theories. Zucker, Ross.

Unfathomed Knowledged, Unmeasured Worth and Growth?. Hauptli, Bruce.

Unification as an Epistemological Problem in Advances in Scientific Philosophy, Schurz, Gerhard (ed). Kanitscheider, Bernulf.

Universals and Universalisability: An Interpretation of Oddie's Discussion of Supervenience. Forrest, Peter.

Unreckoned Misleading Truths and Lehrer's Theory of Undefeated Justification. Bender, John W.

Using Analytical Philosophy in Philosophical Counselling. Lahav, Ran.

Utilitarianism and Infinite Utility. Vallentyne, Peter.

Vagueness and Ignorance—I. Williamson, Timothy.

Vagueness and Ignorance—II. Simons, Peter.

Validities: A Political Science Perspective. Beer, Francis A.

Van Brakel and the Not-So-Naked Emperor. Hardin, C L.

Verdade e Demonstraçao. Tarski, A and Paula Assis, J (trans).

Verdade e Interesse na Cosmogonia de Descartes. Araujo, Cícero R R.

Verificationism, Scepticism, and Consciousness. Seager, William.

Vicissitudes of Laboratory Life. Weinert, Friedel.

Virtual Symposium on Virtual Mind. Hayes, Patrick (& others).

Virtues and Relativism. Perry, Michael J.

Vision and Experience: the Causal Theory and the Disjunctive Conception. Child, William.

Vision, Causation and Occlusion. Hyman, John.

Visualizing as a Means of Geometrical Discovery. Giaquinto, Marcus.

Wahre performative Selbstwidersprüche. Steinhoff, Uwe.

Walrasian Marxism Once Again: A Reply to Joe Roemer. Devine, James and Dymski, Gary.

Was Carnap Entirely Wrong, After All?. Stein, Howard.

Was George Herbert Mead a Feminist?. Aboulafia, Mitchell.

Was ist Phänomenologie? (Nachdruck). Stein, Edith.

Was trägt die Sprachanalyse zur Philosophie der Biologie bei?. Simons, Peter M.

Wat is rationaliteit en wat is er zo goed aan?. Derksen, Ton.

Ways of Knowing: The Creative Process and the Design of Technology. Glynn, Simon.

Weeks, Spinoza's God and Epistemic Autonomy. Leavitt, Frank J.

Weighing Risk. McClennen, Edward and Found, Peter G.

West's Evasion of Pragmatism. Brodsky, G M.

What Does the Double Hermeneutic Explain/Justify?. Lynch, William.

What Does the Scientist of Man Observe?. Broughton, Janet.

What Epistemic Values Should We Reclaim for Religion and Science? A Response to J Wesley Robbins. Van Huyssteen, J Wentzel.

What Impressions of Necessity?. Flew, Antony.

What Is at Stake Between Putnam and Rorty?. Forster, Paul.

What Is Color Vision?. Hilbert, David.

What Is Cooperation?. Tuomela, Raimo.

What is Postmodernism?. Brann, Eva T H.

What Isn't Wrong with Folk Psychology. Dretske, Frederick.

What Walrasian Marxism Can and Cannot Do. Roemer, John.

What We Love. Leighton, S R.

What Wisdom is According to Heraclitus the Obscure. George, Marie.

What's a Theory to Do...with Seeing? or Some Empirical Considerations for Observation and Theory. Gilman, Daniel.

What's Postmodern, Anyway. Münz, Peter.

What's the Good of Trying?. Lee, Richard T.

What-Being: Chuang Tzu versus Aristotle. Li, Chenyang.

When is a Picture?. Scholz, Oliver R.

Why Believe What People Say?. Stevenson, Leslie.

Why Bother? Defending Derrida and the Significance of Writing. Ferrell, Robyn.

Why I Am Not a Physicalist. Kwame, Safro.

Why I Know About As Much As You: A Reply to Hardwig. Webb, Mark Owen.

Why Is There a Discussion of False Belief in the *Theaetetus*?. Benson, Hugh H.

Why Patronize Feminists? A Reply to Stove on Mill. Brecher, Bob.

Why We Believe in Induction: Standards of Taste and Hume's Two Definitions of Causation. Helm, Bennet W.

Why We Listen to Lunatics: Antifoundational Theories and Feminist Politics. Bickford, Susan.

Why We Need Proper Function. Plantinga, Alvin.

Wild Being, the Prepredicative and Expression: How Merleau-Ponty Uses Phenomenology to Develop an Ontology. Godway, Eleanor M.

William H Poteat: *A Laudatio*. Scott, R Taylor.

William James's Concrete Analysis of Experience. Seigfried, Charlene Haddock.

William James's Theory of Truth. Chisholm, Roderick M.

Wissen, Glauben, Nicht-Wissen: Freuds Vexierspiel für die epistemische Logik. Stephan, Achim.

Wittgenstein and Derrida on Meaning. Rowlands, Mark.

Wittgenstein and Infinite Linguistic Competence. Niles, Ian.

Wittgenstein and Knowledge: Beyond Form and Content. Hookway, Christopher.

Wittgenstein and the Cartesian Subject (in Czechoslovakian). Kotatko, P.

Wittgenstein and the End of Philosophy?. Jolley, Kelly D.

Wittgenstein and W C Fields. Cohen, Daniel H.

Wittgenstein In Between—A Fragment in Criss-Crossing A Philosophical Landscape, Schulte, Joachim (ed). Haller, Rudolf.

Wittgenstein on Rule Following. Srinivas, K.

Wittgenstein on Understanding. Goldfarb, Warren.

Wittgenstein y Apel sobre la crítica del sentido: de la lógica a la antropología?. Conill, J.

Wittgenstein's Woodcutters: The Problem of Apparent Irrationality. Risjord, Mark W.

Wittgenstein, Art and Rule-Following. Oinam, Bhagat.

Works, Works Better. Schwartz, Robert.

Worlds and Modality. Roy, Tony.

Writing with Davidson: Some Afterthoughts after Doing *Blind Time IV: Drawing with Davidson*. Morris, Robert.

Wynn on Mathematical Empiricism. Galloway, David.

Yan Fu's Philosophy of Evolution and the Thought of Lao Zi and Zhuang Zi. Dayong, Yang.

You Know What You Falsely Believe (Or: Pollock, Know Theyself!). Shope, Robert K.

Zalta on Sense and Substitutivity. Deutsch, Harry.

Zijn wij ooit modern geweest?. Pels, D.

Zur Inkonsistenz der konstruktivistischen Abstraktionslehre. Siegwart, Geo.

Zwischen Epistemologie und Ethik. Liebsch, Burkhard.

'Epistemological' and 'Narrativist' Philosophies of History in Objectivity, Method and Point of View, Van Der Dussen, W J (ed). Fell, Albert P.

'Hume's Theorem' Concerning Miracles. Millican, Peter.

'Intuition Pumps' and Contemporary Philosophy. MacLean-Tollefsen, Laurie.

'Les Immatériaux' and the Postmodern Sublime in Judging Lyotard, Benjamin, Andrew (ed). Crowther, Paul.

EQUAL OPPORTUNITY

The Dialogue of Justice: Towards a Self-Reflective Society. Fishkin, James S.

Equality of Opportunity as a Sensible Educational Ideal. Burwood, Les.

EQUALITY

see also Egalitarianism

"Yes, But...": Principles and Caveats in American Racial Attitudes. Hochschild, Jennifer L and Herk, Monica.

An Approach to Political Philosophy: Locke in Contexts. Tully, James.

Beyond Equality and Difference. Bock, Gisela (ed) and James, Susan (ed).

Beyond Methodology: Feminist Scholarship as Lived Research. Fonow, Mary Margaret (ed) and Cook, Judith A (ed).

Blacks and Social Justice (Revised Edition). Boxill, Bernard R.

Compassionate Authority: Democracy and the Representation of Women. Jones, Kathleen B.

Democracy. Harrison, Ross.

Exploitation, Unequal Exchange and Dependency: A Dialectical Development. Otubusin, Paul.

Gender Politics and Post-Communism: Reflections from Eastern Europe and the Former Soviet Union. Funk, Nanette (ed) and Mueller, Magda (ed).

Hegel, Freedom, and Modernity. Westphal, Merold.

Hypatia Reborn: Essays in Feminist Philosophy. Al-Hibri, Azizah Y (ed) and Simons, Margaret A (ed).

John Dewey and American Democracy. Westbrook, Robert B.

Law and the Human Sciences. Kevelson, Roberta (ed).

Liberal Rights: Collected Papers 1981-1991. Waldron, Jeremy.

Marxism Recycled. Van Parijs, Philippe.

On the Track of Reason. Beehler, Rodger G (ed), Copp, David (ed) and Szabados, Bela (ed).

Partial Visions: Feminism and Utopianism in the 1970s. Bammer, Angelika.

Peirce's Esthetics of Freedom: Possibility, Complexity, and Emergent Value. Kevelson, Roberta.

Political Liberalism. Rawls, John.

Politics, Gender, and Genre: The Political Thought of Christine de Pizan. Brabant, Margaret (ed).

The Animals Issue: Moral Theory in Practice. Carruthers, Peter.

The Origins of Our Delusions (in Hungarian). Ludassy, Mária.

The Quality of Life. Nussbaum, Martha C (ed) and Sen, Amartya (ed).

The Tanner Lectures On Human Values, V13. Peterson, Grethe B (ed).

Theoretical Perspectives on Sexual Difference. Rhode, Deborah L (ed).

Transforming Power: Domination, Empowerment, and Education. Kreisberg, Seth.

Unreason Within Reason: Essays on the Outskirts of Rationality. Graham, A C.

A Liberal's Brief Against *Meyer* and *Pierce*. Wenz, Peter S.

A Pragmatic Theory of Responsibility for the Egalitarian Planner. Roemer, John E.

A Right to Health Care. McCarrick, Pat Milmoe.

After Libertarianism: Rejoinder to Narveson, McCloskey, Flew, and Machan. Friedman, Jeffrey.

American Democracy and the Majority Rule. Riley, Jonathan.

Another Go at 'Equal Educational Opportunity'. Moulder, James.

Are Human Rights Based on Equal Human Worth?. Pojman, Louis.

Aristotle and Respect for Persons in Essays in Ancient Greek Philosophy, IV, Anton, John P (ed). Preus, Anthony.

Beyond Equality: Gender, Justice and Difference in Beyond Equality and Difference, Bock, Gisela (ed). Flax, Jane.

Citizenship and Equality: The Place for Toleration. Galeotti, Anna Elisabetta.

Commentators on Cohen and Sen in The Quality of Life, Nussbaum, Martha C (ed). Korsgaard, Christine.

Competitive Equality of Opportunity. Dahan, Yossi and Yonah, Yossi.

EQUALITY

Corporeal Archetypes and Power: Preliminary Clarifications and Considerations of Sex. Sheets-Johnstone, Maxine.

Critical Notice: Thomas Nagel's *Equality and Partiality*. Hooker, Bradford.

Deconstructing Speciesism: The Domain Specific Character of Moral Judgments. Paden, Roger K.

Democracy, Socialism, and the Globe in On the Track of Reason, Beehler, Rodger G (ed). Cunningham, Frank.

Democratic Theory and the Democratic Agent. Meyers, Diana.

Difference and Domination: Reflections on the Relation Between Pluralism and Equality. Carens, Joseph H.

Dissent from "The New Consensus": Reply to Friedman. Flew, Antony.

Does Compensation Restore Equality?. Gaus, Gerald.

Educational Ability and Social Justice: What Should the Relationship Be?. Ericson, David P and Ellett Jr, Frederick S.

Egalitarianism and Natural Lottery. Sesardic, Neven.

Electoral Power, Group Power, and Democracy. Levine, Andrew.

Equal Respect among Unequal partners: Gender Difference and the Constitution of Moral Subjects. Herrera, María.

Equality and Difference in National Socialist Racism in Beyond Equality and Difference, Bock, Gisela (ed). Bock, Gisela.

Equality and Sexual Difference in Beyond Equality and Difference, Bock, Gisela (ed). Cavarero, Adriana.

Equality of Opportunity as a Sensible Educational Ideal. Burwood, Les.

Equality of What? in The Quality of Life, Nussbaum, Martha C (ed). Cohen, G A.

Equality Revisited. Wilson, John.

Equality, Difference, Subordination in Beyond Equality and Difference, Bock, Gisela (ed). Pateman, Carole.

Equality, Inequality and the Market. Nalezinski, Alix.

Equity as an Economic Objective in Applied Philosophy, Almond, Brenda (ed). Le Grand, Julian.

Ethnicity and the Problem of Equality. Blanchard Jr, Kenneth C.

Fifteen Years After "Animal Liberation": Has the Animal Rights Movement Achieved Philosophical Legitimacy?. Tuohey, John and Ma, Terence P.

Hobbes and the Equality of All Under the One. Mitchell, Joshua.

If Pornography Is the Theory, Is Inequality the Practice?. McCormack, Thelma.

In Good Standing? The Position of Women in Higher Education. McConnell, David H.

Incentives, Inequality, and Community in The Tanner Lectures On Human Values, V13, Peterson, Grethe B (ed). Cohen, G A.

Individuo y sociedad civil. Vásquez, Eduardo.

Justice and Health Care Rationing in On the Track of Reason, Beehler, Rodger G (ed). Daniels, Norman.

Justice as Social Freedom in On the Track of Reason, Beehler, Rodger G (ed). Miller, Richard.

Liberals, Communitarians, and Political Theory. Allen, Jonathan.

MacIntyre and the Liberal Tradition (in Dutch). Serfontein, Paula.

Market Equality and Social Freedom in Applied Philosophy, Almond, Brenda (ed). Hollis, Martin.

Mary Wollstonecraft and Women's Rights. Larson, Elizabeth.

Measuring Quality of Life in Theory and in Practice: A Dialogue Between Philosophical and Psychological Approaches. Boddington, Paula and Podpadec, Tessa.

Minimal Statism and Metamodernism: Reply to Friedman. McCloskey, Donald N.

Misunderstanding the Democratic 'We': Richard Rorty's Liberalism and the Radical Urge for a Philosophical Foundation. Moussa, Mario.

Nietzsche et l'égalité des droits: De l'usage juridique d'un concept religieux chrétien. Ledure, Yves.

Perfectionism and Equality in On the Track of Reason, Beehler, Rodger G (ed). Hurka, Thomas M.

Pluralism and Equality: The Status of Minority Values in a Democracy. Simon, Robert L.

Political Equality. Christiano, Thomas.

Preferential Treatment and Social Justice in Terrorism, Justice and Social Values, Peden, Creighton (ed). Mosley, Albert.

Reflections on the Idea of Equality in On the Track of Reason, Beehler, Rodger G (ed). Rachels, James.

Rousseauisme et jacobinisme: l'idéal de "l'honnête médiocrité". Roy, Jean.

S Stur's "Treatise on Life" (in Czechoslovakian). Uher, J.

Spencer, Steiner and Hart on the Equal Liberty Principle. Gray, Tim.

The Challenge of Multiculturalism in Political Ethics. Gutmann, Amy.

The Concept of an Equal Educaitonal Opportunity. White, Ronald.

The Demise of the Confessional State and the Rise of the Idea of a Legitimate Minority. Heim, Joseph Charles.

The Politics of Equilibrium. Grant, Robert A D.

The Power and Poverty of Libertarian Thought. Cornuelle, Richard.

The Problem of Religion in Liberalism. Sherlock, Richard and Barrus, Roger.

The Spirit of Simone Weil's Law in Simone Weil's Philosophy of Culture, Bell, Richard (ed). Collins, Ronald K L and Nielsen, Finn E.

The Subjection of John Stuart Mill. Stove, D.

The 'Critique': A View from the Labor Movement in Sartre Alive, Aronson, Ronald (ed). Lennon, Alan.

Three Fallacies Concerning Majorities, Minorities, and Democratic Politics. Shapiro, Ian.

Two Conceptions of Needs in Marx's Writings in On the Track of Reason, Beehler, Rodger G (ed). Braybrooke, David.

Virtue Without Gender in Socrates. Scaltas, Patricia Ward.

Women and the Quality of Life in The Quality of Life, Nussbaum, Martha C (ed). Annas, Julia.

World Poverty, Justice and Equality in International Justice and the Third World, Attfield, Robin (ed). Belsey, Andrew.

'Bread First, then Morals' in Socialism and Morality, McLellan, David (ed). Arblaster, Anthony.

EQUATION

A Word Problem for Normal and Regular Equations. Graczynska, Ewa.

Complexity of Equational Theory of Relational Algebras with Projection Elements. Mikulás, Szabolcs, Sain, Ildikó and Simon, András.

On the Computational Complexity of Integral Equations. Ko, Ker-I.

EQUILIBRIUM

A Reply to Professor Weintraub's "But Doctor Salanti, Bumblebees Really Do Fly". Salanti, Andrea.

A Set of Axioms for Neoclassical Economics and the Methodological Status of the Equilibrium Concept. Vilks, Arnis.

But Doctor Salanti, Bumblebees Really Do Fly. Weintraub, E Roy.

Endogenizing the Order of Moves in Matrix Games. Hamilton, Jonathan H and Slutsky, Steven M.

Is Entropy Relevant to the Asymmetry Between Retrodiction and Prediction?. Barrett, Martin and Sober, Elliott.

Modern and Postmodern Challenges to Game Theory. Varoufakis, Yanis.

The Futility of Multiple Utility. Brennan, Timothy J.

The Indefinitely Iterated Prisoner's Dilemma: Reply to Becker and Cudd. Carroll, John W.

The Utility of Multiple Utility: A Comment on Brennan. Lutz, Mark A.

Über Wünsche, Lust und Rationalität—Eine Auseinandersetzung mit der Gleichgewichtstheorie von Anna Kusser. Piller, Christian.

EQUITY

"Engendering Equity...". Morgan, K P.

Eighteenth-Century Hermeneutics: Philosophy of Interpretation in England from Locke to Burke. Weinsheimer, Joel C.

En/Gendering Equity: Emancipatory Programs or Repressive "Regimes of Truth". De Castell, Suzanne and Bryson, Mary.

En/Gendering Equity: On Some Paradoxical Consequences of Institutionalized Programs of Emancipation. Bryson, Mary and De Castell, Suzanne.

Equity and Mercy. Nussbaum, Martha C.

Equity and Solidarity: The Context of Health Care in The Netherlands. Ten Have, Henk and Keasberry, Helen.

Equity as an Economic Objective in Applied Philosophy, Almond, Brenda (ed). Le Grand, Julian.

From Justified Discrimination to Responsive Hiring. Hall, Pamela.

Real Men in Rethinking Masculinity, May, Larry (ed). LaFollette, Hugh.

The *Lex Talionis* Before and After Criminal Law. Van Den Haag, Ernest.

The Concept, and Conceptions, of Justice in Applied Philosophy, Almond, Brenda (ed). Flew, Antony.

EQUIVALENCE

A Puzzle About Logical Equivalence. Dobrosavljevic, Stojan T.

Aristote et la séparation. Bastit, Michel.

Determination Underdeterred: Reply to Kukla. Leplin, Jarrett and Laudan, Larry.

Justification without Good Reasons. Katzoff, Charlotte.

Laudan, Leplin, Empirical Equivalence and Underdetermination. Kukla, André.

Logical Equivalence and Inductive Equivalence. Deb, Amiyansu.

Single Axioms for the Left Group and the Right Group Calculi. McCune, William W.

EQUIVOCATION

A Thirteenth-Century Interpretation of Aristotle on Equivocation and Analogy. Ashworth, E J.

ERIKSON, E

Trust, the Heart of Religion: A Sketch. Godfrey, Joseph J.

ERIUGENA

Studies in Augustine and Eriugena. O'Meara, John J and Halton, Thomas (ed).

From Dionysius to Eriugena: A Bridge for Voluntarism or "Divine Freedom"?. King-Farlow, John.

Theophanie und Schöpfungsgrund: Der Beitrag des Johannes Scotus Eriugena zum Verständnis *der creatio ex nihilo*. Hoeps, Reinhard.

ERMATH, E

Sequel to History: Postmodernism and the Crisis of Historical Time. Carr, David.

EROS

Rhetoric and Reality in Plato's 'Phaedrus'. White, David A.

The Hymn to Eros. Mitchell, Robert Lloyd.

Truth and Eros: Foucault, Lacan, and the Question of Ethics. Rajchman, John.

Commentary on Halperin's "Plato and the Metaphysics of Desire". Nussbaum, Martha C.

Plato and the Metaphysics of Desire. Halperin, David M.

The Family and Ethics: The Metaphysics of Eros in Emmanuel Levinas's *Totality and Infinity*. Cohen, Richard A.

EROTETIC LOGIC

Erotetic Arguments: A Preliminary Analysis. Wisniewski, Andrzej.

EROTICISM

Erotic Welfare: Sexual Theory and Politics in the Age of Epidemic. Singer, Linda.

Rhetoric and Reality in Plato's 'Phaedrus'. White, David A.

An Ethos of Lesbian and Gay Existence. Blasius, Mark.

Augustine's Erotic Ascent. Kinz, Susan.

Jewish Lesbian Writing: A Review Essay. Scheman, Naomi.

Plato and the Metaphysics of Desire. Halperin, David M.

ERROR

The Errors of the Philosophers (in Hungarian). Romanus, Aegidius.

The Problem of Error: A Surd Spot in Rational Intentionalism. McGeer, V L.

ESCHATOLOGY

Disputed Questions in Theology and the Philosophy of Religion. Hick, John.

Hegel's Grand Synthesis: A Study of Being, Thought, and History. Berthold-Bond, Daniel.

Paul Ricoeur. Clark, Stephen.

By Their Fruit You Shall Know Them: Eschatological and Legal Elements in Peirce's Philosophy in Peirce and Law, Kevelson, Roberta. Schultz, Lorenz.

Chiliasmus and Eschatology or Partnership with the Nature (in Czechoslovakian). Neubauer, Z.

Ipotesi di metafisica: Modello matematico, creazione, eschaton—Una lettura dell' opera di Jean Ladrière. Natale, M R.

The End of History. Schroeder, Steven.

ESCHER, M

Escher and Parmigianino: A Study in Paradox. Duran, Jane.

ESCOUBAS, E

Three Questions to Jacques Derrida in Ethics and Danger, Dallery, Arleen B (ed). Dastur, Françoise.

ESSAY

Montaigne and Melancholy: The Wisdom of the "Essays". Screech, M A.

R G Collingwood: A Bibliographic Checklist. Dreisbach, Christopher.

ESSE

see Being

ESSENCE

see also Form

The Structure of Value. Allen, R T.

A Woman and a Man as Prime Analogical Beings. Allen, Prudence.

Autocoscienza e conoscenza nel 'primo Rosmini'. De Lucia, Paolo.

Da Tebe ad Atene e da Atene a Tebe. Caramuta, Ersilia.

De l'ontologie à la théologie: Lecture du livre Z de la "Métaphysique" d'Aristote. Gérard, Gilbert.

Essential Thinking: Reflections on Heidegger's *Beiträge zur Philosophie. Grieder, Alfons.*

Existence and Essence: Kierkegaard and Hegel. Subramanian, Sharada.

Il romanzo dell'identità: Metafisica ed ermeneutica. Sainati, Vittorio.

L'inno della perla: Una risposta al problema gnostico. Nosari, Sara.

La experiencia noética de Dios (Interpretación sobre textos de Santo Tomás). Rodriguez Valls, F.

Locke on Real Essence and Internal Constitution. Vienne, Jean-Michel.

Natura e uomo in Giulio Cesare Vanini. Marcialis, Maria Teresa.

Some Puzzles on Essence in Analecta Husserliana, XXXIV, Tymieniecka, Anna-Teresa (ed). García-Baró, Miguel.

Species, Essences and the Names of Natural Kinds. Wilkerson, T E.

The Aesthetic Essence of Art. Lind, Richard W.

ESSENTIALISM

A Metalogical Theory of Reference: Realism and Essentialism in Semantics. Vergauwen, Roger.

Modalities: Philosophical Essays. Marcus, Ruth Barcan.

The Republic of Art and Other Essays. Diffey, T J.

Toward Non-Essentialist Sociolinguistics. Janicki, Karol.

Additional Thoughts on Perspective. Gombrich, E H.

Alienation, Cultural Differences, and Moral Judgment. McLane, Janice.

Can Art Ever Be Just about Itself?. McAdoo, Nick.

Carving Nature at the Joints. Khalidi, Muhammad Ali.

Edith Stein: Essential Differences. McAlister, Linda L.

Exclusion and Essentialism in Feminist Theory: The Problem of Mothering. DiQuinzio, Patrice.

Human Functioning and Social Justice: In Defense of Aristotelian Essentialism. Nussbaum, Martha C.

Is It Necessary that Water is H20? in The Philosophy of A J Ayer, Hahn, Lewis Edwin (ed). Putnam, Hilary.

Kripke's Essentialist Argument Against the Identity Theory. Della-Rocca, Michael.

Leibnizian Essentialism, Transworld Identity, and Counterparts. Cover, J A and Hawthorne, John.

Non-Essentialistic Modal Logic, or Meaning and Necessity Revisited. Burdick, Howard.

Philosophische Zeitdiagnose im Zeichen des Postmodernismus. Ollig, Hans-Ludwig.

Phylogenetic Definitions and Taxonomic Philosophy. De Queiroz, Kevin.

Pure Historicism and the Heritage of Hero(in)es: Who Grows in Phillis Wheatley's Garden?. Silvers, Anita.

Richard Rorty's Failed Politics. Haber, Honi.

Splitting the Self: Thoughts on Rortyian Education. Beatham, Mark.

The Quest for Certainty in Feminist Thought. Clark, Ann.

Theorizing about Art. Leddy, Thomas W.

Three Conceptions of 'Voice' and their Pedagogical Implications. Scahill, John H.

Transcendence and Conversation: Two Conceptions of Objectivity. D'Agostino, Fred.

ESTHETICS

see Aesthetics

ESTLUND, D

Could Political Truth be a Hazard for Democracy? in The Idea of Democracy, Copp, David (ed). Copp, David.

ETCHEMENDY, J

Anti-Foundation and Self-Reference. McLarty, Colin.

The Grounds for the Model-Theoretic Account of the Logical Properties. Sánchez-Miguel, Manuel G-C.

ETERNAL

Genius and Talent: Schopenhauer's Influence on Wittgenstein's Early Philosophy. Weiner, David Avraham.

Actual Infinity: A Contradiction?. Senna, Peter.

Attunement and Thinking in Heidegger: A Critical Reader, Dreyfus, Hubert L (ed). Haar, Michel.

Ontological Platonism in Whiteheadian Philosophy of God (in Polish). Zycinski, Jozef.

Plotinus on Matter. Raiger, Michael.

Simultaneity and God's Timelessness. Oddie, Graham and Perrett, Roy W.

Temporality and Divinity: An Analytic Hurdle. Oakes, Robert.

The Contribution of Advaita Vedanta to the Quest for an Effective Reassertion of the Eternal. Schultz, Walter.

The Other Nietzsche in Nietzsche and Asian Thought, Parkes, Graham R (ed). Stambaugh, Joan.

ETERNAL RECURRENCE

Eternal Recurrence, Identity and Literary Characters. Conter, David.

Nietzsche's Superman: The Necessity of Reconsidering the Question of Man (in Dutch). Visser, Gerard.

ETERNALITY

The Deleuze Reader. Boundas, Constantin V (ed).

God, Eternality, and the View from Nowhere in Logic, God and Metaphysics, Harris, James F (ed). Harris, James F.

ETERNITY

Eternity and Time's Flow. Neville, Robert Cummings.

Ethics and Danger. Dallery, Arleen B (ed), Scott, Charles E (ed) and Roberts, P Holley (ed).

Schöpfung und Geist. Günther, Dorothea.

Wittgenstein, Ethics and Aesthetics: The View From Eternity. Tilghman, Benjamin R.

Creazione ed eternità del mondo. Molinaro, A.

Does the Eternity of the World Entail an Actual Infinite? Yes!. Tacelli, Ronald.

Eternity and Special Theory of Relativity. Padgett, Alan.

Eternity, Awareness, and Action. Stump, Eleonore and Kretzmann, Norman.

Metaphysical Presence in Ethics and Danger, Dallery, Arleen B (ed). Chanter, Tina.

Mind Eternity in Spinoza. Rice, Lee C.

On the Mereology of Boethian Eternity. Quinn, Philip L.

Prophecy, Past Truth, and Eternity in Philosophical Perspectives, 5: Philosophy of Religion, 1991, Tomberlin, James E (ed). Stump, Eleonore and Kretzmann, Norman.

Scenes from My Childhood in The Impulse to Philosophise, Griffiths, A Phillips (ed). Magee, Bryan.

Temporal Impermanence and the Disparity of Time and Eternity. Polk, Danne W.

The Concept of Time. Singh, Chhatrapati.

ETHICAL RELATIVISM

see Emotivism

ETHICAL THEORY

Human Nature and Ethical Standards. Luizzi, Vincent.

ETHICS

see also Altruism, Bioethics, Business Ethics, Egoism, Happiness, Humanism, Idealism, Justice, Medical Ethics, Morality, Normative Ethics, Political Phil, Social Phil, Utilitarianism, Voluntarism

"Bergson Resartus" and T S Eliot's Manuscript. Habib, M A R.

"Brother, You Can't Go to Jail for What You're Thinking": Motives, Effects and "Hate Crime" Laws. Gellman, Susan.

"Es ist uns aber bestimmt, von Überzeugungen, die wir aus innerer Notwendigkeit denken, zu leben". Kern, Udo.

"I Can Wait 40 or 400 Years": Gandhian *Satyagraha* West and East. Starosta, William J and Chaudhary, Anju G.

"Ought" Never Is: A Response to Oliver A Johnson. Goldthwait, John T.

"The Will to Believe" and James's "Deontological Streak". O'Connell, Robert.

Ατοπια and Plato's *Gorgias.* Turner, Jeffrey S.

Μεγαλοϕυια in *Nocomachean Ethics iv.* Held, Dirk T D.

A Case For Legal Ethics: Legal Ethics as a Source for a Universal Ethic. Luizzi, Vincent.

A History of Western Ethics. Becker, Lawrence C (ed) and Becker, Charlotte B (ed).

Aesthetic Judgment and the Moral Image of the World: Studies in Kant. Henrich, Dieter.

African-American Perspectives on Biomedical Ethics. Flack, Harley E (ed) and Pellegrino, Edmund D (ed).

Altruism. Paul, Ellen Frankel (ed), Miller, Fred D (ed) and Paul, Jeffrey (ed).

An Ethic of Care: Feminist and Interdisciplinary Perspectives. Larrabee, Mary Jeanne (ed).

An Historical Introduction to Moral Philosophy. Wagner, Michael (ed).

An Introduction to Ethics. Thomas, Geoffrey.

Analecta Husserliana, XXXI. Tymieniecka, Anna-Teresa (ed).

Applied Philosophy. Almond, Brenda (ed) and Hill, Donald (ed).

Aquinas on Human Action: A Theory of Practice. McInerny, Ralph.

Arguing About Abortion. Schwartz, Lewis M.

Aristotle on the Perfect Life. Kenny, Anthony.

Automatism, Insanity, and the Psychology of Criminal Responsibility: A Philosophical Inquiry. Schopp, Robert F.

ETHICS

Balance and Refinement: Beyond Coherence Methods of Moral Inquiry. DePaul, Michael.

Bettering Our Condition: Work, Workers and Ethics in British and German Economic Thought. Chmielewski, Philip J.

Between Philosophy and Social Science: Selected Early Writings. Horkheimer, Max and Hunter, G Frederick (& other trans).

Bibliography of Bioethics, V18. Walters, LeRoy (ed) and Kahn, Tamar Joy (ed).

Bioethics Yearbook, Volume 2—Regional Developments in Bioethics: 1989-1991. Lustig, B Andrew (& other eds).

Biomedical Ethics (Third Edition). Mappes, Thomas A and Zembaty, Jane S.

Biomedical Ethics Reviews 1992. Humber, James M (ed) and Almeder, Robert F (ed).

Birth, Suffering, and Death: Catholic Perspectives at the Edges of Life. Wildes, Kevin W (ed), Abel, Francesc (ed) and Harvey, John C (ed).

Bodies that Matter: On the Discursive Limits of 'Sex'. Butler, Judith.

Buddhism, Sexuality, and Gender. Cabezón, José I (ed).

Burdens of Proof in Modern Discourse. Gaskins, Richard H.

Business, Ethics, and the Environment: The Public Policy Debate. Hoffman, W Michael (ed), Frederick, Robert (ed) and Pentry, Edward S (ed).

Case Studies in Business Ethics (Third Edition). Donaldson, Thomas and Gini, Al.

Case Studies in Business, Society, and Ethics (Third Edition). Beauchamp, Tom L.

Cases in Bioethics: Selections from the Hastings Center Report (Second Edition). Crigger, Bette-Jane (ed).

Changing To National Health Care: Ethical and Policy Issues. Huefner, Robert P (ed) and Battin, Margaret P (ed).

Changing Values in Medical and Health Care Decision Making. Jensen, Uffe Juul (ed) and Mooney, Gavin (ed).

Character Development in Schools and Beyond (Second Edition). Ryan, Kevin (ed) and Lickona, Thomas (ed).

Chinese Foundations for Moral Education and Character Development. Van Doan, Tran (ed), Shen, Vincent (ed) and McLean, George F (ed).

Collected Works of Bernard Lonergan, V10. Doran, Robert M (ed) and Crowe, Frederick E (ed).

Contemporary Issues in Paediatric Ethics. Burgess, Michael M (ed) and Woodrow, Brian E (ed).

Contractarian Liberal Ethics and the Theory of Rational Choice. Park, Jung Soon.

Cross, Crescent, and Sword. Johnson, James Turner (ed) and Kelsay, John (ed).

Cruzan and the Constitutionalization of American Life. Schneider, Carl E.

Culture and Democracy: Social and Ethical Issues in Public Support for the Arts and Humanities. Buchwalter, Andrew.

Dialogue and the Human Image: Beyond Humanistic Psychology. Friedman, Maurice S.

Dialogue with Heidegger on Values: Ethics for Times of Crisis. Joós, Ernest.

Die Welt des Menschen. Kessler, Herbert.

Dirty Hands: The Problem of Political Morality. Buckler, Steve.

Discovering Philosophy. White, Thomas I.

Drawing the Line: Life, Death, and Ethical Choices in an American Hospital. Gorovitz, Samuel.

Ecology, Economics, Ethics: The Broken Circle. Bormann, Herbert F (ed) and Kellert, Stephen R (ed).

Emerson and Thoreau: The Contemporary Reviews. Myerson, Joel (ed).

Environmental Philosophy: From Animal Rights to Radical Ecology. Zimmerman, Michael (& other eds).

Epistemic Virtue and Doxastic Responsibility. Montmarquet, James.

Erotic Welfare: Sexual Theory and Politics in the Age of Epidemic. Singer, Linda.

Essays in Ancient Greek Philosophy, IV. Anton, John P (ed) and Preus, Anthony (ed).

Essays in Quasi-Realism. Blackburn, Simon W.

Essays on Henry Sidgwick. Schultz, Bart (ed).

Essays on the Philosophy of Socrates. Benson, Hugh H (ed).

Ethical Dimensions of Legal Theory. Sadurski, Wojciech (ed).

Ethical Essays, Volume I. Harrison, Jonathan.

Ethical Essays, Volume II. Harrison, Jonathan.

Ethical Issues in Business: A Philosophical Approach (Fourth Edition). Donaldson, Thomas J and Werhane, Patricia H.

Ethical Issues: Perspectives for Canadians. Soifer, Eldon (ed).

Ethical Theory and Business (Fourth Edition). Beauchamp, Tom L and Bowie, Norman E.

Ethics and Danger. Dallery, Arleen B (ed), Scott, Charles E (ed) and Roberts, P Holley (ed).

Ethics and Politics. Paton, Calum.

Ethics and the Conduct of Business. Boatright, John R.

Ethics and the Environment. Hart, Richard E (ed).

Ethics in an Aging Society. Moody, Harry R.

Ethics of Environment and Development: Global Challenge, International Response. Engel, J Ronald (ed) and Engel, Joan Gibb (ed).

Ethics: Studying the Art of Moral Appraisal. Littlejohn, Ronnie L.

Feminine and Feminist Ethics. Tong, Rosemarie.

Feminist Perspectives In Medical Ethics. Holmes, Helen Bequaert (ed) and Purdy, Laura M.

Foundations of Kierkegaard's Vision of Community. Connell, George B (ed) and Evans, C Stephen (ed).

Frames of Deceit: A Study of the Loss and Recovery of Public and Private Trust. Johnson, Peter.

From Morality to Virtue. Slote, Michael.

From Patients to Persons: The Psychiatric Critiques of Thomas Szasz, Peter Sedgwick and R D Laing. Vice, Janet.

Frontiers in American Philosophy, Volume I. Burch, Robert W (ed) and Saatkamp, Herman J Jr (ed).

God and Existence (in Hungarian). Joós, Ernő.

Gulliver's Travels: The Stunting of a Philosopher. Burrow, Richard.

Hart's Legal Philosophy: An Examination. Bayles, Michael D.

Holistic Health and Biomedical Medicine: A Countersystem Analysis. Lyng, Stephen.

In Search of the Ethical: Moral Theory in Twentieth Century America. Edel, Abraham.

Injustice and Restitution: The Ordinance of Time. Ross, Stephen D.

Jen and Li in the Analects. Shun, Kwong-Loi.

Jurisculture: China. Dorsey, Gray L.

Justice: Interdisciplinary Perspectives. Scherer, Klaus R (ed).

Kant and the Experience of Freedom: Essays on Aesthetics and Morality. Guyer, Paul.

Kants Begründung der praktischen Philosophie. Freudiger, Jürg.

Kierkegaard and Kant: The Hidden Debt. Green, Ronald M.

La Dialettica dell'Etico. Li Vigni, Fiorinda.

Law and the Human Sciences. Kevelson, Roberta (ed).

Liberal Rights: Collected Papers 1981-1991. Waldron, Jeremy.

Life and Death: Philosophical Essays in Biomedical Ethics. Brock, Dan W.

Life-Sharing for a Creative Tomorrow. Barral, Mary-Rose.

Malum Vitandum: The Role of Intentions in First-Order Morality. Sullivan, Thomas D and Atkinson, Gary.

Max Scheler's Concept of the Person: An Ethics of Humanism. Perrin, Ron.

Modernity and Authenticity: A Study of the Social and Ethical Thought of Jean-Jacques Rousseau. Ferrara, Alessandro.

Moral Aspects of Legal Theory. Lyons, David.

Moral Boundaries: A Political Argument for an Ethic of Care. Tronto, Joan C.

Moral Controversies: Race, Class, and Gender in Applied Ethics. Gold, Steven Jay.

Moral Education and the Liberal Arts. Mitias, Michael H (ed).

Moral Matters. Narveson, Jan.

Moral Philosophy: A Reader. Pojman, Louis (ed).

Moral Reasoning: Ethical Theory and Some Contemporary Moral Problems (Second Edition). Grassian, Victor.

Morality and the Emotions. Oakley, Justin.

Morality, Prudence, and Nuclear Weapons. Lee, Steven.

Natural Reasons: Personality and Polity. Hurley, S L.

Natural Reasons: Personality and Polity: Review. Jackson, Frank.

Peirce's Esthetics of Freedom: Possibility, Complexity, and Emergent Value. Kevelson, Roberta.

Per un' etica del discorso antropologico. Borutti, Silvana.

Philosophical Foundations for Moral Education and Character Development: Act and Agent (Second Edition). McLean, George F and Ellrod, Frederick E.

Philosophical Perspectives, 6: Ethics, 1992. Tomberlin, James E (ed).

Philosophy and Theology in the Middle Ages. Evans, G R.

Philosophy of Mind: An Introduction. Graham, George.

Plato and Platonism. Moravcsik, Julius.

Poetics of Imagining: From Husserl to Lyotard. Kearney, Richard.

Political Theory and Postmodernism. White, Stephen K.

Postnational Identity: Critical Theory and Existential Philosophy in Habermas, Kierkegaard, and Havel. Matustik, Martin J.

Practical Ethics (Second Edition). Singer, Peter.

Practical Knowledge—Yves R Simon. Mulvaney, Robert J (ed) and Simon, Yves R.

Practices of Reason: 'Aristotle's Nicomachean Ethics'. Reeve, C D C.

Psychological Foundations of Moral Education and Character Development: An Integrated Theory of Moral Development (Second Edition). McLean, George F (ed) and Knowles, Richard T (ed).

Ptolemy's Universe: The Natural Philosophical and Ethical Foundations of Ptolemy's Astronomy. Taub, Liba.

Pursuing Parenthood: Ethical Issues in Assisted Reproduction. Lauritzen, Paul.

Quality of Life, Health and Happiness. Nordenfelt, Lennart.

Reading Heidegger: Commemorations. Sallis, John (ed).

Reading Kristeva: Unraveling the Double-bind. Oliver, Kelly.

Rediscovering the Moral Life. Gouinlock, James.

Reflections on Philosophy. McHenry, Leemon (ed) and Adams, Frederick (ed).

Regulating Death, Carlos F Gomez. Cantor, Norman L.

Religion from Tolstoy to Camus. Kaufmann, Walter (ed).

Rethinking Goodness. Wallach, Michael A and Wallach, Lise.

Rhetoric and Reality in Plato's 'Phaedrus'. White, David A.

Risks and Wrongs. Coleman, Jules L.

Royce's Mature Ethics. Oppenheim, Frank.

Shadow of Spirit. Berry, Philippa (ed) and Wernick, Andrew (ed).

Sharing without Reckoning. Schumaker, Millard.

Sobor and Sobornost'. Tulaev, Pavel.

Sobre Virtudes y Vicios. García Bacca, Juan David.

Spinoza's Ethics: The View from Within. Schipper, Lewis.

Taking Sides: Clashing Views on Controversial Bioethical Issues (Fifth Edition). Levine, Carol.

Taking Sides: Clashing Views on Controversial Issues in Human Sexuality (Third Edition). Francoeur, Robert.

ETHICS

ETHICS

ETHICS

ETHICS

Reply to Westra's "Response—Dr Frankenstein and Today's Professional Bio-technologist". Dandekar, Natalie and Zlotkowski, Edward.

Reply—Rawls: Rejecting Utilitarianism and Animals. Russow, Lilly-Marlene.

Reproductive Technologies and the "Survival" of the "Human Subject". Levesque-Lopman, Louise.

Respect for Autonomy in the Practice of Rehabilitation. Howie, John.

Responsabilidad colectiva y reduccionismo. Welch, John R.

Response to Alexander's "Voluntary Acts: The Child/Davidson Trilemma". Child, James.

Response to Diamond's 'The Importance of Being Human' in Human Beings, Cockburn, David (ed). McNaughton, David.

Response to Lester Hunt's Comments. Welshon, Robert.

Response to McNaughton's 'The Importance of Being Human' in Human Beings, Cockburn, David (ed). Diamond, Cora.

Response—Dr Frankenstein and Today's Professional Biotechnologist: A Failed Analogy?. Westra, Laura.

Response: Of Pigs and Primitive Notions. Detmer, David J.

Responsibility and the Self-made Self. Waller, Bruce N.

Restoration Romanticism. Tamás, G M.

Rethinking Resistance: Environmentalism, Literature, and Poststructural Theory. Quigley, Peter.

Rethinking the Heidegger-Deep Ecology Relationship. Zimmerman, Michael E.

Rethinking the Responsibility of International Corporations: A Response to Donaldson. Koehn, Daryl.

Retribution, Arbitrariness and the Death Penalty. Calvert, Brian.

Retributivism in Hegel as Modern Natural Law. Gardner, Stephen L.

Review Essay: The Best Intuitionistic Theory Yet! Thomson On Rights. Smith, M B E.

Revolutionary Writing, Moral Philosophy, and Universal Benevolence in the Eighteenth Century. Radcliffe, Evan.

Rights and Norms in Frontiers in American Philosophy, Volume I, Burch, Robert W (ed). Singer, Beth.

Rights, Duties and Responsibilities in Health Care. Emson, H E.

Rights, Moral Values and Natural Facts: A Reply to Mary Midgley on the Problem of Child- Abuse. Archard, David.

Risking Extinction: An Axiological Analysis. James, David N.

Ritual, Cosmology, and Ontology: Chang Tsai's Moral Philosophy and Neo- Confucian Ethics. Chow, Kai-wing.

Rolston on Intrinsic Value: A Deconstruction. Callicott, J Baird.

Ross, Promises and the Intrinsic Value of Acts. Brennan, Susan K.

Rule Following, Rule Scepticism and Indeterminacy in Law: A Conventional Account. Drahos, Peter and Parker, Stephen.

Sartre's Early Ethics and the Ontology of 'Being and Nothingness' in Sartre Alive, Aronson, Ronald (ed). Anderson, Thomas C.

Sartre's Student and the Captain of the HMS Indomitable. Dowling, Keith W.

Sartrean Ethics in The Cambridge Companion to Sartre, Howells, Christina (ed). Simont, Juliette.

Satisfied Pigs and Dissatisfied Philosophers: Schlesinger on the Problem of Evil. Grover, Stephen.

Schofield's The Stoic Idea of the City. Annas, Julia.

Scientific Collecting. Loftin, Robert W.

Scientific, Public Policy, and Ethical Implications of the Nuclear Waste Policy Act and Its Amendments. Lemons, John and Malone, Charles.

Second Thoughts About Bluffing. Carson, Thomas.

Self-Defence and Forcing the Choice between Lives. Miller, Seumas.

Self-Defense, Justification, and Excuse. Alexander, Larry.

Self-Forgiveness. Snow, Nancy E.

Selflessness and the Loss of Self. Hampton, Jean.

Set-Asides, Reparations, and Compensatory Justice. Paul, Ellen Frankel.

Sexual Archetypes in Transition. Francoeur, Robert T.

Sexual Ethics in the Age of Epidemic. Young, Iris.

Shakespeare's Demonic Prince. Mindle, Grant B.

Shakespeare's Richard III and the Soul of the Tyrant. Frisch, Morton J.

Shame, Forgiveness, and Juvenile Justice. Moore, David B.

Should a Brain-Dead Pregnant Woman Carry Her Child to Full Term? The Case of the "Erlanger Baby". Anstötz, Christoph.

Should Computer Programs Be Ownable?. Carey, David.

Should Environmentalists Be Organicists?. Norton, Bryan G.

Should Kantians Care about Moral Worth?. Schaller, Walter E.

Should Physicians Be Bayesian Agents?. Cooper, M Wayne.

Should We Genetically Engineer Hogs?. Comstock, Gary L.

Sidgwick and the History of Ethical Dualism in Essays on Henry Sidgwick, Schultz, Bart (ed). Frankena, William K.

Sidgwick on Ethical Judgment in Essays on Henry Sidgwick, Schultz, Bart (ed). Deigh, John.

Simone Weil and the Civilisation of Work in Simone Weil's Philosophy of Culture, Bell, Richard (ed). Fischer, Clare B.

Slippery Slopes and Moral Reasoning. Devettere, Raymond.

Sobre las bases éticas de la democracia. Ferrari, María Aparecida.

Social Control, Efficiency Control and Ethical Control in Different Political Institutions: Education. Natale, Samuel M (& others).

Social Ethic of Mahatma Gandhi and Martin Buber. Henry, Sarojini.

Social Exclusion, Moral Reflection, and Rights. Meyers, Diana Tietjens.

Social Morality as Expressed in Law. Petev, Valentin.

Sociobiology, Ethics and Human Nature in New Horizons in the Philosophy of Science, Lamb, David (ed). Frith, Lucy.

Socrate: Il demone e il risveglio—Sul senso dell'etica socratica. De Bernardi, P.

Socratic Legal Obligation in the Crito. Kusyk, Douglas A.

Solidarité et disposition du corps humain. Hottois, Gilbert.

Solidarity and Moral Community. Hostetler, Karl.

Some Further Thoughts on "Thought Crimes". Weinstein, James.

Some Questions About the Justification of Morality in Philosophical Perspectives, 6: Ethics, 1992, Tomberlin, James E (ed). Railton, Peter A.

Some Virtues of Resident Alienation. Baier, Annette.

Some Ways that Technology and Terminology Distort the Euthanasia Issue. Herrera, Christopher.

Speculative Logic, Deconstruction, and Discourse Ethics. Cutrofello, Andrew.

Speech, Conscience, and Work. Lippke, Richard L.

Spinoza on Self-Consciousness and Nationalism. Freeman, David A.

Statutory Definitions of Death and the Management of Terminally Ill Patients Who May Become Organ Donors after Death. Cole, David.

Stove on Gene Worship. Levin, Michael E.

Strong Utilitarianism in Mo Tzu's Thought. Vorenkamp, Dirck.

Subjectivism and Toleration in A J Ayer Memorial Essays, Griffiths, A Phillips (ed). Williams, Bernard.

Sulle tracce del postmoderno (I). Pellecchia, Pasquale.

Surrendering and Cathcing in Poetry and Sociology. Ward, John Powell.

Surrogate Consent. Richards, Norvin W.

Surrogate Motherhood: Politics and Privacy. Callahan, Joan.

Susan Gellman Has It Right. Brown, Ralph.

Sustainability and the Moral Community. George, Kathryn Paxton.

Sustainability and the Right to Development in International Justice and the Third World, Attfield, Robin (ed). Dower, Nigel.

Synthesis: The Larger Perspective in Contemporary Issues in Paediatric Ethics, Burgess, Michael M (ed). O'Driscoll, Herbert.

Taking Family Seriously. Nelson, James Lindemann.

Taking Morality Seriously. Almond, Brenda.

Teachers Should Disclose Their Moral Commitments in Moral Education and the Liberal Arts, Mitias, Michael H (ed). Ammon, Theodore G.

Teaching Bioethics as a New Paradigm for Health Professionals. Tealdi, Juan Carlos.

Teaching Bioethics to Future Health Professionals: A Case-Based Clinical Model. Macklin, Ruth.

Teaching Ethical Decision-Making. Pfeiffer, Raymond S.

Teaching Ethics in Higher Education: Goals, and the Implications of the Empirical Research on Moral Development. Annis, David B.

Technical Decisions: Time to Rethink the Engineer's Responsibilities?. Davis, Michael.

Techno-Thanatology: Moral Consequences of Introducing Brain Criteria for Death. Bayertz, Kurt.

Technology and Culture and the Problem of the Homeless. Lovekin, David.

Teleology in Spinoza's Ethics. League, Kathleen.

The Gedankenexperiment Method of Ethics. Jackson, M W.

The Lex Talionis Before and After Criminal Law. Van Den Haag, Ernest.

The Narod and the Intelligentsia: From Dissociation to Sobornost'. Klechenov, Gennadii.

The Narod, the Intelligentsia, and the Individual. Kovalev, Vitalii.

The ADL Hate Crime Statute and the First Amendment. Alexander, Larry.

The Advent of Liberalism and the Subordination of Agrarian Thought in the United States. Theobald, P.

The Aim and Structure of Applied Research. Niiniluoto, Ilkka.

The Allied Health Care Professions: New Fields for Philosophical Explorations. Hull, Richard T.

The American Marketing Association Code of Ethics: Instructions for Marketers. O'Boyle, Edward J and Dawson Jr, Lyndon E.

The Apories of Ethics of the Human Environment (in Czechoslovakian). Hubik, S.

The Archimedean Point and Eccentricity: Hannah Arendt's Philosophy of Science and Technology. Tijmes, Pieter.

The Attractive and the Imperative in Essays on Henry Sidgwick, Schultz, Bart (ed). White, Nicholas P.

The Authentic Tele of Politics: A Reading of Aristotle. Swazo, N K.

The Autonomy Imperative of Behavioral Research. Herrera, Christopher.

The Book of the Philosophic Life. Butterworth, Charles E (trans), Muhammad, Abū Bakr and Al-Razi, Zakariyya.

The Call of the Wild. Katz, Eric.

The Case for Letting Vegetative Patients Die. Jennett, Bryan.

The Challenge of Multiculturalism in Political Ethics. Gutmann, Amy.

The Characteristics of a Valid "Empirical" Slippery-Slope Argument. Ozar, David.

The Commonality of Loyalty and Tolerance. Fletcher, George P.

The Compatibility of Eco-Centric Morality. Fieser, James.

The Concept of Ethical Life in Hegel's Philosophy of Right. Kierans, Kenneth.

The Concept of Intrinsic Value and Transgenic Animals. Verhoog, H.

The Concept of Medically Indicated Treatment. Miller, Franklin G.

The Concept of Quackery in Early Nineteenth Century British Medical Periodicals. Carter, K Codell.

The Concept of the Highest Good in Kant's Moral Theory. Engstrom, Stephen.

The Concept of the Person in the Parens Patriae Jurisdiction over Previously Competent Persons. Payton, Sallyanne.

The Connection Between Prudential and Moral Goodness. Vallentyne, Peter.

The Conservative Misinterpretation of the Educational Ecological Crisis. Bowers, C A.

The Constitution and the Nature of Law. Robison, Wade.

The Continuity of Chinese Humanism in the Shang-Chou Period. Wong, Yeu-Guang.

The Courtship of the Paying Patient. Braithwaite, Susan S.

The Dead Donor Rule: Should We Stretch It, Bend It, or Abandon It?. Arnold, Robert M and Youngner, Stuart J.

ETHICS

ETHICS

The Very Idea of Sustainability. Blatz, Charlie V.

The Virtue of Modesty. Ben-Ze'ev, Aaron.

The Virtues of Common Pursuit. Sherman, Nancy.

The Virtues of Thrasymachus. Chappell, T D J.

The Work Ethic and the Work Ethos: The Importance of Ethical Arguments for the Politics of Transition to the Market. Büscher, M.

The Young Heidegger, Aristotle, Ethics in Ethics and Danger, Dallery, Arleen B (ed). Van Buren, E John.

The Young Philosophers. Liverani, Mary Rose.

Theism and Moral Objectivity. Jacobs, Jonathan and Zeis, John.

Theology, Praxis and Ethics in the Thought of Juan Luis Segundo. Zimbelman, Joel.

Thinking as a Team: Towards an Explanation of Nonselfish Behavior. Sugden, Robert.

Thinking Critically in Medicine and Its Ethics in Applied Philosophy, Almond, Brenda (ed). Moros, Daniel A (& others).

Thinking Like a Lawyer in Ethical Dimensions of Legal Theory, Sadurski, Wojciech (ed). Krygier, Martin.

Thinking Morality Interpersonally: A Reply to Burgess-Jackson. Walker, Margaret Urban.

Thomas Aquinas on the Justification of Revolution. Fay, Thomas A.

Thomson and the Trolley. Fisher, John and Ravizza, Martin.

Time-Frames, Voluntary Acts, and Strict Liability. Husak, Douglas N and McLaughlin, Brian P.

Toward a Consistent View of Abortion and Unwanted Pregancy. Williams, Courtney.

Toward a Model of Professional Responsibility. Hollander, Rachelle D.

Toward an Ontology of Virtue Ethics. Savarino, Mary Ella.

Toward the Moral Considerability of Species and Ecosystems. Johnson, Lawrence E.

Towards a More Expansive Moral Community. Bernstein, Mark.

Towards a Postmodern Ethics: Sir Isaiah Berlin and John Caputo. McKinney, Ronald H.

Towards a World Morality. Chethimattam, J B.

Tradition, Friendship and Moral Knowledge. Dinan, Stephen A.

Transcendent Man in the Limited City: The Political Philosophy of Charles N R McCoy. Schall, James V.

Transplantation through a Glass Darkly. Nelson, James Lindemann.

Triage in the ICU. Truog, Robert D.

Troeltsch's Treatment of the Thomist Synthesis. Dietrich, Wendell S.

True to Oneself. Sobel, J Howard.

Trusting People in Philosophical Perspectives, 6: Ethics, 1992, Tomberlin, James E (ed). Baier, Annette.

Truth, Adequacy and Being in Spinoza's *Ethics*. Richey, Lance B.

Two Key Elements in Francis J McConnell's Social Ethics. Burrow Jr, Rufus.

Über das Verhältnis zwischen Immanuel Kants Rechts-und Moralphilosophie. Jacobsen, Mogens Chrom.

Über die Rationalität von Prozeduren und Resultaten. Dorschel, Andreas.

Understanding the Real "Character Issue:" A Review of the Latest Work of Clarence Walton (*The Moral Manager*, and *Corporate Encounters*). Cooke, Robert.

Unequal Property and Subjective Personality in Liberal Theories. Zucker, Ross.

Universalismo e particolarismo nell'etica contemporanea. Guariglia, Osvaldo.

Unravelling the Problems in Ecofeminism. Cuomo, Christine J.

Unrequested Termination of Life: Is It Permissible?. Van Der Wal, Gerrit.

Unsystematic Ethics and Politics in Shadow of Spirit, Berry, Philippa (ed). Cupitt, Don.

Using the Fact/Value Problem to Teach Ethical Theory. Birsch, Douglas.

Utilitarian Ethics and Democratic Government in The Utilitarian Response, Allison, Lincoln (ed). Riley, Jonathan.

Utilitarianism and Retributivism: What's the Difference. Michael, Mark A.

Utilitarianism and Self-Respect. Scarre, Geoffrey.

Utilitarianism on Environmental Issues Reexamined. Holbrook, Daniel.

Value Hierarchies in Scheler and Von Hildebrand. Gooch, Augusta O.

Valuing Lives. Perrett, Roy W.

Varieties of Postmodernism as Moments in Ethics Action Learning. Nielsen, Richard P.

Vie et spéculation dans *l'Anweisung zum seligen Leben*. Philonenko, Alexis.

Virtue and Oppression. Williams, Joan C.

Virtue and Self-Alienation. Zeis, John.

Virtue Ethics. Megone, Christopher.

Virtue Ethics and Democratic Values. Slote, Michael.

Virtue Ethics and Mandatory Birth Control in Biomedical Ethics Reviews 1992, Humber, James M (ed). Vitek, William.

Virtue Ethics: An Orthodox Appreciation. Woodill, Joseph.

Virtue Ethics: Making a Case as it Comes of Age. Keenan, James F.

Virtue: A Brief Bibliography. Galston, William A.

Virtue: Its Nature, Exigency, and Acquisition. Baechler, Jean.

Virtues and Relativism. Perry, Michael J.

Vlasto's *Socrates: Ironist and Moral Philosopher*. Reeve, C D C.

Voluntary Active Euthanasia. Brock, Dan W.

Voluntary Acts: The Child/Davidson Trilemma. Alexander, Larry.

Warum moralisch sein gegenüber Tieren?. Wolf, Jean-Claude.

Was Immanuel Kant a Humanist?. Hiorth, Finngeir.

Was There a Concept of Rights in Confucian Virtue-Based Morality?. Lee, Seung-Hwan.

Weeping at the Death of Dido: Sorrow, Virtue, and Augustine's *Confessions*. Werpehowski, William.

Welfare, Happiness, and Pleasure. Sumner, L W.

Well-Being and Value. Goldsworthy, Jeffrey.

Wellbeing and Everyday Practice: Theorizing Claimsmaking. Kerans, Patrick and Drover, Glen.

Westernizers and Nativists Today. Aksiuchits, Viktor.

What Bioethics Has to Offer the Developing Countires. Qiu, Ren-Zong.

What Did Descartes Do to Virtue?. Santilli, Paul C.

What Is Cooperation?. Tuomela, Raimo.

What is Moral Maturity? Towards a Phenomenology of Ethical Expertise in Revisioning Philosophy, Ogilvy, James (ed). Dreyfus, Hubert L and Dreyfus, Stuart E.

What is the Moral Basis of the Authority of Family Members to Act as Surrogates for Incompetent Patients?. Brock, Dan W.

What Is the Role of Science in the Dialogue Proposed by William Klink?. Gilbert, Thomas L.

What is Wrong with Kant's Four Examples. Potter, Nelson.

What Laches and Nicias Miss—And Whether Socrates Thinks Courage Merely a Part of Virtue. Penner, Terrence M I.

What the Good Samaritan Didn't Know. MacKenzie, J C.

What We Love. Leighton, S R.

What Wisdom is According to Heraclitus the Obscure. George, Marie.

What's So Special About Medicine?. Sulmasy, Daniel P.

What's Wrong With Murder? Some Thoughts on Human and Animal Killing. Everitt, Nicholas.

What's Wrong with Prostitution?. Primoratz, I.

When Self-Determination Runs Amok. Callahan, Daniel.

Where Deathless Horses Weep in Reading Heidegger: Commemorations, Sallis, John (ed). Krell, David Farrell.

Where Ethics Come From and What to Do About It. Elliott, Carl.

Who are the Beneficiaries?. Tännsjö, Torbjörn.

Who Can Accept Moral Dilemmas?. Ohlsson, Ragnar.

Who Can Be Morally Obligated to Be a Vegetarian?. Pluhar, Evelyn.

Who Discovered The Will? in Philosophical Perspectives, 6: Ethics, 1992, Tomberlin, James E (ed). Irwin, T H.

Who or What Has Moral Standing?. Schönfeld, Martin.

Why A Telological Defense of Rights Needn't Yield Welfare Rights. Smith, Tara.

Why Be Moral? A Reply to Donahue and Tierno. Hull, Richard T.

Why Business is Talking About Ethics: Reflections on Foreign Conversations in Revisioning Philosophy, Ogilvy, James (ed). Ciulla, Joanne B.

Why Does Proximity Make a Moral Difference?. Vetlesen, Arne Johan.

Why Lesbian Ethics?. Hoagland, Sarah Lucia.

Why Rational Egoism is Not Consistent. Marshall Jr, John.

Why the Deterrence Argument for Capital Punishment Fails. Reitan, Eric.

Why There Are No Objective Values: A Critique of Ethical Intuitionism from an Evolutionary Point of View. Geiger, Gebhard.

Why We Would Not Understand a Talking Lion. Levvis, Gary W.

William James and Our Moral Lives in Frontiers in American Philosophy, Volume I, Burch, Robert W (ed). Putnam, Ruth Anna.

William Temple and the Bombing of Germany: An Exploration in Just War Tradition. Lammers, Stephen.

Wise Maxims/Wise Judging. Sherman, Nancy.

Wittgenstein and Moral Realism. Werhane, Patricia H.

Wittgenstein's Concept of Showing in Criss-Crossing A Philosophical Landscape, Schulte, Joachim (ed). Pears, David.

Women and the New Casuistry. Sichol, Marcia.

Works by Renato Treves. Velicogna, Nella Gridelli and Segre, Vera.

Yet Another Look at Cognitive Reason and Moral Action in Hume's Ethical System. Johnson, Clarence Sholé.

Young Kids Search for the Philosophers' Stone. Neave, Phillippa.

Zwischen Epistemologie und Ethik. Liebsch, Burkhard.

'Eudemian' Ethical Method in Essays in Ancient Greek Philosophy, IV, Anton, John P (ed). Jost, Lawrence J.

'Is' and 'Ought' in Context: MacIntyre's Mistake. MacBeth, Murray.

'Ought' and Well-being. Gillett, Grant.

'Safe Enough in his Honesty and Prudence': The Ordinary Conduct of Government in the Thought of John Locke. Anderson, Christopher.

'The Very Culture of the Feelings': Poetry and Poets in Mill's Moral Philosophy. Burnstone, Daniel.

ETHNICITY

An Approach to Political Philosophy: Locke in Contexts. Tully, James.

Can There Be a Supranational Identity?. Cerutti, Furio.

Education: Anti-racist, Multi-ethnic and Multi-cultural in Logical Foundations, Mahalingam, Indira (ed). Flew, Antony.

Ethics and the Praise of Diversity: Review of *Workforce America*. Weber, Leonard J.

Ethnicity and the Problem of Equality. Blanchard Jr, Kenneth C.

Moments of Danger: Race, Gender, and Memories of Empire. Ware, Vron.

Secession: The Caes of Quebec. Nielsen, Kai.

The Democratic Solution to Ethnic Pluralism. Singer, Beth.

Westernizers and Nativists Today. Aksiuchits, Viktor.

What are Intellectuals For: A Foucaultian Model of Intellectual Responsibility. Blacker, David.

ETHNOCENTRISM

Philosophical Interventions in the Unfinished Project of Enlightenment. Honneth, Axel (& other eds).

A Rortyian Dilemma of Conversation. Gbocho, Akissi.

Aesthetics and Ethnocentrism in Cultural Relativism and Philosophy, Dascal, Marcelo (ed). Sobrevilla, David.

Is Hermeneutics Ethnocentric? in The Interpretive Turn, Hiley, David R (ed). Hoy, David C.

Philosophy and Social Practice in Philosophical Interventions in the Unfinished Project of Enlightenment, Honneth, Axel (& other eds). McCarthy, Thomas A.

Rationality and Ethnocentrism. Barnhart, J E.

Relativism versus Ethnocentrism?. Van Niekerk, Anton.

ETHNOGRAPHY

Respuesta a lo ajeno: Sobre la relación entre la cultura propia y la cultura ajena. Waldenfels, Bernhard.

Wittgenstein's Woodcutters: The Problem of Apparent Irrationality. Risjord, Mark W.

ETHNOLOGY

Conscience et Culture. Lalèyê, Issiaka-Prosper.

ETHNOMETHODOLOGY

The Role of the Ethnomethodological Experiment in the Empirical Investigation of Social Norms and Its Application to Conceptual Analysis. Place, Ullin T.

ETHOLOGY

Ethics and Animals: A Brief Review. Jamieson, Dale.

Farm Animal Welfare: A Historical Overview. Ewbank, Roger.

ETHOS

Hermeneutics and Human Finitude: Toward a Theory of Ethical Understanding. Smith, P Christopher.

ETIOLOGY

Dispositions or Etiologies? A Comment on Bigelow and Pargetter. Mitchell, Sandra.

Functional Analysis and Etiology. McClamrock, Ron.

ETYMOLOGY

Aristotle on 'ΕΝΤΕΛΕΧΕΙΑ: A Reply to Daniel Graham. Blair, George A.

ETZIONI, A

A Critical Evaluation of Etzioni's Socioeconomic Theory: Implications for the Field of Business Ethics. Swanson, Diane.

Deontology and Economics. Broome, John.

EUCLID

The Theory of Odd and Even in the Ninth Book of Euclid's Elements. Becker, Heribert and Oliver, Charles (trans).

Zur Mathematik in den Werken von Albertus Magnus: Versuch einer Zussammenfassung. Ineichen, Robert.

EULER, L

Defensa de la revelación divina contra las objeciones del librepensador. Arana, Juan (trans) and Euler, L.

EUROCENTRICISM

Eurocentric Elements in the Idea of "Surrender-and-Catch". Moon, Seungsook.

Respuesta a lo ajeno: Sobre la relación entre la cultura propia y la cultura ajena. Waldenfels, Bernhard.

EUROPEAN

see also East European

Bioethics Yearbook, Volume 2—Regional Developments in Bioethics: 1989-1991. Lustig, B Andrew (& other eds).

Changing To National Health Care: Ethical and Policy Issues. Huefner, Robert P (ed) and Battin, Margaret P (ed).

Gender Politics and Post-Communism: Reflections from Eastern Europe and the Former Soviet Union. Funk, Nanette (ed) and Mueller, Magda (ed).

Hans-Georg Gadamer on Education, Poetry, and History: Applied Hermeneutics. Misgeld, Dieter (ed) and Nicholson, Graeme (ed).

Herder's Aesthetics and the European Enlightenment. Norton, Robert E.

Il "Peccato" in Cina: Bene e male nel Neoconfucianismo dalla metà del XIX secolo, by Paolo Santangelo. Elvin, Mark.

Nietzsche and Modern Times. Lampert, Laurence.

Persona ou la Justice au Double Visage. Trigeaud, Jean-Marc.

Poetics of Imagining: From Husserl to Lyotard. Kearney, Richard.

The Enlightenment. Hampson, Norman.

Transition to Modernity: Essays on Power, Wealth and Belief. Hall, John A (ed) and Jarvie, I C (ed).

Ancora sull'idea d'Europa: Il Medioevo como matrice di una coscienza europea. Baldassarre, M R.

Appearance and Reality in Buddhist Metaphysics from a European Philosophical Point of View. Chung, Bongkil.

Border Disputes and the Right of National Self-Determination. Beran, Harry.

Children's Philosophy in Europe. De Bruijn, Jan.

Early European Feminism and American Women in Women's Rights and the Rights of Man, Arnaud, A J. Goldstein, Leslie Friedman.

Europe, Truth, and History: Husserl and Voegelin on Philosophy and the Identity of Europe. Levy, David J.

Foucault and Bentham: A Defence of Panopticism. Semple, Janet.

Hegels Idee von Europa. Innerarity, Daniel.

Heimat und das Fremde. Tani, T.

Institutions, Nationalism, and the Transition Process in Eastern Europe. Pejovich, Svetozar.

Kulturen als Inseln. Richter, Steffi.

National Sovereignty and Ciceronian Political Thought: Aeneas Silvius Piccolomini and the Ideal of Universal Empire in Fifteenth-Century Europe. Nederman, Cary J.

Nationalism and the Idea of Europe: How Nationalists Betray the Nation State. Mosher, Michael A.

Nietzsche's Trans-European Eye in Nietzsche and Asian Thought, Parkes, Graham R (ed). Sprung, G M C.

Nuclear Cities: The Bastille Analogy in Sartre Alive, Aronson, Ronald (ed). Stone, Robert.

On Constructing a European Cultural Identity by Doing Philosophy with Children. Moriyon, Felix Garcia.

On the Problem of Value Reconstruction in Chinese Philosophy under the Impact from European Thought. Liu, Shu-Hsien.

Post-Totalitarian Politics and European Philosophy. Palous, Martin.

Reply to Chakrabarti: Some Comments on Contraposition in European and Indian Logic. Dravid, N S.

Secret, Heresy and Responsibility: Patocka's Europe (Conclusion) (in Czechoslovakian). Derrida, Jacques.

Secret, Heresy and Responsibility: The Europe of Patocka (Part I) (in Czechoslovakian). Derrida, Jacques.

Specific Cultures and the Coexistence of Alternative Rationalities: A Case Study of the Contact of Indian and Greco-European Cultures. Shekhawat, V.

The End of the Russian Idea. Shlapentokh, Dmitry.

The European Cultural Tradition and the Limits of Growth. Klíma, Ivan.

The Intellectual Basis of Bioethics in Southern European Countries. Gracia, Diego.

The Problem of the Body in Nietzsche and Dōgen in Nietzsche and Asian Thought, Parkes, Graham (ed). Parkes, Graham R (trans) and Kōgaku, Arifuku.

Toward 1992: Utilitarianism as the Ideology of Europe. Bluhm, William T.

Wanderers in the Shadow of Nihilism: Nietzsche's 'Good Europeans'. Parkes, Graham R.

'Scattered over Europe': Transcending National Frontiers in the Seventeenth Century. Southgate, Beverley C.

EUTHANASIA

see also Letting Die

Cases in Bioethics: Selections from the Hastings Center Report (Second Edition). Crigger, Bette-Jane (ed).

Cruzan and the Constitutionalization of American Life. Schneider, Carl E.

Ethics in an Aging Society. Moody, Harry R.

Life and Death: Philosophical Essays in Biomedical Ethics. Brock, Dan W.

Moral Matters. Narveson, Jan.

Moral Personhood: An Essay in the Philosophy of Moral Psychology. Scott, G E.

Regulating Death, Carlos F Gomez. Cantor, Norman L.

A German Attack on Applied Ethics: A Statement by Peter Singer. Singer, Peter.

Advance Directives for Voluntary Euthanasia: A Volatile Combination?. Francis, Leslie Pickering.

Against the Right to Die. Velleman, J David.

Altruism and Physician Assisted Death. Gunderson, Martin and Mayo, David J.

Causing, Intending, and Assisting Death. Brody, Howard.

Conscience, Referral, and Physician Assisted Suicide. Wildes, Kevin W.

Courting Euthanasia? Tony Bland and the Law Lords. Keown, John.

Criteria for Death: Self-Determination and Public Policy. Sass, Hans-Martin.

Die konsequenzialistische Begründung des Lebensschutzes. Pöltner, Günther.

Doctors Must Not Kill. Pellegrino, Edmund.

Euthanasia and the Distinction between Acts and Omissions. Nesbitt, Winston.

Healing and Killing, Harming and Not Harming: Physician Participation in Euthanasia and Capital Punishment. Loewy, Erich H.

Is the Killing/Letting-Die Distinction Normatively Neutral?. Winkler, Earl.

Is There a Right to Die?. Kass, Leon R.

Learning to Do No Harm. Gillet, Grant R.

Living with Euthanasia: A Futuristic Scenario. Jonsen, Albert R.

More on Euthanasia: A Response to Pauer-Studer. Singer, Peter and Kuhse, Helga.

Persons and Death: What's Metaphysically Wrong with Our Current Statutory Definition of Death?. Lizza, John.

Peter Singer and Non-Voluntary 'Euthanasia': Tripping Down the Slippery Slope. Uniacke, Suzanne and McCloskey, H J.

Peter Singer on Euthanasia. Pauer-Studer, Herlinde.

Physician Assisted Death and Hard Choices. Mayo, David J and Gunderson, Martin.

Physician-Assisted Dying: Theory and Reality. Meier, Diane E.

Some Ways that Technology and Terminology Distort the Euthanasia Issue. Herrera, Christopher.

The Limits of Consent: A Note on Dr Kevorkian. Kleinig, John.

The Medicalization of Dying. Burgess, Michael M.

The Mercy Argument for Euthanasia: Some Logical Considerations. Walton, Richard E.

The Method of 'Principlism': A Critique of the Critique. Lustig, B Andrew.

The Patient in a Persistent Vegetative State: An Ethical Re-Appraisal. Schotsmans, P.

The Patient Self Determination Act and "Dax's Case". Gelwick, Richard.

The Right to Die as a Case Study in Third-Order Decisionmaking. Schauer, Frederick.

The Right to Die: A Justification of Suicide. Meyers, Chris D.

Unrequested Termination of Life: Is It Permissible?. Van Der Wal, Gerrit.

Voluntary Active Euthanasia. Brock, Dan W.

When Self-Determination Runs Amok. Callahan, Daniel.

EVALUATION

Knowledge and Belief. Schmitt, Frederick.

An Evolutionary Context for the Cognitive Unconscious. Reber, Arthur S.

Evaluations as Assessments, Part I: Properties and Their Signifiers. Magnell, Thomas.

EVALUATIVE

Reply to Garrard and McNaughton. Burton, Stephan L.

EVANGELISM

God, Creation, and Revelation: A Neo-Evangelical Theology. Jewett, Paul K.

Democractic Evasions: Cornel West and the Politics of Pragmatism. Westbrook, Robert B.

West's Evasion of Pragmatism. Brodsky, G M.

EVANS, D

Trust, the Heart of Religion: A Sketch. Godfrey, Joseph J.

EVANS, G

Making Sense of Indexicals. Anderson, Michael.

The Molyneux Problem. Lievers, Menno.

EVANS, J

The Voice that Keeps Reading: Evan's *Strategies of Deconstruction*. Kates, Joshua.

EVENT

Was sind Ereignisse? Eine Studie zur Analytischen Ontologie. Stoecker, Ralf.

A Note on Smith on Attempts and Internal Events. Rickard, Maurice.

Causation: One Thing Just Happens After Another in The Philosophy of A J Ayer, Hahn, Lewis Edwin (ed). Honderich, Ted.

Counterfactuals and Event Causation. Cross, Charles B.

Criteria of Identity and the Individuation of Natural-Kind Events. Savellos, Elias.

Events, Counterfactuals, and Speed. Lombard, Lawrence Brian.

La concezione dell'"evento" nella *Stella della redenzione* di Franz Rosenzweig e nel pensiero di Martin Heidegger. Casper, Bernhard.

Nomic Dependence and Causation. Clendinnen, F John.

On the Experience of Tenseless Time. Oaklander, L Nathan.

The Basic Ontological Categories in Language, Truth and Ontology, Mulligan, Kevin (ed). Chisholm, Roderick M.

The Foundations of Probability and Quantum Mechanics. Milne, Peter.

Thresholds, Transitivity, Overdetermination, and Events. Hausman, Daniel.

EVIDENCE

Another Day for an Old Dogma. Levy, Robert.

Einstein's Attitude Towards Experiments: Testing Relativity Theory 1907-1927. Hentschel, Klaus.

Evidence Against Anti-Evidentialism in Our Knowledge of God, Clark, Kelly James (ed). Kretzmann, Norman.

Explanation and "Old Evidence". Achinstein, Peter.

God and Perceptual Evidence. Draper, Paul.

Historical Evidence and Epistemic Justification: Thucydides as a Case Study. Kosso, Peter.

Observations, Theories and the Evolution of the Human Spirit. Bogen, Jim and Woodward, Jim.

On Novel Confirmation. Kahn, James A, Landsburg, Steven E and Stockman, Alan C.

Peirce and the Nature of Evidence. O'Neill, Len.

Some Complexities of Experimental Evidence. Morrison, Margaret.

Toward an Ethic of Evidence—and Beyond: Observations on Technology and Illness. Miké, Valerie.

Weight of Evidence, Resiliency and Second-Order Probabilities in Probability and Rationality, Eells, Ellery (ed). Logue, James.

EVIDENTIALISM

Evidentialism and Theology: A Reply to Kaufman. Shalkowski, Scott A.

EVIL

see also Theodicy

Beyond Hegel and Dialectic: Speculation, Cult, and Comedy. Desmond, William.

Goodness and Rightness in Thomas Aquinas's "Summa Theologiae". Keenan, James F.

Hell: The Logic of Damnation. Walls, Jerry.

Identity/Difference: Democratic Negotiations of Political Paradox. Connolly, William E.

Il "Peccato" in Cina: Bene e male nel Neoconfucianismo dalla metà del XIX secolo, by Paolo Santangelo. Elvin, Mark.

Philosophy of Religion: A Universalist Perspective. Sterling, Marvin.

Reasoned Faith. Stump, Eleonore (ed).

Speaking of a Personal God: An Essay in Philosophical Theology. Brümmer, Vincent.

The Metaphysics of Death. Fischer, John Martin (ed).

The Morality Maze: An Introduction To Moral Ecology. Daniels, Neil M.

What is God? The Selected Essays of Richard R La Croix. Lucey, Kenneth (ed).

A New Look at the Problem of Evil. Gellman, Jerome I.

A Note on Samkara's Theodicy. Matilal, Bimal Krishna.

Alpha-Claims and the Problem of Evil. Schellenberg, J L.

Antitheism: A Reflection. New, Christopher.

Banalité du mal et sens du devoir chez les administrateurs de l'extermination. Joos, Jean-Ernest.

Beyond Good and Evil. Leiter, Brian.

Beyond Good and Evil: Arendt, Nietzsche, and the Aestheticization of Political Action. Villa, Dana R.

Beyond Good and Evil: The Ethical Sensibility of Michel Foucault. Connolly, William E.

Blijenbergh's Tussing with Evil and Spinoza's Response (in Dutch). Klever, W.

Comment on Langtry's 'God, Evil and Probability'. Chrzan, Keith.

Comparative Oughts and Comparative Evils. Anderson, Robert.

Conditions of Evil in Deconstruction and the Possibility of Justice, Cornell, Durcilla (ed). Schürmann, Reiner and Janssen, Ian (trans).

Courageous Optimism: Augustine on the Good of Creation. Burt, Donald X.

Design and the Anthropic Principle. Leslie, John.

Deus Ex Machina. Arnheim, Rudolf.

Epistemic Probability and Evil in Our Knowledge of God, Clark, Kelly James (ed). Plantinga, Alvin.

Evil and the Concept of God. Bishop, John.

Evil and the Love of God. McCullagh, C Behan.

Extraordinary Evil or Common Malevolence? in Applied Philosophy, Almond, Brenda (ed). Lackey, Douglas.

God and Evil: Polarities of a Problem. Adams, Marilyn McCord.

God and Forgiveness. Londey, David.

Going Astray: Weakness, Perversity, or Evil? in Selves, People, and Persons, Rouner, Leroy S (ed). James, Edward.

How Good/Bad is Middle Knowledge? A Reply to Basinger. Hasker, William.

If There Be a God, From Whence Proceed So Many Evils?. Chakraborty, Nirmalya N.

Imaginary Evil: A Sceptic's Wager. Taliaferro, Charles.

Inductive Argument from Evil and the Human Cognitive Condition in Philosophical Perspectives, 5: Philosophy of Religion, 1991, Tomberlin, James E (ed). Alston, W P.

Kant and Radical Evil in German Philosophy and Jewish Thought, Greenspan, Louis (ed). McRobert, Laurie.

La estética y lo siniestro II. Estrada Mora, Olga C.

Making a Better World: Revisiting David Hume with Ian Markham. Loughlin, Gerard.

Non-Organic Theories of Value and Pointless Evil. O'Leary-Hawthorne, John.

Obligaiton, Loyalty, Exile. Shklar, Judith N.

Omniscience And The Problem of Evil. Hutcheson, Peter.

Ontological Arguments for Satan and Other Sorts of Evil Beings. Power, William L.

Philosophy of Religion Today. Jordan, Jeff.

Plantinga and the Two Problems of Evil. Monasterio, Xavier O.

Prevost, Probability, God and Evil. Milne, Peter.

Probabilistic Arguments From Evil. Draper, Paul.

Problem of Evil, Problem of Air, and the Problem of Silence in Philosophical Perspectives, 5: Philosophy of Religion, 1991, Tomberlin, James E (ed). Van Inwagen, Peter.

Process Theism and Physical Evil. Chew, Ho Hua.

Process Theism Versus Free-Will Theism: A Response to Griffin. Basinger, David.

Providence and the Problem of Evil in Christian Philosophy, Flint, Thomas P (ed). Stump, Eleonore.

Radical Freedom, Radical Evil and the Possibility of Eternal Damnation. Pestana, Mark Stephen.

Raimond Gaita's *Good and Evil*: An Absolute Conception. Hertzberg, Lars.

Ricoeur and Hick on Evil: Post-Kantian Myth?. Anderson, Pamela.

Ruminations About Evil in Philosophical Perspectives, 5: Philosophy of Religion, 1991, Tomberlin, James E (ed). Rowe, William.

Sartre on Evil in Sartre Alive, Aronson, Ronald (ed). Royle, Peter.

Sartre's Ontology of Evil and the Poverty of the Social Sciences. Gordon, Haim and Gordon, Rivca.

Satisfied Pigs and Dissatisfied Philosophers: Schlesinger on the Problem of Evil. Grover, Stephen.

Seeing through CORNEA. Howard-Snyder, Daniel.

Should God Not Have Created Adam?. Fales, Evan.

Social Evil: A Response to Adams. Quinn, Philip.

Suárez and the Problem of Positive Evil. Davis, Douglas P.

Temporal Wholes and the Problem of Evil. Nelson, Mark T.

The Anthropic Coincidences, Evil and the Disconfirmation of Theism. Smith, Quentin.

The Argument from Evil in Philosophical Perspectives, 5: Philosophy of Religion, 1991, Tomberlin, James E (ed). Tooley, Michael.

The Epistemology of Evil Possibilities. Tidman, Paul.

The Inscrutable Evil Defense Against the Inductive Argument from Evil. Sennett, James F.

The Intrinsic Value of Pain. Drum, Peter.

The Locked Door: An Analysis of the Problem of the Origin of the Soul in St Augustine's Thought. Waddell, Michael M.

The Problem of Evil in Paul Ricoeur: An Aporetic Exploration. Mongin, Olivier.

The Problem of Hell: A Problem of Evil for Christians in Reasoned Faith, Stump, Eleonore (ed). Adams, Marilyn McCord.

The Roots of All Evil: Lessons of an Epigram. Harries, Karsten.

Theodizee oder Kulturgeschichte des Bösen? Anmerkungen zum gegenwärtigen Diskurs. Geyer, Carl-Friedrich.

Tra narcisismo e regressione: la crisi dell'uomo contemporaneo. Franchi, A.

Two Concepts of Theodicy. Schuurman, Henry J.

Victimization and the Problem of Evil: A Response to Ivan Karamazov. Tracy, Thomas F.

Whitehead's God and the Problem of Evil. Thero, Daniel.

Zähmung des Bösen? Überlegungen zu Kant vor dem Hintergrund der Leibnizschen Theodizee. Schönrich, Gerhard.

EVOLUTION

see also Darwinism

Charles S Peirce's Evolutionary Philosophy. Hausman, Carl R.

Cosmos, Bios, Theos: Scientists Reflect on Science, God, and the Origins of the Universe, Life, and "Homo sapiens". Margenau, Henry (ed) and Varghese, Roy Abraham (ed).

New Horizons in the Philosophy of Science. Lamb, David (ed).

Nurturing Evolution: The Family as a Social Womb. Carter, Richard B.

Philosophy and the Origin and Evolution of the Universe. Agazzi, Evandro (ed) and Cordero, Alberto (ed).

Search for a Naturalistic World View: Volume II. Shimony, Abner.

A Naturalistic and Evolutionary Account of Content in Analecta Husserliana, XXXIV, Tymieniecka, Anna-Teresa (ed). Potrc, Matjaz.

Additivity and the Units of Selection. Godfrey-Smith, Peter.

An Evolutionary Account of Science: A Response to Rosenberg's Critical Notice. Hull, David L.

Aristotle and Hegel on Nature: Some Similarities. Santoro-Brienza, Liberato.

Charles F Potter: On Evolution and Religious Humanism in God, Values, and Empiricism, Peden, Creighton (ed). Olds, W Mason.

Consciousness: The Cartesian Enigma and its Contemporary Resolution in Wittgenstein's Intentions, Canfield, John V (ed). Coulter, Jeff.

Criticism and Survival: An Interpretation of Popper's Theory of Evolution. Tangwa, Godfrey B.

EVOLUTION

Darwin's Argument in the *Origin*. Hodge, M J S.

Emergence and Reduction in Morphogenetic Theories in Philosophy and the Origin and Evolution of the Universe, Agazzi, Evandro (ed). Artigas, M.

Epistemological Foundations of the Evolution of Science According to Carl F Von Weizäcker (in Polish). Maczka, Janusz.

Ethics and Evolution: The Biological Basis of Morality. Bradie, Michael.

Evolution and Emanation of Spirit in Hegel's *Philosophy of Nature*. Drees, Martin.

Evolution and Special Creation. McMullin, Ernan.

Evolution, Altruism, and the Prisoner's Dilemma. Haji, Ishtiyaque.

Evolution, Teleology and Theology. Soontiëns, Frans.

Evolutionary Anthropology and the Non-Cognitive Foundation of Moral Validity. Geiger, Gebhard.

Evolutionary Epistemology as an Overlapping, Interlevel Theory. Gray Hardcastle, Valerie.

Evolutionary Epistemology on Universals as Innate in Greek Studies in the Philosophy and History of Science, Nicolacopoulos, Pantelis (ed). Krimbas, Costas B.

Evolutionary Epistemology: What Phenotype is Selected and Which Genotype Evolves?. Falk, Raphael.

Evolutionary Explanations of Human Behaviour. Sterelny, Kim.

Evolutionary Ideas and Contemporary Naturalism in Philosophy and the Origin and Evolution of the Universe, Agazzi, Evandro (ed). Cordero, Alberto.

Evolutionary Synthesis: A Search for the Strategy. Tuomi, Juha.

Extending Art Historically. Levinson, Jerrold.

Freiheit und Evolution. Titze, Hans.

Genesis and Evolution in Reasoned Faith, Stump, Eleonore (ed). Van Inwagen, Peter.

Heritability and Causality. Sesardic, Neven.

How to Make Oneself Nature's Spokesman? A Latourian Account of Classification in Eighteenth- and Early Nineteenth-Century Natural History?. Stemerding, Dirk.

Implications of Environment-Trial Interaction for Evolutionary Epistemology. Scott, Jeffrey L.

Is Natural Science 'Natural' Enough? A Reply to Phillip Allport. Cartwright, Nancy.

Liever geen wetenschapsfilosofische supertheorieën. Van Der Steen, Wim J.

Neo-Rationalism Versus Neo-Darwinism: Integrating Development and Evolution. Smith, Kelly C.

Oikeiosis-jenseits von Herder und Darwin. Rohs, Peter.

On the Evolution of Natural Laws. Balashov, Yury V.

Origin and Evolution of the Universe and Mankind in Philosophy and the Origin and Evolution of the Universe, Agazzi, Evandro (ed). Quesada, Francisco Miró.

Peace and Becoming: An Evolutionary Global Struggle. Hetzler, Florence M.

Pre-Theoretical Assumptions in Evolutionary Explanations of Female Sexuality. Lloyd, Elisabeth.

Science and Creation: Big Bang Cosmology and Thomas Aquinas. Carroll, William E.

Sexual Differences: The Contingent and the Necessary. Wilson, John.

Should Environmentalists Be Organicists?. Norton, Bryan G.

Sociocultural Evolution or the Social Evolution of Practical Reason: Eder's Critique of Habermas. Strydom, Piet.

Stephen Jay Gould and the Contingent Nature of History. McRae, Murdo William.

Taking Evolution Seriously. Sheets-Johnstone, Maxine.

Telling the Tree: Narrative Representation and the Study of Evolutionary History. O'Hara, Robert J.

The "Other" Postmodern Theorist: Owen Barfield's Concept of the Evolution of Consciousness. Hocks, Richard A.

The Dimensions of Selection. Godfrey-Smith, Peter and Lewontin, Richard.

The Evolution and Devolution of Personhood. Hughen, Richard.

The Evolution of Altruism: Correlation, Cost, and Benefit. Sober, Elliott.

The Evolution of Human Altruism. Kitcher, Philip.

The Existence of God and the Creation of the Universe. Carloye, Jack C.

The Land Ethic Today. Callicott, J Baird.

The Possibility of an Evolutionary Semantics. Sheets-Johnstone, Maxine.

The Rise and Fall of Evolutionary Thinking Among American Philosophers. Auxier, Randall.

The Synthetic Theory of Evolution and the Neutral Theory and Punctuated Equilibria (in Polish). Kloskowski, K.

The World as One of a Kind: Natural Necessity and Laws of Nature. Bigelow, John, Ellis, Brian and Lierse, Caroline.

The 'Evolutionary Paradigm' and Constructional Biology in New Horizons in the Philosophy of Science, Lamb, David (ed). Goodwin, Brian, Webster, Gerry and Smith, Joseph Wayne.

Theology in an Evolutionary Mode. Schmitz-Moormann, Karl.

Yan Fu's Philosophy of Evolution and the Thought of Lao Zi and Zhuang Zi. Dayong, Yang.

EVOLUTIONISM

A New Religion. Stove, David.

A Simple Theory of Evolution By Natural Selection. Brandon, Robert N.

De opkomst en de ontwikkeling van het evolutionisme en de probleemhistorische methode van Vollenhoven. Bril, K A.

Memes and the Exploitation of Imagination. Dennett, Daniel C.

Neo-Classical Economics and Evolutionary Theory: Strange Bedfellows?. Rosenberg, Alex.

Relationships between Scientific Analysis and the World View of Pierre Teilhard de Chardin. Galleni, Lodovico.

The Egg Came Before the Chicken. Sorensen, Roy.

The Heuristic Bent. Agassi, Joseph.

Why There Are No Objective Values: A Critique of Ethical Intuitionism from an Evolutionary Point of View. Geiger, Gebhard.

EXACTNESS

Exactness and Philosophy in Advances in Scientific Philosophy, Schurz, Gerhard (ed). Koj, Leon.

Why We Cherish Exactness in Advances in Scientific Philosophy, Schurz, Gerhard (ed). Bunge, Mario.

EXAMINATION

Inescapable Surprises and Acquirable Intentions. Goldstein, Laurence.

EXAMPLE

A Presentation Without an Example?. Zuboff, Arnold.

EXCELLENCE

Athletes, Excellence, and Injury: Authority in Moral Jeopardy. Harmer, Peter A.

Excellence as a Guide to Educational Conversation. Noddings, Nel.

Hume on Human Excellence. Martin, Marie A.

Response to "Excellence as a Guide to Educational Conversation". Arnstine, Barbara.

EXCHANGE

Exploitation, Unequal Exchange and Dependency: A Dialectical Development. Otubusin, Paul.

Given Time: I. Counterfeit Money—Jacques Derrida. Derrida, Jacques and Kamuf, Peggy (trans).

La Charpente Modale du Sens. Brandt, Per Aage.

Philosophy of Economics: On the Scope of Reason in Economic Inquiry. Roy, Subroto.

The Logical Foundations of the Marxian Theory of Value. Garcia de la Sienra, Adolfo.

A Political and Economic Case for the Democratic Enterprise. Bowles, Samuel and Gintis, Herbert.

A Set of Axioms for Neoclassical Economics and the Methodological Status of the Equilibrium Concept. Vilks, Arnis.

Asymmetrical Reciprocity in Market Exchange: Implications for Economies in Transition. Buchanan, James M.

Commentator on 'Life-Style and the Standard of Living' in The Quality of Life, Nussbaum, Martha C (ed). Sen, Amartya.

Game Theory and the History of Ideas about Rationality: An Introductory Survey. Cudd, Ann.

Is It Rational To Be Polite?. Kingwell, Mark.

Marx on Some Phases of Communism in On the Track of Reason, Beehler, Rodger G (ed). Ware, Robert.

The Exchange and Allocation of Decision Power. Philipson, Tomas.

The Problem of Social Cost: Coase's Economics Versus Ethics. Hanly, Ken.

EXCLUDED MIDDLE

Petrus Aureoli and His Contemporaries on Future Contingents and Excluded Middle. Normore, Calvin G.

EXCLUSION

The Diversity of Religions: A Christian Perspective. DiNoia, J A.

Exclusion and Abstraction in Descartes' Metaphysics. Murdoch, Dugald.

Social Exclusion, Moral Reflection, and Rights. Meyers, Diana Tietjens.

The Morality of Inclusion. Buchanan, Allen.

EXISTENCE

see also Being, Dasein, Ontology, Reality

Discovering Philosophy. White, Thomas I.

Divine Hiddenness and Human Reason. Schellenberg, J L.

God and Existence (in Hungarian). Joós, Ernó.

L'Utopia di Fourier. Tundo, Laura.

La Comparution/The Compeareance: From the Existence of "Communism" to the Community of "Existence". Nancy, Jean-Luc and Strong, Tracy B (trans).

Our Knowledge of God. Clark, Kelly James (ed).

Person and Being. Clarke, W Norris.

Rediscovering the Moral Life. Gouinlock, James.

The Metaphysics of Death. Fischer, John Martin (ed).

The Moral Life. Luper-Foy, Steven.

Truth and Existence—Jean-Paul Sartre. Sartre, Jean Paul, Van Den Hoven, Adrian (trans) and Aronson, Ronald (ed).

Weaving: An Analysis of the Constitution of Objects. Swindler, James K.

A Classical Misunderstanding of Anselm's Argument. Schufreider, Gregory.

A Reply to Joseph C Flay's "Hegel's Metaphysics". Houlgate, Stephen.

A Reply to Paul Helm. Gale, Richard.

Anscombe on Coming Into Existence and Causation. Gordon, David.

Ayer and Ontology in The Philosophy of A J Ayer, Hahn, Lewis Edwin (ed). Quinton, Anthony.

Basic Principles of Differentiating of Conception of God (in Polish). Gogacz, Mieczyslaw.

Beyond Representation in The Impulse to Philosophise, Griffiths, A Phillips (ed). Palmer, Anthony.

Big Bangs, Plural: A Heretical View. Pecker, Jean-Claude.

Calobiotic or the Art of Aesthetic Life (in Czechoslovakian). Lorenzova, Helena.

Christsein im Denken: Zu Heideggers Kritik der 'christlichen Philosophie'. Haeffner, Gerd.

Classical Physical Abstraction. Adams, Ernest W.

Consistent Reism in Kotarbinski: Logic, Semantics and Ontology, Wolenski, Jan (ed). Grzegorczyk, Andrzej.

El conocimiento de Dios según Malebranche. Fernández, José Luis.

Evidence Against Anti-Evidentialism in Our Knowledge of God, Clark, Kelly James (ed). Kretzmann, Norman.

Existence and Comedy: An Interpretation of the Concluding Unscientific Postscript. Swindle, Stuart.

EXPERIENCE

EXTERNALISM

Boghossian on Externalism and Inference in Rationality in Epistemology, Villanueva, Enrique (ed). Schiffer, Stephen.

Burge on Content. Elugardo, Reinaldo.

Continuity, Consciousness, and Identity in Hume's Philosophy. Yandell, Keith E.

Delightful, Delovely and Externalist. Duran, Jane.

Experience and Externalism: A Reply to Peter Smith. Robinson, Howard.

Externalism (in Chinese). Huang, Yih-mei.

Externalism and Influence in Rationality in Epistemology, Villanueva, Enrique (ed). Boghossian, Paul.

Externalism and Mental Causality (in French). Jacob, Pierre.

Externalism and Mental Causation. Jacob, Pierre.

Externalism and the Explanatory Relevance of Broad Content. Jacob, Pierre.

Externalism and Token Identity. Seager, William.

Externalism for Internalists in Rationality in Epistemology, Villanueva, Enrique (ed). Dancy, Jonathan.

Externalism, Internalism and Moral Scepticism. Goldsworthy, Jeffrey.

Externalist Explanation. Peacocke, Christopher.

Fallibilismus: Ein Paradoxon. Lehrer, Keith.

Hume's Internalism. Coleman, Dorothy.

Object-Dependent Thoughts in Mental Causation, Heil, John (ed). Noonan, H W.

On the Need for a Metaphysics of Justification. Bradshaw, D E.

Privileged Self-Knowledge and Externalism are Compatible. Warfield, Ted A.

Reply to Schiffer in Rationality in Epistemology, Villanueva, Enrique (ed). Boghossian, Paul.

Semantic Externalism and Conceptual Competence. Rey, Georges.

Skepticism and Externalism. Brueckner, Anthony.

Skepticism and Reasoning to the Best Explanation in Rationality in Epistemology, Villanueva, Enrique (ed). Fumerton, Richard.

Some of the Difference in the World: Crane on Intentional Causation. Seymour, Daniel.

The Exorcist's Nightmare: A Reply to Crispin Wright. Tymoczko, Thomas and Vogel, Jonathan.

The Very Idea of the Phenomenological. McCulloch, Gregory.

Thought and Syntax. Seager, William.

Three Varieties of Knowledge in A J Ayer Memorial Essays, Griffiths, A Phillips (ed). Davidson, Donald.

Toward a Compatibility Theory for Internalist and Externalist Epistemologies. Sennett, James F.

Was Carnap Entirely Wrong, After All?. Stein, Howard.

What-Being: Chuang Tzu versus Aristotle. Li, Chenyang.

EXTRASENSORY PERCEPTION

Het visuele argument in de 'psychical research'. Draaisma, Douwe.

EXTRATERRESTRIAL

Big Numbers and Induction in the Case for Extra-Terrestrial Intelligence. Mash, Roy.

Ethics and the Extraterrestrial Environment. Marshall, Alan.

EXTRINSIC

Almost Indiscernible Twins. Baber, Harriet E.

Goodness and Truth. Gaita, Raimond.

What Isn't Wrong with Folk Psychology. Dretske, Frederick.

FABRO, C

La valenza critica della partecipazione nell'opera di C Fabro. Pellecchia, P.

FACKENHEIM, E

Fackenheim and Christianity in German Philosophy and Jewish Thought, Greenspan, Louis (ed). Baum, Gregory.

Fackenheim as Zionist in German Philosophy and Jewish Thought, Greenspan, Louis (ed). Greenspan, Louis.

Reason and Existence in Schelling and Fackenheim in German Philosophy and Jewish Thought, Greenspan, Louis (ed). Burbidge, John W.

Revelation and Resistance: A Reflection on the Thought of Fackenheim in German Philosophy and Jewish Thought, Greenspan, Louis (ed). Munk, Reinier.

FACT

Explanatory Understanding and Contrastive Facts. Grimes, Thomas R.

God and the Status of Facts. Peterson, John.

Martin on the Meaninglessness of Religious Language. Hughes, Charles T.

Natural Meaning. Denkel, Arda.

Nonfactualism about Normative Discourse. Railton, Peter A.

Real Facts in Advances in Scientific Philosophy, Schurz, Gerhard (ed). Hieke, Alexander.

Reply to Sinnott-Armstrong. Gibbard, Allan F.

Rorty and I. Bencivenga, Ermanno.

The Tarasoff Case. Farbstein, Aviva.

Using the Fact/Value Problem to Teach Ethical Theory. Birsch, Douglas.

FACTUALITY

Metafisica e pensiero iniziale: Aspetti della Kehre alle origini del pensiero heideggeriano. Samonà, Leonardo.

FAIRCHILD, D

Fields of Dreams and Men of Straw: Philosophical Reflections on Performance-Enhancers in Sport. Meier, Klaus V.

FAIRNESS

Criminal Desert and Unfair Advantage: What's the Connection?. Davis, Michael.

Fairness and Cores: A Comment on Laden. Gauthier, David.

Fairness and Self-Defense. Draper, George.

Fairness in Hierarchical and Entrepreneurial Firms. Green, Michael K.

Games Philosophers Play: A Reply to Gauthier. Laden, Anthony Simon.

Justice and Insider Trading. Lippke, Richard L.

Loyalties, and Why Loyalty Should be Ignored. Ewin, R E.

QALYs, Age and Fairness. Kappel, Klemens and Sandoe, Peter.

Rationing Fairly: Programmatic Considerations. Daniels, Norman.

FAITH

see also Belief, Fideism, Will To Believe

Boundary Ways: On the Philosophy of the Later Ludwig Wittgenstein (in Hungarian). Neumer, Katalin.

Consent: The Means to an Active Faith According to St Thomas Aquinas. Barad, Judith.

Contemporary Perspectives on Religious Epistemology. Geivert, R Douglas (ed) and Sweetman, Brendan (ed).

Hegel on Logic and Religion: The Reasonableness of Christianity. Burbidge, John W.

Judging in Good Faith. Burton, Steven J.

Making Sense of It All. Morris, Thomas V.

Pistis ed Episteme: A Proposito di una lettura "diacritica" di 1 Cor 2, 3. Campanale, Domenico.

Religion and Philosophy. Warner, Martin (ed).

The Faith of a Liberal—Morris Raphael Cohen. Cohen, Morris R.

The Trinity: An Analysis of St Thomas Aquinas' 'Expositio' of the 'De Trinitate' of Boethius. Hall, Douglas.

A Reply to Paul Helm. Gale, Richard.

Abraham's Silence Aesthetically Considered in Kierkegaard on Art and Communication, Pattison, George (ed). Perkins, Robert L.

Aquinas on Theological Predication: A Look Backward and a Look Forward in Reasoned Faith, Stump, Eleonore (ed). Alston, W P.

Bad Faith, Good Faith, and the Faith of Faith in Sartre Alive, Aronson, Ronald (ed). Mirvish, Adrian M.

Belief vs Commitment, Validity vs Value: A Response to Ward Goodenough. Brink, T L.

Christian Faith in Reasoned Faith, Stump, Eleonore (ed). MacDonald, Scott.

Christsein im Denken: Zu Heideggers Kritik der 'christlichen Philosophie'. Haeffner, Gerd.

Congetture e confutazioni. Milano, A.

Descartes' Debt to Augustine in Philosophy, Religion and the Spiritual Life, McGhee, Michael (ed). Clark, Stephen R L.

Duns Scotus, Demonstration, and Doctrine. Mann, William E.

El estatuto epistemológico de la fe: Un diálogo con Kant. Odero, José Miguel.

Existence and Essence: Kierkegaard and Hegel. Subramanian, Sharada.

F H Bradley and Religious Faith. Carr, Stephen.

Faith and Fidelity as Interpreted by Gabriel Marcel (in Chinese). Kwan, Wing-chung.

Faith and Philosophy. Vaught, Carl G.

Faith and Science in Advances in Scientific Philosophy, Schurz, Gerhard (ed). Bochenski, Joseph M.

Faith Seeks, Understanding Finds in Christian Philosophy, Flint, Thomas P (ed). Kretzmann, Norman.

Faith, Belief, and Rationality in Philosophical Perspectives, 5: Philosophy of Religion, 1991, Tomberlin, James E (ed). Audi, Robert.

Faith, Probability and Infinite Passion. Koons, Robert C.

Faith, Reason, and Ascent to Vision in Saint Augustine. O'Connell, Robert.

Il posto della metafisica nel sapere umano: Il pensiero di Maimonide e eil suo influsso su S Tommaso d'Aquino. Pangallo, Mario.

Kierkegaard's Ironic Ladder to Authentic Faith. Golomb, Jacob.

Kierkegaard's View of Faith in Terrorism, Justice and Social Values, Peden, Creighton (ed). Smorowski, Michael A.

La foi messianique de Hugo Bermann. Kluback, William.

Note sul concetto di alienazione in Hegel. Alfano, G.

Pierre Gassendi nel IV centenario della nascita. Gregory, Tullio.

Reason and Faith—I in Religion and Philosophy, Warner, Marin (ed). Bambrough, Renford.

Reason and Faith—II in Religion and Philosophy, Warner, Marin (ed). Trigg, Roger.

Religiöser Glaube und Gödels ontologischer Gottesbeweis. Muck, Otto.

Religion and Civic Virtue. Budziszewski, J.

Religious Pluralism and the Ground of Religious Faith in Logic, God and Metaphysics, Harris, James F (ed). Long, Eugene T.

Sartre on the Self-Deceiver's Translucent Consciousness. Morris, Phyllis Sutton.

Seeing (Just) Is Believing: Faith and Imagination. Ferreira, M Jamie.

Some Problems with Loyalty: The Metaethics of Commitment. Cochran, Ruth B.

Teología y pluralismo teológico en Etienne Gilson. Moya Obradors, Pedro Javier.

The Dimensions of Faith and the Demands of Reason in Reasoned Faith, Stump, Eleonore (ed). Audi, Robert.

The Examined Life Re-examined in The Impulse to Philosophise, Griffiths, A Phillips (ed). Radford, Colin.

The God of Abraham and the God of the Philosophers: A Reading of Emmanuel Levinas's "Dieu et la Philosophie". Bergo, Bettina.

The Proofs of Natural Theology and the Unbeliever. Sparrow, M F.

The Sentiment of Pragmatism: From the Pragmatism Maxim to a Pragmatic Faith. Ochs, Peter.

Truth and Faith in Paul Tillich's Thought: The Criteria and Values of Ultimacy. Grean, Stanley.

When Christians Become Naturalists. Robbins, J Wesley.

William James and the Logic of Faith. Pappas, Gregory.

FAITHFULNESS

Love's Constancy. Martin, Mike W.

FALES, E

Reply to Fales's 'Are Causal Laws Contingent?' in Ontology, Causality and Mind: Essays in Honour of D M Armstrong, Bacon, John (ed). Armstrong, D M.

FREE WILL

see also Determinism

Anthropologische Geschichtsphilosophie: Für eine Philosophie der Geschichte in der Zeit der Postmoderne. Ignatow, Assen.

Die Rolle der Physiologie in der Philosophie Epikurs. Manolidis, Georgios.

Henry of Ghent: Quodlibetal Questions on Free Will. Teske, Roland (trans).

Open Questions: An Introduction to Philosophy (Concise Edition). Barcalow, Emmett.

The Experience of Philosophy (Second Edition). Kolak, Daniel and Martin, Raymond.

What is God? The Selected Essays of Richard R La Croix. Lucey, Kenneth (ed).

A Chaotic Approach to Free Will and Determinism. Till, Gregory J.

A Definitive Non-Solution of the Free-Will Problem. Brunton, Alan.

Aktuelle Themen und Positionen deutschsprachiger Religionsphilosophie. Engstler, Achim.

Applied Ethics and Free Will: Some Untoward Results of Independence. Machan, Tibor R.

Ayer on Free Will and Determinism in The Philosophy of A J Ayer, Hahn, Lewis Edwin (ed). O'Connor, D J.

Compatibilism and the Free Will Defence. Bishop, John.

Craig on the Possibility of Eternal Damnation. Talbott, Thomas.

Did James Deceive Himself about Free Will?. Smilansky, Saul.

Free Will and the Genome Project. Greenspan, P S.

Free Will in Psychopaths in Analecta Husserliana, XXXI, Tymieniecka, Anna-Teresa (ed). González, Manuel Riobó.

Free-Will and Determinism in Logical Foundations, Mahalingam, Indira (ed). Ayer, A J.

Freiheit und Determinismus (Teil I). Seebass, Gottfried.

Freiheit und Determinismus (Teil II). Seebass, Gottfried.

Freiheit und Evolution. Titze, Hans.

How Rational Must Free Will Be?. Double, Richard.

Incompatibilism, Nondeterministic Causation, and the Real Problem of Free Will. Francken, Patrick.

Indeterminism and Free Agency: Three Recent Views. O'Connor, Timothy.

La question du libre arbitre en France, de la Révolution à la Restauration. Baertschi, Bernard.

Leibniz and the Compatibilist of Free Will. Borst, Clive.

Of One's Own Free Will. Stampe, Dennis W and Gibson, Martha I.

Presciencia divina y libre arbitrio: Boecio de Consolatione V, 3 y Seneca epistulae ad lucilium II, 16. Tursi, Antonio D.

Process Theism Versus Free-Will Theism: A Response to Griffin. Basinger, David.

Self-Identity and Free Will are Beyond our Control. Hunt, Ralph and Hartz, Glenn A.

Some Limits to Freedom. Hughes, Liam.

The Doctrine of Conservation and Free-Will Defence. Jordan, Jeffrey.

The Principle of Rational Explanation Defended. Double, Richard.

Theological Fatalism and Modal Confusion. Talbott, Thomas.

FREEDOM

see also Liberty

Bettering Our Condition: Work, Workers and Ethics in British and German Economic Thought. Chmielewski, Philip J.

Between Slavery and Freedom: Philosophy and American Slavery. McGary, Howard and Lawson, Bill E.

Community at Loose Ends. Miami Theory Collect (ed).

Compassionate Authority: Democracy and the Representation of Women. Jones, Kathleen B.

Contractarian Liberal Ethics and the Theory of Rational Choice. Park, Jung Soon.

Democracy and Complexity: A Realist Approach. Zolo, Danilo and McKie, David (trans).

Democracy. Harrison, Ross.

Environmental Philosophy: From Animal Rights to Radical Ecology. Zimmerman, Michael (& other eds).

Epistemic Virtue and Doxastic Responsibility. Montmarquet, James.

Erotic Welfare: Sexual Theory and Politics in the Age of Epidemic. Singer, Linda.

Essays on Kant's Political Philosophy. Williams, Howard (ed).

Eternity and Time's Flow. Neville, Robert Cummings.

Ethical Essays, Volume I. Harrison, Jonathan.

Fichte's "Wissenschaftslehre" of 1794: A Commentary on Part I. Seidel, George J.

Freedom by Orlando Patterson. King, Richard H.

Hegel, Freedom, and Modernity. Westphal, Merold.

Hermeneutics Ancient and Modern. Bruns, Gerald L.

History, Religion, and American Democracy (New Edition). Wohlgelernter, Maurice (ed).

Identity/Difference: Democratic Negotiations of Political Paradox. Connolly, William E.

Jean-Paul Sartre: Freedom and Commitment. Hill, Charles G.

John Dewey and American Democracy. Westbrook, Robert B.

Justice and Interpretation. Warnke, Georgia.

Justice: Interdisciplinary Perspectives. Scherer, Klaus R (ed).

Kant and the Experience of Freedom: Essays on Aesthetics and Morality. Guyer, Paul.

Kants Begründung der praktischen Philosophie. Freudiger, Jürg.

Law and the Human Sciences. Kevelson, Roberta (ed).

Liberal Rights: Collected Papers 1981-1991. Waldron, Jeremy.

Logical Foundations. Mahalingam, Indira (ed) and Carr, Brian (ed).

Metaphysics (Fourth Edition). Taylor, Richard.

Morality and Moral Controversies (Third Edition). Arthur, John (ed).

Nietzsche: The Politics of Power. Okonta, Ike.

Open Institutions: The Hope for Democracy. Murphy, John W (ed) and Peck, Dennis L (ed).

Partial Visions: Feminism and Utopianism in the 1970s. Bammer, Angelika.

Peirce's Esthetics of Freedom: Possibility, Complexity, and Emergent Value. Kevelson, Roberta.

Philosophisches Denken: Einübungen. Berlinger, Rudolph.

Philosophy of Economics: On the Scope of Reason in Economic Inquiry. Roy, Subroto.

Politics/Sense/Experience: A Pragmatic Inquiry into the Promise of Democracy. Kaufman-Osborn, Timothy V.

Secession: The Morality of Political Divorce from Fort Sumter to Lithuania and Quebec. Buchanan, Allen.

Speech, Crime, and the Uses of Language. Greenawalt, Kent.

The Desire To Be God: Freedom and the Other in Sartre and Berdyaev. McLachlan, James Morse.

The Dialogue of Justice: Towards a Self-Reflective Society. Fishkin, James S.

The Discipline of Taste and Feeling. Wegener, Charles.

The Idea of Democracy. Copp, David (ed), Hampton, Jean (ed) and Roemer, John E (ed).

The Manifestation of Analogous Being in the Dialectic of the Space-Time Continuum: A Philosophical Study in Freedom. Harris, David A.

The Morality Maze: An Introduction To Moral Ecology. Daniels, Neil M.

The Morality of Pluralism. Kekes, John.

The Origins of Our Delusions (in Hungarian). Ludassy, Mária.

The Philosopher of Free Religion: Francis Ellingwood Abbot, 1836-1903. Peden, W Creighton.

The Philosophy of Freedom: Ideological Origins of the Bill of Rights. Rudolph, Samuel B (ed).

The Problem of Hell. Kvanvig, Jonathan L.

The Rationality of Feeling: Understanding the Arts in Education. Best, David.

To Make the Punishment Fit the Crime: Essays in the Theory of Criminal Justice. Davis, Michael.

Transition to Modernity: Essays on Power, Wealth and Belief. Hall, John A (ed) and Jarvie, I C (ed).

Unreason Within Reason: Essays on the Outskirts of Rationality. Graham, A C.

A Coherence Theory of Autonomy. Ekstrom, Laura Waddell.

A Reconstruction of Hegel's Account of Freedom of the Will. Moellendorf, Darrel F.

Abortion and "Choice". Gallagher, Kenneth.

Academic Freedom. O'Reilly, Paul.

Addiction and the Value of Freedom. Oddie, Graham.

After Libertarianism: Rejoinder to Narveson, McCloskey, Flew, and Machan. Friedman, Jeffrey.

Against Couples in Applied Philosophy, Almond, Brenda (ed). Gregory, Paul.

Berlin on the Nature and Significance of Liberty in Terrorism, Justice and Social Values, Peden, Creighton W (ed). Paden, Roger K.

Beyond Negative and Positive Freedom: T H Green's View of Freedom. Simhony, Avital.

Child Liberationism and Legitimate Interference. Lipson, Morrice and Vallentyne, Peter.

Choice and Utility in The Utilitarian Response, Allison, Lincoln (ed). Brittan, Samuel.

Citizenship and Equality: The Place for Toleration. Galeotti, Anna Elisabetta.

Coerced Birth Control, Individual Rights, and Discrimination in Biomedical Ethics Reviews 1992, Humber, James M (ed). Kuo, Lenore.

Comic Illusion and Illusion in Comedy in Aesthetic Illusion, Burwick, Frederick (ed). Pape, Walter.

Conceptions of 'Civil Society'. Honneth, Axel.

Conditionals of Freedom and Middle Knowledge. Gaskin, R.

Conflicting Values in American Higher Education: Development of the Concept of Academic Freedom. Tandy, Charles.

Consciousness and the Experience of Freedom in John Searle and His Critics, LePore, Ernest (ed). Hannay, Alastair.

Could Kant Have Been a Utilitarian. Hare, R M.

Das Ideal des philosophischen Lebens bei G W Leibniz. Rensoli, Lourdes.

Das Problem der Freiheit in der Psychologie von William James. Herzog, Max.

Deformatives: Essentially Other Than Truth in Reading Heidegger: Commemorations, Sallis, John (ed). Sallis, John.

Der gegenwärtige Schelling: Positionen der heutigen Schelling-Forschung—Ein Bericht. Orzechowski, Axel.

Devlin, Hart, and the Proper Limits of Legal Coercion. Nattrass, Mark S.

Die Freiheit des Richters. Schubarth, Martin.

Dissent from "The New Consensus": Reply to Friedman. Flew, Antony.

Divine Self-Limitation in Swinbourne's Doctrine of Omniscience. Fouts, Avery.

Duns Scotus and the Experience of Freedom. Incandela, Joseph M.

Educating the Passions: Reconsidering David Hume's Optimistic Appraisal of Commerce. Schuler, Jeanne A and Murray, Patrick.

Endgame. McCarney, Joseph.

Equality of What? in The Quality of Life, Nussbaum, Martha C (ed). Cohen, G A.

Ethics and Negotiation: The Search for Value and Freedom In Hollywood. Harrison, Harvey E.

Ethnicity and the Problem of Equality. Blanchard Jr, Kenneth C.

Feeling and Freedom: Kant on Aesthetics and Morality. Guyer, Paul.

Fichte's New Wine. Harris, H S.

FUNCTIONAL
Invariance and Structural Dependence. Odelstad, Jan.

FUNCTIONAL COMPLETENESS
Functional Completeness for Subsystems of Intuitionistic Propositional Logic. Wansing, Heinrich.

Zero-Place Operations and Functional Completeness, and the Definition of New Connectives. Humberstone, I L.

FUNCTIONALISM
Block's Challenge in Ontology, Causality and Mind: Essays in Honour of D M Armstrong, Bacon, John (ed). Jackson, Frank.

Defining "Art": The Functionalism/Proceduralism Controversy. Stecker, Robert A.

Functional Analysis and Etiology. McClamrock, Ron.

Functional Explanation and the State in Marx's Theory of History, Wetherly, Paul. Carter, Alan.

Functionalism and Personal Identity. Fuller, Gary.

Intentions, Concepts of Intention, and the "Final Solution". Lang, Berel.

Kein Platz für phänomenale Qualitäten und Leib- Umwelt- Interaktion?. Pohlenz, Gerd.

Leaving Man in Society. Krausz, Ernest.

Mental Causation and Mental Reality. Crane, Tim.

Modernity and Self-Identity: Self and Society in the Late Modern Age. Gluck, Mary.

Philosophical Premises of Functional Anthropology. Brozi, Krzysztof J.

Proper Functionalism. Feldman, Richard.

Proper Functionalism and Virtue Epistemology. Sosa, Ernest.

Reply to Jackson's 'Block's Challenge' in Ontology, Causality and Mind: Essays in Honour of D M Armstrong, Bacon, John (ed). Armstrong, D M.

Truth, Activation Vectors and Possession Conditions for Concepts. Putnam, Hilary.

Two More Proofs of Present Qualia. Wright, Edmond.

Understanding the Phenomenal Mind: Are We All Just Armadillos? in Consciousness: Psychological and Philosophical Essays, Davies, Martin (ed). Van Gulick, Robert.

Why I Am Not a Physicalist. Kwame, Safro.

Why We Need Proper Function. Plantinga, Alvin.

FUNDAMENTALISM
Empiricism, Fideism and The Nature of Religious Belief. Sweet, William and O'Connell, Colin.

Ricoeur and Hick on Evil: Post-Kantian Myth?. Anderson, Pamela.

The Intolerance of Religious Pluralism. Donovan, Peter.

FURLEY, D
Aristotelian Rainfall or the Lore of Averages. Wardy, Robert.

FUTURE
A Future for Aesthetics. Danto, Arthur C.

Commentary on Martin's "Fate and Futurity in the Greco-Roman World". Boedeker, Deborah.

Dewey and Democracy at the Dawn of the Twenty-First Century. Feinberg, Walter.

Does Continental Ethics Have a Future? in Ethics and Danger, Dallery, Arleen B (ed). Wyschogrod, Edith.

Fatalism and Truth about the Future. Felt, James W.

Fate and Futurity in the Greco-Roman World. Martin, Luther H.

Is the Future Really Real?. Faye, Jan.

Knowledge of the Past and Future. Feinberg, Gerald.

Marxism and the Logic of Futural Discourse: A Brief Reflection. O'Connell, Colin.

Modern Chinese Thought: A Retrospective View and a Look into the Future. Lai, Chen.

Petrus Aureoli and His Contemporaries on Future Contingents and Excluded Middle. Normore, Calvin G.

Sailing through the Sea Battle. Bäck, Allan.

Scenes from My Childhood in The Impulse to Philosophise, Griffiths, A Phillips (ed). Magee, Bryan.

The Body of the Future in The Body in Medical Thought and Practice, Leder, Drew (ed). Cassell, Eric J.

The Past Just Ain't What It Used To Be: A Response to Kevin Staley and Ronald Tacelli. Baldner, Steven.

The Prelude to the Philosophy of the Future: The Art of Reading and the Genealogical Methods in Nietzsche. Sax, Benjamin C.

Thinking for Tomorrow: Reflections on Avner de-Shalit. Marshall, Peter.

Twenty Years Before the End of the World: Political Remarks About the Meaning of Our Epoch. Dzarasov, Ruslan.

FUTURE GENERATION
Engineering Ethics and Hazardous Waste Management: Why Should We Care About Future Generations?. Gunn, Alastair S.

Future Generations: Present Harms. O'Neill, John.

Lebensrecht und Überlebeninteresse: Darstellung und Kritik einiger Thesen von Norbert Hoerster. Viefhues, Ludger.

On Obligations to Future Generations. Reichenbach, Bruce R.

Regarding Future Neighbours: Thomas Aquinas and Concern for Posterity. George, William P.

GADAMER, H
Hans-Georg Gadamer on Education, Poetry, and History: Applied Hermeneutics. Misgeld, Dieter (ed) and Nicholson, Graeme (ed)

Hermeneutics and Human Finitude: Toward a Theory of Ethical Understanding. Smith, P Christopher.

A Critique of Gadamer (in Hebrew). Ben-NaftaliBerkowitz, Michal.

Etica Actual: Una Doble Perspectiva. Mauri, Margarita.

Is Hermeneutics Ethnocentric? in The Interpretive Turn, Hiley, David R (ed). Hoy, David C.

L'herméneutique d'Austin Farrer: un modèle participatoire. Bigger, Charles B.

Mead, Gadamer, and Hermeneutics in Frontiers in American Philosophy, Volume I, Burch, Robert W (ed). Moran, Jon S.

On Interpreting Kant's Architectonic in Terms of the Hermeneutic Model. Nuyen, A T.

Schleiermacher's Hermeneutic and Its Critics. Corliss, Richard.

Sulle tracce del postmoderno (I). Pellecchia, Pasquale.

Sulle tracce del postmoderno (II). Pellecchia, Pasquale.

The Idea of Enablement. Martin, Bill.

Truth Without Methodologism: Gadamer and James. Fairfield, Paul.

GAITA, R
Raimond Gaita's *Good and Evil*: An Absolute Conception. Hertzberg, Lars.

Taking Morality Seriously. Almond, Brenda.

GALE, R
Richard Gale's *On the Nature and Existence of God*. Helm, Paul.

GALEN
Galien et le stoïcisme. Manuli, Paola.

GALILEO
Galilei e la fisica del Collegio Romano. Dollo, Corrado.

Galileo, Aristotelian Science, and the Rotation of the Earth. Reitan, Eric A.

Paolo Foscarini's *Letter to Galileo*: The Search for Proofs of the Earth's Motion. Kelter, Irving A.

To Save the Phenomena: Duhem on Galileo. Finocchiaro, M A.

GALLI, C
Modernità: esperienza e schemi concettuali. Marrone, P.

GALLOIS, A
Restricted Rigidity: The Deeper Problem. Ramachandran, Murali.

GALLOP, D
Aristotle on Sleep and Dreams. Woods, Michael.

GALLOWAY, D
Issues Concerning a Nativist Theory of Numerical Knowledge. Wynn, Karen.

GALSTON, W
Liberal Philanthropy. Riley, Jonathan.

GAMBLING
Gambling: A Preliminary Inquiry. Newton, Lisa.

GAME
A Fruitless Definition. Harris, N G E.

Business and Games. Heckman, Peter.

Endogenizing the Order of Moves in Matrix Games. Hamilton, Jonathan H and Slutsky, Steven M.

Eventual Periodicity and "One-Dimensional" Queries. McColm, Gregory L.

Explanatory Instability. Batterman, Robert W.

Fairness and Cores: A Comment on Laden. Gauthier, David.

Game Sentences and Ultrapowers. Jin, Renling and Keisler, H Jerome.

Games Philosophers Play: A Reply to Gauthier. Laden, Anthony Simon.

Language Games, Expression and Desire in the Work of Deleuze. Heaton, John M.

Language Without Conversation. Malcolm, Norman.

On the Logic of Informational Independence and Its Applications. Sandu, Gabriel.

Playing with Language: Language-Games Reconsidered in Wittgenstein's Intentions, Canfield, J V (ed). Frohmann, Bernd.

Relative Separation Theorems. Tuuri, Heikki.

Stable Cooperation in Iterated Prisoners' Dilemmas. Sober, Elliott.

The Definition of 'Game'. Rowe, M W.

The Turing Test as a Novel Form of Hermeneutics. Clark, Timothy.

Trouble with Leprechauns. Hollis, Martin.

GAME THEORY
Artificial Morality: Virtuous Robots for Virtual Games. Danielson, Peter.

Exploitation, Unequal Exchange and Dependency: A Dialectical Development. Otubusin, Paul.

The Grounds and Limits of Political Obligation. Capriotti, Emile.

Are There Internal Prisoner's Dilemmas? A Comment on Kavka's Article. Moreh, J.

Game Theory and the History of Ideas about Rationality: An Introductory Survey. Cudd, Ann.

Hintikka's Game of Language. Kanthamani, A.

Internal Prisoner's Dilemma Vindicated. Kavka, Gregory.

Learning to Cooperate with Pavlov: An Adaptive Strategy for the Iterated Prisoner's Dilemma with Noise. Kraines, David and Kraines, Vivian.

Modern and Postmodern Challenges to Game Theory. Varoufakis, Yanis.

Numerical Quantifiers in Game-Theoretical Semantics. Klima, Gyula and Sandu, Gabriel.

Rationality in Action. Hollis, Martin and Sugden, Robert.

The Dream of Captain Carib. Farley, Jonathan.

The Essence of David Gauthier's Moral Philosophy. Messerly, John.

Three Pseudo-Paradoxes in 'Quantum' Decision Theory: Apparent Effects of Observation on Probability and Utility. Marinoff, Louis.

GANDHI
"I Can Wait 40 or 400 Years": Gandhian *Satyagraha* West and East. Starosta, William J and Chaudhary, Anju G.

Pacifism: A Philosophical Exploration. Filice, Carlo.

Pacifism: A Reply to Professor Narveson. Filice, Carlo.

Professor Filice's Defense of Pacifism: A Comment. Narveson, Jan.

Social Ethic of Mahatma Gandhi and Martin Buber. Henry, Sarojini.

The Tagore-Gandhi Controversy Revisited, I. Singh, Ajay and Singh, Shakuntala.

The Tagore-Gandhi Controversy Revisited, II. Singh, Ajai and Singh, Shakuntala.

GANGESA
The Nyaya Theory of Linguistic Performance: A New Interpretation of Tattvacintamani. Mukhopadhyay, P K.

GANS, E

Resentment and Apophasis: The Trace of the Other in Levinas, Derrida and Gans in Shadow of Spirit, Berry, Philippa (ed). Foshay, Toby.

GARCIA, J

Response to Jorge Garcia in African-American Perspectives on Biomedical Ethics, Flack, Harley E (ed). Beauchamp, Tom L.

GARNHAM, A

Logicism, Mental Models and Everyday Reasoning: Reply to Garnham. Chater, Nick and Oaksford, Mike.

GARRARD, E

Reply to Garrard and McNaughton. Burton, Stephan L.

GARRETT, B

Losing Track of Nozick. Brueckner, Anthony.

GARVER, E

Commentary on Garver's "Making Discourse Ethical". Griswold, Charles L.

GAS

From Gases and Liquids to Fluids in Greek Studies in the Philosophy and History of Science, Nicolacopoulos, Pantelis (ed). Gavroglu, Kostas.

GASS, M

Reply to Gass's "Abortion and Moral Character: A Critique of Smith". Smith, Janet E.

GASSENDI

Gassendi interprete di Cavalieri. Festa, Egidio.

Pierre Gassendi nel IV centenario della nascita. Gregory, Tullio.

GATENS, M

Recent Work in Feminist Philosophy. Mendus, Susan.

GAUTHIER, D

Artificial Virtues and the Equally Sensible Non-Knaves: A Response to Gauthier. Baier, Annette.

Games Philosophers Play: A Reply to Gauthier. Laden, Anthony Simon.

On Contractarian Constitutional Democracy in The Idea of Democracy, Copp, David (ed). Morris, Christopher.

Preference-Revision and the Paradoxes of Instrumental Rationality. MacIntosh, Duncan.

Straight Versus Constrained Maximization. Sobel, J Howard.

The Essence of David Gauthier's Moral Philosophy. Messerly, John.

The Rational Justification of Moral Restraint. Hill, Greg.

The Rationality of Conditional Cooperation. Den Hartogh, Govert.

GEACH, P

The Analogy Theory of Thinking. Haaparanta, Leila.

GEERTSMA, H

Transcendentie en Schepping. De Boer, T.

GEERTZ, C

Is Hermeneutics Ethnocentric? in The Interpretive Turn, Hiley, David R (ed). Hoy, David C.

Relativism versus Ethnocentrism?. Van Niekerk, Anton.

GEMES, K

Hypothetico-Deductivism, Content, and the Natural Axiomatization of Theories. Gemes, Ken.

GENDER

"Engendering Equity...". Morgan, K P.

"Maleness" Revisited. Bordo, Susan.

An Ethic of Care: Feminist and Interdisciplinary Perspectives. Larrabee, Mary Jeanne (ed).

Beyond Equality and Difference. Bock, Gisela (ed) and James, Susan (ed).

Beyond Methodology: Feminist Scholarship as Lived Research. Fonow, Mary Margaret (ed) and Cook, Judith A (ed).

Bodies that Matter: On the Discursive Limits of 'Sex'. Butler, Judith.

Buddhism, Sexuality, and Gender. Cabezón, José I (ed).

Compassionate Authority: Democracy and the Representation of Women. Jones, Kathleen B.

Discovering Philosophy. White, Thomas I.

Elemental Passions—Luce Irigaray. Irigaray, Luce, Collie, Joanne (trans) and Still, Judith (trans).

Engendering the Subject: Gender and Self-Representation in Contemporary Women's Fiction. Robinson, Sally.

Engenderings: Constructions of Knowledge, Authority, and Privilege. Scheman, Naomi.

Erotic Welfare: Sexual Theory and Politics in the Age of Epidemic. Singer, Linda.

Feminine and Feminist Ethics. Tong, Rosemarie.

Feminist Epistemologies. Alcoff, Linda (ed) and Potter, Elizabeth (ed).

From Mastery to Analysis: Theories of Gender in Psychoanalytic Feminism. Elliot, Patricia.

Gender Politics and Post-Communism: Reflections from Eastern Europe and the Former Soviet Union. Funk, Nanette (ed) and Mueller, Magda (ed).

Hypatia Reborn: Essays in Feminist Philosophy. Al-Hibri, Azizah Y (ed) and Simons, Margaret A (ed).

Impressionism: A Feminist Reading. Broude, Norma.

Je, Tu, Nous: Toward a Culture of Difference. Irigaray, Luce and Martin, Alison (trans).

Moral Controversies: Race, Class, and Gender in Applied Ethics. Gold, Steven Jay.

Personal Love. Fisher, Mark.

Philosophy of Mind: An Introduction. Graham, George.

Politics, Gender, and Genre: The Political Thought of Christine de Pizan. Brabant, Margaret (ed).

Reason and Responsibility (Eighth Edition). Feinberg, Joel.

Rethinking Masculinity. May, Larry (ed) and Strikwerda, Robert (ed).

Shadow of Spirit. Berry, Philippa (ed) and Wernick, Andrew (ed).

Subject to History: Ideology, Class, Gender. Simpson, David (ed).

The Quality of Life. Nussbaum, Martha C (ed) and Sen, Amartya (ed).

Theoretical Perspectives on Sexual Difference. Rhode, Deborah L (ed).

Toward a Feminist Epistemology. Duran, Jane.

Transformations: Recollective Imagination and Sexual Difference. Cornell, Drucilla.

Varieties of Moral Personality: Ethics and Psychological Realism. Flanagan, Owen.

Woman and Modernity: The (Life)styles of Lou Andreas-Salomé. Martin, Biddy.

A Critique of Androgeny. Fouché, Fidéla.

A Question of Evidence. Nelson, Lynn Hankinson.

An Inquiry into Gender Considerations and Gender Conscious Reflectivity in Early Buddhism. Rajapakse, Vijitha.

Antigone's Mirrors: Reflections on Moral Madness. Pritchard, Annie.

Beautiful and Sublime: Gender Totemism in the Constitution of Art. Mattick Jr, Paul.

Beyond Equality: Gender, Justice and Difference in Beyond Equality and Difference, Bock, Gisela (ed). Flax, Jane.

Classical Theism, Panentheism, and Pantheism: On the Relation between God Construction and Gender Construction. Frankenberry, Nancy.

Commentator on 'Justice, Gender, and International Boundaries' in The Quality of Life, Nussbaum, Martha C (ed). Nussbaum, Martha C.

Commentator on 'Women and the Quality of Life' in The Quality of Life, Nussbaum, Martha C (ed). Valdés, Margarita M.

Communal Crisis in Community at Loose Ends, Miami Theory Collect, (ed). Andermatt Conley, Verena.

Community, Autonomy and Justice: The Gender Politics of Identity and Relationship. Caust, Lesley.

De deconstructie van het kleine verschil. Everts, Saskia I.

Difference and Domination: Reflections on the Relation Between Pluralism and Equality. Carens, Joseph H.

Duction, Or the Archaeology of Rape. Rendall, Steven.

En/Gendering Equity: Emancipatory Programs or Repressive "Regimes of Truth". De Castell, Suzanne and Bryson, Mary.

En/Gendering Equity: On Some Paradoxical Consequences of Institutionalized Programs of Emancipation. Bryson, Mary and De Castell, Suzanne.

Equal Respect among Unequal partners: Gender Difference and the Constitution of Moral Subjects. Herrera, María.

Equality and Sexual Difference in Beyond Equality and Difference, Bock, Gisela (ed). Cavarero, Adriana.

Feminist Aesthetics and the Spectrum of Gender. Morse, Marcia.

Formation of Theories and Policy of Difference of the Sexes (in Czechoslovakian). List, Elisabeth.

Gender and Epistemic Negotiation in Feminist Epistemologies, Alcoff, Linda (ed). Potter, Elizabeth F.

Gender and the Problem of Personal Identity. Dixon, Beth A.

Gender Treachery: Homophobia, Masculinity, and Threatended Identities in Rethinking Masculinity, May, Larry (ed). Hopkins, Patrick D.

Gender Trouble: Notes on One Book (in Czechoslovakian). Smejkalova, J.

Gender, Metaphor, and the Definition of Economics. Nelson, Julie A.

Gender, Subjectivity and Language in Beyond Equality and Difference, Bock, Gisela (ed). Violi, Patrizia.

Has Her(oine's) Time Now Come?. Silvers, Anita.

If Pornography Is the Theory, Is Inequality the Practice?. McCormack, Thelma.

Justice, Gender and International Boundaries in International Justice and the Third World, Attfield, Robin (ed). O'Neill, Onora.

Justice, Gender, and International Boundaries in The Quality of Life, Nussbaum, Martha C (ed). O'Neill, Onora.

Moments of Danger: Race, Gender, and Memories of Empire. Ware, Vron.

Natural Law and Gender Relations in Women's Rights and the Rights of Man, Arnaud, A J. Conti Odorisio, Ginerva.

One or Two Worlds: Separation or Coexistence? (in Czechoslovakian). LeDoeuff, Michèle.

Oppressive Texts, Resisting Readers and the Gendered Spectator: The New Aesthetics. Devereaux, Mary.

Post Communism's "Lost Treasure": Rethinking Political Agency in a Shifting Public Sphere. Mische, Ann.

Pre-Theoretical Assumptions in Evolutionary Explanations of Female Sexuality. Lloyd, Elisabeth.

Renaissance Madonnas and the Fantasies of Freud. Wiseman, Mary.

Reply to Richard Rorty's "Feminism and Pragmatism": Richard Rorty—Knight Errant. Skillen, Tony.

Sex and Social Roles in Rethinking Masculinity, May, Larry (ed). Grim, Patrick.

Standpoint Reflections on Original Position Objectivity. Bellon, Christina.

The Man Without a Penis: Libidinal Economies that (Re)cognize the Hypernature of Gender. Nash, Margaret M.

The Opinions of Men and Women: Toward a Different Configuration of Moral Voices. Holland, Nancy.

The Politics of Paradigms: Gender Difference and Gender Disadvantage in Beyond Equality and Difference, Bock, Gisela (ed). Rhode, Deborah L.

The Power and Powerlessness of Women in Beyond Equality and Difference, Bock, Gisela (ed). Elshtain, Jean Bethke.

The Right to Privacy versus Uniformitarianism. Machan, Tibor R.

GEOMETRY

On the Automorphism Groups of Finite Covers. Evans, David M and Hrushovski, Ehud.

Projective Geometries of Algebraically Closed Fields of Characteristic Zero. Holland, Kitty L.

Space-Time and Isomorphism. Mundy, Brent.

St Thomas on the Continuum: The Nature of Points in Physics and Geometry. Pearson, Paul A.

Substance and System: Perplexities of the Geometric Order. Wilson, Margaret D.

The Geometric Structure of the Universe in Philosophy and the Origin and Evolution of the Universe, Agazzi, Evandro (ed). Torretti, R.

The Hypotheses of Mathematics in Plato's 'Republic' in Greek Studies in the Philosophy and History of Science, Nicolacopoulos, Pantelis (ed). Karasmanis, Vassilis.

Three Diverse Sciences in Hobbes: First Philosophy, Geometry, and Physics. Sacksteder, William.

Visualizing as a Means of Geometrical Discovery. Giaquinto, Marcus.

Visualizing in Arithmetic. Giaquinto, M.

Vlastos on Elenchus and Mathematics. Seeskin, Kenneth.

GERGEN, J

Acceptance of a Theory: Justification or Rhetoric?. Chow, Siu L.

GERIATRICS

Ethics in an Aging Society. Moody, Harry R.

GERMAN

Bettering Our Condition: Work, Workers and Ethics in British and German Economic Thought. Chmielewski, Philip J.

Contemporary Political Culture. Gibbins, John R (ed).

Die Wirtschaftspolitik des Philosophen Jacobi. Hammacher, Klaus and Hirsch, Hans.

Directions and Misdirections (in Hungarian). Fehér, István M (ed).

Fichte's "Wissenschaftslehre" of 1794: A Commentary on Part I. Seidel, George J.

German Philosophy and Jewish Thought. Greenspan, Louis (ed) and Nicholson, Graeme (ed).

Herder's Aesthetics and the European Enlightenment. Norton, Robert E.

Philosophy and Philosophers: An Introduction to Western Philosophy. Shand, John.

Reappraisals: Shifting Alignments in Postwar Critical Theory. Hohendahl, Peter Uwe.

The Roots of Critical Rationalism. Wettersten, John R.

A German Attack on Applied Ethics: A Statement by Peter Singer. Singer, Peter.

A Reply to My Critics: A Testament of Thought (Includes Bibliography) in German Philosophy and Jewish Thought, Greenspan, Louis (ed). Fackenheim, Emil L.

Argumentation in Germany and Austria: An Overview of the Recent Literature. Kienpointner, Manfred.

Autonomy, Self-Consciousness and National Moral Responsibility. Wells, George Geoffrey.

Berlin on the Nature and Significance of Liberty in Terrorism, Justice and Social Values, Peden, Creighton W (ed). Paden, Roger K.

Bioethics in a Low Key: A Report from Germany. Leist, Anton.

Carl Schmitt, Hans Freyer and the Radical Conservative Critique of Liberal Democracy in the Weimar Republic. Muller, Jerry Z.

Das unerledigte Metaphysikproblem: Anmerkungen zur jümgsten Metaphysikdiskussion im deutschen Sprachraum. Ollig, Hans- Ludwig.

Dismantling Our Own Foundations: A German Perspective on Contemporary Philosophy of Education. Almond, Brenda.

Hegel, des années de jeunesse à la fondation du premier système. Depré, Olivier.

Hegel, Idealism, and Robert Pippin. Westphal, Kenneth.

Historicity, Historicism, and Self-Making in German Philosophy and Jewish Thought, Greenspan, Louis (ed). Dray, W H.

L'idéalisme allemand face à la raison théologique. Maesschalck, Marc.

La "Dialectique" de Schleiermacher. Brito, Emilio.

Liberalism and Nationalism in the Thought of Max Weber. Bellamy, Richard.

Looking at Carl Schmitt from the Vantage Point of the 1990s. Herz, John H.

Nietzsche and Nationalism. Diethe, Carol.

Philosophie et révélation dans l'idéalisme allemand: Un bilan. Maesschalck, Marc.

Questioning One's 'Own' from the Perspective of the Foreign in Nietzsche and Asian Thought, Parkes, Graham R (ed). Parkes, Graham R (trans) and Scheiffele, Eberhard.

The Early Phase in Spengler's Political Philosophy. Farrenkopf, John.

The Impact of Nationalist Ideology on Political Philosophy: The Case of Max Weber and Wilhelmine Germany. Wilson, H T.

The Origins of Social Darwinism in Germany, 1859-1895. Weikart, Richard.

The Problem of Leo Strauss: Religion, Philosophy and Politics. Reinecke, Volker and Uhlaner, Jonathan.

The Roots of All Evil: Lessons of an Epigram. Harries, Karsten.

Tragic Thought: Romantic Nationalism in the German Tradition. Simpson, Patricia Anna.

Über einen vermeintlichen Bruch im "Ältesten Systemprogramm des deutschen Idealismus". Hansen, Frank-Peter.

Vitalism, Empiricism, and the Quest for Reality in German and English Philosophy in The Crisis in Modernism, Burwick, Frederick (ed). Klein, Jürgen.

William Temple and the Bombing of Germany: An Exploration in Just War Tradition. Lammers, Stephen.

Work and *Weltanschauung* in Heidegger: A Critical Reader, Dreyfus, Hubert L (ed). Habermas, Jürgen.

GERVAIS, K

Recent Work on Death and the Meaning of Life. Fischer, John M.

GESTALT

Bad Faith, Good Faith, and the Faith of Faith in Sartre Alive, Aronson, Ronald (ed). Mirvish, Adrian M.

Gestalt Switching: Hanson, Aronson, and Harré. Wright, Edmond.

Kuhn Reconstructed: Incommensurability Without Relativism. Malone, Michael E.

Philosophy as a Sign-Producing Activity: The Metastable Gestalt of Intentionality in Analecta Husserliana, XXXIV, Tymieniecka, Anna-Teresa (ed). Gandelman, Claude.

Tacit Knowing, Gestalt Theory, and the Model of Perceptual Consciousness. Innis, Robert E.

The Gestalt Controversy: The Development of Objects of Higher Order in Meinong's Ontology. Sweet, Dennis J.

The Thinker and the Painter in Merleau-Ponty Vivant, Dillon, M C (ed). Taminiaux, Jacques M.

GESTURE

How Do Gestures Succeed? in John Searle and His Critics, LePore, Ernest (ed). Bennett, Jonathan.

The Future of Dance Aesthetics. Sparshott, Francis.

GETTIER, E

Gettier and Scepticism. Hetherington, Stephen Cade.

Induction and the Gettier Problem. Creath, Richard.

You Know What You Falsely Believe (Or: Pollock, Know Theyself!). Shope, Robert K.

GEYER, C

Die Aktualität der Metaphysik: Perspektiven der deutschen Gegenwartsphilosophie. Ollig, Hans- Ludwig.

GIACOMETTI

Giacometti's Art as a Judgment on Culture. Bell, Richard H.

GIAQUINTO, M

Certainty, Reliability, and Visual Images. Kirby, Kris N.

The Origins of Psychological Axioms of Arithmetic and Geometry. Wynn, Karen.

GIBBARD, A

Choice and Conditional Expected Utility. Rawling, Piers.

Critical Notice of Allan Gibbard *Wise Choices, Apt Feelings: A Theory of Normative Judgment*. Campbell, Richmond M.

Gibbard on Morality and Sentiment. Hill Jr, Thomas E.

Gibbard on Normative Logic. Blackburn, Simon W.

Gibbard's Conceptual Scheme for Moral Philosophy. Carson, Thomas.

Gibbard's Theory of Norms. Horwich, Paul.

Morality and Thick Concepts—II, Through Thick and Thin. Blackburn, Simon W.

Nonfactualism about Normative Discourse. Railton, Peter A.

Nonmoral Explanations in Philosophical Perspectives, 6: Ethics, 1992, Tomberlin, James E (ed). Sturgeon, Nicholas.

On the Importance of Conversation. Morris, Christopher.

Some Problems for Gibbard's Norm- Expressivism. Sinnott-Armstrong, Walter.

GIBSON, J

Determining the Primary Problem of Visual Perception: A Gibsonian Response to the 'Correlation' Objection. Glotzbach, Philip A.

Merleau-Ponty, Gibson, and the Materiality of Meaning. Sanders, John T.

Relativism in Gibson's Theory of Picture Perception. Boynton, David M.

GIBSON, W

Cyberspace: First Steps. Benedikt, Michael (ed).

GIDDENS, A

Giddens on Subjectivity and Social Order. Wagner, Gerhard.

Modernity and Self-Identity: Self and Society in the Late Modern Age. Gluck, Mary.

Reflexive Traditions: Anthony Giddens, High Modernity, and the Contours of Contemporary Religiosity. Mellor, Philip A.

GIERE, R

Natural Laws and the Problem of Provisos. Lange, Marc.

Ronald Giere's "Explaining Science: A Cognitive Approach". Resnik, David B.

GIFFORD, F

The New Problem of Genetics: A Response to Gifford. Smith, Kelly C.

GIFT

Given Time: I. Counterfeit Money—Jacques Derrida. Derrida, Jacques and Kamuf, Peggy (trans).

GILBERT, A

Power Rivalry-Motivated Democracy: A Response to Stephen Krasner. Gilbert, Alan.

GILES OF ROME

Giles of Rome on the Instant of Change. Trifogli, Cecilia.

GILES, J

James Giles on Personal Identity. Flew, Antony.

GILKEY, L

What Religious Naturalism Can Learn from Langdon Gilkey in God, Values, and Empiricism, Peden, Creighton (ed). Stone, Jerome.

GILL, C

Minds Ancient and Modern. Taylor, C C W.

GILLETT, G

Gillett on Consciousness and the Comatose. Serafini, Anthony.

Reply to Gillett's "Consciousness, Intentionality and Internalism". Velmans, Max.

GILLIGAN, C

An Ethic of Care: Feminist and Interdisciplinary Perspectives. Larrabee, Mary Jeanne (ed).

Caring about Justice. Dancy, Jonathan.

GOD

Empiricism, Fideism and The Nature of Religious Belief. Sweet, William and O'Connell, Colin.

Enthusiasm and Its Critics: Historical and Modern Perspectives. Wilson, Catherine.

Epistemic Probability and Evil in Our Knowledge of God, Clark, Kelly James (ed). Plantinga, Alvin.

Eternity and Special Theory of Relativity. Padgett, Alan.

Ethics with God and Ethics Without in On the Track of Reason, Beehler, Rodger G (ed). Penelhum, Terence.

Ethics: Religious and Secular. Pojman, Louis.

Evidence Against Anti-Evidentialism in Our Knowledge of God, Clark, Kelly James (ed). Kretzmann, Norman.

Evil and the Concept of God. Bishop, John.

Evil and the Love of God. McCullagh, C Behan.

Existing by Convention. Ferguson, Kenneth.

Experience and Natural Theology in Prospects for Natural Theology, Long, Eugene Thomas (ed). Long, Eugene Thomas.

Exploring the Concept of Spirit as a Model for the God-World Relationship in the Age of Genetics. Eaves, Lindon and Gross, Lora.

F E Abbot: Science, Nature, and God in God, Values, and Empiricism, Peden, Creighton (ed). Peden, W Creighton.

Faith and Fidelity as Interpreted by Gabriel Marcel (in Chinese). Kwan, Wing-chung.

Faith and Philosophy. Vaught, Carl G.

False Prophecy Versus True Quest: A Most Challenge to Contemporary Relativists. Agassi, Joseph.

Feminist Christian Philoosphy?. Johnson, Patricia Altenbernd.

Filial Gratitude and God's Right to Command. Lombardi, Joseph.

Finally Forgiveness in Foundations of Kierkegaard's Vision of Community, Connell, George B (ed). Berry, Wanda Warren.

From the Profane to the Transcendent: Japa in Tukārām's Mysticism. Pandharipande, Rajeshwari.

Gesetz, Befehle und Theorien der Kausalität. Hampe, Michael.

Getting Isaac Back in Foundations of Kierkegaard's Vision of Community, Connell, George B (ed). Mooney, Edward.

Gli influssi del Platonismo sul Neostoicismo senecano. Natali, Monica.

God Among the Signifiers. Crownfield, David.

God and Concept-Formation in Simone Weil in Simone Weil's Philosophy of Culture, Bell, Richard H (ed). Phillips, D Z.

God and Evil: Polarities of a Problem. Adams, Marilyn McCord.

God and Forgiveness. Londey, David.

God and Freedom: Reply to Jordan. Davies, Brian.

God and Perceptual Evidence. Draper, Paul.

God and Privacy. Falls-Corbitt, Margaret and McClain, F Michael.

God and Process in Logic, God and Metaphysics, Harris, James F (ed). Edwards, Rem B.

God and the Foundation of Moral Value. Tierno, Joel Thomas.

God and the Initial Cosmological Singularity: A Reply to Quentin Smith. Craig, William Lane.

God and the Problem of Loneliness. McGraw, John.

God and the Status of Facts. Peterson, John.

God and Time in Reasoned Faith, Stump, Eleonore (ed). Swinburne, Richard.

God as the Ultimate Meaning is the Primordial Source of All Meanings. Reck, Andrew J.

God's Estate. Taliaferro, Charles.

God's General Concurrence with Secondary Causes in Philosophical Perspectives, 5: Philosophy of Religion, 1991, Tomberlin, James E (ed). Freddoso, Alfred.

God's Obligations in Philosophical Perspectives, 6: Ethics, 1992, Tomberlin, James E (ed). Stump, Eleonore.

God, Determinism and Liberty: Hume's Puzzle. Wolfe, Julian.

God, Eternality, and the View from Nowhere in Logic, God and Metaphysics, Harris, James F (ed). Harris, James F.

God, Foreknowledge and Responsibility (in Chinese). Bar-On, A Zvie.

God, Greed, and Flesh: Saint Paul, Thomas Hobbes, and the Nature/Nurture Debate. Kramer, Matthew H.

Gott und Ereignis—Heideggers Gegenparadigma zur Onto-Theologie. Thurnher, Rainer.

Habermas: An Unstable Compromise. Meynell, Hugo.

Hartshorne and Creel on Impassibility. Shields, George W.

Hartshorne, God, and Relativity Physics. Griffin, David R.

Hasker on Middle Knowledge. Bertolet, Rod.

Hegel and the Gods of Postmodernity in Shadow of Spirit, Berry, Philippa (ed). Williams, Rowan.

Hegel on Religion and Philosophy in The Cambridge Companion to Hegel, Beiser, Frederick C (ed). Dickey, Laurence.

Herbert of Cherbury: A Much-Neglected and Misunderstood Figure in God, Values, and Empiricism, Peden, Creighton (ed). Pailin, David A.

Hold Not Thy Peace At My Tears: Methodological Reflections on Divine Impassibility in Our Knowledge of God, Clark, Kelly James (ed). Clark, Kelly James.

Homo capax Dei?. Klaghofer-Treitler, Wolfgang.

Hope in Reasoned Faith, Stump, Eleonore (ed). Mann, William E.

How Are Souls Related to Bodies? A Study of John Buridan. Zupko, Jack.

How Good/Bad is Middle Knowledge? A Reply to Basinger. Hasker, William.

How to Avoid Speaking of God: The Violence of Natural Theology in Prospects for Natural Theology, Long, Eugene Thomas (ed). Caputo, John D.

Hume on Natural Belief and Original Principles. Gorman, Michael M.

Ian Weeks's Disproof of God. Stainsby, H V.

If There Be a God, From Whence Proceed So Many Evils?. Chakraborty, Nirmalya N.

Il *Filebo* come una 'summa' del pensiero metafisico platonico. Bonagura, P.

Il posto della metafisica nel sapere umano: Il pensiero di Maimonide e eil suo influsso su S Tommaso d'Aquino. Pangallo, Mario.

Immortality: Objective, Subjective, or Neither? in God, Values, and Empiricism, Peden, Creighton (ed). Shaw, D W D.

In Defense of a Kind of Natural Theology in Prospects for Natural Theology, Long, Eugene Thomas (ed). Clarke, Bowman L.

Inductive Argument from Evil and the Human Cognitive Condition in Philosophical Perspectives, 5: Philosophy of Religion, 1991, Tomberlin, James E (ed). Alston, W P.

Inference to the Best Explanation and the New Teological Argument. Johnson, Jeffery L.

Infinite Return: Two Ways of Wagering with Pascal. Wetzel, James.

Infinity and Proofs for the Existence of God. Staley, Kevin.

Infinity in Theology and Mathematics. Le Blanc, Jill.

Innate Ideas and Cartesian Dispositions. Flage, Daniel and Bonnen, Clarence A.

Interrelating Nature, Humanity, and the Work of God: Some Issues for Future Reflection. Peters, Karl E.

Intolerable But Moral? Thinking About Hell. Jensen, Paul T.

Is a Natural Theology Still Viable Today? in Prospects for Natural Theology, Long, Eugene Thomas (ed). Clarke, W Norris.

Is God a Utilitarian?. Holley, David M.

Is God Good By Definition?. Oppy, Graham.

Is There a System in the Theology of Nicholas Lash?. Lamadrid, Lucas.

Islamic Ethical Vision. Michel, Thomas.

J L Mackie's Disposal of Religious Experience. Naulty, R A.

James Ross on the Divine Ideas: A Reply. Maurer, Armand A.

Jephthah's Plight: Moral Dilemmas and Theism in Philosophical Perspectives, 5: Philosophy of Religion, 1991, Tomberlin, James E (ed). Mann, William E.

Johannes Taulers Auffassung vom Menschen. Egerding, Michael.

John Duns Scotus on *Ens Infinitum*. Catania, Francis J.

John Locke's *Questions Concerning the Law of Nature*: A Commentary. Zuckert, Michael (ed) and Horwitz, Robert.

Judge William's Theonomous Ethics in Foundations of Kierkegaard's Vision of Community, Connell, George B (ed). Connell, George B.

Kann Gott reale Beziehungen zu den Geschöpfen haben? Logisch-theologische Betrachtungen im Anschluss an Thomas von Aquin. Liske, Michael-Thomas.

Kant, Wittgenstein e l'argomento ontologico. Paltrinieri, Gian Luigi.

Kants Weg von der Theodizee zur Anthropodizee und retour: Verspätete Kritik an Odo Marquard. Cavallar, Georg.

Kierkegaard's Ironic Ladder to Authentic Faith. Golomb, Jacob.

Kierkegaard's Teleological Suspension of Religious B in Foundations of Kierkegaard's Vision of Community, Connell, George B (ed). Westphal, Merold.

Knowing and Community in On Community, Rouner, Leroy S (ed). Moltmann, Jürgen.

Knowledge, and Our Position Regarding God. Baxter, Anthony.

L'antropologia teologica: Definizione, obiettivi, punto di partenza, metodo, divisione. Mondin, B.

L'interpretazione di Plotino della teoria platonica dell'anima. Szlezák, T A.

La compréhension chrétienne de Dieu comme amour et sagesse selon Schleiermacher. Brito, Emilio.

La experiencia noética de Dios (Interpretación sobre textos de Santo Tomás). Rodriguez Valls, F.

La metafisica del soggetto e l'origine dello spiritualismo filosofico occidentale. Masi, Giuseppe.

La Persona y su mundo: la cultura, la moral, el derecho y la sociedad familiar y política (III). Derisi, Octavio N.

La pro-fanazione Heideggeriana di Dio. Pellecchia, Pasquale.

Language, Interpretation and Worship—I in Religion and Philosophy, Warner, Marin (ed). Warner, Martin.

Language, Interpretation and Worship—II in Religion and Philosophy, Warner, Marin (ed). Lamarque, Peter.

Le ragioni del deismo in Voltaire's e nell'Enciclopedia. Nicolosi, Salvatore.

Leibniz and the Miracle of Freedom. Paull, R Cranston.

Leibnizian Essentialism, Transworld Identity, and Counterparts. Cover, J A and Hawthorne, John.

Leo Strauss's Understanding of Aquinas's Natural Law Theory. Kries, Douglas.

Logical Construction, Whitehead, and God in Logic, God and Metaphysics, Harris, James F (ed). Clarke, Bowman L.

MacMurray's World Community as Antidote to Kant's Theism. Lauder, Robert.

Making a Better World: Revisiting David Hume with Ian Markham. Loughlin, Gerard.

Malebranche, Models, and Causation in Causation in Early Modern Philosophy, Nadler, Steven (ed). Watson, Richard A.

Man and God in Philo: Philo's Interpretation of Genesis 1:26. Arieti, James.

Marx, God, and Praxis in Shadow of Spirit, Berry, Philippa (ed). Tavor Bannet, Eve.

Metafisica della soggettività e filosofia della libertà. Ciancio, Claudio.

Metaphorical Non Sequitur. Sontag, Fred.

Metaphysical Explanation and "Particularization" in Maimonides' *Guide of the Perplexed*. Goldin, Owen.

Métaphysique et politique: Le singe de Dieu, l'homme. Benoist, Jocelyn.

Middle Actions. Howsepian, A A.

Middle Knowledge and the Doctrine of Infallibility in Philosophical Perspectives, 5: Philosophy of Religion, 1991, Tomberlin, James E (ed). Flint, Thomas.

Miracles and Conservation Laws. MacGill, Neil Whyte.

Miracles and Conservation Laws: A Reply to Professor MacGill. Larmer, Robert A H.

Misologia ed irenismo: A proposito di un dialogo dottrinale e di ateismo in K Marx. Gnemmi, Angelo.

GOD

St Thomas, God's Goodness and God's Morality. Dewan, Lawrence.

St Thomas, James Ross, and Exemplarism: A Reply. Dewan, Lawrence.

Standing Alone Together: Silence, Solitude, and Radical Conversion. Staab, Janice.

Suárez and the Problem of Positive Evil. Davis, Douglas P.

Taking Morality Seriously. Almond, Brenda.

Temporal Actualism and Singular Foreknowledge in Philosophical Perspectives, 5: Philosophy of Religion, 1991, Tomberlin, James E (ed). Menzel, Christopher.

Temporal Consciousness. Grimbergen, Elizabeth.

Temporal Wholes and the Problem of Evil. Nelson, Mark T.

Temporality and Divinity: An Analytic Hurdle. Oakes, Robert.

That to Philosophise is to Learn How to Die. Lyas, Colin.

The Aesthetic Dimensions of Religious Experience in Logic, God and Metaphysics, Harris, James F (ed). Hartshorne, Charles.

The Analogy of Religion. Crosson, Frederick.

The Anselmian 'Single-Divine-Attribute Doctrine'. Hestevold, H Scott.

The Apocalypse of Community in On Community, Rouner, Leroy S (ed). Keller, Catherine.

The Argument from Evil in Philosophical Perspectives, 5: Philosophy of Religion, 1991, Tomberlin, James E (ed). Tooley, Michael.

The Birth of God in God, Values, and Empiricism, Peden, Creighton (ed). Sontag, Frederick.

The Book of the Philosophic Life. Butterworth, Charles E (trans), Muhammad, Abū Bakr and Al-Razi, Zakariyya.

The Concept of Kartrtva in the Nyaya-Vaisesika Philosophy. Sen, Brinda.

The Concept of Reading and the 'Book of Nature' in Simone Weil's Philosophy of Culture, Bell, Richard H (ed). Allen, Diogenes.

The Creator and the Integrity of Creation in the Fathers of the Church, Especially in Saint Augustine. Van Bavel, Tarsicius.

The Desire to Be God: Subjective and Objective in Nagel's *The View From Nowhere* and Sartre's *Being and Nothingness*. Wider, Kathleen.

The Doctrine of Conservation and Free-Will Defence. Jordan, Jeffrey.

The Eloquent Silence of Zarathustra in Nietzsche and Asian Thought, Parkes, Graham (ed). Parkes, Graham R (trans), Aihara, Setsuko (trans) and Muneto, Sonoda.

The Epistemology of Evil Possibilities. Tidman, Paul.

The Ethics of Santeria. Canizares, Raul J.

The Existence of God and the Creation of the Universe. Carloye, Jack C.

The Face of Chaos. Stenger, Victor J.

The Genealogy of God's Freedom in Spinoza's *Ethics*. Richey, Lance B.

The God of Abraham and the God of the Philosophers: A Reading of Emmanuel Levinas's "Dieu et la Philosophie". Bergo, Bettina.

The God of Love. Schmitz, Kenneth L.

The Gods above the Gods: Can the High Gods Survive? in Reasoned Faith, Stump, Eleonore (ed). Mavrodes, George I.

The Heidegger Controversy—Updated and Appraised. Wright, Kathleen.

The Incarnation and the Natural Law. McMahon, Kevin.

The Inscrutable Evil Defense Against the Inductive Argument from Evil. Sennett, James F.

The Intensity of Theism. Taliaferro, Charles.

The Intrinsic Value of Pain. Drum, Peter.

The Laws of Nature and of Nature's God. Crosson, Frederick.

The Limits of Theistic Experience: An Epistemic Basis of Theistic Pluralism. McLeod, Mark S.

The Locked Door: An Analysis of the Problem of the Origin of the Soul in St Augustine's Thought. Waddell, Michael M.

The Logic of Mysticism—I in Religion and Philosophy, Warner, Marin (ed). McCabe, Herbert.

The Meaning of 'God'—I in Religion and Philosophy, Warner, Marin (ed). Durrant, Michael.

The Meaning of 'God'—II in Religion and Philosophy, Warner, Marin (ed). Geach, Peter.

The Medieval Approach to Aardvarks, Escalators, and God. Rogers, Katherine A.

The Metaphilosophy of Meaning. Shalom, Albert.

The Miracle of Minimal Foundationalism: Religious Experience and Justified Belief. Bagger, Matthew C.

The Nature of God's Love and Forgiveness. Drabkin, Douglas.

The Necessary Non-Existence of God in Simone Weil's Philosophy of Culture, Bell, Richard H (ed). Williams, Rowan.

The Necessity of Theology and the Scientific Study of Religious Beliefs. D'Agostino, Fred.

The Occasionalist Proselytizer in Philosophical Perspectives, 5: Philosophy of Religion, 1991, Tomberlin, James E (ed). McCann, Hugh J and Kvanvig, Jonathan L.

The Ontology of the Eucharist. Sullivan, T D and Reedy, Jeremiah.

The Person as Resonating Existential. Connor, Robert A.

The Possibility of Power Beyond Possibility in Philosophical Perspectives, 5: Philosophy of Religion, 1991, Tomberlin, James E (ed). Conee, Earl.

The Primacy of God's Will in Christian Ethics in Philosophical Perspectives, 6: Ethics, 1992, Tomberlin, James E (ed). Quinn, Philip.

The Principle of Necessary Reason. O'Leary-Hawthorne, J and Cortens, A.

The Problem and Prospects of a Christian Philosophy—Then and Now. Veatch, Henry B.

The Problem of Divine Exclusivity. Jordan, Jeff.

The Problem of Service to Unjust Regimes in Augustine's *City of God*. Burnell, Peter.

The Rationality of Religious Belief. Rowe, William.

The Relevance of Philosophy to Life in Frontiers in American Philosophy, Volume I, Burch, Robert W (ed). Lachs, John.

The Religious Significance of Ricoeur's Post-Hegelian Kantian Ethics. Bourgeois, Patrick and Herbert, Gary.

The Revelation of the Holy Other as the Wholly Other: Between Barth's Theology of the Word and Levinas's Philosophy of Saying. Ward, Graham.

The Right to Welfare and the Virtue of Charity. Den Uyl, Douglas.

The Roles of Moral Dispositions in the Cognitional Theories of Newman and Lonergan. Miller, Edward Jeremy.

The Scope of Human Autonomy in Our Knowledge of God, Clark, Kelly James (ed). Schlesinger, George.

The Search for Implicit Axioms behind Doctrinal Texts. Ritschi, Dietrich.

The Status and Function of Divine Simpleness in *Summa Theologia* 1a, 2-13. Burns, Peter.

The Status of Politics in St Augustine's *City of God*. Burnell, Peter J.

The Suspension of the Ethical and the Religious Meaning of Ethics in Kierkegaard's Thought. Sagi, Avi.

The Tantalizing Absence of God. Dinan, Stephen A.

The Temptation of God Incarnate. Werther, David.

The Tragic and the Religious: Openness to the Mystery in Caputo's Radical Hermeneutics. Krantz, Susan F L.

The Use of Sophiology. Martz, Erin.

The Value of Harmony in Causation in Early Modern Philosophy, Nadler, Steven (ed). Frankel, Lois.

Theodicy: The Case for a Theologically Inclusive Model of Philosophy in Prospects for Natural Theology, Long, Eugene Thomas (ed). Dupré, Louis.

Theodizee oder Kulturgeschichte des Bösen? Anmerkungen zum gegenwärtigen Diskurs. Geyer, Carl-Friedrich.

Theological Clearances: Foreground to a Rational Recovery of God in Prospects for Natural Theology, Long, Eugene Thomas (ed). Schmitz, K L.

Theology and the Heisenberg Uncertainty Principle: I. Cardoni, Albert.

Theology and the Heisenberg Uncertainty Principle: II. Mooney, Christopher P.

Theology in an Evolutionary Mode. Schmitz-Moormann, Karl.

Theology, Praxis and Ethics in the Thought of Juan Luis Segundo. Zimbelman, Joel.

Theophanie und Schöpfungsgrund: Der Beitrag des Johannes Scotus Eriuguena zum Verständnis *der creatio ex nihilo*. Hoeps, Reinhard.

Thomas Aquinas on What Philosophers Can Know About God. Wippel, John F.

Thomas Aquinas' Double Metaphysics of Simplicity and Infinity. Sweeney, Eileen C.

Thomas, Thomisms and Truth. Marshall, Bruce D.

Thus Spoke Augustine. Frosolono, Anne-Marie.

Tillich's Implicit Ontological Argument. Russell, John M.

Timelessness, Omniscience, and Tenses. Garcia, Laura L.

Together Bound: A New Look at God's Discrete Actions in History. Kirkpatrick, Frank G.

Transcendence in Theism and Pantheism. Levine, Michael.

Transcendence, Instantiation and Incarnation—An Exploration. Durrant, Michael.

Transcendentie en Schepping. De Boer, T.

Transitions to and from Nature in Hegel and Plato. Browning, Gary K.

Triadische Götter-Ordnungen: klassisch-antiker und neuplatonischer Ansatz. Beck, Heinrich.

Trust, the Heart of Religion: A Sketch. Godfrey, Joseph J.

Trusting People in Philosophical Perspectives, 6: Ethics, 1992, Tomberlin, James E (ed). Baier, Annette.

Twelfth-Century Nominales: The Posthumous School of Peter Abelard. Iwakuma Y.

Two Concepts of Theodicy. Schuurman, Henry J.

Two Key Elements in Francis J McConnell's Social Ethics. Burrow Jr, Rufus.

V V Rozanov: An Interview with V G Sukach. Skorobogatko, Nataliia.

Victimization and the Problem of Evil: A Response to Ivan Karamazov. Tracy, Thomas F.

Visions of Narcissism in Merleau-Ponty Vivant, Dillon, M C (ed). Levin, David Michael.

Was Hume an Atheist?. Andre, Shane.

What Religious Naturalism Can Learn from Langdon Gilkey in God, Values, and Empiricism, Peden, Creighton (ed). Stone, Jerome.

What Went Before?. Rothman, Milton.

Whitehead's God and the Dilemma of Pure Possibility in God, Values, and Empiricism, Peden, Creighton W (ed). Crosby, Donald A.

Whitehead's God and the Problem of Evil. Thero, Daniel.

Who is Heidegger's Nietzsche? in Heidegger: A Critical Reader, Dreyfus, Hubert (ed). Havas, Randall.

Who Sets the Task? in Foundations of Kierkegaard's Vision of Community, Connell, George B (ed). Dunning, Stephen N.

Why Does God Allow This? An Empirical Approach to the Theodicy Question through the Themes of Suffering and Meaning. Hutsebaut, Dirk.

Why Does the Universe Exist?. Parfit, Derek.

Why Five Ways?. Johnson, Mark.

Why God is Not a Consequentialist. Chappell, T D J.

Why Heidegger's Godot Might not be Worth the Wait. Bruin, John.

Why Think There are any True Counterfactuals of Freedom?. Sennett, James F.

Why This World?. Brooks, David.

William of Auvergne on *De re* and *De dicto* Necessity. Teske, Roland J.

William of Ockham and Adam Wodeham. White, Graham.

Wittgenstein, Solipsism, and Religious Belief. Huff, Douglas.

Wohlverhalten und Wohlergehen: Der moralische Gottesbeweis in den Schriften Kants. Sala, Giovanni B.

Zagzebski on Power Entailment. Hasker, William.

'Ik geloof in God, de Vader, de Almachtige, Schepper van de hemel en van de aarde'. Geerstema, H G.

'The Wisdom of the Egyptians' and the Secularisation of History in the Age of Newton in The Uses of Antiquity, Gaukroger, Stephen (ed). Gascoigne, John.

GREENWOOD, J
In Defense of the Quine-Duhem Thesis: A Reply to Greenwood. Klee, Robert.

GREGORY OF PALAMAS
Visions of the Self in Late Medieval Christianity: Some Cross-Disciplinary Reflections. Coakley, Sarah.

GREY, W
A Critique of Deep Ecology? Response to William Grey in Applied Philosophy, Almond, Brenda (ed). Drengson, Alan R.

GRICE, P
Meaning and Expression in Mind, Meaning and Metaphysics, Mulligan, Kevin (ed). Liedtke, Frank.

GRIEF
On History, Charm, and Grief. Petricek Jr, Miroslav.

GRIFFIN, D
Process Theism Versus Free-Will Theism: A Response to Griffin. Basinger, David.

GRIMSHAW, J
Gender and Other Categories. Fisher, Linda.

GRISEZ, G
Consequentialism, Incoherence and Choice. Simpson, Peter and McKim, Robert.
Is Contraception Contralife? A Critique of Grisez et al. Rickert, Kevin.

GRISWOLD, C
Four Kinds of Metaphilosophy: Griswold on Platonic Dialogue. Quirk, Michael J.

GROARKE, L
Sources of Knowledge of Sextus Empiricus in Hume's Time. Popkin, Richard H.

GROSSMAN, M
Festive Celebration of Life as One of Santayana's Prime Values: A Comment on M Grossman's Presentation of Santayana's Ultimate. Saatkamp Jr, Herman J.

GROTESQUE
Dislocating the Everyday: David Lynch's Wild at Heart as Cinema of the Grotesque. Olivier, Bert.

GROTIUS
Philosophy and Government, 1572-1651. Tuck, Richard.
The law of War: Grotius, Sidney, Locke and the Political Theory of Rebellion. Scott, Jonathan.

GROUP
Sharing Responsibility. May, Larry.
Complete and Atomic Algebras of the Infinite Valued Lukasiewicz Logic. Cignoli, R.
Joint Action. Miller, Seumas.
Justice between Generations: Compensation, Identity, and Group Membership. Fishkin, James S.
Maximal Subgroups of Infinite Symmetric Groups. Baumgartner, James E, Shelah, Saharon and Thomas, Simon.
More on R. Wagner, Frank O.
On the Automorphism Groups of Finite Covers. Evans, David M and Hrushovski, Ehud.
On the Schur-Zassenhaus Theorem for Groups of Finite Morley Rank. Borovik, Alexandre V and Nesin, Ali.
On the Undecidability of Some Classes of Abelian-By-Finite Groups. Marcja, Annalisa, Prest, Mike and Toffalori, Carlo.
Single Axioms for the Left Group and the Right Group Calculi. McCune, William W.
There is No Sharp Transitivity on $q6$ When q is a Type of Morley Rank 2. Gropp, Ursula.
Undimensional Modules: Uniqueness of Maximal Non-Modular Submodules. Pillay, Anand and Rothmaler, Philipp.

GROWTH
Paradigma e visione in Thomas Kuhn. Meretti, Francesco.
Population Ethics: On Parfit's Views Concerning Future Generations. Pulvertaft, W Robert.
Russell and Whitehead on the Process of Growth in Education. Woodhouse, Howard.

GRUENBAUM, A
The Concepts of "Beginning" and "Creation" in Cosmology. Narlikar, Jayant V.
The Name of the Game: An Analysis of the Grünbaum Debate. Bos, Jaap and Maier, Robert.
The Origin and Creation of the Universe: A Reply to Adolf Grünbaum. Craig, William Lane.

GUARDINI, R
Incontro tra filosofia e teologia nella "Christliche Weltanschauung" di Romano Guardini. Bezzini, L.
Sulle tracce del postmoderno (I). Pellecchia, Pasquale.

GUATTARI, F
Nomads and Revolutionaries. Plant, Sadie.

GUENTHER
Basic Questions about Metaphysics of Technology: Spangler, Heidegger, Günther. Bammé, Arno, Kotzmann, Ernst and Oberheber, Ulrike.

GUEROULT, M
La philosophie de l'histoire de la philosophie de Martial Gueroult. Bernhardt, Jean.

GUIDANCE
Classical Taoism, the I Ching and Our Need for Guidance. Dixon, Paul W.

GUILT
Paul Ricoeur. Clark, Stephen.
A Plea on Behalf of the Innocent. Thompson, Janna.
Guilt as an Identificatory Mechanism. Greenspan, P S.
Guilt, Remorse, and the Sense of Justice. Kyte, Richard.
Il motivo della caduta dell'uomo primordiale nell'interpretazione di Carl Gustav Jung. Zuanazzi, G.
Innocence. Wolgast, Elizabeth H.

GUNN, J
Being Interested in Time: Autobiography and Repetition. Dupuy, Edward J.

GUNTHER, K
Application Discourse and the Special Case-Thesis. Dwars, Ingrid.
Justification and Application of Norms. Alexy, Robert.

GUPTA, A
A Boolean-Valued Version of Gupta's Semantics. Reyes, Marie La Palme and Reyes, Gonzalo E.
On Gupta's Book The Logic of Common Nouns. Bressan, Aldo.

GURU
The Tibetan Tshogs Zhing (Field of Assembly): General Notes on its Function, Structure and Contents. Jackson, Roger R.

GURWITSCH, A
Gurwitsch's Interpretation of Kant: Reflections of a Former Student. Allison, Henry E.
The Field of Consciousness: James and Gurwitsch. Arvidson, P Sven.

GUSTAVSON, J
Ethics from a Theocentric Perspective: A Critical Review of the Thought of James M Gustafson. Hoekema, David A.

GUY, A
The Torn Human Activity: A Response to Alfred Guy's "The Role of Aristotle's Praxis Today". Balaban, Oded.

GUYER, P
Kant's Aesthetics Between 1980 and 1990: A Bibliography in Kant's Aesthetics, Meerbote, Ralf (ed). Cicovacki, Predrag.

HAACK, S
On "Peirce and Logicism": A Response to Haack. Houser, Nathan.

HABERMAS, J
Los Limites de la Comunidad. Thiebaut, Carlos.
Postnational Identity: Critical Theory and Existential Philosophy in Habermas, Kierkegaard, and Havel. Matustik, Martin J.
The Emancipative Theory of Jürgen Habermas and Metaphysics. McLean, George F (ed) and Badillo, Robert Peter.
An Allegory of Modernity/Postmodernity in Working Through Derrida, Madison, Gary B (ed). Bernstein, Richard J.
Antimetaphysics and the Liberal Quandary. Kaplan, Leonard.
Applied Nietzsche: The Problem of Reflexivity in Habermas, A Postmodern Critique. Pickard, Dean.
Autonomy, Self-Consciousness and National Moral Responsibility. Wells, George Geoffrey.
Crisis and Life-World in Husserl and Habermas in Crises in Continental Philosophy, Dallery, Arleen B (ed). Baynes, Kenneth.
Das unerledigte Metaphysikproblem: Anmerkungen zur jüngsten Metaphysikdiskussion im deutschen Sprachraum. Ollig, Hans- Ludwig.
De-Divinization and the Vindication of Everyday-Life: Reply to Rorty. Bernstein, J M.
Deconstruction, Postmodernism and Philosophy: Habermas on Derrida in Derrida: A Critical Reader, Wood, David (ed). Norris, Christopher.
Derrida and Habermas on the Subject of Political Philosophy in Crises in Continental Philosophy, Dallery, Arleen B (ed). Thorp, Thomas R.
Explaining Technology and Society: The Problem of Nature in Habermas. Parsons, Stephen D.
Habermas and Pluralist Political Theory. Walker, Brian.
Habermas and Transcendental Arguments: A Reappraisal. Power, Michael.
Habermas on Heidegger and Foucault: Meaning and Validity in the Philosophical Discourse of Modernity. Visker, Rudi.
Habermas versus Lyotard in Judging Lyotard, Benjamin, Andrew (ed). Steuerman, Emilia.
Habermas, Adorno and the Possibility of Immanent Critique. Nuyen, A T.
Habermas: An Unstable Compromise. Meynell, Hugo.
Habermas: teoría del conocimiento y teoría de la sociedad. Aguirre Oraa, J M.
Heidegger and Habermas on Criticism and Totality. Kolb, David.
Historical Materialism Revisited in Terrorism, Justice and Social Values, Peden, Creighton W (ed). Murray, J Patrick and Schuler, Jeanne.
Jürgen Habermas on the Legacy of Jean-Paul Sartre: Interview. Wolin, Richard.
MacIntyre and Habermas on the Practical Reason. Doody, John A.
Métapsychologie et théorie de la communication Freud versus Habermas. Assoun, P L.
Neumann versus Habermas: The Frankfurt School and the Case of the Rule of Law. Scheuerman, Bill.
New Science, New Nature: The Habermas-Marcuse Debate Revisited. Vogel, Steven M.
Normatively Grounding 'Critical Theory' in Philosophical Interventions in the Unfinished Project of Enlightenment, Honneth, Axel (& other eds). Apel, Karl Otto.
Persoon, substantie en gemeenschap: Over de innerlijke samenhang tussen de positie van de liberals en de communitarians. Cobben, Paul.
Raison, argumentation et légitimation: Habermas, Apel et les apories de la communication. Cometti, Jean-Pierre.
Response: Meaning, Intentionality, and Speech Acts in John Searle and His Critics, LePore, Ernest (ed). Searle, John R.
Review: Bernstein, McCarthy and the Evolution of Critical Theory. Couture, Tony.
Sociocultural Evolution or the Social Evolution of Practical Reason: Eder's Critique of Habermas. Strydom, Piet.

HABERMAS, J

Staging the Life-World: Habermas and the Recuperation of Austin's Speech Act Theory. Kujundzic, Nebojsa and Buschert, William.

Sulle tracce del postmoderno (I). Pellecchia, Pasquale.

The Debate over Performative Contradiction in Philosophical Interventions in the Unfinished Project of Enlightenment, Honneth, Axel (& other eds). Jay, Martin.

The Problem of Community. Crocker, Nancy.

Thinking about Democracy and Exclusion: Jurgen Habermas' *Theory of Communicative Action* and Contemporary Politics. Hanks, Craig.

Universal Pragmatics and the Formation of Western Civilization: A Critique of Habermas's Theory of Human Moral Evolution. Whitton, Brian J.

Women and the "Public Use of Reason". Fleming, Marie.

HABIT

Paradigms and Barriers: How Habits of Mind Govern Scientific Beliefs. Margolis, Howard.

La virtù della giustizia: da "habitudo" ad "habitus": A proposito della giustizia "metaphorice dicta" in Alberto Magno e Tommaso d'Aquino. Canavero, A Tarabochia.

Suárez and the Unity of a Scientific Habit. Doyle, John P.

HACKING, I

Astronomy and Antirealism. Shapere, Dudley.

Sociology and Hacking's Trousers. Schmaus, Warren S.

HAINES, V

Further Fire: Reply to Haines. Levinson, Jerrold.

HALDANE, J

Science, Philosophy, and Politics in the Work of J B S Haldane, 1922-1937. Sarkar, Sahotra.

Theory, Taxonomy and Methodology: A Reply to Haldane's *Understanding Folk*. Churchland, Paul M.

HALLIWELL, S

Commentary on Halliwell's "The Importance of Plato and Aristotle for Aesthetics". Nehamas, Alexander.

HALPER, E

Commentary on Halper's "Some Problems in Aristotle's Mathematical Ontology". Cleary, John J.

HALPERIN, D

Commentary on Halperin's "Plato and the Metaphysics of Desire". Nussbaum, Martha C.

HAMLYN, D

D W Hamlyn's *Being a Philosopher*. Copleston, F C.

Unpacking the Black Box of Cognition. Gillett, Grant.

HAMMOND, D

Response to Hammond's "Expressivist Account of Educational Development". Eisenberg, John A.

HAMPSHIRE, S

Filosofia della mente ed etica in Stuart Hampshire. Reichlin, M.

HANDICAPPED

Disability, Handicap, and the Environment. Amundson, Ron.

HANSLICK, E

Something I've Always Wanted to Know About Hanslick. Kivy, Peter.

HANSON, N

Gestalt Switching: Hanson, Aronson, and Harré. Wright, Edmond.

HAPPINESS

see also Hedonism, Pleasure

Aristotle on the Perfect Life. Kenny, Anthony.

Government, Justice, and Contempt. Lane, Gilles.

La Città della Ragione: Per Una Storia Filosofica del Settecento Francese. Postigliola, Alberto.

Quality of Life, Health and Happiness. Nordenfelt, Lennart.

The Morality of Happiness. Annas, Julia.

Bertrand Russell's Characterization of Benevolent Love. Kohl, Marvin.

Can a Person be Happily Wicked? (Some Problems with Joel Feinberg's Contended Moral Defective). Ducharme, H M.

Clinical Ethics and Happiness. Devettere, Raymond J.

Comprehending *Anna Karenina*: A Test for THeories of Happiness. Hudson, Deal W.

Is God a Utilitarian?. Holley, David M.

Kant's Concepts of Duty and Happiness. Wahidur Rahman, A N M.

The Concept of the Highest Good in Kant's Moral Theory. Engstrom, Stephen.

The Happy Man in Criss-Crossing A Philosophical Landscape, Schulte, Joachim (ed). Schulte, Joachim.

The Moral Status of 'the Many' in Aristotle. Garrett, Jan.

Welfare, Happiness, and Pleasure. Sumner, L W.

HARBERS, H

Reply to Harbers and De Vries. Lynch, William.

What Does the Double Hermeneutic Explain/Justify?. Lynch, William.

HARDIN, R

Social Choice and Democracy in The Idea of Democracy, Copp, David (ed). Christiano, Thomas.

HARDING, S

Feminist Epistemology: Rethinking the Dualisms of Atomic Knowledge. Sells, Laura.

HARDWIG, J

Hardwig on Proxy Decision Making. Brody, Baruch A.

Justice within Intimate Spheres. Carse, Alisa.

Why I Know About As Much As You: A Reply to Hardwig. Webb, Mark Owen.

HARDY, G

The Physiology of Desire. Butler, Keith.

HARE, R

Ethical Essays, Volume II. Harrison, Jonathan.

Imagination in Practical Reason. Ray, Chad.

Kant's Dubious Disciples: Hare and Rawls. Papa, Edward.

Martha Nussbaum and the Need for Novels. Diamond, Cora.

Moral Realism and Objective Theories of the Right. Sherline, Edward.

Moral Rules, Utilitarianism and Schizophrenic Moral Education. McDonough, Kevin.

On Reasoning Morally about the Environment—Response to R M Hare in Applied Philosophy, Almond, Brenda (ed). Hill, Donald.

HARM

Accumulative Harms and the Interpretation of the Harm Principle. Kernohan, Andrew.

Future Generations: Present Harms. O'Neill, John.

Is It Less Wrong to Harm the Vulnerable than the Secure?. Howard-Snyder, Frances.

Learning to Do No Harm. Gillet, Grant R.

HARMAN, G

A Critique of Harman's Empiricistic Relativism. Haines, Byron L.

HARMONY

The Value of Harmony in Causation in Early Modern Philosophy, Nadler, Steven (ed). Frankel, Lois.

Two Interpretations of the Pre-established Harmony in the Philosophy of Leibniz. Kulstad, Mark.

HARNACK, A

Harnack and Hellenization in the Early Church. Rowe, W V.

HARNAD, S

Reaping the Whirlwind: Reply to Harnad's Other Bodies, Other Minds. Hauser, Larry.

HARPER, W

Choice and Conditional Expected Utility. Rawling, Piers.

HARRE, R

Gestalt Switching: Hanson, Aronson, and Harré. Wright, Edmond.

Il Realismo Epistemologico di Rom Harré (parte seconda). Musso, Paolo.

Structural Inquiry, Human Agency and the Contribution of Harré and Bhaskar: A Case Study of Wright's "Classes". Adkins, Barbara.

HARRINGTON, J

"The Commonwealth of Oceana" and "A System of Politics"—James Harrington. Pocock, J G A (ed) and Harrington, James.

HARRIS, E

Reply to Harris: On Formal and Dialectical Logic. Gordon, David.

HARRIS, L

Response to Leonard Harris in African-American Perspectives on Biomedical Ethics, Flack, Harley E (ed). Pellegrino, Edmund.

HARRIS, R

Comments on R Baine Harris's "Can We Have a World Philosophy?". Hubert, Jerzy Z.

HART, H

Hart's Legal Philosophy: An Examination. Bayles, Michael D.

Dworkin and Hart on The Law. Peak Jr, Ira H.

Spencer, Steiner and Hart on the Equal Liberty Principle. Gray, Tim.

HARTMANN

A Philosophical Appreciation. Pinkard, Terry P.

La teoría del objeto puro de A Millán Puelles. López, Jesús García.

HARTMANN, N

Document: Le Concept mégarique et aristotélicien de possibilité. Hartmann, Nicolaï and Narbonne, Jean-Pierre (trans).

Giovanni: Der Ethiker Nicolai Hartmann und die Religion. Hürlimann, Kaspar.

HARTSHORNE, C

Trinity and Process: A Critical Evaluation and Reconstruction of Hartshorne's Di-Polar Theism Towards a Trinitarian Metaphysics. Boyd, Gregory.

Asymmetrical Relations, Identity and Abortion. Dombrowski, Daniel A.

Charles Hartshorne and Subjective Immortality. Suchocki, Marjorie H.

Charles Hartshorne in Founders of Constructive Postmodern Philosophy, Griffin, David Ray (& others). Griffin, David Ray.

Hartshorne and Creel on Impassibility. Shields, George W.

Hartshorne, God, and Relativity Physics. Griffin, David R.

Hartshorne, Metaphysics and the Law of Moderation. Dombrowski, Daniel.

Infinitesimals and Hartshorne's Set-Theoretic Platonism. Shields, George W.

Is Human Existence in Itself Not of Ultimate Significance? A Challenge to Hartshorne's Idea of Ultimate Reality and Meaning. Sia, Santiago.

Musings of a Psychologist-Theologian: Reflections on the Method of Charles Hartshorne. Moore, Mary Elizabeth.

Process Theism and Physical Evil. Chew, Ho Hua.

Some Not Ungrateful But Perhaps Inadequate Comments About Comments on My Writings and Ideas. Hartshorne, Charles.

St Thomas Aquinas and Charles Hartshorne's Process Philosophy. Baldner, Steven.

The Philosophy of Charles Hartshorne. Cobb Jr, John B.

HARVEY, C

Phenomenology, Possible Worlds and Negation. Krysztofiak, Wojciech.

HASKER, W

Hasker on Middle Knowledge. Bertolet, Rod.

Rejoinder to Hasker. Zagzebski, Linda.

Should Peter Go To the Mission Field?. Craig, William Lane.

HEIDEGGER

Heidegger and the World in an Artwork. Singh, R Raj.

Heidegger and the World-Yielding Role of Language. Singh, R Raj.

Heidegger and Theology in The Cambridge Companion to Heidegger, Guignon, Charles (ed). Caputo, John D.

Heidegger et la poésie: De "Sein und Zeit" au premier cours sur Hölderlin. Vandevelde, Pol.

Heidegger in Dialogue with Hegel (Thanksgiving of W Biemel) (in Czechoslovakian). Biemel, W.

Heidegger on Realism and the Correspondence Theory of Truth. Tietz, John.

Heidegger on the Connection between Nihilism, Art, Technology, and Politics in The Cambridge Companion to Heidegger, Guignon, Charles (ed). Dreyfus, Hubert L.

Heidegger's Sache: A Family Portrait. Van Buren, E John.

Heidegger's Autobiographies. Van Buren, E John.

Heidegger's Concept of Truth: Semantics and Relativism. Holtu, Nils.

Heidegger's Interpretation of Kant's Concept of Metaphysics. Bandyopadhayay, Krishna Bala.

Heidegger's Logic of Disproportionality. Schalow, Frank.

Heidegger's Question of Being and the 'Augustinian Picture' of Language. Philipse, Herman.

Heidegger's Truth and Politics in Ethics and Danger, Dallery, Arleen B (ed). Richardson, William J.

Heidegger, Buddhism, and Deep Ecology in The Cambridge Companion to Heidegger, Guignon, Charles (ed). Zimmerman, Michael E.

Heidegger, Schizophrenia and the Ontological Difference. Sass, Louis A.

Heidegger, Vattimo y la deconstrucción. Berciano, Modesto.

Heidegger—The Work and the World-View (in Czechoslovakian). Habermas, Jürgen.

Heidegger: Between Idealism and Realism. Stepanich, Lambert V.

Husserl and Heidegger as Phenomenologists. Gorner, Paul.

I limiti della decostruzione del "soggetto" nella critica filosofica "postmoderna". Bosio, Franco.

L'ermeneutica e il problema della fine: A proposito di due contributi recenti. Fabris, Adriano.

L'Origine de la Responsabilité ou De la "Voix de la Conscience" à la Pensée de la "Promesse". Guest, Gérard.

La concezione dell'"evento" nella Stella della redenzione di Franz Rosenzweig e nel pensiero di Martin Heidegger. Casper, Bernhard.

La filosofia di Edith Stein. Ales Bello, A.

La Morale Bouleversée: La Question de l'Éthique chez Martin Heidegger. Moyse, Danielle.

La pro-fanazione Heideggeriana di Dio. Pellecchia, Pasquale.

La résurgence de l'aristotélisme de la Renaissance dans la philosophie politique de Cassirer. Rudolph, Enno.

Lacan's Philosophical Reference: Heidegger of Kojève?. Van Haute, Philippe.

Lask, Heidegger and the Homelessness of Logic. Crowell, Steven Galt.

Le Chemin et les tournants. Crétella, Henri.

Logos come fondamento: il superamento della metafisica nella riflessione heideggeriana su Leibniz. Di Bartolo, Luigi.

Metafisica e pensiero iniziale: Aspetti della Kehre alle origini del pensiero heideggeriano. Samonà, Leonardo.

Metaphysical Presence in Ethics and Danger, Dallery, Arleen B (ed). Chanter, Tina.

Metaphysics, Fundamental Ontology, Metontology 1925-1935. McNeill, William.

Mind/Action for Wittgenstein and Heidegger. Schatzki, Theodore R.

Mozart und Heidegger—Die Musik und der Ursprung des Kunstwerkes. Pöltner, Günther.

Mythe et révélation dans l'Étoile de la Rédemption: Contemporanéité de Franz Rosenzweig. Bienenstock, Myriam.

Of Derrida's Spirit in Of Derrida, Heidegger, and Spirit, Wood, David (ed). Rose, Gillian.

Ontology of Language and Ontology of Translation in Heidegger in Reading Heidegger: Commemorations, Sallis, John (ed). Escoubas, Eliane.

Parallels in the Conception of Science of Heidegger and Kuhn (in Hungarian). Schwendtner, Tibor.

Per una soggettività non più "animale": Heidegger critico di Husserl. Regina, Umberto.

Phenomenological Research as Destruktion: The Early Heidegger's Reading of Dilthey. Bambach, Charles.

Phenomenology and Metaphysics: Husserl, Heidegger, and Merleau-Ponty in Merleau-Ponty Vivant, Dillon, M C (ed). Margolis, Joseph.

Philosophy and Religion in the Thought of Kierkegaard. Weston, Michael.

Philosophy Beyond the Limits of Politics (in Dutch). Heyde, L.

Poetizing and Thinking in Heidegger's Thought. O'Connor, Tony.

Privilege of Presence?. Boeder, Heribert.

Psychological and Spiritual Freedoms: Reflections Inspired by Heidegger. Todres, Leslie A.

Questioning Heidegger's Silence in Ethics and Danger, Dallery, Arleen B (ed). Babich, Babette E.

Reading a Life in The Cambridge Companion to Heidegger, Guignon, Charles B (ed). Sheehan, Thomas.

Reading and Thinking: Heidegger and the Hinting Greeks in Reading Heidegger: Commemorations, Sallis, John (ed). Maly, Kenneth R.

Rechnendes Denken und besinnendes Denken: Heidegger und die Herausforderung der Leibnizschen Monadologie am Beispiel des Satzes vom Grund. Cristin, Renato.

Rethinking the Heidegger-Deep Ecology Relationship. Zimmerman, Michael E.

Rouse's Knowledge and Power: A Note. Dauenhauer, Bernard.

Soggettività e metafisica. Chiereghin, Franco.

Spirit's Living Hand in Of Derrida, Heidegger, and Spirit, Wood, David (ed). McNeill, Will.

Spiriting Heidegger in Of Derrida, Heidegger, and Spirit, Wood, David (ed). Krell, David Farrell.

Strumenti analitici per la comprensione della filosofia continentale. Marrone, P.

Sulle tracce del postmoderno (II). Pellecchia, Pasquale.

The Actualization of Philosophy and the Logic of 'Geist' in Of Derrida, Heidegger, and Spirit, Wood, David (ed). Wood, David.

The Computer as Component: Heidegger and McLuhan. Heim, Michael.

The Concept of Technique in Heidegger (in Chinese). Chang, Wing-wah.

The Development of Time Consciousness from Husserl to Heidegger in Analecta Husserliana, XXXI, Tymieniecka, Anna-Teresa (ed). Thomas, V C.

The Finitude of the World in Ethics and Danger, Dallery, Arleen B (ed). Held, Klaus.

The Heidegger Controversy—Updated and Appraised. Wright, Kathleen.

The Hermeneutics of the Technological World. Pöggeler, Otto.

The Justice of Mercy in Analecta Husserliana, XXXI, Tymieniecka, Anna-Teresa (ed). Doyle, David.

The Never Setting Sun (in Dutch). Oudemans, T C W.

The Problem of Closure in Derrida (Part Two). Critchley, Simon.

The Question of Being in The Cambridge Companion to Heidegger, Guignon, Charles B (ed). Frede, Dorothea.

The Rigour of Heidegger's Thought. Weatherston, Martin.

The Roots of All Evil: Lessons of an Epigram. Harries, Karsten.

The Temporality of an Original Ethics. Schalow, Frank.

The Trouble with Truth: Heidegger on Aletheia, Buddhist Thinkers on Satya. Kapstein, Matthew.

The Unity of Heidegger's Thought in The Cambridge Companion to Heidegger, Guignon, Charles B (ed). Olafson, Frederick A.

The Young Heidegger, Aristotle, Ethics in Ethics and Danger, Dallery, Arleen B (ed). Van Buren, E John.

Time and Phenomenology in Husserl and Heidegger in The Cambridge Companion to Heidegger, Guignon, Charles B (ed). Dostal, Robert J.

Ways of Knowing: The Creative Process and the Design of Technology. Glynn, Simon.

What Does "To Avoid" Mean? On Derrida's De l'Esprit. David, Pascal.

What Price Deconstruction? Derrida on Heidegger and the Question of Nazims: A Critical Study. Nevo, Isaac.

Whitehead, Heidegger, and the Paradoxes of the New. Bradley, J A.

Why Heidegger Wasn't Shocked by the Holocaust: Philosophy and its Defense System. Watson, James R.

Why Heidegger's Godot Might not be Worth the Wait. Bruin, John.

Wittgenstein + Heidegger on the Stream of Life. Schatzki, Theodore R.

Wittgenstein, Heidegger, and the Reification of Language in The Cambridge Companion to Heidegger, Guignon, Charles (ed). Rorty, Richard.

HEINTZ, R

The PSDA and the Depressed Elderly: "Intermittent Competency" Revisited. Shamoo, Adil E and Irving, Dianne N.

HEISENBERG

A Matter of Order in Greek Studies in the Philosophy and History of Science, Nicolacopoulos, Pantelis (ed). Goudaroulis, Yorgos.

The Hermeneutics of the Technological World. Pöggeler, Otto.

Theology and the Heisenberg Uncertainty Principle: II. Mooney, Christopher P.

HEJDANEK, L

L Hejdanek's Meontology: An Attempt of a Critical Explanation (in Czechoslovakian). Sousedik, S.

HEKMAN, S

Feminist Epistemology: Rethinking the Dualisms of Atomic Knowledge. Sells, Laura.

HELL

Belfagor: Machiavelli's Short Story. Sumberg, Theodore A.

Hell: The Logic of Damnation. Walls, Jerry.

The Problem of Hell. Kvanvig, Jonathan L.

Craig on the Possibility of Eternal Damnation. Talbott, Thomas.

Intolerable But Moral? Thinking About Hell. Jensen, Paul T.

The Problem of Hell: A Problem of Evil for Christians in Reasoned Faith, Stump, Eleonore (ed). Adams, Marilyn McCord.

HELLENISM

Ancient Concepts of Philosophy. Jordan, William.

Aristotle Transformed: The Ancient Commentators and Their Influence. Sorabji, Richard (ed).

Athens and Jerusalem: The Role of Philosophy in Theology. Bonsor, Jack A.

Collected Writings—Leonard E Woodbury. Brown, Christopher G (& other eds) and Woodbury, Leonard E.

Greek Philosophers of the Hellenistic Age. Kristeller, Paul O and Woods, Gregory (trans).

Thrasyllan Platonism. Tarrant, Harold.

A Theophrastean Excursus on God and Nature and its Aftermath in Hellenistic Thought. Mansfeld, Jaap.

Commentary on Martin's "Fate and Futurity in the Greco-Roman World". Boedeker, Deborah.

Converging Theory and Practice: Example Selection in Moral Philosophy. Vitek, William.

Doentes, Doença, Médicos e Medicina em Luciano de Samósata. Brandao, Jacynthos Lins.

Fate and Futurity in the Greco-Roman World. Martin, Luther H.

Nationalism and Transnationalism in Cicero. Nicgorski, Walter.

Philosophy and the Bible: The Areopagus Speech. Adams, Marilyn McCord.

HESTEVOLD, H
On the Experience of Tenseless Time. Oaklander, L Nathan.

HETEROSEXUALITY
Bodies that Matter: On the Discursive Limits of 'Sex'. Butler, Judith.
Woman and Modernity: The (Life)styles of Lou Andreas-Salomé. Martin, Biddy.

HEURISTICS
Natural Heuristics for Proof Construction: Part I—Classical Propositional Logic. Batens, Diderik.
Popper: fallibilismo o scetticismo?. Motterlini, Matteo.

HICK, J
Creenciay Racionalidad: Lecturas de Filosofía de la Religión. Romerales, Enrique (ed).
Ricoeur and Hick on Evil: Post-Kantian Myth?. Anderson, Pamela.
The Pluralistic Hypothesis, Realism, and Post-Eschatology. Heim, S Mark.
The Real or the real? Chardin or Rothko?. O'Hear, Anthony.

HIERARCHY
The Corporation as Anomaly. Schrader, David.
Fairness in Hierarchical and Entrepreneurial Firms. Green, Michael K.
Hierarchical Inductive Inference Methods. Koppel, Moshe.
Hierarchical Semantics for Relevant Logics. Brady, Ross T.
High and Low Thinking about High and Low Art. Cohen, Ted.
Higher Goods and the Myth of Tithonus. Lemos, Noah M.
Realms and Hierarchies. Kerr-Lawson, Angus.
Value Hierarchies in Scheler and Von Hildebrand. Gooch, Augusta O.

HIGHER EDUCATION
All the King's Horses and All the King's Men: Justifying Higher Education. Mendus, Susan.
Competence, Knowledge and Education. Hyland, Terry.
Conflicting Values in American Higher Education: Development of the Concept of Academic Freedom. Tandy, Charles.
Do the Poor Really Pay for the Higher Education of the Rich?. George, Rolf.
In Good Standing? The Position of Women in Higher Education. McConnell, David H.
In Search of a Calling. Buford, Thomas O.
Listening for the Call: Response to Professor Buford. Carbone Jr, Peter F.
The Nature of University Education Reconsidered (A Response to Ronald Barnett's *The Idea of Higher Education*). Aviram, Aharon.

HIGHER ORDER LOGICS
A Critical Appraisal of Second-Order Logic. Jané, Ignacio.
A Functional Partial Semantics for Intensional Logic. Lapierre, Serge.
Cantor's Power-Set Theorem Versus Frege's Double-Correlation Thesis. Cocchiarella, N B.
Eventual Periodicity and "One-Dimensional" Queries. McColm, Gregory L.
Is Higher Order Vagueness Coherent?. Wright, Crispin.
Montague's Semantics for Intensional Logic. Palme Reyes, Marie La and Reyes, Gonzalo E.
On Gupta's Book *The Logic of Common Nouns*. Bressan, Aldo.
Periodic Points and Subsystems of Second-Order Arithmetic. Friedman, Harvey, Simpson, Stephen G and Yu, Xiaokang.
Pure Second-Order Logic. Denyer, Nicholas.
The Analytical Completeness of Dzhaparidze's Polymodal Logics. Boolos, George.
The Interpretability of Robinson Arithmetic in the Ramified Second-Order Theory of Dense Linear Order. Hazen, A P.

HILBERT, D
Hilberts Methode der Idealen Elemente und Kants regulativer Gebrauch der Ideen. Majer, Ulrich.
Peirce, Turing and Hilbert: A Sketch of Pragmatism vs Formalism. Stewart, Arthur F.
Rappresentazione hilbertiana delle logiche quantistiche. Laudisa, Federico.

HILDEBRAND, D
Value Hierarchies in Scheler and Von Hildebrand. Gooch, Augusta O.

HILEY, B
Interpretation and Identity in Quantum Theory. Butterfield, Jeremy.

HILL, K
Nietzsche and MacIntyre: Against Individualism. Starrett, Shari N.

HILL, T
Environmental Virtue Ethics: A New Direction for Environmental Ethics. Frasz, Geoffrey B.

HILPINEN, R
On Peirce's Theory of Propositions: A Response to Hilpinen. Houser, Nathan.

HIMMELFARB, G
Gertrude Himmelfarb: A Historian Considers Heroes and Their Historians. Feuer, Lewis S.

HINDUISM
see also Karma, Reincarnation, Sankara, Yoga
"I Can Wait 40 or 400 Years": Gandhian *Satyagraha* West and East. Starosta, William J and Chaudhary, Anju G.
Gautama's Nyaya-Sutra with Vatsyayana's Commentary. Gangopadhyaya, M.
The Nyaya Theory of Linguistic Performance: A New Interpretation of Tattvacintamani. Mukhopadhyay, P K.
A Hindu Response to Derrida's View of Negative Theology in Derrida and Negative Theology, Coward, Harold (ed). Coward, Harold.
An Early Neo-Hindu Reception of Nietzsche by Sri Aurobindo Ghose (1872-1950) (in Dutch). Van Dijk, A M G.
Consecration in Igbo Traditional Religion: A Definition. Onwurah, Emeka.

From the Profane to the Transcendent: Japa in Tukārām's Mysticism. Pandharipande, Rajeshwari.
Indra's Postmodern Net. Loy, David.
Is "Adhikāra" Good Enough for 'Rights'?. Bilimoria, Purushottama.
Is *Anubhava a Pramana* According to Sankara?. Sharma, Arvind.
Italian Studies on Far Eastern Thought in Comparative Philosophy. Santangelo, Paolo.
Knowledge and the 'Real' World: Sri Harsa and the *Pramanas*. Ram-Prasad, C.
On Knowing by Being Told. Chakrabarti, Arindam.
On Matilal's Understanding of Indian Philosophy. Mohanty, Jitendra N.
Religious Concepts of 'World': Comparative Metaphysical. Pratt, Douglas.
Soft Natural Theology in Prospects for Natural Theology, Long, Eugene Thomas (ed). Smart, Ninian.
The *Trimūrti* of *Smrti* in Classical Indian Thought. Larson, Gerald James.
The Dignity and Indignity of Service: The Role of the Self in Hindu 'Bhakti' in Selves, People, and Persons, Rouner, Leroy S (ed). Carman, John B.
The Karmic A Priori in Indian Philosophy. Potter, Karl H.
Towards a World Morality. Chethimattam, J B.
Valmiki's Ramayana Revisited: Worship by Confrontation—Vidvesha-Bhakti. Amodio, Barbara A.

HINTIKKA, J
Hintikka *et* Sandu versus Frege *in re* Arbitrary Functions. Burgess, John P.
Hintikka's Game of Language. Kanthamani, A.
In Search of Explanations: From Why-Questions to Shakespearean Questions. Sintonen, Matti.
Phenomenology, Possible Worlds and Negation. Krysztofiak, Wojciech.
Reply to Hintikka and Sandu: Frege and Second-Order Logic. Heck Jr, Richard and Stanley, Jason.
The Cogito *cira* AD 2000. Smith, David Woodruff.

HIPPOCRATES
Alcmeon's and Hippocrates's Concept of 'Aetia' in Greek Studies in the Philosophy and History of Science, Nicolacopoulos, Pantelis (ed). Andrioupoulos, D Z.

HIRING
From Justified Discrimination to Responsive Hiring. Hall, Pamela.
Reasonableness, Bias, and the Untapped Power of Procedure. Adler, Jonathan.

HIRSCH, E
Reply to Reviewers. Van Inwagen, Peter.

HISTORIAN
Gertrude Himmelfarb: A Historian Considers Heroes and Their Historians. Feuer, Lewis S.

HISTORICAL MATERIALISM
see also Dialectical Materialism
A Critique of the Technological Interpretation of Historical Materialism. Duquette, David A.
Duquette and the Primacy Thesis. Shaw, William H.
Historical Materialism and Ethics: Eduard Bernstein's Revisionist Perspectives. Steger, Manfred.

HISTORICISM
"Historismus" e mondo moderno: Dilthey e Troeltsch. Cacciatore, Giuseppe.
Analecta Husserliana, XXXI. Tymieniecka, Anna-Teresa (ed).
Beyond Hegel and Dialectic: Speculation, Cult, and Comedy. Desmond, William.
Extensions: Essays on Interpretation, Rationality, and the Closure of Modernism. Watson, Stephen.
Hermeneutics Ancient and Modern. Bruns, Gerald L.
How Memory Shapes Narratives: A Philosophical Essay on Redeeming the Past. Plantinga, Theodore.
Praxiologies and the Philosophy of Economics: The International Annual of Practical Philosophy and Methodology. Auspitz, J Lee (ed), Gasparski, Wojciech W (ed) and Mlicki, Marek K (ed).
The Battle of the Books: History and Literature in the Augustan Age. Levine, Joseph M.
Ambiguity and Originality in the Context of Discursive Relations in Objectivity, Method and Point of View, Van Der Dussen, W J (ed). Boucher, David.
Being, Time, and Politics: The Strauss-Koljève Debate. Pippin, Robert B.
Comment and Publications in Objectivity, Method and Point of View, Van Der Dussen, W J (ed). Dray, W H.
De postmoderniteit en haar geschiedenis: Kanttekeningen bij Stephen Toulmins *Kosmopolis*. Tollebeek, Jo.
Deconstruction and the Teaching Historian. Anderson, Mary R.
Feyerabend, Realism, and Historicity. Yates, Steven A.
Hegel's Historicism in The Cambridge Companion to Hegel, Beiser, Frederick C (ed). Beiser, Frederick.
Historicism and Architectural Knowledge. O'Hear, Anthony.
Historicism and Universalism in Philosophy in Cultural Relativism and Philosophy, Dascal, Marcelo (ed). Quesada, Francisco Miró.
Historicity and Objectivity in Objectivity, Method and Point of View, Van Der Dussen, W J (ed). Rubinoff, M Lionel.
Historicity, Historicism, and Self-Making in German Philosophy and Jewish Thought, Greenspan, Louis (ed). Dray, W H.
Identità dello storicismo. Sorge, V.
Ideologies and Mentalities. Gordon, Daniel.
In the Tracks of the Historicist Movement: Re-assessing the Carnap-Kuhn Connection. Axtell, Guy S.
Methodology: History and Its Philosophy in Objectivity, Method and Point of View, Van Der Dussen, W J (ed). Atkinson, R F.

HISTORICISM

Naturalized Historicism and Hegelian Ethics. Pinkard, Terry P.

On Defining Art Historically. Oppy, Graham.

On Whether History has a Meaning in Objectivity, Method and Point of View, Van Der Dussen, W J (ed). Hunter, J F M.

Patterns of Historical Interpretation in Objectivity, Method and Point of View, Van Der Dussen, W J (ed). Christianson, Paul.

Pure Historicism and the Heritage of Hero(in)es: Who Grows in Phillis Wheatley's Garden?. Silvers, Anita.

The Historian and His Evidence in Objectivity, Method and Point of View, Van Der Dussen, W J (ed). Van Der Dussen, W J.

The Ironist's Utopia: Can Rorty's Liberal Turnip Bleed?. Phillips, Hollibert.

The New Historicism and Shakespearean Criticism: A Marxist Critique. Siegel, Paul N.

Voices of Silence: On Gregory Vlastos' Socrates. Nehamas, Alexander.

HISTORICITY

Die Gegenwart der Geschichtlichkeit: Neuere Arbeiten zur Heideggerschen Philosophie. Figal, Günter.

The Role of Historicity in Man's Creative Experience in Analecta Husserliana, XXXI, Tymieniecka, Anna-Teresa (ed). Kule, Maija.

W H Dray and the Critique of Historical Thinking in Objectivity, Method and Point of View, Van Der Dussen, W J (ed). Rubinoff, M Lionel.

HISTORIOGRAPHY

Soviet Marxism and Analytical Philosophies of History—Eero Loone. Pearce, Brian (trans) and Loone, Eero.

De opkomst en de ontwikkeling van het evolutionisme en de probleemhistorische methode van Vollenhoven. Bril, K A.

Doxographie, historiographie philosophique et historiographie historique de la philosophie. Frede, Michael.

Hegel and the Dialects of American Literary Historiography in Theorizing American Literature, Cowan, Bainard (ed). Jay, Gregory S.

Hume and the Historiography of Science. Wertz, S K.

Identità dello storicismo. Sorge, V.

La posizione storiografica del pensiero di Carlo Mazzantini. Rizza, Aldo.

Les principles d'Eduard Zeller concernant l'histoire de la philosophie. Steindler, Larry.

Non-Marxist Historiography of Today: The Evolution of Its Theoretical and Methodological Principles. Mogilnitsky, B G.

The Secret of the Man of Forty. Aronowicz, Annette.

Vico's Road and Hegel's Owl as Historiographies of Renaissance Philosophy. Verene, Donald Phillip.

Vollenhoven's Legacy for Art Historiography. Seerveld, Calvin S.

Vollenhovens probleemhistorische methode tegen de achtergrond van zijn systematisch denken. Tol, A.

HISTORY

"Les Fondateurs" and "La Découverte de l'Histoire": Two Short Pieces Excluded from "Everywhere and Nowhere," by Maurice Merleau-Ponty. Davis, Duane H (trans).

"Historismus" e mondo moderno: Dilthey e Troeltsch. Cacciatore, Giuseppe.

"Value" in Turn-of-the-Century Philosophy and Sociology. Blegvad, Mogens.

(Postmodern) Tales from the Crypt: The Night of the Zombie Philosophers. Maker, William A.

"An Essay on the Principle of Population"—T R Malthus. Winch, Donald (ed) and Malthus, T R.

"The Commonwealth of Oceana" and "A System of Politics"—James Harrington. Pocock, J G A (ed) and Harrington, James.

A Companion to Aesthetics. Cooper, David E (ed).

A History of Buddhist Philosophy. Kalupahana, David J.

A History of Western Ethics. Becker, Lawrence C (ed) and Becker, Charlotte B (ed).

An Essay In Post-Romantic Literary Theory: Art, Artifact, and the Innocent Eye. Fleming, Bruce.

An Historical Introduction to Moral Philosophy. Wagner, Michael (ed).

An Introduction to the Syllogism and the Logic of Proportional Quantifiers. Thompson, Bruce E R.

An Introductory Guide to Cultural Theory and Popular Culture. Storey, John.

Anthropologische Geschichtsphilosophie: Für eine Philosophie der Geschichte in der Zeit der Postmoderne. Ignatow, Assen.

Anti-Foundationalism: Old and New. Singer, Beth (ed) and Rockmore, Tom (ed).

Ascetic Figures Before and In Early Buddhism: The Emergence of Gautama as the Buddha. Wiltshire, Martin G.

Athens and Jerusalem: The Role of Philosophy in Theology. Bonsor, Jack A.

Between Philosophy and Social Science: Selected Early Writings. Horkheimer, Max and Hunter, G Frederick (& other trans).

Between Slavery and Freedom: Philosophy and American Slavery. McGary, Howard and Lawson, Bill E.

Bioethics Yearbook, Volume 2—Regional Developments in Bioethics: 1989-1991. Lustig, B Andrew (& other eds).

Central Readings in the History of Modern Philosophy: Descartes to Kant. Cummins, Robert (ed) and Owen, David (ed).

Chronotypes: The Construction of Time by John Bender and David E Wellbery. O'Malley, Michael.

Collected Works of Bernard Lonergan, V10. Doran, Robert M (ed) and Crowe, Frederick E (ed).

Common Sense, Science and Scepticism: A Historical Introduction to the Theory of Knowledge. Musgrave, Alan.

Contemplating Music: Source Readings in the Aesthetics of Music, Volume IV— Community of Discourse. Katz, Ruth (ed) and Dahlhaus, Carl (ed).

Contemporary Political Culture. Gibbins, John R (ed).

Context for Meaning and Analysis. Callaway, H G.

Critical Thought Series: 2—Critical Essays on Michel Foucault. Burke, Peter (ed).

Cultural-Political Interventions in the Unfinished Project of Enlightenment. Honneth, Axel (& other eds).

Democracy. Harrison, Ross.

Dialectical Social Theory and Its Critics. Smith, Tony.

East Asian Philosophy: With Historical Background and Present Influence. Ho, John E.

Empirical Theology: A Handbook. Miller, Randolph Crump (ed).

Encounters and Dialogues with Martin Heidegger: 1929-1976 — Heinrich Wiegand Petzet. Emad, Parvis (trans), Wiegand Petzet, Heinrich and Maly, Kenneth (trans).

Essais hérétiques sur la philosophie de l'histoire by Jan Patocka. Tucker, Aviezer.

Essays on Henry Sidgwick. Schultz, Bart (ed).

Explaining Explanation. Ruben, David-Hillel.

Fiat vita, pereat veritas: Nietzsche's Untimely Reflections on Hegel's Dialectic of History. Axiotis, Ares.

Fichte's "Wissenschaftslehre" of 1794: A Commentary on Part I. Seidel, George J.

Foundations of Philosophy of Science: Recent Developments. Fetzer, James.

Freedom by Orlando Patterson. King, Richard H.

Frontiers in American Philosophy, Volume I. Burch, Robert W (ed) and Saatkamp, Herman J Jr (ed).

G A Rauche: Selected Philosophical Papers. Louw, T J G.

Gender Politics and Post-Communism: Reflections from Eastern Europe and the Former Soviet Union. Funk, Nanette (ed) and Mueller, Magda (ed).

Government: Servant or Master?. Radnitzky, Gerard (ed) and Bouillon, Hardy (ed).

Greek Philosophers of the Hellenistic Age. Kristeller, Paul O and Woods, Gregory (trans).

Greek Studies in the Philosophy and History of Science. Nicolacopoulos, Pantelis (ed).

Hans-Georg Gadamer on Education, Poetry, and History: Applied Hermeneutics. Misgeld, Dieter (ed) and Nicholson, Graeme (ed).

Hegel and His Critics. Desmond, William J (ed).

Hegel on Logic and Religion: The Reasonableness of Christianity. Burbidge, John W.

Hegel's Grand Synthesis: A Study of Being, Thought, and History. Berthold-Bond, Daniel.

Hegel: Three Studies. Adorno, Theodor W and Nicholsen, Shierry Weber (trans).

History, Religion, and American Democracy (New Edition). Wohlgelernter, Maurice (ed).

Homo Religiosus ou L'Homme Vertical. Rostenne, Paul.

Hypatia Reborn: Essays in Feminist Philosophy. Al-Hibri, Azizah Y (ed) and Simons, Margaret A (ed).

Il "Peccato" in Cina: Bene e male nel Neoconfucianismo dalla metà del XIX secolo, by Paolo Santangelo. Elvin, Mark.

Il Destino della Famiglia Nell'Utopia. Colombo, Arrigo (ed) and Quarta, Cosimo.

Interpretation and Overinterpretation: Umberto Eco. Collini, Stefan (ed).

Isaiah Berlin: A Celebration. Margalit, Edna (ed) and Margalit, Avishai (ed).

John Dewey and American Democracy. Westbrook, Robert B.

Kierkegaard and Kant: The Hidden Debt. Green, Ronald M.

La Théorie qui n'en est pas une, or, Why Clio Doesn't Care. Steedman, Carolyn.

Liberalism and Modern Society: A Historical Argument. Bellamy, Richard.

Marx's Theory of History. Wetherly, Paul.

Melancholy Dialectics. Pensky, Max.

Metaphysics: An Outline of the Theory of Being. Sandok, Theresa (trans) and Krapiec, Mieczyslaw Albert.

Moral Philosophy: A Reader. Pojman, Louis (ed).

Nationalism, Colonialism, and Literature. Eagleton, Terry, Jameson, Fredric and Said, Edward W.

Nietzsche and Modern Times. Lampert, Laurence.

Objectivity, Method and Point of View. Van Der Dussen, W J (ed) and Rubinoff, Lionel (ed).

Our Knowledge of the External World. Russell, Bertrand.

Paradigms and Barriers: How Habits of Mind Govern Scientific Beliefs. Margolis, Howard.

Partial Visions: Feminism and Utopianism in the 1970s. Bammer, Angelika.

Persona ou la Justice au Double Visage. Trigeaud, Jean-Marc.

Perspectives on the History of Mathematical Logic. Drucker, Thomas (ed).

Phenomenology and Deconstruction, Volume II: Method and Imagination. Cumming, Robert Denoon.

Philosophical Interventions in the Unfinished Project of Enlightenment. Honneth, Axel (& other eds).

Philosophy and Government, 1572-1651. Tuck, Richard.

Philosophy of History (Second Edition). Dray, William H.

Philosophy—A Myth?. Verster, Ulrich.

Postnational Identity: Critical Theory and Existential Philosophy in Habermas, Kierkegaard, and Havel. Matustik, Martin J.

Reality, Knowledge, and the Good Life: A Historical Introduction to Philosophy. DeVries, Willem A.

Religion from Tolstoy to Camus. Kaufmann, Walter (ed).

Revisioning Philosophy. Ogilvy, James (ed).

Revolution and Continuity. Barker, Peter (ed) and Ariew, Roger (ed).

HISTORY

Postmodern Jameson in Postmodernism/ Jameson/ Critique, Kellner, Douglas M (ed). Donougho, Martin J.

Pre-History: The Debate Before Cohen in Marx's Theory of History, Wetherly, Paul. Cowling, Mark and Manners, Jon.

Presence in The Language of Art History, Kemal, Salim (ed). Lyotard, Jean-Françoise.

Probability and the Evidence of Our Senses in A J Ayer Memorial Essays, Griffiths, A Phillips (ed). Mellor, D H.

Pseudoethica Epidemica: How Pagans Talk to the Gods. Readings, Bill.

Questioning One's 'Own' from the Perspective of the Foreign in Nietzsche and Asian Thought, Parkes, Graham R (ed). Parkes, Graham R (trans) and Scheiffele, Eberhard.

Race and the Modern Philosophy Course. Immerwahr, John.

Rational Theology, Moral Faith, and Religion in The Cambridge Companion to Kant, Guyer, Paul (ed). Wood, Allen.

Raymond Aron: Kantian Critique of the 20th Century. Foblets, Marie-Claire.

Recognizing the Past. Jurist, Elliot L.

Refining Art Historically. Levinson, Jerrold.

Refining Not Defining Art Historically. Haines, Victor.

Reflections on *After Virtue* after Auschwitz. Chansky, James D.

Reflections on the Life and Works of Scotus. Wolter, Allan B.

Reid and Lehrer: Metamind in History. Schulthess, Daniel.

Remarks on the History of Science and the History of Philosophy in World Changes, Horwich, Paul (ed). Friedman, Michael.

Reply to Chakrabarti: Some Comments on Contraposition in European and Indian Logic. Dravid, N S.

Reply to Daniel Schulthess's "Reid and Lehrer: Metamind in History". Lehrer, Keith.

Romanticism and Revolution. Cranston, Maurice.

Romanticist and Realist Elements in Nationalist Thinking in the 19th Century. Kemiläinen, Aira.

Rousseau and the Problem of Community: Nationalism, Civic Virtue, Totalitarianism. Simon-Ingram, Julia.

Ruling Memory. Norton, Anne.

Russia and the West: The Quest for Russian National Identity. Groys, Boris.

Santayana's Whitman Revisited. Tejera, V.

Sartre and the Poetics of History in The Cambridge Companion to Sartre, Howells, Christina (ed). Flynn, Thomas R.

Sartre's 'Morality and History': A First Look at the Notes for the Unpublished 1965 Cornell Lectures in Sartre Alive, Aronson, Ronald (ed). Stone, Robert and Bowman, Elizabeth A.

Sartrean Structuralism? in The Cambridge Companion to Sartre, Howells, Christina (ed). Caws, Peter.

Secret, Heresy and Responsibility: The Europe of Patocka (Part I) (in Czechoslovakian). Derrida, Jacques.

Sequel to History: Postmodernism and the Crisis of Historical Time. Carr, David.

Shadow History. Popkin, Richard H.

Shadow History in Philosophy. Watson, Richard A.

Significación lógica del cambio de estructura de *El Capital* entre 1857 y 1866. Delgado, Manuel.

Skrach's Trace in the History of Czech Thought (in Czechoslovakian). Karola, J E.

Sobre predicciones y relatos. Fernández, Oscar.

Social Justice on Trial: The Verdict of History in Analecta Husserliana, XXXI, Tymieniecka, Anna-Teresa (ed). McBride, William.

Socrates' Two Concepts of the Polis. Yonezawa, Shigeru.

Some Recent Essays in the History of the Philosophy of Mathematics: A Critical Review. Tait, William.

Some Remarks on Science, Method and Nationalism in John Locke. Heyd, Thomas.

Sources of Knowledge of Sextus Empiricus in Hume's Time. Popkin, Richard H.

Specific Cultures and the Coexistence of Alternative Rationalities: A Case Study of the Contact of Indian and Greco-European Cultures. Shekhawat, V.

Spirit's Living Hand in Of Derrida, Heidegger, and Spirit, Wood, David (ed). McNeill, Will.

Sport: An Historical Phenomenology. Skillen, Anthony.

Stephen Jay Gould and the Contingent Nature of History. McRae, Murdo William.

Still More of My Life in The Philosophy of A J Ayer, Hahn, Lewis E (ed). Ayer, A J.

Stump, Kretzmann, and Historical Blindness. Griffiths, Paul J.

Terrorism and the Epochal Transformation of Politics. Allen, Wayne.

The Blasphemy of Alfonso X in Revolution and Continuity, Barker, Peter (ed). Goldstein, Bernard.

The Body in the City. Swensen, Cole.

The Body of the Future in The Body in Medical Thought and Practice, Leder, Drew (ed). Cassell, Eric J.

The Cards of Confusion: Reflections on Historical Communism at the 'End of History'. Elliott, Gregory.

The Changing Critical Fortunes of *The Second Sex*. Pilardi, Jo-Ann.

The Computer as Component: Heidegger and McLuhan. Heim, Michael.

The Concept of Quackery in Early Nineteenth Century British Medical Periodicals. Carter, K Codell.

The Continuity of Chinese Humanism in the Shang-Chou Period. Wong, Yeu-Guang.

The Development of Advaita Vedanta as a School of Philosophy. Potter, Karl H.

The Development of 'Jihad' in Islamic Revelation and History in Cross, Crescent, and Sword, Johnson, James Turner (ed). Sachedina, Abdulaziz A.

The Dignity of the History (in Hungarian). Cotroneo, Girolamo.

The Early Phase in Spengler's Political Philosophy. Farrenkopf, John.

The Early Reception of Nietzsche's Philosophy in Japan in Nietzsche and Asian Thought, Parkes, Graham (ed). Parkes, Graham R.

The Embodiment and Durations of Artworks. Krukowski, Lucian.

The Emergence of Nationalism as a Political Philosophy. Frisch, Morton J.

The End of History. Schroeder, Steven.

The End of History and the Last Man. Roth, Michael S.

The End of History in Hegel. Harris, H S.

The Errors of Linguistic Contextualism. Bevir, Mark.

The Face in the Sand in Philosophical Interventions in the Unfinished Project of Enlightenment, Honneth, Axel (& other eds). Schnädelbach, Herbert.

The First Twenty Years of Critique in The Cambridge Companion to Kant, Guyer, Paul (ed). DiGiovanni, George.

The Foundations of Axiology (in Czechoslovakian). Zboril, B.

The Future of Dance Aesthetics. Sparshott, Francis.

The Heidegger Controversy—Updated and Appraised. Wright, Kathleen.

The History of Philosophy and the Reputation of Philosophers. Rogers, G A J.

The History of the Theory of Natural Sciences in Greek Studies in the Philosophy and History of Science, Nicolacopoulos, Pantelis (ed). Noutsos, Panayiotis.

The Idea of a Female Ethic. Grimshaw, Jean.

The Idea of Enablement. Martin, Bill.

The Idea of Philosophical History. Loptson, Peter J.

The Impact of Nationalist Ideology on Political Philosophy: The Case of Max Weber and Wilhelmine Germany. Wilson, H T.

The Interrelations between the Philosophy, History and Sociology of Science in Thomas Kuhn's Theory of Scientific Development. Hoyningen-Huene, Paul.

The New Historicism and Shakespearean Criticism: A Marxist Critique. Siegel, Paul N.

The Orientation of the Nietzschean Text in Nietzsche and Asian Thought, Parkes, Graham R (ed). Parkes, Graham R.

The Origins of Social Darwinism in Germany, 1859-1895. Weikart, Richard.

The Possibility of Historical Knowledge. Pompa, Leon.

The Problem and Prospects of a Christian Philosophy—Then and Now. Veatch, Henry B.

The Problem of Service to Unjust Regimes in Augustine's *City of God*. Burnell, Peter.

The Question of *The Question of Hu*. Mazlish, Bruce.

The Secret of the Man of Forty. Aronowicz, Annette.

The Social Construction of Homosexuality. Thorp, John.

The Status of Politics in St Augustine's *City of God*. Burnell, Peter J.

The Story of Art is the Test of Time. Silvers, Anita.

The Troubled History of Part II of the 'Investigations' in Criss-Crossing A Philosophical Landscape, Schulte, Joachim (ed). Von Wright, George Henrik.

The Truth of Being and the History of Philosophy in Heidegger: A Critical Reader, Dreyfus, Hubert L (ed). Okrent, Mark.

The Voice of the Past in Kotarbinski's Writings in Kotarbinski: Logic, Semantics and Ontology, Wolénski, Jan (ed). Zarnecka-Bialy, Ewa.

The Wisdom of the Many: An Analysis of the Arguments of Books III and IV of Aristotle's *Politics*. Bookman, J T.

Thomists and Thomas Aquinas on the Foundation of Mathematics. Maurer, Armand A.

To Write in Latin or in the Vernacular: The Intellectual Dilemma in an Age of Transition—The Case of Descartes. Limbrick, Elaine.

Tocqueville and Democracy in The Idea of Democracy, Copp, David (ed). Holmes, Stephen.

Tragic Thought: Romantic Nationalism in the German Tradition. Simpson, Patricia Anna.

Twenty Years Before the End of the World: Political Remarks About the Meaning of Our Epoch. Dzarasov, Ruslan.

Two Trends in Modern Polish Thought. Kolakowski, Andrzej.

Un libro tedesco su Gramsci. Maggi, Michele.

Universal Pragmatics and the Formation of Western Civilization: A Critique of Habermas's Theory of Human Moral Evolution. Whitton, Brian J.

V V Rozanov: An Interview with V G Sukach. Skorobogatko, Nataliia.

Ventriloquism: Ecstatic Exchange and the History of the Artwork. Goldblatt, David A.

Vollenhovens probleemhistorische methode tegen de achtergrond van zijn systematisch denken. Tol, A.

Wanderers in the Shadow of Nihilism: Nietzsche's 'Good Europeans'. Parkes, Graham R.

When the Child is the Father of the Man: Work, Sexual Difference, and the Guardian-State in Third Republic France. Schafer, Sylvia.

Who Is Nietzsche's Epicurus?. Lampert, Laurence A.

Whose History? What Ideas? in Isaiah Berlin: A Celebration, Margalit, Edna (ed). Tamir, Yael.

Why Art History Has a History. Carrier, David.

Why Heidegger Wasn't Shocked by the Holocaust: Philosophy and its Defense System. Watson, James R.

Why Liberty is Devoured by Reason in History: Re-Reading Merleau-Ponty During the Days of the Soviet Revolution. Feher, Fererr.

William Temple and the Bombing of Germany: An Exploration in Just War Tradition. Lammers, Stephen.

Wreckage upon Wreckage: History, Documentary, and the Ruins of Memory. Rabinowitz, Paula.

Writing Music History: A Review Essay. Goehr, Lydia.

Writing the Holocaust/Writing Travel: The Space of Representation in Jorge Semprun's Le grand voyage. Silk, Sally M.

'Ces Petits Différends': Lyotard and Horace in Judging Lyotard, Benjamin, Andrew (ed). Bennington, Geoffrey.

'Scattered over Europe': Transcending National Frontiers in the Seventeenth Century. Southgate, Beverley C.

'The Wisdom of the Egyptians' and the Secularisation of History in the Age of Newton in The Uses of Antiquity, Gaukroger, Stephen (ed). Gascoigne, John.

HISTORY OF PHILOSOPHY

Good and Bad Shadow History of Philosophy. Livingston, Donald W.

La philosophie et son histoire: quelques réflexions à propos d'un livre récent de W J Courtenay. Lusignan, Serge.

Shadow History. Popkin, Richard H.

Shadow History in Philosophy. Watson, Richard A.

The History of Philosophy and the Reputation of Philosophers. Rogers, G A J.

HISTORY OF SCIENCE

Duhem and Continuity in the History of Science. Ariew, Roger and Barker, Peter.

Duhem face au post-positivisme. Brenner, Anastasios.

Historia de la ciencia y comunidades científicas. Schuster, Félix G.

HITLER

Hell on Earth: Hannah Arendt in the Face of Hitler. Dews, Peter (trans) and Rogozinski, Jacob.

Toward a Kierkegaardian Understanding of Hitler, Stalin, and the Cold War in Foundations of Kierkegaard's Vision of Community, Connell, George B (ed). Bellinger, Charles.

HOAGLAND, S

In Praise of Blame. Houston, Barbara.

Queer Ethics, or The Challenge of Bisexuality to Lesbian Ethics. Däumer, Elizabeth.

Why Lesbian Ethics?. Hoagland, Sarah Lucia.

HOBBES

Hobbes and Human Nature. Green, Arnold W.

Hobbes and the Social Contract Tradition by Jean Hampton. Zenzinger, Theodore.

Leviathan—Thomas Hobbes. Hobbes, Thomas and MacPherson, C B (ed).

Philosophy and Government, 1572-1651. Tuck, Richard.

Virtues and Rights: The Moral Philosophy of Thomas Hobbes. Ewin, R E.

Contexte des rapports intellectuels entre Hobbes et Locke. Rogers, John.

Filmer, Hobbes, Locke: Les cassures dans l'espace de la théorie politique. Lessay, Franck.

God, Greed, and Flesh: Saint Paul, Thomas Hobbes, and the Nature/Nurture Debate. Kramer, Matthew H.

Hobbes and Ethical Naturalism in Philosophical Perspectives, 6: Ethics, 1992, Tomberlin, James E (ed). Hampton, Jean.

Hobbes and the Equality of All Under the One. Mitchell, Joshua.

Hobbes and the State of Nature: Where are the Women?. McKinney, Audrey.

Hobbes on Opinion, Private Judgment and Civil War. Lund, William R.

Hobbes Without Doubt. Sorell, Tom.

Hobbes's Shortsightedness Account of Conflict. Murphy, Mark C.

Hobbes, Locke, Franzwa on the Paradoxes of Equality. Soles, David E.

Hume's Hobbism and His Anti-Hobbism. Flage, Daniel.

La Propriété chez Hobbes. Zarka, Yves Charles.

La 'Déclaration des droits de l'homme et du citoyen' (1789). Stucki, Pierre-André.

Le discours mental selon Hobbes. Pécharman, Martine.

Le roman philosophique de l'humanité chez Hobbes et chez Locke. Tricaud, François.

Science, Prudence, and Folly in Hobbes's Political Theory. Hanson, Donald W.

The Nature of Mind. Lucash, Frank S.

The Paradox of Power: Hobbes and Stoic Naturalism in The Uses of Antiquity, Gaukroger, Stephen (ed). Kassler, Jamie C.

The Rational Justification of Moral Restraint. Hill, Greg.

Three Diverse Sciences in Hobbes: First Philosophy, Geometry, and Physics. Sacksteder, William.

HOCKING, E

Selfhood, Nature, and Society: Ernest Hocking's Metaphysics of Community in On Community, Rouner, Leroy S (ed). Rouner, Leroy.

HODEIR, A

The Theory of Jazz Music "It Don't Mean a Thing...". Brown, Lee B.

HOEFFE, O

Das wiedergewonnene Paradigma: Otfried Höffes moderne Metaphysik der Politik. Gerhardt, Volker.

HOELDERLIN

El asesinato de la historia. D'Hondt, Jacques.

Heidegger et la poésie: De "Sein und Zeit" au premier cours sur Hölderlin. Vandevelde, Pol.

New and Old Histories: The Case of Hölderlin and Württemberg Pietism. Hayden-Roy, Priscilla.

The Roots of All Evil: Lessons of an Epigram. Harries, Karsten.

The 'Overcoming' of Metaphysics in the Hölderlin Lectures in Reading Heidegger: Commemorations, Sallis, John (ed). Janicaud, Dominique.

Über einen vermeintlichen Bruch im "Ältesten Systemprogramm des deutschen Idealismus". Hansen, Frank-Peter.

HOERSTER, N

Lebensrecht und Überlebensinteresse: Darstellung und Kritik einiger Thesen von Norbert Hoerster. Viefhues, Ludger.

HOESLE, V

Objektiver Idealismus und ökosoziale Marktwirtschaft. Melle, Ulrich.

HOFSTADTER, D

The Origins of Social Darwinism in Germany, 1859-1895. Weikart, Richard.

HOGARTH, M

Forever is a Day: Supertasks in Pitowsky and Malament-Hogarth Spacetimes. Earman, John and Norton, John D.

HOHFELD, W

Précis of *The Realm of Rights*. Thomson, Judith Jarvis.

Stringency of Rights and "Ought". Harman, Gilbert.

HOLISM

After the Demise of the Tradition: Rorty, Critical Theory, and the Fate of Philosophy. Nielsen, Kai.

Donald Davidson and the Mirror of Meaning. Malpas, J E.

Holistic Health and Biomedical Medicine: A Countersystem Analysis. Lyng, Stephen.

Précis of Holism: A Shopper's Guide. LePore, Ernest and Fodor, Jerry.

The Human Person: Animal and Spirit. Braine, David.

Atomism and Holism in the Vienna Circle in Advances in Scientific Philosophy, Schurz, Gerhard (ed). Haller, Rudolf.

Confirmational Holism and Bayesian Epistemology. Christensen, David.

Continuing Empiricist Epistemology: Holistic Aspects in James's Pragmatism. Nevo, Isaac.

Holism and Meaning. Young, James O.

Holism without Skepticism: Contextualism and the Limits of Interpretation in The Interpretive Turn, Hiley, David R (ed). Bohman, James F.

Holism, Hyper-analyticity and Hyper-compositionality. Block, Ned.

Holism, Interest-Identity, and Value. Morito, Bruce.

Holism: Revolution or Reminder?. Sapontzis, Steve F.

Holomovement Metaphysics and Theology. Sharpe, Kevin J.

Idealist Organicism: Beyond Holism and Individualism. Simhony, A.

Idealized Conceptual Roles. Rey, Georges.

La concepción estructural de las ciencias como forma de holismo. Moulines, C Ulises.

Le discours théologique et son objet: perspectives néo-pragmatistes. Viau, Marcel.

Le métier de médecin. Piguet, J Claude.

Mach's Razor, Duhem's Holism, and Bell's Theorem. Rohatyn, Dennis A and Labson, Sam.

Meaning Holism and Semantic Realism. Callaway, H G.

Moral Consideration and the Environment: Perception, Analysis, and Synthesis. Goodpaster, Kenneth E.

On the Body in Medical Self-Care and Holistic Medicine in The Body in Medical Thought and Practice, Leder, Drew (ed). Weston, Anthony.

Reply to Block and Boghossian. Fodor, Jerry and LePore, Ernie.

Reply to Critics. LePore, Ernest and Fodor, Jerry.

Sette paradigmi cosmologici: L'animale, la scala, il fiume, la nuvola, la macchina, il libro e il sistema dei sistemi. Bunge, Mario.

Should Environmentalists Be Organicists?. Norton, Bryan G.

State-Space Semantics and Meaning Holism. Churchland, Paul M.

The Ecology of Cultural Space in Cultural Relativism and Philosophy, Dascal, Marcelo (ed). Dascal, Marcelo.

Who or What Has Moral Standing?. Schönfeld, Martin.

Wittgenstein's Woodcutters: The Problem of Apparent Irrationality. Risjord, Mark W.

HOLMES, O

Justice Holmes and Judicial Virtue. Luban, David.

Peirce and Holmes in Peirce and Law, Kevelson, Roberta. Valauri, John T.

HOLMES, S

Tocqueville, Commerce, and Democracy in The Idea of Democracy, Copp, David (ed). Satz, Debra M.

HOLOCAUST

"One Isaac Waiting to Be Slaughtered": Halpern Leivick, The Holocaust, and Responsibility. Goodhart, Sandor.

Extraordinary Evil or Common Malevolence? in Applied Philosophy, Almond, Brenda (ed). Lackey, Douglas.

Fackenheim as Zionist in German Philosophy and Jewish Thought, Greenspan, Louis (ed). Greenspan, Louis.

Hannah Arendt and the Etiology of the Desk Killer: The Holocaust as Portent. Milchman, Alan.

Response to Douglas P Lackey's 'Extraordinary Evil or Common Malevolence?' in Applied Philosophy, Almond, Brenda (ed). Krizan, M.

Why Does Proximity Make a Moral Difference?. Vetlesen, Arne Johan.

Why Heidegger Wasn't Shocked by the Holocaust: Philosophy and its Defense System. Watson, James R.

Writing the Holocaust/Writing Travel: The Space of Representation in Jorge Semprun's *Le grand voyage*. Silk, Sally M.

HOLTON, G

Einstein, Michelson, and the Crucial Experiment Revisited. Adam, A M.

HOLY

Experience of the Holy in the Technological Age. Ott, Heinrich.

HOME

Heimat und das Fremde. Tani, T.

The Home as the Metaphysical Horizon of Human Life (in Czechoslovakian). Janat, B.

HOMELESS

Technology and Culture and the Problem of the Homeless. Lovekin, David.

HOMER

The Preservation of Homeric Tradition: Heroic Re-Performance in the *Republic* and the *Odyssey*. Klonoski, Richard.

War and Grace: The Force of Simone Weil on Homer. Poole, Adrian.

HOMOGENEITY

Rethinking Objective Homogeneity: Statistical Versus Ontic Approaches. Burnor, Richard.

Some Disquiet about "Difference". Sypnowich, C A.

HOMOLOGY

On the Necessity of an Archetypal Concept in Morphology: With Special Reference to the Concepts of "Structure" and "Homology". Young, Bruce A.

HOMONYMY
Ahnlichkeit, Analogie und Homonymie bei Aristoteles. Rapp, Christof.

HOMOPHOBIA
A Critique of Androgeny. Fouché, Fidéla.

Abjection and Oppression in Crises in Continental Philosophy, Dallery, Arleen B (ed). Young, Iris Marion.

Gender Treachery: Homophobia, Masculinity, and Threatended Identities in Rethinking Masculinity, May, Larry (ed). Hopkins, Patrick D.

Who is that Masked Woman? Reflections on Power, Privilege, and Home-ophobia in Revisioning Philosophy, Ogilvy, James (ed). Scheman, Naomi.

HOMOSEXUALITY
Buddhism, Sexuality, and Gender. Cabezón, José I (ed).

Moral Controversies: Race, Class, and Gender in Applied Ethics. Gold, Steven Jay.

Morality and Moral Controversies (Third Edition). Arthur, John (ed).

An Ethos of Lesbian and Gay Existence. Blasius, Mark.

Aquinas on Disordered Pleasures and Conditions. Daly, Anthony C.

Gay Jocks: A Phenomenology of Gay Men in Athletics in Rethinking Masculinity, May, Larry (ed). Pronger, Brian.

Homosexuality: Right or Wrong?. Ruse, Michael E.

Love and Lust Revisited in Applied Philosophy, Almond, Brenda (ed). Stafford, J Martin.

The Social Construction of Homosexuality. Thorp, John.

HONDERICH, T
Anomalous Monism and Epiphenomenalism: A Reply to Honderich. Smith, Peter.

Conservatism: A Reply to Ted Honderich. O'Sullivan, Noel.

HONESTY
Development of Ethical Awareness: A Model for a Community Business Ethics Forum. Cleary, Claudia M and Kendree, Jack M.

L'aspect de l'esthétique de l'honnête homme (in Japanese). Shihara, Nobuhiro.

'Safe Enough in his Honesty and Prudence': The Ordinary Conduct of Government in the Thought of John Locke. Anderson, Christopher.

HONNEFELDER, L
Die Aktualität der Metaphysik: Perspektiven der deutschen Gegenwartsphilosophie. Ollig, Hans- Ludwig.

HONOR
Honor: Emasculation and Empowerment in Rethinking Masculinity, May, Larry (ed). Harris, Leonard.

HOOKE, R
Robert Hooke, Physico-Mythology, Knowledge of the World of the Ancients and Knowledge ... in The Uses of Antiquity, Gaukroger, Stephen (ed). Birkett, Kirsten and Oldroyd, David.

HOOKS, B
Piecings from a Second Reader. Alexander, Natalie.

HOOSE, B
Liberty Under the Moral Law: On B Hoose's Critique of the Grisez-Finnis Theory of Human Good. George, Robert P.

HOPE
Hope in Reasoned Faith, Stump, Eleonore (ed). Mann, William E.

HORGAN, T
Reply to Reviewers. Van Inwagen, Peter.

HORIZON
Husserl's Concept of Horizon: An Attempt at Reappraisal in Analecta Husserliana, XXXI, Tymieniecka, Anna-Teresa (ed). Kwan, Tze-Wan.

HOROWITZ, I
The Pragmatic Psyche. Bogdan, Radu J.

HORROR
Carl Schmitt: The Conservative Revolutionary Habitus and the Aesthetics of Horror. Wolin, Richard.

Horror, Helplessness, and Vulnerability: A Reply to Robert Solomon. Carroll, Noël.

Noël Carroll's The Philosophy of Horror or Paradoxes of the Heart. Levinson, Jerrold.

Nuclear Holocaust in American Films. Byrne, Edmund F.

HORWICH, P
Critical Notice: Paul Horwich's Truth. Field, Hartry.

On the Coherence of Instrumentalism. Kukla, Andre.

HOSPITAL
Drawing the Line: Life, Death, and Ethical Choices in an American Hospital. Gorovitz, Samuel.

The Role of the Hospital in the Evolution of Elite Cultures of Medicine. Dixon, Kathleen.

Triage in the ICU. Truog, Robert D.

HOSPITALITY
Education as Hospitality: The Reclamation of Cultural Metaphor and Narrative. Losito, William F.

Hospitality and Its Discontents: A Response to Losito. Mulvaney, Robert J.

HOSTETLER, K
Deconstructing Solidarity: Or, A Funny Thing Happened On the Way to Unity. Kohli, Wendy R.

HOULGATE, S
Reply to Houlgate and Pinkard. Wood, Allen.

HOUSTON, B
On Children's Rights: A Response to Barbara Houston. Glass, Ronald.

HOWARD, H
Henry Howard and the Lawful Regiment of Women. Shephard, Amanda.

HOWSON, C
Howson and Franklin on Prediction. Maher, Patrick.

HSUN TZU
Mengzi and Xunzi: Two Views of Human Agency. Van Norden, Bryan.

HUAI-NAN-TZU
The Huai-nan Tzu Alteration. Alt, Wayne.

HUBERT, J
A Note on J Hubert's "Towards a Positive Universalism". Myers, William.

HUGHES, C
Miracles, Laws of Nature and Causation—II. Adams, Robert Merrihew.

HUI SHIH
Hui Shih and Kung Sun Lung an Approach from Contemporary Logic. Lucas, Thierry.

HUIZINGA, J
Historical Interpretation and Mental Images of Culture (in Dutch). Kuiper, Mark.

HUMAN
see also Man, Person

Aquinas on Human Action: A Theory of Practice. McInerny, Ralph.

De re and de corpore (in French). Casati, Roberto.

Divine Hiddenness and Human Reason. Schellenberg, J L.

Homo Religiosus ou L'Homme Vertical. Rostenne, Paul.

Human Beings. Cockburn, David (ed).

The Ethics and Politics of Human Experimentation. McNeill, Paul M.

The Human Person: Animal and Spirit. Braine, David.

The Structure of Value. Allen, R T.

Animal Minds. Sorabji, Richard.

Are People Programmed to be Normal? in Probability and Rationality, Eells, Ellery (ed). Scigala, Ireneusz T.

Artificial Decision-Making and Artificial Ethics: A Management Concern. Khalil, Omar E.

Conscience and Norm. Rotenstreich, Nathan.

Culture as a Human Form of Life: A Romantic Reading of Wittgenstein. Lurie, Yuval.

Evolutionary Explanations of Human Behaviour. Sterelny, Kim.

How Many Selves Make Me?—II in Human Beings, Cockburn, David (ed). Wilkes, Kathleen V.

Human Finitude, Ineffability, Idealism, Contingency. Moore, A W.

Imagination and the Sense of Identity in Human Beings, Cockburn, David (ed). Hertzberg, Lars.

La metafisica della vita secondo A T Tymieniecka. Barral, Mary-Rose.

Liberty Under the Moral Law: On B Hoose's Critique of the Grisez-Finnis Theory of Human Good. George, Robert P.

Mind's Crisis: On Anaxagoras' Nous. Laks, André.

Moral Sensibilities and Moral Standing: Caplan on Xenograft "Donors". Nelson, James Lindemann.

Nature and Value in Aristotle's Nichomachean Ethics. Sim, May.

Necesidad de una renovación ética. López Quintás, Alfonso.

Personsein und Menschendwürde bei Thomas von Aquin and Martin Luther. Schockenhoff, Eberhard.

Real Selves: Persons as a Substantial Kind in Human Beings, Cockburn, David (ed). Lowe, E J.

Reply to André Laks on Anaxagoras' Nous. DeFilippo, Joseph G.

Response to "The Nature and Evolution of Human Language: Commentary". Sheets-Johnstone, Maxine.

Response to Diamond's 'The Importance of Being Human' in Human Beings, Cockburn, David (ed). McNaughton, David.

Response to McNaughton's 'The Importance of Being Human' in Human Beings, Cockburn, David (ed). Diamond, Cora.

The Early Marx on Needs. Chitty, Andrew.

The Human Being as a Logical Thinker. Balzer, Noel.

The Importance of Being Human—I in Human Beings, Cockburn, David (ed). Diamond, Cora.

The Importance of Being Human—II in Human Beings, Cockburn, David (ed). McNaughton, David.

The Incommunicability of Human Persons. Crosby, John F.

The Nature and Evolution of Human Language: Commentary. Bishop, Michael A.

The Rise and Fall of Evolutionary Thinking Among American Philosophers. Auxier, Randall.

The Risks of Going Natural. Storl, Heidi.

Theophrastus and Aristotle on Animal Intelligence in Theophrastus, Fortenbaugh, W W (ed). Cole, Eve.

Vita Humana: Hannah Arendt zu den Bedingungen tätigen Menschseins. Splett, Jörg.

What's Wrong With Murder? Some Thoughts on Human and Animal Killing. Everitt, Nicholas.

Wittgenstein on Voluntary Actions. Arregui, Jorge V.

HUMAN CONDITION
Gabriel Marcel's Philosophy of Human Nature. Hammond, Julien.

Johannes Taulers Auffassung vom Menschen. Egerding, Michael.

St Augustine's View of the Original Human Condition in De Genesi contra Manichaeos. Teske, Roland J.

HUMAN NATURE
A Case For Legal Ethics: Legal Ethics as a Source for a Universal Ethic. Luizzi, Vincent.

A Progress of Sentiments: Reflections on Hume's "Treatise". Baier, Annette.

HUMAN NATURE

A Treatise of Human Nature—David Hume. Mossner, Ernest C (ed).

Dialogues Concerning Natural Religion—David Hume. Hume, David and Bell, Martin (ed).

Éléments d'une Philosophie Politique. Trigeaud, Jean-Marc.

Hobbes and Human Nature. Green, Arnold W.

In Search of the Ethical: Moral Theory in Twentieth Century America. Edel, Abraham.

Leviathan—Thomas Hobbes. Hobbes, Thomas and MacPherson, C B (ed).

Method—Towards a Study of Humankind, Volume I: The Nature of Nature. Morin, Edgar and Bélanger, J L Roland (trans).

Rediscovering the Moral Life. Gouinlock, James.

The Ethical Foundations of Hume's Theory of Politics. Kolin, Andrew.

The Human Person: Animal and Spirit. Braine, David.

The Metaphysics of Edmund Burke. Pappin III, Joseph L.

Thucydides: On Justice, Power, and Human Nature. Woodruff, Paul B (ed & trans) and Thucydides.

Understanding Non-Western Philosophy: Introductory Readings. Bonevac, Daniel A and Phillips, Stephen.

Varieties of Moral Personality: Ethics and Psychological Realism. Flanagan, Owen.

A Hermeneutic Reconstruction of the Child in the Well Example. Allinson, Robert E.

Aquinas on Disordered Pleasures and Conditions. Daly, Anthony C.

Can Neuroscience Provide a Complete Account of Human Nature? A Reply to Roger Sperry. Jones, James W.

Claves para la paz. Mauri, Margarita.

Continuity, Consciousness, and Identity in Hume's Philosophy. Yandell, Keith E.

Duhkha: An Analysis of Buddhist Clue to Understand Human Nature. Chinchore, Mangala R.

Gabriel Marcel's Philosophy of Human Nature. Hammond, Julien.

God and Evil: Polarities of a Problem. Adams, Marilyn McCord.

Human Nature and Ethical Standards. Luizzi, Vincent.

Human Nature and Human Education in Chinese Foundations for Moral Education and Character Development, Van Doan, Tran (ed). Fu, Pei-Jung.

Human Nature as the Foundation of Moral Obligation. Hicks, Alan.

Hume and the Contexts of Politics. Dees, Richard.

Le système chez Hume: une écriture stratégique et théâtrale. Biziou, Michaël.

Leibniz and the Miracle of Freedom. Paull, R Cranston.

Machiavelli's Momentary "Machiavellian Moment": A Reconsideration of Pocock's Treatment of the *Discourses*. Sullivan, Vickie B.

Machiavelli, Violence, and History. Minter, Adam.

Mencius and Kant on Moral Failure. Kerman, Deborah E.

Mengzi and Xunzi: Two Views of Human Agency. Van Norden, Bryan.

Minimal Naturalism. Eggerman, Richard W.

On the Relation between Existence and Value (in Chinese). Fu, Pei-jung.

On There Being Philosophical Knowledge. Nielsen, Kai.

Sociobiology, Ethics and Human Nature in New Horizons in the Philosophy of Science, Lamb, David (ed). Frith, Lucy.

The Ironist's Utopia: Can Rorty's Liberal Turnip Bleed?. Phillips, Hollibert.

The Laws of Nature and of Nature's God. Crosson, Frederick.

The Use of Sophiology. Martz, Erin.

HUMAN RIGHTS

Aesthetic Judgment and the Moral Image of the World: Studies in Kant. Henrich, Dieter.

The Origins of Our Delusions (in Hungarian). Ludassy, Mária.

A Critique of Henry Veatch's "Human Rights: Fact or Fancy?". Lee, Sander H.

Are Human Rights Based on Equal Human Worth?. Pojman, Louis.

Can We Afford International Human Rights?. Brenkert, George G.

Community and the Rights of Future Generations: A Reply to Robert Elliot. De-Shalit, Avner.

Die Zerstückelung des Fu-Tschu-Li. Kohler, Georg.

Global Rights and Regional Jurisprudence. Jackson, Kevin T.

Human Rights and Nature's Rightness. Kohak, Erazim.

Human Rights between Universalism and Relativism. Scholze, Wolfgang.

In Search of a Workable and Lasting Constitutional Change in South Africa. Ramose, Mogobe B, Maphala, T G T and Makhabane, T E.

The Basis for Recoghnition of Human Rights. Duquette, David A.

The Right of National Self Determination. George, David.

Zur Kritik des kritischen Rationalismus. Bader, Erwin.

HUMAN SCIENCES

Law and the Human Sciences. Kevelson, Roberta (ed).

Is the Paradigm Concept Compatible with the Human Sciences? (in Dutch). Antonites, A J.

Zwischen Wissenschaftskritik und Hermeneutik: Foucaults Humanwissenschaften. Teichert, Dieter.

HUMAN SUBJECT

Autonomie, don et partage dans la problématique de l'expérimentation humaine. Fagot-Largeault, Anne.

Solidarité et disposition du corps humain. Hottois, Gilbert.

HUMANISM

"Les Fondateurs" and *"La Découverte de l'Histoire"*: Two Short Pieces Excluded from *"Everywhere and Nowhere,"* by Maurice Merleau-Ponty. Davis, Duane H (trans).

Agents and Lives: Moral Thinking in Literature. Goldberg, S L.

Business, Ethics, and the Environment: The Public Policy Debate. Hoffman, W Michael (ed), Frederick, Robert (ed) and Pentry, Edward S (ed).

Dialogue and the Human Image: Beyond Humanistic Psychology. Friedman, Maurice S.

Humanisme de la Liberté et Philosophie de la Justice. Trigeaud, Jean-Marc.

Persona ou la Justice au Double Visage. Trigeaud, Jean-Marc.

Philosophy and Government, 1572-1651. Tuck, Richard.

Practical Knowledge—Yves R Simon. Mulvaney, Robert J (ed) and Simon, Yves R.

Rethinking Goodness. Wallach, Michael A and Wallach, Lise.

The Battle of the Books: History and Literature in the Augustan Age. Levine, Joseph M.

The Pluralistic Philosophy of Stephen Crane. Dooley, Patrick K.

Truth and Existence—Jean-Paul Sartre. Sartre, Jean Paul, Van Den Hoven, Adrian (trans) and Aronson, Ronald (ed).

William James: Pragmatism in Focus. Olin, Doris (ed).

A Neopragmatist Perspective on Religion and Science. Robbins, J Wesley.

America's Leading Humanist Philosopher: Remembering John Dewey. Kurtz, Paul.

Anarchy and the Condition of Contemporary Humanism. Palmer, Lucia M.

Charles F Potter: On Evolution and Religious Humanism in God, Values, and Empiricism, Peden, Creighton (ed). Olds, W Mason.

Confucius, The First 'Teacher' of Humanism?. Rogers, Gerald F.

Dewey on the Humanist Movement. Smith, Warren Allen.

Dialectic: The Science of Humanism. Anderson, Albert A.

Ecocentric Ethics. Lawler, James.

Ecologies et philosophies. Goffi, Jean-Yves.

Ecology and Human Emancipation. Hayward, Tim.

Environmentalism as a Humanism. Solomon, Robert C.

Environmentalism Humanized. Machan, Tibor R.

Humanism and Environmentalism. Passmore, John.

Humanism and Ethics at the School of St Victor in the Early Twelfth Century. Jaeger, C Stephen.

Humanism's Thorn: The Case of the Bright Believers. Pasquarello, Tony.

In Defense of Secular Humanism. Grünbaum, Adolf.

Introduction to the Methodology of Paraphronesis, With Example: Religion and Education in Postmodern America. Tandy, Charles.

La résurgence de l'aristotélisme de la Renaissance dans la philosophie politique de Cassirer. Rudolph, Enno.

Making it with Death: Remarks on Thanatos and Desiring-Production. Land, Nick.

Orientalism and After: An Interview with Edward Said. Beezer, Anne and Osborne, Peter.

Paradigms for an Open Philosophy. Polis, Dennis F.

Politics beyond Humanism in Working Through Derrida, Madison, Gary B (ed). Bernasconi, Robert.

René Descartes et Pierre Charron. Adam, M.

Science and Humanism in the Renaissance in World Changes, Horwich, Paul (ed). Swerdlow, N M.

Searching for Humanistic Truth. Louch, Alfred R.

The Continuity of Chinese Humanism in the Shang-Chou Period. Wong, Yeu-Guang.

The Moral Foundations of African-American Culture in African-American Perspectives on Biomedical Ethics, Flack, Harley E (ed). Wiredu, Kwasi.

The Politics of Fredric Jameson's Literary Theory in Postmodernism/ Jameson/ Critique, Kellner, Douglas (ed). Goldstein, Philip.

The Problem of Closure in Derrida (Part Two). Critchley, Simon.

The Teaching of *Centesimus Annus*. Schall, James V.

Toward a New Enlightenment: A Response to the Postmodernist Critiques of Humanism. Kurtz, Paul.

Una voz por la paz en el siglo XV: La noción humanística de concordia. Magnavacca, Silvia.

Universal Speciesism. Clements, Tad.

Us and Them, Nature and Humanism. Scott, Eugenie C.

Was Immanuel Kant a Humanist?. Hiorth, Finngeir.

What's Wrong With Murder? Some Thoughts on Human and Animal Killing. Everitt, Nicholas.

HUMANITARIANISM

The Empire of Progress: Bacon's Improvement Upon Machiavelli. Faulkner, Robert K.

HUMANITIES

Culture and Democracy: Social and Ethical Issues in Public Support for the Arts and Humanities. Buchwalter, Andrew.

Moral Education and the Liberal Arts. Mitias, Michael H (ed).

Philosophy and Knowledge: A Commentary on Plato's "Theaetetus". Polansky, Ronald.

Revolutions in Knowledge: Feminism in the Social Sciences. Zalk, Sue Rosenberg (ed) and Gordon-Kelter, Janice (ed).

On Why Philosophers Redefine their Subject. Brown, Stuart.

The Humanities and an Ethics of Care in Moral Education and the Liberal Arts, Mitias, Michael H (ed). Sichel, Betty A.

The Humanities, Moral Education, and the Contemporary World in Moral Education and the Liberal Arts, Mitias, Michael H (ed). Ginsberg, Robert.

Truth and the Humanities. Kohak, Erazim.

HUMANITY

A Hylomorphic Theory of Mind. Cooney, Brian.

A Progress of Sentiments: Reflections on Hume's "Treatise". Baier, Annette.

A Treatise of Human Nature—David Hume. Mossner, Ernest C (ed).

Analecta Husserliana, XXXI. Tymieniecka, Anna-Teresa (ed).

Applied Philosophy. Almond, Brenda (ed) and Hill, Donald (ed).

Aristotle on the Perfect Life. Kenny, Anthony.

Cosmos, Bios, Theos: Scientists Reflect on Science, God, and the Origins of the Universe, Life, and "Homo sapiens". Margenau, Henry (ed) and Varghese. Roy Abraham (ed).

HUMANITY

HUME

The No-Self Theory: Hume, Buddhism, and Personal Identity. Giles, James.

The Rational Warrant for Hume's General Rules. Martin, Marie A.

The Self of Book 1 and the Selves of Book 2. Penelhum, Terence.

The Theater of Personal Identity: From Hume to Derrida. Gallagher, Shaun.

Unidentified Awareness: Hume's Perceptions of Self. Campolo, Christian.

Was Hume an Atheist?. Andre, Shane.

What Does the Scientist of Man Observe?. Broughton, Janet.

What Impressions of Necessity?. Flew, Antony.

Why We Believe in Induction: Standards of Taste and Hume's Two Definitions of Causation. Helm, Bennet W.

Yanal and Others on Hume and Tragedy. Neill, Alex.

Yet Another Look at Cognitive Reason and Moral Action in Hume's Ethical System. Johnson, Clarence Sholé.

'Hume's Theorem' Concerning Miracles. Millican, Peter.

'Is' and 'Ought' in Context: MacIntyre's Mistake. MacBeth, Murray.

HUMILITY

Environmental Virtue Ethics: A New Direction for Environmental Ethics. Frasz, Geoffrey B.

Humility as a Virtue in Teaching. Hare, William.

HUNT, L

Response to Lester Hunt's Comments. Welshon, Robert.

HURLBUTT, R

Hurlbutt, Hume, Newton and the Design Argument. Tweyman, Stanley.

HUSSERL

An Introduction to Husserlian Phenomenology. Bernet, Rudolf, Kern, Iso and Marbach, Eduard.

Analecta Husserliana, XXXI. Tymieniecka, Anna-Teresa (ed).

Analecta Husserliana, XXXIV. Tymieniecka, Anna-Teresa (ed).

Husserl's Transcendental Phenomenology—Elisabeth Ströker. Hardy, Lee (trans) and Ströker, Elisabeth.

Phenomenology and Deconstruction, Volume II: Method and Imagination. Cumming, Robert Denoon.

Poetics of Imagining: From Husserl to Lyotard. Kearney, Richard.

Theology and Difference: The Wound of Reason. Lowe, Walter.

A Critique of Husserl's Notion of Crisis in Crises in Continental Philosophy, Dallery, Arleen B (ed). Buckley, R Philip.

Beiträge zu einer phänomenologischen Theorie des negativen Urteils. Lohmar, Dieter.

Categorial Intuition and the Understanding of Being in Husserl and Heidegger in Reading Heidegger: Commemorations, Sallis, John (ed). Watanabe, Jiro.

Commentary on "Husserl's Critique of Hegel" in Hegel and His Critics, Desmond, William (ed). Duquette, David A.

Conocimiento y concepto. Mayol, Víctor Velarde.

Constitution and Ontology: Some Remarks on Husserl's Ontological Position in the *Logical Investigations*. Zahavi, D.

Crisis and Life-World in Husserl and Habermas in Crises in Continental Philosophy, Dallery, Arleen B (ed). Baynes, Kenneth.

Debate between Husserl and Voigt Concerning the Logic of Content and Extensional Logic in Analecta Husserliana, XXXIV, Tymieniecka, Anna-Teresa (ed). Hamacher-Hermes, Adelheid.

Der Familienname von Edmund Husserl. Wagner, Norbert.

Dialektik als Letzbegründung bei Hegel. Pleines, Jürgen-Eckardt.

Die Selbstintentionalität der Welt in Analecta Husserliana, XXXIV, Tymieniecka, Anna-Teresa (ed). Pavic, Zeljko.

Does Husserl have a Philosophy of History in *The Crisis of European Sciences*?. Mann, Doug.

Edmund Husserl: Intersubjectivity between Epoché and History in Analecta Husserliana, XXXI, Tymieniecka, Anna-Teresa (ed). D'Ippolito, Bianca Maria.

Ein Zeitzeuge über die Anfänge der phänomenologischen Bewegung: Theodor Conrads Bericht aus dem Jahre 1954. Avé-Lallemant, Eberhard and Schuhmann, Karl.

Europe, Truth, and History: Husserl and Voegelin on Philosophy and the Identity of Europe. Levy, David J.

Fathers, Kings, and Promises: Husserl and Reinach on the A Priori. Zelaniec, Wojciech.

Fundamental Ontology and Regional Ontology of Humanities. Ginev, Dimitri.

H Conrad-Martius und E Stein Husserls Schülerinen und aristotelisch-thomistische Philosophie (in Polish). Machnacz, J.

Heimat und das Fremde. Tani, T.

Husserl. Mohanty, J N.

Husserl and Analytic Philosophy and Husserlian Intentionality and Non-Foundational Realism. Sokolowski, Robert.

Husserl and Heidegger as Phenomenologists. Gorner, Paul.

Husserl and the Anthropological Vocation of Phenomenology in Analecta Husserliana, XXXIV, Tymieniecka, Anna-Teresa (ed). Kelkel, Arion L.

Husserl and the Deconstruction of Time. Brough, John B.

Husserl and the Heritage of Transcendental Philosophy in Analecta Husserliana, XXXIV, Tymieniecka, Anna-Teresa (ed). Siemek, Marek J.

Husserl e il linguaggio. Costa, Filippo.

Husserl und die Vorstruktur des Bewusstseins in Analecta Husserliana, XXXIV, Tymieniecka, Anna-Teresa (ed). Ogawa, Tadashi.

Husserl vs Dilthey—A Controversy over the Concept of Reason in Analecta Husserliana, XXXIV, Tymieniecka, Anna-Teresa (ed). Walczewska, Slawomira.

Husserl y las aporías de la intersubjetividad. Finke, S R S.

Husserl's Account of Syncategorematic Terms. Lampert, Jay.

Husserl's Complex Concept of the Self and the Possibility of Social Criticism in Crises in Continental Philosophy, Dallery, Arleen B (ed). Harvey, Charles W.

Husserl's Concept of Horizon: An Attempt at Reappraisal in Analecta Husserliana, XXXI, Tymieniecka, Anna-Teresa (ed). Kwan, Tze-Wan.

Husserl's Concept of the World in Crises in Continental Philosophy, Dallery, Arleen B (ed). Bernet, Rudolf.

Husserl's Conception of Formal Ontology. Poli, Roberto.

Husserl's Critique of Empiricism and the Phenomenological Account of Reflection. Drabinski, John.

Husserl's Critique of Hegel in Hegel and His Critics, Desmond, William (ed). Rockmore, Tom.

Husserl's Critique of Reason in Analecta Husserliana, XXXIV, Tymieniecka, Anna-Teresa (ed). Haney, Kathleen.

Husserl's Intentionality and "Mind" in Chinese Philosophy. Zhang, Xian.

Husserl's Phenomenology and the Motives of Its Transformation (Final Part) (in Czechoslovakian). Landgrebe, L.

Husserl, Child Education, and Creativity in Analecta Husserliana, XXXI, Tymieniecka, Anna-Teresa (ed). Morselli, Graziella.

Husserl, Linguistic Meaning, and Intuition. Owens, Wayne.

Intentional and Material Phenomenology (in German). Kühn, Rolf.

Intersubjectivity in Phenomenology. Tripathy, L K.

Is There a Dichotomy in Husserl's Thought? in Analecta Husserliana, XXXIV, Tymieniecka, Anna-Teresa (ed). Di Stefano, Anna Escher.

Kurt Gödel and Phenomenology. Tieszen, Richard.

L'immagine della donna secondo Ortega y Gasset. Savignano, Armando.

La teoría del objeto puro de A Millán Puelles. López, Jesús García.

Le choix du métier: sur le "rationalisme" de Husserl. Benoist, Jocelyn.

Les figures de l'intersubjectivité: Études des Husserliana XIII-XIV-XV. Depraz, Natalie.

Logical Cognition: Husserl's *Prolegomena* and the Truth in Psychologism. Hanna, Robert.

Man within the Limit of the I in Analecta Husserliana, XXXI, Tymieniecka, Anna-Teresa (ed). Finocchi, Nadia.

Method and Ontology: Reflections on Edmund Husserl in Analecta Husserliana, XXXIV, Tymieniecka, Anna-Teresa (ed). Rossi, Osvaldo.

Mind, Consciousness, and Cognition: Phenomenology versus Cognitive Science. Chokr, Nader N.

Notes on Husserl and Kant in Analecta Husserliana, XXXIV, Tymieniecka, Anna-Teresa (ed). Romani, Romano.

On Contradiction in Analecta Husserliana, XXXIV, Tymieniecka, Anna-Teresa (ed). Corte-Real, Maria L.

Per una soggettività non più "animale": Heidegger critico di Husserl. Regina, Umberto.

Persona, hábito y tiempo: La constitución de la identidad personal. Vigo, Alejandro.

Phenomenology and Metaphysics: Husserl, Heidegger, and Merleau-Ponty in Merleau-Ponty Vivant, Dillon, M C (ed). Margolis, Joseph.

Phenomenology and Teleology: Husserl and Fichte in Analecta Husserliana, XXXIV, Tymieniecka, Anna-Teresa (ed). Valalas, Theresa Pentzopoulou.

Phenomenology of Life and the New Critique of Reason in Analecta Husserliana, XXXIV, Tymieniecka, Anna-Teresa (ed). Tymieniecka, Anna-Teresa.

Phenomenology, Possible Worlds and Negation. Krysztofiak, Wojciech.

Potenzialità conoscitive del trascendentale di Husserl. O'Dwyer Bellinetti, L.

Prolegomena to Phenomenology: Intuition or Argument. Adler, Pierre.

Psychologism and Description in Husserl's Phenomenology in Analecta Husserliana, XXXIV, Tymieniecka, Anna-Teresa (ed). Sodeika, Tomas.

Radical Empiricism and Phenomenology: Philosophy and the Pure Stuff of Experience. Drabinski, John E.

Respuesta a lo ajeno: Sobre la relación entre la cultura propia y la cultura ajena. Waldenfels, Bernhard.

Role-Playing: Sartre's Transformation of Husserl's Phenomenology in The Cambridge Companion to Sartre, Howells, Christina (ed). Cumming, Robert D.

Strumenti analitici per la comprensione della filosofia continentale. Marrone, P.

Sur la liberté et les pouvoirs du langage. Christoff, Daniel.

Temporal Impermanence and the Disparity of Time and Eternity. Polk, Danne W.

The Archeology of Modalization in Husserl in Analecta Husserliana, XXXIV, Tymieniecka, Anna-Teresa (ed). Di Pinto, Luigia.

The Cogito *cira* AD 2000. Smith, David Woodruff.

The Development of Time Consciousness from Husserl to Heidegger in Analecta Husserliana, XXXI, Tymieniecka, Anna-Teresa (ed). Thomas, V C.

The Entelechy and Authenticity of Objective Spirit: Reflections on Husserliana XXVII. Hart, J G.

The Finitude of the World in Ethics and Danger, Dallery, Arleen B (ed). Held, Klaus.

The Foundationalist Conflict in Husserl's Rationalism in Analecta Husserliana, XXXIV, Tymieniecka, Anna-Teresa (ed). Overvold, Gary E.

The Light at the End of the Tunnel Is Coming Right at Me in Analecta Husserliana, XXXVIII, Tymieniecka, Anna-Teresa (ed). Feshbach, Sidney.

The Meaning of Thought's Nearness to Meaning in Husserlian Phenomenology in Analecta Husserliana, XXXIV, Tymieniecka, Anna-Teresa (ed). Pozo, Antonio Gutiérrez.

The Meaning of 'Radical Foundation' in Husserl: The Outline of an Interpretation in Analecta Husserliana, XXXIV, Tymieniecka, Anna-Teresa (ed). Cantista, Maria José.

The Myth of Absolute Consciousness in Crises in Continental Philosophy, Dallery, Arleen B (ed). Evans, J Claude.

The Organizing Principle of the Cognitive Process or the Mode of Existence in Analecta Husserliana, XXXIV, Tymieniecka, Anna-Teresa (ed). Dawidziak, Piotr.

The Phenomenology of Edmund Husserl and the Natural Sciences in Analecta Husserliana, XXXIV, Tymieniecka, Anna-Teresa (ed). Motroshilova, Nelya.

The Rationality of Culture and the Culture of Rationality: Some Husserlian Proposals. Hart, James G.

IDENTITY
Theseus' Clothes-Pin. Chandler, Hugh S.
Thinking About Gender. Nelson, Julie.
Unidentified Awareness: Hume's Perceptions of Self. Campolo, Christian.
What-Being: Chuang Tzu versus Aristotle. Li, Chenyang.
Works, Works Better. Schwartz, Robert.
Wounded Attachments. Brown, Wendy.

IDENTITY THEORY
Power for Realists in Ontology, Causality and Mind: Essays in Honour of D M Armstrong, Bacon, John (ed). Martin, C B.
Reply to Martin's 'Power for Realists' in Ontology, Causality and Mind: Essays in Honour of D M Armstrong, Bacon, John (ed). Armstrong, D M.

IDEOLOGY
Ideology and False Consciousness: Marx and his Historical Progenitors. Pines, Christopher.
Ideology and Modern Culture: Review of J B Thompson. Van Veuren, Pieter.
Ideology: An Introduction. Eagleton, Terry.
Image and Ideology in Modern/PostModern Discourse. Downing, David B (ed) and Bazargan, Susan (ed).
Subject to History: Ideology, Class, Gender. Simpson, David (ed).
A Critical Discussion of Karl Mannheim's Views on Sociology of Knowledge. Mondal, Sunil Baran.
Feminism, Ideology, and Deconstruction: A Pragmatist View. Rorty, Richard.
Hannah Arendt and the Ideological Structure of Totalitarianism. Allen, Wayne.
Marx's Deficient Promise. Ormell, Christopher.
Philosophy and Nationalism. Hejdánek, L.
Science and Ideology via Development. Kebede, Messay.
The Burden of Ideological Masks in *Ideolgiekritik*: On Trying to View Faith Scientifically. Nielsen, Kai.
The Social Divided. Mykkänen, Juri.
The Tagore-Gandhi Controversy Revisited, II. Singh, Ajai and Singh, Shakuntala.
Whitman's 'Convertible Terms' in Theorizing American Literature, Cowan, Bainard (ed). Lindberg, Kathryne V.
Women's Lives/Feminist Knowledge: Feminist Standpoint as Ideology Critique. Hennessy, Rosemary.
'Denken über Ideologie': eine praktische Begründung der Erneuerung der post-sowjetischen Philosophie?. Swiderski, E M.

IF
Blending Semantics for *If* As a One-Place Nonassertive with Semantics for the Conditional. Sylvan, Richard.
The Meaning of 'If' in Conditional Propositions. Hunter, Geoffrey.

IGNORANCE
Infallibility, Error, and Ignorance. Kretzmann, Norman.
Nonfallacious Arguments from Ignorance. Walton, Douglas N.
Vagueness and Ignorance—I. Williamson, Timothy.
Vagueness and Ignorance—II. Simons, Peter.

ILLICH, I
Ivan Illich and the Radical Critique of Tools. Weston, Anthony.

ILLNESS
see also Mental Illness
The Meaning of Illness: A Phenomenological Account of the Different Perspectives of Physician and Patient. Toombs, S Kay.
Can We Talk? Contexts of Meaning for Interpreting Illness. Mount Jr, Eric.
Eating Disorders: The Feminist Challenge to the Concept of Pathology in The Body in Medical Thought and Practice, Leder, Drew (ed). Bordo, Susan R.
Historique des recherches sur la différenciation des Hépatites A & B. Meyer, Jean-Luc.
Statutory Definitions of Death and the Management of Terminally Ill Patients Who May Become Organ Donors after Death. Cole, David.
The Irreversibility of Death: Reply to Cole. Tomlinson, Thomas.
The Metamorphosis: The Nature of Chronic Illness and Its Challenge to Medicine. Toombs, S Kay.

ILLUMINATION
Le ragioni del deismo in Voltaire's e nell'Enciclopedia. Nicolosi, Salvatore.

ILLUSION
Aesthetic Illusion. Burwick, Frederick (ed) and Pape, Walter (ed).
Aesthetic and Illusion of Daily Life in Aesthetic Illusion, Burwick, Frederick (ed). Blanchard, Marc E.
Aesthetic Illusion in the Eighteenth Century in Aesthetic Illusion, Burwick, Frederick (ed). Schulte-Sasse, Jochen.
Appearance in Poetry: Lyric Illusion? in Aesthetic Illusion, Burwick, Frederick (ed). Thomke, Hellmut.
Comic Illusion and Illusion in Comedy in Aesthetic Illusion, Burwick, Frederick (ed). Pape, Walter.
Illusion and Imagination in Aesthetic Illusion, Burwick, Frederick (ed). Shaffer, Elinor S.
Perception and Illusion. Sen, Madhucchanda.
The Grotesque: Illusion versus Delusion in Aesthetic Illusion, Burwick, Frederick (ed). Burwick, Frederick.
The Illusion of 'Illusion' in Aesthetic Illusion, Burwick, Frederick (ed). Watzlawick, Paul.
The Virtues of Illusion. Hardin, C L.
'Fantastic' Images in Aesthetic Illusion, Burwick, Frederick (ed). Stafford, Barbara Maria.

ILYENKOV, E
Re-Reading Soviet Philosophy: Bakhurst on Ilyenkov. Larvor, Brendan.

IMAGE
see also Mental Image
Image and Ideology in Modern/PostModern Discourse. Downing, David B (ed) and Bazargan, Susan (ed).
An Unappreciated Iconology: Aby Warburg and the Hermeneutics of Image (in Japanese). Kato, Tetsuhiro.
André Bazin on Automatically Made Images. Brubaker, David.
Image et mimesis chez Platon (in Japanese). Sekimura, Makoto.
Imaging the Imageless: Symbol and Perception in Early Chinese Thought. Doeringer, Franklin M.

IMAGERY
Speaking about the Unspeakable: Plato's Use of Imagery. Tecusan, Manuela.
The Image of Women in Film: A Defense of a Paradigm. Carroll, Noël.
The Imagery Debate. Eilan, Naomi.

IMAGINARY
Imaginary Evil: A Sceptic's Wager. Taliaferro, Charles.
Impersonal Imagining: A Reply to Jerrold Levinson. Currie, Gregory.
On the Elimination of Imaginaries from Certain Valued Fields. Scowcroft, Philip and Macintyre, Angus.
Seeing, Imaginarily, at the Movies. Levinson, Jerrold.

IMAGINATION
Extensions: Essays on Interpretation, Rationality, and the Closure of Modernism. Watson, Stephen.
Imagination and Chance: The Difference Between the Thought of Ricoeur and Derrida. Lawlor, Leonard.
Kant's Aesthetics. Meerbote, Ralf (ed).
Poetics of Imagining: From Husserl to Lyotard. Kearney, Richard.
Wittgenstein's Philosophy of Psychology. Budd, Malcolm.
Creative Imagination and Dream in Analecta Husserliana, XXXVIII, Tymieniecka, Anna-Teresa (ed). Balzer, Carmen.
Illusion and Imagination in Aesthetic Illusion, Burwick, Frederick (ed). Shaffer, Elinor S.
Imagination and Judgment in the Critical Philosophy in Kant's Aesthetics, Meerbote, Ralf (ed). Posy, Carl J.
Imagination and Myth. Degenaar, Johan.
Imagination and the Sense of Identity in Human Beings, Cockburn, David (ed). Hertzberg, Lars.
Imagination créatrice et connaissance selon Théodule Ribot. Meletti-Bertolini, Mara.
Imagination in Practical Reason. Ray, Chad.
Imagination—The Very Idea. Sparshott, Francis.
Imagined Worlds and the Real One: Plato, Wittgenstein, and Mimesis. Harrison, Bernard.
Mathesis und Phantasie: Die Rolle der Einbildungskraft im Umfeld der Descartesschen *Regulae*. Pasini, Enrico.
Memes and the Exploitation of Imagination. Dennett, Daniel C.
Method of Imaginative Variation in Phenomenology in Thought Experiments in Science and Philosophy, Horowitz, Tamara (ed). Mohanty, J N.
Mistica o filosofia? A proposito della dottrina dell'immagine di Meister Eckhart. Sturlese, Loris.
Perception as Cooperation of Schematization and Figurative Synthesis (in Dutch). Lohmar, D.
Religious Imagination. Hepburn, Ronald W.
Religious Imagination in Philosophy, Religion and the Spiritual Life, McGhee, Michael (ed). Hepburn, Ronald W.
Sense and Sensibility: Wittgenstein on the *Golden Bough*. Margalit, Avishai.
The Moral Imagination and the Aesthetics of Human Existence in Moral Education and the Liberal Arts, Mitias, Michael H (ed). Alexander, Thomas M.
The Road from Nice to Necessary: Broudy's Rationale for Art Education. DiBlasio, Margaret Klempay.
The Role of Aesthetic Emotion in R G Collingwood's Conception of Creative Activity. Anderson, Douglas R and Hausman, Carl R.
The Tiger and His Stripes. Lyons, William.
Vico, Imagination and Education. Iheoma, Eugene O.
What is an Anlogical Imagination?. Conradie, Ernst.

IMITATION
see also Mimesis
Amateurs Imitate, Professionals Steal. Bailey, George W S.
Imagination—The Very Idea. Sparshott, Francis.
Mead's Voices: Imitation as Foundation, or, The Struggle against Mimesis. Leys, Ruth.
Rousseau's Socraticism: The Political Bearing of "On Theatrical Imitation". Sorenson, Leonard R.

IMMANENCE
Immanenz und Absolutheit: Zy Y—Yovels Studie "Spinoza and Other Heretics". Graeser, Andreas.

IMMATERIAL SUBSTANCE
Where Have All the Angels Gone?. Clark, Stephen R L.

IMMATERIALISM
Modern Immaterialism. Luüf, Reginald and Tijmes, Pieter.

IMMORALITY
Kantian Duties and Immoral Agents. Harris, N G E.
Nonmoral Explanations in Philosophical Perspectives, 6: Ethics, 1992, Tomberlin, James E (ed). Sturgeon, Nicholas.
The Immorality of Promising. Fox, Richard M and Demarco, Joseph P.

IMMORTALITY
see also Reincarnation
Bolzano-Forschung: 1989-1991. Berg, Jan and Morscher, Edgar.

IMMORTALITY

Eternity and Time's Flow. Neville, Robert Cummings.
Homo Religiosus ou L'Homme Vertical. Rostenne, Paul.
Philoponus: On Aristotle on the Intellect. Charlton, William (trans).
Augustine's Numbering Numbers and the Immortality of the Human Soul. Ramirez, J Roland.
Averroes, Aristotle, and the Qur'an on Immortality. Mohammed, Ovey N.
Charles Hartshorne and Subjective Immortality. Suchocki, Marjorie H.
D Z Phillips, Self-Renunciation and the Finality of Death. Thomas, Emyr Vaughan.
Immortality: Objective, Subjective, or Neither? in God, Values, and Empiricism, Peden, Creighton (ed). Shaw, D W D.
L'argument par "affinité" dans le "phédon". Rowe, Christopher.
Sempiternity, Immortality and the Homunculus Fallacy. Thornton, Stephen P.

IMMUNOLOGY

How Not to Explain the Errors of the Immune System. Melander, Peter.
In Defense of the Quine-Duhem Thesis: A Reply to Greenwood. Klee, Robert.

IMPARTIALITY

see also Objectivity
Love and Impartiality. Adams, Don.

IMPERATIVES

Are Methodological Rules Hypothetical Imperatives?. Resnik, David B.
Counting the Formulas of the Categorical Imperative: One Plus Three Makes Four. Nuyen, A T.
Imperatives in Merleau-Ponty Vivant, Dillon, M C (ed). Lingis, Alphonso F.
Relevance and "Pseudo-Imperatives". Clark, Billy.
The Rational Imperative to Believe. Gordon, Jeffrey.

IMPERIALISM

Nationalism, Colonialism, and Literature. Eagleton, Terry, Jameson, Fredric and Said, Edward W.
Art and Culture in a Changing World. Degenaar, J J.
Intelligibility, Imperialism, and Conceptual Scheme. Hurley, S L.
Liberalism and Nationalism in the Thought of Max Weber. Bellamy, Richard.

IMPLICATION

see also Material Implication
Approximations and Logic. Marquis, Jean-Pierre.
Extending the Curry-Howard Interpretation to Lienar, Relevant and Other Resource Logics. Gabbay, Dov M and De Queiroz, R J G B.
Lattices of Implicational Logics. Karpenko, Alexander S.
Linearizing Intuitionistic Implication. Lincoln, Patrick, Scedrov, Andre and Shankar, Natarajan.
On Structural Completeness of Implicational Logics. Wojtylak, Piotr.

IMPOSSIBILITY

Possible Versus Potential Universes. Kerszberg, Pierre.

IMPRESSION

Hume on the Ordinary Distinction Between Objective and Subjective Impressions. Kornegay, R Jo.
Hume's Classification of the Passions and Its Precursors. Fieser, James.
Hume's Demarcation Project. Losee, John.

IMPRESSIONISM

Impressionism: A Feminist Reading. Broude, Norma.

IMPROVISATION

Do Composers Have To Be Performers Too?. Spade, Paul Vincent.
When Composers Have To Be Performers. Alperson, Philip A.

IN VITRO FERTILIZATION

Pursuing Parenthood: Ethical Issues in Assisted Reproduction. Lauritzen, Paul.
The Ethics of Reproductive Technology. Alpern, Kenneth D (ed).
Access to In Vitro Fertilization: Costs, Care and Consent. Overall, Christine.
Who are the Beneficiaries?. Tännsjö, Torbjörn.

INCARNATION

The Incarnation and the Natural Law. McMahon, Kevin.
The Temptation of God Incarnate. Werther, David.
Transcendence, Instantiation and Incarnation—An Exploration. Durrant, Michael.

INCENTIVE

Justice Within the Limits of Incentive Alone (in Hebrew). Kasher, Hannah.

INCLUSION

The Morality of Inclusion. Buchanan, Allen.

INCOME

Do Physicians Make Too Much Money?. Curzer, Howard J.

INCOMMENSURABILITY

Deontology, Incommensurability and the Arbitrary. Ellis, Anthony.
Hard Choices: A Sociological Perspective on Value Incommensurability. Cohen, Eric and Ben-Ari, Eyal.
Propiedades modelísticas del concepto de reducción. Ibarra, Andoni and Mormann, Thomas.
The Images of Enslavement and Incommensurability in Plato's *Meno*. Turner, Jeffrey S.

INCOMMUNICABILITY

The Incommunicability of Human Persons. Crosby, John F.

INCOMPLETENESS

see also Completeness
On the Interpretation of Church's Thesis. Cotogno, Paolo.

INCONGRUITY

Das Phänomen der inkongruenten Gegenstücke aus Kantischer und heutiger Sicht. Mühlhölzer, Felix.

INCONSISTENCY

Aquinas and Natural Human Fulfillment: Inconsistencies. Hayden, R Mary.
Rational Inconsistency and Reasoning. Brown, Bryson.
Regular Modal Logics. Swirdowicz, Kazimierz.
Response. Rescher, Nicholas.

INDEPENDENCE

Independence in Democratic Theory: A Virtue? A Necessity? Both? Neither?. Goodin, Robert E.
Independence, Randomness and the Axiom of Choice. Van Lambalgen, Michiel.
Les transcendantalistes: indépendance et infini. Chaput, Sylvie.
On the Logic of Informational Independence and Its Applications. Sandu, Gabriel.

INDETERMINACY

"From Natural Function to Indeterminate Content". Sullivan, Sonja R.
Basic Concepts—Martin Heidegger. Aylesworth, Gary E (trans) and Heidegger, Martin.
Donald Davidson and the Mirror of Meaning. Malpas, J E.
Judging in Good Faith. Burton, Steven J.
New Philosophy of Social Science. Bohman, James F.
Asymmetry and Non-Existence. Belshaw, Christopher.
Discussion: Massey and Kirk on the Indeterminacy of Translation. Hitchcock, Christopher R.
Ex Post Facto Explanations. Hobbs, Jesse.
Indeterminacy and the Construction of Personal Knowledge. McWilliams, Spencer A.
Indeterminacy of Interpretation, Idealization, and Norms. Kirk, Robert.
John Cage's 4'33": Using Aesthetic Theory to Understand a Musical Notion. Campbell, Mark Robin.
Merleau-Ponty's Destruction of Logocentrism in Merleau-Ponty Vivant, Dillon, M C (ed). Madison, G B.
Microphysical Indeterminacy and Freedom: Bergson and Peirce in The Crisis in Modernism, Burwick, Frederick (ed). Capek, Milic.
Minimalist Historical Materialism in On the Track of Reason, Beehler, Rodger (ed). Cohen, Joshua.
On Two Arguments for the Indeterminacy of Personal Identity. Cartwright, Helen Morris.
Owen's Proof in the *Peri Ideon* and the Indeterminacy of Sensibles in Plato. Curry, D C K.
Paradox Regained. Rice Jr, Martin A.
Parfit on What Matters in Survival. Brueckner, Anthony.
Rule Following, Rule Scepticism and Indeterminacy in Law: A Conventional Account. Drahos, Peter and Parker, Stephen.
Semantic Indeterminacy and the Realist Stance. Wilburn, Ronald.
Semantic Supervenience and Referential Indeterminacy. Van Cleve, James.
The Chaotic Law of Tort in Peirce and Law, Kevelson, Roberta. Brion, Denis J.
The Egg Came Before the Chicken. Sorensen, Roy.
The Indeterminacy of Identity: A Reply to Brueckner. Parfit, Derek.
Wittgenstein's Private Language Argument and Quine's Indeterminacy Thesis. Lenka, Laxminarayan.

INDETERMINISM

Indeterminism and Free Agency: Three Recent Views. O'Connor, Timothy.
Time and the Anthropic Principle. Leslie, John.

INDEX

El Index Thomisticus y la semántica lingüística. De Gandolfi, M C Donadío M.

INDEXICAL

Demonstratives and Intentions, Ten Years Later. Bertolet, Rod.
Keeping a Happy Face on Exportation. Kapitan, Tomis.
Making Sense of Indexicals. Anderson, Michael.
Perry on Indexical Semantics and Belief States. Roberts, Lawrence D.

INDEXICALITY

A Here-Now Theory of Indexicality. Plumer, Gilbert.
Indexicality and Deixis. Nunberg, Geoffrey.

INDIAN

see also Buddhism, Hinduism, Jainism, Yoga
Nietzsche and Asian Thought. Parkes, Graham R (ed).
Reason and Tradition in Indian Thought: An Essay on the Nature of Indian Philosophical Thinking. Mohanty, Jitendra N.
The Roles of Sense and Thought in Knowledge. De, P K.
A Comparison of the Chinese Buddhist and Indian Buddhist Modes of Thought. Litian, Fang.
Binary Numbers in Indian Antiquity. Van Nooten, B.
Comments on " The Development of Advaita Vedanta as a School of Philosophy". Sharma, R M.
Comments on "The Development of Advaita Vedanta as a School of Philosophy". Venkatachalam, V.
Das Tal der Sachlichkeit: Albert Schweitzer über Indien. Waligora, Melitta.
Deconstruction and Breakthrough in Nietzsche and Nagarjuna in Nietzsche and Asian Thought, Parkes, Graham R (ed). Martin, Glen T.
Gangesa on Characterizing Veridical Awareness. Phillips, Stephen H (trans).
Human Embodiment: Indian Perspectives in Self as Body in Asian Theory and Practice, Kasulis, Thomas P (ed). Koller, John M.
Indian Bodies in Self as Body in Asian Theory and Practice, Kasulis, Thomas P (ed). Staal, Frits.
Jabir, the Buddhist Yogi. Walter, Michael.
Nietzsche and the Suffering of the Indian Ascetic in Nietzsche and Asian Thought, Parkes, Graham R (ed). Parkes, Graham R (trans) and Hulin, Michel.
Nietzsche's Early Encounters with Asian Thought in Nietzsche and Asian Thought, Parkes, Graham R (ed). Parkes, Graham R (trans) and Figl, Johann.

INDIAN

Nietzsche's Trans-European Eye in Nietzsche and Asian Thought, Parkes, Graham R (ed). Sprung, G M C.

On Knowing by Being Told. Chakrabarti, Arindam.

On Matilal's Understanding of Indian Philosophy. Mohanty, Jitendra N.

Reductionist and Nonreductionist Theories of Persons in Indian Buddhist Philosophy. Duerlinger, James.

Reply to Chakrabarti: Some Comments on Contraposition in European and Indian Logic. Dravid, N S.

Some Remarks on the Gunagunibhedabhanga Chapter in Udayana's Ātmatattvaviveka. Laine, Joy E.

Specific Cultures and the Coexistence of Alternative Rationalities: A Case Study of the Contact of Indian and Greco-European Cultures. Shekhawat, V.

The Development of Advaita Vedanta as a School of Philosophy. Potter, Karl H.

The Incorporation of American Indian Philosophy into Undergraduate Philosophy Courses. Holly, Marilyn.

The Poverty of Indian Political Theory. Parekh, Bhikhu.

The Tagore-Gandhi Controversy Revisited, I. Singh, Ajay and Singh, Shakuntala.

Towards a Creative Synthesis of Cultures. Gopalan, S.

Tradition and the Indian Writer. Parthasarathy, R.

Truth-False Asymmetry in the Logic of Dharmakirti. Simakov, M.

INDIFFERENCE

Care and Indifference in the Moral Domain. Miller, George.

INDISCERNIBILITY

On a Quasi-Set Theory. Krause, Décio.

INDIVIDUAL

see also Person

"Le sens optus" and "Unintentionality" (in Czechoslovakian). Grygar, Mojmir.

An Historical Introduction to Moral Philosophy. Wagner, Michael (ed).

Community at Loose Ends. Miami Theory Collect (ed).

Democracy and Complexity: A Realist Approach. Zolo, Danilo and McKie, David (trans).

Frames of Deceit: A Study of the Loss and Recovery of Public and Private Trust. Johnson, Peter.

Friendship: A Philosophical Reader. Badhwar, Neera Kapur (ed).

Hegel on Want and Desire: A Psychology of Motivation. Forbes, Kipling D.

Justice and Interpretation. Warnke, Georgia.

Max Scheler's Concept of the Person: An Ethics of Humanism. Perrin, Ron.

Modernity and Authenticity: A Study of the Social and Ethical Thought of Jean-Jacques Rousseau. Ferrara, Alessandro.

On Community. Rouner, Leroy S (ed).

Sharing Responsibility. May, Larry.

The Concept of Political Judgment. Steinberger, Peter J.

The Discipline of Taste and Feeling. Wegener, Charles.

The Grounds and Limits of Political Obligation. Capriotti, Emile.

The Moral Life. Luper-Foy, Steven.

The Person and the Common Life. Hart, James G.

The Practice of Moral Judgment. Herman, Barbara.

Understanding Persons: Personal and Impersonal Relationships (Second Edition). Berenson, F M.

Bindings, Shackles, Brakes in Cultural-Political Interventions in the Unfinished Project of Enlightenment, Honneth, Axel (& other eds). Offe, Claus.

Christian Wolff on Individuation. Gracia, Jorge J E.

Community as Ritual Participation in On Community, Rouner, Leroy S (ed). Deutsch, Eliot.

Convivir con la inidentidad. Innerarity, Daniel.

Diagnosing the Takings Problem. Radin, Margaret Jane.

Distributive Justice: A Third World Response to Recent American Thought (Part I). Rao, A P.

Don Quixote and Kierkegaard's Understanding of the Single Individual.... in Foundations of Kierkegaard's Vision of Community, Connell, George B (ed). Ziolkowski, Eric J.

Ethics in the Psyche's Individuating Development towards the Self in Analecta Husserliana, XXXI, Tymieniecka, Anna-Teresa (ed). Rocci, Giovanni.

Hegel and Marx on the Human Individual in Hegel and His Critics, Desmond, William J (ed). Mulholland, Leslie A.

Identidad individual y personalidad jurídica. Aymerich, Ignacio.

Individuo y sociedad: En Duns Scot y en Tomás de Aquino. De Gandolfi, M C Donadío M.

Joint Action. Miller, Seumas.

La idea de la comunidad en la Filosofía Hegeliana del Derecho. Penette, Sonia.

La identidad del sujeto individual según Aristóteles. Inciarte, Fernando.

Leaving Man in Society. Krausz, Ernest.

Leibniz on Properties and Individuals in Language, Truth and Ontology, Mulligan, Kevin (ed). Lenzen, Wolfgang.

Leibnizian Essentialism, Transworld Identity, and Counterparts. Cover, J A and Hawthorne, John.

Moral Sense, Community, and the Individual in Analecta Husserliana, XXXI, Tymieniecka, Anna-Teresa (ed). Loiskandl, Helmut H.

On Conventions. Miller, Seumas.

On the "Subjects" of Knowing and Willing and the "I" in Shcopenhauer. Aquila, Richard E.

Persons and Values. Garrett, Brian.

Rawls's Savings Principle (in Hebrew). Attas, Daniel.

Sartre and Our Identity as Individuals in Human Beings, Cockburn, David (ed). Dilman, Ilham.

Social Relations and the Individuation of Thought. Antony, Michael V.

St Thomas Aquinas on Explaining Individuality. Coulter, Gregory J.

The *Narod*, the Intelligentsia, and the Individual. Kovalev, Vitalii.

The Absent Ontology of Society: Response to Juckes and Barresi. Manicas, Peter T.

The Apocalypse of Community in On Community, Rouner, Leroy S (ed). Keller, Catherine.

The Comparative Study of the Self in Selves, People, and Persons, Rouner, Leroy S (ed). Deutsch, Eliot.

The Environmental Implications of Liberalism. Taylor, Roger.

The Subjective-Objective Dimension in the Individual-Society Connection: A Duality Perspective. Juckes, Tim J and Barresi, John.

Truth, Meaning, and Functional Understanding: A Post-Sartrean Meditation. Barbiero, Daniel.

Vom Risiko der Positivität: Pihlosophieren nach dem Tod des Subjekts. Konersmann, Rolf.

INDIVIDUALISM

Democracy and Complexity: A Realist Approach. Zolo, Danilo and McKie, David (trans).

Natural Reasons: Personality and Polity. Hurley, S L.

Philosophy of the Social Sciences III: Groundwork for Social Dynamics. Wisdom, J O.

Rethinking Goodness. Wallach, Michael A and Wallach, Lise.

Revisioning Philosophy. Ogilvy, James (ed).

Selves, People, and Persons. Rouner, Leroy S (ed).

The Common Mind: An Essay on Psychology, Society, and Politics. Pettit, Philip.

The Corporation as Anomaly. Schrader, David.

The Metaphysics of Edmund Burke. Pappin III, Joseph L.

Toward a Genealogy of Individualism. Shanahan, Daniel.

Virtues and Rights: The Moral Philosophy of Thomas Hobbes. Ewin, R E.

A Convergence of Pragmatisms in Frontiers in American Philosophy, Volume I, Burch, Robert W (ed). Margolis, Joseph.

A Personal View of Percy W Bridgman, Physicist and Philosopher. Holton, Gerald.

Accumulative Harms and the Interpretation of the Harm Principle. Kernohan, Andrew.

Against *A Priori* Arguments for Individualism. Wilson, Robert A.

Altruism Versus Self-Interest: Sometimes a False Dichotomy. Badhwar, Neera Kapur.

Authority, Autonomy and the Legitimate State. Paterson, R W K.

Autonomy and Responsibility: The Social Basis of Ethical Individualism in Revisioning Philosophy, Ogilvy, James (ed). Bellah, Robert N.

Barring Corporations from the Moral Community: the concept and the Cost. Wilson, Paul Eddy.

Between Individuality and Universality: An Explication of Chuang Tzu's Theses of Chien-tu and Ch'i-wu. Hara, Wing-Han.

Beyond Individualism and Collectivism in Revisioning Philosophy, Ogilvy, James (ed). Ogilvy, James.

Collective War and Individualistic Ethics: Against the Conscription of "Self-Defense". Zohar, Noam.

Comment on Davies: A General Dilemma?. Stoneham, Tom.

Cooperating with Cooperators. Rabinowicz, Wlodek.

Criticism and Tradition in Popper, Oakeshott and Hayek. O'Hear, Anthony.

Evolutionary Individualism. Franzwa, Gregg E.

Functional Explanation and Metaphysical Individualism. Schwartz, Justin.

How Can Individualists Share Responsibility?. Baier, Annette.

Idealist Organicism: Beyond Holism and Individualism. Simhony, A.

In Defense of Explanatory Ecumenism. Jackson, Frank and Pettit, Philip.

Individualism, Computation and Perceptual Content. Egan, Frances.

Individuality in Sartre's Philosophy in The Cambridge Companion to Sartre, Howells, Christina (ed). Fretz, Leo.

Inscrutability of Reference, Monism, and Individuals in Psychoanalysis, Mind and Art, Hopkins, Jim (ed). Ishiguro, Hidé.

Is the Biosphere a Luxury?. Midgley, Mary.

Locke on Government in Logical Foundations, Mahalingam, Indira (ed). Atkinson, R F.

MacIntyre's Nietzsche: A Critique. Hill, R Kevin.

Mechanisms, Methodological Individualism and Marxism: A Response to Elster in Marx's Theory of History, Wetherly, Paul. Wetherly, Paul.

Misunderstanding the Democratic 'We': Richard Rorty's Liberalism and the Radical Urge for a Philosophical Foundation. Moussa, Mario.

Natural Law, Liberal Religion, and Freedom of Association: James Luther Adams on the Problem of Jurisprudence. Sturm, Douglas.

New Trends in Russian Philosophy. Fluri, Philippe H.

Nietzsche and MacIntyre: Against Individualism. Starrett, Shari N.

Nietzsche's Philosopher of the Future as an Ethicist: Experimentalism in Ethics. Windham, Mary Elizabeth.

Object-Dependent Thoughts in Mental Causation, Heil, John (ed). Noonan, H W.

Perceptual Content and Local Supervenience. Davies, Martin.

Personal Integrity, Practical Recognition, and Rights. Mack, Eric.

Piecings from a Second Reader. Alexander, Natalie.

Pragmatism and the Normative Sciences in Frontiers in American Philosophy, Volume I, Burch, Robert W (ed). Lieb, Irwin C.

Private Life, Private Interest, Private Property. Zamoshkin, I A.

Scottish Communitarianism, Lockean Individualism, and Women's Moral Development in Women's Rights and the Rights of Man, Arnaud, A J. Cooper, David E.

Secret, Heresy and Responsibility: Patocka's Europe (Conclusion) (in Czechoslovakian). Derrida, Jacques.

Semantic Externalism and Conceptual Competence. Rey, Georges.

INTELLECT

Infinite Intellect and Human Cognition in Spinoza (in Dutch). Bartuschat, W.

Mathematical Construction, Symbolic Cognition and the Infinite Intellect: Reflections on Maimon and Maimonides. Lachterman, David.

Theophrastus on the Intellect in Theophrastus, Fortenbaugh, W W (ed). Devereux, Daniel.

INTELLECTUALISM

The Decline from Authority: Kierkegaard on Intellectual Sin. Aiken, David W.

The Unity of the Virtues in Plato's *Protagoras* and *Laches*. Devereux, Daniel T.

What Did Socrates Teach and To Whom Did He Teach It?. Nehamas, Alexander.

INTELLIGENCE

Are Souls Unintelligible? in Philosophical Perspectives, 5: Philosophy of Religion, 1991, Tomberlin, James E (ed). Hoffman, Joshua and Rosenkrantz, Gary.

Big Numbers and Induction in the Case for Extra-Terrestrial Intelligence. Mash, Roy.

Can Intelligence Be Artificial?. Dretske, Fred.

Comments on "Can Intelligence Be Artificial?". McNamara, Paul.

Il *Filebo* come una 'summa' del pensiero metafisico platonico. Bonagura, P.

Il posto della metafisica nel sapere umano: Il pensiero di Maimonide e eil suo influsso su S Tommaso d'Aquino. Pangallo, Mario.

Reaping the Whirlwind: Reply to Harnad's Other Bodies, Other Minds. Hauser, Larry.

Sex and Social Roles in Rethinking Masculinity, May, Larry (ed). Grim, Patrick.

The Rationality of Intelligence in Probability and Rationality, Eells, Ellery (ed). Lopes, Lola L and Oden, Gregg C.

Theophrastus and Aristotle on Animal Intelligence in Theophrastus, Fortenbaugh, W W (ed). Cole, Eve.

INTELLIGENTSIA

Sobor and *Sobornost'*. Tulaev, Pavel.

Landmarks: An Unheard Warning. Gaidenko, P P.

The *Narod* and the Intelligentsia: From Dissociation to *Sobornost'*. Klechenov, Gennadii.

The *Narod*, the Intelligentsia, and the Individual. Kovalev, Vitalii.

INTELLIGIBILITY

Intelligibility, Imperialism, and Conceptual Scheme. Hurley, S L.

Relativité du vrai, relativisme de l'intelligible. Thom, René.

The Structure-Nominative Reconstruction and the Intelligibility of Cognition. Burgin, Mark and Kuznetsov, Vladimir.

INTENSION

Inadequacies of Intension and Extension in Advances in Scientific Philosophy, Schurz, Gerhard (ed). Simons, Peter.

Inadequacies of Peter and Paul in Advances in Scientific Philosophy, Schurz, Gerhard (ed). Morscher, Edgar.

Intentions and Demonstrations. Bach, Kent.

Wittgenstein's Intentions in Wittgenstein's Intentions, Canfield, J V (ed). Canfield, J V.

INTENSIONAL LOGIC

A Functional Partial Semantics for Intensional Logic. Lapierre, Serge.

Critical and Pre-Critical Phases in Kant's Philosophy of Logic. Nussbaum, Charles.

Montague's Semantics for Intensional Logic. Palme Reyes, Marie La and Reyes, Gonzalo E.

INTENSIONALISM

The New Intensionalism. Katz, Jerrold.

INTENSIONALITY

Réalisme et anti-réalisme en logique. Nef, Frédéric.

INTENTION

Automatism, Insanity, and the Psychology of Criminal Responsibility: A Philosophical Inquiry. Schopp, Robert F.

Malum Vitandum: The Role of Intentions in First-Order Morality. Sullivan, Thomas D and Atkinson, Gary.

Wittgenstein's Intentions. Canfield, J V (ed) and Shanker, Stuart G (ed).

Categorial Intuition and the Understanding of Being in Husserl and Heidegger in Reading Heidegger: Commemorations, Sallis, John (ed). Watanabe, Jiro.

Causing, Intending, and Assisting Death. Brody, Howard.

Demonstratives and Intentions, Ten Years Later. Bertolet, Rod.

Does Intention Define Action? (in French). Neuberg, Marc.

Explaining Intentions: Critical Review of *Explaining Behaviour*. Gillett, Grant.

Inescapable Surprises and Acquirable Intentions. Goldstein, Laurence.

Intention Detecting. Holton, Richard.

Intention in Wittgenstein. Bhat, P R.

Manifesto di un movimento ermeneutico universale. Mathieu, Vittorio.

Objects of Intention. Vermazen, Bruce.

On Logical Form of Action Sentences. Goswami, Chinmoy.

Still More in Defense of Colorization. Young, James O.

The Body in Action: the Relationship between Action, Intention and Corporal Movement (in French). Dokic, Jérôme.

What Is Cooperation?. Tuomela, Raimo.

INTENTIONAL

Intentional and Material Phenomenology (in German). Kühn, Rolf.

Perspectives on Intentional Realism. Davies, David.

Practical Unreason. Pettit, Philip and Smith, Michael.

Some of the Difference in the World: Crane on Intentional Causation. Seymour, Daniel.

INTENTIONALISM

The Intentionalist Controversy and Cognitive Science. Gibbs Jr, Raymond W.

The Problem of Error: A Surd Spot in Rational Intentionalism. McGeer, V L.

INTENTIONALITY

"From Natural Function to Indeterminate Content". Sullivan, Sonja R.

"Le sens optus" and "Unintentionality" (in Czechoslovakian). Grygar, Mojmir.

Agency in Action: The Practical Rational Agency Machine. Coval, Samuel C and Campbell, P G.

An Essay on Belief and Acceptance. Cohen, L Jonathan.

An Introduction to Husserlian Phenomenology. Bernet, Rudolf, Kern, Iso and Marbach, Eduard.

John Searle and His Critics. LePore, Ernest (ed) and Van Gulick, Robert (ed).

Moral Personhood: An Essay in the Philosophy of Moral Psychology. Scott, G E.

The Crisis of Philosophy. McCarthy, Michael.

The Perceptual System: A Philosophical and Psychological Perspective. Ben-Ze'ev, Aaron.

Wittgenstein's Philosophy of Psychology. Budd, Malcolm.

Acting for Reasons and Acting Intentionally. Mele, Alfred.

An Embarrassing Question about Reproduction. Haldane, John.

An Intentional Explication of Universals. Chisholm, Roderick M.

Art and Intentionality. Kolak, Daniel.

Authors and Artifacts. Hilpinen, Risto.

Brentano's Doctrine of Intentionality of Mental Phenomena. Singh, Ravindra.

Cognitive Models and Representation. Kukla, Rebecca.

Consciousness, Intentionality and Internalism: A Philosophical Perspective on Velmans and His Critics. Gillett, Grant.

Decomposing Intentionality: Perspectives on Intentionality Drawn from Language Research with Two Species of Chimpanzees. Bechtel, William.

Die Selbstintentionalität der Welt in Analecta Husserliana, XXXIV, Tymieniecka, Anna-Teresa (ed). Pavic, Zeljko.

Husserl and Analytic Philosophy and Husserlian Intentionality and Non-Foundational Realism. Sokolowski, Robert.

Husserl's Account of Syncategorematic Terms. Lampert, Jay.

Husserl's Intentionality and "Mind" in Chinese Philosophy. Zhang, Xian.

Intention and Convention in Communications- Reunderstanding Bhartrhari. Patnaik, Tandra.

Intention, Intentionality and Causality (in French). Moya, Carlos.

Intentional Action and Unconscious Reasons. Vollmer, Fred.

Intentional Identity Generalized. King, Jeffrey C.

Intentionality *De Re* in John Searle and His Critics, Lepore, Ernest (ed). McDowell, John.

Intentionality and Madness in Hegel's Psychology of Action. Berthold-Bond, Daniel.

Intentionality and Modern Philosophical Psychology, III—The Appeal to Teleology. Lyons, William.

Intentionality and Teleological Error. Pietroski, Paul.

Intentionality and Tendency: How to Make Aristotle Up-To-Date in Language, Truth and Ontology, Mulligan, Kevin (ed). Johansson, Ingvar.

Intentionality and the Phenomenology of Action in John Searle and His Critics, Lepore, Ernest (ed). Wakefield, Jerome and Dreyfus, Hubert.

Intentionality and World in The Cambridge Companion to Heidegger, Guignon, Charles B (ed). Hall, Harrison B.

Intentionality in Research on Teaching. Noel, Jana R.

Intentionality, Consciousness, and Subjectivity. Natsoulas, Thomas.

Intentionality, Narrativity, and Interpretation in John Searle and His Critics, Lepore, Ernest (ed). Feldman, Carol Fleisher.

Intentionality, Perception, and Causality in John Searle and His Critics, Lepore, Ernest (ed). Armstrong, D M.

Intentions, Concepts of Intention, and the "Final Solution". Lang, Berel.

Intenzionalità e filosofia dell'azione. Marrone, Pierpaolo.

Interpretation, Intention, and Truth. Shusterman, Richard.

Justifying Intentions. Mele, Alfred.

Les expériences de Burge et les contenus de pensée. Seymour, Michel.

Logical Positivism and Intentionality in A J Ayer Memorial Essays, Griffiths, A Phillips (ed). Putnam, Hilary.

Meaning and Intentionality in Wittgenstein's Later Philosophy. McDowell, John.

Meaning Holism and Semantic Realism. Callaway, H G.

Non-consequentialism, the Person as an End-in-Itself, and the Significance of Status. Kamm, F M.

On a Model for Psycho-Neural Coevolution. Kobes, Bernard W.

On Thinking. Rotenstreich, Nathan.

Painting, Parapraxes, and Unconscious Intentions. Geller, Jeffery.

Paradigm Intention. Simester, A P.

Perceptual Realism, Naive and Otherwise in John Searle and His Critics, Lepore, Ernest (ed). Zemach, Eddy M.

Possibilità e stati di fatto in Chisholm. Negro, Matteo.

Postivism, Natural Law Theory and the "Internal Morality of Law". Sweet, William.

Predication as Originary Violence in Working Through Derrida, Madison, Gary B (ed). Willard, Dallas.

Putnam on Intentionality. Haldane, John.

Reply to Gillett's "Consciousness, Intentionality and Internalism". Velmans, Max.

Respones: Reference and Intentionality in John Searle and His Critics, Lepore, Ernest (ed). Searle, John R.

Response: Perception and the Satisfactions of Intentionality in John Searle and His Critics, Lepore, Ernest (ed). Searle, John R.

Response: The Background of Intentionality and Action in John Searle and His Critics, Lepore, Ernest (ed). Searle, John R.

Revisionary Physicalism. Bickle, John.

Searle's Theory of Action in John Searle and His Critics, Lepore, Ernest (ed). O'Shaughnessy, Brian.

Searles Auffassung des Verhältnisses von Geist und Körper und ihre Beziehung zur Ideantitätstheorie. Schröder, Jürgen.

INTENTIONALITY

Strumenti analitici per la comprensione della filosofia continentale. Marrone, P.

The Background of Thought in John Searle and His Critics, Lepore, Ernest (ed). Stroud, Barry G.

The Connection between Intentionality and Consciousness in Consciousness: Psychological and Philosophical Essays, Davies, Martin (ed). Nelkin, Norton.

The Education of Searle's Demon. Bombardi, Ronald J.

The Intentionality of Some Ethological Terms. Thompson, Nicholas S and Derr, Patrick.

The Pragmatic Psyche. Bogdan, Radu J.

Three Bad Arguments for Intentional Property Epiphenomenalism. Van Gulick, Robert.

Vision and Intentional Content in John Searle and His Critics, Lepore, Ernest (ed). Burge, Tyler.

'I Believe that P' in John Searle and His Critics, Lepore, Ernest (ed). Malcolm, Norman.

INTERACTION

Metaphor and Cognition. Indurkhya, Bipin.

INTERACTIONISM

The Problem of Psychophysical Causation. Lowe, E J.

INTERDISCIPLINARY

Possible Worlds Between the Disciplines. Ronen, Ruth.

INTEREST

see also Public Interest, Self-Interest

Holism, Interest-Identity, and Value. Morito, Bruce.

INTERIORITY

L'interiorità cartesiana tra metafisica e fenomenismo. Nicolosi, S.

INTERMEDIATE LOGICS

On Structural Completeness of Implicational Logics. Wojtylak, Piotr.

Refutation Calculi for Certain Intermediate Propositional Logics. Skura, Tomasz.

The Disjunction Property of Intermediate Propositional Logic. Chagrov, Alexander and Zakharyashchev, Michael.

The Disjunction Property of the Logics with Axioms of Only One Variable. Sasaki, Katsumi.

The Gentzen-Kripke Construction of the Intermediate Logic LQ. Akama, Seiki.

INTERNAL

The Human Being as a Logical Thinker. Balzer, Noel.

A Note on Smith on Attempts and Internal Events. Rickard, Maurice.

Keeping a Happy Face on Exportation. Kapitan, Tomis.

INTERNALISM

Knowledge and Belief. Schmitt, Frederick.

Abilities, Concepts, and Externalism in Mental Causation, Heil, John (ed). Sosa, Ernest.

Consciousness, Intentionality and Internalism: A Philosophical Perspective on Velmans and His Critics. Gillett, Grant.

Externalism and Mental Causality (in French). Jacob, Pierre.

Externalism for Internalists in Rationality in Epistemology, Villanueva, Enrique (ed). Dancy, Jonathan.

Externalism, Internalism and Moral Scepticism. Goldsworthy, Jeffrey.

Fallibilismus: Ein Paradoxon. Lehrer, Keith.

Hume's Internalism. Coleman, Dorothy.

Inner States. Odegard, Douglas.

Internalism and Agency in Philosophical Perspectives, 6: Ethics, 1992, Tomberlin, James E (ed). Darwall, Stephen L.

Internalism in Epistemology and the Internalist Regress. Jacobson, Stephen.

Justification in the 20th Century in Rationality in Epistemology, Villanueva, Enrique (ed). Plantinga, Alvin.

Kant on Action and Knowledge. Saugstad, Jens.

La métaphysique de la parole et les faubourgs du langage. Cometti, Jean-Pierre.

Locke on Real Essence and Internal Constitution. Vienne, Jean-Michel.

Moral Relativism, Internalism, and the "Humean" View. Tilley, John.

Persons and Perspectives: A Personalist Response to Nagel. Sayre, Patricia.

Proper Functionalism. Feldman, Richard.

Proper Functionalism and Virtue Epistemology. Sosa, Ernest.

Reply to Gillett's "Consciousness, Intentionality and Internalism". Velmans, Max.

Semantic Externalism and Conceptual Competence. Rey, Georges.

Should We Replace Knowledge by Understanding?—A Comment on Elgin and Goodman's Reconception of Epistemology. Koppelberg, Dirk.

Skepticism and Reasoning to the Best Explanation in Rationality in Epistemology, Villanueva, Enrique (ed). Fumerton, Richard.

Skepticism Naturalized in Rationality in Epistemology, Villanueva, Enrique (ed). Higginbotham, James.

The Egg Came Before the Chicken. Sorensen, Roy.

The Prospects for Natural Theology in Philosophical Perspectives, 5: Philosophy of Religion, 1991, Tomberlin, James E (ed). Plantinga, Alvin.

The Role of Internalism in Moral Theory. Bartkowiak, Julia.

Toward a Compatibility Theory for Internalist and Externalist Epistemologies. Sennett, James F.

INTERNATIONAL

Ethics of Environment and Development: Global Challenge, International Response. Engel, J Ronald (ed) and Engel, Joan Gibb (ed).

Praxiologies and the Philosophy of Economics: The International Annual of Practical Philosophy and Methodology. Auspitz, J Lee (ed), Gasparski, Wojciech W (ed) and Mlicki, Marek K (ed).

The Place of the Person In Social Life. Peachey, Paul (ed), Kromkowski, John (ed) and McLean, George F (ed).

Can We Afford International Human Rights?. Brenkert, George G.

Commentator on 'Distributing Health' in The Quality of Life, Nussbaum, Martha C (ed). Seabright, Paul.

Distributing Health in The Quality of Life, Nussbaum, Martha C (ed). Roemer, John E.

Ethics in Business and Administration: An International and Historical Perspective. Small, Michael W.

International Reflections on Individual Autonomy and Corporate Effectiveness. Moore, Jennifer Mills.

Justice, Gender, and International Boundaries in The Quality of Life, Nussbaum, Martha C (ed). O'Neill, Onora.

Rethinking the Responsibility of International Corporations: A Response to Donaldson. Koehn, Daryl.

Self-Determination in Political Philosophy and International Law. Dahbour, Omar.

Why Philosophy of Art in Cross-Cultural Perspectives?. Moravcsik, Julius.

INTERNATIONAL LAW

International Law and World Peace. Mitias, Michael H.

INTERNATIONAL RELATION

Reinhold Niebuhr and the Ethics of Realism in International Relations. Rich, Paul.

INTERNATIONALISM

Ethical Theory and Business (Fourth Edition). Beauchamp, Tom L and Bowie, Norman E.

INTERPERSONAL

Sobre la negación: En busca de un nuevo argumento contra el origen intrapersonal de ese tipo de pensamiento. Bejarano Fernandez, T.

INTERPOLATION

Amalgamation and Interpolation in Normal Modal Logics. Maksimova, L.

INTERPRETABILITY

A Generalized Notion of Weak Interpretability and the Corresponding Modal Logic. Dzhaparidze, Giorgie.

On Σ1 and Π1 Sentences and Degrees of Interpretability. Lindström, Per.

On the Proofs of Arithmetical Completeness for Interpretability Logic. Zambella, Domenico.

Unary Interpretability Logic. De Rijke, Maarten.

INTERPRETATION

Dialogic Semiosis: An Essay on Signs and Meaning. Johansen, Jorgen Dines.

Extensions: Essays on Interpretation, Rationality, and the Closure of Modernism. Watson, Stephen.

Interpretation and Overinterpretation: Umberto Eco. Collini, Stefan (ed).

On Paul Ricoeur: Narrative and Interpretation. Wood, David (ed).

Philosophy and Biblical Interpretation: A Study in Nineteenth-Century Conflict. Addinall, Peter.

The Interpretive Turn. Hiley, David R (ed), Bohman, James F (ed) and Shusterman, Richard (ed).

A Refiner's Fire: Reply to Sartwell and Kolak. Levinson, Jerrold.

A Sociological Perspective on Disease in New Horizons in the Philosophy of Science, Lamb, David (ed). White, Kevin.

A Study of Part I, Chapters 1-7 of Maimonides' The Guide of the Perplexed. Kleven, Terence.

An Inconsistency between Quantum Mechanics and Its Itnerpretation in Advances in Scientific Philosophy, Schurz, Gerhard (ed). Mittelstaedt, Peter.

Argumentation and Interpretation in Law. MacCormick, Neil.

Beneath Interpretation in The Interpretive Turn, Hiley, David R (ed). Shusterman, Richard.

Can We Talk? Contexts of Meaning for Interpreting Illness. Mount Jr, Eric.

Dante and Machiavelli: A Last Word. Peterman, Larry.

Deconstruction and Legal Interpretation in Deconstruction and the Possibility of Justice, Cornell, Durcilla (ed). Rosenfeld, Michel.

Do We Need a Concept of Disease?. Hesslow, Germund.

Extending the Curry-Howard Interpretation to Lienar, Relevant and Other Resource Logics. Gabbay, Dov M and De Queiroz, R J G B.

Frege's Error. Ruthrof, Horst.

Hermeias on Plato Phaedrus 238d and Synesius Dion 14.2. Dickie, Mathew W.

Hermeneutical Terror and the Myth of Interpretive Consensus. Kent, Thomas.

Historical Interpretation and Mental Images of Culture (in Dutch). Kuiper, Mark.

In Defence of Overinterpretation in Interpretation and Overinterpretation: Umberto Eco, Collini, Stefan (ed). Culler, Jonathan.

Incompatible Interpretations. Stecker, Robert A.

Indeterminacy of Interpretation, Idealization, and Norms. Kirk, Robert.

Innate Ideas and Cartesian Dispositions. Flage, Daniel and Bonnen, Clarence A.

Intentionality, Narrativity, and Interpretation in John Searle and His Critics, Lepore, Ernest (ed). Feldman, Carol Fleisher.

Interpretation and History in Interpretation and Overinterpretation: Umberto Eco, Collini, Stefan (ed). Eco, Umberto.

Interpretation and Identity in Quantum Theory. Butterfield, Jeremy.

Interpretation and Objectivity. Currie, Gregory.

Interpretation as Explanation in The Interpretive Turn, Hiley, David R (ed). Roth, Paul A.

Interprétation et vérité. Ladrière, Jean.

Interpretation in Natural and Human Science in The Interpretive Turn, Hiley, David R (ed). Rouse Jr, Joseph T.

Interpretation, Dialogue and the Just Citizen. Kingwell, Mark.

Interpretation, Intention, and Truth. Shusterman, Richard.

Interpreting Art and Literature. Goldman, Alan H.

Jacques Monod's Scientific Analysis and Its Reductionistic Interpretation. Spassov, Spas.

INTERPRETATION

Language, Interpretation and Worship—I in Religion and Philosophy, Warner, Marin (ed). Warner, Martin.

Language, Interpretation and Worship—II in Religion and Philosophy, Warner, Marin (ed). Lamarque, Peter.

Law-Making and Legal Interpretation. Frosini, Vittorio.

Les avatars du sens profond: Réflexion sur quelques modèles de lecture. Vandendorpe, Christian.

Manifesto di un movimento ermeneutico universale. Mathieu, Vittorio.

Mead's Voices: Imitation as Foundation, or, The Struggle against Mimesis. Leys, Ruth.

Metaphorical Meaning and Its Interpretation (in Hebrew). Kulka, Tomas.

Metaphysics, Semiotics, and Common Sense, a review of *Recovery of the Measure: Interpretation and Nature*, by Robert Cummings Neville. Grange, Joseph.

Moore and Shusterman on Organic Wholes. Leddy, Thomas W.

Naming and Knowing: The *Cratylus* on Images. Spellman, Lynne M.

Nietzsche and Aestheticism. Leiter, Brian.

Oltre l'ermeneutica. Mangiagalli, M.

On the Proof of Solovay's Theorem. De Jongh, Dick, Jumelet, Marc and Montagna, Franco.

On the Relevance and Importance of the Notion of Disease. Nordenfelt, Lennart.

Overinterpreting Texts in Interpretation and Overinterpretation: Umberto Eco, Collini, Stefan (ed). Eco, Umberto.

Patterns of Historical Interpretation in Objectivity, Method and Point of View, Van Der Dussen, W J (ed). Christianson, Paul.

Plato and the Sightlovers of the *Republic*. Stokes, Michael C.

Provability Logics for Natural Turing Progressions of Arithmetical Theories. Beklemishev, L D.

Reinterpreting Interpretation. Margolis, Joseph.

Relational Proof System for Relevant Logics. Orlowska, Ewa.

Skeptical Hypotheses and 'Omniscient' Interpreters. Reynolds, Steven L.

Style and Sense in Aristotle's *Rhetoric* Bk 3. Halliwell, Stephen.

The Authorship of the *Abstract* Revisited. Raynor, David.

The Concept of Reading and the 'Book of Nature' in Simone Weil's Philosophy of Culture, Bell, Richard H (ed). Allen, Diogenes.

The Great Fuss over *Philebus* 15b. Mirhady, David C.

The Interpretability of Robinson Arithmetic in the Ramified Second-Order Theory of Dense Linear Order. Hazen, A P.

The Lacuna at Aristotle's *Poetics* 1457b33. Schenkeveld, Dirk M.

The Meaning of 'Radical Foundation' in Husserl: The Outline of an Interpretation in Analecta Husserliana, XXXIV, Tymieniecka, Anna-Teresa (ed). Cantista, Maria José.

The Phrenetic Calculus: A Logician's View of Disordered Logical Thinking in Schizophrenia. Klee, Robert.

The Rhetoric of Jacques Derrida II: *Phaedrus*. Rinon, Yoav.

The Sign Over the Barber Shop: Annotations on the Problems of Interpretation. Schmitz, Heinz-Gerd.

The Tarasoff Case. Farbstein, Aviva.

The Unnamed Fifth: *Republic* 369d. Page, Carl.

The Wisdom of the Many: An Analysis of the Arguments of Books III and IV of Aristotle's *Politics*. Bookman, J T.

Una nuova edizione italiana di Platone. Bausola, Adriano.

Unifying the *Protagoras*. Rutherford, Richard.

Vlastos's Socrates. Kahn, Charles.

Why Can't a Baby Pretend to Smile? in Wittgenstein's Intentions, Canfield, J V (ed). Von Savigny, Eike.

Wittgenstein's Intentions in Wittgenstein's Intentions, Canfield, J V (ed). Canfield, J V.

INTERROGATION

The Interrogative Model of Inquiry as a General Theory of Argumentation. Hintikka, Jaakko.

INTERSUBJECTIVITY

Autocoscienza, riferimento dell'io e conoscenza di sé: Introduzione ad un dibattito contemporaneo. Ferrarin, Alfredo.

Intersubjectivity in Phenomenology. Tripathy, L K.

Les figures de l'intersubjectivité: Études des Husserliana XIII-XIV-XV. Depraz, Natalie.

Merleau-Ponty on Subjectivity and Intersubjectivity. Low, Douglas.

INTERVAL

Continuity and Common Sense. Baxter, Donald L M.

INTERVIEW

A Generation Apart from Adorno (An Interview). Habermas, Jürgen.

An Interview with A J Ayer. Price, Thomas, Russell, Robert and Kennett, Stephen.

An Interview with A J Ayer in A J Ayer Memorial Essays, Griffiths, A Phillips (ed). Honderich, Ted.

Hilary Putnam: On Mind, Meaning, and Reality. Harlan, Josh.

John Rawls: For the Record (An Interview). Aybar, Samuel R, Harlan, Joshua D and Lee, Won J.

Marxism Today: An Interview with István Mészáros. Arthur, Chris and McCarney, Joseph.

Regarding Postmodernism—A Conversation with Fredric Jameson in Postmodernism/ Jameson/ Critique, Kellner, Douglas M (ed). Stephanson, Anders.

Soviet Philosophy in Transition: An Interview with Vladislav Lektorsky. Bakhurst, David.

That Which Resists, After All. Lyotard, Jean-François and Larochelle, Gilbert.

Umbrellas, Laundry Bills, and Resistance: The Place of Foucault's Interviews in his *Corpus*. Cook, Deborah.

V V Rozanov: An Interview with V G Sukach. Skorobogatko, Nataliia.

'I Am No Longer a Realist': An Interview with Jean-Paul Sartre in Sartre Alive, Aronson, Ronald (ed). Verstraeten, Pierre.

INTIMACY

Male Friendship and Intimacy. May, Larry and Strikwerda, Robert.

Male Friendship and Intimacy in Rethinking Masculinity, May, Larry (ed). Strikwerda, Robert A and May, Larry.

INTRINSIC

Almost Indiscernible Twins. Baber, Harriet E.

Appendage Theory—Pro and Con. Natsoulas, Thomas.

Consciousness: Varieties of Intrinsic Theory. Natsoulas, Thomas.

Goodness and Truth. Gaita, Raimond.

Lockean Ideas and 18th Century British Philosophy. Loptson, Peter J.

Rolston on Intrinsic Value: A Deconstruction. Callicott, J Baird.

Ross, Promises and the Intrinsic Value of Acts. Brennan, Susan K.

The Categories of Value. Allen, R T.

The Ontological Argument Defended. Makin, Stephen.

Toward an Improved Understanding of Sigmund Freud's Conception of Consciousness. Natsoulas, Thomas.

INTRINSIC VALUE

The Concept of Intrinsic Value and Transgenic Animals. Verhoog, H.

INTUITION

Analecta Husserliana, XXXIV. Tymieniecka, Anna-Teresa (ed).

The Cambridge Companion to Kant. Guyer, Paul (ed).

The Concept of Political Judgment. Steinberger, Peter J.

Aristotle's Practical Particularism in Essays in Ancient Greek Philosophy, IV, Anton, John P (ed). Louden, Robert B.

Husserl, Linguistic Meaning, and Intuition. Owens, Wayne.

Intuition and Substance: Two Aspects of Kant's Conception of an Empirical Object. Sweet, Dennis J.

Intuition et intuitionisme. Largeault, Jean.

McAllister on Northrop. Seddon, Fred.

Negations in Conflict. Hand, Michael.

On Some Difficulties Concerning Intuition and Intuitive Knowledge. Parsons, Charles.

Parsons on Mathematical Intuition. Page, James.

Scenarios, Concepts and Perception in The Contents of Experience, Crane, Tim (ed). Peacocke, Christopher.

The Significance of Kant's Framework of Possible Experience. Rajiva, Suma.

Was ist Phänomenologie? (Nachdruck). Stein, Edith.

What Is (or At Least Appears to Be) Wrong with Intuistionic Logic? in Advances in Scientific Philosophy, Schurz, Gerhard (ed). Lenzen, Wolfgang.

INTUITIONISM

Brève note sur l'intuitionnisme de Brouwer. Largeault, Jean.

Compassion, Consensus, and Conflict: Should Caregivers' Needs Influence the Ethical Dialectic?. Dagi, Teo Forcht.

Extending the Curry-Howard Interpretation to Lienar, Relevant and Other Resource Logics. Gabbay, Dov M and De Queiroz, R J G B.

F R Leavis: Intuitionist?. Haynes, Anthony.

How Not to Refute Realism. George, Alexander.

In Defense of Explanatory Ecumenism. Jackson, Frank and Pettit, Philip.

Intuitionistic Concept of Mathematical Language (in Polish). Miszczynski, Ryszard.

L'intuitionisme des mathématiciens avant Brouwer. Largeault, Jean.

La gnoseologia dell'arte in J Maritain. Viganó, A.

Review Essay: The Best Intuitionistic Theory Yet! Thomson On Rights. Smith, M B E.

Sidgwick and Whewellian Intuitionism in Essays on Henry Sidgwick, Schultz, Bart (ed). Donagan, Alan.

Spreads or Choice Sequences?. DeSwart, H C M.

The Intuitionistic Alternative Set Theory. Lano, K.

The Unintended Interpretations of Intuitionistic Logic in Perspectives on the History of Mathematical Logic, Drucker, Thomas (ed). Ruitenburg, Wim.

Why There Are No Objective Values: A Critique of Ethical Intuitionism from an Evolutionary Point of View. Geiger, Gebhard.

INTUITIONISTIC LOGIC

A Representation of Intuitionistic Logic in Partial Information Language. Barba Escriba, Juan.

Classical and Intuitionistic Negation. Hand, Michael.

Classical Logic, Intuitionistic Logic, and the Peirce Rule. Africk, Henry.

Functional Completeness for Subsystems of Intuitionistic Propositional Logic. Wansing, Heinrich.

Hilbert's ε-Operator and Classical Logic. Bell, John L.

Intuitionistic Validity in *T*-Normal Kripke Structures. Buss, Samuel R.

Linearizing Intuitionistic Implication. Lincoln, Patrick, Scedrov, Andre and Shankar, Natarajan.

Matrix-Frame Semantics for ISCI and INT. Lukowski, Piotr.

Nonmonotonic Consequence Based on Intuitionistic Logic. Servi, G F.

On the Unity of Logic. Girard, Jean-Yves.

Rudimentary Kripke Models for the Intuitionistic Propositional Calculus. Dosen, Kosta.

The Continuum and First-Order Intuitionistic Logic. Van Dalen, D.

Two Sequents of Locally Tabular Superintuitionistic Logic. Mardaev, S I.

INVARIANCE

Invariance and Structural Dependence. Odelstad, Jan.

INVENTION

De la "invención" al "descubrimiento" del Nuevo Mundo. Dussel, Enrique.

INVITTO, G

L'esistenzialismo rivisitato. Bello, A G A.

INWOOD, B

Presocratics and Sophists. Wright, M R.

JAPANESE

The Social Self in Japanese Philosophy and American Pragmatism: A Comparative Study of Watsuji Tetsurō and George Herbert Mead. Odin, Steve.

Two Contemporary Japanese Views of the Body: Ichikawa Hiroshi and Yuasa Yasuo in Self as Body in Asian Theory and Practice, Kasulis, Thomas P (ed). Nagatomo, Shigenori.

Whitehead and Japanese Aesthetics. Mayada, Arlene M.

JARVIS, J

Non-consequentialism, the Person as an End-in-Itself, and the Significance of Status. Kamm, F M.

JASPERS

Interpretazione esistenziale della storia della filosofia. Penzo, G.

Karl Jaspers and Scientific Philosophy. Bennett, James O.

JAZZ

Adorno's Critique of Popular Culture: The Case of Jazz Music. Brown, Lee B.

The Theory of Jazz Music "It Don't Mean a Thing...". Brown, Lee B.

JECKER, N

Justice within Intimate Spheres. Carse, Alisa.

JEFFERSON

Rational Infidels: The American Deists. Walters, Kerry S.

The Jeffersonian Option. Dawidoff, Robert.

JEFFREY, F

Francis Jeffrey's Associationist Aesthetics. Christie, W H.

JEFFREY, R

Choice and Conditional Expected Utility. Rawling, Piers.

The Geometry of Opinion: Jeffrey Shifts and Linear Operators. Van Fraassen, Bas C.

JENNINGS, R

Jennings and Zande Logic: A Note. Keita, Lansana.

JESUITS

Conditionals of Freedom and Middle Knowledge. Gaskin, R.

De bijdrage van de jezuïeten tot de filosofische cultuur: La contribution des jésuites à la culture philosophique. Verhaeghe, J.

Kasuistik: Ein wiederentdecktes Kapitel der Jesuitenmoral. Schmitz, Philipp.

Necessitas moralis ad optimum (III). Knebel, Sven K.

Suárez and the Jesuits. Noreña, Carlos.

JESUS

see Christ

JEWISH

see also Hebraic, Judaism

"One Isaac Waiting to Be Slaughtered": Halpern Leivick, The Holocaust, and Responsibility. Goodhart, Sandor.

German Philosophy and Jewish Thought. Greenspan, Louis (ed) and Nicholson, Graeme (ed).

Isaiah Berlin: A Celebration. Margalit, Edna (ed) and Margalit, Avishai (ed).

A Critique of Borowitz's Postmodern Jewish Theology. Samuelson, Norbert M.

A Note on Schadenfreude and Proverbs 17:5. Harvey, Warren Z.

Artificial Reproductive Technologies: The Israeli Scene. Heyd, David.

Authentic Selfhood in Heidegger and Rosenzweig. Cohen, Richard A.

Between the Lines: The Jewish Museum, Berlin. Libeskind, Daniel.

Diaspora: Generation and the Ground of Jewish Identity. Boyarin, Daniel and Boyarin, Jonathan.

Extraordinary Evil or Common Malevolence? in Applied Philosophy, Almond, Brenda (ed). Lackey, Douglas.

Hannah Arendt and the Etiology of the Desk Killer: The Holocaust as Portent. Milchman, Alan.

Isaiah's Marx, and Mine in Isaiah Berlin: A Celebration, Margalit, Edna (ed). Cohen, G A.

Jewish Lesbian Writing: A Review Essay. Scheman, Naomi.

Philosophy, History, and the Jewish Thinker in German Philosophy and Jewish Thought, Greenspan, Louis (ed). Morgan, Michael.

Pragmatic Conditions for Jewish-Christian Theological Dialogue. Ochs, Peter.

Response to Daniel Libeskind. Derrida, Jacques.

Response to Douglas P Lackey's 'Extraordinary Evil or Common Malevolence?' in Applied Philosophy, Almond, Brenda (ed). Krizan, M.

Understanding Fascism? in Isaiah Berlin: A Celebration, Margalit, Edna (ed). Ignatieff, Michael.

Whose History? What Ideas? in Isaiah Berlin: A Celebration, Margalit, Edna (ed). Tamir, Yael.

JOB

On "Philosophy" of Women's Double Role (in Czechoslovakian). Vodakova, Alena.

JOHN

The Beginning of the Gospel According to Saint John: Philosophical Reflections. Mensch, James Richard.

JOHN OF THE CROSS

La pensée et la vie. De Cointet, Pierre.

JOHNSON, D

A Reply to Johnson's Reply to "Should Computer Programs Be Ownable?". Carey, David.

Natural Kinds and Ecological Niches—Response to Johnson's Paper. Hogan, Melinda.

JOHNSON, O

"Ought" Never Is: A Response to Oliver A Johnson. Goldthwait, John T.

JOHNSON, W

Metaphysics, Economics and Progress: A Comment on Glass and Johnson. Hands, D Wade.

JOHNSTON, M

Constitution is Identity. Noonan, Harold W.

Found: the Missing Explanation. Menzies, Peter and Philip, Pettit.

JONES, J

Paradigms of Belief, Theory and Metatheory. Sperry, Roger W.

JONES, O

More on Moore. Welbourne, Michael.

JORDAN, J

God and Freedom: Reply to Jordan. Davies, Brian.

JOURNAL

Student Written Philosophical Journals. Sautter, R Craig.

The Institutionalization of a Discipline: A Retrospective of The Journal of Aesthetics and Art Criticism and the Amer Soc for Aesthetics, 1939-1992. Goehr, Lydia.

The Journal of Aesthetics and Danto's Philosophical Criticism. Herwitz, Daniel A.

JOURNALISM

Philosophical Issues in Journalism. Cohen, Elliot D (ed).

The Journalistic Uses of Philosophy. Audi, Robert.

JOYCE

Ulysses and Vacuous Pluralism. Herman, David.

L'assassin d'Ulysse. Leroux, François.

Six Theories in the Bedroom of The Dead. Garrett, Roland.

JUCKES, T

The Absent Ontology of Society: Response to Juckes and Barresi. Manicas, Peter T.

JUDAISM

Disputed Questions in Theology and the Philosophy of Religion. Hick, John.

Reasoned Faith. Stump, Eleonore (ed).

Simone Weil: Portrait of a Self-Exiled Jew. Nevin, Thomas R.

The Rehabilitation of Myth. Mali, Joseph.

Toward a Genealogy of Individualism. Shanahan, Daniel.

A Critique of Borowitz's Postmodern Jewish Theology. Samuelson, Norbert M.

A Reply to My Critics: A Testament of Thought (Includes Bibliography) in German Philosophy and Jewish Thought, Greenspan, Louis (ed). Fackenheim, Emil L.

Fackenheim and Christianity in German Philosophy and Jewish Thought, Greenspan, Louis (ed). Baum, Gregory.

Framing Redemption in Ethics and Danger, Dallery, Arleen B (ed). Comay, Rebecca.

From Theology to Sociology: Bruno Bauer and Karl Marx on the Question of Jewish Emancipation. Peled, Yoav.

Kaufman on Kaplan and Process Theology: A Post-Positivist Perspective. Alexander, H A.

Mordecai M Kaplan and Process Theology: Metaphysical and Pragmatic Perspectives. Kaufman, William E.

Religious Concepts of 'World': Comparative Metaphysical. Pratt, Douglas.

Revelation and Resistance: A Reflection on the Thought of Fackenheim in German Philosophy and Jewish Thought, Greenspan, Louis (ed). Munk, Reinier.

The Passing of Hegel's Germany in German Philosophy and Jewish Thought, Greenspan, Louis (ed). Nicholson, Graeme.

The Teaching of Centesimus Annus. Schall, James V.

Theodicy in the Book of Job (in Hebrew). Schweid, Eliezer.

JUDEO-CHRISTIAN

Reasoned Faith. Stump, Eleonore (ed).

A New Look at the Problem of Evil. Gellman, Jerome I.

About the Beginning of the Hermeneutics of the Self: Two Lectures at Dartmouth— Michel Foucault. Blasius, Mark (ed).

Divine Simplicity in Philosophical Perspectives, 5: Philosophy of Religion, 1991, Tomberlin, James E (ed). Wolterstorff, Nicholas.

Emanation Ex Deus: A Defense. Oakes, Robert.

Forgiveness: A Developmental View. Enright, Robert D, Gassin, Elizabeth A and Wu, Ching-ru.

God and Time in Reasoned Faith, Stump, Eleonore (ed). Swinburne, Richard.

God's General Concurrence with Secondary Causes in Philosophical Perspectives, 5: Philosophy of Religion, 1991, Tomberlin, James E (ed). Freddoso, Alfred.

God, Eternality, and the View from Nowhere in Logic, God and Metaphysics, Harris, James F (ed). Harris, James F.

Las raíces del machismo en la ideología judeo-cristiana de la mujer. Caponi, Orietta.

On Being Inside/Outside Truth in Modernity and Its Discontents, Marsh, James L (ed). Caputo, John D.

On God's Creation in Reasoned Faith, Stump, Eleonore (ed). Frankfurt, Harry G.

Paradigms for an Open Philosophy. Polis, Dennis F.

The Gods above the Gods: Can the High Gods Survive? in Reasoned Faith, Stump, Eleonore (ed). Mavrodes, George I.

The Intensity of Theism. Taliaferro, Charles.

The Problem of Divine Perfection and Freedom in Reasoned Faith, Stump, Eleonore (ed). Rowe, William.

Three Types of Divine Power. Gier, Nicholas F.

Weeks, Spinoza's God and Epistemic Autonomy. Leavitt, Frank J.

JUDGE

Die Freiheit des Richters. Schubarth, Martin.

Judges and Moral Responsibility in Ethical Dimensions of Legal Theory, Sadurski, Wojciech (ed). Wacks, Raymond.

JUDGING

Judging in Good Faith. Burton, Steven J.

Whose Objectivity? Which Neutrality? The Doomed Quest for a Neutral Vantage Point from Which to Judge Relations. D'Costa, Gavin.

JUSTICE

JUSTIFICATION

Aufgeklärtes Eigeninteresse: Eine Theorie theoretischer und praktischer Rationalität. Gosepath, Stefan.

The Corporation as Anomaly. Schrader, David.

Against Coherence. Fritzman, J M.

Conceptual Development and Relativism: Reply to Siegel. Van Haaften, Wouter.

Double-Aspect Foundherentism: A New Theory of Empirical Justification. Haack, Susan.

Doubt, Scepticism, and a Serious Justification Game. Schramm, Alfred.

Epistemic Desiderata. Alston, W P.

Hard Choices: A Sociological Perspective on Value Incommensurability. Cohen, Eric and Ben-Ari, Eyal.

Historical Evidence and Epistemic Justification: Thucydides as a Case Study. Kosso, Peter.

How To Respond To Terrorism in Terrorism, Justice and Social Values, Peden, Creighton (ed). Smith, Steven A.

Inconsistency: The Coherence Theorist's Nemesis?. Engel, Mylan.

Is Terrorism Every Morally Justified? in Terrorism, Justice and Social Values, Peden, Creighton (ed). Davis, Stephen T.

Justification and the Will. Pink, T L M.

Justification in the 20th Century in Rationality in Epistemology, Villanueva, Enrique (ed). Plantinga, Alvin.

Justification without Good Reasons. Katzoff, Charlotte.

Justified False Belief. Rajotte, Mark J.

Justifying Conceptual Development Claims: Response to Van Haaften. Siegel, Harvey.

Justifying Democracy. Fisk, Milton.

Justifying Intentions. Mele, Alfred.

No Confusion: Some Reflections on TWA Flight 847 in Terrorism, Justice and Social Values, Peden, Creighton (ed). Roth, John K.

On the Need for a Metaphysics of Justification. Bradshaw, D E.

Property in *The Realm of Rights.* Thau, Michael Alan.

Religion as *Weltanschauung*: a Solution to a Problem in the Philosophy of Religion. Riordan, P.

Reply to Alfred Schramm's "Doubt, Scepticism, and a Serious Justification Game". Lehrer, Keith.

Reply to Mylan Engel's "Inconsistency: The Coherence Theorist's Nemesis?". Lehrer, Keith.

Rescher on the Justification of Rationality. Siegel, Harvey.

Self-Defence and Forcing the Choice between Lives. Miller, Seumas.

Self-Defense, Justification, and Excuse. Alexander, Larry.

Sense and Justification. Peacocke, Christopher.

Some Questions About the Justification of Morality in Philosophical Perspectives, 6: Ethics, 1992, Tomberlin, James E (ed). Railton, Peter A.

The Epistemology of Trust and the Politics of Suspicion. Webb, Mark Owen.

The Justification of Induction. Rosenkrantz, R D.

The Purpose of the Proof of Pragmatism in Peirce's 1903 Lectures on Pragmatism. Turrisi, Patricia A.

The Rational Justification of Moral Restraint. Hill, Greg.

Thomas Aquinas on the Justification of Revolution. Fay, Thomas A.

Unreckoned Misleading Truths and Lehrer's Theory of Undefeated Justification. Bender, John W.

What Is an Expert?. Weinstein, Bruce D.

JUTRONIC-TIHOMIROVIC, D

Reply to Dunja Jutronic-Tihomirovic's "Language as Fictitious Consensus". Lehrer, Keith.

JUVENILE

Mental Illness and Juvenile Criminal Justice. Pahel, Kenneth R.

Shame, Forgiveness, and Juvenile Justice. Moore, David B.

KAFKA

Being and Infestation. Mish'alani, James K.

KAGAN, S

Non-consequentialism, the Person as an End-in-Itself, and the Significance of Status. Kamm, F M.

KAHNEMAN, D

Scientific Rationality and Human Reasoning. Solomon, Miriam.

KALINOWSKI, G

Axiomatizar la metafísica? A propósito de "L'impossible métaphysique" de G Kalinowski. Ballesteros, Manuel.

KANDINSKY, W

The Idea of Abstraction in German Theories of the Ornament from Kant to Kandinsky. Morgan, David.

KANT

"Fiat lux": Une philosophie du sublime. Saint Girons, Baldine.

"Was darf ich hoffen?" Zum Problem der Vereinbarkeit von theoretischer und praktischer Vernunft bei Immanuel Kant. Förster, Eckart.

Aesthetic Judgment and the Moral Image of the World: Studies in Kant. Henrich, Dieter.

Central Readings in the History of Modern Philosophy: Descartes to Kant. Cummins, Robert (ed) and Owen, David (ed).

De re and *de corpore* (in French). Casati, Roberto.

Essays on Kant's Political Philosophy. Williams, Howard (ed).

Ethical Essays, Volume II. Harrison, Jonathan.

Il Problema della Modalità nelle Logiche di Hegel. Baptist, Gabriella.

Kant and the Experience of Freedom: Essays on Aesthetics and Morality. Guyer, Paul.

Kant's Aesthetics. Meerbote, Ralf (ed).

Kant's Latin Writings (Second Edition). Beck, Lewis W.

Kants Begründung der praktischen Philosophie. Freudiger, Jürg.

Kierkegaard and Kant: The Hidden Debt. Green, Ronald M.

Lectures on Logic—Immanuel Kant. Young, Michael J (ed & trans).

Metaphysical Aporia and Philosophical Heresy. Ross, Stephen David.

Opus Postumum/Immanuel Kant. Kant, Immanuel, Förster, Eckart (ed & trans) and Rosen, Michael (trans).

Quest for the Absolute: The Philosophical Vision of Joseph Maréchal. Matteo, Anthony M.

Stoff and Nonsense in Kant's First *Critique.* Mosser, Kurt.

The Cambridge Companion to Kant. Guyer, Paul (ed).

The Fate of Art: Aesthetic Alienation from Kant to Derrida and Adorno. Bernstein, J M.

The Love Commandments: Essays in Christian Ethics and Moral Philosophy. Santurri, Edmund N (ed) and Werpehowski, William (ed).

The Natural and the Normative: Theories of Spatial Perception from Kant to Helmholtz. Hatfield, Gary.

The Practice of Moral Judgment. Herman, Barbara.

The Renewal of the Heidegger-Kant Dialogue: Action, Thought, and Responsibility. Schalow, Frank.

The Truth about Postmodernism. Norris, Christopher.

Theology and Difference: The Wound of Reason. Lowe, Walter.

Theoretical Philosophy, 1755-1770—Immanuel Kant. Walford, David (ed & trans).

A Kantian Approach to Codes of Ethics. L'Etang, Jacquie.

A Kantian Perspective on Moral Rules in Philosophical Perspectives, 6: Ethics, 1992, Tomberlin, James E (ed). Hill Jr, Thomas E.

A Note on Kant's First Antinomy. Moore, A W.

A Problem in Kant's Theory of Moral Feeling. Blosser, Philip.

Aggravated Murder and Capital Punishment. Sorell, Tom.

An Engagement With Kant's Theory of Beauty in Kant's Aesthetics, Meerbote, Ralf (ed). Wolterstorff, Nicholas.

Art's Autonomy *Is* Its Momrality: A Reply to Casey Haskins on Kant. Hyman, Lawrence W.

Beneficence and Self-Love: A Kantian Perspective in Altruism, Paul, Ellen Frankel (ed). Hill Jr, Thomas E.

C'è un circolo dell'autocoscienza? Uno schizzo delle posizioni paradigmatiche e dei modelli di autocoscienza da Kant a Heidegger. Düsing, Klaus.

Caring about Justice. Dancy, Jonathan.

Cassirer, Neo-Kantianism and Metaphysics. Krois, John Michael.

Categories and Realities. Carr, Brian.

Christianisme et philosophie dans la première philosophie de Fichte. Goddard, Jean-Christophe.

Conceptual Scheming. Rozema, David.

Consciousness, Self-Consciousness and Episodic Memory. Gennaro, Rocco J.

Could Kant Have Been a Utilitarian. Hare, R M.

Counting the Formulas of the Categorical Imperative: One Plus Three Makes Four. Nuyen, A T.

Critical and Pre-Critical Phases in Kant's Philosophy of Logic. Nussbaum, Charles.

Das Phänomen der inkongruenten Gegenstücke aus Kantischer und heutiger Sicht. Mühlhölzer, Felix.

Das Verhältnis von ästhetischer Theorie und Rhetorik in Kants Kritik der Urteilskraft. Oesterreich, P L.

De Baumgarten à Kant: sur la beauté. Parret, Herman.

Defending Hegel from Kant in Essays on Kant's Political Philosophy, Williams, Howard Lloyd (ed). Smith, Steven B.

Der Sinn des Erhabenen—Kants Theorie des Erhabenen und ihre Bedeutung heute (in Japanese). Murata, Seiichi.

Die akroamatische Dimension der Hermeneutik. Fricke, Christel.

Die Entwicklung der Lehre von Grundsätzen—Hermann Cohens Ästhetik (in Japanese). Akiba, Fuminori.

Die Fichte-inspiratie van de dynamiek van het verlangen bij Jos Maréchal. Verhoeven, Jan.

Die Person als Zweck an sich. Mendonça, W P.

Differend and Agonistics: A Transcendental Argument?. Ruthrof, Horst.

Does Kant Reduce Religion to Morality?. Palmquist, S R.

Does Kant's Ethics Require that the Moral Law Be the Sole Determining Ground of the Will?. Wike, Victoria.

Duty and Desolation. Langton, Rae.

El estatuto epistemológico de la fe: Un diálogo con Kant. Odero, José Miguel.

El problema del sujeto en la *Crítica de la Razón Pura.* González Gallego, Agustín.

Esperanza y desesperanza de la razón en Kant. Grimaldi, Nicolás.

Esthetica en kunstsfilosofie. De Visscher, J.

Etica Actual: Una Doble Perspectiva. Mauri, Margarita.

Feeling and Freedom: Kant on Aesthetics and Morality. Guyer, Paul.

Filosofia della mente ed etica in Stuart Hampshire. Reichlin, M.

Finitude et altérité dans l'esthétique transcendentale. Giovannangeli, Daniel.

Formale Semantik im Verhältnis zur Erkenntnistheorie: Ein Blickwechsel. Hrachovec, Herbert.

From Metaphysics to Physics and Back. Kerszberg, Pierre.

Gesetz, Befehle und Theorien der Kausalität. Hampe, Michael.

Gurwitsch's Interpretation of Kant: Reflections of a Former Student. Allison, Henry E.

Habermas and Transcendental Arguments: A Reappraisal. Power, Michael.

Hannah Arendt on Kant, Truth and Politics in Essays on Kant's Political Philosophy, Williams, Howard Lloyd (ed). Riley, Patrick.

KANT

Thomson's Problems with Kant: A Comment on Kant's Problems with Ugliness. Guyer, Paul.

Thought and Being in The Cambridge Companion to Hegel, Beiser, Frederick (ed). Guyer, Paul.

Time and Change in Kant and McTaggart. Waxman, Wayne.

Totalität oder Zweckmässigkeit: Kants Ringen mit dem Mannigfaltigen der Erfahrung im Ausgag der Vernunftkritik. Schiemann, Gregor.

Two Arguments from Incongruent Counterparts. Murray, Lori.

Über das Verhältnis zwischen Immanuel Kants Rechts-und Moralphilosophie. Jacobsen, Mogens Chrom.

Une philosophie de la grammaire d'après Kant: la *Sprachlehre* d'A F Bernhardi. Thouard, Denis.

Unkantian Notions of Disinterest. Zangwill, Nick.

Was Immanuel Kant a Humanist?. Hiorth, Finngeir.

What Are Kant's Analogies About?. Waxman, Wayne.

What is Wrong with Kant's Four Examples. Potter, Nelson.

Whitehead and Kant on Presuppositions of Meaning. Van Der Veken, Jan.

Wohlverhalten und Wohlergehen: Der moralische Gottesbeweis in den Schriften Kants. Sala, Giovanni B.

Zähmung des Bösen? Überlegungen zu Kant vor dem Hintergrund der Leibnizschen Theodizee. Schönrich, Gerhard.

Zur Probleme um Auslegung der kantischen "Kritik der Urteilskraft" von R Oderbrecht (in Japanese). Ohkuma, Haruo.

KANUNGO, R

Alienation and Moral Imperatives: A Reply to Kanungo. Sweet, Robert T.

KAPLAN, D

Demonstrating with Descriptions. Reimer, Marga.

Demonstrative Reference and Unintended Demonstrata. Hand, Michael.

Demonstratives and Intentions, Ten Years Later. Bertolet, Rod.

Intentions and Demonstrations. Bach, Kent.

Operators in the Paradox of the Knower. Grim, Patrick.

Three Views of Demonstrative Reference. Reimer, Marga.

KAPLAN, M

Kaufman on Kaplan and Process Theology: A Post-Positivist Perspective. Alexander, H A.

Mordecai M Kaplan and Process Theology: Metaphysical and Pragmatic Perspectives. Kaufman, William E.

KAPUR, N

Friendship, Morality, and Special Obligation. Grunebaum, James O.

KARAMAZOV, I

Victimization and the Problem of Evil: A Response to Ivan Karamazov. Tracy, Thomas F.

KARMA

The Karmic A Priori in Indian Philosophy. Potter, Karl H.

KATZ, J

Is There a Perennial Philosophy? in Revisioning Philosophy, Ogilvy, James (ed). Smith, Huston.

KAUFMAN, G

Creative Interchange Between Philosophy and Theology: A Call to Dialogue. Eisenhower, William D.

Evidentialism and Theology: A Reply to Kaufman. Shalkowski, Scott A.

On the Issues Dividing Contemporary Christian Philosophers and Theologians. Keller, James A.

Stump, Kretzmann, and Historical Blindness. Griffiths, Paul J.

KAUFMAN, W

Kaufman on Kaplan and Process Theology: A Post-Positivist Perspective. Alexander, H A.

KAVKA, G

Are There Internal Prisoner's Dilemmas? A Comment on Kavka's Article. Moreh, J.

KAYE, L

Compositional Supervenience Theories and Compositional Meaning Theories. Schiffer, Stephen.

KEANEY, J

Keaney's *Composition of Aristotle's Athenaion Politeia*. Rhodes, P J.

KEENAN, J

Reply to Keenan: Thomson's Argument and Academic Feminism. Beckwith, Francis J.

KELLY, G

A Retrospective on the Political Theory of George Armstrong Kelly: *The Humane Comedy: Constant, Tocqueville and French Liberalism*. Riley, Patrick.

KENNEDY, J

Kennedy and West Virginia in Sartre Alive, Aronson, Ronald (ed). Sartre, Jean-Paul and Bowman, Elizabeth A (trans).

KENNY, A

Emoción. Lyons, William.

Descartes on the Material Falsity of Ideas. Field, Richard.

'Eudemian' Ethical Method in Essays in Ancient Greek Philosophy, IV, Anton, John P (ed). Jost, Lawrence J.

KERDEMAN, D

Akrasia and Education: A Response to Deborah Kerdeman. Pendlebury, Shirley.

Disavowing Community. Stone, Lynda.

Response to "Disavowing Community". Stout, Maureen.

KERFERD, G

Fairness in Socratic Justice—*Republic* I. Scaltsas, Theodore.

KEYNES, J

J M Keynes's Theoretical Approach to Decision-Making Under Conditions of Risk and Uncertainty. Brady, Michael Emmett.

Keynes's Theory of Probability and Its Relevance to His Economics: Three Theses. Cottrell, Allin.

Keynesian Economic Theory and the Revival of Classical Theory in Terrorism, Justice and Social Values, Peden, Creighton W (ed). Walter, Edward F.

KEYSERLING, H

Sinn und Ursprung. Gahlings, Ute.

KIEFER, A

Original Representation and Anselm Kiefer's Postmodernism. Gilmour, John C.

KIERKEGAARD

Foundations of Kierkegaard's Vision of Community. Connell, George B (ed) and Evans, C Stephen (ed).

Kierkegaard and Kant: The Hidden Debt. Green, Ronald M.

Kierkegaard on Art and Communication. Pattison, George (ed).

Passionate Reason: Making Sense of Kierkegaard's "Philosophical Fragments". Evans, C Stephen.

Postnational Identity: Critical Theory and Existential Philosophy in Habermas, Kierkegaard, and Havel. Matustik, Martin J.

Word and Spirit: A Kierkegaardian Critique of the Modern Age. Hall, Ronald L.

Authorship and Authenticity: Kierkegaard and Wittgenstein. Phillips, D Z.

Commentary on "Hegel's Philosophy of God in the Light of Kierkegaard's Criticisms" in Hegel and His Critics, Desmond, William J (ed). Perkins, Robert L.

Despair's Demand: An Appraisal of Kierkegaard's Argument for God. Mehl, Peter J.

Existence and Essence: Kierkegaard and Hegel. Subramanian, Sharada.

Fighting for Narnia: Soren Kierkegaard and C S Lewis in Kierkegaard on Art and Communication, Pattison, George (ed). Watkin, Julia.

Hegel's Philosophy of God in the Light of Kierkegaard's Criticisms in Hegel and His Critics, Desmond, William J (ed). Cullen, Bernard.

Indirect Communication: Hegelian Aesthetic and Kierkegaard's Literary Art in Kierkegaard on Art and Communication, Pattison, George (ed). Thomas, John Heywood.

Kierkegaard and Post-Modernity: Judas as Kierkegaard's Only Disciple. Scheffler Manning, Robert John.

Kierkegaard on the Transformation of the Individual in Conversion. Davis, William C.

Kierkegaard's Ironic Ladder to Authentic Faith. Golomb, Jacob.

Kierkegaard's Place in the Hermeneutic Project. Martinez, Roy.

Kierkegaard's View of Faith in Terrorism, Justice and Social Values, Peden, Creighton (ed). Smorowski, Michael A.

Kierkegaard, the Aesthetic and Mozart's 'Don Giovanni' in Kierkegaard on Art and Communication, Pattison, George (ed). Zelechow, Bernard.

Kierkegaard: Poet of the Religious in Kierkegaard on Art and Communication, Pattison, George (ed). Walsh, Sylvia.

Levinas, Kierkegaard, and the Theological Task. Westphal, Merold.

Malinconia e nichilismo—I: Dalla ferita mortale alla ricomposizione dell'infranto. Bottani, Livio.

Music of the Spheres: Kierkegaardian Selves and Transformations. Mooney, Edward F.

On Being Sidetracked by the Aesthetic in Kierkegaard on Art and Communication, Pattison, George (ed). Bell, Richard H.

Philosophy and Religion in the Thought of Kierkegaard. Weston, Michael.

Philosophy and Religion in the Thought of Kierkegaard in Philosophy, Religion and the Spiritual Life, McGhee, Michael (ed). Weston, Michael.

Reflections on the 'Other' in Dinesen, Kierkegaard and Nietzsche in Kierkegaard on Art and Communication, Pattison, George (ed). Makarushka, Irena.

Rereading *Fear and Trembling*. McLane, Earl.

The Decline from Authority: Kierkegaard on Intellectual Sin. Aiken, David W.

The Fragmented Middle: Hegel and Kierkegaard in German Philosophy and Jewish Thought, Greenspan, Louis (ed). Shearson, William A.

The Role of Folk and Fairy Tales in Kierkegaard's Authorship in Kierkegaard on Art and Communication, Pattison, George (ed). Kjaer, Grethe.

The Suspension of the Ethical and the Religious Meaning of Ethics in Kierkegaard's Thought. Sagi, Avi.

'Keeping Silent through Speaking' in Kierkegaard on Art and Communication, Pattison, George (ed). Rogan, Jan.

KILLING

Is the Killing/Letting-Die Distinction Normatively Neutral?. Winkler, Earl.

Lebensrecht und Überlebeninteresse: Darstellung und Kritik einiger Thesen von Norbert Hoerster. Viefhues, Ludger.

The Replaceability Argument and Abortion. Calef, Scott.

KILVINGTON, R

New Light on Medieval Philosophy: The Sophismata of Richard Kilvington. Ashworth, E J.

KIM, J

Was sind Ereignisse? Eine Studie zur Analytischen Ontologie. Stoecker, Ralf.

Psychophysical Supervenience and Nonreductive Materialism. Marras, Ausonio.

Supervenience and Reducibility: An Odd Couple. Marras, Ausonio.

KIMBALL, B

Philosophers, Orators, and the Role of Science in Liberal Education. Robertson, Emily.

KINCAID, H

Aims and Achievements of the Reductionist Approach in Biochemistry/Molecular Biology/Cell Biology: A Response to Kincaid. Robinson, Joseph D.

KINEMATICS

Generalized Probability Kinematics. Wagner, Carl G.

KNOWLEDGE

The Poetics of Alfarabi and Avicenna. Kemal, Salim.

The Roles of Sense and Thought in Knowledge. De, P K.

The Trinity: An Analysis of St Thomas Aquinas' 'Expositio' of the 'De Trinitate' of Boethius. Hall, Douglas.

The Uses of Antiquity. Gaukroger, Stephen (ed).

Thinking Things Through: An Introduction to Philosophical Issues and Achievements. Glymour, Clark.

Thought Experiments in Science and Philosophy. Horowitz, Tamara (ed) and Massey, Gerald J (ed).

Toward a Feminist Epistemology. Duran, Jane.

Truth and Existence—Jean-Paul Sartre. Sartre, Jean Paul, Van Den Hoven, Adrian (trans) and Aronson, Ronald (ed).

Unreason Within Reason: Essays on the Outskirts of Rationality. Graham, A C.

Way, Learning, and Politics: Essays on the Confucian Intellectual. Wei-ming, Tu.

White Queen Psychology and Other Essays for Alice. Millikan, Ruth Garrett.

Wittgenstein's Intentions. Canfield, J V (ed) and Shanker, Stuart G (ed).

Wittgenstein's 'Philosophical Investigations'. Arrington, Robert L (ed) and Glock, Hans-Johann (ed).

Working Without a Net: A Study of Egocentric Epistemology. Foley, Richard.

World Changes. Horwich, Paul (ed).

A Chaotic Approach to Free Will and Determinism. Till, Gregory J.

A Critical Discussion of Karl Mannheim's Views on Sociology of Knowledge. Mondal, Sunil Baran.

A Defence of Empiricism in A J Ayer Memorial Essays, Griffiths, A Phillips (ed). Ayer, A J.

A Diferença entre as Filosofias de Carnap e Popper. De Araújo Dutra, Luiz Henrique.

A Dilemma for Causal Reliabilist Theories of Knowledge. Lipson, Morris and Savitt, Steven.

A Here-Now Theory of Indexicality. Plumer, Gilbert.

A Mistake about Foundationalism. Rappaport, Steven.

A Moderate Mentalism. Peacocke, Christopher.

A Naturalistic and Evolutionary Account of Content in Analecta Husserliana, XXXIV, Tymieniecka, Anna-Teresa (ed). Potrc, Matjaz.

A Platonist Reading of *Theaetetus* 145-147—I. Sedley, David.

A Plea for the Poetic Metaphor. Muscari, Paul G.

A Problem for Anti-Realism. Rogerson, Kenneth.

A Problem for Naturalizing Epistemologies. Jacobson, Anne Jaap.

A Question of Evidence. Nelson, Lynn Hankinson.

A Reconception of Meaning. Heydrich, Wolfgang.

A Test of the Scientific Method. Mckee, Bill.

A World of Propensities: Two New Views of Causality in Advances in Scientific Philosophy, Schurz, Gerhard (ed). Popper, Karl R.

Acquaintance with Qualia. Bigelow, John and Pargetter, Robert.

Advaita Critique of the Sphota and Sabdabrahman. Manninezhath, Thomas.

Aesthetics and Anti-Aesthetics in the Visual Arts. Mattick, Paul.

Aesthetics for Art's Sake, Nor for Philosophy's!. Silvers, Anita.

After Analytic Philosophy, What's Next?: An Analytic Philosopher's Perspective. Walton, Douglas N.

Afterword in Revisioning Philosophy, Ogilvy, James (ed). Appelbaum, David.

Algunos problemas lógicos de verificación y refutación en ciencias del ser humano. Camacho, Luis A.

An Anti-Molinist Argument in Philosophical Perspectives, 5: Philosophy of Religion, 1991, Tomberlin, James E (ed). Adams, Robert Merrihew.

An Application of Weingartner's Logical Proposal for Rational Belief, Knowledge, Assumption in Advances in Scientific Philosophy, Schurz, Gerhard (ed). Festini, Heda.

An Argument for Leibnizian Metaphysics. Huffman, Tom L.

An Epistemic Principle Which Solves Newcomb's Paradox. Lehrer, Keith and McGee, Vann.

An Inquiry into Religion's Empty World. Martland, Thomas R.

Analytic Phenomenological Deconstruction in Certainty and Surface in Epistemology and Philosophical Method, Martinich, A P (ed). Martinich, A P.

Animal Models in Biomedical Research: Some Epistemological Worries. LaFollette, Hugh and Shanks, Niall.

Anomaly and Folk Psychology. Connolly, John M.

Appearances and Impressions. Barney, Rachel.

Applied Logic: An Aristotelian *Organon* for Critical Thinking in a Theoretical Context. Trundle, Robert C.

Apuleius and the Concept of Philosophical Rhetoric. O'Brien, Maeve.

Aquinas on the Foundations of Knowledge. Stump, Eleonore.

Aquinas's Concept of the Body and Out of Body Situations. Quinn, Patrick.

Are Hybrid Proper Names the Solution to the Completion Problem: A Reply to Wolfgang Künne. Harcourt, Edward.

Are There Foundations for Human Knowledge?. Garrett, K Richard.

Are 'Old Wives' Tales' Justified? in Feminist Epistemologies, Alcoff, Linda (ed). Dalmiya, Vrinda and Alcoff, Linda.

Aristotle and the Uses of Actuality. Charlton, William.

Aristotle on Two Kinds of Memory: Platonic Reminiscences (in Dutch). Van Dorp, P.

Aristotle's Practical Particularism in Essays in Ancient Greek Philosophy, IV, Anton, John P (ed). Louden, Robert B.

Assessing Sabara's Arguments for the Conclusion that a Generic Term Denotes Just a Class Property. Scharf, Peter M.

Assisted Performance. Duran, Jane.

Aufbau and Bauhaus: A Cross-Realm Comparison. Krukowski, Lucian.

Aurobindo on Reality as Value. Prasad, Rajendra.

Axiologic Rather than Logic: Priority of Aesthetic and Ethical Over Semiotic Logic of Scientific Discovery. Helm, Bert P.

Ayer on Other Minds in The Philosophy of A J Ayer, Hahn, Lewis Edwin (ed). Sprigge, T L S.

Barnes, Bloor, and the Sociology of Knowledge. Keita, Lansana.

Basanta Kumar Mallik's Theory of Knowledge. Walker, Mary M.

Bayesian Problem-Solving and the Dispensibility of Truth in Rationality in Epistemology, Villanueva, Enrique (ed). Horwich, Paul.

Bergson and the Discourse of the Moderns in The Crisis in Modernism, Burwick, Frederick (ed). Lehan, Richard.

Berkeley and Scepticism: A Fatal Dalliance. Imlay, Robert A.

Berkeley: How to Make a Mistake. Levine, Michael.

Bernard Lonergan on Primary vs Secondary Qualities. Glowienka, Emerine.

Big Numbers and Induction in the Case for Extra-Terrestrial Intelligence. Mash, Roy.

Bodies and Knowledges: Feminism and the Crisis of Reason in Feminist Epistemologies, Alcoff, Linda (ed). Grosz, Elizabeth.

Boghossian on Externalism and Inference in Rationality in Epistemology, Villanueva, Enrique (ed). Schiffer, Stephen.

Boswell on Johnson's Refutation of Berkeley: Revisiting the Stone. Silver, Bruce S.

Buridan and Skepticism. Zupko, Jack.

Can an Ultimate Foundation of Knowledge Be Non-Metaphysical?. Apel, Karl Otto.

Can Contradictions Be True?—I. Smiley, Timothy.

Can Contradictions Be True?—II. Priest, Graham.

Can Religion Give Science a Heart?. Kozhamthadam, Job.

Can We Have a World Philosophy?. Harris, R Baine.

Can't We Doubt Meaning?. Lenka, Laxminarayan.

Character, Mind, and Politics in Psychoanalysis, Mind and Art, Hopkins, Jim (ed). Rorty, Amélie Oksenberg.

Charles Sanders Peirce's Sociology of Knowledge and Critique of Capitalism in Frontiers in American Philosophy, Volume I, Burch, Robert W (ed). Stikkers, Kenneth W.

Children are Not Meant to be Studied.... Hart, W A.

Chinese Rationality: An Oxymoron?. Ames, Roger T.

Clarifying the "Adequate Evidence Condition" in Educational Issues and Research: A Lakoffian View. Miller, Steven I and Fredericks, Janet.

Classical Christian Philosophy and Temporality: Correcting a Misunderstanding. Centore, F F.

Clearing the Ground: Foundational Questions Once Again. Campbell, Robert L and Bickhard, Mark H.

Cognitivism between Computation and Pragmatics: A Peer Review of 'Some Foundational Questions Concerning Language Studies' by Bickhard and Campbell. Leinfellner, Elisabeth.

Coherence, Probability and Induction in Rationality in Epistemology, Villanueva, Enrique (ed). Skyrms, Brian.

Commentary on "Husserl's Critique of Hegel" in Hegel and His Critics, Desmond, William (ed). Duquette, David A.

Commentary on McPherran's *Ataraxia* and *Eudaimonia* in Ancient Pyrrhonism. Ryan, George E.

Commentary on Reesor's "The Stoic Wise Man". Haase, Wolfgang.

Common Sense at the Foundations in Essays on Henry Sidgwick, Schultz, Bart (ed). Hardin, Russell.

Community Ecology, Scale, and the Instability of the Stability Concept. McCoy, E D and Shrader-Frechette, Kristin.

Competence, Knowledge and Education. Hyland, Terry.

Conceivability and Modal Knowledge in Thought Experiments in Science and Philosophy, Horowitz, Tamara (ed). Hetherington, Stephen Cade.

Conceptual Analysis and the Essence of Knowledge. Taylor, James E.

Conceptual Truth and Aesthetic Truth. Dorter, Kenneth N.

Conditionals of Freedom and Middle Knowledge. Gaskin, R.

Conflicting Views on Practical Reason: Against Pseudo-Arguments in Practical Philosophy. Weinberger, Ota.

Connaissance et réminiscence dans le *Ménon*. Brown, L.

Conocimiento y concepto. Mayol, Víctor Velarde.

Conscious Experience. Dretske, Frederick.

Consciousness and Concepts—I. Kirk, Robert.

Consciousness and Concepts—II. Carruthers, Peter.

Consciousness and Self-Knowledge in Aquinas's Critique of Averroe's Psychology. Black, Deborah.

Constructivism Liberalized. Velleman, Daniel.

Contextualism and Knowledge Attributions. De Rose, Keith.

Contingency, A Priority and Acquaintance. Ryckman, Thomas C.

Continuing the Dialogue on Measuring the Quality of Life in Philosophy and Psychology. Anstötz, Christoph.

Contra Hume: On Making Things Happen in Logical Foundations, Mahalingam, Indira (ed). Wright, Colin B.

Coping With Ambiguity and Uncertainty in Patient- Physician Relationships: II — *Traditio Argumentum Respectus*. Rodning, Charles B.

Corrugated Subjects: The Three Axes of Personhood. Clifford, Michael.

Counting the Formulas of the Categorical Imperative: One Plus Three Makes Four. Nuyen, A T.

Credere e sapere. Iwand, Hans Joachim.

Criteria of Acceptance: Comments on Bickhard and Campbell, 'Some Foundational Questions Concerning Language Studies'. Yngve, V H.

Critical Notice of James Robert Brown's *The Rational and the Social*. Matheson, Carl.

Critical Notice of W V Quine's *Pursuit of Truth*. Woods, John.

Cross-Cultural Translation in Cultural Relativism and Philosophy, Dascal, Marcelo (ed). Meehan, Eugene J.

KNOWLEDGE

LANGUAGE

LANGUAGE

LANGUAGE

Three Views of Demonstrative Reference. Reimer, Marga.

Three-Way Games. Leclerc, Jean-Jacques.

Thresholds of the Sign in Theorizing American Literature, Cowan, Bainard (ed). Riddel, Joseph N.

Time and Narrative: Reflections from Paul Ricoeur. Jasper, David.

Time Out of Joint: Reflections on Anachronism. Barnes, Annette and Barnes, Jonathan.

Toward a Compatibility Theory for Internalist and Externalist Epistemologies. Sennett, James F.

Towards a Unified Theory of Higher-Level Predication. Williams, C J F.

Transition and Contradiction. McKie, John.

Transitivity, Torts and Kingdom Loss. Gibson, Kevin.

Translation and Content—Footnotes on Moravcsik's 'All A's are B's'. Hofmann, T R.

Translation and Foreign Cultures. Collin, Finn.

Translation and Languagehood. Sankey, Howard.

Trouble in Paradise? in Criss-Crossing A Philosophical Landscape, Schulte, Joachim (ed). Wedin, Michael V.

Troubles for New Wave Moral Semantics: The 'Open Question Argument' Revived. Horgan, Terence and Timmons, Mark.

True Figures: Metaphor, Social Relations, and the Sorites in The Interpretive Turn, Hiley, David R (ed). Wheeler III, Samuel C.

Truth Makers, Truth Predicates, and Truth Types in Language, Truth and Ontology, Mulligan, Kevin (ed). Hochberg, Herbert I.

Truth, Rightness, and Permanent Acceptability. Künne, Wolfgang.

Two Concepts of Truth. Hugly, Philip G and Sayward, Charles.

Two Problems with Tarski's Theory of Consequence. McGee, Vann.

Una semántica computacional del idioma español usando las teorías de R Montague. Hack, Haroldo G (& others).

Una traduzione sfortunata della "Scienza Nuova". Mastrolianni, Giovanni.

Understanding Language. Smith, Barry C.

Understanding the Committed Writer in The Cambridge Companion to Sartre, Howells, Christina (ed). Goldthorpe, Rhiannon.

Une philosophie de la grammaire d'après Kant: la Sprachlehre d'A F Bernhardi. Thouard, Denis.

Unidentified Awareness: Hume's Perceptions of Self. Campolo, Christian.

Unifying the Protagoras. Rutherford, Richard.

Unity and Logos: A Reading of Theaetetus 201c-210a. Miller, Mitchell.

Universals. Bealer, George.

Unpacking the Black Box of Cognition. Gillett, Grant.

Validities: A Political Science Perspective. Beer, Francis A.

Variable-Free Semantics for Anaphora. Böttner, Michael.

Verdade e Demonstraçao. Tarski, A and Paula Assis, J (trans).

Vérité et sens: retour à Frege. Schmitz, François.

Vision and Intentional Content in John Searle and His Critics, Lepore, Ernest (ed). Burge, Tyler.

Vocalism, Nominalism and the Commentaries on the Categories from the Earlier Twelfth Century. Marenbon, John.

Was Carnap Entirely Wrong, After All?. Stein, Howard.

Was Frege Right about Variable Objects? in Language, Truth and Ontology, Mulligan, Kevin (ed). Santambrogio, Marco.

Was Meinong Only Pretending?. Kroon, Frederick W.

Was trägt die Sprachanalyse zur Philosophie der Biologie bei?. Simons, Peter M.

What Does "To Avoid" Mean? On Derrida's De l'Esprit. David, Pascal.

What Is a Pragmatic Theory of Meaning? in Philosophical Interventions in the Unfinished Project of Enlightenment, Honneth, Axel (& other eds). Wellmer, Albrecht.

What Is the Model-Theoretic Argument?. Anderson, David L.

What is the Role of Model Theory in the Study of Meaning?. Robering, Klaus.

What Must One Have an Opinion About. Ebbesen, Sten.

What's Postmodern, Anyway. Münz, Peter.

Whately's Distinction Between Inferring and Proving. Bitzer, Lloyd F.

Why a Proper Name has a Meaning in Mind, Meaning and Metaphysics, Mulligan, Kevin (ed). Gabriel, Gottfried.

Why Believe What People Say?. Stevenson, Leslie.

Why Can't a Baby Pretend to Smile? in Wittgenstein's Intentions, Canfield, J V (ed). Von Savigny, Eike.

Why Is There So Little Sense in Grundgesetze?. Simons, Peter.

Why Semantic Innocence?. Oppy, Graham.

Why the New Theory of Reference Does Not Entail Absolute Time and Space. Rynasiewicz, Robert.

Why We Would Not Understand a Talking Lion. Levvis, Gary W.

William H Poteat: A Laudatio. Scott, R Taylor.

Wittgenstein and Derrida on Meaning. Rowlands, Mark.

Wittgenstein and Infinite Linguistic Competence. Niles, Ian.

Wittgenstein and Psychology in Wittgenstein Centenary Essays, Griffiths, A Phillips (ed). Shotter, John.

Wittgenstein and Social Science in Wittgenstein Centenary Essays, Griffiths, A Phillips (ed). Trigg, Roger.

Wittgenstein and the Availability of a Transcendental Critique. Pradhan, R C.

Wittgenstein and the Cartesian Subject (in Czechoslovakian). Kotatko, P.

Wittgenstein and the End of Philosophy?. Jolley, Kelly D.

Wittgenstein and W C Fields. Cohen, Daniel H.

Wittgenstein In Between—A Fragment in Criss-Crossing A Philosophical Landscape, Schulte, Joachim (ed). Haller, Rudolf.

Wittgenstein on Believing in 'Philosophical Investigations' Part II in Wittgenstein's Philosophical Investigations, Arrington, Robert T (ed). Hunter, J F M.

Wittgenstein on Freud's 'Abdominable Mess' in Wittgenstein Centenary Essays, Griffiths, A Phillips (ed). Cioffi, Frank.

Wittgenstein on Mathematical Proof in Wittgenstein Centenary Essays, Griffiths, A Phillips (ed). Wright, Crispin.

Wittgenstein on Rule Following. Srinivas, K.

Wittgenstein on Understanding. Goldfarb, Warren.

Wittgenstein über Zeit. Kaspar, Rudolf F and Schmidt, Alfred.

Wittgenstein's Concept of Showing in Criss-Crossing A Philosophical Landscape, Schulte, Joachim (ed). Pears, David.

Wittgenstein's Influence: Meaning, Mind and Method in Wittgenstein Centenary Essays, Griffiths, A Phillips (ed). Grayling, A C.

Wittgenstein's Private Language Argument and Quine's Indeterminacy Thesis. Lenka, Laxminarayan.

Wittgenstein, Anti-Realism and Mathematical Propositions in Criss-Crossing A Philosophical Landscape, Schulte, Joachim (ed). Bouveresse, Jacques.

Wittgenstein, Heidegger, and the Reification of Language in The Cambridge Companion to Heidegger, Guignon, Charles (ed). Rorty, Richard.

Wittgenstein: Whose Philosopher? in Wittgenstein Centenary Essays, Griffiths, A Phillips (ed). Anscombe, G E M.

Worlds and States of Affairs: How Similar Can They Be? in Language, Truth and Ontology, Mulligan, Kevin (ed). Forbes, Graeme R.

Writing with Davidson: Some Afterthoughts after Doing Blind Time IV: Drawing with Davidson. Morris, Robert.

Yu and Your Mind. Priest, Graham.

Zalta on Sense and Substitutivity. Deutsch, Harry.

Zalta's Intensional Logic. Anderson, C Anthony.

'Bring Me a Slab!': Meaning, Speakers, and Practices in Wittgenstein's Philosophical Investigations, Arrington, Robert L (ed). Ring, Merrill.

'Ces Petits Différends': Lyotard and Horace in Judging Lyotard, Benjamin, Andrew (ed). Bennington, Geoffrey.

'Das Wollen ist auch nur eine Erfahrung' in Wittgenstein's Philosophical Investigations, Arrington, Robert T (ed). Candlish, Stewart.

'I Hard a Plaintive Melody' in Wittgenstein Centenary Essays, Griffiths, A Phillips (ed). Hanfling, Oswald.

'Intuition Pumps' and Contemporary Philosophy. MacLean-Tollefsen, Laurie.

'No Matter How No Matter Where': The Unlit in S Beckett's Not I and Stirrings Still in Analecta Husserliana, XXXVIII, Tymieniecka, Anna-Teresa (ed). Oppenheim, Lois.

'Person' as an Essentially Contested Concept in the Commonwealth of Discourse. Merrill, S A.

'Philosophical Investigations' Section 122: Neglected Aspects in Wittgenstein's Philosophical Investigations, Arrington, Robert L (ed). Baker, Gordon.

'Philosophical Investigations' Section 128: in Wittgenstein's Philosophical Investigations, Arrington, Robert L (ed). Glock, Hans-Johann.

'Some Foundational Questions Concerning Language Studies': Commentary. Hertzberg, Lars.

'Tormenting Questions' in 'Philosophical Investigations' in Wittgenstein's Philosophical Investigations, Arrington, Robert L (ed). Hilmy, S Stephen.

LAO TZU

Tao Teh King By Lao Tzu: Interpreted as Nature and Intelligence. Bahm, Archie.

Tao Teh King—Lao Tzu. Tzu, Lao and Bahm, Archie J (trans).

LARMER, R

Miracles and Conservation Laws. MacGill, Neil Whyte.

LASCH, C

Lasch on Sport and the Culture of Narcissism: A Critical Reappraisal. Morgan, William J.

LASH, N

Is There a System in the Theology of Nicholas Lash?. Lamadrid, Lucas.

LASK, E

Lask, Heidegger and the Homelessness of Logic. Crowell, Steven Galt.

Schelling—Lask—Sartre: Die zweifache Unbegreiflichkeit der nackten Existenz. Wetz, Franz Josef.

LATIN

Kant's Latin Writings (Second Edition). Beck, Lewis W.

Aristotle's Peri hermeneias in Medieval Latin and Arabic Philosophy: Logic and the Linguistic Arts. Black, Deborah.

Latin Aristotle Commentaries: Supplementary Renaissance Authors. Lohr, Charles H.

Renaissance Latin Aristotle Commentaries: A Supplement to Lohr's "Latin Aristotle Commentaries". Darowski, Roman.

To Write in Latin or in the Vernacular: The Intellectual Dilemma in an Age of Transition—The Case of Descartes. Limbrick, Elaine.

LATIN AMERICAN

Bibliographia Missionalia Augustiniana: America Latina (1533-1993). Lazcano, Rafael.

Bioethics Yearbook, Volume 2—Regional Developments in Bioethics: 1989-1991. Lustig, B Andrew (& other eds).

Cultural Relativism and Philosophy. Dascal, Marcelo (ed).

Begegnung der Kulturen und inkulturierte Philosophie in Lateinamerika. Scannone, Juan Carlos.

Emanzipation und Befreiung: Lateinamerikas problemat—Verhältnis zur Moderne. Vetter, Ulrich Ben.

Esiste una filosofia latinoamericana?. Savignano, Armando.

Hacia una interpretación del discurso independentista. Ciriza, Alejandra and Fernández, Estela.

Hispanic Philosophy: Its Beginning and Golden Age. Gracia, Jorge J E.

Latin American Personalist: Antonio Caso. Haddox, John H.

LIBERALISM

Reconsidering Aquinas as a Postliberal Theologian. Crosson, Frederick.

Responsibility, Reactive Attitudes, and Liberalism in Philosophy and Politics. Scheffler, Samuel.

Responsible and Irresponsible Liberalism: Dostoevsky's Stavrogin. Neumann, Harry.

Restoration Romanticism. Tamás, G M.

Richard Rorty's Failed Politics. Haber, Honi.

Ruling Memory. Norton, Anne.

Self-Ownership and Worldly Resources. Ingram, A.

Social Ecology, Deep Ecology, and Liberalism. Dizerega, Gus.

Socialism as the Extension of Democracy. Arneson, Richard J.

Some Remarks on Science, Method and Nationalism in John Locke. Heyd, Thomas.

Sterba's Reconciliation Project: A Critique. Peffer, Rodney.

T H Green and the Morality of Victorian Liberalism in Victorian Liberalism, Bellamy, Richard (ed). Bellamy, Richard.

The Advent of Liberalism and the Subordination of Agrarian Thought in the United States. Theobald, P.

The Basic Context and Structure of Hegel's 'Philosophy of Right' in The Cambridge Companion to Hegel, Beiser, Frederick (ed). Westphal, Kenneth.

The Cards of Confusion: Reflections on Historical Communism at the 'End of History'. Elliott, Gregory.

The Concept of an Equal Educaitonal Opportunity. White, Ronald.

The Conflictual Agendas of Neo-Liberal Reconstruction and the Rise of Islamic Politics in Turkey. Birtek, Faruk and Toprak, Binnaz.

The Creolization of Liberalism. Bull, Barry L.

The Disconsolation of Theology: Irony, Cruelty, and Putting Charity First. Jackson, Timothy P.

The Economic and Political Liberalization of Socialism: The Fundamental Problem of Property Rights. Riker, William H and Weimer, David L.

The End of History and the Last Man. Roth, Michael S.

The Environmental Implications of Liberalism. Taylor, Roger.

The Essence and Leading Themes of Russian Philosophy. Frank, S L.

The Good-Enough Citizen: Citizenship and Independence in Beyond Equality and Difference, Bock, Gisela (ed). James, Susan.

The Incompatibility of Liberalism and Pluralism. Kekes, John.

The Jeffersonian Option. Dawidoff, Robert.

The Liberal Discourse on Violence in Selves, People, and Persons, Rouner, Leroy S (ed). Parekh, Bhikhu.

The Liberal Virtues. Strauss, David A.

The Limits of Aristotelian Ethics. Larmore, Charles.

The Moral Commitments of Liberalism in The Idea of Democracy, Copp, David (ed). Hampton, Jean.

The Moral Limits of Feinberg's Liberalism. Doppelt, Gerald.

The Moral Vocabulary of Liberalism. Beiner, Ronald.

The New Liberalism and Its Aftermath in Victorian Liberalism, Bellamy, Richard (ed). Freeden, Michael.

The Origin of Liberal Utilitarianism in Victorian Liberalism, Bellamy, Richard (ed). Rosen, Frederick.

The Place of Neutrality in Liberal Political Theory in Terrorism, Justice and Social Values, Peden, Creighton W (ed). Downing, Lyle and Thigpen, Robert B.

The Political Economy of Community. Farr, Richard.

The Politics of Equilibrium. Grant, Robert A D.

The Power of the Right of Education. Heslep, Robert D.

The Problem of Religion in Liberalism. Sherlock, Richard and Barrus, Roger.

The Right to National Self-Determination as an Individual Right. Tamir, Yael.

The Right to Welfare and the Virtue of Charity. Den Uyl, Douglas.

Thoughts Upon Reading Martin's Comments. Haber, Honi.

Understanding Fascism? in Isaiah Berlin: A Celebration, Margalit, Edna (ed). Ignatieff, Michael.

Unequal Property and Subjective Personality in Liberal Theories. Zucker, Ross.

Virtue and Oppression. Williams, Joan C.

Virtue and Repression. Paden, Roger K.

Vulgar Liberalism. Neal, Patrick.

Whigs and Liberals in Victorian Liberalism, Bellamy, Richard (ed). Fontana, Bianca.

Why We Listen to Lunatics: Antifoundational Theories and Feminist Politics. Bickford, Susan.

'Institutional Exploitation' and Workers' Co-operatives—Or How the British Left Persist in Getting Their Concepts Wrong. Carter, Alan.

LIBERATION

Beyond Liberation Theology. Belli, Humberto and Nash, Ronald.

Exploitation, Unequal Exchange and Dependency: A Dialectical Development. Otubusin, Paul.

Das Selbst in der Yoga-Philosophie. Soni, Jayandra.

Esiste una filosofia latinoamericana?. Savignano, Armando.

Quale liberazione per l'uomo dopo il marxismo?. Fidelibus, G.

The Possibility of an Indigenous Philosophy: A Latin American Perspective. Medina, Vicente.

Three Conceptions of 'Voice' and their Pedagogical Implications. Scahill, John H.

LIBERATION THEOLOGY

Questions d'épistémologie en théologie de la libération: A propos de l'ouvrage de Clodovis Boff. Richard, Jean.

LIBERTARIANISM

Marxism Recycled. Van Parijs, Philippe.

Reason and Responsibility (Eighth Edition). Feinberg, Joel.

A Libertarian Critique of H Tristram Engelhardt, Jr's "The Foundations of Bioethics". Fry-Revere, Sigrid.

After Libertarianism: Rejoinder to Narveson, McCloskey, Flew, and Machan. Friedman, Jeffrey.

Compatibilism and the Free Will Defence. Bishop, John.

Compensation and the Bounds of Rights. Lomasky, Loren.

De staat van Nozick. Rozemond, Klaas.

Defending Backwards Causation. Brown, Bryson.

Dissent from "The New Consensus": Reply to Friedman. Flew, Antony.

Egoism, Obligation, and Herbert Spencer. Wilkinson, Martin.

Ethics and the Extraterrestrial Environment. Marshall, Alan.

Free-market versus Libertarian Environmentalism. Sagoff, Mark.

From Libertarianism to Egalitarianism. Schwartz, Justin K.

How Rational Must Free Will Be?. Double, Richard.

Libertarianism, Postlibertarianism, and the Welfare State: Reply to Friedman. Narveson, Jan.

Middle Actions. Howsepian, A A.

Minimal Statism and Metamodernism: Reply to Friedman. McCloskey, Donald N.

Oakeshott and the Practice of Politics. Katzoff, Charlotte.

Politics or Scholarship?. Friedman, Jeffrey.

The Power and Poverty of Libertarian Thought. Cornuelle, Richard.

The Principle of Rational Explanation Defended. Double, Richard.

The Social Individual in Clinical Ethics. Moreno, Jonathan D.

LIBERTY

An Approach to Political Philosophy: Locke in Contexts. Tully, James.

Democracy. Harrison, Ross.

Government, Justice, and Contempt. Lane, Gilles.

Humanisme de la Liberté et Philosophie de la Justice. Trigeaud, Jean-Marc.

Liberty/Liberté: The American and French Experiences. Klaits, Joseph (ed) and Haltzel, Michael (ed).

Post-Liberalism: Studies in Political Thought. Gray, John.

Rational Infidels: The American Deists. Walters, Kerry S.

The Idea of Democracy. Copp, David (ed), Hampton, Jean (ed) and Roemer, John E (ed).

The Philosophy of Freedom: Ideological Origins of the Bill of Rights. Rudolph, Samuel B (ed).

A propos de la liberté chez les juristes. Rossinelli, Michel.

Accumulative Harms and the Interpretation of the Harm Principle. Kernohan, Andrew.

Berlin on the Nature and Significance of Liberty in Terrorism, Justice and Social Values, Peden, Creighton W (ed). Paden, Roger K.

Caring Love and Liberty: Some Questions. Kohl, Marvin.

De 'L'être et le néant' aux 'Cahiers pour une morale': Un enrichissement de la notion sartrienne de liberté 'pour-autrui'. Salzmann, Yvan.

Early Liberalism and Women's Liberty in Women's Rights and the Rights of Man, Arnaud, A J. Pietarinen, Juhani.

El estado hegeliano como individualidad excluyente. De Rojas Raz, Nerva Borda.

For a *Concept* of Negative Liberty—but Which *Conception*?. Kristjánsson, Kristján.

God, Determinism and Liberty: Hume's Puzzle. Wolfe, Julian.

Hospitality and Its Discontents: A Response to Losito. Mulvaney, Robert J.

La conciliazione estetica e l'etica. Gallino, Guglielmo.

La 'Déclaration des droits de l'homme et du citoyen' (1789). Stucki, Pierre-André.

Liberty Under the Moral Law: On B Hoose's Critique of the Grisez-Finnis Theory of Human Good. George, Robert P.

Machiavelli's Momentary "Machiavellian Moment": A Reconsideration of Pocock's Treatment of the *Discourses*. Sullivan, Vickie B.

Metafisica della soggettività e filosofia della libertà. Ciancio, Claudio.

Mill's Antipaternalism. Kultgen, John.

Necesidad de una renovación ética. López Quintás, Alfonso.

On a Supposed Inconsistency in J S Mill's Utilitarianism. Joy, Glenn C and McKinney, Audrey M.

On Deriving Rights to Goods from Rights to Freedom. Smith, Tara.

Paternalismus. Wolf, Jean-Claude.

Rousseau's Socraticism: The Political Bearing of "On Theatrical Imitation". Sorenson, Leonard R.

Rousseauisme et jacobinisme: l'idéal de "l'honnête médiocrité". Roy, Jean.

Secession: The Caes of Quebec. Nielsen, Kai.

Self-Ownership and Worldly Resources. Ingram, A.

Spencer, Steiner and Hart on the Equal Liberty Principle. Gray, Tim.

Sur la liberté et les pouvoirs du langage. Christoff, Daniel.

The Moral Limits of Feinberg's Liberalism. Doppelt, Gerald.

The Right to Private Property: Reply to Friedman. Machan, Tibor R.

The Spirit of Simone Weil's Law in Simone Weil's Philosophy of Culture, Bell, Richard (ed). Collins, Ronald K L and Nielsen, Finn E.

Two Concepts of Liberty in Isaiah Berlin: A Celebration, Margalit, Edna (ed). Dworkin, Ronald.

What Is Wrong with Positive Liberty?. Kristjánsson, Kristján.

Why Liberty is Devoured by Reason in History: Re-Reading Merleau-Ponty During the Days of the Soviet Revolution. Feher, Fererr.

LICHTENBERG

Aphorisms—Georg Christoph Lichtenberg. Lichtenberg, Georg Christoph.

Lichtenberg and Kant on the Subject of Thinking. Zoeller, Guenter.

LIFE

Analecta Husserliana, XXXVIII. Tymienicka, Anna-Teresa (ed).

Aristotle on the Perfect Life. Kenny, Anthony.

Birth, Suffering, and Death: Catholic Perspectives at the Edges of Life. Wildes, Kevin W (ed), Abel, Francesc (ed) and Harvey, John C (ed).

Daimon Life: Heidegger and Life-Philosophy. Krell, David Farrell.

Death and Personal Survival: The Evidence for Life After Death. Almeder, Robert F.

LIFE

Disputed Questions in Theology and the Philosophy of Religion. Hick, John.
Drawing the Line: Life, Death, and Ethical Choices in an American Hospital. Gorovitz, Samuel.
Expressionism in Philosophy: Spinoza. Deleuze, Gilles and Joughin, Martin (trans).
God and Existence (in Hungarian). Joós, Ernó.
Hobbes and Human Nature. Green, Arnold W.
Life and Death: Philosophical Essays in Biomedical Ethics. Brock, Dan W.
Life-Sharing for a Creative Tomorrow. Barral, Mary-Rose.
Method—Towards a Study of Humankind, Volume I: The Nature of Nature. Morin, Edgar and Bélanger, J L Roland (trans).
Philosophy of Religion: A Universalist Perspective. Sterling, Marvin.
Quality of Life, Health and Happiness. Nordenfelt, Lennart.
Rediscovering the Moral Life. Gouinlock, James.
Terra es animata: On Having a Life. Meilaender, Gilbert C.
The Birth Lottery. Boss, Judith A.
The Cambridge Companion to Heidegger. Guignon, Charles B (ed).
The Ethics of Reproductive Technology. Alpern, Kenneth D (ed).
The Metaphysics of Death. Fischer, John Martin (ed).
The Moral Life. Luper-Foy, Steven.
The Person and the Common Life. Hart, James G.
Aristotle and the Ideal Life. Lawrence, Gavin.
Brain Death: A Survey of the Debate and the Position in 1991. Jeffery, Peter.
Callicles' Hedonism. Rudebusch, George H.
Can Philosophy Speak about Life?. Dilham, Ilham.
Can Philosophy Speak about Life? in The Impulse to Philosophise, Griffiths, A Phillips (ed). Dilman, Ilham.
Commentary on "How Much of the Brain Must Die in Brain Death". Dagi, Teo Forcht.
Contemporary Vitalism in The Crisis in Modernism, Burwick, Frederick (ed). Bakhtin, Mikhail.
Culture as a Human Form of Life: A Romantic Reading of Wittgenstein. Lurie, Yuval.
Descartes and Locke on Speciesism and the Value of Life. Squadrito, Kathy.
Divine Intervention and the Origin of Life. Chandler, Hugh S.
Does the Fetus Have a Right to Life?. Wilkins, Burleigh T.
Euthanasia and the Distinction between Acts and Omissions. Nesbitt, Winston.
How Much of the Brain Must Die in Brain Death?. Bernat, James L.
Innovative Lifesaving Treatments in Contemporary Issues in Paediatric Ethics, Burgess, Michael M (ed). Ackerman, Terrence F.
Interpreting Cultural Differences in Medical Intervention: The Use of Wittgenstein's "Forms of Life". Nash, Carol.
La metafisica della vita secondo A T Tymieniecka. Barral, Mary-Rose.
La natura della vita: Una indagine filosofica. Crescini, Angelo.
Le concept de vie dans la Grèce ancienne et le serment d'Hippocrate. Angeletti, Luciana Rita.
Life-Style and the Standard of Living in The Quality of Life, Nussbaum, Martha C (ed). Bliss, Christopher.
Measuring Quality of Life in Theory and in Practice: A Dialogue Between Philosophical and Psychological Approaches. Boddington, Paula and Podpadec, Tessa.
Meta-Neuroanatomy: The Myth of the Unbounded Main/Brain in Philosophy and the Origin and Evolution of the Universe, Agazzi, Evandro (ed). Cherniak, Christopher.
Mind/Action for Wittgenstein and Heidegger. Schatzki, Theodore R.
My Mental Development in The Philosophy of A J Ayer, Hahn, Lewis E (ed). Ayer, A J.
Necesidad de una renovación ética. López Quintás, Alfonso.
On the Mathematization of Life. Fleischhacker, Louk and Brainard, Marcus (trans).
Phenomenology of Life and the New Critique of Reason in Analecta Husserliana, XXXIV, Tymieniecka, Anna-Teresa (ed). Tymieniecka, Anna-Teresa.
Philosophy and the Cult of Irrationalism. Almond, Brenda.
Poesia e verità: Lettere a Clotilde Marghieri. Scaravelli, Luigi.
Private Life, Private Interest, Private Property. Zamoshkin, I A.
Quality of Life and the Death of "Baby M". Kuhse, Helga.
Reading a Life in The Cambridge Companion to Heidegger, Guignon, Charles B (ed). Sheehan, Thomas.
Recent Work on Death and the Meaning of Life. Fischer, John M.
Reflections on the Moral Life. McInerny, Ralph.
S Stur's "Treatise on Life" (in Czechoslovakian). Uher, J.
Scenes from a Newborn Life (in Dutch). Hendriks, Ruud.
Still More of My Life in The Philosophy of A J Ayer, Hahn, Lewis E (ed). Ayer, A J.
The Enigma of Everydayness in Reading Heidegger: Commemorations, Sallis, John (ed). Haar, Michel.
The Idea of Enablement. Martin, Bill.
The Impossibility and the Necessity of Quality of Life Research. Morreim, E Haavi.
The Limits of Consent: A Note on Dr Kevorkian. Kleinig, John.
The Relevance of Philosophy to Life in Frontiers in American Philosophy, Volume I, Burch, Robert W (ed). Lachs, John.
The Search for the New Pineal Gland: Brain Life and Personhood. Moussa, Mario and Shannon, Thomas A.
The Wisdom of Love. Korab-Karpowicz, W J.
Time Topology for Some Classical and Quantum Non-Relativistic Systems (in Polish). Olszewski, S.
Valuing Lives. Perrett, Roy W.
When Self-Determination Runs Amok. Callahan, Daniel.
Withholding/Withdrawing Life-Sustaining Treatment in Contemporary Issues in Paediatric Ethics, Burgess, Michael M (ed). Bartholome, William.
Wittgenstein + Heidegger on the Stream of Life. Schatzki, Theodore R.
'The Triumph of Life': Nietzsche's Verbicide in The Crisis in Modernism, Burwick, Frederick (ed). Amrine, Frederick.

LIFE AFTER DEATH

see Immortality

LIFE STYLE

Commentator on 'Life-Style and the Standard of Living' in The Quality of Life, Nussbaum, Martha C (ed). Sen, Amartya.
Life-Style and the Standard of Living in The Quality of Life, Nussbaum, Martha C (ed). Bliss, Christopher.

LIFE SUPPORT

Forgoing Life-Sustaining Treatment: Limits to the Consensus. Veatch, Robert M.

LIFSIC, M

Una traduzione sfortunata della "Scienza Nuova". Mastrolianni, Giovanni.

LIGHT

Analecta Husserliana, XXXVIII. Tymieniecka, Anna-Teresa (ed).
Descartes on Seeing: Epistemology and Visual Perception. Wolf-Devine, Celia.
Einstein on Simultaneity. Cohen, Michael.
Light and Metpahor in Plotinus and St Thomas Aquinas. Corrigan, Kevin.
Light-Values as Existential Indices in Thomas Pynchon's Extravagant Comic Revery in Analecta Husserliana, XXXVIII, Tymieniecka, Anna-Teresa (ed). Brottman, David.
Metaphor and the Experience of Light in Analecta Husserliana, XXXVIII, Tymieniecka, Anna-Teresa (ed). Haney II, William S.
Relativism in Gibson's Theory of Picture Perception. Boynton, David M.
The Relativity Principle and the Isotropy of Boosts. Budden, Tim.

LIMITS

Los Limites de la Comunidad. Thiebaut, Carlos.
The Philosophy of the Limit. Cornell, Drucilla.
Bindings, Shackles, Brakes in Cultural-Political Interventions in the Unfinished Project of Enlightenment, Honneth, Axel (& other eds). Offe, Claus.
Defensa de la revelación divina contra las objeciones del librepensador. Arana, Juan (trans) and Euler, L.
Divine Self-Limitation in Swinbourne's Doctrine of Omniscience. Fouts, Avery.
L'Epinomide o della religione ricondotta entro i limiti della ragione. Pesce, Domenico.
L'ermeneutica e il problema della fine: A proposito di due contributi recenti. Fabris, Adriano.
La forma e il limite. Gallino, Guglielmo.
Limit and Exhaustibility in the Questions of T'ang. Stevenson, Frank W.
Potenzialità conoscitive del trascendentale di Husserl. O'Dwyer Bellinetti, L.

LINDSTROM, P

The Compactness of First-Order Logic: From Gödel to Lindström. Dawson Jr, John W.

LINEAR

A Decision Algorithm for Linear Sentences on a PFM. Li, L, Li, H and Liu, Y.
Cut Elimination for the Unified Logic. Vauzeilles, Jacqueline.
Extending the Curry-Howard Interpretation to Lienar, Relevant and Other Resource Logics. Gabbay, Dov M and De Queiroz, R J G B.
Linear Diagrams for Syllogisms (With Relationals). Englebretsen, George.
One-Shot Decisions under Linear Partial Information. Kofler, Edward and Zweifel, Peter.
Revealed Preference and Linear Utility. Clark, Stephen A.
The Interpretability of Robinson Arithmetic in the Ramified Second-Order Theory of Dense Linear Order. Hazen, A P.

LINEAR LOGIC

Cut Elimination for the Unified Logic. Vauzeilles, Jacqueline.
Linearizing Intuitionistic Implication. Lincoln, Patrick, Scedrov, Andre and Shankar, Natarajan.

LINGUISTICS

see also Sociolinguistics

A Metalogical Theory of Reference: Realism and Essentialism in Semantics. Vergauwen, Roger.
Belief Base Dynamics. Hansson, Sven Ove.
Bertrand Russell's Philosophy of Logical Atomism. Patterson, Wayne.
Boundary Ways: On the Philosophy of the Later Ludwig Wittgenstein (in Hungarian). Neumer, Katalin.
Direct Reference: From Language to Thought. Rashed, Roshdi.
First Logic. Goodman, Michael.
Foundations of Logic and Language. Sen, Pranab Kumar (ed).
Language and Philosophical Problems. Stenlund, Sören.
Statement and Referent: An Inquiry into the Foundations of Our Conceptual Order. Shwayder, David S.
The Company of Words: Hegel, Language, and Systematic Philosophy. McCumber, John.
The Linguistic Turn: Essays In Philosophical Method. Rorty, Richard (ed).
The Nyaya Theory of Linguistic Performance: A New Interpretation of Tattvacintamani. Mukhopadhyay, P K.
The Rediscovery of the Mind. Searle, John R.
The Title of the Letter: A Reading of Lacan. Nancy, Jean-Luc and Lacoue-Labarthe, Philippe.
Toward Non-Essentialist Sociolinguistics. Janicki, Karol.
Unreason Within Reason: Essays on the Outskirts of Rationality. Graham, A C.
Voices of the Past: The Status of Language in Eighteenth-Century Japanese Discourse. Sakai, Naoki.
What Is Cognitive Science?. Von Eckardt, Barbara.
A Congery of Self-Reference. Rardin, Patrick.
About Indirect Questions and Semi-Questions. Suñer, Margarita.
Any. Kadmon, Nirit and Landman, Fred.

LINGUISTICS

Argumentation, Self-Inconsistency, and Multidimensional Argument Strength. Sillince, J A A and Minors, R H.

Aristotle's *Peri hermeneias* in Medieval Latin and Arabic Philosophy: Logic and the Linguistic Arts. Black, Deborah.

Axiomatizar la metafísica? A propósito de "L'impossible métaphysique" de G Kalinowski. Ballesteros, Manuel.

Charles de Brosses and Diderot: Eighteenth-Century Arguments Concerning Primitive Language, Particular Natural Languages and a National Language. Clark-Evans, Christine.

Chomsky for Philosophers (and Linguists) (in Dutch). Jaspers, D.

Chomsky Versus Quine on the Analytic-Synthetic Distinction. Horwich, Paul.

Comments on Searle: 'Meaning, Communication, and Representation' in John Searle and His Critics, LePore, Ernest (ed). Habermas, Jürgen.

Decomposing Intentionality: Perspectives on Intentionality Drawn from Language Research with Two Species of Chimpanzees. Bechtel, William.

Eine biolinguistische Kritik Wittgensteins. Gesang, Bernward.

El Index Thomisticus y la semántica lingüística. De Gandolfi, M C Donadío M.

Elementary Formal Semantics for English Tense and Aspect. Pendlebury, Michael.

Eliminative Connectionism: Its Implications for a Return to an Empiricist/Behaviorist Linguistics. Place, Ullin T.

Grammar, Logical Grammar and Grammatical Theory in Foundations of Logic and Language, Sen, Pranab Kumar (ed). Moitra, Shefali.

Hintikka's Game of Language. Kanthamani, A.

Husserl, Linguistic Meaning, and Intuition. Owens, Wayne.

Is Intentionality More Basic than Linguistic Meaning? in John Searle and His Critics, LePore, Ernest (ed). Apel, Karl Otto.

It is Generally the Case That. Hellman, Nathan.

Language and Reality. Gopinathan, K.

Making Sense of Indexicals. Anderson, Michael.

Of One's Own Free Will. Stampe, Dennis W and Gibson, Martha I.

On Punctate Content and on Conceptual Role. McLaughlin, Brian.

On the Study of Linguistic Performance in Cognition, Semantics and Philosophy, Ezquerro, Jesús and Sànchez de Zavala, Víctor.

Peirce's "Sign": Its Concept and Its Use. Deledalle, Gérard.

Postmodernism and Language in Postmodernism and Society, Boyne, Roy (ed). Lecercle, Jean-Jacques.

Prolegomena zu einer semiotischen Beschreibung graphischer Darstellungen in Diagrammatik und Philosophie, Gehring, Petra (ed). Kaczmarek, Ludger and Wulff, Hans Jürgen.

Relevance and "Pseudo-Imperatives". Clark, Billy.

Scope and Rigidity. Horsten, Leon.

Searle on Ontological Commitment in John Searle and His Critics, Lepore, Ernest (ed). Van Inwagen, Peter.

Still an Attitude Problem. Saul, Jennifer M.

The Behaviorist Turn in Recent Theories of Language. Andresen, Julie Tetel.

The Errors of Linguistic Contextualism. Bevir, Mark.

The Formal Syntax of Modernism: Carnap and Le Corbusier. Bearn, Gordon C F.

The Indispensability of Translation in Quine and Davidson. Glock, Hans-Johann.

The Linguistic Turn: Shortcut or Detour?. Dilworth, Craig.

The Linguistic Winding Road. Burri, Alex.

The Place of Language—I. Morris, Michael.

The Second Person. Davidson, Donald.

The Sense of Grounding Speech Act on Use. Lenka, Laxminarayan.

The Social Anatomy of Inference. Brandom, Robert.

Thought and Language in the *Tractatus*. Summerfield, Donna M.

Thought Experiments in Linguistics in Thought Experiments in Science and Philosophy, Horowitz, Tamara (ed). Thomason, Sarah G.

Three Views of Demonstrative Reference. Reimer, Marga.

Translation and Foreign Cultures. Collin, Finn.

Truthlikeness without Truth: A Methodological Approach. Zamora Bonilla, Jesús P.

Verdade e Demonstraçao. Tarski, A and Paula Assis, J (trans).

Was Meinong Only Pretending?. Kroon, Frederick W.

Wittgenstein and Infinite Linguistic Competence. Niles, Ian.

'Tormenting Questions' in 'Philosophical Investigations' in Wittgenstein's Philosophical Investigations, Arrington, Robert L (ed). Hilmy, S Stephen.

LIST

Logic-Theological Schools from the Second Half of the 12th Century: A List of Sources. Yukio, Iwakuma and Ebbesen, Sten.

LITERACY

Inductive Logic: Probability and Statistics. Baird, Davis W.

Tradition and Individuality: Essays. Nyíri, J C.

Can You Read? Philosophical Reflections on Labour, Leisure and Literacy. Hunter, Graeme.

Ethical Thinking and the Liberal Arts Tradition in Moral Education and the Liberal Arts, Mitias, Michael H (ed). Holder Jr, John J.

The Moral Imagination and the Aesthetics of Human Existence in Moral Education and the Liberal Arts, Mitias, Michael H (ed). Alexander, Thomas M.

LITERAL

Metaphors and Malapropisms: Davidson on the Limits of the Literal. Rahat, Ehud.

Signification conventionnelle et non-littéralité. Vallée, Richard.

LITERARY

The Work of John Duns Scotus in the Light of Textual Criticism (Conclusion) (in Czechoslovakian). Richter, V.

LITERARY CRITICISM

A Companion to Aesthetics. Cooper, David E (ed).

Agents and Lives: Moral Thinking in Literature. Goldberg, S L.

Matrix and Line: Derrida and the Possibilities of Postmodern Social Theory. Martin, Bill.

The Republic of Art and Other Essays. Diffey, T J.

Video Icons and Values. Olson, Alan M (ed), Parr, Christopher (ed) and Parr, Debra (ed).

Voices of the Past: The Status of Language in Eighteenth-Century Japanese Discourse. Sakai, Naoki.

Crates on Poetic Criticism. Asmis, Elizabeth.

Following in the Footsteps of Aristotle: The Chicago School, the Glue-stick, and the Razor. Groarke, Louis.

Jameson, Marxism, and Postmodernism in Postmodernism/ Jameson/ Critique, Kellner, Douglas M (ed). Kellner, Douglas M.

Kant, Lentricchia and Aesthetic Education. Miller, Paul Allen.

Marion Montgomery and "The Risk of Prophecy". Hudson, Deal.

Revealing the Scapegoat Mechanism: Christianity after Girard. Kerr, Fergus.

The New Historicism and Shakespearean Criticism: A Marxist Critique. Siegel, Paul N.

The Story of the Moral: The Function of Thematizing in Literary Criticism. Seamon, Roger.

The Work of John Duns Scotus in the Light of Textual Criticism (Conclusion) (in Czechoslovakian). Richter, V.

The Work of John Duns Scotus in the Light of Textual Criticism (Part I) (in Czechoslovakian). Richter, V.

LITERARY THEORY

Adorno's Aesthetic Theory: The Redemption of Illusion. Zuidervaart, Lambert.

After the Demise of the Tradition: Rorty, Critical Theory, and the Fate of Philosophy. Nielsen, Kai.

An Essay In Post-Romantic Literary Theory: Art, Artifact, and the Innocent Eye. Fleming, Bruce.

Antonio Gramsci: Beyond Marxism and Postmodernism. Holub, Renate.

Engendering the Subject: Gender and Self-Representation in Contemporary Women's Fiction. Robinson, Sally.

Extensions: Essays on Interpretation, Rationality, and the Closure of Modernism. Watson, Stephen.

Interpretation and Overinterpretation: Umberto Eco. Collini, Stefan (ed).

Jean-Paul Sartre: Freedom and Commitment. Hill, Charles G.

Melancholy Dialectics. Pensky, Max.

Nationalism, Colonialism, and Literature. Eagleton, Terry, Jameson, Fredric and Said, Edward W.

Nietzsche's Philosophical and Narrative Styles. Pettey, John Carson.

Oneself as Another—Paul Ricoeur. Ricoeur, Paul and Blamey, Kathleen (trans).

Phenomenology and Deconstruction, Volume II: Method and Imagination. Cumming, Robert Denoon.

Philosophy and Biblical Interpretation: A Study in Nineteenth-Century Conflict. Addinall, Peter.

Poetics of Imagining: From Husserl to Lyotard. Kearney, Richard.

T S Eliot and American Philosophy: The Harvard Years. Jain, Manju.

The Banalization of Nihilism. Carr, Karen L.

The Dialogics of Critique. Gardiner, Michael.

The Logic of Sense—Gilles Deleuze. Boundas, Constantin V (ed), Lester, Mark (& other trans) and Deleuze, Gilles.

The Step Not Beyond. Nelson, Lycette (trans) and Blanchot, Maurice.

Theoretical Perspectives on Sexual Difference. Rhode, Deborah L (ed).

Theorizing American Literature. Cowan, Bainard (ed) and Kronick, Joseph G (ed).

Theory Now and Then. Miller, J Hillis.

Ut Pictura Poesis: Vermeer's Challenge to Some Renaissance Literary Assumptions. Hurley, Ann.

Woman and Modernity: The (Life)styles of Lou Andreas-Salomé. Martin, Biddy.

Zarathustra Is a Comic Book. Higgins, Kathleen M.

An Allegory of Modernity/Postmodernity in Working Through Derrida, Madison, Gary B (ed). Bernstein, Richard J.

Appearance in Poetry: Lyric Illusion? in Aesthetic Illusion, Burwick, Frederick (ed). Thomke, Hellmut.

Culture, Textuality and Truth. Lewandowski, Joseph D.

F R Leavis: Intuitionist?. Haynes, Anthony.

Fiction: On the Fate of a Concept Betwen Philosophy and Literary Theory in Aesthetic Illusion, Burwick, Frederick (ed). Pfeiffer, K Ludwig.

Fish's Argument for the Relativity of Interpretive Truth. Stecker, Robert A.

Guilty Pleasures: Aesthetic Meta-Response and Fiction. Markowitz, Sally.

Hegel and the Dialects of American Literary Historiography in Theorizing American Literature, Cowan, Bainard (ed). Jay, Gregory S.

Horror, Helplessness, and Vulnerability: A Reply to Robert Solomon. Carroll, Noël.

How Sexist is Sartre?. Burstow, Bonnie.

Ideologies and Mentalities. Gordon, Daniel.

In Praise of True Pluralism. Harris, Wendell V.

Indirect Communication: Hegelian Aesthetic and Kierkegaard's Literary Art in Kierkegaard on Art and Communication, Pattison, George (ed). Thomas, John Heywood.

Interpretation, Intention, and Truth. Shusterman, Richard.

Nietzsche and Aestheticism. Leiter, Brian.

Palimpsest History in Interpretation and Overinterpretation: Umberto Eco, Collini, Stefan (ed). Brooke-Rose, Christine.

Possible Worlds Between the Disciplines. Ronen, Ruth.

Reply in Interpretation and Overinterpretation: Umberto Eco, Collini, Stefan (ed). Eco, Umberto.

LITERATURE

Plato and Performance. Gould, John.

Polanyian Perspectives on the Teaching of Literature and Composition. Wallace, M Elizabeth (& others).

Reading in (Dramatic) Texts in Pre-Hellenistic Greece (in Czechoslovakian). Hlobil, Tomas.

Reexperiencing Fiction and Non-Fiction. Gerrig, Richard J.

Reflections of the Sun: Explanation in the *Phaedo*. Rowe, Christopher.

Reflections on Time. Dunning, William V.

Reply to Richard Eldridge's "Reading for Life": Martha C Nussbaum on Philosophy and Literature. Nussbaum, Martha C.

Response to Stecker's "Goldman on Interpreting Art and Literature". Goldman, Alan H.

Romance and Ressentiment: Saint Genet in Sartre Alive, Aronson, Ronald (ed). Skakoon, Walter S.

Romancing the Stone in Theorizing American Literature, Cowan, Bainard (ed). Rowe, John Carlos.

Seascape with Fog: Metaphor in Locke's "Essay". Vogt, Philip.

Seeing Blake's Illuminated Texts. Bigwood, Carol.

Shakespeare's Demonic Prince. Mindle, Grant B.

Shakespeare's Richard III and the Soul of the Tyrant. Frisch, Morton J.

Simone de Beauvoir's Adieux: A Funeral Rite and a Literary Challenge in Sartre Alive, Aronson, Ronald (ed). Idt, Geneviève.

Six Theories in the Bedroom of *The Dead*. Garrett, Roland.

Still Unconverted: A Reply to Neill. Yanal, Robert J.

Storytelling and Moral Agency. Tirrell, M Lynne.

The Authorship and Sources of the Peri Semeion Ascribed to Theophrastus in Theophrastus, Fortenbaugh, William W (ed). Cronin, Patrick.

The Body in the City. Swensen, Cole.

The Dilemma Facing Contemporary Research in the *Yijing*. Zheng, Liu.

The New Historicism and Shakespearean Criticism: A Marxist Critique. Siegel, Paul N.

The Nothing That Is in Theorizing American Literature, Cowan, Bainard (ed). Butler, Judith.

The Place of Real Emotion in Response to Fiction. Levinson, Jerrold.

The Preservation of Homeric Tradition: Heroic Re-Performance in the *Republic* and the *Odyssey*. Klonoski, Richard.

The Question of *The Question of Hu*. Mazlish, Bruce.

The Resurrectionist, or November in Le Havre in Sartre Alive, Aronson, Ronald (ed). Wilcocks, Robert.

The Rhetoric of Philosophical "Writing": Emphatic Metaphors in Derrida and Rorty. Trembath, Paul.

The Role of Folk and Fairy Tales in Kierkegaard's Authorship in Kierkegaard on Art and Communication, Pattison, George (ed). Kjaer, Grethe.

The Sign Over the Barber Shop: Annotations on the Problems of Interpretation. Schmitz, Heinz-Gerd.

The Story of the Moral: The Function of Thematizing in Literary Criticism. Seamon, Roger.

The Sublime as a Source of Light in the Works of Nicolas Boileau in Analecta Husserliana, XXXVIII, Tymieniecka, Anna-Teresa (ed). Litman, Theodore.

The Voice that Keeps Reading: Evan's *Strategies of Deconstruction*. Kates, Joshua.

The Work of John Duns Scotus in the Light of Textual Criticism (Part I) (in Czechoslovakian). Richter, V.

This Is Not the Real Me. Sparshott, Francis.

Understanding the Committed Writer in The Cambridge Companion to Sartre, Howells, Christina (ed). Goldthorpe, Rhiannon.

Unifying the *Protagoras*. Rutherford, Richard.

What Gilles Deleuze Has to Say to Battered Women. Holland, Nancy.

Whitman's 'Convertible Terms' in Theorizing American Literature, Cowan, Bainard (ed). Lindberg, Kathryne V.

Wittgenstein and W C Fields. Cohen, Daniel H.

Yanal and Others on Hume and Tragedy. Neill, Alex.

'No Matter How No Matter Where': The Unlit in S Beckett's Not I and Stirrings Still in Analecta Husserliana, XXXVIII, Tymieniecka, Anna-Teresa (ed). Oppenheim, Lois.

'The Very Culture of the Feelings': Poetry and Poets in Mill's Moral Philosophy. Burnstone, Daniel.

LITURGY

The Remembrance of Things (Not) Past in Christian Philosophy, Flint, Thomas P (ed). Wolterstorff, Nicholas.

LIVING WILL

Advance Directives for Voluntary Euthanasia: A Volatile Combination?. Francis, Leslie Pickering.

LOCALITY

Locality: A New Enigma for Physics in Greek Studies in the Philosophy and History of Science, Nicolacopoulos, Pantelis (ed). Bitsakis, Eftichios.

LOCKE

A Locke Dictionary. Yolton, John W.

An Approach to Political Philosophy: Locke in Contexts. Tully, James.

Eighteenth-Century Hermeneutics: Philosophy of Interpretation in England from Locke to Burke. Weinsheimer, Joel C.

Contexte des rapports intellectuels entre Hobbes et Locke. Rogers, John.

De staat van Nozick. Rozemond, Klaas.

Descartes and Locke on Speciesism and the Value of Life. Squadrito, Kathy.

Dispute and Conversation: Probability and the Rhetoric of Natural Philosophy in Locke's *Essay*. Walmsley, Peter.

Enseigner la vertu?. Barnes, Jonathan.

Filmer, Hobbes, Locke: Les cassures dans l'espace de la théorie politique. Lessay, Franck.

God's Estate. Taliaferro, Charles.

Hobbes, Locke, Franzwa on the Paradoxes of Equality. Soles, David E.

Hume and the Lockean Background: Induction and the Uniformity Principle. Owen, David.

John Locke's *Questions Concerning the Law of Nature*: A Commentary. Zuckert, Michael (ed) and Horwitz, Robert.

John Locke's Theory of Natural Law. Cvek, Peter P.

John Locke, Natural Law and Colonialism. Arneil, Barbara.

La polémica sobre lo innato en el libro I de los 'Nuevos Ensayos'. Guillén Vera, Tomás.

La propriété dans la philosophie de Locke. Goyard-Fabre, Simone.

La question du libre arbitre en France, de la Révolution à la Restauration. Baertschi, Bernard.

La teoria postcartesiana delle idee nella recente storiografia anglosassone. Marcialis, Maria Teresa.

La 'Déclaration des droits de l'homme et du citoyen' (1789). Stucki, Pierre-André.

Le mythe de l'intériorité chez Locke. Brykman, Geneviève.

Le roman philosophique de l'humanité chez Hobbes et chez Locke. Tricaud, François.

Locke against Democracy: Consent, Representation and Suffrage in the *Two Treatises*. Wood, E M.

Locke and General Knowledge: A Reconstruction. Odegard, Douglas.

Locke and Limits on Land Ownership. Shrader-Frechette, Kristin.

Locke et l'intentionnalité: le problème de Molyneux. Vienne, Jean-Michel.

Locke on Government in Logical Foundations, Mahalingam, Indira (ed). Atkinson, R F.

Locke on Punishment and the Death Penalty. Calvert, Brian.

Locke on Real Essence and Internal Constitution. Vienne, Jean-Michel.

Locke on Solidity and Incompressibility in Logical Foundations, Mahalingam, Indira (ed). Alexander, Peter.

Locke's Empiricism and the Opening Arguments in Hegel's *Phenomenology of Spirit*. Shamsur Rahman, A K M.

Locke's Idea of an Idea in Logical Foundations, Mahalingam, Indira (ed). Langford, Glenn.

Locke's Proposal for Semiotic and the Scholastic Doctrine of Species. Deely, John N.

Locke, Taxation and Reform: A Reply to Wood. Hughes, Martin.

Lockean Aesthetics. Townsend Jr, Dabney.

Lockean Ideas and 18th Century British Philosophy. Loptson, Peter J.

Natural Law, Property, and Justice: The General Justification of Property in Aquinas and Locke. Lustig, Andrew.

Re-Interpretation of Locke's Theory of Ideas. Squadrito, Kathy.

Scottish Communitarianism, Lockean Individualism, and Women's Moral Development in Women's Rights and the Rights of Man, Arnaud, A J. Cooper, David E.

Seascape with Fog: Metaphor in Locke's "Essay". Vogt, Philip.

Self-Reference: The Radicalization of Locke. Rovane, Carol.

The Epistemological Status of Ideas: Locke Compared to Arnauld. Bolton, Martha Brandt.

The Ideological Commitment of Locke: Freemen and Servants in the *Two Treatises of Government*. Becker, Ron.

The law of War: Grotius, Sidney, Locke and the Political Theory of Rebellion. Scott, Jonathan.

The Radical Dimensions of Locke's Political Thought: A Dialogic Essay on the Problems of Interpretation. Ashcraft, Richard.

The Right to Revolution: Locke or Marx? in Terrorism, Justice and Social Values, Peden, Creighton (ed). Stichler, Richard N.

The Transition to Civil Society: Two Interpretations of Locke's Theory of Property Rights. Rogers, Patrick.

'Safe Enough in his Honesty and Prudence': The Ordinary Conduct of Government in the Thought of John Locke. Anderson, Christopher.

LODGE, R

From Triangles to Tripods: Polycentrism in Environmental Ethics. Rabb, J Douglas.

LOEMKER, L

The Personalism of L E Loemker. Mulvaney, Robert J.

LOEWER, B

Response: Applications of the Theory in John Searle and His Critics, Lepore, Ernest (ed). Searle, John R.

LOEWY, E

Physician-Assisted Dying: Theory and Reality. Meier, Diane E.

LOGIC

see also Abstract Logic, Combinatory Logic, Deontic Logic, Epistemic Logic, Formal Logic, Higher Order Logics, Inductive Logic, Infinitary Logic, Informal Logic, Intensional Logic, Intuitionistic Logic, Many-Sorted Logic, Many-Valued Logics, Modal Logic, Paraconsistent Logics, Propositional Logic, Quantum Logic, Relevant Logics, Symbolic Logic, Tense Logic

"Who Sees with Equal Eye,... Atoms or Systems into Ruin Hurl'd?". DeVries, Willem A.

2-Sequent Calculus: A Proof Theory of Modalities. Masini, Andrea.

7+5=12: Analytic or Synthetic?. Tacelli, Ronald.

A Philosophical Companion to First-Order Logic. Hughes, R I G (ed).

A Rulebook for Arguments (Second Edition). Weston, Anthony.

Advances in Scientific Philosophy. Schurz, Gerhard (ed) and Dorn, Georg J W (ed).

Agency in Action: The Practical Rational Agency Machine. Coval, Samuel C and Campbell, P G.

LOGIC

An Introduction to the Syllogism and the Logic of Proportional Quantifiers. Thompson, Bruce E R.

Bayes or Bust? A Critical Examination of Bayesian Confirmation Theory. Earman, John.

Berkeley's Philosophy of Mathematics. Jesseph, Douglas M.

Bertrand Russell's Philosophy of Logical Atomism. Patterson, Wayne.

Betting on Theories: Cambridge Studies in Probability, Induction, and Decision Theory. Maher, Patrick.

Collected Works of Bernard Lonergan, V10. Doran, Robert M (ed) and Crowe, Frederick E (ed).

Criss-Crossing A Philosophical Landscape. Schulte, Joachim (ed) and Sundholm, Göran (ed).

Dimostrazioni e Significato. Moriconi, Enrico.

Discovering Philosophy. White, Thomas I.

EIS for Nilpotent Shifts of Varieties. Graczynska, Ewa.

First Logic. Goodman, Michael.

Forms of Concrescence: Alfred North Whitehead's Philosophy and Computer Programming Structures. Henry, Granville C.

Foundations of Logic and Language. Sen, Pranab Kumar (ed).

Foundations of Philosophy of Science: Recent Developments. Fetzer, James.

G E Moore. Baldwin, Thomas and Honderich, Ted (ed).

Gautama's Nyaya-Sutra with Vatsyayana's Commentary. Gangopadhyaya, M.

Hegel on Logic and Religion: The Reasonableness of Christianity. Burbidge, John W.

Husserl's Transcendental Phenomenology—Elisabeth Ströker. Hardy, Lee (trans) and Ströker, Elisabeth.

Idealization III. Brzezinski, Jerzy (ed) and Nowak, Leszek (ed).

Il Problema della Modalità nelle Logiche di Hegel. Baptist, Gabriella.

Inductive Logic: Probability and Statistics. Baird, Davis W.

Invariance and Structural Dependence. Odelstad, Jan.

Kotarbinski: Logic, Semantics and Ontology. Wolenski, Jan (ed).

Language and Philosophical Problems. Stenlund, Sören.

Language and Time. Smith, Quentin.

Lectures on Logic—Immanuel Kant. Young, Michael J (ed & trans).

Logic and Sin in the Writings of Ludwig Wittgenstein. Shields, Philip.

Logic Primer. Allen, Colin and Hand, Michael.

Logic, God and Metaphysics. Harris, James F (ed).

Logical Foundations. Mahalingam, Indira (ed) and Carr, Brian (ed).

Machinations: Computational Studies of Logic, Language, and Cognition. Spencer-Smith, Richard (ed) and Torrance, Steve (ed).

Mental Causation. Heil, John (ed) and Mele, Alfred (ed).

Modalities: Philosophical Essays. Marcus, Ruth Barcan.

On the Logic of Ordinary Conditionals. McLaughlin, Robert N.

Ontology Without Ultrafilters and Possible Worlds: An Examination of Bolzano's Ontology. Berg, Jan.

Ontology, Causality and Mind: Essays in Honour of D M Armstrong. Bacon, John (ed), Campbell, Keith (ed) and Reinhardt, Lloyd (ed).

Our Knowledge of the External World. Russell, Bertrand.

Perspectives on the History of Mathematical Logic. Drucker, Thomas (ed).

Philosophical Occasions: 1912-1951—Ludwig Wittgenstein. Klagge, James C (ed), Nordmann, Alfred (ed) and Wittgenstein, Ludwig.

Philosophy in Literature, Volumes I and II. Johnson, Charles W.

Probability and Rationality. Eells, Ellery (ed) and Maruszewski, Tomasz (ed).

Reason and Tradition in Indian Thought: An Essay on the Nature of Indian Philosophical Thinking. Mohanty, Jitendra N.

Reasoning: A Practical Guide. Pinto, Robert C and Blair, John Anthony.

Reflections on Philosophy. McHenry, Leemon (ed) and Adams, Frederick (ed).

Renewing Philosophy. Putnam, Hilary.

Situation Theory and Its Applications, Volume 2. Barwise, K Jon (& other eds).

Statement and Referent: An Inquiry into the Foundations of Our Conceptual Order. Shwayder, David S.

Talk About Beliefs. Crimmins, Mark.

Testimony: A Philosophical Study. Coady, C A J.

The Cambridge Companion to Hegel. Beiser, Frederick (ed).

The Contents of Experience. Crane, Tim (ed).

The Human Being as a Logical Thinker. Balzer, Noel.

The Logic of Scientific Discovery. Popper, Karl R.

The Mechanism and Freedom of Logic. Henry, Granville C.

The Physical Basis of Predication. Newman, Andrew.

The Poetics of Alfarabi and Avicenna. Kemal, Salim.

The Revision Theory of Truth. Gupta, Anil and Belnap, Nuel.

Theories of Truth: A Critical Introduction. Kirkham, Richard.

Thinking Logically: Basic Concepts for Reasoning (Second Edition). Freeman, James.

Thrasyllan Platonism. Tarrant, Harold.

Unreason Within Reason: Essays on the Outskirts of Rationality. Graham, A C.

A Δ2/2 Well-Order of the Reals and Incompactness of L(QMM). Abraham, Uri and Shelah, Saharon.

A Boolean-Valued Version of Gupta's Semantics. Reyes, Marie La Palme and Reyes, Gonzalo E.

A Certain Conception of the Calculus of Rough Sets. Bonikowski, Zbigniew.

A Construction of Boolean Algebras from First-Order Structures. Koppelberg, Sabine.

A Contribution to the End-Extension Problem and the Π1 Conservativeness Problem. Adamowicz, Zofia.

A Critical Appraisal of Second-Order Logic. Jané, Ignacio.

A Decision Algorithm for Linear Sentences on a PFM. Li, L, Li, H and Liu, Y.

A Deduction Theorem Schema for Deductive Systems of Propositional Logics. Czelakowski, J and Dziobiak, W.

A Defense of Branching Quantification. Hand, Michael.

A Defense of Propensity Interpretations of Fitness. Richardson, Robert C and Burian, Richard M.

A Diferença entre as Filosofias de Carnap e Popper. De Araújo Dutra, Luiz Henrique.

A Diophantine Definition of Rational Integers over Some Rings of Algebraic Numbers. Shlapentokh, Alexandra.

A Fruitless Definition. Harris, N G E.

A Functional Partial Semantics for Intensional Logic. Lapierre, Serge.

A Generalized Notion of Weak Interpretability and the Corresponding Modal Logic. Dzhaparidze, Giorgie.

A Limiting Frequency Approach to Probability Based on the Weak Law of Large Numbers. Neapolitan, Richard E.

A Linguistic Approach to Frege's Puzzles in Advances in Scientific Philosophy, Schurz, Gerhard (ed). Bellert, Irena.

A Logic of Better. Goble, Lou.

A Modal Analog for Glivenko's Theorem and Its Applications. Rybakov, V V.

A Modal Reduction for Partial Logic. Barba, Juan.

A Model in Which Every Kurepa Tree is Thick. Jin, Renling.

A N Prior's Rediscovery of Tense Logic. Ohrstrom, Peter and Hasle, Per.

A Natural Deduction System for Discourse Representation Theory. Saurer, Werner.

A Necessary Falsehood in the Third Man Argument. Scaltsas, Theodore.

A New Angle on Russell's "Inextricable Tangle" Over Meaning and Denotation. Rodriguez-Consuegra, Francisco A.

A New Approach to the Problem of the Justification of Deduction in Foundations of Logic and Language, Sen, Pranab Kumar (ed). Datta, Srilkeha.

A New Look at Simultaneity. Peacock, Kent A.

A New Strongly Minimal Set. Hrushovski, Ehud.

A Normal Form for Logical Derivations Implying One for Arithmetic Derivations. Mints, G.

A Note About Reism in Kotarbinski: Logic, Semantics and Ontology, Wolenski, Jan (ed). Hiz, Henry.

A Note About the Axioms for Branching-Time Logic. Zanardo, Alberto.

A Note Concerning Irving H Anellis's "Distortions and Discontinuties of Mathematical Progress". Ernest, Paul.

A Note on Naive Set Theory in LP. Restall, Greg.

A Note on Philip Kitcher's Analysis of Mathematical Truth. Norton-Smith, Thomas M.

A Note on Some Weak Forms of the Axiom of Choice. Shannon, Gary P.

A Note on the "Carving Up Content" Principle in Frege's Theory of Sense. Linsky, Bernard.

A Note on the Diagonzalizable Algebras of PA and ZF. Shavrukov, Y.

A Note on the Extension Principle for Relatively Congruence-Distributive Quasivarieties. Czelakowski, Janusz.

A Note on the Interpretability Logic of Finitely Axiomatized Theories. De Rijke, Maarten.

A Note on the Normal Form of Closed Formulas of Interpretability Logic. Hájek, Petr and Svejdar, Vitezslav.

A Note on Unary Rules and a Complete Syntactic Characterization of Propositional Calculi. Zuber, R.

A Plea on Behalf of the Innocent. Thompson, Janna.

A Presentation Without an Example?. Zuboff, Arnold.

A Priori Truth. Azzouni, Jody.

A Problem for Fictionalism About Possible Worlds. Rosen, Gideon.

A Puzzle About Logical Equivalence. Dobrosavljevic, Stojan T.

A Representation of Intuitionistic Logic in Partial Information Language. Barba Escriba, Juan.

A Sequent- or Tableau-Style System for Lewis's Counterfactual Logic VC. Gent, Ian Philip.

A Set Theory Analysis of the Logic of the I Ching. Fleming, Jesse.

A Sharpened Version of McAloon's Theorem on Initial Segments of Models. D'Aquino, Paola.

A Structurally Complete Fragment of Relevant Logic. Slaney, John K and Meyer, Robert K.

A Theory of Truth Based on a Medieval Solution to the Liar Paradox. Epstein, R L.

A Thirteenth-Century Interpretation of Aristotle on Equivocation and Analogy. Ashworth, E J.

A Trinity on a Trinity on a Trinity. Zeis, John.

A Variable-Free Logic for Mass Terms. Purdy, William C.

A Weak Paraconsistent Conditional Logic. Qingyu, Zhang.

A Word Problem for Normal and Regular Equations. Graczynska, Ewa.

Abelard and the School of the Nominales. Normore, C G.

Abilities, Concepts, and Externalism in Mental Causation, Heil, John (ed). Sosa, Ernest.

Actualisation, développement et perfectionnement des calculs logiques arithmético-intensionnels de Leibniz. Sánchez-Mazas, Miguel.

Against Extended Modal Realism. Perszyk, Kenneth J.

Against Pluralism. Hazen, A P.

Akratic Attitudes and Rationality. Dunn, Robert.

Algebraic Logic for Classical Conjunction and Disjunction. Font, J M and Verdú, V.

Algebraizations of Quantifier Logics, An Introductory Overview. Németi, I.

Amalgamation and Interpolation in Normal Modal Logics. Maksimova, L.

An Algebraic Treatment of the Barwise Compactness Theory. Fleischer, Isidore and Scott, Philip.

An Alternative Rule of Disjunction in Modal Logic. Williamson, Timothy.

LOGIC

LOGIC

LOGIC

MACROCOSM

Scienza e filosofia tra microcosmo e macrocosmo: Il problema di Dio in Diderot e Newton. Nicolosi, S.

MACROECONOMICS

Philosophy of Economics: On the Scope of Reason in Economic Inquiry. Roy, Subroto.

MADDY, P

Penelope Maddy's *Realism in Mathematics* and Charles Chihara's *Constructibility and Mathematical Existence*. McCarty, David Charles.

MADHYAMIKA

Explaining Strange Parallels: The Case of Quantum Mechanics and Mādhyamika Buddhism. Balasubramaniam, Arun.

MADNESS

Critical Thought Series: 2—Critical Essays on Michel Foucault. Burke, Peter (ed).
Intentionality and Madness in Hegel's Psychology of Action. Berthold-Bond, Daniel.
Madness and Method. Beehler, Rodger G.
The Decentering of Reason: Hegel's Theory of Madness. Berthold-Bond, Daniel.

MAGIC

Developmental Hypotheses and Perspicuous Representations: Wittgenstein on Frazer's *Golden Bough*. Hacker, P M S.
Multiple Orderings of Tambiah's Thought. Buchowski, Michal.

MAHAYANA

Chinese Bhiksunis in the Ch'an Tradition (in Chinese). Shih, Heng-ching.

MAIMON

Mathematical Construction, Symbolic Cognition and the Infinite Intellect: Reflections on Maimon and Maimonides. Lachterman, David.

MAIMONIDES

A Study of Part I, Chapters 1-7 of Maimonides' *The Guide of the Perplexed*. Kleven, Terence.
Il posto della metafisica nel sapere umano: Il pensiero di Maimonide e eil suo influsso su S Tommaso d'Aquino. Pangallo, Mario.
Maimonides and Kant on Metaphysics and Piety. Friedman, R Z.
Mathematical Construction, Symbolic Cognition and the Infinite Intellect: Reflections on Maimon and Maimonides. Lachterman, David.
Metaphysical Explanation and "Particularization" in Maimonides' *Guide of the Perplexed*. Goldin, Owen.
Natural Theology and Positive Predication: Might Maimonides Be a Guide? in Prospects for Natural Theology, Long, Eugene Thomas (ed). Ferré, Frederick.

MAJORITY

"Yes, But...": Principles and Caveats in American Racial Attitudes. Hochschild, Jennifer L and Herk, Monica.
American Democracy and the Majority Rule. Riley, Jonathan.
Majorities and Minorities: A Classical Utilitarian View. Rosen, Frederick.
Manipulation under Majority Decision-Making When No Majority Suffers and Preferences Are Strict. MacIntyre, I D A.
Mean Variance Preferences and the Heat Equation. Bardsley, Peter.
Pluralism and Equality: The Status of Minority Values in a Democracy. Simon, Robert L.
Public Choice Versus Democracy. Hardin, Russell.
Rights and Majorities: Rousseau Revisited. Waldron, Jeremy.
The Demise of the Confessional State and the Rise of the Idea of a Legitimate Minority. Heim, Joseph Charles.
Three Fallacies Concerning Majorities, Minorities, and Democratic Politics. Shapiro, Ian.

MAKIN, S

Makin's Ontological Argument Again. Oppy, Graham.

MALAMENT, D

Forever is a Day: Supertasks in Pitowsky and Malament-Hogarth Spacetimes. Earman, John and Norton, John D.

MALCOLM, N

A Refutation of the Dream Argument. Shirley, Edward S.
Animal Thoughts. Gaita, Raimond.
Malcolm and Searle on 'Intentional Mental States'. Hacker, P M S.
Norman Malcolm: A Memoir. Serafini, Anthony.

MALE

see also Men
Why Patronize Feminists? A Reply to Stove on Mill. Brecher, Bob.

MALEBRANCHE

Descartes and Malebranche on Mind and Mind-Body Union. Schmaltz, Tad M.
El conocimiento de Dios según Malebranche. Fernández, José Luis.
L'image de l'homme chez Descartes et chez le cardinal de Bérulle. Vieillard-Baron, J L.
Malebranche, Models, and Causation in Causation in Early Modern Philosophy, Nadler, Steven (ed). Watson, Richard A.
Occasionalism and General Will in Malebranche. Nadler, Steven.

MALINOWOSKI, B

Philosophical Premises of Functional Anthropology. Brozi, Krzysztof J.

MALLIK, B

Basanta Kumar Mallik's Theory of Knowledge. Walker, Mary M.

MALTHUS

"An Essay on the Principle of Population"—T R Malthus. Winch, Donald (ed) and Malthus, T R.

MAN

see also Human, Individual, Person, Philosophical Anthropology
"Doctor humanitatis": Implicazioni e sviluppi dell'antropologia tomistica alla luce degli Atti del IX Congresso Tomistico Internazionale. Turco, G.
Basic Concepts—Martin Heidegger. Aylesworth, Gary E (trans) and Heidegger, Martin.
La Filosofia del Hombre. Lorite-Mena, José.
Women's Rights and the Rights of Man. Arnaud, A J and Kingdom, E.
A Woman and a Man as Prime Analogical Beings. Allen, Prudence.
Between Man and Nature. Dreyfus, Hubert L.
Comunión con el Tú absoluto, según G Marcel. Schmidt Andrade, C.
Cusanus's Concept of God and Man in the Light of His Reflections on Time. Fischer, Norbert.
Il motivo della caduta dell'uomo primordiale nell'interpretazione di Carl Gustav Jung. Zuanazzi, G.
L'aspect de l'esthétique de l'honnête homme (in Japanese). Shihara, Nobuhiro.
L'homme et le langage chez Montaigne et Descartes. De Buzon, F.
L'image de l'homme chez Descartes et chez le cardinal de Bérulle. Vieillard-Baron, J L.
Man and God in Philo: Philo's Interpretation of Genesis 1:26. Arieti, James.
Man and Nature. Jeziorowski, Artur.
Nature and the 'Primal Horizon' in Analecta Husserliana, XXXIV, Tymieniecka, Anna-Teresa (ed). Walton, Roberto J.
Nature—Landscape—Man (in Czechoslovakian). Svobodova, H.
Nicolás de Cusa, "De mente": la profundización de la doctrina del hombre-imagen. D'Amico, Claudia.
Nietzsche's Superman: The Necessity of Reconsidering the Question of Man (in Dutch). Visser, Gerard.
Originalità filosofica dei *Pensieri* di Marco Aurelio. Crovi, Luca.
Per una soggettività non più "animale": Heidegger critico di Husserl. Regina, Umberto.
Socrate: Il demone e il risveglio—Sul senso dell'etica socratica. De Bernardi, P.
The Difference Between Man and Animal: Letters of Max Scheler on F J J Buytendijk (in Dutch). Boudier, Henk Struyker.
Tra narcisismo e regressione: la crisi dell'uomo contemporaneo. Franchi, A.

MANAGEMENT

Praxiologies and the Philosophy of Economics: The International Annual of Practical Philosophy and Methodology. Auspitz, J Lee (ed), Gasparski, Wojciech W (ed) and Mlicki, Marek K (ed).
The Corporation as Anomaly. Schrader, David.
Artificial Decision-Making and Artificial Ethics: A Management Concern. Khalil, Omar E.
Comment on "Managers in the Moral Dimension: What Etzioni Might Mean to Corporate Managers". Etzioni, Amitai.
Hostile Takeovers and Methods of Defense: A Stakeholder Analysis. Hanly, Ken.
Machiavelli's Prince as CEO. D'Andrade, Kendall.
Managers in the Moral Dimension: What Etezioni Might Mean to Corporate Managers. Shaw, Bill and Zollers, Frances E.
The "C" Theory: A Chinese Philosophical Approach to Management and Decision-Making. Cheng, Chung-Ying.

MANDELA, N

Politics beyond Humanism in Working Through Derrida, Madison, Gary B (ed). Bernasconi, Robert.

MANET, E

The Work of Art as Psychoanalytical Object: Wollheim on Manet. Herwitz, Daniel A.

MANKIND

Le roman philosophique de l'humanité chez Hobbes et chez Locke. Tricaud, François.
Nature and Silence. Manes, Christopher.

MANNER

The Sources of Morality: Function, Conformity and Aesthetics. O'Connell, James.

MANNHEIM, K

From Karl Mannheim (Second Edition). Wolff, Kurt H (ed).
A Critical Discussion of Karl Mannheim's Views on Sociology of Knowledge. Mondal, Sunil Baran.
Erwin Panofsky and Karl Mannheim: A Dialogue on Interpretation. Hart, Joan.

MANUSCRIPT

R G Collingwood: A Bibliographic Checklist. Dreisbach, Christopher.
Notabilia I: Hinweise auf wichtige Neuerscheinungen aus dem Bereich der mittelalterlichen Philosophie. Imbach, Ruedi.

MANY

see Pluralism

MANY-SORTED LOGIC

A Boolean-Valued Version of Gupta's Semantics. Reyes, Marie La Palme and Reyes, Gonzalo E.

MANY-VALUED LOGICS

A Modal Reduction for Partial Logic. Barba, Juan.
Complete and Atomic Algebras of the Infinite Valued Lukasiewicz Logic. Cignoli, R.
Construction of Monadic Three-Valued Lukasiewicz Algebras. Monteiro, L, Savini, S and Sewald, J.
Cut-Free Systems for Three-Valued Modal Logics. Takano, Mitio.
Distribution in Lukasiewicz Logics. Beavers, Gordon.
On Sequents and Tableaux for Many-Valued Logics. Carnielli, Walter A.
On Two Relatives of the Classical Logic. Nowak, Marek.
Three-Element Nonfinitely Axiomatizable Matrices. Palasinska, Katarzyna.

MARXISM

Quale liberazione per l'uomo dopo il marxismo?. Fidelibus, G.

Realism, Modernism, and the Empty Chair in Postmodernism/ Jameson/ Critique, Kellner, Douglas M (ed). Zuidervaart, Lambert.

Reassessing Sartre. Bok, Sissela.

Religion and Postmodernism in Postmodernism/ Jameson/ Critique, Kellner, Douglas M (ed). O'Neill, John.

Religion as *Weltanschauung*: a Solution to a Problem in the Philosophy of Religion. Riordan, P.

Reports on International Research in Social Epistemology. Kasavin, Ilya.

Romance and Ressentiment: Saint Genet in Sartre Alive, Aronson, Ronald (ed). Skakoon, Walter S.

Russia and the West: The Quest for Russian National Identity. Groys, Boris.

Sartre and Marxist Existentialism in Sartre Alive, Aronson, Ronald (ed). Langer, Monika.

Sartre's Ontology of Evil and the Poverty of the Social Sciences. Gordon, Haim and Gordon, Rivca.

Sartrean Structuralism? in The Cambridge Companion to Sartre, Howells, Christina (ed). Caws, Peter.

Sociocultural Evolution or the Social Evolution of Practical Reason: Eder's Critique of Habermas. Strydom, Piet.

Some Disquiet about "Difference". Sypnowich, C A.

Soviet Philosophy in Transition: An Interview with Vladislav Lektorsky. Bakhurst, David.

The Debate over Performative Contradiction in Philosophical Interventions in the Unfinished Project of Enlightenment, Honneth, Axel (& other eds). Jay, Martin.

The Defeat of the Computational Model of the Mind. Margolis, Joseph.

The End of History. Schroeder, Steven.

The Freedom of the Truth: Marxist Salt for Christian Earth. Zademach, Wieland.

The Future of a Disillusion in Psychoanalysis, Mind and Art, Hopkins, Jim (ed). Cohen, G A.

The Marxism of George Bernard Shaw 1883-1889. Bevir, Mark.

The New Historicism and Shakespearean Criticism: A Marxist Critique. Siegel, Paul N.

The Possibility of Post-Socialist Politics. Bohman, James F.

The Realism of Moralism: The Political Philosophy of Istvan Bibo. Berki, R N.

The Social Philosophy of N Berdiaev in Light of *Perestroika*. Adiushkin, V N.

The Social Significance of Autonomous Art: Adorno and Bürger. Zuidervaart, Lambert.

The Teaching of *Centesimus Annus*. Schall, James V.

Two Hundred Years of Error? The Politics of Democracy. Howard, Dick.

Una traduzione sfortunata della "Scienza Nuova". Mastrolianni, Giovanni.

Walrasian Marxism Once Again: A Reply to Joe Roemer. Devine, James and Dymski, Gary.

West's Evasion of Pragmatism. Brodsky, G M.

What is Alive and What is Dead in Marx and Marxism. Nielsen, Kai.

What Walrasian Marxism Can and Cannot Do. Roemer, John.

Will Aesthetics Be the Last Stronghold of Marxism. Khanin, Dmitry.

Women's Lives/Feminist Knowledge: Feminist Standpoint as Ideology Critique. Hennessy, Rosemary.

MARXIST

Structural Inquiry, Human Agency and the Contribution of Harré and Bhaskar: A Case Study of Wright's "Classes". Adkins, Barbara.

MASCULINITY

Rethinking Masculinity. May, Larry (ed) and Strikwerda, Robert (ed).

The Interpretation of the Flesh: Freud and Femininity. Brennan, Teresa.

Chastity and the (Male) Philosophers. McGhee, Michael.

Education and Thought in Virginia Woolf's *To The Lighthouse*. Sichel, Betty A.

Gay Jocks: A Phenomenology of Gay Men in Athletics in Rethinking Masculinity, May, Larry (ed). Pronger, Brian.

Gender Treachery: Homophobia, Masculinity, and Threatened Identities in Rethinking Masculinity, May, Larry (ed). Hopkins, Patrick D.

Honor: Emasculation and Empowerment in Rethinking Masculinity, May, Larry (ed). Harris, Leonard.

Real Men in Rethinking Masculinity, May, Larry (ed). LaFollette, Hugh.

MASK

Expression and the Mask: The Dissolution of Personality in Noh. Lamarque, Peter.

MASS

A Variable-Free Logic for Mass Terms. Purdy, William C.

Mass Torts and Moral Principles. Strudler, Alan.

MASS MEDIA

Open Institutions: The Hope for Democracy. Murphy, John W (ed) and Peck, Dennis L (ed).

Video Icons and Values. Olson, Alan M (ed), Parr, Christopher (ed) and Parr, Debra (ed).

MASSEY, G

Discussion: Massey and Kirk on the Indeterminacy of Translation. Hitchcock, Christopher R.

MASTRIUS, B

The Possibility of Created Entities in Seventeenth-Century Scotism. Coombs, Jeffrey.

MATERIAL

Précis of Material Beings. Van Inwagen, Peter.

Comments on Peter Van Inwagen's *Material Beings*. Rosenberg, Jay F.

Descartes on the Material Falsity of Ideas. Field, Richard.

On What There Isn't. Horgan, Terence.

Peter Van Inwagen's *Material Beings*. Hirsch, Eli.

Reply to Reviewers. Van Inwagen, Peter.

The Moral Significance of the Material Culture. Borgmann, Albert.

MATERIAL IMPLICATION

Material Support for Material Implication. Cushing, Steven.

MATERIALISM

see also Atomism, Dialectical Materialism, Historical Materialism, Matter

"La Nature, la raison, l'expérience..." ou la réfutation du matérialisme dans l'apologétique chrétienne des Lumières. Boulad-Ayoub, Josiane.

Περιληπσισ in Epicurean Epistemology. Konstan, David.

A Hylomorphic Theory of Mind. Cooney, Brian.

Between Philosophy and Social Science: Selected Early Writings. Horkheimer, Max and Hunter, G Frederick (& other trans).

Marx's Theory of History. Wetherly, Paul.

Marxism Recycled. Van Parijs, Philippe.

Materialist Feminism and the Politics of Discourse. Hennessy, Rosemary.

Renewing Philosophy. Putnam, Hilary.

Subject to History: Ideology, Class, Gender. Simpson, David (ed).

The Human Person: Animal and Spirit. Braine, David.

The Logic of Marx's "Capital": Replies to Hegelian Criticisms. Smith, Tony.

A Common Sense Approach to the Mind-Body Problem: A Critique of Richard Taylor. Lascola, Russell A.

A Refutation of Historical Materialism? in Marx's Theory of History, Wetherly, Paul. Halfpenny, Peter.

Adam Smith on Feudalism, Commerce and Slavery. Salter, John.

Afterword—Marxism and Postmodernism (Including Bibliography) in Postmodernism/ Jameson/ Critique, Kellner, Douglas (ed). Jameson, Fredric.

Against Eliminative Materialism: From Folk Psychology to Völkerpsychologie. Greenwood, John D.

An Analytical Outline of Historical Materialism in Marx's Theory of History, Wetherly, Paul. Wetherly, Paul.

Ancora a proposito di metafisica: Nota in margine ad un recente volume. Piazza, G.

Behavioral Materialism, The Success of Folk Psychology, and the Ambiguous First-Person Case. Stemmer, Nathan.

Comparative Philosophy in the Soviet Union. Lysenko, Victoria G.

Dennett's Mind. Lockwood, Michael.

Der Seinsbegriff in Platons 'Sophistes'. Bordt, Michael.

Eliminative Materialism, Cognitive Suicide, and Begging the Question. Reppert, Victor.

Historical Materialism Revisited in Terrorism, Justice and Social Values, Peden, Creighton W (ed). Murray, J Patrick and Schuler, Jeanne.

Le ragioni del deismo in Voltaire's e nell'Enciclopedia. Nicolosi, Salvatore.

Metamind, Autonomy and Materialism. Lehrer, Keith.

Minimalist Historical Materialism in On the Track of Reason, Beehler, Rodger (ed). Cohen, Joshua.

On the Relation of J L Fischer to Marxist Philosophy (Reply to L Valenta's Polemic Study) (in Czechoslovakian). Tosenovsky, L.

Philosophical Foundations for Functional Sociology in Marx's Theory of History, Wetherly, Paul. MacDonald, Graham.

Philosophy of Mind in Reflections on Philosophy, McHenry, Leemon (ed). Heil, John.

Post-physicalism and Beyond. Vaden House, D and McDonald, Marvin J.

Pragmatism and Pluralism. Singer, Beth.

Pre-History: The Debate Before Cohen in Marx's Theory of History, Wetherly, Paul. Cowling, Mark and Manners, Jon.

Sobre predicciones y relatos. Fernández, Oscar.

Sociocultural Evolution or the Social Evolution of Practical Reason: Eder's Critique of Habermas. Strydom, Piet.

St Thomas Aquinas and the Individuation of Persons. Brown, Montague.

Supervenience and Reductionism. Von Kutschera, Franz.

Swimming Against the Tide. Campbell, Keith.

The Nature of Mind. Lucash, Frank S.

Yan Fu's Philosophy of Evolution and the Thought of Lao Zi and Zhuang Zi. Dayong, Yang.

'Fitness' and 'Altruism': Traps for the Unwary, Bystander and Biologist Alike. Settle, Tom.

MATERIALITY

Material Beings—P Van Inwagen. Mackie, Penelope.

Can Leclerc's Composite Actualities be Substances?. Kronen, John D.

Le corps de la terre. Laurent, Jérôme.

Leibniz' Theory of Space: A Reconstruction. Khamara, Edward J.

Merleau-Ponty, Gibson, and the Materiality of Meaning. Sanders, John T.

Perceptual Consciousness, Materiality, and Idealism in Analecta Husserliana, XXXIV, Tymieniecka, Anna-Teresa (ed). García-Gómez, Jorge.

MATERNALISM

Psychophysical Supervenience and Nonreductive Materialism. Marras, Ausonio.

MATERNITY

Female Identity between Sexuality and Maternity in Beyond Equality and Difference, Bock, Gisela (ed). Vegetti Finzi, Silvia.

MATHEMATICS

see also Addition, Algebra, Calculus, Geometry

A Philosophical Companion to First-Order Logic. Hughes, R I G (ed).

Berkeley's Philosophy of Mathematics. Jesseph, Douglas M.

Bolzano-Forschung: 1989-1991. Berg, Jan and Morscher, Edgar.

Collected Works of Bernard Lonergan, V10. Doran, Robert M (ed) and Crowe, Frederick E (ed).

MEASUREMENT

Schöpfung und Geist. Günther, Dorothea.

Errors of Measurement and Explanation-as-Unification. Forge, John.

Measurement and Principles: The Structure of Physical Theories. Kremer-Marietti, Angèle.

On Standard and Non-standard Models in Theories of Psychological Measurement in Probability and Rationality, Eells, Ellery (ed). Stachowski, Ryszard.

Teoria quantistica della misura in una visione non oggettivista della realtà. Villani, Giovanni.

MECHANICS

see also Quantum Mechanics

L'*Encyclopédie* et les techniques: problèmes théoriques. Kanelopoulos, Charles.

MECHANISM

The Mathematical Soul: An Antique Prototype of the Modern Mathematisation of Psychology. Stachowski, Ryszard.

A Concepçao Estóica de Natureza e a Moderna Física do Contínuo. Abrantes, Paulo C C.

Artistic Control in Collingwood's Theory of Art. Anderson, Douglas R.

Constructive Postmodern Philosophy in Founders of Constructive Postmodern Philosophy, Griffin, David Ray (& others). Griffin, David Ray.

Hands Invisible and Intangible. Brennan, Geoffrey and Pettit, Philip.

How Infinities Cause Problems in Classical Physical Theories. Van Bendegem, Jean Paul.

In Defense of Explanatory Ecumenism. Jackson, Frank and Pettit, Philip.

Is Classical Mechanics Really Time-Reversible and Deterministic?. Hutchison, Keith.

Jean Piaget's Early Critique of Mendelism: 'La notion de l'espèce suivant l'école mendélienne' (A 1913 Manuscript). Vidal, Fernando.

Knowledge of the Past and Future. Feinberg, Gerald.

On Professor Rychlak's Concerns. Moore, Jay.

On the Interpretation of Church's Thesis. Cotogno, Paolo.

Plato's Escape from Mechanism. Innis, William.

Plato's Failure to Escape Mechanism. Perron, Deborah.

Risposta dell'autore. Basti, G Franco.

Selbstorganisation und Entwicklung. Kummer, Christian.

Sette paradigmi cosmologici: L'animale, la scala, il fiume, la nuvola, la macchina, il libro e il sistema dei sistemi. Bunge, Mario.

The Failure of Dennett's Representationalism: A Wittgensteinian Resolution. Ward, Andrew.

The Last Stand of Mechanism. McDonough, Richard.

Theology and the Heisenberg Uncertainty Principle: I. Cardoni, Albert.

Vitalism and Contemporary Thought in The Crisis in Modernism, Burwick, Frederick (ed). Chiari, Joseph.

Zalta on Sense and Substitutivity. Deutsch, Harry.

MEDIA

Erotic Welfare: Sexual Theory and Politics in the Age of Epidemic. Singer, Linda.

Philosophical Issues in Journalism. Cohen, Elliot D (ed).

Questions de Rhétorique. Meyer, Michel.

Culture and Media in Cultural-Political Interventions in the Unfinished Project of Enlightenment, Honneth, Axel (& other eds). Gadamer, Hans-Georg.

Mass Media, Ethical Paradox, and Democratic Freedom: Jacques Ellul's Ethic of the Word. Fasching, Darrell J.

Minima Moralia: The Gulf War in Fragments. Kellner, Douglas M.

Privacy: An Understanding for Embodied Persons. Dandekar, Natalie.

Rethinking Tradition in Essays on Henry Sidgwick, Schultz, Bart (ed). Kloppenberg, James T.

MEDIATION

Considerazioni sul problema della conoscenza. Baccari, Luciano.

Médiation ou immédiation et philosophie chrétienne. Floucat, Y.

MEDICAL ETHICS

see also Abortion, Bioethics, Euthanasia

African-American Perspectives on Biomedical Ethics. Flack, Harley E (ed) and Pellegrino, Edmund D (ed).

Bibliography of Bioethics, V18. Walters, LeRoy (ed) and Kahn, Tamar Joy (ed).

Biomedical Ethics (Third Edition). Mappes, Thomas A and Zembaty, Jane S.

Abortion Through a Feminist Ethics Lens. Sherwin, Susan.

Access to Experimental Therapies and AIDS. Russell, John.

Access to In Vitro Fertilization: Costs, Care and Consent. Overall, Christine.

Advance Directives for Voluntary Euthanasia: A Volatile Combination?. Francis, Leslie Pickering.

Autonomie, don et partage dans les transplantations d'organes et de tissus humains. Parizeau, Marie-Hélène.

Back to Basics: Problems and Prospects for Applied Philosophy. Warren, Bill.

Clinical Ethics and Happiness. Devettere, Raymond J.

Commentator on 'Quality of Life Measures in Health Care and Medical Ethics' in The Quality of Life, Nussbaum, Martha C (ed). Griffin, James.

Defining Death in Applied Philosophy, Almond, Brenda (ed). Browne, Alister.

Éléments pour une eschatologie du zygote. Caspar, Philippe.

Ethical Problems in Clinical Pathology. Baron, D N.

Having a Future. Daniels, Charles.

Identity and the Ethics of Gene Therapy. Elliot, Robert.

Is the Killing/Letting-Die Distinction Normatively Neutral?. Winkler, Earl.

Medical Genetics: Its Presuppositions, Possibilities and Problems. Jochemsen, H.

Patients' Duties. Meyer, Michael J.

Problems with Laws, Defining Death and a New Uniform Proposal. Tierney, Travis S.

Quality of Life Measures in Health Care and Medical Ethics in The Quality of Life, Nussbaum, Martha C (ed). Brock, Dan W.

Quelques réflexions générales sur la normativité; l'éthique et le droit dans le cadre clinique. Baudouin, Jean-Louis.

Scenes from a Newborn Life (in Dutch). Hendriks, Ruud.

The Allied Health Care Professions: New Fields for Philosophical Explorations. Hull, Richard T.

The Concept of Medically Indicated Treatment. Miller, Franklin G.

The Patient in a Persistent Vegetative State: An Ethical Re-Appraisal. Schotsmans, P.

The Priesthood of Bioethics and the Return of Casuistry. Wildes, Kevin W.

The Search for Bioethical Criteria to Select Renal Transplant Recipients: A Response to the Honourable Judge Jean-Louis Baudouin. Spicker, Stuart F.

The Search for the New Pineal Gland: Brain Life and Personhood. Moussa, Mario and Shannon, Thomas A.

The Theory and Practice of Applied Ethics. Hoffmaster, C Barry.

Triage in the ICU. Truog, Robert D.

Voluntary Active Euthanasia. Brock, Dan W.

When Self-Determination Runs Amok. Callahan, Daniel.

Where Ethics Come From and What to Do About It. Elliott, Carl.

MEDICARE

Holistic Health and Biomedical Medicine: A Countersystem Analysis. Lyng, Stephen.

MEDICINE

Ancient Concepts of Philosophy. Jordan, William.

Biomedical Ethics (Third Edition). Mappes, Thomas A and Zembaty, Jane S.

Birth, Suffering, and Death: Catholic Perspectives at the Edges of Life. Wildes, Kevin W (ed), Abel, Francesc (ed) and Harvey, John C (ed).

Changing To National Health Care: Ethical and Policy Issues. Huefner, Robert P (ed) and Battin, Margaret P (ed).

Changing Values in Medical and Health Care Decision Making. Jensen, Uffe Juul (ed) and Mooney, Gavin (ed).

Contemporary Issues in Paediatric Ethics. Burgess, Michael M (ed) and Woodrow, Brian E (ed).

Drawing the Line: Life, Death, and Ethical Choices in an American Hospital. Gorovitz, Samuel.

Erotic Welfare: Sexual Theory and Politics in the Age of Epidemic. Singer, Linda.

Feminist Perspectives In Medical Ethics. Holmes, Helen Bequaert (ed) and Purdy, Laura M.

From Patients to Persons: The Psychiatric Critiques of Thomas Szasz, Peter Sedgwick and R D Laing. Vice, Janet.

Life and Death: Philosophical Essays in Biomedical Ethics. Brock, Dan W.

Problems in Personal Identity. Baillie, James.

The Birth Lottery. Boss, Judith A.

The Body in Medical Thought and Practice. Leder, Drew (ed).

A Tale of Two Bodies: The Cartesian Corpse and the Lived Body in The Body in Medical Thought and Practice, Leder, Drew (ed). Leder, Drew.

Alcmeon's and Hippocrates's Concept of 'Aetia' in Greek Studies in the Philosophy and History of Science, Nicolacopoulos, Pantelis (ed). Andriopoulos, D Z.

Animal Models in Biomedical Research: Some Epistemological Worries. LaFollette, Hugh and Shanks, Niall.

Being a Burden on Others. Jecker, Nancy S.

Bioethics Education: Expanding the Circle of Participants. Thornton, Barbara C, Callahan, Daniel and Nelson, James Lindemann.

Body, Self, and the Property Paradigm. Campbell, Courtney S.

Brain Death and Slippery Slopes. Veatch, Robert M.

Breasted Experience: The Look and the Feeling in The Body in Medical Thought and Practice, Leder, Drew (ed). Young, Iris Marion.

Causing, Intending, and Assisting Death. Brody, Howard.

Commentary on "How Much of the Brain Must Die in Brain Death". Dagi, Teo Forcht.

Contractarianism and the "Trolley" Problem. Rosenberg, Alexander.

Criteria for Death: Self-Determination and Public Policy. Sass, Hans-Martin.

Decision Making in an Incapacitated Patient. Freer, Jack P.

Deficiencies in the National Institute of Health's Guidelines for the Care and Protection of Laboratory Animals. Stephenson, Wendell.

Descartes: Um Naturalista?. Silveira, Lígia Fraga.

Diagnosis as Narrative in Ancient Literature. Pearcy, Lee T.

Disability, Handicap, and the Environment. Amundson, Ron.

Do Physicians Make Too Much Money?. Curzer, Howard J.

Do We Need a Concept of Disease?. Hesslow, Germund.

Doentes, Doença, Médicos e Medicina em Luciano de Samósata. Brandao, Jacynthos Lins.

Does the Philosophy of Medicine Exist?. Caplan, Arthur L.

Doing What the Patient Orders: Maintaining Integrity in the Doctor-Patient Relationship. Blustein, Jeffrey.

Eating Disorders: The Feminist Challenge to the Concept of Pathology in The Body in Medical Thought and Practice, Leder, Drew (ed). Bordo, Susan R.

Epicureanism and Death. Glannon, Walter.

Epistemologies in Religious Healing. Hufford, David J.

Ethical Problems in Clinical Pathology. Baron, D N.

Experience and Causal Explanation in Medical Empiricism in Greek Studies in the Philosophy and History of Science, Nicolacopoulos, Pantelis (ed). Pentzopoulou-Valalas, Theresa.

Fetal Tissue Research. Coutts, Mary Carrington.

Foucault's Clinic. Long, John C.

Foucault's Political Body in Medical Praxis in The Body in Medical Thought and Practice, Leder, Drew (ed). Spitzack, Carole.

Fry's Concept of Care in Nursing Ethics. Curzer, Howard.

MEDICINE

Getting Consent from the Troops? in Biomedical Ethics Reviews 1992, Humber, James M (ed). Fotion, Nicholas.

Gillett on Consciousness and the Comatose. Serafini, Anthony.

Hardwig on Proxy Decision Making. Brody, Baruch A.

Heidegger Among the Doctors in Reading Heidegger: Commemorations, Sallis, John (ed). Richardson, William J.

Hersendood in meervoud. Wackers, Ger.

How Much of the Brain Must Die in Brain Death?. Bernat, James L.

Imagining Ethics: Literature and the Practice of Ethics. Radey, Charles.

Interpreting Cultural Differences in Medical Intervention: The Use of Wittgenstein's "Forms of Life". Nash, Carol.

Is 'Brain Death' Actually Death?. Siefert, Josef.

Justice within Intimate Spheres. Carse, Alisa.

Kausalität als Leitbegriff ärztlichen Denkens und Handelns. Hartmann, Fritz.

Keeping Moral Space Open: New Images of Ethics Consulting. Walker, Margaret.

Le métier de médecin. Piguet, J Claude.

Madness and Method. Beehler, Rodger G.

Measuring Quality of Life in Theory and in Practice: A Dialogue Between Philosophical and Psychological Approaches. Boddington, Paula and Podpadec, Tessa.

Medical Ethics in Times of War and Insurrection: Rights and Duties. Benatar, S R.

Michael Polanyi and the Philosophy of Medicine. Gelwick, Richard.

More on Euthanasia: A Response to Pauer-Studer. Singer, Peter and Kuhse, Helga.

Non-Heart-Beating Donors of Organs: Are the Distinctions Between Direct and Indirect Effects and Between Killing and Lettie Die Relevant and Helpful?. Childress, James F.

On Romanticism, Science and Medicine. Rousseau, G S.

On the Body in Medical Self-Care and Holistic Medicine in The Body in Medical Thought and Practice, Leder, Drew (ed). Weston, Anthony.

On the Relevance and Importance of the Notion of Disease. Nordenfelt, Lennart.

On the Right of "Nondangerous" Incompetent Patients to Leave Psychiatric Units Against Medical Advice. DeGrazia, David.

Parted Bodies, Departed Souls: The Body in Ancient Medicine and Anatomy in The Body in Medical Thought and Practice, Leder, Drew (ed). Zaner, Richard M.

Patients Should Not Always Come First in Treatment Decisions. Strong, Carson.

Perinatal Technology: Answers and Questions. Krauss, Alfred N, Miké, Valerie and Ross, Gail S.

Persons and Death: What's Metaphysically Wrong with Our Current Statutory Definition of Death?. Lizza, John.

Peter Singer on Euthanasia. Pauer-Studer, Herlinde.

Philosophy of Medicine—From a Medical Perspective. Wulff, Henrik R.

Physicians and the American Armed Forces in Biomedical Ethics Reviews 1992, Humber, James M (ed). Elfstrom, Gerard A.

Picture Perfect: The Politics of Prenatal Testing. Kristol, Elizabeth.

Practicing Medicine, Fiduciary Trust Privacy, and Public Moral Interloping after Cruzan. Rie, Michael A.

Problems with Laws, Defining Death and a New Uniform Proposal. Tierney, Travis S.

Psychosomatics, the Lived Body, and Anthropological Medicine in The Body in Medical Thought and Practice, Leder, Drew (ed). Wiggins, Osborne, Northoff, Georg and Schwartz, Michael Alan.

Public Bodies, Private Selves in Applied Philosophy, Almond, Brenda (ed). Marshall, Sandra E.

Quality of Life and the Death of "Baby M". Kuhse, Helga.

Rationale for an Integrated Approach to Genetic Epidemiology. Laberge, Claude M and Knoppers, Bartha Maria.

Rationality and Principles: A Criticism of the Ethic of Care. Foulk, Gary J and Keffer, M Jan.

Relativism and the Social Scientific Study of Medicine. Risjord, Mark.

Reversibility as a Radical Ground for an Ontology of the Body in Medicine. Brannigan, Michael.

Should a Brain-Dead Pregnant Woman Carry Her Child to Full Term? The Case of the "Erlanger Baby". Anstötz, Christoph.

Should Physicians Be Bayesian Agents?. Cooper, M Wayne.

Some Ways that Technology and Terminology Distort the Euthanasia Issue. Herrera, Christopher.

Taking Family Seriously. Nelson, James Lindemann.

The Body in Multiple Sclerosis: A Patient's Perspective in The Body in Medical Thought and Practice, Leder, Drew (ed). Toombs, S Kay.

The Body of the Future in The Body in Medical Thought and Practice, Leder, Drew (ed). Cassell, Eric J.

The Case for Letting Vegetative Patients Die. Jennett, Bryan.

The Concept of Quackery in Early Nineteenth Century British Medical Periodicals. Carter, K Codell.

The Concept of the Person in the Parens Patriae Jurisdiction over Previously Competent Persons. Payton, Sallyanne.

The Doctor as Double Agent. Angell, Marcia.

The Family in Medical Decisionmaking. Blustein, Jeffrey.

The Impending Collapse of the Whole-Brain Definition of Death. Veatch, Robert M.

The Impossibility and the Necessity of Quality of Life Research. Morreim, E Haavi.

The Irreversibility of Death: Reply to Cole. Tomlinson, Thomas.

The Many Faces of Autonomy. Yeide Jr, Harry.

The Medicalization of Dying. Burgess, Michael M.

The Metamorphosis: The Nature of Chronic Illness and Its Challenge to Medicine. Toombs, S Kay.

The Problem of Proxies with Interests of Their Own: Toward a Better Theory of Proxy Decisions. Hardwig, John.

The PSDA and the Depressed Elderly: "Intermittent Competency" Revisited. Shamoo, Adil E and Irving, Dianne N.

The Relation of Philosophy to Sōphrosynē: Zalmoxian Medicine in Plato's Charmides. Coolidge, Jr, Francis P.

The Role of the Hospital in the Evolution of Elite Cultures of Medicine. Dixon, Kathleen.

Thinking Critically in Medicine and Its Ethics in Applied Philosophy, Almond, Brenda (ed). Moros, Daniel A (& others).

Thomson and the Trolley. Fisher, John and Ravizza, Martin.

Toward an Ethic of Evidence—and Beyond: Observations on Technology and Illness. Miké, Valerie.

Unrequested Termination of Life: Is It Permissible?. Van Der Wal, Gerrit.

Velmans on Consciousness, Brain and the Physical World. Wetherick, Norman.

What Is an Expert?. Weinstein, Bruce D.

What's So Special About Medicine?. Sulmasy, Daniel P.

Where Ethics Come From and What to Do About It. Elliott, Carl.

Who are the Beneficiaries?. Tännsjö, Torbjörn.

Why Aren't More Doctors Phenomenologists? in The Body in Medical Thought and Practice, Leder, Drew (ed). Baron, Richard J.

MEDIEVAL

see also Epistemology, Metaphysics, Religion

Bibliographia Missionalia Augustiniana: America Latina (1533-1993). Lazcano, Rafael.

Confucian Discourse and Chu Hsi's Ascendancy. Tillman, Hoyt Cleveland.

Divine Infinity in Greek and Medieval Thought. Sweeney, Leo.

Éléments d'une Philosophie Politique. Trigeaud, Jean-Marc.

Philoponus: On Aristotle's "Physics" 2. Lacey, A R (trans).

Philosophy and Theology in the Middle Ages. Evans, G R.

PSI XIV 1400: A Papyrus Fragment of John Philoponus. MacCoull, L S B and Siorvanes, L.

Sobre el furor divino y otros textos. Ficino, Marsilio.

Sobre la Suposicion—Guillermo de Ockham. Ockham, Guillermo and Guerrero, Luis (ed).

The Portable Medieval Reader. Ross, James Bruce (ed) and McLaughlin, Mary Martin (ed).

A Theory of Truth Based on a Medieval Solution to the Liar Paradox. Epstein, R L.

A Thirteenth-Century Interpretation of Aristotle on Equivocation and Analogy. Ashworth, E J.

Abelard and the School of the Nominales. Normore, C G.

Analogical Concepts: The Fourteenth-Century Background to Cajetan. Ashworth, E J.

Ancora sull'idea d'Europa: Il Medioevo como matrice di una coscienza europea. Baldassarre, M R.

Argument and Experience in a Thirteenth Century Concept of Science (in Hungarian). Bene, László.

Aristotle and the Sacrament of the Altar: A Crisis in Medieval Aristotelianism. Adams, Marilyn McCord.

Aristotle's Peri hermeneias in Medieval Latin and Arabic Philosophy: Logic and the Linguistic Arts. Black, Deborah.

Aristotle's Topics and Medieval Obligational Disputations. Yrjönsuuri, Mikko.

Container Metaphysics According to Aristotle's Greek Commentators. Matthews, Gareth.

De la político "secundum naturam". Bertelloni, Francisco.

Duhem and Continuity in the History of Science. Ariew, Roger and Barker, Peter.

Henry of Oyta's Nominalism and the Principle of Individuation. Gorman, Michael.

Horen, zien en lezen. Pasveer, Bernike.

Humanism and Ethics at the School of St Victor in the Early Twelfth Century. Jaeger, C Stephen.

La noción de 'spiritus' y de 'spiritualis substantia' en la cuestión disputada De spiritualibus creaturis de Santo Tomás de Aquino. Taubenschlag, C A.

La pensée et la vie. De Cointet, Pierre.

La philosophie et son histoire: quelques réflexions à propos d'un livre récent de W J Courtenay. Lusignan, Serge.

Le projet Thomiste de la métaphysique. Gaboriau, F.

Logic-Theological Schools from the Second Half of the 12th Century: A List of Sources. Yukio, Iwakuma and Ebbesen, Sten.

Mediaeval Thought-Experiments in Thought Experiments in Science and Philosophy, Horowitz, Tamara (ed). King, Peter O.

Mistica o filosofia? A proposito della dottrina dell'immagine di Meister Eckhart. Sturlese, Loris.

New Light on Medieval Philosophy: The Sophismata of Richard Kilvington. Ashworth, E J.

Nicolás de Cusa, "De mente": la profundización de la doctrina del hombre-imagen. D'Amico, Claudia.

Nominalism and Grammatical Theory in the Late Eleventh and Early Twelfth Centuries: An Explorative Study. Kneepkens, C H.

Nominalism and Theology Before Abelard: New Light on Roscelin of Compiègne. Mews, Constant J.

Notabilia I: Hinweise auf wichtige Neuerscheinungen aus dem Bereich der mittelalterlichen Philosophie. Imbach, Ruedi.

Notabilia II: Hinweise auf wichtige Neuerscheinungen aus dem Bereich der mittelalterlichen Philosophie. Imbach, Ruedi.

Paul of Venice on Obligations. Sinkler, Georgette.

Peter of Capua as a Nominalist. Courtenay, William J.

Présence et représentation chez Pierre d'Ailly: Quelques problèmes de théorie de la connaissance au xive siècle. Biard, Joël.

Psychologie philosophique et théologie de l'intellect: Pour une histoire de la philosophie allemande au xiv siècle. De Libera, Alain.

MEDIEVAL

Revenir, sortir, demeurer. Labbé, Y.
Saint Thomas lecteur du "Liber de Causis". D'Ancona Costa, C.
San Tommaso e Hegel per una teodicea cristologica. Mangiagalli, Maurizio.
The Age of the Sign: New Light on the Role of the Fourteenth Century in the History of Semiotics. Kaczmarek, Ludger.
The Authentic *Tele* of Politics: A Reading of Aristotle. Swazo, N K.
The Logic of the *Nominales*, or, The Rise and Fall of Impossible *Positio*. Martin, Christopher J.
The Necessity in Deduction: Cartesian Inference and its Medieval Background. Normore, Calvin G.
The Unity of Plato's Political Thought. Shiell, Timothy C.
Transcendentality of Beauty in the Middle Ages (in Czechoslovakian). Aertsen, Jan A.
Twelfth-Century Nominales: The Posthumous School of Peter Abelard. Iwakuma Y.
Una voz por la paz en el siglo XV: La noción humanística de concordia. Magnavacca, Silvia.
Visions of the Self in Late Medieval Christianity in Philosophy, Religion and the Spiritual Life, McGhee, Michael (ed). Coakley, Sarah.
Visions of the Self in Late Medieval Christianity: Some Cross-Disciplinary Reflections. Coakley, Sarah.
Vocalism, Nominalism and the Commentaries on the *Categories* from the Earlier Twelfth Century. Marenbon, John.
What Must One Have an Opinion About. Ebbesen, Sten.
William of Auvergne on *De re* and *De dicto* Necessity. Teske, Roland J.
William of Ockham and Adam Wodeham. White, Graham.
Women Philosophers in the Middle Ages. Leuven, Lienke.

MEDITATION

Facing Truths: Ethics and the Spiritual Life. McGhee, Michael.

MEGARIANS

Chrysippus's Response to Diodorus's Master Argument. Ide, H A.

MEINONG

Lycan on Lewis and Meinong. King, Peter J.
The Gestalt Controversy: The Development of Objects of Higher Order in Meinong's Ontology. Sweet, Dennis J.
Was Meinong Only Pretending?. Kroon, Frederick W.

MEISEL-HESS, G

Toward the Sexual and Economic Emancipation of Women: The Philosophy of Grete Meisel-Hess. Melander, Ellinor.

MELANCHOLY

Melancholy Dialectics. Pensky, Max.
Montaigne and Melancholy: The Wisdom of the "Essays". Screech, M A.
Malinconia e nichilismo—I: Dalla ferita mortale alla ricomposizione dell'infranto. Bottani, Livio.

MELAND, B

Meland's Post-Liberal Empirical Method in Theology in God, Values, and Empiricism, Peden, Creighton (ed). Inbody, Tyron.
Religious Creaturalism and a New Agenda for Theology in God, Values, and Empiricism, Peden, Creighton W (ed). Axel, Larry E.

MELE, A

Defending Historical Autonomy: A Reply to Professor Mele. Christman, John P.
Justification and the Will. Pink, T L M.

MELIA, J

Numbers and Propositions: Reply to Melia. Crane, Tim.

MELISSUS

Eleatic Monism in Zeno and Melissus. Curd, Patricia.

MELLOR, D

Reply to 'Properties and Predicates' by Mellor in Ontology, Causality and Mind: Essays in Honour of D M Armstrong, Bacon, John (ed). Armstrong, D M.

MEMORY

Another Look at Flage's Hume. Friedman, Lesley.
Aristotle on Two Kinds of Memory: Platonic Reminiscences (in Dutch). Van Dorp, P.
Consapevolezza e riferimento oggettivo: Un problema in Descartes, nell'idealismo e nella filosofia contemporanea. Varnier, Giuseppe.
Consciousness and Concepts—I. Kirk, Robert.
Consciousness, Self-Consciousness and Episodic Memory. Gennaro, Rocco J.
Internalistic Foundationalism and the Justification of Memory Belief. Senor, Thomas D.
Mementos, Death and Nostalgia (in Dutch). Breeur, R.
On Friedman's Look. Flage, Daniel.
Perception, Concepts, and Memory. Martin, M G F.
Remembering Directly in Psychoanalysis, Mind and Art, Hopkins, Jim (ed). Wiggins, David.
Reply to Flage's "On Friedman's Look". Friedman, Lesley.
The *Trimūrti* of *Smrti* in Classical Indian Thought. Larson, Gerald James.
Time, the Heaven of Heavens, and Memory in Augustine's *Confessions*. Ross, Don S.
Wreckage upon Wreckage: History, Documentary, and the Ruins of Memory. Rabinowitz, Paula.

MEN

see also Male
Beyond Methodology: Feminist Scholarship as Lived Research. Fonow, Mary Margaret (ed) and Cook, Judith A (ed).
Fatherhood and Nurturance in Rethinking Masculinity, May, Larry (ed). May, Larry and Strikwerda, Robert A.
Male Friendship and Intimacy. May, Larry and Strikwerda, Robert.
Male Friendship and Intimacy in Rethinking Masculinity, May, Larry (ed). Strikwerda, Robert A and May, Larry.
Men, Feminism, and Power in Rethinking Masculinity, May, Larry (ed). Seidler, Victor J.
The Enduring Appeals of Battle in Rethinking Masculinity, May, Larry (ed). Gray, J Glenn.
The Male Lesbian and the Postmodernist Body. Zita, Jacquelyn N.
The Man Without a Penis: Libidinal Economies that (Re)cognize the Hypernature of Gender. Nash, Margaret M.
The Relation of Man and Nature in Modern Philosophy (in Czechoslovakian). Znoj, M, Sobotka, M and Major, L.
The Rights of Man and the Goals of Women in Women's Rights and the Rights of Man, Arnaud, A J. Parker, Richard B.
Why Do Men Enjoy Pornography? in Rethinking Masculinity, May, Larry (ed). Soble, Alan.

MENCIUS

A Hermeneutic Reconstruction of the Child in the Well Example. Allinson, Robert E.
Mencius and Kant on Moral Failure. Kerman, Deborah E.
Mengzi and Xunzi: Two Views of Human Agency. Van Norden, Bryan.

MENCKEN, H

Friedrich Nietzsche—H L Mencken. Flathman, Richard (ed) and Mencken, H L.

MENDEL

Jean Piaget's Early Critique of Mendelism: 'La notion de l'espèce suivant l'école mendélienne' (A 1913 Manuscript). Vidal, Fernando.

MENTAL

Knowledge and Belief. Schmitt, Frederick.
Mental Causation. Heil, John (ed) and Mele, Alfred (ed).
A Moderate Mentalism. Peacocke, Christopher.
Actions, Reasons and Mental Causes (in French). Engel, Pascal.
Agency and Causal Explanation in Mental Causation, Heil, John (ed). Hornsby, Jennifer.
An Embarrassing Question about Reproduction. Haldane, John.
Anomalism, Uncodifiability, and Psychophysical Relations. Child, William.
Appendage Theory—Pro and Con. Natsoulas, Thomas.
Brentano's Doctrine of Intentionality of Mental Phenomena. Singh, Ravindra.
Close Enough to Reference. Martens, David B.
Conscious Experience. Dretske, Frederick.
Externalism and Mental Causality (in French). Jacob, Pierre.
Externalism and the Explanatory Relevance of Broad Content. Jacob, Pierre.
L'esprit des bêtes. Proust, Joëlle.
Le discours mental selon Hobbes. Pécharman, Martine.
Le mythe de l'intériorité chez Locke. Brykman, Geneviève.
Meaning and Mental Representation. Gamble, D D.
Mental Causation in Mental Causation, Heil, John (ed). Audi, Robert.
Mental Events as Structuring Causes of Behavior in Mental Causation, Heil, John (ed). Dretske, Fred.
Metaphysics and Mental Causation in Mental Causation, Heil, John (ed). Baker, Lynne Rudder.
Mice, Shrews, and Misrepresentation. Clark, Austen G.
Reduction, Elimination, and Firewalking. Cheyne, Colin.
Reid's Answer to Abstract Ideas. Castagnetto, Susan V.
Social Relations and the Individuation of Thought. Antony, Michael V.
Species-Specific Properties and More Narrow Reductive Strategies. Endicott, Ronald P.
Spinoza, Method, and Doubt. Steinberg, Diane.
Swimming Against the Tide. Campbell, Keith.
The Non-Reductivist's Troubles with Mental Causation in Mental Causation, Heil, John (ed). Kim, Jaegwon.
The Visual System and Levels of Perception: Properties of Neuromental Organization. Stoerig, Petra and Brandt, Stephan.
Thinking Causes in Mental Causation, Heil, John (ed). Davidson, Donald.

MENTAL ACT

La teoria postcartesiana delle idee nella recente storiografia anglosassone. Marcialis, Maria Teresa.

MENTAL EVENT

Externalism and Token Identity. Seager, William.

MENTAL ILLNESS

A Proposal for the Use of Advance Directives in the Treatment of Incompetent Mentally Ill Persons. Brock, Dan W.
Mental Illness and the Mind-Brain Problem: Delusion, Belief and Searle's Theory of Intentionality. Fulford, K W M.

MENTAL IMAGE

Historical Interpretation and Mental Images of Culture (in Dutch). Kuiper, Mark.

MENTAL STATES

"From Natural Function to Indeterminate Content". Sullivan, Sonja R.
Analysis and Metaphysics: An Introduction to Philosophy. Strawson, Peter.
Consciousness Reconsidered. Flanagan, Owen.
Everything You Always Wanted to Know About Lacan. Zizek, Slavoj (ed).
Metaphysics of Consciousness. Seager, William.
New Foundations of Ontology. Heald, William (ed), Bergmann, Gustav and Allaire, Edwin B.
The Balance of Consciousness: Eric Voegelin's Political Theory. Keulman, Kenneth.
The Perceptual System: A Philosophical and Psychological Perspective. Ben-Ze'ev, Aaron.
The Philosophical Quest. Almond, Brenda.

METAPHYSICS

Hartshorne, God, and Relativity Physics. Griffin, David R.

Hartshorne, Metaphysics and the Law of Moderation. Dombrowski, Daniel.

Has the Ontological Argument Been Refuted?. Vallicella, William F.

Hasker on Middle Knowledge. Bertolet, Rod.

Hegel and Heidegger in Hegel and His Critics, Desmond, William J (ed). Williams, Robert.

Hegel and Sartre in The Cambridge Companion to Sartre, Howells, Christina (ed). Verstraeten, Pierre.

Hegel and Skepticism. Williams, Robert.

Hegel's *Phenomenology of Spirit: 'The Science of the Umkehrung of Consciousness'*. Weiner, Scott E.

Hegel's Metaphysics. Flay, Joseph C.

Hegel's Treatment of Transcendental Apperception in Kant. Sedgwick, Sally S.

Hegel, Marx and the Absolute Infinite. Cristaudo, Wayne.

Heidegger et la poésie: De "Sein und Zeit" au premier cours sur Hölderlin. Vandevelde, Pol.

Heidegger in Dialogue with Hegel (Thanksgiving of W Biemel) (in Czechoslovakian). Biemel, W.

Heidegger on Realism and the Correspondence Theory of Truth. Tietz, John.

Heidegger's Interpretation of Kant's Concept of Metaphysics. Bandyopadhayay, Krishna Bala.

Heidegger's Question of Being and the 'Augustinian Picture' of Language. Philipse, Herman.

Heidegger: Between Idealism and Realism. Stepanich, Lambert V.

Hermeneutik und Metaphysik. Ricken, Friedo.

Het Hegeliaanse begrijpen: problemen en mogelijkheden. De Vos, L.

Hierarchy and Dualism in Aristotelian Psychology. Glas, G.

Higher-Order Thoughts and the Appendage Theory of Consciousness. Rosenthal, David M.

Historicity, Historicism, and Self-Making in German Philosophy and Jewish Thought, Greenspan, Louis (ed). Dray, W H.

How Are Souls Related to Bodies? A Study of John Buridan. Zupko, Jack.

Human Rights and Nature's Rightness. Kohak, Erazim.

Hume and Reid on Common Sense. Rysiew, Patrick.

Hume on Natural Belief and Original Principles. Gorman, Michael M.

Hume's Ideas of Space and Time: As Original As They First Appear. Coughlan, Stephen G.

Hume's Metaphysical Musicians. Van Steenburgh, E W.

Hume's Playful Metaphysics. Moses, Greg.

Hume: Between Leibniz and Kant (The Role of Pre-Established Harmony in Hume's Philosophy). Vasilyev, Vadim.

Hurlbutt, Hume, Newton and the Design Argument. Tweyman, Stanley.

Husserl and Heidegger as Phenomenologists. Gorner, Paul.

Husserl and the Deconstruction of Time. Brough, John B.

Husserl y las aporías de la intersubjetividad. Finke, S R S.

Husserl's Intentionality and "Mind" in Chinese Philosophy. Zhang, Xian.

Husserl's Phenomenology and the Motives of Its Transformation (Final Part) (in Czechoslovakian). Landgrebe, L.

I μεταξυ nella *Repubblica*: loro significato e loro funzione. Marcellino, Claudio.

I Falsely Believe that *P*. Crimmins, Mark.

I limiti della decostruzione del "soggetto" nella critica filosofica "postmoderna". Bosio, Franco.

Idea y abstraccón en Hume. Del Barco, José Luis.

Idéalisme et théisme dans la dernière philosophie de Fichte: La *Doctrine de la Science* de 1813. Vetö, Miklos.

Idealizing Hume. Hausman, Alan and Hausman, David.

Il *Filebo* come una 'summa' del pensiero metafisico platonico. Bonagura, P.

Il concetto cartesiano del pensare e il problema delle altre intelligenze. Messeri, Marco.

Il nulla e l'essere: Leopardi e l'idea di poesia. Lo Bue, Salvatore.

Il pensiero debole e il ritorno alla metafisica. Manno, A G.

Il posto della metafisica nel sapere umano: Il pensiero di Maimonide e eil suo influsso su S Tommaso d'Aquino. Pangallo, Mario.

Il romanzo dell'identità: Metafisica ed ermeneutica. Sainati, Vittorio.

Il soggetto metafisico alla prima e alla seconda potenza. Crescini, Angelo.

Ilustracón y Clasicismo. Alvarez, Angel.

Imagination and Myth. Degenaar, Johan.

Imagination créatrice et connaissance selon Théodule Ribot. Meletti-Bertolini, Mara.

Imaging the Imageless: Symbol and Perception in Early Chinese Thought. Doeringer, Franklin M.

Immediate Experience. Gilbert, Paul.

Imperatives in Merleau-Ponty Vivant, Dillon, M C (ed). Lingis, Alphonso F.

Implications: The 'A' of *Différance*. Tirone, Nicholas D.

Importanza storica e teoretica del pensiero neoplatonico nel *Pensare l'Uno* di Werner Beierwaltes. Gatti, Maria Luisa.

In Defense of Global Supervenience. Paull, R Cranston and Sider, Theodore R.

Individualism, Computation and Perceptual Content. Egan, Frances.

Indra's Postmodern Net. Loy, David.

Induction: A Non-Sceptical Humean Solution. Nelson, John O.

Infinite Intellect and Human Cognition in Spinoza (in Dutch). Bartuschat, W.

Infinity and Proofs for the Existence of God. Staley, Kevin.

Innate Ideas and Cartesian Dispositions. Flage, Daniel and Bonnen, Clarence A.

Inner States. Odegard, Douglas.

Instance Ontology and Avicenna's Arguments. Mertz, Donald W.

Intention Detecting. Holton, Richard.

Intentionality and Madness in Hegel's Psychology of Action. Berthold-Bond, Daniel.

Intenzionalità e filosofia dell'azione. Marrone, Pierpaolo.

Interpretazione e critica di Plotino della concezione del tempo dei suoi predecessori. Trotta, Alessandro.

Intersubjectivity in Phenomenology. Tripathy, L K.

Introduction: *Reconceptions* in Context. Scholz, Oliver R.

Intuition and Substance: Two Aspects of Kant's Conception of an Empirical Object. Sweet, Dennis J.

Ipotesi di metafisica: Modello matematico, creazione, eschaton—Una lettura dell'opera di Jean Ladrière. Natale, M R.

Iris Murdoch's *Metaphysics as a Guide to Morals*. Midgley, Mary.

Is *Prasanga* a form of Deconstruction?. Matilal, Bimal Krishna.

Is Derrida a Transcendental Philosopher? in Working Through Derrida, Madison, Gary B (ed). Rorty, Richard.

Is Human Existence in Itself Not of Ultimate Significance? A Challenge to Hartshorne's Idea of Ultimate Reality and Meaning. Sia, Santiago.

Is Self-Consciousness a Case of 'Présence à Soi? in Derrida: A Critical Reader, Wood, David (ed). Frank, Manfred and Bowie, Andrew (trans).

Is the Future Really Real?. Faye, Jan.

Is the Ontological Argument Ontological? The Argument According to Anselm and Its Metaphysical Interpretation According to Kant. Marion, Jean-Luc.

Jabir, the Buddhist Yogi. Walter, Michael.

Jameson's Strategies of Containment in Postmodernism/ Jameson/ Critique, Kellner, Douglas (ed). Horne, Haynes.

John Bishop's Natural Agency. Marshall, Graeme.

John Buridan and Donald Davidson on *Akrasia*. Saarinen, Risto.

John Dewey's Idea of Ultimate Reality and Meaning: A Mixture of Stability and Uncertainty in Social Transactions of Human Beings. Reck, Andrew J.

John Niemeyer Findlay, un platonico fra i neopositivisti: ritratto biografico. Marchetto, Michele.

Jonathan Edwards' Twelfth Sign. Raposa, Michael L.

Jürgen Habermas on the Legacy of Jean-Paul Sartre: Interview. Wolin, Richard.

Justice, Scheffler and Cicero. Simpson, Peter.

Kant and Dogmatic Idealism: A Defense of Kant's Refutation of Berkeley. Morgan, Vance.

Kant as an Inadvertant Precursor of 18th Century Neospinozism: On Optimism (1759). Nauen, F G.

Kant on Plato and the Metaphysics of Purpose. White, David A.

Kant's Dubious Disciples: Hare and Rawls. Papa, Edward.

Kant's Idealistic Dilemma (in Hebrew). Kollender, Aaron.

Kant's Second Antinomy and Hume's Theory of Extensionless Indivisibles. Jacquette, Dale.

Kantian Ontology. Rogerson, Kenneth.

Kants transzendentale Deduktion der reinen Verstandesbegriffe (B): Ein kritischer Forschungsbericht—Vierter Teil. Baumanns, Peter.

Kausalität und Freiheit: Ein Beispiel für den Zusammenhang von Metaphysik und Lebenspraxis. Krüger, Lorenz.

Kausalität: Eine Problemübersicht. Heidelberger, Michael.

Kein Platz für phänomenale Qualitäten und Leib- Umwelt- Interaktion?. Pohlenz, Gerd.

Kierkegaard's Place in the Hermeneutic Project. Martinez, Roy.

Knowledge and the 'Real' World: Sri Harsa and the *Pramanas*. Ram-Prasad, C.

Knowledge, and Our Position Regarding God. Baxter, Anthony.

Kurt Gödel and Phenomenology. Tieszen, Richard.

L Hejdanek's Meontology: An Attempt of a Critical Explanation (in Czechoslovakian). Sousedik, S.

L'ermeneutica e il problema della fine: A proposito di due contributi recenti. Fabris, Adriano.

L'esprit des bêtes. Proust, Joëlle.

L'expérience métaphysique et le transcendantal. Vieillard-Baron, J L.

L'interiorità cartesiana tra metafisica e fenomenismo. Nicolosi, S.

L'interpretazione di Plotino della teoria platonica dell'anima. Szlezák, T A.

La ceguera según Aristóteles. Quevedo, Amalia.

La concezione dell'"evento" nella *Stella della redenzione* di Franz Rosenzweig e nel pensiero di Martin Heidegger. Casper, Bernhard.

La cosmologie transcendantale de Whitehead: transformation spéculative du concept de construction logique. Bradley, James.

La cultura y la historia frente a la verdad y el bien en Nitezsche. De Vicente Arregui, Gemma.

La Curiosa Doctrina de Ockham en Torno a la Divisibilidad del Continuo. Larre, Olga L and Bolzan, J E.

La dimensión ontológica de la conciencia afectiva según Ferdinand Alquié — Segunda parte. Sodor, A.

La filosofía como tragedia: Nietzsche. Innerarity, Daniel.

La funzione e la portata della critica alle Idee nel *Parmenide* di Platone: Dalla teoria delle Idee alla teoria dei Principi. Pezzolato, Marco.

La identidad del sujeto individual según Aristóteles. Inciarte, Fernando.

La libertad como esencia de toda la realidad en el primer Schelling. Diosado, Concepción.

La metafisica del soggetto e l'origine dello spiritualismo filosofico occidentale. Masi, Giuseppe.

La metafisica della vita secondo A T Tymieniecka. Barral, Mary-Rose.

La metafisica segreta di Kant: Su un recente saggio di Virgilio Melchiorre. Mancini, Sandro.

La métaphysique de la parole et les faubourgs du langage. Cometti, Jean-Pierre.

La métaphysique l'acte et l'un. Gilbert, Paul P.

La natura della vita: Una indagine filosofica. Crescini, Angelo.

La persona y su mundo: la cultura, la moral, el derecho y la sociedad familiar y política (I). Derisi, Octavio N.

METAPHYSICS

METAPHYSICS

MILITARY

Morality, Prudence, and Nuclear Weapons. Lee, Steven.

The Ethics and Politics of Human Experimentation. McNeill, Paul M.

AIDS Victims and Military Service in Biomedical Ethics Reviews 1992, Humber, James M (ed). Hartle, Anthony E and Christopher, Paul P.

Getting Consent from the Troops? in Biomedical Ethics Reviews 1992, Humber, James M (ed). Fotion, Nicholas.

Nuclear Cities: The Bastille Analogy in Sartre Alive, Aronson, Ronald (ed). Stone, Robert.

Physicians and the American Armed Forces in Biomedical Ethics Reviews 1992, Humber, James M (ed). Elfstrom, Gerard A.

Recent Work on the American Professional Military Ethic: An Introduction and Survey. McGrath, James and Anderson III, Gustaf E.

MILL

Aggravated Murder and Capital Punishment. Sorell, Tom.

Is God a Utilitarian?. Holley, David M.

J S Mill's Language of Pleasures. Hoag, Robert.

J S Mill, Liberalism, and Progress in Victorian Liberalism, Bellamy, Richard (ed). Gibbins, John R.

John Stuart Mill and the Catholic Question in 1825. Kinzer, Bruce L.

John Stuart Mill's Liberal Feminism. Donner, Wendy.

Mill's Antipaternalism. Kultgen, John.

Mill's Higher Pleasures and the Choice of Character. Long, Roderick T.

On a Supposed Inconsistency in J S Mill's Utilitarianism. Joy, Glenn C and McKinney, Audrey M.

Paternalismus. Wolf, Jean-Claude.

Philosophical Foundations of Respect for Autonomy. Gauthier, Candace Cummins.

The Logic and Rhetoric of John Stuart Mill. Zappen, James P.

The Subjection of John Stuart Mill. Stove, D.

Why John Stuart Mill Called Himself a Socialist. Ottow, Raimund.

Why Patronize Feminists? A Reply to Stove on Mill. Brecher, Bob.

'Private Judgement', Mill and Tocqueville: An Apology. Gardner, Peter.

'The Very Culture of the Feelings': Poetry and Poets in Mill's Moral Philosophy. Burnstone, Daniel.

MILLAN PUELLES, A

La teoría del objeto puro de A Millán Puelles. López, Jesús García.

MILLER, J

Descrying the Ideal: The Philosophy of John William Miller. Tyman, Stephen.

MILLETT, K

"Take Your Pill Dear": Kate Millett and Psychiatry's Dark Side. Steinbuch, Thomas.

MILLIKAN, R

Knowing What I'm Thinking Of—I. Millikan, Ruth Garrett.

MIMESIS

Image et mimesis chez Platon (in Japanese). Sekimura, Makoto.

MIND

see also Soul, Spirit

"A Mark of the Growing Mind is Veneration of Objects" (Ludwig Wittgenstein). Sawyier, Fay.

Agency in Action: The Practical Rational Agency Machine. Coval, Samuel C and Campbell, P G.

An Essay on Belief and Acceptance. Cohen, L Jonathan.

An Introduction to Husserlian Phenomenology. Bernet, Rudolf, Kern, Iso and Marbach, Eduard.

Analysis and Metaphysics: An Introduction to Philosophy. Strawson, Peter.

Aquinas on Mind. Kenny, Anthony.

Aspects of Mind—Gilbert Ryle. Meyer, René (ed) and Ryle, Gilbert.

Consciousness, Brain and the Physical World: A Reply to Velmans. Rentoul, Robert.

Consciousness: Psychological and Philosophical Essays. Davies, Martin (ed) and Humphreys, Glyn W (ed).

Direct Reference: From Language to Thought. Rashed, Roshdi.

Essays in Quasi-Realism. Blackburn, Simon W.

Everything You Always Wanted to Know About Lacan. Zizek, Slavoj (ed).

Hobbes and Human Nature. Green, Arnold W.

Husserl's Transcendental Phenomenology—Elisabeth Ströker. Hardy, Lee (trans) and Ströker, Elisabeth.

Ideology and False Consciousness: Marx and his Historical Progenitors. Pines, Christopher.

Inductive Inference and Its Natural Ground: An Essay in Naturalistic Epistemology. Kornblith, Hilary.

Instrumental Realism: The Interface between Philosophy of Science and Philosophy of Technology. Ihde, Don.

Irrationality and the Philosophy of Psychoanalysis. Gardner, Sebastian.

Language, Music, and Mind. Raffman, Diana.

Languages of the Mind: Essays on Mental Representation. Jackendoff, Ray.

Metaphysics (Fourth Edition). Taylor, Richard.

Metaphysics of Consciousness. Seager, William.

Mind, Brain, Behavior: The Mind-Body Problem and the Philosophy of Psychology. Carrier, Martin and Mittelstrass, Jürgen.

Mind, Meaning and Metaphysics. Mulligan, Kevin (ed).

Music and Mind: Philosophical Essays on the Cognition and Meaning of Music. Fiske, Harold E.

Naming and Reference. Nelson, R J.

Paradigms and Barriers: How Habits of Mind Govern Scientific Beliefs. Margolis, Howard.

Philosophy of Mind: An Introduction. Graham, George.

Problems in Personal Identity. Baillie, James.

Psychoanalysis, Mind and Art. Hopkins, Jim (ed) and Savile, Anthony (ed).

Psychology and Nihilism: A Genealogical Critique of the Computational Model of Mind. Evans, Fred.

Science, Knowledge, and Mind: A Study in the Philosophy of C S Peirce. Delaney, C F.

Selected Philosophical and Methodological Papers. Meehl, Paul, Anderson, C Anthony (ed) and Gunderson, Keith (ed).

Stoff and Nonsense in Kant's First *Critique*. Mosser, Kurt.

Talk About Beliefs. Crimmins, Mark.

Testimony: A Philosophical Study. Coady, C A J.

The Balance of Consciousness: Eric Voegelin's Political Theory. Keulman, Kenneth.

The Human Person: Animal and Spirit. Braine, David.

The Mind and Its Depths. Wollheim, Richard.

The Nature of True Minds. Heil, John.

The Philosophy of Mind: Classical Problems/Contemporary Issues. Beakley, Brian (ed) and Ludlow, Peter (ed).

The Rediscovery of the Mind. Searle, John R.

Thinking Things Through: An Introduction to Philosophical Issues and Achievements. Glymour, Clark.

What Is Cognitive Science?. Von Eckardt, Barbara.

A Commentary on Oshita O Oshita's Analysis of the Mind-Body Problem in an African World View. Washington, Johnny.

A Common Sense Approach to the Mind-Body Problem: A Critique of Richard Taylor. Lascola, Russell A.

A Discussion of the Mind-Brain Problem. Popper, K R, Lindahl, B I B and Arhem, P.

A Prescription for Generating a New Paradigm in the Context of Science and Theology. Schmitt, Francis O.

A Turing Test Conversation. Jacquette, Dale.

Aangeboren belevingsstructuren, intenties en symbolen. Slurink, Pouwel.

Alexander on *Phantasia*: A Hopeless Muddle or a Better Account?. Modrak, D K W.

André Bazin on Automatically Made Images. Brubaker, David.

Animal Minds. Sorabji, Richard.

Anomalous Monism and the Mind-Body Problem. Salami, Yunusa Kehinde.

Aristotle and Perceptual Realism. Granger, E Herbert.

Aristotle and Supervenience. Caston, Victor.

Aristotle, Searle, and the Mind-Body Problem in John Searle and His Critics, LePore, Ernest (ed). Code, Alan.

Ayer on Other Minds in The Philosophy of A J Ayer, Hahn, Lewis Edwin (ed). Sprigge, T L S.

Because Mere Calculating Isn't Thinking: Comments on Hauser's "Why Isn't My Pocket Calculator a Thinking Thing?". Rapaport, William J.

Bradley and Moral Philosophy in Psychoanalysis, Mind and Art, Hopkins, Jim (ed). Gardiner, Patrick.

Brainwork: A Review of Paul Churchland's *A Neurocomputational Perspective*. McCauley, Robert N.

Brentano and Marty on Content in Mind, Meaning and Metaphysics, Mulligan, Kevin (ed). Chisholm, Roderick M.

Can Intelligence Be Artificial?. Dretske, Fred.

Can Neuroscience Provide a Complete Account of Human Nature? A Reply to Roger Sperry. Jones, James W.

Carnap's Philosophy of Mind. Cicera, Ramon.

Causing, Delaying, and Hastening: Do Rains Cause Fires?. Mackie, Penelope.

Character, Mind, and Politics in Psychoanalysis, Mind and Art, Hopkins, Jim (ed). Rorty, Amélie Oksenberg.

Chisholm on Persons as *Entia Successiva* and the Brain-Microparticle Hypothesis. Jacquette, Dale.

Cognitive Psychology and the Rejection of Brentano. Macnamara, John.

Computers and the Mind-Body Problem: On Ontological and Epistemological Dualism. Drozdek, Adam.

Connectionisme, plasticiteit en de hoop op betere tijden. Meijsing, Monica.

Consciousness and Cosmology: Hyperdualism Ventilated in Consciousness: Psychological and Philosophical Essays, Davies, Martin (ed). McGinn, Colin.

Consciousness and Objectivity in Consciousness: Psychological and Philosophical Essays, Davies, Martin (ed). Biro, John.

Content and Cause in the Aristotelian Mind. Wedin, Michael V.

Continuity, Consciousness, and Identity in Hume's Philosophy. Yandell, Keith E.

Das Leib-Seele-Pentagon und die Kombinatorik attraktiver Vorstellungen—Ein folgenreiches Konzept der Leibnizschen Frühphilosophie. Busche, Hubertus.

Dennett's Mind. Lockwood, Michael.

Dennett's Rejection of Dualism. Foster, John.

Descartes and Malebranche on Mind and Mind-Body Union. Schmaltz, Tad M.

Descartes on Mind-Body Interaction. Holbrook, Daniel.

Descartes on Mind-Body Interaction and the Conservation of Motion. McLaughlin, Peter.

Drawing the Boundary between Subject and Object: Comments on the Mind-Brain Problem. Rosen, Robert.

Ein Grinsen ohne Katze: Von der Vergleichbarkeit zwischen 'künstlicher Intelligenz' und 'getrennten Intelligenzen'. Capurro, Rafael.

El cuerpo como educador del espíritu en la Filosofía de Bergson. Sánchez Rey, María del Carmen.

Eliminatie of reductie van qualia?. Sleutels, J J M.

Eliminative Materialism, Cognitive Suicide, and Begging the Question. Reppert, Victor.

MIRACLE

Again: Hume on Miracles. Ellin, Joseph S.

An Intervention into the Flew/Fogelin Debate. Ferguson, Kenneth.

Authenticating Biblical Reports of Miracles. Wiebe, Phillip H.

Miracles and Conservation Laws. MacGill, Neil Whyte.

Miracles and Conservation Laws: A Reply to Professor MacGill. Larmer, Robert A H.

Miracles, Laws of Nature and Causation—I. Hughes, Christopher.

Miracles, Laws of Nature and Causation—II. Adams, Robert Merrihew.

Neuere Bücher zum Werk David Humes. Klemme, Heiner F.

Schlesinger on Miracles. Otte, Richard.

What is Right with the Miracle Argument: Establishing a Taxonomy of Natural Kinds. Carrier, Martin.

'Hume's Theorem' Concerning Miracles. Millican, Peter.

MISTAKE

Inculpatory and Exculpatory Mistakes and the Fact/Law Distinction: An Essay in Memory of Myke Bayles. Alexander, Larry.

MITCHELL, R

In the Twilight of Modernity: MacIntyre and Mitchell on Moral Traditions and Their Assessment. Mehl, Peter J.

MITSIS, P

Recent Work on Death and the Meaning of Life. Fischer, John M.

MO TZU

Strong Utilitarianism in Mo Tzu's Thought. Vorenkamp, Dirck.

MODAL

Genuine Modal Realism: Still the Only Non-circular Game in Town. Miller, Richard B.

Modal Theistic Arguments. Oppy, Graham.

MODAL LOGIC

2-Sequent Calculus: A Proof Theory of Modalities. Masini, Andrea.

A Boolean-Valued Version of Gupta's Semantics. Reyes, Marie La Palme and Reyes, Gonzalo E.

A Generalized Notion of Weak Interpretability and the Corresponding Modal Logic. Dzhaparidze, Giorgie.

A Logic of *Better*. Goble, Lou.

A Modal Analog for Glivenko's Theorem and Its Applications. Rybakov, V V.

A Modal Reduction for Partial Logic. Barba, Juan.

A Note on the Interpretability Logic of Finitely Axiomatized Theories. De Rijke, Maarten.

A Note on the Normal Form of Closed Formulas of Interpretability Logic. Hájek, Petr and Svejdar, Vitezslav.

A Problem for Fictionalism About Possible Worlds. Rosen, Gideon.

Against Extended Modal Realism. Perszyk, Kenneth J.

Amalgamation and Interpolation in Normal Modal Logics. Maksimova, L.

An Alternative Rule of Disjunction in Modal Logic. Williamson, Timothy.

An Arithmetical Completeness Theorem for Pre-permutations. Tuttas, Friedemann.

Canonical Formulas for *K*4: Part I—Basic Results. Zakharyaschev, Michael.

Counterpart Theory, Quantified Modal Logic, and Extra Argument Places. Lewis, David.

Counterparts and Comparatives. Milne, Peter.

Cut-Free Systems for Three-Valued Modal Logics. Takano, Mitio.

Ease and Difficulty: A Modal Logic with Deontic Applications. Denyer, Nicholas.

Explicit Fixed Points in Interpretability Logic. De Jongh, Dick and Visser, Albert.

Filosofische logica: een status quaestionis. Vergauwen, R.

From Worlds to Probabilities: A Probabilistic Semantics for Modal Logic. Cross, Charles B.

Las lógicas modales en confrontación con los conceptos básicos de la lógica modal de G W Leibniz. Padilla-Gálvez, Jesús.

Modal Semantics. Slater, B H.

Montague's Semantics for Intensional Logic. Palme Reyes, Marie La and Reyes, Gonzalo E.

Negations in Conflict. Hand, Michael.

Non-Essentialistic Modal Logic, or Meaning and Necessity Revisited. Burdick, Howard.

On Compatibility of Theories and Equivalent Translations. Inoué, Takao.

On Gupta's Book *The Logic of Common Nouns*. Bressan, Aldo.

On the Proof of Solovay's Theorem. De Jongh, Dick, Jumelet, Marc and Montagna, Franco.

On the Proofs of Arithmetical Completeness for Interpretability Logic. Zambella, Domenico.

On the Provability Logic of Bounded Arithmetic. Beraducci, Alessandro and Verbrugge, Rineke.

Possible Logics for Belief. Van Der Hoek, W and Meyer, J J C.

Predicate Provability Logic with Non-modalized Quantifiers. Dzhaparidze, Giorgie.

Provability Logics for Natural Turing Progressions of Arithmetical Theories. Beklemishev, L D.

Regular Modal Logics. Swirdowicz, Kazimierz.

Rosser Orderings and Free Variables. De Jongh, Dick and Montagna, Franco.

Some Independence Results in Interpretability Logic. Svejdar, Vitezslav.

Some Unifying Fixed Point Principles. Smullyan, Raymond M.

The Admissibility of γ in R4. Mares, Edwin D and Meyer, Robert K.

The Analytical Completeness of Dzhaparidze's Polymodal Logics. Boolos, George.

The Formalization of Interpretability. Visser, Albert.

The McKinsey Axiom is Not Compact. Wang, Xiaoping.

The Semantics of R4. Mares, Edwin and Meyer, Robert K.

Twenty-Five Basic Theorems in Situation and World Theory. Zalta, Edward N.

Unary Interpretability Logic. De Rijke, Maarten.

MODAL PROOFS

On a Not Quite Yet "Victorious" Modal Version of the Ontological Argument for the Existence of God. Wingard Jr, John C.

MODAL SYLLOGISMS

Semantic Analysis of the Modal Syllogistic. Thomason, S K.

MODAL THEORY

Modal Fictionalism: A Response to Rosen. Brock, Stuart.

Modal Metaphysics and Comparatives. Milne, Peter.

MODALITY

De Re Certainty. McGowan, Neale.

Foundations of Logic and Language. Sen, Pranab Kumar (ed).

Il Problema della Modalità nelle Logiche di Hegel. Baptist, Gabriella.

La Charpente Modale du Sens. Brandt, Per Aage.

Logic, God and Metaphysics. Harris, James F (ed).

Modalities: Philosophical Essays. Marcus, Ruth Barcan.

Ontology, Causality and Mind: Essays in Honour of D M Armstrong. Bacon, John (ed), Campbell, Keith (ed) and Reinhardt, Lloyd (ed).

Thought Experiments in Science and Philosophy. Horowitz, Tamara (ed) and Massey, Gerald J (ed).

An Alternative Semantics for Modal Predicate-Logic. Meixner, Uwe.

An Epistemological Defence of Realism about Necessity. Elder, Crawford L.

Aristotelian *Topoi* as a Cross-Cultural Analytical Tool. Blinn, Sharon Bracci and Garrett, Mary.

Armstrong's New Combinatorialist Theory of Modality in Ontology, Causality and Mind: Essays in Honour of D M Armstrong, Bacon, John (ed). Lycan, William G.

Avicenna's Conception of the Modalities. Bäck, Allan.

Conceivability and Modal Knowledge in Thought Experiments in Science and Philosophy, Horowitz, Tamara (ed). Hetherington, Stephen Cade.

Concern for Counterparts. Miller, Richard.

Critical Notice of D M Armstrong, *A Combinatorial Theory of Possibility*. Lewis, David.

Descartes, Conceivability, and Logical Modality in Thought Experiments in Science and Philosophy, Horowitz, Tamara (ed). Alanen, Lilli.

Descartes, Modalities, and God. Van Den Brink, Gijsbert.

Epistemically-Qualified Judgment: A Nonquantitative Approach. Backman, Wayne.

Fodor's Modal Argument. Adams, Frederick.

Identity Criteria for Properties. Chisholm, Roderick M.

Laws of Nature, Modality and Humean Supervenience in Ontology, Causality and Mind: Essays in Honour of D M Armstrong, Bacon, John (ed). Menzies, Peter.

Leibniz on Creation, Contingency and Per-Se Modality. McNamara, Paul.

Leibnizian Essentialism, Transworld Identity, and Counterparts. Cover, J A and Hawthorne, John.

Lycan on Lewis and Meinong. King, Peter J.

Modality and Ontology. Shapiro, Stewart.

Modality and Possible Worlds in Foundations of Logic and Language, Sen, Pranab Kumar (ed). Sanyal, Indrani.

Models, Modality, and Natural Theology in Logic, God and Metaphysics, Harris, James F (ed). Dunlap, John T.

Possibilism and Object Theory. Menzel, Christopher.

Provability: The Emergence of a Mathematical Modality. Boolos, George and Sambin, Giovanni.

Reference, Modality, and Relational Time. Cover, J A.

Replies to the Critics. Zalta, Edward N.

Reply to Lycan's 'Armstrong's New Combinatorialist Theory...' in Ontology, Causality and Mind: Essays in Honour of D M Armstrong, Bacon, John (ed). Armstrong, D M.

Reply to Menzies' 'Laws of Nature, Modality and Humean...' in Ontology, Causality and Mind: Essays in Honour of D M Armstrong, Bacon, John (ed). Armstrong, D M.

Supervenience and Anomalous Monism: Blackburn on Davidson. Zangwill, Nick.

The Archeology of Modalization in Husserl in Analecta Husserliana, XXXIV, Tymieniecka, Anna-Teresa (ed). Di Pinto, Luigia.

Worlds and Modality. Roy, Tony.

MODE

Modes of Presentation?. Yagisawa, Takashi.

On the Pragmatics of Mode of Reference Selection. Taylor, Kenneth.

Schiffer on Modes of Presentation. Adams, Fred, Stecker, Robert and Fuller, Gary.

The Floyd Puzzle: Reply to Yagisawa. Adams, Fred, Stecker, Robert and Fuller, Gary.

MODEL

"Who Sees with Equal Eye,... Atoms or Systems into Ruin Hurl'd?". DeVries, Willem A.

Agency in Action: The Practical Rational Agency Machine. Coval, Samuel C and Campbell, P G.

The Logical Foundations of the Marxian Theory of Value. Garcia de la Sienra, Adolfo.

A Δ2/2 Well-Order of the Reals and Incompactness of *L*(QMM). Abraham, Uri and Shelah, Saharon.

A Case Study of Normal Research in Theoretical Economics. Lind, Hans.

A Construction of Boolean Algebras from First-Order Structures. Koppelberg, Sabine.

A Contribution to the End-Extension Problem and the Π1 Conservativeness Problem. Adamowicz, Zofia.

A Critical Evaluation of Etzioni's Socioeconomic Theory: Implications for the Field of Business Ethics. Swanson, Diane.

A Functional Partial Semantics for Intensional Logic. Lapierre, Serge.

A Modal Reduction for Partial Logic. Barba, Juan.

MOORE

Troubles for New Wave Moral Semantics: The 'Open Question Argument' Revived. Horgan, Terence and Timmons, Mark.

Two Responses to Moore and Burks on Editing Peirce. Cook, Don L and Kloesel, Christian J W.

MORAL

Agents and Lives: Moral Thinking in Literature. Goldberg, S L.

An Ethic of Care: Feminist and Interdisciplinary Perspectives. Larrabee, Mary Jeanne (ed).

An Historical Introduction to Moral Philosophy. Wagner, Michael (ed).

Applied Philosophy. Almond, Brenda (ed) and Hill, Donald (ed).

Aquinas on Human Action: A Theory of Practice. McInerny, Ralph.

Automatism, Insanity, and the Psychology of Criminal Responsibility: A Philosophical Inquiry. Schopp, Robert F.

Balance and Refinement: Beyond Coherence Methods of Moral Inquiry. DePaul, Michael.

Between Slavery and Freedom: Philosophy and American Slavery. McGary, Howard and Lawson, Bill E.

British Empiricism and American Pragmatism: New Directions and Neglected Arguments. Roth, Robert.

Case Studies in Business Ethics (Third Edition). Donaldson, Thomas and Gini, Al.

Case Studies in Business, Society, and Ethics (Third Edition). Beauchamp, Tom L.

Consent: The Means to an Active Faith According to St Thomas Aquinas. Barad, Judith.

Discovering Philosophy. White, Thomas I.

Essays in Quasi-Realism. Blackburn, Simon W.

Ethical Dimensions of Legal Theory. Sadurski, Wojciech (ed).

Ethical Essays, Volume I. Harrison, Jonathan.

Ethical Issues: Perspectives for Canadians. Soifer, Eldon (ed).

Ethics: Studying the Art of Moral Appraisal. Littlejohn, Ronnie L.

Exploitation, Unequal Exchange and Dependency: A Dialectical Development. Otubusin, Paul.

Frames of Deceit: A Study of the Loss and Recovery of Public and Private Trust. Johnson, Peter.

Friendship: A Philosophical Reader. Badhwar, Neera Kapur (ed).

George Herbert Mead—The Making of a Social Pragmatist. Cook, Gary A.

In Search of the Ethical: Moral Theory in Twentieth Century America. Edel, Abraham.

Judging in Good Faith. Burton, Steven J.

Life and Death: Philosophical Essays in Biomedical Ethics. Brock, Dan W.

Moral Aspects of Legal Theory. Lyons, David.

Moral Matters. Narveson, Jan.

Moral Personhood: An Essay in the Philosophy of Moral Psychology. Scott, G E.

Moral Reasoning: Ethical Theory and Some Contemporary Moral Problems (Second Edition). Grassian, Victor.

Nietzsche's Philosophical and Narrative Styles. Pettey, John Carson.

Peirce's Esthetics of Freedom: Possibility, Complexity, and Emergent Value. Kevelson, Roberta.

Philosophie de l'action. Neuberg, Marc.

Philosophy in Literature, Volumes I and II. Johnson, Charles W.

Practical Knowledge—Yves R Simon. Mulvaney, Robert J (ed) and Simon, Yves R.

Rethinking Goodness. Wallach, Michael A and Wallach, Lise.

Retribution Reconsidered: More Essays in the Philosophy of Law. Murphy, Jeffrie G.

Royce's Mature Ethics. Oppenheim, Frank.

Sharing without Reckoning. Schumaker, Millard.

The Cambridge Companion to Heidegger. Guignon, Charles B (ed).

The Examined Life. Kekes, John.

The Great Gatsby as a Business Ethics Inquiry. McAdams, Tony.

The Idea of Democracy. Copp, David (ed), Hampton, Jean (ed) and Roemer, John E (ed).

The Moral Dimensions of Marriage and Family Therapy. Lageman, August G.

The Moral Economy of Labor: Aristotelian Themes in Economic Theory. Murphy, James Bernard.

The Moral Life. Luper-Foy, Steven.

The Moral Self. Noam, Gil G (ed) and Wren, Thomas (ed).

The Practice of Moral Judgment. Herman, Barbara.

The Problem of Hell. Kvanvig, Jonathan L.

The Renewal of the Heidegger-Kant Dialogue: Action, Thought, and Responsibility. Schalow, Frank.

The Structure of Value. Allen, R T.

To Make the Punishment Fit the Crime: Essays in the Theory of Criminal Justice. Davis, Michael.

Treatise on Ethics (1684). Malebranche, Nicolas and Walton, Craig (trans).

Truth and Eros: Foucault, Lacan, and the Question of Ethics. Rajchman, John.

Varieties of Moral Personality: Ethics and Psychological Realism. Flanagan, Owen.

Virtues and Rights: The Moral Philosophy of Thomas Hobbes. Ewin, R E.

Way, Learning, and Politics: Essays on the Confucian Intellectual. Wei-ming, Tu.

Why Be Moral? (Second Edition). Bahm, Archie.

A Critique of Harman's Empiricistic Relativism. Haines, Byron L.

A Mathematicians' Mutiny, with Morals in World Changes, Horwich, Paul (ed). Heilbron, J L.

A New Argument for Genuine Moral Dilemmas?. Statman, Daniel.

A New Orientation towards Ethical Value—An Approach to the Phenomenological Method (in Chinese). Woo, Kun-yu.

A Origem da Moral em Psicanálise. Gabbi Jr, Osmyr Faria.

A Pie-Model of Moral Responsibility? in Advances in Scientific Philosophy, Schurz, Gerhard (ed). Lenk, Hans and Maring, Matthias.

A Polemic on Principles: Reflections on the Pittsburgh Protocol. Weisbard, Alan J.

A Proposal for the Use of Advance Directives in the Treatment of Incompetent Mentally Ill Persons. Brock, Dan W.

A Riddle Regarding Omissions. Haji, Ishtiyaque.

Abelard on Atonement: 'Nothing Unintelligible, Arbitrary, Illogical, or Immoral about It' in Reasoned Faith, Stump, Eleonore (ed). Quinn, Philip.

Abortion, Abandonment, and Positive Rights in Altruism, Paul, Ellen Frankel (ed). Long, Roderick T.

Abortion, Abandonment, and Positive Rights: The Limits of Compulsory Altruism. Long, Roderick T.

Abortion, Moral Responsibility, and Self-Defense. Huffman, Tom L.

Adam Smith and David Hume: With Sympathy. Van Holthoon, F L.

Agent-Relativity, Reason, and Value. Stewart, Robert M.

Akrasia (Weakness of Will) and the Christian Understanding of Moral Failure. Brown, Robert F.

Alienation and Moral Imperatives: A Reply to Kanungo. Sweet, Robert T.

Alienation, Cultural Differences, and Moral Judgment. McLane, Janice.

Altruism Versus Self-Interest: Sometimes a False Dichotomy. Badhwar, Neera Kapur.

An Appeal for a Christian Virtue Ethic. Kotva Jr, Joseph J.

An Intervention Curriculum for Moral Development. Ries, Steven I.

Anger and Hate. Ben-Ze'ev, Aaron.

Anthropological Foundation of Moral Education in Chinese Foundations for Moral Education and Character Development, Van Doan, Tran (ed). Shen, Vincent.

Applied Ethics and Free Will: Some Untoward Results of Independence. Machan, Tibor R.

Applied Ethics for Teachers: What Is It and How Do We Teach It?. McCarthy, Christine.

Aquinas and the Moral Status of Animals. Drum, Peter.

Are Collectives Morally Responsible? in Advances in Scientific Philosophy, Schurz, Gerhard (ed). Neumaier, Otto.

Aristotelian Friendship: Self-Love and Moral Rivalry. Dziob, Anne Marie.

Aristotle and the Ideal Life. Lawrence, Gavin.

Artificial Reproductive Technologies: The Israeli Scene. Heyd, David.

Augustine's Radiant Confessional—Theatre of Prophecy. Duval, R Shannon.

Barring Corporations from the Moral Community: the concept and the Cost. Wilson, Paul Eddy.

Bioethics and Culture: An African Perspective. Gbadegesin, Segun.

Bioethics and Paediatrics in Contemporary Issues in Paediatric Ethics, Burgess, Michael M (ed). Ost, David.

Bioethics in a Low Key: A Report from Germany. Leist, Anton.

Both the Moral Right and the Moral Duty to Be Educated. Heslep, Robert D.

Bradley and Moral Philosophy in Psychoanalysis, Mind and Art, Hopkins, Jim (ed). Gardiner, Patrick.

Business and Postmodernism: A Dangerous Dalliance. Walton, Clarence C.

Can a Person be Happily Wicked? (Some Problems with Joel Feinberg's Contended Moral Defective). Ducharme, H M.

Causing, Intending, and Assisting Death. Brody, Howard.

Character and Community in the *Defensor Pacis*: Marsiglio of Padua's Adaptation of Aristotelian Moral Psychology. Nederman, Cary J.

Character Development in the Liberal Arts Students in Moral Education and the Liberal Arts, Mitias, Michael H (ed). Giventer, Edwin B.

Chastity and the (Male) Philosophers. McGhee, Michael.

Civilization and Its Dissents: Moral Pluralism and Political Order. Crosby, Donald A.

Collective Responsibility and Moral Vegetarianism. Hudson, Hud.

Combatancy, Noncombatancy, and Noncombatant Immunity in Just War Tradition in Cross, Crescent, and Sword, Johnson, James Turner (ed). Phillips, Robert L.

Comment on "Managers in the Moral Dimension: What Etzioni Might Mean to Corporate Managers". Etzioni, Amitai.

Commentator on 'Explanation and Practical Reason' in The Quality of Life, Nussbaum, Martha C (ed). Nussbaum, Martha C.

Common Ground in Aristotle's and Dewey's Theories of Conduct. Chambliss, J J.

Compensation and Redistribution. Goodin, Robert E.

Compensation Within the Limits of Reliance Alone. Anderson, Elizabeth.

Competitive Equality of Opportunity. Dahan, Yossi and Yonah, Yossi.

Conscientious Objection. Kemp, Kenneth W.

Contractualist Impartiality and Personal Commitments. Powers, G Madison.

Converging Theory and Practice: Example Selection in Moral Philosophy. Vitek, William.

Cosmopolitan Altruism. Galston, William.

Criminal Liability for the Bad Samaritan. Klepper, Howard.

Critical Notice of Annette Baier's *A Progress of Sentiments*. Russell, Paul.

Deconstructing Solidarity: Or, A Funny Thing Happened On the Way to Unity. Kohli, Wendy R.

Degrees of Finality and the Highest Good in Aristotle. Richardson, Henry.

Der Wert von Autonomie. Schaber, Peter.

Descartes and Locke on Speciesism and the Value of Life. Squadrito, Kathy.

Different Voices, Still Lives: Problems in the Ethics of Care. Mendus, Susan.

Discourse or Moral Action? A Critique of Postmodernism. Beyer, Landon E and Liston, Daniel P.

Distrust as a Practical Problem. Govier, Trudy.

Doctors Must Not Kill. Pellegrino, Edmund.

MORALITY

The Ethics of Parts and Wholes. Oldenquist, Andrew G.

The Inter-Relationship of Moral and Aesthetic Excellence. Bontekoe, Ron and Crooks, Jamie.

The Interplay between Science and Theology in Uncovering the Matrix of Human Morality. Schwarz, Hans.

The Legal Profession's Rule Against Vouching for Clients: Advocacy and "The Manner That Is the Man Himself". Shaffer, Thomas L.

The Light, the Word, the Sea, and the Inner Moral Self in Analecta Husserliana, XXXVIII, Tymieniecka, Anna-Teresa (ed). Gorniak-Kocikowska, Krystyna.

The Limits of Aristotelian Ethics. Larmore, Charles.

The Moral Status of Affirmative Action. Pojman, Louis.

The Moral Status of Smoking. Butler, Keith.

The Moral Theories of Kant and Hume: Comparisons and Polemics. King, James T.

The Moral Vocabulary of Liberalism. Beiner, Ronald.

The Morality of Inclusion. Buchanan, Allen.

The Morality of Insider Trading. Rossouw, G J.

The Morality of Law and Economics. Hardin, Russell.

The Morality of Lying in Saint Augustine. Feehan, Thomas.

The Morality of Niceness: Why Educators Have a Duty To Go Beyond Their "Obligations". Suttle, Bruce B.

The Necessity for Particularity in Education and Child-Rearing: the Moral Issue. Smeyers, Paul.

The New Problem of Curriculum. Martin, Jane Roland.

The Perceptual Paradigm of Moral Epistemology. Sandoe, Peter.

The Primacy of Authority. Wilson, John.

The Professionalism Movement: The Problems Defined. Sammons, Jack L.

The Realism of Moralism: The Political Philosophy of Istvan Bibo. Berki, R N.

The Right and the Good. Garcia, Jorge L A.

The Slippery-Slope Argument. Van Der Burg, Wibren.

The Slippery-Slope Argument Reconstructed: Response to Van Der Burg. Freedman, Benjamin.

The Social Importance of Moral Rights in Philosophical Perspectives, 6: Ethics, 1992, Tomberlin, James E (ed). Feinberg, Joel.

The Sources of Morality: Function, Conformity and Aesthetics. O'Connell, James.

The Use and Abuse of Scientific Studies: Reply. George, Kathryn Paxton.

The Virtues of Common Pursuit. Sherman, Nancy.

The 'Possibility' of A Categorical Imperative in Philosophical Perspectives, 6: Ethics, 1992, Tomberlin, James E (ed). Copp, David.

Theism and Moral Objectivity. Jacobs, Jonathan and Zeis, John.

Thinking Morality Interpersonally: A Reply to Burgess-Jackson. Walker, Margaret Urban.

Timelessness, Omniscience, and Tenses. Garcia, Laura L.

Towards a More Expansive Moral Community. Bernstein, Mark.

Über die Rationalität von Prozeduren und Resultaten. Dorschel, Andreas.

Universal Pragmatics and the Formation of Western Civilization: A Critique of Habermas's Theory of Human Moral Evolution. Whitton, Brian J.

Utilitarianism and Retributivism: What's the Difference. Michael, Mark A.

Virtue and Self-Alienation. Zeis, John.

Virtue Without Gender in Socrates. Scaltas, Patricia Ward.

Warum moralisch sein gegenüber Tieren?. Wolf, Jean-Claude.

Was There a Concept of Rights in Confucian Virtue-Based Morality?. Lee, Seung-Hwan.

What Did Descartes Do to Virtue?. Santilli, Paul C.

What is Moral Maturity? Towards a Phenomenology of Ethical Expertise in Revisioning Philosophy, Ogilvy, James (ed). Dreyfus, Hubert L and Dreyfus, Stuart E.

What is the Moral Basis of the Authority of Family Members to Act as Surrogates for Incompetent Patients?. Brock, Dan W.

What Price Deconstruction? Derrida on Heidegger and the Question of Nazims: A Critical Study. Nevo, Isaac.

What's Wrong With Murder? Some Thoughts on Human and Animal Killing. Everitt, Nicholas.

When The Will is Free in Philosophical Perspectives, 6: Ethics, 1992, Tomberlin, James E (ed). Fischer, John M and Ravizza, Mark.

Who Discovered The Will? in Philosophical Perspectives, 6: Ethics, 1992, Tomberlin, James E (ed). Irwin, T H.

Why Does Proximity Make a Moral Difference?. Vetlesen, Arne Johan.

Wittgenstein and Moral Realism. Werhane, Patricia H.

MORAVCSIK, J

Translation and Content—Footnotes on Moravcsik's 'All A's are B's'. Hofmann, T R.

MORE, H

The Neoplatonic Conception of Nature in More, Cudworth, and Berkeley in The Uses of Antiquity, Gaukroger, Stephen (ed). Jacob, Alexander.

MORE, T

Una reinterpretazione dell' 'Utopia'. Moro, Tomiaso.

MOREH, J

Internal Prisoner's Dilemma Vindicated. Kavka, Gregory.

MORPHOLOGY

On the Necessity of an Archetypal Concept in Morphology: With Special Reference to the Concepts of "Structure" and "Homology". Young, Bruce A.

MORRIS, R

Some Comments on Randall Morris' Process Philosophy and Political Ideology. Hartshorne, Charles.

The Third Man. Davidson, Donald.

Writing with Davidson: Some Afterthoughts after Doing Blind Time IV: Drawing with Davidson. Morris, Robert.

MORRIS, T

The Temptation of God Incarnate. Werther, David.

MORTALITY

Towards a Phenomenological Ethics: Ethos and the Life-World. Marx, Werner.

MOSES

The Idolatry of Rules in Deconstruction and the Possibility of Justice, Cornell, Durcilla (ed). Jacobson, Arthur J.

MOTHERHOOD

Elemental Passions—Luce Irigaray. Irigaray, Luce, Collie, Joanne (trans) and Still, Judith (trans).

From Mastery to Analysis: Theories of Gender in Psychoanalytic Feminism. Elliot, Patricia.

Hypatia Reborn: Essays in Feminist Philosophy. Al-Hibri, Azizah Y (ed) and Simons, Margaret A (ed).

Pursuing Parenthood: Ethical Issues in Assisted Reproduction. Lauritzen, Paul.

The Ethics of Reproductive Technology. Alpern, Kenneth D (ed).

Blood Relations: Feminist Theory Meets the Uncanny Alien Bug Mother. Zwinger, Lynda.

Cultural Patterns and the Way of Mother and Son: An Early Qing Case. Birdwhistell, Anne D.

Exclusion and Essentialism in Feminist Theory: The Problem of Mothering. DiQuinzio, Patrice.

Good Intentions and a Great Divide: Having Babies by Intending Them. Roberts, Melinda.

Julian of Norwich on the Tender Loving Care of Mother Jesus in Our Knowledge of God, Clark, Kelly James (ed). Adams, Marilyn McCord.

Mother: The Legal Domestication of Lesbian Existence. Robson, Ruthann.

Multiple Biological Mothers: The Case for Gestation. Feldman, Susan.

Nurturing Fathers—Some Reflections About Caring. Schmitt, Richard.

On "Philosophy" of Women's Double Role (in Czechoslovakian). Vodakova, Alena.

Pragmatists Jane Addams and John Dewey Inform the Ethic of Care. Leffers, M Regina.

Surrogate Motherhood: Politics and Privacy. Callahan, Joan.

The Primordial Myth of The Bad Mother and The Good Mother in Persons and Places and in The Last Puritan. Wenkart, Henny.

MOTHERSILL, M

Beauty in Shards and Fragments. Sircello, Guy.

Kant, Mothersill and Principles of Taste. Dickie, George T.

Some Reflections on Contemporary Epistemology. Tollefsen, Olaf.

MOTION

Anomalism, Uncodifiability, and Psychophysical Relations. Child, William.

Aristotle on the Non-Supervenience of Local Motion. White, Michael J.

Aristotle's Argument from Motion. McNiff II, James F.

Cambridge Mathematics and Cavendish Physics. Warwick, Andrew.

Descartes on Mind-Body Interaction and the Conservation of Motion. McLaughlin, Peter.

Difficulty in Defining Motion. Augros, Michael.

Galilei e la fisica del Collegio Romano. Dollo, Corrado.

Galileo, Aristotelian Science, and the Rotation of the Earth. Reitan, Eric A.

Het projectiel, het kanon. Serres, M.

Paolo Foscarini's Letter to Galileo: The Search for Proofs of the Earth's Motion. Kelter, Irving A.

Pierre Gassendi nel IV centenario della nascita. Gregory, Tullio.

The Foundations of the Calculus and the Conceptual Analysis of Motion: The Case of the Early Leibniz (1670-1676). White, Michael J.

The Intelligibility of Substantial Change in Aristotle's "Physics". Velharticky, Nick.

Transition and Contradiction. McKie, John.

MOTIVATION

Understanding Action: An Essay on Reasons. Schick, Frederic.

Foundedness and Motivation in Analecta Husserliana, XXXIV, Tymieniecka, Anna-Teresa (ed). Wing-Cheuk, Chan.

Hume's Theory of Motivation—Part 2. Shaw, Daniel.

La théorie platonicienne de la motivation humaine. Cooper, John.

Reconstruing Hempelian Motivational Explanations. Derr, Patrick and Thompson, Nicholas S.

Reward Event Systems: Reconceptualizing the Explanatory Roles of Motivation, Desire and Pleasure. Morillo, Carolyn R.

The Socratic Theory of Motivation. Reshotko, Naomi.

Worlds and States of Affairs: How Similar Can They Be? in Language, Truth and Ontology, Mulligan, Kevin (ed). Forbes, Graeme R.

MOUFFE, C

Laclau's and Mouffe's Secret Agent in Community at Loose Ends, Miami Theory Collect, (ed). Smith, Paul.

MOUNCE, H

Mounce and Collingwood on Art and Craft. Allen, R T.

MOUNIER, E

The Role of Jacques Maritain and Emmanuel Mounier in the Creation of French Personalism. Gendreau, Bernard A.

MOVEMENT

Interpretazione e critica di Plotino della concezione del tempo dei suoi predecessori. Trotta, Alessandro.

Los sentidos del acto en Aristóteles. Yepes, Ricardo.

The Body in Action: the Relationship between Action, Intention and Corporal Movement (in French). Dokic, Jérôme.

The Future of Dance Aesthetics. Sparshott, Francis.

The Process/Product Dichotomy and Its Implications for Creative Dance. Bergmann, Sheryle.

NEGATION

The Unintended Interpretations of Intuitionistic Logic in Perspectives on the History of Mathematical Logic, Drucker, Thomas (ed). Ruitenburg, Wim.

Three Zeros: A Comparative Philosophy of Voids. Bahm, Archie.

What Wisdom is According to Heraclitus the Obscure. George, Marie.

NEGATIVE

Beyond Negative and Positive Freedom: T H Green's View of Freedom. Simhony, Avital.

Platon et Plotin sur la doctrine des parties de l'autre. O'Brien, Denis.

Que reste-t-il de la fondation de la raison?. Joos, Jean-Ernest.

NEGLIGENCE

Pure Negligence. Sverdlik, Steven.

Unilateral Neglect and the Objectivity of Spatial Representation. Brewer, Bill.

NEGOTIATION

Ethics and Negotiation: The Search for Value and Freedom In Hollywood. Harrison, Harvey E.

Second Thoughts About Bluffing. Carson, Thomas.

NEHAMAS, A

Nietzsche and Aestheticism. Leiter, Brian.

NEILL, A

Still Unconverted: A Reply to Neill. Yanal, Robert J.

NELSON, E

What Evidence is There that 2^65536 is a Natural Number?. Isles, David.

NELSON, H

Caring: From Philosophical Concerns to Practice. Vezeau, Toni M.

In Defense of Caring. Noddings, Nel.

NELSON, J

Blessed Are the Peacemakers: Commentary on Making Peace in Gestational Conflicts. Rong, Rosemarie.

More Evidence that Hume Wrote the *Abstract*. Norton, David Fate.

On the Authorship of the *Abstract*: A Reply to John O Nelson. Broome, Jeff.

The Authorship of the *Abstract* Revisited. Raynor, David.

NENON, T

The Entelechy and Authenticity of Objective Spirit: Reflections on Husserliana XXVII. Hart, J G.

NEO-HEGELIANISM

A Philosophical Appreciation. Pinkard, Terry P.

NEO-KANTIANISM

A Philosophical Appreciation. Pinkard, Terry P.

Cassirer, Neo-Kantianism and Metaphysics. Krois, John Michael.

Die Überwindung des Marburger Neukantianismus in der Spätphilosophie Natorps. Wetz, Franz Josef.

Sur le néo-Kantisme de E Cassirer. Capeillères, Fabien.

NEO-MARXISM

Krise und Metamorphose der Rationalität. Ponsetto, Antonio.

NEO-PLATONISM

"Averroe quantumque arabo et ignorante di lingua greca...": Note sull'averrosimo di Giordano Bruno. Sturlese, Rita.

"Influxus Physicus" in Causation in Early Modern Philosophy, Nadler, Steven (ed). O'Neill, Eileen.

Athens and Jerusalem: The Role of Philosophy in Theology. Bonsor, Jack A.

Philoponus: On Aristotle on the Intellect. Charlton, William (trans).

Plato and Platonism. Moravcsik, Julius.

PSI XIV 1400: A Papyrus Fragment of John Philoponus. MacCoull, L S B and Siorvanes, L.

Simplicius: On Aristotle's "Physics" 4.1-5, 10-14. Urmson, J O (trans).

The Question of Being: A Reversal of Heidegger. Rosen, Stanley H.

The Uses of Antiquity. Gaukroger, Stephen (ed).

A Concepçao Estóica de Natureza e a Moderna Física do Contínuo. Abrantes, Paulo C C.

Aristote dans l'enseignement philosophique néoplatonicien: Les préfaces des commentaires sur les *Catégories*. Hadot, Ilsetraut.

Importanza storica e teoretica del pensiero neoplatonico nel *Pensare l'Uno* di Werner Beierwaltes. Gatti, Maria Luisa.

La struttura del mondo soprasensibile nella filosofia di Giamblico. Cocco, Giuseppe.

Plotinus's Metaphysics: Emanation or Creation?. Gerson, Lloyd P.

Polanyi's Augustinianism: A Mark of the Future?. Apczynski, John V.

Saint Thomas lecteur du "Liber de Causis". D'Ancona Costa, C.

The Ascent of Spirit: Is Santayana's System a Naturalistic Neo-Platonic Hierarchy?. Kuntz, Paul G.

The Neoplatonic Conception of Nature in More, Cudworth, and Berkeley in The Uses of Antiquity, Gaukroger, Stephen (ed). Jacob, Alexander.

NEO-THOMISM

Giovanni Maria Cornoldi tra neotomismo e intransigentismo cattolico. Quinto, R.

Physik und Neothomismus: Das ontologische Grundproblem der modernen Physik. Mutschler, Hans-Dieter.

NEONATE

Scenes from a Newborn Life (in Dutch). Hendriks, Ruud.

NEOSCHOLASTICISM

La posizione storiografica del pensiero di Carlo Mazzantini. Rizza, Aldo.

NEUMANN, F

Neumann versus Habermas: The Frankfurt School and the Case of the Rule of Law. Scheuerman, Bill.

NEURAL

Color Perception and Neural Encoding: Does Metameric Matching Entail a Loss of Information?. Hatfield, Gary.

Connectionism, Explicit Rules, and Symbolic Manipulation. Hadley, Robert F.

Currents in Connectionism. Bechtel, William.

NEURATH, O

Overcoming Logical Positivism from Within: The Emergence of Neurath's Naturalism in the Vienna Circle's Protocol Sentence Debate. Uebel, Thomas E.

Neurath vs Carnap: Naturalism vs Rational Reconstructionism Before Quine. Uebel, Thomas.

Neuraths Protokollsätze als Antwort auf Kritik seines Fallibilismus. Uebel, Thomas E.

NEUROBIOLOGY

Neurobiology of Subjective Probability in Probability and Rationality, Eells, Ellery (ed). Nosal, Czeslaw S.

NEUROPHYSIOLOGY

The Plasticity of Categories: The Case of Colour. Van Brakel, J.

Van Brakel and the Not-So-Naked Emperor. Hardin, C L.

What Neuropsychology Tells Us about Consciousness. Lahav, Ran.

NEUROPSYCHOLOGY

On a Model for Psycho-Neural Coevolution. Kobes, Bernard W.

NEUROSCIENCE

Mind, Brain, Behavior: The Mind-Body Problem and the Philosophy of Psychology. Carrier, Martin and Mittelstrass, Jürgen.

What Is Cognitive Science?. Von Eckardt, Barbara.

Brainwork: A Review of Paul Churchland's *A Neurocomputational Perspective*. McCauley, Robert N.

Can Neuroscience Provide a Complete Account of Human Nature? A Reply to Roger Sperry. Jones, James W.

Consciousness and the Experience of Freedom in John Searle and His Critics, LePore, Ernest (ed). Hannay, Alastair.

How to Be a Scientifically Respectable "Property-Dualist". Lahav, Ran and Shanks, Niall.

Mind/Brain Science in John Searle and His Critics, LePore, Ernest (ed). Freeman, Walter J and Skarda, Christine A.

Reduction, Explanatory Extension, and the Mind/Brain Sciences. Hardcastle, Valerie Gray.

Social Causation and Cognitive Neuroscience. Gillett, Grant R.

The Search for the New Pineal Gland: Brain Life and Personhood. Moussa, Mario and Shannon, Thomas A.

Theory Structure, Reduction, and Disciplinary Integration in Biology. Schaffner, Kenneth F.

What Price Neurophilosophy?. Saidel, Eric.

NEUTRALITY

White on Autonomy, Neutrality and Well-Being. Clayton, Matthew.

Whose Objectivity? Which Neutrality? The Doomed Quest for a Neutral Vantage Point from Which to Judge Relations. D'Costa, Gavin.

NEVILLE, R

Metaphysics, Semiotics, and Common Sense, a review of *Recovery of the Measure: Interpretation and Nature*, by Robert Cummings Neville. Grange, Joseph.

NEWCOMB'S PARADOX

The Newcomb Paradox and Everyday Problems (in Hebrew). Berkowitz, Yoseph.

NEWCOMB, W

Newcomb's Paradox: A Realist Resolution. Jacobi, N.

Newcomb's Problem as a Thought Experiment in Thought Experiments in Science and Philosophy, Horowitz, Tamara (ed). Horowitz, Tamara.

Reflective Coherence and Newcomb Problems: A Simple Solution. Malinas, Gary.

The Newcomb Paradox and Everyday Problems (in Hebrew). Berkowitz, Yoseph.

NEWMAN, J

The Roles of Moral Dispositions in the Cognitional Theories of Newman and Lonergan. Miller, Edward Jeremy.

NEWTON

The Life of Isaac Newton. Westfall, Richard S.

Animals Versus the Laws of Inertia. Hassing, R F.

Hurlbutt, Hume, Newton and the Design Argument. Tweyman, Stanley.

On Newtonian History in The Uses of Antiquity, Gaukroger, Stephen (ed). Trompf, Garry W.

Scienza e filosofia tra microcosmo e macrocosmo: Il problema di Dio in Diderot e Newton. Nicolosi, S.

The Empiric Experience and the Practice of Autonomy. Ben-Chaim, Michael.

NEWTONIANISM

Buckets of Water and Waves of Space: Why Space-Time is Probably a Substance. Maudlin, Tim.

NEWTONIANS

Realism About What?. Musgrave, Alan.

NICE

The Morality of Niceness: Why Educators Have a Duty To Go Beyond Their "Obligations". Suttle, Bruce B.

The Teacher As Hero: The Exploitation of Niceness. Futernick, Kenneth.

NICHOLAS OF CUSA

Nicholas of Cusa and Ibn 'Arabi: Two Philosophies of Mysticism. Smirnov, Andrey V.

Nicolás de Cusa, "De mente": la profundización de la doctrina del hombre-imagen. D'Amico, Claudia.

OBJECTIVITY

Objectivity in History: Peter Novick and R G Collingwood. Levine, Joseph M.

Objetividad empírica y juicio transcendental. De Mingo Rodríguez, Alicia.

On Judging Sufficiency of Evidence in The Philosophy of A J Ayer, Hahn, Lewis E (ed). Clarke, David S.

Passionate Objectivity. Swain, Corliss.

Positional Objectivity. Sen, Amartya.

Reasonableness, Bias, and the Untapped Power of Procedure. Adler, Jonathan.

Remarks on Logical Empiricism and Some of Ayer's Achievements in The Philosophy of A J Ayer, Hahn, Lewis Edwin (ed). Polikarov, Azarya and Ginev, Dimitri.

Responses to Authors and Writings of Israel Scheffler. Scheffler, Israel.

Rethinking Objective Homogeneity: Statistical Versus Ontic Approaches. Burnor, Richard.

Rethinking Standpoint Epistemology: 'What Is Strong Objectivity?' in Feminist Epistemologies, Alcoff, Linda (ed). Harding, Sandra G.

Skepticism, Objectivity, and Brains in Vats. Ebbs, Gary.

Soggettivismo e oggettivismo agli albori della metafisica greca. Zeppi, Stelio.

Some Problems for Gibbard's Norm- Expressivism. Sinnott-Armstrong, Walter.

Standpoint Reflections on Original Position Objectivity. Bellon, Christina.

Subjectivity/Objectivity and Meaningful Human Behavior in Terrorism, Justice and Social Values, Peden, Creighton W (ed). Armstrong, Robert L.

The Historian and His Evidence in Objectivity, Method and Point of View, Van Der Dussen, W J (ed). Van Der Dussen, W J.

The Objectivity and Invariance of Quantum Predictions. Fleming, Gordon N.

The Objectivity of Color and the Color of Objectivity. Kraut, Robert.

The Passing of Peirce's Realism. Margolis, Joseph.

The Problem of Objectivity in Post-Critical Philosophy. Lewin, Philip.

The Weak, the Strong and the Mild—Readings of Kant's Ontology. Thomson, Garrett.

Theism and Moral Objectivity. Jacobs, Jonathan and Zeis, John.

Theory-ladenness of Observation as a Test Case of Kuhn's Approach to Scientific Inquiry. Hintikka, Jaakko.

Transcendence and Conversation: Two Conceptions of Objectivity. D'Agostino, Fred.

Unilateral Neglect and the Objectivity of Spatial Representation. Brewer, Bill.

Value and History in Objectivity, Method and Point of View, Van Der Dussen, W J (ed). Pompa, L.

Virtue: Its Nature, Exigency, and Acquisition. Baechler, Jean.

W H Dray and the Critique of Historical Thinking in Objectivity, Method and Point of View, Van Der Dussen, W J (ed). Rubinoff, M Lionel.

OBLIGATION

see also Duty

Prima Facie Obligation in John Searle and His Critics, Lepore, Ernest (ed). Loewer, Barry and Belzer, Marvin.

Sharing without Reckoning. Schumaker, Millard.

The Grounds and Limits of Political Obligation. Capriotti, Emile.

Acts in Discourse: From Monological Speech Acts to Dialogical Inter-Acts. Linell, Per and Marková, Ivana.

Alternative Possibilities, Moral Obligation, and Moral Responsibility. Haji, Ishtiyaque.

Egoism, Obligation, and Herbert Spencer. Wilkinson, Martin.

Ethics and Rationality. Clayton, Philip and Knapp, Steven.

Future Generations: Present Harms. O'Neill, John.

Group Membership and Political Obligation. Gilbert, Margaret.

Human Nature as the Foundation of Moral Obligation. Hicks, Alan.

Hume and the Duties of Humanity. Shaver, Robert.

Moral Consideration and the Environment: Perception, Analysis, and Synthesis. Goodpaster, Kenneth E.

Obligaiton, Loyalty, Exile. Shklar, Judith N.

Obligation, Responsibility and Alternate Possibilities. Zimmerman, Michael J.

Paul of Venice on Obligations. Sinkler, Georgette.

Philosophical Scepticism about Moral Obligation. Platts, Mark.

Philosophical Scepticism about Moral Obligation—II. Black, Robert.

Response: Applications of the Theory in John Searle and His Critics, Lepore, Ernest (ed). Searle, John R.

The Logic of Obligation, 'Better' and 'Worse'. Goble, Lou.

The Morality of Niceness: Why Educators Have a Duty To Go Beyond Their "Obligations". Suttle, Bruce B.

The Paradoxes of Feldman's Neo-Utilitarianism. Almeida, Michael J.

The Teacher As Hero: The Exploitation of Niceness. Futernick, Kenneth.

Who Can Accept Moral Dilemmas?. Ohlsson, Ragnar.

OBSERVATION

A Popular Presumption Refuted. Dudman, V H.

Being at Rest. Snyder, Douglas M.

Beyond Representation in The Impulse to Philosophise, Griffiths, A Phillips (ed). Palmer, Anthony.

Carnap's Conventionalism. Creath, J Richard.

Explanation and "Old Evidence". Achinstein, Peter.

Faces, Boundaries, and Thin Layers in Certainty and Surface in Epistemology and Philosophical Method, Martinich, A P (ed). Simons, Peter.

How We Relate Theory to Observation in World Changes, Horwich, Paul (ed). Cartwright, Nancy.

Hume and the Lockean Background: Induction and the Uniformity Principle. Owen, David.

Hume on the Ordinary Distinction Between Objective and Subjective Impressions. Kornegay, R Jo.

In Praise of Observation Sentences. Quine, Willard V.

Keaney's Composition of Aristotle's Athenaion Politeia. Rhodes, P J.

Observations, Theories and the Evolution of the Human Spirit. Bogen, Jim and Woodward, Jim.

Positional Objectivity. Sen, Amartya.

Scientific Realism and the Criteria for Theory-Choice. McAllister, James W.

Seeing Qualia and Positing the World in A J Ayer Memorial Essays, Griffiths, A Phillips (ed). Honderich, Ted.

Shapere on Observation. Linden, Toby.

The Evidence of Your Own Eyes. Kyburg Jr, Henry E.

The Indirect Practical Functions of Explanations. Weber, Erik.

The Key to Interpreting Quine. Gibson, Roger.

The Third Man. Davidson, Donald.

The Underdetermination Thesis in Frontiers in American Philosophy, Volume I, Burch, Robert W (ed). Murphey, Murray G.

What Does the Scientist of Man Observe?. Broughton, Janet.

What Is a Phenomenon? The Concept of Phenomenon in Husserl's Phenomenology in Analecta Husserliana, XXXIV, Tymieniecka, Anna-Teresa (ed). Kienzler, Wolfgang.

What's a Theory to Do...with Seeing? or Some Empirical Considerations for Observation and Theory. Gilman, Daniel.

OCCASIONALISM

Descartes and Occasionalism in Causation in Early Modern Philosophy, Nadler, Steven (ed). Garber, Daniel.

Mechanism as a Silly Mouse in Causation in Early Modern Philosophy, Nadler, Steven (ed). Lennon, Thomas M.

Natures, Laws, and Miracles: The Roots of Leibniz's Critique of Occasionalism in Causation in Early Modern Philosophy, Nadler, Steven (ed). Rutherford, Donald.

Occasionalism and General Will in Malebranche. Nadler, Steven.

The Occasionalism of Louis de la Forge in Causation in Early Modern Philosophy, Nadler, Steven (ed). Nadler, Steven.

The Occasionalist Proselytizer in Philosophical Perspectives, 5: Philosophy of Religion, 1991, Tomberlin, James E (ed). McCann, Hugh J and Kvanvig, Jonathan L.

OCCIDENTAL

"I Can Wait 40 or 400 Years": Gandhian Satyagraha West and East. Starosta, William J and Chaudhary, Anju G.

A History of Western Ethics. Becker, Lawrence C (ed) and Becker, Charlotte B (ed).

Anti-Foundationalism: Old and New. Singer, Beth (ed) and Rockmore, Tom (ed).

The Emancipative Theory of Jürgen Habermas and Metaphysics. McLean, George F (ed) and Badillo, Robert Peter.

Toward a Genealogy of Individualism. Shanahan, Daniel.

Analytic and Continental Philosophies in Overall Perspective. Owens, Joseph.

Aporias, Ways and Voices in Derrida and Negative Theology, Coward, Harold (ed). Derrida, Jacques.

Approaches to Limits on War in Western Just War Discourse in Cross, Crescent, and Sword, Johnson, James Turner (ed). Lammers, Stephen E.

Aristotle and the Roots of Western Rationality. Lath, Mukund.

Axes du Temps en Afrique et en Occident. Bwele, Guillaume.

Body in Social Theory in Self as Body in Asian Theory and Practice, Kasulis, Thomas P (ed). Dissanayake, Wimal.

Can Western Philosophers Understand Asian Philosophies? in Revisioning Philosophy, Ogilvy, James (ed). Walsh, Roger.

Comments on " The Development of Advaita Vedanta as a School of Philosophy". Sharma, R M.

Comments on "The Development of Advaita Vedanta as a School of Philosophy". Pandey, S L.

D W Hamlyn's Being a Philosopher. Copleston, F C.

From Post-Communism to Civil Society: The Reemergence of History and the Decline of the Western Model. Gray, John.

Jennings and Zande Logic: A Note. Keita, Lansana.

Mysticism and Ethics in Western Mystical Traditions. Katz, Steven T.

New Trends in Russian Philosophy. Fluri, Philippe H.

Nothingness and Freedom: Sartre and Krishnamurti. Agarwal, M M.

The Concept of the Body in Self as Body in Asian Theory and Practice, Kasulis, Thomas P (ed). Deutsch, Eliot.

The Development of Advaita Vedanta as a School of Philosophy. Potter, Karl H.

The Orientation of the Nietzschean Text in Nietzsche and Asian Thought, Parkes, Graham R (ed). Parkes, Graham R.

The Poverty of Indian Political Theory. Parekh, Bhikhu.

The Practice of Education and the Courtship of Youthful Sensibility. Hogan, Pádrig.

Transcendence East and West. Loy, David.

Universal Pragmatics and the Formation of Western Civilization: A Critique of Habermas's Theory of Human Moral Evolution. Whitton, Brian J.

Yan Fu's Philosophy of Evolution and the Thought of Lao Zi and Zhuang Zi. Dayong, Yang.

OCCUPATION

Can Schools Provide the E-Ticket Ride?. Alston, Kal.

Dewey on the Pedagogy of Occupations: The Social Construction of the Hyper-Real. Palermo, James.

OCCURRENCE

What are Occurrences of Expressions?. Wetzel, Linda.

OCKHAM

Sobre la Suposicion—Guillermo de Ockham. Ockham, Guillermo and Guerrero, Luis (ed).

William of Ockham: A Short Discourse on Tyrannical Government. McGrade, Arthur Stephen (ed) and Kilcullen, John (trans).

El "Nuevo" Platon (Continuación). Juárez, Agustín Uña.

ORDINALS

Fixed Points in Peano Arithmetic with Ordinals. Jäger, Gerhard.

Proof-Theoretic Investigations on Kruskal's Theorem. Rathjen, Michael and Weiermann, Andreas.

ORGAN DONOR

A Polemic on Principles: Reflections on the Pittsburgh Protocol. Weisbard, Alan J.

Analogical Reasoning and Easy Rescue Cases. Young, Thomas.

Autonomie, don et partage dans la problématique de l'expérimentation humaine. Fagot-Largeault, Anne.

Autonomie, don et partage dans les transplantations d'organes et de tissus humains. Parizeau, Marie-Hélène.

Non-Heart-Beating Donors of Organs: Are the Distinctions Between Direct and Indirect Effects and Between Killing and Lettie Die Relevant and Helpful?. Childress, James F.

Solidarité et disposition du corps humain. Hottois, Gilbert.

The Dead Donor Rule: Should We Stretch It, Bend It, or Abandon It?. Arnold, Robert M and Youngner, Stuart J.

The Market for Bodily Parts in Applied Philosophy, Almond, Brenda (ed). Chadwick, Ruth F.

The Search for Bioethical Criteria to Select Renal Transplant Recipients: A Response to the Honourable Judge Jean-Louis Baudouin. Spicker, Stuart F.

Transplantation through a Glass Darkly. Nelson, James Lindemann.

ORGAN TRANSPLANT

Autonomie, don et partage dans les transplantations d'organes et de tissus humains. Parizeau, Marie-Hélène.

Moral Sensibilities and Moral Standing: Caplan on Xenograft "Donors". Nelson, James Lindemann.

Organ Transplants, Death, and Policies for Procurement. Lamb, David.

Organ Transplants, Foreign Nationals, and the Free Rider Problem. Davis, Dena S.

Techno-Thanatology: Moral Consequences of Introducing Brain Criteria for Death. Bayertz, Kurt.

The Search for Bioethical Criteria to Select Renal Transplant Recipients: A Response to the Honourable Judge Jean-Louis Baudouin. Spicker, Stuart F.

ORGANIC

Pragmaticism and Perspectivism on Organic Wholes. Shusterman, Richard.

ORGANICISM

Idealist Organicism: Beyond Holism and Individualism. Simhony, A.

ORGANISM

Ensayo de axiomatización de la teoría tisular y su reducción a la teoría celular. De Asúa, Miguel and Klimovsky, Gregorio.

ORGANIZATION

Associations and Democracy. Cohen, Joshua and Rogers, Joel.

Ethical Foundations of Management in Public Service. Geuras, Dean and Garofalo, Charles.

Mythos "Selbstorganisation". Mutschler, Hans-Dieter.

Organization Ethics from a Perspective of Praxis. Nielsen, Richard P.

Selbstorganisation und Entwicklung. Kummer, Christian.

ORIENTAL

see also Asian, Chinese, Indiam, Japanese

An Introductory Guide to Cultural Theory and Popular Culture. Storey, John.

East Asian Philosophy: With Historical Background and Present Influence. Ho, John E.

Tao Teh King By Lao Tzu: Interpreted as Nature and Intelligence. Bahm, Archie.

Tao Teh King—Lao Tzu. Tzu, Lao and Bahm, Archie J (trans).

Understanding Non-Western Philosophy: Introductory Readings. Bonevac, Daniel A and Phillips, Stephen.

Analytic and Continental Philosophies in Overall Perspective. Owens, Joseph.

Aporias, Ways and Voices in Derrida and Negative Theology, Coward, Harold (ed). Derrida, Jacques.

Italian Studies on Far Eastern Thought in Comparative Philosophy. Santangelo, Paolo.

New Trends in Russian Philosophy. Fluri, Philippe H.

Nothingness and Freedom: Sartre and Krishnamurti. Agarwal, M M.

Of Deserts and Doors: Methodology of the Study of Mysticism. Forman, Robert K C.

On Certain Intellectual Stereotypes in Buddhist Studies as Exemplified in T Stcherbatsky's Works. Lysenko, Victoria.

On Matilal's Understanding of Indian Philosophy. Mohanty, Jitendra N.

Orientalism and After: An Interview with Edward Said. Beezer, Anne and Osborne, Peter.

Studying Zen as Studying Philosophy. Murungi, John.

The Eloquent Silence of Zarathustra in Nietzsche and Asian Thought, Parkes, Graham (ed). Parkes, Graham R (trans), Aihara, Setsuko (trans) and Muneto, Sonoda.

The Orientation of the Nietzschean Text in Nietzsche and Asian Thought, Parkes, Graham R (ed). Parkes, Graham R.

The Problem of the Body in Nietzsche and Dōgen in Nietzsche and Asian Thought, Parkes, Graham (ed). Parkes, Graham R (trans) and Kōgaku, Arifuku.

Transcendence East and West. Loy, David.

ORIGIN

Cosmos, Bios, Theos: Scientists Reflect on Science, God, and the Origins of the Universe, Life, and "Homo sapiens". Margenau, Henry (ed) and Varghese, Roy Abraham (ed).

Storia del Buddhismo Ch'an. Arena, Leonardo Vittorio.

The Fine Art of Repetition: Essays in the Philosophy of Music. Kivy, Peter.

Big Bangs, Plural: A Heretical View. Pecker, Jean-Claude.

Divine Intervention and the Origin of Life. Chandler, Hugh S.

Emergence and Reduction in Morphogenetic Theories in Philosophy and the Origin and Evolution of the Universe, Agazzi, Evandro (ed). Artigas, M.

On the Origins of Idealization in the Social Experience in Idealization III, Brzezinski, Jerzy (ed). Sojka, Jacek.

Origin and Evolution of the Universe and Mankind in Philosophy and the Origin and Evolution of the Universe, Agazzi, Evandro (ed). Quesada, Francisco Miró.

Oswald Veblen and the Origins of Mathematical Logic at Princeton in Perspectives on the History of Mathematical Logic, Drucker, Thomas (ed). Aspray, William.

The Locked Door: An Analysis of the Problem of the Origin of the Soul in St Augustine's Thought. Waddell, Michael M.

The Nature and Evolution of Human Language: Commentary. Bishop, Michael A.

The Origin and Creation of the Universe: A Reply to Adolf Grünbaum. Craig, William Lane.

The Origin of 'The Origin of the Work of Art' in Reading Heidegger: Commemorations, Sallis, John (ed). Taminiaux, Jacques M.

The Roots of Philosophy. White, John.

ORIGINAL SIN

Augustine and Aquinas on Original Sin and the Function of Political Authority. Weithman, Paul.

ORIGINALITY

St Augustine's View of the Original Human Condition in De Genesi contra Manichaeos. Teske, Roland J.

ORNAMENT

The Idea of Abstraction in German Theories of the Ornament from Kant to Kandinsky. Morgan, David.

ORTEGA

Freedom, Power, and Culture in Ortega y Gasset's Philosophy of Technology. Dust, Patrick H.

L'immagine della donna secondo Ortega y Gasset. Savignano, Armando.

ORUKA, H

Beyond Universalism and Relativism. Procee, Henk.

ORWELL, G

Orwell and the Anti-Realists. Clark, Stephen R L.

OSTERBERG, J

True to Oneself. Sobel, J Howard.

OSTROW, J

A First Response to the Preceding Essays. Wolff, Kurt H.

OTHER

Life-Sharing for a Creative Tomorrow. Barral, Mary-Rose.

Oneself as Another—Paul Ricoeur. Ricoeur, Paul and Blamey, Kathleen (trans).

The Critical Turn. Angus, Ian (ed) and Langsdorf, Lenore (ed).

The Diversity of Religions: A Christian Perspective. DiNoia, J A.

De 'L'être et le néant' aux 'Cahiers pour une morale': Un enrichissement de la notion sartrienne de liberté 'pour-autrui'. Salzmann, Yvan.

Discontinuing Becomings: Deleuze on the Becoming-Woman of Philosophy. Braidotti, Rosi.

Foreclosure of the Other: From Sartre to Deleuze. Boundas, Constantin V.

Levinas on Desire, Dialogue and the Other. Jopling, David.

Panoptican: A World Order through Education or Education's Encounter with the Other/Difference. Kazmi, Yedullah.

Pouvoir de la singularité: le pathos du visage dans le texte d'Emmanuel Lévinas. Saint-Germain, Christian.

Ricoeur's Ethics of Method. Abel, Olivier.

Slagter's Nek: Imitatio Christi in the Construction of the Other/Self (in Dutch). Praeg, L.

The Instant and the Living Present: Ricoeur and Derrida Reading Husserl. Bourgeois, Patrick.

The Other is My Hell; the Other is My Home. Wu, Kuang-Ming.

The Self as an Other. Reagan, Charles E.

The System and Its Fractures: Gilles Deleuze on Otherness. May, Todd G.

Words of Others and Sightings/Citings/Sitings of Self in The Critical Turn, Angus, Ian (ed). Langsdorf, Lenore.

OTHERNESS

To the Other: An Introduction to the Philosophy of Emmanuel Levinas. Peperzak, Adriaan.

Platon et Plotin sur la doctrine des parties de l'autre. O'Brien, Denis.

OTT, H

Experience of the Holy in the Technological Age. Ott, Heinrich.

OTTE, R

The Unanimity Theory and Probabilistic Sufficiency. Carroll, John W.

OTTO, R

Numinous Experience and Religious Language. Schlamm, Leon.

OUGHT

Comparative Oughts and Comparative Evils. Anderson, Robert.

What the Good Samaritan Didn't Know. MacKenzie, J C.

'Is' and 'Ought' in Context: MacIntyre's Mistake. MacBeth, Murray.

OVER, D

The Objective Dimension of Believing De Re. Kvart, Igal.

OVERDETERMINATION

Thresholds, Transitivity, Overdetermination, and Events. Hausman, Daniel.

OWEN, G

Owen's Proof in the Peri Ideon and the Indeterminacy of Sensibles in Plato. Curry, D C K.

PARADOX
Bertrand Russell's Philosophy of Logical Atomism. Patterson, Wayne.
Language and Time. Smith, Quentin.
Logical Foundations. Mahalingam, Indira (ed) and Carr, Brian (ed).
The Human Being as a Logical Thinker. Balzer, Noel.
The Revision Theory of Truth. Gupta, Anil and Belnap, Nuel.
Theories of Truth: A Critical Introduction. Kirkham, Richard.
Weaving: An Analysis of the Constitution of Objects. Swindler, James K.
A Buridanian Discussion of Desire, Murder and Democracy. Goldstein, Laurence.
A Deflationary Resolution of the Surprise Event Paradox. Jacquette, Dale.
A Presentation Without an Example?. Zuboff, Arnold.
An Alternative Rule of Disjunction in Modal Logic. Williamson, Timothy.
An Epistemic Principle Which Solves Newcomb's Paradox. Lehrer, Keith and McGee, Vann.
Another Window Into Zeno's Antinomies. Gerber, William.
Aspects of the Fin-de-Siècle Decadent Paradox. Marvick, Louis W.
Backward-Induction Arguments: A Paradox Regained. Sobel, Jordan Howard.
Comment on Keith Lehrer and Vann McGee's Solution of Newcomb's Problem. Piller, Christian.
Confirmation without Paradoxes in Advances in Scientific Philosophy, Schurz, Gerhard (ed). Sylvan, Richard and Nola, Roberta.
Curry's Paradox and *Modus Ponens*. Urbas, Igor.
Defending Backwards Causation. Brown, Bryson.
Deontic Tense Logic in Advances in Scientific Philosophy, Schurz, Gerhard (ed). Aqvist, Lennart.
Fences and Celings: Schrödinger's Cat and Other Animals in Logical Foundations, Mahalingam, Indira (ed). Post, Heinz.
I Falsely Believe that *P*. Crimmins, Mark.
Idling Rules. Guetti, James.
Inescapable Surprises and Acquirable Intentions. Goldstein, Laurence.
Inquiry in the "Meno" in The Cambridge Companion to Plato, Kraut, Richard H (ed). Fine, Gail.
Is Higher Order Vagueness Coherent?. Wright, Crispin.
Many, but Almost One in Ontology, Causality and Mind: Essays in Honour of D M Armstrong, Bacon, John (ed). Lewis, David.
More on Moore. Welbourne, Michael.
Newcomb's Paradox: A Realist Resolution. Jacobi, N.
On Paradoxes in Naive Set Theory. Laraudogoitia, Jon Perez.
On the Sense of the Socratic Reply to Meno's Paradox. Jenks, Rod.
Ontology and Pragmatic Paradox. Haslanger, Sally.
Rechnendes Denken und besinnendes Denken: Heidegger und die Herausforderung der Leibnizschen Monadologie am Beispiel des Satzes vom Grund. Cristin, Renato.
Remarks on the Current Status of the Sorites Paradox. DeWitt, Richard.
Reply to Carl G Wagner's "Simpson's Paradox and the Fisher-Newcomb Problem". Lehrer, Keith.
Reply to Christian Piller's "Comment on Keith Lehrer and Vann McGee's Solution of Newcomb's Problem". McGee, Vann.
Reply to Lewis's 'Many, but Almost One' in Ontology, Causality and Mind: Essays in Honour of D M Armstrong, Bacon, John (ed). Armstrong, D M.
Simpson's Paradox and the Fisher-Newcomb Problem. Wagner, Carl G.
Some Problems with Chisholm and Potter's Solution to the Paradox of Analysis. Thomason, Neil.
Sorites Paradoxes and the Transition Question. Sainsbury, Mark.
Super Pragmatic Paradoxes in Logical Foundations, Mahalingam, Indira (ed). Ackermann, Robert.
The First Russell Paradox in Perspectives on the History of Mathematical Logic, Drucker, Thomas (ed). Anellis, Irving H.
The Liar and Sorites Paradoxes: Toward a Unified Treatment. Tappenden, Jamie.
The Logical Sense of παραδοξον in Aristotle's *Sophistical Refutations*. Boger, George.
The Paradoxes of Indicative Conditionals in Logical Foundations, Mahalingam, Indira (ed). Carr, Brian.
Three Pseudo-Paradoxes in 'Quantum' Decision Theory: Apparent Effects of Observation on Probability and Utility. Marinoff, Louis.

PARENT
Between Parents and Children. Machan, Tibor R.
Defective Newborns: Parental Obligation and the Law. Golash, Deirdre.
For All Its Children. Noddings, Nel.
Parental Rights in Applied Philosophy, Almond, Brenda (ed). Page, Edgar.

PARENTHOOD
Pursuing Parenthood: Ethical Issues in Assisted Reproduction. Lauritzen, Paul.

PARFIT, D
Indivisible Selves and Moral Practice. Haksar, Vinit.
Functionalism and Personal Identity. Fuller, Gary.
Identity, Psychological Continuity, and Rationality. Bushnell, Dana E.
On Two Arguments for the Indeterminacy of Personal Identity. Cartwright, Helen Morris.
Parfit on Persons. Cassam, Quassim.
Parfit on What Matters in Survival. Brueckner, Anthony.
Parfit's Arguments for the Present-Aim Theory. Hooker, Brad.
Persons, Plants and Insects: On Surviving Reincarnation. Laine, Joy E.
Persoonlijke identiteit in de analytische wijsbegeerte. Cuypers, Stefaan E.
Population Ethics: On Parfit's Views Concerning Future Generations. Pulvertaft, W Robert.
Reasons and Reductionism. Johnston, Mark.

Recent Work on Personal Identity. Baillie, James.
Social, Moral and Metaphysical Identities (A Response to Joy Laine). Clark, Stephen R L.
The Problematic Nature of Parfitian Persons. Storl, Heidi.
The Relations Between Moral Theory and Metaphysics. Stern, Robert A.

PARGETTER, R
Dispositions or Etiologies? A Comment on Bigelow and Pargetter. Mitchell, Sandra.

PARKER, T
Ralph Waldo Emerson and Theodore Parker: A Comparative Study. Madden, Edward H.

PARMENIDES
Collected Writings—Leonard E Woodbury. Brown, Christopher G (& other eds) and Woodbury, Leonard E.
El oráculo de Narciso. Lomba, Joaquin.
The Presocratic Philosophers: An Annotated Bibliography. Navia, Luis E.
A Note on Barnes's Parmenides. Ketchum, Richard J.
Alētheia and Oblivion's Field in Ethics and Danger, Dallery, Arleen B (ed). Fóti, Véronique.
Deception and Belief in Parmenides' *Doxa*. Curd, Patricia Kenig.
El poema de Parménides y la analogía según Santo Tomás de Aquino. Casaubón, Juan A.
L'unité de l'Etre parménidien. Pasqua, Hervé.
Les multiples lectures du Poème de Parménide. Lafrance, Yvon.
Metaphysics' Forgetfulness of Time in Philosophical Interventions in the Unfinished Project of Enlightenment, Honneth, Axel (& other eds). Theunissen, Michael.
Parmenides and Empedocles in Porphyry's *History of Philosophy*. Kohlschitter, Silke.
Partendo da Parmenide. Frerari, V.
Why Parmenides Wrote in Verse. Floyd, Edwin D.

PARSONS, C
Parsons on Mathematical Intuition. Page, James.

PARSONS, T
The End of Functionalism: *Parsons, Merton, and Their Heirs*. Turner, Stephen.

PARTIAL
A Functional Partial Semantics for Intensional Logic. Lapierre, Serge.
A Modal Reduction for Partial Logic. Barba, Juan.
Partial Functions in Type Theory. Lepage, François.

PARTIALITY
Morality and Partiality in Philosophical Perspectives, 6: Ethics, 1992, Tomberlin, James E (ed). Wolf, Susan.

PARTICIPATION
La valenza critica della partecipazione nell'opera di C Fabro. Pellecchia, P.
Participation et prédication chez Platon. Brisson, Luc.
Plotinus' Account of Participation in *Ennead* VI.4-5. Strange, Steven.
The Ambiguities of Education for Active Citizenship. Wringe, Colin.

PARTICULARITY
Aristotle's Practical Particularism in Essays in Ancient Greek Philosophy, IV, Anton, John P (ed). Louden, Robert B.
Moraliteit en magie?: In reactie op Dieter Lesage. Schuurman, Paul.
The Necessity for Particularity in Education and Child-Rearing: the Moral Issue. Smeyers, Paul.
Universal and Particular in Atonement Theology. Gunton, Colin.

PARTICULARS
Instance Ontology and Avicenna's Arguments. Mertz, Donald W.

PASCAL
Making Sense of It All. Morris, Thomas V.
Blaise Pascal e la problematicità dell'io: Ragione forte e pensiero debole. Todisco, O.
Credere e sapere. Iwand, Hans Joachim.
Infinite Return: Two Ways of Wagering with Pascal. Wetzel, James.
Metafisica e soggettività: Alle origini della filosofia moderna—Descartes, Pascal, Spinoza. Deregibus, Arturo.

PASKE, G
Dilemmas and Incommensurateness. McConnell, Terrance.

PASSION
Faith, Probability and Infinite Passion. Koons, Robert C.
From Passions to Sentiments: The Structure of Hume's *Treatise*. Rorty, Amélie Oksenberg.
Hume on Tranquilizing the Passions. Immerwahr, John.
Hume's Classification of the Passions and Its Precursors. Fieser, James.
L'"akrasia" nell'Etica Nicomachea. Mauri Alvarez, M.
Passionate Objectivity. Swain, Corliss.
Pleasure, Passion and Truth. Tiles, James E.
Reverence and the Passions of Inquiry. Bitting, Paul F and Southworth, Cheryl.
Sympathy, Self, and Reflective Freedom. Paske, Gerald H.
Thomas von Aquins Lehre von der Liebe als menschlicher Grundleidenschaft. Oesterreich, Peter L.

PASSIVITY
Hold Not Thy Peace At My Tears: Methodological Reflections on Divine Impassibility in Our Knowledge of God, Clark, Kelly James (ed). Clark, Kelly James.

PASSMORE, J
Aesthetics for Art's Sake, Nor for Philosophy's!. Silvers, Anita.

PAST
How Memory Shapes Narratives: A Philosophical Essay on Redeeming the Past. Plantinga, Theodore.

PERCEPTION

La polémica sobre lo innato en el libro I de los 'Nuevos Ensayos'. Guillén Vera, Tomás.

Marty on Grounded Relations in Mind, Meaning and Metaphysics, Mulligan, Kevin (ed). Johansson, Ingvar.

McTaggart on Perception. Sharma, Ramesh Kumar.

Mead and Merleau-Ponty: 'Meaning, Perception, and Behavior' in Analecta Husserliana, XXXI, Tymieniecka, Anna-Teresa (ed). Rosenthal, Sandra and Bourgeois, Patrick L.

Negation and Absence. Hardy, Gilbert (trans) and Lavelle, Louis.

Paradigma e visione in Thomas Kuhn. Meretti, Francesco.

Perception and Illusion. Sen, Madhucchanda.

Perception as Cooperation of Schematization and Figurative Synthesis (in Dutch). Lohmar, D.

Perception, Concepts, and Memory. Martin, M G F.

Perceptual Consciousness and Perceptual Evidence. Baergen, Ralph.

Perceptual Consciousness, Materiality, and Idealism in Analecta Husserliana, XXXIV, Tymieniecka, Anna-Teresa (ed). García-Gómez, Jorge.

Perceptual Content and Local Supervenience. Davies, Martin.

Perceptual Realism, Naive and Otherwise in John Searle and His Critics, Lepore, Ernest (ed). Zemach, Eddy M.

Photography, Painting and Perception. Currie, Gregory.

Realizing. Smith, Steven G.

Relativism in Gibson's Theory of Picture Perception. Boynton, David M.

Response: Perception and the Satisfactions of Intentionality in John Searle and His Critics, Lepore, Ernest (ed). Searle, John R.

Scenarios, Concepts and Perception in The Contents of Experience, Crane, Tim (ed). Peacocke, Christopher.

Surface Knowledge in Certainty and Surface in Epistemology and Philosophical Method, Martinich, A P (ed). Alexander Jr, Henry A.

Tacit Knowing, Gestalt Theory, and the Model of Perceptual Consciousness. Innis, Robert E.

The Causal Theory of Perception. Hyman, John.

The Diversity and Unity of Action and Perception in The Contents of Experience, Crane, Tim (ed). O'Shaughnessy, Brian.

The Evidence of Your Own Eyes. Kyburg Jr, Henry E.

The Exorcist's Nightmare: A Reply to Crispin Wright. Tymoczko, Thomas and Vogel, Jonathan.

The Imagery Debate. Eilan, Naomi.

The Nonconceptual Content of Experience in The Contents of Experience, Crane, Tim (ed). Crane, Tim.

The Perceptual Paradigm of Moral Epistemology. Sandoe, Peter.

The Problem of the Unconscious in the Later Thought of L Binswanger in Analecta Husserliana, XXXI, Tymieniecka, Anna-Teresa (ed). Mishara, Aaron L.

The Relativity of Perceptual Knowledge. Boardman, William S.

The Thinker and the Painter in Merleau-Ponty Vivant, Dillon, M C (ed). Taminiaux, Jacques M.

The Virtues of Illusion. Hardin, C L.

The Visual System and Levels of Perception: Properties of Neuromental Organization. Stoerig, Petra and Brandt, Stephan.

Theory-Ladenness of Perception Arguments. Bishop, Michael A.

Vision, Causation and Occlusion. Hyman, John.

Wahrnehmung als "Lektüre". Kühn, Rolf.

What Is Color Vision?. Hilbert, David.

PERESTROIKA

Perestroika, Too, Is Developed Socialism. Radzihkovskii, L A.

The Social Philosophy of N Berdiaev in Light of Perestroika. Adiushkin, V N.

PERFECTION

Aristotle on the Perfect Life. Kenny, Anthony.

The Perfection of the Universe According to Aquinas: A Teleological Cosmology. Blanchette, Oliva.

An Answer on Behalf of Guanilo. Landau, Iddo.

On Divine Perfection in Logic, God and Metaphysics, Harris, James F (ed). Power, William L.

Perfection and Creation in Reasoned Faith, Stump, Eleonore (ed). Morris, Thomas V.

Perfectionism and Equality in On the Track of Reason, Beehler, Rodger G (ed). Hurka, Thomas M.

The Problem of Divine Exclusivity. Jordan, Jeff.

The Problem of Divine Perfection and Freedom in Reasoned Faith, Stump, Eleonore (ed). Rowe, William.

PERFORMANCE

Fields of Dreams and Men of Straw: Philosophical Reflections on Performance-Enhancers in Sport. Meier, Klaus V.

How To Do Things On Stage. Saltz, David Z.

Identity and Relationship in Teaching as Performance. Thompson, Audrey.

Plato and Performance. Gould, John.

The Constantive-Performance Distinction in a Justificatory Perspective. Lenka, Laxminarayan.

The Preservation of Homeric Tradition: Heroic Re-Performance in the Republic and the Odyssey. Klonoski, Richard.

Violins or Viols?—A Reason to Fret. Davies, Stephen.

PERFORMATIVES

Le statut du serment et de la promesse dans la Déclaration des Droits de 1789. Fauré, Christine.

Peut-on parler de vérité et de fausseté pour les propositions performatives?. Gardies, Jean-Louis.

Wahre performative Selbstwidersprüche. Steinhoff, Uwe.

PERFORMING

Ethics and Evidence. Botkin, Jeffrey R.

PERINATAL

Ethics and Evidence. Botkin, Jeffrey R.

Perinatal Technology: Answers and Questions. Krauss, Alfred N, Miké, Valerie and Ross, Gail S.

PERIOD

Aesthetic Discrimination: Evaluation of Pieces by Style, Period, and Site. Duran, Jane.

PERIODICITY

Eventual Periodicity and "One-Dimensional" Queries. McColm, Gregory L.

PERMUTATION

An Arithmetical Completeness Theorem for Pre-permutations. Tuttas, Friedemann.

PERRY, J

On the Pragmatics of Mode of Reference Selection. Taylor, Kenneth.

Perry on Indexical Semantics and Belief States. Roberts, Lawrence D.

Twenty-Five Basic Theorems in Situation and World Theory. Zalta, Edward N.

PERSON

see also Human, Individual

Human Beings. Cockburn, David (ed).

Indivisible Selves and Moral Practice. Haksar, Vinit.

Material Beings—P Van Inwagen. Mackie, Penelope.

Max Scheler's Concept of the Person: An Ethics of Humanism. Perrin, Ron.

Person and Being. Clarke, W Norris.

Person and Religion: An Introduction to the Philosophy of Religion. Sandok, Theresa (trans) and Zdybicka, Zofia J.

Philosophie Juridique Européenne les Institutions. Trigeaud, Jean-Marc.

Selves, People, and Persons. Rouner, Leroy S (ed).

The Human Person: Animal and Spirit. Braine, David.

The Person and the Common Life. Hart, James G.

The Place of the Person In Social Life. Peachey, Paul (ed), Kromkowski, John (ed) and McLean, George F (ed).

Understanding Persons: Personal and Impersonal Relationships (Second Edition). Berenson, F M.

A Commentary on Oshita O Oshita's Analysis of the Mind-Body Problem in an African World View. Washington, Johnny.

A Response to Daniel Holbrook's 'Descartes on Persons' and Doug Anderson's 'The Legacy of Bowne's Empiricism'. Littlejohn, Ronnie L.

A Sufficient Condition for Personhood. Goodman, Michael.

Chisholm, Persons and Identity. Noonan, Harold W.

Die Person als Zweck an sich. Mendonça, W P.

Ecologia categoria etica. Salmona, B.

El descubrimiento del yo según David Hume. Elósegui, María.

Emotions and Rationality. Berenson, F.

Francesco Vito: Economia e personalismo. Riccio, S.

Freiheit und Determinismus (Teil II). Seebass, Gottfried.

From Social Subject to the 'person': The Belated Tranformation in Latter-Day Soviet Philosophy. Swiderski, Edward M.

Giving the Devil His Due. Thomas, Janice.

Hacia una concepción no atomista de la identidad personal. Cuypers, Stefaan.

History and Personal Autonomy. Mele, Alfred.

Identity, Psychological Continuity, and Rationality. Bushnell, Dana E.

Indeterminateness of the Concept of a Person. Chaturvedi, Vibha.

L'embrione e la sua natura. Marra, B.

L'opera di Pietro Piovani. Galasso, Giuseppe.

La identidad del sujeto individual según Aristóteles. Inciarte, Fernando.

La persona y su mundo: la cultura, la moral, el derecho y la sociedad familiar y política (I). Derisi, Octavio N.

Machine Persons. Adams, Frederick.

Machines as Persons?—I in Human Beings, Cockburn, David (ed). Cherry, Christopher.

Machines as Persons?—II in Human Beings, Cockburn, David (ed). Hanfling, Oswald.

Maritain on "the Common Good": Reflections on the Concept. Kalumba, Kibujjo M.

Moralité et magie. Lesage, Dieter.

Non-consequentialism, the Person as an End-in-Itself, and the Significance of Status. Kamm, F M.

Person as Locus of Permanence: Towards Albert Shalom's Metaphysics. Boltuc, Piotr.

Person as the Mask of Being. Tassi, Aldo.

Persona, hábito y tiempo: La constitución de la identidad personal. Vigo, Alejandro.

Personal Identity and the Idea of a Human Being in Human Beings, Cockburn, David (ed). Madell, Geoffrey.

Personhood, Potentiality, and the Temporarily Comatose Patient. Rogers, Katherin A.

Persons and Perspectives: A Personalist Response to Nagel. Sayre, Patricia.

Persons and the Satisfaction of Preferences: Problems in the Rational Kinematics of Values. MacIntosh, Duncan.

Persons, Plants and Insects: On Surviving Reincarnation. Laine, Joy E.

Personsein und Menschendwürde bei Thomas von Aquin und Martin Luther. Schockenhoff, Eberhard.

Persoon, substantie en gemeenschap: Over de innerlijke samenhang tussen de positie van de liberals en de communitarians. Cobben, Paul.

Radical Critique, Scepticism and Commonsense in Human Beings, Cockburn, David (ed). Gaita, Raimond.

PHILOSOPHER

PHILOSOPHER-KING

PHILOSOPHICAL ANTHROPOLOGY

PHILOSOPHICAL PSYCHOLOGY

PHILOSOPHY

see also Metaphilosophy, Process Philosophy

PHILOSOPHY

Nietzsche's Case: Philosophy as/and Literature. Magnus, Bernd, Stewart, Stanley and Mileur, Jean-Pierre.

Nietzsche's Philosophical and Narrative Styles. Pettey, John Carson.

Ontology, Causality and Mind: Essays in Honour of D M Armstrong. Bacon, John (ed), Campbell, Keith (ed) and Reinhardt, Lloyd (ed).

Open Questions: An Introduction to Philosophy (Concise Edition). Barcalow, Emmett.

Opus Postumum/Immanuel Kant. Kant, Immanuel, Förster, Eckart (ed & trans) and Rosen, Michael (trans).

Paul Ricoeur. Clark, Stephen.

Per un' etica del discorso antropologico. Borutti, Silvana.

Person and Religion: An Introduction to the Philosophy of Religion. Sandok, Theresa (trans) and Zdybicka, Zofia J.

Philoponus: On Aristotle on the Intellect. Charlton, William (trans).

Philosophical Occasions: 1912-1951—Ludwig Wittgenstein. Klagge, James C (ed), Nordmann, Alfred (ed) and Wittgenstein, Ludwig.

Philosophical Perspectives, 6: Ethics, 1992. Tomberlin, James E (ed).

Philosophical Universes. Verster, Ulrich.

Philosophie de l'action. Neuberg, Marc.

Philosophy and Artificial Intelligence. Moody, Todd C.

Philosophy and Feminist Criticism. Cole, Eve Browning.

Philosophy and Government, 1572-1651. Tuck, Richard.

Philosophy and Knowledge: A Commentary on Plato's "Theaetetus". Polansky, Ronald.

Philosophy and Philosophers: An Introduction to Western Philosophy. Shand, John.

Philosophy and Theology in the Middle Ages. Evans, G R.

Philosophy in Literature, Volumes I and II. Johnson, Charles W.

Philosophy of History (Second Edition). Dray, William H.

Philosophy of Physics. Sklar, Lawrence.

Philosophy of Religion: A Universalist Perspective. Sterling, Marvin.

Philosophy, Religion and the Spiritual Life. McGhee, Michael (ed).

Philosophy, Rhetoric, and the End of Knowledge: The Coming of Science and Technology Studies. Fuller, Steve.

Philosophy—A Myth?. Verster, Ulrich.

Pistis ed *Episteme*: *A Proposito di una lettura "diacritica" di 1 Cor 2, 3*. Campanale, Domenico.

Plato: "Theaetetus". Williams, Bernard (ed) and Levett, M J (trans).

Psychoanalysis, Mind and Art. Hopkins, Jim (ed) and Savile, Anthony (ed).

Quest for the Absolute: The Philosophical Vision of Joseph Maréchal. Matteo, Anthony M.

R G Collingwood: A Bibliographic Checklist. Dreisbach, Christopher.

Reality, Knowledge, and the Good Life: A Historical Introduction to Philosophy. DeVries, Willem A.

Reason and Tradition in Indian Thought: An Essay on the Nature of Indian Philosophical Thinking. Mohanty, Jitendra N.

Reflections on Philosophy. McHenry, Leemon (ed) and Adams, Frederick (ed).

Renewing Philosophy. Putnam, Hilary.

Revisioning Philosophy. Ogilvy, James (ed).

Science, Knowledge, and Mind: A Study in the Philosophy of C S Peirce. Delaney, C F.

Search for a Naturalistic World View: Volume I. Shimony, Abner.

Selected Philosophical and Methodological Papers. Meehl, Paul, Anderson, C Anthony (ed) and Gunderson, Keith (ed).

Self as Body in Asian Theory and Practice. Kasulis, Thomas P (ed).

Simone Weil: Portrait of a Self-Exiled Jew. Nevin, Thomas R.

Soviet Marxism and Analytical Philosophies of History—Eero Loone. Pearce, Brian (trans) and Loone, Eero.

Speaking of a Personal God: An Essay in Philosophical Theology. Brümmer, Vincent.

T S Eliot and American Philosophy: The Harvard Years. Jain, Manju.

Tao Teh King By Lao Tzu: Interpreted as Nature and Intelligence. Bahm, Archie.

Tao Teh King—Lao Tzu. Tzu, Lao and Bahm, Archie J (trans).

Taoist Mystical Philosophy: The Scripture of Western Ascension, by Livia Kohn. Chan, Alan K L.

The Advancement of Science: Science without Legend, Objectivity without Illusions. Kitcher, Philip.

The Blackwell Dictionary of Twentieth-Century Social Thought. Outhwaite, William (ed) and Bottomore, Tom (ed).

The Butterfly as Companion: Meditations on the First Three Chapters of the Chuang Tzu: Review. Kjellberg, Paul.

The Contents of Experience. Crane, Tim (ed).

The Crisis of Philosophy. McCarthy, Michael.

The Dialogics of Critique. Gardiner, Michael.

The Essays—Francis Bacon. Bacon, Francis and Pitcher, John (ed).

The Examined Life. Kekes, John.

The Experience of Philosophy (Second Edition). Kolak, Daniel and Martin, Raymond.

The Impulse to Philosophise. Griffiths, A Phillips (ed).

The Life of Irony and the Ethics of Belief. Wisdo, David.

The Life of Isaac Newton. Westfall, Richard S.

The Linguistic Turn: Essays In Philosophical Method. Rorty, Richard (ed).

The Manifestation of Analogous Being in the Dialectic of the Space-Time Continuum: A Philosophical Study in Freedom. Harris, David A.

The Mechanism and Freedom of Logic. Henry, Granville C.

The Philosophy of A J Ayer. Hahn, Lewis E (ed).

The Pluralistic Philosophy of Stephen Crane. Dooley, Patrick K.

The Portable Nietzsche. Kaufmann, Walter (ed).

The Quotable Bertrand Russell. Eisler, Lee (ed).

The Rediscovery of the Mind. Searle, John R.

The Revision of Psychoanalysis—Eric Fromm. Fromm, Erich.

The Step Not Beyond. Nelson, Lycette (trans) and Blanchot, Maurice.

Theoretical Philosophy, 1755-1770—Immanuel Kant. Walford, David (ed & trans).

Thought Experiments in Science and Philosophy. Horowitz, Tamara (ed) and Massey, Gerald J (ed).

Time and Transcendence: Secular History, the Catholic Reaction and the Rediscovery of the Future. Motzkin, Gabriel.

Truth in Philosophy. Allen, Barry G.

Value and Understanding: Essays for Peter Winch: Critical Notice. Palmer, Anthony.

Voices of Wisdom: A Multicultural Philosophy Reader. Kessler, Gary E.

Weaving: An Analysis of the Constitution of Objects. Swindler, James K.

William James: Pragmatism in Focus. Olin, Doris (ed).

World Changes. Horwich, Paul (ed).

Worlds Without Content: Against Formalism. O'Neill, John.

Writing Philosophy Papers. Seech, Zachary.

A Bibliography of Works by and on Anton Marty in Mind, Meaning and Metaphysics, Mulligan, Kevin (ed). Bokhove, Niels W and Raynaud, Savina.

A Commentary on Oshita O Oshita's Analysis of the Mind-Body Problem in an African World View. Washington, Johnny.

A Confucian Perspective on Embodiment in The Body in Medical Thought and Practice, Leder, Drew (ed). Wei-ming, Tu.

A Convergence of Pragmatisms in Frontiers in American Philosophy, Volume I, Burch, Robert W (ed). Margolis, Joseph.

A Critique of Borowitz's Postmodern Jewish Theology. Samuelson, Norbert M.

A Critique of Gadamer (in Hebrew). Ben-NaftaliBerkowitz, Michal.

A Diferença entre as Filosofias de Carnap e Popper. De Araújo Dutra, Luiz Henrique.

A Few Notes on the Relation of Philosophy and Ecology (in Czechoslovakian). Kolarsky, R.

A la recherche de vérités éthiques (le réalisme moral dans la philosophie analytique). Ogien, Ruwen.

A Libertarian Critique of H Tristram Engelhardt, Jr's "The Foundations of Bioethics". Fry-Revere, Sigrid.

A Necessary Falsehood in the Third Man Argument. Scaltsas, Theodore.

A New Direction in Confucian Scholarship: Approaches to Examining the Differences between Neo-Confucianism and *Tao-hsüeh*. Tillman, Hoyt Cleveland.

A Nonary of Priorities in Revisioning Philosophy, Ogilvy, James (ed). Panikkar, Raimundo.

A Personal View of Percy W Bridgman, Physicist and Philosopher. Holton, Gerald.

A Question of Style: Nelson Goodman and the Writing of Theory. Engström, Timothy H.

A Response to M A Stewart's 'Berkeley's Introduction Draft'. Belfrage, Bertil.

A Thirteenth-Century Interpretation of Aristotle on Equivocation and Analogy. Ashworth, E J.

Adam Smith and David Hume: With Sympathy. Van Holthoon, F L.

Aesthetics in Reflections on Philosophy, McHenry, Leemon (ed). Stecker, Robert A.

African Philosophy and the Sociological Thesis. Pearce, Carole.

After Analytic Philosophy, What's Next?: An Analytic Philosopher's Perspective. Walton, Douglas N.

Afterthoughts on My Carus Lectures: Philosophy as Anthropology. Putnam, Hilary.

Afterword in Revisioning Philosophy, Ogilvy, James (ed). Appelbaum, David.

Afterwords in World Changes, Horwich, Paul (ed). Kuhn, Thomas S.

American Naturalism from a Non-American Perspective. Karimsky, Anyur M.

American Philosophy Today. Rescher, Nicholas.

An Argument for a Metaphysical Reading of Charles Sanders Peirce's Pragmatic Maxim. Wells, Kelley J.

An Exploration of the Concept of *Zhong* in the Teachings of Confucianism. Rongjie, Chen and Chan, Wing-Tsit.

An Interview with A J Ayer. Price, Thomas, Russell, Robert and Kennett, Stephen.

An Old Way of Looking at New Things: Modern Science, Technology, and the Philosophy of Science. Del Giudice, Denis.

Analogy as a Guide to Philosophical Thinking. Fethe, Charles.

Analytic and Continental Philosophies in Overall Perspective. Owens, Joseph.

Animal Thoughts. Gaita, Raimond.

Applied Phenomenology in Philosophical Counseling. Lahav, Ran.

Approaching Distance. Hanson, Karen.

Apuleius and the Concept of Philosophical Rhetoric. O'Brien, Maeve.

Aquinas on the Active Intellect. Haldane, John.

Aristote et la séparation. Bastit, Michel.

Aristotle and Aquinas on Cognition. Owens, Joseph.

Aristotle and Hellenistic Philosophy. Sharples, Bob.

Aristotle's Philosophy of Mathematics. Apostle, Hippocrates.

Aspects of a Philosophy of Technique. Hottois, Gilbert.

Aspects of French Hegelianism. Rockmore, Tom.

Authenticity in Rousseau (in Hebrew). Golomb, Jacob.

Autonomy and the Philosopher. Agassi, Joseph.

Ayer and the Vienna Circle in The Philosophy of A J Ayer, Hahn, Lewis Edwin (ed). Hung, Tscha.

Ayer's Place in the History of Philosophy in A J Ayer Memorial Essays, Griffiths, A Phillips (ed). Quinton, Anthony.

PHILOSOPHY

PHILOSOPHY

Issues in African Philosophy Re-examined. Okafor, Fidelis U.

Jabir, the Buddhist Yogi. Walter, Michael.

John Rawls: For the Record (An Interview). Aybar, Samuel R, Harlan, Joshua D and Lee, Won J.

Kant e a Filosofia Analítica. Loparic, Zeljko.

Kant's Idealistic Dilemma (in Hebrew). Kollender, Aaron.

Karl Jaspers and Scientific Philosophy. Bennett, James O.

Keaney's *Composition of Aristotle's Athenaion Politeia*. Rhodes, P J.

Knowing Why: Integrating Theory and Practice. Engel, David.

Kurt Gödel and Phenomenology. Tieszen, Richard.

La filosofía como tragedia: Nietzsche. Innerarity, Daniel.

La philosophie et son histoire: quelques réflexions à propos d'un livre récent de W J Courtenay. Lusignan, Serge.

La problemática filosofía de la historia: Anotaciones a una interminable disputa. Gil, Tomás.

La suggestione delle filosofie di moda e il richiamo al senso comune: Tra Vico e Pareyson. Russo, F.

Language and Philosophy in Logical Foundations, Mahalingam, Indira (ed). Burbidge, John W.

Language Without Conversation. Malcolm, Norman.

Le concept de philosophie première dans la "Métaphysique" d'Aristote. Follon, Jacques.

Le relation mente-corpore in le filosofia e in le scientia contemporanee. Blandino, Giovanni.

Leibniz's Vorstellungen über den Zusammenhang von Meteorologie und Anthropologie: "physica specialis cum medicina provisionalis". Obst, Godehard.

Logic in Reflections on Philosophy, McHenry, Leemon (ed). Brenner, William H.

Martha Nussbaum's *Loves Knowledge: Essays on Philosophy and Literature*. Sirridge, Mary.

Marty and the Lvov-Warsaw School in Mind, Meaning and Metaphysics, Mulligan, Kevin (ed). Wolenski, Jan.

Measuring Quality of Life in Theory and in Practice: A Dialogue Between Philosophical and Psychological Approaches. Boddington, Paula and Podpadec, Tessa.

Médiation ou immédiation et philosophie chrétienne. Floucat, Y.

Mein philosophischer Ausgangspunkt. Nishitani, Keiji.

Memories of Michael Polanyi in Manchester. Calvin, Michael.

Metafisica della soggettività e filosofia della libertà. Ciancio, Claudio.

Metaphilosophy in Wittgenstein's City. Jacquette, Dale.

Metaphysics in Reflections on Philosophy, McHenry, Leemon (ed). McHenry, Leemon.

Methodology: History and Its Philosophy in Objectivity, Method and Point of View, Van Der Dussen, W J (ed). Atkinson, R F.

Michael Dummett's *Frege*. Heck Jr, Richard G.

Michael Polanyi and the History of Science. Holton, Gerald.

Michael Polanyi and the Philosophy of Medicine. Gelwick, Richard.

Michel Foucault's Archaeology, Enlightenment, and Critique. Mahon, Michael.

Mistica o filosofia? A proposito della dottrina dell'immagine di Meister Eckhart. Sturlese, Loris.

Modern Chinese Thought: A Retrospective View and a Look into the Future. Lai, Chen.

Moral Flourishing in an Unjust World. Thomas, Laurence.

More Evidence that Hume Wrote the *Abstract*. Norton, David Fate.

Motions of the Mind in Psychoanalysis, Mind and Art, Hopkins, Jim (ed). Hart, W D.

Mystik und Philosophie. Margreiter, Reinhard.

Narrative and Philosophical Experience in On Paul Ricoeur: Narrative and Interpretation, Wood, David (ed). Rée, Jonathan.

Neuer Aufbruch in die Moderne? Beobachtungen zur gegenwärtigen russischen Philosophie. Franz, Margret.

New Trends in Russian Philosophy. Fluri, Philippe H.

Nietzschean Philosophers. Schroeder, William R.

Non-Africans on African Philosophy: Steps to a Difficult Dialogue. Kimmerle, Heinz.

Norman Malcolm: A Memoir. Serafini, Anthony.

Not Lesbian Philosophy. Trebilcot, Joyce.

Notes on Husserl and Kant in Analecta Husserliana, XXXIV, Tymieniecka, Anna-Teresa (ed). Romani, Romano.

Nothingness and Freedom: Sartre and Krishnamurti. Agarwal, M M.

Of Dances and Dreams: Philosophical Projects in the Current Age. O'Connor, Terence.

On an Alleged Inconsistency in Whitehead. Capek, Milic.

On Christian Philosophy: *Una Vera Philosophia?*. Ross, James F.

On Contradiction in Analecta Husserliana, XXXIV, Tymieniecka, Anna-Teresa (ed). Corte-Real, Maria L.

On Matilal's Understanding of Indian Philosophy. Mohanty, Jitendra N.

On Newtonian History in The Uses of Antiquity, Gaukroger, Stephen (ed). Trompf, Garry W.

On Norms of Competence. Bulygin, Eugenio.

On Plato's *Sophist*. Benardete, Seth.

On the Confines of Theology and Philosophy: A Reflection on the Book of T De Boer (in Dutch). Vandenbulcke, Jaak.

On the Deification of Confucius. Gier, Nicholas.

On the Endangered Species of the *Metaphysics*. Malcolm, John F.

On the Interpretation Circle of Philosophy. Guiquan, Zhang.

On the Problem of Value Reconstruction in Chinese Philosophy under the Impact from European Thought. Liu, Shu-Hsien.

On the Proper Function of the Moral Philosopher: Kant and Rawls on Theory and Practice. Nasr, Wassah N.

On the Right Use of Contradiction According to Simone Weil in Simone Weil's Philosophy of Culture, Bell, Richard H (ed). Devaux, André a.

On Time. Priest, Graham.

On Why Philosophers Redefine their Subject. Brown, Stuart.

On Why Philosophers Redefine their Subject in The Impulse to Philosophise, Griffiths, A Phillips (ed). Brown, Stuart.

Orestes Brownson and Christian Philosophy. Maurer, Armand A.

Originalità filosofica dei *Pensieri* di Marco Aurelio. Crovi, Luca.

Particle Labels and the Theory of Indistinguishable Particles in Quantum Mechanics. Redhead, Michael and Teller, Paul.

Paul Weingartner: Philosophy at Work in Advances in Scientific Philosophy, Schurz, Gerhard (ed). Zecha, Gerhard.

Peirce's Contribution to Ethics in Frontiers in American Philosophy, Volume I, Burch, Robert W (ed). Colapietro, Vincent.

Penelope's Web: Reconstruction of Philosophy and the Relevance of Reason. Rockmore, Tom.

Peripatetic Dialectic in the 'De Sensibus' in Theophrastus, Fortenbaugh, W W (ed). Baltussen, Han.

Persuasion. Winch, Peter G.

Phenomenology in Russia: The Contribution of Gustav Shpet. Scanlan, James P.

Philosophical and Methodological Foundations of Kotarbinski's Praxiology in Kotarbinski: Logic, Semantics and Ontology, Wolenski, Jan (ed). Pszczolowski, Tadeusz.

Philosophical Biography: The American Scene. Madden, Edward H and Madden, Marian C.

Philosophical Plumbing. Midgley, Mary.

Philosophical Plumbing in The Impulse to Philosophise, Griffiths, A Phillips (ed). Midgley, Mary.

Philosophical Prose and Practice. McCleary, Richard C.

Philosophical Self-Portrait in Kotarbinski: Logic, Semantics and Ontology, Wolenski, Jan (ed). Kotarbinski, Tadeusz.

Philosophical Studies (Sinology and Indology) in St Petersburg (Leningrad), 1985-1990. Torchinov, E A.

Philosophie et révélation dans l'idéalisme allemand: Un bilan. Maesschalck, Marc.

Philosophie transcendentale et praxis politique chez Fichte. Radrizzani, Ives.

Philosophieren in Brasilien—oder: Wie tief ist der Abgrund zwischen Theorie und Realität?. Kesselring, Thomas.

Philosophy and *Weltanschauung*. Nielsen, Kai.

Philosophy and Evolution of Consciousness in Revisioning Philosophy, Ogilvy, James (ed). McDermott, Robert.

Philosophy and Fascism. Gilbert, Paul.

Philosophy and Fiction. Anderson, Susan Leigh.

Philosophy and Frontier Science in New Horizons in the Philosophy of Science, Lamb, David (ed). Woodhouse, Mark B.

Philosophy and Its History. Copleston, F C.

Philosophy and Literature: Settling a Quarrel?. Halliwell, Stephen.

Philosophy and Nationalism. Hejdánek, L.

Philosophy and Religion in the Thought of Kierkegaard. Weston, Michael.

Philosophy and Religion in the Thought of Kierkegaard in Philosophy, Religion and the Spiritual Life, McGhee, Michael (ed). Weston, Michael.

Philosophy and Sociology of Law in the Work of Renato Treves. Ferrari, Vincenzo and Velicogna, Nella Gridelli.

Philosophy and the Cult of Irrationalism. Almond, Brenda.

Philosophy and the Cult of Irrationalism in The Impulse to Philosophise, Griffiths, A Phillips (ed). Almond, Brenda.

Philosophy and the Future in a Global Context. Khatchadourian, Haig A.

Philosophy and the Outlandishness of Reason. Page, Carl.

Philosophy and the Search for Wisdom. Nielsen, Kai.

Philosophy as a Sign-Producing Activity: The Metastable Gestalt of Intentionality in Analecta Husserliana, XXXIV, Tymieniecka, Anna-Teresa (ed). Gandelman, Claude.

Philosophy Beyond the Limits of Politics (in Dutch). Heyde, L.

Philosophy for Children and Mathematics Education. English, Lyn.

Philosophy for Children: A Note of Warning. Wilson, John.

Philosophy of Medicine—From a Medical Perspective. Wulff, Henrik R.

Philosophy of Religion in Reflections on Philosophy, McHenry, Leemon (ed). Pletcher, Galen K.

Philosophy of Science and Its Rational Reconstructions: Remarks on the VPI Program for Testing Philosophies of Science. Richardson, Alan W.

Philosophy versus Mysticism in Philosophy, Religion and the Spiritual Life, McGhee, Michael (ed). Leaman, Oliver.

Philosophy versus Mysticism: an Islamic Controversy. Leaman, Oliver.

Philosophy, History, and the Jewish Thinker in German Philosophy and Jewish Thought, Greenspan, Louis (ed). Morgan, Michael.

Philosophy, Literature, and Intellectual Responsibility. Rockmore, Tom.

Philosophy/Philosophy, an Untenable Dualism. Haack, Susan.

Plato and the Method of Science. Stekeler-Weithofer, Pirmin.

Plato and the Sightlovers of the *Republic*. Stokes, Michael C.

Plato: The Intellectual Background in The Cambridge Companion to Plato, Kraut, Richard H (ed). Irwin, T H.

Political Philosophy in Reflections on Philosophy, McHenry, Leemon (ed). Hooker, Brad.

Postmodern Grief. Hix, Harvey L.

Postmodernism and 'The End of Philosophy'. Cooper, David E.

Postmodernism: Old and New. Stuhr, John.

Precisationes varie sur questiones de filosofia. Blandino, Giovanni.

Presocratics and Sophists. Wright, M R.

Pseudoscience as Nonsense. Lugg, Andrew.

Race and the Modern Philosophy Course. Immerwahr, John.

Raiders of the Lost Distinction: Richard Rorty and the Search for the Last Dichotomy. Rosenberg, Jay F.

PHILOSOPHY

PHILOSOPHY

Vico's Road and Hegel's Owl as Historiographies of Renaissance Philosophy. Verene, Donald Phillip.

Vincenzo's Portrayal of Nietzsche's Socrates. Domino, Brian.

Virtue and Repression. Paden, Roger K.

Vlastos's Socrates. Kahn, Charles.

Vollenhovens probleemhistorische methode tegen de achtergrond van zijn systematisch denken. Tol, A.

What is Consciousness?. Nelkin, Norton.

What is Moral Maturity? Towards a Phenomenology of Ethical Expertise in Revisioning Philosophy, Ogilvy, James (ed). Dreyfus, Hubert L and Dreyfus, Stuart E.

What Price Neurophilosophy?. Saidel, Eric.

Who Is Nietzsche's Epicurus?. Lampert, Laurence A.

Why Heidegger Wasn't Shocked by the Holocaust: Philosophy and its Defense System. Watson, James R.

Why Philosophy for Children Now?. Kennedy, David.

Why Philosophy of Art in Cross-Cultural Perspectives?. Moravcsik, Julius.

Why Spinoza Had No Aesthetics. Morrison, J C.

Wittgenstein and the End of Philosophy?. Jolley, Kelly D.

Women Philosophers in Antiquity. Leuven, Lienke.

Women Philosophers in the Middle Ages. Leuven, Lienke.

Works by Renato Treves. Velicogna, Nella Gridelli and Segre, Vera.

Yan Fu's Philosophy of Evolution and the Thought of Lao Zi and Zhuang Zi. Dayong, Yang.

Young Kids Search for the Philosophers' Stone. Neave, Phillippa.

'Denken über Ideologie': eine praktische Begründung der Erneuerung der post-sowjetischen Philosophie?. Swiderski, E M.

'Place' in Context in Theophrastus, Fortenbaugh, W W (ed). Algra, Keimpe.

PHILOSOPHY OF EDUCATION

see Education

PHILOSOPHY OF HISTORY

see History

PHILOSOPHY OF LANGUAGE

see Language

PHILOSOPHY OF LAW

see Law

PHILOSOPHY OF MIND

see Mind

PHILOSOPHY OF RELIGION

see Religion

PHILOSOPHY OF SCIENCE

see Science

PHOTOGRAPHY

André Bazin on Automatically Made Images. Brubaker, David.

Frontiers of Utopia: Past and Present. Marin, Louis.

Looking at Art Through Photographs. Savedoff, Barbara.

McTaggart at the Movies. Currie, Gregory.

Photography. Levin, Thomas Y (trans) and Kracauer, Siegfried.

Photography, Painting and Perception. Currie, Gregory.

Scruton and Reasons for Looking at Photographs. King, William L.

Talbot's Technologies: Photographic Depiction, Detection, and Reproduction. Maynard, Patrick L.

The Third Man. Davidson, Donald.

Transforming Images: Photographs of Representations. Savedoff, Barbara.

PHRONESIS

The Place of Phronesis in Postomdern Hermeneutics. Gallagher, Shaun.

PHYSICAL

Lawlikeness. Lange, Marc.

Reconstruction from Recollection and the Refutation of Idealism: A Kantian Theme in the *Aufbau*. Webb, Judson.

Substances, Physical Systems, and Quantum Mechanics in Advances in Scientific Philosophy, Schurz, Gerhard (ed). Scheibe, Erhard.

PHYSICAL OBJECT

Some Remarks on the Object of Physical Knowledge. Nelson, Ralph (trans) and Simon, Yves R.

PHYSICAL REALITY

La relazione di connessione in A N Whitehead: aspetti matematici. Gerla, Giangiacomo and Tortora, Roberto.

The Theories of Relativity and Einstein's Philosophical Turn. Katsumori, Makoto.

PHYSICAL RESEARCH

Het visuele argument in de 'psychical research'. Draaisma, Douwe.

PHYSICAL SYSTEM

Substances, Physical Systems, and Quantum Mechanics in Advances in Scientific Philosophy, Schurz, Gerhard (ed). Scheibe, Erhard.

PHYSICAL THEORY

A Reappraisal of Duhem's Conception of Scientific Progress. Baigrie, Brian S.

Duhem et l'atomisme. Maiocchi, Roberto.

Measurement and Principles: The Structure of Physical Theories. Kremer-Marietti, Angèle.

To Save the Phenomena: Duhem on Galileo. Finocchiaro, M A.

PHYSICALISM

Mental Causation. Heil, John (ed) and Mele, Alfred (ed).

Metaphysics of Consciousness. Seager, William.

New Horizons in the Philosophy of Science. Lamb, David (ed).

Acquaintance with Qualia. Bigelow, John and Pargetter, Robert.

Adding Potential to a Physical Theory of Causation. Zangari, Mark.

Confirmation and the Computational Paradigm (Or: Why Do You Think They Call It *Artificial* Intelligence?). Buller, David J.

Design and the Anthropic Principle. Leslie, John.

Drawing the Boundary between Subject and Object: Comments on the Mind-Brain Problem. Rosen, Robert.

Naturalism and the Mental. Tye, Michael.

Nothing Like Experience. Mellor, D H.

On Leaving Out What It's Like in Consciousness: Psychological and Philosophical Essays, Davies, Martin (ed). Levine, Joseph.

Once Again on the Meaning of Physical Concepts in Greek Studies in the Philosophy and History of Science, Nicolacopoulos, Pantelis (ed). Baltas, Aristides.

Outstanding Problems: Replies to ZiF Critics. Elgin, Catherine Z.

Physicalism, Consciousness and the Antipathetic Fallacy. Papineau, David.

Post-physicalism and Beyond. Vaden House, D and McDonald, Marvin J.

Revisionary Physicalism. Bickle, John.

Some Problems for Fodor's Theory of Content. Myin, Erik.

Tarski's Physicalism. Kirkham, Richard L.

The Recent Case Against Physicalist Theories of Mind in New Horizons in the Philosophy of Science, Lamb, David (ed). Smith, Joseph Wayne.

Thinking Causes in Mental Causation, Heil, John (ed). Davidson, Donald.

Why I Am Not a Physicalist. Kwame, Safro.

PHYSICIAN

Drawing the Line: Life, Death, and Ethical Choices in an American Hospital. Gorovitz, Samuel.

Feminist Perspectives In Medical Ethics. Holmes, Helen Bequaert (ed) and Purdy, Laura M.

Life and Death: Philosophical Essays in Biomedical Ethics. Brock, Dan W.

The Body in Medical Thought and Practice. Leder, Drew (ed).

The Meaning of Illness: A Phenomenological Account of the Different Perspectives of Physician and Patient. Toombs, S Kay.

A Response to a Purported Ethical Difficulty with Randomized Clinical Trials Involving Cancer Patients. Freedman, Benjamin.

Caveats Regarding Slippery Slopes and Physicians' Moral Conscience. Howe, Edmund G.

Conscience, Referral, and Physician Assisted Suicide. Wildes, Kevin W.

Consent, Ethics, and Community. Loewy, Erich H.

Coping With Ambiguity and Uncertainty in Patient- Physician Relationships: II — Traditio Argumentum Respectus. Rodning, Charles B.

Courting Euthanasia? Tony Bland and the Law Lords. Keown, John.

Definitions of Personhood: Implications for the Care of PVS Patients. Gormally, Luke.

Do Physicians Make Too Much Money?. Curzer, Howard J.

Doctors Must Not Kill. Pellegrino, Edmund.

Doentes, Doença, Médicos e Medicina em Luciano de Samósata. Brandao, Jacynthos Lins.

Double Agency and the Ethics of Rationing Health Care: A Response to Marcia Angell. Menzel, Paul T.

Healing and Killing, Harming and Not Harming: Physician Participation in Euthanasia and Capital Punishment. Loewy, Erich H.

Obtaining Consent from the Family: A Horizon for Clinical Ethics. Spinsanti, Sandro.

Physician Assisted Death and Hard Choices. Mayo, David J and Gunderson, Martin.

Physician-Assisted Dying: Theory and Reality. Meier, Diane E.

Physicians and the American Armed Forces in Biomedical Ethics Reviews 1992, Humber, James M (ed). Elfstrom, Gerard A.

Should Physicians Be Bayesian Agents?. Cooper, M Wayne.

Slippery Slopes and Moral Reasoning. Devettere, Raymond.

The Characteristics of a Valid "Empirical" Slippery-Slope Argument. Ozar, David.

The Doctor as Double Agent. Angell, Marcia.

The Ethics of HIV Testing by Physicians. Murphy, Timothy F.

The Many Faces of Autonomy. Yeide Jr, Harry.

The Mercy Argument for Euthanasia: Some Logical Considerations. Walton, Richard E.

The Physician, the Family, and the Truth. Cattorini, Paolo and Reichlin, Massimo.

The Slippery-Slope Argument. Van Der Burg, Wibren.

The Slippery-Slope Argument Reconstructed: Response to Van Der Burg. Freedman, Benjamin.

What is the Moral Basis of the Authority of Family Members to Act as Surrogates for Incompetent Patients?. Brock, Dan W.

Why Aren't More Doctors Phenomenologists? in The Body in Medical Thought and Practice, Leder, Drew (ed). Baron, Richard J.

PHYSICS

see also Psychophysics

Discovering Philosophy. White, Thomas I.

Essays in Quasi-Realism. Blackburn, Simon W.

Greek Studies in the Philosophy and History of Science. Nicolacopoulos, Pantelis (ed).

Homo Metaphisicus. Pezzimenti, Rocco.

New Horizons in the Philosophy of Science. Lamb, David (ed).

Philosophy of Physics. Sklar, Lawrence.

Physikai doxai et problemata physica d'Aristote à Aétius (et au-delà). Mansfeld, Jaap.

Revolution and Continuity. Barker, Peter (ed) and Ariew, Roger (ed).

Search for a Naturalistic World View: Volume I. Shimony, Abner.

The Impulse to Philosophise. Griffiths, A Phillips (ed).

PLURALISM

The Idea of Democracy. Copp, David (ed), Hampton, Jean (ed) and Roemer, John E (ed).

The Morality of Pluralism. Kekes, John.

The Pluralistic Philosophy of Stephen Crane. Dooley, Patrick K.

The Quality of Life. Nussbaum, Martha C (ed) and Sen, Amartya (ed).

Towards a Phenomenological Ethics: Ethos and the Life-World. Marx, Werner.

Ulysses and Vacuous Pluralism. Herman, David.

Value in Ethics and Economics. Anderson, Elizabeth.

A Monistic Interpretation of Whitehead's Creativity. Wilcox, John R.

A 'Counterfactualist' Four-Dimensional Theory of Power. Carter, Alan.

Against Pluralism. Hazen, A P.

Against Polemics, For Disarming Communication. Arcilla, René.

Beyond Universalism and Relativism. Procee, Henk.

Civilization and Its Dissents: Moral Pluralism and Political Order. Crosby, Donald A.

Commentator on 'Pluralism and the Standard of Living' in The Quality of Life, Nussbaum, Martha C (ed). Parfit, Derek.

Confucianism as Political Philosophy: A Postmodern Perspective. Jung, Hwa Yol.

Culture and Rationality: An Interpretation. Roy, Krishna.

Democracy, Difference, and Re-Cognition. Wolin, Sheldon S.

Difference and Domination: Reflections on the Relation Between Pluralism and Equality. Carens, Joseph H.

Discourse or Moral Action? A Critique of Postmodernism. Beyer, Landon E and Liston, Daniel P.

Doctrines and the Virtues of Doctrine: The Problematic of Religious Plurality. Griffiths, Paul J.

El legado categorial de la ciencia griega presocrática. Céspedes, Guillermo Coronado.

Eliminative Pluralism. Ereshefsky, Marc.

From Triangles to Tripods: Polycentrism in Environmental Ethics. Rabb, J Douglas.

Habermas and Pluralist Political Theory. Walker, Brian.

How Determinism Refutes Compatibilism. Settle, Thomas W.

In Praise of True Pluralism. Harris, Wendell V.

Justice, Gender and International Boundaries in International Justice and the Third World, Attfield, Robin (ed). O'Neill, Onora.

Kuhn's Paradigms and Neoclassical Economics. Argyrous, George.

Liberal Discourse and Ethical Pluralism: An Educational Agenda. Strike, Kenneth.

Metaphysical Pluralism. Price, Huw.

Metaphysics and the Good Life: Some Reflections on the Further Point of Morality. Staley, Kevin.

Minimal, Moderate, and Extreme Moral Pluralism. Wenz, Peter.

Moral Pluralism. Gaut, Berys.

Moral Pluralism and Democracy. Galvin, Richard F.

Moral Pluralism and Political Consensus in The Idea of Democracy, Copp, David (ed). Cohen, Joshua.

Moral Pluralism, Intellectual Virtue, and Academic Culture in Moral Education and the Liberal Arts, Mitias, Michael H (ed). Gouinlock, James.

Morality and Cooperation. Korthals, Michiel.

Naturalized Philosophy of Science with a Plurality of Methods. Stump, David.

On Not Being Ashamed of the Gospel: Particularity, Pluralism, and Validation. Yoder, John Howard.

On Plural Reference and Elementary Set Theory. Cartwright, Helen Morris.

Outstanding Problems: Replies to ZiF Critics. Elgin, Catherine Z.

Philosophical Specialization and General Philosophy. O'Connor, David.

Philosophische Zeitdiagnose im Zeichen des Postmodernismus. Ollig, Hans-Ludwig.

Plantinga, Epistemic Permissiveness, and Metaphysical Pluralism. Christian, Rose Ann.

Pluralism and Equality: The Status of Minority Values in a Democracy. Simon, Robert L.

Pluralism and the Priority of Right (in Chinese). Lin, Huo-wang.

Pluralism and the Problem of God in God, Values, and Empiricism, Peden, Creighton W (ed). Dean, William.

Pluralism and the Standard of Living in The Quality of Life, Nussbaum, Martha C (ed). Seabright, Paul.

Pluralism for Education: An Ethics of Care Perspective. Diller, Ann.

Pluralism in Environmental Ethics. Marietta Jr, Don E.

Polishness in a Universalistic Perspective: Pluralism— Dialogue— Synthesis. Kuczynski, Janusz.

Pragmatism and Pluralism. Singer, Beth.

Radicalizing Pluralism. Thompson, Audrey.

Religious Pluralism and the Ground of Religious Faith in Logic, God and Metaphysics, Harris, James F (ed). Long, Eugene T.

Religious Pluralism and the Rationality of Religious Belief. Hick, John.

Religious Story, Religious Truth, Religious Pluralism: A Prolegomenon to Religious Faith. Lauder, Robert.

Respect for Other Religions: A Christian Antidote to Colonialist Discourse. Tanner, Kathryn.

Richard Rorty's Failed Politics. Haber, Honi.

Rootedness: Culture and Value in Simone Weil's Philosophy of Culture, Bell, Richard H (ed). Springsted, Eric.

Rorty on Derrida in Ethics and Danger, Dallery, Arleen B (ed). Bell, Roger.

Secession: The Caes of Quebec. Nielsen, Kai.

Some Philosophical Problems Concerning Culture and Rationality. Bhattacharyya, Sibajiban.

Some Problems in Recent Pragmatism. Rockmore, Tom.

Teología y pluralismo teológico en Etienne Gilson. Moya Obradors, Pedro Javier.

The Challenge of Multiculturalism in Political Ethics. Gutmann, Amy.

The Creolization of Liberalism. Bull, Barry L.

The Demise of the Confessional State and the Rise of the Idea of a Legitimate Minority. Heim, Joseph Charles.

The Democratic Solution to Ethnic Pluralism. Singer, Beth.

The Diverse Styles of Social Pluralism. Milligan, Charles S.

The Incompatibility of Liberalism and Pluralism. Kekes, John.

The Intolerance of Religious Pluralism. Donovan, Peter.

The Limits of Aristotelian Ethics. Larmore, Charles.

The Limits of Theistic Experience: An Epistemic Basis of Theistic Pluralism. McLeod, Mark S.

The Many Faces of Autonomy. Yeide Jr, Harry.

The Moral Commitments of Liberalism in The Idea of Democracy, Copp, David (ed). Hampton, Jean.

The Pluralistic Hypothesis, Realism, and Post-Eschatology. Heim, S Mark.

The Priesthood of Bioethics and the Return of Casuistry. Wildes, Kevin W.

Thinking about Democracy and Exclusion: Jurgen Habermas' *Theory of Communicative Action* and Contemporary Politics. Hanks, Craig.

Viewpoints: Body, Spirit, and Democracy in Revisioning Philosophy, Ogilvy, James (ed). Johnson, Don Hanlon.

What is an Anlogical Imagination?. Conradie, Ernst.

Will Aesthetics Be the Last Stronghold of Marxism. Khanin, Dmitry.

PLURALITY

Pluralità delle culture e universalità del diritto. Calogero, F.

Soggettività e metafisica. Chiereghin, Franco.

POCOCK, J

Critical Response to "Machiavelli's Sisters" by Linda Zerilli. Brodribb, Somer.

Machiavelli's Momentary "Machiavellian Moment": A Reconsideration of Pocock's Treatment of the *Discourses*. Sullivan, Vickie B.

PODPADEC, T

Continuing the Dialogue on Measuring the Quality of Life in Philosophy and Psychology. Anstötz, Christoph.

POET

Kierkegaard: Poet of the Religious in Kierkegaard on Art and Communication, Pattison, George (ed). Walsh, Sylvia.

POETICS

Poetic Truth and Transvaluation in Nietzsche's Zarathustra: A Hermeneutic Study. Joós, Ernest.

Theorizing American Literature. Cowan, Bainard (ed) and Kronick, Joseph G (ed).

Aesop's Lessons in Literary Realism. Skillen, Anthony.

Crates on Poetic Criticism. Asmis, Elizabeth.

Jan Patocka et le phénomène de l'écriture littéraire. Declève, Henri.

La forme du mouvement (sur la notion de rythme). Bourassa, Lucie.

Poetics, Theory, and the Defense of History: Philippe Carrard, *Poetics of the New History*. Carroll, David.

The Question of the End of Art and the Poetic Character of the World (in Czechoslovakian). Axelos, K.

Thresholds of the Sign in Theorizing American Literature, Cowan, Bainard (ed). Riddel, Joseph N.

Tradition and the Indian Writer. Parthasarathy, R.

POETRY

"Liebe, die im Geist mir redet...": Dantes Dame Philosophie. Splett, Jörg.

Hans-Georg Gadamer on Education, Poetry, and History: Applied Hermeneutics. Misgeld, Dieter (ed) and Nicholson, Graeme (ed).

Kant's Latin Writings (Second Edition). Beck, Lewis W.

Mathesis e costruzione tra geometria antica e moderna. Ferrarin, Alfredo.

T S Eliot and American Philosophy: The Harvard Years. Jain, Manju.

The Birth to Presence. Nancy, Jean-Luc.

The Essays—Francis Bacon. Bacon, Francis and Pitcher, John (ed).

The Poetics of Alfarabi and Avicenna. Kemal, Salim.

A Plea for the Poetic Metaphor. Muscari, Paul G.

Amore per la parola (Antologia). Splett, Jörg.

An Academy Inscription: A Retracted Exile? Poetry and *Republic* 614b2. Brumbaugh, Robert.

Appearance in Poetry: Lyric Illusion? in Aesthetic Illusion, Burwick, Frederick (ed). Thomke, Hellmut.

Being Interested in Time: Autobiography and Repetition. Dupuy, Edward J.

Crates on Poetic Criticism. Asmis, Elizabeth.

Da Tebe ad Atene e da Atene a Tebe. Caramuta, Ersilia.

Frail Memorials: "Essays Upon Epitaphs" and Wordsworth's Economy of Reference. Brigham, Linda C.

Headaches of Headless: Who is Poet Enough?. Stratton, Teri.

I poeti nel tempo della povertà. Mazzarella, Arturo.

Inspiration and *Mimēsis* in Plato. Murray, Penelope.

Philosophical Plumbing. Midgley, Mary.

Plato and the New Rhapsody. Baltzly, Dirk.

Plato on Poetic Creativity in The Cambridge Companion to Plato, Kraut, Richard (ed). Asmis, Elizabeth.

Poesia e verità: Lettere a Clotilde Marghieri. Scaravelli, Luigi.

Poetizing and Thinking in Heidegger's Thought. O'Connor, Tony.

S T Coleridge: El papel de la imaginación en el acto creador. Fonseca, Clotilde.

Santayana's Whitman Revisited. Tejera, V.

Seeing Blake's Illuminated Texts. Bigwood, Carol.

Six Theories in the Bedroom of The Dead. Garrett, Roland.

Six Variations in Isaiah Berlin: A Celebration, Margalit, Edna (ed). Spender, Stephen.

POLITICAL PHIL

Hobbes on Opinion, Private Judgment and Civil War. Lund, William R.

Jacob Burckhardt's Liberal-Conservatism. Sigurdson, Richard.

John Locke, Natural Law and Colonialism. Arneil, Barbara.

John Rawls' Ethical Foundations of Politics: A Critical Approach (in Dutch). Devos, Rob.

Kant's Idealization of the Republic (in French). Bergeois, B.

Kant, Arendt e il giudizio politico. Colonnello, P.

Killing, Confiscating, and Banishing at *Gorgias* 466-468. Weiss, Roslyn.

L'assassin d'Ulysse. Leroux, François.

L'État, le mythe, les totalitarismes. DeLaunay, Marc B.

L'homme exorbité: Réflexion sur la notion de fatique culturelle chez Hubert Aquin. Jacques, Daniel.

La fonction du droit et la question du lien social chez Hume et Montesquieu. Autin, Pierre-Louis.

La fondation des lois civiles. Goyard-Fabre, Simone.

La question du libre arbitre en France, de la Révolution à la Restauration. Baertschi, Bernard.

La résurgence de l'aristotélisme de la Renaissance dans la philosophie politique de Cassirer. Rudolph, Enno.

La 'Déclaration des droits de l'homme et du citoyen' (1789). Stucki, Pierre-André.

Le "déprimé explosif". Morin, Michel.

Le chemin de l'immanence. Couture, Yves.

Le statut du serment et de la promesse dans la Déclaration des Droits de 1789. Fauré, Christine.

Leituras de Barthes: II—Compromiso discreto, luita contínua. Soto, Luis García.

Lenin's Reformulation of Marxism: The Colonial Question as a National Question. Seth, Sanjay.

Lenin, Hegel and Western Marxism: From the 1920s to 1953. Anderson, Kevin.

Locke against Democracy: Consent, Representation and Suffrage in the *Two Treatises*. Wood, E M.

Maritain on "the Common Good": Reflections on the Concept. Kalumba, Kibujjo M.

Marx—From the Abolition of Labour to the Abolition of the Abolition of Labour. Cohen, Avner.

Marxism Today: An Interview with István Mészáros. Arthur, Chris and McCarney, Joseph.

Mass Torts and Moral Principles. Strudler, Alan.

Mein philosophischer Ausgangspunkt. Nishitani, Keiji.

Misunderstanding the Democratic 'We': Richard Rorty's Liberalism and the Radical Urge for a Philosophical Foundation. Moussa, Mario.

Moralität und Frieden: Kants Gesetz der Freiheit in der Welt der Staaten. Römpp, Georg.

Nationalism and Nations (in Dutch). Van De Putte, A.

Natural Law and Positive Law: Forever Irresolvable? Discussion. Black, Virginia (ed).

Neuere nordamerikanische Arbeiten über Kants Rechts-und politische Philosophie. Cavallar, Georg.

New "True" Socialism. Baxter, David.

Nietzsche, Spengler, and the Politics of Cultural Despair. Farrenkopf, John.

Pacifying Politics: Resistance, Violence, and Accountability in Seventeenth-Century Contract THeory. Baumgold, Deborah.

Paternalismus. Wolf, Jean-Claude.

Persönliche Freiheitsrechte in Polen. Kedzia, Zdzislaw.

Philosophy and Nationalism. Hejdánek, L.

Philosophy Beyond the Limits of Politics (in Dutch). Heyde, L.

Pierre Teilhard de Chardin und die ökologische Frage. Modler, Peter.

Political Equality. Christiano, Thomas.

Politique, morale et droit: Enjeux autour de la reproduction humaine et de l'avortement. Hudon, Edith D-R.

Polybius and His Theory of *Anacyclosis* Problems of Not Just Ancient Political Theory. Podes, Stephan.

Positive Law Versus Natural Law—A Comment in Response to Percy Black—Natural Law and Positive Law: Forever Irresolvable?. Bjarup, Jes.

Positivism and Natural Law: A "Reconciliation". Shiner, R A.

Postmetaphysics and Democracy. Dallmayr, Fred.

Power and Wealth in a Competitive Capitalist Economy. Bowles, Samuel and Gintis, Herbert.

Power Rivalry-Motivated Democracy: A Response to Stephen Krasner. Gilbert, Alan.

Public Choice Versus Democracy. Hardin, Russell.

Re-Reading Soviet Philosophy: Bakhurst on Ilyenkov. Larvor, Brendan.

Reinhold Niebuhr and the Ethics of Realism in International Relations. Rich, Paul.

Reply to George Allan's "Environmental Philosophizing and Environmental Activism". Durbin, Paul T.

République et Régicide chez Kant. Beyssade, M Jean-Marie.

Responsibility, Reactive Attitudes, and Liberalism in Philosophy and Politics. Scheffler, Samuel.

Rights and Majorities: Rousseau Revisited. Waldron, Jeremy.

Rousseau's Socraticism: The Political Bearing of "On Theatrical Imitation". Sorenson, Leonard R.

Rousseauisme et jacobinisme: l'idéal de "l'honnête médiocrité". Roy, Jean.

Russia's Movement Toward a Market Civilization and the Russian National Character. Smirnov, P I.

Self-Defeating Civic Republicanism. Christodoulidis, Emilios A.

Sobre la legitimidad de la conquista de América: Las Casas y Sepúlveda. Muller, Alfredo Gómez.

Socrates' Two Concepts of the Polis. Yonezawa, Shigeru.

Soviet Philosophy in Transition: An Interview with Vladislav Lektorsky. Bakhurst, David.

Sympathie et individualité dans la philosophie politique de David Hume. Brahami, Frédéric.

T H Green's 'Analysis of Hegel'. Jakubowski, Marek N.

The "Living Center" of Martin Buber's Political Theory. Avnon, Dan.

The *Education of Cyrus* as Xenophon's "Statesman". Ray, John.

The Basis for Recoghnition of Human Rights. Duquette, David A.

The Cards of Confusion: Reflections on Historical Communism at the 'End of History'. Elliott, Gregory.

The Demise of the Confessional State and the Rise of the Idea of a Legitimate Minority. Heim, Joseph Charles.

The Early Phase in Spengler's Political Philosophy. Farrenkopf, John.

The First Crisis of Modernity: Leo Strauss on the Thought of Rousseau. Gildin, Hilail.

The law of War: Grotius, Sidney, Locke and the Political Theory of Rebellion. Scott, Jonathan.

The Methodological Compatibility of Natural Law Theory and Legal Positivism. Magtrayo, Carlos R.

The Morality of Law and Economics. Hardin, Russell.

The Nation: From Nationalism to Post-national Identity (in Dutch). De Wachter, F.

The New World Order and the Public Trust. Brown, Peter G.

The Philosopher's Interest. Vernezze, Peter.

The Possibility of Post-Socialist Politics. Bohman, James F.

The Poverty of Indian Political Theory. Parekh, Bhikhu.

The Radical Dimensions of Locke's Political Thought: A Dialogic Essay on the Problems of Interpretation. Ashcraft, Richard.

The Tagore-Gandhi Controversy Revisited, I. Singh, Ajay and Singh, Shakuntala.

The Unanimity Standard. Kagan, Shelly.

The Wisdom of the Many: An Analysis of the Arguments of Books III and IV of Aristotle's *Politics*. Bookman, J T.

Theorizing about Responsibility and Criminal Liability. Baker, Brenda M.

Thinking about Democracy and Exclusion: Jurgen Habermas' *Theory of Communicative Action* and Contemporary Politics. Hanks, Craig.

Three Fallacies Concerning Majorities, Minorities, and Democratic Politics. Shapiro, Ian.

Tra 'kratos' e 'petsis': La funzione della legge in Platone. Piscione, E.

Transcendent Man in the Limited City: The Political Philosophy of Charles N R McCoy. Schall, James V.

Twenty Years Before the End of the World: Political Remarks About the Meaning of Our Epoch. Dzarasov, Ruslan.

Two Hundred Years of Error? The Politics of Democracy. Howard, Dick.

Tyranny: Ancient and Modern. Bradshaw, Leah.

Un libro tedesco su Gramsci. Maggi, Michele.

Virtue, Commerce and Moderation in the 'Tale of the Troglodytes': Montesquieu's *Persian Letters*. Desserud, Donald A.

What is Alive and What is Dead in Marx and Marxism. Nielsen, Kai.

Why John Stuart Mill Called Himself a Socialist. Ottow, Raimund.

Why Legal Positivism Cannot Be Proved to Be True. Ott, Walter.

Why Punish the Deserving?. Husak, Douglas N.

POLITICAL SCIENCE

Validities: A Political Science Perspective. Beer, Francis A.

POLITICAL THEORY

Essays on Kant's Political Philosophy. Williams, Howard (ed).

From Marx to Mises. Steele, David Ramsay.

Hannah Arendt: A Reinterpretation of Her Political Thought. Canovan, Margaret.

Interpreting Tocqueville's "Democracy in America". Masugi, Ken (ed).

John Dewey and American Democracy. Westbrook, Robert B.

Justice and Interpretation. Warnke, Georgia.

La Comparution/The Compearance: From the Existence of "Communism" to the Community of "Existence". Nancy, Jean-Luc and Strong, Tracy B (trans).

Liberalism and Modern Society: A Historical Argument. Bellamy, Richard.

Modern Political Theory and Contemporary Feminism: A Dialectical Analysis. Ring, Jennifer.

Moral Boundaries: A Political Argument for an Ethic of Care. Tronto, Joan C.

Politica Sacra et Civilis—George Lawson. Lawson, George and Condren, Conal (ed).

Political Theory and Postmodernism. White, Stephen K.

Risks and Wrongs. Coleman, Jules L.

Secession: The Morality of Political Divorce from Fort Sumter to Lithuania and Quebec. Buchanan, Allen.

Terrorism, Justice and Social Values. Peden, W Creighton (ed) and Hudson, Yeager (ed).

The Balance of Consciousness: Eric Voegelin's Political Theory. Keulman, Kenneth.

The Dialogue of Justice: Towards a Self-Reflective Society. Fishkin, James S.

The Ethical Foundations of Hume's Theory of Politics. Kolin, Andrew.

The Idea of Democracy. Copp, David (ed), Hampton, Jean (ed) and Roemer, John E (ed).

The Logic of Marx's "Capital": Replies to Hegelian Criticisms. Smith, Tony.

The Morality of Pluralism. Kekes, John.

The Revision of Psychoanalysis—Eric Fromm. Fromm, Erich.

A Critique of the Liberal Discourse on Violence in Socialism and Morality, McLellan, David (ed). Parekh, Bhikhu.

A Political and Economic Case for the Democratic Enterprise. Bowles, Samuel and Gintis, Herbert.

A Response to Zerilli and Brodribb. Pocock, J G A.

A Retrospective on the Political Theory of George Armstrong Kelly: *The Humane Comedy: Constant, Tocqueville and French Liberalism*. Riley, Patrick.

PLURALISM

Citizenship and Equality: The Place for Toleration. Galeotti, Anna Elisabetta.

Constituting Democracy in The Idea of Democracy, Copp, David (ed). Gauthier, David.

Contemporary Aristotelianism. Wallach, John R.

Contexte des rapports intellectuels entre Hobbes et Locke. Rogers, John.

Conversations with Phocion: The Political Thought of Mably. Wright, J K.

Defending Hegel from Kant in Essays on Kant's Political Philosophy, Williams, Howard Lloyd (ed). Smith, Steven B.

Defensible Anarchy?. Harriott, Howard.

Does Aristotle's Political Theory Rest on a 'Blunder'?. Chan, Joseph.

Electoral Power, Group Power, and Democracy. Levine, Andrew.

Filmer, Hobbes, Locke: Les cassures dans l'espace de la théorie politique. Lessay, Franck.

Functioning and Capability: The Foundations of Sen's and Nussbaum's Development Ethic. Crocker, David A.

Habermas and Pluralist Political Theory. Walker, Brian.

Hegel's Justification of Hereditary Monarchy. Tunick, M.

Hume's Critique of the Contract Theory. Buckle, S and Castiglione, D.

Idealist Organicism: Beyond Holism and Individualism. Simhony, A.

Integrity and Disrespect: Principles of a Conception of Morality Based on the Theory of Recognition. Honneth, Axel.

Is Reflective Equilibrium a Coherentist Model?. Ebertz, Roger.

John Stuart Mill's Liberal Feminism. Donner, Wendy.

Liberals, Communitarians, and Political Theory. Allen, Jonathan.

Locke, Taxation and Reform: A Reply to Wood. Hughes, Martin.

Looking at Carl Schmitt from the Vantage Point of the 1990s. Herz, John H.

Pluralism and Equality: The Status of Minority Values in a Democracy. Simon, Robert L.

Political Rhetoric as Political Theory in Terrorism, Justice and Social Values, Peden, Creighton W (ed). Geise, Jack P.

Political Theory and Political Education. Esquith, Stephen L.

Polybius and His Theory of Anacyclosis Problems of Not Just Ancient Political Theory. Podes, Stephan.

Public Policy and Environmental Risk. Gillroy, John Martin.

Relativism: The Return of the Repressed. Gunnell, John G.

Restoration Romanticism. Tamás, G M.

Rethinking Tradition in Essays on Henry Sidgwick, Schultz, Bart (ed). Kloppenberg, James T.

Rousseau and the Problem of Community: Nationalism, Civic Virtue, Totalitarianism. Simon-Ingram, Julia.

Science, Prudence, and Folly in Hobbes's Political Theory. Hanson, Donald W.

Social Criticism After Rawls. Couture, Tony.

Socialism, Utopianism and the 'Utopian Socialists'. Lovell, David W.

Socrates' Two Concepts of the Polis. Yonezawa, Shigeru.

Soviet Philosophy in Transition: An Interview with Vladislav Lektorsky. Bakhurst, David.

The "Living Center" of Martin Buber's Political Theory. Avnon, Dan.

The Authentic Tele of Politics: A Reading of Aristotle. Swazo, N K.

The Context of Community. Alexander, Thomas M.

The Demise of the Confessional State and the Rise of the Idea of a Legitimate Minority. Heim, Joseph Charles.

The Ideological Commitment of Locke: Freemen and Servants in the Two Treatises of Government. Becker, Ron.

The law of War: Grotius, Sidney, Locke and the Political Theory of Rebellion. Scott, Jonathan.

The Night in Which All Cows are Black: Ethical Absolutism in Plato and Hegel. Browning, Gary K.

The Poverty of Indian Political Theory. Parekh, Bhikhu.

The Radical Dimensions of Locke's Political Thought: A Dialogic Essay on the Problems of Interpretation. Ashcraft, Richard.

The Realism of Moralism: The Political Philosophy of Istvan Bibo. Berki, R N.

The Revolution in the Concept of Politics. Viroli, Maurizio.

The Unanimity Standard. Kagan, Shelly.

The Unity of Plato's Political Thought. Shiell, Timothy C.

Two Concepts of Liberty in Isaiah Berlin: A Celebration, Margalit, Edna (ed). Dworkin, Ronald.

Virtue, Commerce and Moderation in the 'Tale of the Troglodytes': Montesquieu's Persian Letters. Desserud, Donald A.

Vulgar Liberalism. Neal, Patrick.

'Ought' and Well-being. Gillett, Grant.

POLITICS

"Teacher Thinking, Teacher Change, and the 'Capricious Seamstress'"—A Response. Greene, Maxine.

"Young Hegelian" Richard Rorty and the "Foucauldian Left". Cutrofello, Andrew.

"An Essay on the Principle of Population"—T R Malthus. Winch, Donald (ed) and Malthus, T R.

"The Commonwealth of Oceana" and "A System of Politics"—James Harrington. Pocock, J G A (ed) and Harrington, James.

A Companion to Contemporary Political Philosophy. Goodin, Robert E (ed) and Pettit, Philip (ed).

A Dictionary of Philosophical Quotations. O'Grady, Jane (ed) and Ayer, A J (ed).

Aesthetic Judgment and the Moral Image of the World: Studies in Kant. Henrich, Dieter.

An Approach to Political Philosophy: Locke in Contexts. Tully, James.

An Inquiry Into the Nature and Causes of the Wealth of Nations—Adam Smith. Smith, Adam.

An Introductory Guide to Cultural Theory and Popular Culture. Storey, John.

Analytical and Dialectical Marxism. Hunt, Ian.

Anthropologische Geschichtsphilosophie: Für eine Philosophie der Geschichte in der Zeit der Postmoderne. Ignatow, Assen.

Antologia della filosofia cinese. Arena, Leonardo Vittorio.

Antonio Gramsci: Beyond Marxism and Postmodernism. Holub, Renate.

Beyond Equality and Difference. Bock, Gisela (ed) and James, Susan (ed).

Bodies that Matter: On the Discursive Limits of 'Sex'. Butler, Judith.

British Empiricism and American Pragmatism: New Directions and Neglected Arguments. Roth, Robert.

Compassionate Authority: Democracy and the Representation of Women. Jones, Kathleen B.

Contemporary Political Culture. Gibbins, John R (ed).

Cultural-Political Interventions in the Unfinished Project of Enlightenment. Honneth, Axel (& other eds).

Culture and Democracy: Social and Ethical Issues in Public Support for the Arts and Humanities. Buchwalter, Andrew.

Democracy and Complexity: A Realist Approach. Zolo, Danilo and McKie, David (trans).

Dialectical Investigations. Ollman, Bertell.

Dirty Hands: The Problem of Political Morality. Buckler, Steve.

Engenderings: Constructions of Knowledge, Authority, and Privilege. Scheman, Naomi.

Ethics and Danger. Dallery, Arleen B (ed), Scott, Charles E (ed) and Roberts, P Holley (ed).

Ethics and Politics. Paton, Calum.

Ethics and the Environment. Hart, Richard E (ed).

Frames of Deceit: A Study of the Loss and Recovery of Public and Private Trust. Johnson, Peter.

G A Rauche: Selected Philosophical Papers. Louw, T J G.

Gender Politics and Post-Communism: Reflections from Eastern Europe and the Former Soviet Union. Funk, Nanette (ed) and Mueller, Magda (ed).

Hannah Arendt: A Reinterpretation of Her Political Thought. Canovan, Margaret.

Hans-Georg Gadamer on Education, Poetry, and History: Applied Hermeneutics. Misgeld, Dieter (ed) and Nicholson, Graeme (ed).

Identity/Difference: Democratic Negotiations of Political Paradox. Connolly, William E.

Ideology: An Introduction. Eagleton, Terry.

Injustice and Restitution: The Ordinance of Time. Ross, Stephen D.

Invitation to Philosophy: Issues and Options (Sixth Edition). Honer, Stanley M, Hunt, Thomas C and Okholm, Dennis L.

Judging in Good Faith. Burton, Steven J.

Justice for an Unjust Society. Lötter, H P P.

Keeping Faith: Philosophy and Race in America. West, Cornell.

Leviathan—Thomas Hobbes. Hobbes, Thomas and MacPherson, C B (ed).

Liberalism and Modern Society: A Historical Argument. Bellamy, Richard.

Marxism Recycled. Van Parijs, Philippe.

Materialist Feminism and the Politics of Discourse. Hennessy, Rosemary.

Matrix and Line: Derrida and the Possibilities of Postmodern Social Theory. Martin, Bill.

Method—Towards a Study of Humankind, Volume I: The Nature of Nature. Morin, Edgar and Bélanger, J L Roland (trans).

Modern Political Theory and Contemporary Feminism: A Dialectical Analysis. Ring, Jennifer.

Moral Boundaries: A Political Argument for an Ethic of Care. Tronto, Joan C.

Morality, Prudence, and Nuclear Weapons. Lee, Steven.

Mythos and Logos in Platonic Politeiai. Freydberg, Bernard D.

Nietzsche's Case: Philosophy as/and Literature. Magnus, Bernd, Stewart, Stanley and Mileur, Jean-Pierre.

Nietzsche: The Politics of Power. Okonta, Ike.

Of Derrida, Heidegger, and Spirit. Wood, David (ed).

On Intersubjectivity and Cultural Creativity—Martin Buber. Eisenstadt, S N (ed) and Buber, Martin.

Peirce's Esthetics of Freedom: Possibility, Complexity, and Emergent Value. Kevelson, Roberta.

Philosophy and Theology in the Middle Ages. Evans, G R.

Political Liberalism. Rawls, John.

Political Theory and Postmodernism. White, Stephen K.

Politics, Gender, and Genre: The Political Thought of Christine de Pizan. Brabant, Margaret (ed).

Politics/Sense/Experience: A Pragmatic Inquiry into the Promise of Democracy. Kaufman-Osborn, Timothy V.

Post-Liberalism: Studies in Political Thought. Gray, John.

Postmodernism and Society. Boyne, Roy (ed) and Rattansi, Ali (ed).

Psychoanalysis, Mind and Art. Hopkins, Jim (ed) and Savile, Anthony (ed).

Radical Fragments. Marsh, James.

Reading Kristeva: Unraveling the Double-bind. Oliver, Kelly.

Reason and Responsibility (Eighth Edition). Feinberg, Joel.

Rethinking Masculinity. May, Larry (ed) and Strikwerda, Robert (ed).

Sartre Alive. Aronson, Ronald (ed) and Van Den Hoven, Adrian (ed).

Secession: The Morality of Political Divorce from Fort Sumter to Lithuania and Quebec. Buchanan, Allen.

Shadow of Spirit. Berry, Philippa (ed) and Wernick, Andrew (ed).

Sobre la Suposicion—Guillermo de Ockham. Ockham, Guillermo and Guerrero, Luis (ed).

POLITICS

Multiples: On the Contemporary Politics of Subjectivity. Flax, Jane.

Must We Say What "We" Means? The Politics of Postmodernism. Cutrofello, Andrew.

National Sovereignty and Ciceronian Political Thought: Aeneas Silvius Piccolomini and the Ideal of Universal Empire in Fifteenth-Century Europe. Nederman, Cary J.

Negative Campaigning. Wright, William A.

Neumann versus Habermas: The Frankfurt School and the Case of the Rule of Law. Scheuerman, Bill.

Not Exactly Politics or Power?. Lash, Nicholas.

Oakeshott and the Practice of Politics. Katzoff, Charlotte.

Obligaiton, Loyalty, Exile. Shklar, Judith N.

Of Lingering Eyes and Talking Things: Adorno and Deleuze on Philosophy Since Auschwitz. Toole, David.

Of Tennis, Persons and Politics. Springsted, Eric O.

On Castigating Constructivists. Phillips, D C.

On the Social Acceptability of Modern Technology: New Challenges for Politicians and Scientists in a World of Risks. Lompe, Klaus.

On the Three Major Characteristics of Ethical Thought in Traditional China. Gujia, Chen.

One or Two Worlds: Separation or Coexistence? (in Czechoslovakian). LeDoeuff, Michèle.

Orwell and the Anti-Realists. Clark, Stephen R L.

Our Longest Lie: Irrelgious Thoughts on the Relation Between Metaphysics and Politics. Kramer, Matthew H.

Philosophie transcendentale et praxis politique chez Fichte. Radrizzani, Ives.

Philosophy and Feminism: The Case of Susan Bordo. Bernick, Susan.

Picture Perfect: The Politics of Prenatal Testing. Kristol, Elizabeth.

Plato's Later Political Thought in The Cambridge Companion to Plato, Kraut, Richard (ed). Saunders, Trevor J.

Political Philosophy in Reflections on Philosophy, McHenry, Leemon (ed). Hooker, Brad.

Politics and Cuture in Cultural-Political Interventions in the Unfinished Project of Enlightenment, Honneth, Axel (& other eds). Eder, Klaus.

Politics and Religion. Graham, Gordon.

Politics and Religion in Kierkegaard's Thought in Foundations of Kierkegaard's Vision of Community, Connell, George B (ed). Nicoletti, Michele.

Politics and the Polis: How to Study Greek Moral and Political Philosophy. Euben, J Peter.

Politics and the Reconstruction in Cultural-Political Interventions in the Unfinished Project of Enlightenment, Honneth, Axel (& other eds). Cohen, Jean and Arato, Andrew.

Politics beyond Humanism in Working Through Derrida, Madison, Gary B (ed). Bernasconi, Robert.

Politics or Scholarship?. Friedman, Jeffrey.

Politics, Freedom, and Order in The Cambridge Companion to Kant, Guyer, Paul (ed). Kersting, Wolfgang.

Politique, morale et droit: Enjeux autour de la reproduction humaine et de l'avortement. Hudon, Edith D-R.

Post-Totalitarian Politics and European Philosophy. Palous, Martin.

Postmodern Philosophy and Politics. Magnus, Bernd.

Postmodern Theory and Feminist Art Practice in Postmodernism and Society, Boyne, Roy (ed). Wolff, Janet.

Poststructuralism Politics in Postmodernism/ Jameson/ Critique, Kellner, Douglas (ed). Radhakrishnan, R.

Power Rivalry-Motivated Democracy: A Response to Stephen Krasner. Gilbert, Alan.

Power, Politics, Autonomy in Cultural-Political Interventions in the Unfinished Project of Enlightenment, Honneth, Axel (& other eds). Castoriadis, Cornelius.

Power, Rights and Education: A Tale of Two Traditions. Giarelli, James M.

Practical Weakness and Political Institutions. Rost, Marie.

Protected Space: Politics, Censorship, and the Arts. Devereaux, Mary.

Pseudoethica Epidemica: How Pagans Talk to the Gods. Readings, Bill.

Radical Environmentalism and the Political Roots of Postmodernism. Frodeman, Robert.

Reason and Politics in the Kantian Enterprise in Essays on Kant's Political Philosophy, Williams, Howard (ed). O'Neill, Onora.

Reports on International Research in Social Epistemology. Kasavin, Ilya.

Responsibility, Reactive Attitudes, and Liberalism in Philosophy and Politics. Scheffler, Samuel.

Rethinking the Heidegger-Deep Ecology Relationship. Zimmerman, Michael E.

Rhetoric in Postmodern Feminism: Put-Offs, Put-Ons, and Political Plays in The Interpretive Turn, Hiley, David R (ed). Buker, Eloise A.

Rights and the Rise of Informational Society: The Origins and Ends of Behavioral Rights. Luke, Timothy W.

Russia and the West: The Quest for Russian National Identity. Groys, Boris.

Sailing Through the *Republic*. Stalley, R F.

Sartre's 'Morality and History': A First Look at the Notes for the Unpublished 1965 Cornell Lectures in Sartre Alive, Aronson, Ronald (ed). Stone, Robert and Bowman, Elizabeth A.

Science, Philosophy, and Politics in the Work of J B S Haldane, 1922-1937. Sarkar, Sahotra.

Self-Determination in Political Philosophy and International Law. Dahbour, Omar.

Situating Hannah Arendt on Action and Politics. Isaac, Jeffrey C.

Social Control, Efficiency Control and Ethical Control in Different Political Institutions: Education. Natale, Samuel M (& others).

Social Ethic of Mahatma Gandhi and Martin Buber. Henry, Sarojini.

Socrates on the Decline and Fall of Regimes: Books 8 and 9 of the *Republic*. Coby, Patrick.

Some Comments on Randall Morris' Process Philosophy and Political Ideology. Hartshorne, Charles.

Some Rules of Constitutional Design. Ordeshook, Peter C.

Speculation and Judgment. Taminiaux, Jacques M.

Surrogate Motherhood: Politics and Privacy. Callahan, Joan.

Tactics of Appropriation and the Politics of Recognition in Late Modern Democracies. Coombe, Rosemary J.

Teacher Thinking, Teacher Change, and the "Capricious Seamstress"—Memory. Buchmann, Margret.

Terrorism and Morality in Applied Philosophy, Almond, Brenda (ed). Khatchadourian, Haig A.

Terrorism and the Epochal Transformation of Politics. Allen, Wayne.

The Ambiguities of Education for Active Citizenship. Wringe, Colin.

The Aristotelian *Politeia* and the Athenian Society (in Czechoslovakian). Bartfai, Edit.

The Challenge of Multiculturalism in Political Ethics. Gutmann, Amy.

The Concept of Ethical Life in Hegel's *Philosophy of Right*. Kierans, Kenneth.

The Conflictual Agendas of Neo-Liberal Reconstruction and the Rise of Islamic Politics in Turkey. Birtek, Faruk and Toprak, Binnaz.

The Domain of the Political and Overlapping Consensus in The Idea of Democracy, Copp, David (ed). Rawls, John.

The Economic and Political Liberalization of Socialism: The Fundamental Problem of Property Rights. Riker, William H and Weimer, David L.

The Emergence of Nationalism as a Political Philosophy. Frisch, Morton J.

The Empire of Progress: Bacon's Improvement Upon Machiavelli. Faulkner, Robert K.

The Feminist "Sexuality Debates" and the Transformation of the Political. Bar On, Bat-Ami.

The French Derrideans in Working Through Derrida, Madison, Gary B (ed). Fraser, Nancy.

The Future of a Disillusion in Psychoanalysis, Mind and Art, Hopkins, Jim (ed). Cohen, G A.

The Heidegger Controversy—Updated and Appraised. Wright, Kathleen.

The Impact of Nationalist Ideology on Political Philosophy: The Case of Max Weber and Wilhelmine Germany. Wilson, H T.

The Nature and Meaning of Work. Kovacs, George.

The New Liberalism and Its Aftermath in Victorian Liberalism, Bellamy, Richard (ed). Freeden, Michael.

The Oppression Debate in Sexual Politics in Rethinking Masculinity, May, Larry (ed). Clatterbaugh, Kenneth.

The Ordinary Experience of Civilized Life in Essays on Henry Sidgwick, Schultz, Bart (ed). Collini, Stefan.

The Origins of Al-Razi's Political Philosophy. Butterworth, Charles E.

The Place of Neutrality in Liberal Political Theory in Terrorism, Justice and Social Values, Peden, Creighton W (ed). Downing, Lyle and Thigpen, Robert B.

The Political Economy of Community. Farr, Richard.

The Politics of Agonism. Honig, Bonnie.

The Politics of Art: The Domination of Style and the Crisis in Contemporary Art. Wartofsky, Marx.

The Politics of Equilibrium. Grant, Robert A D.

The Politics of Fredric Jameson's Literary Theory in Postmodernism/ Jameson/ Critique, Kellner, Douglas (ed). Goldstein, Philip.

The Politics of Paradigms: Gender Difference and Gender Disadvantage in Beyond Equality and Difference, Bock, Gisela (ed). Rhode, Deborah L.

The Politics of Skepticism: Readong Montaigne. Hiley, David R.

The Politics of Spirituality: The Spirituality of Politics in Shadow of Spirit, Berry, Philippa (ed). Finn, Geraldine.

The Politics of the Common Good. Buell, John.

The Pornography/Civil Rights Ordinance versus The BOG: And the Winner Is...?. Vadas, Melinda.

The Possibility of Post-Socialist Politics. Bohman, James F.

The Postmodern Return, With a Vengeance, of Subjectivity in Postmodernism/ Jameson/ Critique, Kellner, Douglas (ed). Huhn, Thomas.

The Power of the Right of Education. Heslep, Robert D.

The Problem of Leo Strauss: Religion, Philosophy and Politics. Reinecke, Volker and Uhlaner, Jonathan.

The Problem of Religion in Liberalism. Sherlock, Richard and Barrus, Roger.

The Revolution in the Concept of Politics. Viroli, Maurizio.

The Spirit of Simone Weil's Law in Simone Weil's Philosophy of Culture, Bell, Richard (ed). Collins, Ronald K L and Nielsen, Finn E.

The Status of Politics in St Augustine's *City of God*. Burnell, Peter J.

The System and Its Fractures: Gilles Deleuze on Otherness. May, Todd G.

The Teaching of *Centesimus Annus*. Schall, James V.

The Theory and Politics of Postmodernism in Postmodernism and Society, Boyne, Roy (ed). Boyne, Roy and Rattansi, Ali.

The Work Ethic and the Work Ethos: The Importance of Ethical Arguments for the Politics of Transition to the Market. Büscher, M.

The 'Critique': A View from the Labor Movement in Sartre Alive, Aronson, Ronald (ed). Lennon, Alan.

Thoughts Upon Reading Martin's Comments. Haber, Honi.

Transcendent Man in the Limited City: The Political Philosophy of Charles N R McCoy. Schall, James V.

Two Hundred Years of Error? The Politics of Democracy. Howard, Dick.

Two Paradoxes for Machiavelli in Terrorism, Justice and Social Values, Peden, Creighton W (ed). Belliotti, Raymond and Jacobs, William S.

Universalism and the Politicalisation of the World Problem. Philippides, Elias.

Unsystematic Ethics and Politics in Shadow of Spirit, Berry, Philippa (ed). Cupitt, Don.

Utilitarianism: What Is It and Why Should It Respond? in The Utilitarian Response, Allison, Lincoln (ed). Allison, Lincoln.

Was George Herbert Mead a Feminist?. Aboulafia, Mitchell.

POSTMODERNISM

The Role of Rhetorical Devices in Postmodernist Discourse. Nuyen, A T.

The System and Its Fractures: Gilles Deleuze on Otherness. May, Todd G.

The Tacit Victory and the Unfinished Agenda. Rutledge, David (& others).

The Theory and Politics of Postmodernism in Postmodernism and Society, Boyne, Roy (ed). Boyne, Roy and Rattansi, Ali.

The Use and Abuse of Modernity: Postmodenrism and the American Philosophic Tradition. Ryder, John J.

These New Components of the Spectacle in Postmodernism and Society, Boyne, Roy (ed). Wilson, Elizabeth.

Thinking the Thought of that Which is Strictly Speaking Unthinkable: On the Thematization of Alterity in Nishida-Philosophy. Haver, William.

Thoughts Upon Reading Martin's Comments. Haber, Honi.

Three Questions to Jacques Derrida in Ethics and Danger, Dallery, Arleen B (ed). Dastur, Françoise.

Three-Way Games. Leclerc, Jean-Jacques.

Toward a New Enlightenment: A Response to the Postmodernist Critiques of Humanism. Kurtz, Paul.

Towards a Postmodern Ethics: Sir Isaiah Berlin and John Caputo. McKinney, Ronald H.

Tradition, Modernity, and Confucianism. Dallmayr, Fred.

Unsettled Borders: Envisioning Critique at the Postmodern Site in The Critical Turn, Angus, Ian (ed). Angus, Ian and Langsdorf, Lenore.

Unsystematic Ethics and Politics in Shadow of Spirit, Berry, Philippa (ed). Cupitt, Don.

Validities: A Political Science Perspective. Beer, Francis A.

Varieties of Postmodernism as Moments in Ethics Action Learning. Nielsen, Richard P.

What Epistemic Values Should We Reclaim for Religion and Science? A Response to J Wesley Robbins. Van Huyssteen, J Wentzel.

What is a "Postmodern" Education and What Does It Have to Do With Lifelong Learning?. Owen, Roderick.

What Is Feminist Philosophy? (in Czechoslovakian). Nagl-Docekalova, Herta.

What is Postmodernism?. Brann, Eva T H.

What's Postmodern, Anyway. Münz, Peter.

Who Is Afraid of Feminist Philosophy? (in Czechoslovakian). Havelkova, Hana.

Writing Music History: A Review Essay. Goehr, Lydia.

'Les Immatériaux' and the Postmodern Sublime in Judging Lyotard, Benjamin, Andrew (ed). Crowther, Paul.

POSTSTRUCTURALISM

Ideology: An Introduction. Eagleton, Terry.

Marine Lover of Friedrich Nietzsche—Luce Irigaray. Irigaray, Luce and Gill, Gillian C (trans).

Postmodernism and Society. Boyne, Roy (ed) and Rattansi, Ali (ed).

Psychology and Nihilism: A Genealogical Critique of the Computational Model of Mind. Evans, Fred.

The Body in Medical Thought and Practice. Leder, Drew (ed).

Jameson, Totality, and the Poststructuralist Critique in Postmodernism/ Jameson/ Critique, Kellner, Douglas (ed). Best, Steven.

Merleau-Ponty Alive. Madison, G B.

On the Dialectics of Postdialectical Thinking in Community at Loose Ends, Miami Theory Collect, (ed). Terdiman, Richard.

Patterns of Dissonance: Women and/In Philosophy. Braidotti, Rosi.

Postructuralism and the Epistemological Basis of Anarchism. Koch, Andrew M.

Poststructuralism, Difference, and Marxism. Fisk, Milton T.

Rethinking Resistance: Environmentalism, Literature, and Poststructural Theory. Quigley, Peter.

The Body with AIDS: A Post-Structuralist Approach in The Body in Medical Thought and Practice, Leder, Drew (ed). Murphy, Julien S.

The Debate over Performative Contradiction in Philosophical Interventions in the Unfinished Project of Enlightenment, Honneth, Axel (& other eds). Jay, Martin.

The Politics of Fredric Jameson's Literary Theory in Postmodernism/ Jameson/ Critique, Kellner, Douglas (ed). Goldstein, Philip.

The Theater of Personal Identity: From Hume to Derrida. Gallagher, Shaun.

POSTULATE

Belief Contraction Without Recovery. Hansson, Sven Ove.

McAllister on Northrop. Seddon, Fred.

POTEAT, W

William H Poteat: *A Laudatio*. Scott, R Taylor.

POTENCY

Gassendi interprete di Cavalieri. Festa, Egidio.

POTENTIALITY

Possible Versus Potential Universes. Kerszberg, Pierre.

The Actualization of Potentialities in Contemporary Quantum Theory. Fleming, Gordon N.

POTTER, C

Charles F Potter: On Evolution and Religious Humanism in God, Values, and Empiricism, Peden, Creighton (ed). Olds, W Mason.

POTTER, K

Tat tvam asi as Advaitic Metaphor. Myers, Michael.

Comments on "The Development of Advaita Vedanta as a School of Philosophy". Sharma, R M.

Comments on "The Development of Advaita Vedanta as a School of Philosophy". Venkatachalam, V.

POVERTY

International Justice and the Third World. Attfield, Robin (ed) and Wilkins, Barry (ed).

I poeti nel tempo della povertà. Mazzarella, Arturo.

Poverty Lines, Social Participation, and Welfare Rights. Jones, John D.

Technology and Culture and the Problem of the Homeless. Lovekin, David.

World Poverty, Justice and Equality in International Justice and the Third World, Attfield, Robin (ed). Belsey, Andrew.

POWER

"Engendering Equity...". Morgan, K P.

"Power in the Service of Love": John Dewey's *Logic* and the Dream of a Common Language. Hart, Carroll Guen.

"Yes, But...": Principles and Caveats in American Racial Attitudes. Hochschild, Jennifer L and Herk, Monica.

A Companion to Contemporary Political Philosophy. Goodin, Robert E (ed) and Pettit, Philip (ed).

Bodies that Matter: On the Discursive Limits of 'Sex'. Butler, Judith.

Burdens of Proof in Modern Discourse. Gaskins, Richard H.

Compassionate Authority: Democracy and the Representation of Women. Jones, Kathleen B.

Critical Thought Series: 2—Critical Essays on Michel Foucault. Burke, Peter (ed).

Democracy and Complexity: A Realist Approach. Zolo, Danilo and McKie, David (trans).

Disciplining Foucault: Feminism, Power, and the Body. Sawicki, Jana.

Engenderings: Constructions of Knowledge, Authority, and Privilege. Scheman, Naomi.

Expressionism in Philosophy: Spinoza. Deleuze, Gilles and Joughin, Martin (trans).

Feminist Epistemologies. Alcoff, Linda (ed) and Potter, Elizabeth (ed).

Foucault's Nietzschean Genealogy: Truth, Power, and the Subject. Mahon, Michael.

Frames of Deceit: A Study of the Loss and Recovery of Public and Private Trust. Johnson, Peter.

Government: Servant or Master?. Radnitzky, Gerard (ed) and Bouillon, Hardy (ed).

Hannah Arendt: A Reinterpretation of Her Political Thought. Canovan, Margaret.

Injustice and Restitution: The Ordinance of Time. Ross, Stephen D.

Je, Tu, Nous: Toward a Culture of Difference. Irigaray, Luce and Martin, Alison (trans).

Leviathan—Thomas Hobbes. Hobbes, Thomas and MacPherson, C B (ed).

Materialist Feminism and the Politics of Discourse. Hennessy, Rosemary.

Michel Foucault, Philosopher. Armstrong, Timothy J (trans) and Foucault, Michel.

Moral Boundaries: A Political Argument for an Ethic of Care. Tronto, Joan C.

Morality, Prudence, and Nuclear Weapons. Lee, Steven.

Nietzsche's Philosophical and Narrative Styles. Pettey, John Carson.

Nietzsche: The Politics of Power. Okonta, Ike.

Open Institutions: The Hope for Democracy. Murphy, John W (ed) and Peck, Dennis L (ed).

Philosophy—A Myth?. Verster, Ulrich.

Political Theory and Postmodernism. White, Stephen K.

Simone Weil's Philosophy of Culture. Bell, Richard H (ed).

The Corporation as Anomaly. Schrader, David.

The Desire To Be God: Freedom and the Other in Sartre and Berdyaev. McLachlan, James Morse.

The Sickness unto Death in Foundations of Kierkegaard's Vision of Community, Connell, George B (ed). Crites, Stephen.

The Understanding of Difference in Heidegger and Derrida. Donkel, Douglas L.

The Veil of Black: (Un)Masking the Subject of African-American Modernism's "Native Son". Benston, Kimberly W.

Thucydides: On Justice, Power, and Human Nature. Woodruff, Paul B (ed & trans) and Thucydides.

Toward a Feminist Epistemology. Duran, Jane.

Transforming Power: Domination, Empowerment, and Education. Kreisberg, Seth.

Transition to Modernity: Essays on Power, Wealth and Belief. Hall, John A (ed) and Jarvie, I C (ed).

Truth's Debt to Value. Weissman, David.

A Musical Retrieve of Heidegger, Nietzsche, and Technology: Cadence, Concinnity, and Playing Brass. Babich, Babette E.

A 'Counterfactualist' Four-Dimensional Theory of Power. Carter, Alan.

Abstract Principles, Mid-Level Principles, and the Rule of Law. Henley, Kenneth.

Act and Maxim: Value-Discrepancy and Two Theories of Power. Oddie, Graham.

Allmacht in der postmodernen Philosophie. Fink-Eitel, Hinrich.

Bread and Butter Ethics in Marx's Theory of History, Wetherly, Paul. Carling, Alan.

Cantor's Power-Set Theorem Versus Frege's Double-Correlation Thesis. Cocchiarella, N B.

Carl Schmitt: The Conservative Revolutionary Habitus and the Aesthetics of Horror. Wolin, Richard.

Catastrophe Theory and its Critics. Boutot, Alain.

Causal Powers and Conceptual Connections. Christensen, David.

Communicative Virtues and Educational Relations. Rice, Suzanne and Burbules, Nicholas C.

Considerazioni sul *De mundo* e analisi critica delle tesi di Paul Moraux. Bos, A P.

Contested Power in The Idea of Democracy, Copp, David (ed). Moene, Karl Ove.

Corporeal Archetypes and Power: Preliminary Clarifications and Considerations of Sex. Sheets-Johnstone, Maxine.

Difference and Domination: Reflections on the Relation Between Pluralism and Equality. Carens, Joseph H.

Discourse Competence; or, How to Theorize Strong Women Speakers. Mills, Sara.

Divine Foreknowledge and the Libertarian Conception of Human Freedom. Linville, Mark D.

POWER

Does Hume Have a Theory of Justice?. Reidy, David.

E Burke and the Natural Law: About the Foundations of Conservatisim (in Dutch). Van De Putte, A.

Electoral Power, Group Power, and Democracy. Levine, Andrew.

Elite Culture, Popular Culture and the Politics of Hegemony. Jones, Gary.

Equality Revisited. Wilson, John.

Exploring *The Realm of Rights*. Russell, Bruce.

Feminism and Postmodernism in Postmodernism and Society, Boyne, Roy (ed). Lovibond, Sabina.

Feminist Politics and Foucault in Crises in Continental Philosophy, Dallery, Arleen B (ed). Alcoff, Linda.

Foucault's Analytics of Power in Crises in Continental Philosophy, Dallery, Arleen B (ed). McWhorter, Ladelle.

Foucault, Ethics, and the Fragmented Subject. Scott, Charles E.

Foucault: Critique as a Philosophical Ethos in Philosophical Interventions in the Unfinished Project of Enlightenment, Honneth, Axel (& other eds). Bernstein, Richard J.

Freedom, Power, and Culture in Ortega y Gasset's Philosophy of Technology. Dust, Patrick H.

Gay Jocks: A Phenomenology of Gay Men in Athletics in Rethinking Masculinity, May, Larry (ed). Pronger, Brian.

Goods of the Mind, Goods of the Body and External Goods. Gobetti, Daniela.

Hegel on Slavery and Domination. Smith, Steven B.

Hobbes's Shortsightedness Account of Conflict. Murphy, Mark C.

Honor: Emasculation and Empowerment in Rethinking Masculinity, May, Larry (ed). Harris, Leonard.

Il soggetto metafisico alla prima e alla seconda potenza. Crescini, Angelo.

Immodest Proposals II: Give Children the Vote. Wallace, Vita.

In Search of a Workable and Lasting Constitutional Change in South Africa. Ramose, Mogobe B, Maphala, T G T and Makhabane, T E.

Kant's Concept of the State in Essays on Kant's Political Philosophy, Williams, Howard (ed). Kersting, Wolfgang.

Killing, Confiscating, and Banishing at *Gorgias* 466-468. Weiss, Roslyn.

Knowledge, Power, and a Professional Ethic. Di Norcia, V.

La funzione e la portata della critica alle Idee nel *Parmenide* di Platone: Dalla teoria delle Idee alla teoria dei Principi. Pezzolato, Marco.

La noción de *'spiritus'* y de 'spiritualis substantia' en la cuestión disputada *De spiritualibus creaturis* de Santo Tomás de Aquino. Taubenschlag, C A.

Men, Feminism, and Power in Rethinking Masculinity, May, Larry (ed). Seidler, Victor J.

Michel Foucault and the Question of Rhetoric. Biesecker, Barbara.

Michel Foucault's Archaeology, Enlightenment, and Critique. Mahon, Michael.

Monstrous Reflections in Crises in Continental Philosophy, Dallery, Arleen B (ed). Olkowski, Dorothea.

Mosaic Fragment: If Derrida were an Egyptian... in Derrida: A Critical Reader, Wood, David (ed). Bennington, Geoffrey.

Nietzsche's 'Will to Power' and Chinese 'Virtuality' (De) in Nietzsche and Asian Thought, Parkes, Graham R (ed). Ames, Roger T.

Not Exactly Politics or Power?. Lash, Nicholas.

Overcoming Metaphysics: Elias and Foucault on Power and Freedom. Burkitt, Ian.

Philosophy and the Cult of Irrationalism. Almond, Brenda.

Plato on Poetic Creativity in The Cambridge Companion to Plato, Kraut, Richard (ed). Asmis, Elizabeth.

Poststructuralism and the Epistemological Basis of Anarchism. Koch, Andrew M.

Power and Wealth in a Competitive Capitalist Economy. Bowles, Samuel and Gintis, Herbert.

Power, Politics, Autonomy in Cultural-Political Interventions in the Unfinished Project of Enlightenment, Honneth, Axel (& other eds). Castoriadis, Cornelius.

Power, Rights and Education: A Tale of Two Traditions. Giarelli, James M.

Précis of *The Realm of Rights*. Thomson, Judith Jarvis.

Purpose, Power, and Agency. Colapietro, Vincent.

Quelques questions autour de la notion leibnizienne de puissance. De Gaudemar, Martine.

Racism: Flew's Three Concepts of Racism. Skillen, Anthony.

Rejoinder to Hasker. Zagzebski, Linda.

Rouse's *Knowledge and Power*: A Note. Dauenhauer, Bernard.

Sadomasochism and Exclusion. Saxe, Lorena Leigh.

Seeing (Just) Is Believing: Faith and Imagination. Ferreira, M Jamie.

Structural Inquiry, Human Agency and the Contribution of Harré and Bhaskar: A Case Study of Wright's "Classes". Adkins, Barbara.

Subjects, Power and Knowledge: Description and Prescription in Feminist Philosophies of Science in Feminist Epistemologies, Alcoff, Linda (ed). Longino, Helen.

Subversive Rationalization: Technology, Power, and Democracy. Feenberg, Andrew.

The Amazing Predictive Power of Folk Psychology. Lahav, Ran.

The Exchange and Allocation of Decision Power. Philipson, Tomas.

The Face in the Sand in Philosophical Interventions in the Unfinished Project of Enlightenment, Honneth, Axel (& other eds). Schnädelbach, Herbert.

The Feminist "Sexuality Debates" and the Transformation of the Political. Bar On, Bat-Ami.

The Genealogy of God's Freedom in Spinoza's *Ethics*. Richey, Lance B.

The Modern Democratic Revolution in Judging Lyotard, Benjamin, Andrew (ed). Keane, John.

The Paradox of Power: Hobbes and Stoic Naturalism in The Uses of Antiquity, Gaukroger, Stephen (ed). Kassler, Jamie C.

The Place of Real Emotion in Response to Fiction. Levinson, Jerrold.

The Possibility of Power Beyond Possibility in Philosophical Perspectives, 5: Philosophy of Religion, 1991, Tomberlin, James E (ed). Conee, Earl.

The Power and Poverty of Libertarian Thought. Cornuelle, Richard.

The Power and Powerlessness of Women in Beyond Equality and Difference, Bock, Gisela (ed). Elshtain, Jean Bethke.

The Power of the Right of Education. Heslep, Robert D.

The Primacy of Authority. Wilson, John.

The Right to Privacy versus Uniformitarianism. Machan, Tibor R.

The Unanimity Standard. Kagan, Shelly.

Three Conceptions of 'Voice' and their Pedagogical Implications. Scahill, John H.

Three Types of Divine Power. Gier, Nicholas F.

Who is that Masked Woman? Reflections on Power, Privilege, and Home-ophobia in Revisioning Philosophy, Ogilvy, James (ed). Scheman, Naomi.

Zagzebski on Power Entailment. Hasker, William.

'Even a Nation of Devils Needs the State': the Dilemma of Natural Justice in Essays on Kant's Political Philosophy, Williams, Howard (ed). Höffe, Otfried.

PRACTICAL

Kants Begründung der praktischen Philosophie. Freudiger, Jürg.

Doute pratique et doute spéculatif chez Montaigne et Descartes. Rodis-Lewis, G.

Universalismo e particolarismo nell'etica contemporanea. Guariglia, Osvaldo.

PRACTICAL REASON

Audi on Practical Reasoning. Foley, Richard.

Audi's Theory of Practical Reasoning. Barker, John A.

Practical Unreason. Pettit, Philip and Smith, Michael.

Raison, argumentation et légitimation: Habermas, Apel et les apories de la communication. Cometti, Jean-Pierre.

The Nature and Assessment of Practical Reasoning: A Reply to John A Barker and Richard Foley. Audi, Robert.

PRACTICE

"Was darf ich hoffen?" Zum Problem der Vereinbarkeit von theoretischer und praktischer Vernunft bei Immanuel Kant. Förster, Eckart.

Converging Theory and Practice: Example Selection in Moral Philosophy. Vitek, William.

Discourses as the Reflective Educator. Walsh, Paddy.

Ideality and Ontology in the Practice of History in Objectivity, Method and Point of View, Van Der Dussen, W J (ed). Krausz, Michael.

Introduction to the Methodology of Paraphronesis, With Example: Religion and Education in Postmodern America. Tandy, Charles.

Philosophical Prose and Practice. McCleary, Richard C.

Philosophy for Children: Curriculum and Practice. Morehouse, Mort.

PRAGMATIC

Explanatory Understanding and Contrastive Facts. Grimes, Thomas R.

PRAGMATICISM

"Experience and Philosophic Method": Does Dewey's View of Method Speak to the Needs of Philosophy Today?. Garrett, Roland.

"Power in the Service of Love": John Dewey's *Logic* and the Dream of a Common Language. Hart, Carroll Guen.

Frontiers in American Philosophy, Volume I. Burch, Robert W (ed) and Saatkamp, Herman J Jr (ed).

George Herbert Mead: The Making of a Social Pragmatist. Cook, Gary A.

A Convergence of Pragmatisms in Frontiers in American Philosophy, Volume I, Burch, Robert W (ed). Margolis, Joseph.

A Pragmatic Health Care Policy Tradition: Dewey, Franklin and Social Reconstruction. Miller, Irwin.

A Question of Evidence. Nelson, Lynn Hankinson.

Charlotte Perkins Gilman: Instrumentalism Beyond Dewey. Upin, Jane.

Difference Without the Flux: Pragmatic versus Romantic Conceptions of Alterity. Nevo, Isaac.

Feminism and Pragmatism. Miller, Marjorie C.

Feminism, Ideology, and Deconstruction: A Pragmatist View. Rorty, Richard.

Fences and Celings: Schrödinger's Cat and Other Animals in Logical Foundations, Mahalingam, Indira (ed). Post, Heinz.

Heidegger, Contingency, and Pragmatism in Heidegger: A Critical Reader, Dreyfus, Hubert (ed). Rorty, Richard.

Kaufman on Kaplan and Process Theology: A Post-Positivist Perspective. Alexander, H A.

Mead's Voices: Imitation as Foundation, or, The Struggle against Mimesis. Leys, Ruth.

Peirce and the Threat of Nominalism. Forster, Paul.

Pragmatism and Constitutional Interpretation: Deconstruction Without Nihilism. McNicollis, C F.

Pragmatism and Pluralism. Singer, Beth.

Pragmatism and the Context of Rationality: Part I. Singer, Marcus G (ed) and Murphy, Arthur E.

Pragmatism and the Normative Sciences in Frontiers in American Philosophy, Volume I, Burch, Robert W (ed). Lieb, Irwin C.

Pragmatism or Crude Utility: A Critique of the Education with Production Movement in Contemporary Africa. Lungu, Gatian F.

Pragmatism or Hermeneutics? Epistemology after Foundationalism in The Interpretive Turn, Hiley, David R (ed). Guignon, Charles B.

Pragmatism, Prudence, and Morality in Frontiers in American Philosophy, Volume I, Burch, Robert W (ed). Kolenda, Konstantin.

Pragmatists Jane Addams and John Dewey Inform the Ethic of Care. Leffers, M Regina.

Purpose, Power, and Agency. Colapietro, Vincent.

Super Pragmatic Paradoxes in Logical Foundations, Mahalingam, Indira (ed). Ackermann, Robert.

PROBABILITY

Being Knowingly Incoherent. Foley, Richard.

Bell's Inequality, Information Transmission, and Prism Models. Maudlin, Tim.

Cartwright, Capacities, and Probabilities. Irzik, Gürol.

Causation, Probability, and the Monarchy. Rosenberg, Alexander.

Coherence, Probability and Induction in Rationality in Epistemology, Villanueva, Enrique (ed). Skyrms, Brian.

Comment on Keith Lehrer and Vann McGee's Solution of Newcomb's Problem. Piller, Christian.

Comment on Langtry's 'God, Evil and Probability'. Chrzan, Keith.

Critical Notice: Itamar Pitowsky's *Quantum Probability-Quantum Logic*. Malament, David B.

Dispute and Conversation: Probability and the Rhetoric of Natural Philosophy in Locke's *Essay*. Walmsley, Peter.

Doom and Probabilities. Leslie, John.

Exchangeability and Predictivism. Wechsler, Sergio.

Explanation and "Old Evidence". Achinstein, Peter.

Explanatory Instability. Batterman, Robert W.

From a Historical Point of View in Probability and Rationality, Eells, Ellery (ed). Cohen, L Jonathan.

From Worlds to Probabilities: A Probabilistic Semantics for Modal Logic. Cross, Charles B.

General Causal Propensities, Classical and Quantum Probabilities. Sapire, David.

Generalized Probability Kinematics. Wagner, Carl G.

Getting the Constraints on Popper's Probability Functions Right. Leblanc, Hugues and Roeper, Peter.

Gleason's Theorem is Not Constructively Provable. Hellman, Geoffrey.

Heuristic Novelty and the Asymmetry Problem in Bayesian Confirmation Theory. Nunan, Richard.

Inductive Support in Advances in Scientific Philosophy, Schurz, Gerhard (ed). Dorn, Georg J W.

Jonathan Cohen and Thomas Bayes on the Analysis of Chains of Reasoning in Probability and Rationality, Eells, Ellery (ed). Schum, David A.

Kausalität: Eine Problemübersicht. Heidelberger, Michael.

Keynes's Theory of Probability and Its Relevance to His Economics: Three Theses. Cottrell, Allin.

Kings and Prisoners (and Aces). Sobel, Jordan Howard.

La logique interne de la théorie des probabilités. Gauthier, Yvon.

Les fonctions de probabilité: la question de leur définissabilité récursive. Leblanc, Hugues and Roeper, Peter.

Local Utility Functions. Bardsley, Peter.

Logical Atomism and Its Ontological Refinement: A Defense in Language, Truth and Ontology, Mulligan, Kevin (ed). Simons, Peter.

Models for Belief Revision in Rationality in Epistemology, Villanueva, Enrique (ed). Morado, Raymundo.

Neurobiology of Subjective Probability in Probability and Rationality, Eells, Ellery (ed). Nosal, Czeslaw S.

Newcomb's Paradox: A Realist Resolution. Jacobi, N.

Objectivism Without Objective Probabilities. Weintraub, Ruth.

On a Problem About Probability and Decision. Cargile, James Thomas.

On Relativity Theory and Openness of the Future. Maxwell, Nicholas.

On the Reduction of Process Causality to Statistical Relations. Dowe, Phil.

On the Strength of a Causal Chain. Bessie, Joseph D.

Peirce and the Nature of Evidence. O'Neill, Len.

Prevost, Probability, God and Evil. Milne, Peter.

Probabilistic Causality Reexamined. Ray, Greg.

Probabilities and Conditionals: Distinctions By Example. Butterfield, Jeremy.

Probability and Assertion. Dudman, V H.

Probability and Direct Reference: Three Puzzles of Probability Theory. Nida-Rümelin, Martine.

Probability and the Evidence of Our Senses in A J Ayer Memorial Essays, Griffiths, A Phillips (ed). Mellor, D H.

Probability Functions: The Matter of Their Recursive Definability. Leblanc, Hugues and Roeper, Peter.

Probability Theory and the Doomsday Argument. Eckhardt, William.

Radical Probabilism, (Prospectus for a User's Manual) in Rationality in Epistemology, Villanueva, Enrique (ed). Jeffrey, Richard.

Regression Analysis: Classical and Bayesian. Urbach, Peter.

Reply to Carl G Wagner's "Simpson's Paradox and the Fisher-Newcomb Problem". Lehrer, Keith.

Reply to Christian Piller's "Comment on Keith Lehrer and Vann McGee's Solution of Newcomb's Problem". McGee, Vann.

Simpson's Paradox and the Fisher-Newcomb Problem. Wagner, Carl G.

Some Comments by L J C in Probability and Rationality, Eells, Ellery (ed). Cohen, L Jonathan.

The Ancient Legal Sources of Seventeenth-Century Probability in The Uses of Antiquity, Gaukroger, Stephen (ed). Franklin, James.

The Foundations of Probability and Quantum Mechanics. Milne, Peter.

The Geometry of Opinion: Jeffrey Shifts and Linear Operators. Van Fraassen, Bas C.

The Non-Existence of Probabilistic Inductive Support in Logical Foundations, Mahalingam, Indira (ed). Popper, Karl R.

The Rationality of Intelligence in Probability and Rationality, Eells, Ellery (ed). Lopes, Lola L and Oden, Gregg C.

The Unanimity Theory and Probabilistic Sufficiency. Carroll, John W.

Three Pseudo-Paradoxes in 'Quantum' Decision Theory: Apparent Effects of Observation on Probability and Utility. Marinoff, Louis.

Validity, Uncertainty and Vagueness. Edgington, Dorothy.

What's Wrong with Salmon's History: The Third Decade. Fetzer, James H.

PROBLEM

see also Social Problems

The Heuristic Bent. Agassi, Joseph.

PROCEDURALISM

Defining "Art": The Functionalism/Proceduralism Controversy. Stecker, Robert A.

PROCEDURE

Reasonableness, Bias, and the Untapped Power of Procedure. Adler, Jonathan.

Über die Rationalität von Prozeduren und Resultaten. Dorschel, Andreas.

PROCESS

EEEE: Set Theory and Wholeness. Blizard, Wayne D.

La storia e il processi al passato. Del Vecchio, D.

Process Causality and Asymmetry. Dowe, Phil.

The Styles of Art History: Entities or Processes?. MacDonald, Ray A.

PROCESS PHILOSOPHY

Some Not Ungrateful But Perhaps Inadequate Comments About Comments on My Writings and Ideas. Hartshorne, Charles.

PROCESS THEOLOGY

Mordecai M Kaplan and Process Theology: Metaphysical and Pragmatic Perspectives. Kaufman, William E.

Process Theism Versus Free-Will Theism: A Response to Griffin. Basinger, David.

PROCLUS

The Metaphysical Aspect of Tenses in Proclus. Plass, Paul.

PRODUCTION

Essays on Philosophy and Economic Methodology. Hausman, Daniel M.

Bread and Butter Ethics in Marx's Theory of History, Wetherly, Paul. Carling, Alan.

C J Arthur on Marx and Hegel on Alienation. Duquette, David A.

Economics of Production in Crises in Continental Philosophy, Dallery, Arleen B (ed). Schmidt, Dennis J.

New "True" Socialism. Baxter, David.

Process and Product: A Theory of Art. Sartwell, Crispin.

The Incoherence of the Aesthetic Response. Slater, Hartley.

The Problem of Social Cost: Coase's Economics Versus Ethics. Hanly, Ken.

PROFESSION

The Allied Health Care Professions: New Fields for Philosophical Explorations. Hull, Richard T.

The Professionalism Movement: The Problems Defined. Sammons, Jack L.

PROFESSIONAL

Amateurs Imitate, Professionals Steal. Bailey, George W S.

PROFESSIONAL CODE

Can Engineers Hold Public Interests Paramount?. Broome Jr, Taft H.

La transformation des pratiques professionnelles: quelques conséquences pour l'éthique. Bourgeault, Guy.

PROFESSIONAL ETHICS

La transformation des pratiques professionnelles: quelques conséquences pour l'éthique. Bourgeault, Guy.

PROFESSIONALISM

Knowledge, Power, and a Professional Ethic. Di Norcia, V.

PROFIT

Ethical Issues in Business: A Philosophical Approach (Fourth Edition). Donaldson, Thomas J and Werhane, Patricia H.

PROFUNDITY

Profundity: A Universal Value. Harrell, Jean Gabbert.

Musical Profundity Misplaced. Levinson, Jerrold.

Toward a Theory of Profundity in Music. White, David A.

PROGRAMMING

Teaching Formal Logic as Logic Programming in Philosophy Departments. Tieszen, Richard L.

PROGRESS

A Note Concerning Irving H Anellis's "Distortions and Discontinuties of Mathematical Progress". Ernest, Paul.

A Reappraisal of Duhem's Conception of Scientific Progress. Baigrie, Brian S.

Individual, Institution, Nation-Building and Obligation: A Review Essay. Sen, Gautum.

J S Mill, Liberalism, and Progress in Victorian Liberalism, Bellamy, Richard (ed). Gibbins, John R.

La cultura y los valores tradicionales en el desarrollo. Goulet, Denis.

On the Justification of Societal Development Claims. Korthals, Michiel.

Sartre on Progress in The Cambridge Companion to Sartre, Howells, Christina (ed). Aronson, Ronald.

The Tagore-Gandhi Controversy Revisited, II. Singh, Ajai and Singh, Shakuntala.

Two Notions of Progress in Terrorism, Justice and Social Values, Peden, Creighton (ed). DeSchrenk, Laura Mues.

PROGRESSIVISM

The Chicago Pragmatists and American Progressivism. Feffer, Andrew.

PROHIBITION

Deontic Problems with Prohibition Dilemmas. Almeida, Michael J.

PROJECTION

Complexity of Equational Theory of Relational Algebras with Projection Elements. Mikulás, Szabolcs, Sain, Ildikó and Simon, András.

PROJECTIVE GEOMETRY

Projective Geometries of Algebraically Closed Fields of Characteristic Zero. Holland, Kitty L.

PROMISCUITY

Against Couples in Applied Philosophy, Almond, Brenda (ed). Gregory, Paul.

PSYCHOANALYSIS

PSYCHOLOGISM

PSYCHOLOGY

see also Behaviorism, Philosophical Psychology, Psychiatry, Psychoanalysis

PSYCHOLOGY

On Professor Rychlak's Concerns. Moore, Jay.

On Standard and Non-standard Models in Theories of Psychological Measurement in Probability and Rationality, Eells, Ellery (ed). Stachowski, Ryszard.

On the Phases of Reism in Kotarbinski: Logic, Semantics and Ontology, Wolénski, Jan (ed). Smith, Barry.

Ontology and the Construction of Systems. Küng, Guido.

Perceptual Consciousness and Perceptual Evidence. Baergen, Ralph.

Precisationes varie sur questiones de filosofia. Blandino, Giovanni.

Psicologia e Crítica Sartreana do Cogito Cartesiano. Simon, Paul Albert.

Psychological Egoism: *Noch Einmal*. Johnson, Wayne G.

Question-Begging Psychological Explanations. Ward, Andrew.

Questioning Hume's Theory of Meaning. Groothuis, Douglas.

Reduction, Explanatory Extension, and the Mind/Brain Sciences. Hardcastle, Valerie Gray.

Reply to Anstötz: What We Can Learn from People with Learning Difficulties. Boddington, Paula and Podpadec, Tessa.

Reply to Russow's "Fodor, Adams and Causal Properties". Adams, Frederick.

Reward Event Systems: Reconceptualizing the Explanatory Roles of Motivation, Desire and Pleasure. Morillo, Carolyn R.

Robustness and Integrative Survival in Significance Testing: The World's Contribution to Rationality. Trout, J D.

Sartre's Moral Psychology in The Cambridge Companion to Sartre, Howells, Christina (ed). Jopling, David A.

Self-Kowledge: Looking in the Wrong Direction. Greenwood, John D.

Socializing Naturalized Philosophy of Science. Downes, Stephen M.

Some Content is Narrow in Mental Causation, Heil, John (ed). Jackson, Frank and Pettit, Philip.

The Amazing Predictive Power of Folk Psychology. Lahav, Ran.

The Desire to Be God: Subjective and Objective in Nagel's *The View From Nowhere* and Sartre's *Being and Nothingness*. Wider, Kathleen.

The Intentionality of Some Ethological Terms. Thompson, Nicholas S and Derr, Patrick.

The Metaphysics and Metapsychology of Personal Identity. Kolak, Daniel.

The Phrenetic Calculus: A Logician's View of Disordered Logical Thinking in Schizophrenia. Klee, Robert.

The Self of Book 1 and the Selves of Book 2. Penelhum, Terence.

The Thinker and the Painter in Merleau-Ponty Vivant, Dillon, M C (ed). Taminiaux, Jacques M.

Theory, Realism and Common Sense: A Reply to Paul Churchland. Haldane, John.

Theory, Taxonomy and Methodology: A Reply to Haldane's *Understanding Folk*. Churchland, Paul M.

Thinking that One Thinks in Consciousness: Psychological and Philosophical Essays, Davies, Martin (ed). Rosenthal, David.

Three Types of Projectivism in Psychoanalysis, Mind and Art, Hopkins, Jim (ed). Price, A W.

Two Factor Theories, Meaning Wholism and Intentionalistic Psychology: A Reply to Fodor. Senor, Thomas D.

Two Routes to Narrow Content: Both Dead Ends. Manfredi, Pat A.

Unpacking the Black Box of Cognition. Gillett, Grant.

Using Analytical Philosophy in Philosophical Counselling. Lahav, Ran.

Velmans on *Consciousness, Brain and the Physical World*. Wetherick, Norman.

What Happens When Someone Acts?. Velleman, J David.

What is Consciousness?. Nelkin, Norton.

What is Wrong with the Appendage Theory of Consciousness. Natsoulas, Thomas.

What Isn't Wrong with Folk Psychology. Dretske, Frederick.

What Price Neurophilosophy?. Saidel, Eric.

William James in Founders of Constructive Postmodern Philosophy, Griffin, David Ray (& others). Ford, Marcus P.

William James's Concrete Analysis of Experience. Seigfried, Charlene Haddock.

Wittgenstein on Believing in 'Philosophical Investigations' Part II in Wittgenstein's Philosophical Investigations, Arrington, Robert T (ed). Hunter, J F M.

Zwischen Epistemologie und Ethik. Liebsch, Burkhard.

'Ieder ding op zijn eigen plaats'. Schwegman, Marjan.

'Narrow'-Mindedness Breeds Inaction. Buller, David J.

PSYCHOPATHY

Free Will in Psychopaths in Analecta Husserliana, XXXI, Tymieniecka, Anna-Teresa (ed). González, Manuel Riobó.

Hacia un concepto significativo de lo patologico y lo sano, de lo anomal y lo normal in Analecta Husserliana, XXXI, Tymieniecka, Anna-Teresa (ed). Jarquin, Miguel C.

Moral Insanity and Practical Reason. Elliot, Carl and Gillett, Grant.

Some Epistemological Aspects of Present-Day Psychopathology in Analecta Husserliana, XXXI, Tymieniecka, Anna-Teresa (ed). Callieri, Bruno.

PSYCHOPHYSICS

The Problem of Psychophysical Causation. Lowe, E J.

PSYCHOSIS

The Emotional Residence: An Italian Experience of the Treatment of Chronic Psychosis in Analecta Husserliana, XXXI, Tymieniecka, Anna-Teresa (ed). Mencacci, Claudio and Goldfluss, Enrica.

PTOLEMAIC

Paradigms and Barriers: How Habits of Mind Govern Scientific Beliefs. Margolis, Howard.

Did King Alfonso of Castile Really Want to Advise God Against the Ptolemaic System? The Legend in History. Franssen, Maarten.

PTOLEMY

Ptolemy's Universe: The Natural Philosophical and Ethical Foundations of Ptolemy's Astronomy. Taub, Liba.

PUBLIC

Frames of Deceit: A Study of the Loss and Recovery of Public and Private Trust. Johnson, Peter.

Ethical Foundations of Management in Public Service. Geuras, Dean and Garofalo, Charles.

Language, Literature and Publikum: Herder's Quest for Organic Enlightenment. Redekop, Benjamin W.

Public Choice Versus Democracy. Hardin, Russell.

Public Choice Versus Democracy in The Idea of Democracy, Copp, David (ed). Hardin, Russell.

The Diversity Criterion in Public Administration. Stever, James A.

The New World Order and the Public Trust. Brown, Peter G.

PUBLIC GOOD

Law as a Public Good: The Economics of Anarchy. Cowen, Tyler.

Philosophizing as a Public Good in Frontiers in American Philosophy, Volume I, Burch, Robert W (ed). Durbin, Paul T.

Private Corporations and Public Welfare. Brenkert, George G.

PUBLIC INTEREST

Can Engineers Hold Public Interests Paramount?. Broome Jr, Taft H.

PUBLIC POLICY

Business, Ethics, and the Environment: The Public Policy Debate. Hoffman, W Michael (ed), Frederick, Robert (ed) and Pentry, Edward S (ed).

Case Studies in Business, Society, and Ethics (Third Edition). Beauchamp, Tom L.

The Moral Dimensions of Public Policy Choice: Beyond the Market Paradigm. Gillroy, John Martin (ed) and Wade, Maurice (ed).

The Utilitarian Response. Allison, Lincoln (ed).

A New Contractarian View of Tax and Regulatory Policy in the Emerging Market Economies. Frank, Robert H.

Applied Ethics and Free Will: Some Untoward Results of Independence. Machan, Tibor R.

Is There a Right to Die?. Kass, Leon R.

Moral Philosophy and Public Policy: The Case of the New Reproductive Technologies. Kymlicka, Will.

Public Policy and Environmental Risk. Gillroy, John Martin.

Risk and Public Decision-Making: Constructivism and the Postpositivist Challenge. Valverde Jr, L James.

Science, Democracy, and Public Policy. Shrader-Frechette, Kristin.

Understanding Conflicts between North and South in Cultural Relativism and Philosophy, Dascal, Marcelo (ed). Lacey, Hugh M.

PUBLICATION

A Locke Dictionary. Yolton, John W.

De Productie, Distributie en Consumptie Van Cultuur. Kloek, J J and Mijnhardt, W W.

Bibliography of Paul Weingartner's Publications 1961-1991 in Advances in Scientific Philosophy, Schurz, Gerhard (ed). Stieringer, Eva.

PUNCH, J

The Possibility of Created Entities in Seventeenth-Century Scotism. Coombs, Jeffrey.

PUNCTUATION

On Punctate Content and on Conceptual Role. McLaughlin, Brian.

PUNISHMENT

Hart's Legal Philosophy: An Examination. Bayles, Michael D.

The Problem of Hell. Kvanvig, Jonathan L.

To Make the Punishment Fit the Crime: Essays in the Theory of Criminal Justice. Davis, Michael.

A Solution to the Problem of Moral Luck. Browne, Brynmor.

Crime and Punishment: Abortion as Murder?. Mathieu, Deborah.

Criminal Desert and Unfair Advantage: What's the Connection?. Davis, Michael.

Economic, Retributive and Contractarian Conceptions of Punishment. Avio, K L.

Is There a Duty to Accept Punishment?. Michael, Mark.

Kant's Theory of Punishment in Essays on Kant's Political Philosophy, Williams, Howard (ed). Fleischacker, Samuel.

Locke on Punishment and the Death Penalty. Calvert, Brian.

Penance as a Model for Punishment. Baker, Brenda M.

Punishment—A Tale of Two Islands. Walker, M T.

Reward Event Systems: Reconceptualizing the Explanatory Roles of Motivation, Desire and Pleasure. Morillo, Carolyn R.

Shame, Forgiveness, and Juvenile Justice. Moore, David B.

The Utilitarian Ethics of Punishment and Torture in The Utilitarian Response, Allison, Lincoln (ed). Allison, Lincoln.

Utilitarianism and Retributivism: What's the Difference. Michael, Mark A.

Why Punish the Deserving?. Husak, Douglas N.

PUPIL

see Student

PURE REASON

The Conclusion of the *Critique of Pure Reason*. Grondin, Jean.

PURITANISM

Jonathan Edwards: Puritan, Preacher, Philosopher. Smith, John E.

The Primordial Myth of The Bad Mother and The Good Mother in *Persons and Places* and in *The Last Puritan*. Wenkart, Henny.

PURITY

Kants Begründung der praktischen Philosophie. Freudiger, Jürg.

A Note on Contraries and the Incorruptibility of the Human Soul in St Thomas Aquinas. Wilhelmsen, Frederick.

PURITY

Autocoscienza e conoscenza nel 'primo Rosmini'. De Lucia, Paolo.
The Pure and the Non-Pure (in Hebrew). Senderowicz, Y and Dascal, M.
The Purity of Aesthetic Value. Lorand, Ruth.

PURPOSE

see also Aim
Autonomy and the Philosopher. Agassi, Joseph.
Kant on Plato and the Metaphysics of Purpose. White, David A.
Purpose and Content. Whyte, J T.

PUTNAM, H

A Moderate Mentalism. Peacocke, Christopher.
Abilities, Concepts, and Externalism in Mental Causation, Heil, John (ed). Sosa, Ernest.
Activation Vectors versus Propositional Attitudes: How the Brain Represents Reality. Churchland, Paul M.
Brains in a Vat, Subjectivity, and the Causal Theory of Reference. Ludwig, Kirk.
Commentator on 'Objectivity and the Science-Ethics Distinction' in The Quality of Life, Nussbaum, Martha C (ed). Krüger, Lorenz.
Conceiving One's Envatment While Denying Metaphysical Realism. Brueckner, Anthony.
Conceptual Scheming. Rozema, David.
Formale Semantik im Verhältnis zur Erkenntnistheorie: Ein Blickwechsel. Hrachovec, Herbert.
Hilary Putnam: On Mind, Meaning, and Reality. Harlan, Josh.
John Dewey and the Moral Imagination: Beyond Putnam and Rorty toward a Postmodern Ethics. Alexander, Thomas M.
Kein Platz für phänomenale Qualitäten und Leib- Umwelt- Interaktion?. Pohlenz, Gerd.
Les expériences de Burge et les contenus de pensée. Seymour, Michel.
Meaning Holism and Semantic Realism. Callaway, H G.
On Putnam's Proof That We Are Not Brains-In-A-Vat. Wright, Crispin.
Putnam and the Relativist Menace. Rorty, Richard.
Putnam on Intentionality. Haldane, John.
Putnam on Truth. Rorty, Richard.
Putnam's Brains. McIntyre, Jane.
Putnam's Resolution of the Popper-Kuhn Controversy. Gupta, Chhanda.
Rigidity, Ontology, and Semantic Structure. Sidelle, Alan.
Skepticism, Objectivity, and Brains in Vats. Ebbs, Gary.
Some Objections to Putnam's "Consistency Objection". Humphrey, John A.
What Is at Stake Between Putnam and Rorty?. Forster, Paul.

PUZZLE

Advances in Scientific Philosophy. Schurz, Gerhard (ed) and Dorn, Georg J W (ed).
Boundary Ways: On the Philosophy of the Later Ludwig Wittgenstein (in Hungarian). Neumer, Katalin.
Essays on Philosophy and Economic Methodology. Hausman, Daniel M.
Modalities: Philosophical Essays. Marcus, Ruth Barcan.
Talk About Beliefs. Crimmins, Mark.
A Deflationary Resolution of the Surprise Event Paradox. Jacquette, Dale.
A Linguistic Approach to Frege's Puzzles in Advances in Scientific Philosophy, Schurz, Gerhard (ed). Bellert, Irena.
A Specious Puzzle. Bencivenga, Ermanno.
An Epistemic Principle Which Solves Newcomb's Paradox. Lehrer, Keith and McGee, Vann.
An Epistemic Solution to Goodman's New Riddle of Induction. Rheinwald, Rosemarie.
Because Mere Calculating Isn't Thinking: Comments on Hauser's "Why Isn't My Pocket Calculator a Thinking Thing?". Rapaport, William J.
Causing, Delaying, and Hastening: Do Rains Cause Fires?. Mackie, Penelope.
Competitive Equality of Opportunity. Dahan, Yossi and Yonah, Yossi.
Contractarianism and the "Trolley" Problem. Rosenberg, Alexander.
Daniel C Dennett's The Intentional Stance. Lumsden, David.
Death's Badness. Brueckner, Anthony and Fischer, John Martin.
Dutch Strategies for Diachronic Rules: When Believers See the Sure Loss Coming. Armendt, Brad.
Equity and Mercy. Nussbaum, Martha C.
Fear Without Belief. Morreall, John.
Howson and Franklin on Prediction. Maher, Patrick.
Intentions, Concepts of Intention, and the "Final Solution". Lang, Berel.
Jonathan Westphal's Colour. Broackes, Justin.
Kings and Prisoners (and Aces). Sobel, Jordan Howard.
Kuhn's Paradigms and Neoclassical Economics. Argyrous, George.
Many, but Almost One in Ontology, Causality and Mind: Essays in Honour of D M Armstrong, Bacon, John (ed). Lewis, David.
On Being One's Own Worst Enemy. Champlin, T S.
Particle Labels and the Theory of Indistinguishable Particles in Quantum Mechanics. Redhead, Michael and Teller, Paul.
Probability and Direct Reference: Three Puzzles of Probability Theory. Nida-Rümelin, Martine.
Remarks on the Current Status of the Sorites Paradox. DeWitt, Richard.
Reply to Christian Piller's "Comment on Keith Lehrer and Vann McGee's Solution of Newcomb's Problem". McGee, Vann.
Reply to Lewis's 'Many, but Almost One' in Ontology, Causality and Mind: Essays in Honour of D M Armstrong, Bacon, John (ed). Armstrong, D M.
Robust Deflationism. Kraut, Robert.
Some Puzzles on Essence in Analecta Husserliana, XXXIV, Tymieniecka, Anna-Teresa (ed). García-Baró, Miguel.
The Collapse of Collective Defeat: Lessons from the Lottery Paradox. Korb, Kevin B.

The Dream of Captain Carib. Farley, Jonathan.
The Education of Searle's Demon. Bombardi, Ronald J.
The Puzzle of Experience in The Contents of Experience, Crane, Tim (ed). Valberg, J J.
The Sense of 'Thinking'. Hauser, Larry.
Thomson and the Trolley. Fisher, John and Ravizza, Martin.
Trouble with Leprechauns. Hollis, Martin.
Truth, Omniscience, and Cantorian Arguments: An Exchange. Plantinga, Alvin and Grim, Patrick.
Visual Qualia and Visual Content in The Contents of Experience, Crane, Tim (ed). Tye, Michael.
Why Is There a Discussion of False Belief in the *Theaetetus*?. Benson, Hugh H.
Why Isn't My Pocket Calculator a Thinking Thing?. Hauser, Larry.

PYNCHON, T

Light-Values as Existential Indices in Thomas Pynchon's Extravagant Comic Revery in Analecta Husserliana, XXXVIII, Tymieniecka, Anna-Teresa (ed). Brottman, David.

PYNE, W

Subject to History: Ideology, Class, Gender. Simpson, David (ed).

PYRRHONISM

Ataraxia and *Eudaimonia* in Ancient Pyrrhonism: Is the Skeptic Really Happy?. McPherran, Mark L.
Commentary on McPherran's *Ataraxia* and *Eudaimonia* in Ancient Pyrrhonism. Ryan, George E.

PYTHAGORAS

The Presocratic Philosophers: An Annotated Bibliography. Navia, Luis E.

PYTHAGOREANS

Thrasyllan Platonism. Tarrant, Harold.
The World Made of Sound: Whitehead and Pythagorean Harmonics in the Context of Veda and the Science of Mantra. Amodio, Barbara A.

QUALIA

Acquaintance with Qualia. Bigelow, John and Pargetter, Robert.
Ayerian 'Qualia' and the Empiricist Heritage in The Philosophy of A J Ayer, Hahn, Lewis Edwin (ed). Park, Désirée.
Epiphenomena in Certainty and Surface in Epistemology and Philosophical Method, Martinich, A P (ed). Vendler, Zeno.
Seeing Qualia and Positing the World in A J Ayer Memorial Essays, Griffiths, A Phillips (ed). Honderich, Ted.
Some New Problems for Constructive Speculation in Logic, God and Metaphysics, Harris, James F (ed). Chiaraviglio, Lucio.
The Elimination of Experience. Seager, William.
Two More Proofs of Present Qualia. Wright, Edmond.
Visual Qualia and Visual Content in The Contents of Experience, Crane, Tim (ed). Tye, Michael.

QUALITY

see also Primary Quality, Secondary Quality
Quality of Life, Health and Happiness. Nordenfelt, Lennart.
Bernard Lonergan on Primary vs Secondary Qualities. Glowienka, Emerine.
Forms, Qualities, Resemblance. Deutscher, Max.
Life-Style and the Standard of Living in The Quality of Life, Nussbaum, Martha C (ed). Bliss, Christopher.
Particulars, Individual Qualities, and Universals in Language, Truth and Ontology, Mulligan, Kevin (ed). Lehrer, Keith and McGee, Vann.
Secondary Qualities and Representation. Brooks, D H M.
The Epistemic Role of Qualitative Content. Schick Jr, Theodore W.
The Impossibility and the Necessity of Quality of Life Research. Morreim, E Haavi.
Valla's Dialectic in the North 2: Further Commentaries. Mack, P.

QUALITY OF LIFE

Capability and Well-Being in The Quality of Life, Nussbaum, Martha C (ed). Sen, Amartya.
QALYs—A Threat to our Quality of Life?. Haydock, Anne.
Technology, the Natural Environment, and the Quality of Life. De Cózar, José M.

QUANTIFICATION

An Introduction to the Syllogism and the Logic of Proportional Quantifiers. Thompson, Bruce E R.
Modalities: Philosophical Essays. Marcus, Ruth Barcan.
A Defense of Branching Quantification. Hand, Michael.
Compacidad *via* eliminación de cuantificadores. Naishtat, Francisco.
Counterpart Theory, Quantified Modal Logic, and Extra Argument Places. Lewis, David.
La natura della vita: Una indagine filosofica. Crescini, Angelo.
Philosophie du langage et réalisme aristotélicien. Balmès, Marc.
Thought Experiments in the Philosophy of Physical Science in Thought Experiments in Science and Philosophy, Horowitz, Tamara (ed). Forge, John.
Variables im Tractatus. Von Kibéd, Matthias Varga.

QUANTIFIER

A Philosophical Companion to First-Order Logic. Hughes, R I G (ed).
Algebraizations of Quantifier Logics, An Introductory Overview. Németi, I.
Intermediate Quantifiers for Finch's Proportions. Peterson, Philip L.
On the Logic of Informational Independence and Its Applications. Sandu, Gabriel.
Questions and Quantifiers. Brown, Mark.
Surface Reasoning. Purdy, William C.
The Hanf Numbers of Stationary Logic II: Comparison with Other Logics. Shelah, Saharon.

QUANTITY

Gassendi interprete di Cavalieri. Festa, Egidio.

RATIONALISM

RATIONALITY

REALISM

A New Perspective on Pictorial Reprsentation. Gilman, Daniel J.
A Problem for Anti-Realism. Rogerson, Kenneth.
A Problem for Fictionalism About Possible Worlds. Rosen, Gideon.
A Problem With Constructivist Epistemology. Matthews, Michael R.
A Test of the Scientific Method. Mckee, Bill.
Aesop's Lessons in Literary Realism. Skillen, Anthony.
Against Extended Modal Realism. Perszyk, Kenneth J.
An Artistic Misunderstanding. Dickie, George T.
An Epistemological Defence of Realism about Necessity. Elder, Crawford L.
An Interpretation of the Formalism of Quantum Mechanics in Terms of Epistemological Realism. Jabs, Arthur.
Aristotle and Perceptual Realism. Granger, E Herbert.
Aristotle's Perceptual Realism. Broadie, Sarah.
Astronomy and Antirealism. Shapere, Dudley.
Bayesian Conditionalization Resolves Positivist/Realist Disputes. Dorling, Jon.
Burial by Fire of a Phoenix: Metaphysics, Epistemology, and Realism Under Attack in On the Track of Reason, Beehler, Rodger (ed). Martin, C B.
Categories and Realities. Carr, Brian.
Causal Explanation and Scientific Realism. Hitchcock, Christopher Read.
Causality and Realism in the EPR Experiment. Chang, Hasok and Cartwright, Nancy.
Conceiving One's Envatment While Denying Metaphysical Realism. Brueckner, Anthony.
Conceptual Scheming. Rozema, David.
Concern for Counterparts. Miller, Richard.
Convergent Realism and Approximate Truth. Resnik, David B.
David Armstrong and Realism about Colour in Ontology, Causality and Mind: Essays in Honour of D M Armstrong, Bacon, John (ed). Campbell, Keith.
Deleuze's Bergson: Bergson Redux in The Crisis in Modernism, Burwick, Frederick (ed). Douglass, Paul.
Dignity in Difference in On Community, Rouner, Leroy S (ed). Smith, Huston.
Direct Realism, Indirect Realism, and Epistemology. Brown, Harold I.
Does Orthodox Quantum Theory Undermine, or Support, Scientific Realism?. Maxwell, Nicholas.
Early Heidegger on Being, the Clearing, and Realism in Heidegger: A Critical Reader, Dreyfus, Hubert L (ed). Schatzki, Theodore R.
Eliminative Naturalism and Artistic Meaning. Pylkkö, Pauli.
Epistemology and Realism. Grayling, A C.
Evolution and the Naked Truth in Cultural Relativism and Philosophy, Dascal, Marcelo (ed). Munevar, Gonzalo.
Feyerabend, Realism, and Historicity. Yates, Steven A.
Fichte's Anti-Dogmatism. Martin, Wayne M.
Formulating a Plausible Relativism. Edwards, Steve.
Found: the Missing Explanation. Menzies, Peter and Philip, Pettit.
Genuine Modal Realism: Still the Only Non-circular Game in Town. Miller, Richard B.
Gestalt Switching: Hanson, Aronson, and Harré. Wright, Edmond.
Hayek, Realism and Spontaneous Order. Peacock, Mark S.
Hegel's Idealism in The Cambridge Companion to Hegel, Beiser, Frederick (ed). Wartenberg, Thomas E.
Hegel's Original Insight. Pippin, Robert B.
Heidegger on Realism and the Correspondence Theory of Truth. Tietz, John.
Heidegger: Between Idealism and Realism. Stepanich, Lambert V.
How Not to Refute Realism. George, Alexander.
Human Functioning and Social Justice: In Defense of Aristotelian Essentialism. Nussbaum, Martha C.
Husserl and Analytic Philosophy and Husserlian Intentionality and Non-Foundational Realism. Sokolowski, Robert.
I poeti nel tempo della povertà. Mazzarella, Arturo.
Il Realismo Epistemologico di Rom Harré (parte seconda). Musso, Paolo.
Image-Talk: The Myth in the Mirror. Rankin, K W.
Instance Ontology and Avicenna's Arguments. Mertz, Donald W.
Is Dennett a Disillusioned Zimbo?. Sprigge, T L S.
Is God Good By Definition?. Oppy, Graham.
Is There a Problem about Realism? (in Czechoslovakian). Searle, J R.
La cosmologie transcendantale de Whitehead: transformation spéculative du concept de construction logique. Bradley, James.
La métaphysique de la parole et les faubourgs du langage. Cometti, Jean-Pierre.
La teoria postcartesiana delle idee nella recente storiografia anglosassone. Marcialis, Maria Teresa.
Logical Positivism and Intentionality in A J Ayer Memorial Essays, Griffiths, A Phillips (ed). Putnam, Hilary.
Mathematics and Indispensability. Sober, Elliott.
McAllister on Northrop. Seddon, Fred.
Metaphor and Realism in Aesthetics. Zangwill, Nick.
Minds, Memes, and Rhetoric. Clark, Stephen R L.
Modal Fictionalism: A Response to Rosen. Brock, Stuart.
Moral Realism and Objective Theories of the Right. Sherline, Edward.
Moral Tales. Sharpe, R A.
Mundus est fabula: Descartes und das Problem der Repräsentation in Diagrammatik und Philosophie, Gehring, Petra (ed). Keutner, Thomas.
Neurale netwerken en het wetenschappelijk realisme van de waarheid. De Regt, Herman C D G.
Normative Institutionalism and Normative Realism: A Comparison. Faralli, Carla.
Nota sobre el concepto de realismo epistemológico. Cassini, Alejandro.
On Castigating Constructivists. Phillips, D C.
On Natural Properties in Metaphysics. Taylor, Barry.
On the Improvement of Our Moral Portrait: Moral Realism, History of Subjectivity, and Expressivist Language. Thiebaut, Carlos.

Orwell and the Anti-Realists. Clark, Stephen R L.
Penelope Maddy's Realism in Mathematics and Charles Chihara's Constructibility and Mathematical Existence. McCarty, David Charles.
Perception and Illusion. Sen, Madhucchanda.
Perceptual Realism, Naive and Otherwise in John Searle and His Critics, Lepore, Ernest (ed). Zemach, Eddy M.
Perspectives on Intentional Realism. Davies, David.
Philosophie du langage et réalisme aristotélicien. Balmès, Marc.
Philosophy and Experience. Deely, John N.
Pseudoscience as Nonsense. Lugg, Andrew.
Putnam's Resolution of the Popper-Kuhn Controversy. Gupta, Chhanda.
Quietism. Zangwill, Nick.
Realism about Aesthetic Properties. Goldman, Alan H.
Realism About Laws. Woodward, James.
Realism About What?. Musgrave, Alan.
Realism and Empiricism in Contemporary Physics. Dieks, Dennis.
Realism and Folk Psychology in the Ascription of Concepts. Franks, Bradley.
Realism and Idealism in Peirce's Cosmogony. Anderson, Douglas R.
Realism and Methodological Change. Leplin, Jarrett.
Realism and the Principle of the Common Cause. Stone, Mark A.
Realism, Modernism, and the Empty Chair in Postmodernism/ Jameson/ Critique, Kellner, Douglas M (ed). Zuidervaart, Lambert.
Realism, Psychologism, and Intermediary-Shadows in Wittgenstein's Tractatus. Borst, Clive.
Realism, Relativism, and Naturalized Meta-Epistemololgy. Maffie, James.
Réalisme et anti-réalisme en logique. Nef, Frédéric.
Reflections Upon Roy Bhaskar's 'Critical Realism'. Suchting, Wal.
Reinhold Niebuhr and the Ethics of Realism in International Relations. Rich, Paul.
Reply to Campbell's 'David Armstrong and Realism about Colour' in Ontology, Causality and Mind: Essays in Honour of D M Armstrong, Bacon, John (ed). Armstrong, D M.
Resemblance: An Account of Realism in Painting. McKee, Patrick L.
Rethinking the Teaching of Philosophy. Kolenda, Konstantin.
Romanticist and Realist Elements in Nationalist Thinking in the 19th Century. Kemiläinen, Aira.
Ronald Giere's "Explaining Science: A Cognitive Approach". Resnik, David B.
Rule Following and Wright's Social Assessment: Towards Wittgenstein's "Anti-Idiolectic" Understanding. Behera, Satrughna.
Schopenhauer and Direct Realism. Henle, R J.
Science, Realization and Reality: The Fundamental Issues. Radder, Hans.
Scientific Realism and Invariance in Rationality in Epistemology, Villanueva, Enrique (ed). Ghins, Michael.
Scientific Realism and the Criteria for Theory-Choice. McAllister, James W.
Semantic Indeterminacy and the Realist Stance. Wilburn, Ronald.
Some Reflections on Contemporary Epistemology. Tollefsen, Olaf.
Suárez and Metaphysical Mentalism: The Last Visit. Gracia, Jorge J E.
Surface Knowledge in Certainty and Surface in Epistemology and Philosophical Method, Martinich, A P (ed). Alexander Jr, Henry A.
The Anti-Realist's Master Argument. Brueckner, Anthony.
The Argument from Agreement and Mathematical Realism. Garavaso, Pieranna.
The Limits of Pragmatism and the Limits of Realism. Murphy, Nancey.
The Lure of the Ideal in Peirce and Law, Kevelson, Roberta. Bernstein, Richard J.
The Metaphysics of Anti-Realism. Young, James O.
The Method of Possible Worlds. Beck, Simon.
The New Science and the Old: Complexity and Realism in the Social Sciences. Reed, Michael and Harvey, David L.
The Passing of Peirce's Realism. Margolis, Joseph.
The Pluralistic Hypothesis, Realism, and Post-Eschatology. Heim, S Mark.
The Role of Internalism in Moral Theory. Bartkowiak, Julia.
The Role of Limits in Aristotle's Concept of Place. Mariña, Jacqueline.
Theory, Realism and Common Sense: A Reply to Paul Churchland. Haldane, John.
Theory-Conjunction and Mercenary Reliance. Trout, J D.
Three Types of Projectivism in Psychoanalysis, Mind and Art, Hopkins, Jim (ed). Price, A W.
Time and Change. Teichmann, Roger.
Truth and Freedom. Bedell, Gary.
Verificationism, Scepticism, and Consciousness. Seager, William.
What is Right with the Miracle Argument: Establishing a Taxonomy of Natural Kinds. Carrier, Martin.
Why Local Realistic Theories Violate, Nontrivially, the Quantum Mechanical EPR Perfect Correlations. Elby, Andrew.
Wittgenstein and Moral Realism. Werhane, Patricia H.
Wittgenstein, Anti-Realism and Mathematical Propositions in Criss-Crossing A Philosophical Landscape, Schulte, Joachim (ed). Bouveresse, Jacques.
Zum Wesen des Common Sense: Aristoteles und die naive Physik. Smith, Barry.
'I Am No Longer a Realist': An Interview with Jean-Paul Sartre in Sartre Alive, Aronson, Ronald (ed). Verstraeten, Pierre.

REALITY

see also Being, Existence, Ontology, Physical Reality
A Study of Concepts. Peacocke, Christopher.
Ad Litteram: Authoritative Texts and Their Medieval Readers. Jordan, Mark D (ed) and Emery, Jr, Kent (ed).
Aesthetic Judgment and the Moral Image of the World: Studies in Kant. Henrich, Dieter.
Analecta Husserliana, XXXVIII. Tymieniecka, Anna-Teresa (ed).
Analysis and Metaphysics: An Introduction to Philosophy. Strawson, Peter.
Basic Concepts—Martin Heidegger. Aylesworth, Gary E (trans) and Heidegger, Martin.

REALITY

Two Concepts of Truth. Hugly, Philip G and Sayward, Charles.

Two Sources of Knowledge. Simakov, M.

Una nuova edizione italiana di Platone. Bausola, Adriano.

Varieties of Meaning and Truth in The Philosophy of A J Ayer, Hahn, Lewis E (ed). Agazzi, Evandro.

Vision, Causation and Occlusion. Hyman, John.

Vitalism, Empiricism, and the Quest for Reality in German and English Philosophy in The Crisis in Modernism, Burwick, Frederick (ed). Klein, Jürgen.

What are We Looking for When We Search for Meaning?. Längle, Alfried.

What-Being: Chuang Tzu versus Aristotle. Li, Chenyang.

Whitehead and Kant on Presuppositions of Meaning. Van Der Veken, Jan.

Who is Heidegger's Nietzsche? in Heidegger: A Critical Reader, Dreyfus, Hubert (ed). Havas, Randall.

Why Do Idealizational Statements Apply to Reality? in Idealization III, Brzenzinski, Jerzy (ed). Paprzycka, Katarzyna.

Why This World?. Brooks, David.

William James's Theory of the Self. Cooper, W E.

Wittgenstein and Derrida on Meaning. Rowlands, Mark.

Wittgenstein's Concept of Showing in Criss-Crossing A Philosophical Landscape, Schulte, Joachim (ed). Pears, David.

'Les Immatériaux' and the Postmodern Sublime in Judging Lyotard, Benjamin, Andrew (ed). Crowther, Paul.

'Philosophical Investigations' Section 128: in Wittgenstein's Philosophical Investigations, Arrington, Robert L (ed). Glock, Hans-Johann.

REALIZABILITY

Multiple Realizability and Psychophysical Reduction. Bickle, John.

REALIZATION

see also Self-Realization

Realizing. Smith, Steven G.

REASON

see also Practical Reason, Rationalism, Theoretical Reason

"Es ist uns aber bestimmt, von Überzeugungen, die wir aus innerer Notwendigkeit denken, zu leben". Kern, Udo.

"Influxus Physicus" in Causation in Early Modern Philosophy, Nadler, Steven (ed). O'Neill, Eileen.

"Unreasons' Reason": Cervantes at the Frontiers of Difference. Wilson, Diana de Armas.

"Was darf ich hoffen?" Zum Problem der Vereinbarkeit von theoretischer und praktischer Vernunft bei Immanuel Kant. Förster, Eckart.

7+5=12: Analytic or Synthetic?. Tacelli, Ronald.

A Progress of Sentiments: Reflections on Hume's "Treatise". Baier, Annette.

Against Relativism: A Philosophical Defense of Method. Harris, James F.

Altruism. Paul, Ellen Frankel (ed), Miller, Fred D (ed) and Paul, Jeffrey (ed).

America's Philosophical Vision—John E Smith. Colapietro, Vincent.

An Essay on Belief and Acceptance. Cohen, L Jonathan.

An Introduction to Ethics. Thomas, Geoffrey.

Analecta Husserliana, XXXIV. Tymieniecka, Anna-Teresa (ed).

Aufgeklärtes Eigeninteresse: Eine Theorie theoretischer und praktischer Rationalität. Gosepath, Stefan.

Back to the Rough Ground. Dunne, Joseph.

Bayes or Bust? A Critical Examination of Bayesian Confirmation Theory. Earman, John.

Contemporary Perspectives on Religious Epistemology. Geivert, R Douglas (ed) and Sweetman, Brendan (ed).

Divine Hiddenness and Human Reason. Schellenberg, J L.

Eighteenth-Century Hermeneutics: Philosophy of Interpretation in England from Locke to Burke. Weinsheimer, Joel C.

Essays on Kant's Political Philosophy. Williams, Howard (ed).

Ethical Dimensions of Legal Theory. Sadurski, Wojciech (ed).

Feminist Epistemologies. Alcoff, Linda (ed) and Potter, Elizabeth (ed).

Fiat vita, pereat veritas: Nietzsche's Untimely Reflections on Hegel's Dialectic of History. Axiotis, Ares.

Forms of Concrescence: Alfred North Whitehead's Philosophy and Computer Programming Structures. Henry, Granville C.

Herder's Aesthetics and the European Enlightenment. Norton, Robert E.

In the Throe of Wonder: Intimations of the Sacred in a Post-Modern World. Miller, Jerome A.

Injustice and Restitution: The Ordinance of Time. Ross, Stephen D.

Irrationality and the Philosophy of Psychoanalysis. Gardner, Sebastian.

Kierkegaard and Kant: The Hidden Debt. Green, Ronald M.

La Città della Ragione: Per Una Storia Filosofica del Settecento Francese. Postigliola, Alberto.

La Filosofia del Hombre. Lorite-Mena, José.

Lectures on Logic—Immanuel Kant. Young, Michael J (ed & trans).

Machinations: Computational Studies of Logic, Language, and Cognition. Spencer-Smith, Richard (ed) and Torrance, Steve (ed).

Malum Vitandum: The Role of Intentions in First-Order Morality. Sullivan, Thomas D and Atkinson, Gary.

Metaphor and Cognition. Indurkhya, Bipin.

Metaphysical Aporia and Philosophical Heresy. Ross, Stephen David.

Moral Reasoning: Ethical Theory and Some Contemporary Moral Problems (Second Edition). Grassian, Victor.

Natural Reasons: Personality and Polity. Hurley, S L.

Norms of Rhetorical Culture. Farrell, Thomas B.

On the Track of Reason. Beehler, Rodger G (ed), Copp, David (ed) and Szabados, Bela (ed).

Passionate Reason: Making Sense of Kierkegaard's "Philosophical Fragments". Evans, C Stephen.

Person and Religion: An Introduction to the Philosophy of Religion. Sandok, Theresa (trans) and Zdybicka, Zofia J.

Philosophy of Economics: On the Scope of Reason in Economic Inquiry. Roy, Subroto.

Philosophy—A Myth?. Verster, Ulrich.

Political Liberalism. Rawls, John.

Practices of Reason: 'Aristotle's Nicomachean Ethics'. Reeve, C D C.

Praxiologies and the Philosophy of Economics: The International Annual of Practical Philosophy and Methodology. Auspitz, J Lee (ed), Gasparski, Wojciech W (ed) and Mlicki, Marek K (ed).

Prima Facie Obligation in John Searle and His Critics, Lepore, Ernest (ed). Loewer, Barry and Belzer, Marvin.

Psychoanalysis, Mind and Art. Hopkins, Jim (ed) and Savile, Anthony (ed).

Reason and Argument. Feldman, Richard.

Reason and Responsibility (Eighth Edition). Feinberg, Joel.

Reason and Tradition in Indian Thought: An Essay on the Nature of Indian Philosophical Thinking. Mohanty, Jitendra N.

Reasoned Faith. Stump, Eleonore (ed).

Reasoning: A Practical Guide. Pinto, Robert C and Blair, John Anthony.

Religion and Philosophy. Warner, Martin (ed).

Revisioning Philosophy. Ogilvy, James (ed).

Scepticism. Hookway, Christopher.

Sharing without Reckoning. Schumaker, Millard.

Social and Personal Ethics. Shaw, William H.

The Concept of Political Judgment. Steinberger, Peter J.

The Mathematical Soul: An Antique Prototype of the Modern Mathematisation of Psychology. Stachowski, Ryszard.

The Mechanism and Freedom of Logic. Henry, Granville C.

The Metaphysics of Death. Fischer, John Martin (ed).

The Persistence of Modernity: Essays on Aesthetics, Ethics, and Postmodernism. Midgley, David N (trans) and Wellmer, Albrecht.

The Place of Emotion in Argument. Walton, Douglas N.

The Principle of Reason—Martin Heidegger. Heidegger, Martin and Lilly, Reginald (trans).

The Renewal of the Heidegger-Kant Dialogue: Action, Thought, and Responsibility. Schalow, Frank.

The Resources of Rationality: A Response to the Postmodern Challenge. Schrag, Calvin.

The Roles of Sense and Thought in Knowledge. De, P K.

Theology and Difference: The Wound of Reason. Lowe, Walter.

Thinking Logically: Basic Concepts for Reasoning (Second Edition). Freeman, James.

Understanding Action: An Essay on Reasons. Schick, Frederic.

Unreason Within Reason: Essays on the Outskirts of Rationality. Graham, A C.

What Computers "Still" Can't Do: A Critique of Artificial Reason (Rev Ed). Dreyfus, Hubert L.

A Discourse-Theoretical Conception of Practical Reason. Alexy, Robert.

A Matemática como Paradigma da Construçao Filosófica de Descartes: Do Discurso do Método e da Tematizaçao do Cogito. Spinelli, Miguel.

Abduction, Legal Reasoning, and Reflexive Law in Peirce and Law, Kevelson, Roberta. Uusitalo, Jyrki.

Acting for Reasons and Acting Intentionally. Mele, Alfred.

Actions, Reasons and Mental Causes (in French). Engel, Pascal.

Adelheid and the Bishop—What's the Game? in Wittgenstein's Philosophical Investigations, Arrington, Robert L (ed). Schulte, Joachim.

Agency and Causal Explanation in Mental Causation, Heil, John (ed). Hornsby, Jennifer.

Alpha-Claims and the Problem of Evil. Schellenberg, J L.

An Intervention Curriculum for Moral Development. Ries, Steven I.

An Optimist's Pessimism: Conversation and Conjunction in Probability and Rationality, Eells, Ellery (ed). Adler, Jonathan.

Analogical Reasoning and Easy Rescue Cases. Young, Thomas.

Analogical Reasoning: A Logical Inquiry About "Archaic Thought". Van Dormael, Jan.

Anamnestic Reason in Cultural-Political Interventions in the Unfinished Project of Enlightenment, Honneth, Axel (& other eds). Metz, Johann Baptist.

Anchoring Conceptual Content: Scenarios and Perception in Cognition, Semantics and Philosophy, Ezquerro, Jesús (ed). Peacocke, Christopher.

Apollo, Music, and Cross-Cultural Rationality. Higgins, Kathleen M.

Aristotle and Hegel on Nature: Some Similarities. Santoro-Brienza, Liberato.

Aristotle on Reason, Practical Reason, and Living Well in Essays in Ancient Greek Philosophy, IV, Anton, John P (ed). Modrak, D K W.

Aristotle's Practical Particularism in Essays in Ancient Greek Philosophy, IV, Anton, John P (ed). Louden, Robert B.

Artificial Virtues and the Sensible Knave. Gauthier, David.

Berkeley and Scepticism: A Fatal Dalliance. Imlay, Robert A.

Beyond Reason: The Importance of Emotion in Philosophy in Revisioning Philosophy, Ogilvy, James (ed). Solomon, Robert C.

Beyond the Virtues-Principles Debate. Keat, Marilyn S.

Bodies and Knowledges: Feminism and the Crisis of Reason in Feminist Epistemologies, Alcoff, Linda (ed). Grosz, Elizabeth.

Causal Laws and the Foundations of Natural Science in The Cambridge Companion to Kant, Guyer, Paul (ed). Friedman, Michael.

RELEVANT LOGIC

On Interpreting Truth Tables and Relevant Truth Table Logic. Sylvan, Richard.

Read Reduced Models for Relevant Logics Without WI. Giambrone, Steve.

Relational Proof System for Relevant Logics. Orlowska, Ewa.

Relevant Consequence and Empirical Inquiry. Osherson, Daniel N and Weinstein, Scott.

The Admissibility of γ in R4. Mares, Edwin D and Meyer, Robert K.

The First Axiomatization of Relevant Logic. Dosen, Kosta.

The Semantics of R4. Mares, Edwin and Meyer, Robert K.

RELIABILISM

A Dilemma for Causal Reliabilist Theories of Knowledge. Lipson, Morris and Savitt, Steven.

Causality, Reliabilism, and Mathematical Knowledge. Casullo, Albert.

Generic Reliabilism and Virtue Epistemology in Rationality in Epistemology, Villanueva, Enrique (ed). Sosa, Ernest.

RELIABILITY

Reliability in Mathematical Physics. Liston, Michael.

Why Believe What People Say?. Stevenson, Leslie.

RELIGION

see also Agnosticism, Atheism, Buddhism, Christianity, Deism, Dogma, Evil, Faith, Fideism, God, Hinduism, Humanism, Immorality, Jainism, Judaism, Metaphysics, Miracle, Mysticism, Pantheism, Pietism, Theism

"He spak to [T]hem that wolde lyve parfitly:" Thomas Aquinas, the Wife of Bath and the Two Senses of Religion. Sommers, Mary C.

"Liebe, die im Geist mir redet...": Dantes Dame Philosophie. Splett, Jörg.

"New Creation"—the Christian Symbol of Universalism and Our Steps Towards Its Realization. Hummel, Gert.

"Nietzsche im christlichen Denken—am Beispiel Bernhard Weltes". Kienzler, Klaus.

"Saisir Dieu en son vestiaire": L'articulation theologique du sens chez Maître Eckhart. Malherbe, Jean-François.

"The Will to Believe": James's Defense of Religious Intolerance. Gordon, Jeffrey.

"Was darf ich hoffen?" Zum Problem der Vereinbarkeit von theoretischer und praktischer Vernunft bei Immanuel Kant. Förster, Eckart.

A History of Buddhist Philosophy. Kalupahana, David J.

Ad Litteram: Authoritative Texts and Their Medieval Readers. Jordan, Mark D (ed) and Emery, Jr, Kent (ed).

Al-Farabi and His School. Netton, Ian.

America's Philosophical Vision—John E Smith. Colapietro, Vincent.

Antologia della filosofia cinese. Arena, Leonardo Vittorio.

Aquinas on Human Action: A Theory of Practice. McInerny, Ralph.

Aquinas on Mind. Kenny, Anthony.

Aquinas: An Introduction to the Life and Work of the Great Medieval Thinker. Copleston, F C.

Ascetic Figures Before and In Early Buddhism: The Emergence of Gautama as the Buddha. Wiltshire, Martin G.

Athens and Jerusalem: The Role of Philosophy in Theology. Bonsor, Jack A.

Augustine's "De Civitate Dei": An Annotated Bibliography of Modern Criticism, 1960-1990. Donnelly, Dorothy F and Sherman, Mark A.

Axiology: The Science of Values. Bahm, Archie.

Belfagor: Machiavelli's Short Story. Sumberg, Theodore A.

Beyond Liberation Theology. Belli, Humberto and Nash, Ronald.

Birth, Suffering, and Death: Catholic Perspectives at the Edges of Life. Wildes, Kevin W (ed), Abel, Francesc (ed) and Harvey, John C (ed).

Buddhism, Sexuality, and Gender. Cabezón, José I (ed).

Catalyst for Controversy: Paul Carus of Open Court. Henderson, Harold.

Causation in Early Modern Philosophy. Nadler, Steven (ed).

Charles Sanders Peirce: A Life. Brent, Joseph.

Christian Philosophy. Flint, Thomas P (ed).

Confucianism, Buddhism, Daoism, Christianity and Chinese Culture. McLean, George F (ed) and Yi-Jie, Tang.

Consent: The Means to an Active Faith According to St Thomas Aquinas. Barad, Judith.

Contemporary Perspectives on Religious Epistemology. Geivert, R Douglas (ed) and Sweetman, Brendan (ed).

Cosmos, Bios, Theos: Scientists Reflect on Science, God, and the Origins of the Universe, Life, and "Homo sapiens". Margenau, Henry (ed) and Varghese, Roy Abraham (ed).

Creenciay Racionalidad: Lecturas de Filosofía de la Religión. Romerales, Enrique (ed).

Dialogues Concerning Natural Religion—David Hume. Hume, David and Bell, Martin (ed).

Die Welt des Menschen. Kessler, Herbert.

Disputed Questions in Theology and the Philosophy of Religion. Hick, John.

Divine Hiddenness and Human Reason. Schellenberg, J L.

Divine Infinity in Greek and Medieval Thought. Sweeney, Leo.

Empirical Theology: A Handbook. Miller, Randolph Crump (ed).

Eternity and Time's Flow. Neville, Robert Cummings.

Ethical Essays, Volume I. Harrison, Jonathan.

Ethical Essays, Volume II. Harrison, Jonathan.

Fides Quaerens Intellectum: St Anselm's Method in Philosophical Theology. Adams, Marilyn McCord.

Forms of Concrescence: Alfred North Whitehead's Philosophy and Computer Programming Structures. Henry, Granville C.

Frontiers in American Philosophy, Volume I. Burch, Robert W (ed) and Saatkamp, Herman J Jr (ed).

George Berkeley: Alciphron in Focus. Berman, David (ed).

God and Existence (in Hungarian). Joós, Ernó.

God and the Knowledge of Reality. Molnar, Thomas.

God, Creation, and Revelation: A Neo-Evangelical Theology. Jewett, Paul K.

God, Values, and Empiricism. Peden, W Creighton (ed) and Axel, Larry E (ed).

Goodness and Rightness in Thomas Aquinas's "Summa Theologiae". Keenan, James F.

Hegel on Logic and Religion: The Reasonableness of Christianity. Burbidge, John W.

Hegel, Freedom, and Modernity. Westphal, Merold.

Hell: The Logic of Damnation. Walls, Jerry.

Henry of Ghent: Quodlibetal Questions on Free Will. Teske, Roland (trans).

History, Religion, and American Democracy (New Edition). Wohlgelernter, Maurice (ed).

Hobbes and Human Nature. Green, Arnold W.

Homo Religiosus ou L'Homme Vertical. Rostenne, Paul.

In the Throe of Wonder: Intimations of the Sacred in a Post-Modern World. Miller, Jerome A.

Invitation to Philosophy: Issues and Options (Sixth Edition). Honer, Stanley M, Hunt, Thomas C and Okholm, Dennis L.

Jonathan Edwards: Puritan, Preacher, Philosopher. Smith, John E.

Just War and the Gulf War. Johnson, James Turner and Weigel, George.

Kierkegaard and Kant: The Hidden Debt. Green, Ronald M.

Kierkegaard on Art and Communication. Pattison, George (ed).

L'Utopia nella Storia: La Rivoluzione Inglese. Colombo, Arrigo (ed) and Schiavone, Giuseppe.

Liberal Rights: Collected Papers 1981-1991. Waldron, Jeremy.

Logic and Sin in the Writings of Ludwig Wittgenstein. Shields, Philip.

Making Sense of It All. Morris, Thomas V.

Moral Philosophy: A Reader. Pojman, Louis (ed).

Naming and Reference. Nelson, R J.

Nature and Spirit: An Essay in Ecstatic Naturalism. Corrington, Robert S.

Nietzsche and Asian Thought. Parkes, Graham R (ed).

Nietzsche and Modern Times. Lampert, Laurence.

On Feeling, Knowing, and Valuing: Selected Writings—Max Scheler. Scheler, Max.

On Intersubjectivity and Cultural Creativity—Martin Buber. Eisenstadt, S N (ed) and Buber, Martin.

Our Knowledge of God. Clark, Kelly James (ed).

Passionate Reason: Making Sense of Kierkegaard's "Philosophical Fragments". Evans, C Stephen.

Person and Being. Clarke, W Norris.

Person and Religion: An Introduction to the Philosophy of Religion. Sandok, Theresa (trans) and Zdybicka, Zofia J.

Perspectives on the History of Mathematical Logic. Drucker, Thomas (ed).

Philosophical Perspectives, 5: Philosophy of Religion, 1991. Tomberlin, James E (ed).

Philosophy and Biblical Interpretation: A Study in Nineteenth-Century Conflict. Addinall, Peter.

Philosophy and Theology in the Middle Ages. Evans, G R.

Philosophy in Literature, Volumes I and II. Johnson, Charles W.

Philosophy of Religion: A Universalist Perspective. Sterling, Marvin.

Philosophy, Religion and the Spiritual Life. McGhee, Michael (ed).

Pistis et Episteme: A Proposito di una lettura "diacritica" di 1 Cor 2, 3. Campanale, Domenico.

Postmodernism/ Jameson/ Critique. Kellner, Douglas M (ed).

Practical Knowledge—Yves R Simon. Mulvaney, Robert J (ed) and Simon, Yves R.

Profundity: A Universal Value. Harrell, Jean Gabbert.

Prospects for Natural Theology. Long, Eugene Thomas (ed).

Radical Fragments. Marsh, James.

Rational Infidels: The American Deists. Walters, Kerry S.

Reasoned Faith. Stump, Eleonore (ed).

Reflections on Philosophy. McHenry, Leemon (ed) and Adams, Frederick (ed).

Religion and Philosophy. Warner, Martin (ed).

Religion from Tolstoy to Camus. Kaufmann, Walter (ed).

Renewing Philosophy. Putnam, Hilary.

San Juan de la Cruz: Mysticism and Sartrean Existentialism. Ellis, Robert Richmond.

Santayana, Pragmatism, and the Spiritual Life. Levinson, Henry Samuel.

Self as Body in Asian Theory and Practice. Kasulis, Thomas P (ed).

Shadow of Spirit. Berry, Philippa (ed) and Wernick, Andrew (ed).

Socialism and Morality. McLellan, David (ed) and Sayers, Sean (ed).

Speaking of a Personal God: An Essay in Philosophical Theology. Brümmer, Vincent.

Spinoza's Ethics: The View from Within. Schipper, Lewis.

Standing In Your Own Way: Talks On the Nature of Ego. Damiani, Anthony.

Status y verificación de la creencia religiosa. Tomasini Bassols, Alejandro.

Storia del Buddhismo Ch'an. Arena, Leonardo Vittorio.

Studies in Augustine and Eriugena. O'Meara, John J and Halton, Thomas (ed).

T S Eliot and American Philosophy: The Harvard Years. Jain, Manju.

Terra es animata: On Having a Life. Meilaender, Gilbert C.

The Beginning of the Gospel According to Saint John: Philosophical Reflections. Mensch, James Richard.

The Cambridge Companion to Hegel. Beiser, Frederick (ed).

RELIGION

The Challenge of Pluralism: Education, Politics, and Values. Power, F Clark (ed) and Lapsley, Daniel K (ed).

The Diversity of Religions: A Christian Perspective. DiNoia, J A.

The Emancipative Theory of Jürgen Habermas and Metaphysics. McLean, George F (ed) and Badillo, Robert Peter.

The Epistemology of Religious Experience. Yandell, Keith E.

The Life of Irony and the Ethics of Belief. Wisdo, David.

The Love Commandments: Essays in Christian Ethics and Moral Philosophy. Santurri, Edmund N (ed) and Werpehowski, William (ed).

The Perfection of the Universe According to Aquinas: A Teleological Cosmology. Blanchette, Oliva.

The Philosopher of Free Religion: Francis Ellingwood Abbot, 1836-1903. Peden, W Creighton.

The Portable Medieval Reader. Ross, James Bruce (ed) and McLaughlin, Mary Martin (ed).

The Problem of Hell. Kvanvig, Jonathan L.

The Quotable Bertrand Russell. Eisler, Lee (ed).

The Rehabilitation of Myth. Mali, Joseph.

The Sickness unto Death in Foundations of Kierkegaard's Vision of Community, Connell, George B (ed). Crites, Stephen.

The Trinity: An Analysis of St Thomas Aquinas' 'Expositio' of the 'De Trinitate' of Boethius. Hall, Douglas.

The Uses of Antiquity. Gaukroger, Stephen (ed).

Theology and Difference: The Wound of Reason. Lowe, Walter.

Theory Now and Then. Miller, J Hillis.

Time and Transcendence: Secular History, the Catholic Reaction and the Rediscovery of the Future. Motzkin, Gabriel.

Treatise on Ethics (1684). Malebranche, Nicolas and Walton, Craig (trans).

Treatise on the Intellect and the Intelligible. Führer, M L (trans).

Trinity and Process: A Critical Evaluation and Reconstruction of Hartshorne's Di-Polar Theism Towards a Trinitarian Metaphysics. Boyd, Gregory.

Understanding Non-Western Philosophy: Introductory Readings. Bonevac, Daniel A and Phillips, Stephen.

What is God? The Selected Essays of Richard R La Croix. Lucey, Kenneth (ed).

Wittgenstein Centenary Essays. Griffiths, A Phillips (ed).

Wittgenstein's Intentions. Canfield, J V (ed) and Shanker, Stuart G (ed).

A "Just", A Human Society: A Christian- Marxist- Confucian Dialogue. Swindler, Leonard.

A Big Bang Cosmological Argument for God's Nonexistence. Smith, Quentin.

A Classical Misunderstanding of Anselm's Argument. Schufreider, Gregory.

A Comparison of the Chinese Buddhist and Indian Buddhist Modes of Thought. Litian, Fang.

A Contradiction in Saint Thomas's Teaching on Creation. Kondoleon, Theodore J.

A Critique of Borowitz's Postmodern Jewish Theology. Samuelson, Norbert M.

A Defence of Christian Revelation. Byrne, Peter.

A Hegelian/Whiteheadian Critique of Whitehead's Dipolar Theism. Christensen, Darrel E.

A Latter-Day Look at the Foreknowledge Problem. Pike, Nelson.

A Neopragmatist Perspective on Religion and Science. Robbins, J Wesley.

A New Look at the Problem of Evil. Gellman, Jerome I.

A New Religion. Stove, David.

A Note on Barth and Aquinas. Roy, Louis.

A Note on Contraries and the Incorruptibility of the Human Soul in St Thomas Aquinas. Wilhelmsen, Frederick.

A Note on Samkara's Theodicy. Matilal, Bimal Krishna.

A Note on Schadenfreude and Proverbs 17:5. Harvey, Warren Z.

A Origem da Moral em Psicanálise. Gabbi Jr, Osmyr Faria.

A Reply to Paul Helm. Gale, Richard.

A Reply to Robert O'Connell's "Faith, Reason, and Ascent to Vision in Saint Augustine". Van Fleteren, Frederick.

A Spinozistic Vision of God. Leslie, John.

A Study of Part I, Chapters 1-7 of Maimonides' *The Guide of the Perplexed*. Kleven, Terence.

A Theophrastean Excursus on God and Nature and its Aftermath in Hellenistic Thought. Mansfeld, Jaap.

A Theory of Personal Language and Implications for Logos Theology. Crewdson, Joan.

Abraham's Silence Aesthetically Considered in Kierkegaard on Art and Communication, Pattison, George (ed). Perkins, Robert L.

Academic Freedom. O'Reilly, Paul.

Advice from a Thomist. Synan, Edward A.

Aesthetics and Religion in Kierkegaard on Art and Communication, Pattison, George (ed). Polka, Brayton.

Agatheism: A Justification of the Rationality of Devotion to God. Creel, Richard E.

Akrasia (Weakness of Will) and the Christian Understanding of Moral Failure. Brown, Robert F.

Aktuelle Themen und Positionen deutschsprachiger Religionsphilosophie. Engstler, Achim.

Albert the Great and the Hierarchy of Sciences. Jordan, Mark D.

Albert the Great in the Renaissance: Cristoforo Landino's Use of Albert on the Soul. McNair, Bruce.

All This, and God Too? Postmodern Alternatives to Don Cupitt. Cowdell, Scott.

Alpha-Claims and the Problem of Evil. Schellenberg, J L.

Altruism and Christian Love. Browning, Don.

An Alternative Form of Theological Knowing. Newman, Elizabeth.

An Answer on Behalf of Guanilo. Landau, Iddo.

An Anthropological Vision of CHristian Marriage. Martinez, German.

An Appeal for a Christian Virtue Ethic. Kotva Jr, Joseph J.

An Early Neo-Hindu Reception of Nietzsche by Sri Aurobindo Ghose (1872-1950) (in Dutch). Van Dijk, A M G.

An Inquiry into Gender Considerations and Gender Conscious Reflectivity in Early Buddhism. Rajapakse, Vijitha.

An Inquiry into Religion's Empty World. Martland, Thomas R.

An Intervention into the Flew/Fogelin Debate. Ferguson, Kenneth.

An Interview with A J Ayer in A J Ayer Memorial Essays, Griffiths, A Phillips (ed). Honderich, Ted.

An Introduction to *Theology and Social Theory*. Burrell, David B.

Anamnestic Reason in Cultural-Political Interventions in the Unfinished Project of Enlightenment, Honneth, Axel (& other eds). Metz, Johann Baptist.

Anselm on Praising a Necessarily Perfect Being. Rogers, K A.

Anselm, Plantinga and the Ontological Argument. Esmail, K H A.

Antitheism: A Reflection. New, Christopher.

Aquinas and Natural Human Fulfillment: Inconsistencies. Hayden, R Mary.

Aquinas on the Resurrection of the Body. Brown, Montague.

Aquinas's Arguments for Spirit. Foster, David R.

Aquinas's Changing Evaluation of Platon on Creation. Johnson, Mark.

Aquinas's Concept of the Body and Out of Body Situations. Quinn, Patrick.

Aristotle and the Sacrament of the Altar: A Crisis in Medieval Aristotelianism. Adams, Marilyn McCord.

Atonement and Reconciliation. Brümmer, Vincent.

Attention, Extension, and Ecstasis in Augustine's Account of Time. Pawelski, James.

Augustine's Erotic Ascent. Kinz, Susan.

Augustine's Own Examples of Lying. Feehan, Thomas.

Augustine's Radiant Confessional—Theatre of Prophecy. Duval, R Shannon.

Augustinian Christian Philosophy. Plantinga, Alvin.

Authenticating Biblical Reports of Miracles. Wiebe, Phillip H.

Averroes, Aristotle, and the Qur'an on Immortality. Mohammed, Ovey N.

Ayer and World Views in A J Ayer Memorial Essays, Griffiths, A Phillips (ed). Copleston, F C.

Basic Goods and the Human Good in Recent Catholic Moral Theology. Porter, Jean.

Basic Principles of Differentiating of Conception of God (in Polish). Gogacz, Mieczyslaw.

Begegnung der Kulturen und inkulturierte Philosophie in Lateinamerika. Scannone, Juan Carlos.

Belief vs Commitment, Validity vs Value: A Response to Ward Goodenough. Brink, T L.

Belief-In and Belief In God. Williams, John N.

Bibliographie P Josef de Vries S J (1898-1989). Scheit, Herbert.

Big Bangs, Plural: A Heretical View. Pecker, Jean-Claude.

Blijenbergh's Tussing with Evil and Spinoza's Response (in Dutch). Klever, W.

Brain Death: A Survey of the Debate and the Position in 1991. Jeffery, Peter.

Bruce Marshall's Reading of Aquinas. Roy, Louis.

By Their Fruit You Shall Know Them: Eschatological and Legal Elements in Peirce's Philosophy in Peirce and Law, Kevelson, Roberta. Schultz, Lorenz.

Call and Conscience in Tauler and Heidegger. Sikka, Sonya.

Call Me Ishmael—Call Everybody Ishmael in Foundations of Kierkegaard's Vision of Community, Connell, George B (ed). Kirmmse, Bruce.

Can Metaphysics Solve the Problem of Skepticism? in Rationality in Epistemology, Villanueva, Enrique (ed). Foley, Richard.

Can Religion Give Science a Heart?. Kozhamthadam, Job.

Character Consequentialism and Early Confucianism. Ivanhoe, Philip.

Charles F Potter: On Evolution and Religious Humanism in God, Values, and Empiricism, Peden, Creighton (ed). Olds, W Mason.

Chinese Bhiksunis in the Ch'an Tradition (in Chinese). Shih, Heng-ching.

Christian Philosophy: Sociological Category or Oxymoron?. Dougherty, Jude P.

Christian Religious Discourse. Sokolowski, Robert.

Christian Wolff's Criticism of Spinoza. Morrison, J C.

Christianisme et philosophie dans la première philosophie de Fichte. Goddard, Jean-Christophe.

Christianity at the End of the Story or the Return of the Master-Narrative. Loughlin, Gerard.

Christology and its Philosophical Complexities in the Thought of Leontius of Byzantium. Moutafakis, Nicholas J.

Christsein im Denken: Zu Heideggers Kritik der 'christlichen Philosophie'. Haeffner, Gerd.

Classical Christian Philosophy and Temporality: Correcting a Misunderstanding. Centore, F F.

Classical Theism, Panentheism, and Pantheism: On the Relation between God Construction and Gender Construction. Frankenberry, Nancy.

Coercion and the Hiddenness of God. Murray, Michael J.

Comment on Langtry's 'God, Evil and Probability'. Chrzan, Keith.

Commentary on Martin's "Fate and Futurity in the Greco-Roman World". Boedeker, Deborah.

Confidence as a Work of Love in Kierkegaard on Art and Communication, Pattison, George (ed). Andic, Martin.

Consciousness and the Trinity. Lonergan, Bernard J F and Croken, Robert C (ed).

Consecration in Igbo Traditional Religion: A Definition. Onwurah, Emeka.

Consequences of William James's Pragmatism in Religion in God, Values, and Empiricism, Peden, Creighton W (ed). Frankenberry, Nancy.

Converting Time. Wilson, Jackson.

Could Horace Talk with the Hebrews? Translatability and Moral Disagreement in MacIntyre and Stout. Fowl, Stephen E.

RHETORIC

Whately's Distinction Between Inferring and Proving. Bitzer, Lloyd F.

Words of Others and Sightings/Citings/Sitings of Self in The Critical Turn, Angus, Ian (ed). Langsdorf, Lenore.

RHODE, D

Discrimination and Disadvantage in Feminist Legal Theory: A Review of Deborah Rhode's *Justice and Gender*. Smith, Patricia G.

RHYTHM

La forme du mouvement (sur la notion de rythme). Bourassa, Lucie.

RICCI, M

Die Renaissance und ihr Bild vom Konfuzianismus. Kodera, Sergius.

RICH, A

Surviving to Speak New Language: Mary Daly and Adrienne Rich. Hedley, Jane.

RICHARD, M

Reply to Marks. Forbes, Graeme R.

RICHARDSON, H

Moving Forward in Bioethical Theory: Theories, Cases, and Specified Principlism. Degrazia, David.

RICKEN, F

Zu Hermeneutik und Metaphysik: Eine Antwort an Friedo Ricken. Coreth, Emerich.

RICOEUR, P

El discurso filosófico: Análisis desde la obra de Paul Ricoeur. Villaverde, Marcelino Agís.

Imagination and Chance: The Difference Between the Thought of Ricoeur and Derrida. Lawlor, Leonard.

On Paul Ricoeur: Narrative and Interpretation. Wood, David (ed).

Oneself as Another—Paul Ricoeur. Ricoeur, Paul and Blamey, Kathleen (trans).

Paul Ricoeur. Clark, Stephen.

Converting Time. Wilson, Jackson.

Grand Narratives in On Paul Ricoeur: Narrative and Interpretation, Wood, David (ed). Bernstein, J M.

Imagination and Myth. Degenaar, Johan.

Philosophical Antecedents to Ricoeur's 'Time and Narrative' in On Paul Ricoeur: Narrative and Interpretation, Wood, David (ed). Vanhoozer, Kevin J.

Review of Paul Ricoeur's *Oneself as Another*: Personal Identity, Narrative Identity and "Selfhood" in the Thought of Paul Ricoeur. Pucci, Edi.

Ricoeur and Hick on Evil: Post-Kantian Myth?. Anderson, Pamela.

Ricoeur on Narrative in On Paul Ricoeur: Narrative and Interpretation, Wood, David (ed). Carr, David, Taylor, Charles and Ricoeur, Paul.

Ricoeur's Ethics of Method. Abel, Olivier.

Ricoeur, Proust and the Aporias of Time in On Paul Ricoeur: Narrative and Interpretation, Wood, David (ed). Goldthorpe, Rhiannon.

Semiotics and the Deconstruction of Presence: A Ricoeurian Alternative. Bourgeois, Patrick.

Taylor and Ricoeur on the Self. Dauenhauer, Bernard.

The Instant and the Living Present: Ricoeur and Derrida Reading Husserl. Bourgeois, Patrick.

The Preconscious, the Unconscious and the Subconscious: A Phenomenological Critique of the Hermeneutics of the Latent. Seebohm, Thomas M.

The Problem of Evil in Paul Ricoeur: An Aporetic Exploration. Mongin, Olivier.

The Religious Significance of Ricoeur's Post-Hegelian Kantian Ethics. Bourgeois, Patrick and Herbert, Gary.

The Self as an Other. Reagan, Charles E.

Time and Narrative: Reflections from Paul Ricoeur. Jasper, David.

RIEDEL, M

Die akroamatische Dimension der Hermeneutik. Fricke, Christel.

RIEMANN

Le rôle de l'abstrait dans l'oeuvre de B Riemann. Gattico, Emilio.

RIGHT

see also Good, Left, Natural Right, Virtue

La Dialettica dell'Etico. Li Vigni, Fiorinda.

A Consequentialist Case for Rejecting the Right. Howard-Snyder, Frances and Norcross, Alastair.

Abortion and Embodiment. Mackenzie, Catriona.

Apparent Circularity in Aristotle's Account of Right Action in the *Nicomachean Ethics*. Peterson, Sandra.

Asymmetrical Relations, Identity and Abortion. Dombrowski, Daniel A.

Cultural Rights Again: A Rejoinder to Kymlicka. Kukathas, Chandran.

La fonction du droit et la question du lien social chez Hume et Montesquieu. Autin, Pierre-Louis.

La revendication écocentriste d'un droit de la nature. Bégin, Luc.

Law as Idea of Reason in Essays on Kant's Political Philosophy, Williams, Howard (ed). Weinrib, Ernest J.

Mary Wollstonecraft and Women's Rights. Larson, Elizabeth.

Nelson Goodman on Truth. Nader N, Chokr.

Patients' Duties. Meyer, Michael J.

Strong Utilitarianism in Mo Tzu's Thought. Vorenkamp, Dirck.

The Basic Context and Structure of Hegel's 'Philosophy of Right' in The Cambridge Companion to Hegel, Beiser, Frederick (ed). Westphal, Kenneth.

The Fallacy of the Slippery Slope Argument on Abortion. Li, Chenyang.

The Ideology of Fair Use: Xeroxing and Reproductive Rights. Roof, Judith.

The Importance of Knowing What Is Right and Wrong. Daniels, Charles.

The Moral Legitimacy of Intellectual Property Claims: American Business and Developing Country Perspectives. Steidlmeier, Paul.

The Right and the Good. Garcia, Jorge L A.

The Right to Genetic Information: Some Reflections on Dutch Developments. Van Leeuwen, Evert and Hertogh, Cees.

The State, Marriage and Divorce. Trainor, Brian T.

Unequal Property and Subjective Personality in Liberal Theories. Zucker, Ross.

Who Can Be Morally Obligated to Be a Vegetarian?. Pluhar, Evelyn.

RIGHT TO DIE

Against the Right to Die. Velleman, J David.

The Right to Die: A Justification of Suicide. Meyers, Chris D.

RIGHT TO LIFE

Cruzan and the Constitutionalization of American Life. Schneider, Carl E.

Lebensrecht und Überlebeninteresse: Darstellung und Kritik einiger Thesen von Norbert Hoerster. Viefhues, Ludger.

The Right to Die as a Case Study in Third-Order Decisionmaking. Schauer, Frederick.

Who Can Be Morally Obligated to Be a Vegetarian?. Pluhar, Evelyn.

RIGHTEOUSNESS

Ethical Reflection and Righteous Indignation in Essays in Ancient Greek Philosophy, IV, Anton, John P (ed). Burger, Ronna C.

RIGHTNESS

Distinguishing Charity as Goodness and Prudence as Rightness: A Key to Thomas's *Secunda Pars*. Keenan, James F.

On the Rightness of Certain Counterfactuals. Adams, Ernest W.

Should Kantians Care about Moral Worth?. Schaller, Walter E.

RIGHTS

see also Civil Right, Human Rights

An Approach to Political Philosophy: Locke in Contexts. Tully, James.

Arguing About Abortion. Schwartz, Lewis M.

Disciplining Foucault: Feminism, Power, and the Body. Sawicki, Jana.

Essais de Philosophie du Droit. Trigeaud, Jean-Marc.

Government, Justice, and Contempt. Lane, Gilles.

Hart's Legal Philosophy: An Examination. Bayles, Michael D.

Je, Tu, Nous: Toward a Culture of Difference. Irigaray, Luce and Martin, Alison (trans).

Liberal Rights: Collected Papers 1981-1991. Waldron, Jeremy.

Moral Aspects of Legal Theory. Lyons, David.

Morality and Moral Controversies (Third Edition). Arthur, John (ed).

Philosophie Juridique Européenne les Institutions. Trigeaud, Jean-Marc.

Taking Sides: Clashing Views on Controversial Bioethical Issues (Fifth Edition). Levine, Carol.

The Birth Lottery. Boss, Judith A.

The Ethics of Abortion (Revised Edition). Baird, Robert M (ed) and Rosenbaum, Stuart E (ed).

The Ethics of Reproductive Technology. Alpern, Kenneth D (ed).

The Grounds and Limits of Political Obligation. Capriotti, Emile.

The Moral Dimensions of Public Policy Choice: Beyond the Market Paradigm. Gillroy, John Martin (ed) and Wade, Maurice (ed).

The Philosophy of Freedom: Ideological Origins of the Bill of Rights. Rudolph, Samuel B (ed).

The Place of the Person In Social Life. Peachey, Paul (ed), Kromkowski, John (ed) and McLean, George F (ed).

Transformations: Recollective Imagination and Sexual Difference. Cornell, Drucilla.

Virtues and Rights: The Moral Philosophy of Thomas Hobbes. Ewin, R E.

Women's Rights and the Rights of Man. Arnaud, A J and Kingdom, E.

A Critique of Henry Veatch's "Human Rights: Fact or Fancy?". Lee, Sander H.

A propos de la liberté chez les juristes. Rossinelli, Michel.

A Right to Health Care. McCarrick, Pat Milmoe.

Abortion Logic and Paternal Responsibility: One More Look at Judith Thomson's "A Defense of Abortion". Pavlischek, Keith J.

Abortion, Abandonment, and Positive Rights in Altruism, Paul, Ellen Frankel (ed). Long, Roderick T.

Abortion, Abandonment, and Positive Rights: The Limits of Compulsory Altruism. Long, Roderick T.

Academic Freedom and Employee Rights in Terrorism, Justice and Social Values, Peden, Creighton (ed). Grcic, Joseph.

Accumulative Harms and the Interpretation of the Harm Principle. Kernohan, Andrew.

Acts in Discourse: From Monological Speech Acts to Dialogical Inter-Acts. Linell, Per and Marková, Ivana.

Against Caring. Nelson, Hilde L.

An Analysis of the Use of Rights Language in Pre-Modern Catholic Social Thought. Brady, Bernard V.

Animal Welfare, Science, and Value. Rollin, Bernard E.

Animals in the Agrarian Ideal. Thompson, Paul B.

Animals in the Original Position. Russow, Lilly-Marlene.

Are Children's Rights Wrong Rights?. Houston, Barbara.

Blessed Are the Peacemakers: Commentary on Making Peace in Gestational Conflicts. Rong, Rosemarie.

Both the Moral Right and the Moral Duty to Be Educated. Heslep, Robert D.

Child Liberationism and Legitimate Interference. Lipson, Morrice and Vallentyne, Peter.

Coerced Birth Control, Individual Rights, and Discrimination in Biomedical Ethics Reviews 1992, Humber, James M (ed). Kuo, Lenore.

Community and the Rights of Future Generations: A Reply to Robert Elliot. De-Shalit, Avner.

Compensation and Government Takings of Private Property. Munzer, Stephen R.

Compensation and the Bounds of Rights. Lomasky, Loren.

SCEPTICISM

Skeptics, Cynics, Pessimists, and Other Malcontents. Godlovitch, Stan.

Some Reflections on Contemporary Epistemology. Tollefsen, Olaf.

Stroll's Answer to Skepticism in Certainty and Surface in Epistemology and Philosophical Method, Martinich, A P (ed). Popkin, Richard H.

Switched-Words Skepticism: A Case Study in Semantical Anti-Skeptical Argument. Christensen, David.

Teachers Should Disclose Their Moral Commitments in Moral Education and the Liberal Arts, Mitias, Michael H (ed). Ammon, Theodore G.

The Construction of the Physical World in The Philosophy of A J Ayer, Hahn, Lewis E (ed). Foster, John.

The Curricular Role of Russell's Scepticism. Rockler, Michael J.

The Impossibility of Massive Error. Carrier, L S.

The Last Stand of Mechanism. McDonough, Richard.

The Naturalists versus the Skeptics: The Debate Over a Scientific Understanding of Consciousness. Hardcastle, Valerie Gray.

The Perceptual Paradigm of Moral Epistemology. Sandoe, Peter.

The Politics of Skepticism: Readong Montaigne. Hiley, David R.

The Relativity of Perceptual Knowledge. Boardman, William S.

The Significance of Kant's Framework of Possible Experience. Rajiva, Suma.

Verificationism, Scepticism, and Consciousness. Seager, William.

Why Think There are any True Counterfactuals of Freedom?. Sennett, James F.

SCHAFFNER, K

Additional Notes on Integration. Van Der Steen, Wim J.

SCHEDLER, G

Response to Schedler: Why This Policy Is Wrong. Dandekar, Natalie.

SCHEFFLER, I

Objectivity and Rationality in Epistemology and Education: Scheffler's Middle Road. Neiman, Alven and Siegel, Harvey.

On Some Worldly Worries. Goodman, Nelson.

On 'What is Said to Be'. Schwartz, Robert.

Rationality and Democracy: A Critical Appreciation of Israel Scheffler's Philosophy of Education. Arnstine, Donald and Arnstine, Barbara.

Reasonableness, Bias, and the Untapped Power of Procedure. Adler, Jonathan.

Reconstruction in Pragmatism. Hanson, Karen.

Responses to Authors and Writings of Israel Scheffler. Scheffler, Israel.

Scheffler's Symbols. Elgin, Catherine Z.

The New Problem of Curriculum. Martin, Jane Roland.

SCHEFFLER, S

Agent-Relativity, Reason, and Value. Stewart, Robert M.

Justice, Scheffler and Cicero. Simpson, Peter.

SCHELER

Max Scheler's Concept of the Person: An Ethics of Humanism. Perrin, Ron.

On Feeling, Knowing, and Valuing: Selected Writings—Max Scheler. Scheler, Max.

Es la Muerte un acontecimiento de la vida?. Arregui, Jorge Vicente.

Incontro tra filosofia e teologia nella "Christliche Weltanschauung" di Romano Guardini. Bezzini, L.

The Difference Between Man and Animal: Letters of Max Scheler on F J J Buytendijk (in Dutch). Boudier, Henk Struyker.

Value Hierarchies in Scheler and Von Hildebrand. Gooch, Augusta O.

SCHELLING

Der gegenwärtige Schelling: Positionen der heutigen Schelling-Forschung—Ein Bericht. Orzechowski, Axel.

Die Überwindung des Marburger Neukantianismus in der Spätphilosophie Natorps. Wetz, Franz Josef.

Eine Metaphysik des Schwebens: Zum philosophischen Werk von Walter Schulz. Wandschneider, Dieter.

Esthetica en kuntsfilosofie. De Visscher, J.

La "dialectique" de Schleiermacher et l'absolu schellingien. Brito, Emilio.

La libertad como esencia de toda la realidad en el primer Schelling. Diosado, Concepción.

Le point sur les recherches schellingiennes. Tilliette, Xavier.

Mythe et révélation dans l'*Étoile de la Rédemption*: Contemporanéité de Franz Rosenzweig. Bienenstock, Myriam.

Philosophie et révélation dans l'idéalisme allemand: Un bilan. Maesschalck, Marc.

Reason and Existence in Schelling and Fackenheim in German Philosophy and Jewish Thought, Greenspan, Louis (ed). Burbidge, John W.

Schelling—Lask—Sartre: Die zweifache Unbegreiflichkeit der nackten Existenz. Wetz, Franz Josef.

SCHEMATA

A Deduction Theorem Schema for Deductive Systems of Propositional Logics. Czelakowski, J and Dziobiak, W.

SCHEMATISM

Perception as Cooperation of Schematization and Figurative Synthesis (in Dutch). Lohmar, D.

SCHEMATIZATION

La metafisica segreta di Kant: Su un recente saggio di Virgilio Melchiorre. Mancini, Sandro.

SCHEME

Conceptual Scheming. Rozema, David.

SCHENK, D

The World's Features and their Pure Appreciation: A Reply to Schenk. Smith, Quentin.

SCHIFFER, S

Folk-Psychological Ceteris Paribus Laws?. Warfield, Ted A.

Meaning, Truth-Conditions, Proposition: Frege's Doctrine of Sense Retrieved, Resumed and Redeployed in the Light of Certain Recent Criticisms. Wiggins, David.

Reply to Schiffer in Rationality in Epistemology, Villanueva, Enrique (ed). Boghossian, Paul.

Schiffer on Modes of Presentation. Adams, Fred, Stecker, Robert and Fuller, Gary.

Semantic Compositionality: Still the Only Game in Town. Kaye, Lawrence J.

The Floyd Puzzle: Reply to Yagisawa. Adams, Fred, Stecker, Robert and Fuller, Gary.

SCHILLER

La conciliazione estetica e l'etica. Gallino, Guglielmo.

Schiller über das Erhabene. Petrus, Klaus.

SCHINDLER, O

Oskar Schindler and Moral Theory in Applied Philosophy, Almond, Brenda (ed). Jackson, M W.

SCHIZOPHRENIA

Heidegger, Schizophrenia and the Ontological Difference. Sass, Louis A.

The Phrenetic Calculus: A Logician's View of Disordered Logical Thinking in Schizophrenia. Klee, Robert.

SCHLEGEL

Schlegel's Irony: "Hoverings". Weislogel, Eric L.

SCHLEIERMACHER

Deux théries de l'esprit: Hegel et Schleiermacher. Brito, Emilio.

La "Dialectique" de Schleiermacher. Brito, Emilio.

La "dialectique" de Schleiermacher et l'absolu schellingien. Brito, Emilio.

La compréhension chrétienne de Dieu comme amour et sagesse selon Schleiermacher. Brito, Emilio.

Schleiermacher's Hermeneutic and Its Critics. Corliss, Richard.

SCHLESINGER, A

The Diverse Styles of Social Pluralism. Milligan, Charles S.

SCHLESINGER, G

Satisfied Pigs and Dissatisfied Philosophers: Schlesinger on the Problem of Evil. Grover, Stephen.

Schlesinger on Miracles. Otte, Richard.

SCHLICK

Schlick's Epistemology and Its Contrib to Modern Empiricism in Greek Studies in the Philosophy and History of Science, Nicolacopoulos, Pantelis (ed). Avgelis, Nikolaos.

SCHMIDT, H

Morality or Prudence?. Williams, Howard.

SCHMITT, C

Carl Schmitt, Hans Freyer and the Radical Conservative Critique of Liberal Democracy in the Weimar Republic. Muller, Jerry Z.

Carl Schmitt: The Conservative Revolutionary Habitus and the Aesthetics of Horror. Wolin, Richard.

Die Zerstückelung des Fu-Tschu-Li. Kohler, Georg.

Looking at Carl Schmitt from the Vantage Point of the 1990s. Herz, John H.

Modernist Anti-Modernism: Carl Schmitt's Concept of the Political. Scheuerman, Bill.

The Emergence of Nationalism as a Political Philosophy. Frisch, Morton J.

SCHMITZ, H

Leibanwesenheit und primitive Gegenwart. Kühn, Rolf.

SCHOENBERG, A

An Outline of Some Problems in the Philosophy of Music Composition. Trivedi, Saam.

SCHOFIELD, M

Schofield's *The Stoic Idea of the City*. Annas, Julia.

SCHOLARSHIP

Transformations of Hegelianism, 1805-1846 in The Cambridge Companion to Hegel, Beiser, Frederick C (ed). Toews, John.

SCHOLASTICISM

see also Thomism

Cantor and the Scholastics. Small, Robin.

Francisco Suárez: The Man in History. Gracia, Jorge J E.

The Importance of the Concept of Substantial Unity in Suárez's Argument for Hylomorphism. Kronen, John D.

SCHOLZ, H

Aus dem Dunklen ins Helle: Wissenschaft und Theologie im Denken von Heinrich Scholz. Molendijk, A L.

SCHOOL

Character Development in Schools and Beyond (Second Edition). Ryan, Kevin (ed) and Lickona, Thomas (ed).

Meaning, Communication and Understanding in the Classroom. Sainsbury, Marian Jane.

Transforming Power: Domination, Empowerment, and Education. Kreisberg, Seth.

Beyond Comprehension: Why "Hard Reading" Is Too Easy. Bogdan, Deanne and Cunningham, James.

Economic Ends and Educational Means at the White House: A Case for Citizenship and Casuistry. Sullivan, B Todd.

Goodness and Greatness: Broudy on Music Education. Colwell, Richard.

Humanism and Ethics at the School of St Victor in the Early Twelfth Century. Jaeger, C Stephen.

Logic-Theological Schools from the Second Half of the 12th Century: A List of Sources. Yukio, Iwakuma and Ebbesen, Sten.

Philosophy of Education in Canada. Hare, William F.

SCHOOL

Pragmatism or Crude Utility: A Critique of the Education with Production Movement in Contemporary Africa. Lungu, Gatian F.

Privacy, Rights, and Education. Pepperell, Keith.

Private Schools and Public Schools: A Critical Response to the Privatization Debate. Enslin, Penny.

Recreating Classroom Relationships: Mutual Mentoring Joins Critical Hermeneutics and Composition Theory. Abscal-Hildebrand, Mary and Mullins, Joan.

Research on Broudy's Theory of the Uses of Schooling. Schmitz, John G.

School Governors: Conceptual and Practical Problems. Golby, Michael.

Tadeusz Kotarbinski and the Lvov Warsaw School. Wolenski, Jan.

The Myth of Easy Reading. Raitz, Keith L.

The Road from Nice to Necessary: Broudy's Rationale for Art Education. DiBlasio, Margaret Klempay.

Two Rhetorics of Cynicism in Curriculum Deliberation, or Two Riders in a Barren Land. St Maurice, Henry.

What is a "Postmodern" Education and What Does It Have to Do With Lifelong Learning?. Owen, Roderick.

SCHOOLING

Civic Virtue, Markets and Schooling: Lessons from Hegel's Education State. Blacker, David.

Foucault and Rousseau on Teaching in Modern Technocratic Schooling. McKinney, Joseph and Garrison, Jim.

Inventing Postmodern Education: Lifelong Learning or Childhood Schooling? A Proposal for Local Action. Tandy, Charles.

The Modern Quest for Civic Virtues: Issues of Identity and Alienation. Williams, Dilafruz R.

SCHOPENHAUER

Genius and Talent: Schopenhauer's Influence on Wittgenstein's Early Philosophy. Weiner, David Avraham.

On the Will in Nature — Schopenhauer. Schopenhauer, Arthur and Payne, E F J (trans).

Beautiful Truths: Schopenhauer's Philosophy of Art. Johnson, Kenneth M.

La reflexión sobre la negación o afirmación de la vida en Schopenhauer, Feuerbach, Wagner y Nietzsche. Cabada Castro, M.

On the "Subjects" of Knowing and Willing and the "I" in Shcopenhauer. Aquila, Richard E.

Schopenhauer and Buddhism. Abelsen, Peter.

Schopenhauer and Direct Realism. Henle, R J.

Schopenhauer's Circle and the Principle of Sufficient Reason. Jacquette, Dale.

Schopenhauer's Naturalization of Kant's A Priori Forms of Empirical Knowledge. Wicks, Robert.

The Conscious Body: Schopenhauer's Difference from Fichte in Relation to Kant. Chansky, James.

SCHRAMM, A

Reply to Alfred Schramm's "Doubt, Scepticism, and a Serious Justification Game". Lehrer, Keith.

SCHREBER, D

Law and Gynesis: Freud vs Schreber in Shadow of Spirit, Berry, Philippa (ed). O'Neill, John.

SCHRODER, E

The Origin of Relation Algebras in the Development and Axiomatization of the Calculus of Relations. Maddux, R D.

SCHULTHESS, D

Reply to Daniel Schulthess's "Reid and Lehrer: Metamind in History". Lehrer, Keith.

SCHULZ, W

Das unerledigte Metaphysikproblem: Anmerkungen zur jümgsten Metaphysikdiskussion im deutschen Sprachraum. Ollig, Hans- Ludwig.

SCHUMPETER, J

Why John Stuart Mill Called Himself a Socialist. Ottow, Raimund.

SCHWARTZ, J

Reduction, Elimination, and Firewalking. Cheyne, Colin.

SCHWEITZER

"Es ist uns aber bestimmt, von Überzeugungen, die wir aus innerer Notwendigkeit denken, zu leben". Kern, Udo.

Das Tal der Sachlichkeit: Albert Schweitzer über Indien. Waligora, Melitta.

SCIENCE

see also Anthropology, Biology, Chemistry, Economics, Empirical Science, Human Sciences, Matter, Medicine, Natural Sciences, Physics, Political Science, Quantum Mechanics, Relativity, Scientific Method, Social Sciences, Sociology, Space, Time

"From Natural Function to Indeterminate Content". Sullivan, Sonja R.

"More on Einstein, Michelson, and the 'Crucial' Experiment". Holton, Gerald.

A Dictionary of Philosophical Quotations. O'Grady, Jane (ed) and Ayer, A J (ed).

A Hylomorphic Theory of Mind. Cooney, Brian.

A Study of Concepts. Peacocke, Christopher.

Advances in Scientific Philosophy. Schurz, Gerhard (ed) and Dorn, Georg J W (ed).

An Essay on Belief and Acceptance. Cohen, L Jonathan.

Analecta Husserliana, XXXI. Tymieniecka, Anna-Teresa (ed).

Aphorisms—Georg Christoph Lichtenberg. Lichtenberg, Georg Christoph.

Artificial Morality: Virtuous Robots for Virtual Games. Danielson, Peter.

Aspects of Mind—Gilbert Ryle. Meyer, René (ed) and Ryle, Gilbert.

Bayes or Bust? A Critical Examination of Bayesian Confirmation Theory. Earman, John.

Betting on Theories: Cambridge Studies in Probability, Induction, and Decision Theory. Maher, Patrick.

Burdens of Proof in Modern Discourse. Gaskins, Richard H.

Cognition, Semantics and Philosophy. Ezquerro, Jesús (ed) and Larrazabal, Jesús (ed).

Common Sense, Science and Scepticism: A Historical Introduction to the Theory of Knowledge. Musgrave, Alan.

Consciousness Reconsidered. Flanagan, Owen.

Consciousness, Brain and the Physical World: A Reply to Velmans. Rentoul, Robert.

Consciousness: Psychological and Philosophical Essays. Davies, Martin (ed) and Humphreys, Glyn W (ed).

Cosmos, Bios, Theos: Scientists Reflect on Science, God, and the Origins of the Universe, Life, and "Homo sapiens". Margenau, Henry (ed) and Varghese, Roy Abraham (ed).

Creativity and Consciousness: Philosophical and Psychological Dimensions. Brzezinski, Jerzy (& other eds).

Cyberspace: First Steps. Benedikt, Michael (ed).

Dialogue and the Human Image: Beyond Humanistic Psychology. Friedman, Maurice S.

Dialogue with Heidegger on Values: Ethics for Times of Crisis. Joós, Ernest.

Ecology, Economics, Ethics: The Broken Circle. Bormann, Herbert F (ed) and Kellert, Stephen R (ed).

Empirical Theology: A Handbook. Miller, Randolph Crump (ed).

Empiricist Research on Teaching: A Philosophical and Practical Critique of its Scientific Pretensions. Chambers, John H.

Essays in Quasi-Realism. Blackburn, Simon W.

Ethics and the Environment. Hart, Richard E (ed).

Ethics of Environment and Development: Global Challenge, International Response. Engel, J Ronald (ed) and Engel, Joan Gibb (ed).

Explaining Explanation. Ruben, David-Hillel.

Foundations of Philosophy of Science: Recent Developments. Fetzer, James.

Glossary of Cognitive Science. Dunlop, Charles E M and Fetzer, James H.

Glossary of Epistemology/ Philosophy of Science. Fetzer, James H and Almeder, Rober F.

Greek Studies in the Philosophy and History of Science. Nicolacopoulos, Pantelis (ed).

Hegel: Three Studies. Adorno, Theodor W and Nicholsen, Shierry Weber (trans).

Homo Metaphisicus. Pezzimenti, Rocco.

Husserl's Transcendental Phenomenology—Elisabeth Ströker. Hardy, Lee (trans) and Ströker, Elisabeth.

Idealization III. Brzezinski, Jerzy (ed) and Nowak, Leszek (ed).

Injustice and Restitution: The Ordinance of Time. Ross, Stephen D.

Instrumental Realism: The Interface between Philosophy of Science and Philosophy of Technology. Ihde, Don.

Kierkegaard and Kant: The Hidden Debt. Green, Ronald M.

Machinations: Computational Studies of Logic, Language, and Cognition. Spencer-Smith, Richard (ed) and Torrance, Steve (ed).

Mathesis e costruzione tra geometria antica e moderna. Ferrarin, Alfredo.

Mind, Brain, Behavior: The Mind-Body Problem and the Philosophy of Psychology. Carrier, Martin and Mittelstrass, Jürgen.

Mythology: From Ancient to Post-Modern. Kleist, Jürgen (ed) and Butterfield, Bruce (ed).

New Horizons in the Philosophy of Science. Lamb, David (ed).

Nurturing Evolution: The Family as a Social Womb. Carter, Richard B.

Open Institutions: The Hope for Democracy. Murphy, John W (ed) and Peck, Dennis L (ed).

Opus Postumum/Immanuel Kant. Kant, Immanuel, Förster, Eckart (ed & trans) and Rosen, Michael (trans).

Paradigms and Barriers: How Habits of Mind Govern Scientific Beliefs. Margolis, Howard.

Person and Religion: An Introduction to the Philosophy of Religion. Sandok, Theresa (trans) and Zdybicka, Zofia J.

Philosophy and Artificial Intelligence. Moody, Todd C.

Philosophy and Knowledge: A Commentary on Plato's "Theaetetus". Polansky, Ronald.

Philosophy and the Origin and Evolution of the Universe. Agazzi, Evandro (ed) and Cordero, Alberto (ed).

Philosophy of Physics. Sklar, Lawrence.

Philosophy of Science. Fetzer, James.

Philosophy of Technology: An Introduction. Ihde, Don.

Philosophy, Rhetoric, and the End of Knowledge: The Coming of Science and Technology Studies. Fuller, Steve.

Practices of Reason: 'Aristotle's Nicomachean Ethics'. Reeve, C D C.

Probability and Rationality. Eells, Ellery (ed) and Maruszewski, Tomasz (ed).

Problems in Personal Identity. Baillie, James.

Psychology and Nihilism: A Genealogical Critique of the Computational Model of Mind. Evans, Fred.

Ptolemy's Universe: The Natural Philosophical and Ethical Foundations of Ptolemy's Astronomy. Taub, Liba.

Reasoning: A Practical Guide. Pinto, Robert C and Blair, John Anthony.

Representation, Meaning, and Thought. Gillett, Grant.

Revolution and Continuity. Barker, Peter (ed) and Ariew, Roger (ed).

Science, Knowledge, and Mind: A Study in the Philosophy of C S Peirce. Delaney, C F.

Search for a Naturalistic World View: Volume I. Shimony, Abner.

SCIENCE

SCIENCE

SCIENCE

SCIENCE

SCIENCE

SELF

The Other is My Hell; the Other is My Home. Wu, Kuang-Ming.

The Other Nietzsche in Nietzsche and Asian Thought, Parkes, Graham R (ed). Stambaugh, Joan.

The Possibility of an Unbodily Self: In Response to Richard Combes. Gough, Martin.

The Priority of the Personal: An 'Other' Tradition in Modern Continental Philosophy. Surber, Jere P.

The Problem of Personal Identity in *Being and Time* (in Hebrew). Fuchs, Yuval.

The Problem of the Body in Nietzsche and Dōgen in Nietzsche and Asian Thought, Parkes, Graham (ed). Parkes, Graham R (trans) and Kōgaku, Arifuku.

The Reality of the Moral Self. Thomas, Laurence.

The Relational Self in Selves, People, and Persons, Rouner, Leroy S (ed). Oliver, Harold H.

The Revelation of the Holy Other as the Wholly Other: Between Barth's Theology of the Word and Levinas's Philosophy of Saying. Ward, Graham.

The Revolutionary Hero Revisited in Sartre Alive, Aronson, Ronald (ed). Verstraeten, Pierre.

The Right of National Self Determination. George, David.

The Right to Welfare and the Virtue of Charity. Den Uyl, Douglas.

The Rigour of Heidegger's Thought. Weatherston, Martin.

The Self as an Other. Reagan, Charles E.

The Self of Book 1 and the Selves of Book 2. Penelhum, Terence.

The Self-So and Its Traces in the Thought of Guo Xiang. Ziporyn, Brook.

The Social Self in Japanese Philosophy and American Pragmatism: A Comparative Study of Watsuji Tetsurō and George Herbert Mead. Odin, Steve.

The Space of Love and Garbate. Erickson, Stephen A.

The System and Its Fractures: Gilles Deleuze on Otherness. May, Todd G.

Through Metaphysics to Values and about Being (in Czechoslovakian). Dokulil, M.

Toward a Pragmatic Metaphysics: Comments on a Speculative Approach. Littleford, Michael S.

True to Oneself. Sobel, J Howard.

Truth, Meaning, and Functional Understanding: A Post-Sartrean Meditation. Barbiero, Daniel.

Unidentified Awareness: Hume's Perceptions of Self. Campolo, Christian.

Unity, Theism, and Self in Plotinus. Blakeley, Donald N.

Vico as Educator: Values, Self-Development, and Synthesis. Craig, Robert.

Visions of the Self in Late Medieval Christianity in Philosophy, Religion and the Spiritual Life, McGhee, Michael (ed). Coakley, Sarah.

Visions of the Self in Late Medieval Christianity: Some Cross-Disciplinary Reflections. Coakley, Sarah.

What's "I" Got To Do With It?. Bernstein, Susan David.

Whitman's 'Convertible Terms' in Theorizing American Literature, Cowan, Bainard (ed). Lindberg, Kathryne V.

William James's Theory of the Self. Cooper, W E.

Words of Others and Sightings/Citings/Sitings of Self in The Critical Turn, Angus, Ian (ed). Langsdorf, Lenore.

SELF-ACTUALIZATION

Hegel's Ethical Thought. Houlgate, Stephen.

SELF-AWARENESS

L'interpretazione di Plotino della teoria platonica dell'anima. Szlezák, T A.

Plotino e Ficino: l'autorelazione del pensiero. Beierwaltes, Werner.

SELF-CONSCIOUSNESS

Autocoscienza, riferimento dell'io e conoscenza di sé: Introduzione ad un dibattito contemporaneo. Ferrarin, Alfredo.

C'è un circolo dell'autocoscienza? Uno schizzo delle posizioni paradigmatiche e dei modelli di autocoscienza da Kant a Heidegger. Düsing, Klaus.

Consapevolezza e riferimento oggettivo: Un problema in Descartes, nell'idealismo e nella filosofia contemporanea. Varnier, Giuseppe.

Consciousness, Self-Consciousness and Episodic Memory. Gennaro, Rocco J.

Las máscaras del sí mismo. Choza, Jacinto.

Spinoza on Self-Consciousness and Nationalism. Freeman, David A.

SELF-CONTRADICTION

On Being False by Self-Refutation. Page, Carl.

Wahre performative Selbstwidersprüche. Steinhoff, Uwe.

SELF-CONTROL

Irrationality: An Essay on 'Akrasia', Self-Deception, and Self-Control. Mele, Alfred.

The Examined Life. Kekes, John.

Akrasia, Self-Control, and Second-Order Desires. Mele, Alfred.

The Origin and Development of Peirce's Concept of Self-Control. Petry, Jr, Edward S.

SELF-DECEPTION

A Spinozistic Account of Self-Deception: NASS Monograph #1 (1993). Ablondi, Frederick R.

Overcoming Rationalization and Self-Deception: The Cultivation of Critical Thinking. Whisner, William N.

SELF-DEFENSE

Abortion, Moral Responsibility, and Self-Defense. Huffman, Tom L.

Are Active Pacifists Really Just-Warists in Disguise?. Smithka, Paula J.

Fairness and Self-Defense. Draper, George.

Killing in Self-Defense. Miller, Seumas.

Self-Defence and Forcing the Choice between Lives. Miller, Seumas.

Self-Defense, Justification, and Excuse. Alexander, Larry.

SELF-DETERMINATION

Criteria for Death: Self-Determination and Public Policy. Sass, Hans-Martin.

Is Personal Autonomy the First Principle of Education?. Cuypers, Stefaan.

La conciliazione estetica e l'etica. Gallino, Guglielmo.

Self-Determination in Political Philosophy and International Law. Dahbour, Omar.

The Patient Self Determination Act and "Dax's Case". Gelwick, Richard.

The Right to National Self-Determination as an Individual Right. Tamir, Yael.

Truth and Freedom. Bedell, Gary.

When Self-Determination Runs Amok. Callahan, Daniel.

SELF-ESTEEM

Self-Assessment, Self-Esteem and Self-Acceptance. Statman, Daniel.

Self-Esteem and Moral Virtue. Nesbitt, Winston.

Self-Trust, Autonomy, and Self-Esteem. Govier, Trudy.

The Appropriateness of Self-Esteem: A Response to Nesbitt and Statman. Dewhurst, David.

SELF-IDENTITY

Convivir con la inidentidad. Innerarity, Daniel.

El descubrimiento del yo según David Hume. Elósegui, María.

Giving the Devil His Due. Thomas, Janice.

Husserl y las aporías de la intersubjetividad. Finke, S R S.

Identidad individual y personalidad jurídica. Aymerich, Ignacio.

Is Personal Autonomy the First Principle of Education?. Cuypers, Stefaan.

Las máscaras del sí mismo. Choza, Jacinto.

Modernity and Self-Identity: Self and Society in the Late Modern Age. Gluck, Mary.

Persona, hábito y tiempo: La constitución de la identidad personal. Vigo, Alejandro.

Tomás de Aquino y la identidad personal. Martin, Christopher F J.

SELF-INTEREST

Ethical Essays, Volume II. Harrison, Jonathan.

Cosmopolitan Altruism in Altruism, Paul, Ellen Frankel (ed). Galston, William.

Do Plato's Philosopher-Rulers Sacrifice Self-Interest to Justice?. Mahoney, Timothy.

Parfit's Arguments for the Present-Aim Theory. Hooker, Brad.

Religion and Self-Interest. Drum, Peter.

Self-Interest and Survival. Martin, Raymond.

SELF-KNOWLEDGE

Bewusstsein als Durchleben: Eine Antwort auf Ursula Wolf. Pothast, Ulrich.

Importanza storica e teoretica del pensiero neoplatonico nel *Pensare l'Uno* di Werner Beierwaltes. Gatti, Maria Luisa.

L'inno della perla: Una risposta al problema gnostico. Nosari, Sara.

Privileged Self-Knowledge and Externalism are Compatible. Warfield, Ted A.

Self-Kowledge: Looking in the Wrong Direction. Greenwood, John D.

'Know Thyself': What Kind of an Injunction?. Williams, Rowan.

'Know Thyself': What Kind of an Injunction? in Philosophy, Religion and the Spiritual Life, McGhee, Michael (ed). Williams, Rowan.

SELF-LOVE

Aristotelian Friendship: Self-Love and Moral Rivalry. Dziob, Anne Marie.

Beneficence and Self-Love: A Kantian Perspective. Hill Jr, Thomas E.

Friendship, Self-Love and Knowledge. Jacobs, Jonathan.

SELF-REALIZATION

Approaching Distance. Hanson, Karen.

Master Chu's Self-Realization: The Role of *Ch'eng*. Berthrong, John.

Whitehead, Heidegger, and the Paradoxes of the New. Bradley, J A.

SELF-REFERENCE

A Congery of Self-Reference. Rardin, Patrick.

Anti-Foundation and Self-Reference. McLarty, Colin.

Deviant Logic and the Paradoxes of Self Reference. Restall, Greg.

Provability: The Emergence of a Mathematical Modality. Boolos, George and Sambin, Giovanni.

Self, Reference and Self-reference. Lowe, E J.

Self-Reference: The Radicalization of Locke. Rovane, Carol.

Split Self-Reference and Personal Survival. Pears, David.

SELF-REFUTATION

On Being False by Self-Refutation. Page, Carl.

SELF-RESPECT

How to Lose Your Self-Respect. Dillon, Robin.

Self-Respect, Morality, and Justice in Terrorism, Justice and Social Values, Peden, Creighton (ed). Pullman, Daryl.

Utilitarianism and Self-Respect. Scarre, Geoffrey.

SELF-SACRIFICE

Asymmetry and Self-Sacrifice. Sider, Theodore R.

SELF-SUFFICIENCY

Slote on Self-Sufficiency. Hursthouse, Rosalind.

The Riddle of Self-Sufficiency. Stuke, Kurt.

SELFISHNESS

Altruism and the Argument from Offsetting Transfers. Cowen, Tyler.

Altruism Versus Self-Interest: Sometimes a False Dichotomy in Altruism, Paul, Ellen Frankel (ed). Badhwar, Neera Kapur.

Psychological Egoism: *Noch Einmal*. Johnson, Wayne G.

Selflessness and the Loss of Self. Hampton, Jean.

Selflessness and the Loss of Self in Altruism, Paul, Ellen Frankel (ed). Hampton, Jean.

Thinking as a Team: Towards an Explanation of Nonselfish Behavior. Sugden, Robert.

SELLARS, W

Properties as Processes: A Synoptic Study of Wilfrid Sellars' Nominalism. Seibt, Johanna.

The Analogy Theory of Thinking. Haaparanta, Leila.

SELVAGGI, F

Il mio itinerario filosofico. Selvaggi, Filippo.

SEMANTICS

SENSUALISM

Le continuum corps-esprit dans l'économie de notre être selon Bonnet. O'Neal, John.

SENTENCE

see also Proposition, Statement

A Metalogical Theory of Reference: Realism and Essentialism in Semantics. Vergauwen, Roger.

Dimostrazioni e Significato. Moriconi, Enrico.

Direct Reference: From Language to Thought. Rashed, Roshdi.

First Logic. Goodman, Michael.

How Memory Shapes Narratives: A Philosophical Essay on Redeeming the Past. Plantinga, Theodore.

Language and Time. Smith, Quentin.

On the Logic of Ordinary Conditionals. McLaughlin, Robert N.

Overcoming Logical Positivism from Within: The Emergence of Neurath's Naturalism in the Vienna Circle's Protocol Sentence Debate. Uebel, Thomas E.

A Decision Algorithm for Linear Sentences on a PFM. Li, L, Li, H and Liu, Y.

A Defense of Branching Quantification. Hand, Michael.

A Popular Presumption Refuted. Dudman, V H.

Any. Kadmon, Nirit and Landman, Fred.

Attitudes in Context. Richard, Mark E.

Causal Facts as Logical Entailments of Action Statements. Lauer, Henle.

Classical Logic and Truth-Value Gaps. Hugly, Philip G and Sayward, Charles.

Content and Context: The Paratactic Theory Revisited and Revised. Rumfitt, Ian.

Cuestiones Fundamentales de una Teoría del Significado. Schirn, Matthias.

Does an Inferential Role Semantics Rest Upon a Mistake?. Boghossian, Paul.

Elementary Formal Semantics for English Tense and Aspect. Pendlebury, Michael.

Epistemically-Qualified Judgment: A Nonquantitative Approach. Backman, Wayne.

Existence Presuppositions and Background Knowledge. Lasersohn, Peter.

Explanatory Coherence and Data Sentences in Frontiers in American Philosophy, Volume I, Burch, Robert W (ed). Pappas, George S.

Fodorian Semantics, Pathologies, and "Block's Problem". Adams, Fred and Aizawa, Kenneth.

Folk-Psychological Ceteris Paribus Laws?. Warfield, Ted A.

Game Sentences and Ultrapowers. Jin, Renling and Keisler, H Jerome.

Hempel Revisited. Dale, A J.

In Praise of Observation Sentences. Quine, Willard V.

Is There a Need for a Distinction Between Meaning and Sense?. Trivedi, Saam.

Knowing What One Was Intending to Say in Wittgenstein's Intentions, Canfield, John V (ed). Hunter, J F M.

Languages of Empirical Theories and Their Semantics. Przelecki, Marian.

Making Sense of Indexicals. Anderson, Michael.

Narrative and Style. Danto, Arthur C.

On Logical Form of Action Sentences. Goswami, Chinmoy.

On the Sense of Unsaturated Expressions. Diller, Antoni.

Rational Reconstruction as Elucidation? Carnap in the Early Protocol Sentence Debate. Uebel, Thomas.

Realism, Psychologism, and Intermediary-Shadows in Wittgenstein's Tractatus. Borst, Clive.

Reply to Marks. Forbes, Graeme R.

Reply to Sinnott-Armstrong. Gibbard, Allan F.

Robust Deflationism. Kraut, Robert.

Russelem. Williams, C J F.

Sceptical Overkill: On Two Recent Arguments Against Scepticism. O'Hara, Kieron.

Scheffler's Symbols. Elgin, Catherine Z.

Scope and Rigidity. Horsten, Leon.

Semantic Emphasis in Causal Sentences. Stern, Cindy D.

Sensational Sentences in Consciousness: Psychological and Philosophical Essays, Davies, Martin (ed). Rey, Georges.

So-Labeled Neo-Fregeanism. Crimmins, Mark.

Solving the Iteration Problem. Forbes, Graeme R.

Some Unifying Fixed Point Principles. Smullyan, Raymond M.

Suppose, Suppose. Morton, Adam.

Thank Goodness That's Non-Actual. Percival, Philip.

The Anti-Realist's Master Argument. Brueckner, Anthony.

The Context Principle, Universals and Primary States of Affairs. Puntel, Lorenz.

The Date-Analysis of Tensed Sentences. Williams, Clifford.

The Emergence of Meaning. Gärdenfors, Peter.

The Liar and Sorites Paradoxes: Toward a Unified Treatment. Tappenden, Jamie.

The Liar Paradox and Many-Valued Logic. Bhave, S V.

The Logical Structure of Action Sentences (Part I) (in Czechoslovakian). Kolar, P and Svoboda, V.

The Logical Structure of Action Sentences: Two Analytical Exercises (Conclusion) (in Czechoslovakian). Kolar, P and Svoboda, V.

The Logical Structure of Action Sentences: Two Analytical Exercises (Part II) (in Czechoslovakian). Kolar, P and Svoboda, V.

The Meaning of 'If' in Conditional Propositions. Hunter, Geoffrey.

The Metaphysical Aspect of Tenses in Proclus. Plass, Paul.

The Second Person. Davidson, Donald.

Towards a Unified Theory of Higher-Level Predication. Williams, C J F.

Translation and Content—Footnotes on Moravcsik's 'All A's are B's'. Hofmann, T R.

Two Problems with Tarski's Theory of Consequence. McGee, Vann.

Understanding Language. Smith, Barry C.

Verdade e Demonstraçao. Tarski, A and Paula Assis, J (trans).

Was Meinong Only Pretending?. Kroon, Frederick W.

Zalta on Sense and Substitutivity. Deutsch, Harry.

SENTENTIAL CALCULUS

see Propositional Logic

SENTIENCE

Who or What Has Moral Standing?. Schönfeld, Martin.

SENTIMENT

A Progress of Sentiments: Reflections on Hume's "Treatise". Baier, Annette.

Critical Notice of Annette Baier's A Progress of Sentiments. Russell, Paul.

From Passions to Sentiments: The Structure of Hume's Treatise. Rorty, Amélie Oksenberg.

Gibbard on Morality and Sentiment. Hill Jr, Thomas E.

Poesia e verità: Lettere a Clotilde Marghieri. Scaravelli, Luigi.

SENTIMENTALISM

Hume's Moral Sentimentalism. Shaw, Daniel.

SEPARATION

Aristote et la séparation. Bastit, Michel.

Relative Separation Theorems. Tuuri, Heikki.

SEPP, H

The Entelechy and Authenticity of Objective Spirit: Reflections on Husserliana XXVII. Hart, J G.

SEQUENCE

Two Sequents of Locally Tabular Superintuitionistic Logic. Mardaev, S I.

SEQUENT CALCULUS

2-Sequent Calculus: A Proof Theory of Modalities. Masini, Andrea.

A Normal Form for Logical Derivations Implying One for Arithmetic Derivations. Mints, G.

A Sequent- or Tableau-Style System for Lewis's Counterfactual Logic VC. Gent, Ian Philip.

Classical Logic, Intuitionistic Logic, and the Peirce Rule. Africk, Henry.

Coherence in Category Theory and the Church-Rosser Property. Jay, C Barry.

Cut Elimination for the Unified Logic. Vauzeilles, Jacqueline.

Cut-Free Systems for Three-Valued Modal Logics. Takano, Mitio.

Fixed Points in Peano Arithmetic with Ordinals. Jäger, Gerhard.

Functional Completeness for Subsystems of Intuitionistic Propositional Logic. Wansing, Heinrich.

Linearizing Intuitionistic Implication. Lincoln, Patrick, Scedrov, Andre and Shankar, Natarajan.

On Sequents and Tableaux for Many-Valued Logics. Carnielli, Walter A.

Relation Algebras of Every Dimension. Maddux, Roger D.

The Contraction Rule and Decision Problems for Logics Without Structural Rules. Ono, Hiroakira.

The Gentzen-Kripke Construction of the Intermediate Logic LQ. Akama, Seiki.

Two Formal Systems for Situation Semantics. Escriba, Juan Barba.

SEQUENZ CALCULUS

On the Unity of Logic. Girard, Jean-Yves.

SERAFINI, A

Coma, Death and Moral Dues: A Response to Serafini. Gillett, Grant.

SERRES, M

Kreukels in de tijd, kennis zonder centrum. Willems, Dick.

Michel Serres: eigenzinnig/bemiddelaar. Mol, Annemarie.

Paradigma einer Methode in Diagrammatik und Philosophie, Gehring, Petra (ed). Gehring, Petra.

SERVICE

The Dignity and Indignity of Service: The Role of the Self in Hindu 'Bhakti' in Selves, People, and Persons, Rouner, Leroy S (ed). Carman, John B.

SET

see also Class

EIS for Nilpotent Shifts of Varieties. Graczynska, Ewa.

Ontology Without Ultrafilters and Possible Worlds: An Examination of Bolzano's Ontology. Berg, Jan.

A New Strongly Minimal Set. Hrushovski, Ehud.

Cantor's Power-Set Theorem Versus Frege's Double-Correlation Thesis. Cocchiarella, N B.

Compactness and Normality in Abstract Logics. Caicedo, Xavier.

Generic Degrees are Complemented. Kumabe, M.

Loeb Extensions and Ultrapowers of Measures on Fragments. Ng, Siu-Ah.

Ramsey Sets, the Ramsey Ideal, and Other Classes Over R. Corazza, Paul.

Spreads or Choice Sequences?. DeSwart, H C M.

Total Sets and Objects in Domain Theory. Berger, Ulrich.

SET THEORY

Advances in Scientific Philosophy. Schurz, Gerhard (ed) and Dorn, Georg J W (ed).

A $\Delta 2/2$ Well-Order of the Reals and Incompactness of $L(QMM)$. Abraham, Uri and Shelah, Saharon.

A Certain Conception of the Calculus of Rough Sets. Bonikowski, Zbigniew.

A Critical Appraisal of Second-Order Logic. Jané, Ignacio.

A Model in Which Every Kurepa Tree is Thick. Jin, Renling.

A Note on Naive Set Theory in LP. Restall, Greg.

A Note on Some Weak Forms of the Axiom of Choice. Shannon, Gary P.

A Set Theory Analysis of the Logic of the I Ching. Fleming, Jesse.

Anti-Foundation and Self-Reference. McLarty, Colin.

Arithmetized Set Theory. Strauss, Paul.

Critical Notice: David Lewis's Parts of Classes. Potter, M D.

EEEE: Set Theory and Wholeness. Blizard, Wayne D.

Forcing Disabled. Stanley, M C.

Generic Models of the Theory of Normal Z-Rings. Otero, Margarita.

Graham Oppy on the Kalam Cosmological Argument. Craig, William Lane.

Independence, Randomness and the Axiom of Choice. Van Lambalgen, Michiel.

Indispensability and Practice. Maddy, Penelope.

Iterative Set Theory. Potter, M D.

Laws of Nature as a Species of Regularities in Ontology, Causality and Mind: Essays in Honour of D M Armstrong, Bacon, John (ed). Smart, J J C.

Maximal Subgroups of Infinite Symmetric Groups. Baumgartner, James E, Shelah, Saharon and Thomas, Simon.

Natural Predicates and Topological Structures of Conceptual Spaces. Mormann, Thomas.

On *NFU*. Crabbé, Marcel.

On a Quasi-Set Theory. Krause, Décio.

On Paradoxes in Naive Set Theory. Laraudogoitia, Jon Perez.

On Plural Reference and Elementary Set Theory. Cartwright, Helen Morris.

On Potential Embedding and Versions of Martin's Axiom. Fuchino, Sakaé.

On the Sense of Unsaturated Expressions. Diller, Antoni.

Questions and Quantifiers. Brown, Mark.

Relevance, Relatedness and Restricted Set Theory in Advances in Scientific Philosophy, Schurz, Gerhard (ed). Smith, Barry.

Reply to Bigelow's 'Sets Are Haecceities' in Ontology, Causality and Mind: Essays in Honour of D M Armstrong, Bacon, John (ed). Armstrong, D M.

Reply to Smart's 'Laws of Nature as a Species of Regularities' in Ontology, Causality and Mind: Essays in Honour of D M Armstrong, Bacon, John (ed). Armstrong, D M.

Sets Are Haecceities in Ontology, Causality and Mind: Essays in Honour of D M Armstrong, Bacon, John (ed). Bigelow, John.

Singular σ-Dense Trees. Landver, Avner.

Some Remarks Concerning the Notion of Set (in Polish). Lemanska, A.

Sorites Paradoxes and the Transition Question. Sainsbury, Mark.

Symmetric Submodels of a Cohen Generic Extension. Sureson, Claude.

Systems of Combinatory Logic Related to Predicative and 'Mildly Impredicative' Fragments of Quine's 'New Foundations'. Holmes, M Randall.

The Axiom of Choice for Countable Collections of Countable Sets Does Not Imply the Countable Union Theorem. Howard, Paul E.

The Intuitionistic Alternative Set Theory. Lano, K.

The Skeleton in Frege's Cupboard: The Standard Versus Nonstandard Distinction. Hintikka, Jaakko and Sandu, Gabriel.

The Strength of the Δ-System Lemma. Howard, Paul and Solski, Jeffrey.

Why Russell's Paradox Won't Go Away. Moorcroft, Francis.

SEVENTEENTH CENTURY

see Modern

SEX

An Ethic of Care: Feminist and Interdisciplinary Perspectives. Larrabee, Mary Jeanne (ed).

Bodies that Matter: On the Discursive Limits of 'Sex'. Butler, Judith.

Elemental Passions—Luce Irigaray. Irigaray, Luce, Collie, Joanne (trans) and Still, Judith (trans).

Moral Matters. Narveson, Jan.

Rethinking Masculinity. May, Larry (ed) and Strikwerda, Robert (ed).

A Critique of Androgeny. Fouché, Fidéla.

Arousal and the Ends of Desire. Jacobsen, Rockney.

Corporeal Archetypes and Power: Preliminary Clarifications and Considerations of Sex. Sheets-Johnstone, Maxine.

Good Love and Bad Love: A Way of Evaluation. McMurtry, John.

Sex and Social Roles in Rethinking Masculinity, May, Larry (ed). Grim, Patrick.

Sexual Differences: The Contingent and the Necessary. Wilson, John.

Sexual Education and Morality. Spiecker, Ben.

Surviving Sexual Violence. Brison, Susan J.

The Image of Woman in Religious Consciousness: Past, Present, and Future. Stepaniants, M T.

The Man Without a Penis: Libidinal Economies that (Re)cognize the Hypernature of Gender. Nash, Margaret M.

Women's Emancipation and the Theology of Sex in Nineteenth-Century Russia. Polyakov, L V.

SEXISM

Beyond Methodology: Feminist Scholarship as Lived Research. Fonow, Mary Margaret (ed) and Cook, Judith A (ed).

Compassionate Authority: Democracy and the Representation of Women. Jones, Kathleen B.

Abjection and Oppression in Crises in Continental Philosophy, Dallery, Arleen B (ed). Young, Iris Marion.

How Sexist is Sartre?. Burstow, Bonnie.

Modern Feminism and Marx. Kain, Philip J.

Real Men in Rethinking Masculinity, May, Larry (ed). LaFollette, Hugh.

SEXTUS EMPIRICUS

Scepticism. Hookway, Christopher.

Appearances and Impressions. Barney, Rachel.

SEXUAL HARASSMENT

Ethical Theory and Business (Fourth Edition). Beauchamp, Tom L and Bowie, Norman E.

A Feminist Definition of Sexual Harassment. Superson, Anita M.

Justice, Sexual Harassment, and the Reasonable Victim Standard. Wells, Deborah L and Kracher, Beverly J.

SEXUALITY

Buddhism, Sexuality, and Gender. Cabezón, José I (ed).

Critical Thought Series: 2—Critical Essays on Michel Foucault. Burke, Peter (ed).

Dialogue and the Human Image: Beyond Humanistic Psychology. Friedman, Maurice S.

Erotic Welfare: Sexual Theory and Politics in the Age of Epidemic. Singer, Linda.

From Mastery to Analysis: Theories of Gender in Psychoanalytic Feminism. Elliot, Patricia.

Hypatia Reborn: Essays in Feminist Philosophy. Al-Hibri, Azizah Y (ed) and Simons, Margaret A (ed).

Materialist Feminism and the Politics of Discourse. Hennessy, Rosemary.

Personal Love. Fisher, Mark.

Sexual Democracy: Women, Oppression, and Revolution. Ferguson, Ann.

Speculum of the Other Woman—Luce Irigaray. Irigaray, Luce and Gill, Gillian C (trans).

Studies in Augustine and Eriugena. O'Meara, John J and Halton, Thomas (ed).

Taking Sides: Clashing Views on Controversial Issues in Human Sexuality (Third Edition). Francoeur, Robert.

The Logic of Sense—Gilles Deleuze. Boundas, Constantin V (ed), Lester, Mark (& other trans) and Deleuze, Gilles.

The Revision of Psychoanalysis—Eric Fromm. Fromm, Erich.

Theoretical Perspectives on Sexual Difference. Rhode, Deborah L (ed).

Transformations: Recollective Imagination and Sexual Difference. Cornell, Drucilla.

Against Couples in Applied Philosophy, Almond, Brenda (ed). Gregory, Paul.

An Anthropological Vision of CHristian Marriage. Martinez, German.

Antigone's Mirrors: Reflections on Moral Madness. Pritchard, Annie.

Chastity and the (Male) Philosophers. McGhee, Michael.

De deconstructie van het kleine verschil. Everts, Saskia I.

Discontinuing Becomings: Deleuze on the Becoming-Woman of Philosophy. Braidotti, Rosi.

Equality and Sexual Difference in Beyond Equality and Difference, Bock, Gisela (ed). Cavarero, Adriana.

Female Identity between Sexuality and Maternity in Beyond Equality and Difference, Bock, Gisela (ed). Vegetti Finzi, Silvia.

Formation of Theories and Policy of Difference of the Sexes (in Czechoslovakian). List, Elisabeth.

Foucault's Aesthetics of Existence. Thacker, Andrew.

Gender Trouble: Notes on One Book (in Czechoslovakian). Smejkalova, J.

Is Sexual Desire Raced?: The Social Meaning of Interracial Prostitution. Shrage, Laurie J.

Jeffner Allen: A Lesbian Portrait. Zita, Jacquelyn N.

Plato and the Metaphysics of Desire. Halperin, David M.

Pornography and the Alienation of Male Sexuality in Rethinking Masculinity, May, Larry (ed). Brod, Harry.

Pre-Theoretical Assumptions in Evolutionary Explanations of Female Sexuality. Lloyd, Elisabeth.

Queer Ethics, or The Challenge of Bisexuality to Lesbian Ethics. Däumer, Elizabeth.

Sexual Archetypes in Transition. Francoeur, Robert T.

Sexual Differences: The Contingent and the Necessary. Wilson, John.

Sexual Ethics in the Age of Epidemic. Young, Iris.

The Feminist "Sexuality Debates" and the Transformation of the Political. Bar On, Bat-Ami.

The Oppression Debate in Sexual Politics in Rethinking Masculinity, May, Larry (ed). Clatterbaugh, Kenneth.

Tomb of the Sacred Prostitute: 'The Symposium' in Shadow of Spirit, Berry, Philippa (ed). Bell, Shannon.

Toward the Sexual and Economic Emancipation of Women: The Philosophy of Grete Meisel-Hess. Melander, Ellinor.

SHADOW

Author's Reply. Watson, Richard A.

Good and Bad Shadow History of Philosophy. Livingston, Donald W.

Shadow History. Popkin, Richard H.

Shadow History in Philosophy. Watson, Richard A.

The History of Philosophy and the Reputation of Philosophers. Rogers, G A J.

SHAFTESBURY

Estetica e cosmologia in Shaftesbury. Gatti, Andrea.

SHAKESPEARE

Shakespeare's Demonic Prince. Mindle, Grant B.

Shakespeare's Richard III and the Soul of the Tyrant. Frisch, Morton J.

The New Historicism and Shakespearean Criticism: A Marxist Critique. Siegel, Paul N.

SHALOM, A

Person as Locus of Permanence: Towards Albert Shalom's Metaphysics. Boltuc, Piotr.

SHAME

Guilt as an Identificatory Mechanism. Greenspan, P S.

SHAPERE, P

Shapere on Observation. Linden, Toby.

SHAPIRO, D

Hermeneutics of Suspicion. Fisher, Linda.

SHARING

Altruism. Paul, Ellen Frankel (ed), Miller, Fred D (ed) and Paul, Jeffrey (ed).

Life-Sharing for a Creative Tomorrow. Barral, Mary-Rose.

Sharing without Reckoning. Schumaker, Millard.

Altruism Versus Self-Interest: Sometimes a False Dichotomy in Altruism, Paul, Ellen Frankel (ed). Badhwar, Neera Kapur.

Communities of Collaboration: Shared Commitments/Common Tasks in On Community, Rouner, Leroy S (ed). Rupp, George.

SOCIAL CONTRACT

Hume, Bentham, and the Social Contract. Wolff, Jonathan.

La fonction du droit et la question du lien social chez Hume et Montesquieu. Autin, Pierre-Louis.

Pacifying Politics: Resistance, Violence, and Accountability in Seventeenth-Century Contract THeory. Baumgold, Deborah.

SOCIAL CRITICISM

Social Criticism After Rawls. Couture, Tony.

SOCIAL ETHICS

Applied Ethics and Free Will: Some Untoward Results of Independence. Machan, Tibor R.

SOCIAL ORDER

Giddens on Subjectivity and Social Order. Wagner, Gerhard.

SOCIAL PHIL

see also Anarchism, Authority, Communism, Conservatism, Equality, Ethics, Freedom, Political Phil, Progress, Punishment, Society, Toleration, Utopia

"At Risk": Development of Personhood. Nowell, Linda.

"Brother, You Can't Go to Jail for What You're Thinking": Motives, Effects and "Hate Crime" Laws. Gellman, Susan.

"Feminist" Sympathy and Other Serious Crimes: A Reply to Swindle. Mills, Patricia Jagentowicz.

"Justice, Caring, and Animal Liberation": Commentary. Menta, Timothy.

"Le sens optus" and "Unintentionality" (in Czechoslovakian). Grygar, Mojmir.

"Maleness" Revisited. Bordo, Susan.

"One Isaac Waiting to Be Slaughtered": Halpern Leivick, The Holocaust, and Responsibility. Goodhart, Sandor.

"Power in the Service of Love": John Dewey's Logic and the Dream of a Common Language. Hart, Carroll Guen.

"Take Your Pill Dear": Kate Millett and Psychiatry's Dark Side. Steinbuch, Thomas.

"The Dog in the Lifeboat Revisited": Commentary. Finsen, Susan.

"Without a Truly Socialist Society the World of Today and of Tomorrow Is Unthinkable". Wohl, Andrzej.

"Yes, But...": Principles and Caveats in American Racial Attitudes. Hochschild, Jennifer L and Herk, Monica.

"An Essay on the Principle of Population"—T R Malthus. Winch, Donald (ed) and Malthus, T R.

A Companion to Contemporary Political Philosophy. Goodin, Robert E (ed) and Pettit, Philip (ed).

A Progress of Sentiments: Reflections on Hume's "Treatise". Baier, Annette.

A Treatise of Human Nature—David Hume. Mossner, Ernest C (ed).

Action and Agency. Kevelson, Roberta (ed).

Against Relativism: A Philosophical Defense of Method. Harris, James F.

Altruism. Paul, Ellen Frankel (ed), Miller, Fred D (ed) and Paul, Jeffrey (ed).

An Ethic of Care: Feminist and Interdisciplinary Perspectives. Larrabee, Mary Jeanne (ed).

An Inquiry Into the Nature and Causes of the Wealth of Nations—Adam Smith. Smith, Adam.

Analecta Husserliana, XXXI. Tymieniecka, Anna-Teresa (ed).

Analytical and Dialectical Marxism. Hunt, Ian.

Applied Philosophy. Almond, Brenda (ed) and Hill, Donald (ed).

Arguing About Abortion. Schwartz, Lewis M.

Aspects of Mind—Gilbert Ryle. Meyer, René (ed) and Ryle, Gilbert.

Automatism, Insanity, and the Psychology of Criminal Responsibility: A Philosophical Inquiry. Schopp, Robert F.

Bettering Our Condition: Work, Workers and Ethics in British and German Economic Thought. Chmielewski, Philip J.

Betting on Theories: Cambridge Studies in Probability, Induction, and Decision Theory. Maher, Patrick.

Between Philosophy and Social Science: Selected Early Writings. Horkheimer, Max and Hunter, G Frederick (& other trans).

Beyond Equality and Difference. Bock, Gisela (ed) and James, Susan (ed).

Beyond Methodology: Feminist Scholarship as Lived Research. Fonow, Mary Margaret (ed) and Cook, Judith A (ed).

Blacks and Social Justice (Revised Edition). Boxill, Bernard R.

Bodies that Matter: On the Discursive Limits of 'Sex'. Butler, Judith.

Breaking Out Again: Feminist Ontology and Epistemology (Second Edition). Stanley, Liz and Wise, Sue.

British Empiricism and American Pragmatism: New Directions and Neglected Arguments. Roth, Robert.

Changing To National Health Care: Ethical and Policy Issues. Huefner, Robert P (ed) and Battin, Margaret P (ed).

Changing Values in Medical and Health Care Decision Making. Jensen, Uffe Juul (ed) and Mooney, Gavin (ed).

Community at Loose Ends. Miami Theory Collect (ed).

Compassionate Authority: Democracy and the Representation of Women. Jones, Kathleen B.

Confucianism, Buddhism, Daoism, Christianity and Chinese Culture. McLean, George F (ed) and Yi-Jie, Tang.

Contemporary Political Culture. Gibbins, John R (ed).

Contractarian Liberal Ethics and the Theory of Rational Choice. Park, Jung Soon.

Critical Thought Series: 2—Critical Essays on Michel Foucault. Burke, Peter (ed).

Cross, Crescent, and Sword. Johnson, James Turner (ed) and Kelsay, John (ed).

Cultural-Political Interventions in the Unfinished Project of Enlightenment. Honneth, Axel (& other eds).

Democracy. Harrison, Ross.

Dialectical Investigations. Ollman, Bertell.

Dialectical Social Theory and Its Critics. Smith, Tony.

Directions and Misdirections (in Hungarian). Fehér, István M (ed).

Dirty Hands: The Problem of Political Morality. Buckler, Steve.

Disciplining Foucault: Feminism, Power, and the Body. Sawicki, Jana.

Drawing the Line: Life, Death, and Ethical Choices in an American Hospital. Gorovitz, Samuel.

Drug Legalization: For and Against. Evans, Rod L (ed) and Berent, Irwin M (ed).

Ecology, Economics, Ethics: The Broken Circle. Bormann, Herbert F (ed) and Kellert, Stephen R (ed).

Elemental Passions—Luce Irigaray. Irigaray, Luce, Collie, Joanne (trans) and Still, Judith (trans).

Emerson and Thoreau: The Contemporary Reviews. Myerson, Joel (ed).

Engendering the Subject: Gender and Self-Representation in Contemporary Women's Fiction. Robinson, Sally.

Erotic Welfare: Sexual Theory and Politics in the Age of Epidemic. Singer, Linda.

Essays on Kant's Political Philosophy. Williams, Howard (ed).

Essays on Philosophy and Economic Methodology. Hausman, Daniel M.

Ethical Issues: Perspectives for Canadians. Soifer, Eldon (ed).

Ethics and Politics. Paton, Calum.

Ethics in an Aging Society. Moody, Harry R.

Exploitation, Unequal Exchange and Dependency: A Dialectical Development. Otubusin, Paul.

Feminine and Feminist Ethics. Tong, Rosemarie.

Feminist Perspectives In Medical Ethics. Holmes, Helen Bequaert (ed) and Purdy, Laura M.

Foucault's Nietzschean Genealogy: Truth, Power, and the Subject. Mahon, Michael.

Founders of Constructive Postmodern Philosophy. Griffin, David Ray (& others).

Frames of Deceit: A Study of the Loss and Recovery of Public and Private Trust. Johnson, Peter.

Friedrich Nietzsche—H L Mencken. Flathman, Richard (ed) and Mencken, H L.

Friendship: A Philosophical Reader. Badhwar, Neera Kapur (ed).

From Marx to Mises. Steele, David Ramsay.

From Mastery to Analysis: Theories of Gender in Psychoanalytic Feminism. Elliot, Patricia.

G A Rauche: Selected Philosophical Papers. Louw, T J G.

Gender Politics and Post-Communism: Reflections from Eastern Europe and the Former Soviet Union. Funk, Nanette (ed) and Mueller, Magda (ed).

George Herbert Mead—The Making of a Social Pragmatist. Cook, Gary A.

George Herbert Mead: The Making of a Social Pragmatist. Cook, Gary A.

Government, Justice, and Contempt. Lane, Gilles.

Government: Servant or Master?. Radnitzky, Gerard (ed) and Bouillon, Hardy (ed).

Hannah Arendt: A Reinterpretation of Her Political Thought. Canovan, Margaret.

Hegel and His Critics. Desmond, William J (ed).

Hegel on Want and Desire: A Psychology of Motivation. Forbes, Kipling D.

Hegel: Three Studies. Adorno, Theodor W and Nicholsen, Shierry Weber (trans).

History, Religion, and American Democracy (New Edition). Wohlgelernter, Maurice (ed).

Hypatia Reborn: Essays in Feminist Philosophy. Al-Hibri, Azizah Y (ed) and Simons, Margaret A (ed).

Identity/Difference: Democratic Negotiations of Political Paradox. Connolly, William E.

Ideology and False Consciousness: Marx and his Historical Progenitors. Pines, Christopher.

Ideology and Modern Culture: Review of J B Thompson. Van Veuren, Pieter.

Il Destino della Famiglia Nell'Utopia. Colombo, Arrigo (ed) and Quarta, Cosimo.

Image and Ideology in Modern/PostModern Discourse. Downing, David B (ed) and Bazargan, Susan (ed).

Impressionism: A Feminist Reading. Broude, Norma.

In the Throe of Wonder: Intimations of the Sacred in a Post-Modern World. Miller, Jerome A.

International Justice and the Third World. Attfield, Robin (ed) and Wilkins, Barry (ed).

Je, Tu, Nous: Toward a Culture of Difference. Irigaray, Luce and Martin, Alison (trans).

Jean-Paul Sartre: Freedom and Commitment. Hill, Charles G.

John Dewey and American Democracy. Westbrook, Robert B.

Judging in Good Faith. Burton, Steven J.

Judging Lyotard. Benjamin, Andrew (ed).

Justice and Interpretation. Warnke, Georgia.

Justice for an Unjust Society. Lötter, H P P.

Justice: Interdisciplinary Perspectives. Scherer, Klaus R (ed).

Keeping Faith: Philosophy and Race in America. West, Cornell.

L'Utopia di Fourier. Tundo, Laura.

La Comparution/The Compearance: From the Existence of "Communism" to the Community of "Existence". Nancy, Jean-Luc and Strong, Tracy B (trans).

La Théorie qui n'en est pas une, or, Why Clio Doesn't Care. Steedman, Carolyn.

Law and the Human Sciences. Kevelson, Roberta (ed).

Liberalism and Modern Society: A Historical Argument. Bellamy, Richard.

Liberty/Liberté: The American and French Experiences. Klaits, Joseph (ed) and Haltzel, Michael (ed).

Life and Death: Philosophical Essays in Biomedical Ethics. Brock, Dan W.

Life-Sharing for a Creative Tomorrow. Barral, Mary-Rose.

SOCIAL PHIL

Los Limites de la Comunidad. Thiebaut, Carlos.

Marine Lover of Friedrich Nietzsche—Luce Irigaray. Irigaray, Luce and Gill, Gillian C (trans).

Marx's Theory of History. Wetherly, Paul.

Marxism Recycled. Van Parijs, Philippe.

Materialist Feminism and the Politics of Discourse. Hennessy, Rosemary.

Matrix and Line: Derrida and the Possibilities of Postmodern Social Theory. Martin, Bill.

Metaphysical Aporia and Philosophical Heresy. Ross, Stephen David.

Method—Towards a Study of Humankind, Volume I: The Nature of Nature. Morin, Edgar and Bélanger, J L Roland (trans).

Modern Political Theory and Contemporary Feminism: A Dialectical Analysis. Ring, Jennifer.

Moral Boundaries: A Political Argument for an Ethic of Care. Tronto, Joan C.

Moral Controversies: Race, Class, and Gender in Applied Ethics. Gold, Steven Jay.

Moral Personhood: An Essay in the Philosophy of Moral Psychology. Scott, G E.

Morality and Moral Controversies (Third Edition). Arthur, John (ed).

Morality, Prudence, and Nuclear Weapons. Lee, Steven.

Mythology: From Ancient to Post-Modern. Kleist, Jürgen (ed) and Butterfield, Bruce (ed).

Nationalism, Colonialism, and Literature. Eagleton, Terry, Jameson, Fredric and Said, Edward W.

Natural Reasons: Personality and Polity. Hurley, S L.

New Philosophy of Social Science. Bohman, James F.

New Reflections on the Revolution of Our Time. Laclau, Ernesto.

Nietzsche: The Politics of Power. Okonta, Ike.

On Community. Rouner, Leroy S (ed).

On Intersubjectivity and Cultural Creativity—Martin Buber. Eisenstadt, S N (ed) and Buber, Martin.

On the Track of Reason. Beehler, Rodger G (ed), Copp, David (ed) and Szabados, Bela (ed).

Open Institutions: The Hope for Democracy. Murphy, John W (ed) and Peck, Dennis L (ed).

Partial Visions: Feminism and Utopianism in the 1970s. Bammer, Angelika.

Peirce and Law. Kevelson, Roberta.

Persona ou la Justice au Double Visage. Trigeaud, Jean-Marc.

Personal Love. Fisher, Mark.

Philosophical Issues in Journalism. Cohen, Elliot D (ed).

Philosophy and Feminist Criticism. Cole, Eve Browning.

Philosophy and Government, 1572-1651. Tuck, Richard.

Philosophy of Economics: On the Scope of Reason in Economic Inquiry. Roy, Subroto.

Philosophy of Technology: An Introduction. Ihde, Don.

Philosophy of the Social Sciences III: Groundwork for Social Dynamics. Wisdom, J O.

Pianificazione e teoria critica. Campani, Carlos.

Politica Sacra et Civilis—George Lawson. Lawson, George and Condren, Conal (ed).

Political Liberalism. Rawls, John.

Political Theory and Postmodernism. White, Stephen K.

Politics, Gender, and Genre: The Political Thought of Christine de Pizan. Brabant, Margaret (ed).

Politics/Sense/Experience: A Pragmatic Inquiry into the Promise of Democracy. Kaufman-Osborn, Timothy V.

Post-Liberalism: Studies in Political Thought. Gray, John.

Postmodernism and Society. Boyne, Roy (ed) and Rattansi, Ali (ed).

Postnational Identity: Critical Theory and Existential Philosophy in Habermas, Kierkegaard, and Havel. Matustik, Martin J.

Praxiologies and the Philosophy of Economics: The International Annual of Practical Philosophy and Methodology. Auspitz, J Lee (ed), Gasparski, Wojciech W (ed) and Mlicki, Marek K (ed).

Pursuing Parenthood: Ethical Issues in Assisted Reproduction. Lauritzen, Paul.

Quality of Life, Health and Happiness. Nordenfelt, Lennart.

Radical Fragments. Marsh, James.

Rational Infidels: The American Deists. Walters, Kerry S.

Reading Kristeva: Unraveling the Double-bind. Oliver, Kelly.

Reappraisals: Shifting Alignments in Postwar Critical Theory. Hohendahl, Peter Uwe.

Reason and Responsibility (Eighth Edition). Feinberg, Joel.

Relations Between Cultures. McLean, George F (ed) and Kromkowski, John (ed).

Rethinking Goodness. Wallach, Michael A and Wallach, Lise.

Rethinking Masculinity. May, Larry (ed) and Strikwerda, Robert (ed).

Retribution Reconsidered: More Essays in the Philosophy of Law. Murphy, Jeffrie G.

Revolutions in Knowledge: Feminism in the Social Sciences. Zalk, Sue Rosenberg (ed) and Gordon-Kelter, Janice (ed).

Risks and Wrongs. Coleman, Jules L.

Santayana, Pragmatism, and the Spiritual Life. Levinson, Henry Samuel.

Sartre Alive. Aronson, Ronald (ed) and Van Den Hoven, Adrian (ed).

Scepticism. Hookway, Christopher.

Secession: The Morality of Political Divorce from Fort Sumter to Lithuania and Quebec. Buchanan, Allen.

Selves, People, and Persons. Rouner, Leroy S (ed).

Semiotics in the United States. Sebeok, Thomas A.

Sexual Democracy: Women, Oppression, and Revolution. Ferguson, Ann.

Sharing Responsibility. May, Larry.

Sharing without Reckoning. Schumaker, Millard.

Simone Weil's Philosophy of Culture. Bell, Richard H (ed).

Simone Weil: Portrait of a Self-Exiled Jew. Nevin, Thomas R.

Sinn und Ursprung. Gahlings, Ute.

Sobor and Sobornost'. Tulaev, Pavel.

Social and Personal Ethics. Shaw, William H.

Socialism and Morality. McLellan, David (ed) and Sayers, Sean (ed).

Speculum of the Other Woman—Luce Irigaray. Irigaray, Luce and Gill, Gillian C (trans).

Speech, Crime, and the Uses of Language. Greenawalt, Kent.

Standing In Your Own Way: Talks On the Nature of Ego. Damiani, Anthony.

Subject to History: Ideology, Class, Gender. Simpson, David (ed).

T S Eliot and American Philosophy: The Harvard Years. Jain, Manju.

Taking Sides: Clashing Views on Controversial Bioethical Issues (Fifth Edition). Levine, Carol.

Taking Sides: Clashing Views on Controversial Issues in Human Sexuality (Third Edition). Francoeur, Robert.

Terrorism, Justice and Social Values. Peden, W Creighton (ed) and Hudson, Yeager (ed).

The Animals Issue: Moral Theory in Practice. Carruthers, Peter.

The Balance of Consciousness: Eric Voegelin's Political Theory. Keulman, Kenneth.

The Banalization of Nihilism. Carr, Karen L.

The Blackwell Dictionary of Twentieth-Century Social Thought. Outhwaite, William (ed) and Bottomore, Tom (ed).

The Challenge of Pluralism: Education, Politics, and Values. Power, F Clark (ed) and Lapsley, Daniel K (ed).

The Chicago Pragmatists and American Progressivism. Feffer, Andrew.

The Common Mind: An Essay on Psychology, Society, and Politics. Pettit, Philip.

The Concept of Political Judgment. Steinberger, Peter J.

The Crisis in Modernism. Burwick, Frederick (ed) and Douglass, Paul (ed).

The DC-10 Case: A Study in Applied Ethics, Technology, and Society. Fielder, John H and Birsch, Douglas.

The Desire To Be God: Freedom and the Other in Sartre and Berdyaev. McLachlan, James Morse.

The Dialogue of Justice: Towards a Self-Reflective Society. Fishkin, James S.

The Dilemma of Narcissus. Gairdner, W T (trans) and Lavelle, Louis.

The Ethics of Deconstruction: Derrida and Levinas. Critchley, Simon.

The Faith of a Liberal—Morris Raphael Cohen. Cohen, Morris R.

The Grounds and Limits of Political Obligation. Capriotti, Emile.

The Idea of Democracy. Copp, David (ed), Hampton, Jean (ed) and Roemer, John E (ed).

The Interpretation of the Flesh: Freud and Femininity. Brennan, Teresa.

The Logic of Marx's "Capital": Replies to Hegelian Criticisms. Smith, Tony.

The Logical Foundations of the Marxian Theory of Value. Garcia de la Sierra, Adolfo.

The Moral Dimensions of Marriage and Family Therapy. Lageman, August G.

The Moral Dimensions of Public Policy Choice: Beyond the Market Paradigm. Gillroy, John Martin (ed) and Wade, Maurice (ed).

The Morality Maze: An Introduction To Moral Ecology. Daniels, Neil M.

The Morality of Happiness. Annas, Julia.

The Morality of Pluralism. Kekes, John.

The Nature and Process of Law: An Introduction to Legal Philosophy. Smith, Patricia (ed).

The Origins of Our Delusions (in Hungarian). Ludassy, Mária.

The Persistence of Modernity: Essays on Aesthetics, Ethics, and Postmodernism. Midgley, David N (trans) and Wellmer, Albrecht.

The Person and the Common Life. Hart, James G.

The Philosopher of Free Religion: Francis Ellingwood Abbot, 1836-1903. Peden, W Creighton.

The Philosophy of Freedom: Ideological Origins of the Bill of Rights. Rudolph, Samuel B (ed).

The Philosophy of the Limit. Cornell, Drucilla.

The Place of Morality in Foreign Policy. Oppenheim, Felix E.

The Place of the Person In Social Life. Peachey, Paul (ed), Kromkowski, John (ed) and McLean, George F (ed).

The Practice of Moral Judgment. Herman, Barbara.

The Quality of Life. Nussbaum, Martha C (ed) and Sen, Amartya (ed).

The Renewal of the Heidegger-Kant Dialogue: Action, Thought, and Responsibility. Schalow, Frank.

The Resources of Rationality: A Response to the Postmodern Challenge. Schrag, Calvin.

The Revision of Psychoanalysis—Eric Fromm. Fromm, Erich.

The Self Between: From Freud to the New Social Psychology of France. Webb, Eugene.

The Theory-Death of the Avant-Garde. Mann, Paul.

The Utilitarian Response. Allison, Lincoln (ed).

The Veil of Black: (Un)Masking the Subject of African-American Modernism's "Native Son". Benston, Kimberly W.

Theoretical Perspectives on Sexual Difference. Rhode, Deborah L (ed).

SOCIAL PHIL

SOCIAL PHIL

Professor Filice's Defense of Pacifism: A Comment. Narveson, Jan.

Property as Wealth, Property as Propriety. Rose, Carol M.

Property in *The Realm of Rights*. Thau, Michael Alan.

Punishment—A Tale of Two Islands. Walker, M T.

QALYs—A Threat to our Quality of Life?. Haydock, Anne.

Queer Ethics, or The Challenge of Bisexuality to Lesbian Ethics. Däumer, Elizabeth.

Quinn on Doing and Allowing. Fischer, John M.

Race and Culture: A Response to Levin and Thomas. Pojman, Louis.

Race and the Modern Philosophy Course. Immerwahr, John.

Racial Discrimination is Distinct, If Not "Special". Herrera, Christopher.

Racism and Affirmative Action. Corlett, J Angelo.

Racism and Rationality in Hegel's Philosophy of Subjective Spirit. Moellendorf, Darrel F.

Racism: Flew's Three Concepts of Racism. Skillen, Anthony.

Radical Environmentalism and the Political Roots of Postmodernism. Frodeman, Robert.

Rational Altruism or the Secession of Successful?: A Paradox of Social Choice. Nelson, Julianne.

Rationality and Ethnocentrism. Barnhart, J E.

Rationality in Action. Hollis, Martin and Sugden, Robert.

Rationality, Relativism, and Rorty. Allen, Jonathan G.

Rationalization and Responsibility: A Reply to Whisner. Martin, Mike W.

Rawls's Communitarianism. Alejandro, Roberto.

Rawls's Savings Principle (in Hebrew). Attas, Daniel.

Reading Bartky: Identity, Identification, and Critical Self Reflection. Bar On, Bat-Ami.

Realizing Love and Justice: Lesbian Ethics in the Upper and Lower Case. Martindale, Kathleen and Saunders, Martha.

Reason Without Emotion. Jones, Carol.

Reconciliation Reaffirmed: A Reply to Peffer. Sterba, James.

Reflections on Feminist Scepticism, the "Maleness" of Philosophy and Postmodernism. Milligan, Maureen.

Reflections on Personhood: Developing a Sense of Self through Community of Inquiry. Glaser, Jen.

Refusing to Draw the Circle Around 'the Self': The Quest for Community in the Work of Basehart and Berenson. Downing, Fred.

Relativism: The Return of the Repressed. Gunnell, John G.

Religion and Civic Virtue. Budziszewski, J.

Reply to Beckwith: Abortion—Whose Agenda Is It Anyway?. Keenan, James F.

Reply to Commentators on *Femininity and Domination*. Bartky, Sandra.

Reply to Gass's "Abortion and Moral Character: A Critique of Smith". Smith, Janet E.

Reply to Keenan: Thomson's Argument and Academic Feminism. Beckwith, Francis J.

Reply to Richard Rorty's "Feminism and Pragmatism": How Did the Dinosaurs Die Out? How Did the Poets Survive?. Wilson, Catherine.

Reply to Richard Rorty's "Feminism and Pragmatism": Richard Rorty—Knight Errant. Skillen, Tony.

Reports on International Research in Social Epistemology. Kasavin, Ilya.

Reproductive Technologies and the "Survival" of the "Human Subject". Levesque-Lopman, Louise.

Resolving the Tension in Graham and Laird. Guston, David.

Response to Alexander's "Voluntary Acts: The Child/Davidson Trilemma". Child, James.

Response to Bordo's "Feminist Skepticism and the 'Maleness' of Philosophy". Butler, Judith.

Response to Schedler: Why This Policy Is Wrong. Dandekar, Natalie.

Responses to Race Differences in Crime. Levin, Michael.

Responsible and Irresponsible Liberalism: Dostoevsky's Stavrogin. Neumann, Harry.

Restoration Romanticism. Tamás, G M.

Rethinking Resistance: Environmentalism, Literature, and Poststructural Theory. Quigley, Peter.

Retribution, Arbitrariness and the Death Penalty. Calvert, Brian.

Review Article of Ann Ferguson's *Sexual Democracy: Women, Oppression, and Revolution*. Soble, Alan.

Review Essay: The Best Intuitionistic Theory Yet! Thomson On Rights. Smith, M B E.

Richard Rorty's Failed Politics. Haber, Honi.

Rights and the Rise of Informational Society: The Origins and Ends of Behavioral Rights. Luke, Timothy W.

Rights in Social Context. Fisk, Milton T.

Rights, Friends, and Egoism. Smith, Tara.

Rights, Law, and the Right. Sparrow, Edward G.

Risk and Public Decision-Making: Constructivism and the Postpositivist Challenge. Valverde Jr, L James.

Romanticist and Realist Elements in Nationalist Thinking in the 19th Century. Kemiläinen, Aira.

Rousseau and the Problem of Community: Nationalism, Civic Virtue, Totalitarianism. Simon-Ingram, Julia.

Rousseau on the Foundation of National Cultures. Kelly, Christopher.

Rousseau Turned Upright: Technology and Paternalism. Wojciechowski, Krzysztof.

Rules, Principles, Algorithms and the Description of Legal Systems. Utz, Stephen.

Ruling Memory. Norton, Anne.

Russell on Chinese Civilization. Dong, Yu.

Russia and the West: The Quest for Russian National Identity. Groys, Boris.

S Stur's "Treatise on Life" (in Czechoslovakian). Uher, J.

Sadomasochism and Exclusion. Saxe, Lorena Leigh.

Sailing Through the *Republic*. Stalley, R F.

Santo Tomás y el origen de la sociedad. De Stier, María L Lukac.

Sartre's Ontology of Evil and the Poverty of the Social Sciences. Gordon, Haim and Gordon, Rivca.

Scenes from a Newborn Life (in Dutch). Hendriks, Ruud.

Science, Democracy, and Public Policy. Shrader-Frechette, Kristin.

Science, Prudence, and Folly in Hobbes's Political Theory. Hanson, Donald W.

Secession: The Caes of Quebec. Nielsen, Kai.

Self-Defence and Forcing the Choice between Lives. Miller, Seumas.

Self-Determination in Political Philosophy and International Law. Dahbour, Omar.

Self-Interest and Survival. Martin, Raymond.

Self-Ownership and Worldly Resources. Ingram, A.

Self-Trust, Autonomy, and Self-Esteem. Govier, Trudy.

Set-Asides, Reparations, and Compensatory Justice. Paul, Ellen Frankel.

Sexual Archetypes in Transition. Francoeur, Robert T.

Shifting Subjects Shifting Ground: The Names and Spaces of the Post-Colonial. Ray, Sangeeta.

Significación lógica del cambio de estructura de *El Capital* entre 1857 y 1866. Delgado, Manuel.

Situating Hannah Arendt on Action and Politics. Isaac, Jeffrey C.

Skrach's Trace in the History of Czech Thought (in Czechoslovakian). Karola, J E.

Slagter's Nek: Imitatio Christi in the Construction of the Other/Self (in Dutch). Praeg, L.

Slote on Self-Sufficiency. Hursthouse, Rosalind.

Sobre predicciones y relatos. Fernández, Oscar.

Social Choice Theory: Formalism Infatuation and Policy Making Realities. Iannone, A Pablo.

Social Control, Efficiency Control and Ethical Control in Different Political Institutions: Education. Natale, Samuel M (& others).

Social Criticism After Rawls. Couture, Tony.

Social Ecology, Deep Ecology, and Liberalism. Dizerega, Gus.

Socialism as the Extension of Democracy. Arneson, Richard J.

Socialism, Utopianism and the 'Utopian Socialists'. Lovell, David W.

Sociocultural Evolution or the Social Evolution of Practical Reason: Eder's Critique of Habermas. Strydom, Piet.

Sociology in the Economic Mode. Janssen, Maarten C W.

Socrates on the Decline and Fall of Regimes: Books 8 and 9 of the *Republic*. Coby, Patrick.

Solitary Rule-Following. Champlin, T S.

Some Aspects of Person in an African Tradition Thought System. Oshita, Oshita O.

Some Disquiet about "Difference". Sypnowich, C A.

Some Further Thoughts on "Thought Crimes". Weinstein, James.

Some Problems with Loyalty: The Metaethics of Commitment. Cochran, Ruth B.

Some Rules of Constitutional Design. Ordeshook, Peter C.

Some Virtues of Resident Alienation. Baier, Annette.

Speaking to Trees. Kohák, Erazim.

Special Ties and Natural Duties. Waldron, Jeremy.

Spencer, Steiner and Hart on the Equal Liberty Principle. Gray, Tim.

Sport: An Historical Phenomenology. Skillen, Anthony.

State and Nation. Cauchy, Venant.

Statistical Badness. Thomas, Laurence.

Sterba's Reconciliation Project: A Critique. Peffer, Rodney.

Strong Utilitarianism in Mo Tzu's Thought. Vorenkamp, Dirck.

Structural Inquiry, Human Agency and the Contribution of Harré and Bhaskar: A Case Study of Wright's "Classes". Adkins, Barbara.

Subversive Rationalization: Technology, Power, and Democracy. Feenberg, Andrew.

Surrendering and Cathcing in Poetry and Sociology. Ward, John Powell.

Surviving Sexual Violence. Brison, Susan J.

Surviving to Speak New Language: Mary Daly and Adrienne Rich. Hedley, Jane.

Susan Gellman Has It Right. Brown, Ralph.

Tactics of Appropriation and the Politics of Recognition in Late Modern Democracies. Coombe, Rosemary J.

Talking about Talking about Nature: Nurturing Ecological Consciousness. Michael, Mike and Grove-White, Robin.

Teasing Feminist Sense from Experience. Kaufman-Osborn, Timothy V.

Technology and Mother Earth: The Rousseauian Roots of the Debate. Malcolmson, Patrick and Myers, Richard.

Technology and the Civil Epistemology of Democracy. Ezrahi, Yaron.

Technology, the Natural Environment, and the Quality of Life. De Cózar, José M.

Technopraxiology and Development. Tobar-Arbulu, José Felix.

Terrorism and the Epochal Transformation of Politics. Allen, Wayne.

The "C" Theory: A Chinese Philosophical Approach to Management and Decision-Making. Cheng, Chung-Ying.

The *Narod* and the Intelligentsia: From Dissociation to *Sobornost'*. Klechenov, Gennadii.

The *Narod*, the Intelligentsia, and the Individual. Kovalev, Vitalii.

The Absent Ontology of Society: Response to Juckes and Barresi. Manicas, Peter T.

The ADL Hate Crime Statute and the First Amendment. Alexander, Larry.

The Authentic *Tele* of Politics: A Reading of Aristotle. Swazo, N K.

The Big Lie: Human Restoration of Nature. Katz, Eric.

The Body in the City. Swensen, Cole.

The Call of Nature: A Reply to Ted Benton and Tim Hayward. Reid, Michael.

The Challenge of Multiculturalism in Political Ethics. Gutmann, Amy.

The Conflictual Agendas of Neo-Liberal Reconstruction and the Rise of Islamic Politics in Turkey. Birtek, Faruk and Toprak, Binnaz.

The Constitution and the Nature of Law. Robison, Wade.

The Context of Community. Alexander, Thomas M.

The Continuity of Chinese Humanism in the Shang-Chou Period. Wong, Yeu-Guang.

The Correlativity of Duties and Rights. Fieser, James.

SOCIETY

SOCIOLOGY

Emergence of a Radical Sociology of Scientific Knowledge. Zibakalam, Saeid.

From Theology to Sociology: Bruno Bauer and Karl Marx on the Question of Jewish Emancipation. Peled, Yoav.

Is There a Duty to Accept Punishment?. Michael, Mark.

Leaving Man in Society. Krausz, Ernest.

On Understanding Disaster. Simissen, Herman.

Philosophical Foundations for Functional Sociology in Marx's Theory of History, Wetherly, Paul. MacDonald, Graham.

Philosophy and Sociology of Law in the Work of Renato Treves. Ferrari, Vincenzo and Velicogna, Nella Gridelli.

Relativism and the Social Scientific Study of Medicine. Risjord, Mark.

Reply to Harbers and De Vries. Lynch, William.

Reply to Lynch's "What Does the Double Hermeneutic Explain/Justify?". Harbers, Hans and De Vries, Gerard.

Reproductive Technologies and the "Survival" of the "Human Subject". Levesque-Lopman, Louise.

Ronald Giere's "Explaining Science: A Cognitive Approach". Resnik, David B.

Sociology and Hacking's Trousers. Schmaus, Warren S.

Sociology in the Economic Mode. Janssen, Maarten C W.

Surrendering and Cathcing in Poetry and Sociology. Ward, John Powell.

The End of Functionalism: *Parsons, Merton, and Their Heirs*. Turner, Stephen.

The Interrelations between the Philosophy, History and Sociology of Science in Thomas Kuhn's Theory of Scientific Development. Hoyningen-Huene, Paul.

The Phenomenal World of Kurt H Wolff. Horowitz, Irving Louis.

Three Dimensional Social Science. Armstrong, Robert L.

What Does the Double Hermeneutic Explain/Justify?. Lynch, William.

Zur Notwendigkeit von Religion aus der Sicht Durkheims und seiner Erben. Steunebrink, Gerrit A J.

SOCIOLOGY OF KNOWLEDGE

Historia de la ciencia y comunidades científicas. Schuster, Félix G.

Unfathomed Knowledged, Unmeasured Worth and Growth?. Hauptli, Bruce.

SOCRATES

Ancient Concepts of Philosophy. Jordan, William.

Collected Writings—Leonard E Woodbury. Brown, Christopher G (& other eds) and Woodbury, Leonard E.

Early Socratic Dialogues—Plato. Saunders, Trevor J (ed).

Essays on the Philosophy of Socrates. Benson, Hugh H (ed).

Socrates' Second Sailing. Tejera, Victorino.

The Hymn to Eros. Mitchell, Robert Lloyd.

Commentary on Sedley's "Teleology and Myth in the *Phaedo*. Fine, Gail.

Commentary on Vlastos' "Socratic Piety". Lefkowitz, Mary R.

Deontologism and Moral Weakness. Peterson, John.

Diagrams: Socrates and Meno's Slave. Lloyd, Marcus.

Die Wahrheit und das Gute: Sokrates und die Geburt der Metaphysik. Splett, Jörg.

Fairness in Socratic Justice—*Republic* I. Scaltsas, Theodore.

Giustizia e "carità" nel pensiero greco-romano (I). Pizzorni, R.

How Significant is Socrates' Midwifery?. Mazumdar, Rinita.

In Search of Socrates. Scaltsas, Theodore.

Inquiry in the "Meno" in The Cambridge Companion to Plato, Kraut, Richard H (ed). Fine, Gail.

Killing, Confiscating, and Banishing at *Gorgias* 466-468. Weiss, Roslyn.

Malinconia e nichilismo—I: Dalla ferita mortale alla ricomposizione dell'infranto. Bottani, Livio.

On the Place of Validity. Price, Robert G.

On the Sense of the Socratic Reply to Meno's Paradox. Jenks, Rod.

Pictures of Socrates. Thompson, Caleb.

Poverty and Sincerity in the *Apology*. Seeskin, Kenneth.

Sailing Through the *Republic*. Stalley, R F.

Socrate: Il demone e il risveglio—Sul senso dell'etica socratica. De Bernardi, P.

Socrates and Plato. Graham, Daniel W.

Socrates and Rhetoric: The Problem of Nietzsche's Socrates. Vincenzo, Joseph P.

Socrates and the Early Dialogues in The Cambridge Companion to Plato, Kraut, Richard H (ed). Penner, Terrence M I.

Socrates on the Decline and Fall of Regimes: Books 8 and 9 of the *Republic*. Coby, Patrick.

Socrates' Two Concepts of the Polis. Yonezawa, Shigeru.

Socratic Legal Obligation in the *Crito*. Kusyk, Douglas A.

Socratic Piety. Vlastos, Gregory.

Teleology and Myth in the *Phaedo*. Sedley, David.

The Book of the Philosophic Life. Butterworth, Charles E (trans), Muhammad, Abü Bakr and Al-Razi, Zakariyya.

The Conclusion of the *Meno*. Snider, Eric W.

The Examined Life. Dalton, Peter C.

The Origins of Al-Razi's Political Philosophy. Butterworth, Charles E.

The Socratic Theory of Motivation. Reshotko, Naomi.

The Unity of the Virtues in Plato's *Protagoras* and *Laches*. Devereux, Daniel T.

The Virtues of Thrasymachus. Chappell, T D J.

Vincenzo's Portrayal of Nietzsche's Socrates. Domino, Brian.

Virtue Ethics. Megone, Christopher.

Virtue Without Gender in Socrates. Scaltas, Patricia Ward.

Vlasto's *Socrates: Ironist and Moral Philosopher*. Reeve, C D C.

Vlastos's Socrates. Kahn, Charles.

Voices of Silence: On Gregory Vlastos' Socrates. Nehamas, Alexander.

What Did Socrates Teach and To Whom Did He Teach It?. Nehamas, Alexander.

What Laches and Nicias Miss—And Whether Socrates Thinks Courage Merely a Part of Virtue. Penner, Terrence M I.

Why is Annihiliation a Great Gain for Socrates? The Argument of *Apology* 40c3-e2. Calef, Scott.

SOCRATIC METHOD

L'argument par "affinité" dans le "phédon". Rowe, Christopher.

Socratic Questioning, Logic and Rhetoric. Hintikka, Jaakko.

SOFTWARE

A Reply to Johnson's Reply to "Should Computer Programs Be Ownable?". Carey, David.

Should Computer Programs Be Ownable?. Carey, David.

SOLIDARITY

Deconstructing Solidarity: Or, A Funny Thing Happened On the Way to Unity. Kohli, Wendy R.

Solidarité et disposition du corps humain. Hottois, Gilbert.

Solidarity and Moral Community. Hostetler, Karl.

The Ironist's Utopia: Can Rorty's Liberal Turnip Bleed?. Phillips, Hollibert.

SOLIPSISM

Conditions for Interpersonal Communication. Agassi, Joseph.

Il mistero e la persona nell'opera di Edith Stein. D'Ambra, M.

Sind Tiere Bewussthaber? Über die Quelle unserer Du-Evidenz. Schmitz, Hermann.

Wittgenstein, Solipsism, and Religious Belief. Huff, Douglas.

'Narrow'-Mindedness Breeds Inaction. Buller, David J.

SOLITUDE

Approaching Distance. Hanson, Karen.

Soggetto metafisicoe metafisica del sociale. Laganà, Antonino.

SOLOMON, G

Sources of Knowledge of Sextus Empiricus in Hume's Time. Popkin, Richard H.

SOLOMON, R

Horror, Helplessness, and Vulnerability: A Reply to Robert Solomon. Carroll, Noël.

SOLT, K

Escher and Parmigianino: A Study in Paradox. Duran, Jane.

SOMMERS, F

On the Question 'Do We Need Identity?'. Purdy, William C.

SOPHISM

Divine Infinity in Greek and Medieval Thought. Sweeney, Leo.

The Cambridge Companion to Plato. Kraut, Richard H (ed).

Aristotle and Hellenistic Philosophy. Sharples, Bob.

How Significant is Socrates' Midwifery?. Mazumdar, Rinita.

Introduction to the Study of Plato in The Cambridge Companion to Plato, Kraut, Richard H (ed). Kraut, Richard H.

On Plato's *Sophist*. Benardete, Seth.

Plato's "Sophist" on False Statements in The Cambridge Companion to Plato, Kraut, Richard (ed). Frede, Michael.

Presocratics and Sophists. Wright, M R.

The Logical Sense of παραδοξον in Aristotle's *Sophistical Refutations*. Boger, George.

The Night in Which All Cows are Black: Ethical Absolutism in Plato and Hegel. Browning, Gary K.

William of Auvergne on *De re* and *De dicto* Necessity. Teske, Roland J.

SOPHISMATA

New Light on Medieval Philosophy: The Sophismata of Richard Kilvington. Ashworth, E J.

SOPHOCLES

Antigone's Mirrors: Reflections on Moral Madness. Pritchard, Annie.

SORABJI, R

Aristotle and Aquinas on Cognition. Owens, Joseph.

Aristotle and Perceptual Realism. Granger, E Herbert.

SORELL, T

Critical Notice of Tom Sorell *Scientism: Philosophy and the Infatuation with Science*. Lugg, Andrew and McDonald, J F.

SORENSEN, R

A Deflationary Resolution of the Surprise Event Paradox. Jacquette, Dale.

Rationality and Epistemic Paradox. Kroon, Frederick.

SORITES

An Alternative Rule of Disjunction in Modal Logic. Williamson, Timothy.

Is Higher Order Vagueness Coherent?. Wright, Crispin.

SORROW

Weeping at the Death of Dido: Sorrow, Virtue, and Augustine's *Confessions*. Werpehowski, William.

SOSA, E

Why We Need Proper Function. Plantinga, Alvin.

SOUL

see also Mind

A Reading of Hegel's "Phenomenology of Spirit" (Revised Edition). Lauer, Quentin.

Aquinas on Mind. Kenny, Anthony.

Philoponus: On Aristotle on the Intellect. Charlton, William (trans).

Pondus Meum amor meus: the Weight-Metaphor in Saint Augustine's Early Philosophy. Torchia, Joseph.

Schöpfung und Geist. Günther, Dorothea.

The Birth to Presence. Nancy, Jean-Luc.

The Dilemma of Narcissus. Gairdner, W T (trans) and Lavelle, Louis.

The Mathematical Soul: An Antique Prototype of the Modern Mathematisation of Psychology. Stachowski, Ryszard.

SOUL

Understanding Non-Western Philosophy: Introductory Readings. Bonevac, Daniel A and Phillips, Stephen.

A Note on Contraries and the Incorruptibility of the Human Soul in St Thomas Aquinas. Wilhelmsen, Frederick.

Albert the Great in the Renaissance: Cristoforo Landino's Use of Albert on the Soul. McNair, Bruce.

Aquinas's Arguments for Spirit. Foster, David R.

Are Souls Unintelligible? in Philosophical Perspectives, 5: Philosophy of Religion, 1991, Tomberlin, James E (ed). Hoffman, Joshua and Rosenkrantz, Gary.

Aristotle and the Concept of Supervenience. Granger, E Herbert.

Augustine's Numbering Numbers and the Immortality of the Human Soul. Ramirez, J Roland.

Autocoscienza e conoscenza nel 'primo Rosmini'. De Lucia, Paolo.

Brain Death: A Survey of the Debate and the Position in 1991. Jeffery, Peter.

Clarke's Extended Soul. Vailati, Ezio.

Comments on Robert Welshon's "Nietzsche's Peculiar Virtues and the Health of the Soul". Hunt, Lester.

Das Leib-Seele-Pentagon und die Kombinatorik attraktiver Vorstellungen—Ein folgenreiches Konzept der Leibnizschen Frühphilosophie. Busche, Hubertus.

Edith Stein: Essential Differences. McAlister, Linda L.

Hierarchy and Dualism in Aristotelian Psychology. Glas, G.

How Are Souls Related to Bodies? A Study of John Buridan. Zupko, Jack.

Interpretazione e critica di Plotino della concezione del tempo dei suoi predecessori. Trotta, Alessandro.

L'Ane. Jonckheere, L.

L'argument par "affinité" dans le "phédon". Rowe, Christopher.

L'interpretazione di Plotino della teoria platonica dell'anima. Szlezák, T A.

La ceguera según Aristóteles. Quevedo, Amalia.

La théorie platonicienne de la motivation humaine. Cooper, John.

Leibanwesenheit und primitive Gegenwart. Kühn, Rolf.

Mistica o filosofia? A proposito della dottrina dell'immagine di Meister Eckhart. Sturlese, Loris.

Nietzsche's Peculiar Virtues and the Health of the Soul. Welshon, Robert.

On the Simplicity of the Soul in Philosophical Perspectives, 5: Philosophy of Religion, 1991, Tomberlin, James E (ed). Chisholm, Roderick M.

Personal Identity in Reflections on Philosophy, McHenry, Leemon (ed). Fuller, Gary.

Rereading *Fear and Trembling*. McLane, Earl.

Response to Lester Hunt's Comments. Welshon, Robert.

Self, Sameness, and Soul in "Alcibiades I" and the "Timaeus". Goldin, Owen M.

Soul as Attunement: An Analogy or a Model? in Greek Studies in the Philosophy and History of Science, Nicolacopoulos, Pantelis (ed). Scaltsas, Theodore.

Soul, Rational Soul and Person in Thomism. La Plante, Harry.

Spinoza's Argument for the Identity Theory. Della-Rocca, Michael.

St Augustine's View of the Original Human Condition in *De Genesi contra Manichaeos*. Teske, Roland J.

Surviving Souls. Moser, Paul K and Vander Nat, Arnold.

The Locked Door: An Analysis of the Problem of the Origin of the Soul in St Augustine's Thought. Waddell, Michael M.

The Role of the 'Ergon' Argument in Aristotle's 'Nicomachean Ethics' in Essays in Ancient Greek Philosophy, IV, Anton, John P (ed). Achtenberg, Deborah.

The Soul in the Explanation of Life: Aristotle Against Reductionism. Baldner, Steven.

The Unity of Platonic Epistemology: Divine Madness in Plato's *Phaedrus*. Coolidge, Jr, Francis P.

The Unnamed Fifth: *Republic* 369d. Page, Carl.

Writing and Painting: The Soul as Hermeneut in The Language of Art History, Kemal, Salim (ed). Rosen, Stanley H.

SOUND

Discovery, Creation, and Musical Works. Fisher, John Andrew.

Plato and the Sightlovers of the *Republic*. Stokes, Michael C.

Sound and Epistemology in Film. Branigan, Edward.

The World Made of Sound: Whitehead and Pythagorean Harmonics in the Context of Veda and the Science of Mantra. Amodio, Barbara A.

SOUNDNESS

The Minimal System *L'o*. Wang, Xuegang.

SOURCE

Logic-Theological Schools from the Second Half of the 12th Century: A List of Sources. Yukio, Iwakuma and Ebbesen, Sten.

The Authorship and Sources of the Peri Semeion Ascribed to Theophrastus in Theophrastus, Fortenbaugh, William W (ed). Cronin, Patrick.

Virtue: A Brief Bibliography. Galston, William A.

SOUTH AFRICAN

Gerhard A Rauche's Philosophy of Actuality: The Work and Thought of an Individualist South African Philosopher. Louw, Tobias J G.

Private Schools and Public Schools: A Critical Response to the Privatization Debate. Enslin, Penny.

SOUTH AMERICAN

Sinn und Ursprung. Gahlings, Ute.

SOVEREIGNTY

Leviathan—Thomas Hobbes. Hobbes, Thomas and MacPherson, C B (ed).

Hobbes and the Equality of All Under the One. Mitchell, Joshua.

Kant's Idealization of the Republic (in French). Bergeois, B.

SOVIET

Gender Politics and Post-Communism: Reflections from Eastern Europe and the Former Soviet Union. Funk, Nanette (ed) and Mueller, Magda (ed).

Perestroika, Too, Is Developed Socialism. Radzihkovskii, L A.

Sobor and *Sobornost'*. Tulaev, Pavel.

Soviet Marxism and Analytical Philosophies of History—Eero Loone. Pearce, Brian (trans) and Loone, Eero.

Comparative Philosophy in the Soviet Union. Lysenko, Victoria G.

Die Entstehung einer Personalistischen philosophie im heutigen Russland. Solov'ëv, Erich Jurevich.

Do We Have a Scientific Conception of the History of Philosophy? Polemical Notes. Donskikh, O A and Kochergin, A N.

From Social Subject to the 'person': *The Belated Tranformation in Latter-Day Soviet Philosophy*. Swiderski, Edward M.

Is Philosophy a Science?. Nikiforov, A L.

Landmarks: An Unheard Warning. Gaidenko, P P.

Lenin, Hegel and Western Marxism: From the 1920s to 1953. Anderson, Kevin.

Marxism and Actually Existing Socialism in Socialism and Morality, McLellan, David (ed). Sayers, Sean.

Marxism and Russian Philosophy. Zamaleev, A F.

Phenomenology in Russia: The Contribution of Gustav Shpet. Scanlan, James P.

Philosophical Studies (Sinology and Indology) in St Petersburg (Leningrad), 1985-1990. Torchinov, E A.

Private Life, Private Interest, Private Property. Zamoshkin, I A.

Re-Reading Soviet Philosophy: Bakhurst on Ilyenkov. Larvor, Brendan.

Reports on International Research in Social Epistemology. Kasavin, Ilya.

Russia's Movement Toward a Market Civilization and the Russian National Character. Smirnov, P I.

Soviet Philosophy in Transition: An Interview with Vladislav Lektorsky. Bakhurst, David.

The *Narod* and the Intelligentsia: From Dissociation to *Sobornost'*. Klechenov, Gennadii.

The *Narod*, the Intelligentsia, and the Individual. Kovalev, Vitalii.

The Work Ethic and the Work Ethos: The Importance of Ethical Arguments for the Politics of Transition to the Market. Büscher, M.

Westernizers and Nativists Today. Aksiuchits, Viktor.

Women's Emancipation and the Theology of Sex in Nineteenth-Century Russia. Polyakov, L V.

'Denken über Ideologie': eine praktische Begründung der Erneuerung der post-sowjetischen Philosophie?. Swiderski, E M.

SPACE

"A Mark of the Growing Mind is Veneration of Objects" (Ludwig Wittgenstein). Sawyier, Fay.

An Introduction to Husserlian Phenomenology. Bernet, Rudolf, Kern, Iso and Marbach, Eduard.

Cyberspace: First Steps. Benedikt, Michael (ed).

Descartes on Seeing: Epistemology and Visual Perception. Wolf-Devine, Celia.

Philosophical Universes. Verster, Ulrich.

Philosophy of Physics. Sklar, Lawrence.

The Deleuze Reader. Boundas, Constantin V (ed).

The Manifestation of Analogous Being in the Dialectic of the Space-Time Continuum: A Philosophical Study in Freedom. Harris, David A.

The Natural and the Normative: Theories of Spatial Perception from Kant to Helmholtz. Hatfield, Gary.

Theoretical Philosophy, 1755-1770—Immanuel Kant. Walford, David (ed & trans).

A New Look at Simultaneity. Peacock, Kent A.

A Note on Kant's First Antinomy. Moore, A W.

Buckets of Water and Waves of Space: Why Space-Time is Probably a Substance. Maudlin, Tim.

Classical Physical Abstraction. Adams, Ernest W.

Compactness and Normality in Abstract Logics. Caicedo, Xavier.

Constructive Mathematics and Quantum Mechanics: Unbounded Operators and the Spectral Theorem. Hellman, Geoffrey.

Das Phänomen der inkongruenten Gegenstücke aus Kantischer und heutiger Sicht. Mühlhölzer, Felix.

Degrees of Convex Dependence in Recursively Enumerable Vector Spaces. Nevins, Thomas A.

Forever is a Day: Supertasks in Pitowsky and Malament-Hogarth Spacetimes. Earman, John and Norton, John D.

Frontiers of Utopia: Past and Present. Marin, Louis.

Gleason's Theorem is Not Constructively Provable. Hellman, Geoffrey.

Hume's Ideas of Space and Time: As Original As They First Appear. Coughlan, Stephen G.

Husserl's Concept of Horizon: An Attempt at Reappraisal in Analecta Husserliana, XXXI, Tymieniecka, Anna-Teresa (ed). Kwan, Tze-Wan.

Kant's Relational Theory of Absolute Space. Carrier, Martin.

La philosophie de l'espace chez Ernst Cassirer. Ferrari, Massimo.

La scoperta di nuovi documenti sulla vita di Bruno: Su *Giordano Bruno and the Embassy Affair* di John Bossy. Mancini, Sandro.

Leibniz' Theory of Space: A Reconstruction. Khamara, Edward J.

Limit and Exhaustibility in the Questions of T'ang. Stevenson, Frank W.

Marty on Grounded Relations in Mind, Meaning and Metaphysics, Mulligan, Kevin (ed). Johansson, Ingvar.

Marty on Time in Mind, Meaning and Metaphysics, Mulligan, Kevin (ed). Simons, Peter.

Marty's Theory of Space in Mind, Meaning and Metaphysics, Mulligan, Kevin (ed). Egidi, Rosaria.

On an Alleged Inconsistency in Whitehead. Capek, Milic.

STABILITY

Community Ecology, Scale, and the Instability of the Stability Concept. McCoy, E D and Shrader-Frechette, Kristin.

More on *R*. Wagner, Frank O.

On Consensus and Stability in Science. Baigrie, Brian S and Hattiangadi, J N.

On the Undecidability of Some Classes of Abelian-By-Finite Groups. Marcja, Annalisa, Prest, Mike and Toffalori, Carlo.

Stability Among R.E. Quotient Algebras. Love, John.

The Difference Model of Voting. Hansson, Sven Ove.

There is No Sharp Transitivity on *q*6 When *q* is a Type of Morley Rank 2. Gropp, Ursula.

Triviality, NDOP and Stable Varieties. Hart, B, Pillay, A and Starchenko, S.

STALEY, K

The Past Just Ain't What It Used To Be: A Response to Kevin Staley and Ronald Tacelli. Baldner, Steven.

STALIN

Toward a Kierkegaardian Understanding of Hitler, Stalin, and the Cold War in Foundations of Kierkegaard's Vision of Community, Connell, George B (ed). Bellinger, Charles.

STALINISM

Hannah Arendt: A Reinterpretation of Her Political Thought. Canovan, Margaret.

Has History Refuted Marxism?. Hudelson, Richard.

STALNAKER, R

Getting the Constraints on Popper's Probability Functions Right. Leblanc, Hugues and Roeper, Peter.

STANISLAVSKI, K

Tolstoy, Stanislavski, and the Art of Acting. Hughes, R I G.

STARR, W

A Kantian Approach to Codes of Ethics. L'Etang, Jacquie.

STATE

see also Mental States

Hegel on Want and Desire: A Psychology of Motivation. Forbes, Kipling D.

Politica Sacra et Civilis—George Lawson. Lawson, George and Condren, Conal (ed).

The Grounds and Limits of Political Obligation. Capriotti, Emile.

The Origins of Our Delusions (in Hungarian). Ludassy, Mária.

Abstract Principles, Mid-Level Principles, and the Rule of Law. Henley, Kenneth.

Authority, Autonomy and the Legitimate State. Paterson, R W K.

Between Church and State: Nietzsche, Deleuze and the Genealogy of Psychoanalysis. Schrift, Alan D.

Conciencia subjetiva y Estado ético en Hegel. De Meyer, Luisa Herrera.

El estado hegeliano como individualidad excluyente. De Rojas Raz, Nerva Borda.

Ethnic Diversity and the Nation State. Jayal, Niraja Gopal.

Forms of Abstract "Community": From Tribe and Kingdom to Nation and State. James, Paul.

From Social Subject to the 'person': *The Belated Tranformation in Latter-Day Soviet Philosophy*. Swiderski, Edward M.

Functional Explanation and the State in Marx's Theory of History, Wetherly, Paul. Carter, Alan.

Hegel, Modernity, and Civic Republicanism. Buchwalter, Andrew.

Hobbes's Shortsightedness Account of Conflict. Murphy, Mark C.

Introduction to the Methodology of Paraphronesis, With Example: Religion and Education in Postmodern America. Tandy, Charles.

Kant on the State, Law, and Obedience to Authority in the Alleged 'Anti-Revolutionary' Writings. Westphal, Kenneth.

Kant's Concept of the State in Essays on Kant's Political Philosophy, Williams, Howard (ed). Kersting, Wolfgang.

L' "Antibancor" e la filosofia del danaro. Pinottini, Marzio.

La Propriété chez Hobbes. Zarka, Yves Charles.

Moralität und Frieden: Kants Gesetz der Freiheit in der Welt der Staaten. Römpp, Georg.

Nature versus the State? Markets, States, and Environmental Protection. Weale, Albert.

Socrates on the Decline and Fall of Regimes: Books 8 and 9 of the *Republic*. Coby, Patrick.

Socrates' Two Concepts of the Polis. Yonezawa, Shigeru.

State and Nation. Cauchy, Venant.

The Factory Acts in Marx's Theory of History, Wetherly, Paul. Wetherly, Paul.

The State, Marriage and Divorce. Trainor, Brian T.

The Unanimity Standard. Kagan, Shelly.

When the Child is the Father of the Man: Work, Sexual Difference, and the Guardian-State in Third Republic France. Schafer, Sylvia.

STATEMENT

see also Necessary Statements

On the Logic of Ordinary Conditionals. McLaughlin, Robert N.

Overcoming Logical Positivism from Within: The Emergence of Neurath's Naturalism in the Vienna Circle's Protocol Sentence Debate. Uebel, Thomas E.

A New Theory of Comparative and Noncomparative Justice. Hoffman, Joshua.

Contingency, A Priority and Acquaintance. Ryckman, Thomas C.

STATES OF AFFAIRS

Possibilità e stati di fatto in Chisholm. Negro, Matteo.

The Hidden Consequentialist Assumption. Hurley, Paul E.

STATIONARY LOGIC

The Hanf Numbers of Stationary Logic II: Comparison with Other Logics. Shelah, Saharon.

STATISTICS

Inductive Logic: Probability and Statistics. Baird, Davis W.

Bell's Inequality, Information Transmission, and Prism Models. Maudlin, Tim.

Doom and Probabilities. Leslie, John.

On the Reduction of Process Causality to Statistical Relations. Dowe, Phil.

Perspectives on Decisions263-. Segerberg, Krister.

Probability Theory and the Doomsday Argument. Eckhardt, William.

Regression Analysis: Classical and Bayesian. Urbach, Peter.

Rethinking Objective Homogeneity: Statistical Versus Ontic Approaches. Burnor, Richard.

Statistical Badness. Thomas, Laurence.

Wesley Salmon's Process Theory of Causality and the Conserved Quantity Theory. Dowe, Phil.

What's Wrong with Salmon's History: The Third Decade. Fetzer, James H.

STATUS

Aquinas and the Moral Status of Animals. Drum, Peter.

STCHERBATSKY, T

On Certain Intellectual Stereotypes in Buddhist Studies as Exemplified in T Stcherbatsky's Works. Lysenko, Victoria.

STEBBINS, S

Comments on "Anthropomorphism". Hilbert, David.

STECKER, R

Response to Stecker's "Goldman on Interpreting Art and Literature". Goldman, Alan H.

STEIN, E

Edith Stein's Philosophy of Community. Baseheart, Mary Catharine.

Edith Stein: Essential Differences. McAlister, Linda L.

Edith Stein: La dottrina degli Angeli. Tilliette, X.

H Conrad-Martius und E Stein Husserls Schülerinen und aristotelisch-thomistische Philosophie (in Polish). Machnacz, J.

Il mistero e la persona nell'opera di Edith Stein. D'Ambra, M.

La filosofia di Edith Stein. Ales Bello, A.

Refusing to Draw the Circle Around 'the Self': The Quest for Community in the Work of Basehart and Berenson. Downing, Fred.

STEIN, G

Modern Times: Stein, Bergson, and the Ellipses of 'American' Writing in The Crisis in Modernism, Burwick, Frederick (ed). Riddel, Joseph N.

STEIN, H

On Relativity Theory and Openness of the Future. Maxwell, Nicholas.

STEIN, R

A Note on Schadenfreude and Proverbs 17:5. Harvey, Warren Z.

STEINBERG, L

Erwin Panofsky, Leo Steinberg, David Carrier: The Problem of Objectivity in Art Historical Interpretation. Carrier, David.

STEINER, G

Tragedy as Subclause: George Steiner's Dialogue with Donald MacKinnon. Ward, Graham.

STEINER, H

Spencer, Steiner and Hart on the Equal Liberty Principle. Gray, Tim.

STERBA, J

Sterba's Reconciliation Project: A Critique. Peffer, Rodney.

STEWART, M

A Response to M A Stewart's 'Berkeley's Introduction Draft'. Belfrage, Bertil.

STICH, S

Epistemic Normativity. Kornblith, Hilary.

Furthering Stich's Fragmentation. Hetherington, Stephen Cade.

In Defense of Truth and Rationality. Jacobson, Stephen.

Mental Content. Allen, Colin.

STIPULATION

A Note on Philip Kitcher's Analysis of Mathematical Truth. Norton-Smith, Thomas M.

STOCK MARKET

The Morality of Insider Trading. Rossouw, G J.

STOICISM

Greek Philosophers of the Hellenistic Age. Kristeller, Paul O and Woods, Gregory (trans).

The Uses of Antiquity. Gaukroger, Stephen (ed).

And the Idea Turned into History (in Czechoslovakian). Gelenczey-Mihaltz, Aliran.

Commentary on Reesor's "The Stoic Wise Man". Haase, Wolfgang.

Eine Korrektur des Poseidonios-Bildes. Forschner, Maximilian.

Galien et le stoïcisme. Manuli, Paola.

L'opera di Pietro Piovani. Galasso, Giuseppe.

Nationalism and Transnationalism in Cicero. Nicgorski, Walter.

Originalità filosofica dei *Pensieri* di Marco Aurelio. Crovi, Luca.

Rediscovering Some Stoic Arguments in Greek Studies in the Philosophy and History of Science, Nicolacopoulos, Pantelis (ed). Ierodiakonou, Katerina.

Religion and the Failures of Determinism in The Uses of Antiquity, Gaukroger, Stephen (ed). Sutton, John.

Schofield's *The Stoic Idea of the City*. Annas, Julia.

The Attractive and the Imperative in Essays on Henry Sidgwick, Schultz, Bart (ed). White, Nicholas P.

The Paradox of Power: Hobbes and Stoic Naturalism in The Uses of Antiquity, Gaukroger, Stephen (ed). Kassler, Jamie C.

The Stoic Analysis of the Sorites. Mignucci, Mario.

The Stoic Division of Philosophy. Ierodiakonou, Katerina.

STYLE

Architecture and Nihilism: On the Philosophy of Modern Architecture. Cacciari, Massimo and Sartarelli, Stephen (trans).

Nietzsche As Educator. Lemco, Gary.

Treatise on Style—Louis Aragon. Aragon, Louis and Waters, Alyson (trans).

A Question of Style: Nelson Goodman and the Writing of Theory. Engström, Timothy H.

Aesthetic Discrimination: Evaluation of Pieces by Style, Period, and Site. Duran, Jane.

Descartes philosophe et écrivain. Lafond, J.

La stylométrie et la question de "Métaphysique" K. Rutten, Christian.

Plato and the Computer. Robinson, T M.

The Formal Syntax of Modernism: Carnap and Le Corbusier. Bearn, Gordon C F.

The Politics of Art: The Domination of Style and the Crisis in Contemporary Art. Wartofsky, Marx.

SUAREZ

Esse Cognitum and Suárez Revisited. Wells, Norman J.

Francisco Suárez: The Man in History. Gracia, Jorge J E.

La reducción suareciana de los transcendentales. Sanz, Víctor.

Moral Virtue and the Demise of Prudence in the Thought of Francis Suárez. Treloar, John L.

Suárez and Metaphysical Mentalism: The Last Visit. Gracia, Jorge J E.

Suárez and the Jesuits. Noreña, Carlos.

Suárez and the Problem of Positive Evil. Davis, Douglas P.

Suárez and the Unity of a Scientific Habit. Doyle, John P.

Suárez's Conception of Metaphysics: A Step in the Direction of Mentalism?. Gracia, Jorge J E.

The Importance of the Concept of Substantial Unity in Suárez's Argument for Hylomorphism. Kronen, John D.

SUBCONSCIOUS

The Preconscious, the Unconscious and the Subconscious: A Phenomenological Critique of the Hermeneutics of the Latent. Seebohm, Thomas M.

SUBJECT

Foucault's Nietzschean Genealogy: Truth, Power, and the Subject. Mahon, Michael.

Aristotle and the Overcoming of the Subject-Object Dichotomy. Mensch, James.

Constituting the Political Subject, Using Foucault. Seitz, Brian.

Critical Rhetoric and the Possibility of the Subject in The Critical Turn, Angus, Ian (ed). McKerrow, Raymie E.

Foucault, Ethics, and the Fragmented Subject. Scott, Charles E.

I limiti della decostruzione del "soggetto" nella critica filosofica "postmoderna". Bosio, Franco.

Il soggetto metafisico alla prima e alla seconda potenza. Crescini, Angelo.

Inherence and Primary Substance in Aristotle's *Categories.* Devereux, Daniel T.

La metafisica del soggetto e l'origine dello spiritualismo filosofico occidentale. Masi, Giuseppe.

Object-Dependent Thoughts in Mental Causation, Heil, John (ed). Noonan, H W.

Soggetto metafisico e metafisica del sociale. Laganà, Antonino.

The Crisis of the Subject: From Baroque to Postmodern. Van Reijen, Willem.

The Origins of the Theory of the Subject in Philosophical Interventions in the Unfinished Project of Enlightenment, Honneth, Axel (& other eds). Henrich, Dieter.

The Philosophy of Language of Port-Royal and the Ontological Square: On Substantives and Adjectives (in Dutch). De Jong, R.

Vom Risiko der Positivität: Pihlosophieren nach dem Tod des Subjekts. Konersmann, Rolf.

William H Bernhardt's Value Hypothesis: A Systematic Approach in God, Values, and Empiricism, Peden, Creighton W (ed). Brush, Francis.

SUBJECTIVE

Consciousness Reconsidered. Flanagan, Owen.

Charles Hartshorne and Subjective Immortality. Suchocki, Marjorie H.

Hume on the Ordinary Distinction Between Objective and Subjective Impressions. Kornegay, R Jo.

Immortality: Objective, Subjective, or Neither? in God, Values, and Empiricism, Peden, Creighton (ed). Shaw, D W D.

Racism and Rationality in Hegel's Philosophy of Subjective Spirit. Moellendorf, Darrel F.

Subjective Experience and Points of View. Francescotti, Robert M.

The Subjective-Objective Dimension in the Individual-Society Connection: A Duality Perspective. Juckes, Tim J and Barresi, John.

SUBJECTIVISM

Betting on Theories: Cambridge Studies in Probability, Induction, and Decision Theory. Maher, Patrick.

Eternity and Time's Flow. Neville, Robert Cummings.

Ethical Essays, Volume I. Harrison, Jonathan.

Natural Reasons: Personality and Polity. Hurley, S L.

Truth and Eros: Foucault, Lacan, and the Question of Ethics. Rajchman, John.

Aesthetics and Adjudication: Intersubjective Requirements and Juridical Judgment. Purviance, Susan.

Animadversions on the Causal Theory of Perception. Vision, Gerald.

Ayer's Ethical Theory in A J Ayer Memorial Essays, Griffiths, A Phillips (ed). Wiggins, David.

Berkeley and Scepticism: A Fatal Dalliance. Imlay, Robert A.

Does Transcendental Subjectivity Meet Transcendental Grammar?. Kanthamani, A.

Empiricism, Difference, and Common Life. Fosl, Peter S.

Ethics and Subjectivity Today in Analecta Husserliana, XXXI, Tymieniecka, Anna-Teresa (ed). Rossi, Osvaldo.

Exchangeability and Predictivism. Wechsler, Sergio.

Hermeneutics and Genre: Bakhtin and the Problem of Communicative Interaction in The Interpretive Turn, Hiley, David R (ed). Kent, Thomas.

Human Functioning and Social Justice: In Defense of Aristotelian Essentialism. Nussbaum, Martha C.

Husserl y las aporías de la intersubjetividad. Finke, S R S.

L'Exisgence d'une phénoménologie asubjective et la noematique in Analecta Husserliana, XXXIV, Tymieniecka, Anna-Teresa (ed). Sivak, Josef.

Le principe éthique d'universalité et discussion. Canivet, Michel.

Moral Realism and Objective Theories of the Right. Sherline, Edward.

Neurobiology of Subjective Probability in Probability and Rationality, Eells, Ellery (ed). Nosal, Czeslaw S.

On Deafness in the Mind's Ear: John Dewey and Michael Polanyi. Tiles, James E.

Response: Subjective Arbitrariness. Machan, Tibor R.

Subjectivism and Toleration in A J Ayer Memorial Essays, Griffiths, A Phillips (ed). Williams, Bernard.

The Desire to Be God: Subjective and Objective in Nagel's *The View From Nowhere* and Sartre's *Being and Nothingness.* Wider, Kathleen.

The Postmodern Return, With a Vengeance, of Subjectivity in Postmodernism/ Jameson/ Critique, Kellner, Douglas (ed). Huhn, Thomas.

Unequal Property and Subjective Personality in Liberal Theories. Zucker, Ross.

SUBJECTIVITY

Mathesis e costruzione tra geometria antica e moderna. Ferrarin, Alfredo.

Merleau-Ponty Vivant. Dillon, M C (ed).

On Intersubjectivity and Cultural Creativity—Martin Buber. Eisenstadt, S N (ed) and Buber, Martin.

Asceticism/Askēsis in Ethics and Danger, Dallery, Arleen B (ed). McWhorter, Ladelle.

Authentic Selfhood in Heidegger and Rosenzweig. Cohen, Richard A.

Brains in a Vat, Subjectivity, and the Causal Theory of Reference. Ludwig, Kirk.

Edmund Husserl: Intersubjectivity between Epoché and History in Analecta Husserliana, XXXI, Tymieniecka, Anna-Teresa (ed). D'Ippolito, Bianca Maria.

Eine Metaphysik des Schwebens: Zum philosophischen Werk von Walter Schulz. Wandschneider, Dieter.

Embodiment, Sexual Difference, and the Nomadic Subject. Braidotti, Rosi.

Esperienza della soggettività e affermazione della trascendenza. Penati, Giancarlo.

Essere e spirito. Cavaciuti, Santino.

Fichte's New Wine. Harris, H S.

Gender, Subjectivity and Language in Beyond Equality and Difference, Bock, Gisela (ed). Violi, Patrizia.

Giddens on Subjectivity and Social Order. Wagner, Gerhard.

Husserl's Critique of Empiricism and the Phenomenological Account of Reflection. Drabinski, John.

Il concetto cartesiano del pensare e il problema delle altre intelligenze. Messeri, Marco.

Intentionality, Consciousness, and Subjectivity. Natsoulas, Thomas.

La dimensión ontológica de la conciencia afectiva según Ferdinand Alquié — Segunda parte. Sodor, A.

Merleau-Ponty Alive. Madison, G B.

Merleau-Ponty on Subjectivity and Intersubjectivity. Low, Douglas.

Metafisica della soggettività e filosofia della libertà. Ciancio, Claudio.

Metafisica e soggettività: Alle origini della filosofia moderna—Descartes, Pascal, Spinoza. Deregibus, Arturo.

Multiples: On the Contemporary Politics of Subjectivity. Flax, Jane.

On the Improvement of Our Moral Portrait: Moral Realism, History of Subjectivity, and Expressivist Language. Thiebaut, Carlos.

On the Possibility and Impossibility of Christian Existentialism. Toeplitz, Karol.

Per una soggettività non più "animale": Heidegger critico di Husserl. Regina, Umberto.

Positioning Subjects and Objects: Agency, Narration, Relationality. Taylor, Carole Anne.

Possibilities for a Nondominated Female Subjectivity. McLaren, Margaret.

Religionsphilosophie im Spannungsfeld von Wissenschaft und Innerlichkeit. Wuchterl, Kurt.

Reversible Subjectivity in Merleau-Ponty Vivant, Dillon, M C (ed). Davis, Duane.

Soggettivismo e oggettivismo agli albori della metafisica greca. Zeppi, Stelio.

Soggettività e metafisica. Chiereghin, Franco.

Soggettualità del fondamento. Incardona, Nunzio.

Subjectivity and the Arts: How Hepburn Could Be an Objectivist. Reddiford, Gordon.

Subjectivity and Worlds in *Works of Love* in Foundations of Kierkegaard's Vision of Community, Connell, George B (ed). Keeley, Louise Carroll.

Subjectivity in the Making. Ford, Lewis S.

Subjectivity/Objectivity and Meaningful Human Behavior in Terrorism, Justice and Social Values, Peden, Creighton W (ed). Armstrong, Robert L.

Taking Subjectivity into Account in Feminist Epistemologies, Alcoff, Linda (ed). Code, Lorraine.

The Construction of Subjectivity in Analecta Husserliana, XXXIV, Tymieniecka, Anna-Teresa (ed). Montero, Fernando.

Tradition, Modernity, and Confucianism. Dallmayr, Fred.

Truth and Subjectivity in Reasoned Faith, Stump, Eleonore (ed). Adams, Robert Merrihew.

Visions of Narcissism in Merleau-Ponty Vivant, Dillon, M C (ed). Levin, David Michael.

Vom Risiko der Positivität: Pihlosophieren nach dem Tod des Subjekts. Konersmann, Rolf.

SUBLIME

"Fiat lux": Une philosophie du sublime. Saint Girons, Baldine.

Kant and the Experience of Freedom: Essays on Aesthetics and Morality. Guyer, Paul.

SUBLIME

The Truth about Postmodernism. Norris, Christopher.

Analytic Aesthetics and Feminist Aesthetics: Neither/Nor?. Waugh, Joanne B.

Beautiful and Sublime: *Gender Totemism* in the Constitution of Art. Mattick Jr, Paul.

Corporality, Ethics, Experimentation: Lyotard in the Eighties. Lindsay, Cecile.

Der Sinn des Erhabenen—Kants Theorie des Erhabenen und ihre Bedeutung heute (in Japanese). Murata, Seiichi.

Intensity and Its Audiences: Notes Towards a Feminist Perspective on the Kantian. Gould, Timothy.

La conciliazione estetica e l'etica. Gallino, Guglielmo.

Schiller über das Erhabene. Petrus, Klaus.

Taste, Sublimity, and Genius in The Cambridge Companion to Kant, Guyer, Paul (ed). Schaper, Eva.

The Sublime as a Source of Light in the Works of Nicolas Boileau in Analecta Husserliana, XXXVIII, Tymieniecka, Anna-Teresa (ed). Litman, Theodore.

'Les Immatériaux' and the Postmodern Sublime in Judging Lyotard, Benjamin, Andrew (ed). Crowther, Paul.

SUBORDINATION

Friendship and Subordination in Earthly Societies. Burt, Donald X.

SUBSTANCE

see also Attribute, Immaterial Substance, Matter, Spiritual Substance

Il Problema della Modalità nelle Logiche di Hegel. Baptist, Gabriella.

The Ecological Self. Mathews, Freya.

Blaise Pascal e la problematicità dell'io: Ragione forte e pensiero debole. Todisco, O.

De l'ontologie à la théologie: Lecture du livre Z de la "Métaphysique" d'Aristote. Gérard, Gilbert.

Descartes on Persons. Holbrook, Daniel.

Existence and Substance (in Chinese). Chen, Wen-shiow.

Husserl e il linguaggio. Costa, Filippo.

I μεταξυ nella *Repubblica*: loro significato e loro funzione. Marcellino, Claudio.

Il mio itinerario filosofico. Selvaggi, Filippo.

Le concept de philosophie première chez Aristote: Note complémentaire. Follon, Jacques.

Matter against Substance. Gill, Mary Louise.

Metaphysics and the Eucharist in the Early Leibniz. Fouke, Daniel.

On the Endangered Species of the *Metaphysics*. Malcolm, John F.

Pantheism, Substance and Unity. Levine, Michael P.

Peirce on "Substance" and "Foundations". Potter, Vincent.

Real Selves: Persons as a Substantial Kind in Human Beings, Cockburn, David (ed). Lowe, E J.

Senses of Being in Aristotle's *Nichomachean Ethics*. Sim, May.

Substance and System: Perplexities of the Geometric Order. Wilson, Margaret D.

Substance Without Substratum. Denkel, Arda.

The Human Being as Substance and as Actual Entity. Welten, W.

The Importance of the Notion of Being for Philosophical Theology in God, Values, and Empiricism, Peden, Creighton W (ed). Chapman, Harley.

The Legacy of Russell's Idealism for His Later Philosophy: The Problem of Substance. Griffin, Nicholas.

Two Interpretations of the Pre-established Harmony in the Philosophy of Leibniz. Kulstad, Mark.

SUBSTANTIVALISM

Rings, Holes and Substantivalism: On the Program of Leibniz Algebras. Rynasiewicz, Robert.

SUCCESS

Try, Succeed and Fail: A Critique of Empirical Theories of Action (in French). Buekens, Filip.

SUFFERING

A History of Buddhist Philosophy. Kalupahana, David J.

Birth, Suffering, and Death: Catholic Perspectives at the Edges of Life. Wildes, Kevin W (ed), Abel, Francesc (ed) and Harvey, John C (ed).

Aquinas on the Sufferings of Job in Reasoned Faith, Stump, Eleonore (ed). Stump, Eleonore.

Deficiencies in the National Institute of Health's Guidelines for the Care and Protection of Laboratory Animals. Stephenson, Wendell.

Ethics and Animals: A Brief Review. Jamieson, Dale.

Leiden unter der Herrschaft der Zeit: Zu Michael Theunissens "Negativer Theologie der Zeit". Haeffner, Gerd.

Why Does God Allow This? An Empirical Approach to the Theodicy Question through the Themes of Suffering and Meaning. Hutsebaut, Dirk.

SUFFICIENT CONDITION

On the Nature of *Inus* Conditionality. Denise, Theodore C.

SUFFICIENT REASON

Rings, Holes and Substantivalism: On the Program of Leibniz Algebras. Rynasiewicz, Robert.

SUFFRAGE

Locke against Democracy: Consent, Representation and Suffrage in the *Two Treatises*. Wood, E M.

SUGDEN, R

Backward-Induction Arguments: A Paradox Regained. Sobel, Jordan Howard.

SUICIDE

Cruzan and the Constitutionalization of American Life. Schneider, Carl E.

Ethics in an Aging Society. Moody, Harry R.

Against the Right to Die. Velleman, J David.

Causing, Intending, and Assisting Death. Brody, Howard.

Conscience, Referral, and Physician Assisted Suicide. Wildes, Kevin W.

Doctors Must Not Kill. Pellegrino, Edmund.

Euthanasia and the Distinction between Acts and Omissions. Nesbitt, Winston.

Is There a Right to Die?. Kass, Leon R.

Living with Euthanasia: A Futuristic Scenario. Jonsen, Albert R.

Peter Singer and Non-Voluntary 'Euthanasia': Tripping Down the Slippery Slope. Uniacke, Suzanne and McCloskey, H J.

Physician-Assisted Dying: Theory and Reality. Meier, Diane E.

Practicing Medicine, Fiduciary Trust Privacy, and Public Moral Interloping after *Cruzan*. Rie, Michael A.

The Concept of the Person in the *Parens Patriae* Jurisdiction over Previously Competent Persons. Payton, Sallyanne.

The Jaina Ethic of Voluntary Death. Bilimoria, Purushottama.

The Limits of Consent: A Note on Dr Kevorkian. Kleinig, John.

The Right to Die as a Case Study in Third-Order Decisionmaking. Schauer, Frederick.

The Right to Die: A Justification of Suicide. Meyers, Chris D.

Unrequested Termination of Life: Is It Permissible?. Van Der Wal, Gerrit.

Voluntary Active Euthanasia. Brock, Dan W.

SUKACH, V

V V Rozanov: An Interview with V G Sukach. Skorobogatko, Nataliia.

SUNSTEIN, C

Beyond Compensatory Justice?. Johnston, David.

Compensation and Rights in the Liberal Conception of Justice. Barnett, Randy E.

Must Preferences Be Respected in a Democracy? in The Idea of Democracy, Copp, David (ed). Ferejohn, John.

SUPEREROGATION

The Suberogatory. Driver, Julia.

SUPERLATIVES

Formalizing the Logic of Positive, Comparative, and Superlative. Adams, Ernest.

SUPERMAN

Nietzsche's Superman: The Necessity of Reconsidering the Question of Man (in Dutch). Visser, Gerard.

SUPERNATURAL

The Supernatural. Cockburn, David.

SUPERNATURALISM

Refined and Crass Supernaturalism. Sprigge, T L S.

Refined and Crass Supernaturalism in Philosophy, Religion and the Spiritual Life, McGhee, Michael (ed). Sprigge, T L S.

SUPERVENIENCE

Mental Causation. Heil, John (ed) and Mele, Alfred (ed).

Metaphysics of Consciousness. Seager, William.

Natural Reasons: Personality and Polity: Review. Jackson, Frank.

Ontology, Causality and Mind: Essays in Honour of D M Armstrong. Bacon, John (ed), Campbell, Keith (ed) and Reinhardt, Lloyd (ed).

The Nature of True Minds. Heil, John.

The Physical Basis of Predication. Newman, Andrew.

Aristotle and Supervenience. Caston, Victor.

Aristotle and the Concept of Supervenience. Granger, E Herbert.

Aristotle on the Non-Supervenience of Local Motion. White, Michael J.

Block's Challenge in Ontology, Causality and Mind: Essays in Honour of D M Armstrong, Bacon, John (ed). Jackson, Frank.

Causation, Probability, and the Monarchy. Rosenberg, Alexander.

Compositional Supervenience Theories and Compositional Meaning Theories. Schiffer, Stephen.

Content, Causation, and Psychophysical Supervenience. Owens, Joseph.

Externalism and Token Identity. Seager, William.

Identity without Supervenience. Gibbons, John.

In Defense of Global Supervenience. Paull, R Cranston and Sider, Theodore R.

Laws of Nature, Modality and Humean Supervenience in Ontology, Causality and Mind: Essays in Honour of D M Armstrong, Bacon, John (ed). Menzies, Peter.

Leibniz's Phenomenalisms. Hartz, Glenn A.

Long Live Supervenience. Zangwill, Nicholas.

Mental Causation in Mental Causation, Heil, John (ed). Audi, Robert.

Perceptual Content and Local Supervenience. Davies, Martin.

Psychophysical Supervenience and Nonreductive Materialism. Marras, Ausonio.

Reply to Jackson's 'Block's Challenge' in Ontology, Causality and Mind: Essays in Honour of D M Armstrong, Bacon, John (ed). Armstrong, D M.

Reply to Menzies' 'Laws of Nature, Modality and Humean...' in Ontology, Causality and Mind: Essays in Honour of D M Armstrong, Bacon, John (ed). Armstrong, D M.

Semantic Supervenience and Referential Indeterminacy. Van Cleve, James.

Supervenience and Anomalous Monism: Blackburn on Davidson. Zangwill, Nick.

Supervenience and Computational Explanation in Vision Theory. Morton, Peter.

Supervenience and Reducibility: An Odd Couple. Marras, Ausonio.

Supervenience and Reductionism. Von Kutschera, Franz.

Supervenience and the 'Science of the Beautiful'. Wicks, Robert.

The Nature of Naturalism—I. Macdonald, Graham.

The Nature of Naturalism—II. Pettit, Philip.

Universals and Universalisability: An Interpretation of Oddie's Discussion of Supervenience. Forrest, Peter.

Who's in Charge Here? And Who's Doing All the Work? in Mental Causation, Heil, John (ed). Van Gulick, Robert.

SUPREME COURT

"Brother, You Can't Go to Jail for What You're Thinking": Motives, Effects and "Hate Crime" Laws. Gellman, Susan.

First Amendment Challenges to Hate Crime Legislation: Where's the Speech?. Weinstein, James.

TEMPORALITY

The Familiar and the Strange in Heidegger: A Critical Reader, Dreyfus, Hubert L (ed). Fell, Joseph P.

The Metaphysical Aspect of Tenses in Proclus. Plass, Paul.

The New Paradox of Temporal Transience. Buller, David J and Foster, Thomas R.

The Temporality of an Original Ethics. Schalow, Frank.

Things Change. Heller, Mark.

Unmasking Bergson's Idealism. Howe, Lawrence W.

Whitehead, Heidegger, and the Paradoxes of the New. Bradley, J A.

Zeilicovici on Temporal Becoming. Oaklander, Nathan.

TEMPTATION

Temptation. Day, J P.

The Last Temptation of Zarathustra. Cartwright, David.

The Temptation of God Incarnate. Werther, David.

TENNANT, F

Personhood: F R Tennant and Peter Bertocci in the Light of Contemporary Physics. Knott, T Garland.

TENNANT, N

On Interpreting Truth Tables and Relevant Truth Table Logic. Sylvan, Richard.

TENSE

Language and Time. Smith, Quentin.

Comment on Le Poidevin. Lowe, E J.

Elementary Formal Semantics for English Tense and Aspect. Pendlebury, Michael.

Lowe on McTaggart. Le Poidevin, Robin.

Temporal Adverbials, Tenses and the Perfect. Vlach, Frank.

The Date-Analysis of Tensed Sentences. Williams, Clifford.

The Metaphysical Aspect of Tenses in Proclus. Plass, Paul.

TENSE LOGIC

A Note About the Axioms for Branching-Time Logic. Zanardo, Alberto.

Filosofische logica: een status quaestionis. Vergauwen, R.

Nominal Tense Logic. Blackburn, Patrick.

The Minimal System L'o. Wang, Xuegang.

TENSION

Participating in the Tension. Laird, Frank.

Resolving the Tension in Graham and Laird. Guston, David.

The Essential Tension in Science and Democracy. Guston, David.

The Necessity of the Tension. Graham Jr, George J.

TENURE

Conflicting Values in American Higher Education: Development of the Concept of Academic Freedom. Tandy, Charles.

TERM

A Variable-Free Logic for Mass Terms. Purdy, William C.

Antilogia. Incardona, Nunzio.

Leibniz on Private and Primitive Terms. Lenzen, Wolfgang.

On the Question 'Do We Need Identity?'. Purdy, William C.

TERMINAL ILLNESS

Statutory Definitions of Death and the Management of Terminally Ill Patients Who May Become Organ Donors after Death. Cole, David.

The Irreversibility of Death: Reply to Cole. Tomlinson, Thomas.

TERMINOLOGY

On Theoretical Terms in Greek Studies in the Philosophy and History of Science, Nicolacopoulos, Pantelis (ed). Papagounos, G.

Some Ways that Technology and Terminology Distort the Euthanasia Issue. Herrera, Christopher.

TERRITORY

The Concept of 'Region' in the Sociospatial Sciences: An Instance of the Social Production of Nature. Rambanapasi, C O.

TERRORISM

Applied Philosophy. Almond, Brenda (ed) and Hill, Donald (ed).

Cross, Crescent, and Sword. Johnson, James Turner (ed) and Kelsay, John (ed).

Terrorism, Justice and Social Values. Peden, W Creighton (ed) and Hudson, Yeager (ed).

How To Respond To Terrorism in Terrorism, Justice and Social Values, Peden, Creighton (ed). Smith, Steven A.

Irregular Warfare and Terrorism in Islam in Cross, Crescent, and Sword, Johnson, James Turner (ed). Sonn, Tamara.

Is Terrorism Every Morally Justified? in Terrorism, Justice and Social Values, Peden, Creighton (ed). Davis, Stephen T.

No Confusion: Some Reflections on TWA Flight 847 in Terrorism, Justice and Social Values, Peden, Creighton (ed). Roth, John K.

Primoratz on Terrorism. Dardis, Tony.

Terrorism and Morality in Applied Philosophy, Almond, Brenda (ed). Khatchadourian, Haig A.

Terrorism and the Epochal Transformation of Politics. Allen, Wayne.

TEST

A Turing Test Conversation. Jacquette, Dale.

In Defense of the Quine-Duhem Thesis: A Reply to Greenwood. Klee, Robert.

Nomic Dependence and Causation. Clendinnen, F John.

Robustness and Integrative Survival in Significance Testing: The World's Contribution to Rationality. Trout, J D.

The Unanimity Theory and Probabilistic Sufficiency. Carroll, John W.

Who's Afraid of the Turing Test?. Jacquette, Dale.

TESTABILITY

Truth Versus Testability in Quantum Logic. Garola, Claudio.

TESTIMONY

Testimony: A Philosophical Study. Coady, C A J.

TESTING

Idealization III. Brzezinski, Jerzy (ed) and Nowak, Leszek (ed).

Picture Perfect: The Politics of Prenatal Testing. Kristol, Elizabeth.

Testing and Correspondence in Idealization III, Brzenzinski, Jerzy (ed). Kupracz, Andrzej.

The Ethics of HIV Testing by Physicians. Murphy, Timothy F.

TETENS, J

Tetens et la crise de la métaphysique allemande en 1775. Puech, Michel.

TETSURO, W

The Social Self in Japanese Philosophy and American Pragmatism: A Comparative Study of Watsuji Tetsurō and George Herbert Mead. Odin, Steve.

TEXT

Argument and Analysis: An Introduction to Philosophy. Curd, Martin.

Critical Thinking: An Introduction to the Basic Skills. Hughes, William H.

Image and Ideology in Modern/PostModern Discourse. Downing, David B (ed) and Bazargan, Susan (ed).

Logic Primer. Allen, Colin and Hand, Michael.

Lyric Philosophy. Zwicky, Jan.

Reality, Knowledge, and the Good Life: A Historical Introduction to Philosophy. DeVries, Willem A.

The Portable Nietzsche. Kaufmann, Walter (ed).

The Truth about Postmodernism. Norris, Christopher.

A Response to M A Stewart's 'Berkeley's Introduction Draft'. Belfrage, Bertil.

Authorship and Authority. Pappas, Nickolas.

Between Author and Text in Interpretation and Overinterpretation: Umberto Eco, Collini, Stefan (ed). Eco, Umberto.

Doublings in Derrida: A Critical Reader, Wood, David (ed). Sallis, John.

Elliptical Sense in Derrida: A Critical Reader, Wood, David (ed). Nancy, Jean-Luc and Connor, Peter (trans).

Hermeias on Plato Phaedrus 238d and Synesius Dion 14.2. Dickie, Mathew W.

Life in Quest of Narrative in On Paul Ricoeur: Narrative and Interpretation, Wood, David (ed). Ricoeur, Paul.

More Evidence that Hume Wrote the Abstract. Norton, David Fate.

More Truth Than Fact: Storytelling as Critical Understanding in the Writings of Hannah Arendt. Disch, Lisa J.

Object Language and Meta-Language in the Gongsun-long-zi. Vierheller, Ernstjoachim.

Operationale Aufmerksamkeit in der textimmanenten Auslegung. Schobinger, Jean-Pierre.

Passions: 'An Oblique Offering' in Derrida: A Critical Reader, Wood, David (ed). Derrida, Jacques and Wood, David (trans).

Peripatetic Dialectic in the 'De Sensibus' in Theophrastus, Fortenbaugh, W W (ed). Baltussen, Han.

Reply in Interpretation and Overinterpretation: Umberto Eco, Collini, Stefan (ed). Eco, Umberto.

Text and the New Hermeneutics in On Paul Ricoeur: Narrative and Interpretation, Wood, David (ed). Ihde, Don.

The Authorship of the Abstract Revisited. Raynor, David.

The Dilemma Facing Contemporary Research in the Yijing. Zheng, Liu.

The Great Fuss over Philebus 15b. Mirhady, David C.

The Problem of the Authorship of the Yogasutrabhasyavivaranam. Rukmani, T S.

The Text of the Speaking Subject: From Merleau-Ponty to Kristeva in Merleau-Ponty Vivant, Dillon, M C (ed). Silverman, Hugh J.

The Troubled History of Part II of the 'Investigations' in Criss-Crossing A Philosophical Landscape, Schulte, Joachim (ed). Von Wright, George Henrik.

The Unbearable Slyness of Deconstruction. Nuyen, A T.

The Visual Room in Wittgenstein's Philosophical Investigations, Arrington, Robert L (ed). Kemmerling, Andreas.

Truth Without Methodologism: Gadamer and James. Fairfield, Paul.

Why Art History Has a History. Carrier, David.

Why Bother? Defending Derrida and the Significance of Writing. Ferrell, Robyn.

Xenophanes or Theophrastus? in Theophrastus, Fortenbaugh, W W (ed). Runia, David.

'Das Wollen ist auch nur eine Erfahrung' in Wittgenstein's Philosophical Investigations, Arrington, Robert T (ed). Candlish, Stewart.

'Philosophical Investigations' Section 122: Neglected Aspects in Wittgenstein's Philosophical Investigations, Arrington, Robert L (ed). Baker, Gordon.

TEXTBOOK

A Rulebook for Arguments (Second Edition). Weston, Anthony.

Reflections on Philosophy. McHenry, Leemon (ed) and Adams, Frederick (ed).

Writing Philosophy Papers. Seech, Zachary.

TEXTUAL CRITICISM

Operationale Aufmerksamkeit in der textimmanenten Auslegung. Schobinger, Jean-Pierre.

TEXTUALITY

System and Writing in the Philosophy of Jacques Derrida. Johnson, Christopher.

The Dialogics of Critique. Gardiner, Michael.

Voices of the Past: The Status of Language in Eighteenth-Century Japanese Discourse. Sakai, Naoki.

Culture, Textuality and Truth. Lewandowski, Joseph D.

Poverty and Sincerity in the Apology. Seeskin, Kenneth.

The Violence of the Masquerade in Working Through Derrida, Madison, Gary B (ed). Cornell, Drucilla.

THALES

The Presocratic Philosophers: An Annotated Bibliography. Navia, Luis E.

THEOLOGY

Aristotle and the Sacrament of the Altar: A Crisis in Medieval Aristotelianism. Adams, Marilyn McCord.

Atonement and Reconciliation. Brümmer, Vincent.

Aus dem Dunklen ins Helle: Wissenschaft und Theologie im Denken von Heinrich Scholz. Molendijk, A L.

Basic Goods and the Human Good in Recent Catholic Moral Theology. Porter, Jean.

Bernard Loomer's Concept of 'Interconnectedness' in God, Values, and Empiricism, Peden, Creighton W (ed). Fox, Douglas.

Bernhardt's Analysis of the Function of Religion in God, Values, and Empiricism, Peden, Creighton (ed). Tremmel, William C.

Conditionals of Freedom and Middle Knowledge. Gaskin, R.

Creative Interchange Between Philosophy and Theology: A Call to Dialogue. Eisenhower, William D.

Demea's Departure. Dye, James W.

Derrida and Madhyamika Buddhism: From Linguistic Deconstruction to Criticism of Onto-Theologies. Zong-qi, Cai.

Deux paradigmes pour penser le rapport de la théologie aux sciences humaines: herméneutique et narratologie. Fortin-Melkevik, Anne.

Diremption of Spirit in Shadow of Spirit, Berry, Philippa (ed). Rose, Gillian.

Divine Agriculture. Taliaferro, Charles.

Duns Scotus, Demonstration, and Doctrine. Mann, William E.

Eine philosophisch-historische Hermeneutik des Christentums. Pannenberg, Wolfhart.

Empirical Theology in the Light of Science. Peters, Karl E.

Estetica, teologia e antropologia nel pensiero di Tommaso d'Aquino. Simi Varanelli, E.

Ethics from a Theocentric Perspective: A Critical Review of the Thought of James M Gustafson. Hoekema, David A.

Eugen Drewermann: Una lettura in prospettiva filosofica. Giustiniani, P.

Evidentialism and Theology: A Reply to Kaufman. Shalkowski, Scott A.

Evolution, Teleology and Theology. Soontiëns, Frans.

Experience and Natural Theology in Prospects for Natural Theology, Long, Eugene Thomas (ed). Long, Eugene Thomas.

Finally Forgiveness in Foundations of Kierkegaard's Vision of Community, Connell, George B (ed). Berry, Wanda Warren.

Fire and Roses: Or the Problem of Postmodern Religious Thinking in Shadow of Spirit, Berry, Philippa (ed). Raschke, Carl.

For the Common Good?. Heyne, Paul.

Foucault on Continuity: The Postmodern Challenge to Tradition. Byrne, James M.

From Dionysius to Eriugena: A Bridge for Voluntarism or "Divine Freedom"?. King-Farlow, John.

From Theology to Sociology: Bruno Bauer and Karl Marx on the Question of Jewish Emancipation. Peled, Yoav.

God and Evil: Polarities of a Problem. Adams, Marilyn McCord.

Gott und Ereignis—Heideggers Gegenparadigma zur Onto-Theologie. Thurnher, Rainer.

Heidegger and Theology in The Cambridge Companion to Heidegger, Guignon, Charles (ed). Caputo, John D.

Henry Howard and the Lawful Regiment of Women. Shephard, Amanda.

Hermeneutic Philosophy and Natural Theology in Prospects for Natural Theology, Long, Eugene Thomas (ed). Kockelmans, Joseph J.

Holomovement Metaphysics and Theology. Sharpe, Kevin J.

Homo capax Dei?. Klaghofer-Treitler, Wolfgang.

How to Avoid Speaking of God: The Violence of Natural Theology in Prospects for Natural Theology, Long, Eugene Thomas (ed). Caputo, John D.

Human Finitude and the Concept of Women's Experience. Allik, Tiina.

Hurlbutt, Hume, Newton and the Design Argument. Tweyman, Stanley.

In Defense of a Kind of Natural Theology in Prospects for Natural Theology, Long, Eugene Thomas (ed). Clarke, Bowman L.

In Good Standing? The Position of Women in Higher Education. McConnell, David H.

Incommensurability and Aquinas's Metaphysics. Knasas, John F X.

Incontro tra filosofia e teologia nella "Christliche Weltanschauung" di Romano Guardini. Bezzini, L.

Infinity in Theology and Mathematics. Le Blanc, Jill.

Is a Natural Theology Still Viable Today? in Prospects for Natural Theology, Long, Eugene Thomas (ed). Clarke, W Norris.

Is There a System in the Theology of Nicholas Lash?. Lamadrid, Lucas.

Islamic Ethical Vision. Michel, Thomas.

Kierkegaard the Theologian in Foundations of Kierkegaard's Vision of Community, Connell, George B (ed). Plekon, Michael.

L'idéalisme allemand face à la raison théologique. Maesschalck, Marc.

La compréhension chrétienne de Dieu comme amour et sagesse selon Schleiermacher. Brito, Emilio.

La teoría del objeto puro de A Millán Puelles. López, Jesús García.

La théologie comme science et la vocation de savant d'après Max Weber. Gendron, Pierre.

La verdad del otro y la práctica ecuménica en Leibniz. Salas Ortueta, Jaime.

Language, Newspeak and Logic in A J Ayer Memorial Essays, Griffiths, A Phillips (ed). Sutherland, S R.

Le discours théologique et son objet: perspectives néo-pragmatistes. Viau, Marcel.

Leiden unter der Herrschaft der Zeit: Zu Michael Theunissens "Negativer Theologie der Zeit". Haeffner, Gerd.

Levels of the Natural Law. Henle, R J.

Levinas, Kierkegaard, and the Theological Task. Westphal, Merold.

Light and Metaphor in Plotinus and St Thomas Aquinas. Corrigan, Kevin.

Logic-Theological Schools from the Second Half of the 12th Century: A List of Sources. Yukio, Iwakuma and Ebbesen, Sten.

Ludwig Feuerbach and the Political Theology of Restoration. Breckman, Warren.

Maimonides and Kant on Metaphysics and Piety. Friedman, R Z.

Mass Media, Ethical Paradox, and Democratic Freedom: Jacques Ellul's Ethic of the Word. Fasching, Darrell J.

Meister Eckhart e la condanna del 1329. Siena, R M.

Meland's Post-Liberal Empirical Method in Theology in God, Values, and Empiricism, Peden, Creighton (ed). Inbody, Tyron.

Metaphysics in Search of Theology. Gerson, Lloyd P.

Middle Actions. Howsepian, A A.

Mind Forming and Manuductio in Aquinas. George, Marie.

Musings of a Psychologist-Theologian: Reflections on the Method of Charles Hartshorne. Moore, Mary Elizabeth.

Natural Religion, Morality and Lessing's Ditch. Schmitz, K L.

Natural Theology and Positive Predication: Might Maimonides Be a Guide? in Prospects for Natural Theology, Long, Eugene Thomas (ed). Ferré, Frederick.

Nature, Technology, and Theology. Klink, William H.

Nominalism and Grammatical Theory in the Late Eleventh and Early Twelfth Centuries: An Explorative Study. Kneepkens, C H.

Nominalism and Theology Before Abelard: New Light on Roscelin of Compiègne. Mews, Constant J.

Not Exactly Politics or Power?. Lash, Nicholas.

On the "Use" of Neopragmatism. Clayton, Philip.

On the Confines of Theology and Philosophy: A Reflection on the Book of T De Boer (in Dutch). Vandenbulcke, Jaak.

On the Issues Dividing Contemporary Christian Philosophers and Theologians. Keller, James A.

On the Very Strongest Arguments in Prospects for Natural Theology, Long, Eugene Thomas (ed). Mavrodes, George I.

Ordeal and Repetition in Kierkegaard's Treatment of Abraham and Job in Foundations of Kierkegaard's Vision of Community, Connell, George B (ed). Taylor, Mark Lloyd.

Peter Lombard and Abelard: The Opinio Nominalium and Divine Transcendence. Colish, Marcia L.

Philosophical Theology and Provincialism in God, Values, and Empiricism, Peden, Creighton (ed). Roth, John K.

Philosophy of Religion in Reflections on Philosophy, McHenry, Leemon (ed). Pletcher, Galen K.

Philosophy, Aesthetics, and Theology: A Review of Hans Urs von Balthasar's The Glory of the Lord. Wood, Robert.

Post-Marx: Theological Themes in Baudrillard's 'America' in Shadow of Spirit, Berry, Philippa (ed). Wernick, Andrew.

Pragmatic Conditions for Jewish-Christian Theological Dialogue. Ochs, Peter.

Pragmatisme et théologie pratique. Viau, Marcel.

Prospects for Natural Theology. Smith, John E.

Providence and the Problem of Evil in Christian Philosophy, Flint, Thomas P (ed). Stump, Eleonore.

Psychologie philosophique et théologie de l'intellect: Pour une histoire de la philosophie allemande au xiv siècle. De Libera, Alain.

Questions d'épistémologie en théologie de la libération: A propos de l'ouvrage de Clodovis Boff. Richard, Jean.

Reason and Reliance: Adjusted Prospects for Natural Theology in Prospects for Natural Theology, Long, Eugene Thomas (ed). Ross, James F.

Reference and the Refutation of Naturalism in Our Knowledge of God, Clark, Kelly James (ed). Forrest, Peter.

Reflections on the Life and Works of Scotus. Wolter, Allan B.

Rejoinder to Bruce Marshall. Crosson, Frederick.

Relationships between Scientific Analysis and the World View of Pierre Teilhard de Chardin. Galleni, Lodovico.

Religious Creaturalism and a New Agenda for Theology in God, Values, and Empiricism, Peden, Creighton W (ed). Axel, Larry E.

Religious Story, Religious Truth, Religious Pluralism: A Prolegomenon to Religious Faith. Lauder, Robert.

Reply to Brinton's '"Following Nature" in Butler's Sermons'. Millar, Alan.

Resistance to the Rule of Time or a "Post-Metaphysical Metaphysics": Michael Theunissen's Negative Theology of Time. Penta, Leo J.

Response to Maurer and Dewan. Ross, James F.

Rethinking Empiricism in Theology in God, Values, and Empiricism, Peden, Creighton (ed). Miller, Randolph.

Richard Gale's On the Nature and Existence of God. Helm, Paul.

Saint Anselm the Student. Fortin, John.

San Tommaso e Hegel per una teodicea cristologica. Mangiagalli, Maurizio.

Simultaneity and God's Timelessness. Oddie, Graham and Perrett, Roy W.

Social Evil: A Response to Adams. Quinn, Philip.

Soft Natural Theology in Prospects for Natural Theology, Long, Eugene Thomas (ed). Smart, Ninian.

Some Comments on Weingartner's Concept of a Scientific Theology in Advances in Scientific Philosophy, Schurz, Gerhard (ed). Ganthaler, Heinrich.

Some Reflections on Michael Polanyi and Catholic Thought. Kroger, Joseph.

Storied Others and Possibilities of Caritas: Milbank and Neo-Nietzschean Ethics. Coles, Romand.

Technology and Change in Religious Belief. Sweet, William.

The Propositio Famosa Scoti: Duns Scotus and Ockham on the Possibility of a Science of Theology. Dumont, Stephen.

The Argument from Evil in Philosophical Perspectives, 5: Philosophy of Religion, 1991, Tomberlin, James E (ed). Tooley, Michael.

The Ballad of Clyde the Moose in Thought Experiments in Science and Philosophy, Horowitz, Tamara (ed). Camp Jr, Joseph L.

TIME

Marty's Theory of Space in Mind, Meaning and Metaphysics, Mulligan, Kevin (ed). Egidi, Rosaria.

Metafisica e pensiero iniziale: Aspetti della *Kehre* alle origini del pensiero heideggeriano. Samonà, Leonardo.

Metaphysical Presence in Ethics and Danger, Dallery, Arleen B (ed). Chanter, Tina.

Metaphysics' Forgetfulness of Time in Philosophical Interventions in the Unfinished Project of Enlightenment, Honneth, Axel (& other eds). Theunissen, Michael.

Mind Eternity in Spinoza. Rice, Lee C.

On Some Worldly Worries. Goodman, Nelson.

On the Acausality of Time, Space, and Space-Time. Le Poidevin, Robin.

On the Experience of Tenseless Time. Oaklander, L Nathan.

On Time. Priest, Graham.

Personal Identity and Time. Smith, Quentin.

Philosophical Antecedents to Ricoeur's 'Time and Narrative' in On Paul Ricoeur: Narrative and Interpretation, Wood, David (ed). Vanhoozer, Kevin J.

Process Causality and Asymmetry. Dowe, Phil.

Propensity and Possibility. Meixner, Uwe.

Que sont donc l'espace et le temps? Les hypothèses considérées par Kant et la lancinante objection de la "troisième possibilité". Chenet, François-Xavier.

Reference, Modality, and Relational Time. Cover, J A.

Reflections on Time. Dunning, William V.

Reiterating the Temporal in Reading Heidegger: Commemorations, Sallis, John (ed). Wood, David.

Reply to Smith: On the Finitude of the Past. Craig, William Lane.

Resistance to the Rule of Time or a "Post-Metaphysical Metaphysics": Michael Theunissen's *Negative Theology of Time*. Penta, Leo J.

Ricoeur on Narrative in On Paul Ricoeur: Narrative and Interpretation, Wood, David (ed). Carr, David, Taylor, Charles and Ricoeur, Paul.

Ricoeur, Proust and the Aporias of Time in On Paul Ricoeur: Narrative and Interpretation, Wood, David (ed). Goldthorpe, Rhiannon.

Ruling Memory. Norton, Anne.

Scenes from My Childhood. Magee, Bryan.

Scenes from My Childhood in The Impulse to Philosophise, Griffiths, A Phillips (ed). Magee, Bryan.

Sequel to History: Postmodernism and the Crisis of Historical Time. Carr, David.

Simultaneity and God's Timelessness. Oddie, Graham and Perrett, Roy W.

Sobre el espacio-tiempo. Baldomir, Daniel.

Space, Time, Discreteness. Kilmister, C W.

Space-Time and Isomorphism. Mundy, Brent.

Spirit and Danger in Ethics and Danger, Dallery, Arleen B (ed). Caputo, John D.

Temporal Impermanence and the Disparity of Time and Eternity. Polk, Danne W.

The Concept of Time. Singh, Chhatrapati.

The Development of Time Consciousness from Husserl to Heidegger in Analecta Husserliana, XXXI, Tymieniecka, Anna-Teresa (ed). Thomas, V C.

The End of History and the Last Man. Roth, Michael S.

The Geometry of Space-Time: From Einstein to Penrose. Tempczyk, Michael.

The Inscription of the Moment: Zarathustra's Gate. Silverman, Hugh J.

The New Paradox of Temporal Transcience. Buller, David J and Foster, Thomas R.

The Past Just Ain't What It Used To Be: A Response to Kevin Staley and Ronald Tacelli. Baldner, Steven.

The Problem of Personal Identity in *Being and Time* (in Hebrew). Fuchs, Yuval.

The Problem of Persons. Janusz, Sharon and Webster, Glenn.

The Reality and Structure of Time in Analecta Husserliana, XXXI, Tymieniecka, Anna-Teresa (ed). Bar-On, A Zvie.

The Rise and Fall of Time-Symmetrized Quantum Mechanics. Sharp, W David and Shanks, Niall.

The Role of Limits in Aristotle's Concept of Place. Mariña, Jacqueline.

The Story of Art is the Test of Time. Silvers, Anita.

The Unreality of Time. Sprigge, T L S.

Time and Change. Teichmann, Roger.

Time and Change in Kant and McTaggart. Waxman, Wayne.

Time and Division. Dainton, Barry F.

Time and Narrative: Reflections from Paul Ricoeur. Jasper, David.

Time and Phenomenology in Husserl and Heidegger in The Cambridge Companion to Heidegger, Guignon, Charles B (ed). Dostal, Robert J.

Time and the Anthropic Principle. Leslie, John.

Time and World in Mayan and Nahuatl Thought in Cultural Relativism and Philosophy, Dascal, Marcelo (ed). De La Garza, Mercedes.

Time Topology for Some Classical and Quantum Non-Relativistic Systems (in Polish). Olszewski, S.

Time, the Heaven of Heavens, and Memory in Augustine's *Confessions*. Ross, Don S.

Time, Truth, and Culture in Husserl and Hegel in Analecta Husserliana, XXXI, Tymieniecka, Anna-Teresa (ed). Molchanov, Victor.

Timelessness, Omniscience, and Tenses. Garcia, Laura L.

Transition and Contradiction. McKie, John.

Whitehead and Alexander. Emmet, Dorothy.

Why the New Theory of Reference Does Not Entail Absolute Time and Space. Rynasiewicz, Robert.

Wittgenstein über Zeit. Kaspar, Rudolf F and Schmidt, Alfred.

World Enough and Space-Time. Savitt, Steven.

'Being and Time' and 'The Basic Problems of Phenomenology' in Reading Heidegger: Commemorations, Sallis, John (ed). Von Herrmann, Friedrich-Wilhelm.

'The Darkness of This Time': Wittgenstein and the Modern World in Wittgenstein Centenary Essays, Griffiths, A Phillips (ed). Bouveresse, J.

TOCQUEVILLE, A

Interpreting Tocqueville's "Democracy in America". Masugi, Ken (ed).

Participating in the Tension. Laird, Frank.

Resolving the Tension in Graham and Laird. Guston, David.

The Essential Tension in Science and Democracy. Guston, David.

The Necessity of the Tension. Graham Jr, George J.

Tocqueville and Democracy in The Idea of Democracy, Copp, David (ed). Holmes, Stephen.

Tocqueville, Commerce, and Democracy in The Idea of Democracy, Copp, David (ed). Satz, Debra M.

'Private Judgement', Mill and Tocqueville: An Apology. Gardner, Peter.

TOGETHERNESS

Bonhoeffer on Heidegger and Togetherness. Marsh, Charles.

TOLERANCE

"The Will to Believe": James's Defense of Religious Intolerance. Gordon, Jeffrey.

The Diversity of Religions: A Christian Perspective. DiNoia, J A.

The Pluralistic Philosophy of Stephen Crane. Dooley, Patrick K.

Interreligious Dialogue and the Unity of Humanity. Knitter, Paul F.

Pragmatic Conditions for Jewish-Christian Theological Dialogue. Ochs, Peter.

Radicalizing Pluralism. Thompson, Audrey.

The Commonality of Loyalty and Tolerance. Fletcher, George P.

The Intolerance of Religious Pluralism. Donovan, Peter.

TOLERATION

Ethical Essays, Volume I. Harrison, Jonathan.

Liberal Rights: Collected Papers 1981-1991. Waldron, Jeremy.

Subjectivism and Toleration in A J Ayer Memorial Essays, Griffiths, A Phillips (ed). Williams, Bernard.

TOLSTOY

Religion from Tolstoy to Camus. Kaufmann, Walter (ed).

A Note on Heidegger's Death Analytic: The Tolstoyian Correlative in Analecta Husserliana, XXXVIII, Tymieniecka, Anna-Teresa (ed). Pratt, Alan.

Tolstoy, Stanislavski, and the Art of Acting. Hughes, R I G.

TONALITY

The Theory of Tone Semantics: Concept, Foundation, and Application. Leman, Marc.

TOOL

Ivan Illich and the Radical Critique of Tools. Weston, Anthony.

TOOLEY, M

Realism About Laws. Woodward, James.

TOPOLOGY

An Omitting Types Theorem for Saturated Structures. Greif, A D and Laskowski, M C.

Compactness and Normality in Abstract Logics. Caicedo, Xavier.

TORT

Contracts and Torts. Coleman, Jules L.

Mass Torts and Moral Principles. Strudler, Alan.

TOTALITARIANISM

Government: Servant or Master?. Radnitzky, Gerard (ed) and Bouillon, Hardy (ed).

Hannah Arendt: A Reinterpretation of Her Political Thought. Canovan, Margaret.

Faceless Women and Serious Others in Ethics and Danger, Dallery, Arleen B (ed). Vasey, Craig R.

Hannah Arendt and the Ideological Structure of Totalitarianism. Allen, Wayne.

Has History Refuted Marxism?. Hudelson, Richard.

Het Hegeliaanse begrijpen: problemen en mogelijkheden. De Vos, L.

Kritik der Hegelschen Formalismusthese. Freier, F V.

L'État, le mythe, les totalitarismes. DeLaunay, Marc B.

More Truth Than Fact: Storytelling as Critical Understanding in the Writings of Hannah Arendt. Disch, Lisa J.

Post-Totalitarian Politics and European Philosophy. Palous, Martin.

Rousseau and the Problem of Community: Nationalism, Civic Virtue, Totalitarianism. Simon-Ingram, Julia.

Totalitarianism "with a Human Face": A Methodological Essay. Poliakov, Leonid.

Totalitarianism and the Problems of a Work Ethic. Davydov, I N.

Two Hundred Years of Error? The Politics of Democracy. Howard, Dick.

TOTALITY

To the Other: An Introduction to the Philosophy of Emmanuel Levinas. Peperzak, Adriaan.

Heidegger and Habermas on Criticism and Totality. Kolb, David.

Home on the Range: Planning and Totality. Kolb, David.

Jameson, Totality, and the Poststructuralist Critique in Postmodernism/ Jameson/ Critique, Kellner, Douglas (ed). Best, Steven.

L'émergence du concept de totalité chez Lukács (II). Pelletier, Lucien.

La métaphysique, l'acte et l'un. Gilbert, Paul P.

New "True" Socialism. Baxter, David.

Total Sets and Objects in Domain Theory. Berger, Ulrich.

Totalität oder Zweckmässigkeit: Kants Ringen mit dem Mannigfaltigen der Erfahrung im Ausgang der Vernunftkritik. Schiemann, Gregor.

TOTEMISM

Zur Notwendigkeit von Religion aus der Sicht Durkheims und seiner Erben. Steunebrink, Gerrit A J.

TOULMIN, S

De postmoderniteit en haar geschiedenis: Kanttekeningen bij Stephen Toulmins *Kosmopolis*. Tollebeek, Jo.

TOURNIER, M

The Logic of Sense—Gilles Deleuze. Boundas, Constantin V (ed), Lester, Mark (& other trans) and Deleuze, Gilles.

UTILITARIANISM

Heavenly Order, Sagehood and Tao-t'ung—Some Discussions on the Neo- Confucian View of Values (in Chinese). Chang, Jun-chun.

Hume, Bentham, and the Social Contract. Wolff, Jonathan.

Individual Choice and the Retreat from Utilitarianism in The Utilitarian Response, Allison, Lincoln (ed). Reeve, Andrew.

Is God a Utilitarian?. Holley, David M.

J S Mill's Language of Pleasures. Hoag, Robert.

Jeremy Bentham and the Real Property Commission of 1828. Sokol, Mary.

Justice and Utility in Health Care in The Utilitarian Response, Allison, Lincoln (ed). Day, John.

Kant's Dubious Disciples: Hare and Rawls. Papa, Edward.

Majorities and Minorities: A Classical Utilitarian View. Rosen, Frederick.

Mill's Higher Pleasures and the Choice of Character. Long, Roderick T.

Moral Conflict and Political Commitment. Horton, John.

Moral Rules, Utilitarianism and Schizophrenic Moral Education. McDonough, Kevin.

More on Euthanasia: A Response to Pauer-Studer. Singer, Peter and Kuhse, Helga.

Moving Forward in Bioethical Theory: Theories, Cases, and Specified Principlism. Degrazia, David.

On a Supposed Inconsistency in J S Mill's Utilitarianism. Joy, Glenn C and McKinney, Audrey M.

On Obligations to Future Generations. Reichenbach, Bruce R.

On the Consistency of Act- and Motive- Utilitarianism: A Reply to Robert Adams. Feldman, Fred.

Peter Singer and Non-Voluntary 'Euthanasia': Tripping Down the Slippery Slope. Uniacke, Suzanne and McCloskey, H J.

Peter Singer on Euthanasia. Pauer-Studer, Herlinde.

Philosophical Foundations of Respect for Autonomy. Gauthier, Candace Cummins.

Rawls On Act Utilitarianism and Rules in Terrorism, Justice and Social Values, Peden, Creighton (ed). Walter, Edward F.

Reply—Rawls: Rejecting Utilitarianism and Animals. Russow, Lilly-Marlene.

Rethinking Tradition in Essays on Henry Sidgwick, Schultz, Bart (ed). Kloppenberg, James T.

Retributivism in Hegel as Modern Natural Law. Gardner, Stephen L.

Ross, Promises and the Intrinsic Value of Acts. Brennan, Susan K.

Sidgwick and Nineteenth-Century British Ethical Thought in Essays on Henry Sidgwick, Schultz, Bart (ed). Singer, Marcus G.

Sidgwick and the Rationale for Rational Egoism in Essays on Henry Sidgwick, Schultz, Bart (ed). Brink, David O.

Strong Utilitarianism in Mo Tzu's Thought. Vorenkamp, Dirck.

Structures of Normative Theories. Dreier, James.

Taking Morality Seriously. Almond, Brenda.

The Ethics of Parts and Wholes. Oldenquist, Andrew G.

The Origin of Liberal Utilitarianism in Victorian Liberalism, Bellamy, Richard (ed). Rosen, Frederick.

The Paradoxes of Feldman's Neo-Utilitarianism. Almeida, Michael J.

The Structure of Normative Ethics in Philosophical Perspectives, 6: Ethics, 1992, Tomberlin, James E (ed). Kagan, Shelly.

The Unhappy Conclusion and the Life of Virtue. Mulgan, Tim.

The Utilitarian Ethics of Punishment and Torture in The Utilitarian Response, Allison, Lincoln (ed). Allison, Lincoln.

Toward 1992: Utilitarianism as the Ideology of Europe. Bluhm, William T.

Towards a World Morality. Chethimattam, J B.

Utilitarian Ethics and Democratic Government in The Utilitarian Response, Allison, Lincoln (ed). Riley, Jonathan.

Utilitarianism and Education: A Reply to James Tarrant. Miles, T G.

Utilitarianism and Infinite Utility. Vallentyne, Peter.

Utilitarianism and Moral Education: Comment on Sanford Levy's Paper. Hare, R M.

Utilitarianism and Retributivism: What's the Difference. Michael, Mark A.

Utilitarianism and Self-Respect. Scarre, Geoffrey.

Utilitarianism on Environmental Issues Reexamined. Holbrook, Daniel.

Utilitarianism, Conservatism and Social Policy in The Utilitarian Response, Allison, Lincoln (ed). Gibbins, John R.

Utilitarianism: What Is It and Why Should It Respond? in The Utilitarian Response, Allison, Lincoln (ed). Allison, Lincoln.

Welfare, Happiness, and Pleasure. Sumner, L W.

Wellbeing and Everyday Practice: Theorizing Claimsmaking. Kerans, Patrick and Drover, Glen.

UTILITY

Altruism and the Argument from Offsetting Transfers in Altruism, Paul, Ellen Frankel (ed). Cowen, Tyler.

Choice and Conditional Expected Utility. Rawling, Piers.

Choice and Utility in The Utilitarian Response, Allison, Lincoln (ed). Brittan, Samuel.

Game Theory and the History of Ideas about Rationality: An Introductory Survey. Cudd, Ann.

Local Utility Functions. Bardsley, Peter.

Persons and the Satisfaction of Preferences: Problems in the Rational Kinematics of Values. MacIntosh, Duncan.

Pragmatism or Crude Utility: A Critique of the Education with Production Movement in Contemporary Africa. Lungu, Gatian F.

Preference-Revision and the Paradoxes of Instrumental Rationality. MacIntosh, Duncan.

QALYs, Age and Fairness. Kappel, Klemens and Sandoe, Peter.

Realism and Methodological Change. Leplin, Jarrett.

Recenti studi fichtiani. Rotta, Graziella.

Revealed Preference and Linear Utility. Clark, Stephen A.

Straight Versus Constrained Maximization. Sobel, J Howard.

The Aim and Structure of Applied Research. Niiniluoto, Ilkka.

The Categories of Value. Allen, R T.

The Futility of Multiple Utility. Brennan, Timothy J.

The Rationality of Conditional Cooperation. Den Hartogh, Govert.

The Relativity of the Welfare Concept in The Quality of Life, Nussbaum, Martha C (ed). Van Praag, B M S.

The Utility of Multiple Utility: A Comment on Brennan. Lutz, Mark A.

Utilitarianism and Infinite Utility. Vallentyne, Peter.

UTOPIA

From Marx to Mises. Steele, David Ramsay.

Il Destino della Famiglia Nell'Utopia. Colombo, Arrigo (ed) and Quarta, Cosimo.

L'Utopia di Fourier. Tundo, Laura.

L'Utopia nella Storia: La Rivoluzione Inglese. Colombo, Arrigo (ed) and Schiavone, Giuseppe.

Partial Visions: Feminism and Utopianism in the 1970s. Bammer, Angelika.

Psychoanalysis, Mind and Art. Hopkins, Jim (ed) and Savile, Anthony (ed).

Una reinterpretazione dell' 'Utopia'. Moro, Tomiaso.

Aristotle and the Ideal Life. Lawrence, Gavin.

Between Tradition and Utopia: The Hermeneutical Problem of Myth in On Paul Ricoeur: Narrative and Interpretation, Wood, David (ed). Kearney, Richard.

Fine della modernità o nascita di una nuova modernità?. Nicolosi, Salvatore.

L'ironia e il soggetto nascosto. Gallino, Guglielmo.

L'utopie législative de Platon. Laks, André.

La città armoniosa di Péguy: Profezia della speranza o utopia dell'illusione. Nicolosi, Salvatore.

Martin Buber—Critic of Karl Marx. Yassour, Avraham.

Nationalist Nightmares and Postmodernist Utopias: Irish Society in Transition. Smyth, Jim.

Socialism, Utopianism and the 'Utopian Socialists'. Lovell, David W.

Utopia and Fantasy in Psychoanalysis, Mind and Art, Hopkins, Jim (ed). Burnyeat, M F.

Utopia: Fail-Safe or Safe-Fail in Terrorism, Justice and Social Values, Peden, Creighton (ed). Roque, Alicia.

UTOPIANISM

Architecture and Nihilism: On the Philosophy of Modern Architecture. Cacciari, Massimo and Sartarelli, Stephen (trans).

La scoperta dell'America: Tra la realtà e l'utopia di un "nuovo mondo". Bonilla, Alcira B.

VAGUENESS

Is Higher Order Vagueness Coherent?. Wright, Crispin.

Les concepts vagues sont-ils sans frontières?. Engel, Pascal.

Vagueness and Ignorance—I. Williamson, Timothy.

Vagueness and Ignorance—II. Simons, Peter.

Validity, Uncertainty and Vagueness. Edgington, Dorothy.

VAISESIKA

The Concept of Kartrtva in the Nyaya-Vaisesika Philosophy. Sen, Brinda.

VALENTA, L

On the Relation of J L Fischer to Marxist Philosophy (Reply to L Valenta's Polemic Study) (in Czechoslovakian). Tosenovsky, L.

VALIDITY

Belief vs Commitment, Validity vs Value: A Response to Ward Goodenough. Brink, T L.

Habermas on Heidegger and Foucault: Meaning and Validity in the *Philosophical Discourse of Modernity*. Visker, Rudi.

Interprétation et vérité. Ladrière, Jean.

Introducing Validity. Hannan, Barbara.

Intuitionistic Validity in *T*-Normal Kripke Structures. Buss, Samuel R.

On the Place of Validity. Price, Robert G.

Validities: A Political Science Perspective. Beer, Francis A.

Validity, Uncertainty and Vagueness. Edgington, Dorothy.

VALLA, L

Il rinnovamento della filosofia nella *Dialectica* di Lorenzo Valla. Laffranchi, Marco.

Valla's Dialectic in the North 2: Further Commentaries. Mack, P.

VALUATION

Dewey's Contribution to the Theory of Valuation. Dziemidok, Bohdan.

VALUE

see also Intrinsic Value

"Bergson Resartus" and T S Eliot's Manuscript. Habib, M A R.

"Ought" Never Is: A Response to Oliver A Johnson. Goldthwait, John T.

"Value" in Turn-of-the-Century Philosophy and Sociology. Blegvad, Mogens.

Axiology: The Science of Values. Bahm, Archie.

Changing Values in Medical and Health Care Decision Making. Jensen, Uffe Juul (ed) and Mooney, Gavin (ed).

Chinese Foundations for Moral Education and Character Development. Van Doan, Tran (ed), Shen, Vincent (ed) and McLean, George F (ed).

Critical Theoretical Inquiry on the Notion of Act in the Metaphysics of Aristotle and Saint Thomas Aquinas. Lu, Matthias.

Die Wirtschaftspolitik des Philosophen Jacobi. Hammacher, Klaus and Hirsch, Hans.

Ethics and the Environment. Hart, Richard E (ed).

God, Values, and Empiricism. Peden, W Creighton (ed) and Axel, Larry E (ed).

Identity, Consciousness and Value. Unger, Peter.

Jurisculture: China. Dorsey, Gray L.

Knowledge and Belief. Schmitt, Frederick.

Moral Philosophy: A Reader. Pojman, Louis (ed).

VIENNA CIRCLE

Ethics of the Vienna Circle and the Lvov-Warsaw School. Holowka, Jacek.

L'explication en tant que généralisation théorique. Ibarra, Andoni and Mormann, Thomas.

VILLA, D

Situating Hannah Arendt on Action and Politics. Isaac, Jeffrey C.

The Politics of Agonism. Honig, Bonnie.

VINCENZO, J

Vincenzo's Portrayal of Nietzsche's Socrates. Domino, Brian.

VIOLATION

Does Business Ethics Make Economic Sense?. Sen, Amartya.

VIOLENCE

see also Nonviolence

Gulliver's Travels: The Stunting of a Philosopher. Burrow, Richard.

A Critique of the Liberal Discourse on Violence in Socialism and Morality, McLellan, David (ed). Parekh, Bhikhu.

First Amendment Challenges to Hate Crime Legislation: Where's the Speech?. Weinstein, James.

How to Avoid Speaking of God: The Violence of Natural Theology in Prospects for Natural Theology, Long, Eugene Thomas (ed). Caputo, John D.

Machiavelli, Violence, and History. Minter, Adam.

Morality and Coercion-By-Violence in Terrorism, Justice and Social Values, Peden, Creighton (ed). Kucheman, Clark A.

Pacifying Politics: Resistance, Violence, and Accountability in Seventeenth-Century Contract THeory. Baumgold, Deborah.

Predication as Originary Violence in Working Through Derrida, Madison, Gary B (ed). Willard, Dallas.

Primoratz on Terrorism. Dardis, Tony.

René Girard's Theory of Violence: An Introduction. Grote, Jim.

Surviving Sexual Violence. Brison, Susan J.

The Liberal Discourse on Violence in Selves, People, and Persons, Rouner, Leroy S (ed). Parekh, Bhikhu.

VIRTUALITY

Nietzsche's 'Will to Power' and Chinese 'Virtuality' (De) in Nietzsche and Asian Thought, Parkes, Graham R (ed). Ames, Roger T.

VIRTUE

Μεγαλοψυχια in Nocomachean Ethics iv. Held, Dirk T D.

An Historical Introduction to Moral Philosophy. Wagner, Michael (ed).

An Introduction to Ethics. Thomas, Geoffrey.

Aristotle on the Perfect Life. Kenny, Anthony.

Dialogue with Heidegger on Values: Ethics for Times of Crisis. Joós, Ernest.

Epistemic Virtue and Doxastic Responsibility. Montmarquet, James.

Essays on the Philosophy of Socrates. Benson, Hugh H (ed).

Ethical Essays, Volume II. Harrison, Jonathan.

From Morality to Virtue. Slote, Michael.

Kierkegaard and Kant: The Hidden Debt. Green, Ronald M.

Moral Philosophy: A Reader. Pojman, Louis (ed).

Morality and the Emotions. Oakley, Justin.

Philosophy and Knowledge: A Commentary on Plato's "Theaetetus". Polansky, Ronald.

Plato and Platonism. Moravcsik, Julius.

Psychological Foundations of Moral Education and Character Development: An Integrated Theory of Moral Development (Second Edition). McLean, George F (ed) and Knowles, Richard T (ed).

Sobre Virtudes y Vicios. García Bacca, Juan David.

The Examined Life. Kekes, John.

The Moral Life. Luper-Foy, Steven.

The Morality Maze: An Introduction To Moral Ecology. Daniels, Neil M.

The Morality of Happiness. Annas, Julia.

The Philosophical Quest. Almond, Brenda.

Treatise on Ethics (1684). Malebranche, Nicolas and Walton, Craig (trans).

Varieties of Moral Personality: Ethics and Psychological Realism. Flanagan, Owen.

Virtues and Rights: The Moral Philosophy of Thomas Hobbes. Ewin, R E.

Working Without a Net: A Study of Egocentric Epistemology. Foley, Richard.

A Critique of Henry Veatch's "Human Rights: Fact or Fancy?". Lee, Sander H.

Abstract Principles, Mid-Level Principles, and the Rule of Law. Henley, Kenneth.

Adam Smith and the Virtues of Commerce. Berry, Christopher J.

An Appeal for a Christian Virtue Ethic. Kotva Jr, Joseph J.

An Italian View of the Debate on Virtue. Kennedy, Terence.

Applied Ethics for Teachers: What Is It and How Do We Teach It?. McCarthy, Christine.

Aristotelian Deliberation is Not of Ends in Essays in Ancient Greek Philosophy, IV, Anton, John P (ed). Tuozzo, Thomas M.

Aristotle and Respect for Persons in Essays in Ancient Greek Philosophy, IV, Anton, John P (ed). Preus, Anthony.

Aristotle on Temperance in Essays in Ancient Greek Philosophy, IV, Anton, John P (ed). Young, Charles M.

Aristotle on the Good of Virtue-Friendship. Schroeder, D N.

Aristotle's Distinction Between Moral Virtue and Practical Wisdom in Essays in Ancient Greek Philosophy, IV, Anton, John P (ed). Fortenbaugh, W W.

Artificial Virtues and the Equally Sensible Non-Knaves: A Response to Gauthier. Baier, Annette.

Artificial Virtues and the Sensible Knave. Gauthier, David.

Autonomy, Obligation, and Virtue in The Cambridge Companion to Kant, Guyer, Paul (ed). Schneewind, Jerome.

Beyond the Virtues-Principles Debate. Keat, Marilyn S.

Calling all Knaves: Hume on Moral Motivation. Dimock, Susan.

Charting Liberal Virtues. Macedo, Stephen.

Civic Virtue, Markets and Schooling: Lessons from Hegel's Education State. Blacker, David.

Commentary on Michael Slote's "Virtue Ethics and Democratic Values". Swanton, Christine.

Commentator on 'Non-Relative Virtues' in The Quality of Life, Nussbaum, Martha C (ed). Hurley, Susan.

Comments on Robert Welshon's "Nietzsche's Peculiar Virtues and the Health of the Soul". Hunt, Lester.

Creating the Kingdom of Ends in Philosophical Perspectives, 6: Ethics, 1992, Tomberlin, James E (ed). Korsgaard, Christine.

Dialektik als Letzbegründung bei Hegel. Pleines, Jürgen-Eckardt.

Doctrines and the Virtues of Doctrine: The Problematic of Religious Plurality. Griffiths, Paul J.

Does Hume Have a Theory of Justice?. Reidy, David.

Educating the Virtues: A Problem in the Social Development of Consciousness?. Jonathan, Ruth.

Emotional and Moral Evaluations. Ben-Ze'ev, Aaron.

Emotions Among the Virtues of the Christian Life. Roberts, Robert C.

Enseigner la vertu?. Barnes, Jonathan.

Environmental Virtue Ethics: A New Direction for Environmental Ethics. Frasz, Geoffrey B.

Epistemic Virtue and Doxastic Responsibility. Montmarquet, James.

Ethics for Inquisitors. Harriman, Charles J.

Fanning the Embers of Civic Virtue: Toward a (Chastened) Politics of Character. Budziszewski, J.

From Passions to Sentiments: The Structure of Hume's Treatise. Rorty, Amélie Oksenberg.

Gemeinschaft als Grundwert der Aristotelischen Ethik. Ricken, Friedo.

Generic Reliabilism and Virtue Epistemology in Rationality in Epistemology, Villanueva, Enrique (ed). Sosa, Ernest.

Hartshorne, Metaphysics and the Law of Moderation. Dombrowski, Daniel.

Hegel's Concept of Virtue. Buchwalter, Andrew.

Hospitality and Its Discontents: A Response to Losito. Mulvaney, Robert J.

Hume on Human Excellence. Martin, Marie A.

Impersonality, Character, and Moral Expressivism. Moran, Richard A.

Independence in Democratic Theory: A Virtue? A Necessity? Both? Neither?. Goodin, Robert E.

Integrity or "He Who Steals My Purse". Witmer, Judith T.

Is Care a Virtue for Health Care Professionals?. Curzer, Howard J.

Judicial Virtue and Democratic Politics. Pinkard, Terry P.

Justice and Care in Close Associations. Udovicki, Jasminka.

Justice Holmes and Judicial Virtue. Luban, David.

Justice without Virtue. Shklar, Judith N.

Kant's Different "Publics" and the Justice of Publicity. Davis, Kevin R.

Knowing about Virtue. Sher, George.

La théorie platonicienne de la motivation humaine. Cooper, John.

Le paradoxe de Ménon et l'Ecole d'Oxford. O'Brien, D.

Love's Constancy. Martin, Mike W.

Loyalty and Virtues. Ewin, R E.

Machiavelli's Momentary "Machiavellian Moment": A Reconsideration of Pocock's Treatment of the Discourses. Sullivan, Vickie B.

MacIntyre on Rationality and Tradition. Santilli, Paul C.

McDowell, Hypothetical Imperatives and Natural Law. Weithman, Paul.

Moral Incapacity. Shields, Christopher.

Moral Pluralism, Intellectual Virtue, and Academic Culture in Moral Education and the Liberal Arts, Mitias, Michael H (ed). Gouinlock, James.

Moral Virtue and the Demise of Prudence in the Thought of Francis Suárez. Treloar, John L.

More About Hume's Debt to Spinoza. Klever, Wim.

Nietzsche's Peculiar Virtues and the Health of the Soul. Welshon, Robert.

No Ethics, No Text. Haines, Victor Yelverton.

Non-Relative Virtues: An Aristotelian Approach in The Quality of Life, Nussbaum, Martha C (ed). Nussbaum, Martha C.

On Care and Justice Within the Family. Wong, David B.

On the Good of Knowing Virtue. Smith, Rogers M.

On the Sense of the Socratic Reply to Meno's Paradox. Jenks, Rod.

On the Three Major Characteristics of Ethical Thought in Traditional China. Gujia, Chen.

On Why Patriotism Is Not A Virtue. Dombrowski, Daniel.

Oskar Schindler and Moral Theory in Applied Philosophy, Almond, Brenda (ed). Jackson, M W.

Plain Persons and Moral Philosophy: Rules, Virtues and Goods. MacIntyre, Alasdair.

Plato and Personhood. Hall, Robert W.

Quasi-Obligation and the Failure to Be Virtuous. Mellema, Gregory.

Religion and Civic Virtue. Budziszewski, J.

Reply to Brinton's '"Following Nature" in Butler's Sermons'. Millar, Alan.

Response to "Integrity or 'He Who Steals My Purse'". Eaker, Deborah J.

Response to Lester Hunt's Comments. Welshon, Robert.

Satisficing and Virtue. Swanton, Christine.

Self-Esteem and Moral Virtue. Nesbitt, Winston.

Selflessness and the Loss of Self. Hampton, Jean.

Shakespeare's Demonic Prince. Mindle, Grant B.

Socrate prend-il au sérieux le paradoxe de Ménon?. Scott, D.

Some Virtues of Resident Alienation. Baier, Annette.

VIRTUE

The Analogy of Religion. Crosson, Frederick.

The Chinese Notion of "Blandness" As a Virtue: A Preliminary Outline. Parkes, Graham R (trans) and Julien, François.

The Concept of the Highest Good in Kant's Moral Theory. Engstrom, Stephen.

The Difference of Virtue and the Difference It Makes: Courage Exemplified. Hauerwas, Stanley.

The Ethical Project of Alasdair MacIntyre: "A Disquieting Suggestion". Keating, Daniel.

The Fragility of Fortune. Bellamy, Richard.

The Idea of a Female Ethic. Grimshaw, Jean.

The Incompatibility of the Virtues. Walker, A D M.

The Liberal Virtues. Strauss, David A.

The Limits of Aristotelian Ethics. Larmore, Charles.

The Modern Quest for Civic Virtues: Issues of Identity and Alienation. Williams, Dilafruz R.

The Moral Vocabulary of Liberalism. Beiner, Ronald.

The Reality of the Moral Self. Thomas, Laurence.

The Role of the 'Ergon' Argument in Aristotle's 'Nicomachean Ethics' in Essays in Ancient Greek Philosophy, IV, Anton, John P (ed). Achtenberg, Deborah.

The Unhappy Conclusion and the Life of Virtue. Mulgan, Tim.

The Unity of the Virtues in Plato's *Protagoras* and *Laches*. Devereux, Daniel T.

The Virtue of Modesty. Ben-Ze'ev, Aaron.

The Virtues of Common Pursuit. Sherman, Nancy.

The Virtues of Thrasymachus. Chappell, T D J.

Toward an Ontology of Virtue Ethics. Savarino, Mary Ella.

Virtue and Oppression. Williams, Joan C.

Virtue and Repression. Paden, Roger K.

Virtue and Self-Alienation. Zeis, John.

Virtue Ethics. Megone, Christopher.

Virtue Ethics and Democratic Values. Slote, Michael.

Virtue Ethics and Mandatory Birth Control in Biomedical Ethics Reviews 1992, Humber, James M (ed). Vitek, William.

Virtue Ethics: An Orthodox Appreciation. Woodill, Joseph.

Virtue Ethics: Making a Case as it Comes of Age. Keenan, James F.

Virtue Without Gender in Socrates. Scaltas, Patricia Ward.

Virtue, Commerce and Moderation in the 'Tale of the Troglodytes': Montesquieu's *Persian Letters*. Desserud, Donald A.

Virtue: A Brief Bibliography. Galston, William A.

Virtue: Its Nature, Exigency, and Acquisition. Baechler, Jean.

Virtues and Relativism. Perry, Michael J.

Weeping at the Death of Dido: Sorrow, Virtue, and Augustine's *Confessions*. Werpehowski, William.

What Did Descartes Do to Virtue?. Santilli, Paul C.

What Is an Expert?. Weinstein, Bruce D.

What Laches and Nicias Miss—And Whether Socrates Thinks Courage Merely a Part of Virtue. Penner, Terrence M I.

Wise Maxims/Wise Judging. Sherman, Nancy.

'Ought' and Well-being. Gillett, Grant.

VISION

see also Seeing

"Magic Buffalo" and Berkeley's *Theory of Vision*: Learning in Society. Levy, David M.

A Reply to Robert O'Connell's "Faith, Reason, and Ascent to Vision in Saint Augustine". Van Fleteren, Frederick.

Continuity and Discontinuity in Visual Experience. Biggs, Michael A R.

Empedocles' Theory of Vision and Theophrastus' 'De Sensibus' in Theophrastus, Fortenbaugh, W W (ed). Sedley, David N.

Faith, Reason, and Ascent to Vision in Saint Augustine. O'Connell, Robert.

La ceguera según Aristóteles. Quevedo, Amalia.

Sight and Touch in The Contents of Experience, Crane, Tim (ed). Martin, Michael.

Supervenience and Computational Explanation in Vision Theory. Morton, Peter.

Where the Difference Still Lies. O'Connell, Robert.

VISUAL

Consciousness: Psychological and Philosophical Essays. Davies, Martin (ed) and Humphreys, Glyn W (ed).

Descartes on Seeing: Epistemology and Visual Perception. Wolf-Devine, Celia.

Certainty, Reliability, and Visual Images. Kirby, Kris N.

Colors, Cultures, and Practices. MacIntyre, Alasdair.

Determining the Primary Problem of Visual Perception: A Gibsonian Response to the 'Correlation' Objection. Glotzbach, Philip A.

Escher and Parmigianino: A Study in Paradox. Duran, Jane.

Frontiers of Utopia: Past and Present. Marin, Louis.

How to Speak of the Colors. Johnston, Mark.

Novel Colours. Thompson, Evan.

On Cognitive Illusions and Rationality in Probability and Rationality, Eells, Ellery (ed). Gigerenzer, Gerd.

Sound and Epistemology in Film. Branigan, Edward.

The Imagery Debate. Eilan, Naomi.

The Objectivity of Color and the Color of Objectivity. Kraut, Robert.

The Origins of Psychological Axioms of Arithmetic and Geometry. Wynn, Karen.

The Third Man. Davidson, Donald.

The Visual System and Levels of Perception: Properties of Neuromental Organization. Stoerig, Petra and Brandt, Stephan.

Vision and Experience: the Causal Theory and the Disjunctive Conception. Child, William.

Visual Qualia and Visual Content in The Contents of Experience, Crane, Tim (ed). Tye, Michael.

Visualizing as a Means of Geometrical Discovery. Giaquinto, Marcus.

Visualizing in Arithmetic. Giaquinto, M.

What Is Color Vision?. Hilbert, David.

Writing with Davidson: Some Afterthoughts after Doing *Blind Time IV: Drawing with Davidson*. Morris, Robert.

VISUAL ART

"With Skin and Hair": Kracauer's Theory of Film, Marseille 1940. Hansen, Miriam.

Engenderings: Constructions of Knowledge, Authority, and Privilege. Scheman, Naomi.

The Language of Art History. Kemal, Salim (ed) and Gaskell, Ivan (ed).

A New Perspective on Pictorial Reprsentation. Gilman, Daniel J.

Additional Thoughts on Perspective. Gombrich, E H.

Aesthetics and Anti-Aesthetics in the Visual Arts. Mattick, Paul.

Baxandall and Goodman in The Language of Art History, Kemal, Salim (ed). Lord, Catherine and Benardete, José A.

Differences (The Presidential Address). Kivy, Peter.

Drawing from Life in Psychoanalysis, Mind and Art, Hopkins, Jim (ed). Phillips, Antonia.

Fear, Fiction and Make-Believe. Neill, Alex.

Instruments of the Eye: Shortcuts to Perspectives. Korsmeyer, Carolyn.

Looking at Art Through Photographs. Savedoff, Barbara.

On Looking at a Picture in Psychoanalysis, Mind and Art, Hopkins, Jim (ed). Budd, Malcolm.

Or What Should Not Be Said About Representation. Goodman, Nelson.

Painting, Parapraxes, and Unconscious Intentions. Geller, Jeffery.

Photography. Levin, Thomas Y (trans) and Kracauer, Siegfried.

Photography, Painting and Perception. Currie, Gregory.

Pictorial Ambiguity. Scheffler, Israel.

Pictorial Quotation. Bailey, George W S.

Postmodernism in the Visual Arts in Postmodernism and Society, Boyne, Roy (ed). Crowther, Paul.

Presence in The Language of Art History, Kemal, Salim (ed). Lyotard, Jean-Françoise.

Resemblance: An Account of Realism in Painting. McKee, Patrick L.

Scruton and Reasons for Looking at Photographs. King, William L.

Seeing-In and Seeing Fictionally in Psychoanalysis, Mind and Art, Hopkins, Jim (ed). Walton, Kendall L.

Some Questions about E H Gombrich on Perspective. Turner, Norman.

Talbot's Technologies: Photographic Depiction, Detection, and Reproduction. Maynard, Patrick L.

The Rationale of Restoration. Savile, Anthony.

Transforming Images: Photographs of Representations. Savedoff, Barbara.

Two Women by Giovanni Bellini. Wiseman, Mary Bittner.

When is a Picture?. Scholz, Oliver R.

VISUALIZATION

Introduction to Re-Thinking Representation: Anselm and Visual Thinking. Kromm, Jane.

VITALISM

The Crisis in Modernism. Burwick, Frederick (ed) and Douglass, Paul (ed).

Bergson and the Politics of Vitalism in The Crisis in Modernism, Burwick, Frederick (ed). Schwartz, Sanford.

Bergson's Vitalism in the Light of Modern Biology in The Crisis in Modernism, Burwick, Frederick (ed). Wolsky, Maria de Issekutz and Wolsky, Alexander A.

Contemporary Vitalism in The Crisis in Modernism, Burwick, Frederick (ed). Bakhtin, Mikhail.

Minds and Machines. Casey, Gerard.

Sir Charles Bell and the Vitalist Controversy in the Early Nineteenth Century in The Crisis in Modernism, Burwick, Frederick (ed). Burwick, Frederick.

The Perpetual Crisis of Modernism and the Traditions of Enlightenment Vitalism in The Crisis in Modernism, Burwick, Frederick (ed). Rousseau, George.

Vitalism and Contemporary Thought in The Crisis in Modernism, Burwick, Frederick (ed). Chiari, Joseph.

Vitalism, Empiricism, and the Quest for Reality in German and English Philosophy in The Crisis in Modernism, Burwick, Frederick (ed). Klein, Jürgen.

'The Triumph of Life': Nietzsche's Verbicide in The Crisis in Modernism, Burwick, Frederick (ed). Amrine, Frederick.

VITO, F

Francesco Vito: Economia e personalismo. Riccio, S.

VIVES, J

Juan Luis Vives y Charles S Peirce. Nubiola, Jaime.

VIVISECTION

Dedicated to Descartes' Niece: The Women's Movement in the Nineteenth Century and Anti-Vivisection. Kalechofsky, Roberta.

VLASTOS, G

Commentary on Vlastos' "Socratic Piety". Lefkowitz, Mary R.

Gregory Vlastos. Burnyeat, M F.

In Search of Socrates. Scaltsas, Theodore.

The *Meno* and the Mysteries of Mathematics. Lloyd, G E R.

Vlasto's *Socrates: Ironist and Moral Philosopher*. Reeve, C D C.

Vlastos on Elenchus and Mathematics. Seeskin, Kenneth.

Vlastos's Socrates. Kahn, Charles.

Voices of Silence: On Gregory Vlastos' Socrates. Nehamas, Alexander.

VOCABULARY

Lenguaje jurídico, lenguaje documental y tesauro. Aguiló Regla, Josep.

VOEGELIN, E

The Balance of Consciousness: Eric Voegelin's Political Theory. Keulman, Kenneth.

Europe, Truth, and History: Husserl and Voegelin on Philosophy and the Identity of Europe. Levy, David J.

WESTERN CIVILIZATION
Freedom by Orlando Patterson. King, Richard H.

WESTPHAL, J
Jonathan Westphal's *Colour*. Broackes, Justin.

WESTPHAL, K
Hegel's Original Insight. Pippin, Robert B.

WESTPHAL, M
A Final Word (Eight Famous Ones) in Modernity and Its Discontents, Marsh, James L (ed). Caputo, John D.

WETHERICK, N
The World as Perceived, the World as Described in Physics: A Reply to Rentoul and Wetherick. Velmans, Max.

WHATLEY, R
Whately's Distinction Between Inferring and Proving. Bitzer, Lloyd F.

WHISTLEBLOWING
Ethical Theory and Business (Fourth Edition). Beauchamp, Tom L and Bowie, Norman E.
Corporate Attorney Whistle-Blowing: Devising a Proper Standard. Dunfee, Thomas W and Maurer, Virginia G.

WHITE, J
White on Autonomy, Neutrality and Well-Being. Clayton, Matthew.

WHITEHEAD
Comprensione e creatività: La filosofia di Whitehead. Arena, Leonardo Vittorio.
Forms of Concrescence: Alfred North Whitehead's Philosophy and Computer Programming Structures. Henry, Granville C.
George Herbert Mead—The Making of a Social Pragmatist. Cook, Gary A.
A Hegelian/Whiteheadian Critique of Whitehead's Dipolar Theism. Christensen, Darrel E.
A Monistic Interpretation of Whitehead's Creativity. Wilcox, John R.
A N Whitehead, R G Collingwood and the Status of Metaphysics (in Dutch). Vanheeswijck, Guido.
Alfred North Whitehead in Founders of Constructive Postmodern Philosophy, Griffin, David Ray (& others)165-196. Cobb Jr, John B.
Can Whitehead's God be Rescued from Process Theism? in Logic, God and Metaphysics, Harris, James F (ed). Ford, Lewis S.
Creativity and the Extensive Continuum as the Ultimate Ground in Alfred North Whitehead's Philosophy of Becoming. Bracken, Joseph A.
La cosmologie transcendantale de Whitehead: transformation spéculative du concept de construction logique. Bradley, James.
La relazione di connessione in A N Whitehead: aspetti matematici. Gerla, Giangiacomo and Tortora, Roberto.
Logical Construction, Whitehead, and God in Logic, God and Metaphysics, Harris, James F (ed). Clarke, Bowman L.
On an Alleged Inconsistency in Whitehead. Capek, Milic.
Ontological Platonism in Whiteheadian Philosophy of God (in Polish). Zycinski, Jozef.
Russell and Whitehead on the Process of Growth in Education. Woodhouse, Howard.
The Human Being as Substance and as Actual Entity. Welten, W.
The Problem of Persons. Janusz, Sharon and Webster, Glenn.
The World Made of Sound: Whitehead and Pythagorean Harmonics in the Context of Veda and the Science of Mantra. Amodio, Barbara A.
Whitehead and Alexander. Emmet, Dorothy.
Whitehead and Dewey on Experience and System in Frontiers in American Philosophy, Volume I, Burch, Robert W (ed). Sherburne, Donald W.
Whitehead and Japanese Aesthetics. Mayada, Arlene M.
Whitehead and Kant on Presuppositions of Meaning. Van Der Veken, Jan.
Whitehead's God and the Dilemma of Pure Possibility in God, Values, and Empiricism, Peden, Creighton W (ed). Crosby, Donald A.
Whitehead's God and the Problem of Evil. Thero, Daniel.
Whitehead, Heidegger, and the Paradoxes of the New. Bradley, J A.
'Principia Mathematica' and the Development of Autonomated Theorem Proving in Perspectives on the History of Mathematical Logic, Drucker, Thomas (ed). O'Leary, Daniel J.

WHITMAN
Santayana's Whitman Revisited. Tejera, V.
Whitman's 'Convertible Terms' in Theorizing American Literature, Cowan, Bainard (ed). Lindberg, Kathryne V.

WHOLENESS
EEEE: Set Theory and Wholeness. Blizard, Wayne D.

WHOLISM
The Concept of Whole in the Structuralist Theory of Art (in Czechoslovakian). Grygar, Mojmir.
Two Factor Theories, Meaning Wholism and Intentionalistic Psychology: A Reply to Fodor. Senor, Thomas D.

WICKEDNESS
Can a Person be Happily Wicked? (Some Problems with Joel Feinberg's Contended Moral Defective). Ducharme, H M.

WICKS, R
Long Live Supervenience. Zangwill, Nicholas.

WIEHL, R
Die Aktualität der Metaphysik: Perspektiven der deutschen Gegenwartsphilosophie. Ollig, Hans- Ludwig.

WIEMAN, H
A God of Power or a God of Value in God, Values, and Empiricism, Peden, Creighton (ed). Templin, J Alton.

WIGGINS, D
The Method of Possible Worlds. Beck, Simon.

WILL
"The Will to Believe": James's Defense of Religious Intolerance. Gordon, Jeffrey.
Aquinas on Mind. Kenny, Anthony.
Aspects of Mind—Gilbert Ryle. Meyer, René (ed) and Ryle, Gilbert.
Consent: The Means to an Active Faith According to St Thomas Aquinas. Barad, Judith.
Epistemic Virtue and Doxastic Responsibility. Montmarquet, James.
Ethical Essays, Volume I. Harrison, Jonathan.
Kants Begründung der praktischen Philosophie. Freudiger, Jürg.
Nietzsche's Philosophical and Narrative Styles. Pettey, John Carson.
Nietzsche: The Politics of Power. Okonta, Ike.
On the Will in Nature — Schopenhauer. Schopenhauer, Arthur and Payne, E F J (trans).
The Person and the Common Life. Hart, James G.
Truth and Eros: Foucault, Lacan, and the Question of Ethics. Rajchman, John.
Understanding Action: An Essay on Reasons. Schick, Frederic.
A Musical Retrieve of Heidegger, Nietzsche, and Technology: Cadence, Concinnity, and Playing Brass. Babich, Babette E.
A Reconstruction of Hegel's Account of Freedom of the Will. Moellendorf, Darrel F.
Does Kant's Ethics Require that the Moral Law Be the Sole Determining Ground of the Will?. Wike, Victoria.
Duns Scotus and the Experience of Freedom. Incandela, Joseph M.
Freedom, Dependence, and the General Will. Neuhouser, Frederick.
Il pensare è spontaneo?. Rosen, Stanley H.
John Buridan and Donald Davidson on *Akrasia*. Saarinen, Risto.
Justification and the Will. Pink, T L M.
Kritik der Hegelschen Formalismusthese. Freier, F V.
L'oggettivismo etico rosminiano. Nebuloni, R.
La virtù della giustizia: da "habitudo" ad "habitus": A proposito della giustizia "metaphorice dicta" in Alberto Magno e Tommaso d'Aquino. Canavero, A Tarabochia.
Natural Law and the Higher Will. Ryn, Claes G.
Nietzsche's Earliest Essays: Translation and Commentary on "Fate and History" and "Freedom of Will and Fate". Stack, George.
Nietzsche's 'Will to Power' and Chinese 'Virtuality' (De) in Nietzsche and Asian Thought, Parkes, Graham R (ed). Ames, Roger T.
Occasionalism and General Will in Malebranche. Nadler, Steven.
On the "Subjects" of Knowing and Willing and the "I" in Shcopenhauer. Aquila, Richard E.
Peter Lombard and Abelard: The *Opinio Nominalium* and Divine Transcendence. Colish, Marcia L.
Schopenhauer's Circle and the Principle of Sufficient Reason. Jacquette, Dale.
The Primacy of God's Will in Christian Ethics in Philosophical Perspectives, 6: Ethics, 1992, Tomberlin, James E (ed). Quinn, Philip.
Transcending the Natural: Duns Scotus on the Two Affections of the Will. Boler, John F.
Was William James a Closet Nihilist: A Further Contribution to URAM William James Studies (*URAM* 2:40-58, 73-78). Crosby, Donald A.
When The Will is Free in Philosophical Perspectives, 6: Ethics, 1992, Tomberlin, James E (ed). Fischer, John M and Ravizza, Mark.
Who Discovered The Will? in Philosophical Perspectives, 6: Ethics, 1992, Tomberlin, James E (ed). Irwin, T H.
Wittgenstein on Voluntary Actions. Arregui, Jorge V.
'Das Wollen ist auch nur eine Erfahrung' in Wittgenstein's Philosophical Investigations, Arrington, Robert T (ed). Candlish, Stewart.

WILL TO BELIEVE
"The Will to Believe" and James's "Deontological Streak". O'Connell, Robert.
The Rational Imperative to Believe. Gordon, Jeffrey.

WILLIAM OF AUVERGNE
William of Auvergne on *De re* and *De dicto* Necessity. Teske, Roland J.

WILLIAMS, B
External Reasons and the Foundations of Morality: Mother Teresa versus Thrasymachus. Hajdin, Mane.
Who Can Accept Moral Dilemmas?. Ohlsson, Ragnar.

WILLIAMS, C
Russelm or Anselm?. Anscombe, G E M.

WILLIAMS, G
The Slippery-Slope Argument. Van Der Burg, Wibren.

WILLIAMS, R
Commentary on "Hegel and Heidegger" in Hegel and His Critics, Desmond, William (ed). Von Der Luft, Eric.

WILLIAMSEN, T
Vagueness and Ignorance—II. Simons, Peter.

WILLING
Trying Without Willing. Cleveland, Timothy.

WILSON, E
Edmund Wilson and the Problem of Marx: History, Biography, and *To The Finland Station*. Corkin, Stanley.

WINCH, P
Value and Understanding: Essays for Peter Winch: Critical Notice. Palmer, Anthony.
Relativism versus Ethnocentrism?. Van Niekerk, Anton.
Sartre's Student and the Captain of the HMS Indomitable. Dowling, Keith W.

WITTGENSTEIN

Wittgenstein on Believing in 'Philosophical Investigations' Part II in Wittgenstein's Philosophical Investigations, Arrington, Robert T (ed). Hunter, J F M.

Wittgenstein on Freud's 'Abdominable Mess' in Wittgenstein Centenary Essays, Griffiths, A Phillips (ed). Cioffi, Frank.

Wittgenstein on Mathematical Proof in Wittgenstein Centenary Essays, Griffiths, A Phillips (ed). Wright, Crispin.

Wittgenstein on Religious Belief in On Community, Rouner, Leroy S (ed). Putnam, Hilary.

Wittgenstein on Rule Following. Srinivas, K.

Wittgenstein on Understanding. Goldfarb, Warren.

Wittgenstein on Voluntary Actions. Arregui, Jorge V.

Wittgenstein über Zeit. Kaspar, Rudolf F and Schmidt, Alfred.

Wittgenstein versus James and Russell on the Nature of Willing in Wittgenstein's Intentions, Canfield, John V (ed). Shanker, Stuart G.

Wittgenstein y Apel sobre la crítica del sentido: de la lógica a la antropología?. Conill, J.

Wittgenstein's Concept of Showing in Criss-Crossing A Philosophical Landscape, Schulte, Joachim (ed). Pears, David.

Wittgenstein's Doctrine of Silence. McDonough, Richard.

Wittgenstein's Influence: Meaning, Mind and Method in Wittgenstein Centenary Essays, Griffiths, A Phillips (ed). Grayling, A C.

Wittgenstein's Intentions in Wittgenstein's Intentions, Canfield, J V (ed). Canfield, J V.

Wittgenstein's Metaphysics of Contingency. Marcotte, Edward J.

Wittgenstein's Private Language Argument and Quine's Indeterminacy Thesis. Lenka, Laxminarayan.

Wittgenstein's Woodcutters: The Problem of Apparent Irrationality. Risjord, Mark W.

Wittgenstein, Anti-Realism and Mathematical Propositions in Criss-Crossing A Philosophical Landscape, Schulte, Joachim (ed). Bouveresse, Jacques.

Wittgenstein, Art and Rule-Following. Oinam, Bhagat.

Wittgenstein, Heidegger, and the Reification of Language in The Cambridge Companion to Heidegger, Guignon, Charles (ed). Rorty, Richard.

Wittgenstein, Rationality and Relativism in Greek Studies in the Philosophy and History of Science, Nicolacopoulos, Pantelis (ed). Tsinorema, Stavroula F.

Wittgenstein, Solipsism, and Religious Belief. Huff, Douglas.

Wittgenstein: Mind, Body, and Society. Schatzki, Theodore R.

Wittgenstein: Whose Philosopher? in Wittgenstein Centenary Essays, Griffiths, A Phillips (ed). Anscombe, G E M.

'The Darkness of This Time': Wittgenstein and the Modern World in Wittgenstein Centenary Essays, Griffiths, A Phillips (ed). Bouveresse, J.

'Too Low!': Frank Cioffi on Wittgenstein's Lectures on Aesthetics. Schroeder, Severin.

WODEHAM, A

William of Ockham and Adam Wodeham. White, Graham.

WOLF, S

Natural Autonomy and Alternative Possibilities. Waller, Bruce N.

Understanding and Blaming: Problems in the Attribution of Moral Responsibility. Vogel, Lawrence.

WOLF, U

Bewusstsein als Durchleben: Eine Antwort auf Ursula Wolf. Pothast, Ulrich.

WOLFF

Christian Wolff on Individuation. Gracia, Jorge J E.

Christian Wolff's Criticism of Spinoza. Morrison, J C.

WOLFF, K

About Survival and Sociology. Bakan, Mildred B.

Eurocentric Elements in the Idea of "Surrender-and-Catch". Moon, Seungsook.

Surrendering and Cathcing in Poetry and Sociology. Ward, John Powell.

The Phenomenal World of Kurt H Wolff. Horowitz, Irving Louis.

WOLFF, R

Authority, Autonomy and the Legitimate State. Paterson, R W K.

WOLLHEIM, R

Psychoanalysis, Mind and Art. Hopkins, Jim (ed) and Savile, Anthony (ed).

Acting on Phantasy and Acting on Desire in Psychoanalysis, Mind and Art, Hopkins, Jim (ed). Segal, Hanna.

Aggression, Love, and Morality in Psychoanalysis, Mind and Art, Hopkins, Jim (ed). Dent, N J H.

An Artistic Misunderstanding. Dickie, George T.

Drawing from Life in Psychoanalysis, Mind and Art, Hopkins, Jim (ed). Phillips, Antonia.

Individual Style. Carney, James D.

Inscrutability of Reference, Monism, and Individuals in Psychoanalysis, Mind and Art, Hopkins, Jim (ed). Ishiguro, Hidé.

Knowing and Valuing in Psychoanalysis, Mind and Art, Hopkins, Jim (ed). Cavell, Marcia.

Motions of the Mind in Psychoanalysis, Mind and Art, Hopkins, Jim (ed). Hart, W D.

Painting, Beholder and the Self in Psychoanalysis, Mind and Art, Hopkins, Jim (ed). Savile, Anthony.

Psychoanalysis, Interpretation, and Science in Psychoanalysis, Mind and Art, Hopkins, Jim (ed). Hopkins, Jim.

Remembering Directly in Psychoanalysis, Mind and Art, Hopkins, Jim (ed). Wiggins, David.

Seeing-In and Seeing Fictionally in Psychoanalysis, Mind and Art, Hopkins, Jim (ed). Walton, Kendall L.

The Work of Art as Psychoanalytical Object: Wollheim on Manet. Herwitz, Daniel A.

Utopia and Fantasy in Psychoanalysis, Mind and Art, Hopkins, Jim (ed). Burnyeat, M F.

WOLLSTONECRAFT, M

Mary Wollstonecraft and Women's Rights. Larson, Elizabeth.

WOMAN

see also Female, Feminism, Women

A Woman and a Man as Prime Analogical Beings. Allen, Prudence.

L'immagine della donna secondo Ortega y Gasset. Savignano, Armando.

WOMEN

"Engendering Equity...". Morgan, K P.

"Maleness" Revisited. Bordo, Susan.

"Power in the Service of Love": John Dewey's Logic and the Dream of a Common Language. Hart, Carroll Guen.

Arguing About Abortion. Schwartz, Lewis M.

Beyond Equality and Difference. Bock, Gisela (ed) and James, Susan (ed).

Beyond Methodology: Feminist Scholarship as Lived Research. Fonow, Mary Margaret (ed) and Cook, Judith A (ed).

Breaking Out Again: Feminist Ontology and Epistemology (Second Edition). Stanley, Liz and Wise, Sue.

Buddhism, Sexuality, and Gender. Cabezón, José I (ed).

Compassionate Authority: Democracy and the Representation of Women. Jones, Kathleen B.

De Productie, Distributie en Consumptie Van Cultuur. Kloek, J J and Mijnhardt, W W.

Disciplining Foucault: Feminism, Power, and the Body. Sawicki, Jana.

Elemental Passions—Luce Irigaray. Irigaray, Luce, Collie, Joanne (trans) and Still, Judith (trans).

Engendering the Subject: Gender and Self-Representation in Contemporary Women's Fiction. Robinson, Sally.

Engenderings: Constructions of Knowledge, Authority, and Privilege. Scheman, Naomi.

Erotic Welfare: Sexual Theory and Politics in the Age of Epidemic. Singer, Linda.

Feminist Epistemologies. Alcoff, Linda (ed) and Potter, Elizabeth (ed).

Feminist Perspectives In Medical Ethics. Holmes, Helen Bequaert (ed) and Purdy, Laura M.

From Mastery to Analysis: Theories of Gender in Psychoanalytic Feminism. Elliot, Patricia.

Gender Politics and Post-Communism: Reflections from Eastern Europe and the Former Soviet Union. Funk, Nanette (ed) and Mueller, Magda (ed).

Hypatia Reborn: Essays in Feminist Philosophy. Al-Hibri, Azizah Y (ed) and Simons, Margaret A (ed).

Je, Tu, Nous: Toward a Culture of Difference. Irigaray, Luce and Martin, Alison (trans).

La Théorie qui n'en est pas une, or, Why Clio Doesn't Care. Steedman, Carolyn.

Marine Lover of Friedrich Nietzsche—Luce Irigaray. Irigaray, Luce and Gill, Gillian C (trans).

Materialist Feminism and the Politics of Discourse. Hennessy, Rosemary.

Modern Political Theory and Contemporary Feminism: A Dialectical Analysis. Ring, Jennifer.

Partial Visions: Feminism and Utopianism in the 1970s. Bammer, Angelika.

Philosophy and Feminist Criticism. Cole, Eve Browning.

Politics, Gender, and Genre: The Political Thought of Christine de Pizan. Brabant, Margaret (ed).

Revisioning Philosophy. Ogilvy, James (ed).

Revolutions in Knowledge: Feminism in the Social Sciences. Zalk, Sue Rosenberg (ed) and Gordon-Kelter, Janice (ed).

Sexual Democracy: Women, Oppression, and Revolution. Ferguson, Ann.

Simone Weil: Portrait of a Self-Exiled Jew. Nevin, Thomas R.

Speculum of the Other Woman—Luce Irigaray. Irigaray, Luce and Gill, Gillian C (trans).

The Birth Lottery. Boss, Judith A.

The Ethics of Abortion (Revised Edition). Baird, Robert M (ed) and Rosenbaum, Stuart E (ed).

The Ethics of Reproductive Technology. Alpern, Kenneth D (ed).

The Interpretation of the Flesh: Freud and Femininity. Brennan, Teresa.

The Quality of Life. Nussbaum, Martha C (ed) and Sen, Amartya (ed).

Theoretical Perspectives on Sexual Difference. Rhode, Deborah L (ed).

Toward a Feminist Epistemology. Duran, Jane.

Transformations: Recollective Imagination and Sexual Difference. Cornell, Drucilla.

Woman and Modernity: The (Life)styles of Lou Andreas-Salomé. Martin, Biddy.

Women's Rights and the Rights of Man. Arnaud, A J and Kingdom, E.

A Debate Between a Philosopher and a Historian on the Women's Question in Bohemia (in Czechoslovakian). Peskova, Jaroslava and Horska, Pavla.

A Note on Feminist Theories of Representation: Questions Concerning the Autonomy of Art. Leibowitz, Flo.

A Question of Evidence. Nelson, Lynn Hankinson.

A Response to Zerilli and Brodribb. Pocock, J G A.

Abortion and "Choice". Gallagher, Kenneth.

Abortion and the Right to Privacy. Langer, Richard.

Abortion Logic and Paternal Responsibility: One More Look at Judith Thomson's "A Defense of Abortion". Pavlischek, Keith J.

Abortion, Moral Responsibility, and Self-Defense. Huffman, Tom L.

Against Caring. Nelson, Hilde L.

Analytic Aesthetics and Feminist Aesthetics: Neither/Nor?. Waugh, Joanne B.

Antigone's Mirrors: Reflections on Moral Madness. Pritchard, Annie.

Applying the Concept of Gender: Unsettled Questions. Upin, Jane.

Are 'Old Wives' Tales' Justified? in Feminist Epistemologies, Alcoff, Linda (ed). Dalmiya, Vrinda and Alcoff, Linda.

WOMEN

WOMEN

The Rights of Man and the Goals of Women in Women's Rights and the Rights of Man, Arnaud, A J. Parker, Richard B.

The Role of Feminist Aesthetics in Feminist Theory. Hein, Hilde.

The Subjection of John Stuart Mill. Stove, D.

The Tacit Victory and the Unfinished Agenda. Rutledge, David (& others).

The Use of Sophiology. Martz, Erin.

The 'Physical Organisation', Education, and Inferiority of Women in Diderot's 'Refutation ... in Women's Rights and the Rights of Man, Arnaud, A J. Gianformaggio, Letizia.

These New Components of the Spectacle in Postmodernism and Society, Boyne, Roy (ed). Wilson, Elizabeth.

Thinking Morality Interpersonally: A Reply to Burgess-Jackson. Walker, Margaret Urban.

Thinking with Fraser about Rorty, Feminism, and Pragmatism. Fritzman, J M.

Toward a Consistent View of Abortion and Unwanted Pregancy. Williams, Courtney.

Toward the Sexual and Economic Emancipation of Women: The Philosophy of Grete Meisel-Hess. Melander, Ellinor.

Two Women by Giovanni Bellini. Wiseman, Mary Bittner.

Unravelling the Problems in Ecofeminism. Cuomo, Christine J.

Virtue Without Gender in Socrates. Scaltas, Patricia Ward.

Visions and Voices. Briscoe, Felecia.

Was George Herbert Mead a Feminist?. Aboulafia, Mitchell.

What Gilles Deleuze Has to Say to Battered Women. Holland, Nancy.

What's Wrong with Prostitution?. Primoratz, I.

When the Child is the Father of the Man: Work, Sexual Difference, and the Guardian-State in Third Republic France. Schafer, Sylvia.

Who is that Masked Woman? Reflections on Power, Privilege, and Home-ophobia in Revisioning Philosophy, Ogilvy, James (ed). Scheman, Naomi.

Whose Body Is It, Anyway? in Philosophical Perspectives, 6: Ethics, 1992, Tomberlin, James E (ed). Smith, Holly M.

Why Do Men Enjoy Pornography? in Rethinking Masculinity, May, Larry (ed). Soble, Alan.

Why Feminists Thought Take the *Phenomenology of Spirit* Seriously. Swindle, Stuart.

Why Patronize Feminists? A Reply to Stove on Mill. Brecher, Bob.

Why We Listen to Lunatics: Antifoundational Theories and Feminist Politics. Bickford, Susan.

Woman and Space According to Kristeva and Irigaray in Shadow of Spirit, Berry, Philippa (ed). Berry, Philippa.

Women and the "Public Use of Reason". Fleming, Marie.

Women and the New Casuistry. Sichol, Marcia.

Women and the Quality of Life in The Quality of Life, Nussbaum, Martha C (ed). Annas, Julia.

Women as Ends—Women as Means in the Enlightenment in Women's Rights and the Rights of Man, Arnaud, A J. Scaltsas, Theodore.

Women in Political Thought. Pringle, Helen.

Women Philosophers in Antiquity. Leuven, Lienke.

Women Philosophers in the Middle Ages. Leuven, Lienke.

Women's Emancipation and the Theology of Sex in Nineteenth-Century Russia. Polyakov, L V.

Yes, There Are African-American Perspectives on Bioethics in African-American Perspectives on Biomedical Ethics, Flack, Harley E (ed). Dula, Annette.

'Pretty, Witty and Wise': Courtesans in Athenaeus' *Deipnosophistai* Book 13. Hawley, R.

WONDER

In the Throe of Wonder: Intimations of the Sacred in a Post-Modern World. Miller, Jerome A.

Reverence and the Passions of Inquiry. Bitting, Paul F and Southworth, Cheryl.

Science, Wonder and the Lust of the Eyes. O'Neill, John.

The Wonder of the Poet; The Wonder of the Philosopher. George, Marie.

WOOD, A

Hegel's Ethical Thought. Houlgate, Stephen.

WOOD, E

Locke, Taxation and Reform: A Reply to Wood. Hughes, Martin.

WOOLF, V

Education and Thought in Virginia Woolf's *To The Lighthouse*. Sichel, Betty A.

Men and Women: Ball-in-Socket Story?. Gordon, Sophie Haroutunian.

WOOZLEY, A

A D Woozley and the Concept of Right Answers in Law. Bix, Brian.

WORD

Direct Reference: From Language to Thought. Rashed, Roshdi.

Languages of the Mind: Essays on Mental Representation. Jackendoff, Ray.

Word and Spirit: A Kierkegaardian Critique of the Modern Age. Hall, Ronald L.

A Word Problem for Normal and Regular Equations. Graczynska, Ewa.

Aristotle on 'ΕΝΤΕΛΕΧΕΙΑ: A Reply to Daniel Graham. Blair, George A.

How to Undo Things with Words: Spinoza's Criterion for Limiting Freedom of Expression. Madanes, Leiser.

Representation in Words and in Drama in Aesthetic Illusion, Burwick, Frederick (ed). Krieger, Murray.

The Constantive-Performance Distinction in a Justificatory Perspective. Lenka, Laxminarayan.

The Ethos of Epideictic Encounter. Sullivan, Dale L.

The Power of Words. Radford, Colin.

The Referent of Words: Universal or Individual, the Controversies Between Mimamsakas and Naiyayikas. Vattanky, John.

'Intuition Pumps' and Contemporary Philosophy. MacLean-Tollefsen, Laurie.

WORDSWORTH

Frail Memorials: "Essays Upon Epitaphs" and Wordsworth's Economy of Reference. Brigham, Linda C.

Wordsworth and the Recovery of Hope. Fischer, Michael.

WORK

Bettering Our Condition: Work, Workers and Ethics in British and German Economic Thought. Chmielewski, Philip J.

La Dialettica dell'Etico. Li Vigni, Fiorinda.

Alienation and Moral Imperatives: A Reply to Kanungo. Sweet, Robert T.

Democractic Rights at National and Workplace Levels in The Idea of Democracy, Copp, David (ed). Arneson, Richard J.

La città armoniosa di Péguy: Profezia della speranza o utopia dell'illusione. Nicolosi, Salvatore.

Meaningful Work and the Rights of the Worker: A Commentary on *Rerum Novarum* and *Laborem Exercens*. Gini, Al.

Simone Weil and the Civilisation of Work in Simone Weil's Philosophy of Culture, Bell, Richard (ed). Fischer, Clare B.

Speech, Conscience, and Work. Lippke, Richard L.

Vita Humana: Hannah Arendt zu den Bedingungen tätigen Menschseins. Splett, Jörg.

WORK ETHIC

The Work Ethic and the Work Ethos: The Importance of Ethical Arguments for the Politics of Transition to the Market. Büscher, M.

Totalitarianism and the Problems of a Work Ethic. Davydov, I N.

WORKER

Meaningful Work and the Rights of the Worker: A Commentary on *Rerum Novarum* and *Laborem Exercens*. Gini, Al.

'Institutional Exploitation' and Workers' Co-operatives—Or How the British Left Persist in Getting Their Concepts Wrong. Carter, Alan.

WORKING CLASS

Dialectical Investigations. Ollman, Bertell.

Liberal Political Theory and Working-Class Radicalism in Nineteenth-Century England. Ashcraft, Richard.

WORLD

see also External World, Possible World

Aesthetic Judgment and the Moral Image of the World: Studies in Kant. Henrich, Dieter.

Bioethics Yearbook, Volume 2—Regional Developments in Bioethics: 1989-1991. Lustig, B Andrew (& other eds).

Boundary Ways: On the Philosophy of the Later Ludwig Wittgenstein (in Hungarian). Neumer, Katalin.

Dialogue with Heidegger on Values: Ethics for Times of Crisis. Joós, Ernest.

Die Welt des Menschen. Kessler, Herbert.

Fiat vita, pereat veritas: Nietzsche's Untimely Reflections on Hegel's Dialectic of History. Axiotis, Ares.

Husserl's Transcendental Phenomenology—Elisabeth Ströker. Hardy, Lee (trans) and Ströker, Elisabeth.

Philosophical Universes. Verster, Ulrich.

Search for a Naturalistic World View: Volume I. Shimony, Abner.

Search for a Naturalistic World View: Volume II. Shimony, Abner.

The Ecological Self. Mathews, Freya.

A Critique of Husserl's Notion of Crisis in Crises in Continental Philosophy, Dallery, Arleen B (ed). Buckley, R Philip.

An Inquiry into Religion's Empty World. Martland, Thomas R.

Ancora a proposito di metafisica: Nota in margine ad un recente volume. Piazza, G.

Aristotelian Rainfall or the Lore of Averages. Wardy, Robert.

Aristotle's Perceptual Realism. Broadie, Sarah.

Categories and Realities. Carr, Brian.

Comments on R Baine Harris's "Can We Have a World Philosophy?". Hubert, Jerzy Z.

Conceptual Relativism and Philosophy in the Americas in Cultural Relativism and Philosophy, Dascal, Marcelo (ed). Olivé, León.

Considerazioni sul *De mundo* e analisi critica delle tesi di Paul Moraux. Bos, A P.

Cosmic Doing and Undoing Without End: Chauncey Wright's Idea of Ultimate Reality and Meaning. Madden, Edward H.

Creazione ed eternità del mondo. Molinaro, A.

Das Ideal des philosophischen Lebens bei G W Leibniz. Rensoli, Lourdes.

Does the Eternity of the World Entail an Actual Infinite? Yes!. Tacelli, Ronald.

Gerold Prauss—Die Welt und Wir. Sandkaulen, Birgit.

Heidegger and the World in an Artwork. Singh, R Raj.

Heidegger and the World-Yielding Role of Language. Singh, R Raj.

Heidegger—The Work and the World-View (in Czechoslovakian). Habermas, Jürgen.

How I See Philosophy in Certainty and Surface in Epistemology and Philosophical Method, Martinich, A P (ed). Stroll, Avrum.

Husserl e il linguaggio. Costa, Filippo.

Husserl's Concept of the World in Crises in Continental Philosophy, Dallery, Arleen B (ed). Bernet, Rudolf.

Imagined Worlds and the Real One: Plato, Wittgenstein, and Mimesis. Harrison, Bernard.

Intentionality and World in The Cambridge Companion to Heidegger, Guignon, Charles B (ed). Hall, Harrison B.

Justice and Insider Trading. Lippke, Richard L.

Lycan on Lewis and Meinong. King, Peter J.

Making Categories or Making Worlds, II in Frontiers in American Philosophy, Volume I, Burch, Robert W (ed). Wallace, Kathleen.

Guidance on the Use of the Author Index With Abstracts

Each entry in this section begins with the author's name and contains the complete title of the article or book, other bibliographic information, and an abstract if available. The list is arranged in alphabetical order with the author's last name first. Articles by multiple authors are listed under each author's name. Names preceded by the articles De, La, Le, etc. or the prepositions Da, De, Van, Von, etc. are usually treated as if the article or preposition were a part of the last name.

Almost all of the abstracts are provided by the authors of the articles and books; where an abstract does not appear, it was not received from the author prior to the publication of this edition. The staff of the *Index* prepares some abstracts. These abstracts are followed by "(staff)".

In order to locate all the articles and books written by a given author, various spellings of the author's name should be checked. This publication uses the form of the author's name given in the article or book. Hence, variations of an author's name may appear in this index. Particular care should be given to names that have a space, a dash, or an apostrophe in them. Because the computer sorts on each character, the names of other authors may be filed between different spellings of a given author's name.

Aaron, Daniel. George Santayana and the Genteel Tradition in Frontiers in American Philosophy, Volume I, Burch, Robert W (ed). College Station, Texas A&M Univ Pr, 1992.

Abbarno, John M. Interview of Peter A French. *J Value Inq*, 27(1), 113-118, Ja 93.

Abe, Masao and Fredericks, James L (trans). "Inverse Correspondence" in the Philosophy of Nishida: The Emergence of the Notion. *Int Phil Quart*, 32(3), 325-344, S 92.

Abel, Francesc (ed) and Wildes, Kevin W (ed) and Harvey, John C (ed). *Birth, Suffering, and Death: Catholic Perspectives at the Edges of Life*. Dordrecht, Kluwer, 1992.

Abel, Olivier. Ricoeur's Ethics of Method. *Phil Today*, 37(1), 23-30, Spr 93.

A method is always the vehicle of ethical presuppositions. And ethics truly appears when its methodology itself becomes an ethical exercise, an exercise in responsibility. This text begins with the role of the "aporia" in Ricoeur's thought. It then underscores the respect brought to the questions put by others, and thus to the plurality of possible questions. Further on, Ricoeur's treatment of the "remainder", that which each method leaves at its edges, is focused upon. Finally, these various figures are interpreted in the perspective of the implicit anthropology of this ethics.

Abelsen, Peter. Schopenhauer and Buddhism. *Phil East West*, 43(2), 255-278, Ap 93.

Ablondi, Frederick R. *A Spinozistic Account of Self-Deception: NASS Monograph #1 (1993)*. Milwaukee, No Amer Spinoza Soc, 1993.

This work is an attempt to demonstrate how Spinoza's psychology can account for the phenomena of self-deception. Taking as a starting point the standard 4-point clinical definition of self-deception put form by Sackeim and Gur, it is shown how the Spinozistic conception of the human mind allows for each of the four criteria.

Abou El Fadl, Khaled. 'Ahkam al-Bughat': Irregular Warfare and the Law of Rebellion in Islam in Cross, Crescent, and Sword, Johnson, James Turner (ed). Westport, Greenwood Pr, 1990.

Aboulafia, Mitchell. Mead and the Social Self in Frontiers in American Philosophy, Volume I, Burch, Robert W (ed). College Station, Texas A&M Univ Pr, 1992.

Aboulafia, Mitchell. Was George Herbert Mead a Feminist?. *Hypatia*, 8(2), 145-158, Spr 93.

George Herbert Mead was a dedicated progressive and internationalist who strove to realize his political convictions through participation in numerous civic organizations in Chicago. These convictions informed and were informed by his approach to philosophy. This article addresses the bonds between Mead's philosophy, social psychology, and his support of women's rights through an analysis of a letter he wrote to his daughter-in-law regarding her plans for a career.

Abraham, Uri and Shelah, Saharon. A Δ2/2 Well-Order of the Reals and Incompactness of *L*(QMM). *Annals Pure Applied Log*, 59(1), 1-32, Ja 93.

Abrantes, Paulo C C. A Concepçao Estóica de Natureza e a Moderna Física do Contínuo. *Cad Hist Filosof Cie*, 2(1), 33-65, Ja-Je 90.

This paper investigates the participation of two methodological orientations, that we can name "mechanicism" and "dynamism", on some modern scientific research programmes, specially on the origins of the "field" concept, central to the electromagnetic theory developed by Maxwell in the second half of the 19th century. First, the cosmological conceptions of the stoics are exposed as a synthesis of various dynamic intuitions in ancient natural philosophy. The second part is concerned with the influential work of Sambursky's *Physics of the Stoics*. His main theses are presented along with a methodological critique of his historiography. In the third part the influence of stoicism and neoplatonism is investigated, mainly on Newtonian "dynamism" and 18th century British natural philosophy that inherited Newtonian images of nature and science. Faraday's matter theory is then viewed as directly motivated by 18th century Newtonian dynamism.

Abscal-Hildebrand, Mary and Mullins, Joan. Recreating Classroom Relationships: Mutual Mentoring Joins Critical Hermeneutics and Composition Theory. *Phil Stud Educ*, 1, 69-81, 1990.

Achinstein, Peter. Explanation and "Old Evidence". *Philosophica*, 51(1), 125-137, 1993.

Achtenberg, Deborah. On the Metaphysical Presuppositions of Aristotle's *Nicomachean Ethics*. *J Value Inq*, 26(3), 317-340, Jl 92.

Achtenberg, Deborah. The Role of the 'Ergon' Argument in Aristotle's 'Nicomachean Ethics' in Essays in Ancient Greek Philosophy, IV, Anton, John P (ed). Albany, SUNY Pr, 1991.

The main conclusion of the essay is that the *ergon* argument is central to Aristotle's *Nicomachean Ethics* because, according to Aristotle, virtue is the completion of a thing's proper *ergon* and completion of things different in kind are themselves different. Since the *ergon* of human beings is different than the *ergon* of plants and of non-human animals, the virtue of human beings is different than the virtue of plants and non- human animals. Aristotle's *Nicomachean Ethics* account of virtue reflects this difference in *erga*.

Ackerman, Felicia. Does Philosophy Only State What Everyone Admits? A Discussion of the Method of Wittgenstein's *Philosophical Investigations*. *Midwest Stud Phil*, 17, 246-254, 1992.

Ackerman, Terrence F. Innovative Lifesaving Treatments in Contemporary Issues in Paediatric Ethics, Burgess, Michael M (ed). Lewiston, Mellen Pr, 1991.

Ackermann, Robert. Super Pragmatic Paradoxes in Logical Foundations, Mahalingam, Indira (ed). New York, St Martin's Pr, 1991.

Adam, A M. Einstein, Michelson, and the Crucial Experiment Revisited. *Method Sci*, 25(3), 117-128, 1992.

The topic of crucial experiment is an important one that would lend itself to potentially interesting discussion in both philosophy of science and history of science. The present paper discusses a standard account of that topic written by Holton ("Einstein, Michelson, and the Crucial Experiment", *ISIS*, 60, 133-197, 1969) and finds that Holton's paper is so deeply flawed in its overall conception that it needs to be revisited. Yet, Holton's account is now standard. Thus, for example, in Zahar's *Einstein's Revolution*, Holton's account is quoted uncritically. The primary problems with Holton's account of crucial experiment are that it is erroneous as a historical account of what Michelson and Morley's experiment was, as an account of what a crucial experiment is, and as an account of what Einsteins's understanding of a (crucial) experiment is (this will be discussed in my first two sections). The remainder of the business of this paper is to explain what Michelson and Morley's experiment is, if not a crucial experiment.

Adam, M. René Descartes et Pierre Charron. *Rev Phil Fr*, 4, 467-483, O-D 92.

Pierre Charron (1541-1603), ami de Montaigne, a voulvu donner une philosophie alliant le scepticisme des *Essais* et le dogmatisme des Stoïciens. Il est la transition vers Descartes qui connaissait bien son oeuvre. L'épistémologie et surtout la morale de Descartes sont remplies de nombreuses réminiscences de Charron. La conception de la sagesse de Charron reste humaniste, alors que Descartes l'associe à privilégier la pensée active du sujet; Descartes prolonge ceci en y insérant un projet mathématique, principe de sa méthode. Alors, Charron, n'ayant pas perçu l'importance de la science à venir, paissera Descartes achever ce qu'il avait commencé.

Adamowicz, Zofia. A Contribution to the End-Extension Problem and the Π1 Conservativeness Problem. *Annals Pure Applied Log*, 61(1-2), 3-48, My 93.

The paper concerns the end-extension problem from bounded arithmetic. The problem is whether any countable model for bounded arithmetic plus the collection scheme for bounded formulas has a proper end-extension to a model of bounded arithmetic. We show that the answer is negative if we enlarge bounded arithmetic by its consistency (in an appropriate formulation). Since it is similarly for bounded arithmetic enlarged by the axiom of exponentiation, we show that consistency can play a similar role as exponentiation.

Adams, Don. Love and Impartiality. *Amer Phil Quart*, 30(3), 223-234, Jl 93.

Recently it has been argued on several different grounds that strict moral impartiality conflicts with genuine friendship and love, and that because of this conflict, moral theories should somehow permit certain exceptions to the demand that we be strictly impartial. Against this I argue that these objections rest on misconceptions of impartiality and that in fact there is no conflict between strict moral impartiality and love.

Adams, E M. Rationality and Morality. *Rev Metaph*, 46(4), 683-697, Je 93.

The purpose of the article is to challenge widely accepted views of the relationship among rationality, morality, and prudence. It contends that we cannot understand either the rational or the moral enterprise without a correct philosophical view of the human self, and that such a view of the self is impossible without taking account of the rational and the moral enterprises themselves. The paper concludes that the moral point of view is anchored in the nature of selfhood so that one can be neither rational and immoral nor prudent and immoral.

Adams, Ernest. Formalizing the Logic of Positive, Comparative, and Superlative. *Notre Dame J Form Log*, 34(1), 90-99, Wint 93.

A formalism is introduced for symbolizing positives, comparatives, and superlatives like "old", "older", and "oldest" in such a way as to show their interdependence, as in "The youngest old man is a young old man". Formal principles are stated for determining logical properties of such propositions, e.g., whether "All young old men are young men" is logically true. These allow for the fact that adjectives like "young" and "old" may not only be vague and indefinable in terms of their corresponding comparatives, but they may also be relative, so that to be young *for an old man* is not necessarily to be young *for a young man*.

Adams, Ernest W. Classical Physical Abstraction. *Erkenntnis*, 38(2), 145-167, Mr 93.

An informal theory is set forth of relations between abstract entities, including *colors, physical quantities, times, and places in space*, and the concrete things that *have* them, or are *at* or *in* them, based on the assumption that there are close analogies between these relations and relations between abstract *sets* and the concrete things that are *members* of them. It is suggested that even standard scientific usage of these abstractions presupposes principles that are analogous to postulates of abstraction, identity, and other fundamental principles of set theory. Also discussed is the significance of important disanalogies between sets and physical abstractions, including especially *modal* and *temporal* aspects of physical abstractions, which is related to the problem of the characterizing *constancy*, of colors, physical attributes, and locations in space.

Adams, Ernest W. On the Rightness of Certain Counterfactuals. *Pac Phil Quart*, 74(1), 1-10, Mr 93.

That inferences with counterfactual premises, like "Senator A is absent, because Senator B is presiding, and *if Senator A were present he would be presiding*", have factual conclusions suggests that what makes the counterfactuals *right* is itself a matter of fact. But it is argued that this rightness is a matter of probability rather of truth, and inconclusive comments are made on the 'right probabilities' of counterfactuals, i.e., probabilities that lead to right factual conclusions, and on the relation between these probabilities and intuitive feelings of rightness.

Adams, Fred and Aizawa, Kenneth. Fodorian Semantics, Pathologies, and "Block's Problem". *Mind Mach*, 3(1), 97-104, F 93.

In two recent books, Jerry Fodor has developed a set of sufficient conditions for an object "X" to non-naturally and non-derivatively mean X. In an earlier paper we presented three reasons for thinking Fodor's theory to be inadequate. One of these problems we have dubbed the "Pathologies Problem". In response to queries concerning the relationship between the Pathologies Problem and what Fodor calls "Block's Problem", we argue that, while Block's Problem does not threaten *Fodor's view*, the Pathologies Problem does.

Adams, Fred and Enç, Berent. Functions and Goal Directedness. *Phil Sci*, 59(4), 635-654, D 92.

We examine two approaches to functions: etiological and forward-looking. In the context of functions, we raise the question, familiar to philosophers of mind, about the explanatory role of properties that are *not* supervenient on the mere dispositional features of a system. We first argue that the question has no easy answer in either of the two approaches. We then draw a parallel between functions and goal directedness. We conclude by proposing an answer to the question: The explanatory importance of nonsupervenient properties (like having the function of doing something, or like being goal-directed) does not lie in any special causal mechanism through which these properties bring about their effects; it lies rather in the different classification of the explananda types that these properties generate.

Adams, Fred and Fuller, Gary. Names, Contents, and Causes. *Mind Lang*, 7(3), 205-221, Autumn 92.

Can cognitive science run on broad content alone? Yes, but only if Twin-Earth and the names puzzles are solved. Al and Twin-Al share behavior but not broad content. How? Similarly, Al and John behave differently even though they share the same broad thoughts (Tony Curtis/Bernie Schwartz is here). How? We argue elsewhere that Twin-Earth puzzles are easily solved with broad content alone. In this paper, we argue that names puzzles also are solved with broad content alone. It is a good thing, because narrow content is incapable of solving the names puzzles facing cognitive science.

Adams, Fred and Fuller, Gary and Stecker, Robert. Thoughts Without Objects. *Mind Lang*, 8(1), 90-104, Spr 93.

This paper answers objections to object-dependent thoughts (thoughts identified by their objects). We claim that such thoughts exist and are needed to explain behavior in many circumstances. Objections to object-dependent thoughts invoke vacuous singular thoughts (say, of an hallucinated attacker). Such thoughts have no objects (no attacker), hence such thoughts cannot explain behavior in virtue of their object-dependent content. We show that appeals to vacuous thoughts do not diminish the need for object dependent thoughts in non-vacuous situations. We also compare this debate to the broad/narrow content debate and show that the content needed to explain behavior when thoughts are vacuous is not narrow content.

Adams, Fred and Stecker, Robert and Fuller, Gary. Schiffer on Modes of Presentation. *Analysis*, 53(1), 30-34, Ja 93.

Since Lois likes Kent and believes that Kent cannot fly, she would plead with him not to leap from a tall building. Though Lois also likes Superman, she would not plead with him not to leap. If modes of presentation were syntactic items in a language of thought, we could explain that Lois thinks of the same individual once under the mode of "Kent" and later under the mode of "Superman", without thinking "Kent = Superman". In a number of recent writings, Schiffer has proposed a roadblock to this neat explanation. In this paper we argue that the view that modes are syntactic items in a language of thought survives Schiffer's objections.

Adams, Fred and Stecker, Robert and Fuller, Gary. The Floyd Puzzle: Reply to Yagisawa. *Analysis*, 53(1), 36-40, Ja 93.

We defended the view that modes of presentation are syntactic items in the language of thought. Yagisawa argues that our defense of this view did not handle Schiffer's Floyd puzzle. The following truths are supposed to make a rational Floyd irrational (on our account): 1) Floyd believes that Lois believes that Superman flies, 2) Floyd believes that Lois does not believe that Clark Kent flies, and 3) Floyd does not believe that Clark Kent is not Superman. We remain unconvinced. We present not one but two interpretations on which Floyd is not irrational on our view and on which our view survives Schiffer's Floyd puzzle.

Adams, Fred and Stecker, Robert and Fuller, Gary. The Semantics of Thought. *Pac Phil Quart*, 73(4), 375-389, D 92.

This paper accepts that the task of a semantics of thoughts is to explain how thoughts convey information about the world and how behavior can be explained in virtue of the content of thoughts. We defend direct reference theories of meaning against Devitt's charge that such semantic theories cannot give a satisfactory semantics for the problems of identity sentences, opaque contexts, or positive and negative existence sentences. We reply to Devitt's charge, examine and reject Devitt's alternative non-descriptive sense theory, and offer a new account of the semantics of positive and negative existential sentences.

Adams, Frederick. Epistemology in Reflections on Philosophy, McHenry, Leemon (ed). New York, St Martin's Pr, 1993.

This essay introduces epistemology; not by surveying different approaches (coherentism, foundationalism, reliabilism, etc.), although the reader is referred to alternatives, but by motivating, explaining, and defending a reliability theory of knowledge (though not of justification). The essay relies heavily on examples, and on replies to attempted counterexamples and to the challenge of skepticism. The justification for this approach is the attempt to increase understanding of the value of epistemology; to introduce clearly a theory believed likely to be true, rather than risk losing the student in a bewildering array of complexity. A glossary of terms is provided.

Adams, Frederick. Fodor's Modal Argument. *Phil Psych*, 6(1), 41-56, 1993.

What we do, intentionally, depends upon the intentional contents of our thoughts. For about ten years Fodor has argued that intentional behavior causally depends upon the narrow intentional content of thoughts (not broad). His main reason is a causal powers argument—brains of individuals A and B may differ in broad content, but, if A and B are neurophysically identical, their thoughts cannot differ in causal power, despite differences in broad content. Recently Fodor (Fodor, 1991) presents a new 'modal' version of this causal powers argument. I argue that Fodor's argument (in old or new dress) is a *non sequitur*. It neither establishes the existence of narrow content nor the need for a content other than broad content to explain intentional behavior.

Adams, Frederick. Machine Persons. *Personalist Forum*, 8/1(Supp), 47-55, Spr 92.

Why did not Alan Turing or Hilary Putnam solve the problem of personal identity—Al is the same person over time if and only if he is the same Turing machine in the same token run of the same total cognitive program? My method here forty-three years after Turing's classic paper "Computing Machinery and Intelligence" and thirty-three years after Putnam's classic "Minds and Machines" is to determine what we can learn about the identity of human persons by asking similar questions about the identity of machine persons (if we could build them). I conclude that, indeed, the above criteria may determine the identity over time of human and machine persons.

Adams, Frederick. Reply to Russow's "Fodor, Adams and Causal Properties". *Phil Psych*, 6(1), 63-65, 1993.

In 'Fodor's Modal Argument' I claim that Fodor's latest defence of narrow content does not work. I claim that Fodor's modal argument is an unsuccessful resurrection of the Logical Connection Argument. Russow claims that my arguments fail because I confuse cause properties with causal powers, focus on events rather than properties, and overlook the fact that Fodor is trying only to explain *narrow* behavior. In this paper, I plead 'not guilty' to all of Fodor's charges. Narrow content still does not exist.

Adams, Frederick (ed) and McHenry, Leemon (ed). *Reflections on Philosophy*. New York, St Martin's Pr, 1993.

This book contains a collection of eleven original essays intended to introduce students to the main core areas of philosophy. The introductory chapter defines important concepts and attempts to provide a working definition of philosophy. The remaining ten chapters consider the major areas of philosophy, aesthetics, philosophy of religion, personal identity, philosophy of mind, and cognitive science.

Adams, Marilyn McCord. Fides Quaerens Intellectum: St Anselm's Method in Philosophical Theology. *Faith Phil*, 9(4), 409-435, O 92.

This paper argues that Anselm's method in philosophical theology is shaped by five fundamental factors. They are: 1) his appreciation of the ontological incommensuration between god and creatures; 2) his commitment to the infallible authority of Scripture as interpreted through the creeds and conciliar pronouncements; 3) his conviction that humans are made in God's image; 4) his conception of inquiry as essentially a Divine-human collaboration; and 5) his understanding of human inquiry as holistic and developmental.

Adams, Marilyn McCord. Aristotle and the Sacrament of the Altar: A Crisis in Medieval Aristotelianism. *Can J Phil*, Supp(17), 195-249, 1991.

Adams, Marilyn McCord. God and Evil: Polarities of a Problem. *Phil Stud*, 69(2-3), 167-186, Mr 93.

Adams, Marilyn McCord. Julian of Norwich on the Tender Loving Care of Mother Jesus in Our Knowledge of God, Clark, Kelly James (ed). Dordrecht, Kluwer, 1992.

Adams, Marilyn McCord. Philosophy and the Bible: The Areopagus Speech. *Faith Phil*, 9(2), 135-150, Ap 92.

Philosophy does not get much coverage in the Bible, but what there is seems to give it a bad press. If Colossians 2:8 seems to lump philosophy with deceitful human tradition, the harmonization of Paul's experience at Athens (in Acts 17) with I Corinthians 1-2 has seemed to many to imply that philosophical apologetics is wrong-headed, and should yield the field exclusively to kerygmatic preaching. This interpretation challenges the legitimacy of the Society of Christian Philosophers' main aim: to integrate faith with philosophy! In this paper, I apply the methods of Biblical criticism to the Areopagus speech, and concede (from an examination of parallels and sources) that the speech does attempt to meet philosophers on their own ground. On the other hand, I argue that attention to the normative structure of the Acts-speeches and to their deployment of proof texts, suggests a missionary strategy that—so far from being inimical to the methods and purposes of our society—can be seen to coincide with them!

Adams, Marilyn McCord. Sin as Uncleanness in Philosophical Perspectives, 5: Philosophy of Religion, 1991, Tomberlin, James E (ed). Atascadero, Ridgeview, 1991.

Adams, Marilyn McCord. The Problem of Hell: A Problem of Evil for Christians in Reasoned Faith, Stump, Eleonore (ed). Ithaca, Cornell Univ Pr, 1993.

Adams, Robert Merrihew. An Anti-Molinist Argument in Philosophical Perspectives, 5: Philosophy of Religion, 1991, Tomberlin, James E (ed). Atascadero, Ridgeview, 1991.

The paper proposes an alternative version of an argument, due to William Hasker, against Molina's Theory of Middle Knowledge.

Adams, Robert Merrihew. Miracles, Laws of Nature and Causation—II. *Aris Soc*, Supp(66), 207-224, 1992.

Adams, Robert Merrihew. Truth and Subjectivity in Reasoned Faith, Stump, Eleonore (ed). Ithaca, Cornell Univ Pr, 1993.

Adams, Todd. Agency Theory: The Dilemma of Thomas C Upham. *Trans Peirce Soc*, 28(3), 547-568, Sum 92.

Thomas Upham was an American follower of Thomas Reid's commonsense realism. In this article I examine Upham's views on agency as they appeared in his *A Philosophical and Practical Treatise on the Will* (1834). Upham attempted to show that we act freely but also that our actions are caused. He rejected Reid's agent causality because it led to indeterminism. Motives must be understood as causes, yet the will is not determined. The key is to distinguish between preparative and effective causes. Upham's attempt is interesting, but does not succeed. His theory is virtually identical with Reid's agent causality.

Addelson, Kathryn Pyne. Knower/Doers and Their Moral Problems in Feminist Epistemologies, Alcoff, Linda (ed). New York, Routledge, 1993.

Addinall, Peter. *Philosophy and Biblical Interpretation: A Study in Nineteenth-Century Conflict*. New York, Cambridge Univ Pr, 1991.

This study explores the nature of the conflict between science and religion. It shows through a detailed examination of this conflict as it was manifested in nineteenth-century Britain that religion and science, properly understood, cannot co-exist in mutual harmony. The legacy of their conflict has been passed on, greatly to the detriment of religious belief. In its effort to demarcate the outlines of a genuine biblical theology, the book casts light on important questions of biblical interpretation, and demands a radical reassessment of the meaning of science for society.

Adiushkin, V N. The Social Philosophy of N Berdiaev in Light of *Perestroika*. *Sov Stud Phil*, 30(4), 48-63, Spr 92.

Adjukiewicz, Kazimierz. Kotarbinski's 'Elements of the Theory of Knowledge, Formal Logic ...' in Kotarbinski: Logic, Semantics and Ontology, Wolenski, Jan (ed). Dordrecht, Kluwer, 1990.

AUTHOR INDEX WITH ABSTRACTS 389 Aiken, David W

Adkins, Barbara. Structural Inquiry, Human Agency and the Contribution of Harré and Bhaskar: A Case Study of Wright's "Classes". *J Theor Soc Behav*, 23(2), 157-173, Je 93.

Wright's work, *Classes*, and the debate surrounding this research are used as a case study in which to explore the place of agent-centered explanation in structural inquiry. It is argued that the insights provided by Harre and Bhaskar help to clarify the purpose of structural analysis and to identify stages in the process. The paper suggests that questions of agency apply at each stage of inquiry and that the role of questions of agency becomes clearer if we consider these at the level of actual studies of structural determination.

Adler, Jonathan. An Optimist's Pessimism: Conversation and Conjunction in Probability and Rationality, Eells, Ellery (ed). Amsterdam, Rodopi, 1991.

A critical analysis is offered of the interpretation of studies of probabilistic reasoning, especially with conjunction. I argue that a conversational account can go far toward explaining the results. I then challenge the usual framework for understanding the debate about such studies. The framework treats it as an opposition between pessimists, who hold that subjects are involved in deep-seated violations of rationality, and optimists, who deny that such violations are possible. Instead, the proper framework for evaluation is multifaceted, subjects' judgments are criticizable and rational.

Adler, Jonathan. Crime Rates by Race and Causal Relevance: A Reply to Levin. *J Soc Phil*, 24(1), 176-184, Spr 93.

In a recent article, Michael Levin concludes that since "young black males are significantly more likely to commit crimes against persons than are members of any other racially identified group" we are justified in avoiding them in isolated circumstances and the government is warranted in using its coercive power to detain and, presumably, search them without specific evidence of wrongdoing. Levin's arguments rest upon the assumption that probability alone, and not causal relevance (or lawfulness), is a sufficient factual basis for drawing his conclusions. I argue against this assumption.

Adler, Jonathan. Reasonableness, Bias, and the Untapped Power of Procedure. *Synthese*, 94(1), 105-125, Ja 93.

Reasonableness as an ideal involves commitment to impartial procedures to adjudicate disputes. The commitment can be criticized for being too weak, since it does not eliminate disagreements, and too strong, since it enforces uniformity. I argue against these criticisms via an illustration (the hiring procedures of an academic department) meant to show how even those committed to rigorous procedures, rarely meet up to their own standards. One obstacle is an interest in personal understanding at the expense of real understanding. In conclusion, I attempt to resolve the puzzle that, though reasonableness is minimally demanding and universally avowed, it is uncommon.

Adler, Pierre. Prolegomena to Phenomenology: Intuition or Argument. *Grad Fac Phil J*, 16(1), 3-76, 1993.

The paper examines the conceptually originative moments of phenomenology, particularly Husserl's critique of psychologism (i.e., his undoing of the reduction of logic to psychology), which forms the centerpiece of his "prolegomena to pure logic." Close scrutiny of this critique will reveal it to be hybrid, i.e., to be both an ontological and a linguistic one. In conclusion, it will be shown that the latter and its implications render one-sided Husserl's institution of intuition as the sole proper provider of evidence within his method, and inadequate his understanding of language and reflection.

Adorno, Theodor W and Nicholsen, Shierry Weber (trans). *Hegel: Three Studies*. Cambridge, MIT Pr, 1993.

Adriaensen, M. Entre la mort et la vie: d'une comparaison entre l'homme et la machine. *Commun Cog*, 25(1), 53-72, 1992.

Adrian, Lynne M. Emma Goldman and the Spirit of Artful Living in Frontiers in American Philosophy, Volume I, Burch, Robert W (ed). College Station, Texas A&M Univ Pr, 1992.

Emma Goldman, the self-educated anarchist orator, is an important, though neglected, figure of the classical period of American philosophy. I explorer two related concepts in Goldman's thought. First how her aesthetic concept—"artful living", or life as a form of art—is both related to specific views of Dewey, *and* reflects the contemporary progressive artistic community's changed view of art as a *process* rather than art as a *product*. Secondly, I show how this concept of "artful living" reflects several key differences in the use of organicism from the Transcendental sources from which it was drawn.

Aertsen, Jan A. Transcendentality of Beauty in the Middle Ages (in Czechoslovakian). *Estetika*, 28(4), 193-203, 1991.

Africk, Henry. Classical Logic, Intuitionistic Logic, and the Peirce Rule. *Notre Dame J Form Log*, 33(2), 229-235, Spr 92.

A simple method is provided for translating proofs in Gentzen's LK into proofs in Gentzen's LJ with the Peirce rule adjoined. A consequence is a simpler cut elimination operator for LJ + Peirce that is primitive recursive.

Agarwal, M M. Nothingness and Freedom: Sartre and Krishnamurti. *J Indian Counc Phil Res*, 9(1), 45-58, S-D 91.

Agassi, Joseph. Autonomy and the Philosopher. *Method Sci*, 25(1), 1-10, 1992.

Undeniably Wittgenstein endorsed the Socratic concern for people's souls and in its light condemned traditional philosophical doctrines as detrimental to individual autonomy and self-education. Regrettably he refrained from saying so, implying it in his theory of meaning. Now that Quine's critique of all past theories of meaning prevails, it is time to return to explicit statement of variants of the Socratic doctrine, e.g., Karl Popper's *The Open Society*, and debate them. Is this in accord with the teaching of Richard Rorty?

Agassi, Joseph. Conditions for Interpersonal Communication. *Method Sci*, 26(1), 8-17, 1993.

The traditional dichotomy between truth by nature and truth by convention or between appearances and reality leave communication outside the universe of discourse. This permitted the Cartesian classical thought experiment that could and perhaps did land philosophy in a hopeless solipsism. Solipsism is not a serious philosophy and it need not be refuted. Rather what is required is the amendment of the background knowledge that had led to its imposition on philosophy. What is required is a communication theory that will grapple with communication problems and with the fact that communication often breaks down, not only in philosophical contexts.

Agassi, Joseph. False Prophecy Versus True Quest: A Most Challenge to Contemporary Relativists. *Phil Soc Sci*, 22(3), 285-312, S 92.

A good theory of rationality should accommodate debates over first principles, such as those of rationality. The modest challenge made in this article is that relativists try to explain the (intellectual) value of some debates about first principles (absolute presuppositions, basic assumptions, intellectual frameworks, intellectual commitments, and paradigms). Relativists claim to justify moving with relative ease from one framework to another, translating chunks of one into the other; this technique is essential for historians, anthropologists, and others. Thus ideas concerning false prophecy are transferable to contemporary discussions. Ancient false prophets offered illusions of overcoming difficult problems cheaply; relativists do that too. The problem that relativism purports to solve cheaply is that of legitimizing pluralism. As the absolutist theory of truth is intuitively problematic, relativism seems intuitively more acceptable, but this intuitive advantage vanishes when it manifests as false prophecy.

Agassi, Joseph. The Heuristic Bent. *Phil Rhet*, 26(1), 9-30, 1993.

Karl Popper compares the amoeba with Einstein as problem solvers yet contrasts the astrologer with Einstein—even though every human is more intelligent than any amoeba. Popper thus invites an evolutionary scale of adaptation, which is neither historicist nor inductive. Different ideas, from animal psychology, child psychology, cognitive science, linguistics, and artificial intelligence should unite in one scheme of evolutionary methodology, as outlined in this essay.

Agazzi, Evandro. The Universe as a Scientific and Philosophical Problem in Philosophy and the Origin and Evolution of the Universe, Agazzi, Evandro (ed). Norwell, Kluwer, 1991.

Agazzi, Evandro. Varieties of Meaning and Truth in The Philosophy of A J Ayer, Hahn, Lewis E (ed). Peru, Open Court, 1992.

The paper considers Ayer's conception of meaning and truth and tries to see whether this is compatible with certain enlargements of the strict empiricist criteria originally stipulated by him. Such enlargement is only partially possible due to the exclusion of "intentionality" which is typical of Ayer's approach. By taking intentionality into consideration it is possible to accept a reasonable enlargement of meaning and truth able to cover, besides descriptive sentences, also the truth of theories, or moral statements, and of value judgements.

Agazzi, Evandro (ed) and Cordero, Alberto (ed). *Philosophy and the Origin and Evolution of the Universe*. Norwell, Kluwer, 1991.

Aguiló Regla, Josep. Lenguaje jurídico, lenguaje documental y tesauro. *Theoria (Spain)*, 5(12-13), 31-65, N 90.

The aim of this paper is twofold. On the one hand, it tries to analyze and systematize some of the concepts used when approaching the linguistic problems concerning the legal documentation automatic systems: legal language, documentary language, linguistic coordination (*a priori* and *a posteriori*) and thesaurus. On the other hand, it intends to carry out a detailed study of the legal thesauri, focusing basically on its structural elements: the vocabulary and the paradigmatic relationships.

Aguirre Oraa, J M. Habermas: teoría del conocimiento y teoría de la sociedad. *Pensamiento*, 188(47), 415-448, O-D 91.

El artículo analiza el programa "epistemológico-social" de Jürgen Habermas en *su primera etapa*, hasta mediados de los años setenta, antes de su posterior desplazamiento profundizador del paradigma de la filosofía de la conciencia al paradigma de la acción comunicativa. La reflexión de Habermas y sus análisis históricos y epistemológicos van orientados a demostrar la tesis de que una críticia radical del conocimiento sólo es posible imbricándola en una teoría de la sociedad. Este programa epistemológico de textura "materialista-transcendental" desarrolla fundamentalmente la relación existente entre el *conocimiento*, el *interés* y la *emancipación* e intenta recuperar la función y el sentido de la reflexión y de la autoreflexión.

Ahlberg, Lars-Olof. The Nature and Limits of Analytic Aesthetics. *Brit J Aes*, 33(1), 5-16, Ja 93.

Analytical aesthetics conceives aesthetics as a meta-philosophical investigation of the central concepts of aesthetics. The conviction that the concept of art cannot be defined in terms of necessary and jointly sufficient properties is taken by some writers (Shusterman, Lüdeking) to be characteristic of *all* analytical philosophy of art. This view is unacceptable, since many aestheticians working in the analytic tradition have offered definitions of art (Beardsley, Osborne, Dickie). The analytical aesthetician's exclusive interest in conceptual analysis has led to a disregard for the historical and evaluative dimensions of art.

Aihara, Setsuko (trans) and Parkes, Graham R (trans) and Muneto, Sonoda. The Eloquent Silence of Zarathustra in Nietzsche and Asian Thought, Parkes, Graham (ed). Chicago, Univ of Chicago Pr, 1991.

Aiken, David W. The Decline from Authority: Kierkegaard on Intellectual Sin. *Int Phil Quart*, 33(1), 21-35, Mr 93.

This essay has a twofold purpose: First, to examine Kierkegaard's critique of the intellectual life; second, to show that this critique does not necessarily entail epistemological subjectivism, particularly in light of his distinctive conception of religious authority. An exposition of how Anti-Climacus indicts speculative thought forms the point of departure for a discussion of "intellectual insubordination," a central theme in Kierkegaard's neglected *Book on Adler*. The issue of religious authority having been broached, the essay then explores Kierkegaard's insightful and prophetic schema for interpreting the stages through which the self-deceiving intellect passes in its flight from intellectual obedience.

Airaksinen, Timo. Original Populations and Environmental Rights in Applied Philosophy, Almond, Brenda (ed). New York, Routledge, 1992.

Aizawa, Kenneth. Cognitive Science in Reflections on Philosophy, McHenry, Leemon (ed). New York, St Martin's Pr, 1993.

This book chapter provides an elementary introduction to cognitive science for first-year philosophy students. It discusses the computationalist and connectionist approaches, suggesting some of the appeal and some of the limitations of each.

Aizawa, Kenneth and Adams, Fred. Fodorian Semantics, Pathologies, and "Block's Problem". *Mind Mach*, 3(1), 97-104, F 93.

In two recent books, Jerry Fodor has developed a set of sufficient conditions for an object "X" to non-naturally and non-derivatively mean X. In an earlier paper we presented three reasons for thinking Fodor's theory to be inadequate. One of these problems we have dubbed the "Pathologies Problem". In response to queries concerning the relationship between the Pathologies Problem and what Fodor calls "Block's Problem", we argue that, while Block's Problem does not threaten *Fodor's view*, the Pathologies Problem does.

Ajvaz, Michal. The Secret of Books (in Czechoslovakian). *Estetika*, 28(4), 224-227, 1991.

Akama, Seiki. The Gentzen-Kripke Construction of the Intermediate Logic LQ. *Notre Dame J Form Log*, 33(1), 148-153, Wint 92.

Akiba, Fuminori. Die Entwicklung der Lehre von Grundsätzen—Hermann Cohens Ästhetik (in Japanese). *Bigaku*, 43(2), 15-24, Fall 92.

H Cohen erklärt den Prozess des Kunstschaffens durch die Entwicklung des ästhetische Gefühl. Das reine Gefühl entsteht in der Ausgleichung der Gegenbewegung von Naturerkenntnis und sittlicher Erkenntnis. Die Absicht meiner Abhandlung besteht darin, durch die Analyse der beiden Erkenntnisse die Tatsache zu argumentieren, dass das reine Gefühl-im Gegensatz zur bisherigen Auslegung-sich nicht seiner empirischen und faktischen Bedingtheiten entreissen lässt. Naturerkenntnis. In seiner "Logik," basierend auf Kants Lehre von den Grundsätzen, erklärt Cohen die naturwissenschaftliche Erkenntnis als die undenlichewechselseitige Bewegung von Empfindung und Denken (Kategorien). Eine neue Zusammenwirkung der Kategorien entdeckt die bis dahin verborgene Möglichkeit der Empfindung. Die sittliche Erkenntnis ist begründet in der Liebe zur Natur des Menschen als Durchdringung von Leib und Seele. Sie pendelt bald nach der einen (Leib), bald nach der anderen (Seele) Seite, Die sittliche Erkenntnis also ist ebenso geschichtlich bedingt wie die Naturerkenntnis.

Akins, Kathleen A. A Bat without Qualities? in Consciousness: Psychological and Philosophical Essays, Davies, Martin (ed). Cambridge, Blackwell, 1993.

Aksiuchits, Viktor. Westernizers and Nativists Today. *Russian Stud Phil*, 31(4), 83-94, Spr 93.

Al-Hibri, Azizah Y (ed) and Simons, Margaret A (ed). *Hypatia Reborn: Essays in Feminist Philosophy*. Bloomington, Indiana Univ Pr, 1990.

Al-Razi, Zakariyya and Muhammad, Abū Bakr and Butterworth, Charles E (trans). The Book of the Philosophic Life. *Interpretation*, 20(3), 227-236, Spr 93.

Alanen, Lilli. Descartes, Conceivability, and Logical Modality in Thought Experiments in Science and Philosophy, Horowitz, Tamara (ed). Lanham, Rowman & Littlefield, 1991.

This paper examines Descartes' controversial theory of the creation of eternal truths and the views of modality attributed to Descartes in recent interpretations of it. It shows why attempts to make Descartes' view intelligible by distinctions of different kinds of modality fail to do justice to his theory, which is radical indeed without being incoherent or involving universal possibilism or irrationalism. Descartes' opposition to traditional rationalist views of modality, it suggests, can be seen instead as foreshadowing contemporary views prefixed, logical structure of reality or of the divine intellect.

Alcoba, Manuel Luna. El concepto de emanación en Leibniz. *Themata*, 8, 29-44, 1991.

Alcoff, Linda (ed). Bibliography of Feminist Epistemologies in Feminist Epistemologies, Alcoff, Linda (ed). New York, Routledge, 1993.

Alcoff, Linda. Feminist Politics and Foucault in Crises in Continental Philosophy, Dallery, Arleen B (ed). Albany, SUNY Pr, 1990.

Along with many feminist theorists I find Foucault's social analysis very useful. His concerns intersect with feminists in exploring the social constitution of sexuality as well as relations of power and domination that exist in the so-called sphere of "private life". However, in this paper I want to mark out two obstacles Foucault puts in the path of feminist work: subjectivity and political practice. His social ontology, I argue precludes an adequate theory of resistance by undercutting the possibility of agency, and his prescriptions for practice disallow the creation of an effective opposition movement that contests for discursive dominance.

Alcoff, Linda and Dalmiya, Vrinda. Are 'Old Wives' Tales' Justified? in Feminist Epistemologies, Alcoff, Linda (ed). New York, Routledge, 1993.

Alcoff, Linda (ed) and Potter, Elizabeth (ed). *Feminist Epistemologies*. New York, Routledge, 1993.

Aldaz Gazolaz, Antonio F. El racionalismo en Espinosa. *Themata*, 8, 11-27, 1991.

Alejandro, Roberto. Rawls's Communitarianism. *Can J Phil*, 23(1), 75-99, Mr 93.

This essay offers a discussion of John Rawls's understanding of community as it was presented in *A Theory of Justice* and its implications for a pluralist society. It also addresses Michael Sandel's critique of the "individuated subject" that, in his view, underlies justice as fairness. Rawls's communitarianism doesnot depend upon the original position, but on his understanding of associations, institutions, and moral psychology. In Rawls's communitarianism, the priority of the self over its ends is either denied or substantially modified to the extend that the individual confirms his/her own worth, not by standards he/she has created, but by norms and criteria accepted by his/her associates. Likewise, the Rawlsian self needs both institutitions and "the actions of others" to develop a mature sense of justice. Rawls's paradigm rests on the monopoly justice exercises over institutions and the individual's character. The complexity of the human condition challenges that monopoly. Rawls's community is not one of diversity, but uniformity. It is not Kantian, but Platonic.

Alemany, Francisco Salto. In Continuity: A Reflection on the Passive Synthesis of Sameness in Analecta Husserliana, XXXIV, Tymieniecka, Anna-Teresa (ed). Dordrecht, Kluwer, 1992.

An analysis of individuation, sameness and numerical identity from a phenomenological standpoint is purported in the work. Mainly, two arguments are developed in the paper concluding: a) two paradoxes arise from the study of the "Urphänomen" of contrast within the framework of passive synthesis, b) Husserl's own study of such preaffective passive synthesis is insufficient, a precise notion of synthesis in the here relevant sense is defined and applied to both formal (temporal) and internal conditions for an individual phenomenon.

Ales Bello, A. La filosofia di Edith Stein. *Aquinas*, 34(3), 575-580, S-D 91.

Alexander, H A. Kaufman on Kaplan and Process Theology: A Post-Positivist Perspective. *Process Stud*, 20(4), 200-203, Wint 91.

This paper responds to William Kaufman's comparison of the theologies of M Kaplan and Alfred North Whitehead. It argues that Kaufman is correct in viewing Kaplan as a pragmatist who has much in common with Whitehead but that he fails to note how Whitehead moved beyond the naive positivism inherent in Kaplan's thought.

Alexander, Larry. Inculpatory and Exculpatory Mistakes and the Fact/Law Distinction: An Essay in Memory of Myke Bayles. *Law Phil*, 12(1), 33-70, F 93.

In this article I deal with the law/fact distinction in the context of the criminal law's treatment of exculpatory and inculpatory mistakes. I conclude that the difficulty in drawing a distinction between mistakes of law and mistakes of fact does not pose a serious problem for the criminal law's exculpatory doctrines, but it does pose a serious problem for the law of attempts, where mistakes inculpate. I show that none of the approaches that have been put forward to deal with inculpatory mistakes are completely satisfactory.

Alexander, Larry. Practical Reason and Statutory Interpretation. *Law Phil*, 12(3), 319-328, Ag 93.

I examine the "practical reason" approach to statutory interpretation, according to which the interpreter should look not only to text, legislative history, and other indicia of legislative intent, but also to post-enactment history and current values. I argue that if "practical reason" represents an epistemology of statutory interpretation, its proponents owe us an account of statutory ontology, without which their claims cannot be evaluated. On the other hand, if the practical reason approach claims to be itself an account of statutory ontology, then it is implausible. Facts and values cannot be ontologically blended in the way the approach describes.

Alexander, Larry. Self-Defense, Justification, and Excuse. *Phil Pub Affairs*, 22(1), 53-66, Wint 93.

In this article I argue, contrary to Judith Thomson, that there is no general right not to be killed that we possess until we forfeit it through aggression or waive it. Thus, many homicides that Thomson labels as justifiable self-defense because they prevent killings of innocent persons by the victims of the homicides I regard as at most excusable homicides. I argue that the justifiability of homicides that save others' lives is a complex matter involving many more factors than Thomson considers.

Alexander, Larry. The ADL Hate Crime Statute and the First Amendment. *Crim Just Ethics*, 11(2), 49-51, Sum-Fall 92.

In this article I argue that hate crime statutes, those that enhance the punishment for certain crimes when those crimes are committed for bigoted motives, raise some deep first amendment problems. Although the underlying crimes are not conduct that is constitutionally protected, the Supreme Court has recently reaffirmed that unprotected conduct cannot be selectively punished based on the message it conveys if the message itself is constitutionally protected. Thus, the constitutional status of hate crime statutes turns on whether the enhanced punishment is based on an otherwise constitutionally protected message conveyed by the crime and its motive. I argue that some of the rationales for the hate crime statutes are based on protected messages.

Alexander, Larry. Voluntary Acts: The Child/Davidson Trilemma. *Crim Just Ethics*, 11(2), 98-99, Sum-Fall 92.

James Childs attempts to square the criminal law's voluntary act requirement with the existence of negligence and strict liability crimes by relying on Donald Davidson's analysis of action ("intentiona; under some description"). I argue that either the Childs/Davidson approach renders the voluntary act requirement too easily satisfied, or it requires a culpable state of mind to mark the onset of the criminal act, thus making negligence and strict liability crimes problematic.

Alexander, Natalie. Piecings from a Second Reader. *Hypatia*, 7(2), 177-187, Spr 92.

A new collection of critical essays from bell hooks takes as its theme the deep longing for a critical voice. I explore some motifs that operate across the divergent topics of her essays. She writes of the dangers of commodification, of "reassuring" images, of individualism. I also explore the paths of Hooks's uniquely black postmodernism: her critique of various essentialisms, her philosophically important conception of subjectivity, and her beautiful and powerful transformations of multiple discourses.

Alexander, Peter. Locke on Solidity and Incompressibility in Logical Foundations, Mahalingam, Indira (ed). New York, St Martin's Pr, 1991.

This paper begins from the question whether two material objects could occupy the same place at the same time. The author considers some views of David Sanford with particular reference to his use of Locke's views and argues that he has misunderstood Locke on solidity and incompressibility. The author puts what he takes to be Locke's real view about this matter.

Alexander, Ronald G. Personal Identity and Self-Constitution. *Personalist Forum*, 8/1(Supp), 83-89, Spr 92.

In addressing the concept of self-constitution in his book, *I: The Philosophy and Psychology of Personal Identity*, Jonathan Glover defends a folk-psychological interpretation of the ego, finds Freudian psychology helpful in his analysis of self-constitution, and puts the preceding in a "narrative" or existentialistic context. I raise the following problems: 1) Does self-constitution contribute to reidentification? Yes—if taken only from a third-person point of view. 3) If 'person' encompasses more than the term 'human being', then is there something "more" than physical and psychological properties? Yes. The self is supervenient.

Alexander, Thomas M. Dewey and the Metaphysical Imagination. *Trans Peirce Soc*, 28(2), 203-215, Spr 92.

Metaphysics for Dewey involves the use of *imagination* as well as reason. Imagination for pragmatists is seeing the actual in light of the possible. This is a temporal mode of awareness which is related to our active embodiment in the world. Metaphysics is thus a necessary part of wisdom, the art of living well.

Alexander, Thomas M. John Dewey and the Moral Imagination: Beyond Putnam and Rorty toward a Postmodern Ethics. *Trans Peirce Soc*, 29(3), 369-400, Sum 93.

Alexander, Thomas M. Santayana's Unbearable Lightness of Being: Aesthetics as a Prelude to Ontology. *Bull Santayana Soc*, 11, 1-10, Fall 93.

This essay argues that our understanding of the aesthetic and our aesthetics of experience may determine the ontology we have. As examples I show how both Santayana and Dewey made the aesthetic mode of experience absolutely central, and yet, because of their very different views of it, created very different ontologies. Santayana's formalistic aesthetics led to modified Platonism whereas Dewey's contextual aesthetics led to an embodied naturalism.

Alexander, Thomas M. The Context of Community. *SW Phil Stud*, 14, 16-25, Spr 92.

Discussions in ethics and social-political theory start with a series of dichotomies: individual-state, moral-political, self-society, etc. Such discussions have terminated in the (let's face it) dead-end debate of utilitarian and deontological ethics. I propose an alternative approach which *begins* with the primacy of *community* and then proceeds to treat the topics of individuality, the state, and the rest from that context. We grow up as members of communities, not as absolute individuals or members of collective wholes, so this option has the advantage of beginning with real experience.

Alexander, Thomas M. The Moral Imagination and the Aesthetics of Human Existence in Moral Education and the Liberal Arts, Mitias, Michael H (ed). Westport, Greenwood Pr, 1992.

Against the attacks on liberalism as an educational philosophy made by Bloom and Hersch, I argue that Dewey has provided a better defense for the humanities by showing the centrality of imagination and aesthetic understanding for our moral intelligence.

Alexander Jr, Henry A. Surface Knowledge in Certainty and Surface in Epistemology and Philosophical Method, Martinich, A P (ed). Lewiston, Mellen Pr, 1991.

Alexy, Robert. A Discourse-Theoretical Conception of Practical Reason. *Ratio Juris*, 5(3), 231-251, D 92.

Contemporary discussions about practical reason or practical rationality invoke four competing views which can be named as follows by reference to their historical models: Aristotelian, Hobbesian, Kantian and Nietzschean. The subject-matter of this article is a defence of the Kantian conception of practical rationality in the interpretation of discourse theory. At the heart, lies the justification and the application of the rules of discourse. The three parts are as follows: a transcendental-pragmatic argument; and argument which takes account of the maximization of individual utility and an empirical premise about an interest in correctness. Within the framework of the problem of application, the article outlines a justification of human rights and of the basic institutions of the democratic constitutional state on the basis of discourse theory.

Alexy, Robert. Justification and Application of Norms. *Ratio Juris*, 6(2), 157-170, Jl 93.

According to the author there is no doubt that one has to distinguish between the justification and the application of norms. Problems are seen only to arise if one asks what exactly the distinction is and which consequences have to be drawn from it. Recently, Klaus Günther, in particular, has searched for this distinction and connected it with far-reaching conclusions concerning the theory of norms, arguments, and morals. His theses are the object of the author's considerations.

Alfano, G. Note sul concetto di alienazione in Hegel. *Sapienza*, 44(4), 447-459, 1991.

Algra, Keimpe. 'Place' in Context in Theophrastus, Fortenbaugh, W W (ed). New Brunswick, Transaction Books, 1992.

Allaerts, Wilfried. Inquiry Into the Spatio-Temporal Contingency of Cellular Communication Systems. *Commun Cog*, 25(4), 277-294, 1992.

Allaire, Edwin B and Bergmann, Gustav and Heald, William (ed). *New Foundations of Ontology*. Madison, Univ of Wisconsin Pr, 1992.

Bergmann's last book length manuscript represents his final attempt to propose and defend a system of categories appropriate for a realistic ontology rich enough to account for the existence of minds and an adequate grounding of mathematics. An extension of Bergmann's phenomenological atomism, the book also includes a vigorous attempt to show that "formal facts," including not only analytic facts, but also the possessing of syntactical forms by all facts, are "objective" features of a world whose fundamental core consists of atomic facts and the particular and universal "things" of which they are composed.

Allan, George. Environmental Philosophizing and Environmental Activism. *Res Phil Technol*, 12, 119-127, 1992.

Paul Durbin says environmentally concerned philosophers and scientists are morally obliged to be political activists. But we also need what Dewey called pragmatic intelligence to determine if our goals are de jure goods and our methods suitable. And we need speculative intelligence to reshape our cultural traditions, worldviews, where they support practices detrimental to the environment, and to create perspectives able to reconcile current polarities in our thinking. We need to do environmental metaphysics, so as in the long run to fashion transformative interpretations able to guide well our environmental practices.

Allan, James. Justice, Language and Hume: A Reply to Matthew Kramer. *Hume Stud*, 18(1), 81-94, Ap 92.

The author defends the coherence of Hume's convention-based picture of the origins of justice. Bearing in mind the sceptical Humean view of reason as motivationally inert, there are no grounds for holding that the escape to justice needs to be driven by reason. If that be granted, it also follows that the escape need not pre-suppose or rely on a language which is already in place and widely understood. Criticisms of Hume which take such a line fail.

Allchin, Douglas. How Do You Falsify a Question? Crucial Tests versus Crucial Demonstrations. *Proc Phil Sci Ass*, 1, 74-88, 1992.

I highlight a category of experiment—what I am calling 'demonstrations'—that differs in justificatory mode and argumentative role from the more familiar 'crucial tests'. 'Tests' are constructed such that alternative results are equally and symmetrically informative; they help discriminate between alternative solutions within a problem-field, where questions are shared. 'Demonstrations' are notably asymmetrical (for example, "failures" are often not telling), yet they are effective, if not "crucial," in interparadigm dispute, to legitimate questions themselves. The Ox-Phos Controversy in bioenergetics serves as an integral case study.

Allen, Barry G. Difference Unlimited in Working Through Derrida, Madison, Gary B (ed). Evanston, Northwestern Univ Pr, 1993.

Traditionally the sign is secondary in an ontological sense, deriving its identity and existence from something that is not a sign, something more originally determined than any sign, like nature or intentional consciousness. I trace this theme from Aristotle to Husserl, presenting an overview of Derrida's semiology. I discuss the implications of his argumentation for linguistics before and after Saussure, arguing that identity, meaning, and truth-value cannot be settled, not even in principle, by a science or logic or philosophy of language indifferent to historical and political differences of power.

Allen, Barry G. *Truth in Philosophy*. Cambridge, Harvard Univ Pr, 1993.

Offers an overview of the problem of truth from antiquity to the present, discussing Greek and early-modern philosophy, Nietzsche, James, Heidegger, Derrida, Wittgenstein, and Foucault. The argument is organized around two philosophical questions: What is wrong with a correspondence theory of truth, and (Nietzsche's question) what good is truth, why its claim to a superior value? The author identifies and attacks the assumptions of correspondence, presenting a powerful argument for the immanence of truth in practice. The book is clearly and carefully written, and should equally interest philosophers of analytic or continental persuasion.

Allen, Colin. Mental Content. *Brit J Phil Sci*, 43(4), 537-553, D 92.

Daniel Dennett and Stephen Stich have independently argued that the contents of mental states cannot be specified precisely enough for the purposes of scientific prediction and explanation. Dennett takes this to support his view that the proper role for mentalistic terms in science is heuristic. Stich takes it to support his view that cognitive science should be done without reference to mental content at all. I defend a realist understanding of mental content against these attacks by Dennett and Stich. I argue that they both mistake the difficulty of making contents ascriptions precise for the impossibility of doing so.

Allen, Colin and Hand, Michael. *Logic Primer*. Cambridge, MIT Pr, 1992.

Logic Primer presents a complete introduction to natural deduction systems for sentential logic and first order predicate logic, including truth tables and model theory. These topics are presented without superfluous discussion, allowing the instructor to choose how to present them. The text includes over 500 exercises and an appendix with solutions to more than half of them.

Allen, Diogenes. The Concept of Reading and the 'Book of Nature' in Simone Weil's Philosophy of Culture, Bell, Richard H (ed). New York, Cambridge Univ Pr, 1993.

The chapter has two principle aims. It seeks to examine Simone Weil's concept of reading (or *lecture*) from the point of view of its interconnections with other concepts in her thought, namely, necessity, order, suffering, work, and decreation. The other concern is with her claim that the visible things of nature are adumbrations of the invisible God. She claims that by undergoing an apprenticeship, we are able "to read necessity behind sensation, to read order behind necessity, to read God behind order." The chapter presents the apprenticeship that enables us to make these progressively higher readings until we are able to read nature religiously.

Allen, Jonathan. Liberals, Communitarians, and Political Theory. *S Afr J Phil*, 11(4), 77-90, N 92.

In this article, I suggest an interpretation of the current liberal-communitarian debate which may assist in clarifying some of the confusions which have grown up around it. I begin by presenting the 'strong' communitarianism of MacIntyre and Sandel as a critique of liberal theory and liberal practice, and as an attempt to relate the two. In the second section of the article, I argue that the 'strong' communitarian critique fails as a result of its conflation of liberal theory and liberal practice and its 'intellectualist' tendency to criticize the latter on the basis of a critique of the former. In the final section, I attempt to identify the core of this debate in a disagreement concerning the character and function of political theory.

Allen, Jonathan G. Rationality, Relativism, and Rorty. *S Afr J Phil*, 11(3), 52-61, Ag 92.

In this essay, I consider the claim that non-foundational, or anti-foundational, conceptions of rationality result in a relativism which, because of its lack of critical force, encourages existing patterns of injustice. In order to do this, I examine Richard Rorty's influential version of anti-foundationalism. I begin by reconstructing his assessment, and dismissal of foundationalism. Finally, I argue that although Rorty's thought does result in an insufficiently critical endorsement of the values and practices of his society, this does not result from his anti-foundationalist perspective, but rather from a mistaken restriction of the role of rationality and a misleading model of social interaction.

Allen, Prudence. A Woman and a Man as Prime Analogical Beings. *Amer Cath Phil Quart*, 66(4), 465-482, Autumn 92.

M A Krapiec' theory of analogy is applied to the related identities of woman and man. First, in an examination of infraontic analogy the ways in which an individual woman or man can be considered as analogical with herself or himself, as a particular kind of human being who has an identity of structure which persists through change is described. Then we consider inter-ontic analogy, or how women are analogous to one another or men are analogous to one another. Finally, we turn to a consideration of how a man and a woman might be considered as analogous to one another as prime analogical beings.

Allen, R T. Flew, Marx and Gnosticism. *Philosophy*, 68(263), 94-98, Ja 93.

Marx failed to give an 'index of alienation', which Flew says that he should have given because, ultimately, alienation is something that men cannot escape. For it is not just a function of the division of labour and class, but of particularity, differentiation, and finitude. It is a metaphysical malady for which there can be no cure. Marx took this notion of alienation from Hegel who inherited it from the Gnostics. But for Marx there is no way out of the world into which we have fallen.

Allen, R T. Mounce and Collingwood on Art and Craft. *Brit J Aes*, 33(2), 173-176, Ap 93.

Collingwood's distinction between art and craft is defended against Mounce's criticisms which misconceive what Collingwood meant by 'expression' and treat all intentional actions as the use of means to achieve ends beyond themselves.

Allen, R T. The Categories of Value. *J Speculative Phil*, 6(4), 277-300, 1992.

Instead of the usual distinction of 'intrinsic' and 'instrumental' value, four categories of value are distinguished: utility or instrumentality, foundational-value, ingredience, and performer—and performance value. All these arise from the fundamental category of activity. Activities set standards for performers and performances of them, for ingredients in them, for their foundations and for what is useful for them. Sub-categories of value (e.g., fulfillment, success, adequacy) are ways in which those standards are fulfilled. Consequently, all values arise from activities, the spheres of life and mind. The dichotomy of fact and value collapses. For the categories of value are both axiological and ontological, and performers and performances of activities are necessarily achievements of value or failures to achieve value.

Allen, R T. *The Structure of Value*. Brookfield, Avebury, 1993.

A study of all types of value, non moral and moral. Values are shown necessarily to arise from the activities of living and conscious beings, which project fields of value around them and are themselves achievers of value in the successful performance of their functions and other activities. Those activities also form the frames of reference by which they are evaluated. The alleged dichotomies of act and value, and of description and evaluation, are shown to be false. All descriptions of living and conscious beings and their operations are evaluations. The same is also shown to be true of human actions, which are exercises of pre-moral and moral responsibility.

Allen, Wayne. Hannah Arendt and the Ideological Structure of Totalitarianism. *Man World*, 26(2), 115-129, Ap 93.

Hannah Arendt's *The Origins of Totalitarianism* prompted controversy and acclaim. One reason for this was her methodology. Another reason is the centrality she gives to ideology. Her methodology is a vicarious attack on the scientism of modernity, which itself laid the groundwork for her formulation of ideology. Indeed, the modern claims to "know" the world led to the totalitarian effort to reshape man as a thinking animal. It is the effort to reshape the thinking mind that leads to totalitarian terror and destroys politics as a realm of discourse and opinion-getting.

Allen, Wayne. Terrorism and the Epochal Transformation of Politics. *Pub Affairs Quart*, 6(2), 133-154, Ap 92.

The spate of articles and books on terrorism that have appeared recently dwell on techniques, consequences, or even intentions. But little effort has been made to locate the metaphysical sources of the phenomenon, to isolate the mentality of those who promote or practice such monstrous acts. This article seeks to identify the provenance of terrorism in epochal shifts of political self-definition. From the classical period to the present, terrorism paradigmatically reflects a new ordering principle of public life. As the principle has shifted so has the quality and magnitude of the terrorism.

Allik, Tiina. Human Finitude and the Concept of Women's Experience. *Mod Theol*, 9(1), 67-86, Ja 93.

The essay argues that the use of the concept of women's experience to refer to a gender-specific awareness of some aspect of reality that is not mediated by concepts provided by particular communities implies a view of human persons that does not acknowledge the full scope of human finitude. This use undercuts the efforts of feminist theorists to affirm the value of human finitude. Explanations of gender differences in terms of the sensitivity of human beings to their social environment, on the other hand, use conceptualizations of human person-hood that acknowledge human finitude more adequately.

Allinson, Robert E. A Hermeneutic Reconstruction of the Child in the Well Example. *J Chin Phil*, 19(3), 297-308, S 92.

Allinson, Robert E. The Golden Rule as the Core Value in Confucianism and Christianity: Ethical Similarities and Differences. *Asian Phil*, 2(2), 173-185, 1992.

One side of this paper is devoted to showing that the Golden Rule, understood, rather than graded, familial love. In this respect Confucianism and Christianity are similar. The other side of this paper is devoted to arguing contra 18 centuries of commentators that the negative sentential formulation of the Golden Rule as found in Confucius cannot be converted to an affirmative sentential formulation (as is found in Christianity are different).

Allison, Henry E. Gurwitsch's Interpretation of Kant: Reflections of a Former Student. *Kantstudien*, 83(2), 208-221, 1992.

Allison, Lincoln. The Utilitarian Ethics of Punishment and Torture in The Utilitarian Response, Allison, Lincoln (ed). Newbury Park, Sage, 1990.

Allison, Lincoln (ed). *The Utilitarian Response*. Newbury Park, Sage, 1990.

Allison, Lincoln. Utilitarianism: What Is It and Why Should It Respond? in The Utilitarian Response, Allison, Lincoln (ed). Newbury Park, Sage, 1990.

Allport, P P. Are the Laws of Physics 'Economical with the Truth'?. *Synthese*, 94(2), 245-290, F 93.

The author sets out to counter several anti-realist arguments against laws. In particular, he draws on his own experience as a researcher in high energy physics to repudiate claims made about the actual practice of scientific research.

Almeder, Rober F and Fetzer, James H. *Glossary of Epistemology/ Philosophy of Science*. New York, Paragon House, 1993.

This glossary is intended to provide clear and concise definitions for the most important concepts that appear in the theory of knowledge and in the philosophy of science. Among the most important notions that occur in this context are alternative conceptions of inference and argument, of truth and confirmation, of probability and induction, of knowledge and justification, of scientific theories and scientific explanations, of rationalism and empiricism, together with brief sketches of some of the most important historical (Plato, Aristotle, etc.) and contemporary (Russell, Tarski, etc.) thinkers in these fields.

Almeder, Robert F. *Blind Realism: An Essay on Human Knowledge and Natural Science*. Lanham, Rowman & Littlefield, 1992.

This book is a defense of *Blind Realism*, i.e., the view that a) there is an external world, and b) some of our beliefs about such a world (including our theoretical belief) are correct descriptions of such a world, and c) there is no effective decision procedure for determining which of our confirmed beliefs actually succeed in correctly describing the external world.

Almeder, Robert F. *Death and Personal Survival: The Evidence for Life After Death*. Lanham, Rowman & Littlefield, 1992.

We examine non-standard books of evidence for ... in post-mortem survival. The book argues for *post mortem* survival after examining recent evidence from research on reincarnation, apparitional experiences, near-death and out-of-body experiences, and trance mediumship. Sceptical responses and problems with Cartesian egos are also examined.

Almeder, Robert F (ed) and Humber, James M (ed). *Biomedical Ethics Reviews 1992*. Clifton, Humana Pr, 1993.

Biomedical Ethics Reviews: 1992 is the tenth volume in a series of texts designed to review and update the literature on issues of central importance in bioethics today. Two topics are discussed in this volume: 1) Bioethics and the Military, and; 2) Compulsory Birth Control. Three articles deal with issues relevant to #1 (e.g., Should Soldiers Who Test Positive for HIV be Mustered Out of the Service?), while five articles discuss various issues relevant to #2 (e.g., Is It Permissible to Require Use of Birth Control as a Condition of Probation or Parole?)

Almeida, Michael J. Deontic Problems with Prohibition Dilemmas. *Log Anal*, 32, 163-175, S-D 89.

I show, first, that for any normal system of deontic logic, prohibition dilemmas present the very same problems as obligation dilemmas. They both involve the rejection of several plausible deontic axioms. Second, I show that even non-normal systems of deontic logic do not permit the types of prohibition dilemmas thought most plausible.

Almeida, Michael J. The Paradoxes of Feldman's Neo-Utilitarianism. *Austl J Phil*, 70(4), 455-468, D 92.

The semi-formal logic of obligation developed by Fred Feldman embodies a principle of individual moral obligation, MO, according to which moral agents are required to do the best that they can do. I consider the principle, MO, the logic on which it is based, DBWC, and (i) provide a formal model for DBWC and discuss some characteristic theses, (ii) show that five distinct versions of MO are susceptible to several serious paradoxes and (iii) conclude that there is good reason to reject MO as a fundamental normative principle.

Almond, Brenda. Dismantling Our Own Foundations: A German Perspective on Contemporary Philosophy of Education. *J Phil Educ*, 26(2), 265-270, 1992.

This article is a review of Wolfgan Grezinka's *Philosophy of Educational Knowledge*. Brezinka represents a conservative position in German educational philosophy and his philosophical outlook is empiricist and analytic. He describes this work which, is divided into educational theory, educational philosophy and pedagogics, as a metatheory of education. Brezinka believes the function of the educational system is to promote social cohesion and continuity rather than criticism, scepticism and challenges to tradition and to established values.

Almond, Brenda. Human Bonds in Applied Philosophy, Almond, Brenda (ed). New York, Routledge, 1992.

There are three kinds of bonds between human beings: biological and natural; legal and artificial; social and voluntary. Three philosophical conceptions favor unbonding, or detachment from emotional ties: the Stoic, the existentialist, and the feminist. It is concluded that whatever forms they take, personal bonds have fundamental moral priority in the lives of human beings.

Almond, Brenda. Philosophy and the Cult of Irrationalism. *Philosophy*, 33(Supp), 201-217, 1992.

Irrationalism pervades all the main areas of philosophy today—epistemology, ethics, philosophy of science—and has disastrous consequences in practical areas such as education and biomedicine. The Postmodernist rejection of the Enlightenment values of universal truth and a common human morality combines with the fragmentation of philosophy to produce a flawed and incoherent relativism. Feminists have attempted to incorporate this perspective into a feminist social analysis by arguing that the notions of reason and of universal morality are gender-based, but such a position is destructive of feminism.

Almond, Brenda. Philosophy and the Cult of Irrationalism in The Impulse to Philosophise, Griffiths, A Phillips (ed). New York, Cambridge Univ Pr, 1992.

Irrationalism pervades all the main areas of philosophy today—epistemology, ethics, philosophy of science—and has disastrous consequences in practical areas such as education and biomedicine. The postmodernist rejection of the Enlightenment values of universal truth and a common human morality combines with the fragmentation of philosophy to produce a flawed and incoherent relativism. Feminists have attempted to incorporate this perspective into a feminist social analysis by arguing that the notions of reason and of universal morality are gender-based, but such a position is destructive of feminism.

Almond, Brenda. Taking Morality Seriously. *J Applied Phil*, 9(1), 117-118, 1992.

A new trend in ethics, as evidenced by some new publications, takes morality seriously, attacking moral scepticism and views which create a gulf between moral judgment and moral action. This new tendency relates morality to human nature and its needs, including spiritual needs. A survey of recent literature suggests that moral philosophy can no longer be equated with either utilitarianism or the impersonal analysis of moral language.

Almond, Brenda. *The Philosophical Quest*. New York, Penguin USA, 1988.

A personal exploration of the main areas of contemporary philosophy - ethics, politics, logic, philosophy of mind and language, metaphysics - presented in the form of a quest. The book is written in the first person, including letters from a correspondent, Sophia. It starts with personal ethical reflection, sets this in a wider public and political context and then extends discussion to broader epistemological issues. It concludes by linking the logical holism of contemporary philosophers to earlier metaphysical approaches, before returning to its starting-point —the ethical and the applied.

Almond, Brenda (ed) and Hill, Donald (ed). *Applied Philosophy*. New York, Routledge, 1992.

This collection of papers brings the concepts and methods of philosophy to bear on specific, pressing, practical concerns; topics include the environment, personal relationships, war, terrorism, concepts of justice and equality and issues in medical ethics.

Alpern, Kenneth D (ed). *The Ethics of Reproductive Technology*. New York, Oxford Univ Pr, 1992.

This anthology examines normative and conceptual issues raised by recent technological and social innovations in human reproduction such as in vitro fertilization, embryo transfer, and parenting through contract (surrogate motherhood). The approach of the anthology is decidedly philosophical in that it focuses on fundamental conceptual relations that underlie popular debates. The sections of the anthology are: Biological, Technological, and Psychological Background; Conflicting Perspectives: Issues, Positions, and Arguments; Why Have Children—Meaning and Significance; Making and Selling Bavies: Production and Commerce; Reproductive Technology and Women— Opportunity or Oppression?; Constitutional Rights, Law, and Public Policy; Professional Responsibilities; Case Studies.

Alperson, Philip A. The Arts of Music. *J Aes Art Crit*, 50(3), 217-230, Sum 92.

Peter Kivy has argued that pure instrumental ("absolute") music is not an art in the sense of that term most likely to be applied to it in the present day, i.e., as a fine art, but it is, rather, a decorative art. In this paper, I argue that there are at least two "fine arts" of instrumental music (one of which accommodates the understanding of instrumental music as a decorative art), as well as other arts of instrumental music. I examine the sorts of appreciation appropriate to several such arts and the underlying values of these practices. I conclude with general observations about the implications of adopting a pluralist view of the arts of music.

Alperson, Philip A. When Composers Have To Be Performers. *J Aes Art Crit*, 49(4), 369-373, Fall 91.

In an earlier paper entitled, "On Musical Improvisation," I argued that, in general, musical composition and musical performance are interdependent activities, and that, in general, composition is dependent upon performance. In this paper I defend these claims against criticisms by Paul Vincent Spade by developing a version what I call the Interdependence Thesis, maintaining in particular that composition typically involves imaginary performances that count as performances of the work notwithstanding the fact that they are not fully determined. I defend an ontology of the objects of performance and composition, respectively, and of the musical work that is consistent with my view of composition and performance.

Alston, Kal. Can Schools Provide the E-Ticket Ride?. *Proc Phil Educ*, 48, 187-190, 1992.

Alston, W P. Aquinas on Theological Predication: A Look Backward and a Look Forward in Reasoned Faith, Stump, Eleonore (ed). Ithaca, Cornell Univ Pr, 1993.

Much of the paper is devoted to an attempt to get clear as to the exact character of Aquinas' position. That is not as easy as it might seem. Aquinas holds, primarily on the basis of divine simplicity, that no term can be applied univocally to God and creatures, with respect to either the "perfection signified" or the "mode of signification". As for the former, I argue that the position depends on an unwarranted assumption that the meaning of the term must match the ontology of what it denotes. Suggestions are made as to how we might move forward from Aquinas.

Alston, W P. Epistemic Desiderata. *Phil Phenomenol Res*, 53(3), 527-551, S 93.

There are endless disputes over alleged necessary conditions for epistemic justice, e.g., that the belief is *based on* adequate grounds and that the justifier is accessible on reflection. But perhaps it is a mistake to suppose that there is some unique status, "justification" concerning the necessary conditions for which they are arguing. If we abandon that view we can reconstrue this part of epistemology as a study of epistemic desiderata, their nature, viability, and importance for various interests and purposes.

Alston, W P. Inductive Argument from Evil and the Human Cognitive Condition in Philosophical Perspectives, 5: Philosophy of Religion, 1991, Tomberlin, James E (ed). Atascadero, Ridgeview, 1991.

Rowe and others have argued that since there are cases of suffering that, so far as we can see, God would have no sufficient reason to permit, it is reasonable to conclude that God does not exist. In opposition, I contend that our cognitive situation is such that we are not able to show that various suggested reasons are not reasons that God might have. I consider a variety of theodicies and argue in each case that we are not in a position to exclude the possibility that the theodicy might embody at least part of God's reason for permitting the suffering in question.

Alston, W P. Searle on Illocutionary Acts in John Searle and His Critics, LePore, Ernest (ed). Cambridge, Blackwell, 1991.

Though in broad agreement with Searle's approach, I am critical of the details of the execution. Searle's analysis of promising, as the most extended sample of his account, is subjected to detailed critical analysis. The upshot of this to suggest an analysis of illocutionary act concepts that features the speaker's "taking responsibility" for the satisfaction of various conditions. Problems are raised with respect to some of Searle's main categories, such as "direction of fit" and "conditions of satisfaction".

Alston, William. The Place of Experience in the Grounds of Religious Belief in Our Knowledge of God, Clark, Kelly James (ed). Dordrecht, Kluwer, 1992.

Assuming that an experience of the presence of God is a ground of religious belief, the paper seeks to relate it to other grounds, e.g., other sorts of religious experience, revelation, and natural theology. These are reduced to two main types: experiential presentation and inference to the best explanation. These grounds interact not only by adding up to a total case greater than any of its components, but also in more intimate ways, e.g., by one ground contributing to the background system presupposed by another, and by one helping to remove doubts about another.

Alt, Wayne. The Huai-nan Tzu Alteration. *J Chin Phil*, 20(1), 73-85, Mr 93.

Contra Charles LeBlanc in *Huai Nan Tzu: Philosophical Synthesis in Early Han Thought*, I argue that the significance of the Lute Passage from chapter twenty-four of the *Chuang Tzu* is axiological, not metaphysical. A modified version of the Lute Passage in chapter six of the *Haai Nan Tzu* is indeed metaphysical. But the *Chuang Tzu* version was not intended to suggest a realm beyond *Yin* and *Yang*. If anything, it suggests that the distinction between *shih* "right" and *Fei* "wrong" is bogus.

Altekar, Eknath V. A Critique of Hume's Theory of Moral Epistemology. *Indian Phil Quart*, 20/1(Supp), 7-18, Ja 93.

Alvarez, Angel. Ilustracón y Clasicismo. *Agora (Spain)*, 11(1), 183-198, 1992.

Alvarez-Calderón, Luz Maria. Truth, Authenticity, and Culture in Analecta Husserliana, XXXI, Tymieniecka, Anna-Teresa (ed). Dordrecht, Kluwer, 1990.

The purpose is to analyze human realization considering the different ontological strata of reality with their laws and values, and the need to integrate them for building up each's own personality. Conclusions: 1) Need to recognize stages in the development of consciousness in its growing capacity for objective valuation. 2) Positive role of psychoneurosis in the achievement of this process. Importance of culture for authentic education and need for a free space in the individual's interiority to allow an authentic recognition and assumption of superior objective values to shape each's own personality. 4) Unique role of individual consciousness in the elevation of collective moral. (edited)

Amato, Joseph. Death, and the Stories We Don't Have. *Monist*, 76(2), 252-269, Ap 93.

The author argues that death, as we humans experience it, compels us to write narratives and tell stories, whereas Western philosophy with its standing preference for logic and rational explanation has been on the whole anti-theoretical to stories about death, dying, the death, and the afterlife. The essay concludes hoping the philosophers and their allies will recognize that metaphor and narrative are distinct and necessary means to explain life and temporality. Neither can be reduced to serving explanation; neither can be expected to exhaust or even to fathom death, whose endless meanings are inseparable from the even greater endless meanings of life.

Ambrose, Alice. On Certainty in Logical Foundations, Mahalingam, Indira (ed). New York, St Martin's Pr, 1991.

This paper is directed against the thesis that mathematical proofs are "only provisional" and mathematics a "quasi-empirical science", and its concomitant, that no distinction can be made between analytic and synthetic propositions, despite general agreement in some cases on their application. The main support of the thesis is that the similarity between the practice of mathematicians preceding rigorous proof and of natural scientists makes the result plausible but not certain. Computer proofs of theorems, in lacking criteria for the reliability of their programming, are held to yield uncertain results because error is possible. However calculation, by human or machine, does not show a result sometimes holds, but as Wittgenstein pointed out, shows what the result *must* be. This paper argues that dissimilarities between experimental- and proof-steps undercut the view that these are "quasi-empirical".

Ambrose, Alice. Transfinite Numbers in Wittgenstein's Intentions, Canfield, J V (ed). Hamden, Garland, 1993.

The thesis developed here is that the controversy over transfinite numbers is only apparently a controversy over the existence of a realm of abstract entities. Following Wittgenstein, to claim that "there are aleph null integers" expresses a necessary truth about integers, is to urge in a way concealed by the indicative form of speech the acceptance of a convention, here, that "aleph null integers" have a use. M Lazerowitz' account of the connection of necessary propositions with a verbal matter provides a basis for displacing the attempt at solving the Platonic problem of deciding where truth lies with making it disappear.

Ambrose, Alice (ed) and Moore, G E. *Lectures on Metaphysics, 1934-1935: G E Moore*. New York, Lang, 1992.

Ameriks, Karl. The Critique of Metaphysics in The Cambridge Companion to Kant, Guyer, Paul (ed). New York, Cambridge Univ Pr, 1992.

This article is about the relation between traditional ontology and Kant's critique of metaphysics. Kant's criticisms of traditional metaphysics in the Dialectic of the *Critique of Pure Reason* are surveyed and put in the context of Kant's treatment of Baumgarten in his lectures on metaphysics and later writings directly attacking the Leibnizian tradition. The article ends with a focus on the issue of interaction in order to indicate that on some traditional metaphysical issues it is remarkable difficult to draw a sharp line between Kant's Critical position and that of his rationalist predecessors or his own earlier work.

Ames, Roger T. Chinese Rationality: An Oxymoron?. *J Indian Counc Phil Res*, 9(2), 95-119, Ja-Ap 92.

Ames, Roger T. Nietzsche's 'Will to Power' and Chinese 'Virtuality' (De) in Nietzsche and Asian Thought, Parkes, Graham R (ed). Chicago, Univ of Chicago Pr, 1991.

Ames, William L. Bhāvaviveka's *Prajnapradipa* (A Translation of Chapter One: "Examination of Causal Conditions"). *J Indian Phil*, 21(3), 209-259, S 93.

Ammon, Theodore G. Teachers Should Disclose Their Moral Commitments in Moral Education and the Liberal Arts, Mitias, Michael H (ed). Westport, Greenwood Pr, 1992.

Amodio, Barbara A. The World Made of Sound: Whitehead and Pythagorean Harmonics in the Context of Veda and the Science of Mantra. *J Dharma*, 17(3), 233-266, Jl-S 92.

Amodio, Barbara A. Valmiki's Ramayana Revisited: Worship by Confrontation—Vidvesha-Bhakti. *J Dharma*, 16(4), 337-367, O-D 91.

Pursues root meanings of metaphysical, mystical, psychological and ethical symbols in the original Ramayana. Elaborates the tale as unified psychodrama. Focuses on deeper meanings of the unusual but valid ethical worship by Ravana, the archvillain. Shows that the psychodrama parallels the supraconscious mental development Patanjali describes. Verifies Patanjali's Yoga psychology in Ravana with clinical appraisals of the physiology, chemistry and language of feelings displayed by Ravana in ethical dilemmas. Recovers positive ethical functions for "enemies." Universalizes and restores cosmological grounding for the term "warrior" across gender and social status. Isolates the ethico-psychological "transition" from warrior/soldier to Brahmin/saint for which the Ramayana is justly famous. Advanced a unified view of the Indological traditions.

Amrine, Frederick. 'The Triumph of Life': Nietzsche's Verbicide in The Crisis in Modernism, Burwick, Frederick (ed). New York, Cambridge Univ Pr, 1992.

Despite Nietzsche's express desire to beocme a 'Lebensphilosoph,' his characterizations of 'life' are shown to be a series of primitive tautologies strung together by breathtaking illogic. In place of 'life' as a philosophical construct, Nietzsche offers an insubstantial semantic halo, an empty metaphysics that hides its inadequacy behind an anti-metaphysical facade. Into this vacuum rushes an exceedingly sinister political discourse that anticipates the 'blond vitalism' of Nazis.

Amundson, Ron. Disability, Handicap, and the Environment. *J Soc Phil*, 23(1), 105-119, Spr 92.

Although philosophers are familiar with the civil rights issues surrounding feminism and ethnic and racial minorities, there is almost no discussion of the concepts underlying the disability rights movement. This paper introduces to philosophical discussion such concepts as the minority model of disability and the environmental concept of handicap. Most accounts of the special ethical importance of health care issues also imply the importance of specifically disability-related issues. Nevertheless, mainstream medical ethicists' discussions of disability can be seen to be impoverished by the lack of familiarity with the relevant disability rights concepts.

Anagnostopoulos, Georgios. Some Thoughts on Explanation in Ancient Philosophy in Greek Studies in the Philosophy and History of Science, Nicolacopoulos, Pantelis (ed). Dordrecht, Kluwer, 1990.

Anapolitanos, D A. Leibniz on Density and Sequential or Cauchy Completeness in Greek Studies in the Philosophy and History of Science, Nicolacopoulos, Pantelis (ed). Dordrecht, Kluwer, 1990.

Anapolitanos, D A. Thought Experimentsand Conceivability Conditions in Thought Experiments in Science and Philosophy, Horowitz, Tamara (ed). Lanham, Rowman & Littlefield, 1991.

Andereggen, Ignacio E M. La relación de Hegel con el catolicismo según algunas menciones de K Rosenkranz. *Sapientia*, 47(183), 67-72, 1992.

Andermatt Conley, Verena. Communal Crisis in Community at Loose Ends, Miami Theory Collect, (ed). Minneapolis, Univ of Minnesota Pr, 1991.

In this article, I reflect on the disruptive effects postmodern economic and teleological relations are wreaking on communities, but especially on an intellectual and artistic community blind to its own powerlessness even as it prescribes to its own the urgency of being both "affirmative and contestatory." This "crisis" in intellectual life can only be resolved and the high-tech world of "infotainment" be resisted if theorists face up to the powerful ubiquity of an economic genre of "which we are also a part." I intimate that the inaugural situation of ethics is itself already situated within the economic situation that we associate today with postindustrial capitalism, and whose basic exploitative mechanisms and effects have manifestly transcended the realm of the traditionally or strictly economical to pervade the "new" postmodern markets of aesthetics, sexuality, and knowledge, one the domains of nonquantitive concerns.

Anders, Laura. Desire and Receptivity. *Cont Phil*, 15(1), 1-3, Ja-F 93.

Anderson, Albert A. Dialectic: The Science of Humanism. *Dialec Hum*, 17(3), 113-124, 1990.

Anderson, C Anthony. Zalta's Intensional Logic. *Phil Stud*, 69(2-3), 221-229, Mr 93.

This paper critically discusses Edward Zalta's system of intensional logic, as described in his book Intensional Logic and the Metaphysics of Intentionality (Cambridge, MIT Press, 1988). Two main defects are explained. 1) Constraints on a "comprehension principle" restrict property existence in such a way as to limit the applicability of the system. 2) A schema which incorporates a version of Cantor's Theorem is provable about the logic. One instance of the schema yields the odd result that there are "undistinguished objects", distinct objects which have all their properties in common. It also follows that the system is incompatible with set theory.

Anderson, C Anthony (ed) and Meehl, Paul and Gunderson, Keith (ed). *Selected Philosophical and Methodological Papers*. Minneapolis, Univ of Minn Pr, 1991.

This is a collection of articles by a psychologist-philosopher on social science methodology and philosophy of mind. The widely varied topics include theory-testing, open concepts, determinism, emergence, psychoanalytic inference, insanity defense, civil commitment, telepathy, teleology in psychopathology, and the mind-body identity theory.

Anderson, Christopher. 'Safe Enough in his Honesty and Prudence': The Ordinary Conduct of Government in the Thought of John Locke. *Hist Polit Thought*, 13(4), 605-630, Wint 92.

Anderson, David. False Stability in Rawlsian Liberalism. *Cont Phil*, 14(5), 11-16, S-O 92.

In this paper I build on the work of feminist social scientist and philosophers in order to criticize Rawlsian liberalism. I argue that many American men and women would be motivated by largely unconscious reasons to support the original position procedure of justification. I show that unconscious fear and anxiety based largely on the process of socialization would motivate people. Special attention is given to Rawls's old and new arguments for stability. A justificatory morality is inimical to positive social change because it builds in the oppressive features of our stable but inhumane society.

Anderson, David L. What Is the Model-Theoretic Argument?. *J Phil*, 90(6), 311-322, Je 93.

In a recent article, James Van Cleve joins a growing throng who have argued that Hilary Putnam's model-theoretic argument (and his "just more theory" response) begs the question against those who hold externalist theories of reference. Van Cleve has misinterpreted Putnam's argument. Putnam does not demand that the statements which make up the causal theory of reference must, themselves, do the reference-fixing. That would be question-begging. Rather, Putnam's argument is a *reductio*, which can only be blocked with a theory of reference that is both substantive and plausible. Putnam argues that there is no interpretation of "causality" that meets both conditions.

Anderson, Douglas R. American Loss in Cavell's Emerson. *Trans Peirce Soc*, 29(1), 69-89, Wint 93.

Stanley Cavell's reading of Emerson has placed Emerson in line with traditions in British and Continental philosophy. However, Cavell overlooks Emerson's influence on James and Dewey. I argue here that this oversight involves Cavell in a misreading of both Emerson and the American pragmatic tradition.

Anderson, Douglas R. Artistic Control in Collingwood's Theory of Art. *J Aes Art Crit*, 48(1), 53-59, Wint 90.

In this paper I try to show how Collingwood suggests a conception of artistic control that stands between traditional mechanistic and teleological conceptions of control. His notion of "attending" within a totally imaginative experience provides the basis for a looser teleology in expression.

Anderson, Douglas R. Realism and Idealism in Peirce's Cosmogony. *Int Phil Quart*, 32(2), 185-192, Je 92.

Peirce's cosmogony involves an apparent tension concerning the status of initial ideas. They appear both dependent and independent. Peirce appears to resolve this tension, maintaining elements of both his realism and his idealism in his cosmogony, by asserting that God serves as a necessary condition for the reality of the initial ideas and by holding, through his agapasticism, that the ideas, as firsts, retain an element of spontaneity or freedom. From another angle, it is plausible to suggest that for Peirce God functions as a continuum of other continua. Such a view allows Peirce to understand evolution as a developmental teleology in which both order and spontaneity play significant roles.

Anderson, Douglas R. The Legacy of Bowne's Empiricism. *Personalist Forum*, 8/1(Supp), 1-8, Spr 92.

This essay argues for a fundamental similarity in the American philosophies of personalism and pragmatism. It focuses on Borden Bowne's organic interactionism between "mind" and "body" and shows the social and political upshots of this interactionism. Thus, while Bowne's personalism, as idealism, is remote from pragmatism, as a radical empiricism, it is closely related to pragmatism.

Anderson, Douglas R and Hausman, Carl R. The Role of Aesthetic Emotion in R G Collingwood's Conception of Creative Activity. *J Aes Art Crit*, 50(4), 299-305, Fall 92.

Anderson, Elizabeth. Compensation Within the Limits of Reliance Alone. *Nomos*, 33, 178-185, 1991.

Robert Goodin argues that considerations of reliance constitute the basic justification for practices of compensatory justice. This author disputes Goodin's thesis: practices of compensatory justice serve a plurality of aims, such as satisfying needs and securing autonomy, which are distinct from the aim of enabling people to carry out their already conceived plans. Goodin's arguments exemplify the flaws of parsimony in ethical theorizing. We should not confine our ethical principles to the minimum set needed to generate intuitively acceptable outcomes, for ethical principles play expressive roles not fulfilled by the minimum set

Anderson, Elizabeth. *Value in Ethics and Economics*. Cambridge, Harvard Univ Pr, 1993.

This book articulates a pluralist theory of value, which claims that goods differ in kind if they are properly valued in different ways, such as respect, love, and use. Practical reason is exercised in *expressing* these different modes of valuation in action. This pluralist-expressivist theory of value and practical reason offers a systematic alternative to consequentialist theories of rational choice and monistic theories of value. It also explains why some goods should not be sold on the market or otherwise treated as commodities. Cases discussed include prostitution, contract pregnancy, school vouchers, health and environmental safety.

Anderson, Kevin. Lenin, Hegel and Western Marxism: From the 1920s to 1953. *Stud Soviet Tho*, 44(2), 79-129, S 92.

Lenin's 1914-15 notes on Hegel influenced several leading Western Marxists. Although he later repudicated Lenin, Karl Korsch placed a statement from Lenin on Hegel as the frontpiece to his *Marxism and Philosophy* (1923). After the first German translation of Lenin's Hegel Notebooks appeared in 1932, George Lukács in his *The Young Hegel* (1948) and Ernst Bloch in his *Subjekt-Objekt* (1949) also commented on them. Henri Lefebvre and Norbert Guterman's 130-page introduction to a French translation of the Notebooks was published in 1938. In the US in the 1940s, Raya Dunayevskaya, C L R James, and Grace Lee (Boggs) commented extensively on Dunayevskaya's unpublished English translation of the Notebooks.

Anderson, Mary R. Deconstruction and the Teaching Historian. *Hist Euro Ideas*, 14(4), 567-574, Jl 92.

This article's purpose is to explore specific uses of Jacques Derrida's theory of deconstruction in the professional work of a teaching historian. For the historian in the classroom, deconstruction poses the challenges of explication, integration, and new views of context and meaning. After elucidating aspects of Derrida's deconstruction theory most useful to the historian, the author applies these to the ideology of transition in Late Victorian England. The concept of transition was available to the Late Victorians in an uneasy blend of the hierarchical opposition change-stasis. The language of ideology becomes the space where the Victorian self is constituted. In this Derridean reading of the Late Victorian experience, transition is reinscribed by being bound to change-stasis and meaning-experience.

Anderson, Michael. Making Sense of Indexicals. *Lyceum*, 4(1), 39-82, Spr 92.

The article deals with whether or not indexical terms can have a Fregean Sense. The answer to this question is bound up with an analysis of what a Fregean Sense *is*. The paper defends and extends an interpretation given by Gareth Evans ("Understanding Demonstratives") that a Sense is a 'way of thinking about a referent', on which interpretation indexicals may have a Sense. However, the interpretation entails that all meaningful propositions must be about particular objects, and that the ability to make sense (to grasp thoughts) requires of the language user very specific epistemological competencies and connections to the world.

Anderson, Olive. The Feminism of T H Green: A Late-Victorian Success Story?. *Hist Polit Thought*, 12(4), 671-693, Wint 91.

Although hitherto neglected, Green's feminism was as explicit as Mill's and perhaps even more consistent and categorical. In theory and practice Green was deeply committed to 'positive equality' and autonomy for women. He altogether rejected patriarchy and the double standard, and worked with other activists, including radicals like Josephine Butler and Elizabeth Wolstenholme, for the more equal conditions women needed 'to make their own career in life'. His charismatic message that ethical fulfillment comes through active citizenship diffused a service motivated ethic of feminine self-development and self-determination which encouraged feminine advance in Britain well into the 1950s.

Anderson, Pamela. Ricoeur and Hick on Evil: Post-Kantian Myth?. *Cont Phil*, 14(6), 15-20, N-D 92.

Although highly critical—even dismissive—of Paul Ricoeur's *The Symbolism of Evil* in a 1969 review, John Hick has since undergone a Kantian revolution, which I contend, suggests a possible rapprochement between the two men. My paper, first, reassesses Ricoeur's post-Kantian approach to evil with the recent Hick in mind; and second, confronts Ricoeur and Hick with appropriate feminist challenges to their still essentially male conceptions of evil and God. In concluding, the dominance of patriarchal symbols and myths is exposed in their respective theodicies; yet direction is also given for transforming language which marginalizes women under patriarchy.

Anderson, Robert. Comparative Oughts and Comparative Evils. *J Value Inq*, 27(1), 69-73, Ja 93.

This article shows in several ways that paradoxically both event-centered and agent-centered moral theories entail comparative ought-statements which say that we would be better off morally were a vice or two added to our inventory of bad habits or a wrong now and again added to our list of sins. That is, it shows that sometimes we ought to two wrongs rather than just one because two wrongs are better than one.

Anderson, Susan Leigh. Philosophy and Fiction. *Metaphilosophy*, 23(3), 203-213, Jl 92.

The author considers (a) whether anything worthwhile philosophically can be accomplished in a work of fiction, (b) if so, whether there are any limitations as to what can be done philosophically in a work of fiction, (c) whether one can express philosophical ideas as well or even *better* in a work of fiction and (d) what the pitfalls are that one should be aware of in attempting to combine philosophy and fiction.

Anderson, Thomas C. Sartre's Early Ethics and the Ontology of 'Being and Nothingness' in Sartre Alive, Aronson, Ronald (ed). Detroit, Wayne St Univ Pr, 1991.

For decades there has been controversy over whether Sartre's ontology in *Being and Nothingness* is compatible with an ethics. This article maintains that Sartre's posthumous *Notebooks for an Ethics* is in fact a viable morality based on BN's ontology. NE clearly states that BN presented only "ontology before conversion." NE offers coherent reasons for Sartre's selection of freedom as his primary moral value, notwithstanding his rejection of objective values. Thus it shows that BN's ontology was never meant to doom human existence to inevitable failure. Finally, NE demonstrates that Sartre never held that conflict was inevitable in human relations. Crucial to Sartre's ethics is conversion from the project to be God.

Anderson III, Gustaf E and McGrath, James. Recent Work on the American Professional Military Ethic: An Introduction and Survey. *Amer Phil Quart*, 30(3), 187-208, Jl 93.

We offer a comprehensive philosophical introduction to the professional ethic of the individual American soldier. After critically surveying relevant military periodicals, recent books, and professional conferences, we present and interpret an inclusive selection of the basic traditional documents that constitute the profession's formal ethic. An informal ethic of military virtues and values, especially obedience, competence, character, honor and the warrior ethos, is also described.

Andic, Martin. Confidence as a Work of Love in Kierkegaard on Art and Communication, Pattison, George (ed). New York, St Martin's Pr, 1992.

Andic, Martin. Discernment and the Imagination in Simone Weil's Philosophy of Culture, Bell, Richard H (ed). New York, Cambridge Univ Pr, 1993.

Andler, Daniel. Is Context a Problem?. *Proc Aris Soc*, 93, 279-296, 1993.

Andre, Shane. Was Hume an Atheist?. *Hume Stud*, 19(1), 141-166, Ap 93.

Although theistic interpretations of Hume's philosophy of religion have been advanced by others, the major innovation of my interpretation is to approach the title question by way of a conceptual analysis of the terms "theism" and "atheism," leading me to distinguish three forms of theism, "standard," "extended," and "limited." Hume is placed as a doubtly limited theist, his form of theism being limited both as to content (as compared with standard theism and certain forms of deism) and as to strength of belief.

Andresen, Julie Tetel. The Behaviorist Turn in Recent Theories of Language. *Behavior Phil*, 20(1), 1-19, Spr-Sum 92.

Andriopoulos, D Z. Alcmeon's and Hippocrates's Concept of 'Aetia' in Greek Studies in the Philosophy and History of Science, Nicolacopoulos, Pantelis (ed). Dordrecht, Kluwer, 1990.

Anellis, Irving H. The First Russell Paradox in Perspectives on the History of Mathematical Logic, Drucker, Thomas (ed). Basel, Birkhauser, 1991.

After sorting through the debates on the chronology of origin of the Russell paradox and on the connections of the Russell paradox with the other set-theoretic paradoxes, especially the Cantor and Burali Forti paradoxes with which the Russell paradox is linked in the historical literature, unpublished documents are used to show that Russell obtained a version of his paradox earlier than has been commonly assumed, and with the aid of a 1973 work of Crossley in which the Russell paradox was derived directly from the Cantor paradox, it is shown how Russell had done the same, as early as December 1900.

Anellis, Irving H. The Löwenheim-Skolem Theorem, Theories of Quantification, and Proof Theory in Perspectives on the History of Mathematical Logic, Drucker, Thomas (ed). Basel, Birkhauser, 1991.

Angeletti, Luciana Rita. Le concept de vie dans la Grèce ancienne et le serment d'Hippocrate. *Rev Phil Louvain*, 90(86), 156-179, My 92.

During the fifth century B C the general meaning of Plato suggests rules for a stable birth-rate, considered as a State good. In the same period, the influence of Orphism, which forbade destruction of life, and the biological thought of Aristotle, who believes that life cannot be destroyed when there is sensitivity, seem to agree with the ethical concept of the Hippocratic Oath. Passages on the prohibition of abortive remedies are carved also in stones of few temples, such as in the temple of Asclepius in the Akropolis of Athens, confirming the existence of an ethical view on respect of life in the pre-Christian time.

Angelica. Enrico De Negri interprete di Hegel'65-85. *Teoria*, 11(2), Nuzzo, 1991.

Angell, Marcia. The Doctor as Double Agent. *Kennedy Inst Ethics J*, 3(3), 279-286, S 93.

American doctors in the 1990s are being asked to serve as "double agents," weighing competing allegiances to patients' medical needs against the monetary costs to society. This situation is a reaction to rapid cost increases for medical services, themselves the result of the haphazard development since the 1920s of an inherently inflationary, open-ended system for funding and delivering health care. The answer to an inefficient system, however, is not to stint on care, but rather to restructure the system to remove the inflationary pressures. As long as we are spending enormous resources on an inherently inefficient and inflationary system we cannot justify asking doctors to withhold beneficial care to save money for third-party payers. Doing so serves a largely political agenda and endangers the patient-centered ethic that is central to medicine.

Angus, Ian. Learning to Stop: A Critique of General Rhetoric in The Critical Turn, Angus, Ian (ed). Carbondale, So Illinois Univ Pr, 1993.

The essay makes a contribution to the "end of philosophy" debate by arguing that the turn to a performative conception of language allows a new conception of "general rhetoric" in which the mutual translation of language games replaces a foundationalist discourse. The essay thus defends a conception of philosophy through the notion of a discourse that prepares for its own end. Silence is thus the key "discursive" moment of philosophy.

Angus, Ian (ed) and Langsdorf, Lenore (ed). *The Critical Turn*. Carbondale, So Illinois Univ Pr, 1993.

Due to the discursive turn in philosophy and the human sciences, philosophy and rhetoric have begun to converge, though without becoming identical. The original essays collected in this volume, by a number of well-known rhetoricians and philosophers, address this convergence from a number of angles. Together, they make a contribution to the philosophy of the human sciences and to the rhetoric of the human sciences literatures.

Angus, Ian and Langsdorf, Lenore. Unsettled Borders: Envisioning Critique at the Postmodern Site in The Critical Turn, Angus, Ian (ed). Carbondale, So Illinois Univ Pr, 1993.

Annas, Julia. Ancient Ethics and Modern Morality in Philosophical Perspectives, 6: Ethics, 1992, Tomberlin, James E (ed). Atascadero, Ridgeview, 1992.

The article argues that ancient ethical theories, despite the differences in their structure and concerns, are recognizably theories of morality. Several different reasons for claiming that they are not, are considered and rejected.

Annas, Julia. Schofield's *The Stoic Idea of the City. Polis*, 11(1), 95-101, 1992.

This review of Schofield's book, while fully appreciating its contributions to a neglected area, also tries to relate stoic concern with the city to wider issues of stoic political philosophy.

Annas, Julia. *The Morality of Happiness*. New York, Oxford Univ Pr, 1993.

This book presents the basic structure of ancient ethical theory, in a way based on extensive scholarship but accessible to the general reader. It argues that ancient ethical theories are not egoistic, and that they are recognizably theories of morality. Cast in the framework, unfamiliar to us, of happiness and virtue.

Annas, Julia. Women and the Quality of Life in The Quality of Life, Nussbaum, Martha C (ed). New York, Oxford Univ Pr, 1993.

Annis, David B. Teaching Ethics in Higher Education: Goals, and the Implications of the Empirical Research on Moral Development. *Metaphilosophy*, 23(1-2), 187-202, Ja-Ap 92.

The goals of teaching ethics within higher education are critically examined. The empirical research on moral development and conduct is reviewed, and inferences are drawn from this research about effective ways of teaching ethics in higher education.

Annis, David B and Bohanon, Cecil E. Desert and Property Rights. *J Value Inq*, 26(4), 537-546, O 92.

Some philosophers have argued that personal desert is a basis of ownership. Thus, a person's effort in producing an item may make him or her deserving of significant property rights in it. In this essay we support desert as an important basis of ownership.

Anscombe, G E M. Russelm or Anselm?. *Phil Quart*, 43(173), 500-504, O 93.

Anscombe, G E M. Wittgenstein: Whose Philosopher? in Wittgenstein Centenary Essays, Griffiths, A Phillips (ed). New York, Cambridge Univ Pr, 1991.

Anstötz, Christoph. Continuing the Dialogue on Measuring the Quality of Life in Philosophy and Psychology. *Bioethics*, 6(4), 356-360, O 92.

Anstötz, Christoph. Should a Brain-Dead Pregnant Woman Carry Her Child to Full Term? The Case of the "Erlanger Baby". *Bioethics*, 7(4), 340-349, Jl 93.

Anton, John P. Santayana and Greek Philosophy. *Bull Santayana Soc*, 11, 15-29, Fall 93.

The article explores Santayana's views on Greek philosophy and his evaluation of the Greek thinkers that best represent the classical mind: Heraclitus, Democritus, Plato, and Aristotle. His early views on Greek philosophy, traceable in the 1889 Dissertation on Lotze, were revised and formalized in *The Life of Reason*, and finalized in his *Apologia pro mente sua* (1951). The principles that figure dominantly in Santayana's philosophy, materialism, scepticism, and the theory of essences, also pervade his interpretation and critical treatment of Greek philosophy. For all his admiration and love of Greek philosophy, Santayana's naturalistic approach remained close to James' pragmatism.

Anton, John P. The Unity of Scientific Inquiry and Categorical Theory in Greek Studies in the Philosophy and History of Science, Nicolacopoulos, Pantelis (ed). Dordrecht, Kluwer, 1990.

Aristotle developed the concept of unity of the sciences as interrelated domains of inquiry. Though not a principle of system of systems, it functioned to exhibit the continuity between being and knowledge, fact and value. The requirement for axioms, special theses and hypotheses underlies the Aristotelian conception of the unity of the sciences, as in the *Posterior Analytics*. The article discusses in historical context the philosophical significance of Aristotle's theory of wholes and the attendant principle of their irreducibility that together validate the mode of explanation in accord with the tenets of Aristotle's categorial theory of being.

Anton, John P (ed) and Preus, Anthony (ed). *Essays in Ancient Greek Philosophy, IV*. Albany, SUNY Pr, 1991.

A collection of papers by classicists and philosophers presented at the meetings of the Society for Ancient Greek scholarship and textual exegesis. The essays are arranged according to several unifying themes and deal with fundamental issues and concepts in Aristotle's ethical and political writings and other related works, with special attention to problems of virtue and character, moral reasoning and persons and property. A special feature reflecting a pervasive concern in the essays printed here is Aristotle's methodology. Most of the papers are published here for the first time.

Antonites, A J. Is the Paradigm Concept Compatible with the Human Sciences? (in Dutch). *S Afr J Phil*, 11(2), 25-31, My 92.

The Kuhnian paradigm concept has its origin in Kuhn's background in the natural sciences. Because it has remarkable impact, it is rather widely used by human scientists, and the author accepts that there is a substantial difference between the natural and human sciences. The aim in this article is to ascertain whether the paradigm concept is compatible with the human sciences. This is done by measuring the human sciences against the most important criteria for the existence of a paradigm, namely: 1) crisis and revolution; 2) paradigmatic monopoly; 3) degree of scientific development; and 4) paradigms as perspectives. It is deduced that the paradigm concept is indeed compatible especially in terms of the most important criterion, namely, 4. As a result a radical counter-question can be asked whether the paradigm concept is not really a concept that belongs to the human sciences in which the hermeneutic dimension plays an important role.

Antony, Michael V. Social Relations and the Individuation of Thought. *Mind*, 102(406), 247-261, Ap 93.

Tyler Burge has argued that a necessary condition for individual's having many of the thoughts he has is that he bear certain relations to other language users. Burge's conclusion is based on a thought experiment in which an individual's social relations are imagined, counterfactually, to differ from how they are actually. The result is that it seems, counterfactually, the individual cannot be attributed many of the thoughts he can be actually. In the article, an alternative interpretation of Burge's thought experiment is offered on which the intuitions Burge evokes can be accepted while his conclusion about the social character of thought is denied. The alternative interpretation given, it is then argued that it is preferable to Burge's.

Apczynski, John V. Polanyi's Augustinianism: A Mark of the Future?. *Tradition Discovery*, 20(1), 27-40, 1993-94.

The aim of this essay is to display a congruence between several important features of Augustine's theory of knowledge, including our knowledge of the world (*sapientia*) and our knowledge of the standards guiding our thought (*sapientia*), and Michael Polanyi's theory of personal knowledge. Its purpose is to commend an interpretation of Polanyi's thought which situates his major insights within an Augustinian intellectual tradition and which thereby offers fruitful possibilities for theological reflection, particularly on the reality of God.

Apel, Karl Otto. Can an Ultimate Foundation of Knowledge Be Non-Metaphysical?. *J Speculative Phil*, 7(3), 171-190, 1993.

Apel, Karl Otto. Is Intentionality More Basic than Linguistic Meaning? in John Searle and His Critics, LePore, Ernest (ed). Cambridge, Blackwell, 1991.

Apel, Karl Otto. Normatively Grounding 'Critical Theory' in Philosophical Interventions in the Unfinished Project of Enlightenment, Honneth, Axel (& other eds). Cambridge, MIT Pr, 1992.

Apostle, Hippocrates. Aristotle's Philosophy of Mathematics. *Lyceum*, 2(1), 31-44, Spr 90.

Apostle, Hippocrates. Subject, Unity, and Method in Aristotle's Metaphysics. *Lyceum*, 1(2), 19-30, Fall 89.

Appelbaum, David. Afterword in Revisioning Philosophy, Ogilvy, James (ed). Albany, SUNY Pr, 1992.

An exploration of vision in philosophical activity. A common occurrence in perceptual and conceptual realms is that vision calls forth what abides in hiddenness. Novelty is the result of the action of vision. Revisioning philosophy, therefore, calls for an attitude of meeting the continual closure of thought with an acknowledgment of thought's fixity. The awareness capable of this encounter—which stems from the heart of self-recognition, is alone capable of providing the renewing force for philosophy.

Apter, Andrew. Depersonalization, the Experience of Prosthesis, and Our Cosmic Insignificance: The Experimental Phenomenology of an Altered State. *Phil Psych*, 5(3), 257-285, 1992.

Aquila, Richard E. On the "Subjects" of Knowing and Willing and the "I" in Shcopenhauer. *Hist Phil Quart*, 10(3), 241-260, Jl 93.

A state of consciousness is an occurrence of an irreducibly "mental" form. Its material is a direct embodiment of will in various of its grades. Its form is the "pure knowing subject" which is one and the same in everyone. It is reflected in the phenomenal world as a perceivable aspect of it, namely, its pure "presence." This suggestion is related to debates regarding sense and reference of 'I.' It is also used to distinguish two ways of reifying consciousness and the unconscious and, consistently with his own surface/depth metaphor, to interpret Schopenhauer's assertion that the will "comes into consciousness from within," not "below."

Aqvist, Lennart. Deontic Tense Logic in Advances in Scientific Philosophy, Schurz, Gerhard (ed). Amsterdam, Rodopi, 1991.

The paper discusses a version of the Chisholm Contrary-to-Duty Imperatives Paradox within the framework of the system DARB of *deonic tense logic*, due to Åqvist and Hoepleman in their contribution to R Hilpinen (ed) *New Studies in Deontic Logic* (Reidel, 1981). The author insists that there are at least three or four alternative ways of translating into DARB the characteristic contrary-to-duty premiss in Chisholm's argument, all of which turn out to be equivalent in DARB. A distinction between two compound operators is strongly emphasized, viz., the one between, on the one had, "it will be at the next time that it ought to be that" and, on the other, "it ought (now) to be that it will be at the next time that", going back to earlier work by the author on von Wright's tense logic (see Äqvist in *Logique et Analyse 9* (1966) pp 231-251.

Aragaki, Hiro. Communicative Ethics and the Morality of Discourse. *Praxis Int*, 13(2), 154-171, Jl 93.

Aragon, Louis and Waters, Alyson (trans). *Treatise on Style—Louis Aragon*. Lincoln, Univ of Nebraska Pr, 1991.

Arana, Juan (trans) and Euler, L. Defensa de la revelación divina contra las objeciones del librepensador. *Themata*, 8, 195-219, 1991.

Against the great mass of his scientific production, Euler has published an alone apologetic opuscle, although Theologie was an important part of his studies and he had a continuous interest for Religion along his life. All this increases the importance of the Defense of divine dispensation, in which appear some lucid considerations about the limits of knowledge and the kind of certainty attainable to men.

Arato, Andrew and Cohen, Jean. Politics and the Reconstruction in Cultural-Political Interventions in the Unfinished Project of Enlightenment, Honneth, Axel (& other eds). Cambridge, MIT Pr, 1992.

Araujo, Cícero R R. Verdade e Interesse na Cosmogonia de Descartes. *Cad Hist Filosof Cie*, 2, 1-103, Ja-D 90.

This text presents two interpretations of Descartes's cosmogonic theory. Those interpretations, notwithstanding their divergences, state that it is a deliberately false hypothesis, but necessary for satisfying Cartesian interests of thought. According to those views, Descartes's aim was not the knowledge of the progressive formation of celestial bodies (the explicit object that the theory investigates). After an introduction, the present work presents a synthesis of the main points and the different forms by which the French philosopher refers his cosmogony. The third chapter exposes and introduces a criticism of the "speculative interest" interpretation of this cosmogony. The fourth chapter presents and criticizes the "practical-technical interest" interpretation of the cosmogony. The author proposes his own interpretation and completes his criticism.

Arblaster, Anthony. 'Bread First, then Morals' in Socialism and Morality, McLellan, David (ed). New York, St Martin's Pr, 1990.

Archard, David. Rights, Moral Values and Natural Facts: A Reply to Mary Midgley on the Problem of Child-Abuse. *J Applied Phil*, 9(1), 99-104, 1992.

Mary Midgley asserts that my argument concerning the problem of child-abuse was inappropriately framed in the language of rights, and neglected certain pertinent natural facts. I defend the view that the use of rights-talk was both apposite and did not misrepresent the moral problem in question. I assess the status and character of the natural facts Midgley adduces in criticism of my case, concluding that they do not obviously establish the conclusions she believes they do. Finally, I briefly respond to the charge that my suggestions were illiberal.

Arcilla, René. Against Polemics, For Disarming Communication. *Proc Phil Educ*, 48, 45-48, 1992.

Arcilla, René Vincente. Must Private Selves Be Ironists? A Response to Van Hook. *Metaphilosophy*, 24(1-2), 179-182, Ja-Ap 93.

Arcilla, René Vincente. Tragic Absolutism in Education. *Educ Theor*, 42(4), 473-481, Fall 92.

Ardis, Ann. Presence of Mind, Presence of Body: Embodying Positionality in the Classroom. *Hypatia*, 7(2), 167-176, Spr 92.

This essay focuses on how we embody the language we speak: how an audience "reads" the body of a speaker as it both constructs the positionality of that speaking subject and construes that subject's discursive authority. Building on the work of Linda Brodkey and Michelle Fine, I explore what is at stake when university students harass a faculty member by accusing that teacher of not embodying authority in the proper form (body).

Arena, Leonardo Vittorio. *Antologia della filosofia cinese*. Milan, Arnoldo Mondadori, 1990.

Translations are provided with a theoretical introduction to each philosopher and bibliographical notes. General Outline of Chinese Thinking; The Anthology: *I Ching*; Confucius; Lato-tzu; Meng-tzu; Hsün-tzu; Mo-tzu; Chuang-tzu; Hui Shih and Kung-sun Lung; Han-fei-tzu and the Legalism; Huai-nan-tzu; Lieh-tzu; Tung Chung-shu; Chi-tsang and the Buddhism of Void; T'an-ch'iao; Ch'an Buddhism; Chou Tun-i; Wang Ch'ung; Chu Hsi; Wang Yang-ming; K'ang Yu-wei; Mao Tse-tung.

Arena, Leonardo Vittorio. *Comprensione e creatività: La filosofia di Whitehead*. Milan, Angeli, 1989.

The Structure of Natural World; Foundations of Gnoseology; Creativity and Process; Philosophical Understanding; Modes of Time; The Infinite Openness of Divine; Appendix: On Aesthetic Values; Bibliography.

Arena, Leonardo Vittorio. *Storia del Buddhismo Ch'an*. Milan, Arnoldo Mondadori, 1991.

The Origins of Buddhism; The Great Vehicle; Chinese Buddhism; The Origins of Ch'an; Principal Currents of Ch'an; The Development of Ch'an after Hui-neng; The "Five Houses"; Sung Syncretism and Decline of Ch'an in China; Conclusions. Appendixes: Chronology of Chinese Dynasties; Chronology of Ch'an Masters; Bibliography.

Argyrous, George. Kuhn's Paradigms and Neoclassical Economics. *Econ Phil*, 8(2), 231-248, O 92.

This article argues that Kuhn's notion of 'paradigm' has been misinterpreted in the literature. Kuhn intended 'paradigm' to mean an exemplar of good scientific behavior, and not a general world-view as it has commonly been interpreted. The analytical insight gained by the narrower concept of paradigm-as-exemplar is illustrated with reference to the development of the neoclassical consumption function. The history of the Life Cycle/Permanent Income Hypotheses is traced to show that it represents a normal scientific tradition based on the elaboration of the exemplars contained in the classic work of Modigliani and Friedman. The article concludes with a discussion of the relationship between this narrower notion of paradigm-as-exemplar and the broader notion of paradigm-as-world-view.

Arhem, P and Lindahl, B I B and Popper, K R. A Discussion of the Mind-Brain Problem. *Theor Med*, 14(2), 167-180, Je 93.

In this paper Popper formulates and discusses a new aspect of the theory of mind. This theory is partly based on his earlier developed interactionistic theory. It takes as its point of departure the observation that mind and physical forces have several properties in common, at least the following six: both are (i) located, (ii) unextended, (iii) incorporeal, (iv) capable of acting on bodies, (v) dependent upon body, (vi) capable of being influenced by bodies. Other properties such as intensity and extension in time may be added. It is argued that a fuller understanding of the nature of forces is essential for the analysis of the mind-brain problem. The relative autonomy and indeterministic nature of mind is stressed. Indeterminism is treated in relation to a theorem of Hadamard. The computer theory of mind and the Turing test are criticized. Finally the evolution of mind is discussed.

Arieti, James. Man and God in Philo: Philo's Interpretation of Genesis 1:26. *Lyceum*, 4(1), 1-18, Spr 92.

"Let us make man in our image, after our likeness." These words, hardly mentioned among Jewish writers, are quoted by virtually all the Church Fathers, who derive their interpretation from the discussions of Philo, who takes literally Plato's Demiurge (despite evidence that Plato is writing parody). Philo's treatment of other questions—whether there can be a finite image of an infinite God, how a spiritual image of God could sin, how the image was transformed into the Logos—show Philo so adjusting both his Platonism and Hebraism that Eusebius could claim him as a Father of the Catholic Church.

Ariew, Roger. A New Science of Geology in the Seventeenth Century? in *Revolution and Continuity*, Barker, Peter (ed). Washington, Cath Univ Amer Pr, 1991.

Using Leibniz's "Protogaea" I discuss two questions of early modern geology: (i) what are fossils and how are they produced? and (ii) how is it that one can find fossils (or shells) on the tops of mountains? Ultimately this latter question asks about the mechanism for the flood or floods. I compare Leibniz's answers with those of the authors he mentions, from contemporaries he cites with approbation and uses as authorities, to contemporaries and older naturals whom he chooses to dispute. These comparisons enable me to decide whether early modern geology is a new science of geology.

Ariew, Roger and Barker, Peter. Duhem and Continuity in the History of Science. *Rev Int Phil*, 46(182), 323-343, 1992.

We examine the reception of Duhem's claim that medieval science is continuous with modern science, from Antonio Favaro to Peter Dear. After sketching the development of Duhem's views on the history of medieval science, we suggest that a commitment to metaphysically driven revolutionary change in science led Alexandre Koyré and Anneliese Maier to read Duhem's work as an unsatisfactory revolutionary account, rather than one in which the influence of metaphysics is specifically excluded and revolutionary change is denied. (edited)

Ariew, Roger (ed) and Barker, Peter (ed). *Revolution and Continuity*. Washington, Cath Univ Amer Pr, 1991.

This book presents new work in history and historiography of science, linked by a concern to understand the content of early modern science in its own context, and muting the sharp intellectual and institutional discontinuities of earlier histories. The editors' Introduction examines several myths about the Copernican revolution perpetuated by the neglect of context, undermining the presumption of discontinuity in most contemporary history and philosophy of science. (edited)

Aristotle and Tancred, Hugh-Lawson (trans). *The Art of Rhetoric—Aristotle*. New York, Penguin USA, 1991.

Armendt, Brad. Dutch Strategies for Diachronic Rules: When Believers See the Sure Loss Coming. *Proc Phil Sci Ass*, 1, 217-229, 1992.

Two criticisms of Dutch strategy arguments are considered: One says that the arguments fail because agents who know the arguments can use that knowledge to avoid Dutch strategy vulnerability, even though they violate the norm in question. The second consists of cases alleged to be counterexamples to the norms that Dutch strategy arguments defend. Reflection and its Dutch strategy argument are discussed, but most attention is given to two rules: conditionalization and Jeffrey's probability kinematics. I argue that the first criticism should be rejected, and that the second presents no counterexamples to the rationality of commitment to those rules.

Armstrong, D M. Intentionality, Perception, and Causality in John Searle and His Critics, Lepore, Ernest (ed). Cambridge, Blackwell, 1991.

It is argued against Searle that intentionality is neither logically (conceptually) nor ontologically irreducible. Searle's view that perception is intentional is welcomed, as is his view that we have direct experience of causation. It is argued against Searle that there are no inner phenomenal properties involved in perception.

Armstrong, D M. Properties in Language, Truth and Ontology, Mulligan, Kevin (ed). Dordrecht, Kluwer, 1992.

It is argued that we must admit objective properties (and relations) into our ontology, although there are many predicates which do not pick out such properties. Should these properties and relations be taken to be universals or particulars? That issue is delicate, although the author would plump for universals.

Armstrong, D M. Reply to Bigelow's 'Sets Are Haecceities' in Ontology, Causality and Mind: Essays in Honour of D M Armstrong, Bacon, John (ed). New York, Cambridge Univ Pr, 1993.

Against Bigelow's view that sets are Haecceities (singular and plural), Armstrong defends the view that many-membered classes are mereological wholes whose parts are the unit-sets of the members of the class, while unit-sets are states of affairs where the member has the property of unithood, which supervenes on some unit-making property.

Armstrong, D M. Reply to Campbell's 'David Armstrong and Realism about Colour' in Ontology, Causality and Mind: Essays in Honour of D M Armstrong, Bacon, John (ed). New York, Cambridge Univ Pr, 1993.

Armstrong first protests against Campbell interpreting him as holding a physicalized version of a Lockean theory of color (a current physicalist orthodoxy). Against this, he upholds a view which makes color-qualia properties of external things, identifying these properties as purely physical, though at the same time idiosyncratic and likely to be thoroughly disjunctive.

Armstrong, D M. Reply to Fales's 'Are Causal Laws Contingent?' in Ontology, Causality and Mind: Essays in Honour of D M Armstrong, Bacon, John (ed). New York, Cambridge Univ Pr, 1993.

Armstrong and Fales agree that laws of nature are relations of universals. Against Fales' view that these laws are necessary, Armstrong argues that they are contingent. He says that Fales does not show that contingent laws would not sustain counterfactuals and does not show that contingent laws could change. Armstrong also discusses Fales' defense of uninstantiated universals and the view that laws, though necessary, are external.

Armstrong, D M. Reply to Forrest's 'Just Like Quarks?' in Ontology, Causality and Mind: Essays in Honour of D M Armstrong, Bacon, John (ed). New York, Cambridge Univ Pr, 1993.

Forrest and Armstrong agree in accepting the existence of universals, but Forrest accepts, and Armstrong rejects, *uninstantiated* universals. This reply to Forrest is mainly concerned to meet certain difficulties that Forrest thinks are best resolved by introducing uninstantiated universals.

Armstrong, D M. Reply to Jackson's 'Block's Challenge' in Ontology, Causality and Mind: Essays in Honour of D M Armstrong, Bacon, John (ed). New York, Cambridge Univ Pr, 1993.

In this reply, Armstrong registers his fairly complete agreement with Jackson's reply to an argument of Block's against a behavioral/functional account of intelligence.

Armstrong, D M. Reply to Lewis's 'Many, but Almost One' in Ontology, Causality and Mind: Essays in Honour of D M Armstrong, Bacon, John (ed). New York, Cambridge Univ Pr, 1993.

In this reply, Armstrong reiterates his idea (accepted by Lewis) that overlap and the part/whole relation should be seen as partial identity. He goes on to argue that there is another sense of identity, Bishop Butler's "Loose and Popular" identity, and links this concept with Geach's treatment of relative identity.

Armstrong, D M. Reply to Lycan's 'Armstrong's New Combinatorialist Theory...' in Ontology, Causality and Mind: Essays in Honour of D M Armstrong, Bacon, John (ed). New York, Cambridge Univ Pr, 1993.

Lycan directs criticism of Armstrong's combinatorialist theory of possibility particularly at the fictionalist nature of the theory. In reply, Armstrong argues that the combinatorialism can be used to regiment the fiction, so that it can be a *useful* one, as, for instance, the physicist's phase-spaces are useful fictions.

Armstrong, D M. Reply to Martin's 'Power for Realists' in Ontology, Causality and Mind: Essays in Honour of D M Armstrong, Bacon, John (ed). New York, Cambridge Univ Pr, 1993.

Armstrong argues against Martin's view that particulars have properties, categorical properties, that are further associated with irreducible powers, which may not be manifested, to interact with other particulars. First he suggests that Martin would do best to give up the view that these properties are particulars in favor of the view that they are universals. Further, he argues that the operation of these properties should be seen as the manifestation of contingent connections of these universals rather flowing necessarily from powers.

Armstrong, D M. Reply to Menzies' 'Laws of Nature, Modality and Humean...' in Ontology, Causality and Mind: Essays in Honour of D M Armstrong, Bacon, John (ed). New York, Cambridge Univ Pr, 1993.

Armstrong tries to meet what Van Fraassen calls the identification problem can be solved if we have direct experience of singular causation, particularly in awareness of pressure on our own body. Menzies tries to show that there is no such direct awareness, and Armstrong seeks to rebut Menzies' arguments.

Armstrong, D M. Reply to Smart's 'Laws of Nature as a Species of Regularities' in Ontology, Causality and Mind: Essays in Honour of D M Armstrong, Bacon, John (ed). New York, Cambridge Univ Pr, 1993.

In this reply Armstrong welcomes Smart's conversion, announced in his paper, to a theory of properties, conceived of as non-semantic entities. He continues to argue against Smart's regularity theory of laws, upholding against it a theory of laws as relationships of universals.

Armstrong, D M. Reply to 'Properties and Predicates' by Mellor in Ontology, Causality and Mind: Essays in Honour of D M Armstrong, Bacon, John (ed). New York, Cambridge Univ Pr, 1993.

Although Mellor and Armstrong have many deep agreements about properties and the different relations in which they may stand to predicates, Armstrong in this reply concentrates on some differences, in particular Mellor's rejection of complex properties.

Armstrong, D M. The Identification Problem and the Inference Problem. *Phil Phenomenol Res*, 53(2), 421-422, Je 93.

The object is to answer Van Fraassen's criticism, in his *Laws and Symmetry*, of the view that laws of nature are relationships of properties. Such a view, Van Fraassen holds, must either fail to make clear what is the law-making relation (the Identity problem) or else fail to tell us about "what happens and what things are like" (the inference problem). The answer proposed begins with the claim that there is direct perception of singular causal connection.

Armstrong, David M and Place, Ullin T. A Debate on Dispositions, Their Nature and Their Role in Causation—Part I—The Armstrong-Place Debate. *Conceptus*, 25(66), 3-44, 1991.

When we ascribe a dispositional property, such as brittleness, to an entity, such as a pane of glass, at least *part* of what we are saying is that, if certain conditions are fulfilled, if the unprotected glass is stuck with a moderate degree of force, it will behave in a certain way, the glass will break. Like any other empirical proposition, a disposition-ascribing sentence requires a *truthmaker*, an event or state of affairs which is specified by the sentence and which, if it exists, makes the proposition ture. But in the case of a disposition-ascribing sentence, the truthmaker cannot be an event or state of affairs, such as the breaking of the glass, in which the disposition is *manifested*. For it can be true that an entity possesses the property, that the glass is brittle, even though no manifestation of the disposition, no breaking of the glass, ever has occurred or existed in the past or will in fact occur or exist in the future. (edited)

Armstrong, Robert L. Subjectivity/Objectivity and Meaningful Human Behavior in Terrorism, Justice and Social Values, Peden, Creighton W (ed). Lewiston, Mellen Pr, 1990.

I argue that both schools of contemporary philosophy, linguistic analysis and continental phenomenology, mount attacks on strict dichotomy and seek to establish the cognitive legitimacy of a realm of intersubjectivity that is the proper arena of meaningful human behavior. The differences of the two movements in both style and philosophical origin are acknowledged, but it is argued that both use linguistic practice as a paradigm for meaning. (edited)

Armstrong, Robert L. Three Dimensional Social Science. *Cont Phil*, 15(3), 1-3, My-Je 93.

This paper summarizes three versions of social science as presented by David Braybrooke in his *Philosophy of Social Science*. These are: Interpretive Social Science (understanding people from the inside), Naturalistic Social Science (statistical analysis of structural economic forces) and Critical Social Science (critique of ideology). It is argued that it is possible to view the social sciences in a way which displays conceptual unity, a way which differs from Braybrooke's reductive analysis.

Armstrong, Timothy J (trans) and Foucault, Michel. *Michel Foucault, Philosopher*. New York, Routledge, 1992.

Arnason, Johann P. World Interpretation/Mutual Understanding in Cultural-Political Interventions in the Unfinished Project of Enlightenment, Honneth, Axel (& other eds). Cambridge, MIT Pr, 1992.

Arnaud, A J and Kingdom, E. *Women's Rights and the Rights of Man*. Oxford, Aberdeen, 1990.

Arndt, Stephen W. The Justification of Lonergan's Cognitional and Volitional Process. *Amer Cath Phil Quart*, 65(1), 45-61, Wint 91.

Arneil, Barbara. John Locke, Natural Law and Colonialism. *Hist Polit Thought*, 13(4), 587-603, Wint 92.

Arneson, Richard J. Democractic Rights at National and Workplace Levels in The Idea of Democracy, Copp, David (ed). New York, Cambridge Univ Pr, 1993.

Arneson, Richard J. Socialism as the Extension of Democracy. *Soc Phil Pol*, 10(2), 145-171, Sum 93.

Arnheim, Rudolf. Deus Ex Machina. *Brit J Aes*, 32(3), 221-226, Jl 92.

The consistent development of a dramatic story may be violated by the fiat of a superior power that solves the problem by forces not belonging to the given constellation of the play. Superior powers, such as a god's or king's will or a social or physical major force, may serve legitimately as given initial conditions, but the solution of the problem must be due exclusively to the factors set by the dramatic "game".

Arnheim, Rudolf. From Pleasure to Contemplation. *J Aes Art Crit*, 51(2), 195-197, Spr 93.

In the *Nicomachean Ethics*, Aristotle draws a useful distinction between pleasure and happiness. He describes pleasure as an immature means of motivating the conduct of life, whereas happiness comes about by the virtue of contemplation. As he describes the conditions for contemplation, Aristotle overcomes the fruitless but persistent theory of hedonism.

Arnold, Peter J. Sport as a Valued Human Practice: A Basis for the Consideration of Some Moral Issues in Sport. *J Phil Educ*, 26(2), 237-255, 1992.

It is argued that sport, like science or medicine, is a valued human practice and is characterised as much by the moral manner in which its participants conduct themselves as by the pursuit of its own skills, standards and excellences. Virtues, such as justice, honesty and courage, are not only necessary to pursue its goals but to protect it from being corrupted by external interests. After explicating the practice view of sport in contrast to the sociological view, the nature of competition in sport is discussed before examining two related issues: winning at all costs and the taking of performance-enhancing drugs. The importance of practices to education and the good life is also outlined.

Arnold, Robert M and Youngner, Stuart J. The Dead Donor Rule: Should We Stretch It, Bend It, or Abandon It?. *Kennedy Inst Ethics J*, 3(2), 263-278, Je 93.

The dead donor rule — that patients must be dead before their organs are taken — is a central part of the moral framework underlying organ procurement. Efforts to increase the pool of transplantable organs have been forced to either redefine death (e.g., anencephaly) or take advantage of ambiguities in the current definition of death (e.g., the Pittsburgh protocol). Society's growing acceptance of circumstances in which health care professionals can hasten a patient's death also may weaken the symbolic importance of the dead donor rule. We consider the implications of these efforts to continually revise the line between life and death and ask whether it would be preferable to abandon the dead donor rule and rely entirely on informed consent as a safeguard against abuse.

Arnstine, Barbara. Response to "Excellence as a Guide to Educational Conversation". *Proc Phil Educ*, 48, 17-21, 1992.

Arnstine, Barbara and Arnstine, Donald. Rationality and Democracy: A Critical Appreciation of Israel Scheffler's Philosophy of Education. *Synthese*, 94(1), 25-41, Ja 93.

This essay discusses Israel Scheffler's contributions to the philosophy of education, raising critical questions along the way. First, while Scheffler conceives philosophy of education as the analysis of educational discourse, we ask whether a practically useful analysis must not proceed from an analysis of the everyday conditions of schooling. Second Scheffler's remorseless defense of rationality in schooling leaves implications for curriculum ambiguous. Third, while accepting many of Dewey's pragmatic educational views, Scheffler's view of school "standing apart from life" opposes Dewey's socially active schooling.

Arnstine, Donald. The Educator's Impossible Dream: Knowledge As An Educational Aim. *Proc Phil Educ*, 48, 255-264, 1992.

Arnstine, Donald and Arnstine, Barbara. Rationality and Democracy: A Critical Appreciation of Israel Scheffler's Philosophy of Education. *Synthese*, 94(1), 25-41, Ja 93.

This essay discusses Israel Scheffler's contributions to the philosophy of education, raising critical questions along the way. First, while Scheffler conceives philosophy of education as the analysis of educational discourse, we ask whether a practically useful analysis must not proceed from an analysis of the everyday conditions of schooling. Second Scheffler's remorseless defense of rationality in schooling leaves implications for curriculum ambiguous. Third, while accepting many of Dewey's pragmatic educational views, Scheffler's view of school "standing apart from life" opposes Dewey's socially active schooling.

Arntzenius, Frank. How to Discover that the Real Is Unreal. *Erkenntnis*, 38(2), 191-202, Mr 93.

The measurement problem in quantum mechanics is presented in a completely non-technical way by means of the results of some very simple experiments. These experimental results themselves, rather than the formalism of quantum theory, are shown to be extremely hard to incorporate in a sensible state-space picture of the world. A novel twist is then added which makes the problem even harder than it appears to be in other presentations of the measurement problem.

Aronowicz, Annette. The Secret of the Man of Forty. *Hist Theor*, 32(2), 101-118, 1993.

Aronson, Ronald. Deciphering the Israeli-Palestinian Conflict in Sartre Alive, Aronson, Ronald (ed). Detroit, Wayne St Univ Pr, 1991.

Aronson, Ronald. Sartre on Progress in The Cambridge Companion to Sartre, Howells, Christina (ed). New York, Cambridge Univ Pr, 1992.

Aronson, Ronald (ed) and Van Den Hoven, Adrian (ed). *Sartre Alive*. Detroit, Wayne St Univ Pr, 1991.

Aronson, Ronald (ed) and Van Den Hoven, Adrian (trans) and Sartre, Jean Paul. *Truth and Existence—Jean-Paul Sartre*. Chicago, Univ of Chicago Pr, 1992.

Arregui, Jorge V. Wittgenstein on Voluntary Actions. *Int Phil Quart*, 32(3), 299-311, S 92.

Following the thought of Wittgenstein, the paper criticizes the idea that a voluntary action is an action caused by an "act of the will" and puts forward an Aristotelian interpretation of Wittgenstein's insights. Against this interpretation of what is a voluntary action, it is maintained that: (a) willing is not a basic action; (b) a voluntary action is not an action nomologically caused by an act of the will; (c) the will is not a mental experience or a psychological event; and (d) a voluntary action is an action originated by *me*. The arguments developed in the paper lead to the thesis that the will is not a faculty—or operative principle—of the soul parallel to the intellect.

Arregui, Jorge Vicente. Es la Muerte un acontecimiento de la vida?. *Themata*, 8, 141-159, 1991.

It is sometimes said, against an Epicurean treatment of death, that death is not only the terminus of human life, cutting it from outside, but rather than dying is the end *act* by which human existence closes itself, the *act* of expiring which makes of human life a closed whole. The paper discusses this idea, such as it is developed by Tolstoy, Rilke, Scheler and Heidegger, from an existentialist and analytical point of view, and claims that even if death is not merely extrinsic to life, because human life is in every moment a *mortal* one, and even if there exist an appropriation of death, and consequently death has a biographical dimension and not only a biological one, it cannot be considered, as Wittgenstein wrote, as "an act of life". It is argued that the appropriation of death that arises necessarily from human behaviour with regard to it has an unsurmountable limit, because, even if death in not *only* a biological process, it is *also* a biological process.

Arrington, Robert L. Making Contact in Language in Wittgenstein's Philosophical Investigations, Arrington, Robert T (ed). New York, Routledge, 1991.

Arrington, Robert L. The Autonomy of Language in Wittgenstein's Intentions, Canfield, J V (ed). Hamden, Garland, 1993.

Arrington, Robert L (ed) and Glock, Hans-Johann (ed). *Wittgenstein's 'Philosophical Investigations'*. New York, Routledge, 1991.

Art, Brad. Isolation, Loneliness and the Falsification of Reality. *Int J Applied Phil*, 7(1), 31-36, Sum 92.

Loneliness is at once the defining feature of human awareness, and the fundamental question of human existence. Each of us seeks to be in touch with reality with a specific set of basic assumptions about reality, coupled with socially influenced values, and personal history. Using Joseph Soloveitchik's typologies of human nature from "The Lonely Man of Faith," the paper suggests how ontological and axiological analyses can help us understand the systematic distortions of reality created by each vision of living. These analyses are particularly helpful in the area of psychotherapy where the therapist's first goal is to understand the client's sense of reality.

Arthur, Chris and McCarney, Joseph. Marxism Today: An Interview with István Mészáros. *Rad Phil*, 62, 27-34, Autumn 92.

Arthur, John (ed). *Morality and Moral Controversies (Third Edition)*. Englewood Cliffs, Prentice Hall, 1993.

Artigas, M. Emergence and Reduction in Morphogenetic Theories in Philosophy and the Origin and Evolution of the Universe, Agazzi, Evandro (ed). Norwell, Kluwer, 1991.

The paper refers to some difficulties of the classical analysis of reductionism, and suggests that the problem of reduction may be replaced by the analysis of the relations between levels. These reflections are afterwards applied to the examination of some morphogenetic theories, namely non-linear thermodynamics, synergetics, catastrophe theory and deterministic chaos, and finally to the problem of ontological emergence, including an evaluation of some ideas about the origin of the universe and mankind. It is argued that the very existence of natural activity poses problems whose philosophical aspects are not exhausted by scientific explanations.

Artigas, Mariano. Conocimiento humano, fiabilidad y falibilismo. *Anu Filosof*, 25(2), 277-294, 1992.

Fallibilism is a common view in contemporary epistemology. However, an examination of its philosophical basis and consequences show that it requires some non trivial qualifications about its meaning.

Arvidson, P Sven. The Field of Consciousness: James and Gurwitsch. *Trans Peirce Soc*, 28(4), 833-856, Fall 92.

The purpose is to explore the similarities and differences of James and Gurwitsch on the structure of the field of consciousness. The perspective used is Gurwitsch's critique of James on this issue. In articulating Gurwitsch's emendation of James, the possibility of a three versus a two part structure of the field of consciousness is discussed in light of the former's notion of thematic field and Gestalt connection, and the latter's notion of temporality, margin, and fringe.

Ash, C J. Generalizations of Enumeration Reducibility Using Recursive Infinitary Propositional Sentences. *Annals Pure Applied Log*, 58(3), 173-184, N 92.

We consider the relation between sets A and B that for every set S if A is sigma-zero-alpha in S then B is sigma-zero-beta in S. We show that this is equivalent to the condition that B is definable from A in a particular way involving recursive infinitary propositional sentences. When alpha=beta=1, this condition is that B is enumeration reducible to A. We establish further generalizations involving infinitely many sets and ordinals.

Ashcraft, Richard. Liberal Political Theory and Working-Class Radicalism in Nineteenth-Century England. *Polit Theory*, 21(2), 249-272, My 93.

Ashcraft, Richard. The Radical Dimensions of Locke's Political Thought: A Dialogic Essay on the Problems of Interpretation. *Hist Polit Thought*, 13(4), 703-772, Wint 92.

Ashworth, E J. A Thirteenth-Century Interpretation of Aristotle on Equivocation and Analogy. *Can J Phil*, Supp(17), 85-101, 1991.

This paper is a case study of how Aristotle's remarks about equivocation were read in the thirteenth century. I analyze the divisions of equivocation and analogy found in an anonymous commentary on the *Sophistici Elenchi* written in Paris between 1270 and 1280; and I show the part played by four sources: 1) the Greek commentators of late antiquity; 2) the new translations of Aristotle's *Physics* and *Metaphysics*; 3) Arabic works, particularly those of Averroes; 4) new grammatical doctrines, notably *modi significandi*.

Ashworth, E J. Analogical Concepts: The Fourteenth-Century Background to Cajetan. *Dialogue (Canada)*, 31(3), 399-413, Sum 92.

Cajetan attacked three views of the concept of being: that it is a disjunction of concepts; that it is an ordered group of concepts; and that it is a single, separate concept which is unequally participated by substances and accidents. I discuss these views as they were presented by the 14th-century philosopher Peter Aureol, Hervaeus Natalis, and John of Jandun. I thereby shed light on medieval theories of analogy, of signification, and of the so-called objective concept.

Ashworth, E J. New Light on Medieval Philosophy: The Sophismata of Richard Kilvington. *Dialogue (Canada)*, 31(3), 517-521, Sum 92.

In this review-article of a recent edition and translation of the sophismata of the 14th-century English philosopher and theologian, Richard Kilvington, I place sophismata (i.e., puzzle-sentences) in their literary, institutional, and philosophical context. Kilvington's sophismata are particularly characterized by their use of the mathematical language of proportion and the analysis of continuous magnitudes and processes, as well as by their focus on the syntactico-semantic properties of terms. They have important implications for theories of reference.

Asike, Joseph I. Contemporary African Philosophy: The Search for a Method or Rediscovery of its Content?. *Indian Phil Quart*, 19(1), 23-39, Ja 92.

The paper examines the background to the current debate on the nature of African philosophy. It appears that the more substantive issues of reconstructing the philosophy has either been neglected or abandoned. If the Diopian model is to have any credence, then the task should be how to reconstruct the history of African philosophy from antiquity to post colonial Africa.

Asmis, Elizabeth. Crates on Poetic Criticism. *Phoenix*, 46(2), 138-169, Sum 92.

Asmis, Elizabeth. Plato on Poetic Creativity in The Cambridge Companion to Plato, Kraut, Richard (ed). New York, Cambridge Univ Pr, 1992.

Aspray, William. Oswald Veblen and the Origins of Mathematical Logic at Princeton in Perspectives on the History of Mathematical Logic, Drucker, Thomas (ed). Basel, Birkhauser, 1991.

Assoun, P L. Métapsychologie et théorie de la communication Freud versus Habermas. *Commun Cog*, 25(1), 11-28, 1992.

Atienza, Manuel. Practical Reason and Legislation. *Ratio Juris*, 5(3), 269-287, D 92.

The author's starting point is Bobbio's theoretical approach to the problems of the relations between law and reason. He then appraises the meanings of reason and the concept of theoretical and practical rationality in the application of law. He examines the complex problem of the rationality of legislation and distinguishes five levels of rationality.

Atkins, John. Common-Sense or Non-Sense. *Phil Invest*, 15(4), 346-356, O 92.

Wittgenstein's attitude towards epistemology and 'grammar' in his later work has, I think, been widely misunderstood. This perhaps has been because not always was he consistent himself? Greater confusion though seems to have been generated by commentators viewing his work not as a radical departure from the philosophical tradition, but rather as just another approach within it. This short paper seeks to emphasize this point and clarify some aspects of Wittgenstein's thought on these matters.

Atkinson, Gary and Sullivan, Thomas D. *Malum Vitandum*: The Role of Intentions in First-Order Morality. *Int J Phil Stud*, 1(1), 99-110, Mr 93.

"First-Order Morality" in the title refers to moral judgments about actions in contrast to judgments about agents. A number of critics have contended either that the distinction between intended versus merely foreseen consequences makes no sense, or that the agent's intentions should not enter into "first-order morality". We explore and respond to criticisms brought by Roderick Chisholm, Douglas Lackey, and Jonathan Bennett in our defense of the vital role intentions play in the moral assessment of human acts.

Atkinson, Norman. Philosophy for Children Comes to Africa. *Thinking*, 10(3), 13-14, 1993.

In the current world situation, prospects for social and economic development in Africa are more favorable than at any time in the past. The author argues that the crucial need now is for the inculcation of the skills and attitudes of critical thought as a means to responsible decision-making. He believes that the foundations of critical thought must be laid in the school curriculum.

Atkinson, R F. Kant's Moral and Political Rigorism in Essays on Kant's Political Philosophy, Williams, Howard Lloyd (ed). Chicago, Univ of Chicago Pr, 1992.

An attempt to establish: what exactly were Kant's opinions about lying, rebellion, and capital punishment; and the degrees to which they were determined by his theory, his judgement on particular issues, or features of his upbringing and situation. It is concluded that they were mainly influenced by features of his moral theory, and can rather be defended as simple good sense not disregarded as accidental aberrations. Their merits are obscured rather than enhanced by the ethical system in which Kant enfolded them.

Atkinson, R F. Locke on Government in Logical Foundations, Mahalingam, Indira (ed). New York, St Martin's Pr, 1991.

The question is how much of O'Connor's conception of Locke as the liberal and egalitarian apologist for 1658 can survive the findings of more recent scholarship. The conclusion, based on an examination of Locke's account of consent, property and slavery, is that much remains acceptable. Locke's notion of consent, though misused in relation to property, has significant content; and, though he is not in practice egalitarian, he is more liberal than his contemporaries in regard to religious toleration. Locke's views, even when thoroughly contextualised, retain some relevance for later periods.

Atkinson, R F. Methodology: History and Its Philosophy in Objectivity, Method and Point of View, Van Der Dussen, W J (ed). Leiden, Brill, 1991.

The analytical character of philosophy of history is stressed, as is its continuity with philosophy generally, which is a unitary study, prompted by a distinctive form of curiosity, of various subject matters: history, science, morality etc. Procedure should be explicitly comparative, respectful of the practice of historians, though not committed to accepting their categories as beyond criticism. Philosophers study history for their own purposes, and their own conclusions can, but need not be interesting or useful to historians. History is a rich and distinctive mode of enquiry from which philosophers can learn much.

Attas, Daniel. Rawls's Savings Principle (in Hebrew). *Iyyun*, 41, 383-412, O 92.

Attfield, Robin. Development and Environmentalism in International Justice and the Third World, Attfield, Robin (ed). New York, Routledge, 1992.

It is argued that morality and consistency oblige environmentalists to support sustainable development and developmentalists to support some of the "deeper" kinds of environmentalism. This project involves sifting the developmentalist critique of the causes of underdevelopment and the environmentalist critique of anthropocentrism; since each critique neglects the other, both are held to need supplementation.

Attfield, Robin (ed) and Wilkins, Barry (ed). *International Justice and the Third World*. New York, Routledge, 1992.

This book consists of eight papers which discuss notions of global justice and explore their implications for the Third World. They relate Third World development to sustainability, issues of gender, environmentalism and Third World debt, questioning throughout the sufficiency of market mechanisms to cope with these issues. The ability of Liberal and Marxist theories to account for global justice is considered, and various theoretical models of development are critically examined. As many millions of women in the Third World suffer special oppression, it is stressed that any adequate theory must respond to their plight.

Audi, Robert. Faith, Belief, and Rationality in Philosophical Perspectives, 5: Philosophy of Religion, 1991, Tomberlin, James E (ed). Atascadero, Ridgeview, 1991.

Audi, Robert. Mental Causation in Mental Causation, Heil, John (ed). New York, Clarendon/Oxford Pr, 1993.

Audi, Robert 400 AUTHOR INDEX WITH ABSTRACTS

Audi, Robert. The Dimensions of Faith and the Demands of Reason in Reasoned Faith, Stump, Eleonore (ed). Ithaca, Cornell Univ Pr, 1993.

Audi, Robert. The Journalistic Uses of Philosophy. *J Soc Phil*, 23(3), 51-63, Wint 92.

Audi, Robert. The Nature and Assessment of Practical Reasoning: A Reply to John A Barker and Richard Foley. *Behavior Phil*, 19(2), 73-81, Fall-Wint 91.

This paper briefly summarizes the approach of Audi's *Practical Reasoning* (Routledge, 1989 and 1991) and responds to critical studies of the book (published in the same issue) by John Barker and Richard Foley. The paper stresses the nature of practical reasoning as an inferential process; its role in providing reasons for action; its explanatory scope; its connections with desire, belief, and rational action; and the similarities and differences between practical and theoretical reasoning. The essay also explores some of the logical criteria for adequate practical reasoning, some standards for the rationality of actions based on such reasoning, and the extent to which the normative position taken in the book is cognitivist, realist, and naturalistic.

Augros, Michael. Difficulty in Defining Motion. *Lyceum*, 2(1), 53-63, Spr 90.

Auspitz, J Lee (ed) and Gasparski, Wojciech W (ed) and Mlicki, Marek K (ed). *Praxiologies and the Philosophy of Economics: The International Annual of Practical Philosophy and Methodology*. New Brunswick, Transaction Books, 1992.

Autin, Pierre-Louis. La fonction du droit et la question du lien social chez Hume et Montesquieu. *Rev Phil Fr*, 2, 147-172, Ap-Je 92.

Auxier, Randall. The Rise and Fall of Evolutionary Thinking Among American Philosophers. *SW Phil Rev*, 9(1), 135-150, Ja 93.

In the last forty years epistemologists and philosophers of science have shunned the true implications of the Darwinian revolution. The complete adoption of evolution as a metaphysical principle subverts logic-centered epistemology in the following ways: (1) knowledge of the natural world becomes, at best, a matter of probabilities; (2) all knowledge claims arise from a cultural/historical context which the philosophy of science is ill-suited to elucidate (and hence, the philosophy of history and culture must be taken as the ground of any philosophy of science); and, (3) values become the ground of facts instead of the reverse. Dewey's theory of inquiry, or something like it, offers the best hope for making the philosophy of science truly evolutionary.

Avé-Lallemant, Eberhard and Schuhmann, Karl. Ein Zeitzeuge über die Anfänge der phänomenologischen Bewegung: Theodor Conrads Bericht aus dem Jahre 1954. *Husserl Stud*, 9(2), 77-90, 1992.

Averill, Edward Wilson. The Relational Nature of Color. *Phil Rev*, 101(3), 551-588, Jl 92.

This is an essay on the ontology of color. There are two sorts of color properties, relational-color properties and sensuous-color properties. Our use of "yellow" to refer to a relational-color has two suppressed argument places: x is yellow for a certain population in a certain environment. The relational-colors are constructed from sensuous-colors using the relation x-and-y -look- the- same- in- sensuous-color- to- subject- S- under- circumstances- C and some assumptions. Many of the ontological problems involving color are solved by assuming that only relational-colors are instantiated in the actual world.

Avery, Jon. Three Types of American Neo-Pragmatism. *J Phil Res*, 18, 1-13, 1993.

The issue of this paper is the extend to which historicism excludes metaphysics in the contemporary revival of American philosophical pragmatism. I have isolated three types of neo-pragmatism: philosophical, theological, and religious. My thesis is that religious pragmatism is a dialectical compromise between theological pragmatism and philosophical pragmatism. William Dean is correct that Rorty's commitment to human solidarity implies a metaphysics, for human solidarity is valuable only because natural reality is so harsh. (edited)

Avgelis, Nikolaos. Schlick's Epistemology and Its Contrib to Modern Empiricism in Greek Studies in the Philosophy and History of Science, Nicolacopoulos, Pantelis (ed). Dordrecht, Kluwer, 1990.

Avio, K L. Economic, Retributive and Contractarian Conceptions of Punishment. *Law Phil*, 12(3), 249-286, Ag 93.

This paper seeks to identify the theory of punishment that provides the "best" underlying foundation for the criminal law. Economic and Kantian models are discussed and rejected; the former models (Becker-Posner tradition) provide efficiency at the cost of justice, whereas the latter (early Rawls-Hart-Byrd tradition) provide justice at the cost of efficiency. A constitutional-contractarian account simultaneously addresses allocative questions and moral concerns. This account is seen to conform more closely to the idealized criminal law than do alternative models.

Aviram, Aharon. The Nature of University Education Reconsidered (A Response to Ronald Barnett's *The Idea of Higher Education*). *J Phil Educ*, 26(2), 183-200, 1992.

The paper is a response to the present crisis of higher education as reflected in the fragmentation of the university, and its increasingly performative character. It is based on a criticism of Ronald Barnett's recent attempt to tackle this problem. While agreeing with Barnett's fundamentally radical approach to higher education, the paper criticizes Barnett's view on three levels: the methodological, theoretical, and practical. It ends with guidelines for an alternative radical approach which avoids the practical problems besetting Barnett's proposal.

Avnon, Dan. The "Living Center" of Martin Buber's Political Theory. *Polit Theory*, 21(1), 55-77, F 93.

Throughout the mature period of his intellectual life Buber maintained that genuine community originates in a person's (or group of persons') newfound perception of the nature of being. Such a community develops around a "living center." The essay illustrates the importance of Buber's nonpolitical writings as indirect communicators of his idea of the living, human center of community; Buber uses myths and symbols as vehicles for presenting society with a paradigms of personal conduct and communal life. These paradigmatic images become historical metaphors for the mythical reality he envisions. Buber may thus be best described as a political thinker whose primary vocation is the creation of social and political symbols and images.

Awalt, H Mike. Reply to Clifford and Gallagher. *Personalist Forum*, 8/1(Supp), 4346, Spr 92.

This paper responds to Shaun Gallagher's "The Theory of Personal Identity: From Hume to Derrida" and Michael Clifford "Corrugated Subjects: Three Axes of Personhood" showing that they make the same claim about their respective subjects (Derrida and Foucault): They radically decenter the self and reveal that nothing lurks behind the mask of personhood. The paper raises two questions. First, does Clifford's presentations of Foucault's concept of the decentered self solve the problem Clifford raises via the introduction of Jeremy Bentham's 'presence' at the University of London and second, does Derrida deconstruct the possibility of personal identity in a more radical way than Foucault?

Axel, Larry E. Religious Creaturalism and a New Agenda for Theology in God, Values, and Empiricism, Peden, Creighton W (ed). Macon, Mercer Univ Pr, 1989.

Axel, Larry E (ed) and Peden, W Creighton (ed). *God, Values, and Empiricism*. Macon, Mercer Univ Pr, 1989.

God, Values and Empiricism, (Mercer University Press, 1989) is a collection of essays presented at the First International Conference on Philosophical Theology at Oxford University in 1988. The Conference was sponsored by the Highlands Institute for American Religious Thought. The volume reflects the interests of the Institute in liberal religious thought, themes relevant to the "Chicago School" of theology, naturalism in American theology, and in the interface of theology and classical American philosophy. Persons interested in American philosophy and theology will find these strong, scholarly essays of special import.

Axelos, K. The Question of the End of Art and the Poetic Character of the World (in Czechoslovakian). *Filozof Cas*, 40(4), 605-619, 1992.

The author wants to examine the "poetic character" of the world starting from the question of "the end of art." He considers this a key question, the same as it was for Hegel or for Kant. Starting from Kant and Hegel, and working through Marx and Freud to Heidegger—and linking up with his well-known studies—Kostas Axelos examines the "historically" and philosophically equivocal, contradictory and complex relationships of art to a reality. If he is right, that by and through these relationships a clearly metaphysical language game is being played, then he is also right that for "the questioning of thought"—hence for the one philosophy still possible today—the conceptions of such a language must be examined in detail. (edited)

Axiotis, Ares. *Fiat vita, pereat veritas*: Nietzsche's Untimely Reflections on Hegel's Dialectic of History. *Bull Hegel Soc Gt Brit*, 23-24, 61-78, 1991.

Only the renegade classical philologist Nietzsche exposes the performative contradiction in which history is enmeshed, its double game of truth and lie, as a manifestation of the gigantomachy between dialectic and rhetoric. The split memory of history defines a genre whose excellence, only fully attained by Hegel, is to forget its own literariness through the forgetfulness of theory. The more history attains to the status of absolute science as dialectical anamnesis, the more its dissimulating amnesia at the heart of its signification is perfected.

Axtell, Guy S. In the Tracks of the Historicist Movement: Re-assessing the Carnap-Kuhn Connection. *Stud Hist Phil Sci*, 24(1), 119-146, Mr 93.

Aybar, Samuel R and Harlan, Joshua D and Lee, Won J. John Rawls: For the Record (An Interview). *Harvard Rev Phil*, 1(1), 38-48, Spr 91.

Ayer, A J. A Defence of Empiricism in A J Ayer Memorial Essays, Griffiths, A Phillips (ed). New York, Cambridge Univ Pr, 1991.

Ayer, A J. Free-Will and Determinism in Logical Foundations, Mahalingam, Indira (ed). New York, St Martin's Pr, 1991.

Ayer, A J. My Mental Development in The Philosophy of A J Ayer, Hahn, Lewis E (ed). Peru, Open Court, 1992.

Ayer, A J. Still More of My Life in The Philosophy of A J Ayer, Hahn, Lewis E (ed). Peru, Open Court, 1992.

Ayer, A J (ed) and O'Grady, Jane (ed). *A Dictionary of Philosophical Quotations*. Cambridge, Blackwell, 1992.

Aylesworth, Gary E (trans) and Heidegger, Martin. *Basic Concepts—Martin Heidegger*. Bloomington, Indiana Univ Pr, 1993.

Aymerich, Ignacio. Identidad individual y personalidad jurídica. *Anu Filosof*, 26(2), 395-413, 1993.

According to some of Foucault's proposals, this paper deals with the historical constitution of individual identity forms through juridic practices. Concretely the results of the transformation of modern law from the state monopolization of the legislative functions, a process considered to be based on social contract theories. The constitution of social order according to a successive scheme: from the pre-social individuals to supra-individual society. The juridical individualism derives from this model, and the critical approach on its made from the contemporary sciences of human behavior.

Ayuso Torres, M. Francisco Canals y la Escuela tomista de Barcelona. *Pensamiento*, 189(48), 78-82, Ja-Mr 92.

Azzouni, Jody. A Priori Truth. *Erkenntnis*, 37(3), 327-346, N 92.

Babbitt, Susan E. Feminism and Objective Interests: The Role of Transformation Experiences in Rational Deliberation in Feminist Epistemologies, Alcoff, Linda (ed). New York, Routledge, 1993.

Baber, Harriet E. Almost Indiscernible Twins. *Phil Phenomenol Res*, 52(2), 365-382, Je 92.

Babich, Babette E. A Musical Retrieve of Heidegger, Nietzsche, and Technology: Cadence, Concinnity, and Playing Brass. *Man World*, 26(3), 239-260, Jl 93.

The constructive value of Heidegger's philosophy of technology is obscured where Heidegger articulates his questioning of technology as a deliberate misprision of Nietzsche's philosophy of nihilism. Heidegger represents Nietzsche's notion of the will to technological power as the will to dominion over the earth. A more nuanced exposition (*Auseinandersetzung*) of Heidegger's reading of Nietzsche is presented not to advance Nietzsche's perspective as superior but to permit a genuine recollection of Heidegger's philosophic project of questioning in the wake of technology and the spirit of Nietzsche's perspective on value and culture, power and delight.

Babich, Babette E. Commentary: Michael Green, "Nietzsche on Pity and *Ressentiment*". *Int Stud Phil*, 24(2), 71-76, 1992.

In this commentary, I observe that the issue of Nietzsche's views on pity and *ressentment* are not resolvable via the niceties of linguistic or grammatical logic or any discursive focus. Instead pity for Nietzsche corresponds to the will to power of the weak and in its place Nietzsche recommends what this nihilistic will denies; the "great health" of the artist of life. Thus, as a "physician of culture", Nietzsche affirms that while the culture of pity has been essential to the development of Western culture, the challenge of overcoming this culture is the challenge of overcoming nihilism.

Babich, Babette E. Questioning Heidegger's Silence in Ethics and Danger, Dallery, Arleen B (ed). Albany, SUNY Pr, 1992.

Heidegger's silence on the question of the Holocaust is reviewed as either a private silence (contemptuously, shamefully complicit with Nazism) or as a stammering, ringing stillness (correspondent to authentic disclosure in language). Interpreting silence as a kind of reticence that speaks from the side of forbearance and solicitous concern expresses the thinking that has learned how to listen as the condition for a genuinely pluralistic human community. This interpretation enables what Benjamin could have named a weak redemption of Heidegger's thinking in terms of what Reiner Schürmann has named the bifrontal essence of Heidegger's thinking on technology.

Baccari, Luciano. Considerazioni sul problema della conoscenza. *Aquinas*, 35(3), 561-586, S-D 92.

Baccarini, Elvio. Rational Consensus and Coherence Methods in Ethics. *Grazer Phil Stud*, 40, 151-159, 1991.

The method of *reflective equilibrium* implies that moral principles received from philosophical reasoning and *considered moral judgments* received intuitively are finally justified if they cohere with each other. This idea is combined with the proposal of *rational consensus* (Lehrer), which shows the way in which divergences of judgments could be made to converge. This second method is used to the end of rendering more plausible the intuitions used in *reflective equilibrium*, and, so, to show the appropriateness of the coherentist method in ethics.

Bach, Kent. Intentions and Demonstrations. *Analysis*, 52(3), 140-146, Jl 92.

I defend David Kaplan recent claim that demonstrative gestures, functioning merely as 'aids to communication', are without semantic significance-speaker intentions determine the demonstratum. Against this Marga Reimer has argued that demonstrations can and do play an essential semantic role and that intentions are not decisive. She may be correct about such intentions as she considers, but she overlooks the referential intentions specific to communication. It turns out that although demonstrations contribute in a way to what is said, this does not make them semantically significant. For what is said, to the extent that it is not fixed by linguistic meaning, is determined by aspects of the speaker's intention, including, in demonstrative cases, the intention to refer to what one is demonstrating.

Backhaus, Wilfried K. Hume and the Politics of Reason. *Dialogue (Canada)*, 31(1), 65-69, Wint 92.

Backman, Wayne. Epistemically-Qualified Judgment: A Nonquantitative Approach. *J Phil Res*, 17, 1-27, 1992.

The author describes a formal system for interpreting and generating epistemically-qualified judgments, that is, judgments qualified by phrases like "it is certain that", "it is almost certain that", "it is plausible that", and "it is doubtful that". The system has two noteworthy properties. First, the system's qualifiers are purely qualitative. Second, the system is based on epistemic warranting conditions, not truth conditions. (edited)

Bacon, Francis and Pitcher, John (ed). *The Essays—Francis Bacon*. New York, Penguin USA, 1985.

Bacon, John (ed) and Campbell, Keith (ed) and Reinhardt, Lloyd (ed). *Ontology, Causality and Mind: Essays in Honour of D M Armstrong*. New York, Cambridge Univ Pr, 1993.

This Festschrift is a collection of papers on questions central to the philosophy of D M Armstrong, each followed by a reply from Armstrong. Topics covered include universals, dispositions, the combinatorial approach to modality, individuation, causality, laws of nature, consciousness, and color. The contributors are William G Lycan, David Lewis, Peter Forrest, John Bigelow, D H Mellor, Evan Fales, J J C Smart, C B Martin, Peter Menzies, Frank Jackson, and Keith Campbell. A complete bibliography of Armstrong's works up to 1992 closes the book.

Baden, John A. Economic Perspectives on Bioethics. *J Med Phil*, 18(4), 389-397, Ag 93.

Wendell Stephenson argues that the National Institutes of Health's standards for the treatment of laboratory animals fail to give any guidance concerning human well-being nor do they balance human well-being and animal well-being. Stephenson fails, however, to demonstrate how such a balance is to be known. In arguing for reform he implies greater state control without showing that such control would improve the situation. Indeed there are good reasons to think that such control may be harmful.

Bader, Erwin. Zur Kritik des kritischen Rationalismus. *Conceptus*, 25(65), 105-113, 1991.

Ethics has suffered a severe crisis since the advent of Positivism. This fact leads to a reduction of the ethical dimension of the sciences. Hans Albert's attempt to treat norms in a scientific way is interpreted in the above article as a theoretical regress behind René Marcic's theory of "prepositive law." Marcic's theory serves as a basis of human rights, proclaiming the priority of the freedom and dignity of man. The attempt of Popper's to overcome positivism has not met with widespread acceptance so far and has been even less advanced. The above treatise tries to give an impulse in this direction. As point of departure serves the principal theoretical basis of Popper's critical rationalism, which—according to his own word—consists in an ethically motivated and therefore metaphysical-irrational pre-decision. On the basis of this concept of reason, he doesn't acknowledge the possibility for a rational foundation of ethics. (edited)

Badhwar, Neera Kapur. Altruism Versus Self-Interest: Sometimes a False Dichotomy. *Soc Phil Pol*, 10(1), 90-117, Wint 93.

Contrary to the usual view, rationally self-interested motivation *can* have moral worth. I argue that 1) self-interest includes the interest in affirming oneself by affirming one's central dispositions, and that 2) a whole-heartedly altruistic action is one that is motivated, in part, by an agent's interest in affirming the altruistic dispositions central to her self. To support these points I use the example of rescuers of Jews in Nazi Europe. I conclude by arguing that altruism is a virtue only in an individual who is also rationally self-interested (as, conversely, self-interest is a virtue only in an individual who is also rationally altruistic).

Badhwar, Neera Kapur. Altruism Versus Self-Interest: Sometimes a False Dichotomy in Altruism, Paul, Ellen Frankel (ed). New York, Cambridge Univ Pr, 1993.

Contrary to the usual view, rationally self-interested motivation *can* have moral worth. I argue that 1) self-interest includes the interest in affirming oneself by affirming one's central dispositions, and that 2) a whole-heartedly altruistic action is one that is motivated, in part, by an agent's interest in affirming the altruistic dispositions central to her self. To support these points I use the example of rescuers of Jews in Nazi Europe. I conclude by arguing that altruism is a virtue only in an individual who is also rationally self-interested (as, conversely, self-interest is a virtue only in an individual who is also rationally altruistic).

Badhwar, Neera Kapur (ed). *Friendship: A Philosophical Reader*. Ithaca, Cornell Univ Pr, 1993.

This anthology brings together some of the best recent work on friendship. Together, the 15 articles provide a general idea of 1) the nature and personal value of friendship, ii) the moral significance of friendship and the response to this significance by Aristotelian, Christian, Kantian, and consequentialist theories, and c) the importance of personal and civic friendship in a good society. The thirty-six page introduction offers the reader an integrated, critical overview of these issues and their location in the larger philosophical picture by relating the articles to each other, as well as to historical and contemporary discussions not included in the anthology.

Badillo, Robert Peter and McLean, George F (ed). *The Emancipative Theory of Jürgen Habermas and Metaphysics*. Washington, CRVP, 1991.

Though Habermas does not develop the metaphysical themes latent in his own work, in articulating a model of communicating subjects for the exercise of their emancipatory potential, he opens a space which points toward the further reaches of his own philosophical compass. This study argues that Habermas's philosophy of emancipation may be viewed as a new optic for elaborating the notion of being as *esse* by examining the sense in which Habermas's categories of *dialogical* (versus monological) *paradigm, communicative action*, and *emancipation* enrich the transcendental properties of being as *esse* — unity, truth, and goodness — as well as the manner in which Habermas's proposal is itself enriched when understood from the classical metaphysical point of view.

Baechler, Jean. Virtue: Its Nature, Exigency, and Acquisition. *Nomos*, 34, 25-48, 1992.

Virtue is a permanent and deliberate disposition to pursue the good; it is the upper echelon in a scale graduated by non-vice, vice, non-virtue, corruption and perversion. All grades are objective, because the ends of human actions are objective. Virtue and non-vice are requested regarding oneself, others, and groups. Virtue is acquired by teaching and practice, non-vice through the constraints imposed by nature and society. This humanist interpretation of ethics and virtue contrasts with the utilitarian one by showing that it has only a local validity.

Bäck, Allan. Avicenna's Conception of the Modalities. *Vivarium*, 30(2), 217-255, N 92.

Bäck, Allan. Sailing through the Sea Battle. *Ancient Phil*, 12(1), 133-151, Spr 92.

I wish to present a simple resolution of the problem of the sea battle treated in Aristotle's *On Interpretation 9*. Though my model is simple, the task is not. I am going to have to battle with the text and to wade through a sea of secondary literature. Let me, then, first present the solution, and then face these labors. I shall conclude with some reflections about certain problems that my solution makes.

Baergen, Ralph. Perceptual Consciousness and Perceptual Evidence. *Phil Papers*, 21(2), 107-119, Ag 92.

There are compelling empirical reasons for thinking that perceptual evidence is not exhausted by the perceptual consciousness. Segments of the empirical evidence are reviewed, and it is argued that some beliefs based upon unconscious perceptual processing seem to warrant positive epistemic evaluation. Also, many epistemically significant influences upon perception are unconscious. It is argued further that taking all perceptual evidence to be conscious leaves one with a dilemma regarding dreams and hallucinations.

Baertschi, Bernard. La question du libre arbitre en France, de la Révolution à la Restauration. *Stud Phil (Switzerland)*, 49, 103-129, 1990.

At the beginning of the XIXth century, French philosophy is dominated by *Idéologie*, a movement inspired by Condillac and Diderot. Their main figures, Destutt de Tracy and Cabanis, defend a deterministic conception of man, based on a physiologically minded materialism. This position encounters the critics of another philosopher, Maine de Biran: for him, the *Idéologues* neglect the psychological point of view, which teaches man he is free. I examine this opposition, in which we see a first contrast between the objective and subjective point of view.

Baeten, Elizabeth M. Myth and Freedom. *Thought*, 67(266), 324-338, S 92.

Bagger, Matthew C. The Miracle of Minimal Foundationalism: Religious Experience and Justified Belief. *Relig Stud*, 29(3), 297-312, S 93.

Bahlul, Raja. Identity and Necessary Similarity. *Can J Phil*, 22(4), 531-546, D 92.

In this paper I formulate, and offer two arguments in support of a principle which is closely related to the familiar Principle of the Identity of Indiscernibles. The new principle is called "The Identity of Necessary Similarity". I briefly discuss the relevance of both principles to the problem of individuation, and suggest that the new principle offers a more plausible view of the relation between numerical diversity and qualitative difference.

Bahlul, Raja. Leibniz, Aristotle, and the Problem of Individuation. *Pac Phil Quart*, 73(3), 185-199, S 92.

Leibniz and Aristotle offer diametrically opposed accounts of what it is for ordinary particulars to be numerically diverse. Leibniz, through his Principle of the Identity of Indiscernibles (PII), affirms that numerically diverse particulars must have different qualities, whereas Aristotle insists that such particulars are different on account of their "matter". In this paper I seek to bridge the gap between these two rival accounts by means of a (PII)-like principle which seems to be a consequence of the Aristotelian position.

Bahm, Archie. *Axiology: The Science of Values*. Amsterdam, Rodopi, 1993.

This book has two purposes: to help establish axiology as a science and to urge its recognition by philosophers and the scientific community. Distinguishing between intrinsic and instrumental values, it makes clear that intrinsic values, as feelings of enjoyment and suffering, including pleasures and pains, satisfactions and frustrations, enthusiasm and apathy, and contentment and disturbance, are experienced intuitively by every one, so each person can test the theory with certainty.

Bahm, Archie. *Tao Teh King By Lao Tzu: Interpreted as Nature and Intelligence*. Albuquerque, World Books, 1986.

A Second Edition testifies to the popularity of this Great Book of China by adding 50 new titles of translations published between 1958 and 1992 to the 44 listed for 1868 to 1955. Corrections of misleading section titles of my comments about Tao and Teh and comparisons of the philosophies of Lao Tzu and Confucius should prevent possible misunderstanding. The text of the interpretation is presented before the (usually introductory) comments because the doctrine as presented is so simple, clear and obvious that it is its own best introduction.

Bahm, Archie. Three Zeros: A Comparative Philosophy of Voids. *Int Phil Quart*, 32(4), 499-500, D 92.

"Three zeros" refers to three kinds of negation emphasized in three civilizations, Western, Indian, and Chinese: absence of being, absence of difference, absence of exclusion. In the West, "zero being" is nonentity. "Being is; non-being is not". In India, being is, and cannot not be. Nirguna Brahman, pure being, is void of distinctions. Its "zero" is zero difference. In China, being is, and cannot be. Tao (being) is permeated by distinctions (*yin* and *yang*) as mutually immanent opposites. It's "zero" is absence of exclusion. Implications for logical negation: exclusive negation, negation of all negation, and negation of exclusion.

Bahm, Archie. *Why Be Moral? (Second Edition)*. Albuquerque, World Books, 1992.

An introduction to ethical theory, including individual ethics (15 chs.), social ethics (15 chs.) and final ethics (4 chs.). It locates intrinsic value in feelings of enjoyment and suffering, oughtness in the power that apparently greater good has over and apparently lesser good in compelling our choices, and rightness in seeking what is best for oneself in the long run because conceiving self as essentially social, and organically interdependent. Includes principles for choosing and ten principles for promoting self-interest.

Bahm, Archie J (trans) and Tzu, Lao. *Tao Teh King—Lao Tzu*. Albuquerque, World Books, 1986.

Baier, Annette. *A Progress of Sentiments: Reflections on Hume's "Treatise"*. Cambridge, Harvard Univ Pr, 1991.

The book relates Hume's version of our cognitive abilities and disabilities, in *Treatise* Book One, to his account and selective endorsement of our repertoire of passions and sentiments, in Books Two and Three. The role of reflexivity in arriving at normative rules (of causal inference, of justice) is emphasized. "Reason" in a narrow rationalist sense failed the test of reflexivity in Book One, but the more social, natural, and lively "reason," which is in place by the end of the *Treatise*, can survive its own survey and is included among the virtues.

Baier, Annette. Artificial Virtues and the Equally Sensible Non-Knaves: A Response to Gauthier. *Hume Stud*, 18(2), 429-439, N 92.

Hume's response to the sensible knave is exactly what his own moral theory requires—neither a capitulation to that selfish style of thinking nor a false boast of being able to convert knaves. Since Hume's theory bases morality on the sentiment of humanity, it does not expect its appeal to reach those who are devoid of this sentiment. Justice, a virtue which regulates natural self-interest, depends upon the other social virtues for its possibility. The knave lacks these, so has unfitted himself to understand the rewards of justice to just people.

Baier, Annette. How Can Individualists Share Responsibility?. *Polit Theory*, 21(2), 228-248, My 93.

"Individualism" is a term used by Tocqueville for what he found to be a typically American vice, a retreat from community ties and responsibilities. Most social philosophy in the US is still prone to this vice. The appeal to Kant by thinkers such as Rawls is to be a philosopher whose thought displays a tension between extreme individualism and an insistence that each person be seen as a member of a community of rational beings. Kantian thinking has no real place for shared responsibility for such evils as racism and sexism.

Baier, Annette. Some Virtues of Resident Alienation. *Nomos*, 34, 291-308, 1992.

If one is, perhaps for work-related reasons, a resident alien, is one condemned to being a non-political animal? Should one keep to oneself any criticisms one has of one's country of residence? Resident aliens, as aliens know some other country. As residents, they know this one. They are in a good position to make some informed political comparisons. Like field anthropologists and naturalized citizens, their inside knowledge of more than one culture gives them a political perspective which can usefully supplement that of native residents. Might they not be spies for their native land? Smart spies would choose better cover than that of resident aliens, who are comparatively closely monitored.

Baier, Annette. Trusting People in Philosophical Perspectives, 6: Ethics, 1992, Tomberlin, James E (ed). Atascadero, Ridgeview, 1992.

What difference does the design of a social role make to the appropriateness of

trusting the person who occupies that role? We may sometimes trust another just because her face reassures us, but usually social role and institutional setting play an important part in creating the conditions in which trust is reasonably given, and successfully sustained.

Baier, Annette C. Trust in The Tanner Lectures On Human Values, V13, Peterson, Grethe B (ed). Salt Lake City, Univ of Utah Pr, 1992.

Trust is the willingness to give discretionary powers, in the care of something that matters to us, to those we trust. The pathologies of trust range from foolish overestimation of others' trustworthiness in particular contexts, and too generous a willingness to forgive let-downs, to refusal ever to give others a second chance, and crippling refusal to trust. Institutions often provide settings which encourage such faults. Rules to guide us to give appropriate trust and distrust are hard to find, but we can develop powers to judgment as to where institutional reform is needed, and where personal trust is our best bet. Appropriate trust is trust which sustains rather than undermines a climate of trust.

Baigrie, Brian S. A Reappraisal of Duhem's Conception of Scientific Progress. *Rev Int Phil*, 46(182), 344-360, 1992.

For Duhem, the history of science consists principally in the gradual development of physical theory towards a true description of relations among natural entities, a process that he portrayed as a "progressive evolution." What I suggest is that, while this conception of scientific progress is consistent with Duhem's restricted view of physical science as essentially the refinement of theory, it clashes with a more robust account of scientific practice which considers the relationship between theory, the experimental practices of scientists, and the range of phenomena that are adapted to particular theories and experimental practices.

Baigrie, Brian S and Hattiangadi, J N. On Consensus and Stability in Science. *Brit J Phil Sci*, 43(4), 435-458, D 92.

Bailey, Charles. Enterprise and Liberal Education: Some Reservations. *J Phil Educ*, 26(1), 99-106, 1992.

The paper responds to Professor Bridge's paper: 'Enterprise and liberal education', the thesis of which is taken to be that enterprise education is not only compatible with liberal education, but a necessary part of it. A number of reasons are urged against this claim. In particular, it is argued that being enterprising is neither necessarily generalizable nor always desirable; that enterprise education is inextricably, though ambiguously, related to 'the enterprise society', yet ignores the harmful aspects of such a society; and that the claim that enterprise education is liberal because it uses progressive pedagogic methods, is unsustainable.

Bailey, George W S. Amateurs Imitate, Professionals Steal. *J Aes Art Crit*, 47(3), 221-227, Sum 89.

Kostabi sells as authentic Kostabi's paintings he neither designed nor painted. Notions of authenticity based in two theories of art are examined as possible grounds for denying the authenticity of these paintings. It is shown that Nelson Goodman's theory of art cannot be used to answer questions about authenticity because the theory implies that there is no significant sense in which any painting can be held to be a work of art. Next, it is shown that Arthur Danto's theory of art actually supports the thesis that objects Kostabi neither designed nor painted are authentic works of art by Kostabi.

Bailey, George W S. Pictorial Quotation. *Int Stud Phil*, 25(1), 1-8, 1993.

Arthur Danto and W E Kennick appeal to the notion of pictorial quotation in an attempt to show that exact copies cannot be works of art. The theory Danto and Kennick use in explaining pictorial quotation is a variant of what Donald Davidson calls the standard theory. After raising objections to the standard theory, I argue that a copy is analogous to a direct quotation only if it instantiates (all or part of) the work copied. I then examine the possibility that copies are analogous to indirect quotations. I argue that only inexact copies can be analogous to indirect quotations.

Baillie, James. *Problems in Personal Identity*. New York, Paragon House, 1993.

This book discusses the nature of personhood, and proposed criteria of personal identity. After surveying historical material by Locke, Butler, Reid, and Hume, I assess contemporary work by Parfit, Williams, Nozick, Lewis, Shoemaker, Swinburne, and Unger. Following Wilkes, I then criticise the unrestricted use of thought-experiments, arguing that this methodology has produced a distorted view of the issues, and that questions regarding personal identity are more profitably studied by focussing on actual cases. Thus, I examine problems arising from amnesia, commissurotomy, and Multiple Personality Disorder.

Baillie, James. Recent Work on Personal Identity. *Phil Books*, 34(4), 193-206, O 93.

I survey recent research in personal identity, with emphasis on work published within the last ten years. Issues summarized include Reductionism versus Non-Reductionism, Physical and Psychological Criteria, what matters in survival, quasi-Memory, and the legitimacy of thought-experiments. While putting Derek Parfit at center stage, other authors discussed include Unger, Williams, Wilkes, Shoemaker, Johnston, and Schechtman. The article includes extensive references and bibliography.

Baird, Davis W. *Inductive Logic: Probability and Statistics*. Englewood Cliffs, Prentice Hall, 1990.

Inductive Logic: Probability and Statistics was designed to serve as a text, presenting the elements of several varieties of statistical inference as methods of inductive logic. Thus, *Inductive Logic* also provides a sustained discussion of the variety of ways probability and statistics grapple with the problem of induction. By looking at a variety of ways to approach the problem of induction with concepts from probability and statistics, the text urges an eclectic yet formal approach to inductive inference. (edited)

Baird, Robert M (ed) and Rosenbaum, Stuart E (ed). *The Ethics of Abortion (Revised Edition)*. Buffalo, Prometheus, 1993.

This revised collection of essays reflecting a variety of positions in the abortion debate includes many new essays and an altered organizational structure. The essays are arranged in clusters under the following titles: Abortion and the Constitution, Abortion and Feminism, Abortion and Christianity, and Abortion and Moral Philosophy. In addition to the Roe vs Wade decision, the collection now contains versions of the court's decisions in Webster vs Reproductive Health Services and Planned Parenthood of Southeastern Pennsylvania vs Casey. Among the authors included are Robert Bork, Ronald Dworkin, Daniel Maguire, Stanley Hauerwas, Judith Jarvis Thomson, John Wilcox, and Mary Warren.

Bakan, Mildred B. About *Survival and Sociology*. *Human Stud*, 16(3), 341-352, Jl 93.

Baker, Brenda M. Empire-Building. *Dialogue (Canada)*, 32(1), 149-162, Wint 93.

This is a critical review of Ronald Dworkin's Law's Empire (Harvard 1986). After outlining the book's central argument, the review examines Dworkin's account of positivism, the value of his interpretive model, and the success of his claims for integrity. I argue that Dworkin's initial account of positivism as committed to the plain fact view of the law misrepresents it, and relies on a model of disagreement that need not be adopted. His account of interpretation throws light on history, law and literature, but is less suitable for conceptualizing and understanding social practices. And his account of integrity in adjudication is open to objections on the score of both fit with practice and normative appeal.

Baker, Brenda M. Penance as a Model for Punishment. *Soc Theor Pract*, 18(3), 311-332, Fall 92.

This paper criticizes the view of R A Duff in his *Trials and Punishments* (Cambridge, 1986) that legal punishment can be ideally conceived on a model of penance, as a self-imposed suffering which expresses contrition and is socially restorative. I argue that the conditions needed to justify the coercive imposition of penances, and to motivate voluntary penitence, are met in some religious settings, but are not appropriate as regulative ideals for membership in modern secular societies. Penance aims to be reformative and restorative, while legal punishment necessarily has different social objectives, and a system of criminal law can sufficiently respect individual autonomy and rationality without having to construe its penalties as being morally deserved penances.

Baker, Brenda M. Theorizing about Responsibility and Criminal Liability. *Law Phil*, 11(4), 403-430, 1992.

This paper is a critical notice of C T Sistare's *Responsibility and Criminal Liability* (Kluwer 1989). I agree with Sistare's central claim that the capacities model, which focuses on the individual's capacity to conform to the law, is a superior model for legal liability to the cognitive model favoured by many jurisprudents. The latter construes responsible agency as being marked by conscious choice and exhibited in our aware and intentional behaviour. I offer a critical appraisal of the book's theses about the conditions needed for legal liability. These include Sistare's account of imputative responsibility; of the meaning, scope and justification of the "act doctrine" and its implications for omission liability; of voluntariness or the ability of agents to control their behaviour, in comparison with A White's in *Grounds of Liability*; of intentionality as a mode of agent control over events which is insufficiently captured by standard legal formulations of *mens rea*; and of her plausible account of negligence.

Baker, Gordon. Some Remarks on 'Language' and 'Grammar' in Criss-Crossing A Philosophical Landscape, Schulte, Joachim (ed). Amsterdam, Rodopi, 1992.

To clarify Wittgenstein's status as an analytic philosopher, we must study his use of the expressions 'language', 'grammar', etc. We tend to take 'language' as an abstract mass-noun and to generalize quite specific remarks. We overlook the possibility of taking 'our grammar' to refer to our particular description of the use of words rather than to what we describe. Preserving the ambiguity of 'Sprache' between language and speech calls for a neutral translation, e.g., 'what we say'. Wittgenstein's 'descriptions of the grammar of our language' are more varied and purpose-specific than usually recognized.

Baker, Gordon. 'Philosophical Investigations' Section 122: Neglected Aspects in Wittgenstein's Philosophical Investigations, Arrington, Robert L (ed). New York, Routledge, 1991.

Baker, John Robert. The Epistemological Veil of Scientific Creationism. *SW Phil Rev*, 8(1), 173-181, Ja 92.

At the center of Scientific Creationism (S.C.) is an epistemological maneuver common to various forms of skepticism. In S.C. the catastrophe of the Noahic Flood serves to bifurcate historical and scientific inference such that unrestricted inferences from present processes to the Antediluvian period are deemed spurious, the manifestation of uniformitarian assumptions. I argue that S.C. is itself vulnerable to a similar skeptical maneuver such that S.C. is now seen to harbor uniformitarian assumptions vis-a-vis the new skepticism.

Baker, Lynne Rudder. Metaphysics and Mental Causation in Mental Causation, Heil, John (ed). New York, Clarendon/Oxford Pr, 1993.

Bakhtin, Mikhail. Contemporary Vitalism in The Crisis in Modernism, Burwick, Frederick (ed). New York, Cambridge Univ Pr, 1992.

Bakhurst, David. Soviet Philosophy in Transition: An Interview with Vladislav Lektorsky. *Stud Soviet Tho*, 44(1), 33-50, Jl 92.

A transcription of an interview conducted in May, 1991 with Vladislav Lektorsky, editor-in-chief of *Voprosy filosofii*, the Soviet Union's principal philosophy journal. Topics discussed include: the fate of Marxism in the USSR, the problem of reforming the Soviet philosophical world, *Voprosy filosofii*'s role under *glasnost* and *perestroika*, and the recent revival of interest in Russian religious philosophy.

Balaban, Oded. The Torn Human Activity: A Response to Alfred Guy's "The Role of Aristotle's *Praxis* Today". *J Value Inq*, 27(2), 231-234, Ap 93.

Aristotle's distinction between *praxis* and *poesis* is a distinction between activities performed for their own sake, and activities performed as means to an end. It is sustained that these activities are incompatible each with the other, even though human activity *is* often mixed, that is, includes both kinds of activity as its components. Mixed activity in fact encompasses contradiction.

Balashov, Yuri V. Transcendental Background to the Anthropic Reasoning in Cosmology. *Man World*, 25(2), 115-132, Ap 92.

Balashov, Yury V. On the Evolution of Natural Laws. *Brit J Phil Sci*, 43(3), 343-370, S 92.

Poincarés argumentation in favor of essential invariability of the fundamental laws of nature is critically examined. It is contended that within the realist framework Poincarés arguments lost their apodictical force. In this sense the assumption of inconstancy of even the fundamental laws of nature is methodologically legitimate.

Balasubramaniam, Arun. Explaining Strange Parallels: The Case of Quantum Mechanics and Mādhyamika Buddhism. *Int Phil Quart*, 32(2), 205-223, Je 92.

Baldassarre, M R. Ancora sull'idea d'Europa: Il Medioevo como matrice di una coscienza europea. *Sapienza*, 44(4), 443-446, 1991.

Baldner, Steven. St Thomas Aquinas and Charles Hartshorne's Process Philosophy. *Lyceum*, 1(2), 1-18, Fall 89.

Baldner, Steven. The Past Just Ain't What It Used To Be: A Response to Kevin Staley and Ronald Tacelli. *Lyceum*, 4(2), 1-4, Fall 92.

On the question of whether an eternal temporal duration in the past would imply an actual infinity, I argue that past duration, even if infinite, could not be *actually* infinite, because past duration is not actual. Kevin Staley concedes a kind of actuality to the past, but argues that an infinite past would not, because of its very infinity, be an actually infinite past. Ronald Tacelli holds that the past is actual and that an eternal past would imply an actual infinity. This discussion is relevant to arguments for the existence of God such as the Kalam Cosmological Argument.

Baldner, Steven. The Soul in the Explanation of Life: Aristotle Against Reductionism. *Lyceum*, 3(2), 1-14, Fall 91.

Baldomir, Daniel. Sobre el espacio-tiempo. *Agora (Spain)*, 11(1), 31-42, 1992.

In this paper we show some of the space-time characteristics that we put forward as answers to questions concerning their properties: dependency of both concepts after the relativistic formalism, its physical composition not only as "synthetic apriori", what is the highest accuracy we may get to measure them, how, when and from what have they arisen; and finally, whether they have a privileged direction in the Universe. (edited)

Baldwin, Thomas. The Projective Theory of Sensory Content in The Contents of Experience, Crane, Tim (ed). New York, Cambridge Univ Pr, 1992.

The intuitive idea behind the projective theory is that in sense experience we 'project' sensible qualities, such as color, into an external space. No such projection can be literally time; but the theory implies that sense experience involves a primitive intentionality whereby, for example, sensing bluely with respect to the upper region of the visual field is the appearance that there is something blue up above one.

Baldwin, Thomas and Honderich, Ted (ed). G E Moore. New York, Routledge, 1992.

This is a critical investigation of the philosophical writings of G E Moore. The book includes a study of Moore's alleged refutation of idealism and his early realist philosophy, a detailed discussion of *Principia Ethica* and his ethical theory, and an examination of the issues raised by Moore's mature philosophy - especially by his treatments of philosophical analysis, perception, scepticism, and common sense. Throughout Moore's arguments are compared with those of his contemporaries—especially, Bradley, Russell, Wittgenstein; and there is frequent use of previosly unpublished material.

Balibar, M Étienne. "Ego Sum, Ego Existo": Descartes au point·d'hérésie. *Bull Soc Fr Phil*, 86(3), 81-123, Jl-S 92.

Descartes' *Meditationes de prima philosophia* were published 350 years ago. During all that time, it seems that nobody explicitly observed that the famous argument known as *cogito* derives from a well-known sacred "model" or "pattern" in the Scripture: namely the *Ego sum* from St John, 8, 21 sq., which itself is supposed to repeat God's self-nomination *sum qui sum* (Ex., 3, 14). In other terms, consciously or not, the pioneering self-assertion or self-recognition of "the subject" in Modern Philosophy must cross a signifying chain which is as old as Judeo-Christian religious tradition itself: that of the Divine Names as "First Person." (edited)

Ballesteros, Manuel. Axiomatizar la metafísica? A propósito de "L'impossible métaphysique" de G Kalinowski. *Anu Filosof*, 25(3), 515-530, 1992.

Kalinowski conceives metaphysics as a set of propositions which can be axiomatized. This paper exposes the typical rules of an axiomatic system comparing them with the metaphysical system developed by Kalinowski. These rules are linguistic rules, but also admission-rules and transformation-rules. They always refer to the metaphysical propositions (which are first or second propositions, as it is usual in logical systems). This paper tries to evaluate Kalinowski's attempt.

Balmès, Marc. Philosophie du langage et réalisme aristotélicien. *Rev Thomiste*, 92(2), 503-517, Ap-J 92.

Baltas, Aristides. Once Again on the Meaning of Physical Concepts in Greek Studies in the Philosophy and History of Science, Nicolacopoulos, Pantelis (ed). Dordrecht, Kluwer, 1990.

Baltussen, Han. Peripatetic Dialectic in the 'De Sensibus' in Theophrastus, Fortenbaugh, W W (ed). New Brunswick, Transaction Books, 1992.

The nature and purpose of the *De sensibus* have remained unstudied ever since the text was printed as a fragment of the lost (so-called) *Physikon doxai* in H Diels's *Doxographi graeci* (1879). In this paper its general structure and argumentative blue-print are studies from a 'Peripatetic point of view' by using recent insights in Aristotle's use of dialectic. This procedure provides tools for testing 'reputable views' (*endoxa*), which may then serve as a starting-point for a systematic exposition. It is shown that Theophratus also makes use of dialectical moves to examine the theories on perception.

Baltzly, Dirk. Plato and the New Rhapsody. *Ancient Phil*, 12(1), 29-52, Spr 92.

This paper poses the question: Is it possible to discover a Platonic theory and practice of the interpretation of poetic texts? I argue that neither the *Protagoras* nor the *Ion* should be taken to exclude the possibility of such a reformed rhapsody. The latter part of the paper isolates two different perspectives from which Socrates engages in the interpretation and criticism of poetry.

Balzer, Carmen. Creative Imagination and Dream in Analecta Husserliana, XXXVIII, Tymieniecka, Anna-Teresa (ed). Dordrecht, Kluwer, 1992.

Balzer, Noel. *The Human Being as a Logical Thinker*. Amsterdam, Rodopi, 1993.

The aim of this book is to explain human rationality. The fundamental principles of human thought are stated in terms of Balzer's Principles, and their operations in everyday life are illustrated. The natural numbers are defined and explained in a fresh fashion. Paradoxes, including those of class theory and material implication, which have signaled that all is not well in our logical systems, are laid to rest here. The explanation of human rationality has more than logical interest, for it touches upon the human values embedded in our rationality. The book carries the message that all human beings are fundamentally equal.

Balzer, Noel. The Human Being as a Logical Thinker. *J Value Inq*, 26(4), 547-556, O 92.

The purpose of this paper is to exclaim the general principles of human thought. These are stated to be: "an instance of a class is the class" and "a class is an instance of itself". While the claim "a cat is a cat" may sound like an idle truism, we are hard put to account for the claim "a cat is an animal" without these principles. Only through use of the classes, truth and falsity, are we able to know whether or not different classes are necessarily connected.

Bambach, Charles. Phenomenological Research as *Destruktion*: The Early Heidegger's Reading of Dilthey. *Phil Today*, 37(2), 115-132, Sum 93.

Bambrough, Renford. Fools and Heretics in Wittgenstein Centenary Essays, Griffiths, A Phillips (ed). New York, Cambridge Univ Pr, 1991.

Bambrough, Renford. Reason and Faith—I in Religion and Philosophy, Warner, Marin (ed). New York, Cambridge Univ Pr, 1992.

Bamford, Greg. Popper's Explication sof *Ad Hoc*ness: Circularity, Empirical Content, and Scientific Practice. *Brit J Phil Sci*, 44(2), 335-355, Je 93.

Popper's explications of 'ad hoc' in relation to hypotheses or explanations turn out to be either trivial, confused or mistaken. One such explication I discuss at length is circularity; another is reduction in empirical content. I argue that non-circularity is preferable to non-*ad hoc*ness for an acceptable explanation or *explanans*, and I isolate some persistent errors in his analysis. Second, Popper is barking up the wrong tree in proscribing reductions in empirical content in novel hypotheses. Such reductions may constitute scientific progress. He fails to show that *ad hoc* hypothesis are the threat to science he imagines.

Bammé, Arno and Kotzmann, Ernst and Oberheber, Ulrike. Basic Questions about Metaphysics of Technology: Spangler, Heidegger, Günther. *J Speculative Phil*, 7(2), 143-158, 1993.

Bammer, Angelika. *Partial Visions: Feminism and Utopianism in the 1970s*. New York, Routledge, 1991.

Utopianism—the belief that reality not only must, but can, be changed—is one of the most vital impulses of feminist politics. Drawing on feminist and Marxist critical theory (in particular the work of Ernst Bloch), *Partical Visions* traces the articulation of this impulse in literary texts produced within the context of the American, French, and German women's movements between 1969 and 1979. Through both close and contextualized readings, Bammer examines the transformative potential as well as ideological blindspots of Western feminisms of this decade. She argues that in terms of a radical utopianism Western feminism not only continued where the Left foundered but went a decisive step further by reconceptualizing the possible meanings of both "political" and "utopian." Feminist utopianism, Bammer concludes, is not just visionary, but myopic—time—and culture—bound—as well. It is this double edge that *Partical Visions* emphasizes.

Bandyopadhayay, Krishna Bala. Heidegger's Interpretation of Kant's Concept of Metaphysics. *Indian Phil Quart*, 19(2), 139-146, Ap 92.

Martin Heidegger has tried to evaluate Kant's view relating to metaphysics quite differently from his own philosophical perspective. In this article, a brief review on Heidegger's interpretation of Kant's doctrine has been offered. Heidegger thinks that Kant's purpose in the *Critique* is not to construct a theory of knowledge but precisely to lay foundation for metaphysics. Heidegger's attempt is to rediscover Kant in that light. Here I have also dealt with Professor E Cassirer's reaction against such view.

Bang, Jens. The Significance of Some Experimental Tests of Quantum Mechanics. *Dan Yrbk Phil*, 27, 93-108, 1992.

The roles of the argumentation of Einstein, Podolsky and Rosen, Bell's inequalities and the experiment of Aspect in the debate about foundations of quantum mechanics are assessed. It is argued that the significance of Aspect's achievements is mainly pedagogical.

Banner, William A. Is There an African-American Perspective on Biomedical Ethics? in African-American Perspectives on Biomedical Ethics, Flack, Harley E (ed). Washington, Georgetown Univ Pr, 1992.

Banner, William A. Response to Jorge Garcia in African-American Perspectives on Biomedical Ethics, Flack, Harley E (ed). Washington, Georgetown Univ Pr, 1992.

Baptist, Gabriella. *Il Problema della Modalità nelle Logiche di Hegel*. Genova, Pantograf, 1993.

Bar On, Bat-Ami. Marginality and Epistemic Privilege in Feminist Epistemologies, Alcoff, Linda (ed). New York, Routledge, 1993.

Bar On, Bat-Ami. Reading Bartky: Identity, Identification, and Critical Self Reflection. *Hypatia*, 8(1), 159-163, Wint 93.

Remarks on Sandra Lee Bartky's "Femininity and Domination".

Bar On, Bat-Ami. The Feminist "Sexuality Debates" and the Transformation of the Political. *Hypatia*, 7(4), 45-58, Fall 92.

In this essay I examine the history of the sexuality debates among feminists. In both the nineteenth century and the recent sexuality debates the personal is taken to be foundational for a political stance, while simultaneously the debates tranform feminist understandings of the extent to which the personal is political. I suggest that this transformation undermines the epistemological assumptions of the debates, resulting in a feminism that cannot be radical.

Bar-On, A Zvie. God, Foreknowledge and Responsibility (in Chinese). *Phil Rev (Taiwan)*, 15, 163-180, Ja 92.

Bar-On, A Zvie. The Reality and Structure of Time in Analecta Husserliana, XXXI, Tymieniecka, Anna-Teresa (ed). Dordrecht, Kluwer, 1990.

Barad, Judith. *Consent: The Means to an Active Faith According to St Thomas Aquinas*. New York, Lang, 1992.

This study analyzes Aquinas' account of faith by emphasizing his distinction between assent and consent. According to Aquinas, although the assent of the intellect is a necessary condition of faith, the consent of the will is required for faith's completion. In consenting to an end, an individual follows a course of action specified by his intellect and directed by his will. In matters of faith consent issues acts of charity, which completes faith in its movement towards God. Aquinas' doctrine of consent shows that faith requires moral activity for the completion of faith to be accomplished.

Barad, Judith. The Dog in the Lifeboat Revisited. *Between Species*, 8(2), 114-117, Spr 92.

Those students in my Ethics and Animals course who are predisposed to animals having rights find *The Case for Animal Rights* by Tom Regan very convincing. However, their happy response is altered upon reading the passage describing four adults and a dog in a lifeboat, one of whom must be sacrificed or all will die. Regan argues that the dog should be sacrificed, adding that this choice should be make even if the decision were between four humans and a million dogs, though all have equal values. This paper will explore whether or not my students' agitation at this passage can be philosophically supported.

Barba, Juan. A Modal Reduction for Partial Logic. *J Phil Log*, 22(4), 429-435, Ag 93.

This paper presents a four-valued logic whose non-standard truth-values can be soundly interpreted as "undefined" and "incoherent." Then, an embedding in the Modal System S4 is proposed and its adequacy proven. Finally, it is shown that if the "incoherent" value is omitted, the embedding yields the McKinsey System S4.1.

Barba Escriba, Juan. A Representation of Intuitionistic Logic in Partial Information Language. *Log Anal*, 32, 211-214, S-D 89.

In a former paper (J Barba "A modal embedding for partial information semantics", *Logique it Analyse* 125-126, 131-137) a generalization PIL (Partial Information Language) of Data Semantics was presented and embedded in the modal S4. This result, together with Gödel's embedding of propositional logic in S4, is used here to prove an embedding of propositional intuitionistic logic into PIL.

Barbiero, Daniel. Truth, Meaning, and Functional Understanding: A Post-Sartrean Meditation. *Man World*, 26(4), 355-372, O 93.

Sartre's posthumously published Verite et existence is not an epistemology in the narrow sense of a theory intended to explain the relations between statements and states of affairs. Sartre instead presents a theory of meaning, or appropriative relational worth, on both the individual and intersubjective planes. I argue that Sartre's theory, while useful, is incomplete and in need of grounding in a conception of intelligibility as a pre-existing, acculturated set of practices embodied in a kind of functional understanding more fundamental than, and prior to, subjectivity as such.

Barbone, Steven. Are There Discrepancies between Aristotle's *Generation and Corruption* II and *Metereology* IV. *Dialogue (PST)*, 35(1), 7-13, O 92.

Aristotle gives an explanation of the formation of simple compounds in the second book of *Generation and Corruption*. A careful reader will notice what appears to be a different theory in the fourth book of *Meteorology*. Rather than attribute carelessness to Aristotle, I suggest that the differences merely point to his being able to develop a more mature theory of coming-to-be that offers greater explanatory power.

Barcalow, Emmett. *Open Questions: An Introduction to Philosophy (Concise Edition)*. Belmont, Wadsworth, 1992.

Bardsley, Peter. Local Utility Functions. *Theor Decis*, 34(2), 109-118, Mr 93.

In Machina's approach to generalised expected utility theory, decision makers maximize a choice functional which is smooth but not linear in the probabilities. When evaluating small changes, the choice functional can be approximated by the expectation of a local utility function. This local utility function is not however invariant under large changes in risk. This paper gives a simple explicit formula which can be used to write down the local utility functions of some common decision rules.

Bardsley, Peter. Mean Variance Preferences and the Heat Equation. *Theor Decis*, 35(2), 199-202, S 93.

Chipman (1979) proves that for an expected utility maximizer choosing from a domain of normal distributions with mean μ and variance σ 2 the induced preference function $V(\mu, \sigma)$ satisfies a differential equation known as the heat equation. The purpose of this note is to provide a generalization and simple proof of this result which does not depend on the normality assumption.

Barker, Evelyn. Personal Identity and Concrete Values in Analecta Husserliana, XXXI, Tymieniecka, Anna-Teresa (ed). Dordrecht, Kluwer, 1990.

This paper contrasts the phenomenology of an instance of abstract value with that of a concrete value, that is, an identified being felt by a person to be unique and irreplaceable; then it argues that concrete values play an important moral role in personal identity.

Barker, John A. Audi's Theory of Practical Reasoning. *Behavior Phil*, 19(2), 49-58, Fall-Wint 91.

Barker, Peter and Ariew, Roger. Duhem and Continuity in the History of Science. *Rev Int Phil*, 46(182), 323-343, 1992.

We examine the reception of Duhem's claim that medieval science is continuous with modern science, from Antonio Favaro to Peter Dear. After sketching the development of Duhem's views on the history of medieval science, we suggest that a commitment to metaphysically driven revolutionary change in science led Alexandre Koyré and Anneliese Maier to read Duhem's work as an unsatisfactory revolutionary account, rather than one in which the influence of metaphysics is specifically excluded and revolutionary change is denied. (edited)

Barker, Peter (ed) and Ariew, Roger (ed). *Revolution and Continuity*. Washington, Cath Univ Amer Pr, 1991.

This book presents new work in history and historiography of science, linked by a concern to understand the content of early modern science in its own context, and muting the sharp intellectual and institutional discontinuities of earlier histories. The editors' Introduction examines several myths about the Copernican revolution perpetuated by the neglect of context, undermining the presumption of discontinuity in most contemporary history and philosophy of science. (edited)

Barker, Stephen F. Beauty and Induction in Kant's Third "Critique" in Kant's Aesthetics, Meerbote, Ralf (ed). Atascadero, Ridgeview, 1991.

Barnes, Annette. On Deceiving Others. *Amer Phil Quart*, 29(2), 153-162, Ap 92.

It is argued that in interpersonal deception deceivers must know or truly believe that something they intentionally get the deceived to believe is false. An attempt is made to give a characterization of this requirement that is both specific and correct.

Barnes, Annette and Barnes, Jonathan. Time Out of Joint: Reflections on Anachronism. *J Aes Art Crit*, 47(3), 253-261, Sum 89.

If a philosopher analyzes the Aristotelian syllogism in terms of material implication, is this grounds for dismissing the analysis? Do the anachronisms in Shakespeare blemish his work? Would a corsetless Cleopatra or a Bedlam-free Lear be preferable? In the course of their attempt to determine whether the anachronisms that occur in these sorts of places are necessarily or typically defects, the authors provide a characterization of what an anachronism is.

Barnes, Eric. Explanatory Unifcation and the Problem of Asymmetry. *Phil Sci*, 59(4), 558-571, D 92.

Philip Kitcher has proposed a theory of explanation based on the notion of unification. Despite the genuine interest and power of the theory, I argue here that the theory suffers from a fatal deficiency: It is intrinsically unable to account for the asymmetric structure of explanation, and thus ultimately falls prey to a problem similar to the one which beset Hempel's D-N model. I conclude that Kitcher is wrong to claim that one can settle the issue of an argument's explanatory force merely on the basis of considerations about the unifying power of the argument pattern the argument instantiates.

Barnes, Eric C. Explanatory Unification and Scientific Understanding. *Proc Phil Sci Ass*, 1, 3-12, 1992.

Philip Kitcher has proposed a theory of explanation based on the notion of unification. Despite the genuine interest and power of the theory, I argue here that the theory suffers from a fatal deficiency: It is intrinsically unable to account for the asymmetric structure of explanation, and thus ultimately falls prey to a problem similar to the one which beset Hempel's D-N model. I conclude that Kitcher is wrong to claim that one can settle the issue of an argument's explanatory force merely on the basis of considerations about the unifying power of the argument pattern the argument instantiates.

Barnes, Hazel. Sartre's Ontology in The Cambridge Companion to Sartre, Howells, Christina (ed). New York, Cambridge Univ Pr, 1992.

As an activity of intending objects, Sartrean consciousness must be carefully distinguished from nothingness and the embodied for-itself. Consciousness does not create its objects as in idealism. It creates being in the sense of psychic in-itself (Pucciani's term) by imposing a psychic overlay on matter-in worked matter and in the work of art-and in producing its ego. Consciousness is never one with the Ego but of necessity continually creates and recreates it. Sanity and good faith require that consciousness recognize its true relation with its ego. Consciousness' interplay with the psychic structures it brings into being is the central motif of Sartre's philosophy.

Barnes, Hazel. The Role of the Ego in Reciprocity in Sartre Alive, Aronson, Ronald (ed). Detroit, Wayne St Univ Pr, 1991.

Sartre, in the *Notebooks*, while still seeing the ego as the product of consciousness, grants it a more positive role as "my practical objectification in the world." He opposes the idea of the ego as a self-image regulating action, but he acknowledges the inevitable presence of an ego, "always open and always in suspense", existing in order to be lost." As the body individualizes a consciousness without determining it, so a consciousness, by meant of the ego, makes us persons. Both the body and the ego of the other are key elements in authentic love.

Barnes, Jonathan. Enseigner la vertu?. *Rev Phil Fr*, 4, 571-589, O-D 91.

Barnes, Jonathan and Barnes, Annette. Time Out of Joint: Reflections on Anachronism. *J Aes Art Crit*, 47(3), 253-261, Sum 89.

If a philosopher analyzes the Aristotelian syllogism in terms of material implication, is this grounds for dismissing the analysis? Do the anachronisms in Shakespeare blemish his work? Would a corsetless Cleopatra or a Bedlam-free Lear be preferable? In the course of their attempt to determine whether the anachronisms that occur in these sorts of places are necessarily or typically defects, the authors provide a characterization of what an anachronism is.

Barnes, Michael. Tracy in Dialogue: Mystical Retrieval and Prophetic Suspicion. *Heythrop J*, 34(1), 60-65, Ja 93.

Barnett, Randy E. Compensation and Rights in the Liberal Conception of Justice. *Nomos*, 33, 311-329, 1991.

Arguing that the liberal conception of justice underlying the Anglo- American common law is rights-based not compensation-based, Barnett contends that Cass Sunstein's thesis that the common law is incompatible with theories of recovery based on "nonsubordination" or "risk- management" implicitly concedes that the reigning conception of entitlements is liberal. Barnett explains why the burden is properly placed on proponents of these novel legal theories to establish that they will not afoul of the pervasive social problems of knowledge, interest, and power currently handled by the liberal conceptions of justice and the rule of law that they would supplant.

Barney, Rachel. Appearances and Impressions. *Phronesis*, 37(3), 283-313, 1992.

How can we reconcile the Pyrrhonian sceptic's readiness to say how things appear to him with his disavowal of dogmatism? This paper argues that we need not attribute to the sceptic a conception of appearances as 'impressions' unrelated to one's beliefs about the world. An examination of appearances and impressions in earlier philosophies confirms that the idea of an appearance unrelated to belief is itself a dogmatic creation. Instead, the sceptic uses the language of appearance to express a profound and well-founded distrust of his own processes of belief formation.

Barnhart, J E. Rationality and Ethnocentrism. *SW Phil Stud*, 14, 26-33, Spr 92.

Baron, D N. Ethical Problems in Clinical Pathology. *J Applied Phil*, 9(2), 189-202, 1992.

The much discussed ethical problems of clinicians, who have direct care of patients, are mainly within their responsibilities to the 'index' patient with whom they are immediately concerned. When pathologists are practicing clinical pathology they are responsible for performing and interpreting tests on specimens from patients at the request of clinicians, and advising on these tests. Their ethical problems, as they do not have direct care of patients, mainly lie between their obligations to the requesting clinician, to the index patient under investigation in the laboratory, and also to other patients, and to their staff. These problems are largely ignored in the literature both of medical ethics and of pathology. The ethical principles of: (1) respect for autonomy; (2) non-maleficence; (3) beneficence; and (4) justice, are discussed. Ethical problems that arise in the course of a pathologist's receiving, investigating, and reporting and advising on, a patient's specimen are examined on the basis of the above principles. An attempt is made to offer guidance on the problems. (edited)

Baron, Richard J. Why Aren't More Doctors Phenomenologists? in The Body in Medical Thought and Practice, Leder, Drew (ed). Dordrecht, Kluwer, 1992.

Barral, Mary Rose. The Phenomenologico-Sociological Conception of the Human Being on the Brink of Existence in Analecta Husserliana, XXXI, Tymieniecka, Anna-Teresa (ed). Dordrecht, Kluwer, 1990.

The purpose of the work is: to show the human being's absolute need of inter-personal relations for a healthy, conscious life; to see how society is caring for the persons whose conscious existence is threatened by psychological withdrawal from human interaction. Human beings, born into relations — family, society, world — need society's support; a new approach to socio-communal psychiatry (Binswanger, Gramsci, Basaglia) looks at a possible rehabilitation of the sick within society itself, instead of attempting to cure the psyche in isolation.

Barral, Mary Rose. The Truth and Identity of a Person and of a People in Analecta Husserliana, XXXI, Tymieniecka, Anna-Teresa (ed). Dordrecht, Kluwer, 1990.

The purpose is to uncover the reality of a person and of a people. For philosophers and metaphysicians, the truth of an entity is its essence, its being, its identity. This truth-identity can be uncovered by the individual only within the larger entity within which human life evolves, society, itself an identifiable reality. The truth-identity of both individual and society must be preserved if the person is to achieve the full scope of human life, physical, intellectual, moral and spiritual.

Barral, Mary-Rose. La metafisica della vita secondo A T Tymieniecka. *Aquinas*, 35(2), 397-404, My-Ag 92.

Barral, Mary-Rose. *Life-Sharing for a Creative Tomorrow*. New York, Lang, 1992.

Barresi, John and Juckes, Tim J. The Subjective-Objective Dimension in the Individual-Society Connection: A Duality Perspective. *J Theor Soc Behav*, 23(2), 197-216, Je 93.

A duality perspective of the individual-society connection is proposed, which recognizes the irreducibility and the interdependence of individual and society. Individuals, as autonomous agents with subjective orientations to the society of which they are a part, and social structure, as an objective order of material social forces, dialectically interact and jointly produce social change. The model differs from others in recognizing an objective and a subjective aspect to both individual and society. Social structure affects individual agents through the subjectification of the material structure as culture, and individual agents affect structure through the objectification of their action in social positions.

Barrett, Cyril. The Logic of Mysticism—II in Religion and Philosophy, Warner, Marin (ed). New York, Cambridge Univ Pr, 1992.

Barrett, J Edward. Ethical Monotheism and National Usurpation in God, Values, and Empiricism, Peden, Creighton W (ed). Macon, Mercer Univ Pr, 1989.

Barrett, Martin and Sober, Elliott. Conjunctive Forks and Temporally Asymmetric Inference. *Austl J Phil*, 70(1), 1-23, Mr 92.

In *The Direction of Time*, Hans Reichenbach claims that there are conjunctive forks open to the future but none open to the past, and that this asymmetry explains why we know more about the past than about the future. We argue that conjunctive forks open to the past are rare but not impossible. We also propose a new argument for thinking that the common causes discovered by (as yet incomplete) science often form conjunctive forks with their joint effects. We then explore the circumstances under which a conjunctive fork open to the future allows one to know more about the past than about the future.

Barrett, Martin and Sober, Elliott. Is Entropy Relevant to the Asymmetry Between Retrodiction and Prediction?. *Brit J Phil Sci*, 43(2), 141-160, J 92.

The idea that the changing entropy of a system is relevant to explaining why we know more about the system's past than about its future has been criticized on several fronts. This paper assesses the criticisms and clarifies the epistemology of the inference problem. It deploys a Markov process model to investigate the relationship between entropy and temporally asymmetric inference.

Barron, Anne. Lyotard and the Problem of Justice in Judging Lyotard, Benjamin, Andrew (ed). New York, Routledge, 1992.

Barrus, Roger and Sherlock, Richard. The Problem of Religion in Liberalism. *Interpretation*, 20(3), 285-308, Spr 93.

Barry, Norman. The Social Market Economy. *Soc Phil Pol*, 10(2), 1-25, Sum 93.

This article considers the possible economic structures for the regimes emerging from communism. A parallel is drawn with West Germany in the immediate post-war period. Here the free market was introduced subject to important qualifications, e.g., that state action was required to prevent its developing into a system of monopolies and cartels. However, the system degenerated: excessive welfare and regulation sapped the market's vitality. The earlier version of the social market is recommended for part-communist regimes. It is argued that the establishment of predictable legal order is the first priority.

Barry, Robert. Unilateral Nuclear Disarmament and Bilateral Nuclear Sieges. *Amer Cath Phil Quart*, 65(4), 483-501, Autumn 91.

The purpose of this article is to investigate the ethics of nuclear deterrance from the perspective of the classical moral and legal principles that governed siege warfare. This article contends that not all uses of nuclear weapons can be considered immoral when the laws of siege warfare strictly apply.

Barten, Sybil S. The Language of Musical Instruction. *J Aes Educ*, 26(2), 53-61, Sum 92.

Bartfai, Edit. The Aristotelian *Politeia* and the Athenian Society (in Czechoslovakian). *Magyar Filozof Szemle*, 6, 795-804, 1991.

The subject of this essay is to analyze the best regime ("politeia") of Aristotle and comparing this to real contemporary social relations. The theoretical importance of the best regime is not its direct meaning. Its main thesis is the specific combination of the oligarchical economic independence *and* democratic political equality, freedom. The author interprets Aristotle's best regime's oligarchical elements as pre-marks of the "civil society" and its democratic elements as the "political state" separated partially from society. This interpretation can be verified by Athens's social and economic history.

Bartholome, William. Withholding/Withdrawing Life-Sustaining Treatment in Contemporary Issues in Paediatric Ethics, Burgess, Michael M (ed). Lewiston, Mellen Pr, 1991.

Bartkowiak, Julia. The Role of Internalism in Moral Theory. *Auslegung*, 19(1), 47-61, Wint 93.

David O Brink, in various writings, claims that moral theorists should be moral realists. However, his argument in favor of the acceptance of moral realism includes an argument to reflect internalism, and Brink claims that *all* versions of internalism fail; moral theorists must accept both realism and externalism. Brink is correct, no version of internalism can provide up with an adequate moral theory. Thus, any internalist must defend his or her theory from Brink's criticisms, and such a defense will be given in this paper. I will argue that Brink's claim that externalism, not internalism, "...is the appropriate way to represent the practical or action guiding character of morality" is false.

Bartky, Sandra. Reply to Commentators on *Femininity and Domination*. *Hypatia*, 8(1), 192-196, Wint 93.

Sandra Bartky's reply to the paper in the Symposium on her book *Femininity and Domination*.

Barton, Mary. Japanese American Relocation: Who Is Responsible?. *J Soc Phil*, 23(2), 142-156, Fall 92.

Bartuschat, W. Infinite Intellect and Human Cognition in Spinoza (in Dutch). *Tijdschr Filosof*, 54(3), 493-521, S 92.

This article contains an investigation of the meaning of Spinoza's thesis that the human mind is a part of the infinite intellect. Because it is such a part, no matter whether it perceives inadequately or adequately, the modes of human cognition cannot be explicated on the basis of the status of the mind as such a part. Its being a part only guarantees the correspondence between idea and object. It guarantees the truth of an idea but not its adequacy; its adequacy must be ascertained by man under conditions of his own finitude. The import of the theory of the infinite intellect is in the main an ontological one, while the theory of human cognition has been developed with reference to specific elements of human finitude. Only so it is significant to make use of human cognition as the basis of an ethic that is concerned with the well-being of man as a finite mode.

Barwise, K Jon (& other eds). *Situation Theory and Its Applications, Volume 2*. Menlo Park, CSLI, 1991.

Baseheart, Mary Catharine. Edith Stein's Philosophy of Community. *Personalist Forum*, 8/1(Supp), 163-173, Spr 92.

This paper presents the philosophy of community developed by Edith Stein (1891-1942), a remarkable Jewish-Christian phenomenologist of the Husserlian Circle at the Universities of Göttingen and Freiburg, teacher and writer on philosophy, who died at Auschwitz. It presents the findings regarding community — what it is and how it is lived — which she uncovered in her phenomenological investigations of the human person and community, published in her early works. The paper explores the outcomes of Stein's analyses of the phenomena of community in our *Umwelt*.

Basinger, David. Feminism and Epistemology: A Response to Code. *J Phil Res*, 17, 29-37, 1992.

There have been many calls recently for philosophers to rethink what philosophy is and how it should be practiced. Among the most vocal critics is an influential group of feminist philosophers who argue that since current philosophical activity is based primarily on a conception of reason that is both inherently inadequate and oppressive to women, it is imperative that our understanding of the nature and practice of philosophy be significantly modified. I argue that this criticism is fundamentally misguided. Specifically, it seems to me that while philosophers may at times need to rethink the role of the traditional philosophical method of inquiry in the context of general societal debate and rethink the techniques used to help others understand and apply this methodology, this method of inquiry, itself, is not in need of abandonment or major modification.

Basinger, David. Process Theism Versus Free-Will Theism: A Response to Griffin. *Process Stud*, 20(4), 204-220, Wint 91.

David Griffin has argued that free-will theists cannot offer a plausible response to the evil we encounter daily. In response, I argue that Griffin fails to stipulate a set of 'unprivileged' criteria by which the plausibility of a theodicy can be ascertained in as objective, nonquestion-begging sense and, thus, does not successfully demonstrate that a free-will theodicy cannot justifiably be considered plausible.

Bassiry, G R and Jones, Marc. Adam Smith and the Ethics of Contemporary Capitalism. *J Bus Ethics*, 12(8), 621-628, Ag 93.

This paper presents a theoretical elaboration of the ethical framework of classical capitalism as formulated by Adam Smith in reaction to the dominant mercantilism of his day. It is seen that Smith's project was profoundly ethical and designed to emancipate the consumer from a producer and state dominated economy. Over time, however, the various dysfunctions of a capitalist economy—e.g., concentration of wealth, market power—became manifest and the utilitarian ethical basis of the system eroded. Contemporary capitalism, dominated as it is by large corporations, entrenched political interests and persistent social pathologies, bears little resemblance to the system which Smith envisioned would serve the common man. Most critiques of capitalism are launched from a Marxian-based perspective. We find, however, that by illustrating the wide gap between the reality of contemporary capitalism and the model of a *moral* political economy developed by Smith, the father of capitalism proves to be the most trenchant critic of the current order.

Basti, G Franco. Risposta dell'autore. *Aquinas*, 35(1), 155-165, Ja-Ap 92.

Bastit, Michel. Aristote et la séparation. *Rev Phil Louvain*, 90(87), 297-316, Ag 92.

Basu, Arabinda. Language of the Absolute: A Contemporary Indian Interpretation. *J Dharma*, 17(3), 203-209, Jl-S 92.

Batens, Diderik. Natural Heuristics for Proof Construction: Part I—Classical Propositional Logic. *Log Anal*, 32, 337-363, S-D 89.

Batterman, Robert W. Defining Chaos. *Phil Sci*, 60(1), 43-66, Mr 93.

This paper considers definitions of classical dynamical chaos that focus primarily on notions of predictability and computability, sometimes called algorithmic complexity definitions of chaos. I argue that accounts of this type are seriously flawed. They focus on a likely consequence of chaos, namely, randomness in behaviour which gets characterized in terms of the unpredictability of uncomputability of final given intitial states. In doing so, however, they can overlook the definitive feature of dynamical chaos — the fact that the underlying motion generating the behaviour exhibits extreme trajectory instability. I formulate a simple criterion of adequacy for any definition of chaos and show how such accounts fail to satisfy it.

Batterman, Robert W. Explanatory Instability. *Nous*, 26(3), 325-348, S 92.

In this paper it is argued that there exist phenomena ubiquitous in classical physics that require, for their explanations, a model of statistical explanation that is fundamentally different from current accounts. In particular, Peter Railton's Deductive-Nomological-Probabilistic model, as well as Hempel's Inductive-Statistical model, fail to provide the correct explanation for these phenomena. Fully deterministic classical systems can exhibit behavior requiring statistical explanation of a sort completely ignored by the received models. This behavior is the result of instabilities found, in various forms, in the motions of dynamical systems. A sketch of the form an appropriate model for statistical explanation in these cases should take is offered.

Battin, Margaret P (ed) and Huefner, Robert P (ed). *Changing To National Health Care: Ethical and Policy Issues*. Salt Lake City, Univ of Utah Pr, 1992.

Baudouin, Jean-Louis. Quelques réflexions générales sur la normativité; l'éthique et le droit dans le cadre clinique. *Dialogue (Canada)*, 30(3), 419-423, Sum 91.

Baugh, Bruce. Deleuze and Empiricism. *J Brit Soc Phenomenol*, 24(1), 15-31, Ja 93.

Baugh, Bruce. Limiting Reason's Empire: The Early Reception of Hegel in France. *J Hist Phil*, 31(2), 259-275, Ap 93.

Baugh, Bruce. Prolegomena to Any Aesthetics of Rock Music. *J Aes Art Crit*, 51(1), 23-29, Wint 93.

Traditional, formalist criteria of musical aesthetics are inapplicable to rock music. In rock music, the issue of composition or form is secondary in importance to performance-based values, which have to do with how music affects the listener, rather than with a disinterested contemplation of the work's form. The chief criteria of excellence in rock music have to do with: rhythm, loudness and the sound of individual tunes, the "matter" of music.

Baugh, Bruce. Transcendental Empiricism: Deleuze's Response to Hegel. *Man World*, 25(2), 133-148, Ap 92.

Deleuze sees empiricism as a way out of Hegel's dialectics. Empiricism involves: the priority of the a posteriori over the a priori; a logic of externalty (terms are external to their relations), the actual as the condition of the possible, the non-deducibility of the actual from the possible, the conditional nature of all actual conditions, and a relation of immanence between condition and conditioned. Each actual "this" is a "virtual multiplicity" in virtue of its genealogy.

Baum, Gregory. Fackenheim and Christianity in German Philosophy and Jewish Thought, Greenspan, Louis (ed). Toronto, Univ of Toronto Pr, 1992.

Baumanns, Peter. Kants transzendentale Deduktion der reinen Verstandesbegriffe (B): Ein kritischer Forschungsbericht—Vierter Teil. *Kantstudien*, 83(2), 185-207, 1992.

Die kritische Präsentation von 30 Interpretationen der B-Deduktion schliesst mit den folgenden Feststellungen: In der einschlägigen Literatur lassen sich zwei Hauptströmungen erkennen, in Gestalt eines erfahrungs- bzw. wissenschafts-theoretischen und eines apper- zeptions- bzw. bewusstseins- theoretischen Ansatzes. In der Frage der Gliederung der Deduktion gruppiert man um 20 zwei Teile gemäss vier Einteilungsgesichtspunkten, die auch untereinander kombiniert werden. Die Standardinterpretation gliedert die Deduktion der objektiven Gültigkeit der Kategorien in eine Wie- und eine Dass- Untersuchung. Es fehlt eine adäquate Darstellung des Vorgehens von Kant, der mit einer Dass- Wie- Untersuchung den kategorialen Verstand in der ursprünglichen Evidenz der transzendentalen Identität der Apperzeption fundiert. Die in den letzten 20 Jahren meistdiskutierte Interpretation, die die Beweisstruktur der Deduktion in die Aufhebung einer Restriktion der kategorialen Gültigkeit setzt, wurde schon von älteren Interpreten als undurchführbar erkannt.

Baumer, Michael R. Chasing Aristotle's Categories Down the Tree of Grammar. *J Phil Res*, 18, 341-449, 1993.

This paper addresses the problem of the origin and principle of Aristotle's distinctions among the categories. It explores the possibilities of reformulating and reviving the "grammatical" theory, generally ascribed first to Trendelenburg. The paper brings two new perspectives to the grammatical theory: that of Aristotle's own theory of syntax and that of contemporary linguistic syntax and semantics. I put forth a provisional theory of Aristotle's categories in which 1) I propose that the *Categories* sets forth a theory of lexical structure, with the ten categories emerging as lexical or semantic categories, and 2) I suggest conceptual links, both in Aristotle's writings and in actuality, between these semantic categories and certain grammatical inflections.

Baumgartner, James E and Shelah, Saharon and Thomas, Simon. Maximal Subgroups of Infinite Symmetric Groups. *Notre Dame J Form Log*, 34(1), 1-11, Wint 93.

We prove that it is consistant that there exists a subgroup of the symmetric group Sym(λ) which is not included in a maximal proper subgroup of Sym(λ). We also consider the question of which subgroups of Sym(λ) stabilize a nontrivial ideal on λ.

Baumgold, Deborah. Pacifying Politics: Resistance, Violence, and Accountability in Seventeenth-Century Contract THeory. *Polit Theory*, 21(1), 6-27, F 93.

Bausola, Adriano. Una nuova edizione italiana di Platone. *Riv Filosof Neo-Scolas*, 84(2-3), 249-260, Ap-S 92.

Baxandall, Michael. The Language of Art Criticism in The Language of Art History, Kemal, Salim (ed). New York, Cambridge Univ Pr, 1991.

Baxter, Anthony. Knowledge, and Our Position Regarding God. *Heythrop J*, 34(2), 137-159, Ap 93.

Baxter, David. New "True" Socialism. *Auslegung*, 18(2), 97-111, Sum 92.

Baxter, Donald L M. Continuity and Common Sense. *Int Stud Phil*, 24(3), 93-97, 1992.

I propose a common sense, local anti-realism for the ordinary concept of continuity. Whether or not something, e.g., a trail, is continuous ordinarily depends on people's purposes and capabilities. This dependence entails that there is no fact of the matter whether something is continuous. Relativizing continuity to gain a fact of the matter, unacceptable fragments our ordinary concept, and makes it false that we given new information can change our minds when applying the concept.

Bayertz, Kurt. Techno-Thanatology: Moral Consequences of Introducing Brain Criteria for Death. *J Med Phil*, 17(4), 407-417, Ag 92.

This paper is based on the hypothesis that the effort to establish new criteria for diagnosing human death, which has been taking place over the past twenty years or more, can be viewed as a paradigm case for the impact of scientific and technological progress on morality. This impact takes the form of three tendencies within the change in morality, which may be characterized as 'denaturalization', 'functionalization', and 'homogenization'. The paper concludes with the view that these tendencies do not indicate a decline of morality, as feared by some authors, but rather a structural change.

Bayles, Michael D. *Hart's Legal Philosophy: An Examination*. Dordrecht, Kluwer, 1992.

This work presents, interprets, and largely defends the legal philosophy of H L A Hart, except for his account of causation. Hart is considered by many persons to be the most important English writer on jurisprudence in the 20th century. The book considers his general theory of law, this theory of rights and of the enforcement of morality, and his analysis of the conditions of legal responsibility and the justification of punishment.

Baynes, Kenneth. Crisis and Life-World in Husserl and Habermas in Crises in Continental Philosophy, Dallery, Arleen B (ed). Albany, SUNY Pr, 1990.

Bazargan, Susan (ed) and Downing, David B (ed). *Image and Ideology in Modern/PostModern Discourse*. Albany, SUNY Pr, 1991.

This book addresses the function and status of the visual and verbal image as it relates to social, political, and ideological issues. The authors first articulate some of the lost connections between image and ideology, then locate their argument within the modernist/postmodernist debates. They examine the multiple, trans-disciplinary problems arising from the ways cultures, authors, and texts mobilize particular images in order to confront, conceal, work through, or resolve contradictory ideological conditions. The book contains seventeen essays, many by such well-known critics as W J T Mitchell, Jean Baudrillard, Kristina Straud, Richard Pearce, and others.

Beakley, Brian (ed) and Ludlow, Peter (ed). *The Philosophy of Mind: Classical Problems/Contemporary Issues*. Cambridge, MIT Pr, 1991.

This collection of essays in the philosophy of mind ranges from Plato, Aristotle, and Aquinas to Chomsky, Putnam, and the PDP Research Group. Part I covers the classic positions on the mind-body problem, questions of reduction and scientific methodology, and the notion of "contingent identity". Part II concerns the possibility of mental causation. Part III covers arguments for and against mental imagery. Part IV surveys views on associationist and connectionist mental models, and Part V deals with philosophical and scientific evidence concerning innate ideas. The collection is thorough enough to prove useful to students and researchers alike.

Bealer, George. The Incoherence of Empiricism—I. *Aris Soc*, Supp(66), 99-138, 1992.

Bealer, George. Universals. *J Phil*, 90(1), 5-32, Ja 93.

Beardsworth, Richard. On the Critical 'Post' in Judging Lyotard, Benjamin, Andrew (ed). New York, Routledge, 1992.

The article re-evaluates "postmodernist" receptions of Lyotard's work in the Anglophone world by focusing on the question of judgment from *justgaming* to *the differend*. The article critically trails Lyotard's elaboration of philosophy, literature and art as post-Kantian forms of "reflective judgement" and suggests, thereby, that Lyotard's concerns with a non-descriptive justice, a negative "aesthetics" and a "pagan" juridical criticism" are best considered in terms of his understanding of an *event*.

Bearn, Gordon C F. Still Looking for Proof: A Critique of Smith's Relativism. *J Aes Art Crit*, 49(4), 297-306, Fall 91.

Bearn, Gordon C F. The Formal Syntax of Modernism: Carnap and Le Corbusier. *Brit J Aes*, 32(3), 227-241, Jl 92.

Beatham, Mark. Splitting the Self: Thoughts on Rortyian Education. *Phil Stud Educ*, 1, 41-53, 1991.

Beauchamp, Tom L. *Case Studies in Business, Society, and Ethics (Third Edition)*. Englewood Cliffs, Prentice Hall, 1993.

Beauchamp, Tom L. Response to Jorge Garcia in African-American Perspectives on Biomedical Ethics, Flack, Harley E (ed). Washington, Georgetown Univ Pr, 1992.

Beauchamp, Tom L and Bowie, Norman E. *Ethical Theory and Business (Fourth Edition)*. Englewood Cliffs, Prentice Hall, 1993.

Beavers, Gordon. Distribution in Lukasiewicz Logics. *Bull Sec Log*, 21(4), 140-146, D 92.

In Lukasiewicz Logics with both A and B serving as disjunction and both K and L as conjunction there are many possible distributive laws. Proofs from the axioms of the infinite valued system are provided for the distribution of K over A, L over A, A over K, and B over K. The remaining combinations are invalid.

Becchi, Paolo. Las raíces de la ética de la convicción. *Cuad Etica*, 13, 57-79, Je 92.

The paper deals with the problematics of conviction Ethics in a given period of German philosophical and political history (late 18th siecle, and early 19th). Starting from Kant's considerations (KrV, 848-859: *About opinion, knowledge and Faith*), it analyzes the opposition of Fries and the activism of his disciples (Sand, Follen and de Wette), and concludes with Hegelian critic to Ethics of conviction. The prologue to the *Lectures on Philosophy of Right* (1818 and 1820) and other passages of the *Philosophy of Right* are being commented. Hegel could be denouncing the "Fanatism of destruction" in that subjective practical conviction, which despises reason and knowledge, admitting, in the other hand, subjectivity as sign of modernity.

Bechtel, William. Currents in Connectionism. *Mind Mach*, 3(2), 125-153, My 93.

This paper reviews four significant advances on the feedforward architecture that has dominated discussions of connectionism: the use of modular expert networks, the use of recurrent connections, the construction of compressed representations, and the use of backpropagation not only to change weights but also to change input patterns. These advantages significantly increase the usefulness of connectionist networks for modeling human cognitive performance by, among other things, providing tools for explaining the productivity and systematicity of some mental activities and developing representations that are sensitive to the content they are to represent.

Bechtel, William. Decomposing Intentionality: Perspectives on Intentionality Drawn from Language Research with Two Species of Chimpanzees. *Biol Phil*, 8(1), 1-32, Ja 93.

In philosophy the term "intentionality" refers to the feature possessed by mental states of being *about* things other than themselves. A serious question has been how to explain the intentionality of mental states. This paper starts with linguistic representations, and explores how an organism might use linguistic symbols to represent other things. Two research projects of Sue Savage-Rumbaugh, one explicitly teaching two *pan troglodytes* to use lexigrams intentionally, and the other exploring the ability of several members of *pan paniscus* to learn lexigram use and comprehension of English speech spontaneously when raised in an appropriate environment, are examined to explore the acquisition process. (edited)

Bechtel, William. Integrating Sciences by Creating New Disciplines: The Case of Cell Biology. *Biol Phil*, 8(3), 277-299, Jl 93.

Many studies of the unification of science focus on the theories of different disciplines. The model for integration is the theory reduction model. This paper argues that the embodiment of theories in scientists, and the institutions in which scientists work and the instruments they employ, are critical to the sort of integration that actually occurs in science. This paper examines the integration of scientific endeavors that emerged in cell biology in the period after World War II when the development of cell fractionation and electron microscopy made serious investigations of cell organelles possible. One surprising feature of such integration is that it generated further disintegration as the new institutions of cell biology separated the practitioners of the new discipline from other, closely related biological disciplines.

Bechtel, William. The Case for Connectionism. *Phil Stud*, 71(2), 119-154, Ag 93.

This paper begins with a relatively introductory presentation of connectionist approaches to cognitive modeling and then offers an argument that one contribution of connectionism is to expand our conception of cognition. The bulk of the paper then explores strategies connectionists might pursue in answering one of the major objections to connectionism — that it cannot account for the productivity and systematicity of thought — and suggesting a way in which it might account for the intentionality of thought.

Beck, Clive M. Female Identity and Difference. *Proc Phil Educ*, 48, 286-289, 1992.

Beck, Heinrich. Triadische Götter-Ordnungen: klassisch-antiker und neuplatonischer Ansatz. *Theol Phil*, 67(2), 230-245, 1992.

Beck, Lewis W. *Kant's Latin Writings (Second Edition)*. New York, Lang, 1992.

This volume contains translations of all of Kant's extant Latin writings, with extensive commentaries and notes. Only two of them have ever appeared in English. The Latin writings of the pre-critical period are a substantial addition to the better known German works already translated into English. The later occasional pieces (aesthetics, 1777; medical theory, 1781) have been wholly neglected by Kant scholars (even in German). The first edition has been revised and corrected. The book is a product of a collaborative project by Beck, Mary Gregor, Ralf Meerbote, and John A Reuscher.

Beck, Simon. Counterfactuals and the Law. *S Afr J Phil*, 12(3), 62-65, Ag 93.

This article is concerned with the place counterfactual reasoning occupies in South African law, and how philosophy might be able to help the law. I point out some of the more important and unavoidable uses of counterfactual reasoning in our law. Following this I make some suggestions as to how philosophy, and especially informal logic, can be of help to the law. Finally, I make some suggestions as to how the law in its turn can help philosophy.

Beck, Simon. The Method of Possible Worlds. *Metaphilosophy*, 23(1-2), 119-131, Ja-Ap 92.

Becker, Charlotte B (ed) and Becker, Lawrence C (ed). *A History of Western Ethics*. Hamden, Garland, 1992.

The chapters of this book are surveys originally written for the Encyclopedia of Ethics (Garland, 1992). They are republished here unchanged. 1) Presocratic Greek Ethics (Charles H Kahn); 2) Classical Greek Ethics (John M Cooper); 3) Hellenistic Ethics (A A Long); 4) Roman Ethics (A A Long); 5) Early Medieval Ethics (Scott Davis); 6) Later Medieval Ethics (Scott MacDonald); 7) Renaissance Ethics (Jill Kraye); 8) Seventeenth and Eighteenth Century Ethics (J B Schneewind); 9) Nineteenth-Century British Ethics (Marcus G Singer); 10) Nineteenth-Century Continental Ethics (Richard Schacht); 11) Twentieth-Century Continental Ethics, 1 (Joseph J Kochelmans); 12) Twentieth-Century Continental Ethics, 2 (William R Schroeder); 13) Twentieth-Century Anglo-American Ethics (Alan Donagan).

Becker, Heribert and Oliver, Charles (trans). The Theory of Odd and Even in the Ninth Book of Euclid's Elements. *Grad Fac Phil J*, 16(1), 87-110, 1993.

Becker, Lawrence C (ed) and Becker, Charlotte B (ed). *A History of Western Ethics*. Hamden, Garland, 1992.

The chapters of this book are surveys originally written for the Encyclopedia of Ethics (Garland, 1992). They are republished here unchanged. 1) Presocratic Greek Ethics (Charles H Kahn); 2) Classical Greek Ethics (John M Cooper); 3) Hellenistic Ethics (A A Long); 4) Roman Ethics (A A Long); 5) Early Medieval Ethics (Scott Davis); 6) Later Medieval Ethics (Scott MacDonald); 7) Renaissance Ethics (Jill Kraye); 8) Seventeenth and Eighteenth Century Ethics (J B Schneewind); 9) Nineteenth-Century British Ethics (Marcus G Singer); 10) Nineteenth-Century Continental Ethics (Richard Schacht); 11) Twentieth-Century Continental Ethics, 1 (Joseph J Kochelmans); 12) Twentieth-Century Continental Ethics, 2 (William R Schroeder); 13) Twentieth-Century Anglo-American Ethics (Alan Donagan).

Becker, Ron. The Ideological Commitment of Locke: Freemen and Servants in the *Two Treatises of Government*. *Hist Polit Thought*, 13(4), 631-656, Wint 92.

In the most well-known of recent studies on Locke's political thought his ideological placement ranges across the spectrum. Ashcraft believes Locke's thought is that of a radical left-wing revolutionary, while Macpherson argues that the Second Treatise provides a conservative justification for the class rule of the rising bourgeoisie. Ideological analysis of Locke's text and context shows that his proper position is on the right. The distinction between freemen and free men in the Two Treatises allows Locke to argue that when a government is dissolved political authority reverts to the "freemen" of the community, the propertied class. Thus, the right to political participation is explicitly restricted and popular sovereignty highly qualified in Locke's political theory.

Beckermann, Ansgar. States, State Types, and the Causation of Behavior. *Erkenntnis*, 36(3), 267-282, M 92.

After some introductory remarks concerning (a) the origins of the new debate on the causal efficacy of the mental and (b) the notions of states and state types it is argued that mental state types must be causally inert—at least if functionalism is correct. First, according to functionalism a state belongs to a certain mental state type iff it has a certain causal role. Having such a causal role, however, is certainly not a causally efficacious property. And second, according to functionalism a mental state M is realized by a physical state P iff P has the causal role that is characteristic for M. Realization, therefore, implies that it is P that is causally efficacious and not M.

Beckwith, Francis J. Reply to Keenan: Thomson's Argument and Academic Feminism. *Int Phil Quart*, 32(3), 369-376, S 92.

Among his many criticisms of Judith Jarvis Thomson's argument for abortion rights, Francis Beckwith argues that Thomson's libertarian argument is inconsistent with statist feminism as well as the feminist view that pregnant women are not incapacitated so that they are incapable of functioning in the workplace (IPQ 32 [1]). In response, James Keenan argues that Beckwith misrepresents feminism in addition to ignoring prolife feminism (IPQ 32 [2]). In this reply to Keenan, Beckwith argues that Keenan misses the point of his critique of Thomson's argument as well as overstating the influence of prolife feminism.

Bedau, Mark. Where's the Good in Teleology?. *Phil Phenomenol Res*, 52(4), 781-806, D 92.

Bedell, Gary. Truth and Freedom. *Mod Sch*, 70(1), 53-62, N 92.

Arguing from the presupposition of a realist interpretation of the nature of truth, I conclude that, although statements about the past, once true or false always remain true or false, statements about authentic ontological future contingencies are neither true nor false before the occurrence of those events. Since the natural freedom of self-determination, freedom of choice, presupposes ontological future contingencies, such freedom is not compatible with the unqualified assertion that truth does not change.

Bedford, David. John Dewey's Logical Project. *J Prag*, 19(5), 453-468, My 93.

This article reviews the main themes of Dewey's various logical writings. It contends that Dewey's project was to determine the logical condition necessary for science. The scientific enterprise requires the satisfaction of both correspondence and coherence criteria. This means that the logic of science must have a verificationist and a transformational aspect. In addition, a logic of science must also be able to account for certain essential non-truth functional activities. The unique feature of Dewey's logic is the central place it accords to these pragmatic operations.

Beehler, Rodger G. Madness and Method. *Philosophy*, 68(265), 369-388, Jl 93.

The clinical findings reported in the writings of Oliver Sacks provoke the question

how far persons elect those various states referred to by the expressions 'psychosis', 'insanity', 'madness'. This possibility is explored by examining some data from R D Laing's 1960s researches reported in *The Divided Self*. An interpretation of this data is offered that opposes in important respects Laing's theory of psychosis, and supports the possibility implied by Sacks' findings. The general intelligibility of such an election of madness is discussed briefly at the end.

Beehler, Rodger G (ed) and Copp, David (ed) and Szabados, Bela (ed). *On the Track of Reason*. Boulder, Westview Pr, 1992.

This book is a dedicatory volume of essays by friends and colleagues of Kai Nielsen. The subjects addressed range from the foundations of ethics (E J Bond, T Hurka, R Miller, J Rachels), religious belief and morals (T Penelhum), the justice of Oregon's health care rationing policies (N Daniels), Marx on needs (D Braybrooke), history (J Cohen), and metaphilosophical issues (M Hanen and C B Martin). In the case of the Hurka and Miller contributions, their essays iterate succinctly the positions argued in their recent books.

Beer, Francis A. Validities: A Political Science Perspective. *Soc Epistem*, 7(1), 85-105, Ja-Mr 93.

Validity is a central legitimating word in the lexicon of political science, suggesting the connection of scientific theory and research with the political world. Validity is constrained by uncontrolled and uncontrollable variance in sampling, context, text, and analysis. Judgments of validity include scientific and political dimensions, implying serious anomalies. These may be partly dissolved by more complex definition and decomposition into multiple, parallel, switchable validities.

Beezer, Anne and Osborne, Peter. Orientalism and After: An Interview with Edward Said. *Rad Phil*, 63, 22-32, Spr 93.

Bégin, Luc. La nature comme sujet de droit? Réflexions sur deux approches du problème. *Dialogue (Canada)*, 30(3), 265-275, Sum 91.

There are two ways to answer the question "Should we grant legal rights to natural objects?". The first way consists in evaluating the effectiveness of granting legal rights as a means to protect the environment. A second way considers that the main point to be debated is the acknowledgement or not of environment's intrinsic value. The solution to this problem, characteristic of the anthropocentrism/ ecocentrism debate, would determine the answer to our question. This paper shows that the subordination of the environmental rights debate to the broader debate concerning anthropocentrism and ecocentrism indicates a confusion which omits essential reflections for the environmental debate.

Bégin, Luc. La revendication écocentriste d'un droit de la nature. *Laval Theol Phil*, 48(3), 397-414, O 92.

L'idée d'une reconnaissance juridique de la nature (droit *de* la nature plutôt que droit à un environnement sain) fait progressivement son chemi dans certains milieux juridiques et philosophiques. L'auteur examine ici la revendication écocentriste d'un tel droit de la nature. Plus précisément, il critique l'affirmation selon laquelle une telle revendication s'inscrirait dans la continuité de l'histoire de nos institutions juridiques et de l'idéal démocratique qui est au fondement de ces institutions.

Begum, Hasna. Family Planning and the Social Position of Women. *Bioethics*, 7(2-3), 218-223, Ap 93.

Behera, Satrughna. Rule Following and Wright's Social Assessment: Towards Wittgenstein's "Anti-Idiolectic" Understanding. *Indian Phil Quart*, 19/1(Supp), 9-16, Ja 92.

Behr, John. Shifting Sands: Foucault, Brown and the Framework of Christian Asceticism. *Heythrop J*, 34(1), 1-21, Ja 93.

Beierwaltes, Werner. Plotino e Ficino: l'autorelazione del pensiero. *Riv Filosof Neo-Scolas*, 84(2-3), 293-324, Ap-S 92.

Beiner, Ronald. The Moral Vocabulary of Liberalism. *Nomos*, 34, 145-184, 1992.

The essay seeks to challenge the dominant liberal vocabulary of rights, autonomy, and value pluralism by juxtaposing it to an Aristotelian language of the virtues drawn from Book 1 of the *Nicomachean Ethics*. The aim is to show that the moral self-understanding of liberalism would be strengthened if it were to shift from a Kantian discourse of rights and individual autonomy to an Aristotelian discourse of virtues and character formation.

Beiser, Frederick. Hegel's Historicism in The Cambridge Companion to Hegel, Beiser, Frederick C (ed). New York, Cambridge Univ Pr, 1993.

Beiser, Frederick. Kant's Intellectual Development: 1746-1781 in The Cambridge Companion to Kant, Guyer, Paul (ed). New York, Cambridge Univ Pr, 1992.

Beiser, Frederick (ed). *The Cambridge Companion to Hegel*. New York, Cambridge Univ Pr, 1993.

Bejarano Fernandez, T. Sobre la negación: En busca de un nuevo argumento contra el origen intrapersonal de ese tipo de pensamiento. *Pensamiento*, 188(47), 469-479, O-D 91.

Negative statement rejects a false belief, which belongs: 1) to somebody else, or; 2) to oneself in the past. Can the filo- and ontogenetic appearance of the type 2 happen without dependence on the type 1? We propose that an affirmative answer implies to accept that mere perception is syntactic, i.e., that the perceptive content of the present is the erroneous or less finished content of the past plus the correction. But the perception arose in the evolution as a guide for action: Can it possess any complexity useless for that role?

Beklemishev, L D. Provability Logics for Natural Turing Progressions of Arithmetical Theories. *Stud Log*, 50(1), 107-128, Mr 91.

Provability logics with many modal operators for progressions of theories obtained by iterating their consistency statements are introduced. The corresponding arithmetical completeness theorem is proved.

Bélanger, J L Roland (trans) and Morin, Edgar. *Method—Towards a Study of Humankind, Volume I: The Nature of Nature*. New York, Lang, 1992.

This book is the first of several volumes exposing Edgar Morin's general systems view on life and society. This volume maintains that the organization of all life and society necessitates the simultaneous interplay of order and disorder. All systems, physical, biological, social, political and informational, incessantly reshape part and whole through feedback, thereby generating increasingly complex systems. For continued evolution, these simultaneously complementary, concurrent, and antagonistic systems require a priority of love over truth, of subject over object, of Sybernetics over cybernetics. (staff)

Belfrage, Bertil. A Response to M A Stewart's 'Berkeley's Introduction Draft'. *Berkeley News*, 12, 1-10, 1991-92.

M A Stewart is critical of my view that Berkeley offers a position in the *Manuscript Introduction* which is abandoned or denied in the published Introduction to the *Principles*. But he is driven into the absurd opinion that the particular objects of experience and thought are *not ideas* according to Berkeley's *Manuscript Introduction* (which indeed would indicate a remarkable doctrinal clash between the two Introductions). And his attempt at presenting a new dating is based on an erroneous description of the manuscript, actually supporting the view he tried to attack.

Bell, Desmond. Culture and Politics in Ireland: Postmodern Revisions. *Hist Euro Ideas*, 16(1-3), 141-146, Ja 93.

This paper explores the recent debate in Ireland around national identity and uses the Irish case to discuss the framing of issues of identity within postmodernist theory. The refractory character of Irish historical experience with regards the universal thrust of traditional social theory has weakened the position of enlightenment rooted intellectual discourse in Ireland and correspondingly strengthened the hold of literary and romanticised accounts of Irish specificity. Postmodernism has attempted to listen to voices from the periphery, is a critical regionalism of social theory possible on the basis of Irish experience?

Bell, Desmond. Michel Foucault: A Philosopher for All Seasons?. *Hist Euro Ideas*, 14(3), 331-346, My 92.

In this paper I examine Foucault relation to philosophy as a discipline and a calling. I explore his intellectual formation against the backdrop of French philosophy in the post-war period and in the light of his search for a more historically informed philosophical practice. Foucault's archeology of the human sciences leads him to radically reflect on the nature of knowledge, power, and subjectivity, but in place of a coherent theory of knowledge and political action he offers us an aesthetics of self suggestive of postmodernist narcissism rather than a critical philosophy.

Bell, John L. Hilbert's ε-Operator and Classical Logic. *J Phil Log*, 22(1), 1-18, F 93.

Bell, Martin (ed) and Hume, David. *Dialogues Concerning Natural Religion—David Hume*. New York, Penguin USA, 1990.

Bell, Richard H. Giacometti's Art as a Judgment on Culture. *J Aes Art Crit*, 47(1), 15-20, Wint 89.

A look at the non-conceptual nature of Giacometti's Art and how its particularly visual qualities, or how it reflects his way of seeing the world, contributes to the viewer's own judgments on culture. A general conclusion is made about the significance of the sensible in art.

Bell, Richard H. On Being Sidetracked by the Aesthetic in Kierkegaard on Art and Communication, Pattison, George (ed). New York, St Martin's Pr, 1992.

Kierkegaard suggests that we must put aside the aesthetic for the religious or else be side-tracked by the aesthetic. This presents a practical paradox for Kierkegaard since we all live most of the time in the aesthetic and the ethical. I explore how one can express the religious through the aesthetic and that the key to embracing both lies in placing the aesthetic under the governance of the religious.

Bell, Richard H. Reading Simone Weil on Rights, Justice, and Love in Simone Weil's Philosophy of Culture, Bell, Richard (ed). New York, Cambridge Univ Pr, 1993.

An analysis of Simone Weil's concept of Justice. It shows the differences she discusses between "Rights" language and justice related to love and compassion. The conclusion is that Simone Weil sees justice as a "new virtue"—a "supernatural virtue"—which originates in God and is measured out in specific acts of love. When this love is recognized by the world governed by rights, justice is considered as "mad".

Bell, Richard H (ed). *Simone Weil's Philosophy of Culture*. New York, Cambridge Univ Pr, 1993.

The book presents a comprehensive interpretation of the philosophy of Simone Weil and how her thought can illuminate issues of contemporary importance such as work, justice, the law, war and peace, and matters of more general moral and theological concerns. In addition to focusing on how Weil's thought may apply to social and cultural issues, it offers critical interpretations of the following notions in her philosophy: reading, decreation, imagination, beauty, God, and contradiction. Fourteen essays by thirteen well-known international Weil scholars.

Bell, Roger. Rorty on Derrida in Ethics and Danger, Dallery, Arleen B (ed). Albany, SUNY Pr, 1992.

Bell, Shannon. Tomb of the Sacred Prostitute: 'The Symposium' in Shadow of Spirit, Berry, Philippa (ed). New York, Routledge, 1992.

Bellah, Robert N. Autonomy and Responsibility: The Social Basis of Ethical Individualism in Revisioning Philosophy, Ogilvy, James (ed). Albany, SUNY Pr, 1992.

Bellamy, Richard. Defending the Liberal Community. *Hist Euro Ideas*, 17(2-3), 325-331, Mr-My 93.

This article reviews the attempts by Will Kymlicka and Stephen Macedo to overcome the liberal-communitarian debate by injecting a reserve of communitarians into liberalism. Whilst neither attempt is judged successful, Kymlicka's approach is seen as more fruitful than Macedo's.

Bellamy, Richard. *Liberalism and Modern Society: A Historical Argument*. University Park, Penn St Univ Pr, 1992.

Bellamy, Richard. Liberalism and Nationalism in the Thought of Max Weber. *Hist Euro Ideas*, 14(4), 499-507, Jl 92.

Max Weber is often characterised as a typical exemplar of the German bourgeoisie. Supposedly disabused of their ethical ideals for social progress and individual freedom by their failure to unite the nation without the support of Bismarck, the German middle classes are held to have sacrificed the political goals of liberalism to

the pursuit of economic and national expansion by a Junker dominated state. This interpretation fails to distinguish two sorts of nationalism within the German political tradition. The first was intimately linked to the creation of a dynamic capitalist economy and liberal democratic institutions. The second was tied to an authoritarian state structure which sought to stave off social and political reform with military success and imperial expansion. (edited)

Bellamy, Richard. T H Green and the Morality of Victorian Liberalism in Victorian Liberalism, Bellamy, Richard (ed). New York, Routledge, 1990.

Rather than seeing Green's philosophy as attempting to generate liberal conclusions from certain abstract pressures, this paper regards it as a self-conscious attempt to express the public language of contemporary political discourse in philosophical terms. Green's political thought is limited, therefore, by the Victorian standpoint.

Bellamy, Richard. The Fragility of Fortune. *Phil Invest*, 16(1), 36-45, Ja 93.

Bellamy, Richard (ed). *Victorian Liberalism*. New York, Routledge, 1990.

Victorian liberalism brings together leading political theorists and historians in order to examine the interplay of theory and ideology in nineteenth century liberal thought and practice. Drawing as a wide range of source material, the authors discuss liberal thinkers and politicians from Adam Smith, Jeremy Betham and J S Mill to William Gladstone and Joseph Chamberlain. Connections are drawn throughout between the different languages which made up liberal discourse and the relations between their vocabularies and the political movements and the changing social reality they sought to explain.

Bellert, Irena. A Linguistic Approach to Frege's Puzzles in Advances in Scientific Philosophy, Schurz, Gerhard (ed). Amsterdam, Rodopi, 1991.

There has been a long and unresolved dispute in the literature on Frege's puzzles concerning so called identity statements, in particular when embedded in epistemic contexts (e.g., "John believes that Hesperus is Phosphorus"). Leibniz's Law of the substitutivity of identity seems to fail in these cases. Many logicians have dealt with those puzzles and presented partial solutions to the problems involved. Quine treats all names as general terms, whereas Kripke treats them all as rigid designators. The solution proposed by Bellert, based on linguistic criteria of distributivity, goes half way between Quine's and Kripke's theory: names function as rigid designators, but only in syntactic position of full NPs (arguments), and they function as general terms in predicative position. The 'rigidity' of names depends thus on their syntactic position.

Belli, Humberto and Nash, Ronald. *Beyond Liberation Theology*. Grand Rapids, Baker Book, 1992.

Bellinger, Charles. Toward a Kierkegaardian Understanding of Hitler, Stalin, and the Cold War in Foundations of Kierkegaard's Vision of Community, Connell, George B (ed). Atlantic Highlands, Humanities Pr, 1992.

Drawing primarily on *The Concept of Anxiety, Philosophical Fragments*, and *The Sickness Unto Death*, I attempt in this essay to show how Kierkegaard's thought can help us to understand the basic motives that impel human beings to violence. This analysis of Kierkegaard's psychology lays the groundwork for subsequent comments on Naziism, Stalinism, and the Cold War. The theory of violence implicit in Kierkegaard's works is compared briefly with the theories of Carl Jung, Ernest Becker, Alice Miller, and René Girard. Throughout, I argue that Kierkegaard's insights into violence grow out of his interpretation of the Christian doctrine of creation.

Belliotti, Raymond and Jacobs, William S. Two Paradoxes for Machiavelli in Terrorism, Justice and Social Values, Peden, Creighton W (ed). Lewiston, Mellen Pr, 1990.

We examine and resolve two paradoxical positions Machiavelli takes in his writings. We argue that the first paradox—his appreciation of an absolute monarch in *The Prince* and his advocacy of a republic in *The Discourses*—actually is the key to understanding his notion of public morality. Next, we argue that the second paradox—his claim that *virtu* remains constant in the world but that good laws and good arms can alter the amount of *virtu* in a particular state—actually is a statement of a simple truth. As a result, we present Machiavelli as a somewhat more consistent thinker than he is often taken to be.

Bello, A G A. L'esistenzialismo rivisitato. *Aquinas*, 35(3), 647-652, S-D 92.

Bellon, Christina. Standpoint Reflections on Original Position Objectivity. *SW Phil Rev*, 9(1), 105-113, Ja 93.

Belnap, Nuel and Gupta, Anil. *The Revision Theory of Truth*. Cambridge, MIT Pr, 1993.

This book explains how our concept of truth works in both ordinary and pathological contexts (e.g., contexts generating the Liar Paradox). Its central claim is that truth is a circular concept. In support of this claim the book provides a widely applicable general theory ("the revision theory") of definitions. The theory makes sense of arbitrary systems of mutually interdependent concepts of which circular concepts, such as truth, are but a special case. Under the revision theory, when one sees truth as circular, both ordinary and pathological features of truth fall into a simple understandable pattern.

Belsey, Andrew. World Poverty, Justice and Equality in International Justice and the Third World, Attfield, Robin (ed). New York, Routledge, 1992.

This paper criticizes claims that as far as "we" (the inhabitants of wealthy first-world countries) are concerned, the interests of people in the third world are overridden by special obligations we have towards people who are geographically or genetically closer to us. Instead, the paper argues that third-world poverty is the product of an exploitative global system that benefits the wealthy at the expense of the poor, and that part of the remedy is the adoption of a global conception of justice, based on equality and need.

Belshaw, Christopher. Asymmetry and Non-Existence. *Phil Stud*, 70(1), 103-116, Ap 93.

Why is post-mortem non-existence, but not prenatal non-existence, bad? Why do we want to die later, but not to have been born earlier? Bruckner and Fischer argue that we are biased towards the future, and indifferent to the past. I deny the second claim, and present an alternative account. We do not want to have been born earlier, because we believe (rightly or wrongly) our identity depends on the past being much as it was. We are past-preservers. Is there future bias? This matter is not settled.

Belzer, Marvin and Loewer, Barry. *Prima Facie* Obligation in John Searle and His Critics, Lepore, Ernest (ed). Cambridge, Blackwell, 1991.

Ben-Ari, Eyal and Cohen, Eric. Hard Choices: A Sociological Perspective on Value Incommensurability. *Human Stud*, 16(3), 267-297, Jl 93.

Ben-Chaim, Michael. The Empiric Experience and the Practice of Autonomy. *Stud Hist Phil Sci*, 23(4), 533-555, D 92.

Prompted by recent discussions concerning empiricism and the experimental practices of scientific research, the paper poses the following question: how is learning from experience achieved, and what does it accomplish? The paper presents a comparative study of two contributions to experimental science in the early modern period: Isaac Newton's research on light and colours, and Stephen Gray's research in electricity. Its main argument, elaborated through a detailed examination of their experience, is the attainment of individual intellectual autonomy, and that the autonomous participation in public discourse is the underlying principle of conceptual innovations in empirical research.

Ben-NaftaliBerkowitz, Michal. A Critique of Gadamer (in Hebrew). *Iyyun*, 41, 441-456, O 92.

Ben-Yami, Hannoch. A Note on the Chinese Room. *Synthese*, 95(2), 169-172, My 93.

Searle's Chinese Room was supposed to prove that computers can't understand: the man in the room, following, like a computer, syntactical rules alone, though indistinguishable from a genuine Chinese speaker, doesn't understand a word. But such a room is impossible: the man won't be able to respond correctly to questions like 'What is the time?', even though such an ability is indispensable for a genuine Chinese speaker. Several ways to provide the room with the required ability are considered, and it is concluded that for each of these the room will have understanding. Hence, Searle's argument is invalid.

Ben-Ze'ev, Aaron. Anger and Hate. *J Soc Phil*, 23(2), 85-110, Fall 92.

The paper examines some negative emotions toward other agents' actions and traits. It concentrates upon anger and hate, but other emotions, e.g., resentment and contempt, are discussed as well. Understanding the unique nature of these emotions is important for the purpose of determining their moral value and knowing the kind of education and activities that may reduce their extent and intensity.

Ben-Ze'ev, Aaron. Emotional and Moral Evaluations. *Metaphilosophy*, 23(3), 214-229, Jl 92.

Evaluations are important components in both emotional and moral attitudes. The paper compares the types of evaluations involved in these attitudes. It is claimed that the main difference between them concerns their generality: moral evaluations are more general than emotional evaluations in all senses of generality. This difference has important implications concerning the nature of moral behavior and the dispute about ethical universalism and ethical particularism.

Ben-Ze'ev, Aaron. Envy and Pity. *Int Phil Quart*, 33(1), 3-19, Mr 93.

At first sight pity and envy appear to be very different; pity seems to be a basically positive state, highly valued in human relations, while envy seems to be a basically negative state we try to avoid. A closer examination of pity and envy reveals that from a psychological viewpoint, the two states are similar in some important aspects. Discussing this similarity is useful for understanding the nature of envy and pity.

Ben-Ze'ev, Aaron. *The Perceptual System: A Philosophical and Psychological Perspective*. New York, Lang, 1993.

The book presents an original comprehensive approach to some of the most difficult problems concerning sense-perception and other mental states. After rejecting prevailing approaches, the author presents his own viewpoint which may be characterized as direct, critical realism. Basing his conclusions on conceptual analysis, psychological evidence, and historical considerations, the author is able to offer new insights into traditionally unsolved problems concerning the nature of perceptual states, the ontological status of perceptual environment, the cognitive mechanism in perception, and the explanation of perceptual mistakes. The book also discusses the implications of this approach for other mental states such as memory and consciousness.

Ben-Ze'ev, Aaron. The Virtue of Modesty. *Amer Phil Quart*, 30(3), 235-246, Jl 93.

Modesty seems to be an important virtue. Its characterization, however, is problematic and has received little philosophical attention. This essay clarifies some of the issues concerning modesty. In particular it rejects three cognitive accounts of modesty which explain modesty by referring to either the agent's insincerity, ignorance, or realistic knowledge. The essay suggests an evaluative account claiming that the modest person evaluates his or her fundamental human worth as similar to that of other people.

Benardete, José A and Lord, Catherine. Baxandall and Goodman in The Language of Art History, Kemal, Salim (ed). New York, Cambridge Univ Pr, 1991.

Benardete, Seth. On Plato's *Sophist*. *Rev Metaph*, 46(4), 747-780, Je 93.

In the first part, it is argued that the Stranger has employed in his divisions both eikastic and phantastic speech, and that the issue of being arises because Theaetetus fails to recognize Socrates as the philosopher. In the second part, it is argued that phantastic speech as the experience of eikastic speech is false opinion, and that the double account of logos, as the weaving together of species and of agent and action, corresponds respectively to that which makes speech possible, the other, and that which determines truth and falsehood in terms of whether the agent is other than the action.

Benatar, S R. Medical Ethics in Times of War and Insurrection: Rights and Duties. *J Med Human*, 14(3), 137-147, Fall 93.

Bencivenga, Ermanno. A Specious Puzzle. *Erkenntnis*, 38(1), 131-133, Ja 93.

Frege's celebrated puzzle about identity generalizes to all predications. And it doesn't justify the introduction of senses.

Bencivenga, Ermanno. Rorty and I. *Phil Forum*, 24(4), 307-318, Sum 93.

Can philosophy be done with a smile, as Rorty suggests? Is doing philosophy with a smile a way of protecting others from harm—or of harming them irreparably?

Bencivenga, Ermanno. The Electronic Self in Advances in Scientific Philosophy, Schurz, Gerhard (ed). Amsterdam, Rodopi, 1991.

According to the author, transgression and play are essential traits of subjectivity. So, as these traits emerge in the behavior of computer networks, a new, electronic subject also emerges, of impressive power and scope. The *Übermeusch* will not necessarily be an *organic* structure.

Bender, John and Blocker, Gene H. *Contemporary Philosophy of Art*. Englewood Cliffs, Prentice Hall, 1993.

An anthology of outstanding analytic aesthetics, mostly from the last twenty years, along with extended treatment of the "Post-Modern" challenge to that tradition. Ten topical chapters, with critical introductions. Upper undergraduated and graduate use.

Bender, John W. Unreckoned Misleading Truths and Lehrer's Theory of Undefeated Justification. *J Phil Res*, 17, 465-481, 1992.

According to Keith Lehrer's coherence theory, knowledge is true acceptance whose justification is undefeated by a falsehood. It has recently become clear that Lehrer's handling of important Gettier-inspired problems depends upon his position that only falsehoods *accepted by the subject* can act as defeaters of knowledge. I argue against this and present an example in which an *unreckoned truth*—one neither believed nor believed to be false by the subject—defeats knowledge. I trace the negative implications of this matter for the coherence theory.

Bene, László. Argument and Experience in a Thirteenth Century Concept of Science (in Hungarian). *Magyar Filozof Szemle*, 3, 263-284, 1991.

Benedikt, Michael (ed). *Cyberspace: First Steps*. Cambridge, MIT Pr, 1991.

Benedikt, Michael. Expressionism, Romanticism and Postmodernism: Heidegger's Nationalistic Career. *Hist Euro Ideas*, 16(4-6), 795-800, Ja 93.

Benesch, Walter. The Euclidean Egg, the Three Legged Chinese Chicken: "Contextual versus Formal Approaches to Reason and Logics". *J Chin Phil*, 20(2), 109-131, Je 93.

Benhabib, Seyla. Autonomy, Modernity, and Community in Cultural-Political Interventions in the Unfinished Project of Enlightenment, Honneth, Axel (& other eds). Cambridge, MIT Pr, 1992.

Benjamin, Andrew (ed). *Judging Lyotard*. New York, Routledge, 1992.

Benjamin, Martin. Judgment and the Art of Compromise. *Thinking*, 10(1), 2-7, 1992.

Benn, Piers. My Own Death. *Monist*, 76(2), 235-251, Ap 93.

This article discusses the belief that there is an insurmountable difficulty about conceiving of one's own death from a first-personal point of view. A distinction is made between 'conceiving of' and 'conceiving of what it is like', and it is admitted that one's own death is inconceivable in the latter sense, though not in the former. A comparison is made between this problem and Nagel's remarks on 'particular subjectivity'. It is argued that although Nagel is mistaken in thinking that facts about who I am cannot be accommodated in a token-reflexive account of the truth of the relevant utterances, nevertheless his ideas have important connections to our main problem.

Bennett, James O. Karl Jaspers and Scientific Philosophy. *J Hist Phil*, 31(3), 437-453, Jl 93.

Jaspers was a lifelong critic of *wissenschaftliche Philosophie*, and he sought to correct its flaws with his own conception of philosophy. However, I find in his work not one but two views of philosophy in its relationship to *wissenschaft*—what I term "the exclusive view" and "the dual aspect view." The first view precludes the legitimacy of academic philosophy. I argue that the second view is preferable, insofar as it grounds his criticism of the practice of philosophy as wholly impersonal inquiry, while still allowing some place for the institutionalized aspects of philosophy.

Bennett, Jonathan. How Do Gestures Succeed? in John Searle and His Critics, LePore, Ernest (ed). Cambridge, Blackwell, 1991.

This paper criticizes John Searle's "Meaning, Communication, and Representation". Where Grice ties meaning to an intention to affect hearers, Searle ties it to an intention to represent—this having the advantage that it does not have to explain away cases of meaning where there is no intended hearer. It is argued here that those cases do not constitute much of an obstacle to Grice's theory of meaning, and that in any case Searle's concept of "representation" is not sound. Searle defines it in terms of the notion of the "success" of an action, which is left unexplained and apparently unexplainable.

Bennington, Geoffrey. Mosaic Fragment: If Derrida were an Egyptian... in Derrida: A Critical Reader, Wood, David (ed). Cambridge, Blackwell, 1992.

Bennington, Geoffrey. Spirit's Spirit Spirits Spirit in Of Derrida, Heidegger, and Spirit, Wood, David (ed). Evanston, Northwestern Univ Pr, 1993.

Bennington, Geoffrey. 'Ces Petits Différends': Lyotard and Horace in Judging Lyotard, Benjamin, Andrew (ed). New York, Routledge, 1992.

Benoist, Jocelyn. Le choix du métier: sur le "rationalisme" de Husserl. *Rev Phil Louvain*, 91(89), 66-89, F 93.

In the *Kaizo*-papers (1923-1924), Husserl looks as a rationalist philosopher of the 19th century, facing to the initial cataclysm of our modernity: the first World War. Husserl's ethical rationalism comes here into his crucial experience, and appears as a critical one, connected with the phenomenology such as Husserl understood it. Did the author succeed in giving to the ethical position a phenomenological meaning, or is it only a metaphysical residue? To this question are relative the possibility of an *other* phenomenology, which should not ask the being, but the value, and also the definitive meaning of Husserl's rationalist attitude.

Benoist, Jocelyn. Métaphysique et politique: Le singe de Dieu, l'homme. *Arch Phil*, 56(2), 231-250, Ap-Je 93.

The author tries to show how the Cartesian train of thought may have political consequences. The ontology of power which it institutes may found the politics of power, just as it appears in the shape of absolutism in the classic age. Against the temptation of transposing the structure, really self-founding, from Descartes's God to the one of State that is self-founding only in a fantasmatical sense, the author uses

Spinozist criticism of politics as a re-rooting of it into society and history completely ignored by Cartesianism. Against any absolutisation of the politics, he chooses an ethical concept of the politics.

Benso, Silvia. Monica's Grin of Tension. *Cont Phil*, 15(2), 5-10, Mr-Ap 93.

The paper explores the philosophical modernity of Monica, Augustine's mother. A tension never resolved but always lived thoroughly sustains her figure. Phenomenologically, the tension points to all directions of the spacial horizon: upward—the tension between God and Monica, outward—the tension between Monica and her *milieu*, inward—the tension between Monica and Monica. Ontologically, it suggests a model of relation between parts and whole that is neither holistic nor individualistic, but rather communitarian. The notion of community allows for a concept of wholeness that escapes the accusations of being ontotheological, totalitarian, product of the metaphysics either of will or of substance.

Benson, Hugh H (ed). *Essays on the Philosophy of Socrates*. New York, Oxford Univ Pr, 1992.

The last two decades have witnessed a virtual explosion of research in Socratic philosophy. This anthology offers essays representing the range and diversity of that vast literature, including historical and philosophical essays, essays devoted to a single Platonic dialogue, and essays devoted to the Socratic method, Socratic epistemology, and Socratic ethics. It includes lists of suggested further readings, an extensive bibliography of recent Socratic research, and an index locorum. It seeks to be a useful resource both for students and scholars.

Benson, Hugh H. Why Is There a Discussion of False Belief in the *Theaetetus*?. *J Hist Phil*, 30(2), 171-199, Ap 92.

I argue that the false belief passage in the *Theaetetus* (187c-200d) is not a digression. Rather, it is an argument against Theaetetus' definition that knowledge is true belief. After considering two recent interpretations of the puzzle concerning false belief at 187e-188c, I offer an alternative interpretation appealing to premises that are Platonic and making use of Theaetetus' definition. Thus, the puzzle is a Platonic argument to the effect that if knowledge is true belief, then false belief is impossible. But, Plato has already argued for the possibility of true belief (160e-183c). Knowledge, then, cannot be true belief.

Benson, Keith R. Experimental Ecology on the Pacific Coast: Victor Shelford and His Search for Appropriate Methods. *Hist Phil Life Sci*, 14(1), 73-91, Ja 92.

Victor Shelford spent many of his summers between 1914 and 1932 attempting to apply the methods of physiological animal ecology, especially those he pioneered in his studies in the Midwest of the US, to the study of marine organisms in the Pacific intertidal. Working at the Puget Sound Biological Station in Washington State, Shelford soon recognized that the experimental methods of this approach had severe limitations in the new environment. He then abandoned this search for causal explanations of animal distribution in favor of descriptive studies of the different intertidal communities. Shelford's struggle to understand intertidal ecology, therefore, represents an interesting dynamic between descriptive and experimental approaches; indeed, this case study reveals serious limitations to the historical assumptions that American biologists abandoned descriptive approaches in favor of the more productive experimental method.

Benson, Robert W. Peirce and Critical Legal Studies in Peirce and Law, Kevelson, Roberta. New York, Lang, 1991.

Benston, Kimberly W. *The Veil of Black*: (Un)Masking the Subject of African-American Modernism's "Native Son". *Human Stud*, 16(1-2), 69-99, Ap 93.

Beraducci, Alessandro and Verbrugge, Rineke. On the Provability Logic of Bounded Arithmetic. *Annals Pure Applied Log*, 61(1-2), 75-93, My 93.

Beran, Harry. Border Disputes and the Right of National Self-Determination. *Hist Euro Ideas*, 16(4-6), 479-486, Ja 93.

Berciano, Modesto. Heidegger, Vattimo y la deconstrucción. *Anu Filosof*, 26(1), 9-45, 1993.

Postmodern philosophy, as expressed in Vattimo's thought, tries to build a philosophy that rejects all foundation and all that is immovable or absolute. It gives value to life, history and events. Nietzsche and Heidegger are considered forerunners of postmodernism.

Berenson, F. Emotions and Rationality. *Personalist Forum*, 8/1(Supp), 175-185, Spr 92.

The purpose of this paper is to show that emotions, contrary to widespread belief, play an essential part in provoking our understanding. I bring out the central role which emotions play both itself and other understanding thus showing why I take it as mistaken to treat of emotions as purely or necessarily passive phenomena which are also, therefore, irrational. The picture of a man which emerges from such a view seems fraught with serious conceptual difficulties. On this view we are asked to regard emotions as something that happens to a creature who would be intelligible to us as a human agent quite independently of this important emotional dimension.

Berenson, F M. *Understanding Persons: Personal and Impersonal Relationships (Second Edition)*. Lewiston, Mellen Pr, 1992.

Berent, Irwin M (ed) and Evans, Rod L (ed). *Drug Legalization: For and Against*. Peru, Open Court, 1992.

The purpose of this anthology is to introduce readers to the arguments for and against drug legalization used by the major participants in the debate. The work represents the most significant essays written when the debate was first receiving wide coverage in the mainstream media. It gives not only "both sides" but also a number of intermediate positions between the drug laws we have now and a completely free market in drugs. In addition, it is multidisciplinary, containing arguments from such fields as legislation (Charles Rangel), law (Ethan Nadelmann), public policy (James Q Wilson), economics (Milton Friedman), and psychiatry (Thomas Szasz). A forward is included by Linus Pauling and an introduction by Hugh Downs.

Berg, Jan. *Ontology Without Ultrafilters and Possible Worlds: An Examination of Bolzano's Ontology*. Sankt Augustin, Academia, 1992.

Berg, Jan and Morscher, Edgar. *Bolzano-Forschung: 1989-1991*. Sankt Augustin, Academia, 1992.

Bergadano, Francesco. Machine Learning and the Foundations of Inductive Inference. *Mind Mach*, 3(1), 31-51, F 93.

The problem of valid induction could be stated as follows: are we justified in accepting a given hypothesis on the basis of observations that frequently confirm it? The present paper argues that this question is relevant for the understanding of Machine Learning, but insufficient. Recent research in inductive reasoning has prompted another, more fundamental question: there is not just one given rule to be tested, there are a large number of possible rules, and many of these are somehow confirmed by the date—how are we to restrict the space of inductive hypotheses and choose effectively some rules that will probably perform well on future examples? We analyze if and how this problem is approached in standard accounts of induction and show the difficulties that are present. Finally, we suggest that the explanation-based learning approach and related methods of knowledge intensive induction could be, if not a solution, at least a tool for solving some of these problems.

Bergeois, B. Kant's Idealization of the Republic (in French). *Tijdschr Filosof*, 55(2), 293-306, Je 93.

According to Kant there is not just a current 'republican morality', as if a republic could be anything else but morality. The republican state *is* the morality of politics. However, this does not mean that politics has to be made subservient to the ethical order. In itself the state implies for everybody the absolute requirement of submission to the *law*. Republican morality might and should inspire whichever political body, since the republic is neither a structure (a form of sovereignty) nor a practice (a form of government): it is nothing but the will to establish public law on the general will. Although Kant pays tribute to the republican idea, in a way his republicanism is opposed to that of Rousseau as he stresses the disconnection of the rational general will from the empirical will of all. Against popular sovereignty his theory is one of representative sovereignty.

Berger, Ulrich. Total Sets and Objects in Domain Theory. *Annals Pure Applied Log*, 60(2), 91-117, Ap 93.

Total sets and objects generalizing total functions are introduced into the theory of effective domains of Scott and Ersov. Using these notions Kreisel's Density Theorem and the Theorem of Kreisel-Lacombe-Shoenfield are generalized. As an immediate consequence we obtain the well-known continuity of computable functions on the constructive reals as well as a domain-theoretic characterization of the Heriditarily Effective Operations.

Bergmann, Gustav and Heald, William (ed) and Allaire, Edwin B. *New Foundations of Ontology*. Madison, Univ of Wisconsin Pr, 1992.

Bergmann's last book length manuscript represents his final attempt to propose and defend a system of categories appropriate for a realistic ontology rich enough to account for the existence of minds and an adequate grounding of mathematics. An extension of Bergmann's phenomenological atomism, the book also includes a vigorous attempt to show that "formal facts," including not only analytic facts, but also the possessing of syntactical forms by all facts, are "objective" features of a world whose fundamental core consists of atomic facts and the particular and universal "things" of which they are composed.

Bergmann, Sheryle. The Process/Product Dichotomy and Its Implications for Creative Dance. *J Aes Educ*, 26(2), 103-108, Sum 92.

"Process—Not Product" is a slogan touted by many teachers of creative dance. However, it is not always clear what is meant by the terms process and product. Ambiguity at this level results in the postulating of creative dance aims that appear at times to be diametrically opposed to the aims of dance as a performance art. I propose that this dichotomy is a false one and that its dissolution would have positive implications for the teaching of creative dance.

Bergo, Bettina. The God of Abraham and the God of the Philosophers: A Reading of Emmanuel Levinas's "Dieu et la Philosophie". *Grad Fac Phil J*, 16(1), 113-164, 1993.

The present article traces the unfolding of Levinas's critique of onto-theology in "Dieu et la Philosophie." It then proceeds to examine the language he develops to approach transcendence without treating it as a part of the economy of being and beings. The language of Levinas, his use of tropes and figures, bears resemblance to the language of mystics such as Surin and John of the Cross. Without claiming that Levinas's is mystical thought, I examine stylistic intersections between these two languages, asking whether, and in what sense, they share a common objective: a communication of the unthematizable as "ethical" relation.

Bergström, Lars. Quine, Underdetermination, and Skepticism. *J Phil*, 90(7), 331-358, Jl 93.

The underdetermination thesis says, roughly, that radically different scientific theories may be equally supported by all possible evidence. The thesis may well be true, but there is not much support for it. Quine's different reactions to the thesis are not satisfactory. It leads to a kind of skepticism, which Quine's naturalism cannot prevent.

Berki, R N. The Realism of Moralism: The Political Philosophy of Istvan Bibo. *Hist Polit Thought*, 13(3), 513-534, Autumn 92.

Berkowitz, Yoseph. The Newcomb Paradox and Everyday Problems (in Hebrew). *Iyyun*, 42, 323-331, Ap 93.

Berlin, Isaiah. Reply to Ronald H McKinney, "Towards a Postmodern Ethics: Sir Isaiah Berlin and John Caputo". *J Value Inq*, 26(4), 557-560, O 92.

In correcting some misunderstandings of his position, Berlin clarifies his own ethical views. His empirically based conception of common human values sets a minimum standard of tolerable life, and thus a limit to the range of conflicting moral and cultural options open to men and societies. Everyone is entitled to resist whatever falls outside this wide, variegated 'human horizon'. Berlin sharply distinguishes pluralism and relativism, and rejects all a priori views of value. He explains his attitude to those who reject humanity's shared values. He suggests when such dissenters should be regarded as deranged, and when as criminal.

Berlinger, Rudolph. *Philosophisches Denken: Einübungen*. Amsterdam, Rodopi, 1993.

Der Titel "Philosophisches Denken, Einübungen" zielt nicht auf eine Philosophie, die gegeben ist wie irgend ein Ding, dessen Gebrauch man erlernen kann. Wir entwerfen vielmehr Philosophie, deren Achse die gestaltbildende Seinsnatur des menschlichen Geistes ist. Wäre das morphopoietische Sein des Menschen nicht von Grund auf bildnerisch, so vermöchte der Mensch sie nicht als Philosoph künstlerisch zu erproben, indem er eine Welt in Philosophie und Kunst bildet. Hat der Mensch sich aber so als Welt zu begreifen und zu tätigen gelernt, dann ist dies keine Leistung einer zufälligen Beliebigkeit, sondern die Notwendigkeit des endlichen Geistes, die ihren währenden Ausdruck darin findet, dass der Mensch nach Ursprung und Grund seines möglichen Seins fragt, bewegt von dem Verlangen, begründet und gegründet wissen zu wollen. Dieses Wissen wird als Sprache vernehmbar, die der Mensch durch seine dialogische Weltnatur verlautbart. (edited)

Berman, David (ed). *George Berkeley: Alciphron in Focus*. New York, Routledge, 1993.

Alciphron (1732) is Berkeley's most sustained work of philosophical theology; it also presents his final statements on vision, free-will and language. This edition contains the four most important dialogues, together with essays and extracts on it from the 18th to the 20th centuries, including pieces by Francis Hutcheson, Lord Bolingbroke, J S Mill and J O Urmson, and Antony Flew. In the introduction, I try to show that *Alciphron* has a closer connection with Berkeley's Immaterialist philosophy than is generally thought.

Bermejo-Barrera, José C. Explicating the Past: In Praise of History. *Hist Theor*, 32(1), 14-24, 1993.

Since the very beginnings of philosophy, the multifaceted problem of time has constituted one of the central concerns of philosophers and other thinkers. It is of course beyond the reach of a single article to tackle the problem of time in its entirety. Here, I shall concentrate on a single very specific aspect: the definition of the past and the question of whether the past has any explicative value. It is largely on the answer to this question that the possibility of maintaining the coherent identity of history as a branch of knowledge depends. (edited)

Bermudo, J M. Platón y Hume: Cercanos en los importante. *Agora (Spain)*, 11(1), 149-162, 1992.

It is considered that the basic question in political theory is "why law and not rather anarchy"? We discuss here the thesis which says that whenever the philosophy is done by philosophers, they necessarily have to answer another more interesting and exciting question: "How is it possible to have a governor love law?" Both Plato and Hume understood that the problem of faith in a just society went through the possibility of governors loving law, not people: on their side, only obedience is important. We consider this reason important enough as to justify a parallel reading of Plato and Hume. We have nonetheless taken into consideration other common problems, especially the importance they both give to *desire*. (edited)

Bernasconi, Robert. Justice and the Twilight Zone of Morality in Reading Heidegger: Commemorations, Sallis, John (ed). Bloomington, Indiana Univ Pr, 1992.

This paper gathers the various pieces of a surprising history of justice that is scattered through Heidegger's lectures and essays from the period 1935 to 1946. Although Heidegger's account of the history of the essence of truth is more developed, there is some suggestion that Heidegger believed that the thought of justice exceeded that of truth. Not only does justice play an important role in Heidegger's understanding of Plato's *Republic*, Heidegger also dwells on the interpretations of justice to be found both at the beginning of thinking in the Anaximander fragment and Parmenides, and at the end of metaphysics in Nietzsche.

Bernasconi, Robert. No More Stories, Good or Bad: de Man's Criticisms of Derrida on Rousseau in Derrida: A Critical Reader, Wood, David (ed). Cambridge, Blackwell, 1992.

This paper takes up the question of the relation between narration, critique and deconstruction through an examination of De Man's criticisms of Derrida's reading of Rousseau in *Of Grammatology*. The author clarifies the difference between critique and deconstruction by showing how Derrida's exposition of the logic of supplementarity in Rousseau works not as a critique, but as a double reading. This decisive difference provides the basis for a brief exploration of the difficulties of criticizing Derrida. The article ends with some reflections on the parasitic character of deconstructive discourse particularly in connection with the ethico-political motivation for deconstruction.

Bernasconi, Robert. Politics beyond Humanism in Working Through Derrida, Madison, Gary B (ed). Evanston, Northwestern Univ Pr, 1993.

This paper explores the debate about the political dimension of deconstruction in two different but related contexts. "The Ends of Man" is examined to clarify deconstructive strategies with particular reference to the question of Heidegger and humanism. Then Derrida's essays on apartheid and Nelson Mandela, "Racism's Last Word" and "The Laws of Reflection," are scrutinized, with particular attention to the way in which Derrida reads Mandela in terms of Rousseau. The author concludes with a discussion of the way in which deconstructive logic can help elucidate the necessity of positive discrimination as a means to combat racism and the limits of that logic in such a context.

Bernat, James L. How Much of the Brain Must Die in Brain Death?. *J Clin Ethics*, 3(1), 21-26, Spr 92.

The permanent cessation of functioning of the whole brain (cerebral hemispheres, thalamus, hypothalamus, brain stem) is the best criterion of death because it is both a necessary and sufficient condition for death defined as the permanent cessation of functioning of the organism as a whole. Not all brain neurons must die in brain death; only the currently unknown critical number and array that execute the clinical functions of the organism. Purely laboratory-measured minor neuroendocrine function and rudimentary EEG activity that do not contribute to the clinical functions of the organism may persist despite brain death.

Bernet, Rudolf. Husserl's Concept of the World in Crises in Continental Philosophy, Dallery, Arleen B (ed). Albany, SUNY Pr, 1990.

Bernet, Rudolf and Kern, Iso and Marbach, Eduard. *An Introduction to Husserlian Phenomenology*. Evanston, Northwestern Univ Pr, 1993.

The book presents Husserl's philosophy in its chronological development, but also emphasizes the unity of the whole project by showing the systematic interconnections between the basic themes and notions. The authors elucidate Husserl's conceptual development by way of relating his own publications to his many research manuscripts, depicting the broadening of the research program from the early static-descriptive to the genetic-explanatory phenomenology, and presenting Husserl's overall conception of philosophy.

Bernhardt, Jean. La philosophie de l'histoire de la philosophie de Martial Gueroult. *Rev Phil Fr*, 1, 33-48, Ja-Mr 93.

Bernick, Susan. Philosophy and Feminism: The Case of Susan Bordo. *Hypatia*, 7(3), 188-196, Sum 92.

In this paper I lay out what I take to be the crucial insights in Susan Bordo's "Feminist Skepticism and the 'Maleness' of Philosophy" and point out some additional difficulties with the skeptical position. I call attention to an ambiguity in the nature or content of the "maleness" of philosophy that Bordo identifies. Finally, I point out that, unlike some feminist skeptics, Bordo never loses sight in her work of women's loved experiences.

Bernstein, J M. De-Divinization and the Vindication of Everyday-Life: Reply to Rorty. *Tijdschr Filosof*, 54(4), 668-692, D 92.

This essay originated as a reply to Richard Rorty's "Habermas, Derrida, and the Functions of Philosophy". In it, I contest Rorty's deployment of the categories of private self-creation and the collective political enterprise of increasing freedom, first developed in *Contingency, Irony and Solidarity*, to demonstrate that the philosophical projects of Habermas and Derrida are complementary rather than antagonistic. The focus of my critique is two-fold: firstly, I contend that so-called critiques of metaphysics are always simultaneously engaging with some form of social domination or disintegration (e.g., nihilism or societal rationalization); secondly, I argue that the fault-line in Rorty's thought that structures his categories is his, Davidson inspired, naturalized philosophy of language. This philosophy of language falls afoul of Heidegger's analysis of the present-to-hand.

Bernstein, J M. Grand Narratives in On Paul Ricoeur: Narrative and Interpretation, Wood, David (ed). New York, Routledge, 1991.

Bernstein, J M. *The Fate of Art: Aesthetic Alienation from Kant to Derrida and Adorno*. University Park, Penn St Univ Pr, 1992.

Bernstein argues that Kant's attempt to provide a priori validation for the distinction between cognitive and aesthetic judgements fails. If reflective judgements provide the necessary subjective conditions for determinate judgements of the understanding, then even the deployment of the categories depends upon 'aesthetic' conditions. Hence, the modern experience of the autonomy of art and aesthetics from truth-only cognition - an experience here termed 'aesthetic alienation' - belies their categorial entwinement. Bernstein tracks the emergence of this thought in the writings of Heidegger, Derrida and Adorno. In each a term of art drawn from Kant's *Critique of Judgement* underlies their aesthetic critique of truth-only cognition and modern, instrumental rationality.

Bernstein, Mark. Towards a More Expansive Moral Community. *J Applied Phil*, 9(1), 45-52, 1992.

I argue for a broader understanding of the morally considerable. I propose a neo-Aristotelian account of individuals wherein some entities, often precluded from those deserving of moral consideration, are deemed proper subjects of such treatment. The criterion suggested is, roughly, that of self-regulatory development, a teological notion, that I argue should not be viewed as archaic and useless. Not only do many non-human animals then become legitimate subjects of moral consideration, but objects outside the animal kingdom, such as plants and trees, also are to be included in our ethical arena.

Bernstein, Richard J. An Allegory of Modernity/Postmodernity in Working Through Derrida, Madison, Gary B (ed). Evanston, Northwestern Univ Pr, 1993.

Bernstein, Richard J. Foucault: Critique as a Philosophical Ethos in Philosophical Interventions in the Unfinished Project of Enlightenment, Honneth, Axel (& other eds). Cambridge, MIT Pr, 1992.

Bernstein, Richard J. The Lure of the Ideal in Peirce and Law, Kevelson, Roberta. New York, Lang, 1991.

Bernstein, Susan David. What's "I" Got To Do With It?. *Hypatia*, 7(2), 120-147, Spr 92.

Confessional modes of self-representation have become crucial in feminist epistemologies that broaden and contextualize the location and production of knowledge. In some versions of confessional feminism, the insertion of "I" is reflective, the product of an uncomplicated notion of experience that shuttles into academic discourse a personal truth. In contrast to reflective intrusions of the first person, reflexive confessing is primarily a questioning mode that imposes self-vigilance on the process of self positioning.

Berry, Christopher J. Adam Smith and the Virtues of Commerce. *Nomos*, 34, 69-88, 1992.

The two foci are the role Smith allots to desire in a rejection of the philosophical anthropology of classical thought and his account of the moral coherence of commercial society. This coherence relies on the primacy of justice, not on the political virtue of citizens. For Smith in the modern world of strangers we must look to the public realm for rules to govern us and to the private for virtue. Smith's argument thus exemplifies what contemporary communitarian critics of liberalism both object to and seek to overcome.

Berry, Kenneth. Abstract Art and Education. *Brit J Aes*, 32(3), 266-268, Jl 92.

This paper is primarily my response to certain issues raised by Philip Meeson in his paper, 'The Influence of Modernism on Art Education'. The purpose of my work is to increase understanding of the writings on aesthetics, and of the works in general, of major modern painters. My particular concern is that the personal or subjective element in art should be further explored, and the conclusion of my paper, I feel, is that aesthetics benefits from a broadly based approach which is both metaphysical and epistemological, and a multidisciplinary method drawing contrasts and comparisons from various extant sources of study.

Berry, Philippa. Woman and Space According to Kristeva and Irigaray in Shadow of Spirit, Berry, Philippa (ed). New York, Routledge, 1992.

This essay discusses the importance of concepts of spatiality in recent postmodern thought and shows how a feminist appropriation of such concepts has been central to the theoretical writings of Tulia Kristeva and Luce Irigaray, while the interests of Derrida and Baudrillard in "spacing" is discussed, special emphasis is placed upon Heidegger's thought as the chief source of these postmodern and feminist concerns.

Berry, Philippa (ed) and Wernick, Andrew (ed). *Shadow of Spirit*. New York, Routledge, 1992.

By illuminating the striking affinity between the most innovative aspects of postmodern thought and religious or mystical discourse, *Shadow of Spirit* challenges the long-established assumption that Western thought is committed to Nihilism. The collection explores the implications of that fascination with the "sacred" "divine" or "infinite" which characterizes the work of Derrida, Baudrillard, Lyotard, Irisarty and others.

Berry, Wanda Warren. Finally Forgiveness in Foundations of Kierkegaard's Vision of Community, Connell, George B (ed). Atlantic Highlands, Humanities Pr, 1992.

Bertelloni, Francisco. De la político "secundum naturam". *Pat Med*, 12, 3-32, 1991.

This paper deals with Albert's reception of Aristotle's *Politics*. First the author analyzes the notion of politics within the context of the division of the *philosophia moralis* in *ethica, oeconomica and politica* in the *divisiones philosophiae* between 1230 and 1250, in which dominates a *legal* conception of politics. Secondly he follows the Albert's dependency on this political conception. Thirdly, an attempt is made to demonstrate that Albert overcomes this legal conception of politics because of the lecture of Aristotle's *Politics*.

Berteloot, Stéphane. Emile et Robinson. *Rev Phil Fr*, 1, 3-10, Ja-Mr 93.

Berthold-Bond, Daniel. *Hegel's Grand Synthesis: A Study of Being, Thought, and History*. Albany, SUNY Pr, 1989.

The main purpose of this book is to investigate Hegel's attempt to demonstrate the ultimate unity of thought and being—consciousness and reality, self and world—through the vicissitudes of his epistemology, metaphysics, and philosophy of history. It is argued that Hegel's 'grand synthesis" of thought and being creates a basic tension and ambiguity that reaches its most acute formulation in his eschatological language of a final completion or fulfillment of history. It is concluded that this tension can be resolved, but only given a substantially new approach to Hegel's eschatology.

Berthold-Bond, Daniel. Intentionality and Madness in Hegel's Psychology of Action. *Int Phil Quart*, 32(4), 427-441, D 92.

The aim of this article is to show how Hegel's theory of action relies on an anatomy of "unintentional" or unconscious motives. The article looks at the way this theme comes to light in Hegel's critique of purely intentional (non-consequentialist) ethical positions, in his ontology of alienation, in his philosophy of language, and in his theory of madness (Verrücktheit). Various comparisons are made to the views of Nietzsche and Freud on the importance of the unconscious.

Berthold-Bond, Daniel. The Decentering of Reason: Hegel's Theory of Madness. *Int Stud Phil*, 25(1), 9-25, 1993.

Hegel's theory of madness (Verrücktheit), as articulated in his *Encyclopedia* "Anthropology", has been largely neglected. I give an overview of this theory, then turn to a comparison of the phenomenological structures of madness with those of the developed or "healthy" consciousness. I conclude by showing that madness, for Hegel, represents a failed or distorted form of idealism, and compare this with Hegel's own commitment to an idealist metaphysics.

Berthrong, John. Master Chu's Self-Realization: The Role of Ch'eng. *Phil East West*, 43(1), 39-64, Ja 93.

Berti, Enrico. Metafisica e dialettica nel *Commento* di Giacomo Zabarella agli *Analitici posteriori*. *G Metaf*, 14(2), 225-243, My-Ag 92.

By his commentary to *Posterior Analytics*, I 9, 76 a 16-25, and I 11, 77 a 26-35, Zabarella contributes to create image of metaphysics as an universal demonstrative science, capable to demonstrate the proper principles of particular sciences, and the correspondent image of dialectics as a form of probable argumentation, completely lacking of scientific value. This interpretation does not correspond to the results of most recent studies, which on the contrary emphasize the dialectical character of metaphysics and the value of dialectic for scientific knowledge.

Bertolet, Rod. Demonstratives and Intentions, Ten Years Later. *Commun Cog*, 26(1), 3-16, 1993.

In this paper I explore, again, the question of the role of speaker intentions in the reference of demonstratives. David Kaplan initially claimed that such intentions were irrelevant to the determination of the reference of demonstratives, and then completely reversed himself in his essay "Afterthoughts". My own more modest view is that such intentions determine speaker reference, but not semantic reference. I examine both positions in light of some recent examples due to Marga Reimer, tentatively concluding that neither Kaplan's view nor my own is refuted by these examples.

Bertolet, Rod. Hasker on Middle Knowledge. *Faith Phil*, 10(1), 3-17, Ja 93.

This paper disputes two arguments William Hasker gives against the doctrine of middle knowledge in his book *God, Time and Knowledge*. Hasker argues that middle knowledge cannot ground counterfactuals of freedom, and that the standard account of counterfactuals is inapplicable to counterfactuals of freedom. I maintain that the first argument quite inconclusive, and that the second is wrong to deny that the standard semantics for counterfactuals applies to counterfactuals of freedom. I further suggest that reliance on the standard semantics for such counterfactuals is not something that the proponents of middle knowledge need accept.

Bessie, Joseph D. On the Strength of a Causal Chain. *Pac Phil Quart*, 74(1), 11-36, Mr 93.

This paper presents an analysis and response to Salmon's criticism (1980) of I J

Good's theory of probabilistic causality. Specifically, the paper considers the question whether the strength of a causal chain can be defined in terms of the strengths of the individual links which compose it, and employs formally defined Markov chains in an effort to defend Good's positive response against Salmon's criticism. In addition, the paper aims to exhibit the utility of focusing more precisely on the mathematical details of assumptions implicit in current theories of probabilistic causality.

Best, David. *The Rationality of Feeling: Understanding the Arts in Education*. Bristol, Falmer Pr, 1992.

Best, Steven. Jameson, Totality, and the Poststructuralist Critique in Postmodernism/ Jameson/ Critique, Kellner, Douglas (ed). Washington, Maisonneuve Pr, 1989.

Betz, Joseph M. An Introduction to the Thought of Hannah Arendt. *Trans Peirce Soc*, 28(3), 379-422, Sum 92.

The basis of Arendt's political thought is shown in the labor/work/action and private/social/public distinctions. Subsequent sections, in this order, delineate her thought about the world and space; love for the world; appearing; politics and action; revolution; authority, religion, and tradition; civil disobedience, power and violence; history and ideology; totalitarianism; European Jewry in the Nazi period; and thinking and judging. The author hazards his opinion on why Arendt was both widely admired and widely criticized.

Beuchot, Mauricio. The Limits of Cultural Relativism in Cultural Relativism and Philosophy, Dascal, Marcelo (ed). Leiden, Brill, 1991.

Beukes, E P and Fourie, F C V N. Government in the Economy: Outlines of a Reformational Rethink. *Phil Reform*, 57(1), 57-77, Ja 92.

Bevir, Mark. Ernest Belfort Bax: Marxist, Idealist, and Positivist. *J Hist Ideas*, 54(1), 119-135, Ja 93.

Bax was the leading philosopher of the socialist revival in Britain during the 1880's. He saw Marxism as an economic and historical science that lacked a philosophical and ethical basis. Consequently, he tried to justify the Marxian dialectic by using a philosophy indebted to German idealism to show that the dialectic was a fact about reality itself, and he also tried to provide an ethical defence of Marxism in terms of a positivist ethic enshrining the goals of the French Revolution. Such an understanding of Bax's philosophy makes his political activities appear more rational than historians have previously thought.

Bevir, Mark. The Errors of Linguistic Contextualism. *Hist Theor*, 31(3), 276-298, 1992.

This article argues against both hard linguistic contextualists who believe that paradigms give meaning to a text and soft linguistic contextualists who believe that we can grasp authorial intentions only by locating them in a contemporaneous conventional context. Instead it is proposed that meanings come from intentions and that there can be no fixed way of recovering intentions. On these grounds the article concludes first that we can declare some understandings of texts to be unhistorical though not illegitimate, and second that good history depends solely on accurate and reasonable evidence, not on adopting a particular method.

Bevir, Mark. The Marxism of George Bernard Shaw 1883-1889. *Hist Polit Thought*, 13(2), 299-318, Sum 92.

Biographers acknowledge Shaw's debt to Marx, but intellectual historians belittle this debt. The gap can be closed by placing Shaw's Marxism in its contemporary context—Shaw shared most of the Marxist beliefs of the members of the Social Democratic Federation. A study of Shaw's Marxism shows that he was not an anarchist, that secularism played an important role in his thought, and that George's intellectual influence was not as great as is normally thought. Shaw rejected Marxism when he turned to Jevonian economics, but even then much of his Marxism remained intact and divided him from other leading Fabians.

Bewaji, J A I. Empiricism Versus Pragmatism: Truth Versus Results. *Indian Phil Quart*, 20(3), 203-242, Jl 93.

This essay examines the concept of "truth" from empiricist and pragmatist perspectives. This not without reference to other theories. The concern is to see how the ascendancy of pragmatism has affected humanity and may continue to affect humanity, the so-called objectivity in the practice of science and philosophy and the relationships between the diverse peoples of the world. An analysis of the pragmatist's preference for usefulness, rather than truth, it is argued, accounts for the deleterious consequences of pragmatism for humankind in its almost irrational substitution of usefulness for truth.

Beyer, Landon E and Liston, Daniel P. Discourse or Moral Action? A Critique of Postmodernism. *Educ Theor*, 42(4), 371-393, Fall 92.

Beyssade, M Jean-Marie. République et Régicide chez Kant. *Bull Soc Fr Phil*, 87(1), 1-44, Ja-Mr 93.

Kant denies both all counter- revolutionary appraisal and any right to revolution. In order to construe his various statements on what we too readily call 'the French revolution', we have to couple two unusual distinctions. First, a theoretical distinction between two concepts of change, *Wechsel*, i.e., substitution of one thing or state of affairs for another, and *Veränderung*, i.e., the continued identity of a substance throughout its modal transformations. Second, a practical political distinction: the representative idea, which is the principle of republicanism, versus democracy, which is necessarily despotism. (edited)

Bezuidenhout, Anne L. Demonstrative Modes of Presentation. *Commun Cog*, 26(1), 17-36, 1993.

I argue that demonstratives are associated with senses or modes of presentation, though I assume that these senses are non-descriptive in nature. That is, I grant that Kripke and others have shown the inadequacies of classical Fregean sense theories. But direct reference theories cannot deal with the problems of cognitive significance that drove Frege to posit senses. I argue that the two major strategies (which I call the Russellian and the Pragmatic) used by direct reference theorists to deal with these problems are inadequate. Thus, by elimination, only a theory which posits demonstrative senses can satisfactorily deal with these problems.

Bezzini, L. Incontro tra filosofia e teologia nella "Christliche Weltanschauung" di Romano Guardini. *Sapienza*, 45(2), 171-190, 1992.

Bhalla, R S. Possession: Common Sense and Law. *Ratio Juris*, 5(1), 79-91, Mr 92.

This article is written with a view to clarifying the following points: First, to understand the nature of possession, its origin must be kept in mind. Possession is not a legal invention, it is a pre-legal fact. Second, possession whether in law or in common sense is a *de facto* control. There is no difference between possession in law and possession in fact. Third, different types of rules and policies of law to deal with possession, do not change the contents of possession. They merely represent the situations is which possession is found under different circumstances.

Bhat, P R. Intention in Wittgenstein. *Indian Phil Quart*, 20(3), 279-308, Jl 93.

Bhattacharyya, Sibajiban. Comments on "The Development of Advaita Vedanta as a School of Philosophy". *J Indian Counc Phil Res*, 9(2), 175-178, Ja-Ap 92.

The purpose of this paper is to examine Professor Karl Potter's theory of development of Advaita Vedanta as a system of Indian philosophy. The origin of this system is obscure, traceable to early upanisads if not to the Vedas. In the second stage of development there are arguments against different philosophical systems. But the first stage of discovery may reappear after the second and even the third stage, as in the case of Navya-Navya. It is not clear what the practical concerns of a system are. There are stated concerns and unstated concerns with which the systems actually deal.

Bhattacharyya, Sibajiban. Some Philosophical Problems Concerning Culture and Rationality. *J Indian Counc Phil Res*, 9(2), 5-24, Ja-Ap 92.

The purpose of this paper is to examine different concepts of culture and rationality and show their inter-relations. Culture has been conceived in two ways. In the comprehensive way, culture is all-inclusive behaviour pattern of a people. In a narrower way, it is the excellence in different spheres, specially the moral and valuational. Rationality is either absolute and universal or relative to cultures. In either sense rationality is an ingredient of culture, but cannot be the whole of it. Even in the so-called science-culture, which is apparently universal, there is cultural relativity of rationality.

Bhave, S V. The Liar Paradox and Many-Valued Logic. *Phil Quart*, 42(169), 465-479, O 92.

Biard, Joël. Présence et représentation chez Pierre d'Ailly: Quelques problèmes de théorie de la connaissance au xive siècle. *Dialogue (Canada)*, 31(3), 459-474, Sum 92.

Bickford, Susan. Why We Listen to Lunatics: Antifoundational Theories and Feminist Politics. *Hypatia*, 8(2), 104-123, Spr 93.

In this essay, I argue that Richard Rorty's version of pragmatism focuses too much on community, and gives insufficient attention to the workings of power and the necessary relation between theory and practice. I then turn briefly to the work of Michel Foucault for a better understanding of power relations. Finally, I argue for the value of learning from a group of writers who connect theory and practice in a way that attends to both community and power relations.

Bickhard, Mark H and Campbell, Robert L. Clearing the Ground: Foundational Questions Once Again. *J Prag*, 17(5-6), 557-602, Je 92.

We undertake a reply to 16 commentaries on our target article "Some foundational questions concerning language studies." We rebut objections to our critique of encoding-based conceptions of representation and defend our alternative, which is based on interactive differentiation and implicit definition. We show that the consequences of interactivism for language studies are far-reaching: semantics cannot be distinguished from pragmatics in the customary way, syntax cannot be autonomous, and language comprehension and understanding cannot be the processing of derivative encodings. We discuss similarities and differences between Prague School functionalism and our conception of language as a system of operators that transform situation conventions. We respond to positivist critiques of our enterprise, on the one hand, and objections based on Continental philosophy, on the other; we deal with the careless thinking in the linguistic community that gives rise to misapprehensions such as the view that our program is based on behaviorism. (edited)

Bickhard, Mark H and Campbell, Robert L. Some Foundational Questions Concerning Language Studies: With a Focus on Categorial Grammars and Model-Theoretic Possible Worlds Semantics. *J Prag*, 17(5-6), 401-433, Je 92.

Bickle, John. Mental Anomaly and the New Mind-Brain Reductionism. *Phil Sci*, 59(2), 217-230, Je 92.

Davidson's principle of the anomalousness of the mental was instrumental in discrediting once-popular versions of mind-brain reductionism. In this essay I argue that a novel account of intertheoretic reduction, which does not require the sort of cross-theoretic bridge laws that Davidson's principle rules out, allows a version of mind-brain reductionism which is immune from Davidson's challenge. In the final section, I address a second worry about reductionism, also based on Davidson's principle, that survives this response. I argue that new reductionists should revise some significant details of the program, particularly the conception of theories, to circumvent this more pontent Davidson-inspired worry.

Bickle, John. Multiple Realizability and Psychophysical Reduction. *Behavior Phil*, 20(1), 47-58, Spr-Sum 92.

The argument from multiple realizability is that, because quite diverse physical systems are capable of giving rise to identical psychological phenomena, mental states cannot be reduced to physical states. This influential regiment depends upon a theory of reduction that has been defunct in the philosophy of science for at least fifteen years. Better theories are now available.

Bickle, John. Revisionary Physicalism. *Biol Phil*, 7(4), 411-430, O 92.

The focus of much recent debate between realists and eliminativists about the propositional attitudes obscures the fact that a spectrum of positions lies between these celebrated extremes. Appealing to an influential theoretical development in cognitive neurobiology, I argue that there is reason to expect such an "intermediate" outcome. The ontology that emerges is a *revisionary* physicalism. The argument draws lessons about revisionistic reductions from an important historical example, the reduction of equilibrium thermodynamics to statistical mechanics, and applies them to the relationship developing between propositional attitude psychology and this potential neuroscientific successor. It predicts enough conceptual change to rule out a straightforward realism about the attitudes; but at the same time it also resists the eliminativist's comparison of the fate awaiting the propositional attitudes to that befalling caloric fluid, phlogiston, and the like.

Biemel, W. Heidegger in Dialogue with Hegel (Thanksgiving of W Biemel) (in Czechoslovakian). *Filozof Cas*, 40(4), 649-660, 1992.

Biemel, Walter. Elucidations of Heidegger's Lecture 'The Origin of Art and the Destination of Thinking' in Reading Heidegger: Commemorations, Sallis, John (ed). Bloomington, Indiana Univ Pr, 1992.

Bienenstock, Myriam. Mythe et révélation dans l'*Étoile de la Rédemption*: Contemporanéité de Franz Rosenzweig. *Arch Phil*, 55(1), 17-34, Ja-Mr 92.

Franz Rosenzweig (1887-1929) was not only an outstanding Hegelscholar-his thesis on Hegel and the state is still highly respected-he also developed a philosophy of revelation in which the experience of dialogue and, more generally, communication by means of language play a fundamental role. The present article studies the philosophical (especially Schellingian) sources as well as the historical and political context of Rosenzweig's philosophy of revelation and thereby shows him to be our contemporary.

Bienenstock, Myriam. Rosenzweig's Hegel. *Owl Minerva*, 23(2), 177-182, Spr 92.

This paper shows that Franz Rosenzweig's *Hegel und der Staat*, whose impact upon the scholarship of Hegel's philosophy was considerable, embodies an understanding of political and historical life which significantly departs from Hegel's own conception. It also shows that some of the ideas Rosenzweig ascribes to Hegel in this book recur in his later masterpiece of Jewish philosophy, *The Star of Redemption*. This recurrence sheds light upon Rosenzweig's later attitude toward history and politics, but also upon the very way in which he turned to religion.

Bieri, Peter. Trying Out Epiphenomenalism. *Erkenntnis*, 36(3), 283-309, M 92.

Different lines of argument for epiphenomenalism are laid out. The proposals in the literature to ensure mental causation are analyzed and shown to be insufficient. It is explored how mentalistic explanations of behavior might be understood if epiphenomenalism were true.

Biesecker, Barbara. Coming to Terms with Recent Attempts to Write Women into the History of Rhetoric. *Phil Rhet*, 25(2), 140-161, 1992.

Biesecker, Barbara. Michel Foucault and the Question of Rhetoric. *Phil Rhet*, 25(4), 351-364, 1992.

Biesecker, Barbara. Negotiating with Our Tradition: Reflecting Again (Without Apologies) on the Feminization of Rhetoric. *Phil Rhet*, 26(3), 236-241, 1993.

Bigelow, John. Sets Are Haecceities in Ontology, Causality and Mind: Essays in Honour of D M Armstrong, Bacon, John (ed). New York, Cambridge Univ Pr, 1993.

Bigelow, John and Ellis, Brian and Lierse, Caroline. The World as One of a Kind: Natural Necessity and Laws of Nature. *Brit J Phil Sci*, 43(3), 371-388, S 92.

This paper elaborates and defends the view that the world is an instance of a natural kind. It argues that all laws of nature, including the most general ones, are dependent on the essential natures of natural kinds. The causal and statistical laws of nature are said to depend on the essences of the natural kinds of things which exist in the world. The most fundamental laws of nature are argued to depend on the kind of world in which we live. This theory of scientific laws derives from the basic idea that things must behave as they do because of what they are made of, how they are made, and what their circumstances are. (edited)

Bigelow, John and Pargetter, Robert. Acquaintance with Qualia. *Theoria*, 61(3), 129-147, 1990.

Bigger, Charles B. L'herméneutique d'Austin Farrer: un modèle participatoire. *Arch Phil*, 55(1), 49-76, Ja-Mr 92.

During his long and productive career Austin Farrer moved from a voluntaristic and neo-scholastic defence of rational theology to a <post-modern> dialogical model of faith to which God discloses Himself in hermeneutic of images. With Gadamer's help he constructs from this a non-structuralist narrative theology in which we are underway together through a dialectic of these images. The way is cleared by the Good, not by Heidegger's ontological difference. My understanding of this dialectic owes a considerable debt to Emmanuel Lévinas.

Biggs, Michael A R. Continuity and Discontinuity in Visual Experience. *Critica*, 24(70), 3-15, Ap 92.

The article discusses the diverse role of diagrams in Wittgenstein's writings in contrast to an underlying continuity of descriptions based on visual experience. Their use in the Tractatus is compared with their use in the Investigations. These uses are discontinuous inasmuch as the former functions by visual analogy, having a projection relationship to the text, whilst the latter mainly functions metaphorically, for example in 'seeing as'. The underlying continuity is demonstrated by the family resemblance of the concepts 'showing', 'ostension', and 'seeing-as' throughout Wittgenstein's accounts of understanding. This continuity thesis is finally described as a depth-grammar.

Bigwood, Carol. Seeing Blake's Illuminated Texts. *J Aes Art Crit*, 49(4), 307-315, Fall 91.

With the help of Merleau-Ponty and Heidegger, I phenomenologically investigate the experience of reading William Blake's illuminated texts, focusing on the interrelationship of cognition and perception. I show how Blake's texts frustrate the usual cognitive reading and encourage a fuller perceptual experience. His books, thereby, alert us to the restrictive character of our usual reading and thinking, and intimate a move flexible reading that is at once more insightful and more open to the prelinguistic movements of perception.

AUTHOR INDEX WITH ABSTRACTS 415 Black, Deborah

Bilimoria, Purushottama. Is "Adhikāra" Good Enough for 'Rights'?. *Asian Phil*, 3(1), 3-13, Mr 93.

The paper considers the question of whether 'rights' as we have it in modern Western thinking has an equivalence within the Indian framework of *Dharma*. Under Part I we look at *purusarthas* to see if the desired human goals imply rights by examining the tension between aspired 'values' and the 'ought' of duty. Next, a potential cognate in the term *'adhikara'* is investigated via the derivation of a refined signification of 'entitlements', especially in the exegetical hermeneutics of the Mimamsa. Finally, *adhikara's* re-emergence in the *Bhagavadgita* is considered. We suggest that while the boundary is significantly extended, the *Gita* too appears to be circumspect in opening up the discourse in the more abstract and absolute sense which the terms 'rights' nowadays enjoys.

Bilimoria, Purushottama. The Jaina Ethic of Voluntary Death. *Bioethics*, 6(4), 331-355, O 92.

Bilimoria, Purusottama. Evidence in Testimony and Tradition. *J Indian Counc Phil Res*, 9(1), 73-84, S-D 91.

Testimony is a much neglected area in modern theories of knowledge. There are however a few philosophers keenly working on re-examining the epistemological basis of testimony (e.g., Coady). The paper presents another response, drawn from classical Indian theories, but moderated to take into account recent critical formulations suggested by Leslie Stevenson. Two additional conditions of yogayata (linguistic competency) and samarthya (pragmatic viability) are incorporated to strengthen the 'evidential' base of testimony. It is argued that 'tradition' is one of the key sources of such claims and can thus be a valid form of testimony.

Billault, Alain. The Rhetoric of a "Divine Man": Apollonius of Tyana as Critic of Oratory and as Orator According to Philostratus. *Phil Rhet*, 26(3), 227-235, 1993.

In his biography by Philostratus, Apollonius of Tyana champions philosophy and derogates rhetoric. He criticizes orators for showing no regard to truth and making an irresponsible use of speech. He also displays a rhetoric of authority. He speaks as a man who knows the truth thanks to his close relationship with the gods and whose mission is to reveal it to ordinary men who take no part in its discovery. In this basically unequal relationship with his audience, he exemplifies the type of the Divine Man. Thus we may read Philostratus's narrative as spiritual and philosophical record.

Birdwhistell, Anne D. Cultural Patterns and the Way of Mother and Son: An Early Qing Case. *Phil East West*, 42(3), 503-516, Jl 92.

This article addresses the question of cultural patterns of thought and behavior and their underlying theoretical assumptions. A specific case is examined, the Chinese relation called the "way of mother and son." Not one of the five cardinal relations, which gain a privileged position form their importance to the political structure, the way of mother and son was found to have relevance in other (non-political) frames of reference. This relation was especially supported by three theoretical patterns, those called beginning and completing, teaching and transforming, and the standard and the adaptive, all of which have applications in a variety of spaciotemporal contexts.

Birkett, Kirsten and Oldroyd, David. Robert Hooke, Physico-Mythology, Knowledge of the World of the Ancients and Knowledge ... in The Uses of Antiquity, Gaukroger, Stephen (ed). Dordrecht, Kluwer, 1991.

Robert Hooke (1635-1702) developed a theory of the Earth which explained geological changes by supposed changes in the polar axis. He tried, unsuccessfully, to find astronomical evidence for this theory, and so turned to ancient myths for evidence. Analyzing Hooke's investigations, it is shown that he sought to interpret ancient myths as indicators of actual historical events, and as "testimony" for his catastrophist geological theory. By analogy with the term physico-theology, the term "physico-mythology" is coined for this kind of exegesis. Synoptic analyses of Hooke's interpretations of Pling, Strabo, Seneca, Virgil, Ovid, Plato, Hanno, and scripture are provided. An appendix analyzes the contents of Hooke's personal library.

Birmingham, Peg. Building from Ruins: The Wandering Space of the Feminine. *Res Phenomenol*, 22, 73-79, 1992.

Birmingham, Peg. Ever Respectfully Mine in Ethics and Danger, Dallery, Arleen B (ed). Albany, SUNY Pr, 1992.

Birnbacher, Dieter. New Foundations for Environmental Ethics. *Dialec Hum*, 17(1), 88-101, 1990.

The contribution presents an overview of the field of ecological ethics stressing the diversity of philosophical viewpoints underlying, for the most part, a converging set of practical principles and concrete proposals. A priority thesis is argued for according to which "want- regarding" principles should be given precedence over "ideal- regarding" ones, favouring anthropocentric and pathocentric arguments in the field of conservation and preservation.

Birnbacher, Dieter. Rechte des Menschen oder Rechte der Natur? Die Stellung der Freiheit in der ökologischen Ethik. *Stud Phil (Switzerland)*, 49, 61-80, 1990.

The contribution discusses the many-faceted role of the idea of human freedom in environmental ethics. Starting from the consideration that extensions of ethical concern into new areas usually imply additional restrictions of human freedom by increased moral pressure and support for extended state regulation the consequences for freedom of the competing approaches to environmental ethics are subjected to critical examination. "Biocentric" approaches such as that of Paul W Taylor's are criticised for their moral rigorism and their neglect of the high value of individual choice of life-style.

Biro, John. Consciousness and Objectivity in Consciousness: Psychological and Philosophical Essays, Davies, Martin (ed). Cambridge, Blackwell, 1993.

The goal of this paper is to gain some clarity concerning the notion of objectivity involved in the arguments of those (Nagel, Jackson, et al.) who claim that scientific theories are, because of their objectivity, incapable of capturing the "essentially subjective" facts of experience. After some discussion of different senses of 'objective', it is argued that none of them is such that it can sustain the claim in question. It is further suggested that inferring, as the arguments being discussed do, (likely) qualitative differences in experience from physiological differences (such as bats' sonar equipment) embodies the very reductionism whose rejection is their aim.

Birsch, Douglas. Using the Fact/Value Problem to Teach Ethical Theory. *Teach Phil*, 15(3), 217-230, S 92.

The teaching strategy discussed in this essay centers around the fact/value problem, and uses it to make ethical theories more interesting, easier to understand, and to deal with the problem of "student relativism." The method builds on the common student belief that ethics is a matter of opinion. It helps the students transform their idea into something more philosophically interesting, shows them important problems with it, and presents ethical theories as alternatives to their view.

Birsch, Douglas and Fielder, John H. *The DC-10 Case: A Study in Applied Ethics, Technology, and Society*. Albany, SUNY Pr, 1992.

Birtek, Faruk and Toprak, Binnaz. The Conflictual Agendas of Neo-Liberal Reconstruction and the Rise of Islamic Politics in Turkey. *Praxis Int*, 13(2), 192-210, Jl 93.

Bishop, Anne H and Scudder Jr, John R. Recovering the Moral Sense of Health Care from Academic Reification in Analecta Husserliana, XXXI, Tymieniecka, Anna-Teresa (ed). Dordrecht, Kluwer, 1990.

Bishop, John. Compatibilism and the Free Will Defence. *Austl J Phil*, 71(2), 104-120, Je 93.

This paper 1) argues that libertarians are virtually as badly off as compatibilists in the face of the objection to the Free Will Defence that omnipotent God could have ensured that all free beings always but freely did right, and 2) explores the prospects for an "upgraded" Free Will Defense which takes freedom merely as a necessary condition for a further higher good which logically could not be achieved if God employed any of the available strategies—under both compatibilist and libertarian assumptions—for creating morally free beings without the risk of moral evil.

Bishop, John. Evil and the Concept of God. *Phil Papers*, 22(1), 1-15, Ap 93.

This paper argues that, though the Argument from Evil does indeed show that it is unreasonable to believe that there exists an omnipotent, morally perfect, creator *ex nihilo*, theists may have available a more satisfactory alternative to this "omniGod theory". An attempt is made to reflect on the "Concrete Case" version of the Argument from Evil in order to develop an approach to an alternative, but arguably still theistic, concept of God. The paper incorporates a taxonomy and assessment of the most central theodicies.

Bishop, Michael A. The Nature and Evolution of Human Language: Commentary. *Between Species*, 8(2), 95-97, Spr 92.

Bishop, Michael A. Theory-Ladenness of Perception Arguments. *Proc Phil Sci Ass*, 1, 287-299, 1992.

My first aim is to adduce a framework for understanding theory-ladenness of perception arguments. My second aim is to begin to assess an important cluster of theory-ladenness arguments—those that begin with some psychological phenomenon and conclude that scientific controversies are resolved without appeal to theory-neutral observations. Three of the arguments (from expectation effects, ambiguous figures, and inverting lenses) turn out to be either irrelevant to or subversive of theory-ladenness. And even if we grant the premises of the fourth argument (from the penetrability of the visual system), it supports at best a mild version of theory-ladenness.

Bitsakis, Eftichios. Locality: A New Enigma for Physics in Greek Studies in the Philosophy and History of Science, Nicolacopoulos, Pantelis (ed). Dordrecht, Kluwer, 1990.

Bitting, Paul F and Southworth, Cheryl. Reverence and the Passions of Inquiry. *Thinking*, 10(2), 13-18, 1992.

Bitzer, Lloyd F. Whately's Distinction Between Inferring and Proving. *Phil Rhet*, 25(4), 311-340, 1992.

Bix, Brian. A D Woozley and the Concept of Right Answers in Law. *Ratio Juris*, 5(1), 58-66, Mr 92.

In the debates about legal determinacy, an important but often neglected issue is what is meant in the legal context by saying that a question has a right answer. By way of a critique of A.D. Woozley's discussion of "right answers," I try to show how this issue is connected with issues of legal truth, legal mistake, and precedent.

Biziou, Michaël. Le système chez Hume: une éecriture stratégique et théâtrale. *Rev Phil Fr*, 2, 173-199, Ap-Je 92.

Bjarup, Jes. Positive Law Versus Natural Law—A Comment in Response to Percy Black—Natural Law and Positive Law: Forever Irresolvable?. *Vera Lex*, 11(2), 22-24, 1991.

There is an ever-going controversy between natural law theorists and positive law theorists. It seems to me that the dividing line is rather between moral cognitivism and moral non-cognitivism. Natural lawyers usually adopt moral cognitivism. The same holds for some legal positivists. By contrast, some positivists adhere to a non-cognitivist view leading to moral scepticism. This is an important issue where there is room for controversy. Professor Black's plea is for a psychological inquiry to solve the issue. My thesis is that this issue can only be dealt with by a philosophical inquiry into the stated reasons, held by the parties to justify their positions.

Black, Deborah. Aristotle's *Peri hermeneias* in Medieval Latin and Arabic Philosophy: Logic and the Linguistic Arts. *Can J Phil*, Supp(17), 25-83, 1991.

This paper compares the views of a number of Arabic and thirteenth-century Latin commentators on Aristotle's *Peri Hermeneias* on the status of logic as a linguistic art and its relation to grammar. The discussion considers the commentators' general positions on the logician's treatment of linguistic topics, and their attempts to reconcile the dual claim of logic to be both a linguistic and a rational art. These general principles are then traced through the treatment of a number of particular themes in the *Peri Hermeneias's* linguistic sections: The definition of the noun, the cases of the noun, and the indefinite or infinite noun (i.e., of the form non-X). The article concludes that, although there are basic differences between the Latin and Arabic traditions stemming from the presence in the Latin world of a philosophical theory of grammar, authors in both traditions are adamant that a balance must be maintained between the linguistic and rational characterizations of logic.

Black, Deborah. Consciousness and Self-Knowledge in Aquinas's Critique of Averroe's Psychology. *J Hist Phil*, 31(3), 349-385, Jl 93.

Black, Robert. Philosophical Scepticism about Moral Obligation—II. *Aris Soc*, Supp(67), 195-212, 1993.

How much of our ordinary moral thought can we make sense of using a model of practical reason in which value is seen as subjective? There are already problems with showing strength of will not to be irrational. If social obligations are conceived of instrumentally as in a tradition running from Hobbes through Hume to Mackie, and if we employ our strength of will to sacrifice our individual projects in favor of them, the problems become insuperable.

Black, Virginia (ed). Natural Law and Positive Law: Forever Irresolvable? Discussion. *Vera Lex*, 11(2), 30-35, 1991.

Blackburn, Patrick. Nominal Tense Logic. *Notre Dame J Form Log*, 34(1), 56-83, Wint 93.

This paper considers the logical consequences of making Priorean tense logic referential by sorting its atomic symbols. A second sort of atomic symbol, the *nominal*, is introduced and these are constrained to be true at exactly one point in any model. The resulting gain in expressive power is examined, and a number of logics are axiomatized and shown to be decidable. The relevance of the extension to the semantics of natural language is briefly noted.

Blackburn, Simon W. *Essays in Quasi-Realism*. New York, Oxford Univ Pr, 1993.

This book collects together the main papers I have written on the theme of realism and its competitors. It includes addenda discussing reactions and exploring further avenues, and a scene-setting introduction.

Blackburn, Simon W. Gibbard on Normative Logic. *Phil Phenomenol Res*, 52(4), 947-952, D 92.

The point of this paper is to compare and evaluate the different approaches to normative logic revealed in the work of Allan Gibbard, and in my own apparently different approach to the issue. I argue that although in Chapter 5 of his *Wise Choices, Apt Feelings* Gibbard may seem to make use of illegitimate resources, bringing in extra materials (some of which are in other chapters) keeps the theory afloat, and brings the two theories substantially into line.

Blackburn, Simon W. Morality and Thick Concepts—II, Through Thick and Thin. *Aris Soc*, Supp(66), 1992.

Thick concepts have both a descriptive and an evaluative element. But do standard examples, such as the names of the virtues, qualify? I argue that the semantic story is much more complex, and urge the importance of other features, such as intonation, as vehicles of attitude.

Blacker, David. Allowing Educational Technologies to Reveal: A Deweyan Perspective. *Educ Theor*, 43(2), 181-194, Spr 93.

Blacker, David. Civic Virtue, Markets and Schooling: Lessons from Hegel's Education State. *Proc Phil Educ*, 48, 105-113, 1992.

Blacker, David. What are Intellectuals For: A Foucaultian Model of Intellectual Responsibility. *Phil Stud Educ*, 1, 131-144, 1991.

Blair, George A. Aristotle on 'ΕΝΤΕΛΕΧΕΙΑ: A Reply to Daniel Graham. *Amer J Philo*, 114(1), 91-97, Spr 93.

Daniel Graham, in "The Etymology of *Entelecheia*," proposes that Aristotle's term means "perfection" or "being at an end," though he says that Aristotle himself (who coined it) thinks that it means "having one's end inside (oneself)." However, 1) it would be psychologically impossible for someone who coined a word to mistake its components, 2) Aristotle already used many other words meaning "perfection," and had no need to coin a new one, and 3) Graham's meaning reduces several texts to incoherence, while "having the end inside" all contexts nicely. Hence *entelecheia* means "possessing one's end within" and not "being *at* one's end."

Blair, John Anthony and Pinto, Robert C. *Reasoning: A Practical Guide*. Englewood Cliffs, Prentice Hall, 1993.

Blake, Nigel. A Position in Society, an Intimate Constraint. *J Phil Educ*, 26(2), 271-276, 1992.

Blake, Nigel. Modernity and the Problem of Cultural Pluralism. *J Phil Educ*, 26(1), 39-50, 1992.

A curriculum that reflects a pluralist, multi-cultural society in a characteristically 'Western' way may seem to militate against traditionalist sub-cultures, but this outcome is less 'Western' than 'modern', in Habermas's sense. 'Modernisation', involving the institutionalisation of rationality and the decentering of consciousness, and thus acceptance of the 'Western' solution, is possible within any culture, regardless of its content. In a Western society all are economically compelled to a partial 'modernisation', and in Habermas's view all cultures in modern societies suffer erosion by the extension and intrusion of economic and administrative sub-systems. Cultural modernisation affords the strongest available resistance to this erosion. Thus, a supposedly 'Western' curriculum approach would strengthen sub-cultures, notwithstanding the demise of traditionalism.

Blakeley, Donald N. Unity, Theism, and Self in Plotinus. *Phil Theol*, 7(1), 53-80, Autumn 92.

This paper examines the theistic interpretation of Plotinus's conception of unity as presented in the work of John Rist. Three types of unity are identified: unity-with-difference unity-with -out-difference, and unity-and -difference. I argue that the theistic interpretation encounters significant difficulties and cannot respond to the distinction that Plotinus himself observes in his analysis of unity.

Blamey, Kathleen (trans) and Ricoeur, Paul. *Oneself as Another—Paul Ricoeur*. Chicago, Univ of Chicago Pr, 1992.

Blanchard, Marc E. Aesthetic and Illusion of Daily Life in Aesthetic Illusion, Burwick, Frederick (ed). Hawthorne, de Gruyter, 1990.

Blanchard Jr, Kenneth C. Ethnicity and the Problem of Equality. *Interpretation*, 20(3), 309-324, Spr 93.

Blanchette, Oliva. *The Perfection of the Universe According to Aquinas: A Teleological Cosmology*. University Park, Penn St Univ Pr, 1992.

This is a philosophical exposition of Aquinas's conception of the universe as the totality of all things, which is closely connected with the idea of perfection. This idea calls not only for a certain completion in the basic make-up of the universe but also for a certain diversity along with a certain interaction among beings, through which the final perfection of the universe is constituted with human being as the pivotal being. The actual interaction is understood in terms of a threefold order: the order of physical arrangement, the order of generation and time, and the order of reason and intelligence.

Blanchot, Maurice and Nelson, Lycette (trans). *The Step Not Beyond*. Albany, SUNY Pr, 1992.

This translation of Maurice Blanchot's work is of major importance to late 20th-century literature and philosophy studies. Using the fragmentary form, Blanchot challenges the boundaries between the literary and the philosophical. With the obsessive rigor that has always marked his writing, Blanchot returns to the themes that have haunted his work since the beginning: writing, death, transgression, the neuter. But here his discussion turns around the figures of Hegel and Nietzsche rather than Mallarmé and Kafka. (staff)

Blandino, Giovanni. Le relation mente-corpore in le filosofia e in le scientia contemporanee. *Aquinas*, 35(1), 141-155, Ja-Ap 92.

This article is written in Interlingua. There is the exposition of the two principal trends of thought in Christian Philosophy about the relation between body and soul. The A supports the conception (of Augustinian and Cartesian line) that the soul is the Self. *I am the soul*. I have a body which continuously changes, nevertheless I remain constant, the same. Many other argumentations taken from modern science are expounded.

Blandino, Giovanni. Precisationes varie sur questiones de filosofia. *Aquinas*, 35(2), 317-340, My-Ag 92.

Blasius, Mark (ed). About the Beginning of the Hermeneutics of the Self: Two Lectures at Dartmouth—Michel Foucault. *Polit Theory*, 21(2), 198-227, My 93.

Blasius, Mark. An Ethos of Lesbian and Gay Existence. *Polit Theory*, 20(4), 642-671, N 92.

Blattner, William D. Existential Temporality in *Being and Time* in Heidegger: A Critical Reader, Dreyfus, Hubert L (ed). Cambridge, Blackwell, 1992.

In this essay I argue that the originary or existential temporality of *Being and Time* is neither authentic nor inauthentic, and that it is a nonsequential manifold of future, present, and past. To say that it is nonsequential means, e.g., that the originary future is not later than the originary present or past. Still, there is a sequential manifold of the pragmatically significant future, present, and past (circumspective or pragmatic temporality), which depends upon originary temporality. This dependence of pragmatic upon existential temporality illuminates an important way in which Heidegger was not a pragmatist.

Blatz, Charles V. Ethics, Ecology and Development: Styles of Ethics and Styles of Agriculture. *J Agr Environ Ethics*, 5(1), 59-85, 1992.

Blatz, Charlie V. The Very Idea of Sustainability. *Agr Human Values*, 9(4), 12-28, Fall 92.

Discussions of the desirability and ethical justifiability of sustainable agriculture are frequently impeded, if not derailed by the variety of meanings attached to the term "sustainable." This paper suggests a taxonomy of different notions of sustainability distinguishing between agricultural product and process sustainability, in both static and dynamic forms, pursued by reductive (extractive), compensatory, regenerative, and induced homeostatis strategies. The discussion then goes on to argue that ethics demand sustainable agriculture. Finally, the paper tries to identify just which types of sustainable agriculture will meet the ethical demands. I conclude with reasons for living sustainably in the present, as opposed to trying to orient agriculture by reference to the rights of future generations.

Blau, U. Nāgārjuna und die Mengenlehre. *Dialectica*, 46(3-4), 297-311, 1992.

If there is truth, there is formal truth and finally truth in the set universe... Confiding in formal truth and reflecting this confidence we are led beyond all set and class theories to the Absolute Indefinite and formal inexpressibility of the *whole* concept of formal truth—a logical path to Mahāyāna Buddhism.

Blegvad, Mogens. "Value" in Turn-of-the-Century Philosophy and Sociology. *Dan Yrbk Phil*, 26, 51-96, 1991.

That "value" became a prominent term in philosophy and sociology around 1900 is due to many factors. One is the shift in economic value theory connected with the marginalist revolution in the 1870s. Close ties existed between the marginalist Austrian school of Carl Menger and his pupils, and philosophers like Brentano, Meinong and von Ehrenfels who tried to develop a general theory of value. Another factor is the revival of Kantianism. The Baden school of Neo-Kantianism (Windelband, Rickert) also put "value" in the centre, and it had profound influence on Max Weber. By analysis of the theories of the scholars mentioned, as well as those of Simmel and Pareto, the ambiguities of the term value is demonstrated, and doubt is cast on the legitimacy of treating economic, aesthetic, ethical, etc. values as species of a general concept of value.

Blinn, Sharon Bracci and Garrett, Mary. Aristotelian *Topoi* as a Cross-Cultural Analytical Tool. *Phil Rhet*, 26(2), 93-112, 1993.

Bliss, Christopher. Life-Style and the Standard of Living in The Quality of Life, Nussbaum, Martha C (ed). New York, Oxford Univ Pr, 1993.

Blizard, Wayne D. EEEE: Set Theory and Wholeness. *Log Anal*, 32, 215-239, S-D 89.

The acronym EEEE abbreviates "everything enfolds everything else" where the word 'enfolds' means 'contains within itself'. A theory in which some interpretation of the EEEE principle holds, is said to possess (the property of) *wholeness*; that is, each part contains, within itself, the whole (more precisely, the near-whole: every other part). We first discuss classical set theory and wholeness. We then interpret EEEE set theoretically and investigate whole set theory. A method is described by which classical set theory can be made to manifest a degree of wholeness, and further lines of investigation are suggested. A brief discussion of various examples of the EEEE principle is given in the Appendix.

Block, Ned. Holism, Hyper-analyticity and Hyper-compositionality. *Mind Lang*, 8(1), 1-26, Spr 93.

Holism says that the meaning of every word depends on every other word. If language is compositional, the meaning of a sentence is a function of the meanings of its words and their arrangement. But if a language is both holistic and compositional — as, arguably, ours is — it seems that the meaning of only one of the words is sufficient to determine the meaning of the entire sentence. The language is hyper-compositional. The paper discusses these ideas in the context of Fodor's and LePore's criticism of my views.

Blocker, Gene H and Bender, John. *Contemporary Philosophy of Art*. Englewood Cliffs, Prentice Hall, 1993.

An anthology of outstanding analytic aesthetics, mostly from the last twenty years, along with extended treatment of the "Post-Modern" challenge to that tradition. Ten topical chapters, with critical introductions. Upper undergraduated and graduate use.

Blosser, Philip. A Problem in Kant's Theory of Moral Feeling. *Lyceum*, 3(2), 27-39, Fall 91.

I argue that a fundamental incongruity exists between Kant's rich phenomenology of moral feeling and his metaphysic of noumenal purism. Textual support exists both for the view that the moral feeling of respect for the law is 1) an affective response objectively determined *by the will* (as a "legislative" faculty), and for the view that it is 2) a practical incentive serving as a subjective determining ground *of the will* (as an "executive" faculty). But is moral feeling phenomenal or noumenal? Is it pure or is it part of our pathological system? Within the dualist strictures of the Kantian metaphysic, it cannot be both.

Blount, Jackie. Response to Competency, Mastery and the Destruction of Meaning. *Proc S Atlantic Phil Educ Soc*, 36, 95-97, 1991.

Bluhm, William T. Toward 1992: Utilitarianism as the Ideology of Europe. *Hist Euro Ideas*, 16(4-6), 487-494, Ja 93.

Benthamite conceptions of interest aggregation, 1), through the market and 2), through the artificial identification of interests, underlie the functionalist practices of the European Community. The natural identity of interests that the market presupposes is expressed in the single European market, while the idea of artificially identifying interests is embodied in the harmonization efforts of the European Commission (Bentham's "legislator"), and in those of the European Parliament (Benthamite democracy). Problematic for the successful culmination of European unification is the absence of a Benthamite boundary concept to define the system territorially, as well as lack of a principle of legitimacy in utilitarian culture.

Blunt, Paul K. A Defense of Folk Psychology. *Int Phil Quart*, 32(4), 487-498, D 92.

Blustein, Jeffrey. Doing What the Patient Orders: Maintaining Integrity in the Doctor-Patient Relationship. *Bioethics*, 7(4), 289-314, Jl 93.

Critical to a proper appreciation of the significance of the conflict between patient self-determination and physician values is the distinction between medical paternalism and physician integrity. This paper begins by clarifying the nature and import of appeals to conscience. Next, it considers whether compromise with the conflicting values of patients or surrogates is possible without loss of physician integrity. Finally, the common practice of patient referral when conscience does not permit treatment oneself is subjected to critical examination.

Blustein, Jeffrey. The Family in Medical Decisionmaking. *Hastings Center Rep*, 23(3), 6-13, My-Je 93.

This paper focuses on medical decision-making for competent patients and on the question of whether the authority to make treatment decisions should be extended to include the patient's family. Arguments from fairness and communitarian concerns are considered and are shown not to justify such a curtailment of patient autonomy. The paper concludes with remarks on the importance of family involvement in the process of decision-making.

Boardman, William S. The Relativity of Perceptual Knowledge. *Synthese*, 94(2), 145-169, F 93.

I begin by arguing for Austin's claim that perceptual knowledge must not be understood as an inference based upon sensory data. Dretske's non-inferential account of perceptual knowledge can therefore escape skeptical attack, but only if his distinction between a merely logical possibility and any "relevant" possibility that one be mistaken is justified. I argue that this distinction cannot be defended. Finally, following a controversial claim of Austin's, I sketch and defend a more radical account, that a claim of knowledge of any particular matter is relative to a context in which questions about the matter have been raised.

Boatright, John R. *Ethics and the Conduct of Business*. Englewood Cliffs, Prentice Hall, 1993.

This comprehensive textbook for a college-level or MBA course in business ethics uses ethical theory to provide a foundation for discussion of a wide range of problems in business. It adopts an integrated approach that considers the economic and legal points of view and includes relevant economic literature and the reasoning behind business law. Beginning with coverage of utilitarianism, Kantian ethics, and theories of rights and justice, the book also covers such topics as whistle-blowing, conflict of interest, privacy, discrimination, advertising, marketing, unjust dismissal, occupational health and safety, corporate social responsibility, and international business.

Bochenski, Joseph M. Faith and Science in Advances in Scientific Philosophy, Schurz, Gerhard (ed). Amsterdam, Rodopi, 1991.

Bock, Gisela. Equality and Difference in National Socialist Racism in Beyond Equality and Difference, Bock, Gisela (ed). New York, Routledge, 1992.

Bock, Gisela (ed) and James, Susan (ed). *Beyond Equality and Difference*. New York, Routledge, 1992.

Boddington, Paula and Podpadec, Tessa. Measuring Quality of Life in Theory and in Practice: A Dialogue Between Philosophical and Psychological Approaches. *Bioethics*, 6(3), 201-217, Jl 92.

The paper aims at a dialogue between philosophical and psychological approaches to measuring quality of life, focusing on learning difficulties, and addressing implications for the valuing of individual lives. The practical, detailed methodology of some psychological work is of great potential benefit to some philosophical

accounts of quality of life, and in particular some work may help to undo implicit bias in these accounts against certain people, notably those with intellectual disabilities. However, psychological work often suffers from lack of explicit theoretical base and philosophical theory may be usefully applied here.

Boddington, Paula and Podpadec, Tessa. Reply to Anstötz: What We Can Learn from People with Learning Difficulties. *Bioethics*, 6(4), 361-364, O 92.

This paper replies to criticisms of our paper in *Bioethics* 6.3 "Measuring the Quality of Life in Theory and in Practice". Philosophy and psychology take differing approaches to issues concerning people with learning difficulties or mental handicap. Philosophy questions ethical assumptions others may take for granted and the methodological and practical work of psychologists may help philosophers in their aims and in adjusting their theoretical stances. People should be seen as individuals not as members of a homogenous group. Other misunderstandings of our work are addressed.

Bodnár, István M. Anaximander on the Stability of the Earth. *Phronesis*, 37(3), 336-342, 1992.

Boedeker, Deborah. Commentary on Martin's "Fate and Futurity in the Greco-Roman World". *Proc Boston Colloq Anc Phil*, 5, 312-320, 1989.

Luther Martin addresses an important question about differences between Greek and Hebraic worldviews, namely their respective concepts of "futurity". In contrasting the attitudes toward Cyrus the Great in Deutero- Isaiah and Herodotus, however, Martin fails to consider the differences in genre (prophecy vs. historiography) which may account for much of the variation in attitude. Moreover, although oracles in Herodotus often do seem authoritative, implying that the future is pre-ordained, their unintelligibility is even more striking; it is this quality which interests Herodotus more. Even in Greek culture, the future is not fully closed.

Boeder, Heribert. Privilege of Presence?. *Grad Fac Phil J*, 16(1), 77-86, 1993.

As is well-known, Derrida has taken up the Heideggerian confrontation with what he has seen as the privilege of presence in our metaphysical tradition. As for presence itself in the Greek tradition, the fundamental distinction of the sense of *Anwesen* is neglected—to be present at something and something being present to someone with a presence of mind. As for the wider sense of Being, already Heidegger confuses being present with appearing with the enormous consequence, that he interprets the early understanding of *Alätheta* in terms of *Physis*. Moreover, Being is understood in the Medium Epoch not as presence, but as giveness; in the Last Epoch of metaphysics, as positing.

Boehm, Beth A. Feminist Histories: Theory Meets Practice. *Hypatia*, 7(2), 202-214, Spr 92.

Fox-Genovese, Kaminer, and Riley all write the history of feminism as a history of conflict between feminists who desire to deny difference in favor of equality and those who desire to celebrate difference. And they all ask what this contradiction lying at the heart of feminist theory implies for the practice of feminist politics. These works reveal the need for feminist who engage this debate to be self-conscious in their formulations.

Böttner, Michael. Variable-Free Semantics for Anaphora. *J Phil Log*, 21(4), 375-390, N 92.

Bogdan, Deanne and Cunningham, James. Beyond Comprehension: Why "Hard Reading" Is Too Easy. *Proc Phil Educ*, 48, 124-129, 1992.

Bogdan and Cunningham address the charge by Keith Raitz that treating communication as a purpose of reading violates the "communication contract" according to which communication is the necessary and sufficient condition of reading. They point out that it is possible to treat communication as a purpose without falling into adherence to a "conduit theory" of textual meaning or subscribing to "the myth of easy reading". Further, they argue for a "constructionist model' of reading which, while recognizing the meaning making and decoding responsibilities of readers articulated in Reddy's "reconstructionist model", establishes wider criteria for successful reading than the reconstruction of authorial meaning.

Bogdan, Radu J. The Pragmatic Psyche. *Phil Phenomenol Res*, 53(1), 157-158, Mr 93.

In a recent article ("Semantics and the Psyche", *Phil Phenomenol Res*, 52, 1992, 395-399), Dascal and Horowitz criticize two claims I made in "Does Semantics Run the Psyche?" (*Phil and Phenomenol Res*, 49, 1989, 687-700) about Fodor's psychosemantic project. One claim was that the semantics does not run the psyche, the other that Fodor's naturalization of content assumes rather than explains intentionality. I show, first, that my claims survive their criticisms, and second, that that it is because intentionality is left unexplained that the semantics appears to run the psyche.

Bogen, Jim and Woodward, Jim. Observations, Theories and the Evolution of the Human Spirit. *Phil Sci*, 59(4), 590-611, D 92.

Standard philosophical discussions of theory-ladeness assume that observational evidence consists of perceptual outputs (or reports of such outputs) that are sentential or propositional in structure. Theory-ladeness is conceptualized as having to do with logical or semantical relationships between such outputs or reports and background theories held by observers. Using the recent debate between Fodor and Churchland as a point of departure, we propose an alternative picture in which much of what serves as evidence in science is not perceptual outputs or reports of such outputs and is not sentential in structure.

Boger, George. The Logical Sense of παραδοξον in Aristotle's *Sophistical Refutations*. *Ancient Phil*, 13(1), 55-78, Spr 93.

Aristotle is found to use 'paradoxon' (paradox) in Sophistical Refutations in a way very close to how modern logicians use it. He takes a paradoxon to be an argumentation involving several propositions and not (as is commonly believed) to be a single proposition. Examining the text shows that a paradoxon appears to a participant to deduce a false proposition from true propositions. In fact, a paradoxon is a species of phainomenos sullogismos (apparent deduction) and thus is required solution (lusis), scilicet a change in a participant's beliefs about the truth of the premises, the falsity of the conclusion, or the cogency of the reasoning. This interpretation is confirmed by observing that Aristotle treats instances of paradoxa in this way in Nicomachean Ethics and Metaphysics.

Boghossian, Paul. Does an Inferential Role Semantics Rest Upon a Mistake?. *Mind Lang*, 8(1), 27-40, Spr 93.

Jerry Fodor and Ernie Lepore have argued that an inferential role semantics essentially depends upon a distinction between analytic and synthetic inferences, a distinction that Quine has shown to be untenable. My paper refutes their argument. First, I argue that Quine didn't undermine the distinction. Second, I show that our IRS doesn't depend on it.

Boghossian, Paul. Externalism and Influence in Rationality in Epistemology, Villanueva, Enrique (ed). Atascadero, Ridgeview, 1992.

The paper argues that externalism allows for the coherent description of a sort of case that has not been previously recognized: two of a thinker's mental expressions of the same syntactic type have distinct meanings, but the thinker is not able to introspect that fact. The paper goes on to explore the implications of this case for our notions of inference and rationality.

Boghossian, Paul. Reply to Schiffer in Rationality in Epistemology, Villanueva, Enrique (ed). Atascadero, Ridgeview, 1992.

Bogue, Ronald. Gilles Deleuze: The Aesthetics of Force. *J Brit Soc Phenomenol*, 24(1), 56-65, Ja 93.

The contemporary French philosopher Gilles Deleuze identifies the common problem of the arts as the "harnessing of forces," a thesis that is explored first through an examination of Deleuze's study of the painter Francis Bacon and then through a consideration of the relation of Deleuze's views on painting to his treatments of music and cinema. This aesthetics of force may finally be described as an experimental affective physics, in which each art experiments with the body of sensations, defined by Deleuze as the "body without organs," or the unorganized body-world of non-formed elements and anonymous affective forces.

Boguslawski, Andrzej. Regress is Anathema, Yes. *J Prag*, 17(5-6), 441-445, Je 92.

This is a "peer review" of M Bickhard and R Campbell's paper on foundations of theory of language (the same volume). The author shows that the paper accuses, without any proof, nearly all theorists of language of holding an "encodingist" view of language, i.e., of committing a self-contradiction (as the nonce term "encodingism" is explained by the scholars, the theorists are guilty of regarding some items as both "encodings" and "non-encodings"). The author rejects the materialist conception of language advanced in the paper as involving itself as infinite regress against which the scholars rightly warn. He claims that adopting a basis of semantically primitive concepts is the proper way of countering this danger.

Bohanon, Cecil E and Annis, David B. Desert and Property Rights. *J Value Inq*, 26(4), 537-546, O 92.

Some philosophers have argued that personal desert is a basis of ownership. Thus, a person's effort in producing an item may make him or her deserving of significant property rights in it. In this essay we support desert as an important basis of ownership.

Bohman, James F. Holism without Skepticism: Contextualism and the Limits of Interpretation in The Interpretive Turn, Hiley, David R (ed). Ithaca, Cornell Univ Pr, 1991.

Holism is any view of interpretation that sees it as indeterminate, contextual, and circular. "Strong holism" concludes from these features of interpretation that there is no such thing as "correct" interpretations or that interpretations cannot constitute claims to knowledge based on evidence. "Weak holism" denies such interpretive skepticism. Weak holism can be defended by showing that strong holists commit an error in transcendental argumentation; they confuse formal, enabling conditions of interpretation with its material, limiting conditions. Such fallacies can be found in the writings of ethnographers and sociologists of science. Weak holism also suggests ways in which interpretive claims may be well-warranted forms of practical social knowledge.

Bohman, James F. *New Philosophy of Social Science*. Cambridge, MIT Pr, 1992.

The aim of this work is to develop a post-empiricist philosophy of the social sciences by reconstructing their actual practices of explanation and interpretation. By reconstructing successful, "core" explanations in on-going research programs, criteria for the adequacy of explanations can be established for the basic problems of the social sciences: causality, rules, interpretation, macrosociology and social criticism. The unifying theme of these three programs is their common emphasis on the importance of knowledgeable, reflective social actors. This emphasis results in a fundamental problem for social science: the indeterminacy of social action which successful explanations and interpretations can accommodate.

Bohman, James F. The Possibility of Post-Socialist Politics. *Mod Sch*, 70(3), 217-224, Mr 93.

The recent collapse of socialism has brought with it many attempts to rethink the economic and political basis of emancipatory social theory. Some critics of socialism now reject conceptions of "radical democracy" from Marx to Rousseau, including Lefort, Castoriadis, and Howard. This essay responds to such criticism of participatory democratic theories, particularly the false claim that they are inherently "totalitarian." Properly understood, radical democracy still provides the basis for a post-socialist politics, as can be seen in new demands for political equality and participation in recent social movements.

Bohman, James F (ed) and Hiley, David R (ed) and Shusterman, Richard (ed). *The Interpretive Turn*. Ithaca, Cornell Univ Pr, 1991.

In philosophy, the sciences and such diverse fields as anthropolgy, law, and social history, the turn to interpretative methods has challenged fundamental assumptions about the status of knowledge claims. The book addresses these challenges in fifteen new essays by a variety of scholars on topics about the relationship between the natural and human sciences, normative issues of interpretation, and interpretive practices in various disciplines.

Boisvert, Raymond D. Metaphysics as the Search for Paradigmatic Instances. *Trans Peirce Soc*, 28(2), 189-202, Spr 92.

This essay goes beyond the Deweyan articulation of metaphysics as seeking the "generic traits of existence". It argues that Dewey's metaphysics seeks to answer the question "what is most real". The modern responses to this question have been eliminative and reductionistic: the most real are those underlying elements out of which things are composed. Dewey's view is the opposite of this. The most real is the most inclusive. The paradigmatic instance for what is real is "the social". Speaking in terms of paradigmatic instances avoids the sharp bifurcation into reality and appearance. Pluralism can thereby be preserved without a metaphysical relativism.

Bok, Sissela. Commentator on 'Value, Desire, and Quality of Life' in The Quality of Life, Nussbaum, Martha C (ed). New York, Oxford Univ Pr, 1993.

Bok, Sissela. Reassessing Sartre. *Harvard Rev Phil*, 1(1), 48-52, Spr 91.

Bokhove, Niels W and Raynaud, Savina. A Bibliography of Works by and on Anton Marty in Mind, Meaning and Metaphysics, Mulligan, Kevin (ed). Dordrecht, Kluwer, 1990.

Bole III, Thomas J. Taking Hegel's Logic Seriously. *SW Phil Rev*, 9(1), 51-61, Ja 93.

My thesis is that the *Logic* justifies the basic categories of being by means of the dialectic, by showing that they are elements necessary to an account of explanatory thought, and therefore to the explanadum, being. I say how the *Logic* provides a structured explication of those categories that show that being, if it is distinguishable from nothingness, is explainable. I state what categories can thereby by justified. And I indicate why the *Logic*, it reads transcendentally, permits one to see what is and is not viable among the details of the *Logic* and of Hegel's philosophy of the real.

Boler, John F. Transcending the Natural: Duns Scotus on the Two Affections of the Will. *Amer Cath Phil Quart*, 67(1), 109-126, Wint 93.

The paper investigates the "inborn freedom" (*libertas ingenita*) Scotus attributes to the presence of an *affectio justitiae* in the will, allowing the rational agent to rise above the range of *affectio commodi* (the "natural" appetite to realize the potential of the agent's intellectual nature). The thesis is that *libertas ingenita* derives from Scotus's beliefs about the character of morality itself rather than metaphysical or psychological presuppositions concerning freedom of the will. The implicit criticism of an Aristotelian eudaimonist ethics is discussed.

Bolton, Martha Brandt. The Epistemological Status of Ideas: Locke Compared to Arnauld. *Hist Phil Quart*, 9(4), 409-424, O 92.

Bolton, Robert. Aristotle on the Objectivity of Ethics in Essays in Ancient Greek Philosophy, IV, Anton, John P (ed). Albany, SUNY Pr, 1991.

Boltuc, Piotr. Person as Locus of Permanence: Towards Albert Shalom's Metaphysics. *Dialec Hum*, 17(2), 213-233, 1990.

Opposition between irreducibly, fundamental nature of subjectivity and objectivity advocated by Nagel, can be grasped within an approach to the mind-body problem proposed by Shalom. Shalom sees a man as a unitary being perceiving himself under two modalities: 1) The physical perspective (seeing oneself as a body) which gives rise to the ontology. 2) The mental or consciousness-based one (seeing oneself as a mind, e.g., Cartesianism), which gives rise to epistemological approach. Personal identity is understood as a fundamental, phenomenological manifestation of a unity of these two, complementary aspects of a person. Shalom understands a potential, constant element of consciousness (a kind of transcendental subject, though a passive one) as a "locus of timelessness." This leads to the idea of immortality as a final level of the process of internalization. I argue that the passive self is more like a locus of nothingness which mirrors the world of existence from the outside.

Bolzan, J E and Larre, Olga L. La Curiosa Doctrina de Ockham en Torno a la Divisibilidad del Continuo. *Rev Filosof (Mexico)*, 24(71), 142-158, My-Ag 91.

Bombardi, Ronald J. The Education of Searle's Demon. *Ideal Stud*, 23(1), 5-18, Wint 93.

The paper argues against the position adopted by John Searle in his 1980 article, "Minds, Brains, and Programs." On Searle's view, the very idea of artificial intelligence is incoherent; I contend that this view is seriously flawed in two respects: 1) Searle's paradigmatic example for illustrating why computational machinery cannot possess cognitive states actually illustrates the contrary case; and 2) Searle radically misrepresents the functionalist theory of mind underlying most current research in artificial intelligence.

Bonagura, P. Il *Filebo* come una 'summa' del pensiero metafisico platonico. *Riv Filosof Neo-Scolas*, 82(4), 543-577, O-D 90.

Bond, E J. Morality and Reason in On the Track of Reason, Beehler, Rodger G (ed). Boulder, Westview Pr, 1992.

Bonevac, Daniel A and Phillips, Stephen. *Understanding Non-Western Philosophy: Introductory Readings*. Mountain View, Mayfield, 1993.

Bonikowski, Zbigniew. A Certain Conception of the Calculus of Rough Sets. *Notre Dame J Form Log*, 33(3), 412-421, Sum 92.

We consider the family of rough sets in the present paper. In this family we define, by means of a minimal upper sample, the operations of rough addition, rough multiplication, and pseudocomplement. We prove that the family of rough sets with the above operations is a complete atomic stone algebra. We prove that the family of rough sets, determined by the unions of equivalence classes of the relation R with the operations of rough addition, rough multiplication, and complement, is a complete atomic Boolean algebra. If the relation R determines a partition of set U into one-element equivalence classes, then the family of rough sets with the above operations is a Boolean algebra that is isomorphic with a Boolean algebra of subsets of universum U.

Bonilla, Alcira B. La scoperta dell'America: Tra la realtà e l'utopia di un "nuovo mondo". *Aquinas*, 35(2), 389-397, My-Ag 92.

The author is placed at the viewpoint of a phenomenological philosophy of history with ethical and political implications. This article shows that the 12th October, 1492 signals the beginning of a definitive phase for the history of mankind. This phase has not reached its fulfillment yet. The starting points for this analysis are the concepts of "utopia" and "reality", dialectically interwoven throughout the article with those of "discovery" ("descubrimiento"), "concealing" ("encubrimiento") and "rediscovery" ("redescubrimiento"). The attitude of same XVI century Spanish humanist offers a model for the present and new utopia of "rediscovery" of America.

Boniolo, Giovanni. Theory and Experiment: The Case of Eötvös' Experiments. *Brit J Phil Sci*, 43(4), 459-486, D 92.

By analysing the historical case of the proportionality between inertia and gravitation, it is possible to reconstruct one of the most relevant moments in the history of physics, that is to say, the one linked with Eötvös' experiments. At the same time, this reconstruction offers the opportunity to carry out philosophical considerations about the relationship between theory and experiment and about the concept of incommensurability.

Bonnen, Clarence A and Flage, Daniel. Innate Ideas and Cartesian Dispositions. *Int Stud Phil*, 24(1), 65-80, 1992.

Commentators on Descartes's theory of innate ideas argue either that nonoccurrent innate ideas are distinct, actual ideas that exist in the mind like unperceived cards in a file, or they argue that innate ideas are dispositions to form occurrent ideas with particular objective contents. This paper shows that the textual evidence is consistent with the dispositional account of nonoccurrent innate ideas and answers several philosophical objections to that interpretation. It concludes by attempting to unpack the notion of a Cartesian disposition.

Bonsor, Jack. Creatures of Truth. *Thomist*, 56(4), 647-668, O 92.

Bonsor, Jack A. *Athens and Jerusalem: The Role of Philosophy in Theology*. Mahwah, Paulist Pr, 1993.

Bontekoe, Ron and Crooks, Jamie. The Inter-Relationship of Moral and Aesthetic Excellence. *Brit J Aes*, 32(3), 209-220, Jl 92.

The process of artistic creation is a matter of progressively narrowing in on some worthwhile experience the possibility of which the artist has caught a glimpse. This process involves the artist in an attempt to capture the inner necessity governing her subject. Because a bad moral vision is one which gets something significantly wrong about the human condition, if an artist *chooses* to deal with moral issues, and does so badly (i.e., fails to do justice to the inner necessity governing her subject), her work can be criticized as having failed to meet *aesthetic* as well as moral criteria of excellence.

Bontekoe, Ronald. Metaphysics: Should It Be Revisionary or Descriptive?. *Int Phil Quart*, 32(2), 147-160, Je 92.

Hilary Putnam's internal realist conception of what is involved in the pursuit of truth is preferable to Donald Davidson's view because it implies no unwarranted confidence in the truth of our current beliefs, and thus does not tempt us to draw premature conclusions about "the large features of reality". The endeavor to clarify and sharpen our beliefs exactly as they are now (on the Davidsonian assumption that they must be largely true) is the wrong program for metaphysicians to adopt, since it freezes into immobility an inquiry that should be progressing towards new levels of understanding.

Bookman, J T. The Wisdom of the Many: An Analysis of the Arguments of Books III and IV of Aristotle's *Politics*. *Hist Polit Thought*, 13(1), 1-12, Spr 92.

In Books III and IV of *The Politics*, Aristotle examines six arguments made on behalf of rule by the many. These arguments anticipate those made by more contemporary proponents of democracy. There are difficulties in them all, but under less than ideal circumstances and in the absence of men of perfect excellence, Aristotle finds them sufficiently compelling to conclude that a government under law in which the many participate is the best of the imperfect forms. Such a government will not directly promote the good life. It does offer the best chance of stability and moderation—conditions propitious for the individual pursuit of the good life.

Boolos, George. Basic Law (V)—I: Whence the Contradiction?. *Aris Soc*, Supp(67), 213-233, 1993.

Boolos, George. The Analytical Completeness of Dzhaparidze's Polymodal Logics. *Annals Pure Applied Log*, 61(1-2), 95-111, My 93.

The bimodal provability logics of analysis (second-order arithmetic) for ordinary provability and provability by (unrestricted application of) the ω-rule are shown to be fragments of certain 'polymodal' logics introduced by G K Dzhaparidze. In addition to modal axiom schemes expressing Löb's theorem for the two kinds of provability, the logics treated here contain a scheme expressing that if a statement is consistent, then the statement that it is consistent is provable by the *ω-rule.*

Boolos, George and Sambin, Giovanni. Provability: The Emergence of a Mathematical Modality. *Stud Log*, 50(1), 1-23, Mr 91.

Boonin-Vail, David. The Vegetarian Savage: Rousseau's Critique of Meat Eating. *Environ Ethics*, 15(1), 75-84, Spr 93.

Contemporary defenders of philosophical vegetarianism are too often unaware of their historical predecessors. In this paper, I contribute to the rectification of this neglect by focusing on the case of Rousseau. In part one, I identify and articulate an argument against meat eating that is implicitly present in Rousseau's writings, although it is never explicitly developed. In part two, I consider and respond to two objections that might be made to the claim that this argument should be attributed to Rousseau. In part three, I consider how Rousseau's argument might fit into a general typology of recent discussions of vegetarianism, and argue that the eclectic nature that is revealed in doing so shows that the argument is worthy of further consideration.

Booth, David. Logical Feedback. *Stud Log*, 50(2), 225-239, Je 91.

Just as non-well-founded sets extend the usual sets of ZF, so do root reflexive propositional formulas extends the usual class of Boolean expressions. Though infinitary, these formulas are generated by finite patterns. They possess transition functions instead of truth values and have applications in electric circuit theory.

Boothby, Richard. Lacanian Castration in Crises in Continental Philosophy, Dallery, Arleen B (ed). Albany, SUNY Pr, 1990.

Bordo, Jonathan. Ecological Peril, Modern Technology and the Postmodern Sublime in Shadow of Spirit, Berry, Philippa (ed). New York, Routledge, 1992.

Modern technology releases the sublime, and every effort to manage the sublime by reiterated technological means seems merely to increase the indeterminacy, rendering our experience more inchoate and defenceless in face of it. This theoretical resultant is reached through a problematizing of the classical aesthetics of the sublime (Burke and Kant) and Heidegger's *The Question* against the background of technologically induced ecological threats.

Bordo, Susan. "Maleness" Revisited. *Hypatia*, 7(3), 197-207, Sum 92.

My response to the preceding commentaries draws on recent events such as the Thomas/Hill hearings to illustrate some of my central arguments in "Feminist Skepticism and the 'Maleness' of Philosophy." I also attempt to clarify frequently misunderstood aspects of my use of gender as an analytical category, and discuss why, in my opinion, we should continue to care about the "maleness" of philosophy.

Bordo, Susan R. Eating Disorders: The Feminist Challenge to the Concept of Pathology in The Body in Medical Thought and Practice, Leder, Drew (ed). Dordrecht, Kluwer, 1992.

Bordt, Michael. Der Seinsbegriff in Platons 'Sophistes'. *Theol Phil*, 66(4), 493-529, 1991.

The article provides, first, a survey of the scholarly debate about the meaning of 'to be' in Plato's Sophistes, starting from Cornford, centering on Michael Frede and Owen, and leading up to the present day discussion. Then, Plato's criticism of dualism, monism, idealism, 2nd materialism (Soph. 242b6-249d5) is given detailed analysis. The scope of this analyse is to substantiate the hypothesis that Plato distinguishes two types of propositions in Sophistes, i.e., those of predication and a particular kind of identity. Each type uses 'is' differently. However, even when criticizing traditional ontologies, Plato does not use 'is' to mean 'exists'.

Borgmann, Albert. The Moral Significance of the Material Culture. *Inquiry*, 35(3-4), 291-300, S-D 92.

Ethics as a philosophical discipline has always been preoccupied with theory to the detriment of practice and the exclusion of material culture. Lately, practice has been rehabilitated, but material culture continues to be ignored. Cultural critics and sociologists have attended to it but have also refrained from a moral assessment of it. The findings of Csikszentmihalyi and Rochberg-Halton, however, reflect two kinds of cultural realities that sponsor two kinds of conduct. The first, represented by musical instruments, I call commanding reality. It invites social and physical engagement and provides orientation within the world. The second kind, exemplified by stereos, consists of consumable commodities and conduces to a life of distraction and disorientation. (edited)

Bormann, Herbert F (ed) and Kellert, Stephen R (ed). *Ecology, Economics, Ethics: The Broken Circle*. New Haven, Yale Univ Pr, 1991.

Borovik, Alexandre V and Nesin, Ali. On the Schur-Zassenhaus Theorem for Groups of Finite Morley Rank. *J Sym Log*, 57(4), 1469-1477, D 92.

Borst, Clive. Leibniz and the Compatibilist of Free Will. *Stud Leibniz*, 24(1), 49-58, 1992.

Der Aufsatz zielt auf eine nähere Präzisierung der üblicherweise gegebenen Bestimmung, Leibniz sei "Kompatibilist" gewesen. Willensfreiheit ist für Leibniz mit Gottes Vorherwissen und Vorherbestimmung sowie mit dem Prinzip des zureichenden Grundes kompatibel, keineswegs jedoch mit Indifferenz. Um die Vereinbarkeit der Willensfreiheit mit vollständigen individullen Begriffen zu zeigen, scheint der Rekurs auf Gegenstücke in anderen möglichen Welten unerlässlich. Es wird argumentiert, dass Willensfreiheit für Leibniz nicht mit der prinzipiellen Vorhersagbarkeit von Willensentscheidungen durch einen menschlichen Beobachter oder durch einen Laplaceschen Dämon kompatibel ist.

Borst, Clive. Realism, Psychologism, and Intermediary-Shadows in Wittgenstein's *Tractatus*. *Philosophia (Israel)*, 22(1-2), 119-138, Ja 93.

Whether to give a realist or a non-realist, and again a psychologistic or a non-psychologistic interpretation of the *Tractatus*, crucially affects not only our understanding of it, but also the issue of the extent of continuity in Wittgenstein's thought. I adduce a variety of considerations in favour of a realist combined with a psychologistic reading. Elementary sentences have as their sense: states of affairs which correspond (*entsprechen*) to them. These thought-contents are possibilities having the status of shadowy intermediaries between language and actuality. Independent evidence for discontinuity lends further support to the interpretation advanced.

Borutti, Silvana. *Per un' etica del discorso antropologico*. Milano, Guerini, 1993.

This book raises, in relation to anthropological studies, some theoretical and epistemological problems. For example, how can we obtain knowledge in the domain of human phenomena (i.e., of meanings, values, actions, etc.)? Is it really possible to speak of objectivity when knowledge is linked to vital acts? How does our idea of reason relate to the reasons of others? The main thesis of this book concerns the dilemma of the knowledge of others. Against both a monological and a relativistic idea of rationality, the author maintains that knowing in human sciences is a continuing mediation between our *epistemic will* of objectifying and our *ethical will* of respecting the difference of the other.

Bos, A P. Considerazioni sul *De mundo* e analisi critica delle tesi di Paul Moraux. *Riv Filosof Neo-Scolas*, 82(4), 587-606, O-D 90.

Bos, A P. Teologia cosmica e metacosmica nella filosofia greca e nello gnosticismo. *Riv Filosof Neo-Scolas*, 84(2-3), 369-382, Ap-S 92.

After A J Festugière many scholars, in discussing the problem of the origin of Gnosticism, stressed the influence of Greek philosophy, especially of Platonism. In this article it is argued that the double theology of Gnosticism with its transcendent, good God and a lower, (even bad) Demiurge or Worldarchon can only be understood against the background of the double theology of Aristotle's lost dialogues.

Bos, Jaap and Maier, Robert. The Name of the Game: An Analysis of the Grünbaum Debate. *Commun Cog*, 25(4), 295-323, 1992.

This paper aims at analyzing the discussions in "Behavioral and Brain Sciences", vol. 25, nr. 4 (1992) about the 1984 book "The Foundations of Psycho-Analysis" by A Grünbaum. In a "normative method of classification in four steps", the authors discern a number of different argumentative attitudes (mediative, judicious, contentious and irrelevant). The main results of this study are: 1) many of those

Bosio, Franco 420 **AUTHOR INDEX WITH ABSTRACTS**

invited to deliver a contribution does not in fact enter the arena of debate, 2) all contributions contain polemic devices, and 3) only a very limited number of participants enter into a 'real argumentation' with Grünbaum.

Bosio, Franco. I limiti della decostruzione del "soggetto" nella critica filosofica "postmoderna". *G Metaf*, 14(1), 85-90, Ja-Ap 92.

Boss, Judith A. Pro-Child/Pro-Choice: An Exercise in DoubleThink?. *Pub Affairs Quart*, 7(2), 85-91, Ap 93.

The assumption that children actually benefit from a policy which allows abortion-on-demand has rarely been questioned by pro-choice advocates. The evidence not only fails to bear out this assumption, but suggests that such a policy may actually be contributing to an overall decline in children's well-being since 1973.

Boss, Judith A. *The Birth Lottery*. Chicago, Loyola Univ Pr, 1993.

This book is a discussion of the ethics of prenatal diagnosis and selective abortion. Topics covered include the types of genetic disorders, the medical technology involved in prenatal diagnosis and selective abortion, and the different arguments—biomedical, social burden, family burden and "quality of life"—for selective abortion.

Botkin, Jeffrey R. Ethics and Evidence. *J Clin Ethics*, 3(1), 63-64, Spr 92.

Bottani, L. Di due diverse filosofie scettiche. *Sapienza*, 45(1), 83-92, 1992.

Bottani, Livio. Malinconia e nichilismo—I: Dalla ferita mortale alla ricomposizione dell'infranto. *Filosofia*, 43(2), 269-293, My-Ag 92.

Bottomore, Tom (ed) and Outhwaite, William (ed). *The Blackwell Dictionary of Twentieth-Century Social Thought*. Cambridge, Blackwell, 1993.

Twentieth-Century social thought rages widely from the social sciences to philosophy, political theories and doctrines, cultural ideas and movements, and the influence of the natural sciences. This Dictionary aims to provide a reliable and comprehensive overview of the main themes of social thought, principal schools and movements of thought and those institutions that have been the subject of social analysis or engendered significant doctrines and ideas. Long entries cover major currents of thought, philosophical and cultural trends and the individual social sciences. These are supplemented by shorter accounts of specific concepts and phenomena.

Boucher, David. Ambiguity and Originality in the Context of Discursive Relations in Objectivity, Method and Point of View, Van Der Dussen, W J (ed). Leiden, Brill, 1991.

Boudier, Henk Struyker. Helmuth Plessner als Philosophischer Wegweiser für F J J Buytendijk. *Man World*, 26(2), 199-207, Ap 93.

Am 4 September 1992 wurde der hundertste Geburtstag des Philosophen Helmuth Plessner gefeiert. Dem Jahrhundertfest seiner Geburt vorgreifend hat Henk Struyker Boudier die Ausgabe der Korrespondenz von F J J Buytendijk mit Helmuth Plessner vorbereitet und eingeleitet. Plessner aktuelle Bedeutung liegt in seinen Auffassungen über die deutsche Frage, die im Hinblick auf den politischen Zusammenschluss Europas noch immer starke Beachtung finden. Er ist ein philosophischer Wegweiser für jeden, der an den Problemen um Rasse und Volk, Nation und Staat interessiert ist, zum Beispiel im Zusammenhang mit dem Asylrecht. (edited)

Boudier, Henk Struyker. The Difference Between Man and Animal: Letters of Max Scheler on F J J Buytendijk (in Dutch). *Bijdragen*, 53(3), 312-322, 1992.

The subject of this article is the difference between man and animal, viewed from a historical perspective. Two unpublished letters (1922) of Mac Scheler to F J J Buytendijk are used. They illustrate the position of both authors on the subject at the beginning of the 20th century. Both, Scheler and Buytendijk, deal with the difference between man and animal in a phenomenological manner.

Bouillon, Hardy (ed) and Radnitzky, Gerard (ed). *Government: Servant or Master?*. Amsterdam, Rodopi, 1993.

The book is a plea for arresting, or if possible reversing, the long-standing trend of the growth of government, of state interventionism and dirigisme into every corner of our lives. It provides theoretical analyses of the dynamics prevalent in log-rolling special interest democracies. They are followed by case studies. The problems raised by the volume are urgent. They will be of interest to all those who would like to see a transition to a more prosperous society, a society with more economic freedoms and civil liberties. Socialism may perhaps be dead — at least full-scale, avowed socialism — but the question of how to tame Leviathan looms as large as ever.

Boulad-Ayoub, Josiane. "La Nature, la raison, l'expérience..." ou la réfutation du matérialisme dans l'apologétique chrétienne des Lumières. *Dialogue (Canada)*, 31(1), 19-32, Wint 92.

In the context of ideological discursive analysis, we bring out the polemical and political determinations of the refutation of *Système de la nature* made by the catholic priest Bergier in his *Examen du matérialisme* (1771). We emphasize how the author uses concepts shared in common by both materialists and idealist philosophers of the Enlightenment. However, Bergier's theses are only to uphold the Christian representations on these crucial issues—Nature, Man and Society—then discussed. While analyzing the scientific, ontological and ethical aspects of the oppositions which articulate the debate, we evaluate their theoretical pertinence as well as their political impact.

Boulet, Geneviéve. Philosophy and the Teaching of Mathematics. *Eidos*, 10(1), 5-20, J-Jl 91.

Boulting, Noel E. Charles S Peirce's Idea of Ultimate Reality and Meaning Related to Humanity's Ultimate Future as Seen through Scientific Inquiry. *Ultim Real Mean*, 16(1-2), 9-26, Mr-Je 93.

Boundas, Constantin V. Foreclosure of the Other: From Sartre to Deleuze. *J Brit Soc Phenomenol*, 24(1), 32-43, Ja 93.

This essay discusses the place occupied by Sartre in the writings of Deleuze. It places in a critical context Deleuze's praise of Sartre for his attempt to purify the transcendental field from the vestiges of the Husserlian ego, and for his decision to introduce (at least initially) otherness as a structure, instead of indulging in an all-too-empirical preoccupation with the saga of the self as subject or the other self as object. In the sequence, the essay discusses Deleuze's criticisms of Sartre for not questioning the privilege that phenomenology assigns to natural perception, for failing to displace consciousness (in the wake of the displacement of the ego), and for continuing the disastrous politics of negativity and lack.

Boundas, Constantin V (ed). *The Deleuze Reader*. New York, Columbia Univ Pr, 1993.

This volume brings together excerpts from Deleuze's texts, with the intention to offer its readers a comprehensive introduction to the work of this French philosopher. The excerpts are organized into five parts (Rhizomatics, Difference and Repetition, Desire and Schizoanalysis, Minor Languages and Nomad Art, Politics). Although most of the included material has appeared before, the volume contains "The Signs of Madness: Proust", "Painting and Sensation", "The Diagram", and "One Manifesto Less", in English translation for the first time. The book includes a useful introduction by the editor and a good bibliography of Deleuze's work published before 1992.

Boundas, Constantin V (ed) and Lester, Mark (& other trans) and Deleuze, Gilles. *The Logic of Sense—Gilles Deleuze*. New York, Columbia Univ Pr, 1990.

In the opus of Deleuze, *The Logic of Sense* holds the place that *The Archaeology of Knowledge* did in that of Foucault: the latter, being a discourse about discourse, articulates Foucault's methodology which permitted him to examine discursive formations, discursive practices and nondiscursive space surrounding discursive fields; the former, working out the logic of the invention of concepts, assembles around it all the other works of Deleuze and permits him to show how thinking should be understood and discussed, if it is to be a thinking of events, singularities and haecceities. In thirty-four series and five appendices, Deleuze displays his usual virtuosity as he discusses becoming and the paradoxes it generates, sense as the fourth dimension of the proposition, events in the context of two complementary readings of time, the ethics of the event and his early responses to Lacan.

Bourassa, Lucie. La forme du mouvement (sur la notion de rythme). *Horiz Phil*, 3(1), 103-120, Autumn 92.

Bourgeault, Guy. La transformation des pratiques professionnelles: quelques conséquences pour l'éthique. *Dialogue (Canada)*, 30(3), 285-295, Sum 91.

Bourgeois, Bernard. Lo bello y el bien en Kant. *Anu Filosof*, 26(1), 139-154, 1993.

Theory of beauty exposed in Kant's *Critique of Judgment* is neither an epilogue nor the cornerstone of Kantian system. Kant's solution to the problem of delight in beauty illustrates the meaning given to practical reasoning and its absolute dominance in the life of the spirit.

Bourgeois, Patrick. Semiotics and the Deconstruction of Presence: A Ricoeurian Alternative. *Amer Cath Phil Quart*, 66(3), 361-380, 1992.

A critique of Derrida's "semiological reductionism" and the flux of time as discrete on which it is founded provides a context for a viable alternative which does not succumb to the facile distinction of Sassure, or to Derrida's collapse of signs to the relations of differences within the system and the reduction of language to the play of difference. Rather, an alternative emerging from the philosophy of Paul Ricoeur is able adequately to account for duration and continuity in the living present as the basis for language as discourse. (edited)

Bourgeois, Patrick. The Instant and the Living Present: Ricoeur and Derrida Reading Husserl. *Phil Today*, 37(1), 31-37, Spr 93.

This essay will attempt to ascertain whether, beyond Husserl's quasi naive philosophy of presence, phenomenological philosophy is adequate to reflect on the duration of the object in the present, or whether such a philosophy of presence must be rejected because of Derrida's deconstruction which points to an alterity constitutive of the present. After a brief account of the ambiguity and tension within Husserl's analysis of the living present and the instant, Derrida's own deconstruction of Husserl's view of this relation will be brought into focus. Then a contrast of Ricoeur's interpretation of Husserl's analyses with that of Derrida will indicate that Ricoeur's clarification, while allowing for some of Derrida's points, in fact provides a broader and more insightful reading of Husserl. Finally, an attempt will be made to bring Ricoeur's critique of Derrida to a point that even Ricoeur fails to reach, by exposing the assumption and implication of Derrida's deconstruction of Husserl's distinction.

Bourgeois, Patrick and Herbert, Gary. The Religious Significance of Ricoeur's Post-Hegelian Kantian Ethics. *Amer Cath Phil Quart*, 65, 133-144, 1991.

This paper attempts to unfold the religious significance of the ethical in what Ricoeur refers to as his post-Hegelian Kantianism. The expanded ethics, in Ricoeur's terms, takes its bearings by its appropriation of the ethics of Kant and Hegel "by thinking them together—one against the other, and one by means of the other." It is an ethics which is liberated from the lifeless duties of inner freedom of will, an ethics which anchors will in the institutions and events of the concrete world, yet does not restrict the will to retrospective descriptions of a fully developed, final "totality." It is in part the Hegelian element in Ricoeur's thought that enables him to expand ethics beyond the narrowness of Kant's morality of duty to a more concrete concern for freedom. This extension of Kantian ethics to a more concrete, less abstract involvement in the world is accomplished by inserting "the religious" into the core of Ricoeur's overall ethical approach to human activity in the world. This religious core culminates with a God who manifests himself through the imagination of hope, in the creative interpretation of indirect language, such as the open-ended parables as a gift of the imagination of hope.

Bourgeois, Patrick L and Rosenthal, Sandra. Mead and Merleau-Ponty: 'Meaning, Perception, and Behavior' in Analecta Husserliana, XXXI, Tymieniecka, Anna-Teresa (ed). Dordrecht, Kluwer, 1990.

Mead's pragmatic focus on habit as the foundation of meaning is usually viewed in sharp contrast with Merleau-Ponty's phenomenological examination of meaning within experience. This paper attempts to show the way in which the explicit focus of each philosopher's position is latent within that of the other. For Mead and Merleau-Ponty alike, the content of human awareness at all levels is inseparably linked with the structure of human behavior. And, for both, such a structure is permeated throughout by the "living meaning" of anticipatory habit or vital intentionality.

AUTHOR INDEX WITH ABSTRACTS 421 Bradshaw, D E

Boutot, Alain. Catastrophe Theory and its Critics. *Synthese*, 96(2), 167-200, Ag 93.

Catastrophe theory has been sharply criticized because it does not seem to have practical applications nor does it seem to allow us to increase our power over Nature. I want to 'rehabilitate' the theory by foregoing the controversy raised by scientists about its practical efficiency. After a short exposition of the theory's mathematical formalism and a detailed analysis of the main objections that have been raised against it, I argue that theory is not only to be judged on its practical 'results', which are in fact limited, but also on its epistemological and philosophical implications. Catastrophe theory indeed represents a real revolution in science: it announces the coming of a more theoretical, less practical, science, having more to do with understanding reality than with acting on it, and, from that point of view, it may be considered as the modern philosophy of Nature.

Bouveresse, J. 'The Darkness of This Time': Wittgenstein and the Modern World in Wittgenstein Centenary Essays, Griffiths, A Phillips (ed). New York, Cambridge Univ Pr, 1991.

Bouveresse, Jacques. Wittgenstein, Anti-Realism and Mathematical Propositions in Criss-Crossing A Philosophical Landscape, Schulte, Joachim (ed). Amsterdam, Rodopi, 1992.

Wittgenstein is generally supposed to have abandoned in the 1930s a realistic conception of the meaning of mathematical propositions. It is argued that for Wittgenstein, mathematical propositions, which are, as he says, "grammatical" propositions, have a meaning and a role which differ to a much greater degree from those of ordinary propositions than either platonistic realism or intuitionistic anti-realism would admit.

Bowers, C A. The Conservative Misinterpretation of the Educational Ecological Crisis. *Environ Ethics*, 14(2), 101-128, Sum 92.

Conservative educational critics (e.g., Allan Bloom, Mortimer Adler, and E D Hirsch, Jr.) have succeeded in framing the debate on the reform of education in a manner that ignores the questions that should be asked about how our most fundamental cultural assumptions are contributing to the ecological crisis. In this paper, I examine the deep cultural assumptions embedded in their reform proposals that further exacerbate the crisis, giving special attention to their view of rational empowerment, the progressive nature of change, and their anthropocentric view of the universe. I argue that their form of conservatism must be supplanted by the more biocentric conservatism of such thinkers as Aldo Leopold, Wendell Berry, and Gary Snyder.

Bowie, Andrew (trans) and Frank, Manfred. Is Self-Consciousness a Case of 'Présence à Soi? in Derrida: A Critical Reader, Wood, David (ed). Cambridge, Blackwell, 1992.

Bowie, Norman E and Beauchamp, Tom L. *Ethical Theory and Business (Fourth Edition)*. Englewood Cliffs, Prentice Hall, 1993.

Bowker, Geoffrey C. Constructing Science, Forging Technology and Manufacturing Society. *Stud Hist Phil Sci*, 24(1), 147-155, Mr 93.

Bowles, Samuel and Gintis, Herbert. A Political and Economic Case for the Democratic Enterprise. *Econ Phil*, 9(1), 75-100, Ap 93.

We consider two reasons why firms should be owned and run democratically by their workers. The first concerns accountability: because the employment relationship involves the exercise of power, its governance should on democratic grounds be accountable to those most directly affected. The second concerns efficiency: the democratic firm uses a lower level of inputs per unit of output than the analogous capitalist firm. We demonstrate that the employer has power over the worker (in a conventionally defined sense) even in a perfectly competitive economy, and provide a consistent explanation of the failure of worker owned firms to proliferate in a competitive environment despite their superior efficiency.

Bowles, Samuel and Gintis, Herbert. A Political and Economic Case for the Democratic Enterprise in The Idea of Democracy, Copp, David (ed). New York, Cambridge Univ Pr, 1993.

Bowles, Samuel and Gintis, Herbert. Power and Wealth in a Competitive Capitalist Economy. *Phil Pub Affairs*, 21(4), 324-353, Fall 92.

Bowman, Elizabeth A (trans) and Sartre, Jean-Paul. Kennedy and West Virginia in Sartre Alive, Aronson, Ronald (ed). Detroit, Wayne St Univ Pr, 1991.

Bowman, Elizabeth A and Stone, Robert. Sartre's 'Morality and History': A First Look at the Notes for the Unpublished 1965 Cornell Lectures in Sartre Alive, Aronson, Ronald (ed). Detroit, Wayne St Univ Pr, 1991.

Boxer, P and Kenny, V. Lacan and Maturana: Constructivist Origins for a Third-Order Cybernetics. *Commun Cog*, 25(1), 73-100, 1992.

We examine some difficulties in the use made of second-order cybernetics, and the absence within radical constructivism of a theory of the subject. We introduce Lacan's approach to the subject particularly in the structure of discourse. We consider the implications this conception has both in the need for a third-order cybernetics, and for a formulation of an ethics based on calling into question the subject's relation to this third order as it manifests itself in transference.

Boxill, Bernard R. *Blacks and Social Justice (Revised Edition)*. Lanham, Rowman & Littlefield, 1992.

Boxill, Bernard R. On Some Criticisms of Consent Theory. *J Soc Phil*, 24(1), 81-102, Spr 93.

Boya, Luis J. Desarrollo científico: El caso de la física moderna. *Agora (Spain)*, 11(1), 43-50, 1992.

The subject of this paper is scientific progress, taking as example the development of physics in this century.

Boyarin, Daniel and Boyarin, Jonathan. Diaspora: Generation and the Ground of Jewish Identity. *Crit Inquiry*, 19(4), 693-725, Sum 93.

Boyarin, Jonathan and Boyarin, Daniel. Diaspora: Generation and the Ground of Jewish Identity. *Crit Inquiry*, 19(4), 693-725, Sum 93.

Boyd, Gregory. *Trinity and Process: A Critical Evaluation and Reconstruction of Hartshorne's Di-Polar Theism Towards a Trinitarian Metaphysics*. New York, Lang, 1992.

Boyd, Richard (ed) and Gasper, Philip (ed) and Trout, J D (ed). *The Philosophy of Science*. Cambridge, MIT Pr, 1991.

Boydston, Jo Ann. The Dewey Center and *The Collected Works of John Dewey*. *Free Inq*, 13(1), 19-24, Wint 92-93.

Boyer, Alain. Physique de croyant? Duhem et l'autonomie de la science. *Rev Int Phil*, 46(182), 311-322, 1992.

Boyer, Pascal. Causal Thinking and Its Anthropological Misrepresentation. *Phil Soc Sci*, 22(2), 187-213, Je 92.

The study of causal inferences is an essential part of the study of other cultures. It is therefore crucial to describe the cognitive mechanisms whereby subjects are led to find specific causal explanations plausible and "natural". In the anthropological literature, specific causal connections are described as the result produced by applying a general "conception of causation" or some general "theories" to specific events; the essay aims to show that these answers are either trivial or false. The "naturalness" of explanations must be examined in the context of concept acquisition and belief-fixation. On the basis of an ethnographic example, it is possible to show how certain presumptions (e.g., about the use of certain categories as natural kind terms) can be involved in the processes whereby certain explanations are made cognitively salient.

Boyne, Roy (ed) and Rattansi, Ali (ed). *Postmodernism and Society*. New York, St Martin's Pr, 1990.

Boyne, Roy and Rattansi, Ali. The Theory and Politics of Postmodernism in Postmodernism and Society, Boyne, Roy (ed). New York, St Martin's Pr, 1990.

Boynton, David M. Relativism in Gibson's Theory of Picture Perception. *J Mind Behav*, 14(1), 51-69, Wint 93.

J J Gibson's ecological approach to depiction is compared with Nelson Goodman's relativist theory of representation. Goodman's commitment to radical relativism and Gibson's to direct realism would make these thinkers unlikely candidates for comparison if Goodman himself has not indicated a substantial body of agreement with Gibson in the area of picture perception. The present study analyzes this agreement through systematic discussion of the following theses: realism in representation is not a function of geometrical optics, physical similarity to what is depicted, or deception; pictures differ in density and articulation from words, so that picturing has no explicit vocabulary; and artists can teach us new ways to see the world. The agreement between Goodman and Gibson has wide-ranging implications for the further development of what might be called a Gibsonian relativism.

Brabant, Margaret (ed). *Politics, Gender, and Genre: The Political Thought of Christine de Pizan*. Boulder, Westview Pr, 1992.

This international collection of essays breaks new ground in Christine de Pizan scholarship as well as in the fields of political and feminist theory. The essays offer balanced interpretations of Christine's influence upon Western thought. Several essays challenge our historical understanding of the term "feminism" and encourage scholars and students to search the fifteenth, rather than the nineteenth century, for the roots of feminism. This book provides a focused and thorough analysis of the Christine's literary talents and contributions to the development of late medieval political theory.

Bracken, Joseph A. Creativity and the Extensive Continuum as the Ultimate Ground in Alfred North Whitehead's Philosophy of Becoming. *Ultim Real Mean*, 16(1-2), 110-119, Mr-Je 93.

Creativity is the metaphysical ultimate for A N Whitehead in *Process and Reality*. Yet Creativity does not exist in itself but only in and through actual entities. Accordingly, God is "the aboriginal instance" of creativity and "the aboriginal condition" of its action. Linked with another Whiteheadian category, the extensive continuum, creativity constitutes the underlying nature of the triune God which is at the same time the ground of being for all finite actual entities. Together, they constitute a "force-field" out of which the three divine persons and all creatures continuously emerge as members of an all-embracing cosmic society.

Bradie, Michael. Ethics and Evolution: The Biological Basis of Morality. *Inquiry*, 36(1-2), 199-217, Mr 93.

In his recent book, *The Biology of Moral Systems*, R D Alexander seeks to carefully circumscribe what biology can and cannot tell us about the nature of morality. Alexander's fundamental thesis is that whereas philosophical analyses of morality recognize, in general, that moral and ethical issues arise out of conflicts of interest, such analyses fail to clarify the true nature of human interests. Considerations from evolutionary biology, Alexander argues, show that these interests are ultimately reproductive. Nevertheless, Alexander is no crude reductionist. I sketch his position and make some critical remarks about its scope and limits.

Bradley, J A. Whitehead, Heidegger, and the Paradoxes of the New. *Process Stud*, 20(3), 127-150, Fall 91.

Bradley, James. La cosmologie transcendantale de Whitehead: transformation spéculative du concept de construction logique. *Arch Phil*, 56(1), 3-28, Ja-Mr 93.

Whitehead is unusual among modern theorists of event or difference in maintaining the possibility of a categorial and analogical analysis of becoming in the rationalist manner. However, this does not make him the metaphysical realist he is often thought to be. By means of a redefinition of his own early concept of "logical construction," he transforms the nature and status of the traditional apparatus of metaphysical analysis, combining pre- and post-Kantian thought in a unique way.

Bradley, James. Relations, intelligibilité et non-contradiction dans la métaphysique du sentir de F H Bradley: une réinterprétation (II). *Arch Phil*, 55(1), 77-91, Ja-Mr 92.

Bradshaw, D E. On the Need for a Metaphysics of Justification. *Metaphilosophy*, 23(1-2), 90-106, Ja-Ap 92.

While Bergmann's claim that epistemology is 'but the ontology of the knowing situation' might be too strong, some epistemologists have gone to the other extreme, shunning metaphysics altogether. First, I defend the claim that, without some metaphysical elucidation, BonJour's coherentist account of empirical justification (and any internalist account sufficiently like it) is unacceptable. I then consider whether such metaphysical theorizing in epistemology is not seriously at odds with the historical tradition and clarify why metaphysics is especially important for an internalist account. Finally, I sketch a metaphysics of justification of the sort required for a fully articulated internalist coherentist account.

Bradshaw, Leah. Tyranny: Ancient and Modern. *Interpretation*, 20(2), 187-203, Wint 92-93.

Bradstock, Andrew. A Christian Contribution to Revolutionary Praxis? in Socialism and Morality, McLellan, David (ed). New York, St Martin's Pr, 1990.

Brady, Bernard V. An Analysis of the Use of Rights Language in Pre-Modern Catholic Social Thought. *Thomist*, 57(1), 97-121, Ja 93.

The purpose of this essay is to trace the roots of the use of rights language in Catholic social thought. From Aquinas to Suarez, rights language in Catholic thought most often follows the paradigm: The object of justice is right, and rights specify certain conditions of justice based on one's "holdings." Rights are not independent moral claims to do things; they are rather specific claims based on one's social position. I argue that Vitoria pioneered what has become an organizing theme in contemporary Catholic social thought; namely, he used rights language, specifically human rights, to defend the powerless in the face of injustice caused by the powerful.

Brady, Michael Emmett. J M Keynes's Theoretical Approach to Decision-Making Under Conditions of Risk and Uncertainty. *Brit J Phil Sci*, 44(2), 357-376, Je 93.

The paper demonstrates how Keynes' interval estimate approach to probability, combined with his c coefficient, can help resolve the paradoxes and anomalies of modern subjective expected utility theory. It is also established that Keynes' analysis of expectations, risk and uncertainty in his *General Theory* was built on the logical and mathematical analysis of the *Treatise on Probability*.

Brady, Ross T. Hierarchical Semantics for Relevant Logics. *J Phil Log*, 21(4), 357-374, N 92.

I convert depth relevance considerations, introduced in an earlier paper, into a semantical form, which I call hierarchical semantics. The levels of the hierarchy are essentially cumulative degrees so that only formulae of degree less than or equal to i are evaluated at level i. Depth considerations do feature in the evaluation of a subformula of a given formula in that the level of such a valuation must be greater than or equal to the degree of the formula minus the depth of the subformula in it.

Brague, R. Critique de l'*anamnésis*. *Rev Phil Fr*, 4, 621-625, O-D 91.

Brahami, Frédéric. Sympathie et individualité dans la philosophie politique de David Hume. *Rev Phil Fr*, 2, 201-227, Ap-Je 92.

Braidotti, Rosi. Discontinuing Becomings: Deleuze on the Becoming-Woman of Philosophy. *J Brit Soc Phenomenol*, 24(1), 44-55, Ja 93.

This article analyzes Gilles Deleuze's notion of 'becoming', especially of 'becoming-woman', in the framework of feminist concerns about female subjectivity. Special reference is made to the theory of an alternative female feminist subject, developed by Luce Irigaray. The article outlines a pattern of paradoxical avoidance of the issue of sexual difference in Deleuze's work: the recognition of the primordial importance of this issue alternates with its dismissal, in the name of a sexually undifferentiated 'becoming-minority'. Using the example of reproductive technologies, it is concluded that feminists stand in a dissymetrical relationship to the postmodern decline of gender-dualism, which Deleuze advocates.

Braidotti, Rosi. Embodiment, Sexual Difference, and the Nomadic Subject. *Hypatia*, 8(1), 1-13, Wint 93.

This article deals with sexual difference as a philosophy of subjectivity which, however inspired by postructuralism, was further developed by feminists. The main features of this philosophy are outlined both in terms of its style and of its vision of woman as subject. The notion of 'difference' is analyzed in details, as the central concept that sustains the feminist nomadic philosophy of a subject that is both complex and situated, politically empowered and epistemologically legitimate.

Braidotti, Rosi. On the Female Feminist Subject, or: from 'She-Self' to 'She-Other' in Beyond Equality and Difference, Bock, Gisela (ed). New York, Routledge, 1992.

In this article, the central question is: have feminist critiques of theoretical reason as a regulative principle resulted in approaching the notion of sexual difference as laying the foundations for an alternative model of female subjectivity. Thus defined, the problem of feminist theory also implies the questioning of the notion of equality, one of the pillars of Enlightenment thinking. In my understanding, the feminist is a critical thinker, unveiling the modalities of power and domination implicit in all theoretical discourse, including her own.

Braidotti, Rosi. Patterns of Dissonance: Women and/In Philosophy. *Filozof Cas*, 40(5), 839-850, 1992.

This article presents a feminist analysis of contemporary French post-structuralist readings of the "death of the author" and the crisis of the rational subject of philosophy. Special emphasis is placed on the work of Foucault, Derrida and Deleuze. (edited)

Brainard, Marcus (trans) and Fleischhacker, Louk. On the Mathematization of Life. *Grad Fac Phil J*, 16(1), 245-258, 1993.

The article aims at showing the philosophical backgrounds of mathematical models of the processes of organic life. It is pointed out that various claims at reconstructability and simulability of such processes necessarily have metaphysical presupposition of a Cartesian nature. On the other hand, the holistic approach of investigators such as R Sheldrake is shown to be based on essentially the same presuppositions. Finally, a philosophical conception of life is indicated, which enables us to investigate the phenomenon of life without explaining it away altogether.

Brainard, Marcus (trans) and Várdy, Péter. Technology in the Age of Automata. *Grad Fac Phil J*, 16(1), 209-226, 1993.

The paper investigates: 1) the tendency of technical development, illustrated by the history of the lathe from a tool in Egyptian antiquity to the CNC automation; 2) the metaphysical foundations and the philosophical significance of automation.

Braine, David. *The Human Person: Animal and Spirit*. Notre Dame, Univ Notre Dame Pr, 1992.

The book re-establishes a holistic view of human beings as animals, drawing on insights of Aristotle, Aquinas, Ryle, Wittgenstein, and Merleau-Ponty. Carefully analysing features like perception, emotion and action from desire, shared with animals, it demonstrates that understanding these features mechanistically in terms of brain-body relation involves all the mistakes of Descartes' dualism—thereby refuting in detail the materialism of most contemporary analytical philosophers. It then proceeds to examine the nature of language, from this to give a second refutation of mechanism, and finally to show how human beings, still animals, transcend the body in their thought and existence.

Braithwaite, Susan S. The Courtship of the Paying Patient. *J Clin Ethics*, 4(2), 124-133, Sum 93.

This article argues for a prohibition on the courtship of the paying patient by individual practitioners, groups, institutions, and corporations. Our society fails to provide universal access to health care. The author, however, writing from the point of view of the physician, has analyzed the question in terms of a conflict between the economic interest of the physician and the trustworthiness of the profession. The courtship of the paying patient represents a failure of the professional virtues of truthfulness, loyalty, and respect for persons.

Brandao, Jacynthos Lins. Doentes, Doença, Médicos e Medicina em Luciano de Samósata. *Cad Hist Filosof Cie*, 2(2), 145-164, Jl-D 90.

This paper attempts to describe and interpret the medical allusions in Lucian of Samosata's works. In this way my aim is to analyse some aspects of Lucian's attitude towards ill people, disease, physicians and Medicine, focusing on 1) the relation between Medicine and magic, 2) the disease's connections with social class, and 3) the physician's status in hellenistic society.

Brandl, Johannes. Skepsis in der Sprachphilosophie. *Conceptus*, 25(66), 111-120, 1991.

This paper critically reviews some recent attempts at saving the concept of meaning from sceptical arguments. Most of these contributions rely on a reading of Wittgenstein that runs contrary to Kripke's interpretation. It is argued that, whatever the correct reading of Wittgenstein may be, meaning scepticism is a serious challenge to the idea that what we mean by using words is strictly determined by facts that are recognizable for us, e.g., by Cartesian facts about our inner states. Accepting an underdetermination of meaning, as Quine suggests, is more reasonable than reverting to facts that are unrecognizable for the language user.

Brandl, Johannes. Some Remarks on the 'Slingshot' Argument in Advances in Scientific Philosophy, Schurz, Gerhard (ed). Amsterdam, Rodopi, 1991.

The paper first reviews the history of the argument that Barwise and Perry have called 'The Slingshot'. The argument is then connected with the problem of individuating facts as the correlates of sentences. It is proposed that fact-bundles, not individual facts, should be taken as truth-makers also for atomic sentences. This leaves the Slingshot Argument untouched, but blocks its application against an ontology of facts.

Brandom, Robert. Heidegger's Categories in *Being and Time* in Heidegger: A Critical Reader, Dreyfus, Hubert L (ed). Cambridge, Blackwell, 1992.

This essay offers an interpretation of three of Heidegger's conceptual innovations: his conceiving of ontology in terms of self-adjudicating anthropological categories, as summed up in the slogan that "fundamental ontology is the regional ontology of Dasein," his corresponding anti-traditional assertion of the ontological priority of the category of readiness-to-hand to that of presence-at-hand (and hence of objectivity as just one category or kind of social significance), and the non-Cartesian account of awareness and classificatory consciousness in terms of social practices.

Brandom, Robert. The Social Anatomy of Inference. *Phil Phenomenol Res*, 53(3), 661-666, S 93.

In response to Fodor and Lepore's arguments against holism, it is argued that there are good reasons to demarcate specifically *conceptual* contentfulness by its *inferential* articulation. If that is right, possession of such content must be 'anatomic' in their sense. It is claimed further that conceiving conceptual contents in terms of inferential roles does not by itself commit one to a 'two-factor' approach, in which truth and reference are added on as independent elements. Nor does such an approach preclude meaningful talk of shared conceptual contents.

Brandon, Robert N. A Simple Theory of Evolution By Natural Selection. *Phil Sci*, 59(2), 276-281, Je 92.

Kary (1990) defends the view that evolution by natural selection can be adequately explained in terms of a theory incorporating only a single level of selection. Here I point out some of the inherent inadequacies of such a theory.

Brandt, Per Aage. *La Charpente Modale du Sens*. Amsterdam, J Benjamins, 1992.

This book contains the main part of the author's Thése d'Etat defended in 1987 at the Sorbonne. It introduces Catastrophe Theory in Greimas' theory of modality and modal meaning in narrative patterns. It then transcribes Greimas' theory as a whole in terms of a dynamic semiotics. Deep Semiotics is presented as modal structure underlying narrativity, discursive investment, and enunciation. Temporal, aspectual, quantificational, and logical schemata are reformulated in dynamic terms. The result is a semio-linguistic model of meaning, relevant to cognitive as well as to cultural studies. A central concern is for modal patterns in interaction.

Brandt, Per Aage. Remarks on M H Bickhard and R L Campbell, 'Some Fundational Questions Concerning Language Studies'. *J Prag*, 17(5-6), 435-440, Je 92.

The title of this paper—the Sources of Meaning—stresses the problem: interpretation leads to a circular thinking, if meaning is not founded. A principle for this is the dynamic structure of modality (cf my Thesis: La Charpente modale du sens, Amsterdam/Philadelphia 1992, J Benjamins). Two sources are then detected: perception and interaction, both modally structured, and therefore cognition and pragmatics must cooperate. Finally, I propose three levels of organization: psychological, sociological, and informational,—corresponding to verbal semantics. But I stress that meaning composition operates transversally, both bottom-up and top-down.

Brandt, Stephan and Stoerig, Petra. The Visual System and Levels of Perception: Properties of Neuromental Organization. *Theor Med*, 14(2), 117-135, Je 93.

To see whether the mental and the neural have common attributes that could resolve some of the traditional dichotomies, we review neuroscientific data on the visual system. The results show that neuronal and perceptual function share a parallel and hierarchial architecture which is manifest not only in the anatomy and physiology of the visual system, but also in normal perception and in the deficits caused by lesions in different parts of the system. Based on the description of parallel hierarchical levels of active information processing in the visual brain, we suggest a concept of dissociable levels of perception, advocating that the phenomenal perception and recognition is realized in the functional integrity of a network of reciprocal cortico-cortical connections. The properties shared by neuronal and perceptional functions provide a basis for a neuromental monism in which both functions are attributed a causal role.

Brandwood, Leonard. Stylometry and Chronology in The Cambridge Companion to Plato, Kraut, Richard H (ed). New York, Cambridge Univ Pr, 1992.

Branigan, Edward. Sound and Epistemology in Film. *J Aes Art Crit*, 47(4), 311-324, Fall 89.

Brann, Eva T H. What is Postmodernism?. *Harvard Rev Phil*, 2(1), 4-8, Spr 92.

The purpose of the article is to distinguish between postmodernism as a general mode and postmodernism as a current movement. The means is an analysis of the term itself, and the conclusion is that one should resist any movement presented as an irresistible historical necessity.

Brannigan, Michael. Reversibility as a Radical Ground for an Ontology of the Body in Medicine. *Personalist Forum*, 8/1(Supp), 219-224, Spr 92.

Branson, Herman. Africa, African-Americans, and the Origin of a Universal Ethic in African-American Perspectives on Biomedical Ethics, Flack, Harley E (ed). Washington, Georgetown Univ Pr, 1992.

Bratman, Michael. Shared Cooperative Activity. *Phil Rev*, 101(2), 327-341, Ap 92.

You and I might sing a duet together, or build something together. In many such cases ours will be a shared cooperative activity. This essay focuses on shared cooperative activities that involve only a pair of participating agents and are not the activities of complex institutions with structures of authority. Concerning such cases this essay emphasizes an important kind of interdependence of intention. It is argued that shared cooperative activity involves mutual responsiveness—of intention and in action—in the service of appropriately stable, inter-locking, reflexive and mutually non-coerced intentions in favor of the joint activity.

Braun, Carlos Rodriguez and Schwartz, Pedro. Bentham on Spanish Protectionism. *Utilitas*, 4(1), 121-132, My 92.

Braybrooke, David. Two Conceptions of Needs in Marx's Writings in On the Track of Reason, Beehler, Rodger G (ed). Boulder, Westview Pr, 1992.

Marx makes abundant use of two senses of "needs": one generalizes the term to cover any desire for goods and services; the other restricts the term to means of subsistence. Desire needs expand under capitalism in ways distorted by commercialization; they will expand under socialism, too, but in ways more fulfilling and less conflicting. The reduction of conflict presupposes assured consistent provision that capitalism cannot give for needs in the restrictive sense; and the ineluctability of the restrictive sense will extend to more things under socialism, for example, to labor's becoming "the prime necessity of life."

Brearley, Michael. Psychoanalysis: A Form of Life? in Wittgenstein Centenary Essays, Griffiths, A Phillips (ed). New York, Cambridge Univ Pr, 1991.

Brecher, Bob. Why Patronize Feminists? A Reply to Stove on Mill. *Philosophy*, 68(265), 397-400, Jl 93.

David Stove criticizes J S Mill's Feminism ("The Subjection of J S Mill", *Philosophy* 68, January 1993) on the grounds that he was mistaken in arguing that, although women's nature was presently unknown, nevertheless the oppression of women was unnatural: but Stove is himself mistaken, since a modicum of negative knowledge suffices the argument to go through. More importantly, as Mill himself recognized in 'On Nature', "naturalness" or otherwise is not the point — which, contra Stove's insistence that 'all feminists... remain convinced... that women's subjection is unnatural', is precisely what many feminist argue. A number of Stove's more minor points against Mill Subjection are also rebutted.

Breckman, Warren. Ludwig Feuerbach and the Political Theology of Restoration. *Hist Polit Thought*, 13(3), 437-462, Autumn 92.

Bredin, Hugh. Metaphorical Thought. *Brit J Aes*, 32(2), 97-109, Ap 92.

Metaphorical thought consists in a state of mind in which two types of thing are assimilated, rather than likened, to one another. Thus, "man is a wolf" can be paraphrased as "man is a man-as-wolf". From this we can deduce three logical characteristics of metaphor: first, that the alteration of meaning in an expression used metaphorically is extensional; second, that metaphorical expressions are asymmetrical; third, that metaphors are descriptions rather than names. We can also deduce a classification of metaphors into surface and deep metaphors, with a further subdivision of the latter into deep subject and deep predicate metaphors.

Breeur, R. Mementos, Death and Nostalgia (in Dutch). *Tijdschr Filosof*, 55(2), 217-240, Je 93.

Our memory has an obvious cognitive value: it provides us with information about our past. But memory also has another role: what we remember is in some cases not only information about the past, but also evocation. The interpretation I give here of this phenomenon heavily relies on Roland Barthes' notion of 'punctum' in *Camera Lucidea* and also remarks make by Proust on memory and death. The evocative power in virtue of which some past event is vividly present to our minds also makes us aware of an irremediable loss and of the unavoidability of forgetting: we remember that we forget. This experience can, as is shown by Proust, reconcile us with our own finitude.

Breitwieser, Mitchell. Early American Antigone in Theorizing American Literature, Cowan, Bainard (ed). Baton Rouge, Louisiana St Univ Pr, 1991.

Brendle, Jörg and Judah, H and Shelah, S. Combinatorial Properties of Hechler Forcing. *Annals Pure Applied Log*, 58(3), 185-199, N 92.

Using a notion of rank, we investigate combinatorial properties of Hechler forcing—this is a ccc forcing notion adding a dominating real. In particular, we study the effect of adding a Hechler real on the cardinal invariants in Cichón's diagram—these are cardinals related to the ideals of meager and measure zero (null) sets.

Brenkert, George G. Can We Afford International Human Rights?. *J Bus Ethics*, 11(7), 515-521, Jl 92.

In *The Ethics of International Business*, Tom Donaldson argues that multinational corporations (as well as individuals and nation-states) must, at a minimum, respect international human rights. For a purported right to be such a fundamental right it must satisfy three conditions. Donaldson calls the third condition the "fairness-affordability" condition. The affordability part of this condition holds that moral agents must be capable of paying for the burdens and responsibilities that a proposed human right would impose. If this is impossible, then the purported right is not an international human right. I argue that Donaldson's affordability condition is subject to four objections which reveal its untenability as one of the conditions upon which identification of international human rights must rest. I offer another way of treating problems of affordability and capability when it comes to such rights that all moral agents must respect.

Brenkert, George G. Private Corporations and Public Welfare. *Pub Affairs Quart*, 6(2), 155-168, Ap 92.

Private corporations are often said to have a responsibility to aid those deficient in public welfare. Though objections have been raised against this claim from the side of the private corporation, this paper explores the objection that corporations illegitimately encroach upon the public domain when they undertake to do so. Four arguments are presented that private corporate provision of public welfare runs afoul of various conditions, standards, and characteristics crucial to the public realm.

Brennan, Geoffrey and Pettit, Philip. Hands Invisible and Intangible. *Synthese*, 94(2), 191-225, F 93.

Under an invisible hand regime, people intentionally perform actions that have a certain unforseen aggregate effect. Under what we describe as an intangible hand regime, they nonintentionally form attitudes—attitudes, generically, of approval or disapproval of certain forms of behaviour—that have a similar unforseen aggregate effect. We describe the two forms of ordering mechanism and we explore the interesting differences between them.

Brennan, Susan K. Ross, Promises and the Intrinsic Value of Acts. *Lyceum*, 1(2), 43-56, Fall 89.

W D Ross's deontological theory of *prima facie* duties appears to be an attractive alternative to utilitarianism, but on some plausible interpretations of Ross's view, the theory does not mandate any different actions than would a sophisticated version of ideal act-utilitarianism. If the act of keeping a promise has intrinsic value in itself, there may be an explanation of why it is usually right to keep promises even if utilitarianism is correct. I argue that Ross's deontological view has no advantage over a version of ideal act-utilitarianism which recognizes the intrinsic value of some actions.

Brennan, Teresa. *The Interpretation of the Flesh: Freud and Femininity*. New York, Routledge, 1992.

Brennan, Timothy J. The Futility of Multiple Utility. *Econ Phil*, 9(1), 155-164, Ap 93.

"Multiple utility" (MU) choice models offer few if any advantages over economics' "single utility" (SU) framework. SU models are no more malleable than MU variants. Psychological tension accompanying choice may reflect opportunity cost rather than inability to compare. Paradoxical preferences for fewer options could reflect costs of choosing or of avoiding error. Arguments that SU ignores weakness of will or into disequilibria, preference change, or nonpecuniary objectives. MU advocates may divert critical attention away from more important shortcomings of failures of economics.

Brenner, Anastasios. Duhem face au post-positivisme. *Rev Int Phil*, 46(182), 390-404, 1992.

The endeavor to develop a historical philosophy of science is a central problem in Duhem; it is also a major issue in current postpositivism. A comparison between the French philosopher and contemporary authors, such as Laudan and his collaborators, shows that Duhem's influence goes far beyond what Anglo-American philosophers have been willing to admit; yet his strictures on the relativist tendencies of the pragmatism of his day lead him to a conception of scientific growth totally opposed to that proposed by most theorists today, thus providing us with a critical standpoint from which to evaluate current claims.

Brenner, William H. Logic in Reflections on Philosophy, McHenry, Leemon (ed). New York, St Martin's Pr, 1993.

Brent, Joseph. *Charles Sanders Peirce: A Life*. Bloomington, Indiana Univ Pr, 1992.

Bres, Yvon. Platon et la "ΔeinothΣ" Tragique. *Rev Phil Fr*, 4, 435-462, O-D 91.

Bressan, Aldo. On Gupta's Book *The Logic of Common Nouns*. *J Phil Log*, 22(4), 335-383, Ag 93.

Breton, Stanislas. Sophistique et ontologie. *Rev Phil Louvain*, 90(87), 279-296, Ag 92.

Book *Gamma* of Aristotle's *Metaphysics* is still the basic text which any serious thought on ontology takes and must take into consideration. B Cassin and M Narcy's book entitled *La décision du sens* offers an outstanding opportunity to return to this fundamental work. Now in Book *Gamma* it is above all else a matter of "wanting to say something." That is the decision required by Aristotle of any man who wishes to be a man. This decision, which the Sophist must make his own, if he agrees to speak, is thus that which brought about the existence of ontology.

Brewer, Bill. Unilateral Neglect and the Objectivity of Spatial Representation. *Mind Lang*, 7(3), 222-239, Autumn 92.

"Unilateral Neglect" is the name given to a cluster of spatially constrained deficits of certain brain damaged patients, who are, in some sense, unaware of, or seem to ignore, things to their left, or the left sides of things around them. I argue that neither

Bridges, David 424 **AUTHOR INDEX WITH ABSTRACTS**

of the two standard interpretations of Unilateral Neglect, as a spatial bias in attention or as a systematic, non-attentional disorder in the processing of representations, is capable on its own of explaining all the data whilst remaining faithful to the central role of normal spatial perception in a person's thought about himself as one thing among many in an objective world.

Bridges, David. Enterprise and Liberal Education. *J Phil Educ*, 26(1), 91-98, 1992.

Recent initiatives from the Employment Department in the UK have promoted 'enterprise education'. This paper discusses the relationship of enterprise education to the more established notion of a liberal education. It is argued that enterprise education should be understood not as replacing the aspirations of a liberal education, but rather as supporting or extending them. It does this (i) by helping pupils to understand what is arguably a significant form of life; (ii) by developing understanding of the economic conditions of our social functioning; and (iii) by developing personal qualities which equip us practically to pursue our chosen paths in a competitive and sometimes hostile world.

Brigham, Linda C. Frail Memorials: "Essays Upon Epitaphs" and Wordsworth's Economy of Reference. *Phil Lit*, 16(1), 15-31, Ap 92.

Bril, K A. De opkomst en de ontwikkeling van het evolutionisme en de probleemhistorische methode van Vollenhoven. *Phil Reform*, 58(1), 28-48, Ja 93.

This study of the rise of evolutionism makes use of the problem-historical method of D H T Vollenhoven (1892-1978). This method distinguishes between types and currents. Types are traditions of thought, and are similar to metaphysical paradigms; currents are historical periods, and are similar to episteme's. Types are related to views concerning the structure of man and world (dualisms, monisms, etc.), while currents pertain to changing views of normativity. Darwin was the first to bring about a transformation from idealism to positivism (currents) within a biologistic tradition of thought (type). Others followed, such as Haeckel, in other types.

Brink, David O. A Puzzle About the Rational Authority of Morality in Philosophical Perspectives, 6: Ethics, 1992, Tomberlin, James E (ed). Atascadero, Ridgeview, 1992.

The paper examines the rational authority of morality in terms of four claims that can seem individually plausible but are incompatible. I. Moral requirements— including other regarding obligations— apply to agents independently of their aims or interests; II. Moral requirements provide agents with reasons for action; III. Reasons for action are dependent on the aims or interests of the agent who has them; IV. There is no necessary connection between other-regarding action and any aim or interest of the agent. The paper represents familiar positions as solutions to this puzzle and discusses their resources, limitations, and interrelations.

Brink, David O. Sidgwick and the Rationale for Rational Egoism in Essays on Henry Sidgwick, Schultz, Bart (ed). New York, Cambridge Univ Pr, 1992.

Rational egoism treats intertemporal and interpersonal distribution asymmetrically; it is temporally-neutral, but agent-relative. This asymmetrical character may seem arbitrary. If so, fully neutral and fully relative rivals may seem more plausible. Sidgwick finds a rationale for egoism's asymmetrical character in the separateness of persons. The paper explains this rationale and argues, against Parfit, that this rationale is metaphysically robust, in particular, that it is entirely compatible with so-called reductionist accounts of personal identity.

Brink, T L. Belief vs Commitment, Validity vs Value: A Response to Ward Goodenough. *Zygon*, 28(2), 283-286, Je 93.

This paper is on Ward Goodenough's recent article (27:3), suggesting that his points can be clarified by reiterating the distinction between the realms of meaning and relevance. Religion's "truth" is in the form of its *value*; the "proof" which it requires is *vindication*; and the resulting "faith" must be understood as *commitment*.

Brion, Denis J. The Chaotic Law of Tort in Peirce and Law, Kevelson, Roberta. New York, Lang, 1991.

Two polar concepts of the common law process are prominent in legal discourse. One holds that common law doctrine is chaotic in that it is the needs of the power holders in society rather than legal doctrines that determine the outcomes to disputes. The other holds that doctrine properly converges toward a coherent rational structure. The reality of the law of tort is somewhere in between—the pattern of judicial outcomes strongly resembles the patterns described by Chaos Theory: particular dispute outcomes abductively determine particular doctrines, which tend to cluster in patterns similar to the Strange Attractors of Chaos Theory.

Briscoe, Felecia. Visions and Voices. *Phil Stud Educ*, 1, 90-103, 1991.

Brison, Susan J. Surviving Sexual Violence. *J Soc Phil*, 24(1), 5-22, Spr 93.

This article focuses on sexual assault from the point of view of a philosopher who survived a near-fatal attack. Philosophical issues raised by sexual violence, which have been largely ignored by the discipline, are examined. These include the nature and extent of the harm to the victim, the effects of trauma on personal identity, the incompatibility of fear and anger (directed against an assailant), the functions of denial and victim-blaming in maintaining the observer's world view, and the implications of sexual assault for gender equality.

Brisson, Luc. Participation et prédication chez Platon. *Rev Phil Fr*, 4, 557-569, O-D 91.

Brito, Emilio. Deux théries de l'esprit: Hegel et Schleiermacher. *Rev Phil Louvain*, 91(89), 31-65, F 93.

The present article compares, on the one hand, Hegel's philosophy of Subjective Spirit and Objective Spirit to the psychology and ethics of Schleiermacher, and on the other hand Hegel's philosophy of Absolute Spirit to Schleiermacher's conception of art, religion, and dialectic. Both authors seek to express the totality of human activity as the self-manifestation of Spirit. However, instead of arranging the different spiritual domains hierarchically as different moments in a teleological process which overcomes their limits, culminating in one supreme negative identity, as does the Hegelian system, Schleiermacher's system, without either base or final summit, grasps these spiritual domains as a constellation of spheres possessing the same magnitude; respecting equally the formation of subjectivity in its particularity, as well as the autonomous consistency of the diverse ethical institutions.

Brito, Emilio. La "Dialectique" de Schleiermacher. *Dialogue (Canada)*, 32(1), 41-58, Wint 93.

La *Dialectique* de Schleiermacher partage avec les grands systems idéalistes le souci de supprimer la séparation de la logique et de la métaphysique. Héritière de la philosophie chrétienne et attentive à la limite de toute autoanalyse monologique de la raison, elle renonce cependant au "point de vue" absolu et se borne à répérer les présuppositions et les règles du savoir réel. Toutefois, sa façon d'articuler la corrélation de Dieu et du monde n'est pas exempte d'une certaine orientation panthéistique.

Brito, Emilio. La "dialectique" de Schleiermacher et l'absolu schellingien. *Riv Filosof Neo-Scolas*, 84(1), 61-87, Ja-Mr 92.

Bien qu'elle exhibe l'influence du système schellingien de l'identité, aussi bien au niveau du vocabulaire que de la conception systématique, la dialectique de Schleiermacher s'en distingue si nettement—notamment dans la façon de concevoir le rapport de Dieu et du monde, et l'articulation de la philosophie et de la religion—qu'on doit la considérer comme une théorie indépendante, plutôt que comme un simple éclectisme.

Brito, Emilio. La compréhension chrétienne de Dieu comme amour et sagesse selon Schleiermacher. *Laval Theol Phil*, 48(3), 315-342, O 92.

Bien qu'il s'éloigne de Hegel par son incapacité de penser l'autocommunication comme évéement en Dieu lui-même, d'admettre que l'amour désigne l'essence divine comme Dieu-pour-Dieu, Schleiermacher s'en rapproche par sa façon de subordonner la sagesse de Dieu à son amour, en d'autres mots l'élément historique à la communiation intime: chez les deux auteurs, le *Deus pro nobis* tend à se réduire à un simple présupposé du *Deus in nobis*. Enfin, quoique Schleiermacher identifie la sagesse divine avec l'Esprit, et non pas, à l'instar de Hegel, avec le Logos, on constate, dans la manière dont l'un et l'autre relient la sagesse divine et le gouvernement providentiel du monde, une semblable méconnaissance de la contingence du monde.

Brittan, Samuel. Choice and Utility in The Utilitarian Response, Allison, Lincoln (ed). Newbury Park, Sage, 1990.

Broackes, Justin. Jonathan Westphal's *Colour*. *Phil Quart*, 43(171), 233-238, Ap 93.

Broadie, Sarah. Aristotle's Perceptual Realism. *S J Phil*, 31(Supp), 137-159, 1992.

Brock, Dan W. A Proposal for the Use of Advance Directives in the Treatment of Incompetent Mentally Ill Persons. *Bioethics*, 7(2-3), 247-256, Ap 93.

Brock, Dan W. *Life and Death: Philosophical Essays in Biomedical Ethics*. New York, Cambridge Univ Pr, 1993.

Brock, Dan W. Quality of Life Measures in Health Care and Medical Ethics in The Quality of Life, Nussbaum, Martha C (ed). New York, Oxford Univ Pr, 1993.

Brock, Dan W. Voluntary Active Euthanasia. *Hastings Center Rep*, 22(2), 10-22, My-Je 92.

Brock, Dan W. What is the Moral Basis of the Authority of Family Members to Act as Surrogates for Incompetent Patients?. *J Clin Ethics*, 3(2), 121-123, Sum 92.

Brock, Stuart. Modal Fictionalism: A Response to Rosen. *Mind*, 102(405), 147-150, Ja 93.

Gideon Rosen, in his paper 'Modal Fictionalism' (*Mind*, 1990) puts forward and defends what is intended to be an ontologically neutral alternative to modal realism. I argue that Rosen does not achieve this goal. His fictionalism entails realism about possible worlds. Moreover, any attempts to modify the analysis results in an undesirable multiplication of the modal primitives, a problem faced by those who take the standard modal operators as primitive.

Brockway, George. Limited Paternalism and the Salesperson: A Reconsideration. *J Bus Ethics*, 12(4), 275-80, Ap 93.

Given that a salesperson has *some obligation* to keep their customer from suffering harm in their transactions, this article attempts to establish the grounds for such an obligation. It concludes that the most defensible—and fruitful—grounds lie in seeing the salesperson-client relationship as fundamentally one of dependency and trust, and one freely entered into. Such a perspective not only helps explain where and how the basic obligation arises but also what the salesperson is *not* obligated to in the sales encounter.

Brod, Harry. Pornography and the Alienation of Male Sexuality in Rethinking Masculinity, May, Larry (ed). Lanham, Rowman & Littlefield, 1992.

This paper examines relations between pornography and male sexuality, using feminist and Marxist theory. Just as capitalists are alienated under capitalism, so men are alienated under patriarchy. Relevant parallels include objectification of the body, denial of human needs, abstract possessiveness, and thwarting of desired reciprocity in relationships. The paper takes issue with Soble's *Pornography* to argue that pornography shows men's lack of personal power but their domination of public power. Pornography is imperialism of the body, and anti-pornography activism is consumer activism for product safety.

Brodribb, Somer. Critical Response to "Machiavelli's Sisters" by Linda Zerilli. *Polit Theory*, 20(2), 332-336, My 92.

Brodsky, G M. West's Evasion of Pragmatism. *Praxis Int*, 13(1), 14-31, Ap 93.

Brody, Baruch A. Hardwig on Proxy Decision Making. *J Clin Ethics*, 4(1), 66-67, Spr 93.

Hardwig has argued that proxy decision makers should not apply the substituted judgment standard because an exclusively patient-centred ethic must be abandoned. I accept his premise and generalize it, but I argue that his conclusion does not follow. Proxy decision makers must continue to speak for the patient while other decision makers must represent interests that are not patient-centred.

Brody, Howard. Causing, Intending, and Assisting Death. *J Clin Ethics*, 4(2), 112-117, Sum 93.

Brogan, Walter. Heidegger and Aristotle in Crises in Continental Philosophy, Dallery, Arleen B (ed). Albany, SUNY Pr, 1990.

This article attempts to show through an interpretation of the phronesis-praxis structure in the *Nicomachean Ethics* that praxis for Aristotle means that way in which the human being factually chooses to be for its own sake. This apparent retreat form everyday practical involvements back into a concern for one's own being is neither for Aristotle no for Heidegger a form of solipsism, but the only basis for human community and for a genuine relationship to nonhuman beings. Aristotle's treatment of justice, courage and the mean are examined in terms of this understanding of phronesis and praxis.

Brooke-Rose, Christine. Palimpsest History in Interpretation and Over-interpretation: Umberto Eco, Collini, Stefan (ed). New York, Cambridge Univ Pr, 1992.

Brooks, D H M. Secondary Qualities and Representation. *Analysis*, 52(3), 174-179, Jl 92.

Secondary qualities have peculiarities which are thought to threaten physicalism. It is argued that these peculiarities are only to be expected in a physicalist universe in virtue of the essential characteristics of a representing device. Any device representing the world such as a camera will have depictional qualities. Secondary qualities are a subset of these.

Brooks, David. Why This World?. *Phil Papers*, 21(3), 259-273, N 92.

Three different philosophical questions: Why should this world exist? Why should there be something rather than nothing (and the problem of induction turn out to be at bottom the same)? Why should one possible world rather than another be actual? The problem seems insoluble; it seems only too possible that another world might exist. Attempts to solve the problem seem to be question-begging. However, it may be solvable *a posteriori* if this is the only naturally possible world. The relevant notion of natural possibility is intermediate between logical and physical necessity.

Broome, Jeff. On the Authorship of the *Abstract*: A Reply to John O Nelson. *Hume Stud*, 18(1), 95-103, Ap 92.

Until the discovery, in this century, of a copy of *An Abstract of a Treatise of Human Nature*, it had been commonly assumed that Adam Smith had been the author of the *Abstract*. But in the introduction accompanying its publication in 1938, it was forcefully argued by Keynes and Sraffa that Hume, and not Smith, was the author. John O Nelson, however, has argued that Smith is the author. I take up the debate at this point, interpreting important passages in Hume's letters, to show that Hume indeed is the author of the *Abstract*, of which he hoped to publish an Irish edition.

Broome, John. Deontology and Economics. *Econ Phil*, 8(2), 269-282, O 92.

In *The Moral Dimension*, Etzioni claims that people often act for deontological motives. He claims that economics should take account for this fact, and that it would be greatly altered by doing so. This paper examines what it means for people to be motivated by deontological morality, how far it is true that they are, and what significance it would have for economics if it was true. It concludes that deontological motivations would indeed conflict fundamentally with the conventional methods of economics, but other forms of moral motivation would not.

Broome Jr, Taft H. Can Engineers Hold Public Interests Paramount?. *Res Phil Technol*, 9, 3-11, 1989.

The purpose of this paper is to consider whether public paramountcy rules are consistent with defensible conceptions about the nature of engineering. The main arguments are: 1) while these rules are consistent with conventional applied science conceptions of engineering, these conceptions are not defensible, and; 2) ordinary meanings of public paramountcy are not consistent with a new defensible conception of engineering. Instead of suggesting that these rules be repealed from engineering codes of ethics, qualifications for the meaning given to public paramountcy are presented.

Brottman, David. Light-Values as Existential Indices in Thomas Pynchon's Extravagant Comic Revery in Analecta Husserliana, XXXVIII, Tymieniecka, Anna-Teresa (ed). Dordrecht, Kluwer, 1992.

Broude, Norma. *Impressionism: A Feminist Reading*. New York, Rizzoli, 1991.

Brough, John B. Husserl and the Deconstruction of Time. *Rev Metaph*, 46(3), 503-536, Mr 93.

The essay examines the place of presence and absence in Husserl's phenomenology of time and time-consciousness against the background of deconstruction. Deconstruction views the traditional conception of time as metaphysical, meaning that it privileges the present and understands time to be a one-dimensional series of now-points. The deconstructionist largely assimilates Husserl's phenomenology of time to this model. The essay argues to the contrary, that the Husserlian account of time embraces temporal absence as equally primordial with temporal presence, in the process doing justice to our phenomenal experience of the present without falling into the "metaphysical" trap feared by the deconstructionist.

Broughton, Janet. What Does the Scientist of Man Observe?. *Hume Stud*, 18(2), N 92.

I argue that in the *Treatise*, Hume does not begin by supposing that the "perceptions" he studies are Lockean ideas. Realizing this helps us to interpret some otherwise puzzling claims Hume makes about memory and about innate ideas.

Brown, Bryson. Defending Backwards Causation. *Can J Phil*, 22(4), 429-443, D 92.

Brown, Bryson. Rational Inconsistency and Reasoning. *Inform Log*, 14(1), 5-10, Wint 92.

Nicholas Rescher has argued we must tolerate inconsistency because of our cognitive limitations. He has also produced, together with R Brandom, a serious attempt at exploring the logic of inconsistency. Inconsistency tolerance calls for a systematic rewriting of our logical doctrines: it requires a paraconsistent logic. However, having given up all aggregation of premises, Rescher's proposal for a paraconsistent logic fails to account for the reductive reasoning Rescher appeals to in his account of inconsistency tolerance. A non-adjunctive logic developed by P K Schotch and R E Jennings provides just what Rescher's logic is lacking: It allows a tolerant attitude toward inconsistency while giving an account of reductive reasoning.

Brown, Christopher G (& other eds) and Woodbury, Leonard E. *Collected Writings—Leonard E Woodbury*. Atlanta, Scholars Pr, 1991.

Brown, Curtis. Direct and Indirect Belief. *Phil Phenomenol Res*, 52(2), 289-316, Je 92.

Brown, Harold I. Direct Realism, Indirect Realism, and Epistemology. *Phil Phenomenol Res*, 52(2), 341-363, Je 92.

I argue that direct realism does not leave us in a better situation than indirect realism for learning the nature of the physical world. In either case, claims about physical objects must be justified by the hypothetico-deductive procedures that provide the basis for all justifications of scientific theories. The main metaphysical thesis of direct realism is accepted in this paper and the heart of the paper consists of a reconstruction of two traditional arguments against direct realism—the arguments from illusion and from causality—as arguments for an epistemological, rather than a metaphysical, conclusion.

Brown, Harvey R and Sypel, Roland. When is a Physical Theory Relativistic?. *Proc Phil Sci Ass*, 1, 507-514, 1992.

Considerable work within the modern 'space-time theory' approach to relativity physics has been devoted to clarifying the role and meaning of the principle of relativity. Two recent discussions of the principle within this approach, due to Arntzenius (1990) and Friedman (1983), are found to contain difficulties.

Brown, James R. Thought Experiments: A Platonic Account in Thought Experiments in Science and Philosophy, Horowitz, Tamara (ed). Lanham, Rowman & Littlefield, 1991.

Different types of thought experiments are discussed. It is claimed that one type gives us a priori knowledge of nature. The account is tied to realism about laws of nature and likened to Platonism in mathematics.

Brown, L. Connaissance et réminiscence dans le *Ménon*. *Rev Phil Fr*, 4, 603-619, O-D 91.

Brown, Lee B. Adorno's Critique of Popular Culture: The Case of Jazz Music. *J Aes Educ*, 26(1), 17-31, Spr 92.

While Adorno gets credit for claims about popular music, it is argued that they are weakened by, 1) a failure to heed important differences between jazz and popular music in general, and; 2) by an assumption that "serious" music is more "interesting" than popular music, which in turn is based upon an absolutism in conflict with the general principles of Adorno's aesthetics. Adorno's views are distorted both by, 1) Eurocentric prejudices; 2) by a (surprising) "primitivist" prejudice, and; 3) by an assumption that jazz is reducible to its cultural in-puts, rather than having an emergent status.

Brown, Lee B. The Theory of Jazz Music "It Don't Mean a Thing...". *J Aes Art Crit*, 49(2), 115-127, Spr 91.

The paper examines André Hodeir's attempt to define jazz in terms of *sonorité*, "hot" playing, and swing—but *not* improvisation. Special attention is given to Hodeir's strictures upon the concept of necessary condition. (A feature must not merely be universally present in the extention of the class of things being defined, but must contribute to the music in a *jazz* way.) Of particular interest is an interesting type of *reductio* argument latent in his writing that is telling against any "purism" that try to define jazz in terms of its *earliest* forms, a view that has implications for any view of jazz as *either* an inherently African or an inherently African art form.

Brown, Mark. Questions and Quantifiers. *Theoria*, 56(1-2), 62-84, 1990.

Brown, Montague. Aquinas on the Resurrection of the Body. *Thomist*, 56(2), 165-207, Ap 92.

Aquinas arrives at his position on the resurrection of the body by reflecting on what it is to be human. On the one hand, we exercise an immaterial activity, thinking, which means that we have a faculty whose operation transcends the body and therefore is not corrupted when the body is. Thus, the rational soul is an incorruptible substance is the form of the body, naturally requiring the body for its perfection. Aquinas acknowledges both evidences and finds in them reason to affirm the resurrection of the body.

Brown, Montague. St Thomas Aquinas and the Individuation of Persons. *Amer Cath Phil Quart*, 65(1), 29-44, Wint 91.

In this paper it is argued that the absolute respect owed to human beings is based on the fact that they are individuals and not reducible to the species. Aquinas's teaching helps us to understand what it is that makes us individuals. While he admits that human beings are individuals by matter (like all material things) and by esse (like all things), it is the rational soul which is the ultimate principle of individuation. A rational being is, in a way all things, and thus the respect owed to individual rational beings is akin to the respect owed to all reality.

Brown, Peter G. The New World Order and the Public Trust. *Nat Forum*, 72(4), 20-22, Fall 92.

Brown, Ralph. Susan Gellman Has It Right. *Crim Just Ethics*, 11(2), 46-48, Sum-Fall 92.

Brown, Robert F. Akrasia (Weakness of Will) and the Christian Understanding of Moral Failure. *Cont Phil*, 14(6), 10-14, N-D 92.

The ancient problem of *akrasia* is still debated. Davidson holds that free agents sometimes choose contrary to their best judgment, whereas Carrier holds that inappropriate choice is *prima facie* evidence that full consideration was lacking. I argue that Christian thought should align itself with the "Davidson" account; it should renounce its ties with the Platonic-Aristotelian assumption that choosing is coerced by the inherent attractiveness of appetible goods, and should affirm instead that free will includes the power to determine freely what at least some of our incentives will be, even contrary to what we know the rational good to be.

Brown, Stuart. On Why Philosophers Redefine their Subject. *Philosophy*, 33(Supp), 41-57, 1992.

Brown, Stuart. On Why Philosophers Redefine their Subject in The Impulse to Philosophise, Griffiths, A Phillips (ed). New York, Cambridge Univ Pr, 1992.

Brown, Wendy. Wounded Attachments. *Polit Theory*, 21(3), 390-410, Ag 93.

This essay reflects upon the contemporary formation of politicized identity in the US as comprised by specific economic, political and cultural developments. Exploring in particular the consequences of developing identity at the site of a wound, and codifying it through liberal and disciplinary discourses, it uses Nietzsche's account of *ressentiment* to understand the recriminatory speech and moralizing rancor characteristic of some moments in contemporary identity politics. It concludes with some speculative ideas on what might be required to loosen identity from this rancorous moral economy.

Browne, Alister. Defining Death in Applied Philosophy, Almond, Brenda (ed). New York, Routledge, 1992.

Browne, Brynmor. A Solution to the Problem of Moral Luck. *Phil Quart*, 42(168), 345-356, Jl 92.

The idea that a person is only responsible for that which is under his control is central to the account of responsibility which gives rise to the problem of moral luck. But the 'condition of control' is a misnomer which helps us to misconstrue the problem of moral luck which has at its heart an incoherent model of agency. This incoherent view of agency only seems attractive because it helps to justify certain attitudes and practices such as punishment which we believe are central to morality, but which are, in fact, morally wrong.

Browning, Don. Altruism and Christian Love. *Zygon*, 27(4), 421-436, D 92.

Sociobiological theories have had little impact on Christian concepts of neighbor love. Since sociobiological theories of altruism depict love as a form of egoistic interest in enhancing one's general fitness, they are often thought to contradict Christian theories of love. However, altruism as defined by sociobiology has more affinity with Roman Catholic views of Christian love as *caritas* that Protestant views of extreme *agape*. Sociobiological views of altruism may provide more updated models for defining the orders and priorities of love, which has been an important aspect of Roman Catholic ethics. The family's role in mediating between kin altruism and wider love for the community is investigated.

Browning, Douglas. Necessity in Dewey's "Logic" in Frontiers in American Philosophy, Volume I, Burch, Robert W (ed). College Station, Texas A&M Univ Pr, 1992.

In his *Logic: The Theory of Inquiry* John Dewey proposes to defend the hypothesis that all logical forms are instances of a functional relation in properly controlled inquiry. But certain logical forms, namely, those of analytic necessity between meanings of terms in a proposition and of implicative necessity between propositions, resist this characterization. It is argued that Dewey is forced by his own considerations to the conclusion that such forms are neither reducible to nor explainable by reference to the functions or operations of inquiry.

Browning, Gary K. The Night in Which All Cows are Black: Ethical Absolutism in Plato and Hegel. *Hist Polit Thought*, 12(3), 391-404, Fall 91.

Browning, Gary K. Transitions to and from Nature in Hegel and Plato. *Bull Hegel Soc Gt Brit*, 26, 1-12, Autumn-Wint 92.

Brozi, Krzysztof J. Philosophical Premises of Functional Anthropology. *Phil Soc Sci*, 22(3), 357-369, S 92.

The philosophical roots of Malinowski's functionalism are in the academic circles of Krakow, where three figures seem to have exerted a particularly strong influence: Pawlicki, Straszewski, and Heinrich. The predominant trend in philosophy at that time was empiriocriticism, as developed by Mach and Avenarius. Also important were F A Lange's interpretation of Marburg neo-Kantianism. It should be noted that the historical philosophy field was extremely broad and diverse. Functionalism, a philosophically open concept, cannot be subordinated to any one philosophical system, although the "openness" of functionalism is not absolute but complemented by its "closedness" to certain other philosophies. *Praxism* pervades functionalist theory and even creates its foundation. Malinowski's approach is entirely scientific, but functionalism is never just empirical. Malinowski realized that pure experience is as impossible as pure reasoning.

Brubaker, David. André Bazin on Automatically Made Images. *J Aes Art Crit*, 51(1), 59-67, Wint 93.

Brueckner, Anthony. Conceiving One's Envatment While Denying Metaphysical Realism. *Austl J Phil*, 70(4), 469-474, D 92.

Putnam maintains that a Grain in a vat cannot truly state that it is a Grain in a vat. The semantic consideration underlying this claim can be used against metaphysical realism (understood as the view that it is possible for an epistemically ideal theory to be false). I defend Putnam against the objection that the fact that one can conceive of being a brain in a Grain in a vat shows that metaphysical realism is true.

Brueckner, Anthony. Genova, Davidson and Content-Scepticism. *Analysis*, 52(4), 228-231, O 92.

This paper is a discussion of A C Genova's defense of Davidson's Omniscient Interpreter anti-skeptical argument (*Analysis*, 1991).

Brueckner, Anthony. Losing Track of Nozick. *Ratio*, 5(2), 194-198, D 92.

This paper is a response to some criticisms directed against Nozick's anti-skeptical strategy. The criticisms are given by Brian Garrett in "Keeping Track of Nozick's Trackers", *Ratio*, 1992.

Brueckner, Anthony. One More Failed Transcendental Argument. *Phil Phenomenol Res*, 53(3), 633-636, S 93.

This paper is a critical discussion of an argument (by Douglas C Long) to show that if one knows that one is the subject of various mental states, then one has knowledge that this subject is a material thing.

Brueckner, Anthony. Parfit on What Matters in Survival. *Phil Stud*, 70(1), 1-22, Ap 93.

This paper is a critical discussion of Parfit's argument (in *Reasons and Persons*) to show that psychological continuity is the proper focus of the concern one normally attaches to personal identity. One focus is the role of the indeterminacy of identity in Parfit's reasoning.

Brueckner, Anthony. Semantic Answers to Skepticism. *Pac Phil Quart*, 73(3), 200-219, S 92.

I defend an argument against certain forms of skepticism which stems from externalist views about semantics and thought-content. I also discuss the relation between externalism and self-knowledge.

Brueckner, Anthony. Singular Thought and Cartesian Philosophy. *Analysis*, 53(2), 110-115, Ap 93.

This is a critical discussion of John McDowell's claims about the epistemological significance of singular thoughts.

Brueckner, Anthony. Skepticism and Externalism. *Philosophia (Israel)*, 22(1-2), 169-171, Ja 93.

Suppose that some form of externalism in the theory of knowledge is correct (such as Nozick's tracking analysis of knowledge). It is argued that under this assumption, the skeptic cannot easily show that I do not *know that I know* that I am sitting.

Brueckner, Anthony. The Anti-Realist's Master Argument. *Midwest Stud Phil*, 17, 214-223, 1992.

This is a critical discussion of one of Dummett's arguments to show that a speaker's understanding of a sentence does not consist in his grasping of the sentence's truth-conditions.

Brueckner, Anthony and Fischer, John Martin. Death's Badness. *Pac Phil Quart*, 74(1), 37-45, Mr 93.

In this paper we defend the claim that it is rational to hold asymmetric attitudes towards death and pre-natal non-existence (against a criticism which I Haji directs against an earlier paper of ours—"Why Is Death Bad?", *Philosophical Studies* 1986—in his "Pre-Vital and Post-Vital Times", *Pacific Philosophical Quarterly* 1991).

Brueckner, Anthony and Fischer, John Martin. The Asymmetry of Early Death and Late Birth. *Phil Stud*, 71(3), 327-331, S 93.

In this paper, we defend the claim that a rational asymmetry in our attitudes towards past and future pleasures explains why we do not regret the fact that we were not born earlier. The paper is a response to Christopher Belshaw's "Asymmetry and Non-Existence", *Philosophical Studies* 1993, which contained a criticism of our earlier paper "Why Is Death Bad?", *Philosophical Studies* 1986.

Brümmer, Vincent. Atonement and Reconciliation. *Relig Stud*, 28(4), 435-452, D 92.

Atonement (at-one-ment) means reconciliation, i.e. restoration of a broken relationship with God. The nature of this reconciliation depends on the kind of relationship which has to be restored, and the variety of theories of atonement in Christian theology derive from the variety of conceptual models on terms of which this relationship has usually been interpreted in the Christian tradition. In this paper three basic relation models are analyzed and their implications for the theory of atonement are traced.

Brümmer, Vincent. *Speaking of a Personal God: An Essay in Philosophical Theology*. New York, Cambridge Univ Pr, 1993.

This book explains and defends the use of the analytical tools of philosophers in dealing with issues in systematic theology, like those involved in understanding the meaning of our lives in terms of a personal relationship with God. Does this understanding imply that we are personal agents able to resist the grace of God, and that God is a personal agent able to do evil? And can God act in the world through the things which we do? And what does this entail for the problem of evil and for the possibility of religion consoling us in affliction?

Bruin, John. Heidegger and the World in the Work of Art. *J Aes Art Crit*, 50(1), 55-56, Wint 92.

In this critical response (to R Maj Singh, "Heidegger and the World in an Artwork," *JAAC* 48, 1990, I draw attention to the ambiguity in Heidegger's use of the term "work" in his *Origin of the Work of Art*. Heidegger speaks of the "work of art" and the "artwork." The two, I argue, are not the same. The expression "the work of art" conveys something like "the labour, or the efficacy, or the achievement of art." This ontological activity includes, but involves something much more than, the presence of an artwork, which is an entity of sorts.

Bruin, John. Why Heidegger's Godot Might not be Worth the Wait. *Mod Sch*, 70(2), 143-152, Ja 93.

I take to task the underlying claim made in George Kovacs's recent work, *The Question of God in Heidegger's Phenomenology*. Kovacs runs the argument that short of measuring up to the Heideggerian requirements of an ontological setting, authentic religious existence cannot really be achieved. I argue that this view offers an impoverished phenomenology of religion. It too casually makes light of, in fact comes close to disdaining, the "ontic" matrix within which religious existence comes into its own.

Brumbaugh, Robert. An Academy Inscription: A Retracted Exile? Poetry and Republic 614b2. *Ancient Phil*, 12(1), 171-173, Spr 92.

Brunk, Conrad G and Haworth, Lawrence and Lee, Brenda. Is a Scientific Assessment of Risk Possible? Value Assumptions in the Canadian Alachlor Controversy. *Dialogue (Canada)*, 30(3), 235-247, Sum 91.

Brunkhorst, Hauke. Culture and Bourgeois Society in Cultural-Political Interventions in the Unfinished Project of Enlightenment, Honneth, Axel (& other eds). Cambridge, MIT Pr, 1992.

Bruns, Gerald L. *Hermeneutics Ancient and Modern*. New Haven, Yale Univ Pr, 1992.

Brunschwig, J. Pouvoir enseigner la vertu?. *Rev Phil Fr*, 4, 591-602, O-D 91.

Brunton, Alan. A Definitive Non-Solution of the Free-Will Problem. *Phil Invest*, 16(3), 231-242, Jl 93.

The purpose of the article is, firstly, to cast doubt on libertarian or compatibilist solutions. The libertarian gives the "I" strange powers for a referential centre. The compatibilist confuses the true propositions that we have the *general* power to act otherwise, and that we do as we choose, with the dubious proposition that, *on a given occasion*, we could have acted otherwise. Since the central "I" is without content, yet is needed for the legitimacy of moral judgments, we are, as moral beings, stuck with a problem.

Brush, Francis. William H Bernhardt's Value Hypothesis: A Systematic Approach in God, Values, and Empiricism, Peden, Creighton W (ed). Macon, Mercer Univ Pr, 1989.

Bryans, Joan. Substitution and the Explanation of Action. *Erkenntnis*, 37(3), 365-376, N 92.

This paper examines a potential problem area for theories of direct reference: that of the substitution of co-referential names within the belief context of a belief attribution used to explain an action. Of particular interest are action explanations which involve cases of repetition—wherein beliefs are held which, though about one (other) individual, are mistakenly thought to concern two different people. It is argued that, despite the commonly held view to the contrary, no problem is posed by substitution in such circumstances to theories of direct reference.

Brykman, Geneviève. Le mythe de l'intériorité chez Locke. *Arch Phil*, 55(4), 575-586, O-D 92.

The way in which Locke stresses the privacy of our ideas at the beginning of the Essay, Book III, does not imply that our experience is utterly private. So that a close examination of Locke's conception of language learning, give some reasons to resist making the confusion between the traditional mental discourse and Wittgenstein's notion of a private language.

Bryson, Mary and De Castell, Suzanne. En/Gendering Equity: Emancipatory Programs or Repressive "Regimes of Truth". *Proc Phil Educ*, 48, 357-371, 1992.

Bryson, Mary and De Castell, Suzanne. En/Gendering Equity: On Some Paradoxical Consequences of Institutionalized Programs of Emancipation. *Educ Theor*, 43(3), 341-356, Sum 93.

Brzezinski, Jerzy (& other eds). *Creativity and Consciousness: Philosophical and Psychological Dimensions*. Amsterdam, Rodopi, 1993.

Brzezinski, Jerzy (ed) and Nowak, Leszek (ed). *Idealization III*. Amsterdam, Rodopi, 1992.

Buber, Martin and Eisenstadt, S N (ed). *On Intersubjectivity and Cultural Creativity—Martin Buber*. Chicago, Univ of Chicago Pr, 1992.

Bubner, Rüdiger. Hegel and the End of History. *Bull Hegel Soc Gt Brit*, 23-24, 15-23, 1991.

The Hegel School argued that philosophy should care about the future (Cieszkowski) or should restrict all claims of knowledge to the past (Droysen). Hegel himself believed that the intellectual activity of integrating the concrete facts of history into an understandable unity is a continuous task. In retrospective, reason looks at history as a whole but it never can bring the actual processes to a final end.

Buchanan, Allen. *Secession: The Morality of Political Divorce from Fort Sumter to Lithuania and Quebec*. Boulder, Westview Pr, 1991.

Buchanan, Allen. The Morality of Inclusion. *Soc Phil Pol*, 10(2), 233-257, Sum 93.

Buchanan, James H. Merleau-Ponty's Political Passage. *Hist Euro Ideas*, 16(4-6), 909-914, Ja 93.

Buchanan, James M. Asymmetrical Reciprocity in Market Exchange: Implications for Economies in Transition. *Soc Phil Pol*, 10(2), 51-64, Sum 93.

In a market economy, sellers of goods seek and try to satisfy buyers; in a command economy by contrast, consumers must seek and try to satisfy suppliers. Recognition that the reciprocity in markets is not symmetrical helps to explain some of the difficulties encountered in those economies in transition to market organization.

Buchmann, Margret. Reason and Romance in Argument and Conversation. *Proc S Atlantic Phil Educ Soc*, 36, 1-17, 1991.

The need to approach knowledge and action through the structures of language requires consideration of the forms of communication. While dramatic, forceful, and historically dominant, the argumentative model is predicated upon a military analogy, with victory superseding goals of understanding, including sensitivity and openness to alternative views. Conversation, by contrast, encourages participation, and it accepts stories, feelings, and other contributions that do not conform to the demands of traditional logical rigor. Awareness of conversation's limitations is crucial, however, and helps ward off erratic and facile tendencies of conversation. Still, in being more flexible and more compatible with the conditions of effective persuasion, yet capable of incorporating stretches or argument, the conversational model offers a more inclusive approach to addressing questions of knowledge, understanding, and action.

Buchmann, Margret. Teacher Thinking, Teacher Change, and the "Capricious Seamstress"—Memory. *Proc Phil Educ*, 48, 290-299, 1992.

Buchowski, Michal. Multiple Orderings of Tambiah's Thought. *Phil Soc Sci*, 23(1), 84-96, Mr 93.

Stanley J Tambiah's view on magic, science, religion, and the problem of rationality is criticized. Three main points are raised. First, that mere historical contextualization of various modes of thought cannot differentiate them as magical, religious or scientific. The actor's recognition of the status and mutual relation between symbolic and causal elements in the systems of belief is proposed as useful for making such distinction. Second, Tambiah's view that beliefs about practical and social domains are, respectively, amenable and non-amenable to rational evaluation is denied. Third, the unaware confusion of epistemological and anthropological discourses is indicated.

Buchwald, Jed Z. Design for Experimenting in World Changes, Horwich, Paul (ed). Cambridge, MIT Pr, 1993.

Buchwalter, Andrew. *Culture and Democracy: Social and Ethical Issues in Public Support for the Arts and Humanities*. Boulder, Westview Pr, 1992.

Buchwalter, Andrew. Hegel's Concept of Virtue. *Polit Theory*, 20(4), 548-583, N 92.

This paper examines what Hegel understands variously as civic virtue, republican sentiment, or patriotism. For Hegel, civic virtue is defensible under modern conditions not by appealing, as did the ancient Greeks, to a public concept of human nature, but by reflecting on the meaning of individual rights. This *cognitive* approach is shown to accommodate the "organicism" and "trust" common to conventional patriotism. It also allows how modern social complexity, while precluding any "direct" revival of Greek civic virtue, not only permits republicanism but accommodates its modern and general realization. In conclusion, Hegel's position is related to contemporary discussions of patriotism.

Buchwalter, Andrew. Hegel, Modernity, and Civic Republicanism. *Pub Affairs Quart*, 7(1), 1-12, Ja 93.

Buck, Ross W. Epistemological Fundamentals: Knowledge by Acquaintance and Spontaneous Communication. *J Prag*, 17(5-6), 447-454, Je 92.

This article extends the notion of non-encoding forms of knowledge (knowledge-by-acquaintance) to communication in a suggested resolution of the Problem of Other Minds. In spontaneous communication a receiver has biologically-based *direct access* to certain "mental states" (feelings, desires) of the sender. Displays expressing those states evolved in senders, and preattunements sensitive to those displays evolved in receivers, as phylogenetic adaptations. This is not an advanced function but rather is ancient, as demonstrated by spontaneous communication in single-celled slime molds. In humans spontaneous communication is a conversation between limbic systems, reflecting innate passions for communication that, with appropriate cognitive capacities, underlie language.

Buckle, S and Castiglione, D. Hume's Critique of the Contract Theory. *Hist Polit Thought*, 12(3), 457-480, Fall 91.

Buckler, Steve. *Dirty Hands: The Problem of Political Morality*. Brookfield, Avebury, 1993.

The problem of dirty hands in politics is analyzed and following critical analysis of influential attempts to solve the problem, it is argued that the experience of dirty hands is to be taken on its own terms as a moral burden to be borne by political agents and citizens. The nature of the burden and its implication are explored by reference to historical and literary examples and a basis is found for asserting the relevance of moral sensitivity in the political realm.

Buckley, R Philip. A Critique of Husserl's Notion of Crisis in Crises in Continental Philosophy, Dallery, Arleen B (ed). Albany, SUNY Pr, 1990.

In the first part of the paper, I point out that the "crisis" is not merely a theme that arose at the end of Husserl's life, but rather that *all* of his philosophical efforts arose out of a sense of crisis, beginning with the concern for the proper foundation of arithmetical concepts. Attention is also given to certain historical and social events which led to the broader concept of the general crisis of culture. In the second part of the paper, two different sorts of criticism are made of Husserl's view of the crisis, one from the standpoint of fundamental ontology, another from the work of the later Heidegger. With these criticisms in mind, we are able to see how closely a notion of crisis is linked to a thinker's pre-suppositions regarding philosophy itself.

Buckman, Ken. Is Art Dead for Hegel?. *SW Phil Stud*, 14, 34-49, Spr 92.

Budd, Malcolm. Music and the Communication of Emotion. *J Aes Art Crit*, 47(2), 129-138, Spr 89.

Negatively, a critique of a number of conceptions of and claims about the musical expression of emotion. Positively, 1) an account of the musical expression of emotion in terms of imagining music, or one's experience of it, as being an experience of emotion, and 2) an account of the nature of emotional reactions to music that is heard as being expressive of emotion.

Budd, Malcolm. On Looking at a Picture in Psychoanalysis, Mind and Art, Hopkins, Jim (ed). Cambridge, Blackwell, 1992.

An examination of Richard Wollheim's account of pictorial perception in terms of a species of seeing that he calls 'seeing-in'. The conclusion is that 'seeing-in' is ill-defined and an alternative account of pictorial perception is required.

Budd, Malcolm. *Wittgenstein's Philosophy of Psychology*. New York, Routledge, 1991.

Budden, Tim. The Relativity Principle and the Isotropy of Boosts. *Proc Phil Sci Ass*, 1, 528-541, 1992.

A class of theories which satisfy the Relativity Principle has been overlooked. The kinematics for these theories is derived by relaxing the 'boost isotropy' symmetry normally invoked, and the role the dynamical fields play in determining the inertial coordinate systems is emphasized, leading to a criticism of Friedman's (1983) practice of identifying them via the absolute objects of a spacetime theory alone. Some theories complete with 'boost anisotropic' dynamics are given.

Budge, Ian. Can Utilitarianism justify Democracy? in The Utilitarian Response, Allison, Lincoln (ed). Newbury Park, Sage, 1990.

Budziszewski, J. Fanning the Embers of Civic Virtue: Toward a (Chastened) Politics of Character. *Pub Affairs Quart*, 7(2), 93-112, Ap 93.

Budziszewski, J. Religion and Civic Virtue. *Nomos*, 34, 49-68, 1992.

This work clarifies and emphasizes differences between secular and religious understandings of virtue. "Faith vs Reason" is a false dichotomy, for the issue is not whether to have faith, but what to have faith in. Different choices result in radically different *interpretations* of some moral traits and practices, such as tolerance and civic education, and in radically different *evaluations* of others, such as patriotism and "civil religion." As part of its discussion of justice, the article also shows that the relation between rules and virtues was mapped in prophetic and apostolic utterances millennia before its rediscovery by contemporary secular ethicists.

Buekens, Filip. Try, Succeed and Fail: A Critique of Empirical Theories of Action (in French). *Rev Theol Phil*, 124(3), 231-248, 1992.

What is meant by the attempt, the success or the failure of an action? Using Davidson's philosophy of action, I elaborate a theory which admits that every action contains in embryo a possibility of failure. This does not imply that every action is accompanied by an attempt to act, which is only an empiricist prejudice. Attempts are intentional actions. Attempts which fail are actions whose envisioned outcome has not been fulfilled.

Buell, John. The Politics of the Common Good. *Res Phil Technol*, 11, 105-117, 1991.

Bürger, Peter. Art and Rationality in Philosophical Interventions in the Unfinished Project of Enlightenment, Honneth, Axel (& other eds). Cambridge, MIT Pr, 1992.

Starting from the results of his book *Prosa der Moderne* (Frankfort: Suhrkamp 1988) the author specifies the position of art vis-à-vis rationality, taken as the dominant paradigm of action in bourgeois society, by confronting the unity of sign and significance in the symbol with their separation in the allegory. Brecht's return to allegorical form and Benjamin's attempt to rehabilitate it against the idealistic esthetics of the symbol let it seem reasonable to consider the allegory as the modern form par excellence. The essay shows that this is not the case, that the concept of the symbol, in spite of its theological origins, cannot be abandoned.

Büscher, M. The Work Ethic and the Work Ethos: The Importance of Ethical Arguments for the Politics of Transition to the Market. *Russian Stud Phil*, 32(1), 76-82, Sum 93.

The transition process from a planned to a liberal, competitive market economy often is based on an economic model which assumes similar normative, socio-cultural and historical prerequisites in the Russian context as in market economies of a liberal western type. This article argues that this assumption is wrong. The argument exemplarily concentrates on the work ethos as a factor that stands for the fact that for a sustainable transition process contextual prerequisites are crucial.

Buford, Thomas O. In Search of a Calling. *Proc S Atlantic Phil Educ Soc*, 36, 23-30, 1991.

The American college has abandoned its mission to educate students to find and prepare for what they are to do and to be. To reclaim that mission we must recall from our collective memory and refurbish a framework for thinking about persons and their education that has fallen from use in the American college. That way of thinking is Calling. But, since the middle of the nineteenth century colleges have increasingly ignored the moral lives of their students and aided in routinizing and rationalizing their practical identity, splintering it. To educate for rich identity, for moral and practical identity, colleges must reinterpret the biblical and humanist traditions, reformulate calling or callings into contemporary language, and place the education for callings at the center of their mission.

Buker, Eloise A. Rhetoric in Postmodern Feminism: Put-Offs, Put-Ons, and Political Plays in The Interpretive Turn, Hiley, David R (ed). Ithaca, Cornell Univ Pr, 1991.

This essay examines three themes found in postmodern feminist conversations: 1) a critical view that argues that postmodernism is dangerous for feminist scholarship because of its depoliticizing discourse; 2) an exploration of the ways in which postmodernism constructs identities and deconstructs the mind/body dichotomy; 3) the ways in which postmodernism enables feminists to employ play as a strategy for political change. The essay argues that the rhetoric and metaphorical moves made by postmodern feminism enable a radical hermeneutics that develops from the postmodern feminist's focus on the politics of language. This focus can enhance feminist theories and empower feminist politics.

Bulger, Ruth Ellen (ed) and Heitman, Elizabeth (ed) and Reiser, Stanley Joel (ed). *The Ethical Dimensions of the Biological Sciences*. New York, Cambridge Univ Pr, 1993.

This collection contains a variety of classic essays and seminal works by researchers from many disciplines, as well as policy statements and research guidelines from professional and government bodies. Among the issues considered are: the norms of ethical conduct in science and their origins; scientific honesty, skepticism, and self-deception; the ethical standards of laboratory practice; the use of human and animal subjects; the qualifications for authorship and publication; the ethics of learning and teaching; and the relationships of science, industry, and society. (edited)

Bull, Barry L. The Creolization of Liberalism. *Proc Phil Educ*, 48, 237-240, 1992.

Buller, David J. Confirmation and the Computational Paradigm (Or: Why Do You Think They Call It *Artificial* Intelligence?). *Mind Mach*, 3(2), 155-181, My 93.

The idea that human cognitive capacities are explained by computational models is often conjoined with the idea that, while the states postulated by such models are in fact realized by brain states, there are no type-type correlations between the states postulated by computational models and brain states (a corollary of token physicalism). I argue that these ideas are not jointly tenable. I discuss the kinds of empirical evidence available to cognitive scientists for (dis)confirming computational models of cognition and argue that none of these kinds of evidence can be relevant to a choice among competing computational models unless there are in fact type-type correlations between the states postulated by computational models and brain states. Thus, I conclude, research into the computational procedures employed in human cognition must be conducted hand-in-hand with research into the brain processes which realize those procedures.

Buller, David J. 'Narrow'-Mindedness Breeds Inaction. *Behavior Phil*, 20(1), 59-70, Spr-Sum 92.

Discussion of Fodor's doctrine of 'methodological solipsism' and Stich's principle of autonomy has been concerned to show that these principles are incompatible with psychological theories which appeal to states with content (e.g., beliefs and desires). Concern with these issues, and the subsequent attempt to develop a notion of 'narrow' content which is solipsistic or autonomous, has, I believe, obscured a more fundamental issue: No theory which satisfies these principles would ever be able to explain behavior under descriptions which are in fact important to psychology. But I do not simply argue that there are descriptions under which psychological theories will not in fact explain behavior; I argue that descriptions under which psychological theories *do* explain behavior are not compatible with solipsistic principles. I develop several thought experiments to demonstrate this.

Buller, David J and Foster, Thomas R. The New Paradox of Temporal Transcience. *Phil Quart*, 42(168), 357-366, Jl 92.

McTaggart raised a famed paradox regarding the transientist (or dynamic) conception of time, the standard resolution of which involves abandoning the dynamic conception in favor of a static conception of time. Schlesinger, however, recently attempted an ingenious transientist solution to McTaggart's paradox. We argue that Schlesinger's solution to McTaggart's paradox itself gives rise to a new, yet perfectly parallel, paradox which can only be resolved by abandoning the dynamic view of time.

Bulygin, Eugenio. On Norms of Competence. *Law Phil*, 11(3), 201-216, 1992.

Norms conferring public or private powers, i.e., the competence to issue other norms, play a very important role in law. But there is no agreement among legal philosophers about the nature of such norms. There are two main groups of theories, those that regard them as a kind of norms of conduct (either commands or permissions) and those that regard them as non-reducible to other types of norms. I try to show that reductionist theories are not quite acceptable; neither the command-variety (Kelsen, Alf Ross in *On Law and Justice*), nor the permission-variety (von Wright, Kanger, Lindahl) provide a satisfactory account of competence norms. (edited)

Bunge, Mario. Sette paradigmi cosmologici: L'animale, la scala, il fiume, la nuvola, la macchina, il libro e il sistema dei sistemi. *Aquinas*, 35(2), 219-235, My-Ag 92.

Seven major cosmological models or paradigms are described and examined: the world as an animal, a ladder, a river, a cloud, a machine, a book, and the system of all systems. The last one is preferred, and it is argued that it contains some of the insights of three earlier models: the ladder or chain of being, the river (dynamicism), and the cloud (atomism). It is also argued that the zoomorphic and the hermeneutic models are utterly wrong.

Bunge, Mario. Why We Cherish Exactness in Advances in Scientific Philosophy, Schurz, Gerhard (ed). Amsterdam, Rodopi, 1991.

Burbidge, John W. *Hegel on Logic and Religion: The Reasonableness of Christianity*. Albany, SUNY Pr, 1992.

In response to Lessing's challenge that there is a nasty, broad ditch between the eternal truths of reason and the contingent truth of history, Hegel argues that contingency is rationally necessary, and that time and history, especially the events reported in Christian tradition, incarnate a sophisticated rational pattern. Consideration is also given to the forms of rational thought (transition, reflection and understanding), to Schelling's counter-proposal, and to the role of death and unhappy consciousness in the *Phenomenology*. A final chapter asks whether Hegel is a Christian.

Burbidge, John W. Hegel's Conception of Logic in The Cambridge Companion to Hegel, Beiser, Frederick (ed). New York, Cambridge Univ Pr, 1993.

Hegel's *Science of Logic* does not fit the conventional conception of a book on logic. Nonetheless it reproduces a disciplined thinking about the processes of logical thought. Hegel identifies inferential moves so elementary that most people never notice them. Thus the criticisms of Frege and Russell presuppose the very psychologism and reliance on contradiction that they attack. On the other hand, Hegel's three operations—understanding, dialectic and speculation—are common to much reflective discourse and as well reflect the dynamic of the cosmos. The paper concludes with a review of the systematic development in the *Logic*.

Burbidge, John W. Language and Philosophy in Logical Foundations, Mahalingam, Indira (ed). New York, St Martin's Pr, 1991.

Does the structure of the language we speak affect the nature or direction of the way we reason philosophically? A procedure is suggested for correlating the syntax and philosophical reasoning in different cultures, and then used to compare German and English. Texts from Thomas Mann and Jane Austen are used to illustrate syntax; then works by Hans-Georg Gadamer and Gilbert Ryle are analyzed in terms of their arguments. The results of these investigations are correlated and tentative conclusions drawn.

Burbidge, John W. Reason and Existence in Schelling and Fackenheim in German Philosophy and Jewish Thought, Greenspan, Louis (ed). Toronto, Univ of Toronto Pr, 1992.

In his early essays, Fackenheim argued that Schelling did not successfully bridge the gap between the universal truths of reason and the contingency of existence. This becomes the motif of his subsequent writings, both those devoted to German philosophy and those concerned with the contemporary Jewish situation. While Hegel's double representation offers a model adaptable to Jewish thought, Heidegger's existentialism is historically conditioned just where it pretends to transcend existence. For Fackenheim one lives between incomplete narration, where one is confronted with mystery, and absolute imperative—the commanding voice of Auschwitz.

Burbules, Nicholas C and Rice, Suzanne. Communicative Virtues and Educational Relations. *Proc Phil Educ*, 48, 34-44, 1992.

Burch, Robert W (ed) and Saatkamp, Herman J Jr (ed). *Frontiers in American Philosophy, Volume I*. College Station, Texas A&M Univ Pr, 1992.

Burdick, Howard. Non-Essentialistic Modal Logic, or Meaning and Necessity Revisited. *Philosophia (Israel)*, 22(1-2), 87-93, Ja 93.

Burge, Tyler. Frege on Knowing the Third Realm. *Mind*, 101(404), 633-650, O 92.

Burge, Tyler. Mind-Body Causation and Explanatory Practice in Mental Causation, Heil, John (ed). New York, Clarendon/Oxford Pr, 1993.

Burge, Tyler. Vision and Intentional Content in John Searle and His Critics, Lepore, Ernest (ed). Cambridge, Blackwell, 1991.

Burger, Ronna C. Ethical Reflection and Righteous Indignation in Essays in Ancient Greek Philosophy, IV, Anton, John P (ed). Albany, SUNY Pr, 1991.

Righteous indignation or *"nemesis"*—being pained at the undeserved good fortune of one's neighbors—concludes the list of virtues in Book II of the *Nicomachean Ethics*, although, like shame, it is said to be a mean between two extremes without being itself a virtue; it belongs to the one triad in the list which disappears entirely from the longer discussion of the virtues and vices in Books III and IV. This essay explores the possible significance of that disappearance for the argument of the *Ethics* by examining the fundamental presupposition of righteous indignation, that there should be a precise match between fortune and character.

Burgess, John P. Hintikka *et* Sandu versus Frege *in re* Arbitrary Functions. *Phil Math*, 1, 50-65, Mr 93.

Hintikka and Sandu have recently claimed that Frege's notion of function was substantially narrower than that prevailing in real analysis today. In the present note, their textual evidence for this claim is examined in the light of relevant historical and biographical background and judged insufficient.

Burgess, Michael. Mature Minors in Contemporary Issues in Paediatric Ethics, Burgess, Michael M (ed). Lewiston, Mellen Pr, 1991.

Analysis of the basis for moral respect of children supports a more active role for children in health care activities than is currently the case. Early in childhood, the focus ought to be on strong emotional support and attention to expressions of opposition. Attempts to communicate to children their health status and implications of treatment and research must increase with children's maturity until their participation in the decisions displace that of the parents. Consents with are given by comprehending young persons cannot be ignored simply because they are below an arbitrary age limit.

Burgess, Michael M. The Medicalization of Dying. *J Med Phil*, 18(3), 269-280, Je 93.

Physician assisted suicide or active euthanasia is analyzed as a medicalization of the needs of persons who are suffering interminably. As with other medicalized responses to personal needs, the availability of active euthanasia will likely divert attention and resources from difficult social and personal aspects of the needs of dying and suffering persons, continuing the pattern of privatization of the costs of caregiving for persons who are candidates for active euthanasia, limiting the ability of caregivers to assist suffering persons to make their continued suffering tolerable, and casting doubt on the voluntariness of the choice of active euthanasia.

Burgess, Michael M (ed) and Woodrow, Brian E (ed). *Contemporary Issues in Paediatric Ethics*. Lewiston, Mellen Pr, 1991.

This anthology addresses practical issues in the provision of health care to children: David Ost surveys the moral dimensions of caring for children. William Bartholome argues for the importance of best interest judgments by all caregivers when withholding or withdrawing life support. Terry Acherman defends children's strong claim to society's resources in the support of innovative lifesaving therapies. Michael Burgess argues for greater involvement of children in their health care. Susan Sherwin argues against characterizing parents' resistance to medical recommendations as neglect. Reverend Herbert O'Driscoll poetically reflects upon these discussions in a broader context.

Burgess-Jackson, Keith. The Problem with Contemporary Moral Theory. *Hypatia*, 8(3), 160-166, Sum 93.

Feminists, especially radical feminists, have reason to be dissatisfied with contemporary moral theory, but they are understandably reluctant to abandon the theoretical project until it is seen as unsalvageable. The problem is not, however, as Margaret Urban Walker claims, that theory is abstract, that it seeks to guide conduct, or that it postulates moral knowledge. The problem is that contemporary moral theory is foundational.

Burgin, Mark and Kuznetsov, Vladimir. Model Part of a Scientific Theory. *Epistemologia*, 15(1), 41-64, Ja-Je 92.

From the viewpoint of the structure-nominative program in the philosophy of science, we study the model-representing subsystem of a scientific theory. Various conceptual models of objects from the theory's domain occupy the central place in this subsystem. A description of the links between models and the hierarchy of laws is given. Some aspects of theory development are studied.

Burgin, Mark and Kuznetsov, Vladimir. The Structure-Nominative Reconstruction and the Intelligibility of Cognition. *Epistemologia*, 15(2), 219-238, Jl-D 92.

From the structure-nominative view we propose an unified treatment of levels of common and scientific cognition. We also introduce several cognitive schemes giving new kinds of hermeneutic circles. All this develops and deepens some ideas of E Agazzi (1992) concerning the nature and structure of scientific knowledge and cognition.

Burian, Richard M. Unification and Coherence as Methodological Objectives in the Biological Sciences. *Biol Phil*, 8(3), 301-318, Jl 93.

In this paper I respond to Wim van der Steen's arguments against the supposed current overemphasis on norms of *coherence* and *interdisciplinary integration* in biology. On the normative level, I argue that these are *middle-range norms* which, although they may be misapplied in short-term attempts to solve (temporarily?) intractable problems, play a guiding role in the longer-term treatment of biological problems. This stance is supported by a case study of a *partial* success story, the development of the one gene—one enzyme hypothesis. As that case shows, the *goal* of coherent interdisciplinary integration not only provides guidance for research, but also provides the standard for recognizing *failed* integrations of the sort that van der Steen criticizes.

Burian, Richard M and Richardson, Robert C. A Defense of Propensity Interpretations of Fitness. *Proc Phil Sci Ass*, 1, 349-362, 1992.

We offer a systematic examination of propensity interpretations of fitness, which emphasizes the role that fitness plays in evolutionary theory and takes seriously the probabilistic character of evolutionary change. We distinguish questions of the probabilistic character of fitness from the particular interpretations of probability which could be incorporated. The roles of selection and drift in evolutionary models support the view that fitness must be understood within a probabilistic framework, and the specific character of organism/environment interactions supports the conclusion that fitness must be understood as a propensity rather than as a limiting frequency.

Burke, Peter (ed). *Critical Thought Series: 2—Critical Essays on Michel Foucault*. Brookfield, Scolar Pr, 1992.

Burkitt, Ian. Overcoming Metaphysics: Elias and Foucault on Power and Freedom. *Phil Soc Sci*, 23(1), 50-72, Mr 93.

In their respective analyses of Western civilisations, both Norbert Elias and Michel Foucault were concerned to overcome metaphysical notions of power and freedom, seeing them as relations rather than properties. This essay explores the similarities in their understanding of power and freedom, and also the differences between them—most importantly the Nietzschean philosophy that is the foundation of Foucault's analysis. The author argues that Nietzschean concepts such as "agonism" reintroduce metaphysics to Foucault's genealogy. Alternatively, Elias's work is based on a sociological ontology from which truly relational concepts of power and freedom can be devised.

Burnell, Peter. The Problem of Service to Unjust Regimes in Augustine's *City of God*. *J Hist Ideas*, 54(2), 177-188, Ap 93.

Augustine taught that civil justice can be achieved in some degree, and that we must not shirk our civil duties. Reputedly he at the same time forbade revolution. Actually he forbade it in practice; but the City of God, which contains his most developed theoretical treatments of such issues, shows that in principle he accepted that the structure of society might rightly be changed by political intervention.

Burnell, Peter J. The Status of Politics in St Augustine's *City of God*. *Hist Polit Thought*, 13(1), 13-29, Spr 92.

The current orthodoxy is that Augustine regarded politics not as natural to the human make-up, but as a response to our fallen condition, serving ephemeral ends. The classic passages from the City of God show that Augustine regarded politics as natural to man: certain kinds of just things only a state can do. From our condition arises the co-ercion constantly entailed. Despite original sin the rectitude of the civil state (Divine Grace assumed) is in principle the pre-eminent natural form of human virtue. Practically, however, Christianity for Augustine shows little, though a little, politically reformative influence.

Burnor, Richard. Rethinking Objective Homogeneity: Statistical Versus Ontic Approaches. *Phil Stud*, 71(3), 307-325, S 93.

Burns, Peter. The Status and Function of Divine Simpleness in *Summa Theologia* 1a, 2-13. *Thomist*, 57(1), 1-26, Ja 93.

Burnstone, Daniel. 'The Very Culture of the Feelings': Poetry and Poets in Mill's Moral Philosophy. *Utilitas*, 4(1), 81-104, My 92.

Burnyeat, M F. Gregory Vlastos. *Phronesis*, 37(2), 137-140, 1992.

A memorial address on the life and work of Gregory Vlastos.

Burnyeat, M F. Utopia and Fantasy in Psychoanalysis, Mind and Art, Hopkins, Jim (ed). Cambridge, Blackwell, 1992.

The repeated claims in Plato's *Republic* that the ideal city is a practical possibility are to be taken seriously. The fantasy theme, and the reminiscences of Aristophanes' *Ecclesiazousae*, are designed to help us take them seriously. We need to indulge in fantasy in order to see that the ideal city is as practicable as it is desirable.

Buroker, Jill Vance. The Port-Royal Semantics of Terms. *Synthese*, 96(3), 455-475, S 93.

Although the *Port-Royal Logic* of Antoine Arnauld and Pierre Nicole was the most influential logic textbook up through the nineteenth-century, relatively little attention has been paid to it. This article examines the Port-Royal theory of judgment and its foundation in the Cartesian theory of ideas against the backdrop of Fregean semantics. The first part shows how the theory of judgment incorporates the classical notions of conception, negation, and categorical subject-predicate forms. The second half gives an overview of the Port-Royal semantics of general terms, focussing on the ways in which the authors collapse the distinction between naming and predicating.

Burrell, David B. An Introduction to *Theology and Social Theory*. *Mod Theol*, 8(4), 319-329, Oct 92.

It is the sustained thesis of this wide-ranging and erudite study that the "new science of politics", conceived in modern times as an alternative to theological differences, in fact offers an alternative *theological* proposal for human destiny. And that must logically be the case, since the social sciences must presume to offer a *telos* (or *end*) for human existence, which can only be asserted and believed by its proponents. By showing how inherently theological are the proposed alternatives to faith, the author renders invaluable critical readings of Durkheim and Weber, Hegel and Marx, Nietzsche, Heidegger, Derrida, Deleuze, Lyotard and Foucault, within a neo-Augustinian perspective.

Burri, Alex. The Linguistic Winding Road. *Dialectica*, 46(3-4), 215-224, 1992.

Burrow, Richard. *Gulliver's Travels*: The Stunting of a Philosopher. *Interpretation*, 21(1), 41-57, Fall 93.

Burrow Jr, Rufus. Two Key Elements in Francis J McConnell's Social Ethics. *Personalist Forum*, 8(2), 73-87, Fall 92.

Burrows, Mark S. Naming the God Beyond Names: Wisdom from the Tradition on the Old Problem of God-Language. *Mod Theol*, 9(1), 37-53, Ja 93.

This essay explores the problem of naming God within the Christian tradition, bringing a Wittgensteinian approach to language into conversation with the apophatic tradition of medieval Christian mysticism. Particular attention is paid to the "negative theology" of Pseudo-Dionysius, on one hand, and to the analogical understanding of language as articulated by Thomas Aquinas, on the other. In contrast to an approach that would evaluate God-names in strictly socio-cultural terms, this essay suggests that we understand such names not as objective in an ontological sense, but as referential or metaphorical and as incarnational in a functional sense.

Burstow, Bonnie. How Sexist is Sartre?. *Phil Lit*, 16(1), 32-48, Ap 92.

Burt, Donald X. Courageous Optimism: Augustine on the Good of Creation. *Augustin Stud*, 21, 55-66, 1990.

This article explores St Augustine's response to the problem of evil existing in a world controlled by a loving God. The conclusion is that despite the pain from natural evils and the malice reflected in moral evil, there is no contradiction in a good God creating a world in which such evils exist. Indeed, this is the "best possible world".

Burt, Donald X. Friendship and Subordination in Earthly Societies. *Augustin Stud*, 22, 83-123, 1991.

This article argues that St. Augustine believed that friendship should be the foundation of every human society. After a discussion of his thoughts on friendship, application is made to his vision of the ideal family, state, and religious community. Subordination of ruler to ruled in each of these is softened by the fact that it is a relationship between friends.

Burton, Stephan L. Reply to Garrard and McNaughton. *Analysis*, 53(1), 59-61, Ja 93.

Burton, Steven J. *Judging in Good Faith*. New York, Cambridge Univ Pr, 1992.

This book analyzes the grounds, content and force of a judge's legal and moral duties to uphold the law. It defends two primary theses. The good faith thesis holds that judges are bound in law to uphold the law, even when they have discretion, by acting only on reasons warranted by the conventional law as grounds for judicial decisions. The permissible discretion thesis holds that, when exercised in good faith, judicial discretion is compatible with the legitimacy of adjudication in a constitutional democracy under the rule of law.

Burwick, Frederick. Sir Charles Bell and the Vitalist Controversy in the Early Nineteenth Century in The Crisis in Modernism, Burwick, Frederick (ed). New York, Cambridge Univ Pr, 1992.

Burwick, Frederick. The Grotesque: Illusion versus Delusion in Aesthetic Illusion, Burwick, Frederick (ed). Hawthorne, de Gruyter, 1990.

Burwick, Frederick (ed) and Douglass, Paul (ed). *The Crisis in Modernism*. New York, Cambridge Univ Pr, 1992.

Burwick, Frederick (ed) and Pape, Walter (ed). *Aesthetic Illusion*. Hawthorne, de Gruyter, 1990.

Burwood, Les. Equality of Opportunity as a Sensible Educational Ideal. *J Phil Educ*, 26(2), 257-259, 1992.

John Wilson argued, in a recent paper, that equality of opportunity is neither coherent nor reasonable. It seems that we can better understand Wilson's points if we distinguish between what one might call perfect equality of opportunity and greater equality of opportunity. Further, the familiar notions of formal opportunity and substantive opportunity still seem crucial to an understanding of the issues.

Busch, Thomas W. Ethics and Ontology: Levinas and Merleau-Ponty. *Man World*, 25(2), 195-202, Ap 92.

Busche, Hubertus. Das Leib-Seele-Pentagon und die Kombinatorik attraktiver Vorstellungen—Ein folgenreiches Konzept der Leibnizschen Frühphilosophie. *Z Phil Forsch*, 46(4), 489-507, O-D 92.

Leibniz's as yet unnoticed hieroglyph of the *mind-body-pentagon* from his early student years is a secret key to his whole later metaphysics. The pentagon symbolizes the human organism with its five senses. The centre represents the mind or intellectual *point of view* as a focal point in the brain, wherein the impressions from the outward things concur. In the intellectual focus the radiuses of the *sensible species* get transformed into *intelligible species* and become selected and combined according their different attractive force for the will. With this geometrical scheme of visual point and angles Leibniz clarifies the causal relations between neuronal activities and mental acts. With the two circles (*sphaera sensus* and *sphaera intellectus*) he explains the difference between the *confuse* and the *distinct*, between mere *perception* and *apperception*.

Buschert, William and Kujundzic, Nebojsa. Staging the Life-World: Habermas and the Recuperation of Austin's Speech Act Theory. *J Theor Soc Behav*, 23(1), 105-116, Mr 93.

The intuitive seed which occasioned J L Austin's cultivation of speech act theory—what we characterize as the "situationist," performative character of language—has been largely sighted, we suggest, in the subsequent literature of speech act theory, in particular in the work of John Searle. In this paper we seek first to re-examine Austin's distinctive understanding of the speech act and, thereafter, to apply this understanding to some aspects of Jürgen Habermas's theory of communicative action with a view towards sketching a possible "dramaturgical" phenomenology and semiotics of speech acts.

Bushnell, Dana E. Identity, Psychological Continuity, and Rationality. *J Phil Res*, 18, 15-24, 1993.

Derek Parfit claims that all that rationally matters for a person is psychological connectedness or continuity, even without identity. A psychological replica of a person whose body is destroyed upon the replication rationally should be considered just as valuable as the original person. I argue against this, maintaining that any such copying procedure would be objectionable. First, I argue that a copy of an original person does not preserve identity to the original person. And second, I argue that because a copy does not retain the identity of the original, it is *not* irrational to regard a copy as of less value than the original.

Buss, Samuel R. Intuitionistic Validity in *T*-Normal Kripke Structures. *Annals Pure Applied Log*, 59(3), 159-173, F 93.

Let *T* be a first-order theory. A *T*-normal Kripke structure is one in which every world is a classical model of *T*. This paper gives a characterization of the intuitionistic theory *HT* of sentences intuitionistically valid (forced) in all *T*-normal Kripke structures and proves the corresponding soundness and completeness theorems. For Peano arithmetic (*PA*), the theory *HPA* is a proper subtheory of Heyting arithmetic (*HA*), so *HA* is complete but not sound for *PA*-normal Kripke structures.

Butler, Judith. *Bodies that Matter: On the Discursive Limits of 'Sex'*. New York, Routledge, 1993.

Butler, Judith. Commentary on "Hegel, Derrida and Bataille's Laughter" in Hegel and His Critics, Desmond, William (ed). Albany, SUNY Pr, 1989.

Butler, Judith. Response to Bordo's "Feminist Skepticism and the 'Maleness' of Philosophy". *Hypatia*, 7(3), 162-165, Sum 92.

Bordo argues that the "theoretics of heterogeneity" taken too far prevents us from being able make generalizations or broadly conceptual statements about women. I argue that the political efficacy of feminism does not depend on the capacity to speak from the perspective of "women" and that the insistence on the heterogeneity of the category of women does not imply an opposition to abstraction but rather moves abstract thinking in a self- critical and democratizing direction.

Butler, Judith. The Nothing That Is in Theorizing American Literature, Cowan, Bainard (ed). Baton Rouge, Louisiana St Univ Pr, 1991.

Butler, Keith. On Clark on Systematicity and Connectionism. *Brit J Phil Sci*, 44(1), 37-44, Mr 93.

In *Microcognition*, Andy Clark offers a rich and compelling response to Fodor and Pylyshyn's charge that connectionism cannot explain the systematicity of cognition. The present paper examines Clark's account and concludes that it is ultimately unsuccessful.

Butler, Keith. The Moral Status of Smoking. *Soc Theor Pract*, 19(1), 1-26, Spr 93.

This paper considers moral aspects of smoking. Smokers, it is argued, routinely violate the rights of others to be free from harm. The basic argument exploits the fact that smokers do something to nonsmokers, while the reverse is not true. The basic argument divides into three subarguments, corresponding to three levels of harm, each differing in strength and scope. Attention to the details of real-world situations reveals additional moral problems. Some policy considerations are also taken up.

Butler, Keith. The Physiology of Desire. *J Mind Behav*, 13(1), 69-88, Wint 92.

I argue, contrary to wide-spread opinion, that belief-desire psychology is likely to reduce smoothly to neuroscientific theory. I therefore reject P M Churchland's (1981) eliminativism and Fodor's (1976) nonreductive materialism. The case for this claim consists in an example reduction of the desire construct to a suitable construct in neuroscience. A brief account of the standard view of intertheoretic reduction is provided at the outset. An analysis of the desire to construct in belief-desire psychology is then undertaken. Armed with these tools, the paper moves to an examination of the neural structures responsible for the production of motor behavior. This examination provides the basis for a theory of the neurophysiology of desire. A neurophysiological state is isolated and claimed to be type-identical to the state of desiring.

Butterfield, Bruce (ed) and Kleist, Jürgen (ed). *Mythology: From Ancient to Post-Modern*. New York, Lang, 1992.

This book is a collection of sixteen essays by scholars who participated in a Mythology Symposium at the State University of New York, College at Plattsburgh in March, 1991. The essays are presented under four subject titles: Ancient Myths in Modern Contexts (Ulysses, Don Quixote, Don Juan, Amazonian Indians), Myth and Society (French-Canadian Messianism, American Exceptionalism, German-Jewish Tolerance, and Socialism), Myth and the Human Condition (in works of Camus, Ionesco, and Beckett), and Myth, Science, and Technology (the Gaia-concept, artificial intelligence, post-nuclear Re-Creation, and the film "Back to the Future, Part II").

Butterfield, Jeremy. Interpretation and Identity in Quantum Theory. *Stud Hist Phil Sci*, 24(3), 443-476, Ag 93.

I consider briefly Bohm's causal interpretation of quantum theory (QT); and at much greater length, van Fraassen's modal interpretation, in his book "Quantum Mechanics". I argue for three main points about identical particles. The first two concern QT with a fixed number of particles. 1) One can take the particles to be individuals. 2) QT violates even a very weak form of Identity of Indiscernibles. 3) In quantum field theory, the system itself is the individual, with particle and field aspects.

Butterfield, Jeremy. Probabilities and Conditionals: Distinctions By Example. *Proc Aris Soc*, 92, 251-272, 1992.

A single example exhibits the distinction between conditional probability, the probability of a conditional, and a conditional with a probabilistic consequent. And it shows this for a range of interpretations of the conditional connective, and of probability. Namely, for the strict conditional, and the Stalnaker-Lewis counterfactual conditional; and for probability as subjective or objective—and whether or not objective probability is taken to require indeterminism. Finally, I present a condition under which the distinctions collapse.

Butterworth, Charles E. Al-Farabi's Statecraft in Cross, Crescent, and Sword, Johnson, James Turner (ed). Westport, Greenwood Pr, 1990.

Philosophers writing within the medieval Islamic tradition were ever mindful of the horizon revelation places upon expression. Pre-eminent among them is al-Fārābī. Here, his thought is examined to see how it contributes to the later Christian debate about just war. For him, this question arises only within the context of a broader inquiry into the features of excellent political rule. By subordinating his investigation of the character of just war to that of the well-ordered regime in this manner, al-Fārābī presents primarily an account of statecraft.

Butterworth, Charles E. The Origins of Al-Razi's Political Philosophy. *Interpretation*, 20(3), 237-257, Spr 93.

The medieval Baghdad-based philosopher, al-Rāzi (865-925), presents the outlines of a political teaching in a small treatise entitled *Book of the Philosophic Life*. An English translation of the treatise is followed by a detailed analysis that shows how al-Rāzi's novel portrait of Socrates enlarges the sphere of philosophy. Claiming that in his mature years Socrates took philosophy beyond its conventional ethical and metaphysical bounds to examine human affairs, al-Rāzi argues that this is the true understanding of the philosophic life. In the process, he also shows how close he has come to this Socratic understanding.

Butterworth, Charles E (trans) and Muhammad, Abū Bakr and Al-Razi, Zakariyya. The Book of the Philosophic Life. *Interpretation*, 20(3), 227-236, Spr 93.

Button, Graham and Sharrock, Wes. A Disagreement over Agreement and Consensus in Constructionist Sociology. *J Theor Soc Behav*, 23(1), 1-25, Mr 93.

Butts, Robert E. Kant's Theory of Musical Sound: An Early Exercise in Cognitive Science. *Dialogue (Canada)*, 32(1), 3-24, Wint 93.

Bwele, Guillaume. Axes du Temps en Afrique et en Occident. *Quest*, 5(2), 48-62, D 91.

The take-off point for this reflection acknowledges the differences in the conceptualisation of time in Africa and the West, and seeks to establish that this present era, seen as modern, should lead to a great new synthesis under the imperatives of *openness* to the two cultures and civilisations that conduce to the instauration of new stabilizing factors, necessary for peoples and societies that have 'broken down' (en panne) on both sides and who should in any case, seek to avoid a certain 'radical emptiness' (depaysement radical).

Bybee, Michael D. Logic in Rhetoric—And Vice Versa. *Phil Rhet*, 26(3), 169-190, 1993.

Scholars traditionally study the principles of reasoning (logic) separately from the techniques of persuasion (rhetoric). Some philosophers, however, have attempted to reduce rhetoric to logic, and more recently some rhetoricians have advocated discarding logic as vacuous and tyrannical formalism. All these notions rest on systematic and profound misunderstandings of both rhetoric and logic dating from the time of Aristotle, confusions that contemporary investigations have only compounded. Sorting through these misapprehensions leads to a comprehensive general theory of both logic and rhetoric that accounts for the strengths of each and describes their interrelatedness.

AUTHOR INDEX WITH ABSTRACTS 431 **Callaway, H G**

Byrne, Edmund F. Nuclear Holocaust in American Films. *Res Phil Technol*, 9, 13-21, 1989.

The chances of our species' surviving might be improved if films portrayed nuclear holocaust as realistically as horror movies do small scale carnage. American films, however, grossly understate the catastrophic dimensions of a nuclear attack before, during, and after its occurrence. This cosmetization is regrettably consistent with the pro-military myth that a nuclear war is winnable; and the resulting disinformation does far more damage than would a diminished commitment to esthetic indirection. For what is at issue is the downfall not just of some worthy personage, as in classical tragedy, but of the entire world as we know it.

Byrne, James M. Foucault on Continuity: The Postmodern Challenge to Tradition. *Faith Phil*, 9(3), 335-352, Jl 92.

The work of Michel Foucault poses a challenge to all thinking which situates itself in the context of a tradition. This article outlines this challenge by reference to Foucault's views on the continuity/discontinuity problem in history. When Foucault's own position is clarified in relation to a position of absolute discontinuity it can be seen to offer possibilities for theological thinking. The article concludes with some suggestions on the contributions which Foucault's notion of history and tradition can offer to theology on the formal levels of methodology, hermeneutics, discourse, and the body.

Byrne, Peter. A Defence of Christian Revelation. *Relig Stud*, 29(3), 381-394, S 93.

The article is an extended critical discussion of Richard Swinburne's *Revelation: from Metaphor to Analogy*. It explores the extent to which Swinburne's defence of Christianity depends on showing its content to be a priori probable. Reasons are offered against this conclusion and against many of the detailed contentions in Swinburne's case.

Cabada Castro, M. La reflexión sobre la negación o afirmación de la vida en Schopenhauer, Feuerbach, Wagner y Nietzsche. *Pensamiento*, 188(47), 385-414, O-D 91.

En este artículo se intenta hacer un seguimiento analítico del pensamiento de los autores indicados en el título en torno al tema de fondo de la actitud filosófica, afirmadora o negadora, ante la experiencia de la vida humana. Se intenta poner de relieve y valorar las dependencias o influjos mutuos ideológicos y, al mismo tiempo, las mutuas críticas sistemáticas al respecto. Con ello aparecerá que hay un nexo de continuidad y profundización en el tratamiento de una cuestión que tiene una indudable importancia sistemática para la comprensión del vivir humano.

Cabezón, José I (ed). *Buddhism, Sexuality, and Gender*. Albany, SUNY Pr, 1992.

This book explores historical, textual, and social questions relating to the position and experience of women and gay people in the Buddhist world from India and Tibet to Sri Lanka, China, and Japan. It focuses on four key areas: Buddhist history, contemporary culture, Buddhist symbols, and homosexuality, and it covers Buddhism's entire history, from its origins to the present day. The result of original and innovative research, the authors offer new perspectives on the history of the attitudes toward, and of the self-perception of, women in both ancient and modern Buddhist societies. They explore key social issues such as abortion, examine the use of rhetoric and symbols in Buddhist texts and cultures, and discuss the neglected subject of Buddhism and homosexuality.

Cabrera, Julio. Contra la Condenación Universal de los Argumentos Ad Hominem. *Manuscrito*, 15(1), 129-150, Ap 92.

A defense of a certain kind of *ad hominem* arguments is proposed here. It is shown that, in certain cases, considering the personal characteristics of the proponent of an argument is relevant for the assessment of its objective truth-content. Contemporary formal logic's—both classical and non-classical—inability to provide an adequate account of all aspects of the validity of argumentation is criticized, taking as an illustration the problem of the so-called *"ad hominem fallacies"*.

Cacciari, Massimo and Sartarelli, Stephen (trans). *Architecture and Nihilism: On the Philosophy of Modern Architecture*. New Haven, Yale Univ Pr, 1993.

Cacciari studies the relation between philosophy and modern architecture and applies the thinking of avantgarde architects, artists, and writers to the social and political problems raised by technological society. He begins by defining the modern metropolis, using the terms and ideas of Georg Simmel and Max Weber, but revealing where their frameworks are limited. He then examines the work of Adolf Loos and other architects and designers in early twentieth-century Vienna, showing how their architecture and criticism expose the alienation and utopianism in notions of the organic city.

Cacciatore, Giuseppe. "Historismus" e mondo moderno: Dilthey e Troeltsch. *G Crit Filosof Ital*, 71(1), 14-48, Ja-Ap 92.

Cadó, Valdemar. L'esprit dans la philosophie de René Le Senne. *Laval Theol Phil*, 48(3), 343-350, O 92.

La notion d'esprit occupe une place centrale dans la philosophie de René Le Senne. L'esprit est ou l'essence ou l'origine de tout ce qui existe. Réfléchissant sur notre propre expérience personnelle, Le Senne définit l'esprit comme une "unité opératoire d'une relation en exercice". L'esprit est un et plusieurs. En lui se retrouvent aussi bien les esprits finis que l'Esprit infini. Le Senne reçoit la notion d'esprit de la tradition chrétienne néo-platonicienne et de l'hégélianisme, mais le rôle de ces deux apports dans la synthése finale qu'il en tire reste problématique. Le Senne est surtout intéressé par la dynamique de la vie de l'esprit humain qui a pour caractéristique, selon lui, d'être tourné vers l'infini.

Cadwallader, Eva H. From Greek to Globalist: Seven Valuational Attitudes toward Transnationalism. *Hist Euro Ideas*, 16(4-6), 495-500, Ja 93.

Philosophical foundations (rather than the *praxis*) of nationalism and transnationalism are addressed. Nicolai Hartmann's aretaic method, in which an ethos is described in terms of the virtues characterizing its ideals, is expanded to show the relevance of seven ethea in Western history. The seven ethea are the Greco-Roman, Judaic, Christian, Nietzschean, (contemporary) American, Marxist and Globalist. Transnationalism based upon a globalist ethos is viewed as potentially the most constructive attitude our planet has yet seen.

Cahoone, Lawrence. Limits of the Social and Rational Self in Selves, People, and Persons, Rouner, Leroy S (ed). Notre Dame, Univ Notre Dame Pr, 1992.

Caicedo, Xavier. Compactness and Normality in Abstract Logics. *Annals Pure Applied Log*, 59(1), 33-43, Ja 93.

Calef, Scott. The Replaceability Argument and Abortion. *Amer Cath Phil Quart*, 66(4), 447-463, Autumn 92.

Classical Utilitarian proponents of animal liberation agree that pain is evil, whether human or animal. Nevertheless, some suggest that it is permissible to painlessly kill a happy animal if the slain animal is replaced by another, equally happy animal which would not otherwise have existed. This is the "Replaceability" Argument. I discuss implications of this argument for the abortion debate. After drawing comparisons between sentient fetuses and non-human animals, I argue that the consistent Utilitarian position is to affirm the moral permissibility of late term abortion only if the fetus is replaced by another which would not otherwise exist.

Calef, Scott. Why is Annihiliation a Great Gain for Socrates? The Argument of *Apology* 40c3-e2. *Ancient Phil*, 12(2), 285-297, Fall 92.

At *Apology* 40c-e, Socrates argues that if death is dreamless sleep, it is "an advantage." This is problematic, since Socrates is pursuing virtue and believes that the philosophical life is worthwhile. After examining arguments for a rhetorical reading and resolutions suggested by Brickhouse and Smith, Xenophon, West, and Armleder, I propose that annihilation is a gain because it enables Socrates to escape corruption. The only alternative to death following his sentencing is unjust escape into exile. Annihilation enables Socrates to avoid this fate. I conclude by showing how this reading harmonizes well with the *Apology's* other passages concerning death.

Calek, Oldrich. The Hermeneutic of Art as Being-in-the-World (in Czechoslovakian). *Estetika*, 29(4), 36-51, 1992.

Callahan, Daniel. When Self-Determination Runs Amok. *Hastings Center Rep*, 22(2), 52-55, My-Je 92.

Callahan, Daniel and Thornton, Barbara C and Nelson, James Lindemann. Bioethics Education: Expanding the Circle of Participants. *Hastings Center Rep*, 23(1), 25-29, Ja-F 93.

The Hastings Center Project on Bioethics Education identifies and describes the core components of a bioethics curriculum as well as key issues regarding the education of clinicians, ethics committee members and policy- makers in the many diverse settings in which learning about bioethics now takes place. The challenge of translating theory into action as well as the political and practical realities of developing bioethics programs is discussed. Evaluation of existing courses and programs in bioethics is recommended while certification of programs is considered premature.

Callahan, Joan. Surrogate Motherhood: Politics and Privacy. *J Clin Ethics*, 4(1), 82-91, Spr 93.

Callan, Eamonn. Finding a Common Voice. *Educ Theor*, 42(4), 429-441, Fall 92.

Recent feminist scholarship purports to disclose a moral orientation at odds with justice. The alleged alternative orientation, which gives salience to caring rather that respect for rights, suggests a new understanding of moral progress and moral education. But the bifurcation of morality into distinct phenomena of caring and justice is a mistaken. Neither the caring nor the justice worth having can be adequately characterized in abstraction from the other. Justice is needed even when caring attachments are deep and unselfish. Furthermore, approaches to moral education which ignore the importance of caring attachments endanger the motivational efficacy of justice.

Callaway, H G. *Context for Meaning and Analysis*. Amsterdam, Rodopi, 1993.

This book is a critical study of the analytic tradition in the philosophy of language from Frege and Russell to Quine and Davidson. It focuses on issues central to the concepts of meaning and analysis. The guiding conviction is that the philosophy of language, in its scientifically oriented versions, culminates in the philosophy of mind. Connections are drawn between the analytic tradition and pragmatic and naturalistic themes found in Dewey's work. The book is completed by a humanistic approach to questions of values and democracy.

Callaway, H G. Democracy, Value Inquiry, and Dewey's Metaphysics. *J Value Inq*, 27(1), 13-27, Ja 93.

This essay proposes a re-evaluation of Dewey's work with emphasis upon the ability of his philosophy to effect a realistic reformulation and development of America's tradition of humanistic liberalism. Dewey combines the tough-minded realism (or naturalism), congenial to the scientific orientation of American philosophy, with a firm conviction of the need for values and revaluation in community life. I draw on recent work of Hilary Putnam on Dewey and argue for the viability of Dewey's conception of value inquiry. Included here is a rejection of the fact-value distinction, as usually understood, and criticism of cultural relativism. (edited)

Callaway, H G. Does Language Determine Our Scientific Ideas?. *Dialectica*, 46(3-4), 225-242, 1992.

This paper argues that the influence of language on science, philosophy and other field is mediated by communicative practices. Where communications is more restrictive, established linguistic structures exercise a tighter control over innovations and scientifically motivated reforms of language. The viewpoint here centers on the thesis that argumentation is crucial in the understanding and evaluation of proposed reforms and that social practices which limit argumentation serve to erode scientific objectivity. Thus, a plea is made for a sociology of scientific belief designed to understand and insure social-institutional conditions of the possibility of knowledge and its growth. A chief argument draws on work of Axelrod concerning the evolution of cooperation.

Callaway, H G. Meaning Holism and Semantic Realism. *Dialectica*, 46(1), 41-59, 1992.

Reconciliation of semantic holism with interpretation of individual expressions is advanced here by means of a relativization of sentence meaning to object language theories viewed as idealizations of belief-systems. Fodor's view of the autonomy of the special sciences is emphasized and this is combined with detailed replies to his recent criticisms of meaning holism. The argument is that the need for empirical evidence requires a holistic approach to meaning. Thus, semantic realism requires semantic holism.

Callicott, J Baird. Rolston on Intrinsic Value: A Deconstruction. *Environ Ethics*, 14(2), 129-144, Sum 92.

Central to Holmes Rolston's *Environmental Ethics* is the theoretical quest of most environmental philosophers for a defensible concept of intrinsic value for nonhuman natural entities and nature as a whole. Rolston's theory is similar to Paul Taylor's in rooting intrinsic value in conation, but dissimilar in assigning value bonuses to consciousness and self-consciousness and value dividends to organic wholes and elemental nature. I argue that such a theory of intrinsic value flies in the face of the subject/ object and fact/ value dichotomies of the metaphysical foundations of modern science — a problem Rolston never directly confronts. The *modern* scientific view is obsolete. A *post-modern* scientific world view provides for a range of *potential* values in nature actualizable upon interaction with consciousness. The best that a modern scientific world view can provide are subject - generated — though not necessarily subject - centered — values in nature.

Callicott, J Baird. The Land Ethic Today. *Topoi*, 12(1), 41-51, Mr 93.

Has the shift in ecology from a static organismic paradigm to a dynamic individualistic paradigm rendered the Leopold land ethic obsolete in contemporary conservation philosophy? No. Though a life-long advocate of wilderness preservation, Leopold's eventual philosophy of conversation called for a human harmony with nature through "sustainable development", i.e., human economic initiatives limited by ecological exigencies. Leopold explored the concept of "land health" as an objective norm that any development must meet in order to qualify as sustainable.

Callicott, John B. La Nature est morte, vive la nature!. *Hastings Center Rep*, 22(5), 17-23, S-O 92.

Contrary to recent reports, the death of nature is much exaggerated. Rather, the modern *idea* of nature as a pristine realm untrammelled by human contrivances is dead. A new more dynamic, processive, organic idea of nature that includes human beings and our works as entirely natural components is taking shape. The new concept of nature may trickle down into the mass mind through its expression in the current and future generation of postmodern technologies.

Callieri, Bruno. Some Epistemological Aspects of Present-Day Psychopathology in Analecta Husserliana, XXXI, Tymieniecka, Anna-Teresa (ed). Dordrecht, Kluwer, 1990.

Callinicos, Alex. Reactionary Postmodernism? in Postmodernism and Society, Boyne, Roy (ed). New York, St Martin's Pr, 1990.

Calogero, F. Pluralità delle culture e universalità del diritto. *Sapienza*, 46(1), 92-94, 1993.

Calvert, Brian. Locke on Punishment and the Death Penalty. *Philosophy*, 68(264), 211-229, Ap 93.

This paper argues that Locke's justification for the use of the death penalty can be seen as a blend of retributive and utilitarian features though Locke does not make it clear which of these features should be given priority when conflicts arise between them. In addition, while Locke has sometimes been taken as endorsing the use of execution as a punishment for a wide variety of offences, the paper claims that Locke is much more sparing in its application and regards it as a measure to be employed only in the most desperate circumstances.

Calvert, Brian. Retribution, Arbitrariness and the Death Penalty. *J Soc Phil*, 23(3), 140-165, Wint 92.

If we say that the penalty should fit the crime and that death is significantly more severe than other penalties, the imposition of the death penalty is only justifiable if there is a significant difference between crimes for which death is the penalty and crimes for which it is not. Retentionists contend that for execution to be deserved murders must be "different in kind" from murders which do not deserve execution - implying that a clear distinction can be drawn between them. This article denies that any clear distinction exists and claims that the imposition of the death penalty is arbitrary.

Calvin, Michael. Memories of Michael Polanyi in Manchester. *Tradition Discovery*, 18(2), 40-42, 1991-92.

Camacho, Luis A. Algunos problemas lógicos de verificación y refutación en ciencias del ser humano. *Rev Filosof (Costa Rica)*, 30(71), 7-16, J 92.

A demarcation criterion to distinguish between social and natural sciences is here proposed on the basis of the different relation between the knower and the known in each case. Problems of verification in the human sciences are connected to this difference.

Cambiano, Giuseppe. Remarques sur Platon et la *technè*. *Rev Phil Fr*, 4, 407-416, O-D 91.

Camp Jr, Joseph L. The Ballad of Clyde the Moose in Thought Experiments in Science and Philosophy, Horowitz, Tamara (ed). Lanham, Rowman & Littlefield, 1991.

Campanale, Domenico. *Pistis* e d *Episteme*: A Proposito di una lettura "diacritica" di 1 Cor 2, 3. *G Metaf*, 14(2), 331-340, My-Ag 92.

Campani, Carlos. *Pianificazione e teoria critica*. Napoli, Liguori Ed, 1992.

Campbell, Courtney S. Body, Self, and the Property Paradigm. *Hastings Center Rep*, 22(5), 34-42, S-O 92.

Is the body property? Do persons own their bodies? This essay uses the debate over a commercial market in transplantable organs to examine the moral significance of a property paradigm of the human body. This paradigm is constituted by principles of integrity, alienability, and empowerment. Public policies, including policies about organ selling, supported by the property paradigm will reflect a dialection relation between the body as "other" and as "identified" with the self.

Campbell, Courtney S. Moral Responsibility and Irregular War in Cross, Crescent, and Sword, Johnson, James Turner (ed). Westport, Greenwood Pr, 1990.

Campbell, James. Ayer and Pragmatism in The Philosophy of A J Ayer, Hahn, Lewis E (ed). Peru, Open Court, 1992.

This paper first explores some of the aspects of Ayer's discussion of Pragmatism, with a focus on William James's understanding of truth. Then it considers a major aspect of Pragmatism that Ayer does not consider—its attempt to integrate facts and values. Finally, I attempt to show the root of this mission in different senses of the nature of the philosophic endeavor.

Campbell, James. DuBois and James. *Trans Peirce Soc*, 28(3), 569-581, Sum 92.

This paper examines the relationship between the Harvard philosopher and psychologist, William James (1842-1910), and the American activist and social scientist, William Edward Burghardt Du Bois (1868-1963), who studied at Harvard between the years 1888-1892. The first section details the historical aspects of this relationship, and the second section discounts the likelihood that Du Bois derived his social stance from James. The final section explores four parallel aspects of their thought in an attempt to uncover the nature of Du Bois's attraction to James.

Campbell, James. George Herbert Mead on Social Fusion and the Social Critic in Frontiers in American Philosophy, Volume I, Burch, Robert W (ed). College Station, Texas A&M Univ Pr, 1992.

This paper is an examination of the ongoing problem of maintaining individuality in the face of social pressure as interpreted through the work of G H Mead. After an initial consideration of the ideas of H D Thoreau about resisting social fusion, his views are rejected in favor of Mead's sounder analysis of human nature. Finally, some suggestions are made for social action and for re-interpreting Thoreau.

Campbell, Keith. David Armstrong and Realism about Colour in Ontology, Causality and Mind: Essays in Honour of D M Armstrong, Bacon, John (ed). New York, Cambridge Univ Pr, 1993.

This paper points to the history of empirical research as providing successive refutations of realism about color, taking the story as far as Land's theory and Opponent Processing theory. Taking a lead from Hardin's *Color for Philosophers*, it presents a case against Armstrong's reductive realism which appeals to the phenomenology of color mixtures, and a new version of the spectrum-shift argument. To avoid dualism of an almost Cartesian strength, it seems that a full-scale error theory, according to which there are, in reality, no colors, either in objects or in experiences, may have to be embraced.

Campbell, Keith. Swimming Against the Tide. *Inquiry*, 36(1-2), 161-177, Mr 93.

This is a Review Discussion of John Foster, The Immaterial Self: A Defence of the Cartesian Dualist Conception of the Mind whose main theses are that all materialist reductions of mentality are demonstrable invalid, and that the mind is no mere Humean bundle, but an authentic substance. The review takes issue with Foster on three major grounds: (i) the argument proceeds too directly, being insufficiently willing to re-open issues when new considerations arise, (ii) there is a poor appreciation of scientific thought, and (iii) there is too much confidence in the deliverances of intuition, and in our capacity to discern real essences.

Campbell, Keith (ed) and Bacon, John (ed) and Reinhardt, Lloyd (ed). *Ontology, Causality and Mind: Essays in Honour of D M Armstrong*. New York, Cambridge Univ Pr, 1993.

This Festschrift is a collection of papers on questions central to the philosophy of D M Armstrong, each followed by a reply from Armstrong. Topics covered include universals, dispositions, the combinatorial approach to modality, individuation, causality, laws of nature, consciousness, and color. The contributors are William G Lycan, David Lewis, Peter Forrest, John Bigelow, D H Mellor, Evan Fales, J J C Smart, C B Martin, Peter Menzies, Frank Jackson, and Keith Campbell. A complete bibliography of Armstrong's works up to 1992 closes the book.

Campbell, Mark Robin. John Cage's 4'33": Using Aesthetic Theory to Understand a Musical Notion. *J Aes Educ*, 26(1), 83-91, Spr 92.

Campbell, P G and Coval, Samuel C. *Agency in Action: The Practical Rational Agency Machine*. Dordrecht, Kluwer, 1992.

Campbell, Richmond M. Critical Notice of Allan Gibbard Wise Choices, Apt Feelings: A Theory of Normative Judgment. *Can J Phil*, 23(2), 299-323, Je 93.

On Gibbard's theory of normative judgment, to say that something is rational is to express one's acceptance of norms that permit it, not to make a true or false statement. Though the theory is an advance over earlier noncognitivisms, it faces three serious problems: 1) what the theory implies about norm acceptance conflicts with the analysis it gives of the meaning of contexts which embed normative content; 2) the truth of what it implies about normative authority is called into question by the very terms of the theory; 3) the theory appears committed to an implausibly strong form of normative internalism.

Campbell, Robert L and Bickhard, Mark H. Clearing the Ground: Foundational Questions Once Again. *J Prag*, 17(5-6), 557-602, Je 92.

We undertake a reply to 16 commentaries on our target article "Some foundational questions concerning language studies." We rebut objections to our critique of encoding-based conceptions of representation and defend our alternative, which is based on interactive differentiation and implicit definition. We show that the consequences of interactivism for language studies are far-reaching: semantics cannot be distinguished from pragmatics in the customary way, syntax cannot be autonomous, and language comprehension and understanding cannot be the processing of derivative encodings. We discuss similarities and differences between Prague School functionalism and our conception of language as a system of operators that transform situation conventions. We respond to positivist critiques of our enterprise, on the one hand, and objections based on Continental philosophy, on the other; we deal with the careless thinking in the linguistic community that gives rise to misapprehensions such as the view that our program is based on behaviorism. (edited)

Campbell, Robert L and Bickhard, Mark H. Some Foundational Questions Concerning Language Studies: With a Focus on Categorial Grammars and Model-Theoretic Possible Worlds Semantics. *J Prag*, 17(5-6), 401-433, Je 92.

Campbell, Tom D. Unlawful Discrimination in Ethical Dimensions of Legal Theory, Sadurski, Wojciech (ed). Amsterdam, Rodopi, 1991.

In the interest of an effective legal formulation of anti-discrimination law in the light of its moral purpose, it is argued that motive-neutral legal definitions of unlawful discrimination are instrumentally well adapted to the role of anti-discrimination law in combatting prejudice-based disfavoring provided that discriminatory classifications are confined to those which identify groups which are on the receiving end of systematic and serious prejudiced disadvantage.

Campolo, Christian. Unidentified Awareness: Hume's Perceptions of Self. *Auslegung*, 18(2), 157-166, Sum 92.

When Hume discusses personal identity in the *Treatise*, he insists that there is no impression, and so no idea, of the self. But when he discusses the passions, especially those of pride and humility, he insists on the importance of our impressions and ideas of ourselves. The appearance of inconsistency is an unfortunate result of Hume's use of similar terminology in referring to two very different features of the self. One of these features, a Cartesian version of personal identity, Hume firmly rejects. The other feature involves a notion of self-awareness which is crucial to his naturalistic account of human nature.

Canavan, Francis. Natural Law and Judicial Review. *Pub Affairs Quart*, 7(4), 277-286, O 93.

Judicial review in the United States is the power of courts to declare acts of the other branches of government void when they conflict with the constitution. The question addressed here is not whether there is a natural law that binds governments, but whether judges are empowered to enforce it through judicial review. The answer is that they are not. The constitution includes certain natural law principles in its text, but it is itself a positive law, and the power of judges does reach beyond enforcing what is clearly in its text.

Canavero, A Tarabochia. La virtù della giustizia: da "habitudo" ad "habitus": A proposito della giustizia "metaphorice dicta" in Alberto Magno e Tommaso d'Aquino. *Riv Filosof Neo-Scolas*, 84(4), 608-631, O-D 92.

After reading the fifth book of the *Nicomeachean Ethics*, Albertus the Great modified his definition of "justice", no more *habitudo* (i.e., right order of the faculties of the anima), but *habitus* (i.e., tendency of the man to keep or to restore fair relations with other men). For this reason, St. Thomas, following his master, asserts that only in a metaphorical sense (*secundum metaphoram*) the "justice" is founded "in the same man".

Candlish, Stewart. 'Das Wollen ist auch nur eine Erfahrung' in Wittgenstein's Philosophical Investigations, Arrington, Robert T (ed). New York, Routledge, 1991.

Wittgenstein's discussion of the will in *Philosophical Investigations* has received the usual treatment by commentators: individual passages have been quarried, then discussed or developed in isolation. The curious opacity of the whole has gone largely unremarked, and many of its odder passages are ignored or explained away superficially. I argue that this opacity results from over-refinement; a clearer perception of the discussion's point is obtained by investigating rougher, more discursive texts lying in the historical background. The *Investigations* discussion is mostly negative; but remarks in *Zettel* contain the sketch of a positive view which, unlike Wittgenstein's parallel views in other areas, has never been taken seriously.

Canévet, Mariette. Culture païenne et foi chrétienne aux racines de l'Europe: La "Cité de Dieu" d'Augustin. *Gregorianum*, 74(1), 5-16, 1993.

When in 410 the hordes of Ilaric entered Rome, Augustine found himself in a situation somewhat similar to ours; that, namely, of a culture already christianized, faced with hostile assaults from outside. The reflections found in *The City of God* can help us to see what characterizes today's Europe: is it a human culture or a Christian culture? There exists, according to Augustine, a culture "according to man" which possesses its own values; but, unless reference is made to the "last ends", such values bear in themselves the principle of their own corruption: pride, the instinct of domination, a freedom which develops to the cost of others. Christianity is not to be confounded with any culture: it directs them towards what saves from morality. Two contemporary texts show the abiding validity of the criteria put forward by Augustine for a Christian evaluation of "the future of Europe".

Canfield, J V. Private Language: 'Philosophical Investigations' Section 258 and Environs in Wittgenstein's Philosophical Investigations, Arrington, Robert L (ed). New York, Routledge, 1991.

Canfield, J V. Wittgenstein's Intentions in Wittgenstein's Intentions, Canfield, J V (ed). Hamden, Garland, 1993.

Canfield, J V (ed) and Shanker, Stuart G (ed). *Wittgenstein's Intentions*. Hamden, Garland, 1993.

Canivet, Michel. Le principe éthique d'universalité et discussion. *Rev Phil Louvain*, 90(85), 32-49, F 92.

The principle of universality may be understood in a deductive or in an intersubjective way depending on whether it requires the universal applicability of maxims (Kant) or their universal acceptability (Rawls, Habermas). The intersubjective interpretation, however, remains monological if acceptance by all reasonable beings is merely thought. The ethic of discussion (Habermas) avoids this objection when it submits norms to real discussions. However, these discussions are always particular and universality implies their infinity. The ethic of discussion accordingly can only reply to the historical urgency of decisions by reintroducing, within certain limitations, the monological principle of universality. These limitations are analogous to those in politics that legitimately limit the influence of the majority rule.

Canizares, Raul J. The Ethics of Santeria. *J Dharma*, 16(4), 368-374, O-D 91.

In this article, the author contends that part of the reason the Afro-Cuban religion Santeria is misunderstood in the West is that its values, ethics, and morality are markedly different from those of the Judeo-Christian/Islamic traditions. Abrahamic religions exhibit a duality (good/evil) not found in African traditional religions—the two are compared and contrasted.

Cannon, Dale. Toward the Recovery of Common Sense in a Post-Critical Intellectual Ethos. *Tradition Discovery*, 19(1), 5-15, 1992-93.

The modern critical tradition's strategy for defeating the demon of self doubt and securing certainty, as Hannah Arendt has written, restricts serious candidates for belief to those whose conditions of truth can be rendered wholly immanent to focal consciousness within a point of view that is simply taken for granted. Thereby it forecloses the possibility of recognizing the partiality of its own perspective vis-a-vis that of others, taking into account the relevant perspectives of other persons, and reaching any kind of sense in common between perspectives. The institutionalization of this strategy in 20th century academic life is amply and insightfully documented in Bruce Wilshire's *Moral Collapse of the University*. Michael Polanyi, in his writings, adumbrates a post-critical intellectual ethos in which the making of sense in common between persons of differing perspective is central to the enterprise of teaching, learning, and research. Key elements of such an intellectual ethos are articulated and explored.

Canovan, Margaret. *Hannah Arendt: A Reinterpretation of Her Political Thought*. New York, Cambridge Univ Pr, 1992.

Making extensive use of unpublished material, this new interpretation shows that Arendt's thought is both more complex and more deeply preoccupied with totalitarianism (Stalinist as well as Nazi) than is usually appreciated. *The Human Condition* and *On Revolution* read very differently once their links with *The Origins of Totalitarianism* are elucidated. New Light is thrown on many aspects of Arendt's thought, including her theory of action, her views on 'the social question' and her comments on morality in politics. Her tragic view of the human predicament and her anti-foundationalist political theory of 'plurality' have a great deal of relevance to the post-modern era.

Cantista, Maria José. The Meaning of 'Radical Foundation' in Husserl: The Outline of an Interpretation in Analecta Husserliana, XXXIV, Tymieniecka, Anna-Teresa (ed). Dordrecht, Kluwer, 1992.

Canto-Sperber, M. Le paradoxe du *Ménon* et la connaissance définitionnelle. *Rev Phil Fr*, 4, 659-663, O-D 91.

Cantor, Norman L. *Regulating Death*, Carlos F Gomez. *Crim Just Ethics*, 12(1), 71-78, Wint-Spr 93.

Cantrick, Robert. Is the Constructionalist Program Still Relevant?. *J Aes Art Crit*, 51(1), 71-72, Wint 93.

A time quale, according to Nelson Goodman in *Structure of Appearance*, is a time when, i.e., a temporal position. The question arises: is a time quale in music identified by a music notation referring to the same musical event at different performances or by a conductor referring to some musical event at different performances or by a conductor referring to some musical event at just one performance? Goodman has not mooted a fundamental problem for music theory and philosophy of music but sharpened it: how can a temporal position in music be identified?

Capaldi, Nicholas. The Dogmatic Slumber of Hume Scholarship. *Hume Stud*, 18(2), 117-135, N 92.

The standard view of Hume is sketched and then traced to its origin. Its origin lies in the way analytic philosophy has imposed its views on the history of modern philosophy. I conclude with a point by point refutation of the analytic reading of Hume.

Capeillères, Fabien. Sur le néo-Kantisme de E Cassirer. *Rev Metaph Morale*, 97(4), 517-546, O-D 92.

Based on an examination of the functional definition of "neokantianism," explicated by Cassirer in a paper of 1928, this article focuses on his Philosophy of Symbolic Forms, addressing its relationship to this definition and to several historical proponents of neokantianism.

Capek, Milic. Microphysical Indeterminacy and Freedom: Bergson and Peirce in The Crisis in Modernism, Burwick, Frederick (ed). New York, Cambridge Univ Pr, 1992.

On the request of the editor of the volume *The Crisis in Modernism* I allowed them to include Chapter 12 of my book *Bergson and Modern Physics*. I allowed them to incorporate some texts of the quotations into the text itself of the chapter.

Capek, Milic. On an Alleged Inconsistency in Whitehead. *Process Stud*, 20(3), 175-178, Fall 91.

The article deals with the claim made by John D Barrow and Frank J Opler, both authors of *The Anthropic Cosmological Principle* (Oxford Univ Press, 1980, p 216) on the inconsistency of Whitehead's two views about the nature of time: In *The Concept of Time*, he insists on "the global nature of time", and in his *Science and Modern World*, he denies the existence of the unique present. In my book, *Bergson and Modern Physics*, to which both authors refer (pp 252-3), I pointed out that the non-metrical character of Whitehead's "creative nature of time" is compatible with his denial of the absoluteness of one present instant. In other words, "contemporaneity" is different from alleged "co-instantaneity."

Caplan, Arthur L. Does the Philosophy of Medicine Exist?. *Theor Med*, 13(1), 67-77, Mr 92.

Despite the fact that there is a great deal of literature which is classified by the label "Philosophy of Medicine" it is not clear that such a field actually exists. To constitute a field, a line of inquiry must be integrated with other cognate inquiries, have an established canon, and a set of distinctive defining problems and issues. The philosophy of medicine as it currently exists fails to satisfy these criteria and thus does not yet exist.

Caponi, Orietta. Las raíces del machismo en la ideología judeo-cristiana de la mujer. *Rev Filosof (Costa Rica)*, 30(71), 37-44, J 92.

Applying the analysis of the dialectical relation between the mitical and social order we will study the effects of the Judaism and Christianity that have been negative to women. We will show how the Judaic and Christian myths have justified and perpetuated the patriarchal structure presenting the women's inferiority as plausible, rational and inevitable.

Capriotti, Emile. *The Grounds and Limits of Political Obligation*. New York, Lang, 1992.

This book deals with the question of whether citizens have an obligation to states or political entities generally. The argument of the book attempts to show that the individual receives benefits form the state that form both the grounds and also the limits of that obligation to the state. It revises and updates the State of Nature theory of classical social contract philosophy in the light of developments in game theory and economics. It offers an original theory of the relationship between the individual and the state based upon two principals of political obligation: The Nonaggression Principle and The Public Goods Principle.

Capurro, Rafael. Ein Grinsen ohne Katze: Von der Vergleichbarkeit zwischen 'künstlicher Intelligenz' und 'getrennten Intelligenzen'. *Z Phil Forsch*, 47(1), 93-102, Ja-Mr 93.

The purpose of the article is to analyze some similarities and differences between 'artificial intelligence' and the medieval representation of 'separate intelligences' on the basis of Thomas Aquinas' conception of higher (holy) intelligences. The similarity rests upon the conception of mind and matter as distinct and divisible entities which is a common basis to strong functionalism and to metaphysical dualism on the one hand, and on the idea of a higher intelligence on the other hand. The differences are shown on three levels: substantiality, knowledge and will.

Caputo, John D. A Final Word (Eight Famous Ones) in Modernity and Its Discontents, Marsh, James L (ed). Bronx, Fordham Univ Pr, 1992.

Caputo, John D. Heidegger and Theology in The Cambridge Companion to Heidegger, Guignon, Charles (ed). New York, Cambridge Univ Pr, 1993.

Caputo, John D. How to Avoid Speaking of God: The Violence of Natural Theology in Prospects for Natural Theology, Long, Eugene Thomas (ed). Washington, Cath Univ Amer Pr, 1992.

Caputo, John D. On Being Inside/Outside Truth in Modernity and Its Discontents, Marsh, James L (ed). Bronx, Fordham Univ Pr, 1992.

Caputo, John D. On Not Circumventing the Quasi-Transcendental in Working Through Derrida, Madison, Gary B (ed). Evanston, Northwestern Univ Pr, 1993.

Caputo, John D. Spirit and Danger in Ethics and Danger, Dallery, Arleen B (ed). Albany, SUNY Pr, 1992.

Caputo, John D. The Difficulty of Life: A Reply to Ronald H McKinney. *J Value Inq*, 26(4), 561-564, O 92.

Caputo, John D and Marsh, James L and Westphal, Merold. A Philosophical Dialogue in Modernity and Its Discontents, Marsh, James L (ed). Bronx, Fordham Univ Pr, 1992.

Caputo, John D (ed) and Marsh, James L (ed) and Westphal, Merold (ed). *Modernity and Its Discontents*. Bronx, Fordham Univ Pr, 1992.

Caramuta, Ersilia. Da Tebe ad Atene e da Atene a Tebe. *G Metaf*, 14(3), 373-442, S-D 92.

Carbone Jr, Peter F. Listening for the Call: Response to Professor Buford. *Proc S Atlantic Phil Educ Soc*, 36, 31-33, 1991.

Cardoni, Albert. Theology and the Heisenberg Uncertainty Principle: I. *Heythrop J*, 34(3), 247-273, Jl 93.

Carens, Joseph H. Difference and Domination: Reflections on the Relation Between Pluralism and Equality. *Nomos*, 32, 226-250, 1990.

This essay critically examines the claim that pluralism requires us to reject egalitarianism on the grounds that cultural differences between groups will inevitably lead to social and economic inequalities. The essay argues that most inequalities between groups are not due to cultural differences and that inequalities that *do* result from cultural differences are not legitimate if the cultural differences are themselves the product of domination by other groups. To distinguish inequality- generating cultural differences that deserve respect from those that do not, the essay takes up four cases: Asian-Americans, the Amish, American blacks, and women. Overall, the essay concludes that pluralism and equality are usually compatible and often mutually reinforcing.

Carey, David. A Reply to Johnson's Reply to "Should Computer Programs Be Ownable?". *Metaphilosophy*, 24(1-2), 91-96, Ja-Ap 93.

Carey's thesis is that *some* algorithms should be ownable. Johnson holds that *no* algorithm should be owned. The purpose of this paper is to show that we can by-pass the problem of defining what an algorithm is if we can agree about what features of algorithms are relevant. The main argument is this: If the ownership of x contributes to the public good more than the non-ownership of x does, then x should be owned. The ownership of some algorithms contributes to the public good more than non-ownership of them would. Therefore some algorithms should be ownable.

Carey, David. Should Computer Programs Be Ownable?. *Metaphilosophy*, 24(1-2), 76-84, Ja-Ap 93.

Deborah Johnson has proposed that although source code and object code may be protected as intellectual property by copyright, patent, or trade secrecy law, software algorithms should not be owned. Carey examines the two lines of ethical and legal argument, Lockean and utilitarianism, by which Johnson defends her proposal. He concludes that Johnson has not succeeded in ruling out the ownership of algorithms, that the Lockean approach fails, and that the utilitarian approach requires further empirical research. Karmarkar's algorithm, the Hindu-Arabic numeral system, Posner's principle of wealth maximization, Stallman's GNU, and arbitration between IBM and Fujitsu illustrate the discussion.

Cargile, James Thomas. On a Problem About Probability and Decision. *Analysis*, 52(4), 211-216, O 92.

The problem is choosing between two envelopes, given only that a sum was put in e1 and an unbiased coin tossed to determine whether twice or half that amount is put in e2. On the assumption that this means that the probability that e2 has the larger amount is 1/2, we can derive contradictory results using the standard method for calculating expected utilities. I argue that this assumption is false and that this case favors a propensity view of probability over a subjectivist or a frequency view.

Carley, Kathleen M and Kaufer, David S. Condensation Symbols: Their Variety and Rhetorical Function in Political Discourse. *Phil Rhet*, 26(3), 201-226, 1993.

Carling, Alan. Bread and Butter Ethics in Marx's Theory of History, Wetherly, Paul. Brookfield, Avebury, 1992.

Brecht said "Bread first, then ethics". This is seriously misleading as an expression of the Marxian attitude to ethical questions. If ethics are part of the social superstructure, they are explicable by the base, and they will be explicable by the base only if they have a stabilizing effect upon it (according to the view advance by

G.A. Cohen). Ethics therefore figure in Marxist theory only in so far as they are socially efficacious, contrary to what Brecht's aphorism implies. The ethics which act to stabilize the distribution of forces of production may be called 'Bread and Butter Ethics'.

Carling, Alan. Marx, Cohen and Brenner in Marx's Theory of History, Wetherly, Paul. Brookfield, Avebury, 1992.

G A Cohen proposes a version of the Marxist theory of history based on functional explanation, focused on the effect of technology. Robert Brenner proposes a different version based on rational-choice explanation and class struggle. It is possible to reconcile the accounts of the transition from feudalism to capitalism put forward by these two approaches: the origin of capitalism is explained in terms of the probabilistic outcome of medieval class struggle; its subsequent success by the functional superiority given to capitalism by its technological edge over its rivals.

Carloye, Jack C. The Existence of God and the Creation of the Universe. *Zygon*, 27(2), 167-185, Je 92.

Kant argues that any argument for a transcendent God presupposes the logically flawed ontological argument. The teleological argument cannot satisfy the demands of reason for a complete explanation of the meaning and purpose of our universe without support from the cosmological argument. I avoid the assumption of a perfect being, and hence the ontological argument, in my version of the cosmological argument. The necessary being can be identified with the creator of the universe by adding analogical mental relations. The creation of the universe is then shown to reflect modern scientific cosmology as well as stories and metaphors in the Eastern and Western religious traditions and to resolve the problem of evil.

Carlson, Allen. Aesthetics and Engagement. *Brit J Aes*, 33(3), 220-227, Jl 93.

This essay is a consideration of Arnold Berleant's recent attack on traditional aesthetics. I argue that his position is unsuccessful in two ways: First, it fails in its attempt to refute the traditional framework of modern aesthetics: the three dogmas that art i) involves objects which ii) have a special status, and iii) must be viewed in a special way. Second, it fails in its attempt to provide a new theoretical framework—an "aesthetics of engagement" intended both to replace the three dogmas and to underwrite anew the participatory appreciation of art which Berleant rightly favors.

Carlson, David Gray. On the Margins of Microeconomics in Deconstruction and the Possibility of Justice, Cornell, Durcilla (ed). New York, Routledge, 1992.

This article examines price theory from a Derridean perspective. It shows that price theory is a philosophy of presence. The perfect market against which economic propositions are tested cannot account for its own origin. Its origin in fact is in oligopoly — market imperfection — because only the existence of an economic rent can explain why a positive competitive rate of return exists as part of the marginal cost of production. The perfect market expels time, so that time itself is a market imperfection.

Carlson, David Gray (ed) and Rosenfeld, Michel (ed) and Cornell, Durcilla (ed). *Deconstruction and the Possibility of Justice*. New York, Routledge, 1992.

Carman, John B. The Dignity and Indignity of Service: The Role of the Self in Hindu 'Bhakti' in Selves, People, and Persons, Rouner, Leroy S (ed). Notre Dame, Univ Notre Dame Pr, 1992.

Carney, James D. Individual Style. *J Aes Art Crit*, 49(1), 15-22, Wint 91.

Carnielli, Walter A. On Sequents and Tableaux for Many-Valued Logics. *J Non-Classical Log*, 8(1), 59-76, My 91.

Carr, Brian. Categories and Realities. *Indian Phil Quart*, 19(4), 293-310, O 92.

Carr, Brian. The Paradoxes of Indicative Conditionals in Logical Foundations, Mahalingam, Indira (ed). New York, St Martin's Pr, 1991.

Carr, Brian (ed) and Mahalingam, Indira (ed). *Logical Foundations*. New York, St Martin's Pr, 1991.

The essays in this collection were written to mark the occasion of D J O'Connor's 75th birthday. They constitute a celebration of his work in philosophy as a major defender of the logical empiricist tradition which has its roots in the philosophy of John Locke and David Hume. These essays—with very few exceptions—were specially written for this volume. Each essay takes up a central question of philosophy such as logical paradox, deductive and inductive inference, language and rationality, machine intelligence, human freedom and issues in social philosophy.

Carr, David. Education, Learning and Understanding: The Process and the Product. *J Phil Educ*, 26(2), 215-225, 1992.

Recent educational theorising about the nature of teaching, learning and assessment has made much of a distinction between processes and products and of so-called process models of education and curriculum. Following on from reflections on the historical provenance and subsequent evolution of process talk in psychology and the philosophy of mind it is argued in this article that such talk can only import serious conceptual confusion and ambiguity into our attempts to understand clearly and adequately the business of human learning. In the light of this it would be altogether better for us to expunge the language of process from the discourse of education.

Carr, David. Sequel to History: Postmodernism and the Crisis of Historical Time. *Hist Theor*, 32(2), 179-187, 1993.

Carr, David and Taylor, Charles and Ricoeur, Paul. Ricoeur on Narrative in On Paul Ricoeur: Narrative and Interpretation, Wood, David (ed). New York, Routledge, 1991.

Carr, Karen L. *The Banalization of Nihilism*. Albany, SUNY Pr, 1992.

This work is an analysis of some of the interpretations of nihilism in the last century, focusing in particular on Friedrich Nietzsche, Karl Barth, and Richard Rorty. It seeks, first, to show that significant changes have occurred in the appraisal of nihilism; in at least some circles, nihilism is losing its crisis connotations and becoming simply an unobjectionable characteristic of human life. Second, it explores the implications of this change, which are largely negative in the author's mind.

Carr, Stephen. F H Bradley and Religious Faith. *Relig Stud*, 28(3), 371-386, S 92.

The article examines the nature of Bradley's attitude to religious belief, especially in the context of the wider logical and metaphysical arguments of his philosophy. The central place of faith in Bradley's philosophical enterprise is made clear. Towards the end of the article an attempt is made to connect the discussion with various contemporary questions of philosophy and theology, including pragmatism, the nature of philosophy as a practice, the idea of narrative identity in ethics and the argument over internal and external relations. Some sense of the continuing significance of Bradley's philosophy is given.

Carrier, David. Erwin Panofsky, Leo Steinberg, David Carrier: The Problem of Objectivity in Art Historical Interpretation. *J Aes Art Crit*, 47(4), 333-347, Fall 89.

Carrier, David. Why Art History Has a History. *J Aes Art Crit*, 51(3), 299-312, Sum 93.

Carrier, L S. The Impossibility of Massive Error. *Phil Phenomenol Res*, 53(2), 405-409, Je 93.

Kirk Ludwig thinks that Davidson's anti-skeptical argument is designed to show the *logical* impossibility of massive error, which begs the question against the skeptic. Ludwig's criticism can be overcome by interpreting Davidson as arguing, instead, for its *epistemic* impossibility: massive error is inconsistent with many things that we know, including our knowledge of language, its intertranslatability, and its being learned in the presence of that which our words describe. If the skeptic responds that we lack knowledge of these things, Davidson's position is best defended by denying that the only good reasons for believing factual claims are experiential reasons.

Carrier, Martin. Aspekte und Probleme kausaler Beschreibungen in der gegenwärtigen Physik. *Neue Hefte Phil*, 32-33, 82-104, 1992.

The article gives a review of the characteristics and difficulties of causal descriptions in contemporary physics. Problems posed by the quantum measurement paradox and the EPR-correlations are at the focus of the discussion. The result is that no comprehensive causal description of nature is available and that the chief threat to causality stems from the quantum mechanical treatment of coupled systems.

Carrier, Martin. Kant's Relational Theory of Absolute Space. *Kantstudien*, 83(4), 399-416, 1992.

The article contains a new interpretation of Kant's views on the nature of space as expressed in his *Metaphysical Foundations of Natural Science*. The following claims are made: Kant believed that Newtonian mechanics allowed for the conception of "true relative motion". This was supposed to include rectilinear motion; in this case "motion" was intended to refer to "velocity". Kant thought he could demonstrate on this basis that the center-of-mass of the universe is truly at rest. Moreover, Kant believed he could show that rotation can always be reconstructed as relative motion.

Carrier, Martin. What is Right with the Miracle Argument: Establishing a Taxonomy of Natural Kinds. *Stud Hist Phil Sci*, 24(3), 391-409, Ag 93.

The paper addresses the issue of scientific realism. A realism of kinds is introduced and defended. It is claimed that science-on distinguished occasions-succeeds in collecting phenomena into equivalence classes that reflect truly existing similarity relations among these phenomena. This claim is buttressed by appealing to the "Miracle Argument" according to which distinguished instances of scientific success are mysterious unless it is assumed that the corresponding theory has grasped something correctly.

Carrier, Martin and Mittelstrass, Jürgen. *Mind, Brain, Behavior: The Mind-Body Problem and the Philosophy of Psychology*. Hawthorne, de Gruyter, 1991.

Carroll, David. Poetics, Theory, and the Defense of History: Philippe Carrard, *Poetics of the New History*. *Clio*, 22(3), 273-289, Spr 93.

Carroll, John W. The Indefinitely Iterated Prisoner's Dilemma: Reply to Becker and Cudd. *Theor Decis*, 34(1), 63-72, Ja 93.

It is argued that, without a controversial and arguably mistaken assumption, Becker and Cudd's (1990) objections do not undermine the challenge raised by my (1987) model of iterated prisoner's dilemmas for the arguments of Taylor (1976, 1987) and others. Furthermore, it is argued that, even granting this assumption, there is an alternative model that avoids their objections.

Carroll, John W. The Unanimity Theory and Probabilistic Sufficiency. *Phil Sci*, 59(3), 471-479, S 92.

The unanimity theory is an account of property-level causation requiring that causes raise the probability of their effects in specified test situations. Richard Otte (1981) and others have presented counterexamples in which one property is probabilistically sufficient for at least one other property. Given the continuing discussion (e.g., Cartwright 1989; Cartwright and Dupré 1988; Eells 1988a,b), many apparently think that these problems are minor. By considering the impact of Otte's cases on recent versions of the theory, by raising several new examples, and by criticizing natural replies, I argue that the problems for the unanimity theory are severe.

Carroll, Mary Ann and Van Der Bogert, Frans. Art, Ethics and the Law: Where Should the Law End?. *Metaphilosophy*, 24(1-2), 147-154, Ja-Ap 93.

Carroll, Noël. Anglo-American Aesthetics and Contemporary Criticism: Intention and the Hermeneutics of Suspicion. *J Aes Art Crit*, 51(2), 245-252, Spr 93.

Carroll, Noël. Historical Narratives and the Philosophy of Art. *J Aes Art Crit*, 51(3), 313-326, Sum 93.

Carroll, Noël. Horror, Helplessness, and Vulnerability: A Reply to Robert Solomon. *Phil Lit*, 17(1), 110-118, Ap 93.

This is a response to Robert Solomon's critical discussion of *The Philosophy of Horror* in *Philosophy and Literature* 16 (1992). Herein, I stress that Solomon's theory of horror is commmendatory whereas mine is descriptive.

Carroll, Noël. The Image of Women in Film: A Defense of a Paradigm. *J Aes Art Crit*, 48(4), 349-360, Fall 90.

Carroll, William E. Metaphysics, Embryology, and Medieval Aristotelianism. *Lyceum*, 3(1), 1-14, Spr 91.

Carroll, William E. Science and Creation: Big Bang Cosmology and Thomas Aquinas. *Lyceum*, 1(1), 1-4, Wint 89.

Carruthers, Peter. Consciousness and Concepts—II. *Aris Soc*, Supp(66), 41-59, 1992.

This paper contrasts two theories of consciousness. First, it criticizes Robert Kirk's theory that conscious states are those that are available to the organisms' main decision-making processes. Second, it presents and defends an alternative reflexive thinking theory, according to which conscious states are those that are available to thinking that is regularly made available to further thinking, where this availability is in dual mode—it is not just the content of the state, but also the fact that it is occurring, which is available to reflexive thought.

Carruthers, Peter. *The Animals Issue: Moral Theory in Practice*. New York, Cambridge Univ Pr, 1992.

This book is both an introduction to moral theory and an attack on the animal rights movement. It explores a variety of moral theories, bringing out the implausibility of those that would grant animals rights, and defending a contractualist approach (in the tradition of Kant and Rawls) that would deny moral standing to animals. It will be of interest to teachers of moral philosophy (and their students), since it will help them to bring out why theoretical issues in ethics matter, and also to all those whose work may involve killing or experimenting on animals.

Carse, Alisa. Justice within Intimate Spheres. *J Clin Ethics*, 4(1), 68-70, Spr 93.

Though families and friendships are ideally closely knit, mutually concerned social units, they do not therefore represent social spheres in which justice is unnecessary. But how are we properly to construe the nature of justice within intimate spheres? This question is addressed in the context of end-of-life medical treatment, focussing critically on the views of N Jecker and J Hardwig.

Carson, Robert N. A Model for Liberal Education in a Scientific Society. *Proc Phil Educ*, 48, 270-274, 1992.

Carson, Thomas. Friedman's Theory of Corporate Social Responsibility. *Bus Prof Ethics J*, 12(1), 3-32, Spr 93.

I argue that there are very substantial differences between the theory of corporate social responsibility Friedman presents in *Capitalism and Freedom* and the theory he defends in his later essay "Social Responsibility of Business." I also formulate and criticize Friedman's main arguments in support of his theory. In the final section of the paper, I raise what I take to be a very serious objection to Friedman's theory and formulate a revised version of the theory which avoids the objection. I believe that this modified theory is preferable to Friedman's own theory; it is also consistent with the libertarian spirit of Friedman's view.

Carson, Thomas. Gibbard's Conceptual Scheme for Moral Philosophy. *Phil Phenomenol Res*, 52(4), 953-956, D 92.

Carson, Thomas. Second Thoughts About Bluffing. *Bus Ethics Quart*, 3(4), 317-341, O 93.

Suppose that I tell a prospective buyer that $90,000 is absolutely the lowest price that I will accept for my house, when I know that I am willing to accept as little as $80,000. I defend the following claims: a) Statements of this sort generally do not constitute lying. (I attack standard definitions of lying and defend an alternative definition at length.) b) Such statements are usually permissible if one has good reason to think that one's negotiating partner is misstating her negotiating position and usually impermissible if one does not have good reason to think that the other party is misstating her negotiating position.

Carson, Thomas L. Does the Stakeholder Theory Constitute a New Kind of Theory of Social Responsibility?. *Bus Ethics Quart*, 3(2), 171-176, A 93.

In a recent paper, Kenneth Goodpaster formulates three versions of the stakeholder theory of corporate social responsibility. He rejects the first two versions and endorses the third. I argue that the theory that Goodpaster defends under the name "stakeholder theory" is a version (albeit a somewhat different version) of Milton Friedman's theory of corporate social responsibility. I also argue that the first two formulations of the stakeholder theory which Goodpaster discusses are at most only slight modifications of other theories. I conclude by formulating a fourth version of the stakeholder theory which I believe does constitute a substantial departure from earlier theories of social responsibility.

Carter, Alan. A 'Counterfactualist' Four-Dimensional Theory of Power. *Heythrop J*, 33(2), 192-203, Ap 92.

Carter, Alan. Functional Explanation and the State in Marx's Theory of History, Wetherly, Paul. Brookfield, Avebury, 1992.

G A Cohen employs functional explanations to defend Marx's theory of history. In criticising Cohen, this article develops an alternative to Marxist theory—an alternative which, like analytical Marxism, employs functional explanations to situate the state, productive forces, and relations of production within a theory of historical transition. However, this alternative theory, in contradiction to analytical Marxism, accords explanatory primacy to the state rather than to forces of production and, from its standpoint, Marxist assumptions about the role of a revolutionary vanguard and the "withering away" of a "transitional" revolutionary state are shown to be highly problematic.

Carter, Alan. 'Institutional Exploitation' and Workers' Co-operatives—Or How the British Left Persist in Getting Their Concepts Wrong. *Heythrop J*, 33(4), 426-433, O 92.

In an earlier article, I argued that the concept 'self-exploitation' is incoherent and that its current use in Britain leads to a far too hasty opposition by the Left to workers' co-operatives. In a recent reply, John O'Neill, while accepting that 'the concept of "self-exploitation" is, understood literally, incoherent', nevertheless insists that 'the claims that some of the users of this term are making can be made conceptually respectable.' This can be accomplished, O'Neill argues, by understanding the concept 'self-exploitation' in terms of the concept 'institutional exploitation.'

Carter, K Codell. The Concept of Quackery in Early Nineteenth Century British Medical Periodicals. *J Med Human*, 14(2), 89-97, Sum 93.

Carter, Richard B. *Nurturing Evolution: The Family as a Social Womb*. Lanham, Univ Pr of America, 1993.

The author cites several fields of knowledge in order to more comprehensively understand the identity of a human being as a political animal. He asserts that the adult nurturing of a newborn, especially during the year after birth, is a true extension of the evolutionary processes which controlled the development of that baby during the nine months before its birth. The "social womb" that replaces the biological one includes living, functioning human adults and those political entities designed to protect and nourish the institutions of human nurture. Carter examines the biologically definite extensions of uterine development during that period.

Cartwright, David. The Last Temptation of Zarathustra. *J Hist Phil*, 31(1), 49-69, Ja 93.

I analyze Zarathustra's "last sin," pity for the higher men, in Nietzsche's *Thus Spoke Zarathustra* and explain Zarathustra's overcoming of pity as the basis for reorientation towards life that prepared the way for his striving for *Übermenschlichkeit*. I detail Schopenhauer's morality of pity and theory of salvation, Nietzsche's analysis of pity, and pity's function in *Zarathustra* as an expression of a bad love of self, others, and life. I conclude that by highlighting pity as Zarathustra's last temptation, Nietzsche illustrated the life-denying dimensions of altruistic morality, the seductive power of this tradition, and the strengths needed to transcend it.

Cartwright, Helen Morris. On Plural Reference and Elementary Set Theory. *Synthese*, 96(2), 201-254, Ag 93.

The view that plural reference is reference to a set is examined in light of George Boolos' treatment of second-order quantifiers and Richard Sharvy's theory of plural and mass descriptions. I argue that any sentence that properly translates a second-order formula in Boolos' treatment has a first-order formulation in what I call D-mereology, a theory that incorporates Sharvy's. Singular descriptions are added to D-mereology by introducing a primitive predicate for the relation of the referent of a singular description to that of its plural, and the result is a natural basis for a 'pluralized' Zermelo set theory. However, this theory is inconsistent, unless it is recast as a second order theory of sets interpreted in Boolos' way.

Cartwright, Helen Morris. On Two Arguments for the Indeterminacy of Personal Identity. *Synthese*, 95(2), 241-273, My 93.

Both arguments are based on the breakdown of normal criteria of identity in science fictional circumstances. In one case, normal criteria would support the identity of person A with each of two other persons, B and C, and it is argued that, in the imagined circumstances, 'A = B' and 'A = C' have no truth value. In the other, a series or 'spectrum' of cases is tailored to a sorites argument. At one end of the spectrum, persons A and B are such that 'A = B' is true; at the other end, this identity is clearly false. In between, normal criteria of identity leave the truth or falsehood of the identity undecided, and it is argued that it has no true value. These arguments are to be understood counterfactually; and my thesis is that, so understood, neither establishes its conclusion.

Cartwright, Nancy. How We Relate Theory to Observation in World Changes, Horwich, Paul (ed). Cambridge, MIT Pr, 1993.

Kuhn upholds the view that the laws and theoretical claims of physics are symbolic generalizations to be contrasted with the more specific descriptions of them needed to treat real physical situations. In this paper I outline an account of the relationship between these symbolic generalizations and the more specific versions of them used to deal with actual physical situations. My view is that models function like fables to make the general and abstract symbolic laws of physics more concrete and visualizable by providing specific content for them.

Cartwright, Nancy. In Defence of 'This Worldly' Causality: Comments on Van Fraassen's *Laws and Symmetry*. *Phil Phenomenol Res*, 53(2), 423-429, Je 93.

Van Fraassen argues that there are no laws of nature worth having. In this paper I argue that Fraassen's criticisms of laws are based on a misconception of what laws are supposed to do. Laws do not necessitate and explain as Fraassen assumes; causes do. Although Fraassen does not want to allow causality in his models, I argue that if his models have either the objects of modern physics or objects of the ordinary world in them, they will already contain causal processes as well.

Cartwright, Nancy. Is Natural Science 'Natural' Enough? A Reply to Phillip Allport. *Synthese*, 94(2), 291-301, F 93.

Allport argues that complications and limitations in the scope of the fundamental laws of physics are compatible with their simplicity, universality and truth. He insists that unless failure is guaranteed a priori, laws are not deceitful with the truth as I have maintained. In reply I urge a project of natural science which guarantees nothing a priori. Complications and limitations may be compatible with simplicity, universality and truth, but we ought to gather our beliefs about nature from the appearance of things. And if modern science doesn't provide our best evidence for the structure of nature, what can?

Cartwright, Nancy and Chang, Hasok. Causality and Realism in the EPR Experiment. *Erkenntnis*, 38(2), 169-190, Mr 93.

We argue against the common view that it is impossible to give a causal account of the distant correlations that are revealed in EPR-type experiments. We take a realistic attitude about quantum mechanics which implies a willingness to modify our familiar concepts according to its teachings. We object to the argument that the violation of factorizability in EPR rules our causal accounts, since such an argument is at best based on the desire to retain a classical description of nature that consists of processes that are continuous in space and time. We also do not think special relativity prohibits the superluminal propagation of causes in EPR, for the phenomenon of quantum measurement may very well fall outside the domain of application of special relativity. It is possible to give causal accounts of EPR as long as we are willing to take quantum mechanics seriously, and we offer two such accounts.

Cary, Phillip. On Behalf of Classical Trinitarianism: A Critique on Rahner on the Trinity. *Thomist*, 56(3), 365-405, Jl 92.

Through a critique of Karl Rahner and an exegesis of John of Damascus, the article argues that there is no difference in essential logic between Greek and Latin Trinitarianism. In particular, both traditions establish an epistemic gap between the doctrine of the immanent Trinity and the doctrine of the economic Trinity, which (contrary to prevailing theological opinion) is well-placed, but does not imply that the inner self of the Trivine God remains hidden and unknown in the economy of salvation.

Casati, Roberto. De re and de corpore (in French). *Rev Theol Phil*, 124(3), 271-289, 1992.

The author analyses 'de corpore' concepts, concepts belonging to the structure of the attempt to move a part of the body. A famous argument of Kant suggests that the concepts of left and right are 'de re': they refer to a part of absolute space. In showing — in opposition to Kant — that this space is not physical but phenomenal, one can argue for the existence of phenomenal individuals. Since the concepts of left and right are inescapable when describing certain human actions, one can conclude that some 'de corpore' concepts are 'de re'; and some 'de re' concepts are not necessarily external.

Casaubón, Juan A. El poema de Parménides y la analogía según Santo Tomás de Aquino. *Sapientia*, 47(183), 65-66, 1992.

Casement, William. Michael Polanyi's Defense of Spontaneous Order in Terrorism, Justice and Social Values, Peden, Creighton W (ed). Lewiston, Mellen Pr, 1990.

Casey, Edward S. 'The Element of Voluminousness:' Depth and Place Reexamined in Merleau-Ponty Vivant, Dillon, M C (ed). Albany, SUNY Pr, 1991.

Casey, Gerard. Minds and Machines. *Amer Cath Phil Quart*, 66(1), 57-80, Wint 92.

Cashman, Tyrone. Epistemology and the Extinction of Species in Revisioning Philosophy, Ogilvy, James (ed). Albany, SUNY Pr, 1992.

Caspar, Philippe. Éléments pour une eschatologie du zygote. *Rev Thomiste*, 92(2), 460-481, Ap-J 92.

Casper, Bernhard. La concezione dell'"evento" nella *Stella della redenzione* di Franz Rosenzweig e nel pensiero di Martin Heidegger. *Teoria*, 11(2), 47-64, 1991.

Cassam, Quassim. Parfit on Persons. *Proc Aris Soc*, 93, 17-37, 1993.

It is argued that Parfit's claim that personal identity is not what matters depends for much of its plausibility on the assumption that persons are not substances, on either a realist or conceptualist view of substance. It is suggested that the main challenge facing Parfit is to explain why thinking of ourselves as non-substantial is better than the best non-reductionist conception of ourselves, namely, animalism.

Cassell, Eric J. The Body of the Future in The Body in Medical Thought and Practice, Leder, Drew (ed). Dordrecht, Kluwer, 1992.

Cassini, Alejandro. Nota sobre el concepto de realismo epistemológico. *Rev Filosof (Argentina)*, 6(1-2), 87-93, N 92.

Castagnetto, Susan V. Reid's Answer to Abstract Ideas. *J Phil Res*, 17, 39-60, 1992.

This paper shows how Reid uses abstractions to give accounts of universals, concepts and concept formation that are ability-based. Reid replaces abstract ideas with "general conception," in three senses. As universals, they are non-mental objects of acts of abstraction and conception. They are distinguished by the faculty of abstraction, not produced by it. Second, general conceptions are mental acts whose objects are universals. Such acts are made possible by general conceptions in the third sense—general concepts. I argue that Reid intends these as particular abilities to distinguish general features of objects and use general terms as other language users do.

Casti, John L. The Cognitive Revolution?. *Ideal Stud*, 23(1), 19-38, Wint 93.

Just as the development of relativity theory and quantum mechanics have been the defining events of twentieth-century science, the burgeoning field of cognitive science is often trumpeted as being a glimpse into the future of the center of science in the coming century. In this paper, we examine this claim, asking whether the so-called cognitive "revolution" is indeed revolutionary or, on the other hand, is merely a flash-in-the-pan, scientifically speaking. As a point of perspective on this question, the paper looks at the claims and accomplishments of artificial intelligence, as well as the research agenda of workers in the currently fashionable field of artificial life. The paper concludes with some speculations about what directions the "cognitive revolution" is likely to take over the coming decade or two.

Castiglione, D and Buckle, S. Hume's Critique of the Contract Theory. *Hist Polit Thought*, 12(3), 457-480, Fall 91.

Caston, Victor. Aristotle and Supervenience. *S J Phil*, 31(Supp), 107-135, 1992.

Castoriadis, Cornelius. Power, Politics, Autonomy in Cultural-Political Interventions in the Unfinished Project of Enlightenment, Honneth, Axel (& other eds). Cambridge, MIT Pr, 1992.

The essay tries to dispel a contemporary confusion surrounding the term "the political". The political relates to whatever, in every society, has to do with organized, explicit collective power (not to be confused with the "State"). Politics, on the other hand, is the lucid collective activity aiming at the alteration of existing institutions. Its birth is simultaneous with that of democracy (and philosophy), and its ultimate object the establishment of an autonomous, truly self-governing society—an object inseparable of that of bringing up autonomous individuals.

Casullo, Albert. Causality, Reliabilism, and Mathematical Knowledge. *Phil Phenomenol Res*, 52(3), 557-584, S 92.

Paul Benacerraf has argued that plausible causal constraints on knowledge preclude the possibility of knowledge of statements whose truth conditions involve abstract entities. There are two prevalent replies for this charge. The first is to maintain that if the causal constraints are correctly understood they do not preclude knowledge of abstract entities. The second is to maintain that an adequate account of knowledge does not involve the problematic causal constraints. The primary purpose of this paper is to argue that neither reply succeeds.

Catania, Francis J. John Duns Scotus on *Ens Infinitum*. *Amer Cath Phil Quart*, 67(1), 37-54, Wint 93.

The usual interpretation of Duns Scotus's discussion of "Infinite Being" links that concept with his well-known position on the univocity of being. The latter concept is viewed as the basis for continuity between ordinary experience and the transcendent use of a concept. The interpretation of Scotus fosters the image of "parts": one part shared; one part differentiating. Even though Scotus's language supports this interpretation, I suggest that rather than conceiving of "parts," we look at Scotus's concept of being as ultimate subject from two points of view: now abstractively recognized as limited in a potentially variable way; now imaginatively constructed as so intensified as to include in a unitary way the full range of compossible perfections. (edited)

Cattanei, E. Un'ipotesi sul concerto aristotelico di astrazione. *Riv Filosof Neo-Scolas*, 82(4), 578-586, O-D 90.

Cattorini, Paolo and Reichlin, Massimo. The Physician, the Family, and the Truth. *J Clin Ethics*, 3(3), 219-220, Fall 92.

Cauchy, Venant. State and Nation. *Dialec Hum*, 17(1), 56-67, 1990.

The purpose is to enquire into the ontological foundations of society and to explain briefly how a given society must reflect the reality of the individuals who make it up. The distinction between society and community (Gemeinschaft and Gesellschaft) is considered. Society should provide for the fullest satisfaction of individual needs and aspirations in a spirit of valued continuity with the past.

Caust, Lesley. Community, Autonomy and Justice: The Gender Politics of Identity and Relationship. *Hist Euro Ideas*, 17(5), 639-650, S 93.

This paper questions the ontological assumptions of liberalism and Marxism from a feminist perspective. I argue that justice involves considering subjects as persons-in-context with a specific sexual identity. In this sense, prior notions of community and autonomy central to much justice discourse are founded on thin conceptions of the subject. Feminist contributions have posed new and refreshing ways of understanding subjectivity and have thus put 'identity politics' on the political agenda. It is within this fluid framework of feminist theorizing that I posit a notion of transformative autonomy. This is a conception of autonomy that goes beyond the individual/community debate and focuses upon the 'self-in-relations'.

Cavaciuti, Santino. Essere e spirito. *G Metaf*, 14(1), 143-154, Ja-Ap 92.

Cavallar, Georg. Kants Weg von der Theodizee zur Anthropodizee und retour: Verspätete Kritik an Odo Marquard. *Kantstudien*, 84(1), 90-102, 1993.

In 1965, Odo Marquard set up the thesis that the idealistic philosophy of Kant, Fichte and Schelling had found a radical solution to the problem of theodicy. The ongoing discussion is said to have come to a complete stop between 1781 to 1800. The article argues that Marquard was mistaken. Kant did indeed change theodicy into 'anthropodicy', making humans responsible for their actions (and giving the theistic philosopher the opportunity to blame them for the evil in the world). In his 1791 essay on theodicy (*Über das Misslingen aller philosophischen Versuche in der Theodizee*) Kant, however, returns to traditional theodicy, trying to transform it into an authentic and critical article of faith for the religious believer.

Cavallar, Georg. Neuere nordamerikanische Arbeiten über Kants Rechts-und politische Philosophie. *Z Phil Forsch*, 46(2), 266-277, Ap-J 92.

The essay reviews four recent book son Kant's legal and political philosophy. D Howard, "The Politics of Critique", Univ of Minn Pr, 1988; Macmillan 1989; H Van Der Linden, "Kantian Ethics and Socialism", Hackett, 1988; A D Rosen, "Kant's Theory of Justice", Cornell Univ Pr, 1989; L A Mulholland, "Kant's System of Rights", Columbia Univ Pr, 1990. Rosen's thesis is interesting for arguing that Kant advocated a state taking care of the welfare of its citizens, although he adds that this duty 'must always take a back seat to the scrupulous observance of rights'. Mulholland provides probably the best study available in English, unfolding the systematic structure of Kant's legal philosophy.

Cavarero, Adriana. Equality and Sexual Difference in Beyond Equality and Difference, Bock, Gisela (ed). New York, Routledge, 1992.

The purpose of the work is to show how the reality of sexual difference remains totally stronger to the traditional political categories. In Aristotle the political sphere is reserved to man, the universal paradigm of rationality, while the woman is designated to the household. In modern political thought, on the other hand, the female sexual difference is absorbed into the abstract and equalitarian paradigm of the masculine individual. Modernity testifies an immanent schizophrenia between the ancient sexual hierarchy and an onologating-formal system based upon the male as universal model. In order to affirm sexual difference a feminist critique to the juridicial universalism and to the abstract individualism is necessary.

Cavell, Marcia. Knowing and Valuing in Psychoanalysis, Mind and Art, Hopkins, Jim (ed). Cambridge, Blackwell, 1992.

Against Richard Wollheim's view that Freud lends weight to a view of valuing as a kind of projection of subjective experiences onto the world, Cavell argues for a reading of Freud—admittedly less obvious in his writings—according to which certain developmental stages, culminating in "the Oedipal complex", mark simultaneously the *discovery* of value and of other persons as other from oneself.

Caws, Peter. Sartrean Structuralism? in The Cambridge Companion to Sartre, Howells, Christina (ed). New York, Cambridge Univ Pr, 1992.

In spite of a defensible impression that Sartre and structuralism have little in common (and where they do intersect tend to contradict one another), this essay shows, on the basis of evidence drawn mainly (but not only) from Sartre's posthumously published writings, that Sartre had an understanding of the social fully compatible with the essential (as opposed to the ideologically accidental) tenets of structuralism, and that some of his formulations of structuralist positions were better than those of its avowed exponents. What separated Sartre and the structuralists was more political than philosophical; together they deserve further attention.

Caygill, Howard. Architectural Postmodernism in Postmodernism and Society, Boyne, Roy (ed). New York, St Martin's Pr, 1990.

Cebik, L B. Fiction and History: A Common Core?. *Int Stud Phil*, 24(1), 47-63, 1992.

The argument—made most prominent by Hayden White—that history and fiction are rhetorically indistinguishable and therefore structured on aesthetic ground is untenable. Since narrative discourse is logically and epistemically prior to the aesthetic-non-aesthetic distinction, neither element in the distinction can explain narrative itself. Proper categories for narrative theories lie in other directions.

Cebik, L B. On the Suspicion of an Art Forgery. *J Aes Art Crit*, 47(2), 147-156, Spr 89.

Unlike knowledge of an art forgery, suspicion of an art forgery provides insights into the art viewer, the one having the suspicion. In the end, what turns out to be at stake is not so much the art work and its authorship, but the art viewer in relationship to himself or herself.

Cebik, L B. Seeing Aspects and Art: Tilghman and Wittgenstein. *S J Phil*, 30(4), 1-16, Wint 92.

In "But Is It Art?", B R Tilghaman argues in effect that art's necessary paraciticism on other areas of human activity and interest follows from the condition that artistic and aesthetic perceptions are matters of experiencing aspects. However, aspect-seeing is so common in many avenues of human endeavor that it fails to justify a special artistic paraciticism. The realm of art has a language which must be understood in its own right, as is the case for any social realm which dominates a portion of language as a whole.

Cebik, L B. The World Is Not a Novel. *Phil Lit*, 16(1), 68-87, Ap 92.

Examining the theories of fictions of both Bentham and Vaihinger reveals that they provide no grounds for Iser's attempt to rest his theory of fictional literature on a more general idea of fictions. Rather, fictional literature might be better understood by reference to its relationship to reality.

Centore, F F. Classical Christian Philosophy and Temporality: Correcting a Misunderstanding. *Monist*, 75(3), 393-405, Jl 92.

Process philosophy and theology are very popular today. This is because it is generally assumed that being and becoming, time and eternity, are incompatible. The article traces out some of the recent history of this belief as seen in Dilthey, Heidegger, Gadamer, and Kueng. It then outlines how, in Classical Christian Philosophy, this was not assumed to be the case, either in philosophy or theology. In philosophy there is no reason why one must accept Greek Being as the only definition of being, while in theology the Scriptures themselves emphasize the intersection of the fixed and the changeable.

Cenzer, Douglas (& others). Countable Thin ÇP0/1 Classes. *Annals Pure Applied Log*, 59(2), 79-193, Ja 93.

A Pi-0-1 class P is said to be thin if every Pi-0-1 subclass of P is relatively open in P. Thin classes are constructed and the degrees of members of thin classes are studied. In particular, there is an r.e. degree which contains no member of any thin class. The connection between Pi-0-1 classes, logical theories and Boolean algebras is explored. For example, an axiomatizable theory is said to be Martin — Pour-El if every axiomatizable extension is generated by a single new proposition. Then there is a r.e. degree d such that no complete extension of any Martin — Pour-El theory has degree d.

Cepl, Vojtech. The Road Out of Serfdom. *Vera Lex*, 12(1), 4-7, 1992.

Cerutti, Furio. Can There Be a Supranational Identity?. *Phil Soc Crit*, 18(2), 147-162, 1992.

Cerutti, Furio. Ethics and Politics in the Nuclear Age: The End of Deterrence?. *Praxis Int*, 12(4), 387-404, Ja 93.

Céspedes, Guillermo Coronado. El legado categorial de la ciencia griega presocrática. *Rev Filosof (Costa Rica)*, 30(71), 45-52, J 92.

This paper deals with the categorical legacy of Presocratic Science. Three topics are regarded as fundamental. They are the reductionistic thesis, the pitagorical emphasis on mathematical structures, and the pluralism approach as explanatory strategy. Besides, as a condition for analysis, the thesis of the "Greek miracle" is rejected.

Chadwick, Ruth F. The Market for Bodily Parts in Applied Philosophy, Almond, Brenda (ed). New York, Routledge, 1992.

The demand for bodily parts is increasing, and individuals in certain circumstances are offering them for sale. Is there anything wrong in this? Kant had arguments to suggest that we have duties towards our own bodies, including the duty not to sell parts of them. His reasons for this are examined, together with Rom Harre's revision of Kant's argument. Both are rejected in favor of an argument that it does make sense to speak of duties regarding our own bodies, grounded in the duty to promote the flourishing of human beings. This provides a reason for opposing the sale of bodily parts and the market ethic in health care.

Chagrov, Alexander and Zakharyashchev, Michael. The Disjunction Property of Intermediate Propositional Logic. *Stud Log*, 50(2), 189-216, Je 91.

This paper is a survey of results concerning the disjunction property, Halldén-completeness, and other related properties of intermediate propositional logics and normal modal logics containing S4.

Chakrabarti, Arindam. On Knowing by Being Told. *Phil East West*, 42(3), 421-439, Jl 92.

Chakrabarti, Susanta. Heuristic Approach to Scientific Theory-Confirmation. *Indian Phil Quart*, 20(2), 189-197, Ap 93.

Chakraborti, Sadhan. Michael Dummett on Truth. *Indian Phil Quart*, 20(1), 1-16, Ja 93.

There are some serious misconceptions about the Dummettian notion of truth and its place in his philosophy of language. My aim in this paper is to explain what exactly the Dummettian notion of truth is and the role it plays in his philosophy of language. Dummett subscribes to a verificationist theory of meaning, intuitionistic logic and anti-realism. In each of these different aspects of his philosophy of language, i.e., in (a) the theory of meaning, (b) logic and (c) the semantic theory, the notion of truth plays a crucial role: the notion of truth introduced by him is opposed to the classical notion of truth.

Chakraborty, Nirmalya N. If There Be a God, From Whence Proceed So Many Evils?. *Indian Phil Quart*, 20(2), 125-143, Ap 93.

The chief aim of this paper is to critically assess the arguments for and against the compatibility of an omnipotent, omniscient and wholly good God with the existence of evils in the world. The discussion starts with a brief exposition of Hume's analysis of the problem and then goes on to J L Mackie and his opponent A Plantinga. Neither Mackie's nor Plantinga's arguments are flawless. I argue that the theistic beliefs are not inconsistent which Mackie alleges, nor do they involve vicious circularity as many critics think.

Chalmers, Alan. So the Laws of Physics Needn't Lie. *Austl J Phil*, 71(2), 196-205, Je 93.

In her book *How the Laws of Physics Lie*, Nancy Cartwright argues that the fundamental laws of physics cannot be construed as literally true given the way they are used and argued for in the actual practice of physics. In this paper it is argued that Cartwright's arguments do not hold once fundamental laws are interpreted as characterising something like powers or propensities, and, furthermore, that this is precisely the implications of Nancy Cartwright's second book, *Nature's Capacities and Their Measurement*.

Chambers, John H. *Empiricist Research on Teaching: A Philosophical and Practical Critique of its Scientific Pretensions*. Dordrecht, Kluwer, 1992.

The book suggests that there has been a pervasive misunderstanding in research on teaching. In attempting to be *scientific*, researchers have been *empiricist*. Moreover, because they have used a very restricted kind of empiricist method, their results have been only moderately useful. Until the difference between scientific and empiricist activity is recognized and until empiricist research as presently practised is radically modified, this disappointing situation must continue. Through a consideration of the diverse forms of theory, and through case studies, the immense differences between scientific and empiricist research are demonstrated — such as the confusion of abstract and general concepts, and of scientific and statistical experiments.

Chambliss, J J. Common Ground in Aristotle's and Dewey's Theories of Conduct. *Educ Theor*, 43(3), 249-260, Sum 93.

An exploration of Aristotle's and Dewey's theories of conduct leads us to claim that Dewey is correct in holding that Aristotle's vision was limited by his objectivism. Yet the method in Aristotle's approach to the study of conduct may be taken to be a way of overcoming his limitations. To act according to Aristotle's method would bring Aristotle's theory of conduct closer to Dewey's own claim that moral theory is "action in idea" than Dewey recognized. Dewey's moral theory reminds us of Aristotle's distinction between knowing what virtue is and becoming good.

Champagne, Shaun A. Leibniz on Innate Ideas. *Lyceum*, 5(1), 61-65, Spr 93.

This paper aims to get clear about the arguments G W Leibniz had put forth in support of innate ideas. He addressed this topic in his book, *New Essays on Human Understanding*, which when looked at closely depicts a clash between Rationalists (Leibniz) and the Empiricists (Locke). There are two main distinctions which are necessary to make: 1) It is important to distinguish between potential and actual knowledge (what it means "to be in the understanding"). 2) It is equally as important to distinguish between the origin of necessary truths and of truths of fact.

Champlin, T S. On Being One's Own Worst Enemy. *Phil Invest*, 15(4), 324-328, O 92.

If someone who is his own worst enemy believes something to be true of his own worst enemy, is his belief about himself? A simple substitution test would appear to show that the answer is 'Of course' but I argue that the answer is, 'No'. The logician who proffers 'x is the worst enemy of x' as a suitable notation for 'x is his own worst enemy' confuses being one's own worst enemy (scoring own goals through one's own unforced errors) with temporarily taking over the role of an enemy (playing and beating oneself at chess, for example).

Champlin, T S. Solitary Rule-Following. *Philosophy*, 67(261), 285-306, Jl 92.

Can one person who has lived all his life alone on a desert island follow a rule? Although it can be his rule to do something, he cannot bring it about on his own that it is the rule on his island to do anything. Following a rule is, as Wittgenstein suggested, like following a custom. It can be the total solitary's custom to do something but he cannot create a custom. A rule is like a fashion. The total solitary can make and wear his clothes in a certain fashion but what he wears cannot be in or out of fashion.

Chan, Alan K L. *Taoist Mystical Philosophy: The Scripture of Western Ascension*, by Livia Kohn. *Phil East West*, 43(2), 313-321, Ap 93.

A review of Livia Kohn's *Taoist Mystical Philosophy: The Scripture of Western Ascension*, the discussion focuses, first of all, on the origins of the *Scripture of Western Ascension*. Certain textual issues, Kohn's translation, and her claim that the scripture represents the earliest mature formulation of Taoist mystical philosophy are then examined.

Chan, Joseph. Does Aristotle's Political Theory Rest on a 'Blunder'?. *Hist Polit Thought*, 13(2), 189-202, Sum 92.

It has recently been argued that Aristotle's naturalistic approach to politics, which finds its expression in the claim that the polis is a natural community, is consistent with his emphasis on the role of human agency in politics. There is, therefore, a blunder at the root of Aristotle's political theory. This paper argues that the blunder is not real. To show this, I introduce two pairs of distinctions, first between the external conditions of a natural thing which facilitates its occurrence *and* its inner principle which determines its typical change, and second between the political community as a type *and* as a particular form of type.

Chan, Wing-Tsit and Rongjie, Chen. An Exploration of the Concept of *Zhong* in the Teachings of Confucianism. *Chin Stud Phil*, 24(3), 72-100, Spr 93.

Chandler, Hugh S. Divine Intervention and the Origin of Life. *Faith Phil*, 10(2), 170-180, Ap 93.

The 'Intervention Argument' purports to show that God created life on our planet by supernatural intervention. One of its characteristic premises is the claim that if things had been allowed to take their 'natural' course, living organisms would probably not have come into existence here. This paper clarifies the argument and assesses its worth. The upshot is that its plausibility depends upon our estimate of the prior probability of God's intervention, and our guess as to the likelihood that life would have developed naturally on this planet in the absence of such intervention.

Chandler, Hugh S. Some Ontological Arguments. *Faith Phil*, 10(1), 18-32, Ja 93.

The principal arguments considered are in some ways similar to those offered in Anselm's *Proslogium*, Chapters II and III. In addition, two 'quick' versions of the ontological argument are examined. Finally, I worry a bit about the ineffable One. The general line of attack is similar to a procedure employed by David Lewis in discussing *Proslogium II*. My approach to *Proslogium III* is based upon the idea that the appropriate modal logic for these matters is much weaker than the standard S5. The hope is that this alternative perspective reveals features worthy of notice.

Chandler, Hugh S. Theseus' Clothes-Pin. *Analysis*, 44(2), 55-58, Mr 84.

The problem concerns the names of individuals lacking fully determinate re-identification conditions across possible worlds—clothes-pins, frogs, and probably people too. Can such names be 'rigid designators'? Consider a clothes-pin named 'Alice', and a possible world in which each of her two 'legs' is replaced one after the other. We could sharpen the presently fuzzy re-identification conditions for clothes-pins in such a way as to guarantee her survival or, alternatively, in such a way as to guarantee her demise in these circumstances. I conclude that the proper name 'Alice' isn't (now) rigid.

Chang, Hasok and Cartwright, Nancy. Causality and Realism in the EPR Experiment. *Erkenntnis*, 38(2), 169-190, Mr 93.

We argue against the common view that it is impossible to give a causal account of the distant correlations that are revealed in EPR-type experiments. We take a realistic attitude about quantum mechanics which implies a willingness to modify our familiar concepts according to its teachings. We object to the argument that the violation of factorizability in EPR rules our causal accounts, since such an argument is at best based on the desire to retain a classical description of nature that consists of processes that are continuous in space and time. We also do not think special relativity prohibits the superluminal propagation of causes in EPR, for the phenomenon of quantum measurement may very well fall outside the domain of application of special relativity. It is possible to give causal accounts of EPR as long as we are willing to take quantum mechanics seriously, and we offer two such accounts.

Chang, Jun-chun. Heavenly Order, Sagehood and Tao-t'ung—Some Discussions on the Neo-Confucian View of Values (in Chinese). *Phil Rev (Taiwan)*, 15, 143-162, Ja 92.

Chang, Wing-wah. The Concept of Technique in Heidegger (in Chinese). *Phil Rev (Taiwan)*, 15, 209-250, Ja 92.

Chansky, James. The Conscious Body: Schopenhauer's Difference from Fichte in Relation to Kant. *Int Stud Phil*, 24(3), 25-44, 1992.

Understanding Nietzsche's difference from Hegel entails understanding Schopenhauer's difference from Hegel, and this is established here by way of an examination of Schopenhauer's difference from Fichte in relation to Kant. I begin by setting forth the Kantian context out of which both Fichte and Schopenhauer worked, move on to present Fichte's position and Schopenhauer's criticism of it, and then to Schopenhauer's intensification of the Kantian Critique of Reason, his opposition to the "ontological intellectualism" of post-Kantian Idealism and to a priori metaphysics, and, most importantly, his critique and rejection of morality as the practical activity of Reason.

Chansky, James D. Reflections on *After Virtue* after Auschwitz. *Phil Today*, 37(3), 247-256, Fall 93.

By way of an examination of MacIntyre's methodology in *After Virtue*, I argue that the history of morals and morality includes evil ideas and acts no less than good ones. A history that excludes evil, as I claim MacIntyre's does, is an inadequate history of morals and morality. To exclude evil from this history is to presuppose that the difference at least between good and evil is clear, that the former is always what is reasonably sought, and begs at the end of such a history the very question with which one began.

Chanter, Tina. Metaphysical Presence in Ethics and Danger, Dallery, Arleen B (ed). Albany, SUNY Pr, 1992.

Part one of the article gives an account of Heidegger's early view of temporality. Part two explains the view of time expounded in Heidegger's discussion of Nietzsche in *What Is Called Thinking?*. Parts three and four focus upon the problems of eternity and presence respectively. Heidegger claims that the traditional conception of time is contradictory. It is conceptualized as essentially transitory, while at the same time it is assumed that time stands still. The contradiction has not been brought to light, according to Heidegger, because philosophers have consistently failed to see that the question of Being is integral to time.

Chapman, Harley. The Importance of the Notion of Being for Philosophical Theology in God, Values, and Empiricism, Peden, Creighton W (ed). Macon, Mercer Univ Pr, 1989.

The notion of being should be taken as the central concept of philosophical theology because it best accounts for a) the experienced referent, however vaguely understood, and b) the experience of ontological shock. The referent is best interpreted as the unity or integration of mystery, meaning, and power. Ontological shock occurs when a thing, including oneself, is experienced as existing when it otherwise might not be. A theory of ontological creativity, in which contingent beings facing possible non-being are somehow made to be, best accounts for this situation. Finally, the vulnerabilities of this theory are briefly discussed.

Chappell, T D J. The Virtues of Thrasymachus. *Phronesis*, 38(1), 1-17, 1993.

What exactly is Thrasymachus' position on *Republic* Book 1? I consider a variety of answers (Howani, Keferd, MacIntyre, Shorey, Foot) and come up with my own: that Thrasymachus is not an immoralist, but is just as concerned as Socrates with the question "What character traits are needed for a good life?" Unlike Socrates, however, he thinks of justice neither as a virtue, nor as a vice, but as a *device*, used by those of practical cunning to bend others to their will.

Chappell, T D J. Why God is Not a Consequentialist. *Relig Stud*, 29(2), 239-243, Je 93.

The God of Christian belief is not a consequentialist because a consequentialist aims at maximizing the goodness of states of affairs. But God's own existence maximizes the goodness of states of affairs, since God is infinitely good. Thus God's creative finite amounts of further goodness, such as a word, has no consequentialist rationale, even if that world has no evil in it. But (says Christian doctrine) God did create a word. So in creation God did not act on consequentialist reasons. Therefore God is not a consequentialist unless God is inconsistent. (From this it further follows that, if this God exists, consequentialism is false.)

Chaput, Sylvie. Les transcendantalistes: indépendance et infini. *Horiz Phil*, 2(1), 107-114, 1991.

This paper was originally written for an audience of researchers in history of Quebec philosophy. Using examples from the life and works of Thoreau, Fuller and Emerson, the author suggests that transcendentalists, though they invited Americans to express their own thoughts, were not much interested in defining what an American philosophy could be. Yet being oneself was a question that literally obsessed them. Transcendentalism was a reflexion on what enchains or oppresses the self; a quest for independence; a search for an access to the infinite of the world and the infinite that lies in every human being.

Charlton, William. Aristotle and the Uses of Actuality. *Proc Boston Colloq Anc Phil*, 5, 1-22, 1989.

Aristotle uses the terms *dunamis* and *entelecheia* or *energeia* to express a number of different contrasts: between being potentially and being actually something, between a power and its exercise or actualisation, between two positions which may be adopted with regard to infinity, and between possibility and fulfilment. The last is the most important but the most elusive. I suggest that Aristotle may have introduced it to deal with difficulties about the one and the many mentioned by Plato in the *Parmenides* and *Philebus*.

Charlton, William (trans). *Philoponus: On Aristotle on the Intellect*. Ithaca, Cornell Univ Pr, 1991.

Chater, Nick and Oaksford, Mike. Logicism, Mental Models and Everyday Reasoning: Reply to Garnham. *Mind Lang*, 8(1), 72-89, Spr 93.

Chatterjee, Amita. Regimentation—Its Problems and Prospects in Foundations of Logic and Language, Sen, Pranab Kumar (ed). New Delhi, Allied, 1990.

The paper is mainly polemical. Here the author explores in detail the aim, necessity, possibility, and the actual mode of regimentation of loosely-structured natural language sentences and concludes that complete regimentation of a natural language is not possible within the framework of the First Order Predicate Calculus with Identity. To regiment recalcitrant locutions, it is required to extend the logical framework and to enrich the notational system. The paper also highlights the debate over naturalism and constructionism in regimentation, controversy between the 'extensionalists' and the 'intensionalists', a non-Fregean reading of the notion of intension and Montague's system of logic (IL).

Chatterjee, Tara. Moksa, the Parama Purusartha. *J Indian Counc Phil Res*, 9(1), 85-107, S-D 91.

Chattopadhyaya, D P. Rationality: Transparent, Cultural, and Transcendental. *Phil East West*, 42(4), 561-579, O 92.

Chaturvedi, Girdharilal. The Scope of Verbal Testimony (Sabda Pramana). *Indian Phil Quart*, 20/1(Supp), 1-6, Ja 93.

The paper examines the Nyaya definition of sabdapramana (verbal testimony) along with some other definitions with a view to 1) trace the volution of the concept, and 2) identify its scope in up-to-date contexts. As a result of the study, the scope of sabda pramana, i.e, the area of its operation, may be identified as follows: 1) The information from reliable persons including media reports. 2) The necessary or self-evident truths entailed by the analysis of meaning. 3) The knowledge of value. 4) The knowledge of trans-sensual entities, heaven, etc.

Chaturvedi, Vibha. Believer Versus Unbeliever: Reflections on the Wittgensteinian Perspective. *Indian Phil Quart*, 20(2), 173-187, Ap 93.

The paper analyses and examines Wittgenstein's news on disagreement between a believer (B) and unbeliever (UB). It proposes that the use of 'believer' is context dependent. Disagreement between B and UB is not merely a matter a regulating/not regulating one's life by certain pictures but also of having different interpretation of life and the world. Some interpretations of Wittgenstein's views are discussed to show that none of them rule out the possibility of UB contradicting B.

Chaturvedi, Vibha. Indeterminateness of the Concept of a Person. *Indian Phil Quart*, 19(2), 115-125, Ap 92.

The paper concludes that the concept of a person is indeterminate and loose. It is argued that Strawsonian proposal, namely that the concept of a person is of a subject to which both M and P predicates can be ascribed, is basically correct. But it leaves the concept underdetermined. It gives the necessary condition of being a person but not a sufficient condition. The concept demands that some specific type of M predicates and also certain kinds of p predicates be ascribable to a subject. It is, however, not easy to clarify which p-predicates must figure in this context so as not to make the concept too narrow or too wide.

Chaudhary, Anju G and Starosta, William J. "I Can Wait 40 or 400 Years": Gandhian *Satyagraha* West and East. *Int Phil Quart*, 33(2), 163-172, Je 93.

The analysis concerns Mohandas K Gandhi's 1930 Salt March, a satyagraha campaign. The paper first considers the event through western eyes, as a case of civil disobedience or street rhetoric. This is posed as an "etic" perspective. The paper then adopts an indigenous Indian frame of reference, or "emic" view of the events. While both the emic and etic accounts serve to interpret the event, and offer plausible understandings, neither account suffices, taken alone, to "explain" satyagraha.

Chen, Wen-shiow. Existence and Substance (in Chinese). *Phil Rev (Taiwan)*, 15, 17-34, Ja 92.

I explore the concepts of existence and substance in the present paper. "To be" is the pivotal concept of ontology. Aristotle says that "there is a science which investigates being as being and the attributes which belong to this in virtue of its own nature." Descartes treats being as a perfection, but Kant claims that "to be" is not a real predicate. In the practice of modern logic, "to be" is distinguished between the following three senses: identity, predication, and existence. (edited)

Chenet, François-Xavier. Que sont donc l'espace et le temps? Les hypothèses considérées par Kant et la lancinante objection de la "troisième possibilité". *Kantstudien*, 84(2), 129-153, 1993.

Cheney, Jim and Warren, Karen J. Ecosystem Ecology and Metaphysical Ecology: A Case Study. *Environ Ethics*, 15(2), 99-116, Sum 93.

We critique the metaphysical ecology developed by J Baird Callicott in "The Metaphysical Implications of Ecology" in light of what we take to be the most viable attempt to provide an inclusive theoretical framework for the wide variety of extant ecosystem analyses—namely, hierarchy theory. We argue that Callicott's metaphysical ecology is not consonant with hierarchy theory and is, therefore, an unsatisfactory foundation for the development of an environmental ethic.

Cheng, Chung-Ying. The "C" Theory: A Chinese Philosophical Approach to Management and Decision-Making. *J Chin Phil*, 19(2), 125-153, Je 92.

This is an innovative philosophy of management based on an integration of the rationalistic view of management from the West and the humanistic view of management from the East as represented by China and Japan.

Chennakesavan, Sarasvati. Yoga Sūtras. *Asian Phil*, 2(2), 147-155, 1992.

The yoga system accepts the Sāṅkhya metaphysics, the fundamental variation being that consciousness is held to be supreme. The goal to be achieved is to attain this final state of pure consciousness. All obstacles, mental and physical, are subjugated and transcended. The method is the development of concentration by controlling all thought modes. It starts by the purification of the body by the control of posture and breathing. The mind is purified by the rejection of hindrances to the development of concentration. Both require a mandatory practice of the ethical ideals prescribed. The final goal of samādhi is not a post-mortem state but realisable here and now. (edited)

Cherniak, Christopher. Meta-Neuroanatomy: The Myth of the Unbounded Main/Brain in Philosophy and the Origin and Evolution of the Universe, Agazzi, Evandro (ed). Norwell, Kluwer, 1991.

Cherry, Christopher. Machines as Persons?—I in Human Beings, Cockburn, David (ed). New York, Cambridge Univ Pr, 1991.

Much discussion of machine intelligence turns upon the presence of 'inner states' in human beings (and other conspicuously sentient creatures) and whether or not analogous states are intelligibly ascribable to artifacts. The author calls into question the basis of the antithesis 'inner-outer' and the nature of the relationship commonly proposed between the two. He argues for the unitary nature of the person and for the centrality of this notion to a proper understanding of what is and must be involved in sentience ascription.

Chethimattam, J B. Towards a World Morality. *J Dharma*, 16(4), 317-336, O-D 91.

Chew, Ho Hua. Process Theism and Physical Evil. *Sophia (Australia)*, 31(3), 16-27, 1992.

Process theism has been in the limelight for the past few decades for its controversial and refreshing conception of God. One aspect of process theism that has received increasing attention is process theodicy. However, in regard to this problem, it must be said that none of the process philosophers had devoted more attention to it than Charles Hartshorne. This paper reviews Hartshorne's strategy for a process solution of physical evil. The conclusion is that Hartshorne's attempt to collapse the problem of physical evil into the problem of moral evil via the free-will defence and pan-psychism is bogged down by a serious hitch.

Cheyne, Colin. Reduction, Elimination, and Firewalking. *Phil Sci*, 60(2), 349-357, Je 93.

Schwartz (1991) argues that the worry that successful reduction would eliminate rather than conserve the mental is a needless worry. He examines cases of reduction from the natural sciences and claims that if reduction of the mental is like any of these cases then it would not be a case of elimination. I discuss other cases of scientific reduction which do involve elimination. Schwartz has not shown that reduction of the mental could not be like such cases, so his argument is not sufficient to dispel the worry of elimination.

Chiaraviglio, Lucio. Some New Problems for Constructive Speculation in Logic, God and Metaphysics, Harris, James F (ed). Dordrecht, Kluwer, 1992.

Chiari, Joseph. Vitalism and Contemporary Thought in The Crisis in Modernism, Burwick, Frederick (ed). New York, Cambridge Univ Pr, 1992.

Chiereghin, Franco. Soggettività e metafisica. *G Metaf*, 14(1), 11-27, Ja-Ap 92.

The theme of the metaphysical relevance of subjectivity must examine the most elementary manifestations of subjective vitality before the search of the metaphysical characters of human subjectivity. The inquiry into the subjectivity of life as proved indispensable to grasp the evidence of such characters as the autoregulation, the independence, the self-sufficiency of the individual which find a complete realization in human subjectivity. The metaphysical character of human subjectivity becomes evident in the self manifestation of liberty.

Child, James. Donald Davidson and Section 2.01 of the *Model Penal Code*. *Crim Just Ethics*, 11(1), 31-43, Wint-Spr 92.

Child, James. Response to Alexander's "Voluntary Acts: The Child/Davidson Trilemma". *Crim Just Ethics*, 11(2), 99-100, Sum-Fall 92.

Child, William. Anomalism, Uncodifiability, and Psychophysical Relations. *Phil Rev*, 102(2), 215-245, Ap 93.

The doctrine of the anomalism of the mental is often thought to be compatible with psychophysical token identities, but in tension with the supervenience of mental properties on physical properties. It is argued that the reverse is true. The core of Davidson's argument for anomalism is traced to the thesis that rationality is uncodifiable. This is shown to be compatible with the determination of mental properties by physical, and with psychophysical supervenience. But uncodifiability rules out two popular views about psychophysical correlations: "common-sense functionalism"; and the view that each token mental state or event is a physical state or event.

Child, William. Vision and Experience: the Causal Theory and the Disjunctive Conception. *Phil Quart*, 42(168), 297-316, Jl 92.

Some philosophers have argued that the causal theory of vision is committed to a Cartesian conception of visual experience; since that conception is objectionable, they say, the causal theory must be abandoned. A three- stage response to that argument is presented. (i) A non-Cartesian "disjunctive" conception of experience is explained and defended. (ii) This disjunctive conception is shown to be compatible with a causal view of vision. (iii) It is shown that, as long as we think of vision as a way of finding out about an objective world, the idea of causation is essential to our concept of vision.

Childress, James F. Non-Heart-Beating Donors of Organs: Are the Distinctions Between Direct and Indirect Effects and Between Killing and Lettie Die Relevant and Helpful?. *Kennedy Inst Ethics J*, 3(2), 203-216, Je 93.

Chinchore, Mangala R. Duhkha: An Analysis of Buddhist Clue to Understand Human Nature. *Indian Phil Quart*, 20(1), 37-83, Ja 93.

The paper aims at articulating clues to understand human nature through an analysis and defense of *Duhkha*, together with *Dyadesanidana* as given by the Buddha and some of his prominent followers. The paper has three sections. The first demarcates the philosophical approach to *Duhkha* from the non-philosophical ones. The second distinguishes the Buddhist approach to *Duhkha* from that of the non-Buddhist philosophical traditions of the Indian origin and articulates the respective rationales they were backed by. The last brings out some of the crucial implications of the Buddhist approach to *Duhkha*.

Chisholm, Roderick M. Act, Content and the Duck-Rabbit in Wittgenstein's Intentions, Canfield, J V (ed). Hamden, Garland, 1993.

Chisholm, Roderick M. An Intentional Explication of Universals. *Conceptus*, 25(66), 45-48, 1991.

The term "universal" is here taken to mean the same as "attribute" or "property." It is contended in this paper that attributes should be understood both intensionally and intentionally. I say *"intensionally,"* meaning that these entities should *not* be taken *extensionally*; for attributes that have the same instances may yet be different attributes. And I say *"intentionally,"* meaning that intentionality is essential to the concept of an attribute. The nature of an attribute lies in the fact that it is an *ens rationis*—the kind of entity that can be grasped and made the content of thinking and believing. Criteria of identity for attributes require the concept of the intentional *content* of an act of believing: an attribute A is identical with an attribute B, if and only if, A and B are necessarily such that whoever has A as content also has B as content, and whoever has B as content also has A as content.

Chisholm, Roderick M. Brentano and Marty on Content in Mind, Meaning and Metaphysics, Mulligan, Kevin (ed). Dordrecht, Kluwer, 1990.

This is a discussion of a theory of reference developed by Franz Brentano in the final years of his life. In every mental act one is oneself the direct object of one's thinking. If one thinks of another individual, then for some relation that one bears uniquely to that other individual, one thinks of that other individual as bearing that relation to oneself. With this view, Brentano was able to find a synthesis between his earlier views and those of Anton Marty.

Chisholm, Roderick M. Identity Criteria for Properties. *Harvard Rev Phil*, 2(1), 14-17, Spr 92.

Chisholm, Roderick M. On the Simplicity of the Soul in Philosophical Perspectives, 5: Philosophy of Religion, 1991, Tomberlin, James E (ed). Atascadero, Ridgeview, 1991.

Chisholm, Roderick M. The Basic Ontological Categories in Language, Truth and Ontology, Mulligan, Kevin (ed). Dordrecht, Kluwer, 1992.

The theory of categories that is set forth here is Cartesian and Platonic. It is Cartesian in implying the existence of substance and in its concept of rationality. It is Platonistic in implying the existence of abstract objects. Such objects, moreover include attributes that are not and cannot be exemplified. The theory makes use of four undefined metaphysical concepts and of one undefined intentional concept.

Chisholm, Roderick M. William James's Theory of Truth. *Monist*, 75(4), 569-579, O 92.

Chitty, Andrew. The Early Marx on Needs. *Rad Phil*, 64, 23-31, Sum 93.

Chmielewski, Philip J. *Bettering Our Condition: Work, Workers and Ethics in British and German Economic Thought*. New York, Lang, 1992.

This study draws on the writings of crucial British (Smith, Ricardo, Marshall) and German (Hegel, Marx, Schmoller) political economists in order to derive a contemporary social ethic appropriate in the economic world and to indicate the requirements for economic concepts instrumental in reaching the common good. The book also discusses the works of two prominent modern figures (Pesch and Nell-Breuning) of Roman Catholic social teacher who explored the relation of principled values to economic analysis. (edited)

Chokr, Nader N. Mind, Consciousness, and Cognition: Phenomenology versus Cognitive Science. *Husserl Stud*, 9(3), 179-197, 1992.

With the explosion in recent years of the "cognitive revolution," there has been a renewed and sometimes frenetic interest in the nature of the *mind, consciousness,* and *cognition*. Various philosophical and scientific proposals have been made to explain these "last frontiers" in the advance of human knowledge and understanding. In this essay, I chart and delineate one particular context in which these issues are discussed: the debate between phenomenology and cognitive science. Despite their apparently irreconcilable differences, I argue essentially that these two approaches have a lot more to contribute to each other than is often believed.

Cholak, Peter and Downey, Rod. Lattice Nonembeddings and Intervals of the Recursively Enumerable Degrees. *Annals Pure Applied Log*, 61(3), 195-221, Je 93.

Let b and c be r.e. Turing degrees such that b c. We show that there is an r.e. degree a such that b a c and all lattices containing a critical triple, including the lattice 1-3-1, cannot be embedded into the interval [c,a].

Chow, Kai-wing. Ritual, Cosmology, and Ontology: Chang Tsai's Moral Philosophy and Neo-Confucian Ethics. *Phil East West*, 43(2), 201-228, Ap 93.

Current studies of Chinese thought of the Sung period (960-1279) have concentrated on metaphysics without giving due attention to its relationship with social ethics. Using Chang Tsai as an example, this paper seeks to show that the moral philosophy of Chang and of Sung neo-Confucians emphasize ritual in their teaching about moral cultivation. Chang's program of moral cultivation underscores the need to develop proper habitual behavior through ritual practice. In the light of Chang's concern for ritual, his cosmology and ontology are reinterpreted to take note of the rupture between ontological unity and human existence. Despite ontological unity of mankind, the individual is endowed with varying physical nature, which has been molded by "evil" social practices. To Chang, Buddhism is the major source of social evils. Moral cultivation therefore involves first the extirpation of old Buddhist practices/habits, and learning the correct Confucian rituals.

Chow, Siu L. Acceptance of a Theory: Justification or Rhetoric?. *J Theor Soc Behav*, 22(4), 447-474, D 92.

It is argued that acceptance of a psychological theory should be based on specially collected evidence, not on rhetoric. This position is defended with the understanding that all observations are inevitably theory-dependent. The case in favor of objective, non-circular empirical evidence in support of theories implicating unobservable hypothetical mechanisms is based on the following four distinctions between: 1) to-be-validated theory and the theory which defines the identity of evidential data, 2) prior and evidential data, 3) non-experimental research and theory-corroboration experimentation, and 4) a descriptive characterization and the criteria underlying the characterization. The *rhetoric analysis* critique of the role of evidential data is attractive if non-conceptual criteria of theory assessment are adopted.

Choza, Jacinto. Las máscaras del sí mismo. *Anu Filosof*, 26(2), 375-394, 1993.

The masks of the self. The rising of human self-consciousness is developed in six steps: 1) looking at the face; 2) visible and audible masks; 3) tattoos and acting; 4) the mask of the 'Proto-agonist'; 5) the mirror of Narcissus; 6) feelings speculations. Eros and psyche.

Christensen, Darrel E. A Hegelian/Whiteheadian Critique of Whitehead's Dipolar Theism. *Phil Theol*, 7(1), 23-51, Autumn 92.

A critique of Whitehead's concept of God from the standpoint of absolute idealism in general and of Hegel and Whitehead's relation of Hegel in particular.

Christensen, David. Causal Powers and Conceptual Connections. *Analysis*, 52(3), 163-168, Jl 92.

In "A Modal Argument for Narrow Content" (*Journal of Philosophy*, LXXXVIII, 1991, pp 5-26), Jerry Fodor proposes a necessary condition for the distinctness of causal powers. He uses this condition to support psychological individualism. I show that Fodor's argument relies on inconsistent interpretations of his condition on distinct causal powers. Moreover, on no consistent interpretation does Fodor's condition yield the results claimed for it.

Christensen, David. Confirmational Holism and Bayesian Epistemology. *Phil Sci*, 59(4), 540-557, D 92.

Much contemporary epistemology is informed by a kind of confirmational holism, and a consequent rejection of the assumption that all confirmation rests on experiential certainties. Another prominent theme is that belief comes in degrees, and that rationality requires apportioning one's degrees of belief reasonably. Bayesian confirmation models based on Jeffrey Conditionalization attempt to bring together these two appealing strands. I argue, however, that these models cannot account for a certain aspect of confirmation that would be accounted for in any adequate holistic confirmation theory. I then survey the prospects for constructing a formal epistemology that better accommodates holistic insights.

Christensen, David. Skeptical Problems, Semantical Solutions. *Phil Phenomenol Res*, 53(2), 301-321, Je 93.

Semantical answers to the skeptic have attracted much attention recently. They strike many as suspect, roughly because they seem to use purely linguistic considerations to answer substantive questions about the extralinguistic world. I defend the legitimacy of this anti-skeptical strategy, showing that the worries that have been expressed about it in the literature are without foundation. I then argue that precisely this sort of anti-skeptical argument must play a crucial role in epistemology. It provides our only defense against a very simple form of skeptical challenge which would, if unchecked, undermine our knowledge in virtually every area.

Christensen, David. Switched-Words Skepticism: A Case Study in Semantical Anti-Skeptical Argument. *Phil Stud*, 71(1), 33-58, Jl 93.

The paper argues that apparent "mere notational variants" of a theory can be truly incompatible with the original theory. Such alternative theories can then be used to generate interesting skeptical challenges. These challenges can typically be answered, however, by semantical arguments bearing interesting similarities to Putnam's semantical refutation of brain-in-vat skepticism. A common structure for this type of argument is developed, a structure which is independent of any particular account of reference. This type of semantical anti-skepticism is defended as epistemologically important, and is seen to place an interesting constraint on theories of reference.

Christian, Rose Ann. Plantinga, Epistemic Permissiveness, and Metaphysical Pluralism. *Relig Stud*, 28(4), 553-573, D 92.

This paper asks whether Plantinga's religious epistemology, couched in terms of "proper basicality," is overly permissive. His reply to the "Great Pumpkin Objection" is evaluated, and the components and structure of his epistemological program analyzed. The conclusion drawn is that it is not so much permissiveness as pluralism that raises questions for Plantinga's defense of the rationality of theistic belief. This is because Plantinga, in his explication of a broadly inductive "particularist" approach to the identification of properly basic belief, suggests a condition for assessing rationality that his own nonevidentialist religious epistemology cannot meet.

Christiano, Thomas. Political Equality. *Nomos*, 32, 151-183, 1990.

Christiano, Thomas. Sidgwick on Desire, Pleasure, and the Good in Essays on Henry Sidgwick, Schultz, Bart (ed). New York, Cambridge Univ Pr, 1992.

Christiano, Thomas. Social Choice and Democracy in The Idea of Democracy, Copp, David (ed). New York, Cambridge Univ Pr, 1993.

Christianson, Paul. Patterns of Historical Interpretation in Objectivity, Method and Point of View, Van Der Dussen, W J (ed). Leiden, Brill, 1991.

Christie, Drew. Comments on Bechtel's "The Case for Connectionism". *Phil Stud*, 71(2), 155-162, Ag 93.

Connectionism is put in perspective by summarizing the most discussed strengths and weaknesses of three approaches to computer models of the mind: symbolic processing, connectionism, and general skepticism. While Bechtel successfully presents the strengths of connectionism, its widely acknowledged difficulties cannot be overlooked. For example, do connectionist programs evidence "systematicity"? Is "systematicity" a matter of degree or of kind? Bechtel's external symbol approach is, at best, a preliminary partial solution. If Bechtel is right that a learning robot has intentionality, one must question whether it matters if the architecture is connectionist or symbolic.

Christie, W H. Francis Jeffrey's Associationist Aesthetics. *Brit J Aes*, 33(3), 257-270, Jl 93.

Christman, John P. Defending Historical Autonomy: A Reply to Professor Mele. *Can J Phil*, 23(2), 281-289, Je 93.

In "History and Personal Autonomy" (*Canadian Journal of Philosophy*, 23(2)) Alfred Mele criticizes the approach to the concept of autonomy I defended in an earlier article by claiming that, among other things, it cannot maintain its "historical" character. In particular, he claims, there are factors relevant to autonomy which are not aspects of the past processes by which agents have come to have the desires and values they do. In this reply, I concede that some conditions central to autonomy are no historical factors, and hence I modify my original model of autonomy to take account of these points. I claim, however, that the view of autonomy which results is still "historical" in an interesting sense since its central conditions focus on the manner by which a person's character is formed and develops.

Christodoulidis, Emilios A. Self-Defeating Civic Republicanism. *Ratio Juris*, 6(1), 64-85, Mr 93.

The author discusses the recent attempt by constitutional theorists to develop a theory about the empowerment of political community through law. Having outlined the civic republican position, he then examines Ackerman's example of the difference between marriage and love, as an analogy for law and politics, or in republican terminology, "constitutional" and "ordinary" politics respectively. These oppositions are set up around the purchase they offer to the question of community. In turning Ackerman's example against him, his objective is to show that the language of law inhibits rather than facilitates the quest for community.

Christoff, Daniel. Sur la liberté et les pouvoirs du langage. *Stud Phil (Switzerland)*, 49, 19-38, 1990.

Christopher, Paul P and Hartle, Anthony E. AIDS Victims and Military Service in Biomedical Ethics Reviews 1992, Humber, James M (ed). Clifton, Humana Pr, 1993.

The entry evaluates the policies of the US military services in treating and retiring AIDS victims. At the time of writing, each service had a different policy. The article concludes that the US Army's policy, which permitted service members to remain in active duty assignments as long as the individual was capable of performing required duties, was more equitable than those of the Navy and Air Force. The authors show that arguments against such a policy collapse under analysis. (Since the book went to the publisher, the Department of Defense adopted a policy reflecting the authors' position.)

Chrzan, Keith. Comment on Langtry's 'God, Evil and Probability'. *Sophia (Australia)*, 32(2), 54-58, Jl 93.

Chung, Bongkil. Appearance and Reality in Buddhist Metaphysics from a European Philosophical Point of View. *J Chin Phil*, 20(1), 57-72, Mr 93.

Arguments for the ideality of the phenomenal world are introduced from some Western philosophers, leaving differences among them out of discussion. Then arguments for the ideality of the phenomenal world are invited from some Buddhist philosophers, again leaving the differences among them unexamined. Some comparisons are made between the two philosophical traditions, concluding that the arguments for the ideality of the phenomenal world were, one way or another, all anticipated in the writings of the Buddhist philosophers. I take a side with anti-realists saying that the phenomenal world as we experience depends on our sentience just as objects in the dark can only be seen if there is light.

Churchland, Paul M. Activation Vectors versus Propositional Attitudes: How the Brain Represents Reality. *Phil Phenomenol Res*, 52(2), 419-424, Je 92.

Churchland, Paul M. State-Space Semantics and Meaning Holism. *Phil Phenomenol Res*, 53(3), 667-672, S 93.

Churchland, Paul M. Theory, Taxonomy and Methodology: A Reply to Haldane's *Understanding Folk*. *Proc Aris Soc*, 93, 313-319, 1993.

Chvatik, Kvetoslav. Artifact and Artistic Object (in Czechoslovakian). *Estetika*, 29(2), 1-14, 1992.

Ciancio, Claudio. Metafisica della soggettività e filosofia della libertà. *G Metaf*, 14(1), 29-35, Ja-Ap 92.

Cicera, Ramon. Carnap's Philosophy of Mind. *Stud Hist Phil Sci*, 24(3), 351-358, Ag 93.

Cicovacki, Predrag. Kant's Aesthetics Between 1980 and 1990: A Bibliography in Kant's Aesthetics, Meerbote, Ralf (ed). Atascadero, Ridgeview, 1991.

The compiled bibliography provides an extensive list of the secondary literature on Kant's aesthetics that appeared between 1980 and 1990. The bibliography includes books and articles devoted entirely to Kant's aesthetics, as well as books and articles on some related topics. Most of the references cited are in English, German, and French, but there is a considerable number of references to relevant publications in other languages as well.

Cignoli, R. Complete and Atomic Algebras of the Infinite Valued Lukasiewicz Logic. *Stud Log*, 50(3-4), 375-385, S-D 91.

The infinite-valued logic of Lukasiewicz was originally defined by means of an infinite-valued matrix. Lukasiewicz took special forms of negation and implication as basic connectives and proposed an axiom system that he conjectured would be sufficient to derive the valid formulas of the logic; this was eventually verified by M Wajsberg. The algebraic counterparts of this logic have become known as *Wajsberg algebras*. In this paper we show that a Wajsberg algebra is complete and atomic (as a lattice) if and only if it is a direct product of finite Wajsberg chains. The classical characterization of complete and atomic Boolean algebras as fields of sets is a particular case of this result.

Cinelli, Albert. Nietzsche, Relativism and Truth. *Auslegung*, 19(1), 35-45, Wint 93.

The paper provides a reading of the question of truth in Nietzsche's texts from "On Truth and Lies in a Nonmoral Sense" to *Twilight of the Idols*. The focus is on relation of the perspectival elements of Nietzsche's discussion of truth to the paradox of epistemological relativism: the claim that the statement "all truth is relative" (an implication of perspectivism) is self-refuting. I contend that in opposing any fixed and absolute doctrine of truth, even a perspectival one, Nietzsche avoids the paradox since he does not declare "all truth is relative" to be a universally true statement.

Cioffi, Frank. Congenital Transcendentalism and 'the Loneliness Which is the True About Things'. *Philosophy*, 33(Supp), 125-138, 1992.

This paper attempts an elucidation of what it might mean to say, as Wittgenstein said, and many have repeated after him, that what solipsism means is true but unsayable. It distinguishes various sources of denial or doubt as to the shareability the world and settles on the major source as an attempt to convey a sense of the strangeness of what is nevertheless intermittently recognised as a banality—the egocentric predicament— Husserl's 'magnificent fact'. This banality which finds misleading expression as solipsistic doubt affects some temperaments, in some moods as profoundly revelatory, and may indeed be so.

Cioffi, Frank. Congenital Transcendentalism and 'the Loneliness Which is the Truth about Things' in The Impulse to Philosophise, Griffiths, A Phillips (ed). New York, Cambridge Univ Pr, 1992.

This paper attempts an elucidation of Wittgenstein's observation that what solipsism means is true but cannot be said. (Tractatus 5.62). It argues that the 'state of affairs' to which Wittgenstein calls attention sometimes confusedly finds expression in solipsistic doubt whereas its correct expression is Ortega's 'radical solitude' and Husserl's 'transcendental revelation'. Attempts to convey this revelation have been impugned as logically incoherent whereas they might better be seen as rhetorically inept. It also characterises such attempts that not only are there many for whom their content is permanently unintelligible but that its graspability waxes and wanes even for those in whom it intermittently provokes startled recognition.

Cioffi, Frank. Wittgenstein on Freud's 'Abdominable Mess' in Wittgenstein Centenary Essays, Griffiths, A Phillips (ed). New York, Cambridge Univ Pr, 1991.

Ciriza, Alejandra and Fernández, Estela. Hacia una interpretación del discurso independentista. *Rev Filosof (Costa Rica)*, 30(71), 97-101, J 92.

This paper, inserted in the perspective of a Latin American history of ideas, attempts to interpret the articulation between the different social groups that brought about independence, as the effect of the construction of a peculiar ideological device. Through this device, a class fraction—the emergent Creole bourgeoisie—would succeed in summoning the popular sectors to pursue a project presented as the expression of the general concerns of the American people.

Ciulla, Joanne B. Why Business is Talking About Ethics: Reflections on Foreign Conversations in Revisioning Philosophy, Ogilvy, James (ed). Albany, SUNY Pr, 1992.

This paper explores some of the social, political and economic conditions that make business ethics a topic of conversation in different parts of the world. It looks at the following two questions: What conditions make the discussion of business ethics possible today?, and What does the current discussion of business ethics mean in terms of the way that people in various cultures think about morality? The paper is based on conversations that the author has had with business people in different countries. The major themes that emerged from these conversations are political conservatism, deregulation, moral pluralism, and globalization.

Clark, Ann. The Quest for Certainty in Feminist Thought. *Hypatia*, 8(3), 84-93, Sum 93.

In this paper I argue that the essentialism/antiessentialism debate among feminists is a variety of the idealist/realist split that Dewey addressed in The Quest for Certainty. I attempt to use Dewey's thought to subvert this opposition so that we can remove the feminist discussion from the structure of an idealist/realist either/or.

Clark, Austen G. Mice, Shrews, and Misrepresentation. *J Phil*, 90(6), 290-309, Je 93.

Clark, Billy. Relevance and "Pseudo-Imperatives". *Ling Phil*, 16(1), 79-121, F 93.

"Pseudo-imperatives" are constructions which seem to have imperative syntax but which pose problems for many existing semantic analyses of imperatives. It has often been suggested that they are examples of some form of "disguised conditional". This paper looks at a range of constructions which have been described as "pseudo-imperatives" and proposes a straightforward, non-conditional analysis based on the semantic analysis of imperatives proposed by Wilson and Sperber (1988) and a relevance-theoretic account of utterance-interpretation (Sperber and Wilson 1986). The proposed analysis accounts for all but a small range of the examples under consideration for which a separate semantic analysis is proposed.

Clark, Kelly James. Hold Not Thy Peace At My Tears: Methodological Reflections on Divine Impassibility in Our Knowledge of God, Clark, Kelly James (ed). Dordrecht, Kluwer, 1992.

Recent work on the divine nature has criticized the traditional conception of divine impassibility, the doctrine that God is not affected by happenings in the world. A corollary, is that an impassible being cannot suffer. From all sides, the doctrine has been criticized. Recent philosophical theologians Nicholas Wolterstorff and Richard Creel take opposing sides on these issues. Their views are examined for their philosophical and theological methodology. What role do extra-Biblical tradition, philosophy, and religious experience play? In the end, the author tentatively defends divine impassibility on the basis of inference to best explanation.

Clark, Kelly James (ed). *Our Knowledge of God*. Dordrecht, Kluwer, 1992.

This book is a collection of essays on the rationality of religious belief, reason and revelation, the attributes of God and divine benevolence and the problem of eternal punishment. The authors are Norman Kretzmann, Alvin Plantinga, Peter Forrest, William Alston, Richard Swinburne, Nicholas Wolterstorff, Tom Flint, Kelly James Clark, Marilyn McCord Adams and George N Schlesinger.

Clark, Mary T. An Inquiry Into Personhood. *Rev Metaph*, 46(1), 3-28, S 92.

The article aims to retrieve the philosophical background of the contemporary concept of person, and to note the contributions to a fuller understanding of personhood made by the theology of the Trinity and of the Incarnation. The article concludes that although the ancient thinkers did not apply the term "person" with the terms used, they associated important human characteristics such as rationality, responsibility, substantiality, and individuality. Nevertheless, the metaphysical foundation for these personal characteristics was not offered until Thomas Aquinas taught that to be real is to be (esse) and to be is to act. Being at its highest intensity is completely self-communicative, namely, God or Personal Being. Embodied beings not limited by a material form are more self-communicative than bodily things and do so by knowing, loving, and by physical action. They relate to things, other persons, and God. Since individual human being is present always, it is always an actual instance of human being; no lack of observable characteristics eliminates personhood at any state of its development, early or late.

Clark, Michael. On Wanting to be Morally Perfect. *Analysis*, 53(1), 54-56, Ja 93.

Clark, Peter. Basic Law (V)—II: Sets and Indefinitely Extensible Concepts and Classes. *Aris Soc*, Supp(67), 235-249, 1993.

The paper takes issue with Dummett's claim that the source of the contradiction in Frege's *Grundegesetze* is Frege's neglect of indefinitely extensible concepts. It characterizes one possible sense of indefinite extensibility for concepts ('classes') and criticizes Dummett's notion of intrinsic infinity. Finally it argues that there is a well-founded notion of indefinite extensibility to be found in Parson's relativization of the distinction between set and proper class.

Clark, Stephen. *Paul Ricoeur*. New York, Routledge, 1991.

Clark, Stephen A. Revealed Preference and Linear Utility. *Theor Decis*, 34(1), 21-46, Ja 93.

We study a Linear Axiom of Revealed Preference (LARP) that characterizes the consistency of a choice function with respect to a preference order satisfying the independence axiom. In addition, LARP characterizes lexicographic linear utility rationality when the choice space is a convex subset of a finite-dimensional real vector space, and LARP characterizes linear utility rationality when the choice space corresponds to a finite choice experiment.

Clark, Stephen R L. Descartes' Debt to Augustine. *Philosophy*, 32(Supp), 73-88, 1992.

Clark, Stephen R L. Descartes' Debt to Augustine in Philosophy, Religion and the Spiritual Life, McGhee, Michael (ed). New York, Cambridge Univ Pr, 1992.

The usual effect of academic commentary on the classical philosophical texts (for example, Descartes' Meditations) is to encourage scepticism. The proper task of philosophy is to realize ourselves as thinking being faced by a truth that always exceeds our grasp. Descartes' (perhaps unconscious) debt to Augustion, and the thought of Jonathan Edwards, are identified as clues to a decent reading of the texts.

Clark, Stephen R L. How Many Selves Make Me?—I in Human Beings, Cockburn, David (ed). New York, Cambridge Univ Pr, 1991.

Reports of 'multiple personality disorder' are sometimes cited as evidence against any simple, "Cartesian" view of the self. In fact, they should be examined more skeptically, and are, even if correctly reported, compatible with traditional accounts of the mind and personality. I argue that a Plotinian distinction between Self and Personality accommodates whatever is reliable in these reports.

Clark, Stephen R L. Minds, Memes, and Rhetoric. *Inquiry*, 36(1-2), 3-16, Mr 93.

Dennett's *Consciousness Explained* presents, but does not demonstrate, a fully naturalized account of consciousness that manages to leave out the very consciousness he purports to explain. If he were correct, realism and methodological individualism would collapse, as would the very enterprise of giving reasons. The metaphors he deploys actually testify to the power of metaphoric imagination that can no more be identified with the metaphors it creates than minds can be identified with memes. That latter equation, of minds with meme-complexes, rests for its meaning on the existence of real minds, which are not to be equated with the thoughts they have.

Clark, Stephen R L. Orwell and the Anti-Realists. *Philosophy*, 67(260), 141-154, Ap 92.

The Ingsoc theorists of Orwell's *1984* profess an anti-realism, and practice a linguistic tyranny, that has alarming affinities with fashionably anti-realist philosophies of the present day. 'The purpose of Newspeak was not only to provide a medium of expression for the world-view and mental habits proper to the devotees of Ingsoc, but to make all other modes of thought impossible' (G Orwell *1984*). Three questions present themselves. First, is this strategy a possible one? Second, is it one that anyone is, consciously or otherwise, committed to? Third, is its logocentric idealism (so to speak) really compatible with things that most contemporary philosophers also think are true. I consider these questions and suggest that there are passages in Orwell, and in Chesterton, that give the clue to a possible answer to anti-realist tyranny. (edited)

Clark, Stephen R L. Philosophers and Popular Cosmology. *J Applied Phil*, 10(1), 115-122, 1993.

A brief review of recent work in popular biology, especially Richard Dawkins and Stephen Jay Gould, suggesting that philosophers ought to involve themselves in the attempt to draw moral or metaphysical conclusions for scientific theories.

Clark, Stephen R L. Social, Moral and Metaphysical Identities (A Response to Joy Laine). *Personalist Forum*, 8/1(Supp), 159-161, Spr 92.

I offer three interpretations of Laine's paper: (i) that there are creatures elsewhere who look like us but aren't; (ii) that there is no one set of criteria that everyone should use in identifying people; (iii) that talk of reincarnation or transformation actually embodies assumptions about personal identity that might well be true. The third is probably included, and finds support in major philosophers even of the familiar Western tradition (e.g., Leibniz).

Clark, Stephen R L. Where Have All the Angels Gone?. *Relig Stud*, 28(2), 221-234, Je 92.

Angels, even if there are none, provide useful thought experiments. Reports of angelic visitors identify other forms of existence than material continuity. In particular, angels are moods or aspects of human life which need to be integrated in 'the form of humanity', the divine intellect.

Clark, Timothy. The Turing Test as a Novel Form of Hermeneutics. *Int Stud Phil*, 24(1), 17-32, 1992.

This is a study of the Turing Test on a hermeneutial situation which effectively deconstructs aspects of the thought of Gadamer and Ricoeur. Artificial Intelligence is related to Derrida's concept of the literary.

Clark-Evans, Christine. Charles de Brosses and Diderot: Eighteenth-Century Arguments Concerning Primitive Language, Particular Natural Languages and a National Language. *Hist Euro Ideas*, 16(1-3), 183-188, Ja 93.

The present study compares the position of two eighteenth-century philosophers of language, Charles de Brosses and Denis Diderot, on 1) primitive language, 2) the formation of languages, and 3) early etymology in all languages. It also investigates arguments concerning 4) the etymology of particular languages, their specifically national character, and national identity. De Brosses's *Traité de la formation mécaniquedes langues* (1765) is compared to Diderot's article "Encyclopédie" (1755) and *Lettre sur les sourds et muets* (1751). In their view, particular national languages develop in stages, and non-linguistic factors further widen these differences into a national identity.

Clarke, Bowman L. In Defense of a Kind of Natural Theology in Prospects for Natural Theology, Long, Eugene Thomas (ed). Washington, Cath Univ Amer Pr, 1992.

Clarke, Bowman L. Logical Construction, Whitehead, and God in Logic, God and Metaphysics, Harris, James F (ed). Dordrecht, Kluwer, 1992.

Clarke, David S. On Judging Sufficiency of Evidence in The Philosophy of A J Ayer, Hahn, Lewis E (ed). Peru, Open Court, 1992.

This selection is a review and criticism of Ayer's views on the relationship between the acceptance of a proposition as true and the purposes of an agent. Ayer makes a clear distinction between inquiry directed towards the solution of a practical problem and theoretical inquiry. For practical inquiry cost considerations are relevant, he says, in determining the scope of search for evidence prior to accepting a hypothesis as true. For theoretical inquiry, however, rules of acceptance based on purely epistemic criteria will provide the basis for acceptance. I argue that for theoretical inquiry also the potential cost of error is one of the bases for determining acceptance.

Clarke, W Norris. Is a Natural Theology Still Viable Today? in Prospects for Natural Theology, Long, Eugene Thomas (ed). Washington, Cath Univ Amer Pr, 1992.

The purpose of the essay is to show that one can still today make a well-grounded philosophical affirmation of the existence of God and a small number of key attributes. The ground is first cleared of obstacles thrown in the way coming from empiricism, Kantianism, relativism, and deconstruction — all deriving from an unwarrantably restrictive epistemology. Then several central arguments for the existence of God are given, from the contingency or non-self-sufficiency of the hole finite universe and from order in the world. Then the path to affirming meaningful attributes of God is briefly outlined. The approach is Thomistically inspired but not the classic Five Ways of St. Thomas.

Clarke, W Norris. *Person and Being*. Milwaukee, Marquette Univ Pr, 1993.

The purpose is to work out the implications of St. Thomas's metaphysics of being as existential act for his philosophy of the person. All real beings by nature are active and self-communicative to others. Since action necessarily generates relations, all beings have an intrinsically relational aspect, so that relationality becomes an equally primordial dimension of the real as substantiality. To be is to be substance-in-relation. And since the person is the highest level of being, it must itself manifest par excellence this relational and self-communicative aspect.

Clatterbaugh, Kenneth. The Oppression Debate in Sexual Politics in Rethinking Masculinity, May, Larry (ed). Lanham, Rowman & Littlefield, 1992.

This book surveys the major systematic perspectives on masculinity, that is, perspectives that offer a definition of masculinity, an account of how it is created and maintained, and an evaluation of that masculinity. The perspectives examined are biological and classical conservatism, radical and liberal profeminism, men's rights perspectives, mythopoetic perspectives, socialism, and black and gay perspectives. Each perspective's relationship to feminism is also explored. The book brings out the philosophical assumptions on which these perspectives depend and offers the criticisms with which each must contend. The conclusion of the book indicates some new directions for research and for philosophical inquiry.

Clayton, Matthew. White on Autonomy, Neutrality and Well-Being. *J Phil Educ*, 27(1), 101-112, Sum 93.

John White has recently defended a national curriculum which aims to promote children's well-being and personal autonomy. I argue that there is a sense in which the state can remain neutral between different conceptions of the good life and that White has not established that the state should aim to promote particular conceptions. I contend that the arguments which White offer in defence of his view of well-being are inadequate and that he has failed to justify the promotion of everyone's personal autonomy.

Clayton, Philip. On the "Use" of Neopragmatism. *Zygon*, 28(3), 361-369, S 93.

The present article continues an earlier critique of Robbins's and Rorty's neopragmatism. Their skepticism about the traditional *concept* of correspondence and about the *criteria* for truth are both unjustified, and their own assertion of *meaning as usefulness* either presupposes a prior notion of linguistic reference or fails to qualify as a sufficient criterion for knowledge. The difficulties with neopragmatism have implications for two other areas of the religion/science discussion, postmodernism and empirical theology. Postmodernism shares neopragmatism's mistakes regarding the philosophy of language and can be rejected without endangering one's empiricism, humanism, or naturalism. By contrast, the strengths of empirical theology, and of religious empiricism in general, can be preserved without Robbins's proposed ban on metaphysics.

Clayton, Philip and Knapp, Steven. Ethics and Rationality. *Amer Phil Quart*, 30(2), 151-161, Ap 93.

Ethical obligations cannot be derived directly from the notion of rational agency (contra Kant); yet rationality does place some ethical constraints on human agency (contra Williams). We argue that rational agency requires knowing whether actions are appropriate to one's own self-conception, and that this requires critical feedback from the relevant communities of experts. But, we show, certain ethical principles are entailed by the feedback process itself. Although practical reflection begins with internal reasons, then, there is reason to think it may lead, in the Peircean "long run", to the discovery of constraints that apply to all rational agents.

Cleary, Claudia M and Kendree, Jack M. Development of Ethical Awareness: A Model for a Community Business Ethics Forum. *Bus Prof Ethics J*, 11(3-4), 179-186, Fall-Wint 92.

Based on the premise that ethical awareness begins with understanding through dialogue, the Community Business Ethics Forum was organized. Ten business leaders representing the ethnic, professional and gender diversity of the community were invited and facilitated by a Philosophy and a Business professor. After basic instruction in vocabulary and theory, members brought their own cases to the table for discussion. Community outreach work was achieved. Heightened ethical awareness resulted in members forming ethical sounding boards in their own businesses, two members changing jobs and ethical forums being formed in churches, clubs, etc.

Cleary, John J. Commentary on Halper's "Some Problems in Aristotle's Mathematical Ontology". *Proc Boston Colloq Anc Phil*, 5, 277-290, 1989.

Clements, Tad. Universal Speciesism. *Free Inq*, 13(2), 25-27, Spr 93.

Clendinnen, F John. Nomic Dependence and Causation. *Phil Sci*, 59(3), 341-360, S 92.

The paper proposes an explication of causation in terms of laws and their explanatory systematization. A basic notion is "nomic dependence." The definition given by David Lewis is suitable for deterministic laws, and a general definition drawing on Wesley Salmon's statistical-relevance model of explanation is proposed. A test is offered for re-establishing that one chain of nomically dependent events is more direct than another that ends with the same event by considering the relationship between the two chains when an explanation in terms of more basic laws is sought. The chain to an event can be defined as causal if it is the most direct nomically linked chain leading up to that event.

Cleveland, Timothy. *Metaphysics: The Logical Approach*, by José Benardete. *Philosophia (Israel)*, 22(1-2), 173-193, Ja 93.

This critical study of José Benardete's *Metaphysics: The Logical Approach* focuses on the relationship between the insights of mathematical logic and the concerns of classical metaphysics. This study concentrates on a range of issues including: the metaphysical import of Frege's logic, especially with regard to existential generalization; the principle of identity; and Tarski's view of truth and metaphysical relativism. A question is raised concerning whether insights in symbolic logic should be expected to provide any significant contribution to classical metaphysics after the impact of Quinean holism on logic is realized.

Cleveland, Timothy. Trying Without Willing. *Austl J Phil*, 70(3), 324-342, S 92.

Volitionism is the doctrine that all human intentional actions involve a special kind of event called a 'willing'. In order to establish volitionism, philosophers have focused on cases of people who try to move paralyzed limbs. This paper presents an analysis of these cases based on the notion of *de re* intention which (a) helps provide an understanding of what the main tenets of a substantial version of volitionism are, (b) provides an account of the special cases of trying that does not involve willings, and (c) places this account of trying within a general framework for understanding intentional action. The result is a philosophy of action without willings.

Clifford, Michael. Corrugated Subjects: The Three Axes of Personhood. *Personalist Forum*, 8/1(Supp), 31-41, Spr 92.

Clifford, Michael. Dasein and the Analytic of Finitude in Crises in Continental Philosophy, Dallery, Arleen B (ed). Albany, SUNY Pr, 1990.

Clifton, Robert and Pagonis, Constantine and Pitowsky, Itamar. Relativity, Quantum Mechanics and EPR. *Proc Phil Sci Ass*, 1, 114-128, 1992.

The Einstein-Podolsky-Rosen argument for the incompleteness of quantum mechanics involves two assumptions: one about locality and the other about when it is legitimate to infer the existence of an element-of-reality. Using one simple thought experiment, we argue that quantum predictions and the relativity of simultaneity require that both these assumptions fail, whether or not quantum mechanics is complete.

Coady, C A J. *Testimony: A Philosophical Study*. New York, Clarendon/Oxford Pr, 1992.

The role of testimony in getting and spreading reliable belief or knowledge has been relatively neglected. Traditional epistemology is markedly individualist, stressing individual perception, memory or inference. But most of what any individual knows comes from others: palpably with knowledge of history, geography, or science, more subtly with everyday knowledge. This book discusses the philosophical significance of reliance upon testimony, and, in particular, the scope and depth of this dependency, the difficulty of validating it via inferences from an individual's experience of witness reliability, and certain "applied" problems such as the role of testimony in history, mathematics and the law.

Coakley, Sarah. Visions of the Self in Late Medieval Christianity in Philosophy, Religion and the Spiritual Life, McGhee, Michael (ed). New York, Cambridge Univ Pr, 1992.

This essay compares two Christian spiritual writings of the 14th century: *The Cloud of Unknowing* in the West, and Gregory Palamas' *Triads* in the Byzantine East. It is argued: 1) that the companion reveals an important divergence about the nature of the self, Western spiritual writings exhibiting a new sense of disjunctive *choice* about the final point of reference in the self (intellect or risk), Palamas effecting, a new *synthetic* vision of body and mental formalities; 2) that the Western developments provide foreshadowing of Cartesian 'individuation'; and 3) that Palamas' synthetic view is worthy of attention in the philosophy of religion and of identity.

Coakley, Sarah. Visions of the Self in Late Medieval Christianity: Some Cross-Disciplinary Reflections. *Philosophy*, 32(Supp), 89-103, 1992.

Cobb, William S. Plato's *Theages*. *Ancient Phil*, 12(2), 267-284, Fall 92.

My aim is to provide a thorough refutation of the attacks on the authenticity of this Platonic dialogue, especially those that claim the treatment of Socrates' daimonic sign in it is incompatible with that in clearly authentic dialogues and that claim the dialogue depicts Socrates as having some sort of magical power. I also indicate why this dialogue is worthy of more serious study by Plato scholars.

Cobb Jr, John B. Alfred North Whitehead in Founders of Constructive Postmodern Philosophy, Griffin, David Ray (& others)165-196. Albany, SUNY Pr, 1993.

For Whitehead the modern world originated in a reaction to the excesses of speculation intellect and has been characterized by its progressive limitation of the role of reason. Now its worldview of matter in motion has collapsed. The challenge is to renew disciplined speculation to construct a coherent new vision. This requires a shift form substances with attributes to relational events, from the duality of subjects and objects to entities that are at once subjects for themselves and objects for others, and from the primacy of sensation to that of physical feelings.

Cobb Jr, John B. The Philosophy of Charles Hartshorne. *Process Stud*, 21(2), 75-84, Sum 92.

Hartshorne's extraordinary contribution to twentieth-century philosophy has been recognized by Volume XX of "The Library of Living Philosophers". This volume shows the breadth and depth of his contributions-from philosophical studies of physiological psychology and bird song to metaphysics and philosophy of religion. At the age of ninety-six he is still writing. He differs from Whitehead by adopting a more rationalistic approach. He resolves the dualism of the mental and the physical by opting for physicalism, whereas Whitehead proposes events that are both mental and physical.

Cobben, Paul. Persoon, substantie en gemeenschap: Over de innerlijke samenhang tussen de positie van de *liberals* en de *communitarians*. *Alg Ned Tijdschr Wijs*, 84(4), 237-257, O 92.

In this article the internal coherence of the position of the liberals and the communitarians is developed. Departing from a discussion of the theories of Rawls and Habermas, it is argued that the liberals are not able to determine the freedom of the subject in a positive way. In contrast to them, Hegel is able to do this. But as a consequence the liberal position inverts into a communitarian one. As a criticism of Hegel the thesis is put forward that the common actions of the subjects presuppose an absolute difference: their absolute self-reliance. Therefore both positions are dependent on each other.

Coby, Patrick. Socrates on the Decline and Fall of Regimes: Books 8 and 9 of the *Republic*. *Interpretation*, 21(1), 15-39, Fall 93.

Cocchiarella, N B. Cantor's Power-Set Theorem Versus Frege's Double-Correlation Thesis. *Hist Phil Log*, 13(2), 179-201, 1992.

Frege's thesis that second-level concepts can be correlated with first-level concepts and that the latter can be correlated with their value-ranges is in direct conflict with Cantor's power-set theorem, which is a necessary part of the iterative, but not of the logical, concept of class. Two consistent second-order logics with nominalized predicates as abstract singular terms are described in which Frege's thesis and the logical notion of a class are defended and Cantor's theorem is rejected. Cantor's theorem is not incompatible with the logical notion of class, however. Two alternative similar kinds of logics are also described in which Cantor's theorem and the logical notion of a class are retained and Frege's thesis is rejected.

Cocco, Giuseppe. La struttura del mondo soprasensibile nella filosofia di Giamblico. *Riv Filosof Neo-Scolas*, 84(2-3), 468-493, Ap-S 92.

Cochran, Ruth B. Some Problems with Loyalty: The Metaethics of Commitment. *Dialec Hum*, 17(3), 201-210, 1990.

This paper addressed problem inherent in the concept of Loyalty. Philosophers simply cannot avoid the moral implications which follow from the human proclivity to align themselves with a state, a religion, a tribe, abstract ideas, or to all at once. Included in the discussion were the following subjects: (1) Josiah Royce and *The Philosophy of Loyalty*, (2) Loyalty and Bad faith, (3) Loyalty and Moral Agency, and, (4) the possibility of Loyalty in Good Faith.

Cockburn, David (ed). *Human Beings*. New York, Cambridge Univ Pr, 1991.

What is the importance of the notion of a 'human being'? The contributors to this collection have radically different approaches, some accepting and others denying its validity for a proper understanding of what a person is and for our ethical thought about each other. Contributors on both sides of the divide defend their views in ways which stand in sharp contrast to much current work in moral philosophy and philosophy of mind.

Cockburn, David. The Supernatural. *Relig Stud*, 28(3), 285-301, S 92.

Simone Weil writes: 'Earthly things are the criterion of spiritual things'. The analogy of Wittgenstein's discussion of 'other minds' may throw light on this. Talk of the 'supernatural' might be understood as based on a primitive reaction of wonder in the face of certain extraordinary actions; not on the hypothesis that the action involves a violation of the laws of physics. This approach enables us to do justice to the kind of importance which talk of the 'supernatural' has in people's lives; the objection that it is in some way 'reductionist' rests on a confusion.

Code, Alan. Aristotle, Searle, and the Mind-Body Problem in John Searle and His Critics, LePore, Ernest (ed). Cambridge, Blackwell, 1991.

Code, Lorraine. Taking Subjectivity into Account in Feminist Epistemologies, Alcoff, Linda (ed). New York, Routledge, 1993.

Cohen, Avner. Marx—From the Abolition of Labour to the Abolition of the Abolition of Labour. *Hist Euro Ideas*, 17(4), 485-502, Jl 93.

The work shows the change in Marx's approach to the question of the abolition of labour. In his early writings, Marx called for the abolition of labour. Later after 1850, he vigorously argued against this idea. As theoretically Marx did not gain much of this change, its explanation is to be found in politics. It appears that in consequence of the failure of 1848-1849 revolutions Marx adopted a new political strategy. As the call for abolition of labour was not compatible with this strategy, Marx was forced to withdraw this idea.

Cohen, Daniel H. Wittgenstein and W C Fields. *Lyceum*, 2(1), 15-30, Spr 90.

The career of W C Fields, juggler and comedian, provides a helpful metaphor for Wittgenstein's career in philosophy. The metaphor is used to interpret the particularly cryptic remarks beginning at 5.542 on propositional attitudes in the Tractatus Logico-Philosophicus. The metaphysically rich account of the semantics of belief attributions that emerges is well within the "juggling" spirit of the philosophy of the Tractatus—and well outside the "comic" spirit of Wittgenstein's later Philosophical Investigations.

Cohen, Elliot D (ed). *Philosophical Issues in Journalism*. New York, Oxford Univ Pr, 1992.

Bringing together major contemporary and classical writings on a wide range of provocative issues in press ethics and philosophy underlying much of what we see and hear in today's media, this unique anthology covers topics such as what makes a story newsworthy, journalism and professional ethics, the right of free speech, privacy and news sources, politics and the power of the press, objectivity and bias, and the education of journalists.

Cohen, Eric and Ben-Ari, Eyal. Hard Choices: A Sociological Perspective on Value Incommensurability. *Human Stud*, 16(3), 267-297, Jl 93.

Cohen, G A. Equality of What? in The Quality of Life, Nussbaum, Martha C (ed). New York, Oxford Univ Pr, 1993.

The article criticizes John Rawl's case for rejecting the claims of welfare as the appropriate magnitude for egalitarians to equalize. A different case for rejecting those claims, made by Amartya Sen, is endorsed, and Sen's positive answer to "Equality to what?" is expounded and criticized.

Cohen, G A. Incentives, Inequality, and Community in The Tanner Lectures On Human Values, V13, Peterson, Grethe B (ed). Salt Lake City, Univ of Utah Pr, 1992.

Part I lays out the familiar "incentive argument" for inequality, that paying talented people more than untalented ones rebounds to the benefit of the latter. It also defines a condition for what is called "justificatory community": that policy arguments must pass what is called the "interpersonal test". Part II shows that the incentive argument fails the stated test. Part III applies the preceding results to, and against, John Rawls's use of the difference principle to defend incentives-derived inequality.

Cohen, G A. Isaiah's Marx, and Mine in Isaiah Berlin: A Celebration, Margalit, Edna (ed). Chicago, Univ of Chicago Pr, 1991.

The first several pages of the article recount experiences sustained by the author as a student at Oxford, where Sir Isaiah Berlin was his supervisor. The rest of the article counterposes Berlin's interpretations of certain aspects of Karl Marx's thought to the author's own different interpretations of them.

Cohen, G A. The Future of a Disillusion in Psychoanalysis, Mind and Art, Hopkins, Jim (ed). Cambridge, Blackwell, 1992.

The essay looks at the current standing of socialist doctrine, in the wake of the collapse of the communist world. It begins with a personal narrative, recounting the author's Montreal Jewish Communist childhood and adolescence, and proceeds to distinguish what was sound from what was unsound in the traditional socialist critique of capitalism.

Cohen, Jean and Arato, Andrew. Politics and the Reconstruction in Cultural-Political Interventions in the Unfinished Project of Enlightenment, Honneth, Axel (& other eds). Cambridge, MIT Pr, 1992.

Cohen, Joshua. Freedom of Expression. *Phil Pub Affairs*, 22(3), 207-263, Sum 93.

Cohen, Joshua. Minimalist Historical Materialism in On the Track of Reason, Beehler, Rodger (ed). Boulder, Westview Pr, 1992.

Cohen, Joshua. Moral Pluralism and Political Consensus in The Idea of Democracy, Copp, David (ed). New York, Cambridge Univ Pr, 1993.

Cohen, Joshua and Rogers, Joel. Associations and Democracy. *Soc Phil Pol*, 10(2), 282-312, Sum 93.

Cohen, L Jonathan. *An Essay on Belief and Acceptance*. New York, Clarendon/Oxford Pr, 1992.

Believing something is being disposed to feel that it is true, whereas accepting something is adopting a policy of taking it as a premiss for relevant reasonings. So belief is involuntary and acceptance is voluntary. This distinction helps clarify the difference between causes and reasons, and may be fruitfully applied in analysing the purposes of infant and adult humans, of animals and of human organisations. It also sheds important light on the structure of scientific knowledge, on what jury verdicts declare, on subjectivist accounts of probability, on the difference between statement and assertion, and on some paradoxes about self-deception.

Cohen, L Jonathan. From a Historical Point of View in Probability and Rationality, Eells, Ellery (ed). Amsterdam, Rodopi, 1991.

Cohen offers an autobiographical elucidation of his ideas about the philosophy of probability. At first his aim was to write a book on political philosophy (*The Principles of World Citizenship*, 1954). But he was influenced by acquaintance with developments in empirical linguistics and philosophical logic to move into the philosophy of language (*The Diversity of Meaning*, 1962). Out of this latter work he developed his 'Baconian' inductive logic (*The Implications of Induction*, 1970), with

its application to the jurisprudence of forensic proof (*The Probable and the Provable*, 1977) and to the analysis of experimental results in the psychology of probability-judgment (*The Dialogue of Reason*, 1986).

Cohen, L Jonathan. Some Comments by L J C in Probability and Rationality, Eells, Ellery (ed). Amsterdam, Rodopi, 1991.

Cohen replies to discussions of his ideas about the method of relevant variables, and other modes of scientific reasoning, by Leszek Nowak, Menachen Fisch and Maurice Finocchiaro; to discussions of his ideas about Pascalian and Baconian conceptions of subjective probability, by David Schum, James Logue, Czeslaw Nosal and Ryszard Stachowski; and to discussions of his ideas about rationality and methodological pluralism, by Lola Lopes and Greg Oden, Gerd Gigerenzer, Jonathan Adler, Tomasz Maruszewski and Ireneusz Scigala.

Cohen, Michael. Einstein on Simultaneity. *Philosophy*, 67(262), 543-548, O 92.

Einstein's 'train' Gedankenexperiment fails to explain why moving observers must judge the simultaneity of distant events differently from observers at rest. In Einstein's version of the Gedankenexperiment, observers pass at the moment when, with respect to one of them, signals are emitted from equidistant sources. Einstein's error is to treat as absolute a description which is relative to one of the frames. Sound versions of the Gedankenexperiment are presented. It is argued that the appeal to observers' can easily mislead.

Cohen, Morris R. *The Faith of a Liberal—Morris Raphael Cohen*. New Brunswick, Transaction Books, 1993.

Cohen, Paul A. Cultural China: Some Definitional Issues. *Phil East West*, 43(3), 557-563, Jl 93.

Cohen, Richard A. Authentic Selfhood in Heidegger and Rosenzweig. *Human Stud*, 16(1-2), 111-128, Ap 93.

Heidegger's master work, Being and Time (1927), appeared only six years after Rosenzweig's, The Star of Redemption (1921). Both thinkers developed new and profound epistemologies and ontologies, and original conceptions of selfhood with them. Heidegger's Dasein analytic hinges on differentiating inauthentic fascination with beings form authentic care for the question of being. Rosenzweig similarly distinguishes the superficial persona form deep character, but he goes on to elaborate a third deeper dimension revealed only through love, hence in social life. Distinguishing two types of love: being-loved and loving, he situates true selfhood in the chosen Jewish people and the missionizing Christian communion respectively.

Cohen, Richard A. The Family and Ethics: The Metaphysics of Eros in Emmanuel Levinas's *Totality and Infinity*. *Cont Phil*, 15(4), 1-7, Jl-Ag 93.

Cohen, Ted. High and Low Thinking about High and Low Art. *J Aes Art Crit*, 51(2), 151-156, Spr 93.

Coker, John C. On Being Nemesetikos as a Mean. *J Phil Res*, 17, 61-92, 1992.

Aristotle's several accounts of the praiseworthy mean temperament of nemesis, one in the Nichomachean Ethics and two in the Eudemian Ethics, do not cohere with each other, and each account is internally flawed. Some philosophers have pronounced Aristotle's accounts of nemesis as a mean to be irreparably defective and even a misapplication of the doctrine of the mean. Contrary to such pronouncements, Aristotle's accounts of nemesis as a mean have explicable reparable flaws, and can be brought into coherence. The tools for repair are provided by an interpretation and elaboration of Aristotle's discussion, in the Rhetoric, of emotions and temperaments contrary to pity. Ultimately, nemesis as a praiseworthy mean temperament is constituted by and accounted for in terms of four praiseworthy sub-temperaments, namely proper indignation, proper Schadenfreude, proper pity, and proper gratulation.

Colapietro, Vincent. America's Philosophical Vision—John E Smith. *Int Phil Quart*, 33(3), 355-364, S 93.

This article provides an overview of John E Smith's philosophical project, by focusing on his most recent work (America's Philosophical Vision). In particular, it presents his reconstructed notions of human experience and reason; then, it explores several respects in which this compelling and nuanced reconstruction might, nonetheless, be open to criticism.

Colapietro, Vincent. Peirce's Contribution to Ethics in Frontiers in American Philosophy, Volume I, Burch, Robert W (ed). College Station, Texas A&M Univ Pr, 1992.

This paper explores Peirce's distinctive approach to moral philosophy, paying especially close attention to the relationship between ethics and religion. It begins by considering Peirce's explicit skepticism about the value of reflecting on traditional morality; it concludes with a brief contrast between a Peircean and a Deweyan approach to ethics. But the heart of this paper is an interpretation of Peirce's nuanced account of deliberative agency.

Colapietro, Vincent. Purpose, Power, and Agency. *Monist*, 75(4), 423-444, O 92.

This article re-examines classical American pragmatism in terms of the three themes indicated in the title, placing special emphasis on the way Peirce, James, and Dewey proposed to reconstruct our conception of human agency. It is argued here that what we encounter in the writings of these philosophers is nothing less than a speculatively bold, yet empirically nuanced, vision of our agency - in - the - world. The outlines of this vision are traced; its roots in the very exigencies of agents are also explored.

Colapietro, Vincent. Reply to Anderson: Interpreting the Guess of a Physicist. *Int Phil Quart*, 32(3), 377-384, S 92.

Charles S Peirce described his cosmology as a guess at the riddle of the universe; more precisely, he described it as the guess of a physicist, of someone imbued with the spirit of the natural sciences. Recently, Douglas Anderson has explored in "Realism and Idealism in Peirce's Cosmogony" a tension he sees at the center of Peirce's account of the origin of the cosmos. The "Reply to Anderson" continues this exploration, trying to bring into sharp focus the idealistic, realistic, and pragmatic aspects of Peircean cosmogony.

Colapietro, Vincent. The Critical Appropriation of Our Intellectual Tradition: Toward a Dialogue Between Polanyi and Lonergan. *Tradition Discovery*, 17(1-2), 29-43, 1990-91.

This paper explores some of the important similarities between Michael Polanyi and Bernard Lonergan regarding the way we actually live our intellectual lives and attain a rational outlook. In particular, it identifies the conceptual and rhetorical resources within the writings of these two thinkers for steering between, on the one hand, the ahistoric bias of Enlightenment rationality and, on the other, the relativistic implications of most historicist conceptions of human reason. Both Polanyi and Lonergan are, in a broad sense, historicist thinkers; but neither is, in any compromising sense, a relativist.

Colapietro, Vincent M. *Glossary of Semiotics*. New York, Paragon House, 1993.

This lexicon defines the key terms of semiotic discourse (i.e., semiotics *very* broadly conceived) in such a way as to be, at once, useful to those unfamiliar with this field and informative to those who have an acquaintance (even a deep acquaintance) with the texts of Peirce, Saussure, Morris, Barthes, Eco, Derrida, Kristeva, Irigaray, etc. The entries range from the most concise of definition to brief essays in which historical developments and contemporary controversies are highlighted. The definitions of various neologisms and technical terms (perhaps esp. those of Peirce) will be valuable to philosophers in general, not just those interested in semiotics.

Cole, David. Moore on Skepticism and Common Sense in Certainty and Surface in Epistemology and Philosophical Method, Martinich, A P (ed). Lewiston, Mellen Pr, 1991.

Cole, David. Statutory Definitions of Death and the Management of Terminally Ill Patients Who May Become Organ Donors after Death. *Kennedy Inst Ethics J*, 3(2), 145-155, Je 93.

The law stipulates that death is irreversible. Patients treated in accord with the Pittsburgh protocol have death pronounced when their condition might well be reversed by intervention that is intentionally withheld. Nevertheless, the protocol is in accord with the medical "Guidelines for the Determination of Death". However, the Guidelines fail to capture the intent of the law, which turns out to be a good thing, for the law embodies a faulty definition of death. The inclusion of "irreversible" in the legal definition makes that definition excessively demanding and out of step with the ordinary concept of death. On this basis the protocol is absolved of the moral but not the legal charge that it involves vivisection.

Cole, Eve. Theophrastus and Aristotle on Animal Intelligence in Theophrastus, Fortenbaugh, W W (ed). New Brunswick, Transaction Books, 1992.

In this paper I compare the treatments of non-human animal intelligence given by Theophrastus and Aristotle. Both thinkers manifest a lively interest in the cognitive and moral capabilities of animals, and both also appear somewhat ambivalent about the limits of those capabilities. I resolve some apparent contradictions for both Theophrastus and Aristotle, and interpret Theophrastus' greater charity about animal intelligence to his having adopted Aristotle's own naturalistic principles, and carried them further in the post-Aristotelian Peripatos.

Cole, Eve Browning. *Philosophy and Feminist Criticism*. New York, Paragon House, 1993.

This book introduces readers to the conversation between traditional philosophy and its feminist critics which has been taking place over the past 20 years. It surveys feminist criticisms of traditional treatments of problems in metaphysics, epistemology, and ethics, as well as treating of the fresh approaches in philosophy being made by Black feminists, Lesbian philosophers, American Indian feminists, and ecological feminists. Its main message is that neither philosophy nor feminism thrive when viewed as the property of specialists or in-groups, but that in dialogue and mutual engagement both take on new life.

Coleman, Dorothy. Hume's Internalism. *Hume Stud*, 18(2), 331-347, N 92.

Hume is typically taken to be an internalist, i.e., one who maintains that motivation is built into the acceptance or affirmation of a moral judgment. However, Hume does not provide any systematic defense of the internalist view, and recently it has been argued that he is an externalist, one who maintains that the acceptance of a moral judgment does not itself motivate but requires independent desires to so. This paper defends the traditional view that Hume advocates internalism. Hume believes that moral approval and disapproval are not desires to be virtuous but cause desires to be virtuous. This connection between moral passion and moral motivation is an internal connection in so far as the desires that produce moral actions can be caused by moral passions independent of any external desire. While Hume believed that the desire to be virtuous is related to the desire for happiness, the desire for happiness is not required as an external, triggering motive to be virtuous.

Coleman, Jules L. Contracts and Torts. *Law Phil*, 12(1), 71-93, F 93.

Coleman, Jules L. *Risks and Wrongs*. New York, Cambridge Univ Pr, 1992.

Coles, Romand. Storied Others and Possibilities of *Caritas*: Milbank and Neo-Nietzschean Ethics. *Mod Theol*, 8(4), 331-351, Oct 92.

Coletti, G and Regoli, G. How Can an Expert System Help in Choosing the Optimal Decision?. *Theor Decis*, 33(3), 253-264, N 92.

Colgan, Quentin. On Reasoning About That Than Which Only One Being Can Be Thought Greater. *Amer Cath Phil Quart*, 65, 99-105, 1991.

The paper begins by acknowledging (for the sake of argument), the logical force of Anselm's ontological argument. It next attempts to demonstrate that once the logical force of Anselm's argument is accepted, it necessarily entails the existence as well of "that than which only one being can be thought greater." The paper concludes with several questions concerning the possible impact that such entailment might have upon one's commitment to Anselm's argument.

Colish, Marcia L. Peter Lombard and Abelard: The *Opinio Nominalium* and Divine Transcendence. *Vivarium*, 30(1), 139-156, My 92.

One of a series of conference papers published in this issue of *Vivarium*, this paper supports the claim they document that what "nominalism" meant to twelfth-century thinkers was the doctrine of the univocal signification of nouns and verbs, with their

oblique or tensed forms conveying consignification of the things or actions they signify in the nominative case or present tense, respectively. The paper shows that both Peter Abelard and Peter Lombard called upon this doctrine in their argument over whether God can do better that He does, indicating that nominalism so defined has a perceived utility for exponents of differing logical and theological persuasions at the time.

Collie, Joanne (trans) and Irigaray, Luce and Still, Judith (trans). *Elemental Passions—Luce Irigaray*. New York, Routledge, 1992.

Elemental Passions explores the man/woman relationship in a series of meditations on the senses and the elements. Its form resembles a series of love letters in which, however, the identity — and even the reality — of the addressee is deliberately obscured. French philosopher Luce Irigaray's investigations into the nature of gender, language and identity take place in several modes: the analytic, the essayistic and the lyrical poetic.

Collier, Andrew. Marxism and Universalism: Group Interests or a Shared World? in International Justice and the Third World, Attfield, Robin (ed). New York, Routledge, 1992.

This essay asks the question whether Marxist ethics, based as it is on particular socio-historical groups notion universal principles, can give an account of obligations of groups in the richer countries to the "Third World". It is argued that it can, provided that group ethics is not seen as founded on group interests narrowly conceived, but on a group's status in a shared world (natural, social and political).

Collier, John and Stingl, Michael. Evolutionary Naturalism and the Objectivity of Morality. *Biol Phil*, 8(1), 47-60, Ja 93.

We propose an objective and justifiable ethics that is contingent on the truth of evolutionary theory. We do not argue for the truth of this position, which depends on the empirical question of whether moral functions form a natural class, but for its cogency and possibility. The position we propose combines the advantages of Kantian objectivity with the explanatory and motivational advantages of moral naturalism. It avoids problems with the epistemological inaccessibility of transcendent values, while avoiding the relativism or subjectivism often associated with moral naturalism. Our position emerges out of criticisms of the contemporary sociobiological views of morality found in the writings of Richard Alexander, Michael Ruse, and Robert Richards.

Collin, Finn. Translation and Foreign Cultures. *Dan Yrbk Phil*, 26, 7-31, 1991.

Collini, Stefan (ed). *Interpretation and Overinterpretation: Umberto Eco*. New York, Cambridge Univ Pr, 1992.

Collini, Stefan. The Ordinary Experience of Civilized Life in Essays on Henry Sidgwick, Schultz, Bart (ed). New York, Cambridge Univ Pr, 1992.

Collins, Ardis B. Commentary on "Hegel and the Problem of Difference" in Hegel and His Critics, Desmond, William J (ed). Albany, SUNY Pr, 1989.

Collins, Arthur W. On the Paradox Kripke Finds in Wittgenstein. *Midwest Stud Phil*, 17, 74-88, 1992.

Collins, Clint. Response—From Priest to Tourist: The Phiosopher of Education in a Post-Philosophic Moment. *Phil Stud Educ*, 1, 15-19, 1990.

Collins, Ronald K L and Nielsen, Finn E. The Spirit of Simone Weil's Law in Simone Weil's Philosophy of Culture, Bell, Richard (ed). New York, Cambridge Univ Pr, 1993.

Colombo, Arrigo (ed) and Quarta, Cosimo. *Il Destino della Famiglia Nell'Utopia*. Bari, Dedalo, 1991.

This book deals with the problem of the family, of its evolution, of its future through the great masters of utopia and through utopian experimentation. Utopia is both the aim of the just and fraternal society, and the process that creates that society; the family, in this process, *has been reconstructed* in the sense of justice and love. (edited)

Colombo, Arrigo (ed) and Schiavone, Giuseppe. *L'Utopia nella Storia: La Rivoluzione Inglese*. Bari, Dedalo, 1992.

First, the book recalls the historical significance of utopia, as the design of a just and fraternal society, and the process of its construction, which pervades and inspires and defines the whole of history. Second, to contribute to a *revaluation* of the English Revolution, which is the basis of the modern movement towards freedom. (edited)

Colonnello, P. Kant, Arendt e il giudizio politico. *Sapienza*, 45(1), 93-97, 1992.

Coloubaritsis, Lambros. Le status de l'Un dans la "Métaphysique". *Rev Phil Louvain*, 90(88), 497-522, N 92.

Contrary to the traditional interpretation which holds Being and the One to be convertible, the author maintains that this convertibility is only upheld by Aristotle in extreme cases such as the individual being and the supreme genera. In all other cases the relations between Being and the One are controlled by complementarity, the One ensuring the modes of unity for Being. This status of the One also explains the difference between "principles" and "beings", showing that the question of principles belongs to Henology.

Colquhoun, Alan. *Modernity and the Classical Tradition: Architectural Essays 1980-1987*. Cambridge, MIT Pr, 1989.

Colwell, Richard. Goodness and Greatness: Broudy on Music Education. *J Aes Educ*, 26(4), 37-48, Wint 92.

The article discusses the influence of Harry Broudy on the development of a philosophy of education. The author traces Broudy's career as a philosopher and educator, including the influence of his aesthetic education philosophy on people like Bennet Reimer, Ralph Smith, and Carol Holden; his research work, and published articles. Broudy's impact on the development of a philosophy of music education is highlighted, with a discussion of his controversial proposed curriculum for secondary schools. In conclusion, Broudy has been an inspiration to music educators by helping philosophical ideas fit practices in music education.

Comans, Michael. The Question of the Importance of *Samadhi* in Modern and Classical Advaita Vedanta. *Phil East West*, 43(1), 19-38, Ja 93.

It is commonly assumed that the cultivation and practice of Samádhi is central to the liberation concern of Advaita Vedánta. This paper questions that assumption. The paper reviews the writings of some modern exponents of Advaita on this subject, it then discusses in detail the use of the term Samádhi in the accepted works of Sankara. The conclusion reached is that Samádhi is not of major importance in the thought of Sankara.

Comay, Rebecca. Framing Redemption in Ethics and Danger, Dallery, Arleen B (ed). Albany, SUNY Pr, 1992.

Cometti, Jean-Pierre. La métaphysique de la parole et les faubourgs du langage. *Rev Int Phil*, 46(183), 487-504, 1992.

Cometti, Jean-Pierre. Raison, argumentation et légitimation: Habermas, Apel et les apories de la communication. *Philosophiques*, 19(1), 3-24, 1992.

The possibility of defining the rationality upon the only basis of *communicative actions* and *forms of life* lies at the root of several difficulties, of which Habermas' attempts give a very significant example. *Legitimation* is its touchstone. It is the central point of the Apel-Habermas controversy and the basis of its latest developments. Apel and Habermas are seeking an outcome by looking at "claims to validity" which they consider to be embodied in communicative actions. They appeal to a pragmatist account of rationality and to some *Unconditional*, which is the main source of the dilemmas and disagreements they have to cope with. One may wonder whether the kind of tension which strikes the tie relating *argumentation* to some "transcendant moment" is not built into the very notion of communicative rationality. One may also wonder whether some illumination might not consist in some attempt to investigate the very connections between *Necessary* and *Arbitrary*.

Comstock, Gary L. Pigs and Piety: A Theocentric Perspective on Food Animals. *Between Species*, 8(3), 121-135, Sum 92.

Should Christians with a theocentric perspective on ethics condone the domestication and slaughter of food animals? My essay is autobiographical, telling the story of my attempt to answer this question for myself, trying to reconcile my concern for family farmers, my commitment to Mennonite religious beliefs, and my philosophical conversion to moral vegetarianism.

Comstock, Gary L. Should We Genetically Engineer Hogs?. *Between Species*, 8(4), 196-202, Fall 92.

In 1985, researchers inserted a human growth hormone gene into the chromosome of a pig. Nineteen transgenic swine lived through birth and into maturity, but they developed abnormally and exhibited deformed bodies and skulls. I argue that pigs have basic biological needs, and can take an interest in things in their future, and that it is *prima facie* morally wrong to deprive conscious individuals of the things they must have if their basic biological needs are to be met.

Condren, Conal (ed) and Lawson, George. *Politica Sacra et Civilis—George Lawson*. New York, Cambridge Univ Pr, 1992.

Conee, Earl. The Possibility of Power Beyond Possibility in Philosophical Perspectives, 5: Philosophy of Religion, 1991, Tomberlin, James E (ed). Atascadero, Ridgeview, 1991.

Omnipotence is analyzed as the power to have things be any way at all, possible or impossible. The coherence of this notion of omnipotence is defended, and it is compared to Descartes' view of omnipotence. The Stone paradox and the possibility of multiple omnipotent beings are discussed. It is argued that the defended analysis of omnipotence renders the Free Will Defence ineffective, and fosters an epistemic puzzle about the modal status of the actual world.

Conee, Earl. The Truth Connection. *Phil Phenomenol Res*, 52(3), 657-669, S 92.

A particular conception of the justification condition on knowledge is defended. It is argued that this sort of justification has a certain special bearing on truth.

Conill, J. Wittgenstein y Apel sobre la crítica del sentido: de la lógica a la antropología?. *Pensamiento*, 189(48), 3-31, Ja-Mr 92.

Nos preguntamos por qué K O Apel desde la hermenéutica heideggeriana recurrió a la filosofía lingüística de Wittgenstein y en qué medida se apropió de su crítica del sentido en su transformación de la filosofía. Se expone la especificidad de la crítica del sentido asumida por Apel siguiendo el proceso de autocrítica wittgensteiniano a partir de las insuficiencias del criterio lógico y se pone de relieve el significado hermenéutico y antropológico del criterio pragmática del sentido en Wittgenstein son subsanables en el enfoque hermenéutico y antropológico de Apel.

Connell, George B. Judge William's Theonomous Ethics in Foundations of Kierkegaard's Vision of Community, Connell, George B (ed). Atlantic Highlands, Humanities Pr, 1992.

Kierkegaard's ethical stage, which is most fully represented in the letters of Judge Williams in *Either/Or* 2, is frequently described as broadly Kantian in character. This article contests this view, arguing that Judge William views ethical obligation as grounded in the ethical self's relation to God. The article ends by discussion the ways in which the ethical stage is distinct from Kierkegaard's more decisively religious stages.

Connell, George B (ed) and Evans, C Stephen (ed). *Foundations of Kierkegaard's Vision of Community*. Atlantic Highlands, Humanities Pr, 1992.

Since his emergence as a major philosophical voice, Kierkegaard has routinely been stereotyped as an asocial individualist. This collection of articles challenges this stereotype and highlights the new attention being given to the social dimensions of Kierkegaard's thought. Beginning with essays that treat aspects of Kierkegaard's underlying religious vision and ethical thought, the book goes on to focus on Kierkegaard's understanding of modernity and politics and the implications of his insights for such problems as international conflict and the status of women.

Connolly, John M. Anomaly and Folk Psychology. *Inquiry*, 36(1-2), 179-198, Mr 93.

In *An Introduction to Cognitive Science* (1991) Justin Leiber explores the confrontation of Wittgenstein and Turing in 1939, arguing that, though seemingly at odds, the two were really collaborators in the great task of building the new cognitive science: Wittgenstein "the harrower of the old paradigm" (of the mind) "setting tasks for [Turing,] the engineer of the new." But, *pace* Leiber, Wittgenstein's intent was *not* "to expose" the anomalies of everyday cognitive life." On the contrary, he saw, not anomalies, but only the variegated patterns of *use*. I illustrate my contention by exploring the concept of 'folk psychology.'

Connolly, William E. Beyond Good and Evil: The Ethical Sensibility of Michel Foucault. *Polit Theory*, 21(3), 365-389, Ag 93.

Connolly, William E. *Identity/Difference: Democratic Negotiations of Political Paradox*. Ithaca, Cornell Univ Pr, 1991.

Connor, Peter (trans) and Nancy, Jean-Luc. Elliptical Sense in Derrida: A Critical Reader, Wood, David (ed). Cambridge, Blackwell, 1992.

Derrida's thinking of sense as of a spacing of sense itself, or its alteration.

Connor, Robert A. Relational *Esse* and the Person. *Amer Cath Phil Quart*, 65, 253-267, 1991.

Connor, Robert A. The Person as Resonating Existential. *Amer Cath Phil Quart*, 66(1), 39-56, Wint 92.

Connor, Steven. *Theory and Cultural Value*. Cambridge, Blackwell, 1992.

This book examines theories of the value of culture, art and the aesthetic as they are developed in psychoanalysis, neopragmatism, Marxism, feminism, deconstruction, postmodernism, discourse theory and contemporary ethnography. The book argues that the question of cultural value is inherently paradoxical, since it requires a simultaneous commitment to the principles of absolutism and relativism that are usually taken to be opposites. The function of cultural theory ought to be to find ways of inhabiting and thickening this paradox, rather than seeking to abolish or escape it.

Conradie, Ernst. What is an Anlogical Imagination?. *S Afr J Phil*, 11(4), 103-111, N 92.

In this article three layers of meaning of the concept 'analogical imagination' (as proposed by David Tracy) are analysed. An analogical imagination may firstly be understood as a *de facto* description of (theological) interpretation. The analogical nature of the process of interpretation is explained and the role of the imagination in the identification and expression of analogical relations is discussed at length. The analogical imagination secondly also functions on a *de iure* level. It involves, via a radicalization of the role of the imagination, a call for a creative and imaginative search for analogical relations amidst an existing conflicting plurality. On a third and a more existential level an analogical imagination simply involves an urgent call for dialogue in a pluralist culture.

Constable, Elizabeth (trans) and Lyotard, Jean-François. Mainmise. *Phil Today*, 36(4), 419-427, Wint 92.

Contat, Michel. Sartre by Himself: An Account, an Explanation, a Defense in Sartre Alive, Aronson, Ronald (ed). Detroit, Wayne St Univ Pr, 1991.

Conter, David. Eternal Recurrence, Identity and Literary Characters. *Dialogue (Canada)*, 31(4), 549-566, Autumn 92.

Conti Odorisio, Ginerva. Natural Law and Gender Relations in Women's Rights and the Rights of Man, Arnaud, A J. Oxford, Aberdeen, 1990.

Conway, Daniel W and Young, Phillips E. Ethics in America: A Report from the Trenches. *J Value Inq*, 27(1), 123-130, Ja 93.

This report presents some observations on the strengths and weaknesses of the *Ethics in America* telecourse package. In the three years that we have administered the course in our undergraduate curriculum, we have found it a useful pedagogical tool that targets a traditionally inaccessible audience of videophile students. We wish to convey our experience with the telecourse package, and we offer suggestions for the improvement of the course package itself and for its implementation by interested instructors.

Conway, David A. On the Distinction between Convergent and Linked Arguments. *Inform Log*, 13(3), 145-158, Fall 91.

Most recent writers of informal logic texts draw a distinction between "linked" and "convergent" arguments. According to its inventor, Stephen Thomas, the distinction is of the utmost importance; it " seems crucial to the analysis and evaluation of reasoning in natural language." I argue that the distinction has not been drawn in any way that makes it both clear and of any real originality or importance. Many formulations are obscure or conceptually incoherent. One formulation of the distinction does seem tolerable clear and I develop another, but neither promises to make it matter much. We can well do without it.

Conway, Stephen. Bentham and the Nineteenth-Century Revolution in Government in Victorian Liberalism, Bellamy, Richard (ed). New York, Routledge, 1990.

Cook, Albert. The Canon of Poetry and the Wisdom of Poetry. *J Aes Art Crit*, 49(4), 317-329, Fall 91.

Cook, Daniel J. Den "anderen" Leibniz verstehen. *Stud Leibniz*, 24(1), 59-72, 1992.

Bertrand Russell says of Leibniz that "the best parts of his philosophy are the most abstract and the worst those which most nearly concern human life". Many have agreed with Russell's comments (indeed many would say the same about Russell's thought!) and the treatment of Leibniz by most Anglo-American philosophers in particular during this century is a testimony to his sentiments. Even sympathetic commentators have been dismissive or apologetic of those aspects of Leibniz's thought that "concern human life". My purpose here is not to clear Leibniz of any and all animadversions—personal or philosophical—but to attempt to understand the dissimulation and equivocality that even his admirers ascribe to his non-logical writings. It is my position that such qualities were intrinsic to his thought, and not simply personal quirks or flaws that have to be tolerated or dismissed in any sustained examination of his philosophy.

Cook, Deborah. Umbrellas, Laundry Bills, and Resistance: The Place of Foucault's Interviews in his *Corpus*. *Clio*, 21(2), 145-155, Wint 92.

As he became well-known in France, Foucault was able to make extensive use of the media. In interviews and dialogues disseminated by newspapers and television, Foucault put forward his ideas concerning social and political issues and linked his historical and theoretical work to such issues. Political motives informed Foucault's use of the media and the ideas Foucault expressed in interviews supplement his texts in interesting and important ways. To marginalize the interviews, as many commentators have done, leads to a distorted view of Foucault's work.

Cook, Don L and Kloesel, Christian J W. Two Responses to Moore and Burks on Editing Peirce. *Trans Peirce Soc*, 28(2), 303-309, Spr 92.

Cook, Gary A. *George Herbert Mead—The Making of a Social Pragmatist.* Champaign, Univ of Illinois Pr, 1993.

This book traces the genesis of Mead's social-psychological and philosophical ideas by analyzing his journal articles and posthumously published writings. The author draws on unpublished correspondence and other documents to shed light on Mead's early education, his academic career at the universities of Michigan and Chicago, and his leadership in social and educational reform organizations in Chicago. Included are an overview of Mead's contributions to the pragmatic tradition and a detailed account of his involvement, during the final years of his life, in a controversy between University of Chicago President Robert Maynard Hutchins and the school's department of philosophy.

Cook, Gary A. George Herbert Mead: An Unpublished Essay on Royce and James. *Trans Peirce Soc*, 28(3), 583-592, Sum 92.

This previously unpublished manuscript begins with Mead's reflections on his initial exposure to philosophy at Oberlin College, and then records the impressions Royce and James made upon him during his academic year at Harvard in 1887-88. The essay is noteworthy because of its impressionistic descriptions of Royce and James as they were in the late 1880's, and because of the autobiographical light it sheds upon an important early stage in Mead's intellectual development.

Cook, Gary A. *George Herbert Mead: The Making of a Social Pragmatist.* Champaign, Univ of Illinois Pr, 1993.

This book traces the genesis of Mead's social-psychological and philosophical ideas by analyzing his journal articles and posthumously published writings. The author draws on unpublished correspondence and other documents to shed light on Mead's early education, his academic career at the Universities of Michigan and Chicago, and his leadership in social and educational reform organizations in Chicago. Included are an overview of Mead's contributions to the pragmatic tradition and a detailed account of his involvement, during the final years of his life, in a controversy between University of Chicago President Robert Maynard Hutchins and the school's department of philosophy.

Cook, Harold. Physick and Natural History in Seventeenth-Century England in Revolution and Continuity, Barker, Peter (ed). Washington, Cath Univ Amer Pr, 1991.

Cook, J Thomas. Do Persons Follow from Spinoza's God?. *Personalist Forum*, 8/1(Supp), 243-248, Spr 92.

Spinoza says that, "From the necessity of the divine nature there must follow infinitely many things in infinitely many ways (modi)—that is, everything which can fall under an infinite intellect." I interpret this to mean that there must exit any and all things of which there can be an adequate idea in the mind of God. The question is then "Are persons the sorts of things of which there can be adequate ideas?" After some argument I regretfully conclude that the answer to the title question is in the negative.

Cook, John W. Religious Belief in Wittgenstein's Intentions, Canfield, J V (ed). Hamden, Garland, 1993.

Cook, Judith A (ed) and Fonow, Mary Margaret (ed). *Beyond Methodology: Feminist Scholarship as Lived Research.* Bloomington, Indiana Univ Pr, 1991.

Cooke, Robert. Understanding the Real "Character Issue:" A Review of the Latest Work of Clarence Walton (*The Moral Manager*, and *Corporate Encounters*). *Bus Ethics Quart*, 3(3), 307-313, Jl 93.

Coolidge, Jr, Francis P. The Relation of Philosophy to Sōphrosynē: Zalmoxian Medicine in Plato's *Charmides. Ancient Phil*, 13(1), 23-36, Spr 93.

The dialogue about *sophrosyne* in Plato's *Charmides* ostensibly ends in *aporia*. This paper examines Socrates' suggestive account of Zalmoxian medicine near its beginning. An interpretation is developed which seeks to explain, first, why Socrates agrees to be introduced to Charmides as a doctor, second, the inconsistencies in Socrates' account, third, what his account implies about the meaning of *sophrosyne*, and fourth, the relationship between Socrates' philosophical inquiry and Zalmoxian medicine (which is said to engender *sophrosyne*).

Coolidge, Jr, Francis P. The Unity of Platonic Epistemology: Divine Madness in Plato's *Phaedrus. SW Phil Rev*, 8(1), 99-108, Ja 92.

The Platonic dialogues offer two contrasting discussions of how the soul knows the forms: the recollection and purification accounts. The recollection account offers an explanation of knowing based on the immanence of the forms; by contrast, the purification account explains knowledge on the basis of the soul's perception of the transcendent forms (the soul's purification). The discussion of divine madness in the *Phaedrus*, however, suggests how these two accounts have unity. This paper argues that the philosopher's knowing is a kind of oscillation between purification and recollection with recollection completing the process of knowing that begins with purification.

Coombe, Rosemary J. Tactics of Appropriation and the Politics of Recognition in Late Modern Democracies. *Polit Theory*, 21(3), 411-433, Ag 93.

The article considers two forms of cultural politics that appropriate commodified cultural texts (legally protected as trademarks) in articulations of identify and expressions of anxiety in the condition of postmodernity. Looking first at tactics of appropriation that construct identities and compel political recognition by using official insignia, and then at subaltern rumors surrounding corporate trademarks which counter the invisibility of corporate hegemony, the author argues that tactics of appropriation borrow the modes of signification characteristic of the power they counter in a manner that nonetheless disrupts its discursive address. The law operates as both a generative condition and prohibitive boundary for these forms of hegemonic articulation.

Coombs, Jeffrey. The Possibility of Created Entities in Seventeenth-Century Scotism. *Phil Quart*, 43(173), 447-459, O 93.

I present the views of two Scotists, the Irishman John Punch (1603-1672/73) and the Italian Bartholomew Mastrius (1602-73), both Franciscans, on the ontological basis for the distinction between the possible and the impossible. John Punch proposed that there is a type of being called "diminished being" which all possible beings possess independently of any divine creative act and which distinguishes the possibles from the impossibles. Mastrius attacked Punch's view because it introduced a type of being which was neither God nor created by God. Mastrius held instead that possible beings have a "real possibility" which is generated by God's thought about creation.

Cooney, Brian. *A Hylomorphic Theory of Mind.* New York, Lang, 1991.

This book presents a contemporary application of Aristotle's metaphysical concepts to the domains of biology and psychobiology. Professor Cooney reconstructs the form/matter or hylomorphic analysis of organisms and mental functions by linking Aristotle's concept of form to that of information in biological control systems. The resulting hylomorphic theory challenges the orthodoxy of contemporary philosophy by offering an alternative to both materialism and dualism. Professor Cooney makes his book accessible to a wide audience by providing clear digests of the scientific information and philosophical issues relevant to his arguments.

Cooper, David E (ed). *A Companion to Aesthetics.* Cambridge, Blackwell, 1992.

Cooper, David E. Postmodernism and 'The End of Philosophy'. *Int J Phil Stud*, 1(1), 49-59, Mr 93.

Cooper, David E. Scottish Communitarianism, Lockean Individualism, and Women's Moral Development in Women's Rights and the Rights of Man, Arnaud, A J. Oxford, Aberdeen, 1990.

Cooper, David E. Truth and 'Status Rerum' in Logical Foundations, Mahalingam, Indira (ed). New York, St Martin's Pr, 1991.

Cooper, John. La théorie platonicienne de la motivation humaine. *Rev Phil Fr*, 4, 517-543, O-D 91.

Cooper, M Wayne. Should Physicians Be Bayesian Agents?. *Theor Med*, 13(4), 349-361, D 92.

Because physicians use scientific inference for the generalizations of individual observations and the application of general knowledge to particular situations, the Bayesian probability solution to the problem of induction has been proposed and frequently utilized. Several problems with the Bayesian approach are introduced and discussed. These include: subjectivity, the favoring of a weak hypothesis, the problem of the false hypothesis, the old evidence/new theory problem, and the observation that physicians are not currently Bayesians. (edited)

Cooper, Richard and Franks, Bradley. Interruptibility as a Constraint on Hybrid Systems. *Mind Mach*, 3(1), 73-96, F 93.

It is widely mooted that a plausible computational cognitive model should involve both symbolic and connectionist components. However, sound principles for combining these components within a hybrid system are currently lacking; the design of such systems is often *ad hoc*. In an attempt to ameliorate this we provide a framework of types of hybrid systems and constraints therein, within which to explore the issues. In particular, we suggest the use of "system independent" constraints, whose source lies in general considerations about cognitive systems, rather than in particular technological or task-based considerations. We illustrate this through a detailed examination of an interruptibility constraint: handling interruptions is a fundamental facet of cognition in a dynamic world. Aspects of interruptions are delineated, as are their precise expression in symbolic and connectionist systems. We illustrate the interaction of the various constraints from interruptibility in the different types of hybrid systems. The picture that emerges of the relationship between the connectionist and the symbolic within a hybrid system provides for sufficient flexibility and complexity to suggest interesting general implications for cognition, thus vindicating the utility of the framework.

Cooper, W E. William James's Theory of the Self. *Monist*, 75(4), 504-520, O 92.

Copeland, B J. The Curious Case of the Chinese Gym. *Synthese*, 95(2), 173-186, My 93.

Searle has recently used two adaptations of his Chinese room argument in an attack on connectionism. I show that these new forms of the argument are fallacious. First I give an exposition of and rebuttal to the original Chinese room argument, and then a brief introduction to the essentials of connectionism.

Copleston, F C. *Aquinas: An Introduction to the Life and Work of the Great Medieval Thinker.* New York, Penguin USA, 1991.

This book was written for a series edited by A J Ayer and intended mainly for an educated readership, interested in philosophical themes. The author aimed at making Aquinas's thought intelligible for readers who knew little of medieval cultural life, and also at relating Aquinas's ideas and theories to philosophical problems as discussed today. Originally published in 1955, the book has been frequently reprinted, while remaining substantially unchanged.

Copleston, F C. Ayer and World Views in A J Ayer Memorial Essays, Griffiths, A Phillips (ed). New York, Cambridge Univ Pr, 1991.

When invited to contribute to this volume, I chose metaphysics as a theme, as A J Ayer and I had already discussed the subject publicly, particularly in our 1949 radio debate. I wished to examine the extent to which Ayer had come to modify his original dismissal of metaphysics as 'nonsense'. It seems to me that though he came to recognize the need for a rather more discriminating assessment of the nature and significance of metaphysics, his basic attitude underwent no very marked change.

Copleston, F C. D W Hamlyn's *Being a Philosopher. Phil Quart*, 43(173), 505-512, O 93.

Copleston, F C. Philosophy and Its History. *Philosophy*, 67(261), 357-356, Jl 92.

Copp, David. Could Political Truth be a Hazard for Democracy? in The Idea of Democracy, Copp, David (ed). New York, Cambridge Univ Pr, 1993.

If we believe there are truths about what society ought to do, can we believe that societies ought to be democratic? Or must we agree with Plato, that the wise should rule? To resist Plato's ideal, we must not rest our support for democracy in its epistemic virtues, as David Estlund has argued. Instead, our support for democracy should rest on arguments either about the justice of democracy or else about its beneficial indirect effects. I defend arguments of the latter kind from an influential objection of Jon Elster's to the effect that they are "self-defeating".

Copp, David. The 'Possibility' of A Categorical Imperative in Philosophical Perspectives, 6: Ethics, 1992, Tomberlin, James E (ed). Atascadero, Ridgeview, 1992.

In part III of the *Groundwork*, Kant attempted to show "the possibility of a categorical imperative". He thought he needed to show this possibility in order to escape a kind of skepticism. Some relative of Kant's "possibility problem" must be faced by any

Copp, David 448 AUTHOR INDEX WITH ABSTRACTS

non-skeptical moral philosophy. This paper aims to show how Kant saw the problem, to show how it arose in the context of his moral philosophy, and to explain his unsuccessful attempt to solve it. The paper explores Kant's argument in *Groundwork* III, as well as two recent reconstructions of it.

Copp, David (ed) and Beehler, Rodger G (ed) and Szabados, Bela (ed). *On the Track of Reason*. Boulder, Westview Pr, 1992.

This book is a dedicatory volume of essays by friends and colleagues of Kai Nielsen. The subjects addressed range from the foundations of ethics (E J Bond, T Hurka, R Miller, J Rachels), religious belief and morals (T Penelhum), the justice of Oregon's health care rationing policies (N Daniels), Marx on needs (D Braybrooke), history (J Cohen), and metaphilosophical issues (M Hanen and C B Martin). In the case of the Hurka and Miller contributions, their essays iterate succinctly the positions argued in their recent books.

Copp, David (ed) and Hampton, Jean (ed) and Roemer, John E (ed). *The Idea of Democracy*. New York, Cambridge Univ Pr, 1993.

Essays on democratic theory accompanied by critical comments, with an introduction by the editors. Contributors: Richard J Arneson, Pranab Bardhan, Samuel Bowles and Herbert Gintis, Thomas Christiano, Joshua Cohen, David Copp, David Estlund, John Ferejohn, David Gauthier, Jean Hampton, Russell Hardin, Stephen Holmes, Michael S McPherson, Karl Ove Moene, Christopher W Morris, John Rawls, John E Roemer, Debra Satz, John D Stephens, Robert Sugden, Cass R Sunstein.

Corazón, Rafael. Naturaleza de las ideas innatas cartesianas. *Anu Filosof*, 26(1), 47-75, 1993.

Innate ideas are not objective ideas which have ceased to be doubtful. They are not ideas of attributes of modes but rather true realities. Therefore, they are simple, clear, and distinct. These ideas are not possible to analyze. Innate ideas are not conceived when thinking of "something" but when the real world is felt. Therefore, they correspond with objective ideas.

Corazza, Paul. Ramsey Sets, the Ramsey Ideal, and Other Classes Over R. *J Sym Log*, 57(4), 1441-1468, D 92.

We improve results of Marczewski, Frankiewicz, Brown, and other comparing the σ-ideals of measure zero, meager, Marczewski measure zero, and completely Ramsey null sets; in particular, we remove CH from the hypothesis of many of Brown's constructions of sets lying in some of these ideals but not in others. We improve upon work of Marczewski by constructing, without CH, a nonmeasurable Marczewski measure zero set lacking the property of Baire. We extend our analysis of σ-ideals to include the completely Ramsey null sets relative to a Ramsey ultrafilter and obtain all 32 possible examples of sets in some ideals and not others.

Corbí, Josep E. Classical and Connectionist Models: Levels of Description. *Synthese*, 95(2), 141-168, My 93.

To begin, I introduce an analysis of interlevel relations that allows us to offer an initial characterization of the debate about the way classical and connectionist models relate. Subsequently, I examine a compatibility thesis and a conditional claim on this issue. With respect to the compatibility thesis, I argue that, even if classical and connectionist models are not necessarily incompatible, the emergence of the latter seems to undermine the best arguments for the Language of Thought Hypothesis, which is essential to the former. (edited)

Corcos, Alain F and Monaghan, Floyd V. The Real Objective of Mendel's Paper: A Response to Falk and Sarkar's Criticism. *Biol Phil*, 8(1), 95-98, Ja 93.

This paper was a detailed response to the criticisms offered by Falk and Sarkar of a previous paper of ours, *The Real Objective of Mendel's Paper*, *Biol Phil*, 6, 447-452, 1990. Our responses are intelligible only in the context of the original paper to which the reader is referred. The basic argument of the original paper was the following: Mendel's experiments were not aimed at finding the laws of inheritance, but were concerned with the finding of empirical laws which describe the formation of hybrids and the development of their offspring over several generations. This led to the creation of an explanatory scheme adequate to explain the form and contents of the laws.

Cordero, Alberto. Evolutionary Ideas and Contemporary Naturalism in Philosophy and the Origin and Evolution of the Universe, Agazzi, Evandro (ed). Norwell, Kluwer, 1991.

This paper is about recent naturalist programs in the philosophy of science. The chief concern is the debate between naturalists who advocate the elimination of the idea of 'reason' from epistemology and their most cogent aprioristic critics. More coherent scientific conceptions of naturalism are suggested. It is argued that, relative to present knowledge, the fate of philosophy of science, whether in the end it is naturalized or not, will almost certainly be determined by the results of science, not by any necessary or transcendental truth about naturalization.

Cordero, Alberto (ed) and Agazzi, Evandro (ed). *Philosophy and the Origin and Evolution of the Universe*. Norwell, Kluwer, 1991.

Coreth, Emerich. Zu Hermeneutik und Metaphysik: Eine Antwort an Friedo Ricken. *Theol Phil*, 65(1), 74-78, 1990.

Coreth clarifies his position in a few points: 1) Anything we know is immediate as well as mediated; so there is 2) a reciprocal mediation (or condition) of Hermeneutic and Metaphysics, but 3) the fundamental, most universal problem of philosophy remains the question of being, even comprehending the question for sense or meaning.

Corish, Denis. Postmodernism as Modernism. *Harvard Rev Phil*, 2(1), 17-20, Spr 92.

Postmodernism is a form of modernism of the type propounded by Eliot and Pound. The urge to appear to be as modern as possible was characteristic—the urge to imitate science and find the "emotional equivalent of thought." The postmodern, as the emphasis on "post" reveals, is governed by a similar urge. The result has been a despairing, narrowing, search for the yet more modern in an area in which it should be recognized that modernity is superficial upon human nature, and that poetry is ancestral to science rather than needing to be emulative of it.

Corkin, Stanley. Edmund Wilson and the Problem of Marx: History, Biography, and *To The Finland Station*. *Clio*, 22(2), 129-144, Wint 93.

Corlett, J Angelo. Racism and Affirmative Action. *J Soc Phil*, 24(1), 163-175, Spr 93.

It has been argued that affirmative action depends on individual African- Americans receiving special treatment merely because they are members of a group: African-Americans. For affirmative action, some argue, distributes benefits and burdens on the basis of group membership. I argue that affirmative action need not be defended on the grounds that an African-American person deserves something simply because she is a member of a group severely harmed by racism. As a matter of compensatory justice, affirmative action is justified as a partial means of compensating *her* as an individual African- American. (edited)

Corliss, Richard. Schleiermacher's Hermeneutic and Its Critics. *Relig Stud*, 29(3), 363-379, S 93.

The fact that the critics of Schleiermacher are many and his defenders few is due in part to the fact that his hermeneutic has not been understood very well. Schleiermacher asks the question, "What is it that enables us to understand one another by means of language?" and his hermeneutic seeks to answer that question. This paper outlines Schleiermacher's answer to that question and shows that it has some things in common with speech act theory and the work of John Searle and H P Grice.

Cornell, Drucilla. Commentary on "Hegel Versus the New Orthodoxy" in Hegel and His Critics, Desmond, William (ed). Albany, SUNY Pr, 1989.

Cornell, Drucilla. *The Philosophy of the Limit*. New York, Routledge, 1992.

Cornell, Drucilla. The Philosophy of the Limit in Deconstruction and the Possibility of Justice, Cornell, Durcilla (ed). New York, Routledge, 1992.

Cornell, Drucilla. The Violence of the Masquerade in Working Through Derrida, Madison, Gary B (ed). Evanston, Northwestern Univ Pr, 1993.

Cornell, Drucilla. *Transformations: Recollective Imagination and Sexual Difference*. New York, Routledge, 1993.

In this book the author argues for a new understanding of social change that focuses on the tie between political and individual transformation. She explores the social fantasies that keep gender and race hierarchies in place, and she shows how such fantasies work against transformation in the direction of egalitarian democracy.

Cornell, Durcilla (ed) and Rosenfeld, Michel (ed) and Carlson, David Gray (ed). *Deconstruction and the Possibility of Justice*. New York, Routledge, 1992.

Cornuelle, Richard. The Power and Poverty of Libertarian Thought. *Crit Rev*, 6(1), 1-10, Wint 92.

The collapse of the communist economies put to rest one of the great unsettled questions of modern times. Now the libertarian idea that the invisible hand of the market is a more reliable organizer of economic life of nations than the visible hand of the state is the newest universal. The dialog is shifting to ground for which libertarians are unprepared. There is no very distinct libertarian vision of community outside the state. Nor have libertarians confronted the disabling hypocrisy of the capitalist rationale: that while capitalists must have extensive freedom of action, their employees may have much less.

Corrigan, Kevin. Light and Metpahor in Plotinus and St Thomas Aquinas. *Thomist*, 57(2), 187-199, Ap 93.

Corrington, Robert S. Hermeneutics and Loyalty in Frontiers in American Philosophy, Volume I, Burch, Robert W (ed). College Station, Texas A&M Univ Pr, 1992.

An analysis of Royce's concept of loyalty to loyalty as it transforms hermeneutic theory and redefines the semiotic self.

Corrington, Robert S. *Nature and Spirit: An Essay in Ecstatic Naturalism*. Bronx, Fordham Univ Pr, 1992.

This book is concerned with reawakening a sense of the ubiquity of nature in any understanding of the self, its communities, and the divine natures. The method employed is that of ordinal phenomenology, which brings metaphysical categories into the phenomenological enterprise so that the so-called "transcendental standpoint" can be radically overcome. The animating metaphysics is that of ecstatic naturalism that starts from the recognition of the fundamental divide within nature of *natura naturans* and *natura naturata*. A semiotic theory is developed that locates all forms of signification within the contest of worldhood and a self-transforming nature. Finally, four aspects of the divine life are probed as they relate to nature.

Corry, Leo. Kuhnian Issues, Scientific Revolutions and the History of Mathematics. *Stud Hist Phil Sci*, 24(1), 95-117, Mr 93.

Various possible versions of Kuhn's theory of scientific revolutions are analyzed, and criteria are provided for assessing their relative value and usefulness as tools for historians and philosophers of science. In those terms, the existence of "interesting" revolutions do not exist in the body of mathematical knowledge, but that they may occur regarding the 'images of knowledge.' Some examples are analysed.

Corte-Real, Maria L. On Contradiction in Analecta Husserliana, XXXIV, Tymieniecka, Anna-Teresa (ed). Dordrecht, Kluwer, 1992.

Cortens, A and O'Leary-Hawthorne, J. The Principle of Necessary Reason. *Faith Phil*, 10(1), 60-67, Ja 93.

Cosmological arguments have fallen on hard times of late. The main reason for this is that such arguments have traditionally deployed the problematic Principle of Sufficient Reason. In this paper, we explore a different strategy for constructing a cosmological argument. In part 1, we first briefly explain why the Principle of Sufficient Reason is highly questionable. Second, we introduce and motivate the Principle of Necessary Reason. In part 2, we construct an argument that deploys the latter principle, refining it in the face of a number of objections.

Cosculluela, Victor. Peirce on Tychism and Determinism. *Trans Peirce Soc*, 28(4), 741-755, Fall 92.

Costa, Filippo. Husserl e il linguaggio. *G Metaf*, 14(2), 193-224, My-Ag 92.

Cotogno, Paolo. On the Interpretation of Church's Thesis. *Epistemologia*, 15(2), 315-349, Jl-D 92.

Cotroneo, Girolano. The Dignity of the History (in Hungarian). *Magyar Filozof Szemle*, 3, 348-380, 1991.

AUTHOR INDEX WITH ABSTRACTS 449 Craig, William Lane

Cottingham, John. The Cartesian Legacy. *Aris Soc*, Supp(66), 1-21, 1992.

The standard pictures of Descartes is that he is an apriorist about knowledge, a necessitarian about causal explanation, an epistemological foundationalist and a grand optimist about the possibility of our reaching a guaranteed absolute conception of truth and reality. The paper challenges each of these interpretation in turn, and argues that Descartes's actual philosophical goals are much less overweening. The ambitious 'Cartesian rationalism' of the standard picture gives way, on examination of Descartes's actual writings, to a more nuanced account in which his thought is seen as prefiguring, in important respects, some of the ideas of Hume and Kant.

Cottrell, Allin. Keynes's Theory of Probability and Its Relevance to His Economics: Three Theses. *Econ Phil*, 9(1), 25-51, Ap 93.

The recent literature contains several positive assessments of Keynes's theory of probability, along with the argument that Keynes's economics must be understood in the context of that theory. This paper challenges that view, advancing the following three theses: 1) there are severe problems in Keynes's conception of probability, in particular 2) in the relationship between this conception of Keynes's concept of 'weight' of argument; yet 3) these problems do not undercut Keynes's economic conclusions, since the connection between his theory of probability and his economics is not as intimate as some have supposed.

Coughlan, Stephen G. Hume's Ideas of Space and Time: As Original As They First Appear. *Eidos*, 10(2), 143-160, D 92.

Coulter, Gregory J. St Thomas Aquinas on Explaining Individuality. *Amer Cath Phil Quart*, 65, 169-178, 1991.

Coulter, Jeff. Consciousness: The Cartesian Enigma and its Contemporary Resolution in Wittgenstein's Intentions, Canfield, John V (ed). Hamden, Garland, 1993.

Courtenay, William J. Peter of Capua as a Nominalist. *Vivarium*, 30(1), 157-172, My 92.

Courtine, Jean-François. Phenomenology and/or Tautology in Reading Heidegger: Commemorations, Sallis, John (ed). Bloomington, Indiana Univ Pr, 1992.

Cousineau, Robert H. *Zarathustra and the Ethical Ideal*. Amsterdam, J Benjamins, 1991.

A dialogical itinerary with Zarathustra shapes some "Timely Meditations on Philosophy" (subtitle) and, through the phenomena of the strange and familiar, of laughter and fear, offers a symbiotic text of human existence. A hermeneutical exploration gradually expresses its own principles and, since such interpretation exists as action, it entails an exegesis towards an ethical ideal. We discover how we ourselves are parables "to ride to every truth," an horizon open only to noble morality. Renunciation ("amor fati") surpasses resignation which is a failed deconstruction; and, in this manner, Nietzsche's ethical stance is superior to Heidegger's.

Coutts, Mary Carrington. Fetal Tissue Research. *Kennedy Inst Ethics J*, 3(1), 81-101, Mr 93.

Couture, Tony. Review: Bernstein, McCarthy and the Evolution of Critical Theory. *Phil Soc Crit*, 19(1), 59-75, 1993.

Richard Bernstein's *The New Constellation* and Thomas McCarthy's *Ideals and Illusions* are examples of the convergence of critical theory and Anglo-American philosophy. Combining the pragmatic ethos and practical reasoning of analytic philosophy with a new level of self-awareness about the theory of social criticism is a necessary step in the continuing evolution of political philosophy. I discuss how Heidegger, Foucault, Derrida, Habermas and Rorty should be understood as participants in an organic network of critical possibilities.

Couture, Tony. Social Criticism After Rawls. *Phil Soc Crit*, 18(1), 61-80, 1992.

I investigate Rawls' conception of "reflective equilibrium" by contrasting Norman Daniels' idealized interpretation with my own pragmatic view (based on Ronald Dworkin, Rorty and Walzer). After discussing the three elements involved in this procedure of justification, I show that Daniels assumes that there should be a perfect balance among them. It is more likely that critics emphasize one element at the expense of others. I reject Rawls' distinction between ideal and nonideal theory, and support particularistic critics rather that a Super-critic.

Couture, Yves. Le chemin de l'immanence. *Horiz Phil*, 3(1), 59-75, Autumn 92.

Coval, Samuel C and Campbell, P G. *Agency in Action: The Practical Rational Agency Machine*. Dordrecht, Kluwer, 1992.

Cover, J A. Reference, Modality, and Relational Time. *Phil Stud*, 70(3), 251-277, Je 93.

In this paper I examine an argument for the claim that the *New Theory of* (direct, rigid) *Reference* entails the *Absolute Theory of Time*: if relationalist times are sets of events standing in the simultaneity relation, then counterfactual claims to the effect that 'Jones could have done otherwise at *t*' emerge as necessarily false. I claim that this argument can be resisted by (i) attending more closely to the metaphysical commitments of new theories of reference, and by (ii) allowing for eliminative versions of relationalism. Three ways in which counterpart-theoretic and modal realist maneuvers assist the relational theorist of time are also broached.

Cover, J A and Hawthorne, John. Leibnizian Essentialism, Transworld Identity, and Counterparts. *Hist Phil Quart*, 9(4), 425-444, O 92.

The standard view of Leibnizian modality reckons Leibniz committed to superessentialism and to denying trans-world identity. We present historical and philosophical arguments against the standard view. In particular, we argue that Leibnizian essentialism is *consistent* with trans-world identity, and that his modal metaphysics allows for the possibility of a counterpart semantics for *de re* moral predication.

Cowan, Bainard (ed) and Kronick, Joseph G (ed). *Theorizing American Literature*. Baton Rouge, Louisiana St Univ Pr, 1991.

Coward, Harold. A Hindu Response to Derrida's View of Negative Theology in Derrida and Negative Theology, Coward, Harold (ed). Albany, SUNY Pr, 1992.

This chapter compares Derrida's view of negative theology with Hindu thought as found in the Vedas, in Sanbarra, in Bhartrhari, and in the role of silence. Significant parallels and differences are uncovered.

Coward, Harold (ed) and Foshay, Toby (ed). *Derrida and Negative Theology*. Albany, SUNY Pr, 1992.

The book explores the thought of Jacques Derrida as it relates to negative theology and philosophy in both Western and Eastern thought. Derrida's two main essays on negative theology are included as is a conclusion in which Derrida responds to the analysis offered.

Cowdell, Scott. All This, and God Too? Postmodern Alternatives to Don Cupitt. *Heythrop J*, 33(3), 267-282, Jl 92.

Cowell, Mark. Ecological Restoration and Environmental Ethics. *Environ Ethics*, 15(1), 19-32, Spr 93.

Restoration ecology has recently emerged as a branch of scientific ecology that challenges many of the traditional tenets of environmentalism. Because the restoration of ecosystems, "applied ecology," has the potential to advance theoretical understanding to such an extent that scientists can extensively manipulate the environment, it encourages increasingly active human participation within ecosystems and could inhibit the preservation of areas from human influences. Despite the environmentally dangerous possibilities that this form of science and technology present, restoration offers an attractive alternative for human interaction with the environment. (edited)

Cowen, Tyler. Altruism and the Argument from Offsetting Transfers. *Soc Phil Pol*, 10(1), 225-245, Wint 93.

The author considers the argument of Robert Barro, Gary Becker, and others. This argument alleges that changes in private sector gifts and transfers will offset certain government policies to redistribute wealth, such as welfare payments or the deficit. A closer look at the argument shows that private transfers of wealth and government transfers are not perfect substitutes. Transfers differ in their paternalistic motivations, may attempt to influence behavior in different ways, or may involve goods that cannot be redistributed once granted, such as education. When many individuals give to each other, coordination problems may prevent the correct offsetting transfers from being made.

Cowen, Tyler. Altruism and the Argument from Offsetting Transfers in Altruism, Paul, Ellen Frankel (ed). New York, Cambridge Univ Pr, 1993.

Cowen, Tyler. Law as a Public Good: The Economics of Anarchy. *Econ Phil*, 8(2), 249-267, O 92.

I consider the libertarian anarchist claim that protection and law enforcement services can be provided exclusively through markets. Under what conditions is anarchy a stable equilibrium, and what kind of industry structure for protection services does stability require? Anarchy can be stable, but stable versions of anarchy tend to reevolve into government. The same factors that allow stable anarchy also allow private protection agencies to exercise monopoly power and collude. Adjudication of disputes creates an externalities problem. Although this externalities problem can be solved by private contracts, these same contracts allow private protection agencies to collude successfully.

Cowling, Mark and Manners, Jon. Pre-History: The Debate Before Cohen in Marx's Theory of History, Wetherly, Paul. Brookfield, Avebury, 1992.

This article is part of a volume devoted to a discussion of Cohen's account of historical materialism as a form of technological determinism, using functionalist explanation. The article reviews six alternative theories to Cohen's, demonstrating that they have at least some textual foundation in Marx's writings. The alternatives to Cohen which are reviewed are economic determinism, relations of production determinism, scepticism, class unitarianism, praxis approaches and the organic totality model. The article acts as a reminder rather than arguing an original case of its own.

Cox, Chana Berniker. On Michael Levin's "Responses to Race Differences in Crime". *J Soc Phil*, 24(1), 155-162, Spr 93.

Crabbé, Marcel. On *NFU*. *Notre Dame J Form Log*, 33(1), 112-119, Wint 92.

We first describe a general method for building models of *NFU*, i.e., *NF* with atoms, without the help of Ramsey's theorem. Then, we show that *NFU* has essentially the same strength as *NF* without the axiom of extensionality. Further, we consider axioms stating that there is a set extensionally equivalent to every nonextensional object. By using a variant of the technique of permutations, we prove the consistency of such axioms of weak extensionality with the stratifiable axioms of comprehension. Finally, we show that there is an axiom of weak extensionality that implies full extensionality.

Craig, Robert. Vico as Educator: Values, Self-Development, and Synthesis. *J Thought*, 28(1-2), 7-12, Spr-Sum 93.

Craig, William Lane. God and the Initial Cosmological Singularity: A Reply to Quentin Smith. *Faith Phil*, 9(2), 238-248, Ap 92.

Q Smith contends (i) an atheistic interpretation of the Big Bang is better justified than a theistic interpretation because the latter is inconsistent with the standard Big Bang model and (ii) his atheistic interpretation offers a coherent and plausible account of the origin of the universe. But Smith's argument for (i) is multiply flawed, depending on premisses which are false or at least mootable and a key invalid inference. Smith's attempt to demonstrate the plausibility of the atheistic interpretation on the basis of its greater simplicity is based on false parallels between God and the initial cosmological singularity. Smith's effort to prove that the atheist's contention that the universe came into being uncaused out of absolutely nothing is coherent rests upon a confusion between inconceivability and unimaginability and assumes without argument that the causal principle could not be a metaphysically necessary a posteriori truth. In any case, there are good grounds for taking the principle to be a metaphysically necessary, synthetic, a priori truth, in which case the atheistic interpretation is incoherent.

Craig, William Lane. Graham Oppy on the Kalam Cosmological Argument. *Sophia (Australia)*, 32(1), 1-11, Mr 93.

Craig, William Lane. Reply to Smith: On the Finitude of the Past. *Int Phil Quart*, 33(2), 225-231, Je 93.

Craig, William Lane. Should Peter Go To the Mission Field?. *Faith Phil*, 10(2), 261-265, Ap 93.

In a recent article in *Faith and Philosophy* 8 (1991), pp. 380-89, William Hasker related the cases of a veteran missionary, Paul, and a prospective missionary, Peter, who were each reflecting upon the implications of a middle knowledge perspective on the exclusivity of salvation through Christ for their missionary tasks. Peter, in some confusion, wrote to Paul for advice concerning whether he should leave his successful pastorate for the foreign field. Paul's response to Peter's letter has been obtained and is here published.

Craig, William Lane. The Origin and Creation of the Universe: A Reply to Adolf Grünbaum. *Brit J Phil Sci*, 43(2), 233-240, J 92.

This article analyzes Grünbaum's objections to inferring the universe's creation from its temporal origin. It is shown that his objections are largely aimed at straw men or otherwise misconceived. His further claim that the Big Bang cannot have a cause is based on the false assumption that all causes precede temporally their effects.

Crane, Tim. Mental Causation and Mental Reality. *Proc Aris Soc*, 92, 185-202, 1992.

A belief in mental causation is central to any naturalistic theory of the mind. But recent work in the philosophy of mind has challenged the reality of mental causation for at least four reasons: (1) the anomalism of the mental; (2) the causal 'closure' of the physical; (3) the inefficacy of functional properties; and (4) the inefficacy of semantic properties. These reasons are scrutinized and found to be largely independent of each other. it is then argued that only (4) presents a serious problem for causal or functionalist theories of the mind.

Crane, Tim. Numbers and Propositions: Reply to Melia. *Analysis*, 52(4), 253-256, O 92.

Crane, Tim (ed). *The Contents of Experience*. New York, Cambridge Univ Pr, 1992.

Crane, Tim. The Nonconceptual Content of Experience in The Contents of Experience, Crane, Tim (ed). New York, Cambridge Univ Pr, 1992.

Cranston, Maurice. Romanticism and Revolution. *Hist Euro Ideas*, 17(1), 19-30, Ja 93.

Crasnow, Sharon L. Can Science Be Objective?: Longino's Science as Social Knowledge. *Hypatia*, 8(3), 194-201, Sum 93.

In *Science as Social Knowledge*, Helen Longino offers a contextual analysis of evidential relevance. She claims that this "contextual empiricism" reconciles the objectivity of science with the claim that science is socially constructed. I argue that while her account does offer key insights into the role that values play in science, her claim that science is nonetheless objective is problematic.

Creath, J Richard. Carnap's Conventionalism. *Synthese*, 93(1-2), 141-165, N 92.

Creath, Richard. Induction and the Gettier Problem. *Phil Phenomenol Res*, 52(2), 401-404, Je 92.

Creel, Richard E. Agatheism: A Justification of the Rationality of Devotion to God. *Faith Phil*, 10(1), 33-48, Ja 93.

First I argue that evidentialism, fideism, and consequentialism are unsatisfactory ways of evaluating the rationality of devotion to God. Next I argue that an adequate evaluation of the rationality of such devotion must be an axiological enterprise. But given the perfect-being conception of God as infinitely perfect goodness, it follows that no individual could be a greater good or would ensure greater good than God. Therefore, it seems rational to hope that and live as though God exists as long as there is no conclusive proof that God does not exist.

Crescini, Angelo. Il soggetto metafisico alla prima e alla seconda potenza. *G Metaf*, 14(1), 113-124, Ja-Ap 92.

Crescini, Angelo. La natura della vita: Una indagine filosofica. *G Metaf*, 14(2), 277-330, My-Ag 92.

Cresswell, Roger. Spreading Thoughts. *Thinking*, 10(3), 29-34, 1993.

Many teachers in Australia are unaware of Matthew Lipman's approach to teaching philosophy in schools and materials available for that purpose. The report provides an account of a project to create interest in the Institute for the Advancement of Philosophy for Children program. The conclusion is reached that once teachers are familiar with the IACP program and feel competent to use the materials in their classrooms considerable benefits occur, particularly with regard to the development of pupils' critical thinking skills.

Crétella, Henri. Le Chemin et les tournants. *Heidegger Stud*, 8, 147-165, 1992.

The article develops a two fold argument. First, it established *against Hugo Ott's inquisitorial paradigm* that no thinking can be "biographically", *egologically* explained; on the contrary, a true thinker's biography must move from a proper understanding of the *Thought* which was *leading* him. This applies eminently to Heidegger whose thinking must be understood according to its cross-shaped, *staurological* form: not only in an ontological way, but especially in a *renewed* theological one. The point can now be settled thanks to *F W von Herrmann's discovery of several "turns" on the Heideggerian "way of thinking" together with Gérard Guest's analysis of the first of them.*

Crewdson, Joan. A Theory of Personal Language and Implications for Logos Theology. *Tradition Discovery*, 17(1-2), 21-28, 1990-91.

Michael Polanyi's theory of personal knowledge is also a theory of personal language, with implications for Christian *Logos* doctrine. Language is not an arbitrary convention. It links subjectivity and objectivity by reflecting the knowing mind and the reality communicated. Knowing is a mode of being. Speech is an extension of being, a theory about reality in which the mind dwells. For Christians, God in his inner relations and what he is externally in the *Logos* are one. I conclude that Polanyi's theory of personal language illuminates the idea that Christ, the *Logos* of God, provides an interpretative key to the cosmos.

Crigger, Bette-Jane (ed). *Cases in Bioethics: Selections from the Hastings Center Report (Second Edition)*. New York, St Martin's Pr, 1993.

The sixty case studies collected in this volume—all previously published in the Hastings Center Report—illustrate how thoughtful individuals of differing academic and professional backgrounds and varying ethical traditions approach moral in medicine and the life sciences. Individual sections of the relationship between

caregivers and patients, reproductive issues, death and dying, human subjects research, mental incompetence, and allocation and policy issues contain brief introductory essays and selected topical bibliographies. Volume includes glossary and alternate topical table of contents.

Crimmins, Mark. I Falsely Believe that *P. Analysis*, 52(3), 191, Jl 92.

I present a counterexample to the claim that it is never true to say "I falsely believe that so-and-so."

Crimmins, Mark. So-Labeled Neo-Fregeanism. *Phil Stud*, 69(2-3), 265-280, Mr 93.

I explain and criticize a theory of beliefs and of belief sentences offered by Graeme Forbes.

Crimmins, Mark. Tacitness and Virtual Beliefs. *Mind Lang*, 7(3), 240-263, Autumn 92.

I agree with many philosophers that we believe many things without having *explicit beliefs* —concrete cognitive entities representing the propositions believed. After canvassing and rejecting accounts of tacitly believing in terms of dispositions to believe or obvious-consequence relations, I propose and defend the view that at-least-tacitly believing something is being cognitively as if one has an explicit belief in it.

Crimmins, Mark. *Talk About Beliefs*. Cambridge, MIT Pr, 1992.

Cristaldi, Rosario Vittorio. Gustavo Bontadini: Pensieri e ricordi. *G Metaf*, 13(1), 109-119, Ja-Ap 91.

Cristaudo, Wayne. Hegel, Marx and the Absolute Infinite. *Int Stud Phil*, 24(1), 1-16, 1992.

This paper argues that some of the core features of Hegel's metaphysic of the absolute infinite not only resurface at some critical junctures in the logical pattern of Marx's thinking, but they contribute to Marx repeating the very error of hypostasis that he ascribes to Hegel.

Cristin, Renato. Rechnendes Denken und besinnendes Denken: Heidegger und die Herausforderung der Leibnizschen Monadologie am Beispiel des Satzes vom Grund. *Stud Leibniz*, 24(1), 92-100, 1992.

La critique de Heidegger à l'endroit de Leibniz est connue et il suffit de renvoyer à la Marburger Vorlesung de 1928 et à *Der Satz vom Grund* de 1957. Mais l'ensemble de l'interprétation de Heidegger révèle une double attitude: d'une part une attaque contre le rationalisme (Leibniz aurait réduit la pensée à la ratio), d'autre part une défense du sens de l'être-là contenue dans le principe de la raison suffisante. Sur la base de cette ambiguïté on peut reconsidérer l'influence de Leibniz sur la pensée de Heidegger, revoir l'interprétation unilatérale et montrer que, d'une certaine façon, Heidegger s'approche à certains thèmes monadologiques fondamentaux. Tout ceci peut amener à entrevoir la présence de Leibniz aussi bien chez Heidegger même que dans la phénoménologie de la péiode après-Husserl, surtout pour ce qui concerne les problèmes de l'intersubjectivité et du rapport au monde.

Critchley, Simon. *The Ethics of Deconstruction: Derrida and Levinas*. Cambridge, Blackwell, 1992.

In opposition to the polemics claiming that the work of Jacques Derrida is a species of nihilistic textual free play that suspends all questions of value and is therefore immoral and politically pernicious, this book argues that Derridian deconstruction can and indeed should be understood as an ethical demand, provided that ethics is understood in the particular and radical sense given to it in the work of Emmanuel Levinas. Levinas's work, whose full philosophical importance is only now beginning to be recognized, is given a much needed introduction in this book. Levinas has exerted a powerful and continuous influence on the development of Derrida's thinking, and by following the textual dialogue between Levinas and Derrida, one can see how the question of ethics can be compellingly raised within deconstruction.

Critchley, Simon. The Problem of Closure in Derrida (Part Two). *J Brit Soc Phenomenol*, 23(2), 127-145, My 92.

This essay attempts to give a thorough account of the concepts of closure in Derrida's work. The essay traces this concept to Derrida's early readings of Husserl and shows the emergence of the reason of the closure of metaphysics. This is extended through a lengthy discussion of the relation between Derrida and Heidegger. In conclusion, I attempt to develop a notion of *clôtural* reading, giving the examples of Derrida's 'violence and metaphysics' and *Speech and Phenomena*.

Critchley, Simon. The Question of the Question: An Ethico-Political Response to a Note in Derrida's 'De l'esprit' in Of Derrida, Heidegger, and Spirit, Wood, David (ed). Evanston, Northwestern Univ Pr, 1993.

Within the context of a broader argument as to the ethical and political significance of deconstruction, this essay gives a careful reading of a long footnote to Derrida's *Of Spirit*, which shows both how deconstruction addresses the issue of responsibility and the limitations of this concept of responsibility at the level of political thinking.

Crites, Stephen. *The Sickness unto Death* in Foundations of Kierkegaard's Vision of Community, Connell, George B (ed). Atlantic Highlands, Humanities Pr, 1992.

Crocker, David A. Functioning and Capability: The Foundations of Sen's and Nussbaum's Development Ethic. *Polit Theory*, 20(4), 584-612, N 92.

Crocker, Nancy. The Problem of Community. *SW Phil Stud*, 14, 50-62, Spr 92.

In this paper I discuss the problem of creating and maintaining communities in modernity. The motivation for exploring this problem is the recognition that ethical agency is informed by values which are embodied in the institutions and practices of communities. I draw on work in feminist philosophy and on work by Jürgen Habermas. I conclude that a discourse ethics is possible which can be the basis of coherent individual and collective action. This possibility is premised on the recognition of group membership and the ability of the group and the individuals who belong to the group to communicate their standpoint successfully on a par with other groups.

Croken, Robert C (ed) and Lonergan, Bernard J F. Consciousness and the Trinity. *Phil Theol*, 7(1), 3-22, Autumn 92.

Cronin, Patrick. The Authorship and Sources of the Peri Semeion Ascribed to Theophrastus in Theophrastus, Fortenbaugh, William W (ed). New Brunswick, Transaction Books, 1992.

The purpose of this paper is to establish through an analysis of the language of the text and the arrangement of its contents whether or not the *Peri Semeion* is a genuine work of Theophrastus. The author concludes that it is the work of an anonymous Peripatetic, probably and pupil of Theophrastus, who had recourse to (a) two written sources, (b) oral weather lore, and (c) his own experience, and that it was probably composed c. 300 BC.

Crook, Stephen. The End of Radical Social Theory? in Postmodernism and Society, Boyne, Roy (ed). New York, St Martin's Pr, 1990.

Crooks, Jamie and Bontekoe, Ron. The Inter-Relationship of Moral and Aesthetic Excellence. *Brit J Aes*, 32(3), 209-220, Jl 92.

The process of artistic creation is a matter of progressively narrowing in on some worthwhile experience the possibility of which the artist has caught a glimpse. This process involves the artist in an attempt to capture the inner necessity governing her subject. Because a bad moral vision is one which gets something significantly wrong about the human condition, if an artist *chooses* to deal with moral issues, and does so badly (i.e., fails to do justice to the inner necessity governing her subject), her work can be criticized as having failed to meet *aesthetic* as well as moral criteria of excellence.

Crosby, Donald A. Civilization and Its Dissents: Moral Pluralism and Political Order. *J Soc Phil*, 23(2), 111-126, Fall 92.

Moral pluralism is defined under six headings: irreducible plurality of moral theories; incompleteness of moral decision; perspectivity of moral outlooks; complementarity of moral perspectives; overlaps of moral perspectives; and objectivity of moral judgments. Three arguments for the claim that advocacy and practice of moral pluralism would seriously *undermine* political order are countered, and it is argued instead that a pluralistic approach to moral problems is much more likely to *strengthen* political order in today's hetereogeneous societies than are the alternatives of moral absolutism and moral relativism.

Crosby, Donald A. Was William James a Closet Nihilist: A Further Contribution to URAM William James Studies (*URAM* 2:40-58, 73-78). *Ultim Real Mean*, 16(1-2), 141-148, Mr-Je 93.

James's reasons for not distinguishing truth from the means of its justification are first presented. Then his view is defended against Jeffrey Stout's contention that an identification of truth with justification is epistemologically and morally nihilistic because it precludes the possibility of truth (which Stout conceives as invariant and unconditioned, in contrast with justification processes that may change over time or be relative to particular contexts of inquiry). Finally, the question is considered of whether James's view undermines the possibility of true claims about any sort of so-called ultimate. Four reasons are given to show that it does not.

Crosby, Donald A. Whitehead's God and the Dilemma of Pure Possibility in God, Values, and Empiricism, Peden, Creighton W (ed). Macon, Mercer Univ Pr, 1989.

This essay focuses on a basic role of God in the metaphysics of Alfred North Whitehead: God as the foundation of pure possibility and, hence, of metaphysical order. It is first shown that this role requires omniscience in God, and that this requirement is one factor leading to Whitehead's insistence on a nontemporal aspect of God. The essay then critically analyzes this function of God and concludes that a fundamental dilemma it poses can only be resolved by its complete elimination from Whitehead's system. Finally, implication of this resolution are drawn for a new conception of the metaphysical character and status of possibility.

Crosby, John F. The Incommunicability of Human Persons. *Thomist*, 57(3), 403-442, Jl 93.

I defend and develop the proposition that persons do not exist as replaceable specimens or as mere instances of some ideal or type, but exist rather for their own sakes, each existing as incommunicably his or her own. I also introduce the idea of supreme or divine incommunicability, and show how human persons indeed approach to, but then fall short of, such ultimate incommunicability. I try to find a new approach to what is called the dignity of human persons by exploring the relation between dignity and incommunicability. Finally, I look for particularly revealing expressions of incommunicability in the acting of persons.

Crosby, John F. The Personhood of the Human Embryo. *J Med Phil*, 18(4), 399-418, Ag 93.

My interlocutor is anyone who denies personhood to the embryo on the grounds that a human person can exist only in conscious activity and that in the absence of consciousness a person cannot exist at all. I probe personal consciousness to the point at which the distinction between the *being* and the *consciousness* of the human person appears, and argue on the basis of this distinction that the being of a person can exist in the absence of any consciousness. I proceed to argue that it is not only entirely *possible* for the embryo to be a human person, but that, given the embodied personhood of us human beings, this is the only reasonable assumption which we can make.

Cross, Charles B. Counterfactuals and Event Causation. *Austl J Phil*, 70(3), 307-323, S 92.

My aim here is to rehabilitate and clarify the connection between counterfactual dependence and event causation. Both the Humean counterfactual analysis of causation and David Lewis' revision of it seem too strong in at least some cases of causal overdetermination while seeming too weak in at least some cases where two events have a common cause. I show that both kinds of case are handled correctly if the relevant counterfactual is evaluated not at the actual world but at a set of possible worlds in which suitable "test conditions" obtain.

Cross, Charles B. From Worlds to Probabilities: A Probabilistic Semantics for Modal Logic. *J Phil Log*, 22(2), 169-192, Ap 93.

I develop a probabilistic semantics for modal logic that generalizes the quantificational apparatus of Kripke models. Soundness and completeness theorems are proved for propositional M, B, S4, and S5. My semantics formalizes the idea that uncertainty about modal claims like *Possibly*-A arises from the fact that thought experiments which test the intelligibility of A may be inconclusive for a given

agent. On this view, an agent who is uncertain about *Possibly*-A assigns at least as much credibility to *Possibly*-A as she assigns to A in any of the inconclusive thought experiments, but not more.

Cross, Rod. On the Foundations of Hysteresis in Economic Systems. *Econ Phil*, 9(1), 53-74, Ap 93.

This paper examines the conceptual and analytical foundations of hysteresis, and argues that hysteresis is endemic in economic systems. The term hysteresis was coined by Ewing in 1881, but the concept itself has a longer history, the techniques invented by the Krasnosel'skii Group for analyzing systems with hysteresis are outlined, and applied to explain how economic systems react to aggregate shocks. Non-linearities and heterogeneities are the key elements, yielding remanence and selective memory.

Crosson, Frederick. Reconsidering Aquinas as a Postliberal Theologian. *Thomist*, 56(3), 481-498, Jl 92.

A response to Bruce Marshall's attempt to read Aquinas as one whose language about God exhibits "intrasystematic truth". This would entail, inter alia, that any discourse about God must cohere with the "broader norms of Christian belief", so that pagan philosophers like Aristotle, when using the term 'God', could not possibly have meant the same as Aquinas did. The response tries to show that this argument misreads Aquinas' texts in several fundamental ways, notably in construing a demonstrated conclusion as one that is "believed" and in confusing the revelation of the Oneness of God with the demonstration that God is one.

Crosson, Frederick. Rejoinder to Bruce Marshall. *Thomist*, 57(2), 299-303, Ap 93.

Crosson, Frederick. The Analogy of Religion. *Amer Cath Phil Quart*, 65, 1-15, 1991.

Unlike Kant, Aquinas thought that religiousness was a virtue because it inclined to actions specific to itself, not just to the regarding of all our moral duties as divine commands. Aquinas appropriates Cicero's definition of religion as the offering of service and cult to a superior nature, but he has to add that it is a virtue—good for us—only if it is directed toward the true God. This raises the question of whether any form of religiousness not in the Biblical tradition can be a virtue. I argue that it can by an analogy of proportion and discuss Hinduism as such an example.

Crosson, Frederick. The Laws of Nature and of Nature's God. *Vera Lex*, 11(2), 10-11, 1991.

A brief conspectus of the notion of "natural law"—an oxymoron for the Greek and Roman philosophers—why it emerged only in the matrix of the Biblical tradition, and how it lost its evidence as the attempt was made to elicit it from the modern notion of nature.

Crovi, Luca. Originalità filosofica dei *Pensieri* di Marco Aurelio. *Riv Filosof Neo-Scolas*, 84(2-3), 515-538, Ap-S 92.

Crowe, Frederick E (ed) and Doran, Robert M (ed). *Collected Works of Bernard Lonergan, V10*. Toronto, Univ of Toronto Pr, 1993.

Topics in Education, volume 10 of Collected Works of Bernard Lonergan, presents an edited transcript of ten lectures on the philosophy of education delivered by Lonergan at Xavier University, Cincinnati, in 1959. The task Lonergan sets himself is to develop an alternative to traditionalist and modernist notions of education. The context is set by an extensive analysis of the human good and of the 'new learning' first in mathematics and science and then in the study of the human subject. The basis of the alternative lies in the theory of operations that Lonergan's major works have presented. On this basis Lonergan also engages Piaget and presents his views on art and history.

Crowell, Steven Galt. Lask, Heidegger and the Homelessness of Logic. *J Brit Soc Phenomenol*, 23(3), 222-239, O 92.

The article reconstructs a problem in the context of Heidegger's earliest work (1912-1916) which provided the primary conceptual background for Heidegger's later formulation of the Ontological Difference. The problem concerns the "place" of logic in the neo-Kantian system of sciences. The "object" of logic appeared "homeless," belonging neither to the physical, psychical, nor metaphysical orders. The article first examines Emil Lasks's responses to the problem—the object of logic is "meaning" (*Sinn*), which does not "exist" but holds (*gilt*)—and then shows how Heidegger both adopts and transforms Lasks's view by way of transcendental phenomenology. Criticism of lacunae in Heidegger's early position point toward his development of a more adequate non-entitative conception of meaning/Being and *Being and Time*.

Crownfield, David. God Among the Signifiers. *Man World*, 26(1), 83-91, Ja 93.

The signifier "God" participates in an exonomy of differences that is disseminated and drifting; to fix its "mastery" erases its effects. Marking the telos of self-as-desire (Augustine) "God" tacitly haunts secular self-theories, even Lacan. Marking the claim of the other (Torah, neighbor-love) its modern erasure protects (conceals) the site of autonomy-as-mastery. The retrievable site of the God-trace is text, as promise and demand. In creative repetition and prolepsis (whether of god's return or final exit) the signifier may be not erased but reinscribed (perhaps as past?) in moral and discursive practice.

Crowther, Paul. Postmodernism in the Visual Arts in Postmodernism and Society, Boyne, Roy (ed). New York, St Martin's Pr, 1990.

Crowther, Paul. 'Les Immatériaux' and the Postmodern Sublime in Judging Lyotard, Benjamin, Andrew (ed). New York, Routledge, 1992.

Csepregi, Gabor. Corps et culture. *Laval Theol Phil*, 49(1), 121-129, F 93.

L'intention de cet essai est d'amorcer une réflexion sur le sort du corps humain dans let systèmes éducatifs contemporains. Sous l'influence d'une coneption dualiste de l'être humain et d'une valorisation excessive des capacités intellectuelles, la dimension corporelle de l'enfant est encore ignorée ou occultée. Paradoxalement, en considérant l'activité corporelle comme un tremplin permettant d'atteindre des objectifs d'ordre moral ou intellectuel, l'éducation physique semble également entretenir une telle logique de l'oubli ou du refus. Face à cette orientation, ceraines approches récentes tentent de surmonter toute ségrégation dualiste et de favoriser chez l'enfant la découverte et la conscience accrue de son propre corps.

Cua, A S. The Idea of Confucian Tradition. *Rev Metaph*, 45(4), 803-840, Je 92.

Cubitt, Robin P. On the Possibility of Rational Dilemmas: An Axiomatic Approach. *Econ Phil*, 9(1), 1-23, Ap 93.

This paper addresses two connected questions concerning the nature of rationality: 1) whether or not there is anything about the concept of rationality itself which prevents its dictates from conflicting in an irreconcilable way 2) whether or not there is anything about it which guarantees either the existence or the uniqueness of a rational choice in a decision problem. Using axioms, inspired by those of deontic logic, governing the nature of rational permission it characterises and discusses three conceptions of rationality which differ according to the answer which they give to these questions.

Cudd, Ann. Game Theory and the History of Ideas about Rationality: An Introductory Survey. *Econ Phil*, 9(1), 101-134, Ap 93.

In this paper I argue that there is a clear trail to follow that links theories of instrumental rationality from Aristotle to the nineteenth-century marginalist economists and ultimately to von Neumann and Morgenstern and contemporary game theorists, historically grounding game theory as a model of rational interaction. I proceed by analyzing the three main developments in the history of ideas about rationality that led to the development of game theory: 1) the idea that rationality is utility maximization; 2) the idea that rational beliefs and rational expectations can be formalized with probability theory; and 3) the idea that rational interaction is strategic.

Cullen, Bernard. Hegel's Philosophy of God in the Light of Kierkegaard's Criticisms in Hegel and His Critics, Desmond, William J (ed). Albany, SUNY Pr, 1989.

Culler, Jonathan. In Defence of Overinterpretation in Interpretation and Overinterpretation: Umberto Eco, Collini, Stefan (ed). New York, Cambridge Univ Pr, 1992.

Cumming, Robert D. Role-Playing: Sartre's Transformation of Husserl's Phenomenology in The Cambridge Companion to Sartre, Howells, Christina (ed). New York, Cambridge Univ Pr, 1992.

Cumming brings out the adjustments in Husserl's phenomenological method which are involved in the phenomenon of role-playing—entirely alien to Husserl's philosophy—becoming a critical phenomenon in Sartre's.

Cumming, Robert Denoon. *Phenomenology and Deconstruction, Volume II: Method and Imagination*. Chicago, Univ of Chicago Pr, 1992.

By analyzing how Sartre transforms Husserl's phenomenological method, Cumming provides an introduction at once to phenomenology and to the ways in which a previous philosophy can be refurbished in a later philosophy. Phenomenology, which was for Husserl a theory of knowledge in which "we can always presume sincerity," becomes in Sartre a phenomenology in which imagination, self-deception, role playing are crucial phenomena. Cumming also shows that conversion is not only a predisposition of Sartre, which is manifest in his initial conversion to phenomenology and later to Heidegger, and finally to a version of Marxism, but that is a philosophical preoccupation too, most notable when it is "conversion to the imaginary," whereby Sartre explains how he himself, as well as Genet and Faubert, become writers.

Cummins, Robert (ed) and Owen, David (ed). *Central Readings in the History of Modern Philosophy: Descartes to Kant*. Belmont, Wadsworth, 1992.

This is a book of readings for standard mid-level undergraduate courses on the history of early modern philosophy. It provides, in a single volume, the major texts of the most studied figures of the period: Descartes' *Meditations*, Spinoza's *Ethics (Books I and II)*, Leibniz' *Monadology*, Locke's *Essay Concerning Human Understanding* (abridged) and *Three Dialogues*, Hume's *An Enquiry Concerning Human Understanding* and Kant's *Critique of Pure Reason* (abridged). Editing is minimal, complete texts being used in most cases. Even where texts are abridged, the sections used are always complete in themselves. Sample syllabi are provided as guides for using this book in different sorts of courses.

Cunningham, Frank. Democracy, Socialism, and the Globe in On the Track of Reason, Beehler, Rodger G (ed). Boulder, Westview Pr, 1992.

Drawing on theories of the egalitarian socialist, G A Cohen, and C B Macpherson's critique of possessive individualism, a democratic-socialist interpretation of "sustainable development" is recommended, and some of the political consequences of it are drawn out.

Cunningham, James and Bogdan, Deanne. Beyond Comprehension: Why "Hard Reading" Is Too Easy. *Proc Phil Educ*, 48, 124-129, 1992.

Bogdan and Cunningham address the charge by Keith Raitz that treating communication as a purpose of reading violates the "communication contract" according to which communication is the necessary and sufficient condition of reading. They point out that it is possible to treat communication as a purpose without falling into adherence to a "conduit theory" of textual meaning or subscribing to "the myth of easy reading". Further, they argue for a "constructionist model' of reading which, while recognizing the meaning making and decoding responsibilities of readers articulated in Reddy's "reconstructionist model", establishes wider criteria for successful reading than the reconstruction of authorial meaning.

Cuomo, Christine J. Unravelling the Problems in Ecofeminism. *Environ Ethics*, 14(4), 351-363, Wint 92.

Karen Warren has argued that environmental ethics must be feminist and that feminist ethics must be ecological. Hence, she endorses ecofeminism as an environmental ethic with power and promise. Recent ecofeminist theory, however, is not as powerful as one might hope. In fact, I argue, much of this theory is based on values that are potentially damaging to moral agents, and that are not in accord with feminist goals. My intent is not to dismantle ecofeminism, but to analyze and clarify some of the philosophical problems with recent ecofeminist work and to point out a more promising direction for ecofeminist ethics.

Cupitt, Don. Unsystematic Ethics and Politics in Shadow of Spirit, Berry, Philippa (ed). New York, Routledge, 1992.

Postmodern people are suspicious of traditional dreams of systematic unity, mastery and control. They are becoming floating voters, who prefer to put together a package of good causes to support, rather than join a political party of the traditional sort. We are learning to live with the idea that the moral order is continually being renegotiated.

Curd, Martin. *Argument and Analysis: An Introduction to Philosophy*. St Paul, West, 1992.

Argument and Analysis is a textbook intended for introductory philosophy courses. The book is divided into five parts: (1) the rationality of theistic belief, (2) the foundations of morality, (3) the nature of mind, (4) determinism and free will, and (5) knowledge, skepticism, and causation. After the readings in each part there are discussions that explain key aspects of the readings and guide the student through the issues. Important arguments are isolated and analyzed at some length. The book also contains a short introduction to logic and reasoning, a glossary of philosophical terms, and suggestions for further reading.

Curd, Patricia. Eleatic Monism in Zeno and Melissus. *Ancient Phil*, 13(1), 1-22, Spr 93.

While many modern histories of ancient philosophy treat Zeno and Melissus as sympathetic followers of Parmenides, certain of their arguments, reported by the ancient commentators, can be interpreted as expressing anti-Parmenidean sentiments. I contend that the arguments are consistent with Parmenides' claims. By exploring more fully the nature and implications of Parmenides' predicational monism, Zeno and Melissus not only argue in support of Parmenides, they also expand the Parmenidean attack on certain types of pluralism.

Curd, Patricia Kenig. Deception and Belief in Parmenides' *Doxa*. *Apeiron*, 25(2), 109-134, Je 92.

An examination and account of Parmenides' *Doxa*. There is deception in the *Doxa*, in the dualistic account of Light and Night; but Parmenides does not renounce all human belief. While Parmenides does not give the account, a story about the sensible world that is consistent with the *Alêtheia* can be told. While the particular account given in the *Doxa* fails, the *Doxa* has something positive to say about mortal belief. Parmenides supposes that a trustworthy cosmology may be possible and discloses what such a theory might be like and how it could be tested.

Currie, Gregory. Aliens, Too. *Analysis*, 53(2), 116-118, Ap 93.

Historical theories of art claim that it is part of our concept of art that something is art only if it is related in some way to those objects which constitute the remote ancestry of our actual art. I argue that there are possible cases of objects falling under our concept of art that are not related in any substantial way to our art ancestors.

Currie, Gregory. Impersonal Imagining: A Reply to Jerrold Levinson. *Phil Quart*, 43(170), 79-82, Ja 93.

I have argued that the imagining made appropriate by works in visual media is not imagining seeing. Jerrold Levinson disagrees, appealing to a distinction between observers inside and outside the world of the fiction. I argue that Levinson's distinction does not support the thesis of imagining seeing. I argue further that we can account for a distinctively visual form of imagining without appeal to imagining seeing.

Currie, Gregory. Interpretation and Objectivity. *Mind*, 102(407), 413-428, Jl 93.

I characterize objectivity in interpretation as the possibility of rational agreement across interpretive points of view. I note that there can be degrees of such agreements, depending on how heavily conditional the statements agreed on need to be. I argue that different conceptions of the "implied author" weaken the prospects for agreement, and that the role of interpretations in the exploration of value make objectivity more difficult still.

Currie, Gregory. McTaggart at the Movies. *Philosophy*, 67(261), 343-355, Jl 92.

It is generally accepted that the standard mode of engagement with a fiction film is for the view to imagine herself watching the events the film depicts. I argue that this hypothesis is hard to square with the existence of anachronies—flashes back and forward—in film. But for anyone who claims, as I do, that the viewer does not imagine the fictional events happening here and now, there is the difficulty that the concept of anachrony seems to presuppose the concept of presentness. I argue that this in fact not the case, and that we can give an account of anachrony employing only tenseless temporal notions.

Currie, Gregory. Photography, Painting and Perception. *J Aes Art Crit*, 49(1), 23-29, Wint 91.

Is photography distinctive in that it gives us perceptual access to things themselves, as mirrors and lenses do, rather than merely to representations of those things, as sketches and paintings do. Kendall Walton's answer is yes. I review his arguments and decide that none of them establishes the conclusion he wants.

Currie, Gregory. The Long Goodbye: The Imaginary Language of Film. *Brit J Aes*, 33(3), 207-219, Jl 93.

The idea that there is a language, or something interestingly like a language of film is one that refuses to die. I propose to finish it off by looking carefully at the distinctive features of linguistic meaning and arguing that they have no counterpart in film. I conceed that there is a kind of meaning in film that may be called literal meaning, but this just shows that not all literal meaning is linguistic.

Curry, Charles. The Naturalness of the Cosmological Constant in the General Theory of Relativity: A Response to Ray. *Stud Hist Phil Sci*, 23(4), 657-660, D 92.

The issue of whether the cosmological constant is an *ad hoc* modification of Einstein's field equations is reexamined. Using a result known for some time in the literature, it is noted that although the field equations *without* the cosmological constant term constitute the minimal covariant formulation of general relativity, the equations *with* the term are the *only* allowable alteration. It is thereby argued that the constant is not *ad hoc*, and that the most compelling argument for a zero cosmological constant remains that from astronomical observation.

Curry, D C K. Owen's Proof in the *Peri Ideon* and the Indeterminacy of Sensibles in Plato. *Ancient Phil*, 12(2), 351-373, Fall 92.

In this paper I argue that G E L Owen's reading of the "argument from relatives" in the *Peri Ideon*, when taken as indicative of Platonic arguments for Forms, is seriously misleading. Owen argues that proof turns on the notion of incomplete predication and upon Plato's confusion about such predicates. I argue that it is, rather, a concern with the mutability and indeterminacy of the sensible world which motivates the argument, and offer an account of Platonic indeterminacy in the middle dialogues.

Curtis, Ronald. Does Science Belong to Its Elite?. *Phil Soc Sci*, 23(1), 77-83, Mr 93.

Curtis, Ronald. The Essential Nature of the Method of the Natural Sciences: Response to A T Nuyen's "Truth, Method, and Objectivity". *Phil Soc Sci*, 23(1), 73-76, Mr 93.

Curzer, Howard. Fry's Concept of Care in Nursing Ethics. *Hypatia*, 8(3), 174-183, Sum 93.

Sara T Fry maintains that care is a central concept for nursing ethics. This requires, among other things, that care is a virtue rather than a mode of being. But if care is a central virtue of ethics and medical ethics then the claim that care is a central concept for nursing ethics is trivial. Otherwise, it is implausible.

Curzer, Howard J. Do Physicians Make Too Much Money?. *Theor Med*, 13(1), 45-65, Mr 92.

The average net income of physicians in the USA is more than four times the average net income of people working in all domestic industries in the USA. When critics suggest that physicians make too much money, defenders typically appeal to the following four prominent principles of economic justice: Aristotle's Income Principle, the Free Market Principle, the Utilitarian Income Principle, and Rawls' Difference Principle. I shall show that no matter which of these four principles is assumed, the present high incomes of physicians cannot be defended.

Curzer, Howard J. Is Care a Virtue for Health Care Professionals?. *J Med Phil*, 18(1), 51-70, F 93.

Care is widely thought to be a role virtue for health care professionals (HCPs). It is thought that in their professional capacity, HCPs should not only take care of their patients, but should also care for their patients. I argue against this thesis. First I show that the character trait of care causes serious problems both for caring HCPs and for cared-for patients. Then I show that benevolence plus caring action causes fewer and less serious problems. My surprising conclusion is that care is a vice rather than a virtue for HCPs. In their professional capacity HCPs should not care for their patients. Instead HCPs should be benevolent and act in a caring manner toward their patients.

Cushing, James T. Historical Contingency and Theory Selection in Science. *Proc Phil Sci Ass*, 1, 446-457, 1992.

A major, overarching cluster of problems central to the philosophy of science and certainly underlying much of the debate in the recent literature is how scientific theories are constructed, how they are judged or selected, and what type of knowledge they give us. There are two aspects of answers to any of these three questions: what has actually occurred according to the historical record and what is the rational status of each of these activities or of the knowledge produced. The purpose of the present monograph is to use an extensive and detailed case study of a research program in modern theoretical physics to examine how theories are constructed, selected and justified in actual scientific practice. The book is intended both for philosophers of science and for interested physicists.

Cushing, Steven. Material Support for Material Implication. *J Prag*, 18(1), 88-89, Jl 92.

Cussins, Adrian. Content, Embodiment and Objectivity: The Theory of Cognitive Trails. *Mind*, 101(404), 651-688, O 92.

The possibility of a new kind of representational theory is demonstrated: a theory which explains concepts and thoughts in terms of the nonconceptual, embodied contents of experience. The theory is neither empiricist nor rationalist as it adopts a symmetric metaphysics in which mind and world are explained as the logical genesis of objectivity. The notion of "cognitive trails through environmental experience" is introduced, and objective content is formalised as a dynamic construction within a two-dimensional space whose axes are given by the perspective dependence of the cognitive trails, and by their degree of stabilization.

Cutrofello, Andrew. "Young Hegelian" Richard Rorty and the "Foucauldian Left". *Metaphilosophy*, 24(1-2), 136-146, Ja-Ap 93.

Rorty's articulation and critique of the position he identifies as that of "the Foucauldian left" recalls Marx's argument against the young Hegelians. However, on the basis of Rorty's own defense of William James' idea of the "will to believe," it is possible to construe the strategy of the Foucauldian left as taking up a comparably defensible "will to disbelieve." Instead of an anti-utopianism, such a position can be construed as a proto utopian call to question the apparent adequacy of present liberal democratic frameworks. Viewed from this perspective, it is Rorty's position which is guilty of aiming solely at interpretation and not at praxis.

Cutrofello, Andrew. Must We Say What "We" Means? The Politics of Postmodernism. *Soc Theor Pract*, 19(1), 93-109, Spr 93.

In a discussion of three recent books which focus on social theory and postmodernity, the author attempts to steer a middle course between a politics of identity and a politics of difference. Toward this end, the possibility of rethinking Hegel's attempt to articulate the conditions for the possibility of saying "we" is considered. Most helpful in this regard is the theoretical work on radical community developed in Bill Martin's *Matrix and Line: Derrida and the Possibilities of Postmodern Social Theory*, published by SUNY Press.

Cutrofello, Andrew. Quine and the Inscrutibility of Languages. *Int Stud Phil*, 24(1), 33-46, 1992.

Because there is no formal procedure for determining to which language a given expression belongs, it is impossible to limit indeterminacy and inscrutability "at home" by appealing to the principle of ontological relativity. Not only is it impossible to ostend a unique language to which a particular expression would belong, it is impossible even to determine rigorously the boundaries which separate one language from another. Languages are themselves inscrutable.

Cutrofello, Andrew. Speculative Logic, Deconstruction, and Discourse Ethics. *Phil Forum*, 24(4), 319-330, Sum 93.

Hegel's speculative logic differs from Derrida's deconstructions in that the former involves a series of localized strategies for "coping" with the disseminative effects of *différance*. In speculatively determining the equivocity it generates, Hegel's *Logic* generates conditions that can govern considerations of legitimation. Reading Hegel this way suggests an alternative to the tradition of Kantian discourse ethics that has been developed in the work of Rawls and Habermas.

Cutting-Gray, Joanne. Hannah Arendt, Feminism, and the Politics of Alterity: "What Will We Lose If We Win?". *Hypatia*, 8(1), 35-54, Wint 93.

Hannah Arendt's early biography of Rahel Varnhagen, an eighteenth-century German-Jew, provides a revolutionary feminist component to her political theory. In it, Arendt grapples with the theoretical constitution of a female subject and relates Jewish alterity, identity, and history to feminist politics. Because she understood the "female condition" of difference as belonging to the political subject rather than an autonomous self, her theory entails a "politics of alterity" with applications for feminist practice.

Cuypers, Stefaan. Hacia una concepción no atomista de la identidad personal. *Anu Filosof*, 26(2), 223-248, 1993.

This paper argues that the classical debate on personal identity in analytical philosophy implicitly rests upon the untenable doctrine of philosophical atomism. Both the Cartesian Ego Theory and the Empiricist Bundle Theory are built upon the indefensible epistemological presupposition that the self is a private object of introspective knowledge. It is suggested that Peter Strawson's descriptive metaphysics of the person as a public agent contains the essential preliminaries for a non-atomistic view of personal identity.

Cuypers, Stefaan. Is Personal Autonomy the First Principle of Education?. *J Phil Educ*, 26(1), 5-17, 1992.

It is suggested that the current hierarchical (Franklin-Dworkin) model of personal autonomy in philosophical anthropology gives expression to the fundamental presupposition of self-determination in much educational practice and pedagogical theory. Radical criticisms are made of the notions of self-identification and self-evaluation which are of the utmost importance to this model. Instead of relying on such 'acts of the will' as decision and choice for the explanation of self-identification and self-evaluation, the non-intentional as well as the non-individualistic character of these processes is stressed and analysed in terms of volitional necessity and social dependence. The consequence of this criticism is the substitution of the concept of extreme personal autonomy by that of caring about oneself as the first principle of education.

Cuypers, Stefaan E. Davidson and Wittgenstein on Human Action (in Dutch). *Bijdragen*, 53(3), 291-311, 1992.

This article discusses two prominent theories of intentional action in the analytical philosophy of mind. First, the psychological theory of Donald Davidson—based on reasons for action—is presented in connection with his anomalous monism. After a specification of three important problems in this intentional psychology, secondly, the social theory of Ludwig Wittgenstein—based on the observance of a rule—is introduced in an attempt to overcome these problems. But because of the intimate relationship between reasons and rules, the conclusion is that only a hybrid theory of intentional action can constitute the necessary as well as the sufficient conditions for an analysis of human action.

Cuypers, Stefaan E. Persoonlijke identiteit in de analytische wijsbegeerte. *Alg Ned Tijdschr Wijs*, 84(3), 194-205, Jl 92.

It is argued that the classical debate on personal identity in analytical philosophy leads to an aporetic result. Neither the Bundel Theory nor the Ego Theory can adequately account for both the nature and the importance of personal identity. The empiricist Bundel Theory gives rise to a destructive conventionalism whereas the dualist Ego Theory involves a miraculous essentialism. Therefore the problem of personal identity still remains unresolved.

Cvek, Peter P. John Locke's Theory of Natural Law. *Vera Lex*, 12(1), 15-18, 1992.

Czelakowski, J and Dziobiak, W. A Deduction Theorem Schema for Deductive Systems of Propositional Logics. *Stud Log*, 50(3-4), 385-391, S-D 91.

Czelakowski, Janusz. A Note on the Extension Principle for Relatively Congruence-Distributive Quasivarieties. *Bull Sec Log*, 21(3), 92-96, O 92.

D'Agostino, Fred. The Necessity of Theology and the Scientific Study of Religious Beliefs. *Sophia (Australia)*, 32(1), 12-30, Mr 93.

In this paper, I defend two claims:—1) that there are questions which social scientists have an obligation to answer which they cannot answer within the limits of competence associated with the very role which generates the obligation; *and* 2) that those who face these questions are in grave moral peril, there being very considerable risks associated both with a policy of trying to answer them and with a policy of refusing to try to answer them (or of ignoring them). The questions I have in mind are ones which are associated with the explanation of religious beliefs.

D'Agostino, Fred. Transcendence and Conversation: Two Conceptions of Objectivity. *Amer Phil Quart*, 30(2), 87-108, Ap 93.

D'Agostino, Fred. 'Demographic' Factors in Revolutionary Science: The Wave Model. *Method Sci*, 26(1), 41-52, 1993.

D'Ambra, M. Il mistero e la persona nell'opera di Edith Stein. *Aquinas*, 34(3), 581-592, S-D 91.

D'Amico, Claudia. Nicolás de Cusa, "De mente": la profundización de la doctrina del hombre-imagen. *Pat Med*, 12, 53-67, 1991.

D'Ancona Costa, C. Saint Thomas lecteur du "Liber de Causis". *Rev Thomiste*, 92(4), 785-817, O-D 92.

D'Andrade, Kendall. Machiavelli's Prince as CEO. *Bus Ethics Quart*, 3(4), 395-404, O 93.

The Machiavellian model is often praised as a realistic description of modern corporate life. My analysis of *The Prince* follows Rousseau in arguing that the prince can survive and prosper most easily by creating an environment in which almost all the citizens prosper. Far from licensing unrestrained self-aggrandizement, in this model success only comes from providing real value to almost every citizen for the entire period of one's leadership. Translation from the early sixteenth to the late twentieth century is far from simple; for example, the CEO is in many ways far less powerful than a Medici prince. The closest approximation is a far less bureaucratic organization with very small units possessing maximum autonomy. Also, deciding who is, and who is not, a citizen is not nearly as straightforward as it was for Machiavelli; it probably includes every stakeholder on whom the corporation has a major impact.

D'Aquino, Paola 454 AUTHOR INDEX WITH ABSTRACTS

D'Aquino, Paola. A Sharpened Version of McAloon's Theorem on Initial Segments of Models. *Annals Pure Applied Log*, 61(1-2), 49-62, My 93.

D'Costa, Gavin. Whose Objectivity? Which Neutrality? The Doomed Quest for a Neutral Vantage Point from Which to Judge Relations. *Relig Stud*, 29(1), 79-95, Mr 93.

A critical review of the proposals advanced by Harold Netland and Keith Ward regarding the possibility of judging religions from a universally acceptable starting-point. My argument is that such a venture is doomed, as all starting-points of judgment are tradition-specific. Analysing Netland's and Ward's proposals in detail illustrate this contention. The position adopted here draws upon the work of Alistair MacIntyre. (Reference is also made to the work of John Hick.)

D'Hondt, Jacques. El asesinato de la historia. *Cuad Etica*, 13, 19-45, Je 92.

Philological analysis and correct contextuation of *"Communismus der Geister"*, attributed to Hölderlin, confirm the hypothesis of a "communism" in the youth writings of Hölderlin and Hegel that, far from lacking interest, turns to be important for the interpretation of those works. The "communism of writings" of these authors, which did not distinguish in their youth between "mine" and "yours", testifies a "communism of spirit", and the spirit of a period. This paper remarks the novelty of this test of youth (1790), which J D'Hondt himself translates masterly to French, shows its philosophico-political aspects, and notes its exemplary potency for our times.

D'Ippolito, Bianca Maria. Edmund Husserl: Intersubjectivity between Epoché and History in Analecta Husserliana, XXXI, Tymieniecka, Anna-Teresa (ed). Dordrecht, Kluwer, 1990.

Da Costa, N C A and Doria, F A. On the Existence of Very Difficult Satisfiability Problems. *Bull Sec Log*, 21(4), 122-133, D 92.

We present some results on undecidability and incompleteness in the theory of computability. Our basic tool is the concept of complexity in the sense of Kolmogorov, Chaitin and Manin.

Da Costa, N C A and Doria, Francisco Antonio. On the Incompleteness of Axiomatized Models for the Empirical Sciences. *Philosophica*, 50(2), 73-100, 1992.

This is an expository paper in which we discuss our recent results on the incompleteness and undecidability of physical theories, in particular of Hamiltonian mechanics and chaos theory.

Da Costa, Newton C A and Puga, Leila and Vernengo, Robert J. Derecho, moral y preferencias valorativas. *Theoria (Spain)*, 5(12-13), 9-29, N 90.

We study some propositional systems of the logic of preference containing two kinds of deontic operators: juridical and ethical. These logics are important for the formalization of certain theories of law, such as the three-dimensional theory as developed by the Brasilian jurist, Muiguel Reale.

Däumer, Elizabeth. Queer Ethics, or The Challenge of Bisexuality to Lesbian Ethics. *Hypatia*, 7(4), 91-105, Fall 92.

Due to its problematic political and social position between two opposed sexual cultures, bisexuality has often been ignored by feminist and lesbian theorists both as a concept and a realm of experiences. The essay argues that bisexuality, precisely because it transgresses bipolar notions of fixed gendered and sexed identities, is usefully explored by lesbian and feminist theorists, enhancing our efforts to devise an ethics of difference and to develop nonoppressive ways of responding to alterity.

Dagi, Teo Forcht. Commentary on "How Much of the Brain Must Die in Brain Death". *J Clin Ethics*, 3(1), 27-28, Spr 92.

Dagi, Teo Forcht. Compassion, Consensus, and Conflict: Should Caregivers' Needs Influence the Ethical Dialectic?. *J Clin Ethics*, 3(3), 214-218, Fall 92.

In response to the claim that the dialectic surrounding a difficult ethical dilemma must reflect the caregivers' personal needs, this paper contends that the essence of professionalism precludes such needs from influencing the dialectic.

Dahan, Yossi and Yonah, Yossi. Competitive Equality of Opportunity. *Iyyun*, 41, Jl 92.

Dahbour, Omar. Self-Determination in Political Philosophy and International Law. *Hist Euro Ideas*, 16(4-6), 879-884, Ja 93.

This article makes a distinction between two concepts of self-determination: 1) Popular Self-Determination, a principle of international law that expresses the right of self-government for peoples in already existing states, and 2) National Self-Determination, a concept found in nationalist political philosophies that asserts the right of nationalities to states of their own. Criticizing the idea of self-determination for nationalities, especially as it is defended in some recent writings of Joseph Raz and Avishai Margalit, an argument is made for the restriction of the concept of self-determination to peoples, a restriction that accords with current practice in international law.

Dahlhaus, Carl (ed) and Katz, Ruth (ed). *Contemplating Music: Source Readings in the Aesthetics of Music, Volume IV—Community of Discourse*. Stuyvesant, Pendragon Pr, 1993.

Dahlstrom, Daniel O. The Dialectic of Conscience and the Necessity of Morality in Hegel's *Philosophy of Right*. *Owl Minerva*, 24(2), 181-190, Spr 93.

This article takes issue with liberal and Christian criticisms of Hegel's characterization of the necessary emptiness of "conscience" in the pivotal transition from the individual sphere of morality to the communal sphere of ethical life in the *Philosophy of Right*.

Daiber, Hans. The Meteorology of Theophrastus in Syriac and Arabic Translation in Theophrastus, Fortenbaugh, W W (ed). New Brunswick, Transaction Books, 1992.

Theophrastus' meterology of which the Greek original is lost, came to us in a fragmentary Syriac translation from the 9th century and two Syriac-Arabic translations from the 10th century. These versions are published together with an English translation of the most complete Arabic version by Ibn Al-Khammar. Numerous parallels with available Greek meteorological texts show the great influence of Theophrastus who differed from his teacher Aristotle in many details. He laid more emphasis on empirical observations and liked many causes of one meteorological phenomenon.

Dainian, Zhang. The Impact of the Thought of the School of Confucianism and the School of Daoism on the Culture of China. *Chin Stud Phil*, 24(4), 65-85, Sum 93.

Dainton, Barry F. Time and Division. *Ratio*, 5(2), 102-128, D 92.

What would happen to a person if they were to divine into two? It is argued that personal fission (of the problematic sort) is equivalent to a branching in "personal time". When viewed thus, fission is no longer problematic, for it is no longer absurd to hold that a person remains strictly identical with both the people they divine into. Personal fission is one instance of the more general phenomenon of the time of a person's life (the time generated by the relationships between the different stages of their life) diverging from the time of the world as a whole.

Dale, A J. Hempel Revisited. *Analysis*, 44(2), 90-92, Mr 84.

Dalla Chiara, Maria Luisa. Epistemic Logic Without Logical Omniscience in Advances in Scientific Philosophy, Schurz, Gerhard (ed). Amsterdam, Rodopi, 1991.

Dallery, Arleen B (ed) and Scott, Charles E (ed) and Roberts, P Holley (ed). *Crises in Continental Philosophy*. Albany, SUNY Pr, 1990.

Dallery, Arleen B (ed) and Scott, Charles E (ed) and Roberts, P Holley (ed). *Ethics and Danger*. Albany, SUNY Pr, 1992.

Dallmayr, Fred. Hermeneutics and the Rule of Law in Deconstruction and the Possibility of Justice, Cornell, Durcilla (ed). New York, Routledge, 1992.

Dallmayr, Fred. Postmetaphysics and Democracy. *Polit Theory*, 21(1), 101-127, F 93.

Dallmayr, Fred. Tradition, Modernity, and Confucianism. *Human Stud*, 16(1-2), 203-211, Ap 93.

Dalmiya, Vrinda and Alcoff, Linda. Are 'Old Wives' Tales' Justified? in Feminist Epistemologies, Alcoff, Linda (ed). New York, Routledge, 1993.

Dalton, Peter C. The Examined Life. *Metaphilosophy*, 23(1-2), 159-171, Ja-Ap 92.

Daly, Anthony C. Aquinas on Disordered Pleasures and Conditions. *Thomist*, 56(4), 583-612, O 92.

Contrary to the analysis of Gerald D Coleman ("The Vatican Statement on Homosexuality," *Theological Studies*, 48, 1987, pp 727-734). Aquinas argues that certain individuals suffer from a "distortion" at the constitutional level and certain pleasures are strictly unnatural. Pleasures, habits, and conditions are bound together, so that unnatural pleasures are in a way natural to unnatural states. The main ingredients of today's view of homosexuality are implicit in *Summa Theologiae* 1a2ae,31,7, and in Aquinas's commentaries on the *Nicomachean Ethics*, and on the *Epistle to the Romans*.

Dambska, Izydora. Lukasiewicz and Wittgenstein on the Principle of Contradiction. *Dialec Hum*, 17(1), 25-29, 1990.

This paper compares Lukasiewicz's and Wittgenstein's views on the principle of contradiction. The first part describes Lukasiewicz's in particular, his distinction of three meanings of the principle of contradiction: ontological, logical and psychological, and his account of the logical status of the principle as not necessary truth. Wittgenstein was not interested in the ontological principle of contradiction. However, he also regarded this principle as not universal and necessary. Both Lukasiewicz and Wittgenstein justified the principle by its practical significance.

Damiani, Anthony. *Standing In Your Own Way: Talks On the Nature of Ego*. Burdett, Larson, 1993.

Dancy, Jonathan. Caring about Justice. *Philosophy*, 67(262), 447-466, O 92.

I examine the contrast between 'caring' and 'justice' approaches to ethics, arguing that Gilligan misconceived this contrast and that her misconceptions have been persistent. Such complaints as may reasonably be made about the 'justice' approach in *general* do not lead to much in the way of a genuinely alternative position. I suggest that ethical particularism captures most of what is valuable in the 'caring' approach. I also offer a new interpretation of Jake and Amy.

Dancy, Jonathan. Externalism for Internalists in Rationality in Epistemology, Villanueva, Enrique (ed). Atascadero, Ridgeview, 1992.

This paper attempts to reconcile the intuitions underlying internalism and externalism in the theory of justification with a suggestion that a similar reconciliation may be available in ethics.

Dandekar, Natalie. Privacy: An Understanding for Embodied Persons. *Phil Forum*, 24(4), 331-348, Sum 93.

Legal decisions reveal deep divisions about the meaning of privacy, the extent to which it deserves legal protection and the grounds on which this protection should be determined. Philosophic reflection also appears deeply divided. After reviewing the strengths and weaknesses of alternative theoretical understandings of privacy, I show that strengths are retained and weaknesses better answered by grounding privacy rights on the concept of persons as embodied beings who define themselves in social relationships. I argue for conceiving privacy as pertaining to embodied persons, noting that doing so forces us to rethink previously accepted civility rules.

Dandekar, Natalie. Response to Schedler: Why This Policy Is Wrong. *Soc Theor Pract*, 18(3), 333-346, Fall 92.

What makes a social policy minimally just? Where a social policy asks present persons to undertake sacrifices for the sake of future generations, such a policy must, minimally, meet two criteria: 1) enactment must be fair; 2) the policy must provide the most effective means of preventing harm taking into account other values affected and other means available. By these criteria, Schedler's suggestion that the policy of forcing drug addicted pregnant women to undergo abortion is shown to be simply wrong.

Dandekar, Natalie and Zlotkowski, Edward. Moral Issues Associated with Bioengineered Species: Stewardship, Abuse and Sustainability. *Between Species*, 8(4), 209-216, Fall 92.

Mary Shelley's *Frankenstein* provides a fictive exploration of ethical dilemmas springing from a realization of the scientific power to create bioengineered species.

We use the novel as a fictive platform for analyzing what loci of value command human respect and the manner in which such matters are to be decided. We concluded that Dr Fankenstein's wrongdoing involves three specific evasions, in that he pursues exploitation of scientific possibility as if unhindered by a) the need for moral reflection on probable consequences, b) respect for the sensibilities of the nonscientific public and c) any sense that the nonhuman might itself be owed respect. We stress the continuing importance of remedying all three of these psycho-cultural blindspots.

Dandekar, Natalie and Zlotkowski, Edward. Reply to Westra's "Response—Dr Frankenstein and Today's Professional Biotechnologist". *Between Species*, 8(4), 222-223, Fall 92.

We respond to Westra's Comment by pointing out four respects in which use of literary analogy can usefully provide a standpoint from which one can discover insights than contribute to current ecological discourse.

Daniels, Charles. Having a Future. *Dialogue (Canada)*, 31(4), 661-665, Autumn 92.

This article critically dissects the premises of an argument of Don Marquis: A) to deprive someone of the value of his or her future is prima facie wrong, B) the future an adult has is included in the future of the fetus it developed from, C) abortion deprives the fetus of the value of its future, D) therefore, abortion is prima facie wrong.

Daniels, Charles. The Importance of Knowing What Is Right and Wrong. *Dialec Hum*, 17(1), 107-114, 1990.

It is argued that (a) we ought to do what is required to find out what we ought to do. We ought to act so as to gain the knowledge, including the know-how, skill, mastery, and power, needed for doing what we ought to do, and (b) we ought to act to create a climate in which each of us views others as collaborators in a search for truth and power.

Daniels, Charles B and Scully, Sam. Pity, Fear, and Catharsis in Aristotle's Poetics. *Nous*, 26(2), 204-217, Je 92.

The question addressed in this paper is whether Aristotle's analysis of tragedy the production of pity, fear, and a catharsis of these emotions *in audiences*—readers, auditors, or viewers—is *essential* to works of dramatic tragedy, or to good ones. Taking Aristotle passage by passage, the authors argue that it is not. Among the distinctions brought to bear are (1) real life actions and responses in contradistinction to make-believe ones and (2) felt emotions in contradistinction to typically felt emotions or emotional characterizations of actions, events, incidents, and situations.

Daniels, Neil M. *The Morality Maze: An Introduction To Moral Ecology*. Buffalo, Prometheus, 1991.

Daniels, Norman. Justice and Health Care Rationing in On the Track of Reason, Beehler, Rodger G (ed). Boulder, Westview Pr, 1992.

Daniels, Norman. Rationing Fairly: Programmatic Considerations. *Bioethics*, 7(2-3), 224-233, Ap 93.

Danielson, Peter. *Artificial Morality: Virtuous Robots for Virtual Games*. New York, Routledge, 1992.

The philosophical question whether morality is rational can be focussed by asking: should one cooperate in a one-shot Prisoner's Dilemma? We extend and criticize Gauthier's account of morally constrained choice by constructing players modeled as Prolog programs. At this procedural level we learn that conditional strategies are coherent but less constrained players do better than Gauthier's constrained maximizer. We build mechanisms for learning and communicating moral principles and explore the costs of the new methods our moral players deploy. In particular, in the game of Chicken morally useful devices of communication and commitment can be used for amoral purposes.

Danto, Arthur C. A Future for Aesthetics. *J Aes Art Crit*, 51(2), 271-277, Spr 93.

Danto, Arthur C. Narrative and Style. *J Aes Art Crit*, 49(3), 201-209, Sum 91.

Dardis, Anthony B. Sunburn: Independence Conditions on Causal Relevance. *Phil Phenomenol Res*, 53(3), 577-598, S 93.

Dardis, Tony. Primoratz on Terrorism. *J Applied Phil*, 9(1), 93-97, 1992.

In "What is Terrorism?" Igor Primoratz defines terrorism as "the deliberate intimidating them, or other people, into a course of action they would not otherwise take" In this article I argue that Primoratz is wrong a) to posit a necessary connection between terrorism and terror or intimidation, b) to argue that terrorism is directed solely against people, and not, for example, property, and c) to argue that the targets of terrorism proper are 'the innocent'.

Darling, John. Rousseau as Progressive Instrumentalist. *J Phil Educ*, 27(1), 27-38, Sum 93.

In *Emile* Rousseau emphasises four pedagogical principles which have become associated with child-centered education. Rousseau's conception of education, however, is utilitarian. This combination of principles and overall conception anticipates one particular strand of policy thinking today: the 'new vocationalism'. As a postscript, this paper asks why little work in the history of philosophy of education has been done, and identifies the early arguments of RS Peters as responsible for this failure.

Darowski, Roman. Renaissance Latin Aristotle Commentaries: A Supplement to Lohr's "Latin Aristotle Commentaries". *Frei Z Phil Theol*, 40(1-2), 169-180, 1993.

Darwall, Stephen L. Internalism and Agency in Philosophical Perspectives, 6: Ethics, 1992, Tomberlin, James E (ed). Atascadero, Ridgeview, 1992.

In moral philosophical debates between internalists and externalists, it is often unclear exactly what is at issue and what the underlying rationales for contending positions are. I begin with some distinctions between different things referred to as "internalism". I then focus on the following "metaphysical" version: its being the case that an agent ought to do something is constituted by existence of (conclusive) motives for her so acting. I then discuss two different philosophical rationales for this thesis, which mark out two different traditions of thought: philosophical naturalism and a view about the connection between 'ought' and autonomy.

Dascal, M and Senderowicz, Y. The Pure and the Non-Pure (in Hebrew). *Iyyun*, 41, 457-476, O 92.

Dascal, Marcelo (ed). *Cultural Relativism and Philosophy*. Leiden, Brill, 1991.

Fifteen original essays by North American and Latin American philosophers and social scientists address the conceptual and practical issues of cultural relativism across the Americas and their history. The book contains and introduction, name and subject indexes, and four parts: "Relativism: Transformation or death?"; "A Glimpse of variety: Philosophical experiences and worldviews in Latin America"; "Nature, culture, and art"; and "Crossing conceptual frameworks". Contributors: J Margolis, L Peña, L Olivé, L E Goodman, M de la Garza, R E Longacre, F Miró Quesada, M Beuchot, G Munévar, H B Sarles, D Sobrevilla, M Krausz, H Lacey, E J Meehan, M Dascal.

Dascal, Marcelo. Pragmatics and Foundationalism. *J Prag*, 17(5-6), 455-460, Je 92.

Bickhard and Campbell's ("Some foundational questions concerning language studies") argument to the effect that pragmatics is *foundational* for language and mind is discussed. The argument is criticized on a number of counts: 1) It overlooks the distinction between basic and derivative representations; 2) It employs an obscure notion of 'epistemic domains'; 3) It conflates the question of how contents (or meanings) arise in the first place with the question of how, once established, they are used. The conclusion is that their brand of pragmatism, which seeks to reduce semantics to pragmatics, remains in need of a proper foundation.

Dascal, Marcelo. The Ecology of Cultural Space in Cultural Relativism and Philosophy, Dascal, Marcelo (ed). Leiden, Brill, 1991.

It is argued that the traditional ways of conceiving of cultures in terms of spatial metaphors leads to *invidious comparison* between cultures. This, in turn, is perhaps the key source of the ethnocentrism that hampers universalist and relativist positions alike in the debate about cultural relativism. It is suggested that, in order to allow for a non-paternalistic and non-invidious attitude towards other cultures, a radical shift in the metaphorical conceptualization of culture is needed.

Dascal, Marcelo and Horowitz, Amir. Semantics and the Psyche. *Phil Phenomenol Res*, 52(2), 395-399, Je 92.

The paper criticizes two contentions of Bogdan concerning psychosemantics (in "Does Semantic Run the Psyche?", *Phil and Phenomenal Res*, 49 (1992):395-399). Bogdan claims that the content of an attitude has psychological causal powers *qua* pragmatic and not *qua* semantic, and then argues that Fodor's program of naturalizing psychosemantics actually *assumes* intentionality and naturalizes only the conditions of its semantic success. After rebutting Bogdan's first criticism, the paper tries to show why Fodor, within the framework of his theory, does not have to naturalize intentionality, but that nevertheless he does not assume it.

Dastur, Françoise. Language and 'Ereignis' in Reading Heidegger: Commemorations, Sallis, John (ed). Bloomington, Indiana Univ Pr, 1992.

Dastur, Françoise. Three Questions to Jacques Derrida in Ethics and Danger, Dallery, Arleen B (ed). Albany, SUNY Pr, 1992.

Datta, Srilkeha. A New Approach to the Problem of the Justification of Deduction in Foundations of Logic and Language, Sen, Pranab Kumar (ed). New Delhi, Allied, 1990.

Dauenhauer, Bernard. Rouse's *Knowledge and Power*: A Note. *Res Phil Technol*, 11, 179-182, 1991.

Dauenhauer, Bernard. Taylor and Ricoeur on the Self. *Man World*, 25(2), 211-225, Ap 92.

David, Marian. On the Roles of Trustworthiness and Acceptance. *Grazer Phil Stud*, 40, 93-107, 1991.

Our trust in our own trustworthiness as evaluators of truth plays a uniquely important role in Lehrer's recent work in epistemology. Lehrer has claimed that a person who trusts in her own trustworthiness has a reason for accepting everything she accepts, including that she is trustworthy. This claim is too bold, trust in our trustworthiness cannot play the epistemic role Lehrer assigns to it. Neither does a suitably revised version of the claim succeed in assigning any important epistemic role to our own trustworthiness as evaluators of truth.

David, Pascal. What Does "To Avoid" Mean? On Derrida's *De l'Esprit*. *Heidegger Stud*, 8, 15-27, 1992.

This Heidegger study aims at showing how deeply Derrida's De L'Esprit [On Spirit] misunderstood Heidegger's purpose and achievement. Because 'to avoid' does not mean, phenomologically, 'to exclude'. Avoidance in Heidegger (*Being and Time*) (Section 10) aims clearly enough at laying the foundations of what is avoided for a while on a way of thinking.

Davidson, Donald. The Second Person. *Midwest Stud Phil*, 17, 255-267, 1992.

It is argued that to have thoughts, and so to mean anything in speaking, it is necessary to understand, and be understood by, a second person. If Wittgenstein held that language is necessarily social, then the central thesis of this paper is Wittgensteinian. But it is denied that communication requires that one person speak as others do. Rather, the objectivity which thought and language demand depends on the mutual and simultaneous responses of two or more creatures to common distal stimuli and to one another's responses.

Davidson, Donald. The Third Man. *Crit Inquiry*, 19(4), 607-616, Sum 93.

This paper was written for the catalogue accompanying an exhibit of Robert Morris' pictures. The pictures were made blind. Each picture displays the directions Morris gave himself, and a quotation from Davidson's writings. The paper finds surprising relations between the paintings and the quotations.

Davidson, Donald. Thinking Causes in Mental Causation, Heil, John (ed). New York, Clarendon/Oxford Pr, 1993.

This article defends the view that events and objects described in mental or psychological terms can also be described in physical terms without this fact implying 1) that mental terms can be defined in physical terms or 2) that mental terms are related by strict laws to events described in physical terms or 3) that mental

Davidson, Donald 456 AUTHOR INDEX WITH ABSTRACTS

events are causally ineffectual. It is argued that the supervenience of mental concepts on physical concepts does not justify or render intelligible such idioms as "events are causes only as they instantiate physical laws"; on the contrary, causal relations, unlike causal explanations, are extensional.

Davidson, Donald. Three Varieties of Knowledge in A J Ayer Memorial Essays, Griffiths, A Phillips (ed). New York, Cambridge Univ Pr, 1991.

There are three basic varieties of empirical knowledge: knowledge of our own minds, knowledge of other minds, and knowledge of the external world. None of these can be reduced to another, and none can be attained prior to the others. It is argued in particular that knowledge of other minds is essential to all knowledge, since the sense of objectivity depends on it. But knowledge of other minds cannot be prior to knowing our own minds or knowing elementary truths about the shared environment.

Davies, Brian. God and Freedom: Reply to Jordan. *Sophia (Australia)*, 31(3), 124-125, 1992.

Davies, David. Perspectives on Intentional Realism. *Mind Lang*, 7(3), 264-285, Autumn 92.

Davies, Martin. Aunty's Own Argument for the Language of Thought in Cognition, Semantics and Philosophy, Ezquerro, Jesús (ed). Norwell, Kluwer, 1992.

Davies, Martin. Perceptual Content and Local Supervenience. *Proc Aris Soc*, 92, 21-45, 1992.

Davies, Martin (ed) and Humphreys, Glyn W (ed). *Consciousness: Psychological and Philosophical Essays*. Cambridge, Blackwell, 1993.

Davies, Stephen. Mozart's *Requiem*? A Reply to Levinson. *Brit J Aes*, 32(3), 254-257, Jl 92.

Jerrold Levinson argues that two composers independently writing the same notes produce two musical works. Peter Kivy, by contrast, suggests that a single work then is produced. The first view assumes that authorship affects artistically significant properties and, accordingly, work-identity. I agree that differences in the time or place, where these mark differences in musical cultures, affect the identity of works written. But I hold that, just as two people might invent something independently, so two composers sharing a cultural tradition at a given time might independently write a single work, even if, later, only the one person's work is known, influential etcetera.

Davies, Stephen. Violins or Viols?—A Reason to Fret. *J Aes Art Crit*, 48(2), 147-151, Spr 90.

Musicians pursuing authentic performance use replicas of instruments from the period of the work they play. Is this, as Peter Kivy would have it, because these offer incidentally the best means for producing the required sound-structure, or is it, as Jerrold Levinson claims, that authenticity in performance depends essentially on their use? I favor a conventionalist view. The use of the specified instruments is mandatory only where the conventions of the time accept such specifications as definitive. Composers' instructions about performance-means became mandatory in classical notated music by the 19th century; in other kinds of music and before that time, composers' specifications are recommendations only.

Davis, Dena S. Organ Transplants, Foreign Nationals, and the Free Rider Problem. *Theor Med*, 13(4), 337-347, D 92.

This essay examines the philosophical basis for the free rider argument, and compares that with the empirical data about organ donation in the United States. The free rider argument ought not to be used to exclude foreign nationals because it is based on fallacious assumptions about group membership, and how the 'giving community' is defined. Polls show that even among the seventy-five per cent of Americans who support organ donation, only seventeen per cent had taken the small step of filling out donor cards. Therefore, it goes against logic to define the giving community as coextensive with American residency, while excluding foreigners who might well have become donors had they lived in countries which provided that option. (edited)

Davis, Douglas P. Suárez and the Problem of Positive Evil. *Amer Cath Phil Quart*, 65(3), 361-372, Sum 91.

Davis, Duane. Reversible Subjectivity in Merleau-Ponty Vivant, Dillon, M C (ed). Albany, SUNY Pr, 1991.

Davis, Duane H (trans). "*Les Fondateurs*" and "*La Découverte de l'Histoire*": Two Short Pieces Excluded from "Everywhere and Nowhere," by Maurice Merleau-Ponty. *Man World*, 25(2), 203-209, Ap 92.

Davis, Kevin R. Kant's Different "Publics" and the Justice of Publicity. *Kantstudien*, 83(2), 170-184, 1992.

Davis, Michael. Criminal Desert and Unfair Advantage: What's the Connection?. *Law Phil*, 12(2), 133-156, My 93.

The "fairness theory of criminal desert" would proportion (maximum) legal punishment according to the unfair advantage the criminal takes by his crime. Dolinko, Duff, Scheid, and von Hirsch have recently criticized the theory for failing to provide a plausible explanation of the connection between its central notion, unfair advantage, and retributivism's central concern, desert. This paper attempts to provide that explanation and to answer the criticisms of Dolinko, et al.

Davis, Michael. Technical Decisions: Time to Rethink the Engineer's Responsibilities?. *Bus Prof Ethics J*, 11(3-4), 41-55, Fall-Wint 92.

The received view seems to be that the highly compartmentalized environment in which engineers work generally makes them mere tools of their employer. Lacking the control necessary for responsibility, engineers cannot be responsible for what they help bring about. Our research found instead a highly fluid process in which meetings and less formal exchange of information across even departmental lines was normal. Engineers were expected to serve as advocates for safety and quality. Decision was generally by consensus. What are the consequences for philosophy of engineering?

Davis, Michael. *To Make the Punishment Fit the Crime: Essays in the Theory of Criminal Justice*. Boulder, Westview Pr, 1992.

While everyone may agree that the punishment should fit the crime, saying what that means in specific cases is much harder. Philosophical treatments of punishment, which tend to emphasize the nature or justification of punishment, generally offer little help in dealing with practical questions like how much to punish habitual offenders, whether unsuccessful attempts at crime should be punished as much as a completed crime, or whether the criminal law should hold persons strictly liable. This book deals with such questions within a general retributive framework in which punishment takes back the unfair advantage the criminal took by breaking the law.

Davis, Stephen T. Is Terrorism Every Morally Justified? in Terrorism, Justice and Social Values, Peden, Creighton (ed). Lewiston, Mellen Pr, 1990.

Davis, Thomas A. The *Deinon* of Yielding at the End of Metaphysics in Crises in Continental Philosophy, Dallery, Arleen B (ed). Albany, SUNY Pr, 1990.

Davis, Whitney. Beginning the History of Art. *J Aes Art Crit*, 51(3), 327-350, Sum 93.

Davis, William C. Kierkegaard on the Transformation of the Individual in Conversion. *Relig Stud*, 28(2), 145-163, Je 92.

Davydov, I N. Totalitarianism and the Problems of a Work Ethic. *Russian Stud Phil*, 32(1), 67-76, Sum 93.

Dawidoff, Robert. The Jeffersonian Option. *Polit Theory*, 21(3), 434-452, Ag 93.

Dawidziak, Piotr. The Organizing Principle of the Cognitive Process or the Mode of Existence in Analecta Husserliana, XXXIV, Tymieniecka, Anna-Teresa (ed). Dordrecht, Kluwer, 1992.

Dawson Jr, John W. The Compactness of First-Order Logic: From Gödel to Lindström. *Hist Phil Log*, 14(1), 15-37, 1993.

Though regarded today as one of the most important results in logic, the compactness theorem was largely ignored until nearly two decades after its discovery. This paper describes the vicissitudes of its evolution and transformation during the period 1930-1970, with special attention to the roles of Kurt Gödel, A I Maltsev, Leon Henkin, Abraham Robinson, and Alfred Tarski.

Dawson Jr, John W. The Reception of Gödel's Incompleteness Theorems in Perspectives on the History of Mathematical Logic, Drucker, Thomas (ed). Basel, Birkhauser, 1991.

This paper examines the extent to which Gödel's incompleteness theorems were understood and accepted at the time of their enunciation. It is concluded that Gödel's Proofs were most persuasive to formalists; others raised objections on technical or philosophical grounds. Reactions of Skolem, von Neumann, Finsler, Zermelo, Russell and Wittgenstein are discussed in some detail.

Dawson Jr, Lyndon E and O'Boyle, Edward J. The American Marketing Association Code of Ethics: Instructions for Marketers. *J Bus Ethics*, 11(12), 921-930, D 92.

This article addresses the two main obstacles—ignorance and conflict—that block the pathway to ethically proper conduct, both generally in business and specifically in marketing. It begins with a brief examination of theories of the moral good which emphasizes the Greco-Roman humanistic tradition and the Judeo-Christian religious tradition. A professional code of ethics, such as the code of the American Marketing Association, is meaningful only if human beings are regarded as making moral judgments that, objectively speaking, are morally wrong; that is, only when the code is considered a set of moral absolutes. (edited)

Day, J P. More on Moral Dilemmas. *Philosophy*, 67(261), 399-406, Jl 92.

This discussion completes 'Moral Dilemmas, Compromise and Compensation' (*Philosophy*, Vol. 66. No. 257, July 1991). In correction of the earlier discussion, the claim that resolution of moral dilemmas by compromise is always preferable to resolution by compensation, is withdrawn. In a particular case, the decision which is preferable requires judgment (Subsec. 3.8). In amplification of the earlier discussion, it is observed that another way of resolving moral conflicts is what M P Follett calls 'Integration'. In this, the one claimant is made better off and the other claimant is made no worse off. This is in fact an application of a principle of Pareto's. Here again, in a particular case, the decision whether resolution by integration is preferable to resolution by compromise, requires judgment (Subsec. 3.5).

Day, J P. Temptation. *Amer Phil Quart*, 30(2), 175-181, Ap 93.

Temptation is important both in the supernatural sphere and in the mundane sphere. In the former, the Tempter is God's Adversary. In the latter, there is the great moral evil of bribery and corruption. There are two meanings of 'to tempt'. 'To tempt(1)' means 'to test'. But 'to tempt(2)' means 'to try to induce to do something wrong by offering something truly believed to please the temptee'. Tempting(2) is one way of tempting(1), but another way of tempting(1) is provoking. Both tempting(2) and being tempted(2) are immoral. Christians, following St Paul, hold that there are no irresistible temptations(2) and no intolerable provocations. But is argued that this is false, since A can compel B to do X by tempting(2) B irresistibly to do X or by provoking B intolerably to do X. It is argued further that when A thus compels B to do X it is immoral to punish or blame B for doing X. But this is inconsistent both with our moral judgments in particular cases and with the practice of the Anglo-American Criminal Law.

Day, John. Justice and Utility in Health Care in The Utilitarian Response, Allison, Lincoln (ed). Newbury Park, Sage, 1990.

Dayong, Yang. Yan Fu's Philosophy of Evolution and the Thought of Lao Zi and Zhuang Zi. *Chin Stud Phil*, 24(1), 55-84, Fall 92.

De, P K. *The Roles of Sense and Thought in Knowledge*. Calcutta, Bagchi, 1992.

The present volume is a genuine and sincere attempt to bring to light the core of the problem concerning the roles that sense and thought play in perceptual knowledge. This problem has been analysed carefully by bringing the certain key concepts which play significant and important roles in the presentation of empiricism and rationalism as two rival schools of Western philosophy. For example, the concepts of 'sensation', 'simple apprehension', 'sense-organ', etc. and also 'Vikalpa', 'reason', 'understanding', etc. have been analysed with a view to determine the exact meanings of 'sense' and 'thought'.

De Araújo Dutra, Luiz Henrique. A Diferença entre as Filosofias de Carnap e Popper. *Cad Hist Filosof Cie*, 1(1), 7-31, Ja-Je 91.

Carnap and Popper give different solutions to the problem of demarcation between science and metaphysics. Carnap seeks to distinguish meaningful scientific sentences from meaningless metaphysical expressions. And Popper tries to separate falsifiable systems (empirical sciences) from non-falsifiable ones (metaphysics or philosophy). This difference in solving the problem of demarcation is due to the opposite conceptions Carnap and Popper hold on fundamental questions of philosophy of science, such as: knowledge, logic, and philosophy itself. These basic differences between their philosophies are discussed here.

De Armey, Michael H. Experimental Inquiry and Democracy: 'Working Union' of Ideal and Real. *Ultim Real Mean*, 16(1-2), 130-134, Mr-Je 93.

De Asúa, Miguel and Klimovsky, Gregorio. Ensayo de axiomatización de la teoría tisular y su reducción a la teoría celular. *Theoria (Spain)*, 5(12-13), 129-140, N 90.

The conceptual framework of this paper is the structural conception of theories as formulated by Sneed-Stegmüller. We present an informal set-theoretical axiomatization of M F Xavier Bichat's theory of the constitution of the organism, which conceived the tissue as the ultimate constitutive element of the living beings, and a reformulation of our previous axiomatization of the cell theory. We propose a tentative relation of reduction between both theories which possibilities the derivation of the axioms of the tissue theory from those of the cell theory. The limits and problems of the axiomatization are discussed and brief reference is being made to some historical aspects of the reception of the cell theory.

De Bary, W T. The Uses of Neo-Confucianism: A Response to Professor Tillman. *Phil East West*, 43(3), 541-556, Jl 93.

The question is whether Neo-Confucianism, a well-established Western term for the major new development of Confucian thought that arose in the twelfth century, is still serviceable or should be replaced by romanized Chinese terms more specific to period and school. This article argues in favor of keeping "Neo-Confucianism" as an overall rubric for a variety of trends and schools, all emanating from the Sung discourse as principally formulated by Shu Hsi, that reached Korea, Japan and Vietnam, and served as a common cultural denominator throughout pre-modern East Asia.

De Bernardi, P. Socrate: Il demone e il risveglio—Sul senso dell'etica socratica. *Sapienza*, 45(4), 425-443, 1992.

De Boer, T. Transcendentie en Schepping. *Phil Reform*, 57(2), 159-168, Ja 92.

The concept of transcendence must not be conceived of, in the biblical tradition, as an instance beyond space and time or beyond relativity and transitoriness, but as the authority of goodness transcending the ordinary wisdom of man and the generally accepted laws of society. Something similar is true of the concept of creation. It is not making something out of nothing, but rather the laborious struggle against and dominance over the powers of chaos and nothingness. The agony of Christ is a paradigm. The two concepts, understood in this sense, have an experiential basis in everyday life.

De Bruijn, Jan. Children's Philosophy in Europe. *Teach Phil*, 15(3), 255-265, S 92.

'Children's Philosophy in Europe' contains a review of four publications on philosophizing with children. It notes that the subject has received increased attention in recent years. It also notes a distinct departure from American forerunner Matthew Lipman's example. Lastly, it expresses a mild reservation concerning the application of philosophy as a fixed part of elementary school curricula. Such an application is found to seem hypocritical because it introduces pretensions to 'openness' and 'freedom' in a mandatory context.

De Buzon, F. L'homme et le langage chez Montaigne et Descartes. *Rev Phil Fr*, 4, 451-466, O-D 92.

De Castell, Suzanne and Bryson, Mary. En/Gendering Equity: Emancipatory Programs or Repressive "Regimes of Truth". *Proc Phil Educ*, 48, 357-371, 1992.

De Castell, Suzanne and Bryson, Mary. En/Gendering Equity: On Some Paradoxical Consequences of Institutionalized Programs of Emancipation. *Educ Theor*, 43(3), 341-356, Sum 93.

De Cointet, Pierre. La pensée et la vie. *Rev Thomiste*, 93(2), 304-312, Ap-Je 93.

De Cózar, José M. Technology, the Natural Environment, and the Quality of Life. *Res Phil Technol*, 12, 67-81, 1992.

The relationship between technology, environment, and the quality of life is commonly conceptualized as follows: the enhancement of the quality of life is the goal, and technology is the means or instrument by which we transform the environment to achieve, by fulfilling our needs, this goal. The purpose of the paper is to discuss this overly simplistic view, paying close attention to the idea of the quality of life and its relationship to the concept of needs. An alternative, integrated approach to the quality of life is proposed in order to correct the excessive techno-economic bias of current accounts.

De Gandolfi, M C Donadío M. El Index Thomisticus y la semántica lingüística. *Sapientia*, 47(185), 229-234, 1992.

De Gandolfi, M C Donadío M. Individuo y sociedad: En Duns Scot y en Tomás de Aquino. *Sapientia*, 47(185), 209-220, 1992.

De Gandt, François. Cavalieri's Indivisibles and Euclid's Canons in Revolution and Continuity, Barker, Peter (ed). Washington, Cath Univ Amer Pr, 1991.

De Gaudemar, Martine. Quelques questions autour de la notion leibnizienne de puissance. *Stud Leibniz*, 24(2), 216-220, 1992.

Es werden Beziehungen zwischen den Begriffen der potentia, der Existenz und der besten aller möglichen Welten untersucht.

De George, Richard. Business Ethics and the Liberal Arts in Moral Education and the Liberal Arts, Mitias, Michael H (ed). Westport, Greenwood Pr, 1992.

Business ethics can be taught as a subject in the liberal arts. Although often used as a tool for indoctrination, business ethics at it best takes a critical, though not necessarily antagonistic, look at business practices. It can sensitize students to issues, help them become morally articulate, and aid them in thinking through moral problems.

De Jong, R. The Philosophy of Language of Port-Royal and the Ontological Square: On Substantives and Adjectives (in Dutch). *Tijdschr Filosof*, 55(2), 241-264, Je 93.

According to the grammar of Port-Royal it is possible to convert the noun 'homme' ('man') into the adjective 'humain' ('human') by adding a confused signification or connotation. Strangely enough it is stipulated that by the reversal of this process (i.e., stripping the confused signification) the adjective 'human' is converted into the substantive 'humanité' ('humanity') rather than the original noun 'homme'. In this article I argue that the treatment of adjectives and substantives in the Port-Royal grammar depends strongly on the traditional Aristotelian ontology as summarized in the so-called ontological square and the theory of the predicables. In connection with this it is shown that according to the port-Royalists corresponding concrete and abstract nouns like 'homme' and 'humanité', should be in some sense equivalent.

De Jongh, Dick and Jumelet, Marc and Montagna, Franco. On the Proof of Solovay's Theorem. *Stud Log*, 50(1), 51-69, Mr 91.

De Jongh, Dick and Montagna, Franco. Rosser Orderings and Free Variables. *Stud Log*, 50(1), 71-80, Mr 91.

It is shown that for arithmetical interpretations that may include free variables it is not the Guaspari-Solovay system *R* that is arithmetically complete, but their system *R*-. This result is then applied to obtain the nonvalidity of some rules under arithmetical interpretations including free variables, and to show that some principles concerning Rosser orderings with free variables cannot be decided, even if one restricts oneself to "usual" proof predicates.

De Jongh, Dick and Visser, Albert. Explicit Fixed Points in Interpretability Logic. *Stud Log*, 50(1), 39-49, Mr 91.

The problem of Uniqueness and Explicit Definability of Fixed Points for *Interpretability Logic* is considered. It turns out that Uniqueness is an immediate corollary of a theorem of Smorynski.

De La Garza, Mercedes. Time and World in Mayan and Nahuatl Thought in Cultural Relativism and Philosophy, Dascal, Marcelo (ed). Leiden, Brill, 1991.

De Libera, Alain. Psychologie philosophique et théologie de l'intellect: Pour une histoire de la philosophie allemande au xiv siècle. *Dialogue (Canada)*, 31(3), 377-397, Sum 92.

De Lucia, Paolo. Autocoscienza e conoscenza nel 'primo Rosmini'. *Riv Filosof Neo-Scolas*, 84(1), 88-122, Ja-Mr 92.

De Meyer, Luisa Herrera. Conciencia subjetiva y Estado ético en Hegel. *Cuad Etica*, 13, 9-18, Je 92.

Traditionally, an opposition has been seen between the State that Hegel conceives as ethical and the role, within the same State, of subjective moral conscience. A correct interpretation of the problem requires that analysis and comparison of Hegel's *dicta* in *Philosophy of Right* with those in his lectures about the subject, both before and after the publication of *PR*, due to political conditionings. In correct hermeneutics of the genuine Hegelian conception of the State, this last does not only exclude subjective conscience, but accepts it and gives it concrete possibilities of effectuating itself as autonomy. But, beyond Hegelian conception, between both terms there remains an irreducible tension, which cannot be annihilated without paying the cost of a deficit of a critic rationality in the ethical consideration of the problem.

De Mingo Rodríguez, Alicia. Objetividad empírica y juicio transcendental. *Themata*, 8, 181-190, 1991.

De Nys, Martin J. Understanding and Difference in Modernity and Its Discontents, Marsh, James L (ed). Bronx, Fordham Univ Pr, 1992.

De Pace, Anna. Le Matematiche e il Mondo: Ricerche su un dibattito in Italia nella seconda metà del Cinquecento. Milano, FrancoAngeli, 1993.

The publication of Proclus' Commentary on Euclid's Elements aroused a debate about the certainty and dignity of mathematics in the hierarchy of sciences and its suitability for reflecting the truth of natural world. In order to reconsider the 16th century roots of scientific revolution and Galilei's cultural background, the book reconstructs significant lines of that debate, following the connexion of logical, metaphysical and gnoseological aspects in authors as Alessandro Piccolomini, Pereira, Barozzi, Catena, Tartaglia, Mazzoni, and pointing out contaminations and revisions of themes from Platonic and Aristotelian traditions. In the 'Appendix' are published the Lectures Barozzi delivered in 1559 at Padua University on Proclus' Commentary.

De Pisón y Cavero, José Martínez. David Hume: La solidez del artificio. *Agora (Spain)*, 11(1), 133-147, 1992.

In his earliest work, *A Treatise of Human Nature*, Hume attempts an analysis of the forms of social cooperation and the necessity of the establishment of "rules of justice", concluding that the possibility of establishing a basic normative system requires the previous "artificial" production of reasons for acting. Among human beings, there is no natural reason to carry out acts of justice beyond benevolence, altruism and selfishness. In order to defend this thesis Hume develops an interesting syllogism, a model of analysis, by means of which he refutes contemporary theories. As a result of his treatment, rights, society and the basic schemes of justice necessary for cooperation are the offsprings of the peculiarities of human mind and the species specific necessities in what he, happily for philosophy, called "circumstances of justice", and the interest and the principle of sympathy. The author of this paper goes over each of the aspects of his argumentation and makes a brief commentary.

De Queiroz, Kevin. Phylogenetic Definitions and Taxonomic Philosophy. *Biol Phil*, 7(3), 295-313, Jl 92.

An examination of the post-Darwinian history of biological taxonomy reveals an implicit assumption that the definitions of taxon names consist of lists of organismal traits. That assumption represents a failure to grant the concept of evolution a central role in taxonomy, and it causes conflicts between traditional methods of defining taxon names and evolutionary concepts of taxa. Phylogenetic definitions of taxon names grant the concept of common ancestry a central role in the definitions of taxon names and thus constitute an important step in the development of phylogenetic taxonomy. By treating phylogenetic relationships rather than organismal traits as necessary and sufficient properties, phylogenetic definitions remove conflicts between the definitions of taxon names and evolutionary concepts of taxa.

De Queiroz, R J G B and Gabbay, Dov M. Extending the Curry-Howard Interpretation to Lienar, Relevant and Other Resource Logics. *J Sym Log*, 57(4), 1319-1365, D 92.

The so-called Curry-Howard interpretation is known to provide a rather neat term-functional account of intuitionistic implication. Could one refine the interpretation to obtain an almost as good account of other neighboring implications, including the so-called 'resource' implications (e.g., linear, relevant, etc.)? We answer this question positively by demonstrating that just by working with side conditions on the rule of assertability conditions for the connective representing implication one can characterize those 'resource' logics.

De Regt, Herman C D G. Neurale netwerken en het wetenschappelijk realisme van de waarheid. *Alg Ned Tijdschr Wijs*, 85(1), 96-112, F 93.

In this article I explore the consequences of Paul Churchland's philosophical connectionism for scientific realism in general and more specifically for Churchland's own scientific realism. The evaluation of Churchland's position must not be interpreted as a *reductio ad absurdum*, strange though his theory might seem. I argue that his realism is an internalist scientific realism.

De Rijke, Maarten. A Note on the Interpretability Logic of Finitely Axiomatized Theories. *Stud Log*, 50(2), 241-250, Je 91.

In Chapter 6, Albert Visser shows that *ILP* completely axiomatizes all schemata about provability and relative interpretability that are provable in finite axiomatized theories. In this paper we introduce a system called *ILPω* that completely axiomatizes the arithmetically valid principles of provability in and interpretability over such theories. To prove the arithmetical completeness of *ILPω* we use a suitable kind of tail models; as a byproduct we obtain a somewhat modified proof of Visser's completeness result.

De Rijke, Maarten. Unary Interpretability Logic. *Notre Dame J Form Log*, 33(2), 249-272, Spr 92.

We extend the modal logic of provability with a unary operator simulating unary interpretability over a given arithmetical theory. Complete axiomatizations are given of the (unary) interpretability logics underlying Peano Arithmetic and Gödel-Bernays set theory. The paper also represents interpolation and fixed point theorems for the newly defined logics.

De Rojas Raz, Nerva Borda. El estado hegeliano como individualidad excluyente. *Cuad Etica*, 13, 47-55, Je 92.

The analysis proposes to read Hegel from the experience of a non-European people that is seeking its freedom. The thought is presided by the principle that man are not reducible to men, neither are peoples to peoples. The State in Hegel's Philosophy of Right is shaped through an ethic way which makes it determine itself as an excluding individuality that, when meeting other States, cannot continue its proper ethical task. Relations between States are defined on the basis of contingency and arbitrariness. The unavoidable end is war and the imperium of the stronger. The closed State of Philosophy of Right is mediated from Philosophy of History, re-opening the dialectical highway through the "spirit of the people". My analysis notes that modern spirit is not able to experience a just liberty, which impedes it to emancipate from the violent state that presides the world.

De Rose, Keith. Contextualism and Knowledge Attributions. *Phil Phenomenol Res*, 52(4), 913-929, D 92.

De Rose, Keith. Descartes, Epistemic Principles, Epistemic Circularity, and Scientia. *Pac Phil Quart*, 73(3), 220-238, S 92.

De Santamaría, Pilar López. "Pienso, luego no existo": La constitución del sujeto en Wittgenstein. *Anu Filosof*, 26(2), 261-269, 1993.

Wittgenstein's examination of Private Language Argument and Solipsism in the *Philosophical Investigations* implies no critics to his earlier theory maintained in the *Tractatus*. On the contrary, both are inspired by the same idea, the impossibility of finding a thinking subject merely on the grounds of thought itself.

De Souza, Roberta Lima. O Método de Análise da Geometria Grega. *Cad Hist Filosof Cie*, 2(1), 67-83, Ja-Je 90.

This paper presents the method of analysis as a method of discovery used by ancient Greek geometers in looking for proofs of theorems and of constructions to solve problems. The controversy concerning the interpretation of this method came from different approaches given to the Pappusian description of analysis. In dealing with this problem, we try to show that there is a justificationist methodology inherent in the view of historians of mathematics. So according to this view we can remark that analysis might have a certain degree of certainty, though the meaning and field of application of the method be narrowed. Also on the basis of Pappus's account, new possibilities of interpretation of geometrical analysis as a heuristic method come to light by using other historical evidence. Among the main reasons for the loss of the primitive sense of this method, when we follow the lead of historians, there is a subjacent previous conception of rationality.

De Stier, María L Lukac. Santo Tomás y el origen de la sociedad. *Sapientia*, 47(185), 221-228, 1992.

De Vicente Arregui, Gemma. La cultura y la historia frente a la verdad y el bien en Nitezsche. *Themata*, 8, 115-140, 1991.

Setting up the notions of truth and goodness means to revindicate the will to nothingness. Nietzsche tries to affirm the perpetual change of life and to bless what actually happens. Culture and history replace truth and goodness. However, Nietzsche's scheme strikes upon a metaphysics that declares false the anthropologically reached and considers lie as condition of life.

De Visscher, J. Esthetica en kuntsfilosofie. *Tijdschr Filosof*, 55(1), 130-140, Mr 93.

De Vos, L. Het Hegeliaanse begrijpen: problemen en mogelijkheden. *Tijdschr Filosof*, 55(2), 330-343, Je 93.

De Vries, Gerard and Harbers, Hans. Empirical Consequences of the 'Double Hermeneutic'. *Soc Epistem*, 7(2), 183-192, Ap-Je 93.

De Vries, Gerard and Harbers, Hans. Reply to Lynch's "What Does the Double Hermeneutic Explain/Justify?". *Soc Epistem*, 7(2), 205-208, Ap-Je 93.

De Wachter, F. The Nation: From Nationalism to Post-national Identity (in Dutch). *Tijdschr Filosof*, 55(1), 48-71, Mr 93.

The problem of the nation is articulated as the philosophical problem of the relation between the political and the non-political in the context of modernity. When the political relevance of traditional non-political bonds is removed, a new cohesion needs to be found between free and equal individuals.

De Wachter, Maurice. Ethical Aspects of Germline Gene Therapy. *Bioethics*, 7(2-3), 166-177, Ap 93.

De Wolf, Jan (ed) and Van Vucht Tijssen, Lieteke (ed) and Raven, Diederick (ed). *Cognitive Relativism and Social Science*. New Brunswick, Transaction Books, 1992.

Modern epistemology has been dominated by an empiricist theory of knowledge that assumes a direct individualistic relationship between the knowing subject and the object of knowledge. Truth is held to be universal, and non-individualistic social and cultural factors are considered sources of distortion of true knowledge. Since the late 1950s, this view has been challenged by a cognitive relativism asserting that what is true is socially conditioned. This volume examines the far-reaching implications of this development for the social sciences. (edited)

De-Shalit, Avner. Community and the Rights of Future Generations: A Reply to Robert Elliot. *J Applied Phil*, 9(1), 105-115, 1992.

It is widely recognized that we hold certain moral obligations to future generations. Robert Elliot argues that we can base these obligations on the rights of future people. I accept his argument that future people are moral agents who possess rights. However, I argue that the main question for political and moral philosophers is whether it is possible to find the balance between the obligations to, and the rights of, contemporaries, and the obligations to, and the rights of, future people. By analyzing the notions of 'human rights' and 'welfare rights' of future people, I argue that this question can be tackled only in terms of welfare rights. But the latter make sense only in the context of community of provision. This implies that we must first examine the 'trans-generational' community that includes contemporaries and future generations. Thus a theory of justice between generations cannot be purely 'rights-based'. However, by describing the 'trans-generational community' I argue that it can serve as the moral grounds for our obligations to future generations.

Dean, William. Pluralism and the Problem of God in God, Values, and Empiricism, Peden, Creighton W (ed). Macon, Mercer Univ Pr, 1989.

Deb, Amiyansu. Logical Equivalence and Inductive Equivalence. *Indian Phil Quart*, 19(2), 91-104, Ap 92.

Declève, Henri. Jan Patocka et le phénomène de l'écriture littéraire. *Laval Theol Phil*, 49(1), 3-26, F 93.

L'article présente un livre encore récent du philosophe Jan Patocka (1907-1977), L'écrivain, son "objet". *Essais*. Traduit du tchèque et de l'allemand par Erika Abrams, Paris, POL, 1990, 291 p. Une courte bibliographie des oeuvres de cet auteur disponibles en français est suivie d'une mise en situation de son parcours philosophique et de son rôle politique. Disciple de Husserl et de Heidegger, Patocka a entrepris une relecture critique des "deux grands de la phénoménologie", comme il disait, tout en ressaisissant avec une perspicacité cratrice ce qui est en jeu dans l'hisoire de la métaphysique. Son enquete le conduit à s'interroger sur la signification du phénomène littéraire depuis Homère jusqu'au roman et à la poésie moderne. Témoin de la fidélité à la sérénité, pour laisser se créer le sens de la finitude.

Deely, John N. Locke's Proposal for Semiotic and the Scholastic Doctrine of Species. *Mod Sch*, 70(3), 165-188, Mr 93.

Deely, John N. Philosophy and Experience. *Amer Cath Phil Quart*, 66(3), 299-320, 1992.

Deely, John N. The Supplement of the Copula. *Rev Metaph*, 46(2), 251-277, 1992.

Dees, Richard. Hume and the Contexts of Politics. *J Hist Phil*, 30(2), 219-242, Ap 92.

Most accounts of Hume's politics ignore the contextual subtleties of his arguments in his historical and political works. By looking at what Hume does and not just at what he says when he makes political judgments, the article shows that Hume is more sensitive to the peculiarities of situations than we are led to expect from his strictly philosophical works. This understanding of his politics puts Hume's philosophy in a new perspective, one in which Hume's view of human nature is much more flexible than most commentators have realized. Indeed, his view of politics is best characterized as contextual.

DeFilippo, Joseph G. Reply to André Laks on Anaxagoras' *Nous*. *S J Phil*, 31(Supp), 39-48, 1992.

This paper examines André Laks' argument that the separating function of *nous* in Anaxagoras' cosmogony provides a model for his theory of intellection. Laks is right to emphasize the parallel structures of *nous'* motive and cognitive functions. Nevertheless, this is not enough to generate a properly philosophical theory of intellection, nor does Anaxagoras need one. Fragment B12 offers an inchoate design argument for an intelligent first cause of the cosmos. Given this purpose, it needs a theory of *nous'* intellection no more than it needs to explain how *nous* causes motion.

Degenaar, J J. Art and Culture in a Changing World. *S Afr J Phil*, 12(3), 51-56, Ag 93.

The purpose of this article is to look at the meanings of the terms culture, art, and changing South Africa and to discuss some of the relationships between them. I argue that the change taking place in South Africa is a complex one but basic to this complexity is the transition from an apartheid culture to, hopefully, a democratic culture. In this article I demonstrate how difficult the road to democracy is—in particular in a multi-cultural set-up—and how inappropriate all forms of imperialism are in the spheres of culture, art, and politics.

Degenaar, Johan. Imagination and Myth. *S Afr J Phil*, 11(3), 67-74, Ag 92.

Various uses of the term imagination are explored with the purpose of throwing light on the ability of the imagination to produce metaphors and models which function as heuristic fictions which enable us to redescribe reality. On the basis of a discussion

AUTHOR INDEX WITH ABSTRACTS 459 Dent, N J H

of the views of Kant and Ricoeur the nature of imagination is illustrated by the creative role it plays in fiction and, through fiction, in the way it enriches human experience and enhances the quality of life. This develops into a discussion of the role of imagination in the production and interpretation of myths.

Degrazia, David. Moving Forward in Bioethical Theory: Theories, Cases, and Specified Principlism. *J Med Phil*, 17(5), 511-539, O 92.

The field of bioethics has deployed different models of justification for particular moral judgments. The best known models are those of deductivism, casuistry, and principlism (under one, rather limited interpretation). Each of these models, however, has significant difficulties that are explored in this essay. An alternative model, suggested by the work of Henry Richardson, is presented. It is argued that specified principlism is the most promising model of justification in bioethics.

DeGrazia, David. On the Right of "Nondangerous" Incompetent Patients to Leave Psychiatric Units Against Medical Advice. *Cont Phil*, 14(5), 1-5, S-O 92.

Deigh, John. Sidgwick on Ethical Judgment in Essays on Henry Sidgwick, Schultz, Bart (ed). New York, Cambridge Univ Pr, 1992.

Del Barco, José Luis. Idea y abstraccón en Hume. *Anu Filosof*, 25(3), 463-492, 1992.

Hume propounds the aporetic principle of correspondence between impressions and ideas, in order to solve the problem of the genesis of the ideas. This principle, which lacks universal validity, reduces the idea to image and deprives it of universality. In this way is postulated a rigorous and universal nominalism, which converts the ideas into non referential unities the same as the Urimpressions (Husserl) and sets aside the possibility of metaphysics.

Del Barco, José Luis. La sensibilidad postmoderna. *Agora (Spain)*, 11(1), 119-131, 1992.

Some aspects of the present cultural situation seem to announce the end of an epoch and the appearance of a new sensitivity. The depletion of the utopic energies, the disillusion for the consequences of progress without direction and the ecologic consciousness are the most outstanding manifestations of the new sensitivity. In most cases this new phenomenon has adopted the position of a antimodern revolt. Moreover it has renounced to explain rationally the reality as a whole and has succumbed to the breaking up of post-Hegelian thinking. In front of the temptation of *il pensiero debole* the author claim for the necessity of an integral way of thinking, which is placed at a distance from the rationalistic universalization and from the postmodern breaking up.

Del Giudice, Denis. An Old Way of Looking at New Things: Modern Science, Technology, and the Philosophy of Science. *Gnosis*, 4(1), 39-64, 1992.

Del Vecchio, D. Caos, frattali ed altro. *Sapienza*, 46(1), 99-100, 1993.

Del Vecchio, D. La storia e il processi al passato. *Sapienza*, 45(4), 449-450, 1992.

Delaney, C F. Peirce on the Hypothesis of God. *Trans Peirce Soc*, 28(4), 725-739, Fall 92.

Focusing on his notion of "the hypothesis of God," this paper explores the methods of logical continuity between Peirce's scientific beliefs and his religious beliefs.

Delaney, C F. *Science, Knowledge, and Mind: A Study in the Philosophy of C S Peirce*. Notre Dame, Univ Notre Dame Pr, 1993.

This book is a critical study of Peirce's philosophy of science, epistemology and philosophy of mind in their interrelation. His views on truth and realism are discussed in the context of his account of scientific inquiry, and his classic critique of Cartesianism is articulated against this background. His more speculative views in the area of philosophy of mind are sketched to complete his overall vision of science and reality. The study concludes with an exploration of several junctures at which Peirce's vision can be profitably introduced into our present philosophical discussions.

DeLaunay, Marc B. L'État, le mythe, les totalitarismes. *Rev Metaph Morale*, 97(4), 553-558, O-D 92.

Deledalle, Gérard. Peirce's "Sign": Its Concept and Its Use. *Trans Peirce Soc*, 28(2), 289-301, Spr 92.

Deleuze, Gilles and Joughin, Martin (trans). *Expressionism in Philosophy: Spinoza*. Cambridge, MIT Pr, 1992.

Deleuze, Gilles and Lester, Mark (& other trans) and Boundas, Constantin V (ed). *The Logic of Sense—Gilles Deleuze*. New York, Columbia Univ Pr, 1990.

In the opus of Deleuze, *The Logic of Sense* holds the place that *The Archaeology of Knowledge* did in that of Foucault: the latter, being a discourse about discourse, articulates Foucault's methodology which permitted him to examine discursive formations, discursive practices and nondiscursive space surrounding discursive fields; the former, working out the logic of the invention of concepts, assembles around it all the other works of Deleuze and permits him to show how thinking should be understood and discussed, if it is to be a thinking of events, singularities and haecceities. In thirty-four series and five appendices, Deleuze displays his usual virtuosity as he discusses becoming and the paradoxes it generates, sense as the fourth dimension of the proposition, events in the context of two complementary readings of time, the ethics of the event and his early responses to Lacan.

Delgado, Manuel. Significación lógica del cambio de estructura de *El Capital* entre 1857 y 1866. *Rev Filosof (Costa Rica)*, 30(71), 73-80, J 92.

Between 1857-1866, Karl Marx changed the structure of his main work, starting it with the presentation of his theory of value. With this change Marx tried to explain the economic phenomenon in its development, and to demonstrate the real, historical (and not only logical) existence of value.

Della-Rocca, Michael. Kripke's Essentialist Argument Against the Identity Theory. *Phil Stud*, 69(1), 101-112, Ja 93.

In *Naming and Necessity*, Kripke famously argues that mental events are not identical with physical events. I argue that one of Kripke's premises requires more defense than he offers and that there are only two potential ways to provide the needed defense. Unfortunately for Kripke, the first strategy would undermine another premise of his argument and the second strategy would render his argument question-begging. Thus there is no way for Kripke's argument to succeed.

Della-Rocca, Michael. Spinoza's Argument for the Identity Theory. *Phil Rev*, 102(2), 183-213, Ap 93.

Although Spinoza's claim that the mind and body are one and the same thing seems to amount to an identity theory, this interpretation has been challenged by Bennett, Delahunty and others. In this paper, I defend the identity interpretation by showing that Spinoza employs a notion of referential opacity that infects causal and other related contexts. I then show how this broad range of opacity provides Spinoza with an intriguing argument for his claim of identity.

Demarco, Joseph P and Fox, Richard M. The Immorality of Promising. *J Value Inq*, 27(1), 81-84, Ja 93.

If the duty of promise-keeping is interpreted strictly, it overrides other moral duties, committing the promisor to violate them if necessary. If the duty is interpreted in a weaker, prima facie sense, it allows the duty of promise-keeping to be overridden, and hence ceases to provide genuine assurance. Thus promising is immoral in the first case, because it ignores other moral responsibilities, and in the second, because its appearance of assurance is illusory and deceptive. We explore both sides of this dilemma and conclude that various attempts to morally sanction promise-making fail.

Dempster, Douglas. Renaturalizing Aesthetics. *J Aes Art Crit*, 51(3), 351-361, Sum 93.

Den Hartogh, Govert. Rehabilitating Legal Conventionalism. *Law Phil*, 12(2), 233-247, My 93.

The main obstacle for developing a conventionalist theory of the law (Hume, Lewis) is the fact that most of the patterns of interaction regulated by law are not pure coordination games. In his book *A Conventionalist Theory of Institutions*, Helsinki, 1989, Eerik Lagerspetz shows that systems of mutual believes, having the property of being collectively non-corrigible, can be self-reinforcing in other games as well. And even Prisoner's Dilemma games may be tranformed into Assurance Games if the players can ascribe to each other a moral motive. I argue that his case can be strengthened by a more detailed analysis of the structure of patterns of mutual beliefs, and of the role moral motives play in stabilizing them. The results are not nearly as supportive of Hartian positivism as Lagerspetz would like them to be.

Den Hartogh, Govert. The Rationality of Conditional Cooperation. *Erkenntnis*, 38(3), 405-427, My 93.

In *Morals by Agreement*, David Gauthier (1986) argues that it is rational to intend to cooperate, even in single-play Prisoner's Dilemma games, provided 1) your co-player has a similar intention; 2) both intentions can be revealed to the other player. To this thesis four objections are made. a) In a strategic decision the parameters on which the argument relies cannot be supposed to be given. b) Of each pair of *a*-symmetric intentions at least one is not rational. But it is impossible to form symmetric intentions to cooperate conditionally. For the condition on which the decision depends cannot be fulfilled without deciding. c) If one's intention has to be ascertained on the basis of information about one's past performance, it is straightforwardly rational to intend to cooperate, but there is no reason to do so in a single-play PD. d) The argument cannot be extended to *n*-person games which are Gauthier's principal concern.

Den Uyl, Douglas. The Right to Welfare and the Virtue of Charity. *Soc Phil Pol*, 10(1), 192-224, Wint 93.

In this essay I examine the claim that people have a right to welfare by looking at the concept of charity and the ways in which that concept contrasts with that right. The paper considers charity in its full historical context and discusses its role within liberal political theory. The main thesis of the paper is to argue that classical charity is consistent with classical liberalism, especially is the virtue of charity is conceived within the framework of classical ethics.

Den Uyl, Douglas. The Right to Welfare and the Virtue of Charity in Altruism, Paul, Ellen Frankel (ed). New York, Cambridge Univ Pr, 1993.

Denise, Theodore C. On the Nature of *Inus* Conditionality. *Analysis*, 44(2), 49-52, Mr 84.

The thesis of this paper is that J L Mackie's classic definition of an *insufficient* but *necessary* part of a condition that is itself *unnecessary* but *sufficient* for a result (an INUS condition) is too broad. I propose and defend an amendment that not only narrows the classic definition appropriately but also preserves its basic structure.

Denkel, Arda. Natural Meaning. *Austl J Phil*, 70(3), 296-306, S 92.

Natural meaning deserves closer attention than it has so far received. A better understanding of it will not only provide reliable boundaries for nonnatural meaning and thus subserve Grice's analysis; it will also satisfy independent interest. First, if drawn clearly, the distinction between natural and nonnatural meanings is the most promising method for delimiting what one may call 'typically human (or artificial) communication', and second it affords a fuller grasp of the basic and common features meaning bears, both in human languages and in the contexts of animal communication and natural signs. It will emerge in what follows that the received notion of natural meaning is not as clear and satisfactory as it should be for securing such ends. My purpose is to try to cast light on a number of aspects and varieties of natural meaning.

Denkel, Arda. Substance Without Substratum. *Phil Phenomenol Res*, 52(3), 705-711, S 92.

Dennett, Daniel C. Living on the Edge. *Inquiry*, 36(1-2), 135-159, Mr 93.

Dennett, Daniel C. Memes and the Exploitation of Imagination. *J Aes Art Crit*, 48(2), 127-135, Spr 90.

Richard Dawkins' concept of a *meme*, a replicating unit of cultural evolution, has been largely overlooked by humanists, who would prefer not to think of their domains in evolutionary terms. I demonstrate the power of the concept in a variety of contexts, and recommend the evolutionary vision it enables.

Dent, N J H. Aggression, Love, and Morality in Psychoanalysis, Mind and Art, Hopkins, Jim (ed). Cambridge, Blackwell, 1992.

Dent, N J H. Ophir's *Plato's Invisible Cities*. *Polis*, 11(1), 83-87, 1992.

Denyer, Nicholas. Ease and Difficulty: A Modal Logic with Deontic Applications. *Theoria*, 56(1-2), 42-61, 1990.

Ease and difficulty are given a possible worlds semantics, using pleonotetic quantifiers. Just as the possible is done in some accessible worlds, the easy is done in many. Relational propositions like 'It is difficult for Kasparov to beat Short, but easy for Short to be beaten by Kasparov' demand a triadic accessibility: from the actual world Kasparov has access to few worlds in which Kasparov beats Short, while Short has access to many. A symbolism developed for this can also be interpreted deontically. This solves various puzzles about conflicting obligations, Good Samaritans, etc.

Denyer, Nicholas. Pure Second-Order Logic. *Notre Dame J Form Log*, 33(2), 220-224, Spr 92.

Pure second-order predicate calculus is a predicate calculus where the only variables are predicate variables. In it, logical truth is decidable, and semantic consequence is compact. Pure second-order functional calculus is a functional calculus where the only variables are function variables. In it, semantic consequence is not compact, and there is no complete proof procedure for logical truth.

DePaul, Michael. *Balance and Refinement: Beyond Coherence Methods of Moral Inquiry*. New York, Routledge, 1993.

Something like coherentism offers the only rational approach to moral inquiry. But the method of balance and refinement that I defend does not share the mechanical, intellectualist conception of moral inquiry that is common to other versions of coherentism. While arguments surely have an important place in any philosophical inquiry into morality, they are not the whole story. A significant part of moral inquiry is concerned with refining our ability to make sensitive moral judgments. Once we realize this certain things stand out that we previously were unable to see: moral conversions, the possibility of naivete and corruption, and the significant, nearly essential, role of life experience and experience with literature, film, theater, music and art in moral inquiry.

Depraz, Natalie. Les figures de l'intersubjectivité: Études des Husserliana XIII-XIV-XV. *Arch Phil*, 55(3), 479-498, Jl-S 92.

After going through the base of the three volumes formed by Husserl's manuscripts which are available in Leuven but also in Paris (Ulm) and in which prevails, though the multiplicity of the groups of manuscripts put together and their dissemination among these three volumes, the E group, the author undertakes to convey the substantial content of I Kern's introductions to these volumes and to account for the relevance and the coherence of the edition. It is then possible on this basis to attempt to review and analyze Husserl's early (1905-1910) and durable (till in the thirties) interest for the question of intersubjectivity, as also the plurality of forms it takes. Three different figurations of this theme tend to appear, which *grosso modo* coincide with the three ways of the Husserlian phenomenology: *Einfühlung* (Cartesian way), intersubjective reduction (way of psychology), spiritual common world (way of the *Lebenswelt*).

Depré, Olivier. Hegel, des années de jeunesse à la fondation du premier système. *Rev Phil Louvain*, 91(89), 111-125, F 93.

Deregibus, Arturo. Metafisica e soggettività: Alle origini della filosofia moderna—Descartes, Pascal, Spinoza. *G Metaf*, 14(1), 51-65, Ja-Ap 92.

This essay understands the subjectivity and the metaphysics, linked with the new scientific methodology, as the critic foundation of the modern philosophy. It then reflects upon the continuity of the theories of Descartes' "cogito", Pascal's "coeur" and Spinoza's "absolute", although unavoidably different; and it at last underlines the essential and standing speculative validity, critic and "spiritual" at once, of the Cartesian "cogito".

Derisi, Octavio N. La persona y su mundo: la cultura, la moral, el derecho y la sociedad familiar y política (I). *Sapientia*, 47(183), 5-8, 1992.

Derisi, Octavio N. La Persona y su mundo: la cultura, la moral, el derecho y la sociedad familiar y política (III). *Sapientia*, 47(185), 163-168, 1992.

La moral es el orden que Dios impone al hombre para la gloria divina y para el propio bien humano. Es el camino del perfeccionaminto humano trazado por la Ley eterna de Dios íntimamente vinculado a la gloria de Dios y al tema de la persona.

Derksen, A A. Paul Churchland: filosofie en connecitonisme. *Alg Ned Tijdschr Wijs*, 85(1), 7-23, F 93.

In his *Scientific realism and the plasticity of mind* (1979), that is, before his move to connectionism, Churchland already argued in favour of the plasticity of perception, the dangerous grip of folk psychology and the necessity of a non-sentential model of knowledge, topics which play a crucial role in his recent connectionistically inspired philosophy. In this paper I briefly discuss these older *philosophical arguments*. At the end I criticize his "connectionism" at its weakest spot, namely at its (non-) treatment of rationality. I argue that Churchland's non-sentential conception of knowledge is not tenable. On top of the non-sentential basis we need something like the sentential model. Connectionism and neurosciences have much to offer to philosophy, but a philosophy oriented to connectionism and the neurosciences will have to be sensitive to "ecological" aspects.

Derksen, Ton. Wat is rationaliteit and wat is er zo goed aan?. *Alg Ned Tijdschr Wijs*, 84(4), 258-286, O 92.

The irrationalist points out that the rationalist's choice for rationality cannot be rational. He has no independent reason to support this choice. Call this the circle of rationality. So the question is what is so good about rationality. To answer this question I first present an analysis of rationality. This analysis brings to the fore two more—unjustly neglected—circles within the domain of rationality. The one circle crops up when we apply our analysis to rational considerations. In the analyses a not analysed reference to rationality reappears. We come across the other circle in the analysis of a rational person. In the analysans we face a reference to what may be reasonably expected. I argue that all three circles can be removed. Having achieved this I show what is so good about rationality.

Derr, Patrick and Thompson, Nicholas S. Reconstruing Hempelian Motivational Explanations. *Behavior Phil*, 20(1), 37-46, Spr-Sum 92.

When motivational explanations are cast in the Hempelian form, motivations and other mental states usually play the role of antecedent conditions. This leads to two objections: 1) that there is a question-begging connection between the explanandum and the antecedent conditions referring to mental states, and 2) that the intentional character of motivational explanations prevents them from being scientifically useful. These objections are mooted if claims about motivational states are construed as covering laws rather than as statements of antecedent conditions.

Derr, Patrick and Thompson, Nicholas S. The Intentionality of Some Ethological Terms. *Behavior Phil*, 20/2(21/1), 15-24, 1993.

The apparent incompatibility of mental states with physical explanations has long been a concern of philosophers of psychology. This incompatibility is thought to arise from the intentionality of mental states. But, Brentano notwithstanding, intentionality is an ordinary feature of higher order behavior patterns in the classical literature of ethology.

Derrida, Jacques. Aporias, Ways and Voices in Derrida and Negative Theology, Coward, Harold (ed). Albany, SUNY Pr, 1992.

Derrida, Jacques. Force of Law in Deconstruction and the Possibility of Justice, Cornell, Durcilla (ed). New York, Routledge, 1992.

Derrida, Jacques. Heidegger's Ear: Philopolemology ('Geschlecht' IV) in Reading Heidegger: Commemorations, Sallis, John (ed). Bloomington, Indiana Univ Pr, 1992.

Derrida, Jacques. Response to Daniel Libeskind. *Res Phenomenol*, 22, 88-94, 1992.

Derrida, Jacques. Secret, Heresy and Responsibility: Patocka's Europe (Conclusion) (in Czechoslovakian). *Filozof Cas*, 40(5), 857-867, 1992.

Derrida, Jacques. Secret, Heresy and Responsibility: The Europe of Patocka (Part I) (in Czechoslovakian). *Filozof Cas*, 40(4), 551-573, 1992.

Derrida, Jacques and Kamuf, Peggy (trans). *Given Time: I. Counterfeit Money—Jacques Derrida*. Chicago, Univ of Chicago Pr, 1991.

Derrida, Jacques and Wood, David (trans). Passions: 'An Oblique Offering' in Derrida: A Critical Reader, Wood, David (ed). Cambridge, Blackwell, 1992.

DeSchrenk, Laura Mues. Two Notions of Progress in Terrorism, Justice and Social Values, Peden, Creighton (ed). Lewiston, Mellen Pr, 1990.

Deslauriers, Marguerite. Tensions and 'Anamalous' Passages: Aristotle's *Metaphysics* and Science, Method and Practice. *Apeiron*, 25(3), 189-207, S 92.

Desmond, William. *Beyond Hegel and Dialectic: Speculation, Cult, and Comedy*. Albany, SUNY Pr, 1992.

This book is a defense of speculative philosophy in the wake of Hegelian dialectic. It rejects the notion of the end of speculative metaphysics. Though Hegel is the author's primary interlocutor, there is extensive discussion of other major figures like Aristophanes, Socrates, Plato, Augustine, Descartes, Kant, Nietzsche, Heidegger, Derrida. In a set of related, wide-ranging meditative essays, the themes treated include speculation and historicism, cult and representation, evil and dialectic, logos, and the comedy of failure. Desmond pits his own metaxological notion of being and philosophy (also developed in other works) against Hegel's dialectical way.

Desmond, William J (ed). *Hegel and His Critics*. Albany, SUNY Pr, 1989.

This book deals with fundamental problems in Hegel and with Hegel in relation to Kierkegaard, Marx, Nietzsche, Russell, Heidegger, Husserl, Derrida, and Bataille. It reveals Hegel's power to provoke both critical and creative thought across the complete spectrum of philosophical questions.

Despland, Michel. On Not Solving Riddles Alone in Derrida and Negative Theology, Coward, Harold (ed). Albany, SUNY Pr, 1992.

Negative theology is interpreted as a textual virtuosity aiming at the realisation that the writer is using language. Some Greek philosophical and literary virtuosities (Homer, Sophocles) are examined: they show how intelligence lives on after encountering its limits. The argument is that Greek reason is not always logocentric and that the common attack on "logocentric" reason is not necessarily a nihilistic attack on reason.

Desserud, Donald A. Virtue, Commerce and Moderation in the 'Tale of the Troglodytes': Montesquieu's *Persian Letters*. *Hist Polit Thought*, 12(4), 605-626, Wint 91.

Montesquieu's "Tale of the Troglodytes" (*Persian Letters*) has traditionally been seen as a rejection of the Hobbes in favour of Shaftesbury. An alternative interpretation is offered. The regime based upon commerce (sequel) is presented as a regime in which the pursuit of individual desires leads to beneficial consequences for the community as a whole. In this way, the *Persian Letters* becomes an important prequel to the *Spirit of the Laws* and may help us resolve some of the apparent contradictions between commerce and virtue in the *Spirit of the Law*.

Destrée, Pierre. "Physique" et "métaphysique" chez Aristote. *Rev Phil Louvain*, 90(88), 424-444, N 92.

DeSwart, H C M. Spreads or Choice Sequences?. *Hist Phil Log*, 13(2), 203-213, 1992.

Intuitionistically, a set has to be given by a finite construction or by a construction-project generating the elements of the set in the course of time. Quantification is only meaningful if the range of each quantifier is a well-circumscribed set. Thinking upon the meaning of quantification, one is led to insights-in particular, the so-called continuity principles-which are surprising from a classical point of view. We believe that such considerations lie at the basis of Brouwer's reconstruction of mathematics. The predicate 'x is lawless' is not acceptable, the lawless sequences do not form a well-circumscribed intuitionistic set, and quantification over lawless sequences does not make sense.

Detels, Claire. History and the Philosophies of the Arts. *J Aes Art Crit*, 51(3), 363-375, Sum 93.

This essay challenges the assumptions contained under the rubric, "Philosophy and the Arts" (used by the 1991 NEH Institute co-sponsored by the American Society for Aesthetics) as diminishing the true complexity of history as an approach from which to understand art. It also includes a survey and critique of the theories of some current historically-oriented philosophers of art, such as Arthur Danto, Jerrold

AUTHOR INDEX WITH ABSTRACTS 461 DeWitt, Richard

Levinson, Noel Carroll, Anita Silvers, and Joseph Margolis. Its conclusion is that history and philosophy must draw much closer together if they are to aid in the understanding of the problems and questions posed by the complex art cultures of the past and present.

Detlefsen, Michael. Poincaré vs Russell on the Rôle of Logic in Mathematics. *Phil Math*, 1, 24-49, Mr 93.

In the early years of this century, Poincaré and Russell engaged in a debate concerning the nature of mathematical reasoning. Siding with Kant, Poincaré argued that mathematical reasoning is characteristically non-logical in character. Russell urged the contrary view, maintaining that 1) the plausibility originally enjoyed by Kant's view was due primarily to the underdeveloped state of logic in his (i.e., Kant's) time, and that 2) with the aid of recent developments in logic, it is possible to demonstrate its falsity. This refutation of Kant's views consists in showing that every known theorem of mathematics can be proven by purely logical means from a basic set of axioms. (edited)

Detmer, David J. Response: Of Pigs and Primitive Notions. *Between Species*, 8(4), 203-208, Fall 92.

Many people believe that nonhuman animals occupy a vastly lower moral status, and thus rightly command significantly less moral consideration and respect, than do human beings. In this paper I consider and reject several popular arguments in support of this belief. I then go on to consider, and once again reject, the claim that such a belief should be accepted as intuitively obvious even if it cannot legitimately be sustained by argument. My objection is not that such an appeal to intuition is improper, however. Rather, I argue that intuition undermines conventional beliefs about the moral insignificance of animals.

Deutsch, Eliot. Community as Ritual Participation in On Community, Rouner, Leroy S (ed). Notre Dame, Univ Notre Dame Pr, 1992.

In this paper I argue, by way of an analysis of the general concepts of "ceremonial action," "power" and "nondominace" that a community is rightly established by way of the ritual participation of persons acting in a spirit of what I call "creative anarchism". This involves a non-coercive coming together of persons who share common needs and interests in a manner that aims to enhance their dignity and to achieve a celebrative harmony.

Deutsch, Eliot. The Comparative Study of the Self in Selves, People, and Persons, Rouner, Leroy S (ed). Notre Dame, Univ Notre Dame Pr, 1992.

Deutsch, Eliot. The Concept of the Body in Self as Body in Asian Theory and Practice, Kasulis, Thomas P (ed). Albany, SUNY Pr, 1992.

Deutsch, Harry. Zalta on Sense and Substitutivity. *Phil Stud*, 69(2-3), 209-219, Mr 93.

This paper raises some questions about Zalta's treatment of propositional attitudes in his book *Intensional Logic and the Metaphysics of Intentionality.*

Deutscher, Max. Forms, Qualities, Resemblance. *Philosophy*, 67(262), 523-541, O 92.

The paper questions terms current in 'neo-traditionalist' metaphysics. Plato's Socrates posited 'Forms' because he ignored diverse origins of knowledge. Nevertheless, the 'Forms' are developed to show why they dismember themselves. In contrast, neotraditionalism proceeds as if metaphysical language was sound and plain. The paper shows the twists of meaning within *quality, characteristic, property, and resemblance*. To replace *universal by resemblance*, is to treat *resemblance* as a universal. But the sense of the whole cluster—*resemblance, semblance, quality, characteristic, property and universal*—can be revised by attention to etymology, phenomenology and actual use.

Devaux, André a. On the Right Use of Contradiction According to Simone Weil in Simone Weil's Philosophy of Culture, Bell, Richard H (ed). New York, Cambridge Univ Pr, 1993.

Devereaux, Mary. Oppressive Texts, Resisting Readers and the Gendered Spectator: The *New* Aesthetics. *J Aes Art Crit*, 48(4), 337-347, Fall 90.

Traditional aesthetics has recently come under attack by feminists. "Oppressive Texts, Resisting Readers and the Gendered Spectator: The 'New' Aesthetics" examines key elements of the feminist critique of art, particularly as that critique applies to film. It seeks, first, to make clear how claims about the "male gaze" of the cinematic text are to be understood and second, to analyze the far-reaching implications of such claims for traditional aesthetics.

Devereaux, Mary. Protected Space: Politics, Censorship, and the Arts. *J Aes Art Crit*, 51(2), 207-215, Spr 93.

Current Anglo-American aesthetics is embroiled in two debates: one centered on the National Endowment for the Arts and taking place in the "real world" of politics and art; the other centered on specifically philosophical issues and taking place within the progression of aesthetics. Both debates manifest an underlying struggle between political and non-political conceptions of art. Both debates give rise to the same dilemma: forcing us to chose between *either* a formalist conception of art which protects art from the exigencies of changing political fashion but isolates art from life, *or* various political conceptions of art which integrate art with life but sacrifice its autonomy. This dilemma turns on a misunderstanding of autonomy, a misunderstanding that can, I argue, be resolved by a reconceptualization of autonomy as "protected space."

Devereux, Daniel. Theophrastus on the Intellect in Theophrastus, Fortenbaugh, W W (ed). New Brunswick, Transaction Books, 1992.

Devereux, Daniel T. Inherence and Primary Substance in Aristotle's *Categories*. *Ancient Phil*, 12(1), 113-131, Spr 92.

I argue that Aristotle is committed to 'non-substantial particulars' in the *Categories*, i.e. entities predicable of one, but not more than one, substance. I also offer an account of what Aristotle means by 'in a subject' which allows for universal as well as particular attributes to be in a subject. The key element in the account offered is using the way in which parts of a substance can exist separately (i.e., on their own) as a guide for understanding the inseparability of things 'in a subject'. Things in a subject cannot exist *on their own*, apart from the subject in which they inhere; this sort of inseparability applies to universal as well as particular attributes. Towards the end, I discuss some implications of the *Categories* doctrine that parts of primary substances (especially the soul and body) are themselves primary substances.

Devereux, Daniel T. The Unity of the Virtues in Plato's *Protagoras* and *Laches*. *Phil Rev*, 101(4), 765-789, O 92.

Devettere, Raymond. Slippery Slopes and Moral Reasoning. *J Clin Ethics*, 3(4), 297-301, Wint 92.

Devettere, Raymond J. Clinical Ethics and Happiness. *J Med Phil*, 18(1), 71-90, F 93.

Most contemporary accounts of clinical ethics do not explain why clinicians should be ethical. Those few that do attempt an explanation usually claim that clinicians should be ethical because ethical behavior provides an important good for the patient-better care. Both these approaches ignore the customary traditional reason for being ethical, namely, the good of the moral agent. This good was commonly called 'happiness'. The following article shows how the personal happiness of the moral agent provided a major reason for being ethical in the ancient philosophical and biblical traditions and how it continues to play a role in the more modern rights-based, Kantian and utilitarian theories. This history suggests that the personal happiness of the clinician, rightly understood, is a legitimate and important goal of clinical ethics.

Devine, James and Dymski, Gary. Walrasian Marxism Once Again: A Reply to Joe Roemer. *Econ Phil*, 8(1), 157-162, Ap 92.

Devitt, Michael. Localism and Analyticity. *Phil Phenomenol Res*, 53(3), 641-646, S 93.

In their discussion of semantic holism, Fodor and Lepore claim that Quine showed that any inferential properties constituting a meaning cannot be distinguished on epistemic grounds like apriority. But they often write as if Quine showed that such properties cannot be distinguished at all. The paper argues that Quine did not show the latter. It goes on to propose a criterion for distinguishing the constitutive properties: they are the ones that determine reference. Fodor is not in a position to reject this criterion since he already uses an analogous one in his own theory.

Devos, Rob. John Rawls' Ethical Foundations of Politics: A Critical Approach (in Dutch). *Bijdragen*, 53(4), 407-424, 1992.

This article is a critical analysis of John Rawls' *A Theory of Justice*. The first part argues that Rawls' concept of justice is purely procedural. The second part of the article comments on Rawls' basic principles, the principle of freedom and the principle of difference, which he justifies by referring to an amended social contract model, i.e., by deriving those principles from the original position. Our major point of criticism relates to Rawls' model. To begin with, his theory suffers from the weaknesses of every formalistic approach to ethics. A second set of problems center around the question whether Rawls' theory should not be qualified as a suggestive rhetoric rather than as a rational way of reasoning. However, the most important problem is to what extent it is possible for a social contract model, even if it has been amended, to provide a solid basis for the development of political ethics.

DeVries, Willem A. "Who Sees with Equal Eye,... Atoms or Systems into Ruin Hurl'd?". *Phil Stud*, 71(2), 191-200, Ag 93.

This paper comments on Brian McLaughlin's defense of "classical" theories of cognitive structures (also in this issue). Questions are raised about whether there are the kind of atomic capacities classicism presupposes, whether cognitive capacities are independently identifiable in the way that classicism requires, whether systematicity has been confused with generality in at least a number of cases, and what it would really mean for a connectionist system to implement a classical structure.

DeVries, Willem A. *Reality, Knowledge, and the Good Life: A Historical Introduction to Philosophy*. New York, St Martin's Pr, 1991.

Dewan, Lawrence. St Thomas, God's Goodness and God's Morality. *Mod Sch*, 70(1), 45-51, N 92.

Is God "obliged" to create anything at all? "Ought" he to create? Thomas Aquinas discusses this issue in various places, especially in *SCG* 2, 28. Is there any "*debitum*" (something owing), pertaining to the divine act of creation of reality? In the paper, I examine his teaching on this issue, using, as a means of clarifying it somewhat, remarks he makes in the context of strictly human morals, on the distinction between "legal obligation" (*debitum legale*) and the lesser "moral obligation" (*debitum morale*).

Dewan, Lawrence. St Thomas, James Ross, and Exemplarism: A Reply. *Amer Cath Phil Quart*, 65(2), 221-234, Spr 91.

Against Ross, I defend the reading of Thomas as a "photo-exemplarist". 1) Thomas, in a succession of presentations, works hard to explain that God, in knowing his own simplicity, is knowing in their distinctness a multiplicity of diverse objects; 2) God's view of never-created creatables (mere possibles) is genuinely practical, i.e., is of the things in their entire fitness for actual existence outside a mind; 3) the multitude of such divine knowns is infinite, prior to any choice to create.

Dewhurst, D W. The Teaching of Controversial Issues. *J Phil Educ*, 26(2), 153-163, 1992.

The article criticizes certain subjectivist and isolationist stances on controversial issues, and construes the teaching of controversial issues as an interpersonal task. On this view the teacher (1) encourages students to enter into the perspectives of others; (2) establishes points of contact which make reasoned discourse possible; and (3) inducts students into a wider domain where they are provided with knowledge about controversies as well as the skills for handling those controversies. All of this requires considerable intervention on the part of the teacher. Current doubts about such intervention are unjustified.

Dewhurst, David. The Appropriateness of Self-Esteem: A Response to Nesbitt and Statman. *J Moral Educ*, 22(1), 63-65, 1993.

DeWitt, Richard. Remarks on the Current Status of the Sorites Paradox. *J Phil Res*, 17, 93-118, 1992.

The past twenty or so years have seen the sorites paradox receive a good deal of philosophical air-time. Yet, in what is surely a sign of a good puzzle, no consensus has emerged. It is perhaps a good time to stop and take stock of the current status of the sorites paradox. My main contention is that the proposals offered to date as ways of blocking the paradox are seriously deficient, and hence there is, at present, no acceptable solution to the sorites. In the final section I argue that, although vagueness is the source of the threat to *modus ponens* engendered by the sorites, it is also vagueness that protects *modus ponens* from clear counterexample.

Dews, Peter 462 **AUTHOR INDEX WITH ABSTRACTS**

Dews, Peter. Foucault and the French Tradition of Historical Epistemology. *Hist Euro Ideas*, 14(3), 347-363, My 92.

The article examines the relation of Michel Foucault's work on the history of the sciences to the thought of Gaston Bachelard and Georges Cawguilhem, contrary to a widespread assumption, both Bachelard and Cawguilhem are committed to a conception of scientific progress, and Foucault therefore breaks with this tradition in adopting a relativist stance.

Dews, Peter (trans) and Rogozinski, Jacob. Hell on Earth: Hannah Arendt in the Face of Hitler. *Phil Today*, 37(3), 257-274, Fall 93.

This article considers Hannah Arendt's theory of fascism in her book on *Totalitarianism*. The modern denial of transcendence is seen as enabling fascist ideology, and the consequent drive to liquidate the 'other' is explored with the aid of psychoanalytical categories.

Dhooghe, Paul F and Peeters, Guido. The Principle of the Topical Localization of Symbols and the Meaning of the 'Ultimate Meaning'. *Ultim Real Mean*, 15(4), 296-305, D 92.

At the deep structure level of meaning topological localisation of formal symbols, which are subjected to the algebraic operations of 'accentuation' and 'denegation', are used as an ansatz for the development of a formalisation of syntagmatics and paradigmatics. The topological localisation formalises the concept of relation as primitive of 'semiotic schemes' the way they were conceived by L Hjelmslev. The topology of the localisation of the symbols imposes well-defined constraints on the semantic schemes. The development of the theory stresses denegation as a necessary step in the syntagmatic process that leads from actual understanding towards a higher level of understanding. It would follow that the furthest point we can reach in our search for the ultimate meaning will have the character of a 'neutral term'.

Di Bartolo, Luigi. Logos come fondamento: il superamento della metafisica nella riflessione heideggeriana su Leibniz. *G Metaf*, 14(3), 505-539, S-D 92.

Di Norcia, V. Knowledge, Power, and a Professional Ethic. *Bus Ethics Quart*, 3(2), 185-195, A 93.

Di Pinto, Luigia. The Archeology of Modalization in Husserl in Analecta Husserliana, XXXIV, Tymieniecka, Anna-Teresa (ed). Dordrecht, Kluwer, 1992.

Di Stefano, Anna Escher. Is There a Dichotomy in Husserl's Thought? in Analecta Husserliana, XXXIV, Tymieniecka, Anna-Teresa (ed). Dordrecht, Kluwer, 1992.

Diamond, Cora. Martha Nussbaum and the Need for Novels. *Phil Invest*, 16(2), 128-153, Ap 93.

Diamond, Cora. Response to McNaughton's 'The Importance of Being Human' in Human Beings, Cockburn, David (ed). New York, Cambridge Univ Pr, 1991.

Diamond, Cora. The Importance of Being Human—I in Human Beings, Cockburn, David (ed). New York, Cambridge Univ Pr, 1991.

DiBlasio, Margaret Klempay. The Road from Nice to Necessary: Broudy's Rationale for Art Education. *J Aes Educ*, 26(4), 21-35, Wint 92.

Dickey, Laurence. Hegel on Religion and Philosophy in The Cambridge Companion to Hegel, Beiser, Frederick C (ed). New York, Cambridge Univ Pr, 1993.

Dickie, George. Reply to Ryckman's "Dickie on Artifactuality". *J Aes Art Crit*, 47(2), 177, Spr 89.

Dickie, George T. An Artistic Misunderstanding. *J Aes Art Crit*, 51(1), 69-71, Wint 93.

Dickie, George T. Kant, Mothersill and Principles of Taste. *J Aes Art Crit*, 47(4), 375-376, Fall 89.

Dickie, Mathew W. Hermeias on Plato *Phaedrus* 238d and Synesius *Dion* 14.2. *Amer J Philo*, 114(3), 421-440, Fall 93.

Dieks, Dennis. Realism and Empiricism in Contemporary Physics. *Method Sci*, 26(2), 53-73, 1993.

The tension between realism and empiricism in the philosophy of physics is discussed. Van Fraassen's "constructive empiricism" seems suited to bridge the gap. The difficulties involved in giving a realistic interpretation of quantum mechanics are also discussed. However, the position is defended that these difficulties can be overcome, and that quantum theory is capable of the same range of philosophical interpretation as older physical theories.

Diethe, Carol. Nietzsche and Nationalism. *Hist Euro Ideas*, 14(2), 227-234, Mr 92.

I distinguish between Nietzsche's views of the state and of the nation. Nietzsche recognized the state's function of control but was more interested in how this had an impact on a nation's cultural life. At first, influenced by Wagner and by many of the tenets of Romanticism (in spite of his disclaimers), Nietzsche looked forward to the re-emergence of the German spirit, but after his rift with Wagner (1878), he set his face against the Germans and hoped Europe would provide a counter-balance to German philistinism. The final section gives an overview of the (mis)appropriation of Nietzsche's attitude to Nationalism this century.

Dietrich, Wendell S. Troeltsch's Treatment of the Thomist Synthesis. *Thomist*, 57(3), 381-402, Jl 93.

Díez Calzada, José A. Estructura y cinemática de teorías. *Agora (Spain)*, 11(1), 51-68, 1992.

This paper has a twofold aim. The main goal is to introduce, with some slight modification, the structuralist analysis of a type of diachronic phenomenon of science: the *intratheoretic* change, the evolution of theories, of each theory as time goes by; this phenomenon should be carefully distinguished from the *intertheoretic* change, i.e., the evolution of scientific disciplines by the succession of *different* theories. Although expository purpose is fundamental, it is not the only one. I believe that a correct account of the structuralist analysis of intratheoretical change is useful to correctly evaluate the relevancy of previous episodes of the metascientific reflexion. I will first develop this topic as a preface in order to frame the general metascientific context within which the structuralist analysis is to be located. (edited)

Diffey, T J. On American and British Aesthetics. *J Aes Art Crit*, 51(2), 169-175, Spr 93.

American and British philosophical aesthetics (Anglo-American aesthetics) of the last thirty years (1960-1990) are compared. The paper concludes with an analysis of the contents of the *Journal of Aesthetics and Art Criticism* (JAAC) and the *British Journal of Aesthetics* (BJA) for the decade of the 1980s.

Diffey, T J. *The Republic of Art and Other Essays*. New York, Lang, 1991.

This book brings together in a single collection eighteen of the author's papers in aesthetics on the topics of: the definability of art; the institutional theory of art; morality and literacy criticism; aesthetic judgement; value and evaluation; aesthetic experience; natural beauty; the aesthetics of Schopenhauer and of Collingwood. Sixteen of the papers have been published elsewhere between 1967 and 1993. The unpublished papers are on the perception of literature and on Collingwood's aesthetics and philosophical method (which may be published in a projected volume of papers on Collingwood).

DiGiovanni, George. The First Twenty Years of Critique in The Cambridge Companion to Kant, Guyer, Paul (ed). New York, Cambridge Univ Pr, 1992.

The reception of Kant in the first twenty years after the publication of the *Critique of Pure Reason* was to a large extent determined by the difficulty in the new critical system of mediating reflective thought with immediate experience. Kant himself tried different strategies to cope with this difficulty, and so did his would-be disciples. A crucial factor in this process of interpretation was Jacobi's attack on speculative metaphysics, which he considered as necessarily Spinozistic in character because it denied the possibility of individuality. The essay deals with such figures as Reinhold, the early Fichte and Schelling, G E Schulze, Schiller.

Diller, Ann. Pluralism for Education: An Ethics of Care Perspective. *Proc Phil Educ*, 48, 22-29, 1992.

Diller, Antoni. On the Sense of Unsaturated Expressions. *Phil Papers*, 22(1), 71-79, Ap 93.

Frege drew a distinction between two broad categories of expression, namely those that are complete or saturated and those that are unsaturated or incomplete. He also drew a distinction between three realms, namely the linguistic, the ontological and the realm of sense. In this paper two interpretations of Frege's notion of the sense of an unsaturated expression are discussed. These are Geach's, in which such a sense is seen as a function in the realm of sense, and Dummett's, in which such a sense is thought of as a pattern. It is argues that Geach's interpretation is the better one.

Dillon, M C (ed). *Merleau-Ponty Vivant*. Albany, SUNY Pr, 1991.

This is a collection of essays by M C Dillon, Edward S Casey, Duane H Davis, David Michael Levin, Alphonso Lingis, G B Madison, Joseph Margolis, Hugh J Silverman, and Jacques Taminiaux. The collection demonstrates the relevance of Merleau-Ponty's thought to main themes of philosophical discourse at the end of the twentieth century as postmodernism falls into historical perspective and contemporary thinking searches for new directions. The essays address a wide range of topics: postmodernism and deconstruction, spatiality, subjectivity, psychology, metaphysics, ethics and value theory, philosophy of art.

Dillon, Martin C. The Metaphysics of Presence in Working Through Derrida, Madison, Gary B (ed). Evanston, Northwestern Univ Pr, 1993.

This paper presents an analysis of Derrida's deconstruction of the metaphysics of presence. It attempts to show that the deconstruction comes to rest in Derrida's critique of the aporetic conception of time he sees underlying the genesis of Western onto-theology and its founding concepts of being (*ousia, Anwesen*. It then purports to show that this critique depends on a demonstrably mistaken Eleatic conception of time and its relation to being. It concludes with a resumé of the implications inherent in the differences between Derrida's conception of time and a proposed alternative.

Dillon, Robin. How to Lose Your Self-Respect. *Amer Phil Quart*, 29(2), 125-139, Ap 92.

That self-respect has great personal and moral value is clear; what is less clear is precisely what self-respect is and why it has that value. This article seeks to understand the nature and importance of self-respect by examining a wide variety of ways in which it can be lost, or otherwise lacking, damaged, or compromised. This perusal of deficiencies provides the basis for a multi partite account of self-respect; a number of varieties of self-respect are identified and discussed. The analysis further reveals self-respect to be not only richly complex but also profoundly moral, for it is tightly bound up with such morally important things as personhood, rights, agency, autonomy, responsibility, integrity, identity, and character. The article concludes with a discussion of some of the ways in which self-respect matters morally.

Dilman, Ilham. Can Philosophy Speak about Life?. *Philosophy*, 33(Supp), 109-123, 1992.

One may get the impression from Wittgenstein's work that he thinks that philosophy has nothing positive to say about anything. The paper argues that this is a misunderstanding. One doesn't always say something by making a positive statement. Wittgenstein had something to say both about the nature and treatment of the questions he discussed and their subject matter—much in the sense that great literary writers have something to say about life in what they write, though the saying takes different forms in the two cases. The paper argues that life itself can give rise to philosophical questions and that both philosophers and literary writers have something to contribute to these in their own way.

Dilman, Ilham. Can Philosophy Speak about Life? in The Impulse to Philosophise, Griffiths, A Phillips (ed). New York, Cambridge Univ Pr, 1992.

One may get the impression from Wittgenstein's work that he thinks that philosophy has nothing positive to say about anything. The paper argues that this is a misunderstanding. One doesn't always say something by making a positive statement. Wittgenstein had something to say both about the nature and treatment of the questions he discussed and their subject matter—much in the sense that great literary writers have something to say about life in what they write, though the saying takes different forms in the two cases. The paper argues that life itself can give rise to philosophical questions and that both philosophers and literary writers have something to contribute to these in their own way.

Dilman, Ilham. Sartre and Our Identity as Individuals in Human Beings, Cockburn, David (ed). New York, Cambridge Univ Pr, 1991.

Dilworth, Craig. The Linguistic Turn: Shortcut or Detour?. *Dialectica*, 46(3-4), 201-214, 1992.

The aim of this paper is to put the linguistic turn into a broader context.

Dimock, Susan. Calling all Knaves: Hume on Moral Motivation. *Eidos*, 10(2), 179-197, D 92.

A controversy has arisen in recent Hume scholarship, concerning whether or not Hume was an internalist about moral motivation. I argue here that Hume was an internalist about the natural virtues (i.e., it is a conceptual truth that the natural virtues motivate) but an externalist about the artificial virtues.

Dinan, Stephen A. The Tantalizing Absence of God. *Amer Cath Phil Quart*, 65, 87-98, 1991.

In this paper, presented at the 1991 meeting of the American Catholic Philosophical Association, I examine the nature of one's experience of God's absence and compare it to the experience of God's presence. I then argue that the experience of God's absence may have a positive dimension to it, and not merely a negative one. By opening up the possibility that God is really present but at least temporarily "out of reach," it may force the believer to reflect on his or her historicity and to critically confront the traditions within which an understanding of God and God's relationship to the world has been formed. For the traditions within which God's presence has been made known are the same traditions within which it has become possible for God's presence to be masked by evil and other phenomena which often support unbelief.

Dinan, Stephen A. Tradition, Friendship and Moral Knowledge. *Amer Cath Phil Quart*, 65(4), 445-464, Autumn 91.

In this paper I investigate the rather significant role that friendship plays in the communication of moral knowledge, a communication which takes place in the social process called "tradition." I attempt to defend the claim that without friendship, the transmission of moral knowledge in tradition, as well as the continued development of such knowledge, would be impossible. Ever since the Enlightenment criticized what it perceived to be the irrationality of tradition, the properly *cognitive* function of tradition has been largely ignored if not rejected outright. (edited)

DiNoia, J A. *The Diversity of Religions: A Christian Perspective*. Washington, Cath Univ Amer Pr, 1992.

Diosado, Concepción. La libertad como esencia de toda la realidad en el primer Schelling. *Themata*, 8, 163-172, 1991.

Since its beginning Schelling's philosophy can be regarded as a philosophy of freedom. Freedom appears in his very early works as an expression of self and nature's essence. Such a notion is understood as a principle of self-generation and activity which makes it possible for knowledge to find its right sense beyond a theoretical round.

DiQuinzio, Patrice. Exclusion and Essentialism in Feminist Theory: The Problem of Mothering. *Hypatia*, 8(3), 1-20, Sum 93.

Accounts of mothering have both contributed to feminist theory's development and depended on certain of its central concepts. Some of its critics, however, argue that feminist theory is undermined by the problems of exclusion and essentialism. Here I distinguish between these two problems and consider their implications for questions about mothering. I conclude that exclusion and essentialism do not present insurmountable obstacles to theorizing motherhood, but do suggest new directions for such theorizing.

Disch, Lisa J. More Truth Than Fact: Storytelling as Critical Understanding in the Writings of Hannah Arendt. *Polit Theory*, 21(4), 665-694, N 93.

Dissanayake, Wimal. Body in Social Theory in Self as Body in Asian Theory and Practice, Kasulis, Thomas P (ed). Albany, SUNY Pr, 1992.

Dissanayake, Wimal. Self and Body in Theravada Buddhism in Self as Body in Asian Theory and Practice, Kasulis, Thomas P (ed). Albany, SUNY Pr, 1992.

Dixon, Beth A. Gender and the Problem of Personal Identity. *Personalist Forum*, 8/1(Supp), 259-263, Spr 92.

In this paper I am concerned with how the issue of gender bears on the problem of personal identity. I present a thought experiment sometimes used to motivate the memory criterion. Then, I vary the example by changing the genders of the subjects involved, and argue that the memory criterion must be revised to accommodate this example.

Dixon, Kathleen. The Role of the Hospital in the Evolution of Elite Cultures of Medicine. *J Med Human*, 14(4), 179-201, Wint 93.

Dixon, Paul W. Classical Taoism, the *I Ching* and Our Need for Guidance. *J Chin Phil*, 20(2), 147-157, Je 93.

Classical Taoism teaches that truth is found in the One as does Parmenides in his ontogeny of being. Yet we are met with the pervasive angst which is symptomatic of the modern weltanschaung. The *I Ching*, as a work of philosophical and historical wisdom, offers a kind of projective guidance based on a 64 byte code as is also found in the periodic chart of the elements, the DNA molecule and the musical scale. It is concluded, that the *I Ching* offers a comprehensive rational — emotive and cognitive — behavioral means of guidance as a useful bridge between the immanence of being and the transitory nature of ever changing reality.

Dixsaul, Monique. "Ousia", "eidos" et "idea" dans le "Phédon". *Rev Phil Fr*, 4, 479-500, O-D 91.

Dizerega, Gus. Social Ecology, Deep Ecology, and Liberalism. *Crit Rev*, 6(2-3), 305-370, Spr-Sum 92.

Murray Bookchin unites leftist critiques of liberal democratic society with contemporary environmental concerns. His efforts fail in part by false comparisons

between markets and ecosystems. He fails to understand that these systems operate in a like fashion as self-organizing processes. In the market the self-organizing process facilitates cooperation and exchange, but also rewards instrumental relations towards natural communities. Deep ecologists correctly criticize this failure to recognize values other than instrumental. Their challenge can be incorporated in the liberal tradition extending from David Hume to F A Hayek.

Doble, Elizabeth Ann. Interweaving Feminist Frameworks. *J Aes Art Crit*, 48(4), 381-394, Fall 90.

"Interweaving Feminist Frameworks" applies feminist philosophy to the work of artist Nancy Spero. The essay illustrates how three perspectives which situate sexual difference in experience, position in discourse and psychoanalysis, can be theoretically compatible. By treating the frameworks as complements rather than as rivals, one can establish a more productive reading of images.

Dobrochotov, Alexander. Metaphysik und Herrschaft: die 'Russische Idee' als Ursprung einer Kultur des autoritären Denkens und Handelns. *Stud Soviet Tho*, 44(3), 203-209, N 92.

Dobrosavljevic, Stojan T. A Puzzle About Logical Equivalence. *Analysis*, 44(2), 67-69, Mr 84.

Dobson, John. Ethics in Financial Contracting. *Bus Prof Ethics J*, 11(3-4), 93-127, Fall-Wint 92.

This paper is concerned with the value-base of financial economics as portrayed in financial-contracting models. It addresses the question of whether financial economics has, is capable of having, or should have, a value base. First, both normative and positive arguments are presented to support the premise that theoretical finance *has* a value base, and therefore *should* consider ethical values. Second, this paper accounts for the failure of theoretical finance to consider ethics that will facilitate such consideration in the future.

Docherty, Thomas. Criticism, History, Foucault. *Hist Euro Ideas*, 14(3), 365-378, My 92.

Dodson, Kevin E. Kant's Perpetual Peace: Universal Civil Society or League of States?. *SW Phil Stud*, 15, 1-9, Spr 93.

Kant argues that the ultimate end of politics and history is the abolition of war and the establishment of a just and enduring peace. As the means of attaining this end, Kant proposes the creation of a league of states that would be dedicated to the preservation of peace among its members and their collective defense against external aggression. In this paper, I examine Kant's proposal and relate it to his conception of the social contract. It is my contention that Kant's proposed league is incompatible with the idea of the social contract, which, properly understood, requires the creation of a universal civil society.

Doeringer, Franklin M. Imaging the Imageless: Symbol and Perception in Early Chinese Thought. *J Chin Phil*, 20(1), 5-28, Mr 93.

Dokic, Jérôme. The Body in Action: the Relationship between Action, Intention and Corporal Movement (in French). *Rev Theol Phil*, 124(3), 249-270, 1992.

This is an investigation into the ontological nature of action. In opposition to the "internalist" point of view, whereby action occurs in a separate psychological world from the non-psychological changes it effects, I try to show that action is an essentially "psycho-physical"" process of control. More precisely, I draw out a natural structure of action by defining two different types of control. The description of this structure and the introduction of the general notion of control will help, I hope, to clarify how the mind can "change the world".

Dokulil, M. Through Metaphysics to Values and about Being (in Czechoslovakian). *Filozof Cas*, 39(6), 1027-1035, 1991.

Dolis, John. Narrating the Self in Analecta Husserliana, XXXI, Tymieniecka, Anna-Teresa (ed). Dordrecht, Kluwer, 1990.

Dollo, Corrado. Galilei e la fisica del Collegio Romano. *G Crit Filosof Ital*, 71(2), 161-200, My-Ag 92.

Dombrowski, Daniel. Hartshorne, Metaphysics and the Law of Moderation. *Process Stud*, 21(3), 152-165, Fall 92.

In this article the features of virtue ethics relevant to an understanding of Hartshorne's thought and the features of Hartshorne's thought relevant to an understanding of virtue ethics are examined; the virtue of moderation is the focus of the article, a virtue exhibited in Hartshorne's stance regarding abortion.

Dombrowski, Daniel. On Why Patriotism Is Not A Virtue. *Int J Applied Phil*, 7(1), 1-4, Sum 92.

In this article I dispute Alasdair MacIntyre's claim that there are good reasons for thinking that patriotism is a virtue; my defense of liberalism includes the adoption of impersonal moral standards that do not leave one a deracinated citizen of nowhere.

Dombrowski, Daniel A. Asymmetrical Relations, Identity and Abortion. *J Applied Phil*, 9(2), 161-170, 1992.

I freely use the thought of Charles Hartshorne to defend the ethical permissibility of abortion in the early stages of pregnancy. In the later stages of pregnancy the fetus has an ethical status similar to that of a sentient yet non-rational animal, a status which should generate in us considerable ethical respect. The distinctiveness of this Hartshornian approach lies in the effort to bring metaphysics to bear on a controversial issue in applied ethics. In particular, the metaphysical issue of temporal relations is crucial to consider in the effort to ascertain the ethical status of the fetus. Two symmetrical (immoderate) theories of temporal relations are criticised, one of which provides the basis for opposition to abortion, a theory wherein one is internally related both to one's past and to one's future. An asymmetrical (moderate) theory of temporal relations is defended, a theory wherein one is internally related to one's past yet externally related to the future. This latter theory would permit abortion in the early stages of pregnancy.

Domino, Brian. Vincenzo's Portrayal of Nietzsche's Socrates. *Phil Rhet*, 26(1), 39-47, 1993.

In his "Socrates and Rhetoric: The Problem of Nietzsche's Socrates," (*Philosophy and Rhetoric* 25:2), Joseph Vincenzo argues that Nietzsche uncritically accepts the inveterate portrayal of Socrates as hyper-rational. In my response, I demonstrate that Nietzsche intentionally exaggerates Socrates' rationality because he interprets Socrates as a sympton of what he calls *décadence*. As a *décadent*, Socrates lacks the volitional resources necessary to make key decisions; thus, *pace* Vincenzo, Nietzsche does not impute any moral failings onto Socrates.

Donagan, Alan. Can Anybody in a Post-Christian Culture Rationally Believe the Nicene Creed? in Christian Philosophy, Flint, Thomas P (ed). Notre Dame, Univ Notre Dame Pr, 1990.

Donagan, Alan. Sidgwick and Whewellian Intuitionism in Essays on Henry Sidgwick, Schultz, Bart (ed). New York, Cambridge Univ Pr, 1992.

Donaldson, Thomas and Gini, Al. *Case Studies in Business Ethics (Third Edition)*. Englewood Cliffs, Prentice Hall, 1993.

Donaldson, Thomas J and Werhane, Patricia H. *Ethical Issues in Business: A Philosophical Approach (Fourth Edition)*. Englewood Cliffs, Prentice Hall, 1993.

Dong, Yu. Russell on Chinese Civilization. *Russell*, 12(1), 22-49, Sum 92.

Some inaccurate, inconsistent and superficial aspects of Russell's view of Chinese tradition and culture are discussed on the basis of a brief review of some main features of this tradition. Underlying conflicts between Russell's praise of "Confucian Virtues" and his suggestions for China's social reconstruction are revealed. It is found, however, that many of his ideas and insights with respect to the development of civilizations are still valuable. One example is a methodology of evaluating traditions based on a distinction between traditions per se and traditions as restricting paradigms for social progress.

Donkel, Douglas L. *The Understanding of Difference in Heidegger and Derrida*. New York, Lang, 1992.

This study examines the complex relationship between Heidegger's concept of Difference and Derrida's neologism *Différance* in light of the problem of Being. Set in a theological context, it argues that Derrida's reflections call into question Heidegger's account of Difference, thus problematizing the *Seinsfrage* and forestalling any theological appropriation of Being. Further, it argues that Derrida's discourse on *Différance* is itself paradoxical, indicating its status is logically undecidable. Inspired by Heidegger's charge to think the Difference, this work characterizes Derrida's thought as a response to this mandate, and takes as its own task the further thinking through of the problematics of Difference in these thinkers.

Donnelly, Dorothy F and Sherman, Mark A. *Augustine's "De Civitate Dei": An Annotated Bibliography of Modern Criticism, 1960-1990*. New York, Lang, 1991.

This reference guide includes 64 modern works devoted to the study of Augustine's *De Civitate Dei* that appeared in America and Canada between 1960-1990. There are two important section which supplement the main bibliography — a group of 18 studies published in English by foreign publishers and 13 studies published prior to 1960. The entries in all three sections provide full bibliographic citations and 200- to 500-word annotations. The annotations offer a descriptive analysis of the arguments detailed in each work. The book also includes a chronologically arranged bibliography of Augustine's writings, and a selected bibliography of general studies on Augustine and his works.

Donner, Wendy. John Stuart Mill's Liberal Feminism. *Phil Stud*, 69(2-3), 155-166, Mr 93.

In this paper I defend some aspects of Mill's liberal feminism and its foundation in his utilitarian moral philosophy. Liberal feminist theories have been the subject of intense scrutiny in current debates among feminist scholars. In this paper I look at some recent critiques of liberal feminism and argue that Mill's conceptions of the self, individualism and self-development meet many of the concerns raised by critics of liberal feminism whose concerns are more correctly focused on other models of liberalism. I end with an examination of some of the problems of communitarian feminism which are mitigated by an appeal to liberal values.

Donougho, Martin J. Postmodern Jameson in Postmodernism/ Jameson/ Critique, Kellner, Douglas M (ed). Washington, Maisonneuve Pr, 1989.

Donovan, Heather Catherine. Can One Get Beyond Foundationalism and the Coherence Theory?: A Critique of Kornblith's Epistemic Account. *Dialogue (PST)*, 35(2-3), 41-46, Ap 93.

This essay scrutinizes Hilary Kornblith's normative naturalized epistemology in "Beyond Foundationalism and the Coherence Theory"; and naturalizing epistemology in general. The article argues that Kornblith creates a problematic middle ground position and he shows neither that the traditional account fails nor that naturalism must replace it. It is concluded that naturalizing results in loss of ability to talk about what constitutes a justified true belief because normativity loses meaning.

Donovan, Michael. Suspending Meaninglessness: Style, Philosophy, and the Recent Writings of Erazim Kohák. *Lyceum*, 4(2), 5-25, Fall 92.

Donovan, Peter. The Intolerance of Religious Pluralism. *Relig Stud*, 29(2), 217-229, Je 93.

In attacking a pluralistic approach to religions, defenders of "Christian uniqueness" invoke current post-modernist critiques of the Enlightenment tradition of intellectual liberalism. Pluralism, they claim, far from being religiously tolerant, is coercive and destructive of otherness. In reply, a distinction is drawn between *ideological* and *epistemic* pluralism, with the latter being argued to be entirely consistent with the post-modernists' viewpoint, despite their apparently anti-liberal rhetoric. The anti-pluralism stance is, however, a timely reminder that few participants in interreligious dialogue are likely to share the liberal's view of the priority of epistemic over other considerations.

Donskikh, O A and Kochergin, A N. Do We Have a Scientific Conception of the History of Philosophy? Polemical Notes. *Russian Stud Phil*, 31(1), 26-47, Sum 92.

Doody, John A. MacIntyre and Habermas on the Practical Reason. *Amer Cath Phil Quart*, 65(2), 143-158, Spr 91.

Dooley, Patrick K. *The Pluralistic Philosophy of Stephen Crane*. Champaign, Univ of Illinois Pr, 1993.

Stephen Crane (1871-1900) noted novelist and celebrated journalist was a thinker who absorbed and reacted to an agenda of intellectual issues that other nineteenth-century Americans confronted. In the process his poetry and prose engaged the issues that his philosopher counterparts addressed. Accordingly, this study is an exposition and analysis of his philosophy from a consideration of his entire body of work — early, middle and late, novels, sketches, short stories, news dispatches, and poems. Although the criterion for selection has been a work's underlying philosophical content, countless items in the Crane corpus proved worthy of both literary and philosophical study. The book aims at a sustained, direct discussion of Crane's philosophy as well as consideration of his remarkable observations on philosophical matters.

Doppelt, Gerald. The Moral Limits of Feinberg's Liberalism. *Inquiry*, 36(3), 255-286, S 93.

This essay explores Joel Feinberg's conception of liberalism and the moral limits of criminal law. Feinberg identifies liberty with the absence of law. He defends a strong liberal presumption against law, except where it is necessary to prevent wrongful harm or offense to others. Drawing on Rawlsian, Marxian, and feminist standpoints, I argue that there are injuries to individual liberty rooted not in law, but in civil society. Against Feinberg, I defend a richer account of liberalism and liberty, linking them to human dignity, and a more positive role for law.

Doran, Robert M (ed) and Crowe, Frederick E (ed). *Collected Works of Bernard Lonergan, V10*. Toronto, Univ of Toronto Pr, 1993.

Topics in Education, volume 10 of Collected Works of Bernard Lonergan, presents an edited transcript of ten lectures on the philosophy of education delivered by Lonergan at Xavier University, Cincinnati, in 1959. The task Lonergan sets himself is to develop an alternative to traditionalist and modernist notions of education. The context is set by an extensive analysis of the human good and of the 'new learning' first in mathematics and science and then in the study of the human subject. The basis of the alternative lies in the theory of operations that Lonergan's major works have presented. On this basis Lonergan also engages Piaget and presents his views on art and history.

Doria, F A and Da Costa, N C A. On the Existence of Very Difficult Satisfiability Problems. *Bull Sec Log*, 21(4), 122-133, D 92.

We present some results on undecidability and incompleteness in the theory of computability. Our basic tool is the concept of complexity in the sense of Kolmogorov, Chaitin and Manin.

Doria, Francisco Antonio and Da Costa, N C A. On the Incompleteness of Axiomatized Models for the Empirical Sciences. *Philosophica*, 50(2), 73-100, 1992.

This is an expository paper in which we discuss our recent results on the incompleteness and undecidability of physical theories, in particular of Hamiltonian mechanics and chaos theory.

Dorling, Jon. Bayesian Conditionalization Resolves Positivist/Realist Disputes. *J Phil*, 89(7), 362-382, Jl 92.

Dorn, Georg J W. Inductive Support in Advances in Scientific Philosophy, Schurz, Gerhard (ed). Amsterdam, Rodopi, 1991.

The Popper/Miller anti-induction proof of 1983 is reconstructed within an axiomatic theory of genuine inductive support. The reconstruction is discussed with special attention to relevance criteria.

Dorn, Georg J W (ed) and Schurz, Gerhard (ed). *Advances in Scientific Philosophy*. Amsterdam, Rodopi, 1991.

Papers in honor of Paul Weingartner's 60th Birthday. I, "Advances in Philosophical Logic", relevance logic (Sylvan and Nola, B Smith, Schurz), epistemic logic (Dalla Chiara, Gochet and Gillet, Festini), temporal and intuitionistic logics (Aqvist, Orlowska, Lenzen); II, "Current Challenges in Philosophy of Science", a section of Objectivity in Quantum Mechanics (Enz, Mittlestaedt, Scheibe), Reduction and Unification (Stöckler, Kanitscheider, Haller), the structuralist view of theories (Przelecki, Kuipers, Moulines) and probability (Popper, Dorn); III, "Recent Debates in Semantic and Ontology" (Kutschera, Simons, Morscher, Brandl, Hieke); IV, "Epistemological and Ethical Problems with Society" (Klevakina, Tuomela, Lenk and Maring, Heumaier, Bencivenga); V, "Analytical Philosophy of Religion (Bochenski, Nieznanski, Ganthaler); VI, "Methods of Philosophy" (Kreisel, Bunge, Koj); VII, a bio- and bibliography of Weingartner.

Dorschel, Andreas. Über die Rationalität von Prozeduren und Resultaten. *Int Stud Phil*, 24(3), 1-14, 1992.

The subject of this paper is the rationality of procedures on the one hand and of results on the other hand. Its particular interest is the significance of the incongruity between both with regard to ethics. Procedural rationality cannot be defined in terms of the rationality of results; rather a procedure is rational if it is in accordance with a certain rational principle. Although it seems thoroughly possible that irrational procedures can lead to results which are more rational than the results of rational procedures, I try to show that there is a kind of precedence of procedural rationality over the rationality of results, because *that* a result is rational can only be found out by way of a rational procedure.

Dorsey, Gray L. *Jurisculture: China*. New Brunswick, Transaction Books, 1993.

In this volume, Dorsey extends to China his comparative, historical study of the organization and regulation of societies in relation to prevailing views of reality. He finds that from the Han dynasties (202BCE-220CE) until the present century, the Chinese ideal society was a balance of power, interest and morality as understood in a unique Chinese consciousness that had been developing from earliest times. He traces the development of that consciousness, taking into account the extensive archaeological discoveries of this century and the monumental work of Joseph Needham on Chinese science.

Dorter, Kenneth N. Conceptual Truth and Aesthetic Truth. *J Aes Art Crit*, 48(1), 37-51, Wint 90.

Dorter, Kenneth N. Nussbaum on Transcendence in Plato and Aristotle. *Dialogue (Canada)*, 32(1), 105-116, Wint 93.

Nussbaum argues for welcoming life's messy conflicts rather than placing some values above others. Aristotle and Plato are the respective champions of these alternatives: Plato lovelessly advocates inflexible utilitarian rules, while Aristotle champions pluralism and humanism. But Nussbaum approaches these philosophers in precisely the manner that she rejects for life itself, reducing each to a one-dimensional principle and ignoring the "messy conflicts" that other parts of their texts create for her principle. She completely ignores the humane side of Plato's thought in order to paint him as cold and controlling, and either ignores or dismisses the transcendent side of Aristotle's thought in order to paint him as humanistic and pluralistic in a Sartrean sense.

Dosen, Kosta. Rudimentary Kripke Models for the Intuitionistic Propositional Calculus. *Annals Pure Applied Log*, 62(1), 21-49, Je 93.

Dosen, Kosta. The First Axiomatization of Relevant Logic. *J Phil Log*, 21(4), 339-356, N 92.

This is a review, with historical and critical comments, of a paper by I E Orlov form 1928, which gives the oldest known axiomatization of the implication-negation fragment of the relevant logic R Orlov's paper also foreshadows the modal translation of systems with an intuitionistic negation into S4-type extensions of systems with a classical, involutive, negation. Orlov introduces the modal postulates of S4 before Becker, Lewis and Gödel. Orlov's work, which seems to be nearly completely ignored, is related to the contemporaneous work on the axiomatization of intuitionistic logic.

Dostal, Robert J. Friendship and Politics: Heidegger's Failing. *Polit Theory*, 20(3), 399-423, Ag 92.

Heidegger's philosophy is not solipsistically antisocial. Communality is essential to being human. Yet the way he characterizes communality ("Being-with", *Mitsein*) is incompatible with an appropriate politics because he inadequately provides for friendship in the strong sense as well as for the necessary and important political relationships between citizens. This failing becomes clear if we compare Heidegger's understanding of living- together with Aristotle on friendship and politics and to Plato's critique of the statesman as shepherds. Both Heidegger and Plato suggest that this is importantly a religious role. Heidegger, unlike Plato and Aristotle, reduces the political to the religious.

Dostal, Robert J. Time and Phenomenology in Husserl and Heidegger in The Cambridge Companion to Heidegger, Guignon, Charles B (ed). New York, Cambridge Univ Pr, 1993.

This paper presents a general overview of the theme of time in the phenomenologies of Husserl and Heidegger. This paper shows how Heidegger's account of time and temporality in *Being and Time* both follows Husserl's account and differs from it. The paper argues that Heidegger's early project gets caught up in methodological and ontological problems similar to those in Husserl's philosophy. Of particular importance for this account are the concepts of nature and extantness.

Double, Richard. How Rational Must Free Will Be?. *Metaphilosophy*, 23(3), 268-278, Jl 92.

The metaphilosophical view that there exists, or at least could exist, a unified class of choices that are designated by the term "free will" is challenged. By examining a wide range of examples, it is argued that sometimes we place high demands upon the practical reasoning that produces free will, but sometimes we think that such demands are unwarranted. Hence, by attending to the question of how satisfactory practical reasoning must be to produce free will, we can see that no non-contradictory account can capture our intuitions regarding freedom, and that "free will" has no specifiable criteria of application. Hence, there can be no such class of entities as free choices.

Double, Richard. The Principle of Rational Explanation Defended. *S J Phil*, 31(2), 133-142, Sum 93.

I reply to two criticisms of my Principle of Rational Explanation (PRE) provided by Robert Kane and Randolph Clarke. I show that this principle, though in need of clarification, is undefeated by these critics. PRE is not established, however; I also show that the views underlying the criticisms of PRE that Kane and Clarke make cannot be refuted. This impasse over PRE turns out to be an important fact about the free will debate, one that lends support to my radical thesis (developed in *The Non-Reality of Free Will*, Oxford University Press, 1991) that both compatibilist and incompatibilist accounts of free will and moral responsibility are bound to fail.

Dougherty, Daniel J. Closed Categories and Categorial Grammar. *Notre Dame J Form Log*, 34(1), 36-49, Wint 93.

Inspired by Lambek's work on categorial grammar, we examine the proposal that the theory of biclosed monoidal categories can serve as a foundation for a formal theory of natural language. The emphasis throughout is on the derivation of the axioms for these categories from linguistic intuitions. When Montague's principle that there is a homomorphism between syntax and semantics is refined to the principle that meaning is a functor between a syntax-category and a semantics-category, the fundamental properties of biclosed categories induce a rudimentary computationally oriented theory of language.

Dougherty, Jude P. Christian Philosophy: Sociological Category or Oxymoron?. *Monist*, 75(3), 283-290, Jl 92.

The first thesis to be entertained here can be set forth simply. To address the question, "Is there Christian philosophy?", it is necessary, first, to acknowledge that there is no such thing as "Christianity". As a sociological category "Christianity" may have some content. People the world over profess to be Christian. But, when we look to the content of belief we find so little in common between professed Christians that the designation becomes almost meaningless. The second is that, logically and chronologically, philosophy is prior to Christianity.

Douglass, Paul. Deleuze's Bergson: Bergson Redux in The Crisis in Modernism, Burwick, Frederick (ed). New York, Cambridge Univ Pr, 1992.

This essay examines the use to which Deleuze has put Bergsonian ideas in his *Bergsonism* and *Cinema* volumes. It views his film theory as both a critique and an *apologia*—one that purports to out-Bergson Bergson. The essay shows how Deleuze adapted Bergonian ideas of intuition and time and the "self" for his own purposes. It contends that through Bergson, Deleuze found a "deconstructive method."

Douglass, Paul (ed) and Burwick, Frederick (ed). *The Crisis in Modernism*. New York, Cambridge Univ Pr, 1992.

Doull, Floy Andrews. Leibniz's Logical System of 1686-1690. *Theoria (Spain)*, 6(14-15), 9-28, O 91.

Logical works of this period, beginning with *Generales Inquisitiones* and ending with the two dated pieces of August 1, 1690 and August 2, 1690, are read as a sustained effort, finally successful, to develop a set of axioms and an appropriate schema for the expression of categorical propositions faithful to traditional syllogistic. This same set of axioms is shown to be comprehensive of the propositional calculus of *Principia Mathematica*, providing that 'some A is A' is not a *thesis* in an unrestricted sense. There is no indication in the works of this period that Leibniz understood just how significant is this logical system he developed. But it is undeniable that he held tenaciously to this particular set of axioms throughout the period, a set of axioms of great power.

Dowe, Phil. On the Reduction of Process Causality to Statistical Relations. *Brit J Phil Sci*, 44(2), 325-327, Je 93.

Papineau's (1989) defense of the possibility of reducing causal relations to statistical relevance relations is contested. Papineau's claim is that alleged counterexamples to this reduction (where particular 'causes' lower the probability of their 'effects') are not cases of cause and effect, but cases where the second event occurs *despite* the first. Implausibly, this entails that a mechanism, relevantly similar to a causal mechanism, is nevertheless not causal.

Dowe, Phil. Process Causality and Asymmetry. *Erkenntnis*, 37(2), 179-196, S 92.

Process theories of causality seek to explicate causality as a property of individual causal processes. This paper examines the capacity of such theories to account for the asymmetry of causation. Three types of theories of asymmetry are discussed; the subjective, the temporal, and the physical, the third of these being the preferred approach. Asymmetric features of the world, namely the entropic and Kaon arrows, are considered as possible sources of causal asymmetry and a physical theory of asymmetry is subsequently developed with special reference to the questions of objectivity and backwards causation.

Dowe, Phil. Wesley Salmon's Process Theory of Causality and the Conserved Quantity Theory. *Phil Sci*, 59(2), 195-216, Je 92.

This paper examines Wesley Salmon's "process" theory of causality, arguing in particular that there are four areas of inadequacy. The theory is circular, that it is too vague at a crucial point, that statistical forks do not serve their intended purpose, and that Salmon has not adequately demonstrated that the theory avoids Hume's structures about "hidden powers". A new theory is suggested, based on "conserved quantities", which fulfills Salmon's broad objectives, and which avoids the problems discussed.

Dower, Nigel. Sustainability and the Right to Development in International Justice and the Third World, Attfield, Robin (ed). New York, Routledge, 1992.

Is there, as the United Nations Declaration of 1986 suggests, a right to development? On the face of it, if development is a process whereby more people achieve their basic rights, it would appear "yes." But if there are limits on development, imposed by environmental problems and the need for sustainability, there can be no right to development if its definition is left to nation-states and their governments. A limited right to development, based on cosmopolitan rather than internationalist principles, is defended.

Dowling, Keith W. Sartre's Student and the Captain of the HMS Indomitable. *S Afr J Phil*, 12(1), 1-5, F 93.

Some time ago, both A MacIntyre and P Winch offered examples of ostensibly moral judgements—those that result in the context of moral dilemmas—which they claimed do not require universalization. Their claims have been hotly disputed in the philosophical literature yet never completely defeated. The problem with most of the objections, as I will show in this paper, is that both MacIntyre's and Winch's case against the universalizability rule can be stated independently of them. There is one point in this debate however that has been overlooked. If in certain moral dilemmas there are no universalizable grounds for judging between conflicting courses of action A or B, (as MacIntyre and Winch claim), then this *does* imply a universalizable meta-moral judgment, namely, 'In such cases no one should make a judgment in favor of either courses A or B.' Even in these difficult cases, one way or another we are constrained by the universalizability rule.

Downes, Stephen M. Socializing Naturalized Philosophy of Science. *Phil Sci*, 60(3), 452-468, S 93.

I propose an approach to naturalized philosophy of science that takes the social nature of scientific practice seriously. I criticize several prominent naturalistic approaches for adopting "cognitive individualism", which limits the study of science to an examination of the internal psychological mechanisms of scientist. I argue that this limits the explanatory capacity of these approaches. I then propose a three-level model of the social nature of scientific practice, and use the model to defend the claim that scientific knowledge is socially produced.

Downes, Stephen M. The Importance of Models in Theorizing: A Deflationary Semantic View. *Proc Phil Sci Ass*, 1, 142-153, 1992.

I critically examine the semantic view of theories to reveal the following results. First, models in science are not the same as models in mathematics, as holders of the semantic view claim. Second, when several examples of the semantic approach are examined in detail no common thread is found between them, except their close attention to the details of model building in each particular science. These results lead me to propose a deflationary semantic view, which is simply that model construction is an important component of theorizing in science. This deflationary view is consistent with a naturalized approach to the philosophy of science.

Downey, James Patrick. On Omniscience. *Faith Phil*, 10(2), 230-234, Ap 93.

Traditionally, omniscience has been taken to imply knowing all true propositions. Recently, it has been suggested that there are some true propositions that God cannot possibly know. There may well be propositional content in certain knowledge of "what it is like." For instance, we may be able to fill in the blank in 'Being ignorant is like _____' so that this expresses a true proposition. Selmer Bringsjord has considered certain assumptions about what is required in order to have such knowledge, and has suggested that having this knowledge is not logically possible for God. Paralleling revised definitions of omnipotence, he suggests re-defining omniscience in terms of what God can possibly know. I argue that on the assumptions he considers, this new definition will still require that God do what it is logically impossible that God do. I suggest that the assumptions be questioned.

Downey, Rod. Every Recursive Boolean Algebra is Isomorphic to One with Incomplete Atoms. *Annals Pure Applied Log*, 60(3), 193-206, My 93.

The theorem of the title is proven, solving an old question of Remmel. The method of proof uses an algebraic technique of Remmel-Vaught combined with a complex tree of strategies argument where the true path is needed to figure out the final isomorphism.

Downey, Rod and Cholak, Peter. Lattice Nonembeddings and Intervals of the Recursively Enumerable Degrees. *Annals Pure Applied Log*, 61(3), 195-221, Je 93.

Let b and c be r.e. Turing degrees such that b c. We show that there is an r.e. degree a such that b a c and all lattices containing a critical triple, including the lattice 1-3-1, cannot be embedded into the interval [c,a].

Downey, Rod and Stob, M. Friedberg Splittings of Recursively Enumerable Sets. *Annals Pure Applied Log*, 59(3), 175-199, F 93.

Properties of the automorphism group of the lattice of recursively enumerable sets are studied. In particular, the authors analyse interactions of the degrees, automorphisms and Friedberg splittings.

Downing, David B (ed) and Bazargan, Susan (ed). *Image and Ideology in Modern/PostModern Discourse*. Albany, SUNY Pr, 1991.

This book addresses the function and status of the visual and verbal image as it relates to social, political, and ideological issues. The authors first articulate some of the lost connections between image and ideology, then locate their argument within the modernist/postmodernist debates. They examine the multiple, trans-disciplinary problems arising from the ways cultures, authors, and texts mobilize particular images in order to confront, conceal, work through, or resolve contradictory ideological conditions. The book contains seventeen essays, many by such well-known critics as W J T Mitchell, Jean Baudrillard, Kristina Straud, Richard Pearce, and others.

Downing, Fred. Refusing to Draw the Circle Around 'the Self': The Quest for Community in the Work of Basehart and Berenson. *Personalist Forum*, 8/1(Supp), 187-189, Spr 92.

Downing, Lyle and Thigpen, Robert B. The Place of Neutrality in Liberal Political Theory in Terrorism, Justice and Social Values, Peden, Creighton W (ed). Lewiston, Mellen Pr, 1990.

Doyle, David. The Justice of Mercy in Analecta Husserliana, XXXI, Tymieniecka, Anna-Teresa (ed). Dordrecht, Kluwer, 1990.

Doyle, John P. Suárez and the Unity of a Scientific Habit. *Amer Cath Phil Quart*, 65(3), 311-334, Sum 91.

Draaisma, Douwe. Het visuele argument in de 'psychical research'. *Kennis Methode*, 17(1), 30-55, 1993.

Drabinski, John. Husserl's Critique of Empiricism and the Phenomenological Account of Reflection. *SW Phil Rev*, 9(1), 91-104, Ja 93.

The purpose of this essay is to give an exposition of Husserl's phenomenological account of reflection within the context of his critique of traditional empiricism. Out of this context, Husserl clearly distinguishes his account of reflection from the traditional characterization of reflection as inner-perception. Against the empiricist tradition, Husserl's conception of reflection is shown to characterize its reflected objects in terms of the descriptive marks of the thematized object, manifest in the reflective turn, thus freeing his conception of reflection from the metaphysical pre-suppositions of the tradition.

Drabinski, John E. Radical Empiricism and Phenomenology: Philosophy and the Pure Stuff of Experience. *J Speculative Phil*, 7(3), 226-242, 1993.

Drabkin, Douglas. The Nature of God's Love and Forgiveness. *Relig Stud*, 29(2), 231-238, Je 93.

1) I suggest that God, a being good in the best possible combination of ways, loves us by promoting our true good — the moral life — while being disposed to feel joy when we are good, and sorrow when we are evil. I defend this view against Creel, who argues that God cannot suffer, since suffering is neither intrinsically good nor good in virtue of its consequences. 2) I argue, against Minas, that God will forgive us, by feeling joy on our account and ceasing to suffer, provided we repent and commit to becoming good. 3) I argue that emotional change is compatible with omniscience.

Drahos, Peter and Parker, Stephen. Rule Following, Rule Scepticism and Indeterminacy in Law: A Conventional Account. *Ratio Juris*, 5(1), 109-119, Mr 92.

Genuine rule scepticism, the paper claims, has not been developed within traditional legal philosophy. Recently within general philosophy, however, Saul Kripke has proposed an argument which attempts to show that rules do not exist. The paper discusses one possible solution to Kripke's attack on rules and then considers how this solution helps to illuminate the vital role of conventions in legal reasoning. Finally, the paper considers how the systems thinking of Luhmann might help us to come to a better understanding of the role of conventions in law.

Draper, George. Fairness and Self-Defense. *Soc Theor Pract*, 19(1), 73-92, Spr 93.

Draper, Paul. God and Perceptual Evidence. *Int J Phil Relig*, 32(3), 149-165, D 92.

Many theists have nonsensory but phenomenologically perceptual experiences that they believe to be genuine perceptions of God. The perceptual character of these "theistic experiences" gives rise to at least two different arguments for God's existence. One of these is based on the premise that the analogy between theistic experiences and sense experiences is very close. The other is based on the principle that perceptual experiences are, epistemologically speaking, "innocent until proven guilty." I show that neither of these arguments is successful and, more generally, that theistic experiences do not by themselves make God's existence more probable than not.

Draper, Paul. Probabilistic Arguments From Evil. *Relig Stud*, 28(3), 303-317, S 92.

Many philosophers claim that, although the evil in the world doesn't prove that (traditional) theism is false, it does make the falsity of theism probable. Alvin Plantinga challenges these philosophers to support this claim—to establish by argument that theism is improbable on some true statement about evil. I examine two different strategies for attempting to meet Plantinga's challenge, one used by most contemporary proponents of arguments from evil against theism and one used by David Hume in Part XI of *Dialogues Concerning Natural Religion*. I defend the position that Hume's strategy is the more promising of the two.

Dravid, N S. Reply to Chakrabarti: Some Comments on Contraposition in European and Indian Logic. *Int Phil Quart*, 32(4), 515-518, D 92.

Dray, W H. Comment and Publications in Objectivity, Method and Point of View, Van Der Dussen, W J (ed). Leiden, Brill, 1991.

Dray, W H. Historicity, Historicism, and Self-Making in German Philosophy and Jewish Thought, Greenspan, Louis (ed). Toronto, Univ of Toronto Pr, 1992.

Dray, William H. *Philosophy of History (Second Edition)*. Englewood Cliffs, Prentice Hall, 1993.

Drees, Martin. Evolution and Emanation of Spirit in Hegel's *Philosophy of Nature*. *Bull Hegel Soc Gt Brit*, 26, 52-61, Autumn-Wint 92.

Dreier, James. Structures of Normative Theories. *Monist*, 76(1), 22-40, Ja 93.

The paper investigates the structure of normative theories, in particular the contrasts between agent-centered and agent-neutral theories and between consequentialist and non-consequentialist theories. It argues that the first distinction is a more proper focus of contrast. Mistaking one contrast for the other leads to significant logical errors, especially in arguments against allegedly non-consequentialist theories. Second, the paper suggests that the best hope for adjudicating disputes between agent-neutral theories and agent-centered ones is to be found in one or another meta-ethical perspective. Three meta-ethical theories (Ideal Observer, Contractualism, and Virtue Theory) are investigated as examples.

Dreisbach, Christopher. *R G Collingwood: A Bibliographic Checklist*. Bowling Green, Philosophy Doc Ctr, 1993.

Drengson, Alan R. A Critique of Deep Ecology? Response to William Grey in Applied Philosophy, Almond, Brenda (ed). New York, Routledge, 1992.

William Grey criticized the environmental philosophy of supporters of the deep ecology movement for having an inadequate critique of the source of environmental degradation-destruction, and also for their alternative philosophy based on ecosophy, i.e., ecological harmony and wisdom. This article is a defense of the use of paradigm shifts in ecophilosophical analysis in support of the deep ecology movement. It presents a strong defense of a nonanthropocentric, ecological philosophy of (ecocentric) values and practices. A longer version, which goes into the institutional role of science, is available from the author.

Dretske, Fred. Can Intelligence Be Artificial?. *Phil Stud*, 71(2), 201-216, Ag 93.

Intelligence requires, as a minimal condition, the governance of action by thought. What it means for thought to govern action is that meaning or content, *what it is one thinks*, figures in the explanation of the behavior. What rationalizes the act must explain the act. It is impossible, therefore, to build intelligent systems unless one can make meaning or content do some causal work in the determination of output. This, though, seems impossible with machines. Without the right history, meaning is irrelevant. With the right history, we no longer have a machine.

Dretske, Fred. Mental Events as Structuring Causes of Behavior in Mental Causation, Heil, John (ed). New York, Clarendon/Oxford Pr, 1993.

Causal explanations can be broadly classified into those that cite *triggering* causes and those that cite *structuring* causes. A structuring cause brings about conditions that enable triggering causes to be effective. Wiring a button to a bell (structuring cause) causes depression of the button (triggering cause) to ring the bell. Wiring the button to the bell, then is a structuring cause of bell-ringing. Psychological explanations of behavior, those that cite an agent's reasons for behaving, are structuring explanations of behavior. They explain, not why the body moves the way it does, but why certain internal events cause the body to move the way it does.

Dretske, Fred. The Nature of Thought. *Phil Stud*, 70(2), 185-199, My 93.

Some have argued that thought has a social character—that thought cannot exist unless there also exists other conscious beings. While endorsing an externalist view of content according to which the content of thoughts is extrinsic to the thinker, it is argued that the relations underlying content need not be relations to other conscious beings. A learning episode is described in which (it is claimed) an animal acquires a capacity to represent (think about?) the objects it perceives without the need for other beings.

Dretske, Fred. Two Conceptions of Knowledge: Rational versus Reliable Belief. *Grazer Phil Stud*, 40, 15-30, 1991.

There are two ways to think about knowledge: From the *bottom-up* point of view, knowledge is an early arrival on the evolutionary scene; it is what animals need in order to coordinate their behavior with the environmental conditions. The *top-down* approach, departing from Descartes, considers knowledge constituted by a justified belief which gains its justification only in so far as the process by means of which it is reached conforms to canons of scientific inference and rational theory choice. Keith Lehrer's epistemology is analyzed as a *top-down* internalist position and criticised with examples that show that in certain cases obviously knowledge is attained without meeting the standards for reliability of sources and processing of the required information.

Dretske, Frederick. Conscious Experience. *Mind*, 102(406), 263-283, Ap 93.

Perceptual awareness of things (seeing a tree) involves experience, but not necessarily belief. Perceptual awareness of facts (seeing that it is a tree), on the other hand, essentially involves belief. On this basis it is argued that there can be aspects of conscious experience of which a person is not conscious. This, in turn, implies that what makes a mental state conscious—and, hence, what it means for a mental state to be conscious—is not some higher order consciousness of it.

Dretske, Frederick. What Isn't Wrong with Folk Psychology. *Metaphilosophy*, 23(1-2), 1-13, Ja-Ap 92.

Folk psychology regards human beings (and some animals) as extrinsic systems—systems whose behavior (some of it anyway) is explained by content, an extrinsic property that does not supervene on the physical constitution of the system whose behavior is being explained. It is argued that there is nothing scientifically wrong or (even) unusual about this form of explanation. The behavior of artifacts and plants is often explained in exactly the same way. This, then, is something that is *not* wrong with folk psychology.

Dreyfus, Hubert and Wakefield, Jerome. Intentionality and the Phenomenology of Action in John Searle and His Critics, Lepore, Ernest (ed). Cambridge, Blackwell, 1991.

Dreyfus, Hubert L. Between Man and Nature. *Harvard Rev Phil*, 1(1), 6-19, Spr 91.

Dreyfus, Hubert L. Heidegger on the Connection between Nihilism, Art, Technology, and Politics in The Cambridge Companion to Heidegger, Guignon, Charles (ed). New York, Cambridge Univ Pr, 1993.

Dreyfus, Hubert L. Heidegger's History of the Being of Equipment in Heidegger: A Critical Reader, Dreyfus, Hubert L (ed). Cambridge, Blackwell, 1992.

Dreyfus, Hubert L. *What Computers "Still" Can't Do: A Critique of Artificial Reason (Rev Ed)*. Cambridge, MIT Pr, 1992.

Dreyfus, Hubert L and Dreyfus, Stuart E. What is Moral Maturity? Towards a Phenomenology of Ethical Expertise in Revisioning Philosophy, Ogilvy, James (ed). Albany, SUNY Pr, 1992.

Dreyfus, Hubert L (ed) and Hall, Harrison (ed). *Heidegger: A Critical Reader*. Cambridge, Blackwell, 1992.

Dreyfus, Stuart E and Dreyfus, Hubert L. What is Moral Maturity? Towards a Phenomenology of Ethical Expertise in Revisioning Philosophy, Ogilvy, James (ed). Albany, SUNY Pr, 1992.

Driver, Julia. Caesar's Wife: On the Moral SIgnificance of Appearing Good. *J Phil*, 89(7), 331-343, Jl 92.

Driver, Julia. The Suberogatory. *Austl J Phil*, 70(3), 286-295, S 92.

Drover, Glen and Kerans, Patrick. Wellbeing and Everyday Practice: Theorizing Claimsmaking. *Praxis Int*, 13(2), 172-191, Jl 93.

Drozdek, Adam. Computers and the Mind-Body Problem: On Ontological and Epistemological Dualism. *Ideal Stud*, 23(1), 39-48, Wint 93.

There seems to exist an indirect link between computer science and theology via psychology, which is founded on dualism. First, these theories from psychology, computer science and theology are considered that acknowledge the existence of (at least) two different kinds of reality, or, possibly, two different realms of the same reality. In order to express a root of incompatibility of science and theology, a distinction is drawn between ontological and epistemological dualism. It seems that computer science combines ontological monism with epistemological monism, theology combines ontological and epistemological dualism, and psychology takes a position of epistemological monism and is quite hesitant about the ontological status of the phenomena it analyzes. A direct transition from the computer metaphor to theology is almost impossible: there is no overlap of platforms between these domains.

Drucker, Thomas (ed). *Perspectives on the History of Mathematical Logic*. Basel, Birkhauser, 1991.

Drum, Peter. Aquinas and the Moral Status of Animals. *Amer Cath Phil Quart*, 66(4), 483-488, Autumn 92.

Drum, Peter. Religion and Self-Interest. *Sophia (Australia)*, 32(2), 50-53, Jl 93.

In *Reasons and Persons*, Derek Parfit claims that Christian writers — and almost all of the other principal religious traditions — accept the self-interested theory of rational action. I argue that this is not the case at least in respect to the theory of rational action of one important Christian writer, namely St Thomas Aquinas.

Drum, Peter. The Intrinsic Value of Pain. *Sophia (Australia)*, 31(1-2), 97-99, 1992.

Dubiel, Helmut. Domination or Emancipation? in Cultural-Political Interventions in the Unfinished Project of Enlightenment, Honneth, Axel (& other eds). Cambridge, MIT Pr, 1992.

Ducharme, H M. Can a Person be Happily Wicked? (Some Problems with Joel Feinberg's Contended Moral Defective). *Personalist Forum*, 8/1(Supp), 281-284, Spr 92.

Feinberg argues that a person can be happily wicked; that one can be flourishing, fulfilled and content in being wicked. He offers three arguments to support the position that harm to self is wholly want-regarding concept: 1) Platonic moral sickness of the soul cannot be presupposed, 2) there are actual cases of remorselessly wicked, flourishing people, and 3) flourishing and harm can be reduced, without any moral remainder, to want-fulfillment and want-frustration. These three arguments are briefly evaluated.

Dudman, V H. A Popular Presumption Refuted. *J Phil*, 89(8), 431-440, Ag 92.

Dudman, V H. Probability and Assertion. *Analysis*, 52(4), 204-211, O 92.

It is urged that 'assertibility', whether of atomic statements or 'indicative conditionals', is unrelated to high subjective probability. For each case a situation is described in which a given sentence is found to be unassertible despite enormous probability. In the course of this it emerges that 'Someone will shoot Kennedy; therefore if Oswald does not shoot Kennedy someone else will' is not a valid argument.

Duerlinger, James. Reductionist and Nonreductionist Theories of Persons in Indian Buddhist Philosophy. *J Indian Phil*, 21(1), 79-101, Mr 93.

Düsing, Klaus. C'è un circolo dell'autocoscienza? Uno schizzo delle posizioni paradigmatiche e dei modelli di autocoscienza da Kant a Heidegger. *Teoria*, 12(1), 3-29, 1992.

Dufour, Adrian. Ontología del cambio. *Anu Filosof*, 25(2), 379-388, 1992.

Through an analysis of change based in the logical laws of Contradiction and of Excluded Middle, it's possible to demonstrate that the existence of the total state of the world at the present instant does not derive directly from the states of the world of any previous instant.

Dula, Annette. Yes, There Are African-American Perspectives on Bioethics in African-American Perspectives on Biomedical Ethics, Flack, Harley E (ed). Washington, Georgetown Univ Pr, 1992.

Dulckeit, Katharina. Hegel's Revenge on Russell in Hegel and His Critics, Desmond, William J (ed). Albany, SUNY Pr, 1989.

Dummett, Michael. The Metaphysics of Verificationism in The Philosophy of A J Ayer, Hahn, Lewis E (ed). Peru, Open Court, 1992.

Dumont, Stephen. The *Propositio Famosa Scoti*: Duns Scotus and Ockham on the Possibility of a Science of Theology. *Dialogue (Canada)*, 31(3), 415-429, Sum 92.

Dumouchel, Paul. Gilbert Simondon's Plea for a Philosophy of Technology. *Inquiry*, 35(3-4), 407-421, S-D 92.

This paper argues that most contemporary philosophy of technology hardly lives up to its name. What goes by that name gives nearly exclusive attention to the social and political consequences of technological innovations, leaving unattended the properly philosophical questions related to the nature and mode of existence of technical objects. After reviewing some of the reasons for this situation, I argue that over thirty years ago, Gilbert Simondon offered a stimulating analysis of these problems which is still relevant today. (edited)

Dunfee, Thomas W and Maurer, Virginia G. Corporate Attorney Whistle-Blowing: Devising a Proper Standard. *Bus Prof Ethics J*, 11(3-4), 3-39, Fall-Wint 92.

A consequentialistic model of corporate attorney whistle-blowing is developed and then applied to determine the parameters of a legitimate professional ethical norm controlling corporate attorney disclosures of illicit actions by clients. Current practice reveals variety in norms among the states, with some prohibiting attorneys from revealing serious criminal activities except in narrowly defined circumstances. Application of the model supports a standard of broad permissibility while rejecting the extremist norms of total prohibition or of broadly mandated disclosure. Corporate attorneys should be allowed substantial moral free space in choosing whether or not to disclose wrong-doing.

Dunlap, John T. Models, Modality, and Natural Theology in Logic, God and Metaphysics, Harris, James F (ed). Dordrecht, Kluwer, 1992.

Dunlop, Charles E M and Fetzer, James H. *Glossary of Cognitive Science*. New York, Paragon House, 1993.

The purpose of this work is to help the non-specialist gain access to the terminology of cognitive science, by offering clear, nontechnical definitions of its basic vocabulary. Drawing primarily from philosophy, psychology, linguistics, and artificial intelligence, the glossary contains 433 entries, ranging from 25 to 250 words in length. Cross-listings of related terms are easy to track, and many entries are supplemented with illuminating examples. Short biographical entries for many of the key people in cognitive science are also included, along with synopses of their major contributions. References for further reading appear at the end of the book.

Dunn, Robert. Akratic Attitudes and Rationality. *Austl J Phil*, 70(1), 24-39, Mr 92.

The issue in this paper is which principles of rationality provide principles of continence for mental attitudes. The paper argues that the rationality of attitudes is bi-dimensional—reflecting the difference between object-related and attitude-related reasons for mental attitudes— and that akratic havers of attitudes violate principles of attitude-related rationality.

Dunne, Joseph. *Back to the Rough Ground*. Notre Dame, Univ Notre Dame Pr, 1993.

This book aims to provide a philosophical context for limiting the jurisdiction of technical rationality and vindicating practitioner's knowledge in areas such as education, psychotherapy and politics. It explores the retrieval of the Aristotelian distinction between *techne* and *phronesis* in a variety of spheres by five modern thinkers—Newman, Collingwood, Arendt, Gadamer, and Habermas—and then examines these concepts in detail in Aristotle's texts. They are shown to open up themes (e.g., experience, language, finitude) central both to defending the integrity of practical domains and understanding much that is at issue in current debates about modernity and postmodernism.

Dunning, Stephen N. Who Sets the Task? in Foundations of Kierkegaard's Vision of Community, Connell, George B (ed). Atlantic Highlands, Humanities Pr, 1992.

This essay disputes the claim that Kierkegaard was an authoritarian thinker. For him, faith precedes and supports all claims to authority, a relation that can never be reversed. The primary texts analyzed are *On Authority and Revelation* and "Of the Difference between a Genius and an Apostle".

Dunning, William V. Postmodernism and the Construct of the Divisible Self[. *Brit J Aes*, 33(2), 132-141, Ap 93.

Dunning ended an earlier article, *The Concept of Self and Postmodern Painting*, by noting that John Passmore interprets the poststructuralism more accurately assumes the end of the continuity and the *indivisibility* of the Cartesian self and compares it to the divided sense of self inherent in tribal societies. This non-European construct is then related to the current fragmentation of self — presaged by Freud and Lacan — and the impact this has on postmodern painters such as Anselm Kiefer, as evidenced by the focus on myth, religion, and cyclic time.

Dunning, William V. Reflections on Time. *J Aes Educ*, 26(1), 93-99, Spr 92.

The way a culture measures time influences the way it perceives time. A review of the changing methods that various societies used to measure time from hunter-gatherer societies to the present, and the societal changes that generated each new method, explains the abiding interest in the element of time in art, science, and literature. The conclusion is that our mastery of time has rendered us servants to time: our ability to split a second into thirty billion precise increments has created a resentful fragmented culture that is starved for time, and these characteristics are manifest in postmodern art.

Dunning, William V 468 **AUTHOR INDEX WITH ABSTRACTS**

Dunning, William V. The Concept of Self and Postmodern Painting: Constructing a Post-Cartesian Viewer. *J Aes Art Crit*, 49(4), 331-336, Fall 91.

The Cartesian sense of an autonomous individual "self" has essentially disappeared. The postmodern concept of a collective self, which reflects the post-Cartesian culture that generated it, is reflected in postmodern painting. Renaissance and even modern paintings were spatially unified due to their single viewpoint—which implied a single point of view and a single and separate viewer. Due to the fragmentation of current society and the growth of interest in the ideas of Charles Sanders Peirce and Saussure, however, postmodern paintings are fragmented by multiple viewpoints and thus imply a pluralist point of view and a pluralist viewer.

Dupré, Louis. Theodicy: The Case for a Theologically Inclusive Model of Philosophy in Prospects for Natural Theology, Long, Eugene Thomas (ed). Washington, Cath Univ Amer Pr, 1992.

Duprè, John. *The Disorder of Things: Metaphysical Foundations of the Disunity of Science*. Cambridge, Harvard Univ Pr, 1993.

This book offers an extended critique of the mechanistic metaphysics that continues to be assumed by much philosophy, science, and philosophy of science. Detailed criticisms of essentialism, physicalist reductionism, and deterministic or quasi-deterministic accounts of causation, are developed. The close connections between these positions are also exposed. A pluralistic metaphysics, referred to as "promiscuous realism" is developed as an alternative. Concluding chapters address more generally the question of the unity of science, and the role of values in scientific theory.

Dupuy, Edward J. Being Interested in Time: Autobiography and Repetition. *Listening*, 28(2), 141-157, Spr 93.

Duquette, David A. A Critique of the Technological Interpretation of Historical Materialism. *Phil Soc Sci*, 22(2), 157-186, Je 92.

This essay examines and criticizes G A Cohen's interpretation of Marx's materialistic conception of history as presented in Cohen's book *Karl Marx's Theory of History*. In particular, the author attacks Cohen's Primacy Thesis, the claim that (for Marx) human technology is the primary explanatory factor for economic and social change and for historical development generally. The focus of the attack is Cohen's way of distinguishing between the material and social characteristics, or the content and form, of a system of production. The argument is that Cohen's distinctions are defective and therefore fail to provide adequate support for the Primacy Thesis and that, moreover, the position that Cohen defends is not Marx's.

Duquette, David A. C J Arthur on Marx and Hegel on Alienation. *Auslegung*, 19(1), 75-85, Wint 93.

In this article I examine C J Arthur's views on Marx's conception of alienation in the *Paris Manuscripts* and his assessment of Marx's critique of Hegel. In particular, I argue that to take Marx's criticisms of Hegel on the subject of alienation uncritically, as Arthur does, is to ignore some misinterpretations of Hegel by Marx and to perpetuate some confusions about the relation between externalization and estrangement in Hegel's philosophy. In the course of discussion I raise some epistemological issues concerning the relation of self and world as this bears on the topic of alienation.

Duquette, David A. Commentary on "Husserl's Critique of Hegel" in Hegel and His Critics, Desmond, William (ed). Albany, SUNY Pr, 1989.

In my commentary to Tom Rockmore's "Husserl's Critique of Hegel" I suggest that Husserl's inadequate understanding of Hegel on romanticism, reason, naturalism, and historicism (all noted by Rockmore) are evidence that his critique of Hegel was not particularly insightful. Moreover, I argue that Husserl's critique of reason is weakened by his failure to go beyond a Kantian, formalistic ("ratiocinative") treatment of presuppositions and of truth, and thus stands in contrast with Hegel's project of actualizing philosophy concretely. Ironically, if Husserl's critique of Hegel is valuable, it is in revealing the deficiencies in the thought of the critic.

Duquette, David A. The Basis for Recoghnition of Human Rights. *SW Phil Rev*, 8(1), 49-56, Ja 92.

In this essay I discuss the basis for recognition of human rights, in particular whether or not, or to what extent, there must be some sort of institutional ground for the existence of human rights. A theory of rights I have in mind is Joel Feinberg's conception of rights as valid claims and Rex Martin's attempt to use this model to articulate human rights in terms of civil rights. I challenge Martin's thesis that the concept of a human right includes not only the idea of a morally valid claim but also practices of recognition and maintenance by governments. Moreover, I argue that this view diminishes the morally critical significance of human rights.

Duran, Jane. Aesthetic Discrimination: Evaluation of Pieces by Style, Period, and Site. *J Aes Educ*, 26(1), 67-74, Spr 92.

The conclusion that notions of aesthetic style and/or period—as opposed to site—are relatively unexamined and in need of further analysis is supported by two major lines of argument. The first draws on work by Bass and asks us (taking comparative analyses of the stonework of India and Indonesia as exemplary) to consider the notion that what he terms "cognitive difference" may constitute all of the relevant difference between these allegedly distinctive styles. The second utilizes Bailey's analysis of work by Kostabi, and helps support, again, the conclusion that the alleged or purported stylistic distinction is no genuine distinction at all. Work by Krukowski is alluded to, and relevant material from a National Gallery catalogue and Bussagli and Sivaramamurti cited.

Duran, Jane. Assisted Performance. *Int J Applied Phil*, 7(2), 19-23, Wint 92.

A focus on models of assisted performance currently in use in educational circles reveals that many of the models implicitly rely on cognitive interaction theory which posits knowledge acquisition as being social and interpersonal rather than intrasubjective. The paper focuses extensively on one such model (Tharp and Gallimore, 1988), and makes an effort to relate the model to other research in teaching, and also to work in cognitive science.

Duran, Jane. Delightful, Delovely and Externalist. *Critica*, 24(70), 65-82, Ap 92.

Three major lines of argument are developed to support an externalist model of epistemic justification and of knowledge. The first line asks us to recall the origins of internalist models; a second line points out deficiencies in the analysis of externalism in the work of Bonjour, and also alludes to work by Goldman. A third line develops Kornblith's notion that we are hardwired to acquire knowledge in certain sorts of ways, many of which are unconscious processes not susceptible to first-person explication. It is concluded that internalist attacks on externalism fail to grasp the difficulties of the internalist plight and the comparative strengths of the externalist view.

Duran, Jane. Escher and Parmigianino: A Study in Paradox. *Brit J Aes*, 33(3), 239-245, Jl 93.

Commentary on the notion of visual paradox, although highly suggestive, has indicated that this category might well be thought of as the empty set. In three major lines of analysis, I examine the work of Parmigianino and then Escher preparatory to analyzing the notion of the "paradoxical". I conclude that what is important about this notion is closely analogous to the parallel concept in language, and that—whether or not the analogy hits completely home—the concept of the paradoxical is a useful one in examining works of art, and not misplaced in an analysis of these artists.

Duran, Jane. The Intersection of Feminism and Pragmatism. *Hypatia*, 8(2), 159-171, Spr 93.

I cite areas of pragmatism and feminism that have an intersection with or an appeal to the other, including the notions of the universal and/or normative, and foundationalist lines in general. I deal with three areas from each perspective and develop the notion of their intersection. Finally, the paper discusses the importance of a pragmatic view for women's lives and the importance of psychoanalytic theory for finding another area where pragmatism and feminism mesh.

Duran, Jane. *Toward a Feminist Epistemology*. Lanham, Rowman & Littlefield, 1990.

Much of the recent work in feminist theory of knowledge has proceeded without reference to recent advances in contemporary epistemology. Drawing on new work in a naturalized vein, the author constructs and defends a feminist epistemology that is sufficiently rigorous to meet the standards of analytic philosophy. A great deal of the work of the past decade in general feminist theory and the feminist critique of science is made use of.

Durbin, Paul T. Environmental Ethics and Environmental Activism. *Res Phil Technol*, 12, 107-117, 1992.

Encourages cooperation between environmental ethicists and environmental activists, including ecologists and other environmental scientists. Argument based on the inadequacy of environmental ethics analyses alone to deal with the issues of concern to philosophers involved in environmental ethics.

Durbin, Paul T. Philosophizing as a Public Good in Frontiers in American Philosophy, Volume I, Burch, Robert W (ed). College Station, Texas A&M Univ Pr, 1992.

Aims to show that, and how, philosophers of various schools can contribute to the discussion of social problems. Opposes the view that analytical philosophies of various sorts, but especially analytical approaches to applied ethics problems, have any privilege of place in this endeavor. Champions philosophical activism in the name of John Dewey and George Herbert Mead but concludes, using examples, that all sorts of philosophers can contribute in various ways to the solution of current social problems.

Durbin, Paul T. Reply to George Allan's "Environmental Philosophizing and Environmental Activism". *Res Phil Technol*, 12, 129-132, 1992.

Corrects misunderstandings and attempts to sharpen the real differences between the author and Allan. Continues plea for activism in solving environmental problems.

Durrant, Michael. The Meaning of 'God'—I in Religion and Philosophy, Warner, Marin (ed). New York, Cambridge Univ Pr, 1992.

In this paper I (i) examine the claim that 'God' has reference only and no 'sense'; I reject this claim; (ii) contend that non-descriptive uses of 'God' rest upon a descriptive use; (iii) face the problem that 'God' in Christian thought appears to have no single descriptive use but a variety of uses some of which seem to be incompatible with each other. I consider four approaches to this problem, reject all of them and suggest a path forward.

Durrant, Michael. Transcendence, Instantiation and Incarnation—An Exploration. *Relig Stud*, 29(3), 337-352, S 93.

This paper is exploratory. It raises the questions: 1) How is it possible that that which is of its *nature* transcendent should become immanent or incarnate?; 2) How is it possible for one and the same individual to be both *fully* God and *fully* man? As concerns 1) an answer is offered by appeal to Geach's account of Aquinas's doctrine of "Form"; as concerns 2) a sketch answer is supplied on the basis of 1) It is held that a paradox only arises if it were required that God the Son took on the "non-formal" predicates expressing the essence of the Godhead in the *very same sense* as they apply to God himself.

Duska, Ronald F. Aristotle: A Pre-Modern Post-Modern? Implications for Business Ethics. *Bus Ethics Quart*, 3(3), 227-249, Jl 93.

The paper asserts that post-modernisms's rejection of "modern" ethical-theoretical accounts as unacceptable meta-narratives concurs with Aristotelian critiques of contemporary ethical theories, since in some ways Aristotelian critiques are similar to post-modern critiques. However, the paper also points out significant differences between Aristotelian and post-modern approaches, based on different criteria of what counts as ethical knowledge. The paper shows how business ethicists might adopt the approach to ethics Aristotle outlines in the *Nichomachean Ethics* and fully elaborates in the discourses about the just and good in the *Rhetoric*, an approach which avoids the relativism of post-modernism, while accommodating its multi-perspectival approach.

Dussel, Enrique. De la "conquista" a la "colonización" del mundo de la vida (Lebenswelt). *Frei Z Phil Theol*, 39(3), 279-293, 1992.

Dussel, Enrique. De la "invención" al "descubrimiento" del Nuevo Mundo. *Frei Z Phil Theol*, 39(3), 264-278, 1992.

Dust, Patrick H. Freedom, Power, and Culture in Ortega y Gasset's Philosophy of Technology. *Res Phil Technol*, 11, 119-153, 1991.

Technocrats accept the anthropological truth that man is an ever-increasing power and freedom but they underestimate the destructive tendencies of human hubris. *Conservative* approaches to technology—Heidegger, Ellul, Daniel Bell—overreact to that hubris and end by condemning human power and taking refuge in transcendental "solutions" that leave man and history behind. *Ortega's* philosophy of technology offers us a middle ground: it avoids the nihilism implicit in previous understandings of technology and it suggests a positive program in the existential here and now for dealing with the problem. Culture as ontological courage is the most human response to the crisis.

Dutton, Denis. Tribal Art and Artifact. *J Aes Art Crit*, 51(1), 13-22, Wint 93.

In a recent discussion of primitive art, Arthur Danto presents us with an example. Imagine two tribes, he asks, which produce (to us) indistinguishable baskets and pots which nevertheless have in the lives of the tribes radically different cultural significance. I explore the implications of Danto's brilliant example in order to show that it imports into a tribal context aesthetic ideas that have no application there. In interesting and aesthetically significant ways, Danto's example is impossible. Understanding why tell us something about so-called primitive arts in general.

Duval, R Shannon. Augustine's Radiant Confessional—Theatre of Prophecy. *Cont Phil*, 15(2), 1-4, Mr-Ap 93.

This article suggests that an aesthetic reading of Augustine's *Confessions* underlies the traditional religious reading of the text. I suggest this aesthetic reading brings into sharp relief the relationship we are meant to form with both the author and the text. Further, I suggest it is the aesthetic reading that "re-humanizes" Monica—the central female character in the text. In making this argument I make use of Nietzsche's writing on the aesthetic and aesthetic sensibility. The article is also relevant to current feminist concerns as it addresses the alienation engendered towards Monica on a religious as opposed to an aesthetic reading of the *Confessions*.

Dwars, Ingrid. Application Discourse and the Special Case-Thesis. *Ratio Juris*, 5(1), 67-78, Mr 92.

Klaus Günther's (1988) book developed the distinction between two kinds of discourse, the foundation discourse and the application discourse. In an article (Günther 1989a) following the publication of the book, he used this basic distinction as the starting point for a criticism of the special case-thesis as defended by Robert Alexy (1978, 32ff., Alexy 1989, 16ff., 213ff.). The aim of this article is to criticize this criticism in its turn and to show that the special case-thesis does not need the reformulation which Günther proposed. It should be clear from the outset that this concerns an internal discussion in the field of discourse theory; certain discourse-theoretical premises are taken for granted. In order to understand Günther's criticism I will first give a brief account of the distinction he has made.

Dworkin, Ronald. Two Concepts of Liberty in Isaiah Berlin: A Celebration, Margalit, Edna (ed). Chicago, Univ of Chicago Pr, 1991.

Dye, James W. Demea's Departure. *Hume Stud*, 18(2), 467-481, N 92.

Demea's departure at the end of Part XI of the *Dialogues* is insufficiently motivated by Philo's presentation of the problem of evil, given Demea's cooperation in elaborating that problem. Two more specific developments provoke his leaving: 1) Philo's use of Demea's own cosmological argument form (from Part IX) to conclude that God is the cause of evil, which clashes with Demea's conviction (from Part X) that theistic belief is grounded in the hope that God will redeem us from evil, and 2) Philo's claim that Demea's theology, despite its pretense to be non-anthropomorphic, differs only stylistically from Cleanthes', both being tailored to persuade certain audiences rather than to establish truths.

Dyer, Allen R. Polanyi and Post-Modernism. *Tradition Discovery*, 19(1), 31-38, 1992-93.

Post-modernism is receiving much attention, but it is often seen as merely an extrapolation of modernism. Michael Polanyi's post-critical epistemology offers a useful way of understanding post-modernism. The modern objectivism of critical thought leads to a dead-end dehumanization. Polanyi offers a recovery of the human dimension by demonstrating the ways in which all knowing, especially scientific discovery, requires human participation. An analogy is drawn with post-modern art and architecture, which similarly attempt to recover the human form and traditional or classical ornamentation in a way which goes beyond the sterile abstractness of modernism.

Dymski, Gary and Devine, James. Walrasian Marxism Once Again: A Reply to Joe Roemer. *Econ Phil*, 8(1), 157-162, Ap 92.

Dzarasov, Ruslan. Twenty Years Before the End of the World: Political Remarks About the Meaning of Our Epoch. *Praxis Int*, 12(4), 421-432, Ja 93.

Dzhaparidze, Giorgie. A Generalized Notion of Weak Interpretability and the Corresponding Modal Logic. *Annals Pure Applied Log*, 61(1-2), 113-160, My 93.

Dzhaparidze, Giorgie. Predicate Provability Logic with Non-modalized Quantifiers. *Stud Log*, 50(1), 149-160, Mr 91.

Predicate modal formulas with non-modalized quantifiers (call them Q'-formulas) are considered as schemata of arithmetical formulas, where "necessary" is interpreted as the provability predicate of some fixed correct extension *T* of arithmetic. A method of constructing 1) non-provable in *T* and 2) false arithmetical examples for Q'-formulas by Kripke-like countermodels of certain type is given. Assuming the means of *T* to be strong enough to solve the (undecidable) problem of derivability in Q' GL, the Q'-fragment of the predicate version of the logic GL, we prove the recursive enumerability of the sets of Q'-formulas all arithmetical examples of which are: 1) *T*-provable, 2) true. In particular, the first one is shown to be exactly Q' GL and the second one to be exactly the Q'-fragment of the predicate version of Solovay's logic *S*.

Dziemidok, Bohdan. Artistic Formalism: Its Achievements and Weaknesses. *J Aes Art Crit*, 51(2), 185-193, Spr 93.

Dziemidok, Bohdan. Dewey's Contribution to the Theory of Valuation. *Free Inq*, 13(1), 28-30, Wint 92-93.

Dziob, Anne Marie. Aristotelian Friendship: Self-Love and Moral Rivalry. *Rev Metaph*, 46(4), 781-801, Je 93.

Dziobiak, W and Czelakowski, J. A Deduction Theorem Schema for Deductive Systems of Propositional Logics. *Stud Log*, 50(3-4), 385-391, S-D 91.

Eagleton, Terry. *Ideology: An Introduction*. New York, Verso, 1991.

Eagleton, Terry and Jameson, Fredric and Said, Edward W. *Nationalism, Colonialism, and Literature*. Minneapolis, Univ of Minnesota Pr, 1990.

Eaker, Deborah J. Response to "Integrity or 'He Who Steals My Purse'". *Proc S Atlantic Phil Educ Soc*, 36, 81-84, 1991.

Eames, Elizabeth R. A J Ayer's Philosophical Method in The Philosophy of A J Ayer, Hahn, Lewis E (ed). Peru, Open Court, 1992.

This contribution to the Library of Living, Philosophers volume *The Philosophy of A J Ayer* traces the changes in Ayer's conception of philosophy and his use of philosophical methods through his career. It raises questions concerning consistency and compatibility among these changing themes. Between the scope of the analytic definitions and the limits of his empiricism is an area of philosophical challenge for Ayer. Informal logical arguments employing counter-examples as thought experiments provide the basis for some criticisms and queries regarding the outcome of Ayer's philosophical methods.

Earls, C Anthony. Zen and the Art of John Dewey. *SW Phil Rev*, 8(1), 165-172, Ja 92.

Earman, John. *Bayes or Bust? A Critical Examination of Bayesian Confirmation Theory*. Cambridge, MIT Pr, 1992.

Earman, John. Carnap, Kuhn, and the Philosophy of Scientific Methodology in World Changes, Horwich, Paul (ed). Cambridge, MIT Pr, 1993.

Earman, John. In Defense of Laws: Reflections on Bas Van Fraassen's *Laws and Symmetry*. *Phil Phenomenol Res*, 53(2), 413-419, Je 93.

Earman, John and Norton, John D. Forever is a Day: Supertasks in Pitowsky and Malament-Hogarth Spacetimes. *Phil Sci*, 60(1), 22-42, Mr 93.

The standard theory of computation excludes computations whose completion requires an infinite number of steps. Malament-Hogarth spacetimes admit observers whose pasts contain entire future-directed, timelike half-curves of infinite proper length. We investigate the physical properties of these spacetimes and ask whether they and other spacetimes allow the observer to know the outcome of a computation with infinitely many steps.

Eaves, Lindon and Gross, Lora. Exploring the Concept of Spirit as a Model for the God-World Relationship in the Age of Genetics. *Zygon*, 27(3), 261-286, S 92.

The cultural impact of genetics focuses the intellectual and moral challenge of science to theology. Many traditional images of God and the God-world relation are inadequate to represent religious ideas in a world whose self-understanding has been transformed by genetics. Such images also lack the power to help in approaching the ethical challenges of this new era. The way conceptions of the God-world relation can be modified in the light of genetic knowledge is explored by examining how far a new conception of Spirit can function alongside contemporary genetic views of human life in nature. The relationship between genetic theories of human behavior and evolution is related to the revised conception of Spirit.

Ebbesen, Sten. What Must One Have an Opinion About. *Vivarium*, 30(1), 62-79, My 92.

Ebbesen, Sten and Yukio, Iwakuma. Logic-Theological Schools from the Second Half of the 12th Century: A List of Sources. *Vivarium*, 30(1), 173-210, My 92.

Ebbs, Gary. Skepticism, Objectivity, and Brains in Vats. *Pac Phil Quart*, 73(3), 239-266, S 92.

Ebertz, Roger. Is Reflective Equilibrium a Coherentist Model?. *Can J Phil*, 23(2), 193-214, Je 93.

John Rawls' notion of reflective equilibrium is attractive to those who emphasize the role of coherence in justification. This paper looks at the use of reflective equilibrium to justify principles of justice and asks whether it constitutes a model for coherentist approaches to justification. After a brief exposition of 'reflective equilibrium' I argue that although Rawls emphasizes coherence, his use of reflective equilibrium does not provide a coherentist model, and in fact involves a kind of modest foundationalist account of reflective equilibrium could be applied to the moral domain and draw out three important general epistemological insights which arise out of our discussion of reflective equilibrium.

Echeverría, Javier. Cálculos Geométricos en Leibniz. *Theoria (Spain)*, 6(14-15), 29-54, O 91.

In a letter of September 1679 to Huygens, Leibniz proposed a *calculus situs* directly applicable to geometric relations without use of magnitudes. His research on this kind of geometric calculus were developed along all his life, but, unfortunately, only a few of Leibniz's writings on these matters had been published by Gerhardt and Couturat. They were closely connected to his own researches on logic calculus. From a chronological point of view, the unpublished manuscript *Circa Geometrica Generalia* (CGG) (1682) may be considered as the third most important Leibniz's contribution on *Calculus Situs*. CGG summarizes several results obtained by Leibniz from 1679 to 1682 and contains some interesting ideas concerning set theory, geometric axioms, general topology (connexion, frontier, continuous transformations, etc.), and logic foundations of geometry.

Echeverría, Javier (ed & trans). Circa Geometrica Generalia—G W Leibniz. *Theoria (Spain)*, 6(14-15), 55-66, O 91.

Eckhardt, William. Probability Theory and the Doomsday Argument. *Mind*, 102(407), 483-488, Jl 93.

John Leslie has published an argument that our own birth rank among all who have lived can be used to make inferences about all who will ever live, and hence about the expected survival time for the human race. It is found to be shorter than usually supposed. The assumptions underpinning the argument are criticized, especially the unwarranted one that the argument's sampling is equiprobable from among all who ever live. A mathematical derivation shows that Leslie's argument is correct only if there exists a correlation of our birth rank to the event of doomsday. Such correlation is highly improbable.

Eco, Umberto. Between Author and Text in Interpretation and Overinterpretation: Umberto Eco, Collini, Stefan (ed). New York, Cambridge Univ Pr, 1992.

Eco, Umberto. Interpretation and History in Interpretation and Overinterpretation: Umberto Eco, Collini, Stefan (ed). New York, Cambridge Univ Pr, 1992.

Eco, Umberto. Overinterpreting Texts in Interpretation and Overinterpretation: Umberto Eco, Collini, Stefan (ed). New York, Cambridge Univ Pr, 1992.

Eco, Umberto. Reply in Interpretation and Overinterpretation: Umberto Eco, Collini, Stefan (ed). New York, Cambridge Univ Pr, 1992.

École, Jean. La question du statut ontologique du monde dans la métaphysique lavellienne. *Arch Phil*, 56(2), 267-275, Ap-Je 93.

According to Lavelle, there are two kinds of beings radically different: those endowed with consciousness and freedom, which are objects of creation and agents of participation, and those which are only instruments or means of creation as they are deprived of such faculties. His description of the last ones which make the world raises the question: does he not reduce the world to means to be rather than to a real being? Not at all. Total or absolute Being grants to it, as to the particular beings of the first kind, its very being which is totally present in it as well as in them; therefore, together with them, it is part of being and of the same being.

Edel, Abraham. *In Search of the Ethical: Moral Theory in Twentieth Century America*. New Brunswick, Transaction Books, 1993.

The book samples the rich variety of ethical theories in twentieth century America through studies of William James' moral theory, Dewey's ethics, ethical relativism and emotivism, theories of Rawls and Nozick. It explores concepts of value, ethical naturalism and moral change, as well as procedures in moral reasoning. Its aim is to focus on both the structure of moral theories and the process by which theories have practical force in the social culture as well as in personal life.

Edelberg, Walter. Intentional Identity and the Attitudes. *Ling Phil*, 15(6), 561-596, D 92.

Three strategies for theorizing about propositional attitudes are compared. The first attempts to reduce intentional identity to theoretical resources motivated exclusively by ordinary de dicto and de re attitudes. Arguable, this popular strategy is doomed to failure. The second strategy is non-reductive. The third favors a reduction opposite that of the first: de re attitudes are reduced to theoretical resources motivated exclusively by intentional identity and de dicto attitudes. The third approach, which amounts to a form of idealism, yields a much simpler and far more unified explanation of logical puzzles about propositional attitudes than the second strategy permits.

Eder, Klaus. Politics and Cuture in Cultural-Political Interventions in the Unfinished Project of Enlightenment, Honneth, Axel (& other eds). Cambridge, MIT Pr, 1992.

The paper is an attempt to link the reality of political participation and its normative legitimation to differences in social positions, to class structures. This is done by applying a Bourdienan perspective to central assumptions of Habermas' political philosophy. A theory of socio-cultural types of political participation is proposed and its implications for a normative idea political participation in the public space are discussed.

Edgington, Dorothy. Changing Beliefs Rationally: Some Puzzles in Cognition, Semantics and Philosophy, Ezquerro, Jesús (ed). Norwell, Kluwer, 1992.

Edgington, Dorothy. Validity, Uncertainty and Vagueness. *Analysis*, 52(4), 193-204, O 92.

Edgley, Roy. Marxism, Morality and Mr Lukes in Socialism and Morality, McLellan, David (ed). New York, St Martin's Pr, 1990.

Edwards, Paul. A Reply to Crude and Reckless Distortions. *Philosophy*, 67(261), 381-385, Jl 92.

This article is a reply to "In Defense of Heidegger" by S Janusz and G Webster (*Philosophy*, July 1991) which is an attack on my "Heidegger's Quest for Being" (*Philosophy*, October 1989). The most important of the distortions by Janusz and Webster concern my explanation but, contrary to what Heidegger maintains, "exists" is not the name of a characteristic but a logical constant. This criticism is supposed to be based on my assumption of "the fundamentality of formal logic". In fact, it is not based on any such assumption but on an analysis of how "exists" functions in *ordinary* discourse. I am also accused of using Heidegger's political record as an argument against his philosophy. This is not so. The article by Janusz and Webster contains numerous other misrepresentations including attributions to me *in quotation marks* of statements made by others.

Edwards, Rem B. God and Process in Logic, God and Metaphysics, Harris, James F (ed). Dordrecht, Kluwer, 1992.

I examine Bowman Clarke's views that: God is a single, everlasting, non-temporal actual entity, there is no time in God, God has no future, and God and the world do not interact causally. God's being a non-temporal actual entity may mean that (1) God's concrescence is completed, or (2) it is continuous. Clarke holds the former, I the latter. Because completed, God has no future, according to Clarke. I argue that Clarke's position loses all of the advances of process theology, against his claim that God pretends the world non-causally, and for the view that God and the world interact causally.

Edwards, Steve. Formulating a Plausible Relativism. *Philosophia (Israel)*, 22(1-2), 63-74, Ja 93.

This paper constitutes a critical enquiry into the possibility of formulating a plausible relativism. Two kinds of relativism are distinguished, strong and weak. It is argued that the latter proves the more plausable. Weak relativism is seen to require the truth of the following conjunction: 1) that sense can be made of the notion of a conceptual scheme, and 2) that there can be a plurality of such schemes. The relationship between relativism and realism is then examined and it is concluded that relativism requires the truth of realism. Given the latter conclusion, the relationship between relativism and anti-realism is considered. The conclusion reached here is that relativism and anti-realism are mutually exclusive theses.

Eells, Ellery (ed) and Maruszewski, Tomasz (ed). *Probability and Rationality*. Amsterdam, Rodopi, 1991.

In this volume, the works of L Jonathan Cohen are discussed, both critically and in the way of exposition of his views. Following a foreword is an essay by Cohen himself, delineating the development of his thought in various areas, including political philosophy, philosophy of language, philosophy of law, and human rationality. Following this are twelve essays by authors from around the world on Cohen's work on methodology in psychology, on probabilistic reasoning, and on methodological pluralism in the investigation of human rationality. The volume concludes with comments by Cohen on these contributions to the volume.

Efron, Arthur. Residual Asymmetrical Dualism: A Theory of Mind-Body Relations. *J Mind Behav*, 13(2), 113-136, Spr 92.

Progress in understanding the mind-body problem can be made without attempting to solve it as one unified problem, which it is not. Pepper's "Identity Theory" solution to the problem is now seen as not necessarily clarifying for the question of dualism. Residual asymmetrical dualism is proposed as a theory offering one very good way to think about this set of problems in a variety of modes of inquiry. These include neurophysiological research on the amygdala by LeDoux, research in the phenomenon of hearing and learning while under general anesthetic, Gendlin's methods of focusing upon the body during therapeutic procedures and during creative composition of poetry, and Dewey's position concerning "primary experience" versus a "secondary pseudo-environment" inhabited by the civilized human. Residual asymmetrical dualism is not a value-neutral theory: it is based on a determination that bodily intelligence must ultimately guide mental functioning if survival and well-being are to be secured. It leads to taking actions within society to carry out whatever steps are needed to alleviate the mind-body split whenever such a split is harmful to human interaction.

Egan, Frances. Individualism, Computation and Perceptual Content. *Mind*, 101(403), 443-459, Jl 92.

Computational theories of cognition are individualistic—the states they characterize are shared by physical duplicates. It is argued that representational contents play a role in computational psychology analogous to the role played by explanatory models in the physical sciences. The contents assigned to states in explanatory models of computational theories of perception are typically wide, that is, they are individuated by reference to the subject's normal environment. Hence, computational theories of perception are both individualistic and externalist.

Egerding, Michael. Johannes Taulers Auffassung vom Menschen. *Frei Z Phil Theol*, 39(1-2), 105-129, 1992.

Eggerman, Richard W. Minimal Naturalism. *SW Phil Rev*, 8(1), 1-17, Ja 92.

Naturalism is conceived as that position in moral reasoning which authorizes employment of various facts about human nature as unmediated reasons in support of evaluative conclusions. This paper defends minimal naturalism, the assertion that such unmediated fact-to-value inferences are legitimate metaethically, but normatively are to be employed to the smallest extent necessary. It argues, against formalistic positions, that some such inferences are essential, but, against more richly naturalistic approaches such as utilitarianism, that they should be employed sparingly. Gewirth and Rawls are identified as good examples of practitioners of minimal naturalism in normative ethics.

Egidi, Rosaria. Marty's Theory of Space in Mind, Meaning and Metaphysics, Mulligan, Kevin (ed). Dordrecht, Kluwer, 1990.

Egidi, Rosaria. Meaning and Action in Criss-Crossing A Philosophical Landscape, Schulte, Joachim (ed). Amsterdam, Rodopi, 1992.

The paper aims at analyzing Wittgenstein's arguments on voluntary action as they are developed in Part II of PI in Z and eventually in RPPI-II. Special attention is paid to the scrutiny of arguments which could be characterized as the *pars destruens* and the *pars construens* of Wittgenstein's grammar of action. (edited)

Eilan, Naomi. The Imagery Debate. *Phil Books*, 34(3), 137-142, Jl 93.

Eisenberg, John A. Response to Hammond's "Expressivist Account of Educational Development". *Proc Phil Educ*, 48, 352-356, 1992.

Eisenhower, William D. Creative Interchange Between Philosophy and Theology: A Call to Dialogue. *Faith Phil*, 9(3), 353-368, Jl 92.

A novel situation has been created by the sympathetic treatment present-day philosophers are giving traditional Christian themes. What does this mean for the relationship between philosophy and theology? I begin my answer by defining terms and comparing two articles on methodology, one by a philosopher, the other by a theologian. Next I identify four conditions which must be met for creative interchange between the two disciplines to take place. I conclude with a critique of Gordon Kaufman's recent call for dialogue in *Faith and Philosophy*, finding that it fails to satisfy the conditions I have specified.

Eisenstadt, S N (ed) and Buber, Martin. *On Intersubjectivity and Cultural Creativity—Martin Buber*. Chicago, Univ of Chicago Pr, 1992.

Eisler, Lee (ed). *The Quotable Bertrand Russell*. Buffalo, Prometheus, 1992.

Ekstrom, Laura Waddell. A Coherence Theory of Autonomy. *Phil Phenomenol Res*, 53(3), 599-616, S 93.

This paper presents a conception of the self partially in terms of a particular notion of preference. It develops a coherentist account of when one's preferences are *authorized*, or sanctioned as one's own, and presents a coherence theory of autonomous action. The view presented solves certain problems with hierarchical accounts of freedom, such as Harry Frankfurt's.

Elby, Andrew. Why Local Realistic Theories Violate, Nontrivially, the Quantum Mechanical EPR Perfect Correlations. *Brit J Phil Sci*, 44(2), 213-230, Je 93.

Using the Kochen-Specker contradiction, I prove that 'local realistic' theories predict nontrivial violations of the quantum mechanical EPR-type perfect anticorrelations. The proof invokes the same stochastic local realism conditions used in Bell arguments. For a class of theories called 'orthodox spin theories', the perfect anticorrelations used in the proof emerge from rotational symmetry. Therefore, an orthodox spin theorist must abandon either the spirit of relativity, as encoded by local realism, or the letter of relativity, which demands rotational invariance.

Elder, Crawford L. An Epistemological Defence of Realism about Necessity. *Phil Quart*, 42(168), 317-336, Jl 92.

Realists about necessity think there is a difference, independent of our habits of thought, between A's uniformly happening to have property P, and A's necessarily having P—or, again, between property F's merely *accompanying* property G, in A's, and its *causing* A's to have G. *What* differences? Existing answers make the differences seem *so* independent of our thought that we could neither detect them nor assert them. This paper shows that by avoiding the answer about the first difference that is offered by Lewis and "modal realists", and the answer about the second difference that is offered by Dretske, Tooley, and Armstrong, realists can meet these challenges.

Eldridge, Richard T. "Reading for Life": Martha C Nussbaum on Philosophy and Literature. *Arion*, 2(1), 187-197, Wint 92.

A critical review-essay on Martha C Nussbaum's *Love's Knowledge*: the essay describes and praises Nussbaum's project, while suggesting that its execution might better be less Greek, more Kantian, and more library than it is.

Eley, Lothar. Was ist und was leistet eine phänomenologische Theorie der sozialen Welt? in Analecta Husserliana, XXXIV, Tymieniecka, Anna-Teresa (ed). Dordrecht, Kluwer, 1992.

Elfstrom, Gerard A. Physicians and the American Armed Forces in Biomedical Ethics Reviews 1992, Humber, James M (ed). Clifton, Humana Pr, 1993.

Physicians generally believe they are obligated to be healers, that is, to practice medicine and protect the health of individual patients. However, American military physicians are officers whose responsibility is defined by military needs, which sometimes conflict with their healer's role. If the ultimate justification of both medical and military activity is preservation of life, the claims of each can be weighed. The article concludes that military needs may outweigh those of medicine in exceptional cases, but usually human life is best protected by giving primacy to physician's role as healers, and this primacy should be codified in military doctrine.

Elgin, Catherine Z. Outstanding Problems: Replies to ZiF Critics. *Synthese*, 95(1), 129-140, Ap 93.

Answers set the stage for new questions. Reconfigured terrains require new maps. We ended *Reconceptions* with the words "constructionalism always has plenty to do". The papers in this volume prove our point. They raise issues and disclose avenues that merit further investigations. In what follows, I venture some brief replies that answer objections and indicate areas that deserve further study.

Elgin, Catherine Z. Scheffler's Symbols. *Synthese*, 94(1), 3-12, Ja 93.

'Scheffler's Symbols' provides an overview of Israel Scheffler's wide-ranging contributions to philosophy, showing how they are engendered by and figure in a powerful nominalistic theory of symbols.

Elgin, Catherine Z. Understanding: Art and Science. *Synthese*, 95(1), 13-28, Ap 93.

The arts and the sciences perform many of the same cognitive functions, both serving to advance understanding. This paper explores some of the ways exemplification operates in the two fields. Both scientific experiments and works of art highlight, underscore, display, or convey some of their own features. They thereby focus attention on them, and make them available for examination and projection. Thus, the Michelson-Morley experiment exemplifies the constancy of the speed of light. Jackson Pollock's *Number One* exemplifies the viscosity of paint. Despite their similarities, science and art might seem to differ in their attitude toward facts. Science is said to adhere to facts; art, to be indifferent to them. Such, I urge, is not the case. Science, like art, often scorns facts to advance understanding through fiction. Thought experiments, I contend, are scientific fictions; literary and pictorial fictions, aesthetic thought experiments.

Elkins, James. From Original to Copy and Back Again. *Brit J Aes*, 33(2), 113-120, Ap 93.

Elkins, James. The "Fundamental Concepts" of Pictures. *J Speculative Phil*, 6(2), 143-151, 1992.

Ellett Jr, Frederick S and Ericson, David P. Educational Ability and Social Justice: What Should the Relationship Be?. *Proc Phil Educ*, 48, 216-225, 1992.

Ellin, Joseph S. Again: Hume on Miracles. *Hume Stud*, 19(1), 203-212, Ap 93.

What does Hume argue in the essay on miracles (*First Enquiry*, sec. 10)? An overly-strong interpretation (Fogelin's) is that Hume argues a priori that miracles are impossible; an overly-weak view (Flew's) is that Hume claims only that the evidence against any miracle is always strong enough to counter the evidence for the miracle, and therefore to 'check' (rationally prevent) belief. An intermediate thesis, defended here against Flew's several variants, is that Hume argues that the standard of proof required to make miracle claims plausible must be so high that the evidence against a miracle must always be overwhelmingly strong, and that therefore belief in any miracle is irrational.

Elliot, Carl and Gillett, Grant. Moral Insanity and Practical Reason. *Phil Psych*, 5(1), 53-67, 1992.

The psychopathic personality disorder historically has been thought to include an insensitivity to morality. Some have thought that the psychopath's insensitivity indicates that he does not understand morality, but the relationship between the psychopath's defects and moral understanding has been unclear. We attempt to clarify this relationship, first by arguing that moral understanding is incomplete without concern for morality, and second, by showing that the psychopath demonstrates defects in frontal lobe activity which indicate impaired attention and adaptation to environmental conditions which are relevant to the formation of complex intentions. We argue that these frontal lobe defects can help to explain both the psychopath's apparent insensitivity to morality and his characteristic imprudence.

Elliot, Patricia. *From Mastery to Analysis: Theories of Gender in Psychoanalytic Feminism*. Ithaca, Cornell Univ Pr, 1991.

Elliot, Robert. Identity and the Ethics of Gene Therapy. *Bioethics*, 7(1), 27-40, Ja 93.

Certain metaphysical issues pertaining to the manipulation of genetic material in gametes and conception are discussed. Their implications for ethics are then set out. In particular, genetic manipulation does not necessarily disrupt identity and so some such manipulations may be defended by appeal to person-regarding principles.

Elliott, Carl. Where Ethics Come From and What to Do About It. *Hastings Center Rep*, 22(4), 28-35, Jl-Ag 92.

Elliott, Gregory. A Just War? The Left and the Moral Gulf. *Rad Phil*, 61, 10-13, Sum 92.

Elliott, Gregory. The Cards of Confusion: Reflections on Historical Communism at the 'End of History'. *Rad Phil*, 64, 3-12, Sum 93.

Ellis, Anthony. Deontology, Incommensurability and the Arbitrary. *Phil Phenomenol Res*, 52(4), 855-875, D 92.

Non-absolutist deontology holds that certain acts are prohibited unless the consequences of not performing them are sufficiently bad. I argue that we cannot give an account of what 'sufficiently' means in this formulation, and that this destroys such a theory. The problem is that of specifying 'cutoff points'. I argue that such a theory cannot specify such cutoff points without arbitrariness. Nor will it solve the problem to hold that there *is* no cutoff point, or only a vague one. I then gesture towards one moral theory which responds to at least some of the motivations behind non-absolutist deontology but which does not encounter this problem.

Ellis, Brian and Bigelow, John and Lierse, Caroline. The World as One of a Kind: Natural Necessity and Laws of Nature. *Brit J Phil Sci*, 43(3), 371-388, S 92.

This paper elaborates and defends the view that the world is an instance of a natural kind. It argues that all laws of nature, including the most general ones, are dependent on the essential natures of natural kinds. The causal and statistical laws of nature are said to depend on the essences of the natural kinds of things which exist in the world. The most fundamental laws of nature are argued to depend on the kind of world in which we live. This theory of scientific laws derives from the basic idea that things must behave as they do because of what they are made of, how they are made, and what their circumstances are. (edited)

Ellis, Ralph. A Thought Experiment Concerning Universal Expansion. *Philosophia (Israel)*, 21(3-4), 257-275, Ap 92.

This paper argues that (1) distance and sizes have meaning only in comparison to other distances in the universe. (2) Therefore, if the universe expands, then the size of local objects, in comparison with other distances in the universe, becomes smaller. (3) The mass of objects does not change as their distance from each other varies. (4) Since the size of objects becomes smaller as the universe expands, yet their mass remains unaffected, then their mass-density increases in the process. (5) Since this increase in mass-density is a purely logical consequence of the expansion of the universe, it occurs instantaneously and makes it appear that objects are in instantaneous (faster-than-light) communication. (6) At earlier stages of universal expansion, the continual readjustment of gravitational and other physical relationships thus caused would have set up patterns of vibration and oscillation in sub-atomic particles, including 'strings'.

Ellis, Robert Richmond. *San Juan de la Cruz: Mysticism and Sartrean Existentialism*. New York, Lang, 1992.

This study analyzes San Juan de la Cruz from the perspective of Sartrean existentialism, exploring the existential affinities he shares with Golden Age Spanish writers as well as the principal exponents of western apophatic mysticism. In contrast to the cataphatic theology of the scholastics, Sanjuanist mysticism expresses many of the fundamental intuitions of modern secular existentialism. Yet it differs from the Sartrean system with regard to the question of nothingness. The Sanjuanist "dark night" is a contrary of being whereas the Sartrean *néant* is the contradictory. Herein lies the ontological foundation of San Juan's belief and Sartre's atheism.

Ellrod, Frederick E and McLean, George F. *Philosophical Foundations for Moral Education and Character Development: Act and Agent (Second Edition)*. Washington, CRVP, 1992.

Ellul, Jacques. The Search for Ethics in a Technicist Society. *Res Phil Technol*, 9, 23-36, 1989.

Elósegui, María. El descubrimiento del yo según David Hume. *Anu Filosof*, 26(2), 303-326, 1993.

This paper deals with Hume's criticism to Cartesian self and his account of a social self discovered through emotions, pride and sympathy. It wants to give possible solutions to Hume's contradictions on personal identity.

Elshtain, Jean Bethke. The Power and Powerlessness of Women in Beyond Equality and Difference, Bock, Gisela (ed). New York, Routledge, 1992.

Elugardo, Reinaldo. Burge on Content. *Phil Phenomenol Res*, 53(2), 367-384, Je 93.

Elvin, Mark. *Il "Peccato" in Cina: Bene e male nel Neoconfucianismo dalla metà del XIX secolo,* by Paolo Santangelo. *Phil East West*, 43(2), 289-301, Ap 93.

Emad, Parvis. Thinking More Deeply into the Question of Translation in Reading Heidegger: Commemorations, Sallis, John (ed). Bloomington, Indiana Univ Pr, 1992.

This paper outlines the directives for grasping the philosophical problem of translation as a problem that relates to the root-unfolding (Wesen) of language. The questions raised and discussed, all stem from Heidegger's analyses of language, interlingual translation, and the correlation of being (Sein) and language.

Emad, Parvis (trans) and Wiegand Petzet, Heinrich and Maly, Kenneth (trans). *Encounters and Dialogues with Martin Heidegger: 1929-1976 — Heinrich Wiegand Petzet*. Chicago, Univ of Chicago Pr, 1993.

This book is the memoir of the art-historian and literary critique Heinrich-Wiegand Petzet. In recounting his memoirs, Petzet tells the story of his friendship with Martin Heidegger. He focuses on numerous encounters with Heidegger and many dialogues with him. The latter covers topics as diverse as "metaphysics", "art", "modern painting", and "technology". In addition to recounting his dialogues with Heidegger, the book also sheds light on Heidegger's involvement in the politics of national socialism. The introduction to the English edition of Petzet's book takes up the questions concerning Heidegger's political involvement and updates this controversial issue.

Emery, Jr, Kent 472 AUTHOR INDEX WITH ABSTRACTS

Emery, Jr, Kent (ed) and Jordan, Mark D (ed). *Ad Litteram: Authoritative Texts and Their Medieval Readers*. Notre Dame, Univ Notre Dame Pr, 1992.

Emmet, Dorothy. Whitehead and Alexander. *Process Stud*, 21(3), 137-148, Fall 92.

The original English version of an article "Whitehead and Alexander" published in a German translation by M Hampe in *Die Gifford Lectures und ihre Deutung* herausgegeben Hampe und Massen, Suhrkamp, Frankfurt-am-Main 1991. A comparison of the metaphysics of the two philosophers as both claiming to be very general descriptions of pervasive features of reality extending outward form science. Particular notice is drawn to their views of Space and Time, events, the mind-body relation, their realist epistemologies, and their views on values.

Emson, H E. Rights, Duties and Responsibilities in Health Care. *J Applied Phil*, 9(1), 3-11, 1992.

The value of autonomy is generally stated to be of prime importance in relation to health care. Arising out of this, rights of the patient to and in health care have been extensively discussed and stated, and have found expression in law. There have been minimal statements of the rights of others involved in health care, such as caregivers, and minimal discussion of duties and responsibilities in relation to rights claimed and conferred. The author suggests that no claim to rights in health care should now be accepted without consideration of related duties and responsibilities.

Enç, Berent and Adams, Fred. Functions and Goal Directedness. *Phil Sci*, 59(4), 635-654, D 92.

We examine two approaches to functions: etiological and forward-looking. In the context of functions, we raise the question, familiar to philosophers of mind, about the explanatory role of properties that are *not* supervenient on the mere dispositional features of a system. We first argue that the question has no easy answer in either of the two approaches. We then draw a parallel between functions and goal directedness. We conclude by proposing an answer to the question: The explanatory importance of nonsupervenient properties (like having the function of doing something, or like being goal-directed) does not lie in any special causal mechanism through which these properties bring about their effects; it lies rather in the different classification of the explananda types that these properties generate.

Endicott, Ronald P. Species-Specific Properties and More Narrow Reductive Strategies. *Erkenntnis*, 38(3), 303-321, My 93.

A critical evaluation of the "narrow reductive strategy" (NRS) whereby mental types are relativized to specific domains in order to avoid the phenomenon of multiple realization. The logic of the NRS is explored by examining two forms of domain-specific bridge law, the role of disjunctive properties, and the application of approximate reduction. Also discussed is the problem of plasticity within such domains, species, even individuals. Conclusions reached: the NRS is best construed as a form of replacement, not reduction; and it can only replace/reduce token structural events or abstract particulars, not types or properties.

Engel, David. Knowing Why: Integrating Theory and Practice. *Phil Stud Educ*, 1, 115-124, 1990.

The central concern of this paper is to examine ways of knowing which might relate to and clarify the knowledge base of educational administration. Building on Gilbert Ryles' distinction between factual knowledge and performative knowledge/skill, a third epistemological category is developed: knowing-why or the ability to devise and articulate rationales for action.

Engel, J Ronald (ed) and Engel, Joan Gibb (ed). *Ethics of Environment and Development: Global Challenge, International Response*. Tucson, Univ of Arizona Pr, 1990.

Engel, Joan Gibb (ed) and Engel, J Ronald (ed). *Ethics of Environment and Development: Global Challenge, International Response*. Tucson, Univ of Arizona Pr, 1990.

Engel, Mylan. Inconsistency: The Coherence Theorist's Nemesis?. *Grazer Phil Stud*, 40, 113-130, 1991.

The relationship between inconsistency and Lehrerian coherence is scrutinized. Like most coherence theorists of epistemic justification, Lehrer contends that consistency is necessary for coherence. Despite this contention, minimally inconsistent belief-sets prove coherent and rationally acceptable on Lehrer's account of coherence. Lehrer is left with the following dilemma: If consistency *is* necessary for coherence, then 1) he must revise his account of coherence accordingly and, more importantly, 2) such coherence is *not* necessary for justification, since intuitively we are justified in accepting such minimally inconsistent belief-sets. If, on the other hand, minimally inconsistent acceptance systems can be coherent, then to prevent pairwise inconsistent statements from readily cohering with such systems, Lehrer must deny that rational acceptance is closed under deduction.

Engel, Pascal. Actions, Reasons and Mental Causes (in French). *Rev Theol Phil*, 124(3), 305-321, 1992.

One of the main difficulties with contemporary materialism is the risk of epiphenomenalism: if mental properties systematically depend on physical properties, how can they have causal efficiency? Davidson's 'anomalous monism' only solves this problem through a "feeble" understanding of the individuation of events and with relative imprecision as to the pertinence of causal explanations formulated in psychological terms. Nor do other conceptions of the individuation of events and the causal power of mental states, as that of Kim and of Jackson and Pettit, solve the problem. It will not then be solved by modifying the theory of the individuation of events.

Engel, Pascal. Les concepts vagues sont-ils sans frontières?. *Rev Int Phil*, 46(183), 527-538, 1992.

The paper argues that vagueness is not a matter of fuzzy boundaries of concepts, but a matter of there being no boundary at all. Higher-order vagueness must be acknowledged as a real phenomenon.

Engelhardt Jr, H Tristram. Personhood, Moral Strangers, and the Evil of Abortion: The Painful Experience of Post-Modernity. *J Med Phil*, 18(4), 419-421, Ag 93.

The epistemological and sociological consequences of post-modernity include the inability to show moral strangers, in terms they can see as binding, the moral wrongness of activities such as abortion. Such activities can be perceived as morally disordered within a content-full moral narrative, but not outside of the context it brings. Though one can salvage something of the Enlightenment project of justifying a morality that can bind moral strangers, one is left with moral and metaphysical views that can be recognized as impoverished and incomplete by those who live their lives within the embrace of a content-full moral narrative. The cardinal dualism of post-modernity is not that which separates mind from body, but the gulf between the morality binding moral strangers and that binding moral friends.

Englebretsen, George. Linear Diagrams for Syllogisms (With Relationals). *Notre Dame J Form Log*, 33(1), 37-69, Wint 92.

A system for diagramming syllogisms is developed here. Unlike Venn, and other planar diagrams, these diagrams are linear. This allows one to diagram inferences which exceed the virtual four term limit on nonlinear systems. It also can be extended (by the use of vectors) to inferences involving all kinds of relational expressions.

English, Lyn. Philosophy for Children and Mathematics Education. *Thinking*, 10(1), 15-16, 1992.

The article highlights some ways in which the *Philosophy for Children* program can be used in the teaching of mathematics. Ideas from the program are used to establishing a community of inquiry in the mathematics classroom where divergent and flexible mathematical thinking is encouraged. Students examine the nature of thinking and mathematical thinking in particular, and also examine their personal identity, especially with respect to their perception of their mathematical abilities. The program addresses a number of thinking skills and problem-solving strategies which students apply to the working of novel mathematical problems.

English, Parker. Affirmative Action and Philosophy Instruction. *Teach Phil*, 15(4), 311-327, D 92.

When students in Logic and in Introductory Philosophy at Kutztown University first confronted the issue of affirmative action in class, they used analogical arguments to discuss it. This helpful explicate several standard criteria used to evaluate analogical reasoning. It also helped to explicate several of Sidney Hook's remarks about the sort of welfare capitalism practiced in the US, another issue raised in the course on Introductory Philosophy.

Engstler, Achim. Aktuelle Themen und Positionen deutschsprachiger Religionsphilosophie. *Z Phil Forsch*, 46(2), 278-294, Ap-J 92.

In current philosophy of religion a tendency is observable to give 'weak' answers to classical questions. Three recently published German works on theodicy, the existence of God, and the rationality of religious belief are viewed as exemplifying this tendency. Instead of a theodicy, a phenomenology of pain experiences is delivered. Instead of a proof of the existence of God, evidence for the non-contradictoriness of belief in God shall do. And instead of an objective proof of the rationality of religious belief, the possibility of a subjective rational decision for religious belief is pointed out.

Engström, Timothy H. A Question of Style: Nelson Goodman and the Writing of Theory. *Metaphilosophy*, 23(4), 329-349, O 92.

Engstrom, Stephen. The Concept of the Highest Good in Kant's Moral Theory. *Phil Phenomenol Res*, 52(4), 747-780, D 92.

Kant claims that the concept of the highest good, the idea of happiness in proportion to virtue, is grounded in the moral law. But this claim has often been challenged. How can Kant justify including happiness in the highest good? Why should only the virtuous be worth of happiness? This paper argues that when the moral law is interpreted as the criterion for valid application of the concept of the good, the concept of the highest good does indeed follow from the moral law. It also argues that the duty to promote the highest good harmonizes with other duties.

Ennis, Robert. Critical Thinking: What Is It?. *Proc Phil Educ*, 48, 76-80, 1992.

Among other things, Ennis argues that empirical research cannot tell us what critical thinking is. In doing so, he sees similarities among 'good' ("the most general adjective of commendation"), 'justice' (fairness), and 'critical thinking' (reasonable reflective thinking focuses on deciding what to believe or do), all of which are labels for concepts, the conceptualizations of which involve values.

Enright, Robert D and Gassin, Elizabeth A and Wu, Ching-ru. Forgiveness: A Developmental View. *J Moral Educ*, 21(2), 99-114, 1992.

The concept of interpersonal forgiveness is described first through an examination of ancient writings and contemporary philosophical and psychological discourse. Two psychological models are then described. The first concerns developmental patterns in how people think about forgiving another. The second describes how people may go about forgiving another. Implications for counseling and education are drawn.

Enslin, Penny. Private Schools and Public Schools: A Critical Response to the Privatization Debate. *S Afr J Phil*, 11(3), 62-66, Ag 92.

In this article the author responds to the claim by progressive commentators that a process of privatization is taking place in South African schooling. It is argued that the distinction between public and private, especially in education, is a complex one, and that private schooling is characterized by a greater degree of publicness than state schools. Against this background it is argued that so far there is little evidence that a process of privatization is taking place in South African education.

Enz, Charles P. Quantum Theory in the Light of Modern Experiments in Advances in Scientific Philosophy, Schurz, Gerhard (ed). Amsterdam, Rodopi, 1991.

As an introduction it is observed that while the ancient Greek atomists realized the impossibility of indefinite subdivision of objects, they failed to have an idea about the size of their atoms. It is then emphasized that today the limit of subdivisibility and hence of localization is determined by Planck's constant which is the fundamental yardstick of quantum mechanics. The new role of the observer in this theory as an active participant in a measurement is then described and modern quantum experiments are discussed to illustrate these new notions.

Epstein, R L. A Theory of Truth Based on a Medieval Solution to the Liar Paradox. *Hist Phil Log*, 13(2), 149-177, 1992.

Buridan (Sophismata, Chapter 8, translated and commented on by George Hughes) gave a resolution of the liar paradox in which 'what I am now saying is false' is a proposition, every proposition is true or false though not both, and the classical laws of logic hold. Proposition, however, are tokens, and Tarski's Convention T is abandoned in favor or a principle that a proposition is true if it states what is the case and it is consistent to assume that. A formal theory is presented based on Buridan's views, with the informal principles discussed in many examples.

Ereshefsky, Marc. Eliminative Pluralism. *Phil Sci*, 59(4), 671-690, D 92.

This paper takes up the cause of species pluralism. An argument for species pluralism is provided and standard monist objections to pluralism are answered. A new form of species pluralism is developed and shown to be an improvement over previous forms. This paper also offers a general foundation on which to base a pluralistic approach to biological classification.

Erickson, Glenn W and Fossa, John A. Os Sólidos Regulares na Antigüidade. *Cad Hist Filosof Cie*, 2(1), 85-101, Ja-Je 90.

In the *Timaeus*, Plato associates the four material elements—fire, air, water and earth—with the tetrahedron, octahedron, icosahedron, and cube, respectively. The dodecahedron is assigned to the form of the universe. Herein, we try to reconstitute a compelling theory for the given associations. For the most part, the phenomenological (physical) reasons behind the association are discussed in the *Timaeus*; the mathematical reasons, however, are only hinted at, hence we try to explicate these reasons further. By combining these two types of reasons, we are able to outline a theory that makes the Platonic association quite appropriate.

Erickson, Stephen A. The Space of Love and Garbate. *Harvard Rev Phil*, 2(1), 33-40, Spr 92.

Ericson, David P and Ellett Jr, Frederick S. Educational Ability and Social Justice: What Should the Relationship Be?. *Proc Phil Educ*, 48, 216-225, 1992.

Erin, Charles A and Harris, John. AIDS: Ethics, Justice and Social Policy. *J Applied Phil*, 10(2), 165-173, 1993.

Principles of justice and equality demand that HIV seropositive individuals and those with AIDS should not be discriminated against in any area of social provision. If social policy on AIDS is constructed in terms of *reciprocal* obligations, that is if obligations *to* the HIV seropositive individual and obligations of the HIV seropositive individual are given equal weight, the civil rights of HIV seropositive individuals may be secured and this may create a climate in which HIV seropositive individuals will more readily notify partners, and others at risk of infections, of their HIV status. It is conceivable that such a climate could facilitate greater control of the spread of HIV/AIDS.

Ernest, Paul. A Note Concerning Irving H Anellis's "Distortions and Discontinuties of Mathematical Progress". *Philosophica*, 50(2), 123-125, 1992.

Esbjornson, Carl D. Once and Future Farming: Some Meditations on the Historical and Cultural Roots of Sustainable Agriculture in the United States. *Agr Human Values*, 9(3), 20-30, Sum 92.

American agricultural history, literature, and thought reveal historical circumstances that have often been unfavorable to the development of a sustainable agriculture in the United States. Further critical examination of these historical and cultural roots reveals that sustainable agriculture is an evolving concept that can be traced to the tradition of agrarian idealism, scientific and organic agriculture, and the recent history of ecological ideas, beginning with the "Dust Bowl" and extending to the present.

Escoubas, Eliane. Ontology of Language and Ontology of Translation in Heidegger in Reading Heidegger: Commemorations, Sallis, John (ed). Bloomington, Indiana Univ Pr, 1992.

Escriba, Juan Barba. Two Formal Systems for Situation Semantics. *Notre Dame J Form Log*, 33(1), 70-88, Wint 92.

We are going to present two formal systems intended to capture some of the basic features of Barwise and Perry's situation semantics. The first one is a multidimensional system which allows formal counterparts of situations (including incoherent ones), the relational theory of meaning, and the strong consequence relation. Our second system is an extension of the former one and considers a set of actual situations, so that the notion of constraint can be expressed in it. Soundness, completeness, and compactness will be proven for both systems.

Esmail, K H A. Anselm, Plantinga and the Ontological Argument. *Sophia (Australia)*, 31(3), 39-47, 1992.

The paper entitled 'Anselm, Plantinga and the Ontological Argument' considers, first of all, the ontological argument of Anselm's *Proslogian*, Chapter 2 (as it is stated by Alvin Plantinga), and it considers, secondly, Alvin Plantinga's (principal) criticisms of that argument in his work *God and Other Minds*. With regard to the argument itself, the paper re-states it and argues that it fails as it stands. With regard to Plantinga's criticisms, the paper argues that these are misplaced. (Incidentally, the re-statement of the argument provides an alternative-and, it is suggested, a better-interpretation to the one provided by Plantinga.

Espinoza, Miguel. Critique de la science anti-substantialiste. *Theoria (Spain)*, 5(12-13), 67-84, N 90.

A negative conclusion, like R Feynman's sentence "nature is uncomprehensible", forces us to examine the value of contemporary science from the point of view of understanding. As a contribution to this task, I criticize some of the philosophical presuppositions of experimentalism. The I try to place some stepping-stones towards metaphysics, conceived as a rational extension of science, and devoted to the search for intelligibility.

Espinoza, Miguel. Les quatre causes: de Bunge à Aristote. *Rev Phil Fr*, 3, 297-316, Jl-S 92.

Esquith, Stephen L. Political Theory and Political Education. *Polit Theory*, 20(2), 247-273, My 92.

Liberal political theory, especially the work of John Stuart Mill and John Rawls, should be read *as* a form of political education. These theories have mediated trust in expert authority by virtue of their particular methods of practical reasoning. Despite their humane intentions, they can be criticized for domesticating the voices of citizens within neo-corporatist liberal democracies.

Esser, Piet H. Some Difficulties of Modern Science. *Method Sci*, 25(4), 153-169, 1992.

Esterhuyse, Willie. Nietzsche's Interpretation of Metaphysics as a Closed System of Stale Metaphors (in Dutch). *S Afr J Phil*, 12(2), 38-47, My 93.

In this article the author argues that Nietzsche reduces the possibility of metaphysical thinking to a seduction of language. He demonstrates this point in terms of two interlinking aspects of Nietzsche's attack on maetaphysics, namely the genealogical method Nietzsche employs and the position he takes on the nature and function of language. Central to Nietzsche's genealogical criticism of metaphysical thinking is his understanding of language in general as a 'mobile army of metaphors' and concepts in particular as 'metaphors of metaphors', something which is 'forgotten' in metaphysical thinking which treats concepts as having a representational function. On this basis Nietzsche destroys the (methaphysical) correspondence theory of truth and representational theory of meaning.

Estlund, David. Making Truth Safe for Democracy in The Idea of Democracy, Copp, David (ed). New York, Cambridge Univ Pr, 1993.

Is truth anti-democratic? I argue that the following worry is prevalent: if there is truth about, for example, what is just, there must be experts, and the experts must be the appropriate leaders; hence authoritarianism. I argue that even if there are such truths and experts, their authority would not be legitimate. Truth is an appropriate guide only within the constraints of respect for reasonable disagreements, and some reasonable citizens could deny any expert's moral expertise. The challenge is to restore truth, within these liberal bounds, to the theory of democratic legitimacy.

Estrada Mora, Olga C. La estética y lo siniestro II. *Rev Filosof (Costa Rica)*, 30(71), 63-72, J 92.

The basic problem we deal with is the sinister's origin, its undesirable presence, the anguishing experience it provokes, its negative force, which is experienced with a great sense of impotence by human beings. The sinister is understood as a limiting, anguishing, terrific, instantaneous, inexplicable, and negative experience. The sinister is described and explained, in a critic and exemplifying way, starting from its origins, and continuing with its permanence in history. This permanence is due to the fact that human beings are always confronted with their reality. This last approach enables us to understand the sinister as a universal experience.

Etzioni, Amital. Comment on "Managers in the Moral Dimension: What Etzioni Might Mean to Corporate Managers". *Bus Ethics Quart*, 3(2), 169-170, A 93.

Etzioni suggests seven ways in which the article by Shaw and Zoller's advances socio-economic thought. He cites the need to develop a constructive alternative approach to the neoclassical paradigm while recognizing that socio-economics can subsume some elements of the neoclassical model. Socio-economists should work together to create one paradigm rather than compete on related but separate theories. Furthermore, they must specify the action implications of their paradigm and create a practical model to teach managers, executives, and economists. Etzioni concludes by emphasizing that socio-economists have a responsibility to remember the ethical implications of their recommendations and teachings.

Euben, J Peter. Politics and the Polis: How to Study Greek Moral and Political Philosophy. *Polis*, 11(1), 3-26, 1992.

Using a recent collection of essays entitled "Politics and the Polis: Essays in Greek Moral and Political Philosophy" as an example, the essay asks whether the sort of academic training of classical philosophers in the Anglo-American tradition receive can be a hindrance to understanding classical notions of philosophy, politics and morality. Using Nietzsche as a springboard and relying on examples drawn from tragedy and Plato's *Apology of Socrates* and *Gorgias*, the essay looks critically at what seems to be the book's seemingly unproblematic claim that scholarship on Greek moral and political philosophy should be "sensible and coherent," "plausible," and engage in "close analysis."

Euler, L and Arana, Juan (trans). Defensa de la revelación divina contra las objeciones del librepensador. *Themata*, 8, 195-219, 1991.

Against the great mass of his scientific production, Euler has published an alone apologetic opuscle, although Theologie was an important part of his studies and he had a continuous interest for Religion along his life. All this increases the importance of the Defense of divine dispensation, in which appear some lucid considerations about the limits of knowledge and the kind of certainty attainable to men.

Evans, C Stephen. *Passionate Reason: Making Sense of Kierkegaard's "Philosophical Fragments"*. Bloomington, Indiana Univ Pr, 1992.

Through a careful reading of *Philosophical Fragments Passionate Reason* looks at the tension between faith and reason as Kierkegaard understands it so as to rethink the nature of reason itself. It sees Kierkegaard as developing a conception of reason that challenges both the rationalist assumptions of modernity and the relativistic conclusions of post-modernism. Such a view of reason helps us make sense of the intellectual viability of historical Christian faith in the contemporary world.

Evans, C Stephen (ed) and Connell, George B (ed). *Foundations of Kierkegaard's Vision of Community*. Atlantic Highlands, Humanities Pr, 1992.

Since his emergence as a major philosophical voice, Kierkegaard has routinely been stereotyped as an asocial individualist. This collection of articles challenges this stereotype and highlights the new attention being given to the social dimensions of Kierkegaard's thought. Beginning with essays that treat aspects of Kierkegaard's underlying religious vision and ethical thought, the book goes on to focus on Kierkegaard's understanding of modernity and politics and the implications of his insights for such problems as international conflict and the status of women.

Evans, David M and Hrushovski, Ehud. On the Automorphism Groups of Finite Covers. *Annals Pure Applied Log*, 62(2), 83-112, Jl 93.

Evans, Fred. *Psychology and Nihilism: A Genealogical Critique of the Computational Model of Mind*. Albany, SUNY Pr, 1993.

After arguing that the computer model of mind cannot account for our cognitive competence, I show that its persistence as an explanation is due to three levels of intellectual entrapment: analytic discourse, technocratic rationality, and what Nietzsche calls "passive nihilism." An examination of phenomenological and poststructuralist alternatives shows that cognitive agency cannot be identified with either subjects or language. Rather, cognitive agency and competence is located in an irreducible "interplay of voices." This structure of the linguistic community provides the foundation for a "genealogical psychology" and suggests how the passive nihilism of both cognitive psychology and technocracy might be overcome.

Evans, G R. *Philosophy and Theology in the Middle Ages*. New York, Routledge, 1993.

This study, designed for student use, surveys the relationship of philosophy and theology from Augustine to the Reformation in the West. It covers issues of language, and the problems of the existence and nature of God, the creation of the world, incarnation and redemption, the sacraments, the doctrine of man, and ethics and politics.

Evans, J Claude. The Myth of Absolute Consciousness in Crises in Continental Philosophy, Dallery, Arleen B (ed). Albany, SUNY Pr, 1990.

Evans, R J and Penfold, H B and Hooker, C A. Control, Connectionism and Cognition: Towards a New Regulatory Paradigm. *Brit J Phil Sci*, 43(4), 517-536, D 92.

Evans, Rod L (ed) and Berent, Irwin M (ed). *Drug Legalization: For and Against*. Peru, Open Court, 1992.

The purpose of this anthology is to introduce readers to the arguments for and against drug legalization used by the major participants in the debate. The work represents the most significant essays written when the debate was first receiving wide coverage in the mainstream media. It gives not only "both sides" but also a number of intermediate positions between the drug laws we have now and a completely free market in drugs. In addition, it is multidisciplinary, containing arguments from such fields as legislation (Charles Rangel), law (Ethan Nadelmann), public policy (James Q Wilson), economics (Milton Friedman), and psychiatry (Thomas Szasz). A forward is included by Linus Pauling and an introduction by Hugh Downs.

Everitt, Nicholas. What's Wrong With Murder? Some Thoughts on Human and Animal Killing. *Int J Applied Phil*, 7(1), 47-54, Sum 92.

I investigate why the painless killing of a human being should be regarded as seriously wrong while the painless killing of a non-human animal is not so regarded. Attempts to justify this difference are explored, invoking (among other considerations) rights, and biological and mental differences between humans and animals. These attempts are rejected as unsatisfactory, and finally a criterion is suggested in terms of a capacity for self-conscious thought, which would explain why some animal killing is permissible. But the criterion does have the consequence, unacceptable to many, that killing some humans is equally permissible.

Everts, Saskia I. De deconstructie van het kleine verschil. *Kennis Methode*, 16(2), 206-214, 1992.

Ewbank, Roger. Farm Animal Welfare: A Historical Overview. *J Agr Environ Ethics*, 6/1(Supp), 82-86, 1993.

One result of Ruth Harrison's 1964 book *Animal Machines* was the UK Brambell Committee report on the welfare of animals kept under intensive livestock husbandry systems. The Council of Europe took on, from the Brambell Committee evidence, the idea that animals have ethological needs. The concept of rights is somewhat foreign to the UK, but the government's Farm Animal Welfare Council has suggested that farm stock should be kept so that they enjoy the so-called New Five Freedoms — including freedom from suppression of "normal" behavior. Currently two conflicting forces act in the animal welfare area: the seemingly high need of consumers for cheap high-quality animal protein foods and the demand, by the animal rightists, that man should not use animals at all.

Ewin, R E. Corporate Loyalty: Its Objects and Its Grounds. *J Bus Ethics*, 12(5), 387-396, My 93.

Disloyalty is always a vice, but loyalty is not always a virtue, so ethical management should not seek simply whatever loyalty it can get. Loyalty can make it possible for us to trust each other, and, when it takes appropriate objects and does not take extreme or improper forms, it can lie at the heart of much of what makes life worthwhile. Hence, it is understandable that corporations and management seek loyalty despite the fact that it can so easily go wrong. This paper deals with the issues of the grounds and objects of the employee loyalty that it is appropriate for management to seek.

Ewin, R E. Loyalties, and Why Loyalty Should be Ignored. *Crim Just Ethics*, 12(1), 36-42, Wint-Spr 93.

This paper continues an investigation of the claims loyalty has to being a virtue. It argues that, despite the importance of loyalty to and identification with others, moral assessment must be of particular loyalties and their objects rather than of loyalty as such.

Ewin, R E. Loyalty and Virtues. *Phil Quart*, 42(169), 403-419, O 92.

This paper takes up the issue of whether loyalty is a virtue. People can exhibit their loyalty in exhibiting other virtues, and loyalty might be a necessary condition of exhibiting those virtues. Loyalty can be exhibited in some vices. Loyalty is neither virtue nor vice, but is the emotional raw material from which virtues and vices can be constructed.

Ewin, R E. *Virtues and Rights: The Moral Philosophy of Thomas Hobbes*. Boulder, Westview Pr, 1991.

Hobbes's method is often misunderstood. Understood correctly, it shows his moral philosophy to be a virtues theory (as his contemporaries realised) and a rights theory, each dependant on the other. Hobbes himself was misled by the virtues. When that misconstruction is removed, it becomes clear that the more unwelcome aspects of Hobbes's theory of sovereignty are not necessary: people for whom government is possible on Hobbes's account are people who can sort out many things for themselves and do not need an unlimited sovereign.

Eylon, Yuval. Objects as Causes of Emotions (in Hebrew). *Iyyun*, 41, 413-431, O 92.

Ezquerro, Jesús (ed) and Larrazabal, Jesús (ed). *Cognition, Semantics and Philosophy*. Norwell, Kluwer, 1992.

Ezrahi, Yaron. Technology and the Civil Epistemology of Democracy. *Inquiry*, 35(3-4), 363-376, S-D 92.

In analogy with Rousseau's concept of "civil religion" as a system of "positive dogmas", "without which," as he observed, "a man cannot be a good citizen," this paper advances the concept of "civil epistemology" as the positive dogmas without which the agents of government actions cannot be held accountable by democratic citizens. (edited)

Fabris, Adriano. L'ermeneutica e il problema della fine: A proposito di due contributi recenti. *Teoria*, 12(2), 41-50, 1992.

The author discusses some contemporary developments of philosophical hermeneutics in Italy. The works of Mario Ruggenini (*I fenomeni e le parole*: Phenomenons and Words) and Vincenzo Vitiello (*Topologia del moderno*: Topology of Modern Age) are here especially examined. According to his book *Esperienza e paradosso* (Experience and Paradox) Fabris asserts that contemporary hermeneutics has exhausted her possibilities of development: therefore, the philosophical theory of interpretation can only consider its own limits, but not the things. Rethinking the problem of experience can be the way out of these difficulties.

Fackenheim, Emil L. A Reply to My Critics: A Testament of Thought (Includes Bibliography) in German Philosophy and Jewish Thought, Greenspan, Louis (ed). Toronto, Univ of Toronto Pr, 1992.

Factor, R Lance. Regions, Boundaries, and Points in Logic, God and Metaphysics, Harris, James F (ed). Dordrecht, Kluwer, 1992.

In this paper I examine some applications of the calculus of individuals based upon 'connection' as the primitive predicate. Special attention is given to the problems of defining boundaries and of defining points. These topics are central to the characterization of the 'extensive continuum' proposed by A N Whitehead in Part IV of *Process and Reality*. I indicate how the calculus both fulfills and departs from the Whiteheadian project.

Fagot-Largeault, Anne. Autonomie, don et partage dans la problématique de l'expérimentation humaine. *Dialogue (Canada)*, 30(3), 355-363, Sum 91.

Fairchild, David L. The Days Were Longer Then: Some Simple Thoughts About Sports—Philosophy?. *J Phil Sport*, 18, 59-73, 1991.

Fairfield, Paul. Truth Without Methodologism: Gadamer and James. *Amer Cath Phil Quart*, 67(3), 285-298, Sum 93.

Methodological questions have been far from central to philosophical hermeneutics; Gadamer has stated that his project is not primarily to devise criteria by which to adjudicate between conflicting interpretations but to describe what understanding itself is. It remains, however, that the search for such criteria is a legitimate hermeneutical enterprise and must be carried out in order for adjudication to be possible. I argue that the pragmatism of William James provides us with methodological criteria while steering clear of methodologism. James's theory may be incorporated into Gadamerian hermeneutics without running afoul of the basic tenets of the latter.

Fales, Evan. Are Causal Laws Contingent/ in Ontology, Causality and Mind: Essays in Honour of D M Armstrong, Bacon, John (ed). New York, Cambridge Univ Pr, 1993.

Armstrong's contention that laws of nature are contingent, although grounded in relations of necessitation between universals, is examined in detail. I argue that some of the advantages Armstrong claims for his view over the Regularity theory—in particular, its supposed ability to explain why laws sustain counterfactuals—do not succeed unless the necessitation relation is taken to be noncontingent. The paper then shows how noncontingency supplies an argument for Platonism with respect to universals, and considers how such noncontingency of causal relations is to be conceived; viz., whether as an internal relation between universals, or an external one.

Fales, Evan. Should God Not Have Created Adam?. *Faith Phil*, 9(2), 193-209, Ap 92.

The free will defense shows that God cannot be held responsible, in general, for the existence of manmade evil. But, I argue, the defense fails to exculpate God if it can be shown that there are ways God could have fashioned human nature, consistent with our freedom (or increasing it), that would have resulted in our being less evil. I discuss two such ways. The second half of the paper considers various defenses of the free will defense against this challenge, including two more general responses to the argument from evil due to Wykstra and Marilyn McCord Adams.

Fales, Evan and Wasserman, Edward A. Causal Knowledge: What Can Psychology Teach Philosophers?. *J Mind Behav*, 13(1), 1-27, Wint 92.

Theories of how organisms learn about cause-effect relations have a history dating back at least to the associationist/mechanistic hypothesis of David Hume. Some contemporary theories of causal learning are descendents of Hume's mechanistic models of conditioning, but others impute principled, rule-based reasoning. Since even primitive animals are conditionable, it is clear that there are built-in mechanical algorithms that respond to cause/ effect relations. The evidence suggests that humans retain the use of such algorithms, which are surely adaptive when causal judgments must be rapidly made. But we know very little about what these algorithms are and about when and with what ratiocinative procedures they are sometimes replaced. Nor do we know how the concept of causation originates in humans. To clarify some of these issues, this paper surveys the literature and explores the behavioral predictions made by two contrasting theories of causal learning: the mechanical Rescorla-Wagner model and the sophisticated reasoning codified in Bayes' Theorem.

Falguera, José Luis. La noción de modelo en los análisis de la concepción estructuralista. *Agora (Spain)*, 11(1), 97-106, 1992.

The basic unity of analysis for the Structuralist View of Philosophy of Science is the notion of "model" of the formal semantics. The way this notion must be understood is exposued by Balzer-Moulines-Sneed at the beginning of *An Architectonic for Science*. In this paper, I discuss the way they present the notion of "model" which is used in their analysis of empirical sciences and I offer another form to understand it, which is more adequate with their proper use.

Falk, Arthur. New Wrinkles in Old Fatalisms in Foundations of Logic and Language, Sen, Pranab Kumar (ed). New Delhi, Allied, 1990.

I present several formalized arguments for fatalism, expose their assumptions about modality, and evaluate their soundness. The new wrinkles are arguments against free choice that use counterfactual logics. I conclude that, while D Lewis's and Bennett's strictures on the use of counterfactual conditionals will block the fatalistic conclusions, they are open to a fatalist's criticism, and the debate is a stand-off. The new wrinkles deepen our understanding of deliberation and its use of seemingly gerrymandered temporally dependent modalities, which is hard to reconcile with modal realism.

Falk, Barrie. Consciousness, Cognition and the Phenomenol—I. *Aris Soc*, Supp(67), 55-73, 1993.

A current view holds that my mental states are conscious just in case I have a thought of their occurrence. I oppose this, the old idea that sensory states, as well as being items we are conscious of, also constitute our initial consciousness of the world. This cannot be defended. But I develop a notion of sophisticated phenomenal states, the product of complex (and not just sensory) interaction between world and perceiver. This yields a defensible version of the idea that we are aware of our presence in the world in a way that is additional to having the thought that this is so.

Falk, Raphael. Evolutionary Epistemology: What Phenotype is Selected and Which Genotype Evolves?. *Biol Phil*, 8(2), 153-172, Ap 93.

Much of the literature on evolutionary epistemology claimed that knowledge in general, and science as its epitome in particular, evolved along lines analogous to organic biological evolution. I refer here only to the view of knowledge as an extension of material biological evolution. These theories of evolutionary epistemology, contrary to the relativist notions of naturalized epistemology, adopted strict realist positions. (edited)

Falls-Corbitt, Margaret and McClain, F Michael. God and Privacy. *Faith Phil*, 9(3), 369-386, Jl 92.

Contemporary reflection about God which includes certain assumptions raises for us the issue of God and privacy. Some philosophers believe that there is no obligation to respect privacy grounded in our basic moral duty to respect the autonomous choices of persons. If this is correct, and if it is correct to think of God as one whose actions perfectly accord with moral duties, then there is a *prima facie* case for thinking that God respects our privacy. We explore this thesis by considering the most plausible objections to it, including matters of religious practice.

Fantini, Bernardino. The Development of a Scientific Specialty: The Case of Microbial Genetics—A Review of *The Emergence of Bacterial Genetics* by Thomas D Brock. *Hist Phil Life Sci*, 14(1), 137-143, Ja 92.

Faralli, Carla. Normative Institutionalism and Normative Realism: A Comparison. *Ratio Juris*, 6(2), 181-189, Jl 93.

MacCormick and Weinberger's normative institutionalism, or neo-institutionalist theory, is propounded as "a socially realistic development of normativism." This theory blends normativism and realism and represents the coherent outcome of two components of each author's thought: normativism from the standpoint of legal theory; neo-empiricism from the standpoint of philosophy generally. Scandinavian legal realism, or normative realism, is the only school of jurisprudence that can be understood as a direct offspring of one of the philosophical currents (i.e., the Uppsala school) belonging to contemporary new-empiricism. This is why it inevitably becomes a touchstone for those legal theories — like MacCormick and Weinberger's new-institutionalist theory — which are not direct offshoots, but owe much to the principles and methods of new-empiricism.

Farbstein, Aviva. The Tarasoff Case. *Gnosis*, 4(1), 117-123, 1992.

Farley, Jonathan. The Dream of Captain Carib. *Harvard Rev Phil*, 1(1), 53-58, Spr 91.

Farr, Richard. Normative Ethics: Bad News for the Sensible Compromise?. *S J Phil*, 31(2), 143-160, Sum 93.

'Pure' consequentialism is unattractive for a variety of reasons, but few people have thought that consequentialist thinking has no role to play in moral deliberation. Not surprisingly, a strategy of compromise so dominates contemporary thinking that it has become a philosophical platitude. Nevertheless that strategy is, in all its recent manifestations, unworkable.

Farr, Richard. The Political Economy of Community. *J Soc Phil*, 23(3), 118-139, Wint 92.

Communitarianism has enjoyed only a very brief prominence, perhaps because it has been so poorly connected with any examination of, let alone allegiance to, actual communities. One important writer who conspicuously avoids this shortcoming, but who so far has been ignored by academic social philosophers, is Wendell Berry. Here I attempt to derive from his writings on agriculture a concrete picture of what constitutes the difference between the success of 'community' and its failure.

Farrell, Thomas B. *Norms of Rhetorical Culture*. New Haven, Yale Univ Pr, 1993.

Norms of Rhetorical Culture presents a philosophical investigation and defense of rhetoric as an art of practical reason. Against traditions of European philosophy that have disjoined rhetoric from foundational projects of Enlightenment reason, Farrell argues that rhetoric presents a unique and necessary mode of posing and proposing practical questions. The body of analysis forges a synthesis between an amended Aristotelian rhetoric and the critical theory of communication of Jürgen Habermas. The result is a contemporary philosophy of civic discourse and social knowledge.

Farrelly, John. Developmental Psychology and Knowledge of Being in Chinese Foundations for Moral Education and Character Development, Van Doan, Tran (ed). Washington, CRVP, 1991.

Farrenkopf, John. Nietzsche, Spengler, and the Politics of Cultural Despair. *Interpretation*, 20(2), 165-185, Wint 92-93.

Farrenkopf, John. The Early Phase in Spengler's Political Philosophy. *Hist Polit Thought*, 13(2), 319-338, Sum 92.

Fasching, Darrell J. Mass Media, Ethical Paradox, and Democratic Freedom: Jacques Ellul's Ethic of the Word. *Res Phil Technol*, 11, 77-103, 1991.

Faulkner, Robert K. The Empire of Progress: Bacon's Improvement Upon Machiavelli. *Interpretation*, 20(1), 37-62, Fall 92.

Fauré, Christine. Le statut du serment et de la promesse dans la Déclaration des Droits de 1789. *Philosophiques*, 19(1), 75-86, 1992.

The meaning and the function of the *Declaration of the rights of Men and Citizen* has been discussed for a long time. We prefer, among different lectures (juridical and sociological) of the text, the method contrived for an explanation of performative utterances, by the English philosopher J L Austin: it can enable us to discover on what convention a good reception of the Declaration is based, what rules of conducts the "constituants" have chosen. These conventions oath and promise — appear in the text as mere indications. The intensity of the political rupture hide them. To decode the "constituant's" intentions, a contextual analysis is needed, that is both immediate socio-historical context and conceptual context.

Fay, Thomas A. Thomas Aquinas on the Justification of Revolution. *Hist Euro Ideas*, 16(4-6), 501-506, Ja 93.

This article examines the theory of the justification of revolution in the writings of Thomas Aquinas. In his earliest writing, the *Scriptum super libros Sententiarum*, Aquinas seems to make a rather strong case for a right to rebellion against a tyrannous government. Later, in his middle years, for example in the *De Regimine Principum*, he seems to take the view that ordinarily, if the tyranny is not extreme, it is better to tolerate it, because in trying to overthrow the tyrannical government it frequently happens that the peace is disturbed so inordinately that the situation following the rebellion is even worse than the conditions under the regime that preceded it. The examples furnished by several revolutions, e.g., the French, the Russian, the Cuban, etc. make for interesting test cases to which the principles of Thomas may be applied. It will be argued that in fact history shows that the conditions after a revolution are, for the most part, worse than the conditions that preceded it. Thomas Aquinas's theory of revolution, it will be argued, offers a very balanced approach to the question of revolution. While he does not proscribe the possibility of revolution in principle, he sanctions it only with great reluctance because of the difficulty in controlling the violence of the forces it unleashes. His position seems to be vindicated by the history of modern revolutions.

Faye, Jan. Is the Future Really Real?. *Amer Phil Quart*, 30(3), 259-269, Jl 93.

Featherstone, Mike. Postmodernism, Cultural Change, and Social Practice in Postmodernism/ Jameson/ Critique, Kellner, Douglas M (ed). Washington, Maisonneuve Pr, 1989.

Feehan, Thomas. Augustine's Own Examples of Lying. *Augustin Stud*, 22, 165-190, 1991.

Feehan, Thomas. The Morality of Lying in Saint Augustine. *Augustin Stud*, 21, 67-81, 1990.

Feenberg, Andrew. Subversive Rationalization: Technology, Power, and Democracy. *Inquiry*, 35(3-4), 301-322, S-D 92.

This paper argues, against technological and economic determinism, that the dominant model of industrial society is politically contingent. The idea that technical decisions are significantly constrained by 'rationality'—either technical or economic—is shown to be groundless. Constructivist and hermeneutic approaches to technology show that modern societies are inherently available for a different type of development in a different cultural framework. It is possible that, in the future, those who today are subordinated to technology's rhythms and demands will be able to control it and to determine its evolution. I call the process of creating such a society 'subversive rationalization' because it requires technological advances that can only be made in opposition to the dominant hegemony.

Feffer, Andrew. *The Chicago Pragmatists and American Progressivism*. Ithaca, Cornell Univ Pr, 1993.

An intellectual biography of the Chicago pragmatists (John Dewey, George H Mead, James H Tufts) that retraces the story of their personal involvement in reform movements and examines how they revised contemporary political rhetoric and social theory in order to reestablish the foundations of democracy in productive and rewarding work. Also includes an account of certain elitist and anti-democratic assumptions of pragmatist theory, in particular the pragmatists' implicit mistrust of the political impulses of the industrial workers they championed.

Feher, Fererr. Why Liberty is Devoured by Reason in History: Re-Reading Merleau-Ponty During the Days of the Soviet Revolution. *Phil Soc Crit*, 18(2), 135-146, 1992.

Fehér, István M (ed). *Directions and Misdirections (in Hungarian)*. Budapest, Atlantisz, 1991.

The volume, linked up with the series of commentaries on Heidegger, brings forth all the papers delivered at the German-Hungarian Heidegger symposium held in November 1989. Eminent experts discuss different aspects of his oeuvre: its connection with phenomenology, or possible parallels with the philosophical doctrines of Lukács and Wittgenstein. The other group of papers in the collection inquiries into the question of hermeneutics. A German scholar analyses, on the basis of documents, one of the most embarrassing questions of Heidegger's reception, namely the circumstances of his rectorship under Nazi Germany; on other paper discusses Heidegger as a significant representative of post-modernism. The book is intended to readers learned in philosophy, though, as a whole, it is a useful companion for those who wish to get acquainted with Heidegger's oeuvre, as well.

Feinberg, Gerald. Knowledge of the Past and Future. *J Phil*, 89(12), 607-642, D 92.

Feinberg, Joel. *Reason and Responsibility (Eighth Edition)*. Belmont, Wadsworth, 1993.

Feinberg, Joel. The Social Importance of Moral Rights in Philosophical Perspectives, 6: Ethics, 1992, Tomberlin, James E (ed). Atascadero, Ridgeview, 1992.

Philosophers have voiced various kinds of scepticism about rights, particularly about *moral* rights, that is rights whose existence is prior to and independent of legal enactment. I distinguish these various forms of scepticism and try to defend moral rights from each of them, but the emphasis in this paper is on the charge that consciousness of one's moral rights fosters selfishness, sits poorly with loving relationships, are by their very nature a threat to worthwhile community. I also discuss the charge that "moral power," as opposed to physical power, has no value.

Feinberg, Walter. Dewey and Democracy at the Dawn of the Twenty-First Century. *Educ Theor*, 43(2), 195-216, Spr 93.

The essay reviews Robert Westbrook's *John Dewey and American Democracy*, Ithica: Cornell University Press, and gives the book high marks for synthesizing a large amount of material. However, the book fails in its understanding the limits of Dewey's contribution to the concept of democracy. The problem is the failure on Dewey's part to make a clear distinction between political and educational democracy. This failure lead to his inability to examine the rights that non-democratic groups have in a democratic society. It is argued that a clearer distinction between non-democratic and anti-democratic helps sharpen Dewey's ideas of Democracy.

Feingold, Mordechai. Tradition versus Novelty in Revolution and Continuity, Barker, Peter (ed). Washington, Cath Univ Amer Pr, 1991.

Feldman, Carol Fleisher. Intentionality, Narrativity, and Interpretation in John Searle and His Critics, Lepore, Ernest (ed). Cambridge, Blackwell, 1991.

Feldman, Fred. On the Consistency of Act- and Motive- Utilitarianism: A Reply to Robert Adams. *Phil Stud*, 70(2), 201-211, My 93.

In *Motive Utilitarianism*, Adams tried to show that there are situations in which the requirements of act utilitarianism (AU) are incompatible with those of motive utilitarianism (MU). Adams' argument, if successful, would suggest that we cannot coherently think that utilitarianism can be applied across the board to all objects of moral appraisal. After explaining Adams' argument, I present improved formulations of AU and MU. These are based on the formulations presented in my *Doing the Best We Can*. I then show that these doctrines are consistent. Contrary to what Adams claimed, there cannot be a case in which the requirements of AU and MU (properly formulated) are incompatible.

Feldman, Fred. The Enigma of Death. *Philosophia (Israel)*, 21(3-4), 163-181, Ap 92.

According to "the Standard Analysis" death may be defined as the cessation of life. In spite of the popularity of this analysis, it confronts a number of difficulties. Organisms that go into suspended animation cease (temporarily) to live, yet they sometimes do not die. Organisms that reproduce by fission cease to exist when they divide; hence, they also cease to live when they divide. It is counterintuitive to say that they then die. In this paper, I discuss several proposed analyses of the concept of death, and attempt to show that each fails. I conclude that death remains enigmatic.

Feldman, Richard. Proper Functionalism. *Nous*, 27(1), 34-50, Mr 93.

In this paper I reply to some objections Alvin Plantinga raises to recent theories of epistemic justification in *Warrant: The Current Debate* and I raise objections to the theory Plantinga defends in *Warrant and Proper Function*. Plantinga's view is roughly that a belief has epistemic warrant provided it has been produced by properly functioning cognitive faculties in an appropriate environment. I argue that this theory is subject to a problem similar to the generality problem that affects reliabilism. I also argue that given Plantinga's view that something is functioning properly when it is functioning as it supposed or designed to function, his theory runs into objections arising from consideration of poorly designed beings.

Feldman, Richard. *Reason and Argument*. Englewood Cliffs, Prentice Hall, 1993.

Reason and Argument is a textbook for use in courses on reasoning, critical thinking, or informal logic. The first main section contains chapters on truth, rationality, and the basic concepts used in argument evaluation. The second main section develops a general method for identifying, reconstructing, and evaluating arguments. The final section shows how to apply this method to arguments about testimonial, statistical, causal, and moral issues. The method of argument analysis developed in the book discourages simplistic labeling and categorizing of arguments and encourages careful and constructive analysis of arguments.

Feldman, Susan. Multiple Biological Mothers: The Case for Gestation. *J Soc Phil*, 23(1), 98-104, Spr 92.

Dealing with custody cases in which a child has two mothers (genetic and gestational), this paper argues for the primacy of claims made by the gestational mother, on the following grounds: 1) the preference in favor of the genetic mother involves a misunderstanding of the role of genes in development. 2) Pregnancy is work performed by women which society undervalues, yet its quality is crucial to the health of newborns. 3) Preference for gestational mother can be part of a recognition of the value of women's work in pregnancy, thus raising the likelihood of both healthier babies and greater respect for women.

Fell, Albert P. Epistemological and Ontological Queries Concerning David Carr's *Time, Narrative, and History*. *Phil Soc Sci*, 22(3), 370-380, S 92.

David Carr's account of human existence emphasizes its implicit narrative character as something distinct from the subsequent comprehension of it within historical narratives. This helps to reconcile two unwilling partners, epistemologists who have been slow to acknowledge the ubiquity of interpretation in historical inquiry, and radical hermeneuticists who have too quickly jetisoned the epistemological problematic. It is argued, also, that Carr is too reluctant to argue for (a) the universality of the narrative construction of identities in individual and social life, and (b) the possibility of formulating general narratives which establish our common humanity.

Fell, Albert P. 'Epistemological' and 'Narrativist' Philosophies of History in Objectivity, Method and Point of View, Van Der Dussen, W J (ed). Leiden, Brill, 1991.

F R Ankersmit claims (*History and Theory*, 30, 4) that philosophy of history in the Anglo-Saxon tradition faces a dilemma of sticking with the epistemological problematic and becoming "an odd positivist fossil," or displacing that approach with an innovative narrativist or interpretivist one. But I argue that this is a false dichotomy because the productive work of "narrativists" such as Hayden White is quite compatible with, indeed cries out for, complementary reflection on the characteristics of historical knowledge. Philosophy cannot do justice to historiography without analysing its central cognitive claims.

Fell, Joseph P. The Familiar and the Strange in Heidegger: A Critical Reader, Dreyfus, Hubert L (ed). Cambridge, Blackwell, 1992.

Felsenthal, Dan S and Machover, Moshé. Sequential Voting by Veto: Making the Mueller-Moulin Algorithm More Versatile. *Theor Decis*, 33(3), 223-240, N 92.

Felt, James W. Fatalism and Truth about the Future. *Thomist*, 56(2), 209-227, Ap 92.

Is fatalism entailed if propositions referring to the future are already true or false? The answer is yes, not by reason of logic, as is sometimes supposed, but because this would entail causal determinism. But such antecedent truth is neither logically required nor metaphysically believable, given the processive nature of becoming. Strictly speaking, propositions referring to the future are neither true nor false, and if they were, fatalism would be unavoidable.

Fenner, David. Modest Aesthetic Naturalism. *J Aes Art Crit*, 50(4), 283-289, Fall 92.

Is psychology relevant to aesthetics? The answer is yes, and more than in simple ancillary ways. This is argued on the basis of i) answering the traditional difficulties raised by anti-naturalists, and ii) ontological and explanatory economy. The second half of the paper describes and defends a program of modest aesthetic naturalism. What makes the naturalism 'modest' is that, where a value reduction or identity is sought, the naturalist offers argument to justify the connection between value and fact. A simple positing of the connection is incomplete.

Ferejohn, John. Must Preferences Be Respected in a Democracy? in The Idea of Democracy, Copp, David (ed). New York, Cambridge Univ Pr, 1993.

Ferguson, Ann. *Sexual Democracy: Women, Oppression, and Revolution*. Boulder, Westview Pr, 1991.

Ferguson, Kenneth. An Intervention into the Flew/Fogelin Debate. *Hume Stud*, 18(1), 105-112, Ap 92.

Robert Fogelin has forcefully argued that Hume intended to produce an *a priori* argument to show that miracles are logically impossible, while Anthony Flew is noted for a conflicting view that Hume intended merely to urge caution in accepting miracles solely on the basis of testimony. I furnish text (*Enquiry*, Chapter X) which lends aid and comfort to both. But Fogelin's interpretation forbids "miracles" only under a strict definition, whereas the empirical arguments favored by Flew are also needed if particular marvelous reports are to be legitimately dismissed.

Ferguson, Kenneth. Existing by Convention. *Relig Stud*, 28(2), 185-194, Je 92.

I contend that Anselm's famous premise that God is "that than which no greater can be conceived" is actually reducible to either a conventionally popular definition or else a conventionally derived "conceptual truth" about God. If correct, the most that Anselm may show is that within such a conventional framework, consistency demands that God's existence be accepted as an implication. But outside this convention, nothing at all would follow about God's existence.

Fernández, Estela and Ciriza, Alejandra. Hacia una interpretación del discurso independentista. *Rev Filosof (Costa Rica)*, 30(71), 97-101, J 92.

This paper, inserted in the perspective of a Latin American history of ideas, attempts to interpret the articulation between the different social groups that brought about independence, as the effect of the construction of a peculiar ideological device. Through this device, a class fraction—the emergent Creole bourgeoisie—would succeed in summoning the popular sectors to pursue a project presented as the expression of the general concerns of the American people.

Fernández, José Luis. El conocimiento de Dios según Malebranche. *Anu Filosof*, 25(2), 295-319, 1992.

This article seeks to explain one of the four modes of knowledge developed by Malebranche: immediate knowledge of God, which reveals to us that God exists but not what God is.

Fernández, Oscar. Sobre predicciones y relatos. *Rev Filosof (Costa Rica)*, 30(71), 17-26, J 92.

In this article the author attempts to analyze some of the consequences derived from the unsuccessful predictions and promises contained in the historic materialism, the latter being defined as grand story telling, which exerted a luminous influence on the Latin American sociological field for the last decades. Hence, the author proposes the abandonment of great predications and the development of a more explicative and less pretentious theoretical work.

Ferrara, Alessandro. *Modernity and Authenticity: A Study of the Social and Ethical Thought of Jean-Jacques Rousseau*. Albany, SUNY Pr, 1992.

Ferrari, G R F. Platonic Love in The Cambridge Companion to Plato, Kraut, Richard H (ed). New York, Cambridge Univ Pr, 1992.

Plato does not have a comprehensive theory of love. Rather, he diverts certain received opinions about love to his own peculiarly philosophic ends. He is not interested in telling us what it would be like to live with someone as a platonic lover. In the *Symposium*, the cliché that Plato turns to metaphysical advantage is "love promotes virtue." In the *Phaedrus*, it is "love is wild."

Ferrari, María Aparecida. Sobre las bases éticas de la democracia. *Sapientia*, 47(185), 201-208, 1992.

Ferrari, Massimo. La philosophie de l'espace chez Ernst Cassirer. *Rev Metaph Morale*, 97(4), 455-477, O-D 92.

Ferrari, Vincenzo and Velicogna, Nella Gridelli. Philosophy and Sociology of Law in the Work of Renato Treves. *Ratio Juris*, 6(2), 202-215, Jl 93.

After giving account of the main events in R Treves' life, the article describes the basic events in his philosophy and in his sociology of law. Treves' approach to philosophy of law is essentially de-constructivist, in that he transforms the philosophical reflection into a methodology and asserts the compatibility of the most diverse theories from a perspectivist viewpoint. It is precisely this vision which led Treves to building up a modern kind of sociology of law, where theorizing, empirical observation and critical evaluation of values are connected.

Ferrarin, Alfredo. *Mathesis* e costruzione tra geometria antica e moderna. *Teoria*, 11(2), 87-104, 1991.

Ferrarin, Alfredo. Autocoscienza, riferimento dell'io e conoscenza di sé: Introduzione ad un dibattito contemporaneo. *Teoria*, 12(1), 111-153, 1992.

AUTHOR INDEX WITH ABSTRACTS 477 Fieser, James

Ferré, Frederick. Natural Theology and Positive Predication: Might Maimonides Be a Guide? in Prospects for Natural Theology, Long, Eugene Thomas (ed). Washington, Cath Univ Amer Pr, 1992.

If even the great "negative theologian," Maimonides, cannot in practice do without some positive predicates for God and actually offers rules for their use, then positive natural theology may take encouragement. I show that Maimonides allow two types of positive talk about God: for the pious community he affirms positive predicates contained in authorized prayers; for theoretical argument he accepts Aristotle's metaphysical affirmations about the First Mover, I conclude that Quine's model of a "total science," attached by numerous strands to experience but avoiding literal correspondence claims, is implicit in Maimonides' practice and best for natural theology today.

Ferreira, M Jamie. Seeing (Just) Is Believing: Faith and Imagination. *Faith Phil*, 9(2), 151-167, Ap 92.

Appeal to a 'leap' of faith has popularly been both used in defense of faith by some and roundly criticized by others. Descriptions of such conversions are often understood to refer to an exercise of 'will-power'— an intentional (not merely voluntary) selection from a set of options which seem equally 'real' (or even one which goes against the more attractive option). In what follows I challenge such a reading of the transition involved by examining a variety of (mostly autobiographical) descriptions of coming to faith and, conversely, turning away from faith, in the light of accounts (by S T Coleridge and William James) of leap and volition in non-religious contexts. I will argue that the 'leaps' or transitions described in these religious accounts are more appropriately understood in terms of imaginative activity than in terms of either 'acts of will-power' or ineffable happenings.

Ferrell, Robyn. Why Bother? Defending Derrida and the Significance of Writing. *Austl J Phil*, 71(2), 121-131, Je 93.

My discussion begins from a curious question of John Searle's in relation to fictional discourse: 'Why bother?'. I argue that deconstruction is necessary to an understanding of the significance of that question in Anglo-American philosophy, currently.

Ferry, Luc. Aesthetics (in Czechoslovakian). *Filozof Cas*, 40(4), 591-604, 1992.

In his study, the author examines the term *aesthetics*, as developed by modern aestheticians. This first appeared with the advent of the modern era (modernity), which he characterizes as the birth of the modern subject: individual and individualized. The author traces, step by step, the special transformation which occurred in the perception of the artistic work: it ceases to be perceived as an imitation of the objective world that is as perfect as possible, and becomes the product of a definite artist, as far as possible a gifted one, but in every case given by individual taste. Only in exactly this historical moment did "aesthetics" become possible. (edited)

Feshbach, Sidney. The Light at the End of the Tunnel Is Coming Right at Me in Analecta Husserliana, XXXVIII, Tymieniecka, Anna-Teresa (ed). Dordrecht, Kluwer, 1992.

Festa, Egidio. Gassendi interprete di Cavalieri. *G Crit Filosof Ital*, 71(2), 289-300, My-Ag 92.

Festini, Heda. An Application of Weingartner's Logical Proposal for Rational Belief, Knowledge, Assumption in Advances in Scientific Philosophy, Schurz, Gerhard (ed). Amsterdam, Rodopi, 1991.

The author's purpose is to stress that several of Wittgenstein's works support and strengthen Weingartner's realistic epistemic system in his theorems for rational belief, knowledge and assumption. They are motivated by reference to everyday usage and are arrived at within the framework of many-valued semantics by means of finite matrices, building them in such a way that Weingartner's system is not only consistent, but also decidable.

Fethe, Charles. Analogy as a Guide to Philosophical Thinking. *Teach Phil*, 16(1), 59-68, Mr 93.

This article defends the use of analogies as a fundamental tool for promoting philosophical thinking in introductory courses. It surveys some of the major types of analogies, demonstrates how they can be used in the classroom, and offers examples of how philosophers in the past have used analogies to add strength and rhetorical appeal to their arguments.

Fetzer, James. *Foundations of Philosophy of Science: Recent Developments*. New York, Paragon House, 1993.

This collection of twenty-five articles focuses on the crucial theoretical problems fundamental to the philosophy of science today. Included are classic studies by Hempel, Salmon, Popper, Carnap, Quine, Goodman, Kuhn, Lakatos, and many others, as well as contemporary selections reflecting recent developments within the field and discussing their importance. Review questions and suggestions for further reading are provided. The anthology is systematically correlated with a companion text, *Philosophy of Science*, authored by the editor, where the two books may be used independently or in combination as appropriate.

Fetzer, James. *Philosophy of Science*. New York, Paragon House, 1993.

By emphasizing the importance of methodological commitments to the study of science and the significance of interpretations of probability to understanding laws of nature and scientific explanations, this book provides a framework for investigating the most recent work and the most promising solutions to the central problems that define the philosophy of science today. Science is characterized as an attempt to construct a model of the world and philosophy of science as an attempt to construct a model of science, especially by discovering principles and procedures by means of which science might fulfill its aims and thus qualify as rational.

Fetzer, James H. What's Wrong with Salmon's History: The Third Decade. *Phil Sci*, 59(2), 246-262, Je 92.

My purpose here is to elaborate the reasons I maintain that Salmon has not been completely successful in reporting the history of work on explanation. The most important limitation of his account is that it does not emphasize the critical necessity to embrace a suitable conception of probability in the development of the theory of probabilistic explanation.

Fetzer, James H and Almeder, Rober F. *Glossary of Epistemology/ Philosophy of Science*. New York, Paragon House, 1993.

This glossary is intended to provide clear and concise definitions for the most important concepts that appear in the theory of knowledge and in the philosophy of science. Among the most important notions that occur in this context are alternative conceptions of inference and argument, of truth and confirmation, of probability and induction, of knowledge and justification, of scientific theories and scientific explanations, of rationalism and empiricism, together with brief sketches of some of the most important historical (Plato, Aristotle, etc.) and contemporary (Russell, Tarski, etc.) thinkers in these fields.

Fetzer, James H and Dunlop, Charles E M. *Glossary of Cognitive Science*. New York, Paragon House, 1993.

The purpose of this work is to help the non-specialist gain access to the terminology of cognitive science, by offering clear, nontechnical definitions of its basic vocabulary. Drawing primarily from philosophy, psychology, linguistics, and artificial intelligence, the glossary contains 433 entries, ranging from 25 to 250 words in length. Cross-listings of related terms are easy to track, and many entries are supplemented with illuminating examples. Short biographical entries for many of the key people in cognitive science are also included, along with synopses of their major contributions. References for further reading appear at the end of the book.

Feuer, Lewis S. Gertrude Himmelfarb: A Historian Considers Heroes and Their Historians. *Phil Soc Sci*, 23(1), 5-25, Mr 93.

Ficino, Marsilio. *Sobre el furor divino y otros textos*. Barcelona, Anthropos, 1993.

Fidelibus, G. Quale liberazione per l'uomo dopo il marxismo?. *Sapienza*, 44(4), 379-426, 1991.

Field, Hartry. Critical Notice: Paul Horwich's *Truth*. *Phil Sci*, 59(2), 321-330, Je 92.

Field, Hartry. The Conceptual Contingency of Mathematical Objects. *Mind*, 102(406), 285-299, Ap 93.

Field, Richard. Descartes on the Material Falsity of Ideas. *Phil Rev*, 102(3), 309-334, Jl 93.

Descartes claims in the Third Meditation that ideas of sense might be materially false. While an accurate interpretation of this claim has the potential of providing some valuable insights into Descartes's theory of ideas in general and his understanding of the epistemic status of sensations in particular, the explanation Descartes provides of the material falsity of ideas is itself obscure and misleading, making accurate interpretation difficult. In this paper an interpretation of material falsity is offered which identifies the fault of materially false ideas in the logical incoherence of their objective content. The implications of this interpretation are also discussed.

Fielder, John H and Birsch, Douglas. *The DC-10 Case: A Study in Applied Ethics, Technology, and Society*. Albany, SUNY Pr, 1992.

Fieser, James. Callicott and the Metaphysical Basis of Ecocentric Morality. *Environ Ethics*, 15(2), 171-180, Sum 93.

According to the theory of ecocentric morality, the environment and its many ecosystems are entitled to a direct moral standing, and not simply a standing derivative from human interests. J Baird Callicott has offered two possible metaphysical foundations for ecocentrism that attempt to show that inherent goodness can apply to environmental collections and not just to individual agents. I argue that Callicott's first theory fails because it relies on a problematic theory of moral sentiments and that his second theory fails because it rests on an unsupported parallel between the breakdown of the subject-object dichotomy suggested by quantum theory and an alleged actualization of morality upon the interaction of environmental collections with consciousness. Finally, I argue that Callicott overrates the need for a metaphysical grounding of inherent value, and that the metaphysical question has little bearing on the normative issue of ecocentrism.

Fieser, James. Hume's Classification of the Passions and Its Precursors. *Hume Stud*, 18(1), 1-17, Ap 92.

Many aspects of Hume's taxonomy of the passions in the *Treatise* follows traditional classifications. I first sketch the traditional Stoic and Thomistic accounts of the passions. I then argue that Hume's account is traditional insofar he grounds all passions in a class of eight primitive passions, four of which parallel the Stoic account. Hume also appears indebted to Hutcheson's explanation of the calm-violent distinction between passions. The uniqueness of Hume's theory consists in his account of the indirect passions. Finally, I criticize the interpretations of Hume's classification offered by Kemp Smith, Ardal, and Loeb, and suggest what I believe is the most textually sound classification.

Fieser, James. Moore, Spencer, and the Naturalistic Fallacy. *Hist Phil Quart*, 10(3), 271-276, Jl 93.

In Chapter 2 of *Principia Ethica*, Moore presents two criticisms of Spencer's evolutionary ethics. This first is that Spencer wrongly uses the terms "more evolved" (a natural term), and "higher" and "better" (ethical terms) as though they were equivalent, and thereby commits the naturalistic fallacy. The second is that since Spencer believes that pleasure is the same as goodness, then he is once again committing the naturalistic fallacy, It will be argued here that both of Moore's attacks fail since he misunderstood Spencer's meanings of the terms "higher" and "good". In light of Moore's failure, it is suggested that the naturalistic fallacy must be qualified so it does not reduce simply to an allegation that an ethical theory denies moral realism.

Fieser, James. The Compatibility of Eco-Centric Morality. *Int J Applied Phil*, 7(1), 37-40, Sum 92.

According to eco-centric morality, the environment is entitled to a direct moral standing and not merely a standing derived from human interests. Eco-centrism is unique in its attempt to introduce a new principle into our value system rather than the traditional attempt to draw implications from previously accepted principles. By examining Leopold's principle of eco-centrism in his essay "The Land Ethic", I consider whether his principle, or similar principles, can be introduced into our value system without serious conflict with our traditional human oriented obligations, such as prohibitions against stealing. I conclude that only a well qualified *prima facie* principle of eco-centrism will be consistent with traditional normative principles.

Fieser, James. The Correlativity of Duties and Rights. *Int J Applied Phil*, 7(2), 1-7, Wint 92.

The correlativity of duties and rights states that one person's duty entails another person's rights. The correlativity thesis is often criticized with three counter instances where the relation seems not to hold: duties of obedience, duties of charity, and duties to collective entities. I defend the correlativity thesis by addressing these counter instances. Obedience is resolved since it stems from the need to develop habits which do not lead to the infringement of future persons' rights. Duties of charity entail corresponding rights to charity insofar as these duties and rights are graduated according to social proximity. Duties toward species preservation entail corresponding rights to token members, graduated according to the endangerment of the species as a whole.

Fieser, James. The Logic of Natural Law in Aquinas's *Treatise on Law*. *J Phil Res*, 17, 155-172, 1992.

Against recent commentators such as Armstrong, D'Arcy, Copleston, O'Connor, Bourke, and Grisez, I argue that the logic referred to by Thomas in his "Treatise on Law" should not be understood metaphorically. Instead, it involves a chain of syllogisms, beginning with the synderesis principle, followed by primary, secondary, and tertiary principles, and ends with a practical syllogism. In showing this, I attack the view that the synderesis principle, "good ought to be done and evil avoided", is tautological. Second, I show the syllogistic relation between this and the more subordinate moral principles. Finally, I argue that the practical syllogism also involves a logical deduction, where the minor premise is a propositional attitude of perception, and the conclusion is an action which expresses a proposition. What emerges is a more precise account of how actions are related to natural law.

Figal, Günter. Die Gegenwart der Geschichtlichkeit: Neuere Arbeiten zur Heideggerschen Philosophie. *Phil Rundsch*, 39(4), 293-303, 1992.

Figl, Johann and Parkes, Graham R (trans). Nietzsche's Early Encounters with Asian Thought in Nietzsche and Asian Thought, Parkes, Graham R (ed). Chicago, Univ of Chicago Pr, 1991.

Filice, Carlo. Pacifism: A Philosophical Exploration. *J Phil Res*, 17, 119-153, 1992.

I argue in this paper that pacifism is a live moral option. I do this in four steps. First, I try to make the case that the backing of thinkers and prophets of the stature of Gandhi and Jesus lends pacifism some prima-facie moral legitimacy. Second, I try to determine what the ethical-metaphysical preconditions that would justify pacifism would justify pacifism would have to be—and I conclude that some consequentialist soul-exposing scheme would be required. Third, I argue that such a scheme would be able to sustain pacifism against rights-based criticisms, like those advanced by Narveson. Fourth, I defend the possibility of such a required ethical-metaphysical scheme.

Filice, Carlo. Pacifism: A Reply to Professor Narveson. *J Phil Res*, 17, 493-495, 1992.

Finch, H L. Simone Weil: Harbinger of a New Renaissance? in Simone Weil's Philosophy of Culture, Bell, Richard (ed). New York, Cambridge Univ Pr, 1993.

Findlay, John N. Commentary on "Hegel's Revenge on Russell" in Hegel and His Critics, Desmond, William J (ed). Albany, SUNY Pr, 1989.

Findlay, L M. Imagining Epistemology: Plato and Romantic Luminaries in Analecta Husserliana, XXXVIII, Tymieniecka, Anna-Teresa (ed). Dordrecht, Kluwer, 1992.

Fine, Gail. Commentary on Sedley's "Teleology and Myth in the *Phaedo*. *Proc Boston Colloq Anc Phil*, 5, 384-398, 1989.

Fine, Gail. Inquiry in the "Meno" in The Cambridge Companion to Plato, Kraut, Richard H (ed). New York, Cambridge Univ Pr, 1992.

Fink, Eugen and Seibert, Charles H (trans) and Heidegger, Martin. *Heraclitus Seminar*. Evanston, Northwestern Univ Pr, 1993.

In the winter semester of 1966-67 at the University of Freiburg, Martin Heidegger and Eugen Fink conducted an extraordinary seminar on the fragments of Heraclitus. This book records those conversations, documenting the imaginative and experimental character of the multiplicity of interpretations offered and providing an invaluable portrait of Heidegger involved in active discussion and explication. (staff)

Fink-Eitel, Hinrich. Allmacht in der postmodernen Philosophie. *Phil Rundsch*, 39(4), 278-285, 1992.

Finke, S R S. Husserl y las aporías de la intersubjetividad. *Anu Filosof*, 26(2), 327-358, 1993.

This article considers the treatment of intersubjectivity as the core of Husserl's transcendental phenomenology. From this standpoint it identifies the problematic of Husserl's theory of the "experience of the Other", which Husserl exposes in his commentaries on Descartes V Meditation. The paper draws a parallel between Husserl and Kant in order to clarify the Husserlian notions, and finally shows the difficulties of Husserl's approach due to his assumption of the premises of the "*Subjektsphilosophie*".

Finn, Geraldine. The Politics of Spirituality: The Spirituality of Politics in Shadow of Spirit, Berry, Philippa (ed). New York, Routledge, 1992.

Finocchi, Nadia. Man within the Limit of the I in Analecta Husserliana, XXXI, Tymieniecka, Anna-Teresa (ed). Dordrecht, Kluwer, 1990.

Finocchiaro, M A. To Save the Phenomena: Duhem on Galileo. *Rev Int Phil*, 46(182), 291-310, 1992.

Finocchiaro, Maurice A. Induction and Intuition in the Normative Study of Reasoning in Probability and Rationality, Eells, Ellery (ed). Amsterdam, Rodopi, 1991.

Finsen, Susan. "The Dog in the Lifeboat Revisited": Commentary. *Between Species*, 8(2), 118-120, Spr 92.

Fisch, Menachem. Learning from Experience in Probability and Rationality, Eells, Ellery (ed). Amsterdam, Rodopi, 1991.

Fischer, Clare B. Simone Weil and the Civilisation of Work in Simone Weil's Philosophy of Culture, Bell, Richard (ed). New York, Cambridge Univ Pr, 1993.

Fischer, John M. Quinn on Doing and Allowing. *Phil Rev*, 101(2), 343-352, Ap 92.

Warren Quinn has argued for a particular understanding of the distinction between doing and allowing. We argue that his analysis is inadequate.

Fischer, John M. Recent Work on Death and the Meaning of Life. *Phil Books*, 34(2), 65-74, Ap 93.

Fischer, John M. Snapshot Ockhamism in Philosophical Perspectives, 5: Philosophy of Religion, 1991, Tomberlin, James E (ed). Atascadero, Ridgeview, 1991.

I lay out a precise formulation of the Ockhamist position on the relationship between God's foreknowledge and human freedom. I respond to an interesting criticism of my previous work by David Widerker.

Fischer, John M and Ravizza, Mark. The Inevitable. *Austl J Phil*, 70(4), 388-404, D 92.

We critically evaluate various accounts of moral responsibility for consequences of what agents do. We sketch our own approach. On this approach, an agent can be held accountable for an inevitable consequence.

Fischer, John M and Ravizza, Mark. When The Will is Free in Philosophical Perspectives, 6: Ethics, 1992, Tomberlin, James E (ed). Atascadero, Ridgeview, 1992.

Peter van Inwagen has argued that acceptance of a modal principle employed in the standard argument for incompatibilism entails that (even if causal determinism is false) we are rarely, if ever, free to do otherwise. We present an argument against van Inwagen.

Fischer, John Martin. Hard Properties. *Faith Phil*, 10(2), 161-169, Ap 93.

Parallel to the distinction between hard (temporally non-relational) and soft (temporally relational) facts about times is the distinction between hard (temporally non-relational) and soft (temporally relational) properties. David Widerker has criticized a suggested account of the distinction between hard and soft properties. In this paper the criticism is presented and a refined suggestion for an account of the distinction is developed. I claim that this proposal avoids the problems adduced by Widerker.

Fischer, John Martin. Recent Work on God and Freedom. *Amer Phil Quart*, 29(2), 91-109, Ap 92.

This is a survey of recent work on God and human freedom. A version of the "basic" argument for the incompatibility of God's omniscience and human freedom is presented. Various possible responses are developed and discussed.

Fischer, John Martin (ed). The Metaphysics of Death. Stanford, Stanford Univ Pr, 1993.

Fischer, John Martin and Brueckner, Anthony. Death's Badness. *Pac Phil Quart*, 74(1), 37-45, Mr 93.

In this paper we defend the claim that it is rational to hold asymmetric attitudes towards death and pre-natal non-existence (against a criticism which I Haji directs against an earlier paper of ours—"Why Is Death Bad?", *Philosophical Studies* 1986—in his "Pre-Vital and Post-Vital Times", *Pacific Philosophical Quarterly* 1991).

Fischer, John Martin and Brueckner, Anthony. The Asymmetry of Early Death and Late Birth. *Phil Stud*, 71(3), 327-331, S 93.

In this paper, we defend the claim that a rational asymmetry in our attitudes towards past and future pleasures explains why we do not regret the fact that we were not born earlier. The paper is a response to Christopher Belshaw's "Asymmetry and Non-Existence", *Philosophical Studies* 1993, which contained a criticism of our earlier paper "Why Is Death Bad?", *Philosophical Studies* 1986.

Fischer, Michael. Wordsworth and the Recovery of Hope. *Phil Lit*, 16(2), 292-303, O 92.

In M H Abrams' influential reading of Wordsworth's response to the failure of the French Revolution, Wordsworth does not abandon his hope for social change but transfers that hope from political action to literature. Recent critics of romanticism, however, have suggested that even the early Wordsworth recants his political radicalism. According to this view, he opts for a militant quietism and personal account of freedom that makes him impervious to political disappointment. "Wordsworth and the Recovery of Hope" analyzes Wordsworth's reaction to the David Hume-like skepticism that overtakes him in *The Prelude* when the revolution fails. Drawing on Stanley Cavell's treatment of skepticism, I argue that *The Prelude* does not solve the problem of achieving change but keeps the problem alive. In writing *The Prelude* Wordsworth learns not to get over his disgust with history but to maintain it.

Fischer, Norbert. Cusanus's Concept of God and Man in the Light of His Reflections on Time. *Ultim Real Mean*, 15(4), 252-274, D 92.

After remarks about Cusanus' life and today's researching, the question is posed: What are the conditions for the possibility of thinking man and God, considering the incompatibility of the infinite with the finite and the incapability of comprehending finite things in their own precision. The answer is: Man as temporal being has to transform its being in time from possibility to actuality. So perceiving needs a temporal process in order to become what it is possible to be. At this being-between, an act is required raising above time, being sudden and spontaneous. This human designing itself towards a possible perfection is temporal self-realization, where a perfection of time appears suggesting a thinking of absolute perfection (God).

Fishburn, Peter C. The Axioms and Algebra of Ambiguity. *Theor Decis*, 34(2), 119-137, Mr 93.

This paper continues a study of event ambiguity as a primitive concept. Axioms are described for a comparative ambiguity relation on an arbitrary event set that are necessary and sufficient for a representation of the relation by a functional that is nonnegative, vanishes at the empty event, and satisfies complementary equality and submodularity. Uniqueness characteristics of representing functionals are discussed. The theory is extended to multifactor events, where marginal ambiguity and additive representations arise.

Fisher, Alec. Re-engaging with Real Arguments. *Philosophy*, 33(Supp), 89-107, 1992.

This book aims to help college students to think critically about the kind of sustained, theoretical arguments which they commonly encounter in their studies—arguments about the natural world, society, policy, philosophy, etc. The method explained in the book applies to reasoning expressed in natural language and is unusual in employing the "Assertibility Question" (what *would* establish P?) in extracting and evaluating arguments and is applying to 'suppositional reasoning'. Many examples are analysed and there are many exercises. A little formal logical and a chapter on scientific method is also included.

Fisher, Alec. Re-engaging with Real Arguments in The Impulse to Philosophise, Griffiths, A Phillips (ed). New York, Cambridge Univ Pr, 1992.

Formal logic has almost no application to the analysis and evaluation of real reasoning (reasoning which is or has been used with a view to convincing others)—except in mathematics. It rarely applies to philosophical argument either. So why teach formal logic to philosophy students. What is needed is a new 'science of reasoning' which studies real reasoning.

Fisher, John and Ravizza, Martin. Thomson and the Trolley. *J Soc Phil*, 23(3), 64-87, Wint 92.

We set out a version of the Trolley Problem and criticize Judith Thomson's recent suggestion for a solution. Finally, we suggest an explanation for this failure.

Fisher, John Andrew. Discovery, Creation, and Musical Works. *J Aes Art Crit*, 49(2), 129-136, Spr 91.

Fisher, Linda. Gender and Other Categories. *Hypatia*, 7(3), 173-179, Sum 92.

In my discussion of Bordo's paper I leave aside the particulars of her detailed critique of Grimshaw and the issue of the "maleness" of philosophy and focus instead on some questions raised by her analysis of heterogeneity and generality. I find this analysis very persuasive, particularly her counterarguments to the "theoretics of heterogeneity." However, I am less persuaded by her concluding points and suggestions for future directions.

Fisher, Linda. Hermeneutics of Suspicion. *Phil Lit*, 16(1), 106-114, Ap 92.

Following up on a recent discussion comparing the psychologies of the postmodernist and the paranoid, this paper develops this idea by exploring the connection with the "hermeneutics of suspicion". Rather than constituting a rupture with the tradition, postmodernism is continuous with this hermeneutic employment of suspicion and critique which, when intensified into hypersuspicion, leads to the paranoia of postmodernism. Unfolding the implications of this analysis reveals the fundamentally self-contradictory, if not self-destructive, nature of postmodernism.

Fisher, Mark. *Personal Love*. London, Duckworth, 1990.

The book proposes a unified account of all forms of personal love, including adult sexual love, friendship and parents' love of children and children's love of parents. It is a narrative or process account. The process proposed is the development of a fused self, encouraged into being by the lover's tendency to take the beloved's good as the beloved sees it for her own good. Distinctions are drawn between this process and others often confused with it and thought to be love, and an attempt is made to explain the good of the process in the lover's life. Relations, and want of relations, between love and sex are discussed, and the gender-blindness of love is argued. The account is applied to love of children, and the role of jealousy in love is explained. Finally God's love and human love of the dead are sympathetically considered but dismissed.

Fishkin, James S. Justice between Generations: Compensation, Identity, and Group Membership. *Nomos*, 33, 85-96, 1991.

Fishkin, James S. *The Dialogue of Justice: Towards a Self-Reflective Society*. New Haven, Yale Univ Pr, 1993.

Fisk, Milton. Justifying Democracy. *Can J Phil*, 22(4), 463-483, D 92.

Fisk, Milton T. Poststructuralism, Difference, and Marxism. *Praxis Int*, 12(4), 323-340, Ja 93.

Fisk, Milton T. Rights in Social Context. *J Soc Phil*, 23(2), 65-74, Fall 92.

Fiske, Harold E. *Music and Mind: Philosophical Essays on the Cognition and Meaning of Music*. Lewiston, Mellen Pr, 1990.

The work demonstrates that music cognition is limited to the realization of three pattern types. It is shown that pattern types are the product of a finite set of decision-tasks arranged hierarchically. The hierarchy is generic and therefore universal. Thus music cognition is a semantically closed, self-reference system. Musical meaning is a measure of decision-hierarchy penetration by the perceiver; this is separate from "appearance-value" connotations attached to a musical experience by the listener following pattern-type identification.

Fix, Andrew. Balthasar Bekker and the Crisis of Cartesianism. *Hist Euro Ideas*, 17(5), 575-588, S 93.

This paper investigates the late 17th century debate in Holland over the temporal activity of good and evil spirits within the context of the development of Cartesian philosophy. Focussing on the work of the Dutch Reformed pastor Balthasar Bekker, who in his book The World Bewitched (Amsterdam 1691) used arguments drawn from Cartesian dualism to deny the temporal activity of spirits, the paper maintains that the spirit controversy has been largely misunderstood by historians who have seen it as a clash between philosophical rationalism and its conservative opponents within the Dutch Reformed church who rejected Bekker's arguments in favor of traditional belief in spirits. (edited)

Flack, Harley E (ed) and Pellegrino, Edmund D (ed). *African-American Perspectives on Biomedical Ethics*. Washington, Georgetown Univ Pr, 1992.

Flage, Daniel. Descartes's Three Hypothetical Doubts. *Mod Sch*, 70(3), 201-208, Mr 93.

Many commentators treat Descartes's three hypothetical doubts at the end of the First Meditation—the deceiver-God hypothesis, the cause less than God hypothesis, and the malicious demon hypothesis—as a single "deceiver argument." The paper shows that Descartes raised distinct doubts by each argument and used each argument as a heuristic device to either 1) draw the reader away from the

supposition that the world is wholly corporeal and known by means of sense experience, 2) provide something to which to reply in subsequent meditations, or 3) provide a foil against which Descartes can test the certainty of his subsequent conclusions.

Flage, Daniel. Hume's Hobbism and His Anti-Hobbism. *Hume Stud*, 18(2), 369-382, N 92.

The author argues that the Hume of the *Treatise* was a mitigated Hobbist. Like Hobbes, Hume held that the notions of justice and obligation rest on a set of conventional social rules. Hume distinguished himself from Hobbes primarily with respect to questions of moral value. Though Hume provided an account of moral obligation, this was secondary to and parasitic upon his considerations of moral value.

Flage, Daniel. On Friedman's Look. *Hume Stud*, 19(1), 187-197, Ap 93.

The article continues the discussion of David Hume's theory of memory by responding to Lesley Friedman's criticisms of the relative ideas interpretation of Humean memory.

Flage, Daniel and Bonnen, Clarence A. Innate Ideas and Cartesian Dispositions. *Int Stud Phil*, 24(1), 65-80, 1992.

Commentators on Descartes's theory of innate ideas argue either that nonoccurrent innate ideas are distinct, actual ideas that exist in the mind like unperceived cards in a file, or they argue that innate ideas are dispositions to form occurrent ideas with particular objective contents. This paper shows that the textual evidence is consistent with the dispositional account of nonoccurrent innate ideas and answers several philosophical objections to that interpretation. It concludes by attempting to unpack the notion of a Cartesian disposition.

Flanagan, Owen. *Consciousness Reconsidered*. Cambridge, MIT Pr, 1992.

Flanagan, Owen. *Varieties of Moral Personality: Ethics and Psychological Realism*. Cambridge, Harvard Univ Pr, 1991.

Flannery, Maura. Using Science's Aesthetic Dimension in Teaching Science. *J Aes Educ*, 26(1), 1-15, Spr 92.

Stressing the aesthetic dimensions of science is an approach to improving science education which has not been given sufficient attention. This article is a survey of the aesthetics of science—the beauty of science found in the object of study, in the process of inquiry, and in the products of that process—and how it relates to science teaching. An enhanced perception of nature is the common thread running through the arguments for the advantages of including the aesthetic dimension in science courses, and therefore this dimension can enhance students' views not only of science but of art.

Flathman, Richard (ed) and Mencken, H L. *Friedrich Nietzsche—H L Mencken*. New Brunswick, Transaction Books, 1993.

Flax, Jane. Beyond Equality: Gender, Justice and Difference in Beyond Equality and Difference, Bock, Gisela (ed). New York, Routledge, 1992.

Feminist theorists are committed to ending gender-based relations of domination. They disagree on the most useful strategies and theories to approach this end. Recently debate has centered on equality vs difference approaches. Both have fatal flaws. Each and the choice posed reflect assumptions intrinsic to a liberalism that is a contributor to rather than a cure for domination. I propose moving to a different terrain — theories and practices of justice. These must be process rather than procedurally or rationalistically oriented. I draw on D S Winnecott rather than John Rawls to outline more promising approaches to justice.

Flax, Jane. Multiples: On the Contemporary Politics of Subjectivity. *Human Stud*, 16(1-2), 33-49, Ap 93.

The modern subject carries enormous political and philosophic weight. Debates about the nature of subjectivity and its possible relations to emancipatory action thus occupy a central place in contemporary discourse. Two current claims about subjectivity are wrong: emancipatory action requires the sort of unitary self capable of autonomy that Enlightenment philosophers from Kant to Habermas describe; and the decentered postmodernist self cannot engage in effective struggles against domination. There can be forms of subjectivity that are simultaneously fluid, multicentered and politically responsible. These subjects are best equipped to recognize and struggle against relations of domination.

Flay, Joseph C. Hegel's Metaphysics. *Owl Minerva*, 24(2), 145-152, Spr 93.

I argue that Hegel has a metaphysics which takes account of the transcendental turn in Kant and thus differs radically from any metaphysics prior to him and most metaphysical systems which have come after. The interpretation given allows us both to take account of "non-metaphysical" interpretations (K Hartmann) and to sort out his systems from other metaphysical systems. The essay also offers a critique of Stephen Houlgate's recent attempts to make sense of Hegel's system.

Flay, Joseph C. Hegel, Derrida and Bataille's Laughter in Hegel and His Critics, Desmond, William (ed). Albany, SUNY Pr, 1989.

I look at Derrida's treatment of Hegel in two sources: "Violence and Metaphysics" and "From Restricted to General Economy." I argue that there is something insightful in Derrida's deconstruction of Hegel but that, as Derrida himself admits, Hegel was aware of the distinction made between mastery and sovereignty. I then show how, in a way different from that suggested by Derrida/Bataille, sovereignty is taken up by Hegel in order to get us to his metaphysics. Hegel, with his own insight about sovereignty, has another path to the "place" to which Derrida wishes to lead us.

Flay, Joseph C. Hegel, Heidegger, Derrida in Ethics and Danger, Dallery, Arleen B (ed). Albany, SUNY Pr, 1992.

I attempt to show how Hegel's reconstructive retrieval of the tradition not only "completed" metaphysics, but by that very fact also laid the ground for Heidegger's destructive retrieval of the tradition and Derrida's deconstructive retrieval. I then argue that in this Hegelian opening of a "beyond" of metaphysics we also have the grounds for the positive side of the thought of Heidegger and Derrida.

Fleischacker, Samuel. Kant's Theory of Punishment in Essays on Kant's Political Philosophy, Williams, Howard (ed). Chicago, Univ of Chicago Pr, 1992.

Fleischer, Isidore and Scott, Philip. An Algebraic Treatment of the Barwise Compactness Theory. *Stud Log*, 50(2), 217-223, Je 91.

A theorem on the extendability of certain subsets of a Boolean algebra to ultrafilters which preserve countably many infinite meets (generalizing Rasiowa-Sikorski) is used to pinpoint the mechanism of the Barwise proof in a way which bypasses the set theoretical elaborations.

Fleischhacker, Louk and Brainard, Marcus (trans). On the Mathematization of Life. *Grad Fac Phil J*, 16(1), 245-258, 1993.

The article aims at showing the philosophical backgrounds of mathematical models of the processes of organic life. It is pointed out that various claims at reconstructability and simulability of such processes necessarily have metaphysical presupposition of a Cartesian nature. On the other hand, the holistic approach of investigators such as R Sheldrake is shown to be based on essentially the same presuppositions. Finally, a philosophical conception of life is indicated, which enables us to investigate the phenomenon of life without explaining it away altogether.

Fleming, Bruce. *An Essay In Post-Romantic Literary Theory: Art, Artifact, and the Innocent Eye*. Lewiston, Mellen Pr, 1991.

Fleming, Gordon N. The Actualization of Potentialities in Contemporary Quantum Theory. *J Speculative Phil*, 6(4), 259-276, 1992.

Fleming, Gordon N. The Objectivity and Invariance of Quantum Predictions. *Proc Phil Sci Ass*, 1, 104-113, 1992.

A recent argument by Pitowsky (1991), leading to the relativity (as opposed to objectivity) of quantum predictions, is refuted. The refutation proceeds by taking into account the hyperplane dependence of the quantum predictions emerging from the three mutually space-like separated measurements, performed on an entangled state of three spin 1/2 particles, that Pitowsky considers. From this hyperplane dependence one finds that the logical step of conjoining the predictions from distinct measurements is ineffective since those predictions apply either, locally, to sets of points with an intersection that is inaccessible to the particles, or globally, to sets of hyperplanes with an intersection that is empty. We also see how explicit reference to the hyperplane dependence of the predictions gives covariant expression to the invariant content of the predictions, which are thereby shown to be objective.

Fleming, Jesse. A Set Theory Analysis of the Logic of the *I Ching*. *J Chin Phil*, 20(2), 133-146, Je 93.

The *I Ching* (the *Book of Changes*) is too often ignored by Western philosophers due to its apparently absurd and arbitrary arrangement of images and symbols. In fact, embedded in its kaleidoscopic mosaic is an implicit logic which can contribute to modern philosophy of logic in the areas of modal logic, many-valued logic, and set theory. The main conclusion is that the deviant logic employed in the *I Ching* (a "dream logic", or "logic of the unconscious") offers an interesting alternative to the traditional Aristotelian laws of excluded middle and non-contradiction.

Fleming, Marie. Women and the "Public Use of Reason". *Soc Theor Pract*, 19(1), 27-50, Spr 93.

This essay critically examines Jürgen Habermas's idea of the "public use of reason" and assesses his (1962) analysis of the public sphere of modernity in the context of contemporary feminism. I argue that his model of the public sphere's internal dynamic is constituted by the category of gender, even though it rests formally upon the category of class, and that the model cannot theorize gender freedom because it presupposes gender exclusion. Nonetheless, Habermas's identification of an "intimate" sphere offers important insights for the feminist investigation of the public and private spheres of modernity.

Fletcher, George P. The Commonality of Loyalty and Tolerance. *Crim Just Ethics*, 12(1), 68-78, Wint-Spr 93.

Flew, Antony. Dissent from "The New Consensus": Reply to Friedman. *Crit Rev*, 6(1), 83-96, Wint 92.

This 'Dissent' accuses Part II of Friedman's "The New Consensus" of systematically and misleadingly abusing all the key terms. His Positive Libertarianism is no more a sort of libertarianism than imaginary cows are a sort of cows, and what he calls morality is light years away from the domestic decencies of what would normally be accounted moral conduct. Friedman also mistakes the option rights of the American Declaration of Independence to presuppose an ideal of equality far more substantial than the simple equality of common humanity and thinks the intended consequences of actions irrelevant to their morality.

Flew, Antony. Education: Anti-racist, Multi-ethnic and Multi-cultural in Logical Foundations, Mahalingam, Indira (ed). New York, St Martin's Pr, 1991.

The aim is to introduce or restore unmade or allapsed distinctions: between race, culture, and ethnicity; and between three different understandings of 'racism'. It is not, as is now widely assumed, necessarily true but certainly false to say that a multi-racial society, must be multi-cultural. Racism as advantaging or disadvantaging individuals for no other or better reason than that they are members of this racial set and not that is manifestly wrong. Its repudiation requires neither that talents be equally distributed among all racial sets now that every racial set be proportionally represented in every field of employment or activity.

Flew, Antony. James Giles on Personal Identity. *Philosophy*, 67(261), 394-398, Jl 92.

In his 'Bodily Theory and Theory of the Body' (Philosophy, July 1991) James Giles assumed that people are (presumably incorporeal) substances in principle separable from their own equally substantial bodies. Since the ordinary use of person words is to refer to members of a very special yet altogether familiar sort of creatures of flesh and blood, it behooves those who thus wish to speak of persons as substances separable from their own bodies to explain how these are identifiable and re-identifiable as the same individuals. No easy task, or even possible.

Flew, Antony. The Concept, and Conceptions, of Justice in Applied Philosophy, Almond, Brenda (ed). New York, Routledge, 1992.

This paper first distinguishes the traditional concept of justice from what are today offered as conceptions of social justice and then goes on to argue that, by misrepresenting the imposition of some greater even if never complete equality of outcome as the enforcement of mandates of justice, many aficionados of such 'social justice' unwittingly imply that they are presently in possession of property and enjoying incomes stolen from persons worse off than themselves.

Flew, Antony. What Impressions of Necessity?. *Hume Stud*, 18(2), N 92.

The thesis—developed of course with particular reference to Hume's treatment of necessary connection—is that the idea of such connection (and the closely associated ideas of physical necessity, physical impossibility and counterfactual conditionality) are and could only be derived from our experience of being able to make some things happen but being unable to prevent others. What is above all crucial is our experience of the difference between those bodily movements which can be initiated or inhibited at will and those which cannot.

Flint, Thomas. Middle Knowledge and the Doctrine of Infallibility in Philosophical Perspectives, 5: Philosophy of Religion, 1991, Tomberlin, James E (ed). Atascadero, Ridgeview, 1991.

Middle knowledge, though much discussed recently, has infrequently been applied to specific theological topics. This paper suggests that middle knowledge might illuminate the Roman Catholic belief in papal infallibility, for one objection to that doctrine—that the pope, as a free human being, is as liable to error as is anyone—can be defused if we view God as employing his middle knowledge in selecting only popes who will *freely* refrain from issuing erroneous *ex cathedra* pronouncements. Though the paper shows that there are some unexpected complications with this view, the contention that Molinism is helpful here is ultimately endorsed.

Flint, Thomas P (ed). *Christian Philosophy*. Notre Dame, Univ Notre Dame Pr, 1990.

Christian Philosophy contains seven essays that provide ample evidence of the diversity of subjects properly considered part of Christian philosophy today. Originally presented at a Conference on Christian and Theistic Philosophy held at the University of Notre Dame in 1988, these essays represent the efforts of seven of the major thinkers in the field to reflect upon and/or exhibit what they take to be Christian philosophy. Included are papers by Norman Kretzmann, Richard Purtill, Eleonore Stump, Alan Donagan, Nicholas Wolterstorff, Jorge Garcia, and Merold Westphal, along with an introduction by the editor.

Flint, Tom. Prophecy, Freedom and Middle Knowledge in Our Knowledge of God, Clark, Kelly James (ed). Dordrecht, Kluwer, 1992.

Floucat, Y. Médiation ou immédiation et philosophie chrétienne. *Rev Thomiste*, 92(3), 727-755, Jl-S 92.

Floyd, Edwin D. Why Parmenides Wrote in Verse. *Ancient Phil*, 12(2), 251-265, Fall 92.

Parmenides chose verse (instead of prose) for its many resonances highlighting deception. *Prophron* at 1.22, for example, has an apparently straightforward meaning "kindly", but in Homer it is used in contexts of divine disguise. Later on in Parmenides' poem, the focus on the immobility of Being (8.37-38) recalls Athene's fateful deception of Hektor in *Iliad*, book 22. Even more clearly, Doxa shows the pattern too, since the transition from Aletheia at 8.52 parallels a context (Solon, fr l.2, West) in which feigned madness brings about the Athenians's regaining Salamis.

Fluri, Philippe H. New Trends in Russian Philosophy. *Indian Phil Quart*, 20(1), 109-114, Ja 93.

Fluxman, Tony. Freud, Drives, and the 'Social'. *S Afr J Phil*, 12(3), 57-61, Ag 93.

Appel has objected to my argument that Freud was wrong to claim that there is a necessary clash between drives and civilization. In this article I answer Appel's charge that I have misunderstood Freud's theory of drive causality. I also argue that psychoanalysis is better off without drive theory, since the latter fails to account adequately for the social dimension of human reality. Finally, I set out the core of an alternative psychoanalytic approach, known as 'object relations', which I believe offers a more useful framework for doing social theory.

Flynn, Thomas R. Sartre and the Poetics of History in The Cambridge Companion to Sartre, Howells, Christina (ed). New York, Cambridge Univ Pr, 1992.

I reflect on Sartre as a philosopher of the imagination the better to describe and assess his approach to the philosophy of history. Sartre likens the intelligibility of history to that of an artwork because he considers the former as much the product of creative freedom as the latter. Major theses from his *The Psychology of Imagination, War Diaries,* and *Notebooks for an Ethics* are found to be employed in both volumes of the *Critique of Dialectical Reason* and *The Family Idiot*. Thus, we can understand Sartre's claim that history in general and his Flaubert study in particular constitute "a novel that is true" (*un roman vrai*).

Foblets, Marie-Claire. Raymond Aron: Kantian Critique of the 20th Century. *Dialec Hum*, 17(1), 154-165, 1990.

Fodor, Jerry and LePore, Ernest. *Précis of* Holism: A Shopper's Guide. *Phil Phenomenol Res*, 53(3), 637-640, S 93.

Fodor, Jerry and LePore, Ernest. Reply to Critics. *Phil Phenomenol Res*, 53(3), 673-682, S 93.

Fodor, Jerry and LePore, Ernie. Reply to Block and Boghossian. *Mind Lang*, 8(1), 41-48, Spr 93.

Förster, Eckart. "Was darf ich hoffen?" Zum Problem der Vereinbarkeit von theoretischer und praktischer Vernunft bei Immanuel Kant. *Z Phil Forsch*, 46(2), 168-185, Ap-J 92.

Förster, Eckart (ed & trans) and Kant, Immanuel and Rosen, Michael (trans). *Opus Postumum/Immanuel Kant*. New York, Cambridge Univ Pr, 1993.

Foley, Richard. Audi on Practical Reasoning. *Behavior Phil*, 19(2), 59-72, Fall-Wint 91.

Foley, Richard. Being Knowingly Incoherent. *Nous*, 26(2), 181-203, Je 92.

Sometimes the rational strategy is one that we know to be less than ideal. This is so for beliefs as well as actions, and it is for degrees of beliefs as well as for beliefs. One upshot of this is that it can be rational for us to have degrees of belief that we know to be incoherent.

Foley, Richard. Can Metaphysics Solve the Problem of Skepticism? in Rationality in Epistemology, Villanueva, Enrique (ed). Atascadero, Ridgeview, 1992.

Foley, Richard. Rationality and Perspective. *Analysis*, 53(2), 65-68, Ap 93.

Foley, Richard. The Epistemology of Belief and the Epistemology of Degrees of Belief. *Amer Phil Quart*, 29(2), 111-124, Ap 92.

Foley, Richard. *Working Without a Net: A Study of Egocentric Epistemology*. New York, Oxford Univ Pr, 1993.

In this book, I defend an epistemology that takes seriously the perspectives of individual thinkers. I argue that having rational opinions is a matter of meeting our own internal standards rather than standards that are somehow imposed upon us from the outside. It is a matter of making ourselves invulnerable to intellectual self-criticism.

Follon, Jacques. Le concept de philosophie première chez Aristote: Note complémentaire. *Rev Phil Louvain*, 91(89), 5-13, F 93.

In this note the author attempts to show that the reading *achôrista* in Aristotle's *Metaphysics* 1026 a 14 does not, as some might hold, affect the traditional interpretation of Aristotle's concept of "first philosophy", which the author defended in an article published in the last issue of the *Revue philosophique de Louvain*.

Follon, Jacques. Le concept de philosophie première dans la "Métaphysique" d'Aristote. *Rev Phil Louvain*, 90(88), 387-421, N 92.

In this article the author inquires into the meaning of "first philosophy" in Aristotle's *Metaphysics*. In his view, attentive examination of the passages in which the nature of this discipline is mentioned (essentially *Alpha* 1-2, *Gamma* 1-3 and *Epsilon* 1) shows rather clearly that the Stagirite meant by "first philosophy" the science of first causes and hence necessarily of divine substances, which are causes of this kind. In other words, first philosophy, being the supreme aitiology, was theology for him, as the traditional interpretation always held. But, being the science of first causes, it was equally the science of being *qua* being in his eyes, as first causes are precisely those of being *qua* being. The author thus concludes, contrary to the hermeneutic deriving from Suarez, that it is inappropriate to maintain a duality of inspiration and of subject-matter in the *Metaphysics*, and that there is no "onto-theological" ambiguity in Aristotle's view of first philosophy.

Fonow, Mary Margaret (ed) and Cook, Judith A (ed). *Beyond Methodology: Feminist Scholarship as Lived Research*. Bloomington, Indiana Univ Pr, 1991.

Fonseca, Clotilde. S T Coleridge: El papel de la imaginación en el acto creador. *Rev Filosof (Costa Rica)*, 30(71), 89-96, J 92.

Samuel Taylor Coleridge combines poetic genius and capacity to think through the creative act. The present work is focuses on how Coleridge views the role of the imagination in the creative genesis, his concept of form in art, of beauty and aesthetic pleasure. It deals with the way in which these, according to Coleridge, finally lead to truth.

Font, J M and Verdú, V. Algebraic Logic for Classical Conjunction and Disjunction. *Stud Log*, 50(3-4), 391-419, S-D 91.

In this paper we study the relations between the fragment L of classical logic having just conjunction and disjunction and the variety D of distributive lattices, within the context of Algebraic Logic. We prove that these relations cannot be fully expressed either with the tools of Blok and Pigozzi's theory of algebraizable logics or with the use of reduced matrices for L. However, these relations can be naturally formulated when we introduce a new notion of model of a sequent calculus. When applied to a certain natural calculus for L, the resulting models are equivalent to a class of abstracts logics (in the sense of Brown and Suszko) which we call *distributive*. Among other results, we prove that D is exactly the class of the algebraic reducts of the reduced models of L, that there is an embedding of the theories of L into the theories of the equational consequence (in the sense of Blok and Pigozzi) relative to D, and that for any algebra A of type (2,2) there is an isomorphism between the D-congruence of A and the models of L over A. In the second part of this paper (which will be published separately) we will also apply some results to give proofs with a logical flavour for several new or well-known lattice-theoretical properties.

Fontan, P. En Marge de Descartes. *Rev Thomiste*, 92(4), 834-842, O-D 92.

Fontana, Bianca. Whigs and Liberals in Victorian Liberalism, Bellamy, Richard (ed). New York, Routledge, 1990.

Forbes, Graeme R. Reply to Marks. *Phil Stud*, 69(2-3), 281-295, Mr 93.

This paper is a response to two other papers, by Mark Richard and Mark Crimmins respectively, which critically discuss my "logophoric" semantics for propositional attitude ascriptions.

Forbes, Graeme R. Solving the Iteration Problem. *Ling Phil*, 16(3), 311-330, Je 93.

This paper investigates the problem of the logical form of iterated attitude ascriptions. The author's "Logophoric" Semantics is applied to yield a solution.

Forbes, Graeme R. Worlds and States of Affairs: How Similar Can They Be? in Language, Truth and Ontology, Mulligan, Kevin (ed). Dordrecht, Kluwer, 1992.

This paper critically discusses Nathan Salmon's view that possible worlds may be distinct but distinguished only by the identity of some of the things they contain, so long as such worlds differ with respect to their accessibility relations.

Forbes, Kipling D. Hegel on Want and Desire: A Psychology of Motivation. Durango, Longwood Acad, 1991.

This highly systematic work considers two Hegelian texts, *The Phenomenology of Mind* and the *Philosophy of Right*. The dialectic of want and desire found in those works is explicated as a phenomenological psychology of motivation, when this psychology of motivation is taken as the ground of an Hegelian philosophy of education and psychology of learning. The work lays the theoretical foundations for a sociopolitical philosophical psychology of human intelligence and intellectual development, and contains—in an appendix—results of empirical social science research which appear to corroborate some of Hegel's conclusions and predictions about the growth of *"theoretical reason."*

Ford, Lewis S. Can Whitehead's God be Rescued from Process Theism? in Logic, God and Metaphysics, Harris, James F (ed). Dordrecht, Kluwer, 1992.

Bowman Clarke interprets all concrescence as nontemporal, which renders freedom problematic and treats the satisfaction as coextensive with its concrescence. This

theory of concrescence is applied to God in order to distinguish Whitehead's theism form Hartshorne, but it means that God experiences the world in terms of noncausal mutual pretensions. The difficulties this causes with respect to omniscience and becoming and transition in God are explored, as well as the question whether the divine consequence concrescence can be pretended.

Ford, Lewis S. Subjectivity in the Making. *Process Stud*, 21(1), 1-24, Spr 92.

By examining how Whitehead came to fashion the concept of 'subjective aim', we can discern the shifting conceptions of subjectivity which underlie the composition of *Process and Reality*. He had early rejected a substance model of subjectivity, and sought its replacement. Initially the single datum from which concrescence springs provided the being underlying the becoming of the concrescence. When the original datum was replaced by a plurality of past occasions, the unity was placed in the superjective outcome, but how could this retroactively bestow being upon the concrescence? Instead of becoming based on being, as former conceptions had assumed, becoming is now conceived as capable of producing being. Even though only being can causally affect its successors, it must derive its existence from that which has the primary existence, which can only be becoming in all its subjective privacy. (edited)

Ford, Marcus P. William James in Founders of Constructive Postmodern Philosophy, Griffin, David Ray (& others). Albany, SUNY Pr, 1993.

The thesis of this book is that there exists a group of philosophers, Peirce, James, Bergson, Whitehead, and Hartshorne, who, while rejecting many of the defining assumptions of modern philosophy, did not go the route that has become identified as "deconstructive postmodernism" or, simply, "postmodernism". Constructive postmodernism is neither dualistic, nor materialistic; it replaces enduring substances with events and process; it rejects sense empiricism with what James termed "radical empiricism"; and, while rejecting classical concepts of God, adheres to some type of natural theology.

Forge, John. Errors of Measurement and Explanation-as-Unification. *Philosophia (Israel)*, 22(1-2), 41-61, Ja 93.

Forge, John. How Should We Explain Remote Correlations?. *Philosophica*, 51(1), 83-103, 1993.

The aim of the paper is to discuss remote (Bell-type) correlations in the context of the ontic conceptions of explanation. It is then argued that the majority position, the causal-mechanical theory, cannot account for the correlations. An 'unofficial' version is then sketched, and it is argued that remote correlations can then be given a 'structural explanation'.

Forge, John. Thought Experiments in the Philosophy of Physical Science in Thought Experiments in Science and Philosophy, Horowitz, Tamara (ed). Lanham, Rowman & Littlefield, 1991.

Forgie, J William. Kant on the Relation between the Cosmological and Ontological Arguments. *Int J Phil Relig*, 34(1), 1-12, Ag 93.

Kant maintained that the cogency of the cosmological argument depends on that of the ontological, and that the appeal to experience in the former is therefore superfluous. I sketch a way of looking at both arguments which allows one to reject Kant's charges. Central to that sketch is regarding the common conclusion of both arguments, viz., that there (necessarily) exists an *ens realissimum* (or supreme being, or God), as a necessary, but a posteriori, proposition. The cosmological arguer can thus quite coherently reject the ontological argument and also maintain that empirical, a posteriori, premisses are indispensable in any proof of a supreme being.

Forman, Robert K C. Of Deserts and Doors: Methodology of the Study of Mysticism. *Sophia (Australia)*, 32(1), 31-44, Mr 93.

Two warring methodological approaches have dominated the study of mysticism for the last several decades: perennialism and constructivism. Recently, however, several colleagues and I have tried to articulate a new methodological approach which I believe is quite promising. In what follows, I will describe perennialism and constructivism, showing the main strengths and problems of each. Then I will summarize this new methodology, and show how it has begun to articulate a place between these two. Finally I will conclude with a few observations about this new middle ground.

Forrest, Peter. Just Like Quarks? in Ontology, Causality and Mind: Essays in Honour of D M Armstrong, Bacon, John (ed). New York, Cambridge Univ Pr, 1993.

Forrest, Peter. Reference and the Refutation of Naturalism in Our Knowledge of God, Clark, Kelly James (ed). Dordrecht, Kluwer, 1992.

This paper is an argument against Naturalism, by modus tollens: 1) If Naturalism is correct then reference is grossly under-determined. 2) But reference is not grossly under-determined. 3) So Naturalism is not correct. My case for 2) is mainly an appeal to intuition. I support 1), however, by criticizing various prima facie plausible naturalistic attempts at resisting the Putnamesque argument for the gross under-determination of reference. In addition to arguing against Naturalism I argue that our capacity to refer provides a precedent for a capacity for non-inferential knowledge of God.

Forrest, Peter. Universals and Universalisability: An Interpretation of Oddie's Discussion of Supervenience. *Austl J Phil*, 70(1), 93-98, Mr 92.

This is a reply to Oddie's 'Supervenience and Higher-Order Universals' (Australasian Journal of Philosophy, 1991, pp. 20-47.) which is, in turn, a discussion of some ideas presented in Forrest's 'Supervenience: The Grand- Property Hypothesis', (Australasian Journal of Philosophy, 1988, pp. 1-12.) Forrest claimed that non-reductive supervenience was possible if various natural properties were properties of the natural properties, thought of as universals. Oddie uses possible world semantics to argue that strong supervenience would collapse into reduction. In Forrest's reply, he submits that strong supervenience need not collapse provided possible and consistent worlds are distinguished.

Forschner, Maximilian. Eine Korrektur des Poseidonios-Bildes. *Phil Rundsch*, 39(4), 319-329, 1992.

Forster, Michael. Hegel's Dialectical Method in The Cambridge Companion to Hegel, Beiser, Frederick (ed). New York, Cambridge Univ Pr, 1993.

Forster, Paul. Peirce and the Threat of Nominalism. *Trans Peirce Soc*, 28(4), 691-724, Fall 92.

Peirce's philosophy is interpreted as a systematic response to the empiricist-liberalism of the nineteenth century that Peirce calls Nominalism. Nominalism is presented as an integrated philosophy of knowledge, values, and politics. The threat this view poses to Peirce is summarized. Peirce's theories of inquiry and experience are discussed and their implications for Nominalism are detailed. It is concluded that Peirce's campaign against the epistemological theses of Nominalism is part and parcel of an attempt to establish an alternative moral and social ideal.

Forster, Paul. What Is at Stake Between Putnam and Rorty?. *Phil Phenomenol Res*, 52(3), 585-603, S 92.

This paper examines the debate between Hilary Putnam and Richard Rorty. Rorty's pragmatism is defended from Putnam's objection that it is a form of self-refuting relativism, and is also shown to be immune from difficulties with Putnam's limit theory of truth. The central argument is based on Rorty's view of interpretation.

Fortenbaugh, W W. Aristotle's Distinction Between Moral Virtue and Practical Wisdom in Essays in Ancient Greek Philosophy, IV, Anton, John P (ed). Albany, SUNY Pr, 1991.

Aristotle's ethical theory has at its very core a distinction between moral virtue and practical wisdom. This distinction is elucidated by an investigation of passages found outside the ethical treatises. In particular, attention is given to discussions of character (*êthos*) and thought (*dianoia*) occurring in the *Poetics, Rhetoric and Politics*. The procedure is encouraged by Aristotle's own statements in *EN* I.3, 2.1 and 6.I, and makes clear why Aristotle frequently assigns special importance to moral virtue.

Fortenbaugh, W W (ed) and Gutas, Dimitri (ed). *Theophrastus*. New Brunswick, Transaction Books, 1992.

The contents includes two new critical editions: Theophrastus' *Meteorology* and his work *On Fish*. Both editions are accompanied by an English translation and commentary. Also included in the volume are discussions of Theophrastus' work *On Sense Perception*, his *Physical Doctrines* and the Spurious treatise *On Signs*. Finally there are articles on Theophrastus' notion of place, of intellect and of animal intelligence.

Forth, Christopher E. Nietzsche, Decadence, and Regeneration in France, 1891-95. *J Hist Ideas*, 54(1), 97-117, Ja 93.

Fortin, John. Saint Anselm the Student. *Lyceum*, 1(1), 33-41, Wint 89.

This article offers a basic, introductory discussion of the intellectual formation of Saint Anselm. It focuses on the authorities and texts which he would have studied in the course of his education as determined by specific references and literary illusions in his writings as well as by the academic curriculum which was current at his time.

Fortin-Melkevik, Anne. Deux paradigmes pour penser le rapport de la théologie aux sciences humaines: herméneutique et narratologie. *Laval Theol Phil*, 49(2), 223-231, Je 93.

Quel est le statut de la théologie dans la modernité? Quels sont les paramétres du rapport entre la théologie et les sciences humaines? La présente étude examinera deux courants dominants dans la théologie contemporaine, le courant herméneutique et le courant narratologique nord-américain, qui répondent de façon diamétralement différente à ces questions. La divergence entre ces deux courants se résume autour de l'opposition suivante: la tâche de la théologie consiste-t-elle à *interpréter* les textes bibliques, ou plutôt à se mettre à *l'écoute* des récits bibliques? L'oeuvre de Paul Ricoeur, au confluent de l'herméneutique et de la narratologie, se veut une tentative de conciliation permettant l'élaboration d'une théologie des récits bibliques qui allie les intuitions de la phénoménologie, de l'herméneutique et de la narratologie.

Foshay, Toby. Resentment and Apophasis: The Trace of the Other in Levinas, Derrida and Gans in Shadow of Spirit, Berry, Philippa (ed). New York, Routledge, 1992.

Foshay, Toby (ed) and Coward, Harold (ed). *Derrida and Negative Theology*. Albany, SUNY Pr, 1992.

The book explores the thought of Jacques Derrida as it relates to negative theology and philosophy in both Western and Eastern thought. Derrida's two main essays on negative theology are included as is a conclusion in which Derrida responds to the analysis offered.

Fosl, Peter S. Empiricism, Difference, and Common Life. *Man World*, 26(3), 319-328, Jl 93.

This review essay assesses Gilles Deleuze's *Empiricism and Subjectivity*. Deleuze's book is admirable for 1) articulating Hume's criticisms of subjectivity and 2) undermining the narrow naturalistic-psychologistic reading of Hume's work in favor of an attention to considerations of practice and passion. The way in which this text sheds light on the development of Deleuze's own thought is also addressed. Deleuze, however, underrates the importance of skepticism in Hume's thought and illegitimately imports Kantian perspectives. He also fails to appreciate the role the notion of "common life" plays in Hume's work and neglects the contemporary context in which Hume wrote.

Fossa, John A and Erickson, Glenn W. Os Sólidos Regulares na Antigüidade. *Cad Hist Filosof Cie*, 2(1), 85-101, Ja-Je 90.

In the *Timaeus*, Plato associates the four material elements—fire, air, water and earth—with the tetrahedron, octahedron, icosahedron, and cube, respectively. The dodecahedron is assigned to the form of the universe. Herein, we try to reconstitute a compelling theory for the given associations. For the most part, the phenomenological (physical) reasons behind the association are discussed in the *Timaeus*; the mathematical reasons, however, are only hinted at, hence we try to explicate these reasons further. By combining these two types of reasons, we are able to outline a theory that makes the Platonic association quite appropriate.

Foster, David R. Aquinas's Arguments for Spirit. *Amer Cath Phil Quart*, 65, 235-252, 1991.

This article categorizes and critiques Aquinas's arguments for the immateriality of the intellect, which are the key arguments for a spiritual soul. Of the thirty-six arguments he gives, thirty of them can be collected under five types: 1) knower knows all things, 2) knower knows universals, 3) knower possesses the known, 4) knower knows itself, 5) knower possesses contraries. Although the first type, which is based on *De anima* 3,4 has pride of place in Thomas, it seems a poor argument. Type 2, from the knower's grasp of the object in an immaterial manner, and type 4, from the knower's self-consciousness, seems to most promising for use in the present day.

Foster, John. Dennett's Rejection of Dualism. *Inquiry*, 36(1-2), 17-31, Mr 93.

In *Consciousness Explained*, Dennett elaborates and defends a materialist-functionalist account of the human mind, and of consciousness in particular. This defence depends crucially on his prior rejection of dualism. Dennett rejects this dualist alternative on three grounds: first that its version of mind-to-body causation is in conflict with what we know, or have good reason to believe, from the findings of physical science; second, that the very notion of dualistic psychophysical causation is incoherent; and third, that dualism puts the mind beyond the reach of scientific investigation. In each case, his reasoning is unconvincing, and indeed leaves the dualist entirely unscathed. In contrast, without an adequate basis for his rejection of dualism, Dennett himself is left with a theory which is vulnerable to a number of familiar objections.

Foster, John. The Construction of the Physical World in The Philosophy of A J Ayer, Hahn, Lewis E (ed). Peru, Open Court, 1992.

Foster, Thomas R and Buller, David J. The New Paradox of Temporal Transcience. *Phil Quart*, 42(168), 357-366, Jl 92.

McTaggart raised a famed paradox regarding the transientist (or dynamic) conception of time, the standard resolution of which involves abandoning the dynamic conception in favor of a static conception of time. Schlesinger, however, recently attempted an ingenious transientist solution to McTaggart's paradox. We argue that Schlesinger's solution to McTaggart's paradox itself gives rise to a new, yet perfectly parallel, paradox which can only be resolved by abandoning the dynamic view of time.

Foster, Thomas R and Morton, Luise. Goodman, Forgery, and the Aesthetic. *J Aes Art Crit*, 49(2), 155-159, Spr 91.

Fóti, Véronique. Alētheia and Oblivion's Field in Ethics and Danger, Dallery, Arleen B (ed). Albany, SUNY Pr, 1992.

The essay maintains that Heidegger's lecture course on Parmenides (1941-42) develops important aspects of his own thought on historiality and the political. Notably, it offers a critique of nationalism and totalization. In the essay, the philosophical and historico-political bearing of the "indications" Heidegger gleans from the Parmenidean notion of *aletheia* are traced out, with particular attention to the *polis* as the essential figure of the political. The identification of a (quasi-Platonic) "Oblivion's Field" as the "counteressence" of the *polis* is problematized, in view of the inversionary schema that conceives of the nadir of desolation as a destinal turning point.

Fotion, Nicholas. Getting Consent from the Troops? in Biomedical Ethics Reviews 1992, Humber, James M (ed). Clifton, Humana Pr, 1993.

During the recent Gulf War the US military wanted to use experimental drugs on the troops to help protect them from Iraqi use of experimental chemical and biological weapons. Should consent have been obtained from the troops as it would certainly have been if these drugs were employed in a civilian setting? I argue "no". The military is not required to get consent here anymore than it is required to get consent to use an experimental helmet.

Foucault, Michel and Armstrong, Timothy J (trans). *Michel Foucault, Philosopher*. New York, Routledge, 1992.

Fouché, Fidéla. A Critique of Androgeny. *S Afr J Phil*, 11(4), 91-95, N 92.

The author, in order to evaluate the ideal of androgyny, examines the theory or theories of gender presupposed in this concept. She discusses Jean Bethke Elshtain's 'Against androgyny' and tries to indicate the strengths and weaknesses of Elshtains's critique. Whereas Elshtain asserts the inseparability of sex and gender, the writer attempts to show that androgyny is more effectively undermined by a dialectical theory of sex and gender.

Fouke, Daniel. Metaphysics and the Eucharist in the Early Leibniz. *Stud Leibniz*, 24(2), 145-159, 1992.

The author argues that, whereas the early efforts of Leibniz to link the intelligibility of the Mechanical Philosophy to theism leads him to emphasize God as First Mover, his increasing desire to defend the intelligibility of Transubstantiation inspires the development of deeper metaphysical analysis of the sources of substantiality and modes of divine union with the world. However, as Leibniz's mathematical, metaphysical and theological preoccupations further develop during his years in Paris, there is an increasing tension between the direction of his metaphysics and his desire to defend Transubstantiation. The reasons for this tension are linked to the development of the Principle of Equipollence and the increasingly central Leibnizian preoccupation with the intelligibility and autonomy of nature.

Foulk, Gary J. Teaching, Philosophy, and Audience. *Phil Stud Educ*, 1, 57-65, 1990.

In *The Closing of the American Mind* Allan Bloom says that teaching can be a threat to philosophy, that philosophers should never look to an audience, and that it is too much to ask that teachers be philosophers (p.20). This work points out that teaching and both the prospect and actuality of an alert and critical audience can be a stimulus to good philosophy, and that although it is too much to ask that teachers in other fields be philosophers, the extent to which these other fields presuppose philosophical issues and knowledge requires that they at least be informed laymen about philosophy, related to philosophers in the way that first aid givers are related to physicians.

Foulk, Gary J and Keffer, M Jan. Rationality and Principles: A Criticism of the Ethic of Care. *Int J Applied Phil*, 7(1), 15-19, Sum 92.

This work defends the necessity of reason, principles, and traditional metaethical and normative ethical theory in clinical nursing ethics against the claim, exemplified by Randy Spreen Parker's "Nurses' Stories: The Search for a Relational Ethic of Care," in *Advances in Nursing Science* (1990, 13, 1, 31-40), that such concerns tend to obscure the important factors of caring and emotion. By recalling such standard points as the distinction between interested and disinterested interests and the blindness of the raw data of experience and emotion without the light of reason and concepts, it is shown that the appeal to an ethic of care rests on confusion and error.

Found, Peter G and McClennen, Edward. Weighing Risk. *J Soc Phil*, 24(2), 155-175, Fall 93.

Fourie, F C V N and Beukes, E P. Government in the Economy: Outlines of a Reformational Rethink. *Phil Reform*, 57(1), 57-77, Ja 92.

Fouts, Avery. Divine Self-Limitation in Swinbourne's Doctrine of Omniscience. *Relig Stud*, 29(1), 21-26, Mr 93.

In his book, *The Coherence of Theism*, Richard Swinburne argues that God as an omniscient being must engage in cognitive self-limitation in order to preserve the freedom of both divine and human future actions. I argue that the notion of a self-limiting God results in a contradiction for Swinburne. On Swinburne's own grounds, God is necessarily free. I argue thereby that God must be necessarily limited with regard to future knowledge. Talk of "choice" and self-limitation becomes highly problematic.

Fowl, Stephen E. Could Horace Talk with the Hebrews? Translatability and Moral Disagreement in MacIntyre and Stout. *J Relig Ethics*, 19(1), 1-20, Spr 91.

Working from a standpoint which understands Christian ethics as a tradition-bound discourse, this essay provides a critical analysis and assessment of Alasdair MacIntyre and Jeffrey Stout on the problem of translatability between and among ethical traditions. Taking issue with both MacIntyre on the level of agreement needed for translatability and Stout on the idea of a thin conception of the good, the essay argues for a constructive position on the relation of Christian ethics to liberal society which lies between the positions of MacIntyre and Stout.

Fox, Douglas. Bernard Loomer's Concept of 'Interconnectedness' in God, Values, and Empiricism, Peden, Creighton W (ed). Macon, Mercer Univ Pr, 1989.

Bernard Loomer contends that the physically observable is all we can know and the referent for "God" must be concrete, ambivalent, imminent and in process. This process is marked by a drive toward increased value and its chief objective is complex interconnectedness. God's "size" (and ours) is measured by the range and intensity of often contrasting relationships, with "love" the supreme value. The purpose of this discussion of Loomer is to be critical but appreciative of his bold contribution to American theology. Thus it questions aspects of his empiricism and several of its implications, such as the espousal of unselective pantheism but distinctions of value.

Fox, Richard M and Demarco, Joseph P. The Immorality of Promising. *J Value Inq*, 27(1), 81-84, Ja 93.

If the duty of promise-keeping is interpreted strictly, it overrides other moral duties, committing the promisor to violate them if necessary. If the duty is interpreted in a weaker, prima facie sense, it allows the duty of promise-keeping to be overridden, and hence ceases to provide genuine assurance. Thus promising is immoral in the first case, because it ignores other moral responsibilities, and in the second, because its appearance of assurance is illusory and deceptive. We explore both sides of this dilemma and conclude that various attempts to morally sanction promise-making fail.

Franceschelli, O. Oltre "disincanto" e "nichilismo": A proposito di un recente volume di etical filosifca. *Sapienza*, 45(3), 293-297, 1992.

Francescotti, Robert M. Subjective Experience and Points of View. *J Phil Res*, 18, 25-36, 1993.

Thomas Nagel contends that facts regarding the qualitative character of conscious experience can be grasped from only a single point of view. This feature, he claims, is what renders conscious experience *subjective* in character, and it is what makes facts about the qualitative experience *subjective facts*. While much has been written regarding the ontological implications of the *'point of view account'* relatively little has been said on whether the account itself successfully defines the subjectivity of the mental. In this paper, I show that considerations of what can be grasped from only a single point of view provide neither necessary nor sufficient conditions for subjective experience.

Franchi, A. I filosofi contro la filosofia: la filosofia control i filosofi. *Sapienza*, 45(1), 3-27, 1992.

Franchi, A. Tra narcisismo e regressione: la crisi dell'uomo contemporaneo. *Sapienza*, 46(1), 32-52, 1993.

Francis, Leslie Pickering. Advance Directives for Voluntary Euthanasia: A Volatile Combination?. *J Med Phil*, 18(3), 297-322, Je 93.

Defenders of patient autonomy have successfully supported the legal adoption of advance directives. More recently, some defenders of patient autonomy have also supported the legalization of voluntary active euthanasia. This paper explores the wisdom of combining both practices. If euthanasia were to become legal, should it be permitted by advance directives? The paper juxtaposes the most significant doubts about advance directives, with the most significant doubts about euthanasia. It argues that the doubts together raise more concern about the combined practices than about either euthanasia or advance directives separately. Not all cases of voluntary euthanasia by advance directive are equally problematic, however. Advance directives can help in the defense of euthanasia for patients who make the request in advance and reaffirm it under circumstances of severe suffering.

Francken, Patrick. Incompatibilism, Nondeterministic Causation, and the Real Problem of Free Will. *J Phil Res*, 18, 37-63, 1993.

I argue that there cannot be a sense attached to "could have done otherwise" that is both compatible with the truth of determinism and relevant to the question of free will. Then I develop an incompatibilist response to the common objection that the incompatibilist requires of free actions that they have no causes and therefore cannot be anything for which an agent can be responsible. In the process, I bring out a similarity between compatibilism and incompatibilism in respect of where their problem lies.

Franco, Eli. Did Dignāga Accept Four Types of Perception?. *J Indian Phil*, 21(3), 295-299, S 93.

Francoeur, Robert. *Taking Sides: Clashing Views on Controversial Issues in Human Sexuality (Third Edition)*. Guilford, Dushkin, 1991.

Francoeur, Robert T. Sexual Archetypes in Transition. *Free Inq*, 12(2), 40-44, Spr 92.

Compares concepts of 1) human personhood, 2) human origins and Body-Spirit relationships, 3) sex and transcendence, 4) sexual pleasure, and 5) the control of sexual behaviors in Judaeo-Christian and Taoist-Tantric sexual archetypes. Practical applications are discussed in terms of our current pre-figurative culture in which traditional Judaeo-Christian archetypes have lost their sustaining power and new archetypes have yet to emerge or be developed. Several examples of new evolutionary archetypes are discussed. Conclusion: we may not develop a new mythology for a long time to come because things are changing too fast to become mythologized.

Frank, Manfred and Bowie, Andrew (trans). Is Self-Consciousness a Case of 'Présence à Soi? in Derrida: A Critical Reader, Wood, David (ed). Cambridge, Blackwell, 1992.

Frank, Robert H. A New Contractarian View of Tax and Regulatory Policy in the Emerging Market Economies. *Soc Phil Pol*, 10(2), 258-281, Sum 93.

Contractarians explain social institutions by asking what constraints rational, self-interested actors might deliberately impose upon themselves. Self-interest, however, is only one of many important human motives. In this paper, I sketch a more general version of contractarianism, one based on a broader conception of motivation. Without abandoning the essence of contractarian analysis, this alternative approach promises a more complete and coherent account of the activities of the state. It also recommends tax and regulatory policies that are substantially different from the ones most commonly employed in the Western market economies.

Frank, S L. The Essence and Leading Themes of Russian Philosophy. *Sov Stud Phil*, 30(4), 28-47, Spr 92.

Frankel, Lois. The Value of Harmony in Causation in Early Modern Philosophy, Nadler, Steven (ed). University Park, Penn St Univ Pr, 1993.

Frankena, William K. Sidgwick and the History of Ethical Dualism in Essays on Henry Sidgwick, Schultz, Bart (ed). New York, Cambridge Univ Pr, 1992.

Frankenberg, Günter. Disorder Is Possible in Cultural-Political Interventions in the Unfinished Project of Enlightenment, Honneth, Axel (& other eds). Cambridge, MIT Pr, 1992.

Frankenberry, Nancy. Classical Theism, Panentheism, and Pantheism: On the Relation between God Construction and Gender Construction. *Zygon*, 28(1), 29-46, Mr 93.

The argument of this article is that, philosophically, there are but three broad conceptual models that Western thought employs in thinking about the meaning of *God*. At the level of greatest generality, these are the models known as classical theism, pantheism, and panentheism. The essay surveys and updates these three conceptual models in light of recent writings, finds more flaws in classical theism and panentheism than in pantheism, and suggests a feminist response to each.

Frankenberry, Nancy. Consequences of William James's Pragmatism in Religion in God, Values, and Empiricism, Peden, Creighton W (ed). Macon, Mercer Univ Pr, 1989.

Frankfurt, Harry G. On God's Creation in Reasoned Faith, Stump, Eleonore (ed). Ithaca, Cornell Univ Pr, 1993.

Franklin, James. The Ancient Legal Sources of Seventeenth-Century Probability in The Uses of Antiquity, Gaukroger, Stephen (ed). Dordrecht, Kluwer, 1991.

Both the logical/epistemic and the stochastic/frequency kinds of probability have long histories before Pascal. Both are considered in the legal tradition, mainly in Justinian's *Digest* and commentaries on it; in, respectively, sections on the law of evidence and on aleatory contracts. The *Digest* was still the authoritative text of (continental) law in the seventeenth century, and its thinking on evidence and risk informed the thinking of Pascal, Fermat, Huygens and Leibniz, all of whom had legal backgrounds. The 'probability' of scientific theories spoken of by Galileo and Depler also owes a good deal to the *Digest*, though less directly.

Franks, Bradley. Realism and Folk Psychology in the Ascription of Concepts. *Phil Psych*, 5(4), 369-390, 1992.

This paper discusses some requirements on a folk-psychological, computational account of concepts. Although most psychological views take the folk-psychological stance that concept-possession requires capacities of both representation and classification, such views lack a philosophical context. In contrast, philosophically motivated views stress one of these capacities at the expense of the other. This paper seeks to provide some philosophical motivation for the (folk-) psychological stance. (edited)

Franks, Bradley and Cooper, Richard. Interruptibility as a Constraint on Hybrid Systems. *Mind Mach*, 3(1), 73-96, F 93.

It is widely mooted that a plausible computational cognitive model should involve both symbolic and connectionist components. However, sound principles for combining these components within a hybrid system are currently lacking; the design of such systems is often *ad hoc*. In an attempt to ameliorate this we provide a framework of types of hybrid systems and constraints therein, within which to explore the issues. In particular, we suggest the use of "system independent" constraints, whose source lies in general considerations about cognitive systems, rather than in particular technological or task-based considerations. We illustrate this through a detailed examination of an interruptibility constraint: handling interruptions is a fundamental facet of cognition in a dynamic world. Aspects of interruptions are delineated, as are their precise expression in symbolic and connectionist systems. We illustrate the interaction of the various constraints from interruptibility in the different types of hybrid systems. The picture that emerges of the relationship between the connectionist and the symbolic within a hybrid system provides for sufficient flexibility and complexity to suggest interesting general implications for cognition, thus vindicating the utility of the framework.

Franssen, Maarten. Did King Alfonso of Castile Really Want to Advise God Against the Ptolemaic System? The Legend in History. *Stud Hist Phil Sci*, 24(3), 313-325, Ag 93.

The tradition of the legend of King Alfonso's so-called blasphemy, which is presented by Kuhn in *The Structure of Scientific Revolutions* as evidence of a pre-Copernican feeling of crisis toward Ptolemaic astronomy, is tracked from the early 14th century onward. Its astronomical interpretation is seen to have emerged only in the late 17th century.

Franz, Margret. Neuer Aufbruch in die Moderne? Beobachtungen zur gegenwärtigen russischen Philosophie. *Z Phil Forsch*, 47(2), 296-300, Ap-Je 93.

Franzwa, Gregg E. Evolutionary Individualism. *SW Phil Stud*, 14, 1-15, Spr 92.

Fraser, Nancy. The French Derrideans in Working Through Derrida, Madison, Gary B (ed). Evanston, Northwestern Univ Pr, 1993.

Does deconstruction have any political implications? Is it possible — and desirable — to articulate a deconstructive politics? Or is there already a politics implicit in deconstruction? I consider three different answers to these questions: 1) an anti-imperialist politics that would destabilize "the West" by deconstructing its metaphysics; 2) an anti-utopian politics that would deconstruct the metaphysics of revolution; and 3) a quasi-transcendental interrogation of "the essence of the political" that would deconstruct the latter philosophical underpinnings. I focus especially on the third approach, as developed in the early 1980's in France by Philippe Lacoue-Labarthe and Jean-Luc Nancy. I argue that the project is conceptually incoherent, and I show how that assessment was borne out by its subsequent history.

Frasz, Geoffrey B. Environmental Virtue Ethics: A New Direction for Environmental Ethics. *Environ Ethics*, 15(3), 259-274, Fall 93.

In this essay, I first extend the insights of virtue ethics into environmental ethics and examine the possible dangers of this approach. Second, I analyze some qualities of character that an environmentally virtuous person must possess. Third, I evaluate "humility" as an environmental virtue, specifically, the position of Thomas E Hill, Jr. I conclude that Hill's conception of "proper" humility can be more adequately explicated by associating it with another virtue, environmental "openness".

Freddoso, Alfred. God's General Concurrence with Secondary Causes in Philosophical Perspectives, 5: Philosophy of Religion, 1991, Tomberlin, James E (ed). Atascadero, Ridgeview, 1991.

After an exposition of some key concepts in scholastic ontology, this paper examines four arguments presented by Francisco Suarez for the thesis, commonly held by Christian Aristotelians, that God's causal contribution to effects occurring in the ordinary course of nature goes beyond His merely conserving created substances along with their active and passive causal powers. The postulation of a further causal contribution, known as God's general concurrence (or general concourse), can be viewed as an attempt to accommodate an element of truth present in occasionalist accounts of divine causality.

Frede, Dorothea. Disintegration and Restoration: Pleasure and Pain in Plato's "Philebus" in The Cambridge Companion to Plato, Kraut, Richard (ed). New York, Cambridge Univ Pr, 1992.

The unity and inner coherence of Plato's dialogue *Philebus* is often questioned by contemporary commentators, because the treatment of its main topic, the nature of pleasure and knowledge and their claim to be the supreme human good, seems to make little use of the long clarifications of the problem of the One and Many and the method of dialectic in the first part of the dialogue. This essays purpose is to establish the dialogue's inner coherence by pointing out that the results of the dialogue's first part are in fact used to define pleasure and knowledge and make possible their final evaluation as goods in human life.

Frede, Dorothea. The Question of Being in The Cambridge Companion to Heidegger, Guignon, Charles B (ed). New York, Cambridge Univ Pr, 1993.

The article traces the importance and meaning of the question of being in Heidegger's work, from his youth, when he first caught a glimpse of the problem through reading Brentano's *On the Several Senses of Being in Aristotle*, to his fully developed conception of that question in *Being and Time*. It points out how this question emerges in his early writings and explains his final break with Husserl's phenomenology, because for Heidegger abstract introspection of consciousness cannot capture the meaning of being, which he equates with the *sense* that underlies human beings' encounter with the world and all that it contains, including others and the own self.

Frede, Michael. Doxographie, historiographie philosophique et historiographie historique de la philosophie. *Rev Metaph Morale*, 97(3), 311-325, Jl-S 92.

Frede, Michael. Plato's "Sophist" on False Statements in The Cambridge Companion to Plato, Kraut, Richard (ed). New York, Cambridge Univ Pr, 1992.

Frederick, Robert (ed) and Hoffman, W Michael (ed) and Pentry, Edward S (ed). Business, Ethics, and the Environment: The Public Policy Debate. Westport, Greenwood Pr, 1990.

Frederick, Robert (ed) and Hoffman, W Michael (ed) and Petry, Edward S (ed). The Corporation, Ethics, and the Environment. Westport, Greenwood Pr, 1990.

Fredericks, James L (trans) and Abe, Masao. "Inverse Correspondence" in the Philosophy of Nishida: The Emergence of the Notion. *Int Phil Quart*, 32(3), 325-344, S 92.

Fredericks, Janet and Miller, Steven I. Clarifying the "Adequate Evidence Condition" in Educational Issues and Research: A Lakoffian View. *Educ Theor*, 42(4), 461-472, Fall 92.

The article is an attempt to clarify and extend Scheffler's notion of the "adequate evidence condition". Using the framework of an Idealized Cognitive Model, developed by the cognitive-linguist, George Lakoff, various ideas of "evidence" are developed and analyzed. The analysis reveals that our models of adequate evidence influence our traditional epistemological views concerning correspondence and coherence views of "truth". Attempts are made to show the significance of the evidence condition for policy formulation in the human sciences.

Freeden, Michael. The New Liberalism and Its Aftermath in Victorian Liberalism, Bellamy, Richard (ed). New York, Routledge, 1990.

Freedman, Benjamin. A Response to a Purported Ethical Difficulty with Randomized Clinical Trials Involving Cancer Patients. *J Clin Ethics*, 3(3), 231-233, Fall 92.

The ethical foundations of randomized clinical trials (RCTs) have in recent years been under frequent and vigorous attack. Responses to these challenges, particularly some mounted by some major British figures in the realm of clinical trials and statistics, imprudently (and mistakenly) assuming they thereby may speak with authority on the ethics of their practice, have further cast doubt upon the possibility of ethically conducting RCTs. Here, I briefly review the reasons why and conditions under which RCTs are ethical, describe and dispel common erroneous beliefs about the meaning of a doctor's obligation to provide optimal care to patients, the purported conflict posed by RCTs between rights of individuals and collectivities, and the application of Kant to RCTs.

Freedman, Benjamin. The Slippery-Slope Argument Reconstructed: Response to Van Der Burg. *J Clin Ethics*, 3(4), 293-297, Wint 92.

Freeman, David A. Spinoza on Self-Consciousness and Nationalism. *Hist Euro Ideas*, 16(4-6), 915-920, Ja 93.

Freeman, James. *Thinking Logically: Basic Concepts for Reasoning (Second Edition)*. Englewood Cliffs, Prentice Hall, 1993.

This is an informal logic text. We begin by distinguishing the functions of language and discussing problems of meaning. We then introduce the notion of argument. Distinguishing the persuasive force form the logically convincing character of arguments leads to a discussion of various emotional appeal fallacies. A full discussion of argument diagramming via a circle and arrow technique follows. We then turn to the three central issues in argument evaluation-premise acceptability, relevance, and adequate weight. The last includes both inductive and deductive consideration. We conclude with an overall argument evaluation procedure.

Freeman, Walter J and Skarda, Christine A. Mind/Brain Science in John Searle and His Critics, LePore, Ernest (ed). Cambridge, Blackwell, 1991.

Searle's philosophy is distinguished by his refusal of functionalism and his embrace of neuroscience. We focus on four aspects of his views. We agree that brains are self-organizing neural masses, not rule-driven symbol manipulators. We agree on the need for levels of description, but assert that the crucial distinction is between neurons and interactive systems, not between neural and mental functioning, which constitutes a hidden form of dualism. We reject Searle's notion that mental events cause neural events and vice versa, seeing these as opposing sides of the same coin. We see perception as self-organized, not as generated by stimuli.

Freer, Jack P. Decision Making in an Incapacitated Patient. *J Clin Ethics*, 4(1), 55-57, Spr 93.

A clinical case is presented as a focus for a discussion concerning medical decision-making in incapacitated patients. A young male drug abuser has given very specific instructions concerning life-sustaining treatment, but these are difficult to interpret once he becomes incapacitated because of suspicion that the statements were made to obtain prescription drugs for illicit use. Guidance principles for decision-making are then analyzed in this light (advance directives, substituted judgement, and best interests). Application of these principles to individual cases is noted to be a complex process, but can successfully guide decision-making in difficult cases.

Freier, F V. Kritik der Hegelschen Formalismusthese. *Kantstudien*, 83(3), 304-323, 1992.

Frerari, V. Partendo da Parmenide. *Sapienza*, 45(4), 421-424, 1992.

Fretz, Leo. Individuality in Sartre's Philosophy in The Cambridge Companion to Sartre, Howells, Christina (ed). New York, Cambridge Univ Pr, 1992.

Freudiger, Jürg. *Kants Begründung der praktischen Philosophie*. Berne, Haupt, 1993.

Eine Interpretation von Kants *Grundlegun zur Metaphysik der Sitten*, welche die systematische Stellung dieser Schrift in Kants praktischer Philosophie, ihre Methode sowie die entscheidenden Interpretationsprobleme erörtert. Mittels sorgfältiger Rekonstruktion der Kantischen Argumente versucht diese Studie, den Ausführungen Kants Kohärenz und Plausibilität zu verleihen. Ausgehend vom aktuellen Forschungsstand wirft die Arbeit neues Licht auf Themen wie: Enthalten *Grundlegung* und *Kritik der praktischen Vernunft* verschiedene Ansätze? Ist das Sittengesetz ein präskriptiver Satz? Was leistet die Deduktion des kategorischen Imperativs? Worin besteht der vermeintliche Zirkel im dritten Abschnitt? (edited)

Frey, R G. *William James Durant: An Intellectual Biography*. Lewiston, Mellen Pr, 1991.

Freydberg, Bernard D. Mythos and Logos in Platonic Politeiai. *Hist Euro Ideas*, 16(4-6), 607-612, Ja 93.

The paper argues that for Plato, the attempt to expel *mythos* from the city is impossible, comic. An appropriate reading of the relevant sections of the *Republic* and of the *Timaeus* reveals the necessary presence in a city of the dark matters treated in myths, which resurface even in the most intense efforts to suppress them. *Mythos* is as essential to any *politeia* as *logos*.

Fricke, Christel. Die akroamatische Dimension der Hermeneutik. *Phil Rundsch*, 39(4), 304-308, 1992.

Fried, Lewis L B and Schultz, William R. *Jacques Derrida: An Annotated Primary and Secondary Bibliography*. Hamden, Garland, 1992.

The book attempts to be comprehensive rather than selective, and is extensively annotated. It lists primary and secondary works from the year of Derrida's Master's thesis (1954) and extends into 1991.

Friedman, Harvey and Simpson, Stephen G and Yu, Xiaokang. Periodic Points and Subsystems of Second-Order Arithmetic. *Annals Pure Applied Log*, 62(1), 51-64, Je 93.

Friedman, Jeffrey. After Libertarianism: Rejoinder to Narveson, McCloskey, Flew, and Machan. *Crit Rev*, 6(1), 113-152, Wint 92.

Friedman, Jeffrey. Politics or Scholarship?. *Crit Rev*, 6(2-3), 429-445, Spr-Sum 92.

Environmental issues imperil the libertarian utopia of a society in which the individual is completely sovereign over his or her private domain. Taken seriously, this aspiration would lead to an environmentalism so extreme that it would preclude human life, since most human activity entails incursions against the sovereign realms of other human beings. The fallback position many libertarians have adopted — free-market environmentalism — retreats from libertarian ideals by permitting some of the physical aggression of pollution to continue. Neither libertarianism nor free-market environmentalism can culminate in anything close to the abolition of the modern state.

Friedman, Lesley. Another Look at Flage's Hume. *Hume Stud*, 19(1), 177-186, Ap 93.

In recent articles, Daniel Flage offers an interpretation of Humean memory-ideas as relative ideas: ideas of memory are analogous to definite descriptions insofar as they single out exactly one entity. Consequently, Flage argues that Hume has provided an adequate distinction between ideas generated by memory and ideas generated by imagination. It is my contention that Flage's reading is neither consonant with Hume's remarks in the *Treatise* nor successful in reducing the number of difficulties with Hume's theory of memory. I argue that (i) it is not clear that all memory-ideas are complex (an assumption necessary for Flage's interpretation); (ii) Flage construes all memory as episodic, he overlooks semantic memory; and (iii) there is a distinction between mis-remembering and imagining which Flage's account cannot accommodate. In my reply to Flage, I focus on giving further textual evidence for the claim that Hume believed one can have, and remember, a simple idea in its simplicity.

Friedman, Lesley. Reply to Flage's "On Friedman's Look". *Hume Stud*, 19(1), 199-202, Ap 93.

In recent articles, Daniel Flage offers an interpretation of Humean memory-ideas as relative ideas: ideas of memory are analogous to definite descriptions insofar as they single out exactly one entity. Consequently, Flage argues that Hume has provided an adequate distinction between ideas generated by memory and ideas generated by imagination. It is my contention that Flage's reading is neither consonant with Hume's remarks in the *Treatise* nor successful in reducing the number of difficulties with Hume's theory of memory. I argue that (i) it is not clear that all memory-ideas are complex (an assumption necessary for Flage's interpretation); (ii) Flage construes all memory as episodic, he overlooks semantic memory; and (iii) there is a distinction between mis-remembering and imagining which Flage's account cannot accommodate. In my reply to Flage, I focus on giving further textual evidence for the claim that Hume believed one can have, and remember, a simple idea in its simplicity.

Friedman, Maurice S. *Dialogue and the Human Image: Beyond Humanistic Psychology*. Newbury Park, Sage, 1992.

If it is to develop meaningfully, humanistic psychology must not only recognize that it is a human science but also that human potential and self-actualization are *by-products* of our dialogue with what is not ourselves. Part three discusses Dialogical and Contextual (Intergenerational) Family Therapy, Part four the image of the human and psychotherapy, including implications of literature for anxiety, sex and love, freedom and compulsion, the crisis of motives, existential shame, guilt, and trust.

Friedman, Michael. Causal Laws and the Foundations of Natural Science in The Cambridge Companion to Kant, Guyer, Paul (ed). New York, Cambridge Univ Pr, 1992.

Friedman, Michael. Epistemology in the *Aufbau*. *Synthese*, 93(1-2), 15-57, N 92.

Friedman, Michael. Remarks on the History of Science and the History of Philosophy in World Changes, Horwich, Paul (ed). Cambridge, MIT Pr, 1993.

Friedman, R Z. Maimonides and Kant on Metaphysics and Piety. *Rev Metaph*, 45(4), 773-801, Je 92.

Frisch, Morton J. Shakespeare's Richard III and the Soul of the Tyrant. *Interpretation*, 20(3), 275-284, Spr 93.

It must be emphasized that, from Shakespeare's point of view, the soul of the tyrant, given its highest expression in his *Richard III*, represents the darker side of human nature. Richard represents a disposition by no means that uncommon if we are to take seriously Socrates' remark that "surely some terrible, savage and lawless form of desires is in every man, even in some of us who seem to be ever so measured." It would seem as though Shakespeare wanted to show utter depravity as it might be experienced in a human soul, the soul of a tyrant, revealing the inadequacy of the tyrant's conception of what constitutes human happiness.

Frisch, Morton J. The Emergence of Nationalism as a Political Philosophy. *Hist Euro Ideas*, 16(4-6), 885-890, Ja 93.

Frith, Lucy. Sociobiology, Ethics and Human Nature in New Horizons in the Philosophy of Science, Lamb, David (ed). Brookfield, Avebury, 1992.

Fritscher, Bernhard. Kant und Werner: Zum Problem einer Geschichte der Natur und zum Verhältnis von Philosophie und Geologie um 1800. *Kantstudien*, 83(4), 417-435, 1992.

It is dealt with the methodological parallels between Kant's concept of a history of nature (i.e., his distinction between "Naturgeschichte" and "Naturbeschreibung") and the distinction between "Geognosie" and "Oryktognosie" by the German mineralogist A G Werner (1749-1817). By relating those parallels to the introduction of Kant's "Metaphysical Foundations of Natural Science", the paper shows some scarcely considered scientific roots of his epistemology.

Fritzman, J M. Against Coherence. *Amer Phil Quart*, 29(2), 183-191, Ap 92.

Coherentism is a species of foundationalism. Coherentism and traditional foundationalism differ only in their understandings of the nature of foundations. In addition, coherentism ultimately is incoherent by its own criteria for coherence. However, coherence is not necessarily a virtue, and so should not be privileged over incoherence in every context.

Fritzman, J M. Escaping Hegel. *Int Phil Quart*, 33(1), 57-68, Mr 93.

A rhetorical reading of the Hegelian corpus shows that—while Hegel assumes that the end of communication is agreement—consensus is not the goal of communication, but rather its death. Discourse remains alive because dissensus is its end. Recognizing disagreement as the *telos* of communication allows a transversing of the Hegelian dialectic that succeeds in escaping its recuperative moment.

Fritzman, J M. Thinking with Fraser about Rorty, Feminism, and Pragmatism. *Praxis Int*, 13(2), 113-125, Jl 93.

Frodeman, Robert. Radical Environmentalism and the Political Roots of Postmodernism. *Environ Ethics*, 14(4), 307-319, Wint 92.

I examine the close relationship between radical environmentalism and postmodernism. I argue that there is an incoherence within most postmodernist thought, born of an unwillingness or incapacity to distinguish between claims true from an ontological or epistemological perspective and those appropriate to the exigencies of political life. The failure to distinguish which differences make a difference not only vitiates postmodernist thought, but also runs up against some of the fundamental assumptions of radical environmentalism.

Frohmann, Bernd. Playing with Language: Language-Games Reconsidered in Wittgenstein's Intentions, Canfield, J V (ed). Hamden, Garland, 1993.

Fromm, Erich. *The Revision of Psychoanalysis—Eric Fromm*. Boulder, Westview Pr, 1992.

This book is Fromm's long-expected account of his own personal way of understanding and practicing psychoanalysis. Of special interest to today's readers are his continuing efforts to understand the meaning of sexuality, his critique of Herbert Marcuse's vision of psychoanalysis, and the implications of a Freudian analytical social psychology for the reform of social arrangements. The book is essential reading for psychologists and for social and political theorists in many disciplines. For psychoanalysts, it provides Fromm's most provocative and unique recommendations for the revision of psychoanalysis.

Frosini, Vittorio. Law-Making and Legal Interpretation. *Ratio Juris*, 6(1), 118-123, Mr 93.

The creation of written law is symbolized in the Bible, but it is only with the advent of legislation in Rome, that law is given a pragmatic meaning. The publication of a law is the first step in the process of disseminating the information and regulations it contains. Through judicial and administrative procedures, the wording of law is converted into decision-making and action; the connection between a rule, its interpretation and the facts is a dialectic and structural relationship; the interpretation is complementary to statute wording.

Frosolono, Anne-Marie. Thus Spoke Augustine. *Cont Phil*, 15(1), 4-7, Ja-F 93.

Fry-Revere, Sigrid. A Libertarian Critique of H Tristram Engelhardt, Jr's "The Foundations of Bioethics". *J Clin Ethics*, 3(1), 46-52, Spr 92.

Fu, Pei-jung. On the Relation between Existence and Value (in Chinese). *Phil Rev (Taiwan)*, 15, 127-142, Ja 92.

In dealing with the relation between existence and value, the author first gives an analysis concerning the meaning of existence and value respectively, then bases his argument on the Confucian theory of human nature. (edited)

Fu, Pei-Jung. Human Nature and Human Education in Chinese Foundations for Moral Education and Character Development, Van Doan, Tran (ed). Washington, CRVP, 1991.

Fuchino, Sakaé. On Potential Embedding and Versions of Martin's Axiom. *Notre Dame J Form Log*, 33(4), 481-492, Fall 92.

We give a characterization of versions of Martin's axiom and some other related axioms by means of potential embedding of structures.

Fuchs, Yuval. The Problem of Personal Identity in *Being and Time* (in Hebrew). *Iyyun*, 42, 307-322, Ap 93.

Führer, M L (trans). *Treatise on the Intellect and the Intelligible*. Milwaukee, Marquette Univ Pr, 1992.

Fulford, K W M. Mental Illness and the Mind-Brain Problem: Delusion, Belief and Searle's Theory of Intentionality. *Theor Med*, 14(2), 181-192, Je 93.

Until recently there has been little contact between the mind-brain debate in philosophy and the debate in psychiatry about the nature of mental illness. In this paper some of the analogies and disanalogies between the two debates are explored. It is noted in particular that the emphasis in modern philosophy of mind on the importance of the concept of action has been matched by a recent shift in the debate about mental illness from analyses of disease in terms of failure of functioning to analyses of illness in terms of failure of action. The concept of action thus provides a natural conduit for two-way exchanges of ideas between philosophy and psychiatry. The potential fruitfulness of such exchanges is illustrated with an outline of the mutual heuristic significance of psychiatric work on delusions and philosophical accounts of Intentionality.

Fuller, Gary. Functionalism and Personal Identity. *Personalist Forum*, 8/1(Supp), 133-143, Spr 92.

What is the relation between functionalist accounts of mind and theories of personal identity? Sidney Shoemaker has suggested that functionalism does have implications for personal identity and that what it implies is a version of the psychological continuity theory of personal identity. I shall examine Shoemaker's interesting suggestion and argue that it fails. Functionalism, as a theory about the nature of mental states, has few interesting ramification for personal identity and does not favor a psychological theory over a physical theory.

Fuller, Gary. Personal Identity in Reflections on Philosophy, McHenry, Leemon (ed). New York, St Martin's Pr, 1993.

The purpose of the essay is to provide an introduction, especially aimed at the student, to the topic of personal identity. The essay also atttempts to show philosophy in action through the detailed examination of many examples and counter examples. The essay concentrates mainly on the question of what is involved in the survival of a person over time. Various theories are examined including body, psychological continuity, brain, and soul theories. A modified psychological continuity theory, which requires psychological continuity via within-brain causation, is defended. A final section relates the question of personal identity over time to other philosophical questions about persons.

Fuller, Gary and Adams, Fred. Names, Contents, and Causes. *Mind Lang*, 7(3), 205-221, Autumn 92.

Can cognitive science run on broad content alone? Yes, but only if Twin-Earth and the names puzzles are solved. AI and Twin-AI share behavior but not broad content.

How? Similarly, Al and John behave differently even though they share the same broad thoughts (Tony Curtis/Bernie Schwartz is here). How? We argue elsewhere that Twin-Earth puzzles are easily solved with broad content alone. In this paper, we argue that names puzzles also are solved with broad content alone. It is a good thing, because narrow content is incapable of solving the names puzzles facing cognitive science.

Fuller, Gary and Adams, Fred and Stecker, Robert. Thoughts Without Objects. *Mind Lang*, 8(1), 90-104, Spr 93.

This paper answers objections to object-dependent thoughts (thoughts identified by their objects). We claim that such thoughts exist and are needed to explain behavior in many circumstances. Objections to object-dependent thoughts invoke vacuous singular thoughts (say, of an hallucinated attacker). Such thoughts have no objects (no attacker), hence such thoughts cannot explain behavior in virtue of their object-dependent content. We show that appeals to vacuous thoughts do not diminish the need for object dependent thoughts in non-vacuous situations. We also compare this debate to the broad/narrow content debate and show that the content needed to explain behavior when thoughts are vacuous is not narrow content.

Fuller, Gary and Stecker, Robert and Adams, Fred. Schiffer on Modes of Presentation. *Analysis*, 53(1), 30-34, Ja 93.

Since Lois likes Kent and believes that Kent cannot fly, she would plead with him not to leap from a tall building. Though Lois also likes Superman, she would not plead with him not to leap. If modes of presentation were syntactic items in a language of thought, we could explain that Lois thinks of the same individual once under the mode of "Kent" and later under the mode of "Superman", without thinking "Kent = Superman". In a number of recent writings, Schiffer has proposed a roadblock to this neat explanation. In this paper we argue that the view that modes are syntactic items in a language of thought survives Schiffer's objections.

Fuller, Gary and Stecker, Robert and Adams, Fred. The Floyd Puzzle: Reply to Yagisawa. *Analysis*, 53(1), 36-40, Ja 93.

We defended the view that modes of presentation are syntactic items in the language of thought. Yagisawa argues that our defense of this view did not handle Schiffer's Floyd puzzle. The following truths are supposed to make a rational Floyd irrational (on our account): 1) Floyd believes that Lois believes that Superman flies, 2) Floyd believes that Lois does not believe that Clark Kent flies, and 3) Floyd does not believe that Clark Kent is not Superman. We remain unconvinced. We present not one but two interpretations on which Floyd is not irrational on our view and on which our view survives Schiffer's Floyd puzzle.

Fuller, Gary and Stecker, Robert and Adams, Fred. The Semantics of Thought. *Pac Phil Quart*, 73(4), 375-389, D 92.

This paper accepts that the task of a semantics of thoughts is to explain how thoughts convey information about the world and how behavior can be explained in virtue of the content of thoughts. We defend direct reference theories of meaning against Devitt's charge that such semantic theories cannot give a satisfactory semantics for the problems of identity sentences, opaque contexts, or positive and negative existence sentences. We reply to Devitt's charge, examine and reject Devitt's alternative non-descriptive sense theory, and offer a new account of the semantics of positive and negative existential sentences.

Fuller, Robert C. American Pragmatism Reconsidered: William James' Ecological Ethic. *Environ Ethics*, 14(2), 159-176, Sum 92.

In this paper, I argue that pragmatism, at least in its formulation by William James, squarely addresses the metaethical and normative issues at the heart of our present crisis in moral justification. James gives ethics an empirical foundation that permits the natural and social sciences a clear role in defining our obligation to the wider environment. Importantly, James's pragmatism also addresses the psychological and cultural factors that help elicit our willingness to adopt an ethical posture toward life.

Fuller, Steve. Being There with Thomas Kuhn: A Parable for Postmodern Times. *Hist Theor*, 31(3), 241-275, 1992.

On the thirtieth anniversary of the first edition of Kuhn's *The Structure of Scientific Revolutions*, I trace the origins and consequences of the book's remarkable reception, most of which Kuhn himself did not expect and has disavowed. Kuhn's philosophical approach was grounded in his teaching experience in James Conant's General Education in Science Program at Harvard, which was designed to normalize science's relations with the public in the aftermath of the atomic bomb. Kuhn also mixed the epistemologies of the positivists and Michael Polanyi, with the effect of short-circuiting the comprehensively critical approaches to science that had been promoted by both Popperians and radical social scientists. Contrary to how it has been taken up by sociologists and humanists, Kuhn's book effectively legitimized an "end of ideology" mentality within the academy, as well as in science policy.

Fuller, Steve. David Bloor's *Knowledge and Social Imagery*, (Second Edition). *Phil Sci*, 60(1), 158-170, Mr 93.

Bloor's book launched the "Strong Programme in the Sociology of Scientific Knowledge," which, over the last fifteen years, has caused philosophers of science and epistemologists to rethink their tasks. If science is, in some sense, just another social practice without its own distinctive form of rationality, what should philosophers be doing? This was Bloor's original challenge. It should be seen as a radical version of naturalized epistemology that argues, in late Wittgensteinian fashion, that the philosophical task in understanding science is no different from the historical or sociological task. The Strong Programme, then, is meant as language therapy for philosophers. However, Bloor's conclusions are not the only ones that can be drawn from the Strong Programme. Since his book was first published, social studies of science has embraced constructivist and politicized accounts of science that Bloor himself has opposed.

Fuller, Steve. *Philosophy, Rhetoric, and the End of Knowledge: The Coming of Science and Technology Studies*. Madison, Univ of Wisconsin Pr, 1993.

Most philosophical norms are ignored or rejected because those who would be governed by the norms—scientists, in the case of philosophy of science—do not find it in their interest to abide by them. Fuller regards this as the biggest challenge facing social epistemology. His solution is to admit that norms are always socially constructed, which means that philosophers need to persuade scientists that they stand to benefit by following the norms. Part of this rhetorical task involves getting scientists to reflect more on the ends of their inquiries, thereby breaking the "normal science" mentality. Fuller argues that such reflection would help scientists overcome disciplinary boundaries, ultimately making science accountable to a wider public. Fuller's conclusions are informed by recent work in the sociology of science. The book includes case studies from the social and cognitive sciences as well as pedagogical suggestions.

Fumerton, Richard. Skepticism and Reasoning to the Best Explanation in Rationality in Epistemology, Villanueva, Enrique (ed). Atascadero, Ridgeview, 1992.

I evaluate the extent to which reasoning to the best explanation provides a source of justification that will defeat traditional skeptical arguments after discussing the nature of reasoning to the best explanation, I argue that at both superficial and deeper levels it fails to meet the skeptical challenge.

Funk, Nanette (ed) and Mueller, Magda (ed). *Gender Politics and Post-Communism: Reflections from Eastern Europe and the Former Soviet Union*. New York, Routledge, 1993.

Furlán, Augusto. Spinoza: presencia de la tradión en la modernidad. *Sapientia*, 47(183), 45-64, 1992.

Futernick, Kenneth. The Teacher As Hero: The Exploitation of Niceness. *Proc Phil Educ*, 48, 250-254, 1992.

Fynsk, Christopher. Community and the Limits of Theory in Community at Loose Ends, Miami Theory Collect, (ed). Minneapolis, Univ of Minnesota Pr, 1991.

Gabbay, Dov M and De Queiroz, R J G B. Extending the Curry-Howard Interpretation to Lienar, Relevant and Other Resource Logics. *J Sym Log*, 57(4), 1319-1365, D 92.

The so-called Curry-Howard interpretation is known to provide a rather neat term-functional account of intuitionistic implication. Could one refine the interpretation to obtain an almost as good account of other neighboring implications, including the so-called 'resource' implications (e.g., linear, relevant, etc.)? We answer this question positively by demonstrating that just by working with side conditions on the rule of assertability conditions for the connective representing implication one can characterize those 'resource' logics.

Gabbey, Alan. Innovation and Continuity in the History of Astronomy in Revolution and Continuity, Barker, Peter (ed). Washington, Cath Univ Amer Pr, 1991.

Analyses of discussions pre-Newton of the moon's motion, and of Newton's theory of lunar libration, show that before Newton it was not realized that we see always the same face because the moon rotates with *per se* sidereal motion. Before Newton the (non-epicyclical) moon did not possess any *per se* motion, only the motion *per accidens* of its deferent orb (or causal equivalent). Newton's "dynamical" moon removed the last vestige of the celestial spheres doctrine—the lunar orb itself—and so marked a final stage in the demise of the Ptolemeo-Aristotelian cosmos.

Gabbi Jr, Osmyr Faria. A Origem da Moral em Psicanálise. *Cad Hist Filosof Cie*, 1(2), 129-168, Jl-D 91.

Totem und Tabu is not a work of anthropology. It is an essay on metapsychology that attempts to solve several problems left open after the abandonment of the theory of seduction. In this way, it may be understood as a continuation of the theory of the psychic apparatus contained in the seventh chapter of *traumedeutung*. In addition, one of its consequences is to show the genesis of moral and religious feelings.

Gaboriau, F. Le projet Thomiste de la métaphysique. *Rev Thomiste*, 92(3), 702-726, Jl-S 92.

Gabriel, Gottfried. Gottlob Frege (1848-1925): O Pai da Filosofia Analítica. *Cad Hist Filosof Cie*, 2(1), 21-25, Ja-Je 90.

The following remarks try to make clear that Frege, who counts as the father of modern analytic philosophy, nevertheless belongs to the German tradition of continental philosophy. Though he does his work on the new methodological basis of logical analysis of language, he in fact continues the Kantian (and even Aristotelian) way of doing philosophy as a kind of elucidation of our categorical framework. The "only" difference is that, whereas the categories in Aristotle have an ontological and in Kant an epistemological fundamental, in Frege they have a semantic one.

Gabriel, Gottfried. Why a Proper Name has a Meaning in Mind, Meaning and Metaphysics, Mulligan, Kevin (ed). Dordrecht, Kluwer, 1990.

Gadamer, Hans-Georg. Culture and Media in Cultural-Political Interventions in the Unfinished Project of Enlightenment, Honneth, Axel (& other eds). Cambridge, MIT Pr, 1992.

Gärdenfors, Peter. The Emergence of Meaning. *Ling Phil*, 16(3), 285-309, Je 93.

If one assumes that meaning is determined by the mental states of the language users, then explaining the existence of a common meaning becomes a problem. In this paper a social meaning is seen as emerging from individual notions of meaning. The main factor determining the emergent meaning is who has semantic power. Some general conditions on semantic power are formulated and it is shown how such conditions constrain the possible forms of social meaning. Using some elementary notions from model theory, it is then outlined how the semantic power structure can determine an emergent social meaning. Finally, the analysis explains some aspects of language as a convention.

Gahlings, Ute. *Sinn und Ursprung*. Sankt Augustin, Academia, 1992.

Gaidenko, P P. Landmarks: An Unheard Warning. *Russian Stud Phil*, 32(1), 16-46, Sum 93.

Gairdner, W T (trans) and Lavelle, Louis. *The Dilemma of Narcissus*. Burdett, Larson, 1993.

Gaita, Raimond. Animal Thoughts. *Phil Invest*, 15(3), 227-244, Jl 92.

Gaita, Raimond. Goodness and Truth. *Philosophy*, 67(262), 507-521, O 92.

Gaita, Raimond. Language and Conversation in Wittgenstein Centenary Essays, Griffiths, A Phillips (ed). New York, Cambridge Univ Pr, 1991.

Gaita, Raimond. Radical Critique, Scepticism and Commonsense in Human Beings, Cockburn, David (ed). New York, Cambridge Univ Pr, 1991.

Galasso, Giuseppe. L'opera di Pietro Piovani. *G Crit Filosof Ital*, 71(1), 5-13, Ja-Ap 92.

Gale, Richard. A Reply to Paul Helm. *Relig Stud*, 29(2), 257-263, Je 93.

A response is made to numerous criticisms of my book, *On the Nature and Existence of God* (Cambridge University Press, 1991), by Paul Helm in his review in this issue. Special emphasis is given to possible ways out of St. Augustine's "collapse of time" argument and whether omniscience requires not only knowing every true proposition but also knowing what it is like to be every type of thing, for example, what it is like to be a bat or a temporal creature.

Gale, Richard. On Some Pernicious Thought-Experiments in Thought Experiments in Science and Philosophy, Horowitz, Tamara (ed). Lanham, Rowman & Littlefield, 1991.

It is argued that many thought-experiments, especially the science-fiction type ones that are offered as counter-examples to different analyses of personal identity over time, fail to distinguish between the rules that regulate a normative, rule-governed activity and the empirical prerequisites for our wanting to engage in this practice. Herein an attempt is made to answer Wittgenstein's question of why we give proper names to people but not the chairs in a dining room set.

Gale, Richard. Pragmatism Versus Mysticism: the Divided Self of William James in Philosophical Perspectives, 5: Philosophy of Religion, 1991, Tomberlin, James E (ed). Atascadero, Ridgeview, 1991.

James' pragmatism attempts to reconcile his tough—and tender-minded selves. It does not, however, assuage a deeper conflict between his promethean pragmatic self and his mystical self. It is argued that James' philosophy up until the late 1890's is almost exclusively promethean, being based on his brand of "humanistic" pragmatism, and that his later writings tend, though not without important exceptions, for he never succeeded in becoming a unified self, to give voice to a competing anti-promethean type of mysticism of the sort that will assuage his deep cosmic and personal anxieties by giving him absolute assurance that higher spiritual powers reign supreme and thus all is well.

Galeotti, Anna Elisabetta. Citizenship and Equality: The Place for Toleration. *Polit Theory*, 21(4), 585-605, N 93.

Galewicz, Wlodzimierz. Die Möglichkeit der Selbstwahrnehmung bei Brentano. *Conceptus*, 25(66), 49-57, 1991.

The self-perception as conceived by Brentano would be the perception of the substantial self. The mental substance shows on his view three different aspects. First of all, it is maintained to be a principle of individuality of the subject, then it is also interpreted as its principium identitatis and thirdly, it should constitute a unifying principle for our simultaneous acts of consciousness. However, the individual nature of the mental subject is admitted by Brentano himself to be inaccessible to inner perception. As to the identity of the subject, it cannot be perceived either, because the scope of inner perception does not extend itself, according to his theory, beyond our present experiences. The unity of consciousness, finally, involves a reference of our simultaneous acts to phenomenal rather than substantial ego. So it turns out that none of the aspects of the substantial self, as described by Brentano, is given to us immediately.

Gallagher, Kenneth. Abortion and "Choice". *Pub Affairs Quart*, 7(1), 13-17, Ja 93.

Two questions must be asked with respect to abortion. First, is abortion a morally permissible act on the part of an individual? Second, is abortion, irrespective of its individual morality, an act which the state could rightly refrain from prohibiting or regulating? The facing of the issue in terms of a "woman's right to choose" is seen, upon examination, to render the answer to both questions hopelessly confused. In particular, in respect to the political issue, the mere fact of disagreement is not sufficient to decide the matter of legalization; this requires reasoning based upon political prudence, which seeks to balance the relative weight of objective goods.

Gallagher, Kenneth. Dawkins in Biomorph Land. *Int Phil Quart*, 32(4), 501-513, D 92.

This paper examines the arguments for Darwinian theory which Richard Dawkins presents in *The Blind Watchmaker*, and finds them wanting. The "biomorphs" in his model do not seem to be good simulacra of biological reality. The most pervasive defect is the failure to take into account such aspects as qualitative form and function. This makes it impossible to deal with or even represent the issue of the relation between form and function, which seems central to an adequate theory of evolution. The resulting flaws in argumentation are examined in detail.

Gallagher, Shaun. The Place of Phronesis in Postomdern Hermeneutics. *Phil Today*, 37(3), 298-305, Fall 93.

Lyotard's conception of paralogy motivates a number of questions concerning justice and the moral life. I suggest that Lyotard's account fails to provide an adequate response to these questions. A more satisfactory account of justice in paralogy can be developed by exploring the concept of phronesis, and John Caputo's *Radical Hermeneutics* leads us in this direction. But where Lyotard reduces phronesis to cleverness, Caputo elevates it to "meta-phronesis" by overstating the radicality of the paralogical situation. Gadamer's concept of the hermeneutical situation provides a more moderate conception of paralogy, and a more Aristotelian view of phronesis.

Gallagher, Shaun. The Theater of Personal Identity: From Hume to Derrida. *Personalist Forum*, 8/1(Supp), 21-30, Spr 92.

The author explores the status of personal identity within the context of Derrida's deconstructive approach to the issue of consciousness. Derrida is placed at the most recent point of a philosophical conversation which includes Hume and Husserl insofar as he deconstructs Husserl's attempt to answer the problem of personal identity posed by Hume. The paper focuses on the concepts of time-consciousness, fiction, and theatre to address the questions: Does Derrida lead us back towards Hume's critique of metaphysical identity? Or does Derrida deconstruct the possibility of personal identity in a more radical way than Hume?

Galleni, Lodovico. Relationships between Scientific Analysis and the World View of Pierre Teilhard de Chardin. *Zygon*, 27(2), 153-166, Je 92.

This paper introduces the thought of Pierre Teilhard de Chardin form a perspective neglected until now: a view that builds on the analysis of his scientific work formed part of the "modern synthesis" which laid the foundation of contemporary Darwinism. His main contributions in the field were the definition of a new branch of evolutionary sciences, geobiology; the redefinition of the term *orthogenesis;* and the proposal of the "scale" phyletic tree. Using these new research concepts, Teilhard de Chardin attempted to solve, within a scientific framework, a problem fundamental for his philosophical synthesis: that of evolutionary directionality.

Gallino, Guglielmo. L'ironia e il soggetto nascosto. *Filosofia*, 43(1), 15-57, Ja-Ap 92.

Gallino, Guglielmo. La conciliazione estetica e l'etica. *Filosofia*, 43(2), 215-269, My-Ag 92.

Gallino, Guglielmo. La forma e il limite. *Filosofia*, 43(3), 381-430, S-D 92.

Gallois, André. Ramachandran On Restricting Rigidity. *Mind*, 102(405), 151-155, Ja 93.

Gallois, André. Reply to Ramachandran. *Mind*, 102(405), 159-162, Ja 93.

Gallop, David. *Aristotle on Sleep and Dreams*. Peterborough, Broadview Pr, 1991.

Galloway, David. Wynn on Mathematical Empiricism. *Mind Lang*, 7(4), 333-358, Wint 92.

I discuss Wynn's claim that a Mill-Kitcher style mathematical empiricism is refuted by current work in developmental psychology (see Wynn's article in *Mind and Language*, 7, 4, Winter 1992). I argue that the evidence she cites is fully compatible with Kitcher's position, and has relatively little force against the less sophisticated empiricism of Mill.

Galston, William. Cosmopolitan Altruism. *Soc Phil Pol*, 10(1), 118-134, Wint 93.

Galston, William. Cosmopolitan Altruism in Altruism, Paul, Ellen Frankel (ed). New York, Cambridge Univ Pr, 1993.

Galston, William A. Virtue: A Brief Bibliography. *Nomos*, 34, 387-389, 1992.

Galvin, Richard F. Moral Pluralism and Democracy. *Cont Phil*, 15(3), 8-11, My-Je 93.

Gamble, D D. Meaning and Mental Representation. *Austl J Phil*, 70(3), 343-357, S 92.

Gandelman, Claude. Philosophy as a Sign-Producing Activity: The Metastable Gestalt of Intentionality in Analecta Husserliana, XXXIV, Tymieniecka, Anna-Teresa (ed). Dordrecht, Kluwer, 1992.

The article proposes a visual model corresponding to the concept of "intentionality" in phenomenology. This model is provided by the well-known "metastable" visual illusions such as "The Necker Cube", "The Rubin Goblet", or "The Duck-Rabbit". Just as permanent "gestalt-switches" occur in our perception when viewing these figures, similar gestalt-switches occur in the functioning of phenomenological "intention".

Gangopadhyaya, M. *Gautama's Nyaya-Sutra with Vatsyayana's Commentary*. Calcutta, Bagchi, 1982.

The Indian Philosophical tradition owes to Nyaya the general methodological — and perhaps also the basic conceptual — framework. Its extant sourcebook is the Nyaya-sutra attributed to Gautama, also known as Aksapada. The Sutra's being usually too cryptic to be understood by themselves, one is obliged to depend on the comprehensive commentary on these by Vatsyayana.

Ganthaler, Heinrich. Some Comments on Weingartner's Concept of a Scientific Theology in Advances in Scientific Philosophy, Schurz, Gerhard (ed). Amsterdam, Rodopi, 1991.

Garavaso, Pieranna. The Argument from Agreement and Mathematical Realism. *J Phil Res*, 17, 173-187, 1992.

Traditionally in the philosophy of mathematics, realists claim that mathematical objects exist independently of the human mind, whereas idealists regard them as mental constructions dependent upon human thought. It is tempting for realists to support their view by appeal to our widespread agreement on mathematical results. Roughly speaking, our agreement is explained by the fact that these results are about the *same* mathematical objects. It is alleged that the idealist's appeal to mental constructions precludes any such explanation. (edited)

Garber, Daniel. Descartes and Occasionalism in Causation in Early Modern Philosophy, Nadler, Steven (ed). University Park, Penn St Univ Pr, 1993.

This paper discusses the question as to whether or not Descartes can be considered an occasionalist or not. The author argues that while there are significant affinities between Descartes and later Cartesian occasionalists, there are also important reasons for denying that Descartes was an occasionalist.

Garcia, Jorge L A. African-American Perspectives, Cultural Relativism and Normative Issues in African-American Perspectives on Biomedical Ethics, Flack, Harley E (ed). Washington, Georgetown Univ Pr, 1992.

This paper first analyzes three models for understanding ethnic ethical perspective—cultural relativism, communitarianism, and realism—and argues that the last is the best option for those interested in making use of the idea of such perspective. Second, it explores the metaphor of visual perspective and adapts it to the ethical realm. Third, it tentatively proposes an understanding of African-American ethical perspectives as the perspectives of individuals whose thought is meaningfully influenced by commitments, experiences, etc. that they have had because of their racial classification. Finally, it sketches some implications it might have for medical ethics if ethicists took such perspectives more seriously, and suggests ways in which this perspective's limitation might be modified and transcended.

Garcia, Jorge L A. Love and Absolutes in Christian Ethics in Christian Philosophy, Flint, Thomas P (ed). Notre Dame, Univ Notre Dame Pr, 1990.

Christians believe that morality derives from love. Philosophical Christian ethics should say actions, traits, etc. are good just when rightly connected to love. 'Is this loving in the appropriate way?' becomes the central question. In the first two sections, I sketch a relationalist, virtues-based, intentionalist moral position that meets this test, and I show its advantages in the theories of value and duty. In the third, fourth, and fifth section, I use it to defend, against challenges from Scheffler and others, the claim of traditional Christian ethics that some traditional prohibitions admit no exceptions. I conclude by arguing that moral dilemmas, which would undermine exceptionless norms, have no place within Christian ethics.

Garcia, Jorge L A. The New Critique of Anti-Consequentialist Moral Theory. *Phil Stud*, 71(1), 1-32, Jl 93.

The paper defends anti-consequentialism against criticisms developed in Kagan's *Limits of Morality*. It sketches a moral approach that treats intentions as the focus of our moral assessment of actions, and that ties these intentions to the fulfillment of interpersonal role-relationships. Using some cases, it explains how and why intentionally causing or allowing various evils is more objectionable morally than is causing or allowing them only expecting but not intending that they result. This vindicates the crucial and most controversial element within the "doctrine of double effect." Finally, applying recent value theory and a procedure called "serial consideration," I explain why consideration of the numbers of beneficiaries of an action is not morally decisive in certain cases from the literature.

Garcia, Jorge L A. The Right and the Good. *Philosophia (Israel)*, 21(3-4), 235-256, Ap 92.

This essay treats morally right action and morally good action. The first section considers the familiar fact that the mental state from which an agent acts determines whether it is morally good. The second section critically examines Frankena's and French's views, which divorce an action's moral goodness from its moral rightness. The third section presents a positive account of moral rightness, explaining its relation to moral goodness. I argue that a morally right action must be a morally good one, although the converse thesis is false. The fourth section rebuts an objection concerning responsibility. The fifth section shows how the language of moral rightness, properly understood, indicates that an action's actual or probable consequences are irrelevant to whether it is morally good, right, or dutiful, contrary to what both consequentialists and many of their professed opponents claim.

Garcia, Laura L. Timelessness, Omniscience, and Tenses. *J Phil Res*, 18, 65-82, 1993.

Two major objections to divine atemporality center on supposed tensions between the claim that God is omniscient and the claim that he is timeless. Since most defenders of divine timelessness are even more firmly committed to omniscience, driving a wedge between the two is intended to convert such persons to a temporal view of God. However, I believe that both arguments fail to demonstrate an incompatibility between omniscience and timelessness, and that the objections themselves rest in large part on misunderstandings regarding both the motivation for and substance of the doctrine of divine timelessness.

García Bacca, Juan David. *Sobre Virtudes y Vicios*. Barcelona, Anthropos, 1993.

Garcia de la Sienra, Adolfo. *The Logical Foundations of the Marxian Theory of Value*. Dordrecht, Kluwer, 1992.

The purpose of the book is to provide rigorous axiomatic foundations for the labor theory of value, in order to solve its foundational problems. These problems are thoroughly reviewed in the first two chapters. Chapter 3 introduces the logical methodology, whereas ch 4 discusses the philosophical background of Marxian dialectics. Ch 5 proves the existence of numerical labor values in fairly general economies. Ch 6 contains a rigorous axiomatization of the theory. Ch 7 proves the existence of reproducible equilibria for Marxian economics, and ch 8 reviews the Leoutief model from the vantage point previously developed.

García-Baró, Miguel. Some Puzzles on Essence in Analecta Husserliana, XXXIV, Tymieniecka, Anna-Teresa (ed). Dordrecht, Kluwer, 1992.

García-Gómez, Jorge. Perceptual Consciousness, Materiality, and Idealism in Analecta Husserliana, XXXIV, Tymieniecka, Anna-Teresa (ed). Dordrecht, Kluwer, 1992.

García-Gómez, Jorge. Tymieniecka's Phenomenology of Creative Experience and the Critique of Reason in Analecta Husserliana, XXXIV, Tymieniecka, Anna-Teresa (ed). Dordrecht, Kluwer, 1992.

Gardies, Jean-Louis. Peut-on parler de vérité et de fausseté pour les propositions performatives?. *Frei Z Phil Theol*, 39(1-2), 61-76, 1992.

After having specified what he means by *performative sentences* and having distinguished two kinds—weak and strong—of such expressions, the author gives successively three answers to the question of the possibility of their truth or falsehood: 1) these sentences can actually be true or false; 2) some of them can only be true; 3) strong performative sentences are, besides, truthfunctional.

Gardiner, Michael. *The Dialogics of Critique*. New York, Routledge, 1992.

The book explores Bakhtin's insights on the terrain of critical social and cultural theory, encompassing a broad range of interpretive, methodological and epistemological concerns centering around the theory and critique of ideology. It introduces Bakhtin's core concepts through an interpretive examination of the Bakhtin Circle's major writings. It also discusses Bakhtin's insights into the nature of the text, ideology, the hermeneutic tradition as represented by Gadamer, Habermas and Ricoeur, and the poststructuralism of Barthes and Foucault. Gardiner criticizes Bakhtin's contribution to the social sciences and appraises the value of his legacy.

Gardiner, Patrick. Bradley and Moral Philosophy in Psychoanalysis, Mind and Art, Hopkins, Jim (ed). Cambridge, Blackwell, 1992.

The aim of the article is to examine and assess F H Bradley's views concerning the proper scope and limits of moral philosophy. Bradley is shown to have adopted in *Ethical Studies* a profoundly sceptical attitude towards ethical theories which purport to criticize or correct the intuitions of 'common sense' morality as opposed to seeking to understand their presuppositions and rationale; such accounts are held to involve simplistic or inappropriately rigid models of practical thinking which are conspicuously false to moral psychology and experience. The continuing interest and significance of some of Bradley's claims are emphasized, and their relevance to certain recent philosophical trends briefly indicated.

Gardner, Peter. Should We Teach Children to be Open-Minded? Or is the Pope Open-Minded about the Existence of God?. *J Phil Educ*, 27(1), 39-43, Sum 93.

The recommendation that we encourage children to be open-minded has been

gathering strength. Yet given the everyday meaning of 'being open-minded about something', we may decide to reject this recommendation because it proscribes teaching and learning. There again, recent philosophical accounts of open-mindedness seem to oppose everyday meaning and lead to the absurd conclusion that the Pope is open-minded about the existence of God. This paper suggests two ways of looking at these problems, the second of which reconciles ordinary usage with open-mindedness as a desirable educational objective.

Gardner, Peter. 'Private Judgement', Mill and Tocqueville: An Apology. *J Phil Educ*, 26(1), 113-115, 1992.

This highlights a mistake in an earlier paper, "Personal Autonomy and Religious Upbringing: 'The Problem'" (*J Phil Educ*, 25/1, 69-81, 1991), in which I tried to contrast certain religious fundamentalists and those I called "Tocqueville's Americans." This contrast relied on a quotation from Mill on Tocqueville in R B Friedman's essay, "On the Concept of Authority in Political Philosophy." Though Friedman gives no hint of it, a crucial clause has been removed from the quotation he presents. When this is inserted, the contrast I tried to draw cannot be drawn. My "Apology" points this out.

Gardner, Sebastian. *Irrationality and the Philosophy of Psychoanalysis*. New York, Cambridge Univ Pr, 1993.

The book proposes an analytical reconstruction of psychoanalytic theory. The central claim is that Freudian theory is best viewed as an extension of ordinary (commonsense) psychology, which hinges on its employment of the concepts of wish-fulfillment and fantasy, and makes the validation of psychoanalytic explanation independent from the kinds of requirement put on theories in the natural sciences. Authors whose writings are discussed include, apart from Freud, Melanie Klein, Sartre, Richard Wollheim, Donald Davidson and David Pears.

Gardner, Sebastian. The Nature and Source of Emotion in Psychoanalysis, Mind and Art, Hopkins, Jim (ed). Cambridge, Blackwell, 1992.

Gardner, Stephen L. Retributivism in Hegel as Modern Natural Law. *Vera Lex*, 12(1), 13-14, 1992.

Gargani, Aldo Giorgio. Ethics and Aesthetics in the Definition of the Self in Criss-Crossing A Philosophical Landscape, Schulte, Joachim (ed). Amsterdam, Rodopi, 1992.

Beginning with an analysis of the notion of repetition, some parallels are drawn between psychoanalysis and Wittgensteinian philosophy. The view is put forward that in the case of Freud's concept of neurosis as well as in Wittgenstein's concept of rule-following there is not just a monotonous and unvarying replay of one and the same content but rather a steady modification. Thus, the aesthetical becomes an important aspect. Finally ethical moments are considered in comparing suppression with Wittgenstein's statements on superficial philosophical theorizing.

Garner, Richard T. Are Convenient Fictions Harmful to Your Health?. *Phil East West*, 43(1), 87-106, Ja 93.

Plato was not alone in thinking society may profit from being deceived. Some Buddhists talk of heavens and hells because they impress people who can then be led beyond the need for them. A third device is employed by those who speak of intrinsic value and binding obligation without accepting the objectivist implications of this language. I discuss the Humean projectivism of John Mackie and Simon Blackburn, who claims that while there are no objective moral properties, we can speak, without error, as if there are. I explain how each of these fictions is harmful, survey three reasons for rejecting convenient fictions, and conclude with some remarks about convenient fictions today.

Garnham, Alan. Is Logicist Cognitive Science Possible?. *Mind Lang*, 8(1), 49-71, Spr 93.

This paper responds to Oaksford and Chater's attack on logicist cognitive science (*Mind and Language*, 1991). They argue that a logicist approach, and in particular Fodor and Pylyshyn's, cannot explain everyday reasoning. More specifically, nonmonotonic logics can neither capture the inferences people make, nor provide computationally tractable algorithms for computing them. I argue that Oaksford and Chater's characterization of logicist cognitive science is too narrow, that the empirical inadequacy of nonmonotonic logics makes questions about tractability otiose, that people do not use tractable algorithms, and that a "mental models" account of the successes and failings of everyday reasoning is possible.

Garofalo, Charles and Geuras, Dean. Ethical Foundations of Management in Public Service. *SW Phil Stud*, 15, 10-18, Spr 93.

Garola, Claudio. Truth Versus Testability in Quantum Logic. *Erkenntnis*, 37(2), 197-221, S 92.

We forward an epistemological perspective regarding non-classical logics which restores the universality of logic in accordance with the thesis of "global pluralism." In this perspective every non-classical "truth-theory" is actually a theory of some metalinguistic concept which does not coincide with the concept of truth (described by Tarski's truth theory). We intend to apply this point of view to Quantum Logic (QL) in order to prove that its structure properties derive from properties of the metalinguistic concept of *testability* in Quantum Physics. To this end we construct a classical language Lc and endow it with a classical effective interpretation which is partially inspired by the Ludwig approach to the foundations of Quantum Mechanics. Then we select two subsets of formulas in Lc which can be considered testable because of their interpretation and we show that these subsets have the structure properties of Quantum Logics because of Quantum Mechanical axioms, as desired. Finally we comment on some relevant consequences of our approach (in particular, the fact that no non-classical logic is strictly needed in Quantum Physics).

Garrard, Eve. Thick Concepts Revisited: A Reply to Burton. *Analysis*, 53(1), 57-58, Ja 93.

Garrett, Brian. Persons and Values. *Phil Quart*, 42(168), 337-344, Jl 92.

Garrett, Jan. The Moral Status of 'the Many' in Aristotle. *J Hist Phil*, 31(2), 171-189, Ap 93.

A scrutiny of Aristotle's references to "the Many" (hoi polloi) in the *Nicomachean Ethics* yields a surprising result: His moral psychology includes a character type which does not neatly fall into any type commonly discussed in scholarly literature.

Aristotle holds that typical "mass persons" are neither incontinent nor fully vicious or wretched. Rather, they are like incontinents, but the objects at which their unstable wishes aim are roughly equivalent to the objects pursued by the rebellious passions of (unqualified and qualified) incontinents.

Garrett, K Richard. Are There Foundations for Human Knowledge?. *Behavior Phil*, 19(2), 19-33, Fall-Wint 91.

Epistemology or the Theory of Knowledge has become one of the most complicated and esoteric areas of philosophy. This paper attempts to defend a form of foundationalism in epistemology which does not require the reader to be familiar with the philosophical literature; so, it should be of interest to psychologist concerned with the nature and character of human knowledge as well as, of course, to philosophers. The heart of the foundationalism defended here is the thesis that a belief is epistemically reliable unless it has been shown to be suspect.

Garrett, Mary and Blinn, Sharon Bracci. Aristotelian *Topoi* as a Cross-Cultural Analytical Tool. *Phil Rhet*, 26(2), 93-112, 1993.

Garrett, Roland. "Experience and Philosophic Method": Does Dewey's View of Method Speak to the Needs of Philosophy Today?. *Metaphilosophy*, 23(1-2), 139-146, Ja-Ap 92.

This essay is an analysis and evaluation of the concept of philosophical method put forward by Dewey in the first chapter of *Experience and Nature* (Second Edition). It covers the issues of argument versus categorial structuring, the model of science, the role of "primary experience,' the method of denotation, contextualism, and the commitment to the equal reality of things experienced. Serious conceptual weaknesses or restrictions in scope sharply limit the utility of Dewey's conception of philosophic method today, although there are also promising possibilities suggested in Dewey's analysis that his theory of method does not have the conceptual resources to deploy.

Garrett, Roland. Six Theories in the Bedroom of *The Dead*. *Phil Lit*, 16(1), 115-127, Ap 92.

The bedroom scene at the end of James Joyce's story *The Dead* has been studied through many interpretive perspectives, including psychoanalysis, Marxism, feminism, structuralism, deconstruction, and authorial biography. This paper evaluates and challenges the various approaches from a pragmatic standpoint.

Garrison, James W. Conversation as a Romance of Reason: A Response to Buchmann. *Proc S Atlantic Phil Educ Soc*, 36, 18-22, 1991.

Garrison, Jim and McKinney, Joseph. Foucault and Rousseau on Teaching in Modern Technocratic Schooling. *J Thought*, 28(1-2), 61-82, Spr-Sum 93.

Garry, Anne. Why Care About Gender?. *Hypatia*, 7(3), 155-161, Sum 92.

I address motivations that feminist philosophers have for being concerned about the "maleness" of philosophy and the "problem of difference" within deminist theory. An appropriate motivation for caring about both sets of issues is the desire not to oppress others. In order to be able to understand this motivation and to act on it, we need to retain gender as an analytical category.

Garson, James W. Mice in Mirrored Mazes and the Mind. *Phil Psych*, 6(2), 123-134, 1993.

The computational theory of cognition (CTC) holds that the mind is akin to computer software. This article aims to show that CTC is incorrect because it is not able to distinguish the ability to solve a maze from the ability to solve its mirror image. CTC cannot do so because it only individuates brain states up to isomorphism. It is shown that a finer individuation that would distinguish left-handed from right-handed abilities is not compatible with CTC. The view is explored that CTC correctly individuates in an autonomous domain of the mental, leaving discrimination between left and right to some non-cognitive component of psychology such as physiology. I object by showing that the individuation provided by CTC does not properly describe in any domain. An *embodied* computational taxonomy, rather than software alone, is required for an adequate science of the mind.

Garver, Eugene. Making Discourse Ethical: The Lessons of Aristotle's *Rhetoric*. *Proc Boston Colloq Anc Phil*, 5, 73-96, 1989.

While Aristotle says that the enthymeme is the center of the art of rhetoric, he also observes that character, not the enthymeme, is the most effective cause of belief. By explicating the rhetorical relation between making arguments on the one hand and presenting character on the other, centering on Aristotle's advice on, as he puts it, "making arguments ethical", I can give a more detailed consideration of the relation between *phronesis* and the moral virtues than can be drawn from the less developed remarks in the *Ethics*. Aristotle's treatment of arguments drawn from the character of speaker and audience give a rich sense of the nature of practical argument: rhetorical argument ends in a judgment or conviction, and the need for the ethical shows the insufficiency of the purely logical in generating practical judgment.

Garver, Eugene. Point of View, Bias, and Insight. *Metaphilosophy*, 24(1-2), 47-60, Ja-Ap 93.

Bias and prejudice are terms of abuse; interest and authority are sometimes terms of abuse but sometimes can be declared without reducing the credibility of a claim. Yet we all know that there are times when a particular point of view enables insight instead of distortion. There seems to be no principled, theoretical way of distinguishing between bias, interest and insight. One might conclude that therefore biases are putative insights that one doesn't like. These are phenomena, then, on which critical thinking or a study of rationality would have nothing to say. Instead of trying to define these terms, I prefer to look at the way accusations of bias, interest and insight are defeased and defended. These are rhetorical phenomena, modes of argument, and that is where their interest lies. (edited)

Gasché, Rodolphe. Floundering in Determination in Reading Heidegger: Commemorations, Sallis, John (ed). Bloomington, Indiana Univ Pr, 1992.

Gascoigne, John. 'The Wisdom of the Egyptians' and the Secularisation of History in the Age of Newton in The Uses of Antiquity, Gaukroger, Stephen (ed). Dordrecht, Kluwer, 1991.

The purpose of this paper is to illustrate the way in which the biblical understanding of world history was secularised in the late seventeenth and eighteenth centuries in

a similar manner to the secularisation of the understanding of the working of Nature associated with Newton and his followers. The role of Providence was retained but as a force working through the laws of nature rather that through a series of miraculous 'special Providences'.

Gaskell, Ivan (ed) and Kemal, Salim (ed). *The Language of Art History*. New York, Cambridge Univ Pr, 1991.

The first volume in the series "Cambridge Studies in Philosophy and the Arts" offers a range of responses by distinguished philosophers and art historians to some crucial issues generated by the relationship between the art object and language in art history. Each of the chapters in this volume is a searching response to theoretical and practical questions, in terms accessible to readers of all human science disciplines. The issues they discuss challenge the boundaries to thought that some contemporary theorizing sustains. (edited)

Gaskin, R. Conditionals of Freedom and Middle Knowledge. *Phil Quart*, 43(173), 412-430, O 93.

The doctrine of middle knowledge, developed by the Spanish Jesuits Luis de Molina and Fransisco Suarez in the late 16th century, claims that God can know the truth-value of subjunctive conditionals recording what agents would freely do if place in any hypothetical circumstance ('conditionals of freedom'). The article argues that the doctrine can rebut the charges of incoherence levelled at it by a number of recent writers, including Kenny and Hasker. The article argues that the objections either misunderstand the way in which possible worlds semantics apply to the thesis that God has middle knowledge, or rest on an implausible correspondence theory of truth. (edited)

Gaskin, Richard. Alexander's Sea Battle: A Discussion of Alexander of Aphrodisias *De Fato 10*. *Phronesis*, 38(1), 75-94, 1993.

The article argues that in chapter 10 of his treatise *De Fato* Alexander presupposes an interpretation of Aristotle's *De Interpretatione* 9 according to which Aristotle restricted the principle of bivalence for statements about future contingencies. This reading of Alexander had been challenged on the grounds that Alexander presupposes determinism in arguing against his Stoic opponents, and that this presupposition prevents us from assessing whether Alexander thought necessity is consequential upon the sheer assumption of future truth. But by detailed examination of the text it is shown that the presupposition of determinism does not enter into the specific part of the text where future truth is in question, and that there Alexander does argue for an entailment from future truth to necessity, and hence that he must have supposed that Aristotle restricted the general validity of the principle of bivalence in order to avoid a general necessitarianism.

Gaskins, Richard H. *Burdens of Proof in Modern Discourse*. New Haven, Yale Univ Pr, 1993.

Gasparski, Wojciech W (ed) and Auspitz, J Lee (ed) and Mlicki, Marek K (ed). *Praxiologies and the Philosophy of Economics: The International Annual of Practical Philosophy and Methodology*. New Brunswick, Transaction Books, 1992.

Gasper, Philip. Reduction and Instrumentalism in Genetics. *Phil Sci*, 59(4), 655-670, D 92.

In his important paper "1953 and All That: A Tale of Two Sciences" (1984), Philip Kitcher defends biological antireductionism, arguing that the division of biology into subfields such as classical and molecular genetics is "not simply ... a temporary feature of our science stemming from our cognitive imperfections but (is) the reflection of levels of organization in nature" (p.371). In a recent discussion of Kitcher's views, Alexander Rosenberg has argued, first, that Kitcher has shown that the reduction of classical to molecular genetics is impossible only because of our intellectual limitations and, second, that this kind of antireductionism supports an instrumentalist approach to biological theory. I argue that both of Rosenberg's claims should be rejected despite the fact that Kitcher misdiagnoses the central reason for the failure of reduction.

Gasper, Philip (ed) and Boyd, Richard (ed) and Trout, J D (ed). *The Philosophy of Science*. Cambridge, MIT Pr, 1991.

Gass, Michael. Abortion and Moral Character: A Critique of Smith. *Int Phil Quart*, 33(1), 101-108, Mr 93.

Janet E Smith argues that studies by Carol Gilligan and others reveal that most women act contrary to their moral beliefs in aborting their fetus, thereby harming their moral character by eroding their self-respect. For this reason alone, if not also because of the lethal consequences for their fetus, such women act wrongly in having an abortion, Smith concludes. I argue (a) that Smith's assessment of the causal relationship between abortion and moral character rests on an unjustifiable naive interpretation of what the subjects in the studies she consults report about their moral beliefs; and (b) that the ethical inference which Smith draws from this assessment rests on the unwarranted assumption that it is always wrong to erode one's self-respect.

Gassin, Elizabeth A and Enright, Robert D and Wu, Ching-ru. Forgiveness: A Developmental View. *J Moral Educ*, 21(2), 99-114, 1992.

The concept of interpersonal forgiveness is described first through an examination of ancient writings and contemporary philosophical and psychological discourse. Two psychological models are then described. The first concerns developmental patterns in how people think about forgiving another. The second describes how people may go about forgiving another. Implications for counseling and education are drawn.

Gates, Henry Louis. Statistical Stigmata in Deconstruction and the Possibility of Justice, Cornell, Durcilla (ed). New York, Routledge, 1992.

The "Law and Economics" movement has theorized about "statistical discrimination," viewing racial discrimination as, in many cases, rational and efficient, a strategy for conserving on information costs. At the time, many courts have been reluctant to apply statistical evidence of racial discrimination, rejecting the idea of single-case probability. By contrast, a realist interpretation of probability invites the alternative model, sketched here, of what K A Appiah calls "probabilistic harm," according to which you can harm someone by, say, decreasing his or her chance of receiving some good.

Gatti, Andrea. Estetica e cosmologia in Shaftesbury. *G Crit Filosof Ital*, 71(1), 87-101, Ja-Ap 92.

Gatti, Maria Luisa. Importanza storica e teoretica del pensiero neoplatonico nel *Pensare l'Uno* di Werner Beierwaltes. *Riv Filosof Neo-Scolas*, 84(2-3), 261-292, Ap-S 92.

Gattico, Emilio. Le rôle de l'abstrait dans l'oeuvre de B Riemann. *Rev Theol Phil*, 125(2), 175-190, 1993.

Dire que la connaissance mathématique est réele guère dire que les objets mathématiques soient existants. Ce sont des idées abstraites qui, comme telles, n'ont pas été composées. L'oeuvre de Riemann a été choisie pour montrer que le rôle joué par ces idées est à la création de la physique mathématique. On donne des exemples historiques et on propose des suggestions épistémologiques pour montrer que la catégorie de l'abstrait représent le stade le plus développé de la recherche scientifique.

Gatto, Romano and Palladino, Franco. The "Dutch's Problem" and Leibniz's Point of View on the "Analytic Art". *Stud Leibniz*, 24(1), 73-92, 1992.

In diesem Aufsatz untersuchen wir Leibniz' Ansicht über die "Ars Analytica". Gelegenheit dazu bietet die Diskussion über die Lösung der sogenannten "Probleme eines Holländers". Es geht dabei um 12 Probleme über das Dreieck. Gegeben sind in diesen Problemen: einer der Basiswinkel, die Differenz von Basissegmenten und ein Verhältnis, das bei den einzelnen Problemen variiert zwischen den Seiten des Dreiecks. "Die Probleme des Holländers" sind aus mehreren Gründen wichtig. Sie liefern einen aufschllussreichen Test, den Stand der Mathematik in Italien in der zweiten Hälfte des 17. Jahrhunderts zu prüfen. Sie lassen das Nebeneinanderbestehen unterschiedlicher mathematischer Methoden erkennen, und zwar klassischer und moderner Methoden. Schliessich sind die Probleme sehr interessant für den Stand der Gedanken, die Leibniz zu ihrer Behandlung äussert.

Gaudillières, Jean-Paul. J Monod, S Spiegelman et l'adaptation enzymatique: Programmes de recherche, cultures locals et traditions disciplinaires. *Hist Phil Life Sci*, 14(1), 23-71, Ja 92.

Gauker, Christopher. An Extraterrestrial Perspective on Conceptual Development. *Mind Lang*, 8(1), 105-130, Spr 93.

The network theory of conceptual development represents conceptual development as the construction of a network of linked nodes, representing concepts. The structure of such a network is not determined by experience alone but must evolve in accordance with "abstraction heuristics," which constrain the varieties of network between which experience must decide. This paper criticizes the network theory on the grounds that current proposals regarding these abstraction heuristics all fail, and further, that no viable account of these abstraction heuristics will be possible. In particular, the requisite abstraction heuristics cannot be universal principles of rational thought or species-specific natural conventions.

Gauker, Christopher. The Lockean Theory of Communication. *Nous*, 26(3), 303-324, S 92.

The Lockean theory of communication is here defined as the theory that communication takes place when a hearer grasps some sort of mental object, distinct from the speaker's words, that the speaker's words express. This theory contrasts with the view that spoken languages are the very medium of a kind of thought of which overt speech is the most basic form. This article is a critique of some of the most common motives for adopting a Lockean theory of communication.

Gaukroger, Stephen (ed). *The Uses of Antiquity*. Dordrecht, Kluwer, 1991.

The essays in the collection explore the ways in which antiquity was conceived of, put to use, and reassessed in the 17th century scientific revolution. Topics covered include the symbolic and polemical uses of antiquity, e.g., in Copernicus and in Glanville; the use of antiquity as a fund of ideas or as a source of evidence, e.g., in Hooke and above all in Newton; and the way in which an image of antiquity was constructed and put to use in 17th century disputes in areas as diverse as the nature of free will, astronomy, natural philosophy, geology, and chronology.

Gaus, Gerald. Does Compensation Restore Equality?. *Nomos*, 33, 45-81, 1991.

Gaut, Berys. Moral Pluralism. *Phil Papers*, 22(1), 17-40, Ap 93.

This paper defends moral pluralism, the view that there is a plurality of moral principles and no further principle entailing the ranking of one above the other in all cases where they clash. It argues against views advanced by John Rawls, which purport to show that pluralism is false. Arguments given by Brink and Dancy and an argument from moral reductionism are also rejected. A positive argument for pluralism is advanced, showing that a reflectively improved version of common-sense morality is the best moral position, and that this will be pluralist.

Gauthier, Candace Cummins. Philosophical Foundations of Respect for Autonomy. *Kennedy Inst Ethics J*, 3(1), 21-37, Mr 93.

Understanding the philosophical foundations of the principle of respect for autonomy is essential for its proper application within medical ethics. The foundations provided by Immanuel Kant's principle of humanity and John Stuart Mill's principle of liberty share substantial areas of agreement including: the grounding of respect for autonomy in the capacity for rational agency, the restriction of this principle to rational agents, and the important distinction between influence and control. Their work helps to clarify the scope and role of the principle of respect for autonomy in health care delivery; its implications for truth telling, informed consent, and confidentiality; and its relationship to other moral principles, such as beneficence and distributive justice.

Gauthier, David. Artificial Virtues and the Sensible Knave. *Hume Stud*, 18(2), 401-427, N 92.

Gauthier, David. Constituting Democracy in The Idea of Democracy, Copp, David (ed). New York, Cambridge Univ Pr, 1993.

Gauthier, David. Fairness and Cores: A Comment on Laden. *Phil Pub Affairs*, 22(1), 44-47, Wint 93.

In Anthony Laden's paper "Games, Fairness, and Rawls's *A Theory of Justice*" (*Phil Pub Affairs*, 20, 1991, 189-222) he claims that in a game "the outcomes in the core will not be unfair." I argue that he is mistaken to link fairness to the core of a game. I offer examples of a game with an empty core that has a fair outcome and a game with a non-empty core that has no fair outcomes in its core.

Gauthier, Yvon. La logique interne de la théorie des probabilités. *Dialogue (Canada)*, 32(1), 95-104, Wint 93.

The paper is a reassessment of Reichenbach's probability theory based on E Nelson's novel formulation of infinitesimals in a non-standard probability theory. The author shows how the work of Hilbert and Von Neumann in the foundations of Quantum Mechanics point the direction of an internal logic of probability theory which does not need an infinite support (set) and does not have the classical features of Boolean logic and probability theory.

Gavroglu, Kostas. From Gases and Liquids to Fluids in Greek Studies in the Philosophy and History of Science, Nicolacopoulos, Pantelis (ed). Dordrecht, Kluwer, 1990.

Gawoll, Hans-Jürgen. Das Verschwinden des Originals—Apropos neuerer Forschungen zum sogenannten 'ältesten Systemprogramm' des deutschen Idealismus. *Z Phil Forsch*, 46(3), 413-428, Jl-S 92.

Gawronski, Alfred. Psychologism and the Principle of Relevance in Semantics in Kotarbinski: Logic, Semantics and Ontology, Wolenski, Jan (ed). Dordrecht, Kluwer, 1990.

Gbadegesin, Segun. Bioethics and Culture: An African Perspective. *Bioethics*, 7(2-3), 257-262, Ap 93.

On the assumption that the project of Bioethics requires paying attention to the cultural particularities of peoples, I discuss the world-view of the Yoruba of West Africa. I focus on the concepts of the human person and causation, both of which are important for understanding the attitude of the people to issues such as euthanasia, infertility, adoption and surrogate pregnancy and organ transplantation. I argue, however, that the most crucial issue of Bioethics in Africa in general, and Nigeria in particular, is the problem of access to health care. I conclude that an adequate resolution of this problem requires a full democratization of the political systems.

Gbocho, Akissi. A Rortyian Dilemma of Conversation. *Auslegung*, 18(2), 145-156, Sum 92.

In setting the task of extending the work of Davidson into areas which Davidson has not explored, Richard Rorty seeks to portray Donald Davidson as one of his allies to his own ethnocentrism thesis. In the paper I argue that Rorty goes wrong in his peculiar way of making Davidson right. Either Rorty goes all the way with Davidson; but then his ethnocentrism thesis is untenable; or he does not; but then again his ethnocentrism goes by the board.

Geach, Peter. Names in Kotarbinski's Element in Kotarbinski: Logic, Semantics and Ontology, Wolenski, Jan (ed). Dordrecht, Kluwer, 1990.

Geach, Peter. The Meaning of 'God'—II in Religion and Philosophy, Warner, Marin (ed). New York, Cambridge Univ Pr, 1992.

Geerstema, H G. 'Ik geloof in God, de Vader, de Almachtige, Schepper van de hemel en van de aarde'. *Phil Reform*, 57(2), 132-158, Ja 92.

This article presents a critical analysis of *Th. de Boer, De God van de Pascal (The God of the philosophers and the God of Pascal)*. s'Gravenhage: Meinema, 1989, 1991. It argues mainly three points: 1)The focus of the philosophical reflection but a critique of the theo-ontological tradition from an ethical perspective. One of the results is the return of the Kantian problem of a philosophical argument about God. 2) De Boer is not consistent: a. the same concepts that are rejected as exemplary of the traditional approach are used for the alternative; b. basic elements of the subject-object scheme are combined with the hermeneutical approach which is critical of that scheme. 3) The idea of God's almightiness ignores basic elements of the biblical tradition which De Boer takes as his starting point.

Gehring, Petra (ed). *Diagrammatik und Philosophie*. Amsterdam, Rodopi, 1992.

Gehring, Petra. Paradigma einer Methode in Diagrammatik und Philosophie, Gehring, Petra (ed). Amsterdam, Rodopi, 1992.

It is shown by two examples from the context of French structuralism how the concept of diagram, not the diagram itself, might get its importance in philosophical texts. The semiotic question after what a diagram "is" loses its weight. The diagram makes its appearance more as a significant the general process and the heuristics of signification itself. The differenciation between different sorts of signs known from semiotics is undermined: In between scriptural and pictural images, structures are found, and the name of a form of representation becomes apt as a philosophical metaphor by this in-between position. In the moment of heuristics, *all* graphisms as such are called in question. (edited)

Geiger, Gebhard. Evolutionary Anthropology and the Non-Cognitive Foundation of Moral Validity. *Biol Phil*, 8(2), 133-151, Ap 93.

This paper makes an attempt at the conceptual foundation of descriptive ethical theories in terms of evolutionary anthropology. It suggests, first, that what human social actors tend to accept to be morally valid and legitimate ultimately rests upon empirical authority relations and, second, that this acceptance follows an evolved pattern of hierarchical behavior control in the social animal species. The analysis starts with a brief review of Thomas Hobbes' moral philosophy, with special emphasis on Hobbes' "authoritarian" view of moral validity and of the common political origins and ultimate basis of legitimacy of moral and legal systems. Hobbes' philosophical conceptions are then put into the context of Max Weber's influential empirical theory of legitimacy, especially charismatic revelation and authority as the ultimate source of all moral, legal and religious obligations. (edited)

Geiger, Gebhard. Why There Are No Objective Values: A Critique of Ethical Intuitionism from an Evolutionary Point of View. *Biol Phil*, 7(3), 315-330, Jl 92.

Using concepts of evolutionary game theory, this paper presents a critique of ethical intuitionism, or non-naturalism, in its cognitivist and objectivist interpretation. While epistemological considerations suggest that human rational learning through experience provides no basis for objective moral knowledge, it is argued below that modern evolutionary theory explains *why* this is so, i.e., *why* biological organisms do not evolve so as to experience objective preferences and obligations. The difference between the modes of the cognition of objective and of valuative environmental attributes is explained with reference to different modes of natural selection acting on the cognitive apparatus of the organism. The negative implications are pointed out

AUTHOR INDEX WITH ABSTRACTS 491 George, David

which the observable diversity of intraspecific behavioural adaptations and of cultural values has for the cognitivist, objectivist foundation of ethics. Eventually a non-cognitivist alternative to ethical intuitionism is outlined in terms of empirical authority relations, with the ritualisation of dominance-submission patterns as the evolutionary origin of human charismatic authority.

Geise, Jack P. Political Rhetoric as Political Theory in Terrorism, Justice and Social Values, Peden, Creighton W (ed). Lewiston, Mellen Pr, 1990.

The political theory of liberalism confronts two tasks. First, it must establish that it has a moral point. Second, it must find a rhetorical vehicle that makes its political injunctions persuasive and accessible to citizens. In sum, liberalism has to see its politics as a practical activity. One occasion on which liberalism has succeeded in linking its theoretical injunctions with issues of political and ethical moment, and when it has done so in a persuasive fashion, can be found in M Cuomo's Notre Dame Address on the issue of abortion policy and political responsibility. Cuomo's speech demonstrated that liberal political rhetoric and theory could be convincing, ethical, and practical.

Geivert, R Douglas (ed) and Sweetman, Brendan (ed). *Contemporary Perspectives on Religious Epistemology*. New York, Oxford Univ Pr, 1992.

Gelblum, Tuvia. On 'the Meaning of Life' and the *Bhagavad Gita*. *Asian Phil*, 2(2), 121-130, 1992.

This is a philosophically based rebutter to A L Herman's attempt to demonstrate the inapplicability of the 'Aristotelian' meaning of 'the meaning of life' to the *Bhagavadgita (Asian Philosophy*, Volume 1, Number 1, pp 5-13). Conclusion: *pace* Herman, it is neither goalessness nor desirelessness *simpliciter* that the *Bhagavadgita* attributes to the ideal man, but rather the supersedence of self-interest, as motivation of action, by twin wider goals— (1) individual mystic transcendence (*moksa*); (2) social-moral-cosmic co-operation (*loka-sangraha*)—and the respective entailed desires. *Pari passu* a parallelism is detected in Rudyard Kipling's writings regarding the *yoga* (self-control) of practising heroic equanimity.

Gelenczey-Mihaltz, Aliran. And the Idea Turned into History (in Czechoslovakian). *Magyar Filozof Szemle*, 6, 805-820, 1991.

The tragic course of life of the late third century BC Spartan reformer kings, Agis and Cleomenes has been treated several times. However, relatively slight attention was paid to Sphairos, the Stoic philosopher, who should be considered as the key figure of the Spartan Revolution. Without his Stoicism, the whole character of the revolution would have taken a quite different course. Namely it was Sphairos who, by means of his stoic idealism, helped Lycurgean Sparta—still alive in its utmost dignity in myths of her real, historical Golden Age—to be restored and reanimated. He was neither the first nor the most genuine Greek philosopher who was engaged actively in politics, but *he was the first inspired by a real social movement and motivated by exalted ideas of philosophy to try to change the course of history*. (edited)

Geller, Jeffery. Painting, Parapraxes, and Unconscious Intentions. *J Aes Art Crit*, 51(3), 377-387, Sum 93.

This essay traces the connections between Richard Wollheim's arguments against conventionalism and his argument for a psychoanalytically based account of pictorial meaning. The plausibility of Wollheim's version of intentionalism (as expressed in *Painting as an Art*) hinges on his formulation of a satisfactory theory of "match" (between the pointer's intentions, the painting, and the mental state of the spectator). After examining his theory for potential weaknesses, the current essay concludes that Wollheim's broadened, enriched intentionalism compared favorably to conventionalism and to versions of intentionalism that ignore unconscious intentions.

Gellman, Jerome I. A New Look at the Problem of Evil. *Faith Phil*, 9(2), 210-216, Ap 92.

Philosophers have traditionally considered the problem of evil to be constituted by an *argument*, either deductive or inductive. As a result, the task of furnishing a theodicy has been relegated to the periphery of philosophic concerns. I argue that the problem of evil is first and foremost grounded on a type of experience that provides defeasible grounds for believing in the non-existence of God. Thus the problem of evil bears to the philosophers' versions thereof, the same relationship that religious experience bears to philosophers' proofs for God's existence. On this understanding theodicies become central to the solution of the problem of evil.

Gellman, Jerome I. Naming, and Naming God. *Relig Stud*, 29(2), 193-216, Je 93.

I argue that "God" can be understood as a proper name, fixed by a "path" of reference. So understood, Anselm's ontological argument can be seen to be not a proof of God's existence, but of the existence of the being than which no greater can be thought, which Anselm argues must be God.

Gellman, Susan. "Brother, You Can't Go to Jail for What You're Thinking": Motives, Effects and "Hate Crime" Laws. *Crim Just Ethics*, 11(2), 24-28, Sum-Fall 92.

Gelwick, Richard. Michael Polanyi and the Philosophy of Medicine. *Tradition Discovery*, 18(3), 21-29, 1992.

One of the great contributions of 20th century medicine is Michael Polanyi's philosophy. The importance of Polanyi's medical background is seen in the principles of his theory of knowledge, his terminology, and his examples. "Physician of culture" is the best description of Polanyi's work. Polanyi's philosophy provides a grounding for a more humanistic philosophy of medicine in three ways: 1) a critique of the image of the physician as scientist instead of healer; 2) the integration of medical research with medical practice, and; 3) a view of scientific progress that balances the roles of research with therapy. Polanyi's philosophy of medicine, though Hungarian, resembles the Polish School.

Gelwick, Richard. The Patient Self Determination Act and "Dax's Case". *J Med Human*, 13(3), 177-187, Fall 92.

Based on Lonnie Kliever's book, *Dax's Case*, twelve questions are raised. These questions show the great responsibility involved in working with people who want to formalize their right to die. The challenges are: adequacy of patient's history, the true message in a request to die, opposing individual rights against professional respect and care, the need for dialogue, time limited contracts, quality of life, conflicts of interest, language of self-determination, difference between sufferer and care giver, moral ambiguity of pain, loneliness of rights, and variable meanings of suffering and death.

Gemes, Ken. Hypothetico-Deductivism, Content, and the Natural Axiomatization of Theories. *Phil Sci*, 60(3), 477-487, S 93.

In Gemes (1990) I examined a certain formal version of hypothetico-deductivism (H-D) showing that they have the unacceptable consequence that "Abe is a white raven" confirms "All ravens are black"! In Gemes (1992) I developed a new notion of content that could save H-D from this bizarre consequence. In this paper, I argue that more traditional formulations of H-D also need recourse to this new notion of content. I present a new account of the vexing notion of the natural axiomatization of a theory. The notion is used to construct a form of H-D that allows for the type of selective confirmation without which Glymour (1980a,b) claims H-D is hopeless.

Gemtos, Petros. Law and Economics in Greek Studies in the Philosophy and History of Science, Nicolacopoulos, Pantelis (ed). Dordrecht, Kluwer, 1990.

Gendre, Michael. Transcendence and Judgment in Arendt's Phenomenology of Action. *Phil Soc Crit*, 18(1), 29-50, 1992.

For Arendt, meaning or judgment is possible only in connection with transcendence, the capacity to exceed the merely given. Judgment's centrality (fully recognized by Kant but displaced by Heidegger) culminates in action through the hierarchy labor-work-action and is reached through a phenomenological method involving reduction. 1) Labor, a symbiotic process of bodily contention/appropriation, allows no transcendence vis-a-vis nature; 2) Work involves a sight that transcends appearances; 3) Action takes place in a medium of chain reactions entailing boundlessness, unreliability, and essential frailty. Account is given of the Greek *daimon*, *eudaimonia*, and Pericle's sobriety as fundamentals in the Greek revealing and transcending of appearances in judgment.

Gendreau, Bernard A. The Role of Jacques Maritain and Emmanuel Mounier in the Creation of French Personalism. *Personalist Forum*, 8/1(Supp), 97-108, Spr 92.

Gendron, Pierre. La théologie comme science et la vocation de savant d'après Max Weber. *Laval Theol Phil*, 49(2), 215-222, Je 93.

La question du statut épistémologique de la théologie peut être abordée en fonction du constat que les théologiens, en tant que membres d'une communauté de recherche, sont des acteurs sociaux. Le regard porté sur leur situation est alors celui que porte le sociologue sur les institutions de la science. Or, Max Weber (1864-1920), dans un passage aussi critique que dense, a traité le thème de la théologie comme science à la fin de sa conférence de 1919 sur "Le métier et la vocation de savant" (*Wissenschaft als Beruf*). *L'interprétation qui est tentée ici repose sur la possibilité de lire ce passage en se référant de manière systématique à l'étude sur "La notion de Beruf* chez Luther" que Weber avait placée au début de son célèbre ouvrage de 1905 sur *L'éthique protestante et l'esprit du capitalisme*.

Gennaro, Rocco J. Brute Experience and the Higher-Order Thought Theory of Consciousness. *Phil Papers*, 22(1), 51-69, Ap 93.

Peter Carruthers attacks the natural view that animals have conscious pains and suffer. Thus, brutes do not warrant our moral concern. I defend the "higher-order thought theory of consciousness" as it pertains to brute experience. In sections I and II, I critique Carruthers' analysis of consciousness and show how he mischaracterizes the higher-order theory which is indeed compatible with many brutes having conscious pains. In section III, I show how brutes can have the conceptual sophistication required by the theory. In section IV I offer evidence concerning animal brain structure supporting the conclusion that most animals have conscious pains.

Gennaro, Rocco J. Consciousness, Self-Consciousness and Episodic Memory. *Phil Psych*, 5(4), 333-347, 1992.

My aim in this paper is to show that consciousness entails self-consciousness by focusing on the relationship between consciousness and memory. More specifically, I address the following questions: (1) does consciousness require episodic memory?; and (2) does episodic memory require self-consciousness? With the aid of some Kantian considerations and recent empirical data, it is argued that consciousness does require episodic memory. This is done after defining episodic memory and distinguishing it from other types of memory. An affirmative answer to (2) is also warranted especially in the light of the issues raised in answering (1). I claim that 'consciousness entails self-consciousness' is thereby shown via the route through episodic memory, i.e., via affirmative answers to (1) and (2). My aim is to receive this Kantian thesis and to bring together current psychological research on amnesia with traditional philosophical perspectives on consciousness and memory.

Gent, Ian Philip. A Sequent- or Tableau-Style System for Lewis's Counterfactual Logic VC. *Notre Dame J Form Log*, 33(3), 369-382, Sum 92.

In a 1983 paper, de Swart gave sequent based proof systems for two counterfactual logics: Stalnaker's "VCS" and Lewis's "VC". In this paper I demonstrate that de Swart's system for "VC" is incorrect by giving a counterexample. This counterexample does not affect de Swart's system for "VCS". Then I give a new sequent- or tableau-style proof system for "VC" together with soundness and completeness proofs. The system I give is closely modeled on de Swart's.

George, Alexander. How Not to Refute Realism. *J Phil*, 90(2), 53-72, F 93.

An influential argument for anti-realism holds that a realist construal of the sentences of our language must be rejected on the grounds that no substance can be given to attribution of such an understanding to a speaker. Here, this argument is examined in the context of mathematics. The argument is analyzed in detail and found to beg the question against realists in covertly assuming a conception of the infinite at odds with that which underlies classical mathematics. The paper concludes by sketching a different conception of the philosophical significance of intuitionism. (edited)

George, David. The Right of National Self Determination. *Hist Euro Ideas*, 16(4-6), 507-513, Ja 93.

It is argued that there is no moral counterpart to the legal right of national self determination under international human rights law, because national self determination lacks the necessary universality and fails to confer the special benefits to human flourishing characteristic of such moral rights. Nor is it the subject of a particular moral right since one cannot be derived either from individual moral rights or from the facts of nationhood. Indeed, the lack of an institutional structure in nations entails their inability to exercise or even to bear any kind of collective right, including that of self determination.

George, Kathryn Paxton. Moral and Nonmoral Innate Constraints. *Biol Phil*, 7(2), 189-202, Ap 92.

George, Kathryn Paxton. Sustainability and the Moral Community. *Agr Human Values*, 9(4), 48-57, Fall 92.

Three views of sustainability are juxtaposed with four views about who the members of the moral community are. These provide points of contact for understanding the moral issues in sustainability. Attention is drawn to the preferred epistemic methods of the differing factions arguing for sustainability. Criteria for defining membership in the moral community are explored; rationality and capacity for pain are rejected as consistent criteria. (edited)

George, Kathryn Paxton. The Use and Abuse of Scientific Studies: Reply. *J Agr Environ Ethics*, 5(2), 217-233, 1992.

Detailed analysis shows that Pluhar misappropriates findings and conclusions of studies, makes sweeping generalizations from scanty data, ignores causal explanations, equates hypothesis with fact, draws false cause conclusions, and claims conclusions opposite of what is published. Numerous reviews and textbooks in nutrition show that each of Pluhar's claim is suspect or incorrect. Pluhar has not undermined my central claims: even if animals have rights and well-planned vegetarian diets are safe in industrialized societies, these diets presuppose high levels of wealth, education, and medical care; women, children, the aged and some ill persons are at greater risk on vegan diets.

George, Marie. Mind Forming and Manuductio in Aquinas. *Thomist*, 57(2), 201-213, Ap 93.

This article explains a key concept in Thomistic pedagogy. Manuduction is anything which helps the learner to see a given truth because of its being proportioned to the natural weakness of the human mind. This weakness lies in the fact that the human mind starts from sense experience and aims at the goal of wisdom, i.e., scientific knowledge of all that is, especially of those things having most being. The good teacher does not initially overburden the student with demonstrative arguments which are abstracted, but aids the student by presenting him with sensible examples, arguments by similitude, and other such things which, while not constituting proof render the student more capable of grasping proofs.

George, Marie. The Wonder of the Poet; The Wonder of the Philosopher. *Amer Cath Phil Quart*, 65, 191-202, 1991.

The questions addressed are whether the wonder in poetry is the same or only similar to that in philosophy, and whether the forms of wonder found in poetry is conducive or not to philosophical wonder. We argue that in poetry of three forms of wonder which are different from philosophical wonder are found: 1) that which arises from plot, 2) from fantastical things, 3) from questions concerning human existence. I argue that the first is conducive to philosophical wonder insofar as it involves a problem of sorts, whereas the second is not since it does not motivate one to seek solutions. While the third bears materially on philosophical questions, the kind of answers it provides differs from those of philosophy, and thus it may or may not lead to philosophical wonder.

George, Marie. What Wisdom is According to Heraclitus the Obscure. *Lyceum*, 5(1), 1-19, Spr 93.

One reading of Heraclitus' fragments on the nature of wisdom reveals him to be a humble pursuer of wisdom, rather than the skeptic he is generally thought to be. This reading is plausibly based upon Heraclitus' statements on the divine character of wisdom and on the limited ability of human mind to come to know the mind of God.

George, Marie I. The Notion of Paideia in Aristotle's *De Partibus Animalium*. *Amer Cath Phil Quart*, 67(3), 299-320, Sum 93.

A proper reading of the beginning of *De Partibus Animalium* is of key importance for understanding Aristotle's educational views. There is, however, substantial disagreement as to the interpretation of this text. Matters of dispute include: the nature of particular paideia, the nature of general paideia, the relation of paideia and logic, and the value of paideia. Taking as our starting point the various opposed views of the commentators, we intend to show how the text must be read.

George, Robert P. Liberty Under the Moral Law: On B Hoose's Critique of the Grisez-Finnis Theory of Human Good. *Heythrop J*, 34(2), 175-182, Ap 93.

George, Rolf. Do the Poor Really Pay for the Higher Education of the Rich?. *Dialogue (Canada)*, 30(3), 297-307, Sum 91.

It is often claimed that the poor subsidize the rich through their tax contributions to public higher education. The concept of "subsidy" underlying this claim is criticised, as is the underlying "proportionality assumption", viz that if higher education costs 5% of a state's budget, then a nickel of every tax dollar, regardless of source, is used for that purpose. It is shown, instead, that universities are a good bargain, if the tax on the higher incomes of graduates (in Canada as much as a billion dollars a year for a medium sized university) are viewed as returns on investment.

George, Rolf A. The Tradition of Thought Experiments in Epistemology in Thought Experiments in Science and Philosophy, Horowitz, Tamara (ed). Lanham, Rowman & Littlefield, 1991.

The thought experiment chiefly explored is that of Condillac: what would we know if we had only one sense, what if two, what if we had no memory, what if we did, etc. How would the world appear to us in these various circumstances. Condillac's influence on Kant and others is explored.

George, William P. Regarding Future Neighbours: Thomas Aquinas and Concern for Posterity. *Heythrop J*, 33(3), 283-306, Jl 92.

Gérard, Gilbert. De l'ontologie à la théologie: Lecture du livre Z de la "Métaphysique" d'Aristote. *Rev Phil Louvain*, 90(88), 445-485, N 92.

Book Z constitutes the turning-point of Aristotle's *Metaphysics*. The author shows how Aristotle, by means of a series of reductions that follow one on the other, sets

out from the affirmation of the numerous meanings of being and continues to progress to the threshold of theology envisaged as the site of the final reply to the ontological problem. The heart of this progression, the coherence of which maintains itself from a protological perspective that constantly returns, consists in the characterisation of substance as quiddity, and hence, by means of the essential simplicity of quiddity in the proper sense, as form, while the composite, on the other hand, is only substance in a derived and secondary sense. In the final analysis, this metaphysical procedure when taken inversely, nevertheless raises the crucial question of the capacity of the theological, i.e., of being in its first and supreme meaning, to found being in its totality, which is where the author discovers the prime quandary of Aristotelian metaphysics as an onto-theology.

Geras, Norman. Marxism and Moral Advocacy in Socialism and Morality, McLellan, David (ed). New York, St Martin's Pr, 1990.

The paper identifies some central weaknesses in Marxist thought with respect to ethical issues, and then goes on to argue for a contrasting strength there, via a criticism of contemporary libertarian and liberal thinkers. It is to Marxism's credit that it sought to go beyond abstract appeals to conscience and to root the moral critique of existing society within real oppositional tendencies and social forces.

Gerber, William. Another Window Into Zeno's Antinomies. *Indian Phil Quart*, 20(1), 115-119, Ja 93.

Zeno's antinomies seem to prove that motion is impossible, that a plurality of entities is impossible, etc. Where did his reasoning go astray? I show that his basic assumption should be modified so as to recognize that, when we multiply an infinitesimal number by an infinite number, the result is a finite number.

Gerhardt, Volker. Das wiedergewonnene Paradigma: Otfried Höffes moderne Metaphysik der Politik. *Phil Rundsch*, 39(4), 257-277, 1992.

Gerla, Giangiacomo and Tortora, Roberto. La relazione di connessione in A N Whitehead: aspetti matematici. *Epistemologia*, 15(2), 351-364, Jl-D 92.

In [5], [6] and [7], A N Whitehead presents a particular point of view on the physical world. According to it, the geometric properties of the space-time are reconstructed starting from some primitive objects and relations among them which satisfy a number of intuitive assumptions. Our aim is to translate, as adequately as possible, Whitehead's informal analysis into mathematical axiom systems. This purpose seems to us very interesting, since the approach of Whitehead may give useful tools to some recent researches towards the possibility of building Geometry without using the notion of point as primitive. (edited)

Geroimenko, Wladimir A. Tacit Scientific Knowledge (A Typological Analysis). *Method Sci*, 26(2), 87-97, 1993.

In the article is considered the specificity and interdependence of the most important types and variants of tacit knowledge. The recognition is based on the following phenomena: the subject-bearer, the functions in the cognitive process, the role in the reflective analyses, etc. Tacit knowledge is a many-sided and versatile phenomenon. The consideration of the main gradations of tacit knowledge (personal-paradigmal-objectivized-transsubjective, auxiliary-basic, the means of reflection—the object of reflection, etc.) opens new possibilities for further investigation of its nature and gnosiological functions.

Gerrand, Nicole. Creating Embryos for Research. *J Applied Phil*, 10(2), 175-187, 1993.

The 1987 Amendment to the Infertility (Medical Procedures) Act (Vic) allows the creation of embryos specifically for research purposes, as long as the proposed experiment takes place within 24 hours. The purpose of this paper is to determine whether there is any significant ethical difference between creating embryos specifically for research and using those that are surplus from the new reproductive technologies. The relevant arguments in this debate can be grouped under three heads: those focussing on the embryo; those focussing on the possible consequences of these practices and those focussing on the women who donate the eggs.

Gerrig, Richard J. Reexperiencing Fiction and Non-Fiction. *J Aes Art Crit*, 47(3), 277-280, Sum 89.

Philosophers have often discussed classes of emotional responses that might be—but are not—undermined by the unreality of fiction. This article describes two such phenomena, *anomalous suspense* and *anomalous replotting*. Extant analysis of these phenomena have explained them by reference to special properties of fiction. The current article demonstrates that the phenomena also occur in non-fictional circumstances. A general constraint on memory search during the experience of narrative—the *expectation of uniqueness*—is suggested as a more appropriate causal explanation.

Gerson, Lloyd P. Metaphysics in Search of Theology. *Lyceum*, 2(2), 1-21, Fall 90.

This article explores the relation between a science of being and a science of a first principle of all in antiquity. It distinguishes three positions: those who pursued metaphysics without theology; those who pursued theology without metaphysics; and those who identified the two in some way. It argues for the superiority of the last position.

Gerson, Lloyd P. Plotinus's Metaphysics: Emanation or Creation?. *Rev Metaph*, 46(3), 559-574, Mr 93.

Plotinus' metaphysics is widely regarded as emanationist. This article analyzes various senses of the term 'emanation' and tries to show that none of these accurately reflect the nature and causality exercised by the One, the first principle of all. It is argued that in fact Plotinus' metaphysics is more creationist than emanationist. Creation in Plotinus, however, is instrumental in order to preserve the perfect simplicity of the One.

Gerson, Lloyd P. The Discovery of the Self in Antiquity. *Personalist Forum*, 8/1(Supp), 249-257, Spr 92.

This article describes some of the stages in the development of the concept of a self in antiquity. It focuses on Plotinus and his destruction of an empirical and ideal self and his argument that the ideal self is the agent of self-reflexive cognition.

Gert, Bernard. Transplants and Trolleys. *Phil Phenomenol Res*, 53(1), 173-178, Mr 93.

Gesang, Bernward. Eine biolinguistische Kritik Wittgensteins. *Z Phil Forsch*, 46(4), 584-590, O-D 92.

Biolinguistics (BL) shows that syntactic and semantic aspects of language are innate and are a "reaction" to the structures of the world (cf., E H Lenneberg, E Holenstein). Wittgenstein's theory of language starts from the idea that language is primarily not caused by the world and it maintains that it is language that gives structure to the reality. In Wittgenstein's "Tractatus" the world-creating function lies with logic, it remains central. In his PI meaning is only deduced from the use of language. This is contrary to the discovery of "semantic universals" in BL. If Wittgenstein wants to formulate a theory of language that is empirically correct, he fails for he stresses a structuring function that is empirically less relevant.

Geuras, Dean. In Defence of Divine Forgiveness: A Response to David Londey. *Sophia (Australia)*, 31(1-2), 65-77, 1992.

Geuras, Dean and Garofalo, Charles. Ethical Foundations of Management in Public Service. *SW Phil Stud*, 15, 10-18, Spr 93.

Gewirth, Alan. The Egoist's Objection. *J Value Inq*, 27(1), 101-103, Ja 93.

Each agent logically must extend to all other agents his or her claim to have the generic rights. The ground for this extension presented in my book *Reason and Morality*, pp 116-119, was overlooked by Joseph Schmitt in what he called the 'egoist's objection'.

Geyer, Carl-Friedrich. Theodizee oder Kulturgeschichte des Bösen? Anmerkungen zum gegenwärtigen Diskurs. *Z Phil Forsch*, 46(2), 238-256, Ap-J 92.

Der Literaturbericht nimmt Stellung zu sieben repräsentativen Neuerscheinungen zur Theodizee, vor allem aus dem deutschsprachigen und italienischen Raum, die hinsichtlich der Verwendung des Theodizee*begriffs* befragt werden. Vf plädiert für eine Ablösung dieses Begriffs zugunsten einer Kulturgeschichte des Bösen. Der Aufsatz ist eine Vorwegnahme wesentlicher Thesen des soeben erschinenen Buches des Vf zum gleichen Thema (Die Theodizee, Diskurs, Dokumentation, Transformation, Verlag Franz Steiner, Stuttgart 1992).

Ghins, Michael. Scientific Realism and Invariance in Rationality in Epistemology, Villanueva, Enrique (ed). Atascadero, Ridgeview, 1992.

Giambrone, Steve. Read Reduced Models for Relevant Logics Without WI. *Notre Dame J Form Log*, 33(3), 442-449, Sum 92.

John Slaney, in "Reduced Models for Relevant Logics Without WI", *NDJFL* 28, 1987, 395-407, provides reduced models (ones in which there is but one "real" world) for a number of relevant (and a few irrelevant) logics via certain kinds of frames, as opposed to the conventional Routley-Meyer model structures. This paper corrects some very minor errors (slips) in Slaney's paper and criticizes Slaney's models for being overly syntactic. It is then shown that Slaney's basic results can be used to provide reduced models for most of the same logics (the system E being a notable exception) using the Routley-Meyer model structures which do not suffer from this defect. The paper ends with a brief discussion of the philosophical significance of closing theories (worlds) under certain rules of inference as well as under provable implication. That discussion insists upon the importance of a distinction made by N D Belnap, Jr between primitive/ derivable rules of inference and merely admissible rules.

Gianformaggio, Letizia. The 'Physical Organisation', Education, and Inferiority of Women in Diderot's 'Refutation ... in Women's Rights and the Rights of Man, Arnaud, A J. Oxford, Aberdeen, 1990.

Giaquinto, M. Visualizing in Arithmetic. *Phil Phenomenol Res*, 53(2), 385-396, Je 93.

Focusing on two examples, this paper appraises a couple of objections to the possibility of discovering general arithmetical truths by visualizing. The first objection is that one cannot make a discovery about all numbers of a certain kind by imagining a particular number of items. It is argued that this rests on the false premise that an image of an array of items must be numerically determinate. The second objection is that an image of an array will exclude relevant cases. It is argued that this is sometimes true, but not always. So these objections are not fatal to the possibility of arithmetical discovery by visualizing.

Giaquinto, Marcus. Diagrams: Socrates and Meno's Slave. *Int J Phil Stud*, 1(1), 81-97, Mr 93.

Giaquinto, Marcus. Infant Arithmetic: Wynn's Hypothesis Should Not Be Dismissed. *Mind Lang*, 7(4), 364-366, Wint 92.

This brief paper defends Wynn's hypothesis that infants have some innate arithmetical knowledge for positive integers up to three, based on her experimental work and on the evidence for an underlying mechanism, known as the accumulator. The natural philosophical objections are, it is argued, insufficient ground for rejecting Wynn's claim.

Giaquinto, Marcus. Visualizing as a Means of Geometrical Discovery. *Mind Lang*, 7(4), 382-401, Wint 92.

Can visualizing be an epistemically acceptable way of acquiring a mathematical belief? By detailed consideration of one simple geometrical example, I argue that (a) the answer is 'no' if the visualizing is used to recall past sense experience as evidence for the geometrical belief, (b) 'no' if the visualizing is used as an inner experiment in which images are taken as data, (c) possibly, if visualizing is used in a certain way other than providing visual evidence. I argue that we do sometimes use visualization in a non-evidential way and that this may be a reliable means of acquiring a mathematical belief.

Giarelli, James M. Dewey and the Feminist Successor Pragmatism Project. *Free Inq*, 13(1), 30-31, Wint 92-93.

Important recent work in philosophy explores the many significant congruences between the public and philosophical projects of pragmatism and feminism. This essay provides a brief overview of this work, with particular attention to John Dewey and feminist pragmatists. Dewey's political support of women's suffrage, his professional efforts to challenge traditional sex-role stereotyping in progressive schools, and his recognition of the radical changes which would result in philosophy if women's experience were considered are noted as signs of an historically fruitful exchange between pragmatists and feminists which bears promise for contemporary philosophers.

Giarelli, James M. Power, Rights and Education: A Tale of Two Traditions. *Proc Phil Educ*, 48, 212-215, 1992.

Gibbard, Allan F. Moral Concepts: Substance and Sentiment in Philosophical Perspectives, 6: Ethics, 1992, Tomberlin, James E (ed). Atascadero, Ridgeview, 1992.

Gibbard, Allan F. Morality and Thick Concepts—I, Thick Concepts and Warrant for Feelings. *Aris Soc*, Supp(66), 267-283, 1992.

Gibbard, Allan F. Précis of "Wise Choices, Apt Feelings". *Phil Phenomenol Res*, 52(4), 943-945, D 92.

Gibbard, Allan F. Reply to Blackburn, Carson, Hill, and Railton. *Phil Phenomenol Res*, 52(4), 969-980, D 92.

Gibbard, Allan F. Reply to Sinnott-Armstrong. *Phil Stud*, 69(2-3), 315-328, Mr 93.

Gibbins, John R (ed). *Contemporary Political Culture*. Newbury Park, Sage, 1989.

Gibbins, John R. J S Mill, Liberalism, and Progress in Victorian Liberalism, Bellamy, Richard (ed). New York, Routledge, 1990.

This essay enquires whether Mills defence of Liberalism is coherent and compatible with his ascription to utilitarianism, democracy and female suffrage. The answer reveals tensions between all these elements but suggests that Mill found coherence for himself in the role of philosophical statesman. With certainty about the ultimate end, happiness, and a practical commitment to progress toward this ideal, he felt justified in balancing the claims of competing values, interests, principles, theories thinkers, movements and policies. The resulting evidence of incoherence results from the compromises required.

Gibbins, John R. Utilitarianism, Conservatism and Social Policy in The Utilitarian Response, Allison, Lincoln (ed). Newbury Park, Sage, 1990.

This essay suggests that attempts to unite utility and rights arguments and claims while maintaining the integrity of each and the coherence of the whole, are impossible. Textual analysis of recent Conservative Party policy papers reveals an attempt to benefit from both types of argument with resulting incoherence and conflict. Various attempts at reconciling the claims of utility and rights, principally by John Gray, are assessed critically.

Gibbins, P F. Why the Distributive Law is Sometimes False. *Analysis*, 44(2), 64-67, Mr 84.

Gibbons, John. Identity without Supervenience. *Phil Stud*, 70(1), 59-79, Ap 93.

Tyler Burge has presented an argument against the token identity theory for content-bearing mental events. One premise in the argument is content essentialism: the view that if a mental even has a certain content in one possible world, it has the same content in every world in which it exists. This paper argues against content essentialism. Essentialism is first distinguished from various independent issues about individuation. Two general theories of events are examined, and the one which most strongly suggests content essentialism is rejected on independent grounds. Finally, some intuitive considerations are presented to motivate the rejection.

Gibbs Jr, Raymond W. The Intentionalist Controversy and Cognitive Science. *Phil Psych*, 6(2), 181-205, 1993.

What role do speakers'/authors' communicative intentions play in language interpretation? Cognitive scientists generally assume that listeners'/readers' recognitions of speakers'/authors' intentions is a crucial aspect of utterance interpretation. Various philosophers, literary theorists and anthropologists criticize this intentional view and assert that speakers'/authors' intentions do not provide either the starting point for linguistic interpretation or constrain how texts should be understood. Until now, cognitive scientists have not seriously responded to the current challenges regarding intentions in communication. My purpose is to provide such a response. I briefly describe some of the empirical evidence in cognitive science on the importance of intentions in communication. I then discuss some of the criticisms of the intentional view that have arisen in the humanities and social sciences. I offer a partial resolution to the intentionalist controversy that recognizes the differing views on the idea of linguistic interpretation. (edited)

Gibson, Kevin. Transitivity, Torts and Kingdom Loss. *J Phil Res*, 18, 83-96, 1993.

Here I look at the views of Mackie about the transitivity of causal statements. Mackie suggests that we replace total transitivity with a calculation which assigns a proportional value to partial causes this allows us to work out an overall proportion of a single event in a causal chain. I marry the philosophical discussion with a sketch of tort law by means of an unusual hypothetical. I suggest that Mackie's proportional analysis could have a useful practical application since current tort law regards causality as transitive and that total responsibility may be placed on the originator of connected but distinct events.

Gibson, Martha I and Stampe, Dennis W. Of One's Own Free Will. *Phil Phenomenol Res*, 52(3), 529-556, S 92.

Gibson, Roger. The Key to Interpreting Quine. *S J Phil*, 30(4), 17-30, Wint 92.

There is a key to unlocking a correct interpretation of Quine which many of his critics and commentators have overlooked. That key is Quine's commitment to naturalism. I briefly explain Quine's naturalism, then I sketch what I take to be a correct interpretation of a portion of his philosophy in light of his naturalism, and, finally, I show that four widespread criticisms of Quine's thought arise only because his critics have failed to take seriously Quine's commitment to naturalism.

Gier, Nicholas. On the Deification of Confucius. *Asian Phil*, 3(1), 43-54, Mr 93.

In contrast to Krishna, Gautama, and Jesus, who were deified early be their devotees, Confucius was seen by most Chinese as a great sage only. Recently Roger Ames and David Hall have made the claim that tradition and specific texts demand that Confucius be considered a deity. The two texts, neither from Confucius himself, involve, as I show in Section II, a mistranslation in the first and a misreading of figurative language in the second. Section II contains a discussion of the Confucius triad of heaven, humans, and earth, in which humans are not deified and gods are not humanized. I contend that Christian and Indian incarnational theologies upset the balance of this cosmic harmony.

Gier, Nicholas F. Three Types of Divine Power. *Process Stud*, 20(4), 221-232, Wint 91.

The first type of power discussed is divine omnicausality (DP1), which holds that God is the originative and immediate cause of everything and event. Second, there is DP2, which stipulates that God delegates power of self-regulating nature and self-determining moral agents, but God can override both if he chooses. Third, there is the view of process theism (DP3), in which God is the preeminent power but cannot control nature nor contravene free choices. Using some ingenious electrical analogies, Nelson Pike has tried to make DP2 intelligible, but I argue that he fails. David Basinger contends that he has formulated a type of DP3 without sacrificing the divine control of traditional theism. I argue that Basinger's view is simply another form of DP2, which he desires.

Giere, Ronald. Science and Technology Studies: Prospects for an Enlightened Postmodern Synthesis. *Sci Tech Human Values*, 18(1), 102-112, Wint 93.

I argue that recent attempts to model Technology Studies on Science Studies have consequences for approaches to Science Studies as well. In particular, the move to Technology Studies through Science Studies counts against the existing extreme pictures of science, "enlightenment rationalism" and "constructivism", which I identify with modernism and post-modernism, respectively. I find some components for a moderate "enlightened post-modern synthesis" in naturalism (philosophy of science), interest theory (sociology of science), and systems theory (history of technology).

Gigerenzer, Gerd. On Cognitive Illusions and Rationality in Probability and Rationality, Eells, Ellery (ed). Amsterdam, Rodopi, 1991.

Gil, Tomás. La problemática filosofía de la historia: Anotaciones a una interminable disputa. *Themata*, 8, 173-180, 1991.

The article analyses the main ideas and theorems of the classical philosophy of history and why some of them have become problematic. In an introductory first part it clarifies the concept "classical philosophy of history".

Gilbert, Alan. Power Rivalry-Motivated Democracy: A Response to Stephen Krasner. *Polit Theory*, 20(4), 681-689, N 92.

Gilbert, Margaret. Group Membership and Political Obligation. *Monist*, 76(1), 119-131, Ja 93.

Many people apparently think they have political obligations. What is the presumed source of these obligations? This paper argues that social groups in a central everyday sense involve obligations. Such groups are a function of a 'joint commitment' which involves a special sort of obligation. A prevalent sense of political obligation may well be a sense of obligation through a joint commitment. The common use of phrases such as 'our country' and 'our government' suggests as much. For in a central narrow sense of the pronoun 'we', it is understood to refer to the parties to a joint commitment.

Gilbert, Michael A. The Enthymeme Buster: A Heuristic Procedure for Position Exploration in Dialogic Dispute. *Inform Log*, 13(3), 159-166, Fall 91.

Positions in dialogic dispute are presented enthymematically. It is important to explore the position the disputant holds. A model is offered which relies on the presentation of a counter-example to an inferred missing premiss. The example may be: [A+] embraced as falling under the rule; [A-] rejected as basically changing the position; or, [R] rejected as changing the proffered missing premiss. In each case the offered model indicates the next appropriate action. The focus of the model is on unconvering the position actually held by the disputant as opposed to identifying the "logically correct" enthymematic premiss.

Gilbert, Paul. Criteria of Nationality and the Ethics of Self-Determination. *Hist Euro Ideas*, 16(4-6), 515-520, Ja 93.

The concept of nationhood is clarified by regarding the ability to support a claim to Statehood as partly constitutive of it. The ethnicity model makes nationhood depend upon discoverable facts about people; the allegiance model upon their will to associate politically. Both fail to generate a right to Statehood since neither establishes the desirability of grouping people in accordance with the model. In consequence a 'common good' model of nationhood is proposed which allows people a claim to Statehood if they display in their behaviour a will to live together, (which they may disavow in a plebiscite).

Gilbert, Paul. Immediate Experience. *Proc Aris Soc*, 92, 233-250, 1992.

What philosophical account can we give of the subjective character of experience? Physicalist accounts are rejected as presupposing an unsupported theory of phenomenal content, held to consist of intrinsic properties of experience directly discriminable through their observation. It is noted that Bertrand Russell also rejected "content", and offered an account of experience as supplying basic non-inferential grounds for belief or desire. It is suggested that the subjective character of experience simply consists in its reason giving role, and that this account yields all the advantages of physicalist ones, without their disadvantages.

Gilbert, Paul. Philosophy and Fascism. *J Applied Phil*, 9(2), 245-247, 1992.

Gilbert, Paul P. La métaphysique, l'acte et l'un. *Gregorianum*, 73(2), 291-315, 1992.

Metaphysics enunciates what is the foundation of our experience, while unifying it. Thereby it is tempted to reduce the many to the one. But the one, if it were without inner space, could not be the foundation for what is really plural. In order that the metaphysical enterprise be successful, it must therefore be guided by a model of the one which leaves room for the many; that is to say: the model must be a dynamic relation. Such is the spirit.

Gilbert, Thomas L. What Is the Role of Science in the Dialogue Proposed by William Klink?. *Zygon*, 27(2), 211-220, Je 92.

Gildin, Hilail. The First Crisis of Modernity: Leo Strauss on the Thought of Rousseau. *Interpretation*, 20(2), 157-164, Wint 92-93.

Giles, James. The No-Self Theory: Hume, Buddhism, and Personal Identity. *Phil East West*, 43(2), 175-200, Ap 93.

Gill, Gillian C (trans) and Irigaray, Luce. *Marine Lover of Friedrich Nietzsche—Luce Irigaray*. New York, Columbia Univ Pr, 1991.

Gill, Gillian C (trans) and Irigaray, Luce. *Speculum of the Other Woman—Luce Irigaray*. Ithaca, Cornell Univ Pr, 1985.

Gill, Kathleen. Teaching *Herland*. *Teach Phil*, 15(2), 133-138, J 92.

C P Gilman's *Herland* (1915) is a humorous utopian novel which can be used in introductory-level philosophy courses to discuss feminist issues as well as more standard philosophical problems. I describe a wide variety of ways in which Gilman's ideas can be developed.

Gill, Mary Louise. Matter against Substance. *Synthese*, 96(3), 379-397, S 93.

This paper argues that for Aristotle living organisms are primary substances. This was the *Categories'* position, but that work treats ontological priority as the criterions for substantiality, while the *Metaphysics* focuses on conceptual priority. The question is whether composites can be primary on this criterion. Gill claims that the answer turns on the status of matter in the generation and constitution of composites, and she argues the *Metaphysics* Z-H explores one conception, H.6 and Φ another. On the second conception, composites can be defined with reference to their form alone, and so can succeed as both ontologically and conceptually basic.

Gillet, Eric and Gochet, Paul. On Professor Weingartner's Contribution to Epistemic Logic in Advances in Scientific Philosophy, Schurz, Gerhard (ed). Amsterdam, Rodopi, 1991.

The paper offers an alternative to the system designed by Professor Weingartner to capture a form of weak knowledge (which does not license the inference from A knows that B knows that p to A knows that p.) As opposed to the former system, the new one caters for any finite number of epistemic agents and provides a possible world semantics (with completeness proof) which is easier to handle than the matrix semantics of the initial system.

Gillet, Grant R. Learning to Do No Harm. *J Med Phil*, 18(3), 253-268, Je 93.

The legalisation of euthanasia creates a certain tension when it is compared with those traditional medical principles that seem to embody respect for the sanctity of life. It also creates a real need for us to explore what we mean by harm in relation to dying patients. When we consider that we must train physicians so that they not only understand ethical issues but also show the virtues in their clinical practice, it becomes important for us to strive to train them in virtue rather than mere knowledge. We can only do this by conveying a real sense of the needs of the patient and an ability to relate to patients as people not problems. Such attitudes take shape in a training programme in which practical situations are explored and discussed and the limits of scientific medical responses to those challenges are exposed.

Gillett, Grant. Coma, Death and Moral Dues: A Response to Serafini. *Bioethics*, 6(4), 375-377, O 92.

In this response I defended my earlier views on consciousness against the criticism that patients in irreversible coma have mental states (such as belief) and therefore interests. I deny the coherent ascription of mental states to such people and therefore liken the irreversible comatose to the brain dead (with respect to their ethical status). I conclude that it is justified to withdraw life-sustaining measure from such patients.

Gillett, Grant. Consciousness, Intentionality and Internalism: A Philosophical Perspective on Velmans and His Critics. *Phil Psych*, 5(2), 173-179, 1992.

I argue that there is a common but mistaken tendency to reify the observer-relative and intentional aspects of perception. This yields a doctrine of internal objects which are the real objects of consciousness. This mistaken view leads to the idea that the properties of objects-as-seen are in some sense projected onto them by observers and can ground idealist or social-epistemic forms of scepticism. Defusing the base mistake avoids either of these views.

Gillett, Grant. Explaining Intentions: Critical Review of *Explaining Behaviour*. *Brit J Phil Sci*, 44(1), 157-165, Mr 93.

Dretske offers an account of mental explanation which draws heavily on animal models and our understanding of 'thin' or low-level goal-directed behaviour. I argue from the normative features of mental content and the critical self-reflective abilities of human thinkers that such an account is deeply misleading. The conclusion is that a causal state analysis of human thought and behaviour is likely to be flawed in quite profound ways.

Gillett, Grant. *Representation, Meaning, and Thought*. New York, Oxford Univ Pr, 1992.

'Representation, meaning and thought' are the central topics in any theory of mind and meaning. An account of mind and intentionality based on the later Wittgenstein focusses on rules, practices, and the use of language. This generates a theory of mental content that is closely tied to an understanding of persons and their techniques of relating to things around them. The resulting account of intentionality is naturalistic and anti-reductive. It generates distinctive conceptualisations of mental explanation, personal identity, sense and reference and traditional sceptical doubt.

Gillett, Grant. Unpacking the Black Box of Cognition. *Inquiry*, 35(3-4), 463-472, S-D 92.

This critical review of Hamlyn's *In and out of the black box* is centred on the argument that properly epistemic ascriptions such as X believes that p or y knows that q are not applicable to subpersonal cognitive mechanisms. The inherent normativity and holism (relative) of such ascriptions makes them suited to and justifiable in the case of whole organisms. The resulting synthesis recommends a focus on human contexts of thought and language as the basis of cognition.

Gillett, Grant. 'Ought' and Well-being. *Inquiry*, 36(3), 287-306, S 93.

The idea that there is an inherent incentive in moral judgment or, in Classical terms, that there is an essential relationship between virtue and well-being is sharply criticized in contemporary moral theory. The associated theses that there is a way of living which is objectively good for human beings and that living that way is part of understanding moral truth are equally problematic. The Aristotelian argument proceeded via the premise that a human being was a rational social being. The present reworking of that thesis builds on the internal connection between rationality and concept use.

Gillett, Grant and Elliot, Carl. Moral Insanity and Practical Reason. *Phil Psych*, 5(1), 53-67, 1992.

The psychopathic personality disorder historically has been thought to include an insensitivity to morality. Some have thought that the psychopath's insensitivity indicates that he does not understand morality, but the relationship between the psychopath's defects and moral understanding has been unclear. We attempt to clarify this relationship, first by arguing that moral understanding is incomplete without concern for morality, and second, by showing that the psychopath demonstrates defects in frontal lobe activity which indicate impaired attention and adaptation to environmental conditions which are relevant to the formation of complex intentions. We argue that these frontal lobe defects can help to explain both the psychopath's apparent insensitivity to morality and his characteristic imprudence.

Gillett, Grant R. Social Causation and Cognitive Neuroscience. *J Theor Soc Behav*, 23(1), 27-46, Mr 93.

Social realities such as meanings, roles and values are hard to incorporate in psychological explanations which implicitly accept neuroscience as the scientific base of psychology. Using considerations of rule-following as the basis of meaning and categorisation and exploring connectionist approaches to neuroscience, I am to reconcile social factors with 'hard science' in psychology. Social variables shape brain function to realize meaning and thereby explain behavior but not in a mechanistic way.

Gillroy, John Martin. Public Policy and Environmental Risk. *Environ Ethics*, 14(3), 217-237, Fall 92.

I argue that environmental risk is a strategic situation that places the individual citizen in the position of an *imprisoned rider* who is being exploited without his or her knowledge by the preferences of others. I contend that what is at stake in policy decisions regarding environmental risk is not numerical probabilities or consistent, complete, transitive preferences for individual welfare, but rather respect for the *human agency* of the individual. Human agency is a prerequisite to one's utility function and is threatened and exploited in the strategic situation that produces the imprisoned rider. This problem is created by the policy maker's assumption that his or her task is to assume rational preferences and aggregate them. The guidelines for evaluation and justification of policy should move beyond welfare preferences and involve an active state protecting human agency and empowering the imprisoned rider. Only in this way can we free all citizens (a priori) from fear of exploitation by those who would impose collective and irreversible risk on each of them in violation of their unconditional right to their own agency.

Gillroy, John Martin (ed) and Wade, Maurice (ed). *The Moral Dimensions of Public Policy Choice: Beyond the Market Paradigm*. Pittsburgh, Univ of Pitt Pr, 1992.

Gilman, Daniel. What's a Theory to Do...with Seeing? or Some Empirical Considerations for Observation and Theory. *Brit J Phil Sci*, 43(3), 287-309, S 92.

Criticism of the observation/theory distinction generally supposes it to be an empirical fact that even the most basic human perception is heavily theory-laden. I offer critical examination of experimental evidence cited by Thomas Kuhn and Paul Churchland on behalf of this supposition. I argue that the empirical evidence cited is inadequate support for the claims in question. I further argue that we have empirical grounds for claiming that the Kuhnian discussion of perception is developed within an inadequate conceptual framework and that a version of the observation/ theory distinction is indeed tenable. The connection between cognitive science and epistemology is also discussed.

Gilman, Daniel J. A New Perspective on Pictorial Reprsentation. *Austl J Phil*, 70(2), 174-186, Je 92.

Nelson Goodman, Max Black, Kendall Walton and—with some qualification—Ernst Gombrich have all argued against the possibility of a naturalist account of *mimesis* in pictorial representation. I argue that their critique of the possibility of a naturalist account is problematic. I examine their discussion of pictorial resemblance, pictorial imitation, perspective and pictorial realism. I suggest that a naturalist account may be developed if one considers both the physical properties of pictures and their subjects *as physical stimuli* and the psychological and biological capacities of viewers of pictures *as perceivers of such stimuli*.

Gilmour, John C. Original Representation and Anselm Kiefer's Postmodernism. *J Aes Art Crit*, 46(3), 341-350, Spr 88.

Ginet, Carl. The Dispositionalist Solution to Wittgenstein's Problem About Understanding a Rule: Answering Kripke's Objections. *Midwest Stud Phil*, 17, 53-73, 1992.

The paper explicates a version of dispositionalism and defends it against Kripke's objections (in his *Wittgenstein on Rules and Private Language*) that 1) it leaves out the normative aspect of a rule, 2) it cannot account for the directness of the knowledge one has of what one meant, and 3) regarding rules for computable functions of numbers, a) there are numbers beyond one's capacity to consider and b) there are people who are disposed to make systematic mistakes in computing values of functions they understand perfectly well.

Ginev, D. Do We Need Fixed Methodological Principles?. *Brit J Phil Sci*, 44(2), 329-334, Je 93.

Ginev, Dimitri. Fundamental Ontology and Regional Ontology of Humanities. *Epistemologia*, 15(1), 87-100, Ja-Je 92.

It is the contention of this article that the hermeneutico- phenomenological interpretation of the hermeneutical mode of investigation in humanities reveals the existential structure of the "region" constituted by this mode of theoretical Being-in-the-world. It is suggested that the "regional ontology" is the ontology of "interpretive dialogue" which mediates between the existential ontology and the cognitive structure of humanities. This has consequences for clarifying the relations between phenomenological philosophy and non-objectivistic scientific research.

Ginev, Dimitri and Polikarov, Azarya. Remarks on Logical Empiricism and Some of Ayer's Achievements in The Philosophy of A J Ayer, Hahn, Lewis Edwin (ed). Peru, Open Court, 1992.

Two basic ideas of Ayer's philosophical views, i.e., the necessity of a verifiability criterion, and the importance of a logico-critical analysis of scientific knowledge are discussed. It is argued that Ayer's more liberal 'logicism' does not exclude post-positivistic 'historicism' in philosophy of science, but that both may be considered as complementary approaches. This examination is preceded by an attempt at a quasi-axiomatic presentation and critical evaluation of logical empiricism.

Gini, Al. Meaningful Work and the Rights of the Worker: A Commentary on *Rerum Novarum* and *Laborem Exercens*. *Thought*, 67(266), 225-239, S 92.

Gini, Al and Donaldson, Thomas. *Case Studies in Business Ethics (Third Edition)*. Englewood Cliffs, Prentice Hall, 1993.

Ginsberg, Robert. The Humanities, Moral Education, and the Contemporary World in Moral Education and the Liberal Arts, Mitias, Michael H (ed). Westport, Greenwood Pr, 1992.

Gintis, Herbert and Bowles, Samuel. A Political and Economic Case for the Democratic Enterprise. *Econ Phil*, 9(1), 75-100, Ap 93.

We consider two reasons why firms should be owned and run democratically by their workers. The first concerns accountability: because the employment relationship involves the exercise of power, its governance should on democratic grounds be accountable to those most directly affected. The second concerns efficiency: the democratic firm uses a lower level of inputs per unit of output than the analogous capitalist firm. We demonstrate that the employer has power over the worker (in a conventionally defined sense) even in a perfectly competitive economy, and provide a consistent explanation of the failure of worker owned firms to proliferate in a competitive environment despite their superior efficiency.

Gintis, Herbert and Bowles, Samuel. A Political and Economic Case for the Democratic Enterprise in The Idea of Democracy, Copp, David (ed). New York, Cambridge Univ Pr, 1993.

Gintis, Herbert and Bowles, Samuel. Power and Wealth in a Competitive Capitalist Economy. *Phil Pub Affairs*, 21(4), 324-353, Fall 92.

Ginzberg, Ruth. Audre Lorde's (Nonessentialist) Lesbian Eros. *Hypatia*, 7(4), 73-90, Fall 92.

Audre Lorde reopened the question of the position of the erotic with respect to both knowledge and power in her 1983 essay "Uses of the Erotic: The Erotic as Power." This is not a new question in the philosophical literature; it is a very old one. What is different about Audre Lorde's examination of Eros is that she starts with a decidedly lesbian conception of Eros, in marked contrast to other Western philosophers' work.

Giovannangeli, Daniel. Finitude et altérité dans l'esthétique transcendentale. *Rev Phil Louvain*, 91(89), 14-30, F 93.

Inquiring into the meaning of self-affection in the Kantian problematic, the author examines in particular Heidegger's interpretation and Cassirer's objections to it. Extending the teaching of the transcendental aesthetic he suggests that the pure feeling of respect as accompanied by an indirect presentation of the moral law, is perhaps not itself reducible to the immanence of auto-affection.

Girard, Jean-Yves. On the Unity of Logic. *Annals Pure Applied Log*, 59(3), 201-217, F 93.

We present a single sequent calculus common to classical, intuitionistic and linear logics. The main novelty is that classical, intuitionistic and linear logics appear as *fragments*, i.e., as particular classes of formulas and sequents. For instance, a proof of an intuitionistic formula *A* may use classical or linear lemmas without any restriction: but after cut-elimination the proof of *A* is wholly intuitionistic, what is superficially achieved by the subformula property (only intuitionistic formulas are used) and more deeply by a very careful treatment of structural rules. This approach is radically different from the one that consists in "changing the rule of the game" when we want to change logic, e.g., pass from one style of sequent to another: here, there is only one logic, which—depending on its use—may appear classical, intuitionistic or linear.

Gitik, M and Shelah, S. More on Simple Forcing Notions and Forcings With Ideals. *Annals Pure Applied Log*, 59(3), 219-238, F 93.

Giustiniani, P. Eugen Drewermann: Una lettura in prospettiva filosofica. *Sapienza*, 45(2), 205-209, 1992.

Giventer, Edwin B. Character Development in the Liberal Arts Students in Moral Education and the Liberal Arts, Mitias, Michael H (ed). Westport, Greenwood Pr, 1992.

Gizbert-Studnicki, Tomasz. Conflict of Values in Adjudication in Ethical Dimensions of Legal Theory, Sadurski, Wojciech (ed). Amsterdam, Rodopi, 1991.

Glannon, Walter. Epicureanism and Death. *Monist*, 76(2), 222-234, Ap 93.

Epicurus claimed that death is not bad and should not be of concern to us because we do not exist when it occurs. This Existence Principle has been challenged recently by what may be called the Deprivation of Goods Principle, which says that death is bad to the extent that it deprives a person of the goods he would have enjoyed had he continued to live. This paper argues that the Deprivation of Goods Principle is false and that, as a consequence, the Existence Principle is a more plausible response to the related questions of whether death is bad and whether it is rational to fear death.

Glas, G. Hierarchy and Dualism in Aristotelian Psychology. *Phil Reform*, 57(2), 95-116, Ja 92.

Hierarchical and dualist tendencies in the Aristotelian conception of emotion are outlined. The hierarchical view, as expressed in the hylemorphism of *De Anima*, is confronted with the bipartite psychology of *Nicomachean Ethics, Rhetoric* and *Politics*, with its dualist and instrumentalist overtones. The discussion is build up around two pairs of contrasts, i.e., emotion as a rational versus an irrational phenomenon and emotion as an activity versus a passive affection. It is concluded, that, paradoxically, the exclusive position of the nous (intellectus agens) protects Aristotle's psychology against mere dualism. At the same time, it accounts for ambiguities in the hierarchical view.

Glaser, Jen. Reason and the Reasoner. *Thinking*, 10(2), 23-29, 1992.

Terms such as 'reasoning' and 'critical thinking' have become the rallying points for improving education... yet various programs reflect significant differences in the way in which the term 'reasoning' is to be understood. This paper aims to provide a theory of reasoning that takes into account the relationship between (1) *reasoning*, (2) the *reasoner*, (3) what counts as *success* in reasoning in order to then evaluate the coherency of various programs designed to strengthen/develop reason. Such a theory will take the ethical, social, and dialogical dimensions of reasoning as integral components of the theory of reason itself.

Glaser, Jen. Reflections on Personhood: Developing a Sense of Self through Community of Inquiry. *Thinking*, 10(1), 19-22, 1992.

In this paper, I explore some ideas about the connection between students' interaction within a community of inquiry and their perceptions of themselves and of each other as persons. In order to understand this connection, I suggest we need to explore the role reasoning plays in the development of our self-concept and its connection to such things as self-esteem and autonomy. I argue that our participation in reflective communities of inquiry leads us to understanding of Self and Other through three routes: 1) Through a reflective mode; 2) through the mode of encounter, and; 3) through the development of judgment.

Glass, Ronald. On Children's Rights: A Response to Barbara Houston. *Proc Phil Educ*, 48, 1992.

This paper challenges five arguments against rights often found in feminist ethics: that rights promote conflict rather than community, that rights invoke an inappropriate autonomous individualism, that a rights approach cannot handle difference, that there are no political advantages to children's rights, and that a rights approach has the wrong focus. It argues that children's rights are salient to an ethics of care insofar as they help give voice to the heart's cry at children's suffering and are effectively deployed in struggles to improve children's lives, to provide quality education, to eliminate childhood malnourishment and hunger, and to provide adequate health care and housing for all children.

Globus, Gordon G. Derrida and Connectionism: Différance in Neural Nets. *Phil Psych*, 5(2), 183-198, 1992.

A possible relation between Derrida's deconstruction of metaphysics and connectionism is explored by considering *différance* in neural nets terms. First *différance*, as the crossing of Saussurian difference and Freudian deferral, is modeled and then the fuller 'sheaf' of *différance* is taken up. The metaphysically conceived brain has two versions: in the traditional computational version the brain processes information like a computer and in the connectionist version the brain computes input vector to output vector and transformations nonsymbolically. The 'deconstructed brain' neither processes information nor computes functions but is spontaneously economical.

Glock, Hans-Johann. The Indispensability of Translation in Quine and Davidson. *Phil Quart*, 43(171), 194-209, Ap 93.

How did an exotic phenomenon like radical translation come to be the linchpin of two important philosophical systems? Because both Quine and Davidson claim that *all* linguistic communication rests on such translation. My article attacks this idea. By contrasting the way we use these terms, I cast initial doubts on the assimilation of understanding and translation. Quine and Davidson ignore these differences, because they believe that translation into a 'background language' is a precondition of understanding. This 'indispensability thesis' leads to a vicious regress and the conclusion that understanding is impossible. Against it I adduce a 'transcendental counter-argument', and argue that its conclusion constitutes a *reductio ad absurdum*.

Glock, Hans-Johann. 'Philosophical Investigations' Section 128: in Wittgenstein's Philosophical Investigations, Arrington, Robert L (ed). New York, Routledge, 1991.

The essay discusses Wittgenstein's provocative claim that if one tried to offer theses in philosophy, it would be impossible to debate them because everyone would agree to them. Wittgenstein himself seems to offer highly debatable theses, although some have understood him to take no philosophical position on any topic and merely to engage in therapy. I reject this 'no position'- position, and argue that Wittgenstein's indisputable theses are reminders of grammatical rules, which form part of a dialectic pattern of argument which accuses the opponent of using words according to conflicting rules - a strategy Wittgenstein refers to as 'undogmatic procedure'.

Glock, Hans-Johann (ed) and Arrington, Robert L (ed). *Wittgenstein's 'Philosophical Investigations'*. New York, Routledge, 1991.

Glossop, Ronald J. Toward Democracy for the World Community. *Cont Phil*, 14(5), 6-10, S-O 92.

1) Does world-level democracy require transformation of the UN into a federation? 2) Does world-level democracy require that all nation-states be democracies? 3) Must a democratic world federation begin with a nucleus of mature democracies? It is argued that global democracy requires a world federation, that not all nation-states need to be democracies internally, and that the Binding Triad voting system (count votes in UN General Assembly three times, including once on basis of population and once on basis of financial support for UN provides a concrete and feasible way of instituting democracy at the global level.

Glotzbach, Philip A. Determining the Primary Problem of Visual Perception: A Gibsonian Response to the 'Correlation' Objection. *Phil Psych*, 5(1), 69-94, 1992.

Fodor and Pylyshyn (1981) criticize J J Gibson's ecological account of perception for failing to address what I call the 'correlation problem' in visual perception. That is, they charge that Gibson cannot explain how perceivers learn to correlate detectable properties of the light with perceptible properties of the environment. Furthermore, they identify correlation problem as a crucial issue for any theory of visual perception, what I call a 'primary problem'—i.e., a problem which plays a definitive role in establishing the concerns of a particular scientific research program. If they are correct, Gibson's failure to resolve this problem would cast considerable doubt upon his ecological approach to perception. In response, I argue that both Fodor and Pylyshyn's problem itself and their proposed inferential solution embody a significant mistake which needs to be eliminated from our thinking about visual perception. As part of my response, I also suggest a Gibsonian alternative to Fodor and Pylyshyn's primary problem formulation.

Glouberman, M. Intermediate Possibility and Actuality: Cartesian Error Theory. *Amer Cath Phil Quart*, 65(1), 63-82, Wint 91.

Generically, Berkeley's anti-abstractionism is theoretically similar to Descartes's treatment of the error attributed to the sense-perceiver, viz. the error of subscribing

to a *metaphysically impossible* worldview. Berkeley, however, makes cognitive deviation from the possible a function of words alone, in this way overcoming a problem which arises for Descartes due to the fact that he assigns to the impossible a psycho-cognitive status similar to that accorded 'clear and distinct' cognitions. But while Berkeley's position is theoretically more stable than Descartes's, it is less plausible vis-à-vis the phenomenal data. Arguably, Kant is a dialectical beneficiary of the incapacity of Cartesian theorists of error to manage these data.

Glouberman, Mark. Cogito: Inference and Certainty. *Mod Sch*, 70(2), 81-98, Ja 93.

Descartes concedes that if the cogito-argument were inferential in logical structure, that would upset the certainty of its outcome. Why are inferentiality and certainty at odds? Interpreters usually explain the matter epistemologically: the meditator would have to know the major premise for certain in order for the argument's conclusion to quality. I advance a different, ontological, construal of the idea of inferentiality, one which saves Descartes from the charge of dogmatism usually levelled from the epistemological perspective. In attacking inferentiality, Descartes is attacking what he sees as the pre-scientific and non-realistic Aristotelian way of representing reality. At base, inferentiality clashes for Descartes not with epistemological certainty, but with realistic truth.

Glouberman, Mark. Theory and Form in Descartes' *Meditations*. *Man World*, 26(3), 261-274, Jl 93.

Is Descartes's use of a fictional personage in the *Meditations* theoretically significant? Elsewhere, I have argued the affirmative, on the grounds that some specifics of Descartes's age inform his analysis at the most basic level. Here I argue that descent from the general level is unavoidable for an even deeper reason. While, on the general level, the idea of falsehood can be handled, the idea of error cannot. The fact of error is not however incidental relative to the very idea of cognitive activity. So something belonging to the lesser level of generality is unavoidable in any adequate epistemology. Since Descartes tries theoretically to handle the phenomenon of error in fully general terms, the *Meditations* is more perspicuous in this regard even than its own author (who also wrote the very undramatic *Principles of Philosophy*) believes.

Glouberman, Mark. Transcendental Idealism and the End of Philosophy. *Metaphilosophy*, 24(1-2), 97-112, Ja-Ap 93.

The first *Critique*, Kant states inaugurates 'a perfectly new science'. But this 'transcendental philosophy', for dealing in possibilities, not actualities, does not qualify as philosophy in the traditional sense. What Kant dubs 'transcendental idealism' *is* however an (ontological) doctrine about things. Kant's doctrinal stand is thus inconsistent with his description of transcendental enquiry. Since transcendental idealism gets its meaning from the contrast with Cartesian realism, it follows that Kant must implicitly be granting that in some measure at least the earlier metaphysicians did what they said they were doing. Indeed, Kant must be relying on some part of what they did. It follows that if there is a *via media* between traditional Cartesian metaphysics and Hume's backgammon, Kant does not locate it.

Glowienka, Emerine. Bernard Lonergan on Primary vs Secondary Qualities. *SW Phil Stud*, 14, 63-73, Spr 92.

After noting inconsistencies in adherents of the distinction between primary and secondary qualities, Bernard Lonergan, *Insight* (1957), showed that the distinction is untenable. Both of the so-called "qualities" are only sensory data accompanied by intellectual viewpoints. On the level of direct experience and verification (common sense) the various interpretations are those of *description*; on the level of indirect, but verifiable, experience, the various interpretations are those of *explanation*. In this Lonergan antedated Hilary Putnam and Richard J Bernstein. Lonergan also antedated Hans-George Gadamer in speaking of "viewpoint" before Gadamer coined the new term "horizon" which Lonergan subsequently adopted.

Gluck, Mary. Modernity and Self-Identity: Self and Society in the Late Modern Age. *Hist Theor*, 32(2), 214-220, 1993.

Glymour, Clark. *Thinking Things Through: An Introduction to Philosophical Issues and Achievements*. Cambridge, MIT Pr, 1992.

Glymour, Clark and Kelly, Kevin T. Inductive Inference from Theory Laden Data. *J Phil Log*, 21(4), 391-444, N 92.

A familiar conception of scientific inquiry portrays the scientist as attempting to converge to the truth about some hypothesis under study. Formal learning theorists attempt to determine when there exists a method that is guaranteed to do so and when there does not. Learning theoretic analysis assumes, however, that there is a fixed language of inquiry and that the scientist receives data whose meaning and truth value is fixed. Philosophical relativists hold, to the contrary, that truth, meaning, and observability can shift as a function of what the process of inquiry does, or of what the inquirer believes. In this paper, we propose a generalization of the learning-theoretic framework in which the aim of science is to arrive at one's own truth given that the truth depends upon how one conducts inquiry. (edited)

Glynn, Simon. Ways of Knowing: The Creative Process and the Design of Technology. *J Applied Phil*, 10(2), 155-163, 1993.

This paper draws upon the already extensive epistemology of science, both to provide a yardstick of comparison for the emergent epistemology of design, and to establish some starting points from which we might begin to construct the epistemology of design. It employs Heidegger's distinction between 'know-how' and 'knowledge-that', popularised by Ryle, and shows it to be central to the distinction between the implicit processes of design employed by craft technologies, and the explicit processes employed by modern scientific technology. It explores the nature of the phases of analysis or 'deconstruction', synthesis or construction, and evaluation, by which scientifically informed design is supposed to proceed, paying particular attention to the relationship between deconstructive analysis and constructive synthesis, in order to re-construct the creative moment/movement by which designers 'leap' from problem to solution.

Gnemmi, Angelo. Misologia ed irenismo: A proposito di un dialogo dottrinale e di ateismo in K Marx. *Riv Filosof Neo-Scolas*, 84(4), 678-696, O-D 92.

Goad, Candace. Leibniz on Innate Knowledge of Moral Truth. *SW Phil Rev*, 8(1), 109-117, Ja 92.

Contrary to the views of many critics, it is my position that Leibniz propounds a theory of innateness which is both coherent and complete. His view, as I understand it, includes in fact analogous accounts of both innate speculative and innate moral knowledge. This paper offers a preliminary sketch of Leibniz's view of innate moral knowledge.

Goad, Candice. Leibniz and Descartes on Innateness. *SW Phil Rev*, 9(1), 77-89, Ja 93.

Gobetti, Daniela. Goods of the Mind, Goods of the Body and External Goods. *Hist Polit Thought*, 13(1), 31-49, Spr 92.

The article analyzes the historical origins of the modern theory of subjective rights in the works of seventeenth-century natural law thinkers. It argues that their approach to rights is based on the Roman law tradition, which gives particular emphasis to property in things as the blueprint for all right-based social phenomena. One of the consequences of this approach is the difficulty to analyze relations among human beings which regard resources other than material ones, in particular resources that are not separable from the body of the possessor, such as performance of sexual acts, or services. Through an analysis of a passage in Hume's treaty, the author shows the limits of a language of rights that tries to see all resources as analogues of material, or external goods.

Goble, Lou. A Logic of *Better*. *Log Anal*, 32, 297-318, S-D 89.

Deontic functions 'ought', 'ought not', etc. and axiological functions 'good', 'bad', etc. can all be defined in terms of a single binary operation 'better'. This paper presents a formal theory of this connective. First it defines truth conditions for statements 'P would be better than Q' somewhat informally, locating them within a framework of other subjunctive concepts; then it develops a formal model theory and axiomatics for such statements. The axiom system is proved consistent and complete with respect to its semantics.

Goble, Lou. The Logic of Obligation, 'Better' and 'Worse'. *Phil Stud*, 70(2), 133-163, My 93.

Gochet, Paul and Gillet, Eric. On Professor Weingartner's Contribution to Epistemic Logic in Advances in Scientific Philosophy, Schurz, Gerhard (ed). Amsterdam, Rodopi, 1991.

The paper offers an alternative to the system designed by Professor Weingartner to capture a form of weak knowledge (which does not license the inference from A knows that B knows that p to A knows that p.) As opposed to the former system, the new one caters for any finite number of epistemic agents and provides a possible world semantics (with completeness proof) which is easier to handle than the matrix semantics of the initial system.

Gochet, Pual. On Sir Alfred Ayer's Theory of Truth in The Philosophy of A J Ayer, Hahn, Lewis E (ed). Peru, Open Court, 1992.

Goddard, Jean-Christophe. Christianisme et philosophie dans la première philosophie de Fichte. *Arch Phil*, 55(2), 199-220, Ap-Je 92.

In order to solve the problem of the theoretical inadequacy of faith (with which Kant had already copied in his doctrine of postulates and which Forberg used against criticism), Fichte, in his first writings, tried to give Christianism a transcendental basement which took the form of an ascending Christology. The argument proving the practical reality of reason (which was meant to settle any philosophy on firm grounds) owned much to the johanic notion of "love or truth" (i.e., "spirit of truth") already used in 1793 in the defence of the French Revolution.

Godfrey, Joseph J. Trust, the Heart of Religion: A Sketch. *Amer Cath Phil Quart*, 65, 157-167, 1991.

This proposal that trust is the heart of religion is jointly supported by study of religious attitudes as expressed in the key Vedantist, Buddhist, Hebrew, and Christian terms *sraddha, visvasa, bitachon, emunah, pistis*, and by an understanding of trust as four-dimensional: instrumental reliance, I-Thou relation, security, and openness. Trust is more central to religion than will or commitment, love, or belief. This proposal also challenges distinguishing between the truth of beliefs and their usefulness. Trust as one component in religious attitudes has been studied by Donald Evans, Hans Küng, Maurice Friedman and especially Raymond Panikkar.

Godfrey-Smith, Peter. Additivity and the Units of Selection. *Proc Phil Sci Ass*, 1, 315-328, 1992.

"Additive variance in fitness" is an important concept in the formal apparatus of population genetics. Wimsatt and Lloyd have argued that this concept can also be used to decide the "unit of selection" in an evolutionary process. The paper argues that the proposed criteria of Wimsatt and Lloyd are ambiguous, and several interpretations of their views are presented. It is argued that none of these interpretations provide acceptable criteria for deciding units of selection. The reason is that additive variance in fitness can be both a cause of evolution, but also a byproduct of selection at another level.

Godfrey-Smith, Peter and Lewontin, Richard. The Dimensions of Selection. *Phil Sci*, 60(3), 373-395, S 93.

Proponents of genic selectionism have claimed that evolutionary processes normally viewed as selection on individuals can be "represented" as selection on alleles. This paper discusses the relationship between mathematical questions about the formal requirements upon state spaces necessary for the representation of different types of evolutionary processes and causal questions about the units of selection in such processes.

Godlovitch, Stan. Music—What to Do About It. *J Aes Educ*, 26(2), 1-15, Sum 92.

Although music is considered a performing art, little consideration has gone into whether it is so essentially. Furthermore, few have clarified what it means exactly to be a performer. Technology has influenced traditional categories. I argue that technology shows performers to be only contingently related to music and that the concept of a performer no longer draws upon traditional notions of specialized physical skill. Thus music is more properly described as a performed rather than a performing art.

Godlovitch, Stan. Skeptics, Cynics, Pessimists, and Other Malcontents. *Metaphilosophy*, 23(1-2), 14-24, Ja-Ap 92.

However compelling intellectually, philosophical skepticism has little credibility regarding conduct as Aristotle and Hume both realized. However, having a skeptical

attitude is common and advisable in ordinary life. This paper explores the link between philosophical and attitudinal skepticism arguing that the former is a reductio ad absurdum of the latter. The latter is analyzed as not following from the former, but, instead, as being a manifestation of natural wariness which is explainable by appeal to natural selection. As an attitude with dispositional properties, skepticism is more like cynicism or pessimism than it is a 'rational' epistemic stance.

Godway, Eleanor M. Wild Being, the Prepredicative and Expression: How Merleau-Ponty Uses Phenomenology to Develop an Ontology. *Man World*, 26(4), 389-401, O 93.

Merleau-Ponty's ontology depends on a reduction beyond the predicative and calls for philosophical expression which, leaving behind attempts at literal (adequate) description and putting itself in question, allows Wild Being to break through. *Parole originaire*, speech which gives birth to new meanings, is more primordial than literal (secondary) speech, and thus metaphor may be taken as revelatory and not as aberrant description (Ricoeur). Wild Being is "being in dehiscence" and it cannot be wholly present to us or dominated by us (c.f. logo-centrism) but in living thought, feeling and action which are open to a future, we participate in it and bear witness to it as the irreducible horizon of our own being.

Goehr, Lydia. Being True to the Work. *J Aes Art Crit*, 47(1), 55-67, Wint 89.

An investigation of the ramifications of speaking about music in terms of *works*. Two interrelated claims are made, both of which derive from the particular historical thesis that the concept of a musical work first fully emerged in classical musical practice around 1800, and that, since then, it has been employed widely and pervasively. The first claim is that the work-concept is an open concept with paradigmatic and derivative employment; the second claim is that the traditional counterexample method used so often in the search for definitions is undermined in a way hitherto unseen in the philosophical literature.

Goehr, Lydia. The Institutionalization of a Discipline: A Retrospective of The Journal of Aesthetics and Art Criticism and the Amer Soc for Aesthetics, 1939-1992. *J Aes Art Crit*, 51(2), 99-121, Spr 93.

A story of the institutionalization of 'American Aesthetics through its central society and journal. The interpretation focuses on two different relations, the first between a discipline and an institution; the second between aesthetics and philosophy. I tell first the story of how and why the society and journal were founded. I then move on to show why and how the evolution of the ASA and *JAAC* moved away from the original interdisciplinary ambitions of a few central figures to create an aesthetics that was institutionally independent of philosophy, toward an increasing acceptance of aesthetics as a fully dependent part of the philosophical discipline. This development created perpetual but often creative institutional and disciplinary tensions.

Goehr, Lydia. Writing Music History: A Review Essay. *Hist Theor*, 31(2), 182-199, 1992.

Influenced by methodological trends in contemporary cultural history, recent writings in music history now share a common and very basic concern: to reconcile the desire to treat musical works as purely musical entities with value and significance of their own with the desire to account for the fact that such works are conditioned by the historical, social, and psychological contexts in which they are produced. This essay places these modern reconciliations within a broader discussion of the uneasy relations that hold between the domains of the musical and the extra-musical. It shows how both the logic and the history of this relationship has reflected the need to establish borders of the musical domain, and, following upon that, criteria of relevance for determining what is and what is not to be included in the writing of music history.

Goertzel, Ben. Quantum Theory and Consciousness. *J Mind Behav*, 13(1), 29-36, Wint 92.

This article seeks to clarify the relation between consciousness and quantum physics. It is argued that, in order to be consistent with quantum theory, one must never assert that conscious action has caused a given event to occur. Rather, consciousness must be identified with "measurement" or, more concretely, with an increase in the entropy of the probability distribution of possible events. It is suggested that the feeling of self- awareness may be associated with the exchange of entropy between groups of quantum systems which are so tightly coupled as to be, for all practical purposes, an indivisible unit. Such groups of systems may be understood to measure themselves. Two interpretations of the quantum theory of consciousness are distinguished: one in which consciousness is defined as quantum measurement; and one in which this measurement is hypothesized to correlate with a certain biological phenomenon called consciousness.

Goffi, Jean-Yves. Ecologies et philosophies. *Rev Theol Phil*, 125(1), 77-84, 1993.

L'ouvrage incisif de Luc Ferry sur l'éthique de l'environnement (*Le nouvel ordre écologique*) décrit la rupture avec l'humanisme moderne que constituent les courants récents dans lesquels on traite les "êtres de nature" comme des "êtres de liberté". L Ferry fait le tour de ces courants et montre les difficultés auxquelles ils se heurtent, mais il ne parvient pas à entrer en débat avec ses adversaires. Il donne par conséquent un diagnostic plutôt qu'une contribution fondamentale au débat contemporain.

Gogacz, M. Identification philosophique de l'homme (in Polish). *Stud Phil Christ*, 28(1), 7-18, 1992.

Gogacz, Mieczyslaw. Basic Principles of Differentiating of Conception of God (in Polish). *Stud Phil Christ*, 27(2), 7-18, 1991.

The conceptions of God depend on theory of cognition or on theory of being. According to the theory of cognition we can point out theses conceptions of God which depend on the object of cognition. According to the theory of being we can differentiate some conceptions of God dependent of comprehension of being. When we grasp the essence and existence in the being, God appears as the Existence Itself.

Golash, Deirdre. Defective Newborns: Parental Obligation and the Law. *Cont Phil*, 15(4), 16-20, Jl-Ag 93.

Parents are ordinarily morally obligated to provide life-saving treatment for defective infants, unless it would be rational for a person so afflicted to commit suicide. The burden on the parents should be a factor only where home care is necessary to make the child's life worthwhile, and providing it would so burden the parents that their own lives would no longer be worth living. State enforcement is morally justified if the state has fulfilled its own obligations to handicapped children, but is limited by practical considerations.

Golby, Michael. School Governors: Conceptual and Practical Problems. *J Phil Educ*, 26(2), 165-172, 1992.

The new role of school governor poses questions about the proper conduct of these new authorities in regard to the professional work of schools. Schools have unique purposes and for that reason metaphors for their governors' conduct from commerce and from democratic decision-making have important limitations as well as some strengths. Schools need to account for their use of public funds, but they are not institutions whose main purpose is profit. They need to respect the popular will, but this cannot mean the handover of all professional functions to governors. The distinction between management and governance is considered and it is suggested that the jury might be a more appropriate model for school governors' activity.

Gold, Steven Jay. *Moral Controversies: Race, Class, and Gender in Applied Ethics*. Belmont, Wadsworth, 1993.

The book is an applied ethics reader that integrates race, class and gender issues into a traditional format. Problems of abortion, surrogacy, gay rights, euthanasia, testing, death penalty, acquaintance rape, pornography, economic justice and welfare, affirmative action, comparable worth, sexual harassment, animals and the environment, are presented through new material and traditional pieces, conventional and radical perspective, legal decisions and discussion cases. Special attention is paid to the effects public policy decisions have on women and people of color, e.g., racism and the death penalty, justice for Native Americans and farmworkers, feminism and surrogacy, abortion, and ecofeminism.

Goldberg, S L. *Agents and Lives: Moral Thinking in Literature*. New York, Cambridge Univ Pr, 1993.

Goldblatt, David A. The Dislocation of the Architectural Self. *J Aes Art Crit*, 49(4), 337-348, Fall 91.

Goldblatt, David A. Ventriloquism: Ecstatic Exchange and the History of the Artwork. *J Aes Art Crit*, 51(3), 389-398, Sum 93.

Goldfarb, Warren. Wittgenstein on Understanding. *Midwest Stud Phil*, 17, 109-122, 1992.

Goldfluss, Enrica and Mencacci, Claudio. The Emotional Residence: An Italian Experience of the Treatment of Chronic Psychosis in Analecta Husserliana, XXXI, Tymieniecka, Anna-Teresa (ed). Dordrecht, Kluwer, 1990.

Goldin, Owen. Metaphysical Explanation and "Particularization" in Maimonides' *Guide of the Perplexed*. *J Phil Res*, 17, 189-213, 1992.

Within *The Guide of the Perplexed* Maimonides presents an argument that is intended to render probable the temporal creation of the cosmos. In one of these arguments Maimonides adopts the Kalamic strategy of arguing for the necessity of there being a "particularizing" agent. Maimonides argues that even one who grants Aristotelian science can still ask why the heavenly realm is as it is, to which there is no reply forthcoming but "God so willed it". The argument is effective against the Arabic Neoplatonic Aristotelians, but not against Aristotle himself. Aristotle's response to Maimonides would be that the latter is in effect asking, "Why are there the essences there are?", a question that Aristotle would take to be fundamentally misplaced, since he holds that the existence of the theoretical primitives of every science is to be assumed. (edited)

Goldin, Owen M. Self, Sameness, and Soul in "Alcibiades I" and the "Timaeus". *Frei Z Phil Theol*, 40(1-2), 5-19, 1993.

Within the Socratic dialogue *Alcibiades I* reference is made to "the Self Itself," apparently the form of the self. This is thought to serve as the ground of the selfhood of all beings and of the soul's ability to recognize beings as the selves they are. Both *Alcibiades I* and Plato's *Timaeus* take the form of the self (or of the same) to be a basic constituent of soul. But in the *Timaeus* the form of the Different is an equally important constituent of soul. This can be considered a development of the psychology of *Alcibiades I* in light of the results of the *Sophist*.

Goldman, Alan H. Art Historial Value. *Brit J Aes*, 33(1), 17-28, Ja 93.

Many aesthetic properties are had by artworks only relative to standards that vary over time. Some artworks are valuable because of their place in historical narratives, e.g., because they initiate or foreshadow later movements according to these narratives. This article is concerned with ameliorating the relativistic implications of these claims. It takes a realistic view of stylistic developments and the standards implicit in them.

Goldman, Alan H. Interpreting Art and Literature. *J Aes Art Crit*, 48(3), 205-214, Sum 90.

Interpretation of an artwork is inference to an explanation that facilitates appreciation of the work. Interpreters show how elements of works contribute to their artistic values. In all media there are data that can be described without being interpreted and that serve as explananda or constraints on acceptable interpretations. There can be incompatible but equally acceptable interpretations, and honoring the intentions of artists contributes to one major, but not the only, artistic value.

Goldman, Alan H. Realism about Aesthetic Properties. *J Aes Art Crit*, 51(1), 31-37, Wint 93.

This article argues that anti-realists (in regard to aesthetic properties) can better explain agreements and disagreements among critics than can realists. It answers arguments of Zemach that there must be sufficient agreement in use of aesthetic property terms to ground realism, and that scientific realists must be realists about aesthetic properties too. The most plausible realist account refers to responses of ideal critics, but it has no way of explaining why disagreements would persist even among such critics.

Goldman, Alan H. Representation and Make-Believe (Kendall L Walton, *Mimesis as Make-Believe*). *Inquiry*, 36(3), 335-350, S 93.

Goldman, Alan H. Response to Stecker's "Goldman on Interpreting Art and Literature". *J Aes Art Crit*, 49(3), 246-247, Sum 91.

Goldman, Alan H. The Value of Music. *J Aes Art Crit*, 50(1), 35-44, Wint 92.

The value that great musical works share with other art forms is the full engagement of our sensory, perceptual, cognitive, and affective capacities in appreciating their unfolding forms. Such full engagement creates the illusion of another world in which we pursue the musical goals of the composer. The uniqueness of music as an art form lies in the fact that its worlds are completely different from and detached from the real world, uniting us directly through its evanescent sounds to the minds of composers.

Goldman, Alvin and Shaked, Moshe. Commentary on the Scientific Status of Econometrics. *Soc Epistem*, 7(3), 249-253, Jl-S 93.

A target article by Feigenbaum and Levy contributes to the truth-oriented mission of social epistemology by revealing the limited incentives for error-detecting replication studies under current institutional conditions. We draw analogies between their article and our own previous work, in which a model of scientific activity plus assumptions about credit-maximizing motivations have implications for the truth-promoting properties of scientific experimentation.

Goldstein, Bernard. The Blasphemy of Alfonso X in Revolution and Continuity, Barker, Peter (ed). Washington, Cath Univ Amer Pr, 1991.

Goldstein, Laurence. A Buridanian Discussion of Desire, Murder and Democracy. *Austl J Phil*, 70(4), 405-414, D 92.

Sophism 18 of Buridan's *Sophismata* elicits from Buridan an analysis of, and a notation for, speech acts, together with a powerful account of conditional desires. The sophism, I show, has close structural similarities both with James Forrester's 'Paradox of Gentle Murder' and Richard Wollheim's 'Paradox of Democracy.' Buridan's remarkable discussion provides us with the tools for solving these paradoxes. The solution to Forrester's is close to one formalized within temporal deontic logic by Aqvist and Van Eck. The solution to Wollheim's is natural and new and turns on the notion of degrees of strength of belief.

Goldstein, Laurence. Inescapable Surprises and Acquirable Intentions. *Analysis*, 53(2), 93-99, Ap 93.

The teacher says 'There will be an examination tomorrow, but you don't believe that there will be'. The student appropriates this as 'There will be an examination tomorrow, but I don't believe that there will be'. The teacher's claim is OK; the student's is Moore-paradoxical. Wittgenstein has the right solution to Moore's paradox, and what I show is that that solution provides us with the essentials for solving the Surprise Examination, and Kavka's Toxin Paradox too. There can be surprise examinations, and you can get rich by intending to drink poison.

Goldstein, Leon J. Hegel's Methodology: A Reply to Eduardo Vásquez. *Int Stud Phil*, 24(3), 109-111, 1992.

One of the goals of my "Force and the Inverted World is Dialectical Retrospection" (*Int Stud Phil*, 20/3, 13-28, 1988) is to show that Hegelian dialectic does not proceed internally, but that every move requires the impact of something logically contingent with respect to what has been achieved so far. Eduardo Vasquez attempted to refute this contention by citing passages in which Hegel characterizes what he does as what I reject. To this I respond by showing that apart from what Hegel may say about what he does, it is what he actually does that is important, and in the practice of the *Phenomenology* and the *Philosophy of History*, there is neither development or change without the impact of the contingent.

Goldstein, Leslie Friedman. Early European Feminism and American Women in Women's Rights and the Rights of Man, Arnaud, A J. Oxford, Aberdeen, 1990.

Two of the leading feminist theorists of the early nineteenth century, Frances (Fanny) Wright and Harriet Martineau, both participated in the rather widespread nineteenth-century practice of authoring studies of democracy in America. This essay examines these women's reflections on American women, American gender relations, and American democracy. The paper argues that these two authors exemplify what have now come to be viewed as the two alternative intellectual traditions shaping American political history. Wright (despite the radicalism of her communitarian utopian views) evidently shares the heritage of the classical, virtuous republic tradition, while Martineau fits easily into the tradition of liberal individualism that dates back to the doctrine of Hobbes, Locke, and Hume.

Goldstein, Philip. The Politics of Fredric Jameson's Literary Theory in Postmodernism/ Jameson/ Critique, Kellner, Douglas (ed). Washington, Maisonneuve Pr, 1989.

Goldsworthy, Jeffrey. Externalism, Internalism and Moral Scepticism. *Austl J Phil*, 70(1), 40-60, Mr 92.

In "Moral Realism and the Foundations of Ethics", David Brink defends externalist moral realism against Mackie's sceptical arguments, which presuppose some kind of internalism. But Brink confuses the issues by failing to distinguish different kinds of internalism. What he calls conceptual internalism may be false, but Mackie can retreat to sociological internalism, which holds that most people believe moral requirements to be capable of motivating action regardless of pre-existing desires. Brink does not challenge that thesis, which is all that Mackie's sceptical arguments necessarily presuppose.

Goldsworthy, Jeffrey. Well-Being and Value. *Utilitas*, 4(1), 1-26, My 92.

This article discusses four theories of well-being: desire-satisfaction and objectivist theories (briefly), and hedonist and non-cognitivist theories (at greater length). It argues that hedonist theories may be defensible against the common objection that certain things are good for us regardless of their effects on our mental states. The key is to distinguish between what is good *for us* and what is good *simpliciter*, that is, between well-being and value in general. The common objection may refute hedonist theories of value, but not hedonist theories of well-being. If it refutes both, non-cognitivism about well-being seems inescapable.

Goldthorpe, Rhiannon. Ricoeur, Proust and the Aporias of Time in On Paul Ricoeur: Narrative and Interpretation, Wood, David (ed). New York, Routledge, 1991.

Goldthorpe, Rhiannon. Understanding the Committed Writer in The Cambridge Companion to Sartre, Howells, Christina (ed). New York, Cambridge Univ Pr, 1992.

Goldthwait, John T. "Ought" Never Is: A Response to Oliver A Johnson. *J Value Inq*, 26(3), 443-447, Jl 92.

Hume faults moral thinkers for passing "insensibly" from "is"-statements to "ought"-statements in arguments to make moral judgments credible. The basic error made by Johnson and other interpreters of the argument in Hume's Challenge is not in the attempt to side-step a fourth-term fallacy in arguments moving from "is" to "ought", but in attempting to infer a non-truth-bearing proposition from truth-bearing propositions. The "ought" statements are members of a class, value-assertive propositions, that do not and cannot bear truth. Thus we actually cannot "go from is to ought".

Golomb, Jacob. Authenticity in Rousseau (in Hebrew). *Iyyun*, 42, 249-273, Ap 93.

The paper examines three different ways Rousseau suggests to attain authenticity, all inspired by the biological model (in contradistinction to the aesthetic one). These are: 1) the socio-political approach that aims at revolutionary changes (propagated in his *Discourses* and *Social Contract*); 2) the educational-evolutionary way proposed in *Emile*; 3) the solitary individual way of attaining authenticity pictured in his *Les Rêveries du promeneur solitaire*. Rousseau's approach to authenticity and education is compared to Nietzsche's, which is found to be more viable and productive.

Golomb, Jacob. Kierkegaard's Ironic Ladder to Authentic Faith. *Int J Phil Relig*, 32(2), 65-81, O 92.

(1) Kierkegaard's life and writings are a persistent quest for authentic selfhood. (2) He wishes to infuse "The Present Age" with passion. (3) Passion + sincerity of intention = authenticity. (4) The techniques of indirect communication and irony serve as an initial stage of the enticing procedure. (5) Since authentic commitment has no cognitive content he resorts to the indirect arousal of a certain emotional pathos. (6) His thesis that "Truth is subjectivity" means truth as personal authenticity as against truth as the objective value of the propositional content of sentences about reality. His views of authenticity are critically examined and defended against some criticism.

Gombrich, E H. Additional Thoughts on Perspective. *J Aes Art Crit*, 51(1), 69, Wint 93.

Gómez-Lobo, Alfonso. Philosophical Remarks on Thucydides' Melian Dialogue. *Proc Boston Colloq Anc Phil*, 5, 181-203, 1989.

This paper offers first a step by step interpretation of Thucydides V. 86-116. The ideas put forward therein by the Athenians are then compared to Callicles' speech in Plato's *Gorgias*. An effort is made to show that those ideas do not amount to a might-makes-right theory, but rather to a descriptive thesis about the nature of power: the stronger simply dominate because of natural necessity. The question whether this may be unjust does not arise. The paper ends with the suggestion that in the Melian dialogue Thucydides deliberately presented his fellow countrymen in a negative light.

Goncharov, Sergey and Yakhnis, Alexander and Yakhnis, Vladimir. Some Effectively Infinite Classes of Enumerations. *Annals Pure Applied Log*, 60(3), 207-235, My 93.

This research partially answers the question raised by Goncharov about the size of the class of positive elements of a Roger's semilattice. We introduce a notion of effective infinity of classes of computable enumerations. Then, using finite injury priority method, we prove five theorems which give sufficient conditions to be effectively infinite for classes of all enumerations without repetitions, positive undecidable enumerations, negative undecidable enumerations and all computable enumerations of a family of r.e. sets. These theorems permit to strengthen the results of Pour-El, Pour-El and Howard, Ershov and Khutoretskii about existence of enumerations without repetitions and positive undecidable enumerations.

González, Manuel Riobó. Free Will in Psychopaths in Analecta Husserliana, XXXI, Tymieniecka, Anna-Teresa (ed). Dordrecht, Kluwer, 1990.

In the psychopathological classification there are some oligophrenias in order to the mental deficiencies (idiocies), even with some rudimentary sentiment; nevertheless there's also a *moral oligophrenia* suffered by certain psychopathic personalities whose deficiency of moral feelings is exhibited in emotional unbalance and lack of social adaptation (*sociopathy*), that affects manifestly to rightness of moral judgment, as well as their determination with respect to ordinary norms according to law or to customary norms of conduct. The deterioration of his ideoaffectivity affects his *free will*. Thus, their intention acts supporting one *untrue activity*. Considering the psychomatic unity of the human psyche, idiocy seems to be at most a secondary phenomenon for the psychopathic personalities.

González, Wenceslao J. Semántica anti-realista: Intuicionismo matemático y concepto de verdad. *Theoria (Spain)*, 5(12-13), 149-170, N 90.

Among the philosophical problems recently discussed, the question on the anti-realist semantic is outstanding. Its origin arose when M Dummett tries a Wittgenstenian interpretation of the Intuitionistic Mathematics. He uses the concept of justification as the key concept—understood as proof or verification—, and it faces up to a realistic view centered in the notion of truth. But, carefully analyzed, it shows a clear vulnerability, while the realistic position has got serious elements on its favour, and so it is recognized by the supporter of the opposite point of view. Thus, the notion of truth cannot be disregarded.

González Gallego, Agustín. El problema del sujeto en la *Crítica de la Razón Pura*. *Agora (Spain)*, 11(1), 107-117, 1992.

Kant criticizes the "cartesian 'I'" as "subjectum" in the "transcendental doctrine of the elements". From there on, the article exposes, from the value of knowledge, how Kant looks over the empirist and rationalist thesis about the "I". In both redactions of the "transcendental analytic" estabilishes the distinction between the "empiric 'I'" and the "transcendental 'I'". Finally, the article exposes the "rational psychology illusion" the same way as it appears in the "Transcendental Dialectic". That reading of the "Kantian 'I'" exposes how modern the Kantian reflexion was, as, in its moment, Heidegger said, and Kant's critic severity to a possible idealism.

Gonzi, Andrea. Fondazione, creazione e creazione artistica in Sartre. *Filosofia*, 43(1), 59-89, Ja-Ap 92.

Gooch, Augusta O. Value Hierarchies in Scheler and Von Hildebrand. *SW Phil Stud*, 15, 19-27, Spr 93.

Both Max Scheler and Dietrich von Hildebrand seek, ultimately, to overthrow ethical relativism with their value theory. Scheler's central contribution to 20th century phenomenological realism includes his description and elaboration of knowable objective values which motivate human response. Von Hildebrand also builds his ethical theory around value recognition and value response, adding rich philosophical distinctions and intuitive commands. Because of the variety of values and value-families, von Hildebrand demonstrates the need for several kinds of hierarchical order, not just one as Scheler had established. The chart at the end of the paper shows the difference between Scheler's and von Hildebrand's value hierarchies.

Goodchild, Philip. Speech and Silence in the *Mumonkan*: An Examination of Use of Language in Light of the Philosophy of Gilles Deleuze. *Phil East West*, 43(1), 1-18, Ja 93.

This article examines the way in which language is used in the text of the *Mumonkan*, a collection of paradoxical sayings of Zen Masters used for meditation in Rinzai Zen. It draws upon the 'logic of sense' elaborated by Gilles Deleuze to show how the techniques of paradox and negation can express a profound meaning which escapes the normal powers of expression in language. It concludes that there is a dynamic use of language, beyond signification, which directly communicates religious insight.

Goodhart, Sandor. "One Isaac Waiting to Be Slaughtered": Halpern Leivick, The Holocaust, and Responsibility. *Phil Lit*, 16(1), 88-105, Ap 92.

Goodin, Robert E. Compensation and Redistribution. *Nomos*, 33, 143-177, 1991.

Goodin, Robert E. Government House Utilitarianism in The Utilitarian Response, Allison, Lincoln (ed). Newbury Park, Sage, 1990.

Goodin, Robert E. Independence in Democratic Theory: A Virtue? A Necessity? Both? Neither?. *J Soc Phil*, 24(2), 50-56, Fall 93.

Goodin, Robert E (ed) and Pettit, Philip (ed). *A Companion to Contemporary Political Philosophy*. Cambridge, Blackwell, 1992.

There are three sections to this book. The first consists of a series of extended essays on the contributions to political theory of analytical philosophy, continental philosophy, history, sociology, economics, political science and legal studies. The second comprises analyses of current political ideologies: anarchism, conservatism, feminism, liberalism, Marxism and socialism. And the third involves shorter discussions of over twenty-five major concepts, ranging from virtue and equality to sociobiology and environmentalism.

Goodman, Lenn E. Six Dogmas of Relativism in Cultural Relativism and Philosophy, Dascal, Marcelo (ed). Leiden, Brill, 1991.

Against relativism, I argue that 1) the theory dependence of observations creates no stultifying circle, since perception and speculation are activities, not singular propositions, 2) paradigms do not lock us in closed systems; thinking is open-textured, generating internal critiques and responding to external criticisms, so 3) our modes of thought are not incommensurable, for 4) natural languages are not confined to unique, univocal repertoires of categories; indeed, 5) language, being intensional, *permits* categorial distinctions rather than just following them. 6) To be is not just to be the value of a variable. Ontology in earnest is both possible and necessary: there are no sealed systems.

Goodman, Michael. A Sufficient Condition for Personhood. *Personalist Forum*, 8/1(Supp), 75-81, Spr 92.

The principal aim of the article is to offer an account of the necessary and sufficient conditions for moral personhood. It attempts to show that certain proposed conditions are not sufficient (e.g., rationality, self-consciousness, free-will) and proposes that there is a necessary and sufficient condition for moral personhood.

Goodman, Michael. *First Logic*. Lanham, Univ Pr of America, 1993.

The book is an introduction to the basic concepts and techniques of logic, including a number of common informal fallacies of reasoning. The book explores logical analysis applied as the most effective method of deciding for or against an argument. Aristotle called his treatise on logic "Organon", which means organ or instrument; logic is fun and also used every day.

Goodman, Michael and Snyder, Robert A. *Contemporary Readings in Epistemology*. Englewood Cliffs, Prentice Hall, 1993.

This is an edited anthology of previously published essays in contemporary epistemology. The book covers six sections: The Analysis of Knowledge, Epistemic Justification, A Priori Knowledge, Theories of Truth, Skepticism, and Alternate Approaches to Epistemology. It is intended for upper-division undergraduate and graduate students. The essays selected aim at fundamental issues in contemporary epistemology. The last section considers recent challenges to epistemology as traditionally conceived and investigates the social character of knowledge. There is an analytical overview and a selected bibliography for each section.

Goodman, Nelson. On Some Worldly Worries. *Synthese*, 95(1), 9-12, Ap 93.

Israel Scheffler and others have had trouble accepting such drastic theses in my work as that worlds, even old ones, are made by right versions, even new ones, and that two conflicting versions may both be right. But further explication shows how such theses have advantages over the more usual common-sense alternatives.

Goodman, Nelson. Or What Should Not Be Said About Representation. *J Aes Art Crit*, 46(3), 419-420, Spr 88.

Goodpaster, Kenneth E. Moral Consideration and the Environment: Perception, Analysis, and Synthesis. *Topoi*, 12(1), 5-20, Mr 93.

In the opening part of this essay, a model of the decision-making process (individual and institutional) is sketched and separated into two stages: moral consideration and moral engagement. Moral consideration is then subdivided into three parts: perception, analysis, and synthesis. In the remainder of the discussion, concepts like "holism", "impartiality", and "pluralism" are distinguished and associated with questions that arise during the moral consideration process. I argue that environmental ethics needs a communitarian principle beyond stakeholder analysis, and a stewardship principle that regards human beings as "special, but no different" in the moral community.

Goodwin, Brian and Webster, Gerry and Smith, Joseph Wayne. The 'Evolutionary Paradigm' and Constructional Biology in New Horizons in the Philosophy of Science, Lamb, David (ed). Brookfield, Avebury, 1992.

Goodwin, David. The Dialectic of Second-Order Distinctions: The Structure of Arguments about Fallacies. *Inform Log*, 14(1), 11-22, Wint 92.

Arguments about fallacies generally attempt to *distinguish* real from apparent modes of argumentation and reasoning. To examine the structure of these arguments, this paper develops a theory of dialectical distinction. First, it explores the connection between Nicholas Rescher's concept of distinction as a "dialectical countermove" and Chaim Perelman and L Olbrecht-Tyteca's "dissociation of ideas". Next, it applies a theory of distinction to Aristotle's extended arguments about fallacies in *De Sophisticis Elenchis*, primarily with a view to analyzing its underlying strategies of argumentation. Finally, it examines how second-order distinctions (those designed to challenge previously formulated distinctions) underpin current arguments against the Aristotelian or "Standard Treatment" of the fallacies.

Gopalan, S. Towards a Creative Synthesis of Cultures. *J Indian Counc Phil Res*, 9(1), 59-71, S-D 91.

Gopinathan, K. Language and Reality. *Indian Phil Quart*, 19/2(Supp), 25-28, Ap 92.

Gordon, Daniel. Ideologies and Mentalities. *Hist Theor*, 32(2), 196-213, 1993.

This review essay takes Michel Vovelle's *Mentalities and Ideologies* as an occasion to critically analyze the definitions of culture in French historiography. The author charges the Annales School with an excessive materialism and discusses some flaws in recent studies of popular religion, attitudes toward death, and the French Revolution. The method advocated is one informed by hermeneutics and moral philosophy.

Gordon, David. Anscombe on Coming Into Existence and Causation. *Analysis*, 44(2), 52-54, Mr 84.

Gordon, David. Green on Dictators and Democracies. *Analysis*, 44(2), 95-96, Mr 84.

Gordon, David. Reply to Harris: On Formal and Dialectical Logic. *Int Phil Quart*, 32(2), 247-252, Je 92.

Gordon, Haim and Gordon, Rivca. Sartre's Ontology of Evil and the Poverty of the Social Sciences. *Man World*, 26(3), 275-285, Jl 93.

Sartre's biography of Jean Genet, *Saint Genet*, is the major work in which he discusses the ontological status of evil. He immediately shows that this ontology cannot be separated from the reality of evil and from its being a social phenomenon. Evil, Sartre holds, is a projection of the self-castrated "right thinking man." After explaining how Genet developed as an evil being on the basis of the project of the "right thinking man," we indicate that most social scientists today are right thinking men who ignore evil and view society on the basis of the bourgeois seriousness that Sartre despised.

Gordon, Jeffrey. "The Will to Believe": James's Defense of Religious Intolerance. *SW Phil Stud*, 15, 28-36, Spr 93.

Gordon, Jeffrey. The Rational Imperative to Believe. *Relig Stud*, 29(1), 1-19, Mr 93.

Despite his avowed purpose in "The Will to Believe" to defend the legitimacy of religious faith, James makes a cause for a much stronger conclusion. He argues for a rational imperative to believe. In Part I of this paper, I defend this reading of James. In Part II, I defend the soundness of James's newly interpreted argument.

Gordon, Rivca and Gordon, Haim. Sartre's Ontology of Evil and the Poverty of the Social Sciences. *Man World*, 26(3), 275-285, Jl 93.

Sartre's biography of Jean Genet, *Saint Genet*, is the major work in which he discusses the ontological status of evil. He immediately shows that this ontology cannot be separated from the reality of evil and from its being a social phenomenon. Evil, Sartre holds, is a projection of the self-castrated "right thinking man." After explaining how Genet developed as an evil being on the basis of the project of the "right thinking man," we indicate that most social scientists today are right thinking men who ignore evil and view society on the basis of the bourgeois seriousness that Sartre despised.

Gordon, Sophie Haroutunian. Men and Women: Ball-in-Socket Story?. *Proc Phil Educ*, 48, 201-204, 1992.

Gordon-Kelter, Janice (ed) and Zalk, Sue Rosenberg (ed). *Revolutions in Knowledge: Feminism in the Social Sciences*. Boulder, Westview Pr, 1991.

Gormally, Luke. Definitions of Personhood: Implications for the Care of PVS Patients. *Ethics Med*, 9(3), 44-48, Autumn 93.

Gorman, Michael. Henry of Oyta's Nominalism and the Principle of Individuation. *Mod Sch*, 69(2), 135-148, Ja 92.

Henry Totting of Oyta (b. ca. 1330; d. 1397) was an important master at Prague and Vienna. This article examines his views on individuality as they are found in his *Quaestiones in Isagogen Porphyrii*. Drawing on the conceptual framework outlines by Jorge J E Gracia in *Individuality* (1988), the article discusses the intension of 'individual', and the principle of individuation. Henry's somewhat unusual solution to the problem of individuation is a good illustration of the pressures exerted by a nominalist ontology.

Gorman, Michael M. Hume on Natural Belief and Original Principles. *Hume Stud*, 19(1), 103-116, Ap 93.

Gorman, Michael M. Hume's Theory of Belief. *Hume Stud*, 19(1), 89-101, Ap 93.

The paper defends Hume's theory of belief against charges of inconsistency (but does not argue that Hume's theory is correct). It is noted that his statements about belief are actually statements about three different questions: the nature of belief, the effects of belief, and the causes of belief. The question of the nature of belief is

analyzed in the most detail. Hume has two theories, which I call his "manner of conception theory" and his "feeling theory," but on Humean assumptions, these theories turn out to mean the same thing.

Gorman, Michael M. Ontological Priority and John Duns Scotus. *Phil Quart*, 43(173), 460-471, O 93.

The philosophical literature understands ontological priority in two ways, in terms of dependence, and in terms of degrees-of-being. These views are not reconcilable in any straightforward manner. However, they can be reconciled indirectly, if both are seen as instances of higher-level concept that is a modification of John Duns Scotus' notion of essential order. The result is a theory of ontological priority that takes the form of a list of membership criteria for the class of "ontological priority relations", of which dependence and degrees-of-being are just two examples.

Gorner, Paul. Husserl and Heidegger as Phenomenologists. *J Brit Soc Phenomenol*, 23(2), 146-155, My 92.

Gorniak-Kocikowska, Krystyna. The Light, the Word, the Sea, and the Inner Moral Self in Analecta Husserliana, XXXVIII, Tymieniecka, Anna-Teresa (ed). Dordrecht, Kluwer, 1992.

The paper presents some aspects of A T Tymieniecka's *Logos and Life*, Book 3. There are two basic subjects of inquiry. The first being the question of the relation between knowledge and values. The second problem is the static versus dynamic concept of reality. The novels about the sea analyzed by Tymieniecka provide good material for such an inquiry. The conclusion of the article is that the basic value of the West in modern times: freedom, requires a dynamic concept of reality. Freedom manifests itself in creating *visions* according to which humans change reality. However, in that process one discovers that values, too, have a dynamic character. Tymieniecka's views are compared with the philosophy of Nietzsche.

Gorovitz, Samuel. *Drawing the Line: Life, Death, and Ethical Choices in an American Hospital*. New York, Oxford Univ Pr, 1992.

Gosepath, Stefan. *Aufgeklärtes Eigeninteresse: Eine Theorie theoretischer und praktischer Rationalität*. Frankfurt, Suhrkamp, 1992.

The aim of the book is to clarify the concept of rationality. The analysis of usage and of various forms of theoretical and practical rationality yields the result to which the title refers. There is a single meaning of the colloquial expression "rational" in the sense of "justified" and a basic structure of justification common to all forms of rationality. This structure has to do with an optimal choice of aims, actions and even beliefs. The idea of an optimal choice, which differs from the orthodox model of practical rationality by involving enlightenment and reflection, thus proves to be the central ingredient of the concept of rationality.

Gosling, Justin. Mad, Drunk or Asleep?—Aristotle's Akratic. *Phronesis*, 38(1), 98-104, 1993.

Assumptions: use of relevant knowledge suffices for action; use of particular knowledge involves putting it to work with other knowledge. Does comparison with drunkenness mean the akratic suffer failure of belief or understanding? i) The account of use does not entail it. ii) Drunkenness produces general diminution in use; the akratic use their knowledge fully in pursuit of pleasure. The akratic is not deficient in belief or understanding, but they cannot use their knowledge contemporaneously in pursuit of pleasure and of an opposed good. The one actualisation must oust the other.

Goswami, Chinmoy. On Logical Form of Action Sentences. *Indian Phil Quart*, 19(3), 187-198, Jl 92.

The purpose of this paper is to show that the logical form of action sentences are dependent upon the concept of 'agent' that one takes. A thing type of agent leads to the extensional form while a thinking type of agent leads to intentional form of action sentences. Consequently, it is important to note the locus of the describer who himself is also an agent. If the describer is someone other than the agent, the ascription of action is based on a tacit counterfactual. The agent could have done otherwise, implying the agent to be a being-of-the-world, who acts on the things of the world to bring about a change which could not have occurred otherwise.

Gottlob, Rainer. How Scientists Confirm Universal Propositions. *Dialectica*, 46(2), 123-139, 1992.

Scientists regard their inductive hypotheses as confirmed when consistence exists between two or more results obtained by differing methods. Three hierarchical levels of confirmation are applied: 1) No counterinstances; 2) Several "sieves" described in extenso; 3) The network of our entire knowledge into which the hypothesis must fit. Certainty is obtained by the deductive element of the third level. The question of uniformity of nature is less decisive than the question of whether or not the complexity of the processes observed or the limited scope of our senses and instruments permits to see through the causal connections involved.

Goudaroulis, Yorgos. A Matter of Order in Greek Studies in the Philosophy and History of Science, Nicolacopoulos, Pantelis (ed). Dordrecht, Kluwer, 1990.

Gough, Martin. The Possibility of an Unbodily Self: In Response to Richard Combes. *J Speculative Phil*, 6(4), 317-321, 1992.

Combes argues that objects of visual perception and bodily sensations are in the conscious subject's "original position" experienced as not located, but that the tactile perception is more primitive. I explain that the argument is unsound: it relies on questionable empirical data, leading to a somewhat hasty solution to Molyneux's Question. However, the thesis suitably modified, and not dependent on empirical data, has implications for the nature of self-consciousness. A quasi-"Cartesian" concept of self can persist in the "primordial consciousness", which does not involve even implicit reference to oneself as body in the spatial world.

Gouinlock, James. Moral Pluralism, Intellectual Virtue, and Academic Culture in Moral Education and the Liberal Arts, Mitias, Michael H (ed). Westport, Greenwood Pr, 1992.

Gouinlock, James. *Rediscovering the Moral Life*. Buffalo, Prometheus, 1993.

Gould, Carol C. Philosophical Dichotomies and Feminist Thought: Towards a Critical Feminism (in Czechoslovakian). *Filozof Cas*, 40(5), 851-856, 1992.

Recent feminist theory has revealed the one-sidedness of the philosophical tradition in its predominant emphasis on universal rationality and an impartial ethical perspective. However, it seems to me that feminist theory has too often fallen into a one-sidedness of its own which is an exclusionary emphasis on values and characteristics associated with the feminine. In this way, it retains the dichotomy between the masculine and the feminine which it began by criticizing. I critically examine two recent expressions of this one-sidedness in recent feminist ethical theory, and argue for a more mediated view of the relation between ostensibly dichotomous male and female modes of rational or moral thought and action. (edited)

Gould, John. Plato and Performance. *Apeiron*, 25(4), 13-25, D 92.

Gould, Timothy. Emerson's Words, Nietzsche's Writing. *Int Stud Phil*, 24(2), 21-32, 1992.

Gould, Timothy. Intensity and Its Audiences: Notes Towards a Feminist Perspective on the Kantian. *J Aes Art Crit*, 48(4), 305-315, Fall 90.

Goulet, Denis. La cultura y los valores tradicionales en el desarrollo. *Rev Filosof (Costa Rica)*, 30(71), 27-36, J 92.

Development, as conventionally practiced, destroys many precious cultural values and causes great human suffering. This paper argues that the human cost of development need not be so high. Better ways of thinking about development are needed; so are new development strategies which respect traditional values. Development should be redefined to mean the integrally good life, the proper basis for a just society, and the best criterion for relating to the forces of nature. Present concepts of development must be greatly expanded beyond economic growth, institutional modernization, and technological efficiency. (edited)

Govier, T. Trust and Testimony: Nine Arguments on Testimonial Knowledge. *Int J Moral Soc Stud*, 8(1), 21-39, Spr 93.

Since much of our knowledge is based on what other people tell us, much of our knowledge presupposes trust in other people. Believing or accepting evidence from others is reasonable only to the extent that we regard them as reliable, competent, and honest. In this paper I discuss nine arguments purporting to justify our reliance upon the testimony of others. The paper is intended to summarize and evaluate these arguments, paying special attention to the role of trust.

Govier, Trudy. Distrust as a Practical Problem. *J Soc Phil*, 23(1), 52-63, Spr 92.

Basic trust, a sense that even those others who are total strangers, have no intention to harm us, is a necessary condition of a viable social life. But much distrust exists and some is warranted. Given that trust is essential for communication and cooperation, how can we move from warranted distrust to well-founded trust? I describe this problem and describe and evaluate various proposed solutions. I offer a conceptual account of trust and distrust, point to some valid ground for distrust, and explore five approaches to the practical problem.

Govier, Trudy. Self-Trust, Autonomy, and Self-Esteem. *Hypatia*, 8(1), 99-120, Wint 93.

Self-trust is a necessary condition of personal autonomy and self-respect. Self-trust involves a positive sense of the motivations and competence of the trusted person; a willingness to depend on him or her; and an acceptance of vulnerability. It does not preclude trust in others. A person may be rightly said to have too much self-trust; however core self-trust is essential for functioning as an autonomous human being.

Govier, Trudy. What Is a Good Argument?. *Metaphilosophy*, 23(4), 393-409, O 92.

To be epistemically and logically adequate, an argument must meet two sorts of conditions: those concerning its premises and those concerning the inferential link between its premises and its conclusion. We may call such an argument cogent. A survey of pertinent texts and other works reveals at least six different accounts of argument and cogency. These are: classic deductivism, classic positivism, methodological deductivism, pragmatic positivism, the qualified spectrum view, and the pluralist view. The paper explains and appraises these views.

Goyard-Fabre, Simone. La fondation des lois civiles. *Laval Theol Phil*, 49(1), 105-119, F 93.

Goyard-Fabre, Simone. La propriété dans la philosophie de Locke. *Arch Phil*, 55(4), 607-630, O-D 92.

In the Locke's philosophy, the concept of property is polyvalent; in consequence, its interpretation is difficult. Indeed, three figures correspond to this concept: first, the originary property of the earth (communio fundi originaria); secondly, the property which, as original right of mankind, is "a dominion in common"; at last, the property which every man has on his own person (property in) and which becomes, by the means of labour, property on, that is to say the property on goods (res). The problem consists to understand how these three aspects, under the great law of nature, are distinct but interdependent.

Grabinska, T. Determinism and Reductionism in Light of Empirical Mathematics (in Polish). *Stud Phil Christ*, 28(1), 19-30, 1992.

The fractal conceptualization of natural phenomena and its relation to the iterated solutions of nonlinear differential equations are discussed. The traditional connection between determinism and reductionism should be once more revised when fractal methods are taken into account; a holistic coupling of part and the whole is preferred. The consideration of regular solutions of the nonlinear differential equations and their chaotic counterpart implies the Metallman claim about strict and statistic determinism. The indeterminism of chaos, however, cannot be called in question.

Gracia, Diego. The Intellectual Basis of Bioethics in Southern European Countries. *Bioethics*, 7(2-3), 97-107, Ap 93.

Gracia, Jorge J E. Christian Wolff on Individuation. *Hist Phil Quart*, 10(2), 147-164, Ap 93.

The paper is divided into three parts. In the first, I examine briefly the nature of Wolff's *Ontology*, its method, and the place that the discussion of individuality and individuation occupies in the overall structure of the text. In the second, I present and characterize Wolff's view of individuation. Finally, in the third, I explore the extent to which Wolff's theory of individuation displays the influence of the epistemologism

prevalent in modern philosophy. Two main theses are presented in the paper. First, Wolff's theory of individuation is a bundle view with a strong accidental component. Second, the epistemologism of modern philosophy is one of the factors that led Wolff to adopt the view of individuation that he did.

Gracia, Jorge J E. Francisco Suárez: The Man in History. *Amer Cath Phil Quart*, 65(3), 259-266, Sum 91.

This article presents a short summary of Suárez's life, works, and place in history. It argues that, contrary to widespread interpretations, which portray Suárez exclusively as a medieval theologian or a modern philosopher, he is best seen as both.

Gracia, Jorge J E. Hispanic Philosophy: Its Beginning and Golden Age. *Rev Metaph*, 46(3), 475-502, Mr 93.

This article argues for the use of the notion of Hispanic philosophy in the historiography of the philosophy of Iberian and Latin American countries beginning in the 16th century. It proposes an understanding of this notion in terms of historical relations and continuity rather than specific and enduring characteristics. It also argues that it is in the 16th century that Hispanic philosophy began and reached its highest level of achievement.

Gracia, Jorge J E. Suárez and Metaphysical Mentalism: The Last Visit. *Amer Cath Phil Quart*, 67(3), 349-354, Sum 93.

This article is a reply to N J Wells' article "*Esse Cognitum* and Suárez Revisited" (*ACPQ* 67, 3 (1993): 339-348) prompted in turn by my article "Suárez's Conception of Metaphysics: A Step in the Direction of Mentalism?" (*ACPQ* 65 (1991): 287-309). I argue that, contrary to what Professor Wells' believes: First, he has not clarified the status of the objective concept, and, second, he must accept that, if his interpretation were correct, metaphysics, for Suárez, would be concerned with what is in the mind, rather than with what is outside it.

Gracia, Jorge J E. Suárez's Conception of Metaphysics: A Step in the Direction of Mentalism?. *Amer Cath Phil Quart*, 65(3), 287-309, Sum 91.

Mentalism in metaphysics is the view that the object of study of metaphysics is something mental rather than something real. Suárez has been identified as a key figure in the development of mentalism in early modern philosophy. Contrary to this view I argue that Suárez did not take any unambiguous steps toward mentalism and that his position is concordant with the medieval Aristotelian tradition of realism. In the article I examine Suárez's view of the nature of metaphysics, its object, and the ontological status of that object.

Graczynska, Ewa. EIS for Nilpotent Shifts of Varieties. *Bull Sec Log*, 21(2), 72-78, Je 92.

In the paper we prove that the operation *N* preserves the *EIS*-property for varieties of algebras.

Graczynska, Ewa. A Word Problem for Normal and Regular Equations. *Bull Sec Log*, 21(4), 152-155, D 92.

The paper is a continuation of the paper: Ewa Graczynska, "On Normal and Regular Identities", Algebra Universalis 27, 1990, 387-397. We have generalized one of the theorems. Namely, it is noticed that the word problem for free algebras of a given variety of algebras of arbitrary type is solvable if and only if it is solvable for the normal, regular part of that variety. This gives a practical simplification: one needs to deal only with normal, regular identities, instead of all.

Graeser, Andreas. Immanenz und Absolutheit: Zy Y—Yovels Studie "Spinoza and Other Heretics". *Frei Z Phil Theol*, 40(1-2), 217-235, 1993.

Graham, A C. *Unreason Within Reason: Essays on the Outskirts of Rationality*. Peru, Open Court, 1992.

Graham, Daniel W. Socrates and Plato. *Phronesis*, 37(2), 141-165, 1992.

The view that the Socrates of Plato's early dialogues represents the historical Socrates (the Early Dialogue Theory, EDT) must face sceptical objections. A serious problem is how to explain why Plato should simply recreate Socrates' views. We can understand the importance of Socrates to Plato by analogy to the relation between Wittgenstein and his students. Another serious problem for EDT is how to establish a criterion for distinguishing Socratic and Platonic elements. Doctrinal differences between Plato's early and middle dialogues are not sufficient to establish such a criterion; but differences of social attitude, entailing different methods, do provide a criterion. Aristotle's testimony, for which there is confirmation, implies Plato had doctrines incompatible with those of Socrates even when he was writing his early dialogues.

Graham, George. *Philosophy of Mind: An Introduction*. Cambridge, Blackwell, 1993.

Included are such central topics as mind/body, consciousness, and intentionality, as well as other issues less often contained in introductions such as minds of animals and of God, mental illness, and 'after-death' experience. Intended for readers with little or no background in philosophy.

Graham, Gordon. Liberalism and Democracy. *J Applied Phil*, 9(2), 149-160, 1992.

Political liberalism and the democratic ideal together supply the foundation of almost all contemporary political thinking. This essay explores the relation between them. It argues that, despite common parlance, there is an inevitable tension between the two. Futhermore, attempts to resolve this tension by showing that democracy is a good thing in its own right, or that it is the inevitable development of liberal aspirations, or that it is conceptually connected to fundamental liberal ideas, all fail. The conclusion to be drawn is that liberalism requires a pragmatic rather than a principled approach to democratic aspirations.

Graham, Gordon. Politics and Religion. *J Soc Phil*, 24(1), 114-122, Spr 93.

The traditional liberal argument for religious toleration—the neutrality of the state—has frequently been extended to moral questions and has equally frequently been found wanting. This paper argues that, despite such objections, the argument for liberal neutrality with respect to religion is still a convincing one.

Graham, Gordon. Religion, Secularization and Modernity. *Philosophy*, 67(260), 183-197, Ap 92.

This essay re-examines the thesis of secularization and its connections with discussions of modernity. It argues that the thesis of secularization is a variation on

Hegelian conceptions of history and as such can be shown to be erroneous. It further argues that modernity cannot properly be conceived of as non-religious.

Graham Jr, George J. The Necessity of the Tension. *Soc Epistem*, 7(1), 25-34, Ja-Mr 93.

The tension between science and democracy is explored in the context of the tensions within scientific and democratic practices. The focus is on the positions of Alexis de Tocqueville, Machiavelli, Hobbes, Locke, and James Madison in the effort to counter arguments by David Guston. The problem of connecting democracy and science is to maintain the tensions within scientific pluralism and within pluralist democracy (and between the continuing political and scientific processes) to enhance liberal society's commitment to the paradoxes and tensions that refine and redefine its own understandings of democracy, equality, and scientific authority.

Grange, Joseph. Metaphysics, Semiotics, and Common Sense, a review of *Recovery of the Measure: Interpretation and Nature*, by Robert Cummings Neville. *Phil East West*, 43(2), 303-311, Ap 93.

In this article, I maintain that Robert Neville's *Recovery of the Measure* is the first, full scale contemporary metaphysics to defeat the attacks of postmodern deconstructive thought. It is neither logocentric, nor ontotheological nor totalizing. Rather in the tradition of American Naturalism and Process Metaphysics, it sets forth fruitful hypotheses that develop vague but specifiable and important categories for understanding nature and its essential processes. Also it establishes normative metaphysical measures to judge the depth and reach of cultural interpretations concerning the natural world.

Granger, E Herbert. Aristotle and Perceptual Realism. *S J Phil*, 31(Supp), 161-171, 1992.

The paper is the published commentary on Sarah Broadie's paper, 'Aristotle's Perceptual Realism', and both Broadie's paper and the commentary were presented to the 1992 Spindel Conference on ancient theories of psychology. According to Broadie, Aristotle believes that 'secondary qualities' are causally efficacious without their dependence upon primary qualities for their causal efficacy. The commentary noted some passages from the *Parva Naturalia*, wherein primary qualities seem to be the basis for the causal activity of secondary qualities. Also, the commentary concluded that, although Broadie's interpretation respects the causal efficacy of soul, it makes no provision for the immateriality of soul.

Granger, E Herbert. Aristotle and the Concept of Supervenience. *S J Phil*, 31(2), 161-178, Sum 93.

Two reasons are given for thinking that it is wrong to try to cast the relationship between matter and form in terms of supervenience. 1) The notion of supervenience is not clear enough. 2) Even if the notion is limited to what may justly be credited to it, its application to form and matter is inappropriate. For on the standard view of supervenience, the subvenient domain wholly 'Determines' the supervenient domain, and in the effort to view matter and form in terms of supervenience form is alleged to supervene on matter. Yet on Aristotle's view form largely 'determines' the condition of the material domain.

Grant, Robert A D. The Politics of Equilibrium. *Inquiry*, 35(3-4), 423-446, S-D 92.

Review discussion of T Tännsjö's *conservatism for our Time* 1990), which claims that conservatism aims to preserve whatever is 'well established', that including 'actually existing socialism' in the E European communist states of the mid-to-late 1980's. Grant argued that conservatism is a matter of substance rather than form, and that Tännsjö's invocations of sociobiology, economic rationality etc. are misplaced. Legitimacy of any political order rests on consent, rather than on naked force, naked interest, etc.

Grassian, Victor. *Moral Reasoning: Ethical Theory and Some Contemporary Moral Problems (Second Edition)*. Englewood Cliffs, Prentice Hall, 1991.

Grattan-Guinness, I. Russell and Karl Popper: Their Personal Contacts. *Russell*, 12(1), 3-18, Sum 92.

This paper contains transcriptions of the most interesting letters between the two men. These include Russell's testimony on Popper's *The Open Society*, published in full for the first time; a broadcast review in German by Popper of Russell's *History of Western Philosophy*; correspondence at the time over Wittgenstein's approach to Popper with a poker; and Popper's plan (not fulfilled in the end) to dedicate to Russell his *Postscript to the Logic of Scientific Discovery*.

Gray, J Glenn. The Enduring Appeals of Battle in Rethinking Masculinity, May, Larry (ed). Lanham, Rowman & Littlefield, 1992.

Gray, John. From Post-Communism to Civil Society: The Reemergence of History and the Decline of the Western Model. *Soc Phil Pol*, 10(2), 26-50, Sum 93.

Gray, John. *Post-Liberalism: Studies in Political Thought*. New York, Routledge, 1993.

Gray, Tim. Herbert Spencer's Liberalism—from Social Statics to Social Dynamics in Victorian Liberalism, Bellamy, Richard (ed). New York, Routledge, 1990.

Gray, Tim. Spencer, Steiner and Hart on the Equal Liberty Principle. *J Applied Phil*, 10(1), 91-104, 1993.

According to many contemporary observers, including Hillel Steiner, Herbert Hart, John Gray and Isaiah Berlin, the equal liberty principle lies at the heart of liberalism. Yet despite its central place in liberal theory, it has attracted little critical appraisal. This paper seeks to examine the meaning and some of the policy implications of the equal liberty principle, paying particular attention to the elucidations produced by Herbert Spencer, Steiner and Hart—the only systematic analysts of the notion of equal liberty. In part 1, the meaning of the equal liberty principle is discussed, and it is shown to be intrinsically ambivalent. In part 2, where certain policy implications are considered, the conclusion is reached that the equal liberty principle is ambiguous in its policy prescriptions, and requires to be supplemented by some other principle before it can be unequivocally applied.

Gray Hardcastle, Valerie. Evolutionary Epistemology as an Overlapping, Interlevel Theory. *Biol Phil*, 8(2), 173-192, Ap 93.

I examine the branch of evolutionary epistemology which tries to account for the character of cognitive mechanisms in animals and humans by extending the biological theory of evolution to the neurophysiological substrates of cognition. Like Plotkin, I construe this branch as a struggling science, and attempt to characterize the sort of theory one might expect to find this truly interdisciplinary endeavor, an endeavor which encompasses not only evolutionary biology, cognitive psychology, and developmental neuroscience, but also and especially, the computational modeling of "artificial life" programming; I suggest that extending Schaffner's notion of interlevel theories to include both "horizontal" and "vertical" levels of abstraction best fits the theories currently being developed in cognitive science. (edited)

Grayling, A C. Epistemology and Realism. *Proc Aris Soc*, 92, 47-65, 1992.

Grayling, A C. Wittgenstein's Influence: Meaning, Mind and Method in Wittgenstein Centenary Essays, Griffiths, A Phillips (ed). New York, Cambridge Univ Pr, 1991.

The paper has two purposes: to identify Wittgenstein's main contribution to philosophical debate, and to evaluate it. I argue that the private language argument and the rule-following considerations are his main contributions, but that the philosophical psychology that goes with them is deeply unsatisfactory, and that there are strong conclusions implicit in the private-language/rules issues that either Wittgenstein or many of his followers would like.

Grcic, Joseph. Academic Freedom and Employee Rights in Terrorism, Justice and Social Values, Peden, Creighton (ed). Lewiston, Mellen Pr, 1990.

Grean, Stanley. Truth and Faith in Paul Tillich's Thought: The Criteria and Values of Ultimacy. *Ultim Real Mean*, 16(1-2), 149-166, Mr-Je 93.

Paul Tillich's definition of faith implies that anything in theory could be the object of ultimate concern. But can we discriminate between true and false faiths? Are there any criteria of the truth of ultimates? Since symbols are necessary for the expression of faith the question becomes one of the truth of symbols. An attempt is made to describe those criteria that Tillich formulated explicitly as well as drawing out others that are implied. It is concluded that Tillich worked with a model of dynamic faith and a set of values that determined his judgments and controlled what he called "experiential verification" as opposed to experimental or scientific verification.

Greblo, Edoardo. Filosofia della tradizione nascosta, Filosofia e cultura ebraica. *Filosofia*, 43(1), 89-117, Ja-Ap 92.

Greco, John. How to Beat a Sceptic without Begging the Question. *Ratio*, 6(1), 1-15, Je 93.

In this paper I offer a solution to scepticism about the world which neither embraces idealism, nor ends in a stalemate, nor begs the question against the sceptic. In the first part of the paper I explicate the sceptical argument and try to show why it has real force. In the next part of the paper I propose a version of the relevant possibilities approach to scepticism. The central claim of the proposed solution is that a sceptical possibility undermines knowledge only if the possibility is true in some close possible world. But since there is no reason to believe that I am deceived by an evil demon or that I am a brain in a vat in some close possible world, there is no reason to accept an essential premise of the sceptical argument, i.e., that the sceptical scenarios are relevant possibilities. Finally, I argue that the solution proposed does not embrace idealism, end in a stalemate, or beg the question.

Green, Arnold W. *Hobbes and Human Nature*. New Brunswick, Transaction Books, 1993.

Green, Judy. The Problem of Elimination in the Algebra of Logic in Perspectives on the History of Mathematical Logic, Drucker, Thomas (ed). Basel, Birkhauser, 1991.

Green, Karen. Logical Renovations: Restoring Frege's Functions. *Pac Phil Quart*, 73(4), 315-334, D 92.

Through the influence of Russell and Carnap, Frege's sense/reference distinction has been interpreted so that the reference of a predicate is a set and its sense is a property. This ignores the fact that Frege clearly intended the referents of predicate expressions to be functions. This paper explores the implications of reinstating Frege's way of understanding the distinction between the sense and reference of predicate expressions. A slight modification of Frege's doctrine that properties are functions from objects onto truth values is suggested. It is argued that this version of Frege's schema has distinct philosophical advantages.

Green, Michael. Nietzsche on Pity and *Ressentiment*. *Int Stud Phil*, 24(2), 63-70, 1992.

Nietzsche saw the following relationship between pity and *ressentiment*: *Ressentiment* involves a pragmatically inconsistent rejection of values. The rejection is inconsistent because it is motivated solely by the frustration of the values rejected and this frustration presupposes an attachment to the values. Pity is linked to ressentiment because the motivation for aiding the pitied is not a concern for others but an attempt to end the pain of negatively evaluating others. When the frustration of our values concerning others cannot be ended through aid, we attempt to negate these values in *ressentiment*. This is what Nietzsche calls "great pity".

Green, Michael. Perceived Ethical Values of Malaysian Managers. *J Bus Ethics*, 12(4), 323-330, Ap 93.

Green, Michael K. Fairness in Hierarchical and Entrepreneurial Firms. *J Bus Ethics*, 11(11), 877-882, N 92.

Green, Michael K. Kant and Moral Self-Deception. *Kantstudien*, 83(2), 149-169, 1992.

An agent is one who regulates his/her own actions through positive and negative feedback. It is painful for a rational being to set himself a task and then find himself unable to complete it entirely as he/she conceives it. To escape this pain, a person may use self-deception to avoid such negative feedback. When this denial becomes universalized, an agent can no longer function as a self-regulating, cybernetic system, i.e., as an agent who directs his/her own actions. Ten types of moral self-deception are distinguished, and the duty of moral self-knowledge is clarified.

Green, Ronald M. Business Ethics as a Postmodern Phenomenon. *Bus Ethics Quart*, 3(3), 219-225, Jl 93.

This paper contends that work in business ethics participates in two key aspects of the broad philosophical and aesthetic movement known as postmodernism. First, like postmodernists generally, business ethicists reject the "grand narratives" of historical and conceptual justification, especially the narratives embodied in Marxism and Milton Friedman's vision of unfettered capitalism. Second, both in the methods and content of their work, business ethicists share postmodernism's "de-centering" of perspective and discovery of "otherness," "difference" and marginality as valid modes of approach to experience and moral decision.

Green, Ronald M. *Kierkegaard and Kant: The Hidden Debt*. Albany, SUNY Pr, 1992.

This is the first detailed, full-length study of Kierkegaard's reliance on and familiarity with Kant's works. My findings include discovery of an extensive pattern of use of Kantian materials by Kierkegaard, often without acknowledgement and with signs that Kierkegaard sought actively to conceal his debt to Kant. I conclude that Kierkegaard is not only one of Kant's best nineteenth century readers but also the genuine heir to the legacy of Kant's mature ethical and religious thought.

Greenawalt, Kent. *Speech, Crime, and the Uses of Language*. New York, Oxford Univ Pr, 1992.

Greene, Maxine. "Teacher Thinking, Teacher Change, and the 'Capricious Seamstress'"—A Response. *Proc Phil Educ*, 48, 300-302, 1992.

Greenspan, Louis. Fackenheim as Zionist in German Philosophy and Jewish Thought, Greenspan, Louis (ed). Toronto, Univ of Toronto Pr, 1992.

Greenspan, Louis (ed) and Nicholson, Graeme (ed). *German Philosophy and Jewish Thought*. Toronto, Univ of Toronto Pr, 1992.

Greenspan, P S. Free Will and the Genome Project. *Phil Pub Affairs*, 22(1), 31-43, Wint 93.

The Human Genome Project is thought to raise worries about the implications of genetic determination for free will and moral responsibility. I argue that it poses no *special* problems for the standard philosopher's question of free will: freedom versus determinism. Instead I identify a distinct set of worries about the treat posed by science to free will: freedom versus *internal constraint*. I attempt to show how making out behavior as determined by emotional reactive traits would indeed undermine our received picture of moral education and character, the picture that ultimately derives from Aristotle's account of training in virtue.

Greenspan, P S. Guilt as an Identificatory Mechanism. *Pac Phil Quart*, 74(1), 46-59, Mr 93.

I interpret guilt as based on emotional self-punishment on behalf of a victim of one's action in line with Jonathan Edwards' account of "natural conscience." The account is meant to extend a view of guilt found in Rawls and contemporary psychologists as essentially involving concern for others in a way that need not be true of shame and similar alternative reactions to one's own wrongdoing. It allows for overlap insofar as shame and other emotions may be used as forms of self-punishment, but it also explains the special advantages (along with the peculiar pitfalls) of guilt motivation.

Greenwood, John D. Against Eliminative Materialism: From Folk Psychology to Völkerpsychologie. *Phil Psych*, 5(4), 349-367, 1992.

In this paper it is argued that we would not be logically obliged or rationally inclined to reject the ontology of contentful psychological states postulated by folk psychology even if the explanations advanced by folk psychology turned out to be generally inaccurate or inadequate. Moreover, it is argued that eliminativists such as Paul Churchland do not establish that folk psychological explanations are, or are likely to prove, generally inaccurate or inadequate. (edited)

Greenwood, John D. Self-Kowledge: Looking in the Wrong Direction. *Behavior Phil*, 19(2), 35-47, Fall-Wint 91.

In this paper it is argued that none of the empirical studies cited by contemporary philosophical critics of self-knowledge (such as those documented by Nisbett and Ross, 1980) demonstrate the general inaccuracy or unreliability of self-knowledge of psychological states. It is argued that most accounts of self-knowledge are based upon the misguided notion that self-knowledge of psychological states involves a form of theoretical inference to, or theoretically informed perception of, internal states. It is argued that self-knowledge of psychological states is not internally or psychologically directed, but on the contrary, is externally or socially directed.

Greer, W Dwaine. Harry Broudy and Discipline-Based Art Education (DBAE). *J Aes Educ*, 26(4), 49-60, Wint 92.

Broudy's part in the discipline-based revolution taking place in art education is described. His work as a faculty leader in the Getty Institute for Educators on the Visual arts is used to reveal his personality. This personal portrait is interwoven with his ideas that have influenced people from many different areas of education. He is credited with theoretical foundations from philosophy and aesthetic education that have had such wide-ranging impact on the field of art education.

Gregory, Paul. Against Couples in Applied Philosophy, Almond, Brenda (ed). New York, Routledge, 1992.

Gregory, Tullio. Pierre Gassendi nel IV centenario della nascita. *G Crit Filosof Ital*, 71(2), 202-226, My-Ag 92.

Prospettive aperte da Gassendi: legame scetticismo-empiricismo; critica della ragione metafisica (Aristotelico-Scolastica; Cartesiana); tradizione rinascimentale e nuova scienza nella riscoperta dell'atomismo epicureo; i compiti della ragione empirica anche nelle scienze dell'uomo. P Gassendi, Rinascimento, Epicuro, Copernico, Galilei, Descartes, Nuova scienza, Inquisizione.

Greif, A D and Laskowski, M C. An Omitting Types Theorem for Saturated Structures. *Annals Pure Applied Log*, 62(2), 113-118, Jl 93.

Greif, Gary F. Freedom of Choice and the Tyranny of Desire. *J Value Inq*, 27(2), 187-195, Ap 93.

This essay indicates how an individual can exercise some degree of independence over his or her choice of a course of action, given the assumption that everyone must choose what promises to provide the greatest satisfaction to the one choosing. The analysis shows that under some generally specifiable circumstances the choosing individual, by considering realistic implications of carrying out the alternatives for choice, alters the strength of his or her desires to perform the alternatives, thereby influencing which among them will appear the most appealing and be chosen.

Grey, William. A Critique of Deep Ecology in Applied Philosophy, Almond, Brenda (ed). New York, Routledge, 1992.

Our environmental crisis is commonly explained as a product of a set of attitudes and beliefs about the world which have been developed by a post-Cartesian technological society. Deep ecologists claim that the crisis can only be overcome by adopting an alternative non-technological paradigm, such as can be discovered in non-Western cultures. In this paper, I a) reject the claim that a science-based world-view inevitably fosters manipulative and exploitative attitudes to the natural world, b) suggest that non-technological cultures do not necessarily provide exemplary and superior models for relating to the natural world, and c) defend scientific naturalism as a satisfying way of realizing our unity with the natural world.

Grieder, Alfons. Essential Thinking: Reflections on Heidegger's *Beiträge zur Philosophie*. *J Brit Soc Phenomenol*, 23(3), 240-251, O 92.

Griffin, David R. Hartshorne, God, and Relativity Physics. *Process Stud*, 21(2), 85-112, Sum 92.

Griffin, David Ray. Charles Hartshorne in Founders of Constructive Postmodern Philosophy, Griffin, David Ray (& others). Albany, SUNY Pr, 1993.

Griffin, David Ray. Constructive Postmodern Philosophy in Founders of Constructive Postmodern Philosophy, Griffin, David Ray (& others). Albany, SUNY Pr, 1993.

Griffin, David Ray (& others). *Founders of Constructive Postmodern Philosophy*. Albany, SUNY Pr, 1993.

Griffin, James. Commentator on 'Quality of Life Measures in Health Care and Medical Ethics' in The Quality of Life, Nussbaum, Martha C (ed). New York, Oxford Univ Pr, 1993.

This paper, a comment on one by Dan Brock, argues two main points: 1) that the notion of the quality of life fragments into several notions appropriate to different sorts of social decision, and 2) that we need to identify the basic, comprehensive conception of the quality of life (that is, the list of prudential values) both because it is relevant to some social decisions and because it is part of understanding what generates narrower conceptions.

Griffin, Nicholas. The Legacy of Russell's Idealism for His Later Philosophy: The Problem of Substance. *Russell*, 12(2), 186-196, Wint 92-93.

In my book *Russell's Idealist Apprenticeship*, I presented Russell's grounds for rejecting neo-Hegelianism in broadly logical terms as based on the difficulty of adequately treating relations with a neo-Hegelian framework. In this paper, I show that the same story could be told in more traditional metaphysical terms, in which the chief difficulty is one of specifying what counts as a substance, i.e., an item capable of independent existence.

Griffin, Susan. Daring Witness: The Recovery of Female Time in Revisioning Philosophy, Ogilvy, James (ed). Albany, SUNY Pr, 1992.

Griffiths, A Phillips (ed). *A J Ayer Memorial Essays*. New York, Cambridge Univ Pr, 1991.

Griffiths, A Phillips. Religion and Ethics—II in Religion and Philosophy, Warner, Marin (ed). New York, Cambridge Univ Pr, 1992.

Griffiths, A Phillips (ed). *The Impulse to Philosophise*. New York, Cambridge Univ Pr, 1992.

Griffiths, A Phillips (ed). *Wittgenstein Centenary Essays*. New York, Cambridge Univ Pr, 1991.

Griffiths, Paul J. Doctrines and the Virtues of Doctrine: The Problematic of Religious Plurality. *Amer Cath Phil Quart*, 65, 29-44, 1991.

This paper argues that proper attention to the nature and functions of religious doctrine is indispensable if the philosophical dimensions of religious pluralism are to be understood and addressed. Using the distinction between primary and secondary doctrines argued for by William A Christian, Sr, it is suggested, with examples from Buddhism and Christianity, that 'doctrine' is a category that necessarily has inter-religious applicability, and that deploying it properly both allows and requires the development of inter-religious apologetical arguments.

Griffiths, Paul J. Stump, Kretzmann, and Historical Blindness. *Faith Phil*, 10(1), 79-85, Ja 93.

Eleonore Stump and Norman Kretzmann have argued, against Gordon Kaufman, that they are skeptical as to the possibility of constructing an argument that will lend plausibility to the claim that Christianity bears some significant responsibility for any of the major systemic evils of the twentieth century, including the holocaust. This note presents a counter-argument, of a historical kind, which suggests that a significant causal connection does in fact obtain between the classical Christian understanding of Jews and Judaism and the occurrence of the holocaust.

Grim, Patrick. Operators in the Paradox of the Knower. *Synthese*, 94(3), 409-428, Mr 93.

Predicates are term-to-sentence devices, and operators are sentence-to-sentence devices. What Kaplan and Montague's Paradox of the Knower demonstrates is that necessity and other modalities cannot be treated as operators instead. Such is the current wisdom. A number of previous pieces have challenged such a view by showing that a predicative treatment of modalities need *not* raise the Paradox of the Knower. This paper attempts to challenge the current wisdom in another way as well: to show that mere appeal to modal operators in the sense of sentence-to-sentence devices is insufficient to *escape* the Paradox of the Knower. A family of systems is outlined in which closed formulae can encode other formulae and in which the diagonal lemma and Paradox of the Knower are thereby demonstrable for operators in this sense.

Grim, Patrick. Sex and Social Roles in Rethinking Masculinity, May, Larry (ed). Lanham, Rowman & Littlefield, 1992.

The purpose of this piece is to attack familiar chains of reasoning from data on sex differences to the conclusions that social roles should be differentiated along sexual lines. The attack includes (a) some embarrassing questions concerning the data itself, (b) a gain-loss consideration of how to act on the data given our own ignorance, and (c) an argument that standard inferences in this area are neither as direct nor as tight as is commonly assumed. This piece originally appeared in Mary Vetterling-Braggin, ed., *'Femininity', 'Masculinity', and 'Androgyny': A Modern Philosophical Discussion*, Littlefield and Adams, 1982.

Grim, Patrick and Plantinga, Alvin. Truth, Omniscience, and Cantorian Arguments: An Exchange. *Phil Stud*, 71(3), 267-306, S 93.

Grimaldi, Nicolás. Esperanza y desesperanza de la razón en Kant. *Anu Filosof*, 26(1), 79-94, 1993.

The author seeks to establish the strict validity of the composition of the *Critique of Judgement* and how the analysis of the aesthetic judgement prepares for the understanding of the teleological judgement. He shows how the *Critique of Judgement*, especially the statues on art, resolves the opposition between nature and the spirit, the need of liberty, mechanical causality and finality that the first two Critiques had left unsolved.

Grimbergen, Elizabeth. Temporal Consciousness. *Cont Phil*, 15(2), 11-13, Mr-Ap 93.

Grimes, John. Sankara's Siren of Sruti. *J Dharma*, 17(3), 196-202, Jl-S 92.

Grimes, Thomas R. Explanatory Understanding and Contrastive Facts. *Philosophica*, 51(1), 21-38, 1993.

After reviewing pragmatic, inferential, and causal accounts of explanatory understanding, I develop a fourth account based on an analysis of the notion of nomic responsibility. I also give an account of the object of explanation in terms of three types of contrastive facts and show that the conditions nomically responsible for these types of facts are not too numerous to identify.

Grimshaw, Jean. The Idea of a Female Ethic. *Phil East West*, 42(2), 221-238, Ap 92.

Griswold, Charles L. Commentary on Garver's "Making Discourse Ethical". *Proc Boston Colloq Anc Phil*, 5, 97-105, 1989.

Groarke, Louis. Following in the Footsteps of Aristotle: The Chicago School, the Glue-stick, and the Razor. *J Speculative Phil*, 6(3), 190-205, 1992.

The article is a plea against a purported reductionism or monism in contemporary literary criticism. It argues that a principle of explanatory economy (the razor) must be balanced or offset by a principle of explanatory sufficiency (the glue-stick). The critical apparatus of the Chicago School is presented as an alternative both to a reductionist focus on language and an extraneous concern with ideology. Formal elements reveal an aesthetic purpose which must inform and orient our criticism. The article challenges the intentional fallacy and Barthes's notion of "the death of the author" in the light of concrete examples.

Grondin, Jean. The Conclusion of the *Critique of Pure Reason*. *Grad Fac Phil J*, 16(1), 165-178, 1993.

It is well-known that the fundamental problem of Kant's *Critique of Pure Reason* is that of the possibility of metaphysics as science. What is much less known and infinitely less evident, is Kant's answer to this cardinal problem whose urgency he so well signified. This paper argues that this answer has to be found in the decisive and concluding chapter on the "Canon of Pure Reason". It serves, so to speak, as the positive counterpart to the Dialectic, as the arena where one has to find Kant's original solution to the problem of metaphysics that finds itself reoriented towards the practical.

Groothuis, Douglas. Obstinacy in Religious Belief. *Sophia (Australia)*, 32(2), 25-35, Jl 93.

This paper considers the epistemic propriety persistence in Christian belief even in the face of supposed counter-evidence against distinctive Christian truth-claims. I compare C S Lewis's construal of religious belief as the "logic of personal relation" (which makes "obstinacy" in belief legitimate) with Basil Mitchell's treatment of the nature of scientific and other theoretical beliefs. I argue that Mitchell's insights help soften a distinction made by Lewis between religious and scientific beliefs, but that this does not overthrow Lewis's essential insight. I conclude that what I call "tenacity" (as opposed to Lewis's "obstinacy") in Christian belief is epistemically appropriate under certain specified conditions.

Groothuis, Douglas. Questioning Hume's Theory of Meaning. *Kinesis*, 18(2), 27-38, Wint 92.

Hume's empiricism hangs on his understanding of the relationship of impressions to ideas. He argues that ideas are traceable to previous and resembling impressions. This impression-idea thesis is applied by Hume both as a psychological description and as a universal theory of meaning. If any idea—such as self, substance, God—cannot be traced to impressions it must be rejected as meaningless. I argue that Hume's idea—impression thesis, when understood as a theory of meaning, does not fulfill its own truth conditions. It is thus self-defeating and false. I explore several ways Hume might respond to this charge and find them inadequate.

Gropp, Ursula. There is No Sharp Transitivity on *q*6 When *q* is a Type of Morley Rank 2. *J Sym Log*, 57(4), 1198-1212, D 92.

Grosholz, Emily R. Descartes' 'Geometry' and the Classical Tradition in Revolution and Continuity, Barker, Peter (ed). Washington, Cath Univ Amer Pr, 1991.

Grosholz, Emily R. Objects and Structures in the Formal Sciences. *Proc Phil Sci Ass*, 1, 251-260, 1992.

Mathematics and mechanics conceived as a formal science, have their own proper subject matters, their own proper unities, which ground the characteristic way of constituting problems and solutions in each domain, the discoveries that expand and integrate domains with each other, and so in particular allow them, in the end, to be connected in a partial way with empirical fact. Criticizing both empiricist and structuralist accounts of mathematics, I argue that only an account of the formal sciences which attributes to them objects as well as structure, proper semantics as well as syntax, can do justice to their intelligibility, heuristic force and explanatory power.

Grosos, Philippe. La musique et les limites du système. *Arch Phil*, 56(1), 101-121, Ja-Mr 93.

Can any philosophical system give an account of music in its essence? Mastering such a question implies both addressing oneself to philosophy as system and studying how music manifests itself as art. The reflections of German idealism on the subject, which are examined below, maintain that music is always in want of objectivation. Hence, a phenomenology which is open to a non-thematic *pathos* can bring out the inobjectivable character of music, thus making us aware of the limits of the system which is unable for exactly the same reasons to account either for music or for existence.

Gross, David. Marxism and Resistance in Postmodernism/ Jameson/ Critique, Kellner, Douglas M (ed). Washington, Maisonneuve Pr, 1989.

Gross, Lora and Eaves, Lindon. Exploring the Concept of Spirit as a Model for the God-World Relationship in the Age of Genetics. *Zygon*, 27(3), 261-286, S 92.

The cultural impact of genetics focuses the intellectual and moral challenge of science to theology. Many traditional images of God and the God-world relation are inadequate to represent religious ideas in a world whose self-understanding has been transformed by genetics. Such images also lack the power to help in approaching the ethical challenges of this new era. The way conceptions of the God-world relation can be modified in the light of genetic knowledge is explored by examining how far a new conception of Spirit can function alongside contemporary genetic views of human life in nature. The relationship between genetic theories of human behavior and evolution is related to the revised conception of Spirit.

Grossman, Morris. Santayana's Idea of Ultimate Reality and Meaning. *Ultim Real Mean*, 16(1-2), 87-96, Mr-Je 93.

Grosz, Elizabeth. Bodies and Knowledges: Feminism and the Crisis of Reason in Feminist Epistemologies, Alcoff, Linda (ed). New York, Routledge, 1993.

Grote, Jim. René Girard's Theory of Violence: An Introduction. *Res Phil Technol*, 12, 261-270, 1992.

Grove-White, Robin and Michael, Mike. Talking about Talking about Nature: Nurturing Ecological Consciousness. *Environ Ethics*, 15(1), 33-47, Spr 93.

The increasing effort, both lay and academic, to encourage a transition from an "I-It" to an "I-Thou" relation to nature is located within a typology of ways of "knowing nature." This typology provides the context for a particular understanding of human conversation which sees the relation as a cyclical process of "immersion" and "realization" from which a model of the dialectic between "I-It" and "I-Thou" relations to nature can be developed. This model can be used to identify practical measures that can be taken as first steps toward a balance between these relations, both in general and in the context of science-oriented nature conservation organizations such as English Nature in Britain (formerly, the Nature Conservancy Council).

Grover, Stephen. Satisfied Pigs and Dissatisfied Philosophers: Schlesinger on the Problem of Evil. *Phil Invest*, 16(3), 212-230, Jl 93.

I argue that Schlesinger's proposed solution to the problem of evil fails because: 1) the degree of desirability of state of a being is not properly regarded as a trade-off between happiness and potential; 2) degree of desirability of state is not capable of infinite increase; 3) there is no hierarchy of possible beings, but only an ordering of beings by preference; 4) such a hierarchy is anyway morally repulsive. The problem of evil disappears through the recognition of the limits of our concepts of satisfaction and happiness, not through the incoherent claim that satisfaction or happiness is capable of unlimited increase.

Groys, Boris. Russia and the West: The Quest for Russian National Identity. *Stud Soviet Tho*, 43(3), 185-198, My 92.

Grünbaum, Adolf. In Defense of Secular Humanism. *Free Inq*, 12(4), 30-39, Fall 92.

Prompted by recent attacks on secular humanism made in the political arena in the USA, this paper examines the conceptual relations between the theological and moral components of theistic creeds. It argues that theim is morally sterile as such no less than atheism as such is morally barren. Thus, neither doctrine itself imposes any concrete prohibitions on human conduct. The doctrine of divine omnibenevolence is shockingly permissible morally, to the point of sanctioning the justice of the Holocaust. There is no morally asymmetry between theism and atheism.

Grünbaum, Adolf. Pseudo-Creation of the 'Big Bang'. *Free Inq*, 13(1), 14-15, Wint 92-93.

Grünberg, Ludwig. The Phenomenology of Value and the Value of Phenomenology in Analecta Husserliana, XXXI, Tymieniecka, Anna-Teresa (ed). Dordrecht, Kluwer, 1990.

Grunebaum, James O. Friendship, Morality, and Special Obligation. *Amer Phil Quart*, 30(1), 51-61, Ja 93.

Two justifications are discussed of the belief that we owe special duties to our friends or that we ought to treat our friends with special preference. The first examines so-called moral values that constitute friendship, justice and benevolence, which are believed to justify preferential treatment. The second examines the attempts to deduce special treatment from various moral principles. The first strategy fails because either the values that constitute friendship are not moral values or they do not justify the preferential treatment. The second demonstrates that egalitarian moral principles without an assumption of fundamental equality possibly supply a justification.

Grygar, Mojmir. "Le sens optus" and "Unintentionality" (in Czechoslovakian). *Estetika*, 28(4), 204-218, 1991.

Grygar, Mojmir. The Concept of Whole in the Structuralist Theory of Art (in Czechoslovakian). *Estetika*, 29(2), 15-28, 1992.

Mukarovsky distinguished three kinds of totality in the modern theory of art: composition—as a kind of Gestalt quality and semantic context, on the one hand, and structure, on the other. While the former concepts emphasize the totality as a finished whole, i.e., on the mutual relationship of art in the last four decades as well as new methodological impulses of the contemporary semiotics of art open new problems concerning this question. (edited)

Grzegorczyk, Andrzej. Consistent Reism in Kotarbinski: Logic, Semantics and Ontology, Wolenski, Jan (ed). Dordrecht, Kluwer, 1990.

Guariglia, Osvaldo. Universalismo e particolarismo nell'etica contemporanea. *Teoria*, 12(2), 15-40, 1992.

Günther, Dorothea. *Schöpfung und Geist*. Amsterdam, Rodopi, 1993.

Inhalt: Einleitung. 1) Tendere ad esse—tendere ad nihil als Horizont von Zeit. 2) Die Ubiquität der Zeit. 3) Das Problem der Messbarkeit. 4) Zeit im Horizont von Schöpfung und Geist. Resumée und Ausblick. Literaturverzeichnis.

Günther, Klaus. Critical Remarks on Robert Alexy's "Special-Case Thesis". *Ratio Juris*, 6(2), 143-156, Jl 93.

In this paper the author criticizes the way Robert Alexy reconstructs the relationship between legal and practical reasoning. The core of Alexy's argumentation (Alexy 1978) is considered the claim that legal argumentation is a "special case" of general practical discourse. In order to question this claim, the author analyzes three different types of argument: 1) that legal reasoning is needed by general practical discourse itself, 2) that there are similarities between legal argumentation and general practical discourse, 3) that there is a correspondence between certain types of argument in general practical discourse and in legal argumentation.

Guerrero, Luis (ed) and Ockham, Guillermo. *Sobre la Suposicion—Guillermo de Ockham*. Mexico, Univ Panamericana, 1992.

Guest, Gérard. L'Origine de la Responsabilité ou De la "Voix de la Conscience" à la Pensée de la "Promesse". *Heidegger Stud*, 8, 29-62, 1992.

Guetti, James. Idling Rules. *Phil Invest*, 16(3), 179-197, Jl 93.

"Rule-sceptical" philosophical attitudes may be seen to depend upon an inactive apprehension of "idling" concepts. This way of taking rules as interminably interpretable is incommensurate with Wittgenstein's admonition that there is another (more active) way of "grasping a rule which is not an interpretation." But what is most important here is to understand the deceptive vitality of such idle apprehensions, which is not that of working language but which is, apparently, so easily mistaken for it. In this respect the isolated and static "rule" is analogous—in Wittgenstein's treatment in Part 2 of the *Investigations*—to an "aspected image."

Guignon, Charles B. Authenticity, Morl Values, and Psychotherapy in The Cambridge Companion to Heidegger, Guignon, Charles B (ed). New York, Cambridge Univ Pr, 1993.

Psychotherapy theorists who appropriate the early Heidegger's thought tend to treat it as an "existentialist" glorification of authentic individuality. This interpretation conceals the emphasis Heidegger places on our "thrownness" within, and indebtedness to, a shared, value-filled heritage. In this paper, I examine some of the assumptions common to most mainstream psychotherapy theories (including "existentialist" schools). I try to show that these theories usually presuppose an objectified conception of humans, and that they try to avoid taking a substantive position on moral questions. I then lay out Heidegger's view of authentic existence as a life with a specific sort of narrative structure that is embedded in a meaningful social context. Given this picture of the good life, it becomes clear that therapeutic dialogue must have an irreducible evaluative dimension.

Guignon, Charles B. History and Commitment in the Early Heidegger in Heidegger: A Critical Reader, Dreyfus, Hubert L (ed). Cambridge, Blackwell, 1992.

Guignon, Charles B. Pragmatism or Hermeneutics? Epistemology after Foundationalism in The Interpretive Turn, Hiley, David R (ed). Ithaca, Cornell Univ Pr, 1991.

Guignon, Charles B (ed). *The Cambridge Companion to Heidegger*. New York, Cambridge Univ Pr, 1993.

A collection of essays by top scholars, this volume discusses Heidegger's work, its historical roots, and its impact for various disciplines. Three essays deal with Heidegger's life's work as a whole. Four essay deal with *Being and Time*, and others explore Heidegger's relevance for psychotherapy, literary interpretation, ecology, theology, and politics. Essays by Charles Taylor and Richard Rorty give different appraisals of the significance of Heidegger's work. There are several discussions of Heidegger's involvement with the Nazis and of his earliest writings before *Being and Time*. The editor's introduction traces the path from Heidegger's earlier thought to the later *Beiträge zur Philosophie*.

Guillaume, E. La Théorie de la Relativité et le Tempes universel. *Filosofia*, 43(1), 119-161, Ja-Ap 92.

Guillén Vera, Tomás. La polémica sobre lo innato en el libro I de los 'Nuevos Ensayos'. *Theoria (Spain)*, 6(14-15), 67-81, O 91.

Leibniz's *Noveaux Essays* are the exercise of a system's dialogue. It is in the first book, when he speaks about innate ideas, where its bases are set, and where Leibniz propounds the basic ideas of his controvery against Locke. Leibniz is convinced that his system is more perfect than Locke's one and that if Locke solved his contradictions he would approach his own system. The hidden aim of the *Nouveaux Essays* reducation is placed beyond a system dialogue, and it can be seen in it the existence of a vast political dialogue whose purpose is the European entity.

Guiquan, Zhang. On the Interpretation Circle of Philosophy. *Chin Stud Phil*, 24(2), 70-95, Wint 92-93.

Gujia, Chen. On the Three Major Characteristics of Ethical Thought in Traditional China. *Chin Stud Phil*, 24(2), 3-38, Wint 92-93.

Gunderson, Keith (ed) and Anderson, C Anthony (ed) and Meehl, Paul. *Selected Philosophical and Methodological Papers*. Minneapolis, Univ of Minn Pr, 1991.

This is a collection of articles by a psychologist-philosopher on social science methodology and philosophy of mind. The widely varied topics include theory-testing, open concepts, determinism, emergence, psychoanalytic inference, insanity defense, civil commitment, telepathy, teleology in psychopathology, and the mind-body identity theory.

Gunderson, Martin. Birth Control as a Condition of Probation or Parole in Biomedical Ethics Reviews 1992, Humber, James M (ed). Clifton, Humana Pr, 1993.

I argue that court ordered birth control as a condition of parole or probation is justifiable provided that the following conditions are met. 1) The use of birth control is necessary to prevent harm to another child or to assure the success of probation or parole. 2) The criminal agrees to the use of birth control as a condition of probation or parole after receiving adequate information. 3) The criminal is not given a more severe sentence than he or she would have otherwise received in order to coerce the criminal to use birth control as a condition of avoiding the sentence through probation. 4) The use of birth control is not discriminatory on the basis of race, ethnic status, or gender. 5) The use of birth control is *not* motivated in part by considerations of eugenics.

Gunderson, Martin and Mayo, David J. Altruism and Physician Assisted Death. *J Med Phil*, 18(3), 281-296, Je 93.

We assume that a statute permitting physician assisted death has been passed. We note that the rationale for the passage of such a statute would be respect for individual autonomy, the avoidance of suffering and the possibility of death with dignity. We deal with two moral issues that will arise once such a law is passed. First, we argue that the rationale for passing an assistance in dying law in the first place provides a justification for assisting patients to die who are motivated by altruistic reasons as well as patients who are motivated by reasons of self-interest. Second, we argue that the reasons for passing a physician assisted death law in the first place justify extending the law to cover some non-terminal patients as well as terminal patients.

Gunderson, Martin and Mayo, David J. Physician Assisted Death and Hard Choices. *J Med Phil*, 18(3), 329-341, Je 93.

We argue that after the passage of a physician assisted death law some inequities in the health care system which prevent people from getting the medical care they need will become reasons for choosing assisted death. This raises the issue of whether there is compelling moral reason to change those inequities after the passage of an assisted death law. We argue that the passage of an assisted death law will not create additional moral reasons for eliminating inequities *simply* because they become motives for someone to opt for assisted death. We also argue that it is not feasible to eliminate these reasons for opting for assisted death by granting a right to health care because of an intractable scarcity of medical resources.

Gunn, Alastair S. Engineering Ethics and Hazardous Waste Management: Why Should We Care About Future Generations?. *Res Phil Technol*, 12, 135-146, 1992.

Gunn, J A W. Opinion in Eighteenth-Century Thought: What Did the Concept Purport to Explain?. *Utilitas*, 5(1), 17-33, My 93.

Modern studies of public opinion assume both that one's interests lie at the basis of one's opinions and that public opinion can best be understood as an aggregate of individual opinions. These assumptions are sometimes used as well to make sense of what earlier political thinkers thought about interests, opinions and public opinion. Consultation of documents from the eighteenth century and earlier makes clear that the reading back of a modern view is unwarranted. For thinkers who wrote prior to twentieth-century empirical studies, interests belonged to individuals. However, opinions that were politically relevant were those of the community. Detailed treatment of arguments about the basis of the French nobility illustrates the point of this distinction.

Gunnell, John G. Relativism: The Return of the Repressed. *Polit Theory*, 21(4), 563-584, N 93.

The focus on the problem of relativism in philosophy and political theory is a displacement of the practical issue of the relationship between theory and practice or, more generally, the relationship between first and second-order discourses. Relativism is neither a genuine philosophical issue nor a practical dilemma.

Gunter, P A Y. Bergson and Sartre: The Rise of French Existentialism in The Crisis in Modernism, Burwick, Frederick (ed). New York, Cambridge Univ Pr, 1992.

Sartre's and Bergson's philosophies have in common five basic assumptions: 1) the reality and freedom of the individual; 2) the reality of becoming; 3) a dualistic theory of freedom; 4) a critique of scientific intelligence; 5) the appeal to "intuition". They differ (and profoundly) over 6) the concept of negation. Bergson's influence on Sartre is greater than has generally been believed.

Gunter, Pete A Y. Henri Bergson in Founders of Constructive Postmodern Philosophy, Griffin, David Ray (& others). Albany, SUNY Pr, 1993.

The author proposes Bergson's philosophy as an example of constructive post-modernism, stressing Bergson's affiliations with feminism, environmentalism, pacifism, and the search for the "open society". Bergson's philosophy opens the way for new paradigms in the natural sciences, and new, badly needed social and religious values.

Gunton, Colin. Universal and Particular in Atonement Theology. *Relig Stud*, 28(4), 453-466, D 92.

Gupta, Amitabha and Shashidharan, Suryaprabha. Representation *versus* Mirroring: A Cognitivist Response to Rorty. *J Indian Counc Phil Res*, 9(1), 127-138, S-D 91.

Gupta, Anil and Belnap, Nuel. *The Revision Theory of Truth*. Cambridge, MIT Pr, 1993.

This book explains how our concept of truth works in both ordinary and pathological contexts (e.g., contexts generating the Liar Paradox). Its central claim is that truth is a circular concept. In support of this claim the book provides a widely applicable general theory ("the revision theory") of definitions. The theory makes sense of arbitrary systems of mutually interdependent concepts of which circular concepts, such as truth, are but a special case. Under the revision theory, when one sees truth as circular, both ordinary and pathological features of truth fall into a simple understandable pattern.

Gupta, Chhanda. Putnam's Resolution of the Popper-Kuhn Controversy. *Phil Quart*, 43(172), 319-334, Jl 93.

Gupta, Chhanda. Rationality and Culture: Behavior within the Family as a Case Study. *Phil East West*, 42(3), 441-454, Jl 92.

Gupta, R K. Social Atmosphere. *Indian Phil Quart*, 20(3), 309-317, Jl 93.

The primary aim of the paper is to determine the nature of social atmosphere. According to it, it consists in the general feel, general emotive experience, which it offers of itself, as being, for example, relaxed or tense, friendly or hostile, warm or cool, exhilarating or depressing, encouraging or discouraging, spiritual or physical, academic or non-academic, and so on. This general feel or emotive experience which a social setting offers of itself, it offers through the varied expressions of the people who are there in that setting, for example their facial expressions, their words, their actions and even physical objects which they may appropriately use as expressing themselves, like perhaps a display of black to mark a mournful state.

Gurtler, Gary M. Plotinus and the Platonic *Parmenides*. *Int Phil Quart*, 32(4), 443-457, D 92.

Guston, David. Resolving the Tension in Graham and Laird. *Soc Epistem*, 7(1), 47-60, Ja-Mr 93.

The paper responds George Graham's and Frank Laird's comments on "The essential tension in science and democracy." Graham dismisses the tension because science is procedural, as is democracy, and is but one sphere in a pluralistic democracy. I respond that science is not just another pluralist sphere because it claims to pursue the truth, and thus authority over other spheres. Laird acknowledges the tension, but argues that "participatory analysis" can educate citizens in evaluating scientific claims and resolve it. I reply that Laird's proposal will ameliorate but not resolve the tension because choices between scientific and democratic modes will remain.

Guston, David. The Essential Tension in Science and Democracy. *Soc Epistem*, 7(1), 3-23, Ja-Mr 93.

In *Democracy in America*,, Tocqueville claims that democracies will not prevent scientific achievement, but they will bend science toward practical applications. The paper argues that Tocqueville was incorrect. There are three possible tensions between science and democracy—populist, plutocratic, and exclusionary. The exclusionary tension is essential because it is grounded in the exclusionary rationality common to science and liberal democracy. The professionalization of science and the "republic of science" embody this tension, which underlies many current problems in the governance of science. The essential tension means that choices will always need to be made between democratic and scientific modes of choice.

Gutas, Dimitri (ed) and Fortenbaugh, W W (ed). *Theophrastus*. New Brunswick, Transaction Books, 1992.

The contents includes two new critical editions: Theophrastus' *Meteorology* and his work *On Fish*. Both editions are accompanied by an English translation and commentary. Also included in the volume are discussions of Theophrastus' work *On Sense Perception*, his *Physical Doctrines* and the Spurious treatise *On Signs*. Finally there are articles on Theophrastus' notion of place, of intellect and of animal intelligence.

Gutiérrez, J M. On the Gearing Adjustment: An Axiomatic Approach. *Theor Decis*, 33(3), 207-221, N 92.

The gearing adjustment is approached axiomatically. The gearing adjustment defines a capital maintainence concept; the revaluation criteria compatible with it are investigated. It is proved that one and only one kind of revaluation criterion is compatible with the gearing adjustment.

Gutmann, Amy. The Challenge of Multiculturalism in Political Ethics. *Phil Pub Affairs*, 22(3), 171-206, Sum 93.

Guyer, Paul. Feeling and Freedom: Kant on Aesthetics and Morality. *J Aes Art Crit*, 48(2), 137-146, Spr 90.

Guyer, Paul. *Kant and the Experience of Freedom: Essays on Aesthetics and Morality*. New York, Cambridge Univ Pr, 1993.

This collection of essays, six previously published and four new, explores various aspects of the links between Kantian aesthetics and moral philosophy. The first part of the volume places Kant's treatment of disinterestedness and the freedom of the imagination in its historical context. The second part explores specific topics such as the distinction between the beautiful and sublime, genius, and duty and inclination.

Guyer, Paul (ed). *The Cambridge Companion to Kant*. New York, Cambridge Univ Pr, 1992.

This volume surveys the whole of Kant's philosophy in essays by F C Beiser, Charles Parsons, J Michael Young, Paul Guyer, Michael Friedman, Gary Hatfield, Thomas E Wartenberg, Karl Ameriks, Onora O'Neill, J B Schneewind, Wolfgang Kersting, Eva Schaper, Allen W Wood, and George Di Giovanni. It includes an introduction and extensive bibliography by the editor.

Guyer, Paul. The Transcendental Deduction of the Categories in The Cambridge Companion to Kant, Guyer, Paul (ed). New York, Cambridge Univ Pr, 1992.

This essay analyzes the various objectives and proof-strategies of Kant's several versions of the transcendental deduction in a chronological as well as analytical order. It is intended to offer a more perspicuous exposition of the approach originally developed in the author's *Kant and the Claims of Knowledge* (1987).

Guyer, Paul. Thomson's Problems with Kant: A Comment on Kant's Problems with Ugliness. *J Aes Art Crit*, 50(4), 317-319, Fall 92.

Guyer, Paul. Thought and Being in The Cambridge Companion to Hegel, Beiser, Frederick (ed). New York, Cambridge Univ Pr, 1993.

Haack, Susan. Double-Aspect Foundherentism: A New Theory of Empirical Justification. *Phil Phenomenol Res*, 53(1), 113-128, Mr 93.

This paper develops a theory of justification which, like foundationalism and unlike coherentism, allows the relevance of experience to the justification of empirical beliefs, and, like coherentism and unlike foundationalism, requires neither beliefs justified exclusively by experience, nor exclusively one-directional relations of evidential support. To explicate the role of experience, the theory combines causal and evaluative elements. The causal element makes the theory consonant with a very modest style of epistemological naturalism.

Haack, Susan. Peirce and Logicism: Notes Towards an Exposition. *Trans Peirce Soc*, 29(1), 33-56, Wint 93.

Peirce held that mathematics is reducible to logic - even giving, as early as 1867, a definition of cardinal number which anticipated *Principia Mathematica*; and yet he staunchly denied another logicist thesis, that the epistemic foundations of mathematics lie in logic. Part of the explanation why, unlike Frege or Russell, Peirce did not take it for granted that the first of these claims implies the second, is an ambiguity in his use of "logic," between "theory of reasoning" ("logic") and "mathematical formalization of necessary reasoning" ("*logic*"); mathematics is reducible to *logic*, but not epistemically dependent on logic.

Haack, Susan. Philosophy/Philosophy, an Untenable Dualism. *Trans Peirce Soc*, 29(3), 411-426, Sum 93.

Rorty thoroughly misunderstands Peirce, who is unclassifiable in terms of Rorty's false dichotomy of realist, foundationalist philosopher versus "pragmatist" philosopher. In particular: Peirce does not make an idol of science, but neither does he see philosophy as a genre of literature; he does not construe truth as faithful mirroring, but neither does he think that truth is not the kind of thing one should expect to have an interesting theory about; he does not appeal to transcendental principles, but neither does he think that epistemic standards are merely conversational conventions.

Haack, Susan. The Two Faces of Quine's Naturalism. *Synthese*, 94(3), 335-356, Mr 93.

Quine's 'naturalized epistemology' is ambivalent between a modest naturalism according to which epistemology is an a posteriori discipline, an integral part of the web of empirical belief, and a scientistic naturalism according to which epistemology is to be conducted wholly within the natural sciences. This ambivalence is encouraged by Quine's ambiguous use of "science", to mean sometimes, broadly, 'our presumed empirical knowledge' and sometimes, narrowly, 'the natural sciences'. Quine's modest naturalism is reformist, tackling the traditional epistemological problems in a novel way; his scientistic naturalism is revolutionary, requiring restriction and reconceptualization of epistemological problems. In particular, his scientistic naturalism trivializes the question of the epistemic standing of the natural sciences, whereas modest naturalism takes it seriously, and can offer a plausible answer.

Haaparanta, Leila. The Analogy Theory of Thinking. *Dialectica*, 46(2), 169-183, 1992.

The paper deals with a doctrine called the analogy theory of thinking. Its contemporary proponents have been Wilfried Sellars and Peter Geach. The paper is an attempt to give an exact formulation for one answer to the question concerning the relation of thought and speech. That answer is a reduction of Sellar's theory. A semiformal explication of the view is suggested by means of the classical analogy theory and Bochenski's treatment of that theory. It is argued that even if the analogy theory of thinking is subject to serious criticism, it offers us tools for considering some old philosophical problems in a new way.

Haar, Michel. Attunement and Thinking in Heidegger: A Critical Reader, Dreyfus, Hubert L (ed). Cambridge, Blackwell, 1992.

Haar, Michel. The Enigma of Everydayness in Reading Heidegger: Commemorations, Sallis, John (ed). Bloomington, Indiana Univ Pr, 1992.

The phenomenon of everydayness is enigmatic because it includes a first destitution which is prior to being-one's-self. The question is: How can I find myself *against* everydayness? It seems Heidegger repeats platonic schism between the true world and doxa, transposed in the opposition between the hero and the ordinary man.

Haar, Michel and McNeill, Will (trans). The Play of Nietzsche in Derrida in Derrida: A Critical Reader, Wood, David (ed). Cambridge, Blackwell, 1992.

Haarscher, Guy. Law, Reason and Ethics in the Philosophy of Human Rights in Ethical Dimensions of Legal Theory, Sadurski, Wojciech (ed). Amsterdam, Rodopi, 1991.

Haase, Wolfgang. Commentary on Reesor's "The Stoic Wise Man". *Proc Boston Colloq Anc Phil*, 5, 124-134, 1989.

These remarks on Margaret Reesor's paper are intended to contribute to the clarification of certain features of the image of the Stoic sage and to place this image in its entirety in a particular perspective. The features treated are the role of paradox in the Stoic concept of the sage, the kind and extend of his knowledge and abilities outside the field of ethical choice, and the absoluteness of his virtue. Finally, it is contended that the figure of the sage occupies a harmonious, noncontradictory and even necessary place in the Stoic system.

Haber, Honi. Richard Rorty's Failed Politics. *Soc Epistem*, 7(1), 61-74, Ja-Mr 93.

In his book *Contingency, Irony, and Solidarity* Richard Rorty claims to have reconciled liberalism and radical pluralism. Through a close examination of this text I argue that this reconciliation is attempted by means of cultural imperialism and that this results in an elitist and insidious political theory. Central to my critique is his public/private distinction, his disempowering of those not belonging to the ironist elite, and his failure to apply his fundamental postmodern insights to his own political theory. I conclude by suggesting that a Foucauldian understanding of power would be helpful in giving voice to Rorty's oppressive silencings.

Haber, Honi. Thoughts Upon Reading Martin's Comments. *Soc Epistem*, 7(1), 83-84, Ja-Mr 93.

Habermas, Jürgen. A Generation Apart from Adorno (An Interview). *Phil Soc Crit*, 18(2), 119-124, 1992.

Habermas, Jürgen. Comments on Searle: 'Meaning, Communication, and Representation' in John Searle and His Critics, LePore, Ernest (ed). Cambridge, Blackwell, 1991.

Habermas, Jürgen. Heidegger—The Work and the World-View (in Czechoslovakian). *Filozof Cas*, 40(3), 355-381, 1992.

A contribution to the renewed German and French discussion about the important German philosopher of this century, Martin Heidegger, and about his relation to national socialism. To deal with the ideological and personal partake of the thinker in the activity of NSDAP, two points of view deserve our attention. First, Heidegger's attitude towards his own past after 1945 is typical for the spiritual position that continually shaped the history of the Federal Republic of Germany up to the 60's. Second, each tradition, which made people blind to the nazi regime, is to be critically adopted.

Habermas, Jürgen. Work and *Weltanschauung* in Heidegger: A Critical Reader, Dreyfus, Hubert L (ed). Cambridge, Blackwell, 1992.

This article proves internal connections between the development of Heidegger's work and Heidegger's politics between 1933 and 1945.

Habib, M A R. "Bergson Resartus" and T S Eliot's Manuscript. *J Hist Ideas*, 54(2), 255-276, Ap 93.

This paper examines Eliot's unpublished manuscript entitled "Draft of a Paper on Bergson." This shows that Eliot never espoused Bergson's central ideas: durée, the primacy of time over space, the absolute authenticity of immediate experience, and an essential difference between consciousness and the external world. Eliot accepts certain Bergsonian ideas when they overlap with those of Bradley. This is because Eliot sees Bergson work as part of a Romantic tradition whereas he regards Bradley as continuing a classical Greek tradition. The paper finally pursues the possible influence of Bergson on Eliot's literary work.

Hack, Haroldo G (& others). Una semántica computacional del idioma español usando las teorías de R Montague. *Theoria (Spain)*, 5(12-13), 171-191, N 90.

Montague's theory of language is used to present a formal system that can be implemented directly using *Prolog* to obtain a semantic interpreter capable of analysing an important fragment of the Spanish language.

Hacker, P M S. Developmental Hypotheses and Perspicuous Representations: Wittgenstein on Frazer's *Golden Bough*. *Iyyun*, 41, 277-299, Jl 92.

Hacker, P M S. Malcolm and Searle on 'Intentional Mental States'. *Phil Invest*, 15(3), 245-275, Jl 92.

This essay aims to rudicate Norman Malcom's remarks that believing is not a mental state and that Searle's theory of intentionality is a re-run of Wittgenstein's account of internationality in the *Tractatus*. The concept of a mental state is examined in detail. Searle's conceptions of *representational content, fitting, and direction of fit* are anatomised and found wanting. They collapse in the face of Wittgenstein's version of his own early theory. Searle's conception of the neural realization of intentional states is likewise found to be flawed.

Hacker, P M S. The Agreement of Thought and Reality in Wittgenstein's Intentions, Canfield, J V (ed). Hamden, Garland, 1993.

Hacking, Ian. On Kripke's and Goodman's Uses of 'Grue'. *Philosophy*, 68(265), 269-295, Jl 93.

Hacking, Ian. Working in a New World: The Taxonomic Solution in World Changes, Horwich, Paul (ed). Cambridge, MIT Pr, 1993.

Hadden, Richard W. Artful Fiction and Adequate Discourse: *Irony and Social Theories of Science*. *Phil Soc Sci*, 22(4), 421-439, D 92.

This essay argues that recent reflexively oriented critiques of social studies of science, especially those of Steve Woolgar, present a problematic version of instrumental irony. Woolgar's own view is presented as instrumental and his antipathy to theorizing is opposed by arguing for the need to adopt a privileged position in order to carry out his recommended refusal objectivist discourse.

Haddox, John H. Latin American Personalist: Antonio Caso. *Personalist Forum*, 8/1(Supp), 109-118, Spr 92.

The personalist position of Mexican philosopher and educator Antonio Caso (1883-1946) is presented with an analysis of his distinction between life as economic (self-centered and egoistic) and life as ethical (existence as charity). Concerning the latter, Caso affirms our ability to surpass our selfish drives to take, to hate, and to kill with tendencies to give, to love, and to heal. He argues that in fact such ethical activities are the fulfillment of life itself. Only a person can perform such acts, and ones humanity is progressively perfected in so acting.

Hadley, Robert F. Connectionism, Explicit Rules, and Symbolic Manipulation. *Mind Mach*, 3(2), 183-200, My 93.

At present, the prevailing Connectionist methodology for *representing rules* is to *implicitly* embody rules in "neurally-wired" networks. That is, the methodology adopts the stance that rules must either be hard-wired or "trained into" neural structures, rather than represented via explicit symbolic structures. However, arguments are presented herein that humans *sometimes* follow rules which are *very rapidly* assigned *explicit* internal representations, and that humans possess *general* mechanisms capable of interpreting and following such rules. It is further argued that the existence of general-purpose rule following mechanisms strongly indicates that explicit rule following is not an *isolated* phenomenon, but may well be a common and important aspect of cognition. The relationship of the foregoing conclusions to Smolensky's view of explicit rule following is also explored.

Hadot, Ilsetraut. Aristote dans l'enseignement philosophique néoplatonicien: Les préfaces des commentaires sur les *Catégories*. *Rev Theol Phil*, 124(4), 407-426, 1992.

Cet article représente une contribution de plus á ma critique générale des thèses de Praechter selon lesquelles l'école néoplatonicienne dite *d'Alexandrie* s e distinguerait, non seulement par le lieu de son enseignement, de celle dite *d'Athènes*, mais encore et surtout par ses doctrines philosophiques et par son attitude envers l'oeuvre d'Aristote. La comparison entre elles des préfaces des cinq commentaires néoplatoniciens des Catégories d'Aristote, dont l'un, celui de Simplicius, appartiendrait, selon Praechter, à l'ècole d'Alexandrie, fait apparaître la concordance fondamentale de la philosophie néoplatonicienne qui était enseignée à Athènes avec celle qui était enseignée à Alexandrie: toutes deux interprètent la philosophie d'Aristote dans la même perspective néoplatonicienne et la même volonté d'harmoniser Platon et Aristote.

Haeffner, Gerd. Christsein im Denken: Zu Heideggers Kritik der 'christlichen Philosophie'. *Theol Phil*, 68(1), 1-24, 1993.

In Heidegger's eyes, the very concept of a 'Christian philosophy' suffers from an inner contradiction which stems above all from the different existential structure of faiths and of questioning. It is shown, that Heidegger arrives at this thesis by reasons which are not only philosophical, but also theological (and biographical). These reasons are critically discussed. Finally, a possibility is suggested to conceive of a way of philosophy which, despite its essential autonomy, can be called Christian.

Haeffner, Gerd. Leiden unter der Herrschaft der Zeit: Zu Michael Theunissens "Negativer Theologie der Zeit". *Theol Phil*, 67(4), 570-577, 1992.

The essential context of Theunissens's book is presented succinctly: For Theunissens, time is a powerful reality which exercises an alienating domination on us. Happiness is to be had only if we participate in some sort of eternity. Depressive people can be understood as people being haunted by time. The fundamental assumptions of Theunissens are criticized: 1) that philosophical theory can suppose the inner unity of something called 'time'; 2) that possible sufferings as regards time can be derived from being-in-time as such.

Haeger, Jack H. Samuel Taylor Coleridge and the Romantic Background to Bergson in The Crisis in Modernism, Burwick, Frederick (ed). New York, Cambridge Univ Pr, 1992.

Hahn, Lewis E (ed). *The Philosophy of A J Ayer*. Peru, Open Court, 1992.

This is volume 21 of the Library Philosophers with the Library's standard format of Intellectual Autobiography, Critical Essays and Replies, and Bibliography of Ayer's publications. In it Sir Alfred responds to 22 of his ablest critics and engages them in lively interchange. Unfortunately, he passed away before seeing three other papers. The critics represent diverse perspectives and come from nine different countries including Belgium, Bulgaria, Canada, People's Republic of China, Italy, Norway, Peru, United Kingdom, and USA. His Autobiography traces his development and comments on contemporary philosophy. Its addendum provides his reflections on his remarkable brush with death.

Haines, Byron L. A Critique of Harman's Empiricistic Relativism. *J Phil Res*, 18, 97-107, 1993.

In a paper, "Is there a Single True Morality," Gilbert Harman presents an argument for moral relativism that some have found persuasive. Relativism is, Harman argues, the view that is most compatible with a scientific view of the world. The present paper argues that Harman's argument is unsound since it contains at least one false premise. Further, there are considerations to which Harman himself draws attention which count against moral relativism and in favor of moral absolutism, i.e., the view that actions have a moral character that is independent of how individuals or groups think or feel about them.

Haines, Victor. Refining Not Defining Art Historically. *J Aes Art Crit*, 48(3), 237-238, Sum 90.

Recursive definitions of art, which harness the identification of artworks through historical narrative to the relatively complete ways of regard for which artworks in the past were intended, fail because the intentionality of present activity may inadvertently hook into a total way of regard correctly accorded artworks hidden in the past, thus implausibly rendering that activity an artwork with no end to the sort of activities that might be so rendered.

Haines, Victor Yelverton. No Ethics, No Text. *J Aes Art Crit*, 47(1), 35-42, Wint 89.

Hajdin, Mane. External Reasons and the Foundations of Morality: Mother Teresa versus Thrasymachus. *J Value Inq*, 26(3), 433-441, Jl 92.

This essay shows that believing that there are external reasons for action is compatible with taking seriously those who, in the manner of Thrasymachus, refuse to assent to any claim that they have reasons to do things that are not going to contribute to the satisfaction of their desires. It thus eliminates the main source of motivation for the view that there are no external reasons. The way of interpreting 'Thrasymachus' challenge' that is offered in this essay makes it possible to regard relationships between morality and prudence as symmetrical.

Hájek, Petr and Svejdar, Vitezslav. A Note on the Normal Form of Closed Formulas of Interpretability Logic. *Stud Log*, 50(1), 25-28, Mr 91.

Haji, Ishtiyaque. A Riddle Regarding Omissions. *Can J Phil*, 22(4), 485-502, D 92.

I motivate a riddle regarding omissions: some cases appear to show that a person is not morally responsible for failing to bring about something in virtue of the fact that the person could not bring about that thing. Other cases seemingly show that a person *is* responsible for failing to bring about something even though the person could not bring about that thing. What explains the asymmetry in responsibility attributions in these cases involving omissions? I consider some answers to this riddle and explain why they are inadequate. I then sketch my own answer.

Haji, Ishtiyaque. Alternative Possibilities, Moral Obligation, and Moral Responsibility. *Phil Papers*, 22(1), 41-50, Ap 93.

I first challenge David Widerker's argument that rejection of the principle of alternative possibilities requires rejection of the 'ought' implies 'can' principle, by challenging Widerker's thesis that a person is blameworthy for performing an action only if she has an objective moral obligation not to perform that action. I replace this thesis with the alternative that an agent is blameworthy for performing an action only if she has a subjective moral obligation not to perform that action. Finally, I suggest that there may well be a requirement of alternative possibilities for moral responsibility for the class of wrong actions.

Haji, Ishtiyaque. Evolution, Altruism, and the Prisoner's Dilemma. *Biol Phil*, 7(2), 161-175, Ap 92.

I first argue against Peter Singer's exciting thesis that the Prisoner's Dilemma explains why there could be an evolutionary advantage in making reciprocal exchanges that are ultimately motivated by genuine altruism over making such exchanges on the basis of enlightened long-term self-interest. I then show that an alternative to Singer's thesis—one that is also meant to corroborate the view that natural selection favors genuine altruism, recently defended by Gregory Kavka, fails as well. Finally, I show that even granting Singer's and Kavka's claim about the selective advantage of altruism proper, it is doubtful whether that type of claim can be used in a particular sort of sociobiological argument against psychological egoism.

Haksar, Vinit. *Indivisible Selves and Moral Practice*. Edinburgh, Edinburgh Univ Pr, 1991.

Haldane, John. An Embarrassing Question about Reproduction. *Phil Psych*, 5(4), 427-431, 1992.

Standard objections to dualism focus on problems of individuation: what, in the absence of matter, serves to diversify immaterial items? and interaction: how can material and immaterial elements causally affect one another? Given certain ways of conceiving mental phenomena and causation, it is not obvious that one cannot reply to these objections. However, a different kind of difficulty comes into view when one considers the question of the origin of the mental. Here attention is directed upon the case of intentionality. It might seem that the transition between non-intentional and intentional phenomena could be dealt with by adopting a version of Dennett's discharging strategy, but this is argued against. Several responses to the origination problem are identified, including a creationist one.

Haldane, John. Aquinas on the Active Intellect. *Philosophy*, 67(260), 199-210, Ap 92.

It is generally assumed by both analytical philosophers and neo-scholastics that Aquinas takes themes and doctrines from Aristotle and works with them as part of his own theological projects. This is partly true but it omits the important part that in Aquinas's treatment Aristotelian ideas are often considerably changed. The present paper considers this in relation to Aquinas's Cognitive Psychology as this draws upon the Aristotelian distinction between active and passive intellects.

Haldane, John. De Consolatione Philosophiae. *Philosophy*, 32(Supp), 31-45, 1992.

This paper considers two questions: Can any interesting sense be made of the claim that philosophy might be a source of comfort or consolation? And is there reason to believe this claim to be true? Beginning with an examination of Boethius text it proceeds to the idea that a form of consolation might be available from the recognition that in the exercise of this capacity the human mind realizes itself as a power of understanding. These ideas are then related to certain aesthetic and mystical experiences.

Haldane, John. De Consolatione Philosophiae in Philosophy, Religion and the Spiritual Life, McGhee, Michael (ed). New York, Cambridge Univ Pr, 1992.

This essay explores the question of whether any sense can be made of the idea inspiring Boethius's classic that the practice of philosophy may be a source of consolation. Setting aside the notion of mere distraction the arguments of De Consolatione are considered and are shown to rest on certain problematic ontological assumptions. It is suggested that on the basis of a moderate realism of the sort associated with Aristotle it is possible to make sense of the idea of a philosophical experience and this is then connected to a special kind of experience induced by certain art forms.

Haldane, John. Incarnational Anthropology in Human Beings, Cockburn, David (ed). New York, Cambridge Univ Pr, 1991.

This essay is concerned with the drift of recent analytical philosophy of mind away from the view of persons as unified subjects of thought and action—human beings as rational animals—towards various forms of dualism (including materialist dualism) and eliminativism. It raises the question what view of persons would be able to accommodate (even if only as a hypothesis) the idea that human beings are images of God and that God took on a human nature in the person of Jesus Christ? The reply is in terms of a non-dualist, non-physicalist view: 'incarnational anthropology'.

Haldane, John. Putnam on Intentionality. *Phil Phenomenol Res*, 52(3), 671-682, S 92.

In recent publications Hilary Putnam has criticised realist and reductionist accounts of intentionality. He argues that the claim that intentionality is an objective, primitive mind/world relation is demonstrably incoherent. The resent paper identifies several distinct charges in Putnam's writings and in examining them and their presuppositions it argues that the case against intentionalism is not made out. At least one version of realism about intentional content and reference escapes conviction.

Haldane, John. Theory, Realism and Common Sense: A Reply to Paul Churchland. *Proc Aris Soc*, 93, 321-327, 1993.

This response to Paul Churchland's "Theory, Taxonomy and Methodology" (PAS, same number) begins by identifying a point of significant agreement. We both reject the adequacy of anti-realist defenses of folk psychology. However, it is then argued that Churchland misconceives the nature of theories and fails to take the force of the claim that many psychological generalizations are normative and a priori and are thereby distinguished from empirical laws.

Halfpenny, Peter. A Refutation of Historical Materialism? in Marx's Theory of History, Wetherly, Paul. Brookfield, Avebury, 1992.

G A Cohen, in his book *Karl Marx's Theory of History: A Defence* (Oxford University Press, 1978), maintains that (a) historical materialism consists of a set of functional explanations and (b) functional explanations in the social sciences can be successful. Through a critical examination of Cohen's defence of (b) against four common objections, and through a close examination of the conditions under which elaborations of functional explanations are convincing, this article argues that functional explanations can be extended to the social sciences only in the specific guise of purposive explanations, and that these are incompatible with historical materialism.

Hall, David L. Reason and Its Rhyme. *J Indian Counc Phil Res*, 9(2), 25-46, Ja-Ap 92.

Hall, Douglas. *The Trinity: An Analysis of St Thomas Aquinas' 'Expositio' of the 'De Trinitate' of Boethius*. Leiden, Brill, 1992.

Hall, Harrison (ed) and Dreyfus, Hubert L (ed). *Heidegger: A Critical Reader*. Cambridge, Blackwell, 1992.

Hall, Harrison B. Intentionality and World in The Cambridge Companion to Heidegger, Guignon, Charles B (ed). New York, Cambridge Univ Pr, 1993.

The common (mis)interpretation of early Heidegger as a pragmatist rests on an equally common (mis)reading of *Being and Time*. On this reading the *whole* point of that work is to reverse the traditional priority of the theoretical over the practical by means of an elaborate account of human being which shows it to consist essentially of practical doing rather than theoretical knowing. I argue that a careful reading of Division One of *Being and Time* reveals corresponding senses of intentionality and world more fundamental than either the practical or the theoretical. This "more fundamental" understanding of human being is probably the central contribution of *Being and Time*, tying together the two divisions of that work and forming the link between *Being and Time* and Heidegger's later writings. (edited)

Hall, James A. Polanyi and Psychoanalysis. *Tradition Discovery*, 18(2), 5-9, 1991-92.

Hall, John A (ed) and Jarvie, I C (ed). *Transition to Modernity: Essays on Power, Wealth and Belief*. New York, Cambridge Univ Pr, 1992.

Hall, Pamela. From Justified Discrimination to Responsive Hiring. *J Soc Phil*, 24(1), 23-45, Spr 93.

Hall, Robert W. Plato and Personhood. *Personalist Forum*, 8(2), 88-100, Fall 92.

Hall, Ronald L. *Word and Spirit: A Kierkegaardian Critique of the Modern Age*. Bloomington, Indiana Univ Pr, 1993.

By means of a Kierkegaardian critique of postmodernism, Hall argues that the postmodernist flirtation with Kierkegaard ignores the existential import of his thought. *Word and Spirit* offers a novel interpretation of Kierkegaard's conception of the self, according to which spirit is essentially linked to the speech act. The enriched concept of the speech act represented by the Hebrew idea of *dabbar* frames Hall's critique of irony, romanticism, Don Giovanni, Faust, the demonic, music, and, ultimately, postmodernism in a Kierkegaardian mode. The result of the modern suspicion of speech, Hall concludes, is a demonic, musical spiritlessness.

Hallam, Nicholas. An Argument in Favour of Non-Classical Logic for Quantum Theory. *Analysis*, 44(2), 61-64, Mr 84.

Haller, Rudolf. Atomism and Holism in the Vienna Circle in Advances in Scientific Philosophy, Schurz, Gerhard (ed). Amsterdam, Rodopi, 1991.

Haller, Rudolf. Wittgenstein In Between—A Fragment in Criss-Crossing A Philosophical Landscape, Schulte, Joachim (ed). Amsterdam, Rodopi, 1992.

Wittgenstein's attitude toward philosophy and philosophical problems is examined with the result that—in spite of his own strong criticism of his earlier work—the aim of philosophy remains the same throughout his life: clarity for its own sake. Wittgenstein's concept of philosophy is sketched as non-naturalistic and anti-systematic with the recommendation of being unbiased as the only remedy for falling again into the old traps. The criticism of the Russell-Frege view of existential quantification and generalization included in the "Big Typescript" is outlined as well as the position toward verification Wittgenstein maintained in between his beginning to work in philosophy anew and his first attempt of systematizing the results in the "Big Typescript".

Halliwell, Stephen. Philosophy and Literature: Settling a Quarrel?. *Phil Invest*, 16(1), 1-17, Ja 93.

The article discusses Martha Nussbaum's *Fragility of Goodness* (1986) in the context of traditional arguments about the relationship between philosophy and literature. In arguing for qualified acceptance of Nussbaum's central claim for the ethical value of literature, Halliwell examines the contrasts i) between literary and non-literary experience, ii) between concepts of literary nimesis and literary artifice, iii) between literature as 'interpretation of life' and as the production of 'world-like' images.

Halliwell, Stephen. Style and Sense in Aristotle's *Rhetoric* Bk 3. *Rev Int Phil*, 47(184), 50-69, 1993.

Aristotle's discussion of verbal style constructs a scale of discourse, running from 'standard' speech to the most artful forms of poetry. Aristotle takes clarity to be essential to the declarative function of language, and he grades styles in terms of their divergence from the standard. But his analysis of stylistic qualities, including his remarks on metaphor, works against a strictly formal separation of style from sense: style is treated as an expressive dimension of linguistic significance. Despite this, Aristotle displays ambivalence towards the value of style in relation to philosophy.

Halliwell, Stephen. The Importance of Plato and Aristotle for Aesthetics. *Proc Boston Colloq Anc Phil*, 5, 321-348, 1989.

Starting from a challenge to doctrines of aesthetic autonomy, this article examines Plato *Republic 2-3* and Aristotle's *Poetics* as representative of paradigmatic and permanently available positions in aesthetics. It argues that Plato's judgments of art by ethical, truth-related, and psychological standards are legitimately focussed on intrinsic features of art-works. But Plato fails to integrate these life-values with specific requirements for artistic forms and materials. Aristotle's position tries to balance 'internal' and 'external' factors relating to art; but he cannot clinch art's immunity to Platonic appraisal. The quest for 'pure' aesthetic values is concluded to be vain.

Halper, Edward. Some Problems in Aristotle's Mathematical Ontology. *Proc Boston Colloq Anc Phil*, 5, 247-276, 1989.

This paper begins by developing two ontological problems that concern Aristotle's numbers and arise from his metaphysical positions: 1) it seems that each attribute is an attribute of some individual substance, numbers are attributes, but numbers do not belong to individuals; and 2) Aristotle denies that attributes can have attributes, numbers are attributes, but arithmetic investigates the attributes of numbers. The paper uses these problems as touchstones to evaluate several prominent accounts of Aristotelian mathematics. Drawing upon Aristotle's account of the infinite in *Physics I*, I develop an interpretation of Aristotelian arithmetic that resolves these problems. By examing possible objections, I round out the account and bring it to bear on several other problems in Aristotle's mathematical ontology. My account combines realist and constructivist elements, and it suggests a way that Aristotle might have responded to some of Frege's criticisms. (edited)

Halperin, David M. Plato and the Metaphysics of Desire. *Proc Boston Colloq Anc Phil*, 5, 27-52, 1989.

Plato proposed a metaphysical solution to the puzzle of erotic desire. I argue that Plato's metaphysical approach and transcendental solution are defensible both philosophically and intuitively. I attempt to show that Platonic doctrine represents not a sharp break from traditional Greek thinking on the subject of desire but a philosophical elaboration and systematization of one element in it. Finally, I illustrate this thesis by means of a brief if tendentious reading of Homer's *Iliad*.

Halton, Thomas (ed) and O'Meara, John J. *Studies in Augustine and Eriugena*. Washington, Cath Univ Amer Pr, 1992.

Haltzel, Michael (ed) and Klaits, Joseph (ed). *Liberty/Liberté: The American and French Experiences*. Baltimore, Johns Hopkins U Pr, 1991.

The meaning of the word "liberty" has been decidedly different in the United States and France. *Liberty/Liberté* explores these differences, tracing the development of French and American ideas over the past two centuries in seven essays by American and seven by French scholars. The first half of the book examines common patterns in the intellectual backgrounds, political theories, and symbolic practices which have shaped conceptions of liberty and liberalism. The second half stresses the varieties of liberty's formulations in the historical experience of the two countries, examining the comparative development of "liberalism" and its conflict with other political philosophies.

Hamacher-Hermes, Adelheid. Debate between Husserl and Voigt Concerning the Logic of Content and Extensional Logic in Analecta Husserliana, XXXIV, Tymieniecka, Anna-Teresa (ed). Dordrecht, Kluwer, 1992.

In the early 1890's an argument took place between Edmund Husserl and Andreas Voigt in the pages of the *Vierteljahrsschrift für wissenschaftliche Philosophie*. It concerned the relative merits of a logic of content (*Inhaltslogik*) and of a logic of extension (*Umfangslogik*). The analysis and evaluation of this hitherto disregarded debate in the present paper is complemented by a short biography of Volgt whose work and significance as a logician is almost unknown today. Acquaintance with the controversy is indispensable for a deeper understanding of Husserl's attitude towards mathematical theories of logic, in particular the algebra of logic.

Hamilton, Jonathan H and Slutsky, Steven M. Endogenizing the Order of Moves in Matrix Games. *Theor Decis*, 34(1), 47-62, Ja 93.

Players often have flexibility in when they move and thus whether a game is played simultaneously or sequentially may be endogenously determined. For 2x2 games, we analyze this using an extended game. In a stage prior to actual play, players choose in which of two periods to move. A player moving at the second turn learns the first mover's action. If both select the same turn, they play a simultaneous move subgame. If both players have dominant strategies in the basic game, equilibrium payoffs in the basic and extended games are identical. If only one player has a dominant strategy or if the unique equilibrium in the basic game is in mixed strategies, then the extended game equilibrium payoffs differ iff some pair of pure strategies Pareto dominates the basic game simultaneous play payoffs. If so, sequential play attains the Pareto dominating payoffs. The mixed strategy equilibrium occurs only when it is not Pareto dominated by some pair of pure strategies. In an alternative extended game, players cannot observe delay by opponents at the first turn. Results for 2x2 games are essentially the same as with observable delay, differing only when one player has a dominant strategy.

Hamlyn, D W. Knowledge and Rationality in Logical Foundations, Mahalingam, Indira (ed). New York, St Martin's Pr, 1991.

It is argued that only rational creatures can have knowledge. Hence, the aims of naturalized epistemology are unattainable, in that without a place for rationality a reliable process or mechanism is insufficient for knowledge. On the other hand, knowledge does not always require a direct dependence on reason-giving; if the creature in question is rational it can sometimes know things without this depending on justification via reasons. Both extreme these argue that what is true sometimes is true always. But the general rationality that is presupposed by knowledge itself presupposes other features, found in human beings, including non-cognitive ones.

Hammacher, Klaus and Hirsch, Hans. *Die Wirtschaftspolitik des Philosophen Jacobi*. Amsterdam, Rodopi, 1993.

Friedrich Heinrich Jacobi (1743-1819), Philosoph und Schriftsteller, wirkte 1772-1779, bevor er mit dem Spinozastreit (1785/86) als Philosoph berühmt wurde, als Wirtschaftspolitiker in kurfürstlichen Diensten, und zwar als Hofkammerat und Geheimrat in den Rheinlanden (Jülich-Berg)und kurze Zeit in Bayern (1779). Aufbauend auf die Theorien der sog. Physiokraten, z.B. eines Turgot, und der Freihandelslehre Adam Smith kämpfte er, wenn auch mit bescheidenen Erfolgen, für einen von staatlicher Bevormundung freien Markt. Aufgrund bisher unbekannter Dokumente wird diese Tätigkeit minutiös rekonstruiert. Philosophisch eine nicht unbedeutende Komponente in der Ausbildung moderner Vertragstheorien, erscheint sie theoriegeschichtlich als ökonomische Leistung, die nachhaltig auf die Herausbildung moderner Wirtschaftsformen eingewirkt hat.

Hamminga, Bert. Idealization in the Practice and Methodology of Classical Economics in Idealization III, Brzenzinski, Jerzy (ed). Amsterdam, Rodopi, 1992.

Classical economic theories are deductive structures. Their axioms should reflect human nature, and their conclusions should be plausible. Much of the work done by classical economists has the aim of meeting these requirements as well as possible, for instance by removing "undesired" theorems. This is studied in the paper, focusing on a lemma in this deductive structure, the so-called labor theory of value.

Hammond, David. Taking Wittgenstein to School: Toward an Expressivist Account of Educational Development. *Proc Phil Educ*, 48, 342-351, 1992.

Hammond, Julien. Gabriel Marcel's Philosophy of Human Nature. *Dialogue (PST)*, 35(1), 1-5, O 92.

This article studies Gabriel Marcel's philosophy of the human person in light of Leslie Stevenson's four-fold analytical method. It looks at such topics as Marcel's theory of the universe, his theory of the human person, his diagnosis of the human condition, and his prescription for setting it right. The author concludes that "a philosophy of human nature such as Marcel has presented can only be of benefit to the whole human race."

Hampe, Michael. Gesetz, Befehle und Theorien der Kausalität. *Neue Hefte Phil*, 32-33, 15-49, 1992.

The essay gives an abstract of the relations between theories of moral and scientific laws (Hume, Kant, Leibniz, Spinoza, Wittgenstein) and discusses recent theories of Laws. It tries to show that a theory of the origin of laws needs a theory of creative causality and of the instantiation of general rules in individuals. The conceptions of Ryle, Strawson and Armstrong are considered. It is argued that there is no satisfying theory of the instatiation and origin of laws to be found yet, neither in the philosophy of law, nor in the philosophy of science.

Hampshire, Stuart. Nationalism in Isaiah Berlin: A Celebration, Margalit, Edna (ed). Chicago, Univ of Chicago Pr, 1991.

Hampson, Norman. The Enlightenment. New York, Penguin USA, 1990.

Hampton, Jean. Hobbes and Ethical Naturalism in Philosophical Perspectives, 6: Ethics, 1992, Tomberlin, James E (ed). Atascadero, Ridgeview, 1992.

This article evaluates the success of the Hobbesian version of ethical naturalism, and argues that the plausibility of his approach depends upon the covert importation of the very "metaphysical nonsense" it claims to eschew. The author also contends that once the metaphysical problems of Hobbes' type of moral theory are understood, it is possible to reconcile two divergent interpretations of the Hobbesian moral texts. Those who interpret Hobbes as an ethical subjectivist and an instrumentalist about

reason correctly identify the view Hobbes intended to put forward; those who interpret him as a moral objectivist and a non-instrumentalist about reason appreciate the view that he is forced to fall back upon given the theoretical problems with his intended view.

Hampton, Jean. Selflessness and the Loss of Self. *Soc Phil Pol*, 10(1), 135-165, Wint 93.

This essay attempts to explore the sort of "selfless" act that is bad, and the sort of "selfish" conduct that is good, where the terms 'good' and 'bad' here are understood as moral terms. The adjective 'moral' is normally understood to refer to other-regarding actions or traits of character. But this paper attempts to pursue what might be called the "self-regarding" component of morality.

Hampton, Jean. Selflessness and the Loss of Self in Altruism, Paul, Ellen Frankel (ed). New York, Cambridge Univ Pr, 1993.

Sacrificing one's own interests in order to serve another is, in general, supposed to be an example of altruism, the hallmark of morality, and something we should commend to (but, not always require of) the entirely-too-selfish human beings of our society. But not all self-sacrifice is worthy of our respect or moral commendation. Often 'selfless' people are in danger of losing the self they ought to be developing, and as a result, may be indirectly harming the very people for whom they care. This paper explores the sort of "selfless" act that is bad, and the sort of "selfish" conduct that is good.

Hampton, Jean. The Moral Commitments of Liberalism in The Idea of Democracy, Copp, David (ed). New York, Cambridge Univ Pr, 1993.

In his recent work, Rawls has put forward what he calls a "political" brand of liberalism that attempts to be neutral between competing comprehensive views in the society. Central to this conception of liberalism is Rawls's idea that the ruling conception of justice must be an "overlapping consensus" among these views. But is such a consensus merely a politically expedient compromise? This paper argues that in order to avoid interpreting the overlapping consensus as "political in the wrong sense", Rawls must develop it along moral objectivist lines. But by so doing, his brand of liberalism is no longer completely neutral and nonpartisan on moral matters, and no longer methodologically different from the forms of liberalism that preceded it.

Hampton, Jean (ed) and Copp, David (ed) and Roemer, John E (ed). *The Idea of Democracy*. New York, Cambridge Univ Pr, 1993.

Essays on democratic theory accompanied by critical comments, with an introduction by the editors. Contributors: Richard J Arneson, Pranab Bardhan, Samuel Bowles and Herbert Gintis, Thomas Christiano, Joshua Cohen, David Copp, David Estlund, John Ferejohn, David Gauthier, Jean Hampton, Russell Hardin, Stephen Holmes, Michael S McPherson, Karl Ove Moene, Christopher W Morris, John Rawls, John E Roemer, Debra Satz, John D Stephens, Robert Sugden, Cass R Sunstein.

Han, Cheong K. The Positive Contribution of Confucianism to the Modernization of East Asian Business Enterprises. *J Chin Phil*, 19(2), 171-181, Je 92.

Hance, Allen. Pragmatism as Naturalized Hegelianism: Overcoming Transcendental Philosophy?. *Rev Metaph*, 46(2), 343-368, 1992.

In this essay I argue that Richard Rorty's account of Hegel is systematically distorted by his use of the critical conceptual tool of "naturalizing." For Rorty to naturalize a philosophical theory means to eliminate its transcendental presuppositions. After showing that Rorty conflates the "transcendental" with the "foundational," I argue that his naturalizing critique of Hegel misses the target: while many transcendental philosophers have been foundationalists, Hegel was not among them. I conclude that Hegel's antifoundationalist transcendental ontology remains an attractive philosophical alternative to Rorty's neo-pragmatism.

Hand, Michael. A Defense of Branching Quantification. *Synthese*, 95(3), 419-432, Je 93.

Adding branching quantification to a first-order language increases the expressive power of the language, *without adding to its ontology*. The present paper is a defense of this claim against Quine (1970) and Patton (1991).

Hand, Michael. Classical and Intuitionistic Negation. *SW Phil Rev*, 8(1), 157-164, Ja 92.

Hand, Michael. Demonstrative Reference and Unintended Demonstrata. *Commun Cog*, 26(1), 37-48, 1993.

Hand, Michael. Mathematical Structuralism and the Third Man. *Can J Phil*, 23(2), 179-192, Je 93.

Hand, Michael. Negations in Conflict. *Erkenntnis*, 38(1), 115-129, Ja 93.

Hand, Michael and Allen, Colin. Logic Primer. Cambridge, MIT Pr, 1992.

Logic Primer presents a complete introduction to natural deduction systems for sentential logic and first order predicate logic, including truth tables and model theory. These topics are presented without superfluous discussion, allowing the instructor to choose how to present them. The text includes over 500 exercises and an appendix with solutions to more than half of them.

Hands, D Wade. Metaphysics, Economics and Progress: A Comment on Glass and Johnson. *Brit J Phil Sci*, 43(2), 241-244, J 92.

This paper is a critical comment on a paper by Glass and Johnson published in the *BJPS* in 1988. The Glass and Johnson paper attempted to use economics to demonstrate (contra claims by Koertge) the importance of metaphysics in social science. The comment shows how their efforts fail to achieve their goal.

Hanen, Marsha. Reflections on Contemporary Metaphilosophy in On the Track of Reason, Beehler, Rodger (ed). Boulder, Westview Pr, 1992.

Haney, Kathleen. Husserl's Critique of Reason in Analecta Husserliana, XXXIV, Tymieniecka, Anna-Teresa (ed). Dordrecht, Kluwer, 1992.

In the concluding sections of the fifth of his *Cartesian Meditations*, Husserl undertakes phenomenology's self-evaluation which quickly becomes a new critique of reason which reinstates the role of analogy in philosophy. This analysis is generated by the role which intersubjectivity plays in guaranteeing the experience of transcendent reality and the impossibility of direct evidence of the lived experiences of the other. Reason, now as evidence which acknowledges givenness, moves all the early phenomenological analysis from the factual to the eidetic. This critique of reason leads to the existential motif in Husserl's thought while rescuing philosophers from the chains of the modern understanding of reason.

Haney II, William S. Metaphor and the Experience of Light in Analecta Husserliana, XXXVIII, Tymieniecka, Anna-Teresa (ed). Dordrecht, Kluwer, 1992.

Hanfling, Oswald. "'Thinking", A Widely Ramified Concept'. *Phil Invest*, 16(2), 101-115, Ap 93.

Is thinking an activity? Is it a mental activity? I argue that there *is* an activity of thinking, which may be either overt, in the form of speech or other behavior, or mental, in a sense involving no observable speech or behavior. In the latter case, it may consist of words, but need not consist of anything. Did Wittgenstein regard thinking as an activity? In some passages he was uneasy about doing so, but his position on this was less firm that some commentators have thought. However, his main interest lay in the rejection of 'accompaniment' theories of thinking.

Hanfling, Oswald. Healthy Scepticism?. *Philosophy*, 68(263), 91-93, Ja 93.

In a recent article it is claimed that there is no reason for preferring the 'realist hypothesis' to the hypothesis that 'what we perceive' is due to a 'deceitful demon'. I argue that what we perceive can often be verified by means of physical interaction, and that the latter is not itself a species of perception. Secondly, even if the demon hypothesis were allowed to stand, it would not amount to an argument for *scepticism*. Scepticism must mean a denial of the possibility of knowledge, and this possibility is not ruled out by the mere supposition of a deceitful demon.

Hanfling, Oswald. Loving My Neighbour, Loving Myself. *Philosophy*, 68(264), 145-157, Ap 93.

The Biblical injunction to 'love your neighbour as yourself' involves three difficulties. 1) Who is 'my neighbour'? I discuss a) Butler's answer and b) a utilitarian universalist approach. 2) Can love be commanded? We can choose to *behave* lovingly, or to behave in ways that may be conducive to love, but love itself is not subject to choice. Kant's interpretation of the injunction is relevant but not satisfactory. 3) What is meant by 'loving oneself'? Selfishness, concern for self-interest, etc., are not kinds of love. Aristotle and Hume spoke of self-love but also expressed reservations about this notion. Was the Good Samaritan acting from love?

Hanfling, Oswald. Machines as Persons?—II in Human Beings, Cockburn, David (ed). New York, Cambridge Univ Pr, 1991.

Could there be artificial persons, made from artificial materials? It is thought that such beings ('a-people') might *behave* like natural people ('n-people'), but would lack an 'inner life'; and this would prevent us from treating them as real people. But this position is untenable. Scepticism about the feelings of a-people would be no better than that about the feelings of n-people. An a-person subjected to discrimination would be entitled to accuse us of 'artifactism'. In a practical situation, which I sketch in dialogue form, it would be impossible for us to avoid entering into an obligation of promising with an a-person.

Hanfling, Oswald. 'I Hard a Plaintive Melody' in Wittgenstein Centenary Essays, Griffiths, A Phillips (ed). New York, Cambridge Univ Pr, 1991.

Hankinson, R J and Matthen, Mohan P. Aristotle's Universe: Its Form and Matter. *Synthese*, 96(3), 417-435, S 93.

Despite anthropomorphic and animistic elements, much of Aristotle's conception of the universe in the early chapters of *De Caèlo* can be accounted for empirically. And though many moderns allege that Aristotle over-used naive observation, his key ideas originate from theory. It is argued that the doctrine of the universe as a bounded plenum arises from constraints on the explanation of eternal objects, from an anti-reductionist vision of the primacy of the whole, and from the phenomena.

Hanks, Craig. Thinking about Democracy and Exclusion: Jurgen Habermas' *Theory of Communicative Action* and Contemporary Politics. *SW Phil Rev*, 8(1), 145-155, Ja 92.

Hanly, Ken. Hostile Takeovers and Methods of Defense: A Stakeholder Analysis. *J Bus Ethics*, 11(12), 895-913, D 92.

During the last decade, there has been a wave of mergers and hostile takeovers throughout the corporate world. This wave has been accompanied by various defensive strategies of managers to defend target firms from these takeovers. These include: greenmail, golden parachutes, and leveraged management buyouts. This paper examines hostile takeovers and defenses against them from a stakeholder point of view; that is, from a consideration of the various obligations a firm has to the different groups that have a stake in the firm. I conclude that many stakeholders, such as workers and communities, have unjustly suffered as a result of hostile takeovers and the associated defenses, and that their rights as stakeholders have been violated. Finally, I suggest some possible reforms to protect these stakeholders in the future.

Hanly, Ken. The Problem of Social Cost: Coase's Economics Versus Ethics. *J Applied Phil*, 9(1), 77-83, 1992.

Coase's now famous paper, "The Problem of Social Cost", argues that social harms caused by industry are best addressed through a policy which would be optimal in terms of market efficiency. I argue that this narrowly based policy represents a classic example of the failure of many welfare economists to consider adequately the ethical implications of their recommendations. I also indicate the manner in which Coase's recommendations conflict with intuitively well-established ethical principles. I conclude that only an approach that considers many more features than market efficiency can produce an optimal policy for dealing with the social costs of production.

Hanna, Robert. Descartes and Dream Skepticsm Revisited. *J Hist Phil*, 30(3), 377-398, J 92.

In the first of his *Meditations on First Philosophy*, Descartes raises a famous skeptical doubt about perceptual knowledge, on the basis of our inability to distinguish between waking and dreaming; but in the sixth *Meditation* he appears to remove this doubt summarily in a single paragraph. Critics of Descartes (beginning with Hobbes) have been nearly unanimous in claiming that the anti-skeptical argument in the sixth *Meditation* is fallacious and ill-conceived. But this claim is based on a misreading of the texts. In fact, the argument is much stronger and more sophisticated than most have thought. It is possible to give a careful re-reading of the controversial anti-skeptical argument in the sixth *Meditation* which shows (a) that Descartes in fact argues for a much weaker—and therefore more defensible—conclusion than has traditionally been thought, and (b) that the argument makes a crucial appeal to the *causal sources* of waking perceptual experiences, not merely to the *coherence* of waking perceptual experiences.

Hanna, Robert. Logical Cognition: Husserl's *Prolegomena* and the Truth in Psychologism. *Phil Phenomenol Res*, 53(2), 251-275, Je 93.

Frege's devastating attack on logical psychologism leaves philosophers of logic in a quandary: If logical propositions exist altogether independently of human acts of thinking, then *how* can they be grasped by thinkers? Husserl's *Prolegomena to Pure Logic* contains a thorough critique of psychologism, but manages to avoid Frege's problem by developing a plausible theory of logical cognition. Husserl's account entails that a) logical propositions are essentially knowable by finite rational minds, but also b) those propositions are irreducible to individual human minds. Hence Husserl shows that there can be a weak form of psychologism that is perfectly consistent with anti-psychologism.

Hanna, Robert. The Trouble with Truth in Kant's Theory of Meaning. *Hist Phil Quart*, 10(1), 1-20, Ja 93.

The aim of this paper is to explore Kant's theory of empirical truth from the standpoint of his theory of meaning. This exploration produces two conclusions: 1) that Kant identifies the meaning of an empirical judgment with a rule specifying the empirical conditions under which the judgment is true (verificationism); and 2) that his doctrine of empirical truth, according to which "coherence" (*Zusammenhang*) is the criterion of truth, leads him into serious skeptical difficulties. In light of Kant's influence o the origins of 20th century verificationism, his trouble with truth carries problematic consequences for verificationist semantics quite generally.

Hannan, Barbara. Introducing Validity. *Teach Phil*, 15(3), 251-254, S 92.

A method is described of introducing the notion of deductive validity to elementary logic students in such a way that it becomes clear to the student that validity is a formal notion and has no essential connection with the meaning or truth-value of the premises and conclusion of an argument.

Hannay, Alastair. Consciousness and the Experience of Freedom in John Searle and His Critics, LePore, Ernest (ed). Cambridge, Blackwell, 1991.

In his Reith lectures John Searle claims we are endowed evolutionarily with an experience of freedom as a sense of there being alternative possibilities, even though according to our well-supported conception of physical reality that sense must be illusory. The essay argues that evolutionary principles can be drawn on to ease the strain Searle feels in his allegiance to both mentalism and physical determination. We should expect the human organism to be subject to forms of control specifically related to its being conscious, and should therefore also expect there to be a sense of freedom in the sense of being "where the action is", even if this does not yet amount to there being alternative possibilities. But then perhaps the sense of there being such is not essential to the feeling of freedom we actually have.

Hannay, Alastair. New Foundations and Philosophers in Certainty and Surface in Epistemology and Philosophical Method, Martinich, A P (ed). Lewiston, Mellen Pr, 1991.

Classical foundationalism is the view that there are infallible beliefs whose infallibility justifies them, while all other justified beliefs are justified by appeal to these. An alternative "foundational intuition", formulated by Avrum Stroll, asserts a core of unrevisable common-sense beliefs of the kind classical foundationalism finds fallible and in need of justification. The essay examines the conditions under which this intuition deserves to be called foundational, and finds that they include the requirement that certain common-sense distinctions are autonomous and so unreplaceable. The intuition is therefore weakened by any considerations that can show that common sense is revisable, in such cases, in the light of scientific reflection. Such considerations are to be found in the case of perception.

Hansen, Frank-Peter. Über einen vermeintlichen Bruch im "Ältesten Systemprogramm des deutschen Idealismus". *Z Phil Forsch*, 47(1), 103-112, Ja-Mr 93.

Otto Pöggeler maintains that what he calls a "Bruch" in Hegel's "Das älteste Systemprogramm des deutschen Idealismus" is a result of Hölderlin's influence on Hegel. Pöggeler argues that Hölderlin's life, in particular his stance against Fichte was a major influence on Hegel when he arrived in Frankfurt 1797. Taking in consideration Kant's and Schiller's ethical and aesthetical theory, the author demonstrates that the second part of the fragment is not only a *critique* of ethical one-sidedness but an enclosed aesthetical arrangement of the complete human perception abilities.

Hansen, Miriam. "With Skin and Hair": Kracauer's Theory of Film, Marseille 1940. *Crit Inquiry*, 19(3), 437-469, Spr 93.

Hanson, Donald W. Science, Prudence, and Folly in Hobbes's Political Theory. *Polit Theory*, 21(4), 643-664, N 93.

Hanson, Karen. Approaching Distance. *Int Stud Phil*, 24(2), 33-40, 1992.

The focus of this essay is on the surfacing of the notion of distance in Emerson's and Nietzsche's remarks on the self—on the self's nature, on the prospects and proper methods for self-knowledge, self-development, and community, and on what might be identified as the gendered character of the human being. Both Nietzsche and Emerson produce, I suggest, a specifically feminine articulation of the self, but each reads his production with decided ambivalence. Whether this ambivalence marks a personal problem or signals philosophical accuracy is, in each case, a question I leave open.

Hanson, Karen. Reconstruction in Pragmatism. *Synthese*, 94(1), 13-23, Ja 93.

Originally part of an APA symposium, this paper is a discussion of the connections between Israel Scheffler's work and the views of some classic American pragmatists. Among the illustrating topics are Scheffler's treatment of the cognitive/emotive distinction, the relations between thought and action, science and morality, subjectivity and objectivity. In connection with this last, there is some comment on both Scheffler's earlier and his more recent criticisms of the views of Thomas Kuhn and on the difficulties of either sustaining or abandoning the fact/value distinction.

Hansson, Sven Ove. *Belief Base Dynamics*. Uppsala, Acta U Upsaliensis, 1991.

The AGM (Alchourrón-Gärdenfors-Makinson) model of belief change is modified by letting beliefs be represented by sets of sentences (belief bases) that are *not* required to be closed under logical consequence. This makes it possible to distinguish between different inconsistent belief states. Therefore, belief changes that pass through inconsistent states can readily be represented. Two new operations of belief change are introduced, that both require this feature of the formal framework. A model is provided for non-prioritized reception of epistemic input, i.e., reception of new information without allotting to it any special priority due to its novelty.

Hansson, Sven Ove. Belief Contraction Without Recovery. *Stud Log*, 50(2), 251-260, Je 91.

The postulate of recovery is commonly regarded to be the intuitively least compelling of the six basic Gärdenfors postulates for belief contradiction. We replace recovery by the seemingly much weaker postulate of core-retainment, which ensures that if *x* is excluded from "K" when *p* is contracted, then *x* plays some role for the fact that "K" implies *p*. Surprisingly enough, core-retainment together with four of the other Gärdenfors postulates implies recovery for logically closed belief sets. Reasonable contraction operators without recovery do not seem to be possible for such sets. Instead, however, they can be obtained for non-closed belief bases. Some results on partial meet contractions on belief bases are given, including an axiomatic characterization and a non-vacuous extension of the AGM closure condition.

Hansson, Sven Ove. Similarity Semantics and Minimal Changes of Belief. *Erkenntnis*, 37(3), 401-429, N 92.

Different similarity relations on sets are introduced, and their logical properties are investigated. Close relationships are shown to hold between similarity relations that are based on symmetrical difference and operators of belief contraction that are based on relational selection functions. Two new rationality criteria for minimal belief contraction, the maximizing property and the reducing property, are proposed.

Hansson, Sven Ove. The Difference Model of Voting. *Notre Dame J Form Log*, 33(4), 576-592, Fall 92.

A participant in a voting procedure may be concerned not only that the outcome should be as good as possible but also that her own vote should be cast for some alternative that is as good as possible. A high priority for the latter means unwillingness to compromise. Two formal models, one ordinal and one cardinal, are developed for voting in which the individual preferences are combinations of these two types of values. A close relationship is shown to hold between the two models. Formal results are obtained on conditions for voting sequences to be "stable" in the sense that no collection of voters will have incentive to unilaterally defect from the way they voted (Nash equilibria). Furthermore, computer simulations of the three-person case are reported. In these, it is shown how the incidence of instability, multi-stability (more than one stable outcome), and tie-stability (tie as the only stable outcome) varies with different priorities between the two types of values.

Hansson, Sven Ove. The False Promises of Risk Analysis. *Ratio*, 6(1), 16-26, Je 93.

The relatively new discipline of risk analysis promises to provide objective guidance in some of the most controversial issues in modern high-technology societies. Four conditions are discussed that must be satisfied for this promise to be fulfilled. Since none of these conditions is satisfied, risk analysis does not keep its promise. In its attempts to reduce genuinely political issues to technocratic calculations, it neglects many of the factors that should influence decisions on risk acceptance. A list of tentative guidelines is given for numerical decision support that encourages democratic decision-making instead of trying to evade it.

Hanzel, Igor. The Pure Idealizational Law—the Inherent Law—the Inherent Idealizational Law in Idealization III, Brzezinski, Jerzy (ed). Amsterdam, Rodopi, 1992.

The idealizational methodology of science as it has been developed by the Poznan school puts forward provocative problems which are challenging philosophers, methodologists, and students of the concrete sciences. They include the problem of understanding of the idealizational laws. The purpose of this paper is to throw some additional light on the topic, which might clarify issues bearing upon the construal of the idealizational law, essentially the latter's treatment by L Nowak.

Hara, Wing-Han. Between Individuality and Universality: An Explication of Chuang Tzu's Theses of Chien-tu and Ch'i-wu. *J Chin Phil*, 20(1), 87-99, Mr 93.

Harbers, Hans and De Vries, Gerard. Empirical Consequences of the 'Double Hermeneutic'. *Soc Epistem*, 7(2), 183-192, Ap-Je 93.

Harbers, Hans and De Vries, Gerard. Reply to Lynch's "What Does the Double Hermeneutic Explain/Justify?". *Soc Epistem*, 7(2), 205-208, Ap-Je 93.

Harcourt, Edward. Are Hybrid Proper Names the Solution to the Completion Problem: A Reply to Wolfgang Künne. *Mind*, 102(406), 301-313, Ap 93.

Künne argued that if an utterance of an atomic first-person sentence expresses a Fregean thought, the bearer of the sense that completes the sense of the predicate must be a "hybrid proper name" (a token of "I" plut its utterer). This proposal is criticized for theoretical redundancy and the manner of its formulation. It is argued that if, following Dummett, Fregean sense and linguistic meaning are treated as kinds of properties of utterances, Künne's proposal can be seen not to be required by his assumptions, and tokens of "I" themselves regarding as bearers of the Fregean sense in question.

Hardcastle, Valerie Gray. Reduction, Explanatory Extension, and the Mind/Brain Sciences. *Phil Sci*, 59(3), 408-428, S 92.

In trying to characterize the relationship between psychology and neuroscience, the trend has been to argue that reductionism does not work without suggesting a suitable substitute. I offer explanatory extension as a good model for elucidating the complex relationship among disciplines which are obviously connected but which do not share pragmatic explanatory features. Explanatory extension rests on the idea that one field can "illuminate" issues that were incompletely treated in another. In this paper, I explain how this "illumination" would work between psychology and neuroscience.

Hardcastle, Valerie Gray. The Naturalists versus the Skeptics: The Debate Over a Scientific Understanding of Consciousness. *J Mind Behav*, 14(1), 27-50, Wint 93.

There are three basic skeptical arguments against developing a scientific theory of consciousness: 1) theory cannot capture a first person perspective; 2) consciousness is causally inert with respect to explaining cognition; and 3) the notion "consciousness" is too vague to be a natural kind term. Although I am sympathetic to naturalists' counter-arguments, I also believe that most of the accounts given so far of how explaining consciousness would fit into science are incorrect. In this essay, I indicate errors my colleagues on both sides of the fence make in thinking about his issue, as well as outline data relevant to distinguishing conscious states from unconscious ones empirically.

Hardin, C L. The Virtues of Illusion. *Phil Stud*, 68(3), 371-382, D 92.

What ecological advantages do animals gain by being able to detect, extract and exploit wavelength information? What are the advantages of representing that information as hue qualities? The benefits of adding chromatic to achromatic vision, marginal in object detection, become apparent in object recognition and receiving biological signals. It is argued that this improved performance is a direct consequence of the fact that many animals' visual systems reduce wavelength information to combinations of four basic hues. This engenders a simple categorical scheme that permits a rich amount of sensory information to be rapidly and efficiently employed by cognitive machinery of limited capacity.

Hardin, C L. Van Brakel and the Not-So-Naked Emperor. *Brit J Phil Sci*, 44(1), 137-150, Mr 93.

Hardin, Russell. Common Sense at the Foundations in Essays on Henry Sidgwick, Schultz, Bart (ed). New York, Cambridge Univ Pr, 1992.

Sidgwick's common moral reasoning must be similar to practical reasoning more generally. It will turn on the moral knowledge available to the reasoner. That knowledge must have been gained in ways similar to the learning of any other knowledge. For practical reason, the question why we know what we know may be more important than that of how we know it is valid. We require an economic theory of the costs and incentives of coming to know. The rationality and morality of an action depends on what it makes sense for the actor to know at the time of action.

Hardin, Russell. Liberalism: Political and Economic. *Soc Phil Pol*, 10(2), 121-144, Sum 93.

Hardin, Russell. Public Choice Versus Democracy. *Nomos*, 32, 184-203, 1990.

Public choice theory offers two main classes of findings. First, aggregation from individual to collective preferences may not be well-defined. Second, individual motives for action may not fit collective preferences for outcomes even when the latter are well-defined. We may all agree, for example, that we would all be better off if we would all pay extra to reduce pollution, but no one of us would, therefore, have an interest in making the extra expenditure. Not only are we damned if we don't agree on what to do, we may also be damned if we do.

Hardin, Russell. Public Choice Versus Democracy in The Idea of Democracy, Copp, David (ed). New York, Cambridge Univ Pr, 1993.

Hardin, Russell. The Morality of Law and Economics. *Law Phil*, 11(4), 331-384, 1992.

The moral heart of normative law and economics is efficiency, especially dynamic efficiency that takes incentive effects into account. In the economic theory, justificatory argument is inherently at the institutional- or rule-level, not at the individual- or case-level. In *Markets, Morals, and the Law* Jules Coleman argues against the efficiency theory on normative grounds. Although he strongly asserts the need to view law institutionally, he frequently grounds his criticisms of law and economics in arguments from little more than direct moral intuition about individual cases. He evidently holds that consent provides a better normative basis for law than does efficiency and he uses consent arguments to attack recommendations from scholars in law and economics. His own chief contribution, however, is to law and economics rather than to any alternative theory.

Harding, James M. Historical Dialectics and the Autonomy of Art in *Adorno's Asthetische Theorie*. *J Aes Art Crit*, 50(3), 183-195, Sum 92.

Harding, Sandra G. Rethinking Standpoint Epistemology: 'What Is Strong Objectivity?' in Feminist Epistemologies, Alcoff, Linda (ed). New York, Routledge, 1993.

Standpoint epistemology is one of the striking contributions that has emerged from reflection on the research processes through which some of the most important feminist work in the natural and social sciences has been produced. This essay distinguishes standpoint from empiricist theories of knowledge, and then from several alternatives to empiricism to which it is often wrongly assimilated: ethnocentrism, relativism, pluralism, and "identity politics" research. Finally the subject/agent or knowledge and the "strong objectivity" generated by standpoint epistemology is contrasted with the subject of knowledge and only weak standards for maximizing objectivity characteristic of empiricist epistemology.

Hardwick, Charley D. Naturalism and Existentialist Interpretation in God, Values, and Empiricism, Peden, Creighton W (ed). Macon, Mercer Univ Pr, 1989.

Hardwig, John. The Problem of Proxies with Interests of Their Own: Toward a Better Theory of Proxy Decisions. *J Clin Ethics*, 4(1), 20-27, Spr 93.

Medical treatment decisions often dramatically affect the lives of others, especially the patient's family. Consequently, our theory of proxy decisions is mistaken: 1) The best interest of the patient is not the only morally-relevant interest. Proxies who are family members must not be instructed to ignore their own interests. Sometimes the interests of the proxy and/or other family members ought to *override* the interests of the patient. 2) Substituted judgment is often not the appropriate standard for proxy decisions. Proxy deciders should sometimes make decisions *at odds with* the known wishes of a formerly competent patient.

Hardy, Gilbert (trans) and Lavelle, Louis. Negation and Absence. *Int Stud Phil*, 25(1), 37-53, 1993.

The translation features the first chapter of the unfinished work *Reality and the Spirit* by L Lavelle (1883-1951), the leading figure of French Spiritualism between the two world wars. "Negation and Absence" carries both a metaphysical and a moral message in that Lavelle insists that Being is at once absolute Presence and Self-affirming Act. These themes suggest an idealistic undercurrent in Lavelle's thought, recast, however, in an original way, within the perspective of the French school of psycho-metaphysical spiritualism.

Hardy, Lee (trans) and Ströker, Elisabeth. *Husserl's Transcendental Phenomenology—Elisabeth Ströker*. Stanford, Stanford Univ Pr, 1993.

In this work, Professor Ströker offers a unified and critical interpretation of Husserl's transcendental phenomenology as a whole from the standpoint of method. Taking her point of orientation from Husserl's self-professed goal of realizing in his work the ideal of "first philosophy", she tracks the dynamic interplay between the development of Husserl's method and the thematic progression of his research. Along the way she deflects many of the common objections to Husserl's project, while pointing out its conceptual limitations and de facto oversights.

Hare, R M. Could Kant Have Been a Utilitarian. *Utilitas*, 5(1), 1-16, My 93.

It is wrong to assume as it commonly done that Kant was an anti-utilitarian. He argues (unsuccessfully) for some anti-utilitarian practical percepts, because of his rigid early upbringing; but his theory of the Categorical Imperative allows, indeed requires him to be a utilitarian of one sort. The contrary belief rests on misunderstandings of his text and neglect of clear indications of a utilitarian tendency, especially in his *Tugendlehre*. These, and the examples and formulations of the Categorical Imperative in the *Grundlegung*, are discussed. Treating others' ends as my ends, as he enjoins, requires me to be a utilitarian.

Hare, R M. Moral Reasoning about the Environment in Applied Philosophy, Almond, Brenda (ed). New York, Routledge, 1992.

This paper deals in the main with the problem of delimiting the classes of being to which we have moral duties when making environmental decisions, and of how to balance their interests fairly. The relation between having interests, having desires and having value (intrinsic or other) is discussed, and a distinction made between entities which can themselves value and those which can have value. Its conclusion is that duties are owed directly to, and only to, sentient beings, and that these duties can be ascertained by weighing their interest impartially strength for strength. It ends with some suggestions about procedures for doing this. Examples are taken from proposals to develop a beach commercially, and to construct a new road in an environmentally sensitive area.

Hare, R M. Utilitarianism and Moral Education: Comment on Sanford Levy's Paper. *Stud Phil Educ*, 11(3), 197-205, 1992.

Since moral intuitions and language are the product of moral education, intuitionism and naturalism both collapse into cultural relativism. Only morally neutral concepts, such as are common to Kantianism and utilitarianism, can yield a logic for non-question-begging moral argument. My own theory, combining these approaches, gives such a formal, neutral account of the moral concepts. Levy shows that a theory so constructed can use a utilitarian method to select and criticize the prima facie intuitive principles we cultivate in education. These are not 'mere rules of thumb'. He successfully defends this two-level account against Bernard Williams' attack.

Hare, William. Humility as a Virtue in Teaching. *J Phil Educ*, 26(2), 227-236, 1992.

Some have denied that humility is a virtue in teaching, and others have found the idea problematic especially as concerns the teacher's authority and the matter of self-esteem. These difficulties have encouraged the emergence of narrow approaches to teaching, or have spawned simplistic solution which confuse humility with outright scepticism. This discussion links humility with two chief ideals, both requiring careful consideration: deference to reason and evidence and respect for the student's interpretation; and it suggests a connection with the Socratic conception of wisdom, itself often misunderstood. Some tentative suggestions emerge with respect to humility in the practice of teaching.

Hare, William F. Philosophy of Education in Canada. *Eidos*, 10(1), 69-90, J-Jl 91.

This paper traces the development of philosophy of education in Canada in the twentieth century. It argues that there is more continuity to be found than generally recognized, but shows that a new rigour came into the subject in the second half of the century largely as a result of developments in the field in the United States, and to a lesser extent Britain, in the 1940's and 1950's, bringing changes which started to take hold in Canada in the 1960's. Today, philosophy of education is a lively and productive branch of philosophy in Canada.

Harizanov, V S. The Possible Turing Degree of the Nonzero Member in a Two Element Degree Spectrum. *Annals Pure Applied Log*, 60(1), 1-30, F 93.

We construct a recursive model M, a recursive subset R of its domain, and a nonzero Turing degree x less than or equal to 0', which satisfy the following condition. The nonrecursive images of R under all isomorphisms from M to other recursive models are of Turing degree x and cannot be recursively enumerable.

Harlan, Josh. Hilary Putnam: On Mind, Meaning, and Reality. *Harvard Rev Phil*, 2(1), 20-25, Spr 92.

Harlan, Joshua D and Aybar, Samuel R and Lee, Won J. John Rawls: For the Record (An Interview). *Harvard Rev Phil*, 1(1), 38-48, Spr 91.

Harman, Gilbert. Stringency of Rights and "Ought". *Phil Phenomenol Res*, 53(1), 181-185, Mr 93.

Harmer, Peter A. Athletes, Excellence, and Injury: Authority in Moral Jeopardy. *J Phil Sport*, 18, 24-38, 1991.

Much authority in sport is in moral jeopardy because of its failure to supply medical support staff to representative teams. Arguments in favor of supplying staff, including the special relationship between authority and athletes based on duty and obligation, and the rights of injured athletes, are advanced. Arguments (including indifference, supererogation, disavowal, replacement, consent, convention, compulsion, inability, and ignorance) that attempt to defend current practice are repudiated. The moral currency of authority is, thus, claimed suspect, for although authority may act in several ways, to act in a way that denies its obligation to those with who it has a special relationship is morally wrong.

Harrell, Jean Gabbert. *Profundity: A Universal Value*. University Park, Penn St Univ Pr, 1992.

The commonly used valuational criterion of profundity has never before been investigated as have those of the beautiful or the sublime. Rather than attempting a definition of profundity in terms of necessary and sufficient conditions, this book looks at characteristic usage of the word as denoting a quality that is subjective but universal to humans. Two sense patterns that are biologically indigenous to life are seen to recur in music and visual arts of all cultures, and related extensions are made into religion, literature, and ethics, thus placing the most rudimentary of human values as independent of cultural context.

Harries, Karsten. The Roots of All Evil: Lessons of an Epigram. *Int J Phil Stud*, 1(1), 1-20, Mr 93.

The boundary between philosophical and poetic discourse has become blurred in recent years. Representative of such blurring is the work of Heidegger, who came to insist that to understand his thought, we have to understand it as serving poetry, especially the poetry of Holderlin, supposed to possess a unique significance that recalls the authority a Christian philosophy once granted Scripture. Taking its cues from one of Holderlin's epigrams, the essay argues that Heidegger's insistence on such significance, while rooted in his fundamental ontology, rests on a misreading born of what the tradition had called pride. But pride is "The Root of All Evil."

Harriman, Charles J. Ethics for Inquisitors. *SW Phil Stud*, 15, 37-42, Spr 93.

Harrington, James and Pocock, J G A (ed). *"The Commonwealth of Oceana" and "A System of Politics"—James Harrington*. New York, Cambridge Univ Pr, 1992.

Harriott, Howard. Defensible Anarchy?. *Int Phil Quart*, 33(3), 319-340, S 93.

Harris, David A. *The Manifestation of Analogous Being in the Dialectic of the Space-Time Continuum: A Philosophical Study in Freedom*. New York, Lang, 1992.

This book is a formidable work of philosophical synthesis. By introducing dialectical argumentation, it casts the problematic of analogous being in a new light. In the process it illuminates the main issues that arise in classical philosophy. The examination of the Pre-Socratics is especially important as introducing cosrnological categories. These are taken up in a dialectical sequence that culminates in Kepler's Laws. The result is a metaphysical standpoint beyond mechanism. The physical world is understood not as a system of external relations, but as an organic totality, self-determining and free.

Harris, H S. Fichte's New Wine. *Dialogue (Canada)*, 32(1), 129-134, Wint 93.

This is a short critical study of Frederick Neuhouser's *Fichte's Theory of Subjectivity*, Cambridge, United Kingdom, 1990.

Harris, H S. Hegel's Intellectual Development to 1807 in The Cambridge Companion to Hegel, Beiser, Frederick (ed). New York, Cambridge Univ Pr, 1993.

This essay describes Hegel's education at Stuttgart and Tübingen, and traces the development of his own thought from the Tübingen Fragment of 1743 as far as the conception and writing of the *Phenomenology of Spirit* in 1807.

Harris, H S. The End of History in Hegel. *Bull Hegel Soc Gt Brit*, 23-24, 1-14, 1991.

This essay shows that the interpretation of the "End of History" offered by Francis Fukuyama is based upon a mistaken interpretation of Hegel. It offers a more adequately Hegelian interpretation of what the "end of history" meant for Hegel himself; and it argues that the properly Hegelian view shows why the "end of history," as proclaimed by Fukuyama, is bound to be far less final than he believes.

Harris, James F. *Against Relativism: A Philosophical Defense of Method*. Peru, Open Court, 1992.

Recent decades have witnessed the extraordinary growth of radical relativism, according to which, any proposition can be true or false in relation to a chosen framework, the evaluation of fundamental theories of 'paradigms' is beyond argument, there are no universal standards of rationality, and, methodologically, 'Anything goes!' I have selected the strongest and most plausible arguments for relativism within contemporary academic philosophy. I turn the techniques of relativism against relativism itself, showing that it is ultimately self-refuting or otherwise ineffectual. I demonstrate that Quine's rejection of the analytic-synthetic distinction appeals to the very analytic truths Quine tries to dispel; that Kuhn's celebrated account of paradigms must be either self-refuting or unintelligible; that Rorty cannot avoid presupposing the epistemological principles he attacks; and that (although feminist criticisms of science exert a welcome corrective) attempts to develop a distinctively 'feminist science' are misconceived and unhelpful to feminism. In all these discussions, I explain the arguments I am criticizing for the benefit of the non-specialist reader, so that his work can serve as a partisan but fair introduction to some of the most important to present-day philosophical debates.

Harris, James F. God, Eternality, and the View from Nowhere in Logic, God and Metaphysics, Harris, James F (ed). Dordrecht, Kluwer, 1992.

Harris, James F (ed). *Logic, God and Metaphysics*. Dordrecht, Kluwer, 1992.

Harris, John. Is Gene Therapy a Form of Eugenics?. *Bioethics*, 7(2-3), 178-187, Ap 93.

Harris, John and Erin, Charles A. AIDS: Ethics, Justice and Social Policy. *J Applied Phil*, 10(2), 165-173, 1993.

Principles of justice and equality demand that HIV seropositive individuals and those with AIDS should not be discriminated against in any area of social provision. If social policy on AIDS is constructed in terms of *reciprocal* obligations, that is if obligations *to* the HIV seropositive individual and obligations of the HIV seropositive individual are given equal weight, the civil rights of HIV seropositive individuals may be secured and this may create a climate in which HIV seropositive individuals will more readily notify partners, and others at risk of infections, of their HIV status. It is conceivable that such a climate could facilitate greater control of the spread of HIV/AIDS.

Harris, Leonard. Autonomy Under Duress in African-American Perspectives on Biomedical Ethics, Flack, Harley E (ed). Washington, Georgetown Univ Pr, 1992.

I argue that neither a rational choice decision procedure nor a gambling paradigm is sufficient to resolve some controversial cases. The gambling paradigm can tell us the probable benefits a child can receive from a bone marrow transplant, not the risk factors. Rational choice theory cannot tell us whether to counsel a parent to grant priority to the interest of their child over their own when parents are living under duress. In the chronically racist society the importance of kinship bonding in the process of seeking a cure is an important moral consideration. I use an imagined conversation between George W Carver as a eunuch and the AMA personalities, Dr Dick, Dr Death, and Dr Goodbody. I argue that concepts of autonomy do not escape entrapment in a web of meaning.

Harris, Leonard. Honor: Emasculation and Empowerment in Rethinking Masculinity, May, Larry (ed). Lanham, Rowman & Littlefield, 1992.

Honor is a form of reverence, esteem, and deference an individual receives from others. Persons excluded from a moral community, however, are also generally excluded from honor independent of gender. The possibility of honor for an individual is integrally tied to the possibility of their community having honorable status. With examples of castration, lynching, and from the possibility of empowerment across generations. Traits of love, care, compassion, and sacrifice are no less significant as sources of honor than the traits of discipline, tenacity, and aggressiveness. Racism helps account for why honor has been an elusive good for African American males; the type of honor accorded to Dr. M L King is not a counter example to the idea that honor is a social good.

Harris, N G E. A Fruitless Definition. *Philosophy*, 68(265), 389-391, Jl 93.

Harris, N G E. Kantian Duties and Immoral Agents. *Kantstudien*, 83(3), 336-343, 1992.

Kant has been interpreted (e.g., by Gilbert Harman) as holding that when deciding what are the principles of action we should follow we must discount the possibility that the people with whom we are dealing may act immorally. This interpretation leads to absurd consequences. An alternative interpretation of Kant's view is presented. Deciding on what it is our duty to do is a two-stage process: (1) determining what action it would be reasonable for us to consider doing in the circumstances; (2) determining which amongst those actions it is our duty to do. Furthermore, the concept of the Kingdom of Ends is an ideal one only in being of a situation in which everyone rationally chooses to do his duty-it is not of a situation from which all evil has already been removed.

Harris, R Baine. Can We Have a World Philosophy?. *Dialec Hum*, 17(3), 99-107, 1990.

This paper considers some ways that have been proposed for the resolution of human conflict through the unification of thought and concludes that all of them still allow some form of philosophical pluralism. A world philosophy would not be possible apart from some strong political or military force capable of enforcing a given ideology. Some philosophies, however, can be more universal than others if they meet certain general requirements. These requirements are presented and discussed.

Harris, Wendell V. In Praise of True Pluralism. *Phil Lit*, 16(2), 364-372, O 92.

James Battersby's *Paradigms Regained: Pluralism and the Practice of Criticism* is a major contribution to a growing reaction against the celebration of indeterminacy of meaning and the denial of authorial intention which arose in the 1960's. Battersby cogently makes a number of important points for which support can be drawn from sources as diverse as C S Peirce, R S Crane, Kenneth Burke, Charles Morris, E D Hirsch, Nelson Goodman, Hilary Putnam, Donald Davidson, and George Dillon. In brief, the overall position recognizes that human understanding depends on humanly constructed schemes, but denies that we cannot distinguish appropriate actions, translate between schemes, or distinguish between an author's interests and our own.

Harrison, Andrew. A Minimal Syntax for the Pictorial in The Language of Art History, Kemal, Salim (ed). New York, Cambridge Univ Pr, 1991.

Harrison, Bernard. Imagined Worlds and the Real One: Plato, Wittgenstein, and Mimesis. *Phil Lit*, 17(1), 26-46, Ap 93.

Many critics hold that literary language, in Merleau-Ponty's phrase, has "nothing to do with anything but itself". It is frequently taken to follow from this claim that literary language can have no cognitive concern with extralinguistic reality. But does this follow? This paper attempts to show that it does not, drawing its arguments from some reflection upon the *Cratylus* and the *Philosophical Investigations*.

Harrison, Harvey E. Ethics and Negotiation: The Search for Value and Freedom In Hollywood. *Int J Applied Phil*, 7(1), 11-14, Sum 92.

What happens when one negotiates a deal in Hollywood? I will explore this question, first, by a general examination of the negotiation process, and I will conclude that negotiation is, in critical respects, an ethical process. This examination and this conclusion are derived from my years as a professional negotiator in the motion picture and television industry of Hollywood. I will then attempt to support this conclusion with reference to certain ideas from the moral philosophy of Immanuel Kant.

Harrison, Jonathan. *Ethical Essays, Volume I*. Brookfield, Avebury, 1993.

Harrison, Jonathan. *Ethical Essays, Volume II*. Brookfield, Avebury, 1993.

Harrison, Ross. *Democracy*. New York, Routledge, 1993.

The book considers and answers problems posed about the value of democracy as a decision procedure. The problems are first posed historically by considering the theoretical contributions of Plato, Aristotle, Hobbes, Locke, Rousseau, Hume, the Federalists, Bentham, the Mills, Hegel, and Marx. This historical context provides a series of specific problems of how democracy may be compatible with other values, including liberty, equality, knowledge, and welfare. These problems are then considered analytically, on their own terms. In each case it is argued that democracy is compatible; and so may be justified and defended.

Hart, B and Pillay, A and Starchenko, S. Triviality, NDOP and Stable Varieties. *Annals Pure Applied Log*, 62(2), 119-146, Jl 93.

Hart, Carroll Guen. "Power in the Service of Love": John Dewey's *Logic* and the Dream of a Common Language. *Hypatia*, 8(2), 190-214, Spr 93.

While contemporary feminist philosophical discussions focus on the oppressiveness of universality which obliterates "difference," the complete demise of universality might hamper feminist philosophy in its political project of furthering the well-being of all women. Dewey's thoroughly functionalized, relativized, and fallibilized understanding of universality may help us cut universality down to size while also appreciating its limited contribution. Deweyan universality may signify the ongoing search for a genuinely common language in the midst of difference.

Hart, J G. The Entelechy and Authenticity of Objective Spirit: Reflections on Husserliana XXVII. *Husserl Stud*, 9(2), 91-110, 1992.

Hart, James G. *The Person and the Common Life*. Dordrecht, Kluwer, 1992.

This Husserl-based social ethics claims that the properly philosophical life, i.e., one lived within the noetic-noematic field, is not cut off from action. Indeed, the ethical and political dimensions of the person are disclosed through various reductions. At the passive-synthetic level as well as at the higher founded levels of personal constitution, a basic sense of will emerges, the *telos* of which is a godly intersubjective self-ideal. This "truth of will" is inseparably an "ought" and an "is" involving moral categoriality as a way of letting the good of others be part of one's own. Both moral categoriality and the *polis* actuate the latent first-person plural dative of manifestation which emerges with a common world. (edited)

Hart, James G. The Rationality of Culture and the Culture of Rationality: Some Husserlian Proposals. *Phil East West*, 42(4), 643-664, O 92.

Hart, Joan. Erwin Panofsky and Karl Mannheim: A Dialogue on Interpretation. *Crit Inquiry*, 19(3), 534-566, Spr 93.

Hart, Richard E (ed). *Ethics and the Environment*. Lanham, Univ Pr of America, 1992.

This collection of essays provides historical and philosophical background on the issue of environmental ethics. With an eye toward significant change in contemporary ethical theory, these authors supply the expertise and analysis necessary for a sophisticated understanding of the current debate on the environment. Philosophers, humanists, politicians, geologists, chemists and physicists offer a variety of opinions on topics such as property rights, organism and community, nuclear energy, safe water supply and environmental values.

Hart, Richard E. Existential, Literary or Machine Persons?: Analysis of McLachlan, Adams and Steinbeck. *Personalist Forum*, 8/1(Supp), 67-74, Spr 92.

Hart, W A. Children are Not Meant to be Studied.... *J Phil Educ*, 27(1), 17-26, Sum 93.

The project of studying children in order to understand them, which lies at the heart of contemporary thinking about children and their education, is misconceived. It rests, first of all, upon a false belief that we can only come to know something properly by deliberately and systematically pursuing knowledge of it. Secondly, it offers a paradigm of knowing children which justifies parent and teachers in not giving themselves to children. By re-interpreting the problems that adults experience with children as technical, as arising from lack of information about them, it ignores the personal and moral dimension of adults' relations with children and thus further alienates them from one another.

Hart, W D. Motions of the Mind in Psychoanalysis, Mind and Art, Hopkins, Jim (ed). Cambridge, Blackwell, 1992.

Hartle, Anthony E and Christopher, Paul P. AIDS Victims and Military Service in Biomedical Ethics Reviews 1992, Humber, James M (ed). Clifton, Humana Pr, 1993.

The entry evaluates the policies of the US military services in treating and retiring AIDS victims. At the time of writing, each service had a different policy. The article concludes that the US Army's policy, which permitted service members to remain in active duty assignments as long as the individual was capable of performing required duties, was more equitable than those of the Navy and Air Force. The authors show that arguments against such a policy collapse under analysis. (Since the book went to the publisher, the Department of Defense adopted a policy reflecting the authors' position.)

Hartmann, Dirk. Ist die konstruktive Abstraktionstheorie inkonsistent?. *Z Phil Forsch*, 47(2), 271-285, Ap-Je 93.

In the first part of the article the constructive abstraction-procedure is introduced. The second part is concerned with special consequences of the procedure which are often overlooked. One conclusion here is, that the versions of the procedure given by Paul Lorenzen and Christian Thiel are *not* equivalent. In the third part the recent attempts of Geo Siegwart to prove the inconsistency of the constructive theory of abstraction are discussed. The article comes to the conclusion, that Siegwart has *not* succeeded in proving the Lorenzen-version being inconsistent. In fact he *has* proven the inconsistency of the Thiel-version, which was always regarded as being more "elegant".

Hartmann, Fritz. Kausalität als Leitbegriff ärztlichen Denkens und Handelns. *Neue Hefte Phil*, 32-33, 50-81, 1992.

Hartmann, Nicolaï and Narbonne, Jean-Pierre (trans). Document: Le Concept mégarique et aristotélicien de possibilité. *Laval Theol Phil*, 49(1), 131-146, F 93.

Hartshorne, Charles. A Dual Theory of Theological Analogy in God, Values, and Empiricism, Peden, Creighton W (ed). Macon, Mercer Univ Pr, 1989.

Hartshorne, Charles. Some Comments on Randall Morris' Process Philosophy and Political Ideology. *Process Stud*, 21(3), 149-151, Fall 92.

Dr. Morris's criticisms are partly relevant to my political beliefs, but partly not relevant, because they concern beliefs I have never had. He misunderstood a rather unclear paragraph of mine, written fifty years before he criticized it.

Hartshorne, Charles. Some Not Ungrateful But Perhaps Inadequate Comments About Comments on My Writings and Ideas. *Process Stud*, 21(2), 123-129, Sum 92.

Hartshorne, Charles. Some Under- and Over-Rated Great Philosophers. *Process Stud*, 21(3), 166-174, Fall 92.

Overrated: Aristotle and Kant; Underrated: Plato and Bergson. In both cases the ratings were based on the wrong reasons or the wrong portions of the writers' writings.

Hartshorne, Charles. The Aesthetic Dimensions of Religious Experience in Logic, God and Metaphysics, Harris, James F (ed). Dordrecht, Kluwer, 1992.

Hartz, Glenn A. Leibniz's Phenomenalisms. *Phil Rev*, 101(3), 511-549, Jl 92.

Leibniz's mature account of bodies is construed according to three models: (1) perceptual, (2) mereological, and (3) supervenience. On (1) "aggregates" are phenomenal appearances mistakenly judged by the perceiving mind to be extra-mental bodies possessing secondary qualities, unity, and spatial continuity. (2) Says extramentally-considered aggregates are non-unified collections of an infinite number of discrete substances. Arguments are presented against Robert M Adams' claims that these aggregates are spatially continuous and that a "principle of aggregation" determines their arrangements. (3) Claims that both aggregates and "corporeal substances" have a "derivative force" supervening on their constituent substances' "primitive force". These analyses are melded together into an overarching account of the sufficient conditions for Leibnizian bodies.

Hartz, Glenn A and Hunt, Ralph. Self-Identity and Free Will are Beyond our Control. *Personalist Forum*, 8/1(Supp), 197-204, Spr 92.

Evidence from psychology helps show that personal identity and free will are typically handed to us ready-made by the brain. Kinesthesia as well as normal memory *presuppose* a built-in sense of where and who we are. We relate this to Kant's notion that it is an "a priori" matter that we "find ourselves" in a region of space and see our "representations" as states of persisting "I." Finally, free will is addressed: the "inner voice" that seems to be initiating free acts is itself the result of brain activity beyond our control. So the biggest obstacle to genuine free will may be, not the laws of nature or subconscious Freudian forces, but the fact that not one of our thoughts originates with the inner voice.

Harvey, Charles W. Husserl's Complex Concept of the Self and the Possibility of Social Criticism in Crises in Continental Philosophy, Dallery, Arleen B (ed). Albany, SUNY Pr, 1990.

This essay shows that Husserl's complex description of the self allows us to understand how and why the human subject engages in social criticism. It situates Husserl's notion of the self between the idea of a totally attached and embedded self, one ensnared in the world, and a world-purified self, a pure and empty ego and nothing more. The case is made that a person must be both connected and disconnected to social reality in order to effectively criticize it, and that Husserl's fully developed notion of the self shows how and that this is the way we are.

Harvey, David L and Reed, Michael. The New Science and the Old: Complexity and Realism in the Social Sciences. *J Theor Soc Behav*, 22(4), 353-380, D 92.

Harvey, Irene E. Derrida and the Issues of Exemplarity in Derrida: A Critical Reader, Wood, David (ed). Cambridge, Blackwell, 1992.

Harvey, J. Challenging the Obvious: The Logic of Colour Concepts. *Philosophia (Israel)*, 21(3-4), 277-294, Ap 92.

The paper gives a dispositionalist analysis of colour concepts (as applied to physical objects) involving three levels of colour concepts: "perceived colours", the object's "present colour", and the object's "official colour". The concept of an object's present colour depends on there being a rough uniformity of perceived colours within some chosen group of viewers. This empirical requirement leads to the role of "a standard-state viewer". A startling implication as to what constitutes a finer colour discriminator reveals that traditionally we have not maintained consistently these foundations of our anthropocentric colour concepts. Also, some recent attacks on dispositionalist accounts are shown to fail because they lack any clear concept of an object's present colour.

Harvey, John C (ed) and Abel, Francesc (ed) and Wildes, Kevin W (ed). *Birth, Suffering, and Death: Catholic Perspectives at the Edges of Life*. Dordrecht, Kluwer, 1992.

Harvey, Peter. The Mind-Body Relationship in Pāli Buddhism: A Philosophical Investigation. *Asian Phil*, 3(1), 29-41, Mr 93.

The *Suttas* indicates physical conditions for success in meditation, and also acceptance of a not-Self life-principle (primarily *vinnana*) which is (usually) dependent on the mortal physical body. In the *Abhidhamma* and commentaries, the physical acts on the mental through the senses and through the 'basis' for mind-organ and mind-consciousness, which came to be seen as the 'heart-basis'. Mind acts on the body through two 'intimations': fleeting modulations in the primary physical elements. Various forms of *rupa* are also said to originate dependent on *citta* and other types of *rupa*. Meditation makes possible the development of a 'mind-made body' and control over physical, elements through psychic powers. The formless rebirths and the state of cessation are anomalous states of mind-without-body, or body-without-mind, with the latter presenting the problem of how mental phenomena can arise after being completely absent. Does this twin-category process pluralism avoid the problems of substance-dualism?

Harvey, Warren Z. A Note on Schadenfreude and Proverbs 17:5. *Iyyun*, 41, 357-360, Jl 92.

Harvie, Christopher. Gladstonianism, the Provinces, and Popular Political Culture, 1860-1906 in Victorian Liberalism, Bellamy, Richard (ed). New York, Routledge, 1990.

Haskell, Francis. A Puzzle about Italian Art in Isaiah Berlin: A Celebration, Margalit, Edna (ed). Chicago, Univ of Chicago Pr, 1991.

Hasker, William. How Good/Bad is Middle Knowledge? A Reply to Basinger. *Int J Phil Relig*, 33(2), 111-118, Ap 93.

Hasker, William. Zagzebski on Power Entailment. *Faith Phil*, 10(2), 250-255, Ap 93.

In her book, *The Dilemma of Freedom and Foreknowledge*, Linda Zagzebski devotes considerable attention to the "power entailment principles." Acknowledging that these principles make things quite difficult for theological compatibilism, she offers three counterexamples in an attempt to show that the principles are false. In this paper her counterexamples are refuted.

Haskins, Casey. Dewey's *Art as Experience*: The Tension between Aesthetics and Aestheticism. *Trans Peirce Soc*, 28(2), 217-259, Spr 92.

Dewey's *Art as Experience* defends the view that art and life are a unity. But his version of this view exhibits an ambiguity, arising from his tendency to move back and forth in the text between two usages of "art". These two usages allow for two different interpretations of the theme of the unity of art and life: an "aesthetic" interpretation emphasizing the uniqueness of the fine arts as instrumentally valuable sources of aesthetic and consummatory experience, and an "aestheticist" interpretation emphasizing the presence of such experience not only in the fine arts but throughout the spectrum of intelligent practice. Are these interpretations necessarily in tension, or can we read them as part of a single consistent argument about the nature of art in Dewey's text? I argue that we can, but to do so we need to view them dialectically, and with a glance toward a figure whose influence on Dewey is underappreciated in the recent literature: Hegel.

Haskins, Casey. Kant and the Autonomy of Art. *J Aes Art Crit*, 47(1), 43-54, Wint 89.

Haskins, Casey. Kant, Autonomy, and Art for Art's Sake. *J Aes Art Crit*, 48(3), 235-237, Sum 90.

Haslanger, Sally. Ontology and Pragmatic Paradox. *Proc Aris Soc*, 92, 293-313, 1992.

This paper explores whether the injunction to avoid pragmatic paradox or self-defeat provides a basis for positive ontological results. In the first part I offer an account of how such arguments are supposed to work; in the second part I consider an example of the strategy for the conclusion that there are actual enduring things. In particular, I consider whether the nature of inference is such that the rejection of endurance *for reasons* is self-defeating. I argue that the charge is unconvincing, and its failure has broader implications for what we should expect self-defeat arguments to accomplish.

Hasle, Per and Ohrstrom, Peter. A N Prior's Rediscovery of Tense Logic. *Erkenntnis*, 39(1), 23-50, Jl 93.

Hass, Lawrence. Merleau-Ponty and Cartesian Skepticism: Exorcising the Demon. *Man World*, 26(2), 131-145, Ap 93.

It is frequently suggested that Cartesian skepticism is unimpeachable because it does not require any assumptions for its formulation. I argue that this is false, that to believe skepticism holds over perceptual experience is to assume perception to be the very kind of thing Descartes concludes it is in the 2cd Meditation, namely, *judgment*. In addition to identifying this "new Cartesian circle", I argue that Merleau-Ponty's philosophy of perception offers compelling reasons for rejecting the "judgment theory" of perception altogether.

Hassing, R F. Animals Versus the Laws of Inertia. *Rev Metaph*, 46(1), 29-61, S 92.

This paper investigates the laws of motion in Newton and Descartes, focusing initially on the first laws of each (later conjoined in the minds of interpreters in what came to be called the law of inertia). Our analysis leads to the special significance of Newton's third law, and thus to a consideration of Newton's three laws of motion taken as a whole. Principal results are: (1) There is no one law of inertia; Newton's first law is distinct from Descartes's in its implications for our understanding of nature. (2) Force in Newton's laws of motion is not the same as cause of motion. (3) Newton's three laws, unlike Descartes', do not rule out internal causes of motion, and are thus not reductionist, but rather neutral to the issue of holism versus reductionism.

Hatfield, Gary. Color Perception and Neural Encoding: Does Metameric Matching Entail a Loss of Information?. *Proc Phil Sci Ass*, 1, 492-504, 1992.

In metameric matching, spectrophotometrically diverse materials appear the same. Intuitively, this seems like a loss of information. This intuition relies on a implicit conception that the function of color vision is to represent the physical properties of surfaces. The paper presents an alternative conception of the function of color vision, that of partitioning surfaces into discrimination classes.

Hatfield, Gary. Empirical, Rational, and Transcendental Psychology in The Cambridge Companion to Kant, Guyer, Paul (ed). New York, Cambridge Univ Pr, 1992.

This chapter examines Kant's refutation of rational psychology in the Paralogisms, his contrast between empirical psychology and the transcendental philosophy of the Deduction, his implicit appeal to faculty psychology throughout the first *Critique*, and his new definitions for and support of empirical and rational psychology in the Method. Kant's criticism of the possibility of scientific psychology fails, but his distinction between philosophy and psychology is of lasting interest.

Hatfield, Gary. *The Natural and the Normative: Theories of Spatial Perception from Kant to Helmholtz*. Cambridge, MIT Pr, 1991.

This book examines psychological and philosophical theories of mind and of spatial perception in the period from Kant to Helmholtz (including the background from Descartes to Hume). It distinguishes naturalism from materialism, and separates the natural-normative distinction from substance dualism. It argues that Helmholtz responded effectively to Kant's theory of space, but that his refutation was based on physics and not psychology (as he thought).

Hattiangadi, J N and Baigrie, Brian S. On Consensus and Stability in Science. *Brit J Phil Sci*, 43(4), 435-458, D 92.

Hauerwas, Stanley. The Difference of Virtue and the Difference It Makes: Courage Exemplified. *Mod Theol*, 9(3), 249-264, Jl 93.

This article argues that recent communitarian celebration of virtue fails to give an adequate account of the differences between virtue theories in their historical modes. By comparing Aristotle's and Aquinas's accounts of courage, the article exemplifies the difference of paradigmatic examples for the differences of virtue and the difference it makes. In particular, Aristotle's concentration on courage in battle in contrast with Aquinas's understanding of the martyr's courage exemplifies the difference between quite different traditions.

Haugeland, John. Dasein's Disclosedness in Heidegger: A Critical Reader, Dreyfus, Hubert L (ed). Cambridge, Blackwell, 1992.

Haughey, John C. Does Loyalty in the Workplace Have a Future?. *Bus Ethics Quart*, 3(1), 1-16, Ja 93.

Recent economic constraints on business have led to massive layoffs and downsizing. One effect is the widespread feeling that employee loyalty to a business or a boss is finished. The author claims that one kind of loyalty is on its way out and a more mature loyalty is now possible. Inspired by Josiah Royce and Lawrence Kohlberg, the author claims that the three limitations of prior forms of loyalty can now be superseded by loyalties that are less person/place fixed, less tribal and less co-dependent. The new loyalties have a chance of being more principled, discriminating, and common-good oriented.

Hauptli, Bruce. Unfathomed Knowledged, Unmeasured Worth and Growth?. *Phil Soc Sci*, 23(1), 97-102, Mr 93.

Bartley's *Unfathomed Knowledge, Unmeasured Wealth* contends there is little growth of knowledge because university professors are mainly concerned with protecting their property rights to ideas and ensuring that they are consistent with those accepted by professional communities. His "pancritical" rationalism would encourage free market structures which should engender the growth of knowledge by emphasizing the "unfathomable" character of our ideas or theories, the importance of criticism and the economic character of epistemology. Given his contention that the truth is not manifest, however, it is not clear what entitles him to claim that his "pancritical" rationalism fosters the growth of knowledge.

Hauser, Larry. Act, Aim and Unscientific Explanation. *Phil Invest*, 15(4), 313-323, O 92.

"Folk psychology" (FP) is widely held to have the same logical structure and cognitive aims as scientific theories generally. But then it seems FP is bad (imprecise, stagnant) science. This diagnosis misapprehends the cognitive functions, hence the logical form, of FP's central pattern of explanation (of acts by aims). These conform neither to Hempel's Deductive Nomological nor Inductive Statistical types. Conformity to scientific patterns would bar such explanations from having the practical, evaluative uses they do. Thus, FP is not vulnerable to replacement by competing scientific theories and not amenable to scientific improvement—neither would-be nor has-been science.

Hauser, Larry. Reaping the Whirlwind: Reply to Harnad's Other Bodies, Other Minds. *Mind Mach*, 3(2), 219-237, My 93.

Steven Harnad's proposal (in "Other Bodies, Other Minds") for the "robotic upgrade" of Turing's Test from a test of linguistic capacity alone to a Total Turing Test of linguistic and sensorimotor capacity conflicts with his claim that no behavioral test provides even probable warrant for attributions of thought. I agree that wholesale identification of thought with "private experience" *has* the skeptical consequence Harnad accepts—"there is in fact *no evidence* for me that anyone else but me has a mind." I disagree with his *acceptance* of it! Further considerations Harnad offers in favor of his proposed upgrade are unconvincing also.

Hauser, Larry. The Sense of 'Thinking'. *Mind Mach*, 3(1), 21-29, F 93.

William Rapaport objects that the syllogism "Calculating is thinking; Cal (my pocket calculator) calculates, therefore Cal thinks," I propose in *Why Isn't My Pocket Calculator a Thinking Thing* either equivocates on 'thinks' or fails to show Cal thinks in a sufficiently robust way to be philosophically interesting sense. Against this I maintain that there is no distinction of *meaning* or *sense* (only of degree) between what Rapaport calls the "minimal" and "maximal" senses of 'thinking'. Consequently, the syllogism shows Cal thinks in the philosophically interesting sense of being a subject possessed of intentional mental states.

Hauser, Larry. Why Isn't My Pocket Calculator a Thinking Thing?. *Mind Mach*, 3(1), 3-10, F 93.

It seems my pocket calculator (Cal) calculates and that calculating is thinking. Yet these claims together seem to entail a conclusion—Cal thinks—most would deny. If standards of autonomy and self-consciousness are proposed to rule out Cal, these make it impossible to verify whether anything or anyone (save myself?) meets them. While the intentionality of thought or the unity of minds suggest methodologically more credible lines of resistance, available accounts of intentionality and mental unity are insufficient to provide very substantial arguments against Cal's thinking either. Indeed, considerations favoring this conclusion are more formidable than generally appreciated.

Hausman, Alan and Hausman, David. Idealizing Hume. *Hume Stud*, 18(2), 209-218, N 92.

Hausman, Carl R. *Charles S Peirce's Evolutionary Philosophy*. New York, Cambridge Univ Pr, 1993.

A systematic introduction to the philosophy of Charles Peirce. It focuses on his pragmaticism, theory of signs, phenomenology, and theory of continuity (synecism) as these relate to his conception of evolutionary change. The thesis is that Peirce's hope for an architectonic was tied to a unique form of metaphysical realism according to which his dynamical object is a condition that evolves and constrains thought. The final chapter discusses ways Peirce's form of realism responds to those neopragmatists who resist commitments to the view that there are constraints on thought that have their source in something not wholly dependent on linguistic and conceptual perspectives.

Hausman, Carl R. Figurative Language in Art History in The Language of Art History, Kemal, Salim (ed). New York, Cambridge Univ Pr, 1991.

The way art critics use language in interpreting works of art involves the use of metaphors. The essay attempts to show how whole works of art exhibit the kind of structure (interactions of meanings) found in verbal metaphors. It then considers, using examples, how subordinate metaphors are used to apply the distinct aspects of works of are and give specificity to the "overall" metaphor of the work.

Hausman, Carl R and Anderson, Douglas R. The Role of Aesthetic Emotion in R G Collingwood's Conception of Creative Activity. *J Aes Art Crit*, 50(4), 299-305, Fall 92.

Hausman, Daniel. Liberalism, Welfare Economics, and Freedom. *Soc Phil Pol*, 10(2), 172-197, Sum 93.

This essay argues that liberalism is not committed to assessing policies by their impact on individual preferences and that liberals should be wary of contemporary welfare economies. There is a good liberal argument for markets, but there are also good reasons for liberals to be concerned to regulate and limit markets.

Hausman, Daniel. Thresholds, Transitivity, Overdetermination, and Events. *Analysis*, 52(3), 159-163, Jl 92.

This paper argues that in circumstances involving causal thresholds or causal overdetermination one cannot consistently hold both that causation is a transitive relation and that its relata are "coarse-grained" events individuated by their spatial and temporal boundaries.

Hausman, Daniel. Why Don't Effects Explain Their Causes?. *Synthese*, 94(2), 227-244, F 93.

This paper argues that its title is a serious question to which no satisfactory answer has been given. The only answer suggested in the literature is pragmatic, and it is unacceptable. The paper gives some hints concerning the answer.

Hausman, Daniel M. *Essays on Philosophy and Economic Methodology*. New York, Cambridge Univ Pr, 1992.

This is a collection of essays on philosophy of economics, most of which were published previously. Part I addresses issues concerning the appraisal of economic theory. Part II is concerned with the causal structure of economic theories. Part III addresses philosophical problems raised by particular economic theories. Part IV contains reflections on philosophy of economics itself.

Hausman, Daniel M. Linking Causal and Explanatory Asymmetry. *Phil Sci*, 60(3), 435-451, S 93.

This essay defends two theses that jointly establish a link between causal and explanatory asymmetry. The first thesis is that statements specifying facts about effects, unlike statements specifying facts about causes, are not "independently variable". The second thesis is that independent variability among purportedly explanatory factors is a necessary condition on scientific explanations.

Hausman, David and Hausman, Alan. Idealizing Hume. *Hume Stud*, 18(2), 209-218, N 92.

Havas, K G. Do We Tolerate Inconsistencies?. *Dialectica*, 47(1), 27-35, 1993.

It is not the inconsistency in the sense of classical logic (CI) that we have to tolerate. The dialectical reasoning, described by N Rescher, is outside the domain where CI is defined. The apparent contradiction between CI and paraconsistent logic (PL) can be removed by realizing that PL is a widening of the conceptual framework of classical logic. In this new framework the meaning of some words was changed similarly as, according to N Bohr, in quantum mechanics the words "particle" and "wave" have changed their meaning.

Havas, Randall. Who is Heidegger's Nietzsche? in Heidegger: A Critical Reader, Dreyfus, Hubert (ed). Cambridge, Blackwell, 1992.

Havelkova, Hana. Who Is Afraid of Feminist Philosophy? (in Czechoslovakian). *Filozof Cas*, 40(5), 729-741, 1992.

With regard to the fact that this article is an introduction to feminist philosophy which has been lacking in Czech philosophy till now, it concentrates both on the issue of the place of feminist philosophy in the western philosophical discourse and on the issue of its heuristic potential in relation to the Czech milieu and the needs of its reflexion by political philosophy. The themes of feminist philosophy are presented first of all from the viewpoint of their significance for constituting a specific method of feminist philosophy as a critical and practical philosophy which makes it possible to test the universalistic claim of a number of the principles of modernism and postmodernism. It is one of the intentions of this explanation to correct the idea that feminist philosophy is determined by the so-called female question as its exclusive subject. The stress laid on the fact that feminist philosophy is primarily a specific type of philosophizing makes it possible to elucidate both its alternative and parallel position within the framework of philosophy. (edited)

Haver, William. Thinking the Thought of that Which is Strictly Speaking Unthinkable: On the Thematization of Alterity in Nishida-Philosophy. *Human Stud*, 16(1-2), 177-192, Ap 93.

Hawley, R. 'Pretty, Witty and Wise': Courtesans in Athenaeus' *Deipnosophistai* Book 13. *Int J Moral Soc Stud*, 8(1), 73-91, Spr 93.

This paper examines and shows the weaknesses of two traditional conceptions of modern classical scholarship. Firstly, the idea that the classical *hetaira* was distinguished from other prostitutes not only by her beauty, but also by her intellectual accomplishments, is usually based upon texts cited in Athenaeus' *Deipnosophistai*. But a closer reading proves this interpretation to be misleading. 'Wise' *hetairai* are constructed as complementary opposites to 'wise' women philosophers. Secondly, Athenaeus has a poor reputation among scholars as a mere collator, incompetent and unoriginal, whose work lacks a clear structure. An analysis of book 13, On Women, reveals that the quotations are arranged in a dramatic dialogue designed to satirize both the genre of symposium literature and contemporary moralizing on marriage. In a variety of subtle and humorous ways Athenaeus stresses the dangerous deception of love.

Haworth, Lawrence and Brunk, Conrad G and Lee, Brenda. Is a Scientific Assessment of Risk Possible? Value Assumptions in the Canadian Alachlor Controversy. *Dialogue (Canada)*, 30(3), 235-247, Sum 91.

Hawthorne, John and Cover, J A. Leibnizian Essentialism, Transworld Identity, and Counterparts. *Hist Phil Quart*, 9(4), 425-444, O 92.

The standard view of Leibnizian modality reckons Leibniz committed to superessentialism and to denying trans-world identity. We present historical and philosophical arguments against the standard view. In particular, we argue that Leibnizian essentialism is *consistent* with trans-world identity, and that his modal metaphysics allows for the possibility of a counterpart semantics for *de re* moral predication.

Hay, John. The Human Body as a Microcosmic Source of Macrocosmic Values in Calligraphy in Self as Body in Asian Theory and Practice, Kasulis, Thomas P (ed). Albany, SUNY Pr, 1992.

Hay, William H. The Standpoint of the Universe, if It Has One, Is Not that of Our Moral Situation. *Ultim Real Mean*, 16(1-2), 73-86, Mr-Je 93.

After years of reviewing rival claims about ultimate reality, Arthur Edward Murphy abandoned them all concluding that meaning is not "something brought in from a higher reality to save an incoherent world." Rather the answer to the quest for meaning will be "the sense we can find in our own actions, when we know what we are doing and the good of doing it." Because everyone has grown up as a member of some moral community and as a result understands the operation of moral ideas as reasons, everyone can join in the creation of such a community.

Hayden, R Mary. Aquinas and Natural Human Fulfillment: Inconsistencies. *Amer Cath Phil Quart*, 65, 215-233, 1991.

Aquinas's identification of this life's happiness with the contemplation of God seems inconsistent with the inadequacies of natural and metaphysical knowledge of God, the perfection of love, and the human need for moral virtue and friendship. But these textual inconsistencies are only apparent: there is a mediated contemplation of God that as the whole of happiness suffices for the natural last end; necessary conditions of happiness are not to be conflated with its essential constituent; and happiness is predicated analogously of contemplation and the acts of practical reason.

Hayden-Roy, Priscilla. New and Old Histories: The Case of Hölderlin and Württemberg Pietism. *Clio*, 21(4), 369-379, Sum 92.

Haydock, Anne. QALYs—A Threat to our Quality of Life?. *J Applied Phil*, 9(2), 183-188, 1992.

QALY calculations are currently being considered in the UK as a way of showing how the National Health Service (NHS) can do the most good with its resources. After providing a brief summary of how QALY calculations work and the most common arguments for and against using them to set NHS priorities, I suggest that they are an inadequate measure of the good done by the NHS because they refer only to its effects on what will be defined as the 'patient community.' The benefit of the NHS to the wider community is best regarded as a public good—everyone benefits from the general belief that the NHS is there to provide care for those who fall into a state of medical need. QALY ideology threatens this belief because it gives efficiency a higher priority than caring in response to need. It is a fallacy that a QALY maximizing health service will be a greater good to society, because this sort of quest for efficiency threatens the caring basis of the Welfare State as such.

Hayes, Patrick (& others). Virtual Symposium on Virtual Mind. *Mind Mach*, 2(3), 217-238, Ag 92.

Haynes, Anthony. F R Leavis: Intuitionist?. *Brit J Aes*, 33(2), 162-167, Ap 93.

British literary critic F R Leavis described himself as an 'anti-philosopher'. There may, however, be some philosophies to which he was unwittingly allied. Despite Leavis's reputation as a moralist, there has been curiously little attempt to relate his work to the British moral philosophy of his period. Intuitionism provides one point of contact. A comparison of key passages from Levis on R S Eliot's *Four Quartets* and H A Prichard on moral obligation reveal logical parallels. There are also parallels with C D Broad. Leavis's work may not be wholly or consistently intuitionist, but it certainly contains an intuitionist core.

Hayward, Tim. Ecology and Human Emancipation. *Rad Phil*, 62, 3-13, Autumn 92.

Hazen, A P. Against Pluralism. *Austl J Phil*, 71(2), 132-144, Je 93.

It has been argued (by, e.g., George Boolos and David Lewis) that the interpretation of second-order variables as plural terms shows that at least monadic second-order logic is free of ontological commitment to classes. I refute this contention.

Hazen, A P. The Interpretability of Robinson Arithmetic in the Ramified Second-Order Theory of Dense Linear Order. *Notre Dame J Form Log*, 33(1), 101-111, Wint 92.

Ramified Second Order Logic is often thought of as uninterestingly weak: in the sense of Lindstrom's Theorem, it is no more expressively powerful than First Order Logic. In contrast, I show that, although the First Order theory of dense linear order is decidable, its Ramified Second Order theory is essentially undecidable, and argue that there is therefore another sense in which Ramified Second Order languages are more expressive than First Order.

Heald, William (ed) and Bergmann, Gustav and Allaire, Edwin B. *New Foundations of Ontology*. Madison, Univ of Wisconsin Pr, 1992.

Bergmann's last book length manuscript represents his final attempt to propose and defend a system of categories appropriate for a realistic ontology rich enough to account for the existence of minds and an adequate grounding of mathematics. An extension of Bergmann's phenomenological atomism, the book also includes a vigorous attempt to show that "formal facts," including not only analytic facts, but also the possessing of syntactical forms by all facts, are "objective" features of a world whose fundamental core consists of atomic facts and the particular and universal "things" of which they are composed.

Healey, Richard A. Causation, Robustness, and EPR. *Phil Sci*, 59(2), 282-292, Je 92.

In his recent work, Michael Redhead (1986, 1987, 1989, 1990) has introduced a condition he calls robustness which, he argues, a relation must satisfy in order to be causal. He has used this condition to argue further that EPR-type correlations are neither the result of a direct causal connection between the correlated events, nor the result of a common cause associated with the source of the particle pairs which feature in these events. Andrew Elbly (1992) has used this same condition as a premise in an independent argument for the conclusion that EPR-type correlations cannot be causally explained (except, perhaps, by a nonlocal hidden varible theory). I wish to argue here that robustness is itself too fragile a notion to support such conclusions.

Heaton, John M. Language Games, Expression and Desire in the Work of Deleuze. *J Brit Soc Phenomenol*, 24(1), 77-87, Ja 93.

Heck, Richard. On the Consistency of Second-Order Contextual Definitions. *Nous*, 26(4), 491-494, D 92.

The paper argues that the consistency of an arbitrary second-order contextual definition is undecidable, by showing that, given any second- order formula A, there is a contextual definition C(A) with the following property: Every model of A can be extended to a model of C(A), and every model of C(A) is a model of A. Finally, the significance of this fact for relent reconstructions of logicism is discussed.

Heck Jr, Richard and Stanley, Jason. Reply to Hintikka and Sandu: Frege and Second-Order Logic. *J Phil*, 90(8), 416-424, Ag 93.

Heck Jr, Richard G. Michael Dummett's *Frege*. *Phil Quart*, 43(171), 223-232, Ap 93.

This critical study of Dummett's recent book focuses on his discussions of the question whether numbers are objects. It also touches upon the Julius Caesar problem, and Dummett's new argument for intuitionism, based upon the claim that central mathematical concepts are "indefinitely extensible" or, in Russell's phrase, "self-reproductive".

Heckman, Peter. Business and Games. *J Bus Ethics*, 11(12), 933-938, D 92.

This paper responds to the popular argument that business is like a game and is thus insulated from the demands of morality. In the first half of the paper, I offer objections to this argument as it is put forward by John Ladd in his well-known article, 'Morality and the Ideal of Rationality in Formal Organizations'. I argue that Ladd's analysis is flawed both because it deprives us of the ability to assert that a business is acting badly or that its goals are irrational, and because it is internally inconsistent. In the second half of the paper, I give reasons for thinking that business is not like a game.

Heckman, Peter. The Role of Science in *Human-all-too-Human*. *Man World*, 26(2), 147-160, Ap 93.

In this paper, the author considers the odd appearance of *Human-all-too-Human*, in which science is praised, in the wake of Nietzsche's earlier work which deflates scientific aspirations. This work offers science as an alternative to a network of comforting metaphysical beliefs. Ultimately, however, this distinction breaks down as we learn that science ultimately offers a kind of salvation, the installation of humanity within a natural order of innocence. The author argues that the construction of a distinction which ultimately fails is appropriate to an "ironist" thinker such as Nietzsche.

Heckmann, Heinz-Dieter. Mental Events Again—Or What Is Wrong with Anomalous Monism?. *Erkenntnis*, 36(3), 345-373, M 92.

A persistent philosophical worry about Anomalous Monism has been the suspicion that it gives the mental only an epiphenomenal role in mental causation. In a recent lecture Davidson has tried to meet the epiphenomenalism objection. I argue that given the most plausible ontological conception of events there is no way for Anomalous Monism to allay the suspicion.

Hedley, Jane. Surviving to Speak New Language: Mary Daly and Adrienne Rich. *Hypatia*, 7(2), 40-62, Spr 92.

As radical feminists seeking to overcome the linguistic oppression of women, Rich and Daly apparently shared the same agenda in the late 1970s; but they approached the problem differently, and their paths have increasingly diverged. Whereas Daly's approach to the repossession of language is code-oriented and totalizing, Rich's approach is open-ended and context-oriented. Rich has therefore addressed more successfully than Daly the problem of language in use.

Hefner, Philip. Biological Perspectives on Fall and Original Sin. *Zygon*, 28(1), 77-101, Mr 93.

Hehir, J Bryan. Response to Kwasi Wiredu and Laurence Thomas in African-American Perspectives on Biomedical Ethics, Flack, Harley E (ed). Washington, Georgetown Univ Pr, 1992.

Heidegger, Martin and Aylesworth, Gary E (trans). *Basic Concepts—Martin Heidegger*. Bloomington, Indiana Univ Pr, 1993.

Heidegger, Martin and Fink, Eugen and Seibert, Charles H (trans). *Heraclitus Seminar*. Evanston, Northwestern Univ Pr, 1993.

In the winter semester of 1966-67 at the University of Freiburg, Martin Heidegger and Eugen Fink conducted an extraordinary seminar on the fragments of Heraclitus. This book records those conversations, documenting the imaginative and experimental character of the multiplicity of interpretations offered and providing an invaluable portrait of Heidegger involved in active discussion and explication. (staff)

Heidegger, Martin and Lilly, Reginald (trans). *The Principle of Reason—Martin Heidegger*. Bloomington, Indiana Univ Pr, 1992.

Heidelberger, Michael. Kausalität: Eine Problemübersicht. *Neue Hefte Phil*, 32-33, 130-153, 1992.

Heil, John. Philosophy of Mind in Reflections on Philosophy, McHenry, Leemon (ed). New York, St Martin's Pr, 1993.

A discussion of a variety of conceptions of mind (dualist, idealist, and materialist), and the problem of intentionality, designed to introduce the issues to readers unfamiliar with the territory. Topics include: interactionism, parallelism, epiphenomenalism, the identity theory, behaviorism, functionalism, instrumentalism, eliminativism, and internalist and externalist accounts of mental content.

Heil, John. *The Nature of True Minds*. New York, Cambridge Univ Pr, 1992.

Recent work in the philosophy of mind and cognitive science calls into question the traditional Cartesian picture of minds in a way that is nothing short of revolutionary. *Externalists* argue that the significance of thought turns on the circumstances of thinkers; *reductionists* hold that mental characteristics of agents are, at bottom, physical; and *eliminativists* contend that the concept of thought belongs to an outmoded folk theory of behaviour. *The Nature of True Minds* explores these and related claims, argues that they do indeed portend a revolution in our conception of mind, and points the way to a post-Cartesian, naturalistic synthesis.

Heil, John (ed) and Mele, Alfred (ed). *Mental Causation*. New York, Clarendon/Oxford Pr, 1993.

Explaining how mind can make a difference in a material universe has proved challenging. The essays in this volume—each written expressly for it—approach this issue from widely divergent perspectives and offer a cross-section of contemporary responses to the problem of mental causation.

Heilbron, J L. A Mathematicians' Mutiny, with Morals in World Changes, Horwich, Paul (ed). Cambridge, MIT Pr, 1993.

An examination of the threats of some mathematicians to secede from the Royal Society of London in 1784 suggests that people who did not regard themselves as mathematicians brought about the quantification of physics. This finding indicates the impropriety of using words like "physics" and "mathematics" to label branches of knowledge over long periods of time and the need to modify T S Kuhn's concept of mathematical and experimental traditions in the development of physical science.

Heim, Joseph Charles. The Demise of the Confessional State and the Rise of the Idea of a Legitimate Minority. *Nomos*, 32, 11-23, 1990.

Heim, Michael. The Computer as Component: Heidegger and McLuhan. *Phil Lit*, 16(2), 304-319, O 92.

Philosophers will never treat cyberspace and virtual reality so long as the conceptual framework of the AI debate dominates discussion. An essentialist bias haunts questions like, Can computers think?—as if we could locate the essence of a non-interactive machine. Computers now inform a range of activities from writing and planning to art and communication. I suggest a different paradigm based on the existential pragmatics of computing, found in McLuhan and Heidegger. The new paradigm converts the computer-as-opponent to the computer as component of human activity.

Heim, Michael. The Essence of VR. *Ideal Stud*, 23(1), 49-62, Wint 93.

"The Essence of VR" comes from the book *The Metaphysics of Virtual Reality* (Oxford U Press, 1993) where it is chapter 8. The chapter explores in turn the seven key features of virtual reality technology and seeks to pinpoint a single definition of "virual reality" based on the work of VR pioneers. The chapter shows how pivotal metaphysical notions are for VR such as "presence" and "actuality," and the chapter concludes with several suggestions for creating virtual worlds and for employing metaphysicians as part of the design team for virtual environments.

Heim, S Mark. The Pluralistic Hypothesis, Realism, and Post-Eschatology. *Relig Stud*, 28(2), 207-219, Je 92.

Hein, Hilde. The Role of Feminist Aesthetics in Feminist Theory. *J Aes Art Crit*, 48(4), 281-291, Fall 90.

This essay argues that feminism is not about women as such, but about gender as a conceptual frame. Feminist theory entails a new concept of theory, whose objective is to preserve and illuminate multiplicity rather than to reduce it. Feminist aesthetic theory lies at the heart, not the periphery, of theoretical reflection, but is often at odds with or obliquely related to conventional, male-produced theoretical norms. The author shows by illustration how feminist aesthetic reflection reveals errors and sharpens understanding of a world whose perception has been inappropriately fixed to a male-gendered norm. Aesthetic analysis as a tool of feminist theory is a needed corrective.

Heinaman, Robert. Rationality, Eudaimonia and Kakodaimonia in Aristotle. *Phronesis*, 38(1), 31-56, 1993.

I argue that Aristotle does not believe all rational action aims at securing eudaimonia (happiness) for the agent. Intrinsic goods are worth having independently of their promotion of any further ends, including eudaimonia. Aiming for such a good or avoiding evil may be rational even when eudaimonia is impossible and not the agent's goal. *Politics* 1332a7f suggests that even the happy agent may act rationally without aiming for eudaimonia. The final section argues that, given that an immoral agent secures the greatest of evils, an alleged conflict in the *Nicomachean Ethics* between the intellectualist Book X and earlier books disappears.

Heitman, Elizabeth (ed) and Bulger, Ruth Ellen (ed) and Reiser, Stanley Joel (ed). *The Ethical Dimensions of the Biological Sciences*. New York, Cambridge Univ Pr, 1993.

This collection contains a variety of classic essays and seminal works by researchers from many disciplines, as well as policy statements and research guidelines from professional and government bodies. Among the issues considered are: the norms of ethical conduct in science and their origins; scientific honesty, skepticism, and self-deception; the ethical standards of laboratory practice; the use of human and animal subjects; the qualifications for authorship and publication; the ethics of learning and teaching; and the relationships of science, industry, and society. (edited)

Hejdanek, L. Sousedik's Unsuccessful Criticism (in Czechoslovakian). *Filozof Cas*, 40(4), 677-679, 1992.

Hejdánek, L. Philosophy and Nationalism. *Tijdschr Filosof*, 55(1), 1-12, Mr 93.

Unlike the rational political conception of a nation state, the nationalistic view is not so much an idea as it is an ideological construct, based on a certain pseudo-naturalistic approach to community life. In order to explain the success of nationalistic "mythologisms", one has to understand them as surrogates or substitutes for an integrated religious or mythical world view for the great mass of people who have lost their identity and their roots. The real importance of such an ideology does not consist in its being theoretically correct, but in its producing an abstract, often mistaken feeling of a so-called national character. Nationalist ideologies, however, need not be true to have influence, and the fact that masses of people do identify themselves with their nations, easily turns their hypostatical constructs into social and historical realities.

Hekman, Susan. Moral Voices, Moral Selves: About Getting it Right in Moral Theory. *Human Stud*, 16(1-2), 143-162, Ap 93.

Carol Gilligan's exploration of the "different voice" in moral theory raises profound questions about the constitution of moral voices and moral selves. In this paper I argue, first, that there are serious confusions in Gilligan's understanding of the epistemological implications of the different voice, and second, that neither Gilligan nor those who have employed her researches realize the radical implications of her work. Third, I argue that Gilligan's understanding of the constitution of moral voices leads to a radical restructuring of the moral domain. It effectively deconstructs the metanarrative of moral theory and, instead, implies an understanding of morality which presupposes a multiplicity of moral voices. In conclusion I explore the consequences of this conception for feminist moral theory.

Held, Dirk T D. Μεγαλοϖια in *Nocomachean Ethics* iv. *Ancient Phil*, 13(1), 95-110, Spr 93.

Held, Klaus. Fundamental Moods and Heidegger's Critique of Contemporary Culture in Reading Heidegger: Commemorations, Sallis, John (ed). Bloomington, Indiana Univ Pr, 1992.

Held, Klaus. The Finitude of the World in Ethics and Danger, Dallery, Arleen B (ed). Albany, SUNY Pr, 1992.

Heller, Agnes. Rights, Modernity, Democracy in Deconstruction and the Possibility of Justice, Cornell, Durcilla (ed). New York, Routledge, 1992.

Heller, Mark. Things Change. *Phil Phenomenol Res*, 52(3), 695-704, S 92.

A common objection to the temporal parts ontology is that such an ontology is inconsistent with the fact that things survive change. I consider various versions of the objection and argue that they all depend on misunderstanding the temporal parts ontology.

Heller, Michael. Singularities, Quantum Creation, History, and the Existence of the Universe. *Phil Sci (Tucson)*, 5, 33-49, 1993.

Hellman, Geoffrey. Constructive Mathematics and Quantum Mechanics: Unbounded Operators and the Spectral Theorem. *J Phil Log*, 22(3), 221-248, Je 93.

Hellman, Geoffrey. Constructivist Mathematics, Quantum Physics and Quantifiers—I, The Boxer and His Fists. *Aris Soc*, Supp(66), 61-77, 1992.

Hellman, Geoffrey. Gleason's Theorem is Not Constructively Provable. *J Phil Log*, 22(2), 193-203, Ap 93.

Gleason's Theorem characterizes the possible generalized probability measures on the closed subspaces of a Hilbert space of dimension three or greater. They are given by the quantum mechanical pure and mixed states. In addition to ruling out non-contextual hidden variables, the theorem is central in determining how probability can be introduced into quantum mechanics. This paper shows by reduction that even the weakest restriction of the theorem is not constructively provable in the sense of Brouwer or Bishop, i.e., by intuitionistic reasoning. The theorem is shown to reduce the lesser halting problem. This partially answers an open problem posed by Douglas Bridges. It does not say whether any viable constructivist substitute for Gleason's theorem is possible.

Hellman, Nathan. It is Generally the Case That. *Auslegung*, 18(2), 131-143, Sum 92.

Helm, Bennet W. Why We Believe in Induction: Standards of Taste and Hume's Two Definitions of Causation. *Hume Stud*, 19(1), 117-140, Ap 93.

Two interrelated elements of Hume's account of causation are often overlooked. The first is the distinction between the natural and philosophical relations of causation, which is one between why we *in fact* and why we *ought* to make causal inferences. Because these are essentially interrelated, we can see why Hume gives two definitions of causation. The second is that in making causal inferences "we must follow our taste and sentiment." Because the standards for the philosophical relation are not intelligible in terms of demonstrative inference, Hume appeals to a different kind of standard, analogous to standards for aesthetic and moral judgments. This provides him with the tools for a solution to his problem of induction.

Helm, Bert P. Axiologic Rather than Logic: Priority of Aesthetic and Ethical Over Semiotic Logic of Scientific Discovery. *Ultim Real Mean*, 16(1-2), 128-130, Mr-Je 93.

Some recent account of the philosophy of Charles Sanders Peirce (such as that of Noel Boulting) present Peirce as one who is primarily a logician, especially as that logic is displayed semeiotically in the logic of the sciences. Probably, however, a less scholastic approach to Peirce should be taken if we are to comprehend him adequately. His stress on kinds of openness, not closure, would come to the fore. Such an approach would capture Peirce's attention to vagueness, to mystery, to the umbral. Especially where the emphasis falls across value can we see that Peirce's axiologic takes precedence over his logic.

Helm, Paul. Preserving Perseverence. *Int J Phil Relig*, 33(2), 103-109, Ap 93.

Helm, Paul. Richard Gale's *On the Nature and Existence of God*. *Relig Stud*, 29(2), 245-255, Je 93.

Henderson, Harold. *Catalyst for Controversy: Paul Carus of Open Court*. Carbondale, So Illinois Univ Pr, 1993.

Hendley, Brian P. Rorty Revisited. *Metaphilosophy*, 24(1-2), 175-178, Ja-Ap 93.

I have two pet peeves with Rorty. First is his claim to be a "fairly faithful follower of John Dewey" while insisting on a hard and fast dualism between private irony and public liberalism. Second is his arms-length approach to education which is a far cry from Dewey's attempt to intellectualize practice and practicalize intelligence. I conclude with the suggestion that Rorty might find Camus more to his taste than Dewey.

Hendriks, Ruud. Scenes from a Newborn Life (in Dutch). *Kennis Methode*, 16(4), 294-312, 1992.

If there is any place where medical, ethical, legal and lay accounts are intermingled, recent discussions in neonatology—e.g., the Dutch baby Ross case—provide a good case. In their mutual interaction participants constitute a normative order, which surround and pervades neonatal practice. Redefining the neonatal debate amounts to redefine the destiny of the newborn life. Those who want to join in the discussion however, are often confronted with barriers that prevent participation. A semiotics of actor-networks is used to follow participants around as they constitute this order of different degrees of access. It is argued that a redescription of the development of the debate might better the chances for as yet unheard stories.

Henle, R J. Levels of the Natural Law. *Vera Lex*, 11(2), 1-5, 1991.

The basic thesis is that the Natural Law is not innate, is not imposed from without and is simply worked out by human reason and is a fact in all societies. The analysis may be viewed chronologically as the stages of historical development as societies grow more sophisticated or may be regarded as layers existing in all societies, however developed. The business of the philosopher is not to create the Natural Law but to purify, clarify and apply it.

Henle, R J. Schopenhauer and Direct Realism. *Rev Metaph*, 46(1), 125-140, S 92.

Henley, Kenneth. Abstract Principles, Mid-Level Principles, and the Rule of Law. *Law Phil*, 12(1), 121-132, F 93.

The rule of law requires predictability in the application of legal principles. The more abstract a principle is, the more indeterminate its application. Thus mid-level principles, advocated by Michael Bayles for other reasons, also serve the rule of law. Ronald Dworkin's treatment of the principle "no one should profit from his own wrongdoing" is criticized as insufficiently grounded in the history of its use in equity courts. Historical context fills out the meaning of principles.

Hennessy, Rosemary. *Materialist Feminism and the Politics of Discourse*. New York, Routledge, 1993.

Materialist Feminism and the Politics of Discourse shows how the resources of the Marxist feminist tradition can contribute to the current rethinking of the subject of feminism. The book argues that one of feminism's strongest legacies is its critique of social totalities like patriarchy and capitalism. Materialist feminism keeps alive the critique of social totalities without abandoning attention to the differential positioning of women. The book focuses on the problem of the subject, specifically the subject constituted by discourse, and argues that we need to examine the social logics implicit in postmodern theories to see what extent a particular theoretical framework may subvert or enhance feminism's political objectives. Offering critiques of a number of influential thinkers including Foucault, Kristeva, Laclau and Mouffe, the book illustrates that materialist feminism's political aims are most congruent with a theory of discourse as ideology.

Hennessy, Rosemary. Women's Lives/Feminist Knowledge: Feminist Standpoint as Ideology Critique. *Hypatia*, 8(1), 14-34, Wint 93.

Feminist standpoint theory posits feminism as a way of conceptualizing from the vantage point of women's lives. However, in current work on feminist standpoint the material links between lives and knowledges are often not explained. This essay argues that the radical marxist tradition standpoint theory draws on—specifically theories of ideology post-Althusser—offers a systemic mode of reading that can redress this problem and provide the resources to elaborate further feminism's oppositional practice and collective subject.

Henrich, Dieter. *Aesthetic Judgment and the Moral Image of the World: Studies in Kant*. Stanford, Stanford Univ Pr, 1992.

Henrich, Dieter. The Origins of the Theory of the Subject in Philosophical Interventions in the Unfinished Project of Enlightenment, Honneth, Axel (& other eds). Cambridge, MIT Pr, 1992.

Henricks, Joyce E. Ethics in Reflections on Philosophy, McHenry, Leemon (ed). New York, St Martin's Pr, 1993.

This chapter starts with setting out some general "ground rules" for engaging in moral discussion, applying these ground rules to an examination of the relationships between morality, religion, and custom. Utilitarianism and Kantianism are discussed, along with Ross' notion of "prima facie" duties. A brief discussion of some standard justificatory techniques is presented, concluding with the challenge to traditional ethical theory presented by an "ethics of care" perspective. The emphasis throughout the chapter is to help students examine the various perspectives and reach their own conclusions about the relative merits of these perspectives; as such, criticisms are kept to a minimum, and are left up to the instructor to develop.

Henry, D P. The Logical Grammar of the Transcendentals. *Phil Quart*, 43(173), 431-446, O 93.

Reminders of the immense overlap now visible between medieval and contemporary linguistic and logical philosophy are followed by an exemplificatory analysis of a section of Aquinas' *De Veritate*.

Henry, Granville C. *Forms of Concrescence: Alfred North Whitehead's Philosophy and Computer Programming Structures*. Lewisburg, Bucknell Univ Pr, 1993.

Henry, Granville C. *The Mechanism and Freedom of Logic*. Lanham, Univ Pr of America, 1993.

Henry, Sarojini. Social Ethic of Mahatma Gandhi and Martin Buber. *J Dharma*, 16(4), 375-386, O-D 91.

Hentschel, Klaus. Einstein's Attitude Towards Experiments: Testing Relativity Theory 1907-1927. *Stud Hist Phil Sci*, 23(4), 593-624, D 92.

It is shown that contrary to a widespread myth of Einstein as a highbrow theorist, he was extremely curious about experimental results linked to his newly proposed theoretical principles. Hitherto unpublished correspondence demonstrates that he eagerly motivated specialists to search for effects like gravitational redshift and light deflection, actively helped to provide them with adequate institutional backing if needed. In contrast to contemporaries who were willing to carefully modify the theory of relativity and gravitation in the light of apparently contrary evidence, Einstein was not willing to modify his theories but rather to give them up completely. Newly discovered Einstein articles and interviews in the daily press of the mid-20's confirm this.

Hepburn, R W. Values of Art and Values of Community in On Community, Rouner, Leroy S (ed). Notre Dame, Univ Notre Dame Pr, 1992.

This study seeks to identify values of common concern to the aesthetic enterprise and the moral and religious community. In opposition to some influential current theorists, it is argued that freedom, disinterested, contemplative attitudes and respect-for-other-being play vital parts in both fields; and that a reasoned defense of this claim is possible. Discussion is extended to certain overlaps between aesthetic and religious modes of experience. Examples considered here are: 1) the evocation of a sense of "transcendence," and; 2) the dynamic interrelation between concepts of life or creative activity, and of stillness and tranquility. These are thought of as fused in God, at their maximal intensity.

Hepburn, Ronald W. Religious Imagination. *Philosophy*, 32(Supp), 127-143, 1992.

In the field of religion, imagination tends to be given a large and indispensable role: typically carrying the believer from finite and temporal events, experiences, symbols, and rites to the thought of an infinite, eternal, world-transcending being to which these, in various ways, point. But imagination can also be seen as limited and problematic, unable to discriminate between revealing and deceptive pictures of deity. The appraisal of imagination's theological role is attempted through critical discussion particularly of J McIntyre's *Faith, Theology, and Imagination* (1987) and J P Mackey's (ed.) *Religious Imagination* (1986). Finally, some general and fundamental questions are raised about the validation of religious images and symbols.

Hepburn, Ronald W. Religious Imagination in Philosophy, Religion and the Spiritual Life, McGhee, Michael (ed). New York, Cambridge Univ Pr, 1992.

In the field of religion, imagination tends to be given a large and indispensable role: typically carrying the believer from finite and temporal events, experiences, symbols and rites to the thought of an infinite, eternal, world-transcending being to which these, in various ways, point. But imagination can also be seen as limited and problematic, unable to discriminate between reveling and deceptive pictures of deity. The appraisal of imagination's theological role is attempted through critical discussion particularly of J McIntyre's *Faith, Theology and Imagination* (1987) and J P Mackey's (ed) *Religious Imagination* (1986). Finally, some general and fundamental questions are raised about the validation of religious images and symbols.

Herbert, Gary and Bourgeois, Patrick. The Religious Significance of Ricoeur's Post-Hegelian Kantian Ethics. *Amer Cath Phil Quart*, 65, 133-144, 1991.

This paper attempts to unfold the religious significance of the ethical in what Ricoeur refers to as his post-Hegelian Kantianism. The expanded ethics, in Ricoeur's terms, takes its bearings by its appropriation of the ethics of Kant and Hegel "by thinking them together—one against the other, and one by means of the other." It is an ethics which is liberated from the lifeless duties of inner freedom of will, an ethics which anchors will in the institutions and events of the concrete world, yet does not restrict the will to retrospective descriptions of a fully developed, final "totality." It is in part the Hegelian element in Ricoeur's thought that enables him to expand ethics beyond the narrowness of Kant's morality of duty to a more concrete concern for freedom. This extension of Kantian ethics to a more concrete, less abstract involvement in the world is accomplished by inserting "the religious" into the core of Ricoeur's overall ethical approach to human activity in the world. This religious core culminates with a God who manifests himself through the imagination of hope, in the creative interpretation of indirect language, such as the open-ended parables as a gift of the imagination of hope.

Herk, Monica and Hochschild, Jennifer L. "Yes, But...": Principles and Caveats in American Racial Attitudes. *Nomos*, 32, 308-335, 1990.

Herkless, John L. Neo-idealism and Finance Capitalism. *Hist Euro Ideas*, 14(4), 509-530, Jl 92.

Herman, Barbara. *The Practice of Moral Judgment*. Cambridge, Harvard Univ Pr, 1993.

Herman, David. *Ulysses* and Vacuous Pluralism. *Phil Lit*, 17(1), 65-76, Ap 93.

Drawing on Brentano's, Husserl's and others' conception of intentional or "ideal" objects, this paper construes as nonsensical the view that, at any given time, an unconstrained plurality of legitimate interpretations holds for one and the same artifact, situation, event or object. Through discussion of Joyce's *Ulysses*, the argument about interpretation in general is brought to bear on literary texts in particular. Literary interpretation, like other forms of interpretive activity, entails establishing a range of more or less admissible strategies for idealizing or disactualizing—and thus asking about—the interpretandum.

Herman, Stewart W. The Modern Business Corporation and an Ethics of Trust. *J Relig Ethics*, 20(1), 111-148, Spr 92.

Recent theologically grounded contributions to business ethics, though innovative and promising, are flawed by an unrealistic conception of human agency in corporate settings. By drawing upon the resources of organization theory, we can construct a more reliable descriptive anthropology as a foundation for prescriptive judgments. By bringing this reconstructed knowledge into connection with the normative moral arguments of H Richard Niebuhr, we can develop a corporate ethics of trust building that both takes organizational relatities seriously and also guides their transformation.

Hermerén, Göran. Scandinavian Aesthetics. *J Aes Art Crit*, 51(2), 177-183, Spr 93.

Herrera, Christopher. Racial Discrimination is Distinct, If Not "Special". *J Value Inq*, 27(2), 239-242, Ap 93.

Michael Levin alleges that we subvert our better judgment when we provide restitution to victims of racial discrimination or even when we explore the nature of the harm involved. Discrimination, Levin claims, is not "special" indeed, it is far less serious than other harms that receive less restitution or moral attention. Analysis of Levin's arguments reveals, however, that while discrimination does not merit a glorified status in a taxonomy of harms, it remains a distinct form of wrong, and one not easily compared to acts like verbal abuse, physical assault, or murder.

Herrera, Christopher. Some Ways that Technology and Terminology Distort the Euthanasia Issue. *J Med Human*, 14(1), 23-31, Spr 93.

Technology and terminology often detract from a reasoned appraisal of the euthanasia option, especially in those discussions that argue for euthanasia's incorporation into a beneficence-based medical model. "Beneficent euthanasia," assuming there is such a thing, poses special challenges to the traditional provider-patient relationship. These challenges argue for well-defined limits of beneficence and a more equitable distribution of responsibility between participants. We should not allow technology and terminology to generate an unrealistic portrayal of patient death and its ramifications. Participants need to acknowledge their roles in the decision to kill and the obligations that those roles entail. Perhaps we can reach ethical consensus concerning euthanasia by first reasserting our span of control over the technology that can extend the near-death period and by openly discussing euthanasia's implications.

Herrera, Christopher. The Autonomy Imperative of Behavioral Research. *J Soc Phil*, 24(2), 224-234, Fall 93.

Human research subjects in behavioral research transfer their autonomy to the researcher. Deception skews this transfer in the researcher's favor. The deception-debriefing system leaves researchers free to determine the level of respect that subject autonomy receives. For this researchers risk little or nothing, although this imbalance is often justified on the dubious promise that the research results will benefit society. An equitable scenario, one incorporating an "autonomy imperative," would have researchers and subjects agreeing on the conditions of the transfer of autonomy, and acknowledging what both stand to gain from the transfer.

Herrera, María. Equal Respect among Unequal partners: Gender Difference and the Constitution of Moral Subjects. *Phil East West*, 42(2), 263-275, Ap 92.

The ideal of equal respect becomes a problem once we accept that differences among subjects are relevant for moral theory. This problem consists in finding adequate ways to conceptualize the normative recognition of differences. We attempt to suggest a solution via a revised version of Discourse Ethics, moving away from the concept of "argumentation" (Habermas) to a form of moral "conversation" as a form of rational deliberation closer to ordinary linguistic interaction. One in which questions of the identity and historical constitution of moral subjects become central for moral reflection.

Herrnstein Smith, Barbara. Judgment After the Fall in Deconstruction and the Possibility of Justice, Cornell, Durcilla (ed). New York, Routledge, 1992.

The dualistic typology of value judgments (impersonal/personal, universally valid/merely contingent, etc.) crucial to Alisdair MacIntyre's *After Virtue: A Study in Moral Theory*, (1984) yields a dubious myth of the Fall: i.e., the idea that, before modern degeneracy, judgments could be objective because they appealed to truly communal values. The conception of language presupposed by MacIntyre's myth and other dualistic typologies of evaluative discourse ignores the contingent operations of all use of language and obscures the subtle social operations—and thereby the sources of the effectiveness—of all values judgments. Adapted from Smith, *Contingencies of Value: Alternative Perspectives for Critical Theory*, (1988).

Hertogh, Cees and Van Leeuwen, Evert. The Right to Genetic Information: Some Reflections on Dutch Developments. *J Med Phil*, 17(4), 381-393, Ag 92.

New developments in genetics are rapidly spreading over the Western World. The standards of clinical practice differ however according to local value and health-care systems. In this article a short survey is given of Dutch developments in this field. An effort is made to explain the philosophical and ethical background of Dutch policy by concentrating on autonomy, responsibility and the right not to know.

Hertzberg, Lars. Imagination and the Sense of Identity in Human Beings, Cockburn, David (ed). New York, Cambridge Univ Pr, 1991.

A discussion, with reference to Geoffrey Madell and Katherine Wilkes, of the use of appeals to what can be imagined in the context of discussing personal identity. It is argued that something's being imaginable is not a property of the event in itself, but rather depends on what makes sense in the context of the type of discourse in question. Also, the capacity of thought experiments for illuminating the notion of identity is questioned, since they make use of the unwarranted assumption that our current use of language contains rules determining the correct use of our words in radically altered circumstances.

Hertzberg, Lars. Primitive Reactions—Logic or Anthropology. *Midwest Stud Phil*, 17, 24-39, 1992.

A discussion of Wittgenstein's use of the notion of primitive reactions. In calling a reaction primitive, is one to be understood to be making a logical point, simply denying that the reaction is grounded in any form of reasoning previously mastered, or is one committing oneself to a more substantive claim about human nature? An attempt is made to bridge the apparent conflict: what can be intelligibly seen as a primitive reaction in the logical sense is ultimately dependent on the reaction's making sense to us in the context in which it occurs, and thus, on its being a reaction we can share in.

Hertzberg, Lars. Raimond Gaita's *Good and Evil*: An Absolute Conception. *Phil Invest*, 15(4), 357-371, O 92.

Gaita's central concern is with ways in which ethics has been misunderstood. Ethics inescapably contains within itself the tension between being an academic subject and a Socratic activity. The critical vocabulary used in assessing moral judgments is one to which reference to the speaker's relation to her words is essential, hence ethical inquiry must take the form of asking what it is to be serious in speaking about questions of life. The book powerfully criticizes much current moral philosophy; it is rich and bold, though in places obscure. If properly heeded it could have a deep impact on the state of ethics.

Hertzberg, Lars. 'Some Foundational Questions Concerning Language Studies': Commentary. *J Prag*, 17(5-6), 461-465, Je 92.

Herwitz, Daniel A. The Journal of Aesthetics and Danto's Philosophical Criticism. *J Aes Art Crit*, 51(2), 261-270, Spr 93.

Herwitz, Daniel A. The Work of Art as Psychoanalytical Object: Wollheim on Manet. *J Aes Art Crit*, 49(2), 137-153, Spr 91.

This paper discusses Richard Wollheim's psychoanalytical account of paintings as among the best and most original psychological accounts. It thus raises questions about the adequacy of any psychological account. Wollheim (a mixture of connoisseurship and psychoanalysis, looks to the subtle and distinctive visual features of a painting (those features which have traditionally been the preview of the aesthetic or connoisseur) and takes them to signify the deepest expressive in the picture. In this way, Wollheim is really a psychological account of expression in painting. By criticizing his reading of Monet, I challenge the very idea that any perspective (psychological, historical...) is sufficient to explain painting as such.

Herz, John H. Looking at Carl Schmitt from the Vantage Point of the 1990s. *Interpretation*, 19(3), 307-314, Spr 92.

Herzog, Max. Das Problem der Freiheit in der Psychologie von William James. *Stud Phil (Switzerland)*, 49, 131-154, 1990.

"Noetic freedom" is understood as the core concept both for the psychology of William James and his later philosophical writings. The article shows that William James was a forerunner of continental phenomenological psychology. James' psychology integrated subjective and objective methods in empirical psychological research. His approach is exemplified by the mutual dependence of self and body, volition and choice, function and conscious experience. James' psychology may be taken as a corrective against both behaviorism and today's cognitivism.

Heslep, Robert D. Both the Moral Right and the Moral Duty to Be Educated. *Educ Theor*, 42(4), 413-428, Fall 92.

This paper seeks to clarify the logical relationship between the moral right and the moral duty to be educated. It proceeds by analyzing the concepts of moral theory, education, right, and duty. It holds that some dimensions of the moral right and the moral duty to be educated may be independent of and compatible with each other; that no aspect of the right is subordinate or superior to any aspect of the duty; and that a moral theory should comprise both educational rights and duties.

Heslep, Robert D. The Power of the Right of Education. *Proc Phil Educ*, 48, 205-211, 1992.

This paper rejects the cynical position that rights by themselves neither protect nor gain anything for their bearers. More specifically, it argues that at least one right, the right of education, logically implies power for any and all moral agents who are bearers and respecters of the right. The argument opens with an analysis of the right of education with a view to locating the power contained within its structure. It then responds to likely objections from cynics and communitarians.

Hesslow, Germund. Do We Need a Concept of Disease?. *Theor Med*, 14(1), 1-14, Mr 93.

The terms "health", "disease" and "illness" are frequently used in clinical medicine. This has misled philosophers into believing that these concepts are important for clinical thinking and decision making. For instance, it is held that decisions about whether or not to treat someone or whether to relieve someone of moral responsibility depend on whether the person has a disease. In this paper it is argued that the crucial role of the 'disease' concept is illusory. The health/disease distinction is irrelevant for most decisions and represents a conceptual straightjacket. Sophisticated and mature clinical decision making requires that we free ourselves from the concept of disease.

Hestevold, H Scott. The Anselmian 'Single-Divine-Attribute Doctrine'. *Relig Stud*, 29(1), 63-77, Mr 93.

Roughly, the Single-Divine-Attribute Doctrine (SDA) implies that God is "absolutely perfect"—"a being greater than which nothing can be conceived"—and that whatever properties God exemplifies can only be "illuminated" in terms of the concept of absolute perfection. George N Schlesinger uses SDA to defend the coherence of theism, dismissing disputes about the consistency of the divine attributes on grounds that God has whatever properties are required for absolute perfection. This essay offers objections to each of three interpretations of SDA, which suggests that SDA cannot be used to dismiss so easily questions about the coherence of theism.

Hetherington, Stephen Cade. Conceivability and Modal Knowledge in Thought Experiments in Science and Philosophy, Horowitz, Tamara (ed). Lanham, Rowman & Littlefield, 1991.

I argue for an analysis of conceivability as a form of modal knowledge: to conceive of p's being true is to know that "Possibly, p" is true.

Hetherington, Stephen Cade. Epistemology's Psychological Turn. *Metaphilosophy*, 23(1-2), 47-56, Ja-Ap 92.

Epistemology's swing from the logicised to the psychologised is typically motivated by a kind of counterexample in which the epistemic subject, seeking knowledge or justification, gains her belief for the wrong *reasons*. Focussing on a paradigmatic such counterexample, offered by Kornblith, I argue for its underdetermining the psychologistic moral it usually inspires. The underdetermination is revealing: the psychologised epistemologist can draw that moral only about epistemic subjects who are *themselves* epistemologists. This unprofessed self-referentiality in that epistemologist's methodology clashes with one of the professed attractions of her psychologism—namely, its supposed interest in *all* psyches.

Hetherington, Stephen Cade. Furthering Stich's Fragmentation. *Analysis*, 53(1), 40-44, Ja 93.

In his book, *The Fragmentation of Reason*, Stephen Stich argues that there is no good reason for epistemic subjects to value truth in particular. His favoured alternative is a pragmatist account of cognitive value. I turn his argument on its head, arguing that an analogue of his reason for eschewing the quest for truth entails that it is equally unsatisfactory to seek pragmatic ends in particular.

Hetherington, Stephen Cade. Gettier and Scepticism. *Austl J Phil*, 70(3), 277-285, S 92.

Edmund Gettier's famous counterexamples to the sufficiency of justified true belief for knowledge are never thought of as being "sceptical" cases. I argue that they "are" sceptical. I describe what it is for a case to be sceptical, and I argue that Gettier's cases satisfy this description. They are sceptical about being any "epistemological" knowledge of the nature of knowledge.

Hetzler, Florence M. Peace and Becoming: An Evolutionary Global Struggle. *Dialec Hum*, 17(2), 151-162, 1990.

Heyd, David. Artificial Reproductive Technologies: The Israeli Scene. *Bioethics*, 7(2-3), 263-270, Ap 93.

The article presents and analyses the main points of the interim report of a government committee on reproductive technologies in Israel. A special emphasis is put on those aspects and issues which are unique to the Israeli scene, particularly the tension between liberal trends and the important role that the Jewish tradition plays in contemporary Israel. The high value attached by Jewish religions culture to procreation is shown to be instrumental in working out ways to agree on principles for regulating IVF, AID and surrogacy.

Heyd, Thomas. Some Remarks on Science, Method and Nationalism in John Locke. *Hist Euro Ideas*, 16(1-3), 97-107, Ja 93.

Locke's background in the observational/experimental, Baconian sciences and his adherence to the resolutive-compositive method are discussed, as well as those elements of Locke's political philosophy which would endorse nationalist doctrines. I point out that at least some of Locke's claims that underwrite nationalist doctrines seem to result from his scientific experience and, more directly, from his method. I conclude that, since some of those claims are highly objectionable, they call for a re-examination of the method which Locke utilizes.

Heyde, L. Philosophy Beyond the Limits of Politics (in Dutch). *Tijdschr Filosof*, 55(1), 72-99, Mr 93.

According to Hegel there is an inner connection between the modern state and philosophy, which lies in the actuality of one and the same rationality. Therefore

Heydrich, Wolfgang 520 AUTHOR INDEX WITH ABSTRACTS

philosophy and (modern) politics share the same orientation on universality. In this they are opposed to forms of nationalism in which particularity is the guiding principle. Nevertheless this alliance has its limits. An analysis of *Encyclopedy 552* shows that politics remains characterized by elements of particularity. Genuine universality lies beyond the limits of politics. The article concludes with some reflections on the relation between thinking and experience which could perhaps help to understand this peculiar fate of philosophy.

Heydrich, Wolfgang. A Reconception of Meaning. *Synthese*, 95(1), 77-94, Ap 93.

Goodman's proposal for a reconception of meaning consists in replacing the absolute notion of *sameness of meaning* by that of *likeness of meaning* (with respect to pertinent contexts). According to this view, synonymy is a matter of degree (of interreplaceability) with identity of expression as a limiting case. Goodman's demonstration that no two expressions are exactly alike in meaning is shown to be unsuccessful. Although it does not make use of quotational contexts for the test of interreplaceability, it is tantamount to their acceptance. Goodman rejects quotational contexts; I argue that they should be accepted. This move offers two advantages. *Firstly*, and mainly, it allows interlinguistic comparison of meaning, something that has not been deemed possible in the received version of Goodman's account. *Secondly*, it restores the full scale of likeness of meaning damaged by the renunciation of those contexts that guarantee difference in meaning for diverse expressions.

Heyne, Paul. For the Common Good?. *Crit Rev*, 6(2-3), 185-209, Spr-Sum 92.

This essay reviews *For the Common Good*, in which authors Herman Daly and John Cobb argue that the pressure of human population and production on the biosphere will soon compel thoroughgoing social changes, and that we would want radical changes, with more emphasis on community and less on the pursuit of individual advantage, if we correctly understood our own natures. Because they believe that economics has systematically blinded us to the realities of our situation, they focus on the criticism and reform of the discipline, and consequently ignore much of what economics could contribute to the transformation they desire.

Hibbs, Thomas. MacIntyre's Postmodern Thomism. *Thomist*, 57(2), 277-297, Ap 93.

Hick, John. *Disputed Questions in Theology and the Philosophy of Religion*. New Haven, Yale Univ Pr, 1993.

A volume of mainly reprinted papers of the last five years, divided into five parts: Epistemological; Christ and Christianity; Hints from Buddhism; Religious Pluralism; Life and Death. The topics include religious experience, the realist/non-realist issue, an inspiration christology, the Buddhist doctrines of the 'undetermined questions' and 'skillful means', the question of whether Jews, Christians and Muslims worship the same God, and a possible conception of life after death.

Hick, John. Religious Pluralism and the Rationality of Religious Belief. *Faith Phil*, 10(2), 242-249, Ap 93.

The view that religious experience is a valid ground of basic religious beliefs inevitably raises the problem of the apparently incompatible belief-systems arising from different forms of religious experience. David Basinger's and William Alston's responses to the problem present the Christian belief-system as the sole exception to the general rule that religious experience gives rise to false beliefs. A more convincing response presents it as an exemplification of the general rule that religious experience gives rise (subject to possible defeaters) to true beliefs. This requires a 'two-level' conception.

Hicks, Alan. Human Nature as the Foundation of Moral Obligation. *SW Phil Rev*, 8(1), 29-37, Ja 92.

This essay begins with the observation that moral obligation is a basic human experience. It is then argued that various modern attempts to account for this experience are inadequate in that they fail to give an adequate reason or motive for engaging in moral activity. It is concluded that the only sufficient explanation for moral obligation is human nature itself and the good or perfection following upon that nature which we are "compelled" to seek as human beings. Accordingly, moral standards reflect an awareness of what a human being "ought to be, but is [perhaps] not yet."

Hiebeler, David E. Implications of Creation. *Ideal Stud*, 23(1), 63-73, Wint 93.

Hieke, Alexander. Real Facts in Advances in Scientific Philosophy, Schurz, Gerhard (ed). Amsterdam, Rodopi, 1991.

In this paper, conditions are given for singling out sentences which express "real facts". Intuitively, a sentence expresses a real fact if it is true and mirrors the structure of a part of reality. This property is attributed to formulae which are either positive or connected. In order to define these terms the "Program Form" of formulae is introduced. Thus positive and connected formulae can be singled out. Intuitively, true positive formulae depict bundles of atomic facts, and true connected formulae depict bundles of law-like facts. The notions of positive and connected formulae were first explicated by Paul Weingartner, and this paper tries to develop some of his ideas.

Higginbotham, James. Skepticism Naturalized in Rationality in Epistemology, Villanueva, Enrique (ed). Atascadero, Ridgeview, 1992.

Higgins, Kathleen M. *Zarathustra* Is a Comic Book. *Phil Lit*, 16(1), 1-14, Ap 92.

I argue that the comic aspects of *Thus Spoke Zarathustra* can help us to make sense of Nietzsche's many claims that modern humanity could be redeemed through comedy. These aspects can also assist our efforts to understand Nietzsche's suggestion in *Ecce Homo* that he, like Shakespeare, is perhaps a buffoon.

Higgins, Kathleen M. Apollo, Music, and Cross-Cultural Rationality. *Phil East West*, 42(4), 623-641, O 92.

I argue that our Western conception of rationality grows out of aesthetic sources that are often obscured in contemporary discussion. Exploring these sources, we can discover points of commonality with notions of rationality found in certain non-Western cultures. I go on to suggest that we can assist our understandings of other cultures' concepts of rationality through an investigation of the values implicit in their musics and other aesthetic phenomena.

Higgs, E. Musings at the Confluence of the Rivers Techné and Oikos. *Res Phil Technol*, 12, 243-258, 1992.

The philosophy of technology and the philosophy of the environment, as two marked subjects within philosophy, have not been examined significantly for conceptual and practical questions that lie at their confluence. This essay, based on the deliberations of a workshop held in 1990, describes various points of connection, and suggests directions for further research.

Hikins, James W and Zagacki, Kenneth S. Rhetoric, Objectivism, and the Doctrine of Tolerance in The Critical Turn, Angus, Ian (ed). Carbondale, So Illinois Univ Pr, 1993.

Hilbert, David. Comments on "Anthropomorphism". *Phil Stud*, 69(2-3), 123-127, Mr 93.

Hilbert, David. What Is Color Vision?. *Phil Stud*, 68(3), 351-370, D 92.

Hiley, David R. The Politics of Skepticism: Readong Montaigne. *Hist Phil Quart*, 9(4), 379-399, O 92.

Hiley, David R (ed) and Bohman, James F (ed) and Shusterman, Richard (ed). *The Interpretive Turn*. Ithaca, Cornell Univ Pr, 1991.

In philosophy, the sciences and such diverse fields as anthropolgy, law, and social history, the turn to interpretative methods has challenged fundamental assumptions about the status of knowledge claims. The book addresses these challenges in fifteen new essays by a variety of scholars on topics about the relationship between the natural and human sciences, normative issues of interpretation, and interpretive practices in various disciplines.

Hill, Charles G. *Jean-Paul Sartre: Freedom and Commitment*. New York, Lang, 1992.

Hill, Donald. On Reasoning Morally about the Environment—Response to R M Hare in Applied Philosophy, Almond, Brenda (ed). New York, Routledge, 1992.

Hill, Donald (ed) and Almond, Brenda (ed). *Applied Philosophy*. New York, Routledge, 1992.

This collection of papers brings the concepts and methods of philosophy to bear on specific, pressing, practical concerns; topics include the environment, personal relationships, war, terrorism, concepts of justice and equality and issues in medical ethics.

Hill, Greg. The Rational Justification of Moral Restraint. *S J Phil*, 31(2), 179-191, Sum 93.

Hill, Patrick. Religion and the Quest for Community in On Community, Rouner, Leroy S (ed). Notre Dame, Univ Notre Dame Pr, 1992.

Hill, R Kevin. MacIntyre's Nietzsche: A Critique. *Int Stud Phil*, 24(2), 3-12, 1992.

In Alastair MacIntyre's *After Virtue*, Nietzsche is presented as (1) an emotivist, (2) the culmination of the liberal tradition, and (3) fundamentally opposed to Aristotle. All three claims are criticized, thus casting doubt not only on MacIntyre's interpretation of Nietzsche, but also on his larger account of the history of Western ethical theory and practice, as well as on his proposal that we return to the tradition which Nietzsche has called into question.

Hill Jr, Thomas E. A Kantian Perspective on Moral Rules in Philosophical Perspectives, 6: Ethics, 1992, Tomberlin, James E (ed). Atascadero, Ridgeview, 1992.

The paper sketches a broadly Kantian perspective for thinking about how moral rules should be conceived, specified, and applied. The perspective reflects a Kantian view of the commitments of reasonable conscientious agents facing practical moral problems in which familiar rules are relevant but indecisive. The elements of the perspective are drawn from Kant's conception of a good will and several versions of the Categorical Imperative, but they combine in an idea of moral legislation with closest affinities to Kant's "kingdom of ends." The perspective is contrasted others, e.g., rule-utilitarianism and Rawls's original position. Four main problems, and Kantian strategies for response, are briefly considered.

Hill Jr, Thomas E. Beneficence and Self-Love: A Kantian Perspective. *Soc Phil Pol*, 10(1), 1-23, Wint 93.

A Kantian position is contrasted with others regarding the related questions: What, if anything, are we morally required to do on behalf of others? Why is such regard for others a reasonable moral requirement? Is it even possible for us to act altruistically? Emphasis is on the last question, considered from the perspective of a conscientious deliberating agent. Here empirical evidence is relevant but indecisive. For the Kantian the answer depends not on whether one has warm feelings for others but on whether, independently of that, one has good reason to help them.

Hill Jr, Thomas E. Beneficence and Self-Love: A Kantian Perspective in Altruism, Paul, Ellen Frankel (ed). New York, Cambridge Univ Pr, 1993.

Given a practical context of conscientious deliberation, what are Kantian responses to these related questions: What is our duty of beneficence? What are its grounds? Is it even possible for us to act altruistically as this (putative) duty of beneficence would require? A Kantian response to the last question depends on answers to the first two questions. It also turns on the distinction between how one must conceive one's feelings in moral deliberation and how one can conceive them for purposes of empirical explanation.

Hill Jr, Thomas E. Gibbard on Morality and Sentiment. *Phil Phenomenol Res*, 52(4), 957-960, D 92.

Some questions are raised regarding Gibbard's subtle and important defense of noncognitivism. Is our concept of a moral judgment as inclusive as Gibbard's? On Gibbard's analysis, how different are the best objective normative judgments (which supposedly "mimic facts") from other judgments we count as factual? How are we to understand simple moral utterances as expressing endorsement of the agent's whole complex system or norms? Are not norms for feelings too peripheral and problematic for the central role in ethics that Gibbard proposes for them? Are feelings of guilt, as distinct from judgments of guilt, as crucial to morality as Gibbard suggests?

Hilmy, S Stephen. 'Tormenting Questions' in 'Philosophical Investigations' in Wittgenstein's Philosophical Investigations, Arrington, Robert L (ed). New York, Routledge, 1991.

Hilpinen, Risto. Authors and Artifacts. *Proc Aris Soc*, 93, 155-178, 1993.

The paper discusses the conditions under which an object can be said to have an author (a maker). Objects which have no author (or several authors) are called artifacts. The concepts of authorship and artifactuality are characterized by means of 9 conditions. Paradigmatic artifacts are objects whose existence and properties depend on the intentions of their authors. Various borderline cases are discussed.

Hilpinen, Risto. On Peirce's Philosophical Logic: Propositions and Their Objects. *Trans Peirce Soc*, 28(3), 467-488, Sum 92.

According to C S Peirce, every proposition consists of two signs, 1) a subject, an indexical sign which "indicates" some object or objects (the objects of the proposition), and 2) a predicate, an iconic sign whose function is to represent the object (or objects) indicated by the subject. This paper analyzes the ways in which the subject of a proposition indicates its object or objects in simple (atomic) propositions, their truth-functional compounds, quantified propositions, and modal propositions, and discusses Peirce's view of the objects of fictional discourse.

Hintikka, Jaakko. Carnap's Work in the Foundations of Logic and Mathematics in a Historical Perspective. *Synthese*, 93(1-2), 167-189, N 92.

Carnap's philosophy is examined from new viewpoints, including three important distinctions: (i) language as calculus vs language as universal medium; (ii) different senses of completeness: (iii) standard vs nonstandard interpretations of (higher-order) logic. (i)Carnap favored in 1930-34 the "formal mode of speech," a corollary to the universality assumption. He later gave it up partially but retained some of its ingredients, e.g., the one-domain assumption. (ii) Carnap's project of creating a universal self-referential language is encouraged by (ii) and by the author's recent work. (iii) Carnap was aware of (iii) and occasionally used the standard interpretation, but was not entirely clear of the nature of the contrast.

Hintikka, Jaakko. Socratic Questioning, Logic and Rhetoric. *Rev Int Phil*, 47(184), 5-30, 1993.

The earliest form of Aristotle's methodology was a dialectic modelled on the Socratic method of questioning. Logic originated as a study of such answers received in a dialectical game as were necessitated by earlier answers. Even after the ideas of syllogistic and syllogistically organized science were developed, Aristotle's conception of method contained a major dialectical element. Aristotle's conception of method contained a major dialectical element. Aristotle's rhetoric is but another variant of the same dialectical methodology. Several of its main features can be understood better in terms of the logic of dialectical (interrogative) inquiry, for instance Aristotle's comments on the role of the speaker's character in rhetorical persuasion.

Hintikka, Jaakko. The Interrogative Model of Inquiry as a General Theory of Argumentation. *Commun Cog*, 25(2-3), 221-242, 1992.

Hintikka, Jaakko. Theory-ladenness of Observation as a Test Case of Kuhn's Approach to Scientific Inquiry. *Proc Phil Sci Ass*, 1, 277-286, 1992.

Kuhn's basic concepts need closer analysis. For instance, the alleged theory-ladenness of observations has several different interpretation. In one sense, it is trivially built into my interrogative approach to inquiry, in that the consequences of an observational answer by nature depend crucially on the initial theoretical premises. A more interesting sense is obtained by noting the multi-level character of inquiry. A lower-level (experimental or observational) inquiry will on this view depend on earlier results obtained on the higher (theoretical) level.

Hintikka, Jaakko and Sandu, Gabriel. The Skeleton in Frege's Cupboard: The Standard Versus Nonstandard Distinction. *J Phil*, 89(6), 290-315, Je 92.

Henkin formulated the standard versus nonstandard distinction in 1950, but the idea of the standard interpretation of hegher-order variables is virtually equivalent with that of an arbitrary function, which was debated by nineteenth-century mathematicians. Frege's disregard of the latter notion and his criticisms of abstraction show that he opted for a nonstandard interpretation. This would make his system an inadequate foundation for mathematics, even if it were consistent. One reason why the nonstandardness of Frege's interpretation has been overlooked is that he did not identify higher-order existence with definability, which is falsely assumed to be the only possible nonstandard interpretation.

Hiorth, Finngeir. Was Immanuel Kant a Humanist?. *Free Inq*, 12(3), 49-50, Sum 92.

The paper examines to which extent Kant can be regarded as a predecessor of secular humanism. The author concludes that Kant's criticism of the arguments for the existence of God and his attempt to find the basis of ethics in man, and not in God, remain viable elements of his philosophy. Secular humanists may also agree with Kant's statement that we always should treat our fellow beings as ends, not only as means. In spite of many doubtful features in Kant's philosophy, Kant is, with repect to others and important features, one of the many roots of secular humanism.

Hirsch, Eli. Peter Van Inwagen's *Material Beings*. *Phil Phenomenol Res*, 53(3), 687-691, S 93.

Hirsch, Hans and Hammacher, Klaus. *Die Wirtschaftspolitik des Philosophen Jacobi*. Amsterdam, Rodopi, 1993.

Friedrich Heinrich Jacobi (1743-1819), Philosoph und Schriftsteller, wirkte 1772-1779, bevor er mit dem Spinozastreit (1785/86) als Philosoph berühmt wurde, als Wirtschaftspolitiker in kurfürstlichen Diensten, und zwar als Hofkammerat und Geheimrat in den Rheinlanden (Jülich-Berg)und kurze Zeit in Bayern (1779). Aufbauend auf die Theorien der sog. Physiokraten, z.B. eines Turgot, und der Freihandelslehre Adam Smith kämpfte er, wenn auch mit bescheidenen Erfolgen, für einen von staatlicher Bevormundung freien Markt. Aufgrund bisher unbekannter Dokumente wird diese Tätigkeit minutiös rekonstruiert. Philosophisch eine nicht unbedeutende Komponente in der Ausbildung moderner Vertragstheorien, erscheint sie theoriegeschichtlich als ökonomische Leistung, die nachhaltig auf die Herausbildung moderner Wirtschaftsformen eingewirkt hat.

Hitchcock, Christopher Read. Causal Explanation and Scientific Realism. *Erkenntnis*, 37(2), 151-178, S 92.

It is widely believed that many of the competing accounts of scientific explanation have ramifications which are relevant to the scientific realism debate. I claim that the two issues are orthogonal. For definiteness, I consider Cartwright's argument that causal explanations secure belief in theoretical entities. In Section I, van Fraassen's anti-realism is reviewed; I argue that this anti-realism is, *prima facie*, consistent with a causal account of explanation. Section II reviews Cartwright's arguments. In Section III, it is argued that causal explanations do not license the sort of inferences to theoretical entities that would embarass the anti-realist. Section IV examines the epistemic commitments involved in accepting a causal explanation. Section V presents my conclusions: *contra* Cartwright, the anti-realist may incorporate a causal account of explanation into his vision of science in an entirely natural way.

Hitchock, Christopher R. Discussion: Massey and Kirk on the Indeterminacy of Translation. *J Phil Res*, 17, 215-223, 1992.

Gerald Massey has constructed translation manuals for the purposes of illustrating Quine's Indeterminacy Thesis. Robert Kirk has argued that Massey's manuals do not live up to their billing. In this note, I will present Massey's manuals and defend them against Kirk's objections. The implications for Quine's Indeterminacy Thesis will then be briefly discussed.

Hix, Harvey L. Postmodern Grief. *Phil Lit*, 17(1), 47-64, Ap 93.

The "electronic age" has changed the transmission, acquisition, storage and exchange of cognitive materials more drastically and rapidly than did the introduction of the alphabet into ancient Greece. A change so drastic is inevitably also a loss, and the thinkers who describe the change to postmodernism also grieve over the loss of modernism. I argue that the prophecies of the postmoderns can also be viewed as lamentations that follow Elisabeth Kubler-Ross's popular account of five stages of grief.

Hiz, Henry. A Note About Reism in Kotarbinski: Logic, Semantics and Ontology, Wolenski, Jan (ed). Dordrecht, Kluwer, 1990.

Hlobil, Tomas. Reading in (Dramatic) Texts in Pre-Hellenistic Greece (in Czechoslovakian). *Estetika*, 29(2), 50-56, 1992.

Ho, John E. *East Asian Philosophy: With Historical Background and Present Influence*. New York, Lang, 1992.

The purpose of this book is to help readers understand the intellectual foundations, strategies and tactics of East Asians in Japan and the so-called Four Mini-Dragons (Hong Kong, Singapore, South Korea, and Taiwan). In addition, it sets out to help East Asians, especially overseas Asians, understand their own philosophical and cultural tradition. It is the first book published which discusses various aspects, both positive and negative, of the philosophical and cultural heritage of these countries as a whole by tracing their historical development and background.

Hoag, Robert. J S Mill's Language of Pleasures. *Utilitas*, 4(2), 247-278, N 92.

I clarify understanding of Mill's doctrine of qualities of pleasures in Utilitarianism by examining and applying to it accounts of names, attributes (quantity, quality), and kinds in a system of logic. The argument shows illuminating connections between his innovative account of connotative names and of higher pleasures. In addition to dismissing many common criticisms of the latter, the argument shows that the doctrine of pleasures establishes paramount value for simple pleasures associated with activities of distinctly human faculties in practical reasoning.

Hoagland, Sarah Lucia. Why Lesbian Ethics?. *Hypatia*, 7(4), 195-206, Fall 92.

This essay is part of a recent version of a talk I have given by way of introducing Lesbian Ethics. I mention ways in which lesbian existence creates certain conceptual possibilities that can effect conceptual shifts and transform consciousness.

Hobbes, Thomas and MacPherson, C B (ed). *Leviathan—Thomas Hobbes*. New York, Penguin USA, 1993.

Hobbs, Jesse. Ex Post Facto Explanations. *J Phil*, 90(3), 117-136, Mr 93.

A broad class of explanations that are non-predictive in principle yet possess exemplary epistemological credentials is illustrated using recent developments in non-linear dynamics known as chaos theory. They qualify as explanatory in terms of leading ontic theories of explanation, but also appear to satisfy unificationist requirements. They are non-predictive through a combination of indeterminism, computational complexity, and/or epistemic timelags. Examples include the rotation of Saturn's moon Hyperion, the path of billiard in a stadium, meteorological chaos, and the persistence or extinction of species. The relation of chaos theory to neo-Darwinian *ex post facto* explanations is briefly explored.

Hochberg, Herbert I. Truth Makers, Truth Predicates, and Truth Types in Language, Truth and Ontology, Mulligan, Kevin (ed). Dordrecht, Kluwer, 1992.

Hochschild, Jennifer L and Herk, Monica. "Yes, But...": Principles and Caveats in American Racial Attitudes. *Nomos*, 32, 308-335, 1990.

Hocks, Richard A. The "Other" Postmodern Theorist: Owen Barfield's Concept of the Evolution of Consciousness. *Tradition Discovery*, 18(1), 27-38, 1991-92.

This essay presents an overview of the principal ideas of the philosophical thought of Owen Barfield, particularly his doctrines regarding Appearances, Participation, Evolution, and Polarity. The essay concludes that Barfield's work is a fruitful alternative to postmodern thinkers such as Derrida and Foucault. The essay also cites the parallelism of Barfield with Michael Polanyi.

Hodge, Joanna. Against Aesthetics: Heidegger on Art. *J Brit Soc Phenomenol*, 23(3), 263-279, O 92.

Hodge, Joanna. Genealogy for a Postmodern Ethics: Reflections on Hegel and Heidegger in Shadow of Spirit, Berry, Philippa (ed). New York, Routledge, 1992.

Hodge, M J S. Darwin's Argument in the *Origin*. *Phil Sci*, 59(3), 461-464, S 92.

Various claims have been made, recently, that Darwin's argumentation in the *Origin* instantiates and so supports some general philosophical proposal about scientific theorizing, for example, the "semantic view." But these claims are grounded in various incorrect analyses of that argumentation. A summary is given here of an analysis defended at greater length in several papers by the present author. The historical and philosophical advantages of this analysis are explained briefly. Darwin's argument comprises three distinct evidential cases on behalf of natural selection, cases, that is, for its *existence*, its *adequacy* and its *responsibility*. Theorizing, today, about evolution by natural selection involves a similar structure of evidential and explanatory concerns.

Hodgkin, Robin A. The Roots of Culture. *Tradition Discovery*, 18(3), 30-32, 1992.

Human culture springs from the way we—child, parent, community—make sense from (and in) the universe. If we abstract an idea (e.g., a principle; how it works) *from* some complex system and express this in language, we are taking the first step in science. If on the other hand we *embody* an idea (call it 'principle', 'logos', 'fragment of mind') and use this principle to build small parts into a functioning whole (e.g., a machine) then we are taking the first step in technology (= words about good making). So, science primordially, means 'principles in' to material, giving it a new level of orderliness. (See my *Playing and Exploring* (1985) and 'Teche, technology and inventiveness' *Oxford Review of Education* no 2 1990).

Höffe, Otfried. 'Even a Nation of Devils Needs the State': the Dilemma of Natural Justice in Essays on Kant's Political Philosophy, Williams, Howard (ed). Chicago, Univ of Chicago Pr, 1992.

Even a nation of devils — that means: of radical egoists — would choose a type of society that is associated with an implementational force. Indeed, since life is an indispensable condition of man's being able to act, the enlightened self-interest dictates us to prefer not to run the risk of being violently killed to having the possibility to kill whoever we want. But this transcendental interest can be guaranteed only be a reciprocal limitation of our freedom and only on the condition that it happens with no parasitical exploitation. For these reasons, it needs a coercion by the state authority to provide this distributive advantage.

Hoekema, David A. Ethics from a Theocentric Perspective: A Critical Review of the Thought of James M Gustafson. *Vera Lex*, 11(2), 14-16,18, 1991.

A review essay summarizing the contributions of Gustafson's two-volume work to Christian ethics, crediting the work for its originality and thoroughness but criticizing some of its proposed applications and its theological approach.

Hoeps, Reinhard. Theophanie und Schöpfungsgrund: Der Beitrag des Johannes Scotus Eriguena zum Verständnis *der creatio ex nihilo*. *Theol Phil*, 67(2), 161-191, 1992.

Hörl, Christoph. Semantik und Handlungskausalität: Zur Diskussion über die 'künstliche Intelligenz'. *Theol Phil*, 66(2), 192-215, 1991.

A comparison between Searle's "Chinese Room" and Putnam's "Brains in a Vat" leads to the conclusion that semantic reference presupposes non-linguistic interactions between thinkers and the world their thoughts are about. In a second reflection it turns out that this interaction cannot be sufficiently described in terms of observable physical movements but must be explained by a theory of action. A discussion of Davidson's "Anamolous Monism" highlights some requirements for such a theory.

Hoffheimer, Michael H. The Idea of Law (*Recht*) in Hegel's *Phenomenology of Spirit*. *Clio*, 21(4), 345-367, Sum 92.

Hoffman, Joshua. A New Theory of Comparative and Noncomparative Justice. *Phil Stud*, 70(2), 165-183, My 93.

Joel Feinberg has argued that 1) there is a distinction between *comparative* and *noncomparative* justice, ("Noncomparative Justice", *Philosophical Review*, 83, 1974, 297-338), that 2) the basic principle of comparative justice is that like cases are to be treated alike and different cases to be treated differently, and that 3) the basic principle of noncomparative justice is that each person should be treated according to his rights and deserts. In this paper I first dispute both 2) and 3) while accepting 1). I then offer an alternative basis for a theory of comparative and noncomparative justice.

Hoffman, Joshua and Rosenkrantz, Gary. Are Souls Unintelligible? in Philosophical Perspectives, 5: Philosophy of Religion, 1991, Tomberlin, James E (ed). Atascadero, Ridgeview, 1991.

Hoffman, Piotr. Death, Time, History in The Cambridge Companion to Heidegger, Guignon, Charles B (ed). New York, Cambridge Univ Pr, 1993.

Hoffman, W Michael (ed) and Frederick, Robert (ed) and Pentry, Edward S (ed). *Business, Ethics, and the Environment: The Public Policy Debate*. Westport, Greenwood Pr, 1990.

Hoffman, W Michael (ed) and Frederick, Robert (ed) and Petry, Edward S (ed). *The Corporation, Ethics, and the Environment*. Westport, Greenwood Pr, 1990.

Hoffmaster, C Barry. The Theory and Practice of Applied Ethics. *Dialogue (Canada)*, 30(3), 213-234, Sum 91.

Hofmann, James R and Hofmann, Paul A. Darcy's Law and Structural Explanation in Hydrology. *Proc Phil Sci Ass*, 1, 23-35, 1992.

Darcy's law is a phenomenological relationship for fluid flow. Hydrologists apply fundamental principles to idealized conceptual models to generate approximate derivations of Darcy's law. These structural explanations of the law can illuminate the nature and interdependence of selected parameters pertaining to the fluid and its medium. Multiple mutually inconsistent models may be used sequentially to explore the contributions of a wide variety of flow parameters. The idealized conditions incorporated into models make a realist interpretation or application problematic, however. Modeling exercises that support hydrological structural explanations cannot be expected to converge to a single model of optimum accuracy and scope.

Hofmann, Paul A and Hofmann, James R. Darcy's Law and Structural Explanation in Hydrology. *Proc Phil Sci Ass*, 1, 23-35, 1992.

Darcy's law is a phenomenological relationship for fluid flow. Hydrologists apply fundamental principles to idealized conceptual models to generate approximate derivations of Darcy's law. These structural explanations of the law can illuminate the nature and interdependence of selected parameters pertaining to the fluid and its medium. Multiple mutually inconsistent models may be used sequentially to explore the contributions of a wide variety of flow parameters. The idealized conditions incorporated into models make a realist interpretation or application problematic, however. Modeling exercises that support hydrological structural explanations cannot be expected to converge to a single model of optimum accuracy and scope.

Hofmann, T R. Translation and Content—Footnotes on Moravcsik's 'All A's are B's'. *J Prag*, 18(6), 591-596, D 92.

Moravcsik (*J Prag*, 1991) concluded that lawlikeness is based on the state of the knowledge of the community, because it is not an aspect of logical form. However, his notion of logical form reflects arbitrary superficial forms of English and other languages. I argue that: a) some superficial forms of English to mark lawlikeness explicitly, namely negative universals like, "There *are* no A's that are not B's" (all A's are B's) and, "There *can be* no A's that are not B's" (same, but lawlike), without use of the counterfactual subjunctive mood, and thus; b) logical forms can and should show lawlikeness.

Hogan, Melinda. Natural Kinds and Ecological Niches—Response to Johnson's Paper. *Biol Phil*, 7(2), 203-208, Ap 92.

This paper is a response to David M Johnson's "Can Abstractions Be Causes?" (*Biology and Philosophy*, 5, 63, 67) in which it is argued that natural kinds should be construed as 'causally effective niches in nature'. In the present paper it is argued that such a way of construing kinds is not needed to do the explanatory work Johnson wants done. Other types of difficulties for Johnson's specific identification of biological species with ecological niches are discussed.

Hogan, Pádrig. The Practice of Education and the Courtship of Youthful Sensibility. *J Phil Educ*, 27(1), 5-15, Sum 93.

Traditionally, 'education' in Western civilisation has involved those controlling the enterprise securing a privileged status for certain beliefs and outlooks. This proprietorial assumption of rights over the sensibilities of pupils, as it is described here, has, it is argued, survived the Enlightenment spirit of critique of power and enjoyed a renaissance in the recent 'practical' educational reforms in some Western countries. A case is made for saying that understanding educational practice must attend not to disembedded 'concepts' but to what actually befalls our human experience when teaching and learning take place. This experience, it is argued, is inescapably a courtship, but courtships can be honourable or dubious, imprisoning or emancipating. Taking its cue from the historical Socrates, the paper suggests that the articulation and defence of emancipatory cultural courtships are among the most overlooked, promising and practical of tasks for the philosophy of education.

Hohendahl, Peter Uwe. *Reappraisals: Shifting Alignments in Postwar Critical Theory*. Ithaca, Cornell Univ Pr, 1991.

Holbrook, Daniel. Descartes on Mind-Body Interaction. *SW Phil Stud*, 14, 74-83, Spr 92.

In his *Meditations on First Philosophy*, Descartes argues for there being a radical difference between mind and body. Yet, we know that mind and body interest. How is this possible? Descartes's answer to this question is that human nature is a "substantial union" of mind and body. In this essay, Descartes's solution is explained and critically examined.

Holbrook, Daniel. Descartes on Persons. *Personalist Forum*, 8/1(Supp), 9-14, Spr 92.

Descartes concludes that he is essentially a thinking substance. Professors Kenny and Hooker have shown that the Argument from Doubt is insufficient to prove Descartes's conclusion. I argue that Descartes also relies on two metaphysical assumptions—what I call the "Substance-Attribute Principle" and the "Unique Defining Attribute Principle." With these assumptions, Descartes argument becomes valid.

Holbrook, Daniel. Utilitarianism on Environmental Issues Reexamined. *Int J Applied Phil*, 7(1), 41-46, Sum 92.

Recently, several authors have argued that utilitarianism leads to implausible implications when applied to practical and theoretical issues in environmental ethics. The question is, "Does utilitarianism adequately support environmental preservation?" This essay shows that a version of utilitarianism similar to that originally developed by John Stuart Mill does adequately support sound environmental policies. In the course of the argument, problems in basing environmental ethics on the interests of future generations and the enjoyment of Nature as a "higher pleasure" are discussed.

Holder Jr, John J. Ethical Thinking and the Liberal Arts Tradition in Moral Education and the Liberal Arts, Mitias, Michael H (ed). Westport, Greenwood Pr, 1992.

In this essay, I extend John Dewey's naturalistic approach to moral education by using some recent developments in philosophy and cognitive psychology. I suggest that a Deweyan account of moral education should be grounded in a naturalistic theory of experience, and that the key concept, "ethical thinking," can be more fully developed by taking into account Mark Johnson's recent work on the noncognitive structures in the imagination. I then apply the account of "ethical thinking" to the consideration of a liberal arts education. I conclude that a liberal arts education can be as effective as moral education so long as it integrates and balances imaginative inquiry with traditional cultural values.

Holenstein, Elmar. Classical and Modern Work on Universals in Mind, Meaning and Metaphysics, Mulligan, Kevin (ed). Dordrecht, Kluwer, 1990.

According to traditional philosophical doctrines of *grammatica universalis*, linguistic universals are essential, fundamental, central, and logically *a priori* deducible traits of all languages. According to modern universals research, they are contingent, superficial, and peripheral as well as fundamental and central traits of natural human language. They are based on theory-laden empirical research. They concern mainly relational constraints of linguistic variation. Not everything that is logically possible is natural.

Holland, Alan. A Fortnight of My Life is Missing in Applied Philosophy, Almond, Brenda (ed). New York, Routledge, 1992.

The term 'pre-embryo' encapsulates a denial that human beings begin to exist from the moment of conception. The denial rests on two kinds of reason: one is that the pre-embryo lacks the characteristics of a human being; the other is that it lacks what it takes to be an individual human being. I argue that the first embodies an untenable view of what it is to be human, and the second exploits logical difficulties which are of questionable relevance. I conclude that there is no good reason to deny that human beings begin to exist from the moment of conception.

Holland, Kitty L. Projective Geometries of Algebraically Closed Fields of Characteristic Zero. *Annals Pure Applied Log*, 60(3), 237-260, My 93.

Fix an algebraically closed field of characteristically zero and leg G be its geometry of transcendence degree one extensions. Let X be a set of points of G. We show that

X extends to a projective subgeometry of *G* exactly if the partial derivates of the polynomials inducing dependence on its elements satisfy certain separability conditions. This analysis produces a concrete representation of the coordinatizing fields of maximal projective subgeometries of *G*.

Holland, Nancy. The Opinions of Men and Women: Toward a Different Configuration of Moral Voices. *J Soc Phil*, 24(1), 65-80, Spr 93.

This paper compares Carol Gilligan's work on the "different voice" in women's moral reasoning with cross-cultural studies on Lawrence Kohlberg's theory of moral development. These bodies of research suggest that, rather than women, traditional peoples, and non-dominant culture men being less morally mature than European men, the "justice" perspective in Kohlberg's higher levels of moral thinking reflects an historically specific set of intellectual preoccupations, whereas the "care" perspective found in the other groups may be closer to the human norm of moral maturity.

Holland, Nancy. What Gilles Deleuze Has to Say to Battered Women. *Phil Lit*, 17(1), 16-25, Ap 93.

In "Coldness and Cruelty", Deleuze argues for a strong distinction between sadism and masochism. Contrasting this view with traditional theories of "sado-masochism" in Freud and Sartre, I focus on the Hedda Nussbaum/Joel Steinberg case and use the reconceptualization of masochism that Deleuze suggests to explain what is wrong with blaming a supposed masochism in battered women for the crimes committed against them.

Hollander, Rachelle D. Toward a Model of Professional Responsibility. *Res Phil Technol*, 9, 37-44, 1989.

Holley, David M. Is God a Utilitarian?. *Relig Stud*, 29(1), 27-45, Mr 93.

This paper explores the difficulties involved in reconciling utilitarian theory with traditional theism by considering: 1) what divine acceptance of utilitarianism would imply for human ethical thinking, 2) the nature of utilitarian happiness and the kind of happiness a benevolent God would be concerned with, 3) whether benevolence on the part of God implies a concern for happiness which overrides other concerns, and 4) whether a benevolent concern for the individual can be reconciled with the characteristic utilitarian focus on the total result. Finally, the paper discusses the tensions involved in trying to reconcile traditional theism and consequentialist approaches to ethics.

Holley, David M. Presumption and Confession: Augustine, Freud, and Paths to Knowledge. *Cont Phil*, 15(1), 8-10, Ja-F 93.

For Augustine genuine knowledge of God requires submission to a process in which the knower can be altered enough to receive the truth. His view can be profitably compared to the Freudian claim that a therapeutic process is needed to reveal the unconscious self. For both Freud and Augustine the process is a means of overcoming resistances to knowledge, and for both awareness of a transcendent object depends on attending in a particular way to that which is accessible. Such views raise important questions about the ideal of rational autonomy.

Hollis, Martin. Man as a Subject for Social Science in The Philosophy of A J Ayer, Hahn, Lewis E (ed). Peru, Open Court, 1992.

A J Ayer remained Humean about the explanation of action. The paper praises his elegance, especially in 'Man as a Subject for Science', but challenges his approach on three grounds: reasons are not linked to actions by a covering law; strategic reasons in the games people play are not always the instruments of separable passions; understanding (*verstehen*) is more than a heuristic device. But Ayer is right to distance agents from the social rules which they follow.

Hollis, Martin. Market Equality and Social Freedom in Applied Philosophy, Almond, Brenda (ed). New York, Routledge, 1992.

In thinking about freedom and equality, liberals are pulled one way by libertarians and another by social democrats. When we distinguish negative from positive notions of both freedom and equality, freedom 'to pursue our own good in our own way' is a positive idea of freedom, combined with a negative idea of equality as 'equity'. Yet 'equity' is not strong enough to ground public goods. Trust is a crucial public good, essential for markets and dependable only if citizens are morally committed to a positive basic equality.

Hollis, Martin. Trouble with Leprechauns. *Philosophy*, 33(Supp), 25-39, 1992.

Hollis, Martin. Trouble with Leprechauns in The Impulse to Philosophise, Griffiths, A Phillips (ed). New York, Cambridge Univ Pr, 1992.

Leprechauns delight in finding paradoxes at the end of long chains of fine reasoning. For example an analysis of rational choice which starts with Hume's philosophy of mind and ends with Lewis's theory of convention should dispose of the game-theoretic problem of coordination. But leprechauns delight in demonstrating that it does nothing of the sort. Paradoxes are endemic in our attempts to think rationally and often inspire the impulse to philosophy.

Hollis, Martin and Sugden, Robert. Rationality in Action. *Mind*, 102(405), 1-35, Ja 93.

The paper reviews 'the state of the art' in rational choice and game theory, identifying paradoxes of philosophical interest. The first part traces the idea of utility from Hobbes to Savage. The second deploys the game-theoretic notion of strategically rational choice and dissects the problems of coordination, commitment, constrained maximization, promising and 'cheap talk'. The third casts doubt on the assumption of Common Knowledge of Rationality by examining the backward induction paradox. The fourth uncovers the philosophy of mind implicit in utility theory and reflects on Humean, Kantian and Wittgensteinian accounts of motivation.

Holly, Marilyn. The Incorporation of American Indian Philosophy into Undergraduate Philosophy Courses. *Teach Phil*, 15(4), 349-365, D 92.

This article justifies the teaching of North American Indian philosophy as a part of mainstream philosophy courses, identifies core themes as delineated by American Indian writers, presents basic bibliographies for different sorts of philosophy courses, and discusses actual problems encountered by the author in the classroom when using these writings. The author argues that the quincentennial year 1992 requires that the field of philosophy re-evaluate itself and the mainstream culture with respect to ethnocentrism.

Holmes, Helen Bequaert (ed) and Purdy, Laura M. *Feminist Perspectives In Medical Ethics*. Bloomington, Indiana Univ Pr, 1992.

Holmes, M Randall. Systems of Combinatory Logic Related to Predicative and 'Mildly Impredicative' Fragments of Quine's 'New Foundations'. *Annals Pure Applied Log*, 59(1), 45-53, Ja 93.

This paper extends the results of an earlier paper by the author (this journal, 1991). New subsystems of the combinatory logic TRC shown in that paper to be equivalent to NF are introduced; these systems are analogous to subsystems of NF with predicativity restrictions on set comprehension introduced and shown to be consistent by Crabbé. For one of these systems, an exact equivalence in consistency strength and expressive power with the analogous subsystem of NF is established.

Holmes, Stephen. Tocqueville and Democracy in The Idea of Democracy, Copp, David (ed). New York, Cambridge Univ Pr, 1993.

Holmstrom-Hintikka, Ghita. On Argumentation in Legal Contexts. *Commun Cog*, 25(2-3), 259-268, 1992.

Holopainen, Taina and Knuuttila, Simo. Conditional Will and Conditional Norms in Medieval Thought. *Synthese*, 96(1), 115-132, Jl 93.

The historical background of the fourteenth century discussion of conditional norms is elucidated by an analysis of the emergence of the logic of will in early medieval thought (Abelard, Peter of Poitiers, William of Auxerre, Walter Burley). It is also shown that some problems relevant to later medieval deontic logic were discussed in obligations logic (positio dependens, positio cadens, positio renascens).

Holowka, Jacek. Ethics of the Vienna Circle and the Lvov-Warsaw School. *Dialec Hum*, 17(1), 30-39, 1990.

Holton, Gerald. "More on Einstein, Michelson, and the 'Crucial' Experiment". *Method Sci*, 26(1), 6-7, 1993.

Holton, Gerald. A Personal View of Percy W Bridgman, Physicist and Philosopher. *Method Sci*, 26(1), 1-5, 1993.

An assessment of the five main ordering ideas that motivated P W Bridgman's life and work (as physicist and philosopher), based on the author's observations, first as his student and later as his colleague.

Holton, Gerald. Ernst Mach and Paul Carus. *Method Sci*, 25(2), 73-79, 1992.

Holton, Gerald. Michael Polanyi and the History of Science. *Tradition Discovery*, 19(1), 16-30, 1992-93.

This essay is a study of Polanyi's career as scientist and philosopher from the point of view of the history of science, starting with the first step in his academic career helped by an intervention of Albert Einstein. Polanyi's ideas are better understood if placed against the background of then-fashionable philosophical movements, including logical positivism, and his disagreement with Bukharin in 1935. The essay studies the sources and ambitions of Polanyi's notion of the tacit dimension, his attitude to evolution and "emergence," and his contribution to the search for the origins of Einstein's Relativity Theory. His success in the last of these is shown to be an exemplar of Polanyi's own philosophy.

Holton, Richard. Intention Detecting. *Phil Quart*, 43(172), 298-318, Jl 93.

Crispin Wright has argued that our concept of intention is extension-determining, and that this explains why we are so good at knowing our intentions: it does so by subverting the idea that we detect them. This paper has two aims. The first is to make sense of Wright's claim that intention is extension-determining; this is achieved by comparing his position to that of analytic functionalism. The second is to show that it doesn't follow from this that we do not detect our intentions. Wright has conflated two questions. Firstly, do we detect our intentions? Secondly, do we detect the concept of intention itself? The extension-determining account returns a negative answer only to the second.

Holton, Richard. Response-Dependence and Infallibility. *Analysis*, 52(3), 180-184, Jl 92.

Some say that subjects will, in general, be infallible in their application of response-dependent concepts. I show that this is not right. Infallibility will only result if the relevant response meets three further conditions. It must be (i) a judgment, that (ii) concerns the concept in question, and (iii) is made by the very class of people who use the concept.

Holtu, Nils. Heidegger's Concept of Truth: Semantics and Relativism. *Dan Yrbk Phil*, 27, 7-22, 1992.

In this paper I argue that Heidegger has an anti-realist conception of truth and meaning, and that in his theory of knowledge, he is committed to relativism. Heidegger holds that alternative uncoverings of entities are possible within different modes of "Being". This view is combined with a general anti-realist picture of truth. Thus it becomes unclear by which criteria, if any, he can privilege any one proposition, held true within one conceptual horizon, above another incompatible proposition, held true within another conceptual horizon. Furthermore, Heidegger is unable to adopt certain strategies by which to avoid relativism, and I argue that other strategies are either implausible in their own light, or in the context of Heidegger's theory of truth and meaning.

Holtug, Nils. Human Gene Therapy: Down the Slippery Slope?. *Bioethics*, 7(5), 402-419, O 93.

In this article I assess the slippery slope arguments that have been put forward against human gene therapy. I distinguish between two logical versions and an empirical one. It is argued that neither version pulls through; accepting morally unproblematic cases of gene therapy does not logically force us to accept more problematic cases; there seems to be no empirical evidence supporting the claim that we shall in fact slide down the slope if we engage in gene therapy; and if we agreed to ban gene therapy on the empirical argument, we would have to make very undesirable modifications in health care in general, to be consistent.

Holub, Renate. *Antonio Gramsci: Beyond Marxism and Postmodernism*. New York, Routledge, 1992.

Holzhey, Helmut. Gibt es einen natürlichen Anspruch auf Freiheit?. *Stud Phil (Switzerland)*, 49, 81-96, 1990.

The article focuses on the ethical problem of freedom and discusses the question whether there is a justified claim to freedom derived from human nature. It is argued that human nature does not lead to any commitment of freedom. On the contrary, a part of this commitment consists of one's responsibility for the natural conditions of human existence.

Honderich, Ted. An Interview with A J Ayer in A J Ayer Memorial Essays, Griffiths, A Phillips (ed). New York, Cambridge Univ Pr, 1991.

Ayer's philosophical career, at Oxford and University College London, can be regarded as having had four periods. The first, Logical Positivism, had at its center the Verification Principle of Meaning, a criterion for distinguishing statements from non-statements. At the end of his life Ayer was still inclined to it but felt it had not been satisfactorily formulated. The second period was one of Phenomenalism. It too is at best an incomplete program. The third period was one of an epistemological kind, centering on scepticism, and may have contained his best work. The fourth period, constructionism, owed something to the work of Peirce and Quine. The aim in all periods was to get something right in philosophy.

Honderich, Ted. Causation: One Thing Just Happens After Another in The Philosophy of A J Ayer, Hahn, Lewis Edwin (ed). Peru, Open Court, 1992.

A cause is best regarded not as an event but as individual property. Its relation to the effect is stated by the conditionals 'If not C-then not-E', and also 'If C then E'. To the main philosophical question about causation, that of the relation between a causal circumstance (including a cause) and an effect, answers in terms of Humean regularity are unsatisfactory. The relation is one stated by a type of conditional statement: 'If or since CC, even if X, still E.' The conditional can but need not be elaborated in terms of possible worlds. The conditional, which involves a generalization, but not in the Humean way, also expresses nomic or lawlike connection.

Honderich, Ted. Conservatism Not Much Reconsidered. *Utilitas*, 4(1), 145-153, My 92.

The political tradition of Conservatism is unique, not in being self-interested, but in being self-interested and without the support of a general moral principle. The Left in politics, by contrast, is in fact definable in terms of the Principle of Equality. Conservatism is not distinguished as the tradition which advocates freedom: each and every political tradition advocates certain freedoms as against others. Conservatism has been and continues to be reluctant about democracy. Such judgments about it are not in any bad sense rationalistic.

Honderich, Ted. Conservatism, Ideology, Rationale, and a Red Light. *Rad Phil*, 61, 34-36, Sum 92.

The methods of analytic philosophy are excellent methods for making sense of a political ideology. Any alternative methods are at best unclear. With respect to the ideology of conservatism, these methods lead to the conclusion that it has a rationale—like any large political tradition. Its rationale, which is different from the various distinctions of the tradition, is self-interest, unsupported by a general moral principle. That conservatism has a rationale is not put in doubt by diversity within the tradition. Nor, certainly, does diversity give a reason for thinking that a tradition cannot be identified.

Honderich, Ted. Seeing Qualia and Positing the World in A J Ayer Memorial Essays, Griffiths, A Phillips (ed). New York, Cambridge Univ Pr, 1991.

Ayer held that in perceptual experience we perceive or are aware of subjective entities, qualia. This issues in our positing or constructing objective entities, the world. An argument from the premise that we do not see all of what makes something objective does not establish that we perceive subjective entities. The doctrines of qualia and positing are in fact owed to but not established by 1) Mental Realism as distinct from other accounts of mental events and 2) the desire to distinguish perceptual from other mental events. What is needed, a qualia-free account of perception, rules out the proposition that we posit the world.

Honderich, Ted. Smith and the Champion of Mauve. *Analysis*, 44(2), 86-89, Mr 84.

The Champion of Mauve allows that it is the fleece of his mauve bedroom slippers which has the effect of keeping him warm. He allows too that the colour of the slippers is not necessary to the fleece. But he insists on the efficacy of mauve, as he says, on the ground that the slippers with the fleece are identical with the mauve slippers. Compare insisting on the mental efficacy of an event, whose physical property alone is said to be causal with respect to actions, on the ground that the event with the mental property is identical with the event with the physical property. This argument for mental efficacy, used to defend Davidson's Anamalous Monism, seems no better than the argument for mauvish efficacy.

Honderich, Ted. The Union Theory and Anti-Individualism in Mental Causation, Heil, John (ed). New York, Clarendon/Oxford Pr, 1993.

Certain constraints on an adequate philosophy of mind, including psychoneural intimacy and mental indispensability, seem to point to an Identity Theory of mind and brain. But the theory does not satisfy the constraints. The Union Theory does so. However, like other mind-brain theories, it fails if the anti-individualism or externalism of Putnam and Burge is correct. In fact the Union Theory, tested by total plausibility, is superior to anti-individualism.

Honderich, Ted (ed) and Baldwin, Thomas. *G E Moore*. New York, Routledge, 1992.

This is a critical investigation of the philosophical writings of G E Moore. The book includes a study of Moore's alleged refutation of idealism and his early realist philosophy, a detailed discussion of *Principia Ethica* and his ethical theory, and an examination of the issues raised by Moore's mature philosophy - especially by his treatments of philosophical analysis, perception, scepticism, and common sense. Throughout Moore's arguments are compared with those of his contemporaries—especially, Bradley, Russell, Wittgenstein; and there is frequent use of previously unpublished material.

Honer, Stanley M and Hunt, Thomas C and Okholm, Dennis L. *Invitation to Philosophy: Issues and Options (Sixth Edition)*. Belmont, Wadsworth, 1992.

Honig, Bonnie. The Politics of Agonism. *Polit Theory*, 21(3), 528-533, Ag 93.

The essay criticizes the identification of agonism with aestheticism and subjectivism. It argues that the agonism of both Nietzsche and Arendt is a form of institutionalism, built on shared practices of promising, forgiveness and ostracism. Seen this way, agonism becomes a potentially valuable model of democratic action, particularly when informed by Nietzsche's and Arendt's rather different assessments of its promise and power in modern settings.

Honneth, Axel. Conceptions of 'Civil Society'. *Rad Phil*, 64, 19-22, Sum 93.

Honneth, Axel (& other eds). *Cultural-Political Interventions in the Unfinished Project of Enlightenment*. Cambridge, MIT Pr, 1992.

Honneth, Axel. Integrity and Disrespect: Principles of a Conception of Morality Based on the Theory of Recognition. *Polit Theory*, 20(2), 187-201, My 92.

Honneth, Axel. Moral Development and Social Struggle in Cultural-Political Interventions in the Unfinished Project of Enlightenment, Honneth, Axel (& other eds). Cambridge, MIT Pr, 1992.

Honneth, Axel (& other eds). *Philosophical Interventions in the Unfinished Project of Enlightenment*. Cambridge, MIT Pr, 1992.

Hood, Webster F. Dewey and the Technological Context of Directed Practice in Frontiers in American Philosophy, Volume I, Burch, Robert W (ed). College Station, Texas A&M Univ Pr, 1992.

Hooker, Brad. Parfit's Arguments for the Present-Aim Theory. *Austl J Phil*, 70(1), 61-75, Mr 92.

The *Self-Interest Theory* maintains that one has most reason to do what would be best for oneself over the long term. The *Present-aim Theory* claims that one has just as much reason to do what would fulfill one's present desires, even if this is not best for oneself over the long term. Which theory provides a better account of what one has most reason to do apart from moral considerations? Derek Parfit argues that the Present- aim Theory does. This article challenges his arguments.

Hooker, Brad. Political Philosophy in Reflections on Philosophy, McHenry, Leemon (ed). New York, St Martin's Pr, 1993.

This paper is about distributive justice. It notes that the diminishing marginal utility of material goods furnishes utilitarians with a reason for equalizing distribution. It also defends the idea that the need for economic incentives gives utilitarians a reason for favoring systems that won't distribute equally. It then outlines Rawls's conception of just distribution. But many people believe that what people deserve is not a function of utilitarian or Rawlsian considerations. After rehearsing Rawls's well-known reply, the paper defends redistributive programs in a way compatible with this familiar idea that certain people deserve more than others independently of utilitarian and of Rawlsian considerations.

Hooker, Bradford. Critical Notice: Thomas Nagel's *Equality and Partiality*. *Phil Quart*, 43(172), 366-372, Jl 93.

Hooker, C A and Penfold, H B and Evans, R J. Control, Connectionism and Cognition: Towards a New Regulatory Paradigm. *Brit J Phil Sci*, 43(4), 517-536, D 92.

Hookway, Christopher. Belief, Confidence and the Method of Science. *Trans Peirce Soc*, 29(1), 1-32, Wint 93.

Hookway, Christopher. Peirce, a Philosopher for the 21st Century: Part II. *Trans Peirce Soc*, 28(2), 261-288, Spr 92.

Hookway, Christopher. Russell and the Possibility of Scepticism. *J Speculative Phil*, 6(2), 95-110, 1992.

Hookway, Christopher. *Scepticism*. New York, Routledge, 1992.

Hookway, Christopher. Wittgenstein and Knowledge: Beyond Form and Content. *J Speculative Phil*, 7(2), 77-91, 1993.

Hooper, Alan. From Liberal-Radicalism to Conservative Corporatism in Victorian Liberalism, Bellamy, Richard (ed). New York, Routledge, 1990.

Hoopes, James (ed). *Peirce on Signs*. Chapel Hill, Univ N Carolina Pr, 1991.

Hoose, Bernard. Proportionalists, Deontologists and the Human Good. *Heythrop J*, 33(2), 175-191, Ap 92.

The author holds that, although there may appear to be a good deal of agreement, there are in fact major differences between how proportionalists understand the human good and how their opponents in the school of thought headed by Germain Grisez and John Finnis understand it. He goes on to suggest that the proportionalists' supposed problem of incommensurability among goods can be overcome by ceasing to regard the so-called basic goods as separate entities (almost Platonic Ideas). He calls for a greater concentration upon the human person and openness to new knowledge about the same.

Hopkins, Jim. Psychoanalysis, Interpretation, and Science in Psychoanalysis, Mind and Art, Hopkins, Jim (ed). Cambridge, Blackwell, 1992.

Hopkins, Jim (ed) and Savile, Anthony (ed). *Psychoanalysis, Mind and Art*. Cambridge, Blackwell, 1992.

Hopkins, Patrick D. Gender Treachery: Homophobia, Masculinity, and Threatended Identities in Rethinking Masculinity, May, Larry (ed). Lanham, Rowman & Littlefield, 1992.

Horder, Jeremy. Criminal Culpability: The Possibility of a General Theory. *Law Phil*, 12(2), 193-215, My 93.

In this article, I try to do two things. First I analyse critically the suggestion that the principles of criminal culpability can be explained by reference to a single, all-encompassing concept, such as "defiance of the law." I then go on to explain the foundations of criminal culpability by reference to three interlocking theories—the capacity theory, the character theory, and the agency theory. I conclude that even these three theories may not be sufficient to explain the complex structure of culpability, which is shaped as much by shared cultural understanding as by moral theory.

Horgan, Terence. From Cognitive Science to Folk Psychology: Computation, Mental Representation, and Belief. *Phil Phenomenol Res*, 52(2), 449-484, Je 92.

This paper is a critical study of Lynne Rudder Baker's *Saving Belief: A Critique of Physicalism*; Jay Garfield's *Belief in Psychology: A Study in the Ontology of Mind*; and Robert Cummins's *Meaning and Mental Representation*. All three books discuss interconnections between computational cognitive science and common-sense intentional psychology. The paper includes, as groundwork, a critical examination of certain influential views of Jerry Fodor about these matters. One of my central claims is that the relation between the state-types of intentional psychology and those of computational cognitive science is best viewed as realization, not (contra Fodor) as type-identity.

Horgan, Terence. On What There Isn't. *Phil Phenomenol Res*, 53(3), 693-700, S 93.

Peter van Inwagen, in his book *Material Beings*, argues that the only real material entities are physical simples and living organisms. In this symposium paper on *Material Beings*, I first articulate a metaphysical principle which plausibly underwrites van Inwagen's argument; I call it *the non-arbitrariness of composition*. I then argue that this principle generates heavy dialectical pressure against van Inwagen's preferred ontology — and toward an ontological position that repudiates not only the tables, chairs, and other dry goods both natural and artifactual, but also persons and other living organisms. Arguably, even more isn't than van Inwagen claims isn't.

Horgan, Terence and Timmons, Mark. Troubles for New Wave Moral Semantics: The 'Open Question Argument' Revived. *Phil Papers*, 21(3), 153-175, N 92.

We argue that (1) the new wave version of ethical naturalism defended by David Brink, Richard Boyd, Nicholas Sturgeon, and others, rests on a certain view about the semantics of moral terms that stems from the attempt to extend relatively recent developments in the philosophy of language (due to the work of Putnam and Kripke) to the understanding of moral language; but that (2) this new wave semantic view succumbs to an updated version of Moore's 'Open Question Argument' as reveled by a Twin Earth thought experiment. We conclude that, in the end, new wave ethical naturalism is as fatally flawed as its predecessor.

Horkheimer, Max and Hunter, G Frederick (& other trans). *Between Philosophy and Social Science: Selected Early Writings*. Cambridge, MIT Pr, 1993.

Hormigón, Mariano. La pesada herencia de la libertad matemática. *Theoria (Spain)*, 5(12-13), 241-259, N 90.

The debate between the pure or fundamentalist branch of mathematics and the applied one induces to discuss dispassionately the links between *the queen of sciences* and the development of technology. To avoid the existing difficulty in separating the concrete daily problems from the conceptual and theoretic reflections, it generally produces good results to show some elements of the relations between mathematics and technology. The autonomous position, which characterizes the mathematics of absolute freedom, clashes with the quick development of technology, which creates a new structure of mathematics. This development produces a permanent interrogation about what is building and developing anyone who calls himself a mathematician.

Horne, Haynes. Jameson's Strategies of Containment in Postmodernism/Jameson/ Critique, Kellner, Douglas (ed). Washington, Maisonneuve Pr, 1989.

Hornsby, Jennifer. Agency and Causal Explanation in Mental Causation, Heil, John (ed). New York, Clarendon/Oxford Pr, 1993.

Horowitz, Amir and Dascal, Marcelo. Semantics and the Psyche. *Phil Phenomenol Res*, 52(2), 395-399, Je 92.

The paper criticizes two contentions of Bogdan concerning psychosemantics (in "Does Semantic Run the Psyche?", *Phil and Phenomenal Res*, 49 (1992):395-399). Bogdan claims that the content of an attitude has psychological causal powers *qua* pragmatic and not *qua* semantic, and then argues that Fodor's program of naturalizing psychosemantics actually *assumes* intentionality and naturalizes only the conditions of its semantic success. After rebutting Bogdan's first criticism, the paper tries to show why Fodor, within the framework of his theory, does not have to naturalize intentionality, but that nevertheless he does not assume it.

Horowitz, Gad. Groundless Democracy in Shadow of Spirit, Berry, Philippa (ed). New York, Routledge, 1992.

Ernesto Laclau and Chantal Mouffe have put forward a post-structuralist grounding of democracy in and as "negativity", constant undermining of all identities, constant revelation of the groundlessness of all social institutions; the groundlessness of all existents is the ground of democracy. This argument will be subjected to neighborly criticism from the no-position, (the absolute absence of any) position of Buddhist Madhyamika philosophy. It will then be possible to restore the distinction, minimized by post-structuralism, between social and discursive power, and to restore the sundered connection between language and politics on the one hand, and Nature and Value on the other.

Horowitz, Irving Louis. The Phenomenal World of Kurt H Wolff. *Human Stud*, 16(3), 325-328, Jl 93.

This statement was prepared in honor of the publication of K H Wolff's book on *Survival and Sociology*, and delivered before an annual meeting of the Society for the Study of Phenomenology. It is first, a review of the humanistic bases of Wolff's analysis of the tasks of social science; second, an appreciation of the philosophical sources for his work; and third, a critique of the empirical limits of even a well-crafted general approach to the therapeutic values of sociology.

Horowitz, Tamara. Newcomb's Problem as a Thought Experiment in Thought Experiments in Science and Philosophy, Horowitz, Tamara (ed). Lanham, Rowman & Littlefield, 1991.

Horowitz, Tamara (ed) and Massey, Gerald J (ed). *Thought Experiments in Science and Philosophy*. Lanham, Rowman & Littlefield, 1991.

Horska, Pavla and Peskova, Jaroslava. A Debate Between a Philospoher and a Historian on the Women's Question in Bohemia (in Czechoslovakian). *Filozof Cas*, 40(5), 757-768, 1992.

The philosopher Jaroslava Pesková and the historian Pavla Horská try to find out the reasons why the "women's question" has almost never become a form in the Czech history in which the emancipation of an individual in general has been put through. (edited)

Horsten, Leon. Scope and Rigidity. *Commun Cog*, 25(4), 353-372, 1992.

In the appendix to chapter 5 of his classical work "Frege: Philosophy of Language", Dummett argues that Kripke's theory that proper names are rigid designators does no more work for us than the thesis that proper names should always be given wide

scope. Since it is not always clear what his alternative explanations amount to when applied to concrete examples, the present article tries to make them more concrete. When the concept of a prioricity is brought into play, it is found that Dummett's proposal gives rise to consequences which do not accord well with our semantic intuitions.

Horsten, Leon. Two Problems Concerning Frege's Distinction Between Concepts and Objects. *Log Anal*, 32, 267-284, S-D 89.

It is generally believed that Frege's doctrine of incomplete referents is an answer to the following philosophical puzzle: "A sentence is more than a list of names. Therefore not every work of a sentence can stand for an object." In the first part of the paper it is argued that this is a puzzle about meaning rather than about reference. The second part of the paper discusses Frege's two criteria for deciding whether a given expression stands for a concept or an object. It is argued that in particular cases these two criteria are in conflict with each other.

Horton, John. Moral Conflict and Political Commitment. *Utilitas*, 5(1), 109-120, My 93.

A critical review of Steven Lukes's *Moral Conflict and Politics*. Several features of the book are considered but the principal focus of the discussion is on a perceived tension between Lukes's belief in the incommensurability of values and the inerradicability of moral conflict, and his commitment to a strong conception of rational political deliberation and argument.

Horwich, Paul. Bayesian Problem-Solving and the Dispensibility of Truth in Rationality in Epistemology, Villanueva, Enrique (ed). Atascadero, Ridgeview, 1992.

The Bayesian model (that there are *degrees* of belief between zero and one, and that *rational* degrees of belief must satisfy the probability calculus) is at once extremely fruitful, yet almost certainly false. It is argued that this problem should be resolved by regarding the model as helpful idealization containing just the right balance of accuracy and simplicity to enable us to clear away confusions concerning the methodology of science.

Horwich, Paul. Chomsky Versus Quine on the Analytic-Synthetic Distinction. *Proc Aris Soc*, 92, 95-108, 1992.

It is argued that the apparent conflict between Quine's critique of the analytic-synthetic distinction and its postulation within cognitive science is an illusion. For the following central features of Quine's position are unaffected by the scientific situation: (1) that reductionist epistemology (which demanded a determinate analytic-synthetic distinction) is wrong and should be replaced by the 'web of belief' model; (2) that a scientific, fully determinate analytic-synthetic distinction would have no philosophical import; and (3) that the semantic properties to which we ordinarily refer may be heavily indeterminate. Even if those employed in cognitive science are not.

Horwich, Paul. Gibbard's Theory of Norms. *Phil Pub Affairs*, 22(1), 67-78, Wint 93.

It is argued that Gibbard's expressivist (emotivist) account of normative judgment would be improved by the acknowledgement that normative predicates (such as "rational") express properties and that normative claims are true or false. The departure from the traditional formulation of emotivism is motivated by the 'deflationary' (redundancy) perspective on truth, and it facilitates solution of the Frege/Geach 'embedding' problem.

Horwich, Paul (ed). *World Changes*. Cambridge, MIT Pr, 1993.

Horwitz, Robert and Zuckert, Michael (ed). John Locke's *Questions Concerning the Law of Nature*: A Commentary. *Interpretation*, 19(3), 251-306, Spr 92.

Locke's *Question on the Law of Nature*, an early work prepared while he was lecturing on moral philosophy in the 1660s, gives every appearance of being a work much in the tradition of Christian natural law theory, as developed by Thomas Aquinas and revived in Locke's England by thinkers like Richard Hooker and Nathaniel Culverwell. Closer examination of this text, Locke's only extended writing on the law of nature, largely dispels the impression of Locke's allegiance to one or another variety of Christian natural law theory. Contrary to his initial claims, Locke progressively undermines all the grounds of Christian natural law he brings forth. His work thus serves far more as a critique than an endorsement of traditional law of natural doctrine.

Hossack, Keith. Constructivist Mathematics, Quantum Physics and Quantifiers—II, Constructivism and Quantifiers. *Aris Soc*, Supp(66), 79-97, 1992.

Hostetler, Karl. Solidarity and Moral Community. *Proc Phil Educ*, 48, 316-323, 1992.

Habermas, Gadamer, and Rorty all stress the importance of solidarity as a feature of moral community, but there are important differences in their views on the nature and grounds of solidarity. This paper considers how well the views of these writers serve educators in their task of fostering solidarity and moral community among school students, particularly those who are victims of injustice. It recommends a Gadamerian approach to this task. What this means for practice is that "we-centrism" should be the basis from which broader solidarities are created.

Hottois, Gilbert. Aspects of a Philosophy of Technique. *Res Phil Technol*, 9, 45-57, 1989.

Hottois, Gilbert. Solidarité et disposition du corps humain. *Dialogue (Canada)*, 30(3), 3o65-381, Sum 91.

Quatre attitudes générales relatives aux dons et prélèvements d'organes sont analysées: le refus plus ou moins absolu sur base symbolique (religieuse), qui exclut l'argent et la technique; la symbolique du don comme démarche individuelle et élective qui exclut l'argent et subordonne la technique au symbole; la logique du marché (commerce) qui ignore le symbole mais n'est pas sans convergence avec la dynamique technicienne; la solidarité sociale: une tentative de resymbolisation ouverte à l'exploitation du possible technique.

Houlgate, Stephen. A Reply to Joseph C Flay's "Hegel's Metaphysics". *Owl Minerva*, 24(2), 153-161, Spr 93.

This article deals with the relation between Hegel's *Phenomenology* and his *Science of Logic* via a discussion of Joseph Flay's essay, "Hegel's Metaphysics". My claim is that the purpose of Hegel's *Phenomenology* is not to show that thought is embedded in a real *relation* to being (as Flay proposes), but rather to dissolve the very distinction between thought and being upon which the idea of a "relation" between the two rests. The *Phenomenology* should thus be understood as leading to the point at which the form of thought and the form of being are known to be *identical*.

Houlgate, Stephen. Hegel's Ethical Thought. *Bull Hegel Soc Gt Brit*, 25, 1-17, Spr-Sum 92.

This article discusses Allen Wood's *Hegel's Ethical Thought*, (Cambridge University Press, 1990). I contend that Wood provides an excellent account of Hegelian *Sittlichkeit* and shows conclusively that it fulfills, rather than suppresses human individuality. I suggest, however, that Wood misunderstands Hegel's analyses of punishment and poverty in the *Philosophy of Right* because he fails to appreciate the importance of dialectical logic for Hegel's ethico-political philosophy. In conclusion, I argue that close attention to the logic of the *Philosophy of Right* reveals that (*pace* Wood) Hegel does provide a satisfactory justification for punishment and a solution to the problem of poverty.

Houser, Nathan. Charles S Peirce: American Backwoodsman in Frontiers in American Philosophy, Volume I, Burch, Robert W (ed). College Station, Texas A&M Univ Pr, 1992.

Houser, Nathan. On "Peirce and Logicism": A Response to Haack. *Trans Peirce Soc*, 29(1), 57-67, Wint 93.

Houser, Nathan. On Peirce's Theory of Propositions: A Response to Hilpinen. *Trans Peirce Soc*, 28(3), 489-504, Sum 92.

Houser, Nathan. Peirce and the Law of Distribution in Perspectives on the History of Mathematical Logic, Drucker, Thomas (ed). Basel, Birkhauser, 1991.

Houston, Barbara. Are Children's Rights Wrong Rights?. *Proc Phil Educ*, 48, 145-155, 1992.

Houston, Barbara. In Praise of Blame. *Hypatia*, 7(4), 128-147, Fall 92.

Recent writers in feminist ethics have been concerned to find ways to reclaim and augment women's moral agency. This essay considers Sarah Hoagland's intriguing suggestion that we renounce moral praise and blame and pursue what she calls an "ethic of intelligibility." I argue that the eschewal of moral blame would not help but rather hinder our efforts to increase our sense of moral agency. It would, I claim, further intensify our demoralization.

Howard, Dick. Two Hundred Years of Error? The Politics of Democracy. *Phil Soc Crit*, 19(1), 15-24, 1993.

How is one to understand the Revolutions of 1989 in Eastern Europe? I propose to return to the French Revolution of 1789 to see the emergence of modern politics. I then claim that each in its own way liberal capitalism and planned socialism were forms of *anti-politics*. 1989 is thus the return of the political and a renewal of the project of democracy as radical.

Howard, Paul and Solski, Jeffrey. The Strength of the A-System Lemma. *Notre Dame J Form Log*, 34(1), 100-106, Wint 93.

The delta system lemma is not provable in set theory without the axiom of choice nor does it imply the axiom of choice.

Howard, Paul E. The Axiom of Choice for Countable Collections of Countable Sets Does Not Imply the Countable Union Theorem. *Notre Dame J Form Log*, 33(2), 236-243, Spr 92.

A model for the theory ZFU (Zermelo-Fraenkel set theory weakened to permit the existence of atoms) is constructed in which the axiom of choice for countable collections of countable sets is true and the countable union theorem is false. By a transfer theorem of Pincus there is a model of Zermelo-Fraenkel set theory satisfying the same conditions.

Howard-Snyder, Daniel. Seeing through CORNEA. *Int J Phil Relig*, 32(1), 25-49, Ag 92.

Wykstra argued that the atheist doesn't justifiedly believe evil appears not to have a point since it's not reasonable to believe that if there were one, they'd likely discern it. Five problems beset his case: (i) appearing claims are inessential to the atheist's argument, (ii) CORNEA—his epistemic principle—leads to an unpalatable dilemma, (iii) CORNEA is false, (iv) rendered plausible, CORNEA is unemployable since Wykstra's minor premise is unsupported by reasons he adduces in its favor, and (v) supposing that gap filled, his argument is a *nonsequitur*. In closing, I offer a neo-Wykstraen challenge.

Howard-Snyder, Daniel and Howard-Snyder, Frances. The Christian Theodicist's Appeal to Love. *Relig Stud*, 29(2), 185-192, Je 93.

Many Christian theodicists wish to affirm three propositions. 1) God's creating beings with the capacity to love in large part justifies His permitting evil. 2) Love is essential to the internal life of God. 3) God is essentially perfectly good. We argue that 1-3 are prima facie incompatible, and that four attempts at dispelling this air of incompatibility fail.

Howard-Snyder, Frances. Elbow-Room for Consequentialists. *Analysis*, 52(4), 249-, O 92.

Critics argue that consequentialism deprives us of moral autonomy. Seana Shiffrin clarifies this objection like this: consequentialism deprives us of the freedom to perform a non-optimific action without doing wrong. I explore several reasons for thinking this a valuable freedom and find them wanting. The chief reason is that without this freedom we are forced to choose between optimizing and being subject to guilt and blame. I point out that the consequentialist rejects the link between wrongdoing and blameworthiness. There is no inconsistency, for the consequentialist, in saying: "I did less than the best. So I did wrong. But I'm not going to feel guilty about it."

Howard-Snyder, Frances. Is It Less Wrong to Harm the Vulnerable than the Secure?. *J Phil*, 89(12), 643-647, D 92.

In "Agency and Morality" (Journal of Philosophy, April 1991) Richard Brook argues that the fact that someone is unthreatened at a moment gives her a right not to be harmed, and that this right explains the wrongness of killing one to save two or more. He claims that this explains the distinction between deontology and consequentialism. I offer counterexamples to the suggestion that the right of the unthreatened is more stringent than the right of the threatened, pointing out that it seems harsh to claim an extra protection for those who are already lucky enough not to be in harm's way. I argue for an alternative account of the distinction between deontology and consequentialism.

Howard-Snyder, Frances. Rule Consequentialism is a Rubber Duck. *Amer Phil Quart*, 30(3), 271-277, Jl 93.

Like rubber ducks and prairie dogs, rule consequentialism is not what its name suggests: it is not a form of consequentialism. This follows from what is currently the most popular account of the distinction between consequentialism and non-consequentialism, an account that relies crucially on the notion of agent-centeredness. So much the worse for that account, you might say. I argue, however, that there is much to be said for classifying rule consequentialism as a form of deontology rather than consequentialism. Chiefly, it shares both the main strengths and the main weaknesses of deontology relative to consequentialism.

Howard-Snyder, Frances and Howard-Snyder, Daniel. The Christian Theodicist's Appeal to Love. *Relig Stud*, 29(2), 185-192, Je 93.

Many Christian theodicists wish to affirm three propositions. 1) God's creating beings with the capacity to love in large part justifies His permitting evil. 2) Love is essential to the internal life of God. 3) God is essentially perfectly good. We argue that 1-3 are prima facie incompatible, and that four attempts at dispelling this air of incompatibility fail.

Howard-Snyder, Frances and Norcross, Alastair. A Consequentialist Case for Rejecting the Right. *J Phil Res*, 18, 109-125, 1993.

Satisficing and maximizing versions of consequentialism have both assumed that rightness is an all-or-nothing property. We argue that this is inimical to the spirit of consequentialism, and that, from the point of view of the consequentialist, actions should be evaluated purely in terms that admit of degree. We consider the suggestion that rightness and wrongness are a matter of degree. We conclude that the consequentialist can make no sense of the concept of wrongness. (edited)

Howe, Edmund G. Caveats Regarding Slippery Slopes and Physicians' Moral Conscience. *J Clin Ethics*, 3(4), 251-255, Wint 92.

Howe, Lawrence W. Unmasking Bergson's Idealism. *SW Phil Stud*, 15, 43-50, Spr 93.

This paper discusses interpretations of Bergson's metaphysics. Some have argued that Bergson's metaphysics is a vitalism, others have argued that he was a pioneer of process philosophy. While each of these interpretations are in certain respects plausible, they ultimately fail to detect a confusion of terms in Bergson's metaphysics that sponsors a very different interpretation of his position. Reasons are presented for interpreting Bergson as an idealist holding that there is a primitive mind operative in each strata of existence and that the vital impetus and duration are confused modes of mental activity.

Howells, Christina. Sartre and the Deconstruction of the Subject in The Cambridge Companion to Sartre, Howells, Christina (ed). New York, Cambridge Univ Pr, 1992.

The essay pursues a double line of argument, showing first that the subject for Sartre is not the autonomous, self-sufficient foundation his opponents portray it as, but rather divided, non-egoic, never self-identical; and second that the major opponents of a philosophy of the subject in France are now withdrawing from their previous radical positions and attempting to construct a notion of subjectivity that would be comparable with what has been learned from Structuralism and Deconstruction.

Howells, Christina (ed). *The Cambridge Companion to Sartre*. New York, Cambridge Univ Pr, 1992.

This is a comprehensive survey of the philosophy of Sartre, covering his writings on ontology, phenomenology, psychology, ethics and aesthetics as well as his work on history, commitment, and progress; a final section considers Sartre's relationship to structuralism and deconstruction. The essays provide a balanced view of Sartre's philosophy and situate it in relation to contemporary trends in Continental philosophy.

Howie, John. Respect for Autonomy in the Practice of Rehabilitation. *Cont Phil*, 14(5), 21-23, S-O 92.

Respect for autonomy as an ethical principle requires rehabilitation counselors to provide three essential elements: 1) client's freedom from control by others (including "control" by the counselor); 2) client possession of relevant knowledge for independent decision-making, and; 3) the client's ability to employ such knowledge for assessing the situation, planning an action, and acting in accordance with the adopted plan. In providing these essential elements the counselor, on the one hand, must insist upon disclosure and understanding of pertinent information and, on the other, voluntariness and authorization as part of the client's consential agreement.

Howsepian, A A. Middle Actions. *Int J Phil Relig*, 34(1), 13-28, Ag 93.

William Hasker and other theological compatibilists have felt the need to retreat into a doctrine of divine providence—by risk that is theologically repugnant to a large number of traditionally-minded theists. I resist this providence-weakening retreat by appealing to a kenotically motivated action-theoretic analogue of divine middle knowledge, viz, middle actions, which I argue can elegantly mediate robust providential governance within an incompatibilist framework.

Hoy, David C. Is Hermeneutics Ethnocentric? in The Interpretive Turn, Hiley, David R (ed). Ithaca, Cornell Univ Pr, 1991.

Hans-Georg Gadamer's hermeneutical philosophy represents a radical break with Cartesian and Kantian theories of knowledge. My specific concern here is whether his program can be defended against those who infer from the hermeneutical insistence on context-boundedness that hermenuetics necessarily condones ethnocentrism. I argue that Gadamer is a critical pluralist, not a critical monist, and as such he can be defended against Habermas's critique. Ethnocentrism follows not from Gadamer's pluralism, but on the contrary, from the expectation of consensus and convergence.

AUTHOR INDEX WITH ABSTRACTS 527 Hughen, Richard

Hoy, David Couzens. Heidegger and the Hermeneutic Turn in The Cambridge Companion to Heidegger, Guignon, Charles B (ed). New York, Cambridge Univ Pr, 1993.

By making interpretive understanding the central mode of human existence, sections 31 and 32 of Martin Heidegger's *Being and Time* have led to a hermeneutic turn in later philosophy. After situating the accounts of understanding and interpretation in *Being and Time* against the background of traditional hermeneutics as well as of Cartesian and Kantian philosophy, the article goes on to describe the influence of Heidegger's argument on later hermeneutic and deconstructive philosophies.

Hoyningen-Huene, Paul. The Interrelations between the Philosophy, History and Sociology of Science in Thomas Kuhn's Theory of Scientific Development. *Brit J Phil Sci*, 43(4), 487-501, D 92.

The paper deals with the interrelations between the philosophy, sociology, and historiography of science in Thomas Kuhn's theory of scientific development. First, the historiography of science provides the basis for both the philosophy and sociology of science in the sense that the fundamental questions of both disciplines depend on the principles of the form of historiography employed. Second, the fusion of the sociology and philosophy of science, as advocated by Kuhn, is discussed. This fusion consists essentially in a replacement of methodological rules by cognitive values that influence the decisions of scientific communities. As a consequence, the question of the rationality of theory choice arises, both with respect to the actual decisions and to the possible justification of cognitive values and their change.

Hrachovec, Herbert. Formale Semantik im Verhältnis zur Erkenntnistheorie: Ein Blickwechsel. *Z Phil Forsch*, 47(2), 165-183, Ap-Je 93.

Hrushovski, Ehud. A New Strongly Minimal Set. *Annals Pure Applied Log*, 62(2), 147-166, Jl 93.

Hrushovski, Ehud and Evans, David M. On the Automorphism Groups of Finite Covers. *Annals Pure Applied Log*, 62(2), 83-112, Jl 93.

Huang, Yih-mei. Externalism (in Chinese). *Phil Rev (Taiwan)*, 15, 101-126, Ja 92.

One basic problem of epistemic justification is the regress problem. The externalist attempts to solve the regress problem by claiming that the acceptance of beliefs satisfying the externalist conditions is epistemically justified. They claim that the person for whom the belief is justified need not himself have any cognitive grasp at all of the reasons. This paper introduces D M Armstrong's and A Goldman's theories and analyzes the arguments in favor of or against the theories. I argue that externalism is not sufficient for epistemic justification.

Hubert, Jerzy Z. Comments on R Baine Harris's "Can We Have a World Philosophy?". *Dialec Hum*, 17(3), 235-238, 1990.

Hubik, S. The Apories of Ethics of the Human Environment (in Czechoslovakian). *Filozof Cas*, 39(6), 955-964, 1991.

Huby, Pamela M. What did Aristotle Mean by 'Nature does Nothing in Vain'? in Logical Foundations, Mahalingam, Indira (ed). New York, St Martin's Pr, 1991.

The aim is to combat the prevailing view that "[God and] nature do nothing in vain" is just decorative or at best heuristic, and does not reflect Aristotle's real thinking. A detailed study of his use of such expressions shows three groups, in biology, politics, and physics. In the last there is a mass of evidence that Aristotle treated nature as a universal force, sometimes alongside God. Perhaps nature is one aspect of God. Aristotle worried all his life about the relationship between God and the world, and all his arguments about this are to be taken seriously.

Hudelson, Richard. Has History Refuted Marxism?. *Phil Soc Sci*, 23(2), 180-198, Je 93.

This article considers the significance of the fall of communism for the question of the truth of Marxism. It begins by considering some Marxist theories of Stalinism and some Marxist criticisms of Bolshevism. Having rejected the adequacy of those theories, the author goes on to argue that while Stalinism in part rests on a nonmarket vision of socialism derived from Marx, contrary to an argument of Carl Cohen, this vision is not deeply rooted in Marxist philosophy.

Hudon, Edith D-R. Politique, morale et droit: Enjeux autour de la reproduction humaine et de l'avortement. *Aquinas*, 35(3), 613-643, S-D 92.

Hudson, Deal. Marion Montgomery and "The Risk of Prophecy". *Thought*, 67(266), 240-256, S 92.

Marion Montgomery's work, particularly his trilogy *The Prophetic Poet and the Spirit of the Age*, is explored in the context of his concern for applying Thomism to the analysis of American culture and intellectual history. Montgomery is also seen as carrying forward the Fugitive-Agrarian tradition and the legacy of Flannery O'Connor. Montgomery is seen as a prophetic writer himself who has revealed this country's spiritual and philosophical dislocations that have shaped the "spirit of the age."

Hudson, Deal W. Comprehending *Anna Karenina*: A Test for THeories of Happiness. *Int Phil Quart*, 32(3), 285-297, S 92.

Hudson, H W. Could the World Embody God? in Logical Foundations, Mahalingam, Indira (ed). New York, St Martin's Pr, 1991.

Hudson, Hud. Collective Responsibility and Moral Vegetarianism. *J Soc Phil*, 24(2), 89-104, Fall 93.

I begin by charting various approaches to defending a vegetarian diet on moral grounds, finally concentrating on the most plausible arguments in favor of moral vegetarianism as well as on a significant challenge to those arguments. I then develop some results in recent work on theories of collective responsibility, collective inaction, and moral taint, which provide a means of escape from that challenge. Finally, I propose four different arguments for moral vegetarianism which are informed by the results of recent work on collective responsibility, concluding on the basis of my investigation that a respectable version of moral vegetarianism is philosophically defensible.

Hudson, Hud. The Significance of Analytic of the Ugly in Kant's Deduction of Pure Judgments of Taste in Kant's Aesthetics, Meerbote, Ralf (ed). Atascadero, Ridgeview, 1991.

I argue that judgments of taste (of reflection) are either judgments of beauty or judgments of ugliness and, modelling my discussion on the "Analytic of the Beautiful" in the *Critique of Aesthetic Judgment*, I present an "Analytic of the Ugly" in which the ugly is the object of a disinterested, subjectively-universal, conditionally-necessary, disliking, and which is an object's form of subjective contrapurposiveness. I also argue that recognizing the role of judgments of ugliness permits a defense of Kant's deduction of pure judgments of taste from the charge that it leads to the unacceptable consequence that all objects of cognition are beautiful.

Hudson, Yeager. Omnipotence: Must God Be Infinite? in God, Values, and Empiricism, Peden, Creighton (ed). Macon, Mercer Univ Pr, 1989.

The article argues that because there are things most philosophers agree even an omnipotent being cannot do (e.g., logically impossible things, changing the past, determining the free actions of other agents, committing evil, creating outside the realm of possibility) it may be advisable to substitute for the word or 'infinite' or 'omnipotent' words like 'almighty,' or simply to admit that a deity able to create the world we see with its, beauty, grandeur and conduciveness to highest human values is great enough for a devotee to worship or a philosopher to respect even if that deity cannot be called infinite.

Hudson, Yeager (ed) and Peden, W Creighton (ed). *Terrorism, Justice and Social Values*. Lewiston, Mellen Pr, 1990.

This book consists of papers selected from those presented at an international conference of the North American Society for Social Philosophy at Guadalajara, Mexico. The papers address the turbulence and violence of the Twentieth Century, especially issues surrounding the use of terrorism as an instrument in the fight for justice and the promotion of political ideologies and causes. In our times the time-honored principle that innocent by-standers must not be harmed has been openly renounced. Questions about human rights, morality, justice, and social progress are addressed in the context of this change.

Huefner, Robert P (ed) and Battin, Margaret P (ed). *Changing To National Health Care: Ethical and Policy Issues*. Salt Lake City, Univ of Utah Pr, 1992.

Huenemann, Charles. Squaring the Cartesian Circle. *Auslegung*, 19(1), 23-34, Wint 93.

Hürlimann, Kaspar. Giovanni: Der Ethiker Nicolai Hartmann und die Religion. *Frei Z Phil Theol*, 40(1-2), 107-124, 1993.

According to Hartmann philosophical ethics has to be exclusively based on values which can be grasped phenomenologically. Thus it is opposed to ethics founded on theology. There exist unsolvable antinomies between these two conceptions of ethics, such as the antinomy between directedness towards this world and directedness towards the other world, or the antinomy between the humanum and the divinum as the supreme value, or that between autonomy and theonomy, between the human free will and divine providence or between the possibility and impossibility of redemption. Hartmann admits that also the religious conception of ethics cannot be without any empirical or intuitive content, but according to him it can nevertheless not be turned into a rational conception. Religion is not rejected but it is excluded from the realm of pure reason. This presentation is followed by a critical assessment of Hartmann's point of view.

Huff, Douglas. Wittgenstein, Solipsism, and Religious Belief. *Sophia (Australia)*, 31(1-2), 37-52, 1992.

Discourse about religious belief is often faced with the following dilemma: either it is part of all reasonable discourse, and thus open to charges of irrationality and absurdity; or it is immune to rational criticism, which leads to a destructive relativism of language and action. The purpose of this paper is to demonstrate why this dilemma does not arise for Wittgenstein. I argue 1) that Wittgenstein's picture of language does not lead to a destructive relativism, where the distinction between meaningful and meaningless discourse is eliminated; and 2) that this interpretation resolves many of the difficulties surrounding the nature of religious belief.

Huffman, Tom L. Abortion, Moral Responsibility, and Self-Defense. *Pub Affairs Quart*, 7(4), 287-302, O 93.

Many argue that if we assume that fetuses are persons from conception and reason by the principle of the justified use of deadly force in self-defense that this justifies a moderate stance on abortion rights. This paper pays close attention to whether the threatened person is responsible for the threat she faces and what bearing such responsibility would have on abortion rights. Employing a general analysis of moral responsibility the paper concludes that the self-defense model argues *against* a woman's right to obtain an abortion under typical circumstances.

Huffman, Tom L. An Argument for Leibnizian Metaphysics. *Amer Cath Phil Quart*, 67(3), 321-332, Sum 93.

Leibnizian metaphysics is often derided as an instance of enlightenment rationalism run wild. This paper tries to show that Leibniz's most notorious doctrines are based upon only three plausible principles and are supported by rather difficult to refute arguments. Furthermore, this paper seeks to demonstrate that despite well-publicized differences, Leibniz's account of substance and general methodology are essentially cartesian. This suggests that Descartes would have accepted Leibniz's denial of physical substance had he paid more attention to individuation than he did.

Hufford, David J. Epistemologies in Religious Healing. *J Med Phil*, 18(2), 175-194, Ap 93.

Religious beliefs in miraculous healing through prayer remain prevalent in modern society. Most such beliefs do not conflict with medical advice but some do. Conventional views have considered these beliefs incompatible with rational modern thought, predicting their demise and explaining their persistence in terms of non-rational thinking, "special logics" and psychological compartmentalization. However, attention to the actual beliefs of individuals often reveals them to be rationally ordered and empirically founded. Further, they do not usually involve disbelief of medical knowledge. Their differences from each other and from orthodox medical ideas arise from differing assumptions, the crediting of subjective experience, and the particular experiences of believers.

Hughen, Richard. The Evolution and Devolution of Personhood. *Personalist Forum*, 8/1(Supp), 275-280, Spr 92.

This paper considers three arguments that life (ensoulment or personhood) does not begin at conception. In summary, the arguments are that if life begins at conception then: 1) human embryos have little value (in the cosmic sense) because it is wasteful of and demeaning to embryonic-persons, 2) the uniqueness of persons (individuals) would be violated and 3) the definition of human life needs alteration or there is the odd result that live embryonic-persons are also dead babies. The conclusion of the paper is that it is unlikely that personhood is endowed instantaneously at conception or at any other time, but rather that one attains personhood in degrees and stages and one looses personhood similarly; it is a matter of evolution and devolution.

Hughes, Charles T. Martin on the Meaninglessness of Religious Language. *Int J Phil Relig*, 34(2), 95-114, O 93.

In this paper I analyze and reject Michael Martin's recent attempt to rehabilitate and defend a verificationist analysis of religious statements as factually meaningless, as presented in his book *Atheism: A Philosophical Justification*. (Philadelphia: Temple University Press, 1990), Chapter 2. I argue, first, that there remain strong reasons to reject the newly fortified weak verificationist principle which Martin develops and defends against Richard Swinburne's critique of verificationism. Second, I show that, even if we grant Martin his version of the weak verificationist principle, theological statements can still pass its test for factual meaningfulness.

Hughes, Christopher. Miracles, Laws of Nature and Causation—I. *Aris Soc*, Supp(66), 179-205, 1992.

Hughes, Judith. The Philosopher's Child. *Thinking*, 10(1), 38-45, 1992.

Hughes, Liam. Some Limits to Freedom. *Phil Invest*, 15(4), 329-345, O 92.

I state what I take to be the core problem of freedom, namely, to describe the kind of freedom we must have, to be able to make sense of our judgments of responsibility. I identify two pillars of freedom: the ability to envisage possibilities, à la Sartre, and the ability to do what one wants. Together they suffice for responsibility, and are compatible with determinism. Our attributions of responsibility, however, go beyond ontological or factual considerations and raise ethical questions.

Hughes, Martin. Locke, Taxation and Reform: A Reply to Wood. *Hist Polit Thought*, 13(4), 691-702, Wint 92.

In reply to Ellen Wood, I argue that Locke was not committed to the ancestral constitution but to reason, justice and equality: within the limits of an age where it had not occurred to anyone that now — taxpayers should be enfranchised.

Hughes, Paul. Bad Samaritans, Morality, and the Law. *Int J Applied Phil*, 7(2), 9-13, Wint 92.

Bad samaritans are people who fail to help strangers in need when such assistance may be easily rendered at no significant cost to themselves. Because liberal moral and legal theory regards bad samaritans as failing to discharge an *imperfect* duty to render aid, it views the criminalization of such omissions as inappropriate. I argue that the liberal view tells an incomplete story about bad samaritan immorality, that bad samaritans are morally unvirtuous, and that there is no reason in principle why this type of moral judgment cannot provide a rationale for criminalizing bad samaritan failures to aid those in peril.

Hughes, R I G (ed). *A Philosophical Companion to First-Order Logic*. Indianapolis, Hackett, 1993.

Hughes, R I G. Tolstoy, Stanislavski, and the Art of Acting. *J Aes Art Crit*, 51(1), 39-48, Wint 93.

Hughes, William H. *Critical Thinking: An Introduction to the Basic Skills*. Peterborough, Broadview Pr, 1992.

This is a textbook, written for a one semester university course. It adopts the criterial approach to critical thinking, and treats fallacies as violations of the three standard criteria. It begins with discussions of meaning and language, and then sets out the general skills for assessing arguments. It also covers the distinguishing features and weaknesses of inductive and deductive arguments, as well as moral reasoning. It concludes with discussions of strategies for arguing back, irrational techniques of persuasion, and assessing argumentative essays. Each chapter includes one or more self-tests, as well as numerous questions designed for class discussion.

Hugly, Philip G and Sayward, Charles. Classical Logic and Truth-Value Gaps. *Phil Papers*, 21(2), 141-150, Ag 92.

Standard approaches to truth-value gaps involve, in one way or another, deviations from central features of classical logic. Against these standard approaches an account of the logic of languages with truth-value gaps is proposed which leaves the fundamental features of classical logic intact.

Hugly, Philip G and Sayward, Charles. Two Concepts of Truth. *Phil Stud*, 70(1), 35-58, Ap 93.

The redundancy theory of truth concerns the connective 'it is true that'. It is extended by A N Prior to cover a wide variety of further uses of 'true'. It is argued that Prior was right about the scope and limits of the redundancy theory and that the line he drew between those uses of 'true' which are and are not redundant serves to distinguish two important and mutually irreducible types of truth.

Huhn, Thomas. The Postmodern Return, With a Vengeance, of Subjectivity in Postmodernism/ Jameson/ Critique, Kellner, Douglas (ed). Washington, Maisonneuve Pr, 1989.

Hulin, Michel and Parkes, Graham R (trans). Nietzsche and the Suffering of the Indian Ascetic in Nietzsche and Asian Thought, Parkes, Graham R (ed). Chicago, Univ of Chicago Pr, 1991.

Hull, David L. An Evolutionary Account of Science: A Response to Rosenberg's Critical Notice. *Biol Phil*, 7(2), 229-236, Ap 92.

In his critical notice, Rosenberg (1991) raises three objections to my evolutionary account of science: whether it is more than a weak metaphor, the compatibility of my past objections to reduction and my current advocacy of viewing selection in terms of replication and interaction, and finally, the feasibility of identifying appropriate replicators and interactors in biological evolution, let alone conceptual evolution. I discuss each of these objections in turn.

Hull, Richard T. The Allied Health Care Professions: New Fields for Philosophical Explorations. *J Value Inq*, 26(4), 473-482, O 92.

The aim of this essay is to introduce the Allied Health Professions as individually and collectively constituting a rich field of issues for philosophers and other humanists interested in the applied focusing of their fields of inquiry to the medical and health sciences and professions. I do not presume familiarity with Allied Health, and I discuss these professions and their origins before identifying some of the issues I find of greatest interest in them.

Hull, Richard T. Why Be Moral? A Reply to Donahue and Tierno. *J Value Inq*, 27(1), 109-110, Ja 93.

I describe an amoralist who uses moral language for effect, but without endorsing any moral claims, and argue that, *contra* Donahue and Tierno, such an Amoralist is not inconsistent.

Hull, Robert. Epistemology and the Autodevaluation of Morality: Towards an Atheoretical Nietzsche. *SW Phil Rev*, 8(1), 119-125, Ja 92.

Humber, James M (ed) and Almeder, Robert F (ed). *Biomedical Ethics Reviews 1992*. Clifton, Humana Pr, 1993.

Biomedical Ethics Reviews: 1992 is the tenth volume in a series of texts designed to review and update the literature on issues of central importance in bioethics today. Two topics are discussed in this volume: 1) Bioethics and the Military, and; 2) Compulsory Birth Control. Three articles deal with issues relevant to #1 (e.g., Should Soldiers Who Test Positive for HIV be Mustered Out of the Service?), while five articles discuss various issues relevant to #2 (e.g., Is It Permissible to Require Use of Birth Control as a Condition of Probation or Parole?)

Humberstone, I L. Zero-Place Operations and Functional Completeness, and the Definition of New Connectives. *Hist Phil Log*, 14(1), 39-66, 1993.

If the definability, by composition, of all truth-functions on the basis of some set of truth-functions is what is required for that set to be functionally complete, then several sets (e.g., that comprising negation and conjunction) for which functional completeness is claimed in the literature in fact do not merit the description. The trouble arises over the unobtainability of zero-place truth-functions on the basis of such sets. For the claims to be correct, we must understand functional completeness in a more generous way: in terms of what we call liberalized polynomial definability. This concept is closely related to a liberalized version of equational definability employed by Tarski to characterize definitionally equivalent theories in equational logic.

Humbert, David. The Return of Adam: Freud's Myth of the Fall. *Relig Stud*, 29(3), 287-296, S 93.

This paper argues that Freud reformulates the theological myth of the fall in the guise of psychoanalytic theory. By examining the tactics of therapy, the theories of the instincts and of the genesis of religion, the paper shows that Freudian theory rests on a suspicion of nature which it shares with modern technological science. Far from having value-free foundations, psychoanalysis implies a covert moral condemnation of nature which is a secularized version of the doctrine of original sin. The view of human nature articulated in Freudian theory is a modern repetition, a "return", of the myth of Adam.

Humble, P N. Chess as an Art Form. *Brit J Aes*, 33(1), 59-66, Ja 93.

Hume, David and Bell, Martin (ed). *Dialogues Concerning Natural Religion—David Hume*. New York, Penguin USA, 1990.

Hummel, Gert. "New Creation"—the Christian Symbol of Universalism and Our Steps Towards Its Realization. *Dialec Hum*, 17(3), 9-21, 1990.

Universalism is a way of thinking which tries to understand reality-in-totality. The concept of a reality-in-totality is related to a sense-reality or to that "which ultimately concerns us" (P Tillich). The Jewish-Christian symbol of reality-in-totality is the "New Creation," an expected ultimate sense-reality. The relationship between "New Creation" and the finite world-to-be-found is to be determined as a growing process. Theologically, this demands that we think God and the world together. The world is God's body. Thus, in Christian-theological thinking, the problem of universalism is an ethical challenge.

Humphrey, John A. Some Objections to Putnam's "Consistency Objection". *J Phil Res*, 18, 127-141, 1993.

This paper is a critical analysis of Putnam's "consistency objection," an objection made against a particular reading of Wittgenstein's philosophy of mathematics ("up-to-us-ism"). I show that Putnam's objection presupposes a rather unlikely version of Wittgenstein's "up-to-us-ism" and is unable to undermine a more likely anti-Platonist version. I also show that a companion argument, (the "something more" argument) is unable to overturn this more sophisticated anti-Platonist version of Wittgenstein's up-to-us-ism. Along the way I try to clarify Wittgenstein's anti-Platonist account of mathematics, so that others do not repeat Putnam's mistake.

Humphreys, Glyn W (ed) and Davies, Martin (ed). *Consciousness: Psychological and Philosophical Essays*. Cambridge, Blackwell, 1993.

Hundersmarck, Lawrence. More Final Still: Natural Law and Final Teleology. *Vera Lex*, 11(2), 12-13, 1991.

This paper affirms that natural law theory is best grounded in a teleological rather than a mechanical world-view. Although persons seek to be adjusted to the secular order of finite goods, a close analysis of desire indicates that persons seek the absolute good of total human completion. It is this desire that underlies much discourse in the field of Natural Law.

Hung, Tscha. Ayer and the Vienna Circle in The Philosophy of A J Ayer, Hahn, Lewis Edwin (ed). Peru, Open Court, 1992.

Hunt, David P. Omniprescient Agency. *Relig Stud*, 28(3), 351-369, S 92.

Insofar as the alleged incompatibility of divine foreknowledge with divine agency is made to rest on the principle that foreknowledge precludes deliberation, it is vulnerable to the possibility of non-deliberative agency. Recently, however, Tomis Kapitan has endeavored to strengthen the case against divine agency by grounding it in the principle that foreknowledge precludes *intentionality*. His argument has three premises: (i) that agency presupposes intention-acquisition; (ii) that intention-acquisition presupposes openness; and (iii) that openness presupposes ignorance. I maintain to the contrary that the argument suffers from two fatal flaws: premise (i) is false, and there is no univocal sense of 'openness' under which premises (ii) and (iii) are both true.

Hunt, G M K. Is Philosophy a 'Theory of Everything'?. *Philosophy*, 33(Supp), 219-232, 1992.

Hunt, G M K. Is Philosophy a 'Theory of Everything'? in The Impulse to Philosophise, Griffiths, A Phillips (ed). New York, Cambridge Univ Pr, 1992.

The paper investigates whether there could be a "Theory of Everything" and whether such a theory would, or should, be a philosophical theory: and answers both questions in the negative. It does so by examining the regress of explanation involved in a theory of everything looking in particular at the use of epistemological principles to terminate the regress. It examines one candidate — the Church Turing Thesis — and concludes that it is a physical hypothesis, and probably false.

Hunt, Geoffrey. Is There a Conflict Between Environmental Protection and the Development ... in International Justice and the Third World, Attfield, Robin (ed). New York, Routledge, 1992.

Hunt, Ian. *Analytical and Dialectical Marxism*. Brookfield, Avebury, 1993.

This book uses the methods and analytical rigour of 'analytical Marxism' to provide a new dialectical interpretation of Marx's social theory. A chapter on historical materialism uses a model of dialectic to give an interpretation of the key concepts of the theory, thereby showing how philosophical puzzles as to its meaning and consistency can be resolved. Similar puzzles about Marx's theories of capitalism and revolution are also solved. The book stresses the need to understand Marx's social theory properly before assessing it against the facts.

Hunt, Lester. Comments on Robert Welshon's "Nietzsche's Peculiar Virtues and the Health of the Soul". *Int Stud Phil*, 24(2), 91-93, 1992.

Hunt, Ralph and Hartz, Glenn A. Self-Identity and Free Will are Beyond our Control. *Personalist Forum*, 8/1(Supp), 197-204, Spr 92.

Evidence from psychology helps show that personal identity and free will are typically handed to us ready-made by the brain. Kinesthesia as well as normal memory *presuppose* a built-in sense of where and who we are. We relate this to Kant's notion that it is an "a priori" matter that we "find ourselves" in a region of space and see our "representations" as states of persisting "I." Finally, free will is addressed: the "inner voice" that seems to be initiating free acts is itself the result of brain activity beyond our control. So the biggest obstacle to genuine free will may be, not the laws of nature or subconscious Freudian forces, but the fact that not one of our thoughts originates with the inner voice.

Hunt, Thomas C and Honer, Stanley M and Okholm, Dennis L. *Invitation to Philosophy: Issues and Options (Sixth Edition)*. Belmont, Wadsworth, 1992.

Hunter, G Frederick (& other trans) and Horkheimer, Max. *Between Philosophy and Social Science: Selected Early Writings*. Cambridge, MIT Pr, 1993.

Hunter, Geoffrey. The Meaning of 'If' in Conditional Propositions. *Phil Quart*, 43(172), 279-297, Jl 93.

Hunter, Graeme. Can You Read? Philosophical Reflections on Labour, Leisure and Literacy. *Eidos*, 10(1), 47-61, J-Jl 91.

I argue that learning to read presupposes learning to discriminate, i.e., to tell the good from the bad, the high from the low, the excellent from the mediocre. I claim that the growth in illiteracy in the West is inversely proportional to the decline in that discriminatory skill.

Hunter, J F M. Knowing What One Was Intending to Say in Wittgenstein's Intentions, Canfield, John V (ed). Hamden, Garland, 1993.

The paper takes up some exegetical and some philosophical problems that arise primarily in *Philosophical Investigations* pp 633-637. Wittgenstein's first point is that normally there is no moment at which we do not know, hence none at which we have still to find out, and no technique for finding out. When we are unselfconsciously engaged in conversation, we will be making comparisons, drawing inferences, reporting things we have noticed, and so on. We may be distracted momentarily by a noise from the kitchen or a pain in the elbow, but that need not always throw us into confusion, and we may normally continue as before, guided by our sense of what makes a useful or an amusing contribution to the discussion at hand. We will not be working out what we would have said, but just returning to where we were, and continuing from there.

Hunter, J F M. On Whether History has a Meaning in Objectivity, Method and Point of View, Van Der Dussen, W J (ed). Leiden, Brill, 1991.

Hunter, J F M. Wittgenstein on Believing in 'Philosophical Investigations' Part II in Wittgenstein's Philosophical Investigations, Arrington, Robert T (ed). New York, Routledge, 1991.

There are probably more perplexities per page in this chapter of Part II of this *Investigations* than in anything of comparable length that Wittgenstein wrote. The paper is an attempt to make clear sense of the detail of this chapter, and one of the main themes is the view that we do not use the word 'believe' to record the occurrences of any phenomenon.

Hurka, Thomas M. Perfectionism and Equality in On the Track of Reason, Beehler, Rodger G (ed). Boulder, Westview Pr, 1992.

Some classical versions of perfectionism (Plato, Aristotle, Nietzsche) are extremely autiegalitarian, whereas others (Marx, T H Green) favour roughly equal distributions of resources and opportunities. The paper explains how differences in the formulation of perfectionism lead to this divergence about distribution, and argues that, in each case, the more plausible formulation is the one with roughly egalitarian implications.

Hurley, Ann. *Ut Pictura Poesis*: Vermeer's Challenge to Some Renaissance Literary Assumptions. *J Aes Art Crit*, 47(4), 349-357, Fall 89.

Hurley, Paul E. The Hidden Consequentialist Assumption. *Analysis*, 52(4), 241-248, O 92.

Hurley, S L. Intelligibility, Imperialism, and Conceptual Scheme. *Midwest Stud Phil*, 17, 89-108, 1992.

Hurley, S L. *Natural Reasons: Personality and Polity*. New York, Oxford Univ Pr, 1992.

Natural Reasons revives a classical idea about rationality in a modern framework, by developing analogies between the structure of personality and the structure of

society in the context of contemporary work in philosophy of mind, ethics, decision theory, and social choice theory. In light of the philosophies of Wittgenstein and Davidson, it is argued that the value-ladenness of preference dissolves certain standard ways of conceiving issues about objectivity and rationality. Various interpersonal conceptions of rationality are projected onto the intrapersonal case and evaluated, and vice versa. The implications for theories of distributive justice and of democracy are considered.

Hurley, Susan. Commentator on 'Non-Relative Virtues' in The Quality of Life, Nussbaum, Martha C (ed). New York, Oxford Univ Pr, 1993.

Hurnik, J F. Ethics and Animal Agriculture. *J Agr Environ Ethics*, 6/1(Supp), 21-35, 1993.

In the past, value judgments regarding animal agriculture, its techniques and goals, focused predominantly on production efficiency. At the present time, the concept of maximized production is gradually losing ground to a more broader concept of optimal production. Decreasing consumer trust in some animal products, the impact of modern agriculture on the environment, increasing disparities in food production around the globe, loss of family farms, declining self-respect of farmers due to increasing dependence on subsidies, and the decreasing social reputation of farmers due to economic pressures to intensify even at the cost of animal quality of life, should be incorporated in any ethically relevant assessment of modern animal production systems. In its main section, the paper focuses on the quality of life of animals used for food production. It proposes an instrumental definition of animal well-being and discusses a welfare-relevant distinction between satisfaction of animal needs and satisfaction of animal desires.

Hursthouse, Rosalind. Slote on Self-Sufficiency. *J Soc Phil*, 24(2), 57-67, Fall 93.

Husak, Douglas N. Why Punish the Deserving?. *Nous*, 26(4), 447-464, D 92.

I argue that a comprehensive justification for punishing criminals must address why those persons who deserve to be punished should actually be punished, all things considered. Plausible answers to this question reveal deficiencies in pure retributive theories, which deem consequences to be irrelevant to the justification of the distribution of punishment.

Husak, Douglas N and McLaughlin, Brian P. Time-Frames, Voluntary Acts, and Strict Liability. *Law Phil*, 12(1), 95-120, F 93.

Hussey, Edward. Comment on W J Korab-Karpowicz's "Wisdom of Love". *Dialec Hum*, 17(3), 231-232, 1990.

Hutcheon, Pat Duffy. Dewey's Commitment to Science and Democracy. *Free Inq*, 13(1), 26, 28, Wint 92-93.

Hutcheson, Peter. Omniscience and The Problem of Evil. *Sophia (Australia)*, 31(1-2), 53-58, 1992.

Can the problem of evil be avoided by changing the definition of "God?" I think that the answer is "no," and thus agree with P J McGrath, who argues for that conclusion in a recent exchange with various authors in *Analysis*. But what is surprising is that all of the participants in this exchange overlook the fact that one option open to theists is to conceive of God as having limited knowledge. Hence McGrath has not proven that conclusion. In this article I argue that conceiving of God as less-than-omniscient cannot dissolve the problem of evil, either.

Hutchings, Kimberly. Perpetual War/Perpetual Peace: Kant, Hegel and the End of History. *Bull Hegel Soc Gt Brit*, 23-24, 39-50, 1991.

This paper is in three sections. The first part presents a reading of Kant's philosophy of history and war and its problematic consequences. Part two demonstrates how Hegel transforms speculatively Kant's treatment of history and war in The Philosophy of Right, giving us a more fruitful approach to questions of war and peace. Part three critically examines Hayo Krombach's Hegelian Reflections on the Idea of Nuclear War (London, 1991).

Hutchison, Keith. Copernicus, Apollo, and Herakles in The Uses of Antiquity, Gaukroger, Stephen (ed). Dordrecht, Kluwer, 1991.

This paper analyzes the symbolism of Copernicus' personal seal (a near-naked man playing a lyre), and extends the Apolline interpretation of this seal proposed by Mossakowski in 1973. I argue that the clear evidence in favour of Apollo can be paralleled by somewhat stronger evidence that the figure is Herakles—particularly appropriate as an emblem for Copernicus because of his traditional connections with astronomy and harmony. I suggest further that by the time of the Renaissance, the mythologies of Herakles, Apollo (and several other deities) overlap substantially, so each is very much a duplicate of the other.

Hutchison, Keith. Is Classical Mechanics Really Time-Reversible and Deterministic?. *Brit J Phil Sci*, 44(2), 307-323, Je 93.

This essay scrutinizes the claims that classical mechanics is time-reversible and deterministic, and argues that neither is valid in the extremely general senses in which they are usually presumed. The argument uses counter-examples, commonplace mechanical systems which do not exhibit the characteristics in dispute. Some of these counter- examples are already familiar, though it is widely believed they have been answered. So the essay also examines attempts to avoid my examples, arguing that these depend on an equivocation between two quite different claims, confusing a belief that *nature* has time-reversible components, with the characteristics of a *theory*.

Hutsebaut, Dirk. Why Does God Allow This? An Empirical Approach to the Theodicy Question through the Themes of Suffering and Meaning. *Ultim Real Mean*, 15(4), 286-295, D 92.

Christian Theology has developed different models for the solution of the theodicy problem. We distinguish the apathetic God, the retributive God, the planning and controlling God, the therapeutic God, the symbol of the compassionate god, the symbol of the vicarious servant of God, the symbol of the God with whom a mystical unity is sought. By means of an empirical study, carried out on 274 adults: we observed four different important models (apathy, retribution, plan-pedagogy and compassion). The order of the models in the experience of the subjects is influenced by their personal religious belief and by the subjects' image of God.

Hyde, Michael J and Smith, Craig R. Aristotle and Heidegger on Emotion and Rhetoric in The Critical Turn, Angus, Ian (ed). Carbondale, So Illinois Univ Pr, 1993.

Hyland, Terry. Competence, Knowledge and Education. *J Phil Educ*, 27(1), 57-68, Sum 93.

Since the establishment of the National Council for Vocational Qualifications (NCVQ) in 1986, the influence of the *competence-based* approach, which underpins National Vocational Qualifications (NVQs), has spread beyond its original remit and now extends into schools and higher education. Competence strategies are criticised for their *conceptual* imprecision and their *behaviourist* foundation. More significantly, it is argued that the competence approach displays confusion and incoherence in its interpretation and use of the ideas of *'knowledge'* and *'understanding'*, and so should be challenged and resisted by educators committed to these values.

Hyland, Terry. Moral Vocationalism. *J Moral Educ*, 21(2), 139-150, 1992.

After years of neglect attempts have recently been made to introduce the important ethical aspects of educational development into schools and colleges through programmes which emphasize the values of active citizenship and the importance of 'moral competence' in contemporary society. These programmes are described and labelled as examples of 'moral vocationalism' and criticised on the grounds that they have a weak knowledge base, are founded on behaviourist learning principles and are located within an exclusively instrumentalist framework. Such schemes, consequently, fail to meet the criteria for satisfactory moral education and need to be supplemented by the good practice developed in the 1960s and 1970s by, for example, Kohlberg, the Farmington Trust and the Schools Council.

Hylton, Peter. Hegel and Analytic Philosophy in The Cambridge Companion to Hegel, Beiser, Frederick C (ed). New York, Cambridge Univ Pr, 1993.

Hyman, John. Prediction and Predication. *Ratio*, 6(1), 27-35, Je 93.

Nelson Goodman's solution to the new riddle of induction turns of the degree to which predicates are entrenched in our use of language. This solution requires that judgements about relative entrenchment can be made independently of any canon of perceptible similarity, but this requirement cannot be met. The riddle depends on the claim that since 'green' can be defined in terms of 'grue' and 'bleen', positionally is 'an entirely relative matter'. However, a non-positional definition of 'grue', rather than a positional definition of 'green', is needed to establish that positionality is a relative matter. No such definition is possible.

Hyman, John. The Causal Theory of Perception. *Phil Quart*, 42(168), 277-296, Jl 92.

Hyman, John. Vision, Causation and Occlusion. *Phil Quart*, 43(171), 210-214, Ap 93.

Hyman, Lawrence W. Art's Autonomy *Is* Its Momrality: A Reply to Casey Haskins on Kant. *J Aes Art Crit*, 47(4), 376-377, Fall 89.

Iannone, A Pablo. Social Choice Theory: Formalism Infatuation and Policy Making Realities. *Epistemologia*, 15(2), 263-278, Jl-D 92.

This paper argues for seven theses. First, in applying social theory to policy making, the social decision function must be known at decision making time. Second, in significant policy making situations, this requirement leads to disregarding the social process of critical scrutiny and social interaction that helps work out many policy making data. Third, the social choice theory treats policy making decisions as mere logical consequences of data fixed at decision making time. Fourth, this is hopelessly static. Fifth, primarily for this reason, not just a particular social choice theory, but the field of study itself is useless for sound policy making. Sixth, social choice theory is also useless as a source of heuristic models for policy making. Seventh, satisficing theories are better.

Ibarra, Andoni and Mormann, Thomas. L'explication en tant que généralisation théorique. *Dialectica*, 46(2), 151-168, 1992.

Depuis l'époque du Cercle de Vienne on considère l'explication en tant que tâche centrale de la philosophie analytique. Cependent il n'y a pas unanimité autour de la compréhension du concept d'explication. Dans cet article nous suggérons, tout en suivant Bachelard, de considérer une explication d'un concept en tant que sa généralisation propre dans le cadre d'une théorie explicative. Nous examinons notre approche en envisageant l'explication des concepts logiques ("implication"), mathématiques ("nombre" et "ligne droite") et de la philosophie des sciences ("réduction").

Ibarra, Andoni and Mormann, Thomas. Propiedades modelísticas del concepto de reducción. *Agora (Spain)*, 11(1), 69-95, 1992.

Theorists of incommensurability have demonstrated the inherent difficulties in the diverse concepts of reduction suggested in the standard framework. In spite of this, the philosophers of the structuralist view have given an explication of scientific progress, in which the concept of reduction in its diverse variants—exact, approximative, etc.—plays a fundamental role. The aim of this paper is to offer a view of the structuralist studies on reduction. Adequacy conditions for the relation of reduction characterize it basically as a law preserving relation and as an anomaly explaining relation. It is provable that there does not exist a reduction relation that is law preserving *and* anomaly explaining, i.e., for any theory T there cannot exist a reducing theory T', such that T' has greater explanatory power and implies T. To cope with the apparent incompatibility of this fact we propose to introduce a new degree of liberalism in the logical reconstruction of empirical theories to make possible the implementation of different reduction maps simultaneously.

Ide, H A. Chrysippus's Response to Diodorus's Master Argument. *Hist Phil Log*, 13(2), 133-148, 1992.

Chrysippus claims that some propositions perish, including some true conditionals whose consequent is impossible and antecedent is possible, to which he appeals against Diodorus's Master Argument. On the standard interpretation, perished propositions lack truth values, and these conditionals are true at the same time as their antecedents are possible and consequents impossible. But perished propositions are false, and Chrysipus's conditionals are true when their antecedent and consequent are possible, and false when their antecedent is possible and consequent impossible. The claim of the Master Argument that Chrysippus rejects, then, is stronger than usually supposed.

Idt, Geneviève. Simone de Beauvoir's Adieux: A Funeral Rite and a Literary Challenge in Sartre Alive, Aronson, Ronald (ed). Detroit, Wayne St Univ Pr, 1991.

Ierodiakonou, Katerina. Rediscovering Some Stoic Arguments in Greek Studies in the Philosophy and History of Science, Nicolacopoulos, Pantelis (ed). Dordrecht, Kluwer, 1990.

Ierodiakonou, Katerina. The Stoic Division of Philosophy. *Phronesis*, 38(1), 57-74, 1993.

In introductions to Stoicism, Stoic philosophy customarily is discussed under the headings of "logic", "physics", and "ethics"; the evidence, however, shows that the Stoics' own view on the tripartition was more complex. The paper focusses on a passage in Diogenes Laertius (VII 39-41) and deals with the following four points the passage raises: first, according to most Stoics, it is not philosophy, but philosophical discourse, which is divided into three parts. Second, different Stoics used different terms when referring to the three parts. Third, Stoics were not unanimous as to the order of the three parts. Fourth, different similes were used by the Stoics to describe the interrelation of the three parts. It is only by close analysis of these points that we see in what sense Stoic philosophers divided philosophy, and how they understood the unity of the philosophical disciplines underlying their division.

Ignatieff, Michael. Understanding Fascism? in Isaiah Berlin: A Celebration, Margalit, Edna (ed). Chicago, Univ of Chicago Pr, 1991.

Ignatow, Assen. *Anthropologische Geschichtsphilosophie: Für eine Philosophie der Geschichte in der Zeit der Postmoderne*. Sankt Augustin, Academia, 1993.

Ihara, Craig K. Some Thoughts on Confucianism and Modernization. *J Chin Phil*, 19(2), 183-196, Je 92.

This article argues 1) that the impediments to modernization often attributed to Confucianism would themselves be condemned by Confucius, 2) that Confucius would also be highly critical of modernization as we find it in the West, 3) that modernization may be compatible with Confucian ideals, but that its realization is unlikely unless there is a collective effort to apply Confucianism to practical and moral problems faced in contemporary society.

Ihde, Don. Image Technologies and Traditional Culture. *Inquiry*, 35(3-4), 377-388, S-D 92.

The thesis explored here is that 'image technologies' prominent in today's communications technologies are *acidic* to traditional cultures. I parallel examples from the history of early modern science and its optical instrumentation with the rise of cinema and television and other audio-visual technologies to show a similar history and effect. One dominant contemporary phenomenon which occurs through image technologies is the appearance of *pluriculture*, a unique mediation of the multi-cultural. The challenge of pluriculture *vis-á-vis* the contemporary forms of reaction to the phenomenon is also examined.

Ihde, Don. *Instrumental Realism: The Interface between Philosophy of Science and Philosophy of Technology*. Bloomington, Indiana Univ Pr, 1991.

This study begins with the "Kuhnian Revolution" and in the first section examines parallel framework relative developments in the Continental traditions of philosophy (including Husserl, Merleau-Ponty, Foucault) with respect to science, and then an examination of the role of technology vis-a-vis science (Heidegger) in those same traditions. The second part of the book then turns to recent American philosophers whose interests have focused upon instruments and experimentation as 'science's technologies.' Both Anglo-American philosophers of science (Ackermann, Galison, Hacking) and Euro-American philosophers (Dreyfus, Heelan, Ihde, and Latour) are situated with respect to what is claimed as an emergent consensus regarding 'instrumental realism,' a realism which relates to instrumental use in science.

Ihde, Don. *Philosophy of Technology: An Introduction*. New York, Paragon House, 1993.

Designed as an undergraduate textbook in the philosophy of technology, this book parallels, in narrative form, a brief history of the inter-relationship between philosophy and science and the lack of attention to the history of technology and the inter-relationship between science and technology. It outlines a set of basic problems within philosophy of technology, analyzes the major contributions of contemporary philosophers of technology, and makes projections concerning the future development and needs in the philosophy of technology.

Ihde, Don. Text and the New Hermeneutics in On Paul Ricoeur: Narrative and Interpretation, Wood, David (ed). New York, Routledge, 1991.

This essay examines the recent Euro-American preoccupation with writing and the text. It argues that there is a tendency to replace the role of 'world', previously central to this tradition, with 'texts'. The work of Paul Ricoeur is located within this tendency and his work is seen as a corrective which returns the importance of both reference and temporality to the debates. However, Riceour, too, underplays the role of perception in reading and of cross cultural differences. The essay suggests' several variants of non-European cultural processes in which the role of body and perception is seen to play an important role in counterparts to reading.

Iheoma, Eugene O. Vico, Imagination and Education. *J Phil Educ*, 27(1), 45-55, Sum 93.

This paper explores the contribution of Vico's philosophy of imagination to a practical recognition of the importance of the imagination in the conduct of human affairs in general and in education in particular. Vico's claim that the imagination is an essential component of our human nature together with the claim that all human knowledge ultimately has its origins in the imaginative activities of our forebears (a claim which has received empirical support from recent research on the history of oral cultures) provides us with the necessary philosophical basis for establishing a logical connection between imagination and education. If accepted, such a perspective would, in my view, dispel much of the skepticism that still surrounds the role of the imagination in contemporary education.

Ijsseling, Samuel. Mimesis and Translation in Reading Heidegger: Commemorations, Sallis, John (ed). Bloomington, Indiana Univ Pr, 1992.

Translation is both a hermeneutic and mimetic activity. Heidegger takes up its hermeneutical aspect but neglects the mimetic. This reflects a wider reservation in

Heidegger with regard to *mimesis* and its role in the rhetorical tradition, his consideration of *mismesis* being largely confined to the Plato's views on it. Despite this a fundamental *mimetology*, one betraying Platonic traits, seems to be at work in Heidegger. The text concludes by suggesting that a wider consideration of the notion of *mimesis* in Greek thought would shed a different light on the problem of translation on Heidegger's understanding of it.

IJsseling, Samuel. Heidegger and Politics in Ethics and Danger, Dallery, Arleen B (ed). Albany, SUNY Pr, 1992.

Illanes, José Luis. La historia entre el nihilismo y la afirmación del sentido. *Anu Filosof*, 26(1), 95-111, 1993.

The problem of the meaning of history has solicited a lot of different solutions. This article reviews the standard interpretations of the course of the history, emphasizing three approaches to its understanding: the Greek, the Christian and the Modern.

Imbach, Ruedi. Notabilia I: Hinweise auf wichtige Neuerscheinungen aus dem Bereich der mittelalterlichen Philosophie. *Frei Z Phil Theol*, 39(1-2), 180-194, 1992.

The "Notabilia" gives a survey and evaluation of the most important new publishings (1989-1991) in the field of middle-age philosophy.

Imbach, Ruedi. Notabilia II: Hinweise auf wichtige Neuerscheinungen aus dem Bereich der mittelalterlichen Philosophie. *Frei Z Phil Theol*, 40(1-2), 181-216, 1993.

The "Notabilia" give a survey and evaluation of the most important new publishings (1990-1992) in the field of middle age philosophy.

Imlay, Robert A. Berkeley and Scepticism: A Fatal Dalliance. *Hume Stud*, 18(2), 501-510, N 92.

Berkeley in his desire to discredit representational realism and to replace it with a form of the logical phenomenalism employs a sceptical argument, namely one that assimilates all sensible properties to subjective experiences like those of heat and cold. The problem is that by employing such an argument Berkeley commits himself to the scepticism he so despises. He should, then, avoid such an argument but systematic considerations make this impossible for him to do so consistently.

Immerwahr, John. Hume on Tranquilizing the Passions. *Hume Stud*, 18(2), 293-314, N 92.

Hume's preference for calm over the violent passions is a unifying theme that runs through a great deal of his writing, especially his Essays, Moral, Political, and Literary. In personal life, religion and politics, calm passions are the key to moderation and stability. Hume believes that the passions can be softened by playing opposites against one another, and this principle of opposition is a literary strategy in many of his works. Hume's writings, especially his popular works, are intended to produce calm passions in the readers.

Immerwahr, John. Race and the Modern Philosophy Course. *Teach Phil*, 16(1), 21-34, Mr 93.

This article gives several suggestions for philosophy teachers who want to make a course in early modern philosophy more sensitive to issues of race. The article explores some of the connections between empiricism, liberalism, racism and slavery as these ideas played out in philosophers such as Locke, Hume and Descartes.

In-Sing Leung, Thomas. Communication and Hermeneutics: A Confucian Postmodern Point of View. *J Chin Phil*, 19(4), 407-422, D 92.

The post-modern represents a cultural break from the modern. The culture of postmodernity is conditional by information. Meanwhile, postmodernism provides an immanent critique of enlightenment. The focal point of philosophy then is how to communicate and to understand. The confucian concepts of *Jen* (real humanity), *Tao* (the way), *Huseh* (learning, *chih* (understand), *hsing* (actions) are ground for communication and understanding. *Jen* as real humanity provides a process ontology which makes an open hermeneutical process possible. Through reflection and critique on pre-understanding and prejudice, a condition for communication and understanding is provided. In this sense, Confucianism is relevant to the postmodern problems.

Inagaki, H. A Philosophical Analysis of Traditional Japanese Culture. *Phil Reform*, 57(1), 39-56, Ja 92.

Inbody, Tyron. Meland's Post-Liberal Empirical Method in Theology in God, Values, and Empiricism, Peden, Creighton (ed). Macon, Mercer Univ Pr, 1989.

Incandela, Joseph M. Duns Scotus and the Experience of Freedom. *Thomist*, 56(2), 229-256, Ap 92.

Incardona, Nunzio. Antilogia. *G Metaf*, 14(3), 361-372, S-D 92.

Incardona, Nunzio. Soggettualità del fondamento. *G Metaf*, 14(1), 5-10, Ja-Ap 92.

Inciarte, Fernando. La identidad del sujeto individual según Aristóteles. *Anu Filosof*, 26(2), 289-302, 1993.

The paper focuses on the contrast between the ontologies of the subject, such as the Aristotelian one, with the ontologies of the process, such as that of Quine. It attempts to justify the Aristotelian approach paying special attention to Quine's criticism.

Indurkhya, Bipin. *Metaphor and Cognition*. Dordrecht, Kluwer, 1992.

Ineichen, Robert. Zur Mathematik in den Werken von Albertus Magnus: Versuch einer Zussammenfassung. *Frei Z Phil Theol*, 40(1-2), 55-87, 1993.

Im Jahre 1958 ist die Darstellung von B Heyer, "Die mathematischen Schriften des Albertus Magnus", publiziert worden. Im Anschluss daran sind in den letzten Jahrzehnten eine Reihe von Arbeiten erschienen, die sich entweder allgemein mit der Mathematick in den Werken von Albertus Magnus befassen oder dann mit dem sogenannten "Albertus-Kommentar", einem Kommentar zu den ersten vier Büchern von Euklids "Elementen", der mit grösster Wahrscheinlichkeit Albertus Magnus zugeschrieben werden kann. — Der Autor versucht sine Zusammenfassung der Resultate dieser Arbeiten zu geben, die vor allem auch jenen Lesern zugänglich ist, die mit der Mathematik und ihrer Geschichte nicht speziell vertraut sind.

Ingham, Mary Elizabeth. Scotus and the Moral Order. *Amer Cath Phil Quart*, 67(1), 127-150, Wint 93.

Inglis, Fred. Socialism and the Good Life in Socialism and Morality, McLellan, David (ed). New York, St Martin's Pr, 1990.

Ingram, A. Self-Ownership and Worldly Resources. *Int J Moral Soc Stud*, 8(1), 3-20, Spr 93.

Rights theorists often express the principle of individual liberty as a thesis of self-ownership. The idea is that the various liberties and powers associated with private property comprise the rightful control that each person has over her body and personal powers. But self-ownership without access to worldly resources is empty. In this article I examine three leading attempts to combine the principle of self-ownership with access to worldly resources. I argue that the first depends on unshared theological assumptions, the second is not cogent, and the third does not inevitably meet the legitimate claims of the needy. I conclude that the problem is insoluble as long as we continue to think of rights as flowing from a master right of self-ownership.

Ingram, David. The Limits and Possibilities of Communicative Ethics for Democratic Theory. *Polit Theory*, 21(2), 294-321, My 93.

Democracy seldom, if ever, generates rational outcomes or uniquely consistent, maximal rank orderings of preferences of the sort required by a Rousseauist theory of legitimation. The sources of legitimation must reside in just procedure rather than consensus. Habermas's discourse ethics suggests limits and possibilities for such a view. It may mitigate paradoxes of social choice. However, it also seems inadequate to account for strategic political behavior and compromise. Yet there are other vantage points from which the theory can be assessed. It provides a non-metaphysical foundation for rights which does justice to their conventional and historical character. Supplemented with developmental studies and ancilliary argumentation, it supports the expansion of democracy to the workplace.

Ingram, David. The Postmodern Kantianism of Arendt and Lyotard in Judging Lyotard, Benjamin, Andrew (ed). New York, Routledge, 1992.

Innerarity, Daniel. Convivir con la inidentidad. *Anu Filosof*, 26(2), 361-374, 1993.

Modernity has made identity impossible because of its exigency of a perfection that is not compatible with human finitude. This is the reason why since Romanticism it has been generalized the attempt of establishing scopes in which man is freed from this duty. There arises also many phenomena that can be understood as aesthetic instances that defend the individual particularity and promote the cultural variety.

Innerarity, Daniel. Hegels Idee von Europa. *Z Phil Forsch*, 46(3), 381-394, Jl-S 92.

Innerarity, Daniel. La filosofía como tragedia: Nietzsche. *Anu Filosof*, 25(3), 531-541, 1992.

Nietzsche understood philosophy as an activity which arises from a profound passion for truth. This article examines such pathos and tries to show its inconsistencies thus terminating in a philosophy of appearances.

Innis, Robert E. Tacit Knowing, Gestalt Theory, and the Model of Perceptual Consciousness. *Dan Yrbk Phil*, 27, 23-43, 1992.

By studying how Michael Polanyi's epistemological project went beyond the confines of Gestalt theory as such I expose the essential contours of his epistemological model, its fundamental novelty, and selected points of intersection with parallel projects and present problems. To this end the structural analogy between knowledge and skills, the relations between perception and the logic of discovery, the nature of higher forms of tacit integrations that operate in the articulate domain, and the rejection of isomorphism between the physical and the psychic are discussed. Polanyi's cognitional theory is an invitation to cognitional self-appropriation and self-engagement.

Innis, William. Plato's Escape from Mechanism. *Lyceum*, 3(2), 55-62, Fall 91.

Inoué, Takao. On Compatibility of Theories and Equivalent Translations. *Bull Sec Log*, 21(3), 112-119, O 92.

Iranzo Garcia, V. Naturalismo y argumentos "a priori" en la epistemología de W V Quine. *Pensamiento*, 189(48), 33-47, Ja-Mr 92.

La consecuencia principal del giro naturalista en epistemología, tal como Quine lo entiende, es el rechazo de una *filosofía primera*, o lo que es lo mismo, la negativa a acotar un ámbito cognoscitivo separado de la ciencia. Esta tesis rompe con la concepción kantiana de la teoría del conocimiento (la epistemología como fundamentación apriorística de nuestro discurso sobre el mundo) que, con algunos retoques, ha sobrevivido en la filosofía analítica. En este artículo pretendo averiguar si el desarrollo de la epistemología naturalizada implica la existencia de un ámbito de reflexión a priori, esto es, autónomo respecto a las investigaciones empíricas. Creo que puede defenderse un doble nivel argumentativo en la posición guineana sin que ello le comprometa con un discurso legitimador cualitativamente distinto de la ciencia.

Irigaray, Luce and Collie, Joanne (trans) and Still, Judith (trans). *Elemental Passions—Luce Irigaray*. New York, Routledge, 1992.

Elemental Passions explores the man/woman relationship in a series of meditations on the senses and the elements. Its form resembles a series of love letters in which, however, the identity — and even the reality — of the addressee is deliberately obscured. French philosopher Luce Irigaray's investigations into the nature of gender, language and identity take place in several modes: the analytic, the essayistic and the lyrical poetic.

Irigaray, Luce and Gill, Gillian C (trans). *Marine Lover of Friedrich Nietzsche—Luce Irigaray*. New York, Columbia Univ Pr, 1991.

Irigaray, Luce and Gill, Gillian C (trans). *Speculum of the Other Woman—Luce Irigaray*. Ithaca, Cornell Univ Pr, 1985.

Irigaray, Luce and Martin, Alison (trans). *Je, Tu, Nous: Toward a Culture of Difference*. New York, Routledge, 1993.

Irvine, Andrew D. Thought Experiments in Scientific Reasoning in Thought Experiments in Science and Philosophy, Horowitz, Tamara (ed). Lanham, Rowman & Littlefield, 1991.

This paper describes thought experiments in science as specific types of arguments whose role in science has always been central but whose sophistication has increased only with the sophistication of science itself. Thought experiments in science and mathematics from antiquity to the 20th century are discussed, including Galileo's famous thought experiment concerning falling objects and the 18th century thought experiment which gave rise to the now famous Olber's paradox.

Irvine, William B. Teaching Without Books. *Teach Phil*, 16(1), 35-46, Mr 93.

I describe my experiment in teaching introductory philosophy courses without using books or, for that matter, without any assigned readings. I also offer advice for those wishing to participate in the experiment. In the course of my paper, I not only defend the "bookless" approach to teaching philosophy, but criticize the more traditional notion that introductory philosophy is best taught by having students read the works of the great philosophers.

Irving, Dianne N and Shamoo, Adil E. The PSDA and the Depressed Elderly: "Intermittent Competency" Revisited. *J Clin Ethics*, 4(1), 74-79, Spr 93.

Irwin, T H. Eminent Victorians and Greek Ethics in Essays on Henry Sidgwick, Schultz, Bart (ed). New York, Cambridge Univ Pr, 1992.

Irwin, T H. Plato: The Intellectual Background in The Cambridge Companion to Plato, Kraut, Richard H (ed). New York, Cambridge Univ Pr, 1992.

Irwin, T H. Who Discovered The Will? in Philosophical Perspectives, 6: Ethics, 1992, Tomberlin, James E (ed). Atascadero, Ridgeview, 1992.

Irzik, Gürol. Cartwright, Capacities, and Probabilities. *Proc Phil Sci Ass*, 1, 239-250, 1992.

I argue that Nancy Cartwright's largely methodological arguments for capacities and against Hume's regularity account of causation are only partially successful. They are especially problematic in establishing the primacy of singular causation and the reality of mixed-dual capacities. Therefore, her arguments need to be supported by ontological ones, and I propose the propensity interpretation of causal probabilities as a neutral way of doing this.

Isaac, Jeffrey C. Situating Hannah Arendt on Action and Politics. *Polit Theory*, 21(3), 534-540, Ag 93.

Ishiguro, Hidé. Inscrutability of Reference, Monism, and Individuals in Psychoanalysis, Mind and Art, Hopkins, Jim (ed). Cambridge, Blackwell, 1992.

Isles, David. What Evidence is There that 2^65536 is a Natural Number?. *Notre Dame J Form Log*, 33(4), 465-480, Fall 92.

The closure of the natural numbers under exponentiation a^b is a fact which is central to results in metamathematics. The argument which purports to establish this closure involves a simple mathematical induction. An analysis of this proof shows that it may involve a new and subtle form of circularity.

Ivaldo, Marco. Lignes de développement de la pensée transcendentale: La recherche historique et systématique de Reinhard Lauth. *Arch Phil*, 55(2), 177-197, Ap-Je 92.

Reinhard Lauth by the new edition of Fichte has also given excellent studies of transcendental philosophy from Descartes to Kant, Reinhold and Fichte to Karl Marx. Even Dostoïevski is taken in account.

Ivanhoe, Philip. Character Consequentialism and Early Confucianism. *J Relig Ethics*, 19(1), 55-70, Spr 91.

Early Confucian ethics can best be understood as character consequentialism, an ethical theory concerned with the effects actions have upon the cultivation of virtues and which concentrates on certain psychological goods, particularly certain kinship relationships which it regards not only as intrinsically but also instrumentally valuable, as the source of more general social virtues. According to character consequentialism, the way to maximize the good is to maximize the number of virtuous individuals in society, but because human virtues cannot be cultivated by pursuing their good consequences directly, they must be sought as expressions of a life ideal. This ideal entails developing one's nature to fulfill Heaven's design.

Iwakuma Y. Twelfth-Century Nominales: The Posthumous School of Peter Abelard. *Vivarium*, 30(1), 97-109, My 92.

Iwand, Hans Joachim. Credere e sapere. *Teoria*, 12(1), 153-163, 1992.

Izquierdo Labeaga, José Antonio. El hombre entre dos hermenéuticas. *Gregorianum*, 73(3), 523-539, 1992.

After the change of course brought on by positivism, explicit in A Comte's "law of the three states", philosophical anthropology loses its background of the First Causes in the hands of the sciences. Well before Comte, Thomas Aquinas had discovered a "law of the three states". His hermeneutics, however, elaborated from a standpoint more universal and open, are quite different from Comte's. Science is here seen as the fruitful substatum of a superior type of knowledge, which flourishes in metaphysics and theology. They are complementary types of knowledge, not mutually exclusive. (edited)

Jabs, Arthur. An Interpretation of the Formalism of Quantum Mechanics in Terms of Epistemological Realism. *Brit J Phil Sci*, 43(3), 405-421, S 92.

We present an alternative to the Copenhagen interpretation of the formalism of nonrelativistic quantum mechanics. The basic difference is that the new interpretation is formulated in the language of epistemological realism. It involves a change in some basic physical concepts. Elementary particles are considered as extended objects and nonlocal effects are included. The role of the new concepts in the problems of measurement and of the Einstein-Podolsky-Rosen correlations is described. Experiments to distinguish the proposed interpretation from the Copenhagen one are pointed out.

Jackendoff, Ray. Languages of the Mind: Essays on Mental Representation. Cambridge, MIT Pr, 1992.

This is a collection of essays, some new, some previously published, summarizing and extending Jackendoff's theories on the nature of mental representation. The first two chapters summarize the notion of levels of representation and show how conceptual structure can be approached along lines familiar from syntax and phonology. Subsequent chapters develop issues in word meaning (and their pertinence to the Piaget Chomsky debate) and the relation of conceptual structure to the understanding of physical space. Further chapters apply the theory to social

and cultural cognition, psychodynamic phenomena, and the relation of musical parsing to musical affect. The final chapter argues that the philosophical insistence on the intentionality of mental states should abandoned.

Jackson, Frank. *Natural Reasons: Personality and Polity*: Review. *Austl J Phil*, 70(4), 475-488, D 92.

This rich, long and complex book discusses and interconnects issues in ethics, decision theory, philosophy of mind, philosophy of law, and political theory. I am going to concentrate on the substantial and interesting things Susan Hurley has to say in ethics. After describing her position and making some passing comments, I will argue that there is a problem with her treatment of ethical scepticism. I will conclude by taking the liberty of suggesting what in my view she should, and consistently with her overall position, could have said about scepticism.

Jackson, Frank. Block's Challenge in Ontology, Causality and Mind: Essays in Honour of D M Armstrong, Bacon, John (ed). New York, Cambridge Univ Pr, 1993.

This paper is concerned with what kind of supervenience of intelligence on behavior in circumstances survives the challenge of Ned Block's look up tree case.

Jackson, Frank and Pettit, Philip. In Defense of Explanatory Ecumenism. *Econ Phil*, 8(1), 1-21, Ap 92.

Social and other explananda are capable of being explained with greater or lesser attention to the detail of the producing mechanism and a common assumption is that the more fine-grained an explanation, the better. We reject this fine-grain preference and the explanatory individualism which it would support. We argue that explanations of different levels of grain may be interesting in different ways, so that individual-level explanations in social theory, for example, may serve to complement rather than replace structural accounts. This view can be described as a sort of explanatory ecumenism or pluralism.

Jackson, Frank and Pettit, Philip. Some Content is Narrow in Mental Causation, Heil, John (ed). New York, Clarendon/Oxford Pr, 1993.

Is water solubility narrow or broad? In one sense it is broad. What makes a substance water soluble is the way it does or would interact with its environment, not the way it is in itself. In another sense it is narrow. Any two internally identical substances in this world must agree in whether or not they are water soluble. Water solubility passes one version of the Doppelgänger test. We argue that in the second sense of 'narrow' some, but not all, content is narrow.

Jackson, Kevin T. Global Distributive Justice and the Corporate Duty to Aid. *J Bus Ethics*, 12(7), 547-552, Jl 93.

This article challenges an argument from Tom Donaldson's recent book *The Ethics of International Business* with a claim that distributive justice, deemed in many circles to impose a duty of mutual aid on individuals and nations, establishes a basis for holding multinational corporations to such a duty as well. The root idea I advocate is that Rawls' theory of justice can be deployed—beyond its original intent yet in line with its spirit—to underwrite a *prima facie* obligation of international business to render aid to ameliorate suffering on behalf of the inhabitants of developing countries in which they operate.

Jackson, Kevin T. Global Rights and Regional Jurisprudence. *Law Phil*, 12(2), 157-192, My 93.

This article asks whether a "law-as-integrity" approach to human rights adjudication provides a theoretical framework within which to make sense of authoritative regional interpretations of basic human rights for the global community. To focus analysis, I consider U S court interpretations of international human rights as an interpretive context. I argue that, with appropriate modification so as to include the world community as a "community of principle" for purposes of human rights adjudication, the law-as-integrity perspective permits disputes surrounding the legality of human rights to resolve around competing interpretive claims backed up by justifying legal theories, rather than as ideological battles external to a juridical philosophy of rights.

Jackson, M W. Justice and The Cave in Terrorism, Justice and Social Values, Peden, Creighton (ed). Lewiston, Mellen Pr, 1990.

Jackson, M W. Oskar Schindler and Moral Theory in Applied Philosophy, Almond, Brenda (ed). New York, Routledge, 1992.

In this paper the universal rationality of moral philosophy is applied to one case, that of Mr Oscar Schindler. Schindler was an industrialist who worked in German war effort during World War II. He also sheltered as many as one thousand Jews. His story was told in Thomas Keneally's novel *Schindler's Ark*. The criteria of rationality and universality embedded in modern moral theory lead to the conclusion that Schindler's acts on behalf of Jews were not morally good. This conclusion should cause a re-consideration of the meanings of rationality and universality.

Jackson, M W. The *Gedankenexperiment* Method of Ethics. *J Value Inq*, 26(4), 525-535, O 92.

Jackson, Roger R. The Tibetan *Tshogs Zhing* (Field of Assembly): General Notes on its Function, Structure and Contents. *Asian Phil*, 2(2), 157-172, 1992.

The *tshogs zhing*, or field of assembly, is an important subject in Tibetan religious art. Typically, it focuses on one's own guru, seated at the crest of a great tree, with the gurus preceding him ranged in the sky above him and the deities of one's tradition ranged on the tree below him. The *tshogs zhing* is an object of visualization in Tibetan guru yoga practices, and serves as both a 'map' of the Tibetan sacred cosmos and as an index of the guru's crucial role in the tradition as a mediator between the practitioner on the one hand and the diachronic lineage of teachers and the synchronic pantheon of deities, on the other.

Jackson, Timothy P. The Disconsolation of Theology: Irony, Cruelty, and Putting Charity First. *J Relig Ethics*, 20(1), 1-36, Spr 92.

In this essay I reply to Richard Rorty's and Judith Shklar's influential accounts of liberalism, preferring what I call "strong agapism" to Rorty's ironism and Shklar's emphasis on avoidance of cruelty. Strong agapism treats love as a "metavalue," an indispensable source of moral insight and power, yet it admits the genuineness and fragility of goods other than love (for example, health, happiness). The detaching of charity from moral self-sufficiency—as well as from certainty about personal immortality—amounts to a disconsoling doctrine in many respects. I conclude, however, that accent on *agape* betokens a profound philosophical and theological optimism. This optimism stems from the conviction that putting charity first is its own reward, a joyful affirmation of life (and its Creator) that is the basis of all other virtues.

Jacob, Alexander. The Neoplatonic Conception of Nature in More, Cudworth, and Berkeley in The Uses of Antiquity, Gaukroger, Stephen (ed). Dordrecht, Kluwer, 1991.

Jacob, Pierre. Externalism and Mental Causality (in French). *Rev Theol Phil*, 124(3), 323-340, 1992.

According to common sense, beliefs (and propositional attitudes in general) are causes of intentional action and are reasons for what we do. The content of what we believe is held to be a causal property of what we intentionally do. In the externalist conception of most contemporary philosophers, the content of a person's belief depends on his/her environment. The theory of the causal efficacy of the intentional properties of propositional attitudes is subject to two epiphenomenalist threats. 1) If intentional properties are held to be functional properties of a person's brain, their causal efficacy risks being pre-empted by the causal efficacy of the brain's physical properties. 2) If exterminalism is admitted, then intentional properties are not functional properties and they risk being deprived of causal efficacy if one holds that causal properties are local properties.

Jacob, Pierre. Externalism and Mental Causation. *Proc Aris Soc*, 92, 203-219, 1992.

I assume the truth of Externalism. I therefore assume that the contents of an individual's propositional attitudes are not local properties of the individual's brain. Content does not supervene of the physical properties of an individual's brain. Assuming that causally efficacious properties of an individual must supervene of physical properties of his or her brain, I argue that there is a tension between Externalism and the commonsense view that the content of an individual's propositional attitudes causally explains the individual's intentional actions.

Jacob, Pierre. Externalism and the Explanatory Relevance of Broad Content. *Mind Lang*, 8(1), 131-156, Spr 93.

I assume the truth of externalism. The intentional properties—the contents—of an individual's propositional attitudes depend on the individual's environment. I then claim that it becomes puzzling how intentional properties of mutual states can be relevant to the causal explanation of an individual's behavior. I argue that intentional properties of mental states are relevant to *comparative* non-causal explanations.

Jacobi, N. Newcomb's Paradox: A Realist Resolution. *Theor Decis*, 35(1), 1-17, Jl 93.

Jacobs, Jonathan. Friendship, Self-Love and Knowledge. *Amer Cath Phil Quart*, 66(1), 21-38, Wint 92.

Friendship and self-love have normative bases in that their primary forms involve desiring the good of the individual (another or oneself) and doing good for that individual because they are worthy of it. Virtue is the basis of both in that it is virtue that merits them and at the same time, practical wisdom is needed for sound judgment of when friendship and self-love are merited and in what ways. This Aristotelian basis is revised and expanded to address modern issues of subjectivity; and the causal relations between friendship and self-love are explored.

Jacobs, Jonathan and Zeis, John. Theism and Moral Objectivity. *Amer Cath Phil Quart*, 66(4), 429-445, Autumn 92.

Jacobs, William S and Belliotti, Raymond. Two Paradoxes for Machiavelli in Terrorism, Justice and Social Values, Peden, Creighton W (ed). Lewiston, Mellen Pr, 1990.

We examine and resolve two paradoxical positions Machiavelli takes in his writings. We argue that the first paradox—his appreciation of an absolute monarch in *The Prince* and his advocacy of a republic in *The Discourses*—actually is the key to understanding his notion of public morality. Next, we argue that the second paradox—his claim that *virtu* remains constant in the world but that good laws and good arms can alter the amount of *virtu* in a particular state—actually is a statement of a simple truth. As a result, we present Machiavelli as a somewhat more consistent thinker than he is often taken to be.

Jacobsen, Mogens Chrom. Über das Verhältnis zwischen Immanuel Kants Rechts-und Moralphilosophie. *Dan Yrbk Phil*, 27, 72-92, 1992.

Traditional efforts to relate the Kantian conception of right to the categorical imperative has mainly been conceived as a deduction of the principle of rights from the categorical imperative itself. This point of view could be warranted if only "the groundwork to the metaphysics of morals" is taken into consideration. The thesis of this paper is that a quite different view is to be found, i.e., "the metaphysics of morals" itself. The categorical imperative and the principle of rights are two different and independent ways of legislative action, but with a common origin in practical reason. The paper will substantiate this thesis and elaborate on differences, relations and relevance of these forms of practical reason.

Jacobsen, Rockney. Arousal and the Ends of Desire. *Phil Phenomenol Res*, 53(3), 617-632, S 93.

Usual classifications of desires into kinds derive from a prior classification of objects of desire. When this strategy is employed, sexual perversions prevent the recognition of sexual desire as one kind of desire. An alternative classificatory strategy for desires is defended, together with a distinction between desires and (aroused states of) appetites. The definition of sexual desire that results enables us to accommodate two otherwise dubious distinctions from our sexual folklore: a distinction between perverse and nonperverse sex, and a distinction between mutual masturbation and making love.

Jacobson, Anne Jaap. A Problem for Naturalizing Epistemologies. *S J Phil*, 30(4), 31-49, Wint 92.

Every epistemological theory needs to be able to articulate some version of the following principle: If S's belief *q* is to make S's belief *p* justified (or is to make *p* something S knows), then *q* must possess some positive epistemic merit. This paper argues that naturalizing epistemologies do not have access to this principle. The central problem is that of providing a naturalistic account of the notion of a reason-for-which one believes while avoiding internalist commitments. The discussion, which focuses on the work of Alvin Goldman, is part of a general argument against causal accounts of reasons-for-which.

Jacobson, Arthur J. The Idolatry of Rules in Deconstruction and the Possibility of Justice, Cornell, Durcilla (ed). New York, Routledge, 1992.

The purpose of the Essay is to explore the only literate account of the significance of reducing law to writing: the Five Books of Moses. Moses makes ten references to writing in the Five Books, five before and five after the episode of the golden calf. The structure of the array reveals Moses' dilemma: the people need written rules backed by sanctions because they cannot hear the inner ethical voice of the Ten Commandments (literally "Ten Proposition's"), yet putting law into writing risks the idolations worship of rules. The Essay explores the philosophic ramifications of this discovery for other jurisprudences.

Jacobson, Stephen. In Defense of Truth and Rationality. *Pac Phil Quart*, 73(4), 335-346, D 92.

Jacobson, Stephen. Internalism in Epistemology and the Internalist Regress. *Austl J Phil*, 70(4), 415-424, D 92.

In his book *Introduction to Contemporary Epistemology*, Jonathan Dancy defends internalism in epistemology against an infinite regress (which he calls "the internalist regress"). In this paper, I argue that: (i) Dancy's defence of internalism is inadequate; (ii) paradigm internalisms—including skeptical arguments, foundations and coherence theories—fall outside Dancy's conception of internalism and do not generate the internalist regress; (iii) Dancy's conception of internalism is idiosyncratic, because it does not do justice to the evidence condition that is the focus of classical internalist epistemologies.

Jacques, Daniel. L'homme exorbité: Réflexion sur la notion de fatique culturelle chez Hubert Aquin. *Horiz Phil*, 3(1), 1-9, Autumn 92.

Jacques, Robert A. On the Reality of Seconds. *Trans Peirce Soc*, 28(4), 757-766, Fall 92.

An all but universal neglect of exactly *what* in Peirce's realism is real is amended by extensive citation, showing that Peirce identified seconds and secondness as *real* as strongly as thirds and thirdness (seconds being traditionally identified in the literature with existence). Attempts to reconcile this contradiction—by emendation, developmental reconciliation, and Hegelian synthesis—are all unsuccessful. The most significant result is that the synechistic architectonic is impossible, which is confirmed by Peirce's own failure to complete it.

Jacquette, Dale. A Deflationary Resolution of the Surprise Event Paradox. *Iyyun*, 41, 335-349, Jl 92.

The prediction, surprise examination, or executioner paradox is the apparent pragmatic difficulty of being unable truthfully to announce a surprise event to take place at an unspecified particular time within a specified interval of time. A deflationary resolution is offered, according to which the paradox arises through an elementary confusion about knowledge and time, and the limitations of future knowledge at a time. The paradox is shown to obtain only on the mistaken assumption that a victim can soundly judge that the surprise definitely will not occur at any later moment within the remaining announced time limit. This violates intuitive paradox constraints, because it requires relative omniscience about future events in the as yet unexpended portion of the penultimate moment before the surprise occurs.

Jacquette, Dale. A Turing Test Conversation. *Philosophy*, 68(264), 231-233, Ap 93.

This imaginary dialogue between a Turing Test interrogator and two (at first unidentified) minds or machines takes place over a computer video screen by BITNET E-mail. By asking about the truth values of simplified Gödel sentences and their negations, the interrogator distinguishes the first participant as a machine, when it becomes evident through the machine's responses that it can only apply a reformulated general principle by mechanical syntactical intersubstitutions of terms, rather than grasping the principle's meaning or intent. The second participant by contrast passes the test, and the two discuss some logical and philosophical aspects of the Gödel sentence Turing Test.

Jacquette, Dale. Chisholm on Persons as *Entia Successiva* and the Brain-Microparticle Hypothesis. *Mod Sch*, 70(2), 99-113, Ja 93.

The hypothesis that persons are brain-microparticles is critically examined. Chisholm argues that persons are dual-aspect nonsuccessive entities, in accord with phenomenological evidence about the persistence of agents as identical over time. This supports a strict adherence to the principle of mereological essentialism for persons, with the consequence that persons must be material atoms. Susan Leigh Anderson's objections to Chisholm's argument are criticized, and a similar charge, but one arguably more sensitive to the real structure of Chisholm's position as ultimately circular in its rejection of the possibility successiveness of persons, is advanced.

Jacquette, Dale. Contradiction. *Phil Rhet*, 25(4), 365-390, 1992.

A comprehensive analysis of the concept of contradiction is proposed. To contradict is literally to speak against, which can include refutation, inconsistency of assertion and behavior, hypocrisy, double-standard, dialectical collision of thesis and antithesis, self-defeating assertions, incongruity, *contradictio - in - adjecto*, oxymoron, and predicate or color incompatibility. These are contrasted with elementary textbook treatments of contradiction, whose abstract equivocation - insensitive conditions are seldom if ever satisfied in actual discourse. The model stipulates that contradiction occurs when and only when dynamic thoughts, actions, and expressions semantically intend a univocal argument context, and can reasonably be mapped onto corresponding abstract syntactically inconsistent logical images.

Jacquette, Dale. Kant's Second Antinomy and Hume's Theory of Extensionless Indivisibles. *Kantstudien*, 84(1), 38-50, 1993.

In the second antinomy of the *Critique of Pure Reason*, the 'Second Conflict of the Transcendental Ideas', Kant attempts to demonstrate *a priori* that there must and that there cannot possibly exist indivisibles or absolutely simple constituents of extension. The antithesis of the second antinomy, that there cannot exist simples, fails to consider Hume's theory of sensible extensionless indivisibles. Hume avoids the conclusion of the antithesis of Kant's second antinomy by denying the proof's assumption that only extended things are capable of occupying space. Kant's philosophy is known to have been deeply influenced by Hume's writings on metaphysics, but surprisingly Kant evinces no appreciation of the implications of Hume's theory in forestalling the second antinomy.

Jacquette, Dale. Metaphilosophy in Wittgenstein's City. *Int Stud Phil*, 25(1), 27-35, 1993.

Wittgenstein in *Philosophical Investigations* chapter 18 compares language to an ancient city with an original core, additions from various periods, and modern suburbs. Robert Ackermann's (1988) book *Wittgenstein's City* explores this metaphor in fascinating detail, and raises the important question of why Wittgenstein excludes philosophy from the city of language games. Ackermann's answer, that Wittgenstein must restrict philosophy from membership in the city if it is to serve its function as city surveyor and custodian of linguistic confusions, is criticized as inadequate. Four alternative explanations are considered and rejected, leaving the conclusion that there is no fully satisfactory textually defensible solution to the problem.

Jacquette, Dale. Schopenhauer's Circle and the Principle of Sufficient Reason. *Metaphilosophy*, 23(3), 279-287, Jl 92.

Schopenhauer describes the principle of sufficient reason, that 'Nothing is without a ground or reason why it is', as the epistemic foundation of his metaphysics of appearance and the Will. Although he formulates the principle with full generality for every true judgment, he makes an important exception for the principle of sufficient reason itself. The principle cannot be questioned, he believes, without falling into vicious circularity in demanding a proof for the right to demand proof. The circularity argument is critically examined, and, contrary to Schopenhauer's conclusion, and interpretation is offered whereby skepticism about the truth of the principle of sufficient reason is intelligible.

Jacquette, Dale. Who's Afraid of the Turing Test?. *Behavior Phil*, 20/2(21/1), 63-74, 1993.

The Turing Test is a verbal-behavioral operational criterion of artificial intelligence. If a machine can participate in question-and-answer conversation adequately enough to deceive an intelligent interlocutor, then it has intelligent information processing abilities. Robert M French has argued that recent discoveries in cognitive science about subcognitive processes involving associational primings prove that the Turing Test cannot provide a satisfactory criterion of machine intelligence, that Turing's prediction concerning the feasibility of building machines to play the imitation game successfully is false, and that the test should be rejected as ethnocentric and incapable of measuring kinds and degrees of nonhuman intelligence. But French's criticism is flawed, because it requires Turing's sufficient conditional criterion of intelligence to serve as a necessary condition. Turing's Test is defended against these objections, and French's claim that the test ought to be rejected because machines cannot pass it is deemed unscientific, resting on the empirically unwarranted assumption that intelligent machines are possible.

Jadacki, Jacek J. Truth: Its Definition and Criteria. *Dialec Hum*, 17(2), 193-212, 1990.

The author introduces the distinction between the nature (definition) and criteria (characterisation) of something's being true. Then he analyzes, i.e., the following formula: "For every proposition *S* and every event *Z* (if *S* refers to *Z*, the (*S* is true, if *Z* occurs))", considered as the semantic definition of truth in the classical interpretation. This definition does not lead to the paradox of the liar (in Jan Lukasiewicz's version). The classical interpretation of the semantic definition is contrasted with formalistic and nihilistic interpretations, as well as with various interpretations of syntactic and pragmatic definitions. All definitions of truth are finally compared with the specter of respective characterisations (i.e., of evidential, structural, genetic types).

Jäckel, Achim. Das neurophysiologische korrelat des induktiven Denkens. *Theoria (Spain)*, 5(12-13), 141-148, N 90.

This paper presents a new theory of connection between neurophysiological facts and the psychological inductive method. Based on the nature of synaptic transmission as a fundamental principle, this theory offers an explanation of abstraction, inductive thinking and any form of learning.

Jaeger, C Stephen. Humanism and Ethics at the School of St Victor in the Early Twelfth Century. *Med Stud*, 55, 51-79, 1993.

Jäger, Gerhard. Fixed Points in Peano Arithmetic with Ordinals. *Annals Pure Applied Log*, 60(2), 119-132, Ap 93.

This paper deals with some proof-theoretical aspects of fixed point theories over Peano arithmetic with ordinals. It studies three such theories which differ in the principles which are available for induction on the natural numbers and ordinals. The main result states that there is a natural theory in this framework which is a conservative extension of Peano arithmetic.

Jaggar, Alison M. Feminist Ethics: Projects, Problems, Prospects (in Czechoslovakian). *Filozof Cas*, 40(5), 782-801, 1992.

Presently in the United States, there is much talk about so-called feminist ethics. Unfortunately, there is less self-conscious reflection about just what feminist ethics might be, a situation that I hope to remedy, at least partially, in this presentation. My paper is divided into three parts. In the first, I describe the emergence of what has come to be known as feminist ethics in the United States, and identify several distinct enterprises sometimes characterized as feminist ethics. In the second part, I discuss each of these enterprises in turn, noting problems faced by each. I draw on these discussions in the third and final part of the paper to summarize my own understanding of feminist ethics. (edited)

Jain, Manju. *T S Eliot and American Philosophy: The Harvard Years*. New York, Cambridge Univ Pr, 1993.

An innovative study of T S Eliot's Harvard years traces the genesis of his major literary, religious, and intellectual preoccupations in his early work as a student of philosophy, and explores its influence on his poetic and critical practice. His concerns were located within the mainstream of Harvard philosophical debates, especially in relation to the controversy of science versus religion. These questions point forward to important debates in later philosophy and hermeneutics, especially on such issues as the implications of a relativist historiography, the objectivism of the social sciences, the role and status of interpretation, the critique of foundational knowledge, and the revival of pragmatism. (edited)

Jaki, Stanley. The Last Word in Physics. *Phil Sci (Tucson)*, 5, 9-32, 1993.

Jakubowski, Marek N. T H Green's 'Analysis of Hegel'. *Hist Polit Thought*, 13(2), 339-340, Sum 92.

James, David N. Risking Extinction: An Axiological Analysis. *Res Phil Technol*, 11, 49-63, 1991.

This paper examines the philosophical assumptions undergirding Jonathan Schell's *The Fate of the Earth*. After criticizing several of his inadequate arguments, James reformulates and defends Schell's contention that hope and anticipation of the future is a fundamental to a meaningful human life. The key point concerns shared activity: Human extinction threatens the meaning of our current activities by making both intergenerational activities and activities shared with contemporaries incomplete and futile. Hope in the continued existence of a common world filled with worthwhile activities sustains us and enhances the meaning of our lives.

James, Edward. Going Astray: Weakness, Perversity, or Evil? in Selves, People, and Persons, Rouner, Leroy S (ed). Notre Dame, Univ Notre Dame Pr, 1992.

How we appear when we wrong, morally educate, and punish each other, reveals that one can *go astray*, i.e., one oneself can knowingly and willingly choose to do wrong, in three ways—by being overcome through weakness, deceived through perversion, and evil through radical choice. Each of these ways uses one of the terms defining going astray paradoxically—with weakness using "choosing" paradoxically, perversion "knowing", and evil "oneself". These paradoxes can be resolved only by the idea of the self as a bounded mind-body continuum, a unique interrelationship between two extremes that asymptotically approach each other and that cannot be inclusively or exclusively ordered.

James, Paul. Forms of Abstract "Community": From Tribe and Kingdom to Nation and State. *Phil Soc Sci*, 22(3), 313-336, S 92.

Apart from a few notable exceptions, the current retreat from Grand Theory has been accompanied by a reluctance to think about how we might theorize different forms of social formation. The present study began as an attempt to understand one such community form, the nation. However, in delineating an analytical method that allowed the theoretical space for exploring the ontological contradictions endemic to living as part of a national community, it became necessary to work comparatively across history and across different social forms. In doing so, the article argues for a method that conceives the various kinds of human community as formed in the changing and contradictory intersections of (diacritically distinguishable) levels of integration—from the most embodied ties of face-to-face reciprocity to the most abstract relations of strangers-in-association such as exemplified in the electronic communications of "information capitalism".

James, Susan. The Good-Enough Citizen: Citizenship and Independence in Beyond Equality and Difference, Bock, Gisela (ed). New York, Routledge, 1992.

In analyzing the ways in which liberal political theory excludes women from full citizenship, some authors have argued that women lack the required level of independence. Others, exponents of an ethic of care, have claimed that independence is undesirable. In this essay I argue that some emotional independence is a condition of full citizenship, but that we cannot take its existence for granted, as many liberals do. Citizens are expected to be able to speak in their own voices and to exercise a degree of impartiality, but these capacities require a self-esteem which has to be created. Rather than being opposed, emotional dependence and independence are complementary. One grows out of the other.

James, Susan (ed) and Bock, Gisela (ed). *Beyond Equality and Difference*. New York, Routledge, 1992.

Jameson, Fredric. Afterword—Marxism and Postmodernism (Including Bibliography) in Postmodernism/ Jameson/ Critique, Kellner, Douglas (ed). Washington, Maisonneuve Pr, 1989.

Jameson, Fredric and Eagleton, Terry and Said, Edward W. *Nationalism, Colonialism, and Literature*. Minneapolis, Univ of Minnesota Pr, 1990.

Jamieson, Dale. Ethics and Animals: A Brief Review. *J Agr Environ Ethics*, 6/1(Supp), 15-20, 1993.

This essay is a short exposition of the current state of the discussion regarding ethics and animals. The views of various proponents of animal rights and liberation are discussed, along with those of their critics. What emerges is that few moral philosophers today would defend the full extent of our current practices with regard to non-human animals. We have entered a new era in our concerns about animal welfare, and there will be no going back. Animals are now centrally located on the moral map. Ethology has played an important role in this shift, and animal welfare science is an important key to improving the lives of non-human animals and helping us to discharge our moral obligations to them. In these circumstances philosophy and animal welfare science must mutually inform each other.

Janat, B. The Home as the Metaphysical Horizon of Human Life (in Czechoslovakian). *Filozof Cas*, 40(3), 382-394, 1992.

Janaway, Christopher. Arts and Crafts in Plato and Collingwood. *J Aes Art Crit*, 50(1), 45-54, Wint 92.

Collingwood alleges that art and craft are fundamentally distinct, and that Plato wrongly thinks there is a poetic craft. The article argues that Plato's view of poetry is closer to Collingwood's own. Plato suggests poets succeed by inspiration rather than craft-like expertise. Then in the *Gorgias* he assimilates tragic poetry and musical performance to rhetoric, placing them in the class of 'flattery' rather than 'craft'. Because they proceed from no knowledge of general principles, aim at pleasure rather than good, and can give no rational account of themselves, poetry and music are not a matter of craft-expertise for Plato.

AUTHOR INDEX WITH ABSTRACTS 535 Jesseph, Douglas M

Jané, Ignacio. A Critical Appraisal of Second-Order Logic. *Hist Phil Log*, 14(1), 67-86, 1993.

Because of its capacity to characterize mathematical concepts and structures—a capacity which first-order languages clearly lack—second-order languages recommend themselves as a convenient framework for much of mathematics, including set theory. This paper is about the credentials of second-order logic: the reasons for it to be considered logic, its relations with set theory, and especially the efficacy with which it performs its role of the underlying logic of set theory.

Janicaud, Dominique. The 'Overcoming' of Metaphysics in the Hölderlin Lectures in Reading Heidegger: Commemorations, Sallis, John (ed). Bloomington, Indiana Univ Pr, 1992.

Janicki, Karol. *Toward Non-Essentialist Sociolinguistics*. Hawthorne, de Gruyter, 1990.

Janis, Allen I. Can Thought Experiments Fail? in Thought Experiments in Science and Philosophy, Horowitz, Tamara (ed). Lanham, Rowman & Littlefield, 1991.

Three senses in which a real experiment can fail are distinguished: i) it cannot be carried to completion, ii) it gives an incorrect result, and iii) it produces results that, although correct, fail to answer the questions that motivated the experiment. It is argued that thought experiments can also fail in each of these ways. The third type of failure, for both real and thought experiments, is the most interesting, in that it often leads to deeper understanding.

Janney, Richard W. Some Reflections on Foundational Questions. *J Prag*, 17(5-6), 467-475, Je 92.

M L Bickhard and R H Campbell's recent rejection of the action of symbolically enroded linguistic knowledge poses interesting problems for modern pragmatics. The authors offer convincing developmental and epistemological support for the roots of linguistic choice in intersubjective experience. (edited)

Janowski, W K. Discoveries as the Origin of Modern Economic Values. *J Value Inq*, 27(1), 43-48, Ja 93.

The notion of value was introduced by early economists and defined in classical economics. From those times labor was thought to be the source of value. Especially in Marxist philosophy and political economy, labor and only labor is the true origin of every value. That trend survived to modern times and has never been seriously questioned. Some contemporary philosophers and political economists recognize the importance of discoveries for economic growth (Romer, 1990), but this has not been translated into a theory of value.

Janssen, Ian (trans) and Schürmann, Reiner. Conditions of Evil in Deconstruction and the Possibility of Justice, Cornell, Durcilla (ed). New York, Routledge, 1992.

Janssen, Maarten C W. Sociology in the Economic Mode. *Theor Decis*, 34(1), 73-81, Ja 93.

Janssen, Maarten C W and Tan, Yao-Hua. Friedman's Permanent Income Hypothesis as an Example of Diagnostic Reasoning. *Econ Phil*, 8(1), 23-49, Ap 92.

In this paper we analyze the structure of a non-deductive type of explanation called diagnostic reasoning. Diagnostic reasoning is a recent development in artificial intelligence based on default logic. Scientific laws are regarded as default rules of the logic. The relevancy of the approach is illustrated by examining the permanent income hypothesis of the economist Milton Friedman.

Janusz, Sharon and Webster, Glenn. The Problem of Persons. *Process Stud*, 20(3), 151-161, Fall 91.

Jardine, David. The Fecundity of the Individual Case: Considerations of the Pedagogic Heart of Interpretive Work. *J Phil Educ*, 26(1), 51-61, 1992.

Using the example of a beginning teacher's account of the experience of entering her new school for the first time, this paper presents a consideration of the nature of interpretive inquiry in education and how such inquiry treats 'the individual case'. This is compared with how more traditional, quantitative studies might treat such cases. The pedagogic character of interpretive inquiry is then discussed.

Jarquin, Miguel C. Hacia un concepto significativo de lo patologico y lo sano, de lo anomal y lo normal in Analecta Husserliana, XXXI, Tymieniecka, Anna-Teresa (ed). Dordrecht, Kluwer, 1990.

Jarvie, I C (ed) and Hall, John A (ed). *Transition to Modernity: Essays on Power, Wealth and Belief*. New York, Cambridge Univ Pr, 1992.

Jason, Gary. On the Nonexistence of Computer Ethics in Terrorism, Justice and Social Values, Peden, Creighton (ed). Lewiston, Mellen Pr, 1990.

Jasper, David. Time and Narrative: Reflections from Paul Ricoeur. *Heythrop J*, 34(3), 302-306, Jl 93.

Narrative and a particular consciousness of time underpin Ricoeur's writings on biblical hermeneutics. This paper concentrates on *Time and Narrative* Vol 3, linking Ricoeur's Kantian thought with issues in postmodern thinkers on metaphor and narrative. His proposal for a hermeneutics of historical consciousness is anticipated in his earlier work *Biblical Hermeneutics*, published as an issue of *Semeia*, and looks back directly to the gospel narratives in its philosophy of narrative hope.

Jaspers, D. Chomsky for Philosophers (and Linguists) (in Dutch). *Tijdschr Filosof*, 55(2), 265-292, Je 93.

Chomsky's views on natural language regularly fall prey to misrepresentation. Often the confusion involves the creative aspect of language use, an aspect of linguistic performance, which tends to be confounded with the notion recursivity, a property of the grammatical competence system. The present article clears away the most deep-seated confusions and proves that criticism of generative grammar based upon them cannot be upheld. It shows that the existence of metaphors, and deviations from rules more generally, reinforces rather than refutes Chomsky's theory so long as the crucial distinction between knowledge of language and language use is taken heed of. It is argued that theories which deny this distinction and view human language as a set of dispositions or as an ability are misguided. The final section illustrates some properties of Universal Grammar (UG) by means of data from the domain of negative polarity and subject-object asymmetries. (edited)

Jauss, Hans Robert. Tradition, Innovation, and Aesthetic Experience. *J Aes Art Crit*, 46(3), 375-388, Spr 88.

Jay, C Barry. Coherence in Category Theory and the Church-Rosser Property. *Notre Dame J Form Log*, 33(1), 140-143, Wint 92.

Szabo's derivation systems on sequent calculi with exchange and product are not Church-Rosser. Thus, his coherence results for categories having a symmetric product (either monoidal or cartesian) are false.

Jay, Gregory S. Hegel and the Dialects of American Literary Historiography in Theorizing American Literature, Cowan, Bainard (ed). Baton Rouge, Louisiana St Univ Pr, 1991.

Jay, Martin. The Debate over Performative Contradiction in Philosophical Interventions in the Unfinished Project of Enlightenment, Honneth, Axel (& other eds). Cambridge, MIT Pr, 1992.

Jayal, Niraja Gopal. Ethnic Diversity and the Nation State. *J Applied Phil*, 10(2), 147-153, 1993.

The coterminality of nation and state is the central legitimising principle of the modern state, which has recently come to be challenged by a variety of ethnic groups across the world. This essay identifies two such challenges: a) The Claim of Alternative Statehood, which endorses the coterminality of cultural and political community, challenges the political boundaries of existing nation-states, and grounds its secessionist demands in a more precise congruence between nationality and state; and b) The Claim of Alternative Citizenship, which does not threaten the nation-state, and seeks only protection for the special requirements of cultural community, for which it demands autonomy, agency and rights. It is argued that the failed promise of pluralism in modern multi-ethnic societies demands a rethinking of the notion of citizenship. (edited)

Jecker, Nancy S. Being a Burden on Others. *J Clin Ethics*, 4(1), 16-19, Spr 93.

Individuals facing death are sometimes reluctant to exhaust the income and assets they have accumulated over a lifetime in order to pay for end-of-life-care. They also may fear and wish to avoid becoming dependent and reliant on family members for assistance with activities of daily living. This paper argues that reasons of justice can support patients' choices to incorporate such considerations into their personal health-care decisions. I argue that respect for patients' well being and ethical integrity can require others to honor patients' preferences made on this basis.

Jecker, Nancy S. Founding a Family in Biomedical Ethics Reviews 1992, Humber, James M (ed). Clifton, Humana Pr, 1993.

This chapter discusses ethical concerns raised by recent developments in contraception, prenatal genetic testing, and other reproductive technologies. The principal emphasis is on government intervention in reproductive decisions. Part one traces the recent history of government control of reproduction since the nineteenth century. Part two critically examines the question when, if ever, is mandatory contraception ethically permissible. The recent development of Norplant contraception makes this a timely and important question. The author rejects arguments favoring compulsory contraception and sketches an argument showing that the value of personal relationships and family formation justify reproductive privacy.

Jecker, Nancy S. Intergenerational Justice and the Family. *J Value Inq*, 26(4), 495-509, O 92.

This essay investigates the theoretical justification for intergenerational justice. "Generation" refers to successive generations in a family lineage, both extant and future. I argue that intergenerational justice requires a distinct justification, and a modified version of Rawls's theory can provide this. The modification involves extending the motivational assumption of the original position so that parties care not only about successive generations, but also about prior generations. Thus, parties care about their parents and grandparents, as well as their children and grandchildren. I also consider the prospect of incorporating the notion of care more fully under the rubric of justice theories.

Jeffery, Peter. Brain Death: A Survey of the Debate and the Position in 1991. *Heythrop J*, 33(3), 307-323, Jl 92.

Jeffrey, Richard. Radical Probabilism, (Prospectus for a User's Manual) in Rationality in Epistemology, Villanueva, Enrique (ed). Atascadero, Ridgeview, 1992.

Jenks, Rod. On the Sense of the Socratic Reply to Meno's Paradox. *Ancient Phil*, 12(2), 317-330, Fall 92.

At the close of the slave boy section of the Meno, Socrates withdraws his assertion of the priestly story concerning rebirth, a story which, if true, clearly answers Meno's Paradox. I argue that coming to understand this Socratic caveat is crucial to understanding Plato's response to Meno's Paradox, and suggest a conceptual coherence thesis as the Platonic residue of doctrine left over after this Socratic expression of doubt.

Jennett, Bryan. The Case for Letting Vegetative Patients Die. *Ethics Med*, 9(3), 40-43, Autumn 93.

This paper considers the ethical and legal basis of the first decision in an English High Court to declare it lawful to withdraw tube feeding from a vegetative patient. This is seen as a logical extension of the common practice of withholding treatment after a trial has shown it to be of no benefit to the patient. Theologians as well as all nine judges in this case reject the principle that prolongation of life is always the first medical priority. The decision does not recommend treatment withdrawal but indicates that it is ethical and lawful. It brings Britain into line with practice in the US and several other countries.

Jensen, Paul T. Intolerable But Moral? Thinking About Hell. *Faith Phil*, 10(2), 235-241, Ap 93.

Thomas Talbott's recent argument for Hell's nonexistence is a sophisticated version of hard universalism. I suggest some reasons to question his argument and to accept the logical and moral possibility that some humans will not be saved.

Jensen, Uffe Juul (ed) and Mooney, Gavin (ed). *Changing Values in Medical and Health Care Decision Making*. New York, Wiley & Sons, 1992.

Jesseph, Douglas M. *Berkeley's Philosophy of Mathematics*. Chicago, Univ of Chicago Pr, 1993.

This book examines the place of mathematics in Berkeley's philosophy and Berkeley's place in the history of mathematics. Beginning with an account of the traditional "abstractionist" philosophy of mathematics which Berkeley opposed, it examines his case against abstract ideas as well as his differing accounts of arithmetic and geometry. Berkeley's critique of the calculus is also examined in detail, beginning with a historical treatment of the origins of the calculus, proceeding to analyze Berkeley's objections in his 1734 work *The Analyst*, and studying some of the many responses to Berkeley.

Jewett, Paul K. *God, Creation, and Revelation: A Neo-Evangelical Theology*. Grand Rapids, Eerdmans, 1991.

This systematic theology text introduces the doctrines of revelation, the divine nature and attributes, and creation; taking a Protestant, Evangelical, and Reformed point of view and presupposing the normativity of Scripture for the teaching of the church. The author both interacts critically with the ways Scripture has been understood throughout church history and engages the contemporary world of thought in which the church is called to minister; making a particular effort to consider scientific and social issues with which the church is now confronted. The book also contains sermons demonstrating how the various doctrines can be preached.

Jeziorowski, Artur. Man and Nature. *Dialec Hum*, 17(1), 68-71, 1990.

The original act of culture constitution is the need of creating such an area in which projecting determinate meanings of an individual is confronted not with nature but with himself as co-originator of the systems of values. What shapes the interrelation of man and nature is not only primacy of the problem of knowledge about being preceding the problem of being itself, but also the fact that thinking is connected with the socio-communicational function. And this fundamental situation is determined by the relations of man to man. The field of knowledge transcends the natural. Thus nature is not the sufficient condition of a dialogue. The specific mental space must be brought into existence if the dialogue is to be carried on.

Jiadong, Zheng. The Fate of Confucianism and of the New Confucianism: A Philosophical Reflection on the Debate on Culture Since "May Fourth". *Chin Stud Phil*, 24(3), 41-71, Spr 93.

Jin, Renling. A Model in Which Every Kurepa Tree is Thick. *Notre Dame J Form Log*, 33(1), 120-125, Wint 92.

Jin, Renling and Keisler, H Jerome. Game Sentences and Ultrapowers. *Annals Pure Applied Log*, 60(3), 261-274, My 93.

Jochemsen, H. Medical Genetics: Its Presuppositions, Possibilities and Problems. *Ethics Med*, 8(2), 18-30, Sum 92.

Johansen, Jorgen Dines. *Dialogic Semiosis: An Essay on Signs and Meaning*. Bloomington, Indiana Univ Pr, 1993.

Johansson, Ingvar. Intentionality and Tendency: How to Make Aristotle Up-To-Date in Language, Truth and Ontology, Mulligan, Kevin (ed). Dordrecht, Kluwer, 1992.

The aim of the article is to show the need for an accurate delineation of the categories of intentionality and tendency, which both, each in its own way, can be characterized by means of the concept of directedness. Aristotle, it is claimed, wrongly fused the two categories in a concept of *causa sui*. The true contrast between tendency and intentionality makes some peculiar part-whole relationships visible.

Johansson, Ingvar. Marty on Grounded Relations in Mind, Meaning and Metaphysics, Mulligan, Kevin (ed). Dordrecht, Kluwer, 1990.

The author argues that latent in the Swiss philosopher Anton Marty's use of the concept of 'grounded relations' there is a threefold division of such relations into ideal relations, relations grounded on non-real relata, and relations grounded on real relata. This division makes it possible for Marty to claim that space and spatial relations are ontologically different.

Johnson, Charles W. *Philosophy in Literature, Volumes I and II*. Lewiston, Mellen Pr, 1992.

Johnson, Christopher. *System and Writing in the Philosophy of Jacques Derrida*. New York, Cambridge Univ Pr, 1993.

The main purpose of the book is a critical analysis of Derrida's theory of writing and its articulation with the concept of system. The book provides a series of close readings showing the persistence and structural coherence of the theory across a range of texts. While recognizing the importance of recent philosophical re-evaluations of Derrida's work, the book suggests a further recontextualization by situating his theory of system and writing in a wider context, including the development of biology and systems theory in the post-war period.

Johnson, Clarence. Hume's Theory of Moral Responsibility: Some Unresolved Matters. *Dialogue (Canada)*, 31(1), 3-18, Wint 92.

A standard reaction to the theory of moral responsibility that Hume presents is that the theory cannot be reconciled with the account of self Hume had offered in *Treatise* Book One. In addition, it is said, Hume cannot be describing our moral practices in saying that to hold a person responsible for a action is in fact to hold him responsible for his character. On at least these two counts the theory is thought to be implausible. The following reconstruction of Hume's theory demonstrates, among other things, that the theory is quite plausible.

Johnson, Clarence Sholé. Yet Another Look at Cognitive Reason and Moral Action in Hume's Ethical System. *J Phil Res*, 17, 225-238, 1992.

But for a very recent exception, Hume has generally been thought to deny that cognitive reason plays a distinctive role in morality. The cornerstone of this view has been his notorious remark that reason is and ought only to be the slave of passion and can never pretend to any other office that to serve and obey passion. But, this remark notwithstanding, Hume's view about the significance of intention in moral processes suggests that he does assign to cognitive reason a very crucial role in morality. This is what the present study establishes.

Johnson, Deborah. A Reply to "Should Computer Programs Be Ownable?". *Metaphilosophy*, 24(1-2), 85-90, Ja-Ap 93.

Johnson, Deborah G. Do Engineers have Social Responsibilities?. *J Applied Phil*, 9(1), 21-34, 1992.

Most American engineers believe that they have a responsibility for the safety and well-being of society, but whence does this responsibility arise? What does it entail? After describing engineering practice in America as compared with the practice of other professions, this paper examines two standard types of accounts of the social responsibilities of professionals. While neither provides a satisfactory account of the social responsibilities of American engineers, several lessons are learned by uncovering their weaknesses. Identifying the gamework in which professional rights and responsibilities are justified, I argue that an end or primary good is the starting place for conceptualizing a profession, and justifying its existence and shape. Too little attention has been paid to the end(s) of engineering. The social responsibilities of American engineers as defined in the present system of engineering are ambiguous and weak. I indicate how the case for assigning American engineers stronger social responsibilities must be made by starting with the end(s) of engineering. I argue that, at present, American engineers do not have social responsibilities as engineers, though they do have social responsibilities as persons.

Johnson, Dell. Religion Generates Moral Energy in God, Values, and Empiricism, Peden, Creighton (ed). Macon, Mercer Univ Pr, 1989.

Johnson, Don Hanlon. Viewpoints: Body, Spirit, and Democracy in Revisioning Philosophy, Ogilvy, James (ed). Albany, SUNY Pr, 1992.

Johnson, Fred. Counting Functions. *Notre Dame J Form Log*, 33(4), 567-568, Fall 92.

Counting functions are shown to be closed under composition.

Johnson, Fred. Three-membered Domains for Aristotele's Syllogistic. *Stud Log*, 50(2), 181-187, Je 91.

The paper shows that for any invalid polysyllogism there is a procedure for constructing a model with a domain with exactly three members and an interpretation that assigns non-empty, non-universal subsets of the domain to terms such that the model invalidates the polysyllogism.

Johnson, James E and Zechmeister, Eugene B. *Critical Thinking: A Functional Approach*. Belmont, Wadsworth, 1992.

Johnson, James Turner (ed) and Kelsay, John (ed). *Cross, Crescent, and Sword*. Westport, Greenwood Pr, 1990.

Johnson, James Turner and Weigel, George. *Just War and the Gulf War*. Washington, Ethics & Pub Policy, 1991.

Johnson, Jeffery L. Inference to the Best Explanation and the New Teological Argument. *S J Phil*, 31(2), 193-203, Sum 93.

This paper critically investigates the new teleological argument: *Evidence*: The physical universe exhibits exceedingly fine-tuned structure and order. This precise structure and order seem a prerequisite for the evolution of conscious intelligence. *Explanation*: God exists, and designed that physical universe in such a way that intelligent life would eventually evolve. The focus on physical, rather than biological, order and structure in the new version of the argument is immune from the devastating rival explanation provided in the theory of natural selection. The framework of inference to the best explanation is applied through a discussion of naturalist rival explanations of the "cosmic coincidences."

Johnson, Kenneth M. Beautiful Truths: Schopenhauer's Philosophy of Art. *Dialogue (PST)*, 35(1), 14-18, O 92.

Johnson, Lawrence E. *Focusing on Truth*. New York, Routledge, 1992.

Johnson, Lawrence E. Toward the Moral Considerability of Species and Ecosystems. *Environ Ethics*, 14(2), 145-157, Sum 92.

I develop the thesis that species and ecosystems are living entities with morally significant interests in their own right and defend it against leading objections. Contrary to certain claims, it is possible to individuate such entities sufficiently well. Indeed, there is a sense in which such entities define their own nature. I also consider and reject the argument that species and ecosystems cannot have interests or even traits in their own right because evolution does not proceed on that level. Although evolution proceeds on the level of the genotype, those selected are able to cooperate in entities of various higher orders— including species and ecosystems. Having their own nature and interests, species and ecosystems can meaningfully be said to have moral standing.

Johnson, Mark. Aquinas's Changing Evaluation of Platon on Creation. *Amer Cath Phil Quart*, 66(1), 81-88, Wint 92.

Once it is granted that Thomas Aquinas consistently attributed a doctrine of creation to Aristotle, the question arises as to Thomas' evaluation of Plato. The article shows that, while early in his writing's Thomas linked Plato and Anaxagoras together as not holding a doctrine of creation, Thomas later linked Plato and Aristotle together as holding a doctrine of eternal creation.

Johnson, Mark. Does Natural Philosophy Prove the Immaterial? A Rejoinder. *Amer Cath Phil Quart*, 65(1), 97-105, Wint 91.

Continuing a previous discussion with John Knasas, which took place in this journal and in *The Modern Schoolman*, this article insists that a sensitive reading of Thomas' various texts shows him to think that natural philosophy as he understood it does attain to showing that immaterial realities exist.

Johnson, Mark. Why Five Ways?. *Amer Cath Phil Quart*, 65, 107-121, 1991.

If each of St Thomas Aquinas's famous "five ways" for proving God's existence is successful, then why does he provide more than one? This article tries to answer that question on the basis of the theological endeavor of the *Summa Theologiae*.

Johnson, P O. Wholes, Parts, and Infinite Collections. *Philosophy*, 67(261), 367-379, Jl 92.

In *The Principles of Mathematics*, Russell argued that a whole need not be greater than its part where both are infinite quantities. He claimed that this assumption enabled him to resolve the paradox of Achilles and the Tortoise and the Tristram Shandy paradox. In fact, it does not enable him to resolve either of these paradoxes, although they can be resolved by assuming the impossibility of an infinite whole or part. This assumption, which is more acceptable to common-sense than Russell's, also enables one to resolve his notorious paradox concerning the Class of Classes that are Not Members of Themselves.

Johnson, Patricia Altenbernd. Feminist Christian Philoosphy?. *Faith Phil*, 9(3), 320-334, Jl 92.

The paper argues that in order to develop the autonomy, integrity, and boldness that

Plantinga has advised Christian philosophers to develop, we need to listen to the voices of feminist philosophers within and outside of the Christian community. The paper sets out the hermeneutical stance of the Christian philosopher as described by Plantinga and shows how feminist thought contributes to this stance. The paper focuses on how we name and symbolize the sacred, reviews some of the names and symbols used by feminist thought, and makes use of Sara Ruddick's work, *Maternal Thinking*, to explore some of the implications of the name "Mother".

Johnson, Pauline. Feminism and the Enlightenment. *Rad Phil*, 63, 3-12, Spr 93.

Johnson, Peter. *Frames of Deceit: A Study of the Loss and Recovery of Public and Private Trust*. New York, Cambridge Univ Pr, 1992.

Johnson, Wayne G. Psychological Egoism: *Noch Einmal*. *J Phil Res*, 17, 239-264, 1992.

While psychological egoism "A", the theory that all human actions are selfish, is easily defeated, an alternative formulation, "B", is defended: "All deliberate human actions are either self-interested or self-referential". While "B" is not empirically testable, neither is any alternative altruistic theory. "B" escapes criticisms leveled at "A", including those of Joseph Butler. "B" is shown to be theoretically superior to any theory of altruism since it brings coherence to moral theory by explaining the nature of moral motivation.

Johnston, David. Beyond Compensatory Justice?. *Nomos*, 33, 330-354, 1991.

Johnston, Mark. How to Speak of the Colors. *Phil Stud*, 68(3), 221-263, D 92.

Johnston, Mark. Reasons and Reductionism. *Phil Rev*, 101(3), 589-618, Jl 92.

Jolley, Kelly D. Wittgenstein and the End of Philosophy?. *Phil Invest*, 16(4), 327-332, O 93.

Jonathan, Ruth. Educating the Virtues: A Problem in the Social Development of Consciousness?. *J Phil Educ*, 27(1), 115-124, Sum 93.

Review essay of Carr D *Education the Virtues*, 1991, Routledge. This essay endorses the author's dispositional account of morality but argues that he takes insufficient account of the actual conditions of modernity as parameters for moral development. It stresses that contingency and particularity should be construed not merely as providing the possibilities and constraints for conduct, but more importantly for the formation of dispositions. Whilst rejecting, with the author, both foundationalism and relativism in morality, this essay insists on the dialectical relation between individual and social development, and its implications for moral education.

Jonckheere, L. L'Ane. *Commun Cog*, 25(1), 101-106, 1992.

Jones, Carol. Reason Without Emotion. *Rad Phil*, 61, 32-33, Sum 92.

Jones, Gary. Elite Culture, Popular Culture and the Politics of Hegemony. *Hist Euro Ideas*, 16(1-3), 235-240, Ja 93.

Jones, James W. Can Neuroscience Provide a Complete Account of Human Nature? A Reply to Roger Sperry. *Zygon*, 27(2), 187-202, Je 92.

In a recent *Zygon* article (June 1991), Roger Sperry argues for the unification of science and religion based on the principle of emergent causation within the central nervous system. After illustrating Sperry's position with some cerrent experiments, I suggest that his conclusions exceed his argument and the findings of contemporary neuroscience and propose instead a pluralistic, rather than unified, approach to the relations between religion and science necessitated by the incompleteness inherent in any strictly neurological account of human nature.

Jones, John D. Poverty Lines, Social Participation, and Welfare Rights. *Cont Phil*, 15(4), 8-15, Jl-Ag 93.

Jones, Kathleen B. *Compassionate Authority: Democracy and the Representation of Women*. New York, Routledge, 1993.

Jones, L Gregory. The Love Which *Love's Knowledge* Knows Not: Nussbaum's Evasion of Christianity. *Thomist*, 56(2), 323-337, Ap 92.

Jones, Marc and Bassiry, G R. Adam Smith and the Ethics of Contemporary Capitalism. *J Bus Ethics*, 12(8), 621-628, Ag 93.

This paper presents a theoretical elaboration of the ethical framework of classical capitalism as formulated by Adam Smith in reaction to the dominant mercantilism of his day. It is seen that Smith's project was profoundly ethical and designed to emancipate the consumer from a producer and state dominated economy. Over time, however, the various dysfunctions of a capitalist economy—e.g., concentration of wealth, market power—became manifest and the utilitarian ethical basis of the system eroded. Contemporary capitalism, dominated as it is by large corporations, entrenched political interests and persistent social pathologies, bears little resemblance to the system which Smith envisioned would serve the common man. Most critiques of capitalism are launched from a Marxian-based perspective. We find, however, that by illustrating the wide gap between the reality of contemporary capitalism and the model of a *moral* political economy developed by Smith, the father of capitalism proves to be the most trenchant critic of the current order.

Jones, W T. Deconstructing Derrida: Below the Surface of *Differance*. *Metaphilosophy*, 23(3), 230-250, Jl 92.

Jonsen, Albert R. Living with Euthanasia: A Futuristic Scenario. *J Med Phil*, 18(3), 241-251, Je 93.

In 1991 and 1992, citizens of Washington State and California voted on whether "aid-in-dying" should be legalized. In both states, the proposition was defeated. In this article, the author, who participated in the Washington State campaign, imagines what might have happened in the fictitious State of Redwood, had such a proposal passed.

Joos, Jean-Ernest. Banalité du mal et sens du devoir chez les administrateurs de l'extermination. *Philosophiques*, 19(1), 61-74, 1992.

The concept of banality of evil, as proposed by Hannah Arendt in her report on Eichmann's trial, serves the purpose of understanding the role and attitude of German bureaucrats regarding of the Extermination process. This concept relates to a sense of duty lacking of personal judgment and political responsibility. However, the description Raoul Hilberg (an historian) gives of the Bureaucracy of extermination reveals remarkably self-governing actions. How does this self-government and the absence of political intentions can coexists in a same person, in a same institution?

Joos, Jean-Ernest. Que reste-t-il de la fondation de la raison?. *Arch Phil*, 55(3), 369-384, Jl-S 92.

This article will show that Adorno's concept of "negative dialectic" is in fact the elaboration of an aspect of Kant's philosophy. Adorno and Kant have in common the hypothesis on rational legitimation as an unfinished process. Jean-François Lyotard follows the same path as Adorno, as he focuses his reading of Kant on the link between reason and judgment. It will then be shown how Lyotard's reading opens new perspectives, beyond Adorno, and gives a new meaning to the specific notion rational legitimation he inherits from Adorno.

Joós, Ernest. *Dialogue with Heidegger on Values: Ethics for Times of Crisis*. New York, Lang, 1991.

The author's dialogue with Heidegger leads to the positing of his thesis: Heidegger's *Sein und Zeit* and his *Vom Wesen des Grundes (The Essence of Reason)* contain a philosophical anthropology whose essential feature is the rehabilitation of the senses as means of knowing. Dasein must *see* the meanings of entities in the concrete. Such seeing is the seeing of the *degrees* of meaning of an individual entity. Meaning then becomes the measure of values manifested in the *World's Worlding*. The author calls this the *Third Copernican Revolution*.

Joós, Ernest. *Poetic Truth and Transvaluation in Nietzsche's Zarathustra: A Hermeneutic Study*. New York, Lang, 1991.

The author wants to view Nietzsche as a poet. He opposes the universality of abstract truth to the *poetic truth* which is the incarnation of the absolute in the concrete and valid only as *meaning* in a particular context. A large part of the book is devoted to the application of this theory, hence the book is a hermeneutic study and a practical guide for the interpretation of Nietzsche's controversial topics such as the Death of God, marriage, life and death, or—woman and the Superman (*Übermensch*). Part three deals with Hermeneutics and Metaphysics.

Joós, Ernó. *God and Existence (in Hungarian)*. Budapest, Pallwest, 1991.

The immigrant Hungarian author, an economist turned man of letters, then well-known philosopher, designed his book for the Hungarian public with the intention to introduce the reader into the fundamental concepts of philosophy. As a preliminary he tries to guide us to understand the "whys" of philosophy, its starting-points and henceforth its relations to problems of culture, ethics and technology. He illustrates the connection between philosophy and hermeneutics with abundant belletristic references. In the concluding part of the book, raising final questions on the meaning of life, he analyses the essence of the triad of God, existence and metaphysics.

Jopling, David. Levinas on Desire, Dialogue and the Other. *Amer Cath Phil Quart*, 65(4), 405-427, Autumn 91.

Jopling, David A. Sartre's Moral Psychology in The Cambridge Companion to Sartre, Howells, Christina (ed). New York, Cambridge Univ Pr, 1992.

Jordan, Jeff. Philosophy of Religion Today. *Cont Phil*, 14(6), 1-2, N-D 92.

Jordan, Jeff. The Problem of Divine Exclusivity. *Int J Phil Relig*, 33(2), 89-101, Ap 93.

Many theists have claimed that God is an essentially moral perfect being and that God is a gracious being. The first claim, that God is essentially morally perfect, implies that God is a morally unsurpassable being: it is not possible that there be a morally better being than God. The second claim, that God is gracious, is often taken to mean that God freely remits the deserved punishment of some persons (but not all persons) and to those persons, God freely grants an eternal happiness. It is the argument of this paper that these two traditional claims are not compatible.

Jordan, Jeffrey. Pascal's Wager and the Rationality of Devotion to God. *Faith Phil*, 10(1), 49-59, Ja 93.

In this paper, I identify two versions of an objection to Pascal's Wager which claims that any calculation of expected utility which involves infinite utilities will result in a situation of rational indeterminacy. One version holds that the use of infinite utilities results in a decisional indeterminacy since any option which offers an infinite payoff would also have an infinite expected utility. The other version contends that whenever one includes infinite disutilities as well as infinite utilities in a calculation of expected utility, a mathematical indeterminacy results. I argue that neither version of this "indeterminacy objection" is fatal to the Wager since a Pascalian can augment utility maximization with certain other plausible decision-theoretic principles in order to resolve the indeterminacies.

Jordan, Jeffrey. The Doctrine of Conservation and Free-Will Defence. *Sophia (Australia)*, 31(1-2), 59-64, 1992.

Jordan, Mark D. Albert the Great and the Hierarchy of Sciences. *Faith Phil*, 9(4), 483-499, O 92.

The paper follows Albert through three of his discussions of the hierarchy of sciences. The first discussion presents what seems a straightforward account of Aristotle's trichotomy of speculative sciences. It remains unsatisfying so far as it exacerbates tensions latent in Aristotle. In the second discussion, Albert attempts to resolve these tensions by supplying a narrative of the mind's ascent along the hierarchy. But the narrative fails to describe convincingly the power by which the mind is rendered capable of ascending. The description is provided finally by the third discussion. In it, Albert identifies the topmost science as rhetorical theology that wants to persuade its students to advance towards God in faith. By completing the narrative in this way, Albert suggests that any adequate discussion of the hierarchy of sciences will not be a contextless description, but a rhetorically situated exhortation.

Jordan, Mark D (ed) and Emery, Jr, Kent (ed). *Ad Litteram: Authoritative Texts and Their Medieval Readers*. Notre Dame, Univ Notre Dame Pr, 1992.

Jordan, William. *Ancient Concepts of Philosophy*. New York, Routledge, 1992.

Jost, Lawrence J. 'Eudemian' Ethical Method in Essays in Ancient Greek Philosophy, IV, Anton, John P (ed). Albany, SUNY Pr, 1991.

Joughin, Martin (trans) and Deleuze, Gilles. *Expressionism in Philosophy: Spinoza*. Cambridge, MIT Pr, 1992.

Joy, Glenn C and McKinney, Audrey M. On a Supposed Inconsistency in J S Mill's Utilitarianism. *SW Phil Stud*, 14, 84-91, Spr 92.

Joy, Morny. Divine Reservations in Derrida and Negative Theology, Coward, Harold (ed). Albany, SUNY Pr, 1992.

Juárez, Agustín Uña. El "Nuevo" Platon (Continuación). *Rev Filosof (Mexico)*, 24(71), 159-189, My-Ag 91.

Juckes, Tim J and Barresi, John. The Subjective-Objective Dimension in the Individual-Society Connection: A Duality Perspective. *J Theor Soc Behav*, 23(2), 197-216, Je 93.

A duality perspective of the individual-society connection is proposed, which recognizes the irreducibility and the interdependence of individual and society. Individuals, as autonomous agents with subjective orientations to the society of which they are a part, and social structure, as an objective order of material social forces, dialectically interact and jointly produce social change. The model differs from others in recognizing an objective and a subjective aspect to both individual and society. Social structure affects individual agents through the subjectification of the material structure as culture, and individual agents affect structure through the objectification of their action in social positions.

Judah, H and Brendle, Jörg and Shelah, S. Combinatorial Properties of Hechler Forcing. *Annals Pure Applied Log*, 58(3), 185-199, N 92.

Using a notion of rank, we investigate combinatorial properties of Hechler forcing—this is a ccc forcing notion adding a dominating real. In particular, we study the effect of adding a Hechler real on the cardinal invariants in Cichón's diagram—these are cardinals related to the ideals of meager and measure zero (null) sets.

Juhl, Cory. Bayesianism and Reliable Scientific Inquiry. *Phil Sci*, 60(2), 302-319, Je 93.

The inductive reliability of Bayesian methods is explored. The first result presented shows that for any solvable inductive problem of a general type, there exists a subjective prior which yields a Bayesian inductive method that solves the problem, although not all subjective priors give rise to a successful inductive method for the problem. The second result shows that the same does not hold for computationally bounded agents, so that Bayesianism is "inductively incomplete" for such agents. Finally a consistency proof shows that inductive agents do not need to disregard inductive failure on sets of subjective probability 0 in order to be ideally rational. Together the results reveal the inadequacy of the subjective Bayesian norms for scientific methodology.

Julien, François and Parkes, Graham R (trans). The Chinese Notion of "Blandness" As a Virtue: A Preliminary Outline. *Phil East West*, 43(1), 107-111, Ja 93.

Jumelet, Marc and De Jongh, Dick and Montagna, Franco. On the Proof of Solovay's Theorem. *Stud Log*, 50(1), 51-69, Mr 91.

Jung, Hwa Yol. Confucianism as Political Philosophy: A Postmodern Perspective. *Human Stud*, 16(1-2), 213-230, Ap 93.

Jung, Hwa Yol. The Genealogy of Technological Rationality in the Human Sciences. *Res Phil Technol*, 9, 59-82, 1989.

Jurist, Elliot L. Recognizing the Past. *Hist Theor*, 31(2), 163-181, 1992.

The philosophical past, once a thing of the past, is with us again. I examine three recent positions about how to understand the philosophical past: the presentism of Richard Rorty, the traditionalism of Alasdair MacIntyre, and the interpretism of Charles Taylor. Rorty, MacIntyre, and Taylor all acknowledge a Hegelian influence upon their views; thus, I also explore Hegel's own view of the history of philosophy. Finally, I offer my own view that our relation to the past ought to be guided by "recognizing" it. Although the concept of recognition is found in Hegel, I argue that Hegel as well as Rorty and MacIntyre end up conceiving of our relation to the past as one of appropriation. Recognition as I define it eschews such appropriation; rather, it consists in a "working through" of the past in a sense the paper specifies.

Jutronic-Tihomirovic, Dunja. Language as Fictitious Consensus: A Critique of Keith Lehrer's Conception of Language. *Grazer Phil Stud*, 40, 163-179, 1991.

The paper tries to show that Lehrer's attempt to apply his consensual model to social theories of meaning and reference is misconceived and that Lehrer's belief that language is a fictitious consensus is not justified. It is argued that the idiolects are basically fragmented and eccentric. Underlying causal networks establish both speaker and conventional meaning. Experts are not essential for the creation of communal language. Indeterminacy of meaning is epiphenomenal in a sense that language is open to continual modifications but there is an underlying structure that forms our communal language which is stable. It is furthermore argued, that a full-blown causal theory of reference incorporates semantics but with different basic assumptions from those that Lehrer holds.

Kōgaku, Arifuku and Parkes, Graham R (trans). The Problem of the Body in Nietzsche and Dōgen in Nietzsche and Asian Thought, Parkes, Graham (ed). Chicago, Univ of Chicago Pr, 1991.

Kaczmarek, Ludger. The Age of the Sign: New Light on the Role of the Fourteenth Century in the History of Semiotics. *Dialogue (Canada)*, 31(3), 509-515, Sum 92.

Kaczmarek, Ludger and Wulff, Hans Jürgen. Prolegomena zu einer semiotischen Beschreibung graphischer Darstellungen in Diagrammatik und Philosophie, Gehring, Petra (ed). Amsterdam, Rodopi, 1992.

Examples of graphical structural images mainly from linguistics are given to show in which way graphical representations are minimal formal models of their domains.

Kadmon, Nirit and Landman, Fred. Any. *Ling Phil*, 16(4), 353-422, Ag 93.

Kadowaki, Kakichi. Shinto and Christianity: Dialogue for the Twenty-First Century. *Int Phil Quart*, 33(1), 69-89, Mr 93.

Kagan, Shelly. The Structure of Normative Ethics in Philosophical Perspectives, 6: Ethics, 1992, Tomberlin, James E (ed). Atascadero, Ridgeview, 1992.

Kagan, Shelly. The Unanimity Standard. *J Soc Phil*, 24(2), 129-154, Fall 93.

In *Equality and Partiality* Thomas Nagel argues for a particularly stringent standard of justification in political philosophy, the *unanimity standard*, according to which political institutions are morally legitimate only if they are based on principles that no one could reasonably reject. I lay out the various assumptions of Nagel's argument, and argue that despite the intuitive appeal of much of Nagel's position, Nagel in fact fails to provide anything like an adequate defense of the unanimity standard.

Kahn, Charles. Vlastos's Socrates. *Phronesis*, 37(2), 233-258, 1992.

A critical review of Vlastos' important and long-awaited book on the philosophy of Socrates, published shortly before his death. The review identifies two major theses: 1) that the philosophy expressed by Socrates in the earlier dialogues (before the *Meno*) is not only different from but antithetical to the philosophy expressed by the same *persona* in the middle dialogues; and 2) that the philosophy of the earlier works is that of the historical Socrates. Systematic arguments are developed against both theses. The review claims that the notion of elenctic dialogue, on which thesis 1 depends, is a misleading generalization of traits specific to the *Gorgias*.

Kahn, James A and Landsburg, Steven E and Stockman, Alan C. On Novel Confirmation. *Brit J Phil Sci*, 43(4), 503-516, D 92.

Kahn, Tamar Joy (ed) and Walters, LeRoy (ed). *Bibliography of Bioethics, V18*. Washington, Kennedy Inst Ethics, 1992.

Kain, Philip J. Marx, Housework, and Alienation. *Hypatia*, 8(1), 121-144, Wint 93.

For different feminist theorists, housework and child rearing are viewed in very different ways. I argue that Marx gives us the categories that allow us to see why housework and child care can be both a paradigm of unalienated labor and also involve the greatest oppression. In developing this argument, a distinction is made between alienation and oppression and the conditions are discussed under which unalienated housework can become oppressive or can become alienated.

Kain, Philip J. Modern Feminism and Marx. *Stud Soviet Tho*, 44(3), 159-192, N 92.

Marx has been criticized by feminists for many reasons, much of it based upon a misunderstanding of Marx. Many feminists take Marx's view to be that the family, gendered division of labor, and male domination are determined by either purely economic factors of natural biological factors. I try to show that Marx holds neither of these views. I also try to show that reproduction and the oppression of women that arises from men's control of private property, which are often claimed to be matters of peripheral interest to Marx, are, in fact, conceptually most central and important for him.

Kaiser, Matthias. Philosophers Adrift? Comments on the Alleged Disunity of Method. *Phil Sci*, 60(3), 500-512, S 93.

R Laudan and L Laudan (1989) have put forth a new model intended to solve the problem of disagreement, the problem of consensus, and the problem of innovation in science. In support of this model they cite the history of the acceptance of continental drift, or plate tectonics. In this discussion, I claim that this episode does not constitute an instance of their model. The historical evidence does not support this model. Indeed, closer examination seems to weaken it. I also sketch an alternative model.

Kalechofsky, Roberta. Dedicated to Descartes' Niece: The Women's Movement in the Nineteenth Century and Anti-Vivisection. *Between Species*, 8(2), 61-71, Spr 92.

Kalfas, Vassilis. Criteria Concerning the Birth of a New Science in Greek Studies in the Philosophy and History of Science, Nicolacopoulos, Pantelis (ed). Dordrecht, Kluwer, 1990.

Kalumba, Kibujjo M. Maritain on "the Common Good": Reflections on the Concept. *Laval Theol Phil*, 49(1), 93-104, F 93.

Two major theses underly Maritain's position in *The Person and The Common Good*: the thesis that society is whole, and the thesis that, as persons, humans are not parts of, but wholes within, society. In light of these, he criticizes three major approaches to the common good: individualism, communism, and totalitarianism, and proposes an alternative candidate for the concept. To this candidate I propose a succinct characterization which I show to have universal as well as ecclesiastical significance.

Kalupahana, David J. *A History of Buddhist Philosophy*. Honolulu, Univ of Hawaii Pr, 1992.

Kamaryt, J. The Ecological Issue and the Crisis of Metaphysical Reason (in Czechoslovakian). *Filozof Cas*, 39(6), 925-943, 1991.

Kamm, F M. Non-consequentialism, the Person as an End-in-Itself, and the Significance of Status. *Phil Pub Affairs*, 21(4), 354-389, Fall 92.

The article discusses the structure of nonconsequentialism—including options not to maximize the good and restrictions based on the harm/not aid distinction and the intention/foresight distinction—in part by way of consideration of works by Kagan, Quinn, and Thomson. Options are connected with the idea of the person as an aid in itself as are restrictions on harming some to and others. Consideration is also given to when it is permissible to harm some to and others, as in the trolley problem case.

Kamuf, Peggy. On the Limit in Community at Loose Ends, Miami Theory Collect, (ed). Minneapolis, Univ of Minnesota Pr, 1991.

Kamuf, Peggy (trans) and Derrida, Jacques. *Given Time: I. Counterfeit Money—Jacques Derrida*. Chicago, Univ of Chicago Pr, 1991.

Kanelopoulos, Charles. L'*Encyclopédie* et les techniques: problèmes théoriques. *Arch Phil*, 56(1), 69-100, Ja-Mr 93.

The theoretical approach of mechanical arts in the *Encyclopédie* is not an homogeneous one. The *Discours préliminaire* does not delimitate a proper field to these arts; the reference to natural history does not confer them a clear status in the Knowledge system. The specificity of these arts is better explained by Diderot in the *Prospectus* and in the article *Art*, which propounds the idea of a general Treatise of Mechanical Arts and the elaboration of their proper geometry and grammar. The article *Éclectisme* proposes to create an Academy of Arts and to write specialized treatises. These projects go beyond the purposes of the *Encyclopédie* and offer a new theorical prospect.

Kang, Ouyang. Reports on International Research in Social Epistemology in the People's Republic of China. *Soc Epistem*, 7(2), 131-146, Ap-Je 93.

The paper reviews the status of research in Social Epistemology in People's Republic of China today, and expresses the author's own views on Social Epistemology as a relatively independent theory. It is composed of four parts. 1) The social and theoretical background for the emergence of the Social Epistemology as a new field of philosophical research. 2) The rise of the Social Epistemology in China and the main cause of its development. 3) The different opinions as to the nature and meanings of Social Epistemology in contemporary China. 4) As the founding scholar of Social Epistemology in China, the author's own views of Social Epistemology were expressed. They include: the definitions, the theoretical positions, the practical necessity and the possibility of social epistemology research, the major content and the structure of the author's book, *An Introduction to Social Epistemology*, China Social Scientific Publishing House, 1991. (edited)

Kanitscheider, B. The Anthropic Principle and Its Epistemological Status in Philosophy and the Origin and Evolution of the Universe, Agazzi, Evandro (ed). Norwell, Kluwer, 1991.

Kanitscheider, Bernulf. Unification as an Epistemological Problem in Advances in Scientific Philosophy, Schurz, Gerhard (ed). Amsterdam, Rodopi, 1991.

Kant, Immanuel and Förster, Eckart (ed & trans) and Rosen, Michael (trans). *Opus Postumum/Immanuel Kant*. New York, Cambridge Univ Pr, 1993.

Kanthamani, A. Does Transcendental Subjectivity Meet Transcendental Grammar?. *Indian Phil Quart*, 20(3), 321-324, Jl 93.

Kanthamani, A. Hintikka's Game of Language. *Indian Phil Quart*, 20(2), 145-160, Ap 93.

Kapitan, Tomis. Keeping a Happy Face on Exportation. *Phil Stud*, 70(3), 337-346, Je 93.

In *Propositional Attitudes*, Mark Richard criticizes the practice of exporting singular terms outside attitudinal scope as a means of articulating so-called "cognitive theories of content." One of his arguments, based on his well-known Phone Booth example, utilizes a plausible pattern of inference while blocking a *de re* reading of ascriptions containing the indexical 'I' in subject position. To the contrary, I argue that a *de re* reading can be motivated and, in so doing, I defend the exportation of indexical terms from within the apparent scope of a psychological verb whose subject is the indexical 'I'.

Kaplan, Leonard. Antimetaphysics and the Liberal Quandary. *Phil Soc Sci*, 22(4), 492-511, D 92.

Kappel, Klemens and Sandoe, Peter. QALYs, Age and Fairness. *Bioethics*, 6(4), 297-316, O 92.

The QALY method for measuring utility of health improvements assumes that a certain improvement of a person's health has the same utility whether the person is old or young. In addition, proponents of QALY often hold that we should be morally indifferent between giving a certain health improvement to a young or an old person. The paper criticizes these assumptions. It is argued that the benefit to the person of a certain improvement of health depends on how it coheres with the persons life as a whole, including also age. Second it is argued that considerations of fairness speak in favor of giving preferential treatment to the young before the old.

Kapstein, Matthew. The Trouble with Truth: Heidegger on Aletheia, Buddhist Thinkers on Satya. *J Indian Counc Phil Res*, 9(2), 69-85, Ja-Ap 92.

Karandikar, A G. Locations of Inner Self. *Indian Phil Quart*, 19/4(Supp), 17-23, O 92.

The purpose of the work is to put upanisadic concept in correct contemporary language so as to avoid misconceptions. The subject includes knowledge about the states of consciousness as discussed by upanisadic literature. Also the work includes a comparative picture of psychology of upanisadic era and contemporary psychology. It explains how the ionic charge present in the body operates to exhibit various states of consciousness, the process of interpretations of dreams by the brain, etc. The nature of the actual knower to which the hinduic philosophy calls it as the 'purusa' or the personality of a living being in other words.

Karasmanis, Vassilis. The Hypotheses of Mathematics in Plato's 'Republic' in Greek Studies in the Philosophy and History of Science, Nicolacopoulos, Pantelis (ed). Dordrecht, Kluwer, 1990.

Karger, Élizabeth. Syllogistique buridanienne. *Dialogue (Canada)*, 31(3), 445-458, Sum 92.

Karimsky, Anyur M. American Naturalism from a Non-American Perspective. *Trans Peirce Soc*, 28(4), 645-665, Fall 92.

Karola, J E. Skrach's Trace in the History of Czech Thought (in Czechoslovakian). *Filozof Cas*, 40(3), 503-517, 1992.

This treatise is composed as a contribution to the knowledge and just evaluation of the thought import of V K Skrach. (edited)

Karpenko, Alexander S. Lattices of Implicational Logics. *Bull Sec Log*, 21(3), 82-91, O 92.

Recently there has been published several articles that establish an interrelationship among some propositional logics. But it is worth emphasizing that already in 1972 the problem of *classification* of logical systems was considered by V A Smirnov in his book *Formal Inference and Logical Calculus*. The main goal of this paper is to analyze interrelationships between the most interesting implicational logics. It is a very natural task because many logical systems are distinguished only by their implicational fragments.

Kasachkoff, Tziporah. Some Complaints About and Some Defenses of Applied Philosophy. *Int J Applied Phil*, 7(1), 5-9, Sum 92.

This article argues that the field of applied philosophy is not distinguished by its topical nature, for the problems it takes up are not new to philosophy; rather, it is distinguished by the attention it gives to the specific and detailed empirical contexts—institutional and personal—in which the issues it deals with are embedded. Second, the criticisms that have been directed at applied philosophy—that it lacks theoretical credentials and so a systematic approach, that it relies on no ultimate normative principles and so cannot insure against inconsistencies, that it is done "piecemeal" and so presents no unified sense of the whole moral picture—while accurately describing the field, does not give us reason to view it with suspicion.

Kasavin, Ilya. Reports on International Research in Social Epistemology. *Soc Epistem*, 7(2), 109-129, Ap-Je 93.

Kashar, Asa. Some Foundational Rejoinders Concerning Language Studies: With a Focus on Pragmatics. *J Prag*, 17(5-6), 477-482, Je 92.

Kasher, Hannah. Justice Within the Limits of Incentive Alone (in Hebrew). *Iyyun*, 41, 371-382, O 92.

Kaspar, Rudolf F and Schmidt, Alfred. Wittgenstein über Zeit. *Z Phil Forsch*, 46(4), 569-583, O-D 92.

The authors give a survey of Wittgenstein's remarks in connection with problems of time. Wittgenstein never treated the topic systematically — he sometimes used it as an example of how to handle philosophical problems. Working on "Philosophical Remarks", 'time' played a role in the context of the possible truth of solipsism. Also for the later Wittgenstein, problems like "Is only the present moment real?" are interesting, but now Wittgenstein tries to deepen our insight into our common (non-philosophical) concepts of time by construing alternative language games.

Kass, Leon R. Is There a Right to Die?. *Hastings Center Rep*, 23(1), 34-43, Ja-F 93.

Kassler, Jamie C. The Paradox of Power: Hobbes and Stoic Naturalism in The Uses of Antiquity, Gaukroger, Stephen (ed). Dordrecht, Kluwer, 1991.

Kastenbaum, Robert. Last Words. *Monist*, 76(2), 270-290, Ap 93.

Words spoken shortly before a person dies have been accorded a special status in folkway traditions, both East and West. This contextualist inquiry focuses on claims that last words deserve a privileged status from either the epistemological or moral standpoints, i.e., they have a superior truth value, and should be taken as guides for conduct. Both claims are found to be unsupported. It is suggested that symbolization and reification have constructed a "death- beyond- words- about-death" that serves as a distraction from the examination of death within particular contexts of human experience. Death may be as variable as its experiential contexts.

Kasulis, Thomas P (ed). *Self as Body in Asian Theory and Practice*. Albany, SUNY Pr, 1992.

Kasulis, Thomas P. The Body—Japanese Style in Self as Body in Asian Theory and Practice, Kasulis, Thomas P (ed). Albany, SUNY Pr, 1992.

Kates, Joshua. The Voice that Keeps Reading: Evan's *Strategies of Deconstruction*. *Phil Today*, 37(3), 318-335, Fall 93.

This article uses Evans recent book as a springboard to ask after 1) the role of reading in Derrida's work; and 2) the status of the 'voice' in *Speech and Phenomenon*. Evans' critique is taken as representative of a longstanding misreading of Derrida's work, both by traditional Husserlians, and also be Searle and Rorty. The voice is not one medium of communication (breath) among others. Instead, language and its body, sense and the sign, are through it first distinguished. The operation by which this is demonstrated is an instance of Derridean 'reading.'

Kato, Tetsuhiro. An Unappreciated Iconology: Aby Warburg and the Hermeneutics of Image (in Japanese). *Bigaku*, 43(2), 25-35, Fall 92.

Aby Warburg is well-known to us as the founder of modern iconology, but as a matter of fact, in contrast with Panofsky's authorized and internationalized version of iconology, his way of interpretation has been looked upon as rather idiosyncratic. It has not always been justly appreciated. In this paper, I try to make clear the hitherto unnoticed actuality of Warburg's hermeneutics of image by examining his famous concept of "Pathosformel". (edited)

Katsumori, Makoto. The Theories of Relativity and Einstein's Philosophical Turn. *Stud Hist Phil Sci*, 23(4), 557-592, D 92.

Einstein's philosophical turn at the midpoint of his academic career is analyzed in its relation to his modes of thought in the theories of relativity, with a focus on the epistemological differences between the special and the general theories. It is shown that Einstein's philosophical turn may be characterized as a process in which the instrumental and intersubjective dimensions of thought, essential to his early work, were progressively concealed, and that this concealment is closely linked to the philosophical implications of four-dimensional space-time and the tensor formalism.

Katz, Claire Elise. Bridging the Gap. *Thinking*, 10(1), 13-14, 1992.

This article relates Katz's experiences using the Philosophy for Children program with some sixth and seventh grade children at a private school in Maryland. While using this program she brought 26 of these children to one of her college level critical thinking classes at Salisbury State University. A lively dialogue on "animal rights" ensued—a dialogue in which the children had much to contribute. The college students learned a great deal about the capabilities of young children and she became further convinced of the value of the Philosophy for Children program.

Katz, Eric. Environmental Ethics: A Select Annotated Bibliography II, 1987-1990. *Res Phil Technol*, 12, 287-324, 1992.

An annotated bibliography of over 120 books, anthologies, and articles in the field of environmental ethics and environmental philosophy, published from 1987-1990.

Katz, Eric. The Big Lie: Human Restoration of Nature. *Res Phil Technol*, 12, 231-241, 1992.

This paper examines the environmental policy of the restoration of damaged natural environments. I argue against the optimistic view that humanity has the obligation and ability to repair or reconstruct damaged natural systems. Restoration is a deception, a self-imposed lie. A "restored" nature is an artifact created to meet human satisfactions and interests. It is an expression of a fundamental anthropocentrism, the insidious dream of the human domination of the natural world.

Katz, Eric. The Call of the Wild. *Environ Ethics*, 14(3), 265-274, Fall 92.

I use encounters with the white-tailed deer of Fire Island to explore the "call of the wild"—the *attraction to value* that exists in a natural world outside of human control. Value exists in nature to the extent that it avoids modification by human technology. Technology "fixes" the natural world by improving it for human use or by restoring degraded ecosystems. Technology creates a "new world," an artifactual reality that is far removed from the "wilderness" of nature. The technological "fix" of nature thus raises a moral issue: how is an artifact morally different from a natural and wild entity? Artifacts are human instruments; their value lies in their ability to meet human needs. Natural entities have no intrinsic functions; they were not created for any instrumental purpose. To attempt to manage natural entities is to deny their inherent autonomy: a form of domination. The moral claim of the wilderness is thus a claim against human technological domination. We have an obligation to struggle against this domination by preserving as much of the natural world as possible.

Katz, Eric and Oechsli, Lauren. Moving beyond Anthropocentrism: Environmental Ethics, Development, and the Amazon. *Environ Ethics*, 15(1), 49-59, Spr 93.

We argue for the rejection of an anthropocentric and instrumental system of normative ethics. Moral arguments for the preservation of the environment cannot be based on the promotion of human interests or goods. The failure of anthropocentric arguments is exemplified by the dilemma of Third World development policy, e.g., the controversy over the preservation of the Amazon rain forest. Considerations of both utility and justice preclude a solution to the problems of Third World development from the restrictive framework of anthropocentric interests. A moral theory in which nature is considered to be morally considerable in itself can justify environmental policies of preservation, even in the Third World. Thus, a nonanthropocentric framework for environmental ethics should be adopted as the basis for policy decisions.

Katz, Jerrold. The New Intensionalism. *Mind*, 101(404), 689-719, O 92.

From the beginning of the linguistic turn in this century to the present, philosophical discussions of language have consistently assumed that intensionalism, the doctrine that expressions of natural language have sense as well as reference, can only be Fregean intensionalism. In earlier papers, I argued that this widespread assumption is false because there is another form of intensionalism fundamentally different from Frege's, and, further, that the failure to recognize such an alternative has led to the acceptance of criticisms of the intensionalist position which, in fact, are only criticisms of Fregean intensionalism. Since then I have come to think that the assumption is false for a different and deeper reason, namely, that the systematic semantics that Frege developed and that Carnap refurbished is not intensionalism at all. In this paper, I want to explain why I now think this. In the process, I hope to provide a new perspective on the linguistic turn in twentieth century philosophy and a new conception of the relation between the analytic and the necessary and a priori.

Katz, Marilyn. Ideology and "the Status of Women" in Ancient Greece. *Hist Theor*, 31(4), 70-97, 1992.

This essay investigates the constitution of the principal research question on women in ancient Greece, namely, the status of women in ancient Athens, and attempts to formulate a historiography for it under three headings. "Patriarchy and Misogyny" reviews the history of the question, from the time of its canonical formulation by A W Gomme in 1925, back to its initial constitution as a scholarly question by K A Böttiger in 1775, and up to its conceptualization in contemporary and feminist scholarship. (edited)

Katz, Ruth (ed) and Dahlhaus, Carl (ed). *Contemplating Music: Source Readings in the Aesthetics of Music, Volume IV—Community of Discourse*. Stuyvesant, Pendragon Pr, 1993.

Katz, Steven T. Ethics and Mysticism in Eastern Mystical Traditions. *Relig Stud*, 28(2), 253-267, Je 92.

This essay seeks to establish the deep ethical concerns of the Eastern mystical traditions. In contrast to the common view that eastern mystical traditions are unconcerned with ethical behavior, I show that in both Hinduism and Buddhism ethical action is a primary factor leading towards, as well as leading away from, mystical experience. In particular, this essay analyzes the metaphysical arguments of these traditions in order to explain just why it is that ethics has the significant role it does have in these mystical communities. More generally, this essay is another piece in my ongoing project of explicating the contextual nature of mystical experience.

Katz, Steven T. Mysticism and Ethics in Western Mystical Traditions. *Relig Stud*, 28(3), 407-423, S 92.

Katzoff, Charlotte. Justification without Good Reasons. *Phil Papers*, 21(2), 121-131, Ag 92.

I take issue with Richard Feldman's claim that objective justification, *i.e.*, having good reasons to believe *p*, is equivalent to subjective justification, *i.e.*, having good reasons to believe you have good reasons to believe *p*. If having good reasons for a belief means that the belief is very likely to be true, then only having good reasons to believe you have good reasons means that the likelihood of the belief is diminished. I suggest, however, that on a deontological notion of justification, if 5 is justified in believing he is justified, then he is justified.

Katzoff, Charlotte. Oakeshott and the Practice of Politics. *J Phil Res*, 17, 265-277, 1992.

Oakeshott's thesis is that political knowledge is essentially practical: it is not given to propositional formulation and cannot be deliberately exercised, but rather is expressed in conduct and transmitted by example and practice. I argue that this is true primarily of physical skills which depend upon unconscious, automatic physiological processes. Political practice, by contrast, is largely a matter of rule-governed activity. It is an empirical fact that we do have introspective access to many of the rules which govern our political conduct, and there is good evidence for the claim that we can deliberately and reflectively set ourselves to apply them.

Kaufer, David S and Carley, Kathleen M. Condensation Symbols: Their Variety and Rhetorical Function in Political Discourse. *Phil Rhet*, 26(3), 201-226, 1993.

Kaufman, Gordon D. Nature, History, and God: Toward an Integrated Conceptualization. *Zygon*, 27(4), 379-401, D 92.

In this paper I bring the ancient symbol "God" into conceptual relationship with modern understandings of the development of the cosmos, the evolution of life, and the movements of human history. I suggest that the cosmos can quite possibly be interpreted today in terms of two fundamental ideas: 1) a notion of "cosmic serendipitous creativity," 2) the expression of which is through "directional movements" or "trajectories" of various sorts that work themselves out in longer and shorter stretches of time. In a universe understood in these terms, the symbol "God" may be taken to designate the underlying creativity working in and through all things, and in particular working in and through the evolutionary-historical trajectory on which human existence has appeared and by which it is sustained. With this interpretation the symbol "God" continues to perform its important function of helping focus human consciousness, devotion, and work in a way appropriate to the actual world and the enormous problems with which men and women today must come to terms.

Kaufman, William E. Mordecai M Kaplan and Process Theology: Metaphysical and Pragmatic Perspectives. *Process Stud*, 20(4), 192-199, Wint 91.

Kaufman-Osborn, Timothy V. *Politics/Sense/Experience: A Pragmatic Inquiry into the Promise of Democracy*. Ithaca, Cornell Univ Pr, 1991.

This book mobilizes the spirit of pragmatism to explore the vitality of democracy in a technological age. It begins with a genealogy of Western rationalism, extending from its origins in the Greek city-state to its epistemological reformulation in the seventeenth century. This is followed by an examination of the relationship between our received understanding of reason and the crisis of twentieth century liberalism. Finally, the author speculates on the implications of these investigations for the contemporary bureaucratic state, and asks how we might fashion a constitutional order whose democratic form affirms the sense of everyday politics.

Kaufman-Osborn, Timothy V. Teasing Feminist Sense from Experience. *Hypatia*, 8(2), 124-144, Spr 93.

We sometimes experience more than we can say, and often it is the "questions" posed by such nondiscursive reality to which feminist writings speak most profoundly. Feminists should therefore decline Richard Rorty's neopragmatist exhortation to forgo all appeals to "women's experience." Invoking an alternative account of pragmatism's import for feminism, I explore the problematic relationship between the experience of being pregnant and the language we use in talking about it.

Kaufmann, Walter (ed). *Religion from Tolstoy to Camus*. New Brunswick, Transaction Books, 1994.

Kaufmann, Walter (ed). *The Portable Nietzsche*. New York, Penguin USA, 1982.

Kavka, Gregory. Internal Prisoner's Dilemma Vindicated. *Econ Phil*, 9(1), 171-174, Ap 93.

Kawata, Tokiko. On Clement Greenberg's Formalistic Criticism (in Japanese). *Bigaku*, 43(1), 13-23, Sum 92.

Clement Greenberg regarded the history of paintings as the dialectic development periodically fluctuating between the "plastic" and the "painterly". As for Modernism, Greenberg equates its essence with reinforcing "self-criticism". That's why, Greenberg asserts, Modernist art attempted to be a pure art, and Modernist painting increasingly emphasized "flatness". But, in Greenberg's view, such painting cannot be flat enough to be the physical surface of the canvas; inevitably it permit a strictly optical illusion of a third dimension. Greenberg's theory of formalism is based on Kant's aesthetics. According to Kant, aesthetic judgment is first made possible by an intuitive grasp of the formal element of the object in the world of phenomenon, and then by balanced faculties of transcendental cognition. So Greenberg attaches much importance to aesthetic intuition. But on that point, there are some problems, which I would like to investigate. (edited)

Kay, Lily E. Quana of Life: Atomic Physics and the Reincarnation of Phage. *Hist Phil Life Sci*, 14(1), 3-21, Ja 92.

I will use the history of phage to focus on the issue of biological explanations; on the relationship between biology and physics; and on the historical problem of the disciplinary autonomy of biology, versus its reduction, which ultimately seeks to place it within the domain of the physical sciences. Paradoxically, the two physicists I focus on most, Neils Bohr and Max Delbrück, represent attempts to preserve the autonomy of biology, each in a very complex way. Once again the problematique here is the nature of biological systems as a goal-oriented historical phenomena, that is, as teleological explanations rather than mechanistic accounts of life.

Kaye, Lawrence J. Are Most of Our Concepts Innate?. *Synthese*, 95(2), 187-217, My 93.

Fodor has argued that, because acquisition relies on the use of concepts already possessed by the learner, all concepts that cannot be definitionally reduced are innate. Since very few reductive definitions are available, it appears that most concepts are innate. After noting the reasons why we find such radical concept nativism implausible, I explicate Fodor's argument, showing that anyone who is committed to mentalistic explanation should take it seriously. Three attempts at avoiding the conclusion are examined and found to be unsuccessful. I then present an alternative way around Fodor's nativism; I maintain that concepts at a given level of explanation can be semantically primitive, yet at least partially acquired if some of the conditions at a lower level of explanation that are responsible for the concept's presence are themselves acquired.

Kaye, Lawrence J. Semantic Compositionality: Still the Only Game in Town. *Analysis*, 53(1), 17-23, Ja 93.

I defend the compositional approach to theories of meaning for natural (and mental) languages against two counter examples/ arguments from Stephen Schiffer. I show that his cases leave us without an explanation of how we are able to understand indefinitely many semantic types of sentences.

Kaye, Richard. Hilbert's Tenth Problem for Weak Theories of Arithmetic. *Annals Pure Applied Log*, 61(1-2), 63-73, My 93.

Hilbert's tenth problem for a theory T asks if there is an algorithm which decides for a given polynomial with integer coefficients whether it has a root in some model of T. Assuming an affirmative answer, we give new independence results for T=Open Induction and other theories. We apply these methods by providing a negative answer to the above question for the theories of banded existential induction and of parameter-free bounded universal induction.

Kazmi, Yedullah. Panoptican: A World Order through Education or Education's Encounter with the Other/Difference. *Phil Soc Crit*, 19(2), 195-213, 1993.

Keane, John. The Modern Democratic Revolution in Judging Lyotard, Benjamin, Andrew (ed). New York, Routledge, 1992.

Kearney, Richard. Between Tradition and Utopia: The Hermeneutical Problem of Myth in On Paul Ricoeur: Narrative and Interpretation, Wood, David (ed). New York, Routledge, 1991.

Kearney, Richard. Derrida and the Ethics of Dialogue. *Phil Soc Crit*, 19(1), 1-14, 1993.

AUTHOR INDEX WITH ABSTRACTS 541 Kelkel, Arion L

Kearney, Richard. Derrida's Ethical Re-Turn in Working Through Derrida, Madison, Gary B (ed). Evanston, Northwestern Univ Pr, 1993.

Kearney, Richard. *Poetics of Imagining: From Husserl to Lyotard*. New York, Routledge, 1991.

This book offers a rigorous and accessible account of the major theories of imagination in modern European thought. It analyses the contributions made to our understanding of the imaginary life by phenomenology (Husserl, Sartre, Merleau-Ponty, Bachelard), hermeneutics (Heidegger, Ricoeur) and postmodernism (Vattimo, Kristeva, Lyotard). The book asks such questions as: what is imagination? What is the relationship between aesthetics and ethics in a contemporary civilization dominated by the image? Are the claims of artistic creativity and moral responsibility compatible?

Kearney, Richard. Postmodernity, Nationalism and Ireland. *Hist Euro Ideas*, 16(1-3), 147-155, Ja 93.

This article explores how certain postmodern theories (Derrida, Lyotard, Frampton) offer a critique of centralist models of nationalist politics. It applies this critique to contemporary Irish politics and literature with particular attention to the work of Seamus Heaney and John Hewitt.

Keasberry, Helen and Ten Have, Henk. Equity and Solidarity: The Context of Health Care in The Netherlands. *J Med Phil*, 17(4), 463-477, Ag 92.

The current debate on health care resource allocation in the Netherlands is characterized by a social context in which two values are generally and traditionally accepted as being equally fundamental: solidarity and equity. We will present an outline of the distinctive features of the Dutch health care system, and analyze the present state of affairs in the resource allocation debate. The presuppositions of the political call for constraint and (renewed) government supervision and the role of the specific value context in recent proposals for reconstruction of the Dutch health care system will be evaluated.

Keat, Marilyn S. Beyond the Virtues-Principles Debate. *Educ Theor*, 42(4), 443-459, Fall 92.

This essay looks at new foundations for moral education in the partial synthesis of Aristotle's ethics on virtue and Kant's ethics of principle and duty which is found in the moral philosophies of Paul Ricoeur and Hans-Georg Gadamer. This synthesis accounts for not only the conditionedness of moral life, but also the possibility and necessity of transcending situatedness in a morally plural world and appealing to universal principles. Moral education based on this perspective would aim first to lay a groundwork in virtue and awareness of freedom and gradually proceed to a focus on moral autonomy.

Keating, Daniel. The Ethical Project of Alasdair MacIntyre: "A Disquieting Suggestion". *Lyceum*, 4(1), 104-119, Spr 92.

The aim of this paper is to present an introductory explanation of the ethical project of Alasdair MacIntyre and a brief examination of that project in the light of scholarly critique by his peers. MacIntyre's thesis has received comment from experts in many fields of research. His argumentation and his conclusions have received much criticism, but his evaluation of the contemporary moral situation remains persuasive and challenging.

Kebede, Messay. Science and Ideology via Development. *J Value Inq*, 26(4), 483-494, O 92.

A pertinent case of the dichotomy between the subjective and the objective is the opposition between science and ideology. Even for those theoreticians who do not follow the Marxist method, which identifies ideology with deception, the general trend is to derive it from some supra-individual entity, thus turning it into manipulation. Yet, for theoreticians of development, behind secular goals, there are always ideological commitments. The culture change that enables people to get out of underdevelopment is precisely thought to be the suffusion of secular pursuits with ideological beliefs. May it not be, then, that ideology is neither deception nor manipulation, but a necessary attendant of the will whenever a ranking of drives, from which the spirit of achievement springs, is desired?

Kedzia, Zdzislaw. Persönliche Freiheitsrechte in Polen. *Stud Phil (Switzerland)*, 49, 199-215, 1990.

Keeley, Louise Carroll. Subjectivity and Worlds in *Works of Love* in Foundations of Kierkegaard's Vision of Community, Connell, George B (ed). Atlantic Highlands, Humanities Pr, 1992.

Keenan, James F. Distinguishing Charity as Goodness and Prudence as Rightness: A Key to Thomas's *Secunda Pars*. *Thomist*, 56(3), 407-426, Jl 92.

The article presupposes two moral descriptions for all moral activity. First, whether the activity attains or fulfills the moral expectations or demands that are concretely set by the norms of a reasoning community. When these are met, action is described as right; when the action falls short of these demands, the action is called wrong. Second, whether the agent in acting, acts out of a moral motivation like love (in the Christian tradition) or duty (in the Kantian tradition). The article argues that Aquinas had two such descriptions: prudence conforms to contemporary usage of rightness; and charity conforms to goodness.

Keenan, James F. *Goodness and Rightness in Thomas Aquinas's "Summa Theologiae"*. Washington, Georgetown Univ Pr, 1992.

Distinguishing goodness as moral effort or striving from rightness as moral attainment or correctness, the author asks whether Aquinas maintained two distinguishable descriptions for the moral life. First, however, he asks whether Aquinas's description of the relation between the reason and the will provides adequate ground for two demoral descriptions. Then, he treats the notions of act, object, end, intention, virtues (acquired and theological), and sin to ask whether Aquinas's use of these terms belong to the realm of rightness or goodness.

Keenan, James F. Reply to Beckwith: Abortion—Whose Agenda Is It Anyway?. *Int Phil Quart*, 32(2), 239-245, Je 92.

In reply to Francis Beckwith's article in *IPQ*, 1992, 105-118, on abortion and pro-choice arguments, this article presents several feminists who are pro-life and asks whether of identification of feminism with pro-choice positions is a fair assumption. Against Beckwith's assumption that such identification is correct, Keenan argues that a pro-choice position expresses liberal, not necessarily feminist, thought.

Keenan, James F. Virtue Ethics: Making a Case as it Comes of Age. *Thought*, 67(265), 115-127, Je 92.

The article begins by narrating the roots of virtue ethics, describing its attempts to overcome both competitive methods of moral reasoning (deontology and consequentialism), and distinguishing the concepts of moral goodness from moral rightness. It presents the structure of virtue ethics and emphasizes both the importance of community and the importance of establishing ends in determining virtuous courses of action. It concludes suggesting ways that virtue ethics can practically apply.

Keenan, Thomas and Leventure, Albert. A Bibliography of the Works of Jacques Derrida in Derrida: A Critical Reader, Wood, David (ed). Cambridge, Blackwell, 1992.

Keene, G B. Pretending to Infer in Logical Foundations, Mahalingam, Indira (ed). New York, St Martin's Pr, 1991.

Keffer, M Jan and Foulk, Gary J. Rationality and Principles: A Criticism of the Ethic of Care. *Int J Applied Phil*, 7(1), 15-19, Sum 92.

This work defends the necessity of reason, principles, and traditional metaethical and normative ethical theory in clinical nursing ethics against the claim, exemplified by Randy Spreen Parker's "Nurses' Stories: The Search for a Relational Ethic of Care," in *Advances in Nursing Science* (1990, 13, 1, 31-40), that such concerns tend to obscure the important factors of caring and emotion. By recalling such standard points as the distinction between interested and disinterested interests and the blindness of the raw data of experience and emotion without the light of reason and concepts, it is shown that the appeal to an ethic of care rests on confusion and error.

Kegley, Jacquelyn A. Loyalty to Loyalty in Frontiers in American Philosophy, Volume I, Burch, Robert W (ed). College Station, Texas A&M Univ Pr, 1992.

The purpose of this paper is to address the issue of community building in America today as it is presented in works by Robert Bellah, by Amitai Etzioni and the communitarians, and by Psychiatrist Scott Peck. It is argued that the best philosophical base for such community building is to be found in the work of Josiah Royce. In his "Problem of Christianity" and other works, Royce develops a philosophical viewpoint that is person-centered and yet focuses on the conditions of community. Royce's view especially deals with individualistic pursuits of the conflict of multiple interests.

Keisler, H Jerome and Jin, Renling. Game Sentences and Ultrapowers. *Annals Pure Applied Log*, 60(3), 261-274, My 93.

Keita, Lansana. Barnes, Bloor, and the Sociology of Knowledge. *Quest*, 5(2), 90-105, D 91.

Keita, Lansana. Jennings and Zande Logic: A Note. *Brit J Phil Sci*, 44(1), 151-156, Mr 93.

In 'Zande Logic and Western Logic' Richard Jennings argues that contrary to the view of Evans-Pritchard and Tim Triplett the system of logic employed by the Azande is sui generis and distinct from that of Westerners. I argue that this thesis is erroneous because Jennings, following Evans-Pritchard, is at fault in his analysis of the logic of the Azande. Zande thinking on the topic of witchcraft-substance heritability is not contradictory as believed. But even if one assumes that the Azande do reason contradictority on matters of institutional importance, Jennings' thesis on the possibility of incompatible logics still fails because similar instances of contradictory thinking could be found in the West. Although in practical matters all peoples appeal to orthodox logic, in matters of institutional importance the epistemological relativist could be on fertile ground where orthodox logic is in conflict with beliefs that are institutionally grounded.

Kejian, Huang. The Cultural Dilemma of Contemporary China: A Discussion of My Own Views on Culture and Response to Mou Zhongjian. *Chin Stud Phil*, 24(2), 39-69, Wint 92-93.

Kekes, John. Disgust and Moral Taboos. *Philosophy*, 67(262), 431-446, O 92.

The central claim of this paper is that there is a form of disgust that has fundamental moral importance because it is the justified reaction to the violation of moral taboos. Moral taboos prohibit breaking basic moral rules that protect us from evil and constitute part of our identity as moral agents. Since the moral taboos whose violation causes disgust form the bulwark of civilized life against barbarism, the disposition to feel disgust on the appropriate occasions is a sign of justified moral seriousness. Correspondingly, its loss is a sign of a reprehensible weakening of moral commitments.

Kekes, John. *The Examined Life*. University Park, Penn St Univ Pr, 1992.

Kekes, John. The Incompatibility of Liberalism and Pluralism. *Amer Phil Quart*, 29(2), 141-151, Ap 92.

Liberals have claimed and their critics have conceded that there is an intimate connection between liberalism and pluralism. The purpose of this paper is to show that they are both mistaken. There are good reasons for supposing that liberalism and pluralism are incompatible. If pluralism is committed to anything, it must be to the claim that there is no particular value that in conflict with other values always take justifiable precedence over them. Similarly, if liberalism is to avoid the charge of vacuity, it must be committed to holding that in cases of conflict the particular values liberals favor do take justifiable precedence over other values. How, then, could liberalism and pluralism be compatible?

Kekes, John. *The Morality of Pluralism*. Princeton, Princeton Univ Pr, 1993.

The aim of this book is to develop a pluralistic account of values. Values are conceived as possibilities whose realization would make lives good. Their realization, however, is no easy matter because there are many different types of values and it is often impossible to realize them together since they are incompatible, incommensurable, and conflicting. Living a good life requires the resolution of such conflicts, but the resolutions are themselves plural in nature. It is a central claim of the book that the nature of the resolution of conflicts among values nevertheless need not be arbitrary, but can be brought under rational control. The account developed establishes a middle ground between a traditional monistic view, which is committed to there being modern relativistic view, which accepts an unlimited plurality of values and denies that they can be rationally justified.

Kelkel, Arion L. Husserl and the Anthropological Vocation of Phenomenology in Analecta Husserliana, XXXIV, Tymieniecka, Anna-Teresa (ed). Dordrecht, Kluwer, 1992.

Keller, Catherine. The Apocalypse of Community in *On Community*, Rouner, Leroy S (ed). Notre Dame, Univ Notre Dame Pr, 1992.

Keller, James A. On the Issues Dividing Contemporary Christian Philosophers and Theologians. *Faith Phil*, 10(1), 68-78, Ja 93.

Recently Gordon Kaufman published an article in *Faith and Philosophy* in which he gave some reasons why contemporary theologians are not much interested in the issue of evidentialism. Still more recently Eleonore Stump and Norman Kretzmann replied to it. In this paper I argue that their reply does not engage the issue which concerns the theologian. I try to define that issue and show what implications it has for the usefulness to Christian theologians of the work of Christian philosophers of religion.

Kellert, Stephen R (ed) and Bormann, Herbert F (ed). *Ecology, Economics, Ethics: The Broken Circle*. New Haven, Yale Univ Pr, 1991.

Kellner, Douglas. Bartky, Domination, and the Subject. *Hypatia*, 8(1), 145-152, Wint 93.

Bartky's *Femininity and Domination* analyses the social construction of femininity and the ways that it oppresses women. Utilizing phenomenology, Bartky provides illuminating examples of the experience of oppression and how women are constructed to submit to images and models of femininity. I raise questions concerning the standpoint of normative critique from which Bartky criticizes the oppression of women, the model of agency that she utilizes, and the politics she supports to overthrow oppression and domination.

Kellner, Douglas M. Jameson, Marxism, and Postmodernism in *Postmodernism/ Jameson/ Critique*, Kellner, Douglas M (ed). Washington, Maisonneuve Pr, 1989.

The article attempts to trace the itinerary of the thought of Fredric Jameson, generally considered to be the most important living Marxist literary critic. The article provides the first comprehensive overview of Jameson's work and situates his turn to postmodernism within the trajectory of his theoretical project. After exploring the sources and origins of Jameson's Marxism, the article traces his appropriation of French post-structuralist thought and then postmodern theory. (edited)

Kellner, Douglas M. Minima Moralia: The Gulf War in Fragments. *J Soc Phil*, 24(2), 68-88, Fall 93.

"Minima Moralia: The Gulf War in Fragments" is an experimental essay in social theory. Inspired by Adorno's book *Minima Moralia*, I do a critique of the media coverage of the Gulf war through weekly reflections on the course of the war, as it played through out on television. Drawing on research for my book *The Persian Gulf TV War* (Westview, 1992), I utilize fragmentary observations to try to convey a sense of the immorality of the war and the media coverage without resorting to foundationist arguments.

Kellner, Douglas M (ed). *Postmodernism/ Jameson/ Critique*. Washington, Maisonneuve Pr, 1989.

The book interrogates the relations between the work of Fredric Jameson and postmodern theory. Jameson, often considered the most important English-language Marxist literary critic, has attempted to produce syntheses of Marxism and postmodern theory. His article, "Postmodernism, the Cultural Logic of Capital," has been perhaps the most influential article of the past decade and has been a key marker in the debates over postmodernism. The volume contains a series of articles introducing Jameson's thought and criticizing his work from a variety of post-structuralist positions. (edited)

Kellogg, Frederic R. A Pragmatic Theory of Legal Classification in Peirce and Law, Kevelson, Roberta. New York, Lang, 1991.

Kelly, Christopher. Rousseau on the Foundation of National Cultures. *Hist Euro Ideas*, 16(4-6), 521-525, Ja 93.

Rousseau's political thought combines a radical attachment to individualism and a novel endorsement of nationalism. His account of human beings as radically asocial leads him to support the development of unnaturals, and, to some extent arbitrary, feelings as necessary for the foundation of any soical unity. Unlike other supporters of national cultures, Rousseau insists that nations are only preconditions for sound political life which requires, in addition, the self-conscious work of legislators free of national prejudice.

Kelly, David A. The Highest Chinadom in Nietzsche and Asian Thought, Parkes, Graham R (ed). Chicago, Univ of Chicago Pr, 1991.

Through this century, Chinese intellectuals have forged an ethos of moral rebellion from the thought of Nietzsche. Even where it vulgarizes its model, Chinese Nietzscheanism reveals radical dilemmas of Chinese culture: the experience of modernity as a state of continual crisis characterized by nihilism, and an abiding metaphysical hunger which fuels both dictatorship and dreams of liberation. Earlier disciples of Nietzsche—Lu Xun (1881-1936), Lie Shicen (1892-1934), the war-time fascist *Zhanguo Ce* (Warring States) group—are described. An account of the orthodox Communist critique introduces the startling figure of Liu Xiaobo (1955-), a key figure in the Tiananmen tragedy of 1989.

Kelly, Kevin T and Glymour, Clark. Inductive Inference from Theory Laden Data. *J Phil Log*, 21(4), 391-444, N 92.

A familiar conception of scientific inquiry portrays the scientist as attempting to converge to the truth about some hypothesis under study. Formal learning theorists attempt to determine when there exists a method that is guaranteed to do so and when there does not. Learning theoretic analysis assumes, however, that there is a fixed language of inquiry and that the scientist receives data whose meaning and truth value is fixed. Philosophical relativists hold, to the contrary, that truth, meaning, and observability can shift as a function of what the process of inquiry does, or of what the inquirer believes. In this paper, we propose a generalization of the learning-theoretic framework in which the aim of science is to arrive at one's own truth given that the truth depends upon how one conducts inquiry. (edited)

Kelsay, John. Islam and the Distinction between Combatants and Noncombatants in *Cross, Crescent, and Sword*, Johnson, James Turner (ed). Westport, Greenwood Pr, 1990.

"Combatancy" and "noncombatancy" came gradually to be established concepts in Europe as various institutions strove to find a viable way to honor the moral concern to discriminate between the just and the unjust in war. The Islamic tradition underwent a similar development, yet religious considerations particular to Islam led to specifications of "just" and "unjust" different from those of the just war tradition. Islam does not show evidence of a distinction between combatancy and noncombatancy as such. It does, however, develop rules for the conduct of war consistent with the desire to discriminate between the guilty and the innocent on the enemy side.

Kelsay, John (ed) and Johnson, James Turner (ed). *Cross, Crescent, and Sword*. Westport, Greenwood Pr, 1990.

Kelter, Irving A. Paolo Foscarini's *Letter to Galileo*: The Search for Proofs of the Earth's Motion. *Mod Sch*, 70(1), 31-44, N 92.

Kemal, Salim. *The Poetics of Alfarabi and Avicenna*. Leiden, Brill, 1991.

The book undertakes a philosophical analysis of commentaries and essays on Aristotle's *Poetics* by the Medieval Arabic philosophers Alfarabi and Avicenna.

Kemal, Salim (ed) and Gaskell, Ivan (ed). *The Language of Art History*. New York, Cambridge Univ Pr, 1991.

The first volume in the series "Cambridge Studies in Philosophy and the Arts" offers a range of responses by distinguished philosophers and art historians to some crucial issues generated by the relationship between the art object and language in art history. Each of the chapters in this volume is a searching response to theoretical and practical questions, in terms accessible to readers of all human science disciplines. The issues they discuss challenge the boundaries to thought that some contemporary theorizing sustains. (edited)

Kemiläinen, Aira. Romanticist and Realist Elements in Nationalist Thinking in the 19th Century. *Hist Euro Ideas*, 16(1-3), 307-314, Ja 93.

The Idea of Nationalism has often been considered to be an expression of the Romanticist Movement which regarded a nation as individual, emphasized the importance of national language and spoke about national soul. The purpose of this study is to say that the nationalism was brought about by real needs created by the modern development of culture and economic progress. This course of things was possible only by means of close connections between government and citizens. If some population didn't understand the official language and had no school education, they stressed the importance of language and nationality.

Kemmerling, Andreas. The Visual Room in Wittgenstein's Philosophical Investigations, Arrington, Robert L (ed). New York, Routledge, 1991.

This is an attempt at understanding section 398 of the *Philosophical Investigations*. Wittgenstein attacks a conception of what it is to have (visual) ideas. According to this conception, having such ideas is something essentially subjective: necessarily, if somebody has a particular idea, nobody else has it. This can be construed in two different ways. Wittgenstein raises some interesting points against the reading of the subjectivity-thesis in the first paragraph of section 398, he argues unconvincingly against the other reading in the second paragraph, and it is hard to figure out what he is up to in the third paragraph.

Kemp, Kenneth W. Conscientious Objection. *Pub Affairs Quart*, 7(4), 303-324, O 93.

This paper discusses both moral and political aspects of conscientious objection. It attempts to work out the details of exactly when a just-war theorist must refuse to perform military service or to fight. With respect to the political question, the article argues that it is not always necessary for the state to respect what it sees as an erroneous conscience and there are practical problems that must be overcome, especially the determination of sincerity for selective conscientious objectors. Nevertheless, conscience should be respected when possible; we should seek ways of overcoming the practical problems.

Kemp, Peter. Bioethics and Ethics of Nature. *Aquinas*, 35(3), 661-671, S-D 92.

Kendree, Jack M and Cleary, Claudia M. Development of Ethical Awareness: A Model for a Community Business Ethics Forum. *Bus Prof Ethics J*, 11(3-4), 179-186, Fall-Wint 92.

Based on the premise that ethical awareness begins with understanding through dialogue, the Community Business Ethics Forum was organized. Ten business leaders representing the ethnic, professional and gender diversity of the community were invited and facilitated by a Philosophy and a Business professor. After basic instruction in vocabulary and theory, members brought their own cases to the table for discussion. Community outreach work was achieved. Heightened ethical awareness resulted in members forming ethical sounding boards in their own businesses, two members changing jobs and ethical forums being formed in churches, clubs, etc.

Kennedy, David. Why Philosophy for Children Now?. *Thinking*, 10(3), 2-6, 1993.

Kennedy, Ralph. Professor Chisholm and the Problem of the Speckled Hen. *J Phil Res*, 18, 143-147, 1993.

The Problem of the Speckled Hen is a potential stumbling-block for any philosophical treatment of perceptual certainty. Roderick Chisholm argues in the third edition of his *Theory of Knowledge* (Prentice Hall, 1989) that the Speckled Hen is not a problem for the account of the perceptually certain contained in that book. In this note, I argue that Chisholm's defense of his account does not work.

Kennedy, Terence. An Italian View of the Debate on Virtue. *Thomist*, 57(1), 123-130, Ja 93.

Kennett, Stephen and Russell, Robert and Price, Thomas. An Interview with A J Ayer. *Kinesis*, 19(1), 28-55, Spr 93.

Kenny, Anthony. *Aquinas on Mind*. New York, Routledge, 1993.

The aim of the book is to make accessible parts of Aquinas's philosophy of mind which have enduring value. The kernel of the work is a close reading of the sections of the *Summa Theologiae* which are devoted to human intellect and will add to the relationship between soul and body.

Kenny, Anthony. *Aristotle on the Perfect Life*. New York, Clarendon/Oxford Pr, 1992.

In the last twenty years many scholars have discussed Aristotle's ethical reaching on the topic of happiness. Is perfect happiness to be found only in contemplation (as *Nicomachean Ethics* suggests) or in the practice of all the virtues (as some have argued on the basis of NEI)? This book argues that the solution to the problem is to be found in a close study of *Eudemian Ethics*.

Kenny, V and Boxer, P. Lacan and Maturana: Constructivist Origins for a Third-Order Cybernetics. *Commun Cog*, 25(1), 73-100, 1992.

We examine some difficulties in the use made of second-order cybernetics, and the absence within radical constructivism of a theory of the subject. We introduce Lacan's approach to the subject particularly in the structure of discourse. We consider the implications this conception has both in the need for a third-order cybernetics, and for a formulation of an ethics based on calling into question the subject's relation to this third order as it manifests itself in transference.

Kent, Thomas. Hermeneutical Terror and the Myth of Interpretive Consensus. *Phil Rhet*, 25(2), 124-139, 1992.

This article examines Jean-Francois Lyotard's claim that interpretative consensus represents a powerful myth, a species of metadiscourse that partakes of the master-narrative of emancipation. By appealing to the master-narrative of emancipation, consensus—according to Lyotard—becomes a legitimate form of terror in the sense that players in a language-game may be conveniently silenced or omitted entirely if they do not conform to the consensus operating within a discourse community. Finally, consensus requires us to conform and to forget that if we wish to communicate at all, we not only must observe the grammar inherent within a language-game, we also must perform by *employing* the grammar of the language-game.

Kent, Thomas. Hermeneutics and Genre: Bakhtin and the Problem of Communicative Interaction in The Interpretive Turn, Hiley, David R (ed). Ithaca, Cornell Univ Pr, 1991.

Employing an anti-Cartesian or externalist account of language, M M Bakhtin maintains that the speech genre constitutes the most fundamental element of communicative interaction. By concentrating on Bakhtin's conception of communicative interaction, this essay argues that a *genre* corresponds to an open-ended and uncodifiable strategy for hermeneutic guessing which, in turn, requires us to rethink our notions about the possibility of describing discourse production and reception as reductive cognitive processes of one kind or another. This Bakhtinian conception of communicative interaction also requires us to relinquish the hope for hermeneutical certainty or for what some have called interpretive monism.

Keohane, Kieran. Central Problems in the Philosophy of the Social Sciences after Postmodernism. *Phil Soc Crit*, 19(2), 145-169, 1993.

Keown, John. Courting Euthanasia? Tony Bland and the Law Lords. *Ethics Med*, 9(3), 34-36, Autumn 93.

Kerans, Patrick and Drover, Glen. Wellbeing and Everyday Practice: Theorizing Claimsmaking. *Praxis Int*, 13(2), 172-191, Jl 93.

Kerdeman, Deborah. Educating Ethical Behavior: Aristotle's Views on Akrasia. *Proc Phil Educ*, 48, 81-89, 1992.

Kerman, Deborah E. Mencius and Kant on Moral Failure. *J Chin Phil*, 19(3), 309-328, S 92.

Kern, Iso and Bernet, Rudolf and Marbach, Eduard. *An Introduction to Husserlian Phenomenology*. Evanston, Northwestern Univ Pr, 1993.

The book presents Husserl's philosophy in its chronological development, but also emphasizes the unity of the whole project by showing the systematic interconnections between the basic themes and notions. The authors elucidate Husserl's conceptual development by way of relating his own publications to his many research manuscripts, depicting the broadening of the research program from the early static-descriptive to the genetic-explanatory phenomenology, and presenting Husserl's overall conception of philosophy.

Kern, Udo. "Es ist uns aber bestimmt, von Überzeugungen, die wir aus innerer Notwendigkeit denken, zu leben". *Frei Z Phil Theol*, 39(1-2), 77-104, 1992.

Albert Schweitzers elementares ethisches Vernunftdenken ist das Thema: Vernunft ist Erkennen von Leben. Alles Wissen von Leben ist Staunen über das nichtauslotbare Rätsel des Lebens, führt zur Ehrfurcht vor dem Leben. Notwendig ist durch die vielen Einzelnen elementares Denken, das den Willen zum Leben teleogisiert. So wird der Mensch als Denkender und Freier effizienter Träger einer heute weitgehend entbehrten ethischen Kultur. Ethisches Primärsubjekt ist der Einzelne und nicht die Kollektivitäten. Nur durch ethische Vernunftideale kommen wir in ein normales Verhältnis zur Wirklichkeit. Elementares Denken und elementare Religion entsprechen einander. Schweitzer versteht sich als "schlichter Wegbereiter" einer neuen Renaissance, in der das Ethische als "die höchste Wahrheit und Zweckmässigkeit" gilt.

Kernohan, Andrew. Accumulative Harms and the Interpretation of the Harm Principle. *Soc Theor Pract*, 19(1), 51-72, Spr 93.

Accumulative harms, following Feinberg, are harms brought about by the innocuous activities of large numbers of individuals, where the harm cannot be imputed or assigned in any way to the individuals. Multiple source pollution is a good example. This article argues for interpreting the Harm Principle as permitting interference with actions in order to prevent accumulative harms to others, even though the actions in question cannot be imputed any share in the causation of harm. This interpretation is defended against libertarian and other objections.

Kernohan, Andrew. Desert and Self-Ownership. *J Value Inq*, 27(2), 197-202, Ap 93.

Kerr, Fergus. Getting the Subject Back into the World: Heidegger's Version in Human Beings, Cockburn, David (ed). New York, Cambridge Univ Pr, 1991.

Kerr, Fergus. Rescuing Girard's Argument?. *Mod Theol*, 8(4), 385-399, Oct 92.

Kerr, Fergus. Revealing the Scapegoat Mechanism in Philosophy, Religion and the Spiritual Life, McGhee, Michael (ed). New York, Cambridge Univ Pr, 1992.

Kerr, Fergus. Revealing the Scapegoat Mechanism: Christianity after Girard. *Philosophy*, 32(Supp), 161-175, 1992.

Kerr-Lawson, Angus. An Abulensean Pragmatist?. *Bull Santayana Soc*, 10, 17-21, Fall 92.

Several recent commentaries on Santayana have pointed out features of his philosophy which are common to the school of pragmatism. This paper argues that, on balance, very little of Santayana's thought is close to a pragmatist perspective, apart from a certain symbolic account of knowledge.

Kerr-Lawson, Angus. Realms and Hierarchies. *Bull Santayana Soc*, 10, 32-34, Fall 92.

Santayana's later philosophy has a strong ontological focus, as displayed in his four realms of being. To some, this has suggested a hierarchical, comprehensive, platonic philosophy. I argue that the realms are instead applied in a contrastive fashion, where they are stretched as far as possible from each other. This is not compatible with hierarchy.

Kerr-Lawson, Angus. Stripped Down Burch. *Trans Peirce Soc*, 28(3), 523-546, Sum 92.

Kersting, Wolfgang. Kant's Concept of the State in Essays on Kant's Political Philosophy, Williams, Howard (ed). Chicago, Univ of Chicago Pr, 1992.

Kersting, Wolfgang. Politics, Freedom, and Order in The Cambridge Companion to Kant, Guyer, Paul (ed). New York, Cambridge Univ Pr, 1992.

Kerszberg, Pierre. From Metaphysics to Physics and Back. *Phil Books*, 34(4), 207-213, O 93.

Kerszberg, Pierre. Possible Versus Potential Universes. *J Speculative Phil*, 7(1), 1-20, 1993.

Various areas of contemporary natural science are based on the assumption that time is an explanatory factor. The philosophical problems associated with this assumption are examined in relation to recent developments in quantum cosmology, where the concept of "creation" is supposed to receive an explanation in terms of physical categories. A shift from possibility to potentiality is needed in order to justify this explanation. The limits inherent in this shift are evaluated critically.

Kesselring, Thomas. Philosophieren in Brasilien—oder: Wie tief ist der Abgrund zwischen Theorie und Realität?. *Frei Z Phil Theol*, 39(3), 369-390, 1992.

The article deals with: 1) The role of academic philosophy in the Brazilian society—a society divided into two extremely different parts: the rich or educated and the poor or marginals; 2) the history of philosophy in Brazil; 3) its dependency on European and American academic philosophy, and; 4) its search for a genuine South American way of thinking; 5) finally, some suggestions are given concerning the subjects a so-called *Philosophy of Liberation* (inspired by the *Theology of Liberation*) might deal with.

Kesserling, Thomas. Die Krise der Gegenwart und die Verantwortung der Philosophie (Vittorio Hösle). *Frei Z Phil Theol*, 39(1-2), 195-205, 1992.

The article is a review of Professor V Hoesle's book, *Die Krise der Gegenwart und die Verantwortung der Philosophie* (The Present Time's Crisis and the Responsibility of Philosophy), Munique (Beck), 1989. The book contains, first, a severe critique of the widespread relativism preventing the academic philosophy from dealing with the main challenges of present time; second, a reconstruction of K O Apel's 'Transcendental Pragmatics' and, third, an introduction into 'Objective Idealism', presented by Hoesle as a 'synthesis' of Naturalism and Subjective Idealism. The review stresses the author's claim that the total separation of natural sciences and ethics may be one of the ecological crisis' main reasons. But the author's foundation of an 'objective idealistic' ethics is not yet convincing.

Kessler, Gary E. *Voices of Wisdom: A Multicultural Philosophy Reader*. Belmont, Wadsworth, 1992.

This book is designed to be used to introduce students to the study of philosophy in a multicultural framework. In addition to classic Western material, the book presents Buddhist, African, Chinese, Hindu, Native American, African-American, Feminist, Islamic, and Hispanic views in a topical framework. Problems in ethics, political philosophy, metaphysics, epistemology, and religious philosophy are discussed. There are introductions that provide students with necessary background information and a set of reading questions to aid the student in reading the selections.

Kessler, Herbert. *Die Welt des Menschen*. Sankt Augustin, Academia, 1992.

Ketchum, Richard J. A Note on Barnes's Parmenides. *Phronesis*, 38(1), 95-97, 1993.

I argue that the formalized version of Jonathan Barnes' reconstruction of Parmenides argument for the conclusion that whatever any student studies exists [*The Presocratic Philosophers*, Routledge and Kegan Paul (London, 1982) pp. 155-175.] confuses the claim, "it is not the case that everything that anyone studies exists" with "nothing anyone studies exists." I then provide an alternative reconstruction which saves most of what Barnes has to say about the argument including the claim that the argument is valid. I respond to an objection to the reformulation.

Keulman, Kenneth. *The Balance of Consciousness: Eric Voegelin's Political Theory*. University Park, Penn St Univ Pr, 1991.

Keutner, Thomas. Mundus est fabula: Descartes und das Problem der Repräsentation in Diagrammatik und Philosophie, Gehring, Petra (ed). Amsterdam, Rodopi, 1992.

Against the background of his comprehensive history of the controversy between instrumentalism and realism, Pierre Duhem has emphasized the role of Descartes as the champion of the instrumentalistic "esprit geometrique". The article asks whether this evaluation is still valid and whether Duhem's thesis is true, that models have no place in science, in the strict sense.

Kevelson, Roberta (ed). *Action and Agency*. New York, Lang, 1991.

The collection of papers addresses selected critical issues of intention, property relations, reference and authority which relate to the general sociolegal topics of Action and Agency. This collection, form several academic perspectives, is unified under the special viewpoint of legal semiotics. Charles Peirce's philosophy and continental hermeneutics are the two main philosophical approaches represented here.

Kevelson, Roberta 544 AUTHOR INDEX WITH ABSTRACTS

Kevelson, Roberta (ed). *Law and the Human Sciences*. New York, Lang, 1992.

Law and the Human Sciences is a collection of inquiries from the crossdisciplinary, transcultural perspective of legal semiotics, which focuses on the relations between the humanistic sciences as mediated by the many dimensions of law. Theory and practice of the law is regarded as a paradigm for investigating analogous issues in the "human sciences". This volume serves as major reference for studies in the philosophy of signs.

Kevelson, Roberta. Peirce and Community in Peirce and Law, Kevelson, Roberta. New York, Lang, 1991.

Kevelson, Roberta. *Peirce and Law*. New York, Lang, 1991.

Kevelson, Roberta. *Peirce's Esthetics of Freedom: Possibility, Complexity, and Emergent Value*. New York, Lang, 1993.

According to Peirce, the value of the idea of freedom arises only to oppose the idea of necessity. Freedom emerges as a working value, a primary esthetic principle, in response to that which is perceived as fixed, determined, necessary, absolute. The idea of freedom materializes, assumes a million appearances, wears its ten million masks... ...Freedom as the freedom-to-focus is a Peircean esthetic process that becomes realized through the three stages of fragment/fractal, fact, form. This triadic process corresponds to the semiotic functions of icon, index, symbol. Freedom's course is nonlineal, self-corrective, dynamic, open: Freedom is the occasion for chaos, and chaos is the locus of form.

Keyser, Paul. A Proposed Diagram in Aristotle *EN* V3, 1131a24-b20 for Distributive Justice in Proportion. *Apeiron*, 25(2), 135-144, Je 92.

Aristotle's discussion of distributive justice is formulated geometrically. There is an ambiguity in the text (kai to holon pros to holon, 1131b7-8, 14): what terms are combined to yield this whole? Aristotle was using a diagram of two divided lines, one for the persons, the other for their shares. These lines were drawn intersecting at their point of division, which allows one to elucidate the "to holon pros to holon" as meaning "the persons together to their shares together." For the evaluation of persons in distributive justice, Aristotle lists several possibilities (1131a24-9) but never restricts himself to one. But his willingness to treat the worths of persons as additive with shares here suggests he was thinking of wealth.

Keyser, Paul T. Cicero on Optics (Att 2.3.2). *Phoenix*, 47(1), 67-69, Spr 93.

Kfia, Lilianne Rivka. The Ontological Status of Mathematical Entities: The Necessity for Modern Physics of an Evaluation of Mathematical Systems. *Rev Metaph*, 47(1), 19-42, S 93.

Khalidi, Muhammad Ali. Carving Nature at the Joints. *Phil Sci*, 60(1), 100-113, Mr 93.

This paper discusses a philosophical issue in taxonomy. At least one philosopher has suggested the taxonomic principle that scientific kinds are disjoint. An opposing position is defended here by marshalling examples of nondisjoint categories which belong to different, coexisting classification schemes. This denial of the disjointness principle can be recast as the claim that scientific classification is "interest-relative". But why would anyone have held that scientific categories are disjoint in the first place? It is argues that this assumption is needed in one attempt to derive essentialism. This shows why the essentialist and interest-relative approaches to classification are in conflict.

Khalil, Omar E. Artificial Decision-Making and Artificial Ethics: A Management Concern. *J Bus Ethics*, 12(4), 313-321, Ap 93.

The paper addresses an ethical concern when using the currently available expert systems in a decision-making capacity. This concern is basically due to three reasons: expert systems' lack of human intelligence, lack of emotions and values, and possible incorporation of intentional or accidental bias. For these reasons, artificial ethics seems to be science fiction. Consequently, expert systems should be used only in an advising capacity and managers should not absolve themselves from legal and ethical responsibility when using expert systems in decision making.

Khamara, Edward J. Leibniz' Theory of Space: A Reconstruction. *Phil Quart*, 43(173), 472-488, O 93.

The article offers an interpretation of Leibniz' relative theory of space which, while denying the possibility of a spatial world containing no material objects at all, allows for the possibility of unoccupied places, and preserves both the continuity of space and its infinite extent. The author concludes that Leibniz' theory is subtler and more interesting than it is commonly taken to be, and is not open to some of the allegedly serious objections that are currently held against it.

Khanin, Dmitry. Will Aesthetics Be the Last Stronghold of Marxism. *Phil Lit*, 16(2), 266-278, O 92.

The author, formerly a Soviet philosopher, formulates a three-part scheme used by Eastern-bloc theorists for analyses of "bourgeois conceptions." An examination of Terry Eagleton's works serves to prove that the same scheme is at work in Western Marxism. The main conclusion is that because of the methodology they employ Marxists just force new content into worn-out winebags. Exploring new subjects they only attempt the last-ditch defense of Marxist Orthodoxy.

Khatchadourian, Haig A. Philosophy and the Future in a Global Context. *Metaphilosophy*, 23(1-2), 25-33, Ja-Ap 92.

The article proposes a number of global goals for philosophers. They include 1) continued *rapprochement* between Anglo-American and continental philosophy, as well as *rapprochement* between them and Latin American, African and other non-Western philosophy; 2) revival of the Socratic quest for wisdom; and efforts to help create heightened awareness of humanity's oneness on this plant; 3) a return to the philosopher's role as the gadfly of society; 4) participation in worldwide efforts to create a moral and peaceful world; including the formulation of an enlightened universal secular-humanist ethic: a humanism embracing the ideal of man's respect for and harmony with nature everywhere.

Khatchadourian, Haig A. Terrorism and Morality in Applied Philosophy, Almond, Brenda (ed). New York, Routledge, 1992.

The paper addresses the fundamental issue of the morality of terrorism. It distinguishes four types of terrorism — "predatory," "retaliatory," "political" and "moralistic" — and argues that in all of them terrorism (in a "descriptive," value-neutral sense of the word) is always wrong. The paper considers the conceptual problem of defining 'terrorism, with the necessary modifications, of the Principles of Discrimination and of Proportion of "just war" theory. It argues that these conditions support the paper's central contention. Additional support is then found in the concept and principles of human rights. In the final section the paper evaluates Kai Nielsen's act-utilitarian support of so-called "revolutionary terrorism." Throughout the discussion is illustrated by actual examples for the recent past.

Kidd, Ian G. Theophrastus' Metereology, Aristotle and Posidonius in Theophrastus, Fortenbaugh, W W (ed). New Brunswick, Transaction Books, 1992.

The evidence for Theophrastus' *Meteorology* as reported in the fragments from the Syriac and Arabic translations reveals a work different from Aristotle's *Meteorology* in content and form, presenting theories which Aristotle had criticised and rejected, and others which are incompatible with Aristotle's conclusions, hypotheses and arguments. The key form of multiple causal explanation is not doxographic review, but an elemental classification of the variety of occurrence of similar phenomena. In later tradition such multiple explanation appealed to Epicureans and explains the extensive echoes in Lucretius VI. But Stoic and Peripatetic tradition from Posidonius on followed Aristotle not Theophrastus.

Kidd, James W. Dialogal Modes of Universalism. *Dialec Hum*, 17(3), 109-112, 1990.

Kienpointner, Manfred. Argumentation in Germany and Austria: An Overview of the Recent Literature. *Inform Log*, 13(3), 129-136, Fall 91.

This paper gives information about the study of argumentation in Austria and Germany. While there are still relatively few academic institutions in the field of rhetoric and argumentation, a rapidly increasing amount of research is done in disciplines like linguistics, literary criticism, philosophy and law. Relevant work as well as outstanding figures in current research are reviewed. Furthermore, activities such as conferences, the publication of journals and encyclopedias (esp. the historically orientated encyclopedia 'Historisches Wörterbuch der Rhetorik', which is being edited at the Institute of General Rhetoric of the University of Tübingen) are mentioned.

Kienzler, Klaus. "Nietzsche im christlichen Denken—am Beispiel Bernhard Weltes". *Theol Phil*, 66(3), 398-410, 1991.

Der Freiburger Religionsphilosoph Bernhard Welte (+1988) hat Friedrich Nietzsche in die christlichen Theologie als ernsthaften Gesprächspartner eingeführt. Im Sommersemester 1948 hat W eine Öffentliche Vorlesung "Nietzsche und das Problem des Atheismus" an der Universität Freiburg gehalten. Damit stellt sich W in die Reihe der grossen Nietzsche- Interpretationen dieser Zeit von Karl Jaspers einerseits und Martin Heidegger andererseits, mit denen W selbst intensiv im Gespräch war. W trägt dort eine Nietzsche- Interpretation vor, die auch heute noch Bedeutung hat. W hat seine Gedanken überarbeitet und 1958 das Buch "Nietzsches Atheismus und das Christentum" veröffentlicht. Darüber hinaus hat Friedrich Nietzsche zeitlebens für die Religionsphilosophie W's eine grosse Bedeutung behalten.

Kienzler, Wolfgang. What Is a Phenomenon? The Concept of Phenomenon in Husserl's Phenomenology in Analecta Husserliana, XXXIV, Tymieniecka, Anna-Teresa (ed). Dordrecht, Kluwer, 1992.

Kierans, Kenneth. The Concept of Ethical Life in Hegel's *Philosophy of Right*. *Hist Polit Thought*, 13(3), 417-435, Autumn 92.

In this essay I look at Hegel's position in light of the concluding passages of the *Philosophy of Right* on war and the endlessness of conflict within the historical realm. I argue that the seemingly endless freedom of modern society is a necessary element, though only an element, of his philosophical and theological exposition of the state. Commentators have not explained his insistence that modern freedom and ethical life can be both antagonistic and radically one.

Kiesow, Karl-Friedrich. Marty on Form and Content in Language in Mind, Meaning and Metaphysics, Mulligan, Kevin (ed). Dordrecht, Kluwer, 1990.

Kilcullen, John (trans) and McGrade, Arthur Stephen (ed). *William of Ockham: A Short Discourse on Tyrannical Government*. New York, Cambridge Univ Pr, 1992.

Kilmister, C W. Space, Time, Discreteness. *Philosophica*, 50(2), 55-71, 1992.

Kim, Jaegwon. Can Supervenience and 'Non-Strict Laws' Save Anomalous Monism? in Mental Causation, Heil, John (ed). New York, Clarendon/Oxford Pr, 1993.

In "Thinking Causes" (*Mental Causation*, ed John Heil), Davidson attempts to respond to his critics' claim that his "anomalous monism" leads to the causal impotence of mental properties. He does this by invoking mind-body supervenience and the existence of "nonstrict" psychophysical laws that might back mind-body causal claims. This paper examines Davidson's arguments and shows why his attempts do not succeed.

Kim, Jaegwon. The Non-Reductivist's Troubles with Mental Causation in Mental Causation, Heil, John (ed). New York, Clarendon/Oxford Pr, 1993.

Nonreductive physicalism arguably is the "received view" on the mind-body problem. This paper argues that it shares with emergentism many of its core tenents, and like emergentism it is committed to "downward causation". It further argues that downward causation has consequences that no physicalist should, or could, accept.

Kimmel, Larry D. The Sounds of Music: First Movement. *J Aes Educ*, 26(3), 55-65, Fall 92.

Kimmerle, Heinz. Non-Africans on African Philosophy: Steps to a Difficult Dialogue. *Quest*, 6(1), 69-77, Je 92.

King, James T. The Moral Theories of Kant and Hume: Comparisons and Polemics. *Hume Stud*, 18(2), 441-465, N 92.

King, Jeffrey C. Intentional Identity Generalized. *J Phil Log*, 22(1), 61-93, F 93.

Geach's problem of intentional identity concerned sentences such as 'Hob believes that a witch blighted Bob's mare and Nob believes she killed Cob's sow.' This sentence has a reading on which the quantifier in the first sentence ('a witch') takes narrow scope relative to the belief operator there, and on which the pronoun in the second conjunct is nonetheless anaphoric on that quantifier. Geach wondered what the semantic function of the pronoun is on this reading of the sentence. The present paper argues that the sentences noticed by Geach are instances of a more general phenomenon which includes more complex cases. As a result, any account of the pronoun in the Geach sentence (on the reading in question) must generalize to handle the more complex data if it is to be considered successful. Such an account is provided.

King, Peter J. Lycan on Lewis and Meinong. *Proc Aris Soc*, 93, 193-201, 1993.

In "Two — No, Three — Concepts of Possible Worlds" (1991; *Proceedings of the Aristotelian Society*) William Lycan criticises David Lewis's modal realism, arguing that it excludes the philosophically useful notion of impossible worlds. He dismisses Lewis's use of restricting modifiers, drawing upon Meinongian metaphysics. In this paper I counter Lycan's criticism, offering what I take to be a more accurate representation of Meinong's position, and arguing that it can be discussed *within* Lewisian realism without the need for impossibilia. I do not solve Lewis's admitted problem concerning impossible worlds, I merely try to clear the ground for a solution.

King, Peter O. Mediaeval Thought-Experiments in Thought Experiments in Science and Philosophy, Horowitz, Tamara (ed). Lanham, Rowman & Littlefield, 1991.

King, Richard H. *Freedom* by Orlando Patterson. *Hist Theor*, 31(3), 326-334, 1992.

This review-essay of Patterson's *Freedom* places this work in the tradition of Hegelian-inspired histories of the West. The way Patterson derives his "chordal triad" of freedom is examined and questions of a conceptual nature are raised: does Patterson need a positive-negative freedom distinction? Why is civic or participatory freedom relatively underplayed? And why does the biblically-derived idea of collective liveration receive scarcely any attention? How Patterson will complete his study in a planned second volume is unclear but it is safe to assume that the United States will become the main focus for a study of the fate of freedom under the conditions of modernity.

King, William L. Scruton and Reasons for Looking at Photographs. *Brit J Aes*, 32(3), 258-265, Jl 92.

King-Farlow, John. Conceptual Atomism and Nagarjuna's Sceptical Arguments. *Indian Phil Quart*, 19(1), 16-21, Ja 92.

"Conceptual Atomism", as proposed with seminal originality by Richard Bosley, is a term whose coverage includes fallacious reasoning from "A and B are conceptually distinguishable" to "A and B are distinct", to "A and B are separable", to "A and B are separate", etc. Hume's frequent "reductions" of causality to constant conjunction (hence necessity to contingency) underlie attacks on theists' cosmological arguments. Nagarjuna, a brilliant Buddhist sceptic of the Second Century A D, produced many nice arguments against Common Sense and earlier philosophical reasoning. Probing concepts of Separateness, Causality and Co-existence, Change, etc., Nagarjuna sought to undermine human thinking.

King-Farlow, John. From Dionysius to Eriugena: A Bridge for Voluntarism or "Divine Freedom"?. *Laval Theol Phil*, 48(3), 367-378, O 92.

The moving style and apparent echoes of truly Christian Platonism left the works of Dionysius the Pseudo-Areopagite long tempting to identify with nearly authoritative writings by a friend of Saint Paul. The latter would have really lived centuries before. Centuries later the genius of John Scotus Eriugena drew copiously on the Pseudo-Areopagite, Plato, the Scriptures, etc., to provide a dazzling system of philosophy and theology. While these systems are now recovering modern interest, their ontologically Monist character and their confused attempts to uphold God's omnipotence and other perfections by absorbing creatures, merit analytical reproof. Free Will and ontological Pluralism belong with the metaphysics of the Bible. It is hoped to re-introduce the visions of two often neglected heretics.

Kingdom, E and Arnaud, A J. *Women's Rights and the Rights of Man*. Oxford, Aberdeen, 1990.

Kingwell, Mark. Interpretation, Dialogue and the Just Citizen. *Phil Soc Crit*, 19(2), 115-144, 1993.

The liberal project of justification through abstraction — modelled in the priority of right thesis — has come under increasing attack in recent years. In particular, it has been argued that priority-of-right theories empty political life of its *sittlich* meaning. This paper begins with that attack and uses two important aspects of it, the restoration of context and the focus on virtues to motivate a new look at the prospects for liberalism when conceived as an *interpretive* theory. What emerges, through discussions of Habermas and Rorty is a renewed sense of the necessary virtues of citizenship, especially a commitment of civility in the ongoing social dialogue of legitimation.

Kingwell, Mark. Is It Rational To Be Polite?. *J Phil*, 90(8), 387-404, Ag 93.

Kinney, Timothy P. Logic and Psychology: Russell's Theory of Knowledge. *Dialogue (PST)*, 34(2-3), 33-43, Ap 92.

Kinz, Susan. Augustine's Erotic Ascent. *Cont Phil*, 15(1), 11-15, Ja-F 93.

This article attempts to look at the three ascents of Augustine—his neoplatonic ascent of Book 7, the conversion in the garden in Book 8, and the dialogical ascent with Monica in Book 9—through the perspective of the three ascents of Plato's Eros—the divided line and the myth of the cave of the Republic, the myth of the soul in the Phaedrus, and the erotic ascent described by Diotima in the Symposium—in order to uncover the erotic structure underlying Augustine's project and how that structure manifests itself in his relationship with God.

Kinzer, Bruce L. John Stuart Mill and the Catholic Question in 1825. *Utilitas*, 5(1), 49-67, My 93.

The chief purpose of this article is to examine the ways in which Mill's youthful political sectarianism shaped his response to the Catholic Question in the mid-1820s. The examination derives principally from a lengthy article Mill wrote on the subject for the *Parliamentary History and Review*, a short-lived Benthamite journal. The article concludes that Mill's sectarianism led him to adopt a radical and relentless consequentialist position on the various aspects of the issue, a position governed in particular by his preoccupation with the question of who exercised power over whom, and with what results.

Kirby, Brian S. Descartes, Contradiction, and Time. *Hist Phil Quart*, 10(2), 137-145, Ap 93.

Early in the third Meditation, Descartes entertains the thought that although he is presently alive it might some day be true to say that he had never lived. He thinks of this as a "manifest contradiction". In this essay, I propose a way in which an Evil Genius could consistently construct a world in which this situation obtained. The proposal depends upon Descartes' conception of time as consisting of discrete independent moments which depend for their veridical sequential arrangement on the will of God. As a result, manifest contradiction in this case is conceptual impossibility rather than logical contradiction.

Kirby, Kris N. Certainty, Reliability, and Visual Images. *Mind Lang*, 7(4), 402-408, Wint 92.

This article is a brief commentary on another article "Visualizing as a Means of Geometrical Discover", by Marcus Giaquinto (Winter, 1992), *Mind and Language*, 7(4), 364-401.

Kirby, Kris N. Intensity of Stimulation, Necessary Truths, and the Acquisition of Numeracy. *Mind Lang*, 7(4), 359-363, Wint 92.

This article is a brief commentary on another article "Evidence against empiricist accounts of the origins of numerical knowledge", by Karen Wynn (Winter, 1992), *Mind and Language*, 7(4), 315-332. (edited)

Kirk, James. Bernhardt's Philosophy and the Study of World Religions in God, Values, and Empiricism, Peden, Creighton (ed). Macon, Mercer Univ Pr, 1989.

Kirk, Robert. Consciousness and Concepts—I. *Aris Soc*, Supp(66), 23-40, 1992.

Kirk, Robert. Indeterminacy of Interpretation, Idealization, and Norms. *Phil Stud*, 70(2), 213-223, My 93.

In "Real Patterns", Dennett points out that all interpretation involves idealisation. But he is mistaken in assuming that idealisation inevitably makes room for a strong variety of indeterminacy. Intentional interpretations have to satisfy various strong constraints. And when there are norms governing the interpretation of ground-level data, idealisation doesn't necessarily bring indeterminacy with it. Since Dennett's argument from idealisation takes no account of that fact, it fails. He might give up his argument from idealisation and defend the 'domestic' version of Quine's indeterminacy thesis. But that would expose him to my counter-argument in *Translation Determined*.

Kirk, Robert. 'The Best Set of Tools'? Dennett's Metaphors and the Mind-Body Problem. *Phil Quart*, 43(172), 335-343, Jl 93.

In *Consciousness Explained* Dennett offers new 'ways of thinking', new metaphors, which he hopes will let us 'see how the traditional paradoxes and mysteries of consciousness can be resolved'. I argue that his two main metaphors are not much help for philosophical purposes. That of 'Joycean machines' is no use because, among other things, it cannot matter whether the underlying architecture is serial or parallel; nor whether the machine is virtual or hard-wired. The metaphor of 'multiple drafts' is also seriously flawed; and the associated ideas of 'probing' and 'narrative precipitation' are unilluminating.

Kirkeby, O F. Dual Textuality and the Phenomenology of Events: On Some Conceptual Problems in the Article by M H Bickhard and R L Campbell. *J Prag*, 17(5-6), 483-490, Je 92.

To criticize any possibility of a model-theoretic approach in cognitive science. This critical platform is developed by hand of the epistemological assumption that existence is situational and analytically accessible through the conceptual framework of *Dual Textuality*. Both the external and the internal world have textual quality and thus you cannot step outside of the situation in order to formalize without the result of an infinite regression. For a theory of science this should question any possibility of an analytical approach within the social and the human sciences and thus within cognitive science.

Kirkham, Richard. *Theories of Truth: A Critical Introduction*. Cambridge, MIT Pr, 1992.

A study of theories of truth and related topics; including, but not limited to, the correspondence, coherence, pragmatic, performative, prosentential, redundancy, and semantic theories; and the liar paradox, the Davidson program, Dummett, and physicalism. It is argued that when the different projects for which theories of truth are created are disentangled it turns out that many theories of truth often thought to be competitors with one another are not so. The correspondence theory is defended, but is shown to have far fewer metaphysical, epistemological, and semantic implications than is usually thought.

Kirkham, Richard L. Tarski's Physicalism. *Erkenntnis*, 38(3), 289-302, My 93.

Hartry Field has argued that Alfred Tarski desired to reduce all semantic concepts to concepts acceptable to physicalism and that Tarski failed to do this. In the two succeeding decades, Field has been charged with being too lenient with Tarski; but it has been almost universally accepted that an objection at least as strong as Field's is telling against Tarski's theory. Close examination of the relevant literature, most of it printed in this journal in the 1930s, reveals that Field's conception of physicalism is anachronistic. Tarski did succeed in furthering the sort of physicalist program he had in mind.

Kirkpatrick, Frank G. Together Bound: A New Look at God's Discrete Actions in History. *Int J Phil Relig*, 32(3), 129-147, D 92.

Particular divine actions alongside the acts of other agents are often declared to be impossible out of a fear that they will be rendered subject to casual law. This study argues that the understanding of divine action, similar to that of human action, requires a distinction between the free initiation of an act and the casual mechanisms through which it is carried to completion, thus providing a place for freedom in action that neither contradicts casual law nor is subsumable under it. This freedom is attributable to God and, therefore, to specific divine acts in history.

Kirmmse, Bruce. Call Me Ishmael—Call Everybody Ishmael in Foundations of Kierkegaard's Vision of Community, Connell, George B (ed). Atlantic Highlands, Humanities Pr, 1992.

The article examines Kierkegaard's social thought. After situating Kierkegaard in the context of modern individualism, it examines his critique of various modern forms of deification of the social order, giving particular attention to the dangers inherent in the post-1848 "People's Church", with its implication that religion is the property of the sovereign people. Finally, the article examines Kierkegaard's proposed cure, namely that modern society take seriously the full implications of its radical individualism: each of us must exist as an individual before God, seeing our "Neighbor" in the faces of the people we meet. We can thus be individuals without being alone.

Kirscher, Gilbert. La Philosophie Morale d'Eric Weil et la fondation de la loi morale. Arch Phil, 56(1), 29-51, Ja-Mr 93.

Contrary to the contemporary philosophical discourses, E Weil's Philosophie Morale (Paris, 1961) resumes in his essential part of the Kantian idea of the moral law. But E Weil displaces the problem of foundation, proceeding by the method of "genetical analysis" which conciliates "phenomenological development" and "encyclopaedic exposition." The way of apories of the moral reflexion leads into the philosophical self-consciousness of the moral question as a question, and as an irreducible question, in other words as a question stated to a freedom which has, without reason, already chosen the reason.

Kitchener, Richard F. Towards a Critical Philosophy of Science in New Horizons in the Philosophy of Science, Lamb, David (ed). Brookfield, Avebury, 1992.

Kitcher, Philip. Knowledge, Society, and History. Can J Phil, 23(2), 155-1177, Je 93.

Kitcher, Philip. The Advancement of Science: Science without Legend, Objectivity without Illusions. New York, Oxford Univ Pr, 1993.

Kitcher, Philip. The Evolution of Human Altruism. J Phil, 90(10), 497-516, O 93.

Kitromilides, Paschalis M. The Idea of Science in the Modern Greek Enlightenment in Greek Studies in the Philosophy and History of Science, Nicolacopoulos, Pantelis (ed). Dordrecht, Kluwer, 1990.

The study argues that a consideration of the impact of modern scientific ideas on Greek thought in the course of the eighteenth century may prove useful for an understanding of the Enlightenment as a form of cultural criticism. To this end the study surveys the transition from Neo-Aristotelianism to modern science and the embattled reception of Newtonian theories in Greek culture. Special attention is paid to the elaboration of the modern scientific attitude by means of an examination of the views of three major figures of the Modern Greek Enlightenment, Eugenios Voulgaris, Iosipos Moisiodax and Veniamin Lesvios. Reference is also made to the views of other important contributors to the debate on the interpretation of nature in Greek thought, such as Nikiphoros Theotokis and Nicolaos Zerzoulis, Newton's first translator into Greek.

Kivy, Peter. Auditor's Emotions: Contention, Concession and Compromise. J Aes Art Crit, 51(1), 1-12, Wint 93.

It is argued in the present paper that although music has a tendency to arouse sadness when it is sad, happiness when it is happy, this tendency is defeated in the listening experience of many sophisticated listeners who perceive emotions in the music, but do not feel those emotions in so doing.

Kivy, Peter. Differences (The Presidential Address). J Aes Art Crit, 51(2), 123-132, Spr 93.

The philosophical legacy of the eighteenth century, to the discipline of aesthetics, was the task of defining art: finding the common defining property (or properties) of those arts which the century itself formed into what P O Kristeller aptly named "The Modern System of the Arts." It is argued in the present paper that the task as stated may well be impossible because, in certain respects, the "System" is malformed: in particular, absolute music is singled out as not a fine art at all, and the novel not one of the representational arts.

Kivy, Peter. Hutcheson's Idea of Beauty: Simple or Complex?. J Aes Art Crit, 50(3), 243-245, Sum 92.

I have argued in previous publications that for Francis Hutcheson the idea of beauty is a simple idea (in Locke's sense). It has been argued recently by Dabney Townsend that the idea of beauty is a complex idea. In the present paper I defend my position against Townsend's.

Kivy, Peter. Kant and the "Affektenlehre": What He Said, and What I Wish He Had Said in Kant's Aesthetics, Meerbote, Ralf (ed). Atascadero, Ridgeview, 1991.

I argue in the present paper that Kant had at least the vague outline of a new, more plausible way to deal with the emotive content of music, derived from his notion of the aesthetic ideas. But I conclude that, in the end, he did not realize the promise of his insight and cashed it out merely with some kind of "physiological" account, not very much different in principle from the kind many of his lesser contemporaries offered.

Kivy, Peter. Oh Boy! You Too! Aesthetic Emotivism Reexamined in The Philosophy of A J Ayer, Hahn, Lewis Edwin (ed). Peru, Open Court, 1992.

I argue in the present paper that the easy transition Ayer and other ethical emotivists make from ethical to aesthetic emotivism is unwarranted. It is generally assumed, as Ayer does, that the same arguments will serve for both. What I try to show is that things which may seem at least initially plausible in emotivist ethics do not in aesthetics even have that initial plausibility.

Kivy, Peter. Something I've Always Wanted to Know About Hanslick. J Aes Art Crit, 46(3), 413-417, Spr 88.

In a crucial passage of his monograph, The Beautiful in Music, Eduard Hanslick suggests that music can be emotively appropriate or inappropriate to a text, thus seeming to contradict his well-known denial that music can have a definite emotive character. This contradiction is explored and confirmed in the present paper.

Kivy, Peter. The Fine Art of Repetition: Essays in the Philosophy of Music. New York, Cambridge Univ Pr, 1993.

The present volume contains essays by the author ranging over a thirty-year period,

from 1959 to 1993, three of which are published here for the first time. The essays deal, in general, with what might be called "the philosophy of music," and are of two kinds: those which concern themselves with the history of the subject, particularly the eighteenth century, and those directed at current issues in the discipline.

Kjaer, Grethe. The Role of Folk and Fairy Tales in Kierkegaard's Authorship in Kierkegaard on Art and Communication, Pattison, George (ed). New York, St Martin's Pr, 1992.

Kjellberg, Paul. The Butterfly as Companion: Meditations on the First Three Chapters of the Chuang Tzu: Review. Phil East West, 43(1), 127-135, Ja 93.

In his book The Butterfly as Companion, Kwang-ming Wu reads Chuang Tzu as advocating a kind of participatory relativism, which is evident not only in his philosophical ideas themselves but more importantly is his presentation of those ideas. Having delineated various facets of Wu's argument, the latter part of this review raises some concerns about it both as a reading of the text and as a philosophical position in its own right.

Klagge, James C (ed) and Nordmann, Alfred (ed) and Wittgenstein, Ludwig. Philosophical Occasions: 1912-1951—Ludwig Wittgenstein. Indianapolis, Hackett, 1993.

Shorter writings by or deriving from Wittgenstein, in German and English. Brief introductions describe the circumstances of origin of each piece. Contents: Review of Coffey's Science of Logic, Letters to Eccles, Preface to the Wörterbuch, "Some Remarks on Logical Form," Lecture on Ethics, Moore's Lecture Notes, "Remarks on Frazer," Letter to Mind, "Philosophy" (from the Big Typescript), "Notes for Lectures on 'Private Experience' and 'Sense Data'" (reedited and significantly expanded), Rhees' Lecture Notes on Freedom of the Will, "Notes for the 'Philosophical Lecture'" (previously unpublished), Letters to von Wright, and a new edition of von Wright's "The Wittgenstein Papers".

Klaghofer-Treitler, Wolfgang. Homo capax Dei?. Frei Z Phil Theol, 39(1-2), 155-179, 1992.

How can man justify his thinking of and talking about God? Which are the presuppositions of this matter in question? One main issue may serve as a justifiable answer: Beyond the past and present attempts of the mythologies and their dissolutions, of the analogia entis, the "proofs" of God's existence, and the theologia negative we have to watch out for God's self-revelation, and we have to communicate it face to face with philosophical theories of world and man.

Klaits, Joseph (ed) and Haltzel, Michael (ed). Liberty/Liberté: The American and French Experiences. Baltimore, Johns Hopkins U Pr, 1991.

The meaning of the word "liberty" has been decidedly different in the United States and France. Liberty/Liberté explores these differences, tracing the development of French and American ideas over the past two centuries in seven essays by American and seven by French scholars. The first half of the book examines common patterns in the intellectual backgrounds, political theories, and symbolic practices which have shaped conceptions of liberty and liberalism. The second half stresses the varieties of liberty's formulations in the historical experience of the two countries, examining the comparative development of "liberalism" and its conflict with other political philosophies.

Klami, Hannu Tapani. Moral Reasoning and Evidence in Legal Decision-Making in Ethical Dimensions of Legal Theory, Sadurski, Wojciech (ed). Amsterdam, Rodopi, 1991.

Klechenov, Gennadii. The Narod and the Intelligentsia: From Dissociation to Sobornost'. Russian Stud Phil, 31(4), 54-70, Spr 93.

Klee, Robert. Anomalous Monism, Ceteris Paribus and Psychological Explanation. Brit J Phil Sci, 43(3), 389-403, S 92.

Davidson has argued that there can be no laws linking psychological states with physical states. I stress that this argument depends crucially on there being no purely psychological laws. All of this has to do with the holism and indeterminacy of the psychological domain. I criticize this claim by showing how Davidson misconstrues the role of ceteris paribus clauses in psychological explanation. Using a model of how ceteris paribus clauses operate derived from Lakatos, I argue that if Davidson is correct, then there can be no purely physical laws either. This is illustrated with a case from immunology involving interferons. Since there clearly are physical laws, Davidson cannot be correct.

Klee, Robert. In Defense of the Quine-Duhem Thesis: A Reply to Greenwood. Phil Sci, 59(3), 487-491, S 92.

While discussing the work of Kuhn and Hanson, John Greenwood (1990) misidentifies the nature of the relationship between the incommensurability of theories and the theory-ladenness of observation. After pointing out this error, I move on to consider Greenwood's main argument that the Quine-Duhem thesis suffers from a form of epistemological self-defeat if it is interpreted to mean that any recalcitrant observation can always be accommodated to any theory. Greenwood finds this interpretation implausible because some adjustments to auxiliary hypotheses undermine too much of the prior observational evidence for the test theory. I argue that Greenwood mistakes the logico-metaphysical Quine-Duhem thesis for an epistemological one. All the argument he takes to undercut it actually illustrates how well the thesis works on a practical level. This is illustrated with an example from contemporary immunology.

Klee, Robert. The Phrenetic Calculus: A Logician's View of Disordered Logical Thinking in Schizophrenia. Behavior Phil, 20/2(21/1), 49-62, 1993.

This paper contains a preliminary investigation of an experimental, first-order logic with identity which encodes as an inference rule the faulty reasoning which Von Domarus (1944) suggested underwrote much of the bizarre thinking seen in certain forms of Schizophrenia. I begin with a discussion of the "Von Domarus thesis," note its fate under statistical testing, and remark on its continued explanatory power in the hands of certain psychiatrists. I next discuss a proof calculus which contains a rule representing Von Domarus reasoning—the phrenetic calculus—and present several nonstandard theorems which are provable in this system. In an appendix the phrenetic calculus is proven to be absolutely consistent, but unsound, yet complete.

After a brief aside which addresses certain caveats and restrictions required in order to avoid rendering the calculus trivial, I close with a discussion of three of the nonstandard theorems, each of which are consistent in interesting ways with known schizophrenic cognitive deficits.

Kleene, Stephen C. The Writing of *Introduction to Metamathematics* in Perspectives on the History of Mathematical Logic, Drucker, Thomas (ed). Basel, Birkhauser, 1991.

Klein, Ellen R. Is 'Normative Naturalism' an Oxymoron?. *Phil Psych*, 5(3), 289-297, 1992.

In this paper I will examine one argument in favor of a normative naturalism. I will show that such a proposal is inherently problematic and argue that naturalism and normativity are mutually exclusive concepts. Therefore, I suggest that, even in the 'age of cognitive science', epistemologists continue to do traditional epistemology by attempting to develop, a priori, the general criteria for determining the justificatory status of our (scientific) beliefs. (edited)

Klein, Ellen R. Normative Naturalism Undefended: A Response to McCauley's Reply. *Phil Psych*, 5(3), 307-, 1992.

There has been much discussion concerning the consequences of 'going natural', i.e., of replacing *a priori* epistemology with empirical psychology. Traditionalists claim that a naturalized epistemology is not viable—to eliminate the normative from an account of knowledge is to cease to do epistemology at all. Naturalists claim that a naturalized account is the only viable one—assuming, in step with the urgings of Quine, that there are no standards independent of (and external to) science, science itself must act as the sole epistemic norm. In the wake of the above debate some epistemologists have attempted to argue in favor of, and develop, a middle-ground position—*normative naturalism*. In this paper I will examine one argument in favor of a *normative naturalism*. I will show that such a proposal is inherently problematic and argue that naturalism and normativity are mutually exclusive concepts. (edited)

Klein, Jürgen. Vitalism, Empiricism, and the Quest for Reality in German and English Philosophy in The Crisis in Modernism, Burwick, Frederick (ed). New York, Cambridge Univ Pr, 1992.

Kleinig, John. The Limits of Consent: A Note on Dr Kevorkian. *Int J Applied Phil*, 7(2), 63-65, Wint 92.

With regard to legal permissibility, is it sufficient that those whose death Dr Kevorkian has assisted have consented to it? This note canvasses several limitations on the legal maxim, *volenti non fit injuria*, and suggests that the social recognition of his activity would be to give into and to sanction the fragmentation of social relations that has so denuded a life of the sense of worthwhileness that its extinction is deemed desirable.

Kleist, Jürgen (ed) and Butterfield, Bruce (ed). *Mythology: From Ancient to Post-Modern*. New York, Lang, 1992.

This book is a collection of sixteen essays by scholars who participated in a Mythology Symposium at the State University of New York, College at Plattsburgh in March, 1991. The essays are presented under four subject titles: Ancient Myths in Modern Contexts (Ulysses, Don Quixote, Don Juan, Amazonian Indians), Myth and Society (French-Canadian Messianism, American Exceptionalism, German-Jewish Tolerance, and Socialism), Myth and the Human Condition (in works of Camus, Ionesco, and Beckett), and Myth, Science, and Technology (the Gaia-concept, artificial intelligence, post-nuclear Re-Creation, and the film "Back to the Future, Part II").

Klemme, Heiner F. Neuere Bücher zum Werk David Humes. *Z Phil Forsch*, 47(1), 118-131, Ja-Mr 93.

This is a review essay on recent books related to Hume and the Scottish Enlightenment. Authors discussed included Y Kulen Kampff, 'David Hume' (1989); M A Weber, 'David Hume und Edward Gibbon' (1990); M P Levine, 'Hume and the Problem of Miracles: A Solution' (1989) and M A Stewart (ed) 'Studies in the Philosophy of the Scottish Enlightenment' (1990).

Klepper, Howard. Criminal Liability for the Bad Samaritan. *Pub Affairs Quart*, 7(1), 19-28, Ja 93.

Most of the debate about criminalization of failure to perform an easy rescue has centered on the moral equivalence of acts and omissions, and whether omissions can be considered as causes. I claim that a theory-driven approach to that question has not been fruitful, and that the common law rules of causation can accommodate omissions. I then examine the gradations of fault among different types of bad samaritans, and how these fit with the common law categories of homicide and the Model Penal Code categories of *scienter*.

Klevakina, Elena. The Case against Value-Free Belief in Advances in Scientific Philosophy, Schurz, Gerhard (ed). Amsterdam, Rodopi, 1991.

Kleven, Terence. A Study of Part I, Chapters 1-7 of Maimonides' *The Guide of the Perplexed*. *Interpretation*, 20(1), 3-16, Fall 92.

Klever, W. Blijenbergh's Tussing with Evil and Spinoza's Response (in Dutch). *Tijdschr Filosof*, 55(2), 307-329, Je 93.

One of the main items in Spinoza's philosophy is the non-existence of evil in nature. A thing may be good or bad for other finite beings or may be imagined as evil in itself. A scientific analysis, however, forbids us to attribute an ontological value to the moral concepts originating from our comparison of things. The rather extended correspondence between Spinoza and the Calvinistic merchant Willem van Blijenbergh gives us a lively access to all the ins and outs of the traditional philosophical problem of evil. The four letters in which Spinoza reacts to the questions and objections of Christian dogmatics, constitute nothing less than a full treatise on the subject. Never before this part of the correspondence has been the object of a separate study. The result is not only a clarification of the systematic relevance of Spinoza's theory. Research also throws light on the principles of his reasoning and contributes to a better understanding of his hermeneutics as well as of his attitude towards Cartesianism.

Klever, Wim. More About Hume's Debt to Spinoza. *Hume Stud*, 19(1), 55-74, Ap 93.

After the demonstration (*Hume Studies*, vol. XVI) of the influence of Spinoza's critical epistemology (*Ethics*, II) on Hume's theory of the understanding (*Treatise*, Book I), it is now shown, by a careful comparison of various items and the structure of the arguments, that also the second part of the *Treatise On the Passions* is very close to Spinoza's treatise on the same subject (Part III) and must be conceived to be dependent on it.

Klima, Gyula. The Changing Role of *Entia Rationis* in Mediaeval Semantics and Ontology: A Comparative Study with a Reconstruction. *Synthese*, 96(1), 25-58, Jl 93.

This paper argues that while beings of reason for Thomas Aquinas (and for any other "*via antiqua* thinker") were indispensable tools for reducing the apparent ontological commitments of his semantic theory, William Ockham's new semantics rendered them in the old interpretation eliminable. Ockham's new semantics therefore opened the way to a radical reinterpretation of the concept of *ens rationis* and to a new research program for ontology. Through a formal reconstruction of the basic semantic ideas considered, Ockham's innovations are presented as a type-lowering of the signification of categorematic terms, yielding "automatically" the desired ontological reductions.

Klima, Gyula and Sandu, Gabriel. Numerical Quantifiers in Game-Theoretical Semantics. *Theoria*, 61(3), 173-192, 1990.

Klíma, Ivan. The European Cultural Tradition and the Limits of Growth. *Phil Lit*, 17(1), 77-83, Ap 93.

Klimenkova, T A. Feminism and Postmodernism. *Phil East West*, 42(2), 277-285, Ap 92.

Klimovsky, Gregorio and De Asúa, Miguel. Ensayo de axiomatización de la teoría tisular y su reducción a la teoría celular. *Theoria (Spain)*, 5(12-13), 129-140, N 90.

The conceptual framework of this paper is the structural conception of theories as formulated by Sneed-Stegmüller. We present an informal set-theoretical axiomatization of M F Xavier Bichat's theory of the constitution of the organism, which conceived the tissue as the ultimate constitutive element of the living beings, and a reformulation of our previous axiomatization of the cell theory. We propose a tentative relation of reduction between both theories which possibilities the derivation of the axioms of the tissue theory from those of the cell theory. The limits and problems of the axiomatization are discussed and brief reference is being made to some historical aspects of the reception of the cell theory.

Kline, George L. The Use and Abuse of Hegel by Nietzsche and Marx in Hegel and His Critics, Desmond, William J (ed). Albany, SUNY Pr, 1989.

Klinger, Cornelia. Die Französische Revolution und die Frauen: Kommentar. *Stud Phil (Switzerland)*, 49, 233-239, 1990.

Klink, William H. Nature, Technology, and Theology. *Zygon*, 27(2), 203-210, Je 92.

Modern technology presents new challenges and possibilities to the environment and life on earth. It is argued that ecology as the science of the earth as a whole cannot provide the means for making technical decisions pertaining to the environment. An alternative means is suggested in which modern technology provides the medium for communicating with nature, so that a dialogue, an intruding in and listening to nature, becomes the basis both for seeing modern technology in a new light and for living with modern technology in a new way. Some theological ramifications are also explored.

Kloek, J J and Mijnhardt, W W. *De Productie, Distributie en Consumptie Van Cultuur*. Amsterdam, Rodopi, 1991.

Kloesel, Christian J W and Cook, Don L. Two Responses to Moore and Burks on Editing Peirce. *Trans Peirce Soc*, 28(2), 303-309, Spr 92.

Klonoski, Richard. The Preservation of Homeric Tradition: Heroic Re-Performance in the *Republic* and the *Odyssey*. *Clio*, 22(3), 251-271, Spr 93.

The author suggests that Plato was much more ambivalent about the value of Homeric epic poetry than his famous critique of it in the *Republic* seems to indicate. The author argues, by comparing the heroic journeys into Hades enacted by Odysseus in the *Odyssey* and Socrates in the *Republic* that Plato attempts to preserve a Homeric tradition regarding the founding of cities and the foundations of Greek culture. The essay begins and ends with some brief remarks on the theory(ies) of interpretation and/or protocols of reading employed in the author's reading of the *Odyssey* and the *Republic*.

Kloppenberg, James T. Rethinking Tradition in Essays on Henry Sidgwick, Schultz, Bart (ed). New York, Cambridge Univ Pr, 1992.

Klosko, George. Persuasion and Moral Reform in Plato and Aristotle. *Rev Int Phil*, 47(184), 31-49, 1993.

Kloskowski, K. The Synthetic Theory of Evolution and the Neutral Theory and Punctuated Equilibria (in Polish). *Stud Phil Christ*, 28(1), 31-51, 1992.

The considerations in the paper correspond to the findings of such scholars as: J L King, T H Jukes, M Kimura, T Ohta, N Eldredge, S J Gould. The article attempts to answer the question of whether the neutral theory and punctuated equilibria make continuation and development of interpretation of the synthetic theory of evolution or if they are not within its trend. The former stresses the fact that the evolutionary process, to a considerable degree, depends on the mutations which do not undergo the natural selection; so they are dependent on the genetic drift activity. At the same time, the theory explains clearly the mutations which limit to a level of the genetic variability but do not negate the activity of the natural selection. The punctuated equilibria, on the other hand, lays emphasis on the changes in the classes being verifiable on the base of fossil record. (edited)

Kluback, William. La foi messianique de Hugo Bermann. *Arch Phil*, 55(1), 35-48, Ja-Mr 92.

Hugo Bergmann's work embraced that realm of human thought in which man has struggled for generations with the relationship between faith and reason. Bergmann was a believing philosopher. He believed in the traditions of the Fathers, but this belief was neither confining nor exclusive. Faith encompassed every religion which stood humbly and in trust before God. With his faith in Israel, Bergmann turned with love and awe to Christianity, to every thinker and believer who sought not only the ways of reason, but those of faith. Bergmann called for a courageous philosophy, one that was not restricted to conceptualization. He urged the thinker to be a doer, to deserve the truths he enunciated, to be worthy of the humanity he shared with others. The way of each individual was distinct and different, but never could these qualities shut man off from his fellow man. In faith man found not only the self, but a sensitivity to the faith of his fellow man. In the philosopher, the believer finds companionship; in the believer, the philosopher, finds the divine. Why should they live apart from each other?

Kluxen, Wolfgang. Der Übergang von der Physik zur Metaphysik im thomistischen Gottesbeweis. *Frei Z Phil Theol*, 40(1-2), 44-54, 1993.

Knapp, Steven and Clayton, Philip. Ethics and Rationality. *Amer Phil Quart*, 30(2), 151-161, Ap 93.

Ethical obligations cannot be derived directly from the notion of rational agency (contra Kant); yet rationality does place some ethical constraints on human agency (contra Williams). We argue that rational agency requires knowing whether actions are appropriate to one's own self-conception, and that this requires critical feedback from the relevant communities of experts. But, we show, certain ethical principles are entailed by the feedback process itself. Although practical reflection begins with internal reasons, then, there is reason to think it may lead, in the Peircean "long run", to the discovery of constraints that apply to all rational agents.

Knasas, John F X. Incommensurability and Aquinas's Metaphysics. *Amer Cath Phil Quart*, 65, 179-190, 1991.

My paper tackles Bernstein's and Rorty's denials of a common ground, a commensurating framework, for the adjudication of varoius philosophical discourses. I argue that their position on its own merits fails. Also, their arguments for incommensurability fail to apply to Aquinas's metaphysics. First, as a philosophy, Thomistic metaphysics appeals to natural reason, not to tyranny. Second, through masterful strokes of analogy, the view of reality in Thomistic metaphysics leaves ample room for the emerging of novelty. Third, Thomistic metaphysics leads to an ethics in which analogy again is operative for understanding the human good, thus setting the stage for the exercise of decision. Finally, an open and honest look at the real shows it to have a visage.

Knebel, Sven K. Necessitas moralis ad optimum (III). *Stud Leibniz*, 24(2), 182-215, 1992.

Quite contrary to the mainstream history of ideas, Spanish intellectuals play an important part in the 17th century dispute about natural law, physical evidence and the principle of induction. Optimism as taught by Antonio Perez (1599-1649) and Martín Esparza (1606-1689) in Salamanca and Rome has given rise to a sophisticated theological debate of a subject that was to demand philosophers' attention for centuries to come. The features of empiricism brought forward by Bernardo Aldrete (1594-1657) and Antonio Bernaldo de Quiros (1613-1668) will stimulate the research on Hume's scholastic reading.

Knebel, Sven K. Necessitas moralis ad optimum: Die früheste scholastische Absage an den Optimismus. *Theol Phil*, 67(4), 514-535, 1992.

Looking for the sources of Leibniz's Theodicee in the contemporary scholastic thought you should turn towards Sevilla. Optimism has been invented by the Jesuits Ruiz de Montoya (1562-1632) and Granado (1571-1632). The new approach has been accomplished by responding to Jorge Hemelman (1574-1637), who had been the first to attack it when lecturing at Granada in 1616/17: "An providentia voluntasque Dei sit moraliter necessitata et semper velit efficaciter quod est optimum?" The manuscript extant reveals a vigorous and highly sophisticated defense of the rules of consequence against the confusion arising from this very moralization of modalities.

Kneepkens, C H. Nominalism and Grammatical Theory in the Late Eleventh and Early Twelfth Centuries: An Explorative Study. *Vivarium*, 30(1), 34-50, My 92.

Knitter, Paul F. Interreligious Dialogue and the Unity of Humanity. *J Dharma*, 17(4), 282-297, O-D 92.

The fact that the religions of the world have been sources of conflict and disunity has helped create a situation in which they can "redeem" themselves and make a significant contribution to the peace and unity of humankind. There is a new kairos for interreligious dialogue and cooperation; concern for human and ecological well-being can serve as a hermeneutical common ground for a new kind of interreligious discourse. Unless this discourse takes place and religions make their joint contribution to world peace, there will, most likely, be no peace.

Knoppers, Bartha Maria and Laberge, Claude M. Rationale for an Integrated Approach to Genetic Epidemiology. *Bioethics*, 6(4), 317-330, O 92.

Knott, T Garland. Personhood: F R Tennant and Peter Bertocci in the Light of Contemporary Physics. *Personalist Forum*, 8(2), 101-114, Fall 92.

Knott, T Garland. Personhood: F R Tennant and Peter Bertocci in the Light of Contemporary Physics. *Personalist Forum*, 8/1(Supp), 215-217, Spr 92.

Knowles, Richard T (ed) and McLean, George F (ed). *Psychological Foundations of Moral Education and Character Development: An Integrated Theory of Moral Development (Second Edition)*. Washington, CRVP, 1992.

Knuuttila, Simo. Remarks on Induction in Aristotle's Dialectic and Rhetoric. *Rev Int Phil*, 47(184), 78-88, 1993.

Aristotle says in *Top*, VIII, 2 that syllogism should be used in the discussions with dialecticians and induction in the discussions with other people. Why did he not give the same statue to induction in rhetoric? It is argued in the first part of the paper that Aristotle regarded the non-trivial induction as a conceptual analysis which may be connected with difficult problems; presenting them in a speech would be boring and too arduous for the audience. Using the paradigm, the more simple rhetorical induction, does not differ in this respect. If the background analysis is not obvious, the listeners easily say that the cases are not similar.

Knuuttila, Simo and Holopainen, Taina. Conditional Will and Conditional Norms in Medieval Thought. *Synthese*, 96(1), 115-132, Jl 93.

The historical background of the fourteenth century discussion of conditional norms is elucidated by an analysis of the emergence of the logic of will in early medieval thought (Abelard, Peter of Poitiers, William of Auxerre, Walter Burley). It is also shown that some problems relevant to later medieval deontic logic were discussed in obligations logic (positio dependens, positio cadens, positio renascens).

Ko, Ker-I. On the Computational Complexity of Integral Equations. *Annals Pure Applied Log*, 58(3), 201-228, N 92.

The computational complexity of Volterra integral equations of the second kind and of the first kind is investigated. It is proved that if the kernel functions satisfy the Lipschitz condition, then the solutions of Volterra equations of the second kind are polynomial-space computable. If, on the other hand, the kernel functions only satisfy the logical Lipschitz condition with the Lipschitz constants growing in an exponential rate, then the solutions could be exponential-time hard. We identify a class of Volterra equations of the first kind that can be converted to Volterra equations of the second kind satisfying the local Lipschitz condition. The complexity of the solutions of these equations is also proved to be exponential-time hard.

Kobes, Bernard W. On a Model for Psycho-Neural Coevolution. *Behavior Phil*, 19(2), 1-17, Fall-Wint 91.

According to a model of inter-theoretic relations advocated by Patricia S. Churchland, psychology will need to revise its theories so as to fit them for "smooth reduction" to the neurosciences, and this will lead to the elimination of reference to intentional contents from psychology. It is argued that this model is ambiguous; on one reading it is empirically implausible, on the other its methodology is confused. The connectionist program NETtalk, far from exemplifying the model as Churchland claims, suggests a theoretical rationale for employing relations to intentional contents in psychology.

Koch, Andrew M. Postructuralism and the Epistemological Basis of Anarchism. *Phil Soc Sci*, 23(3), 327-351, S 93.

This essay identifies two different methodological strategies used by the proponents of anarchism. In what is termed the "ontological" approach, the rationale for anarchism depends on a particular representation of human nature. That characterization of "being" determines the relation between the individual and the structures of social life. In the alternative approach, the epistemological status of "representation" is challenged, leaving human subjects without stable identities. Without the possibility of stable human representations, the foundation underlying the exercise of institutional power can be challenged. This epistemological discussion is traced from Max Stirner to the twentieth-century movement known as poststructuralism.

Koch, C H. The Correspondence of Ernst Mach with a Young Danish Philosopher. *Dan Yrbk Phil*, 26, 97-112, 1991.

In the article are eight edited and annotated letters from Ernst Mach (1838-1916) to the Danish philosopher Anthon Thomsen (1877-1916), together with excerpts from Thomsen's diary and from his letters to Mach. Five of Mach's letters and the excerpts have not appeared in print before.

Kochergin, A N and Donskikh, O A. Do We Have a Scientific Conception of the History of Philosophy? Polemical Notes. *Russian Stud Phil*, 31(1), 26-47, Sum 92.

Kochumuttom, Thomas. Ethics-Based Society of Buddhism. *J Dharma*, 16(4), 410-420, O-D 91.

Kockelmans, Joseph J. Hermeneutic Philosophy and Natural Theology in Prospects for Natural Theology, Long, Eugene Thomas (ed). Washington, Cath Univ Amer Pr, 1992.

The essay starts with a description of the origin and development of natural theology between Aristotle and Hegel and then explains its concern with proofs for the existence of God. The second section discusses the critique of hermeneutic philosophy in regard to metaphysics and to natural theology as a form of special metaphysics. It is argued that today arguments for God's existence, even if logically valid, are of no real importance philosophically; yet they may be meaningful for the believer. The last section presents ideas about negative theology and the use of analogy and symbolic language in natural theology.

Kodera, Sergius. Die Renaissance und ihr Bild vom Konfuzianismus. *Conceptus*, 25(65), 67-84, 1991.

This article is about the interpretation of Confucianism by Matteo Ricci. It discusses texts which can serve as a documentation of the encounter of two different cultures. The interpretation of the Jesuit missionary (which was accepted by his order for a long time) was not without patterns, which we can trace back to the intellectual culture of the European Renaissance. It was Renaissance - Neoplatonism, which had claimed before, (referring to the tradition of prisca theologia or "Ancient Theology") that Platonic doctrines were reconcilable with the teachings of Christianity. Later, the Jesuit's arguments for an integration of Christianity into Confucian doctrines ran along similar lines. (edited)

Koehn, Daryl. Rethinking the Responsibility of International Corporations: A Response to Donaldson. *Bus Ethics Quart*, 3(2), 177-183, A 93.

This article challenges Thomas Donaldson's theory that the language of rights and duties is better suited than the language of virtue ethics for discussing the moral responsibilities of international corporations. The article shows that Donaldson ignores many strengths of the latter language while minimizing difficulties associated with the language of rights.

Körner, Stephan. On the Relation between Common Sense, Science and Metaphysics in A J Ayer Memorial Essays, Griffiths, A Phillips (ed). New York, Cambridge Univ Pr, 1991.

Kofler, Edward and Zweifel, Peter. One-Shot Decisions under Linear Partial Information. *Theor Decis*, 34(1), 1-20, Ja 93.

This paper purports to make a contribution to the analysis of a class of decisions that has received little attention in the literature, although it appears to be of considerable importance. Certain decisions cannot be repeated but must be made under fuzziness in the sense that state probabilities are not exactly known (LPI-fuzziness). The analysis of Linear Partial Information is applied to the principle of neglecting small probabilities found by Allais (1953), enabling the decision maker to break away from the maxmin criterion. By systematic exploitation of the fuzzy information available, strategies are shown to exist that provide payoffs whose lower bound exceeds the maxmin benchmark with sufficiently high probability. The same methodology is shown to be useful for dealing with the case of only ordinal preference orderings that are so typical of those crucial decisions that may be made only once in a lifetime.

Kogan, L A. The Philosophy of N F Fedorov. *Sov Stud Phil*, 30(4), 7-27, Spr 92.

Kohak, E. Speaking to Trees (in Czechoslovakian). *Filozof Cas*, 39(6), 903-913, 1991.

The author raises the question of the epistemological status of a world view within which speaking to trees would appear as an appropriate behavior. He claims that would be the case in a world perceived as a community of autonomous beings worthy of respect. He contrasts such a perception with the anthropocentric conception of the world as a value free reservoir of raw materials and claims that neither can or should claim descriptive accuracy. Both are equally metaphors and the choice between them must rest on whether they are conducive to ecologically constructive or ecologically destructive behavior. On that basis, he considers speaking to trees a legitimate, speaking of biomechanisms an illegitimate form of verbal behavior.

Kohak, Erazim. Human Rights and Nature's Rightness. *Lyceum*, 2(2), 22-36, Fall 90.

The author seeks to show that there is an inherent contradiction between the conception of humans as "masters of nature" and that of humans as endowed with natural rights. The idea of such rights is intelligible only within a meaningfully ordered cosmos whose order imposes obligations on humans as well. Without a recognition of those obligations and of the order on which they are based—nature's rightness—there is no basis for any claim of human rights. Ecological and humanistic considerations are thus intrinsically linked.

Kohak, Erazim. Selves, People, Persons: An Essay in American Personalism in Selves, People, and Persons, Rouner, Leroy S (ed). Notre Dame, Univ Notre Dame Pr, 1992.

Author surveys the metaphysical and moral conceptions of American personalism and its claim that *person* is the basic metaphysical category. That claim becomes the basis for a *Bildungsphilosophie* and a social critique (the task of moral growth to freedom and responsibility or *personhood*, society as called to support it); for a metaphysics (reality as life-world constituted as community of persons); and for a moral philosophy (respect for personhood of all beings). Author suggests that personalism provides an idiom and a conceptual schema no more or less "true" than those of current common sense but superior as the basis for human moral orientation in the world.

Kohak, Erazim. Truth and the Humanities. *Human Stud*, 16(3), 239-253, Jl 93.

Some assertions in the human sciences can be considered non-trivially T/F iff we treat them not as descriptions but as guidelines for comportment. While to disinterested observer ("theoretical reason") what is may appear compatible with contradictory claims, for purposive agent (in humans, "practical reason") it is value-laden: some things aid, others hinder life—and, as value for itself, life has value in itself. Thus assertions conducive to sustaining life in the multiplicity of its conflicted harmony can be said to be valid independently of human assent.

Kohák, Erazim. Speaking to Trees. *Crit Rev*, 6(2-3), 371-388, Spr-Sum 92.

Speaking to trees constitutes a legitimate form of linguistic behavior if we consider speaking an expression of respect and if we conceive of the world as a community of beings worthy of such respect. Though such a conception may be no more descriptively accurate than an anthropocentric or mechanistic one, it is conducive to more desirable social strategies and so preferable to its alternatives. Speaking to trees is thus not only legitimate but also desirable.

Kohl, Marvin. Bertrand Russell's Characterization of Benevolent Love. *Russell*, 12(2), 117-134, Wint 92-93.

This paper analyzes the characterization of benevolent love found in Bertrand Russell's *What I Believe*. It distinguishes between benevolent and caring love and suggests that each is problematic as a moral ideal. Benevolent love is indefinitely extensible but it cannot save the world; caring love is not indefinitely extensible, but it could save the world if it were. Russell also believed he was advocating a radical reform of society. But in describing some of the means he may have aimed too low. Perhaps in a non-benevolent society, positing an ideal of benevolence is significant reform. But it is not as radical a reform as targeting and explicitly aiming at both benevolence and beneficence.

Kohl, Marvin. Caring Love and Liberty: Some Questions. *Free Inq*, 12(2), 49-51, Spr 92.

This paper describes an empirically manifested type of relationship called "caring love". It explains why this kind of love often requires a form of paternalism. Using Robert J Sternberg's characterization of commitment, it suggests that there is a need to more clearly distinguish between having some commitment and having an unconditional one. Finally it replies, at least in part, to contrary point of view. These include varieties of the agape-like argument that "love demands complete acceptance" and Jan Narveson's argument for relationships based primarily on self-interest.

Kohlenbach, Ulrich. Effective Bounds from Ineffective Proofs in Analysis: An Application of Functional Interpretation and Majorization. *J Sym Log*, 57(4), 1239-1273, D 92.

We show how to extract effective uniform bounds in higher types from ineffective proofs of functional existence theorems in systems of finite type arithmetic relative to a large class of analytical lemmas (which includes, e.g., binary König's lemma WKL). This is done by a new proof-theoretic combination of Gödel's functional interpretation with a pointwise version of Howard's majorizability. As a consequence we obtain new conservation results for WKL. In a subsequent paper the method will be applied to concrete proofs in best approximation theory.

Kohler, Georg. Die Zerstückelung des Fu-Tschu-Li. *Stud Phil (Switzerland)*, 49, 241-254, 1990.

Kohli, Wendy R. Deconstructing Solidarity: Or, A Funny Thing Happened On the Way to Unity. *Proc Phil Educ*, 48, 324-327, 1992.

Kohlschitter, Silke. Parmenides and Empedocles in Porphyry's *History of Philosophy*. *Hermathena*, 150, 43-54, Sum 91.

Kohn, Livia. Selfhood and Spontaneity in Ancient Chinese Thought in Selves, People, and Persons, Rouner, Leroy S (ed). Notre Dame, Univ Notre Dame Pr, 1992.

Contemporary psychology distinguishes between the object self and the observing self, a deficiency-oriented object view of oneself and a being-oriented way of flowing along with nature. In ancient China a similar distinction was made between *ji* and *zi*, both meaning "self." The *ji* or object self was condemned, the *zi* was lauded. Many philosophers emphasized the importance to abandon desire and egotistic striving and instead become part of a larger whole—society, nature, universal love, or the Tao. The Chinese wish to replace the *ji* with the *zi*. To do so, they try to curb individualism and the fulfillment of personality traits, an effort evident in philosophy, law, and literature.

Koj, Leon. Exactness and Philosophy in Advances in Scientific Philosophy, Schurz, Gerhard (ed). Amsterdam, Rodopi, 1991.

Kolak, Daniel. Art and Intentionality. *J Aes Art Crit*, 48(2), 158-162, Spr 90.

Kolak, Daniel. The Metaphysics and Metapsychology of Personal Identity. *Amer Phil Quart*, 30(1), 39-50, Ja 93.

What are the metaphysical and metapsychological boundaries of a person? How do we draw our borders? This much is clear: personal identity without thought experiments is impossible. I develop a new way of conceptualizing physiological and psychological borders leading to a re-evaluation of the problem of personal identity within the contemporary literature, especially Parfit, arguing that we must, necessarily, turn to the conceptual analysis of metaphysical and metapsychological borders. I offer an explanation of the persistence of common sense against philosophical analysis, criticize Wilkes's position, and provide a foundation for the proper use of thought experiments in analytic metapsychology and metaphysics.

Kolak, Daniel and Martin, Raymond. *The Experience of Philosophy (Second Edition)*. Belmont, Wadsworth, 1992.

A collection reflecting the ways philosophy has changed over the last two decades, with an attempt to link philosophy to literature and the physical and social sciences. Contributors include Daniel Dennett, Robert Nozick, Thomas Nagel, Richard Taylor, Douglas Hofstadter, Gary Gutting, Richard Dawkins, Frank Jackson, Paul Churchland, Paul Darris, and Jonathan Glover.

Kolakowski, Andrzej. Two Trends in Modern Polish Thought. *Dialec Hum*, 17(1), 40-55, 1990.

Kolar, P and Svoboda, V. The Logical Structure of Action Sentences (Part I) (in Czechoslovakian). *Filozof Cas*, 40(3), 459-466, 1992.

Kolar, P and Svoboda, V. The Logical Structure of Action Sentences: Two Analytical Exercises (Conclusion) (in Czechoslovakian). *Filozof Cas*, 40(5), 887-905, 1992.

Kolar, P and Svoboda, V. The Logical Structure of Action Sentences: Two Analytical Exercises (Part II) (in Czechoslovakian). *Filozof Cas*, 40(4), 661-671, 1992.

Kolarsky, R. A Few Notes on the Relation of Philosophy and Ecology (in Czechoslovakian). *Filozof Cas*, 39(6), 914-924, 1991.

This article deals with the need and motives of the philosophical thematization of ecological crisis. The author compares different approaches to this problem and sympathizes with A Naess's argumentation that ecology itself is not able to cope with the task of saving the nature and that—apart from scientific cognition—philosophy is also needed for its saving. When considering the question whether the contemporary ecological crisis is a philosophical crisis as well, the author advocates the standpoint that philosophy is deeply touched by this crisis, that it ceases to be possible for philosophy to deal with the interests of man and mankind and not to take into consideration the interests of nature at the same time. As the history of philosophy and the history of the Earth intersect in a new way nowadays, the fate of the Earth will be influenced by the fact to what extent philosophy will assume responsibility for its earthly inhabitance.

Kolb, David. Heidegger and Habermas on Criticism and Totality. *Phil Phenomenol Res*, 52(3), 683-693, S 92.

Habermas's criticizes Heidegger for insulating totalities of meaning form possible overturning by attempts to validate individual claims. This essay first states Habermas's criticism, then elaborates an example from Heidegger concerning Aristotle's physics that supports Habermas's attack. Then the essay defends Heidegger by distinguishing levels of meaning and Heidegger's "world" from Habermas's more propositional "lifeworld." The essay concludes by accepting Habermas's objection restated in terms of the contrast between transcendental and local conditions. If Heidegger is unwilling to pay the price of either Kantian generality or Hegelian unity, he should give up the simple priority of the epochal understandings of being.

Kolb, David. Home on the Range: Planning and Totality. *Res Phenomenol*, 22, 3-11, 1992.

Drawing a parallel between Le Corbusier (on functional divisions in the city and on the need to clear the site for building) and Plato (on how all things are composed of limit and unlimited), this essay examines a gradually wilder set of metaphors that might replace the Platonic/modernist imposition of univocal limits on unlimited material, place, or lives. Settling on the image of an unruly ecology, the essay examines some analogies and disanalogies between the excess of interpretation in deconstructive theory and the excess of nature and social economy that refuse to be schematized into a single system or plan.

Kolenda, Konstantin. Pragmatism, Prudence, and Morality in Frontiers in American Philosophy, Volume I, Burch, Robert W (ed). College Station, Texas A&M Univ Pr, 1992.

Kolenda, Konstantin. Problems with Transcendence in God, Values, and Empiricism, Peden, Creighton (ed). Macon, Mercer Univ Pr, 1989.

Kolenda, Konstantin. Rethinking the Teaching of Philosophy. *Teach Phil*, 15(2), 121-131, J 92.

Kolin, Andrew. *The Ethical Foundations of Hume's Theory of Politics*. New York, Lang, 1992.

The terms nature and artifice date back to the origins of Western political thought. Historically, political philosophers have debated using either nature or artifice to explain the foundations of politics. This book demonstrates it is possible to reconcile nature and artifice, using the arguments presented by the great political philosopher of the Scottish Enlightenment, David Hume. Through a careful analysis of Hume's political writings, it traces how a definition of politics as nature and artifice must be understood in an historical context.

Kollender, Aaron. Kant's Idealistic Dilemma (in Hebrew). *Iyyun*, 41, 432-440, O 92.

Koller, John M. Human Embodiment: Indian Perspectives in Self as Body in Asian Theory and Practice, Kasulis, Thomas P (ed). Albany, SUNY Pr, 1992.

Kondoleon, Theodore J. A Contradiction in Saint Thomas's Teaching on Creation. *Thomist*, 57(1), 51-61, Ja 93.

My article argues that there is an implicit contradiction in what Saint Thomas has to say about the *de fide* character of the world's temporal beginning. In the *Summa Theologiae* (I, Question 46, Article 2), Aquinas argues that the world's temporal beginning cannot be rationally demonstrated but is something that can be accepted only on faith. Yet, in the preceding article of this question, in his replies to objections 6 and 9, he gives as a reason why God created the world with a temporal beginning instead of creating it as something eternal, the fact that we can be led more evidently to a knowledge of the divine creating power, given the world had a beginning (since what does not always exist manifestly has a cause). But this implies that we can know by reason that the world has a beginning, something he denies.

Konersmann, Rolf. Vom Risiko der Positivität: Pihlosophieren nach dem Tod des Subjekts. *Phil Rundsch*, 39(3), 214-235, 1992.

Konstan, David. Περιληϖισ in Epicurean Epistemology. *Ancient Phil*, 13(1), 125-137, Spr 93.

In this paper I argue that the Greek term *perilêpsis* or "comprehension" represents a distinct epistemological category in ancient Epicurean theory, alongside the more familiar concepts of *aisthêsis*, *phantasia*, and *prolêpsis*. Comprehension is a mode of perception associated specifically with delimited or comprehensible quantities or magnitudes. Such percepts are distinguished from incomprehensibly large aggregates, which form a special category in Epicureanism between the comprehensible and the infinite (e.g., the kinds of atoms are incomprehensibly large but not infinite). I suggest that *perilêpsis* accounts in a materialist epistemology for the unitary appearance of compound objects.

Koons, Robert C. Faith, Probability and Infinite Passion. *Faith Phil*, 10(2), 145-160, Ap 93.

I propose an account of Christian faith, inspired by Kierkegaard's *Concluding Unscientific Postscript*, according to which 1) belief involves a relation to factual religious propositions, but 2) the strength of religious belief is measured, not by the degree of one's confidence in the truth of these propositions, but rather by the degree to which the desirability of possible states of the world is affected by whether they include the truth of these propositions. I will defend this Kierkegaardian view by means of two mathematical tools developed in the twentieth century: Frank Ramsey's decision theory, and Robinson's theory of hyper-real numbers. I hope to show that Kierkegaard's hypothesis that Christian faith is an infinite passion can be formulated precisely and shown to be mathematically coherent.

Koppel, Moshe. Hierarchical Inductive Inference Methods. *Log Anal*, 32, 285-295, S-D 89.

We consider the class of all mappings from binary strings to a single bit (representing the predicted next bit). Such mappings are called "inference methods". An inference method which maps every Boolean function of a pair of strings to that function of the images of these strings is said to be "consistent". We show that a principle of indifference in selecting among consistent inference methods, leads to a naive but elegant formulation of Carnap's two prediction criteria — empirical and analytic.

Koppelberg, Dirk. Should We Replace Knowledge by Understanding?—A Comment on Elgin and Goodman's Reconception of Epistemology. *Synthese*, 95(1), 119-128, Ap 93.

Goodman and Elgin have recommended a reconception of philosophy. A central part of their recommendation is to replace knowledge by understanding. According to Elgin, some important internalist and externalist theories of knowledge favor a sort of undesirable cognitive minimalism. Against Elgin I try to show how the challenge of cognitive minimalism can be met. Goodman and Elgin claim that defeat and confusion are built into the concept of knowledge. They demand either its revision or its replacement or its supplement. I show that these are three very different options. While agreeing with the view that there may be good reasons for some revisions and supplements, I strongly disagree with Elgin and Goodman's replacement thesis.

Koppelberg, Sabine. A Construction of Boolean Algebras from First-Order Structures. *Annals Pure Applied Log*, 59(3), 239-256, F 93.

We give a construction assigning classes of Boolean algebras to first-order theories; several classes of Boolean algebras considered previously in the literature can be thus obtained. In particular, it turns out that the class of semigroup algebras can be defined in this way, in fact by Horn theory, and it is the largest class of Boolean algebras defined by a Horn theory.

Korab-Karpowicz, W J. The Wisdom of Love. *Dialec Hum*, 17(3), 211-216, 1990.

Empedocles sees both love and strife as forces active on many levels, from cosmic and organic levels to the level of political and personal life. What we can learn from him is that we are still living in the Iron Age, upon which strife holds its sway. The paper points out a way to a New Age—the Age of Intelligence.

Korb, Kevin B. The Collapse of Collective Defeat: Lessons from the Lottery Paradox. *Proc Phil Sci Ass*, 1, 230-236, 1992.

The Lottery Paradox has been thought to provide a reductio argument against probabilistic accounts of inductive inference. As a result, much work in artificial intelligence has concentrated on qualitative methods of inference, including default logics, which are intended to model some varieties of inductive inference. It has recently been shown that the paradox can be generated within qualitative default logics. However, John Pollock's qualitative system of defeasible inference (named OSCAR), does avoid the Lottery Paradox by incorporating a rule designed specifically for that purpose. I shall argue that Pollock's system instead succumbs to a worse disease: it fails to allow for induction at all (a disease sometimes known as "Conjunctivitis').

Kornblith, Hilary. Epistemic Normativity. *Synthese*, 94(3), 357-376, Mr 93.

This paper examines the source and content of epistemic norms. In virtue of what is it that epistemic norms have their normative force? A semantic approach to this question, due to Alvin Goldman, is examined and found unacceptable. Instead, accounts seeking to ground epistemic norms in our desires are argued to be most promising. All of these accounts make epistemic norms a variety of hypothetical imperative. It is argued that such an account may be offered, grounding our epistemic norms in desire, which nevertheless makes these imperatives universal. The account is contrasted with some recent work of Stephen Stich.

Kornblith, Hilary. *Inductive Inference and Its Natural Ground: An Essay in Naturalistic Epistemology*. Cambridge, MIT Pr, 1993.

Both the epistemology and the underlying metaphysical bases of inductive inference are examined. On the metaphysical side, an account of natural kinds is presented, following Richard Boyd, which identifies natural kinds with homeostatic clusters of properties. On the epistemological side, it is argued that we have certain native conceptual structures, and native inferential tendencies, which dovetail with the causal structure of natural kinds in such a way as to allow for inductive understanding of the world.

Kornblith, Hilary. The Laws of Thought. *Phil Phenomenol Res*, 52(4), 895-911, D 92.

The psychological literature on human inference, if taken at face value, seems to suggest that human beings reason very badly. This body of literature is examined, and it is argued that this pessimistic picture of our inferential abilities is not supported by the data.

Kornegay, R Jo. Hume on the Ordinary Distinction Between Objective and Subjective Impressions. *Can J Phil*, 23(2), 241-269, Je 93.

This paper explores Hume's theory that the ordinary person distinguishes between 1) series of impressions taken to be perceptions of objective events and 2) series of impressions considered mere mental events in terms of the constancy or coherence exhibited by 1), but not 2). It is argued that, although Hume's account of 1) is incomplete, it can be extended to cover problematic cases of non-constant and non-coherent series that are, nonetheless, considered objective. However, the author contends that a fleshed out Humean analysis of 2) is inadequate to account for certain coherent series which are, nonetheless, considered subjective.

Korsgaard, Christine. Commentators on Cohen and Sen in The Quality of Life, Nussbaum, Martha C (ed). New York, Oxford Univ Pr, 1993.

Sen and Cohen propose ways of measuring the quality of life. One may assess such metrics simply as proposals about what constitutes a good life, or for their legitimacy in determining what the state should do for its citizens. For liberals, the purpose of the state is not to produce the good life for its citizens, but rather to provide a sphere in which citizens freely pursue their own conceptions of the good. On this and other grounds, I argue that Sen's "capability" metric, which focuses on the agent's freedom, is more suitable for use in a liberal society than Cohen's "access to advantage" metric.

Korsgaard, Christine. Creating the Kingdom of Ends in Philosophical Perspectives, 6: Ethics, 1992, Tomberlin, James E (ed). Atascadero, Ridgeview, 1992.

Drawing on an account of friendship common to Aristotle and Kant, I argue that personal relations are characterized by an expectation of reciprocity which is only possible between those who hold one another responsible. Holding someone responsible may be understood either as having a belief about her or as taking up a practical attitude towards her. If it is the latter we need practical reasons for holding people responsible. Kant's ethical theory shows us what those reasons are. Holding ourselves and others responsible is a precondition for moral action, and so is what Kant calls a "postulate of practical reason."

Korsgaard, Christine. The Reasons We Can Share in Altruism, Paul, Ellen Frankel (ed). New York, Cambridge Univ Pr, 1993.

The distinction between agent-relative (subjective) and agent-neutral (objective) reasons leaves an important option out: reasons may be intersubjective, or shared. I examine the examples which Nagel, in *The View from Nowhere*, uses to motivate the claim that some reasons are agent-relative: reasons springing from personal projects and deontological reasons. I argue that such reasons are better understood as intersubjective reasons. This is also a better way to understand agent-neutral reasons. The normativity of reasons does not spring from the claims made on us by either our personal projects or objective goods. It springs from the claims we make on one another.

Korsgaard, Christine. The Reasons We Can Share: An Attack on the Distinction between Agent-Relative and Agent-Neutral Values. *Soc Phil Pol*, 10(1), 24-51, Wint 93.

The distinction between agent-relative (subjective) and agent-neutral (objective) reasons leaves an important option out: reasons may be intersubjective, or shared. I examine the examples which Nagel, in *The View from Nowhere*, uses to motivate the claim that some reasons are agent-relative: reasons springing from personal projects and deontological reasons. I argue that such reasons are better understood as intersubjective reasons. This is also a better way to understand agent-neutral reasons. The normativity of reasons does not spring from the claims made on us by either our personal projects or objective goods. It springs from the claims we make on one another.

Korsmeyer, Carolyn. Instruments of the Eye: Shortcuts to Perspectives. *J Aes Art Crit*, 47(2), 139-146, Spr 89.

Nineteenth century America saw a surge of popularity of painting and drawing, accomplishments that were believed to serve not only decorative purposes but also moral and social ends. Manuals for amateurs offered instruction on drawing that passed along ideas about philosophy, aesthetics, and optics which had been developing in European art theory since the Renaissance. This paper examines the dissemination of some of these ideas, focussing on linear perspective, devices recommended for its execution, and the presumptions about vision implicit in their employment.

Korsmeyer, Carolyn. Pleasure: Reflections on Aesthetics and Feminism. *J Aes Art Crit*, 51(2), 199-206, Spr 93.

The first section of this paper reflects upon approaches to philosophy of art that feminists perspectives have fostered, noting points of commonality with other recent theoretical shifts in the field of aesthetics. The second section focuses on the question of aesthetic pleasure. Pleasure is a staple in older traditions of aesthetics that has regained currency from the challenge posed by psychoanalytic feminist theories, including theories of the gaze. The paper concludes by discussing incompatibilities between the latter approach to pleasure and the standard needs of aesthetic theory, suggesting certain avenues for resolution of these difficulties.

Korthals, Michiel. Morality and Cooperation. *J Moral Educ*, 21(1), 17-27, 1992.

Piaget's early theory on moral development and moral education can elucidate some important points in the discussion about a broad or narrow definition of morality and its consequences for educational practice. In the first place, Piaget introduces a concept of morality which transcends the partly misleading dichotomy between broad and narrow morality. Secondly, he conceptualizes the educational relationship as a development of two stages and evades the unfruitful dichotomy between liberal education and transmission of traditions. In this regard, his concept of mutual respect is an important educational device for handling the plurality of cultures in the modern world.

Korthals, Michiel. On the Justification of Societal Development Claims. *Phil Soc Crit*, 19(1), 25-41, 1993.

Recently, some social theoreticians have proposed societal stage development models which claim that later stages are somehow superior to preceding ones. In this article different elements of justification are distinguished and several types of justification are analyzed, inter alia that of the American psychologist Kohlberg, the German social philosopher Habermas and the English anthropologist Gellner. All try to connect the theory of societal development with individual development and therefore have educational relevance as well. The author refutes the nonmoral and individual types of justification, and proposes some kind of transcendental argument instead.

Kosso, Peter. Historical Evidence and Epistemic Justification: Thucydides as a Case Study. *Hist Theor*, 32(1), 1-13, 1993.

Through both a conceptual analysis of historical evidence in general, and a specific study of Thucydides' evidence on the Peloponnesian war, the structure of justification of historical knowledge is described and evaluated. The justification is internal in the sense of being done entirely within a network of evidential and descriptive claims about the past. This forces a coherence form of justification in which the telling epistemic standards are eliminative—indicators of what is *not* likely to be true rather than what is. The epistemological contrast is between justification by coherence among historical claims, or by appeal to epistemic foundations. (edited)

Kotarbinska, Janina. Puzzles of Existence in Kotarbinski: Logic, Semantics and Ontology, Wolenski, Jan (ed). Dordrecht, Kluwer, 1990.

Kotarbinski, Tadeusz. Philosophical Self-Portrait in Kotarbinski: Logic, Semantics and Ontology, Wolenski, Jan (ed). Dordrecht, Kluwer, 1990.

Kotatko, P. Wittgenstein and the Cartesian Subject (in Czechoslovakian). *Filozof Cas*, 40(3), 435-457, 1992.

The paper deals with two Wittgenstein's arguments concerning the problem of rule-following: the argument against private language (PLA), i.e., language whose expressions refer or apply exclusively to private phenomena, and the argument against individual language (ILA), i.e., language whose semantic rules are introduced and fixed by intentions of an isolated speaker. Part I suggests a way of reconstruction of PLA, while part II characterizes Wittgenstein's account of public discourse about mental states in the light of PLA. Parts III-V discuss ILA, especially in its Kripkean version, focussing on its consequences for the account of public communication. (edited)

Kotva Jr, Joseph J. An Appeal for a Christian Virtue Ethic. *Thought*, 67(265), 158-180, Je 92.

Kotzin, Rhoda Hadassa. Bribery and Intimidation: A Discussion of Sandra Lee Bartky's *Femininity and Domination*. *Hypatia*, 8(1), 164-172, Wint 93.

A review of my undergraduate students' commentaries on two of Bartky's essays serves as the occasion for elaborating on Bartky's analyses of factors that sustain and perpetuate the subjection and disempowerment of women. In my elaboration I draw from John Stuart Mill's statement: "In the case of women, each individual of the subject-class is in a chronic state of bribery and intimidation combined". I conclude by raising the question, How is personal transformation possible?

Kotzmann, Ernst and Bammé, Arno and Oberheber, Ulrike. Basic Questions about Metaphysics of Technology: Spangler, Heidegger, Günther. *J Speculative Phil*, 7(2), 143-158, 1993.

Kouba, P. Fragments on Nihilism—Nietzsche (in Czechoslovakian). *Filozof Cas*, 40(4), 625-637, 1992.

Koutougos, Aris. The Plato-Wittgenstein Rte to the Pragmatics of Falsification in Greek Studies in the Philosophy and History of Science, Nicolacopoulos, Pantelis (ed). Dordrecht, Kluwer, 1990.

Kovacs, George. The Nature and Meaning of Work. *Res Phil Technol*, 11, 183-194, 1991.

These reflections analyze the nature and meaning of work (in the light of continental philosophy). They indicate some guidelines for rediscovering the primordial function and meaning of work in contemporary culture and society, for discerning its deep roots in human existence, as well as its determinative political and technological context.

Kovalev, Vitalii. The *Narod*, the Intelligentsia, and the Individual. *Russian Stud Phil*, 31(4), 71-82, Spr 93.

Kow, James P. Hegel, Kolb, and Flay: Foundationalism or Anti-Foundationalism?. *Int Phil Quart*, 33(2), 203-218, Je 93.

To be intelligible, the finite order of human experience, for Hegel, requires infinite absolute spirit. Flay and Kolb overlook this infinite in Hegel's thought.

Notwithstanding their contextualist hints in interpreting Hegel they regard Hegel as even more of a foundationalist than the epistemological foundationalists. But the notion of ground in Hegel's Logic refutes this. Hegel's systemic holism is grounded in the prospective completed infinity of spirit beyond either Foundationalism or Anti-Foundationalism. In the absence of infinite spirit we are consigned to an unnecessarily attenuated human finitude. The mutual career of the Hegelian finite and infinite however frees us from this prospect.

Kozhamthadam, Job. Can Religion Give Science a Heart?. *J Dharma*, 18(2), 139-161, Ap-Je 93.

Modern science has achieved its stupendous progress by distancing itself from other disciplines and by concentrating on certain limited aspects of reality and human life. This has resulted in a science that has become "heartless" and ever threatening to destroy us humans and our planet. It is possible for science to have a heart without losing its head? The paper argues that it is possible and that the injection of certain religious and moral values into science can go a long way towards achieving this goal.

Kracauer, Siegfried and Levin, Thomas Y (trans). Photography. *Crit Inquiry*, 19(3), 421-436, Spr 93.

Kracher, Beverly J and Wells, Deborah L. Justice, Sexual Harassment, and the Reasonable Victim Standard. *J Bus Ethics*, 12(6), 423-432, Je 93.

In determining when sexual behavior at work creates a hostile working environment, some courts have asked, "Would a reasonable *person* view this as a hostile environment? Other courts have asked, "Would a reasonable *victim* view this is as a hostile environment?" There is no consensus in the legal community regarding which of these is just. Using moral theory, businesses can construct just procedures regarding sexually hostile environments. The duty of mutual respect of persons and the duty not to harm the innocent compels use of the reasonable victim standard. A training approach to reducing sexual harassment at work is proposed.

Krämer, Hans. L'interpretazione di Platone della Scuola di Tubinga e della Scuola di Milano. *Riv Filosof Neo-Scolas*, 84(2-3), 203-218, Ap-S 92.

Krämer, Hans-Joachim. Plato and Aristotle: A New Look at Their Relationship — The Historical Place of Aristotelian Metaphysics (in Czechoslovakian). *Magyar Filozof Szemle*, 6, 866-935, 1991.

Krämer, Sybille. Symbolische Erkenntnis bei Leibniz. *Z Phil Forsch*, 46(2), 224-237, Ap-J 92.

Leibniz's conception of "symbolic cognition" is analysed. Leibniz characterizes reasoning as "cogitatio caeca vel symbolica"—"blind or symbolic reasoning". The paradox arises how truth should be achieved by "blind" insight. It is solved by the hypothesis that "cogitatio caeca vel symbolica" is the metaphorical description of an epistemic procedure, which reduces truth to correctness. This reduction is realized by "calculization". But a calculus is not only a medium to represent but to construct its referential objects. Symbolic reasoning is an epistemic procedure not only for representing, but for generating intellectual objects.

Kragh, Helge. Bohr's Quantum Philosophy: On the Shoulders of a Giant?. *Dan Yrbk Phil*, 27, 109-118, 1992.

This is an essay review of Jan Faye's *Niels Bohr: His Heritage and Legacy* (Dordrecht: Kluwer Intl, 1991), focusing on Faye's main claim that the Danish philosopher Harold Hoffding was Bohr's intellectual mentor. It is argued that although Faye presents strong arguments for his claim, he greatly exaggerates Hoffding's influence. Hoffding cannot be considered the spiritual father of the complementarity principle. It is further discussed, in a general way, how to decide such influence claims in the history and philosophy of science.

Kraines, David and Kraines, Vivian. Learning to Cooperate with Pavlov: An Adaptive Strategy for the Iterated Prisoner's Dilemma with Noise. *Theor Decis*, 35(2), 107-150, S 93.

Conflict of interest may be modeled, heuristically, by the iterated Prisoner's Dilemma game. Although several researchers have shown that the Tit-For-Tat strategy can encourage the evolution of cooperation, this strategy can never outscore any opponent and it does poorly against its clone in a noisy environment. Here we examine the family of Pavlovian strategies which adapts its play by positive and negative conditioning, much as many animals do. Mutual cooperation will evolve in a contest with Pavlov against a wide variety of opponents and in particular against its clone. And the strategy is quite stable in a noisy environment. Although this strategy cooperates and retaliates, as does Tit-For-Tat, it is not forgiving; Pavlov will exploit altruistic strategies until he is punished by mutual defection. Moreover, Pavlovian strategies are natural models for many real life conflict-of-interest encounters as well as human and computer simulations.

Kraines, Vivian and Kraines, David. Learning to Cooperate with Pavlov: An Adaptive Strategy for the Iterated Prisoner's Dilemma with Noise. *Theor Decis*, 35(2), 107-150, S 93.

Conflict of interest may be modeled, heuristically, by the iterated Prisoner's Dilemma game. Although several researchers have shown that the Tit-For-Tat strategy can encourage the evolution of cooperation, this strategy can never outscore any opponent and it does poorly against its clone in a noisy environment. Here we examine the family of Pavlovian strategies which adapts its play by positive and negative conditioning, much as many animals do. Mutual cooperation will evolve in a contest with Pavlov against a wide variety of opponents and in particular against its clone. And the strategy is quite stable in a noisy environment. Although this strategy cooperates and retaliates, as does Tit-For-Tat, it is not forgiving; Pavlov will exploit altruistic strategies until he is punished by mutual defection. Moreover, Pavlovian strategies are natural models for many real life conflict-of-interest encounters as well as human and computer simulations.

Krajewski, Stanislaw. One Logic or Many Logics? (Epstein's Set-Assignment Semantics for Logical Calculi). *J Non-Classical Log*, 8(1), 7-33, My 91.

A philosophically motivated uniform semantical framework for various propositional calculae is sketched, following Richard L Epstein's book *The Semantic Foundations of Logic*. The main idea is that a conditional can be true only if there is some connection between its antecedent and its consequent. Also a new concept of translations between logics (a joint work with Epstein) is presented. One theorem from the book is simplified and strengthened. The problem how to extend the approach to the predicate case (also a joint work, not included in the book) is discussed for the most natural system—*the relatedness logic*.

Kramer, Lloyd S. *The Rhetoric of Historical Representation: Three Narrative Histories of the French Revolution* by Ann Rigney. *Hist Theor*, 31(3), 314-325, 1992.

Kramer, Matthew H. God, Greed, and Flesh: Saint Paul, Thomas Hobbes, and the Nature/Nurture Debate. *S J Phil*, 30(4), 51-66, Wint 92.

Numerous scholars in a wide range of disciplines have endorsed the neopragmatist thesis that reality is a "social construct." This essay seeks to expose a common muddle in the debates that surround the social-construction thesis. Stated specifically, the point of confusion lies in the equating of the social-construction principle with the theory of environmental determinism (i.e., the favoring of the "nurture" side in the nature/nurture debate). More generally, the point of confusion lies in the collapsing of metaphysical problems and mundane problems.

Kramer, Matthew H. Our Longest Lie: Irrelgious Thoughts on the Relation Between Metaphysics and Politics. *Phil Today*, 37(1), 89-109, Spr 93.

Krantz, Susan F L. The Tragic and the Religious: Openness to the Mystery in Caputo's Radical Hermeneutics. *Amer Cath Phil Quart*, 65, 75-85, 1991.

Krapiec, Mieczyslaw Albert and Sandok, Theresa (trans). *Metaphysics: An Outline of the Theory of Being*. New York, Lang, 1991.

This book is both a comprehensive introduction to the philosophy of being and a sustained argument for the value of approaching metaphysics from a classical, realistic point of view. The traditional topics addressed in classical metaphysics— the transcendental properties of being, act and potency, substance and accident, essence and existence, etc.— are presented in a contemporary light and related to current philosophical controversies. The book culminates in an extended discussion of the analogical nature of being and cognition.

Krause, Décio. On a Quasi-Set Theory. *Notre Dame J Form Log*, 33(3), 402-411, Sum 92.

Quasi-set theories (QST) were proposed to deal, in set-theoretical terms, with collections of indistinguishable objects. The idea of the paper is to provide the axiomatics of a QST by modifying the concept of identity of the underlying logical apparatus: to a certain kind of atoms, the concept of identity, in a precise sense, cannot be applied. Among other things, it results that some quasi-sets have no ordinal associated to them, but only a cardinal (introduced as a primitive concept). The heuristic motivation is the behaviour of Quantum Elementary Particles, mainly in what concerns to some ideas of E Schrödinger and H Weyl.

Krauss, Alfred N and Miké, Valerie and Ross, Gail S. Perinatal Technology: Answers and Questions. *J Clin Ethics*, 3(1), 56-62, Spr 92.

This article focuses on uncertainty in perinatal medicine. Sources of uncertainty include not only the complexity of premature physiology and related disease mechanisms, but also the lack of proper assessment of many perinatal technologies for their safety and effectiveness. These issues are illustrated by means of two perinatal technologies: transcutaneous oxygen monitoring and neonatal extracorporeal membrane oxygenation (ECMO). They are analyzed in terms of a proposed "ethics of evidence," meaning, in concrete but not exhaustive terms, guidelines for the creation, assessment and dissemination of evidence. Related problem are then discussed in the broader context of contemporary perinatal medicine.

Krausz, Ernest. Leaving Man in Society. *Method Sci*, 25(3), 141-152, 1992.

Two major questions are raised: Is it justified to study social reality by means of aggregated data of social phenomena?; How does individualized behaviour fit into a macro-quantitative explanatory scheme? Conclusions: Although underlying social phenomena there is an element of human volition and choice, this does not destroy a social science based on aggregated data. The choice factor of the individual becomes the chance factor in the statistics which accrue. Again, intentional behaviour is mostly *not unique* behaviour and can be placed in some category, thus giving rise to the patterns and probabilities the sociologist wishes to examine and explain.

Krausz, Michael. Crossing Cultures: Two Universalisms and Two Relativisms in Cultural Relativism and Philosophy, Dascal, Marcelo (ed). Leiden, Brill, 1991.

I distinguish two sets of distinctions to help chart a conceptual landscape in terms of which descriptions of cultural diversity may be placed. I distinguish 'hard' universalism from 'soft' universalism (section II), and I distinguish extreme relativism from rational relativism (section III). These markers should be understood as designating attitudes on a continuum rather than sharply defined and exclusive positions.

Krausz, Michael. Ideality and Ontology in the Practice of History in Objectivity, Method and Point of View, Van Der Dussen, W J (ed). Leiden, Brill, 1991.

Kraut, Richard H. Introduction to the Study of Plato in The Cambridge Companion to Plato, Kraut, Richard H (ed). New York, Cambridge Univ Pr, 1992.

This essay presents an overview of Plato's philosophy and of contemporary scholarship of Plato. Among the topics are discussed are: Plato's philosophical development, the theory of Forms, and the various methodologies scholars have employed for interpreting Plato.

Kraut, Richard H (ed). *The Cambridge Companion to Plato*. New York, Cambridge Univ Pr, 1992.

This volume contains 15 essays, each specially written for it. They cover the entire range of Plato's dialogues and are intended for use by students as well as specialists. Among the topics covered are: alternative strategies for reading Plato, the intellectual background that shaped Plato's philosophy, the chronology of the dialogues, Socrates, the influence of mathematics on Plato, the learner's paradox of the *Meno*, Plato's relation to Greek religion, Platonic love, the theory of Forms, Platonic ethics, Plato's critique of poetry, the third man argument, the *Sophist* on falsity, pleasure in the *Philebus*, and the political thought of the *Laws*.

Kraut, Richard H. The Defense of Justice in Plato's "Republic" in The Cambridge Companion to Plato, Kraut, Richard H (ed). New York, Cambridge Univ Pr, 1992.

This essay attempts to state Plato's argument in the *Republic* that justice is so great a good that a just person is necessarily better off than a just person, regardless of any other differences in their circumstances. The heart of Plato's argument lies in his theory of Forms, and the essay tries to show how the central books of the *Republic* contribute to the single complex argument in defense of justice that begins in Book II and terminates in Book IX.

Kraut, Robert. Robust Deflationism. *Phil Rev*, 102(2), 247-263, Ap 93.

Irrealist explanations are controversial: the requisite distinction between "descriptive" discourse that states facts, and "expressive" discourse that expresses commitments or manifests stances, is difficult to explicate. Nevertheless: Are there regions of discourse which must—on pain of contradiction—be construed realistically? Recent discussions suggest that irrealism about *semantic* discourse—e.g., deflationism about "S has truth conditions"—cannot be coherently conjoined with irrealism about other fragments of discourse. I argue that such discussions are mistaken. I also locate deflationism within a larger philosophical context, and suggest that expressivism about the descriptive/expressive distinction is coherent and plausible.

Kraut, Robert. The Objectivity of Color and the Color of Objectivity. *Phil Stud*, 68(3), 265-287, D 92.

My focus is the metaphysical and semantic categories routinely mobilized in discussions of color. Much of the literature asks whether color has objective status: whether colors are real properties of objects around us (like shape), or whether colors enjoy a merely subjective status (artifacts of conscious experience.) The literature assumes that 'objective,' 'real property,' and 'mind dependence' are clear notions. They are not. In this paper I clarify these metaphysical notions, arguing that they function nondescriptively to express commitments to the explanatory eliminability of certain regions of discourse.

Kreisberg, Seth. *Transforming Power: Domination, Empowerment, and Education*. Albany, SUNY Pr, 1992.

Kreisel, Georg. Suitable Descriptions for Suitable Categories in Advances in Scientific Philosophy, Schurz, Gerhard (ed). Amsterdam, Rodopi, 1991.

Krell, David Farrell. *Das Unheimliche*: Architectural Sections of Heidegger and Freud. *Res Phenomenol*, 22, 43-61, 1992.

The article discusses the importance of the notion of "the uncanny" in the work of Freud and Heidegger. The relevance of the uncanny for architecture is emphasized.

Krell, David Farrell. *Daimon Life: Heidegger and Life-Philosophy*. Bloomington, Indiana Univ Pr, 1992.

The work explores the importance of life-philosophy (Dilthey, Nietzsche, Scheler, Simmel, etc.) for Heidegger's thought. Major way-stations include Heidegger's *Being and Time* (1927), and the lecture course on theoretical biology (1929-1930), as well as later essays on Greek philosophy and on Nietzsche. Heidegger's difficulties in acknowledging life-forms other than the human are also shown to have political consequences.

Krell, David Farrell. Of Spirit and the Daimon in Ethics and Danger, Dallery, Arleen B (ed). Albany, SUNY Pr, 1992.

A meditation on the political scandal of Heidegger's involvement in National Socialism in the 1930's, this article raises the question as to whether, in retrospect, Heidegger should be burned.

Krell, David Farrell. Spiriting Heidegger in Of Derrida, Heidegger, and Spirit, Wood, David (ed). Evanston, Northwestern Univ Pr, 1993.

Krell, David Farrell. Where Deathless Horses Weep in Reading Heidegger: Commemorations, Sallis, John (ed). Bloomington, Indiana Univ Pr, 1992.

A reading of Heidegger's 1929-1930 lectures on theoretical biology in the context of my book *Daimon Life: Heidegger and Life-Philosophy*, 1992.

Kremer, Michael. The Multiplicity of General Propositions. *Nous*, 26(4), 409-426, D 92.

At *Tractatus* 4.0411, Wittgenstein gives examples to illustrate 4.04's claim that a proposition and the situation that it represents share the same "multiplicity." These examples also illustrate the doctrine that what can be shown cannot be said. Hence, 4.0411 is a comment not only on 4.04 (as some have maintained) but also on 4.041 (as Wittgenstein's numbering indicates). This illuminates Wittgenstein's views on generality, on showing and saying, and on multiplicity and logical form. In particular, attempts to say what can only be shown are doubly nonsensical, failing both to *say* anything and to *show* anything; the notions of logical form and multiplicity should be applied to the whole of language rather than to individual propositions; and the doctrine of showing and saying rests in part on this holism.

Kremer-Marietti, Angèle. Measurement and Principles: The Structure of Physical Theories. *Rev Int Phil*, 46(182), 361-375, 1992.

Krettek, Thomas. Actualities, Finalities and Dunamis as Ultimate Realities in the Thought of Paul Weiss. *Ultim Real Mean*, 16(1-2), 97-109, Mr-Je 93.

Kretzmann, Norman. Evidence Against Anti-Evidentialism in Our Knowledge of God, Clark, Kelly James (ed). Dordrecht, Kluwer, 1992.

Kretzmann, Norman. Faith Seeks, Understanding Finds in Christian Philosophy, Flint, Thomas P (ed). Notre Dame, Univ Notre Dame Pr, 1990.

Kretzmann, Norman. Infallibility, Error, and Ignorance. *Can J Phil*, Supp(17), 159-194, 1991.

Kretzmann, Norman and Stump, Eleonore. Eternity, Awareness, and Action. *Faith Phil*, 9(4), 463-482, O 92.

Our article "Eternity" (1981), in which we presented, defended, and applied the traditional doctrine of divine eternity, prompted some criticisms that focus on difficulties in the concept of eternity itself. In the present article we summarize our original account of the doctrine before offering versions of two such criticisms and replying to them. Our replies are intended to clarify and develop further the essential notions of eternity's atemporal duration and of its relationship with time.

AUTHOR INDEX WITH ABSTRACTS 553 Krukowski, Lucian

Kretzmann, Norman and Stump, Eleonore. Prophecy, Past Truth, and Eternity in Philosophical Perspectives, 5: Philosophy of Religion, 1991, Tomberlin, James E (ed). Atascadero, Ridgeview, 1991.

We examine three attempts to show that the doctrine of eternity fails to contribute to a solution to the foreknowledge problem. The first is that of David Widerker, who finds problems for the eternity solution in the traditional doctrine that God occasionally reveals to prophets truths about the future. The second is that of Jonathan Edwards, who bases his objection on the mere possibility of prophecy. And the third is that of Alvin Plantinga, who argues that the problem of foreknowledge and freedom simply can't be resolved by the doctrine of eternity. We argue that none of these criticisms succeeds, if we understand correctly the nature of the relations between an eternal God and temporal creatures.

Krieger, Murray. Representation in Words and in Drama in Aesthetic Illusion, Burwick, Frederick (ed). Hawthorne, de Gruyter, 1990.

The history of literary theory has been largely shaped by the aesthetics of the "natural sign." Since Plato, this history has been characterized by a central distinction in the modes of representation between drama and the other literary genres. What is at stake is the role of dramatic "illusion," which can be traced from the *Republic* to 17th-century French dramatic theory and then to Lessing's *Laokoön* and Johnson's *Preface to Shakespeare*. It is tempting to extend the use of the "natural sign" to the political realm; the literary art—as a self-conscious illusion—may function to alert us to the delusionary consequences of the political appeal to the natural sign.

Krieglstein, Werner. Philosophical Implications of Chaos Theory: Toward a Meta-Critique of Action. *Dialec Hum*, 17(3), 151-156, 1990.

Kries, Douglas. Leo Strauss's Understanding of Aquinas's Natural Law Theory. *Thomist*, 57(2), 215-232, Ap 93.

This article argues that Leo Strauss understood Thomas Aquinas to have altered the classical view of natural rights by introducing the concept of *synderesis* into that theory, by obfuscating the question of the best regime, and by linking natural right theory to the notion of a divine lawgiver. Strauss felt that Thomas thereby rendered the traditional natural right theory inflexible and made it susceptible to attack from modern political philosophy.

Krimbas, Costas B. Evolutionary Epistemology on Universals as Innate in Greek Studies in the Philosophy and History of Science, Nicolacopoulos, Pantelis (ed). Dordrecht, Kluwer, 1990.

Modern population biology is nominalistic, evolution does not permit the acceptance of "types". However, both nominalist and essentialist (realist) positions are not free from difficulties. The concept of *family resemblances* of Wittgenstein is also discussed and its application to Numerical Taxonomy. The author argues that a satisfactory solution to the type problem is provided by evolutionary epistemology: the capacity for forming universals is genetically fixed by natural selection. The acceptance of this provides a satisfactory solution to several logical difficulties.

Kristeller, Paul O and Woods, Gregory (trans). *Greek Philosophers of the Hellenistic Age*. New York, Columbia Univ Pr, 1993.

Kristjánsson, Kristján. For a *Concept* of Negative Liberty—but Which *Conception*?. *J Applied Phil*, 9(2), 221-231, 1992.

The present essay concurs with R Beehler's recent contribution to this journal ('For One Concept of Liberty', (1) 1991) in deeming the concept of negative liberty fully adequate for political discourse. Thus, section 1 indicates a plausible line of reasoning by which the negative concept can be defended against some standard objections. However, sections 2 and 3 argue that, nevertheless, Beehler's traditional conception of negative liberty is inadequate. It does not account correctly for various paradigmatic cases of 'unfreedom', for instance, the curtailment of the liberty of the poor by their lack of economic resources. More precisely, Beehler's account will in many such cases fail to identify the correct constraining agents. The present essay suggests how Beehler's aim may be achieved on the basis of a different conception of negative liberty: the 'responsibility view.'

Kristjánsson, Kristján. What Is Wrong with Positive Liberty?. *Soc Theor Pract*, 18(3), 289-310, Fall 92.

Kristol, Elizabeth. Picture Perfect: The Politics of Prenatal Testing. *Ethics Med*, 9(2), 23-31, Sum 93.

Krizan, M. Response to Douglas P Lackey's 'Extraordinary Evil or Common Malevolence?' in Applied Philosophy, Almond, Brenda (ed). New York, Routledge, 1992.

Kroger, Joseph. Some Reflections on Michael Polanyi and Catholic Thought. *Tradition Discovery*, 18(2), 15-21, 1991-92.

Krois, John Michael. Cassirer, Neo-Kantianism and Metaphysics. *Rev Metaph Morale*, 97(4), 437-453, O-D 92.

Cassirer hat sich—wie der späte Cohen und der späte Natorp—von der Marburger Beschränkung auf Erkenntnistheorie entfernt. In bisher unpublizierten Texten aus der Emigrationszeit befasste Cassirer sich mit dem Problem der Metaphysik. Goethes Lehre von den Urphänomenen und die Gestalttheorie Kurt Goldsteins beeinflussten Cassirers späte Theorie der "Basisphänomene." Diese neue Denkrichtung knüpfte an die Symboltheorie Cassirers an und wies auf ihren Ausgang hin.

Kromkowski, John (ed) and McLean, George F (ed). *Relations Between Cultures*. Washington, CRVP, 1991.

Kromkowski, John (ed) and McLean, George F (ed). *Urbanization and Values*. Washington, CRVP, 1991.

Kromkowski, John (ed) and Peachey, Paul (ed) and McLean, George F (ed). *The Place of the Person In Social Life*. Washington, CRVP, 1991.

Kromm, Jane. Introduction to Re-Thinking Representation: Anselm and Visual Thinking. *Listening*, 28(2), 95-104, Spr 93.

Gives general summary of visual and verbal inter-relations in medieval illuminated manuscripts and texts, including those discussed in recent critical writing. Focuses on the significance of visual thinking in Anselm's theological writings, to the truth claims of the ontological argument in particular, and to his influence on the visual arts of his era.

Kronen, John D. Can Leclerc's Composite Actualities be Substances?. *Process Stud*, 21(1), 25-43, Spr 92.

Since most process metaphysicians have reacted negatively to traditional substance metaphysics it is interesting that one process metaphysician, Ivor Leclerc, has tried to appropriate the concept of substance into a process framework. This paper argues, using the thought of Suarez as a backdrop, that Lecerc's attempt does not succeed because 1) he makes what is an accident, namely relation, into a substance, 2) he allows for wholes that are greater than the sum of their parts, and 3) he allows substances to have more than one substantial being, a contradiction.

Kronen, John D. The Importance of the Concept of Substantial Unity in Suárez's Argument for Hylomorphism. *Amer Cath Phil Quart*, 65(3), 335-360, Sum 91.

The paper analyzes Suarez's arguments for the form-matter nature of material substances based on the need for a substantial principle unifying them. It is shown that Suarez deemphasizes the traditional argument for the form-matter nature of such substances based on change, preferring instead the more metaphysical argument based on unity. Finally the reason's why Suarez prefers such an argument are explained both from the perspective of the age in which he lived and from the perspective of his metaphysical program.

Kronick, Joseph G. Romance and the Prose of the World in Theorizing American Literature, Cowan, Bainard (ed). Baton Rouge, Louisiana St Univ Pr, 1991.

American romance has traditionally been interpreted as a self-reflexive genre that reconciles thought and history. Following Hegel's concept of prosaism as a purely grammatical linking of idea and form rather than a sensory manifestation of the idea in the phenomenon, we can shift the ground of literary representation from aesthetics to a nonreflexive grammatical relation. If we read Hawthorne's romances through Hegel's theory of prosaism, we find that romance is the allegorical undoing of the identity between consciousness and language and between history and nature that lies at the basis of American ideology.

Kronick, Joseph G (ed) and Cowan, Bainard (ed). *Theorizing American Literature*. Baton Rouge, Louisiana St Univ Pr, 1991.

Kroon, Frederick. Rationality and Epistemic Paradox. *Synthese*, 94(3), 377-408, Mr 93.

This paper provides a new solution to the paradox of 'belief-instability', discussed by—among others—Burge, Conee, and Sorensen. The problem involves a rational agent who has good reason to believe the truth of something of the form: (p if and only if it is not the case that I accept p), and who wonders whether or not she should accept p. My solution to the ensuing choice problem claims that in its most serious form the problem wrongly assumes that rational agents are always allowed to assume their own rationality when deciding how they should choose.

Kroon, Frederick W. Was Meinong Only Pretending?. *Phil Phenomenol Res*, 52(3), 499-527, S 92.

In this paper I argue against the usual interpretation of Meinong's argument for nonexistent objects, an interpretation according to which Meinong imported nonexistent objects like *the golden mountain* to account directly for the truth of statements like 'the golden mountain is golden'. I claim instead (using evidence from Meinong's *On Assumptions*) that his argument really involves an ineliminable appeal to the notion of pretense. This appeal nearly convinced Meinong at one stage that he could do without nonexistent objects. The reason, I argue, why he nonetheless embraced an ontology of nonexistents has to do with the phenomenology of representation, and not with semantics.

Krüger, Lorenz. Commentator on 'Objectivity and the Science-Ethics Distinction' in The Quality of Life, Nussbaum, Martha C (ed). New York, Oxford Univ Pr, 1993.

In agreement with Putnam both absolute truth *and* relativism of truth are rejected. But against Putnam a certain version of correspondence is defended: truth relates us to experiential facts which are independent of our actions. Ontological relativity is ruled out on empirical and pragmatic grounds. In contrast, evaluative statements are claimed to derive from human self-determination, so that the realm of rationality is seen to be wider than that of truth. Hence, truth cannot be equated with rational assertability.

Krüger, Lorenz. Kausalität und Freiheit: Ein Beispiel für den Zusammenhang von Metaphysik und Lebenspraxis. *Neue Hefte Phil*, 32-33, 1-14, 1992.

Starting with some historical reflections on the conceptual interrelatedness of causality and agent responsibility it is claimed that the notion of a cause not only presupposes the notion of freedom to act but that free actions are to be viewed as paradigmatic cases of causation. Following the rejection of the regularity view an alternative pragmatically orientated construal of causality is proposed according to which a cause is an event which makes a difference to the regular though indeterministic course of events. Free actions then are opposed to cases of indifferent indeterminism (random) and revealed as genuine causes.

Krukowski, Lucian. Aufbau and Bauhaus: A Cross-Realm Comparison. *J Aes Art Crit*, 50(3), 197-209, Sum 92.

I identify similarities in historical position and program between the philosophical and social context of Rudolph Carnap's "Logische Aufbau der Welt" and the activities of the "Bauhaus", the school of visual design headed by Walter Gropius. I then develop a structural comparison between the constructionalist systems of Carnap, Nelson Goodman and Ludwig Wittgenstein, and the artworks and theoretical writings of the painters Wassily Kandinsky and Piet Mondrian.

Krukowski, Lucian. The Embodiment and Durations of Artworks. *J Aes Art Crit*, 46(3), 39-397, Spr 88.

I view the relationship between the artwork and its physical object as one of "embodiment". I comment on Joseph Margolis's use of the term and develop the temporal variations that are the possible conditions of the pairing. I claim that in the embodiment relationship, the temporal durations of works and their objects need not be identical. As a consequence, both work and object may begin before, coincide with, or endure beyond each other. This generates none variations of the work-object pair. I describe the conditions and offer examples for each variation.

Kruks, Sonia. Simone de Beauvoir: Teaching Sartre about Freedom in Sartre Alive, Aronson, Ronald (ed). Detroit, Wayne St Univ Pr, 1991.

This paper analyzes the philosophical relationship between Beauvoir and Sartre. In her early ethical essays and in *The Second Sex* (1949), Beauvoir developed a significantly different account of human freedom from that proposed by Sartre in *Being and Nothingness* (1943). Like Merleau-Ponty, Beauvoir stressed the socially situated nature of freedom, the interdependence of freedoms, and our consequent vulnerability to oppression. In some of his later works, culminating in *Critique of Dialectical Reason* (1960), Sartre's ideas about freedom gradually shifted towards those of Beauvoir. The traditional view, that Beauvoir was philosophically derivative of Sartre, thus needs to be re-thought.

Krygier, Martin. Thinking Like a Lawyer in Ethical Dimensions of Legal Theory, Sadurski, Wojciech (ed). Amsterdam, Rodopi, 1991.

Krysztofiak, Wojciech. Phenomenology, Possible Worlds and Negation. *Husserl Stud*, 8(3), 205-220, 1991-92.

The explication of the framework for the phenomenological genetic analysis of negation is the main aim of this article. This task is motivated by Charles Harvey's, Jaakko Hintikka's, David Woodruff Smith's and Ronald McIntyre's results concerned with accommodating possible worlds semantics to phenomenological genetic analyses. First, the concept of genetic analysis will be explicated. Subsequently, the main statements of Harvey and Hintikka will be presented. Then, these will be compared with the Husserlian theory of consciousness. Finally, the phenomenological conception of negation—different from Husserl's original theory and its interpretation formulated by Harvey and Hintikka—will be discussed and expressed with the help of categories of possible worlds semantics.

Kucheman, Clark A. Morality and Coercion-By-Violence in Terrorism, Justice and Social Values, Peden, Creighton (ed). Lewiston, Mellen Pr, 1990.

Kuczynski, Janusz. Polishness in a Universalistic Perspective: Pluralism—Dialogue— Synthesis. *Dialec Hum*, 17(2), 93-114, 1990.

Kühn, Rolf. Intentional and Material Phenomenology (in German). *Tijdschr Filosof*, 54(4), 693-714, D 92.

Husserl's phenomenology abandoned the fundamental phenomenological task of investigating pure appearance in favour of research into transcendent knowledge of essences. Thereby, in place of the original *cogitatio* with its capacity for self-giving, the intentional intuition came to present itself as a mode of givenness without a radical phenomenalization of the ontologically pre-given. M Henry, who already elaborated a "material phenomenology" of the original hyletic self-affection as immanence of like, has demonstrated the deficiency of the phenomenological differentiation of appearing from appearance by invoking four principles of phenomenology. These concern the relation between being/appearing, intuition/evidence, method/things in themselves, and reduction/givenness. Regarding this last connection J L Marion's recent phenomenological approach is also worth taking into account. With the "pure appeal", Marion at the same time questions Heidegger's priority of Dasein on behalf of the Ego.

Kühn, Rolf. Leibanwesenheit und primitive Gegenwart. *Z Phil Forsch*, 47(1), 136-141, Ja-Mr 93.

Kühn, Rolf. Wahrnehmung als "Lektüre". *Gregorianum*, 73(3), 499-522, 1992.

Kueker, D W and Laskowski, M C. On Generic Structures. *Notre Dame J Form Log*, 33(2), 175-183, Spr 92.

We discuss many generalizations of Fraissé's construction of countable 'homogeneous-universal' structures. We give characterizations of when such a structure is saturated and when its theory is ω-categorical. We also state very general conditions under which the structure is atomic.

Küng, Guido. Ontology and the Construction of Systems. *Synthese*, 95(1), 29-53, Ap 93.

After drawing attention to the basic importance of Goodman's work *The Structure of Appearance*, this paper turns to a critical analysis of Goodman's claims concerning worldmaking. It stresses that Goodman's acceptance of a multiplicity of actual worlds does *not* involve the belief in an unknowable underlying reality; but that it is due to the non-mysterious fact that constructional systems allow for a multiplicity of disagreeing, right versions. However, from the point of view of truthmaker ontology, most 'worlds' of constructional systems are not genuine worlds; and so far it has *not* been shown that there are genuine truthmaker worlds that disagree. It is suggested that the construction of systems usually involves three conflicting aims; the logical, the ontological, and the psychological. Considering the current interest in cognitive psychology and phenomenology, the implications of the psychological aim, too, deserve to be reexamined.

Künne, Wolfgang. Hybrid Proper Names. *Mind*, 101(404), 721-731, O 92.

Künne, Wolfgang. Truth, Rightness, and Permanent Acceptability. *Synthese*, 95(1), 107-117, Ap 93.

Goodman and Elgin want truth to be demoted and rightness to be promoted. In the first part of this paper the main reasons they offer for this reorientation are discussed. Goodman once suggested that one construe truth as acceptability that is not subsequently lost, but later he quietly dropped this proposal. In the second part of this paper it is argued that ultimate acceptability is indeed neither a necessary nor a sufficient condition for truth.

Kuhn, Thomas S. Afterwords in World Changes, Horwich, Paul (ed). Cambridge, MIT Pr, 1993.

The author closes the volume with comments organized to update central aspects of his present view of scientific development. Finding the basis for incommensurability in local structural difference between the lexicons of kind-terms employed by different communities, he suggests that some propositions evaluable for their truth value within one community cannot be even candidates for true/false in another. There can in principle be no lexically-independent truth towards which science could move ever closer. Cognitive development, like biological, does nevertheless progress, but not without the ever increasing specialization that isolates on community (or species) from another.

Kuhn, Thomas S. The Natural and the Human Sciences in The Interpretive Turn, Hiley, David R (ed). Ithaca, Cornell Univ Pr, 1991.

Intended for an occasion that was to have been an exchange with Charles Taylor, this paper suggests that the interpretive techniques he develops by contrasting the human with the natural sciences are deeply relevant to understanding the natural sciences as well. It closes with inconclusive comments on a resulting problem: how to differentiate the two areas of research.

Kuhse, Helga. Quality of Life and the Death of "Baby M". *Bioethics*, 6(3), 233-250, Jl 92.

I argue that there are good reasons to think that "Baby M" (who was suffering from spina bifida) did not die from "natural causes", as the coroner found. Rather, Baby M died because she was "conservatively" treated, on the basis of her projected quality of life. This 'conservative' approach was supported by members of the Roman Catholic church and by the coroner, and yet it is in stark conflict with the traditional sanctity-of-life approach. I argue quality-of-life decisions can be morally sound, but argue that the law must be charged to make them legally sound.

Kuhse, Helga and Singer, Peter. More on Euthanasia: A Response to Pauer-Studer. *Monist*, 76(2), 158-174, Ap 93.

We reply to Pauer-Studer's critique of our views on euthanasia. The reply is in three parts. First comes a defense of Peter Singer's position in *Practical Ethics*, against criticisms made by Pauer-Studer. This is followed by an account of the weaknesses in what Pauer-Studer says about the distinction between killing and letting die. Finally, we comment on the way in which Pauer-Studer sees the German reaction to the debate over euthanasia that has taken place in that country since 1989.

Kuic, Vukan. Government of Law and Judicial Review. *Vera Lex*, 12(1), 10,22, 1992.

Acting on their belief in a higher natural law and inalienable human rights, the American founders designed judicial review to be to the Constitution what the practice of government of law is to its theory. It is heartening to see that the political and constitutional reforms in Eastern Europe, calling for full independence of the judiciary, are carried out in a similar spirit. It would be a shame if this school of jurisprudence were to succumb completely to the combined encroachments of legal scepticism and positivism in this country.

Kuiper, Mark. Historical Interpretation and Mental Images of Culture (in Dutch). *Tijdschr Filosof*, 54(4), 607-636, D 92.

This article is a search for a position with regards to the question of meaning in history which avoids the ironic stand that meaning is created by narrative, without retreating to the naive strategy which holds that the past itself has a narrative structure. The author concludes that a solution may be found in Johan Huizing's ideas on the importance of historical experience. Although narrative is not a mapping of real structure, it need not be regarded as the source of meaning. Narrative may be seen as the communication of experience, and experience is the moment in which reality presents itself as both real and meaningful.

Kuipers, T A F. Structuralist Explications of Dialectics in Advances in Scientific Philosophy, Schurz, Gerhard (ed). Amsterdam, Rodopi, 1991.

As an example of analytic explication of non-analytic concepts a set of related dialectical concepts is explicated: 'dialectical negation', 'dialectical correspondence', 'double negation', 'thesis-antithesis-synthesis', 'the absolute'. It is claimed to be useful and instructive for dialectical as well as analytical philosophers. The perspective on dialectical concepts is provided by my structuralist approach to the problem of verisimilitude or truthlikeness. It turns out to be possible to explicate the main dialectical concepts on the descriptive level of the actual world as well as on the theoretical level of empirically possible worlds in three different ways: (epistemo-) logical, methodological and ontological.

Kuipers, T A F. Truth Approximation by Concretization in Idealization III, Brzenzinski, Jerzy (ed). Amsterdam, Rodopi, 1992.

First the naive the refined structuralist definitions of truthlikeness are presented and the notion of structurelikeness underlying the refined definition. Then it is shown that the refined notions can be applied to the method of idealization and concretization: it is a special kind of (potential) refined truth approximation. This is also illustrated by the Van der Waals's theory of gases. Moreover, it is indicated how idealization and concretization can function as a strategy in validity research around 'interesting theorems'.

Kuipers, Theo A F. Naive and Refined Truth Approximation. *Synthese*, 93(3), 299-342, D 92.

The naive structuralist definition of truthlikeness is an idealization in the sense that it assumes that all mistaken models of a theory are equally bad. The natural concretization is a refined definition based on an under- lying notion of structurelikeness. In Section 1 the naive definition of truthlikeness of theories is presented, using a new conceptual justification, in terms of instantial and explanatory mistakes. In Section 2 general constraints are formulated for the notions of strcturelikeness and truthlikeness of structures. In Section 3 a refined definition of truthlikeness of theories is presented, based on the notion of structurelikeness, using a sophisticated version of the conceptual justification for the naive definition. In Section 4 it is shown that 'idealization and concretization' is a special kind of potentially truth approximation.

Kujundzic, Nebojsa. Beyond Unity of Science: Churchland and Rorty. *Dialogue (PST)*, 35(2-3), 47-51, Ap 93.

In this paper the two "working agendas" endorsed by Richard Rorty and Paul Churchland are sketched. They serve as a means of convincing readers that their proposed perspectives not only escape possible accusations of "limitation" and "elimination" but that their theories are, in the broadest sense, intrinsically "dynamic." The question of whether they are indeed dynamic, is what I seek to address in this paper.

Kujundzic, Nebojsa and Buschert, William. Staging the Life-World: Habermas and the Recuperation of Austin's Speech Act Theory. *J Theor Soc Behav*, 23(1), 105-116, Mr 93.

The intuitive seed which occasioned J L Austin's cultivation of speech act theory—what we characterize as the "situationist," performative character of language—has been largely sighted, we suggest, in the subsequent literature of speech act theory, in particular in the work of John Searle. In this paper we seek first to re-examine Austin's distinctive understanding of the speech act and, thereafter, to apply this understanding to some aspects of Jürgen Habermas's theory of communicative action with a view towards sketching a possible "dramaturgical" phenomenology and semiotics of speech acts.

Kukathas, Chandran. Cultural Rights Again: A Rejoinder to Kymlicka. *Polit Theory*, 20(4), 674-680, N 92.

Kukla, Andre. Endogenous Constraints on Inductive Reasoning. *Phil Psych*, 5(4), 411-425, 1992.

It is widely recognized that computational theories of learning must posit the existence of a priori constraints on hypothesis selection. The present article surveys the theoretical options available for modelling the dynamic process whereby the constraints have their effect. According to the 'simplicity' theory (exemplified by Fodor's treatment), hypotheses are preference-ordered in terms of their syntactic or semantic properties. It is argued that the same explanatory power can be obtained with a weaker (hence better) theory, the 'minimalist' theory, which dispenses with the preference ordering. According to the 'finitistic' theory, the learner is capable of generating only finitely many hypotheses for evaluation. Chomsky maintains that the occurrence of errorless learning in language acquisition necessitates a finististic explanation. Once again, there is a weaker theory that explains the same data. Finally, Goodman's argument to the effect that there cannot be a computational theory of learning is examined and rejected.

Kukla, Andre. On the Coherence of Instrumentalism. *Phil Sci*, 59(3), 492-497, S 92.

According to a certain type of instrumentalist, we may have good reasons for accepting scientific theories, but never for believing more than their empirical consequences. Horwich (1991) considers several attempts to capture a difference between acceptance and belief, and claims that none of them succeed. He concludes that instrumentation has not been shown to be a coherent position. However, in the course of his discussion, Horwich himself deploys a conceptual apparatus which is sufficient for formulating the instrumentalist doctrine in a coherent manner. The worst accusation that can be laid against instrumentalists is that they have violated common linguistic usage.

Kukla, André. Laudan, Leplin, Empirical Equivalence and Underdetermination. *Analysis*, 53(1), 1-7, Ja 93.

According to Laudan and Leplin, it is a received view that E) there are empirically equivalent rivals to any scientific theory, and that, as a consequence, U) theory choice is radically underdetermined by all possible evidence. Laudan and Leplin reject both E and the claim that E entails U. I agree that E does not entail U. However, I argue that both E and U are true. Whereas Laudan and Leplin claim that underdetermination would not be a problem even if every theory did have empirical equivalents, my view is that underdetermination would still be a problem even if theories did not have empirical equivalents.

Kukla, Rebecca. Causation as a Natural and as a Philosophical Relation. *Eidos*, 10(2), 161-178, D 92.

Kukla, Rebecca. Cognitive Models and Representation. *Brit J Phil Sci*, 43(2), 219-232, J 92.

Several accounts of representation in cognitive systems have recently been proposed. These look for a theory that will establish how a representation comes to have a certain content, and how these representations are used by cognitive systems. Covariation accounts are unsatisfactory, as they make intelligent reasoning and cognition impossible. Cummins' interpretation-based account cannot explain the distinction between cognitive and non- cognitive systems, nor how certain cognitive representations appear to have intrinsic meaning. Cognitive systems can be defined as *model-constructers*, or systems that use information from interpreted models as arguments in the functions they execute. An account based on this definition solves many of the problems raised by the earlier proposals.

Kule, Maija. The Ontological Pre-conditions of Understanding and the Formation of Meaning in Analecta Husserliana, XXXIV, Tymieniecka, Anna-Teresa (ed). Dordrecht, Kluwer, 1992.

The paper deals with the phenomenological and hermeneutical understanding of meaning. From phenomenological point of view the ontological pre-requisites of meaning is subjectivity and its intentional, synthetic activity. Phenomenology develops into hermeneutics, what describes ontology of culture. Author calls to analyze spirituality as ontological pre-condition of the formation of meaning.

Kule, Maija. The Role of Historicity in Man's Creative Experience in Analecta Husserliana, XXXI, Tymieniecka, Anna-Teresa (ed). Dordrecht, Kluwer, 1990.

The purpose of the work is to get answer: Has the notion of the historicity changed in relation to man's creative experience? Author gives a comparative analysis of the ideas of Kant, Fichte, Hegel, Husserl, Heidegger, and Gadamer. In Kant's philosophy man's creative experience remains separate from historical experience, Fichte proposed cognizing subject as a historical subject. Hegel deals with historically-logical process. Philosophy of XX century: Husserl, Heidegger, Gadamer speak about historicity of 1) consciousness, 2) human being (Dasein), and 3) culture and understanding. Being alive to our historicity is not an obstacle to creativity, but it is the condition for it.

Kulka, Tomas. Art and Science: An Outline of Popperian Aesthetics (in Czechoslovakian). *Estetika*, 29(2), 29-40, 1992.

Kulka, Tomas. Metaphorical Meaning and Its Interpretation (in Hebrew). *Iyyun*, 42, 295-306, Ap 93.

Kulstad, Mark. Causation and Preestablished Harmony in the Early Development of Leibniz's Philosophy in Causation in Early Modern Philosophy, Nadler, Steven (ed). University Park, Penn St Univ Pr, 1993.

This article examines Leibniz's development on the questions of causation, mind-body interaction, and pre-established harmony from Leibniz's university years to the composition of the *Discourse on Metaphysics*. Among the issues taken up are the relationship of Leibniz's developing views to those of Descartes, Malebranche,

and notably, Spinoza. Interpretations of scholars such as Belaval, Kabitz, Robinet and Parkinson on these early years are evaluated, and numerous positive theses—often opposed to previous views—are presented and defended. Significant shifts in Leibniz's views during this period are documented. One of these appears to be that Leibniz at least briefly adopted a version of occasionalism a few years after the Paris period.

Kulstad, Mark. Two Interpretations of the Pre-established Harmony in the Philosophy of Leibniz. *Synthese*, 96(3), 477-504, S 93.

A typical, *universal*, interpretation of Leibniz's doctrine of Pre-established Harmony is that each created substance, without interacting with other created substances, generates the sequence of *all* its non-initial states by means of the nature or force that God has given it at creation, with its resulting states corresponding perfectly with those of all other created substances. A *limited* interpretation holds that the nature or force of a created substance is sufficient only for natural (not miraculous) non-initial states of the substance. Although the limited interpretation brings philosophical difficulties with it, its textual support, while not conclusive, is strong.

Kultgen, John. Mill's Antipaternalism. *SW Phil Rev*, 8(1), 57-64, Ja 92.

Recent discussions of paternalism have led some critics to attribute a form of absolute antipaternalism to Mill. This would construe some passages from *On Liberty* in a deontological view. Closer analysis shows that his antipaternalism is qualified and contextual.

Kumabe, M. Generic Degrees are Complemented. *Annals Pure Applied Log*, 59(3), 257-272, F 93.

Let n be greater than or equal to two. Let a be n-generic. Turing degree of unsolvability, i.e., Cohen generic for n-quantifier arithmetic. Let D(a) be the set of degrees less than or equal to a. We show the complementation theorem for D(a). In other words, there is an n-generic c less than a such that the greatest lower bound of b and c is o, and the least upper bound of b ad c is a.

Kummer, Christian. Selbstorganisation und Entwicklung. *Theol Phil*, 66(4), 547-556, 1991.

The double meaning of the prefix 'self' in the term self-organization is pointed out: *spontaneous*, but nevertheless passively mechanistic, or actively *self-causing*. The development of living structures is related to both aspects. During ontogenesis an organism follows a presupposed programme rather than generates its form autonomously, although there are exceptions in the field of neuronal differentiation. The phylogenetic strategy of gaining information, although based on a simple chemical mechanism, supposes individual activity in order to select new and better genetic constellations. So, not complexity by itself, as suggests the concept of physical self-organization, but (increasing) individual autonomy appears as the final cause of evolution.

Kummer, Martin and Stephan, F. Weakly Semirecursive Sets and R E Orderings. *Annals Pure Applied Log*, 60(2), 133-150, Ap 93.

Weakly semirecursive sets have been introduced by Jockusch and Owings (1990). In the present paper their investigation is pushed forward by utilizing r.e. partial orderings, which turn out to be instrumental for the study of degrees of subclasses of weakly semirecursive sets.

Kuntz, Paul G. The Ascent of Spirit: Is Santayana's System a Naturalistic Neo-Platonic Hierarchy?. *Bull Santayana Soc*, 10, 22-31, Fall 92.

There was, said Santayana, a "truly philosophical" center of his work: spirit. The work that flows most directly from "the fountain of spirit" within him is, this paper claims, *Platonism and the Spiritual Life*. Is this then a philosophy that is false to naturalism? No, because a naturalistic critique is needed to red neo-Platonism of the errors of confusing ideas with powers and deriving powers of the realm of matter from the realm of essence. But what then is revealed? The truth of Platonic experience, that "Spirit, since its essence is to aspire, comes to life at the foot of the ladder; it lives by contemplation, by knowing the thing above it." The other error of Platonism, its moralism, is corrected by Christian humility. Hence the book, a response to Dean Inge, also expresses a Christian Neo-Platonism.

Kuo, Lenore. Coerced Birth Control, Individual Rights, and Discrimination in Biomedical Ethics Reviews 1992, Humber, James M (ed). Clifton, Humana Pr, 1993.

Since the introduction of Norplant, an implantable female birth control device, several attempts have been made to coerce its use, either as a condition for parole for certain types of crimes, or through "inducement" programs for welfare recipient. In this article, I argue that such attempts are morally and legally unjustifiable because they constitute "secondary" discrimination, and violate the Harm Principle, the Least Restrictive Remedy Principle, and the Rational Relationship Principle. Ultimately, I argue that coerced birth control could only be justified (at some future time) in a very limited number of instances, to prevent highly probable severe birth defects.

Kuokkanen, Martti. On the Structuralist Constraints in Social Scientific Theorizing. *Theor Decis*, 35(1), 19-54, Jl 93.

It is shown that important structuralist constraints emerge in three cases selected from social scientific theorizing. First of the cases is a purely qualitative theory, the second one is a quantitative theory and the third case is the explanation schema of folk psychology. The related constraints seem to work as idealizing factual assumptions. The three cases, *mutatis mutandis*, covering nearly all types of social scientific theorizing.

Kuokkanen, Martti. Structuralist Constraints and Mathematical Social Theorizing. *Erkenntnis*, 38(3), 351-370, My 93.

Several case studies and theoretical reports indicate that the structuralist concept of a constraint has a central role in the reconstruction of the physical theories. It is surprising that there is, in the literature, only little theoretical discussion on the relevance of constraints for the reconstruction of social scientific theories. Almost all structuralist reconstructions of social theorizing are vacuously constrained. Consequently, constraints are methodologically irrelevant. In this paper I try to show that there really exist constraint-type assumptions in mathematical modelling in the social sciences. Methodologically constraints have exactly the same role in the context of social mathematical modelling as they have in physical theories. In typical cases of mathematical modelling in the social sciences, the related constraints work as empirical hypotheses and should be tested by statistical means.

Kuokkanen, Martti and Tuomivaara, Timo. On the Structure of Idealizations in Idealization III, Brzenzinski, Jerzy (ed). Amsterdam, Rodopi, 1992.

It is argued that the original Poznan view of idealizing laws is too narrow. New types of idealizations, partial idealizations, are introduced via the structuralist approach. It is shown that the original Poznan view is incapable in taking into account such idealizations. The analysis shows that the almost extensional structuralist framework is completely adequate in studying for example the factual and counterfactual content of theories. The result makes unnecessary to study these aspects of theories using intensional languages.

Kupfer, Joseph H. The Ethics of Genetic Screening in the Workplace. *Bus Ethics Quart*, 3(1), 17-25, Ja 93.

This paper clarifies the nature of genetic screening and morally evaluates using it to deny people employment. Four sets of variables determine screening's ability to forecast disorder. Two epistemological limitations concern reliance on markers and linkage analysis. Two refer to genetic causality: the influence of auxiliary genes and certainty of vs. susceptibility to disorder. Considerations of privacy and justice warrant restricting screening to job-specific disorders. Penalizing someone for susceptibility to a disorder is unjust, as is using publicly supported research and technology against members of the public.

Kupracz, Andrzej. Testing and Correspondence in Idealization III, Brzenzinski, Jerzy (ed). Amsterdam, Rodopi, 1992.

Kuroda, S Y. The Categorical and the Thetic Judgement Reconsidered in Mind, Meaning and Metaphysics, Mulligan, Kevin (ed). Dordrecht, Kluwer, 1990.

Kurtz, Paul. America's Leading Humanist Philosopher: Remembering John Dewey. *Free Inq*, 13(1), 16-18, Wint 92-93.

Kurtz, Paul. Toward a New Enlightenment: A Response to the Postmodernist Critiques of Humanism. *Free Inq*, 13(1), 33-37, Wint 92-93.

Kuspit, Donald. *The Cult of the Avant-Garde Artist*. New York, Cambridge Univ Pr, 1993.

Kusyk, Douglas A. Socratic Legal Obligation in the *Crito*. *Dialogue (PST)*, 34(2-3), 54-59, Ap 92.

The purpose of this paper is to carefully examine the argument of the *Crito*, and then to offer an alternative interpretation of the work. The paper also includes a "non-critical" explication of the text. Based on this paper's interpretation Socrates' obligation to Athens is questioned.

Kutash, Emilie. Anaxagoras and the Rhetoric of Plato's Middle Dialogue Theory of Forms. *Phil Rhet*, 26(2), 134-152, 1993.

Kuznetsov, Vladimir and Burgin, Mark. Model Part of a Scientific Theory. *Epistemologia*, 15(1), 41-64, Ja-Je 92.

From the viewpoint of the structure-nominative program in the philosophy of science, we study the model-representing subsystem of a scientific theory. Various conceptual models of objects from the theory's domain occupy the central place in this subsystem. A description of the links between models and the hierarchy of laws is given. Some aspects of theory development are studied.

Kuznetsov, Vladimir and Burgin, Mark. The Structure-Nominative Reconstruction and the Intelligibility of Cognition. *Epistemologia*, 15(2), 219-238, Jl-D 92.

From the structure-nominative view we propose an unified treatment of levels of common and scientific cognition. We also introduce several cognitive schemes giving new kinds of hermeneutic circles. All this develops and deepens some ideas of E Agazzi (1992) concerning the nature and structure of scientific knowledge and cognition.

Kvanvig, Jonathan L. *The Problem of Hell*. New York, Oxford Univ Pr, 1993.

Kvanvig, Jonathan L and McCann, Hugh J. The Occasionalist Proselytizer in Philosophical Perspectives, 5: Philosophy of Religion, 1991, Tomberlin, James E (ed). Atascadero, Ridgeview, 1991.

This paper explores the occasionalist implications of the claim that God not only creates the world, but sustains it throughout its existence. It is argued that both the doctrine of sustenance and that of divine providence indicate that God is directly responsible for everything that occurs. This is incompatible with event causation, if by the latter we understand a process wherein one event is responsible for the existence of another. But this concept of causation is untenable in any case: neither diachronically nor synchronically does any event ever produce another. There are, however, other ways of understanding causation so that it remains a viable concept, and the explanatory force of scientific laws is preserved.

Kvart, Igal. Counterfactuals. *Erkenntnis*, 36(2), 139-179, Mr 92.

In this article I offer an approach to counterfactuals based on a notion of objective probability. It is in the spirit of, though it does not fall squarely under, the metalinguistic model. Thus, it is not developed in terms of possible worlds, or notions parasitic on them (e.g., similarity). Its dominant features are rooted in objective probability and causal relevance (analyzed probabilistically), and thus it is not close in spirit to a maximal similarity or a minimal change approach.

Kvart, Igal. The Objective Dimension of Believing De Re. *Critica*, 24(70), 83-107, Ap 92.

Kwame, Safro. Why I Am Not a Physicalist. *Personalist Forum*, 8/1(Supp), 191-196, Spr 92.

Simply stated, the reason I am not a physicalist, is that I am a quasi-physicalist. Unlike physicalists of the reductive or so called non-reductive school, quasi-physicalists neither identify the mind with processes or properties of physical objects, nor rule out the existence of objects that are not completely physical. If so called non-reductive physicalists such as Quine and Rorty are right, reductive physicalism is dead. But if reductive physicalism is dead, so is non-reductive physicalism. For physicalism will be reductive or, else, not at all.

Kwan, Tze-Wan. Husserl's Concept of Horizon: An Attempt at Reappraisal in Analecta Husserliana, XXXI, Tymieniecka, Anna-Teresa (ed). Dordrecht, Kluwer, 1990.

This paper explains the concept of horizon as one of the most crucial operational

concepts in Husserl's phenomenology. In his writings, Husserl used the work horizon in many different contexts: internal and external horizons, empty horizon, Welthorizont, temporal horizon, Lebenshorizont..., reflecting thus the great versatility of the concept on dealing with the different aspects of phenomenology. At this point the paper argues that natural, unthematic setting. Precisely for this reason, the concept of horizon not only flourished with Husserl, but also has experienced a "renewal" in the subsequent philosophical discussions of Heidegger and Gadamer.

Kwan, Wing-chung. Faith and Fidelity as Interpreted by Gabriel Marcel (in Chinese). *Phil Rev (Taiwan)*, 15, 53-100, Ja 92.

Faith and fidelity, which seem to be two separate items, are nevertheless sprung from the same loving-presence of an "I-Thou Relationship." They simply are two different foci of the same mutual call and response. In addition to the horizontal-human dimension of faith and fidelity between two human persons, we also have the vertical-transcendent dimension of faith and fidelity between man and God. The one cannot be separated from the other any more than love of neighbor can be separated from love of God. (edited)

Kyburg Jr, Henry E. The Evidence of Your Own Eyes. *Mind Mach*, 3(2), 201-218, My 93.

The evidence of your own eyes has often been regarded as unproblematic. But we know that people make mistaken observations. This can be looked on as unimportant if there is *some* class of statements that can serve as evidence for others, or if every statement in our corpus of knowledge is allowed to be no more than probable. Neither of these alternatives is plausible when it comes to machine or robotic observation. Then we must take the possibility of error seriously, and we must be prepared to deal with error quantitatively. The problem of using internal evidence to arrive at error distributions is the main focus of the paper.

Kymlicka, Will. Moral Philosophy and Public Policy: The Case of the New Reproductive Technologies. *Bioethics*, 7(1), 1-26, Ja 93.

This paper discusses to common views about the role that moral philosophers can play in public policy-making bodies, such as government commissions into reproductive technologies. The ambitious view says that philosophers should encourage Commissioners to adopt the best comprehensive moral theory (e.g., utilitarianism or contractarianism), and then to apply it to policy choices. The moderate view says that philosophers should identify inconsistencies within the Commission's arguments, without influencing the underlying theory. I reject the first view as unrealistic, and the second as inadequate to ensure morally responsible recommendations. I then discuss a third "guiding principles" approach that relies less on philosophical sophistication and more on sensitivity to the actual impact of policies on all relevant parties.

Kyte, Richard. Guilt, Remorse, and the Sense of Justice. *Cont Phil*, 14(5), 17-20, S-O 92.

In his 1982 essay, "Love, Guilt, and the sense of Justice," John Deigh argues that Rawls conflates guilt and remorse in Chapter VIII of *A Theory of Justice*. In the present essay, I try to show that even if Deigh is correct, the upshot should not be, as Deigh claims, the rejection of Rawls's account of moral development, but rather the recognition that Rawls explains the development of both guilt and remorse-equally important moral emotions.

L'Etang, Jacquie. A Kantian Approach to Codes of Ethics. *J Bus Ethics*, 11(10), 737-744, O 92.

The paper discusses whether codes of ethics are Kantian notions through an analysis of their intention and structure. The article also discusses some of the ideas put forward by William Starr in his article, 'Codes of Ethics— Towards a Rule-Utilitarian Justification,' *Journal of Business Ethics 2(2) (May 1983).(edited)*

La Plante, Harry. Soul, Rational Soul and Person in Thomism. *Mod Sch*, 70(3), 209-216, Mr 93.

La Torre, Massimo. Institutionalism Old and New. *Ratio Juris*, 6(2), 190-201, Jl 93.

The author deals with the legal theoretical approach that has been labelled "legal institutionalism." An old and a new version of this approach are singled out: The old one is identified with the theory defended by the Italian public lawyer Santi Romano in the first half of this century; the second one is seen in the recent work by Ota Weinberger and Neil MacCormick. After a short presentation of Romano's work, his ideas and the development proposed by MacCormick and Weinberger are compared. Similarities and differences between the two versions of institutional theory are worked out. A coda hints at an ambiguity in the definition of institution proposed by the "new" institutionalism.

Labbé, Y. Revenir, sortir, demeurer. *Rev Thomiste*, 92(3), 642-673, Jl-S 92.

Laberge, Claude M and Knoppers, Bartha Maria. Rationale for an Integrated Approach to Genetic Epidemiology. *Bioethics*, 6(4), 317-330, O 92.

Labson, Sam and Rohatyn, Dennis A. Mach's Razor, Duhem's Holism, and Bell's Theorem. *Phil Sci (Tucson)*, 5, 79-116, 1993.

Lacey, A R (trans). *Philoponus: On Aristotle's "Physics" 2*. Ithaca, Cornell Univ Pr, 1993.

Lacey, Hugh M. Understanding Conflicts between North and South in Cultural Relativism and Philosophy, Dascal, Marcelo (ed). Leiden, Brill, 1991.

Two detailed accounts of recent conflicts in Central America are offered, each displaying a complex interaction among 1) interests (those involved in liberation movements, on the one hand; those of ruling oligarchs, modernizing elites and their first world allies, on the other), 2) understandings (perceptions, descriptions and explanations) of events and of the behavior of self and others, 3) views of legitimacy, 4) analyses of what is possible, and 5) aspirations. Then, four criteria are proposed that must be satisfied by any adequate explanatory account of such conflicts. These criteria clarify the logic of interpretive methodologies.

Lacher, R C. Expert Networks: Paradigmatic Conflict, Technological Rapprochement. *Mind Mach*, 3(1), 53-71, F 93.

A rule-based expert system is demonstrated to have both a symbolic computational network representation and a sub-symbolic connectionist representation. These alternate views enhance the usefulness of the original system by facilitating introduction of connectionist learning methods into the symbolic domain. The connectionist representation learns and stores metaknowledge in highly connected subnetworks and domain knowledge in a sparsely connected expert network superstructure. The total connectivity of the neural network representation approximates that of real neural systems and hence avoids scaling and memory stability problems associated with other connectionist models.

Lachs, John. Law and the Importance of Feelings in Peirce and Law, Kevelson, Roberta. New York, Lang, 1991.

Lachs, John. The Relevance of Philosophy to Life in Frontiers in American Philosophy, Volume I, Burch, Robert W (ed). College Station, Texas A&M Univ Pr, 1992.

Lachterman, David. Mathematical Construction, Symbolic Cognition and the Infinite Intellect: Reflections on Maimon and Maimonides. *J Hist Phil*, 30(4), 497-522, O 92.

Lackey, Douglas. Extraordinary Evil or Common Malevolence? in Applied Philosophy, Almond, Brenda (ed). New York, Routledge, 1992.

Laclau, Ernesto. Community and Its Paradoxes: Rorty's 'Liberal Utopia' in Community at Loose Ends, Miami Theory Collect, (ed). Minneapolis, Univ of Minnesota Pr, 1991.

Laclau, Ernesto. *New Reflections on the Revolution of Our Time*. New York, Verso, 1990.

Lacoue-Labarthe, Philippe and Nancy, Jean-Luc. *The Title of the Letter: A Reading of Lacan*. Albany, SUNY Pr, 1992.

This book is a close reading of Jacques Lacan's seminal essay, "The Agency of the Letter in the Unconscious or Reason Since Freud", selected for the particular light it casts on Lacan's complex relation to linguistics, psychoanalysis, and philosophy. It clarifies the way Lacan renews or transforms the psychoanalytic field, through his diversion of Saussure's theory of the sign, his radicalization of Freud's fundamental concepts, and his subversion of dominant philosophical values. The author's argue, however, that Lacan's discourse is marked by a deep ambiguity: while he invents a new "language", he nonetheless maintains the traditional metaphysical motifs of systemacity, foundation, and truth. (staff)

Laden, Anthony Simon. Games Philosophers Play: A Reply to Gauthier. *Phil Pub Affairs*, 22(1), 48-52, Wint 93.

This article replies to a criticism made by David Gauthier to a game-theoretic account of fairness. It distinguishes between two similar theories, one attributed to the author by Gauthier and one actually advanced by the author. The difference is traced to an underlying disagreement about the proper role of game theory in political philosophy. Gauthier's counter-examples are dealt with.

Ladrière, Jean. Interprétation et vérité. *Laval Theol Phil*, 49(2), 189-199, Je 93.

Längle, Alfried. What are We Looking for When We Search for Meaning?. *Ultim Real Mean*, 15(4), 306-314, D 92.

Laffranchi, Marco. Il rinnovamento della filosofia nella *Dialectica* di Lorenzo Valla. *Riv Filosof Neo-Scolas*, 84(1), 13-60, Ja-Mr 92.

LaFollette, Hugh. Real Men in Rethinking Masculinity, May, Larry (ed). Lanham, Rowman & Littlefield, 1992.

"Ah, for the good old days, when men were men and women were women." Men who express such sentiments long for the world where homosexuals were ensconced in their closets and women were sexy, demure, and subservient. That is a world well lost— though not as lost as I would like. More than a few men still practice misogyny and homophobia. The defects of such attitudes are obvious. My concern in this paper is not to document these defects but to ask how real men, men who reject stereotypical male-female roles—men who are sensitive to the insights of feminism—should relate with women. In particular, how should men and women relate in intimate, sexually oriented, i.e., "romantic," relationships.

LaFollette, Hugh and Shanks, Niall. Animal Models in Biomedical Research: Some Epistemological Worries. *Pub Affairs Quart*, 7(2), 113-130, Ap 93.

The public (and most philosophers) support the widespread use of animals in biomedical research because they are convinced it substantially benefits humans. We acknowledge that animal experimentation has likely benefitted humans. However, we offer historical and methodological ground for deflating researchers' claims about its value. Once the limitations of animal research are recognized, the character of the moral debate concerning its use we change.

Lafond, J. Descartes philosophe et écrivain. *Rev Phil Fr*, 4, 421-438, O-D 92.

Lafont, Cristina. Die Rolle der Sprache in "Sein und Zeit". *Z Phil Forsch*, 47(1), 41-59, Ja-Mr 93.

This article argues that Heidegger's Being and Time implicitly makes use of a certain trait of language, which is not accounted for by its author in his explicit reflections on language in this work. An analysis beginning there shows a hidden conception of language at work which has much more to do with the one affirmed by the later Heidegger than with the one usually attributed to Being and Time. This suggests strong evidence for the view that there is a deep continuity in the totality of Heidegger's work and helps to understand the peculiarities of the "linguistic turn" initiated by Being and Time and developed by Hermeneutics.

Lafrance, Yvon. Les multiples lectures du Poème de Parménide. *Dialogue (Canada)*, 32(1), 117-128, Wint 93.

Following the publication of Etudes sur Parménide, Aubenque, Paris, Vrin, 1987, 2 volumes, this study is concerned with the analytical interpretation of the Parmenides' Poem by G E L Owen as well as the conventional interpretation by P Aubenque. In both cases, the author shows that there is a failure in the historical reconstruction of the context of the Poem. Theses interpreters haven't forgotten the cosmological context of the Presocratic thought. A longer version of this study was published in Spanish in the review Methexis (5, 1992).

Laganà, Antonino. Soggetto metafisicoe metafisica del sociale. *G Metaf*, 14(1), 155-158, Ja-Ap 92.

Lageman, August G. *The Moral Dimensions of Marriage and Family Therapy*. Lanham, Univ Pr of America, 1993.

The issues and dilemmas of professional ethics for therapists who have multiple clients, i.e., families are examined. Moral philosophy is synthesized with family systems approaches by means of four distinct approaches to ethics. Duty-based ethics, begun by Kant and W D Ross are considered in order to clarify the duties of the therapist. Then the issues are examined from the perspective of the "rights" of the clients. Developmental moral theory (Kohlberg and Gilligan) is integrated into the therapeutic process. Finally Lageman examines these issues from the perspective of virtue based ethics—concluding that it is the best approach for family therapists.

Lagerspetz, Olli. Dorothea and Casaubon. *Philosophy*, 67(260), 211-232, Ap 92.

Drawing on an example from Eliot's *Middlemarch*, the author discusses what a 'solution' to a moral dilemma would amount to. Recognising a dilemma involves understanding concrete individuals. The Kantian ideal of disinterested, universalisable judgments is, rather than the general form of morality, simply one form morality may take. Moral utterances are not just descriptions of reality: above all, they are responses. They involve the utteres and make a difference to him. The quest for a universal moral code, rather than being an expression of a personal commitment to morality, may sometimes stem from a wish to escape from it.

Lahav, Ran. Applied Phenomenology in Philosophical Counseling. *Int J Applied Phil*, 7(2), 45-52, Wint 92.

Philosophical Counseling is an approach for treating personal predicaments through philosophical (rather than psychological) means. The Philosophical Counseling movement was born in Europe at the beginning of the eighties, and is now expanding to North America. This paper shows how philosophical methods taken from phenomenological literature can be applied to counseling situations. Two case studies illustrate how phenomenology can be used to investigate the counselee's world view, and to facilitate a change in the counselee's attitude to personal problems.

Lahav, Ran. On Thinking Clearly and Distinctly. *Metaphilosophy*, 23(1-2), 34-46, Ja-Ap 92.

This paper questions the commonly-made presupposition that philosophical knowledge of the world is attained through what I call "a cognitivist attitude": a reflective, disinterested, analytic, and propositional perspective that is isolated from everyday life. It is argued that the writings of Bergson, Heidegger, and others can be interpreted as offering non-cognitivist alternatives, and hence meta-philosophical views about how philosophy ought to be done. The paper then discusses the legitimacy of non-cognitivist approaches, and argues that there is no easy way to disqualify them.

Lahav, Ran. The Amazing Predictive Power of Folk Psychology. *Austl J Phil*, 70(1), 99-105, Mr 92.

One of the arguments offered in favor of the elimination of folk psychology from cognitive science is that it has low predictive success. This paper counters this argument by pointing out that folk psychology has tremendous success in predicting an important type of behaviour that permeates our lives: the continuation and completion of actions.

Lahav, Ran. Using Analytical Philosophy in Philosophical Counselling. *J Applied Phil*, 10(2), 243-251, 1993.

In the past decade, philosophers have started to use philosophical methods of counselling for everyday problems and predicaments, such as decision-making, inter-personal conflicts, occupational dissatisfaction, search for meaning, etc. This paper shows, on the basis of two case studies, how philosophical counselling can utilise analytic methods commonly used in academic philosophy, such as conceptual analysis. The paper also discusses the difference between philosophical counselling and psychological therapy.

Lahav, Ran. What Neuropsychology Tells Us about Consciousness. *Phil Sci*, 60(1), 67-85, Mr 93.

I argue that, contrary to some critics, the notion of conscious experience is a good candidate for denoting a distinct and scientifically interesting phenomenon in the brain. I base this claim mainly on an analysis of neuropsychological data concerning deficits resulting from various types of brain damage as well as some additional supporting empirical evidence. These data strongly point to the hypotheses that conscious experience expresses information that is available for global, integrated, and flexible behavior.

Lahav, Ran and Shanks, Niall. How to Be a Scientifically Respectable "Property-Dualist". *J Mind Behav*, 13(3), 211-232, Sum 92.

We argue that the so-called "property-dualist" theory of consciousness is consistent both with current neurobiological data and with modern theories of physics. The hypothesis that phenomenal properties are global properties that are irreducible to microphysical properties, whose role is to integrate information across large portions of the brain, is consistent with current neurobiological knowledge. These properties can exercise their integration function through action on microscopic structures in the neuron without violating the laws of quantum mechanics. Although we offer no positive argument for the existence of irreducibly global properties, the conclusion is that this view is a scientifically respectable hypothesis that deserves to be investigated.

Lai, Chen. Modern Chinese Thought: A Retrospective View and a Look into the Future. *Chin Stud Phil*, 24(3), 3-24, Spr 93.

Laine, Joy E. Persons, Plants and Insects: On Surviving Reincarnation. *Personalist Forum*, 8/1(Supp), 145-158, Spr 92.

Laine, Joy E. Some Remarks on the Gunagunibhedabhanga Chapter in Udayana's Ātmatattvaviveka. *J Indian Phil*, 21(3), 261-294, S 93.

Laird, Frank. Participating in the Tension. *Soc Epistem*, 7(1), 35-46, Ja-Mr 93.

Laks, André. L'utopie législative de Platon. *Rev Phil Fr*, 4, 417-428, O-D 91.

Laks, André. Mind's Crisis: On Anaxagoras' Nous. *S J Phil*, 31(Supp), 19-38, 1992.

Lalèyê, Issiaka-Prosper. Conscience et Culture. *Quest*, 6(1), 10-27, Je 92.

By investigating the relationship between consciousness and culture, the author exposes the limits of the world-wide culturalist movement. This movement, which has particularly been developed within the UN by UNESCO, aims at eliminating the relations of domination and aggression in the world. (edited)

Lamadrid, Lucas. Is There a System in the Theology of Nicholas Lash?. *Heythrop J*, 33(4), 399-414, O 92.

This article examines the methodological commitments of Nicholas Lash's theology and concludes that they are inconsistent with his thought on knowing and naming God. By examining how Lash employs the categories of narrative, metaphor, and analogy one would expect a fuller descriptive account of how we know and name God. The problem is found in Lash's reticence to allow metaphysics to play the grammatical role he claims it should have. He paradoxically concentrates his energies on developing a system for restricting the place and use of systems in theology. In the process he delimits the strength of the role of narrative by yielding a kataphatic portrait of the God Christians claim in their narrative.

Lamarque, Peter. Expression and the Mask: The Dissolution of Personality in Noh. *J Aes Art Crit*, 47(2), 157-168, Spr 89.

The paper examines, from an analytical perspective, how the portrayal of character is possible in the formal, stylized performance of Noh drama. The underlying conception of character is explored, drawing on the treatises of Zeami Motokiyo; Noh characters have a high degree of abstractness and their successful portrayal relies on the development of mood and suggestiveness. The emphasis is not, as with Western theater and literature, on presenting complex personalities with psychological depth. Instead the special interest of Noh rests on the emotional intensity with which fragments of a personality are presented. Consequences for personal identity and for the theory of fiction are explored.

Lamarque, Peter. Kendall L Walton's *Mimesis as Make-Believe: On the Foundations of the Representational Arts*. *J Aes Art Crit*, 49(2), 161-166, Spr 91.

The main theses of Kendall Walton's Mimesis as Make-Believe are explored, particularly those relating to fictionality. Focus is given to the widespread use by Walton of the intensional idiom 'It is fictional that' and the question raised of how 'watertight' the operator is in distancing what is real from what is fictional. The case of emotional response to fiction (especially 'fearing fictions') is highlighted and Walton is criticized for denying to the reality of some emotional responses. Finally Walton's attempt to explain propositions 'about fictional characters' in terms of games of make-believe is considered and an alternative proposed in terms of more familiar conceptions of propositional content.

Lamarque, Peter. Language, Interpretation and Worship—II in Religion and Philosophy, Warner, Marin (ed). New York, Cambridge Univ Pr, 1992.

Lamarra, Antonio. Théologie, métaphysique, science générale: une lettre inédite de Leibniz à A L Königsmann. *Stud Leibniz*, 24(2), 133-144, 1992.

In August 1712 A L Königsmann sent to Leibniz a copy of his dissertation *De rationali metaphysices cultu* together with a letter. In his answer to Königsmann (dated from Hanover, October 30th) Leibniz underlines, firstly, his rationalistic opinion on the relationship between natural and revealed theology and, in second place, his moderate position regarding the anti-Scholastic polemics. Leibniz's letter, till now unpublished, has been edited and annexed at the bottom of the article.

Lamb, David. Death: The Final Frontier in New Horizons in the Philosophy of Science, Lamb, David (ed). Brookfield, Avebury, 1992.

This survey of philosophical problems raised by the application of neurological criteria for death outlines the concept and criteria for death and stresses their independence from other interests such as the cost of therapy and the need for transplantable organs. Formulations of brain death, including the 'whole brain' and 'higher brain' definitions are considered but the paper concludes with a defense of the brainstem concept of death.

Lamb, David (ed). *New Horizons in the Philosophy of Science*. Brookfield, Avebury, 1992.

This collection of essays celebrates the diversity of post-positivist philosophy of science. Although wide-ranging in subject-matter, with inquiries extending across physics, biology, sociobiology and the social sciences, medicine and the neurophysiological sciences, all of the contributors share the view that philosophy can contribute to scientific practice and that philosophers can take sides in scientific disputes.

Lamb, David. Organ Transplants, Death, and Policies for Procurement. *Monist*, 76(2), 203-221, Ap 93.

Lamb, James W. Evaluative Compatibilism and the Principle of Alternate Possibilities. *J Phil*, 90(10), 517-527, O 93.

What may be called *Evaluative Compatibilism* is the view that the kind of free will that incompatibilists have held to be incompatible with determinism—the counterfactual ability to do otherwise—is not worth having. It is an essential element of the Evaluative Compatibilist's strategy that the Principle of Alternate Possibilities—the principle that a person is morally responsible for something he has done only if he could have done otherwise—be shown false. For if the Principle is true, the counterfactual ability to do otherwise is worth having at least insofar as moral responsibility is worth having. The article defends a version of the Principle of Alternate Possibilities against three kinds of counterexamples and thus undermines the thesis of Evaluative Compatibilism. In the course of the discussion it is argued that Harry Frankfurt's celebrated "counterfactual intervener" counterexample fails because of something akin to a modal fallacy.

Lambert, Karel. Definite Descriptions and the Theory of Objects in Language, Truth and Ontology, Mulligan, Kevin (ed). Dordrecht, Kluwer, 1992.

Lammers, Stephen. William Temple and the Bombing of Germany: An Exploration in Just War Tradition. *J Relig Ethics*, 19(1), 71-92, Spr 91.

This essay examines William Temple's defense of the British bombing of German cities during the Second World War. After detailing Temple's position in defense of the bombing, the essay raises a number of questions from within the just war tradition. First, does the just war tradition have to be understood deontologically, or is it possible to interpret it in a utilitarian fashion? If the former, then considerations of the means of warfare are still important. Second, how should we characterize the relationship of the citizen and the state during modern warfare? Is it as close as Temple claimed, so that we can no longer distinguish between citizens and states? Third, has the practice of deception of citizens by their leaders on questions of the means of warfare led to a situation in which it is no longer prudent to trust political leaders when they report to their peoples on these matters? The paper ends with a suggestion for further discussion on the third question.

Lammers, Stephen E. Approaches to Limits on War in Western Just War Discourse in Cross, Crescent, and Sword, Johnson, James Turner (ed). Westport, Greenwood Pr, 1990.

This essay identifies ways in which thinkers in the just war tradition attempt to limit war. These limits are of two types: upon the occasions of war (*jus ad bellum*), and upon conduct in war (*jus in bello*). Lammers identifies distinctive cultural patterns which provided the background for these limits in the past, patterns not present for the discussions of the limitation of war today. He points out why contemporary theorists focus on *jus in bello* constraints and concludes that more attention ought to be given to *jus ad bellum* considerations as a way of limiting war in our own time.

Lampert, Jay. Husserl's Account of Syncategorematic Terms. *S J Phil*, 30(4), 67-94, Wint 92.

Lampert, Laurence. *Nietzsche and Modern Times*. New Haven, Yale Univ Pr, 1993.

This book is an installment in the new history of philosophy made possible by Friedrich Nietzsche. It provides a new interpretation of modern philosophy by developing Nietzsche's view that genuine philosophers set out to determine the direction of culture through their ideas and that they concealed the radical nature of their thought by their esoteric style. From this Nietzschean perspective Bacon and Descartes can be considered the founders of modernity. Their writings advanced the claims of science in order to destroy the cultural hegemony of Christianity. Nietzsche's cultural aims are as grand as theirs. He is the first thinker to have understood modern times and transcended it in a postmodern view.

Lampert, Laurence A. Who Is Nietzsche's Epicurus?. *Int Stud Phil*, 24(2), 99-105, 1992.

This essay presents Nietzsche's unique interpretation of Epicurus as an installment in his comprehensive revaluation of Western philosophy. Also, the aphoristic, scattered way in which Nietzsche shares his Epicurus with others points to his strategy of communication: the reader grows acquainted with Nietzsche's Epicurus as a late survival of the healthy Hellenism that predated the Socratic turn, and as an opponent of the world- denying religious encouraged by Platonisn, and anti-Christian before the fact. As grateful he is for Epicurus, Nietzsche shows how we must go beyond even him.

Land, Nick. Making it with Death: Remarks on Thanatos and Desiring-Production. *J Brit Soc Phenomenol*, 24(1), 66-76, Ja 93.

Land, Nick. Spirit and Teeth in Of Derrida, Heidegger, and Spirit, Wood, David (ed). Evanston, Northwestern Univ Pr, 1993.

Landau, Iddo. An Answer on Behalf of Guanilo. *Phil Theol*, 7(1), 81-96, Autumn 92.

The ontological proof is wrong because it can be used to prove not only the existence of God, but also of imaginary entities such as spirits of stones and trees, etc. It is faulty because it proves too much; it can be used to prove not only the existence of God, but also the existence of a vast number of imaginary entities to the existence of which theists would not like to commit themselves.

Landau, Iddo. Metafiction as a Rhetorical Device in Hegel's History of Absolute Spirit and Gabriel Garcia Marquez' *One Hund Years of Solitude*. *Clio*, 21(4), 401-410, Sum 92.

Landgrebe, L. Husserl's Phenomenology and the Motives of Its Transformation (Final Part) (in Czechoslovakian). *Filozof Cas*, 40(3), 401-410, 1992.

Landini, Gregory. Russell to Frege, 24 May 1903: "I Believe I Have Discovered That Classes are Entirely Superfluous". *Russell*, 12(2), 160-185, Wint 92-93.

The well-known treatment of class symbols in *Principia Mathematica* was by no means Russell's only "no-classes" theory. There were many false starts. One intriguing episode occurred in May of 1903 shortly after the publication of *The Principles of Mathematics (PoM)*. Russell excitedly telegrammed Whitehead of his "unspeakable relief" in having solved the contradiction. He also sent a letter to Frege and included a few definitions for the solution. Propositional functions are to stand in for classes. Russell's relief was short-lived. Recalling the solution in a 1906 letter to Jourdain, he explained that a contradiction of propositional functions was its undoing. But this is odd. Russell already knew the paradox of functions in *(PoM)*. Appealing to unpublished manuscripts, this paper offers an explanation. Russell's solution was tied to Frege's idea of rejecting Basic Law V.

Landman, Fred and Kadmon, Nirit. Any. *Ling Phil*, 16(4), 353-422, Ag 93.

Landsburg, Steven E and Kahn, James A and Stockman, Alan C. On Novel Confirmation. *Brit J Phil Sci*, 43(4), 503-516, D 92.

Landver, Avner. Singular σ-Dense Trees. *J Sym Log*, 57(4), 1403-1416, D 92.

Lane, Gilles. *Government, Justice, and Contempt*. Lanham, Univ Pr of America, 1993.

Governments could deal more realistically with the demands and aspirations of the citizens, and thus promote the establishment of a more natural social bond, if they took into account 1) the basic element which is contained in all demands for justice, and 2) the deeper object of the human yearning for liberty and a happier life. This study proposes a criterion which would enable each person to discriminate between just and unjust acts, and whose content would show how citizens could live a happy life while promoting a truly social good.

Lang, Berel. Intentions, Concepts of Intention, and the "Final Solution". *J Soc Phil*, 23(3), 105-117, Wint 92.

Lang, Donald L and Malloy, David C. An Aristotelian Approach to Case Study Analysis. *J Bus Ethics*, 12(7), 511-516, Jl 93.

The purpose of this paper is to apply Aristotle's theory of causation to the administrative realm in an attempt to provide the manager/student with a more complete basis for organizational analysis. The authors argue that the traditional approach to administrative case studies limits the manager's/student's perspective to the positivistic world view at the expense of a more encompassing perspective which can be achieved through the use of an Aristotelian approach. Aristotle's four-part theory of causation is juxtaposed with contemporary views of organizational ideology/philosophy, culture, climate and leadership, and staff or personnel. The Mazda automobile plant in Flat Rock, Michigan is provided as a sample case study to demonstrate the comprehensiveness of the Aristotelian method in organizational contexts.

Lange, Marc. Armstrong and Dretske on the Explanatory Power of Regularities. *Analysis*, 52(3), 154-159, Jl 92.

Armstrong and Dretske have argued that an analysis of natural laws as those Humean regularities possessing some further property, "lawlikeness", cannot account for the role that law-statements play in scientific explanations. They charge that in order for a regularity to figure in an explanation of one of its instances, that instance would, in effect, have to be explaining itself. I explain how their argument fails.

Lange, Marc. Lawlikeness. *Nous*, 27(1), 1-21, Mr 93.

It is argued that only generalizations believed "lawlike" (i.e., believed, if true, to state natural laws) can be confirmed "inductively"; induction is distinguished from other ways to confirm a generalization's truth. Evidence for a generalization's truth is contrasted with evidence for its lawlikeness. A generalization following logically from lawlike claims need not be lawlike. An analysis of lawlikeness is proposed to save these phenomena: to believe "All Fs and G" lawlike is to hold that were it true and one believed"... is F," then "... is F" would be an optimal way for one to justify"... is G."

Lange, Marc. Natural Laws and the Problem of Provisos. *Erkenntnis*, 38(2), 233-248, Mr 93.

Hempel and Giere contend that the existence of provisos poses grave difficulties for any regularity account of physical law. However, Hempel and Giere rely upon a mistaken conception of the way in which statements acquire their content. By correcting this mistake, I remove the problem Hempel and Giere identify but reveal a different problem that provisos pose for a regularity account—indeed, for any account of physical law according to which the state of affairs described by a law-statement presupposes a Humean regularity. These considerations suggest a normative analysis of law-statements. On this view, law-statements are not distinguished from accidental generalizations by the kind of Humean regularities they describe because a law-statement need not describe any Humean regularity. Rather, a law-statement says that in certain contexts, one ought to regard the assertion of a given type of claim, if made with justification, as a proper way to justify a claim of a certain other kind.

Langer, Monika. Sartre and Marxist Existentialism in Sartre Alive, Aronson, Ronald (ed). Detroit, Wayne St Univ Pr, 1991.

I argue that Sartre's *Critique of Dialectical Reason* is fundamentally at odds with authentic Marxism—whether classical or revisionist. I claim that Marxism bases itself on an unclarified conception of freedom; and I contend that Sartre's existentialism is unable to provide the requisite philosophical grounding. Yet the flaws in Sartre's position are fruitful in disclosing a possible corresponding weakness in Marxism and underlying the need for an adequate phenomenological analysis of freedom. My reconsideration of Sartre's philosophy sheds light on what remains to be done to provide a genuinely firm footing for Marxism.

Langer, Richard. Abortion and the Right to Privacy. *J Soc Phil*, 23(2), 23-51, Fall 92.

This article seeks to establish guidelines for inferring a rights waiver from a person's conduct and then to apply these guidelines to the case of abortion. Three criteria are given for establishing a rights waiver: causation, voluntariness and foreseeability. Each of these are discussed in some depth and then applied to the case of abortion. It is concluded that in many cases of unwanted pregnancy, there are adequate grounds for inferring a waiver of the woman's right to privacy against the fetus.

Langevin, Lysanne. Prolégomènes à une réflexion sur la problématique: Femme et langage. *Horiz Phil*, 3(1), 121-137, Autumn 92.

This article is about the linguistic approaches and methods available to apprehend different aspects of women's verbal behavior. A review of linguistic notions leads us to conclude that a combination of various disciplines (ethnomethodology, sociolinguistic, pragmatic) and methods (iconographic, prosodic, thematic, pragmatic) is required to realize a complete description of the communicative competence in the conversational process taking into account not only the sexual membership of the speakers but also their role and situation in the controversial exchange.

Langford, Glenn. Locke's Idea of an Idea in Logical Foundations, Mahalingam, Indira (ed). New York, St Martin's Pr, 1991.

The purpose of the paper is to examine Locke's idea of an idea in the light of the gist of his account rather than his explicit definition. The claim that on Locke's account, we are acquainted only with our own ideas and therefore can have no knowledge of their supposed originals, is then criticized. It is argued that, correctly understood, Locke's view is that we are acquainted with reality through our ideas, rather than being separated from it by them; and, indeed, that the idea of an idea, like the idea of a footprint, incorporates a reference to its cause and, unlike a footprint, cannot be understood in any other way.

Langsdorf, Lenore. Words of Others and Sightings/Citings/Sitings of Self in The Critical Turn, Angus, Ian (ed). Carbondale, So Illinois Univ Pr, 1993.

Langsdorf, Lenore (ed) and Angus, Ian (ed). *The Critical Turn*. Carbondale, So Illinois Univ Pr, 1993.

Due to the discursive turn in philosophy and the human sciences, philosophy and rhetoric have begun to converge, though without becoming identical. The original essays collected in this volume, by a number of well-known rhetoricians and philosophers, address this convergence from a number of angles. Together, they make a contribution to the philosophy of the human sciences and to the rhetoric of the human sciences literatures.

Langsdorf, Lenore and Angus, Ian. Unsettled Borders: Envisioning Critique at the Postmodern Site in The Critical Turn, Angus, Ian (ed). Carbondale, So Illinois Univ Pr, 1993.

Langston, Douglas C. Scotus's Doctrine of Intuitive Cognition. *Synthese*, 96(1), 3-24, Jl 93.

The first section of the article uses various texts to present Scotus's doctrine of intuitive cognition: agents perceive their own mental acts through intelligible species and perceive presently existing material singulars through intelligible species and phantasms. The second section draws out certain implications of this doctrine. For example, in intuitive cognition, an agent grasps the property of actual existence. Moreover, Scotus's emphasis on the role of intelligible species in human cognition shows his historical importance for issues surrounding intentionality.

Langton, Rae. Duty and Desolation. *Philosophy*, 67(262), 481-505, O 92.

The correspondence between Kant and Maria von Herbert concerns friendship and secrecy, duty and desire. I discuss the role of these in Kant's philosophy, drawing on the *Doctrine of Virtue*, and the work of Strawson and Korsgaard. Kant's contrast between lying and reticence is illfounded by Kant's own lights: lying can be virtuous. Moreover, Herbert's plight challenges a severe Kantian philosophy, for she, although suicidal, is a Kantian saint. There is a saner Kantian philosophy which has a better answer to her quandary. Following Korsgaard, I consider how a consequentialist Kantianism might apply to Herbert's case.

Langtry, Bruce. Some Internal Theodicies and the Objection from Alternative Goods. *Int J Phil Relig*, 34(1), 29-39, Ag 93.

Many theists try to morally justify God's causing or permitting evils (sin, mental illness, suffering, etc.) by citing the existence of goods which outweigh the evils and for which the evils, or at least God's permitting the evils, are logically necessary. This strategy encounters an objection: surely God could have brought about great alternative goods for which neither the evils nor God's permitting the evils was logically necessary, and in this case the attempted theodicy fails. In this paper I argue that there are 'greater good' theodicies — what I call greater good internal theodicies for classical theism — which survive the objection.

Lanigan, Richard L. The Algebra of History in The Critical Turn, Angus, Ian (ed). Carbondale, So Illinois Univ Pr, 1993.

Subtitled "Merleau-Ponty and Foucault on the Rhetoric of the Person," this article critically analyzes the inaugural lectures of the two philosophers at the College de France, i.e., Merleau-Ponty's Eloge de la Philosophie and Foucault's L'Ordre ju Discours. The article discusses the conjunction of Religion/Lavalle, History/Bergson, and Philosophy/Socrates in Merleau-Ponty and the conjuction of Event/Dumezil, Series/Canguilhem, and Regularity/Socrates in Foucault. Lanigan's method of "semiotic phenomenology" is explicated.

Lano, K. The Intuitionistic Alternative Set Theory. *Annals Pure Applied Log*, 59(2), 141-156, Ja 93.

The Alternative Set Theory, as defined in Vopenka and Sochor, demonstrate how a set theory which avoids actually infinite sets can serve as a framework for much of classical mathematics. This paper defines a theory which can serve as an intuitionistic analogue of AST, and examines motivations for alternative formulations of classical AST from an intuitionistic and finitistic viewpoint. The intuitionistic AST uses appropriate modifications of the concepts of AST, with the notion of *feasibility* replacing *finiteness*, and with new distinctions between alternative definitions of Countable Class and Revealment. Results of classical AST which are still valid in this new system are given, and an interpretation of the corresponding classical system in the intuitionistic system is defined. This shows that the adoption of an intuitionistic logic does not essentially deprive us of classical methods or results for AST.

Lanteigne, Josette. Quelques remarques sur le jugement. *Philosophiques*, 19(1), 25-44, 1992.

The aim is to present this notion from different points of view (logical, pragmatical and transcendental). In the first section, it will be a question not only of synthesis in the Kantian sense which bears upon intuition, but equally of the three syntheses distinguished by Heidegger and Lotsz. The second section, more Wittgensteinian in spirit, asks the question of judgment in the context of the "philosophical grammar". The third section investigates Poulain's idea of a primacy of judgment on the basis of the primacy of theoretical reason over practical reason. At first sight, this thesis of Poulain seems to go against Kant's thesis in the *Critic of Practical Reason*, but we don't have to attribute to him the will to establish a new "theoretical philosophy".

Lapierre, Serge. A Functional Partial Semantics for Intensional Logic. *Notre Dame J Form Log*, 33(4), 517-541, Fall 92.

In this paper a partial semantics for the higher order modal language of Intensional Logic is suggested. Partial semantic values of functional types are defined as monotone functions on partially ordered sets; it is shown that this characterization is materially adequate for representing partial values and that it overcomes the difficulties that arise when we attempt to introduce one-place partial functions in the hierarchy of types. Partial values of any type are related to classical values of the same type by means of a relation of approximation. This allows us to compare partial models with classical models. Classical semantics then appears to be a part of partial semantics to the extend that there exists a bijective mapping from classical models onto totally defined partial models. This also allows us to define, according to the partial semantics, a notion of entailment which is coextensive with the classical notion.

Lappé, Marc A. Justice and the Limitations of Genetic Knowledge. *Nat Forum*, 73(2), 30-34,41, Spr 93.

Lapsley, Daniel K (ed) and Power, F Clark (ed). *The Challenge of Pluralism: Education, Politics, and Values*. Notre Dame, Univ Notre Dame Pr, 1992.

Lara, María Pía. *La Democracia Como Proyecto de Identidad Ética*. Barcelona, Anthropos, 1992.

Laraudogoitia, Jon Perez. On Paradoxes in Naive Set Theory. *Log Anal*, 32, 241-245, S-D 89.

In 1979 Meyer, Routley and Dunn found a new form of Russell's paradox, different from those found by Curry. By means of elementary syntactic transformations it is possible to clarify the relation which these paradoxes have with each other. Also, we find new relationships with important metatheoric results relative to Peano's arithmetic (Gödel's theorem of incompleteness).

Largeault, Jean. Brève note sur l'intuitionnisme de Brouwer. *Rev Phil Fr*, 3, 317-324, Jl-S 92.

Largeault, Jean. Emile Meyerson, philosophe oublié. *Rev Phil Fr*, 3, 273-295, Jl-S 92.

Largeault, Jean. Intuition et intuitionisme. *Arch Phil*, 55(4), 685-690, O-D 92.

Largeault, Jean. L'intuitionisme des mathématiciens avant Brouwer. *Arch Phil*, 56(1), 53-67, Ja-Mr 93.

Pre-intuitionist French mathematicians (as Brouwer called them) in the 1900s had addressed constructivistically minded criticisms to various set theoretical conceptions. They had inquired what the scope and limits of the thinkable are, but they had not systematized their insights about a positive conception of intuition. Their alleged empiricism had its roots in a French tradition of taking psychology as a basis for philosophy.

Larmer, Robert A H. Miracles and Conservation Laws: A Reply to Professor MacGill. *Sophia (Australia)*, 31(1-2), 89-95, 1992.

In a recent article, Neil MacGill criticizes my claim (See *Water Into Wine*, MacGill-Queen's University Press, 1988) that miracles, understood as a transcendent agent overriding the usual course of nature, can conceivably occur without violating or suspending any of the laws of nature. MacGill feels that my account of miracles implies the violation of at least one law of nature, the Principle of the Conservation of Energy. In my reply, I point out that he is mistaken and that my original claim has not, therefore, been refuted.

Larmore, Charles. The Limits of Aristotelian Ethics. *Nomos*, 34, 185-196, 1992.

(Neo-) Aristotelian ethics is inadequate to the task of political philosophy in modern times. The enduring insight of liberal thought is that reasonable people tend naturally to differ and disagree about the nature of the good life. The ideal of a common moral ground amidst profound and abiding disagreement about the good is nowhere to be found in Aristotelian thought.

Larochelle, Gilbert and Lyotard, Jean-François. That Which Resists, After All. *Phil Today*, 36(4), 402-417, Wint 92.

Larrabee, Mary Jeanne (ed). *An Ethic of Care: Feminist and Interdisciplinary Perspectives*. New York, Routledge, 1993.

This volume collects key contributions to the extensive debate on Carol Gilligan's work. It pays particular attention to issues in moral philosophy (care vs justice, autonomy); empirical studies within psychology (sex differences in moral reasoning); and challenges to Gilligan's work that claim it leaves African-American and other cultures out of account. The volume calls for a new look at developmental theory and offers an alternative that would combine dimensions of the voices of care and justice.

Larrazabal, Jesús (ed) and Ezquerro, Jesús (ed). *Cognition, Semantics and Philosophy*. Norwell, Kluwer, 1992.

Larre, Olga L and Bolzan, J E. La Curiosa Doctrina de Ockham en Torno a la Divisibilidad del Continuo. *Rev Filosof (Mexico)*, 24(71), 142-158, My-Ag 91.

Larson, Elizabeth. Mary Wollstonecraft and Women's Rights. *Free Inq*, 12(2), 45-48, Spr 92.

Larson, Gerald James. The *Trimūrti* of *Smṛti* in Classical Indian Thought. *Phil East West*, 43(3), 373-388, Jl 93.

Larson, Richard K and Ludlow, Peter. Interpreted Logical Forms. *Synthese*, 95(3), 305-355, Je 93.

Recently, various authors have suggested that familiar semantic problems with propositional attitude verbs might be resolved by taking such predicates to express relations between agents and interpreted logical forms (ILFs). ILFs are annotated constituency graphs whose nodes pair terminal and nonterminal symbols with a semantic value. In this paper, we present an explicit theory of ILFs and apply it to classical questions regarding propositional attitude semantics. Our formal construction algorithm is embedded within a recursive theory of truth for natural language of the kind advocated by Davidson. We apply ILFs to issues involving substitutivity, demonstratives, general beliefs, and iterated attitude ascriptions.

Laruelle, François. La Science des phénomènes et la critique de la décision phénoméologique in Analecta Husserliana, XXXIV, Tymieniecka, Anna-Teresa (ed). Dordrecht, Kluwer, 1992.

Larvor, Brendan. Re-Reading Soviet Philosophy: Bakhurst on Ilyenkov. *Stud Soviet Tho*, 44(1), 1-31, Jl 92.

Bakhurst argues that Soviet philosophy needs to be studied by means of a method of 'sympathetic identification', and undertakes such a study of the work of Ilyenkov. I take issue with some of the details of Bakhurst's account of Ilyenkov. I discuss Ilyenkov's essentialism and evaluate his polemic against positivism. Finally, I discuss the implications of the collective nature of philosophy for Bakhurst's scholarly method.

Lascola, Russell A. A Common Sense Approach to the Mind-Body Problem: A Critique of Richard Taylor. *J Phil Res*, 17, 279-286, 1992.

In a popular book and a widely anthologized article, Richard Taylor argues for a materialistic account of human nature based on consideration of common sense. While I do not argue against materialism, per se, I offer an extended critique of Taylor's position that common sense unambiguously supports his version of materialism. I also argue that his account of the nature of psychological processes is of dubious philosophical value.

Lasersohn, Peter. Existence Presuppositions and Background Knowledge. *J Semantics*, 10(2), 113-122, 1993.

When a definite noun phrase fails to refer, the statement containing it is often felt to lack a truth value, as in *The king of France is bald*. In other examples, however, the statement seems intuitively false, and not truth-valueless: consider the case of a speaker who points at an obviously empty chair and says *The king of France is sitting in that chair*. The difference appears to depend on the pragmatics of verification; we know the sentence is false because the chair is empty — the question of the existence of the king of France need not even come up. A semantics is sketched for assigning truth values to sentences relative to information states.

Lash, Nicholas. Not Exactly Politics or Power?. *Mod Theol*, 8(4), 353-364, Oct 92.

Laskey, Dallas. The Moral Sense: An Appraisal in Analecta Husserliana, XXXI, Tymieniecka, Anna-Teresa (ed). Dordrecht, Kluwer, 1990.

Traditional phenomenology has been challenged by Anna-Teresa Tymieniecka who is concerned to reformulate phenomenology with cosmic proportions and not restricted to the domain of intentional consciousness. Within this new framework, the concept of the moral sense is now taken to be part of the real and evolutionary process in nature. It has an independent and autonomous sense-bestowing function and claimed to be the source of society and morality. The theory is examined in its details and shown to require clarification especially at the level where the moral sense merges with intentional consciousness.

Laskowski, M C and Greif, A D. An Omitting Types Theorem for Saturated Structures. *Annals Pure Applied Log*, 62(2), 113-118, Jl 93.

Laskowski, M C and Kueker, D W. On Generic Structures. *Notre Dame J Form Log*, 33(2), 175-183, Spr 92.

We discuss many generalizations of Fraissé's construction of countable 'homogeneous-universal' structures. We give characterizations of when such a structure is saturated and when its theory is ω-categorical. We also state very general conditions under which the structure is atomic.

Laskowski, Michael Chris. The Categoricity Spectrum of Pseudo-Elementary Classes. *Notre Dame J Form Log*, 33(3), 332-347, Sum 92.

Latawiec, A. La simulation du point de vue de la thérie des jeux (in Polish). *Stud Phil Christ*, 28(1), 53-68, 1992.

Dans cet article sont présentées les notons de simulation, de modèel et de jeu de simulation. En comparant ces notions il faut soulingner que a Isimulation est comprosise comme application d'un système à l'aide d'un ordinateur. Le jeu de simulation est une expérience qui consiste à faire jouer à plusieurs participants des rôles prévus dans un scéaario créé à partir d'un modèle de simulation. A chaque rôle correspond un ensemble défini de décisions dont dépendent des conséquences définies aussi. On peut donc dire d'un modèle qu'il peut être créé pour lui-même mais qu'il devient une phase intermédiaire dans le cas d'une simulation ou de l'élaboration d ún jeu de simulation. Pour qu'une expérience de simulation soitt effectivement un jeu de simulation il faut que les participants prennent plus d'une décision, sinon il ne s'agirait que d'une définition des variables d'entrée.

Latawiec, Anna. Existe-t-il une théorie de la simulation et la simulation est-elle une théorie? (in Polish). *Stud Phil Christ*, 27(2), 19-30, 1991.

Dans le présent article il s'agit d'essayer de répondre à la question s'il existe une théorie de la simulation et si la simulation est ellemême, une théorie. Après avoir esquissé les principes méthodologiques et avoir passé en revue les problèmes liés à la simulation a été admise la solution suivante. La simulation n'est pas seulement un instrument important ou une méthode de la pratique de la connaissance du monde; c'est aussi une théorie, ou plutôt une description de la théorie qui étabi pour combien les modéles simulationistes sont une application, une projection de leurs prototypes à partir d'un point de vue choisi. En tant qui objet de recherche, ces modèles, ces principes et les relations entre eux déterminent en tant que causes l'existence de plusieurs théories de la simulation qui sont complémentaries ou concurentielles entre elles.

Lath, Mukund. Aristotle and the Roots of Western Rationality. *J Indian Counc Phil Res*, 9(2), 55-68, Ja-Ap 92.

Laudan, Larry and Leplin, Jarrett. Determination Underdeterred: Reply to Kukla. *Analysis*, 53(1), 8-16, Ja 93.

We criticize algorithmic attempts to guarantee, for any theory, the availability of empirically equivalent rivals. Epistemic constraints on the admissability of auxiliaries used to determine what a theory's empirical consequences are must be respected by purported rivals. Accordingly, what algorithms produce are either not rivals or are not theories. Multiplicity of theoretical options cannot be adduced to establish the thesis that theories are inevitably underdetermined by all possible evidence. Nor can this thesis be grounded on an appeal to Bayesian methodology.

Lauder, Robert. MacMurray's World Community as Antidote to Kant's Theism. *Sophia (Australia)*, 31(3), 28-38, 1992.

Scottish personalist John Macmurray created a philosophy of person and God that can be looked upon as a corrective to Kant's theism. Finding Kant's division of the phenomenal and nomenal unacceptable and that Kantian thought did not do justice to the religious aspect of personal existence, Macmurray argued for a world community of persons with God as the center. Believing that modern philosophy, starting with Descartes and including Kant, did not do justice to the relational aspect of personal existence Macmurray created a philosophy that he believed was both personal and practical, a philosophy that included both God as person and the moral dimension of human living.

Lauder, Robert. Religious Story, Religious Truth, Religious Pluralism: A Prolegomenon to Religious Faith. *Amer Cath Phil Quart*, 65, 123-132, 1991.

In this article Robert Lauder argues that while all truth is truth in relation to persons and so to some extent historically conditioned, truth is nevertheless absolute, that is intersubjective and transhistorical. While true meaning is due to human presence, persons do not create true meaning, they are not the sole source of truth. Meaning appears through human person encountering other and truth is the correct articulation of that meaning. Rejecting religious relativism Lauder argues that religious truth is historical but also transhistorical, personal but also intersubjective, related to persons but also absolute.

Laudisa, Federico. Rappresentazione hilbertiana delle logiche quantistische. *Epistemologia*, 15(2), 279-313, Jl-D 92.

The so-called *logical* approach to quantum mechanics was firstly introduced in the

30's by Birkhoff and von Neumann, who pointed out that the deepest branching point between classical and quantum mechanics was the difference between the logico-algebraic structure of the propositions about the physical systems respectively in classical and quantum domains. After two decades the project was revived and the development of a *quantum logic* really started. In the paper the conceptual roots of the logical approach to quantum mechanics are examined, since the pioneering work of Birkhoff and von Neumann up to the fundamental work of Mackey, who settled the main issues of the approach. (edited)

Lauener, Henri. Speaking About Language in Certainty and Surface in Epistemology and Philosophical Method, Martinich, A P (ed). Lewiston, Mellen Pr, 1991.

Claiming that meaning and truth depend on context the author argues that linguistic individuals cannot be identified without regard to the context of their use. Expressions are abstract objects, not (physical) tokens: they are identified on the ground of purely linguistic considerations regarding their grammatical functions and their specific location in a text, whereas the tokens, required merely as a material support, remain utterly irrelevant to the internal semantic workings of a language system. He also warns against the confusion of naming and quoting: the use of so-called quotation names, favoring such a confusion, is placed by a more careful procedure introducing proper names.

Lauer, Henle. Causal Facts as Logical Entailments of Action Statements. *Indian Phil Quart*, 19(4), 283-292, O 92.

Some theorists purport that action statements carry special, quasi-logical causal entailments due to their transitive verb form. But examples suggest this is very often not the case. Undue attention to the 'surface structure' of action sentences obscures the way that causal sequences may in fact be assessed case by every case, as actions done unsuccessfully, ineffectively, creatively, unusually, unintentionally, unwittingly, unpredictably, deftly, and the log.

Lauer, Quentin. *A Reading of Hegel's "Phenomenology of Spirit" (Revised Edition)*. Bronx, Fordham Univ Pr, 1993.

Laurent, E. En quoi l'inconscient freudien est-il savoir?. *Commun Cog*, 25(1), 29-39, 1992.

Laurent, Jérôme. Le corps de la terre. *Arch Phil*, 55(1), 3-16, Ja-Mr 92.

What is properly earth according to Plotinus? This question has often been neglected by commentators who concentrated on problems raised by each of the three hypostasies. But, as Plotinus, against the Gnostics, dislikes the nostalgy of a plerom from which our soul would have fallen, according to the Enneades, the world we inhabit is the only manifestation which imitates the intelligible. But, according to Treatises 47 and 48 (III, 2 and 3) there is a sharp opposition sublunary/supralunary; in Treatise 50 (III, 5) the soul of the earth is compared only to the vulgar Aphrodite whom Pausanias mentions in the Symposion. What about its body? As it is a place for the greatest suffering can it be divine as the bodies of other planets? How can earthly splendour be reconciled with the elementary poverty of the earthly?

Lauritzen, Paul. *Pursuing Parenthood: Ethical Issues in Assisted Reproduction*. Bloomington, Indiana Univ Pr, 1993.

This book explores the ethical issues raised by assisted reproduction by bringing together an analysis of the literature on the morality of assisted reproduction and the author's own experience of infertility. Lauritzen argues that critics of assisted reproduction have too frequently defined parenthood genetically and that we need to move toward a social definition of parenthood. There are chapters on artificial insemination with husband's sperm, in vitro fertilization, donor insemination, surrogate motherhood, and adoption.

Lauterbach, Hanna. Moore-Sätze, Regelfolgen und antiskeptische Strategien in Wittgensteins, Über Gewissheit'. *Theol Phil*, 66(1), 49-74, 1991.

Lauth, B and Zoubek, G. Zur Rekonstruktion des Bohrschen Forschungsprogramms I. *Erkenntnis*, 37(2), 223-247, S 92.

Lauth, B and Zoubek, G. Zur Rekonstruktion des Bohrschen Forschungsprogramms II. *Erkenntnis*, 37(2), 249-273, S 92.

Lavaud, Claudie. Le système impossible: remarques sur l'inachèvement des dialectiques platoniciennes. *Rev Phil Fr*, 4, 545-555, O-D 91.

Lavelle, Louis and Gairdner, W T (trans). *The Dilemma of Narcissus*. Burdett, Larson, 1993.

Lavelle, Louis and Hardy, Gilbert (trans). Negation and Absence. *Int Stud Phil*, 25(1), 37-53, 1993.

The translation features the first chapter of the unfinished work *Reality and the Spirit* by L Lavelle (1883-1951), the leading figure of French Spiritualism between the two world wars. "Negation and Absence" carries both a metaphysical and a moral message in that Lavelle insists that Being is at once absolute Presence and Self-affirming Act. These themes suggest an idealistic undercurrent in Lavelle's thought, recast, however, in an original way, within the perspective of the French school of psycho-metaphysical spiritualism.

Lavine, Thelma Z. Postmodernism and American Pragmatism. *J Speculative Phil*, 7(2), 110-113, 1993.

Lavoie, Don. Democracy, Markets, and the Legal Order: Notes on the Nature of Politics in a Radically Liberal Society. *Soc Phil Pol*, 10(2), 103-120, Sum 93.

The two ideals classical liberalism originally stood for—democracy and markets—have never seemed to fit well with one another, and have each been taken in most doses. Properly understood, however, markets and democracy are applications of a more fundamental principle, "openness." The upshot of this re-interpretation is a critique of liberalism's traditional individualistic and modernistic biases, and an emphasis on the importance of political culture. The two classic principles of liberalism can be radicalized in a way which may make the idea of free-market anarchism more attractive than it now seems to most social theorists.

Lawler, James. Ecocentric Ethics. *Free Inq*, 13(2), 16-17, Spr 93.

Lawler, Peter Augustine. Havel and the Foundaiton of Political Responsibility. *Vera Lex*, 12(1), 8-9, 1992.

Lawlor, Leonard. *Imagination and Chance: The Difference Between the Thought of Ricoeur and Derrida*. Albany, SUNY Pr, 1992.

Lawrence, Gavin. Aristotle and the Ideal Life. *Phil Rev*, 102(1), 1-34, Ja 93.

Many find Aristotle's account of happiness in *Nicomachean Ethics* 10 problematic because they misconstrue his topic. This primarily concerns activity, not value. It seeks to determine the perfect human life—a life unqualifiedly ideal, in being the best way to live in ideal circumstances. Of course we also need to be perfect people—to have the values that enable us to discern and dispose us to do whatever is best whatever our circumstances. These latter are often not ideal. So the best life good people are free to live is often not the ideal one, and only "secondarily" happy.

Lawson, Bill E and McGary, Howard. *Between Slavery and Freedom: Philosophy and American Slavery*. Bloomington, Indiana Univ Pr, 1992.

The American slave experience and philosophical analysis are used to examine six moral and political concepts— oppression, paternalism, resistance, political obligation, citizenship, and forgiveness. This work also demonstrates that the slave narrative, important historical accounts of the predicament of slaves, is equally useful as a means of exploring perplexing philosophical issues.

Lawson, George and Condren, Conal (ed). *Politica Sacra et Civilis—George Lawson*. New York, Cambridge Univ Pr, 1992.

Laymon, Ronald E. Thought Experiments of Stevin, Mach and Gouy in Thought Experiments in Science and Philosophy, Horowitz, Tamara (ed). Lanham, Rowman & Littlefield, 1991.

Lazari-Pawlowska, Ija. The Deductive Model in Ethics. *Dialec Hum*, 17(1), 79-87, 1990.

Lazcano, Rafael. *Bibliographia Missionalia Augustiniana: America Latina (1533-1993)*. Madrid, Ed Revista Agustin, 1993.

El material bibliográfico existente sobre la 'familia agustiniana'(OSA, OAR, OAD y agustinas) referido a su presencia en América Latina, está reunido en la presente obra bibliográfica. Por secciones y en orden alfabético, aparecen agrupadas las fuentes bibliográficas consultadas, las crónicas agustinianas, los estudios generales y locales—sobre conventos, iglesias y actividades-, siguiendo el orden de naciones—16 en total-. En la sección 'Historia personal', la más ámplia del volúmen—ofrece R Lazcano, los escritos "de" y "sobre" las cien-100-figuras agustinas más relevantes en el campo de la evangelización y la cultura latinoamericana. Indices.

Lazcano, Rafael. *Panorama Bibliográfico de Xavier Zubiri*. Madrid, Ed Revista Agustin, 1993.

Esta obra ofrece el primer ensayo bibliográfico completo *de* y *sobre* el útlimo filósofo español, X Zubiri (1898-1983). La obra consta de ocho capítulos, en los que R Lazcano presenta, con método, precisión y claridad, los escritos editado del metafísico X Z (ediciones, traducciones, recensiones); los estudios sobre la vida y obra, aparecidos en forma de libros, artículos y comentarios; las noticias aparecidas en los medios de comunicación (periódicos, semanarios, revistas, etc.). Al final de la obra están los índices: cronológico, temático y onomástico. El prólogo del libro bibliográfico lo firma Carmen Castro de Zubiri.

Le Blanc, Jill. Infinity in Theology and Mathematics. *Relig Stud*, 29(1), 51-62, Mr 93.

God's infinity is sometimes used as an explanation for difficulties in talking about God. We might expect that the source of any difficulties "extending" our concepts from finite objects to infinite objects will be seen clearly in the mathematical concept of the infinite. Through a brief historical survey, I distinguish the mathematical infinite from the theological infinite. The attribution of infinity to God may be seen, not as a literal cause or reason for inexpressibility, but as a metaphorical expression of the mystery, fascination, and wonder attached to the incomprehensibly immense.

Le Grand, Julian. Equity as an Economic Objective in Applied Philosophy, Almond, Brenda (ed). New York, Routledge, 1992.

Political philosophers and economists have recently shown great interest in different conceptions of equity or justice. These have included utilitarianism, Rawls' maximum principle, and envy-free distribution. None of these conceptions command general consensus, and this paper is an attempt to find out why. It is argued that they fail because they do not take account of an essential element of equity and social justice, its relationship to choice. Specifically, outcomes that are the result of individual's. Voluntary choices are equitable. Those that are the result of factors beyond individual control are not. This conception of equity comes closer to meeting the test of moral intuition than any of the others considered.

Le Ny, Jean-François. Cognitive Science and Semantic Representations. *Theoria (Spain)*, 5(12-13), 85-106, N 90.

The main task of cognitive science is to construct concepts and models that would superordinate to knowledge in the various particular cognitive sciences. In particular, one major objective is to formulate a hypergeneral description of representations that could encompass all descriptions given in subordinate domains. A first basic distinction is between natural and rational representations, i.e., given mental entities and representations that are governed by prescriptive rules coming from logical or scientific thought. In addition, representations must be described in respect to several sources of variability, which are tentatively listed here. (edited)

Le Poidevin, Robin. Lowe on McTaggart. *Mind*, 102(405), 163-170, Ja 93.

This paper is in part a reply to E J Lowe's discussion note, 'McTaggart's Paradox Revisited' (*Mind*, 101, 1992). In that note, Lowe develops the theme of an earlier article, in which he argued (a) that McTaggart's attempted proof of the unreality of time makes crucial use of iterated, or higher-order, tenses (e.g., 'it will be the case in the future that *e* is past'); and (b) that iterated tenses are incoherent. In reply, I defend iterated tenses, but also present a version of McTaggart's argument which, I believe, does not employ them.

Le Poidevin, Robin. On the Acausality of Time, Space, and Space-Time. *Analysis*, 52(3), 146-154, Jl 92.

This paper examines the *a priori* basis of the widely-held view that space and time are causally inert. It is suggested that the view depends upon the plausible assumption of homogeneity: that any time (or place) has the same intrinsic properties of any other time (or place). However, General Relativity gives us a reason to doubt homogeneity, since space-time may be variably curved. Provided that we do not think that *affecting* something entails *changing* it, we can coherently suppose that it is possible to causally affect, and be affected by, space-time itself.

Leach, Mary S. "Is The Personal Political?" Take Two: "Being One's Self Is Always An Acquired Taste". *Proc Phil Educ*, 48, 279-285, 1992.

League, Kathleen. Teleology in Spinoza's *Ethics*. *SW Phil Rev*, 8(1), 77-83, Ja 92.

Leal, Fernando and Shipley, Patricia. Deep Dualism. *Int J Applied Phil*, 7(2), 33-44, Wint 92.

Leaman, Oliver. Philosophy versus Mysticism in Philosophy, Religion and the Spiritual Life, McGhee, Michael (ed). New York, Cambridge Univ Pr, 1992.

There is a protracted debate in Islamic philosophy between philosophers and mystics. Philosophers argue that the best way to attain the truth is through the demonstrative methodology offered by philosophy, while mystics argue that this is only capable of attaining partial access to truth. The views of al-Ghazali on this controversy are discussed, and it is suggested that there are problems in moving from the privacy of the mystical experience to the public nature of a religion such as Islam.

Leaman, Oliver. Philosophy versus Mysticism: an Islamic Controversy. *Philosophy*, 32(Supp), 177-187, 1992.

Any view of religion which is defined in terms of its public character finds it difficult to accommodate the mystic. Islamic philosophy was determined to accept a wide variety of routes to God, but the mystical route was often treated with some suspicion. For the philosophers, the nature of reality is essentially knowable, although we cannot grasp it all due to our finitude. Mystics believe that behind what can be known lies a realm of reality which is ineffable, and which may only be approached by a special form of religious experience.

Lear, Jonathan. Inside and Outside the *Republic*. *Phronesis*, 37(2), 184-215, 1992.

Leavitt, Frank J. Weeks, Spinoza's God and Epistemic Autonomy. *Sophia (Australia)*, 31(1-2), 111-118, 1992.

Epistemic autonomy is revealed in the feeling we have that our thoughts are our own and to God's or someone else's. Ian Weeks has an argument which suggests that our epistemic autonomy is incompatible with God's existence. I examine Spinoza's conception of God to see whether it is vitiated by our epistemic autonomy. Spinoza's Johannine Christian concept of God is contrasted with the God of Israel, and a comparison is suggested between Spinoza's Attribute of Thought and Kant's Transcendental Subject.

Leblanc, Hugues and Roeper, Peter. Getting the Constraints on Popper's Probability Functions Right. *Phil Sci*, 60(1), 151-157, Mr 93.

Shown here is that a constraint used by Popper in *The Logic of Scientific Discovery* (1959) for calculating the absolute probability of a universal quantification, and one introduced by Stalnaker in "Probability and Conditionals" (1970, 70) for calculating the relative probability of a negation, are too weak for the job. The constraint wanted in the first case is in Bendall (1979) and that wanted in the second case is Popper (1959).

Leblanc, Hugues and Roeper, Peter. Les fonctions de probabilité: la question de leur définissabilité récursive. *Dialogue (Canada)*, 31(4), 643-659, Autumn 92.

Leblanc, Hugues and Roeper, Peter. Probability Functions: The Matter of Their Recursive Definability. *Phil Sci*, 59(3), 372-388, S 92.

This paper studies the extent to which probability functions are recursively definable. The absolute probability functions considered are those of Kolmogorov and Carnap, and the relative ones are those of Kolmogorov, Carnap, Rényi, and Popper. (edited)

Lecercle, Jean-Jacques. Postmodernism and Language in Postmodernism and Society, Boyne, Roy (ed). New York, St Martin's Pr, 1990.

Leclerc, André. La Grammaire générale classique en tant que programme de recherche scientifique. *Dialogue (Canada)*, 32(1), 77-94, Wint 93.

Leclerc, Jean-Jacques. Three-Way Games. *Phil Today*, 36(4), 336-350, Wint 92.

Leddy, Michael. Limits of Allusion. *Brit J Aes*, 32(2), 110-122, Ap 92.

No essence of allusion is at issue here; as Nelson Goodman suggests, "allusion" itself resists firm definition. I do offer a description of limits implicit in the typical use of allusion-words ("allusion," "allusive," "to allude," "to make an allusion"). I argue that these implicit limits present great difficulties for the extension of allusion-words to music and the visual arts, noting how the typical use of allusion-words undergoes silent and significant alteration when one moves beyond the verbal. I also distinguish allusion from imitation, parody, "mere" quotation, and intra-art relations of form, style, and subject.

Leddy, Thomas W. Moore and Shusterman on Organic Wholes. *J Aes Art Crit*, 49(1), 63-73, Wint 91.

Although G E Moore was sympathetic to the idea that works of art are organic wholes he argued against the radical organicism exemplified by Hegel in which the parts of organic wholes are internally related to other parts and are essentially related to emergent properties of the whole. Richard Shusterman draws from Moore in criticizing Hegel's position as well as Nietzsche and Derrida. Drawing from a discussion of the process of painting, I defend radical organicism against Moore and Shusterman. My position is consistent with Nietzsche's perspectivism, James's pragmatist conception of truth, and the romantic vitalistic conception of organicism.

Leddy, Thomas W. The Socratic Quest in Art and Philosophy. *J Aes Art Crit*, 51(3), 399-410, Sum 93.

I defend a pragmatist form of historicism concerning the question of defining art. I call for an essentialism in which essences are not eternal and unchanging but are entities that correspond to something like the Socratic quest. The question "What is art?" searches for such an essence. I take essences to be what Joe Margolis has called "culturally emergent entities." In this, they are like persons and works of art. The essence of art is emergent upon the practices of artists, critics, art historians and philosophers. This essence changes historically, but is to be distinguished from the concept of art.

Leddy, Thomas W. Theorizing about Art. *J Aes Educ*, 26(1), 33-46, Spr 92.

Tilghman argues against theorizing about art. I reply that the capacity to make essentialist claims is important for such practices as art history, sculpture and aesthetics; and that philosophy of art, the art theory of artists, and the practice of artists are much closer than Tilghman allows. We should abandon the assumption, shared by Tilghman and others, that natural science theories are paradigmatic for theories in general. The use of theory to identify objects as works of art has been overemphasized. Essences are, rather, the "inner natures" of things. I conclude by criticizing a commonly held theory of philosophical "clarity."

Leder, Drew. A Tale of Two Bodies: The Cartesian Corpse and the Lived Body in The Body in Medical Thought and Practice, Leder, Drew (ed). Dordrecht, Kluwer, 1992.

The Cartesian notion of the human body is explored and critiqued with an eye to its influence on medicine. The author contends that Descartes' metaphysics and methodology privileges the *dead body*, and that this reign of the corpse has shaped medical practice in certain deleterious ways. As an alternative, the author presents the phenomenological notion of the "lived body" as discussed by Merleau-Ponty and others. It is suggested that attending to the lived body would lead to a reformulation of medical diagnosis and treatment.

Leder, Drew (ed). *The Body in Medical Thought and Practice*. Dordrecht, Kluwer, 1992.

In the 20th century, social theorists, phenomenologists and feminists have radically challenged our conventional notion of the human body dating back to 17th century Cartesian thought. This volume explores the range of contemporary perspectives on the body, along with historical and cross- cultural studies, and draws out the crucial implications for medicine. The authors suggest that many of the problems of modern medicine — dehumanized treatment, overspecialization, neglect of the mind's healing resources — are traceable to medicine's fundamental paradigm of embodiment. New alternatives are proposed by philosophers and physicians.

Ledermann, E K. Challenge of Ill Health in New Horizons in the Philosophy of Science, Lamb, David (ed). Brookfield, Avebury, 1992.

LeDoeuff, Michèle. One or Two Worlds: Separation or Coexistence? (in Czechoslovakian). *Filozof Cas*, 40(5), 801-817, 1992.

The author, a scientific worker of the French C N R S, reacts in this study to the present sharp discussion concerning the problem of equality of the sexes. The analysis of this problem shows that it has not been by far definitively solved—as it might naively seem—and that it is, on the contrary, alarmingly topical. By stressing the speciality and even the difference of female sex in relation to male sex, the feminist movements fall into a trap laid for them by a discourse which is singularly archaic. M Le Doeuff wants to analyze this very discourse both from the philosophical and historical and—why not—even philological viewpoint. (edited)

Ledure, Yves. Nietzsche et l'égalité des droits: De l'usage juridique d'un concept religieux chrétien. *Arch Phil*, 56(2), 251-265, Ap-Je 93.

Does the notion of right include that of equality as suggests recent juridical usage? According to Nietzsche, such practice which democracy boasts to be its conquest recalls the Christian idea of all men equal before God. But may a theological concept be applied in laws and politics? According to Nietzsche that is wrong and what might be suitable between man and God cannot stand for just relations between men. Equality does not indeed state the right of individuals. Therefore we can ask whether the notion of democracy should be rethought?

Lee, Brenda and Haworth, Lawrence and Brunk, Conrad G. Is a Scientific Assessment of Risk Possible? Value Assumptions in the Canadian Alachlor Controversy. *Dialogue (Canada)*, 30(3), 235-247, Sum 91.

Lee, Jee-Hun and Wringe, Colin. Rational Autonomy, Morality and Education. *J Phil Educ*, 27(1), 69-78, Sum 93.

Some traditional assumptions regarding rational autonomy are examined and criticised. The exclusion of subjective considerations from autonomous choice is shown to be unjustified, as are attempts to identify autonomy with morally desirable conduct. Unexpected implications of these conclusions for education and certain other social institutions are also indicated.

Lee, Richard T. What's the Good of Trying?. *J Phil Sport*, 18, 39-48, 1991.

"Trying to do X" is first construed as an intentional predicate, along the lines of "believing that X". On this view, trying would be related to doing as believing is to believing truly, and doing would be externally related to trying in just the same way truth is related to belief. This analysis is discarded in favor of construing trying as a kind of learning, and the temporal connection between learning and doing is stressed. Finally, I examine some connections between trying, persistence, and exertion and suggest how the different moral values of these activities can be understood in an unforced way, if we adopt a noninternalist view of trying.

Lee, Sander H. A Critique of Henry Veatch's "Human Rights: Fact or Fancy?". *Lyceum*, 3(1), 23-44, Spr 91.

In his book *Human Rights: Fact or Fancy?*(1985), Henry Veatch presents an eloquent defense of a naturalist theory of rights based on his reading of Aristotle. In this paper, I critically analyze Veatch's basic argument in order to show that such a naturalist theory can only be accepted under certain conditions. In order to do this, I first summarize Veatch's argument as I understand it, and then point out its flaws as well as those in similar arguments given by Alan Gewirth and Alasdair MacIntyre. I conclude by defending the notion of an ethical theory based on a Sartrean existentialism.

Lee, Seung-Hwan. Was There a Concept of Rights in Confucian Virtue-Based Morality?. *J Chin Phil*, 19(3), 241-261, S 92.

Lee, Steven. Is the Just War Tradition Relevant in the Nuclear Age?. *Res Phil Technol*, 9, 83-90, 1989.

Does the new destructive dimension in warfare created by the introduction of nuclear weapons require that we alter our moral view of the use of force by states? Some have argued that the just-war principle of discrimination implies that neither the use nor the threatened use of nuclear weapons is morally acceptable, which is the position known as nuclear pacifism, and that nuclear pacifism implies the just war tradition is irrelevant. This paper assesses this argument, examines the sense of irrelevancy it involves, and considers whether the just war theory should be revised in order to avoid its conclusion.

Lee, Steven. *Morality, Prudence, and Nuclear Weapons*. New York, Cambridge Univ Pr, 1993.

This book is the first post-Cold War assessment of nuclear deterrence. It seeks to provide a comprehensive normative understanding of nuclear deterrence policy, examining both its ethical and strategic dimensions. The question is: What kind of nuclear policy, if any, is both morally and prudentially acceptable. The author distinguishes what is essential to the nuclear deterrence relationship, and thus what we can expect to encounter again, from what is accidental, and thus merely a function of the particular political relationship between the US and the former Soviet Union. Throughout, the easy assumption that nuclear deterrence has worked is critically examined.

Lee, Won J and Harlan, Joshua D and Aybar, Samuel R. John Rawls: For the Record (An Interview). *Harvard Rev Phil*, 1(1), 38-48, Spr 91.

Leeds, Jeremy. Problems of Relativism in Psychoanalysis. *Phil Forum*, 24(4), 349-362, Sum 93.

Leffers, M Regina. Pragmatists Jane Addams and John Dewey Inform the Ethic of Care. *Hypatia*, 8(2), 64-77, Spr 93.

Both Jane Addams and John Dewey see human beings as ultimately creative in nature and as radically connected to each other. In this paper I look to these ideas to provide a theoretical model that is able to explain why we are able to extend our care to others outside of our intimate circle of family and friends, and to show us how we can purposefully move to the next higher level of moral reasoning.

Lefkowitz, Mary R. Commentary on Vlastos' "Socratic Piety". *Proc Boston Colloq Anc Phil*, 5, 239-246, 1989.

(1) The gods of conventional belief were not as unpredictable and capricious as Professor Vlastos implies, even though in enacting their justice they must often hurt innocent victims; (2) in insisting that the gods must be good, Socrates was following in a tradition already established by poets (which is not to minimize Socrates' contribution to that tradition, namely, making it systematic); (3) that while there are some precedents for Socrates' notion that piety is doing god's work to benefit human beings, it was revolutionary (and dangerous) to claim that the gods spoke directly to him and told him what was right.

Lehan, Richard. Bergson and the Discourse of the Moderns in The Crisis in Modernism, Burwick, Frederick (ed). New York, Cambridge Univ Pr, 1992.

This essay reads Henri Bergson, especially his *Creative Evolution*, against a background of competing and compatible ideas, especially his response to the Enlightenment and to Darwinian evolution. I focus on the way Bergson was anticipated by such literary figures as Samuel Butler and G B Shaw as well as the ground he shared with such other figures as D H Lawrence, James Joyce, Virginia Woolf. The essay also compares Bergson and Heidegger and Bergson and the systems biology of Bertalannfy and Laszlo.

Lehman, Glen. China After Tiananmen Square: Rawls and Justice. *Praxis Int*, 12(4), 405-420, Ja 93.

Lehman, Hugh. Are Value Judgements Inherent in Scientific Assessment?. *J Agr Environ Ethics*, 6/2(Supp), 60-67, 1993.

In Part I, I discuss the view of Bernard Rollin on the question posed in the title of the paper. In Part II, I make and defend and assumption concerning scientific method. In Part III, I argue that value commitments do enter into the application of scientific method at each stage and so are indeed inherent in science itself. Further, I suggest here that conflicts concerning the nature of scientific method reflect, in part, conflicts among scientist and other people with regard to what values can be considered to be values of science itself. I call attention to the grain of partial truth which is reflected in scientists' claims that science is value free. (edited)

Lehrer, Keith. Fallibilismus: Ein Paradoxon. *Conceptus*, 25(66), 59-68, 1991.

We can always err—even when we have an outstanding justification for accepting something. It is natural to combine the doctrine of fallibilism with the doctrine that we must have a criterion of justification, a criterion that we can apply to determine whether one is justified in accepting something. Assume that RK is a criterion of justification. Two principles are valid for such a criterion. The first says that when a person is justified in accepting that p, then is the person justified in accepting that p. Unfortunately, the doctrine of fallibilism is inconsistent with these two principles. That is the paradox of fallibilism. An externalist could deny the second principle, an internalist could deny the first principle, and a theorist who combined externalism and internalism could reject the principle of fallibilism.

Lehrer, Keith. Knowledge, Coherence and Skepticism in Rationality in Epistemology, Villanueva, Enrique (ed). Atascadero, Ridgeview, 1992.

This article shows that the *relevant alternatives* account of knowledge does not provide an adequate account of *knowledge*. An adequate reply to the skeptic must meet the objections she raises, and such a reply must be based on coherence with a background system. Coherence answers the skeptic, and yields knowledge.

Lehrer, Keith. Metamind, Autonomy and Materialism. *Grazer Phil Stud*, 40, 1-11, 1991.

The human mind is essentially a metamind. Autonomy, knowledge, preference, acceptance, consciousness, and the content of thought all incorporate metamental ascent to a higher level beyond first level belief and desire. The primary function or role of metamental ascent is conflict resolution and higher order evaluation. An infinite regress of metamental ascent is avoided by a mental loop of *keystone* stages which refer back to themselves yielding autonomy and knowledge without paradox. The metamental loop is, moreover, compatible with materialism, even eliminative materialism. Vector activation in the brain averages neural impulses, and conflict resolution in the brain, like interpersonal conflict resolution, is obtained from weighted averaging. The resolution of the conflict is a fixed point vector of integrative weights which yields itself back forming a neural loop. Thus, neurophysiology recapitulates metamentality.

Lehrer, Keith. Reply to Alfred Schramm's "Doubt, Scepticism, and a Serious Justification Game". *Grazer Phil Stud*, 40, 88-91, 1991.

Lehrer, Keith. Reply to Carl G Wagner's "Simpson's Paradox and the Fisher-Newcomb Problem". *Grazer Phil Stud*, 40, 195-196, 1991.

Lehrer, Keith. Reply to Christian Piller's "On Keith Lehrer's Belief in Acceptance". *Grazer Phil Stud*, 40, 62-69, 1991.

Lehrer, Keith. Reply to Daniel Schulthess's "Reid and Lehrer: Metamind in History". *Grazer Phil Stud*, 40, 148-149, 1991.

Lehrer, Keith. Reply to Dunja Jutronic-Tihomirovic's "Language as Fictitious Consensus". *Grazer Phil Stud*, 40, 180-183, 1991.

Lehrer, Keith. Reply to Elvio Baccarini's "Rational Consensus and Coherence Methods in Ethics". *Grazer Phil Stud*, 40, 160-162, 1991.

Lehrer, Keith. Reply to Fred Dretske's "Two Conceptions of Knowledge: Rational versus Reliable Belief". *Grazer Phil Stud*, 40, 31-35, 1991.

Lehrer, Keith. Reply to Marian David's "On the Roles of Trustworthiness and Acceptance". *Grazer Phil Stud*, 40, 108-111, 1991.

Lehrer, Keith. Reply to Mylan Engel's "Inconsistency: The Coherence Theorist's Nemesis?". *Grazer Phil Stud*, 40, 131-133, 1991.

Lehrer, Keith and McGee, Vann. An Epistemic Principle Which Solves Newcomb's Paradox. *Grazer Phil Stud*, 40, 197-220, 1991.

If it is certain that performing an observation to determine whether P is true will in no way influence whether P is true, then the proposition that the observation is performed ought to be probabilistically independent of P. Applying the notion of "observation" liberally, so that a wide variety of actions are treated as observations, this proposed new principle of belief revision yields the result that simple utility maximization gives the correct solution to the Fisher smoking paradox and the two-box solution to Newcomb's paradox.

Lehrer, Keith and McGee, Vann. Particulars, Individual Qualities, and Universals in Language, Truth and Ontology, Mulligan, Kevin (ed). Dordrecht, Kluwer, 1992.

This article develops Thomas Reid's theory of individual qualities and universals connecting his theory with recent work. Reid held that individualities, now called tropes, were the basis for our general conceptions of universals which, however, are not things that exist. His theory is related to prototype theory in psychology and to nominalist ontology.

Leibowitz, Flo. A Note on Feminist Theories of Representation: Questions Concerning the Autonomy of Art. *J Aes Art Crit*, 48(4), 361-364, Fall 90.

A preliminary comparison is made among three feminist analyses of representation—those of Laura Mulvey, Melinda Vadas and Suzanne Kappeler. The three theories seem to apply what is called here a Principle of Worldy Attachment concerning the meaning of a depiction and the role of ideology in meaning, and expression of skepticism about the autonomy of art which limits the effects of art to the effects of representations in other, prior contexts. It is observed further that the three theories are also theories of emotional response to art.

Leibowitz, Flo. Movie Colorization and the Expression of Mood. *J Aes Art Crit*, 49(4), 363-365, Fall 91.

This is a brief discussion of what kind of object a movie is. It is intended to provide added support to Jerrold Levinson's claim that colorizing a movie interferes with a filmmaker's freedom of expression. Movies are pictorial narratives where expressive work is done by the way the pictures look and changing the look can change the movie. The mood of a movie can be changed this way because it is dependent on the pictorialization of a narrative, which colorizing changes. Colorizing thus adds information to a movie which is extraneous at best.

Leighton, S R. What We Love. *Austl J Phil*, 71(2), 145-158, Je 93.

This paper tries to preserve some commonplace intuitions about persons as proper and primary objects of love. In so doing it contrasts a Platonic approach in which abstract properties, universals and features are deemed the primary and more plausible objects of love. The argument studies both the evolution of Plato's view and its influence within contemporary theorizing. I conclude that ancient and recent suggestions get much of their life from a particular orientation to characteristics and their subjects, and that an Aristotelian orientation is one way to avoid these consequences and defend our intuitions.

Leinfellner, Elisabeth. Cognitivism between Computation and Pragmatics: A Peer Review of 'Some Foundational Questions Concerning Language Studies' by Bickhard and Campbell. *J Prag*, 17(5-6), 491-503, Je 92.

Leist, Anton. Bioethics in a Low Key: A Report from Germany. *Bioethics*, 7(2-3), 271-279, Ap 93.

Leiter, Brian. Beyond Good and Evil. *Hist Phil Quart*, 10(3), 261-270, Jl 93.

This essay presents a systematic analysis of Nietzsche's slogan "beyond good and evil" by examining the *three* respects in which the good/evil distinction differs from the good/bad distinction: genetic, evaluative, and metaphysical. For example, while the good/evil distinction evaluates particular actions, and views persons as free agents responsible for those actions, the good/bad distinction evaluates the whole person (as "noble" or "contemptible"), without supposing free agency. Nietzsche's call, then, to move "beyond good and evil" amounts to a rejection of quite particular views of both value and agency.

Leiter, Brian. Nietzsche and Aestheticism. *J Hist Phil*, 30(2), 275-290, Ap 92.

In *Nietzsche: Life as Literature*, Alexander Nehamas attributes to Nietzsche "aestheticism," the view that the world is like a literary text in two respects: 1) the world and literary texts are essentially indeterminate, so that both admit of a plurality of conflicting interpretations; and 2) the world and its occupants have features that we ordinarily associate with literary texts and characters. This essay demonstrates that Nehamas systematically fails to provide adequate textual support for this interpretation; in developing his reading of Nietzsche as "aestheticist," Nehamas appears to leave Nietzsche behind.

Lejewski, Czeslaw. On the Dramatic Stage in the Development of Kotarbinski's Pansomatism in Kotarbinski: Logic, Semantics and Ontology, Wolenski, Jan (ed). Dordrecht, Kluwer, 1990.

Leman, Marc. The Theory of Tone Semantics: Concept, Foundation, and Application. *Mind Mach*, 2(4), 345-363, N 92.

Tone semantics is a psychoacoustic-based theory of Gestalt perception that deals with tone perception and the assignment of functional relationships between tones in the musical context. The theory provides an operational account of semantics in terms of complex dynamic systems theory and forms the basis for non-symbolic research in music imagination. This is illustrated by an application in the automatic recognition of tone centers from acoustical input. An analysis of the basic concepts and related epistemological and methodological principles reveals a promising paradigm for music research.

Lemanska, A. Some Remarks Concerning the Notion of Set (in Polish). *Stud Phil Christ*, 28(1), 69-85, 1992.

The aim of this paper is to present and discuss three different theories of sets. They are: 1) axiomatic systems of set theory based on the Cantor's notion of set; 2) intuitionistic mathematics; 3) the alternative set theory. The main difference between these theories is related to the notion of the infinite.

Lemco, Gary. *Nietzsche As Educator*. Lewiston, Mellen Pr, 1992.

Lemons, John and Malone, Charles. Scientific, Public Policy, and Ethical Implications of the Nuclear Waste Policy Act and Its Amendments. *Res Phil Technol*, 11, 5-32, 1991.

Lemos, Noah M. Higher Goods and the Myth of Tithonus. *J Phil*, 90(9), 482-496, S 93.

This essay attempts to explain what it is for one good to be "higher" than another. It also seeks to defend the view that some goods are higher than others. Roughly, a good A is a higher good than another good B just in case an instance of A is better than any number of instances of B.

Lenk, Hans. Erlebte und erschlossene Realität. *Z Phil Forsch*, 47(2), 286-292, Ap-Je 93.

The perspective of an interpretative constructivist approach to the problem of the criterion of reality is discussed starting from Dilthey's and Scheler's opinion that pragmatic resistance is a criterion of reality and dealing also with the problem of whether or not the "brute facts" which allegedly cannot be conceived of under interpretational perspectives. A discussion with Professor Fellmann (published in Allgemeine Zeitschrift für Philosophie 1990, 15. 2) he is taken up again. The thesis is that even though we will not be able to change some real facts we are encountering there are epistemologically speaking no absolute facta bruta because any fact whatsoever according to the manner in which it is perceived or grasped or even conceived of is at least by the way of circumscription and representation dependent on an interpretative approach. That is even true for seemingly hard facts (facta bruta) and unavoidable experiences of resistance, etc.

Lenk, Hans and Maring, Matthias. A Pie-Model of Moral Responsibility? in Advances in Scientific Philosophy, Schurz, Gerhard (ed). Amsterdam, Rodopi, 1991.

Problems of distributing responsibility are found in highly developed industrial societies. In this context, the so-called pie-model of moral responsibility distribution is discussed: The more people share responsibility, the less each seems to be responsible; responsibility would be diluted by increasing numbers of people—at least as a matter of fact. But also normatively speaking? In general however, moral responsibility cannot be disected and shared like a pie. Moral responsibility is a function of power, impact, and knowledge and the mere fact that others are co-responsible, does not diminish the very responsibility of each partaking individual in contexts of collective or group or even institutional action.

Lenk, Hans and Maring, Matthias. Ecology and Ethics: Notes About Technology and Economic Consequences. *Res Phil Technol*, 12, 157-176, 1992.

More frequently than ever, in highly developed societies individual actions are hidden behind or at least, overridden by collective, corporate and group actions. The individualistic concepts of ethics are generally not sufficient any more to tackle the problem of distributing responsibility for untoward (e.g., ecological) consequences of such actions, especially in social trap constellations. With respect to moral evaluation many participating and contributing individuals have to bear a certain co-responsibility for the supraindividual effects according to their active, potential or formal involvement and impact or influence. A moral re-orientation of individuals to cope with the problems of this new situation is necessary, but not sufficient. We also need structural incentives, social mechanisms for sanctioning, and institutional, e.g., legal and political, measures.

Lenka, Laxminarayan. Can't We Doubt Meaning?. *Indian Phil Quart*, 20/3 (Supp), 1-10, Jl 93.

This is an attempt to show how we can doubt meanings and do that in a scientific way. It endorses to Quine's notion of "background language" and, on the basis of that, distinguishes scientific doubt from philosophical doubt. The important point that has been suggested in this paper is that Quine's indeterminary thesis is a scientific doubt on meaning.

Lenka, Laxminarayan. The Constantive-Performance Distinction in a Justificatory Perspective. *Indian Phil Quart*, 19/3(Supp), 17-26, Jl 92.

The author distinguishes the justificatory perspective of 'how to do things with words' from its explanatory perspective. Then, he views, constative-performative distinction has been refuted by Austin on a justificatory ground.

Lenka, Laxminarayan. The Sense of Grounding Speech Act on Use. *Indian Phil Quart*, 19/2(Supp), 1-18, Ap 92.

The author argues (1) the speech act theories (of Austin, Searle, and Grice) conceptually presuppose language to be an activity and (2) this presupposed feature of language is explained by means of Wittgenstein's 'meaning is in use' rather than be any speech act theory. Suggesting that contextuality, intentionality, and rule following are the other such presuppositions, unexplained but adopted by speech act theory and explained by 'meaning in use', the author concludes that 'use' stands as the explanatory ground for speech act theories.

Lenka, Laxminarayan. Wittgenstein's Private Language Argument and Quine's Indeterminacy Thesis. *J Indian Counc Phil Res*, 9(1), 1-12, S-D 91.

This is an attempt to show foundationalism inside Wittgenstein's Private Language Argument and naturalism inside Quine's Indeterminacy Thesis.

Lennon, Alan. The 'Critique': A View from the Labor Movement in Sartre Alive, Aronson, Ronald (ed). Detroit, Wayne St Univ Pr, 1991.

Lennon, Thomas M. Mechanism as a Silly Mouse in Causation in Early Modern Philosophy, Nadler, Steven (ed). University Park, Penn St Univ Pr, 1993.

Lennox, James. Darwinian Thought Experiments in Thought Experiments in Science and Philosophy, Horowitz, Tamara (ed). Lanham, Rowman & Littlefield, 1991.

Darwin's *Origin* contains numerous 'imaginary illustrations' to strengthen the plausibility of his theory of Natural Selection. These are interpreted as thought experiments. These illustrations allowed Darwin to show how apparent anomalies for his theory could be explained, and allowed his critics a means of critical assessment. What have recently been called Just-so-Stories are best understood, it is argued, as Darwinian Thought Experiments.

Lenzen, Wolfgang. Leibniz on Private and Primitive Terms. *Theoria (Spain)*, 6(14-15), 83-96, O 91.

We first present an edition of the manuscript LH VII, B2 39, in which Leibniz develops a new formalism in order to give rigorous definitions of positive, of private, and of primitive terms. This formalism involves a symbolic treatment of conceptual quantification which differs quite considerably from Leibniz's "standard" theory of "indefinite concepts" as developed, e.g., in the "General Inquiries". In the subsequent commentary, we give an interpretation and a critical evaluation of Leibniz's symbolic apparatus. It turns out that the definition of privative terms and primitive terms lead to certain inconsistencies which, however, can be avoided by slight modifications.

Lenzen, Wolfgang. Leibniz on Properties and Individuals in Language, Truth and Ontology, Mulligan, Kevin (ed). Dordrecht, Kluwer, 1992.

This paper presents a logical reconstruction of Leibniz's idea of God's "creation of the world out of One and Nothing". Starting with the numerals 0 and 1, one first obtains the set of natural numbers. Each of these numbers is then interpreted as representing a specific primary concept. By way of logical combination the larger set of general concepts is obtained. Individual-concepts will then be defined as maximally consistent concepts. Among the set of all possible individuals the relation of compossibility is introduced. Possible worlds are defined as maximal collections of pairwise compossible individuals. The real world is distinguished from its rivals by being the most numerous (and, perhaps, also in some other respect the best) of all possible worlds.

Lenzen, Wolfgang. What Is (or At Least Appears to Be) Wrong with Intuistionic Logic? in Advances in Scientific Philosophy, Schurz, Gerhard (ed). Amsterdam, Rodopi, 1991.

The aim of this paper is to examine whether the standard axiomatization of intuitionistic logic really captures the philosophical (or heuristical) ideas underlying intuitionistic mathematics. Within the framework of a classical meta-language (enriched by a modal operator to be interpreted as 'provability') several interpretations of the intuitionistic sentential connectives are given. It is argued that the Heyting-calculus fails to provide an adequate axiomatization of Brouwerian intuitionism.

Leon, Mark. Rationalising Belief. *Phil Papers*, 21(3), 299-314, N 92.

What are beliefs? Beliefs are states with two central and connected characteristics. Beliefs are truth-sensitive representational internal states. And beliefs are internal states with a causal role in the production of other internal states, typically other beliefs, and in interaction with desires, or behaviour. Beliefs are states which as reasons, or components of reasons, cause other occurrences. They are rational causes. They rationalize certain occurrences. In this paper I examine these two related aspects of belief: the distinctively rational character of beliefs and the way that rational character governs their role in rationalization.

Leopold, A. Ethics of the Earth (Commentary: R Kolarsky) (in Czechoslovakian). *Filozof Cas*, 39(6), 1010-1026, 1991.

Lepage, François. Partial Functions in Type Theory. *Notre Dame J Form Log*, 33(4), 493-516, Fall 92.

Leplin, Jarrett. Realism and Methodological Change. *Proc Phil Sci Ass*, 1, 435-445, 1992.

Recent theories in quantum cosmology cannot be evaluated by prevailing, empiricist standards. The phenomena that might test them are unproducible by foreseeable technology. These theories nevertheless compel wide assent for their explanatory resources and the new connections they forge among phenomena predicted by earlier theories. A tension has arisen between how theories are supposed to be judged and how scientists are inclined to judge them. Methodological change in standards of theory evaluation have occurred historically under such conditions. This paper assesses the prospects for and justification of a new standard capable of warranting current theory.

Leplin, Jarrett and Laudan, Larry. Determination Underdeterred: Reply to Kukla. *Analysis*, 53(1), 8-16, Ja 93.

We criticize algorithmic attempts to guarantee, for any theory, the availability of empirically equivalent rivals. Epistemic constraints on the admissability of auxiliaries used to determine what a theory's empirical consequences are must be respected by purported rivals. Accordingly, what algorithms produce are either not rivals or are not theories. Multiplicity of theoretical options cannot be adduced to establish the thesis that theories are inevitably underdetermined by all possible evidence. Nor can this thesis be grounded on an appeal to Bayesian methodology.

LePore, Ernest and Fodor, Jerry. *Précis* of Holism: A Shopper's Guide. *Phil Phenomenol Res*, 53(3), 637-640, S 93.

LePore, Ernest and Fodor, Jerry. Reply to Critics. *Phil Phenomenol Res*, 53(3), 673-682, S 93.

LePore, Ernest (ed) and Van Gulick, Robert (ed). *John Searle and His Critics*. Cambridge, Blackwell, 1991.

This anthology includes articles from an interdisciplinary group of scholars — philosophers, psychologists, neuro-scientists — and is dedicated to an analysis and assessment of the work of John Searle. Each part of the book is capped with a response from Searle. Topics covered include: Meaning and speech acts; the mind-body problem; perception; intentionality; reference; the background of intentionality and action; social explanation; and ontology.

LePore, Ernie and Fodor, Jerry. Reply to Block and Boghossian. *Mind Lang*, 8(1), 41-48, Spr 93.

Leroux, François. L'assassin d'Ulysse. *Horiz Phil*, 3(1), 11-29, Autumn 92.

Leroux, Georges. *Heidegger et Platon: Le problème du nihilisme* de Alain Boutot. *Philosophiques*, 19(1), 113-122, 1992.

Lesage, Dieter. Moralité et magie. *Rev Phil Louvain*, 90(85), 50-66, F 92.

In the distribution of our interest in, and attention and care for other persons, we generally give priority to persons who, in one way or another, are near to us. From an impersonal and impartial point of view, one may object that this attitude is egocentric and arbitrary. The question whether or not to give moral significance to the proximity of persons who call for our care is at the heart of the debate between universalist and particularist positions in so-called anglo-saxon philosophy. By way of an analysis of the use of the pronoun "my" in the context of symbolic attitudes, this article develops an argument for the idea that, contrary to what has been suggested by William Godwin, the pronoun "my" may very well have a magic significance and that, moreover, this significance unmistakably has a moral bearing.

Leslie, John. A Spinozistic Vision of God. *Relig Stud*, 29(3), 277-286, S 93.

Neoplatonism's God is an ethical requirement for a good world's existence, a requirement guaranteeing its existence, although only with a synthetic, not an analytic necessity. Or (just a verbally different alternative) 'God' names the world which possesses creative ethical requiredness. The name might be particularly appropriate were the world essentially mental. Traditionally, God knows everything. Now, even an infinite mind cannot know exactly how it feels to be you or me, plunged in ignorance, unless it includes limited and ignorant regions which, says Spinoza, are people such as you and me. It could have ethical grounds for giving them immortality.

Leslie, John. Creation Stories, Religious and Atheistic. *Int J Phil Relig*, 34(2), 65-77, O 93.

A possible religious story describes an eternal magician, existing reasonlessly and creating by mere will-power. A contemporary atheistic tale describes an eternally inflating field that gives birth to bubble universes with randomized properties which are sometimes life-permitting. However, even an eternal magician or field calls for explanation. Neoplatonism explains things in terms of an ethical requirement that the good should exist. The requirement needs no help from anything further: it itself acts creatively. Philosophically defensible, this is compatible with scientific findings and with a Spinozistic God, or with a divine person whose existence can be explained.

Leslie, John. Design and the Anthropic Principle. *Biol Phil*, 7(3), 349-354, Jl 92.

Carter's anthropic principle reminds us that intelligent life can find itself only in life-permitting times, places or universes. The principle concerns a possible observational selection effect, not a designing deity. It has no special concern with humans, nor does it say that intelligent life is inevitable and common. Barrow and Tipler, who discuss all this, are not biologically ignorant. As argued in *Universes* (Leslie, 1989) they may well be right in thinking that "fine tuning" of force strengths and particle masses, without which life would be impossible, proves the reality of God or else of multiple universes plus observational selection.

Leslie, John. Doom and Probabilities. *Mind*, 102(407), 489-491, Jl 93.

If the human race survived many more centuries, even at just its present size, the humans of today would have been in a minuscule minority. Carter's doomsday argument, an application of the anthropic principle and of Bayesian thought, seeks to treat our observed temporal position as nothing very special. It concludes that humanity's imminent extinction is more probable than we should otherwise have thought. The article defends the argument against two objections: i) that we could not find ourselves in the future, because future humans are not alive yet, and ii) that the reference class, humans, is specified too arbitrarily.

Leslie, John. Time and the Anthropic Principle. *Mind*, 101(403), 521-540, Jl 92.

B Carter's anthropic principle reminds us that observers are most likely to find themselves in the spatiotemporal regions containing most observers. This could much increase the estimated likelihood that our technological civilization was not the very first in a universe which would include hugely many, or (which is the Carter-Leslie "doomsday argument") that you and I are not in the first 0.1% of the human race, as we would be if it survived long, even if only at its present size. The argument survives numerous ingenious objections, but is weaker in a radically indeterministic world.

Lessay, Franck. Filmer, Hobbes, Locke: Les cassures dans l'espace de la théorie politique. *Arch Phil*, 55(4), 645-660, O-D 92.

It is common practice to lump Hobbes and Filmer together, as advocates of an absolute type of sovereignty, and to oppose them to Locke as the defender of a liberal conception of the State. This habit is caused by a desire to classify, even at the cost of oversimplification. It also results, to a certain extent, from Locke's subtle polemic against Hobbes and Filmer in the *Two Treatises*. The object of this paper is to offer another interpretation of this triangular relationship. The analysis starts from a twofold observation. Filmer's critique of Hobbes could apply to Locke with just as much validity. The political status ascribed by Hobbes to the family argues a complete break with patriarchalism as a way of legitimizing power. No such attitude can be found in Locke. (edited)

Lester, Mark (& other trans) and Boundas, Constantin V (ed) and Deleuze, Gilles. *The Logic of Sense—Gilles Deleuze*. New York, Columbia Univ Pr, 1990.

In the opus of Deleuze, *The Logic of Sense* holds the place that *The Archaeology of Knowledge* did in that of Foucault: the latter, being a discourse about discourse, articulates Foucault's methodology which permitted him to examine discursive formations, discursive practices and nondiscursive space surrounding discursive fields; the former, working out the logic of the invention of concepts, assembles around it all the other works of Deleuze and permits him to show how thinking should be understood and discussed, if it is to be a thinking of events, singularities and haecceities. In thirty-four series and five appendices, Deleuze displays his usual virtuosity as he discusses becoming and the paradoxes it generates, sense as the fourth dimension of the proposition, events in the context of two complementary readings of time, the ethics of the event and his early responses to Lacan.

Leuven, Lienke. Women Philosophers in Antiquity. *Method Sci*, 25(2), 80-90, 1992.

Leuven, Lienke. Women Philosophers in the Middle Ages. *Method Sci*, 25(4), 170-192, 1992.

Leventure, Albert and Keenan, Thomas. A Bibliography of the Works of Jacques Derrida in Derrida: A Critical Reader, Wood, David (ed). Cambridge, Blackwell, 1992.

Levesque-Lopman, Louise. Reproductive Technologies and the "Survival" of the "Human Subject". *Human Stud*, 16(3), 329-340, Jl 93.

Levett, Jonathan. Wittgenstein and the Metaphysics of Propositions. *Phil Invest*, 16(2), 154-162, Ap 93.

It is an attraction of the later Wittgenstein's connection of meaning and use that one can dispense with abstract entities such as propositions, intensions, etc. from the theory of meaning, and restrict oneself to an ontology of words and sentences, whose meaning is to be explained in terms of their use in language-games. It is argued, however, that despite claims to the contrary by Jon Dorbolo and Deborah Jane Orr, Wittgenstein in *On Certainty* commits himself to an ontology of propositions by assigning a semantic/logical role to truths which, due to their special function, are not given explicit linguistic expression.

Levett, M J (trans) and Williams, Bernard (ed). *Plato: "Theaetetus"*. Indianapolis, Hackett, 1992.

Levin, David Michael. Visions of Narcissism in Merleau-Ponty Vivant, Dillon, M C (ed). Albany, SUNY Pr, 1991.

Merleau-Ponty's phenomenology of our visual encounter with others brings out the truth that the initial moment of narcissim in the mirroring stage is ultimately double-crossed by the intertwining and reversibility of gazes, so that this moment is sublimated by (in) a moment of intersubjectivity, deeply transforming the character of the subject. This phenomenology also shows how, correlatively, in the communicative interaction of gazes, and intersubjective rationality can be educed from an initially subject-centered reason. In the reversibility of gazes, a hermeneutical phenomenology can make visible the experiential ground of rational social order: the ethics of reciprocity and the rational principle of justice.

Levin, Joel. The Possibility of Natural Law. *Vera Lex*, 12(1), 1-3, 1992.

Levin, Michael. Reply to Fulda on Animal Rights. *J Value Inq*, 27(1), 111-112, Ja 93.

Fulda would solve the man-vs-animal problem by according animals rights of denumerable strength and men rights of nondenumerable strength. But the problem remains if there are sufficiently many animals and sufficiently few men in the universe. Fulda may have meant that human rights are (weakly) inaccessible and animal rights smaller. My objection to animal rights remains, and I note that even Peter Singer allows that the rights of slum children (but perhaps not others) may conflict with those of rats.

Levin, Michael. Responses to Race Differences in Crime. *J Soc Phil*, 23(1), 5-29, Spr 92.

One out of four black males has spent time in jail for a felony. Blacks are on average about ten times more likely to be violent offenders than are whites. I argue that these statistics make it rational to be apprehensive about blacks. From a moral point of view it is permissible to seek to avoid them in many circumstances. The state is also entitled to use race-conscious screening of potential offenders. Arguments that this approach is "racist" are shown also to imply that affirmative action is "racist."

Levin, Michael E. Stove on Gene Worship. *Philosophy*, 68(264), 240-243, Ap 93.

Stove thinks talk of "gene strategies" is literally and misleading as metaphor because genes do not literally intend. I point out that there is an intermediate sense in which an organism or gene can be said to act "because" of the effects of its action, namely that these effects explain the action non-causally, or teleologically, as Darwin made clear. An important corollary is that persistent but seemingly maladaptive behavior, such as selfishness, must have some fitness characteristic (where "fitness" also means inclusive fitness).

Levin, Thomas Y (trans) and Kracauer, Siegfried. Photography. *Crit Inquiry*, 19(3), 421-436, Spr 93.

Levine, Andrew. Electoral Power, Group Power, and Democracy. *Nomos*, 32, 251-264, 1990.

A discussion of methods for empowering minority voters—including proportional representation—from the standpoint of democratic theory.

Levine, Carol. *Taking Sides: Clashing Views on Controversial Bioethical Issues (Fifth Edition)*. Guilford, Dushkin, 1993.

Levine, Elliott. Anarchy: The State of Our Post-Modern Human Condition. *Hist Euro Ideas*, 16(4-6), 553-559, Ja 93.

Social action is situated within language whose terms are said in many ways. Unpacking multivocity here is the stuff of this paper. It is the ground of speaking truth to power. *"...The prophet said, 'the people suffer for your corruption,' and the king harkened—or not..."* Exiled from the system Anarchy deconstructs false gods, falsifies just these gods, warrants just gods—who standing in need of the warrant, are no longer independent gods, but 'Just'. Humankind survives subjugated to false gods, to hierarch's masquerading Opinion—Justice, counting followed Opinion—Fact.

Levine, Joseph. On Leaving Out What It's Like in Consciousness: Psychological and Philosophical Essays, Davies, Martin (ed). Cambridge, Blackwell, 1993.

Levine, Joseph M. Objectivity in History: Peter Novick and R G Collingwood. *Clio*, 21(2), 109-127, Wint 92.

Levine, Joseph M. *The Battle of the Books: History and Literature in the Augustan Age*. Ithaca, Cornell Univ Pr, 1991.

The *Battle of the Books* describes the climactic episode in the quarrel between the ancients and the moderns in England, c. 1690-1740. The dispute was about the relation between classical learning and modern life; about the proper way to understand and employ the authors of the past; and about the rival claims of history and literature then and now. The issues that surfaced then continued to baffle writers and scholars until they were transformed by the historicism of a later time. This book closely describes the debate and examines the historical thinking and writing of both sides.

Levine, Michael. Berkeley: How to Make a Mistake. *Philosophia (Israel)*, 22(1-2), 29-37, Ja 93.

Berkeley's epistemology is intrinsically linked to his metaphysics. His epistemology is necessary to understanding his idealism and other aspects of his peculiar metaphysics. Berkeley's notion of error must be explained in the context of his theory of justification which, as will be seen, cannot be divorced from his wider idealist position. This paper is limited to an analysis of what I take to be Berkeley's strongly foundationalist position on epistemic justification of empirical knowledge. His explanation of how and when error is possible, and when it is not, follows from this.

Levine, Michael. Deep Structure and the Comparative Philosophy of Religion. *Relig Stud*, 28(3), 387-399, S 92.

Contrary to Ronald Green, I argue that the comparative philosophy of religion should not be concerned with uncovering "deep structure" since such approaches are invariably reductionistic. They are antithetical to both cultural-linguistic and experiential/ expressive analyses of the nature of religion. The possibility of comparative philosophy of religion must be understood in terms of how the purpose of such comparisons can plausibly and normatively be articulated. Any method of comparison presupposes such goals. Suggestions are made as to what the proper goals are. Not surprisingly, they are diverse and contextually specific to particular concerns.

Levine, Michael. Monism and Pantheism. *S J Phil*, 30(4), 95-110, Wint 92.

I discuss general features of the alleged relation between monism and pantheism. I deny that pantheists—in virtue of their pantheism—are necessarily monists. Although some pantheists may also be monists, and although monism may be essential to some versions of pantheism (like Spinoza's), pantheist's are not monists. Like most people they are pluralists. Even in Spinoza's case the explanation of pantheistic Unity in terms of his contention that there is and can be only one substance, merely glosses the more significant—pantheistically speaking—evaluative implications he sees as entailed by that monism for his pantheistic metaphysic.

Levine, Michael. Transcendence in Theism and Pantheism. *Sophia (Australia)*, 31(3), 89-123, 1992.

Pantheism is the view that everything which exists constitutes a unity and that this all-inclusive unity is divine. Since most versions of pantheism deny God is transcendent in a philosophically or religiously relevant sense (e.g., "ontologically"), pantheism can be seen as the most radical solution to a complex set of interrelated issues broadly defined as "the problem of transcendence." Despite pantheism's denial of any God distinct from the all-inclusive divine Unity, I argue that under the view of pantheism as resolving the problem of transcendence is mistaken.

Levine, Michael P. Pantheism, Substance and Unity. *Int J Phil Relig*, 32(1), 1-23, Ag 92.

Levinson, Henry Samuel. *Santayana, Pragmatism, and the Spiritual Life*. Chapel Hill, Univ N Carolina Pr, 1991.

Levinson, Jerrold. A Refiner's Fire: Reply to Sartwell and Kolak. *J Aes Art Crit*, 48(3), 231-235, Sum 90.

This is a reply to two sets of objections to my intentional-historical definition of art (1979, 1989). At issue are how the theory handles deliberate forgeries, art-oblivious artmaking, and art repudiated by its creator.

Levinson, Jerrold. Extending Art Historically. *J Aes Art Crit*, 51(3), 411-423, Sum 93.

This is the third in a series setting out and defending an intentional-historical conception of arthood. (The predecessors were "Defining Art Historically", *BJA* 1979; and "Refining Art Historically", *JAAC* 1989.) In this paper I respond to criticisms of Robert Stecker and Stephen Davies, consider alternate forms of historical definition, and test the bounds of an intentional-historical approach to art.

Levinson, Jerrold. Further Fire: Reply to Haines. *J Aes Art Crit*, 49(1), 76-77, Wint 91.

Levinson, Jerrold. Musical Profundity Misplaced. *J Aes Art Crit*, 50(1), 58-60, Wint 92.

In the last chapter of Peter Kivy's *Music Alone* (1990) a theory of musical profundity is proposed. I criticize this theory as misguided, and sketch the outlines of any adequate approach to the topic.

Levinson, Jerrold. Noël Carroll's *The Philosophy of Horror or Paradoxes of the Heart*. *J Aes Art Crit*, 49(3), 253-258, Sum 91.

A critical notice of Carroll's remarkable book, focussing on his characterization of monsters and our characteristic reaction to them ("art-horror"), and his treatment of the paradoxes of fiction and horror.

Levinson, Jerrold. Refining Art Historically. *J Aes Art Crit*, 47(1), 21-33, Wint 89.

Levinson, Jerrold. Seeing, Imaginarily, at the Movies. *Phil Quart*, 43(170), 70-78, Ja 93.

Levinson, Jerrold. The Place of Real Emotion in Response to Fiction. *J Aes Art Crit*, 48(1), 79-80, Wint 90.

In this short note I indicate how to couple the basic insight of a Waltonian approach to understanding emotional responses to friction with an appreciation of the way real emotion (i.e., not make-believe) enters into the total response as well.

Levmore, Saul. On Compensation and Distribution. *Nomos*, 33, 186-192, 1991.

This comment argues that deterrence and compensation goals of law cannot be easily separated from one another. As a matter of descriptive theory, a variety of foundational legal rules make sense only if their deterrence features, rather than their compensatory or redistributive aspects, are emphasized. Examples involving tort liability and, in particular, "economic losses" (such as lost profits in the restaurant and fishing industries after a negligent oil spill closes down a waterway) are discussed.

Levvis, Gary W. Why We Would Not Understand a Talking Lion. *Between Species*, 8(3), 156-162, Sum 92.

Levvis, Margaret Ayotte. The Value of Judgments Regarding the Value of Animals. *Between Species*, 8(3), 150-155, Sum 92.

Levy, David J. Europe, Truth, and History: Husserl and Voegelin on Philosophy and the Identity of Europe. *Man World*, 26(2), 161-180, Ap 93.

Levy, David M. "Magic Buffalo" and Berkeley's *Theory of Vision*: Learning in Society. *Hume Stud*, 19(1), 223-226, Ap 93.

Berkeley's claim that we learn to perceive distance can be tested by appeal to the experience of people who live in dense rain forests and have no need to learn to separate distance and magnitude.

Levy, David M. Bishop Berkeley Exorcises the Infinite: Fuzzy Consequences of Strict Finitism. *Hume Stud*, 18(2), 511-536, N 92.

If infinitesimals are nonsense then what? Berkeley's doctrine leads to a theory of fuzzy perception. This in turn heavily influences Adam Smith. It is conjectured that histories of mathematics prior to the development of nonstandard analysis have seriously misrepresented the issue in Berkeley's attack on infinitesimals.

Levy, Robert. Another Day for an Old Dogma. *Proc Phil Sci Ass*, 1, 131-141, 1992.

Using probability theory and symbolic logic, I present two interpersonal Bayesian models of the confirmation of hypotheses of the form 'All S is P' by data reports. The models are applicable to both truth-functional and modal hypotheses of universal form. Illustrating the utility of this approach to confirmation, I show how these models treat (1) to the old evidence problem; (2) the raven paradox, and (3) Goodman's grue paradox.

Lewandowski, Joseph D. Culture, Textuality and Truth. *Phil Soc Crit*, 19(1), 43-58, 1993.

Lewin, Philip. The Problem of Objectivity in Post-Critical Philosophy. *Tradition Discovery*, 18(1), 18-26, 1991-92.

This essay demonstrates a series of parallels between Polanyi's conception of "personal knowing" and Heidegger's exploration of *Dasein* to propose an account of scientific objectivity as "passionate appropriation." This account is intended to overcome problems in standard postempiricist versions of objectivity. The essay then suggests a limit in Polanyi's work, raising the question of the degree to which personal knowing is compromised by cultural inscription.

Lewis, David. Counterpart Theory, Quantified Modal Logic, and Extra Argument Places. *Analysis*, 53(2), 69-71, Ap 93.

When we translate 'There might be blue swans' in terms of what goes on in other worlds, should we use novel relational predicates: x is-a-swan-at w, x is-blue-at w? Or will ordinary predicates suffice, without the extra argument place for worlds? Mark Sainsbury alleges that Lewis has changed his mind on this question, having favoured extra arguments places in 'Counterpart Theory and Quantified Modal Logic'. It is shown that this reading is mistaken.

Lewis, David. Critical Notice of D M Armstrong, *A Combinatorial Theory of Possibility*. *Austl J Phil*, 70(2), 211-224, Je 92.

This critical notice discusses four questions: (1) Armstrong's positive and negative views about the range of possibilities; (2) his principle that all truths require truthmakers; (3) whether he succeeds in avoiding primitive modal concepts; and (4) his fictionalism about possibilities.

Lewis, David. Many, but Almost One in Ontology, Causality and Mind: Essays in Honour of D M Armstrong, Bacon, John (ed). New York, Cambridge Univ Pr, 1993.

It is arbitrary where a cloud leaves off. Thanks to boundary vagueness, there are many equally good candidates to be the cloud. Yet we have *one* cloud up there, not many. How so? The method of supervaluation yields one answer. Armstrong's observation that extensive overlap approximates to identity yields another: we have a cloud up there to which all clouds up there are approximately identical. The two answers do not compete; they may usefully be combined.

Lewis, David. Mathematics is Megethology. *Phil Math*, 1, 3-23, Mr 93.

Megethology is the second-order theory of the part-whole relation. It can express such hypotheses about the size of Reality as that there are inaccessibly many atoms. Take a non-empty class to have exactly its non-empty subclasses as parts; hence, its singleton subclasses as atomic parts. Then standard set theory becomes the theory of the member-singleton function—better, the theory of *all* singleton functions—within the framework of megethology. Given inaccessibly many atoms and a specification of which atoms are urelements, a singleton function exists, unique up to isomorphism.

Lewis, David. Meaning Without Use: Reply to Hawthorne. *Austl J Phil*, 70(1), 106-110, Mr 92.

I once claimed that sentences get their meaning in virtue of conventions of truthfulness and trust. John Hawthorne says this won't work in the case of unused sentences, because the probability that these sentences will be uttered is sometimes zero. I argue that the probability will never be quite zero, but that there's a different reason why my proposal won't work for unused sentences. I then defend a method of extapolation: truthfulness and trust give meanings for used sentences, and we may project meanings to unused sentences via rules of syntax and semantics. We must be brave in insisting on our right to use the distinction between 'straight' and 'bent' rules.

Lewontin, Richard and Godfrey-Smith, Peter. The Dimensions of Selection. *Phil Sci*, 60(3), 373-395, S 93.

Proponents of genic selectionism have claimed that evolutionary processes normally viewed as selection on individuals can be "represented" as selection on alleles. This paper discusses the relationship between mathematical questions about the formal requirements upon state spaces necessary for the representation of different types of evolutionary processes and causal questions about the units of selection in such processes.

Leydet, Dominique. L'a priori kantien et sa postérité selon Jean Grondin. *Dialogue (Canada)*, 31(1), 71-82, Wint 92.

Leys, Ruth. Mead's Voices: Imitation as Foundation, or, The Struggle against Mimesis. *Crit Inquiry*, 19(2), 277-307, Wint 93.

Li, Chenyang. The Fallacy of the Slippery Slope Argument on Abortion. *J Applied Phil*, 9(2), 233-237, 1992.

This paper attempts to show that the acorn-oak tree argument against the slippery slope on the personhood of the fetus is valid and William Cooney's attack on this argument fails. I also argue that the slippery slope argument leads to an undesirable conclusion and should not be used as a valid tool in the debate on the personhood of the fetus.

Li, Chenyang. What-Being: Chuang Tzu versus Aristotle. *Int Phil Quart*, 33(3), 341-353, S 93.

An attempt to show how Chuang Tzu's metaphysics is a plausible alternative to Aristotelian metaphysics. First, whereas Aristotle maintains that every primary substance is a definite "this-and-such," Chuang Tzu believes that an object is a "this-and-that." An ox is an ox, but also a pack of flesh and bones. Second, because of this diversity of being, Chuang Tzu does not believe that there is a single objectively correct answer to the question of what an object is primarily. It is correct to say that the object is primarily an ox; it is also correct to say that it is primarily a pack of flesh and bones, depending on the perspective we use. Thirdly, because an object can be both a "this" and a "that," Chuang Tzu suggests that an object can survive a substance sortal concept change.

Li, H and Li, L and Liu, Y. A Decision Algorithm for Linear Sentences on a PFM. *Annals Pure Applied Log*, 59(3), 273-285, F 93.

By PFM, we mean a finitely generated module over a principal ideal domain; a linear sentence is a sentence that contains no disjunctive and negative symbols. In this paper, we present an algorithm which decides the truth for linear sentences on a given PFM, and we discuss its time complexity. In particular, when the principal ideal domain is the ring of integers or a univariate polynomial ring over the field of rationals, the algorithm is polynomial-time. Finally, we consider some applications to Abelian groups.

Li, L and Li, H and Liu, Y. A Decision Algorithm for Linear Sentences on a PFM. *Annals Pure Applied Log*, 59(3), 273-285, F 93.

By PFM, we mean a finitely generated module over a principal ideal domain; a linear sentence is a sentence that contains no disjunctive and negative symbols. In this paper, we present an algorithm which decides the truth for linear sentences on a given PFM, and we discuss its time complexity. In particular, when the principal ideal domain is the ring of integers or a univariate polynomial ring over the field of rationals, the algorithm is polynomial-time. Finally, we consider some applications to Abelian groups.

Li Vigni, Fiorinda. *La Dialettica dell'Etico*. Milano, Guerini, 1993.

Libeskind, Daniel. Between the Lines: The Jewish Museum, Berlin. *Res Phenomenol*, 22, 82-87, 1992.

Lichtenberg, Georg Christoph. *Aphorisms—Georg Christoph Lichtenberg*. New York, Penguin USA, 1990.

Lickona, Thomas (ed) and Ryan, Kevin (ed). *Character Development in Schools and Beyond (Second Edition)*. Washington, CRVP, 1992.

Lieb, Irwin C. Pragmatism and the Normative Sciences in Frontiers in American Philosophy, Volume I, Burch, Robert W (ed). College Station, Texas A&M Univ Pr, 1992.

Liebsch, Burkhard. Zwischen Epistemologie und Ethik. *Phil Rundsch*, 39(3), 186-213, 1992.

Liedtke, Frank. Meaning and Expression in Mind, Meaning and Metaphysics, Mulligan, Kevin (ed). Dordrecht, Kluwer, 1990.

Lierse, Caroline and Ellis, Brian and Bigelow, John. The World as One of a Kind: Natural Necessity and Laws of Nature. *Brit J Phil Sci*, 43(3), 371-388, S 92.

This paper elaborates and defends the view that the world is an instance of a natural kind. It argues that all laws of nature, including the most general ones, are dependent on the essential natures of natural kinds. The causal and statistical laws of nature are said to depend on the essences of the natural kinds of things which exist in the world. The most fundamental laws of nature are argued to depend on the kind of world in which we live. This theory of scientific laws derives from the basic idea that things must behave as they do because of what they are made of, how they are made, and what their circumstances are. (edited)

Lievers, Menno. The Molyneux Problem. *J Hist Phil*, 30(3), 399-416, J 92.

The Molyneux problem as it appears in Locke's *Essay* is usually taken to be a question about the relationship between the ideas acquired by touch and those acquired by sight. In this article it is argued instead, that the problem must be seen first and foremost within the context of the problem of the visual perception of depth. This interpretation is corroborated by contrasting Descartes' theory of depth perception with that of Molyneux and Locke. The article concludes with an attempt to show how Berkeley's treatment of the Molyneux problem has distorted its proper interpretation.

Light, Andrew R F. The Role of Technology in Environmental Questions: Martin Buber and Deep Ecology as Answers to Technological Consciousness. *Res Phil Technol*, 12, 83-104, 1992.

Lilly, Reginald (trans) and Heidegger, Martin. *The Principle of Reason—Martin Heidegger*. Bloomington, Indiana Univ Pr, 1992.

Limbrick, Elaine. To Write in Latin or in the Vernacular: The Intellectual Dilemma in an Age of Transition—The Case of Descartes. *Hist Euro Ideas*, 16(1-3), 75-81, Ja 93.

Descartes' decision to write the *Discourse on Method* in French rather than Latin, the traditional language of philosophical discourse since Cicero, greatly popularized philosophy and science in seventeenth-century France. His choice of a first-person narrative, more suited to lively discussion, indicated a radical change in philosophical perspective: subjective certainty overturned Aristotelian doctrine symbolically encased in Latin. Like his sixteenth-century precursors, Ramus and Montaigne, Descartes, through his use of vernacular, addressed a wider audience of men and women interested in his ideas.

Lin, Huo-wang. Pluralism and the Priority of Right (in Chinese). *Phil Rev (Taiwan)*, 15, 35-52, Ja 92.

John Rawls argues that the concept of right is prior to the concept of the good. He attempts to construct his conception of justice without presupposing any particular comprehensive ideal of the good. This article tries to show that Rawls does assume a controversial conception of the good, namely, the individualistic ideal of the person, as one of the premises in developing his theory of justice. (edited)

Lincoln, Patrick and Scedrov, Andre and Shankar, Natarajan. Linearizing Intuitionistic Implication. *Annals Pure Applied Log*, 60(2), 151-177, Ap 93.

An embedding of the implicational propositional intuitionistic logic (IIL) into the nonmodal fragment of intuitionistic linear logic (IMALL) is given. The embedding preserves cut-free proofs in a proof system that is a variant of IIL. The embedding is efficient and provides an alternative proof of the PSPACE-hardness of IMALL. It exploits several proof-theoretic properties of intuitionistic implication that analyze the use of resources in IIL proofs.

Lind, Hans. A Case Study of Normal Research in Theoretical Economics. *Econ Phil*, 8(1), 83-102, Ap 92.

The main results from this case study of normal research in mainstream theoretical economics are that: the core of the theoretical analysis is proof that certain relations hold in a specific model-economy; the dominating type of contribution is to analyze a model-economy that is more realistic; the model-economy includes restrictive simplifications that prohibit direct conclusions about relations in a real economy; the results of the articles are often described in terms like "increase of understanding" or "show that something can have certain consequences"; no trace is found of the instrumentalistic view; no trace is found of the hypothetico-deductive method.

Lind, Richard W. The Aesthetic Essence of Art. *J Aes Art Crit*, 50(2), 117-130, Spr 92.

There are good reasons to believe that "making a statement," in a broader sense than Danto's, is a *necessary* condition of art. But phenomenological analysis tends to show that an artwork must be *aesthetic* as well as meaningful. Otherwise, what the artist has to say could not be distinguished from many *non*artistic forms of communication. Moreover, its meaning must *subserve* the aesthetic function of the artwork, in a role best described as "*significance*." "Art" must therefore be defined in terms of *the creation of significant aesthetic objects*.

Lindahl, B I B and Popper, K R and Arhem, P. A Discussion of the Mind-Brain Problem. *Theor Med*, 14(2), 167-180, Je 93.

In this paper Popper formulates and discusses a new aspect of the theory of mind. This theory is partly based on his earlier developed interactionistic theory. It takes as its point of departure the observation that mind and physical forces have several properties in common, at least the following six: both are (i) located, (ii) unextended, (iii) incorporeal, (iv) capable of acting on bodies, (v) dependent upon body, (vi) capable of being influenced by bodies. Other properties such as intensity and extension in time may be added. It is argued that a fuller understanding of the nature of forces is essential for the analysis of the mind-brain problem. The relative autonomy and indeterministic nature of mind is stressed. Indeterminism is treated in relation to a theorem of Hadamard. The computer theory of mind and the Turing test are criticized. Finally the evolution of mind is discussed.

Lindberg, Kathryne V. Whitman's 'Convertible Terms' in Theorizing American Literature, Cowan, Bainard (ed). Baton Rouge, Louisiana St Univ Pr, 1991.

Linden, Toby. Shapere on Observation. *Phil Sci*, 59(2), 293-299, Je 92.

In his article "The Concept of Observation in Science and Philosophy" (1982), Dudley Shapere argues for an analysis of what it is for an object to be directly observed (observable). He does so by presenting two contrasting ways of observing the center of the sun. However, his examples, which are probabilistic in nature, are at odds with his analysis, which is absolute. I argue that of the three features of the examples which could serve as the basis of this feature, I show that the analysis still fails to provide a sufficient condition for observation.

Lindgren, J Ralph. Rethinking the Grounds for Reproductive Freedom in Women's Rights and the Rights of Man, Arnaud, A J. Oxford, Aberdeen, 1990.

Lindsay, Cecile. Corporality, Ethics, Experimentation: Lyotard in the Eighties. *Phil Today*, 36(4), 389-401, Wint 92.

Against the claim that Jean-François Lyotard's work exhibits a postmodern malaise divorcing political theory from concrete, practical issues, it is argued that Lyotard demonstrates the power of experimentation in art, science, and literature to constitute a social, ethical force. New technologies now make it possible to experiment with and alter the supposed givens of human embodiment; Lyotard's work in the decade of the eighties proposes an ethics of respect for the multiplicity, mutability, permutability, and indetermination of corporality.

Lindström, Per. On $\Sigma 1$ and $\Pi 1$ Sentences and Degrees of Interpretability. *Annals Pure Applied Log*, 61(1-2), 175-193, My 93.

Linell, Per and Marková, Ivana. Acts in Discourse: From Monological Speech Acts to Dialogical Inter-Acts. *J Theor Soc Behav*, 23(2), 174-195, Je 93.

Lingis, Alphonso F. Imperatives in Merleau-Ponty Vivant, Dillon, M C (ed). Albany, SUNY Pr, 1991.

Linsky, Bernard. A Note on the "Carving Up Content" Principle in Frege's Theory of Sense. *Notre Dame J Form Log*, 33(1), 126-135, Wint 92.

In the *Grundlagen* Frege says that "line *a* is parallel to line *b*" differs from "the direction of *a*=the direction of b" in that "we carve up the content in a way different from the original way". It seems that such recarving is crucial to Frege's logicist program of defining numbers, but it also seems incompatible with his later theory of sense and reference. I formulate a restriction on recarving, in particular, that no names may be introduced that introduce new possibilities of reference failure, which is observed by Frege's examples. This restriction discriminates between various relatives of the "slingshot" argument which rely on a step of recarving. I offer an argument for the restriction based on Fregean principles, which I formalize in Church's "Logic of Sense and Denotation", and briefly discuss various axioms of his "Alternative (0)" which are incompatible with recarving.

Linsky, Bernard. The Logical Form of Descriptions. *Dialogue (Canada)*, 31(4), 677-683, Autumn 92.

This critical notice of Stephen Neale's *Descriptions*, (MIT Press, 1990) summarizes the content of the book and presents several objections to its arguments, as well as praising Neale for showing just how close the linguistic notion of L F is to the analytic philosopher's notion of "logical form". It is claimed that Neale's use of generalized quantifiers to represent definite descriptions from Russell's account by which descriptions are "incomplete symbols". I also argue that his assessment of the Quine/Smullyan exchange about "Necessarily the number of the planets is greater than seven" is incorrect.

Linsky, Leonard. The Unity of the Proposition. *J Hist Phil*, 30(2), 243-273, Ap 92.

Linville, Mark D. Divine Foreknowledge and the Libertarian Conception of Human Freedom. *Int J Phil Relig*, 33(3), 165-186, Je 93.

Lippke, Richard L. Justice and Insider Trading. *J Applied Phil*, 10(2), 215-226, 1993.

I summarise the scholarly debate over the fairness of insider trading and lay bare the assumptions about fairness implicit in that debate. I focus on whether those assumptions can be defended independently of a more comprehensive theory of social justice. Current analyses presuppose that we can intelligently discuss what the social rules regarding insider trading should be while ignoring questions about the broader principles of justice that should be adopted and the extent to which existing institutions realise those principle. I argue that such questions must be addressed. I then employ an egalitarian conception of social justice to analyse insider trading. I thereby illustrate how a more systematic approach, grounded in a comprehensive theory of justice, transforms the debate about the fairness of insider trading.

Lippke, Richard L. Speech, Conscience, and Work. *Soc Theor Pract*, 18(3), 237-258, Fall 92.

Extending David Richards' Kantian-contractarian analysis of rights of free speech and conscience, I argue that employees are entitled to institutionalized protection of work-related exercises of speech and conscience. While I admit that such exercises may legitimately be limited in order to protect other equally weighty interests, I argue against the view that employees have an obligation to first register their dissent in ways internal to the organization. I also consider and attempt to defuse a variety of objections to work-related freedom of speech and conscience.

Lipson, Morrice and Vallentyne, Peter. Child Liberationism and Legitimate Interference. *J Soc Phil*, 23(3), 5-15, Wint 92.

Lipson, Morris and Savitt, Steven. A Dilemma for Causal Reliabilist Theories of Knowledge. *Can J Phil*, 23(1), 55-74, Mr 93.

Lipton, Peter. Is the Best Good Enough?. *Proc Aris Soc*, 93, 89-104, 1993.

According to the argument from 'underconsideration', scientists never have good reason to believe that any of their theories are true, since they can only judge that a theory is the best of the generated competitors and they have no reason to believe that the truth lies in this group. I show that this argument is incoherent. Given the role of background theories is judgements of inductive support, scientists could not reliably rank competing theories unless they also had good reason to believe that some of their theories are true.

Lipton, Peter. Making a Difference. *Philosophica*, 51(1), 39-54, 1993.

This paper sketches a model of contrastive explanation, according to which an explanatory cause must 'make a difference' between and effect and a specific foil. This model brings out one of the reasons we so often ask contrastive why-questions. A specific foil reduces the indeterminacy of the 'backward' counterfactual involved in causal explanation, enabling us to answer the question of how things would have been different earlier, had the effect not occurred.

Liske, Michael-Thomas. Kann Gott reale Beziehungen zu den Geschöpfen haben? Logisch-theologische Betrachtungen im Anschluss an Thomas von Aquin. *Theol Phil*, 68(2), 208-228, 1993.

A relation is weakly real, if an underlying absolute reality of the subject suffices to find this relation. The obtaining of a strongly real relation must also imply a difference in the absolute being of the subject. We can give a temporal-process description of those activities which, like God's creating, transcend their subject insofar as they initiate processes without presupposing God's mutability. This is true only if creating establishes a weakly real relation between God and his creatures without having any effect upon his own being, whereas the creatures are ontologically dependent and therefore strongly related to God.

List, Elisabeth. Formation of Theories and Policy of Difference of the Sexes (in Czechoslovakian). *Filozof Cas*, 40(5), 825-838, 1992.

Modern science presents itself as the most reasonable and the most developed form of human cognition, strictly objective, neutral with a view to values, i.e., without any subjective and social biases. From the feminist viewpoint it becomes evident that sciences do not meet this demand, particularly with regard to the neutral attitude to sex which they proclaim. The feminist research of science has proved that the sexual attitude, particularly the male one, affects three levels: the social and historical level, the psychical level, and the symbolic-cognitive level. (edited)

Liston, Daniel P and Beyer, Landon E. Discourse or Moral Action? A Critique of Postmodernism. *Educ Theor*, 42(4), 371-393, Fall 92.

Liston, Michael. Reliability in Mathematical Physics. *Phil Sci*, 60(1), 1-21, Mr 93.

In this paper I argue three things: 1) that the interactionist view underlying Benacerraf's (1973) challenge to mathematical beliefs renders inexplicable the reliability of most of our beliefs in physics; 2) that examples from mathematical physics suggest that we should view reliability differently; and 3) that abstract mathematical considerations are indispensable to explanations of the reliability of our beliefs.

Liston, Michael. Taking Mathematical Fictions Seriously. *Synthese*, 95(3), 433-458, Je 93.

I argue on the basis of an example, Fourier theory applied to the problem of vibration, that Field's program for nominalizing science is unlikely to succeed generally, since no nominalistic variant will provide us with the kind of physical insight into the phenomena that the standard theory supplies. Consideration of the same example also shows, I argue, that some of the motivation for mathematical fictionalism, particularly the alleged problem of cognitive access, is more apparent than real.

Litian, Fang. A Comparison of the Chinese Buddhist and Indian Buddhist Modes of Thought. *Chin Stud Phil*, 24(4), 3-46, Sum 93.

Litman, Theodore. The Sublime as a Source of Light in the Works of Nicolas Boileau in Analecta Husserliana, XXXVIII, Tymieniecka, Anna-Teresa (ed). Dordrecht, Kluwer, 1992.

Little, J P. Simone Weil's Conception of Decreation in Simone Weil's Philosophy of Culture, Bell, Richard H (ed). New York, Cambridge Univ Pr, 1993.

Littleford, Michael S. Toward a Pragmatic Metaphysics: Comments on a Speculative Approach. *Man World*, 26(3), 339-350, Jl 93.

Littlejohn, Ronnie L. A Response to Daniel Holbrook's 'Descartes on Persons' and Doug Anderson's 'The Legacy of Bowne's Empiricism'. *Personalist Forum*, 8/1(Supp), 15-20, Spr 92.

Littlejohn, Ronnie L. *Ethics: Studying the Art of Moral Appraisal*. Lanham, Univ Pr of America, 1993.

The principal concern of this work is to give careful attention to moral practice and allow our descriptions to reveal the features of moral life found therein. These descriptions include what entities and events are morally appraisable and how we offer responsibility descriptions of justification and excuse, with attention to the use of virtue language. In the process of doing this, the theoretical concerns of philosophy arise quite naturally and their urgency and significance is readily apparent. This leads naturally into conversation about the classical theoretical positions taken on key moral issues and the major positions taken on them.

Liu, Shu-Hsien. On the Problem of Value Reconstruction in Chinese Philosophy under the Impact from European Thought. *J Chin Phil*, 20(1), 45-56, Mr 93.

The problem of value reconstruction is an urgent issue at the present time. Professor Mou Tsung-san, an eminent contemporary Neo-Confucian philosopher, finds affinity in Kant's thought. He appreciates Kant's effort to establish a metaphysics of morals, but criticizes Kant's failure to develop a moral metaphysics. Professor Mou tries to give reinterpretation of the insights of Confucius, Mencius, and Sung-Ming Neo-Confucian philosophers in order to formulate a new philosophy of value. His thoughts may serve as a point for departure for further reflection on the problem.

Liu, Y and Li, H and Li, L. A Decision Algorithm for Linear Sentences on a PFM. *Annals Pure Applied Log*, 59(3), 273-285, F 93.

By PFM, we mean a finitely generated module over a principal ideal domain; a linear sentence is a sentence that contains no disjunctive and negative symbols. In this paper, we present an algorithm which decides the truth for linear sentences on a given PFM, and we discuss its time complexity. In particular, when the principal ideal domain is the ring of integers or a univariate polynomial ring over the field of rationals, the algorithm is polynomial-time. Finally, we consider some applications to Abelian groups.

Liverani, Mary Rose. The Young Philosophers. *Thinking*, 10(1), 10-12, 1992.

Livingston, Donald W. Good and Bad Shadow History of Philosophy. *J Hist Phil*, 31(1), 111-113, Ja 93.

Lizza, John. Multiple Personality and Personal Identity Revisited. *Brit J Phil Sci*, 44(2), 263-274, Je 93.

Lizza, John. Persons and Death: What's Metaphysically Wrong with Our Current Statutory Definition of Death?. *J Med Phil*, 18(4), 351-374, Ag 93.

This paper challenges the recommendation of 1981 President's Commission for the Study of Ethical Problems in Medicine and Biomedical and Behavioral Research that all jurisdictions in the United States should adopt the Uniform Determination of Death Act, which endorses a whole-brain, rather than a higher-brain, definition of death. I argue that the Commission was wrong to reject the "personhood argument" for the higher-brain definition on the grounds that there is no consensus among philosophers or the general population as to what constitutes "personhood". (edited)

Llewelyn, John. Responsibility with Indecidability in Derrida: A Critical Reader, Wood, David (ed). Cambridge, Blackwell, 1992.

From quasi-analysis of paradoxes construed by Derrida, Ponge, Ramsey and Austin it is decided that where responsibility is responsibility to the singularity of the other, respect for whom and for which must not be sacrificed to respect for the universality of the law, i.e., where responsibility is critical co-respondence of reflective and determinant judgment, indecidability is not necessarily without responsibility. For, indecidably limited and unlimited, *before* the law in both senses, responsibility within decidability is responsibility with indecidability.

Lloyd, Elisabeth. Pre-Theoretical Assumptions in Evolutionary Explanations of Female Sexuality. *Phil Stud*, 69(2-3), 139-153, Mr 93.

Through a case study of pre-theoretical bias in evolutionary explanation of female orgasm, this paper challenges the narrowness of predominant frameworks within contemporary philosophy of science. There are two conclusions: gender bias has had a serious and detrimental effect on explanations of human evolution; and, as philosophers, we cannot afford to ignore such social and cultural assumptions in our understanding of science.

Lloyd, G E R. The *Meno* and the Mysteries of Mathematics. *Phronesis*, 37(2), 166-183, 1992.

Lo Bue, Salvatore. Il nulla e l'essere: Leopardi e l'idea di poesia. *G Metaf*, 14(3), 543-566, S-D 92.

Loades, Ann. Simone Weil and Antigone: Innocence and Affliction in Simone Weil's Philosophy of Culture, Bell, Richard (ed). New York, Cambridge Univ Pr, 1993.

The essay fills a gap in Steiner's *Antigones* of 1984 by looking at what Simone Weil made of the Antigone theme. Like Kierkegaard, she explores it to some extent as a self-confessional mask. The essay ends by asking how someone with an implacable conscience can live in our time.

Lockwood, Michael. Dennett's Mind. *Inquiry*, 36(1-2), 59-72, Mr 93.

Drawing on data from contemporary experimental psychology and research in artificial intelligence, Dennett argues for a *multiple drafts* model of human consciousness, which he offers as an alternative to what he calls *Cartesian materialism*. I argue that the considerations Dennett advances do not, in fact, call for the abandonment of Cartesian materialism. Moreover, the theory presented by Dennett does not, as he claims, succeed in explaining *consciousness*; in particular, it fails to do justice to qualia. Illuminating though Dennett's discussion is, in many ways, it nevertheless leaves the traditional mind-body problem intact.

Loeb, Louis E. Causation, Extrinsic Relations, and Hume's Second Thoughts about Personal Identity. *Hume Stud*, 18(2), 219-231, N 92.

According to *Treatise* I.iv.6, the identity of a mind over time consists in a sequence of perceptions related by causation. In both of Hume's two definitions of cause, causation is an external or extrinsic relation. Hume finds this result tolerable. If causation is an extrinsic relation, and personal identity is analyzed in terms of causation, then personal identity is an extrinsic relation as well. I suggest that, in the Appendix, Hume finds this consequence intolerable, and that his finding it so is the source of his famous misgivings in regard to his section on personal identity.

Lötter, H P P. *Justice for an Unjust Society*. Amsterdam, Rodopi, 1993.

Loewer, Barry and Belzer, Marvin. *Prima Facie* Obligation in John Searle and His Critics, Lepore, Ernest (ed). Cambridge, Blackwell, 1991.

Loewy, Erich H. Consent, Ethics, and Community. *J Clin Ethics*, 3(3), 224-228, Fall 92.

Loewy, Erich H. Healing and Killing, Harming and Not Harming: Physician Participation in Euthanasia and Capital Punishment. *J Clin Ethics*, 3(1), 29-34, Spr 92.

Loftin, Robert W. Scientific Collecting. *Environ Ethics*, 14(3), 253-264, Fall 92.

Scientists often collect (kill) organisms in pursuit of human knowledge. When is such killing morally permissible? I explore this question with particular reference to ornithology and against the background of animal liberation ethics and a land ethic, especially Mary Anne Warren's account that finds the two ethics complementary. I argue that the ethical theories offered provide insufficient guidance. As a step toward the resolution of this serious problem, I offer a set of criteria to determine when collecting is morally permissible.

Lofts, Steve. Une nouvelle approche de la philosophie d'Ernst Cassirer. *Rev Phil Louvain*, 90(88), 523-538, N 92.

Logan, Beryl. The Irregular Argument in Hume's Dialogues. *Hume Stud*, 18(2), 483-500, N 92.

In this paper, I argue that there are two arguments in Hume's *Dialogues Concerning Natural Religion*: the 'regular' argument that is articulated in Part 2 and the 'irregular' argument in Part 3, and that the statement of belief that is found in the *Dialogues* is not expressed in the ambiguous, undefined statement that 'the cause or causes of order in the universe probably bear some remote analogy to human intelligence' that results from Cleanthes' 'regular' argument, but is declared by Philo in his 'irregular' argument.

Logue, James. Weight of Evidence, Resiliency and Second-Order Probabilities in Probability and Rationality, Eells, Ellery (ed). Amsterdam, Rodopi, 1991.

Several philosophers have suggested that weight of evidence (the sum of favourable and unfavourable evidence) is as important an element in characterizing states of uncertainty as probability (derived from the preponderance of favourable over unfavourable evidence), and that this undermines any univocal subjectivist theory of probability. This paper argues that subjectivism can defuse such threats by analysing weight as a function of second-order subjective probabilities, themselves functions of the resiliency — stability under Bayesian conditionalization — of first-order probabilities. The analysis is applied to resisting some of L J Cohen's arguments for pluralism in the interpretation of probability in inductive and judicial contexts.

Lohmar, D. Perception as Cooperation of Schematization and Figurative Synthesis (in Dutch). *Tijdschr Filosof*, 55(1), 100-129, Mr 93.

According to Kant the figurative synthesis and the schemata are both serving the mediation of intuition and concept. In this article, I investigate their respective functions and the special manner of their cooperation in the process of knowledge. Kant prefers geometrical concepts as examples for schemata. The schema of a triangle is a rule to construct it, that is a rule which is able to produce an image. The representation of a triangle requires a construction, which is an action of the pure productive imagination: the figurative synthesis connects the manifold in pure intuition following the rules for construction. But important aspects remain hidden in mathematical examples. It is after all the same figurative synthesis which enables us to apprehend an object with the use of empirical concepts (A 244/B 271). This action of imagination and its cooperation with schematization becomes especially clear in the use of empirical concepts.

Lohmar, Dieter. Beiträge zu einer phänomenologischen Theorie des negativen Urteils. *Husserl Stud*, 8(3), 173-204, 1991-92.

Lohmar, Dieter. Kants Wahrnehmungsurteile als Erbe Humes?. *Z Phil Forsch*, 46(2), 186-204, Ap-J 92.

Lohr, Charles H. Latin Aristotle Commentaries: Supplementary Renaissance Authors. *Frei Z Phil Theol*, 40(1-2), 161-168, 1993.

Supplement to the author's inventory of *Latin Aristotle Commentaries*, Volume II. *Renaissance Authors*, Florence, 1988, containing bio-bibliographical information on 35 additional commentators and additional information on 17 commentators already including in the inventory.

Loiskandl, Helmut H. Moral Sense, Community, and the Individual in Analecta Husserliana, XXXI, Tymieniecka, Anna-Teresa (ed). Dordrecht, Kluwer, 1990.

Lomasky, Loren. Compensation and the Bounds of Rights. *Nomos*, 33, 13-44, 1991.

Lomba, Joaquin. *El oráculo de Narciso*. Zaragoza, Pr Univ Zaragoza, 1993.

In his poem Parmenides relates how the Goddess taught him a new way of speaking and thinking about nature, different from myth: rationally by "S is P" articulated on the verb "to be". But since rational judgment cannot be based on itself (it would fall into an interminable process) the Goddess introduced him to the myth "being" with its characteristic terms (sperical, ethernal, full, etc.), representative of the new rational way of thinking and speaking. This becomes much clearer of the Greek language and rationality are compared with other cultures, such as Semitic ones, which do not have the copulative verb "to be".

Lombard, Lawrence Brian. Events, Counterfactuals, and Speed. *Austl J Phil*, 70(2), 187-197, Je 92.

Jonathan Bennett has stressed the idea that counterfactual claims about events bear important relations to claims concerning the properties events have essentially. Bennett illustrates this idea with an argument the soundness of which would show that events can occur more quickly than they actually do. I argue that Bennett's argument, as formulated, is invalid, and so cannot be an illustration of the connection between counterfactuals and essentialist claims about events. I also show that, when supplemented in a way that makes it valid, Bennett's argument cannot be sound, and hence, that it fails to be a demonstration of the view that an event can occur more quickly that it in fact does.

Lombardi, Joseph. Filial Gratitude and God's Right to Command. *J Relig Ethics*, 19(1), 93-118, Spr 91.

Defenders of theistic morality sometimes insist that God's will can impose moral obligation only if God has a right to command. The right is compared to that which parents have over their children and which is thought to derive from a filial debt of gratitude. This essay examines arguments for divine authority based on gratitude which employ the parental analogy. It is argued that neither parental nor divine authority is based on gratitude. An alternative derivation of parental authority is suggested but shown to be unavailable to those who would compare divine to parental rights.

Lompe, Klaus. On the Social Acceptability of Modern Technology: New Challenges for Politicians and Scientists in a World of Risks. *Res Phil Technol*, 11, 33-48, 1991.

Science and technology have become factors that significantly affect the traditional forms of the balance and exercise of power. Questions about the applications of science and technology and their effects on man and the environment have thus become a political issue of central importance. Political decision makers are markedly dependent on scientific input in this regard. Today, scientists are increasingly consulted in the analysis, prognosis, and evaluation of processes which are largely the result of their own work. It seems important, therefore, to allow for an interdisciplinary improvement in the transparency of the political dimensions in the techno-scientific process, to publicly discuss concepts for social acceptability and to make possible appropriate forms of participation for all concerned.

Londey, David. God and Forgiveness. *Sophia (Australia)*, 31(1-2), 101-109, 1992.

Lonergan, Bernard J F and Croken, Robert C (ed). Consciousness and the Trinity. *Phil Theol*, 7(1), 3-22, Autumn 92.

Long, Eugene T. Religious Pluralism and the Ground of Religious Faith in Logic, God and Metaphysics, Harris, James F (ed). Dordrecht, Kluwer, 1992.

Long, Eugene Thomas. Experience and Natural Theology in Prospects for Natural Theology, Long, Eugene Thomas (ed). Washington, Cath Univ Amer Pr, 1992.

Long, Eugene Thomas (ed). *Prospects for Natural Theology*. Washington, Cath Univ Amer Pr, 1992.

Long, John C. Foucault's Clinic. *J Med Human*, 13(3), 119-138, Fall 92.

Foucault's clinic is a discourse that links health with knowledge in the modern period. The clinic is a mode of perception and enunciation that enables us to think about disease when we make statements about birth and death. Within clinical discourse resides understanding of disease visible on the surfaces and hidden within the depths of ailing patients. The truth of disease and placement of that truth in a general plan of the world in Renaissance woodcuts and John Donne's poetry is different from the regime of truth in modern paintings and lithographs and the verse of Walt Whitman and L E Sisman.

Long, Roderick T. Abortion, Abandonment, and Positive Rights in Altruism, Paul, Ellen Frankel (ed). New York, Cambridge Univ Pr, 1993.

Abortion is permissible, while infant abandonment is not. How can this be true, given that abortion seems to be a killing, and abandonment merely a letting-die? It is argued that the ban on using others as mere means rules out basic positive rights but endorses derivative positive rights. Abandonment turns out to be best understood as a killing rather than a letting-die, so the infant has a derivative positive right not to be abandoned, but abortion, though also a killing and so prima facie objectionable, is justified as a derivative positive right on grounds of self-defense.

Long, Roderick T. Abortion, Abandonment, and Positive Rights: The Limits of Compulsory Altruism. *Soc Phil Pol*, 10(1), 166-191, Wint 93.

Abortion is permissible, while infant abandonment is not. How can this be true, given that abortion seems to be a killing, and abandonment merely a letting-die? It is argued that the ban on using others as mere means rules out basic positive rights but endorses derivative positive rights. Abandonment turns out to be best understood as a killing rather than a letting-die, so the infant has a derivative positive right not to be abandoned; but abortion, though also a killing and so prima facie objectionable, is justified as a derivative positive right on grounds of self-defense.

Long, Roderick T. Mill's Higher Pleasures and the Choice of Character. *Utilitas*, 4(2), 279-297, N 92.

Mill's account of pleasure initially seems inconsistent: if the superiority of "higher pleasures" is quantitative, then Mill's higher/lower distinction is superfluous; if their superiority is not quantitative, then Mill's hedonism is compromised. A careful reading of Mill resolves this conflict. The superiority of higher pleasures is indeed quantitative, but only *indirectly* so; in choosing a higher pleasure over a lower one, we are *ipso facto* choosing a nobler character over a baser one, and it is the pleasantness of the noble character, not of the higher pleasure itself, that provides the needed quantitative superiority.

Longino, Helen. Subjects, Power and Knowledge: Description and Prescription in Feminist Philosophies of Science in Feminist Epistemologies, Alcoff, Linda (ed). New York, Routledge, 1993.

A number of the feminist critiques of science argue that the ideal knower presupposed in traditional discussions of science is marked by a position or expectation of domination. They suggest that a different (kind of) knowledge will be produced by knowers with a different relation to power. I argue that they have succeeded in establishing the importance of social location, but have not established the superiority of any one subject position. I argue that an interactively social account of inquiry is required to accommodate the feminist insights about the subjectivity and answer some objections to this account.

Longino, Helen E. Knowledge, Bodies, and Values: Reproductive Technologies and their Scientific Context. *Inquiry*, 35(3-4), 323-340, S-D 92.

This essay sets human reproductive technologies in the context of biological research exploiting the discovery of the structure of the DNA molecule in the early 1950s. By setting these technological developments in this research context and then setting the research in the framework of a philosophical analysis of the role of social values in scientific inquiry, it is possible to develop a perspective on these technologies and the aspirations they represent that is relevant to the concerns of their social critics.

Longxi, Zhang. The Cannibals, the Ancients, and Cultural Critique: Reading Montaigne in Postmodern Perspective. *Human Stud*, 16(1-2), 51-68, Ap 93.

In questioning the self and the tradition of European culture of his time, Montaigne anticipated much of the postmodern cultural critique. In using the New World cannibals as representing the non-Western Other to criticize the Western self, he was also a precursor of postmodernism. But while postmodernist theory overemphasizes cultural difference, Montaigne finally insists on the value of a shared humanity among different cultures and peoples. That is an important lesson we can learn from him, and we cannot afford to abandon our shared humanity if we want to eradicate racism and to avoid further fragmentize our multicultural society.

Loone, Eero and Pearce, Brian (trans). *Soviet Marxism and Analytical Philosophies of History—Eero Loone*. New York, Verso, 1992.

In this, the first of his books to be translated into English, Loone surveys the philosophy of history as practised in the West, and then subjects Marxism to careful analytic scrutiny. He provides both a fresh perspective on familiar non-Marxist writers such as Collingwood, Popper, Kuhn, Modigliano and Plumb and a fruitful reformulation of the Marxist theory of history.

Loparic, Zeljko. Kant e a Filosofia Analítica. *Cad Hist Filosof Cie*, 2(1), 27-32, Ja-Je 90.

Analytic philosophy is an analysis of language that makes use of the tools of formal logic. In this sense, it only begins to exist after Frege's work. Notwithstanding this distinction, one may find in Kant a philosophy of language, although he often uses mentalist descriptions for linguistic conceptions. This article presents some of Kant's contributions to the philosophy of language. It shows that semantic problems play a central role in Kant's philosophy.

Lopes, Lola L and Oden, Gregg C. The Rationality of Intelligence in Probability and Rationality, Eells, Ellery (ed). Amsterdam, Rodopi, 1991.

Lopez, M Carmen. La estética ontológica de M Merleau-Ponty. *Pensamiento*, 189(48), 69-77, Ja-Mr 92.

López, Jesús García. La teoría del objeto puro de A Millán Puelles. *Anu Filosof*, 25(2), 321-347, 1992.

This article studies the "Theory of the Pur Object" of the Spanish philosopher Antonio Millán-Puelles, relating it to the Scholastic and to Husserl and Hartmann.

López Quintás, Alfonso. Necesidad de una renovación ética. *G Metaf*, 14(2), 171-191, My-Ag 92.

López-Escobar, E G K. Global Discharge Conditions for Natural Deduction Systems. *J Non-Classical Log*, 8(1), 39-44, My 91.

It is shown that by adding the rules of *selection* to a natural deduction system the discharging of assumption formulas can be carried out in a uniform way.

Loptson, Peter J. Lockean Ideas and 18th Century British Philosophy. *Theoria*, 56(1-2), 85-106, 1990.

This paper undertakes a re-examination of Locke's concept of idea, arguing that standard interpretations have over-stressed a sensory motivation or component for what Locke has in mind. Ideas for Locke are not sense data but mental contents (thoughts, in the object, not act sense). Essentially deriving from Cartesian usage, Lockean ideas recognizably resemble the ideas of common sense conception. Whatever their final metaphysical analysis may be, there is every reason to regard ideas as real. A progressively transmutation of Lockean ideas into sense data, especially due to Berkeley, is traced. Other 18th century conceptions of ideas are also explored.

Loptson, Peter J. The Idea of Philosophical History. *Dialogue (Canada)*, 31(1), 33-50, Wint 92.

This paper argues for a reconsideration of the idea of universal or philosophical history. Tracing its development from Vico through Herder to Hegel and several 19th century thinkers to Spengler and Toynbee, the major 20th century figures in this tradition, the paper argues that the idea finds interesting contemporary expression in the work of the world historian, William H McNeill. His work is discussed and argued to be a particularly mature—in part because so impressively empirically grounded—representative of this philosophical genre. Some 20th century empiricist analytic positions are argued to give distinctive philosophical plausibility to McNeill's work.

Lorand, Ruth. Bergson's Concept of Order. *J Hist Phil*, 30(4), 579-595, O 92.

The traditional concept of order recognizes only one type of order. In this type of order laws, external to the ordered set, dictate the position of each element within that set. Bergson discerns two types of order: 1) The geometrical, or intellectual, order is a pragmatic order and corresponds to the traditional concept. 2) The vital, or intuitive, order, reflects true experience. It is highly unpredictable, sensitive and governed by internal necessity. Bergson concludes that disorder does not exist, since in the absence of one type of order there is always another type. Although I agree with Bergson's distinction, I argue against his claim that there is no disorder.

Lorand, Ruth. On 'Free and Dependent Beauty'—A Rejoinder. *Brit J Aes*, 32(3), 250-253, Jl 92.

This paper is a reply to two comments on my paper, "On Free and Dependent Beauty: A Puzzling Issue" (*British Journal of Aesthetics*, 29, 1989, 32-40). 1. My reply to R Stecker's criticism is based on the claim that an aesthetic experience cannot be non-conceptual as Kant believes. 2. My reply to K Lord is that an aesthetic evaluation is bound to be comparative. An aesthetic evaluation is singular and addresses the object's individuality. The nature of this individuality can be comprehended only through some kind of comparison.

Lorand, Ruth. The Purity of Aesthetic Value. *J Aes Art Crit*, 50(1), 13-21, Wint 92.

The article examines the idea that aesthetic values are independent of and disconnected from any non-aesthetic values. Having analyzed the various meanings of 'purity', the article discusses Kant's notions of 'pure beauty' and 'dependent beauty' as well as arguments against the detachment of aesthetic from non-aesthetic evaluations. It concludes that aesthetic values are 'pure' in the sense that they are *not derived* from any non-aesthetic concepts. However, aesthetic values must refer to non-aesthetic properties and therefore are effected by them and by their context. It is in this sense that aesthetic values are not 'pure' but 'dependent'.

Lord, Catherine and Benardete, José A. Baxandall and Goodman in The Language of Art History, Kemal, Salim (ed). New York, Cambridge Univ Pr, 1991.

Lorenz, Kuno. Die Selbstorganisation der Philosophie durch das dialogische Prinzip. *Dialectica*, 46(3-4), 191-199, 1992.

Ausgehend von Cassirers Dictum "man is constantly conversing with himself" wird ein Versuch unternommen, die widersprüchliche Erfahrung, sich reflektierend zugleich als ein Subjekt und als ein Objekt vorzufinden, in der dialogischen Verfassung des Menschen zu verankern. Philosophieren als Vollzug und Dartellung menschlicher Selbstbestimmung kann erst in der Rekonstruktion von Handlungs- und Sprachkompetenz mit dialogischen Elementarsituationen ihres Erwerbs einen Begriff von sich selbst entwickeln, der beide Übergänge, den von der Gegendstandsebene zur Darstellungsebene (Distanzierung durch 'Objektivierung') und den umgekehrten (Aneignung durch 'Symbolisierung') als Mittel des Zusammenhangs von 'Praxis' und 'Theorie' (traditionell: 'Körper' und 'Geist') zu begreifen erlaubt.

Lorenzo, Javier. Leibniz-Frege, utopías de la razón conceptual?. *Theoria (Spain)*, 6(14-15), 97-114, O 91.

The dream of Leibniz and that of Frege, to create a *lingua charactierica* in order to demonstrate conceptual thought, incorporates in a wider process, the division and tension between the distinct spheres which the human sup-species have been creating. Spheres which remain hidden by natural language, essentially spoken language. For the creation and demonstration of the conceptual-sphere the establishing of a language of characters has become indispensable, essentially written language.

Lorenzova, Helena. Calobiotic or the Art of Aesthetic Life (in Czechoslovakian). *Estetika*, 29(4), 52-64, 1992.

Lorenzova, Helena. Solar Myth in the Works of Julius Zeyer (in Czechoslovakian). *Estetika*, 28(4), 219-223, 1991.

Lorite-Mena, José. *La Filosofia del Hombre*. Navarra, Ed Verbo Divino, 1992.

The text develops around two questions: *What is man?* and *Who are we?* The first one is formulated by Kant as the articulation's axis of his Pragmatic Anthropology; the second one is proposed by Foucault as a problematic issue derived from the dissolution of the "anthropological dream". The analysis reveals the epistemological supports which makes possible the first interrogation (the distance Newton-Rousseau), the historic inflationary productions of man's representations which allows the second question (empiric anthropologies and "masters of suspicion"), and the challenge this second question represents for us (the possibilities of anthropology in the space of *auto-organization*).

Lorraine, Renée. Musicology and Theory: Where It's Been, Where It's Going. *J Aes Art Crit*, 51(2), 235-244, Spr 93.

Losee, John. Hume's Demarcation Project. *Hume Stud*, 18(1), 51-62, Ap 92.

David Hume sought to exclude certain concepts from the domain of empirically significant discourse. To achieve the desired exclusion he appealed to both a Derivability Principle and a Copy Principle. The Derivability Principle, the Copy Principle, and the position that the "missing shade of blue" is a simple idea constitute an inconsistent set of claims. Moreover, if the missing shade instead is acknowledged to be a complex idea, affirmation of both the Derivability Principle and the Copy Principle leads to a violation of a "Pragmatic Maxim" to which Hume also is committed. A demarcation achieved by application of the Derivability Principle alone also is unsatisfactory, since it fails to exclude the notion of "substance *qua* substratum".

Losito, William F. Education as Hospitality: The Reclamation of Cultural Metaphor and Narrative. *Proc S Atlantic Phil Educ Soc*, 36, 62-69, 1991.

The first part of the paper describes and critically appraises contemporary emphases on school through the metaphor/model of school-as production. The analysis concludes that this model is deficient as an approach to resolving the inherent alienation which characterizes our large, bureaucratized urban educational systems. The second part of the paper identifies and explicates the "hospitality" concept as a theme in our traditional literature. The argument is made, based on the textual analysis along with other references to traditional literature, that the meaning of hospitality is a fruitful concept for reclaiming as a component of an ideal perspective for speculating about worthwhile school environments.

Losoncy, Thomas A. More on an "Elusive" Argument. *Amer Cath Phil Quart*, 66(4), 501-505, Autumn 92.

This article responds to an article by Gregory Schufreider in the same Journal volume to the effect that my earlier article, "St Anselm's Rejection of the Ontological Argument—A Review of the Occasion and Circumstances," does not ultimately recognize that Anselm has an ontological argument in chapter 2 of the *Proslogion*. This response indicates that the information found in chapter 2, cannot be understood without going outside that very chapter. Moreover, when one does clarify chapter 2 by pursuing its outside supporting bases, one finds that any claim that Anselm's argument is "ontological" fails.

Losonsky, Michael. Abstraction, Covariance, and Representation. *Phil Stud*, 70(2), 225-234, My 93.

Losonsky, Michael. Leibniz's Adamic Language of Thought. *J Hist Phil*, 30(4), 523-543, O 92.

Adamicism is characterized as the view that there is an innate, universal, natural, and unambiguous language that human beings have and understand without learning. In the Seventeenth century, these properties were attributed to Adam's language of nature. I argue that in Leibniz the Adamic language of nature just becomes the language of thought.

Louch, Alfred R. Searching for Humanistic Truth. *Phil Lit*, 16(2), 354-363, O 92.

Louden, Robert B. Aristotle's Practical Particularism in Essays in Ancient Greek Philosophy, IV, Anton, John P (ed). Albany, SUNY Pr, 1991.

Many philosophers have agreed with Aristotle's claim that practical and theoretical knowledge differ. We still lack an accurate account of what this difference is. I argue that it lies in the following two theses: (1) Knowledge of action is knowledge of genuine particulars rather than of kinds; (2) Agents cannot know these particulars by inferential or deductive reasoning but only by intuition. In this essay I attempt to demonstrate the strong textual roots of Aristotle's practical particularism, to defend the particularist reading against several recent anti-particularist interpretations, and to show how Aristotle himself attempts to justify it.

Loughlin, Gerard. Christianity at the End of the Story or the Return of the Master-Narrative. *Mod Theol*, 8(4), 365-384, Oct 92.

Loughlin, Gerard. Making a Better World: Revisiting David Hume with Ian Markham. *Mod Theol*, 8(3), 297-303, Jl 92.

Loui, R P. How a Formal Theory of Rationality Can Be Normative. *J Phil*, 90(3), 137-143, Mr 93.

The paper distinguishes implementation from interpretation as a possible case of normative formal theory. It identifies the source of normative force as the intention to implement in a particular way, which it deliberately conflates with a contract. Finally, it discusses constructive theories of reasoning which depend on non-deterministic processes. These theories make little sense from an interpretive point of view, and are becoming more common among implementers.

Louw, T J G. *G A Rauche: Selected Philosophical Papers*. Alice, Fort Hare Univ Pr, 1992.

This voluminous book of 500 pages comprises a selection of 42 philosophical essays by the German born South African philosopher, Gerhard Rauche. Apart from 4 new essays, 38 others have been carefully selected from previously published material. The book is introduced by the editor with a presentation on Rauche's "Philosophy of Actuality" and concluded with a complete *curriculum vitae* and list of publications of the author. The table of contents is divided into eleven themes: introduction to philosophy, anthropology, philosophy of science, ethics, metaphysics, epistemology, Kantian philosophy, social and political philosophy, philosophy in South Africa, philosophy of history, and aesthetics and literature.

Louw, Tobias J G. Gerhard A Rauche's Philosophy of Actuality: The Work and Thought of an Individualist South African Philosopher. *Man World*, 26(2), 181-197, Ap 93.

This essay aims to open a window to the philosophy of Gerhard Rauche. The introductory profile of his life and works is accompanied by an analysis of the development of his thought and concluded with a discussion of his central argument. Rauche has devoted his life to the critical examination of the basic questions of truth and knowledge. His historical-hermeneutical approach to the philosophical dialogue has enabled him to develop his key idea: *contingency*. This concept reveals man's changing experience of reality as the common root of all theory and practice, and explains the contradictory nature of scientific theories and moral practices.

Love, John. Stability Among R.E. Quotient Algebras. *Annals Pure Applied Log*, 59(1), 55-63, Ja 93.

A recursive algebra is recursively stable among r.e. quotient algebras if the graph of each isomorphism from it, to the quotient of a recursive algebra by an r.e. congruence, is r.e. We provide syntactical conditions equivalent to the recursive stability among r.e. quotient algebras of any recursive algebra, assuming it has a recursive existential diagram. A counter-example is provided which demonstrates the necessity of this assumption.

Lovekin, David. Technology and Culture and the Problem of the Homeless. *Phil Forum*, 24(4), 363-374, Sum 93.

Lovell, David W. Early French Socialism and Politics: The Case of Victor Considérant. *Hist Polit Thought*, 13(2), 257-279, Sum 92.

Lovell, David W. Socialism, Utopianism and the 'Utopian Socialists'. *Hist Euro Ideas*, 14(2), 185-201, Mr 92.

French socialists of the period 1830-48 have come to be known as the 'utopian socialists'. But in what respects can they be considered 'utopian'? This paper reveals that the charge was derived chiefly from disputes among the early socialists themselves. Its thrust was concerned with the inadequacy of the means proposed, not with socialism itself. The tendency to treat means as 'utopian' is criticized, and the merits of reserving 'utopian' as a critique of ends are explored. A definition is proposed of 'utopianism' as any monism of values: it points to the common utopianism of Marx and those he described as 'utopians'.

Lovibond, Sabina. Feminism and Postmodernism in Postmodernism and Society, Boyne, Roy (ed). New York, St Martin's Pr, 1990.

Low, Douglas. Merleau-Ponty on Subjectivity and Intersubjectivity. *Int Stud Phil*, 24(3), 45-64, 1992.

This paper explicates Merleau-Ponty's highly original theory of subjectivity and intersubjectivity. Merleau-Ponty challenges traditional philosophy/psychology by rejecting the notion of subjective awareness as an introspective awareness of the private contents of one's own consciousness. For Merleau-Ponty, the subjective is a prereflective, prepersonal bodily openess to an anonymous visibility, a visibility in which both the individual and others participate. Thus, for Merleau-Ponty, the personal/ subjective and the shared/ intersubjective overlap. This view escapes the individualism of the West and the collectivism of authoritarian communism. It provides a balanced theory for both political theory and practice.

Low, Douglas. The Continuity Between Merleau-Ponty's Early and Late Philosophy of Language. *J Phil Res*, 17, 287-311, 1992.

The primary concern of this essay is the similarity and difference between Merleau-Ponty's early *Phenomenology of Perception* and late *The Visible and the Invisible* philosophy of language. While some argue that Merleau-Ponty's late work breaks with the earlier text and foreshadows poststructuralist and deconstructionist philosophy of language, I argue (with others) that there is no significant break in Merleau-Ponty's thought. The essay is cast in the form of a detailed exposition, thus providing a comprehensive essay-length introduction to Merleau-Ponty's philosophy of language.

Lowe, E J. Comment on Le Poidevin. *Mind*, 102(405), 171-173, Ja 93.

Robin Le Poidevin's most recent attempt to rehabilitate McTaggart's argument against the reality of the A-series is criticized as falling foul of the same 'indexical fallacy' as the original. It is argued that the ontological asymmetry between past and future can be perfectly well accommodated in A-series terms and that there is no reason to suppose that tensed utterances can be assigned purely tenseless truth-conditions. But standard tense logic is also criticized.

Lowe, E J. Experience and Its Objects in The Contents of Experience, Crane, Tim (ed). New York, Cambridge Univ Pr, 1992.

In this paper a detailed account is given of the way in which systematic causal dependencies between the qualitative features of perceptual experience and the properties of environmental objects enable human subjects to extract environmental information from their sensory stimulations. An account which presents a distinct alternative to both the 'ecological' and the 'computational' theories of perception currently in favour amongst philosophical psychologists.

Lowe, E J. Real Selves: Persons as a Substantial Kind in Human Beings, Cockburn, David (ed). New York, Cambridge Univ Pr, 1991.

This paper discusses the ontological status of the self, examining three alternative views. One, following Aristotle, treats persons as biological substances (a kind of animal), while another, following Locke, treats them as psychological modes (suitably unified successions of mental states). These are rejected in favour of a (non-Cartesian) version of the view that persons are psychological substances, a version which permits the self to be a bearer of physical as well as mental states.

Lowe, E J. Self, Reference and Self-reference. *Philosophy*, 68(263), 15-33, Ja 93.

An analysis of selfhood is presented which ties this notion to the possession of certain kinds of first-person knowledge, in particular *de re* knowledge of the identity of one's own conscious thoughts and experiences. This leads to an exploration of the nature of demonstrative reference to one's own conscious states and to physical objects, whence it is argued that the semantic distinction between 'direct' and 'indirect' demonstrative reference helps to delineate the metaphysical boundary between oneself and the world.

Lowe, E J. The Problem of Psychophysical Causation. *Austl J Phil*, 70(3), 263-276, S 92.

It is widely supposed that interactionist dualism cannot plausibly be reconciled with the conservation laws of physics. These laws do not, however, imply that the physical universe is a causally closed system. Various dualist systems of psychophysical causation are shown to be consistent with our current knowledge of physical law, the most plausible such system being one in which mental causes impose structure on patterns of physical events without entering directly into chains of physical causation.

Lowe, Scott. Institutions and Debts of Gratitude. *Int J Applied Phil*, 7(2), 57-62, Wint 92.

Many agree that individuals are obligated out of gratitude by being the recipients of benefits produced by others out of the motive of goodwill. Some have argued that a citizen's obligation to obey the law or support other social organizations is owed as the appropriate grateful return for the benefits these organizations provide. This implies that it is possible to owe debts of gratitude to institutions themselves. It is the possibility of owing debts of gratitude to institutions which I deny. Drawing on work from the field of business ethics on the moral responsibility of corporations, I argue that institutions cannot have the motive of goodwill.

Lowe, Walter. *Theology and Difference: The Wound of Reason*. Bloomington, Indiana Univ Pr, 1993.

The book seeks to clarify the meaning of critical, dialectical thinking ("the wound of reason") through an interactive reading of Derrida, Kant — and the early radical theology of Karl Barth. Attention to "the memory of suffering," specifically the mass violence of the twentieth century, leads to a reinterpretation of Kant's critical philosophy in light of the early *question of* theodicy. Deconstruction permits — nay, requires — something like the radical ethical demand epitomized by Kant. Only thus is dialectical thinking impelled and the memory of suffering preserved. The book concludes by examining Barth's ethically important notion of a "memory of God."

Lowy, Richard F. Mental Sociality as Ultimate Reality and Meaning in the Thought of George Herbert Mead. *Ultim Real Mean*, 16(1-2), 56-72, Mr-Je 93.

Loy, David. Indra's Postmodern Net. *Phil East West*, 43(3), 481-510, Jl 93.

Loy, David 572 AUTHOR INDEX WITH ABSTRACTS

Loy, David. The Deconstruction of Buddhism in Derrida and Negative Theology, Coward, Harold (ed). Albany, SUNY Pr, 1992.

Loy, David. Transcendence East and West. *Man World*, 26(4), 403-427, O 93.

This paper argues that the cultural polarity between Indian-influenced cultures and Chinese-Japanese cultures is more significant than that between "East" and "West". Part one outlines the most significant contrasts. Part two adumbrates the pattern in those differences, which reduces to differing attitudes toward *transcendence* (three meanings are distinguished) and asks why a transcendental dimension became important in certain places while not in others. Part three reflects on where "the West" fits into this schema: in the West the transcendental has been gradually internalized into the supposedly autonomous and self-directed *individual*. The conclusion briefly evaluates these three different cultural paradigms.

Loy, David. Trying to Become Real: A Buddhist Critique of Some Secular Heresies. *Int Phil Quart*, 32(4), 403-425, D 92.

The Buddhist denial of self suggests that our fundamental repression is not sex or death but the quite valid intuition that *I am not real*. In this case the "return of the repressed" manifests as a sense of *lack*, and we compensate by trying to make ourselves real. If not blinded by the usual sacred-secular distinction, we can see that fame, money, romance and even technology are ways we symbolically try to fill up this sense of lack. Since we cannot overcome our sense of unreality in this fashion, those pursuits tend to become "demonic": i.e., we keep concluding that we need *more*.

Lu, Matthias. *Critical Theoretical Inquiry on the Notion of Act in the Metaphysics of Aristotle and Saint Thomas Aquinas*. New York, Lang, 1992.

Luban, David. Justice Holmes and Judicial Virtue. *Nomos*, 34, 235-264, 1992.

Lucardie, Paul. A Stage in Moral Development? in The Utilitarian Response, Allison, Lincoln (ed). Newbury Park, Sage, 1990.

Lucas, Hans-Christian. The "Sovereign Ingratitude" of Spirit toward Nature: Logical Qualities, Corporeity, Animal Magnetism, and Madness in Hegel's "Anthropology". *Owl Minerva*, 23(2), 131-150, Spr 92.

Lucas, Thierry. Hui Shih and Kung Sun Lung an Approach from Contemporary Logic. *J Chin Phil*, 20(2), 211-255, Je 93.

Semantical instruments of contemporary logic are applied to the analysis of Hui Shih's "Ten Propositions" and Kung Sun Lung's discourses "On the White Horse", "On Hard and White", "On Indices and Things". The notion of logical interpretation is used to clarify the structure of Hui Shih's argument; coupled with the notion of sorted language, it also allows us to show the logical coherence and common structure of Kung Sun Lung's three discourses.

Lucash, Frank S. The Nature of Mind. *G Metaf*, 13(1), 89-107, Ja-Ap 91.

I present several assumptions needed for a satisfactory theory of the mind/body relation and which I think will be helpful in avoiding traditional difficulties.

Lucey, Kenneth (ed). *What is God? The Selected Essays of Richard R La Croix*. Buffalo, Prometheus, 1993.

Ludassy, Mária. *The Origins of Our Delusions (in Hungarian)*. Budapest, Atlantisz, 1991.

The book, though written in the 80s, contains six studies on issues still relevant. When the author meditates on the over-emphasis of the role of the state, the birth of etatist attitude, the representatives of cultural criticism and national isolationism or the dawn of racial myths, the well-versed reader can immediately "adapt" what she says: etatism, populist attitudes, contempt for an denunciation of otherness are present in public life even now. The presumably most interesting writings of the volume discuss Rousseau's views: the author's analysis strengthens the position of those who find the origins of modern etatism in Rousseau. In the other studies of the volume the question of basic human rights, civil disobedience, Gobineau's essay on racial inequality are brought up. Ludassy's book illustrates how ideas intending to elevate humanity can be distorted and become tools of tyranny.

Ludlow, Peter (ed) and Beakley, Brian (ed). *The Philosophy of Mind: Classical Problems/Contemporary Issues*. Cambridge, MIT Pr, 1991.

This collection of essays in the philosophy of mind ranges from Plato, Aristotle, and Aquinas to Chomsky, Putnam, and the PDP Research Group. Part I covers the classic positions on the mind-body problem, questions of reduction and scientific methodology, and the notion of "contingent identity". Part II concerns the possibility of mental causation. Part III covers arguments for and against mental imagery. Part IV surveys views on associationist and connectionist mental models, and Part V deals with philosophical and scientific evidence concerning innate ideas. The collection is thorough enough to prove useful to students and researchers alike.

Ludlow, Peter and Larson, Richard K. Interpreted Logical Forms. *Synthese*, 95(3), 305-355, Je 93.

Recently, various authors have suggested that familiar semantic problems with propositional attitude verbs might be resolved by taking such predicates to express relations between agents and interpreted logical forms (ILFs). ILFs are annotated constituency graphs whose nodes pair terminal and nonterminal symbols with a semantic value. In this paper, we present an explicit theory of ILFs and apply it to classical questions regarding propositional attitude semantics. Our formal construction algorithm is embedded within a recursive theory of truth for natural language of the kind advocated by Davidson. We apply ILFs to issues involving substitutivity, demonstratives, general beliefs, and iterated attitude ascriptions.

Ludwig, Kirk. Brains in a Vat, Subjectivity, and the Causal Theory of Reference. *J Phil Res*, 17, 313-345, 1992.

This paper evaluates Putnam's argument in the first chapter of *Reason, Truth, and History*, for the claim that we can know that we are not brains in a vat (of a certain sort). A widespread response to Putnam's argument has been that if it were successful not only the world but the meanings of our words (and consequently our thoughts) would be beyond the pale of knowledge, because a causal theory of reference is not compatible with our having knowledge of the meanings of our words. I argue that *this* is not so. I argue also, however, that given *how* Putnam argues (here) for the causal theory of reference, he cannot after all escape this consequence.

Ludwig, Kirk A. Direct Reference in Thought and Speech. *Commun Cog*, 26(1), 49-76, 1993.

This paper offers an epistemological argument for the conclusion that the contents of some of our thoughts are essentially object involving: we could have some of the referential capacities we know we have given our epistemic capacities only if we know that we refer directly in thought to some spatio-temporal particulars. The danger to our first person authority this result threatens is met if we restrict direct reference to the self-at-a-time, which is sufficient to account for the referential capacities which are the basis for the argument for direct reference in thought.

Ludwig, Kirk A. Skepticism and Interpretation. *Phil Phenomenol Res*, 52(2), 317-339, Je 92.

I offer an interpretation and criticism of Donald Davidson's arguments against radical skepticism. I distinguish two lines of argument, the omniscient interpreter argument, and an argument from the necessary publicity of language. I argue the omniscient interpreter argument begs the question, and that the argument from the necessary publicity of language requires a much stronger publicity requirement than is supported any intuitive ... considerations in support of the claim that languages are necessarily public. I conclude with a criticism of the central argument for a coherence theory and a suggestion based on that criticism for an alternative approach to skepticism.

Ludwig, Walter. The Method of Hegel's *Phenomenology of Spirit*. *Owl Minerva*, 23(2), 165-175, Spr 92.

In an earlier article, I argued that the unity between subject and object disclosed in absolute knowing preserves their radical opposition. I now show how this interpretation of absolute knowing sheds new light on Hegel's argument in the Introduction to the *Phenomenology of Spirit*. First, it provides a unique understanding of the process and the standard of the self-examination of consciousness which constitutes the method of the *Phenomenology*. Second, it shows that Hegel's initial polemic concerning cognition is directed against both epistemological realism and epistemological idealism, thus revealing the revolutionary character of Hegel's position.

Lugg, Andrew. Pseudoscience as Nonsense. *Method Sci*, 25(2), 91-101, 1992.

In this paper I defend the view that pseudoscience differs from science in kind rather than degree. I argue that what needs discussing is not so much whether pseudoscientific statements are meaningless (as opposed to merely false) as how their meaninglessness ought to be understood. In this connection I examine—with special reference to Moritz Schlick's "Positivism and Realism"—the relationship of meaningfulness to verifiability and the way in what we mean depends on what we do.

Lugg, Andrew and McDonald, J F. Critical Notice of Tom Sorell *Scientism: Philosophy and the Infatuation with Science*. *Can J Phil*, 23(2), 291-298, Je 93.

This paper focuses on Sorell's critique of scientistic philosophy. We dispute his view that philosophers such as Bacon, Descartes, Wittgenstein, Carnap, and Quine are scientistic because they advocate the extension of the methods of science into nonscientific domains. And we challenge his view that we must embrace metaphysical philosophy if we are to avoid scientism. Our main contention is that both scientistic and metaphysical philosophy should give way to the Kantian approach—dismissed by Sorell—that "the critical path alone is still open".

Lugones, María. On *Borderlands/La Frontera*: An Interpretive Essay. *Hypatia*, 7(4), 31-37, Fall 92.

Borderlands/La Frontera deals with the psychology of resistance to oppression. The possibility of resistance is revealed by perceiving the self in the process of being oppressed as another face of the self in the process of resisting oppression. The new mestiza consciousness is born from this interplay between oppression and resistance. Resistance is understood as social, collective activity, by adding to Anzaldúa's theory the distinction between the act and the process of resistance.

Luizzi, Vincent. *A Case For Legal Ethics: Legal Ethics as a Source for a Universal Ethic*. Albany, SUNY Pr, 1993.

In suggesting that general ethics be modeled on legal ethics, this book is a call for more creativity in our moral experience. Luizzi argues that lawyers regularly re-think their roles and the rules related to these roles. What this says for general ethics is that we are to become active participants in defining our roles. *A Case for Legal Ethics* rejects fixed conceptions of human nature and extends our constructive efforts beyond specific roles to human nature itself and our environments. Luizzi appeals to role modeling, both to keep our constructed conceptions within moral bounds, and to develop the literature on moral education. We must be willing for others to imitate us as we live according to the conceptions we construct.

Luizzi, Vincent. Human Nature and Ethical Standards. *Dialec Hum*, 17(1), 102-106, 1990.

In this essay I examine the ways in which philosophers appeal to human nature to ground their ethical theories. I locate these theories on a spectrum. At one end are ethical theories where it seems that what we ought to do is congruent with what our nature compels us to do. At the other end are ethical theories which obligate us in ways which are within our capabilities but which are in no sense compelled by our nature. I conclude with a discussion of what we can learn about ethical theorizing from this classification.

Luke, Brian. Justice, Caring, and Animal Liberation. *Between Species*, 8(2), 100-108, Spr 92.

The most prominent defenders of animal liberation, Peter Singer and Tom Regan, work within a justice framework. I argue that a caring orientation is more appropriate to animal liberation since: 1) the justice-based arguments are unsound, and; 2) the caring approach is truer to the moral psychology of animal liberationists.

Luke, Timothy W. Rights and the Rise of Informational Society: The Origins and Ends of Behavioral Rights. *J Soc Phil*, 23(1), 89-97, Spr 92.

This paper extends the logic of Marshall's and Bendix's models of how rights are defined and defended through political struggles. It looks at some of the new social movements since the 1960s as political resistance groups, struggling to win "behavioral rights" for new classes of people in postindustrial informationalizing societies.

Luków, Pawel. The Fact of Reason: Kant's Passage to Ordinary Moral Knowledge. *Kantstudien*, 84(2), 204-221, 1993.

The paper gives an interpretation of Kant's doctrine of the fact of reason against the background of a constructivist reading of his philosophy, which does not allow us to appeal to any indubitable facts. The fact of reason is the object of a philosophical account of the moral law forms the quid juris part of deduction or legitimization of the law. A more intuitive grasp of the fact is the phenomenon of reverence for duty which ordinary people grasp in form of a feeling and emotion.

Lukowski, Piotr. Matrix-Frame Semantics for ISCI and INT. *Bull Sec Log*, 21(4), 156-162, D 92.

Lumsden, David. Daniel C Dennett's *The Intentional Stance*. *Erkenntnis*, 39(1), 101-109, Jl 93.

In "True Believers" Dennett explains how his view of intentional states is a *sort* of realism. He speaks of fatalism being almost right and of patterns imposing themselves with great vigor. An interpretation is offered linking this with his theme that a state of a system counts as a representation of the world if it is relatively difficult to fool the system. This pair of themes disappears elsewhere in *The Intentional Stance*. It is argued that his other attempts to articulate that *sort* of realism, which lose the force of these themes, can be adapted to accommodate them.

Lund, William R. Hobbes on Opinion, Private Judgment and Civil War. *Hist Polit Thought*, 13(1), 51-72, Spr 92.

Hobbes treats opinion as an ineradicable determinant of voluntary action. Nonetheless, he argues against particular erroneous opinions, especially the claim that men carry an unqualified right of private judgment from nature to "civil" society. To understand the relationship between *Behemoth* and his abstract political theory, we need to recognize how he blames the Civil War on that opinion and other mistakes that followed from its acceptance. Since men needed to act on true opinions, a history like *Behemoth* could supplement his more philosophical efforts to lead men to self-limitation and peace by vividly illustrating the dangers of private judgment.

Lungu, Gatian F. Pragmatism or Crude Utility: A Critique of the Education with Production Movement in Contemporary Africa. *Quest*, 5(2), 74-89, D 91.

Luntley, Michael. Practice Makes Knowledge?. *Inquiry*, 35(3-4), 447-461, S-D 92.

Luper-Foy, Steven. *The Moral Life*. Fort Worth, Holt Rinehart Winst, 1992.

Lurie, Yuval. Culture as a Human Form of Life: A Romantic Reading of Wittgenstein. *Int Phil Quart*, 32(2), 193-204, Je 92.

The idea that human beings are cultural beings underlies Wittgenstein's thinking. By placing emphasis on *deeds*, Wittgenstein overcomes the metaphysical distinction between culture and nature. This suggests that rules and concepts are abstracted expressions for socially administered deeds. A culture can then be seen as shared forms of life in which organic and communal forces merge, so as to provide human beings with a spiritual bond. In so doing it also provides human beings with a home in place of the one they no longer have in nature. Language, on this reading, is a great cultural work.

Lurie, Yuval. Geniuses and Metaphors. *J Aes Art Crit*, 49(3), 225-233, Sum 91.

Similarities between Wittgenstein's use of the concept of genius and Rorty's use of the concept of metaphor reflect similarities between Romanticism and Pragmatism regarding human nature and culture. Wittgenstein relays on the concept of genius to describe the creative forces in a culture which provide for its spiritual progression. Rorty uses the concept of metaphor to describe the way in which the introduction of new linguistic devices provide for revolutionary innovations which enable human beings to break with tradition and acquire new beliefs. In both cases an inherent indeterminacy is perceived in the creative forces which underlie human cultures.

Luscombe, David. The School of Peter Abelard Revisited. *Vivarium*, 30(1), 127-138, My 92.

Lusignan, Serge. La philosophie et son histoire: quelques réflexions à propos d'un livre récent de W J Courtenay. *Dialogue (Canada)*, 31(3), 495-507, Sum 92.

Lustig, Andrew. Natural Law, Property, and Justice: The General Justification of Property in Aquinas and Locke. *J Relig Ethics*, 19(1), 119-149, Spr 91.

This essay examines the justification of property offered by John Locke, considered as the *locus classicus* of the modern liberal understanding of natural law. I argue that Locke's account of property must be understood in light of the Scholastic discussion of property-in-common, especially in the writings of Thomas Aquinas and Francisco Suarez. Despite very different historical and intellectual settings, I suggest that the Scholastic and Lockean justifications of property share several themes: (1) both discuss the institution of property within the context of foundationally *social* natural law directives; (2) both emphasize the moral priority of individual access to property-in-common according to need; and (3) both employ the language of justice rather than discretionary charity to describe the social constraints upon private acquisition. I conclude by considering the relevance of this interpretation of Locke to recent debates on distributive justice between Nozick and Rawls, as well as its affinities with the understanding of the social obligations of property in Catholic social teaching.

Lustig, B Andrew (& other eds). *Bioethics Yearbook, Volume 2—Regional Developments in Bioethics: 1989-1991*. Dordrecht, Kluwer, 1992.

Volume 2 of *The Bioethics Yearbook* provides a comprehensive summary of recent international and regional developments on the following specific topics: new reproductive technologies, abortion, maternal-fetal conflicts, severely disabled newborns, consent to treatment and experimentation, confidentiality, equitable access to health care, ethical issues in cost-containment, withholding and withdrawing treatment, active euthanasia, the definition of death, and organ donation and transplantation. Internationally respected contributors report on the following sixteen areas: the US, Canada, Latin America, the United Kingdom and Ireland, France, the Netherlands, Germany/Austria/Switzerland, Eastern Europe, Spain/Portugal/Italy, Scandinavia, India, Southeast Asia, China, Japan, Australia/New Zealand, and the Council of Europe/EEC.

Lustig, B Andrew. The Method of 'Principlism': A Critique of the Critique. *J Med Phil*, 17(5), 487-510, O 92.

Lutz, Mark A. The Utility of Multiple Utility: A Comment on Brennan. *Econ Phil*, 9(1), 145-154, Ap 93.

This is a response to T Brennan on the new "multiple utility" frameworks in economics pioneered by Sen and further articulated by Hirschman and Etzioni (among others). In essence, Brennan felt that logic of rational choice theory was unassailable and that any movement in economics that is predicated on questioning the maximization postulate on logical grounds is doomed to failure. Against Brennan, it is argued that a multiple utility conception can be defended on logical grounds, and that it also has relevance in practical applications. It seeks to demonstrate that not all choice situations can be reduced to an algorithmic ranking procedure. This is evident in choices involving simultaneously other-regarding interests and self-interest, thereby causing problems of incompleteness or "overcompleteness." The upshot is that economic rationality has its limits, a conclusion that will undermine "economics imperialism." (edited)

Luüf, Reginald and Tijmes, Pieter. Modern Immaterialism. *Res Phil Technol*, 12, 271-284, 1992.

Lux, David. Societies, Circles, Academies, and Organizations in Revolution and Continuity, Barker, Peter (ed). Washington, Cath Univ Amer Pr, 1991.

Lyas, Colin. That to Philosophise is to Learn How to Die. *Phil Invest*, 16(2), 116-127, Ap 93.

This paper starts with an examination of Montaigne's Dictum that to philosophise is to learn how to die and investigates the ways in which philosophy might bear on the question of a good death.

Lycan, William G. Armstrong's New Combinatorialist Theory of Modality in Ontology, Causality and Mind: Essays in Honour of D M Armstrong, Bacon, John (ed). New York, Cambridge Univ Pr, 1993.

Lyddon, William J and McLaughlin, James T. Constructivist Psychology: A Heuristic Framework. *J Mind Behav*, 13(1), 89-107, Wint 92.

Psychologists representing a broad spectrum of psychological specialties use the term "constructivist" to characterize their theories and underscore individuals' active participation in reality-making. In spite of constructivism's apparent widespread influence on psychology, however, significantly different forms of constructivist metatheory may be identified when constructivist assumptions about causal processes are contrasted. Both Pepper's (1942) worldview framework and Aristotle's four-fold classification of causation in natural phenomena are used to distinguish four forms of constructivism—material, efficient, formal, and final. Salient examples of each form as evident in contemporary psychological theory are given with a discussion of implications of these distinctions for the development of a comprehensive conception of cognition and human knowing.

Lynch, Richard A. Bakhtin's Ethical Vision. *Phil Lit*, 17(1), 98-109, Ap 93.

This paper is an analysis of M M Bakhtin's account of "polyphony". Polyphony is a strongly democratic form of discourse, a dialogue between independent and autonomous individuals with equal rights and free from subordination. Polyphony is found illustrated in Dostoevsky's novels, but can be introduced, Bakhtin suggests, as an ethical standard or ideal in real discourses. This standard facilitates recognition of and action in accord with what some feminists have termed relations of "caring".

Lynch, William. Reply to Harbers and De Vries. *Soc Epistem*, 7(2), 209-211, Ap-Je 93.

Lynch, William. What Does the Double Hermeneutic Explain/Justify?. *Soc Epistem*, 7(2), 193-204, Ap-Je 93.

Lyng, Stephen. *Holistic Health and Biomedical Medicine: A Countersystem Analysis*. Albany, SUNY Pr, 1992.

Lyons, D. Adam Smith's Aesthetic of Conduct. *Int J Moral Soc Stud*, 8(1), 41-60, Spr 93.

Most readers see Smith's *Theory of Moral Sentiments* as a book about ethics. But most of the analysis there is about judgments of splendid vs pathetic conduct (the aesthetics of conduct) rather than about ethical judgments of guilty or innocent conduct. The thesis is defended here that 'moral' in the book's title is equivalent to 'normative': the treatise is about approvals/disapprovals of human conduct whether these are moral or aesthetic judgments. Smith asked precise questions about when admiration or contempt, pride or humiliation, are warranted. An implicit disagreement is uncovered between Smith and Plato over this issue: how should we judge, on reflection, the seeming lustre of traits like bravery and cleverness and self-discipline, when these traits are displayed in imprudent or wicked projects?

Lyons, David. *Moral Aspects of Legal Theory*. New York, Cambridge Univ Pr, 1993.

This volume comprises ten essays in legal philosophy written over a period of twenty years. Five of the essays concern the relations between law and moral principle and emphasize the fragility of connections between law and justice. One essay considers the distinctive claims of classic American jurisprudence. Four essays address problems and current theories of legal interpretation. They argue that law should be interpreted so as to increase the moral justifiability of its applications. The last essay in this collection, previously unpublished, compares Dworkin's "constructive interpretation" with analysis associated with the critical legal studies movement.

Lyons, William. *Emoción*. Barcelona, Anthropos, 1993.

Lyons, William. Intentionality and Modern Philosophical Psychology, III—The Appeal to Teleology. *Phil Psych*, 5(3), 309-326, 1992.

This article is the sequel to 'Intentionality and Modern philosophical psychology, I. The modern reduction of intentionality', (Philosophical Psychology, 3 (2), 1990) which examined the view of intentionality pioneered by Carnap and reaching its apotheosis in the work of Daniel Dennett. In 'Intentionality and modern philosophical psychology, II. The return to representation' (Philosophical Psychology, 4 (1), 1991) I examined the approach to intentionality which can be traced back to the work of Noam Chomsky but which has been given its canonical treatment in the work of Jerry Fodor. In this article, the last in the series, I explore a very recent approach to intentionality which has been associated especially with the work of Ruth Garrett Millikan and Colin McGinn, and might, if the phrase were not so rebarbative, be called "the biologizing of intentionality".

Lyons, William. The Tiger and His Stripes. *Analysis*, 44(2), 93-95, Mr 84.

This article is a response to Dennett's argument, in *Content and Consciousness*, that imagination does not involve anything like images. Against the background of arguing for the general principle, that "one cannot be more sophisticated visually in imagination than one is in perception itself", I argue that it makes no sense at all to try to "read off" the number of stripes from either a perceptual "freeze frame" or a visual-imagination one. To think otherwise is to understand neither perception nor imagination.

Lyotard, Jean-François. A l'insu (Unbeknownst) in Community at Loose Ends, Miami Theory Collect, (ed). Minneapolis, Univ of Minnesota Pr, 1991.

The purpose is to recall that something still remains untractable inside social and political tractations. Contracts do not exhaust community life ties. Nor structures do either. "May 1968" can be viewed as a precary surging of this something.

Lyotard, Jean-François. Sensus Communis in Judging Lyotard, Benjamin, Andrew (ed). New York, Routledge, 1992.

The purpose is to elaborate the status of this notion which is the core of Kantian Analytic of the Beautiful (*Critique of Judgment*) so that the traditionally anthropological reading must be evacuated to the benefit of the idea of a transcendental promise of attunement between the two faculties at work in the judgment of taste, understanding and imagination.

Lyotard, Jean-François and Constable, Elizabeth (trans). Mainmise. *Phil Today*, 36(4), 419-427, Wint 92.

Lyotard, Jean-François and Larochelle, Gilbert. That Which Resists, After All. *Phil Today*, 36(4), 402-417, Wint 92.

Lyotard, Jean-Françoise. Presence in The Language of Art History, Kemal, Salim (ed). New York, Cambridge Univ Pr, 1991.

Lysenko, Victoria. On Certain Intellectual Stereotypes in Buddhist Studies as Exemplified in T Stcherbatsky's Works. *J Indian Counc Phil Res*, 9(2), 87-93, Ja-Ap 92.

Lysenko, Victoria G. Comparative Philosophy in the Soviet Union. *Phil East West*, 42(2), 309-326, Ap 92.

Analyzing the East-West comparisons of some modern Russian orientalists, the author comes to classify them into 1) those revealing the parallels in development of philosophical ideas in different civilizations, 2) those aiming at a more profound understanding of only one particular tradition, while taking others as a kind of unquestioned background. As in Russia today, the East-West problem proves to be a vital matter of cultural self-identification, rather than an issue of purely scholastic interest, the author argues that the majority of Russian orientalists, in much more degree than their Western colleagues, disclose in their comparisons a culturally bounded existential interest.

Ma, Terence P and Tuohey, John. Fifteen Years After "Animal Liberation": Has the Animal Rights Movement Achieved Philosophical Legitimacy?. *J Med Human*, 13(2), 79-89, Sum 92.

Fifteen years ago, Peter Singer published "Animal Liberation: A New Ethics for Our Treatment of Animals". In it, he proposed to end "the tyranny of humans over nonhuman animals" by "thinking through, carefully, and consistently, the question of how we ought to treat animals" (p. ix). On this anniversary of the book's publication, a critical analysis shows that the logic he presents, though popularly appealing, is philosophically flawed. Though influential in slowing and in some cases stopping biomedical research involving animals, the animal rights movement in the United States has yet to offer a clear and compelling argument for the equality of species.

Maas, Jörg F. Zur Rationalität des vermeintlich Irrationalen in Diagrammatik und Philosophie, Gehring, Petra (ed). Amsterdam, Rodopi, 1992.

The historical inspection of iconographic/diagrammatic models and their development shows that their plasticity and propositional conceptibility are commensurable and even follow the same principle of rational structures of thinking and representation.

MacBeth, Murray. 'Is' and 'Ought' in Context: MacIntyre's Mistake. *Hume Stud*, 18(1), 41-50, Ap 92.

I argue that, in 'Hume on "is" and "Ought"', Alasdair MacIntyre fails to appreciate that Hume's account of justice is explanatory rather than justificatory; I further argue that it is a dominant strategy of the *Treatise* to replace justification with explanation; and, since explanation is an 'is' concept and justification an 'ought' concept, MacIntyre's mistake is to fail to heed Hume's warning about the difference between 'is' and 'ought'.

MacCormick, Neil. Argumentation and Interpretation in Law. *Ratio Juris*, 6(1), 16-29, Mr 93.

The author proceeds from a brief elucidation of the concept "argumentation" through a more extended account of substantive reasons in pure practical argumentation and of institutional argumentation applying "authority reasons" as grounds for legal decisions to an initial account of the nature and place of legal interpretative reasoning. Then he explores the three main categories of interpretative arguments, linguistic arguments, systemic arguments and teleological/deontological arguments; and he examines the problem of conflicts of interpretation and their resolution. His conclusion is that legal argumentation is only partly autonomous since it has to be embedded within wider elements of practical argumentation.

MacCoull, L S B and Siorvanes, L. PSI XIV 1400: A Papyrus Fragment of John Philoponus. *Ancient Phil*, 12(1), 153-170, Spr 92.

Macdonald, Graham. The Nature of Naturalism—I. *Aris Soc*, Supp(66), 225-243, 1992.

MacDonald, Graham. Philosophical Foundations for Functional Sociology in Marx's Theory of History, Wetherly, Paul. Brookfield, Avebury, 1992.

MacDonald, Ray A. The Styles of Art History: Entities or Processes?. *J Speculative Phil*, 7(1), 48-63, 1993.

MacDonald, Scott. Christian Faith in Reasoned Faith, Stump, Eleonore (ed). Ithaca, Cornell Univ Pr, 1993.

This paper argues that Christian faith is a complex propositional attitude the primary components of which are a cognitive state (belief that the propositions definitive of Christianity are true) and a volitional state (love for God and commitment to God's purposes) based on the belief that Christianity is true. This analysis is used as a basis for rejecting some common misconceptions, including that having faith requires believing on weak or no evidence, that it requires epistemic certainty, that it is necessarily irrational, and that it requires that one have voluntary control over one's beliefs.

Macedo, Stephen. Charting Liberal Virtues. *Nomos*, 34, 204-232, 1992.

Liberalism contains positive ideals of citizenship, virtue, and community which provide the resources needed to mount a positive response to liberalism's republican and communitarian critics. Liberal theory does not suppose that self-interest or disagreement are the basic facts of social life, rather, it counts on a shared and overriding commitment to the values associated with liberal justice. These shared liberal values, which are far from neutral, splash pervasively across the canvas of a liberal society, shape both private and public life, and allow us to adumbrate a liberal way of life.

MacGill, Neil Whyte. Miracles and Conservation Laws. *Sophia (Australia)*, 31(1-2), 79-87, 1992.

In his book, "Water into Wine," Robert Larmer argues that miracles can occur as divine interventions in the world without involving any change or suspension of the laws of nature. They may do this by the direct creation or destruction of some of the basic 'stuff' of the universe, while it continues to conform to the unaltered laws. This paper, on the contrary, claims that conservation is essential to the concept of the 'stuff' as being basic, and that changes in its total quantity therefore undermine the laws of nature just as seriously as any other conflicting evidence.

Machan, Tibor R. Applied Ethics and Free Will: Some Untoward Results of Independence. *J Applied Phil*, 10(1), 59-72, 1993.

Is free will a necessity or a luxury for an understanding of applied ethics? This paper offers an argument for why it is the former. First some reasons are offered why applied ethics, under the influence of Rawls's metaethics, has eschewed the topic of free will. It is shown why this is a mistake—namely, how applied ethics will falter without such a theory. The paper then argues for a conception of free will and indicates what ethical and public policy implications may flow from this theory.

Machan, Tibor R. Between Parents and Children. *J Soc Phil*, 23(3), 16-22, Wint 92.

The crux of the argument is that by a process of rational reconstruction it is possible to explain that children ought to be raised with their talents and personal developments as the prime objective. Since parents "invite" children into their lives knowing they will be very needy beings, they commit themselves to supporting these children so as to grow up to be functional and possibly successful adults. Since children may be assumed to want to grow up well and this is possible only with parental support, they owe cooperation, obedience, etc.

Machan, Tibor R. Environmentalism Humanized. *Pub Affairs Quart*, 7(2), 131-147, Ap 93.

This is a defense of what may be called classical individualistic anthropocentrism and the environmental ethics/politics that it implies. Human individuals are of supreme importance in nature, it is argued, because of their capacity for the creation and production of a great variety and amount of values, i.e., life-enhancing and developing facilities, circumstances, etc. Human individuals are, thus, at the pinacle of life (so far as we know now) and an environmental ethics must adjust to this fact. Environmental politics, in turn, must adjust to the fact that human individuality is diverse and creative exploratory conduct by human beings, provided it does not involve dumping or trespassing, ought to given full legal protection.

Machan, Tibor R. How to Understand Eastern European Developments?. *Pub Affairs Quart*, 6(2), 169-179, Ap 92.

This paper argues that although Marxism need not consider the recent demise of the USSR's command economic system any sort of refutation of itself, there are independent reasons why Marxism does not suffice to make the best sense of those events. Indeed, the bourgeois individualist conception of human history, whereby individuals make significant, historically decisive choices (and face genuine alternatives from which to make such unpredictable choices), is a theoretically more powerful alternative. Eastern European developments are, then, the result of the combination of choices of individuals faced with the institutions that resulted from previous choices.

Machan, Tibor R. Response: Subjective Arbitrariness. *Vera Lex*, 11(2), 44, 1991.

When economists use "subjective" to designate values they may mean two different things—(a) "their own expressed evaluation of something," or (b) "values for which no objective justification is possible." If they mean (b) the problem arises that their own system will be no more than a bias. And the alternative need not be, as some claim, that values are *intrinsic*, i.e., a property of some goods or services standing entirely independently of those making the evaluation. *Objective* values may be relational, signifying a specific beneficial relationship between some goods or services and agents seeking these.

Machan, Tibor R. Some Reflections on Richard Rorty's Philosophy. *Metaphilosophy*, 24(1-2), 123-135, Ja-Ap 93.

The paper counters Rorty's antifoundationalism, first in terms of some internal problems that position encounters (for example, can one misrepresent Rorty's ideas in terms of his anti-representationalist views?), then with the support of a conception of knowledge modeled on "grasping" or "grabbing," suggested by the German "begriffen." Part 2 addresses Rorty's historicism and his solidarism, arguing that both self-destruct under scrutiny.

Machan, Tibor R. The Right to Privacy versus Uniformitarianism. *J Soc Phil*, 23(2), 75-84, Fall 92.

Catherine MacKinnon urges that the abortion debate not be conducted in terms of the individual rights of women but in terms of political power women as a class should be granted (or should seek and take). This paper argues that such a group or collectivist approach will fail because the individuality that supports the rights perspective is ontologically irreducible and even to attempt to argue it away leads one into paradoxes (e.g., one's individual creativity in proposing solutions and criticizing the work of others reasserts such individuality).

Machan, Tibor R. The Right to Private Property: Reply to Friedman. *Crit Rev*, 6(1), 97-106, Wint 92.

The principle of private property rights is defended based on: a) everyone's social need for a sphere of justidiction (Nozick's "moral space") and; b) the recognition that good judgment regarding available resources (in nature or the marketplace) deserves acknowledgment and social reward. This principle, in turn, is basic to others required for a morally meaningful social life (no free press, religious freedom, or democracy) is possible when it is systematically violated. (That the principle is "absolute" is beside the point—that merely *emphasizes* that it ought to be upheld consistently, fully, whenever possible.)

Machle, Edward. The Mind and the "Shen-ming" in Xunzi. *J Chin Phil*, 19(4), 361-386, D 92.

The article focuses on the sentence in *Xunzi* (Hsün Tzu), 21, "the mind is the ruler of the body *er* the *zhu* of its *shen-ming*," taking issue with the extant translations. The uses of the italicized chinese words are examined at some length, yielding the reading "as for the mind, it can be host to such a divine enhancement since it is a ruler, the ruler of the body". Consequences of such a translation for the interpretation of Xunzi's philosophy are suggested.

Machnacz, J. H Conrad-Martius und E Stein Husserls Schülerinen und aristotelisch-thomistische Philosophie (in Polish). *Stud Phil Christ*, 28(1), 87-103, 1992.

Conrad-Martius und Stein gehören zum Kreis der bagabtesten Husserls Schüler aus seiner Göttingener Zeit. Es ist darum interessante Frage, was haben sie von der aristotelischen und thomistischen Philosophie erhofft (1). Steins Interesse an der Philosophie des hl. Thomas sind durch ihr religiöses und wissenschaftliches Lebens verursacht und geprägt. Sie möchte wissen: mit welcher Methode wird in der Scholastik gearbeitet? Sie versucht zu zeigen, ob und wie weit Zusammenarbeit zwischen Philosophie Husserls und des hl. Thomas möglich ist (4). Conrad-Martius Theorie der transphysischen Wirklichkeit ist eine interessante Interpretation der organischen und unorganischen Natur, man kann sie aber nicht als Erneuerung oder Vertiefung der aristotelisch-thomistischen Philosophie verstehen. (edited)

Machover, Moshé. The Place of Nonstandard Analysis in Mathematics and in Mathematics Teaching. *Brit J Phil Sci*, 44(2), 205-212, Je 93.

The role of Nonstandard Analysis (NSA) as an *applied* branch of pure mathematics is emphasized. It is argued that NSA, while extremely useful as a heuristic and technical tool, cannot replace standard mathematics. This is due to the non-canonicity of nonstandard enlargements, even within a given ambient set theory. Nelson's "Radically Elementary" approach is discussed in this light.

Machover, Moshé and Felsenthal, Dan S. Sequential Voting by Veto: Making the Mueller-Moulin Algorithm More Versatile. *Theor Decis*, 33(3), 223-240, N 92.

MacIntosh, Duncan. Persons and the Satisfaction of Preferences: Problems in the Rational Kinematics of Values. *J Phil*, 90(4), 163-180, Ap 93.

If one can get the targets of one's current wants only by acquiring new wants (as in the Prisoner's Dilemma), is it rational to do so? Maybe not. For this could justify adopting unsatisfiable wants, violating the rational duty to maximize one's utility. Further, why cause a want's target if one will not then want it? And people *are* their wants. So if these change, people will not survive to enjoy their wants' targets. But one rationally need not advance one's future wants, only current ones; rational choice seeks not utility (the co-obtaining of a want and its target), but satisfaction (the eventual obtaining of what is now wanted); and persons survive *rational* changes of values. Otherwise, it would be irrational to care now about what happens after one dies. Thus reflection on the rational revision of values illuminates personal identity and the bases and aims of rational choice.

MacIntosh, Duncan. Preference-Revision and the Paradoxes of Instrumental Rationality. *Can J Phil*, 22(4), 503-529, D 92.

To the normal reasons we think can justify preferring something, *x* (*x* has objectively preferable properties, or ones one prefers things to have, or *x's* obtaining would advance one's preferences), I add: *preferring x* would advance one's preferences; one prefers *x* not because of properties of *x*, but of the *preference for x*. So revising one's preferences is rational in paradoxical choice situations (PCSs) like Kavka's Deterrence Paradox. Objections considered: this is stoicist, incoherent, bad faith; it conflates instrumental and intrinsic value, gives wrong solutions to PCSs, entails vicious regresses of value justification, falsifies value realism, makes valuing *x* unresponsive to *x's* properties, causes value conflict, conflicts with other standards of rationality, violates decision theory, counsels immorality, makes moral paradox, treats value change as voluntary, and conflates first- and second-order values; it is psychologically unrealistic; and PCSs never occur.

MacIntosh, J J. Reincarnation, Closest Continuers, and the Three Card Trick: A Reply to Noonan and Daniels. *Relig Stud*, 28(2), 235-251, Je 92.

This paper is a response to criticisms by Noonan and Daniels of my 'Reincarnation and Relativized Identity'. There I argued that the arguments for a certain kind of 'soul-less' reincarnation not only do but must fail, and in this paper I argue further that Noonan's defences (based on considerations of the closest continuer theory, and the multiple occupancy possibility) also fail. I further argue that Daniels's epistemological remarks, while by and large acceptable, fail to touch the basic position outlined in the earlier paper. Finally I discuss an argument of Davidson's further, albeit somewhat theoretical, difficulty for the reincarnationist.

Macintyre, Angus and Scowcroft, Philip. On the Elimination of Imaginaries from Certain Valued Fields. *Annals Pure Applied Log*, 61(3), 241-276, Je 93.

A nontrivial ring with unit eliminates imaginaries just in case its complete theory has the following property: every definable m-ary equivalence relation $E(x,y)$ may be defined by a formula $f(x)=f(y)$, where f is an m-ary definable function. We show that for certain natural expansions of the field of p-adic numbers, elimination of imaginaries fails or is independent of ZFC. Similar results hold for certain fields of formal power series.

MacIntyre, Alasdair. Colors, Cultures, and Practices. *Midwest Stud Phil*, 17, 1-23, 1992.

What conditions have to be satisfied for objectivity in judgments concerning color to be achieved? Can a solitary language-user achieve objectivity in such judgments? What resources does Wittgenstein provide on these matters? Do variations in the color vocabularies of different cultures provide grounds for relativism? Within what contexts of practice can one color vocabulary be judged superior to another? Answers are proposed to these questions.

MacIntyre, Alasdair. Plain Persons and Moral Philosophy: Rules, Virtues and Goods. *Amer Cath Phil Quart*, 66(1), 3-19, Wint 92.

A discussion of the relationship between the questions, assertions, and arguments of plain persons and those of moral philosophers, concerning how much of and what kind of moral philosopher a plain person needs to be. It is argued that plain persons are potentially Aristotelians, but that this potentiality is often frustrated by cultural circumstance.

MacIntyre, I D A. Manipulation under Majority Decision-Making When No Majority Suffers and Preferences Are Strict. *Theor Decis*, 35(2), 167-178, S 93.

Conditions are defined under the majority voting procedure under which manipulation does no harm to a majority, and when a majority benefit. The effect of introducing interpersonal comparability on the desirability of manipulation is discussed under Rawlsian justice and with preference intensities.

Mack, Eric. Of Transplants and Trolleys. *Phil Phenomenol Res*, 53(1), 163-167, Mr 93.

Mack, Eric. Personal Integrity, Practical Recognition, and Rights. *Monist*, 76(1), 101-118, Ja 93.

Mack, P. Valla's Dialectic in the North 2: Further Commentaries. *Vivarium*, 30(2), 256-275, N 92.

Lorenzo Valla's (1407-1457) *Repastinatio dialecticae et philosophiae* was the most radical revision of Aristotelian logic written in the fifteenth century. This article studies its influence on sixteenth-century logic in northern Europe. The five commentaries show considerable knowledge of Valla's doctrines, but none of them supports his most controversi

al views or presents his system as a whole. Northern logicians thought Valla an important scholar, with valuable opinions on Latin usage, who made many errors in logic. The article includes a list of points of disagreement between Valla and Rudolph Agricola (1444-1485) and a list of Aristotelian views rejected by Valla.

Mackenzie, Catriona. Abortion and Embodiment. *Austl J Phil*, 70(2), 136-155, Je 92.

This article develops a feminist defense of abortion which criticizes and departs from traditional feminist appeals to bodily autonomy that are based on proprietorial models of the body. The author's argument in defense of a woman's right to abortion focuses upon a number of interconnected considerations, including: an account of the kind of moral responsibility exercised in decision-making about abortion; a view of foetal worth as tied to both intrinsic and relational properties; and a phenomenologically-based interpretation of embodiment and bodily autonomy in pregnancy. On the basis of these considerations, she shows how proprietorial accounts of bodily autonomy can justify abortion only as a right to evacuation of the feotus from the uterus, and argues that, on the basis of the view of bodily-autonomy developed in the article, abortion can and should be justified as including the right to demand feotal death, nor merely feotal evacuation.

MacKenzie, J C. What the Good Samaritan Didn't Know. *J Value Inq*, 27(1), 39-41, Ja 93.

Mackey, James P. Moral Values as Religious Absolutes. *Philosophy*, 32(Supp), 145-160, 1992.

This work envisages an epistemology in which knowing how is the major part of knowing that. Since knowing how involves doing, or action under a conscious sense of obligation, it already involves morality. Hence an account of the elusive sense of obligation in action, construed in terms of Platonic Eros, serves as an account of the principal way in which we come to know reality. A different relationship between knowing and being, meaning and truth comes into views, different from that which seems to disintegrate when absolutes need to be envisaged.

Mackey, James P. Moral Values as Religious Absolutes in Philosophy, Religion and the Spiritual Life, McGhee, Michael (ed). New York, Cambridge Univ Pr, 1992.

Mackie, J L. Sidgwick's Pessimism in Essays on Henry Sidgwick, Schultz, Bart (ed). New York, Cambridge Univ Pr, 1992.

Mackie, Penelope. *Material Beings*—P Van Inwagen. *Phil Books*, 34(2), 75-82, Ap 93.

Mackie, Penelope. Causing, Delaying, and Hastening: Do Rains Cause Fires?. *Mind*, 101(403), 483-500, Jl 92.

Jonathan Bennett has pointed out that although we tend to regard hastening something as causing it, we do not tend to regard delaying something as causing it. The paper aims to explain this asymmetry. Following the rejection of various proposed explanations (including those suggested by Bennett and by Lawrence Lombard) it is argued that the asymmetry results from a difference in the ways in which delaying and hastening are related to preventing. The explanation is compatible both with the view that, in general, delaying is not causing, and with a pragmatic account of our reluctance to treat delaying as causing.

MacKinnon, D M. Ayer's Attack on Metaphysics in A J Ayer Memorial Essays, Griffiths, A Phillips (ed). New York, Cambridge Univ Pr, 1991.

Macklin, Ruth. Teaching Bioethics to Future Health Professionals: A Case-Based Clinical Model. *Bioethics*, 7(2-3), 200-206, Ap 93.

Teaching bioethics to future health professionals can take many forms. Based on more than a decade of experience teaching medical students and post-graduate trainees, the author favors a case-based clinical model. Illustrative cases from the author's experience are provided, drawn from prominent bioethical problems facing clinicians from different specialty areas of medicine.

Maclachlan, D L C. Strawson and the Argument for Other Minds. *J Phil Res*, 18, 149-157, 1993.

The classical argument for the existence of other minds begins by ascribing states of consciousness to oneself, and argues to the existence of other conscious beings on the basis of an analogy in bodily constitution and behavior. P F Strawson attacks the foundation of this argument. "One can ascribe states of the consciousness to oneself only if one can ascribe them to others. One can ascribe them to others only if one can identify other subjects of experience." My thesis is that this objection depends on running together the two distinct necessary conditions for ascribing states of consciousness. (edited)

MacLean-Tollefsen, Laurie. 'Intuition Pumps' and Contemporary Philosophy. *Lyceum*, 1(2), 61-67, Fall 89.

MacMillan, Robert. Marshall McLuhan at the Mercy of His Commentators. *Phil Soc Sci*, 22(4), 475-491, D 92.

Readers generally associate Marshall McLuhan with research in the theory of communications processes. Although his work attracted wide interest in the mid 1960s, it fell into comparative obscurity in the late seventies. McLuhan's fall from grace is attributed to theoretical flaws in his work. However, an appraisal of his critics suggests an alternative hypothesis. (edited)

Macnamara, John. Cognitive Psychology and the Rejection of Brentano. *J Theor Soc Behav*, 23(2), 117-137, Je 93.

Franz Brentano characterized the cognitive as those phenomena in which there is reference to something as an object. This is explained by reference to Aristotle. Brentano claimed access to cognitive states mainly through inner perception, which he distinguished from introspection. Inner perception is best understood as intuition. Brentano was set aside by biologically minded psychologists; even more so by behaviorists. Psycholinguistics did not set things to right, because of the emphasis on syntax rather than semantics. Nor did cognitive science with its commitment to computer models, because computers do not interpret their symbols as humans do. A brief sketch of cognition with reference as a primitive is offered.

Macpherson, Brian. Is It Possible that Belief Isn't Necessary?. *Notre Dame J Form Log*, 34(1), 12-28, Wint 93.

There has been a tradition in the history of doxastic logic of treating belief as analogous to necessity. The resulting logics presuppose that believers are "ideal", which is unacceptable in light of various counterexamples discussed in the literature. It is argued that Rantala's proposals to salvage the alleged analogy between necessity and belief fail. In addition, a logic that treats belief as analogous to possibility and a corresponding semantics motivated by Stalnaker's claim that agents can be in more than one belief state are developed. Although this logic and semantics are inconsistency-tolerant, new problems arise. Finally a modest though nontrivial belief logic is proposed which does not treat logic as possibility or necessity and which does not presuppose that agents' beliefs are consistent or deductively closed.

MacPherson, C B (ed) and Hobbes, Thomas. *Leviathan—Thomas Hobbes*. New York, Penguin USA, 1993.

Macquarrie, John. The Logic of Religious and Theological Language. *J Dharma*, 17(3), 169-177, Jl-S 92.

Maczka, Janusz. Epistemological Foundations of the Evolution of Science According to Carl F Von Weizäcker (in Polish). *Stud Phil Christ*, 27(2), 31-47, 1991.

Carl F von Weizsäcker in his theory of the unity of nature formulated general metascientific principles underlying the growth of science. In this approach he avoided both empiricism and radical rationalism to defend a platonically oriented vision of the growth of scientific theories. In expounding the tenets of this approach, the paper places Weizsäcker's philosophic contributions against the background of these metascientific theories that prevail in the contemporary philosophy of science.

Madanes, Leiser. How to Undo Things with Words: Spinoza's Criterion for Limiting Freedom of Expression. *Hist Phil Quart*, 9(4), 401-408, O 92.

Madden, Edward H. Cosmic Doing and Undoing Without End: Chauncey Wright's Idea of Ultimate Reality and Meaning. *Ultim Real Mean*, 16(1-2), 27-44, Mr-Je 93.

I endeavor to clarify Chauncey Wright's concept of ultimate meaning in three areas—cosmology, epistemology, and ethics. He based his naturalistic, non-directional world view on conservation laws and an original interpretation of the second law of thermodynamics. In epistemology he held that sense-data are neutral in nature and are classified as objective or subjective only by reflection upon them. In ethics he stressed the indispensable significance of moral rules.

Madden, Edward H. Ralph Waldo Emerson and Theodore Parker: A Comparative Study. *Trans Peirce Soc*, 29(2), 179-209, Spr 93.

Madden, Edward H and Madden, Marian C. Philosophical Biography: The American Scene. *Trans Peirce Soc*, 28(4), 609-643, Fall 92.

Philosophical biography has been a thriving enterprise in America though scholars have given insufficient attention to conflicing views about what constitutes legitimate philosophical biography. In contention we find the classical view, psychobiography, and milieu analysis, all have diametrically opposed presuppositions. These conflicting views have never been defined carefully, and changes within them have not been carefully noted. Our aim is to rectify, at least to some extent, these long standing deficiencies.

Madden, Marian C and Madden, Edward H. Philosophical Biography: The American Scene. *Trans Peirce Soc*, 28(4), 609-643, Fall 92.

Philosophical biography has been a thriving enterprise in America though scholars have given insufficient attention to conflicing views about what constitutes legitimate philosophical biography. In contention we find the classical view, psychobiography, and milieu analysis, all have diametrically opposed presuppositions. These conflicting views have never been defined carefully, and changes within them have not been carefully noted. Our aim is to rectify, at least to some extent, these long standing deficiencies.

Maddux, R D. The Origin of Relation Algebras in the Development and Axiomatization of the Calculus of Relations. *Stud Log*, 50(3-4), 421-455, S-D 91.

The calculus of relations was created and developed in the second half of the nineteenth century by Augustus De Morgan, Charles Sanders Peirce, and Ernst Schröder. In 1940 Alfred Tarski proposed an axiomatization for a large part of the calculus of relations. In the next decade Tarski's axiomatization led to the creation of the theory of relation algebras, and was shown to be incomplete by Roger Lyndon's discovery of nonrepresentable relation algebras. This paper introduces the calculus of relations and the theory of relation algebras through a review of these historical developments.

Maddux, Roger D. Relation Algebras of Every Dimension. *J Sym Log*, 57(4), 1213-1229, D 92.

An equation of the De Morgan-Peirce-Schröder calculus of relations is said to be "n-provable" (for an integer $n$less than or equal to 3) if the sequent expressing the equation has a proof (in a special sequent calculus designed for such equations) that contains no sequent with more than n variables. It was previous known that for infinitely many integers $n$less than or equal to 3 there are equations that are n-provable but not (n+1)-provable. This paper extends this result to *every* integer $n$less than or equal to 3 by constructing a finite relation algebra of dimension n that is not a relation algebra of dimension n+1.

Maddy, Penelope. Indispensability and Practice. *J Phil*, 89(6), 275-289, Je 92.

This paper examines the efficacy of the familiar indispensability arguments for the existence of mathematical entities. It suggests that these arguments rest on inaccurate portrayals of scientific and mathematical practice.

Madell, Geoffrey. Personal Identity and the Idea of a Human Being in Human Beings, Cockburn, David (ed). New York, Cambridge Univ Pr, 1991.

Madigan, Arthur R. 'Eth Nic 9.8: Beyond Egoism and Altruism? in Essays in Ancient Greek Philosophy, IV, Anton, John P (ed). Albany, SUNY Pr, 1991.

To reconcile self-love and self-sacrifice Aristotle appeals to the noble and to the satisfaction of intellect. Ambiguities in these notions lead to different possible interpretations of his arguments, none fully satisfactory. Aristotle did not solve the problem of egoism and altruism; his notions of nobility and intellect make it difficult even to pose that problem in the first place.

Madigan, Timothy J. John Dewey and *A Common Faith*. *Free Inq*, 13(1), 24-25, Wint 92-93.

John Dewey was a critic of dualisms. Yet his own distinction in "A Common Faith" between "religious" and "religion" was itself a type of dualism.

Madison, G B. Merleau-Ponty Alive. *Man World*, 26(1), 19-44, Ja 93.

Madison, G B. Merleau-Ponty's Destruction of Logocentrism in Merleau-Ponty Vivant, Dillon, M C (ed). Albany, SUNY Pr, 1991.

Madison, Gary B (ed). *Working Through Derrida*. Evanston, Northwestern Univ Pr, 1993.

Männikkö, Nancy Farm. If a Tree Falls in the Forest: A Refutation of Technological Determinism. *Res Phil Technol*, 12, 213-227, 1992.

This paper employs a case study from industrial forestry to debunk the notions of technological determinism and idyllic pastoralism. It is a response to simplistic interpretations of Langdon Winner's book, *Autonomous Technology*, and argues strenuously for the social control of technology and innovation. The author argues that notions such as Albert Borgmann's "device paradigm" serve as rationalizations for the avoidance of individual responsibility. She concludes by emphasizing that problems such as environmental degradation are driven not by technology, but instead by market forces and consumer demand.

Maesschalck, Marc. L'idéalisme allemand face à la raison théologique. *Laval Theol Phil*, 49(2), 309-320, Je 93.

L'auteur se propose d'indiquer comment en arriver à mieux saisir les enjeux épistémologiques des débats de l'idéalisme allemand avec la rationalité théologique.

Maesschalck, Marc. Philosophie et révélation dans l'idéalisme allemand: Un bilan. *Frei Z Phil Theol*, 39(1-2), 39-60, 1992.

The evolution of Fichte's, Schelling's and Hegel's idealistic systems is bound to the way they shall try to conceive, after Kant, the criticism of the relations of the finite conscience with an "absolute manifestation", inherent in Christianity. Therefore, the Christian revelation is considered, from an anthropological angle, as an event befalling in the historical framework of the human destiny, and challenging liberty, in its effort of realization. This approach to the religions phenomenon, according to a philosophy of history, is common to the famous idealists and shall equally arouse the question of the absolute Being in the late Fichte, the one of the absolute will in the late Schelling or the one of the absolute Spirit in the Hegel of maturity. The revelation of the Absolute remains so an essential key to understand those routes of thinking, whether as a source (*archè*), or an aim (*eschaton*), or again, an accomplishment (*parousia*) of the finite existence.

Maffie, James. Realism, Relativism, and Naturalized Meta-Epistemololgy. *Metaphilosophy*, 24(1-2), 1-13, Ja-Ap 93.

Meta-epistemological naturalists look for epistemology in the conjunction of contingent, *a posteriori* facts about human beings and their environment. They eschew appeals to intrinsically rational ends or principles, pre-existing epistemic reality, or divine imperative. Yet without such constraints, relativism appears irresistible. Naturalist epistemic realism cuts between absolutism and relativism by embracing legislative anti-realism plus adjudicative realism. Our legislating epistemic ends is contingent. However subsequent to our legislation there emerges an evidential practice-independent fact of the matter regarding the epistemic status of our cognitive activity. Epistemic properties are neither absolute nor relative but relational.

Magee, Bryan. Scenes from My Childhood. *Philosophy*, 33(Supp), 165-180, 1992.

Magee, Bryan. Scenes from My Childhood in The Impulse to Philosophise, Griffiths, A Phillips (ed). New York, Cambridge Univ Pr, 1992.

The author tells how he became fascinated in childhood by some of the fundamental problems of philosophy without realizing that this is what they were: the antimonies of time and space, the problem of motion, free will, the representative nature of perception, the impossibility of proving the existence of an external world. This paper is also the first chapter and a projected book, whose aim is to tackle basic philosophical problems as existentially encountered rather than as subjects for academic discussion.

AUTHOR INDEX WITH ABSTRACTS 577 Makarushka, Irena

Maggi, Michele. Un libro tedesco su Gramsci. *G Crit Filosof Ital*, 71(1), 119-128, Ja-Ap 92.

The article examines a recent study of Gramsci's thought (J Ranke, *Marxismus und Historismus*, Frankfurt am Main 1989). In Maggi's evaluation, the general research position taken in this book, is relative to the Gramscian theory of the essential characteristics of modern revolutionary ideology in its interweaving of historicism and its choice of palingenesis. It gathers only in part the analyses of the German scholar regarding the relations between the "filosofia della prassi" of Gramsci and the philosophy of Gentile and Croce. In particular, it emphasizes the conceptual difference between the historicism of Gramsci and that of Croce.

Magnavacca, Silvia. Una voz por la paz en el siglo XV: La noción humanística de concordia. *Rev Filosof (Argentina)*, 6(1-2), 37-56, N 92.

Magnell, Thomas. Evaluations as Assessments, Part I: Properties and Their Signifiers. *J Value Inq*, 27(1), 1-11, Ja 93.

The first of two successful articles, Part I sets out two basic distinctions that can be used for rethinking how evaluative assertions differ from non-evaluative assertions. One distinction concerns two ways to signify properties. Properties may be signified either by independent signifiers or by dependent signifiers. The other distinction concerns two kinds of properties, intrinsic properties and extrinsic properties. That distinction is contrasted with three different dichotomies of properties as accidental or essential, as relational or non-relational, and as supervenient or non-supervenient. The distinctions drawn here between properties and their signifiers are put to use in a successive article, "Evaluations as Assessments, Part II: Classifying Adjectives, Distinguishing Assertions, and Instancing Good of a Kind".

Magnell, Thomas. Evaluations as Assessments, Part II: Classifying Adjectives, Distinguishing Assertions, and Instancing Good of a Kind. *J Value Inq*, 27(2), 151-163, Ap 93.

The second of two successive articles, "Evaluations as Assessments, Part II" make use of several distinctions that provide grounds for rethinking just where evaluative assertions fit within the class of assertions. Adjectives are distinguished according to their role and work. Adjectives may play semantically predicative or semantically attributive roles. Adjectives may semantically work extensionally or intensionally. The latter distinction coincides with two distinctions about properties and their signifiers drawn in "evaluations as Assessments, Part I." Together, the three distinctions serve to characterize two types of assertions, claims and assessments. Evaluations using good of a kind share the characteristics of assessments. Non-cognitivists have argued as if the characteristics are peculiarities of evaluative assertions. But many non-evaluative, plainly factual assertions share the characteristics as well. This indicated the philosophical importance of recognizing evaluations as assessments.

Magnus, Bernd. Postmodern Philosophy and Politics. *Hist Euro Ideas*, 16(4-6), 561-567, Ja 93.

Magnus, Bernd and Stewart, Stanley and Mileur, Jean-Pierre. *Nietzsche's Case: Philosophy as/and Literature*. New York, Routledge, 1992.

This jointly-authored study of Nietzsche and his literary interlocutors occupies the interface of philosophy and literature, bringing conventionally marked "philosophical" and "literary" texts into conversation with one another in a way never done before. Nietzsche's texts are brought into productive conversation with the New Testament and texts by Sidney, Bacon, Spenser, Milton, Shakespeare, Browning, Coleridge, Wordsworth, Blake, Caryle, Lawrence, as well as with the standard texts of the philosophical and critical traditions from Plato to Derrida.

Magtrayo, Carlos R. The Methodological Compatibility of Natural Law Theory and Legal Positivism. *Vera Lex*, 11(2), 25-27, 1991.

Mahalingam, Indira. Languageless Creatures and Communication in Logical Foundations, Mahalingam, Indira (ed). New York, St Martin's Pr, 1991.

H P Grice's account of meaning that does not presuppose language as its vehicle in his paper 'Meaning' opens up the possibility of ascribing communication to languageless creatures. The paper examines how sense can be made of communication between languageless creatures on the basis of languageless creatures having a conception of themselves as having intentions and beliefs and a conception of others as like themselves in having intentions and beliefs.

Mahalingam, Indira (ed) and Carr, Brian (ed). *Logical Foundations*. New York, St Martin's Pr, 1991.

The essays in this collection were written to mark the occasion of D J O'Connor's 75th birthday. They constitute a celebration of his work in philosophy as a major defender of the logical empiricist tradition which has its roots in the philosophy of John Locke and David Hume. These essays—with very few exceptions—were specially written for this volume. Each essay takes up a central question of philosophy such as logical paradox, deductive and inductive inference, language and rationality, machine intelligence, human freedom and issues in social philosophy.

Maher, Lisa and Von Hirsch, Andrew. Can Penal Rehabilitationism be Revived?. *Crim Just Ethics*, 11(1), 25-30, Wint-Spr 92.

The article deals with recent proposals to revive rehabilitation as the basis for criminal sentencing. After pointing out that penal treatment programs tend to be effective for only special subgroups of offenders, and that treatment-based sentences are not necessarily milder than proportionate ones, the article deals with the questions of fairness that arise when rehabilitation is made the basis for sentencing. Foremost among those fairness questions, the article points out, is the tendency of rehabilitation-based sentences to disregard the degree of blameworthiness of the conduct in determining the sentence.

Maher, Patrick. *Betting on Theories: Cambridge Studies in Probability, Induction, and Decision Theory*. New York, Cambridge Univ Pr, 1993.

An interpretation of Bayesian decision theory is articulated and defended. It is argued that this decision theory provides the most solid foundations for Bayesian confirmation theory, including principles of diachronic rationality. A notion of acceptance of a theory is then defined and shown to be irreducible to that of probability, yet needed in Bayesian philosophy of science. A decision-theoretic account of rational acceptance is provided, supported by a representation theorem. This account is used to give subjective definitions of such scientific values as information and verisimiltude, and to illuminate the scientific realism debate.

Maher, Patrick. Howson and Franklin on Prediction. *Phil Sci*, 60(2), 329-340, Je 93.

Evidence for a hypothesis typically confirms the hypothesis more if the evidence was predicted than if it was accommodated. Or so I argued in previous papers, where I also developed an analysis of why this should be so. But this was all a mistake if Howson and Franklin (1991) are to be believed. In this paper, I show why they are not to be believed. I also identify a grain of truth that may have been dimly grasped by those Bayesians who deny the confirmatory value of prediction.

Mahon, Joseph. Existentialism, Feminism and Simone de Beauvoir. *Hist Euro Ideas*, 17(5), 651-658, S 93.

There is an influential viewpoint, championed by Mary Warnock among others, that Simone de Beauvoir always remained loyal to an austere 1940s existentialism which Sartre had progressively abandoned in his intellectual and political voyage towards Marxism from the 1950s onwards. But detailed analysis of de Beauvoir's 1940s writings discloses sharp divergences with Sartrian existentialism, as de Beauvoir undertook her own voyage towards existentialist feminism. The extent of the philosophical divergence between them is at least partly responsible, I argue, for de Beauvoir's embarrassed repudiation of some of these writings in her memoirs.

Mahon, Michael. *Foucault's Nietzschean Genealogy: Truth, Power, and the Subject*. Albany, SUNY Pr, 1992.

This is a study of the impact of Nietzsche's writings on the thought of Michel Foucault. Focusing on the notion of genealogy in the thought of both Nietzsche and Foucault, it explores the three genealogical axes—truth, power, and the subject—as they gradually emerge in Foucault's writings. This complex of axes into which Foucault was drawn, especially as a result of his early history of madness, called forth his explicit adoption of a Nietzschean approach to his future work. An examination of Foucault's explicit methodological statements reveals that there is no chase between Foucault's archaeological writings and his genealogies. The work concludes with an analysis of Foucault's final writings on the genealogy of modern subjectivity and an examination of how truth, power, and the subject operate for the modern psychoanalytic subject of desire.

Mahon, Michael. Michel Foucault's Archaeology, Enlightenment, and Critique. *Human Stud*, 16(1-2), 129-141, Ap 93.

Mahoney, Timothy. Do Plato's Philosopher-Rulers Sacrifice Self-Interest to Justice?. *Phronesis*, 37(3), 265-282, 1992.

This paper elucidates the conception of self-interest at work in the *Republic* and demonstrates that being just is essential to one's own self-interest, whether one conceives of justice as a *psychic* virtue, i.e., each part of the soul fulfilling its proper function for the good of the soul as a whole, or as a *social* virtue, i.e., each person in a society fulfilling his or her proper function for the good of society as a whole.

Maier, Robert and Bos, Jaap. The Name of the Game: An Analysis of the Grünbaum Debate. *Commun Cog*, 25(4), 295-323, 1992.

This paper aims at analyzing the discussions in "Behavioral and Brain Sciences", vol. 25, nr. 4 (1992) about the 1984 book "The Foundations of Psycho-Analysis" by A Grünbaum. In a "normative method of classification in four steps", the authors discern a number of different argumentative attitudes (mediative, judicious, contentious and irrelevant). The main results of this study are: 1) many of those invited to deliver a contribution does not in fact enter the arena of debate, 2) all contributions contain polemic devices, and 3) only a very limited number of participants enter into a 'real argumentation' with Grünbaum.

Maiocchi, Roberto. Duhem et l'atomisme. *Rev Int Phil*, 46(182), 376-389, 1992.

Majer, Ulrich. Hilberts Methode der Idealen Elemente und Kants regulativer Gebrauch der Ideen. *Kantstudien*, 84(1), 51-77, 1993.

Hilbert's method of ideal elements is explained and compared with Kant's notion of ideas of reason as regulative principles which unify and simplify a field of operations. To be more concrete: The method of ideal elements is a method of domain-extension in order to eliminate boundary rules to which the operations are submitted in the smaller domain. By this method Hilbert justifies the principle of excluded middle and thereby the notion of the "infinite" as a regulative idea.

Majer, Ulrich. Weyls Kritik an Dedekinds Zahlbegriff. *Dialectica*, 46(2), 141-149, 1992.

Zunächst wird Dedekinds Charakterisierung der Reihe der natürlichen Zahlen als *einfaches unendliches System* mittels des Begriffes der *Kette* vorgestellt und gezeigt, dass diese Charakterisierung einen grossen Vorteil, aber auch einen entscheidenden Nachteil hat: Der Vorteil besteht darin, dass bei Dedekind nicht mehr—wie noch bei Frege—die *einzelne* Zahl, sondern die ganze, *unendliche Reihe* der natürlichen Zahlen zum Gegenstand der logischen Analyse gemacht wird. Der Nachteil besteht darin, dass Dedekind die unendliche Reihe der Zahlen als fertig vorliegende Gesamtheit und nicht als etwas im *Entstehen* befindliches betrachtet. Hieran knüpft Weyls Kritik an. Abschliessend wird argumentiert, dass Dedekind der Weylschen Kritik hätte Rechnung tragen können, ohne den Vorteil der strukturalistischen Kennzeichnung aufgeben zu müssen, wenn er sich an seine eigene frühere, mehr *dynamische* Betrachtungsweise gehalten hätte, dergemäss die Zahlen von uns *erzeugt* und nicht vorgefunden werden.

Major, L and Sobotka, M and Znoj, M. The Relation of Man and Nature in Modern Philosophy (in Czechoslovakian). *Filozof Cas*, 39(6), 975-991, 1991.

Makarushka, Irena. Reflections on the 'Other' in Dinesen, Kierkegaard and Nietzsche in Kierkegaard on Art and Communication, Pattison, George (ed). New York, St Martin's Pr, 1992.

This essay explores two competing views of the 'other' within the context of Dinesen's "Babette's Feast." Kierkegaard and Nietzsche offer competing perspectives on the significance of the 'other.' Whereas Kierkegaard conceives of difference and otherness negatively, Nietzsche affirms difference. The value they attribute the difference or the 'other' informs their attitude toward desire, pleasure and duty and reflects their perception of the role of ambiguity in experience and their understanding of the relationship between art and religious discourse. "Babett's Feast" represents the tension present in the contrasting views of Kierkegaard and Nietzsche. Dinesen's representation of the 'other' suggest an attitude closer to Nietzsche's and echoes a feminist understanding of the relationship between virtue and the creative spirit.

Maker, William A. (Postmodern) Tales from the Crypt: The Night of the Zombie Philosophers. *Metaphilosophy*, 23(4), 311-328, O 92.

This essay argues that certain postmodernists, especially Rorty, can be described as zombie philosophers in the style of Romero's *Night of the Living Dead*: they are dead, because they claim they are not doing philosophy; but alive, because they argue philosophically for the death of philosophy. Additionally, they resurrect physically dead philosophers in order to parade their philosophical demise as a way of recruiting new zombies. I conclude by arguing that the zombie philosophers are themselves stalked by the dead philosophers they wish to enslave as zombies, and suggest a notion of philosophy which can avoid the ghoulish entrapments of these zombies.

Maker, William A. Hegel's Critique of Marx: The Fetishism of Dialectics in Hegel and His Critics, Desmond, William J (ed). Albany, SUNY Pr, 1989.

Marx claims that his philosophy is rooted in the correct understanding of dialectics which he achieved by eliminating Hegel's idealistic errors. This essay turns Marx on his head by showing: 1) That it is Hegel who properly grasps the nature and limits of dialectical theory (although this is usually not recognized). 2) That it is Marx who commits the idealistic fallacy by ignoring these limits in his claim to discover dialectics in reality. 3) That this move fetishizes dialectics and undermines the possibility of a coherent and legitimate critical theory.

Makhabane, T E and Maphala, T G T and Ramose, Mogobe B. In Search of a Workable and Lasting Constitutional Change in South Africa. *Quest*, 5(2), 4-31, D 91.

Makin, Stephen. The Ontological Argument Defended. *Philosophy*, 67(260), 247-255, Ap 92.

Maksimova, L. Amalgamation and Interpolation in Normal Modal Logics. *Stud Log*, 50(3-4), 457-471, S-D 91.

This is a survey of results on interpolation in propositional normal modal logics. Interpolation properties of these logics are closely connected with amalgamation properties of varieties of modal algebras. Therefore, the results on interpolation are also reformulated in terms of amalgamation.

Malament, David B. Critical Notice: Itamar Pitowsky's *Quantum Probability-Quantum Logic*. *Phil Sci*, 59(2), 300-320, Je 92.

A critical overview of Pitowsky's book is offered with particular attention to three topics: (1) Pitowsky's geometric analysis of Bell-type inequalities; (2) his account of "quantum logic"; (3) his claim that the theorems of Kochen-Specker and Bell do *not* rule out all interesting local, non-contextualist hidden variable theories.

Malcolm, John F. On the Endangered Species of the *Metaphysics*. *Ancient Phil*, 13(1), 79-93, Spr 93.

This article undertakes to show that, despite the assertion in Zeta 13 of Aristotle's *Metaphysics* to the effect that no universal is substance, species, though universals, may be considered in the *Metaphysics* to be non-primary substances and hence may be regarded as existent entities therein. My strategy is to explain away those passages which say that universals are not substances as in fact to be claiming that no universals are primary substances. The result is that the doctrines presented in the *Metaphysics* are a development of those in the *Categories* rather than a repudiation thereof.

Malcolm, Norman. Language Without Conversation. *Phil Invest*, 15(3), 207-214, Jl 92.

Malcolm, Norman. 'I Believe that *P*' in John Searle and His Critics, Lepore, Ernest (ed). Cambridge, Blackwell, 1991.

Malcolmson, Patrick and Myers, Richard. Technology and Mother Earth: The Rousseauian Roots of the Debate. *J Dharma*, 18(2), 162-173, Ap-Je 93.

Feminimism and environmentalism have spawned a new enthusiasm for the old pagan idea of "Mother Earth." The thesis of this article is that the main inspiration for this enthusiasm is to be found in Romanticism, and that serious reflection about "Mother Earth" therefore demands a return to the thought of the philosophical founder of Romanticism, Jean-Jacques Rousseau. This study of Rousseau's *Discourse on the Origins of Inequality* suggests that for Rousseau, there is no getting "back to nature" in any more than a superficial way. It also suggests that for Rousseau, technology cannot easily be "revalued" since it is motivated primarily by an ineradicable feature of post-state of nature humanity: *amour-propre*.

Maldamé, J M. Place de l'homme dans la nature. *Rev Thomiste*, 92(4), 871-891, O-D 92.

Malebranche, Nicolas and Walton, Craig (trans). *Treatise on Ethics (1684)*. Dordrecht, Kluwer, 1993.

Malherbe, Jean-François. "Saisir Dieu en son vestiaire": L'articulation theologique du sens chez Maître Eckhart. *Laval Theol Phil*, 49(2), 201-213, Je 93.

L'étude que Jean Ladrière a consacrée au *langage des spirituels* a donné à la lecture que nous avons faite de l'oeuvre allemande de Maître Eckhart ses clés d'intelligibilité: *métaphoricité*, dynamique des contradictions dans la *vection symbolique* et *interanimation sémantique* des phrases. Il en est résulté une approache particulière de la théologie négative qui perçoit la signifiance propre de la prédication du mystique rhénan au travers de l'image du *peintre iconoclaste*: nous ne pouvons pas ne pas mal parler de Dieu, s'est un fait; mais c'est moins une raison de se taire que de continuer à en mal parler en toute lucidité et révérence. Une importance particulière est reconnue au thème de la souffrance conçue non pas comme une substance maléfique à éradiquer de l'existence humaine, mais comme une force à apprivoiser pour en inverser la logique infernale et la transvaluer en *plus rapide coursier vers la perfection*.

Mali, Joseph. *The Rehabilitation of Myth*. New York, Cambridge Univ Pr, 1992.

Malinas, Gary. Reflective Coherence and Newcomb Problems: A Simple Solution. *Theor Decis*, 35(2), 151-166, S 93.

Assignments of greater expected value to dominated options in Newcomb problems are analyzed as manifestations of reflective incoherence. The prospect of a greater reward by choosing a dominated option is illusory, since any "ill gotten", i.e., irrational, gains can be leeched away by submitting the agent to a dynamic Dutch Book. In the Appendix, a proof is given which shows that if the agent is to avoid the Dutch Book in Newcomb situations, his degrees of belief are reflectively coherent if and only if his desirabilities at the time of choice align with his desirabilities at the time of action.

Mall, Ram Adhar. Hermeneutik, Interkulturalität und die Postmoderne. *Conceptus*, 25(65), 3-22, 1991.

The main concern of this paper is a renewed reflection of the intercultural and hermeneutical challenges of the different continents and cultural worlds in our "Weltalter" (World-Age, M Scheler), and to formulate a hermeneutical approach adequate to this situation which *de facto* is hermeneutical. Such an approach has to be situated beyond the concepts of identity (modernism) as well as difference (postmodernism). It consists of the more or less present transitions and overlappings between culturally creative areas. It is the essential insight of this approach that understanding and wanting to be understood are the two sides of the same hermeneutical medal.

Malla, N. Causality, Meaning and Culture. *Indian Phil Quart*, 19(2), 127-137, Ap 92.

The purpose of the work is to present a critical analysis of Pitirim Sorokin's views on culture and society. In fact, the attempt has been made to give a defence to Sorokin by way of explicating his views. Accordingly, the following conclusions have been reached. Culture is a system of meanings or ideas. They are non-material in nature. As such, culture cannot be adequately explained in terms of causality. Culture being non-material in nature, can be adequately understood only through non-causal analysis.

Malloy, David C and Lang, Donald L. An Aristotelian Approach to Case Study Analysis. *J Bus Ethics*, 12(7), 511-516, Jl 93.

The purpose of this paper is to apply Aristotle's theory of causation to the administrative realm in an attempt to provide the manager/student with a more complete basis for organizational analysis. The authors argue that the traditional approach to administrative case studies limits the manager's/student's perspective to the positivistic world view at the expense of a more encompassing perspective which can be achieved through the use of an Aristotelian approach. Aristotle's four-part theory of causation is juxtaposed with contemporary views of organizational ideology/philosophy, culture, climate and leadership, and staff or personnel. The Mazda automobile plant in Flat Rock, Michigan is provided as a sample case study to demonstrate the comprehensiveness of the Aristotelian method in organizational contexts.

Malone, Charles and Lemons, John. Scientific, Public Policy, and Ethical Implications of the Nuclear Waste Policy Act and Its Amendments. *Res Phil Technol*, 11, 5-32, 1991.

Malone, Michael E. Kuhn Reconstructed: Incommensurability Without Relativism. *Stud Hist Phil Sci*, 24(1), 69-93, Mr 93.

On the standard reading of Kuhn's philosophy, the incommensurability of rival paradigms makes rational debate about rivals nearly impossible. If this reflects his real view, then it is prima facie absurd and easily refuted with counterexamples. I argue that the incommensurability thesis *per se* is not easily refutable, but only his gestalt interpretation of it. The gestalt interpretation misrepresents Kuhn's more fundamental ideas on exemplars, and it is in itself confused. I explain and defend the incommensurability thesis without invoking gestalts, and use my reconstruction to dismiss the criticisms of Davidson and Laudan and the endorsement by Barnes.

Malpas, J E. Analysis and Hermeneutics. *Phil Rhet*, 25(2), 93-123, 1992.

This paper is an investigation of the concept of hermeneutic definition and the nature of hermeneutic philosophical practice in general. It takes as its starting point Carl Erik Kühl's discussion of the work of the Norwegian praxeologist Jakob Meloe, but much of the discussion focuses on the work of Heidegger and the later Wittgenstein as exemplary of the hermeneutic approach. That approach is presented as essentially 'disclosive'—it aims at 'showing' rather than deducing or demonstrating—and is contrasted with a more 'analytical' mode in philosophy. It is argued that the difference between these approaches go beyond questions of mere style, but extend to differences about the nature and possibilities of philosophy itself.

Malpas, J E. *Donald Davidson and the Mirror of Meaning*. New York, Cambridge Univ Pr, 1992.

The aim of this book is to provide an articulation and development of Donald Davidson's account of interpretation, and some of the philosophical consequences of that account. The book focuses specifically on the idea of holism in Davidson's thought. Beginning with the origins of his thinking in the work of Quine, successive chapters provide an account of the basics of the Davidsonian position, while also setting out a more developed version that draws upon hermeneutical and phenomenological ideas. Particular attention is paid to topics such as charity, indeterminacy, relativism, and scepticism, and the concluding sections draw a comparison between the Davidsonian and Heideggerian accounts of truth.

Malthus, T R and Winch, Donald (ed). *"An Essay on the Principle of Population"—T R Malthus*. New York, Cambridge Univ Pr, 1992.

Maly, Kenneth (trans) and Wiegand Petzet, Heinrich and Emad, Parvis (trans). *Encounters and Dialogues with Martin Heidegger: 1929-1976 — Heinrich Wiegand Petzet*. Chicago, Univ of Chicago Pr, 1993.

This book is the memoir of the art-historian and literary critique Heinrich-Wiegand Petzet. In recounting his memoirs, Petzet tells the story of his friendship with Martin Heidegger. He focuses on numerous encounters with Heidegger and many dialogues with him. The latter covers topics as diverse as "metaphysics", "art", "modern painting", and "technology". In addition to recounting his dialogues with Heidegger, the book also sheds light on Heidegger's involvement in the politics of national socialism. The introduction to the English edition of Petzet's book takes up the questions concerning Heidegger's political involvement and updates this controversial issue.

Maly, Kenneth R. Reading and Thinking: Heidegger and the Hinting Greeks in Reading Heidegger: Commemorations, Sallis, John (ed). Bloomington, Indiana Univ Pr, 1992.

Mancini, Sandro. La metafisica segreta di Kant: Su un recente saggio di Virgilio Melchiorre. *Riv Filosof Neo-Scolas*, 84(1), 168-177, Ja-Mr 92.

L'articolo discute l'interpretazione del significato dell' analogia nella filosofia Kantiana, proposta da virgilio melchiorre nel sue ultimo libro ("Analogia e Analisi Trascendentale", Mursia, Milano, 1991). Nell' esporre le tesi di fondo del libro, si mostra come esso rientri nel solco di quella linea interpretativa che ma valorizzato positivamente la funzione della metafisica in Kant, da Paulsen a Martinetti, a Maréchal.

Mancini, Sandro. La scoperta di nuovi documenti sulla vita di Bruno: Su *Giordano Bruno and the Embassy Affair* di John Bossy. *Riv Filosof Neo-Scolas*, 84(4), 657-675, O-D 92.

Lo studio esamina le argomentazioni con cui Bossy Afferma di avere scoperto che, con lo pseudonimo di Henry Fagot, Bruno svolse un'attivitá spio. Nistica durante il suo soggiorno londinese a favore della regina Elisabetta. Nell' articolo si prende una decisa posizione a favore della tesi di Bossy, e si avanzano anzi ulteriori argomenti che la rafforzano. Si mostra anche che, con il libro di Bossy, il paradigma interpretativo di F Yates si frantumi definitivamente. L'articolo respinge invece come inguistificata e arbitraria la frettolosa condanna di Bruno con cui Bossy chiude, infelicemente, la sua importante ricerca.

Manes, Christopher. Nature and Silence. *Environ Ethics*, 14(4), 339-350, Wint 92.

A viable environmental ethics must confront "the silence of nature"—the fact that in our culture only humans have status as speaking subjects. Deep ecology has attempted to do so by challenging the idiom of humanism that has silenced the natural world. The approach has been criticized by those who wish to rescue the discourse of reason in environmental ethics. I give a genealogy of nature's silence to show how various motifs of medieval and Renaissance origins have worked together historically to create the fiction of "Man," a character portrayed as sole subject, speaker, and *telos* of the world. I conclude that the discourse of reason, as a guide to social practice, is implicated in this fashion and, therefore, cannot break the silence of nature. Instead, environmental ethics must learn a language that leaps away from the motifs of humanism, perhaps by drawing on the discourse of ontological humility found in primal cultures, postmodern philosophy, and medieval contemplative tradition.

Manfredi, Pat A. Tacit Belief and Other Doxastic Attitudes. *Philosophia (Israel)*, 22(1-2), 95-117, Ja 93.

It is widely supposed that each individual has far too many beliefs to suppose that all of them are represented in the brain. Innumerable mundane facts such as "roasts cannot be cooked in dishwashers" have never been the focus of our attention, but seem to be among our long-standing beliefs. William Lycan calls such beliefs "tacit beliefs." I argue that, appearances to the contrary, there are no tacit beliefs. I propose a four-fold taxonomy for doxastic states in terms of a state's inferential integration with other mental states and its conscious accessibility, and argue that what appear to be tacit beliefs are either dispositions to believe or sub-doxastic states.

Manfredi, Pat A. Two Routes to Narrow Content: Both Dead Ends. *Phil Psych*, 6(1), 3-21, 1993.

If psychology requires a taxonomy that categorizes mental states according to their causal powers, the common sense method of individuating mental states (a taxonomy by intentional content) is unacceptable because mental states can have different intentional content, but identical causal powers. This difference threatens both the vindication of belief/desire psychology and the viability of scientific theories whose posits include intentional states. To resolve this conflict, Fodor has proposed that for scientific purposes mental states should be classified by their narrow content. Such a classification is supposed to correspond to a classification by causal powers. Yet a state's narrow content is also supposed to determine it (broad) intentional content whenever that state is 'anchored' to a context. I Examine the two most plausible accounts of narrow content implicit in Fodor's work, arguing that neither account can accomplish both goals.

Mangiagalli, M. Gilson tra Roma e Lovanio. *Sapienza*, 45(4), 409-419, 1992.

Mangiagalli, M. Oltre l'ermeneutica. *Aquinas*, 34(3), 625-642, S-D 91.

Mangiagalli, M. Una nuova edizione italiana del Trattato aristotelico sulle *Categorie*. *Aquinas*, 34(3), 605-624, S-D 91.

Mangiagalli, Maurizio. San Tommaso e Hegel per una teodicea cristologica. *Aquinas*, 35(2), 307-316, My-Ag 92.

Manicas, Peter T. The Absent Ontology of Society: Response to Juckes and Barresi. *J Theor Soc Behav*, 23(2), 217-228, Je 93.

The essay attacks the dominating dualism in social theory, the bifurcation of 'self' and 'society,' rooted in the bifurcation of 'subject' and 'object' and manifest, e.g., in polarities between 'culture' (or 'experience' or in Marxism, 'superstructure') and social structure (e.g., as in Parsons or Marxist economism). The view is most plausible theorized as a 'dialect' in which 'society' forms 'selves' and 'constrains' action, which at the same time 'determine' social forms. Drawing on Mead and Marx, and more recently on Giddens and Bhaskar, I argue that society exists only as incarnate in the activities of social selves.

Mann, Doug. Does Husserl have a Philosophy of History in *The Crisis of European Sciences*?. *J Brit Soc Phenomenol*, 23(2), 156-166, My 92.

There is a traditional assumption that phenomenology and history are hostile to each other. Although Husserl includes a Hegelian motif of a historical dialectic in his *Crisis of European Sciences*, he also puts forward two contradictory notions of the Life-World that strip this dialectic of any sense of unity. His sense of crisis here is one of a purely intellectual nature; his transcendental reduction is in fact a reduction of history. History is in fact a doxic, a posteriori discipline, and must have a sense of its being an unforeseeable adventure, which Husserl fails to understand.

Mann, Paul. *The Theory-Death of the Avant-Garde*. Bloomington, Indiana Univ Pr, 1991.

Mann, William E. Duns Scotus, Demonstration, and Doctrine. *Faith Phil*, 9(4), 436-462, O 92.

The first question raised in the Prologue to John Duns Scotus's *Commentary on the Sentences of Peter Lombard* is "Whether It Is Necessary for Man in His Present State To Be Supernaturally Inspired With Some Doctrine." Scotus's answer is "Yes," but only after a lengthy discussion of several important epistemological issues connected to understanding and faith. This essay provides some of the background necessary for appreciating Scotus's views. It begins with a discussion of the Aristotelian conception of demonstration, laying emphasis on the distinction between demonstration of a fact and demonstration of the reason for the fact. It then considers the role of authority in generating knowledge that is not demonstrative, the notion of *scientia*, and the difference between Aristotle and Scotus on natural necessity. Special attention is given to Scotus's view on understanding terms, understanding propositions, and being cognitively neutral with respect to a proposition. The essay concludes with a reconstruction of the first of five arguments that Scotus gives for this position. If the reconstruction is correct, then Scotus's argument is even more dependent on revelation than appears initially.

Mann, William E. Hope in Reasoned Faith, Stump, Eleonore (ed). Ithaca, Cornell Univ Pr, 1993.

This essay examines the credentials of hope for one's salvation and its relation to the other two traditional Christian theological virtues of faith and charity. Martin Luther's doctrine of pure love of God, contained in his *Lectures on Romans*, is presented as an example of a religious outlook according to which hope is not a virtue. Luther's doctrine is defended against several philosophical objections. It is ultimately rejected for reasons grounded in St. Thomas Aquinas's *Summa Theologiae*, especially the consideration that without an adequate account of hope, one cannot give an adequate account of charity.

Mann, William E. Jephthah's Plight: Moral Dilemmas and Theism in Philosophical Perspectives, 5: Philosophy of Religion, 1991, Tomberlin, James E (ed). Atascadero, Ridgeview, 1991.

Theists who have tried to ground an ethical theory in God's goodness or God's will have generally supposed that all moral dilemmas must be *secundum quid*; if there is a situation in which the agent cannot avoid doing something wrong, then the agent must have done something culpably wrong to get into the situation. This position is attributed to St. Thomas Aquinas. I argue that there is no evidence to show that Aquinas held it. I then explore theistic ethical theory without the assumption, arguing that many of its distinctive features are compatible with the existence of moral dilemmas.

Manners, Jon and Cowling, Mark. Pre-History: The Debate Before Cohen in Marx's Theory of History, Wetherly, Paul. Brookfield, Avebury, 1992.

This article is part of a volume devoted to a discussion of Cohen's account of historical materialism as a form of technological determinism, using functionalist explanation. The article reviews six alternative theories to Cohen's, demonstrating that they have at least some textual foundation in Marx's writings. The alternatives to Cohen which are reviewed are economic determinism, relations of production determinism, scepticism, class unitarianism, praxis approaches and the organic totality model. The article acts as a reminder rather than arguing an original case of its own.

Manninezhath, Thomas. Advaita Critique of the Sphota and Sabdabrahman. *J Dharma*, 17(3), 178-195, Jl-S 92.

Manning, Richard N. Pragmatism and the Quest for Truth. *Metaphilosophy*, 23(4), 350-362, O 92.

I examine Richard Rorty's arguments against the traditional philosophical quest for Truth and in favor of a post-philosophical culture. I argue that Rorty's rejection of traditional philosophy is ironically founded upon paradigmatical Philosophical grounds. I then turn the tables on Rorty, offering several genuinely pragmatic considerations in favor of traditional philosophy, which, given his self-professed pragmatism, should be especially significant from Rorty's point of view.

Manno, A G. Il pensiero debole e il ritorno alla metafisica. *Sapienza*, 45(1), 39-52, 1992.

Manno, A G. L'insegnamento della logica nelle scuole medie superiori?. *Sapienza*, 45(4), 445-449, 1992.

Manolidis, Georgios. *Die Rolle der Physiologie in der Philosophie Epikurs*. Frankfurt, Athenaum, 1987.

Mansfeld, Jaap. *Physikai doxai* et *problemata physica* d'Aristote à Aétius (et au-delà). *Rev Metaph Morale*, 97(3), 327-363, Jl-S 92.

Mansfeld, Jaap. A Theophrastean Excursus on God and Nature and its Aftermath in Hellenistic Thought. *Phronesis*, 37(3), 314-335, 1992.

Mansfeld, Jaap. Physikai doxai and Problemata Physika from Aristotle to Aëtius (and Beyond) in Theophrastus, Fortenbaugh, W W (ed). New Brunswick, Transaction Books, 1992.

Manuli, Paola. Galien et le stoïcisme. *Rev Metaph Morale*, 97(3), 365-375, Jl-S 92.

Maphala, T G T and Ramose, Mogobe B and Makhabane, T E. In Search of a Workable and Lasting Constitutional Change in South Africa. *Quest*, 5(2), 4-31, D 91.

Mappes, Thomas A and Zembaty, Jane S. *Biomedical Ethics (Third Edition)*. New York, McGraw-Hill, 1991.

Marantz, Haim. Loyalty and Identity: Reflections on and About a Theme in Fletcher's *Loyalty*. *Crim Just Ethics*, 12(1), 63-67, Wint-Spr 93.

Marbach, Eduard and Kern, Iso and Bernet, Rudolf. *An Introduction to Husserlian Phenomenology*. Evanston, Northwestern Univ Pr, 1993.

The book presents Husserl's philosophy in its chronological development, but also emphasizes the unity of the whole project by showing the systematic interconnections between the basic themes and notions. The authors elucidate Husserl's conceptual development by way of relating his own publications to his many research manuscripts, depicting the broadening of the research program from the early static-descriptive to the genetic-explanatory phenomenology, and presenting Husserl's overall conception of philosophy.

Marcellino, Claudio. I μεταξυ nella *Repubblica*: loro significato e loro funzione. *Riv Filosof Neo-Scolas*, 84(2-3), 410-467, Ap-S 92.

Marchetto, Michele 580 AUTHOR INDEX WITH ABSTRACTS

Marchetto, Michele. John Niemeyer Findlay, un platonico fra i neopositivisti: ritratto biografico. *Riv Filosof Neo-Scolas*, 84(2-3), 539-555, Ap-S 92.

Marcialis, Maria Teresa. La teoria postcartesiana delle idee nella recente storiografia anglosassone. *G Crit Filosof Ital*, 71(1), 102-118, Ja-Ap 92.

Marcialis, Maria Teresa. Natura e uomo in Giulio Cesare Vanini. *G Crit Filosof Ital*, 71(2), 227-247, My-Ag 92.

Marcja, Annalisa and Prest, Mike and Toffalori, Carlo. On the Undecidability of Some Classes of Abelian-By-Finite Groups. *Annals Pure Applied Log*, 62(2), 167-173, Jl 93.

Marcotte, Edward J. Wittgenstein's Metaphysics of Contingency. *Metaphilosophy*, 23(1-2), 57-67, Ja-Ap 92.

Marcus, Ruth Barcan. *Modalities: Philosophical Essays*. New York, Oxford Univ Pr, 1993.

Some essays published between 1961 and 1990. Among continuing themes introduced between 1961 and 1970 are 1) The relative nature of principles of extensionality; 2) The necessity of identity as it evolved from a formal proof in 1947; 3) A theory of proper names as directly referential tags; 4) Essentialism characterized and the non-commitment of some modal theories to essentialism; 5) Substitutional quantification and its uses; 6) Interpretation of the Barcan Formula; 7) A modal class theory and class (set) identity. Later essays concern 8) Possibilia and possible worlds; 9) Moral dilemmas and their non-evidence for inconsistency of moral codes; 10) Belief and rationality; 11) Essays on specific figures such as Spinoza, Russell and Quine.

Mardaev, S I. Two Sequents of Locally Tabular Superintuitionistic Logic. *Stud Log*, 50(2), 333-342, Je 91.

A negative solution of the problem posed by Maksimova is given. Two sequences of superintuitionistic logics are axiomatized by using an analogy of the operation ω

Marder, Elissa. Disarticulating Voices: Feminism and Philomela. *Hypatia*, 7(2), 148-166, Spr 92.

By juxtaposing readings of selected feminist critics with a reading of Ovid's account of Philomela's rape and silencing, this essay interrogates the rhetorical, political, and epistemological implications of the feminist "we." As a political intervention that comes into being as a response to women's oppression, feminism must posit a collective "we." But this feminist "we" is best understood as an impersonal, performative pronoun whose political force is not derived from a knowable referent.

Marenbon, John. Vocalism, Nominalism and the Commentaries on the *Categories* from the Earlier Twelfth Century. *Vivarium*, 30(1), 51-61, My 92.

Mares, Edwin and Meyer, Robert K. The Semantics of R4. *J Phil Log*, 22(1), 95-110, F 93.

Mares, Edwin D and Meyer, Robert K. The Admissibility of γ in R4. *Notre Dame J Form Log*, 33(2), 197-206, Spr 92.

Margalit, Avishai. Sense and Sensibility: Wittgenstein on the *Golden Bough*. *Iyyun*, 41, 301-318, Jl 92.

Margalit, Avishai (ed) and Margalit, Edna (ed). *Isaiah Berlin: A Celebration*. Chicago, Univ of Chicago Pr, 1991.

Margalit, Edna (ed) and Margalit, Avishai (ed). *Isaiah Berlin: A Celebration*. Chicago, Univ of Chicago Pr, 1991.

Margenau, Henry (ed) and Varghese, Roy Abraham (ed). *Cosmos, Bios, Theos: Scientists Reflect on Science, God, and the Origins of the Universe, Life, and "Homo sapiens"*. Peru, Open Court, 1992.

Margolis, Howard. *Paradigms and Barriers: How Habits of Mind Govern Scientific Beliefs*. Chicago, Univ of Chicago Pr, 1993.

The book gives an account of just what it is that shifts in a Kuhnian paradigm shift. It argues that what shifts is a particular, identifiable habit of mind: collectively, the "barriers" of the title. Detailed applications are made to Lavoisier/Stahl, Copernicus/Tycho/Ptolemy, the emergence of probability, Hobbes/Boyle, and to the Scientific Revolution in general. This leads to a critique of both positivist and constructivist readings of the history of science.

Margolis, Joseph. A Convergence of Pragmatisms in Frontiers in American Philosophy, Volume I, Burch, Robert W (ed). College Station, Texas A&M Univ Pr, 1992.

Margolis, Joseph. Exorcising the Dreariness of Aesthetics. *J Aes Art Crit*, 51(2), 133-140, Spr 93.

The essay reviews, for the 50th anniversary issue of the *Journal of Aesthetics and Art Criticism*, the thesis of Passmore's "The Dreariness of Aesthetics." Passmore's charge is shown to be mistaken: "dreariness" follows for instance from a failure to come to terms, in a philosophically serious way, with the historicity of pertinent generalization.

Margolis, Joseph. Phenomenology and Metaphysics: Husserl, Heidegger, and Merleau-Ponty in Merleau-Ponty Vivant, Dillon, M C (ed). Albany, SUNY Pr, 1991.

Margolis, Joseph. Reconciling Analytic and Feminist Philosophy and Aesthetics. *J Aes Art Crit*, 48(4), 327-335, Fall 90.

This is a response to a discussion, somewhat along Rortyan lines, of the author's philosophy of art, by Joanne Waugh. It offers reasons for doubting that there can be a distinctive feminist aesthetics, a different matter altogether from the prospects of feminist criticism in the arts and in philosophy. It supports a rapprochement between "analytic" and "feminist" aesthetics, but it shows the dialectical difficulties confronting both analytic and feminist philosophy and aesthetics.

Margolis, Joseph. Reinterpreting Interpretation. *J Aes Art Crit*, 47(3), 237-251, Sum 89.

This was the presidential address of 1988 for the American Society for Aesthetics. Exploring the views of Rosalind Krauss, Roland Barthes, Hans-Georg Gadamer, and Michel Foucault, it demonstrates the coherence and viability of a theory of interpretation that preserves reference and predication while abandoning the fixity of texts. The account accommodates the historicity of artworks, their alterability under interpretation, and the coherence of relativism. It demonstrates, in passing, the compatibility of "readerly" and "writerly" texts and defines a novel sense of "interpret".

Margolis, Joseph. Relativism and the 'Lebenswelt' in Cultural Relativism and Philosophy, Dascal, Marcelo (ed). Leiden, Brill, 1991.

The prospects of relativism are explored in terms of Husserl's view of the confrontation between naturalism and phenomenology. Arguments favoring relativism and flux are drawn out of the internal difficulties of Husserl's own account, particularly along the lines of cultural preformation and history—that is, along the lines of a defensible reading of the *Lebenswelt*. The entire issue is brought to bear on the wider debates of twentieth-century philosophy.

Margolis, Joseph. The Defeat of the Computational Model of the Mind. *Iyyun*, 41, 251-275, Jl 92.

The defeat of the computational model of the mind may be gained by exploring strategies linked to the general thesis, "thinking has (or is) a history." It is shown that the conditions for successful reference and predication, essential for natural-language discourse and linked to that thesis, cannot be algorithmically modeled or defined and that, as a consequence, computationality fails as a reasonable bet. The views of Marx, Churchland, Quine, Goodman, and Edelman are discussed.

Margolis, Joseph. The Passing of Peirce's Realism. *Trans Peirce Soc*, 29(3), 293-330, Sum 93.

Peirce's realism regarding "generals" is examined in terms of the realism/ nominalism controversy and Peirce's treatment of the role of mind. The account is generally supported in terms of its realism, but faulted in terms of its failure to accommodate actual social practices regarding predicables. A solution is offered.

Margonis, Frank. New Problems in Child-Centered Pedagogy. *Proc Phil Educ*, 48, 130-140, 1992.

The child-centered pedagogies of Rousseau and Dewey embody ideals that rightly claim our commitment. But the theories of learning and knowledge Dewey and Rousseau develop in support of those ideals betray the values and ways of thinking of the relatively privileged groups who have created and employed child-centered pedagogies. As a consequence, the character of child-centered pedagogies affirms some students while excluding others. This paper attempts to locate some of the sources of bias in Rousseau's and Dewey's work, and drawing upon the existential phenomenologies of Heidegger and Merleau-Ponty, attempts to ask questions that might lead child-centered educators in a more pluralistic direction.

Margreiter, Reinhard. Mystik und Philosophie. *Phil Rundsch*, 39(3), 161-185, 1992.

Margulies, Martin B. Intent, Motive, and the *R A V* Decision. *Crim Just Ethics*, 11(2), 42-45, Sum-Fall 92.

Marietta Jr, Don E. Pluralism in Environmental Ethics. *Topoi*, 12(1), 69-80, Mr 93.

A number of recent books and articles have claimed that environmental ethics should be plutalistic; in response to these J Baird Callicott has written a strong attack upon moral pluralism. This paper will survey briefly some of the recent work advocating moral pluralism and examine Callicott's defense of moral monism. Then it will examine the justification for building an ethical system upon more than one fundamental source of moral insight. The moral system which succeeds in taking into account all that is morally relevant will be contextualist, and it might need to be pluralistic as well.

Marin, Louis. Frontiers of Utopia: Past and Present. *Crit Inquiry*, 19(3), 397-420, Spr 93.

Mariña, Jacqueline. The Role of Limits in Aristotle's Concept of Place. *S J Phil*, 31(2), 205-216, Sum 93.

Maring, Matthias and Lenk, Hans. A Pie-Model of Moral Responsibility? in Advances in Scientific Philosophy, Schurz, Gerhard (ed). Amsterdam, Rodopi, 1991.

Problems of distributing responsibility are found in highly developed industrial societies. In this context, the so-called pie-model of moral responsibility distribution is discussed: The more people share responsibility, the less each seems to be responsible; responsibility would be diluted by increasing numbers of people—at least as a matter of fact. But also normatively speaking? In general however, moral responsibility cannot be disected and shared like a pie. Moral responsibility is a function of power, impact, and knowledge and the mere fact that others are co-responsible, does not diminish the very responsibility of each partaking individual in contexts of collective or group or even institutional action.

Maring, Matthias and Lenk, Hans. Ecology and Ethics: Notes About Technology and Economic Consequences. *Res Phil Technol*, 12, 157-176, 1992.

More frequently than ever, in highly developed societies individual actions are hidden behind or at least, overridden by collective, corporate and group actions. The individualistic concepts of ethics are generally not sufficient any more to tackle the problem of distributing responsibility for untoward (e.g., ecological) consequences of such actions, especially in social trap constellations. With respect to moral evaluation many participating and contributing individuals have to bear a certain co-responsibility for the supraindividual effects according to their active, potential or formal involvement and impact or influence. A moral re-orientation of individuals to cope with the problems of this new situation is necessary, but not sufficient. We also need structural incentives, social mechanisms for sanctioning, and institutional, e.g., legal and political, measures.

Marinoff, Louis. Three Pseudo-Paradoxes in 'Quantum' Decision Theory: Apparent Effects of Observation on Probability and Utility. *Theor Decis*, 35(1), 55-73, Jl 93.

In quantum domains, the measurement (or observation) of one of a pair of complementary variables introduces an unavoidable uncertainty in the value of that variable's complement. Such uncertainties are negligible in Newtonian worlds, where observations can be made without appreciably disturbing the observed system. Hence, one would not expect that an observation of a non-quantum probabilistic outcome could affect a probability distribution over subsequently possible states, in a way that would conflict with classical probability calculations. This paper examines three problems in which observations appear to affect the probabilities and expected utilities of subsequent outcomes, in ways which may appear paradoxical. Deeper analysis of these problems reveals that the anomalies arise, not from paradox, but rather from faulty inferences drawn from the observations themselves. Thus the notion of 'quantum' decision theory is disparaged.

Marion, Jean-Luc. Is the Ontological Argument Ontological? The Argument According to Anselm and Its Metaphysical Interpretation According to Kant. *J Hist Phil*, 30(2), 201-218, Ap 92.

Marková, Ivana and Linell, Per. Acts in Discourse: From Monological Speech Acts to Dialogical Inter-Acts. *J Theor Soc Behav*, 23(2), 174-195, Je 93.

Markowitz, Sally. Guilty Pleasures: Aesthetic Meta-Response and Fiction. *J Aes Art Crit*, 50(4), 307-316, Fall 92.

Marquis, Jean-Pierre. Approximations and Logic. *Notre Dame J Form Log*, 33(2), 184-196, Spr 92.

Scientists work with approximations almost all the time and have to reason with these approximations. Therefore, it is very natural to wonder if approximations influence logical deduction and if so, how. Our goal in this paper is to present a class of lattices which captures some intuitions concerning propositions expressing numerical approximations and consider how they relate to classical logic.

Marra, B. L'embrione e la sua natura. *Sapienza*, 46(1), 87-89, 1993.

Marras, Ausonio. Psychophysical Supervenience and Nonreductive Materialism. *Synthese*, 95(2), 275-304, My 93.

Jaegwon Kim and others have claimed that (strong) psychophysical supervenience entails the reducibility of mental properties to physical properties. I argue that this claim is unwarranted with respect to epistemic (explanatory) reducibility (either of a 'global' or of a 'local' sort), as well as with respect to ontological reducibility. I then attempt to show that a robust version of nonreductive materialism (which I call 'supervenient token-physicalism') can be defended against the charge that nonreductive materialism leads to epiphenomenalism in failing to account for the causal or explanatory relevance of mental properties.

Marras, Ausonio. Supervenience and Reducibility: An Odd Couple. *Phil Quart*, 43(171), 215-222, Ap 93.

In a series of influential papers, Jaegwon Kim has argued that in order to capture the dependence of the mental on the physical we need a notion of supervenience at least as strong as what he has called 'strong supervenience', which, he has further argued, 'entails the possibility of reducing the supervenient to the subvenient', and thus the mental to the physical. I dispute this latter claim. First I argue that the claim is unwarranted; then I argue that the claim is in fact demonstrably false: any notion of supervenience that captures the intended sense of psychophysical dependence must actually entail the denial of reducibility, and insofar as Kim's 'strong supervenience' captures at least an essential component of such an notion, it cannot entail psychophysical reducibility.

Marrone, P. Modernità: esperienza e schemi concettuali. *Aquinas*, 35(1), 167-179, Ja-Ap 92.

Marrone, P. Strumenti analitici per la comprensione della filosofia continentale. *Aquinas*, 34(3), 593-604, S-D 91.

Marrone, Pierpaolo. Intenzionalità e filosofia dell'azione. *Aquinas*, 35(2), 405-412, My-Ag 92.

Marsh, Charles. Bonhoeffer on Heidegger and Togetherness. *Mod Theol*, 8(3), 263-283, Jl 92.

The author gives a critical reading of Heidegger's celebrated account of being-with others in light of Dietrich Bonhoeffer's social ontology. First, according to Bonhoeffer, Heidegger's description of social relation is unable to appreciate the constitutive otherness of the other, and ultimately consolidates the other with Dasein. The social world is always a referential totality *for the sake of the I* that is Dasein. Second, authentic Dasein as being-towards-death results in the disconnection of any genuine bond between I and other. Bonhoeffer emphasizes that self-relation and relation with others must be mediated in a theologically and ethically meaningful way, rather than in terms of an individualized resoluteness.

Marsh, James. *Radical Fragments*. New York, Lang, 1992.

Marsh, James L. Ambiguity, Language, and Communicative Praxis in Modernity and Its Discontents, Marsh, James L (ed). Bronx, Fordham Univ Pr, 1992.

Marsh, James L. The Gentle and Rigorous Cogency of Communicative Rationality in Modernity and Its Discontents, Marsh, James L (ed). Bronx, Fordham Univ Pr, 1992.

Marsh, James L and Caputo, John D and Westphal, Merold. A Philosophical Dialogue in Modernity and Its Discontents, Marsh, James L (ed). Bronx, Fordham Univ Pr, 1992.

Marsh, James L (ed) and Caputo, John D (ed) and Westphal, Merold (ed). *Modernity and Its Discontents*. Bronx, Fordham Univ Pr, 1992.

Marshall, Alan. Ethics and the Extraterrestrial Environment. *J Applied Phil*, 10(2), 227-236, 1993.

After a brief review of environmental ethics this paper examines how terrestrial environmental values can be developed into policies to protect extraterrestrial environments. Shallow environmentalism, deep environmentalism and the libertarian extension of rights are compared and then applied to the environmental protection of extraterrestrial bodies. Some scientific background is given. The planet Mars is used as a test case from which an ethical argument emerges for the protection of environments beyond Earth. The argument is based on the necessity to recognise the intrinsic value of all living species and natural environments. At present, the treatment of extraterrestrial environments by makers of space policy is ethically undernourished. This paper explains why such an attitude endangers those environments and calls for the policymakers to incorporate non-anthropocentric ethics into extraterrestrial environmental policy.

Marshall, Bruce D. Thomas, Thomisms and Truth. *Thomist*, 56(3), 499-524, Jl 92.

In response to objections raised in the accompanying articles by Profs. Roy and Crossan, this essay defends and extends the interpretation of Aquinas on truth and epistemic justification proposed in my earlier article, "Aquinas as Postliberal Theologian." An important test for this interpretation is whether it can offer an account of Thomas's apparent endorsement of "natural theology" consistent with the claim that for Thomas all beliefs must be tested for truth by ascertaining their coherence with the chief articles of Christian belief; this essay develops such an account, primarily on the basis of Thomas's commentary on Romans 1.

Marshall, Graeme. John Bishop's Natural Agency. *Dialogue (Canada)*, 31(4), 685-690, Autumn 92.

Bishop enters action theory with a sceptical problem about the very possibility of agency in a causally ordered world. His solution is to develop from Davidson an ontologically reductive causal theory of intentional action that rules out any notion of agency not analysable in terms of event causality. In this critical notice it is argued that although such a theory might explain actions as observed in the world it does not accommodate actions as performed and so misses what is essential to us as agents — our engaged acting.

Marshall, Peter. Thinking for Tomorrow: Reflections on Avner de-Shalit. *J Applied Phil*, 10(1), 105-113, 1993.

According to Avner de-Shalit, our relationship with future generations is one of obligation based on welfare rights, not on basic human rights. This is because welfare rights derive from a shared community, and because we and future generations are members of the one 'transgenerational' community. I argue that although it is correct to ground our relations to possible future people in the concept of community, it is wrong to think that rights-talk of any kind is an adequate articulation of that sense of community. To present the issue of our relationship with future generations in terms of a choice between human rights and welfare rights misrepresents the nature of reasoning on these sorts of concerns. In a properly developed communitarian position there is a model of philosophical reasoning that can better articulate and interpret our intuitions about community in general and about our relations to potential future people in particular. Furthermore, such articulations can give those intuitions persuasive force.

Marshall, Sandra E. Public Bodies, Private Selves in Applied Philosophy, Almond, Brenda (ed). New York, Routledge, 1992.

Marshall Jr, John. Why Rational Egoism is Not Consistent. *Rev Metaph*, 45(4), 713-737, Je 92.

Rational egoism is the normative thesis that we ought to make our own happiness our ultimate end. In a variation of G E Moore's argument against egoism the author shows that this thesis is not consistent. In grounding his normative view that he ought to promote his own happiness, the egoist presupposes a conception of goodness that he cannot consistently invoke in the further normative assertion he is also committed to that each person's happiness is good. Thus, he cannot have both the universality and objectivity his normative thesis requires. The author examines several attempts to meet this argument.

Martens, David B. Close Enough to Reference. *Synthese*, 95(3), 357-377, Je 93.

This paper proposes a response to the duplication objection to the descriptive theory of singular mental reference. This objection involves hypothetical cases in each of which there are a pair of qualitatively indistinguishable objects and a thought that apparently refers to only one of the pair, despite the descriptive indistinguishability of the two objects. I identify a concept of reference-likeness or closeness to reference, which is related to the concept of genuine singular reference as the concept of truthlikeness or closeness to truth is related to the concept of truth. My response to the duplication objection is to say that the hypothetical cases it involves establish only that a thought can come close enough to singular reference to a thing despite not genuinely referring to that thing, a consequence that is compatible with the descriptive theory of singular mental reference.

Martin, Alison (trans) and Irigaray, Luce. *Je, Tu, Nous: Toward a Culture of Difference*. New York, Routledge, 1993.

Martin, Biddy. *Woman and Modernity: The (Life)styles of Lou Andreas-Salomé*. Ithaca, Cornell Univ Pr, 1991.

Martin, Bill. Elements of a Derridean Social Theory in Ethics and Danger, Dallery, Arleen B (ed). Albany, SUNY Pr, 1992.

Martin, Bill. Liberalism: Modern and Postmodern. *Soc Epistem*, 7(1), 75-81, Ja-Mr 93.

Martin, Bill. *Matrix and Line: Derrida and the Possibilities of Postmodern Social Theory*. Albany, SUNY Pr, 1992.

Martin, Bill. The Idea of Enablement. *Man World*, 26(4), 457-466, O 93.

Martin, C B. Burial by Fire of a Phoenix: Metaphysics, Epistemology, and Realism Under Attack in On the Track of Reason, Beehler, Rodger (ed). Boulder, Westview Pr, 1992.

Martin, C B. Power for Realists in Ontology, Causality and Mind: Essays in Honour of D M Armstrong, Bacon, John (ed). New York, Cambridge Univ Pr, 1993.

Martin, Christopher F J. Tomás de Aquino y la identidad personal. *Anu Filosof*, 26(2), 249-259, 1993.

The concept of "person" does not determine criteria of identity: the pseudo-concept of "personal identity" is not found in Aquinas. Discussions of immortality and resurrection which use this pseudo-concept have obvious flaws. Neither the affirmation nor the denial of "personal identity through death" have determinate sense.

Martin, Christopher J. The Logic of the *Nominales*, or, The Rise and Fall of Impossible *Positio*. *Vivarium*, 30(1), 110-138, My 92.

Martin, Glen T. Deconstruction and Breakthrough in Nietzsche and Nagarjuna in Nietzsche and Asian Thought, Parkes, Graham R (ed). Chicago, Univ of Chicago Pr, 1991.

This essay explores the relation of each thinker's deconstructive project to his vision of spiritual transfiguration. Both hermeneutically deconstruct our "being" orientation into one of radical "becoming." Yet Nietzsche's symbology expressing his vision of human transformation (in metaphors of alchemy, art, and play) resonates in stark contrast to Nágárjuna's focus on "emptiness" involving a methodological refusal to make any ontological assertions whatsoever (which reflects the very "essence" of the Buddha's enlightenment). Both thinkers, finally, are related to the spiritual crisis of the 20th century and the possibility of a new "fullness-emptiness" as expressed in the thought of Nishitani Keiji.

Martin, Jane Roland. The New Problem of Curriculum. *Synthese*, 94(1), 85-104, Ja 93.

Although 'What should be taught?' has often been called "the" curriculum question, few contemporary philosophers of education have paid it the attention it deserves. One notable exception is Israel Scheffler. In "Justifying Curriculum Decisions," an essay written in 1958, Scheffler provided what is surely one of the most sophisticated accounts we have of the process of content selection. In this paper I summarize Scheffler's position, explore a gap in his text, and propose that the problem of content selection can be more readily solved if it is first constructed in a new way.

Martin, Luther H. Fate and Futurity in the Greco-Roman World. *Proc Boston Colloq Anc Phil*, 5, 291-311, 1989.

This reexamines the conventional thesis that a fully developed historical consciousness was a Hebraic achievement never fully realized by the Greeks or Romans. By examining the collective mentality of Hebraic and Hellenic culture as manifest is 'religious' practice, it is concluded that this thesis is essentially correct, though for reasons other than have usually been given.

Martin, M G F. Perception, Concepts, and Memory. *Phil Rev*, 101(4), 745-763, O 92.

Martin, Marie A. Hume on Human Excellence. *Hume Stud*, 18(2), 383-399, N 92.

This article is intended as an initial step in refocusing our view on the neglected classical aspects of Hume's moral thought. Hume conceives of human excellence as greatness of mind and extensive benevolence, and argues that these are founded on the motivating passions of self-esteem and love. Hume aligns himself with classical virtue ethics both in his view that virtue is an intrinsic good and in his rejection of the modern's view that voluntary action is the focus of moral evaluation.

Martin, Marie A. The Rational Warrant for Hume's General Rules. *J Hist Phil*, 31(2), 245-257, Ap 93.

Various commentators have claimed that Hume's naturalism avoids irrationalism by appealing to general rules, which serve to distinguish rationally warranted from unwarranted judgments. But, according to Hume, general rules are formed according to exactly the same natural propensities as the judgments they regulate. The question addressed in this article is how Hume can defend their normative authority. Hume's answer is that general rules are based on the fundamental, universal, and unavoidable principles inherent in human reasoning, and it is only by the continual adherence to general rules that we achieve a consistent system of orderly, coherent, and stable judgment.

Martin, Michael. Sight and Touch in The Contents of Experience, Crane, Tim (ed). New York, Cambridge Univ Pr, 1992.

Martin, Michael. The Rational Role of Experience. *Proc Aris Soc*, 93, 71-88, 1993.

Martin, Mike W. Love's Constancy. *Philosophy*, 68(263), 63-77, Ja 93.

At its best, marital love is a durable attitude and relationship defined in part by the virtues of caring, honesty, fairness—and faithfulness. Marital faithfulness, which is distinct from the much narrower idea of foregoing adultery, is grounded in a commitment to love. That commitment has unjustifiably been criticized as unintelligible, unreasonable, inhumane, unnecessary, non-binding, and even incompatible with love. Rejecting these criticisms, however, leaves open the question of why faithfulness is a virtue. (edited)

Martin, Mike W. Rationalization and Responsibility: A Reply to Whisner. *J Soc Phil*, 23(2), 176-184, Fall 92.

William Whisner has insightfully explored the importance of self-deceiving rationalization in public life ("Rationalization, Self-Deception, and the Demise of Practical Moral Reason," *Journal of Social Philosophy*, 2, 1992). In this rejoinder I add some clarifications and suggested modifications of his claims about how self-interest warps moral reasoning in the professions and in public service. The concept of self-deception is an important diagnostic tool in understanding irresponsible conduct, but caution is needed in applying it to ambiguous situations where compromises and conflicting value perspectives (rather than corruption) may be at stake.

Martin, Raymond. *Having* the Experience: The Next Best Thing to Being There. *Phil Stud*, 70(3), 305-321, Je 93.

The traditional debate over personal identity focused almost exclusively on specifying the conditions under which identity is preserved. However, since the 1970s many theoriests have been equally concerned to discover what matters primarily in survival (with some still convinced it is identity) and then to specify the conditions under which that (whatever it is) is preserved. My interest is in this newer debae. I argue that there is an important source of self-concern—the anticipation of *having* experiences—that has either been overlooked or seriously underrated by major contributors to this debate and that, as a consequence, theories that were designed to challenge the idea that identity is what matters primarily in survival are much weaker than they could be.

Martin, Raymond. Objectivity and Meaning in Historical Studies: Toward a Post-Analytic View (Review Essay of *Objectivity, Method and Point of View*. *Hist Theor*, 32(1), 25-50, 1993.

Many contemporary historians and philosophers are dissatisfied both with the accounts traditional analytic philosophers have given of the epistemological dimensions of historical studies and also with the ways many continental philosophers more recently have brushed aside the need for any such accounts. Yet no one has yet proposed a unified research program that could serve as the central focus for a better epistemologically-oriented approach. Such a research program would not only address epistemological problems from a perspective that would be of methodological interest to historians but would also be directly responsive to fundamental motivations people have for caring about historical studies in the first place. The main purpose of this review essay is to sketch and then illustrate the main outlines of such a research program. (edited)

Martin, Raymond. Self-Interest and Survival. *Amer Phil Quart*, 29(4), 319-330, O 92.

Recently philosophers concerned with personal identity have been preoccupied with examples in which people who believe they might continue to lead desirable lives nevertheless apparently have, as an expression of their desire to survive, sufficient, *self-interested* reasons to cease to exist. These paradoxical examples have seemed to many to shed light on how much preserving one's identity matters in survival. But there is a neglected problem that not only complicates any attempt to draw a moral from the examples but is, I believe, symptomatic of a deep tension in our understandings of such fundamental notions as self-interest, self-regard, egoism, and survival. The purpose of the present paper is to explain what this problem is, and then to solve it.

Martin, Raymond. Survival of Bodily Death: A Qeustion of Values. *Relig Stud*, 28(2), 165-184, Je 92.

Unlike traditional arguments for survival of bodily death, the argument for reincarnation presented in this paper is compatible with materialism or physicalism, stands or falls on straightforward empirical grounds and dispenses with the assumption that meaningful personal survival requires identity. It is modest also in being only for the temporary survival of some and in resting on admittedly incomplete and fragmentary data. Even so, it is for actual personal survival of bodily death, something most contemporary philosophers regard as completely beyond the pale. The argument is presented to show how survival of bodily death can be argued for most plausibly and in particular to illustrate how dropping the assumption that survival requires identity changes the dynamic of the traditional debate.

Martin, Raymond and Kolak, Daniel. *The Experience of Philosophy (Second Edition)*. Belmont, Wadsworth, 1992.

A collection reflecting the ways philosophy has changed over the last two decades, with an attempt to link philosophy to literature and the physical and social sciences. Contributors include Daniel Dennett, Robert Nozick, Thomas Nagel, Richard Taylor, Douglas Hofstadter, Gary Gutting, Richard Dawkins, Frank Jackson, Paul Churchland, Paul Darris, and Jonathan Glover.

Martin, Wayne M. Fichte's Anti-Dogmatism. *Ratio*, 5(2), D 92.

One of the main points of entry for understanding German Idealism has been Fichte's contrast between idealism and what he calls "dogmatism." This contrast provides one of Fichte's central tools for defining and legitimating his philosophical program. Commentators have uniformly interpreted the term "dogmatism" as Fichte's polemical equivalent for "realism." This assumption has given rise to a number of apparently intractable debates about the content of Fichte's idealism. The paper argues that the identification of dogmatism with realism is fundamentally mistaken. Once we properly understand the question which, according to Fichte, philosophy should answer, we can see that the defining claim of the dogmatic position is not realism but a form of naturalism. Fichte's idealism thus should be seen as consisting not in a rejection of realism but in a commitment to a non-naturalistic account of subjectivity.

Martindale, Kathleen and Saunders, Martha. Realizing Love and Justice: Lesbian Ethics in the Upper and Lower Case. *Hypatia*, 7(4), 148-171, Fall 92.

This essay examines two tendencies in lesbian ethics as differing visions of community, as well as contrasting views of the relationship between the erotic and the ethical. In addition to considering those authors who make explicit claims about lesbian ethics, this paper reflects on the works of some lesbians whose works are less frequently attended to in discussions about lesbian ethics, including lesbians writing from the perspectives of theology and of literature.

Martinez, German. An Anthropological Vision of CHristian Marriage. *Thomist*, 56(3), 451-472, Jl 92.

This essay has attempted to elaborate on the new modern understanding of the person and to show how this has resulted in a paradigm shift in the Christian vision of marriage. The anthropological approach is essential. In fact, the underestimation of the values of marriage or, more precisely, the lack of a personalist anthropology and an adequate theological consideration of sexuality has been at the root of the weakness of the traditional approach to marriage.

Martinez, Roy. Kierkegaard's Place in the Hermeneutic Project. *Laval Theol Phil*, 49(2), 295-308, Je 93.

The basic theme of radical hermeneutics — the effort to restore life to its original difficulty, i.e., to take stock of life in all of its uncertainty and undecidability — draws deeply upon Kierkegaard's project as a writer. The key terms here are "restore" and "original". For if something needs to be restored to its original form or status, the implication is that it has been covered up, bastardized, or falsified. According to radical hermeneutics, the classic Western metaphysics of presence, which takes Being as an abiding permanence (*essentia, natura, eidos, ousia*) has engendered this illusion. It is for this reason that Caputo (in his recent book *Radical Hermeneutics*) endorses Heraclitus, not Parmenides; Aristotle instead of Plato; Nietzsche instead of Hegel. The religious insight that animates radical hermeneutics — its attempt to cope with the sufferings induced by the flux, and its rejection of metaphysics — brings it into a deep and genuine association with Kierkegaard's thought.

Martinich, A P. Analytic Phenomenological Deconstruction in Certainty and Surface in Epistemology and Philosophical Method, Martinich, A P (ed). Lewiston, Mellen Pr, 1991.

Both phenomenology and deconstruction, which are usually associated with continental philosophy, are shown to have an important place within analytic philosophy, especially in the work of Wittgenstein and J L Austin. A careful study of Avrum Stroll's phenomenological and deconstructive work on philosophical views on surfaces is also included.

Martinich, A P (ed) and White, Michael J (ed). *Certainty and Surface in Epistemology and Philosophical Method*. Lewiston, Mellen Pr, 1991.

This book is a collection of essays in honor of Avrum Stroll, with a focus on the connections between certainty, the nature and perception of surfaces, and philosophical method. Some of the essays are "Certainty Made Simple" by Wallace Matson, "New Foundations and Philosophers" by Alastair Hannay, "Stroll's Answer to Scepticism" by Richard Popkin, "Moore on Scepticism and Common Sense" by David Cole, "Epiphenomena" by Zeno Vendler, "Faces, Boundaries, and Thin Layers," by Peter Simons, "Folk Theories and Physical Metrics" by Michael White, "Analytic Phenomenological Deconstruction" by A P Martinich, and "How I See Philosophy" by Avrum Stroll.

Martinot, Steve. L'Esprit Objectif as a Theory of Language. *Man World*, 26(1), 45-62, Ja 93.

In *L'Idiot de la Famille*, Sartre accepts and re-poses certain issues raised by Barthes and Derrida; l'Esprit objectif becomes a partial appropriation of the deconstructive critique of language to the realm of praxis, and as such, presents a theory of language. For Sartre, L'Esprit objectif is an extension of the practico-inert to the realm of culture and writing; this extension constitutes a restructuring of semiosis in the praxos the reading. Sartre develops a theory of reading, as conditioning the writer's construction by cultural tradition, and articulates it using discursive forms homologous to various Derridean structures.

Martins, Roberto D A. A Teoria Aristotélica da Respiraçao. *Cad Hist Filosof Cie*, 2(2), 165-212, Jl-D 90.

Aristotle studied the breathing of animals in his biological works. He concluded that it consists in a refrigeration phenomenon that controls the breath of living beings. He analyses how such a phenomenon takes place in several kinds of animals, using observation, anatomic dissections and experiments. Aristotle offers a consistent theoretical system, well empirically founded. This article describes Aristotle's contribution and discusses his methodology showing that it is similar to the modern scientific method.

Martland, Thomas R. An Inquiry into Religion's Empty World. *J Phil*, 90(9), 469-481, S 93.

Religion's assertions and actions are to reality as geometry's axioms and postulates are to reality. 1) Religion is cognizant of old world responsibilities, but 2) it acts irresponsibly toward them 3) by contributing tools and techniques that make a new reality possible. 4) Its work is not performed by individuals who are 'holy', 5) rather they become 'holy' as they perform and contribute to that new reality. 6) This 'becoming' is religion's one directive: Let go of all content, including this one. 7) This act is the new reality. It is done 'this' day. It is worthy of being honored because by so doing, emptiness is now.

Martz, Erin. The Use of Sophiology. *Sophia (Australia)*, 31(1-2), 129-132, 1992.

Maruszewski, Tomasz. Human Rationality—Fact or Idealizational Assumption in Probability and Rationality, Eells, Ellery (ed). Amsterdam, Rodopi, 1991.

Because "rationality" is a natural concept we have to focus on central cases (exemplars) of that category. The author suggests that it is crucial to distinguish between competence and performance in an analysis of rationality. This differentiation allows to understand apparent discrepancies between theoretical view that man is rational being and his/her irrational behavior/cognitive biases, defense mechanisms. Theory of rationality should be built with the Norm Extraction Method of L J Cohen. This theory may be polymorphous because the following dimensions of a decision situation can determine the form of rational behaviour: emotional valence of the situation; repetitive versus unique character of the situation; descriptive versus affective character of the situation; open situation versus deadlock.

Maruszewski, Tomasz (ed) and Eells, Ellery (ed). *Probability and Rationality*. Amsterdam, Rodopi, 1991.

In this volume, the works of L Jonathan Cohen are discussed, both critically and in the way of exposition of his views. Following a foreword is an essay by Cohen himself, delineating the development of his thought in various areas, including political philosophy, philosophy of language, philosophy of law, and human rationality. Following this are twelve essays by authors from around the world on Cohen's work on methodology in psychology, on probabilistic reasoning, and on methodological pluralism in the investigation of human rationality. The volume concludes with comments by Cohen on these contributions to the volume.

Marvick, Louis W. Aspects of the Fin-de-Siècle Decadent Paradox. *Clio*, 22(1), 1-19, Fall 92.

The late nineteenth-century decadent was a two-sided being who credited himself with a number of solid bourgeois virtues. The chief characteristics of decadent style (oxymoron and a preoccupation with detail) were literary consequences of a more general effort to convince the bourgeois reader that the decadent (the morbid detail) was really the epitome of late nineteenth-century society (the healthy body). Janus, the two-faced god of thresholds, provides a model for conceiving how the decadent could simultaneously confront and turn his back on his time and place. The relatively small literary output of the decadents is accounted for by their reluctance to exchange the perception of paradox for a clear choice of alternatives.

Marx, Werner. *Towards a Phenomenological Ethics: Ethos and the Life-World*. Albany, SUNY Pr, 1992.

Maryniarczyk, A. From the History of the Research Work of a System of Metaphysics (in Polish). *Stud Phil Christ*, 28(1), 105-118, 1992.

The term "system," though found in different contexts of meaning, nevertheless is connected for good with a metaphysics or with a philosophical school. In the history of philosophy, this connection spawned two different theories: 1) the term "system" qualifies the ideal of the philosophical knowledge which is well ordered and describes the whole knowledge about reality and is a method of metaphysical cognition. Or 2) "system" indicates the disease (illness) and a weakness of metaphysical cognition. In this context, we want to see the history of the investigation of a system of metaphysics. (edited)

Mascaró, Joan and Rigau, Gemma. Modularity in Cognition: The Case of Phonetic and Semantic Interpretation of Empty Elements. *Theoria (Spain)*, 5(12-13), 107-128, N 90.

In this paper, we offer an argument in favor of the modular character of mind, based on a more detailed proof of the modular character of the linguistic capacity: in comparing the properties of different components of grammar in a specific area we will draw general consequences about the properties of the cognitive system. More specifically, we analyze and compare the properties, in logical form (LF) and in phonology, of "empty elements"—elements that are "visible" or "full" at some level of representation, but not at another level. (edited)

Mash, Roy. Big Numbers and Induction in the Case for Extra-Terrestrial Intelligence. *Phil Sci*, 60(2), 204-222, Je 93.

Arguments favoring the existence of extraterrestrial intelligence nearly always contain an overt appeal to big numbers, often combined with a covert reliance on generalization from a single instance. In this paper I examine both motifs, and consider whether big numbers might actually make palatable otherwise implausible single-case inductions. In the end, the dispute between believers and skeptics is seen to boil down to a conflict of intuitions which can barely be engaged, let alone resolved, given our present state of knowledge.

Masi, Giuseppe. La metafisica del soggetto e l'origine dello spiritualismo filosofico occidentale. *G Metaf*, 14(1), 91-112, Ja-Ap 92.

Masi, Giuseppe. Le fonti egiziane dello spiritualismo occidentale. *G Metaf*, 13(1), 37-67, Ja-Ap 91.

Masini, Andrea. 2-Sequent Calculus: A Proof Theory of Modalities. *Annals Pure Applied Log*, 58(3), 229-246, N 92.

In this work we propose an extension of the Gentzen sequent calculus in order to deal with modalities. We extend the notion of a sequent obtaining what we call a 2-sequent. For the obtained calculus we prove a cut elimination theorem.

Mason, Andrew. Liberalism and the Value of Community. *Can J Phil*, 23(2), 215-239, Je 93.

This paper focuses on a particular understanding of community which has been neglected in the recent debates between liberals and communitarians: one which regards 'community' as a moral notion, part of the point of which is to mark off relations between people which involve mutual concern, and which are not tainted by systematic exploitation. It is argued that liberals can value community when it is conceived in this way, but that the priority they give to autonomy means that they must sacrifice community for autonomy when the two conflict.

Massey, Barbara. Do All Rational Folk Reason As We Do? in Thought Experiments in Science and Philosophy, Horowitz, Tamara (ed). Lanham, Rowman & Littlefield, 1991.

Using a thought experiment, Frege tried to show classical logic to be privileged by showing that any logically deviant community we can conceive must be conceived of as irrational. His argument fails, because we can construct a richly fleshed-out thought experiment where a logically deviant community has rational justification intelligible to us. If some logical value other than truth is to be preserved through inference, then non-classical inference rules are required.

Massey, Gerald J. Backdoor Analycity in Thought Experiments in Science and Philosophy, Horowitz, Tamara (ed). Lanham, Rowman & Littlefield, 1991.

When they abandoned the analytic-synthetic distinction, analytic philosophers substituted for it uncritical appeals to thought experiments or conceivability arguments. Although the history of philosophy is replete with thought experiments, medieval and early modern philosophers developed sophisticated theories concerning what governs what happens in thought experiments. By contrast, contemporary philosophers subscribe to the thesis of facile conception according to which casual allegations of conceivability or inconceivability are taken as good evidence of possibility or impossibility. Philosophers need to adopt standards of thought experimentation like those found in science and to ground them in a general theory of conceivability.

Massey, Gerald J (ed) and Horowitz, Tamara (ed). *Thought Experiments in Science and Philosophy*. Lanham, Rowman & Littlefield, 1991.

Mastrolianni, Giovanni. Una traduzione sfortunata della "Scienza Nuova". *G Crit Filosof Ital*, 71(2), 308-19, My-Ag 92.

Masugi, Ken (ed). *Interpreting Tocqueville's "Democracy in America"*. Lanham, Rowman & Littlefield, 1991.

Matheson, Carl. Critical Notice of James Robert Brown's The Rational and the Social. *Can J Phil*, 23(1), 125-150, Mr 93.

In *The Rational and the Social*, Brown i) defends the concept of scientific rationality from a number of sociological attacks (Bloor, Barnes, Collins and Latour) and ii) proposes a meta-criterion for the adequacy of any prospective theory of scientific rationality. In this critical notice, the author argues that i) although Brown answers the letter of the sociologist's flawed arguments, he does not address their substantial claim that rationality is non-explanatory, and ii) Brown's own meta-criterion is both unwieldy and prone to generate unwelcome theories of rationality, such as the theory that every scientific decision is necessarily rational.

Mathews, Freya. *The Ecological Self*. Savage, Barnes & Noble, 1991.

Mathieu, Deborah. Crime and Punishment: Abortion as Murder?. *J Soc Phil*, 23(2), 5-22, Fall 92.

Mathieu, Vittorio. L'attualismo di Gentile e la morte dell'arte. *Filosofia*, 43(3), 347-380, S-D 92.

Mathieu, Vittorio. Manifesto di un movimento ermeneutico universale. *Filosofia*, 43(2), 199-213, My-Ag 92.

Matilal, Bimal Krishna. A Note on Samkara's Theodicy. *J Indian Phil*, 20(4), 363-376, D 92.

Matilal, Bimal Krishna. Is Prasanga a form of Deconstruction?. *J Indian Phil*, 20(4), 345-362, D 92.

Matson, Wallace I. Certainty Made Simple in Certainty and Surface in Epistemology and Philosophical Method, Martinich, A P (ed). Lewiston, Mellen Pr, 1991.

Certainty pertains to beliefs (not propositions). Language made possible a kind of belief, hence of certainty, not constrained by the actual nature of things. These imaginative beliefs, being socially important, were protected against confutation. The safeguards failed only once, in Greece, when the beliefs arising from practice coalesced in a world view — science — able to compete with imaginative certainties. Greek skepticism was aimed against imaginative certainties. Modern skepticism, on the contrary, is actually generated by them. It is dissolved once its nature is clearly understood — as is also the irrationalist notion of autonomous, global beliefs systems immune from external criticism.

Matteo, Anthony M. *Quest for the Absolute: The Philosophical Vision of Joseph Maréchal*. DeKalb, No Illinois Univ Pr, 1992.

Matthen, Mohan P and Hankinson, R J. Aristotle's Universe: Its Form and Matter. *Synthese*, 96(3), 417-435, S 93.

Despite anthropomorphic and animistic elements, much of Aristotle's conception of the universe in the early chapters of *De Caèlo* can be accounted for empirically. And though many moderns allege that Aristotle over-used naive observation, his key ideas originate from theory. It is argued that the doctrine of the universe as a bounded plenum arises from constraints on the explanation of eternal objects, from an anti-reductionist vision of the primacy of the whole, and from the phenomena.

Matthews, Gareth. Container Metaphysics According to Aristotle's Greek Commentators. *Can J Phil*, Supp(17), 7-23, 1991.

The neo-Platonism of Aristotle's Greek Commentators leaves them unable to take with full seriousness the *Categories* doctrine that individual organisms like this human being or that horse are the primary realities. Yet these commentators stand with Michael Frede and G E L Owen against John Ackrill in reading 1a24-5 in such a way that Aristotle can really mean what he says when he maintains that all other things besides primary substances are either said of them, or in them, as subjects. Not only are this grey and this color in the old grey mare, grey and color are there, too.

Matthews, Michael R. A Problem With Constructivist Epistemology. *Proc Phil Educ*, 48, 312-315, 1992.

Matthis, Michael J. Nietzsche as Anti-Naturalist. *Phil Today*, 37(2), 170-182, Sum 93.

Mattick, Paul. Aesthetics and Anti-Aesthetics in the Visual Arts. *J Aes Art Crit*, 51(2), 253-259, Spr 93.

Mattick Jr, Paul. Beautiful and Sublime: *Gender Totemism* in the Constitution of Art. *J Aes Art Crit*, 48(4), 293-303, Fall 90.

Matustik, Martin J. *Postnational Identity: Critical Theory and Existential Philosophy in Habermas, Kierkegaard, and Havel*. New York, Guilford, 1993.

This work offers an alternative to the conceptualization of identity based on nationalism that is emerging in eastern Europe, the former Soviet Union, and the US. In synthesizing the critical theory of Habermas and the existential philosophy of Kierkegaard and Havel, Matustik argues for a move from these nationalist and fundamentalist constructions of identity to postnational, open, and multicultural identity. Keying off Habermas's study of Kierkegaard's critique of the national-state, the author, himself a signatory of the *Charta 77*, uses Havel's call for a permanent existential and democratic revolution as a guidepost to emancipation from nationalist and fundamentalist ideologies. As well as offering the most extensive examination of Habermas's and Kierkegaard's critiques of nationalist identity available, it is one of the first works to treat seriously the existential thought of Havel.

Matzko, David M. Postmodernism, Saints and Scoundrels. *Mod Theol*, 9(1), 19-36, Ja 93.

Maudlin, Tim. Bell's Inequality, Information Transmission, and Prism Models. *Proc Phil Sci Ass*, 1, 404-417, 1992.

This paper examines violations of Bell's inequality from an information-theoretic point of view. I derive limits for the least amount of information that must be transmitted to reproduce the quantum predictions. I also demonstrate that Fine's analysis of his prism models is flawed.

Maudlin, Tim. Buckets of Water and Waves of Space: Why Space-Time is Probably a Substance. *Phil Sci*, 60(2), 183-203, Je 93.

This paper sketches a taxonomy of forms of substantivalism and relationism concerning space and time, and of the traditional arguments for these positions. Several natural sorts of relationism are able to account for Newton's bucket experiment. Conversely, appropriately constructed substantivalism can survive Leibniz's critique, a fact which has been obscured by the conflation of two of Leibniz's arguments. The form of relationism appropriate to the Special Theory of Relativity is also able to evade the problems raised by Field. I survey the effect of the General Theory of Relativity and of plenism on these considerations.

Maurer, Armand A. James Ross on the Divine Ideas: A Reply. *Amer Cath Phil Quart*, 65(2), 213-220, Spr 91.

The article is a reply to Ross's criticism of Etienne Gilson for ascribing to Thomas Aquinas the doctrine that God contains many ideas as models for actual and possible creatures. The article shows that Gilson regarded this Thomist doctrine as an accommodation to Augustinism. In fact, Aquinas taught that there is but one divine idea, namely his own essence.

Maurer, Armand A. Orestes Brownson and Christian Philosophy. *Monist*, 75(3), 341-353, Jl 92.

The article shows that Brownson defended the philosopher's free and independent use of reason according to its own nature and laws. He rejected the Traditionalist view of philosophy's resting on authority rather than on reason. Thus, in the Traditionalist sense 'Christian philosophy' is a misnomer and confusion of nature and supernature. But Brownson also rejected rationalism, arguing that Christian revelation can throw light on philosophical issues.

Maurer, Armand A. Thomists and Thomas Aquinas on the Foundation of Mathematics. *Rev Metaph*, 47(1), 43-61, S 93.

The article shows the disagreement among Thomists on the object of mathematics, some claiming that it is real quantity, others that it is quantity as constructed or reconstructed in the imagination and mind. Evidence for both interpretations can be found in Aquinas. In a neglected passage he places the immediate foundation of mathematics in the constructive act of the mind, with real quantity as its remote foundation.

Maurer, Virginia G and Dunfee, Thomas W. Corporate Attorney Whistle-Blowing: Devising a Proper Standard. *Bus Prof Ethics J*, 11(3-4), 3-39, Fall-Wint 92.

A consequentialistic model of corporate attorney whistle-blowing is developed and then applied to determine the parameters of a legitimate professional ethical norm controlling corporate attorney disclosures of illicit actions by clients. Current practice reveals variety in norms among the states, with some prohibiting attorneys from revealing serious criminal activities except in narrowly defined circumstances. Application of the model supports a standard of broad permissibility while rejecting the extremist norms of total prohibition or of broadly mandated disclosure. Corporate attorneys should be allowed substantial moral free space in choosing whether or not to disclose wrong-doing.

Mauri, Margarita. Claves para la paz. *Sapientia*, 47(183), 73-78, 1992.

Mauri, Margarita. Etica Actual: Una Doble Perspectiva. *Rev Filosof (Mexico)*, 24(71), 135-141, My-Ag 91.

This paper treats to present the currey debate between two faces of the foundation of moral decision: virtue or duty. It analyses the most important thesis of philosophers that follow at the present time the ethics of Aristotle and Kant.

Mauri Alvarez, M. L'"akrasia" nell'Etica Nicomachea. *Sapienza*, 46(1), 71-78, 1993.

Mavrodes, George I. On the Very Strongest Arguments in Prospects for Natural Theology, Long, Eugene Thomas (ed). Washington, Cath Univ Amer Pr, 1992.

Mavrodes, George I. The Gods above the Gods: Can the High Gods Survive? in Reasoned Faith, Stump, Eleonore (ed). Ithaca, Cornell Univ Pr, 1993.

Maxwell, Nicholas. Does Orthodox Quantum Theory Undermine, or Support, Scientific Realism?. *Phil Quart*, 43(171), 139-157, Ap 93.

It is usually taken for granted that orthodox quantum theory poses a serious problem for scientific realism, in that the theory is empirically extraordinarily successful, and yet has instrumentalism built into it. This paper stands this view on its head. It is shown that orthodox quantum theory suffers from a number of severe (if not always noticed) defects precisely because of its inbuilt instrumentalism. This defective character of orthodox quantum theory thus undermines instrumentalism, and supports scientific realism. The paper goes on to consider whether there is here the basis for a general argument against instrumentalism.

Maxwell, Nicholas. Induction and Scientific Realism: Einstein Versus Van Fraassen. *Brit J Phil Sci*, 44(1), 61-101, Mr 93.

I expound and defend a conception of science, close to Einstein's, which I call aim-oriented empiricism, and which asserts that science 1) presupposes that the universe is comprehensible in some way or other, and 2) has aims and methods that evolve with evolving knowledge. Aim-oriented empiricism solves the problem of induction, provides decisive grounds for reflecting constructive empiricism, solves the problem of verisimilitude, enables us to interpret successive fundamental physical theories as providing us with improving approximate knowledge of unobservable entities, and provides physics with a rational, if fallible, method of discovery.

Maxwell, Nicholas. Induction and Scientific Realism: Einstein Versus Van Fraassen—Part Three. *Brit J Phil Sci*, 44(2), 275-305, Je 93.

This paper shows how Einstein made essential use of aim-oriented empiricism (expounded and defended in Parts I and II) in discovering special and general relativity. The paper then considers whether the nature Einstein explicitly advocated aim-oriented empiricism.

Maxwell, Nicholas. On Relativity Theory and Openness of the Future. *Phil Sci*, 60(2), 341-348, Je 93.

In a recent paper Stein (1991) makes a number of criticisms of an earlier paper of mine (Maxwell 1985) that explored the question of whether the idea that the future is genuinely "open" in a probabilistic universe is compatible with special relativity. I disagree with almost all of Stein's criticisms.

May, Larry. *Sharing Responsibility*. Chicago, Univ of Chicago Pr, 1992.

The central claim of this book is that people should see themselves as sharing responsibility for various harms perpetrated by, or occurring within, their communities. The book is divided into three main parts, each corresponding to an area of expansion of the domain of responsibility that is warranted once one accepts the notion of shared responsibility. In the first part, I argue for responsibility based on one's attitudes, especially those attitudes that make harm within a community more likely to occur. In the second part, I argue for responsibility based on failures to act, both individual omissions and collective inaction, especially as those failures increase the likelihood and scope of harm that one's community perpetrates. And in the third part, I argue for increased responsibility based on the various roles and positions people assume within their communities.

May, Larry and Strikwerda, Robert. Male Friendship and Intimacy. *Hypatia*, 7(3), 110-125, Sum 92.

Our primary focus is the concept of intimacy, especially in the context of adult American male relationships. We begin with an examination of comradeship, a nonintimate form of friendship, then develop an account of the nature and value of intimacy in friendship. We follow this with discussions of obstacles to intimacy and of Aristotle's views. In the final section, we discuss the process of men attaining intimacy.

May, Larry (ed) and Strikwerda, Robert (ed). *Rethinking Masculinity*. Lanham, Rowman & Littlefield, 1992.

This anthology presents a set of philosophical essays written by men, most of whom call themselves feminists which attempt to come to terms with some issue or question arising out of the authors' experiences of being a male in Western culture. The anthology begins with a reassessment of the data on sex role differences. It then considers men's experiences in war and sports, romance and fatherhood, as well as the problems of intimacy and homophobia. There is also a section on pornography and on empowerment. The authors are: Patrick Grim, J Glenn Gray, Brian Pronger, Hugh LaFollette, Larry May, Robert Strikwerda, Patrick Hopkins, Alan Soble, Harry Brod, Kenneth Clatterbaugh, Leonard Harris, and Victor Seidler.

May, Larry and Strikwerda, Robert A. Fatherhood and Nurturance in Rethinking Masculinity, May, Larry (ed). Lanham, Rowman & Littlefield, 1992.

We argue that fatherhood should today be ideally conceived in terms of nurturance. First, we provide a brief history of modern conceptions of fatherhood. Second, we analyze the notion of nurturance and argue that conceptions of fatherhood that are not drawn in terms of nurturance are quite anemic. Third, we respond to several arguments against our thesis from biology and psychology. And finally, we explore some of the significant advantages to men that will accrue when they see themselves as, and become, nurturers.

May, Larry and Strikwerda, Robert A. Male Friendship and Intimacy in Rethinking Masculinity, May, Larry (ed). Lanham, Rowman & Littlefield, 1992.

Our primary focus is the *concept* of intimacy, especially in the context of adult American male relationships. We begin with an examination of comradeship, a contrasting nonintimate form of friendship. We follow this with a discussion of obstacles to intimacy and a comparison of our views with those of Aristotle. In the final section, we discuss the process of attaining intimacy for men and resources for enhancing that process.

May, Todd G. The Community's Absence in Lyotard, Nancy, and Lacoue-Labarthe. *Phil Today*, 37(3), 275-284, Fall 93.

This paper argues that the project engaged in by Lyotard, Nancy, and Lacoue-Labarthe to conceive a non-totalitarian community on the basis of absence necessarily fails, because such a conception already presupposes a positive communal agreement on the moral disvalue of totalitarianism. The more Foucaultian and Deleuzian conception of community as a contingent whole is offered as an alternative to such an absence-based conception.

May, Todd G. The System and Its Fractures: Gilles Deleuze on Otherness. *J Brit Soc Phenomenol*, 24(1), 3-14, Ja 93.

Like many contemporary French thinkers, Gilles Deleuze is concerned with articulating a philosophical approach that escapes the problems associated with identity. His approach to otherness is distinct, however, in its attempt to conceptualize difference as positive. It is argued that by locating difference in irreducible singularities, however, Deleuze's thought falls into paradox. Another strain of his thought, a holism associated with his "rhizomatic" approach, provides a more fruitful framework for the articulation of otherness.

Mayada, Arlene M. Whitehead and Japanese Aesthetics. *Harvard Rev Phil*, 1(1), 29-37, Spr 91.

Mayer, J R A. A Post-Modern Look at the Tension Between Anarchy and Socialism. *Hist Euro Ideas*, 16(4-6), 591-596, Ja 93.

The contemporary tension between attitudes expecting governments to address and resolve social problems and regulate commerce, health service and education and the view that governance limits individual freedoms, and hence the best government is least government results from the fact that these views are frequently simultaneously and unreflectively help by many. Thus socialism and the "new right," appealing to minimizing the role of government, both seek and find popular support. Post-modernity can be characterized as no longer seeking to find a single coherent alternative by means of a rational process: rather, it sees the tension resulting from the simultaneous appeal of inconsistent positions as fruitful and appropriate for the dynamic development of sociopolitical contexts.

Mayhew, Robert. Aristotle on Property. *Rev Metaph*, 46(4), 803-831, Je 93.

Despite the large amount of work that has been done on Aristotle's political philosophy, relatively little has been written that deals at length with his views on property. In this essay I investigate all the relevant texts on property from the Aristotelian corpus (and most importantly from the *Politics*), beginning with an especially careful look at Aristotle's criticism of Plato's communism of property. I conclude that although Aristotle does not defend absolute property rights, the limits to the use of property are few, especially when considered in their historical context.

Maynard, Patrick L. Talbot's Technologies: Photographic Depiction, Detection, and Reproduction. *J Aes Art Crit*, 47(3), 263-276, Sum 89.

Mayo, David J and Gunderson, Martin. Altruism and Physician Assisted Death. *J Med Phil*, 18(3), 281-296, Je 93.

We assume that a statute permitting physician assisted death has been passed. We note that the rationale for the passage of such a statute would be respect for individual autonomy, the avoidance of suffering and the possibility of death with dignity. We deal with two moral issues that will arise once such a law is passed. First, we argue that the rationale for passing an assistance in dying law in the first place provides a justification for assisting patients to die who are motivated by altruistic reasons as well as patients who are motivated by reasons of self-interest. Second, we argue that the reasons for passing a physician assisted death law in the first place justify extending the law to cover some non-terminal patients as well as terminal patients.

Mayo, David J and Gunderson, Martin. Physician Assisted Death and Hard Choices. *J Med Phil*, 18(3), 329-341, Je 93.

We argue that after the passage of a physician assisted death law some inequities in the health care system which prevent people from getting the medical care they need will become reasons for choosing assisted death. This raises the issue of whether there is compelling moral reason to change those inequities after the passage of an assisted death law. We argue that the passage of an assisted death law will not create additional moral reasons for eliminating inequities *simply* because they become motives for someone to opt for assisted death. We also argue that it is not feasible to eliminate these reasons for opting for assisted death by granting a right to health care because of an intractable scarcity of medical resources.

Mayol, Víctor Velarde. Conocimiento y concepto. *Sapientia*, 47(183), 23-44, 1992.

Mazlish, Bruce. The Question of *The Question of Hu*. *Hist Theor*, 31(2), 143-152, 1992.

The article examines Jonathan Spence's book *The Question of Hu*, asking the central question as to what difference it makes if the book is viewed as history or fiction. (Spence's own question is whether Hu, the Chinese, is mad.) In addition to raising specific questions as to Spence's treatment of his materials, the article addresses the question of the historical novel, following on the work of Georg Lukács and Sir Walter Scott, and concludes that Spence's work is not of this genre. Neither is it a history à la Herodotus or Thucydides, where analysis—the raising of *historical* questions and sharing the evidence and inference with the reader—and narrative must go together. The article concludes that, wonderful as *The Question of Hu* is as literature, it is not a true piece of historical narrative. In coming to this judgment, the article uses Spence's book as a way of reflecting on fundamental questions concerning the nature of history, fiction, analysis, and narrative.

Mazumdar, Rinita. How Significant is Socrates' Midwifery?. *Indian Phil Quart*, 19(4), 311-326, O 92.

Commentators have come up with various interpretations of Socrates's reference to himself as a midwife in the *Theaetetus*. The author discusses several of the moral common interpretations. (edited)

Mazzarella, Arturo. I poeti nel tempo della povertà. *Filosofia*, 43(2), 313-321, My-Ag 92.

McAdams, Tony. *The Great Gatsby* as a Business Ethics Inquiry. *J Bus Ethics*, 12(8), 653-660, Ag 93.

The author argues for the use of F Scott Fitzgerald's novel, *The Great Gatsby*, as a "text" for studying business ethics. The author presents a documented analysis of the major ethics themes in the book including, for example, moral growth, Gatsby's life of illusion, the withering of the American Dream, and the parallels between the 1920s and the 1980s. Fitzgerald's fiction analysis is then tied to the '90s via current social science and philosophical evidence addressing Fitzgerald's 1920s concerns. Data examining the incidence of lying in contemporary American life, a review of Lawrence Kohlberg's theory of moral development, and data-based studies of wealth distribution in America are among those strands of evidence. The article concludes with a brief look at students' responses to *Gatsby* in a legal and social environment of business course. In effect, the author presents a lesson plan for teaching *The Great Gatsby* as a general introduction to ethics and American values. As such, the *Gatsby* discussion is designed to precede a more pragmatic and specific inquiry employing conventional business cases and the like.

McAdoo, Nick. Can Art Ever Be Just about Itself?. *J Aes Art Crit*, 50(2), 131-138, Spr 92.

In this paper, I argue that it is impossible to separate our aesthetic interest in art from its non-aesthetic significancies. Usually, this is because the work's *aesthetic* identity is dependent on its thematic and expressive aspects, but even in characterizing *pure* instrumental music and abstract art, we typically find ourselves borrowing a vocabulary from the "everyday" world. I conclude that not only is the strict disjunction "either aesthetic or non-aesthetic" unworkable, but that without this "built in" connection between aesthetic form and worldly significance, we simply could not explain the seriousness of our interest in art.

McAlister, Linda L. Edith Stein: Essential Differences. *Phil Today*, 37(1), 70-77, Spr 93.

I argue that Edith Stein's work on women has been ignored by feminists because of its obvious essentialism. But feminist thinkers are now beginning to have beyond knee-jerk condemnation of essentialism. I give four examples of this and argue that Stein's brand of essentialism avoids the objection that it erases differences among women. I suggest that her theory of types and of individual difference may make it worthwhile for feminists to look into her work.

McAllister, James W. Scientific Realism and the Criteria for Theory-Choice. *Erkenntnis*, 38(2), 203-222, Mr 93.

The central terms of certain theories which were valued highly in the past, such as the phlogiston theory, are now believed by realists not to refer. Laudan and others have claimed that, in the light of the existence of such theories, scientific realism is untenable. This paper argues in response that realism is consistent with—and indeed is able to explain—such theories' having been highly valued and yet not being close to the truth. It follows that the set of highly-valued past theories cited by Laudan, presumed to miltate against realism, is in fact innocuous to the doctrine. The argument hinges largely on identifying the grounds on which theory-adoption is actually performed.

McBride, William. Social Justice on Trial: The Verdict of History in Analecta Husserliana, XXXI, Tymieniecka, Anna-Teresa (ed). Dordrecht, Kluwer, 1990.

This article notes with satisfaction, and encourages, an apparent change in philosophical focus from theories of justice, especially of the distributive sort emphasized by Rawls, to the phenomenological description and systematic analysis of salient social injustices, including particularly those of global economics. It briefly documents the twin historical failures both of actual societies to realize, and of social theories such as Plato's to "capture", perfect justice, arguing that there is no convincing evidence of the existence of such a thing and that even talk of "nearly just societies" is seriously misleading.

McCabe, Herbert. The Logic of Mysticism—I in Religion and Philosophy, Warner, Marin (ed). New York, Cambridge Univ Pr, 1992.

McCabe, Mary Margaret. Myth, Allegory and Argument in Plato. *Apeiron*, 25(4), 47-67, D 92.

McCann, Hugh J and Kvanvig, Jonathan L. The Occasionalist Proselytizer in Philosophical Perspectives, 5: Philosophy of Religion, 1991, Tomberlin, James E (ed). Atascadero, Ridgeview, 1991.

This paper explores the occasionalist implications of the claim that God not only creates the world, but sustains it throughout its existence. It is argued that both the doctrine of sustenance and that of divine providence indicate that God is directly responsible for everything that occurs. This is incompatible with event causation, if by the latter we understand a process wherein one event is responsible for the existence of another. But this concept of causation is untenable in any case: neither diachronically nor synchronically does any event ever produce another. There are, however, other ways of understanding causation so that it remains a viable concept, and the explanatory force of scientific laws is preserved.

McCarney, Joseph. Endgame. *Rad Phil*, 62, 35-38, Autumn 92.

McCarney, Joseph and Arthur, Chris. Marxism Today: An Interview with István Mészáros. *Rad Phil*, 62, 27-34, Autumn 92.

McCarrick, Pat Milmoe. A Right to Health Care. *Kennedy Inst Ethics J*, 2(4), 389-405, D 92.

The paper provides a brief essay and a compilation of works dating from 1976 concerning whether or not all Americans have a right to receive some level of guaranteed health care. Although not legally established, this concept of a right to health care has gained wide acceptance in the past fifty years. The debate flourished during the 1960s and 1970s, and current literature continues to offer much the same arguments. Annotated citations to government documents, statements by organizations, books, chapters and articles are included.

McCarthy, Christine. Applied Ethics for Teachers: What Is It and How Do We Teach It?. *Phil Stud Educ*, 1, 82-94, 1990.

McCarthy, Christine. Why Be Critical? (or Rational, or Moral?): The Justification of Critical Thinking. *Proc Phil Educ*, 48, 60-68, 1992.

McCarthy, Michael. *The Crisis of Philosophy*. Albany, SUNY Pr, 1989.

McCarthy, Thomas A. Philosophy and Social Practice in Philosophical Interventions in the Unfinished Project of Enlightenment, Honneth, Axel (& other eds). Cambridge, MIT Pr, 1992.

McCarty, David Charles. Penelope Maddy's *Realism in Mathematics* and Charles Chihara's *Constructibility and Mathematical Existence*. *Synthese*, 96(2), 255-291, Ag 93.

McCarty, David Charles. Undoubted Truth. *Proc Phil Educ*, 48, 172-176, 1992.

McCarty, Richard. Kantian Moral Motivation and the Feeling of Respect. *J Hist Phil*, 31(3), 421-435, Jl 93.

The prevailing, "intellectualist" view of Kantian moral motivation is that respect for the moral law is properly conceived as a purely cognitive motivational attitude. While some intellectualist interpreters acknowledge Kant's comments about respect's affective aspect, or "moral feeling," they deny this feeling can play any motivational role in action *from duty*. This article advances an alternative, "affectivist" view of Kantian moral motivation: that Kant assumed the feeling of respect does indeed play a motivational role. Textual evidence form Kant's early lectures in ethics to his final ethical writings supports the affectivist interpretation.

McCauley, Robert. Models of Knowing and Their Relation to Our Understanding of Liberal Education. *Metaphilosophy*, 23(3), 288-309, Jl 92.

Models of direct knowing in some domain have unfortunate proclivities. Extreme versions foreclose on alternatives, squashing opportunities for criticism and imaginative endeavor. Since these models' claims for unmediated knowledge are never themselves unmediated, they are inescapabley hypothetical. Models that reject direct knowing accentuate covert theoretical assumptions and construction and comparison of idealized, overt theories. Models of unmediated knowing analogically, if not directly, encourage "retentive" view of education. While underscoring proficiency with profound positions from the past, comparative models of knowing leave little room for revering anything. The ultimate goals of education on these models concern developing skills for richer living.

McCauley, Robert N. Brainwork: A Review of Paul Churchland's *A Neurocomputational Perspective*. *Phil Psych*, 6(1), 81-96, 1993.

Taking inspiration from developments in neurocomputational modeling, Paul Churchland develops his positions in the philosophy of mind and the philosophy of science. Concerning the former, Churchland relaxes his eliminativism at various points and seems to endorse a traditional identity account of sensory qualia. Although he remains unsympathetic to folk psychology, he no longer seeks the elimination of normative epistemology, but rather its transformation to a philosophical enterprise informed by current developments in the relevant sciences. Churchland supplies suggestive discussions of the character of knowledge, simplicity, explanation, theory, and conceptual change. Many of his treatments turn on his prototype activation model of neural representation, which looks to the notion of a 'prototype' as it is employed in the psychological literature on concept representation, however, this and other features of Churchland's neurocomputational program do not square well with some of his views about cross-scientific relations.

McCauley, Robert N. Defending Normative Naturalism: A Reply to Ellen Klein. *Phil Psych*, 5(3), 299-305, 1992.

Rejecting Klein's claims that normative epistemology and naturalism are mutually exclusive, I defend the normative naturalism of my "Epistemology in an Age of Cognitive Science". When insisting that epistemic standards simultaneously external to, superior to, and independent of those of science do not exist, I hold neither that science exhausts standards of rationality nor that relevant extra-scientific considerations do not exist. Cognitive science may transform how we pose some normative questions in epistemology. Concurring with Klein that the burden of evidence resides with normative naturalism, I explore suggestive proposals that Churchland and Thagard have offered on just this front.

McClain, F Michael and Falls-Corbitt, Margaret. God and Privacy. *Faith Phil*, 9(3), 369-386, Jl 92.

Contemporary reflection about God which includes certain assumptions raises for us the issue of God and privacy. Some philosophers believe that there is no obligation to respect privacy grounded in our basic moral duty to respect the autonomous choices of persons. If this is correct, and if it is correct to think of God as one whose actions perfectly accord with moral duties, then there is a *prima facie* case for thinking that God respects our privacy. We explore this thesis by considering the most plausible objections to it, including matters of religious practice.

McClamrock, Ron. Functional Analysis and Etiology. *Erkenntnis*, 38(2), 249-260, Mr 93.

Cummins (1982) argues that etiological considerations are not only *insufficient* but *irrelevant* for the determination of *function*. I argue that his claim of irrelevance rests on a misrepresentation of the use of functions in evolutionary explanations. I go on to suggest how accepting an *etiological constraint* on functional analysis might help resolve some problems involving the use of functional explanations.

McCleary, Richard C. Philosophical Prose and Practice. *Philosophy*, 68(263), 79-89, Ja 93.

McClennen, Edward and Found, Peter G. Weighing Risk. *J Soc Phil*, 24(2), 155-175, Fall 93.

McCloskey, Donald N. Minimal Statism and Metamodernism: Reply to Friedman. *Crit Rev*, 6(1), 107-112, Wint 92.

Friedman misunderstands postmodernism — or, as it could better be called, metamodernism. Metamodernism is the common sense beyond the lunatic formulas of the Vienna Circle and conventional statistics. It has little to do with the anxieties of Continental intellectuals. It therefore is necessary for serious empirical work on the role of the state.

McCloskey, H J and Uniacke, Suzanne. Peter Singer and Non-Voluntary 'Euthanasia': Tripping Down the Slippery Slope. *J Applied Phil*, 9(2), 203-219, 1992.

This article discusses the nature of euthanasia, and the way in which redevelopment of the concept of euthanasia in some influential recent philosophical writing has led to morally less discriminating killing/letting die/not saving being misdescribed as euthanasia. Peter Singer's defense of non-voluntary 'euthanasia' of defective infants in his influential book *Practical Ethics* is critically evaluated. We argue that Singer's pseudo-euthanasia arguments in *Practical Ethics* are unsatisfactory as approaches to determining the legitimacy of killing, and that these arguments present a total utilitarian improvement policy—not a case for non-voluntary euthanasia.

McColm, Gregory L. Eventual Periodicity and "One-Dimensional" Queries. *Notre Dame J Form Log*, 33(2), 273-290, Spr 92.

We expand on the automata-like behavior of monadic second order relations investigated by Buchi and Ladner. We present a generalization of their representation theorem and use it to separate the intersection of the classes of monadic existential second order and monadic universal second order queries from the class of one-dimensional inductive queries.

McConnell, David H. In Good Standing? The Position of Women in Higher Education. *Phil Stud Educ*, 1, 151-163, 1990.

McConnell, Terrance. Dilemmas and Incommensurateness. *J Value Inq*, 27(2), 247-252, Ap 93.

It is often argued that right-making properties are incommensurate and because of this we must endorse the possibility of moral dilemmas. This paper criticizes that position. It argues that even if basic values are incommensurate, it does not follow that there are genuine moral dilemmas. The analysis provided also shows how foes of dilemmas can handle so-called symmetrical cases.

McCormack, Thelma. If Pornography Is the Theory, Is Inequality the Practice?. *Phil Soc Sci*, 23(3), 298-326, S 93.

An examination of contemporary debate on pornography and censorship within feminist scholarship. Claim is made by pro-censorship groups that pornography degrades women and is, therefore, instrumental for inequality. Paper examines this and finds it false. 1) The image of women used to rationalize structural inequality is the traditional family-centered woman. 2) Confuses degradation and devaluation. Paper also examines claim that a choice must be made between equality and freedom of expression. Rejects on grounds that from a feminist perspective, no such trade-off can be made. Censorship legalizes a social problem and has long-term effects of reenforcing dependency of women.

McCoy, Charles. The Polanyian Revolution: Post-Critical Perspectives for Ethics. *Tradition Discovery*, 18(2), 33-39, 1991-92.

McCoy, E D and Shrader-Frechette, Kristin. Community Ecology, Scale, and the Instability of the Stability Concept. *Proc Phil Sci Ass*, 1, 184-199, 1992.

Conceptual clarification is perhaps the most important key to progress in community ecology. In order to investigate some of the reasons that might explain why community ecology has been unable to arrive at a widely accepted general theory, in this essay we analyze "stability," one of its most important foundational concepts. After reviewing the stability concept and sketching its associated problems, we assess the epistemological status of four difficulties with the concept.

McCullagh, C Behan. Evil and the Love of God. *Sophia (Australia)*, 31(3), 48-60, 1992.

Physical and moral evil seem less inconsistent with God's love when the Biblical account of the nature of his love is considered more carefully. The Bible shows God has a greater concern with our eternal salvation than with our physical comfort. Pain, indeed, has its uses, and its significance is discussed. The Bible also describes a loving God as doing all He can to encourage and enable people to choose the good, by no means indifferent to moral evil.

McCulloch, Gregory. The Spirit of Twin Earth. *Analysis*, 52(3), 168-174, Jl 92.

McCulloch, Gregory. The Very Idea of the Phenomenological. *Proc Aris Soc*, 93, 39-57, 1993.

McCumber, John. *The Company of Words: Hegel, Language, and Systematic Philosophy*. Evanston, Northwestern Univ Pr, 1993.

This book interprets Hegel as the first important philosopher to have made the linguistic turn (so that the famous "Absolute," for example, is a language game). Hegel's approach to language and thought is related to earlier thinkers (Plato, Locke, Kant, and others). It is contrasted with contemporary thinkers who unknowingly followed Hegel in the linguistic turn: Flege, Wittgenstein, Austin, Davidson. Strengths and possibilities are assessed.

McCune, William W. Single Axioms for the Left Group and the Right Group Calculi. *Notre Dame J Form Log*, 34(1), 132-139, Wint 93.

This article is on axiomatizations of the left group calculus and of the right group calculus. The axiomatizations use modus ponens rather than equality substitution as the inference rule. The structures being axiomatized are ordinary free groups, and the sole operation is division. Previous axiomatizations are due to J A Kalman. The article contains single axioms and other simple axiomatizations of the two calculi. An automated theorem-proving program was used extensively to find candidate axiomatizations and to find proofs that candidates are in fact axiomatizations.

McCurdy, William James. Taking Graham Seriously on Taking Chinese Thought Seriously. *J Chin Phil*, 19(3), 329-355, S 92.

McDermott, John J. A Sometime Companion. *Bull Santayana Soc*, 11, 11-14, Fall 93.

McDermott, Robert. Philosophy and Evolution of Consciousness in Revisioning Philosophy, Ogilvy, James (ed). Albany, SUNY Pr, 1992.

This paper aims to illumine the relationship between philosophy and the evolution of consciousness, including a brief sketch of the history of philosophy from its beginnings until its possible eclipse in our time, and suggestions concerning ways in which philosophy can advance the evolution of consciousness. Such an advance can take place by means of a method and practice of philosophical imagination, particularly through applying this meditative philosophic discipline to the workings of philosophy in relation to the evolution of consciousness. When practiced as a spiritual discipline, as meditative thinking, philosophy can and should play a distinctive—perhaps decisive—role in showing the way out of the present crisis of consciousness.

McDonald, J F and Lugg, Andrew. Critical Notice of Tom Sorell *Scientism: Philosophy and the Infatuation with Science*. *Can J Phil*, 23(2), 291-298, Je 93.

This paper focuses on Sorell's critique of scientistic philosophy. We dispute his view that philosophers such as Bacon, Descartes, Wittgenstein, Carnap, and Quine are scientistic because they advocate the extension of the methods of science into nonscientific domains. And we challenge his view that we must embrace metaphysical philosophy if we are to avoid scientism. Our main contention is that both scientistic and metaphysical philosophy should give way to the Kantian approach—dismissed by Sorell—that "the critical path alone is still open".

McDonald, Marvin J and Vaden House, D. Post-physicalism and Beyond. *Dialogue (Canada)*, 31(4), 593-621, Autumn 92.

McDonough, Kevin. Moral Rules, Utilitarianism and Schizophrenic Moral Education. *J Phil Educ*, 26(1), 75-89, 1992.

R M Hare has argued for and defended a 'two-level', view of moral agency. He argues that moral agents ought to rely on the rules of 'intuitive moral thinking' for their 'everyday' moral judgments. When these rules conflict or when we do not have a rule at hand, we ought to ascend to the act-utilitarian, 'critical' level of moral thinking. I argue that since the rules at the intuitive level of moral thinking necessarily conflict much more often than Hare supposes, and since we often do not have ready-made rules for our moral judgments, we must necessarily use critical moral thinking very frequently. However, act-utilitarian judgments at this level will sharply conflict with our strongly held 'intuitive' moral convictions. I show that Hare's attempt to balance these two aspects of moral judgment requires us to simultaneously adopt two conflicting sets of moral standards, and thus an attempt to inculcate such standards constitutes a 'schizophrenic' moral education. Finally, I briefly outline an alternative conception of moral education, based on Aristotelian phronesis.

McDonough, Richard. The Last Stand of Mechanism. *J Speculative Phil*, 6(3), 206-225, 1992.

McGinn concludes that the human mind, and perhaps all minds (including God's) cannot possibly know the mechanisms underlying consciousness. Rather than conclude that there are no such mechanisms, he holds that they *must* exist, but are described by a science which may be *unknowable by all minds!* The emerging partnership between scientism, skepticism and occultism in analytical philosophy is a precise repetition of the occultism which led to the collapse of the French Enlightenment. That collapse paved the way for the German Enlightenment, and the view that skepticism can be avoided only if science is limited by an intelligence which cannot itself be understood in scientific terms.

McDonough, Richard. Wittgenstein's Doctrine of Silence. *Thomist*, 56(4), 695-699, O 92.

McDowell, John. Intentionality *De Re* in John Searle and His Critics, Lepore, Ernest (ed). Cambridge, Blackwell, 1991.

McDowell, John. Meaning and Intentionality in Wittgenstein's Later Philosophy. *Midwest Stud Phil*, 17, 40-52, 1992.

McErlean, Jennifer. Critical Principles and Emergence in Beardsley's Aesthetic Theory. *J Aes Art Crit*, 48(2), 153-156, Spr 90.

In his article "Beardsley, Sibley and Critical Principles" (*The Journal of Aesthetics and Art Criticism* 46(1987):229-237), George Dickie claimed that while Beardsley's distinction between primary and secondary criteria failed to maintain the generality of critical reasons, he believed he could save the distinction by modifying it along lines suggested by Frank Sibley. I argue that Dickie's new definition of "primary positive criteria", a definition that Beardsley in fact comes close to espousing in his later works, does not succeed in preserving generality.

McGary, Howard and Lawson, Bill E. *Between Slavery and Freedom: Philosophy and American Slavery*. Bloomington, Indiana Univ Pr, 1992.

The American slave experience and philosophical analysis are used to examine six moral and political concepts— oppression, paternalism, resistance, political obligation, citizenship, and forgiveness. This work also demonstrates that the slave narrative, important historical accounts of the predicament of slaves, is equally useful as a means of exploring perplexing philosophical issues.

McGee, Vann. Reply to Christian Piller's "Comment on Keith Lehrer and Vann McGee's Solution of Newcomb's Problem". *Grazer Phil Stud*, 40, 229-232, 1991.

McGee, Vann. Two Problems with Tarski's Theory of Consequence. *Proc Aris Soc*, 92, 273-292, 1992.

Two problems arise for the treatment of validity as truth in every model (treating a model as a structured set). First, it is a contingent fact what models there are, whereas it is not contingent what sentences are valid. This is resolved by an ontological argument, relying on the thesis that mathematical objects are necessary existents; second, there may be features of the universe as a whole which are not reflected in any set-sized model. As a possible example, an analogue of Hilbert's completeness axiom is suggested which, if true, gives a categorical second-order characterization of the universe of set theory.

McGee, Vann and Lehrer, Keith. An Epistemic Principle Which Solves Newcomb's Paradox. *Grazer Phil Stud*, 40, 197-220, 1991.

If it is certain that performing an observation to determine whether P is true will in no way influence whether P is true, then the proposition that the observation is performed ought to be probabilistically independent of P. Applying the notion of "observation" liberally, so that a wide variety of actions are treated as observations, this proposed new principle of belief revision yields the result that simple utility maximization gives the correct solution to the Fisher smoking paradox and the two-box solution to Newcomb's paradox.

McGee, Vann and Lehrer, Keith. Particulars, Individual Qualities, and Universals in Language, Truth and Ontology, Mulligan, Kevin (ed). Dordrecht, Kluwer, 1992.

This article develops Thomas Reid's theory of individual qualities and universals connecting his theory with recent work. Reid held that individualities, now called tropes, were the basis for our general conceptions of universals which, however, are not things that exist. His theory is related to prototype theory in psychology and to nominalist ontology.

McGeer, V L. The Problem of Error: A Surd Spot in Rational Intentionalism. *Philosophia (Israel)*, 21(3-4), 295-309, Ap 92.

McGhee, Michael. Chastity and the (Male) Philosophers. *J Applied Phil*, 10(1), 45-57, 1993.

Although sexual continence is no longer considered a necessary condition of the philosophical life, various spiritual traditions favour the development of a form of 'concentration' (*samdhi*) of the person which they claim to depend on such continence, and of which a perceived outcome is a natural state of 'chastity'. Such 'concentration' is insisted upon on the grounds that it is the condition under which the real nature of things is disclosed to the practitioner. Since philosophers are concerned to discover the real nature of things the implication might be thought to be that sexual continence should come back into favour and philosophers become spiritual practitioners. However, a distinction is made between ejaculatory and non-ejaculatory sexual activity and the suggestion made that despite the dominant tradition in the West, the relevant forms of concentration may develop under a regime of non-ejaculation rather than of continence understood as abstinence. (edited)

McGhee, Michael. Facing Truths: Ethics and the Spiritual Life. *Philosophy*, 32(Supp), 229-246, 1992.

McGhee, Michael. Facing Truths: Ethics and the Spiritual Life in Philosophy, Religion and the Spiritual Life, McGhee, Michael (ed). New York, Cambridge Univ Pr, 1992.

McGhee, Michael (ed). *Philosophy, Religion and the Spiritual Life*. New York, Cambridge Univ Pr, 1992.

This is a collection of fourteen essays from the 1991 Royal Institute of Philosophy Conference at Liverpool. The writers include philosophers and theologians who were invited to consider the relations indicated in the title, reflecting on their own experience if they thought it appropriate. Augustine, Boethius, Plato, Kierkegaard, and the classical Tibetan Buddhist thinkers are brought into the discussion.

McGinn, Colin. Consciousness and Cosmology: Hyperdualism Ventilated in Consciousness: Psychological and Philosophical Essays, Davies, Martin (ed). Cambridge, Blackwell, 1993.

McGinn, Marie. Wright's Reply to Benacerraf. *Analysis*, 44(2), 69-72, Mr 84.

Benacerraf has argued that since no single reduction of number-theory to set-theory can be established as uniquely correct, there is no answer to the question which sets numbers really are, and that therefore numbers could not be sets at all. Wright argued that this is just a particular case of Quinean indeterminacy and does not establish that there is a *special* difficulty about the reference of numbers. The author argues that the indeterminacy Benacerraf points to is not Quinean, in that adoption of Zermelo or von-Neumann definitions of number does not require reinterpretation of the numerical sign of identity.

McGowan, Neale. *De Re* Certainty. *Pac Phil Quart*, 73(4), 347-354, D 92.

This paper is an attempt at refuting Frances Howard-Snyder's argument that de re modality entails de re vagueness. Howard-Snyder's argument is 1) the acceptance of de re modality leads to the rejection of temporal parts, and this, in turn, leads to the acceptance of vague theories of composition, and 2) the acceptance of vague theories of composition leads to de re vagueness. I attempt to refute both 1) and 2) with the use of Spinoza's de re modal theories and his theory of language.

McGrade, Arthur Stephen (ed) and Kilcullen, John (trans). *William of Ockham: A Short Discourse on Tyrannical Government*. New York, Cambridge Univ Pr, 1992.

McGrath, James and Anderson III, Gustaf E. Recent Work on the American Professional Military Ethic: An Introduction and Survey. *Amer Phil Quart*, 30(3), 187-208, Jl 93.

We offer a comprehensive philosophical introduction to the professional ethic of the individual American soldier. After critically surveying relevant military periodicals, recent books, and professional conferences, we present and interpret an inclusive selection of the basic traditional documents that constitute the profession's formal ethic. An informal ethic of military virtues and values, especially obedience, competence, character, honor and the warrior ethos, is also described.

McGraw, John. God and the Problem of Loneliness. *Relig Stud*, 28(3), 319-346, S 92.

This article concerns the nature and kinds of loneliness. It suggests how God, largely the Christian version, and Jesus Christ have been related to the problem of loneliness and how they've been deemed or not deemed the solution to each of its types. Ten forms of loneliness are distinguished: metaphysical, epistemological, communicative, ontological, ethical, existential, eros ("emotional"), friendship ("social"), cultural, and cosmic. Loneliness is also compared to solitude and alienation. This essay primarily pertains to philosophy, theology and religion; but sociology, psychology, psychiatry, and literature are also represented in this study of a complex, widespread and often harrowing phenomenon.

McHenry, Leemon. Metaphysics in Reflections on Philosophy, McHenry, Leemon (ed). New York, St Martin's Pr, 1993.

In this general introduction to metaphysics, the author explores issues in contemporary ontology and focuses attention on the contrast between substance and event ontologies. The author argues for the superiority of an event ontology on the basis that this view is more compatible with modern physics and adequately deals with the question of ontological reduction. Unlike recent analyses of events, the author's view does not depend on ordinary language analysis as a guide to determining ontological matters. This essay then concludes with a defense of metaphysics against standard objections from logical positivism and pragmatism.

McHenry, Leemon (ed) and Adams, Frederick (ed). *Reflections on Philosophy*. New York, St Martin's Pr, 1993.

This book contains a collection of eleven original essays intended to introduce students to the main core areas of philosophy. The introductory chapter defines important concepts and attempts to provide a working definition of philosophy. The remaining ten chapters consider the major areas of philosophy, aesthetics, philosophy of religion, personal identity, philosophy of mind, and cognitive science.

McInerny, Ralph. *Aquinas on Human Action: A Theory of Practice*. Washington, Cath Univ Amer Pr, 1992.

McInerny, Ralph. Reflections on the Moral Life. *Lyceum*, 2(1), 1-14, Spr 90.

McInerny, Ralph. The Science We Are Seeking. *Rev Metaph*, 47(1), 3-18, S 93.

McIntyre, Jane. Putnam's Brains. *Analysis*, 44(2), 59-61, Mr 84.

Mckee, Bill. A Test of the Scientific Method. *Phil Sci*, 60(3), 469-476, S 93.

A conventional experiment is proposed to resolve the realist/idealist debate by challenging the premise that double blinding and an attitude of objectivity in general deter the corroborative influence which preconceptions exert on perception. The possibility that objectivity enhances corroboration would not contradict empirical findings, and would account for the success of science.

McKee, Patrick L. Resemblance: An Account of Realism in Painting. *Phil Invest*, 16(4), 298-306, O 93.

It is widely agreed that realism in a painting calls for explanation. Optical congruence with the subject does not explain realism in an image, but resemblance, conceived differently than optical congruence does. To explain realism by citing a resemblance between image and object is not to identify a cause of the realism but to identify the object of the experience of a realistic image. This way of thinking provides a middle way between the semiotic theory and the "copy" theory, avoiding the difficulties of both.

McKerrow, Raymie E. Critical Rhetoric and the Possibility of the Subject in The Critical Turn, Angus, Ian (ed). Carbondale, So Illinois Univ Pr, 1993.

McKie, David (trans) and Zolo, Danilo. *Democracy and Complexity: A Realist Approach*. University Park, Penn St Univ Pr, 1992.

This book is a highly original and provocative contribution to democratic theory. Zolo argues that the increasing complexity of modern societies represents a fundamental challenge to the basic assumptions of the Western democratic tradition and calls for a reformulation of some of the key questions of political theory. Zolo maintains that, as modern societies become more complex and more involved in the "information revolution", they are subjected to new and unprecedented forms of stress. In conclusion, Zolo develops a set of proposals which seek to renew democratic values and to contribute to a fundamental reform of Western political systems. (staff)

McKie, John. Transition and Contradiction. *Philosophica*, 50(2), 19-32, 1992.

This article provides a non-technical exposition of some of the main advantages and disadvantages associated with discrete space and time. This includes discussion of whether an object is moving or at rest at an instant, the idea of an intrinsic state of motion, possible constants of length and duration, and discrete space and time without constants.

McKie, John R. Donnellan's Distinction: Semantics Versus Pragmatics. *Philosophia (Israel)*, 22(1-2), 139-153, Ja 93.

Kripke proposes to account for Donnellan's distinction on pragmatic grounds — in terms of a difference in speech acts — encapsulated in the distinction between semantic reference and speaker's reference. In contrast, Devitt defends the semantic significance of Donnellan's distinction by appealing to the distinction between referential and attributive singular term tokens. This paper defends the latter approach, and attempts to show how several of Kripke's most important arguments in favor of a pragmatic construal of Donnellan's distinction can be dealt with.

McKim, Robert and Simpson, Peter. Consequentialism, Incoherence and Choice. *Amer Cath Phil Quart*, 66(1), 93-98, Wint 92.

The authors charged, in an earlier article in the same journal, that an argument of Boyle, Finnis and Grisez to prove consequentialism incoherent (because it could not account for the making of wrong choices) was fallacious. They repeat that charge here against an attempt of Boyle, Finnis, and Grisez to defend their argument and also point out that the proposed defense falls into other fallacies of its own.

McKinney, Audrey. Hobbes and the State of Nature: Where are the Women?. *SW Phil Stud*, 15, 51-59, Spr 93.

McKinney, Audrey M and Joy, Glenn C. On a Supposed Inconsistency in J S Mill's Utilitarianism. *SW Phil Stud*, 14, 84-91, Spr 92.

McKinney, Joseph and Garrison, Jim. Foucault and Rousseau on Teaching in Modern Technocratic Schooling. *J Thought*, 28(1-2), 61-82, Spr-Sum 93.

McKinney, Ronald H. Towards a Postmodern Ethics: Sir Isaiah Berlin and John Caputo. *J Value Inq*, 26(3), 395-407, Jl 92.

This essay first attempts to formulate an exploratory definition of the "postmodern" moment in literary criticism followed by a critical analysis of the ethical reflections of Sir Isaiah Berlin and John Caputo. Their views are compared and contrasted and then shown to exemplify a "postmodern" perspective in keeping with the deconstructive tenets of Jacques Derrida.

McKinsey, Michael. Curing Folk Psychology of 'Arthritis'. *Phil Stud*, 70(3), 323-336, Je 93.

Burge's thought experiment concerning 'arthritis' is commonly assumed to show that ascriptions of content to cognitive attitudes are dependent for their truth upon facts about the agent's social and linguistic environment. It is shown that neither Burge's initial thought experiment nor a second type of example that Burge describes supports this conclusion. The proper conclusion to draw from Burge's discussion is identified, and it is shown that this conclusion does not pose a serious problem for individualism about the mental. Finally, it is argued that Burge's discussion does not provide a conclusive reason for believing its proper conclusion.

McLachlan, James M. Nicolas Berdyaev's Existentialist Personalism. *Personalist Forum*, 8/1(Supp), 57-65, Spr 92.

The Russian philosopher/theologian Nicholas Berdyaev created one of the most original and non-traditional philosophies of religion in the history of Christianity. Berdyaev's thought is radical and is strongly humanistic. He dispenses with a good deal of what the Christian theological tradition considers normative: creation ex nihilo, the immutability of God, the ontological difference between God and creation. He argues for the humanity of God as including a dramatic inner life. Berdyaev's philosophy expresses its voluntarism through the rejection of ontology as the starting point of metaphysics. Berdyaev claims in existentialist philosophy freedom is prior to being and philosophical reflection must begin with the person.

McLachlan, James Morse. *The Desire To Be God: Freedom and the Other in Sartre and Berdyaev*. New York, Lang, 1992.

Jean-Paul Sartre and Nicholas Berdyaev were contemporaries in the Paris of the thirties and forties. Sartre became the most famous existentialist author and was also a politically active Marxist. Berdyaev had been a Marxist and political activist but converted to Christianity and became one of the inspirations of the French personalist movement and a key exponent of religious existentialism. This study focuses on the central concern of both philosophers: the question of freedom. Sartre argued in *Being and Nothingness* that God is incompatible with human freedom. Berdyaev argued that God is not only compatible but necessary to freedom. This study reveals two ironies: Berdyaev's God is a more radical departure from traditional Western theism than Sartre's atheism. And Berdyaev's idea of freedom presents the more radical alternative to that tradition.

McLane, Earl. Rereading *Fear and Trembling*. *Faith Phil*, 10(2), 198-219, Ap 93.

McLane, Janice. Alienation, Cultural Differences, and Moral Judgment. *Phil Today*, 37(1), 78-88, Spr 93.

McLaren, Margaret. Possibilities for a Nondominated Female Subjectivity. *Hypatia*, 8(1), 153-158, Wint 93.

This essay examines one of the contributions that Sandra Bartky makes to feminist theory. Bartky critiques Foucault for his gender blind treatment of the disciplines and social practices that create "docile bodies". She introduces several gender specific disciplines and practices that illustrate that the production of bodies is itself gender coded. This essay argues that social practices are not monolithic, but are composed of various strands that may be in tension with one another.

McLarty, Colin. Anti-Foundation and Self-Reference. *J Phil Log*, 22(1), 19-28, F 93.

The syntax for self-reference in Barwise and Etchemendy *The Liar* (1987, Oxford) is made isomorphism invariant by just dropping their requirement that the reference relation be a fragment of the iterated membership relation. Aczel's set theory AFA presents no different isomorphism types than ZF or other reasonable set theories, and so this new version is compatible with any of those set theories. Dropping the tie to iterated membership also makes the syntax easier to modify for other views of self-reference.

McLaughlin, Andrew C. The Connectionism/Classical Battle to Win Souls. *Phil Stud*, 71(2), 163-190, Ag 93.

McLaughlin, Brian. On Davidson's Response to the Charge of Epiphenomenalism in Mental Causation, Heil, John (ed). New York, Clarendon/Oxford Pr, 1993.

McLaughlin, Brian. On Punctate Content and on Conceptual Role. *Phil Phenomenol Res*, 53(3), 653-660, S 93.

McLaughlin, Brian P and Husak, Douglas N. Time-Frames, Voluntary Acts, and Strict Liability. *Law Phil*, 12(1), 95-120, F 93.

McLaughlin, James T and Lyddon, William J. Constructivist Psychology: A Heuristic Framework. *J Mind Behav*, 13(1), 89-107, Wint 92.

Psychologists representing a broad spectrum of psychological specialties use the term "constructivist" to characterize their theories and underscore individuals' active participation in reality-making. In spite of constructivism's apparent widespread influence on psychology, however, significantly different forms of constructivist metatheory may be identified when constructivist assumptions about causal processes are contrasted. Both Pepper's (1942) worldview framework and Aristotle's four-fold classification of causation in natural phenomena are used to distinguish four forms of constructivism—material, efficient, formal, and final. Salient examples of each form as evident in contemporary psychological theory are given with a discussion of implications of these distinctions for the development of a comprehensive conception of cognition and human knowing.

McLaughlin, Mary Martin (ed) and Ross, James Bruce (ed). *The Portable Medieval Reader*. New York, Penguin USA, 1977.

McLaughlin, Peter. Descartes on Mind-Body Interaction and the Conservation of Motion. *Phil Rev*, 102(2), 155-182, Ap 93.

The traditional (Leibnizian) reading of Descartes on mind-body interaction is given a more rigorous reformulation, explaining how Descartes could assert that the mind while not affecting the quantity of motion in the world could change its direction. It is shown, contrary to the trend in recent literature, that this reading has a reliable textual base, and it is argued that it attributes to Descartes a philosophical position of more substance and interest. The kind of interpretation favored depends on the status that the reader attributes to the assertion of the causal closer of the material world.

McLaughlin, Robert N. *On the Logic of Ordinary Conditionals*. Albany, SUNY Pr, 1990.

McLaughlin, T H. Citizenship, Diversity and Education: A Philosophical Perspective. *J Moral Educ*, 21(3), 235-250, 1992.

The concept of 'education for citizenship' contains a number of ambiguities and tensions, related to differing interpretations of the notion of 'citizenship'. This paper explores some of the philosophical difficulties which arise from the task of trying to offer a substantial notion of 'education for citizenship' in the context of the diversity of a pluralistic democratic society. One of the central areas requiring attention by philosophers is an account of the public civic virtues which are 'thick' or substantial enough to satisfy the communal demands of citizenship, yet compatible with liberal demands concerning the development of critical rationality by citizens and satisfaction of the demands of justice relating to diversity. It is suggested that a wide ranging debate about these matters at the national level cannot be avoided if 'education for citizenship' is to be conducted defensibly and effectively.

McLean, Edward B. Nature *and* Nature's God: The Divine Source of Natural Law. *Vera Lex*, 11(2), 6-7, 1991.

The article argues that natural law precepts and applications are necessarily devoid of rational or logical support unless they stem from the existence of a transcendent God. Attempts to articulate or apply natural law precepts which are not grounded on the existent God, move inexorably into non-demonstrable and fully relativistic statements. Therefore, natural law arguments which are not based on God's existence differ little from legal positivist arguments, and result in a relativistic set of standards and values.

McLean, George F. The Person and Moral Growth in Chinese Foundations for Moral Education and Character Development, Van Doan, Tran (ed). Washington, CRVP, 1991.

McLean, George F (ed) and Badillo, Robert Peter. *The Emancipative Theory of Jürgen Habermas and Metaphysics*. Washington, CRVP, 1991.

Though Habermas does not develop the metaphysical themes latent in his own work, in articulating a model of communicating subjects for the exercise of their emancipatory potential, he opens a space which points toward the further reaches of his own philosophical compass. This study argues that Habermas's philosophy of emancipation may be viewed as a new optic for elaborating the notion of being as *esse* by examining the sense in which Habermas's categories of *dialogical* (versus monological) *paradigm, communicative action, and emancipation* enrich the transcendental properties of being as *esse* — unity, truth, and goodness — as well as the manner in which Habermas's proposal is itself enriched when understood from the classical metaphysical point of view.

McLean, George F and Ellrod, Frederick E. *Philosophical Foundations for Moral Education and Character Development: Act and Agent (Second Edition)*. Washington, CRVP, 1992.

McLean, George F (ed) and Knowles, Richard T (ed). *Psychological Foundations of Moral Education and Character Development: An Integrated Theory of Moral Development (Second Edition)*. Washington, CRVP, 1992.

McLean, George F (ed) and Kromkowski, John (ed). *Relations Between Cultures*. Washington, CRVP, 1991.

McLean, George F (ed) and Kromkowski, John (ed). *Urbanization and Values*. Washington, CRVP, 1991.

McLean, George F (ed) and Kromkowski, John (ed) and Peachey, Paul (ed). *The Place of the Person In Social Life*. Washington, CRVP, 1991.

McLean, George F (ed) and Shen, Vincent (ed) and Van Doan, Tran (ed). *Chinese Foundations for Moral Education and Character Development*. Washington, CRVP, 1991.

This volume consists of 9 chapters which are divided in three parts: 1) the first part studies the basic characters of morals in the Chinese Classics; 2) the second part offers some modern views on the growth of human characters and morale, while 3) the third part deals specifically with the moral education in modern China. The conclusion reached by the co-authors of this volume is: a moral education should be based on 1) traditional resources and 2) a full understanding of man (human nature, human development etc.).

McLean, George F (ed) and Yi-Jie, Tang. *Confucianism, Buddhism, Daoism, Christianity and Chinese Culture*. Washington, CRVP, 1991.

McLellan, David (ed) and Sayers, Sean (ed). *Socialism and Morality*. New York, St Martin's Pr, 1990.

Examines the relationship between socialism and morality from economic, political, and social aspects. The first half of the book examines the controversial question of how ethics is to be reconciled with a Marxist historical materialism; the second half elaborate the foundations of a socialist morality in the face of that a-moral ravages of the market.

McLeod, Mark S. The Limits of Theistic Experience: An Epistemic Basis of Theistic Pluralism. *Int J Phil Relig*, 34(2), 79-94, O 93.

This essay has three goals. The first is to explore one epistemic basis of the proliferation of descriptions of God. The second is to argue that the problem of theistic pluralism is generated because theistic belief finds its source in experience but experience alone is not enough for what I call "doctrinal accounts" of the supernatural. The third is to suggest that insofar as some contemporary philosophers of religion take experience to ground theistic beliefs as they are embedded in various theological traditions, they are expecting too much from experience alone.

McMahon, Cliff G. The Janus Aesthetic of Duchamp. *J Aes Educ*, 26(2), 41-51, Sum 92.

McMahon, Kevin. The Incarnation and the Natural Law. *Lyceum*, 1(1), 5-11, Wint 89.

McMichael, Alan. Why Physics Can't Be Nominalized. *Analysis*, 44(2), 72-78, Mr 84.

McMullin, Ernan. Evolution and Special Creation. *Zygon*, 28(3), 299-335, S 93.

The logical relationships between the ideas of evolution and of special creation are explored here in the context of a recent paper by Alvin Plantinga claiming that from the perspective of biblical religion it is more likely than not that God acted in a "special" way at certain crucial moments in the long process whereby life developed on earth. I argue against this thesis, asking first under what circumstances the Bible might be thought relevant to an issue of broadly scientific concern. I go on to outline some of the arguments supporting the thesis of common ancestry, and argue finally that from the theistic perspective, special creation ought to be regarded as, if anything, less rather than more likely than its evolutionary alternative.

McMullin, Ernan. Indifference Principle and Anthropic Principle in Cosmology. *Stud Hist Phil Sci*, 24(3), 359-389, Ag 93.

The successes scored by the big bang model of cosmic evolution in the 1960's led to an intensive application of quantum theory to the problem of how the expansion might have begun and what its likely first stages were. It seemed as though an incredibly precise setting of the initial conditions would have been needed in order that a long-lived galactic universe containing heavy elements might develop. One response was to suppose that the fine-tuning could somehow be explained by the presence of humans in the universe. This ran quite counter to the traditional supposition, according to which an initial "chaos" was sufficient. This essay outlines the history of the two principles, argues that the so-called "weak" anthropic principle is banal, distinguishes between two sorts of anthropic explanation, and assesses the prospects of the anthropic turn in cosmology. (edited)

McMullin, Ernan. Rationality and Paradigm Change in Science in World Changes, Horwich, Paul (ed). Cambridge, MIT Pr, 1993.

The notion of paradigm change is central to Kuhn's account of science. There has been a long-standing debate as to the rationality, in Kuhn's eyes, of such change. In this essay, four points are made. First, Kuhn himself stresses that there are reasons for paradigm change, reasons that are, however, not coercive. Second, certain values are to be maximized in theory choice; much depends on how these values themselves are to be grounded. Third, paradigm change can reach to different depths; a "deep" paradigm change is the one that raises the typically "Kuhnian" sort of question. Finally, Kuhn's real challenge is not to the rationality of scientific change, but to scientific realism and traditional notions of scientific truth.

McMurtry, John. Good Love and Bad Love: A Way of Evaluation. *J Speculative Phil*, 6(3), 226-241, 1992.

The article argues that the 2500 year tradition of inquiry into love has lacked philosophical grounding in the biological and social-structural conditions within which love and choices of love take place: presupposing rather than critically addressing the connected problems of patriarchal control, proprietary relations and pathogenic interaction. It shows that these enduring and deep-structural problems of sex-love require us to evaluate it in relation to the larger social and natural systems within which it occurs as a basic form of their reproduction and recreation. (edited)

McNair, Bruce. Albert the Great in the Renaissance: Cristoforo Landino's Use of Albert on the Soul. *Mod Sch*, 70(2), 115-129, Ja 93.

McNamara, Paul. Comments on "Can Intelligence Be Artificial?". *Phil Stud*, 71(2), 217-222, Ag 93.

Doubts are raised about the assumption that an entity can't have a representational state that governs its behavior in virtue of its content unless that internal state has been acquired via appropriate interaction with its environment. The doubts hinge on a subtle distinction between a system's acquiring an internal representational state and a system's internal state acquiring the property of being representational. Employing this distinction, it is suggested that we can pre-load machines with states "destined" to acquire specific, predictable and efficacious representational properties in a manner that is consistent with Dretske's general naturalistic approach.

McNamara, Paul. Does the Actual World Actually Exist?. *Phil Stud*, 69(1), 59-81, Ja 93.

Assuming minimal fine-individuation, on standard actualist frameworks the answer is "No". I specify one fully graspable, purely qualitative maximal consistent state of affairs (MCS), then another necessarily equivalent to the first. So there *could* have been more than one obtaining MCS. I then argue that there *is* more than one obtaining MCS. So the set of worlds is not the set of MCSs. I explore various patch ups. Finally, I compare the actualist and realist notions of worlds and argue that even if the realist is right about world ensembles, necessary truth is not truth in all worlds anyway.

McNamara, Paul. Leibniz on Creation, Contingency and Per-Se Modality. *Stud Leibniz*, 22(1), 48-68, 1990.

Leibniz's first problem with contingency stems from his doctrine of divine creation (not his later doctrine of truth) and is solved via his concepts of necessity per se, etc. (not via his later concept of infinite analysis). I scrutinize some of the earliest texts in which the first problem and its solution occur. I compare his "per se modal concepts" with his concept of analysis and with the traditional concept of metaphysical necessity. I then identify and remove the main obstacle to Leibniz's employment of these concepts by reflecting on his concept of a world and comparing it with contemporary conceptions. Finally I sketch the place that this early problem and its solutions had in the context of his mature philosophy. A disagreement between Sleigh and Adams which hinges on the assumption that there is just one problem with competing solutions is seen to dissolve in this light.

McNaughton, David. McGinn on Experience of Primary and Secondary Qualities. *Analysis*, 44(2), 78-80, Mr 84.

McGinn argues (*The Subjective View*) for an inseparability thesis (IT) about perception: any sense experience must be as of both primary and secondary qualities. I reply that IT is uncontroversially true only of sight. Both smell and hearing can deliver purely secondary quality experience. And Hume's case of the man with a palsied hand (*Treatise* I iv 4) suggests that there might be tactile experience which was only as of primary qualities. I then discuss what it is about sight which distinguishes it from the other senses and makes IT true of it.

McNaughton, David. Reparation and Atonement. *Relig Stud*, 28(2), 129-144, Je 92.

Richard Swinburne (in his *Responsibility and Atonement*) argues for a sacrificial version of the Atonement, in which the individual penitent offers the life of Christ to God in (partial) reparation for his sins. I argue that any version of this account is both conceptually incoherent and morally unsatisfying and offer in its place a version of the exemplary theory of the Atonement which, I claim, meets the conditions he lays down for any satisfactory account.

McNaughton, David. Response to Diamond's 'The Importance of Being Human' in Human Beings, Cockburn, David (ed). New York, Cambridge Univ Pr, 1991.

There are two possible ways of interpreting a disagreement as to whether the severely handicapped have a human life to lead. It may be a disagreement within a practice, or between divergent practices. In either case, I argue, we can offer reasons for our view. These are necessarily reasons from within our point of view, which may engage with the viewpoint of the other. In either case, however, we shall be offering a *justification* for our position; a claim which Diamond denies.

McNaughton, David. The Importance of Being Human—II in Human Beings, Cockburn, David (ed). New York, Cambridge Univ Pr, 1991.

I defend a form of moral realism which leads to particularism about moral judgement. I then apply this doctrine to the notion of being human; sometimes the fact that what I do affects a human, as distinct from some other being, is relevant, and sometimes it is not. Moreover, the manner of its relevance changes from context to context. I then raise critical questions about Cora Diamond's claim that we have a conception of what it is to be human which is 1) non-biological, 2) constituted by our practice(s), 3) such that we do not need to justify the inclusion of the severely handicapped in the practice.

McNaughton, David and Rawling, Piers. Deontology and Agency. *Monist*, 76(1), 81-100, Ja 93.

Constraints are a defining feature of deontologies, but there is considerable debate over how to characterize them. Authors such as Nagel, Parfit and Scheffler see them as generating agent-relative reasons. On this characterization, it is natural to suppose that constraints arise because of an agent's concern with her own agency. Brook and Kamm, however, offer a victim, rather than an agent, focussed rational. We rebut their arguments against agent-focussed views and show that their own accounts fall foul of consequentialist ploys.

McNeill, Paul M. *The Ethics and Politics of Human Experimentation*. New York, Cambridge Univ Pr, 1993.

This book discusses the ethics of medical research and research in the social sciences and asks whether human subjects of research and experimentation are adequately protected from harm and whether their interests are fairly balanced against the interests of researchers and research institutions. It examines the development of review committees and reports on their functioning throughout the world. It takes historical, philosophical, medical and legal approaches and addresses the inherently political nature of committee review. A radically different rationale and model for committee review is suggested which includes the proposal that there be direct representation of research subjects on committees.

McNeill, Will. Spirit's Living Hand in Of Derrida, Heidegger, and Spirit, Wood, David (ed). Evanston, Northwestern Univ Pr, 1993.

A discussion of Derrida's readings of Heidegger in "Geschlecht II: Heidegger's Hand," and *Of Spirit*, focussing on the implicit hermeneutics of the deconstructive gesture.

McNeill, Will (trans) and Haar, Michel. The Play of Nietzsche in Derrida in Derrida: A Critical Reader, Wood, David (ed). Cambridge, Blackwell, 1992.

McNeill, William. Metaphysics, Fundamental Ontology, Metontology 1925-1935. *Heidegger Stud*, 8, 63-79, 1992.

An examination of the relation between metaphysics, fundamental ontology and metontology as conceived by Heidegger from *The History of the Concept of Time* (1925) to *Introduction to Metaphysics* (1935), focussing on the meaning and possibility of metontology.

McNicollis, C F. Pragmatism and Constitutional Interpretation: Deconstruction Without Nihilism. *Gnosis*, 4(1), 65-92, 1992.

McNiff II, James F. Aristotle's Argument from Motion. *Int Phil Quart*, 32(3), 313-323, S 92.

McNulty, T Michael. The Value of Economics: A Response to Robert Charles Graham. *J Value Inq*, 27(2), 235-237, Ap 93.

Robert Charles Graham has criticized a recent writing of mine (J Value Inq 24[1990]) in that it fails to take into account the value of economic advice. I claim that my concern had been with the theoretical basis of that advice, which seems to be based on fatally unrealistic and logically flawed assumptions. I indicate that prominent economists are aware of these problems.

McPeck, John. The Justification of Critical Thinking: A Response to McCarthy. *Proc Phil Educ*, 48, 69-71, 1992.

McPeck, John. Underlying Traits of Critical Thinkers: A Response to Stephen Norris. *Proc Phil Educ*, 48, 58-59, 1992.

McPherran, Mark L. *Ataraxia* and *Eudaimonia* in Ancient Pyrrhonism: Is the Skeptic Really Happy?. *Proc Boston Colloq Anc Phil*, 5, 135-171, 1989.

Despite their purported freedom from all theoretical commitments, the Pyrrhonists—like their Hellenistic brethren—were moral naturalists, reporting that since they possessed an accurate appraisal of human nature, and a therapeutic methodology uniquely sensitive to it, they could deliver what no other school could: *eudaimonia* (happiness) consisting in *ataraxia* (lack of anxiety). On their account, it is

belief in objective moral value that is at the root of human unhappiness, and thus, only through the skeptical purgation of such dogmatic belief can one be happy. This paper interprets and explores these rather paradoxical views, and defends them against recent criticism.

McPherson, Michael S. Alternative Conceptions of Feasibility in The Idea of Democracy, Copp, David (ed). New York, Cambridge Univ Pr, 1993.

McRae, Murdo William. Stephen Jay Gould and the Contingent Nature of History. *Clio*, 22(3), 239-250, Spr 93.

In *Wonderful Life: The Burgess Shale and the Nature of History*, Stephen Jay Gould describes recent paleontological research into the Burgess Shale of British Columbia, the most significant early Cambrian fossil deposit. Although he describes that research as something of a Kuhnian scientific revolution, in which contingency displaces Darwinian gradualism as the key to evolutionary history, his book is more a paradigm in its own right of the problems associated with paradigmatic change. Indebted to the structural implications of traditional linear narrative, his argument for contingency ultimately returns to the notions of progress and predictability it set out to challenge.

McRobert, Laurie. Kant and Radical Evil in German Philosophy and Jewish Thought, Greenspan, Louis (ed). Toronto, Univ of Toronto Pr, 1992.

McWhorter, Ladelle. Asceticism/Askēsis in Ethics and Danger, Dallery, Arleen B (ed). Albany, SUNY Pr, 1992.

McWhorter, Ladelle. Foucault's Analytics of Power in Crises in Continental Philosophy, Dallery, Arleen B (ed). Albany, SUNY Pr, 1990.

McWhorter, Ladelle. Self-Overcoming and the Will to Truth: A Reading of Foucault's *Discipline and Punish*. *Praxis Int*, 12(4), 341-351, Ja 93.

McWilliams, Spencer A. Indeterminacy and the Construction of Personal Knowledge. *Tradition Discovery*, 19(2), 5-11, 1993.

Polanyi's post-critical philosophy contains a tension between the personal commitment of the knower to the apprehension of knowledge and the understanding of the incomplete, or potentially mistaken, nature of current understanding. This essay addresses this tension, both theoretically and practically, by drawing parallels between Polanyi's theory and George Kelly's Personal Construct Psychology. The two approaches share many similar assumptions about the development of knowledge. Application of Kelly's perspective may assist us in developing direct awareness of our active participation in creating knowledge, and helping us to articulate some of our underlying assumptions. Such activities facilitate movement toward more comprehensive understanding.

Medina, Vicente. The Possibility of an Indigenous Philosophy: A Latin American Perspective. *Amer Phil Quart*, 29(4), 373-380, O 92.

The aim of this paper is to explore the controversy over the possibility of an indigenous Latin American philosophy. First, it is argued that this controversy is not only one between *serious philosophy* and *free-spirited philosophy*, but one between philosophy conceived as *moral attitude* and philosophy conceived as *rigorous methodology*. And second, it is argued that the idea of an indigenous Latin American philosophy of liberation is a dubious claim. If this is the case, then it is argued that to uphold the desirability of such a philosophy will be incoherent.

Meehan, Eugene J. Cross-Cultural Translation in Cultural Relativism and Philosophy, Dascal, Marcelo (ed). Leiden, Brill, 1991.

The paper examines the general problem of translation error in cross-cultural translations. In principle, error is unavoidable, but the author suggests that by limiting translations to the knowledge needed for directing human actions on defensible grounds, it can be contained. The solution is to create a generalized analytic/theoretical framework linking purposes sought with the knowledge to the necessary/sufficient conditions for achieving them. That apparatus can then be taught in conjunction with the substantive materials of the field, and used to deal critically with knowledge claims that fall within its boundaries.

Meehl, Paul and Anderson, C Anthony (ed) and Gunderson, Keith (ed). *Selected Philosophical and Methodological Papers*. Minneapolis, Univ of Minn Pr, 1991.

This is a collection of articles by a psychologist-philosopher on social science methodology and philosophy of mind. The widely varied topics include theory-testing, open concepts, determinism, emergence, psychoanalytic inference, insanity defense, civil commitment, telepathy, teleology in psychopathology, and the mind-body identity theory.

Meerbote, Ralf (ed). *Kant's Aesthetics*. Atascadero, Ridgeview, 1991.

Megone, Christopher. Virtue Ethics. *Polis*, 11(1), 52-61, 1992.

This article is a critical discussion of William Prior, Virtue and Knowledge: An Introduction to Ancient Greek Ethics. It is suggested that the framework for Prior's work, the relation between virtue, wisdom, and happiness, may obscure the differences between the approaches considered, from Homer to the Stoics and Epicureans. It is further argued that this book, while lucidly written, might only cautiously be recommended as an introduction to virtue ethics owing to flaws in its interpretation, particularly of Socrates, Plato and Aristotle.

Mehl, Peter J. Despair's Demand: An Appraisal of Kierkegaard's Argument for God. *Int J Phil Relig*, 32(3), 167-182, D 92.

After explicating Kierkegaard's theory of the self and its close relation to his image of the normatively human, I argue that Kierkegaard argues for belief in God on the basis of our experience of despair over realizing this image of the normatively human. It is clear how the individual is compelled to be morally engaged, but what is not clear is how Kierkegaard's demand for nothing less than moral transcendence follows. Yet this strong moral demand is the presupposition for his argument for God; without the ideal Kierkegaard's argument for God loses much, but not all, of its rationale.

Mehl, Peter J. In the Twilight of Modernity: MacIntyre and Mitchell on Moral Traditions and Their Assessment. *J Relig Ethics*, 19(1), 21-54, Spr 91.

This essay compares Alasdair MacIntyre's and Basil Mitchell's recent work in religious ethics and ethical theory. The focus is on the interconnections among theories of human nature, sociocultural context, moral thought, and theories of rationality, all of which have a bearing on our prospects for assessing moral traditions. While I note many of the striking parallels between their positions, I also point out that they differ regarding their appreciation of the impact of social and cultural context on morality. In distinction from MacIntyre, Mitchell combines an appreciation for moral tradition with an awareness that in order to assess traditions we must have some critical resources that are relatively tradition-independent. He finds these in theories of human nature and in general standards of rationality. Furthermore, from Mitchell's perspective, MacIntyre seems to employ similar resources in developing his position.

Meier, Diane E. Physician-Assisted Dying: Theory and Reality. *J Clin Ethics*, 3(1), 35-37, Spr 92.

Meier, Klaus V. Fields of Dreams and Men of Straw: Philosophical Reflections on Performance-Enhancers in Sport. *J Phil Sport*, 18, 74-85, 1991.

Meijering, T C. Neuraal vernunft en gedachteloze kennis: Het moderne pleidooi voor een niet-propositioneel kennismodel. *Alg Ned Tijdschr Wijs*, 85(1), 24-48, F 93.

This paper critically surveys various sources of the common view that knowledge is essentially propositional, such as classical categorization theory, the medieval notion of an *oratio mentalis*, the rise of the modern formal logic, and the development of Chomskyan linguistics. In radical contrast to the received view, however, recent developments in cognitive science seem to converge in suggesting that our cognitive capabilities may be basically *non-propositional* in character. So-called connectionist networks, in particular, provide effective models of such non-propositional knowledge representations. The paper goes on to explore and assess the philosophical ramification implied in the unorthodox view that cognition is to be modeled on pattern recognition. (edited)

Meijsing, Monica. Connectionisme, plasticiteit en de hoop op betere tijden. *Alg Ned Tijdschr Wijs*, 85(1), 49-69, F 93.

Paul Churchland looks upon connectionism as the solution for many — if not all — problems in cognitive science and philosophy. In this article I argue that 1) Churchland's connectionism is highly problematical as a psychological theory; 2) the phrasing of his psychological explanations repeatedly suffers from "homonuculus errors" and 3) his connectionist semantics is only tenable in an empiricist version, a position Churchland explicitly repudiates. By way of conclusion I contrast Churchland's promissory notes for the future with a not very promising observation on the past.

Meilaender, Gilbert C. *Terra es animata*: On Having a Life. *Hastings Center Rep*, 23(4), 25-32, Jl-Ag 93.

The author examines the use of the concept of personhood in bioethics, arguing that the person has been wrongly divorced from the life of the body. If we take seriously the natural trajectory of bodily life as the locus of personal presence, we will be skeptical of attempts (e.g., advance directives) to locate one moment in life as that from which decisions about the entire life of the person should be made.

Meinwald, Constance. Good-bye to the Third Man in The Cambridge Companion to Plato, Kraut, Richard (ed). New York, Cambridge Univ Pr, 1992.

Presents, for the general philosophical reader, applications of the main innovation of the *Parmenides* to handle problems turning on "self-predication". The author's *Plato's Parmenides* (OUP, 1991) argued the dialogue introduced a distinction between two kinds of predication. This paper explains what these are and shows how their possession protects Plato from trouble with the Third Man and the "greatest difficulty". Broadly, the first part of the *Parmenides* calls attention to deficiencies in the presentation of forms in the middle period, and the balance of the dialogue supplies the deficiencies.

Meixner, Uwe. An Alternative Semantics for Modal Predicate-Logic. *Erkenntnis*, 37(3), 377-400, N 92.

The semantical framework is fundamentally intensional: neither possible worlds nor sets as basic entities, but rather, besides individuals, propositions, properties and relations (in intension). Logical truth is defined in terms of logical form (without mentioning this notion) without employing sets of models and the concept of truth in a model. Truth itself is explicitly defined (without recursion); the truth-conditions for the logical constants of the object-language become theorems derivable from the axioms for *to intend*—the basic semantical relation.

Meixner, Uwe. Der ontologische Gottesbeweis in der Perspektive der Analytischen Philosophie. *Theol Phil*, 67(2), 246-262, 1992.

The paper offers a reconstruction of the Ontological Argument which makes it analytically valid. The proof is even found to be convincing (not only analytically valid) for everybody who accepts "God is identical to that entity greater than which noting is possible"; but the truth of this identity-statement may rationally be doubled: the presupposition "There is a *possible* object greater than which nothing is possible" can apparently not be verified without verifying "There is an *existing* object, etc.," — which is problematic prior to the proof

Meixner, Uwe. On Negative and Disjunctive Properties in Language, Truth and Ontology, Mulligan, Kevin (ed). Dordrecht, Kluwer, 1992.

The paper is a defense of negative and disjunctive properties against the criticism of D M Armstrong in part II of *Universals and Scientific Realism*. Given a mereology of properties (properties which are parts of properties) there must be negative and disjunctive properties. Moreover, negations of properties can be causally efficacious, and disjunctions of properties can be identical in different particular; they fulfill Armstrong's own criteria for propertyhood; Hence they are properties in his sense.

Meixner, Uwe. Propensity and Possibility. *Erkenntnis*, 38(3), 323-341, My 93.

The author analyzes necessity in the sense of unchangeability (and hence the correlative possibility) without reference to possible worlds or possibilia of any kind. (edited)

Melander, Ellinor. Toward the Sexual and Economic Emancipation of Women: The Philosophy of Grete Meisel-Hess. *Hist Euro Ideas*, 14(5), 695-713, S 92.

The article introduces a female writer and sexual reformer who created a feminist philosophy of her own. Her name was Grete Meisel-Hess (1879-1922). She lived and worked in Vienna and Berlin. Meisel Hess was influenced by two different kinds of intellectual sources: the women's liberation movement and male philosophers such as Friedrich Nietzsche and Ernst Haeckel. In her own thinking she combined these different influences into a philosophy which tried to widen the intellectual horizon of women. She also broadened the demands of the women's movement to encompass the field of love and sexuality.

Melander, Peter. How Not to Explain the Errors of the Immune System. *Phil Sci*, 60(2), 223-241, Je 93.

According to Mohan Matthen and Edwin Levy, certain immunological processes require explanations in which the immune system is attributed intentional states. This, they think, strengthens the scientific credentials of intentional psychology and undermines the position of those who argue that the scientific treatment of human action should involve the elimination of intentional description. In this paper, I argue that immunology does not and need not employ intentional explanation or description and consequently has nothing to offer those who seek to defend the scientific standing of intentional psychology by looking for other disciplines that "accommodate the intentional".

Melchiorre, Virgilio. L'analogia come chiave di lettura della creazione. *Riv Filosof Neo-Scolas*, 84(4), 563-586, O-D 92.

The theological theme of *creation* is linked, even in the biblical tradition, to the experience of what flowers from nothingness. The idea of nothingness is not at the origins: it could not be thought without the idea of being. Therefore at the origin of every reality there is not nothingness, but Being as pure being, as something which, somehow *pre-contains* every possible reality. All this involves an intimate affinity, an intimate *ontological participation* between everything which exists and what stands at its origin. The concept of participation involves identity and diversity at the same time: in all the realities of the creation, the *identical* Being reveals itself in many *different* ways. The conceptual language, which proceeds through definitions, can hardly express *together* this participation, this unity of identical and diverse. Only the *symbolic language* can help us to understand: that is the reason why the biblical language is *essentially* made up of symbolic images as well as metaphors and parables.

Mele, Alfred. Acting for Reasons and Acting Intentionally. *Pac Phil Quart*, 73(4), 355-374, D 92.

This paper examines the thesis that an agent intentionally *A*-s if and only if she *A*-s for a reason. It is argued that the spirit of this thesis, if not its letter, survives a variety of criticisms — including worries posed by causal deviance, dumb luck, "arational" actions, subsidiary actions, and double effect. The paper's aim is to illuminate the nature of reasons for action, acting for reasons, and acting intentionally.

Mele, Alfred. Akrasia, Self-Control, and Second-Order Desires. *Nous*, 26(3), 281-302, S 92.

Pristine belief/desire psychology has its limitations. Recognizing this, some have attempted to fill gaps by adding more of the same, but at higher levels. This paper's focal question is whether continent and incontinent behavior are properly conceived in terms of the victory or defeat of higher-order desires. The answer defended is 'No'. The problems with traditional 'judgment-centered' conceptions of continent and incontinent behavior can be resolved by means of a proper understanding of practical commitment—one that does not treat such commitment as an essentially second-order phenomenon.

Mele, Alfred. History and Personal Autonomy. *Can J Phil*, 23(2), 271-280, Je 93.

This paper is a critical discussion of John Christman's recent historical account of autonomy relative to a desire (in "Autonomy and Personal History," *Canadian Journal of Philosophy*, 1991). A variety of counterexamples are developed, and some suggestions are offered concerning a more satisfactory account.

Mele, Alfred. *Irrationality: An Essay on 'Akrasia', Self-Deception, and Self-Control*. New York, Oxford Univ Pr, 1992.

Mele, Alfred. Justifying Intentions. *Mind*, 102(406), 335-337, Ap 93.

This is the fourth installment in an exchange between T L M Pink and Alfred Mele on the functions of intentions, including their role in practical reasoning. Mele grants that Pink has located significant difficulties for a traditional view of intentions. Mele argues, however, that if a proper view of intention must do justice not only to intention's contribution to practical planning and coordination but also to intention's place in the initiating, sustaining, and guiding of intentional actions, Pink has failed to advance a worthy successor to the view that he criticizes.

Mele, Alfred (ed) and Heil, John (ed). *Mental Causation*. New York, Clarendon/Oxford Pr, 1993.

Explaining how mind can make a difference in a material universe has proved challenging. The essays in this volume—each written expressly for it—approach this issue from widely divergent perspectives and offer a cross-section of contemporary responses to the problem of mental causation.

Meletti-Bertolini, Mara. Imagination créatrice et connaissance selon Théodule Ribot. *Rev Phil Fr*, 1, 11-25, Ja-Mr 93.

Cet article présente une analyse de l'imagination, de ses formes et de ses fonctions dans la pensée de Th Ribot. Son explication psychologique de la créativité est presentée comme complementaire et parallèle à sa conception de la connaissance scientifique.

Melia, Joseph. A Note on Lewis's Ontology. *Analysis*, 52(3), 191-192, Jl 92.

Lewis has claimed that his theory of possible worlds is qualitatively parsimonious. For Lewis' worlds are the same kind of objects as the actual world—thus his theory is not committed to things of some new kind. I point out that Lewis is committed not only to possible worlds but to the possible objects which compose his possible worlds. Since these possible objects include every possible kind of thing, it follows that Lewis' theory is as qualitatively unparsimonious as a theory could be.

Melle, Ulrich. Objektiver Idealismus und ökosoziale Marktwirtschaft. *Phil Rundsch*, 39(4), 286-292, 1992.

Mellema, Gregory. Quasi-Obligation and the Failure to Be Virtuous. *J Soc Phil*, 24(2), 176-185, Fall 93.

Traditional deontic categories do not leave room for a category of acts which, though they do not qualify as obligatory, are nevertheless morally sub-standard or blameworthy to omit. But it is becoming increasingly common to find philosophers arguing on behalf of such acts. These include Aurel Kolnai, Claudia Card, Neera Badhwar, I M Humberstone, John Whelan, and (with minor qualifications) Judith Jarvis Thomson. It is my suggestion that those who have defended these acts have tended to concentrate too narrowly upon deontic concepts and categories. I argue that a more satisfactory approach takes into account the aretaic dimensions of morality.

Mellor, D H. How to Believe a Conditional. *J Phil*, 90(5), 233-248, My 93.

The paper develops and defends the theory that conditionals express inferential dispositions. It reconciles Lewis's 'triviality' results with Adam's use of conditional credences to measure degrees of acceptance of conditionals. The causes and effects of inferential dispositions are used to distinguish the two main types of conditional, vindicating Dudman's reclassification of them. A realist interpretation of these dispositions is used to deal with counter-examples. Finally Adams's thesis is refuted.

Mellor, D H. Nothing Like Experience. *Proc Aris Soc*, 93, 1-16, 1993.

I argue that knowing what an experience is like is knowing how to recognize and imagine it. Imagining an experience is itself an experience, but one we can't imagine, so we don't know what it's like. We can also imagine many things, e.g., photographable views, that aren't experiences. So there being something X is like, which we can know, is not a good test for X being an experience. I conclude we need no such test! Experiences are just natural phenomena, to be studied like all others.

Mellor, D H. Probability and the Evidence of Our Senses in A J Ayer Memorial Essays, Griffiths, A Phillips (ed). New York, Cambridge Univ Pr, 1991.

It is argued that Ayer's persistent and unsuccessful attempts to explain how our senses justify the beliefs they give us, by postulating sense data, stemmed from his failure to adopt the right conception of probability. This is the objective contingent single case chance which causes give effects and which perceptual causes give the beliefs in them which our senses make them cause and which are thereby justified by being made probably true.

Mellor, D H. Properties and Predicates in Ontology, Causality and Mind: Essays in Honour of D M Armstrong, Bacon, John (ed). New York, Cambridge Univ Pr, 1993.

I argue first that the universals — properties and relations — that exist are those quantified over in a ramsey sentence stating all laws. I then use the predicate 'is red' to show how slight and complex the relation is between the meanings of predicates generally and the universals whose effects cause us to apply these predicates correctly.

Mellor, Philip A. Reflexive Traditions: Anthony Giddens, High Modernity, and the Contours of Contemporary Religiosity. *Relig Stud*, 29(1), 111-127, Mr 93.

Melville, Stephen. Just Between Us. *Phil Today*, 36(4), 367-376, Wint 92.

Mencacci, Claudio and Goldfluss, Enrica. The Emotional Residence: An Italian Experience of the Treatment of Chronic Psychosis in Analecta Husserliana, XXXI, Tymieniecka, Anna-Teresa (ed). Dordrecht, Kluwer, 1990.

Mencken, H L and Flathman, Richard (ed). *Friedrich Nietzsche—H L Mencken*. New Brunswick, Transaction Books, 1993.

Méndez, José M. Exhaustively Axiomatizing RMO with an Appropriate Extension of Anderson and Belnap's "Strong and Natural List of Valid Entailments". *Theoria (Spain)*, 5(12-13), 223-228, N 90.

Mendonça, W P. Die Person als Zweck an sich. *Kantstudien*, 84(2), 167-184, 1993.

Mendus, Susan. All the King's Horses and All the King's Men: Justifying Higher Education. *J Phil Educ*, 26(2), 173-182, 1992.

This article addresses the question 'What is the justification of higher education in modern society?' It takes issue with writers such as Alasdair MacIntyre and Allan Bloom, who argue that the fragmentation of value characteristic of modernity has undermined the possibility of providing a coherent justification of higher education. Against MacIntyre and Bloom, I argue that we should understand education as a means of developing reflective consciousness in students, and that that will require fragmentation and the immanent conflict of traditions rather than a background of agreed values.

Mendus, Susan. Different Voices, Still Lives: Problems in the Ethics of Care. *J Applied Phil*, 10(1), 17-27, 1993.

Recent writings in feminist ethics have urged that the activity of caring is more central to women's lives than are considerations of justice and equality. This paper argues that an ethics of care, so understood, is difficult to extend beyond the local and familiar, and is therefore of limited use in addressing the political problems of the modern world. However, the ethics of care does contain an important insight: if references to care are understood not as claims about women's nature, but as reflections on the extent to which moral obligations are both unchosen and conflicting, then an ethics of care can supplement an ethics of justice, and can also provide a more realistic account of both men's and women's moral life.

Mendus, Susan. Kant: 'An Honest but Narrow-Minded Bourgeois'? in Essays on Kant's Political Philosophy, Williams, Howard (ed). Chicago, Univ of Chicago Pr, 1992.

This paper attempts to elucidate Kant's views on women as citizens. It concentrates on his claim that women are only passive citizens, not active ones, and asks whether this claim merely reflects the prejudices of his time, or whether it is symptomatic of deeper tensions between his moral and political philosophy. The postscript draws attention to Kant's rejection of the principle of self-ownership and compares his position to that of some modern feminist writers, particularly Carole Pateman.

Mendus, Susan. Recent Work in Feminist Philosophy. *Phil Quart*, 43(173), 513-519, O 93.

Mensch, James. Aristotle and the Overcoming of the Subject-Object Dichotomy. *Amer Cath Phil Quart*, 65(4), 465-482, Autumn 91.

Since Descartes's time the problem of the subject-object relation has bedeviled philosophy's attempts to understand the world. His framework is one where we attempt to define knowing in terms of material causality, locating both subject and object within space and time taken as somehow independent of them. I show how, by following Aristotle's relativization of space and time (his making them non-independent attributes of bodies), we can account for knowing without falling into the paradoxes of his framework. After discussing the relation between potentiality and presence, I end with an Aristotelian account of "where" the teacher is when he teaches.

Mensch, James Richard. *The Beginning of the Gospel According to Saint John: Philosophical Reflections*. New York, Lang, 1992.

This book's objective is to provide a sample of a new way of reading the Gospel as well as a definition of what constitutes a sacred text. The Gospel presents a character, Jesus, who claims the transcendence of God. Given that a text which attempts to present the radically transcendence of God. Given that a text which attempts to present the radically transcendent can do so only by disrupting itself, my interpretation focuses not just on the sense conveyed by the Gospel, but also on the breakdown of this sense, on the text's failure to locate, to understand its central character, Jesus. A sacred text is such by having an equally disruptive character.

Menta, Timothy. "Justice, Caring, and Animal Liberation": Commentary. *Between Species*, 8(2), 109-112, Spr 92.

In his article, "Justice, Caring, and Animal Liberation," Brian Luke suggests that the ethical basis of animal liberationism should be understood in terms of caring rather than justice. His claim is that insufficient attention has been paid to the caring orientation due to the fact that the two most influential philosophical defenders of animal rights, Tom Regan and Peter Singer, both work exclusively within the justice framework of moral philosophy. I suggest that: a) justice and caring are by no means mutually exclusive ethical orientations, and; b) it would be more productive to animal liberationism to see caring as a supplement to, or foundation of, the justice approaches, rather than a replacement for them.

Menzel, Christopher. Possibilism and Object Theory. *Phil Stud*, 69(2-3), 195-208, Mr 93.

In his 1988 book *Intentional Logic and the Metaphysics of Intentionality*, Edward Zalta argues that unactualized possibilia are needed for an adequate account of the semantics of modal discourse, and in particular for a proper analysis of the modal operators. In this paper, I begin by clarifying the nature of Zalta's own commitment to possibilia. I then discuss some of the problems of such a commitment from the perspective of actualism. Finally, I argue that Zalta's possibilist account of modal discourse has no advantages over an alternative actualist account and, hence, that his chief argument for commitment to possibilia fails.

Menzel, Christopher. Temporal Actualism and Singular Foreknowledge in Philosophical Perspectives, 5: Philosophy of Religion, 1991, Tomberlin, James E (ed). Atascadero, Ridgeview, 1991.

Theists typically believe that before creation God knew precisely what was to take place in the world he planned to create. Hence, on of the things he knew was that Arthur Prior, say, was to be a philosopher. But how could God have known any such thing? For before creation there was no such person as Prior for God to know anything about. After canvassing and rejecting several proposals, I argue for a new solution to this problem that both preserves the idea that there was no information about Prior before creation, but/still provides a straightforward sense in which it is true nonetheless that God knew that Prior was to be a philosopher.

Menzel, Paul T. Double Agency and the Ethics of Rationing Health Care: A Response to Marcia Angell. *Kennedy Inst Ethics J*, 3(3), 287-292, S 93.

The arguments against doctors as "double agents" that are presented by Marcia Angell in the article "The Doctor as Double Agent" (*Kennedy Institute of Ethics Journal* Vol. 3, No. 3, 279-286) do not defeat the core justification for rationing some relatively high-expense, low-benefit care, and they do not enable us to conclude that clinicians should be barred from any active, substantive role in decisions to limit that care. They do, however, reveal several important conditions that need to govern cost-conscious medical practice in order to preserve an ethic of fidelity to patients: insurers' profits and providers' incomes must be fair, providers must inform patients of any economic reasons that lead to the foregoing of care, and "direct incentive" arrangements must not be used to contain costs.

Menzies, Peter. Laws of Nature, Modality and Humean Supervenience in Ontology, Causality and Mind: Essays in Honour of D M Armstrong, Bacon, John (ed). New York, Cambridge Univ Pr, 1993.

This paper is concerned with the modal character of laws of nature. After reviewing the shortcomings of David Lewis' regularity theory of laws and David Armstrong's necessitation theory, I propose a new theory in terms of a primitive concept of modality which we all must possess in virtue of being decision-makers. The modal concept is that of the possible courses of events which an agent could bring about by performing an action. I argue that a law of nature is a regularity that is experimentally resilient in the sense that it holds in all such possible courses of events.

Menzies, Peter and Philip, Pettit. Found: the Missing Explanation. *Analysis*, 53(2), 100-109, Ap 93.

Mark Johnston has argued that certain realist explanations go missing under response-dependent theories. For example, a familiar response-dependent account of color holds that it is a priori true that something is red if and only if it disposed to look red to a normal observer under normal conditions. Johnston argues that one cannot maintain the a priori truth of this biconditional while advancing the realist explanation that something looks red to normal observers because it is red. In this paper we argue that the response-dependence biconditionals do not cause the corresponding realist explanations to go missing.

Menzies, Peter and Price, Huw. Causation as a Secondary Quality. *Brit J Phil Sci*, 44(2), 187-203, Je 93.

In this paper we answer four standard objections to an agency approach to causation, according to which an event *A* is a cause of a distinct event *B* just in case bringing about *A* would be an effective means by which an agent could bring about *B*. The four objections we discuss all turn on the fact that this approach makes essential reference to human capacities. Our strategy is to draw parallels between the agency approach and philosophical treatments of color as a secondary quality. These parallels suggest replies to the objections in question.

Mercer, Mark Douglas. On a Pragmatic Argument Against Pragmatism in Ethics. *Amer Phil Quart*, 30(2), 163-173, Ap 93.

To be pragmatic is to consider only what one has reason to do, given one's current beliefs and desires, and not what one is ethically required to do. Now it is often said that one who fails to consider what one is ethically required to do runs the risk of becoming nihilistic and, thus, that people have a pragmatic reason not to be entirely pragmatic. The author argues, however, that in fact is those who refuse to become pragmatic who runs the greatest risk of becoming nihilistic.

Meretti, Francesco. Paradigma e visione in Thomas Kuhn. *Epistemologia*, 15(2), 239-262, Jl-D 92.

Several concepts of the Kuhnian phenomenology of scientific "growth" refer to a *psychology of research* which amounts, particularly starting with the *Postscript 1969* added to the second edition of *The Structure of Scientific Revolutions*, to an inquiry concerning the cognitive conditionings from which the "way of seeing" the world adopted by scientists derives. In particular, the notion of "paradigm" appears to be strictly connected to the theory of vision that Kuhn adopted thinking over the question—posed first by Ludwig Wittgenstein and later on by Norwood Hanson—of the distinction between perception and interpretation. (edited)

Merrill, S A. 'Person' as an Essentially Contested Concept in the Commonwealth of Discourse. *Metaphilosophy*, 23(4), 363-377, O 92.

Mertz, Donald W. Instance Ontology and Avicenna's Arguments. *Mod Sch*, 70(3), 189-199, Mr 93.

Meseguer, Alvaro G. Language and Reality. *J Prag*, 17(5-6), 505-509, Je 92.

Human beings are placed in the interface of two worlds, the one external (*physical*, perceived by the human senses) and the other internal (*psychic*); a part of the psychic world is perceived with the body (*affective* world) and another with the mind (*cognitive* world). In the physical and affective worlds, reality is the origin and language the result (*R-L situation*); in the cognitive world, language is the origin and reality the result (*L-R situation*). Language and reality are not linked by a unique relation but by two, one governing what happens in R-L situations, the other governing what happens in L-R situations.

Messeri, Marco. Il concetto cartesiano del pensare e il problema delle altre intelligenze. *G Crit Filosof Ital*, 71(1), 65-86, Ja-Ap 92.

Messerly, John. The Essence of David Gauthier's Moral Philosophy. *Kinesis*, 18(2), 39-55, Wint 92.

This work presents the context of Gauthier's moral philosophy, including his theory of rationality and the Prisoner's Dilemma, and proceeds to explicate the main theses of Gauthier's *Moral By Agreement*. Understanding Gauthier to be advancing ten interconnected theses, I proceed to explicate each in turn. I conclude that Gauthier's theory is most vulnerable regarding the issue of *ex post* compliance.

Metz, Johann Baptist. Anamnestic Reason in Cultural-Political Interventions in the Unfinished Project of Enlightenment, Honneth, Axel (& other eds). Cambridge, MIT Pr, 1992.

Anamnestic reason — as it characterizes the spirit of biblical traditions — is more foundational than communicative reason. It is the intellectual expression of a so-called "anamnestic culture" which guarantees the authenticity and identity of the humanities in the processes of enlightenment.

Mews, Constant J. Nominalism and Theology Before Abelard: New Light on Roscelin of Compiègne. *Vivarium*, 30(1), 4-33, My 92.

Meyer, J J C and Van Der Hoek, W. Possible Logics for Belief. *Log Anal*, 32, 127-128, S-D 89.

The problem of logical omniscience, arising in many (modal) logics for belief, is discussed. Such logics yield belief-sets that are i) consistent, ii) containing all tautologies and iii) closed under logical consequences. It is proposed to modally define belief as a *possibility*, rather than a *necessity*; some of the problems noted earlier then disappear. Then, as a dual of an *awareness* operator, the authors propose to also add a *prejudice* operator to logics for belief: whereas awareness can 'filter out' unwanted beliefs, prejudices can 'spontaneously generate' desirable beliefs. It is argued that combinations of these notions can be interpreted on adjusted Kripke models.

Meyer, Jean-Luc. Historique des recherches sur la différenciation des Hépatites A & B. *Hist Phil Life Sci*, 14(1), 93-111, Ja 92.

The numerous researches devoted to 'jaundice' during the Second World War have brought to light the existence of an infectious type of hepatic jaundice or 'homologous serum jaundice' following parenteral injection of vaccines containing human serum and blood transfusions, which were carried out on a large scale at the time. This type of serum jaundice was then gradually differentiated from 'catarrhal', contagious or epidemic jaundice by clinical trails along with large series of animal studies. Finally, the epidemiological, clinical and biological data obtained made it possible to establish, between 1944 and 1954, the viral etiology of these two types of jaundice: the A virus, present in the patients' blood and stools, was considered to be the agent responsible for epidemic hepatitis; the B virus, present primarily in the blood, was held to be responsible for serum hepatitis.

Meyer, Michael J. Patients' Duties. *J Med Phil*, 17(5), 541-555, O 92.

This paper argues that patients' duties are derivable from the idea which typically grounds the idea of patients' rights: patient autonomy. The autonomous patient, joined in partnership with the health care professional, has self-regarding obligations and obligations to others, including health care professionals. Patients' duties include, but are not limited to: a duty to be honest about why the patient seeks care; a duty to collect information on available treatments and like side-effects; a duty for a patient who has an infectious condition to act on that information which can best prevent further transmission.

Meyer, Michel. *Questions de Rhétorique*. Paris, Lib Gen Francaise, 1993.

Meyer, René (ed) and Ryle, Gilbert. *Aspects of Mind—Gilbert Ryle*. Cambridge, Blackwell, 1993.

This volume consists *inter alia* of eight chapters of not previously published papers by the late Gilbert Ryle, and four chapters of extensive notes of lectures delivered shortly before his retirement. The general drift is a concern with thinking as a typically human phenomenon. The volume amplifies key themes in Ryle's *The Concept of Mind*, e.g., thinking, perceiving, learning and freedom. Contemporary materialists cannot derive comfort from Ryle's work except on pain of confusing "behaviour" as "mere bodily behaviour" with "behaviour proper" (action, conduct). A select bibliography links this volume with Ryle's previously published work on thinking.

Meyer, Robert K and Mares, Edwin. The Semantics of R4. *J Phil Log*, 22(1), 95-110, F 93.

Meyer, Robert K and Mares, Edwin D. The Admissibility of γ in R4. *Notre Dame J Form Log*, 33(2), 197-206, Spr 92.

Meyer, Robert K and Slaney, John K. A Structurally Complete Fragment of Relevant Logic. *Notre Dame J Form Log*, 33(4), 561-566, Fall 92.

Meyer, Susan Sauvé. Aristotle, Teleology, and Reduction. *Phil Rev*, 101(4), 791-825, O 92.

The thesis that Aristotle identifies as the rival to his own thesis of natural teleology is not reductionism, as is commonly supposed. Rather, it is an anti-reductionist thesis which supports the eliminative ontological proposal of his opponents. Understanding this rival thesis allows us to see the close connection, in Aristotle's view, between efficient and final causation. And it shows that, in Aristotle's view, natural teleology does not conflict with the view that natural processes are causally determined by material causal interactions.

Meyers, Chris D. The Right to Die: A Justification of Suicide. *Dialogue (PST)*, 34(2-3), 60-63, Ap 92.

Meyers, Christopher. Maintaining the Violinist: A Mother's Obligations to the Fetus She Decides to Keep. *J Soc Phil*, 23(2), 52-64, Fall 92.

Using a variation upon Judith Jarvis Thomson's example of the famous violinist, I argue that just as a person who decides to maintain the violinist incurs certain obligations toward him, so also does a woman who decides to maintain her developing fetus incur certain obligations toward it. I argue further that acceptance of this view does not reduce the pregnant woman to being a tool for the fetus, though it does demand that women must have genuine reproductive options from which to choose, including affordable and legal abortions.

Meyers, Diana. Democratic Theory and the Democratic Agent. *Nomos*, 32, 126-150, 1990.

After criticizing the individualistic conception of the self underlying public-choice theory and the social conception of the self underlying radical-participation theory, I defend an account of the self-defining agent that makes sense of the respect that democracy accords to individuals. This account provides grounds for rejecting consensus theory and grounds for endorsing majoritarian theory; however, it also argues in favor of counter-majoritarian rights that safeguard individual integrity.

Meyers, Diana Tietjens. Moral Reflection: Beyond Impartial Reason. *Hypatia*, 8(3), 21-47, Sum 93.

This paper considers two accounts of the self that have gained prominence in contemporary feminist psychoanalytic theory and draws out the implications of these views with respect to the problem of moral reflection. I argue that our account of moral reflection will be impoverished unless it mobilizes the capacity to empathize with others and the rhetoric of figurative language. To make my case for this claim, I argue that John Rawls's account of reflective equilibrium suffers from his exclusive reliance on impartial reason.

Meyers, Diana Tietjens. Social Exclusion, Moral Reflection, and Rights. *Law Phil*, 12(2), 217-232, My 93.

This essay explores Martha Minow's treatment of the problem of social exclusion. Although I am sympathetic to Minow's basic approach (outlined in Section 1), I take issue with several of her major claims. Section 2 argues that some forms of difference are not best understood as social constructions resting on illegitimate uses of power and that some social consequences of difference should not be neutralized. Section 3 argues that what Minow calls "social relations analysis" compasses two approaches to moral and legal reflection, impartial reason and empathic thought, and that some forms of the problem of social exclusion are best approached through impartial reason while others are best approached through empathic thought. Section 4 argues that introducing empathic thought does not sever the problem of social exclusion from the discourse of rights.

Meyers, Robert G. Peirce's New Way of Signs. *Trans Peirce Soc*, 28(3), 505-521, Sum 92.

The paper argues that Peirce's theory of signs was an attempt to replace the medieval theory of language as perfected by Locke. Peirce rejects the distinction between simple and complex ideas, and holds that every (mental or linguistic) sign refers to its object by virtue of another sign it implies, viz its interpretant. The paper explains how the resulting theory implies a rejection of analyticity and the doctrine of the determinacy of thought. It is suggested that the theory assumes the intentionality of signs and, contrary to Peirce's intentions, does not explain intentionality.

Meynell, Hugo. Habermas: An Unstable Compromise. *Amer Cath Phil Quart*, 65(2), 189-201, Spr 91.

Habermas's basic epistemological principles, as set out in *Theory of Communicative Action*, are quite largely correct; but they commit him, when followed through, to something much closer to the traditional metaphysics and 'first philosophy' than he is prepared to countenance. In fact, his thinking appears to exhibit a curious oscillation between what is in effect the *proposing of a 'first philosophy', and a denial that such a 'first philosophy' is possible*.

Miami Theory Collect (ed). *Community at Loose Ends*. Minneapolis, Univ of Minnesota Pr, 1991.

Michael, Mark. Is There a Duty to Accept Punishment?. *J Soc Phil*, 24(2), 200-223, Fall 93.

From the perspective of someone who faces the prospect of punishment, the crucial problem in the theory of punishment is whether and under what conditions attempting to avoid or escape punishment is justified. This question has been largely ignored because it has been assumed that the answer is simply entailed by whatever answer one gives to a more theoretical question concerning the justification of punishment. I argue that this assumption is mistaken; significant issues will be encountered in trying to answer questions about evading punishment. In the second part of the paper I offer a theory which incorporates what I call the linked model of escape. On this model evading punishment is justified if one's initial act of lawbreaking was justified.

Michael, Mark A. Utilitarianism and Retributivism: What's the Difference. *Amer Phil Quart*, 29(2), 173-182, Ap 92.

The traditional distinction between utilitarian and retributive justifications of punishment is often explicated in extremely vague and imprecise terms. Several new versions of retributivism such as that found in Herbert Morris's "Persons and Punishment" have further complicated the situation, as they seem to incorporate both utilitarian and retributive elements. A new criterion for marking out this distinction is proposed here based on the relation between the act of punishment and the events/states of affairs which are supposed to justify it.

Michael, Mike and Grove-White, Robin. Talking about Talking about Nature: Nurturing Ecological Consciousness. *Environ Ethics*, 15(1), 33-47, Spr 93.

The increasing effort, both lay and academic, to encourage a transition from an "I-It" to an "I-Thou" relation to nature is located within a typology of ways of "knowing nature." This typology provides the context for a particular understanding of human conversation which sees the relation as a cyclical process of "immersion" and "realization" from which a model of the dialectic between "I-It" and "I-Thou" relations to nature can be developed. This model can be used to identify practical measures that can be taken as first steps toward a balance between these relations, both in general and in the context of science-oriented nature conservation organizations such as English Nature in Britain (formerly, the Nature Conservancy Council).

Michel, Thomas. Islamic Ethical Vision. *J Dharma*, 16(4), 398-409, O-D 91.

Michelsen, John M. George Santayana: A Pyrrhonian Sceptic of Our Time. *Bull Santayana Soc*, 11, 30-40, Fall 93.

Mickett, Carole A. Comments on Sandra Lee Bartky's *Femininity and Domination*. *Hypatia*, 8(1), 173-178, Wint 93.

To illustrate the strength of Bartky's clarity of insight, I focus on her discussion of shame found in two essays in *Femininity and Domination*. I argue that these essays as well as the other in the collection identify and offer a clear analysis of many issues central to feminism and call for Bartky to write a sequel which offers constructive suggestions of ways out.

Midgley, David N (trans) and Wellmer, Albrecht. *The Persistence of Modernity: Essays on Aesthetics, Ethics, and Postmodernism*. Cambridge, MIT Pr, 1991.

These four essays, drawn from two books by one of Germany's foremost philosophers, go to the heart of a number of contemporary issues: Adorno's aesthetics, the nature of a postmodern ethics, and the persistence of modernity in the so-called postmodern age. Albrecht Wellmer defends the general thesis that modernity contains its own critique and that what has been called postmodernism is in fact a further articulation of that critique. More specifically, his essays offer a reinterpretation of Adorno's aesthetics within the framework of a postutopian philosophy of communicative reason, an analysis of the postmodern critique of instrumental reason and its subject that becomes an argument for democratic pluralism and universalism, a discussion of the dialectics of modernism and postmodernism in the context of architecture and industrial design, and a dialogical ethics that is inspired by and yet takes issue with Habermas' discourse ethics.

Midgley, Mary. Iris Murdoch's *Metaphysics as a Guide to Morals*. *Phil Invest*, 16(4), 333-341, O 93.

Midgley, Mary. Is the Biosphere a Luxury?. *Hastings Center Rep*, 22(3), 7-12, My-Je 92.

Midgley, Mary. Philosophical Plumbing. *Philosophy*, 33(Supp), 139-151, 1992.

Midgley, Mary. Philosophical Plumbing in The Impulse to Philosophise, Griffiths, A Phillips (ed). New York, Cambridge Univ Pr, 1992.

Mignucci, Mario. The Stoic Analysis of the Sorites. *Proc Aris Soc*, 93, 231-245, 1993.

Migotti, Mark. Self-Determination, Self-Expression, and Self-Knowledge. *Personalist Forum*, 8/1(Supp), 233-242, Spr 92.

This paper explores an Emersonian conception of the relationship between self-determination and self-expression. I take self-determination to require "fundamental deliberation", deliberation in which one takes as little about oneself and the world for granted as possible. I take Emerson to suggest that what is expressed in self-expressive activity is an inherent nexus of cognitive, conative, and emotional tendencies. I argue that if one takes fluent self-expression as the goal of fundamental deliberation one can avoid the Sartrean paradox of the impossibility of justifying the results of such deliberation.

Mijnhardt, W W and Kloek, J J. *De Productie, Distributie en Consumptie Van Cultuur*. Amsterdam, Rodopi, 1991.

Miké, Valerie. Toward an Ethic of Evidence—and Beyond: Observations on Technology and Illness. *Res Phil Technol*, 9, 101-113, 1989.

Miké, Valerie and Krauss, Alfred N and Ross, Gail S. Perinatal Technology: Answers and Questions. *J Clin Ethics*, 3(1), 56-62, Spr 92.

This article focuses on uncertainty in perinatal medicine. Sources of uncertainty include not only the complexity of premature physiology and related disease mechanisms, but also the lack of proper assessment of many perinatal technologies for their safety and effectiveness. These issues are illustrated by means of two perinatal technologies: transcutaneous oxygen monitoring and neonatal extracorporeal membrane oxygenation (ECMO). They are analyzed in terms of a proposed "ethics of evidence," meaning, in concrete but not exhaustive terms, guidelines for the creation, assessment and dissemination of evidence. Related problem are then discussed in the broader context of contemporary perinatal medicine.

Mikulás, Szabolcs. The Completeness of the Lambek Calculus with Respect to Relational Semantics. *Bull Sec Log*, 21(2), 55-66, Je 92.

We proved that Lambek's calculus of syntactic types is (strongly) sound and complete with respect to the so-called Relational semantics proposed by Johan van Benthem. The idea of this semantics of dynamic nature is that we associate binary relations with types, and set-theoretic operations between relations (such as relational composition) with the connectives of the calculus. The completeness proof is an application of an algebraic representation theorem, where we show that every Lindenbaum-Tarski algebra of the Lambek calculus is isomorphic to an algebra of binary relations.

Mikulás, Szabolcs and Sain, Ildikó and Simon, András. Complexity of Equational Theory of Relational Algebras with Projection Elements. *Bull Sec Log*, 21(3), 103-111, O 92.

In connection with a problem of L Henkin and J D Monk, we show that the equational theory and the first order theory of True Pairing Algebras (TPA's) (Relation Algebras expanded with concrete set theoretic projection functions) are not axiomatizable by any decidable set of axioms. More specifically, the equational theory of TPA's is exactly as complex as the second order universal theory of natural numbers. Finally, we show that the equational theory of the projection-free reducts of TPA's is recursively enumerable but not finitely axiomatizable.

Milam, Michael C. The Misuse of Nietzsche in Literary Theory. *Phil Lit*, 16(2), 320-332, O 92.

It has been claimed by deconstructionist theorists such as Derrida, David B Allison, Paul de Man, and J Hillis Miller that Nietzsche's philosophy is unequivocally nihilistic. These claims are made, however, by ignoring his historical and philosophical context and are also rarely documented well from his texts. Recent philosophical scholarship, on the other hand, has moved toward a more positive and affirmative view of Nietzsche's philosophical enterprise.

Milano, A. Congetture e confutazioni. *Sapienza*, 46(1), 91-92, 1993.

Milbank, John. Problematizing the Secular: The Post-Postmodern Agenda in Shadow of Spirit, Berry, Philippa (ed). New York, Routledge, 1992.

Milchman, Alan. Hannah Arendt and the Etiology of the Desk Killer: The Holocaust as Portent. *Hist Euro Ideas*, 14(2), 213-226, Mr 92.

Miles, T G. Utilitarianism and Education: A Reply to James Tarrant. *J Phil Educ*, 26(2), 261-264, 1992.

This article focuses on Part III of Tarrant's paper, 'Utilitarianism, education and the philosophy of moral insignificance'. His argument that Mill's distinction between higher and lower pleasures appeals to non-utilitarian values is rejected on the grounds that he misconstrues Mill's concept of 'content' and fails to give an adequate critique of Mill's attempt to distinguish between the quantity and quality of pleasures. An improved criticism is offered, and it is argued that utilitarianism fails through the dependence of happiness itself upon non-utilitarian values. It is concluded that utilitarianism would devalue the role of liberal area subjects in sensitizing pupils to the problematic nature of human happiness.

Milet, Matias (trans) and Prado Jr, Plinio Walder. Argumentation and Aesthetics: Reflections on Communication and the Differend. *Phil Today*, 36(4), 351-366, Wint 92.

Mileur, Jean-Pierre and Stewart, Stanley and Magnus, Bernd. *Nietzsche's Case: Philosophy as/and Literature*. New York, Routledge, 1992.

This jointly-authored study of Nietzsche and his literary interlocutors occupies the interface of philosophy and literature, bringing conventionally marked "philosophical" and "literary" texts into conversation with one another in a way never done before. Nietzsche's texts are brought into productive conversation with the New Testament and texts by Sidney, Bacon, Spenser, Milton, Shakespeare, Browning, Coleridge, Wordsworth, Blake, Caryle, Lawrence, as well as with the standard texts of the philosophical and critical traditions from Plato to Derrida.

Millar, Alan. Jerry A Fodor's "A Theory of Content and Other Essays". *Phil Quart*, 42(168), 367-372, Jl 92.

Fodor's atomistic conception of meaning is motivated by his aim to reconcile belief-desire psychology with the claim that there is no principled analytic-synthetic distinction. To avoid having meaning constituted by links between representation Fodor seeks to make meaning dependent on nomic links between representations and the objects which usually produce them. The article raises doubts as to whether the approach can cope with the role of theory in governing the way our representations function. In a discussion of modularity in perception it is suggested that Fodor had better make experiences rather than beliefs the immediate outputs of the perceptual system.

Millar, Alan. Reply to Brinton's '"Following Nature" in Butler's Sermons'. *Phil Quart*, 42(169), 486-491, O 92.

Brinton argued that the interpretation of Butler's moral philosophy in 'Following Nature' exaggerates the importance of adaptation and overplays the role of God in Butler's thought. It is argued, among other things, (1) that Butler explicitly appeals to the notion of our being adapted to virtue in meeting an objection from Wollaston to his claim that virtue consists in following our nature, and (2) that though being adapted to virtue does not entail being made for virtue, within Butler's explanatory framework we are in fact adapted to virtue only insofar as we have been designed by God for virtue.

Miller, David. In Defence of Nationality. *J Applied Phil*, 10(1), 3-16, 1993.

The principle of nationality is widely believed to be philosophically disreputable and politically reactionary. As defined here, it embraces three propositions: national identities are properly part of personal identities; they ground circumscribed obligations to fellow-nationals; and they justify claims to political self-determination. To have a national identity is to think of oneself as belonging to a community constituted by mutual belief, extended in history, active in character, connected to a particular territory, and marked off from others by its members' distinct traits. Such identities are inevitably partly mythical in nature, yet they answer a pressing modern need, the maintenance of solidarity in large, anonymous societies. They are allied to

AUTHOR INDEX WITH ABSTRACTS 595 Milligan, Charles S

no particular political programme. They do not require the suppression of minority cultures within the political community. They do not justify a secessionist free-for-all. Nor finally does recognition of the role of sentiments in constituting national communities commit us to a subjectivist view of social obligations. Philosophers should recognise the value of these loyalties even if they cannot be rationally grounded in a strong sense.

Miller, David James and Schrag, Calvin. Communication Studies and Philosophy in The Critical Turn, Angus, Ian (ed). Carbondale, So Illinois Univ Pr, 1993.

Miller, Edward Jeremy. The Roles of Moral Dispositions in the Cognitional Theories of Newman and Lonergan. *Thought*, 67(265), 128-147, Je 92.

John Henry Newman and Bernard Lonergan both argue that true judgments following upon insight depend not only on sound mental principles and logic but also on the moral dispositions of the thinker. If modern philosophy tends to bifurcate mental acumen from one's personal ethics, Lonergan more recently and Newman a century ago strongly demur. Lonergan argues the role of self-correcting operations of the mind, dependent upon various levels of ethical conversion. Newman, using a more personalist language, describes conscience as a mental *eros* questing for truthfulness in judgment. Thus, an ethical dimension of life affects one's acts of insight and judgment.

Miller, Franklin G. The Concept of Medically Indicated Treatment. *J Med Phil*, 18(1), 91-98, F 93.

The following article examines critically Robert Veatch's argument that respect for patient autonomy invalidates the concept of medically indicated treatment. I contend that when judgments of medically indicated treatment are distinguished from what ought to be done in a given case, all things considered, they are compatible with patient autonomy. Yet there remains a significant danger, which needs to be guarded against, that physicians will use these judgments to dominate their interactions with patients. Medicine would be impoverished, however, if physicians were barred from using clinical judgment to recommend medically indicated treatment.

Miller, Fred D (ed) and Paul, Ellen Frankel (ed) and Paul, Jeffrey (ed). *Altruism*. New York, Cambridge Univ Pr, 1993.

The essays in this volume address the following questions and issues: When deciding what action to take, should an individual give greater weight to others' interests or to his own? Or is it possible to reconcile altruism and egoism, to show that we have self-regarding reasons for acting altruistically? What is the relationship between altruism and rationality? Whether, and under what conditions, may we properly be forced to serve others' interests? What role should government play in regulating our interactions? Confronting crucial and difficult issues, the ten authors whose essays appear in this volume offer fresh perspectives on the nature and value of altruism. Contributors: Thomas E Hill, Jr, Christine M Korsgaard, David Schmidtz, Robert Sugden, Neera Kapur Badhwar, William A Galston, Jean Hampton, Roderick T Long, Douglas J Den Uyl, and Tyler Cowen.

Miller, George. Care and Indifference in the Moral Domain. *J Value Inq*, 27(1), 105-108, Ja 93.

Miller, George. Creativity in the Void. *Phil Stud Educ*, 1, 104-116, 1991.

Miller, George David. The Allegory of the Classrooms. *J Value Inq*, 27(2), 243-246, Ap 93.

Miller, Irwin. A Pragmatic Health Care Policy Tradition: Dewey, Franklin and Social Reconstruction. *Bus Prof Ethics J*, 12(1), 47-57, Spr 93.

Miller, J Hillis. Laying Down the Law in Literature in Deconstruction and the Possibility of Justice, Cornell, Durcilla (ed). New York, Routledge, 1992.

Miller, J Hillis. *Theory Now and Then*. Durham, Duke Univ Pr, 1991.

Miller, Jerome A. *In the Throe of Wonder: Intimations of the Sacred in a Post-Modern World*. Albany, SUNY Pr, 1992.

In the Throe of Wonder is a phenomenology of wonder, honor and awe, and a exploration of their ontological import. It argues that these experiences are not subjective, emotive responses to events that happen in the world but disruptions that fracture the immediacy of the given and, in so doing, radically transform our sense of being itself. Such disruptions undermine not only the metaphysics of presence and representational epistemology but also the pragmatism that is often treated as an alternative to them. While meditative rather than exegetical in its focus, the book improvises on themes opened up by Heidegger, Lonergan, Freud, Rorty and Derrida.

Miller, M C. The Principle of Continuity in C S Peirce and Contemporary ... in Frontiers in American Philosophy, Volume I, Burch, Robert W (ed). College Station, Texas A&M Univ Pr, 1992.

I argue that several of Peirce's conceptions (including the architectonic of the sciences, the nature of inquiry, habit, logic as semiotic, and synechism), interrelated through his principle of continuity, provide a particularly useful approach to the analysis of Decision Support Systems. I propose that the distinctive practical problems emerging in the institutionalization of DSS shed some interesting light on some dangers in the field of decision theory. Decision-theoretic analyses have been too narrowly focused in logic as critic: Peirce's contribution through logic as semiotic can be fully appreciated only if one takes seriously the prime importance of continuity.

Miller, Marjorie C. Feminism and Pragmatism. *Monist*, 75(4), 445-457, O 92.

Rediscovery may be recognized by emergence of vocabulary, categories, distinctions, and problems previously articulated in a powerful philosophy. This may be viewed as "rediscovery" even if those articulating new positions are unaware of debt to the earlier tradition. I defend the claim that just such a rediscovery of the American Tradition is apparent in the work of contemporary feminists in: the problematizing of experience, the critique of "reason", and the conception of philosophy. Feminist's development of these issues, in terms of the way their approaches may be viewed as a "rediscovery" of the "classic tradition", support extending the reconstruction.

Miller, Mitchell. Unity and *Logos*: A Reading of *Theaetetus* 201c-210a. *Ancient Phil*, 12(1), 87-111, Spr 92.

Miller, Paul Allen. Kant, Lentricchia and Aesthetic Education. *Kantstudien*, 83(4), 454-466, 1992.

This paper examines Lentricchia's criticism of Kant's aesthetics, as presented in the *Critique of Judgment* and finds them based on a fundamental misunderstanding of what is meant by "free beauty" (*pulchritudo vaga*). It argues that Kant's formulation can stand as a foundation on which to build a truly dialectical understanding of the value of beauty, and that this understanding, in turn, can provide a renewed rationale for the role of the humanities in education.

Miller, Randolph. Rethinking Empiricism in Theology in God, Values, and Empiricism, Peden, Creighton (ed). Macon, Mercer Univ Pr, 1989.

Miller, Randolph Crump (ed). *Empirical Theology: A Handbook*. Birmingham, Religious Educ Pr, 1992.

Empirical theology, based on the interpretation of experience, especially as developed by the Chicago School, is central. Its historical development, major themes, contrast with empirical methods in the sciences, difference from traditional theology, approach to God, the Spirit, Jesus, the church, humanity, ethics and values, and its approach to ecology are interpreted. Its use in pastoral care and significance for the local congregation conclude the book with the statement that a Christian can be an empiricist and an empirical theologian can be a Christian. Contributors include T Inbody, N Frankenberry, K Peters, M Suchocki, W Dean, B Lee, G Sloyan, W Tremmel, R Corrington, F Ferre, J Cobb Jr, and R C Miller.

Miller, Richard. Concern for Counterparts. *Phil Papers*, 21(2), 133-140, Ag 92.

This paper refutes an old objection to genuine modal realism. The difficulty was first offered by Saul Kripke and has recently been reformulated by Simon Blackburn and Gideon Rosen. This problem alleges that an analysis of counterfactuals in terms of what is true of our counterparts can never adequately capture our sense of immediate and personal concern with the truth of counterfactuals about ourselves because we can never be concerned with what befalls others (our counterparts) the way we are concerned with what happens to ourselves. This objection fails because we have an immediate and personal concern that we should be happier than those to whom we compare ourselves, especially our counterparts. And the truth conditions for counterfactuals about ourselves involve just such comparisons of ourselves with others similar to us.

Miller, Richard. Justice as Social Freedom in On the Track of Reason, Beehler, Rodger G (ed). Boulder, Westview Pr, 1992.

Miller, Richard B. A Purely Causal Solution to One of the Qua Problems. *Austl J Phil*, 70(4), 425-434, D 92.

Miller, Richard B. Genuine Modal Realism: Still the Only Non-circular Game in Town. *Austl J Phil*, 71(2), 159-160, Je 93.

Miller, Seumas. Joint Action. *Phil Papers*, 21(3), 275-297, N 92.

Examples of joint actions are: two people dancing, tradesmen building a house. Joint actions are actions performed by individuals and directed to a collective end. This collective end theory can be elaborated and generalised so as to accommodate a whole range of quasi-joint actions in, for example, free-rider contexts.

Miller, Seumas. Killing in Self-Defense. *Pub Affairs Quart*, 7(4), 325-339, O 93.

I argue against existing accounts of the justification for killing in self-defense, including those of Montague, Teichman, and Thomson. I argue for a fault-based internalist account. You suspend your right not to be killed by me if: 1) you are a deadly threat to me; 2) you intend to kill me and you are responsible for this intention; 3) you do not have a decisive moral justification for killing me, and with respect to a decisive moral justification for killing me, believe that you have it, and believe this with good reason.

Miller, Seumas. On Conventions. *Austl J Phil*, 70(4), 435-444, D 92.

Agents are parties to a convention to *x* iff: 1) each has the procedure to *x*; 2) each has the procedure to *x* because the others have that procedure, and if all (most) have the procedure some collective end is realized; 3) each mutually believes everyone (most) have the procedure to *x*.

Miller, Seumas. Self-Defence and Forcing the Choice between Lives. *J Applied Phil*, 9(2), 239-243, 1992.

In the standard case of justifiable killing in self-defence one agent without provocation tries to kill a second agent and the second agent's only way to avoid death is to kill his attacker. It is widely accepted that such killings in self-defence are morally justifiable, but it has proved difficult to show why this is so. Recently, Montague has put forward an account in terms of forcing a choice between lives, and Teichman has propounded a quasi-Hobbesian rights-based account of self-defence. I argue that neither Montague nor Teichman has succeeded in providing an adequate justification for killing in self-defence.

Miller, Steven I and Fredericks, Janet. Clarifying the "Adequate Evidence Condition" in Educational Issues and Research: A Lakoffian View. *Educ Theor*, 42(4), 461-472, Fall 92.

The article is an attempt to clarify and extend Scheffler's notion of the "adequate evidence condition". Using the framework of an Idealized Cognitive Model, developed by the cognitive-linguist, George Lakoff, various ideas of "evidence" are developed and analyzed. The analysis reveals that our models of adequate evidence influence our traditional epistemological views concerning correspondence and coherence views of "truth". Attempts are made to show the significance of the evidence condition for policy formulation in the human sciences.

Miller Jr, Fred D. Aristotle on Property Rights in Essays in Ancient Greek Philosophy, IV, Anton, John P (ed). Albany, SUNY Pr, 1991.

Millican, Peter. 'Hume's Theorem' Concerning Miracles. *Phil Quart*, 43(173), 489-495, O 93.

Milligan, Charles S. The Diverse Styles of Social Pluralism. *Cont Phil*, 15(3), 16-20, My-Je 93.

At the conclusion of WWII the problem of the future was thought to be that of avoiding conflict between the "great powers," i.e., nation-states. However, since then wars have increasingly been between ethnic, religious, or political factions within nations. Thus management of pluralistic societies has become critical. A typology is proposed for analyzing different modes of governance, based on where determinative power is located with respect to diverse and competing populations within a society. The five styles are: coercive, assimilative, tradition as controlling, community opinion, and legal policy.

Milligan, Charles S. William Bernhardt's Theory of Religious Values in God, Values, and Empiricism, Peden, Creighton (ed). Macon, Mercer Univ Pr, 1989.

The primary purpose is to provide an exposition and analysis of William Bernhardt's theory of religious values. He argued that values are relational, culminative, and satisfying. They are not essences, but modifying attributes of experienced events. As combinations of qualities they are usually experienced as wholenesses. Religious values are those life values which are realized through religious practices and interpretations. They occur in relation to the "nonmanipulable"— when our knowledge and skills are inadequate. The chief religious value is maintenance of morale in the face of demoralizing factors. Three supplementary hypotheses are proposed.

Milligan, Maureen. Reflections on Feminist Scepticism, the "Maleness" of Philosophy and Postmodernism. *Hypatia*, 7(3), 166-172, Sum 92.

Bordo is concerned with what she calls a postmodern "theoretics of heterogeneity" that questions the validity of historical and cultural analyses "along gender-lines." It also challenges the validity of feminist analyses concerning the "maleness" of philosophy. Not surprisingly, this has precipitated debate between postmodernists and those alarmed by its implications for feminist work. At issue is the epistemological and political capacity of feminism to analyze social power and dominance through an analysis of gender.

Millikan, Ruth Garrett. Explanation in Biopsychology in Mental Causation, Heil, John (ed). New York, Clarendon/Oxford Pr, 1993.

I explore implications for the science of psychology of the thesis that the categories of intentional psychology are function categories in the biologist's sense of "function," according to which function is determined by evolutionary history rather than by current dispositions. I explore, first, the general shape of the discipline that is psychology under this interpretation. What is its subject matter? What kinds of explanations does it seek for what kinds of phenomena? Second, I bring these refections to bear on the question what it means to assume that man is a rational animal. I argue that it need not mean that there are psychological laws requiring normal humans to make rational inferences ceteris paribus.

Millikan, Ruth Garrett. Knowing What I'm Thinking Of—I. *Aris Soc*, Supp(67), 91-108, 1993.

I argue that under a very plausible interpretation, knowing what one is thinking of or judging about turns out to be a matter of degree. The lowest degree many be necessary for having thought at all, but the highest degree is never realized. As Gareth Evans saw, grasping the identity of the object of one's thought requires having a concept of that object, which requires, in turn, conforming to what Evans called the 'generality constraint' (1982, p 100). But a concept is an ability, a knowhow, and unlike either know-thats or dispositionists, knowhows come in degrees. One can know how but still fail. Indeed, it is common actually to be mistaken about the object of one's thought.

Millikan, Ruth Garrett. *White Queen Psychology and Other Essays for Alice*. Cambridge, MIT Pr, 1993.

The title essay discusses meaning rationalism and argues that there is no legitimate interpretation under which logical possibility and necessity are known a priori. Nor are there any laws of rational psychology. Rationality is not a lawful occurrence but a biological norm affected in an integrated head-world system under biologically ideal conditions. Other essays clarify the nature of mental representation, explore whether human thought is a product of natural selection, examine the nature of behavior as studied by the behavioral sciences, and discuss the issues of individualism in psychology, psychological explanation, indexicality in thought, what knowledge is, and the realism/antirealism debate.

Mills, Eugene. Dividing without Reducing: Bodily Fission and Personal Identity. *Mind*, 102(405), 37-51, Ja 93.

I reconcile anti-reductionism about persons with the apparent possibility of personal fission. Apparent fission is *merely* apparent, I argue: both fission-survivors must exit before fission as well as after. I accept, however, Derek Parfit's point that if fission-survivors shared a single stream of consciousness before fission, then it cannot be that *both* mental continuity and connectedness *and* identity over time are what matter in survival, as anti-reductionism requires. The proper conclusion is that fission-survivors had distinct streams of consciousness while cohabiting in a single body before fission. I defend this thesis against several objections.

Mills, Patricia Jagentowicz. "Feminist" Sympathy and Other Serious Crimes: A Reply to Swindle. *Owl Minerva*, 24(1), 55-62, Fall 92.

Mills, Sara. Discourse Competence; or, How to Theorize Strong Women Speakers. *Hypatia*, 7(2), 4-17, Spr 92.

In feminist linguistic analysis, women's speech has often been characterized as "powerless" or as "over-polite"; this paper aims to challenge this notion and to question the eliding of a feminine speech style with femaleness. In order to move beyond a position which judges speech as masculine or feminine, which are stereotypes of behavior, I propose the term "discourse competence" to describe speech where cooperative and competitive strategies are used appropriately.

Milne, Peter. Counterparts and Comparatives. *Analysis*, 53(2), 82-92, Ap 93.

Milne, Peter. Modal Metaphysics and Comparatives. *Austl J Phil*, 70(3), 248-262, S 92.

Milne, Peter. Prevost, Probability, God and Evil. *Heythrop J*, 33(4), 434-436, O 92.

Milne, Peter. The Foundations of Probability and Quantum Mechanics. *J Phil Log*, 22(2), 129-168, Ap 93.

Taking as starting point two familiar interpretations of probability, we develop these in a perhaps unfamiliar way to arrive ultimately at an improbable claim concerning the proper axiomatization of probability theory: the domain of definition of a point-valued probability distribution is an orthomodular partially ordered set. Similar claims have been made in the light of quantum mechanics but here the motivation is intrinsically probabilistic. This being so the main task is to investigate what light, if any, this sheds on quantum mechanics. In particular it is important to know under what conditions these point-valued distributions can be thought of as derived from distribution-pairs of upper and lower probabilities on Boolean algebras. Generalising known results this investigation unsurprisingly proves unrewarding. In the light of this failure the next topic investigated is how these generalized probability distributions are to be interpreted.

Mindle, Grant B. Shakespeare's Demonic Prince. *Interpretation*, 20(3), 259-274, Spr 93.

Minors, R H and Sillince, J A A. Argumentation, Self-Inconsistency, and Multidimensional Argument Strength. *Commun Cog*, 25(4), 325-338, 1992.

Nonmonotic and default logics for maintaining consistency of beliefs are only semidecidable, so that in practice heuristics are relied upon. These logics continue to use the concepts of validity. This paper suggests the use of argument strength instead of validity, and outlines a way of getting conflicting agents to carry some of the load usually carried by logics. The paper suggests a data structure which would enable inconsistency to occur, suggests how argument strength would be determined by tactical rules and how attention focus within the shared argument map would be determined by strategic rules, and shows how arguments operate simultaneously on several different levels in a manner analogous to linguistic comprehension.

Minter, Adam. Machiavelli, Violence, and History. *Harvard Rev Phil*, 2(1), 25-33, Spr 92.

Mints, G. A Normal Form for Logical Derivations Implying One for Arithmetic Derivations. *Annals Pure Applied Log*, 62(1), 65-79, Je 93.

A normal form theorem for derivations in the first order arithmetic, having the same consequences as cut-elimination, is usually being proved by model-theoretic arguments. Our proof is a simple modification of the construction of a countermodel of a predicate formula from the open branch of its canonical proof-search tree. It extends to intuitionistic and higher-order systems. The proof of the corresponding normalization theorem uses the passage to the infinitary derivations enriched by the finitary derivations.

Mirhady, David C. The Great Fuss over *Philebus* 15b. *Apeiron*, 25(3), 171-177, S 92.

The previously overlooked introductory working to the vexed passage at *Philebus* 15b describe it as a dispute that results from a "great fuss." A proper appreciation of the ironical aspects of this wording help to interpret 15b, which is read not as two or three distinct 'questions,' but rather as the single statement of the dispute, namely, how to make sense of unities like man, ox, and the good being both one and many.

Mirvish, Adrian M. Bad Faith, Good Faith, and the Faith of Faith in Sartre Alive, Aronson, Ronald (ed). Detroit, Wayne St Univ Pr, 1991.

The phenomenon of bad faith for Sartre is analyzed in terms of worlds of belief, an idea which makes use of the notion of evidence. It is emphasized that misunderstanding can easily arise in the Sartre never explicitly discusses the actual mechanism whereby bad faith can occur, but that this can be explained in terms of principles of Gestalt psychology. Finally, it is shown that Sartre's view of bad faith has to be understood as a reaction to both the orthodox psychoanalysis of Freud and the rationalism of Alain.

Mische, Ann. Post Communism's "Lost Treasure": Rethinking Political Agency in a Shifting Public Sphere. *Praxis Int*, 13(3), 242-267, O 93.

Misgeld, Dieter (ed) and Nicholson, Graeme (ed). *Hans-Georg Gadamer on Education, Poetry, and History: Applied Hermeneutics*. Albany, SUNY Pr, 1992.

This is a collection of essays by Hans-Georg Gadamer, all of which had been untranslated hitherto—with one exception. The editors (who co-translated the essays with Lawrence Schmidt and Monica Reusch) arranged the essays in three groups, introducing each of the three sections with a long and intensive interview with Hans-Georg Gadamer. The parts are: 1) The Philosopher in the University; 2) Hermeneutics, Poetry and Modern Culture; 3) Europe and the Humanities. The interviews discuss Gadamer's relation to his times, from World-War I to Nazism and the post-war era, his relation to Heidegger and others, etc. The essays selected include essays on George and Celan, on the European Humanities, and on Planning the Future, on the German University, its history and limitations. There is a wide-ranging editors' introduction covering these topics.

Mish'alani, James K. Being and Infestation. *Grad Fac Phil J*, 16(1), 227-243, 1993.

This essay is an attempt at a daseinsanalysis of Gregor Samsa in Franz Kafka's *The Metamorphosis*. It claims that the existential predicament in Gregor's metamorphosis into a vermin is one of deranged temporality: being in a state without possibilities. It traces this absurdity to a false inwardness whereby the self evades its being-in-the-world by degrading its dwelling to a condition of infestation. This particular type of evasion of authentic being is shown to be particularly tempting in western modernity.

Mishara, Aaron L. The Problem of the Unconscious in the Later Thought of L Binswanger in Analecta Husserliana, XXXI, Tymieniecka, Anna-Teresa (ed). Dordrecht, Kluwer, 1990.

Miszczynski, Ryszard. Intuitionistic Concept of Mathematical Language (in Polish). *Stud Phil Christ*, 27(2), 49-64, 1991.

The aim of the paper is to discuss the intuitionistic concept of mathematical language, according to ideas of Brouwer, Heyting and van Dantzig. It is compared to other points of view represented in philosophy of mathematics. Intuitionism, rejecting the role of language in mathematics, is the opposition to formalism. The author shows, how the intuitionistic standpoint evolves from Brouwer to Heyting, becoming more realistic. The concept of language, although generating difficulties and unsolved problems, plays the central role in the intuitionistic conception of mathematics, which in turn is an important element of modern philosophy of mathematics. It helps to bring out the role of language in classical mathematics.

Mitcham, Carl. An Introduction to "Basic Questions about Metaphysics of Technology". *J Speculative Phil*, 7(2), 137-142, 1993.

A brief introduction to the thought of Gotthard Günther, which is examined at greater length in a following paper by Arno Bammé, Ernst Kotzmann, and Ulrike Oberheber, with the indicated title, pp 143-158.

Mitchell, Joshua. Hobbes and the Equality of All Under the One. *Polit Theory*, 21(1), 78-100, F 93.

The peculiarities of Hobbes's political theory—his epistemology, his understanding of the magnitude of the problem of pride, and view of sovereignty—can best be understood in the context of the Reformation debate about the meaning of the equality of all under the One. Hobbes's political theory does not rest upon a foundation of reason, but rather Revelation. This is not to say that the theology he invokes is conventional. Nevertheless, without attempting to grasp the way in which Hobbes is entering into the existing debate of his times, his political theory remains opaque.

Mitchell, Robert Lloyd. *The Hymn to Eros*. Lanham, Univ Pr of America, 1993.

Three main dimensions emerge in this attempt at a deep, thoughtful reading of the *Symposium* in its entirety: 1) the story of the rise and fall of the proudest center of Hellenic culture, the city of Athens; 2) an account of the living impulse that constitutes *human* life itself: a complex interplay of two opposing sides that is resolved only in intensely problematic fulfillment; and 3) a confrontation with the *problem* of philosophy, and of Socrates—the two cannot be separated. In place of Platonic "doctrine," this reading indicates why philosophy, in the *Symposium's* sense, can never be doctrine.

Mitchell, Sandra. Dispositions or Etiologies? A Comment on Bigelow and Pargetter. *J Phil*, 90(5), 249-259, My 93.

Bigelow and Pargetter (*J Phil* 84(4), 181-196, Ap 1987) reject the etiological theory of function and defend a dispositional account. They reason by analogy between biological function and fitness. I argue that their negative argument fails by begging the question of causal mechanism. Their positive argument fails by shifting the problem addressed by functional explanations. Functions construed as dispositions explain survival (or selection of a trait). I conclude that dispositional and etiological theories are not proper alternatives, confusion arises when the respective scientific roles of function are conflated.

Mitias, Michael H. Dewey's Theory of Expression. *J Aes Educ*, 26(3), 41-53, Fall 92.

The essay is essentially a defense of Dewey's theory of expression. The author responds to Alan Tormey's criticism of Dewey's version of the Expression Theory of Art. Two points are stressed: (1) Dewey's theory remains a rich source of insight in theorizing about the artistic adventures and achievements of the twentieth century; (2) the concept of expression does shed a light of understanding on the distinctive feature of art works as a class.

Mitias, Michael H. International Law and World Peace. *Dialec Hum*, 17(3), 187-199, 1990.

The paper argues that a necessary condition for promoting World peace is developing a world order erected on a just international law. And in order for this law to be conducive to World Peace, (1) it should be responsive to the needs and concerns of all the nation states; (2) it should be a legal order; and (3) this order should be accepted freely by all the world states.

Mitias, Michael H (ed). *Moral Education and the Liberal Arts*. Westport, Greenwood Pr, 1992.

This book is a critical and evaluative study of the role the humanities can play in the cultivation of character at the college level. The book is composed of nine essays. Each essay deals with a number of question and problems relating to the whole issue of moral education.

Mitias, Michael H. Possibility of Moral Education in the Liberal Arts in Moral Education and the Liberal Arts, Mitias, Michael H (ed). Westport, Greenwood Pr, 1992.

This paper discusses three questions: 1) Can a college foster the moral growth of its students? 2) What moral values can a college teach or foster? 3) How can a college contribute to the moral growth of its students? Moreover, what are the ingredients of moral education? Finally, under what conditions can a college influence the moral character of young people?

Mitias, Michael H. Possibility of World Community. *Dialec Hum*, 17(2), 163-177, 1990.

World Community is a necessary condition for a peaceful world order, but world community is possible only if (1) the world is organized as a legal order; (2) rational channels of world cooperation are established; and (3) the basic principles of democracy govern the political life of the nation states of the world.

Mitra, Kumar. Some Reflections on Noam Chomsky. *Indian Phil Quart*, 19/3(Supp), 1-9, Jl 92.

The purpose of the work is to support the 'mentalism' in Chomskian philosophy of language and to show its social relevance. Chomsky sees human language as creative, in the sense that it is free from external or internal stimuli. We acquire language through some in-built linguistic capacity which is species- specific. If we try to explain human behavior (linguistic or otherwise) as response to stimuli, we fail to get the essence of humanity. Human creativity needs freedom everywhere. The present social order is not much conducive to the realisation of human potentialities. Hence, a different approach to the base-structure is needed, not only in the field of language, but also in the field of society.

Mittelstaedt, Peter. An Inconsistency between Quantum Mechanics and Its Itnerpretation in Advances in Scientific Philosophy, Schurz, Gerhard (ed). Amsterdam, Rodopi, 1991.

Mittelstrass, Jürgen and Carrier, Martin. *Mind, Brain, Behavior: The Mind-Body Problem and the Philosophy of Psychology*. Hawthorne, de Gruyter, 1991.

Mlicki, Marek K (ed) and Gasparski, Wojciech W (ed) and Auspitz, J Lee (ed). *Praxiologies and the Philosophy of Economics: The International Annual of Practical Philosophy and Methodology*. New Brunswick, Transaction Books, 1992.

Modler, Peter. Pierre Teilhard de Chardin und die ökologische Frage. *Theol Phil*, 65(2), 234-245, 1990.

Modrak, D K W. Alexander on *Phantasia*: A Hopeless Muddle or a Better Account?. *S J Phil*, 31(Supp), 173-197, 1992.

Alexander's lengthiest treatment of phantasia, found in his de Anima, is detailed and largely satisfactory but in the de Fato he invokes two different and incompatible notions of phantasia, neither of which is the same as the de Anima's. Does Alexander have a coherent notion of phantasia, or is his position a hopeless muddle of Aristotelian and Stoic notions? In order to answer this question, the paper examines the de Fato, Alexander's commentaries and de Anima and then discusses both the relation between Alexander's conception of phantasia and Aristotle's and the relation between his position and the Stoic's. In the final section, the overall cogency of Alexander's core concept of phantasia is defended.

Modrak, D K W. Aristotle on Reason, Practical Reason, and Living Well in Essays in Ancient Greek Philosophy, IV, Anton, John P (ed). Albany, SUNY Pr, 1991.

From the first line, the *Nicomachean Ethics* is about practical thinking, how we choose or should choose to act and to urge others to act. Thus it is especially disturbing that Aristotle's account of practical thinking is open to the charge of inadequacy on two major fronts: (1) the cogency of his analysis of moral weakness; and (2) the absence of a genuine conceptual niche for *phronesis*, whose work seems to be done by *ethike arete*, by *euboulia*, and by *sophia*. However, these misgivings will be assuaged if we interpret Aristotle's ethical doctrines in light of his conception of the cognitive life of a human being—as I argue we should.

Moellendorf, Darrel F. A Reconstruction of Hegel's Account of Freedom of the Will. *Owl Minerva*, 24(1), 5-18, Fall 92.

The paper examines a reconstructed version of Hegel's *Encyclopedia* account of freedom of the will, and situates it as an attempt to respond to Kant. Hegel's implicit position is that certain forms of human activity, in particular the establishment of rights based polities, can best be explained in terms of free goal-directed activity. Furthermore, Hegel's account of the free will is shown to include elements of both self-determination and compatibilism.

Moellendorf, Darrel F. Racism and Rationality in Hegel's Philosophy of Subjective Spirit. *Hist Polit Thought*, 13(2), 243-255, Sum 92.

This paper exhibits passages of the "Philosophy Subjective Spirit" on race, linking them to Hegel's other claims about African culture and the slave trade. It argues that Hegel's philosophy of spirit is tainted by the causal role which he gives to race. The source of his racism isn't in any of his fundamental claims about spirit; rather it lies in the general ideology of the nineteenth century. Still, understanding how Hegel could hold racist views aids in appreciating both the problems of the Hegelian conception of personhood and the conservative bias built into his method of political philosophy.

Moene, Karl Ove. Contested Power in The Idea of Democracy, Copp, David (ed). New York, Cambridge Univ Pr, 1993.

The aim of the article is to show that Samuel Bowls and Herbert Gintis influential models of contested exchange provide a general theory of a special case. On the basis of a contract theory of contingent renewal Bowles and Gintis derive the concept of short-side power where important agency problems are overlooked. The applicability of the theory as a micro foundation of power relations in market economies is therefore limited. Under some circumstances agents may be locked into specific relationships that give raise to more severe power abuse than that emerging from short-side power.

Mogilka, Judith. Education and the Spirit. *J Thought*, 28(1-2), 13-20, Spr-Sum 93.

Mogilnitsky, B G. Non-Marxist Historiography of Today: The Evolution of Its Theoretical and Methodological Principles. *Clio*, 21(4), 411-427, Sum 92.

Mohammed, Ovey N. Averroes, Aristotle, and the Qur'an on Immortality. *Int Phil Quart*, 33(1), 37-55, Mr 93.

This article questions the correctness of Christian and Jewish scholars concerning Averroes' doctrine of immortality and suggests a hypothesis which it seeks to substantiate: that Averroes' treatment of soul and intellect exemplifies the harmony of faith and reason, but his treatment of the soul, including its immortality, is what the Islamic faith proposes and philosophical reason investigates. The article further shows that this harmony is successful to the extent that it accounts for a system of reward and punishment in the afterlife that is compatible with Aristotle in his *De Anima* and with the teaching of the Qur'an.

Mohanty, J N. Husserl. *J Brit Soc Phenomenol*, 23(3), 280-287, O 92.

Mohanty, J N. Method of Imaginative Variation in Phenomenology in Thought Experiments in Science and Philosophy, Horowitz, Tamara (ed). Lanham, Rowman & Littlefield, 1991.

Mohanty, Jitendra N. On Matilal's Understanding of Indian Philosophy. *Phil East West*, 42(3), 397-406, Jl 92.

Mohanty, Jitendra N. *Reason and Tradition in Indian Thought: An Essay on the Nature of Indian Philosophical Thinking*. New York, Oxford Univ Pr, 1992.

In this book an attempt is made to lay back the concept of theoretical rationality in Indian thought. The topics treated are "Consciousness and Knowledge", "Language and Meaning", "Logic", "Truth", "Being", Time, History and Nature" and the nature of the Indian theory of "pramāna". The concluding chapter denies that Indian and Western philosophies are radically different, while still recognizing that there are important differences. The familiar cliche's about Indian philosophy misconstrue both the differences from and the similarities with Western philosophy.

Moitra, Shefali. Grammar, Logical Grammar and Grammatical Theory in Foundations of Logic and Language, Sen, Pranab Kumar (ed). New Delhi, Allied, 1990.

The paper examines how the study of first order grammar may lead to the search for the essentials of language and how these essentials fit the different natural languages. Alternative theories regarding the solution or dissolution of foundational questions have been discussed. Strawson's grammatical theory has been extrapolated from his writings and cited as a paradigm. Finally, some methodological problems relating to grammatical theory construction and the role of presupposition have been looked at.

Mokrejs, A. A Talk on Democracy and Truth (in Czechoslovakian). *Filozof Cas*, 40(4), 686-689, 1992.

Mokrejs, Antonin. F Nietzsche's Thematization of Art (in Czechoslovakian). *Estetika*, 29(2), 41-49, 1992.

Mol, Annemarie. Michel Serres: eigenzinnig/bemiddelaar. *Kennis Methode*, 16(3), 233-244, 1992.

Molchanov, Victor. Time, Truth, and Culture in Husserl and Hegel in Analecta Husserliana, XXXI, Tymieniecka, Anna-Teresa (ed). Dordrecht, Kluwer, 1990.

Moldau, Juan Hersztajn. On the Lexical Ordering of Social States According to Rawls' Principles of Justice. *Econ Phil*, 8(1), 141-148, Ap 92.

Molendijk, A L. Aus dem Dunklen ins Helle: Wissenschaft und Theologie im Denken von Heinrich Scholz. *Hist Phil Log*, 14(1), 101-108, 1993.

Molinaro, A. Creazione ed eternità del mondo. *Riv Filosof Neo-Scolas*, 82(4), 607-622, O-D 90.

Molnar, Thomas. *God and the Knowledge of Reality*. New Brunswick, Transaction Books, 1993.

Molnar's analysis of the history of philosophy and false mysticism leads him to conclude that a return to a moderate realism will save the philosophical enterprise from a series of epistemological and societal absolutes that are embodied in contemporary rationalism and mysticism alike. Issues that have been systematically excluded from discourse will have to be reintroduced into the discussion of person and providence. Molnar divides the philosophical systems into two groups according to their vision of God, and consequently of reality. One group removes God from the human scope, therefore rendering the world unreal, unknowable, and meaningless. The second group holds that God is immanent in the human soul, thereby emphasizing the human attainment of divine status, and reducing the extra-mental world to a condition of utter imperfection. Either way, the result is a pseudo-mysticism, a denial of the creaturely status of human beings. (edited)

Moltmann, Jürgen. Knowing and Community in On Community, Rouner, Leroy S (ed). Notre Dame, Univ Notre Dame Pr, 1992.

Monaghan, Floyd V and Corcos, Alain F. The Real Objective of Mendel's Paper: A Response to Falk and Sarkar's Criticism. *Biol Phil*, 8(1), 95-98, Ja 93.

This paper was a detailed response to the criticisms offered by Falk and Sarkar of a previous paper of ours, *The Real Objective of Mendel's Paper*, *Biol Phil*, 6, 447-452, 1990. Our responses are intelligible only in the context of the original paper to which the reader is referred. The basic argument of the original paper was the following: Mendel's experiments were not aimed at finding the laws of inheritance, but were concerned with the finding of empirical laws which describe the formation of hybrids and the development of their offspring over several generations. This led to the creation of an explanatory scheme adequate to explain the form and contents of the laws.

Monasterio, Xavier O. Plantinga and the Two Problems of Evil. *Lyceum*, 4(1), 83-103, Spr 92.

Plantinga makes a distinction between two problems of evil: the existential and the philosophical. The former has to do with attitudes towards God, the latter with the rational propriety of believing that God exists. This distinction corresponds to Plantinga's fundamental distinction between belief *in* God and belief *that* God exists, on which the legitimacy of the kind of "philosophical theology" he favors and practices hinges. I attempt to show that neither of the above distinctions makes sense, and that Plantinga's philosophical theology accordingly is a futile undertaking that has nothing to do with the God in whom Christians believe.

Mondal, Sunil Baran. A Critical Discussion of Karl Mannheim's Views on Sociology of Knowledge. *Indian Phil Quart*, 20/2(Supp), 11-16, Ap 93.

This article is an attempt to discuss the crucial point of Karl Mannheim's views on 'Sociology of Knowledge'. Secondly I have tried to show that Mannheim's view is not free from criticism. I have pointed out the drawbacks of his view. Lastly an attempt has been made to compare his view with that of other thinkers (i.e., Karl Marx).

Mondin, B. L'antropologia teologica: Definizione, obiettivi, punto di partenza, metodo, divisione. *Sapienza*, 45(2), 113-135, 1992.

The title speaks for itself: it says what the article is all about, namely: definition, object, point of departure, method and division of theological anthropology. It explains that this branch of theology has to do with man as we know him through revelation in his triple condition: divine origin, fall and redemption. Therefore it has to do with grace (election), sin (original sin), salvation and predestination. The method of theological anthropology is presented as a twofold hermeneutics: the first is the hermeneutics of faith of what man is and is called to be with the help of divine grace and the light of human sciences; the second is the hermeneutics of man and his history through the light of faith. Theological anthropology is the happy combination of these two hermeneutics.

Mongin, Olivier. The Problem of Evil in Paul Ricoeur: An Aporetic Exploration. *Praxis Int*, 12(4), 352-370, Ja 93.

Montagna, Franco and De Jongh, Dick. Rosser Orderings and Free Variables. *Stud Log*, 50(1), 71-80, Mr 91.

It is shown that for arithmetical interpretations that may include free variables it is not the Guaspari-Solovay system *R* that is arithmetically complete, but their system *R*-. This result is then applied to obtain the nonvalidity of some rules under arithmetical interpretations including free variables, and to show that some principles concerning Rosser orderings with free variables cannot be decided, even if one restricts oneself to "usual" proof predicates.

Montagna, Franco and Jumelet, Marc and De Jongh, Dick. On the Proof of Solovay's Theorem. *Stud Log*, 50(1), 51-69, Mr 91.

Montefiore, Alan. The Philosophy of Education? in Logical Foundations, Mahalingam, Indira (ed). New York, St Martin's Pr, 1991.

Monteiro, L and Savini, S and Sewald, J. Construction of Monadic Three-Valued Lukasiewicz Algebras. *Stud Log*, 50(3-4), 473-483, S-D 91.

Montero, Fernando. The Construction of Subjectivity in Analecta Husserliana, XXXIV, Tymieniecka, Anna-Teresa (ed). Dordrecht, Kluwer, 1992.

Montes, Maria J. A Response to Ronald G Alexander's 'Personal Identity and Self-Constitution' and Michael Goodman's 'A Sufficient Condition for Personhood'. *Personalist Forum*, 8/1(Supp), 91-96, Spr 92.

Montmarquet, James. *Epistemic Virtue and Doxastic Responsibility*. Lanham, Rowman & Littlefield, 1993.

This book concerns the ethics of belief, especially in relation to the ethics of action. It argues that moral responsibility in many instances turns on doxastic responsibility (responsibility for belief), and that the latter is dependent ultimately on the exercise of certain qualities of intellectual character—the epistemic virtues and viles.

Montmarquet, James. Epistemic Virtue and Doxastic Responsibility. *Amer Phil Quart*, 29(4), 331-341, O 92.

This paper argues, first, that moral responsibility in many cases depends upon the assignment of responsibility for what one believes, second, that the latter is not in many cases dependent on responsibility for some further action or omission, and third, that such underived doxastic responsibility can be plausibly made out in terms of one's responsibility for exercising certain traits of epistemic character.

Montminy, Martin. Indétermination de la traduction et sous-détermination des théories scientifiques. *Dialogue (Canada)*, 31(4), 623-642, Autumn 92.

The relations between indeterminacy of translation and under-determination of theories are examined. Contrary to what certain authors suggest, recent versions of under-determination make it still comparable with indeterminacy, though it is unclear how they can support it.

Moody, Harry R. *Ethics in an Aging Society*. Baltimore, Johns Hopkins U Pr, 1992.

The ethical dilemmas of an aging society present challenges for both individuals and society. This book examines distinctive questions raised by Alzheimer's Disease and by "rational suicide" on grounds of age. The book proposes a model of "negotiated consent" for ethical issues of long-term care and examines the problem of justice between generations in allocation of health care resources. In methodological terms, the book argues that neither virtue ethics nor the ethics of rules and principles are useful models for geriatric ethics. Instead, the author applies ideas of communicative ethics derived from the Critical Theory of Jürgen Habermas.

Moody, Todd C. *Philosophy and Artificial Intelligence*. Englewood Cliffs, Prentice Hall, 1993.

Moon, Seungsook. Eurocentric Elements in the Idea of "Surrender-and-Catch". *Human Stud*, 16(3), 305-317, Jl 93.

"Surrender" refers to a suspension of received notions including one's tradition, and "catch" means any intellectual-emotional outcome of such an exercise. Wolff argues that although the practice of surrender is cross-cultural, the concept of "surrender-and-catch" is Western because it is marked by a critical attitude toward one's own culture in order to improve this world. The author examines racial and cultural implications of the exclusive Westerness of the idea: First, the static view of one's own tradition and others' ignores (and denies) historical changes and the possibility of change in the "non-Western" world. Second, it creates artificial distinction between "Western" reason which can criticize, and "non-Western" reason which cannot.

Mooney, Christopher P. Theology and the Heisenberg Uncertainty Principle: II. *Heythrop J*, 34(4), 373-386, O 93.

Mooney, Edward. Getting Isaac Back in Foundations of Kierkegaard's Vision of Community, Connell, George B (ed). Atlantic Highlands, Humanities Pr, 1992.

Abraham's decision to sacrifice his son appears to cut him off from any community of understanding, justification, or reason. However in Kierkegaard's view, faith includes the assurance that one is prepared to accept and live in the world of relationship and community. As opposed to the knight of resignation, the knight of faith "welcomes the finite back with open arms." Isaac's restoration is both the restoration of simple worldly life and the acceptance of "the essentially human", construed as a cluster of moral/religious virtues: freedom, responsibility, and trusting receptivity. An analogy with Kant and attention to the shopkeeping knight show faith's essential connection to the social.

Mooney, Edward F. Music of the Spheres: Kierkegaardian Selves and Transformations. *Int Phil Quart*, 32(3), 345-361, S 92.

Kierkegaard describes selfhood (in *Sickness Unto Death*) as a relational field (not an "atomic point" of free will or a composite of items). I elaborate this field musically, taking a performing sextet as an enlightening analogue of Kierkegaard's three-part "relation relating to itself grounded in a power that constitutes it." His view of stage-shift is also elaborated musically on analogy with shifts and dissonance in musical key. A side-benefit of these elaborations is a correction of the popular view (held, for example, by Alastair MacIntyre) that Kierkegaardian stage-shift is a matter of arbitrary choice by an "asocial" "disencumbered" will.

Mooney, Gavin (ed) and Jensen, Uffe Juul (ed). *Changing Values in Medical and Health Care Decision Making*. New York, Wiley & Sons, 1992.

Moorcroft, Francis. Why Russell's Paradox Won't Go Away. *Philosophy*, 68(263), 99-104, Ja 93.

Moore, A W. A Note on Kant's First Antinomy. *Phil Quart*, 42(169), 480-485, O 92.

The author defends an interpretation of Kant's First Antinomy whereby both its thesis and its antithesis depend on a common basic principle, endorsed by Kant, namely that there cannot be any contingent facts about how an infinite region of space or time is occupied. The greatest problem with this interpretation is that Kant explicitly declines to apply counterparts of the temporal arguments in the Antinomy to the world's future. The author argues that this problem is surmountable.

Moore, A W. Human Finitude, Ineffability, Idealism, Contingency. *Nous*, 26(4), 427-446, D 92.

The author attempts to explore connections between the four themes of human finitude, ineffability, idealism, and contingency. These connections can be summed up in the following way: Because of their finitude, humans have certain insights which are ineffable; but, because of an aspiration to be infinite, they are tempted to try to express these insights, and the results include a kind of transcendental idealism, together with the claim that all necessity rests on some deep or transcendent contingency.

Moore, David B. Shame, Forgiveness, and Juvenile Justice. *Crim Just Ethics*, 12(1), 3-25, Wint-Spr 93.

The paper considers the theoretical ramifications of a recently developed scheme for responding to juvenile offending. The scheme, initiated by police and local community consultative committees in Australia's Riverina district, involves young offenders, their victims, and the friends and family of both in the search for appropriate restitution and reparation in the wake of an offense. The designers of the scheme have made substantial use of contemporary social theory. Both the aims of the designers, and some findings from an early evaluation of the scheme, are considered here. It is suggested that the findings raise important issues for both positive and normative social theory. Particular attention is paid to implications of the scheme for republican criminology, for moral philosophy—in the light of affect theory's challenge to cognitive psychology, and for the debate in political philosophy between liberals and communitarians.

Moore, G E and Ambrose, Alice (ed). *Lectures on Metaphysics, 1934-1935: G E Moore*. New York, Lang, 1992.

Moore, Jay. On Private Events and Theoretical Terms. *J Mind Behav*, 13(4), 329-345, Autumn 92.

The conception of a private event as an inferred, theoretical construct is critically examined. The foundation of this conception in logical positivist epistemology is noted, and the basis of the radical behaviorist alternative is presented. Of particular importance is the radical behaviorist stance on the contributions of physiology and private behavioral events to psychological explanations. Two cases are then reviewed to illustrate radical behaviorist concerns about private events, theoretical terms, and the relation between them. The first is the position of cognitive psychology toward internal states and processing mechanisms. The second is the recent suggestion that even radical behaviorists regard the private event as an eferred, theoretical construct (Zuriff, 1985).

Moore, Jay. On Professor Rychlak's Concerns. *J Mind Behav*, 13(4), 359-369, Autumn 92.

Professor Rychlak has thoughtfully responded to my target article that addressed private events and theoretical terms in psychology. I agree with his objections to the mechanistic approaches that dominate contemporary psychology. However, I disagree that Skinner's radical behaviorism is one of those mechanistic approaches. Moreover, the alternative he advocates is heavily influenced by mentalistic traditions. According to the perspective presented here, the value of his approach derives from the extent to which it may be reinterpreted within a comprehensive behavioral framework.

Moore, Jennifer Mills. International Reflections on Individual Autonomy and Corporate Effectiveness. *Bus Ethics Quart*, 3(2), 197-203, A 93.

Moore, Mary Elizabeth. Musings of a Psychologist-Theologian: Reflections on the Method of Charles Hartshorne. *Process Stud*, 21(2), 113-117, Sum 92.

Morado, Raymundo. Models for Belief Revision in Rationality in Epistemology, Villanueva, Enrique (ed). Atascadero, Ridgeview, 1992.

Moran, Jon S. Mead, Gadamer, and Hermeneutics in Frontiers in American Philosophy, Volume I, Burch, Robert W (ed). College Station, Texas A&M Univ Pr, 1992.

The paper argues that there are significant avenues for comparative research involving the philosophies of Mead and Gadamer. First, there are similarities between Mead's view of temporality and Gadamer's view of the interpretation of the past. Second, Mead's concept of sociality and Gadamer's fusion of horizons link interpretation with a contextual view of reality. Third, Mead's view of the self relates favorably to Gadamer's notion of an I-Thou stance taken toward texts. Finally, comparisons of the two thinkers forge relations between pragmatic, scientific methods of historical investigation and the continental tradition in philosophy.

Moran, Richard A. Impersonality, Character, and Moral Expressivism. *J Phil*, 90(11), 578-595, N 93.

The paper concerns certain complexities in the proper understanding of the demand for impersonality in moral thinking, with specific attention to moral thought about one's own character. Certain forms of self-assessment, modeled on the judgment of others, threaten to undermine the very trait that is the basis of one's assessment. A notion of 'self-objectification' is sketched out, which combines a kind of impersonality with a characteristic form of moral evasion.

Moran III, Francis. Between Primates and Primitives: Natural Man as the Missing Link in Rousseau's *Second Discourse*. *J Hist Ideas*, 54(1), 37-58, Ja 93.

Morantz-Sanchez, Regina. Feminist Theory and Historical Practice: Rereading Elizabeth Blackwell. *Hist Theor*, 31(4), 51-69, 1992.

This essay assesses the value of social constructivist theories of science to the history of medicine. It highlights particularly the ways in which feminist theorists have turned their attention to gender as a category of analysis in scientific thinking, producing an approach to modern science that asks how it became identified with "male" objectivity, reason, and mind, set in opposition to "female" subjectivity, feeling, and nature. (edited)

Moravcsik, Julius. *Plato and Platonism*. Cambridge, Blackwell, 1992.

The book challenges the mainstream interpretation, formulated by W D Ross in 1953 that Plato's Forms are just as early version of universals. It presents a new interpretation of Plato's ontology, it shows that the epistemology is centered on insight, not on propositional knowledge, and it presents Plato's ethics as an "ideal ethics", not same as either Kantian or utilitarian ethics. The last part compares Plato's ontology to those of Bernay's, Gödel, and Russell; and the ethics to those of F H Bradley and Wittgenstein.

Moravcsik, Julius. Why Philosophy of Art in Cross-Cultural Perspectives?. *J Aes Art Crit*, 51(3), 425-435, Sum 93.

This paper attacks both current institutional approaches to art, and pessimistic views according to which there can be no uniform ways of talking about art. It suggests that we can talk about art cross-culturally, as a basic human capacity, and identify it in terms of artforms like carving, dance, painting, or music, that seem to pervade most (all?) cultures. A conceptual framework is developed in the paper as the foundation for such cross-cultural treatment of art.

Moreh, J. Are There Internal Prisoner's Dilemmas? A Comment on Kavka's Article. *Econ Phil*, 9(1), 165-170, Ap 93.

Morehouse, Mort. Philosophy for Children: Curriculum and Practice. *Thinking*, 10(3), 7-12, 1993.

This paper explores the suggestion that Philosophy for Children and the whole-language approach to reading might both benefit from closer cooperation. It explores some of the common ground between the two approaches and suggests ways that each could learn from the other. The result of a fruitful dialogue between the two programs might lead to more students developing a greater appreciation for literature and better thinking skills.

Moreno, Jonathan D. The Social Individual in Clinical Ethics. *J Clin Ethics*, 3(1), 53-55, Spr 92.

Moreso, José Juan and Navarro, Pablo Eugenio. Some Remarks on the Notions of Legal Order and Legal System. *Ratio Juris*, 6(1), 48-63, Mr 93.

In this paper, the authors discuss some problems related to the existence and identity of legal norms and legal systems. Firstly, two criteria for identification of legal norms are analyzed: linguistic criteria and non-linguistic criteria. Secondly, the dynamics of legal systems and the distinction between legal system and legal order are examined (close to Raz's distinction between momentary legal system and legal system). Based on the logical relations of membership and inclusion, two ways of analysing the change of legal systems are suggested. Thirdly, a criterion for identification of legal orders (from Bulygin) is discussed and it is shown that this criterion does not explain adequately, on the one hand, the existence of some norms, i.e., unconstitutional norms. The main conclusions of this paper are : a) the concepts of legal system and legal order could not explain the existence of law in a given society; b) the concepts of legal system and legal order could be considered models of rational normative systems.

Morgan, David. The Idea of Abstraction in German Theories of the Ornament from Kant to Kandinsky. *J Aes Art Crit*, 50(3), 231-242, Sum 92.

The modern concept of abstraction is indebted to a theoretical discourse on ornament which was intertwined with some of the most basic themes in nineteenth-century German art theory. Discussions of ornament and the impact of form, style, and empathy on artistic representation are traced from the late eighteenth century to German Expressionist thought in the early twentieth in order to demonstrate how debate concerning ornament contributed to the idea that works of visual art need refer to nothing beyond the abstract forms which they present in order to be meaningful.

Morgan, K P. "Engendering Equity...". *Proc Phil Educ*, 48, 372-378, 1992.

Morgan, Michael. Philosophy, History, and the Jewish Thinker in German Philosophy and Jewish Thought, Greenspan, Louis (ed). Toronto, Univ of Toronto Pr, 1992.

Morgan, Michael. Plato and Greek Religion in The Cambridge Companion to Plato, Kraut, Richard H (ed). New York, Cambridge Univ Pr, 1992.

Morgan, Vance. Kant and Dogmatic Idealism: A Defense of Kant's Refutation of Berkeley. *S J Phil*, 31(2), 217-237, Sum 93.

Kant's treatment of Berkeley in both the *Critique of Pure Reason* and the *Prolegomena* has been criticized as either a gross misreading or deliberate distortion of Berkeley's positions. Such criticisms, however, fail properly to distinguish between the Berkeleian and Kantian conceptions of space. I argue that, given this distinction, Berkeley's "dogmatic idealism" is undermined by Kant's "transcendental idealism" in precisely the way Kant claims.

Morgan, William J. Lasch on Sport and the Culture of Narcissism: A Critical Reappraisal. *J Phil Sport*, 18, 1-23, 1991.

Mori, Gianluca. Il convegno di Lecce e l' 'empiricismo' di Descartes. *G Crit Filosof Ital*, 71(2), 301-307, My-Ag 92.

Mori, Maurizio. Genetic Selection and the Status of the Embryo. *Bioethics*, 7(2-3), 141-148, Ap 93.

Moriconi, Enrico. *Dimostrazioni e Significato*. Milano, FrancoAngeli, 1993.

Morillo, Carolyn R. Reward Event Systems: Reconceptualizing the Explanatory Roles of Motivation, Desire and Pleasure. *Phil Psych*, 5(1), 7-32, 1992.

A developing neurobiological/ psychological theory of positive motivation gives a key causal role to reward events in the brain which can be directly activated by electrial stimulation (ESB). In its strongest form, this Reward Event Theory (RET) claims that all positive motivation, primary and learned, is functionally dependent on these reward events. Some of the empirical evidence is reviewed which either supports or challenges RET. The paper examines the implications of RET for the concepts of 'motivation', 'desire' and 'reward' or 'pleasure'. It is argued 1) that a 'causal base' as opposed to a 'functional' concept of motivation has theoretical advantages; 2) that a causal distinction between the 'focus' and the 'anchor' of desire suggests an ineliminable 'opacity' of desire; and 3) that some *affective* concept, such as 'pleasure', should play a key role in psychological explanation, *distinct from* that of motivational (or cognitive) concepts. A concept of 'reward' or 'pleasure' as *intrinsically positive affect* is defended, and contrasted with the more 'operational' definitions of 'reward' in some of the hypotheses of Roy Wise.

Morin, Edgar and Bélanger, J L Roland (trans). *Method—Towards a Study of Humankind, Volume I: The Nature of Nature*. New York, Lang, 1992.

This book is the first of several volumes exposing Edgar Morin's general systems view on life and society. This volume maintains that the organization of all life and society necessitates the simultaneous interplay of order and disorder. All systems, physical, biological, social, political and informational, incessantly reshape part and whole through feedback, thereby generating increasingly complex systems. For continued evolution, these simultaneously complementary, concurrent, and antagonistic systems require a priority of love over truth, of subject over object, of Sybernetics over cybernetics. (staff)

Morin, Michel. Le "déprimé explosif". *Horiz Phil*, 3(1), 43-58, Autumn 92.

Morito, Bruce. Holism, Interest-Identity, and Value. *J Value Inq*, 27(1), 49-62, Ja 93.

Inverting the traditional axiological scheme is the primary intent of the paper. By applying an evolutionary and ecological analysis to values, it is argued that the liberal assumption that human agents are value-conferring generators of value is a factual misrepresentation of what is actually the case. Values are essentially and internally related to their bearers at some fundamental level of existence. We do not necessarily err therefore when we subject value ascriptions to factual falsification criteria. The fact-value distinction is thereby partially dissolved: an event that makes transition from ecological principle to normative principle possibly intelligible.

Moriyon, Felix Garcia. On Constructing a European Cultural Identity by Doing Philosophy with Children. *Thinking*, 10(2), 2-5, 1992.

Mormann, Thomas. Natural Predicates and Topological Structures of Conceptual Spaces. *Synthese*, 95(2), 219-240, My 93.

In the framework of set theory we cannot distinguish between natural and non-natural predicates. To avoid this shortcoming one can use mathematical structures as conceptual spaces such that natural predicates are characterized as structurally 'nice' subsets. In this paper topological and related structures are used for this purpose. We shall discuss several examples taken from conceptual spaces of quantum mechanics ('orthoframes'), and the geometric logic of refutative and affirmable assertions. In particular we deal with the problem of structurally distinguishing between natural colour predicates and Goodmanian predicates like 'grue' and 'bleen'. Moreover the problem of characterizing natural predicates is reformulated in such a way that its connection with the classical problem of geometric conventionalism becomes manifest. This can be used to shed some new light on Goodman's remarks on the relative entrenchment of predicates as a criterion of projectibility.

Mormann, Thomas and Ibarra, Andoni. L'explication en tant que généralisation théorique. *Dialectica*, 46(2), 151-168, 1992.

Depuis l'époque du Cercle de Vienne on considère l'explication en tant que tâche centrale de la philosophie analytique. Cependent il n'y a pas unanimité autour de la compréhension du concept d'explication. Dans cet article nous suggérons, tout en suivant Bachelard, de considérer une explication d'un concept en tant que sa généralisation propre dans le cadre d'une théorie explicative. Nous examinons notre approche en envisageant l'explication des concepts logiques ("implication"), mathématiques ("nombre" et "ligne droite") et de la philosophie des sciences ("réduction").

Mormann, Thomas and Ibarra, Andoni. Propiedades modelísticas del concepto de reducción. *Agora (Spain)*, 11(1), 69-95, 1992.

Theorists of incommensurability have demonstrated the inherent difficulties in the diverse concepts of reduction suggested in the standard framework. In spite of this, the philosophers of the structuralist view have given an explication of scientific progress, in which the concept of reduction in its diverse variants—exact, approximative, etc.—plays a fundamental role. The aim of this paper is to offer a view of the structuralist studies on reduction. Adequacy conditions for the relation of reduction characterize it basically as a law preserving relation and as an anomaly explaining relation. It is provable that there does not exist a reduction relation that is law preserving *and* anomaly explaining, i.e., for any theory T there cannot exist a reducing theory T', such that T' has greater explanatory power and implies T. To cope with the apparent incompatibility of this fact we propose to introduce a new degree of liberalism in the logical reconstruction of empirical theories to make possible the implementation of different reduction maps simultaneously.

Moro, Tomiaso. *Una reinterpretazione dell' 'Utopia'*. Bari, Dedalo, 1992.

This book, while focusing upon Thomas More's "Utopia", his most subversive work, constitutes a *complete monograph* on his political thought. It is the most complete and up-to-date study on the subject and is the result of extensive research by a specialist in the field of utopia, the author of *Platonic Utopia* published in 1985. This book is a thorough and critical examination of More's political ideas: the central and problematic role of the family; the abolition of property and the community of goods; work, needs, pleasure; the political organization, the aims proposed and the problems posed by it; the pressing need for peace. It aims at nucleating the values transmitted by the tradition of utopia, which are relevant to the *problems we face today* and which can help us to solve them.

Moros, Daniel A (& others). Thinking Critically in Medicine and Its Ethics in Applied Philosophy, Almond, Brenda (ed). New York, Routledge, 1992.

Morreall, John. Fear Without Belief. *J Phil*, 90(7), 359-366, Jl 93.

To launch his theory of fiction as a game of make-believe, Kendall Walton used a puzzle in which he claimed that fear involves the belief that one is in danger. Against this claim, and the whole cognitive theory of fear, I argue three points. First, fear need not have an intentional object. Second, when fear has an intentional object, we need not believe that objects of that kind are dangerous. And third, even when we fear an object knowing that objects of that kind are dangerous, we need not believe that this object of fear is dangerous to us.

Morreall, John. The Contingency of Cuteness: A Reply to Sanders. *Brit J Aes*, 33(3), 283-285, Jl 93.

John Sanders objects to three theses which he attributes to me: that cuteness is 1) a characteristic set of features now common among human infants; 2) a set of features which was attractive to adult members of our ancestor species independently of the fact that infants had them; and 3) a set of features which was selected specifically because of the attractiveness. However, I do not hold 2) or 3). And thought I hold (1), I reject Sanders criticism that this is an uninformative necessary truth. The cuteness of infants, I show, is neither a logical nor a biological necessity.

Morreim, E Haavi. The Impossibility and the Necessity of Quality of Life Research. *Bioethics*, 6(3), 218-232, Jl 92.

Morris, Bernard S. Epitaph for Socialist Internationalism. *Hist Euro Ideas*, 16(4-6), 527-536, Ja 93.

This paper was designed as a summary review of the way in which the Soviets used nationalism and internationalism as tools in their internal and external revolutionary strategy and organization. Within the USSR the policy of indigenisation through universal literacy and education in both the national language and Russian gave way to Russification; externally Soviet policy foundered on the conflict with national communist party and state loyalties. In historical perspective socialist internationalism represents one more failure by man to form a political association that would transcend national boundaries. Alternative forms of political and socioeconomic organization containing a core of socialist humanism do not loom on the horizon. Nationalism is rampant; the free market is enshrined.

Morris, Christopher. On Contractarian Constitutional Democracy in The Idea of Democracy, Copp, David (ed). New York, Cambridge Univ Pr, 1993.

Morris, Christopher. On the Importance of Conversation. *Dialogue (Canada)*, 32(1), 135-148, Wint 93.

A critical notice of *Wise Choices, Apt Feelings*, (Harvard University Press, 1990) by Allan Gibbard.

Morris, Michael. The Place of Language—I. *Aris Soc*, Supp(67), 153-172, 1993.

Morris, Phyllis Sutton. Sartre on the Self-Deceiver's Translucent Consciousness. *J Brit Soc Phenomenol*, 23(2), 103-119, My 92.

Some critics of Sartre, such as M R Haight, claim that Sartre has made self-deception impossible by his claim that consciousness is translucent. After distinguishing translucency from transparency, a reply to those critics is given by identifying four dimensions of consciousness which enable Sartre to describe various subtle strategies of self-deception. However, another problem is found, which undercuts Sartre's claim that persons are totally responsible for all they do.

Morris, Robert. Writing with Davidson: Some Afterthoughts after Doing *Blind Time IV: Drawing with Davidson*. *Crit Inquiry*, 19(4), 617-627, Sum 93.

Morris, Thomas V. *Making Sense of It All*. Grand Rapids, Eerdmans, 1992.

This is a Pascalian book taking up the main issues of the *Pensées* and exploring the plausibility of a Christian worldview. It is written for a broad audience.

Morris, Thomas V. Perfection and Creation in Reasoned Faith, Stump, Eleonore (ed). Ithaca, Cornell Univ Pr, 1993.

I have recently argued that Perfect Being Theology and Creation Theology ought to be brought together. But there is a problem: If a perfect creator would have to create a best possible world, and there can't be such a world, then God can't be both a creator and perfect. I argue that God is not under the alleged and problematic maximization requirement and yet that there can still be a sense in which creation is perfect.

Morrison, J C. Christian Wolff's Criticism of Spinoza. *J Hist Phil*, 31(3), 405-420, Jl 93.

Morrison, J C. Why Spinoza Had No Aesthetics. *J Aes Art Crit*, 47(4), 359-365, Fall 89.

Morrison, Margaret. Some Complexities of Experimental Evidence. *Proc Phil Sci Ass*, 1, 49-62, 1992.

The paper is intended as an extension to some of the recent discussion on the nature of experimental evidence. In particular I examine the role of empirical evidence attained through the use of deductions from phenomena. I discuss a particular formulation of Maxwell's electrodynamics, one he claims was deduced from experimental facts. However, the deduction is problematic in that it is questionable whether one of the crucial parameters of the theory, the displacement current, can be given an empirical foundation. In outlining Maxwell's argument I draw attention to the philosophical implications of the theoretical constraints that arise in this particular case of deduction from phenomena.

Morscher, Edgar. Inadequacies of Peter and Paul in Advances in Scientific Philosophy, Schurz, Gerhard (ed). Amsterdam, Rodopi, 1991.

Morscher, Edgar. Judgement-Contents in Mind, Meaning and Metaphysics, Mulligan, Kevin (ed). Dordrecht, Kluwer, 1990.

Morscher, Edgar and Berg, Jan. *Bolzano-Forschung: 1989-1991*. Sankt Augustin, Academia, 1992.

Morse, Marcia. Feminist Aesthetics and the Spectrum of Gender. *Phil East West*, 42(2), 287-295, Ap 92.

Morselli, Graziella. Husserl, Child Education, and Creativity in Analecta Husserliana, XXXI, Tymieniecka, Anna-Teresa (ed). Dordrecht, Kluwer, 1990.

Morton, Adam. Suppose, Suppose. *Analysis*, 53(1), 61-64, Ja 93.

I describe a type of conditional which is often found when we are thinking in narrative terms. It involves a series of antecedents which have to be evaluated in terms of one another, so that it does not reduce to a complex iteration of a single two-place conditional. One natural expression of this in ordinary language is "Suppose that p1. Then suppose that p2... then q." I give a formal definition of this n-place connective.

Morton, Luise and Foster, Thomas R. Goodman, Forgery, and the Aesthetic. *J Aes Art Crit*, 49(2), 155-159, Spr 91.

Morton, Peter. Supervenience and Computational Explanation in Vision Theory. *Phil Sci*, 60(1), 86-99, Mr 93.

According to Marr's theory of vision, computational processes of early vision rely for their success on certain "natural constraints" in the physical environment. I examine the implications of this feature of Marr's theory for the question whether psychological states supervene on neural states. It is reasonable to hold that Marr's theory is nonindividualistic in that, given the role of natural constraints, distinct computational theories of the same neural processes may be justified in different environments. But to avoid trivializing computational explanations, theories must respect methodological solipsism in the sense that within a theory there cannot be differences in content without a corresponding difference in neural states.

AUTHOR INDEX WITH ABSTRACTS 601 Moussa, Mario

Moser, Johann. Ethical Values in Literature. *Lyceum*, 2(1), 45-52, Spr 90.

Moser, Paul K. Analyticity and Epistemology. *Dialectica*, 46(1), 3-19, 1992.

This paper defends the philosophical importance of analyticity against the influential objections raised by W V Quine. It characterizes analyticity in a way that (a) is nonepistemic, (b) avoids Quine's objections and fits his general strictures, and (c) explains the epistemological importance of analyticity. It also explains why even proponents of Quine's naturalized epistemology should value the epistemological importance of analyticity, in connection with questions about the correctness of their epistemic principles. Given these considerations, this paper may be regarded as having rescued analyticity from the throes of suspicion and myth, as set by "Two Dogmas of Empiricism."

Moser, Paul K. Beyond the Private Language Argument. *Metaphilosophy*, 23(1-2), 77-89, Ja-Ap 92.

Wittgenstein's private language argument receives a rather clear formulation in Peter Hacker's *Insight and Illusion*, 2d ed. This paper shows that Hacker's version of the argument commits us either to an implausible sort of verificationism about correctness or to an uncompelling kind of extreme nominalism. The paper also shows how private languages are genuinely possible.

Moser, Paul K. *Philosophy after Objectivity: Making Sense in Perspective*. New York, Oxford Univ Pr, 1993.

This book contends that we cannot meet skeptics' typical demands for non-questionbegging support for claims to objective truth. It identifies the role of variable semantic commitments and instrumental, purpose-relative considerations in justification. The book treats fundamental methodological issues in ontology, epistemology, the theory of meaning, the philosophy of mind, and the theory of practical rationality.

Moser, Paul K and Vander Nat, Arnold. Surviving Souls. *Can J Phil*, 23(1), 101-106, Mr 93.

This paper shows that Richard Swinburne's Cartesian argument for the conclusion that we have immaterial souls fails, owing to a dilemma concerning the logical possibility of conscious beings' surviving bodily destruction. The paper identifies a non-Cartesian, Humean approach to survival that is not challenged by Swinburne's argument.

Moses, Greg. Hume's Playful Metaphysics. *Hume Stud*, 18(1), 63-78, Ap 92.

This paper argues that the mature Hume allows for playful engagement in a strong king of metaphysics. While remaining an Academic Sceptic on matters susceptible of agreement between reasonable people, he countenances a *Treatise*-like Pyrrhonism beyond such limits. Philo in Hume's *Dialogues* is claimed to engage in just that kind of metaphysics which Hume has ruled out in *Treatise* and *Enquiries*, albeit in a playful 'Pyrrhonian' fashion. Contemporary involvement in metaphysics in this mature Humean style may be useful for plugging intellectual gaps otherwise occupied by "harmful superstitions" of modern secular techo-economic as well as fundamentalist religious or New Age varieties.

Mosher, Michael A. Nationalism and the Idea of Europe: How Nationalists Betray the Nation State. *Hist Euro Ideas*, 16(4-6), 891-897, Ja 93.

This essay explores the simultaneous evolution of the idea of the nation and the idea of Europe in Western political thought, with specific reference to the ideas of Montesquieu, Rousseau, Hegel, and the recent commentators on the French Revolution. It then examines Benedict Anderson's Imagined Communities as an example of recent writing on the subject. The essay concludes by arguing that only where nationalists have not betrayed the nation by insisting on the union of culture and politics, where the technocrats of modernity have not swamped ancient memories, and where God has few public duties has the European nation state idea taken hold.

Mosley, Albert. Preferential Treatment and Social Justice in Terrorism, Justice and Social Values, Peden, Creighton (ed). Lewiston, Mellen Pr, 1990.

Mosley, David L. *Auflösung* in Nineteenth-Century Literature. *J Aes Art Crit*, 51(3), 437-444, Sum 93.

In this article the German term *Auflösung* is examined in the context of 19th century literature, music, and philosophy. As a poetic topic this term signifies transcendence, as a musical device it describes the resolution of a dissonance — or unstable pitch-configuration — to a consonance — or stable pitch- configuration. Also contained in the article is an analysis of F Schubert's Lied "Auflosung" D. 807 in which he sets to music a poem by J Mayrhofer. As a conclusion, the use of *Auflösung* as a philosophical and historical principle in Hegel's *Aesthetics* (1835) is discussed.

Moss, Donald. Obesity, Objectification, and Identity in The Body in Medical Thought and Practice, Leder, Drew (ed). Dordrecht, Kluwer, 1992.

Moss, Lenny. A Kernel of Truth? On the Reality of the Genetic Program. *Proc Phil Sci Ass*, 1, 335-348, 1992.

The idea of a genetic program capable of directing ontogenesis and regulating cellular/organismic function is critically examined. Historical sources are found in the rhetoric of Mendelism, the informationist turn of certain quantum physicists, and the instrumentalism of molecular virology. It is argued, however, that warrant for this new preformationism can be found in neither the legacy of classical embryology nor in contemporary studies. Empirically based cell and molecular models are offered to show that bio-organizational information is *ir*reducible to nucleic acid sequence, and that causal chains run centripetally as well as centrifugally with genetic regulation itself dependent upon the complexities of physiological context.

Moss, Myra M. The Verifiability of Ethical Judgments in Terrorism, Justice and Social Values, Peden, Creighton (ed). Lewiston, Mellen Pr, 1990.

The essay's purpose is to determine whether the expressed intent to terrorize, that is to coerce into submission by violence and threat, the passengers and crew on the June 14, 1985 TWA flight 847 from Athens to Rome amounted to an ethically bad act. The essay concludes that the judgment that the intent to terrorize was an ethically bad one can be verified in terms of the direct experience of ethical disvalue felt by passengers and crew while they were being terrorized. Positive values and disvalues form part of what is immediately experienced, along with colors, sounds, and tactile qualities.

Mosser, Kurt. *Stoff* and Nonsense in Kant's First *Critique*. *Hist Phil Quart*, 10(1), 21-36, Ja 93.

Mossner, Ernest C (ed). *A Treatise of Human Nature—David Hume*. New York, Penguin USA, 1984.

Mosterin, J. What Can We Know about the Universe? in Philosophy and the Origin and Evolution of the Universe, Agazzi, Evandro (ed). Norwell, Kluwer, 1991.

Our knowledge of the universe cannot progress beyond certain fundamental limits and horizons, which are independent of the current state of technology. The aim of this paper is to delineate those horizons of the perceptible, the observable and the theoretical universe. In the case of the observable universe, the limits considered are the special-relativistic horizon, the horizon due to the expansion, the electromagnetic horizons and the information-carrying possibilities of neutrinos and gravitational waves. The whole of reality goes beyond those horizons, but we cannot say anything meaningful about it.

Mothersill, Mary. Aesthetic Laws, Principles and Properties: A Response to Eddy Zemach. *J Aes Art Crit*, 47(1), 77-82, Wint 89.

Mothersill, Mary. The Antinomy of Taste in Kant's Aesthetics, Meerbote, Ralf (ed). Atascadero, Ridgeview, 1991.

Motroshilova, Nelya. The Phenomenology of Edmund Husserl and the Natural Sciences in Analecta Husserliana, XXXIV, Tymieniecka, Anna-Teresa (ed). Dordrecht, Kluwer, 1992.

Motterlini, Matteo. Popper: fallibilismo o scetticismo?. *Epistemologia*, 15(2), 191-218, Jl-D 92.

This article undertakes a critical evaluation of Popper's theory of corroboration, aiming to show that some remnants of inductivism are still to be found in it. Popper and Watkins's answer to their critics on this point is considered, i.e., their statement that the corroboration-appraisal is analytic and does not have predictive implications. Against this, we argue that, thus purified, the degree of corroboration becomes valueless as a measure of pragmatic acceptability of a theory over its rivals. Some such measure, however, is in fact needed for any rational appraisal of and intervention in technological matters. (edited)

Motzkin, Gabriel. *Time and Transcendence: Secular History, the Catholic Reaction and the Rediscovery of the Future*. Dordrecht, Kluwer, 1992.

Mouffe, Chantal. Democratic Citizenship and the Political Community in Community at Loose Ends, Miami Theory Collect, (ed). Minneapolis, Univ of Minnesota Pr, 1991.

Moulder, James. Another Go at 'Equal Educational Opportunity'. *S Afr J Phil*, 11(3), 49-51, Ag 92.

I accept and evaluate Ian Bunting's argument that 'equal educational opportunity' is a technical phrase which gets its sense or meaning from a specific theory of distributive justice. I argue that 'an index of need and achievement' which rides on axioms of equality, compensation and temporal bad luck, as well as on a specification of what must be corrected to achieve equal educational opportunity, yields a simpler theory of distributive justice than 'strong egalitarianism' or 'fair competition'.

Moulines, C Ulises. Desarrollo científico y verdad. *Agora (Spain)*, 11(1), 179-182, 1992.

Moulines, C Ulises. La concepción estructural de las ciencias como forma de holismo. *Agora (Spain)*, 11(1), 9-18, 1992.

This paper discusses what the *sense* of scientific terms really is. To overcome the well-known inadequacies of operationalism, an epistemic-semantic conception nowadays considered to be mistaken, an alternative is proposed: a semantic conception that might be denominated "moderate holism". This conception stems from analysis of structuralist view of scientific theories.

Moulines, C Ulises. Pragmatics in the Structuralist View of Science in Advances in Scientific Philosophy, Schurz, Gerhard (ed). Amsterdam, Rodopi, 1991.

The essay consists of three parts. The first one is a detailed reply to the criticisms made by P Weingartner to the structuralist approach in philosophy of science. The second one offers a summary of the main components of a scientific theory according to structuralism. The third part is an original contribution to the explication of two essential components of a theory according to structuralism: "intended applications" and the "user" of a theory. The essential idea is that intended applications have to be defined as potential models relative to which the user has a particular kind of propositional attitude.

Mount Jr, Eric. Can We Talk? Contexts of Meaning for Interpreting Illness. *J Med Human*, 14(2), 51-65, Sum 93.

In a pluralistic society, is it possible for people of differing religious or non-religious persuasions to find common ground for communication about illness and suffering? Which metaphors offer the most promise—those of mastery, those of fated fellow-suffering or those of "ironical struggle" (M Ignatieff)? This essay examines four interpretive possibilities: 1) psychosomatic self-mastery (B Siegel); 2) philosophical explanation (J Cobb's and D Griffin's process thought); 3) religious confessionalism (S Hauerwas); and 4) phenomenology of the clinical encounter (R Zaner). An appraisal of the strengths and weaknesses of each option reveals the need for a perspective that energizes personal responsibility, nurtures empathy, and recognizes that we are in less than total control of our stories.

Moussa, Mario. Foucault and the Problem of Agency in Ethics and Danger, Dallery, Arleen B (ed). Albany, SUNY Pr, 1992.

Moussa, Mario. Misunderstanding the Democratic 'We': Richard Rorty's Liberalism and the Radical Urge for a Philosophical Foundation. *Phil Soc Crit*, 17(4), 297-312, 1991.

Many leftist critics have assailed Richard Rorty for trying to revivify the liberal distinction between public and private life. Rorty, say these critics, claims that competing political groups could abandon their differences and form a harmonious, liberal "we." By contrast, I argue that Rorty's critics misinterpret his remarks about liberalism. In fact, Rorty wants to show that, from a practical point of view, current political theory, especially what he calls "leftspeak," has become marginal. Left-speaking political theorists are mostly addressing each other. Consequently, their brand of theory distorts politics in its most meaningful sense.

Moussa, Mario and Shannon, Thomas A. The Search for the New Pineal Gland: Brain Life and Personhood. *Hastings Center Rep*, 22(3), 30-37, My-Je 92.

Many ethicists have recently argued that the human fetus, once its brain begins to function, should be considered a person. They find support for this notion of "brain life" in the wide acceptance of the criteria for "brain death." In this essay, by contrast, we attempt to undercut the analogy rests primarily on a simple verbal association (life/death), supported by a philosophical tradition that assumes the mind somehow resides "inside" the body, particularly the brain. In addition, we explore the undesirable social consequences of the "brain life" debate.

Moutafakis, Nicholas J. Christology and its Philosophical Complexities in the Thought of Leontius of Byzantium. *Hist Phil Quart*, 10(2), 99-119, Ap 93.

The paper carefully examines the literature on Leontius of Byzantium in terms of how it has historically focused on theological interpretations of his work. The author endeavors to argue that past commentators have missed the rich philosophical import of Leontius' work especially as it pertains to his adoption of basic Aristotelian ideas to deal with the Christological problem, which was a question of how one rationally explains Christ's dual nature as both divine and humanly physical. The paper explores both the original sources of Leontius' known work and interpretations by Basil Tatakis.

Moya, Carlos. Intention, Intentionality and Causality (in French). *Rev Theol Phil*, 124(3), 293-304, 1992.

Current philosophies of the mind try to envisage intentionality of the basis of causality and/or rationality. Davidson's understanding of the mind stems from these two categories, though their correlation in the human mind remains 'a mystery' for Fodor. This article takes 'primitive intentional behaviour' rather as a starting point, a concept inspired by what Wittgenstein called 'the primitive expression of intention'. The main characteristics of the conception of mind which results from this are shown, as well as the advantages of this conception over those of Davidson and Fodor.

Moya Obradors, Pedro Javier. Teología y pluralismo teológico en Etienne Gilson. *Sapientia*, 47(185), 195-200, 1992.

Moyal, G J D. La première "Critique" de Descartes. *Kantstudien*, 83(3), 257-267, 1992.

The metaphysics of Descartes's *Meditations* are read here as critical philosophy, i.e., as a statement of the *formal conditions* of the possibility of knowledge. The *cogito*, the existence of a veracious God and that of the material world, being formal conditions ('principles') of knowledge, cannot constitute, or be part of, a science, or be founded themselves on the guaranteed veracity of the clear and distinct. Never-defined key epistemic notions are place-markers in this cartography of knowledge. Contrary to the picture Descartes-himself propagates, there is a logical hiatus between metaphysics and the sciences. Some perennial problems of Cartesian exegesis dissolve under this reading.

Moyse, Danielle. La Morale Bouleversée: La Question de l'Éthique chez Martin Heidegger. *Heidegger Stud*, 8, 103-121, 1992.

Doesn't Heidegger indulge in meditating about what man does not control—death in particular—to make a responsible being, or an ethic, conceivable from his work? Nevertheless, as soon as Dasein is involved, it becomes impossible to imagine moral autonomy as a resistance to Nature, as in Kant, or "spirituality" in relationship with an intelligible reality: calling man back to his finite essence, to the "shepherd's poverty", Heidegger drastically changes the data of moral.

Muck, Otto. Eigenschaften Gottes im Licht des Gödelschen Arguments. *Theol Phil*, 67(1), 60-85, 1992.

In his sketch of an Ontological Proof (dated February 10th 1970) Kurt Gödel introduces the concept of a positive property and proves the necessary existence of exact one being which instantiates all positive properties — he calls it 'summun bonum'. Special emphasis in the discussion of this argument is put on the logical structure of positive property and the comparison with the concept of (pure) perfection as it is used in traditional philosophy of God for dealing with divine attributes.

Muck, Otto. Religiöser Glaube und Gödels ontologischer Gottesbeweis. *Theol Phil*, 67(2), 263-267, 1992.

In discussing the rationality of religious belief, Franz von Kutschera (Vernuft und Glaube, 1990) criticises attempts to clarify divine attributes and to demonstrate the existence of God, including Goedel's Ontological Proof. The article argues that the criticism proposed neglects the concept of pure perfection and that the logical structure of this concept can be clarified in further developing Goedel's concept of positive property.

Mudimbe, V Y. From "Primitive Art" to "*Memoriae Loci*". *Human Stud*, 16(1-2), 101-110, Ap 93.

Mühlhölzer, Felix. Das Phänomen der inkongruenten Gegenstücke aus Kantischer und heutiger Sicht. *Kantstudien*, 83(4), 436-453, 1992.

In different phases of his theoretical philosophy, Kant gave different answers to the question concerning the 'ultimate foundation' of the phenomenon of incongruent counterparts (i.e., the fact that an asymmetric object can exist in either of two mirror-image forms). This paper once more examines and assesses Kant's arguments, relates them to what we nowadays would say about incongruent counterparts and, in particular, explains Hermann Weyl's statement that the ultimate foundation of the phenomenon of incongruent counterparts has to be seen in a combinatorial fact, namely in the difference between even and odd permutations.

Mueller, Ian. Mathematical Method and Philosophical Truth in The Cambridge Companion to Plato, Kraut, Richard H (ed). New York, Cambridge Univ Pr, 1992.

Section I sets out some of the evidence connecting the Platonic Academy and mathematical science. Section II explains some methodological terminology used in the discussion of mathematics: analysis, synthesis, *diorismos*, lemma. Sections III-V analyze the well-known passages on hypothetical method in the *Meno, Phaedo, and Republic*. They argue that Plato's hypothetical method is adapted from mathematics, but that the adaptation is importantly influenced by Plato's own philosophical purposes. The stance of the paper is unitarian rather than developmental.

Mueller, Magda (ed) and Funk, Nanette (ed). *Gender Politics and Post-Communism: Reflections from Eastern Europe and the Former Soviet Union*. New York, Routledge, 1993.

Müller, Anselm. Mental Teleology. *Proc Aris Soc*, 92, 161-183, 1992.

The author argues for the existence of a kind of teleology ("unreasoned teleology") not covered by the common dichotomy between natural and intentional teleology. Unreasoned purposiveness is exemplified by practical reasoning (as distinguished from its result), by finding what one is mentally looking for, and by judging something to be the case. Two implications of the author's claim: (1) Such judging is voluntary, though (as opposed to guessing that...) not intentional; (2) Arguments against natural teleology have to be reconsidered.

Münz, Peter. What's Postmodern, Anyway. *Phil Lit*, 16(2), 333-353, O 92.

Postmodernism is rooted in Nietzsche's discovery that the modernist belief that language is a neutral medium, is flawed. Contemporary postmodernists, from the late Wittgenstein to Kuhn, Derrida, Rorty and Lyotard, have over- reacted by assimilating science to poetry. The hub of this over-reaction is the postmodern denial that there can be any over-arching theories or metanarratives which explain and/or order all diverse subjective standpoints. This denial is mistaken because, since all possible subjective standpoints are evolved from a single common origin like the Big Bang or have a common ancestor in "black Eve", there must be a metanarrative to tell the story of this evolution.

Mugerauer, Robert. Architecture as Properly Useful Opening in Ethics and Danger, Dallery, Arleen B (ed). Albany, SUNY Pr, 1992.

Muhammad, Abū Bakr and Butterworth, Charles E (trans) and Al-Razi, Zakariyya. The Book of the Philosophic Life. *Interpretation*, 20(3), 227-236, Spr 93.

Mujumdar, Rinita. Dream Objects, Reference and Naturalized Epistemology. *Indian Phil Quart*, 19(2), 73-89, Ap 92.

Mukhopadhyay, P K. *The Nyaya Theory of Linguistic Performance: A New Interpretation of Tattvacintamani*. Calcutta, Bagchi, 1992.

This new commentary on Tattvacintamani identifies the original contributions of Gangesa and sources in the classical literature of Indian philosophy of some of his ideas. The work stresses the unbroken continuity to date of Nyaya tradition and shows the great relevance which the perspective of Nyaya, as it has been reconstructed here, has in modern times. This book may be found useful also by the scholars who are interested in the problems of epistemology and philosophy of language of the contemporary West.

Mukhopadhyay, Ranjan. Self-Justify Rules in Foundations of Logic and Language, Sen, Pranab Kumar (ed). New Delhi, Allied, 1990.

The paper examines in the content of the problem of justification of deduction the possibility whether rules of inference can be regarded as self-justifying. A rule will be self-justifying if it gives the very meaning of that logical constant for which the rule is framed. The conditions mentioned in the relevant literature for a rule's being meaning-given are those of conservative extension, uniqueness, harmony, stability, and separativeness. These are explained and interconnections among them explored. It is found that separativeness is an extension of the condition of conservative extension, and harmony is the same as conservative extension.

Mulgan, Tim. The Unhappy Conclusion and the Life of Virtue. *Phil Quart*, 43(172), 357-358, Jl 93.

Mulhall, Stephen. Consciousness, Cognition and the Phenomenol—II. *Aris Soc*, Supp(67), 75-89, 1993.

This article responds to a paper by Barrie Falk, contesting his account of the relation between aspect-perception and the cognitive processing model of the mind. It argues that aspect-dawning cannot be understood in terms of a mixture of bottom-up/top-down processing, that aspect-seeing does not presuppose a bodily contribution to visual appearances, that retinal images play no role in psychological processes, and that Wittgenstein's account of seeing aspects renders otiose any invocation of cognitive processing models.

Mulholland, Leslie A. Hegel and Marx on the Human Individual in Hegel and His Critics, Desmond, William J (ed). Albany, SUNY Pr, 1989.

Muller, Alfredo Gómez. Sobre la legitimidad de la conquista de América: Las Casas y Sepúlveda. *Logos (Mexico)*, 20(60), 21-37, S-D 92.

Muller, James W. Collingwood's Embattled Liberalism. *Interpretation*, 20(1), 63-80, Fall 92.

This essay is a review of R G Collingwood, *Essays in Political Philosophy*, ed. David Boucher (Oxford: Clarendon Press, 1990), a new volume of his writings on politics which has appeared almost half a century after Collingwood's death. More than half of them appear in print for the first time. In the theoretical first part of the book, Collingwood combines variations on James Mill's account of utility, Hobbes's account of right, and Hegel's account of duty in a welter of ideas more thought provoking than consistent. In the more practical second part, he advances a trenchant, if not always persuasive view of the dangers facing liberalism.

Muller, Jerry Z. Carl Schmitt, Hans Freyer and the Radical Conservative Critique of Liberal Democracy in the Weimar Republic. *Hist Polit Thought*, 12(4), 695-715, Wint 91.

Mulligan, Kevin (ed). *Language, Truth and Ontology*. Dordrecht, Kluwer, 1992.

This volume brings together new investigations of the ontological credentials of things, events, states of affairs, variable and non-existent objects, properties, tropes and tendencies by a number of leading philosophers.

Mulligan, Kevin. Marty's Philosophical Grammar in Mind, Meaning and Metaphysics, Mulligan, Kevin (ed). Dordrecht, Kluwer, 1990.

Marty's philosophy of language and its relation to his philosophy of mind are expounded. Points of contact between Marty Wittgenstein and later analytic philosophy of language are noted.

Mulligan, Kevin (ed). *Mind, Meaning and Metaphysics*. Dordrecht, Kluwer, 1990.

This volume contains papers on the philosophies of mind and language and on the metaphysics of Anton Marty, a leading figure in the Brentanian tradition. Two hitherto unpublished letters from Marty to Husserl, as well as a full bibliography are also provided.

Mulligan, Kevin and Schuhmann, Karl. Two Letters from Marty to Husserl in Mind, Meaning and Metaphysics, Mulligan, Kevin (ed). Dordrecht, Kluwer, 1990.

Two letters from Marty to Husserl are given together with English translations and a brief commentary. The two letters deal with intentionality and the status of immanent objects.

Mullins, Joan and Abscal-Hildebrand, Mary. Recreating Classroom Relationships: Mutual Mentoring Joins Critical Hermeneutics and Composition Theory. *Phil Stud Educ*, 1, 69-81, 1990.

Mulvaney, Robert J. Hospitality and Its Discontents: A Response to Losito. *Proc S Atlantic Phil Educ Soc*, 36, 70-72, 1991.

Mulvaney, Robert J. The Personalism of L E Loemker. *Personalist Forum*, 9(1), 1-61, Spr 93.

Mulvaney, Robert J (ed) and Simon, Yves R. *Practical Knowledge—Yves R Simon*. Bronx, Fordham Univ Pr, 1991.

Munday, Roderick. Bentham, Bacon and the Movement for the Reform of English Law Reporting. *Utilitas*, 4(2), 299-316, N 92.

Using the Bentham Manuscripts, held at University College London, the article examines Bentham's unpublished scheme to reform eighteenth-century England's chaotic system of law-reporting, a project that would have formed an important element in the compilation of Bentham's *Digest*. Bentham's scheme is evaluated, and the extent of the intellectual debt Bentham owed to Bacon in the elaboration of this work is analysed.

Mundy, Brent. Space-Time and Isomorphism. *Proc Phil Sci Ass*, 1, 515-527, 1992.

Earman and Norton argue that manifold realism leads to inequivalence of Leibniz-shifted space-time models, with undesirable consequences such as indeterminism. I respond that intrinsic axiomatization of space time geometry show the variant models to be isomorphic with respect to the physically meaningful geometric predicates, and therefore certainly physically equivalent because no theory can characterize its models more closely than this. The contrary philosophical arguments involve confusions about identity and representation of space-time points, fostered by extrinsic coordinate formulations and irrelevant modal metaphysics. I conclude that neither the revived Einstein hole argument nor the original Leibniz indiscernibility argument have any force against manifold realism.

Muneto, Sonoda and Aihara, Setsuko (trans) and Parkes, Graham R (trans). The Eloquent Silence of Zarathustra in Nietzsche and Asian Thought, Parkes, Graham (ed). Chicago, Univ of Chicago Pr, 1991.

Munevar, Gonzalo. Evolution and the Naked Truth in Cultural Relativism and Philosophy, Dascal, Marcelo (ed). Leiden, Brill, 1991.

Popper and other philosophers have thought that evolution can serve as a justification of realism. A careful look at evolutionary biology, however, leads to relativism. This evolutionary relativism can be easily defended against Plato's and other traditional objections, the thesis of scientific convergence, and the view that relativism must assume its own (absolute) truth, as well as the competition from internal realism. A theory of relative truth is then suggested. This theory explains and supersedes the correspondence, coherence, and pragmatic theories of truth.

Munk, Reinier. Revelation and Resistance: A Reflection on the Thought of Fackenheim in German Philosophy and Jewish Thought, Greenspan, Louis (ed). Toronto, Univ of Toronto Pr, 1992.

Munzer, Stephen R. Compensation and Government Takings of Private Property. *Nomos*, 33, 195-222, 1991.

Murata, Seiichi. Der Sinn des Erhabenen—Kants Theorie des Erhabenen und ihre Bedeutung heute (in Japanese). *Bigaku*, 43(3), 1-11, Wint 92.

In den heutigen Diskussionen über das Erhabene erregt es Aufmerksamkeit, dass das Erhabene die beiden positiven und negativen Momente eenthält, besonders dass die negativen Momente desselben selbst eine positive Bedeutung in der Kunst der neueren Zeit haben. Kants Theorie des Erhabenen, die eine neue Möglichkeit des Ästhetischen enthält, ist heute noch nüzlich zur theoretischen Begründung der ästhetischen Erfahrung. (edited)

Murdoch, Dugald. Exclusion and Abstraction in Descartes' Metaphysics. *Phil Quart*, 43(170), 38-57, Ja 93.

The paper discusses a neglected, but important, distinction in Descartes' philosophy between *abstraction* (thinking of one idea while ignoring another) and *exclusion* (excluding one idea from another). It is argued that exclusion plays an important role in metaphysical doubt, and in several of the key arguments in the *Meditations*, including the *cogito*, the *res cogitans*, and the ontological argument. Moveover, Descartes' argument for the real distinction between the mind and the body cannot properly be understood unless the role that exclusion plays in it is grasped.

Murphey, Murray G. The Underdetermination Thesis in Frontiers in American Philosophy, Volume I, Burch, Robert W (ed). College Station, Texas A&M Univ Pr, 1992.

Murphy, Arthur E. Pragmatism and the Context of Rationality, Part II. *Trans Peirce Soc*, 29(3), 331-368, Sum 93.

Murphy, Arthur E and Singer, Marcus G (ed). Pragmatism and the Context of Rationality: Part I. *Trans Peirce Soc*, 29(2), 123-178, Spr 93.

Murphy, James Bernard. *The Moral Economy of Labor: Aristotelian Themes in Economic Theory*. New Haven, Yale Univ Pr, 1993.

Ever since Aristotle, there have been many theories of distributive justice but very little in the way of a theory of justice in production. Murphy develops an Aristotelian theory of productive labor through a critique and reconstruction of Aristotle's views on moral and technical reason (*phronésis* and *techné*) as well as Aristotle's views on nature, custom, and reason (*physis, ethos, logos*).

Murphy, James Bernard. The Workmanship Ideal: A Theologico-Political Chimera?. *Polit Theory*, 20(2), 319-326, My 92.

In this essay I attack Locke's theory that labor creates property rights. First, Locke wrongly describes the telos of labor to be the fabrication of an object rather than the satisfaction of a socially-defined human need. Second, Locke's analogy between divine workmanship and human workmanship in Platonic rather than Christian.

Murphy, Jeffrie G. Bias Crimes: What Do Haters Deserve?. *Crim Just Ethics*, 11(2), 20-23, Sum-Fall 92.

Murphy, Jeffrie G. *Retribution Reconsidered: More Essays in the Philosophy of Law*. Dordrecht, Kluwer, 1992.

Murphy, John W (ed) and Peck, Dennis L (ed). *Open Institutions: The Hope for Democracy*. New York, Praeger, 1993.

In this book, the issue of democratization is addressed. The claim is made that before democracy is possible, a democratic culture must be established. Most often this point is raised with regard to logistical considerations, such as voting and parliamentary procedures. But before democracy can be established, knowledge bases, information dissemination systems, and social imagery must be democratized.

Murphy, Julien S. The Body with AIDS: A Post-Structuralist Approach in The Body in Medical Thought and Practice, Leder, Drew (ed). Dordrecht, Kluwer, 1992.

Murphy, Mark C. Hobbes's Shortsightedness Account of Conflict. *S J Phil*, 31(2), 239-253, Sum 93.

Jean Hampton has recently argued that a shortsightedness account of conflict, on which it is the mistaken reasoning of persons in the state of nature that is the cause of most of the fighting, would produce the state of war that Hobbes describes in *Leviathan*; she presents little reason, however to believe that Hobbes had such an account in mind. I present further evidence for the claim that Hobbes advocated such an account, though not of the sort that Hampton proposes. I argue that an Hobbes' view it is not mistaken reasoning that causes shortsightedness, but rather the fact that presently sensed objects have a disproportionate effect on the faculty of desire.

Murphy, Michael. The Evolution of Embodied Consciousness in Revisioning Philosophy, Ogilvy, James (ed). Albany, SUNY Pr, 1992.

Murphy, Nancey. The Limits of Pragmatism and the Limits of Realism. *Zygon*, 28(3), 351-359, S 93.

I argue here for a limited version of pragmatism—called conceptual pragmatism—that recognizes that conceptual systems are to be evaluated according to their usefulness for helping us get around in the world. Once a conceptual system is in place, however, the truth of sentences is a matter of both empirical fit and coherence with the rest of our knowledge. The error of critical realists is to fail to take into account the limited conceptual relativity that is to be expected on the basis of conceptual pragmatism. The conceptual realist thesis applies equally in science and theology.

Murphy, Timothy F. The Ethics of HIV Testing by Physicians. *J Med Human*, 14(3), 123-135, Fall 93.

This essay argues that informed consent remains desirable for both moral and practical reasons in regard to HIV testing by physicians. At the very least, respect for consent preserves patient control over treatment and affords the opportunity for education about the nature of HIV-related disorders. Nevertheless, there do appear to be circumstances under which involuntary testing may occur especially when health care workers may have become occupationally exposed to risk of HIV infection. To eliminate conflicts between health workers and their patients, however, it is desirable to work to eliminate the stigmatizing and discriminatory effects of HIV infection that can induce persons to resist testing.

Murphy, Jr, Cornelius F. Jurisprudence and Natural Law. *Vera Lex*, 12(1), 11-12, 1992.

Murray, J Patrick and Schuler, Jeanne. Historical Materialism Revisited in Terrorism, Justice and Social Values, Peden, Creighton W (ed). Lewiston, Mellen Pr, 1990.

The authors discuss Habermas's revival of historical materialism. Unlike dogmatic Marxists, Habermas's theory resembles the "reconstructive science" of Piaget; it concerns the developmental logic of history. Three interests—technical, communicative, and expressive—underlie the species' evolution. Progress involves an interplay between technical crisis (e.g., the Great Depression) and responses that embody new norms (e.g., more egalitarian social relations). While systems crisis do not necessarily provoke moral growth, Habermas shares Kant's hope in enlightenment. The authors question whether an encompassing framework hinders Habermas's critical project. He also stirs up controversy by presupposing Kohlberg's moral scale—crown with Habermas's discourse ethic—as the yardstick of progress.

Murray, Lori. Two Arguments from Incongruent Counterparts. *SW Phil Rev*, 9(1), 163-169, Ja 93.

Murray, Michael J. Coercion and the Hiddenness of God. *Amer Phil Quart*, 30(1), 27-38, Ja 93.

Atheists often challenge theists to explain why God is a necessary condition of ultimate human fulfillment. I argue that one condition required to preserve creaturely freedom is the absence of coercion by means of a threat. Further, if the Christian God were to be too perspicuous, our beliefs and actions would be originating in the context of a threat sufficient to preclude the exercise of morally significant freedom. Consequently, God must be hidden, to a degree, in order to preserve the good of creaturely freedom.

Murray, Patrick and Schuler, Jeanne A. Educating the Passions: Reconsidering David Hume's Optimistic Appraisal of Commerce. *Hist Euro Ideas*, 17(5), 589-598, S 93.

Murray, Penelope. Inspiration and *Mimēsis* in Plato. *Apeiron*, 25(4), 27-46, D 92.

Murray, Thomas H. Genetics and the Moral Mission of Health Insurance. *Hastings Center Rep*, 22(6), 12-17, N-D 92.

Murris, Karin. Beetle Crushers Lift the Lid on Mindless Behavior. *Thinking*, 10(2), 30-38, 1992.

Murungi, John. Studying Zen as Studying Philosophy. *Man World*, 26(4), 429-441, O 93.

Muscari, Paul G. A Plea for the Poetic Metaphor. *J Mind Behav*, 13(3), 233-245, Sum 92.

What is the future of the poetic figures in a technological and scientific world where a more restricted view appears to be emerging as to what is adequate and relevant about metaphors? What part should the radical trope play in a script where the figures that are heralded are usually those that are perceived as having practical importance, i.e., those that fill in the gaps of existing knowledge? It will be the intent of this paper to show that the current preoccupation of much of philosophy and psychology with structural explanation and cognitive theory has certainly contributed to establishing a coordinated and unified theory of metaphors, but left unto itself such a concern is severely limited and does not adequately explain the full potential of metaphorical expressions.

Musgrave, Alan. *Common Sense, Science and Scepticism: A Historical Introduction to the Theory of Knowledge*. New York, Cambridge Univ Pr, 1993.

Can we know anything for certain? There are those who think we can (traditionally labelled the 'dogmatists') and those who think we cannot (traditionally labelled the 'sceptics'). The theory of knowledge or 'epistemology" is a great debate between the two. This book is an introductory and historically-based survey of these debates. It sides for the most part with the sceptics. It also develops out of scepticism a third view, fallibilism or critical rationalism, which incorporates an uncompromising realism about perception, about science, and about the nature of truth.

Musgrave, Alan. Realism About What?. *Phil Sci*, 59(4), 691-697, D 92.

Roger Jones asks what Newtonian realists should be realists about, given that there are four empirically equivalent formulations of Newtonian mechanics which have different ontological commitments and explanatory mechanisms. A realist answer is sketched: Newtonians should be realists about what the best metaphysical considerations dictate, where the best metaphysical considerations are required within physics, just as they are required to eliminate idealist and surrealist theories which are empirically equivalent to realist ones. Realists must reject the positivist assumption that empirically equivalent theories are explanatory and evidential equivalents, too.

Musschenga, Bert and Van Der Steen, Wim J. The Issue of Generality in Ethics. *J Value Inq*, 26(4), 511-524, O 92.

The methodologies of ethics and empirical science should be similar to a large extent. Unfortunately methodology is underdeveloped in ethics. Due to this ethicists do not realize sufficiently that possibilities for the elaboration of general theories are limited. Methodological analysis shows that the views of researchers aiming at general theories and researchers aiming at casuistry are not as different as the literature suggests. Controversies concerning this are spurious in view of ambiguities in the notion of generality and the notion of theory.

Musso, Paolo. Il Realismo Epistemologico di Rom Harré (parte seconda). *Epistemologia*, 15(1), 101-117, Ja-Je 92.

The aim of this paper is to show the main problems concerned with the form of realism proposed by Rom Harré, which was sketched in a previous paper, attempting to solve them. There are three questions. 1) Which is the meaning of the in-principle revisability of scientific theories? 2) How does the choice of analogues happen? 3) Which is the real *status* of theoretical terms? (edited)

Mutschler, Hans-Dieter. Mythos "Selbstorganisation". *Theol Phil*, 67(1), 86-108, 1992.

Mutschler, Hans-Dieter. Physik und Neothomismus: Das ontologische Grundproblem der modernen Physik. *Theol Phil*, 68(1), 25-51, 1993.

Myers, Michael. *Tat tvam asi* as Advaitic Metaphor. *Phil East West*, 43(2), 229-242, Ap 93.

Tat tvam asi ("That thou art") is the instruction given from father to son in the Chandogya Upanisad. It is generally regarded as one of four central propositions of nondualist Vedanta because it identifies the son with Brahman, the ultimately real. The dualist school of Vedanta argues that the pronouns in the sentence are examples of a metonymy which retains the distinction between son and Brahman. The paper argues that only a nondualist interpretation of the sentence as metaphor is consistent with Upanisadic context. The paper suggests further that the four central propositions generate a nondualist model of religious life.

Myers, Richard and Malcolmson, Patrick. Technology and Mother Earth: The Rousseauian Roots of the Debate. *J Dharma*, 18(2), 162-173, Ap-Je 93.

Feminimism and environmentalism have spawned a new enthusiasm for the old pagan idea of "Mother Earth." The thesis of this article is that the main inspiration for this enthusiasm is to be found in Romanticism, and that serious reflection about "Mother Earth" therefore demands a return to the thought of the philosophical founder of Romanticism, Jean-Jacques Rousseau. This study of Rousseau's *Discourse on the Origins of Inequality* suggests that for Rousseau, there is no getting "back to nature" in any more than a superficial way. It also suggests that for Rousseau, technology cannot easily be "revalued" since it is motivated primarily by an ineradicable feature of post-state of nature humanity: *amour-propre*.

Myers, William. A Note on J Hubert's "Towards a Positive Universalism". *Dialec Hum*, 17(3), 227-228, 1990.

Myers, William. Community and the Global Quasi-Community. *Dialec Hum*, 17(3), j59-69, 1990.

Myerson, Joel (ed). *Emerson and Thoreau: The Contemporary Reviews*. New York, Cambridge Univ Pr, 1992.

Myin, Erik. Some Problems for Fodor's Theory of Content. *Philosophica*, 50(2), 101-122, 1992.

In this paper I will discuss Jerry A Fodor's theory of content. I will first expose it and will then point to some problems for it. More specifically, I will claim that Fodor's theory can't live up to standards Fodor sets for rival theories. The main problems seem to be caused by Fodor's requirements of atomism and of determinancy.

Mykkänen, Juri. The Social Divided. *Phil Soc Crit*, 18(1), 1-27, 1992.

Nadelman, Healther L. Baconian Science in Post-Bellum America: Charles Peirce's "Neglected Argument for the Reality of God". *J Hist Ideas*, 54(1), 79-96, Ja 93.

Nader N, Chokr. Nelson Goodman on Truth. *Dialectica*, 47(1), 55-73, 1993.

I examine Goodman's reasons for why we should do away with "truth" and adopt "rightness" instead, and countenance "radical relativism." In contrast to many critics, and despite a number of outstanding problems, I show in what sense his radical relativism is indeed restrained by "criteria of rightness," and provides thus for "a meaningful and objective evaluation." Goodman's views are best understood in the interface between pragmatism and hermeneutics. Ultimately, they can be seen as a renewed and provocative defense of a position which is not only intuitively appealing, but philosophically desirable, namely, pluralism.

Nadler, Steven (ed). *Causation in Early Modern Philosophy*. University Park, Penn St Univ Pr, 1993.

The essays in this volume all examine the problem of causation as dealt with by several seventeenth century philosophers. They discuss occasionalism and the preestablished harmony as responses to Cartesian and other early modern doctrines of causality. Philosophers discussed include Malebranche, Descartes, Leibniz, Bayle, La Forge, Conway, and more.

Nadler, Steven. Occasionalism and General Will in Malebranche. *J Hist Phil*, 31(1), 31-47, Ja 93.

This paper examines a common misreading of the mechanics of Malebranche's doctrine of divine causal agency, occasionalism, and its roots in a related misreading of Malebranche's theories. God, contrary to this misreading, is for Malebranche constantly and actively causally engaged in the world, and does not just establish certain laws of nature. The key is in understanding just what Malebranche means by 'general volitions'.

Nadler, Steven. The Occasionalism of Louis de la Forge in Causation in Early Modern Philosophy, Nadler, Steven (ed). University Park, Penn St Univ Pr, 1993.

In this paper I examine the nature and extent of the Cartesian Louis de la Forge's commitment to an occasionalist doctrine of causation. I conclude that he really only uses occasionalism to account for body-body interlations, and leaves real causal interaction intact in the mind-body realm.

Naess, Arne. Ayer on Metaphysics, a Critical Commentary by a Kind of Metaphysician in The Philosophy of A J Ayer, Hahn, Lewis Edwin (ed). Peru, Open Court, 1992.

The Greek philosopher Gorgia's slogan "nothing exists" must not be taken at "its face value," nor other metaphysicians' slogans or key sentences. We have to study their texts, if available. Spinoza's text *Ethics* is interpreted and reinterpreted and, for some scholars, most of the text is meaningful. As meaningful as J A Wheeler's general relativity slogan "matter tells space how to curve, and space tells matter how to move." Ayer is wrong in saying that G E Moore looked at metaphysics with the devastating simplicity and candor of a child. He looked at certain separate sentences that way.

Nagatomo, Shigenori. Two Contemporary Japanese Views of the Body: Ichikawa Hiroshi and Yuasa Yasuo in Self as Body in Asian Theory and Practice, Kasulis, Thomas P (ed). Albany, SUNY Pr, 1992.

Nagayama, Misao. On Boolean Algebras and Integrally Closed Commutative Regular Rings. *J Sym Log*, 57(4), 1305-1318, D 92.

We consider properties, related to model-completeness, of the theory of Boolean algebras. We obtain the theorem claiming that in a Boolean algebra, the truth of a prenex sigma-n-formula can be determined by finitely many definable conditions in the language of the Boolean algebras including the first entries of Tarski invariant and n-characteristics. Then we derive two corollaries: An embedding between two Boolean algebras preserving the n-characteristic is a sigma-n-extension. The theory of n-separable Boolean algebras admits elimination of quantifiers in a simple definitional extention of the language of Boolean algebras. Finally we translate these results into the language of commutative regular rings.

Nagl-Docekalova, Herta. What Is Feminist Philosophy? (in Czechoslovakian). *Filozof Cas*, 40(5), 742-756, 1992.

In Part One, which deals with the clarification of conceptions, the author explains what is concerned: it is not a matter of an additional, isolated sub-discipline of philosophy, but of the perspective of research related to the whole discipline. Feminist philosophy is philosophizing which is concerned with the comprehension of woman. Part Two distinguishes different conceptions of the respective problem. On the one hand, historical-critical investigations are needed; it is necessary to restore: 1) the development of philosophy of the relation between the sexes; 2) the latent forms of women's elimination; 3) the concerns of women-philosophers. On the other hand, it is a matter of the creation of an alternative to patriarchal philosophy. Part Three attempts a clear indication of the diverse and debatable starting points of feminist philosophy which have developed since the end of the sixties, particularly in comparison of the Continental and Anglo-Saxon debates. (edited)

Nair, Sreekala M. Plato's Analysis of Knowledge: An Appraisal. *Indian Phil Quart*, 20/3(Supp), 11-18, Jl 93.

Naishtat, Francisco. Compacidad *via* eliminación de cuantificadores. *Rev Filosof (Argentina)*, 6(1-2), 67-86, N 92.

Nalezinski, Alix. Equality, Inequality and the Market. *Dialogue (Canada)*, 32(1), 163-170, Wint 93.

Kenneth Rogerson argues against Dworkin's claim that the free market treats people equally by giving people equality of opportunity. Equality of result is left aside. I examine Rogerson's points and argue that they are false in very important ways. In the end, the free market is vindicated. I also note that Rogerson's attempts to interfere with the market do not treat people equally.

Nancy, Jean-Luc. Of Being-in-Common in Community at Loose Ends, Miami Theory Collect, (ed). Minneapolis, Univ of Minnesota Pr, 1991.

Any ontology, including Heidegger's one, presents being as being of someone, principally alone. It is necessary to think of being as ontologically determined by being-together or in-common.

Nancy, Jean-Luc. *The Birth to Presence*. Stanford, Stanford Univ Pr, 1993.

A collection of essays on literature and philosophy.

Nancy, Jean-Luc and Connor, Peter (trans). Elliptical Sense in Derrida: A Critical Reader, Wood, David (ed). Cambridge, Blackwell, 1992.

Derrida's thinking of sense as of a spacing of sense itself, or its alteration.

Nancy, Jean-Luc and Lacoue-Labarthe, Philippe. *The Title of the Letter: A Reading of Lacan*. Albany, SUNY Pr, 1992.

This book is a close reading of Jacques Lacan's seminal essay, "The Agency of the Letter in the Unconscious or Reason Since Freud", selected for the particular light it casts on Lacan's complex relation to linguistics, psychoanalysis, and philosophy. It clarifies the way Lacan renews or transforms the psychoanalytic field, through his diversion of Saussure's theory of the sign, his radicalization of Freud's fundamental concepts, and his subversion of dominant philosophical values. The author's argue, however, that Lacan's discourse is marked by a deep ambiguity: while he invents a new "language", he nonetheless maintains the traditional metaphysical motifs of systemacity, foundation, and truth. (staff)

Nancy, Jean-Luc and Strong, Tracy B (trans). *La Comparution/*The Compearance: From the Existence of "Communism" to the Community of "Existence". *Polit Theory*, 20(3), 371-398, Ag 92.

Narayan, Uma. What Do Rights Have to Do With It?. *J Soc Phil*, 24(2), 186-199, Fall 93.

I argue that since legal rights (in the Hohfeldian sense) existed in many traditional nonwestern contexts, "rights" are *not* a "western" *concept*. I suggest that it is a more egalitarian distribution of rights, and the normative justifications for this distribution that distinguish contemporary rights-based systems (western and nonwestern) from traditional legal systems. Distinguishing "rights" from "human rights", I explore the relationship between "human rights" and "human dignity". I end by exploring the ways in which different traditional legal framework may or may not have conceptual room for "human rights".

Narayanan, Ajit. The Chinese Room Argument in Logical Foundations, Mahalingam, Indira (ed). New York, St Martin's Pr, 1991.

Narbonne, Jean-Marc. Plotin, Descartes et la notion de *causa sui*. *Arch Phil*, 56(2), 177-195, Ap-Je 93.

This paper tries to show the ancient origin of the concept of *causa sui* in the history of Western philosophy. There are indeed numerous speculations relative to self-causation in Hellenistic philosophy and in Plotinus, a profound and original philosophical reflection on the meaning and limits of the concept. We can thus show that it is Plotinus and not Descartes (Marion) to whom we owe the philosophical use of the concept of *causa sui*. Further, a continued comparison between Plotinus and Descartes shows that, apart from the difference of systems, the *causi sui* argument meets with insurmountable difficulties in both of them. This explains why tradition has preferred the concept of *aseity* in the sense of that which is *without cause*. One can conclude from this that it is really *a-causality* and not *self-causality* (Heidegger, Marion), which expresses the ultimate thought of the foundation.

Narbonne, Jean-Pierre (trans) and Hartmann, Nicolaï. Document: Le Concept mégarique et aristotélicien de possibilité. *Laval Theol Phil*, 49(1), 131-146, F 93.

Narlikar, Jayant V. The Concepts of "Beginning" and "Creation" in Cosmology. *Phil Sci*, 59(3), 361-371, S 92.

The paper is inspired by the arguments raised recently by Grünbaum criticizing the current approaches of many cosmologists to the problem of spacetime singularity, matter creation and the origin of the universe. While agreeing with him that the currently favored cosmological ideas do not indicate the biblical notion of divine creation *ex nihilo*, I present my viewpoint on the same issues, which differs considerably from Grünbaum's. First I show that the symmetry principle which leads to the conservation law of energy is violated when the time axis is terminated at t=0. Next I discuss why this epoch (t=0) is more a mathematical artifact whose supposed significance may disappear when one goes beyond the classical relativistic cosmology. This is illustrated by the example of quantum cosmology.

Narveson, Jan. Libertarianism, Postlibertarianism, and the Welfare State: Reply to Friedman. *Crit Rev*, 6(1), 45-82, Wint 92.

Libertarianism is defended here against several important criticisms by Jeffrey Friedman. I argue that his concept of "positive libertarianism" is not coherent, that libertarianism proper is defensible on familiar contractarian grounds which require no special view of the soul, nor (more surprisingly) the attachment of any special value to freedom as such. It is also neither consequentialist nor nonconsequentialist as those terms are usually employed, for they too are ambiguous. Libertarianism is, in my view, simply founded on each of us being concerned to live the best life we can.

Narveson, Jan. *Moral Matters*. Peterborough, Broadview Pr, 1993.

Moral Matters is a series of essays on the familiar general moral issues, preceded by an unconventional introduction to moral philosophy in a broadly Hobbesian contractarian framework, which criticizes the usual "consequential/deontological" classification. Topics treated: suicide, euthanasia, criminal punishment, war, animal rights, starvation, population control, abortion, sexual ethics (sex, love, marriage, family), pornography, non-discrimination, affirmative action, and obeying the law. A radically liberal ("libertarian") view is argued for each. It is intended to be used with any anthology in which proponents of other viewpoints speak for themselves.

Narveson, Jan. Professor Filice's Defense of Pacifism: A Comment. *J Phil Res*, 17, 483-491, 1992.

Professor Carlo Filice defends pacifism by some familiar arguments: some admirable people have been such, and so on. But in the end he requires "metaphysical" premises to support it. I argue that this very move is morally illegitimate, that morals must be for all, not just for believers in special creeds or schemes, and that fully public defenses of it simply can't wash, especially since pacifism undermines the most central thing about morality: our personal security.

Nash, Carol. Interpreting Cultural Differences in Medical Intervention: The Use of Wittgenstein's "Forms of Life". *J Clin Ethics*, 4(2), 188-191, Sum 93.

There are important differences in how Anglo Americans and persons from other cultures view various forms of medical intervention. This paper outlines the differences as the author has found them regarding a medical intervention program by Canadians in Costa Rica. Suggestions are offered for how these differences might be interpreted from the perspective of Wittgenstein's "forms of life" so as to predict the types of intervention that may be successful and those that are more likely to fail.

Nash, Margaret M. The Man Without a Penis: Libidinal Economies that (Re)cognize the Hypernature of Gender. *Phil Soc Crit*, 18(2), 125-134, 1992.

This article explores the excessive character of gender identity and ways to move outside the feminine/masculine bifurcation. In making the multiplicity which constitutes gender explicitly, I attempt to denaturalize and displace notions of gender tied to phallocentric power configurations.

Nash, Ronald and Belli, Humberto. *Beyond Liberation Theology*. Grand Rapids, Baker Book, 1992.

Nasr, Wassah N. On the Proper Function of the Moral Philosopher: Kant and Rawls on Theory and Practice. *Metaphilosophy*, 23(1-2), 172-179, Ja-Ap 92.

Natale, M R. Ipotesi di metafisica: Modello matematico, creazione, eschaton—Una lettura dell'opera di Jean Ladrière. *Riv Filosof Neo-Scolas*, 84(4), 632-656, O-D 92.

The philosophy of Jean Ladrière, a contemporary Belgian philosopher, was born as a philosophy of mathematics, it evolved as epistemology and comes to fulfillment as a philosophy of action based on a creationist mathematics which is essentially critical-realistic. Firstly, Ladrière investigates the object of mathematics and then by means of this enquiry turns to studying the faculty which guides human knowledge and action, that is reason. According to Ladrière, reason is by definition eschatological. In other words, it is constantly facing what constitutes the end of all reality: the ontological truth of reality. Research into the statute of reason leads Ladrière from the gnoseological to the metaphysical in a continuous theological tension.

Natale, Samuel M (& others). Social Control, Efficiency Control and Ethical Control in Different Political Institutions: Education. *Int J Applied Phil*, 7(2), 25-31, Wint 92.

The technological age demands new skills constantly. Progress is dependent on research, education and training. This mandates the educational system teach students how to learn through life and how to adapt to changing demands. The public education system cannot supply such graduates. It is the product of the nineteenth century, requiring only basic literacy and compliant attitude. Today this is unacceptable. Such a system today effectively enslaves its graduates to lowest level jobs because they do not know how to learn. The learning styles approach teaches all students how to learn in any situation, setting them up for success in school and after.

Natali, Monica. Gli influssi del Platonismo sul Neostoicismo senecano. *Riv Filosof Neo-Scolas*, 84(2-3), 494-514, Ap-S 92.

Nathan, N M L. Democracy. *Proc Aris Soc*, 93, 123-137, 1993.

Nathan, Nicholas. On the Ethics of Belief. *Ratio*, 5(2), 147-159, D 92.

Nathanson, Stephen. Fletcher on Loyalty and Universal Morality. *Crim Just Ethics*, 12(1), 56-62, Wint-Spr 93.

In his book, *Loyalties: An Essay on the Morality of Relationships* (Oxford, 1992), George Fletcher argues for the moral importance of loyalties and claims that taking loyalties seriously requires a rejection of the universal model of morality associated with Kant, Bentham, and others. While agreeing with Fletcher's view that loyalties are morally important, I criticize his claim that this acknowledgement requires a rejection of universal morality. I argue that the special duties generated by loyalties are compatible with reasonable forms of moral universalism.

Natsoulas, Thomas. Appendage Theory—Pro and Con. *J Mind Behav*, 13(4), 371-395, Autumn 92.

Natsoulas, Thomas. Consciousness and Commissurotomy: Iv—Three Hypothesized Dimensions of Deconnected Left-Hemispheric Consciousness. *J Mind Behav*, 13(1), 37-67, Wint 92.

Natsoulas, Thomas. Consciousness: Varieties of Intrinsic Theory. *J Mind Behav*, 14(2), 107-132, Spr 93.

Natsoulas, Thomas. Intentionality, Consciousness, and Subjectivity. *J Mind Behav*, 13(3), 281-308, Sum 92.

Searle restricted intrinsic intentionality (intentional contents, aspectual shapes) to occurrent neurophysiological states that are conscious in the sense that their owner has awareness of them when they occur; all occurrent nonconscious states of the brain have, at most, a derivative intentionality by reliably producing, unless obstructed, conscious intentional states. The grounds for thus restricting intrinsic intentionality are explored, and traced to Searle's conviction that aspectual shapes (intentional contents) must be "manifest" whenever actually exemplified by an instance of any mental brain-occurrence. By "manifest," Searle seems to mean that aspectual shapes must be not only contents but also, at the same time, objects of the very states whose contents they are.

Natsoulas, Thomas. Toward an Improved Understanding of Sigmund Freud's Conception of Consciousness. *J Mind Behav*, 13(2), 171-192, Spr 92.

Natsoulas, Thomas. What is Wrong with the Appendage Theory of Consciousness. *Phil Psych*, 6(2), 137-154, 1993.

The present article distinguishes three kinds of accounts of direct (reflective) awareness (i.e., awareness of one's mental occurrences causally unmediated by any other mental occurrence): mental-eye theory, self-intimational theory and appendage theory. These aim to explain the same phenomenon, though each proposes that direct (reflective) awareness occurs in a fundamentally different way.

Also, I address a crucial problem that appendage theory must solve: how does a direct (reflective) awareness succeed in being awareness specifically of the particular mental-occurrence instance that is its object? Appendage theory is singled out for this attention because psychologists, as they embark on their renewed study of consciousness, are most likely to be attracted by appendage theory for their explanation of direct (reflective) awareness.

Nattrass, Mark S. Devlin, Hart, and the Proper Limits of Legal Coercion. *Utilitas*, 5(1), 91-107, My 93.

Nauen, F G. Kant as an Inadvertant Precursor of 18th Century Neospinozism: On Optimism (1759). *Kantstudien*, 83(3), 268-279, 1992.

Naulin, M Paul. Réflexion et Genèse: Le Non-Dit du Spinozisme. *Bull Soc Fr Phil*, 86(4), 125-149, O-D 92.

Naulty, R A. J L Mackie's Disposal of Religious Experience. *Sophia (Australia)*, 31(1-2), 1-9, 1992.

Navarro, Pablo Eugenio and Moreso, José Juan. Some Remarks on the Notions of Legal Order and Legal System. *Ratio Juris*, 6(1), 48-63, Mr 93.

In this paper, the authors discuss some problems related to the existence and identity of legal norms and legal systems. Firstly, two criteria for identification of legal norms are analyzed: linguistic criteria and non-linguistic criteria. Secondly, the dynamics of legal systems and the distinction between legal system and legal order are examined (close to Raz's distinction between momentary legal system and legal system). Based on the logical relations of membership and inclusion, two ways of analysing the change of legal systems are suggested. Thirdly, a criterion for identification of legal orders (from Bulygin) is discussed and it is shown that this criterion does not explain adequately, on the one hand, the existence of some norms, i.e., unconstitutional norms. The main conclusions of this paper are : a) the concepts of legal system and legal order could not explain the existence of law in a given society; b) the concepts of legal system and legal order could be considered models of rational normative systems.

Navia, Luis E. *The Presocratic Philosophers: An Annotated Bibliography*. Hamden, Garland, 1993.

This is the first comprehensive annotated bibliography on Presocratic philosophy published in English. It provides descriptive bibliographic information on more than 2600 works, with abundant cross-references and an index of authors. The annotated works include books, articles, notices, dissertations, fiction and poetry, and musical compositions on Anaxagoras, Anaximenes, Democritus, Empedocles, Heraclitus, Parmenides, Pythagoras, Thales, Xenophanes, and Zeno. A chapter on the source collection furnishes information of the various books which present the fragments of the Presocratics in the original language and in translation.

Neal, Patrick. Vulgar Liberalism. *Polit Theory*, 21(4), 623-642, N 93.

Neapolitan, Richard E. A Limiting Frequency Approach to Probability Based on the Weak Law of Large Numbers. *Phil Sci*, 59(3), 389-407, S 92.

Von Mises defined a "physical" probability as a strict limit of the relative frequency of occurrence of an event in repeated trials. As a result of a number of criticisms of von Mises's approach, the more favored approach became the "propensity" interpretation. It is argued here that this interpretation is not compelling and that the only problem in von Mises's approach is the assumption that the relative frequency converges in a strict sense. This problem is then remedied by deducing the axioms of probability theory from the assumption that the relative frequency converges only in the sense of the weak law of large numbers.

Neave, Phillippa. Young Kids Search for the Philosophers' Stone. *Thinking*, 10(1), 8-9, 1992.

Nebuloni, R. L'oggettivismo etico rosminiano. *Riv Filosof Neo-Scolas*, 82(4), 623-630, O-D 90.

Nederman, Cary J. Character and Community in the *Defensor Pacis*: Marsiglio of Padua's Adaptation of Aristotelian Moral Psychology. *Hist Polit Thought*, 13(3), 377-390, Autumn 92.

Like his contemporaries, Marsiglio of Padua drew heavily upon the Aristotelian account of moral character. But where previous thinkers limited their use of Aristotle's teachings to an analysis of the special qualities necessary for the good ruler, marsiglio broadens the horizon of Aristotelian psychology in order to explain how the various parts of the fully perfected community are differentiated and formed. In this way, Marsiglio adapts and remolds elements of traditional medieval Aristotelianism to fit his conceptions of an inclusive politics.

Nederman, Cary J. National Sovereignty and Ciceronian Political Thought: Aeneas Silvius Piccolomini and the Ideal of Universal Empire in Fifteenth-Century Europe. *Hist Euro Ideas*, 16(4-6), 537-543, Ja 93.

Aeneas Silvius Piccolomini's *De ortu et auctoritate Imperii Romani*(1446) is usually regarded to be an anachronistic throwback to medieval conceptions of universal empire. But a careful study of the text reveals that his argument exploits and develops a philosophical ambiguity regarding the nature of human society that emerges from Cicero's political thought. Consequently, *De ortu* is far more consistent than has been imagined with the contours of Renaissance political theory.

Nef, Frédéric. Réalisme et anti-réalisme en logique. *Arch Phil*, 55(3), 461-478, Jl-S 92.

In a review of Pascal Engel's *La norme du vrail* (*The Norm of Truth*, Harvester, 1991), the author discusses mainly three issues the philosophy of logic: the opposition between realism and anti-realism in logic, intensionality, and the origins of logical normativity. On the first point, the author shows that the whole discussion has its origins in the inquiry about the nature of logical constraints. He shows all the difficulties of the anti-realist position, even in its weakened version. On intensionality he shows some skepticism towards a strict extensionalism. On logical normativity the author denies to the theories of minimal rationality the capacity of expression and describing the nature of the logical normative as such.

Negrin, Llewellyn. Postmodernism and the Crisis in Criticism. *Phil Soc Crit*, 19(2), 171-193, 1993.

This paper examines several postmodernist critiques of the institution of criticism. After outlining the socio/historical factors which have provoked these challenges I analyze two of them. The first, exemplified by Sontag and Derrida, rejects the notion of criticism as the interpretation of the truth content of works of art, while the second, exemplified by Hohendahl and Eagleton attacks the institutional structure within which criticism takes place. My conclusion is that these responses to the crisis of criticism ultimately serve to promote what they seek to overcome—namely the subjection of the evaluation of art to the art market.

Negro, Matteo. Possibilità e stati di fatto in Chisholm. *Epistemologia*, 15(1), 65-86, Ja-Je 92.

To the modal concept of possibility is nowadays paid an always growing attention. The realism of Roderick M Chisholm—one of the top representatives of American analytical philosophy and a deep expert of Middle-European thought—constitutes an important attempt made in the direction of the refusal of reductionism and nominalism, by means of the acknowledgment of irreducibly abstract properties. Abstract objects are properties, that could reasonably be attributed to contingent things. In our study we consider abstract objects. Among them we find properties and states of affairs. States of affairs are the equivalents of Meinongian "objectives": real abstract objects, expressions of thoughts (that-*p*). (edited)

Nehamas, Alexander. Commentary on Halliwell's "The Importance of Plato and Aristotle for Aesthetics". *Proc Boston Colloq Anc Phil*, 5, 349-383, 1989.

Nehamas, Alexander. Paintings as an Art in Psychoanalysis, Mind and Art, Hopkins, Jim (ed). Cambridge, Blackwell, 1992.

Nehamas, Alexander. Serious Watching in The Interpretive Turn, Hiley, David R (ed). Ithaca, Cornell Univ Pr, 1991.

The essay is on effort to show that "literacy" and "sophistication" have many more dimension than a usually acknowledged. I examine a number of common objections to the idea that the medium of television can produce works of aesthetic value. Through an analysis of *St Elsewhere*, I try to show that such objections are groundless. They presuppose the wrong standards — standards applicable to other media — and prevent them from engaging in the appropriate interpretation and criticism of television, which is also shown to reward serious watching.

Nehamas, Alexander. Voices of Silence: On Gregory Vlastos' Socrates. *Arion*, 2(1), 157-186, Wint 92.

Vlastos's Socrates competes with the portraits of Gotz and Zellar. Yet, the evidence he presents for the reconstruction of the historical figure is not finally compelling. Moreover, Vlastos's understanding of Socratic irony is such that it allows us to construe Socrates as a dogmatist, knowing the truth but keeping it back for purely pedagogical reasons. The result is not acceptable.

Nehamas, Alexander. What Did Socrates Teach and To Whom Did He Teach It?. *Rev Metaph*, 46(2), 279-306, 1992.

This is a defense of Socrates against the charge of "intellectualism"—the charge that he held that intellectual capacities could secure success and happiness and that he neglected the affective aspect of his students' personalities. The defense depends on showing that Socrates was not, and did not present himself, as a teacher of others, at least in Plato's early dialogues. The assumption that he must have been one is due to Plato and to *his* conception of philosophy's mission — a conception which needs to be seriously questioned.

Neill, Alex. Fear, Fiction and Make-Believe. *J Aes Art Crit*, 49(1), 47-56, Wint 91.

Neill, Alex. Fiction and the Emotions. *Amer Phil Quart*, 30(1), 1-13, Ja 93.

This article addresses the issue of what sorts of state we are moved to when we are moved by fiction. It argues that at least some emotions, such as pity, may be founded on an agent's beliefs about what is fictionally the case, and thus may have objects that are known by the agent to be fictional. Other emotions, including fear for oneself and jealousy, cannot be so founded, and hence cannot take objects that the agent knows to be fictional. We can pity fictional characters, but we cannot fear them or be jealous of them.

Neill, Alex. Yanal and Others on Hume and Tragedy. *J Aes Art Crit*, 50(2), 151-154, Spr 92.

Neiman, Alven and Siegel, Harvey. Objectivity and Rationality in Epistemology and Education: Scheffler's Middle Road. *Synthese*, 94(1), 55-83, Ja 93.

In this paper, we describe and defend Israel Scheffler's treatment of objectivity and rationality. We explain how Scheffler's epistemology, developed in works such as *Science and Subjectivity*, provides a "middle road" between fixed foundations, certainty and the given, on the one hand; and subjectivism, relativism and skepticism on the other. We discuss Scheffler's use of this "middle road" in his work on education and teaching. Our goal here is to suggest that this work provides a valuable paradigm for responding to a number of intractable controversies among educational theorists and philosophers, especially those having to do with the state of the university in contemporary culture.

Nelkin, Norton. The Connection between Intentionality and Consciousness in Consciousness: Psychological and Philosophical Essays, Davies, Martin (ed). Cambridge, Blackwell, 1993.

Recently, a number of philosophers have argued that intentionality is essentially connected to consciousness, that intentional states are at the same time phenomenal (or phenomenological) and introspective. The clinical cases and thought experiments presented point, however, to dissociations between intentionality and introspection, and between intentionality and phenomenality, and support the view that we mean three different states by the term "conscious(ness)", that there is no noncomposite, indivisible, turn-the-switch-on state of the kind dreamed of in the view mentioned above. Whatever the correct understanding of intentionality, intentionality is not essentially tied to either of introspection or phenomenality.

Nelkin, Norton. What is Consciousness?. *Phil Sci*, 60(3), 419-434, S 93.

When philosophers and psychologists think about consciousness, they generally focus on one or more of three features: phenomenality (how experiences feel), intentionality (that experiences are "of" something, that experiences *mean* something), and introspectibility (our awareness of the phenomenality and intentionality of experience). Using examples from empirical psychology and neuroscience, I argue that consciousness is not a unitary state, that, instead, these three features characterize *different* and *dissociable* states, which often happen to occur together. Understanding these three features as dissociable from each other will resolve philosophical disputes and facilitate scientific investigation.

Nelson, G C. Constructive Ultraproducts and Isomorphisms of Recursively Saturated Ultrapowers. *Notre Dame J Form Log*, 33(3), 433-441, Sum 92.

Various models of a first order theory T are obtained from given models of that theory by generalizations of the ultraproduct construction. It is demonstrated that for a model complete theory this construction can be carried out using as functions for the ultraproduct exactly those functions defined by terms in an extension of the original language. In this way one obtains countable nonstandard models of T which can be endowed with other desirable properties such as being recursively saturated. These constructions use only the most basic ideas of model theory and recursion theory. Two countable elementarily equivalent models are shown to have recursive ultrapowers which are isomorphic and recursively saturated.

Nelson, Hilde L. Against Caring. *J Clin Ethics*, 3(1), 8-15, Spr 92.

Although caring is a fundamental activity of nursing, the feminine ethics of care articulated by Nel Noddings cannot keep nurses from harming themselves in their interactions with patients, and because it restricts itself to intimates and "proximate strangers," it is equally incapable of providing a basis for nursing-related questions of social justice. Drawing on the work of Simone Weil, Iris Murdoch, and Martha Nussbaum, I recommend instead an ethics of attention that can resist the subjugation of women and that, while sensitive to broader social concerns, is particularly well suited to the special intimacy of the nurse-patient relationship.

Nelson, James Lindemann. Making Peace in Gestational Conflicts. *Theor Med*, 13(4), 319-328, D 92.

Mary Anne Warren's claim that "there is room for only one person with full and equal rights inside a single human skin" calls attention to the vast range of moral conflict engendered by assigning full basic moral rights to fetuses. Thereby, it serves as a goal to thinking about conflicts between pregnant women and their fetuses in a way that emphasizes relationships rather than rights. I sketch out what a 'care orientation' might suggest about resolving gestational conflicts. I also argue that the care orientation, with its commitment to the significance of the partial and the particular, cannot be absorbed within standard, impartialist moral theory.

Nelson, James Lindemann. Moral Sensibilities and Moral Standing: Caplan on Xenograft "Donors". *Bioethics*, 7(4), 315-322, Jl 93.

Interspecies transplantation — or xenograft — must answer the challenge that many nonhumans are on a moral par with mentally handicapped humans, and hence are equally immune from being unwilling sources of vital organs (the so-called "marginal cases" argument). Arthur Caplan has offered perhaps the most interesting counter to this argument, which appeals in part to differences in patterns of sensibility — in brief, humans would tend to suffer more if their children, handicapped or not, were used as organ sources than would nonhuman parents. I argue that his defense cannot fully meet the weight of the strongest moral challenges to xenograft, in part because it does not address the distinction between what we *do* care about, and what we *should* care about.

Nelson, James Lindemann. Taking Family Seriously. *Hastings Center Rep*, 22(4), 6-12, Jl-Ag 92.

As some perceptive commentators are starting to point out, the prevalent ethic of patient autonomy in medicine ignores other morally relevant considerations—for instance, the stake that family members may have in the course of a patient's treatment. This article extends this theme, sets it more explicitly into a context which assigns special significance to intimate relationships, discusses its implications for particular cases, reveals some of the lurking difficulties with the line, and ends with recommendation for appropriate changes in the structure of medical decisionmaking: the competent patient's authority over her own treatment decisions should be seen not as an absolute constraint, but as a strong but rebuttable presumption.

Nelson, James Lindemann. Transplantation through a Glass Darkly. *Hastings Center Rep*, 22(5), 6-8, S-O 92.

Using animals as sources of transplantable organs—"xenograft"—has tempted physicians for decades, and recent developments in immunosuppressant technology have given new life to this long-cherished hope. There are, however, philosophical questions raised by xenograft on which little progress has been made. Until we have a better story on what of moral significance separates xenograft "donors" from xenograft recipients—in other words, unless and until there is a response to what is generally called "The Argument from Marginal Cases"—procuring organs from animals is not an appropriate way of responding to the organ shortfall.

Nelson, James Lindemann and Callahan, Daniel and Thornton, Barbara C. Bioethics Education: Expanding the Circle of Participants. *Hastings Center Rep*, 23(1), 25-29, Ja-F 93.

The Hastings Center Project on Bioethics Education identifies and describes the core components of a bioethics curriculum as well as key issues regarding the education of clinicians, ethics committee members and policy- makers in the many diverse settings in which learning about bioethics now takes place. The challenge of translating theory into action as well as the political and practical realities of developing bioethics programs is discussed. Evaluation of existing courses and programs in bioethics is recommended while certification of programs is considered premature.

Nelson, John O. Induction: A Non-Sceptical Humean Solution. *Philosophy*, 67(261), 307-327, Jl 92.

Nelson, Julianne. Rational Altruism or the Secession of Successful?: A Paradox of Social Choice. *Pub Affairs Quart*, 7(1), 29-46, Ja 93.

Robert Reich has claimed that the wealthiest fifth of the US population "is quietly seceding from the rest of the nation". I observe that Sen's paradox of the "Paretian liberal" has the same formal structure as Reich's secession scenario. I argue that the resolutions to Sen's paradox offered by Nozick, Riley, Suzumura, and Pressler essentially define the problem out of existence and can actually be used to justify

secession. In contrast, the resolution suggested by Gibbard—a form of rational altruism that may be difficult to implement—improves the lot of everyone in society relative to the secession scenario.

Nelson, Julie. Thinking About Gender. *Hypatia*, 7(3), 138-154, Sum 92.

I present a way of thinking about gender that I have found helpful in evaluating various proposed feminist projects. By considering gender and value as independent dimensions, of "difference" can be more clearly perceived as involving relationships of lack, of complementarity, or of perversions. I illustrate the use of my gender/value "compass" with applications to questions of self-edentity, rationality, and knowledge. This way of thinking about gender allows a conceptualization of feminism that neither erases nor emphasizes gender distinctions.

Nelson, Julie A. Gender, Metaphor, and the Definition of Economics. *Econ Phil*, 8(1), 103-125, Ap 92.

Drawing on feminist scholarship regarding the social construction of gender categories and the social construction of the academic disciplines, this article examines the relationship between cultural conceptions of gender and value and the central defining features of contemporary mainstream economics. The culturally dominant hierarchical conception of gender leads to high value being attributed to subjects and methods perceived as masculine, and a parallel devaluing of subjects or methods metaphorically associated with femininity. The ways in which this hierarchical gender metaphor has helped to shape economics, and the implications for economics of the use of an alternative "encompassing" metaphor of gender and value, are explored.

Nelson, Lycette (trans) and Blanchot, Maurice. *The Step Not Beyond*. Albany, SUNY Pr, 1992.

This translation of Maurice Blanchot's work is of major importance to late 20th-century literature and philosophy studies. Using the fragmentary form, Blanchot challenges the boundaries between the literary and the philosophical. With the obsessive rigor that has always marked his writing, Blanchot returns to the themes that have haunted his work since the beginning: writing, death, transgression, the neuter. But here his discussion turns around the figures of Hegel and Nietzsche rather than Mallarmé and Kafka. (staff)

Nelson, Lynn Hankinson. A Question of Evidence. *Hypatia*, 8(2), 172-189, Spr 93.

I outline a pragmatic account of evidence, arguing that it allows us to underwrite two implications of feminist scholarship: that knowledge is socially constructed and constrained by evidence, and that social relations, including gender, race, and class, are epistemologically significant. What makes the account promising is that it abandons any pretense of a view from nowhere, the view of evidence as something only individuals gather or have, and the view that individual theories face experience in isolation.

Nelson, Lynn Hankinson. Epistemological Communities in Feminist Epistemologies, Alcoff, Linda (ed). New York, Routledge, 1993.

I argue that communities, rather than individuals, are the primary loci— the primary generators, repositories, holders, and acquirers— of knowledge, and that multiple, overlapping, and evolving epistemic communities are the appropriate focus of a feminist naturalized epistemology. My arguments for the primacy of epistemological communities and a naturalized epistemology build from a view of evidence as nonfoundational and communal, a view I show to be compatible with and supported by feminist science criticism, as well as post_Quinean philosophy of science, and an alternative to postmodern skepticism about the possibility or desirability of epistemology.

Nelson, Mark T. Temporal Wholes and the Problem of Evil. *Relig Stud*, 29(3), 313-324, S 93.

The argument from evil usually contains the premise that there is much evil in the world. I consider a strategy for rejecting this premise which does not require the implausible claim that the phenomenal world is illusory. I borrow an idea suggested in the fiction of C. S. Lewis that good and evil are retrospective, and then develop the concept of a "temporal whole" to explain Lewis's suggestion that the way things turn out later in one's life may affect the extent to which painful events earlier in one's life really *were* evil.

Nelson, Michael P. A Defense of Environmental Ethics: A Reply to Janna Thompson. *Environ Ethics*, 15(3), 245-258, Fall 93.

Janna Thompson dismisses environmental ethics primarily because it does not meet her criteria for ethics: consistency, non-vacuity, and decidability. In place of a more expansive environmental ethic, she proposes to limit moral considerability to beings with a "point of view." I contend, first, that a point-of-view centered ethic is unacceptable not only because it fails to meet the tests of her own and other criteria, but also because it is precisely the type of ethic that has contributed to our current environmental dilemmas. Second, I argue that the holistic, ecocentric land ethic of Aldo Leopold, as developed by J Baird Callicott, and environmental ethic that Thompson never considers, nicely meets Thompson's criteria for acceptable ethics, and may indeed be the cure for our environmental woes.

Nelson, R J. *Naming and Reference*. New York, Routledge, 1992.

The first half of this book surveys the history of the problem of reference from Locke to Quine and Kripke. The second half contains a theory of reference which takes seriously the causal notion of reference, while at the same time preserving Frege's distinction between sense and reference. The algorithmic theory that results treats reference in explicitly nonsemantical terms. It incorporates or reflects the latest work in computational logic, cognitive science, philosophy of mind, linguistics and brain biology.

Nelson, Ralph (trans) and Simon, Yves R. Some Remarks on the Object of Physical Knowledge. *Int Phil Quart*, 32(3), 275-283, S 92.

Taking the term physical knowledge in a broad sense that would include the philosophy of nature, the author proceeds to examine three formulations of the object of this kind of knowledge—mobile being, sensible being, and material being—in order to establish that the three are equivalent. Theoretical knowledge in its optimal state is certain and explanatory, and physical knowledge would have these notes as well were it perfect. The analysis utilizes distinctions between necessity and contingency, between typological and extensive abstraction, and between the inherently sensible and the accidentally sensible. (The last distinction is ignored in the Berkeleyan account of physical knowledge.) The object of physical knowledge, Simon states, is "the incorruptible formulation of a corruptible reality."

Németi, I. Algebraizations of Quantifier Logics, An Introductory Overview. *Stud Log*, 50(3-4), 485-569, S-D 91.

This paper is an introduction: in particular, to algebras of relations of various ranks, and in general, to the part of algebraic logic algebraizing quantifier logics. The paper has a survey character, too. The most frequently used algebras like cylindric-, relation-, polyadic-, and quasi-polyadic algebras are carefully introduced and intuitively explained for the nonspecialist. Their variants, connections with logic, abstract model theory, and further algebraic logics are also reviewed. Efforts were made to make the review part relatively comprehensive. In some directions we tried to give an overview of the most recent results and research trends, too.

Nesbitt, Winston. Euthanasia and the Distinction between Acts and Omissions. *J Applied Phil*, 10(2), 253-256, 1993.

It is commonly assumed that the view that passive euthanasia is morally preferable to active euthanasia is an implication of the view that killing someone is worse than merely letting her die, and that it is held by its proponents on this ground. Accordingly, attempts to discredit the former often take the form of attempted refutations of the latter. In the present paper, it is argued that such attempts are misguided, since the former view is not in fact implied by the latter.

Nesbitt, Winston. Self-Esteem and Moral Virtue. *J Moral Educ*, 22(1), 51-53, 1993.

David Dewhurst has recently argued that certain apparent problems with the aim of promoting pupils' self-esteem stem from a tendency to think of self-esteem as having a necessary connection with comparison between oneself and others. He argues that there is a kind of self-esteem of which this is not true, and that these problems do not arise if the aim is to promote self-esteem or 'self-acceptance' of this sort. While accepting his central argument, I take issue with his dismissal of the suggestion that we should try to deal with the problems in question in part by placing less emphasis on achievement and competence, and more on qualities like kindness and generosity.

Neschke, Ada. Le degré zéro de la philosophie platonicienne: Platon dans l'*Historia critica philosophiae* de J J Brucker (1742). *Rev Metaph Morale*, 97(3), 377-400, Jl-S 92.

Nesin, Ali and Borovik, Alexandre V. On the Schur-Zassenhaus Theorem for Groups of Finite Morley Rank. *J Sym Log*, 57(4), 1469-1477, D 92.

Nesteruk, Jeffrey and Risser, David T. Conceptions of the Corporation and Ethical Decision Making in Business. *Bus Prof Ethics J*, 12(1), 73-89, Spr 93.

We argue that business decision makers are influenced in the performance of their professional roles by the conceptions they hold of the corporation as a social institution. Two distinct and opposing views of the corporation, *corporations-as-property* and *corporations-as-persons*, are evident in American political culture and serve as the basis for these conceptions. We propose a third view, that of *restricted personhood* for corporations, and suggest the implications of this view for business decision making.

Netton, Ian. *Al-Farabi and His School*. New York, Routledge, 1992.

Using an epistemological focus, this book examines the thought of al-Farabi, Yahya B Adi, Abu Sulayman al-Sijistani, al-Amiri and Abu Hayyan al-Tawhidi. It demonstrates that al-Farabi produced a "school of philosophical thought" to which these four other philosophers adhered, especially from an epistemological point of view. While the thinking of all five thinkers was influenced by that of Plato, Aristotle and Plotinus, it was never a mere copy of any one of these. Dr. Netton identifies 'a fundamental epistemology of salvation' and maintains that its "primary elements were the noetic, the ethical and the soteriological".

Neubauer, Z. Chiliasmus and Eschatology or Partnership with the Nature (in Czechoslovakian). *Filozof Cas*, 39(6), 1001-1008, 1991.

Neuberg, Marc. Does Intention Define Action? (in French). *Rev Theol Phil*, 124(3), 217-229, 1992.

Is it not the case that in the philosophy of action we generally have a highly simplified idea of the physical structure of action? Does not defining action in terms of an intention seem unavoidable simply because we give such an anemic meaning to the notion of bodily movement? But if this notion were adequately analyzed, it would perhaps prove sufficient as a basis for the concept of action.

Neuberg, Marc. *Philosophie de l'action*. Gembloux, Acad Royal Belg, 1993.

Neuhouser, Frederick. Freedom, Dependence, and the General Will. *Phil Rev*, 102(3), 363-395, Jl 93.

Neumaier, Otto. Are Collectives Morally Responsible? in Advances in Scientific Philosophy, Schurz, Gerhard (ed). Amsterdam, Rodopi, 1991.

Neumann, Harry. Responsible and Irresponsible Liberalism: Dostoevsky's Stavrogin. *Hist Euro Ideas*, 16(4-6), 569-575, Ja 93.

Honest liberalism liberates from all morality and politics. Dostoyevsky knew that all serious political conflict is hot (or cold) war over opposing gods (moralities): without theology, no morality and without morality, no politics! Atheist (liberal) politics or morality is an oxymoron. Each faction has its god, its notion of political correctness which it strives to impose on its enemies: there never is respect for "diversity" in politics! An honest liberal (atheist), Stavrogin despises politics. This contempt is anathema to his desires, since desire always wants to politically empower its god, what it feels to be politically correct. Stavrogin's suicide is triggered by the moral indignation of desire's illiberalism (morality, piety) against reason's liberalism (amorality, atheism).

Neumer, Katalin. *Boundary Ways: On the Philosophy of the Later Ludwig Wittgenstein (in Hungarian)*. Budapest, MTA Filoz Int, 1991.

The insight that boundary questions formulated in language, in our "linguistic puzzles" are practically problems of existence and consequently they can be interpreted as the "counterposition of man and the world of things" is a cardinal thesis in Neumer's argument. She thus discusses XIX-XXth century "philosophies of life" (Schopenhauer, Mauthner, Spengler) indicating the influence they possibly exerted on Wittgenstein. In this vein the author realizes that deep in his later works a well-determined ethical intention can be traced highlighting the connections between faith and knowledge, morality and art. The "unspeakable" of the early Tractatus thus appears in a new context as the polarity of reflection and irreflection, sense and senseless. The scholarly study is supplied with a detailed bibliography.

Neville, Robert Cummings. *Eternity and Time's Flow*. Albany, SUNY Pr, 1993.

The book develops the thesis that time's flow can be understood only as the togetherness of past, present, and future in dynamic eternity, as that thesis shapes four topic areas: personal moral identity, a phenomenology, cosmology, and metaphysics of temporality, a theology of God as eternal, and personal eternal life or immortality.

Nevin, Thomas R. *Simone Weil: Portrait of a Self-Exiled Jew*. Chapel Hill, Univ N Carolina Pr, 1991.

Nevins, Thomas A. Degrees of Convex Dependence in Recursively Enumerable Vector Spaces. *Annals Pure Applied Log*, 60(1), 31-47, F 93.

Let W be a recursively enumerable vector space over a recursive ordered field. We show the Turing equivalence of the following sets: the set of all tuples of vectors in W which are linearly dependent; the set of all tuples of vectors in W whose convex closures contain the zero vector; and the set of all pairs (X, Y) of tuples in W such that the convex closure of X intersects the convex closure of Y. We also form the analogous sets consisting of tuples with given numbers of elements, and prove similar results on the Turing equivalence of these.

Nevo, Isaac. Continuing Empiricist Epistemology: Holistic Aspects in James's Pragmatism. *Monist*, 75(4), 458-476, O 92.

Nevo, Isaac. Difference Without the Flux: Pragmatic versus Romantic Conceptions of Alterity. *Man World*, 25(2), 149-164, Ap 92.

Nevo, Isaac. What Price Deconstruction? Derrida on Heidegger and the Question of Nazims: A Critical Study. *Philosophia (Israel)*, 21(3-4), 183-199, Ap 92.

New, Christopher. Antitheism: A Reflection. *Ratio*, 6(1), 36-43, Je 93.

Why is there no sustained tradition of argument concerning the existence of a supreme (omniscient and omnipotent) being who is perfectly evil, as there is about one who is perfectly good? Arguments which are reflections of the ontological, cosmological and teleological arguments, and arguments based on personal experience or the occurrence of antimiracles (harmful events not explicable by science) could have provided at least as good grounds for belief in such a being (i.e., for antitheism) as their originals in fact provide for theism. An imaginary encyclopedia entry, in which fictional antitheistic arguments and thinkers are presented, illustrates this point. The reason for the nonexistence of a tradition of antitheism seems therefore to be that it is merely emotionally, not that it is rationally, less inviting to theism.

Newcomer Scalo, Maria. The Possibility of a Christian Ethic in the Philosophy of Nietzsche. *Dialogue (PST)*, 34(2-3), 50-53, Ap 92.

Newman, Andrew. *The Physical Basis of Predication*. New York, Cambridge Univ Pr, 1992.

This is a book about some of the basic concepts of metaphysics: universals, particulars, causality and possibility. Its aim is to give an account of the real constituents of the world. The author defends a realistic view of universals, characterizing the notion of universal by considering language and logic, possibility, hierarchies of universals, and causation. On the other hand, he argues that logic and languages are not reliable guides to the nature of reality. All assertions and predications about the natural world are ultimately founded on "basic universals", which are the fundamental type of universal and central to causation. A distinction is drawn between unified particulars (which have a natural principle of unity) and arbitrary particulars (which lack such a principle); unified particulars are the terms of causal relations and thus real constituents of the world. Arbitrary particulars such as events, states of affairs, and sets have no ontological significance.

Newman, Elizabeth. An Alternative Form of Theological Knowing. *Tradition Discovery*, 20(1), 13-26, 1993-94.

This essay seeks to incorporate Polanyi's post-critical conception of knowing more fully into theology by emphasizing that all knowing is a personal activity rooted in a particular place. While deconstruction describes itself as post-critical, its assumption that all knowledge is a social "construct" and/or an instrument of social coercion fails to account for the involvement of the person in all acts of knowing. A more genuine post-critical approach takes seriously the cohesion between the knower and the known, and thus allows space for the liturgy to be a form of theological knowing. If how and what we know are internally related, then the liturgy, when faithfully entered into, is a form of theological knowing that needs to be taken seriously.

Newton, Lisa. Gambling: A Preliminary Inquiry. *Bus Ethics Quart*, 3(4), 405-418, O 93.

Why is gambling wrong? A preliminary inquiry rules out the positions that gambling (with one's own money) is a violation of rights, and that gambling (except in special circumstances) is an infliction of harm or detriment to welfare. No case may be made that gambling violates justice. Gambling's chief wrong, it seems, is waste—it is a waste of money, time and human life, and as such violates duties of stewardship. Since "stewardship" is not widely recognized in the contemporary literature of obligations, I sketch its moral grounds and chart its place on the map of duties.

Ng, Siu-Ah. Loeb Extensions and Ultrapowers of Measures on Fragments. *Annals Pure Applied Log*, 60(2), 179-190, Ap 93.

Keisler initiated and provided a detail study of various kinds of measures on T-algebras generated by definable sets. Here we study the ultrapower of a measure on an algebra generated by formulas with parameters from a fixed set. It is shown that the ultrapower is always nonforking. Results dealing with the equivalence of measures, Loeb measures, ultrapowers and Loeb extensions of ultrapowers are proved. Conditions for preservation of these measure constructions are studied.

AUTHOR INDEX WITH ABSTRACTS 609 Nieznanski, Edward

Nguyen, Vinh-De. Avons-nous vraiment besoin d'une éthique de l'environnement?. *Dialogue (Canada)*, 30(3), 249-263, Sum 91.

Ni, Peimin. Changing the Past. *Nous*, 26(3), 349-359, S 92.

Nicgorski, Walter. Nationalism and Transnationalism in Cicero. *Hist Euro Ideas*, 16(4-6), 785-791, Ja 93.

Three facets of Cicero's thought are examined in an effort to understand how his Roman particularism relates to his Stoic universalism. 1) Cicero's explanation of the origin and purpose of political community reveals an understanding of appropriate human development. 2) In this light Rome as center of Cicero's loyalties is an instance of a rationally reinforced attachment. 3) Cicero expects the Roman political community to proceed toward its goal within the ligatures of the universal human community, and it is the latter community as backdrop that reveals Roman defects. If ever reason and context called for new, transnational political communities, Cicero's understanding of human development would leave him appreciative of how effective national bonds can prepare and have prepared humankind for the new political forms.

Nicholsen, Shierry Weber (trans) and Adorno, Theodor W. *Hegel: Three Studies*. Cambridge, MIT Pr, 1993.

Nicholson, Ben. The Grit and Grist of Thinking the Unthinkable House. *Res Phenomenol*, 22, 12-22, 1992.

Nicholson, Graeme. The Passing of Hegel's Germany in German Philosophy and Jewish Thought, Greenspan, Louis (ed). Toronto, Univ of Toronto Pr, 1992.

Nicholson, Graeme (ed) and Greenspan, Louis (ed). *German Philosophy and Jewish Thought*. Toronto, Univ of Toronto Pr, 1992.

Nicholson, Graeme (ed) and Misgeld, Dieter (ed). *Hans-Georg Gadamer on Education, Poetry, and History: Applied Hermeneutics*. Albany, SUNY Pr, 1992.

This is a collection of essays by Hans-Georg Gadamer, all of which had been untranslated hitherto—with one exception. The editors (who co-translated the essays with Lawrence Schmidt and Monica Reusch) arranged the essays in three groups, introducing each of the three sections with a long and intensive interview with Hans-Georg Gadamer. The parts are: 1) The Philosopher in the University; 2) Hermeneutics, Poetry and Modern Culture; 3) Europe and the Humanities. The interviews discuss Gadamer's relation to his times, from World-War I to Nazism and the post-war era, his relation to Heidegger and others, etc. The essays selected include essays on George and Celan, on the European Humanities, and on Planning the Future, on the German University, its history and limitations. There is a wide-ranging editors' introduction covering these topics.

Nicholson, Peter P. Kant, Revolutions and History in Essays on Kant's Political Philosophy, Williams, Howard Lloyd (ed). Chicago, Univ of Chicago Pr, 1992.

It is a familiar charge that Kant, because he apparently condemned all revolution as illegal and immoral yet applauded the French Revolution, is inconsistent. The paper argues that there is no inconsistency. Kant's remarks on revolution on the one hand, and on the French Revolution on the other, are compatible because they belong to fundamentally distinct kinds of discourse: his moral-juridical theory and his philosophy of history respectively.

Nicolacopoulos, Pantelis (ed). *Greek Studies in the Philosophy and History of Science*. Dordrecht, Kluwer, 1990.

The purpose of this volume is to provide an accurate and current picture of the achievements of the Greek community of the history and philosophy of science. Although it draws from the rich tradition of Classical Greek philosophy and science, and it relates some of the contemporary issues to their original Greek expression, it emphasizes the contemporary *problematique* and suggests original solutions to today's outstanding questions and open problems. The 26 essays of the volume represent both the historical and the analytic approaches, balance foundational issues with advanced results, and address a number of sciences and philosophy, demonstrating both the broadness of interests and the depth of analysis of the current research.

Nicoletti, Michele. Politics and Religion in Kierkegaard's Thought in Foundations of Kierkegaard's Vision of Community, Connell, George B (ed). Atlantic Highlands, Humanities Pr, 1992.

Kierkegaard condemns and mingling of politics and religion: religion cannot serve its cause following a secular logic and politics cannot present itself as a masked religion, which pretends to realize heaven on earth. Kierkegaard foresees that the absoluteness of politics, which is typical of his time, will produce a dissolution of politics itself, because the political sphere cannot satisfy the need of infinity. So "it will be seen that in the decisive moment only martyrs are able to rule the world": by refusing every form of absolutization of the political , martyrs restore the world to itself.

Nicolosi, S. L'interiorità cartesiana tra metafisica e fenomenismo. *Sapienza*, 44(4), 353-377, 1991.

Nicolosi, S. Scienza e filosofia tra microcosmo e macrocosmo: Il problema di Dio in Diderot e Newton. *Aquinas*, 34(3), 485-518, S-D 91.

Nicolosi, Salvatore. Fine della modernità o nascita di una nuova modernità?. *Sapienza*, 46(1), 3-29, 1993.

Nicolosi, Salvatore. La città armoniosa di Péguy: Profezia della speranza o utopia dell'illusione. *Aquinas*, 35(3), 517-537, S-D 92.

Nicolosi, Salvatore. Le ragioni del deismo in Voltaire's e nell'Enciclopedia. *Sapienza*, 45(2), 137-170, 1992.

Nida-Rümelin, Martine. Probability and Direct Reference: Three Puzzles of Probability Theory. *Erkenntnis*, 39(1), 51-78, Jl 93.

I discuss three puzzles of probability theory which seem connected with problems of direct reference and rigid designation. The resolution of at least one of them requires referential use of definite descriptions in probability statements. I argue that contrary to common opinion all these puzzles are in a way still unsolved: They seem to exemplify cases in which a change of probabilities is rationally required, even though any specific change presupposes unjustified assumptions.

Nielsen, Finn E and Collins, Ronald K L. The Spirit of Simone Weil's Law in Simone Weil's Philosophy of Culture, Bell, Richard (ed). New York, Cambridge Univ Pr, 1993.

Nielsen, Kai. *After the Demise of the Tradition: Rorty, Critical Theory, and the Fate of Philosophy*. Boulder, Westview Pr, 1991.

Nielsen, Kai. Analytical Marxism: A Form of Critical Theory. *Erkenntnis*, 39(1), 1-21, Jl 93.

Nielsen, Kai. Elster's Marxism. *Phil Papers*, 21(2), 83-106, Ag 92.

Nielsen, Kai. Global Justice, Capitalism and the Third World in International Justice and the Third World, Attfield, Robin (ed). New York, Routledge, 1992.

Nielsen, Kai. On There Being Philosophical Knowledge. *Theoria*, 61(3), 193-225, 1990.

Nielsen, Kai. Philosophy and *Weltanschauung*. *J Value Inq*, 27(2), 179-186, Ap 93.

Nielsen, Kai. Philosophy and the Search for Wisdom. *Teach Phil*, 16(1), 5-20, Mr 93.

Nielsen, Kai. Secession: The Caes of Quebec. *J Applied Phil*, 10(1), 29-43, 1993.

I argue that people have a right to self-determination when they are plainly predominant in a certain territory and do not violate the civil liberties of minorities. But there is no self-determination without the preservation of self-identity and the cultural preservation that goes with its secure existence. So to preserve autonomy and self-determination people must preserve their cultural identity and this cannot be securely sustained in modern conditions without a nation-state concerned to nourish that identity. Such considerations support a right to secession when certain conditions are met. The conditions are that the people in question have a cultural identity, live in a distinct territory which they have inhabited for a long time, form an extensive majority, and respect the civil liberties of the minorities living in that territory (as well as elsewhere). Where they are such a group they have a right to secede from a larger state to which they are historically attached. These conditions, I argue, are met in Quebec.

Nielsen, Kai. The Burden of Ideological Masks in *Ideolgiekritik*: On Trying to View Faith Scientifically. *Metaphilosophy*, 23(3), 251-267, Jl 92.

Nielsen, Kai. What is Alive and What is Dead in Marx and Marxism. *Laval Theol Phil*, 49(2), 277-293, Je 93.

An effort is made to sort out what is alive and what is dead in Marx and Marxism. This is done by way of critically examining Jon Elster's sorting. Elster, a major analytical Marxist, has provided what is arguably the most thorough and sophisticated sorting of Marx and Marxism we have to date. That notwithstanding I contend that there are rational reconstructions of historical materialism and functional explanation that withstand Elster's critique but I further contend that, even if Elster's critique on both accounts is sound, along with his critique of such familiar notions as the labour theory of value, the falling rate of profit and methodological holism, that what Elster finds to be wheat and not chaff in Marx and Marxism is sufficient to keep socialism on the political agenda. There remain important viable elements of a Marxian theory of society after the collapse of Marxist Fundamentalism.

Nielsen, Richard P. Organization Ethics from a Perspective of Praxis. *Bus Ethics Quart*, 3(2), 131-151, A 93.

Organization ethics praxis is theory and method of appropriate action for addressing ethics issues and developing ethical organizations. The perspective of praxis (theory and method of action) is important and different from the perspectives of theoria (theory of understanding), epistemology (ways of knowing), and ontology (ways of being/existing). Praxis is the least developed area within the field of organization ethics.

Nielsen, Richard P. Varieties of Postmodernism as Moments in Ethics Action Learning. *Bus Ethics Quart*, 3(3), 251-269, Jl 93.

Through an international case study, this paper illustrates how a conversation method was used effectively to address a cross-cultural ethics problem. The method included as moments in one continuous process three different dimensions of postmodernism—Gadamer reconstruction, Derrida deconstruction, and Rorty neopragmatism. In addition to including different dimensions of postmodernism, the method combines effective mutual learning and effective action. Strengths and limitations of the approach are discussed. The article demonstrates how it can be beneficial to build bridges between and within the postmodernism and organization ethics literatures. Also, the article demonstrates how postmodernism can be positively ethical and not necessarily aethical or nihilistic.

Nieuwendijk, Arthur. Semantics and Comparative Logic. *J Indian Phil*, 20(4), 377-418, D 92.

The paper takes up the question as to which logical framework is most suitable for a formal interpretation of Navyanyāya logic. It is claimed that, for this purpose, the framework offered by extensional first-order predicate logic is inadequate. This claim is established by discussing three well-known difficulties: the interpretation of the notion of jnāna, the question whether contraposition is a law of Navyanyāya logic, and the interpretation of the Navyanyāya scheme of inference. Next, the interrelatedness of these difficulties is pointed out, and, carrying through the analysis, it is examined whether situation semantics offers a suitable alternative framework.

Nieznanski, Edward. The Beginnings of Formalization in Theology in Advances in Scientific Philosophy, Schurz, Gerhard (ed). Amsterdam, Rodopi, 1991.

In areas where conceptual systems are particularly complex precision created by formalization protects against making syntactic, semantic and sometimes also pragmatic mistakes. All the attempts at formalization in theology have been done within the framework of systematic theology (apologetics, dogmatics). The Thomist proofs of the immortality of the soul, of the existence of God and of the occurrence of certain ontological attributes in God's essence have been formalized. The extent of the applicability of the logic to religion was described, the formal and logical structure of religions text was revealed, the foundation for a logical semiotics of religions language was created and the principles of argumentation for religions theses were presented.

Niiniluoto, Ilkka. The Aim and Structure of Applied Research. *Erkenntnis*, 38(1), 1-21, Ja 93.

The distinction between basic and applied research is notoriously vague, despite its frequent use in science studies and in science policy. In most cases it is based on such pragmatic factors as the knowledge and intentions of the investigator or the type of research institute. Sometimes the validity of the distinction is denied altogether. This paper suggest that there are two ways of distinguishing systematically between basic and applied research: 1) in terms of the "utilities" that define the aims of inquiry, and 2) by reference to the structure of the relevant knowledge claims. An important type of applied research aims at results that are expressed by "technical norms" (in von Wright's sense): if you wish to achieve A, and you believe you are in a situation B, then you should do X. This conception of "design sciences" allows us to re-evaluate many issues in the history, philosophy, and ethics of science.

Nikiforov, A L. Is Philosophy a Science?. *Russian Stud Phil*, 31(1), 8-25, Sum 92.

Nikolic, Zivojin. Cekic and Lukács über die Ontologie des gesellschaftlichen Seins: 'Die Prioritätsfrage' in Analecta Husserliana, XXXI, Tymieniecka, Anna-Teresa (ed). Dordrecht, Kluwer, 1990.

Niles, Ian. Wittgenstein and Infinite Linguistic Competence. *Midwest Stud Phil*, 17, 193-213, 1992.

Many philosophers have argued that linguistic creativity can be explained only by postulating theories of meaning. This argument implicitly presupposes a view of linguistic understanding which is shared by Plato, Locke, Frege, and most contemporary philosophers of language. However, Wittgenstein mounted a formidable, albeit largely ignored, challenge to this view of understanding. The conclusion of this essay is that it is unclear whether linguistic creativity is grounds for positing theories of meaning. Furthermore, there will be clarity on this point only when there is agreement about the nature of linguistic understanding.

Nishitani, Keiji. Mein philosophischer Ausgangspunkt. *Z Phil Forsch*, 46(4), 545-556, O-D 92.

Nissen, Lowell A. Four Ways of Eliminating Mind from Teleology. *Stud Hist Phil Sci*, 24(1), 27-48, Mr 93.

The article examines four strategies for eliminating mentalistic concepts from teleological language in the life sciences: behaviourism, natural selection, metaphor, and negative feedback. It argues that none succeeds and recommends an analysis based on unreduced intentionality.

Noam, Gil G (ed) and Wren, Thomas (ed). *The Moral Self*. Cambridge, MIT Pr, 1993.

Noddings, Nel. Excellence as a Guide to Educational Conversation. *Proc Phil Educ*, 48, 5-16, 1992.

This article, originally the author's presidential address at the Philosophy of Education Society in 1992, makes one major point and three arguments to support it. Excellence, I argue, is a more powerful concept than equity in guiding educational conversation, if it is defined to include: 1) fine programs of study for a full range of human talents, not just traditional academic talent; 2) the quality of present life, not mere preparation for the future, and; 3) common learnings redefined to consider every facet of human life, not the traditional (and outdated) liberal arts.

Noddings, Nel. For All Its Children. *Educ Theor*, 43(1), 15-22, Wint 93.

This article, part of a special issue responding to Jonathan Kozol's *Savage Inequalities*, supports Kozol's work with three arguments: First, a decent society must care for and educate all its children appropriately. We are not excused if parents themselves do not care. Second, we should provide decent school facilities for all our children because it is the right thing to do, not merely so that they "can learn." (This leaves us hostage to test results.) Finally, we must convince the contented majority that it is in their own best interest to relieve poverty and provide all children with decent living conditions.

Noddings, Nel. For All Its Children. *Free Inq*, 13(1), 25-26, Wint 92-93.

This is a brief article in an issue devoted to remembering John Dewey. Its theme is Dewey's warning to America: "What the best and wisest parent wants for his own child, that must the community want for all its children. Any other ideal for our schools is narrow and unlovely; acting upon, it destroys our democracy" (*School and Society*, 1956-1900,). Dewey's vision is contrasted with the realities documented in Jonathan Kozol's *Savage Inequalities* (1991).

Noddings, Nel. In Defense of Caring. *J Clin Ethics*, 3(1), 15-18, Spr 92.

This is a response to Hilde Nelson's "Against Caring" in the same issue. The defense includes 1) classification of caring as vital in the intellectual, emotional, and moral domains — not just the physical; 2) recognition of the dangers of motivational displacement; 3) discussion of engrossment as a form of attention. The article concludes with an exploration of the cases Nelson presented and application of an ethic of care to each of them.

Noel, Jana R. Intentionality in Research on Teaching. *Educ Theor*, 43(2), 123-145, Spr 93.

Rejecting such syntactical notions of intentionality as those of Dennett and Stich, and building on representational notions like Fodor's, this paper develops the following conception of intentionality: a) teachers have contentful states, such as beliefs and desires, which have meaning for teachers, and; b) practical reasoning is the process that turns these intentional components into active decision making. Three established programs of research on teaching—"process-product," "cognitive processing," and "reflective teaching"—are examined for their consideration of this notion of the intentionality of teachers. The paper concludes that none of these three research programs address teachers with the full conception of intentionality developed here.

Noh, Yang-jin. Davidson on the Idea of a Conceptual Scheme. *Kinesis*, 19(2), 4-12, Sum 93.

This paper is to show that Davidson's criticism of the conceptual scheme notion, if successful, does not lead to his claim that we give up the very notion as incoherent. Davidson's criticism is solely directed to the unnecessarily rigid notion of a conceptual scheme that he sets up for his own discussion, which preclude the possibility of a modified notion of it. This suggests that for a more meaningful talk about human understanding, we can have a modified conceptual scheme notion as an open possibility even after Davidson's criticism.

Nola, Roberta and Sylvan, Richard. Confirmation without Paradoxes in Advances in Scientific Philosophy, Schurz, Gerhard (ed). Amsterdam, Rodopi, 1991.

Noonan, H W. Object-Dependent Thoughts in Mental Causation, Heil, John (ed). New York, Clarendon/Oxford Pr, 1993.

Noonan, Harold W. Chisholm, Persons and Identity. *Phil Stud*, 69(1), 35-58, Ja 93.

The purpose of the paper is to survey Chisholm's views on identity and personal identity. It finds in Chisholm important anticipations of arguments of David Lewis and Garth Evens.

Noonan, Harold W. Constitution is Identity. *Mind*, 102(405), 133-146, Ja 93.

The purpose of the article is to defend the view that materially identical objects are identical simpliciter. An argument to the contrary by Mark Johnston is criticized. In the course of the article a Lewisean four dimensional ontology and a counterpart theoretic interpretation of modal predication are defended.

Norcross, Alastair and Howard-Snyder, Frances. A Consequentialist Case for Rejecting the Right. *J Phil Res*, 18, 109-125, 1993.

Satisficing and maximizing versions of consequentialism have both assumed that rightness is an all-or-nothing property. We argue that this is inimical to the spirit of consequentialism, and that, from the point of view of the consequentialist, actions should be evaluated purely in terms that admit of degree. We consider the suggestion that rightness and wrongness are a matter of degree. We conclude that the consequentialist can make no sense of the concept of wrongness. (edited)

Nordenfelt, Lennart. On the Relevance and Importance of the Notion of Disease. *Theor Med*, 14(1), 15-26, Mr 93.

This paper constitutes a defence of the basic philosophical enterprise of characterising concepts such as 'disease' and 'health', as well as other medical concepts. I argue that these concepts play important roles, not only in medical, but also in other scientific and social contexts. In particular, medical decisions about health and diseasehood have important ethical, social and economic consequences. The role played is, however, not always a rational one. But the greater is the need for a reconstruction of this network of concepts for the purpose of efficient and rational communication.

Nordenfelt, Lennart. *Quality of Life, Health and Happiness*. Aldershot, Ashgate, 1993.

This book has two main purposes. One is analytical and one is critical. First, the book sets out to reconstruct the concept of quality of life. It does so mainly through an analysis of the concept of happiness. It traces various dimensions of happiness, for instance the dimension of richness, and ties them together into a unified concept. The analytical part of the book also contains a section where the concepts of happiness and health are related to each other. This analysis constitutes a background for a critical study of some contemporary instruments designed for the purpose of measuring human health and quality of life. The instruments are scrutinized mainly from the point of view of conceptual clarity, consistency and practicality. The general conclusion of the book is that the value of these measuring instruments remains doubtful if their construction has not been preceded by a thorough theoretical analysis of the concepts used.

Nordmann, Alfred (ed) and Klagge, James C (ed) and Wittgenstein, Ludwig. *Philosophical Occasions: 1912-1951—Ludwig Wittgenstein*. Indianapolis, Hackett, 1993.

Shorter writings by or deriving from Wittgenstein, in German and English. Brief introductions describe the circumstances of origin of each piece. Contents: Review of Coffey's *Science of Logic*, Letters to Eccles, Preface to the *Wörterbuch*, "Some Remarks on Logical Form," Lecture on Ethics, Moore's Lecture Notes, "Remarks on Frazer," Letter to *Mind*, "Philosophy" (from the Big Typescript), "Notes for Lectures on 'Private Experience' and 'Sense Data'" (reedited and significantly expanded), Rhees' Lecture Notes on Freedom of the Will, "Notes for the 'Philosophical Lecture'" (previously unpublished), Letters to von Wright, and a new edition of von Wright's "The Wittgenstein Papers".

Noreña, Carlos. Suárez and the Jesuits. *Amer Cath Phil Quart*, 65(3), 267-286, Sum 91.

Norman, Andrew P. Naming, Reference, and Sense: Theoretical and Practical Attitudes at Odds. *Auslegung*, 18(2), 113-121, Sum 92.

The paper examines three philosophical controversies over proper names, specifically, those occasioned by the questions: (1) Do proper names have a sense?; (2) If so, does the sense fix the reference?; (3) Are name-to-name identity-claims about words or their references?—and argues that each is crucially ambiguous. The issues hinge on the interpretations given to 'have', 'fix', and 'about', respectively. Recognizing these ambiguities makes it possible to give disputants on both sides (Frege, Russell, Searle, and Kripke) their due. Proper names do not *possess* a sense, but *carry* one; sense can help fix reference initially, but need not thereafter; and name-to-name identity-claims can *convey information about* words, even though they do not describe them.

Norman, Richard. The Case for Pacifism in Applied Philosophy, Almond, Brenda (ed). New York, Routledge, 1992.

The idea of respect for human life generates a strong, though not necessarily absolute, moral presumption against killing in war. Neither 'just war' theory nor consequentialist claims are successful in overriding this presumption. Despite the strength of the moral case against war, people sometimes say that they have no choice but to fight. This idea is briefly explored in the concluding section of the paper.

Normore, C G. Abelard and the School of the Nominales. *Vivarium*, 30(1), 80-96, My 92.

Normore, Calvin G. Petrus Aureoli and His Contemporaries on Future Contingents and Excluded Middle. *Synthese*, 96(1), 83-92, Jl 93.

Normore, Calvin G. The Necessity in Deduction: Cartesian Inference and its Medieval Background. *Synthese*, 96(3), 437-454, S 93.

Norris, Christopher. Deconstruction, Postmodernism and Philosophy: Habermas on Derrida in Derrida: A Critical Reader, Wood, David (ed). Cambridge, Blackwell, 1992.

This essay raises a number of objections to Habermas's reading of Derrida. It argues that deconstruction cannot be understood as just another form of modish counter-Enlightenment thinking, one that treats philosophy as a "kind of writing" on a level with poetry, rhetoric, literary criticism, etc. What Habermas fails to see — perhaps understandably, given his Kantian assumptions — is that Derrida is still very much engaged with distinctively *philosophical* problems, even while exploiting certain fictive or rhetorical devices which call into question the self-image of "philosophy" as an autonomous discipline of thought. Other thinkers — Austin among them — have likewise managed to complicate the philosophy/literature distinction without thereby ceasing to offer cogent philosophical arguments.

Norris, Christopher. Lost in the Funhouse in Postmodernism and Society, Boyne, Roy (ed). New York, St Martin's Pr, 1990.

This paper offers a critical appraisal of the various arguments (or unargued assertions) advanced by postmodernist thinkers like Jean-Francois Lyotard and Jean Baudrillard. It claims that their reasoning is often philosophically confused, their language a prey to all kinds of unexamined presupposition, and their influence (especially on literary theorists) a compound of various dogmas, fallacies, and modish *idées recues*. The paper attempts to balance this negative bias by suggesting alternative resource - mainly from epistemology, linguistics, and philosophy of science-which provide the wherewithal to criticize such forms of irrationalist and nihilist thinking.

Norris, Christopher. *The Truth about Postmodernism*. Cambridge, Blackwell, 1993.

This book examines some of the errors and misreadings—especially misreadings of Kant—that have characterized recent post-modernist and post-structuralist thought. For these issues have a social and political relevance, Norris argues, far beyond the academic enclaves of philosophy, literary theory, and cultural criticism. Thus he makes large claims for the importance of getting Kant right on the relation between epistemology, ethics and politics, and also for pursuing the Kantian question "What is Enlightenment?" as raised—and symptomatically misconstrued—in Foucault's later writings.

Norris, Stephen P. Bachelors, Buckyballs, and Ganders: Seeking Analogues for Definitions of "Critical Thinking". *Proc Phil Educ*, 48, 49-57, 1992.

In this paper, I propose that the theorizing of philosophers engaged in the study of critical thinking should form the basis of empirical research in the area. Philosophers can provide hypotheses for empirical researchers to test and explanations for the findings empirical research yields. To play this role, philosophers of education must frame their theories of critical thinking so that their empirical implications are clear.

Northoff, Georg and Wiggins, Osborne and Schwartz, Michael Alan. Psychosomatics, the Lived Body, and Anthropological Medicine in The Body in Medical Thought and Practice, Leder, Drew (ed). Dordrecht, Kluwer, 1992.

Norton, Anne. Ruling Memory. *Polit Theory*, 21(3), 453-463, Ag 93.

Norton, Bryan G. Should Environmentalists Be Organicists?. *Topoi*, 12(1), 21-30, Mr 93.

Several versions of "organicism" are distinguished as part of a general argument that, while environmentalists need a new organizing metaphor, versions of "strong organicism" (which identify one level of nature's complex organization as a mental agent and which are teleological) cannot guide environmental thinking or action. Strong organicism has been interpreted too literally (suggesting that ecosystems are like organisms) and it has been taken to have moral force (requiring that we value systems over their parts). A version of "minimal holism", rather, is advocated. Minimal holism is based on the analogy between self-organizing, "dissipative structures", more generally, and ecosystems, avoiding the implication that ecosystems are like persons and avoiding moral implications that have seemed to some to be "Fascistic".

Norton, David Fate. More Evidence that Hume Wrote the Abstract. *Hume Stud*, 19(1), 217-222, Ap 93.

This brief paper adduces additional external and internal evidence that Hume is the author of An Abstract of...A Treatise of Human Nature. It concludes that this evidence, when combined with information previously provided by James Moore and David Raynor, makes the case for Hume's authorship a very strong one.

Norton, John. Thought Experiments in Einstein's Work in Thought Experiments in Science and Philosophy, Horowitz, Tamara (ed). Lanham, Rowman & Littlefield, 1991.

Thought experiments are just arguments of a special type: they posit hypothetical or counterfactual states of affairs and invoke particulars irrelevant to the generality of the conclusion. I illustrate this claim with analysis of thought experiments in thermodynamics, relativity theory and quantum theory drawn from Einstein's work.

Norton, John D and Earman, John. Forever is a Day: Supertasks in Pitowsky and Malament-Hogarth Spacetimes. *Phil Sci*, 60(1), 22-42, Mr 93.

The standard theory of computation excludes computations whose completion requires an infinite number of steps. Malament-Hogarth spacetimes admit observers whose pasts contain entire future-directed, timelike half-curves of infinite proper length. We investigate the physical properties of these spacetimes and ask whether they and other spacetimes allow the observer to know the outcome of a computation with infinitely many steps.

Norton, Robert E. *Herder's Aesthetics and the European Enlightenment*. Ithaca, Cornell Univ Pr, 1991.

Norton-Smith, Thomas M. A Note on Philip Kitcher's Analysis of Mathematical Truth. *Notre Dame J Form Log*, 33(1), 136-139, Wint 92.

Philip Kitcher presents an attractive view of mathematical reality with an attending stipulational account of mathematical truth in The Nature of Mathematical Knowledge. However, if Kitcher's analysis of mathematical statements is correct, then some statements which are referentially true cannot satisfy his stipulational truth conditions. Thus, Paul Benacerraf's objection that stipulational theories of truth do not introduce genuine notions of truth finds Kitcher as a mark.

Nosal, Czeslaw S. Neurobiology of Subjective Probability in Probability and Rationality, Eells, Ellery (ed). Amsterdam, Rodopi, 1991.

The goal of the paper is to pay attention to neurobiological support for a processual interpretation of probabilistic norm formation as the cognitive activity. The neuropsychological results show that in the brain there are separate anatomical structures correlated with the learning of a conditioned reaction to signals with various objectively scheduled probability of reinforcement /neocortex vs. hippocampus/. Another neurobiological results show an important and different role of the left and right hemispheres for probability estimation.

Nosari, Sara. L'inno della perla: Una risposta al problema gnostico. *Filosofia*, 43(3), 431-471, S-D 92.

Noutsos, Panayiotis. The History of the Theory of Natural Sciences in Greek Studies in the Philosophy and History of Science, Nicolacopoulos, Pantelis (ed). Dordrecht, Kluwer, 1990.

This paper reconstructs the thought of the Greek Enlightenment as regards the theoretical approach to the history of the physical sciences. The model of scientificity derives from the re-unification of philosophy with the physical sciences which subjected the date of their empirical investigations to mathematical calculation and concentrated on one specific object of knowledge, within the context of the division of intellectual labour which established the practice of the sciences as a special social institution. The social development of the scientific ideas, which at the level of the individual is marked as freedom of the mind from all kinds of prejudice, presupposes and implies the transition from "Barbarism" to "civilization".

Novitz, David. The Integrity of Aesthetics. *J Aes Art Crit*, 48(1), 9-20, Wint 90.

A critique of the notion of pure aesthetic value.

Nowak, Leszek. On the Concept of Adequacy of Laws: An Idealizational Explication in Idealization III, Brzezinski, Jerzy (ed). Amsterdam, Rodopi, 1992.

Nowak, Leszek. The Idealizational Approach to Science: A Survey in Idealization III, Brzenzinski, Jerzy (ed). Amsterdam, Rodopi, 1992.

Nowak, Leszek. The Method of Relevant Variables and Idealization in Probability and Rationality, Eells, Ellery (ed). Amsterdam, Rodopi, 1991.

L J Cohen (e.g., *The Probable and the Provable*, Oxford, 1977) claims that his method of relevant variables encompasses the method of idealization. The goal of the paper is to prove that this is not the case. L J Cohen discovered, instead, a special counterfactual procedure which has not been yet conceptualized in the terms of the idealizational methodology (cf. L Nowak, The Structure of Idealization, Dordrecht/Boston, 1980). The method is reconstructed in the idealizational terms and the conditions of its applicability are discussed.

Nowak, Leszek (ed) and Brzezinski, Jerzy (ed). *Idealization III*. Amsterdam, Rodopi, 1992.

Nowak, Leszek and Nowakowa, Izabella. 'Truth is a System': An Explication in Idealization III, Brzezinski, Jerzy (ed). Amsterdam, Rodopi, 1992.

Nowak, Marek. On Two Relatives of the Classical Logic. *Bull Sec Log*, 21(3), 97-102, O 92.

In the paper we give a semantics for Hiz logic and an axiomatization of some 3-element matrix whose consequence operation is related to the classical logic in the similar way as Hiz logic.

Nowakowa, Izabella. A Notion of Truth for Idealization in Idealization III, Brzenzinski, Jerzy (ed). Amsterdam, Rodopi, 1992.

Nowakowa, Izabella. The Idea of 'Truth as a Process': An Explication in Idealization III, Brzezinski, Jerzy (ed). Amsterdam, Rodopi, 1992.

Nowakowa, Izabella and Nowak, Leszek. 'Truth is a System': An Explication in Idealization III, Brzezinski, Jerzy (ed). Amsterdam, Rodopi, 1992.

Nowell, Linda. "At Risk": Development of Personhood. *Thinking*, 10(1), 23-26, 1992.

"At-risk" students face a greater threat than the danger of becoming a drop-out statistic—what is "at-risk" is their personhood. Moreover, the threat comes from an educational system that views individuals as objects that can be shaped and managed. In order to counter this threat, we must change the model—to one that creates an environment which views the individual as an active participant who is capable of critically and creatively reflecting on her/his experiences and which provides the individual with the "proper tools" for that encounter. This environment is created within a community of inquiry.

Nubiola, Jaime. Juan Luis Vives y Charles S Peirce. *Anu Filosof*, 26(1), 155-166, 1993.

Connections between J L Vives and C S Peirce are shown. Not only is reflection on language and meaning central in both thinkers, but Peirce also knew Vive's thought especially through W Hamilton and the Scottish common sense school. Peirce credited Vives with being a forerunner of the use of diagrams in logic, and both share a critical view of late medieval nominalistic logicians and a social and hierarchical conception of knowledge.

Nuccetelli, Susana. Speech Acts and Semantics—A Review of "Meaning and Speech Acts: Principles of Language Use". *J Prag*, 18(1), 59-69, Jl 92.

This article offers a discussion of Vanderveken's speech acts theory (1990). This theory tries to accomplish a general semantics, as well as some specific description of English verbs, which is intended to show the applicability of the theory. Two distinct issues are considered: constructing a formal intensional semantics for natural language, and providing a theory of meaning. The reviewer argues that the failure of distinguishing between these two questions undermines the whole project. It is also pointed out that there exists a lack of connection between the theory and its application.

Nunan, Richard. Heuristic Novelty and the Asymmetry Problem in Bayesian Confirmation Theory. *Brit J Phil Sci*, 44(1), 17-36, Mr 93.

Bayesian confirmation theory holds that the degree to which a particular body of evidence increases the epistemic probability of a hypothesis is the same whether the evidence is discovered (or recognized) before or after formulation of the hypothesis. Richmond Campbell and Thomas Vinci recently offered a reinterpretation of Bayes' Theorem under which evidence E will increase the probability of hypothesis H only if it is *heuristically novel* (meaning that *H* was not deliberately designed to explain *E*, or in anticipation of *E*). In this paper it is argued that heuristic novelty has no special effect on theory confirmation, even under Campbell's and Vinci's revisionist interpretation of Bayes' Theorem.

Nunberg, Geoffrey. Indexicality and Deixis. *Ling Phil*, 16(1), 1-43, F 93.

Nunner-Winkler, Gertrud. Knowing and Wanting in Cultural-Political Interventions in the Unfinished Project of Enlightenment, Honneth, Axel (& other eds). Cambridge, MIT Pr, 1992.

Kohlberg's assumption of cognitive-affective parallelism in moral development and his description of the preconventional stage as instrumentalist is contested: Turiel found early understanding of the intrinsic validity of moral rules; also spontaneous altruism in children has been documented. Data are presented (200 children, 4-5 years) to show that in fact there is good moral understanding; yet most children still lack 'moral motivation' as measured by emotion ascriptions to hypothetical wrongdoers. Moral development is conceptualized as a two step learning process: universally children acquire moral knowledge; growth of moral motivation however involves a slow, differentially successful, painful second learning process.

Nussbaum, Charles. Critical and Pre-Critical Phases in Kant's Philosophy of Logic. *Kantstudien*, 83(3), 280-293, 1992.

The transition in Kant's writings form a pre-critical to a critical standpoint has been thoroughly documented with regard to Kant's changing conception of metaphysics, theory of knowledge, and philosophy of mathematics. But a similar alteration in standpoint in Kant's philosophy of logic has received little or no attention. This paper documents the existence of this shift in Kant's philosophy of logic and examines its nature. The resulting analysis provides evidence for the thesis that Kant began with a strictly intensional term logic and with a theory of inference based on the analytic composition of concepts, and ended with a view of logic which, while remaining fundamentally intensional and term-based, shows movement towards a logic of propositions and propositional connectives.

Nussbaum, Martha C. Commentary on Halperin's "Plato and the Metaphysics of Desire". *Proc Boston Colloq Anc Phil*, 5, 53-72, 1989.

Nussbaum, Martha C. Commentator on 'Explanation and Practical Reason' in The Quality of Life, Nussbaum, Martha C (ed). New York, Oxford Univ Pr, 1993.

Nussbaum, Martha C. Commentator on 'Justice, Gender, and International Boundaries' in The Quality of Life, Nussbaum, Martha C (ed). New York, Oxford Univ Pr, 1993.

Nussbaum, Martha C. Equity and Mercy. *Phil Pub Affairs*, 22(2), 83-125, Spr 93.

Nussbaum, Martha C. Human Functioning and Social Justice: In Defense of Aristotelian Essentialism. *Polit Theory*, 20(2), 202-246, My 92.

Nussbaum, Martha C. Non-Relative Virtues: An Aristotelian Approach in The Quality of Life, Nussbaum, Martha C (ed). New York, Oxford Univ Pr, 1993.

Nussbaum, Martha C. Reply to Papers. *Phil Invest*, 16(1), 46-86, Ja 93.

Nussbaum, Martha C. Reply to Richard Eldridge's "Reading for Life": Martha C Nussbaum on Philosophy and Literature. *Arion*, 2(1), 198-207, Wint 92.

Nussbaum, Martha C (ed) and Sen, Amartya (ed). *The Quality of Life*. New York, Oxford Univ Pr, 1993.

Nuyen, A T. Counting the Formulas of the Categorical Imperative: One Plus Three Makes Four. *Hist Phil Quart*, 10(1), 37-48, Ja 93.

Nuyen, A T. Habermas, Adorno and the Possibility of Immanent Critique. *Amer Cath Phil Quart*, 66(3), 331-340, 1992.

Habermas argues that Adorno's critique of reason is a "totalizing critique" and thus internally contradictory insofar as it makes use of the very reason that it criticizes. I defend Adorno by identifying his critique as an immanent critique and arguing that such a critique is possible. Indeed, if Kant is right, such a critique is *necessary*. By contrast, Habermas's conception of critique posits a "transcendental viewpoint." I argue that such a critique is in danger of turning the authority of reason into an authoritarianism of reason.

Nuyen, A T. On Interpreting Kant's Architectonic in Terms of the Hermeneutic Model. *Kantstudien*, 84(2), 154-166, 1993.

When Kant says that reason is "by nature architectonic," he means that reason inevitably constructs a systematic whole which determines *a priori* the scope of the parts as well as their relative positions within the whole. Since the whole includes empirical objects as well as "intelligible" objects, Kant's first task is to solve the antinomies that arise when reason moves from the empirical to the intelligible. That done, Kant shows how the idea of an architectonic whole regulates his account of the elements of the understanding. Finally, the systematic unity of knowledge and understanding is our guarantee of truth.

Nuyen, A T. The Fragility of the Self: From Bundle Theory to Deconstruction. *J Speculative Phil*, 6(2), 111-122, 1992.

Among the targets of post-structuralism is the Cartesian view of the non-material and unified self, capable of achieving self-consciousness, self-certainty and self-possession. The Cartesian self is present to itself in an act of self-reflection. Post-structuralists attempt to "deconstruct" this view, arguing that the self is "split," "fractured," and can never be fully present to itself. As such, it is fragile and can disintegrate. The paper compares and contrast the post-structuralist position with Kant's view and with Hume's bundle theory.

Nuyen, A T. The Role of Rhetorical Devices in Postmodernist Discourse. *Phil Rhet*, 25(2), 183-194, 1992.

The paper is an attempt to defend the writing style of postmodernist/post-structuralist philosophers. Postmodernists emphasize difference (rather than identity), fragmentation (rather than unity), both-and (rather than either-or). Rhetorical devices such as metaphor, irony, metonymy, chiasmus, as well as sheer playfulness are designed to highlight postmodernist themes. Contra Plato, it is argued that style can serve a cognitive function, i.e., it is not purely rhetorical (or alternatively, there is much that is cognitive in the rhetorical).

Nuyen, A T. The Unbearable Slyness of Deconstruction. *Philosophy*, 68(265), 392-396, Jl 93.

Nwodo, C S. The Future of Democracy in Nigeria in Terrorism, Justice and Social Values, Peden, Creighton W (ed). Lewiston, Mellen Pr, 1990.

Nye, Andrea. Frege's Metaphors. *Hypatia*, 7(2), 18-39, Spr 92.

The form of the sentence, as it is understood in contemporary semantics and linguistics, is functional. This paper interprets the metaphors in which Frege shows what the functional sentence means, arguing that Frege's sentence is neither an adequate translation of natural language nor of use in feminist theorizing.

Nye, Andrea. Philosophy: A Woman's Thought or a Man's Discipline? The Letters of Abelard and Heloise. *Hypatia*, 7(3), 1-22, Sum 92.

This paper is part of a larger project of recovering the work of women thinkers. Heloise has traditionally been read as either a foil of Abelard or his intellectual appendage. In this paper, I present her views on love, religious devotion, and language as an alternative to philosophic method as it is conceived by Abelard.

Nyíri, J C. *Tradition and Individuality: Essays*. Dordrecht, Kluwer, 1992.

A volume on the themes of tradition, oral versus literal communication, Wittgenstein, and computers. Wittgenstein is a *traditionalist*, and, along with Heidegger, a philosopher of postmodern—secondary—*orality*, yearning for pre-modern times of *primary* orality. Under conditions of primary orality traditions fulfilled the specific cognitive role of conserving information—a role subsequently taken over by writing, and today by electronic data processing. Western values of individuality and critical thinking are bound up with the technology of *writing*—still a condition of and a foundation for the emerging computer culture.

O'Boyle, Edward J and Dawson Jr, Lyndon E. The American Marketing Association Code of Ethics: Instructions for Marketers. *J Bus Ethics*, 11(12), 921-930, D 92.

This article addresses the two main obstacles—ignorance and conflict—that block the pathway to ethically proper conduct, both generally in business and specifically in marketing. It begins with a brief examination of theories of the moral good which emphasizes the Greco-Roman humanistic tradition and the Judeo-Christian religious tradition. A professional code of ethics, such as the code of the American Marketing Association, is meaningful only if human beings are regarded as making moral judgments that, objectively speaking, are morally wrong; that is, only when the code is considered a set of moral absolutes. (edited)

O'Brien, D. Le paradoxe de Ménon et l'Ecole d'Oxford. *Rev Phil Fr*, 4, 643-658, O-D 91.

O'Brien, Denis. Platon et Plotin sur la doctrine des parties de l'autre. *Rev Phil Fr*, 4, 501-512, O-D 91.

O'Brien, Maeve. Apuleius and the Concept of Philosophical Rhetoric. *Hermathena*, 151, 39-50, Wint 91.

An exposition of how Apuleius makes a sophist's special plea for the primacy of rhetoric. It follows Apuleius as he first revises Plato to construct his own concept of philosophical rhetoric, and then as he characteristically offers an example of how the concept may be popularly illustrated.

O'Brien, Sean M. Fish vs CLS: A Defense of Critical Legal Theory. *J Soc Phil*, 23(1), 64-73, Spr 92.

O'Brien, Wendell. Judgments of Character. *Int J Applied Phil*, 7(2), 15-18, Wint 92.

I argue that in general we should refrain from making judgments about the character and motivation of other persons, and therefore that (for the most part) we should refrain from making charges of bigotry, sexism, and the like. My argument stresses the epistemic difficulties associated with such charges.

O'Connell, Colin. Marxism and the Logic of Futural Discourse: A Brief Reflection. *Indian Phil Quart*, 19(3), 199-206, Jl 92.

O'Connell, Colin and Sweet, William. Empiricism, Fideism and The Nature of Religious Belief. *Sophia (Australia)*, 31(3), 1-15, 1992.

Recent discussion of the nature and meaningfulness of religious belief in Anglo-American religious thought seems polarized between two views: empiricism and fideism. We argue that both positions are inadequate because they fail to reflect what religious belief is and perhaps more importantly, what religious believers do. We sketch out how empiricism and fideism fail in providing an accurate account of the nature of religious belief, and suggest an alternative that preserves the best insights of both empiricism and fideism while also being more faithful to the experience of ordinary believers.

O'Connell, James. The Sources of Morality: Function, Conformity and Aesthetics. *Heythrop J*, 34(2), 160-170, Ap 93.

The ground of morality and the sources of morality are often confused. The paper argues that the ground of morality is respect for the individual. The sources of morality—those areas of conduct from which the content of moral judgments is taken—are, however, three-fold: social function (e.g., procreation), wholeness/community (belonging and identity), and aesthetic taste. These sources provide moral guidelines and content and need to be respected. But if they are used—as happens in many natural law approaches—without reference to individual persons, they deform morality. Moral thinking has to reflect critically on its sources.

O'Connell, Robert. "The Will to Believe" and James's "Deontological Streak". *Trans Peirce Soc*, 28(4), 809-831, Fall 92.

James's ethical thought could frequently be consequentialist, but it could also on occasion show a deontological side, or "streak," as I contended in *William James on the Courage to Believe*. This shows up when he speaks of the "strenuous" as against the "easy-going" moral mood, in "The Moral Philosopher and the Moral Life," and it preserves the precursive intervention of our "passional natures" in "The Will to Believe" from lapsing into "wishful thinking." Toned down slightly, perhaps, in *Varieties of Religious Experience*, it reasserts itself in *Pragmatism*, and, it could be shown, in James's succeeding works as well.

O'Connell, Robert. Faith, Reason, and Ascent to Vision in Saint Augustine. *Augustin Stud*, 21, 83-126, 1990.

This article was in fact composed some ten years ago, but went astray on the road to publication. It aimed to answer a pair of articles in which Dr Van Fleteren had presented a more "porphyrian" interpretation of the early Augustine's views on faith, reason, and ultimate vision, by showing that a "plotinian" perspective on those same matters— accurately understood— might be considered to represent a more coherent and intelligible view of Augustine's efforts.

O'Connell, Robert. Where the Difference Still Lies. *Augustin Stud*, 21, 139-152, 1990.

Here I point out that (in my view) Van Fleteren still remains overdependent on Courcelle's famous "tentatives d'ecstase" view of *Confessions 7*, as well as Courcelle's conviction that the Augustine of A.D. 386 had read only a "very few books" of Plotinus. Hence other key features of Augustine's account, especially his lengthy treatment of the problem of evil, are eclipsed, and so, understandably, is the key feature of Augustine's answer to that problem, the sinful "fall of the soul".

O'Connor, D J. Ayer on Free Will and Determinism in The Philosophy of A J Ayer, Hahn, Lewis Edwin (ed). Peru, Open Court, 1992.

O'Connor, David. Philosophical Specialization and General Philosophy. *Metaphilosophy*, 24(1-2), 113-122, Ja-Ap 93.

The lament has been heard in recent years that academic philosophy, analytic philosophy especially, increasingly had become irrelevant to the intellectual culture at large, to good undergraduate education, and to what Dewey called "the problem of men." This alleged irrelevancy is deemed due to the growth in philosophy of specialization and technicality. I show a serious misunderstanding at the base of the lament and provide a model that shows the relevance of academic philosophy to the intellectual culture at large, to good undergraduate education, and to the problems of men.

O'Connor, David. Sartre on God, Freedom, and Determinism. *Sophia (Australia)*, 31(1-2), 27-35, 1992.

I examine Sartre's atheistic argument from *Existentialism and Humanism*. I show, first, some interesting convergence between Sartre's thinking I that argument and classical theism, and second, that his argument is considerably less implausible than it seems.

O'Connor, Terence. Of Dances and Dreams: Philosophical Projects in the Current Age. *Phil Stud Educ*, 1, 1-19, 1991.

O'Connor, Timothy. Indeterminism and Free Agency: Three Recent Views. *Phil Phenomenol Res*, 53(3), 499-526, S 93.

O'Connor, Timothy. Scotus on the Existence of a First Efficient Cause. *Int J Phil Relig*, 33(1), 17-32, F 93.

In the *Tractatus De Primo Principio*, Duns Scotus offers a lengthy, sophisticated argument for the existence of a first efficient cause. In this paper, I offer an interpretation of the argument and then go on to identify an important defect in the argument's structure. After briefly discussing the resources available to Scotus for attempting to repair it, I suggest that the argument can rather easily be transformed into a purely *ontological* form. I contend that (in virtue of the modesty of its central "possibility" premise) it compares favorably in certain respects with the more attractive varieties of cosmological and ontological arguments.

O'Connor, Tony. Poetizing and Thinking in Heidegger's Thought. *J Brit Soc Phenomenol*, 23(3), 252-262, O 92.

I show that Heideggerian *Denken* rests on a mixed foundation of figurative and literal terms, that appear to carry no absolutely essential meaning, but clusters of associations and entailments that may vary according to the context in which they are used. I argue that the most he may validly establish through his 'thinking of Being', therefore, is contextually relative possibility conditions of meaning, where cross-contextual linkates, if they are possible, must at best be established concretely and by persuasion.

O'Donnell, M G. Economics as Ethics: Bastiat's Nineteenth Century Interpretation. *J Bus Ethics*, 12(1), 57-62, Ja 93.

Frederic Bastiat was an influential economic writer of the middle 1800s. In his work, *Economic Sophisms* (1848), Bastiat proposed a dual system of ethics, containing economic ethics and religious ethics. Bastiat first described the tendency of individuals toward "plunder" as a means of satisfying their economic needs. Men, he held, could work and produce what they needed by toil, but history had shown that men preferred to take what they could from others who had toiled. Bastiat identified two main types of plunder—force and fraud.

O'Driscoll, Herbert. Synthesis: The Larger Perspective in Contemporary Issues in Paediatric Ethics, Burgess, Michael M (ed). Lewiston, Mellen Pr, 1991.

O'Dwyer Bellinetti, L. Potenzialità conoscitive del trascendentale di Husserl. *Aquinas*, 35(1), 59-72, Ja-Ap 92.

O'Grady, Jane (ed) and Ayer, A J (ed). *A Dictionary of Philosophical Quotations*. Cambridge, Blackwell, 1992.

O'Hagan, Timothy. Charles Taylor's Hidden God. *Ratio*, 6(1), 72-81, Je 93.

With tongue half-way in cheek, the author distinguishes, among the post-modernists, an "extremist" tendency (Derrida and his followers), and a "moderate" tendency ("conservative" faction: MacIntyre, Sandel; "progressive" faction: Dworkin). Locating Charles Taylor's *Sources of the Self* on the "moderate-progressive" wing of the movement, he criticizes Taylor for misreading two key authors in his intellectual history. For Taylor, Aristotle is either naively parochial or improperly relativist; and Rawls is wedded to an erroneous, abstract philosophical anthropology. The author argues that both Taylor's charges are mistaken, and undertakes a rapid re-assessment of the two figures. Finally he addresses Taylor's ambiguous theology. It serves to give coherence and significance to human strivings. But, beyond the appellation "Judaeo-Christian", we are given no clue about its sources or content.

O'Hara, Kieron. Sceptical Overkill: On Two Recent Arguments Against Scepticism. *Mind*, 102(406), 315-327, Ap 93.

Recent papers in *Mind*, by Brueckner and Wright, attempt to undermine external world scepticism. This paper shows that these arguments beg questions against the sceptic, since they both assume that the sceptic has available various epistemological warrants. However, the sceptic can insist that these warrants are conditional on his hypothesis being false. In particular, the sceptical premisses, suitably conditionalized, entail that everyone is always cognitively disabled! Wright's response that one could never warrantedly believe the premisses of this new argument removes some of the worry, but, by being consistent with the sceptical hypothesis, fails to undermine the sceptical position.

O'Hara, Robert J. Telling the Tree: Narrative Representation and the Study of Evolutionary History. *Biol Phil*, 7(2), 135-160, Ap 92.

Accounts of the evolutionary past have as much in common with narrative histories as they do with conventional works of science. Narrative phenomena in evolutionary writing include selective attention, perspective, foregrounding and backgrounding, and the establishment of a canon of important events. While these narrative phenomena promote linearity and cohesiveness in conventional stories, they conflict with the underlying chronicle of evolution, which is not linear, but branched, and which does not cohere, but diverges. If we are to understand the true nature of evolutionary history we must practice "tree thinking", and develop new ways of telling the history of life.

O'Hear, Anthony. Criticism and Tradition in Popper, Oakeshott and Hayek. *J Applied Phil*, 9(1), 65-75, 1992.

Popper's attitude to traditions is fundamentally rationalistic. He analyzes traditions, along with other institutions and practices, in terms of their efficiency in promoting goals which can be specified independently of the traditions themselves. Hayek, by contrast, looks at traditions in terms of their contributions to the survival of the culture in which they are embedded, something whose evaluation may be opaque even to people within the culture. Both these approaches are flawed compared to Oakeshott's insistence that traditions are not goal-oriented, and that goals cannot be specified independently of agents' forms of life. Oakeshott's views constitute a *via media* between Popperian rationalism and Hayekian anti-rationalism.

O'Hear, Anthony. Historicism and Architectural Knowledge. *Philosophy*, 68(264), 127-144, Ap 93.

Historicism is the view that history has a definite direction, and that people, including architects, should attempt to follow that direction. Both modernism and post-modernism in architecture are frequently defended on historicist grounds. But the pretensions of the historicist to knowledge are spurious and ethically unacceptable. In architecture knowledge has been gained over the centuries through trial and error attempts to serve human need. Architects should forget historicist explanations and retrieve what has been spontaneously discovered.

O'Hear, Anthony. The Real or the real? Chardin or Rothko?. *Philosophy*, 32(Supp), 47-58, 1992.

The still life painter Chardin concentrates on the detail and beauty of everyday life; the abstract expressionist Rothko produces contentless paintings which engulf the viewer. Rothko's work has often been analysed in religious, quasi-mystical terms. It has something in common with an approach to religious experience, such as that of John Hick, which prescinds from differences between religious and abstracts from content. The danger is that Hich, like Rothko, plays down the specifically human forms of perception and living celebrated by Chardin.

O'Hear, Anthony. The Real or the Real? Chardin or Rothko? in Philosophy, Religion and the Spiritual Life, McGhee, Michael (ed). New York, Cambridge Univ Pr, 1992.

Chardin domestic still-lives have a meaning which Rothko's vast abstract paintings lack. The latter, like some recent speculations in the philosophy of religion, many gesture at the inettably Real, but they do so at the expense of wiping away all that is specifically human in what we bring to the world. The wiping away of the detail of our life and thought may lead to an empty religion, as to an empty aesthetic.

O'Hear, Anthony. Wittgenstein and the Transmission of Traditions in Wittgenstein Centenary Essays, Griffiths, A Phillips (ed). New York, Cambridge Univ Pr, 1991.

It is argued that Wittgenstein's private language argument and what he says about rule following entail a conservative philosophical anthropology. Rule following requires a community to sustain the efforts of the individual rule-follower. Analogous considerations apply to our shared investigations of the empirical world, but relativism need not be the consequence.

O'Leary, Daniel J. 'Principia Mathematica' and the Development of Autonomated Theorem Proving in Perspectives on the History of Mathematical Logic, Drucker, Thomas (ed). Basel, Birkhauser, 1991.

The paper describes and contrasts two approaches to automated theorem proving applied to portions of Russell and Whitehead's *Principia Mathematica* (PM). The Logic Theory Machine by Newell, Shaw, and Simon tried to duplicate the reasoning behind the proofs as a human mathematician might do. Wang's approach uses sequent logic and the computer to prove the theorems. The paper describes both methods in detail. It also resolves an error in PM and in the correspondence between Simon and Russell. The paper concludes that the Logic Theory Machine approach is more satisfying in its attempt to understand the human endeavor that is the basis for PM.

O'Leary-Hawthorne, J and Cortens, A. The Principle of Necessary Reason. *Faith Phil*, 10(1), 60-67, Ja 93.

Cosmological arguments have fallen on hard times of late. The main reason for this is that such arguments have traditionally deployed the problematic Principle of Sufficient Reason. In this paper, we explore a different strategy for constructing a cosmological argument. In part 1, we first briefly explain why the Principle of Sufficient Reason is highly questionable. Second, we introduce and motivate the Principle of Necessary Reason. In part 2, we construct an argument that deploys the latter principle, refining it in the face of a number of objections.

O'Leary-Hawthorne, John. Meaning and Evidence: A Reply to Lewis. *Austl J Phil*, 71(2), 206-211, Je 93.

In response to an earlier paper of mine that focused on his inability to deal with long sentences, David Lewis has recently revised his convention-based account of linguistic meaning. In this paper, I focus on a class of sentences that has long interested philosophers—the evidence-transcendent variety—arguing that neither Lewis' earlier self nor his later self offer a satisfactory account of our mastery of them.

O'Leary-Hawthorne, John. Non-Organic Theories of Value and Pointless Evil. *Faith Phil*, 9(3), 387-391, Jl 92.

In this paper, I shall argue that if a certain theory of value is correct, then there is pointless evil in the world. I shall not try to defend the theory. Nor shall I assume that a justified belief in pointless evil is sufficient epistemic warrant for atheism. Thus I am not arguing for atheism here. This paper is intended rather to help elucidate what it would take to demonstrate that no one is justified in believing in pointless evil. If my thesis is correct, then any successful attempt to show that no belief in pointless evil is justified will, inter alia, have to demonstrate that belief in what I shall call "a non-organic theory of value" is irrational.

O'Malley, Michael. *Chronotypes: The Construction of Time* by John Bender and David E Wellbery. *Hist Theor*, 31(3), 343-354, 1992.

O'Meara, Dominic. The Freedom of the One. *Phronesis*, 37(3), 343-349, 1992.

This is a review article of G Leroux' commentary on Plotinus *Ennead* VI 8 (Paris 1990). The following questions are discussed: What is Plotinus' treatise about? What inspired its writing" Does it represent a new departure in Plotinus' metaphysics?

O'Meara, John J and Halton, Thomas (ed). *Studies in Augustine and Eriugena*. Washington, Cath Univ Amer Pr, 1992.

O'Meara, William M. Marx and Mead on the Social Nature of Rationality and Freedom in Frontiers in American Philosophy, Volume I, Burch, Robert W (ed). College Station, Texas A&M Univ Pr, 1992.

O'Neal, John. Le continuum corps-esprit dans l'économie de notre être selon Bonnet. *Philosophiques*, 19(1), 87-110, 1992.

By "the Economy of our Being," Bonnet means essentially the positive and negative changes in the body, brain, and soul. Simply by using two sensations in his statue, Bonnet calls attention to the dynamic and successive nature of our being. Through them, he not only can explain the faculties of the soul and the generation of ideas, but demonstrates his profound commitment to sensationism and analytic method. Bonnet's method conflates a continuous view of nature with a similar view of human cognition. The Chain of Being has its epistemological counterpart in the successive steps of the cognitive process.

O'Neill, Eileen. "Influxus Physicus" in Causation in Early Modern Philosophy, Nadler, Steven (ed). University Park, Penn St Univ Pr, 1993.

Leibniz claims there are three systems of natural change in created substances: the "hypothesis of occasional causes", his own Pre-established Harmony, and "the common hypothesis of influx" or of "physical influence". But what precisely is this latter system which both the Occasionalists and Leibniz sought to subvert? I begin with an examination of the influx models of natural causation with which Leibniz could have been familiar: Neoplatonic, Scholastic, and an Atomistic- Corpuscularian model, as well as Bacon's Multiplication of Species model. I argue that the Neoplatonic replicative model and the Corpuscular diremptive model picture natural change in terms of transmission. I show that the Multiplication of Species model tries to avoid, but ultimately falls back upon, a transmission picture and that Leibniz saw the Scholastics as equally unable to escape this picture of natural change. I discuss Leibniz's complex relation to the Corpuscularians and ask does Leibniz take Descartes's model of natural change to be that of *influxus physicus*, and is Leibniz correct? (edited)

O'Neill, John. Future Generations: Present Harms. *Philosophy*, 68(263), 35-51, Ja 93.

This paper rejects an assumption shared by the protagonists in the recent philosophical debates on future generations: that there is a special problem concerning our obligations to future generations—that we can benefit or harm them but that they cannot benefit or harm us. I criticize the subjectivist account of well-being that underlies this perspective on the goods and harms that can befall us and explore the social conditions responsible for its prevalence. I show that what happens after death can harm us and outline the implications this has for our obligations to future generations.

O'Neill, John. Law and Gynesis: Freud vs Schreber in Shadow of Spirit, Berry, Philippa (ed). New York, Routledge, 1992.

Freud insists upon homosexualizing Schreber's virgin birth. He ignores Schreber's by-pass of his own father's severe child pedagogy and of the Phallic Principle through the myth of the holy family. The memoirs are the anti-paternal text.

O'Neill, John. Religion and Postmodernism in Postmodernism/ Jameson/ Critique, Kellner, Douglas M (ed). Washington, Maisonneuve Pr, 1989.

A political conservative (Daniel Bell) and a cultural Marxist (Fred Jameson) are found to consider religion (in the Durkheimian sense) the possible anchor against post-modern devaluation. A third direction is suggested in terms of an allegory of the body-politic (O'Neill).

O'Neill, John. Science, Wonder and the Lust of the Eyes. *J Applied Phil*, 10(2), 139-146, 1993.

Is a scientific attitude to the natural world an obstacle to an appreciation of its value? This paper argues that it is not. Following Aristotle and Marx, it maintains that, properly pursued, science has value because it enables us to contemplate that which is wonderful and beautiful. However, the paper concedes that, as actually practised, science can foster a vice described by Augustine as 'the lust of the eyes': knowledge is sought not to open us to the world, but merely to satisfy the itch of curiosity. If scientific knowledge is thus pursued, no limits to the means to it nor to its objects are recognized. Those who thus seek knowledge fail to understand its value.

O'Neill, John. *Worlds Without Content: Against Formalism*. New York, Routledge, 1992.

For the Enlightenment, science represented an ideal of rational argument, behaviour and community against which could be judged other spheres of human practice. This enlightenment ideal runs through much liberal and socialist theory. However, it has appeared to many to be increasingly uncompelling. What explains its apparent decline? One neglected answer proposed by Husserl is that its decline is rooted in the growth of formalism in the sciences. This book criticises defences of such formalism. However, it rejects Husserl's own views on the formalization of the sciences. It shows that the rise of a formalism is founded in the professionalization of modern science, and discusses the significance of this professionalization for the fate of the Enlightenment view of science.

O'Neill, Len. Peirce and the Nature of Evidence. *Trans Peirce Soc*, 29(2), 211-224, Spr 93.

This paper begins by outlining the major contemporary positions on whether, and if so, why, evidence that has been predicted from a previously specified hypothesis is more significant than evidence accommodated by a subsequent hypothesis. It is then argued that while Peirce is committed to the special efficacy of prediction, it is unclear just what support he offers for this. While Peirce hints at a number of approaches, the position of greatest plausibility and contemporary significance is based on recognizing the difference between the *ability to accommodate* data and the *ability to predict* data. The second, but not the first, involves the ability to select true hypotheses. Predictive success is evidence of this ability and consequently of the truth of the hypothesis in question.

O'Neill, Onora. Justice, Gender and International Boundaries in International Justice and the Third World, Attfield, Robin (ed). New York, Routledge, 1992.

Idealized conceptions of boundaries are common in discussions of sovereignty and states; idealized conceptions of autonomy and independence in discussions of women's issues. The problem in each case is not as is often alleged abstraction (which is unavoidable) but reliance on fictitious premisses. These are avoidable, and avoiding them would improve discussions in both domains. Throughout the case of poor women in vulnerable economies is used as a test case for various theoretical positions.

O'Neill, Onora. Justice, Gender, and International Boundaries in The Quality of Life, Nussbaum, Martha C (ed). New York, Oxford Univ Pr, 1993.

Discussions of international and of gender justice demand both that principles of justice abstract from differences between cases and that judgements of justice respond to differences between them. Abstraction and sensitivity to context are often treated as incompatible: abstraction is taken to endorse idealized models of individual and state; sensitivity to human differences is identified with relativism. An account of justice can, however, combine abstract principles with consideration of differences in their application. The case of poor women in impoverished economies - a hard case both for gender and for international justice - illustrates how universal, abstract principles of justice may not only permit but mandate differentiated application.

O'Neill, Onora. Reason and Politics in the Kantian Enterprise in Essays on Kant's Political Philosophy, Williams, Howard (ed). Chicago, Univ of Chicago Pr, 1992.

A critique of reason should show why certain ways of structuring thought and action count as reasoned while others do not. Kant's approach to this central task is surprisingly little discussed, but can be found in the prefaces, dialectic and doctrine of method of the First and Third Critiques, and in certain essays of the 1780s. He presents the demands of reason as a weak, modal constraint: reasoned thought and action should be guided by principles which can be followed by all. Reason is intersubjective, but not relativised to actual beliefs or practices; practical reason is universalisability under a meager, modal interpretation.

O'Neill, Onora. Vindicating Reason in The Cambridge Companion to Kant, Guyer, Paul (ed). New York, Cambridge Univ Pr, 1992.

Did Kant criticize reason, or did he simply take it as given and use it to criticize other matters? This paper sketches Kant's attempt to distinguish the unity he attributes to reason, the vindication he offers for its fundamental principle and to suggest how derivative principles of reason may be related to that principle. It offers a constructivist reading of Kant's account of reason, which locates reason's spare yet demanding authority in the requirement that thought and action not be based on principles others cannot follow. Kantian reason is a matter of double modality, of the *necessity* to rely on principles that are *possible* for others.

O'Reilly, Paul. Academic Freedom. *Lyceum*, 1(1), 25-32, Wint 89.

O'Shaughnessy, Brian. Searle's Theory of Action in John Searle and His Critics, Lepore, Ernest (ed). Cambridge, Blackwell, 1991.

O'Shaughnessy, Brian. The Diversity and Unity of Action and Perception in The Contents of Experience, Crane, Tim (ed). New York, Cambridge Univ Pr, 1992.

O'Sullivan, Noel. Conservatism: A Reply to Ted Honderich. *Utilitas*, 4(1), 133-143, My 92.

O'Toole, Frederick J. Descartes' Problematic Causal Principle of Ideas. *J Phil Res*, 18, 167-191, 1993.

There is a virtual consensus among commentators on Descartes that the causal principle by which he relates the objective reality of his ideas to the formal reality of their causes is indefensible. In particular, Descartes' claim that this principle follows from the general principle which states that the cause must contain at least as much reality as the effect has been examined and rejected as logically implausible. I challenge this view by showing that there is a logically plausible derivation of the causal principle of ideas from the general causal principle. This result has important implications due to the crucial role the causal principle of ideas plays in Descartes' first *a posteriori* argument for the existence of God.

Oakes, Robert. Emanation *Ex Deus*: A Defense. *Amer Phil Quart*, 29(2), 163-171, Ap 92.

Oakes, Robert. Temporality and Divinity: An Analytic Hurdle. *Sophia (Australia)*, 31(1-2), 11-26, 1992.

Oaklander, L Nathan. On the Experience of Tenseless Time. *J Phil Res*, 18, 159-166, 1993.

Defending the tenseless theory of time requires dealing adequately with the experience of temporal becoming. The issue centers on whether the defender of tenseless time can provide an adequate analysis of the presence of experience and the appropriateness of certain of our attitudes toward future and past events. By responding to a recent article, 'Passage and the Presence of Experience', by H Scott Hestevold, I shall attempt to show that adequate analysis of tenseless time is possible.

Oaklander, L Nathan. Thank Goodness It's Over. *Philosophy*, 67(260), 256-258, Ap 92.

In a recent article, "Not Over Yet: Prior's 'Thank Goodness' Argument", Delman Kiernan-Lewis offers a new reading of Prior's much discussed argument against the tenseless theory of time according to which reality (existence) is tenseless. In this note I argue that Kiernan-Lewis's interpretation of Prior's argument does not undermine the tenseless view since it is neither unsound or invalid. I then offer a diagnosis of Kiernan-Lewis's mistakes.

Oaklander, Nathan. Zeilicovici on Temporal Becoming. *Philosophia (Israel)*, 21(3-4), 329-334, Ap 92.

The aim of David Zeilicovici's recent article "Temporal Becoming Minus the Moving Now" is clear and admirable. He wants to develop a theory of temporal becoming that (1) gives full ontological status to B-relations (2) gives full ontological status to the transitory aspect of time and (3) avoids commitment to the moving-NOW and the subsequent (McTaggart's) paradox. It does not seem to me that he succeeds in accomplishing these difficult undertakings and in this paper I attempt to explain why.

Oakley, Justin. Altruistic Surrogacy and Informed Consent. *Bioethics*, 6(4), 269-287, O 92.

A crucial premise in many recent arguments against the moral permissibility of surrogate motherhood arrangements is the claim that a woman cannot *autonomously* consent to gestating and relinquishing a child to another couple, because she cannot be fully informed about her future emotional responses to pregnancy and relinquishment. I argue that such reasoning involves a serious *non sequitur*, since neither autonomous decision-making nor informed consent requires having *this* kind of information about one's future emotional responses. Therefore, a surrogate's failure to foresee the actual emotional responses she will have in proceeding with such an arrangement does not undermine the autonomy of her decision to undertake it.

Oakley, Justin. *Morality and the Emotions*. New York, Routledge, 1991.

This book argues that emotions have moral significance in their own right. We praise others for their emotional capacities, yet we possess deeply-held assumptions about the antipathy of emotions to reason and responsibility. I argue that ethicists who marginalise the emotions often rely on inadequate accounts of what emotions *are*, and that a proper understanding of the nature of emotions enables us to see their fundamental role in our moral lives. I also discuss the extent to which we may be responsible for our emotions, and I argue that we are sometimes rightly blamed on account of our emotions.

Oaksford, Mike and Chater, Nick. Logicism, Mental Models and Everyday Reasoning: Reply to Garnham. *Mind Lang*, 8(1), 72-89, Spr 93.

Oberdan, Thomas J. The Concept of Truth in Carnap's *Logical Syntax of Language*. *Synthese*, 93(1-2), 239-260, N 92.

It is argued that Carnap's repudiation of the concept of truth in The Logical Syntax of Language was founded on his conception of logic —especially metalogic— rather than on epistemological prejudices, like his verificationism, as is usually thought. The argument proceeds by detailing the development of Carnap's *Syntax*-era philosophy and its application to problems in epistemology (e.g., protocol sentences and pseudo-object sentences). Finally, it is shown that the grounds of Carnap's repudiation of truth ultimately lead to the failure of the *Syntax* program, thus paving the way for Carnap's eventual endorsement of semantic methods.

Oberheber, Ulrike and Kotzmann, Ernst and Bammé, Arno. Basic Questions about Metaphysics of Technology: Spangler, Heidegger, Günther. *J Speculative Phil*, 7(2), 143-158, 1993.

Obst, Godehard. Leibniz's Vorstellungen über den Zusammenhang von Meteorologie und Anthropologie: "physica specialis cum medicina provisionalis". *Stud Leibniz*, 24(1), 7-24, 1992.

On the basis of the "principle of the universal connection" Leibniz connected the science of nature, anthropology and meteorology and linked climatic conditions with human diseases. In 1671-76, he put his bioclimatical conception in writing for the first time in the *Directiones*. Stimulated and supported by Caspar Neumann, Bernardo Ramazzini and Friedrich Hoffman, Leibniz since 1690 demanded in several letters and papers bioclimatic observations for Germany. The *Summarische Punctation* is the best paper, where Leibniz named the conditions for an effective bioclimatology. The present paper reports on the philosophical basis and the chronological sequence of Leibniz' bioclimatical project.

Ochs, Peter. Charles Sanders Peirce in Founders of Constructive Postmodern Philosophy, Griffin, David Ray (& others). Albany, SUNY Pr, 1993.

Charles Peirce may be labelled "the logician of postmodernism". This is because, as a *performance*, the development of his logical inquiry displayed identifiably postmodern, or more exactly postcritical, tendencies. In his later work Peirce diagrammed these tendencies, producing logics of relations and of vagueness which postcritical philosophers would find helpful guides for their own work. Interpreted in terms of his own semeiotic, Peirce's postcritical inquiry appears as a) an activity of sign-interpretation, habit-change, and corrective inquiry that b) offers claims about reality and evolution for the sake of c)reintegrating certain isolated individual thinkers into what Peirce hoped would be a universal church of pragmatic scientists.

Ochs, Peter. Pragmatic Conditions for Jewish-Christian Theological Dialogue. *Mod Theol*, 9(2), 123-140, Ap 93.

This essay offers a pragmatic analysis of a particular type of successful Jewish-Christian theological dialogue. The analysis is based on Charles Peirce's claim that pragmatic inquiry seeks to resolve the problems that stimulate it. The type is exemplified by two parallel cases: the Christian theologian George Lindbeck's dialogue with Jewish sources, and the Jewish theologian Michael Wyschogrod's dialogue with Christian sources. The conclusion is that these dialogues are stimulated by complementary problems, which members of the one biblical religion can resolve most readily by learning some specific lesson from practitioners of the other religion. The resulting model of dialogue as "reciprocal pragmatic inquiry" is compared with David Novak's phenomenological model.

Ochs, Peter. The Sentiment of Pragmatism: From the Pragmatism Maxim to a Pragmatic Faith. *Monist*, 75(4), 551-568, O 92.

The uniquely pragmatic aspect of Peirce's pragmatism in a *sentiment* of assurance derived from Jesus' injunction "That ye shall know them by their fruits." As interpreted in the pragmatic maxim, this is an *instruction* both to *trust* that any disputes or conflicts *concerning actual knowledge of this world* will be resolved *and* to look for that resolution in the consequences of those disputes for future conduct in the world. As interpreted in Peirce's pragmaticism, the sentiment also provides for *dialogic* solutions. By way of illustration, a contemporary dispute among historicist and foundationalist *pragmatists* is resolved by redescribing pramaticist inquiry as a dialogue between *pragmatically* historicist and foundationalist interpretive tendencies.

Ockham, Guillermo and Guerrero, Luis (ed). *Sobre la Suposicion—Guillermo de Ockham*. Mexico, Univ Panamericana, 1992.

Oddie, Graham. Act and Maxim: Value-Discrepancy and Two Theories of Power. *Phil Phenomenol Res*, 53(1), 71-92, Mr 93.

Value-discrepancy obtains if the value of each act of maxim-compliance is lower than the value of each act of non-compliance, even though maxim-compliance overall would be best. The focus is a single perduring individual rather than a group of synchronic agents. It is shown that under typical conditions there is a straightforward way for the act consequentialist to harmonize the values of act and maxim, and a simple theorem of 'extensional equivalence' is proved. But this reveals the conditions under which genuine discrepancy arises. Rule-consequentialism can be avoided by the strategy theory of ability: that agents are endowed with non-causal powers over future events by the strategies open to them.

Oddie, Graham. Addiction and the Value of Freedom. *Bioethics*, 7(5), 373-401, O 93.

Is addiction intrinsically bad? A careful analysis of addiction supports a *prima facie* argument—from the possibility of bad cases—against addiction, but the associated disvalue is extrinsic. Any argument for the thesis of the intrinsic disvalue of addiction must turn on loss of freedom, and of the consequent loss of the value of freedom. Weak and a strong theses of freedom's value are distinguished. The strong thesis is implausible. The weak thesis is plausible, but, by bare difference arguments, it is shown that the weak thesis cannot be utilized without begging the question at issue. Particular cases are used to illustrate the conclusions.

Oddie, Graham and Perrett, Roy W. Simultaneity and God's Timelessness. *Sophia (Australia)*, 31(1-2), 123-127, 1992.

We argue that the following *reductio* of God's timelessness is unsound. A timeless omniscient God would know all temporal events "at once". Hence (by transitivity of simultaneity) all temporal events would be simultaneous with one another (contradicting their evident temporal sequence). We argue that, provided simultaneity is a *three*-place relation, between two events and an observer (or point of view), this reductio fails. Relativity theory embodies the idea that simultaneity is a three-place relation, and so if there is something fundamentally wrong with our deflection of the criticism, then so too with the conception of simultaneity within STR.

Odegard, Douglas. Inner States. *Personalist Forum*, 8/1(Supp), 265-273, Spr 92.

We can maintain an asymmetry between the way we stand to some of our own states and the way we stand to the states of others without making excessive epistemic claims about ourselves and without understanding our epistemic claims about others. An inner state is a state such that there must be immediate reason for us to believe that we are in it if we are in it and if we have the appropriate concepts. We can claim to know that we are in such states without having to claim incorrigibility, and we can claim to know that others are in such states without having to treat our knowledge as inferential. Some consequences are sketched for materialism and for our conception of subjects and of mental states.

Odegard, Douglas. Locke and General Knowledge: A Reconstruction. *Hist Phil Quart*, 10(3), 225-239, Jl 93.

John Locke thinks that we know something only if we are certain of it and only if we are certain that nothing will emerge in future to overturn it. As a result, he thinks that our general knowledge must be nonempirical. But it is usually impossible to get nonempirical guarantees about future evidence. Therefore his position needs reconstructing if it is to avoid scepticism. The best reconstruction treats predictions about future evidence as empirical and confines the nonempirical dimension of knowledge to reasons for belief.

Odegard, Douglas. Resolving Epistemic Dilemmas. *Austl J Phil*, 71(2), 161-168, Je 93.

There are cases in which our evidence for holding a belief changes when the belief is adopted such that, whereas initially we have adequate evidence for holding the belief, we cease to have adequate evidence upon adopting it. According to Richard Foley, we are in an epistemic dilemma: we should neither deny the belief nor adopt it nor withhold on it. The dilemma is best resolved by noting that we have two epistemic goals and that one goal is prior to the other.

Odelstad, Jan. *Invariance and Structural Dependence*. New York, Springer-Verlag, 1992.

Structural dependence is a relation holding between attributes. An attribute is viewed as a function which has sets as arguments and set-theoretical structures as values. Different notions of stability are defined. A distinction between dependence in the sense of determination and in the sense of relevance is drawn. Structural dependence both in the sense of determination and relevance can be found in varying degrees, ranging from complete determination and elevance to complete underdetermination and irrelevance. The possibility of different "scales" of determination and relevance is considered. The dependence relations in social choice and group decision theory are studied.

Oden, Gregg C and Lopes, Lola L. The Rationality of Intelligence in Probability and Rationality, Eells, Ellery (ed). Amsterdam, Rodopi, 1991.

Odero, José Miguel. El estatuto epistemológico de la fe: Un diálogo con Kant. *Anu Filosof*, 26(1), 113-137, 1993.

The Epistemological Status of the Faith: A Dialogue with Kant. The Kantian philosophy studies with special care the classic problem of the epistemological situation of the faith, analysing the distinctions between believing, knowing, and meaning. Kant maintains the absolute singularity of the act of faith.

Odin, Steve. The Social Self in Japanese Philosophy and American Pragmatism: A Comparative Study of Watsuji Tetsurō and George Herbert Mead. *Phil East West*, 42(3), 475-501, Jl 92.

Oechsli, Lauren and Katz, Eric. Moving beyond Anthropocentrism: Environmental Ethics, Development, and the Amazon. *Environ Ethics*, 15(1), 49-59, Spr 93.

We argue for the rejection of an anthropocentric and instrumental system of normative ethics. Moral arguments for the preservation of the environment cannot be based on the promotion of human interests or goods. The failure of anthropocentric arguments is exemplified by the dilemma of Third World development policy, e.g., the controversy over the preservation of the Amazon rain forest. Considerations of both utility and justice preclude a solution to the problems of Third World development from the restrictive framework of anthropocentric interests. A moral theory in which nature is considered to be morally considerable in itself can justify environmental policies of preservation, even in the Third World. Thus, a nonanthropocentric framework for environmental ethics should be adopted as the basis for policy decisions.

Oesterreich, P L. Das Verhältnis von ästhetischer Theorie und Rhetorik in Kants Kritik der Urteilskraft. *Kantstudien*, 83(3), 324-335, 1992.

The work focuses on three problems concerning the ambivalent attitude of Kant towards rhetoric. On one hand classical rhetoric (Cicero, Quintilian) delivers outstanding categories of Kant's esthetics, without being mentioned as a source. On the other hand Kant's ambivalence towards theories is shown: the notion of rhetorical art versus praise of artless eloquence. Finally Kant's merits for rhetorical theory are made clear: he gives a transcendental basis to the *sensus-communis* theory and thus makes possible an anthropology of the public self in society.

Oesterreich, Peter L. Thomas von Aquins Lehre von der Liebe als menschlicher Grundleidenschaft. *Theol Phil*, 66(1), 90-97, 1991.

This article represents Thomas Aquinas's theory of *amor*, which is found in the '*passio*-tract' of the *Summa theologica*. After treating the essence and appearance of *amor* the article demonstrates the ontological foundation of the *amor*-concept. Subsequently it elaborates on the implicit aesthetics as well as on the problem of *pulchritudo*. Finally the preeminence of *amor* for all other passions is pointed out.

Offe, Claus. Bindings, Shackles, Brakes in Cultural-Political Interventions in the Unfinished Project of Enlightenment, Honneth, Axel (& other eds). Cambridge, MIT Pr, 1992.

Offen, Karen. Defining Feminism: A Comparative Historical Approach in Beyond Equality and Difference, Bock, Gisela (ed). New York, Routledge, 1992.

Ogawa, Tadashi. Husserl und die Vorstruktur des Bewusstseins in Analecta Husserliana, XXXIV, Tymieniecka, Anna-Teresa (ed). Dordrecht, Kluwer, 1992.

Ogien, Ruwen. A la recherche de vérités éthiques (le réalisme moral dans la philosophie analytique). *Rev Int Phil*, 46(183), 458-486, 1992.

Ogilvy, James. Beyond Individualism and Collectivism in Revisioning Philosophy, Ogilvy, James (ed). Albany, SUNY Pr, 1992.

Ogilvy, James (ed). *Revisioning Philosophy*. Albany, SUNY Pr, 1992.

Ogor, Robert. Das gemeinsame Ziel des Menschengeschlechts in Dantes "Monarchia" und des Averroes Lehre von der Einheit des separaten Intellekts. *Frei Z Phil Theol*, 40(1-2), 88-106, 1993.

Oh, Tai K. Inherent Limitations of the Confucian Tradition in Contemporary East Asian Business Enterprises. *J Chin Phil*, 19(2), 155-169, Je 92.

The Post-Confucian ideology of South Korea, Taiwan, Singapore and Hong Kong has been recognized as a major force behind their rapid economic growth. Confucianism has produced a highly educated, disciplined, obedient work force, but it has also created some liabilities: exclusivity towards those outside the clan, a formalism which tends to create social distance and impede authentic communication, and an undue emphasis on formal education which is not well adapted to expressing the theoretical or to logical reasoning. Also, emphasis on obedience to superiors leads to suppression of negative feelings and lack of conflict resolution.

Ohkuma, Haruo. Zur Probleme um Auslegung der kantischen "Kritik der Urteilskraft" von R Oderbrecht (in Japanese). *Bigaku*, 43(2), 1-14, Fall 92.

R Odebrecht hat in seinem ersten Buch "Grundlegung der ästhetishen Werttheorie" den Standpunkt seiner Ästhetik klar gemacht, und in seinem zweiten Buch "Form und Geist", gebrauchend seinen Begriff, auf dem Gesichtspurkt der Gefühlsästhetik, kantische "Dritte Kritik" kritisiert. Seiner Versuch war von kantischen Ästhetik theoretischen und ethischen oder theologischen Einfluss auszufliessen, und die Reinheit der gefülsästhetischen Region festzustellen. Nach diesem Zweck, hat er die Widerspruche, von kantischer Begriffe, z B "Idea," "Natur," "Genie" u s w, untersucht. (edited)

Ohlsson, Ragnar. Who Can Accept Moral Dilemmas?. *J Phil*, 90(8), 405-415, Ag 93.

Ohrstrom, Peter and Hasle, Per. A N Prior's Rediscovery of Tense Logic. *Erkenntnis*, 39(1), 23-50, Jl 93.

Oinam, Bhagat. Wittgenstein, Art and Rule-Following. *Indian Phil Quart*, 20/2(Supp), 1-10, Ap 93.

The paper discusses three questions regarding aesthetic appreciation: 1) Can art be precisely defined? 2) Does appreciation of a work of art imply following certain rules? 3) Are rules viable only under a logical framework? It is not possible to discuss the essential characteristics of art without invoking Wittgensteinian notion of 'family resemblance' since there are no common similarities among different works of art.

However, public character and intelligibility of art necessarily presuppose 'rule-following' in appreciating the work. Though these rules are not fixed or pre-given, yet they are articulated and applied within a priori logical framework of possible interpretations.

Okafor, Fidelis U. Issues in African Philosophy Re-examined. *Int Phil Quart*, 33(1), 91-99, Mr 93.

The purpose of this work is to draw the attention of our professional colleagues in Africa and elsewhere who have been involved in the debate on African philosophy (Is there an African "philosophy" and if so, what exactly is it?) that their intellectual energies should be better invested in *doing* African philosophy according to their various orientations rather than insisting on reaching a consensus on the nature and method of African philosophy which is an elusive goal. The work affirms the existence of African philosophy and concludes that African philosophy is culture relative and demands a relativity in method which need not conform with the method established by Western Science and philosophy which itself is culture-determined.

Okholm, Dennis L and Hunt, Thomas C and Honer, Stanley M. *Invitation to Philosophy: Issues and Options (Sixth Edition)*. Belmont, Wadsworth, 1992.

Okolo, Chukwudum B. Self as a Problem in African Philosophy. *Int Phil Quart*, 32(4), 477-485, D 92.

The article seeks to discover the status of self in African philosophy. As in naturalism, reality in African philosophy is a series of interactions and interconnections. The African universe appears as a great 'chain of being' with things closely linked to one another. Man, the ontological mean, has necessary connections with beings above and below him. Such a view is bound to do violence to man conceived in most systems as independent, free, and intrinsic. But these values are seriously threatened in African philosophy of man. The paper concludes that African philosophy as a system is defective from this perspective.

Okonta, Ike. *Nietzsche: The Politics of Power*. New York, Lang, 1992.

This work contends that the theory of the will to power culminates in a vision of a new power politics. Although numerous studies on Nietzsche have tried to transform the will to power into a doctrine of self-mastery, evidences abound in Nietzsche's work that he considered the political arena as the realm in which the will to power finds its ultimate expression and realization. If, as most scholars acknowledge, the doctrine of the will to power was designed to undermine the democratic and socialist ideals of equal rights and equal justice, how then does such a doctrine suddenly become transformed into a doctrine of self-mastery?

Okrent, Mark. The Truth of Being and the History of Philosophy in Heidegger: A Critical Reader, Dreyfus, Hubert L (ed). Cambridge, Blackwell, 1992.

Okshevsky, Walter C. Wittgenstein on Agency and Ability: Consequences for Rationality and Criticalness. *Proc Phil Educ*, 48, 161-171, 1992.

Oladipo, Olusegun. The Debate On African Philosophy: A Critical Survey. *Indian Phil Quart*, 19(1), 42-51, Ja 92.

Oladipo, Olusegun. The Yoruba Conception of a Person: An Analytico-Philosophical Study. *Int Stud Phil*, 24(3), 15-24, 1992.

The paper analyzes the nature of the relationship between the various components of a person as postulated by the Yoruba. The author argues that the dichotomy between the material and immaterial components of a person in the Yoruba conception of a person is not the same as the dualism of body and mind which features in Western philosophy. He shows how the postulation of a quasi-material entity—*èmí*—as the categorical basis of life serves to regulate "the course of experience," even though it generates some theoretical difficulties. Finally, he contends that this conception of a person is "this-worldly" in orientation.

Olafson, Frederick A. The Unity of Heidegger's Thought in The Cambridge Companion to Heidegger, Guignon, Charles B (ed). New York, Cambridge Univ Pr, 1993.

Heidegger's philosophical career is often divided into an early and a late period and it is supposed that his preoccupation with human "existence" (*Dasein*) in the former is irreconcilable with the preeminence of being as such in the latter. When being as such is understood as presence (*Anwesen*), however, it becomes apparent that it is in fact complimentary to existence. It is shown that both are integral to Heidegger's thought throughout his career and that the famous "turning" (*Kehre*) through which it passed has to be understood as has his attempt to define the relation between the two more adequately than he had in *Being and Time*

Oldenquist, Andrew G. The Ethics of Parts and Wholes. *Crim Just Ethics*, 12(1), 43-47, Wint-Spr 93.

Oldmeadow, Harry. Sankara's Doctrine of *Maya*. *Asian Phil*, 2(2), 131-146, 1992.

Like all monisms Vedenta posits a distinction between the relatively and the absolutely Real, and a theory of illusion to explain their paradoxical relationship. Sankara's resolution of the problem emerges from his discourse on the nature of māyā which mediates the relationship of the world of empirical, manifold phenomena and the one Reality of Brahman. Their apparent separation is an illusory fissure deriving from ignorance and maintained by 'superimposition'. Māyā, enigmatic from the relative viewpoint, is not inexplicable but only not self-explanatory. Sankara's exposition is in harmony with sapiential doctrines from other religious traditions and implies a profound spiritual therapy.

Oldroyd, David and Birkett, Kirsten. Robert Hooke, Physico-Mythology, Knowledge of the World of the Ancients and Knowledge ... in The Uses of Antiquity, Gaukroger, Stephen (ed). Dordrecht, Kluwer, 1991.

Robert Hooke (1635-1702) developed a theory of the Earth which explained geological changes by supposed changes in the polar axis. He tried, unsuccessfully, to find astronomical evidence for this theory, and so turned to ancient myths for evidence. Analyzing Hooke's investigations, it is shown that he sought to interpret ancient myths as indicators of actual historical events, and as "testimony" for his catastrophist geological theory. By analogy with the term physico-theology, the term "physico-mythology" is coined for this kind of exegesis. Synoptic analyses of Hooke's interpretations of Pling, Strabo, Seneca, Virgil, Ovid, Plato, Hanno, and scripture are provided. An appendix analyzes the contents of Hooke's personal library.

Olds, W Mason. Charles F Potter: On Evolution and Religious Humanism in God, Values, and Empiricism, Peden, Creighton (ed). Macon, Mercer Univ Pr, 1989.

Olejnik, Roman M. Kazimierz Twardwski filosofo e fondatore. *Aquinas*, 35(3), 653-660, S-D 92.

The Scholar, who at the start of this century has indicated the direction towards philosophy not only of the School of Leopoli but, in a certain sense, of the whole Poland, was Kazimierz Twardowski. This study presents briefly his biography and his activity as teacher and as organiser. The knowledge of the setting in which he was formed in the intellectual attitude of the founder of the Philosophical School of Leopoli— Warsaw can facilitate a brief exposition of the theories of Twardowski. He was an excellent Brentanist, and in the development of this doctrine he stands midway between F Brantano and E Husserl. K Twardowski is the founder of the School which represents a relevant trend in modern analytical philosophy.

Olesen, Soren Gosvig. Variation in Analecta Husserliana, XXXIV, Tymieniecka, Anna-Teresa (ed). Dordrecht, Kluwer, 1992.

Olin, Doris (ed). *William James: Pragmatism in Focus*. New York, Routledge, 1992.

This work contains a reprinting of James' *Pragmatism*, along with critical commentary. Both the introduction and the critical discussion focus on the theories of meaning and truth central to Pragmatism. The essays in the discussion selection include classic papers by Moore and Russell, as well as more recent commentary.

Olivé, León. Conceptual Relativism and Philosophy in the Americas in Cultural Relativism and Philosophy, Dascal, Marcelo (ed). Leiden, Brill, 1991.

Oliver, Alex. Classes and Goodman's Nominalism. *Proc Aris Soc*, 93, 179-191, 1993.

Nelson Goodman has argued that classes ought to be rejected because they violate his nominalist principle about composition: 'No distinction of entities without a distinction of content'. The principle is examined and found to be unsupported. David Lewis's argument (in his *Parts of Classes*) that classes do not violate the principle is criticized. Finally, four arguments for the folk metaphysical claim that classes are composed from their members are shown to be wrong, and so, even if Goodman's principle were true, we would have no reason to believe that it applies to classes.

Oliver, Amy A. Values in Modern Mexican Thought. *J Value Inq*, 27(2), 215-230, Ap 93.

Oliver, Charles (trans) and Becker, Heribert. The Theory of Odd and Even in the Ninth Book of Euclid's Elements. *Grad Fac Phil J*, 16(1), 87-110, 1993.

Oliver, Harold H. The Relational Self in Selves, People, and Persons, Rouner, Leroy S (ed). Notre Dame, Univ Notre Dame Pr, 1992.

Oliver, Kelly. Julia Kristeva's Feminist Revolutions. *Hypatia*, 8(3), 94-114, Sum 93.

Julia Kristeva is known as rejecting feminism, nonetheless her work is useful for feminist theory. I reconsider Kristeva's rejection of feminism and her theories of difference, identity, and maternity, elaborating on Kristeva's contributions to debates over the necessity of identity politics, indicating how Kristeva's theory suggests the cause of and possible solutions to women's oppression in Western culture, and, using Kristeva's theory, setting up a framework for a feminist rethinking of politics and ethics.

Oliver, Kelly. *Reading Kristeva: Unraveling the Double-bind*. Bloomington, Indiana Univ Pr, 1993.

This is a recuperative reading of Kristeva's writings that diagnoses the contributions that her writings makes to feminist theory. This text concentrates primarily on her psychoanalytic writings of the 1980's; although it also provides an overview of her work from the late 1960's to the early 1990's. This book provides an accessible introduction to Kristeva's writings as well as a detailed and subtle analysis of that writing.

Olivier, Bert. Dislocating the Everyday: David Lynch's *Wild at Heart* as Cinema of the Grotesque. *S Afr J Phil*, 11(4), 96-102, N 92.

This article is an interpretation of the film *Wild at Heart* in terms of a philosophical-theoretical exploration of the phenomenon of the grotesque. The concept of the grotesque is subjected to historical as well as structural scrutiny—an examination which shows that it is characteristically ambivalent. This ambivalence is fleshed out by means of three pairs of concepts, namely, ideal body/exaggerated body, realism/fantasy and tragedy/comedy, all of which are applied successively to pertinent scenes from the film narrative. The significance of the fact that the grotesque appears in the film in the form of perceivable images, as opposed to literary descriptions, is noted before concluding with a brief consideration of its relevance for human existence and culture.

Olkowski, Dorothea. Monstrous Reflections in Crises in Continental Philosophy, Dallery, Arleen B (ed). Albany, SUNY Pr, 1990.

Ollig, Hans-Ludwig. Das unerledigte Metaphysikproblem: Anmerkungen zur jümgsten Metaphysikdiskussion im deutschen Sprachraum. *Theol Phil*, 65(1), 31-68, 1990.

Having in view reflections by J Habermas, W Schulz and D Henrich the article discusses the question of the legitimacy of metaphysical thinking in the present time. The author does not accept the necessity of abandoning metaphysical thinking as Habermas for one pleads for by appealing to the paradigm shift in present philosophy. The metaphysics of suspense as conceived by Schulz he also perceives as problematic as it is construed at the expense of a complete loss of an orientating dimension of philosophical knowledge. As opposed to these it is the merit of Henrich's ideas about a rehabilitation of the concept of speculation to have opposed with good reasons a theoretical defeatism as regards metaphysics.

Ollig, Hans-Ludwig. Die Aktualität der Metaphysik: Perspektiven der deutschen Gegenwartsphilosophie. *Theol Phil*, 68(1), 52-81, 1993.

Beginning with the thesis by L Honnefelder about the timeliness of the Scotist type of metaphysics, the defense by R Spaemann of a metaphysics of self-being, the attempt by C F Geyer to Contextualize metaphysical thinking at the end of European modernity as well as the stock-taking by R Wiehl of the results of metaphysical endeavours in the 20th century, the article tries to underline the following: Metaphysics remains timely, as philosophy can neither dispense with a reflection on the fundamental philosophical presuppositions on which it is based, nor with a reflection on its relation towards totality that of necessity is implied in human world-orientation, including the ontological and vital consequences that follow from this.

Ollig, Hans-Ludwig. Philosophische Zeitdiagnose im Zeichen des Postmodernismus. *Theol Phil*, 66(3), 338-364, 1991.

The article is concerned with three German variations of post-modernism, i.e., the plea by W Welsch for post-modern pluralism, P Sloterdijk's renunciation of the immobilism of modernity and with P Koslowski's concept of a post-modern essentialism. The author demonstrates that the concept of "post-modernism" in all three authors displays a lack of clarity and enumerated deficiencies of their attempt at a diagnosis of the present time in the light of post-modernism.

Ollman, Bertell. *Dialectical Investigations*. New York, Routledge, 1992.

Dialectical Investigations offer a unique combination of beginner's manual and advanced guide to dialectics, particularly for those who wish to use it in their research. The most distinctive quality of the work is its detailed reconstruction of Marx's process of abstraction, which is presented as the key for "putting dialectics to work". The book also offers seven case studies that illustrate the application of dialectics to a wide range of social and historical phenomena.

Olshewsky, Thomas M. Peirce's Antifoundationalism. *Trans Peirce Soc*, 29(3), 401-409, Sum 93.

Olson, Alan M (ed) and Parr, Christopher (ed) and Parr, Debra (ed). *Video Icons and Values*. Albany, SUNY Pr, 1991.

This collection of essays considers various aspects of television as the most powerful agent of value formation in today's world. The negative and positive implications and consequences of video technology are discussed. Among the more prominent issues and questions: In what ways can television be considered an "agent of value formation?" What is the impact of conventional, commercially formatted, broadcast television on perception and meaning, values and critical judgment? Is the growing problem of *aliteracy* today directly attributable to television? Contributors include: Rebecca Abbott, Dick Hebdige, Gregor Goethals, Renee Hobbs, Lenore Langsdorf, Jeremy Murray-Brown, Alan M Olson, Christopher and Debra Parr, Robert Scholes, and E David Thorp.

Olszewski, S. Time Topology for Some Classical and Quantum Non-Relativistic Systems (in Polish). *Stud Phil Christ*, 28(1), 119-135, 1992.

In this paper, we examined a problem of the topology of the time scale. As an alternative to an open, or linear scale, there are presented arguments for a closed, or circular scale of time. As the first step, we pointed out that the time scale can be a subjective notion dependent on the physical properties of a given system and the perception ability of an observer connected with that system. As a second step, in order to have an idea about the topology of the time scale for microphysical systems, this topology was examined for a non-degenerate quantum-mechanical system perturbed by a small potential. (edited)

Omata, Izumi. L'art comme absence—autour de Foucault (in Japanese). *Bigaku*, 43(2), 36-46, Fall 92.

Le rapport de l'Art à la réalité a été discuté en discours modernes comme le moment positif pour changer dislectiquement l'état social et politique. Posant la (réalité) unique, les pratiques diverses de l'Art devaient présenter à celle-ci la vision idéale ou l'image utopique au-delà de l'Histoire. Cet article a pour but de reconsidérère cette relation entre la réalité et l'art, en examinant la pensée implicite et singulière sur le réel de M Foucault. Autour de son texte *Les mots et les choses* (1966), on peut suivre le développement de cette pensée à travers les usages du mot (être). Il montre la dualité de ce terme et en ce point, dévoilant le processus de (redoulbement) propre à la représentation classique, suggère l'invisibilité ou plutôt l'absence de la chose même. Le (Même) objectif de la représentation est défait par son dualisme de (dédoublement) du visible et l'énoncable. Ainsi la (réalité) totale et unique s'échappera à l'interstice des deux termes. (edited)

Ono, Hiroakira. The Contraction Rule and Decision Problems for Logics Without Structural Rules. *Stud Log*, 50(2), 299-319, Je 91.

This paper shows a role of the contract rule in decision problems for the logics weaker than the intuitionistic logic that are obtained by deleting some or all of structural rules. It is well-known that for such a predicate logic L, if L does not have the contraction rule then it is decidable. In this paper, it will be shown first that the predicate logic FL(subscript)ec with the contraction and exchange rules, but without the weakening rule, is undecidable while the propositional fragment of FL(subscript)ec is decidable. On the other hand, it will be remarked that logics without the contradiction rule are still decidable, if our language contains function symbols.

Onwurah, Emeka. Consecration in Igbo Traditional Religion: A Definition. *J Dharma*, 17(3), 210-219, Jl-S 92.

The paper searches for an interpretative meaning of *Consecration* in the light of Igbo and Western world-views. Issues of methodology are raised. Having established some doubts on the essentialist approach, the dice is cast on the phenomenological approach which is considered suitable because it is situationally oriented and fits into a tripartite description of *Consecration* in Igbo Religion: transcendental, horizontal, and psychological. The author calls for further discussions and probings as he has merely provoked an awareness as to how domestication of words in foreign category can be used to research on some aspect of the traditional religion of Africa.

Oppenheim, Felix E. *The Place of Morality in Foreign Policy*. New York, Lexington Books, 1991.

Oppenheim, Frank. Major Developments in Royce's Ethics after the "Problem" in Frontiers in American Philosophy, Volume I, Burch, Robert W (ed). College Station, Texas A&M Univ Pr, 1992.

Oppenheim, Frank. *Royce's Mature Ethics*. Notre Dame, Univ Notre Dame Pr, 1993.

This work examines Josiah Royce's 1912-1916 ethics by analyzing archival materials—some recently discovered—and published sources. Acknowledging the links of Royce's late logic and ethics, the author clarifies how Royce connects his ethics with his interpretive epistemology and process metaphysics of community guided by the Logos-Spirit. After documenting Royce's integrated ethical method and his art of loyalty, the study identifies the mature Royce's maximal ethical insights: his harmonizing both of Freedom, Good, and Duty and of three species of integrated loyalty, his burdgeoning ethics of responsibility, and the role of hope in true loyalty.

Oppenheim, Lois. 'No Matter How No Matter Where': The Unlit in S Beckett's Not I and Stirrings Still in Analecta Husserliana, XXXVIII, Tymieniecka, Anna-Teresa (ed). Dordrecht, Kluwer, 1992.

This essay describes the topology of creative function and, specifically, delimits the point of juncture of imaginative function with the elemental force of light in Beckett's late work. The compulsion to be seen, and the objectivation of self signified by the doubling of character evident in so many of his texts, is explored in the context of the fading of light which leads, paradoxically, not to the dark as end, but as a starting point for another appearance. The negative productivity of the absence or fading of light in Beckett's mid-to-late work reflects both the process by which the text reveals its own poetic function and an expansion of ontological vision born of minimization: From *Not I* to *Stirrings Still*, each of Beckett's writings, *in enacting the irreducibility of the conundrum of human existence to conceptualization*, contains the whole of our ontological plight.

Oppy, Graham. Is God Good By Definition?. *Relig Stud*, 28(4), 467-474, D 92.

Many people have held that it is a definitional, or necessary, or conceptual truth about God that God is perfectly good. I argue that these people are *a fortiori* committed to an objectionably strong objectivist meta-ethic (of the kind derided by J L Mackie).

Oppy, Graham. Makin's Ontological Argument Again. *Philosophy*, 68(264), 234-239, Ap 93.

This discussion note is a reply to Stephen Makin's "The Ontological Argument Defended", *Philosophy* 67, 1992. In particular, I take issue with some of his criticisms of my "Makin on the Ontological Argument", *Philosophy* 66, 1991, which was a critique of his "The Ontological Argument", *Philosophy* 63, 1988. I argue: 1) that, even in its most robust form, his ontological argument can be parodied to its detriment; and 2) that his ontological argument is vitiated by a fallacy of equivocation.

Oppy, Graham. Modal Theistic Arguments. *Sophia (Australia)*, 32(2), 17-24, Jl 93.

The principal contention advanced in this paper is that theists and non-theists have differing conceptions of the nature of logical space. The main consequence which is claimed to follow from this contention is that *modal* arguments for the existence (or non-existence) of God—exemplified in the work of Plantinga and Leftow, among many others—which depend upon the unargued selection of a favored conception are simply question-begging.

Oppy, Graham. On Defining Art Historically. *Brit J Aes*, 32(2), 153-161, Ap 92.

This paper is a critical study of Jerrold Levinson's "Defining Art Historically", *British Journal of Aesthetics*, 19, 1979, 232-250, and of the subsequent literature generated by this paper. The central claim is that it is very unlikely that any attempted historical definition of "art" will succeed.

Oppy, Graham. On Functional Definitions of Art: A Response to Rowe. *Brit J Aes*, 33(1), 67-71, Ja 93.

In a recent work, M W Rowe argues 1) that art can be defined functionally; and 2) that this definition entails that works of art must achieve a certain level of value. I claim that, if art can be defined functionally—in terms of the proper function of works of art—the definition will not have the consequence which Rowe predicts.

Oppy, Graham. Why Semantic Innocence?. *Austl J Phil*, 70(4), 445-454, D 92.

Many recent semantic theories, e.g., those of Scott Soames, Nathan Salmon, Mark Crimmins and John Perry—have endorsed the principle of semantic innocence. I argue 1) that there is no good argument in favour of adoption of this principle; and 2) that there is reason to prefer theories which do not accept this principle.

Ordeshook, Peter C. Some Rules of Constitutional Design. *Soc Phil Pol*, 10(2), 198-232, Sum 93.

Orlowska, Ewa. Relational Formalization of Temporal Logics in Advances in Scientific Philosophy, Schurz, Gerhard (ed). Amsterdam, Rodopi, 1991.

Orlowska, Ewa. Relational Proof System for Relevant Logics. *J Sym Log*, 57(4), 1425-1440, D 92.

A method is presented for constructing natural deduction-style systems for propositional relevant logics. The method consists in first translating formulas of relevant logics into ternary relations, and then defining deduction rules for a corresponding logic of ternary relations. Proof systems of that form are given for various relevant logics. A class of algebras of ternary relations is introduced that provides a relation-algebraic semantics for relevant logics.

Ormell, Christopher. Is the *Uncertainty* of Mathematics the Real Source of Its Intellectual Charm?. *J Phil Educ*, 27(1), 125-133, Sum 93.

This is a review of a collection of papers on radical constructivism in mathematics education, edited by E von Glaserfeld. The theme of the review is to question the basic premise of "radical constructivism" that mathematics can be made more teachable to reluctant learners by stressing its *uncertainty*. It is suggested that what learners need most is to be shown the *purpose* of "maths" in human contexts; and this, it is argued, can be best done by emphasizing its Peircean applicability.

Ormell, Christopher. Marx's Deficient Promise. *Philosophy*, 67(262), 552-558, O 92.

Marx was not a 'philosopher' in the modern sense. He claimed that we would all be happier if we systematically changed our values. His 'Alternative Social Contract' is not 'falsifiable' in the narrow, scientific sense, but it is, in effect, a 'promise', and it *did* need to deliver what it promised, if it was to retain its potency. The central concept in Marx is 'exploitation': his definition of this entailed the progressive impoverishment of the state, by cutting off rewards for enterprise. Exploitation in the genuine sense still exists and requires a proper logical analysis.

Ormell, Christopher. Values Versus Values. *J Moral Educ*, 22(1), 31-45, 1993.

Close analysis of the word 'values' shows that it covers two quite distinct meanings: a heavier sense in which to possess a value is to accept rigorous obligations to act, and a lighter sense in which it does not. It is suggested that the capital 'V' should be used in the heavier case in written work. Educational Values are not a distinct variety of Values, simply a subset of ordinary Values. It is suggested that schools should be encouraged to adopt distinctive Values, offering a diversity of regimes to the parent population.

Ormiston, Gayle. Postmodern *Différends* in Crises in Continental Philosophy, Dallery, Arleen B (ed). Albany, SUNY Pr, 1990.

This paper presents an attempt to make explicit links between two texts by Jean-Francois Lyotard, *The Postmodern Condition* and *The Differand*. These links are articulated by way of an exegesis of a specific line from *The Differand*: "Reality relays the *differend*". The purpose of this exegesis is to describe the presumptions behind Lyotard's rendering of the phrase "the postmodern condition". Links with other Lyotard texts are made to facilitate the working hypothesis of the paper which is "from the outset, 'the postmodern condition is' is 'schizo'".

Ormiston, Gayle and Sassower, Raphael. From Marx's Politics to Rorty's Poetics: Shifts in the Critique of Metaphysics. *Man World*, 26(1), 63-82, Ja 93.

Using Rorty's distinctions between systematic and edifying discourses, the cultures and vocabularies of Philosophy and post-philosophy, and (more recently) "metaphysics" and "poetry," the paper proceeds in three phases: 1) offering an exploration of Rorty's treatment of Marx as an *edifying* thinker in *Philosophy and the Mirror of Nature*, and then, as a *metaphysician* in *Contingency, irony, solidarity*; 2) exploring Rorty's "critique of metaphysics," in terms of how "metaphysics" is defined and determined by Rorty in his efforts to dismiss all but those who he classifies as liberal ironists, and applying the critique to Rorty's own vocabularies and texts; and 3) examining the concepts of "progress" and "replacement" and the role these concepts play in Rorty's critique of metaphysics. The paper ends questioning the status (ontological or otherwise) of any critique, analysis, or narrative vis-a-vis the topic, problem or question it identifies and the purposes for which that identification has been made.

Orzechowski, Axel. Der gegenwärtige Schelling: Positionen der heutigen Schelling-Forschung—Ein Bericht. *Z Phil Forsch*, 47(2), 301-306, Ap-Je 93.

Osborne, Peter and Beezer, Anne. Orientalism and After: An Interview with Edward Said. *Rad Phil*, 63, 22-32, Spr 93.

Osherson, Daniel N and Weinstein, Scott. Relevant Consequence and Empirical Inquiry. *J Phil Log*, 22(4), 437-448, Ag 93.

A criterion of adequacy is proposed for theories of relevant consequence. According to the criterion, scientists whose deductive reasoning is limited to some proposed subset of the standard consequence relation must not thereby suffer a reduction in scientific competence. A simple theory of relevant consequence is introduced and shown to satisfy the criterion with respect to a formally defined paradigm of empirical inquiry.

Oshita, Oshita O. Some Aspects of Person in an African Tradition Thought System. *J Soc Phil*, 24(2), 235-242, Fall 93.

I address the theme of Person and its attributes within the belief system of the Boki people of South Eastern Nigeria. I examine the functional relation of the personality attributes including the mind and the body. The aim of the work is the exposition of the network of heuristic beliefs within which the Bokis make meaning of their material and spiritual existence. My conclusion is that the Boki belief in the material potency of *d'tiem* (mind) and the spiritual potency of *bikoh* (body) seems to make the traditional Mind/Body problem superfluous.

Osmani, Siddiq. Commentator on 'The Relativity of the Welfare Concept' in The Quality of Life, Nussbaum, Martha C (ed). New York, Oxford Univ Pr, 1993.

Ost, David. Bioethics and Paediatrics in Contemporary Issues in Paediatric Ethics, Burgess, Michael M (ed). Lewiston, Mellen Pr, 1991.

Ost, François and Van Hoecke, Mark. Epistemological Perspectives in Legal Theory. *Ratio Juris*, 6(1), 30-47, Mr 93.

The authors deal with several important epistemological problems in legal theory. The nineteenth century background is analyzed from the emergence of legal science freed from the constraints of natural law and built on the model of the empirical sciences. The authors show how this science of law has been influenced by the social sciences and trends in ideological criticism throughout the twentieth century. The epistemological question central to legal science is tackled, i.e., what kind of "epistemological break" should there be with regard to the object studied? To answer this question, the authors plead for the adoption of a "moderate external point of view" which bears in mind lawyers' "internal point of view."

Otero, Margarita. Generic Models of the Theory of Normal Z-Rings. *Notre Dame J Form Log*, 33(3), 322-331, Sum 92.

Otero, Margarita. The Amalgamation Property in Normal Open Induction. *Notre Dame J Form Log*, 34(1), 50-55, Wint 93.

It is known that open induction (OI), the fragment of Peano arithmetic, fails to have the joint embedding property, a result due to Wilkie. On the other hand we have proved that if we require our models to be normal, that is, to be integrally closed in their fraction fields, the corresponding theory NOI extending OI, has the joint embedding property. Here we prove NOI does not have the amalgamation property.

Otero, Margarita. The Joint Embedding Porperty in Normal Open Induction. *Annals Pure Applied Log*, 60(3), 275-290, My 93.

The models of normal open induction are those discretely ordered rings, integrally closed in their fraction field whose nonnegative part satisfy Peano's induction axioms for open formulas in the language of ordering semirings. It is known that neither open induction nor the usually studied stronger fragments of arithmetic (where induction for quantified formulas is allowed), have the joint embedding property. We prove that normal models of open induction have the joint embedding property.

Otruba, Mojmir. The Prisoner and the Prison in 2: Song of Macha's May (in Czechoslovakian). *Estetika*, 29(4), 18-35, 1992.

Ott, Heinrich. Experience of the Holy in the Technological Age. *J Dharma*, 18(2), 106-113, Ap-Je 93.

Ott, Walter. Why Legal Positivism Cannot Be Proved to Be True. *Vera Lex*, 11(2), 19-22, 1991.

Otte, Richard. Schlesinger on Miracles. *Faith Phil*, 10(1), 93-98, Ja 93.

George Schlesinger has recently presented a reply to Hume's argument concerning miracles. Schlesinger argues that probability theory and some simple assumptions about miracles show that testimony for a miracle increases the probability of God existing; furthermore this testimony can raise the probability of God existing enough that it is rational to believe that God exists. I argue that one of the assumptions that Schlesinger makes is false, and that the justification Schlesinger gives for it does not succeed. Thus I claim Schlesinger's reply to Hume fails.

Ottow, Raimund. Why John Stuart Mill Called Himself a Socialist. *Hist Euro Ideas*, 17(4), 479-483, Jl 93.

The article furnishes a set of explanatory arguments why Mill called himself a socialist in his posthumous autobiography. The stress is laid on the negative reaction of the English establishment provoked by the mounting socialist threat against private property, whereas Mill adhered to his ideas of social reform and accepted experimental socialism.

Otubusin, Paul. *Exploitation, Unequal Exchange and Dependency: A Dialectical Development*. New York, Lang, 1992.

There is no more central concept in contemporary Marxian theory than that of exploitation. Western analytical Marxists have refined and revised the concept. Third World theorists have extended it from class to country. Political regimes have drawn policy conclusions. Dr Otubusin has constructed a framework within which to situate these developments and one which highlights the normative presuppositions of the various theorists. He has managed a synthesis of a vast amount of diverse literature and has offered a cogent critical analysis. Dr. Otubusin has "exploited" his training in both philosophy and political science to produce a compelling piece of work.

Oudemans, T C W. The Never Setting Sun (in Dutch). *Tijdschr Filosof*, 54(3), 424-456, S 92.

This article attempts to interpret an enigmatic statement of Heidegger from his 1966 seminar on Heraclitus (held together with Eugen Fink): "The question is, whether the setting of the sun is a necessary representation, or if there is a possible way of seeing for which the sun never sets." The interpretation given here places the statement in the light of the Copernican revolution and the way this revolution is threatening the sun of daily life and poetry. In doing this, the author enters into dialogue with the 16th fragment of Heraclitus.

Outhwaite, William (ed) and Bottomore, Tom (ed). *The Blackwell Dictionary of Twentieth-Century Social Thought*. Cambridge, Blackwell, 1993.

Twentieth-Century social thought rages widely from the social sciences to philosophy, political theories and doctrines, cultural ideas and movements, and the influence of the natural sciences. This Dictionary aims to provide a reliable and comprehensive overview of the main themes of social thought, principal schools and movements of thought and those institutions that have been the subject of social analysis or engendered significant doctrines and ideas. Long entries cover major currents of thought, philosophical and cultural trends and the individual social sciences. These are supplemented by shorter accounts of specific concepts and phenomena.

Overall, Christine. Access to In Vitro Fertilization: Costs, Care and Consent. *Dialogue (Canada)*, 30(3), 383-397, Sum 91.

What would be a caring approach to providing procedures of artificial reproduction such as in vitro fertilization (IVF)? 1) Liberal theorists suggest that access to IVF is a matter of right. 2) Existing social policies imply that access to IVF is a privilege. 3) Religious conservatives argue that, because of its alleged violation of family values, IVF should not be available at all, while some feminists draw a similar conclusion on the different grounds of IVF's risks and low success rate. After evaluating each view, I offer a feminist alternative, describing a caring and careful means of providing IVF.

Overvold, Gary E. The Foundationalist Conflict in Husserl's Rationalism in Analecta Husserliana, XXXIV, Tymieniecka, Anna-Teresa (ed). Dordrecht, Kluwer, 1992.

Husserl cannot, without contradiction, simultaneously maintain two of his central theses. He cannot both claim that apodicticity is the necessary standard of evidence for a rigorously scientific philosophy and concurrently maintain that philosophy must be free from aprioristic presuppositions about its systematic final structure. Husserl had three options for resolving this dilemma. Of the three, the one he chose most violated the spirit of his phenomenological methods and the one he should have chosen most violated his notion of philosophy as rigorous science. My conclusion is that Heidegger was correct in claiming that phenomenology can only be practiced hermeneutically.

Owen, David. Hume and the Lockean Background: Induction and the Uniformity Principle. *Hume Stud*, 18(2), 179-207, N 92.

Hume's argument concerning induction is often interpreted according to modern conceptions of deductive and inductive reasoning. This article argues that Hume's account of reasoning is derivative from, and a reaction to, Locke's account of reasoning as based on a relation between ideas, and that no notion of deductive validity plays any role in either Locke or Hume's account. Hume's negative argument concerning induction is re-interpreted in this light, and it is argued that its target is very likely Locke's account of probable reasoning.

Owen, David (ed) and Cummins, Robert (ed). *Central Readings in the History of Modern Philosophy: Descartes to Kant*. Belmont, Wadsworth, 1992.

This is a book of readings for standard mid-level undergraduate courses on the history of early modern philosophy. It provides, in a single volume, the major texts of the most studied figures of the period: Descartes' *Meditations*, Spinoza's *Ethics* (Books I and II), Leibniz' *Monadology*, Locke's *Essay Concerning Human Understanding* (abridged) and *Three Dialogues*, Hume's *An Enquiry Concerning Human Understanding* and Kant's *Critique of Pure Reason* (abridged). Editing is minimal, complete texts being used in most cases. Even where texts are abridged, the sections used are always complete in themselves. Sample syllabi are provided as guides for using this book in different sorts of courses.

Owen, Roderick. What is a "Postmodern" Education and What Does It Have to Do With Lifelong Learning?. *Proc S Atlantic Phil Educ Soc*, 36, 123-125, 1991.

Owens, David. *Causes and Coincidences*. New York, Cambridge Univ Pr, 1992.

The book deals with several of the major issues in the philosophy of causation: the direction of causation, the difference between causal and non-causal explanation, the logical form of causal statements and the nature of events, causation and reduction, causation in perception and action. First it is argued that to explain an event we must do more than cite a necessary and sufficient for its occurrence: we must show it is no coincidence as well. Then, the above problems are tackled by equating causation with causal explanation so understood.

Owens, Joseph. Analytic and Continental Philosophies in Overall Perspective. *Mod Sch*, 70(2), 131-142, Ja 93.

During the past six decades, analytic and Continental writers have spread their discussions over most of the traditional problems of western philosophy. Viewed in overall perspective, these thinkers differ from preceding philosophers in their selection of basic starting points. Pre-Cartesian philosophers had located the starting points in things eternal to human cognition, while a modern philosophers had placed them in human ideas or sensations. In contrast, the analytic and Continental philosophers find theirs in language, and proceed in the one case by way of logical analysis and in the other through the historicity involved in human speech.

Owens, Joseph. Aristotle and Aquinas on Cognition. *Can J Phil*, Supp(17), 103-123, 1991.

This book is basically a study of the quantum leaps between philosophies. Bertrand Russell observed that no two philosophers ever understand one another. The reason is that ancient and medieval philosophers take "things in themselves" as the starting points, modern or Enlightenment philosophers place them in ideas, postmodern philosophers seek them in language with the historicity thereby involved. In each of these areas an indefinitely numerous variety of starting points is possible. This renders philosophies as individual as fingerprints or DNA, but with family resemblances. Today's genial pluralism is not a disease. It belongs to philosophy's very nature.

Owens, Joseph. *Cognition: An Epistemological Inquiry*. Houston, Ctr Thomistic Stud, 1992.

After reviewing the meaning and history of epistemology, this study explains the primacy of the external in human cognition. It shows how sensible things, and not our concepts or sensations of them, are basic to our knowledge. No "bridge" to the external world is required, since we are already there cognitionally in priority to awareness of self. Sensations, percepts, concepts, judgments, and reasoning are then examined in both perspectives. Finally, the panorama of the sciences and of the indefinitely numerous philosophies is surveyed, with attention to quantum leaps respectively from ancient to medieval to modern and to postmodern epochs.

Owens, Joseph. Content, Causation, and Psychophysical Supervience. *Phil Sci*, 60(2), 242-261, Je 93.

There is a growing acceptance of the idea that the explanatory states of folk psychology do not supervene on the physical. Even Fodor (1987) seems to grant as much. He argues, however, that this cannot be true of theoretical psychology. Since theoretical psychology offers causal explanations, its explanatory states must be taxonomized in such a way as to supervene on the physical. I use this concession to invert his argument and cast doubt on the received model of folk psychological explanation as causal explanation by intentionally individuated states. This in turn undermines the central model of cognitive theory—causal explanation by representational states.

Owens, Joseph. Value and Practical Knowledge in Aristotle in Essays in Ancient Greek Philosophy, IV, Anton, John P (ed). Albany, SUNY Pr, 1991.

Approach to Aristotelian practical knowledge in terms of value can hardly fail to encounter difficulties today. The difficulties are neither linguistic nor conceptual. Rather, they arise from the Kantian setting in which twentieth-century philosophy has presented the Humean opposition between judgments of value and judgments of fact. On the contrary, with Aristotle every fact has a value of some kind, while to be operative every value has to be there in fact. Against the background Aristotle faces the contrast between the morally good and the morally wrong throughout their respective grades, with practical knowledge as knowledge of the right choice.

Owens, Wayne. Husserl, Linguistic Meaning, and Intuition. *SW Phil Stud*, 15, 60-66, Spr 93.

Ozar, David. The Characteristics of a Valid "Empirical" Slippery-Slope Argument. *J Clin Ethics*, 3(4), 301-302, Wint 92.

Packer, Mark. Dissolving the Paradox of Tragedy. *J Aes Art Crit*, 47(3), 211-219, Sum 89.

The paradox of tragedy involves explaining how a literary work or drama can elicit both pain and pleasure in the same reader or viewer. It is commonly believed that because the contrary emotions occasioned by tragedy are experienced simultaneously or in close temporal proximity, they must have either a causal or intentional relationship. I argue instead that the causes of the tragic affects are separate psychological processes required for the interpretation of the text, and that their intentional objects are not one another, but logically distinct aesthetic properties of the drama.

Paden, Roger. Nature and Morality. *Environ Ethics*, 14(3), 239-251, Fall 92.

In their attempt to develop a nonanthropocentric ethic, many biocentric philosophers have been content to argue for the expansion of the moral community to include natural entities. In doing so, they have implicitly accepted the idea that the conceptions of moral duties developed by anthropocentric philosophers to describe the moral relationships that hold between humans can be directly applied to the human/nature relationship. To make this expansion plausible, they have had to argue that natural entities have traits that are similar to the morally relevant traits of human beings. Not only are these arguments often unconvincing, but it seems implausible that the same moral concepts and principles that govern human relationships also should govern human/nonhuman relationships. Many nonanthropocentric ethics, I argue, are (mistakenly) anthropomorphic. To go beyond this relationship I recommend the development of a nonanthropomorphic biocentric ethic. (edited)

Paden, Roger K. Berlin on the Nature and Significance of Liberty in Terrorism, Justice and Social Values, Peden, Creighton W (ed). Lewiston, Mellen Pr, 1990.

In "Two Concepts of Liberty," Isaiah Berlin distinguishes between two concepts of liberty, "negative" and "positive" liberty, and argues that only one concept, that of negative liberty, can ground a just social order. I argue that two other concepts of liberty lie implicit in Berlin's essay, "absolute" liberty and "reflective" liberty. Moreover, because his argument for negative liberty takes the form of a forced choice argument, the existence of these other concepts renders his argument formally invalid. Furthermore, many of his arguments actually seem to support the idea that the concept of reflective liberty should form the foundation of a just order.

Paden, Roger K. Deconstructing Speciesism: The Domain Specific Character of Moral Judgments. *Int J Applied Phil*, 7(1), 55-64, Sum 92.

The central argument in Singer's book *Animal Liberation* consists of two inconsistent parts, only one of which is utilitarian. In one part, focusing on the term "speciesism," Singer attempts to establish the scope of moral concern by appealing to Bentham's utilitarian "sentience" standard. He argues that it is speciesist to treat equal pains unequally just because they are experienced by members of different species. Having argued for the equal significance of equal treatment of all those entities that experience pain. This position, however, conflicts with utilitarianism, both theoretically and practically.

Paden, Roger K. Virtue and Repression. *Cont Phil*, 15(3), 12-15, My-Je 93.

It is widely held that a concern with moral virtue is incompatible with liberal political theory. This paper disputes that claim. Instead, it is argued, there are some essential connections between several fundamental liberal values and a particular conception of the virtues. It is further argued that, the active promotion of the virtues, so conceived, is essential to liberalism's flourishing. To make this case, two approaches to virtue theory are distinguished. It is then argued that one of these approaches, the *phronesis* approach, is not only consistent with several fundamental liberal values, but that this approach fills a fundamental gap in the psychology of the liberal individual.

Padgett, Alan. Eternity and Special Theory of Relativity. *Int Phil Quart*, 33(2), 219-223, Je 93.

Padilla-Gálvez, Jesús. Las lógicas modales en confrontación con los conceptos básicos de la lógica modal de G W Leibniz. *Theoria (Spain)*, 6(14-15), 115-127, O 91.

In the first section we examine Leibniz's "termini necesitas-possibilitas". In the second section we propose a minimal modal logic, L (subscript) LM, arises from the addition of modal principles. In the final section we examine his complex study towards the interpretation of modal language in the possible worlds. The resulting interplay between the minimal modal logic and the possible world perspective is one of the main charms of semantics.

Page, Carl. On Being False by Self-Refutation. *Metaphilosophy*, 23(4), 410-426, O 92.

Page, Carl. Philosophy and the Outlandishness of Reason. *J Speculative Phil*, 7(3), 206-225, 1993.

In the figure of Socrates, Plato represents philosophy as having to defend itself before the city. The goods of the city and the goods of philosophy both have validity but lack immediate harmony. The dissonance is not a matter of misunderstanding, but follows from the natural dislocativeness of reason. Reason's outlandishness is the precondition for all human culture. Philosophy may not therefore be perfected either entirely within (historicism, sophistry) or entirely outside of politics, but mandates a constant care for the balance of theory and practise that must avoid the laziness of seeking a final, seamless whole.

Page, Carl. The Unnamed Fifth: *Republic* 369d. *Interpretation*, 21(1), 3-14, Fall 93.

At *Republic* 369d Socrates declares that the "most necessary city" is made up of "four or five men." The incompatibility of utmost necessity and Socrates' vague count is explained in terms of care's transcendence of bodily need. But who is the unnamed fifth? Benardete's interpretation that he is a warrior is examined in light of how war emerges for the City in Speech. It is argued that the unnamed fifth is not a warrior but a doctor. Medicine is the *Republic's* metaphor for the preventive and corrective aspects of rule. Some final remarks consider why the issue of rule is suppressed at this early stage of the City in Speech.

Page, Edgar. Donation, Surrogacy and Adoption in Applied Philosophy, Almond, Brenda (ed). New York, Routledge, 1992.

Page, Edgar. Parental Rights in Applied Philosophy, Almond, Brenda (ed). New York, Routledge, 1992.

Page, James. Parsons on Mathematical Intuition. *Mind*, 102(406), 223-232, Ap 93.

Charles Parsons has argued that we have the ability to apprehend, or "intuit", certain kinds of abstract objects; that among the objects we can intuit are some which form a model for arithmetic; and that our knowledge that the axioms of arithmetic are true in this model involves our intuition of these objects. I find a problem with Parson's claim that we know this model is infinite through intuition. Unless this problem can be resolved. I question whether our knowledge that the arithmetical axioms are true can reasonably be called intuitive in the way Parsons intends.

Pagonis, Constantine and Clifton, Robert and Pitowsky, Itamar. Relativity, Quantum Mechanics and EPR. *Proc Phil Sci Ass*, 1, 114-128, 1992.

The Einstein-Podolsky-Rosen argument for the incompleteness of quantum mechanics involves two assumptions: one about locality and the other about when it is legitimate to infer the existence of an element-of-reality. Using one simple thought experiment, we argue that quantum predictions and the relativity of simultaneity require that both these assumptions fail, whether or not quantum mechanics is complete.

Pahel, Kenneth R. Mental Illness and Juvenile Criminal Justice. *J Soc Phil*, 23(1), 120-131, Spr 92.

The paper analyzes a juvenile murder case and reveals numerous flaws in the juvenile justice system in general, and in the Guilty But Mentally Ill verdict in particular. Attempting to balance the public interest in order and security with the interests in protecting the rights and rehabilatative opportunities of juvenile offenders, a number of reforms are recommended.

Paik, Ki-soo. The Aesthetics of Confucius (in Czechoslovakian). *Estetika*, 29(4), 1-17, 1992.

Pailin, David A. Herbert of Cherbury: A Much-Neglected and Misunderstood Figure in God, Values, and Empiricism, Peden, Creighton (ed). Macon, Mercer Univ Pr, 1989.

After noting his complex character, this article considers Herbert of Cherbury's metaphysical thought on truth and his attempt to identify universally recognized religious truths. His epistemology both recognizes the activity of the mind in grasping what is time and endorses the common sense view of truth as the perception of things as they are. The accusation that Herbert was a deist is challenged by reference to his ideas about the reality of God, immortality, revelation, prayer, salvation, the Bible, faith, and history. On the basis of the common notions of religion he sought a reasonable, simple and universal form of theistic belief.

Pal, Jagat. Nyaya Inference: Deductive or Inductive. *Indian Phil Quart*, 20(3), 263-277, Jl 93.

The purpose of this paper is to examine the veracity of the claim, made by some of the Indian thinkers like C D Sharma, M Hiriyanna and Radhakrishnan, that Nyāya Logic is deductive-inductive in character. An attempt has been made to show that inferences in Nyāya, both of the old and the new schools, are not deductive-inductive in character, and those who have claimed it, have done it due to their misconception about the distinction of deductive and inductive inferences.

Palasinska, Katarzyna. Three-Element Nonfinitely Axiomatizable Matrices. *Bull Sec Log*, 21(4), 147-151, D 92.

Palermo, James. Dewey on the Pedagogy of Occupations: The Social Construction of the Hyper-Real. *Proc Phil Educ*, 48, 177-186, 1992.

Palladino, Franco and Gatto, Romano. The "Dutch's Problem" and Leibniz's Point of View on the "Analytic Art". *Stud Leibniz*, 24(1), 73-92, 1992.

In diesem Aufsatz untersuchen wir Leibniz' Ansicht über die "Ars Analytica". Gelegenheit dazu bietet die Diskussion über die Lösung der sogenannten "Probleme eines Holländers". Es geht dabei um 12 Probleme über das Dreieck. Gegeben sind in diesen Problemen: einer der Basiswinkel, die Differenz von Basissegmenten und ein Verhältnis, das bei den einzelnen Problemen variiert zwischen den Seiten des Dreiecks. "Die Probleme des Holländers" sind aus mehreren Gründen wichtig. Sie liefern einen aufschllussreichen Test, den Stand der Mathematik in Italien in der zweiten Hälfte des 17. Jahrhunderts zu prüfen. Sie lassen das Nebeneinanderbestehen unterschiedlicher mathematischer Methoden erkennen, und zwar klassischer und moderner Methoden. Schliessich sind die Probleme sehr interessant für den Stand der Gedanken, die Leibniz zu ihrer Behandlung äussert.

Palme Reyes, Marie La and Reyes, Gonzalo E. Montague's Semantics for Intensional Logic. *Log Anal*, 32, 319-335, S-D 89.

In this paper we shall describe a simplified version of the semantics of Montague for intensional logic as exposed in [6]. We hope that this new version is clearer than the original one and that will help to understand Montague's semantics, its achievements and its limitations. In particular, we discuss problems of identity, possibility and existence and we show some of its shortcomings to cope with these fundamental problems in the philosophy of language. This paper is a companion to [7], where a Boolean-valued version of Gupta's semantics [4] is explained and criticized. These two papers may be viewed both as an introduction and a motivation for a system of intensional logic that we believe free of the shortcomings of both Montague's and Gupta's semantics: the logic of kinds. The interested reader may consult [7] and [8].

Palmer, Anthony. *Value and Understanding: Essays for Peter Winch*: Critical Notice. *Phil Invest*, 15(3), 276-284, Jl 92.

Palmer, Anthony. Beyond Representation. *Philosophy*, 33(Supp), 153-163, 1992.

Palmer, Anthony. Beyond Representation in The Impulse to Philosophise, Griffiths, A Phillips (ed). New York, Cambridge Univ Pr, 1992.

Palmer, Lucia M. Anarchy and the Condition of Contemporary Humanism. *Hist Euro Ideas*, 16(4-6), 577-583, Ja 93.

In this study the author outlines the origin and structure of the philosophical intercontinental "anarchy" which spans Europe and English speaking America. She argues that European and American discourses disclose various alternative types of anarchies and reconstructive humanisms. The main examples of such reconstructed human types are Rorty's liberal ironist, MacIntyre's and Gadamer's virtuous individuals of *phronesis* and praxis and the practical communicative individuals of Habermas.

Palmeri, Frank. The Capacity of Narrative: Scott and Macaulay on Scottish Highlanders. *Clio*, 22(1), 37-52, Fall 92.

Palmquist, S R. Analysis and Synthesis in the Geometry of Logic. *Indian Phil Quart*, 19(1), 1-15, Ja 92.

This article introduces a new way of distinguishing between "analysis" and "synthesis", as referring to types of abstract logical relations, and shows how simple geometrical figures can be used as precise maps for each type. Analytic (twofold) relations are based on the law of noncontradiction and can be mapped directly onto line segments (first level) or crosses (second level). Synthetic (threefold) relations are based on the law of contradiction and can be mapped onto triangles. A way of combining analysis and synthesis in a (twelvefold) "compound relation" is suggested, and mapped onto a circle.

Palmquist, S R. Does Kant Reduce Religion to Morality?. *Kantstudien*, 83(2), 129-148, 1992.

The common misconception that Kant attempted to reduce religion to morality is encouraged by a misleading translation of the title of his *Religion within the Bounds of Bare Reason*, and by a misunderstanding of how its preface places the book in relation to Kant's other works. An overview of these points and of the book's contents reveals that at each stage religion goes beyond and supplements morality, making it possible to reach the otherwise unattainable goal of morality itself. Although Kant attempts a loose, "explanatory" reduction, he intends not to *eliminate religion*, but to *raise morality* to the level of religion.

Palous, Martin. Post-Totalitarian Politics and European Philosophy. *Pub Affairs Quart*, 7(2), 149-164, Ap 93.

The political reality of East European post-communist societies, exposed to the enormous power of the negative of their totalitarian past, is approached as a philosophical problem. The point of departure is the Husserlian phenomenology which aims at the revival of the spirit of Europe in the 20th century by the philosophical anamnesis of subjectivity. The philosophy of Jan Patocka—his analyses of the life-world, his "negative platonism" and the concept of philosophy as "the care about the soul"—is examined. Because the most dynamic factor in post-totalitarian politics is the state of political mind, post-totalitarian political philosophy has to reassume its classical, however in the modernity, forgotten task: to develop its questions in the concrete context of life of the polis, to exert "in the homes of humans" its original maieutical and therapeutic function.

Paltrinieri, Gian Luigi. Kant, Wittgenstein e l'argomento ontologico. *Teoria*, 11(2), 105-130, 1991.

Pande, G C. Comments on "The Development of Advaita Vedanta as a School of Philosophy". *J Indian Counc Phil Res*, 9(2), 164-167, Ja-Ap 92.

Pandey, Ashok Kumar. Kant and the Faculty Psychology. *Indian Phil Quart*, 20/1(Supp), 19-25, Ja 93.

Kant is said to have based his Critical Philosophy upon faculty psychology. But modern psychology, which regards the human mind as an organic unity of interdependent functions, rejects faculty psychology. Thus, Kant's foundation seems to be questioned. The present work attempts to prove that even if we reject faculty psychology, Kant's philosophy is not damaged. He was primarily interested in analysing different operations or activities of the mind. And these activities are not destroyed by the elimination of faculty psychology.

Pandey, S L. Comments on "The Development of Advaita Vedanta as a School of Philosophy". *J Indian Counc Phil Res*, 9(2), 168-170, Ja-Ap 92.

Pandharipande, Rajeshwari. From the Profane to the Transcendent: Japa in Tukārām's Mysticism. *J Dharma*, 17(1), 25-37, Ja-Mr 92.

Pang, Yeuk Yi and Wojciechowicz, Elizabeth. Coordinating the Emotional and Rational in Moral Education. *Eidos*, 10(1), 21-46, J-Jl 91.

Pangallo, Mario. Il posto della metafisica nel sapere umano: Il pensiero di Maimonide e eil suo influsso su S Tommaso d'Aquino. *Gregorianum*, 74(2), 331-352, 1993.

The intellectual training does not begin with Metaphysics according to Maimonides (*The Guide of the Perplexed*, I, 34). There are five main reasons for this: I) A difficulty concerning metaphysical arguments. II) The imperfection of human understanding. III) Necessity of long preparatory study. IV) The inadequacy of individual dispositions. V) Some preoccupations in the daily life. St. Thomas follows Maimonides in this question and develops his arguments. According to St. Thomas, God disclosed the metaphysical truth because otherwise people would not arrive easily at metaphysical knowledge. This question has some implications for pedagogy but also for theoretical philosophy: I) There exists a Christian philosophy; II) Philosophical knowledge is really autonomous; III) Metaphysics presupposes Physics (not vice versa) and opens it to supernatural knowledge; IV) The Metaphysics of Being implies a reflexion about the limits of human knowledge.

Panikkar, Raimundo. A Nonary of Priorities in Revisioning Philosophy, Ogilvy, James (ed). Albany, SUNY Pr, 1992.

Panneerselvam, S. Derrida and the Philosophy of Deconstruction. *Indian Phil Quart*, 19(3), 255-259, Jl 92.

Pannenberg, Wolfhart. Eine philosophisch-historische Hermeneutik des Christentums. *Theol Phil*, 66(4), 481-492, 1991.

Pannenberg, Wolfhart. Fichte und die Metaphysik des Unendlichen: Dieter Henrich zum 65 Geburstag. *Z Phil Forsch*, 46(3), 348-362, Jl-S 92.

Papa, Edward. Kant's Dubious Disciples: Hare and Rawls. *Amer Cath Phil Quart*, 65(2), 159-175, Spr 91.

Papagounos, G. On Theoretical Terms in Greek Studies in the Philosophy and History of Science, Nicolacopoulos, Pantelis (ed). Dordrecht, Kluwer, 1990.

The author proposes an alternative approach to the concept of "theoretical terms". This approach provides a better understanding of such linguistic entities than the traditional "observational- theoretical" polarity. He argues that these terms are used, first, to delineate the realm of the legitimate objects, phenomena, events, relations that the theory investigates and, second, to delimit the ontological domain of that theory by assigning existential status to the entities that the theory is about. He examines the use of such terms using examples from the historical record of science and he discusses the problems which arise in relation to this approach.

Papagounos, G and Tzavaras, Athanase. The Development of Freudian Theory in Greek Studies in the Philosophy and History of Science, Nicolacopoulos, Pantelis (ed). Dordrecht, Kluwer, 1990.

The authors develop the "centric-excentric" approach to account for the diffusion of Freudian theory. This approach explains the phenomenon of the simultaneous production, elaboration and diffusion of the psychoanalytic theory and it further ellucidates the various debates on orthodoxy and heterodoxy concerning the main tenets of the theory and the practice of psychoanalysis which were carried out in North America and the continent. The case of French psychoanalysis and in particular J Lacan is illustrative of the mode of investigation which the approach permits. Greek psychoanalysis provides another illustration of "excentric" characteristics in the case on Andreas Empiricos.

Pape, Walter. Comic Illusion and Illusion in Comedy in Aesthetic Illusion, Burwick, Frederick (ed). Hawthorne, de Gruyter, 1990.

Pape, Walter (ed) and Burwick, Frederick (ed). *Aesthetic Illusion*. Hawthorne, de Gruyter, 1990.

Papenkort, Ulrich. Philosophie und Raum in Diagrammatik und Philosophie, Gehring, Petra (ed). Amsterdam, Rodopi, 1992.

The author tries to show a significant connection between diagrammatics, grammatology, description, systematics, geography and space. It is presupposed that 1) the role of diagrammatics in philosophy can be discussed in a sufficient way only in the context of a philosophical evaluation of graphical technique, of descriptive method, of systematic thinking, and of geography as a science; 2) that in the background of every single such discussion the phenomenon of space and that of visual apperception is present; and 3) that all these moments are still underestimated in philosophical tradition.

Papineau, David. Physicalism, Consciousness and the Antipathetic Fallacy. *Austl J Phil*, 71(2), 169-183, Je 93.

Papineau argues that our ways of thinking about experiences fall into two categories: "first-person" ways, which deploy "secondary versions" of the experiences being thought about, and "third-person" ways, which do not. He argues that the contrast between these two categories is responsible for the widespread intuition that consciousness is non-physical: for there is a seductive use-mention confusion ("the antipathetic fallacy") which takes us, from the true premise that third-person thoughts about experience do not use (versions of) the experiences being referred to, to the false conclusion that they do not mention those experiences at all.

Pappas, George S. Explanatory Coherence and Data Sentences in Frontiers in American Philosophy, Volume I, Burch, Robert W (ed). College Station, Texas A&M Univ Pr, 1992.

Pappas, George S. Perception of the Self. *Hume Stud*, 18(2), 275-280, N 92.

Pappas, Gregory. William James and the Logic of Faith. *Trans Peirce Soc*, 28(4), 781-808, Fall 92.

James tells us that basic to faith is a logic that James often refers to as a faith ladder. In the first section of this paper I attempt to throw some light unto this notion of a "faith ladder" and to correct certain misconceptions of it which have arisen and might arise. Then I consider two distinct kinds of cases, presented throughout James's writings, in which this logic of belief operates. An then, in a final section, I address some philosophical implications on James' view and the belief process.

Pappas, Gregory Fernando. Dewey and Feminism: The Affective and Relationships in Dewey's Ethics. *Hypatia*, 8(2), 78-95, Spr 93.

Dewey provides an ethics that is committed to those aspects of experience that have been associated with the "feminine." In addition to an argument against the devaluation of the affective and of concrete relationships, we also find in Dewey's ethics a thoughtful appreciation of how and why these things are essential to our moral life. In this article I consider the importance of the affective and of relationships in Dewey's ethics and set out aspects of Dewey's ethics that might be useful resources for feminist writers in ethics.

Pappas, Nickolas. Authorship and Authority. *J Aes Art Crit*, 47(4), 325-332, Fall 89.

Foucault's essay "What Is an Author?" is my springboard for asking a methodological question about authorial intentions in place of the traditional epistemological question: Not "How can the author be known?" but "What is the effect on interpretative practice of trying to know it?" By resisting the assumption that knowing the author is necessary, we realize how the author- construct polices readers by legitimizing only certain effects of reading. With the author set aside, knowing intentions becomes one interpretive goal among many; other ways of reading that leave out the author are legitimate, and sometimes more fruitful.

Pappin III, Joseph L. *The Metaphysics of Edmund Burke*. Bronx, Fordham Univ Pr, 1992.

Burke revisionists, forced to acknowledge his use of the "natural law", label such use as a rhetorical means for utilitarian ends. Not only does this work challenge the "utilitarian" view of Burke, it sets out, "to make explicit the implicit metaphysical core of Burke's political thought." Pappin examines both Burke's critics and Burke's own attack on a rationalist, ideologically inspired metaphysics. Drawing from Burke's vast writings, Pappin establishes as his goal "to demonstrate that Burke's political philosophy is grounded in a realist metaphysic, one that is basically consonant with the Aristotelian-Thomistic tradition."

Paprzycka, Katarzyna. Why Do Idealizational Statements Apply to Reality? in Idealization III, Brzenzinski, Jerzy (ed). Amsterdam, Rodopi, 1992.

The essay raises the need to account for the sense in which idealizational statements apply to reality. The relation of holding-for is distinguished from the relation of application. On the positivist conception of application, which effectively identifies these two relations, one must conclude that idealizational statements do not apply to reality but only to abstract models. By suggesting how to understand the relation of application in terms of the relation of holding-for and a non-Aristotelian conception of generality, it is shown that although idealizational statements hold for ideal domains they apply to reality.

Paprzycka, Katarzyna and Paprzycki, Marcin. A Note on the Unitarian Explication of Idealization in Idealization III, Brzezinski, Jerzy (ed). Amsterdam, Rodopi, 1992.

The main function of the procedure of idealization in the sciences is to annul the influence of secondary factors. The most extensive treatment of the procedure is L Nowak's *The Structure of Idealization*. More recently, Nowak suggested an explication of the procedure of idealization as well as of the concept of influence in terms of his unitary metaphysics. It is shown that the explication falls short of explaining how when a factor is idealized its influence on another factor is annulled.

Paprzycka, Katarzyna and Paprzycki, Marcin. Accuracy, Essentiality and Idealization in Idealization III, Brzezinski, Jerzy (ed). Amsterdam, Rodopi, 1992.

According to L Nowak's idealizational reconstruction of science, scientists first propose (idealizational) laws which incorporate only principal factors, and then gradually concretize the laws with respect to secondary factors—in the order of the latter's essentiality. One sense of such methodological rule is investigated: the more essential a factor the more accurate is the statement incorporating it. It is shown that the order of essentiality of factors and the order of accuracy they afford align only under strong assumptions. This suggests that scientists follow two methodological rules: "theoreticians" follow the order of essentiality, "practitioners" follow the order of relative accuracy.

Paprzycki, Marcin and Paprzycka, Katarzyna. A Note on the Unitarian Explication of Idealization in Idealization III, Brzezinski, Jerzy (ed). Amsterdam, Rodopi, 1992.

The main function of the procedure of idealization in the sciences is to annul the influence of secondary factors. The most extensive treatment of the procedure is L Nowak's *The Structure of Idealization*. More recently, Nowak suggested an explication of the procedure of idealization as well as of the concept of influence in terms of his unitary metaphysics. It is shown that the explication falls short of explaining how when a factor is idealized its influence on another factor is annulled.

Paprzycki, Marcin and Paprzycka, Katarzyna. Accuracy, Essentiality and Idealization in Idealization III, Brzezinski, Jerzy (ed). Amsterdam, Rodopi, 1992.

According to L Nowak's idealizational reconstruction of science, scientists first propose (idealizational) laws which incorporate only principal factors, and then gradually concretize the laws with respect to secondary factors—in the order of the latter's essentiality. One sense of such methodological rule is investigated: the more essential a factor the more accurate is the statement incorporating it. It is shown that the order of essentiality of factors and the order of accuracy they afford align only under strong assumptions. This suggests that scientists follow two methodological rules: "theoreticians" follow the order of essentiality, "practitioners" follow the order of relative accuracy.

Parekh, Bhikhu. A Critique of the Liberal Discourse on Violence in Socialism and Morality, McLellan, David (ed). New York, St Martin's Pr, 1990.

This paper seeks to explore a paradox. The liberal society disapproves of violence, yet it commits much violence in practice. The author argues that the explanation lies in many of the hidden assumptions of liberal thought. He identifies eight of them and subjects them to a searching critique. He ends by outlining an alternative mode of discourse on violence.

Parekh, Bhikhu. The Liberal Discourse on Violence in Selves, People, and Persons, Rouner, Leroy S (ed). Notre Dame, Univ Notre Dame Pr, 1992.

Parekh, Bhikhu. The Poverty of Indian Political Theory. *Hist Polit Thought*, 13(3), 535-560, Autumn 92.

The author argues that independent India has thrown up agonising problems relating to equality, justice, national unity, secularism and the nature of modernisation. He contends that these problems have not been theoretically explored by Indian political theorists. As a result post-independence India has thrown up little by way of political theory. The author explains this in terms of such factors as the dominance of a single official political philosophy, the complex nature of Indian political reality, and the ambiguous relationship between the theorist and his subject matter.

Parens, Erik. Kundera, Nietzsche, and Politics: On the Questions of Eternal Return and Responsibility. *Phil Today*, 37(3), 285-297, Fall 93.

Argues that one of the questions at the heart of Kundera's *Unbearable Lightness of Being* is this: What is it like to live in a world where there is no eternal return, yet where people sometimes act as if there were? Further, argues that by asking that question, Kundera keeps in play the difficult problem of the political ramifications of Nietzsche's thought of eternal return.

Parfit, Derek. Commentator on 'Pluralism and the Standard of Living' in The Quality of Life, Nussbaum, Martha C (ed). New York, Oxford Univ Pr, 1993.

Parfit, Derek. The Indeterminacy of Identity: A Reply to Brueckner. *Phil Stud*, 70(1), 23-33, Ap 93.

Parfit, Derek. Why Does the Universe Exist?. *Harvard Rev Phil*, 1(1), 2-5, Spr 91.

Pargetter, Robert and Bigelow, John. Acquaintance with Qualia. *Theoria*, 61(3), 129-147, 1990.

Parizeau, Marie-Hélène. Autonomie, don et partage dans les transplantations d'organes et de tissus humains. *Dialogue (Canada)*, 30(3), 343-353, Sum 91.

The question of organ transplantation is first analyzed from the American perspective in terms of utilitarist values: autonomy, justice, and gift as opposed to commercialization. The continental perspective (France) promotes more Kantian values: integrity and unavailability of the human body which imply gift and solidarity. Both ethical traditions are confronted to the pressure of the market and of the extension of the medical indications. The philosophical issue consist in the status of the human body in link to the nature of the gift. As the trend of technosciences is an objectivization of the parts of the human body into biological material, than what kind of social symbolization can be opposed to allow the survival of the gift which is an ethical foundation to transplantation.

Park, Désirée. Ayerian 'Qualia' and the Empiricist Heritage in The Philosophy of A J Ayer, Hahn, Lewis Edwin (ed). Peru, Open Court, 1992.

Park, Jung Soon. *Contractarian Liberal Ethics and the Theory of Rational Choice*. New York, Lang, 1992.

The book investigates the relationship between morality and rationality in the context of historical and present-day contractarian ethics. From Rawls to Gauthier, contractarians have attempted to construct their methodological foundations on the theory of rational choice. Through a careful study of the nature and limits of the theory of rational choice, Jung Soon Park argues that the theory cannot provide the reliable foundations for contractarian liberal ethics. Consequently, the author takes seriously the question about the future of contractarian liberal ethics: Is it the end or can there be a transformation?

Parker, Richard B. The Rights of Man and the Goals of Women in Women's Rights and the Rights of Man, Arnaud, A J. Oxford, Aberdeen, 1990.

Parker, Stephen and Drahos, Peter. Rule Following, Rule Scepticism and Indeterminacy in Law: A Conventional Account. *Ratio Juris*, 5(1), 109-119, Mr 92.

Genuine rule scepticism, the paper claims, has not been developed within traditional legal philosophy. Recently within general philosophy, however, Saul Kripke has proposed an argument which attempts to show that rules do not exist. The paper discusses one possible solution to Kripke's attack on rules and then considers how

this solution helps to illuminate the vital role of conventions in legal reasoning. Finally, the paper considers how the systems thinking of Luhmann might help us to come to a better understanding of the role of conventions in law.

Parkes, Graham R (ed). *Nietzsche and Asian Thought*. Chicago, Univ of Chicago Pr, 1991.

This volume aims to counterbalance the distinctly Eurocentric bias of most of the literature on Nietzsche. The first several essays deal with general hermeneutic problems concerning his relation to "the foreign." A section on India assesses his engagement with Indian thought and investigates parallels with Indian philosophical ideas. Section on China and Japan discuss the vast impact Nietzsche's philosophy has had in those countries and also engage in comparative studies of its relations to Chinese and Japanese philosophies. The volume as a whole illuminates aspects of Nietzsche's thought that have largely been ignored or overlooked by western commentators.

Parkes, Graham R. The Early Reception of Nietzsche's Philosophy in Japan in Nietzsche and Asian Thought, Parkes, Graham (ed). Chicago, Univ of Chicago Pr, 1991.

The reception of Nietzsche's philosophy in Japan (and, from there, in China) has an interesting history- mostly unknown to scholars in the West which began a few years ago before his death. The initial impact of his ideas in Japan was enormous, and has been sustained to the present day - owing in part to their resonances with the Japanese Buddhist tradition of thought.

Parkes, Graham R. The Orientation of the Nietzschean Text in Nietzsche and Asian Thought, Parkes, Graham R (ed). Chicago, Univ of Chicago Pr, 1991.

Parkes, Graham R. Wanderers in the Shadow of Nihilism: Nietzsche's 'Good Europeans'. *Hist Euro Ideas*, 16(4-6), 585-590, Ja 93.

This short essay presents Nietzsche's attitudes toward nationalism, and their underlying grounds, as an antidote toward contemporary nationalistic tendencies in Europe. He resolutely avoids the temptation to lapse into nationalism as a response to nihilism and "the death of God," evading both traditional "fatherlandishness" and the naive universalism of modernism. He emphasizes the radical multiplicity of the European heritage, and suggests engaging it through a kind of "cultural nomadism"—a wandering (dance), informed by disciplined intelligence and insight, through a range of cultural possibilities. His ideal of the "good European" is of supreme salutary relevance to the current situation in Europe.

Parkes, Graham R (trans) and Aihara, Setsuko (trans) and Muneto, Sonoda. The Eloquent Silence of Zarathustra in Nietzsche and Asian Thought, Parkes, Graham (ed). Chicago, Univ of Chicago Pr, 1991.

Parkes, Graham R (trans) and Figl, Johann. Nietzsche's Early Encounters with Asian Thought in Nietzsche and Asian Thought, Parkes, Graham R (ed). Chicago, Univ of Chicago Pr, 1991.

Parkes, Graham R (trans) and Hulin, Michel. Nietzsche and the Suffering of the Indian Ascetic in Nietzsche and Asian Thought, Parkes, Graham R (ed). Chicago, Univ of Chicago Pr, 1991.

Parkes, Graham R (trans) and Julien, François. The Chinese Notion of "Blandness" As a Virtue: A Preliminary Outline. *Phil East West*, 43(1), 107-111, Ja 93.

Parkes, Graham R (trans) and Kōgaku, Arifuku. The Problem of the Body in Nietzsche and Dōgen in Nietzsche and Asian Thought, Parkes, Graham (ed). Chicago, Univ of Chicago Pr, 1991.

Parkes, Graham R (trans) and Scheiffele, Eberhard. Questioning One's 'Own' from the Perspective of the Foreign in Nietzsche and Asian Thought, Parkes, Graham R (ed). Chicago, Univ of Chicago Pr, 1991.

Parmigiani, Giovanni. Minimax, Information and Ultrapessimism. *Theor Decis*, 33(3), 241-252, N 92.

Discussing the foundations of the minimax principle, Savage (1954) argued that it is "utterly untenable for statistics" because it is "ultrapessimistic" when applied to negative income, but claimed that such objection is not relevant when the principle is applied to regret. In this paper I rebut the latter claim. I first present an example where ultrapessimism, as Savage understood it, applies to minimax regret but not to minimax negative income. Then, for a sequential decision problems with two terminal acts and a finite number of states of nature, I give necessary and sufficient conditions for a decision rule to be ultrapessimistic, and show that for every payoff table with at least three states, be it in regret form or not, there exist an experiment such that the minimax rule is ultrapessimistic. I conclude with some more general remarks on information and the value of experimentation for a minimax agent.

Parr, Christopher (ed) and Olson, Alan M (ed) and Parr, Debra (ed). *Video Icons and Values*. Albany, SUNY Pr, 1991.

This collection of essays considers various aspects of television as the most powerful agent of value formation in today's world. The negative and positive implications and consequences of video technology are discussed. Among the more prominent issues and questions: In what ways can television be considered an "agent of value formation?" What is the impact of conventional, commercially formatted, broadcast television on perception and meaning, values and critical judgment? Is the growing problem of *aliteracy* today directly attributable to television? Contributors include: Rebecca Abbott, Dick Hebdige, Gregor Goethals, Renee Hobbs, Lenore Langsdorf, Jeremy Murray-Brown, Alan M Olson, Christopher and Debra Parr, Robert Scholes, and E David Thorp.

Parr, Debra (ed) and Parr, Christopher (ed) and Olson, Alan M (ed). *Video Icons and Values*. Albany, SUNY Pr, 1991.

This collection of essays considers various aspects of television as the most powerful agent of value formation in today's world. The negative and positive implications and consequences of video technology are discussed. Among the more prominent issues and questions: In what ways can television be considered an "agent of value formation?" What is the impact of conventional, commercially formatted, broadcast television on perception and meaning, values and critical judgment? Is the growing problem of *aliteracy* today directly attributable to television? Contributors include: Rebecca Abbott, Dick Hebdige, Gregor Goethals, Renee Hobbs, Lenore Langsdorf, Jeremy Murray-Brown, Alan M Olson, Christopher and Debra Parr, Robert Scholes, and E David Thorp.

Parra Luna, Francisco. Hacia un replanteamiento epistemológico del problema del paro en España. *Theoria (Spain)*, 5(12-13), 229-240, N 90.

Unemployment is not only an economic problem, but a complex axiological one, the understanding of which cannot be envisaged without dealing with all the social, economic, political and institutional causes. Unemployment in Spain is so high (18% of Active Population). That its solution needs other ways out than those sustained by traditional economicist approaches based mainly on neoliberal economic growth. To be more specific, Spain suffers from three axiological desequilibria (more unemployment, less public services and infrastructures, and less tax pressure) which adequate integration and optimization could solve, not the problem wholely, but at least, by bringing Spain into line with the European rate.

Parret, Herman. De Baumgarten à Kant: sur la beauté. *Rev Phil Louvain*, 90(87), 317-343, Ag 92.

Alexander Baumgarten, still very dependent on the scholastic and Wolffian heritages, deplaces the thought of the beautiful from metaphysics towards a new science called "aesthetics" (*Aesthetica* has been published in 1750). Baumgarten's systematic aesthetics combines two approaches: the one reconstructing the general conditions of aesthetic creativity, and the one determining the general characteristics of the beautiful object. Two philosophical theses of Baumgarten have been taken over by Kant in his *Critique of Judgment*: the aesthetic experience is a judgment, and the aesthetic judgment presupposes a sensitivity of the individual. Without any doubt, Kant transcends Baumgarten by his depth and argumentation. However, it is Baumgarten who created with precision the space itself where Kant's theory of the aesthetic judgment will be developed.

Parsons, Charles. On Some Difficulties Concerning Intuition and Intuitive Knowledge. *Mind*, 102(406), 233-246, Ap 93.

Parsons, Charles. The Transcendental Aesthetic in The Cambridge Companion to Kant, Guyer, Paul (ed). New York, Cambridge Univ Pr, 1992.

Parsons, Stephen D. Explaining Technology and Society: *The Problem of Nature in Habermas*. *Phil Soc Sci*, 22(2), 218-230, Je 92.

Habermas's concept of 'labour' is an attempt to integrate Mary and Kant. It is a category of human existence and an epistemological category. However, this attempted synthesis fails. As an epistemological category, labour both constitutes the object domain of nature, yet must be receptive to nature. Nature is thus constituted through labour, yet must also ground the validity of the act of constitution itself. Labour thus takes the role of Kant's unschematized categories, which neglects the importance of time in Kant's theory.

Parthasarathy, R. Tradition and the Indian Writer. *Brit J Aes*, 32(2), 134-148, Ap 92.

Parusnikova, Zuzana. Against the Spirit of Foundations: Postmodernism and David Hume. *Hume Stud*, 19(1), 1-17, Ap 93.

Pasini, Enrico. Mathesis und Phantasie: Die Rolle der Einbildungskraft im Umfeld der Descartesschen *Regulae*. *Stud Leibniz*, 24(2), 160-176, 1992.

A particular aspect of the confrontation between modern philosophy and the Aristotelian tradition relates to the so-called psychology of faculties. On this basis, it is much harder for modern thought, in comparison to the field of natural sciences, to separate itself from the concepts, theories and terminologies which characterize the still deriding traditional approach. Focusing on the *Regulae ad directionem ingenii* — in which the young Descartes, first writing about method, attempted to lay the foundation of a "mathesis generalis" — these problems are discussed as far as the role of imagination is concerned. There are two main questions: the presence of mental images in thought processes, and the cognitive functions of the imagination. (edited)

Paske, Gerald H. Sympathy, Self, and Reflective Freedom. *SW Phil Rev*, 8(1), 19-28, Ja 92.

Contrary to Hume, the passions sometimes can and ought to bow to reason. The capacity to do so depends upon language. Building upon Jonathan Bennett's distinction between iconic and non-iconic languages, I argue that: (1) Moral concepts are non-iconic. (2) Humean sympathy is inadequate to account for moral motivation. (3) Thoughts about thoughts are necessary for the evaluation of one's own passions. (4) Self evaluation shows that it is the pain of others and not one's sympathy which is morally relevant. (5) Abstract sympathy is the recognition of the moral relevance of another's pain. (6) Morality requires us to consider what we ought to shape our capacity for feeling shows that hedonistic consequentialism is an incomplete moral theory. (8) In shaping our feeling capacities we make the passions bow to reason.

Pasqua, Hervé. L'unité de l'Etre parménidien. *Rev Phil Louvain*, 90(86), 143-155, My 92.

Being exists in an absolute sense, and because it exists it cannot cease to be. In other words non-being is impossible. This is the central thesis of Parmenides' poem. The A. aims to show that this thesis can only be justified in Parmenides' view if Being is considered to be identical with the One. If this is the case, it has an important effect on the interpretation of the Poem, namely that the affirmation of Being does not depend on the denial of Non-being, as many exegetes hold. In this article two recent interpretations are discussed, namely those of N L Cordero and L Couloubaritsis. The A aims to inquire to what extent the true thought of Parmenides does not consist in making the affirmation of Being depend on that of Non-Being, but rather the contrary, by basing his argumentation on the reciprocity of Being and the One.

Pasquarello, Tony. Humanism's Thorn: The Case of the Bright Believers. *Free Inq*, 13(1), 38-42, Wint 92-93.

Exploiting the dilemma: 1) There are bright believers; 2) Bright people don't believe nonsense; 3) Traditional theism is nonsense, the contemporary phenomenon of fundamentalist Christian belief in intellectuals, e.g., professional philosophers, is explored. Typical humanist explanations that believers aren't "bright" or have "compartmentalized" beliefs are rejected, as are believers' potential rejoinders that their stance is either rationally defensible or need not meet the test of reason. How can humanists comprehend this state of affairs without compromising a naturalistic ontology? No solution, other than a call for dialogue is suggested.

Passmore, John. Humanism and Environmentalism. *Free Inq*, 13(2), 13, Spr 93.

Pasveer, Bernike. Horen, zien en lezen. *Kennis Methode*, 17(1), 56-72, 1993.

Patellis, Ioli. Frege: Theory of Meaning or Philosophy of Science? in Greek Studies in the Philosophy and History of Science, Nicolacopoulos, Pantelis (ed). Dordrecht, Kluwer, 1990.

Patellis, Ioli. Patterns of Differences, Sameness and Unity in Some Kantian Principles. *Kantstudien*, 84(1), 78-89, 1993.

The paper examines Kant's manner of forming concepts. It argues that the principles of the formal finality of nature, teleology in physical anthropology, a civil constitution and morality exhibit a common conceptual pattern, since each of them is a result of transformations of the same formal concepts of difference, sameness and unity, which together make up the idea of a system. These transformations are dictated by the requirements of the values informing the domains of application of these principles, each of which thus results from the interplay of the values peculiar to its own domain and the Kantian value of systematicity.

Pateman, Carole. Equality, Difference, Subordination in Beyond Equality and Difference, Bock, Gisela (ed). New York, Routledge, 1992.

To see feminism as divided between advocates of equality and advocates of recognition of women's difference from men misrepresents feminist history; women's freedom not difference is at stake. The paradox is that motherhood (difference) has been the major vehicle of women's incorporation into the political order, but motherhood is seen as the antithesis of citizenship (equality). Arguments about citizens' service and duty to the state ignore motherhood as a political status, equivalent to that of worker or soldier. Women's duties are not considered, yet women, like soldiers, have died in performing their duty of replacing/expanding the population.

Paterson, R W K. Authority, Autonomy and the Legitimate State. *J Applied Phil*, 9(1), 53-64, 1992.

R P Wolff has argued that there is an irreconcilable conflict between the distinguishing mark of every state, viz., to act autonomously by taking moral responsibility for all of their actions. Utilitarian and consent theories which seek to justify the state's claim to possess a monopoly of the rightful use of force are shown to fail and the concept of a 'legitimate state' to be morally incoherent. However, Wolff's version of individualist anarchism does not follow. Human beings are by no means equally rational or homogeneously autonomous. There are 'states' which have a contingent and variable right to enforce obedience over an indefinitely large number of their 'subjects', although not over those who are autonomous because rational in high degree.

Patkos, Judit. Remarks On the Creation of the World (in Czechoslovakian). *Magyar Filozof Szemle*, 6, 821-865, 1991.

Patnaik, Tandra. Intention and Convention in Communications-Reunderstanding Bhartrhari. *Indian Phil Quart*, 19(4), 335-356, O 92.

The paper discusses in detail two ways of analysing the issues of the speaker's intention, the hearer's understanding and the universal ground of communicability—first by the ancient Indian philosopher Bhartrhari and then by Grice, Searle, and Austin. Bhartrhari presupposes the verbal, pre-verbal (mental) and trans-verbal stages to identify the *universal linguistic potency* as the ground of communicability. Whereas the modern philosophers keep their analysis confined to verbal stage, therefore they presuppose *constitutive rules* as the common ground of communication.

Paton, Calum. Ethics and Politics. Brookfield, Avebury, 1992.

This original book seeks to link classic meta-ethical theory with major traditions in political theory. It defends a *modified* view of ethical absolutism, by reference to the work of both Roderick Firth and Thomas Kuhn—while extending their perspectives. Using this framework, it seeks to defend a dialectical tradition in political theory, and establishes the basis for *evolving* political ethics on a non-arbitrary basis. In so doing, analysis of the Hegelian and Marxist tradition is provided.

Paton, R C. Towards a Metaphorical Biology. *Biol Phil*, 7(3), 279-294, Jl 92.

The metaphorical nature of biological language is examined and the use of metaphors for providing the linguistic context in which similarities and differences are made is described. Certain pervasive metaphors which are characterised by systemic properties are noted, and in order to provide some focus to the study, systemic metaphors associated with machine, text, and organism are discussed. Other systemic metaphors such as society and circuit are also reported. Some details concerning interrelations between automation and organism are presented in the light of the previous discussion. An approach towards the analysis of biosystem metaphors is outlined which relates part-whole, organisational level and systemic metaphors in a single model. Examples are provided throughout the discussion and mainly come from computing. The potential for metaphorical transfers between these domains is considered.

Patterson, Dennis M. The Value of a Promise. *Law Phil*, 11(4), 385-402, 1992.

The question "What makes a promise binding?" has received much attention both from philosophers and lawyers. One argument is that promises are binding because the act of making a promise creates expectations in the promisee, which expectations it would be morally wrong to disappoint. Another argument is grounded in the effects engendered by the making of a promise, specifically actions taken in reliance upon the promise. These two positions, the so-called expectation and reliance theories, have traditionally been thought to be incommensurable. In a recent article, 'Promises and Practices", Thomas Scanlon advances a theory of promising developed out of both of these positions. This article argues that Scanlon's argument fails because it cannot avoid the incommensurability of the expectation and reliance principles.

Patterson, Richard. Aristotle's Perfect Syllogisms, Predication, and the *Dictum de Omni*. *Synthese*, 96(3), 359-378, S 93.

Patterson, Wayne. Bertrand Russell's Philosophy of Logical Atomism. New York, Lang, 1993.

The book provides a detailed explication of Russell's philosophy of logical atomism, as presented in his eight lectures of 1919. Though reference is occasionally made to other works by Russell the book is essentially a commentary on the 1919 lectures, with one chapter devoted to each lecture. The book was written for the benefit of students with minimal background in twentieth century Anglo-American philosophy and hopes to achieve two objectives. The first is to explain the complexities of Russell's logical atomism in a way which can be readily grasped by students with little philosophical training. The second is to provide students with a grounding in the tools and methods of modern analytic philosophy. (edited)

Pattison, George (ed). *Kierkegaard on Art and Communication*. New York, St Martin's Pr, 1992.

The work is a collection of twelve essays by British, European and North American scholars, plus introduction by the editor. The essays explore the constant and complex interaction in Kierkegaard's authorship between medium and message, author and reader, text and transcendence. The perspectives are varied and a range of special interests are brought to bear on the interpretation of Kierkegaard. These include: old testament studies, opera, literary theory, the logical hermeneutics, Nietzsche and feminism.

Patton, Michael. Teaching Graduate Students to Teach—An Approach. *Teach Phil*, 15(3), 231-238, S 92.

In this essay, I describe the merits of the system I was a part of as a Teaching Assistant at Syracuse University. This system, due mainly to its developmental approach and its dependence on input from the graduate students involved in it, fostered excellence and interest in teaching. I show that many aspects of the Syracuse model can be adopted at little or no expense in other graduate programs, and argue that the adoption of these techniques will serve to produce Ph.D.'s in Philosophy who are also excellent teachers.

Patton, Thomas E. Quine's Truth: The Unending Pursuit. *Dialogue (Canada)*, 31(1), 107-113, Wint 92.

This is a critical notice of W V Quine's excellent short book *Pursuit of Truth*, which continues Quine's major philosophical project, "to examine the evidential support of science." Its five chapters deal with evidence, reference, meaning, intension and truth. The critical notice charts the surface of each chapter and goes deeper at a few points.

Pauer-Studer, Herlinde. Peter Singer on Euthanasia. *Monist*, 76(2), 135-157, Ap 93.

Singer thinks it is morally permissible to kill severely handicapped infants if their prospects to lead a satisfactory life are minimal. His justification for active euthanasia rests to a large extent on the view that there is a symmetry between killing a person and letting her die (equivalence thesis). It is argued that the equivalence thesis cannot be used to support the moral permissibility of active euthanasia. In the author's view, some of the harsh reactions to Singer's views in German speaking countries express deep worries due to specific historical experiences, that a fully developed moral theory cannot simply ignore.

Paul, Ellen Frankel. Set-Asides, Reparations, and Compensatory Justice. *Nomos*, 33, 97-139, 1991.

An assessment of the utility of the concept of compensatory justice for rectifying real-world instances of injustice. *City of Richmond vs. Crosson*, United States policy toward Japanese internees, German reparations to survivors of Nazi atrocities, and reparations toward victims of Soviet-style regimes are the principal cases examined. Compensatory justice breaks down, it is argued, when one attempts to use it to rectify injustices to generations long dead, to diffuse and not easily identified victims and perpetrators, and to the acts of regimes that take as their raison d'être the wholesale violation of human rights.

Paul, Ellen Frankel (ed) and Miller, Fred D (ed) and Paul, Jeffrey (ed). *Altruism*. New York, Cambridge Univ Pr, 1993.

The essays in this volume address the following questions and issues: When deciding what action to take, should an individual give greater weight to others' interests or to his own? Or is it possible to reconcile altruism and egoism, to show that we have self-regarding reasons for acting altruistically? What is the relationship between altruism and rationality? Whether, and under what conditions, may we properly be forced to serve others' interests? What role should government play in regulating our interactions? Confronting crucial and difficult issues, the ten authors whose essays appear in this volume offer fresh perspectives on the nature and value of altruism. Contributors: Thomas E Hill, Jr, Christine M Korsgaard, David Schmidtz, Robert Sugden, Neera Kapur Badhwar, William A Galston, Jean Hampton, Roderick T Long, Douglas J Den Uyl, and Tyler Cowen.

Paul, Jeffrey (ed) and Miller, Fred D (ed) and Paul, Ellen Frankel (ed). *Altruism*. New York, Cambridge Univ Pr, 1993.

The essays in this volume address the following questions and issues: When deciding what action to take, should an individual give greater weight to others' interests or to his own? Or is it possible to reconcile altruism and egoism, to show that we have self-regarding reasons for acting altruistically? What is the relationship between altruism and rationality? Whether, and under what conditions, may we properly be forced to serve others' interests? What role should government play in regulating our interactions? Confronting crucial and difficult issues, the ten authors whose essays appear in this volume offer fresh perspectives on the nature and value of altruism. Contributors: Thomas E Hill, Jr, Christine M Korsgaard, David Schmidtz, Robert Sugden, Neera Kapur Badhwar, William A Galston, Jean Hampton, Roderick T Long, Douglas J Den Uyl, and Tyler Cowen.

Paula Assis, J (trans) and Tarski, A. Verdade e Demonstraçao. *Cad Hist Filosof Cie*, 1(1), 91-122, Ja-Je 91.

Paull, R Cranston. Leibniz and the Miracle of Freedom. *Nous*, 26(2), 218-235, Je 92.

Paull, R Cranston and Sider, Theodore R. In Defense of Global Supervenience. *Phil Phenomenol Res*, 52(4), 833-854, D 92.

Pauri, M. The Universe as a Scientific Object in Philosophy and the Origin and Evolution of the Universe, Agazzi, Evandro (ed). Norwell, Kluwer, 1991.

The purpose of the work is to defend the thesis that the Universe as a whole cannot be considered as a scientific object in any sense that such words have had in the historical development of physics. It is also argued that there is no justification for relativistic cosmology's claim that it has given or is about to give empirical answers to the traditional "cosmological problems". And this, not on the basis of philosophical reasons alone but also as a consequence of the weakness of its logical and empirical foundations.

Pavic, Zeljko. Die Selbstintentionalität der Welt in Analecta Husserliana, XXXIV, Tymieniecka, Anna-Teresa (ed). Dordrecht, Kluwer, 1992.

Pavlischek, Keith J. Abortion Logic and Paternal Responsibility: One More Look at Judith Thomson's "A Defense of Abortion". *Pub Affairs Quart*, 7(4), 341-361, O 93.

Through a close examination of the logic and thought experiments of Judith Thomson's purportedly moderate defense of abortion in her classic essay, "A Defense of Abortion", I argue that the moderate pro-choice position is in many cases incompatible with a legal requirement that fathers financially support their children. I argue that this lends credence to the feminist pro-life claim that permissive abortion laws simply reaffirm male failings and neglect as well as the broader pro-life claim that the way a culture treats the unborn has serious cultural ramifications for other vulnerable members of society.

Pawelski, James. Attention, Extension, and Ecstasis in Augustine's Account of Time. *Cont Phil*, 15(2), 14-18, Mr-Ap 93.

Paxman, David B. Language and Difference: The Problem of Abstraction in Eighteenth-Century Language Study. *J Hist Ideas*, 54(1), 19-36, Ja 93.

How do peoples derive radically different abstract ideas? To answer this question, Locke, Condillac, Maupertuis, and Herder had to yoke contrarieties within their theories. The general problem was to achieve theories of difference without converting it into mere varieties of sameness. Locke asserted that similar mental processes operating in response to the same external world may result in radically different ideas, but this undercuts the possibilities for difference it seeks to preserve. Condillac asserted that language constitutes thought, but if that were true, could one ever make the assertion? Recognizing these and similar problems, Herder conceptualized the dynamics of sameness and difference in a yet-developing humanity.

Payne, E F J (trans) and Schopenhauer, Arthur. *On the Will in Nature — Schopenhauer*. New York, St Martin's Pr, 1991.

Payton, Sallyanne. The Concept of the Person in the *Parens Patriae* Jurisdiction over Previously Competent Persons. *J Med Phil*, 17(6), 605-645, D 92.

This article reviews the medieval law background of the *parens patriae* jurisdiction of the state as it has been exercised over incompetent persons who formerly were competent adults, concluding that the fiduciary standard implied in the statute *De Prerogative Regis* (1324), which is the basis for modern guardianship status, requires that the court and guardian adopt an attitude of respectful friendship toward the incompetent person, just as though they were to be accountable to the person himself, were he to recover his faculties and become competent once more. The article argues that because the determination of legal incompetence and the consequent transfer of custody of the person and property of an incompetent person to the state would result in a drastic forfeiture of liberty and property interests were it not for the fiduciary obligation owed by the state to the incompetent. (edited)

Peachey, Paul (ed) and Kromkowski, John (ed) and McLean, George F (ed). *The Place of the Person In Social Life*. Washington, CRVP, 1991.

Peacock, Kent A. A New Look at Simultaneity. *Proc Phil Sci Ass*, 1, 542-552, 1992.

By considering a science fictional version of the Twin Paradox due to Robert Heinlein, I argue that the common present of several observers in relative motion, if there could be such a thing, should be associated with certain values of *proper* time (equivalently, constant *action*) of those observers. This defines an invariant notion of simultaneity, which I call *dynamic* or *intrinsic* simultaneity, in contrast to the usual *kinematic* or *extrinsic* Einsteinian notion of simultaneity. If this picture is correct then the relativity of extrinsic simultaneity may be simply irrelevant to the question of the possibility of a globally distinguished "present".

Peacock, Mark S. Hayek, Realism and Spontaneous Order. *J Theor Soc Behav*, 23(3), 249-264, S 93.

The paper examines connections between Hayek and Bhaskar's realism, arguing that Hayek embraces a sufficiently realist view of science on which to base his theory of spontaneous order. However, this theory contains a number of flaws and is compared unfavorably to the social ontologies of Bhaskar and Giddens. Despite this, there remains much in common between Hayek and realism, and the implications of this, for realism, are explored. It is argued that realism, if properly conceived as a philosophical underlaborer, does not stand or fall with any substantive analyses with it may be consistent.

Peacocke, Christopher. A Moderate Mentalism. *Phil Phenomenol Res*, 52(2), 425-430, Je 92.

Peacocke, Christopher. *A Study of Concepts*. Cambridge, MIT Pr, 1992.

A concept is individuated by the condition a thinker must meet to possess it—its possession condition. This general theory, together with constraints relating to reference and truth, is developed to explain various phenomena found for all concepts. Particular possession conditions are developed for observational concepts, logical concepts and the concept of belief, and employed to explain their distinctive phenomena. The book also discusses the ontology of concepts as abstract objects, the normative dimensions of concepts, and the relation between philosophical and psychological theories of concepts. The theory is applied in building a nonverificationist account of the limits of intelligibility.

Peacocke, Christopher. Anchoring Conceptual Content: Scenarios and Perception in Cognition, Semantics and Philosophy, Ezquerro, Jesús (ed). Norwell, Kluwer, 1992.

The content of an experience with spatial representational content is given in part by specifying which ways of filling in the world around the subject are consistent with the correctness of the experience. These ways are spatial types, "scenarious", and constitute a nonconceptual level of amodal content. They can be used in solving several puzzles about the nature of perceptual content. There is also a further level of "propositional" content, needed in the description of perceptual grouping. Each type of content plays an important role in spatial reasoning and in the individuation of observational concepts.

Peacocke, Christopher. Externalist Explanation. *Proc Aris Soc*, 93, 203-230, 1993.

Externally individuated intentional states are capable of explaining, and being explained by, relationally, environmentally individuated states of affairs. These externalist explanations cannot be replaced by internalist explanations supplemented with specifications of the environmental relations of the internal states. Externalist explanations do not violate contingency requirements on explanation, nor the principle that higher-order states cannot be explanatory of their defining effects. A subpersona psychology must involve externalist explanation. A proper understanding of externalist explanation also paves the way for an account of self-knowledge, and for the possibility of knowing the mental states of others.

Peacocke, Christopher. Scenarios, Concepts and Perception in The Contents of Experience, Crane, Tim (ed). New York, Cambridge Univ Pr, 1992.

The content of an experience with spatial representational content is given in part by specifying which ways of filling in the world around the subject are consistent with the correctness of the experience. These ways are spatial types, "scenarios", and constitute a nonconceptual level of amodal content. They can be used in solving several puzzles about the nature of perceptual content. There is also a further level of "protopropositional" content, needed in the description of perceptual grouping. Each type of content plays an important role in spatial reasoning and in the individuation of observational concepts.

Peacocke, Christopher. Sense and Justification. *Mind*, 101(404), 793-816, O 92.

If a pair of Fregean thoughts immediately justify (or are justified by) different thoughts or states of the thinker, they are distinct. The paper aims to explain these links between justification and sense. It considers the *Grundgesetze*, and goes on to propose "the reciprocal conception" of the relation between justification and the individuation of senses by their possession conditions. It is argued that a priori instances of the justification relation are anchored in features of possession conditions; and that the conditions for knowing a content must make reference to an instance of the justification relation so anchored.

Peak Jr, Ira H. Dworkin and Hart on The Law. *Tradition Discovery*, 18(2), 22-32, 1991-92.

Pearce, Brian (trans) and Loone, Eero. *Soviet Marxism and Analytical Philosophies of History—Eero Loone*. New York, Verso, 1992.

In this, the first of his books to be translated into English, Loone surveys the philosophy of history as practised in the West, and then subjects Marxism to careful analytic scrutiny. He provides both a fresh perspective on familiar non-Marxist writers such as Collingwood, Popper, Kuhn, Modigliano and Plumb and a fruitful reformulation of the Marxist theory of history.

Pearce, Carole. African Philosophy and the Sociological Thesis. *Phil Soc Sci*, 22(4), 440-460, D 92.

"African philosophy", when conceived of as ethnophilosophy, is based on the idea that all thought is social, culture-bound, or based in natural language. But ethnophilosophy, whatever its sociological status, makes no contribution to philosophy, which is necessarily invulnerable to the sociological thesis. The sociological thesis must be limited in application to its own proper domain. The conflation of sociological and philosophical discourse arises from the fallacy of misplaced concreteness. This fallacy is responsible, among other things, for the sociological misinterpretation of Wittgenstein. African philosophy, to be thought philosophical, must conceive of itself as addressing universal problems instead of pursuing intellectual apartheid.

Pearcy, Lee T. Diagnosis as Narrative in Ancient Literature. *Amer J Philo*, 113(4), 595-616, Wint 92.

Pears, David. Ayer's Views on Meaning-Rules in The Philosophy of A J Ayer, Hahn, Lewis Edwin (ed). Peru, Open Court, 1992.

Pears, David. On the Parallelism between Theoretical and Practical Reasoning in Psychoanalysis, Mind and Art, Hopkins, Jim (ed). Cambridge, Blackwell, 1992.

Pears, David. Philosophy and the History of Philosophy in Isaiah Berlin: A Celebration, Margalit, Edna (ed). Chicago, Univ of Chicago Pr, 1991.

Pears, David. Split Self-Reference and Personal Survival. *SW Phil Rev*, 8(1), 65-76, Ja 92.

Pears, David. Wittgenstein's Concept of Showing in Criss-Crossing A Philosophical Landscape, Schulte, Joachim (ed). Amsterdam, Rodopi, 1992.

Starting from an analysis of Wittgenstein's reasons for placing all true-seeming sentences about the relation between language and the world in the class of utterances that lack a truth-value and can only communicate in the privileged way, the doctrine of showing is investigated in Wittgenstein's later writings. In contrast to the view that the concept of showing simply disappeared with the abandonment of the picture theory of the sentence it is argued that much of his early doctrine of showing survives in Wittgenstein's later philosophy.

Pearson, Paul A. St Thomas on the Continuum: The Nature of Points in Physics and Geometry. *Aquinas*, 35(3), 673-683, S-D 92.

Pécharman, Martine. Le discours mental selon Hobbes. *Arch Phil*, 55(4), 553-573, O-D 92.

Hobbes's analysis of mental discourse begins by a refutation of mind's substantiality. Mental discourse is nothing but an effect of sensation. However, Hobbes's reductionism is not radical: mental discourse must be distinguished from the infinite series of sensations. Further, the phantasms subsist someway and give matter to an internal reasoning. It is precisely this internal reasoning which prevents any other reduction of mental discourse to a mere series of universal names. Nevertheless,

mental discourse must give place to universal names, so as to be traduced into verbal discourse, but in such a way that the hypothesis of private language becomes impossible.

Peck, Dennis L (ed) and Murphy, John W (ed). *Open Institutions: The Hope for Democracy*. New York, Praeger, 1993.

In this book, the issue of democratization is addressed. The claim is made that before democracy is possible, a democratic culture must be established. Most often this point is raised with regard to logistical considerations, such as voting and parliamentary procedures. But before democracy can be established, knowledge bases, information dissemination systems, and social imagery must be democratized.

Pecker, Jean-Claude. Big Bangs, Plural: A Heretical View. *Free Inq*, 13(1), 10-11, Wint 92-93.

The metaphysical background of the debate around the "big bang" has unfortunately obscured a purely scientific debate. Actually, it seems now impossible to reach a final conclusion about the last evolution of our Universe.

Peczenik, Aleksander. 'Prima-Facie' Values and the Law in Ethical Dimensions of Legal Theory, Sadurski, Wojciech (ed). Amsterdam, Rodopi, 1991.

Optimal interpretation of the law is an as coherent as possible reconstruction of the *prima-facie* law and *prima-facie* moral values. This theory is a synthesis of six pairs of theories, *inter alia* the following: 1) a consensus theory on the *prima-facie* moral level—and a coherence theory on the all-things-considered level; and 2) a *prima-facie* obligation to obey the consensually established law—and an all-things-considered obligation to obey a coherent reconstruction of this law.

Peden, W Creighton. F E Abbot: Science, Nature, and God in God, Values, and Empiricism, Peden, Creighton (ed). Macon, Mercer Univ Pr, 1989.

The essay introduces the philosophical theology of Francis E Abbot, 1836-1903. Abbot was the first American philosopher to come out in support of Darwin's theory of evolution. He relied upon the scientific method for understanding Nature. He is noted as the first philosopher to focus on the relationship between thing, instead of focusing on things separately, as essential for an adequate understanding of Nature. His approach relies on the theory of evolution as providing a new way of contemplating the universe, which is heliocentric and not geocentric. Persons focusing on American philosophy will find Abbot of special interest. Most of this essay appears in The Philosopher of Free Religion: Francis E Abbot, 1836-1903 by W Creighton Peden (Lang, 1992).

Peden, W Creighton. The Philosopher of Free Religion: Francis Ellingwood Abbot, 1836-1903. New York, Lang, 1992.

The Philosopher of Free Religion presents an intellectual biography of Francis E Abbot, 1836-1903. Abbot was a radical figure in the American free thought tradition, being the first philosopher to support in writing the thought of Charles Darwin. Chapters alternate between biographical periods and the philosophical and theological thought of each period. In the conclusion, an evaluation is presented of Abbot's contributions as a philosopher and member of the Metaphysical Club, in social philosophy, and in serving as the prophet of Free Religion.

Peden, W Creighton (ed) and Axel, Larry E (ed). God, Values, and Empiricism. Macon, Mercer Univ Pr, 1989.

God, Values and Empiricism, (Mercer University Press, 1989) is a collection of essays presented at the First International Conference on Philosophical Theology at Oxford University in 1988. The Conference was sponsored by the Highlands Institute for American Religious Thought. The volume reflects the interests of the Institute in liberal religious thought, themes relevant to the "Chicago School" of theology, naturalism in American theology, and in the interface of theology and classical American philosophy. Persons interested in American philosophy and theology will find these strong, scholarly essays of special import.

Peden, W Creighton (ed) and Hudson, Yeager (ed). Terrorism, Justice and Social Values. Lewiston, Mellen Pr, 1990.

This book consists of papers selected from those presented at an international conference of the North American Society for Social Philosophy at Guadalajara, Mexico. The papers address the turbulence and violence of the Twentieth Century, especially issues surrounding the use of terrorism as an instrument in the fight for justice and the promotion of political ideologies and causes. In our times the time-honored principle that innocent by-standers must not be harmed has been openly renounced. Questions about human rights, morality, justice, and social progress are addressed in the context of this change.

Peeters, Guido and Dhooghe, Paul F. The Principle of the Topical Localization of Symbols and the Meaning of the 'Ultimate Meaning'. *Ultim Real Mean*, 15(4), 296-305, D 92.

At the deep structure level of meaning topological localisation of formal symbols, which are subjected to the algebraic operations of 'accentuation' and 'denegation', are used as an ansatz for the development of a formalisation of syntagmatics and paradigmatics. The topological localisation formalises the concept of relation as primitive of 'semiotic schemes' the way they were conceived by L Hjelmslev. The topology of the localisation of the symbols imposes well-defined constraints on the semantic schemes. The development of the theory stresses denegation as a necessary step in the syntagmatic process that leads from actual understanding towards a higher level of understanding. It would follow that the furthest point we can reach in our search for the ultimate meaning will have the character of a 'neutral term'.

Peffer, Rodney. Sterba's Reconciliation Project: A Critique. *J Soc Phil*, 23(1), 132-144, Spr 92.

Pejovich, Svetozar. Institutions, Nationalism, and the Transition Process in Eastern Europe. *Soc Phil Pol*, 10(2), 65-78, Sum 93.

Peled, Yoav. From Theology to Sociology: Bruno Bauer and Karl Marx on the Question of Jewish Emancipation. *Hist Polit Thought*, 13(3), 463-485, Autumn 92.

Most commentators on Marx's essay, *On the Jewish Question*, have regarded it either as an anti-semitic document or as a philosophical tract nor primarily concerned with the Jewish question at all. I argue for a different reading of the essay, one which regards its two aspects—a call for the emancipation of German Jewry and an important advance in the development of historical materialism—as intimately related. My reading is based on a serious consideration of the arguments against Jewish emancipation advanced by Bruno Bauer—something which most commentators have neglected to do—and of Marx's essay as a critique of those arguments. By shifting the debate from the plane of theology to that of sociology, I argue, Marx was able to circumvent one of Bauer most forceful arguments, namely, that as a religion of law, not of faith, Judaism was by its very nature public, hence unsuitable for life in the modern state. This shift also constituted Marx's first treatment of alienation as rooted primarily not in political oppression but in economic activity.

Pellecchia, P. La valenza critica della partecipazione nell'opera di C Fabro. *Aquinas*, 34(3), 459-484, S-D 91.

Pellecchia, Pasquale. La pro-fanazione Heideggeriana di Dio. *Aquinas*, 35(1), 11-46, Ja-Ap 92.

The essay wants to show that the "Thought" of Heideggarian not only doesn't prepare for the coming of God or of Gods, but prevents it. It is impossible to be a Heideggarian follower and theists. This is true both for philosophers and theologians.

Pellecchia, Pasquale. Sulle tracce del postmoderno (I). *Aquinas*, 35(2), 341-379, My-Ag 92.

The essay examines R Guardini's, H Gadamer's, G Vattino's, J Habermas' and C Fabro's thought about the concept of "modernity" and of the needs (for those authors) to go further than modernity.

Pellecchia, Pasquale. Sulle tracce del postmoderno (II). *Aquinas*, 35(3), 469-516, S-D 92.

The essay wants to show how the existential hermetic of Heidegger and the philosophical hermetic of Gadamer, reducing the truth of being, have prepared the "weak thought" of post-modernity.

Pellegrino, Edmund. Doctors Must Not Kill. *J Clin Ethics*, 3(2), 95-102, Sum 92.

Pellegrino, Edmund. Response to Leonard Harris in African-American Perspectives on Biomedical Ethics, Flack, Harley E (ed). Washington, Georgetown Univ Pr, 1992.

Pellegrino, Edmund D (ed) and Flack, Harley E (ed). *African-American Perspectives on Biomedical Ethics*. Washington, Georgetown Univ Pr, 1992.

Pelletier, Lucien. L'émergence du concept de totalité chez Lukács (II). *Laval Theol Phil*, 48(3), 379-396, O 92.

Après avoir exposé dans la première partie de cet article les motivations, le fonctionnement et les sources du concept de totalité dans l'esthétique théorique du jeune Lukács, l'auteur procède maintenant à son évaluation. Il montre que le recours à la catégorie de totalité ne pouvait se satisfaire du cadre néo-Kantien dans lequel Lukács voulait l'enserrer; les apories théoriques ainsi engendrées ont requis le passage à un autre horizon conceptuel.

Pels, D. Zijn wij ooit modern geweest?. *Kennis Methode*, 17(3), 279-304, 1993.

This paper ventures a critique of Bruno Latour's fascinating, but flawed, idea of a 'Modern Constitution' which has fatally divorced the scientific representation of things from the political representation of persons. His account of Hobbes and Boyle as founding fathers of this divide is not symmetrical, and performs a rather idiosyncratic 'translation' of both. The grand distinction between political and scientific representation itself is conceptually overtaxed, collapsing as it does the Science/Politics dualism into the dualism of Nature/Society. In addition, Latour's peculiar *dialectics* of a translation and purification appears to install something like a self-propelling, explosive historical contradiction — thus repeating some doubtful features of Marxian objectivistic teleology in a semiotic framework. For all of such reasons, his conviction that *We have never been modern* (Harvester, 1993) should be moderated and graced with a question mark.

Peña, Lorenzo. Contradictions and Paradigms in Cultural Relativism and Philosophy, Dascal, Marcelo (ed). Leiden, Brill, 1991.

Peña, Lorenzo. De la logique combinatoire des 'Generales Inquisitiones' aux calculs combinatoires contemporains. *Theoria (Spain)*, 6(14-15), 129-159, O 91.

In his 1686 essay, Leibniz undertook to reduce sentences to noun-phrases, truth to being. Such a reduction arose from his equating proof with conceptual analysis. Within limits, Leibniz's logical calculus provides a reasonable way of surmounting the dichotomy, thus allowing a reduction of hypothetical to categorical statements. However it yields the disastrous result that whenever A is possible and so is B there can be an entity being both A and B. Yet, Leibniz was the forerunner of twentieth century combinatory logic, which (successfully!) practices — sometimes for reasons not entirely unlike Leibniz's own grounds — reductions of the same kinds he tried to carry out.

Penati, Giancarlo. Aristotle e Heidegger: Prospettive e momenti di un'interpretazione. *G Metaf*, 14(3), 485-504, S-D 92.

Attraverso il riesame dei costanti e continui incontri di Heidegger con Aristotele, sin dalla lettura giovanile di Brentano e per tutto il corso della sua ricerca, viene qui dimostrato quanto sia essenziale per il senso del "cammino" Heideggeriano il dialogo con lo Stagirita. Benché Heidegger rifiuti il linguaggio apofantico e le sue applicazioni onto-teologiche, egli percorre la via già indicata da Aristotele del linguaggio semantico e, sino al suo culminante sbocco nell'ascolto della impronunziabile "parola assoluta", si confronta col principio, non tacito, ma indimostrabile, del sapere di Aristotele.

Penati, Giancarlo. Esperienza della soggettività e affermazione della trascendenza. *G Metaf*, 14(1), 125-142, Ja-Ap 92.

Poiché il soggetto umano, in quanto cosciente e libero, é immediatamente presente a sé come l'essereche trascende se stesso, è esso a costituire obbligato luogo, centro motore dell'apertura alla trascendenza. Questa perb si colloca al di là di ogni limite del vissuto, dell'espresso e del pensato, come irriducibile alla presenza, come attuale non-presenza: fonte però e sintesi unitaria e originante di tutte le presenze, di tutte le attuali e possibili soggettività; ad essa sono presenti tali soggesttività in quanto essa si configura come puro atto creativo.

Pendlebury, Michael. Elementary Formal Semantics for English Tense and Aspect. *Phil Papers*, 21(3), 215-241, N 92.

This paper is an exercise in interval semantics. It presents and defends a truth-conditional and compositional account of the basic temporal semantics of English verb phrases constructed from "core verb phrases" and one or more of the "basic temporal operators" (the present and past tense operators, the progressive and perfective auxiliaries, and the modal "will" as used to express futurity.) It also includes and makes use of a new interval-based account of the Kenny-Vendler classification of verb phrases into state, activity, accomplishment, and achievement verb phrases.

Pendlebury, Shirley. Akrasia and Education: A Response to Deborah Kerdeman. *Proc Phil Educ*, 48, 90-92, 1992.

Kerdeman argues that Aristotle's account of *akrasia* illuminates the tasks and constraints of moral education. In this response, I consider some mistaken assumptions about *akrasia* and moral education: i) the assumption that *akrasia* is only a moral problem; ii) the assumption that the primary task of moral education is to overcome *akrasia*; and iii) the assumption that pluralism is the main reason why it may be difficult to know what is right. I also sketch a few broader education implications of some recent accounts of *akrasia*.

Penelhum, Terence. Ethics with God and Ethics Without in On the Track of Reason, Beehler, Rodger G (ed). Boulder, Westview Pr, 1992.

In *Ethics Without God*, and elsewhere, Kai Nielsen suggests that if one does not hold a divine-command theory of morals, belief in God has no ethical role. I attempt to explain a role that theism has in ethics for the Christian even without a divine-command theory. It helps determine moral motivation in two ways: 1) The belief that the Kingdom is at-hand allays anxiety and requires complete, rather than conditional, adherence to principle. 2) The belief in the coming of a final fulfillment offsets discouragement in the face of short-run failure.

Penelhum, Terence. The Self of Book 1 and the Selves of Book 2. *Hume Stud*, 18(2), 281-291, N 92.

Hume has often been accused of inconsistency in writing of the self in Book 2 of the *Treatise*, when he has questioned its unity in Book 1. Recent defences of Hume against this charge seem to me successful; but I argue here that his discussions of the self are deeply deficient in failing to account for the fact that each of us distinguishes between himself/herself on the one hand, and other selves on the other—a distinction that is fundamental to his analysis of the passions.

Penette, Sonia. La idea de la comunidad en la Filosofía Hegeliana del Derecho. *Cuad Etica*, 13, 81-93, Je 92.

In this paper, I try to show that, in Hegelian practical philosophy: 1) The idea of community is the background and point of reference that remains through the modalities that the will gives to itself in its realization — from the abstraction and formality of private right and morality, to the effectiveness of its liberty in ethicity. 2) Every possibility of subsistence and realization of the individual takes the community for granted, and that even the illusion of excluding oneself from it, far from being an achievement, leads to hypocrisy, to vanity, or to subjective opinion the three of which destroy the singular itself. 3) The State, not taken in a determined form, but as the organic constitution of the community, must be its effective realization. 4) Freedom is not the banal affirmation of subjective arbitrament, but can only grow in the soil of the rational community.

Penfold, H B and Hooker, C A and Evans, R J. Control, Connectionism and Cognition: Towards a New Regulatory Paradigm. *Brit J Phil Sci*, 43(4), 517-536, D 92.

Penner, Terrence M I. Socrates and the Early Dialogues in The Cambridge Companion to Plato, Kraut, Richard H (ed). New York, Cambridge Univ Pr, 1992.

Penner, Terrence M I. What Laches and Nicias Miss—And Whether Socrates Thinks Courage Merely a Part of Virtue. *Ancient Phil*, 12(1), 1-28, Spr 92.

Pensky, Max. *Melancholy Dialectics*. Amherst, Univ of Mass Pr, 1993.

This book offers a comprehensive interpretation of Walter Benjamin's work, centering on the ideas of mourning and melancholia. For Benjamin melancholia was both a subjective disposition that threatened the individual with incapacitating sadness, and a subtle mode of historical and ultimately theological insight. Through close readings of Benjamin's work on baroque German dogma and the *Arcades* Project, the book argues that this "melancholy dialectics" lies at the heart of Benjamin's mature thought.

Penta, Leo J. Resistance to the Rule of Time or a "Post-Metaphysical Metaphysics": Michael Theunissen's *Negative Theology of Time*. *Phil Today*, 37(2), 211-224, Sum 93.

This article presents an overview of Michael Theunissen's attempt to reclaim metaphysics (in a transformed sense) based on a negative reading of time.

Pentry, Edward S (ed) and Frederick, Robert (ed) and Hoffman, W Michael (ed). *Business, Ethics, and the Environment: The Public Policy Debate*. Westport, Greenwood Pr, 1990.

Pentzopoulou-Valalas, Theresa. Experience and Causal Explanation in Medical Empiricism in Greek Studies in the Philosophy and History of Science, Nicolacopoulos, Pantelis (ed). Dordrecht, Kluwer, 1990.

The article discusses the concept of experience as developed by medical Empiricism. The discussion is based on Galen's works ("On Medical Experience", particularly). Two points are stressed. a) The empiricists centered their theory on key concepts such as experience and observation, whose scope lies beyond the medical sphere. In this sense we might call their theory a consistent empirical theory of knowledge. b) Quenesidemus's criticism of causal explanations (particularly the eight etiological modes in Sextus Empizicus) allows the distinction between science and ideology. The Empizicists rejected ideology.

Penzo, G. Interpretazione esistenziale della storia della filosofia. *Aquinas*, 35(1), 47-58, Ja-Ap 92.

Peperzak, Adriaan. Heidegger and Plato's Idea of the Good in Reading Heidegger: Commemorations, Sallis, John (ed). Bloomington, Indiana Univ Pr, 1992.

Heidegger's interpretation of Plato, as defended in his publications from 1927 until

1932 and in *Plato's Doctrine of Truth* (1942) is analyzed and criticized, especially with regard to *aletheia, paideia, idea* and *to agathon*. Heidegger's characterization of Plato's thinking as "metaphysics" is challenged and some consequences of a different interpretation are indicated.

Peperzak, Adriaan. *To the Other: An Introduction to the Philosophy of Emmanuel Levinas*. West Lafayette, Purdue Univ Pr, 1993.

This study is an introduction into Levinas's oeuvre. After a first chapter on the existential background and key issues of his thought, chapters 2, 3, and 4 concentrate on a short text in English and French, Philosophy and the Idea of the Infinite," which contains the program of Levinas's entire oeuvre. Chapter 5 analyzes the structure of Totality and the Infinite and shoes how its questions and answers adhere together. Chapter 6 is a succinct interpretation of Otherwise Than Being or Beyond Essence as an attempt to lead from phenomenology toward a saying beyond phenomena and (inter-)essence. A selective bibliography is added to facilitate further study.

Pepperell, Keith. Privacy, Rights, and Education. *Phil Stud Educ*, 1, 41-56, 1990.

Percival, Philip. Indices of Truth and Intensional Operators. *Theoria*, 61(3), 148-172, 1990.

This paper provides a general framework in which to assess the use of indices to which semantic concepts like 'truth' are relativized in the meaning-theoretical semantics of intensional operators. But it is particularly concerned to critically compare this approach to an alternative which conducts truth theory in an intensional metalanguage. Focusing on temporal and modal operators, the choice to be made between these approaches is seen to depend on a number of issues, including the indexicality or otherwise of temporal and modal operators, instrumentalism in semantic theory, and the debate between molecularist and holistic approaches to language.

Percival, Philip. Thank Goodness That's Non-Actual. *Phil Papers*, 21(3), 191-213, N 92.

In contrast to Lewis at one extreme, and Prior at the other, Mellor treats time and modality disanalogously by 'spatialising' the former but not the latter. This asymmetrical position requires an argument for not spatialising modality the temporal analogue of which isn't equally persuasive. I consider whether the modal analogue of Prior's 'Thank goodness' argument—which seems to be akin to an argument against Lewis by Adams—is one such. I argue that it isn't. I consider various means of resisting this argument, and show that all are no less cogent than their analogues resisting Prior's original temporal argument. Of these alternatives, the one which refines ideas of Evans is defended in both the temporal and modal cases.

Pereira Martins, Lilian A C. Aristóteles e a Geraçao Espontânea. *Cad Hist Filosof Cie*, 2(2), 213-237, Jl-D 90.

This paper studies Aristotle's ideas about the spontaneous birth (without parents) of some kinds of animals such as eels, oysters and flies. From the analysis of his biological works his theory of spontaneous generation as well as the observations upon which it was based are rebuilt. After a detailed description of his ideas and arguments about spontaneous generation, his methodology is discussed and his methodological flaws are pointed. However, many exemplary aspects of his research are also emphasized.

Perkins, Robert L. Abraham's Silence Aesthetically Considered in Kierkegaard on Art and Communication, Pattison, George (ed). New York, St Martin's Pr, 1992.

The third problem in Kierkegaard's *Fear and Trembling* has been relatively neglected by philosophers in spite of its being the largest section of the book and its inclusion of a large number of aesthetic concepts, among them "immediacy" and "the interesting." The article addresses both terms in the intellectual climate of which Kierkegaard was so critical: Hegelianism and romanticism. Kierkegaard compares and contrasts the loquacity of Socrates with the silence of Abraham in order to separate the ethical from the aesthetic and both from the religious. Abrahamic faith is a "second immediacy" in contrast with both romantic immediacy and Hegelian ethical life. Neither is "the interesting" Abraham's category, for his experience is incommensurable with the common life and the aesthetic as modeled by the German romantics. Abraham has a category of his own: faith.

Perkins, Robert L. Commentary on "Hegel's Philosophy of God in the Light of Kierkegaard's Criticisms" in Hegel and His Critics, Desmond, William J (ed). Albany, SUNY Pr, 1989.

This article is a critique of one by Bernard Cullen, "Hegel's Philosophy of God in the Light of Kierkegaard's Criticisms" in the same volume. Cullent's effort offers a summary of the traditional replies Hegel might have made against Kierkegaard's criticism. Perkins's response argues that Hegel could make no reply to Kierkegaard without changing his method, denying the unity of thought and being, and rejecting the content of the system he spent his life developing. Taken together, Cullen's and Perkins's articles contain a synopsis of the issues between Kierkegaard and Hegel.

Perkins Jr, Raymond K. Tom Regan, G E Moore, and Bishop Butler's Maxim: A Revisitation. *J Value Inq*, 27(1), 93-100, Ja 93.

Regan's 1982 paper is partially defended. Butler's maxim is not a premiss of Moore's naturalistic fallacy argument. But, contrary to what Regan says, Moore regarded the underlying error of the fallacy as logical, not factual.

Perreiah, Alan R. Aristotle's Axiomatic Science: Peripatetic Notation or Pedagogical Plan?. *Hist Phil Log*, 14(1), 87-99, 1993.

To meet a dilemma between the axiomatic theory of demonstrative science in *Posterior analytics* and the non-axiomatic practice of demonstrative science in the physical treatises, Jonathan Barnes has proposed that the theory of demonstration was not meant to guide scientific research but rather scientific pedagogy. The present paper argues that far from contributing directly to oral instruction, the axiomatic account of demonstrative science is a model for the written expression of science. The paper shows how this interpretation accords with related theories in the *Organon*, including the theories of dialectic in *Topics* and of deduction in *Prior analytics*.

Perrett, Roy W. Valuing Lives. *Bioethics*, 6(3), 185-200, Jl 92.

How is the value of a person's life properly measured? I discuss the attempts of economists to put a monetary price on the value of a life. I argue that: (i) it is morally permissible to put a price on a person's life; and (ii) there is a theoretically adequate way of determining such a price.

Perrett, Roy W and Oddie, Graham. Simultaneity and God's Timelessness. *Sophia (Australia)*, 31(1-2), 123-127, 1992.

We argue that the following *reductio* of God's timelessness is unsound. A timeless omniscient God would know all temporal events "at once". Hence (by transitivity of simultaneity) all temporal events would be simultaneous with one another (contradicting their evident temporal sequence). We argue that, provided simultaneity is a *three*-place relation, between two events and an observer (or point of view), this reductio fails. Relativity theory embodies the idea that simultaneity is a three-place relation, and so if there is something fundamentally wrong with our deflection of the criticism, then so too with the conception of simultaneity within STR.

Perrin, Ron. *Max Scheler's Concept of the Person: An Ethics of Humanism*. New York, St Martin's Pr, 1991.

Max Scheler was the only member of the phenomenological school of philosophy to turn the phenomenological method to the study of ethics. Part One of this book is a critical evaluation of that effort with particular attention given to Scheler's attempt to complement the formalism of Kantian ethics with an ethics of material values, i.e., those values that are the intentional objects of acts of preference. After concluding that Scheler was unable to overcome the basic Kantian dichotomy between thought and sensibility, the study proceeds, in Part Two, to argue that Scheler's chief contribution to moral philosophy rests with his attempt make the character of the ethical agent, that is, the Person, the ultimate standard of good and evil.

Perron, Deborah. Plato's Failure to Escape Mechanism. *Lyceum*, 3(2), 63-70, Fall 91.

Perry, Clifton B. Contraception in Biomedical Ethics Reviews 1992, Humber, James M (ed). Clifton, Humana Pr, 1993.

From the 1873 Comstock Act to the 1927 US Supreme Court Case of Buck versus Bell (274 US 200). There have been secular arguments, persuasive at law, for both encouraging and discouraging contraception. In addition, recent criminal cases have referenced contraception. This paper investigates the arguments for the present secular and sectarian policies concerning the use and nonuse of contraception.

Perry, Michael J. Virtues and Relativism. *Nomos*, 34, 117-131, 1992.

Perszyk, Kenneth J. Against Extended Modal Realism. *J Phil Log*, 22(2), 205-214, Ap 93.

Extended modal realism is David Lewis's realism about possible worlds and their inhabitants. Takashi Yagisawa has given the most serious defence in print of the conditional thesis that if Lewisian modal realism is to be accepted, then extended modal realism is to be accepted. He has two (main) arguments for this thesis, what I shall call 'the Parallel-Case Argument' and 'the Theoretical-Benefits Argument'. A central issue in the metaphysics of modality is whether Yagisawa's thesis is right. My aim in this paper is to reject his thesis by rebutting his two arguments in support of it.

Pesce, Domenico. *L'Epinomide* o della religione ricondotta entro i limiti della ragione. *Riv Filosof Neo-Scolas*, 84(1), 3-12, Ja-Mr 92.

The Platonism of *Epinomis* is without a doubt recognizable just from the title itself connecting this dialogue to the *Laws*, which are explicitly mentioned (980a) in order to reaffirm Plato's three theological dogmas. Other Platonic issues in *Epinomis* are the connection *sapience: wisdom* (sophia: phronesis) and the importance attached to the mathematics. This is the basis for an original doctrine which implies on one hand a plain indifference to the ontology and to the dialectics — considered a didactic procedure, not a scientific one — and on another hand a large interest in astronomy — a basis itself for the theology, since the stars are considered visible gods — and religion. The model of the intelligence is not more the Idea but the Law.

Peskova, Jaroslava and Horska, Pavla. A Debate Between a Philospoher and a Historian on the Women's Question in Bohemia (in Czechoslovakian). *Filozof Cas*, 40(5), 757-768, 1992.

The philosopher Jaroslava Pesková and the historian Pavla Horská try to find out the reasons why the "women's question" has almost never become a form in the Czech history in which the emancipation of an individual in general has been put through. (edited)

Pessoa, Jr, Osvaldo. Reversibility and the Interpretation of Mixtures in Quantum Mechanics. *Proc Phil Sci Ass*, 1, 381-392, 1992.

This paper examines the problem of the interpretation of mixtures in quantum mechanics, presenting a survey of the philosophical debate between the ignorance interpretation (Igl) and the instrumentalist approach. An important argument in defense of the Igl is shown not to be valid: "equivalent" mixtures (described by the same density matrix) prepared by different procedures can never be distinguished by measuring particle fluctuations. We present an alternative argument, based on an experiment to test whether the process of mixing is reversible or not. The expected result of this thought-experiment favors a weak version of the Igl.

Pestana, Mark Stephen. Radical Freedom, Radical Evil and the Possibility of Eternal Damnation. *Faith Phil*, 9(4), 500-507, O 92.

Thomas Talbott has recently argued that eternal damnation is incompatible with the notion of self-willed damnation as being incoherent. In may paper I critique this part of his argument by attempting to provide a ground in action theory for the idea of willful separation from God. I elucidate this ground in terms of Duns Scotus' characterization of free agency and a distinction in the intentional ordering of volition. I briefly elaborate the structure of moral evil in terms of these notions. And finally I argue, using these concepts, that the idea of eternal self-willed damnation is not incoherent, even if we consider those blessed with the vision of God.

Peterman, Larry. Dante and Machiavelli: A Last Word. *Interpretation*, 20(1), 17-36, Fall 92.

In a previous article in *Interpretation*, I examined Machiavelli's *Dialogue on Language* on the premise that its indictment of Dante places it in the modern lines in the battle between ancients and moderns. The article emphasizes the political dimension of Machiavelli's charge that by claiming to write in a common "courtly" language rather than Florentine Dante is unpatriotic and verges on "parricide," but in the end I concluded that linguistics and politics do not exhaust the issues between the two Florentines and that to do justice to them would require a systematic look at the performed dialogue from which the *Dialogue* takes its title. In the present article, I return this unfinished business and emend my original premise. Insofar as Machiavelli's account of his dispute with Dante is a true measure of their differences, I now think it fair to say, the dialogue becomes a sourcebook on the origins of the battle between ancients and moderns.

Peters, Karl E. Empirical Theology in the Light of Science. *Zygon*, 27(3), 297-325, S 92.

Empirical theology stands in contrast to science insofar as it seeks to understand the nature and source of human fulfillment and insofar as science seeks to understand the world and human beings regardless of the implications of that knowledge for human welfare. However, empirical theology is like science insofar as it affirms a dynamic, relational naturalism; accepts limitations of the human knower, thereby making all knowledge including religious knowledge tentative; seeks causal explanations as well as religious meaning; and argues that a key criterion for justifying ideas is their ability to explain experience already had and to predict new experiences in Lakatosian-type progressive research programs.

Peters, Karl E. Interrelating Nature, Humanity, and the Work of God: Some Issues for Future Reflection. *Zygon*, 27(4), 403-419, D 92.

This essay suggests some future items for an agenda about human viability, defined as survivability with meaning and purpose, by exploring interrelations between nature, humanity, and the work of God. It argues for intrinsic and creative value in nature, so there is a value kinship, as well as a factual kinship, between humans, nature, and God-working. It considers humans as "webs of culture, life, and cosmos" and suggests some implications of this notion of human nature for viability. And it asks what human fulfillment can be in light of the awesome creative - destroying - recreative - activity that seems to be the ground of an evolving universe.

Peterson, Grethe B (ed). *The Tanner Lectures On Human Values, V13*. Salt Lake City, Univ of Utah Pr, 1992.

Peterson, John. Deontologism and Moral Weakness. *Int Phil Quart*, 33(2), 173-181, Je 93.

Can a person who believes it better to do x than y choose to do y (moral voluntarism (MV)) or not (moral intellectualism (MI))? MI is implied by psychological and ethical eudemonism (PE and EE), psychological and ethical hedonism (PH and EH) and psychological and ethical Nietzscheanism (PN and EN). Since PE, PH and PN are the only plausible psychological generalizations from which MI is deduced, it follows that, if PE, PH and PN are false, then MI goes unsupported. But PE, PH and PN *are* false. MV is justified by a *deontological* definition of "it is better to do x and not y". This is, ED, it is better for a person (s) to do x and not y = df (i) it is right to s to do x and (ii) s's doing y is either wrong or morally neutral. Unlike EE, EH and EN, ED passes the open-question test. But on ED, MI becomes, counterintuitively. "It is not possible for a person s to choose to do x over y when s believes it is right for s to do y and s's doing x is either wrong or morally neutral.

Peterson, John. God and the Status of Facts. *Thomist*, 56(4), 635-646, O 92.

Peterson, Philip L. Intermediate Quantifiers for Finch's Proportions. *Notre Dame J Form Log*, 34(1), 140-149, Wint 93.

In "Validity Rules for Proportionally Quantified Syllogisms", H A Finch gave six complex rules for determining validity and invalidity of syllogism-analogues — argument forms that contain fraction quantifiers applying to each of the terms. The algebraic method for determining validity or invalidity for the 5-quantity and "higher" quantity syllogisms can be extended to cover all the syllogism-analogues which Finch considers, clearing the way for a syllogistically-oriented approach to explaining human reasoning about numbers (wherein intermediate quantifiers are fundamental).

Peterson, Sandra. Apparent Circularity in Aristotle's Account of Right Action in the *Nicomachean Ethics*. *Apeiron*, 25(2), 83-108, Je 92.

The paper argues against the claim, especially as made by J L Ackrill, that Aristotle's account of key notions in the *Nicomachean Ethics* is circular. The paper's argument consists of the exhibition of a non-circular explanatory arrangement for eighteen such notions, including right action, *phronesis*, virtuous action, the right reason, and too much (or too little) of specific emotions and behavior.

Peterzil, Ya'acov. Zilber's Conjecture for Some o-Minimal Structures Over the Reals. *Annals Pure Applied Log*, 61(3), 223-239, Je 93.

Petev, Valentin. Social Morality as Expressed in Law. *Ratio Juris*, 5(1), 104-108, Mr 92.

The article deals with the questions of the relation between law and morality, the obligatory character of law in a pluralistic society, and the possibility of the rational justification of ethical and political conceptions. The criteria on which the law is to be judged cannot be derived from a separate moral sphere, but only from the actual morality of the respective society. In a pluralistic society, only the law makes normative regulation possible. Its binding force is due to its socio-ethical content. The basic principles of law must be justified by a practical discourse within society, taking into account historical (p.t.o.) as well as the particular contemporary practice.

Petricek Jr, Miroslav. On History, Charm, and Grief. *Phil Today*, 36(4), 304-308, Wint 92.

Petrus, Klaus. Schiller über das Erhabene. *Z Phil Forsch*, 47(1), 23-40, Ja-Mr 93.

Mit dem Nachweis, dass 1) Schillers Konzeption des Erhabenen in relevanter Hinsicht über Kants Ansätze hinausweist, ergeben sich Möglichkeiten 2) einer systematischen Verortung des Schönen und Erhabenen in Schillers *Aesthetik*. Die Rekonstruktion des Verhältnisses dieser beiden Kategorien eröffnet zugleich neue Perspektiven 3) auf Schillers *Geschichtsauffassung*.

Petry, Edward S (ed) and Frederick, Robert (ed) and Hoffman, W Michael (ed). *The Corporation, Ethics, and the Environment*. Westport, Greenwood Pr, 1990.

Pétry, A. Stratified Languages. *J Sym Log*, 57(4), 1366-1376, D 92.

Petry, Jr, Edward S. The Origin and Development of Peirce's Concept of Self-Control. *Trans Peirce Soc*, 28(4), 667-690, Fall 92.

Pettersson, Anders. On Walton's and Currie's Analyses of Literary Fiction. *Phil Lit*, 17(1), 84-97, Ap 93.

The article criticizes the theory (in Kendall Walton's *Mimesis as Make-Believe* and Gregory Currie's *The Nature of Fiction*) that reading or viewing representational artworks involves playing games of make-believe. In particular, it is argued that the make-believe theory sheds no light on literary representation, and that imagining, which undoubtedly plays a role in connection with such representation, does not presuppose make-believe in the required sense.

Pettey, John Carson. *Nietzsche's Philosophical and Narrative Styles*. New York, Lang, 1992.

Pettit, Philip. *The Common Mind: An Essay on Psychology, Society, and Politics*. New York, Oxford Univ Pr, 1992.

The Common Mind argues for a naturalistic way of marking off thinking subjects from other intentional systems, natural and artificial. It defends the holistic view that human thinkers require communal resources but denies that such social holism compromises the autonomy of individuals. And it elaborates the significance of this view—this holistic individualism—for social and political theory. Social theory is allowed to deploy intentional interpretation or decision-theoretic reconstruction, structural explanation or rational choice derivation. But political theory is treated less permissively. The framework raises serious questions about contractarian and atomistic modes of thought and it points the way to a republican rethinking of liberal commitments.

Pettit, Philip. The Nature of Naturalism—II. *Aris Soc*, Supp(66), 245-266, 1992.

This paper characterizes naturalism by the slogan 'Outside nature, no salvation', commenting on the various readings of 'nature', 'outside' and 'salvation'. It distinguishes two challenges that the naturalist faces: one, to find room in a scientifically characterized nature for commonsense realities like mind and value; and two, to make space for the commonsense claim to be able to detect realities like causal relations that are already countenanced in the scientific image. The paper attempts, finally, to show how the 'program' model of causal architecture can deal with the second challenge, at least so far as it bears on causal relations.

Pettit, Philip and Brennan, Geoffrey. Hands Invisible and Intangible. *Synthese*, 94(2), 191-225, F 93.

Under an invisible hand regime, people intentionally perform actions that have a certain unforseen aggregate effect. Under what we describe as an intangible hand regime, they nonintentionally form attitudes—attitudes, generically, of approval or disapproval of certain forms of behaviour—that have a similar unforseen aggregate effect. We describe the two forms of ordering mechanism and we explore the interesting differences between them.

Pettit, Philip (ed) and Goodin, Robert E (ed). *A Companion to Contemporary Political Philosophy*. Cambridge, Blackwell, 1992.

There are three sections to this book. The first consists of a series of extended essays on the contributions to political theory of analytical philosophy, continental philosophy, history, sociology, economics, political science and legal studies. The second comprises analyses of current political ideologies: anarchism, conservatism, feminism, liberalism, Marxism and socialism. And the third involves shorter discussions of over twenty-five major concepts, ranging from virtue and equality to sociobiology and environmentalism.

Pettit, Philip and Jackson, Frank. In Defense of Explanatory Ecumenism. *Econ Phil*, 8(1), 1-21, Ap 92.

Social and other explananda are capable of being explained with greater or lesser attention to the detail of the producing mechanism and a common assumption is that the more fine-grained an explanation, the better. We reject this fine-grain preference and the explanatory individualism which it would support. We argue that explanations of different levels of grain may be interesting in different ways, so that individual-level explanations in social theory, for example, may serve to complement rather than replace structural accounts. This view can be described as a sort of explanatory ecumenism or pluralism.

Pettit, Philip and Jackson, Frank. Some Content is Narrow in Mental Causation, Heil, John (ed). New York, Clarendon/Oxford Pr, 1993.

Is water solubility narrow or broad? In one sense it is broad. What makes a substance water soluble is the way it does or would interact with its environment, not the way it is in itself. In another sense it is narrow. Any two internally identical substances in this world must agree in whether or not they are water soluble. Water solubility passes one version of the Doppelgänger test. We argue that in the second sense of 'narrow' some, but not all, content is narrow.

Pettit, Philip and Smith, Michael. Practical Unreason. *Mind*, 102(405), 53-79, Ja 93.

Most approaches to practical unreason treat the phenomenon as a practical failure that is not distinctively a failure of reason—say, as a loss of autonomy or control—or as a failure of reason that is not distinctively practical: say, as a form of inattention or illogic. This paper describes an approach under which the failure can be both a practical failure and a failure of reason. The authors begin with a picture of human psychology under which action is always the product of belief and desire but is also answerable to deliberative judgment. They find room for practical unreason, properly understood, in the gap that can open between the properties that an agent finds deliberatively compelling —the properties that, were he rational and informed, he would want himself to desire—and the properties that actually arouse his desires and move him to action. The possibility of this gap opening up is documented by reference to five broadly different varieties of practical unreason.

Pezzimenti, Rocco. *Homo Metaphisicus*. Sao Paulo, LER, 1992.

Pezzolato, Marco. La funzione e la portata della critica alle Idee nel *Parmenide* di Platone: Dalla teoria delle Idee alla teoria dei Principi. *Riv Filosof Neo-Scolas*, 84(2-3), 383-409, Ap-S 92.

AUTHOR INDEX WITH ABSTRACTS 629 **Piller, Christian**

Pfeifer, Karl. Searle, Strong AI, and Two Ways of Sorting Cucumbers. *J Phil Res*, 17, 347-350, 1992.

This paper defends Searle against the misconstrual of a key claim of "Minds, Brains, and Programs" and goes on to explain why an attempt to turn the tables by using the Chinese Room to argue for intentionality in computers fails.

Pfeiffer, K Ludwig. Fiction: On the Fate of a Concept Betwen Philosophy and Literary Theory in Aesthetic Illusion, Burwick, Frederick (ed). Hawthorne, de Gruyter, 1990.

Pfeiffer, Raymond S. Owing Loyalty to One's Employer. *J Bus Ethics*, 11(7), 535-543, Jl 92.

Neither employer expectations of loyalty, nor good treatment of employees by employers, nor employee appreciation of employers, nor the duty of nonmaleficence, nor the intention to be loyal, nor the duty not to act disloyally provide a basis for a moral or ethical duty of employee loyalty. However, in addition to the law, a pledge to be loyal can obligate one to be loyal. But if the specific content of such a pledge is unstated, the conduct required by the pledge may be indefinite. Moreover, the content and implications of loyalty are fluid, varying from context to context. Consequently, there is only a limited basis for the thesis that employees owe loyalty to their employers.

Pfeiffer, Raymond S. Teaching Ethical Decision-Making. *Teach Phil*, 15(2), 175-184, J 92.

One goal of applied ethics is to help students develop their ability to make responsible decisions. The resolved strategy offers a step-by-step way to address the main questions leading to a decision regarding an ethical conflict in one's personal life. The strategy requires the use of some practical ethical principles, such as Bernard Gert's Moral Rules. The strategy is explained, and a personal ethical conflict is presented along with a student analysis.

Philip, Pettit and Menzies, Peter. Found: the Missing Explanation. *Analysis*, 53(2), 100-109, Ap 93.

Mark Johnston has argued that certain realist explanations go missing under response-dependent theories. For example, a familiar response-dependent account of color holds that it is a priori true that something is red if and only if it disposed to look red to a normal observer under normal conditions. Johnston argues that one cannot maintain the a priori truth of this biconditional while advancing the realist explanation that something looks red to normal observers because it is red. In this paper we argue that the response-dependence biconditionals do not cause the corresponding realist explanations to go missing.

Philippides, Elias. Universalism and the Politicalisation of the World Problem. *Dialec Hum*, 17(3), 125-128, 1990.

Philipse, Herman. Heidegger's Question of Being and the 'Augustinian Picture' of Language. *Phil Phenomenol Res*, 52(2), 251-287, Je 92.

Philipson, Tomas. The Exchange and Allocation of Decision Power. *Theor Decis*, 33(3), 191-206, N 92.

Traditional theories of multi-person choice takes as exogenous data the allocation of decision power, that is, they assume the answer to the question of who-decides-what. This paper applies the standard economic theory of scarce resource allocation to explain observed allocations of decision power using as an illustrative example the allocation of power across committees in the US Congress.

Phillips, Antonia. Drawing from Life in Psychoanalysis, Mind and Art, Hopkins, Jim (ed). Cambridge, Blackwell, 1992.

Phillips, D C. On Castigating Constructivists. *Proc Phil Educ*, 48, 312-315, 1992.

Phillips, D Z. Authorship and Authenticity: Kierkegaard and Wittgenstein. *Midwest Stud Phil*, 17, 177-192, 1992.

Phillips, D Z. God and Concept-Formation in Simone Weil in Simone Weil's Philosophy of Culture, Bell, Richard H (ed). New York, Cambridge Univ Pr, 1993.

Phillips, D Z. Religion in Wittgenstein's Mirror in Wittgenstein Centenary Essays, Griffiths, A Phillips (ed). New York, Cambridge Univ Pr, 1991.

Phillips, D Z. Ten Questions for Psychoanalysis. *Philosophy*, 68(264), 183-192, Ap 93.

Phillips, Hollibert. The Ironist's Utopia: Can Rorty's Liberal Turnip Bleed?. *Int Phil Quart*, 32(3), 363-368, S 92.

The paper first sketches quite briefly Rorty's historicist-ironist position as presented in his *Contingency, Irony, and Solidarity*. It then undertakes to do three related things. It argues: (1) that far from renouncing any view of a common human nature, Rorty's version of "we-intentions", as a working notion, preserves, indeed entails, some such view; (2) that in maintaining that "cruelty is the worst thing we do", Rorty presents a position which is either incoherent or, if coherent, fails to yield any moral obligations; and (3) that his utopian society consisting of "liberal ironists" represents a dubious improvement over one that appeals to the "myth" of the rational grounding of its central beliefs.

Phillips, Robert L. Combatancy, Noncombatancy, and Noncombatant Immunity in Just War Tradition in Cross, Crescent, and Sword, Johnson, James Turner (ed). Westport, Greenwood Pr, 1990.

Phillips, Stephen and Bonevac, Daniel A. *Understanding Non-Western Philosophy: Introductory Readings*. Mountain View, Mayfield, 1993.

Phillips, Stephen H (trans). Gangesa on Characterizing Veridical Awareness. *J Indian Phil*, 21(2), 107-168, Je 93.

Within the context of a causal theory of knowledge, Gangesa, the revolutionary 14th-century Indian logician and epistemologists, considers and reflects about twenty-five definitions of knowledge (in his view, "veridical awareness," *pramā*), and accepts about eight, with one in particular acquiring the status of Plato's "justified true belief" for all later epistemologists (writing in Sanskrit) to the present. This article is an annotated translation, introducing technical notions of Gangesa's system (in particular for an audience of nonsanskritist philosophers). The notes provide some historical context but are devoted chiefly to the question of the success of the project.

Phillips, Winfred George. Rahner's Transcendental Deduction of the *Vorgriff*. *Thomist*, 56(2), 257-290, Ap 92.

Philonenko, Alexis. Vie et spéculation dans *l'Anweisung zum seligen Leben*. *Arch Phil*, 55(2), 243-261, Ap-Je 92.

Life and speculation in 1806 according to the *Anweisung zum seligen Leben*, and dialectics of love and hatred in order to sketch the problems of several perspectives in the *Wissenschaftslehre*.

Piazza, G. Ancora a proposito di metafisica: Nota in margine ad un recente volume. *Sapienza*, 46(1), 79-85, 1993.

Piché, Claude. The Philosopher-Artist: A Note on Lyotard's Reading of Kant. *Res Phenomenol*, 22, 152-160, 1992.

Lyotard's emphasis on Kant's third *Critique* leads to an aestheticization of philosophy based on an understanding of the philosopher's task as that of a genius. This paper examines the textual basis of this interpretation as well as its consequences.

Pickard, Dean. Applied Nietzsche: The Problem of Reflexivity in Habermas, A Postmodern Critique. *Auslegung*, 19(1), 1-21, Wint 93.

I will be concerned here with the issue of the self-referential or reflexive nature of reason that Nietzsche's perspectivism and antifoundationalism illuminates. I will apply Nietzsche's antifoundationalism and his insights about language and reason to a contemporary attempt by Jürgen Habermas to once again ground morality in necessary conditions of reason, this time beyond subjectivist epistemology on purported necessary conditions of reason, this time beyond subjectivist epistemology on purported necessary conditions of speech. The chapter will conclude with a similar application of related insights from Wittgenstein's *Philosophical Investigations and On Certainty*.

Pietarinen, Juhani. Early Liberalism and Women's Liberty in Women's Rights and the Rights of Man, Arnaud, A J. Oxford, Aberdeen, 1990.

Pietroski, Paul. Intentionality and Teleological Error. *Pac Phil Quart*, 73(3), 267-282, S 92.

I discuss Millikan's account of content, according to which a belief (type) B has proposition P as its content, if tokens of B are *supposed* to covary with P; where mental states have such normative properties in virtue of their natural history. But on Millikan's account, an organism can believe that P without having any ability to tell whether P is the case, thus rendering intentional explanations of the organism's behavior very implausible. I conclude that Millikan has not provided a good theory of *content*, and that telelogical approaches to content are suspect in general.

Piguet, J Claude. La Phénoménologie refuse l'abstraction et la formalisation in Analecta Husserliana, XXXIV, Tymieniecka, Anna-Teresa (ed). Dordrecht, Kluwer, 1992.

L'abstraction provient de la tradition "aristotélicienne" occidentale, *via* Boèce. La formalisation provient de la tradition "péripatéticienne" islamique (et judaïque), *via* Avicenne et Maïmonide. Tout constructivisme cherche à construire le concret avec l'abstrait. Or la phénoménologie refuse le constructivisme (elle est holistique). Elle refuse donc l'abstraction et se tourne vers le seul concret ("Zu den Sachen selbst"). Un concept formel (un nombre, un cube) est objet pour la phénoménologie: il est phénomène. Mais de là ne suit pas que les concepts formels soient au service de la méthode phénoménologieque. La phénoménologie doit refuser la formalisation. Ce qui manque encore à sa méthodologie, s'est la rigueur propre d'une épistémologie.

Piguet, J Claude. Le métier de médecin. *Rev Theol Phil*, 125(2), 191-195, 1993.

Ce livre est une contribution à l'épistémologie des sciences médicales. Selon l'auteur, la médecine a deux jambes: *psyché* et *sôma*. De là des conséquences: 1) C'est l'objet du médecin qui est "holistique", ce n'est pas la médecine; 2) Le médecin doit connaître son âmes s'il veut soigner le tout (âme et corps) du malade; 3) Il n'existe pas de théorie psychanalytique séparée de la pratique clinique.

Pike, Nelson. A Latter-Day Look at the Foreknowledge Problem. *Int J Phil Relig*, 33(3), 129-164, Je 93.

Pilardi, Jo-Ann. The Changing Critical Fortunes of *The Second Sex*. *Hist Theor*, 32(1), 51-73, 1993.

This article is a "review of reviews," a study of the critical response to Simone de Beauvoir's book, *The Second Sex (Le Deuxième Sexe)*, published in 1949; it also reports the publishing history and provides some statistical information on the criticism and citations of the book. The claim here is that Beauvoir's work is a "classic" appreciated for its theoretical notion of "woman as absolute Other" and its accompanying description of patriarchal culture as a reflection of that notion. But it is a classic with a mercurial past. Though the book and its author were severely attacked following its French publication, the work received positive reviews four years later upon its translation into English. (edited)

Pillay, A and Hart, B and Starchenko, S. Triviality, NDOP and Stable Varieties. *Annals Pure Applied Log*, 62(2), 119-146, Jl 93.

Pillay, Anand and Rothmaler, Philipp. Undimensional Modules: Uniqueness of Maximal Non-Modular Submodules. *Annals Pure Applied Log*, 62(2), 175-181, Jl 93.

We characterize the non-modular models of a unidimensional first-order theory of modules as the elementary submodels of its prime pure-injective model. We show that in case the maximal non-modular submodel of a given model splits off this is true for every such submodel, and we thus obtain a cancellation result for this situation. Although the theories in question always have models (in every big enough power) whose maximal non-modular submodel do split off, they may as well have others where they don't. We present a corresponding example.

Piller, Christian. Comment on Keith Lehrer and Vann McGee's Solution of Newcomb's Problem. *Grazer Phil Stud*, 40, 221-228, 1991.

Piller, Christian. On Keith Lehrer's Belief in Acceptance. *Grazer Phil Stud*, 40, 37-61, 1991.

Keith Lehrer's notion of acceptance and its relation to the notion of belief in analyzed in a way that a person only accepts some proposition *p* if she decides to believe it in order to reach the epistemic aim. This view of acceptance turns out to be untenable: Under the empirical claim that we don't have the power to decide what to believe it follows that we cannot accept anything. If reaching the truth is the epistemic aim acceptance proves ill-formed, it is impossible to pursue the aim of truth by believing or accepting something because belief itself is a truth-directed attitude. If the epistemic aim is formulated in a weaker sense, combined with other aims, the danger lurks that accepting a proposition *p* is the end loosing any connection with the truth of *p*.

Piller, Christian. Über Wünsche, Lust und Rationalität—Eine Auseinandersetzung mit der Gleichgewichtstheorie von Anna Kusser. *Conceptus*, 25(66), 69-95, 1991.

There are conditions of rationality for desires. Decision theory is a general theory of the rationality of extrinsic desires, and also intrinsic desires can be evaluated in terms of rationality because of their connection with certain beliefs. These results arise from a critique of Anna Kusser's equilibrium theory of rational desires. Kusser's idea that an equilibrium between different kinds of desires is a condition of their rationality and her claim that under certain conditions decision theoretic deliberations lead into a circle are both rejected in this paper.

Pines, Christopher. *Ideology and False Consciousness: Marx and his Historical Progenitors*. Albany, SUNY Pr, 1993.

According to recent interpreters of Marx, 1) Marx did not have a conception of ideology as false consciousness; and 2) Marx's conception of ideology is best understood in a non-epistemological, functionalist was the worldview or political program of a social group. In opposing this contemporary trend of interpretation, I argue that Marx did have an epistemological conception of ideology as false consciousness similar in meaning to Engels. Secondly, I demonstrate that the various meanings of false consciousness found in the writings of Marx and Engels reflect the influence of the views of the Baconian-French Enlightenment and the Hegelian-Feuerbachian philosophies on their thinking. According to these classical theories, false consciousness signified: 1) alienated and misguided thinking; 2) the common mind's social and historical unconsciousness; 3) social delusionary thinking; and 4) a falsified and distorted collective understanding and perception of reality. In spite of the diverse senses of false consciousness, I argue that for Marx what false consciousness generally denotes is a social consciousness which takes certain false things to be true about matters having significance to the outcome of class divided societies.

Pink, T L M. Justification and the Will. *Mind*, 102(406), 329-334, Ap 93.

According to Davidson and Bratman, intentions to do A are pro attitudes towards doing A. That is a) one's justifications for the intention are a simple function of one's justifications for doing A; and b) the psychological states which explain intentions are ones which, at the appropriate time, would also motivate one to do A. It's argued that though (b) is often true, there are counterexamples; and these show that (a) is always false. Forming an intention to do A is like trying to do A—an activity justified by ends which *it* furthers, though often explained by motives for doing A.

Pinkard, Terry P. A Philosophical Appreciation. *Z Phil Forsch*, 46(4), 600-608, O-D 92.

Pinkard, Terry P. Judicial Virtue and Democratic Politics. *Nomos*, 34, 265-282, 1992.

Pinkard, Terry P. Naturalized Historicism and Hegelian Ethics. *Bull Hegel Soc Gt Brit*, 25, 18-33, Spr-Sum 92.

Pinottini, Marzio. L' "Antibancor" e la filosofia del danaro. *Filosofia*, 43(3), 507-513, S-D 92.

Pinto, Robert C and Blair, John Anthony. *Reasoning: A Practical Guide*. Englewood Cliffs, Prentice Hall, 1993.

Pinto De Oliveira, José Carlos. Kuhn e Quine. *Cad Hist Filosof Cie*, 1(1), 33-53, Ja-Je 91.

When he analyzes the relation between languages Quine sees it as involving an indeterminacy of reference. In this paper we attempt to show that for Kuhn scientific theories are languages, and hence, his concept of incommensurability, which calls into question the traditional idea of intertheoretical competition in science, is correctly formulated in terms of indeterminacy of reference.

Pippin, Robert B. Being, Time, and Politics: The Strauss-Koljève Debate. *Hist Theor*, 32(2), 138-161, 1993.

Pippin, Robert B. Hegel's Original Insight. *Int Phil Quart*, 33(3), 285-296, S 93.

Pippin, Robert B. The Modern World of Leo Strauss. *Polit Theory*, 20(3), 448-472, Ag 92.

I draw attention here to Leo Strauss's "wave hypothesis", his claim that the modern experiment should be understood as occuring in three waves—a great instauration attributed mainly to Hobbes (though built on ground well prepared by Machiavelli), a first "crisis" correctly diagnosed but not solved by Rousseau, and a second crisis, the continuing "crisis of our times", correctly diagnosed and ruthlessly explored by Nietzsche. I argue that Strauss's interpretation of the second wave (or first crisis) misinterprets and undervalues the alternatives presented by the German thinkers so influenced by Rousseau, the German Idealists, Kant, Fichte, and Hegel especially. Strauss had a number of reasons for the belief that this tradition must eventually result in a self-undermining historicism, one that intensifies rather than resolves the modern crisis. I disagree with those reasons, and thereby disagree that there is some fatal *aporia* within modernity finally and decisively revealed by Nietzsche.

Pippin, Robert B. You Can't Get There from Here in The Cambridge Companion to Hegel, Beiser, Frederick (ed). New York, Cambridge Univ Pr, 1993.

Piscione, E. Tra 'kratos' e 'petsis': La funzione della legge in Platone. *Sapienza*, 45(1), 53-62, 1992.

Pitcher, John (ed) and Bacon, Francis. *The Essays—Francis Bacon*. New York, Penguin USA, 1985.

Pitowsky, Itamar and Pagonis, Constantine and Clifton, Robert. Relativity, Quantum Mechanics and EPR. *Proc Phil Sci Ass*, 1, 114-128, 1992.

The Einstein-Podolsky-Rosen argument for the incompleteness of quantum mechanics involves two assumptions: one about locality and the other about when it is legitimate to infer the existence of an element-of-reality. Using one simple thought experiment, we argue that quantum predictions and the relativity of

simultaneity require that both these assumptions fail, whether or not quantum mechanics is complete.

Pitt, Joseph C. The Heavens and Earth in Revolution and Continuity, Barker, Peter (ed). Washington, Cath Univ Amer Pr, 1991.

Pizzorni, R. Giustizia e "carità" nel pensiero greco-romano (I). *Sapienza*, 45(3), 233-278, 1992.

Place, U T. A Radical Behaviorist Methodology for the Empirical Investigation of Private Events. *Behavior Phil*, 20/2(21/1), 25-36, 1993.

Skinner had repeatedly asserted that he does not deny either the existence of private events or the possibility of studying them scientifically. But he has never explained how his position in this respect differs from that of the mentalist or provided a practical methodology for the investigation of private events within a radical behaviorist perspective. With respect to the first of these deficiencies, I argue that observation statements describing a public state of affairs in the common public environment of two more observers which those observers confirm as a correct description provide a far more objective and secure foundation for empirical knowledge than statements describing private events in the experience of a single individual. (edited)

Place, Ullin T. Eliminative Connectionism: Its Implications for a Return to an Empiricist/Behaviorist Linguistics. *Behavior Phil*, 20(1), 21-35, Spr-Sum 92.

For the past three decades linguistic theory has been based on the assumption that sentences are interpreted and constructed by the brain by means of computational processes analogous to those of a serial-digital computer. The recent interest in devices based on the neural network or parallel distributed processor (PDP) principle raises the possibility ("eliminative connectionism") that such devices may ultimately replace the S-D computer as the model for the interpretation and generation of language by the brain. An analysis of the differences between the two models suggests that the effect of such a development would be to steer linguistic theory towards a return to the empiricism and behaviorism which prevailed before it was driven by Chomsky towards nativism and mentalism. Linguists, however, will not be persuaded to return to such a theory unless and until it can deal with the phenomenon of novel sentence construction as effectively as its nativist/mentalist rival.

Place, Ullin T. The Role of the Ethnomethodological Experiment in the Empirical Investigation of Social Norms and Its Application to Conceptual Analysis. *Phil Soc Sci*, 22(4), 461-474, D 92.

It is argued that conceptual analysis as practiced by the philosophers of ordinary language, is an empirical procedure that relies on a version of Garfinkel's ethnomethodological experiment. The ethnomethodological experiment is presented as a procedure in which the existence and nature of a social norm is demonstrated by flouting the putative convention and observing what reaction that produces in the social group within which the convention is assumed to operate. Examples are given of the use of ethnomethodological experiments, both in vivo and as a thought experiment, in order to demonstrate the existence of otherwise invisible conventions governing human social behavior. Comparable examples are cited from the writings of ordinary language philosophers of ethnomethodological thought experiments designed to demonstrate the existence of linguistic conventions.

Place, Ullin T and Armstrong, David M. A Debate on Dispositions, Their Nature and Their Role in Causation—Part I—The Armstrong-Place Debate. *Conceptus*, 25(66), 3-44, 1991.

When we ascribe a dispositional property, such as brittleness, to an entity, such as a pane of glass, at least *part* of what we are saying is that, if certain conditions are fulfilled, if the unprotected glass is stuck with a moderate degree of force, it will behave in a certain way, the glass will break. Like any other empirical proposition, a disposition-ascribing sentence requires a *truthmaker*, an event or state of affairs which is specified by the sentence and which, if it exists, makes the proposition ture. But in the case of a disposition-ascribing sentence, the truthmaker cannot be an event or state of affairs, such as the breaking of the glass, in which the disposition is *manifested*. For it can be true that an entity possesses the property, that the glass is brittle, even though no manifestation of the disposition, no breaking of the glass, ever has occurred or existed in the past or will in fact occur or exist in the future. (edited)

Plant, Sadie. Nomads and Revolutionaries. *J Brit Soc Phenomenol*, 24(1), 88-101, Ja 93.

Plantinga, Alvin. Augustinian Christian Philosophy. *Monist*, 75(3), 291-320, Jl 92.

I distinguish four parts to Christian philosophy: philosophical theology, apologetics, both positive and negative, Christian Philosophical Criticism, and Positive Christian Philosophy. The first two are self-explanatory. The third is a matter of criticizing and evaluating various philosophical projects from the perspective of Christianity; and the fourth involves thinking about the various sorts of questions philosophers ask and answer—the nature of substance, the question of human freedom, the nature of universals, causality, the nature of thought, and so on—from a Christian perspective.

Plantinga, Alvin. Epistemic Probability and Evil in Our Knowledge of God, Clark, Kelly James (ed). Dordrecht, Kluwer, 1992.

Plantinga, Alvin. Justification in the 20th Century in Rationality in Epistemology, Villanueva, Enrique (ed). Atascadero, Ridgeview, 1992.

Contemporary concepts of epistemic justification display an enormous and bewildering diversity. I argue that this confusing variety can be understood by tracing these concepts back to the deontological claim—made by Descartes and Locke—that we have epistemic duties and obligations. I go on to argue that internalism in epistemology arises from this deontological claim. Finally, the 'received tradition' in epistemology is a cluster of four ideas; 1) warrant depends on factors internal to the epistemic agent, 2) justification is necessary and nearly sufficient for warrant, the quantity enough of which together with true belief is sufficient for knowledge, 3) justification is a matter of fulfilling intellectual duty, and 4) justification essentially involves a belief's fitting the believers evidence. I argue that this tradition is incoherent; justification and warrant "are not merely uneasy bedfellows; they are worlds apart."

Plantinga, Alvin. The Prospects for Natural Theology in Philosophical Perspectives, 5: Philosophy of Religion, 1991, Tomberlin, James E (ed). Atascadero, Ridgeview, 1991.

Plantinga, Alvin. Why We Need Proper Function. *Nous*, 27(1), 66-82, Mr 93.

This is a reply to Ernest Sosa and Richard Feldman's comments on my two books *Warrant: The Current Debate* and *Warrant and Proper Function* in a 1992 APA Pacific Division Symposium.

Plantinga, Alvin and Grim, Patrick. Truth, Omniscience, and Cantorian Arguments: An Exchange. *Phil Stud*, 71(3), 267-306, S 93.

Plantinga, Carl. Film Theory and Aesthetics: Notes on a Schism. *J Aes Art Crit*, 51(3), 445-454, Sum 93.

Though film theory and philosophical aesthetics sometimes explore identical issues, the two disciplines have not taken advantage of each other's scholarship. Contact between the disciplines, once more common, has recently been rare, and when it does occur, rancorous. This essay accounts for the schism by tracing the history of film studies' turn away from humanistic inquiry, and by describing differences between the disciplines in methodology and basic assumptions about what constitutes important scholarship.

Plantinga, Theodore. *How Memory Shapes Narratives: A Philosophical Essay on Redeeming the Past*. Lewiston, Mellen Pr, 1992.

Plass, Paul. The Metaphysical Aspect of Tenses in Proclus. *Int Phil Quart*, 33(2), 143-151, Je 93.

The NeoPlatonism reality is composed of hierarchical levels from the One down to the spatial-temporal universe. Every aspect of the latter has metaphysical causes at higher planes. Above empirical time lies whole time, which is relatively more complex than Eternity and includes the causes of various tensed divisions of time. The past has a higher level of cause than do the present or future because the flow of events is fixed in the past as it is not in the other two tenses. This primacy reflects a general bias toward the past in Greek culture due to its paradigmatic role.

Platts, Mark. Philosophical Scepticism about Moral Obligation. *Aris Soc*, Supp(67), 175-194, 1993.

Plebe, Armando. La possibilità di una Formalizzazione della Logica Aristotelica degli Entimemi. *Rev Int Phil*, 47(184), 70-77, 1993.

Pleines, Jürgen-Eckardt. Dialektik als Letzbegründung bei Hegel. *Z Phil Forsch*, 46(4), 591-599, O-D 92.

Letzbegründung is in German parlance a novice and the word means "to give the reasons for the last causes" (well-founded). It follows the metaphysical concept of Plato's and the Aristotelian idealism but now under the conditions of reason to all intents and purposes of modern science, culture and literature. The first to represent this idea have been Paul Natorp and Edmund Husserl; but the concept you'll find also in Hegel's interpretation of dialectical or speculative philosophy.

Plekon, Michael. Kierkegaard the Theologian in Foundations of Kierkegaard's Vision of Community, Connell, George B (ed). Atlantic Highlands, Humanities Pr, 1992.

Pletcher, Galen K. Philosophy of Religion in Reflections on Philosophy, McHenry, Leemon (ed). New York, St Martin's Pr, 1993.

Chapter Eight: Philosophy of Religion. This chapter provides an introduction to the following traditional problems in the philosophy of religion: arguments for the existence of god, the analysis of religious experience, naturalistic analyses of religion, the nature of god and of human beings, the relation between religion and morality, and the problem of evil. It introduces these problems as instances of the three traditional concerns of philosophers: epistemology, metaphysics, and ethics. Although the chapter provides provisional evaluations of arguments and positions, its presentation invites further consideration of the issues. There are study questions and suggestions for further reading.

Pluhar, Evelyn. Who Can Be Morally Obligated to Be a Vegetarian?. *J Agr Environ Ethics*, 5(2), 189-215, 1992.

Kathryn George has recently argued that, even if Tom Regan position on animal rights is correct, most humans cannot be morally obligated to be vegetarians. Regan's "liberty principle", she holds, permits us to kill animals for food *if* doing so prevents us from being made worse off. Unlike Regan, George maintains that vegetarianism is unsafe for most humans. I argue that Regan's "liberty principle" either contradicts his "equal rights view" or prohibits such slaughter. I show that an "unequal rights view" would permit this action—against *humans* as well as other animals—to safeguard one's life or health. Finally, I argue that current research does not support George's contention that most humans would suffer if they ceased eating meat and dairy products.

Plumer, Gilbert. A Here-Now Theory of Indexicality. *J Phil Res*, 18, 193-211, 1993.

This paper attempts to define indexicality so as to semantically distinguish indexicals from proper names and definite descriptions. The widely-accepted approach that says that indexical reference is distinctive in being dependent on context of use is criticized. A reductive approach is proposed and defended that takes an indexical to be (roughly) an expression that either is or is equivalent to 'here' or 'now', or is such that a tokening of it refers by relating something to the place and/or time that would have been referred to had 'here' and 'now' been tokened instead. Alternative reductive approaches are criticized.

Pocock, J G A. A Response to Zerilli and Brodribb. *Polit Theory*, 20(4), 672-673, N 92.

Pocock, J G A (ed) and Harrington, James. *"The Commonwealth of Oceana" and "A System of Politics"—James Harrington*. New York, Cambridge Univ Pr, 1992.

Podes, Stephan. Polybius and His Theory of *Anacyclosis* Problems of Not Just Ancient Political Theory. *Hist Polit Thought*, 12(4), 577-587, Wint 91.

The author's approach is to take the micro-macro-level differentiation developed by Coleman within the rational choice concept and apply it to Polybius' theory of anacyclosis. The investigation reveals the following findings: (1) On the micro-level Polybius' theory of anacyclosis is a chain of genetic explanations of constitutional transition; (2) Polybius is mainly concerned with the 'problem of coordination'; (3) Polybius fails to treat the 'problem of transformation' adequately; and (4) A possible solution of this 'problem of transformation' may be found in the theory of political entrepreneurship. The traces of this theory in Polybius are followed up.

Podpadec, Tessa and Boddington, Paula. Measuring Quality of Life in Theory and in Practice: A Dialogue Between Philosophical and Psychological Approaches. *Bioethics*, 6(3), 201-217, Jl 92.

The paper aims at a dialogue between philosophical and psychological approaches to measuring quality of life, focusing on learning difficulties, and addressing implications for the valuing of individual lives. The practical, detailed methodology of some psychological work is of great potential benefit to some philosophical accounts of quality of life, and in particular some work may help to undo implicit bias in these accounts against certain people, notably those with intellectual disabilities. However, psychological work often suffers from lack of explicit theoretical base and philosophical theory may be usefully applied here.

Podpadec, Tessa and Boddington, Paula. Reply to Anstötz: What We Can Learn from People with Learning Difficulties. *Bioethics*, 6(4), 361-364, O 92.

This paper replies to criticisms of our paper in *Bioethics* 6.3 "Measuring the Quality of Life in Theory and in Practice". Philosophy and psychology take differing approaches to issues concerning people with learning difficulties or mental handicap. Philosophy questions ethical assumptions others may take for granted and the methodological and practical work of psychologists may help philosophers in their aims and in adjusting their theoretical stances. People should be seen as individuals not as members of a homogenous group. Other misunderstandings of our work are addressed.

Pöggeler, Otto. The Hermeneutics of the Technological World. *Int J Phil Stud*, 1(1), 21-48, Mr 93.

Pöltner, Günther. Die konsequenzialistische Begründung des Lebensschutzes. *Z Phil Forsch*, 47(2), 184-203, Ap-Je 93.

Kritische Auscinandersetzung mit P Singer und N Hoerster, 1) Dei kinsequenzialistischen Argumente (Vorwurf des Speziesismus; Ablehnung des Potentialitätsarguments, Beginn des Lebensrechts). 2) Die fragwürdigen Voraussetzungen des Konsequnzialismus: Ein reduktionistischer Seinsbergriff (Sein = bedeutungslose Faktizität) und ein unzureichender Personbegriff (Person = selbstbewubtes Individuum). Mensch zu sein ist nicht, wie der Konsequenzialismus behauptet, eine Eigenschaft. 3) Schlubfolgerung: Die Alternative zum biologischen Speziesimus ist nicht der konsequenzialistische Interessenschutz, sodern die These, die Menschenwürde ist mit dem Menschsein selbst gegeben.

Pöltner, Günther. Mozart und Heidegger—Die Musik und der Ursprung des Kunstwerkes. *Heidegger Stud*, 8, 123-145, 1992.

Der Aufsatz versucht, im Ausgang bon Heideggers Kunstwerkaufsatz eine Wesensbestimmung der Musik zu geben und zu begründen, warum der Vorrang der Dichtkunst fragwürdig ist (Doppeldeutigkeit des Begriffs "Erde" im Zusdmmenhang des Sprachkunstwerks: Laut bzw. Wort). In der Musik wird auf urpprügliche Weise Zeit und Welt erfahren. Die Musik ist die Kunst der Gestimmtheit des Menschen. Sie enthullt das Wesen des Menschen, d h den Bezug nov Sein und Mensch. Sie ist im ausgezeichneten Sinn die Kunst des "Ereignisses". Der Aufsatz enthält phänomenologische Analysen der Musik.

Pohlenz, Gerd. Kein Platz für phänomenale Qualitäten und Leib- Umwelt-Interaktion?. *Z Phil Forsch*, 46(3), 363-380, Jl-S 92.

Natural sciences are *implicitly* and basically defined by the *external*-realistic principle of body-environment interaction and the related structure-function principle. A transcendentalistic interpretation of empirical science thus is excluded (not, however, *touching* Kantian theory by theoretical physics). On the other hand, if the modern purely negative characterization of the qualia is completed by a non-trivial tautological definition, we reach an understanding of a systematic core of Kant's theory. According to its specific perspective of empirical observation, qualia are primarily and irreducibly bound to empirical *objects* (which are also a priori defined by 'formal' principles).

Pojman, Louis. Are Human Rights Based on Equal Human Worth?. *Phil Phenomenol Res*, 52(3), 605-622, S 92.

In this paper I examine ten arguments for equal human rights given by contemporary egalitarians: (1) The Presumption Argument; (2) The Properly Basic Belief Strategy; (3) The Existential Strategy; (4) The Libertarian Argument; (5) The Family Argument; (6) The Pragmatic Argument; (7) The Utilitarian Argument; (8) The Coherentist Argument; (9) The Rational Agency Argument; and (10) The Argument from Moral Personality. I argue that in their present form none of them is compelling and that there are reasons to give up egalitarianism altogether.

Pojman, Louis. Do Animal Rights Entail Moral Nihilism?. *Pub Affairs Quart*, 7(2), 165-185, Ap 93.

After outlining the seven positions on the moral status of animals, three of which grant them equal status with ourselves, I argue that these equal status theories entail moral nihilism.

Pojman, Louis. Ethics: Religious and Secular. *Mod Sch*, 70(1), 1-30, N 92.

I argue against the "Standard View", held by the majority of philosophers since Kant, that the content of enlightened secular ethics and religious ethics is essentially the same. I argue that metaphysics does matter, and that there are fundamental differences between the two types of ethical systems. After identify a common core in the historic Christian view, I identify four differences between it and secular systems. They have to do with the concept of obligation, the supremacy of morality, the idea that humans are equal positive worth, and the problem of morality and self-interest.

Pojman, Louis (ed). *Moral Philosophy: A Reader*. Indianapolis, Hackett, 1993.

A new collection of 30 classical and contemporary readings in Ethical Theory, covering eight topics: What is Morally Right Conduct; Moral Relativism; Ethics and Egoism; Value; Utilitarianism, Deontological Ethics; Virtue Ethics; and Ethics and Religion. There is a General Introduction and section introductions by the editor.

Pojman, Louis. Race and Culture: A Response to Levin and Thomas. *J Soc Phil*, 24(1), 152-154, Spr 93.

In this paper I assess the debate between Michael Levin and Laurence Thomas on race and culture. I point out that Thomas misrepresents Levin's argument and hence does not succeed in rebutting him. I go on to put the debate in a broader context.

Pojman, Louis. The Moral Status of Affirmative Action. *Pub Affairs Quart*, 6(2), 181-206, Ap 92.

I distinguish two versions of Affirmative Action (AA): *Weak AA* which involves such measures as the elimination of segregation, widespread advertisement to groups not previously represented in certain privileged positions, and using underrepresentation or a history of past discrimination as a tie breaker when candidates are relatively equal; and *Strong AA* which involves more positive steps to eliminate past injustice, such as reverse discrimination, reparations, and hiring candidates minimally qualified candidates over more qualified ones. After a brief history of affirmative action, I examine several arguments for and against Strong AA and conclude that it is not morally permissible.

Pokriefka, M L. More on Empirical Significance. *Analysis*, 44(2), 92-93, Mr 84.

Polansky, Ronald. *Philosophy and Knowledge: A Commentary on Plato's "Theaetetus"*. Lewisburg, Bucknell Univ Pr, 1992.

This commentary defends to connected views; the *Theaetetus* is complete and its provides a basic answer about what knowledge is. The dialogue attempts four accounts of knowledge: the established sciences, perception, true opinion, and true opinion with an account. The commentary argues that these cover all the real possibilities, so the dialogue is complete. Moreover, since the dialogue seeks an account of knowledge and the final section aims for an account of account, the ending constitutes lucid self-reflection upon the whole discourse. Thus, if not straightforwardly in speech, then in deed, Plato succeeds in presenting human knowledge.

Polanyi, Michael. The Value of the Inexact. *Tradition Discovery*, 18(3), 35-36, 1992.

Poli, Roberto. Husserl's Conception of Formal Ontology. *Hist Phil Log*, 14(1), 1-14, 1993.

The concept of formal ontology was first developed by Husserl. It concerns problems relating to the notions of object, substance, property, part, whole, predication, nominalization, etc. The idea of formal ontology is present in many of Husserl's works, with minor changes. This paper provides a reconstruction of such an idea. Husserl's proposal is faced with contemporary logical orthodoxy and it is presented also an interpretative hypothesis, namely that the original difference between the general perspective of usual model theory and formal ontology is grounded in the fact that this latter starts from an *intended* interpretation and not from the set of all the possible interpretations.

Poliakov, Leonid. Totalitarianism "with a Human Face": A Methodological Essay. *Russian Stud Phil*, 31(3), 40-50, Wint 92-93.

Polikarov, Azarya and Ginev, Dimitri. Remarks on Logical Empiricism and Some of Ayer's Achievements in The Philosophy of A J Ayer, Hahn, Lewis Edwin (ed). Peru, Open Court, 1992.

Two basic ideas of Ayer's philosophical views, i.e., the necessity of a verifiability criterion, and the importance of a logico-critical analysis of scientific knowledge are discussed. It is argued that Ayer's more liberal 'logicism' does not exclude post-positivistic 'historicism' in philosophy of science, but that both may be considered as complementary approaches. This examination is preceded by an attempt at a quasi-axiomatic presentation and critical evaluation of logical empiricism.

Polis, Dennis F. Paradigms for an Open Philosophy. *Metaphilosophy*, 24(1-2), 33-46, Ja-Ap 93.

Our Geometric Paradigm of scientific knowledge has dis-integrated our scientific, humanistic and spiritual world views. Demanding all relevant conclusions be deduced from set postulates closes scientific systems to experiences beyond a pre-defined scope. Two paradigms conducive to open systems are presented. The Projection Paradigm sees all knowledge as valid but limited, and seeks points of correspondence between various projections of reality. It represents the actual practice of physics, psychology and philosophy better than the Geometric Paradigm. The Strophe-Antistrophe Paradigm remains open to the possibility that "meaningless" questions will be meaningful in the antistrophe of a developed system.

Polk, Danne W. Temporal Impermanence and the Disparity of Time and Eternity. *Augustin Stud*, 22, 63-82, 1991.

Given the fact that Husserl credits Augustine for being the first thinker to seriously wrestle with the enigma of time-consciousness, this paper follows Augustine's lead by comparing the *Confessions* with phenomenological descriptions of time. We will discover that for both Husserl and Augustine, we are dealing with the problem of the difference between objectivity and subjectivity, and how this problem correlates to the categorical rift between Being and becoming. We will see that Augustine's great discovery is that an adequate treatment of the reality of time requires an account which will address the fact that time is experienced perspectivally.

Polka, Brayton. Aesthetics and Religion in Kierkegaard on Art and Communication, Pattison, George (ed). New York, St Martin's Pr, 1992.

Pollard, D E B. Literature and Representation: A Note. *Brit J Aes*, 32(2), 166-168, Ap 92.

Pollock, John. Reply to Shope's "You Know What You Falsely Believe". *Phil Phenomenol Res*, 52(2), 411-413, Je 92.

Polsek, Darko. Phenomenology as a Methodological Research Program in Analecta Husserliana, XXXIV, Tymieniecka, Anna-Teresa (ed). Dordrecht, Kluwer, 1992.

Polyakov, L V. Women's Emancipation and the Theology of Sex in Nineteenth-Century Russia. *Phil East West*, 42(2), 297-308, Ap 92.

Pompa, L. Value and History in Objectivity, Method and Point of View, Van Der Dussen, W J (ed). Leiden, Brill, 1991.

The aim of the article is to rebut two claims about the way in which historians' value

judgments necessarily affect their accounts of the way the past really was: by governing the characterisation of such value-laden activities as enter them and by determining the contextualisations required for the attribution of causal responsibility to historical agents. The first claim is rejected on the ground that historical accounts ought to be constrained by what historical evidence licenses and that, although only characterised activities can enter them, the evidence is already characterised and does not need recharacterisation. The second is rejected on the ground that the reason for accepting one contextualisation rather than another must lie in the historical plausibility of the accounts to which they give rise rather than any non-historical judgments on the strength of which they may first have been advanced.

Pompa, Leon. Philosophical History and the End of History. *Bull Hegel Soc Gt Brit*, 23-24, 24-38, 1991.

The aim is to ascertain whether there are grounds in Hegel's philosophy, and particularly his philosophy of history, which commit him to the view that history must come to an end. The conclusions are that there are none and that, on the contrary, he is committed to the view that history cannot come to an end, because of the nature of dialectic. But his claim that the philosophical historian is in possession of a valid viewpoint can be maintained only by a conception of the development of spirit as dialectically determined which commits him to the view that the nature of spirit must be equally determined. His claims are rejected on the grounds that they involve the same mistake as the ontological argument.

Pompa, Leon. The Possibility of Historical Knowledge. *Aris Soc*, Supp(67), 1-16, 1993.

In the first part I argue that historical knowledge is not attainable under current theories because they all involve some form of argument from or to evidence. But data are evidence only under a theory of interpretation and since data are overdetermined by theory, we need a justification for the truth-yielding theory. In the second part I suggest that a justified theory is provided by the historical transmission of truths about the past, resting upon a different theory of knowledge, which constrain theory in such a way as to make historical knowledge possible.

Ponferrada, Gustavo E. Ciencia y filosofía en el tomismo. *Sapientia*, 47(183), 9-22, 1992.

Ponsetto, Antonio. Krise und Metamorphose der Rationalität. *Theol Phil*, 68(2), 161-181, 1993.

Poole, Adrian. War and Grace: The Force of Simone Weil on Homer. *Arion*, 2(1), 1-15, Wint 92.

Poole, Ross. On National Identity: A Reponse to Jonathan Rée. *Rad Phil*, 62, 14-19, Autumn 92.

Popkin, Richard H. Shadow History. *J Hist Phil*, 31(1), 119-122, Ja 93.

Popkin, Richard H. Sources of Knowledge of Sextus Empiricus in Hume's Time. *J Hist Ideas*, 54(1), 137-141, Ja 93.

Popkin, Richard H. Stroll's Answer to Skepticism in Certainty and Surface in Epistemology and Philosophical Method, Martinich, A P (ed). Lewiston, Mellen Pr, 1991.

Popp, Jerome A. The Reflective Thought of Philip G Smith. *Phil Stud Educ*, 1, 125-132, 1990.

Popper, K R and Lindahl, B I B and Arhem, P. A Discussion of the Mind-Brain Problem. *Theor Med*, 14(2), 167-180, Je 93.

In this paper Popper formulates and discusses a new aspect of the theory of mind. This theory is partly based on his earlier developed interactionistic theory. It takes as its point of departure the observation that mind and physical forces have several properties in common, at least the following six: both are (i) located, (ii) unextended, (iii) incorporeal, (iv) capable of acting on bodies, (v) dependent upon body, (vi) capable of being influenced by bodies. Other properties such as intensity and extension in time may be added. It is argued that a fuller understanding of the nature of forces is essential for the analysis of the mind-brain problem. The relative autonomy and indeterministic nature of mind is stressed. Indeterminism is treated in relation to a theorem of Hadamard. The computer theory of mind and the Turing test are criticized. Finally the evolution of mind is discussed.

Popper, Karl R. A World of Propensities: Two New Views of Causality in Advances in Scientific Philosophy, Schurz, Gerhard (ed). Amsterdam, Rodopi, 1991.

Popper, Karl R. Broadcast Review of *History of Western Philosophy*. *Russell*, 12(1), 19-21, Sum 92.

Popper, Karl R. *The Logic of Scientific Discovery*. New York, Routledge, 1992.

Popper, Karl R. The Non-Existence of Probabilistic Inductive Support in Logical Foundations, Mahalingam, Indira (ed). New York, St Martin's Pr, 1991.

Poratti, Armando. Sobre el lenguaje de Heráclito. *Rev Filosof (Argentina)*, 6(1-2), 23-35, N 92.

Porter, Jean. Basic Goods and the Human Good in Recent Catholic Moral Theology. *Thomist*, 57(1), 27-49, Ja 93.

This essay examines the claim that there are self-evident basic goods that serve as the foundation for moral judgments. It argues, contrary to G Grisez and J Finnis, that there are no basic goods of the requisite sort, and concludes that moral judgment presupposes a thicker account of the human good that Grisez and Finnis can allow.

Post, Frederick R and Shaw, Bill. A Moral Basis for Corporate Philanthropy. *J Bus Ethics*, 12(10), 745-752, O 93.

The authors argue that corporate philanthropy is far too important as a social instrument for good to depend on ethical egoism for its support. They claim that rule utilitarianism provides a more compelling, though not exclusive, moral foundation. The authors cite empirical and legal evidence as additional support for their claim.

Post, Heinz. Fences and Celings: Schrödinger's Cat and Other Animals in Logical Foundations, Mahalingam, Indira (ed). New York, St Martin's Pr, 1991.

Post, Stephen G. Justice, Community Dialogue, and Health Care. *J Soc Phil*, 23(3), 23-34, Wint 92.

This article reviews the theory and practice of discerning community values through dialogues that transcend adversarial democracy. The communitarian ideal of a democracy distinct from special interest politics is examined.

Post, Stephen G. The Moral Meaning of Relinquishing an Infant: Reflections on Adoption. *Thought*, 67(265), 207-220, Je 92.

This article considers the experience of birth mothers in relinquishing infants for adoption. Historical discussion is provided as background. Under conditions of freedom, such relinquishment is defended.

Postigliola, Alberto. *La Città della Ragione: Per Una Storia Filosofica del Settecento Francese*. Rome, Bulzoni, 1992.

Posy, Carl J. Imagination and Judgment in the Critical Philosophy in Kant's Aesthetics, Meerbote, Ralf (ed). Atascadero, Ridgeview, 1991.

This paper offers an account of the role of imagination in Kant's theories of theoretical judgment (both synthetic and analytic), ethical judgment and aesthetic judgment. It shows that though imagining is a phenomenological component of the activities underlying each of these kinds of judgment, Kant nevertheless denies any role to imagination in some of these cases. The paper infers from this fact the conclusion that imagination and judgment are to be understood epistemically rather than phenomenologically. This in turn leads to an interpretation of Kant's distinction between reflective and determinative judgments and to an explanation of Kant's theories of the beautiful and the sublime.

Pothast, Ulrich. Bewusstsein als Durchleben: Eine Antwort auf Ursula Wolf. *Z Phil Forsch*, 46(3), 403-412, Jl-S 92.

It is argued that consciousness cannot be interpreted as a process of "living through" a series of episodes, as series of episodes occur in the career of such beings as well which normally are not considered to be "conscious", like plants, primitive organisms, even anorganic entities.

Potrc, Matjaz. A Naturalistic and Evolutionary Account of Content in Analecta Husserliana, XXXIV, Tymieniecka, Anna-Teresa (ed). Dordrecht, Kluwer, 1992.

Content is explained as fitting in the picture of man as organism, whose primary task is survival in its surroundings. A course-grained naturalistic account places content at the intersection of perception and higher cognition, along the lines of the modularity thesis. A fine-grained naturalistic account presents content in predicate notation. Constant part of the content is output of the modular elaboration of perceptual information, a category. Predicate part of the content has its roots in gathering of perceptual aspects, and may be characterized by the help of distributed representations.

Potter, Elizabeth (ed) and Alcoff, Linda (ed). *Feminist Epistemologies*. New York, Routledge, 1993.

Potter, Elizabeth F. Gender and Epistemic Negotiation in Feminist Epistemologies, Alcoff, Linda (ed). New York, Routledge, 1993.

The primary epistemic agent is the community, not the individual, and gender politics can intersect the production of knowledge by a community when epistemic decisions are made, especially when competing beliefs are underdetermined by the data. These decisions can be seen as negotiations and observation of scientific communities reveals that scientists make many epistemic decisions through micro-negotiations, but gender politics can also enter macro-negotiations occurring, for example, in academic journals or among groups of people such as occurred in seventeenth-century England over the nature of air.

Potter, Karl H. The Development of Advaita Vedanta as a School of Philosophy. *J Indian Counc Phil Res*, 9(2), 135-158, Ja-Ap 92.

Potter, Karl H. The Karmic A Priori in Indian Philosophy. *Phil East West*, 42(3), 407-419, Jl 92.

Potter, M D. Critical Notice: David Lewis's *Parts of Classes*. *Phil Quart*, 43(172), 362-366, Jl 93.

Parts of Classes tries to separate the unproblematic part of set theory (mereology) from the problematic part (singletons). In the process several things get lost: an empty set which is really empty; a satisfying account of the paradoxes; and the motivation for the iterative conception of set. Lewis' attack on the coherence of singletons makes it puzzling what he sees his book as doing. Nor is it clear that mereology is as ontologically innocent as Lewis would have us believe.

Potter, M D. Iterative Set Theory. *Phil Quart*, 43(171), 178-193, Ap 93.

The iterative conception of set, which is currently dominant in mathematical practice, can be given a strikingly simple axiomatization (due to Dana Scott and John Derrick), which is summarized here. Hardly anyone seriously doubts the consistency of this axiomatization. But is it sound for arithmetic? The incompleteness of all our first-order characterizations of number theory makes this a live question, to which—it is argued—only the set-theoretic platonist can hope to give an affirmative answers. Reformulating the specifications in second-order terms merely transfers the difficulty from set theory to logic.

Potter, Nelson. What is Wrong with Kant's Four Examples. *J Phil Res*, 18, 213-229, 1993.

Kant gives four examples to illustrate the application of the categorical imperative immediately after introducing its "universal law" formulation in Chapter Two his *Groundwork of the Metaphysics of Morals*. These examples have been much discussed to gain an understanding of how the categorical imperative applies to derive specific duties. It is argued that the discussions found in these examples do not accord well with Kant's fuller account of that application in his later work *The Metaphysics of Morals*. That [later] work has quite different, sometimes better, arguments for the same moral conclusions, and never mentions the argument against making a lying promise (the second example). Giving exclusive or excessive attention to these four examples has distorted our understanding of Kant's moral philosophy.

Potter, Vincent. Peirce on "Substance" and "Foundations". *Monist*, 75(4), 492-503, O 92.

This article suggests that C S Peirce is worth a second look for light he can shed on two controversial philosophical notions presently debated, namely, "substance" and "foundations." Both are currently understood as the Enlightenment philosophers used the terms and have been rightly subjected to severe criticism. Peirce suggests 1) another, older and more viable, view of substance using his categories to show that substance is relational and not an "unknown X" underlying sense of qualities; 2)

another more viable understanding of what grounds our knowledge besides a mysterious "intuition" or some privileged cognitive event which is "self-justifying" and so a "first" principle.

Pouncy, Peter R. Commentary on Gómez-Lobo's "Philosophical Remarks on Thucydides' Melian Dialogue". *Proc Boston Colloq Anc Phil*, 5, 204-211, 1989.

Power, F Clark (ed) and Lapsley, Daniel K (ed). *The Challenge of Pluralism: Education, Politics, and Values*. Notre Dame, Univ Notre Dame Pr, 1992.

Power, Michael. Habermas and Transcendental Arguments: A Reappraisal. *Phil Soc Sci*, 23(1), 26-49, Mr 93.

This paper reappraises Habermas's transcendentalism in *Knowledge and Human Interests*. Prevailing conceptions of strong transcendental arguments, which inform Habermas's critics such as Rorty, cannot be sustained. The analytic reception of Kantian philosophy suggests a more modest and credible role for transcendental arguments which is similar to Habermas's later conception of 'rational reconstruction.' It is argued that Habermas's transcendentalism owes much to Kant's concept of 'regulative idea'. The 'as if' status of regulative ideas allows one to make better sense of the metacritical structure of *Knowledge and Human Interests* and Habermas's transcendental arguments are more hermeneutic than logical in character.

Power, William L. On Divine Perfection in Logic, God and Metaphysics, Harris, James F (ed). Dordrecht, Kluwer, 1992.

One of the most discussed issues among philosophers and theologians of the 20th century is whether the traditional understanding of God is credible or whether it should be revised and to what extent. In this paper, a revised understanding of classical theism is suggested where in a nontemporal concept of divine perfection is developed which builds upon the work of A N Whitehead and William P Alston.

Power, William L. Ontological Arguments for Satan and Other Sorts of Evil Beings. *Dialogue (Canada)*, 31(4), 667-676, Autumn 92.

From time to time it has been suggested that ontological arguments for Satan and other sorts of evil beings can be constructed on the model of Anselm's argument in the *Proslogium*. In this paper I attempt to show that such proposals are improper and unsound. In Section I, I present an interpretation of Anselm's argument as a framework for Section II and III. Section II is an attempt to show the unsoundness of ontological arguments for Satan, and Section III is an attempt to show the unsoundness of ontological arguments for other sorts of evil beings which are purported to be conceivable or possible and necessary.

Powers, G Madison. Contractualist Impartiality and Personal Commitments. *Amer Phil Quart*, 30(1), 63-71, Ja 93.

Some philosophers argue that impartial moral theories suppose an implausible account of human motivation. A commitment to acting only as one's impartial moral theory permits or requires is said to be objectionable in several respects: (i) it is too demanding; (ii) it is incompatible with the motivations essential to friendship and love; (iii) it crowds out non-moral virtues needed for well-being; and (iv) it presents a distorted account of the relation between moral justification and personal motivation. The argument of this article is that a contractualist theory can defeat each of these objections.

Powers, John. On Being Wrong: Kripke's Causal Theory of Reference. *Int Phil Quart*, 32(4), 459-476, D 92.

Pozo, Antonio Gutiérrez. The Meaning of Thought's Nearness to Meaning in Husserlian Phenomenology in Analecta Husserliana, XXXIV, Tymieniecka, Anna-Teresa (ed). Dordrecht, Kluwer, 1992.

Pradhan, R C. Wittgenstein and the Availability of a Transcendental Critique. *Indian Phil Quart*, 19(3), 153-166, Jl 92.

This paper seeks to establish that Wittgenstein's critique of language is transcendental rather that empirical and anthropological. The transcendental critique brings into focus the non-empirical source of grammar and the grammatical rules. In short, it proves the autonomy of grammar. This thesis rejects the received view that Wittgenstein's philosophy of language is anthropocentric and naturalistic. Wittgenstein's is, however, a philosophy of transcendental 'bedrock'.

Prado Jr, Plinio Walder and Milet, Matias (trans). Argumentation and Aesthetics: Reflections on Communication and the Differend. *Phil Today*, 36(4), 351-366, Wint 92.

Praeg, L. Slagter's Nek: Imitatio Christi in the Construction of the Other/Self (in Dutch). *S Afr J Phil*, 12(1), 6-11, F 93.

The Slagter's Nek episode in du Toit's *Die Geskiedenis van ons Land in die Taal van ons Volk* is the subject of this article. The possibility is explored that within the tradition of Afrikaner historiography, this interpretation of the Afrikaner's suffering need not only be seen as an attempt to position the *self* within a historico-teleological frame, but that this text could also be interpreted as a possible origin of the historical structuring of a specific relationship between the *other* (black African) and the *self*. Within the context of Hayden White's genre typology, Du Toit's narrative is defined as a Tragedy, the meaning of which is generated by Du Toit's application of a Manichean allegory as well as the illustration of the working of specific historical causal laws. Further, according to a Hegelian teleology of history, this micro-narrative is situated within the macro-narrative of the Afrikaner's history. Through this positioning, Slagter's Nek acquires the additional meaning of the birth of a moral ideal of self-sacrifice—not only for the sake of the ideal of nationalism, but within the framework of the myth of Predestination, also as an imitatio Christi—that is, a suffering for the sake of the other.

Prasad, Chakravarthi Ram. Dreams and Reality: The Sankarite Critique of Vijnanavada. *Phil East West*, 43(3), 405-456, Jl 93.

The essay concentrates on two passages in the Advaitin Sankara's commentary on the *Brahmasutras*. Against the background of an interpretation of the *pramanas* as a theory of knowledge, it reconstructs an Advaitic understanding of experience of an external world, and the Buddhist idealist denial of externality through an argument from dreaming. It then analyzes Sankara's critique of the idealist argument. It speculates on the way in which his modified version of the argument could contribute to a 'non-realist' metaphysics which accepts the assumption of externality in explaining experience but argues that such externality cannot be a determinate reality.

Prasad, Rajendra. Aurobindo on Reality as Value. *J Indian Counc Phil Res*, 9(1), 33-44, S-D 91.

Pratt, Alan. A Note on Heidegger's Death Analytic: The Tolstoyian Correlative in *Analecta Husserliana*, XXXVIII, Tymieniecka, Anna-Teresa (ed). Dordrecht, Kluwer, 1992.

Critics suggest that the Death Analytic incorporates traces from the thought of Rainer Maria Rilke and Karl Jaspers. In his discussion, however, Heidegger, only references Leo Tolstoy's *The Death of Ivan Ilyich*, significantly the only prose fiction work mentioned in *Being and Time*. Tolstoy's novella made a lasting impression of Heidegger because in it he could find dramatically illustrated most of the characteristic behaviors and evasive attitudes uncovered in his own phenomenology of death. *The Death of Ivan Ilyich*, then, is an illuminating supplement — specific, personal and emotional — to what Heidegger universalized in his philosophy.

Pratt, Douglas. Religious Concepts of 'World': Comparative Metaphysical. *Sophia (Australia)*, 31(3), 74-88, 1992.

Religion is frequently characterised as being "other-worldly", yet religions are also "world-views". Religions both espouse views about the world and also influence the way in which the world is understood and treated. Today's environmental concerns are of global scope. Local issues often have international significance and implications. The religious dimension to all this is significant; it is also diverse. The task of this paper is to explore that diversity, and specifically to identify and suggest some key metaphysical perspectives of the religious world-views that impinge upon, and have relevance for, ecological concern for the physical environment.

Pratt, V. Dynamic Algebras: Examples, Constructions, Applications. *Stud Log*, 50(3-4), 571-605, S-D 91.

Predelli, Stefano. A Czar's Ukase Explained: An Analysis of *Tractatus* 5.54 FF. *Phil Stud*, 71(1), 81-97, Jl 93.

I discuss Wittgenstein's argument in *Tractatus* 5.54ff for the conclusion that attitude attributions do not constitute a counterexample to the principle of extensionality. I focus on Wittgenstein's views on propositions, and I defend the interpretation of Wittgenstein's strategy according to which attitude attributions are not 'proper' propositions.

Prest, Mike. Remarks on Elementary Duality. *Annals Pure Applied Log*, 62(2), 183-205, Jl 93.

Elementary duality between left and right modules over a ring, especially its interpretation in terms of the relevant functor categories, is discussed, as is the relationship between these categories of functors and sorts in theories of modules. A topology on the set of indecomposable pure-injective modules over a ring is introduced. This topology is dual to the Ziegler topology and may be seen as a generalization of the Zariski topology.

Prest, Mike and Marcja, Annalisa and Toffalori, Carlo. On the Undecidability of Some Classes of Abelian-By-Finite Groups. *Annals Pure Applied Log*, 62(2), 167-173, Jl 93.

Preston, Beth. Heidegger and Artificial Intelligence. *Phil Phenomenol Res*, 53(1), 43-69, Mr 93.

A Heideggerian critique of AI does not show that intelligent machines are impossible, but rather that the cognitivist approach of explaining intelligent behavior exclusively in terms of internal representation and computation is misguided. Heidegger's analysis of routine activity suggests that explanation must be in terms of the complex interactions of a relatively simple creature with nonrepresented environmental structures and processes. I call this approach the interactionist alternative. Its adoption is motivated by considerations of computational complexity, and by discussion of successful AI systems which employ it. The methodological implications for further research in cognitive science are indicated.

Preus, Anthony. Aristotle and Respect for Persons in Essays in Ancient Greek Philosophy, IV, Anton, John P (ed). Albany, SUNY Pr, 1991.

Preus, Anthony (ed) and Anton, John P (ed). *Essays in Ancient Greek Philosophy, IV*. Albany, SUNY Pr, 1991.

A collection of papers by classicists and philosophers presented at the meetings of the Society for Ancient Greek scholarship and textual exegesis. The essays are arranged according to several unifying themes and deal with fundamental issues and concepts in Aristotle's ethical and political writings and other related works, with special attention to problems of virtue and character, moral reasoning and persons and property. A special feature reflecting a pervasive concern in the essays printed here is Aristotle's methodology. Most of the papers are published here for the first time.

Price, A W. Three Types of Projectivism in Psychoanalysis, Mind and Art, Hopkins, Jim (ed). Cambridge, Blackwell, 1992.

Price, Huw. Agency and Causal Asymmetry. *Mind*, 101(403), 501-520, Jl 92.

Several writers have attempted to account for causal asymmetry in terms of the so-called "form asymmetry" (roughly, the fact that correlated spatially separated events turn out to be jointly correlated with some event in their common past, and not with an event in their common future). I criticise these attempts, concentrating on that of Lewis. I argue that the most promising alternative lies in the proposal that causation should be explicated in terms of the notion of agency. On this view causal asymmetry becomes anthropocentric, reflecting the asymmetry of means-end deliberation from the agent's point of view.

Price, Huw. Metaphysical Pluralism. *J Phil*, 89(8), 387-409, Ag 92.

The paper argues that semantic and ontological minimalism undercuts the distinction between various non-Humean forms of metaphysical realism and something akin to a Wittgensteinian linguistic pluralism. Moreover, pluralism is the default position, and hence constitutes an important and neglected option in a range of contemporary metaphysical debates.

Price, Huw and Menzies, Peter. Causation as a Secondary Quality. *Brit J Phil Sci*, 44(2), 187-203, Je 93.

In this paper we answer four standard objections to an agency approach to causation, according to which an event *A* is a cause of a distinct event *B* just in case

bringing about *A* would be an effective means by which an agent could bring about *B*. The four objections we discuss all turn on the fact that this approach makes essential reference to human capacities. Our strategy is to draw parallels between the agency approach and philosophical treatments of color as a secondary quality. These parallels suggest replies to the objections in question.

Price, Robert G. On the Place of Validity. *Phil Rhet*, 25(4), 341-350, 1992.

Socrates, after *Phaedo* 89d, offers as a response to misology a safe answer (here discussed as a minimal metaphysics) and a new safe answer (here discussed as a first account of demonstration) and contrasts both with the old answers using arguments based on likelihood (here discussed as rhetorical). The paper develops this trichotomy as it is found in both the *Phaedo* and Aristotle's *Metaphysics, Analytic's* and *Rhetoric*, in order to provide an account of the need for the construction of syllogisms from which conclusions follow of necessity, that is, validly.

Price, Thomas and Russell, Robert and Kennett, Stephen. An Interview with A J Ayer. *Kinesis*, 19(1), 28-55, Spr 93.

Priest, Graham. Can Contradictions Be True?—II. *Aris Soc*, Supp(67), 35-54, 1993.

This paper is a reply to T Smiley, 'Can Contradictions be True?—I', *Proc. Aris. Soc.*, Supp. Vol. 67 (1993), 17-33. It defends dialetheism against Smiley's objections, criticizes his solution to the liar paradox and argues that his three triviality arguments fail.

Priest, Graham. Minimally Inconsistent LP. *Stud Log*, 50(2), 321-331, Je 91.

The paper explains how a paraconsistent logician can appropriate all classical reasoning. This is to take consistency as a default assumption, and hence to work within those models of the theory at hand which are minimally inconsistent. The paper spells out the formal application of this strategy to one paraconsistent logic, first-order LP. The result is a strong non-monotonic paraconsistent logic agreeing with classical logic in consistent situations. It is shown that the logical closure of a theory under this logic is trivial only if its closure under LP is trivial.

Priest, Graham. On Time. *Philosophica*, 50(2), 9-18, 1992.

The paper proposes utilising a Hegelean account of change, according to which a state of change is an intrinsically contradictory one, to solve a number of the puzzles associated with time. Specifically, it is argued that by applying this account of change to time itself, a satisfactory account can be given of the flow of time, the direction of time and the "specious present".

Priest, Graham. Yu and Your Mind. *Synthese*, 95(3), 459-460, Je 93.

This note is a brief reply to the main argument of Qiuen Yu: 1992, 'Consistency, Mechanicalness, and the Logic of the Mind', *Synthese* 90, 145-79.

Primoratz, I. What's Wrong with Prostitution?. *Philosophy*, 68(264), 159-182, Ap 93.

I discuss five lines of argument for the claim that prostitution is wrong: 1) the condemnation of prostitution by positive morality; 2) paternalist objections to it; 3) the claim that some things just aren't for sale and that sex is one of them, which is based either on the view of sex as essentially tied to procreation and marriage, or on the conception of sex as bound up with love; 4) the radical feminist critique of prostitution as a practice that degrades women, and 5) is implicated in the oppression of women. I try to show that none of these objections is valid, and that we still lack a good argument to support the widespread condemnation of prostitution.

Pringle, Helen. Women in Political Thought. *Hypatia*, 8(3), 136-159, Sum 93.

The argument of this paper is that texts in the history of political thought are rather more loquacious on the question of women than has often been supposed. The argument is developed using examples from Plato's *Republic*, notably the sections on injustice and tyranny. The paper concludes by suggesting the general implications of its approach for the concerns and style of political theory, particularly as to the importance of understanding symbolic and mythic elements in works of political thought.

Prisco, Di. Dialettica di fantasia e logos nella nozione di mito secondo Aristotele. *Aquinas*, 35(2), 273-306, My-Ag 92.

Pritchard, Annie. Antigone's Mirrors: Reflections on Moral Madness. *Hypatia*, 7(3), 77-93, Sum 92.

Sophocles's Antigone continues to attract attention for its portrayal of the themes of moral agency and sexual difference. In this paper I argue that the contradictory factors which constitute Antigone's social identity work against the possibility of assessing her actions as either "virtuous" or not. I challenge readings of the play which suggest either that individual moral agency is sexually neutral or that women's action is necessarily and simply in direct opposition to the interests of the public sphere.

Pritscher, Conrad P. Aspects of Chaos Research Related to Teaching. *Phil Stud Educ*, 1, 64-76, 1991.

The purpose of this paper is to attempt to clarify whether or not students fall into a dogmatic slumber when their teachers too often provide them with too much clarity. Part of this paper will attempt to show that we now have an excessive emphasis in schools on specialized concepts and a dearth of emphasis on generalized concepts. The concept of "chaos" is now being used in a variety of fields much as a medical doctor would use a stethoscope, sonogram, or X-rays. The paper attempts to explain aspects of chaos research related to the practices of teaching by restating and integrating ideas from a variety of authors.

Procee, Henk. Beyond Universalism and Relativism. *Quest*, 6(1), 44-55, Je 92.

Pronger, Brian. Gay Jocks: A Phenomenology of Gay Men in Athletics in Rethinking Masculinity, May, Larry (ed). Lanham, Rowman & Littlefield, 1992.

This paper is a critical, phenomenological examination of the relationship between masculine gender power, homosexuality and sport. Exploring some of the themes developed in a larger work by the same author, *The Arena of Masculinity: Sports, Homosexuality and the Meaning of Sex* (St. Martin's Press, 1990), the paper argues that the cultural meanings men find in gender and sexuality are fluid and situational. This often leads to an ironic sensibility for homosexually inclined men. A gay experience of sport and masculinity, therefore, is often an ironic one.

Prosch, Harry. Those Missing "Objects". *Tradition Discovery*, 17(1-2), 17-20, 1990-91.

In this article Prosch enumerates, and denies that he holds any of the five positions attributed to him as his views concerning Michael Polanyi's thought in Maben Poirier's article, "Harry Prosch's Modernism," *Tradition and Discovery*, 16, 1988-89. Prosch states fully what he actually does think Polanyi held in relation to these five philosophic concerns and shows that such unfashionable views as these could not possibly admit him to "modernist" circles. Prosch also suggests that he might not have been as misunderstood had he suggested that Polanyi should have provided the so-called "objects" of his humanities and religious articulations with something like enduring cores analogous to Plato's Forms or Hegel's Concepts.

Protevi, John. The Economy of Exteriority in Derrida's *Speech and Phenomena*. *Man World*, 26(4), 373-388, O 93.

By showing difference at work in the logical (identity/difference), temporal (time/space), and "liminological" (border: inside/outside) fields, the essay shows exteriority in general and the economy of exteriority as deep structures of SP. Exteriority in general allows for grouping into an economy of exteriority four registers: raw space, the tamed space of consciousness, the tamed space of sense, and the spacing of internal time-consciousness. The economy of exteriority is necessary to explain the three moves of SP: Husserl's inability to bracket indication from expression, expression from sense, and the spacing of time.

Proust, Françoise. L'entrelacs du temps. *Arch Phil*, 55(3), 385-408, Jl-S 92.

According to W Benjamin, time is not a sequence of "nows", is not ecstatic (Heidegger) but is an intertwining of many "this time" each of which makes itself an exception out of history and leaves behind it marks on space and time (dates and places) connected with their idea, their mind, their spectrum fated to come back haunting another "this time". Interfering in history means accompanying time in its shadow and dubbings and, *in extremis*, dubbing it instantly in order to turn it over and stop it.

Proust, Joëlle. L'esprit des bêtes. *Rev Int Phil*, 46(183), 418-434, 1992.

This paper explores the criteria according to which an organism may justifiably be attributed mental states. Montaigne's and Descartes' criteria are good representatives of a discontinuist approach of the mental. The Fodorian hypothesis of a language of thought allows the continuists to meet Descartes' objections. Nevertheless, this hypothesis commits us to a slippery slope. Is conditioning a sufficient criterion for the existence of a mind? Plausibly not. The notion of a *psychological scale* is shown to beg the question, and the explanatory benefit of the intentional stance is far from clear in many cases. Another criterion, offered in one of Fodor's papers, in terms of responding to non-nomic stimulus properties is discussed and shown to be finally insufficient.

Przelecki, Marian. Ineffability of Truth in Plato's Philosophy. *Epistemologia*, 15(2), 171-190, Jl-D 92.

The thesis of the inexpressibility of certain kinds of philosophical knowledge, as ascribed to Plato, is subjected to an analysis and, in consequence, interpreted in such a way which does not charge Plato's position with any kind of mysticism or irrationalism. The interpretation propounded assumes that it is only some vague philosophical ideas that are said to be not expressible in a definite way.

Przelecki, Marian. Is the Notion of Truth Applicable to Scientific Theories? in Advances in Scientific Philosophy, Schurz, Gerhard (ed). Amsterdam, Rodopi, 1991.

Some recent trends in the philosophy of science seem to imply that scientific theories are entities to which the notion of truth cannot be meaningfully applied. The paper contains a brief survey of those trends and a discussion of their claims. It is shown, in particular, how the gap between the traditional view of theories as sets of statements and the structuralist view of theories as sets of set-theoretical structures can be bridged.

Przelecki, Marian. Languages of Empirical Theories and Their Semantics. *Dialec Hum*, 17(2), 179-191, 1990.

Przelecki, Marian. Semantic Reasons for Ontological Statements in Kotarbinski: Logic, Semantics and Ontology, Wolenski, Jan (ed). Dordrecht, Kluwer, 1990.

Przelecki, Marian. The Work of Janina Kotarbinska. *Dialec Hum*, 17(1), 5-13, 1990.

Pszczolowski, Tadeusz. Philosophical and Methodological Foundations of Kotarbinski's Praxiology in Kotarbinski: Logic, Semantics and Ontology, Wolenski, Jan (ed). Dordrecht, Kluwer, 1990.

Pucci, Edi. Review of Paul Ricoeur's *Oneself as Another*: Personal Identity, Narrative Identity and "Selfhood" in the Thought of Paul Ricoeur. *Phil Soc Crit*, 18(2), 185-209, 1992.

Puech, Michel. Tetens et la crise de la métaphysique allemande en 1775. *Rev Phil Fr*, 1, 3-29, Ja-Mr 92.

Puga, Leila and Da Costa, Newton C A and Vernengo, Robert J. Derecho, moral y preferencias valorativas. *Theoria (Spain)*, 5(12-13), 9-29, N 90.

We study some propositional systems of the logic of preference containing two kinds of deontic operators: juridical and ethical. These logics are important for the formalization of certain theories of law, such as the three-dimensional theory as developed by the Brasilian jurist, Muiguel Reale.

Pullman, Daryl. Self-Respect, Morality, and Justice in Terrorism, Justice and Social Values, Peden, Creighton (ed). Lewiston, Mellen Pr, 1990.

Although there is plenty of evidence to suggest that "self-respect" was introduced to Rawls' theory of justice as a late amendation to tie together loose theoretical ends, the idea of "self-respect" as a social primary good has assumed central importance in later discussions of Rawls' position. This paper examines the status of self-respect as a social primary good, and argues that self-respect should not been seen this way. In short, self-respect is not a social primary good. Hence a theory of justice should not be concerned with distributing it fairly. The paper goes on to suggest the role that such a notion can and should play in moral theory after all.

Pulvertaft, W Robert. Population Ethics: On Parfit's Views Concerning Future Generations. *Dan Yrbk Phil*, 26, 33-50, 1991.

Puntel, Lorenz. The Context Principle, Universals and Primary States of Affairs. *Amer Phil Quart*, 30(2), 123-135, Ap 93.

This article develops a semantico-ontological approach based on a strong version of the Context Principle: "Only in the context of a sentence do words have any meaning" (Frege). This principle yields an account of sentences according to which one should distinguish between primary and secondary sentences. Primary sentences express primary states of affairs. These entities cannot be explained within the framework of the common view of predication, i.e., in terms of subject-predicate duality. Rather, primary states of affairs are to be defined as realized attributes, without presupposing something like a substratum exemplifying them. They are the only constituents of the categorial furniture of the world.

Purdy, Laura M and Holmes, Helen Bequaert (ed). *Feminist Perspectives In Medical Ethics*. Bloomington, Indiana Univ Pr, 1992.

Purdy, William C. A Variable-Free Logic for Mass Terms. *Notre Dame J Form Log*, 33(3), 348-358, Sum 92.

This paper presents a logic appropriate for mass terms, that is, a logic that does not presuppose interpretation in discrete models. Models may range from atomistic to atomless. This logic is a variation of a logic developed by the author for natural language reasoning. It is suitable for natural language reasoning because the formal language is similar to surface English (i.e., they are 'well-translatable'). Moreover, deduction performed in this logic is similar to syllogistic, and therefore captures an essential characteristic of human reasoning. Absence of variables makes it simpler than a more conventional formalization based on predicate logic. Capability to deal effectively with discrete terms, and in particular with singular terms, can be added to the logic, making it possible to reason about discrete entities and mass entities in a uniform manner.

Purdy, William C. On the Question 'Do We Need Identity?'. *Notre Dame J Form Log*, 33(4), 593-603, Fall 92.

This paper formalizes and extends Sommers's position on identity. This formalization is compared with MPL to define precisely the difference in expressive power. The formal language defined for this investigation is similar to the language of MPL (modern predicate logic). The similarity will not only facilitate comparison, but perhaps will also make this formal language more palatable to readers whose experience and/or predisposition favors MPL. (edited)

Purdy, William C. Surface Reasoning. *Notre Dame J Form Log*, 33(1), 13-36, Wint 92.

Surface reasoning is defined to be deduction conducted in a surface language in terms of certain primitive logical relations. A surface language is a spoken or written natural language (in this paper, English), in contrast to a "base language" or "deep structure" sometimes hypothesized to explain natural language phenomena. The primitive logical relations are inclusion, exclusion, and overlap between classes of entities. A language and a calculus for representing surface reasoning is presented. Then a paradigm for reasoning in this calculus is developed. This paradigm is similar to but more general than syllogistic. Reasoning is represented as construction of fragments (subposets) of lattices. Elements of the lattices are expressions denoting classes of individuals. Strategies to streamline the reasoning process are proposed.

Purtill, Richard L. Justice, Mercy, Supererogation, and Atonement in Christian Philosophy, Flint, Thomas P (ed). Notre Dame, Univ Notre Dame Pr, 1990.

Purviance, Susan. Aesthetics and Adjudication: Intersubjective Requirements and Juridical Judgment. *J Value Inq*, 27(2), 165-178, Ap 93.

Ronald Dworkin's theory of adjudication views law and literature as standing equally in need of interpretive judgments. This paper critiques Dworkin's attempt to meld aesthetics to political and moral philosophy and develops a theory of juridical judgment more suited to his goals, arguing that aesthetic constraints can only be made consistent with his theory by reconceiving the role of regulative ideals in adjudication. The Kantian theory of aesthetic judgment I provide explains how the model of intersubjectively valid judgments mandates respect for the decisions of other judges, while allowing for the possibility of other judges deciding that case differently.

Purviance, Susan M. Age Rationing, the Virtues, and Wanting More Life. *J Med Human*, 14(3), 149-165, Fall 93.

The goal of this paper is to show that Callahan's reasons for withholding life extending care cannot be made out exclusively in terms of contemporary notions of distributive justice and fair allocation. I argue that by relying on a notion of justice which links the merit of the individual with the fairness of a social pattern of shares, Callahan imputes vice to the elderly as he denies them eligibility for life-prolonging care. Aristotle's doctrine of the mean is a useful tool for character evaluation. One can speak meaningfully of a proper disposition of a person of a certain type (an elderly person) with respect to the good of continued life. I claim that the mean of one's disposition with respect to the good of continued life would be relative to one's age group, and would be determined by that principle by which an elderly person of practical wisdom would determine it. This leads to very different conclusions than those drawn by Callahan.

Putnam, Hilary. Afterthoughts on My Carus Lectures: Philosophy as Anthropology. *Lyceum*, 1(2), 40-42, Fall 89.

This paper suggest that the best alternative to the conception of philosophy as description of how things are from a God's Eye View is to view philosophy as an activity of making sense of human life and the human situation in the world from within that life and that situation. (A brief note.)

Putnam, Hilary. Is It Necessary that Water is H20? in The Philosophy of A J Ayer, Hahn, Lewis Edwin (ed). Peru, Open Court, 1992.

This paper argues that the theory of rigid designation requires the notion of physical necessity, but, contrary to Kripke, that it does not require the allegedly stronger notion of "metaphysical necessity." It further argues that the claim that "Water is H2O" is "true in all metaphysically possible worlds" is involved in difficulties similar to those which face the analytic/synthetic distinction.

Putnam, Hilary. James's Theory of Perception in Frontiers in American Philosophy, Volume I, Burch, Robert W (ed). College Station, Texas A&M Univ Pr, 1992.

Putnam, Hilary 636 AUTHOR INDEX WITH ABSTRACTS

Putnam, Hilary. Logical Positivism and Intentionality in A J Ayer Memorial Essays, Griffiths, A Phillips (ed). New York, Cambridge Univ Pr, 1991.

In this paper I argue that the reasons Carnap and Reichenbach gave for regarding the problem of intentionality as a "pseudoproblem" are incoherent, and make it impossible for either of these great positivist philosophers to successfully rebut the charge of solipsism. At the end of the paper I suggest a very different way of undermining the problem, one which may have been Wittgenstein's.

Putnam, Hilary. Objectivity and the Science-Ethics Distinction in The Quality of Life, Nussbaum, Martha C (ed). New York, Oxford Univ Pr, 1993.

Putnam, Hilary. *Renewing Philosophy*. Cambridge, Harvard Univ Pr, 1992.

This book, containing the Gifford Lectures I delivered in 1990, in addition to addressing several topics individually (reference and realism and religion and the foundations of democratic politics), offers a diagnosis of the present situation in philosophy as a whole, and suggest the directions in which we might look for a renewal.

Putnam, Hilary. Truth, Activation Vectors and Possession Conditions for Concepts. *Phil Phenomenol Res*, 52(2), 431-447, Je 92.

Putnam, Hilary. Wittgenstein on Religious Belief in On Community, Rouner, Leroy S (ed). Notre Dame, Univ Notre Dame Pr, 1992.

This paper offers a reading of Wittgenstein's Lectures on Religious Belief which 1) does not claim that religious utterances are "expressive" as opposed to "fact stating", and 2) does not immunize them from attack, although 3) it is claimed that the sorts of religious statements of which Wittgenstein approves are immune to *scientific* attack.

Putnam, Ruth Anna. Commentator on 'Objectivity and Social Meaning' in The Quality of Life, Nussbaum, Martha C (ed). New York, Oxford Univ Pr, 1993.

Walzer's attempt to ground inter-cultural criticism in the theory of the social construction of meaning fails. However, once we reject Walzer's distinction between simple- objects- in- the- world (facts) and objects- that- carry- social- meanings (values), we do not need separate criteria of objectivity. Rather, any belief is objective if its truth or falsehood relative to a conceptual scheme depends on the nature of the world and not on the knower. Rejecting a sharp fact/value dichotomy enhances our resources for inter-cultural discussion and possible agreement, a necessity for those interested in improving the quality of the life world-wide.

Putnam, Ruth Anna. William James and Our Moral Lives in Frontiers in American Philosophy, Volume I, Burch, Robert W (ed). College Station, Texas A&M Univ Pr, 1992.

Pylkkö, Pauli. Eliminative Naturalism and Artistic Meaning. *Phil Today*, 37(2), 183-200, Sum 93.

Pyper, Hugh S. The Apostle, the Genius and the Monkey in Kierkegaard on Art and Communication, Pattison, George (ed). New York, St Martin's Pr, 1992.

Both Kierkegaard's strategy of indirect communication and his analysis of authority, particularly of the biblical text, are exemplified by his interpretation of the biblical account of David's encounter with Nathan in 2 Samuel 12. The authority of the text is demonstrated in its effect of bringing about repentance. The technique involves revealing the errors of the subject's self-perception by evoking a negative judgment on a character who is then exposed as a reflection of the subject.

Qingyu, Zhang. A Weak Paraconsistent Conditional Logic. *J Non-Classical Log*, 8(1), 45-57, My 91.

The weak conditional logic W is presented in Nute's "Topics in Conditional Logic", and many well-known conditional logics are proper extensions of W. In this paper, I will develop a weak paraconsistent conditional logic PIW based on the Nute's preformal intuitions about conditionals. The difference here is that I think the hypothetical situations are paraconsistent. I take the D Batens' paraconsistent system PI as the start of PIW. First, I determine the logic PIW through determining its formal semantics in Section 1. Then, in Section 2, I present the axiomatized system HPIW of PIW and demonstrate the completeness of HPIW with respect to the formal semantics of PIW.

Qiu, Ren-Zong. What Bioethics Has to Offer the Developing Countires. *Bioethics*, 7(2-3), 108-125, Ap 93.

After explaining the intellectual basis of bioethics in developing countries, the bioethical dilemmas facing these countries including four dichotomies of can vs. ought, paternalism vs. autonomy, modernity vs. tradition, universalism vs. relativism, are discussed. It is argued that if bioethics is to take root in these countries, the changes have to be made in its emphasis on rights approach, individualistic orientation, and technological worship, and inadequacies in inquiry into the meaning of life and health and in international cooperation.

Quantz, Richard A. From Priest to Tourist: The Philosopher of Education in a Post-Philosophic Moment. *Phil Stud Educ*, 1, 1-14, 1990.

Quarta, Cosimo and Colombo, Arrigo (ed). *Il Destino della Famiglia Nell'Utopia*. Bari, Dedalo, 1991.

This book deals with the problem of the family, of its evolution, of its future through the great masters of utopia and through utopian experimentation. Utopia is both the aim of the just and fraternal society, and the process that creates that society; the family, in this process, *has been reconstructed* in the sense of justice and love. (edited)

Quesada, Daniel. The Labryinth of Attitude Reports in Cognition, Semantics and Philosophy, Ezquerro, Jesús (ed). Norwell, Kluwer, 1992.

Quesada, Francisco M. Ayer's Philosophy of Logic and Mathematics in The Philosophy of A J Ayer, Hahn, Lewis Edwin (ed). Peru, Open Court, 1992.

Quesada, Francisco Miró. Historicism and Universalism in Philosophy in Cultural Relativism and Philosophy, Dascal, Marcelo (ed). Leiden, Brill, 1991.

Quesada, Francisco Miró. Origin and Evolution of the Universe and Mankind in Philosophy and the Origin and Evolution of the Universe, Agazzi, Evandro (ed). Norwell, Kluwer, 1991.

Quevedo, Amalia. La ceguera según Aristóteles. *Anu Filosof*, 25(2), 349-375, 1992.

The sight is the *ousia* of the eye, just as the soul is to the body: up to what point can the eye not see is only an eye by name. Blindness is the worst of privations in the sensible order, by virtue of the highest sense, to wit: the sight.

Quigley, Peter. Rethinking Resistance: Environmentalism, Literature, and Poststructural Theory. *Environ Ethics*, 14(4), 291-306, Wint 92.

I argue that with the advent of poststructuralism, traditional theories of representation, truth, and resistance have been seriously brought into question. References to the "natural" and the "wild" cannot escape the poststructural attack against foundational concepts and the constituting character of human-centered language. I explore the ways in which environmental movements and literary expression have tended to posit pre- ideological essences, thereby replicating patterns of power and authority. I also point to how environmentalism might be reshaped in light of poststructuralism to challenge power without reference to authority.

Quine, Willard V. In Praise of Observation Sentences. *J Phil*, 90(3), 107-116, Mr 93.

Quinn, Patrick. Aquinas's Concept of the Body and Out of Body Situations. *Heythrop J*, 34(4), 387-400, O 93.

Quinn, Philip. Abelard on Atonement: 'Nothing Unintelligible, Arbitrary, Illogical, or Immoral about It' in Reasoned Faith, Stump, Eleonore (ed). Ithaca, Cornell Univ Pr, 1993.

This paper is devoted to discussion of Abelard's account of the Christian doctrine of the Atonement. It defends his account against charges of Exemplarism and Pelagianism. It also argues that his account contains material that ought to be incorporated into Christian thinking about the Atonement. Abelard's constructive contribution to such thinking is the idea that divine love, made manifest in the life and death of Jesus, has the power to transform human sinners, if they cooperate, in ways that fit them for everlasting life in intimate union with God.

Quinn, Philip. Epistemic Parity and Religious Argument in Philosophical Perspectives, 5: Philosophy of Religion, 1991, Tomberlin, James E (ed). Atascadero, Ridgeview, 1991.

This paper explores the complex notion of epistemic parity. It first tries to show how the intuitive idea of fairness in the ethics of belief can be made precise using the deontological concepts of prescription, permission and prohibition. It then argues for the philosophical utility of its technical machinery by employing it to interpret, analyze and criticize two claims Terence Penelhum has made concerning what parity arguments show about the rationality of religious belief.

Quinn, Philip. Social Evil: A Response to Adams. *Phil Stud*, 69(2-3), 187-194, Mr 93.

This paper is a response to a recent attempt by Marilyn McCord Adams to provide a complete picture of the problem of evil that confronts biblical religions. It argues that her picture does not contain enough detail about distinctively social evils. It also argues that an important difficulty for biblical religions lies in steering between the prideful response to social evils according to which we bear the whole responsibility for uprooting them and the slothful response according to which that responsibility belongs entirely to God.

Quinn, Philip. The Primacy of God's Will in Christian Ethics in Philosophical Perspectives, 6: Ethics, 1992, Tomberlin, James E (ed). Atascadero, Ridgeview, 1992.

This paper begins with an attempt to build a cumulative case for a divine command conception of Christian morality. Like a tripod, the case rests on three legs. They are a strong doctrine of divine sovereignty, a medieval tradition of interpreting the stories in scripture described as the immoralities of the patriarchs, and a Kierkegaardian reading of the love commandments in the Gospels. The paper concludes with an argument to show that this conception is superior to rival virtue theories of Christian morality.

Quinn, Philip L. On the Mereology of Boetheian Eternity. *Int J Phil Relig*, 32(1), 51-60, Ag 92.

This paper criticizes Brian Leftow's attempt in his book, *Time and Eternity*, to explicate the Boethian idea that divine eternity is some sort of atemporal duration in terms of a conception of Quasi-Temporal Eternality. It argues that Leftow's account of Quasi-Temporal Eternality is inconsistent and that his arguments in support of that account fail. Quasi-Temporal Eternality cannot be, as Leftow claims it is, both an extension that has no proper parts and an extension in which points are ordered as earlier and later. In conclusion, some tentative suggestions for revising Leftow's account are set forth.

Quintás, Alfonso Lopez. L'expérience esthétique musicale et la pensée philosophique de Gabriel Marcel. *G Metaf*, 13(1), 3-36, Ja-Ap 91.

Quinto, R. Giovanni Maria Cornoldi tra neotomismo e intransigentismo cattolico. *Riv Filosof Neo-Scolas*, 82(4), 631-636, O-D 90.

Quinton, Anthony. Ayer and Ontology in The Philosophy of A J Ayer, Hahn, Lewis Edwin (ed). Carbondale, So Illinois Univ Pr, 1992.

Quinton, Anthony. Ayer's Place in the History of Philosophy in A J Ayer Memorial Essays, Griffiths, A Phillips (ed). New York, Cambridge Univ Pr, 1991.

Quinton, Lord. Ayer and Ontology in The Philosophy of A J Ayer, Hahn, Lewis Edwin (ed). Peru, Open Court, 1992.

Quirk, Michael J. Four Kinds of Metaphilosophy: Griswold on Platonic Dialogue. *Metaphilosophy*, 23(1-2), 147-158, Ja-Ap 92.

Rabb, J Douglas. From Triangles to Tripods: Polycentrism in Environmental Ethics. *Environ Ethics*, 14(2), 177-183, Sum 92.

Callicott's basic mistake in his much regretted paper "Animal Liberation: A Triangular Affair" is to think of the anthropocentric, zoocentric, and biocentric perspectives as mutually exclusive alternatives. An environmental ethics requires, instead, a polycentric perspective that accommodates and does justice to all three positions in question. I explain the polycentric perspective in terms of an analogy derived from the pioneering work of Canadian philosopher Rupert C Lodge and distinguish it from both pragmatism and moral pluralism.

Rabinowicz, Wlodek. Cooperating with Cooperators. *Erkenntnis*, 38(1), 23-58, Ja 93.

Collective Egoism (CE)—formulated by Jan Österberg in *Self and Others*, 1988—prescribes, roughly, that each member of a group should do his part in the action-pattern that is most beneficial for the group, provided that other members do *their* parts. Österberg pleads for a collectivistic approach to morality. He therefore argues that CE constitutes the most defendable form of ethical egoism. *Pace* Österberg, CE is shown to yield "wrong" prescriptions in certain "free rider"—form of many-persons Prisoners' Dilemmas. Also, it violates the principles of "deontic consequence" and "joint satisfiability" considered by Österberg to be analytical adequacy conditions for ethical theories.

Rabinowitz, Paula. Wreckage upon Wreckage: History, Documentary, and the Ruins of Memory. *Hist Theor*, 32(2), 119-137, 1993.

Rachels, James. Reflections on the Idea of Equality in On the Track of Reason, Beehler, Rodger G (ed). Boulder, Westview Pr, 1992.

Racine, Louis. L'éthique de l'ingénierie: vers un nouveau paradigme. *Dialogue (Canada)*, 30(3), 277-284, Sum 91.

Radcliffe, Evan. Revolutionary Writing, Moral Philosophy, and Universal Benevolence in the Eighteenth Century. *J Hist Ideas*, 54(2), 221-240, Ap 93.

In the British controversy over the French Revolution, universal benevolence was hotly argued, with supporters of France attacking it. The elements of this debate can be traced to previous philosophical discourse. But the 1790s transformed the argument. Earlier, universal benevolence had been a defense of society against egoistic views. But at century's end many thinkers sought to defend society against universal benevolence; they saw in it a subversion of everything local and thus the potential destruction of human nature itself.

Radder, Hans. Experimental Reproducibility and the Experimenters' Regress. *Proc Phil Sci Ass*, 1, 63-73, 1992.

In his influential book, *Changing Order*, H M Collins puts forward three claims concerning experimental replication. i) Replication is rarely practiced by experimentalists; ii) replication cannot be used as an objective test of scientific knowledge claims, because of the occurrence of the so-called experimenters' regress; and iii) stopping this regress at some point depends upon the enculturation in a local community of practitioners, by tacitly learning the relevant skills. In my paper I discuss and assess these claims on the basis of a more comprehensive analysis of experimentation and experimental reproducibility. The main point is that Collins' claims are not, strictly speaking, wrong, but rather one-sided and therefore inadequate. This point also calls for a reconsideration of the radical (social constructivist) conclusions that Collins has draw from his studies of scientific experimentation.

Radder, Hans. Science, Realization and Reality: The Fundamental Issues. *Stud Hist Phil Sci*, 24(3), 327-349, Ag 93.

Many recent studies of science have shown that not only the knowledge of experimental and observational processes and results but even their very existence is essentially dependent on the work done by human beings. But when this is the case, how can scientific knowledge ever be about a human-independent reality? In answering this question it is argued that the reproducibility of experiments and observations entails an ontology of both independently persisting, real potentialities and their historically contingent, local and non-local, realizations. In other words, science and scientific knowledge are at once in and about the world. The ontological views are developed by showing how they relate to and differ from transcendental realist and constructivist alternatives, and how they shed new light on the old debates about the status of universals and about the methodological role of abstraction.

Radey, Charles. Imagining Ethics: Literature and the Practice of Ethics. *J Clin Ethics*, 3(1), 38-45, Spr 92.

Radford, Colin. Emotions and Music: A Reply to the Cognitivists. *J Aes Art Crit*, 47(1), 69-76, Wint 89.

Radford, Colin. Muddy Waters. *J Aes Art Crit*, 49(3), 247-252, Sum 91.

Radford, Colin. The Examined Life Re-examined. *Philosophy*, 33(Supp), 1-23, 1992.

Radford, Colin. The Examined Life Re-examined in The Impulse to Philosophise, Griffiths, A Phillips (ed). New York, Cambridge Univ Pr, 1992.

Radford, Colin. The Power of Words. *Philosophy*, 68(265), 325-342, Jl 93.

Radford, M A. Meaning and Significance in Aesthetic Education. *J Aes Educ*, 26(1), 53-66, Spr 92.

Works of art can only make sense in a context of shared perceptions as to the needs that the work addresses and the parameters within which it does so. As with any system of communication the meaning of a work lies not in any single interpretation or intention, but in the shared perception of audience and artist and the dialogue that follows. The significance of a work lies in the way in which the artist shares the psychological need of the audience and responds to them.

Radhakrishnan, R. Poststructuralism Politics in Postmodernism/ Jameson/ Critique, Kellner, Douglas (ed). Washington, Maisonneuve Pr, 1989.

The purpose of this essay is to enable a critical dialogue between poststructuralist epistemology and a Marxism that is influenced substantively by discourses of the "post-". Fredric Jameson's work is particularly important in this respect since it seeks to retain the political effects and objectives of Marxist thought without denying the legitimacy of poststructuralist interventions. The essay argues that despite Jameson's inclusive attitude towards poststructuralism, his advocacy of Marxist remain totalized and does not acknowledge fully some of the implications of "the politics of difference."

Radice, Roberto. Ordine musica bellezza in Agostino. *Riv Filosof Neo-Scolas*, 84(4), 587-607, O-D 92.

The essay presents the book *Ordine, Musica, Bellezza*, edited by Maria Bettetini (Rusconi, Milano 1992), which contains a translation of the dialogues *De Ordine* and *De musica* by Augustine, and an anthology of Augustinian passages about Beauty. In her *Introduction*, Bettetini explains Augustine's conception of *ordo* and its relations with numbers, proportion and world's harmony. We can find the sources of Augustinian vision of the world in Plato's thought, especially in the so called "not-written doctrines" about the Unity, and in Plotin and Perfirio's works.

Radin, Margaret Jane. Diagnosing the Takings Problem. *Nomos*, 33, 248-278, 1991.

Radnitzky, Gerard (ed) and Bouillon, Hardy (ed). *Government: Servant or Master?*. Amsterdam, Rodopi, 1993.

The book is a plea for arresting, or if possible reversing, the long-standing trend of the growth of government, of state interventionism and dirigisme into every corner of our lives. It provides theoretical analyses of the dynamics prevalent in log-rolling special interest democracies. They are followed by case studies. The problems raised by the volume are urgent. They will be of interest to all those who would like to see a transition to a more prosperous society, a society with more economic freedoms and civil liberties. Socialism may perhaps be dead — at least full-scale, avowed socialism — but the question of how to tame Leviathan looms as large as ever.

Radrizzani, Ives. Philosophie transcendentale et praxis politique chez Fichte. *Rev Theol Phil*, 125(1), 1-20, 1993.

Selon la conception fichtéenne de la philosophie, le philosophe ne peut s'en tenir à sa pure science, mais doit s'engager dans la *praxis* politique, avec tous les risques que cela comporte. Ce passage du plan de l'*a priori* à celui de l'*a posteriori* s'avère problématique. Si Fichte a peu varié dans sa définition de l'Etat idéal, en revanche son jugement quant à la réalisation possible de cet idéal et aux moyens à mettre en oeuvre pour y parvenir ont considérablement évolué. Cette évolution de sa pensée politique, souvent qualifiée de "machiavélisation", peut sans doute être expliquée par des arguments d'ordre tant historique que systématique. Toutefois, elle ne laisse pas de jeter un doute sur le caractère de "science" que Fichte prétend attribuer à la politique, en même temps qu'elle risque de rendre sujette à caution la consistance de la pensée transcendantale en matière de politique.

Radzihkovskii, L A. *Perestroika*, Too, Is Developed Socialism. *Russian Stud Phil*, 32(1), 62-67, Sum 93.

Raff, Charles. Moore's Argument and Scepticism. *Dialogue (Canada)*, 31(4), 691-700, Autumn 92.

Raffman, Diana. *Language, Music, and Mind*. Cambridge, MIT Pr, 1993.

The book invokes recent linguistic and psychological theories to provide a cognitivist account of ineffable musical knowledge. Three kinds of ineffability are isolated. The most important, *nuance ineffability*, is shown to attend our perceptual knowledge of expressive nuances of musical performances. The proposed account is compared to some traditional accounts of musical ineffability, e.g., Cavell's and Goodman's. A detailed comparison is made of linguistic and musical understanding, culminating in an attack on the idea that emotions are musical meanings. A concluding chapter explores some negative implications of the proposed account for Dennett's propositional theory of consciousness.

Rahat, Ehud. Metaphors and Malapropisms: Davidson on the Limits of the Literal. *Philosophia (Israel)*, 21(3-4), 311-327, Ap 92.

Davidson wrote on two issues concerning the limits of the literal, metaphors and malapropisms (lexically wrong uses of words), with few comments about how they relate. This paper compares his views on the two topics, and is intended to clarify these views as well as his notion of literal meaning. Davidson characterizes literal meaning by distinguishing between different levels in the order of a speaker's intentions in communication, placing literal meaning as the first intention in that order. Malapropisms are lexical deviations on that first level of intentions, whereas metaphors concern higher order intentions.

Raiger, Michael. Plotinus on Matter. *Lyceum*, 2(2), 37-51, Fall 90.

Railton, Peter A. Nonfactualism about Normative Discourse. *Phil Phenomenol Res*, 52(4), 961-968, D 92.

Nonfactualism—the model here is Allan Gibbard's highly insightful *Wise Choice, Apt Feelings*— is a very dramatic philosophical response to normative discourse. It requires a nonstandard semantic theory that nonetheless mimics, and dovetails with, standard assertoric semantics. Moreover, it yields a dualism about concepts with explanatory as well as normative uses—e.g., "reason for action", "meaning", "good", and many others (if one assumes meaning holism, language is pervaded with normativity). Gibbard's account may be unable to yield the fact/value distinction he seeks, which is meant to be term-by-term, conservative of the "Galilean core", and itself factual.

Railton, Peter A. Some Questions About the Justification of Morality in Philosophical Perspectives, 6: Ethics, 1992, Tomberlin, James E (ed). Atascadero, Ridgeview, 1992.

Someone asking what to think of morality might want to be shown the advantages of moral conduct, but might have in mind a different question: Is morality just one more ideology? Parallels with logic, aesthetics, and instrumental rationality, are used to develop the idea of a set of standards non-hypothetical in scope with respect to a well-founded domain that possesses actual evaluative impact for us. Such standards would have a normative standing for us quite different from sheer advantage. I then try to show that, on a particular interpretation, moral standards might also have this sort of standing.

Rainbolt, George W. Rights as Normative Constraints on Others. *Phil Phenomenol Res*, 53(1), 93-111, Mr 93.

The article sketches a new theory of what it is to have a right. Because rights are normative constraints on others, one has a right if and only if one has an Hohfeldian claim or an Hohfeldian immunity. Liberty rights and power rights are packages of Hohfeldian relations which are rights because they contain a claim. This claim protects the relation after which the right is named. There are similar packages of relations corresponding to the rest of the Hohfeldian relations, i.e., there are duty rights, disability rights, liability rights and no-claim rights.

Rainey, Lee. The Concept of Ch'i in the Thought of Wang Ch'ung. *J Chin Phil*, 19(3), 263-284, S 92.

Raitz, Keith L. The Myth of Easy Reading. *Proc Phil Educ*, 48, 117-123, 1992.

Rajapakse, Vijitha. An Inquiry into Gender Considerations and Gender Conscious Reflectivity in Early Buddhism. *Int Stud Phil*, 24(3), 65-91, 1992.

Taking due notice of the contemporary philosophic recognition that gender is an influence on human thought, this paper seeks to highlight some characteristic manifestations of the phenomenon as revealed in the Theraváda scriptural tradition, which is a product of early Buddhism. Philosophic analysis of texts pursued here yields three main insights: (1) the doctrinal cure of this tradition is gender-neutral; (2) yet its secondary elaborations encompass some telling instances of gender inflected-thinking which project male biases; (3) though less prominent, Theraváda Scripture, however, also carry distinctive expressions of feminine reflection.

Rajchman, John. *Truth and Eros: Foucault, Lacan, and the Question of Ethics*. New York, Routledge, 1991.

The author isolates the question of ethics in the work of Foucault and Lacan and explores its ramifications and implications for the present day. He argues that in departing from the piety of moral theory, Foucault and Lacan embark on a strange voyage through the historical of ethical thought, that takes them through Cynicism and Platonism; Antigone and Socrates; Aristotle, Kant and Bentham; Nietzsche and Freud. He demonstrates that the question of ethics was at once the most difficult and most intimate question for these two authors. As such, he argues that it belongs to that great tradition that is concerned with the passion or eros of philosophy and of its "will to truth."

Rajiva, Suma. The Significance of Kant's Framework of Possible Experience. *Gnosis*, 4(1), 1-38, 1992.

Rajotte, Mark J. Justified False Belief. *Dialogue (PST)*, 34(2-3), 44-49, Ap 92.

Often, implicit commitments are made, and, consequently, reasoned from in the enterprise of belief formation and revision. Now, the reliability of the implicit commitments made by the cognizer is often taken for granted and, at times, the cause of one's presumed true belief being, in fact, a false belief. This possibility poses a serious question which I address, namely, "Is a belief epistemically justified when formed by a reliable process and false due to a "failure" with the implicit commitment?" Can a false belief be epistemically justified? I propose that a false belief can be epistemically justified within the Theory of Justification, because, in this domain, we are concerned only with the coherence of beliefs in one's own corpus of beliefs. Epistemic justification deals with how the belief is formed and with the status the belief holds in relation to other previously held beliefs. If a belief is formed by a reliable process, not positively undermined, and in reflective equilibrium with other beliefs, then, the belief can be both false and epistemically justified.

Ram-Prasad, C. Knowledge and the 'Real' World: Sri Harsa and the *Pramanas*. *J Indian Phil*, 21(2), 169-203, Je 93.

Sri Harsa argues that no system for attaining knowledge can non-circularly be established as valid; epistemic activity is conducted only on the assumption, transcendentally argued for, that a system for attaining knowledge and that it is possible to establish, prior to inquiry, that some favoured system is valid. Sri Harsa considers arguments in favour of this claim and refutes them, concluding that it can only be argued that epistemic activity is best explained by the assumption of the validity of some favoured system.

Ramachandran, Murali. Restricted Rigidity: The Deeper Problem. *Mind*, 102(405), 157-158, Ja 93.

Rambanapasi, C O. The Concept of 'Region' in the Sociospatial Sciences: An Instance of the Social Production of Nature. *Soc Epistem*, 7(2), 147-182, Ap-Je 93.

The purpose of the article was to unravel the philosophical underpinnings of the multiple definition of the geographical concept of a region which had become accepted by geographers and others as universally competing ideological alternatives. A historical review of paradigmatic shifts in Epistemological Geographies indicated changes in their philosophical foundations accompanying increased socioeconomic development in Europe and North America. This led to the conclusion that a region is an epistemological concept whose definitional variation is philosophically rooted in Epistemological Geographies whose articulation historically represented the concurrence of various stages of national socioeconomic development with the accompanying structuration of geographic space.

Ramirez, J Roland. Augustine's Numbering Numbers and the Immortality of the Human Soul. *Augustin Stud*, 21, 153-161, 1990.

Ramose, Mogobe B and Maphala, T G T and Makhabane, T E. In Search of a Workable and Lasting Constitutional Change in South Africa. *Quest*, 5(2), 4-31, D 91.

Rampley, Matthew. Physiology as Art: Nietzsche on Form. *Brit J Aes*, 33(3), 271-282, Jl 93.

Ramsey, Jeffry L. Towards an Expanded Epistemology for Approximations. *Proc Phil Sci Ass*, 1, 154-164, 1992.

By stressing the act rather than the relation of approximation, I argue that the criteria for praising or blaming approximate results should not be limited to an analysis of the magnitude of the error. Magnitude is a necessary but not sufficient condition for such a judgment. Controllability, the absence of cancelling errors, and the approximation's justification are also important criteria. Boltzmann's discussion of the types of approximations used in the kinetic theory of gases at the turn of the century illustrates the use of these criteria.

Ramsey, William. Belief and Cognitive Architecture. *Dialogue (Canada)*, 31(1), 115-120, Wint 92.

Rankin, K W. Image-Talk: The Myth in the Mirror. *Philosophy*, 67(260), 241-246, Ap 92.

Rao, A P. Distributive Justice: A Third World Response to Recent American Thought (Part I). *Manuscrito*, 15(1), 53-127, Ap 92.

It is shown, by an analysis of the concept of a community, that every individual enjoys two basic rights, a right to survival and a right to participation. It is argued that this implies that underdeveloped communities must give a greater priority to guaranteeing the rights to participation and to survival of all their members than to satisfying any other needs. It is argued that the state has the right to transfer goods in such a way as to guarantee these basic needs. Nozick's arguments that there is no such right are critically examined and rejected. Hayek's claim that the concept of justice can only be applied to individuals, and his rejection of the concept of social justice are criticized. A principle for deciding how basic goods should be distributed is established. The views of Rawls are examined and it is shown that although he correctly sees that the results of natural lotteries are irrelevant to questions of justice he fails to draw the correct conclusions from this insight. Other aspects of Rawls' views are critically examined.

Rapaport, William J. Because Mere Calculating Isn't Thinking: Comments on Hauser's "Why Isn't My Pocket Calculator a Thinking Thing?". *Mind Mach*, 3(1), 11-20, F 93.

This paper is a commentary on Larry Hauser's "Why Isn't My Pocket Calculator a Thinking Thing?" *Minds and Machines*, Vol 3, No 1 (1993). I suggest that on a strong view of thinking, mere calculating is *not* thinking (and pocket calculators don't think), but on a weak, but unexciting, sense of thinking, pocket calculators do think. I close with some observations on the implications of this conclusion.

Raphael, Frederic. Some Philosophers I Have Not Known. *Philosophy*, 33(Supp), 59-72, 1992.

Raphael, Frederic. Some Philosophers I Have Not Known in The Impulse to Philosophise, Griffiths, A Phillips (ed). New York, Cambridge Univ Pr, 1992.

Raposa, Michael L. Jonathan Edwards' Twelfth Sign. *Int Phil Quart*, 33(2), 153-162, Je 93.

Rapp, Christof. Ähnlichkeit, Analogie und Homonymie bei Aristoteles. *Z Phil Forsch*, 46(4), 526-544, O-D 92.

Inasmuch as Aristotle makes use of the universal scheme of genus and species, relations of similarity arise only as a derivative of the membership of kind. As soon as this scheme is incomplete or standards of meticulousness which are usually compulsory cannot be applied, the relation of similarity takes an independent and irreducible function. The essay is concerned with the role of similarity in Aristotelian philosophy under various aspects: similarity as peculiarity of quality, similarity and analogy as types of unity, the syllogism of similarity, the function of similarity in epistemology, and homonymy, paronymy as types of similarity, etc.

Rappaport, Steven. A Mistake about Foundationalism. *S J Phil*, 30(4), 111-125, Wint 92.

Some critics of Foundationalism (for instance, Keith Lehrer) assume that it regards basic beliefs as (a) non-inferential, and (b) self-justified in that no other beliefs play any role in their justification. These critics maintain that even a putative basic belief like my belief that I am sensing green depends for its warrant on other beliefs, and not just on my sense experience. This holistic nature of the justification of putative basic beliefs entails that they are not really self-justified, and so there are not any basic beliefs as understood by foundationalism. My purpose is to show that the critics in question misconstrue foundationalism in ascribing (a) and (b) to basic beliefs.

Rappaport, Steven. Must a Metaphysical Relativist Be a Truth Relativist?. *Philosophia (Israel)*, 22(1-2), 75-85, Ja 93.

Metaphysical relativism holds that there is no unique, objective world order. This is a deduction from the claim that reality does not come pre-sorted; instead, the sorting of reality into kinds is relative to the classification scheme adopted. It may seem that metaphysical relativism *implies* relativism about truth. Truth relativism affirms that statements are not true *simpliciter*, but only relative to something else — a conceptual framework, form of life, or whatever. I argue that, on the contrary, metaphysical relativism does *not* imply truth relativism. For the metaphysical relativist may consistently adopt the disquotational view of truth, and this view of truth conflicts with truth relativism.

Rardin, Patrick. A Congery of Self-Reference. *Auslegung*, 18(2), 123-130, Sum 92.

I present a systematic analysis of Grelling's paradox of heterological adjectives. I question whether the system in which the paradox arises is a genuine or a spurious interpretation of ordinary linguistic usage. Within intuitively acceptable parameters for differentiating genuine and spurious systems, I argue that the system responsible for Grelling's paradox is a spurious interpretation of ordinary linguistic usage. The result in an analysis of the paradox which preserves the integrity of ordinary linguistic usage without introducing either a suspect ontology of properties or an ad hoc proliferation of language hierarchies.

Raschke, Carl. Fire and Roses: Or the Problem of Postmodern Religious Thinking in Shadow of Spirit, Berry, Philippa (ed). New York, Routledge, 1992.

Rashed, Roshdi. *Direct Reference: From Language to Thought*. Cambridge, Blackwell, 1993.

Rasmussen, David M. Business Ethics and Postmodernism: A Response. *Bus Ethics Quart*, 3(3), 271-277, Jl 93.

The author considers the contribution of Ronald Green, David Schmidt, Clarence Walton, Ron Duska, and Richard Neilsen to a special issue of *Business Ethics Quarterly* entitled "Business Ethics and Postmodernism." This essay poses a fundamental question: to what extent can a position which characterizes itself as postmodern be ethical? The paper argues on philosophical grounds that the debate between modernity and postmodernity is a debate over the very possibility of an ethic. The paper concludes that although Jacques Derrida has made the most convincing argument for an ethic within postmodernity, it remains skeptical because such an argument simply presupposes assumptions which owe their origin to modernity.

Rathjen, Michael and Weiermann, Andreas. Proof-Theoretic Investigations on Kruskal's Theorem. *Annals Pure Applied Log*, 60(1), 49-88, F 93.

In this paper, we calibrate the exact proof-theoretic strength of Kruskal's theorem, thereby giving, in some sense, the most elementary proof of Kruskal's theorem. Furthermore, these investigations give rise to ordinal analyses of restricted bar induction.

Rattansi, Ali (ed) and Boyne, Roy (ed). *Postmodernism and Society*. New York, St Martin's Pr, 1990.

Rattansi, Ali and Boyne, Roy. The Theory and Politics of Postmodernism in Postmodernism and Society, Boyne, Roy (ed). New York, St Martin's Pr, 1990.

Rautenberg, W. Axiomatizing Logics Closely Related to Varieties. *Stud Log*, 50(3-4), 607-622, S-D 91.

Raven, Diederick (ed) and Van Vucht Tijssen, Lieteke (ed) and De Wolf, Jan (ed). *Cognitive Relativism and Social Science*. New Brunswick, Transaction Books, 1992.

Modern epistemology has been dominated by an empiricist theory of knowledge that assumes a direct individualistic relationship between the knowing subject and the object of knowledge. Truth is held to be universal, and non-individualistic social and cultural factors are considered sources of distortion of true knowledge. Since the late 1950s, this view has been challenged by a cognitive relativism asserting that what is true is socially conditioned. This volume examines the far-reaching implications of this development for the social sciences. (edited)

Ravizza, Mark and Fischer, John M. The Inevitable. *Austl J Phil*, 70(4), 388-404, D 92.

We critically evaluate various accounts of moral responsibility for consequences of what agents do. We sketch our own approach. On this approach, an agent can be held accountable for an inevitable consequence.

Ravizza, Mark and Fischer, John M. When The Will is Free in Philosophical Perspectives, 6: Ethics, 1992, Tomberlin, James E (ed). Atascadero, Ridgeview, 1992.

Peter van Inwagen has argued that acceptance of a modal principle employed in the standard argument for incompatibilism entails that (even if causal determinism is false) we are rarely, if ever, free to do otherwise. We present an argument against van Inwagen.

Ravizza, Martin and Fisher, John. Thomson and the Trolley. *J Soc Phil*, 23(3), 64-87, Wint 92.

We set out a version of the Trolley Problem and criticize Judith Thomson's recent suggestion for a solution. Finally, we suggest an explanation for this failure.

Ravven, Heidi M. A Response to "Why Feminists Should Take the *Phenomenology of Spirit* Seriously. *Owl Minerva*, 24(1), 63-68, Fall 92.

Stuart Swindle in "Why Feminist Should Take the *Phenomenology of Spirit* Seriously" accuses me of failing —in my article, "Has Hegel Anything to Say to Feminists?"—to interpret the passages in the *Phenomenology* on the family and women in the full context of the progress to Absolute Spirit. I offer here a critique of Swindle's method of interpreting Hegelian texts, exposing its serious flaws. I then conclude with a critique of the implications of Swindle's argument that the progress of Spirit can be characterized as a "feminine form of consciousness."

Rawling, Piers. Choice and Conditional Expected Utility. *Synthese*, 94(2), 303-328, F 93.

The principle that agents should maximize conditional expected utility has been challenged on various grounds. The 'common cause' example is one in which, purportedly, this principle yields an irrational prescription. This apparent failure gives prima facie reason to favor causal decision theory. However, the example can be modified so as to pose difficulties for the latter theory as well—unless careful heed is paid to the distinction between those propositions an agent believes she can choose to make true and those the truth of which she believes she can merely attempt to ensure. But in that case the respective theories are *both* left unscathed.

Rawling, Piers and McNaughton, David. Deontology and Agency. *Monist*, 76(1), 81-100, Ja 93.

Constraints are a defining feature of deontologies, but there is considerable debate over how to characterize them. Authors such as Nagel, Parfit and Scheffler see them as generating agent-relative reasons. On this characterization, it is natural to suppose that constraints arise because of an agent's concern with her own agency. Brook and Kamm, however, offer a victim, rather than an agent, focussed rational. We rebut their arguments against agent-focussed views and show that their own accounts fall foul of consequentialist ploys.

Rawls, John. *Political Liberalism*. New York, Columbia Univ Pr, 1993.

Rawls, John. The Domain of the Political and Overlapping Consensus in The Idea of Democracy, Copp, David (ed). New York, Cambridge Univ Pr, 1993.

Ray, Chad. Imagination in Practical Reason. *SW Phil Rev*, 9(1), 115-121, Ja 93.

Ray, Christopher. Fundamental Laws and *Ad Hoc* Decisions: A Reply to Curry. *Stud Hist Phil Sci*, 23(4), 661-664, D 92.

Whether or not the cosmological constant is an ad hoc addition to the General Theory of Relativity depends in part on historical and empirical considerations and not simply on any mathematical justification.

Ray, Greg. Probabilistic Causality Reexamined. *Erkenntnis*, 36(2), 219-244, Mr 92.

According to Nancy Cartwright, a causal law holds just when a certain *probabilistic condition* obtains in all "test situations" which in turn satisfy a set of *background conditions*. These background conditions are shown to be inconsistent and, on separate account, logically incoherent. I offer a corrective reformulation which also incorporates a strategy for problems like Hesslow's thrombosis case. I also show that Cartwright's recent argument for modifying the condition to appeal to singular causes fails. Proposed modifications of the theory's *probabilistic* condition to handle effects with extreme probabilities (0 or 1) are found unsatisfactory. I propose a unified solution which also handles extreme *causes*. Undefined conditional probabilities give rise to three good, but non-equivalent, ways of formulating the theory. Various formulations appear in the literature. I give arguments to eliminate all but one candidate. Finally, I argue for a crucial new condition clause, and show how to extend the results beyond a simple probabilistic framework.

Ray, John. The *Education of Cyrus* as Xenophon's "Statesman". *Interpretation*, 19(3), 225-242, Spr 92.

Ray, Sangeeta. Shifting Subjects Shifting Ground: The Names and Spaces of the Post-Colonial. *Hypatia*, 7(2), 188-201, Spr 92.

This essay participates in a feminist postcolonial critical historiography/epistemology by providing a critique of *The Post-Colonial Critic: Interviews, Strategies, Dialogues*. The essay considers Spivak's success in interrogating her own position as a leading postcolonial critic as she engages in dialogues with various people. Spivak's commitment to cross-cultural exchanges is undeniable. However, at times the resurgence of her authoritative subject position deflects productive tensions generated by careful scrutiny of the category postcolonial.

Raynaud, Savina and Bokhove, Niels W. A Bibliography of Works by and on Anton Marty in Mind, Meaning and Metaphysics, Mulligan, Kevin (ed). Dordrecht, Kluwer, 1990.

Raynor, David. The Authorship of the *Abstract* Revisited. *Hume Stud*, 19(1), 213-215, Ap 93.

Raz, Joseph. On the Autonomy of Legal Reasoning. *Ratio Juris*, 6(1), 1-15, Mr 93.

The paper argues that reasoning according to law is an instance of moral reasoning. Several ways of understanding this claim are distinguished. A number of arguments to the effect that because of the internal logic of the law, or the special skills it involves legal reasoning should be seen as immune to moral considerations are rejected. Nevertheless, the paper affirms the relative and limited autonomy of legal reasoning, and the *sui generis* role of doctrine in it which is manifested in the many cases in which the moral considerations pertaining to the case underdetermine its result.

Readings, Bill. Pagans, Perverts or Primitives? in Judging Lyotard, Benjamin, Andrew (ed). New York, Routledge, 1992.

Readings, Bill. Pseudoethica Epidemica: How Pagans Talk to the Gods. *Phil Today*, 36(4), 377-388, Wint 92.

This essay considers the impact of Lyotard's account of the "pagan" upon the traditional role of the intellectual and upon conceptions of historical time and political endeavor. It argues for an "inhuman ethics" in which singular judgments are understood as acts of revolutionary prudence. Discussion of Sir Thomas Browne, Machiavelli, and Marxism.

Reagan, Charles E. The Self as an Other. *Phil Today*, 37(1), 3-22, Spr 93.

This article is a thorough exposition of Paul Ricoeur's book, *The Self As An Other* (Chicago: University of Chicago Press, 1993). The article begins with an examination of the question of personal identity and then shows how Ricoeur progressively argues for a concept of personal identity which is inextricably bound up with the concept of the other and the relation between the self and the other. Ricoeur analyzes personal identity through a semantics and pragmatics of the subject, the philosophy of action, narrative identity, and finally through a dialectic between teleological and deontological ethics which ultimately manifests the self as an other.

Reale, Giovanni. Precisazioni metodologiche sulle implicanze e sulle dimensioni storiche del nuovo paradigma ermeneutico nell'interpretazione di Platone. *Riv Filosof Neo-Scolas*, 84(2-3), 219-248, Ap-S 92.

Reber, Arthur S. An Evolutionary Context for the Cognitive Unconscious. *Phil Psych*, 5(1), 33-51, 1992.

This paper is an attempt to put the work of the past several decades on the problems of implicit learning and unconscious cognition into an evolutionary context. Implicit learning is an inductive process whereby knowledge of a complex environment is acquired and used largely independently of awareness of either the process of acquisition or the nature of that which has been learned. Characterized this way, implicit learning theory can be viewed as an attempt to come to grips with the classic epistemological issues of knowledge acquisition, representation and use. The argument is made that the process, despite its seeming cognitive sophistication, is of considerable evolutionary antiquity and that it antedates awareness and the capacity for conscious control of mentation. Various classic heuristics from evolutionary biology are used to substantiate this claim and several specific entailments of this line of argument are outlined.

Reck, Andrew J. God as the Ultimate Meaning is the Primordial Source of All Meanings. *Ultim Real Mean*, 16(1-2), 137-139, Mr-Je 93.

This brief comment on Bracken's "Creativity and the Extensive Continuum as the Ultimate Ground in Whitehead's Philosophy of Becoming" questions the propriety of elevating the extensive continuum to the function Bracken accords it and proposes God instead.

Reck, Andrew J. John Dewey's Idea of Ultimate Reality and Meaning: A Mixture of Stability and Uncertainty in Social Transactions of Human Beings. *Ultim Real Mean*, 16(1-2), 45-55, Mr-Je 93.

After commenting on the paradoxical character of Dewey's philosophy, the author focuses on *Experience and Nature*. He examines Dewey's conception of empirical method in philosophy and explores Dewey's metaphysics. He contends that Dewey sought to provide in his metaphysics as the science of the generic traits of existence the groundmap for the province of criticism, epitomized by philosophy as wisdom or the criticism of criticism. Dewey's metaphysics presents human meanings, found in associated living, to be the stabilizing principles in a world of change and peril. Dewey's later substitution of the concept of transaction for experience is also discussed. The ultimate paradox in Dewey's thought is the very idea of a humanistic naturalism or naturalistic humanism.

Recker, Doren A. Mathematical Demonstration and Deduction in Descartes's Early Methodological and Scientific Writings. *J Hist Phil*, 31(2), 223-244, Ap 93.

Recki, Birgit. Aesthetica und Anaesthetica: Odo Marquards philosophische Überlegungen zur Ästhetik. *Z Phil Forsch*, 46(3), 395-402, Jl-S 92.

The article gives a critical appreciation of Marguard's position in aesthetics. 1) His theory of Fine Art — and aesthetic experience — to overtake important compensatory functions for the losses of modern society's progresses turns out to be a modification of the Hegelian model of development-in-history. But the question for the subject behind the progress, style of Marguard's writing provides in itself an example for one of the functions of the aesthetic, he is theoretically pleading for: releasing tension. Thus it appears to be an attempt towards the traditional claim for unity of matter and form.

Reda, Clementina Gily. Il problema del fondamento e la filosofia italiana del 900: Un convegno a Subiaco. *Filosofia*, 43(2), 305-312, My-Ag 92.

Reddiford, Gordon. Subjectivity and the Arts: How Hepburn Could Be an Objectivist. *J Phil Educ*, 26(1), 107-111, 1992.

Hepburn argues that all education, and so Arts Education, educates a person's subjectivity, his or her Lebenswelt; though the sciences take the 'objectifying way' they too educate our subjectivity. I show why there can be no decision procedures, involving the use of logical operators for interpreting a work or art, but argue that Hepburn's view that music etc. can furnish 'authoritative imaginative realisations', nevertheless presupposes a 'soft' objectivist position. Whilst Hepburn is right in thinking that the subjective provides the context for objectifying procedures in education (and more generally), it cannot be the case, as he implies, that aesthetic criteria could have a role in the selection of preferred scientific explanations and theories. It is, however, argued that the aesthetic can be generative of objectifying ways, or theory- enabling.

Redekop, Benjamin W. Language, Literature and Publikum: Herder's Quest for Organic Enlightenment. *Hist Euro Ideas*, 14(2), 235-253, Mr 92.

The article explores the close relationship between Herder's emphasis on language as a crucial element in human thought, and his notions on the proper role of "enlightener" in helping give rise to a unified and educated German "Publikum" or "citizenry". It is shown that Herder developed an "organic" conception of enlightenment in which prose literature figured as a crucial forum for public discussion and formation, as well as an important medium in the development of an authentic German national consciousness. Herder's literary/philosophical perspective was closely related to his concern with engendering an educated, harmonious and self-conscious German "Publikum".

Redhead, Michael and Teller, Paul. Particle Labels and the Theory of Indistinguishable Particles in Quantum Mechanics. *Brit J Phil Sci*, 43(2), 201-218, J 92.

We extend the work of French and Redhead (1988) further examining the relation of quantum statistics to the assumption that quantum entities have the sort of identity generally assumed for physical objects, more specifically an identity which makes them susceptible to being thought of as conceptually individuable and labelable even though they cannot be experimentally distinguished. We also further examine the relation of such hypothesized identity of quantum entities to the Principle of the Identity of Indiscernibles. We conclude that although such an assumption of identity is consistent with the facts of quantum statistics, methodological considerations show that we should take quantum entities to be entirely unindividuatable, in the way suggested by a Fock space description.

Redish, Martin. Freedom of Thought as Freedom of Expression: Hate Crime Sentencing Enhancement and First Amendment Theory. *Crim Just Ethics*, 11(2), 29-41, Sum-Fall 92.

Rée, Jonathan. Narrative and Philosophical Experience in On Paul Ricoeur: Narrative and Interpretation, Wood, David (ed). New York, Routledge, 1991.

Ricoeur argues very persuasively that novels and history books call upon a phenomenologically fundamental capacity for narrative; but, surprisingly enough, be does not consider whether the same may apply to theoretical works, and in particular to philosophical works such as his own. This article tries to fill this gap, by proposing a concept of philosophical experience and arguing that it has a particular kind of narrative structure. The argument is illustrated by reference to Descartes, Hegel, Bentham, Mill, Berkeley, Spinoza, Kierkegaard, and others.

Reed, Michael and Harvey, David L. The New Science and the Old: Complexity and Realism in the Social Sciences. *J Theor Soc Behav*, 22(4), 353-380, D 92.

Reedy, Jeremiah and Sullivan, T D. The Ontology of the Eucharist. *Amer Cath Phil Quart*, 65(3), 373-386, Sum 91.

Although Suarez agrees with Aquinas's principal conclusions about the ontology of the eucharist, Suarez raises doubts about aspects of Aquinas's reasoning. Particularly troubling is the claim that quantity (by the power of God) can exist without a subject. We probe this and other ontological issues raised by the theological problem Aquinas and Suarez seek to solve.

Reesor, Margaret E. The Stoic Wise Man. *Proc Boston Colloq Anc Phil*, 5, 107-123, 1989.

This is a study of the wise man in early Stoic philosophy. It opens with an investigation of the relation of the wise man to other wise men, and those who were not wise. This is followed by an analysis of passages which assign to the wise man knowledge of all crafts, and an examination of his moral disposition. In the second part, the emotions of the hero Heracles, as they are presented in Euripides' *Heracles*, are compared to those of the wise man. The role of fact, and the qualities of endurance and acceptance are discussed.

Reeve, Andrew. Individual Choice and the Retreat from Utilitarianism in The Utilitarian Response, Allison, Lincoln (ed). Newbury Park, Sage, 1990.

Reeve, C D C. *Practices of Reason: 'Aristotle's Nicomachean Ethics'*. New York, Clarendon/Oxford Pr, 1992.

The book is an exploration of the epistemological, metaphysical, and psychological foundations of the *Ethics*, which exposes the deep connections between it and the *Metaphysics, Posterior Analytics, Topics, De Anima*, and biological writings. It argues that *episteme* is possible in ethics and that dialectic and *nous* play essentially the same role in ethics as in an Aristotelian science. It defends an exclusivist conception of *eudaimonia*, identifying primary *eudaimonia* with theoretical activity, and secondary *eudaimonia* with practical activity.

Reeve, C D C. Vlasto's *Socrates: Ironist and Moral Philosopher*. *Polis*, 11(1), 72-82, 1992.

1) Vlastos does not include the *Euthydemus* and *Lysis* as "Socratic" dialogues for inadequate reasons based on a dubious view of the elenchus. 2) He mischaracterizes the differences between the Socrates of the early and the Socrates of the middle dialogues, because he fails to see how problematic the elenchus is as a source of moral knowledge. 3) He has not faced the problems the *Apology* raises for his portrayal of Socrates as a "complex" ironist.

Reeves, Robert A. Nostalgia and the Nostalgic. *SW Phil Stud*, 14, 92-97, Spr 92.

Nostalgia is connected with the type of memory that isn't merely a "propositional attitude" toward a past event but to some extent recreates past feelings. It is thus a complex emotion which typically has three parts: one, an immediate affective reaction to the event or object that triggers the memory; two, the recreated past emotion; three, a "second-order" present emotion towards the past event. Nostalgia wants, however briefly, to replace the present with the past, and is at the same time conscious that this is impossible. It is both a realistic and a dreamlike feeling, both liberating and tragic.

Regina, Umberto. Per una soggettività non più "animale": Heidegger critico di Husserl. *G Metaf*, 14(1), 67-84, Ja-Ap 92.

Regoli, G and Coletti, G. How Can an Expert System Help in Choosing the Optimal Decision?. *Theor Decis*, 33(3), 253-264, N 92.

Reichenbach, Bruce R. On Obligations to Future Generations. *Pub Affairs Quart*, 6(2), 207-225, Ap 92.

I argue that "obligation" is a referential notion, flowing from actual or potential relationships. Applied to future persons, our relationship with them is established by virtue of the significant effects that our acts will have on them, and this in turn provides the basis of our obligation to them. Referential problems arise particularly in the types of cases where alternative acts bring different people into existence, for here there is no clear referent of the obligation. In such cases a theistic model has an advantage by delineating lines of obligation through God.

Reichlin, M. Filosofia della mente ed etica in Stuart Hampshire. *Riv Filosof Neo-Scolas*, 82(4), 509-542, O-D 90.

Reichlin, Massimo and Cattorini, Paolo. The Physician, the Family, and the Truth. *J Clin Ethics*, 3(3), 219-220, Fall 92.

Reid, Jeffrey. Dialectique et désepoir dans "La fatique culturelle du Canada français". *Horiz Phil*, 3(1), 77-84, Autumn 92.

Reid, Michael. The Call of Nature: A Reply to Ted Benton and Tim Hayward. *Rad Phil*, 64, 13-18, Sum 93.

Reidy, David. Does Hume Have a Theory of Justice?. *Auslegung*, 19(1), 63-74, Wint 93.

The paper first argues that Hume fails to establish a coherent connection between justice and self-interest, because he fails both to state explicitly what he means by self-interest and to consider plausible alternative origins of the artificial virtue of justice. The paper then argues that Hume's conception of justice may plausibly be traced to the power of a few operating indirectly through convention. The argument focuses upon Hume's failure to extend justice to those insufficiently powerful to pose a real threat to others and his erroneous assumption that every particular property regime will serve the self-interest of all because all do better with some property regime rather than no property regime.

Reidy Jr, David A. Hume's System: An Examination of the First Book of his *Treatise* by David Pears. *Auslegung*, 18(2), 179-187, Sum 92.

Pears argues that questions of meaning logically precede questions of truth and that a proper interpretation of Hume's *Treatise* must examine both issues, even if Hume did not. Of course, Hume's phenomenological and naturalistic inquiry into human reasoning does not easily lend itself to the distinction between meaning and truth Pears demands. Consequently, one finds in this work as much, if not more, Pears than Hume. Too often Pears fails to let Hume speak for himself, instead insisting that Hume work within a 20th century philosophical framework. Nonetheless, advanced students of Hume will find Pears's work rewarding.

Reimer, Marga. Demonstrating with Descriptions. *Phil Phenomenol Res*, 52(4), 877-893, D 92.

Reimer, Marga. Incomplete Descriptions. *Erkenntnis*, 37(3), 347-363, N 92.

Standard attempts to defend Russell's Theory of Descriptions against the problem posed by "incomplete" descriptions, are discussed and dismissed as inadequate. It is then suggested that one such attempt, one which exploits the notion of a contextually delimited domain of quantification, may be applicable to "incomplete" quantifier expressions which are typically treated as quantificational: expressions of the form "All F's", "No F's", "Some F's", "Exactly eight F's", etc. In this way, one is able to retain the plausible claim that such expressions ought to receive their usual quantificational analyses. The conclusion tentatively drawn is that perhaps definite descriptions are *not* amenable to a (Russellian) quantificational analysis.

Reimer, Marga. Three Views of Demonstrative Reference. *Synthese*, 93(3), 373-402, D 92.

Three views of demonstrative reference are examined: 'contextual', 'intentional', and 'quasi-intentional'. According to the first, such reference is determined entirely by certain publicly accessible features of the context. According to the second, speaker intentions are 'criterial' in demonstrative reference. And according to the third, both contextual features and intentions come into play in the determination of demonstrative reference. The first two views (both of which enjoy current popularity) are rejected as implausible; the third (originally proposed by Kaplan in'Dthat') is argued to be highly plausible.

Reinecke, Volker and Uhlaner, Jonathan. The Problem of Leo Strauss: Religion, Philosophy and Politics. *Grad Fac Phil J*, 16(1), 189-208, 1993.

Reiner, Richard. Necessary Conditions and Explaining How-Possibly. *Phil Quart*, 43(170), 58-69, Ja 93.

William Dray has argued that historical explanations may take the form of answers to the question "How could the event *E* possibly have occurred?", and that such explanations are not reducible to covering-law form. In this article, it is argued that in Dray's examples only a single member of some hypothetical *jointly* necessary set of conditions has been satisfied. It is further argued that Dray's examples seem convincing only because they suggest a covering-law explanation, and that explanation by necessary conditions is suspect because statements of the form "*E1* is a necessary condition for *E2*" are unfalsifiable.

Reinhardt, Lloyd (ed) and Campbell, Keith (ed) and Bacon, John (ed). *Ontology, Causality and Mind: Essays in Honour of D M Armstrong*. New York, Cambridge Univ Pr, 1993.

This Festschrift is a collection of papers on questions central to the philosophy of D M Armstrong, each followed by a reply from Armstrong. Topics covered include universals, dispositions, the combinatorial approach to modality, individuation, causality, laws of nature, consciousness, and color. The contributors are William G Lycan, David Lewis, Peter Forrest, John Bigelow, D H Mellor, Evan Fales, J J C Smart, C B Martin, Peter Menzies, Frank Jackson, and Keith Campbell. A complete bibliography of Armstrong's works up to 1992 closes the book.

AUTHOR INDEX WITH ABSTRACTS 641 Reyes, Marie La Palme

Reiser, Stanley Joel (ed) and Heitman, Elizabeth (ed) and Bulger, Ruth Ellen (ed). *The Ethical Dimensions of the Biological Sciences*. New York, Cambridge Univ Pr, 1993.

This collection contains a variety of classic essays and seminal works by researchers from many disciplines, as well as policy statements and research guidelines from professional and government bodies. Among the issues considered are: the norms of ethical conduct in science and their origins; scientific honesty, skepticism, and self-deception; the ethical standards of laboratory practice; the use of human and animal subjects; the qualifications for authorship and publication; the ethics of learning and teaching; and the relationships of science, industry, and society. (edited)

Reitan, Eric. Why the Deterrence Argument for Capital Punishment Fails. *Crim Just Ethics*, 12(1), 26-33, Wint-Spr 93.

Reitan, Eric A. Galileo, Aristotelian Science, and the Rotation of the Earth. *Lyceum*, 1(2), 31-39, Fall 89.

Renaut, Alain. Fichte: le droit sans la morale?. *Arch Phil*, 55(2), 221-242, Ap-Je 92.

According to Fichte, in 1793 natural right is included in ethics; in 1796 legal and ethical are independent from one another; in 1807 (Rede an die deutsche Nation) right is unthinkable without ethics. What is the logic of such transformation, how does it affect the political philosophy of Fichte in itself?

Rendall, Steven. Duction, Or the Archaeology of Rape. *Phil Lit*, 17(1), 119-128, Ap 93.

Rensoli, Lourdes. Das Ideal des philosophischen Lebens bei G W Leibniz. *Stud Leibniz*, 24(1), 101-111, 1992.

Leibniz's ideal of philosophical life is based on a unity of the theory of freedom, of ethics and the task of improving the world. Leibniz develops two projects: firstly, the Socratian task to support all men and all nations in finding the most important truths, and secondly, the practical application of these truths, that is, the joint struggle for a 'realm of reason'.

Rentoul, Robert. *Consciousness, Brain and the Physical World*: A Reply to Velmans. *Phil Psych*, 5(2), 163-166, 1992.

Reppert, Victor. Eliminative Materialism, Cognitive Suicide, and Begging the Question. *Metaphilosophy*, 23(4), 378-392, O 92.

Rescher, Nicholas. American Philosophy Today. *Rev Metaph*, 46(4), 717-745, Je 93.

Rescher, Nicholas. Leibniz Finds a Niche. *Stud Leibniz*, 24(1), 25-48, 1992.

Dieser Aufsatz bietet eine Skizze der Umstände, die zu Leibniz' Eintritt in den Dienst am Hannoverschen Hof führten, und untersucht die Gegebenheithn, die er bei seiner Ankunft in Hannover im Jahr 1676 vorfand, insbesondere die soziale Lage und die organisatorischen Einrichtungen, die für Leibniz' Stellung am Hof Herzogs Ernst August massgeblich waren. Ziel der Abhandlung ist, Auskunft zu geben über die berufliche und persöliche Stellung, die Leibniz in den Jahren 1676-1677 am Hannoverschen Hof innehatte.

Rescher, Nicholas. Response. *Inform Log*, 14(1), 53-58, Wint 92.

Rescher, Nicholas. The Promise of Process Philosophy in Frontiers in American Philosophy, Volume I, Burch, Robert W (ed). College Station, Texas A&M Univ Pr, 1992.

Rescher, Nicholas. Thought Experimentation in Presocratic Philosophy in Thought Experiments in Science and Philosophy, Horowitz, Tamara (ed). Lanham, Rowman & Littlefield, 1991.

Reshotko, Naomi. The Socratic Theory of Motivation. *Apeiron*, 25(3), 145-170, S 92.

I construct an account of eight Socratic claims. Along the way, I uncover two major ways in which Socrates' views on human motivation are incompatible with some common folk-psychological assumptions concerning human motivation: first, Socrates holds that individuals are not in a privileged position when it comes to identifying the objects of their own desires; second, Socrates' rigorous requirements for knowledge specify an object of knowledge which is broader than contemporary epistemological theories assume.

Resnik, David B. Are Methodological Rules Hypothetical Imperatives?. *Phil Sci*, 59(3), 498-507, S 92.

This discussion adjudicates a dispute between Larry Laudan and Gerald Doppelt over the nature of methodological rules. Laudan holds that all methodological rules are hypothetical imperatives, while Doppelt argues that a subset of those rules, basic methodological standards, are not hypothetical imperatives. I argue that neither writer offers a satisfactory account of methodological rules and that their reliance on the hypothetical/ nonhypothetical distinction does not advance our understanding of methodological rules. I propose that we dispense with this dubious distinction and develop an alternative account of scientific norms.

Resnik, David B. Convergent Realism and Approximate Truth. *Proc Phil Sci Ass*, 1, 421-434, 1992.

This paper examines the role that approximate truth plays in arguments for convergent realism and diagnoses some of the difficulties that face attempts to defend realism by employing the slippery concept. Approximate truth plays two important roles in convergent realism: it functions as a truth surrogate and it helps explain the success of science. This paper argues that approximate truth cannot perform one but not both of these roles.

Resnik, David B. Do Scientific Aims Justify Methodological Rules?. *Erkenntnis*, 38(2), 223-232, Mr 93.

According to a popular view of scientific methodology, scientific methods are prescriptive rules (methodological rules) which are justified in so far as they realize or promote the aims of science. This paper considers several different interpretations of the phrase "aims of science", arguing that none of these interpretations allow aims to provide a satisfactory justification of methodological rules.

Resnik, David B. Genetic Privacy in Employment. *Pub Affairs Quart*, 7(1), 47-56, Ja 93.

This paper proposes some guidelines for the disclosure of genetic information in employment. It argues that the moral right to provacy allows employees to restrict their employers' access to genetic information in most situations, but that employers may invade an employee's genetic provacy only if such an invasion meets criteria for a legitimate (or justified) invasion.

Resnik, David B. Leo Buss's *The Evolution of Individuality*. *Biol Phil*, 7(4), 453-460, O 92.

In his book *The Evolution of Individuality*, Leo Buss attacks a central dogma of the neo-Darwinian theory of evolution, the idea that the individual is the sole unit of selection, by arguing that individuals themselves emerged as the result of selective forces that regulated the replication of cell lineages for the benefit of the whole organism. This discussion explores Buss's work and argues that despite the revolutionary character of this book, it still reflects the adaptationist thinking associated with the neo-Darwinian approach.

Resnik, David B. Ronald Giere's "Explaining Science: A Cognitive Approach". *Erkenntnis*, 38(2), 261-271, Mr 93.

In *Explaining Science: A Cognitive Approach*, Ronald Giere (1988), proposes what he calls a "cognitive theory of science (p 2)." Giere intends his view to be a "broadly scientific account employing the resources of the cognitive sciences (Giere, 1988, p 2)." This paper argues that Giere does not secure a firm foundation for a cognitive theory of science because he leaves the door wide open for social constructivist interpretations of his views. In order to avoid social constructivism, Giere needs to adopt or develop an objective (i.e., non-conventionalist) concept of similarity.

Restall, Greg. A Note on Naive Set Theory in LP. *Notre Dame J Form Log*, 33(3), 422-432, Sum 92.

Recently there has been much interest in naive set theory in non-standard logics. This note continues this trend by considering a set theory with a general comprehension schema based on the paraconsistent logic LP. We demonstrate the nontriviality of the set theory so formulated, deduce some elementary properties of this system of sets, and also delineate some of the problems of this approach.

Restall, Greg. Deviant Logic and the Paradoxes of Self Reference. *Phil Stud*, 70(3), 279-303, Je 93.

Some take the paradoxes of self reference to give us reasons to abandon classical logic as an account of valid inference. Others seek to retain classical logic, despite the paradoxes. Most often, this is not argued for, but there are some arguments in the literature. In this paper I use these arguments to motivate a re-examination of the philosophy of formal logic and the status of logical truths and rules. I then show that this gives us the means to defend non-classical approaches to the paradoxes against these criticisms.

Reuter, Robert. The Radical Agent: A Deweyan Theory of Causation. *Trans Peirce Soc*, 29(2), 239-257, Spr 93.

This article attempts to construct the beginnings of a theory of causation based primarily on some of Dewey's later works. I argue that the theory is a radical version of the more common agent centered theories of causation because the agent for Dewey plays a much more direct and extensive role in determining events and sequences as causal. But the theory is not radical to the point of making causation wholly agent dependent, which I illustrate through Dewey's brand of realism and the claim that causal connections are necessary connections.

Rey, Georges. Idealized Conceptual Roles. *Phil Phenomenol Res*, 53(3), 647-652, S 93.

Rey, Georges. Semantic Externalism and Conceptual Competence. *Proc Aris Soc*, 92, 315-333, 1992.

Rey, Georges. Sensational Sentences in Consciousness: Psychological and Philosophical Essays, Davies, Martin (ed). Cambridge, Blackwell, 1993.

Rey, Georges. Sensational Sentences Switched. *Phil Stud*, 68(3), 289-319, D 92.

Reyes, Gonzalo E and Palme Reyes, Marie La. Montague's Semantics for Intensional Logic. *Log Anal*, 32, 319-335, S-D 89.

In this paper we shall describe a simplified version of the semantics of Montague for intensional logic as exposed in [6]. We hope that this new version is clearer than the original one and that will help to understand Montague's semantics, its achievements and its limitations. In particular, we discuss problems of identity, possibility and existence and we show some of its shortcomings to cope with these fundamental problems in the philosophy of language. This paper is a companion to [7], where a Boolean-valued version of Gupta's semantics [4] is explained and criticized. These two papers may be viewed both as an introduction and a motivation for a system of intensional logic that we believe free of the shortcomings of both Montague's and Gupta's semantics: the logic of kinds. The interested reader may consult [7] and [8].

Reyes, Gonzalo E and Reyes, Marie La Palme. A Boolean-Valued Version of Gupta's Semantics. *Log Anal*, 32, 247-265, S-D 89.

In this paper we shall describe a Boolean-valued version of the intensional semantics of Gupta [2]. We believe that our presentation clarifies some points left obscure in the original work. Furthermore, we give a complete treatment of individuals with partial existence, thus extending the original semantics to cover this important case. The presentation is then followed by a discussion of the limitations of this semantics to handle some problems of philosophy of language. Our paper is a companion to [3] which deals with the semantics of Montague. These two papers thus motivate a new system of intensional logic, the logic of kinds, that may be found in [4] and [5].

Reyes, Marie La Palme and Reyes, Gonzalo E. A Boolean-Valued Version of Gupta's Semantics. *Log Anal*, 32, 247-265, S-D 89.

In this paper we shall describe a Boolean-valued version of the intensional semantics of Gupta [2]. We believe that our presentation clarifies some points left obscure in the original work. Furthermore, we give a complete treatment of individuals with partial existence, thus extending the original semantics to cover this important case. The presentation is then followed by a discussion of the limitations of this semantics to handle some problems of philosophy of language. Our paper is a companion to [3] which deals with the semantics of Montague. These two papers thus motivate a new system of intensional logic, the logic of kinds, that may be found in [4] and [5].

Reynolds, Steven L. Skeptical Hypotheses and 'Omniscient' Interpreters. *Austl J Phil*, 71(2), 184-195, Je 93.

The paper defends a version of Donald Davidson's omniscient interpreter argument that massive error about the external world is impossible. Objections answered include those by Richard Foley and Richard Fumerton, Colin McGinn, and Bruce Vermazen.

Rheinwald, Rosemarie. An Epistemic Solution to Goodman's New Riddle of Induction. *Synthese*, 95(1), 55-76, Ap 93.

Goodman's *new riddle of induction* can be characterized by the following questions: What is the difference between 'grue' and 'green'?; Why is the hypothesis that all emeralds are grue not lawlike?; Why is this hypothesis not confirmed by its positive instances?; and, Why is the predicate 'grue' not projectible? I argue in favor of epistemological answers to Goodman's questions. The notions of 'lawlikeness', 'confirmation', and 'projectibility' have to be relativized to (actual and counterfactual) epistemic situations that are determined by the available background information. In order to defend this thesis, I discuss an example that is less strange that the grue example. From the general conclusions of this discussion, it follows that 'grue' is not projectible in the actual epistemic situation, but it is projectible in certain counterfactual epistemic situations.

Rhode, Deborah L. The Politics of Paradigms: Gender Difference and Gender Disadvantage in Beyond Equality and Difference, Bock, Gisela (ed). New York, Routledge, 1992.

Rhode, Deborah L (ed). *Theoretical Perspectives on Sexual Difference*. New Haven, Yale Univ Pr, 1992.

Rhodes, P J. Keaney's *Composition of Aristotle's Athenaion Politeia*. *Polis*, 11(1), 89-94, 1992.

This review summarizes Keaney's book, and doubts whether the author of the *Athenaion Politeia* was as consistently careful in his choice and use of words as Keaney maintains.

Riccio, S. Francesco Vito: Economia e personalismo. *Sapienza*, 45(2), 191-204, 1992.

Rice, Lee C. La causalité adéquate chez Spinoza. *Philosophiques*, 19(1), 45-60, 1992.

This study addresses the problem of analyzing two distinct conceptions of causality in Spinoza. According to the first ("emanative") god-nature is the direct cause of every action which occurs at the level of finite things; while, according to the second ("sequential"), every finite action would be part of an infinite chain of causes (each finite) extended into duration. I show that sequential causality is neither illusory nor simply derivative, contrary to the suggestions made by several recent studies of Spinoza. Secondly, I offer a model for sequential causality which assures the possibility that finite beings may function as adequate causes (in Spinoza's sense) within the physical field. Here my analysis is opposed to those commentators who argue for a rupture in Spinoza between the attributes of thought and extension.

Rice, Lee C. Mind Eternity in Spinoza. *Iyyun*, 41, 319-334, Jl 92.

Propositions 23 through 25 of *Ethics V* have been a continuing problem for Scholars. In this essay I do three things. First, I examine and put some order into the variety of interpretations of mind eternity in Spinoza. Secondly, I argue for a number of criteria which I believe any proposed (re)interpretation must meet in order to be successful. Lastly, I suggest a naturalistic interpretation which meets these criteria. The proposed line of solution is not wholly new, since in general outline something like it has already been suggested by Matheron and earlier by Rivaud.

Rice, Suzanne and Burbules, Nicholas C. Communicative Virtues and Educational Relations. *Proc Phil Educ*, 48, 34-44, 1992.

Rice Jr, Martin A. Paradox Regained. *SW Phil Rev*, 8(1), 127-136, Ja 92.

I argue three things concerning Quine's thesis of the Indeterminacy of translation and the inscrutability of reference: (1) that the two theses logical imply each other, (2) either one will entail normative ethical relativism and virtually any variety of conceptual relativism, and (3) either one will entail that no sentence is either true or false in relation to a stipulated translation manual or by acquiescing in a mother tongue. I take this to be a sufficient refutation of both theses.

Rich, Paul. Reinhold Niebuhr and the Ethics of Realism in International Relations. *Hist Polit Thought*, 13(2), 281-298, Sum 92.

This paper examines the evolution of Niebuhr's thought in International Relations. It challenges the view that Niebuhr was simply an apostle of Cold War realism and argues that Niebuhr's concern from the inter-war years with issues of social justice continued to pervade his thought on international issues during the 1950s and 1960s and led him into growing opposition to US involvement in South East Asia. The article concludes by arguing that Niebuhr remains a figure of interest in International Relations theory as he serves as a key figure in the examination of what can be feasible achieved in the area of human rights given the survival of sovereign nation states.

Richard, Jean. Questions d'épistémologie en théologie de la libération: A propos de l'ouvrage de Clodovis Boff. *Laval Theol Phil*, 49(2), 249-275, Je 93.

Cet article poursuit la discussion des questions soulevées dans la thèse de Clodovis Boff. La théologie du politique est considérée ici comme théologie de la culture, en corrélation avec la théologie d'Église. Le rapport à la praxis, propre à la théologie de la libération, signifie l'engagement concret du théologien en faveur des pauvres. Le caractère socialiste-marxiste de cette théologie apparaît alors clairement dans son versant socio-analytique. Auant à l'autre versant, herméneutique, on soutient qu'il implique le rejet de toute pensée supranaturaliste et l'identification réelle de la libération humaine et du salut divin.

Richard, Mark E. Attitudes in Context. *Ling Phil*, 16(2), 123-148, Ap 93.

This paper a) defends the author's *Propositional Attitudes* against criticisms by Crimmins; b) amends the account of representations employed in that book; c) compares the author's and John Perry's and Crimmins' views on logic and context sensitivity; d) criticizes Perry/Crimmins' account of attitude ascription.

Richard, Mark E. Sense, Necessity and Belief. *Phil Stud*, 69(2-3), 243-263, Mr 93.

A critical discussion of some neo-Fregean accounts of modal contexts, belief

ascriptions, and putative examples of contingent *a priori* knowledge. (Originally part of an APA symposium on Graeme Forbes's *Languages of Possibility*.)

Richards, Neil. A Question of Loyalty. *Crim Just Ethics*, 12(1), 48-55, Wint-Spr 93.

Richards, Norvin W. Surrogate Consent. *Pub Affairs Quart*, 6(2), 227-243, Ap 92.

If our guiding assumption is an absolute abhorrence of medical paternalism, what should we take to be the surrogate's role in speaking for patients who are incompetent to speak for themselves? First, I argue, to deliver the patient's last direction on the matter, whether written or oral. Second, in the absence of any such directions, to choose any course not clearly counter to the patient's interests: including, in some cases, letting the patient die. Finally, I argue that the surrogate serves only to offer the patient's voice in what it is to be done, and that this is not necessarily conclusive: there are always other interests to be considered as well.

Richardson, Alan W. Logical Idealism and Carnap's Construction of the World. *Synthese*, 93(1-2), 59-92, N 92.

Richardson, Alan W. Philosophy of Science and Its Rational Reconstructions: Remarks on the VPI Program for Testing Philosophies of Science. *Proc Phil Sci Ass*, 1, 36-46, 1992.

In this paper I argue that the program of L Laudan et al for empirically testing historiographical philosophies of science ("the VPI program") does not succeed in providing a consistent naturalist program in philosophy of science. In particular, the VPI program endorses a nonnaturalist metamethodology that insists on a hypothetico-deductive structure to scientific testing. But hypothetico-deductivism seems to be both inadequate as an account of scientific theory testing in general and fundamentally at odds with most of the historiographic philosophies under test. I sketch an account of testing historiographic philosophies of science more consistent with the views about scientific testing of those philosophies and argue that such a program is neither viciously circular nor necessarily self-refuting.

Richardson, Henry. Degrees of Finality and the Highest Good in Aristotle. *J Hist Phil*, 30(3), 327-352, J 92.

This article develops a uniform interpretation of *pursuit for the sake of an end*, explaining what an "unqualified final" end (sought solely for its own sake) offers that a (merely) final one does not and providing an improved account of what Aristotle means by an "ultimate end". This interpretation sheds light on (1) the regress argument at the outset of *N.E.I.2*, (2) the way Aristotle argues for the existence of a highest good, (3) the special contribution of "self-sufficiency" (autarkeia) within that good, and (4) the potential flexibility of Aristotle's view about the content of the highest good.

Richardson, Robert C and Burian, Richard M. A Defense of Propensity Interpretations of Fitness. *Proc Phil Sci Ass*, 1, 349-362, 1992.

We offer a systematic examination of propensity interpretations of fitness, which emphasizes the role that fitness plays in evolutionary theory and takes seriously the probabilistic character of evolutionary change. We distinguish questions of the probabilistic character of fitness from the particular interpretations of probability which could be incorporated. The roles of selection and drift in evolutionary models support the view that fitness must be understood within a probabilistic framework, and the specific character of organism/environment interactions supports the conclusion that fitness must be understood as a propensity rather than as a limiting frequency.

Richardson, William J. Heidegger Among the Doctors in Reading Heidegger: Commemorations, Sallis, John (ed). Bloomington, Indiana Univ Pr, 1992.

Richardson, William J. Heidegger's Truth and Politics in Ethics and Danger, Dallery, Arleen B (ed). Albany, SUNY Pr, 1992.

Richey, Lance B. The Genealogy of God's Freedom in Spinoza's *Ethics*. *Dialogue (PST)*, 35(2-3), 29-32, Ap 93.

In this article, I trace Spinoza's argument for attributing freedom to God, in addition to power. I conclude that, for Spinoza, God's freedom is derivative from, and not deductively equivalent to His power.

Richey, Lance B. Truth, Adequacy and Being in Spinoza's *Ethics*. *Lyceum*, 5(1), 21-36, Spr 93.

In this article, I explore the distinction Spinoza makes between true and adequate ideas. I conclude that his distinction, and Spinoza's entire epistemology, is a direct outgrowth from his ontology, and should be seen as such.

Richter, Steffi. Kulturen als Inseln. *Conceptus*, 25(65), 57-65, 1991.

"Universalism" is one of today's buzz-words. The lack of "universalism" in Japanese culture sometimes is stated together with linking it to some sort of "provinciality". Conceptualizations of this kind result from comparative studies, and such studies are widely agreed upon to be bound to reflect their own standpoint as well as the contingency of their own view on the other. The second part of this paper describes some aspects of the meeting of Japanese and European cultures, and especially the reflection of this communicative process by the so-called "Dutch-" or "European Studies" (rangaku, yogaku), starting from the beginning of the nineteenth century.

Richter, V. The Work of John Duns Scotus in the Light of Textual Criticism (Conclusion) (in Czechoslovakian). *Filozof Cas*, 40(5), 868-886, 1992.

Richter, V. The Work of John Duns Scotus in the Light of Textual Criticism (Part I) (in Czechoslovakian). *Filozof Cas*, 40(4), 639-648, 1992.

Rickard, Maurice. A Note on Smith on Attempts and Internal Events. *Analysis*, 44(2), 81-83, Mr 84.

Ricken, Friedo. Gemeinschaft als Grundwert der Aristotelischen Ethik. *Theol Phil*, 66(4), 530-546, 1991.

Ricken combines a personal (formal) and a consequentialist approach to moral philosophy. The concept that mediates between them is the Aristotelian concept of community. Moral norms build up human community which is the necessary condition for the realization of all natural, extra-moral goods. But human community is also the necessary condition for the moral goods of self-respect and mutual respect. Usefulness is not the aim but a consequence of moral goodness.

Ricken, Friedo. Hermeneutik und Metaphysik. *Theol Phil*, 65(1), 69-73, 1990.

The paper is a congratulatory address to Emerich Coreth on his 70th birthday. Coreth's philosophy is a reflection on religion which uses two methods: metaphysics and hermeneutics. According to Coreth, hermeneutics presupposes metaphysics. Criticizing Coreth, Ricken first defends the view that in some aspects metaphysics presupposes hermeneutics. He then distinguishes two types of metaphysics: the Platonic metaphysics of the good and the Aristotelian metaphysics of being. Hermeneutics presupposes the Platonic but not the Aristotelian type.

Rickert, Kevin. Is Contraception Contralife? A Critique of Grisez *et al. Lyceum*, 4(1), 19-37, Spr 92.

This article comprises a critical examination of an article recently published by Germain Grisez, John Finnis, Joseph Boyle, and William E. May in which they argue that contraception is morally evil because it is "contralife." The "contralife" argument is shown to be implausible for several reasons: first, because it entails a logical fallacy; second, because it fails to sufficiently distinguish contraception from Natural Family Planning; and third, because it leads to a number of absurdities. Their argument, which purports to be aimed "toward a clearer understanding," is properly seen as an inadequate and confused understanding.

Ricoeur, Paul. Life in Quest of Narrative in On Paul Ricoeur: Narrative and Interpretation, Wood, David (ed). New York, Routledge, 1991.

Ricoeur, Paul. Narrative Identity in On Paul Ricoeur: Narrative and Interpretation, Wood, David (ed). New York, Routledge, 1991.

Ricoeur, Paul and Blamey, Kathleen (trans). *Oneself as Another—Paul Ricoeur.* Chicago, Univ of Chicago Pr, 1992.

Ricoeur, Paul and Taylor, Charles and Carr, David. Ricoeur on Narrative in On Paul Ricoeur: Narrative and Interpretation, Wood, David (ed). New York, Routledge, 1991.

Riddel, Joseph N. Modern Times: Stein, Bergson, and the Ellipses of 'American' Writing in The Crisis in Modernism, Burwick, Frederick (ed). New York, Cambridge Univ Pr, 1992.

Riddel, Joseph N. Thresholds of the Sign in Theorizing American Literature, Cowan, Bainard (ed). Baton Rouge, Louisiana St Univ Pr, 1991.

Ridley, Aaron. Desire in the Experience of Fiction. *Phil Lit*, 16(2), 279-291, O 92.

This article challenges the claim made by Scruton and others that our emotional responses to fictional characters do not involve desires about those characters. I show that an element of desire—properly construed— does indeed enter into our responses; and I go on to argue that the value which we place on certain distressing fictions cannot be understood fully *unless* the role played by desire in our responses is acknowledged.

Ridley, Aaron. Pitiful Responses to Music. *Brit J Aes*, 33(1), 72-74, Ja 93.

This paper is a reply to Derek Matravers's "Art and the Feelings and Emotions", *Brit J Aes*, 31(4), 322-332. I show that Matravers's version of the Arousal Theory of Musical Expression fails on two counts, which are collectively fatal to it.

Rie, Michael A. Practicing Medicine, Fiduciary Trust Privacy, and Public Moral Interloping after *Cruzan. J Med Phil*, 17(6), 647-664, D 92.

The Supreme Court decision in *Cruzan* reaffirmed the power of the states to set procedural standards for due process regarding the individual's exercise of his liberty interest. As a result, to effect an autonomous decision to refuse treatment when one becomes incompetent requires an affirmative articulation by means of an advance directive. This article argues against simplified advance directives in that they fail to enhance individual liberty and responsibility and fail to provide physicians with needed information. A model protective advance directive is advocated with direction to terminate personal and health insurance payments for health care that is not desired by the patient.

Rieber, Steven. Understanding Synonyms Without Knowing that They are Synonymous. *Analysis*, 52(4), 225-228, O 92.

Ries, Steven I. An Intervention Curriculum for Moral Development. *J Moral Educ*, 21(1), 41-58, 1992.

This paper reports a study of an educational intervention curriculum and its facilitative effect upon moral development (Kohlberg, 1984). The approach of the curriculum is to facilitate moral reasoning through conceptualizing and integrating essential philosophical concepts. The curriculum is a system of reasoning discovered by the individual and then applied to any experience in life, specifically moral experiences.

Rigau, Gemma and Mascaró, Joan. Modularity in Cognition: The Case of Phonetic and Semantic Interpretation of Empty Elements. *Theoria (Spain)*, 5(12-13), 107-128, N 90.

In this paper, we offer an argument in favor of the modular character of mind, based on a more detailed proof of the modular character of the linguistic capacity: in comparing the properties of different components of grammar in a specific area we will draw general consequences about the properties of the cognitive system. More specifically, we analyze and compare the properties, in logical form (LF) and in phonology, of "empty elements"—elements that are "visible" or "full" at some level of representation, but not at another level. (edited)

Riker, William H and Weimer, David L. The Economic and Political Liberalization of Socialism: The Fundamental Problem of Property Rights. *Soc Phil Pol*, 10(2), 79-102, Sum 93.

The establishment of more effective property rights systems is a key to the successful economic and political liberalization of post-communist polities. More effective property rights systems have clarify of allocation, alienability, security from trespass, and credibility of persistence. Credibility is especially important for economic growth. It also contributes to political stability by limiting the policy dimensions subject to political debate. Yet credibility is difficult to achieve in the context of political instability. Social science offers little guidance in predicting the transformation of property rights in post-communist polities; the transformation, however, offers a valuable natural experiment for social scientist.

Riley, Jonathan. American Democracy and the Majority Rule. *Nomos*, 32, 267-307, 1990.

Riley, Jonathan. Liberal Philanthropy. *Nomos*, 34, 338-385, 1992.

Riley, Jonathan. Utilitarian Ethics and Democratic Government in The Utilitarian Response, Allison, Lincoln (ed). Newbury Park, Sage, 1990.

Riley, Patrick. A Retrospective on the Political Theory of George Armstrong Kelly: *The Humane Comedy: Constant, Tocqueville and French Liberalism. Polit Theory*, 20(3), 502-510, Ag 92.

Riley, Patrick. Hannah Arendt on Kant, Truth and Politics in Essays on Kant's Political Philosophy, Williams, Howard Lloyd (ed). Chicago, Univ of Chicago Pr, 1992.

Ring, Jennifer. *Modern Political Theory and Contemporary Feminism: A Dialectical Analysis.* Albany, SUNY Pr, 1991.

The book offers an epistemology for feminism that, unlike standard empiricism, acknowledges the impossibility of complete neutrality and, unlike deconstructionism, harnesses conventional epistemology for the purpose of achieving a degree of objectivity. After a critical review of the feminist literature that avoids, on political principle, both traditional epistemological boundaries and conflictual methods, there follows an extended critique of Liberal empiricism, and of Hegelian and Marxian dialectics. In their place Ring advances what she calls "minimalist dialectics", grounded in process and conflict. Truth so arrived at must be regarded as momentary, for the epistemology does not presuppose knowledge of posited political ends.

Ring, Merrill. 'Bring Me a Slab!': Meaning, Speakers, and Practices in Wittgenstein's Philosophical Investigations, Arrington, Robert L (ed). New York, Routledge, 1991.

Section 19(b)-20 of the *Philosophical Investigations* concern the relation between 'Slab!' and 'Bring Me a Slab!' Wittgenstein retained this material through all early versions of the book, although shifting its location. The essay attempts to learn why Wittgenstein thought the material important enough to warrant a long investigation. It turns out that, although the discussion is badly handled in detail, a major point is made: Wittgenstein was exhibiting the role practices would have in subsequent investigations, especially in escaping both mentalism and behaviorism.

Rinon, Yoav. The Rhetoric of Jacques Derrida I: Plato's Pharmacy. *Rev Metaph*, 46(2), 369-386, 1992.

Taking Derrida's article "Plato's Pharmacy" as an example, I try to refute Derrida's claim that a deep understanding of the Platonic corpus leads the reader to acknowledge that the corpus is a phenomenon which cannot decide between two opposed meanings of the Greek word *pharmakon*, poison and remedy. This refutation is focused on the internal contradiction between two necessary conditions of any Derridian reading: any text is both hierarchical and ahierarchical at the same time. The rhetoric of the strategy which successfully blurs this contradiction is exemplified by the definition given by Wittgenstein to his language games.

Rinon, Yoav. The Rhetoric of Jacques Derrida II: Phaedrus. *Rev Metaph*, 46(3), 537-558, Mr 93.

The aim of the article is to criticise one of Derrida's seminal discussions concerning the problematic relationship between writing and speech. In his article "Plato's Pharmacy" which focuses on Plato's *Phaedrus* Derrida claims that Plato's devaluation of writing, on the one hand, and the eulogy of speech, on the other, exemplify a long tradition in Western philosophy in which the logos stands at the highest stage of an ethical hierarchy. However, a closer examination of the dialogue reveals that the Derridian emphasis is misleading, since Plato never devalues writing as such. Both writing and speech are considered to be morally neutral, and the ethical judgment relates to the content of the message regardless of its form. Thus, the Platonic distinction is not, as Derrida claims, between writing and speech but between two kinds of writing, bad and good, as well as the same two kinds of speech. Another aspect of Derrida's argumentation criticised in the article concerns his treatment of the Greek word *Pharmakon*. While Derrida claims for the absolute "metaphysical" independence of the *pharmakon*, I try to show its complete dependence upon the human agent.

Riordan, P. Religion as *Weltanschauung*: a Solution to a Problem in the Philosophy of Religion. *Aquinas*, 34(3), 519-534, S-D 91.

Risjord, Mark. Relativism and the Social Scientific Study of Medicine. *J Med Phil*, 18(2), 195-212, Ap 93.

Does the social scientific study of medicine require a commitment to relativism? Relativism claims that some subject (e.g., knowledge claims or moral judgments) is relative to a background (e.g., a culture or conceptual scheme) and that judgments about the subject are incommensurable. Examining the concept of success as it appears in orthodox and nonorthodox medical systems, we see that judgments of success are relative to a background medical system. Relativism requires the social scientific study of medicine to be value free in the sense that a medical system must be described without evaluating its elements. When social scientists do evaluate the successfulness of a nonorthodox medical system, they give a crucial role to the nonorthodox conception of success. This strategy does not vitiate value-freedom and it entails a relativism about success. The social scientific study of medicine, therefore, does require relativism in the form of a relativism about success.

Risjord, Mark W. Wittgenstein's Woodcutters: The Problem of Apparent Irrationality. *Amer Phil Quart*, 30(3), 247-258, Jl 93.

When a social scientist discovers speech or behavior which seems irrational, she is likely to eliminate the appearance of irrationality by changing her interpretation. What principles guide such changes? This paper suggests that overall explanatory coherence should guide interpretive changes. Since the most coherent alternative might attribute some different standard of rationality to the subjects, we must reject the common thesis that the social scientist must find her subjects rational according to her own norms of rationality. Advantages of the coherence approach are documented by examining realistic cases of apparent irrationality and interpretive change.

Risser, David T and Nesteruk, Jeffrey. Conceptions of the Corporation and Ethical Decision Making in Business. *Bus Prof Ethics J*, 12(1), 73-89, Spr 93.

We argue that business decision makers are influenced in the performance of their professional roles by the conceptions they hold of the corporation as a social institution. Two distinct and opposing views of the corporation, *corporations-as-property* and *corporations-as-persons*, are evident in American political culture and serve as the basis for these conceptions. We propose a third view, that of *restricted personhood* for corporations, and suggest the implications of this view for business decision making.

Risser, James C. Siting Order at the Limits of Construction: Deconstructing Architectural Place. *Res Phenomenol*, 22, 62-72, 1992.

This paper explores the philosophical and architectural problem of order in the twentieth century architectural "styles" of modernism, post-modernism, and deconstructive architecture. Using examples from representative projects, it is argued that a deconstructive architecture, despite appearances to the contrary, is in its own way taking up this problem of order in the articulation of the notion of uncanny space.

Ritchie, Gisela F. Gotthold Ephraim Lessing, A Citizen of the World. *Hist Euro Ideas*, 16(4-6), 815-820, Ja 93.

A study of Lessing's work reveals that the 18th century German author can be regarded as a citizen of the world, who with his ideas prepared the groundwork for the development of a new political course. Lessing who was versed in numerous languages, was familiar with many of the great thinkers through the centuries. From early on, Lessing's writings show him to be a thinker across national boundaries. In the "Dialogues of Ernst and Falk" Lessing hopes that the wisest men of different states would make the barriers between the nations more flexible. He develops this idea further in the "Nathan der Weise", where the representatives of different religions and nations turn out to be one loving family. "Die Erziehung des Menschengeschlechts" displays Lessing's belief in mankind, its progress toward a better world.

Ritschl, Dietrich. The Search for Implicit Axioms behind Doctrinal Texts. *Gregorianum*, 74(2), 207-221, 1993.

Riverso, Emanuele. Ayer's Treatment of Russell in The Philosophy of A J Ayer, Hahn, Lewis Edwin (ed). Peru, Open Court, 1992.

The paper is an exposition and a discussion of the views about Russell's achievements in philosophy that can be found in the works of A J Ayer. The verdict is that such views give an adequate account of the most important topics of Russell's philosophy with the exception of education, but fail to allow for the development of this philosophy from an original *platonism of relations* coupled with sensationalism (the world built up of sense-data and subsisting relations) into a sort of empiricism with universals as mere linguistic implements. The dismissal of relations and logical constants as realities caused Russell to get into trouble in the following development of his thought.

Rizza, Aldo. La posizione storiografica del pensiero di Carlo Mazzantini. *Filosofia*, 43(3), 473-506, S-D 92.

Rizzacasa, Aurelio. The Concept of 'Person' between Existence and the Realm of Life in Analecta Husserliana, XXXI, Tymieniecka, Anna-Teresa (ed). Dordrecht, Kluwer, 1990.

Rizzerio, Laura. Platon l'École de Tübingen et Giovanni Reale. *Rev Phil Louvain*, 91(89), 90-110, F 93.

Robberechts, Edouard. Savoir et mort chez F Rosenzweig. *Rev Phil Louvain*, 90(86), 180-191, My 92.

For Rosenzweig, a certain type of knowledge, characterized by forgetfulness of temporality and by an obliteration of the multiple concreteness of language, is closely connected with what one could call the suicidal tendency in the West. Under the appearance of a search for logical harmony, both globalising and spotless, it is held that there is a rejection of responsibility, a running away from life and the fear of death which traverses it, a fear that is held to inscribe precisely in the very nexus of life the perfect opportunity of opening up to the numerous faces of otherness and to their infinite demands. (edited)

Robbins, J Wesley. A Neopragmatist Perspective on Religion and Science. *Zygon*, 28(3), 337-349, S 93.

Pragmatists, most notably John Dewey and Richard Rorty, propose overcoming the modern split between science and values with a new image of ourselves as language users. In this new self-understanding, both our scientific and evaluative vocabularies are integral parts of self-reliant human problem solving and coping with the larger natural environment. Our language is not the medium of any higher power from which it derives its legitimacy. On this view, the principal matter at issue between pragmatists and realists so far as interaction between religion and science is concerned is the moral one of human self-reliance.

Robbins, J Wesley. When Christians Become Naturalists. *Relig Stud*, 28(2), 195-206, Je 92.

Argues, contrary to Brian Hebblewaite, that there is nothing deceptive or otherwise immoral about re-definition of bey Christian terms by religious naturalists like John Dewey and, more recently, Don Cupitt.

Robering, Klaus. What is the Role of Model Theory in the Study of Meaning?. *J Prag*, 17(5-6), 511-522, Je 92.

The status of model theory within formal semantics is discussed. Model theory in itself is not a formal theory of meaning but has to be supplemented by principles from semantics proper. The failure to see this leads to inappropriate criticism because of overestimation. On the other side, model theory is oftenly underestimated in ignorance of its more recent applications to formal pragmatics. Some of these are sketched in the article.

Roberts, Lawrence D. Perry on Indexical Semantics and Belief States. *Commun Cog*, 26(1), 77-96, 1993.

I discuss John Perry's essential indexicals, their psychological and semantic accounts, and Howard Wettstein's objections to them. Problems in Perry's psychological account derive from a gap in his semantic account: the latter offers no details about how *context* contributes to indexical reference. To remedy this, I propose an explanatory model for indexical reference, the figure-ground model, and use it to deal with Wettstein's objections and with essential indexicals. I also draw a contrast between specificatory and explanatory theories to explain why direct reference semantics fails to provide a basis for psychological theories.

Roberts, Lissa. Condillac, Lavoisier, and the Instrumentalization of Science. *Kennis Methode*, 16(2), 172-190, 1992.

Roberts, Mark S. Necessary Propositions and the Square of Opposition. *Thomist*, 56(3), 427-433, Jl 92.

Roberts, Melinda. Good Intentions and a Great Divide: Having Babies by Intending Them. *Law Phil*, 12(3), 287-317, Ag 93.

This paper argues, on the basis of our obligations to any children to (or for) whom we are in some sense responsible, that various acts involved in the practice of commercial "surrogate motherhood," including, e.g., the enforcement by the courts of the surrogacy agreement, are morally impermissible. Along the way I consider 1) an "intentionalist" theory of parenthood that purports to refute the view that commercial surrogacy is open to certain of the objections that have been raised against "baby-selling" and 2) the argument that surrogacy arrangements are protective of the interests of the surrogacy child, who likely owes its very existence to those arrangements.

Roberts, P Holley (ed) and Scott, Charles E (ed) and Dallery, Arleen B (ed). *Crises in Continental Philosophy*. Albany, SUNY Pr, 1990.

Roberts, P Holley (ed) and Scott, Charles E (ed) and Dallery, Arleen B (ed). *Ethics and Danger*. Albany, SUNY Pr, 1992.

Roberts, Robert C. Emotions Among the Virtues of the Christian Life. *J Relig Ethics*, 20(1), 37-68, Spr 92.

Emotions enter into the structure of Christian virtues in especially central ways because of special features of the Christian virtues-system. Four kinds of virtues can be distinguished—emotion virtues, behavioral virtues, virtues of will power, and attitudinal virtues. A detailed examination of an example of a Christian virtue from each of the last three classes discloses the structural dependency of these virtues on the Christian emotions.

Robertson, Emily. Philosophers, Orators, and the Role of Science in Liberal Education. *Proc Phil Educ*, 48, 275-278, 1992.

Robertson, John E. The Legacy of Adam Smith in Victorian Liberalism, Bellamy, Richard (ed). New York, Routledge, 1990.

Robinson, David B. A Reply to Martha Nussbaum's Reply. *Phil Invest*, 16(1), 87-88, Ja 93.

Robinson, Denis. Epiphenomenalism, Laws and Properties. *Phil Stud*, 69(1), 1-34, Ja 93.

Robinson, Don. Renormalization and the Effective Field Theory Programme. *Proc Phil Sci Ass*, 1, 393-403, 1992.

Since 1980 effective field theories (EFT's) have been the focus of much research by quantum field theorists but their philosophical implications have gone mostly unnoticed. Some authors claim EFT's are approximations to some fundamental theory. Others claim EFT's are ends in themselves, not approximations to some fundamental theory, and that we can use them to bypass the problem of renormalization. In the present work I argue that the EFT program can bypass the problem if ontological commitments only come from theoretical predictions. Since the history of QFT suggests some form of entity realism, the EFT program does not allow us to bypass the problem of renormalization.

Robinson, Guy. Language and the Society of Others. *Philosophy*, 67(261), 329-341, Jl 92.

My aim is to bring out the depth and radical nature of the challenge implicit in Wittgenstein's 'private language argument' as one issued against the individualistic assumptions shaping the world-view dominant in the West since the Reformation. This places him in the company of both Marx and Aristotle in making language out to be an essentially social phenomenon, in disposing of the mythological 'pre-social language-user', invented by political and social theorists, and in making the social prior to the individual. This involves arguing against the common, rather flat interpretation of it as opposing only something called a 'necessarily private' language.

Robinson, Helier J. A Discourse on the Good. *J Value Inq*, 26(3), 409-416, Jl 92.

Robinson, Howard. Experience and Externalism: A Reply to Peter Smith. *Proc Aris Soc*, 92, 221-223, 1992.

Robinson, Jim. A Change in Plato's Conception of the Good. *J Phil Res*, 18, 231-241, 1993.

One of the most interesting passages in the *Republic* is the comparison of the Form of the Good with the Sun. Although this depiction of the Good was never repeated, many hold that the Good retained its privileged place in Plato's metaphysics. I shall argue that there are good reasons for thinking that Plato, when writing the *Sophist*, no longer held his earlier view of the Good. Specifically, I shall contend that he ceased to believe that as the Sun makes its objects visible, so the Good makes the Forms knowable. This being the case, it cannot also be said to illuminate either the Forms or the order they exhibit. (edited)

Robinson, Jim. Teaching the Allegory of the Cave. *Teach Phil*, 15(4), 329-335, D 92.

The Allegory of the Cave is discussed in many different courses, and is frequently included in introductory courses. Often the allegory is presented in isolation from the rest of the dialogue; sometimes it is even discussed in isolation from the Divided Line, even though the two are explicitly related (517a-b). I show that by relating the two (literally mapping the Line onto the Cave), and then considering the relevance of this to the stated purpose of the dialogue, one not only provides a better interpretation, but enhances the opportunities to involve the class in exciting discussions.

Robinson, Joseph D. Aims and Achievements of the Reductionist Approach in Biochemistry/Molecular Biology/Cell Biology: A Response to Kincaid. *Phil Sci*, 59(3), 465-470, S 92.

Kincaid argues that molecular biology provides little support for the reductionist program, that biochemistry does not reveal common mechanisms, indeed that biochemical theory obstructs discovery. These assertions clash with biologists' stated advocacy of reductionist programs and their claims about the consequent unity of experimental biology. This striking disagreement goes beyond differences in meaning granted to the terms. More significant is Kincaid's misunderstanding of what biochemists do, for a closer look at scientific practice—and one of Kincaid's examples—reveals substantial progress toward explaining biological function with biochemical models. With the molecular detail emerge unifying generalizations as well as further aspects of the functional processes.

Robinson, Sally. *Engendering the Subject: Gender and Self-Representation in Contemporary Women's Fiction*. Albany, SUNY Pr, 1991.

Robinson, T M. Plato and the Computer. *Ancient Phil*, 12(2), 375-382, Fall 92.

Robison, Wade. The Constitution and the Nature of Law. *Law Phil*, 12(1), F 93.

It is thought a puzzle that such a concept as the right to privacy should be given Constitutional protection when no one ever thought of the right to privacy until over 100 years after the Constitution was adopted. By Alexander Hamilton's interpretation of the Constitution, such protection would not be puzzling: the rights could readily be added to. That route is now precluded. The way in which language functions makes it perfectly understandable how a concept like equal protection might come to cover school desegregation, for instance. We may understand the concept of equal protection differently than those who wrote the 14th Amendment, and that is no more cause for concern than our having a different, deeper understanding of gravity than Newton's rather truncated conception. (edited)

Robson, Ruthann. Mother: The Legal Domestication of Lesbian Existence. *Hypatia*, 7(4), 172-185, Fall 92.

The legal category "mother" operates restrictively and punitively to "domesticate" lesbian existence. Our domestication is the reason that we have difficulty thinking beyond the category "mother." I explore how "mother" is used by both lesbians and nonlesbians within the legal system. In order to ensure lesbian survival on lesbian terms, we must strategize theories that do not preserve the dominant legal paradigm that codifies "mother," even if that category is expanded to include "lesbian mother."

Rocci, Giovanni. Ethics in the Psyche's Individuating Development towards the Self in Analecta Husserliana, XXXI, Tymieniecka, Anna-Teresa (ed). Dordrecht, Kluwer, 1990.

Roche, Mark W. National Socialism and the Disintegration of Values: Reflections on Nietzsche, Rosenberg, and Broch. *J Value Inq*, 26(3), 367-380, Jl 92.

Nietzsche's perspectivism is logically incoherent and passes over into power positivism. The philosopher of National Socialism, Alfred Rosenberg, is shown to share Nietzsche's position. National Socialism arises not from an absolute philosophy but from a relativistic position that has passed over into power positivism: because there are no universal truths, one subject or group of subjects has the right to assert its irrational truths over others. A literary analogue is evident in Broch's *The Sleepwalkers*, where we see the development from an undermining of truth (Bertrand) to the arbitrary assertion of truth (Esch) and the arbitrary assertion of power (Huguenau).

Rock, Irvin. On Explanation in Psychology in John Searle and His Critics, Lepore, Ernest (ed). Cambridge, Blackwell, 1991.

John Searle maintains that there is no gap to be filled between brain explanations of mind and explanation of the language of intentionality. While agreeing that, from the standpoint of *ontology*, there is no level other than mind and brain, I maintain that there is an indispensable level of *explanation* between the two. Functional explanations, often in the form of hypothetical constructs, that provide an understanding of what kind of process occurs that underlies phenomenal experience or behavior, must precede and supplement brain explanations. Such functional explanations are necessary to understand the meaning of the neuropsysiological cause, to guide us in our brain explorations, and to avoid postulation overly simplistic and premature brain mechanisms.

Rockefeller, Steven C. John Dewey, Spiritual Democracy, and the Human Future in Revisioning Philosophy, Ogilvy, James (ed). Albany, SUNY Pr, 1992.

Rockler, Michael J. The Curricular Role of Russell's Scepticism. *Russell*, 12(1), 50-60, Sum 92.

This article describes the way in which Bertrand Russell's philosophical skepticism can be applied to school curriculum. It examines the development of Russell's perspective and indicates how he applied it to his writings on education. It also suggests how Russell's educational work can be applied to contemporary issues of school curriculum. This article argues that much of Russell's educational thought—partly developed from skepticism—remains relevant today. Russell's skepticism was one of his most significant contributions to modern thought. Contemporary schooling in the twenty-first century would be improved if educators adopted the ideas of this remarkable thinker born in the nineteenth century.

Rockmore, Tom. Aspects of French Hegelianism. *Owl Minerva*, 24(2), 191-206, Spr 93.

Rockmore, Tom. Fichte, Lask, and Lukác's Hegelian Marxism. *J Hist Phil*, 30(4), 557-577, O 92.

Rockmore, Tom. Husserl's Critique of Hegel in Hegel and His Critics, Desmond, William (ed). Albany, SUNY Pr, 1989.

Rockmore, Tom. Penelope's Web: Reconstruction of Philosophy and the Relevance of Reason. *J Speculative Phil*, 7(2), 114-136, 1993.

Rockmore, Tom. Philosophy, Literature, and Intellectual Responsibility. *Amer Phil Quart*, 30(2), 109-121, Ap 93.

Rockmore, Tom. Some Problems in Recent Pragmatism. *Hist Phil Quart*, 10(3), 277-289, Jl 93.

Rockmore, Tom (ed) and Singer, Beth (ed). *Anti-Foundationalism: Old and New*. Philadelphia, Temple Univ Pr, 1992.

While many in the philosophical community today treat antifoundationalism as a "postmodern" phenomenon, this work demonstrates that it has been a major theme throughout the history of Western philosophy. The ten essays included trace this history, dealing with such figures as Anaximander, Plato, Aristotle, Gassendi,

Descartes, Hegel, Nietzsche, Habermas, Chisholm, James, Dewey, Randall, Buchler and Rorty. The contributors are Joseph Margolis, Ronald Polansky, Gary Calore, Fred S Michael, Emily Michael, Wilhelm S Wurzer, Charlene Haddock Seigfried, Sandra B Rosenthal, Kathleen Wallace, and the editors.

Rodeheffer, Jane Kelley. The Call of Conscience and the Call of Language in Crises in Continental Philosophy, Dallery, Arleen B (ed). Albany, SUNY Pr, 1990.

The essay offers a reading of sections 54-60 of Martin Heidegger's *Being and Time* which interprets the central notion of the call of conscience in light of Heidegger's later view of language as calling to human being to dwell within its speaking. The essay suggests that the experience Dasein undergoes in the call of conscience in *Being and Time* is really an experience with language, such that language, not human being, becomes the site of the disclosure of being. It is thus in Dasein's appropriation of the call of conscience in *Being and Time* that passage to Heidegger's later thinking occurs.

Rodis-Lewis, G. Doute pratique et doute spéculatif chez Montaigne et Descartes. *Rev Phil Fr*, 4, 439-449, O-D 92.

Rodning, Charles B. Coping With Ambiguity and Uncertainty in Patient-Physician Relationships: II — *Traditio Argumentum Respectus*. *J Med Human*, 13(3), 147-156, Fall 92.

A methodology of argumentation and a perspective of incredulity are essential ingredients of all intellectual endeavor, including that associated with the art and science of medical care. *Traditio argumentum respectus* (tradition of respectful argumentation) as a principled system of assessing the validity of beliefs, opinions, perceptions, data, and knowledge, is worthy of practice and perpetuation, because assessments of validity are susceptible to incompleteness, incorrectness, and misinterpretation. Since the latter may lead to ambiguity, uncertainty, anxiety, and animosity among the individuals (patients and physicians) involved in such dialogue, objective analyses and criteria are desirable. (edited)

Rodríguez, Virgilio Ruiz. El Aborto y los Derechos Humanos. *Rev Filosof (Mexico)*, 24(71), 126-134, My-Ag 91.

Rodríguez Consuegra, Francisco. La reducción ontológica y sus problemas. *Critica*, 24(70), 17-64, Ap 92.

Rodriguez Rial, Nel. The Moral Act in Analecta Husserliana, XXXI, Tymieniecka, Anna-Teresa (ed). Dordrecht, Kluwer, 1990.

Rodriguez Valls, F. La experiencia noética de Dios (Interpretación sobre textos de Santo Tomás). *Pensamiento*, 188(47), 481-496, O-D 91.

Rodriguez-Consuegra, Francisco A. A New Angle on Russell's "Inextricable Tangle" Over Meaning and Denotation. *Russell*, 12(2), 197-207, Wint 92-93.

This article is a brief study of one of Russell's unpublished writings from 1905: "on fundamentals". The manuscript is very interesting because it provides the background to "on denoting" mainly in two points: 1) the difficult passages in which Russell succeeds in dispensing with the distinction meaning-denotation; 2) the precise formulation of the main definition of the theory of definite descriptions in itself.

Roemer, John. What Walrasian Marxism Can and Cannot Do. *Econ Phil*, 8(1), 149-156, Ap 92.

Roemer, John E. A Pragmatic Theory of Responsibility for the Egalitarian Planner. *Phil Pub Affairs*, 22(2), 146-166, Spr 93.

Contemporary egalitarian theory calls for equalizing opportunities. Opportunity egalitarianism is here interpreted as equalizing outcomes in so far as they are due to causes beyond the control of persons, but allowing outcomes to differ in so far as they are due to causes within the control of persons. A method is proposed for implementing this kind of equality, given the norms that a society has with regard to what actions of persons are deemed to be within their control. Several examples are discussed, and it is shown how the recommended approach differs significantly from the kind of equality recommended by R Dworkin's resource egalitarianism.

Roemer, John E. Distributing Health in The Quality of Life, Nussbaum, Martha C (ed). New York, Oxford Univ Pr, 1993.

How should an international agency, charged with using its budget to reduce infant mortality, allocate it across countries? An axiomatic approach is followed, and axioms are suggested which jointly characterize the lexicographical minimum solution. The author analyzed the budgets of the World Health Organization, and interviewed its officers. It appears as if WHO subscribes to all the substantive axioms, yet its allocation rule is not lexicographical minimum. The ubiquitously used in social choice theory is never suitable for describing the behavior of actual organizations facing allocation problems. Consequently, the results which depend on such an axiom are of questionable political relevance.

Roemer, John E. The Possibility of Market Socialism in The Idea of Democracy, Copp, David (ed). New York, Cambridge Univ Pr, 1993.

The Communist political economies failed due to the conjunction of three characteristics: 1) administrative allocation of resources, 2) non-competitive politics, and 3) public ownership (in the sense of micro-control by the state) of firms. A version of market socialism is proposed in which 1) markets would allocate most commodities, 2) politics would be democratic and competitive, and 3) firms would not be controlled by the state. Nevertheless, the distributive of profit income would be much more egalitarian than in capitalist economies. The essential issue addressed is whether firms would remain innovative and competitive when unlimited private accumulation in stock is not possible.

Roemer, John E (ed) and Hampton, Jean (ed) and Copp, David (ed). *The Idea of Democracy*. New York, Cambridge Univ Pr, 1993.

Essays on democratic theory accompanied by critical comments, with an introduction by the editors. Contributors: Richard J Arneson, Pranab Bardhan, Samuel Bowles and Herbert Gintis, Thomas Christiano, Joshua Cohen, David Copp, David Estlund, John Ferejohn, David Gauthier, Jean Hampton, Russell Hardin, Stephen Holmes, Michael S McPherson, Karl Ove Moene, Christopher W Morris, John Rawls, John E Roemer, Debra Satz, John D Stephens, Robert Sugden, Cass R Sunstein.

Römpp, Georg. Double Vision Idealism. *Man World*, 26(3), 329-338, Jl 93.

Römpp, Georg 646 AUTHOR INDEX WITH ABSTRACTS

Römpp, Georg. Moralität und Frieden: Kants Gesetz der Freiheit in der Welt der Staaten. *Theol Phil*, 65(2), 216-233, 1990.

Roeper, Peter and Leblanc, Hugues. Getting the Constraints on Popper's Probability Functions Right. *Phil Sci*, 60(1), 151-157, Mr 93.

Shown here is that a constraint used by Popper in *The Logic of Scientific Discovery* (1959) for calculating the absolute probability of a universal quantification, and one introduced by Stalnaker in "Probability and Conditionals" (1970, 70) for calculating the relative probability of a negation, are too weak for the job. The constraint wanted in the first case is in Bendall (1979) and that wanted in the second case is Popper (1959).

Roeper, Peter and Leblanc, Hugues. Les fonctions de probabilité: la question de leur définissabilité récursive. *Dialogue (Canada)*, 31(4), 643-659, Autumn 92.

Roeper, Peter and Leblanc, Hugues. Probability Functions: The Matter of Their Recursive Definability. *Phil Sci*, 59(3), 372-388, S 92.

This paper studies the extent to which probability functions are recursively definable. The absolute probability functions considered are those of Kolmogorov and Carnap, and the relative ones are those of Kolmogorov, Carnap, Rényi, and Popper. (edited)

Rössler, Otto E and Rössler, Reimara. Is the Mind-Body Interface Microscopic?. *Theor Med*, 14(2), 153-165, Je 93.

This paper puts forward the hypothesis that consciousness might be linked to matter in a way which is more sophisticated than the traditional macroscopic Cartesian hypothesis suggests. Advances in the biophysics of the nervous system, not only on the level of its macroscopic functioning but also on the level of individual ion channels, have made the question of 'how finely' consciousness is tied to matter and its dynamics more important. Quantum mechanics limits the attainable resolution and puts into doubt the idea of an infinitely fine-woven attachment. A recent approach to physics rekindles such a rationalist hope. 'Endophysics' focuses on the global implications of microscopic computer simulations of chemical and biophysical processes. A complete 'artificial universe' can be set up in the computer.

Rössler, Reimara and Rössler, Otto E. Is the Mind-Body Interface Microscopic?. *Theor Med*, 14(2), 153-165, Je 93.

This paper puts forward the hypothesis that consciousness might be linked to matter in a way which is more sophisticated than the traditional macroscopic Cartesian hypothesis suggests. Advances in the biophysics of the nervous system, not only on the level of its macroscopic functioning but also on the level of individual ion channels, have made the question of 'how finely' consciousness is tied to matter and its dynamics more important. Quantum mechanics limits the attainable resolution and puts into doubt the idea of an infinitely fine-woven attachment. A recent approach to physics rekindles such a rationalist hope. 'Endophysics' focuses on the global implications of microscopic computer simulations of chemical and biophysical processes. A complete 'artificial universe' can be set up in the computer.

Rogan, Jan. 'Keeping Silent through Speaking' in Kierkegaard on Art and Communication, Pattison, George (ed). New York, St Martin's Pr, 1992.

Rogers, G A J. The History of Philosophy and the Reputation of Philosophers. *J Hist Phil*, 31(1), 113-118, Ja 93.

Rogers, Gerald F. Confucius, The First 'Teacher' of Humanism?. *Free Inq*, 13(2), 46-49, Spr 93.

Rogers, Joel and Cohen, Joshua. Associations and Democracy. *Soc Phil Pol*, 10(2), 282-312, Sum 93.

Rogers, John. Contexte des rapports intellectuels entre Hobbes et Locke. *Arch Phil*, 55(4), 531-551, O-D 92.

Despite the many works of comparison between Hobbes and Locke, especially with regard to their political theory, there remain puzzles about their relationship. This paper attempts some illumination by examining how they both stood to Robert Boyle, and especially how their positions compare with regard to Boyle's understanding of scientific method. An examination of the celebrated dispute between Boyle and Hobbes over the possibility of a vacuum is seen as providing a key to some aspects of Locke's response to Hobbes. It is suggested that Locke, in siding with Boyle, placed himself at a distance from Hobbes that hindered Locke recognising the extent of their agreement on central issues.

Rogers, K A. Anselm on Praising a Necessarily Perfect Being. *Int J Phil Relig*, 34(1), 41-52, Ag 93.

Anselm of Canterbury believes that, though rational creatures must be free in the libertarian sense, God necessarily does the best. Otherwise He would not be maximally praiseworthy or the ultimate standard for value. It follows that the actual world is the best and only world God could make, but this conclusion is not incoherent. And though He "cannot do otherwise" we should nevertheless praise God, recognizing that such praise is *worship* having little in common with the praise we give our fellow creatures.

Rogers, Katherin A. Personhood, Potentiality, and the Temporarily Comatose Patient. *Pub Affairs Quart*, 6(2), 245-254, Ap 92.

Are fetuses persons in the moral sense? It is rationality and perhaps other uniquely human qualities which distinguishes the person from the non-person. The example of the temporarily comatose patient shows that present possession of these qualities is not necessary. That the patient had them in the past is not significant morally. It is future possession which grants present personhood. Thus the fetus is a person from conception. The arguments which purport to prove the absurdity of this position, the case of twinning, for example, can all be successfully countered.

Rogers, Katherine A. The Medieval Approach to Aardvarks, Escalators, and God. *J Value Inq*, 27(1), 63-68, Ja 93.

The concept of a maximally perfect being requires the possibility of one hierarchy of value on which everything can be ranked. Some contemporary philosophers say this is absurd. However, there are reasons to adopt the idea of a 'Great Chain of Being' which makes sense of a single scale. If creation is an image of the Creator, everything is commensurate because everything reflects God more or less. Second, the notion that more 'being' means more value jibes well with common moral intuitions. Third, if one scale will serve, it violates Ockham's razor to posit more.

Rogers, Patrick. The Transition to Civil Society: Two Interpretations of Locke's Theory of Property Rights. *SW Phil Stud*, 15, 67-73, Spr 93.

James Tully, in his *A Discourse on Property* offers an interpretation of Locke's theory of property rights in which he claims that Locke did not believe that individuals could have the right to private property in a state of nature, and that Locke is a pure "conventionalist" about property. In *The Right to Private Property*, Jeremy Waldron takes issue with Tully's interpretation, and argues that it rests on a mistaken interpretation of Locke. In this paper I examine both sides of this issue and conclude that Waldron's interpretation is more plausible given the structure of the text and the evidence he introduces.

Rogerson, Kenneth. A Problem for Anti-Realism. *SW Phil Rev*, 9(1), 63-69, Ja 93.

The purpose of this article is to challenge Michael Dummett's criticism of a truth conditional theory of meaning. Dummett's intent is to show that an anti-realist (verificationist) theory of meaning can account for the problematic class of "undecidable" statements where a truth conditional theory cannot. In the present paper Dummett' is criticized on the grounds that once we expose the assumptions an anti-realist needs to account for the meaning of "undecidables" it will turn out that these same assumptions will also allow a truth conditional theory to give a plausible explanation for these cases.

Rogerson, Kenneth. Kantian Ontology. *Kantstudien*, 84(1), 3-24, 1993.

The purpose of this paper is to defend Kant's transcendental idealism. Kant wants to establish that space, time, causality and other "pure concepts of the understanding" can be shown to be the basis for important *a priori* and necessary statements. But further, he also wants to show that if we grant these arguments to *a priority* and necessity we must also grant that the ontological position entitled "transcendental idealism." My project is to show that despite recent criticisms Kant is on tolerably solid ground holding that an idealism (suitably understood) follows from the *a priority* and necessity of space, time, and causality.

Roggerone, Giuseppe A. Dottrina non scritta e limiti della comunicabilità filosofica in Platone. *G Metaf*, 14(2), 245-275, My-Ag 92.

Rogozinski, Jacob and Dews, Peter (trans). Hell on Earth: Hannah Arendt in the Face of Hitler. *Phil Today*, 37(3), 257-274, Fall 93.

This article considers Hannah Arendt's theory of fascism in her book on *Totalitarianism*. The modern denial of transcendence is seen as enabling fascist ideology, and the consequent drive to liquidate the 'other' is explored with the aid of psychoanalytical categories.

Rohatyn, Dennis A and Labson, Sam. Mach's Razor, Duhem's Holism, and Bell's Theorem. *Phil Sci (Tucson)*, 5, 79-116, 1993.

Rohs, Peter. Oikeiosis-jenseits von Herder und Darwin. *Z Phil Forsch*, 47(1), 113-117, Ja-Mr 93.

Rollin, Bernard E. Animal Welfare, Science, and Value. *J Agr Environ Ethics*, 6/2(Supp), 44-50, 1993.

A main component of 20th century scientific ideology is the view that science is "value-free." This notion has dominated the view of animal welfare in the emerging field of animal welfare science. Science, however, is neither value-free in general, nor ethics-free in particular. The value-laden nature of the concept of "animal welfare" is clear, and even what information is considered to count as facts is structured by valuational presuppositions. Animal pain and stress, which were, until recently, viewed strictly in physicalistic terms, have become increasingly viewed in terms of animal subjective experience, as society grows more and more concerned about animal suffering. The new ethic emerging for animals in society is thus calling for a concept of welfare significantly different from traditional views such as the one which equates welfare with productivity.

Rollin, Bernard E. Intrinsic Value for Nature—An Incoherent Basis for Environmental Concern. *Free Inq*, 13(2), 20, Spr 93.

Various philosophers have attempted to argue that environmental ethics should be based in recognition of intrinsic or inherent value for nature. But, as Plato pointed out, ethical progress involves drawing unnoticed conclusions from previously accepted principles. Thus, one can extend the notion of inherent value in humans to other sentient creatures since, in both cases, what we do to the being in question matters to *it*. Such a move cannot, however, be employed regarding non-sentient nature. Further, attempts to provide intrinsic value to nature generally subordinate the interests of "mere individuals" to that of nature, ecosystems, species, etc., leading to what has been called "Eco-Fascism."

Rolnick, Phil. Polanyi's Progress: Transcendence, Universality and Teleology. *Tradition Discovery*, 19(2), 13-31, 1993.

Polanyi's work supports the idea of progress by linking progress to the transcendent, the universal, and the teleological. Polanyi's epistemology is developed in tandem with an implied metaphysics, one which incorporates a tripartite dialectic among the community, the individual, and the transcendent, universal reality which both community and individual progressively seek. Traditions, whether scientific or religious, may rightfully claim a penultimate authority. However, in science just as in religion, only the living God can possess ultimate authority. Hence, traditions may undergo progressive development by breaking out of their current understandings en route to greater understandings. In order to do so, the traditio must continually submit itself to the reality which it seeks to mediate to its members.

Romani, Romano. Notes on Husserl and Kant in Analecta Husserliana, XXXIV, Tymieniecka, Anna-Teresa (ed). Dordrecht, Kluwer, 1992.

The paper deals with Husserl's and Kant's transcendental idealism, i.e., with Kant's and Husserl's criticism intended as an investigation on meaning in speaking-thinking, as well as in action-experiencing. One goes back to the Greek source of Idealism, i.e., Plato and Aristotle. The problems involve: the relationship between philosophy and rhetoric, the art of persuasion and the search for truth, the implications of these relationships with the ones existing, between sciences and philosophy. Husserl's phenomenology and Kant's criticism are investigated from the point of view of Plato's and Aristotle's research on Being, which is the source of every noetic and ethical problem.

Romani, Romano. The Unattainability of the Norm in Analecta Husserliana, XXXI, Tymieniecka, Anna-Teresa (ed). Dordrecht, Kluwer, 1990.

AUTHOR INDEX WITH ABSTRACTS 647 Rosen, Robert

Romanus, Aegidius. The Errors of the Philosophers (in Hungarian). *Magyar Filozof Szemle*, 3, 316-347, 1991.

Romerales, Enrique (ed). *Creenciay Racionalidad: Lecturas de Filosofía de la Religión*. Barcelona, Anthropos, 1992.

Ronen, Ruth. Possible Worlds Between the Disciplines. *Brit J Aes*, 33(1), 29-40, Ja 93.

'Possible Worlds' refers to different concepts in the various disciplines in which they are employed. This paper shows how PW, originating from modal logic and later adopted by aesthetics, literary theory, linguistics, etc., were developed into an interdisciplinary tool by undergoing substantial changes of meaning. This paper aims to expose some incompatibilities between interpretations attached to PW by philosophers on the one hand and by literary theorists (who use PW in order to solve the problem of fictionality) on the other hand.

Rong, Rosemarie. Blessed Are the Peacemakers: Commentary on Making Peace in Gestational Conflicts. *Theor Med*, 13(4), 329-335, D 92.

The purpose of this commentary on James Nelson's article is to advocate introducing the ethics of care into the arena of gestational conflict. Too often the debate gets stalled in a maternal versus fetal rights headlock. Interventionists stress fetal over maternal rights: they believe education, post-birth prosecution or pre-birth seizure of pregnant women may be permissible. In contrast to interventionists, other philosophers stress that favoring fetal rights treats women like 'fetal containers'. I question whether we should really consider issues of moral/parental obligations to children in terms of rights. Rather, the language of care should guide moral conduct vis-a-vis children/fetuses. The particularity of each woman's story-the particulars of her human relationships-inform her story. An individual's ability to care is largely a function of whether community cares for her. We must care for others to enable them to care for themselves and their loved ones-born or unborn.

Rongjie, Chen and Chan, Wing-Tsit. An Exploration of the Concept of *Zhong* in the Teachings of Confucianism. *Chin Stud Phil*, 24(3), 72-100, Spr 93.

Roof, Judith. The Ideology of Fair Use: Xeroxing and Reproductive Rights. *Hypatia*, 7(2), 63-73, Spr 92.

Looking at the metaphorical similarities between abortion statutes and copyright law reveals reproductive laws' stake in property ideologies. "Fair use" provisions in copyright law are analogous to abortion rights, delimiting the extent to which a non-owner (one who copies, a mother) can exert control over material "belonging" to another. The similarity suggests that the way to understand abortion fury is as a manifestation of property rights.

Rooney, Phyllis. Feminist-Pragmatist Revisionings of Reason, Knowledge, and Philosophy. *Hypatia*, 8(2), 15-37, Spr 93.

By tracing a specific development through the approaches of Peirce, James, and Dewey I present a view of (classical) pragmatist epistemology that invites comparison with recent work in feminist epistemology. Important dimensions of pragmatism and feminism emerge from this critical dialectical relationship between them. Pragmatist reflections on the role of reason and philosophy in a changing world encourage us to see that philosophy's most creative and most responsible future must also be a feminist one.

Rooney, Phyllis A. On Values in Science: Is the Epistemic/Non-Epistemic Distinction Useful?. *Proc Phil Sci Ass*, 1, 13-22, 1992.

The debate about the rational and the social in science has sometimes been developed in the context of a distinction between epistemic and non-epistemic values. Paying particular attention to two important discussions in the last decade, by Longino and by McMullin, I argue that a fuller understanding of values in science ultimately requires abandoning the distinction itself. This is argued directly in terms of an analysis of the lack of clarity concerning what epistemic values are. I also argue that the philosophical import of much of the feminist work in philosophy of science is restricted by any kind of strict adherence to the distinction.

Roque, Alicia. Utopia: Fail-Safe or Safe-Fail in Terrorism, Justice and Social Values, Peden, Creighton (ed). Lewiston, Mellen Pr, 1990.

The paradigm for utopian literature to date has been a "fail-safe" drawn from the typological thinking of Plato, for whom only the fixed and unchangeable eidos is ultimately real. Accordingly, most utopias since Plato are designed so as not to be subject to change and, a fortiori, failings. As a result they are intentionally closed, isolated and rigid societies. In contrast, a more desirable "safe-fail" model relying on a paradigm that takes change as fundamental is suggested. Safe-fail societies would aim for resilience, not stability, and in order to achieve those ends would be structured as spatially and temporally heterogeneous societies with flexibly coupled subsystems, characteristics that make them open, engaged and dynamic societies with the capacity for self-renewal.

Rorty, Amélie Oksenberg. Character, Mind, and Politics in Psychoanalysis, Mind and Art, Hopkins, Jim (ed). Cambridge, Blackwell, 1992.

Rorty, Amélie Oksenberg. From Passions to Sentiments: The Structure of Hume's *Treatise*. *Hist Phil Quart*, 10(2), 165-179, Ap 93.

Rorty, Amélie Oksenberg. The Directions of Aristotle's *Rhetoric*. *Rev Metaph*, 46(1), 63-95, S 92.

Rorty, Richard. A Pragmatist View of Rationality and Cultural Difference. *Phil East West*, 42(4), 581-596, O 92.

Rorty, Richard. Feminism and Pragmatism in The Tanner Lectures On Human Values, V13, Peterson, Grethe B (ed). Salt Lake City, Univ of Utah Pr, 1992.

Rorty, Richard. Feminism, Ideology, and Deconstruction: A Pragmatist View. *Hypatia*, 8(2), 96-103, Spr 93.

Neither philosophy in general, nor deconstruction in particular, should be thought of as pioneering, path-breaking, tool for feminist politics. Recent philosophy, including Derrida's, helps us see practices and ideas (including patriarchal practices and ideas) as neither natural nor inevitable—but that is all it does. When philosophy has finished showing that everything is a social construct, it does not help us decide which social constructs to retain and which to replace.

Rorty, Richard. Heidegger, Contingency, and Pragmatism in Heidegger: A Critical Reader, Dreyfus, Hubert (ed). Cambridge, Blackwell, 1992.

Rorty, Richard. Is Derrida a Transcendental Philosopher? in Derrida: A Critical Reader, Wood, David (ed). Cambridge, Blackwell, 1992.

Rorty, Richard. Is Derrida a Transcendental Philosopher? in Working Through Derrida, Madison, Gary B (ed). Evanston, Northwestern Univ Pr, 1993.

Rorty, Richard. Putnam and the Relativist Menace. *J Phil*, 90(9), 443-461, S 93.

Putnam has frequently criticized Rorty as a "cultural relativist", but Rorty finds this description puzzling, and thinks of himself as agreeing with Putnam on practically all issues — particularly in his criticism of Bernard Williams' notion of "how things are anyway". Rorty suggests that the only real difference between him and Putnam may be over the question of whether "correctness is just for a time and a place," and about whether a Darwinian conception of humans as clever animals is adequate.

Rorty, Richard. Putnam on Truth. *Phil Phenomenol Res*, 52(2), 415-418, Je 92.

Rorty, Richard (ed). *The Linguistic Turn: Essays In Philosophical Method*. Chicago, Univ of Chicago Pr, 1992.

Rorty, Richard. The Pragmatist's Progress in Interpretation and Overinterpretation: Umberto Eco, Collini, Stefan (ed). New York, Cambridge Univ Pr, 1992.

Rorty, Richard. Wittgenstein, Heidegger, and the Reification of Language in The Cambridge Companion to Heidegger, Guignon, Charles (ed). New York, Cambridge Univ Pr, 1993.

Wittgenstein and Heidegger passed each other in the night, going in opposite directions. Wittgenstein reified "Language" in the *Tractatus*, as Heidegger was to do after his "turn". For reasons Davidson has offered in his "A Nice Derangement of Epitaphs", such hypostatization is a bad idea. Both *Philosophical Investigations* and *Being and Time* are good examples of how to avoid this reification. Wittgenstein got better in this respect, whereas Heidegger got worse.

Rose, Carol M. Property as Wealth, Property as Propriety. *Nomos*, 33, 223-247, 1991.

This article questions Stephen Munzer's claim that preference-satisfaction, fairness, and desert are pluralistic principles of property; it constructs a model in which preference-satisfaction subsumes both other principles. It then argues that the genuinely divergent elements in modern property arise from the mix of a dominant preference-satisfaction model with remnants of a pre-capitalist understanding of property, where property was thought to belong "properly" to persons and families according to their role in the commonwealth. The article describes this "propriety" version of property in aristocratic Europe and early republican American, and outlines its continued influence in American "takings" law.

Rose, Gillian. Diremption of Spirit in Shadow of Spirit, Berry, Philippa (ed). New York, Routledge, 1992.

Rose, Gillian. Of Derrida's Spirit in Of Derrida, Heidegger, and Spirit, Wood, David (ed). Evanston, Northwestern Univ Pr, 1993.

Rosemann, Philipp W. Nova et vetera: "Le fondement de la morale" de Mgr A Léonard. *Rev Phil Louvain*, 91(89), 126-136, F 93.

"Nova et vetera" — new things and old — is the motto of Louvain's Institute of Philosophy. It encapsulates a Neoscholasticism which is convinced that the Scholastic method consists in the constant effort to create ever richer philosophical syntheses which combine knowledge gained from the tradition with the insights of contemporary thought. Bishop Léonard's book on fundamental ethics is a fine example of this approach, as it enriches Thomism with elements of the Kantian tradition, but also of psychoanalysis and other views emphasizing the aspect of necessity in human conduct. The article is a discussion of Léonard's book.

Rosen, Frederick. Majorities and Minorities: A Classical Utilitarian View. *Nomos*, 32, 24-43, 1990.

Rosen, Frederick. The Origin of Liberal Utilitarianism in Victorian Liberalism, Bellamy, Richard (ed). New York, Routledge, 1990.

Rosen, Gideon. A Problem for Fictionalism About Possible Worlds. *Analysis*, 53(2), 71-81, Ap 93.

Fictionalism about possible worlds is the view that talk about worlds in the analysis of modality is to be construed as ontologically innocent discourse about the content of a fiction. Versions of the view have been defended by D M Armstrong (in *A Combinatorial Theory of Possibility*) and by myself (in "Modal Fictionalism', *Mind* 99, July 1990). The present note argues that fictionalist accounts of modality (both Armstrong's version and my own) fail to serve the fictionalists ontological purposes because they imply that as a matter of necessity there exist many worlds.

Rosen, Michael (trans) and Förster, Eckart (ed & trans) and Kant, Immanuel. *Opus Postumum/Immanuel Kant*. New York, Cambridge Univ Pr, 1993.

Rosen, Robert. Drawing the Boundary between Subject and Object: Comments on the Mind-Brain Problem. *Theor Med*, 14(2), 89-100, Je 93.

Physics says that it cannot deal with the mind-brain problem, because it does not deal in subjectivities, and mind is subjective. However, biologists still claim to seek a material basis for subjective mental processes, which would thereby render them objective. Something is clearly wrong here. I claim that what is wrong is the adoption of too narrow a view of what constitutes 'objectivity', especially in identifying it with what a 'machine' can do. I approach the problem in the light of two cognate circumstances: a) the 'measurement problem' in quantum physics, and b) the objectivity of standard mathematics, even though most of it is beyond the reach of 'machines'. I argue that the only resolution to such problems is in the recognition that closed loops of causation are 'objective'; i.e., legitimate objects of scientific scrutiny.

Rosen, Robert. On Psychomimesis. *Ideal Stud*, 23(1), 87-95, Wint 93.

We review some aspects of the Mind-Brain Problem, as they have been approached from a perspective based on Mimesis. Such studies are usually prefixed by the adjective "artificial", as in "artificial intelligence", "artificial life", etc. The key assertion of such approaches is embodied in the familiar "Turing Test"; that two systems which behave "enough" alike are alike. Specifically, that a properly programmed finite-state device which behaves "sufficiently" intelligently is intelligent; or contrapositively, that any intelligent system is such a device. We put such mimetic assertions into a historical perspective, and conclude that there is no finite threshold, beyond which "enough" commonality of behaviors allows us to draw conclusions like that asserted by the "Turing Test".

Rosen, Stanley H. Il pensare è spontaneo?. *Teoria*, 12(1), 31-59, 1992.

Rosen, Stanley H. *The Question of Being: A Reversal of Heidegger*. New Haven, Yale Univ Pr, 1993.

This book contains a detailed philological and philosophical critique of Heidegger's interpretation of Western metaphysics as Platonism, and in particular of Heidegger's readings of Plato and Nietzsche. There is also a fresh analysis of Platonism, based in large part on a detailed commentary on the *phaedo* passage concerning Socrates' career, as well as a detailed analysis of the connection between philosophy and everyday life.

Rosen, Stanley H. Writing and Painting: The Soul as Hermeneut in The Language of Art History, Kemal, Salim (ed). New York, Cambridge Univ Pr, 1991.

Rosenbaum, Stuart E (ed) and Baird, Robert M (ed). *The Ethics of Abortion (Revised Edition)*. Buffalo, Prometheus, 1993.

This revised collection of essays reflecting a variety of positions in the abortion debate includes many new essays and an altered organizational structure. The essays are arranged in clusters under the following titles: Abortion and the Constitution, Abortion and Feminism, Abortion and Christianity, and Abortion and Moral Philosophy. In addition to the Roe vs Wade decision, the collection now contains versions of the court's decisions in Webster vs Reproductive Health Services and Planned Parenthood of Southeastern Pennsylvania vs Casey. Among the authors included are Robert Bork, Ronald Dworkin, Daniel Maguire, Stanley Hauerwas, Judith Jarvis Thomson, John Wilcox, and Mary Warren.

Rosenberg, Alex. Neo-Classical Economics and Evolutionary Theory: Strange Bedfellows?. *Proc Phil Sci Ass*, 1, 174-183, 1992.

Microeconomic theory and the theory of natural selection share salient features. This has encouraged economics to appeal to the character of evolutionary theory in defending the adequacy of microeconomics, despite its evident weaknesses as an explanatory or predictive theory. This paper explores the differences and similarities between these two theories and the phenomena they treat in order to assess the force of the economist's appeal to evolutionary theory as a model for how economic theory should proceed.

Rosenberg, Alexander. Causation, Probability, and the Monarchy. *Amer Phil Quart*, 29(4), 305-318, O 92.

This paper argues that if the world is indeterministic in its fundamental laws of working, then there casual relations do not obtain among events. Or at least this is the view to which a proponent of Humean supervenience is committed. The argument proceeds by attempting to show that accounts of causation as probability increase fail to account for causal transitivity, causal priority and counterfactual dependency.

Rosenberg, Alexander. Contractarianism and the "Trolley" Problem. *J Soc Phil*, 23(3), 88-104, Wint 92.

The paper argues that the difference in our intuitions about the permissibility of killing one so that five may be saved in Thompson's trolley case and the impermissibility of killing one so that five may be saved in her transplant case can be explained from a contractarian perspective, by showing that a rational self-interested agent would contract for social rules that permitted trolley and forbade transplant. The explanatory power of contractarianism with respect to these intuitions is some evidence for its general plausibility.

Rosenberg, Jay F. Comments on Peter Van Inwagen's *Material Beings*. *Phil Phenomenol Res*, 53(3), 701-708, S 93.

Rosenberg, Jay F. Raiders of the Lost Distinction: Richard Rorty and the Search for the Last Dichotomy. *Phil Phenomenol Res*, 53(1), 195-214, Mr 93.

Rosenfeld, Michel. Deconstruction and Legal Interpretation in Deconstruction and the Possibility of Justice, Cornell, Durcilla (ed). New York, Routledge, 1992.

There is a crisis in legal interpretation. Critical legal studies' challenge has not been met by Dworkin, Posner's law and economics or reliance on "interpretive communities". This crisis can be overcome though a version of deconstruction as involving an ontology and ethics based on an irreconcilable gap between self and other. Stressing intertextual exchange, this deconstructive practice establishes paths of interpretation yielding partially determined meanings. Viewing meaning as intersubjective, this practice leads to a critique of recent more sophisticated versions of legal formalism, and allows for a workable distinction between law, ethics and politics.

Rosenfeld, Michel (ed) and Cornell, Durcilla (ed) and Carlson, David Gray (ed). *Deconstruction and the Possibility of Justice*. New York, Routledge, 1992.

Rosenkrantz, Gary and Hoffman, Joshua. Are Souls Unintelligible? in Philosophical Perspectives, 5: Philosophy of Religion, 1991, Tomberlin, James E (ed). Atascadero, Ridgeview, 1991.

Rosenkrantz, R D. The Justification of Induction. *Phil Sci*, 59(4), 527-539, D 92.

We show there is only one consistent way to update a probability assignment, that given by Bayes' rule. The price of inconsistent updating is a loss of efficiency. The implications of this for the problem of induction are discussed.

Rosenow, Eliyahu. The Teacher: Authority or Deputy? (in Hebrew). *Iyyun*, 42, 275-294, Ap 93.

Rosenthal, David. Thinking that One Thinks in Consciousness: Psychological and Philosophical Essays, Davies, Martin (ed). Cambridge, Blackwell, 1993.

It's generally accepted that, for creatures with the requisite linguistic ability, a mental state is conscious if, and only if, one can report being in that mental state. (This fixes the reference of conscious mental states for linguistic creatures; it doesn't mean that only such creatures have conscious states.) I show that this suffices to establish that a mental state's being conscious consists in its being accompanied by a thought that one is in that state. Rejecting that hypothesis inevitably means that we will conflate what it is to verbally express an intentional state with what it is to report that state.

Rosenthal, David M. Higher-Order Thoughts and the Appendage Theory of Consciousness. *Phil Psych*, 6(2), 155-166, 1993.

Theories of what it is for a mental state to be conscious must answer two questions. We must say how we're conscious of our conscious mental states. And we must explain why we seem to be conscious of them in a way that's immediate. Thomas Natsoulas (1993) distinguishes three strategies for explaining what it is for mental states to be conscious. I show that the differences among those strategies are due to the divergent answers they give to the foregoing questions. Natsoulas finds most promising the strategy that amounts to the higher-order-thought hypothesis that I've defended elsewhere. But he raises a difficulty for it, which he thinks probably can be met only by modifying that strategy. I argue that this is unnecessary. The difficulty is a special case of a general question, the answer to which is independent of any issues about consciousness. So it's no part of a theory of consciousness to address the problem much less solve it. Moreover, the difficulty seems to have intuitive force only given the picture that underlies the other two explanatory strategies, which both Natsoulas and I reject.

Rosenthal, Sandra and Bourgeois, Patrick L. Mead and Merleau-Ponty: 'Meaning, Perception, and Behavior' in Analecta Husserliana, XXXI, Tymieniecka, Anna-Teresa (ed). Dordrecht, Kluwer, 1990.

Mead's pragmatic focus on habit as the foundation of meaning is usually viewed in sharp contrast with Merleau-Ponty's phenomenological examination of meaning within experience. This paper attempts to show the way in which the explicit focus of each philosopher's position is latent within that of the other. For Mead and Merleau-Ponty alike, the content of human awareness at all levels is inseparably linked with the structure of human behavior. And, for both, such a structure is permeated throughout by the "living meaning" of anticipatory habit or vital intentionality.

Ross, Don S. Time, the Heaven of Heavens, and Memory in Augustine's *Confessions*. *Augustin Stud*, 22, 191-205, 1991.

Ross, Gail S and Miké, Valerie and Krauss, Alfred N. Perinatal Technology: Answers and Questions. *J Clin Ethics*, 3(1), 56-62, Spr 92.

This article focuses on uncertainty in perinatal medicine. Sources of uncertainty include not only the complexity of premature physiology and related disease mechanisms, but also the lack of proper assessment of many perinatal technologies for their safety and effectiveness. These issues are illustrated by means of two perinatal technologies: transcutaneous oxygen monitoring and neonatal extracorporeal membrane oxygenation (ECMO). They are analyzed in terms of a proposed "ethics of evidence," meaning, in concrete but not exhaustive terms, guidelines for the creation, assessment and dissemination of evidence. Related problem are then discussed in the broader context of contemporary perinatal medicine.

Ross, James Bruce (ed) and McLaughlin, Mary Martin (ed). *The Portable Medieval Reader*. New York, Penguin USA, 1977.

Ross, James F. On Christian Philosophy: *Una Vera Philosophia?*. *Monist*, 75(3), 354-380, Jl 92.

There is Christian philosophy: 1) when the philosophy has distinctively Christian insights, e.g., "Can a thing be of more than one nature or quiddity?" (Incarnation); 2) when Christian revelation has to be accommodated, negatively or positively, (even if not mentioned); when the issue (of morality, law, cognition, the will or even being) cannot be comprehensively stated *neutrally* to the Christian faith, (what is true human freedom?); and 4) most distinctively, when the whole *Christian Wisdom*, and its resulting civilization, is *compared* to other Wisdoms and Ways, like the pagan philosophies Augustine considered, and other religions (Buddhist, Hindu), ethical systems (Confucian), and other "folk mythologies" (native American), and their civilizations, leading to a judgment like Augustine's, that "*Christianitas est una vera philosophia*", not item by item, but globally.

Ross, James F. Reason and Reliance: Adjusted Prospects for Natural Theology in Prospects for Natural Theology, Long, Eugene Thomas (ed). Washington, Cath Univ Amer Pr, 1992.

Surveying recent accomplishments, I conclude that: Recognition that trust is a means of knowledge has entered epistemology in general and made obvious the rationality of some religious belief; recognition of the role of the will and of feelings in both our discerning meanings and explanations opens further prospect of religious knowledge; acknowledging that there are many standard successful kinds of proofs makes proving the existence of God much easier than was previously contended; and the existence of evil works even better as a reason for believing in God than it does against.

Ross, James F. Response to Maurer and Dewan. *Amer Cath Phil Quart*, 65(2), 235-243, Spr 91.

Fr Maurer most helpfully clarifies Gilson's and his own reading of Aquinas' exemplarism so as to leave no difference between us on that subject. Fr Dewan, in contrast, adroitly argues that Aquinas held a full strength version of Augustine's exemplarism, to preclude God's finding out anything by creating it. Our disagreement is not about what Aquinas is trying to achieve or even about how to understand the words and the examples, taken item by item, but about how he *achieves* the objectives, and, about whether Aquinas is framing a revolutionary view of the divine ideas within accepted Augustinian words. I opted for the revolution.

Ross, Stephen D. *Injustice and Restitution: The Ordinance of Time*. Albany, SUNY Pr, 1993.

This book addresses the nature and injustice of authority, retracing the ideas of reason and law from ancient Greece to the present, pursuing a line of thought begun with Anaximander, who speaks of the ordinance of time as restitution for immemorial injustice, and Heraclitus, who speaks of justice as strife. Predominantly philosophical, exploring the authority of Western philosophy in twentieth-century continental and pragmatist writings, the book explores alternative voices as challenges to authority, in feminist and multicultural writings, in Greek mythology and African narratives, in Greek drama and twentieth-century literature.

AUTHOR INDEX WITH ABSTRACTS 649 Rousseau, George

Ross, Stephen David. *Metaphysical Aporia and Philosophical Heresy*. Albany, SUNY Pr, 1989.

This book addresses the nature and injustice of authority, retracing the ideas of reason and law from Ancient Greece to the present, pursuing a line of thought begun with Anaximander, who speaks of the ordinance of time as restitution for immemorial injustice, and Heraclitus, who speaks of justice as strife. Predominantly philosophical, exploring the authority of Western philosophy in twentieth-century continental and pragmatist writings, the book explores alternative voices as challenges to authority, in feminist and multicultural writings, in Greek mythology and African narratives, in Greek drama and twentieth-century literature.

Rossi, Osvaldo. Ethics and Subjectivity Today in Analecta Husserliana, XXXI, Tymieniecka, Anna-Teresa (ed). Dordrecht, Kluwer, 1990.

Rossi, Osvaldo. Method and Ontology: Reflections on Edmund Husserl in Analecta Husserliana, XXXIV, Tymieniecka, Anna-Teresa (ed). Dordrecht, Kluwer, 1992.

Rossinelli, Michel. A propos de la liberté chez les juristes. *Stud Phil (Switzerland)*, 49, 175-192, 1990.

The author strives to demonstrate that if the individual's rights and liberties are to be found primarily in texts of constitutional value or in international agreements, the position of the constitutional courts is essential both to give force to certain unwritten rights and to give concrete forms to liberties often stated with few words in these texts. The constitutional judges' ultimate horizon is thus a value system. The entire difficulty resides in the perception the judges have of these values and in the way of solving certain conflicts amongst these values. One but has to examine the reports of cases of various constitutional courts to verify that, based on same texts, the solutions are quite different.

Rossouw, G J. The Morality of Insider Trading. *S Afr J Phil*, 12(3), 66-71, Ag 93.

The debate on insider trading remains a very interesting and intriguing one despite the fact that it is legally forbidden in most developed countries. In this article the moral implications of insider trading is dealt with in the following way. First, the phenomenon of insider trading is described and defined. Second, the approach for dealing morally with the issue is explained and justified. Third, the moral implications of insider trading for a variety of interest groups are discussed. In the final section the respective contributions that these interest groups can make in dealing with the issue are suggested.

Rost, Marie. Practical Weakness and Political Institutions. *Dialogue (PST)*, 34(2-3), 25-32, Ap 92.

The thesis of "Practical Weakness and Political Institutions" is that apart from whatever personal responsibility individual politicians bear, governmental structures somehow and in some measure contribute to the perversion of public office that is often blamed solely on individual office holders, especially in the case of interest groups exerting undue influence on the decision-making process. More specifically, the paper demonstrates that these perversions are at least partially caused by a weakness in the governmental structure. This flaw is analagous to the flaw of moral weakness in human character, first discussed by Aristotle.

Rostenne, Paul. *Homo Religiosus ou L'Homme Vertical*. Bordeaux, Biere, 1993.

Rotem, Ornan. Vasubandhu's Idealism: An Encounter Between Philosophy and Religion. *Asian Phil*, 3(1), 15-28, Mr 93.

According to idealism the world, as we perceive it, is in effect a creation of the mind. There are many different forms of idealism and this paper investigates one form of idealism that was advocated by the 4th century Buddhist Yogacarin Vasubandhu and one not unfamiliar in the west, especially in the works of George Berkeley. This paper suggests that when idealism, as a metaphysical theory, is set within a soteriological framework, as is the case with Vasubandhu, it serves to bridge the philosophical endeavour with the religious quest as outlined in Buddhist thought. Idealism is a theory about the borders between mind and matter, and specifically about the demolition of matter. This demolition, in the hands of Vasubandhu, manages to redefine the framework of speculation by incorporating the soteriological within it and thus constructing a viable bridge between philosophy and religion.

Rotenstreich, Nathan. Conscience and Norm. *J Value Inq*, 27(1), 29-37, Ja 93.

Rotenstreich, Nathan. On Thinking. *Man World*, 26(1), 1-18, Ja 93.

Roth, John K. No Confusion: Some Reflections on TWA Flight 847 in Terrorism, Justice and Social Values, Peden, Creighton (ed). Lewiston, Mellen Pr, 1990.

Reflecting on the political and moral implications of airline hijackings, this essay argues that by commission of and complicity in certain acts, men and women forfeit their rights to life. Among the examples included in that proposition are terrorist acts of war in general and hijackings in particular. Even if we are loath to admit it, there is retributive justice. Death is its ultimate instance. One does not punish terrorists to rehabilitate them. One does so to prevent them from hijacking ever again and to insist that a similar fate awaits anyone else who make the attempt. Imperfect thought such strategies may be, they are better than no deterrent at all.

Roth, John K. Philosophical Theology and Provincialism in God, Values, and Empiricism, Peden, Creighton (ed). Macon, Mercer Univ Pr, 1989.

As a philosopher, Josiah Royce was intensely interested in what religions share. That broad concern, however, never led him to lose sight of religion's particularity. To the contrary, when Royce wrote about the social consequences of belief in God, his philosophy included a place for *provincialism*. This paper concentrates on that latter aspect of Royce's thought, focussing on Royce's development of the idea of "wise provincialism" in particular.

Roth, Michael S. The End of History and the Last Man. *Hist Theor*, 32(2), 188-195, 1993.

Roth, Paul A. Interpretation as Explanation in The Interpretive Turn, Hiley, David R (ed). Ithaca, Cornell Univ Pr, 1991.

Roth, Robert. American Pragmatism and Ultimate Reality and Meaning as Seen in Religion. *Ultim Real Mean*, 16(1-2), 120-127, Mr-Je 93.

The article deals with the religious theories of Charles Sanders Peirce, William James, and John Dewey. They shared a common vision of ultimate meaning which included an openness to nature and a commitment to the human community. Peirce and James argued to the reality of God as a reasonable hypothesis for such a vision. Dewey rejected a deity and religion since, in his view, they separated human beings from the world. Yet the common strand was the emphasis on contact with the world, with people, and with social institutions for the full development of the person.

Roth, Robert. *British Empiricism and American Pragmatism: New Directions and Neglected Arguments*. Bronx, Fordham Univ Pr, 1993.

This volume traces the influence of the British Empiricists—John Locke and David Hume—upon the American pragmatists—Charles S Peirce, William James, and John Dewey. But there are significant differences between the two traditions so that it can be said that the pragmatists gave the classical empirical tradition new directions. Heretofore these lines of influence and divergence have been recognized but not sufficiently developed. This movement is illustrated in chapters on experience, necessary connection, personal identity, and moral, social, and political theory. A final chapter indicates the challenges that are still to be addressed by pragmatism.

Rothmaler, Philipp and Pillay, Anand. Undimensional Modules: Uniqueness of Maximal Non-Modular Submodules. *Annals Pure Applied Log*, 62(2), 175-181, Jl 93.

We characterize the non-modular models of a unidimensional first-order theory of modules as the elementary submodels of its prime pure-injective model. We show that in case the maximal non-modular submodel of a given model splits off this is true for every such submodel, and we thus obtain a cancellation result for this situation. Although the theories in question always have models (in every big enough power) whose maximal non-modular submodel do split off, they may as well have others where they don't. We present a corresponding example.

Rothman, Milton. What Went Before?. *Free Inq*, 13(1), 12, Wint 92-93.

Rotta, Graziella. Recenti studi fichtiani. *Teoria*, 12(2), 51-57, 1992.

Rouner, Leroy. Selfhood, Nature, and Society: Ernest Hocking's Metaphysics of Community in On Community, Rouner, Leroy S (ed). Notre Dame, Univ Notre Dame Pr, 1992.

This essay focuses on Ernest Hocking's theory of the relation among the three fundamental objects of human experience: the self, other selves, and physical nature. Hocking argued that natural objects are the necessary content of mind, and that we share a common mind with others through our common perception of these natural objects. The essay concludes with an evaluation of his qualified dualism, which "defend(s) the realism of physical nature as both fact and idea; (and insists) that selves are both individuals and inextricably bound in community; that even God is both whole and unfinished.

Rouner, Leroy S (ed). *On Community*. Notre Dame, Univ Notre Dame Pr, 1992.

The book contains thirteen essays. The first four, by Eliot Deutsch, R W Hepburn, Hilary Putnam, and Leroy S Rouner, examine philosophies of community, emphasizing metaphysical analysis and definition of the nature of community. The second section considers the theme in a cross-cultural context. Merry I White, Katherine Platt, Benjamin Schwartz, and Huston Smith illustrate in this section the various ways in which community is understood and experienced in Japan, North Africa, China, and India. The final section, which contains contributions by Patrick Hill, Jürgen Moltmann, Catherine Keller, and George Rupp, explores the future of community, focusing on community building in Western societies.

Rouner, Leroy S (ed). *Selves, People, and Persons*. Notre Dame, Univ Notre Dame Pr, 1992.

The contributors to *selves, people, and persons* reshape fundamental ideas of the self in such varied fields as theology, biology, psychoanalysis, and political philosophy. Essays by Erazim Kohak, Harold H Oliver, Lawrence E Cahoone, and Edward W James focus on basic issues in the philosophy of selfhood. The second group of essays, by Eliot Deutsch, John G Carman, and Livia Kohn, deal with selfhood in various cultures. The final section includes essays by Krister Stendahl, Alfred I Tauber, John E Mack, and Bhikhu Parekh on the problem of selfhood in theology, biology, psychoanalysis, and political theory.

Rouse Jr, Joseph T. Interpretation in Natural and Human Science in The Interpretive Turn, Hiley, David R (ed). Ithaca, Cornell Univ Pr, 1991.

I extend earlier arguments denying epistemically interesting differences in kind between natural and human sciences. Drawing upon Charles Taylor's own discussion of language and "social reality" as intertwined, and of how empiricist social science makes important political phenomena invisible, I argue against Taylor's attempt to confine these points to the human sciences. "Natural reality" as the object of scientific research cannot be abstracted from the language of scientific practice, and the attempt to do so obscures some important cultural and political concerns and conflicts. Rejecting Taylor's natural/human science dualism, however, yields not a unified science, but a multiplicity of sciences.

Rousseau, G S. On Romanticism, Science and Medicine. *Hist Euro Ideas*, 17(5), 659-664, S 93.

The role of science and medicine in Romantic thinking, fictional as well as philosophical constructions, has been underestimated. New directions in criticism and scholarship must do more than familiarize themselves with the history of science and medicine. Interpretive skills are necessary, especially close reading and biographical sophistication.

Rousseau, George. The Perpetual Crisis of Modernism and the Traditions of Enlightenment Vitalism in The Crisis in Modernism, Burwick, Frederick (ed). New York, Cambridge Univ Pr, 1992.

I demonstrate that Enlightenment vitalism was politically, socially, and ideologically charged, and that, despite its having permeated Anglo-European thought, it was not at all the opposite of mechanical doctrines. A wide variety of scientific, medical, philosophical, and literary writers is discussed. Mikhail Bakhtin's 1926 treatise on neo-vitalism is printed in English translation for the first time, and discussed in its Enlightenment, Kantian, neo-Kantian, Bergsonian, and Russian materialist contexts.

Rovane, Carol. Self-Reference: The Radicalization of Locke. *J Phil*, 90(2), 73-97, F 93.

The psychological view of personal identity, and with it Locke's distinction between 'person' and 'human being', K defended on several grounds. First, psychological relations are necessary and sufficient for the self-directed ethical attitudes of responsibility and self-concern. Second, there are real instances of non-human persons: multiple and corporate persons. Third, McDowell's objections to these instances of non-human persons K refuted, through a consideration of his arguments appealing to identification-free self-reference.

Rowe, Christopher. L'argument par "affinité" dans le "phédon". *Rev Phil Fr*, 4, 463-477, O-D 91.

Rowe, Christopher. Reflections of the Sun: Explanation in the *Phaedo*. *Apeiron*, 25(4), 89-101, D 92.

Essentially a shorter version of 'Explanation in *Phaedo* 99cG-102a8', in *Oxford Studies in Ancient Philosophy, X*, 1993, 49-69, this essay discovers the 'higher hypotheses' of *Phaedo* 101 d-e in the text of the *Phaedo* itself: they are the various different ways an offer of spelling out the 'participation' by particulars in forms.

Rowe, John Carlos. Romancing the Stone in Theorizing American Literature, Cowan, Bainard (ed). Baton Rouge, Louisiana St Univ Pr, 1991.

The essay argues that Herman Melville's romance, *Pierre* (1852), is a critical reading of central concepts in Hegel's philosophy, especially as these concepts contribute to Hegel's social theory. In his critique of Hegel's idealism, Melville complements the work of Marx, although no argument for specific influence is offered. The more general argument of the essay is that romantic idealism (English Romanticism, American Transcendentalism, and German Idealism) contributed to an "aesthetic ideology" that helped alienate subjects from their own powers of representation and thus form their ultimate "labor-power" as producers of social reality.

Rowe, M W. The Definition of 'Game'. *Philosophy*, 67(262), 467-479, O 92.

Rowe, W V. Harnack and Hellenization in the Early Church. *Phil Reform*, 57(1), 78-85, Ja 92.

Rowe, William. Ruminations About Evil in Philosophical Perspectives, 5: Philosophy of Religion, 1991, Tomberlin, James E (ed). Atascadero, Ridgeview, 1991.

Consider the claim that we have good reasons to believe that there exist gratuitous evils (evils that an omnipotent, omniscient being could have prevented without losing some greater good or permitting some evil equally bad or worse.) In this paper I respond to two criticisms of this claim—one by Plantinga and one by Wykstra. I also respond to a criticism by Hasker to the effect that God would be justified in permitting the existence of gratuitous evil.

Rowe, William. The Problem of Divine Perfection and Freedom in Reasoned Faith, Stump, Eleonore (ed). Ithaca, Cornell Univ Pr, 1993.

The aim is to discuss two problems relating to God's absolute perfection and his freedom in selecting a world to create. Both suppose that absolute perfection is an essential property of God and that for him to be free in doing X he must have the power not to do X. The first problem consists in an argument for the conclusion that if there is a morally best world among worlds God can create, God is not free to refrain from creating and not free to create any world other than the best. The second problem arises if we suppose that for every creatable world there is another creatable world that is morally better than it. This problem consists in an argument for the conclusion that in this case God cannot both be morally unsurpassable and a creator. For if a being creates a world when there is some morally better world that it could have created, then it is *possible* that there be a being morally better than it. Therefore, the being would not be morally unsurpassable.

Rowe, William. The Rationality of Religious Belief. *Cont Phil*, 14(6), 3-9, N-D 92.

Belief in God is rational for a person provided it is either properly basic for that person or justified by other beliefs the person holds. A person who upon seeming to see a tree forms the belief that he is seeing a tree may have a properly basic belief. In the normal case, his belief will be properly basic if he has no reason to believe that delusive-making factors are present in his experience. His not knowing of the presence of such factors is *informed* provided he knows what some of these factors are and can tell whether they are present. Otherwise, his not knowing of the presence of such factors is *uninformed*. I argue that in the cases of basic religious beliefs the not knowing of the presence of delusive-making factors is uninformed. I then assess the significance of this point for the rationality of basic religious beliefs.

Rowlands, Mark. Wittgenstein and Derrida on Meaning. *Behavior Phil*, 20/2(21/1), 37-48, 1993.

Roy, Jean. Rousseauisme et jacobinisme: l'idéal de "l'honnête médiocrité". *Dialogue (Canada)*, 31(4), 567-91, Autumn 92.

Roy, Krishna. Culture and Rationality: An Interpretation. *J Indian Counc Phil Res*, 9(2), 47-53, Ja-Ap 92.

Both 'culture' and 'rationality' are open to diverse interpretations. Culture encompasses all that are cultivated by man and is in everything human, yet it is not anything specific; it is the structure of our being. The usage of 'rationality' too differs in different contexts, e.g., epistemic rationality, applicable in natural sciences, may not be significant in human sciences. Rationality, as we understand practice, has to be culture-sensitive. As the cultivated form of rationality, culture is inalienably connected with it. But this relation is not one-dimensional but circular. Whereas rationality makes culture possible, culture continues to influence rationality.

Roy, Louis. A Note on Barth and Aquinas. *Amer Cath Phil Quart*, 66(1), 89-92, Wint 92.

Two passages of the *Church Dogmatics* discuss Aquinas's position on the love of God. The article argues that in his concern to affirm the priority of God's love over the goodness of creation, Barth unfortunately reads into Aquinas's text some modern theologians' views he is rightly determined to oppose. The misunderstanding has something to do with the meaning of the word *inquantum*.

Roy, Louis. Bruce Marshall's Reading of Aquinas. *Thomist*, 56(3), 473-480, Jl 92.

This article opposes Marshall's contention that Aquinas should be viewed as a "post-liberal" theologian and that Lindbeck propounds the same account of truth as Aquinas. It discusses the claim that linguistic and practical coherence (intra systematic truth) are criteria by which correspondence to reality (ontological truth) must be checked; the assertion that, in the case of non-Christians, belief in God does not mean the same thing as in the case of Christian believers; Marshall's misconstruing of Aquinas's first truth.

Roy, Subroto. *Philosophy of Economics: On the Scope of Reason in Economic Inquiry*. New York, Routledge, 1991.

This book may be the first work to have successfully bridged serious economics in the twentieth century with modern Anglo-American philosophy, in particular the work of Wittgenstein. The book raises some of the central philosophical questions facing modern economics, especially to do with the scope of objective reasoning in the making of evaluative judgments, the appropriate role of economic expertise, and the status of the concepts and theorems of mathematical economics.

Roy, Tony. Worlds and Modality. *Phil Rev*, 102(3), 335-362, Jl 93.

What is it in virtue of which metaphysically modal statements are true or false? Some appeal to quantification over possible worlds. But I suggest that there are reasons to wonder whether possible worlds (as developed by Lewis and by Plantinga) are even relevant to modal truth. I then argue that there is a sense in which possible worlds of a certain sort may be seen as relevant to modality. The "worlds" represent combinations allowable under fixed constraints. On my account, for metaphysical modality, the important constraints have to do with the actual structures of non-modal properties.

Royle, Peter. Sartre on Evil in Sartre Alive, Aronson, Ronald (ed). Detroit, Wayne St Univ Pr, 1991.

The object of this work is to clarify Sartre's theory of good and evil and to show how it is relevant to an understanding of evil in the world. For Sartre what I want is, for me, good; and what I don't want is bad. Despite this I can want for myself what I recognize as bad. People who do this may be weak-willed or strong- willed, humble, remorseful, repentant, rebellious, satanic, masochistic, or saintly. What makes such a phenomenon possible is the structure of our consciousness, which does not coincide with itself. Evil is necessarily parasitic on good.

Rozema, David. Conceptual Scheming. *Phil Invest*, 15(4), 293-312, O 92.

In *Reason, Truth and History*, Hilary Putnam describes and defends a philosophical theory which he calls 'internal realism', and in the course of this defence, claims an affinity with the thought of Kant and Wittgenstein. This paper will show that Putnam cannot claim such an affinity for internal realism with the thought of Wittgenstein. Behind this lies a critique of the more general tendency, so prevalent among philosophers nowadays, to see all claims as theoretical.

Rozemond, Klaas. De staat van Nozick. *Alg Ned Tijdschr Wijs*, 84(3), 182-193, Jl 92.

Robert Nozick's main arguments in favor of the minimal state are reconstructed. Special attention is paid to his analysis of risks, which is applied to contract and property rights. The welfare state (the more than minimals state) could be justified, it is held, if the unrestricted use of these rights on the free market leads to unacceptable risks like economic crises.

Ruben, David-Hillel. *Explaining Explanation*. New York, Routledge, 1992.

In the historical section, I give a detailed account of the idea of explanation, as it is developed by Plato, Aristotle, John Stuart Mill, and Carl Hempel. In the second section, I develop certain topics raised by them: the non-extensionality of explanation, whether all singular explanation is causal, the adequacy of the Covering Law model of explanation, and whether explanations are arguments. In conclusion, I offer a 'Realist' theory of explanation.

Ruben, David-Hillel. Simple Attentive Miscalculation. *Analysis*, 52(3), 184-109, Jl 92.

Typically, making a mistake in adding a long column of large numbers consists in somewhere making a mistake adding two single-digit numbers. I call this 'simple miscalculation'. For example, someone may intentionally write 5 as the sum of 4 and 2. Sometimes no inattention is involved in doing this. Which of the agent's beliefs explains this miscalculation? I consider three possibilities: the false belief that 4+2=5, the true belief that 4+2=5, and the denial that every intentional action has a belief as part of its explanation. I find all three possible answers inadequate, and conclude that, although I know that simple attentive miscalculation occurs, I do not know how it is possible.

Rubinoff, Lionel (ed) and Van Der Dussen, W J (ed). *Objectivity, Method and Point of View*. Leiden, Brill, 1991.

Rubinoff, M Lionel. Historicity and Objectivity in Objectivity, Method and Point of View, Van Der Dussen, W J (ed). Leiden, Brill, 1991.

This essay attempts to develop R G Collingwood's claim that history is a school of practical wisdom, the objectivity of which is achieved not in spite of but because of the historian's point of view. The question is thus raised: How is it possible to reconcile recognition of the historicity of historical judgments with claims to objectivity, and how can historical knowledge, so conceived, be regarded as a school of practical wisdom? In addressing this question, a number of sources are drawn upon, including Collingwood and Dray, as well as historians such as A R M Lower and E H Carr, with particular attention being given to Lower's attempt to reconcile the antithetical approaches of English and French Canadian historians to the interpretation of Canadian history.

Rubinoff, M Lionel. W H Dray and the Critique of Historical Thinking in Objectivity, Method and Point of View, Van Der Dussen, W J (ed). Leiden, Brill, 1991.

This essay is intended as a general introduction to W.H. Dray's contributions to the field of analytical philosophy of history, examined in the context of his long-standing

AUTHOR INDEX WITH ABSTRACTS 651 Rychlak, Joseph F

dispute with the covering-law theorists. Special attention is paid to Dray's attempt to reopen the "objectivity debate" in ways that pay attention to the role played by "points-of-view" in the genisis of causal explanations in history. Of central importance in this discussion is Dray's claim that the historian's selection of causes in often determined by prior value judgements concerning the locus of responsibility.

Rudebusch, George H. Callicles' Hedonism. *Ancient Phil*, 12(1), 53-71, Spr 92.

There has been no consensus as to what version of hedonist Callicles is, because there are grave difficulties with the versions which have been suggested. These versions may be classified as prudential, indiscriminate and sybaritic versions of hedonism. In contrast to these, I argue that Callicles is best understood as holding a satisfaction hedonism of felt desire with respect to the intrinsically desirable. I indicate some of the difficulties with the previously suggested alternatives. Then I draw the distinctions needed to understand the hedonism I attribute to Callicles, and argue for its adequacy as an interpretation and importance to philosophy.

Rudolph, Enno. La résurgence de l'aristotélisme de la Renaissance dans la philosophie politique de Cassirer. *Rev Metaph Morale*, 97(4), 479-490, O-D 92.

Ernst Cassirers Kritik an Martin Heideggers existentialer Kritik erschöpft sich nicht in einem Streit um die richtige Auslegung der Philosophie Immanuel Kants, sondern sie enthält auch den Vorwurf, der Philosophie Heideggers ermangele es an einer humanistischen Perspektive. In Cassirers Kulturbegriff als auch in seiner originären Systematisierung der Philosophie der Renaissance verbirgt sich die Konzeption eines humanistischen Paradigmas. Der vorliegende Beitrag versucht dieses Paradigma zu rekonstruieren und diskutiert sowohl seine philosophische als auch seine politische Aktualität.

Rudolph, Katherine. Descartes' Discourse. *Phil Today*, 37(1), 38-51, Spr 93.

Rudolph, Samuel B (ed). *The Philosophy of Freedom: Ideological Origins of the Bill of Rights*. Lanham, Univ Pr of America, 1993.

This book is an elucidation of the philosophical origins of our Bill of Rights. It focuses on the writings of Anglo-American thinkers and statesmen up to the nineteenth century. A collection of original pieces with editor's commentary, it includes British selections from the writings of Locke, Blackstone, Trenchard and Gordon. It proceeds to the early American writings, including those of Otis, Hamilton, Jefferson, Paine, Mason and Madison. It is the editor's conviction that any "original intent" in our Constitution is best captured by going to the words and works of the founders themselves. Only through grasping our roots and origins in this way can we truly know and preserve our heritage of liberty under law.

Ruini, C C. Presentazione "Dizionario Enciclopedico del pensiero di S Tommaso d'Aquino" del P G B Mondin. *Aquinas*, 35(1), 3-10, Ja-Ap 92.

Ruitenburg, Wim. The Unintended Interpretations of Intuitionistic Logic in Perspectives on the History of Mathematical Logic, Drucker, Thomas (ed). Basel, Birkhauser, 1991.

We present an overview of the unintended interpretations of intuitionistic logic that arose after Heyting formalized the "observed regularities" in the use of formal parts of language, in particular, first-order logic and Heyting Arithmetic. We include unintended interpretations of some mild variations on "official" intuitionism, such as intuitionism, such as intuitionistic type theories with full comprehension and higher order logic without choice principles or not satisfying the right choice sequence properties. We conclude with remarks on the quest for a correct interpretation of intuitionistic logic.

Rukmani, T S. The Problem of the Authorship of the *Yogasutrabhasyavivaranam*. *J Indian Phil*, 20(4), 419-423, D 92.

Rumfitt, Ian. Content and Context: The Paratactic Theory Revisited and Revised. *Mind*, 102(407), 429-454, Jl 93.

Davidson has suggested that, for semantical purposes, a report such as 'Galileo said that the earth moved' is best construed as an utterance of two sentences, as in 'Galileo said that. The earth moves'. The article uses modern linguistic theory to meet objections to the suggestion stemming (a) from considerations of ambiguity and (b) from syntactic differences between demonstratives and as complementisers. It advances the explication of the indirect saying relation by permitting the *use* of indexical expressions in the statement of a Davidsonian truth theory. The author thereby reaches an account of propositions whereby a single declarative utterance may express more than one proposition, and concludes by applying this account to Kripke's puzzle about belief.

Runia, David. Xenophanes or Theophrastus? in Theophrastus, Fortenbaugh, W W (ed). New Brunswick, Transaction Books, 1992.

Rupp, George. Communities of Collaboration: Shared Commitments/Common Tasks in On Community, Rouner, Leroy S (ed). Notre Dame, Univ Notre Dame Pr, 1992.

Ruse, Michael E. Homosexuality: Right or Wrong?. *Free Inq*, 13(2), 35-37, Spr 93.

In this paper I consider the morality of homosexuality looking at it from a utilitarian and a Kantian perspective. I argue that there are no good grounds for thinking homosexuality immoral, even though imminent philosophers have thought otherwise.

Ruskola, Teemu H. Moral Choice in the Analects: A Way without a Crossroads?. *J Chin Phil*, 19(3), 285-296, S 92.

Russell, Bertrand. *Our Knowledge of the External World*. New York, Routledge, 1993.

Russell, Bruce. Exploring *The Realm of Rights*. *Phil Phenomenol Res*, 53(1), 159-162, Mr 93.

Russell, John. Access to Experimental Therapies and AIDS. *Dialogue (Canada)*, 30(3), 399-418, Sum 91.

Russell, John M. Tillich's Implicit Ontological Argument. *Sophia (Australia)*, 32(2), 1-16, Jl 93.

Russell, Paul. Critical Notice of Annette Baier's *A Progress of Sentiments*. *Can J Phil*, 23(1), 107-123, Mr 93.

Russell, Robert and Price, Thomas and Kennett, Stephen. An Interview with A J Ayer. *Kinesis*, 19(1), 28-55, Spr 93.

Russo, F. La suggestione delle filosofie di moda e il richiamo al senso comune: Tra Vico e Pareyson. *Sapienza*, 45(1), 77-81, 1992.

Russow, Lilly-Marlene. Animals in the Original Position. *Between Species*, 8(4), 224-229, Fall 92.

Russow, Lilly-Marlene. Fodor, Adams and Causal Properties. *Phil Psych*, 6(1), 57-61, 1993.

Russow, Lilly-Marlene. Reply—Rawls: Rejecting Utilitarianism and Animals. *Between Species*, 8(4), 232-233, Fall 92.

Rustin, Michael. Justice and the Gulf War. *Rad Phil*, 61, 3-9, Sum 92.

Rutherford, Donald. Natures, Laws, and Miracles: The Roots of Leibniz's Critique of Occasionalism in Causation in Early Modern Philosophy, Nadler, Steven (ed). University Park, Penn St Univ Pr, 1993.

Leibniz raises three main objections to the doctrine of occasionalism: 1) it is inconsistent with the supposition of finite substances; 2) it presupposes the occurrence of "perpetual miracles"; 3) it requires that God "disturb" the ordinary laws of nature. At issue in objection 1) is the proper understanding of divine omnipotence, and of the relationship between the power of God and that of created things. I argue that objections 2) and 3), on the other hand, derive from a particular conception of the intelligibility of nature, a conception to which Leibniz is firmly committed and that occasionalists like Malebranche no less firmly reject.

Rutherford, Richard. Unifying the *Protagoras*. *Apeiron*, 25(4), 133-156, D 92.

Ruthrof, Horst. Differend and Agonistics: A Transcendental Argument?. *Phil Today*, 36(4), 324-335, Wint 92.

The paper argues that the useful critical notion of the 'differend' introduced by Jean-Francois Lyotard conceals a transcendental argument. The main steps of Kant's procedure are compared with a reconstruction of Lyotard's implied argument. The paper concludes with an extension of Lyotard's notion beyond the linguistic.

Ruthrof, Horst. Frege's Error. *Phil Today*, 37(3), 306-317, Fall 93.

Rutledge, David (& others). The Tacit Victory and the Unfinished Agenda. *Tradition Discovery*, 18(1), 5-17, 1991-92.

This title includes five presentations from a 1991 conference at Kent State marking the centennial of the birth of Michael Polanyi, scientist/philosopher. Articles discuss how Polanyi's view of the irreducibly personal character of knowledge is bearing fruit, beyond his initial epistemological discussions of "the tacit dimension" of knowing, which has been widely accepted by philosophers. Articles deal with: feminist and ecological issues (D W Rutledge), current epistemological discussions (W B Gulick), Richard Rorty and Polanyi (J V Apczynski), Polanyi's thought in the arts (D Adams), and Polanyi in relation to chaos theory and the work of W H Poteat (J Stines).

Rutten, Christian. La stylométrie et la question de "Métaphysique" K. *Rev Phil Louvain*, 90(88), 486-496, N 92.

Stylometric methods can provide considerable information in regard to the relative chronology of the parts of the *Metaphysics* and their authenticity. In this article some suggestions are made on the problems raised by book K on the basis of the "analysis of the materials". The passage K7, 1064A28-1064B14, in which the science of being as being is assimilated to the science of the divine being, is closer, from a stylometric point of view, to the *Metaphysis* of Theophrastus than to that of Aristotle. The same holds for K10. On the other hand, the classification based on stylometrics corresponds for the other chapters to the evolution which Aristotle's thought underwent in various regards.

Ruzhuang, Xu (trans) and Yanping, Shi. Developments in Chinese Philosophy Over the Last Ten Years. *Phil East West*, 43(1), 113-125, Ja 93.

Ryan, George E. Commentary on McPherran's *Ataraxia* and *Eudaimonia* in Ancient Pyrrhonism. *Proc Boston Colloq Anc Phil*, 5, 172-180, 1989.

Most accounts of the skepticism of Sextus Empiricus assume that he offers as an ideal a life lived without belief or commitment. Such a view contradicts explicit textual evidence to the contrary and makes it difficult to explain the obvious influence and appeal that skepticism possessed in antiquity as an alternative to Dogmatic ways of thinking and living. The ancient skeptic questions a certain attitude towards belief, not belief itself. A better grasp of the skeptic's notion of belief enables us to see how skepticism represented a viable alternative to Dogmatic philosophy and at the same time resulted in the peculiar detachment and passivity that are characteristic of the skeptic's report of "happiness" (ataraxia).

Ryan, Kevin (ed) and Lickona, Thomas (ed). *Character Development in Schools and Beyond (Second Edition)*. Washington, CRVP, 1992.

Ryba, Thomas. Elemental Forms, Creativity and the Transformative Power of Literature in Analecta Husserliana, XXXVIII, Tymieniecka, Anna-Teresa (ed). Dordrecht, Kluwer, 1992.

Rybakov, V V. A Modal Analog for Glivenko's Theorem and Its Applications. *Notre Dame J Form Log*, 33(2), 244-248, Spr 92.

This paper gives a modal analog for Glivenko's Theorem. Namely, it is shown that possibilities of formulas are equivalent in modal Lewis system S5 if necessities of possibilities of these formulas are equivalent in modal system K4. NP-formula is a formula which is built upon its own subformulas which have prefix "necessary that possible that". It is proved that the adding of a finite number of NP-formulas to axioms of a given logic preserves decidability and finite model property.

Rychlak, Joseph F. A Teleologist's Reactions to "On Private Events and Theoretical Terms". *J Mind Behav*, 13(4), 347-357, Autumn 92.

This paper examines the theoretical differences obtaining between a mechanist like Moore and a teologist like the writer. It is shown that mechanistic formulations invariably reduce the account to material and efficient causation, whereas teleologists want to bring in formal-final cause descriptions as well. Mechanists frame their explanations in third-person (extraspective) terms whereas teleologists often seek a first-person (introspective) formulation of behavior. Moore's reference to "private events" are shown to be extraspectively understood. A major theme of this

Ryckman, Thomas C 652 AUTHOR INDEX WITH ABSTRACTS

paper is that Skinner actually capitalized on the intentional nature of human behavior, and that it would be fairly easy to reconceptualize his theory and its empirical support in teleological terms. Careful examination of both the contingency and the discriminative-stimulus constructs are made in support of this contention.

Ryckman, Thomas C. Contingency, A Prioricity and Acquaintance. *Phil Phenomenol Res*, 53(2), 323-343, Je 93.

Ryckman, Thomas C. Dickie on Artifactuality. *J Aes Art Crit*, 47(2), 175-176, Spr 89.

This paper contains a discussion of and a series of counter-examples to the view of artifactuality George Dickie expressed in *The Art Circle*.

Ryder, John J. Contradictions in American Culture in Frontiers in American Philosophy, Volume I, Burch, Robert W (ed). College Station, Texas A&M Univ Pr, 1992.

American culture, like any other, is constituted by a range of contradictory traits, at the material level and at the level of dominant ideology and values. These contradictions appear in, among other places, political affairs, in ethical principles and in social life, and they are especially evident in the contradictory ways our culture treats the individual and freedom. One of the more interesting earlier treatments of this phenomenon is John Dewey's, in which it is argued that the cultural contradictions are best understood as conflicts between material conditions and an outmoded ideology. This approach obscures too much, however, and it is more enlightening to regard current cultural contradictions as reflecting the material realities of contemporary American life.

Ryder, John J. The Use and Abuse of Modernity: Postmodenrism and the American Philosophic Tradition. *J Speculative Phil*, 7(2), 92-102, 1993.

The most influential contemporary phase in philosophy's self-definition is "postmodernism." Postmodernist ideas have been in the air since the mid-nineteenth century in both Europe and America. The American contribution to postmodenrism has been most apparent in Dewey, and as several recent works have argued, in Emerson. In fact, many of the philosophic concepts which define postmodernism are also to be found in Royce, Peirce, James, Santayana and in more recent naturalism. The American tradition helps to clarify the achievements of postmodernism, though despite its achievements postmodernism also suffers from serious philosophic flaws. Its excesses, however, can be avoided, and again the American philosophic tradition, particularly recent naturalism, suggests valuable directions.

Ryklin, Mikhail. The Defeat of Vision: Five Reflections on the Culture of Speech. *Russian Stud Phil*, 31(3), 51-78, Wint 92-93.

Ryle, Gilbert and Meyer, René (ed). *Aspects of Mind—Gilbert Ryle*. Cambridge, Blackwell, 1993.

This volume consists *inter alia* of eight chapters of not previously published papers by the late Gilbert Ryle, and four chapters of extensive notes of lectures delivered shortly before his retirement. The general drift is a concern with thinking as a typically human phenomenon. The volume amplifies key themes in Ryle's *The Concept of Mind*, e.g., thinking, perceiving, learning and freedom. Contemporary materialists cannot derive comfort from Ryle's work except on pain of confusing "behaviour" as "mere bodily behaviour" with "behaviour proper" (action, conduct). A select bibliography links this volume with Ryle's previously published work on thinking.

Ryn, Claes G. Natural Law and the Higher Will. *Vera Lex*, 11(2), 17-18, 1991.

Rynasiewicz, Robert. Rings, Holes and Substantivalism: On the Program of Leibniz Algebras. *Phil Sci*, 59(4), 572-589, D 92.

I argue that the program of Leibniz algebras is subject to radical local indeterminism to the same extent as substantivalism. In fact, for the category of topological spaces of interest in spacetime physics, the program is equivalent to the original spacetime approach. Moreover, the motivation for the program—that isomorphic substantival models should be regarded as representing the same physical situation—is misguided. (edited)

Rynasiewicz, Robert. Why the New Theory of Reference Does Not Entail Absolute Time and Space. *Phil Sci*, 59(3), 508-509, S 92.

I explain why the New Theory of Reference of Marcus, Kripke, Kaplan, Putnam and others does not entail absolute time and space, contrary to what Quentin Smith has recently claimed.

Rysiew, Patrick. Hume and Reid on Common Sense. *Eidos*, 10(2), 123-142, D 92.

The first half of this paper is concerned with drawing out the commonalities—and, more importantly, the differences—between the views of Hume and Reid regarding both the nature of common sense and the epistemological status of the basic deliverances thereof. (Thus, the author seeks to expose the falsity of the claim that Hume and Reid "differed more in words than in opinion.) It is then argued that Reid's conception of common sense is to be preferred over Hume's.

Saarinen, Risto. John Buridan and Donald Davidson on *Akrasia*. *Synthese*, 96(1), 133-154, Jl 93.

The article outlines some medieval views concerning the interpretation of Aristotle's akrasia (weakness of will, incontinence). It is further shown that some important philosophical ideas proposed recently by Donald Davidson, in his article 'How is Weakness of the Will possible', are anticipated in the medieval discussion, especially in John Buridan's Commentary on the Nicomachean Ethics. These ideas include the distinction between 'prima facie' and 'unconditional' judgments and the view that akratic reasoning is based on probabilistic evidence.

Saatkamp Jr, Herman J (ed) and Burch, Robert W (ed). *Frontiers in American Philosophy, Volume I*. College Station, Texas A&M Univ Pr, 1992.

Saatkamp Jr, Herman J. Festive Celebration of Life as One of Santayana's Prime Values: A Comment on M Grossman's Presentation of Santayana's Ultimate. *Ultim Real Mean*, 16(1-2), 134-137, Mr-Je 93.

Sachedina, Abdulaziz A. The Development of 'Jihad' in Islamic Revelation and History in Cross, Crescent, and Sword, Johnson, James Turner (ed). Westport, Greenwood Pr, 1990.

Sacksteder, William. Three Diverse Sciences in Hobbes: First Philosophy, Geometry, and Physics. *Rev Metaph*, 45(4), 739-772, Je 92.

In *De Corpore*, Hobbes discriminates three diverse sciences. Contrary to standard interpretations, no posterior science can be derived from one prior by "deductive moves". First philosophy supplies alone universal principles. These consist in strictly non-causal definitions. Principles peculiar to geometry and physics are adapted to distinctive and special topics diversely proposed by mathematical construction or found among natural particulars. Though expounded by synthetic demonstration, each science has some principles peculiarly its own and employs distinctive analytic operations in ways adapted to its subjects alone. Also, each is correlated with phenomenal data in a way suitable to no other.

Sadurski, Wojciech (ed). *Ethical Dimensions of Legal Theory*. Amsterdam, Rodopi, 1991.

This is a collection of essays which cover the following issues: moral reasoning and evidence in legal decision-making, conflicts of values in adjudication, prima facie values and the law, judges and moral responsibility, philosophy of human rights, unlawful discrimination, and intergenerational justice.

Sagi, Avi. The Suspension of the Ethical and the Religious Meaning of Ethics in Kierkegaard's Thought. *Int J Phil Relig*, 32(2), 83-103, O 92.

Sagoff, Mark. Free-market versus Libertarian Environmentalism. *Crit Rev*, 6(2-3), 211-230, Spr-Sum 92.

Libertarians favor a freemarket for intrinsic reasons—liberty, accountability, consent, cooperation, and other virtues—and, if property rights against trespasses such as pollution are enforced, a free market may also protect the environment. In contrast, Anderson and Leal's *Free Market Environmentalism* favors a free market solely on instrumental grounds; markets allocate resources efficiently. By regarding pollution as a compensable external cost rather than as an enjoinable nuisance and by arguing that the government should auction rather than give public lands to environmental groups Anderson and Leal offer less protection to the environment than libertarians do.

Saha, Sutapa. Indirect Speech and Ontological Commitment in Foundations of Logic and Language, Sen, Pranab Kumar (ed). New Delhi, Allied, 1990.

The paper deals with the problem of the apparent failure of the principle of extensionality in the context of indirect speech. The author considers two main attempts at solving the problem. The one is the Fregean approach and the other Donald Davidson's. A comparative assessment is made. It is noted which of the two views makes least ontological commitment. The author finds a Dummettian version of the Fregean approach least objectionable. However, the novelty of Davidson's concept of *samesaying* is duly appreciated.

Said, Edward W and Jameson, Fredric and Eagleton, Terry. *Nationalism, Colonialism, and Literature*. Minneapolis, Univ of Minnesota Pr, 1990.

Saidel, Eric. What Price Neurophilosophy?. *Proc Phil Sci Ass*, 1, 461-468, 1992.

Recent eliminativist arguments of Paul and Patricia Churchland rely on the power of connectionist models to solve problems facing cognitive science. This paper argues first that their demonstrations of this power do not challenge folk psychology. Implicit in the Churchlands' arguments is the premise that folk psychology will fail to reduce to neuroscience. The remainder of the paper is devoted to arguing that the possible future failure of folk psychology to reduce to neuroscience would not of itself argue for the elimination of folk psychology.

Sain, Ildikó and Mikulás, Szabolcs and Simon, András. Complexity of Equational Theory of Relational Algebras with Projection Elements. *Bull Sec Log*, 21(3), 103-111, O 92.

In connection with a problem of L Henkin and J D Monk, we show that the equational theory and the first order theory of True Pairing Algebras (TPA's) (Relation Algebras expanded with concrete set theoretic projection functions) are not axiomatizable by any decidable set of axioms. More specifically, the equational theory of TPA's is exactly as complex as the second order universal theory of natural numbers. Finally, we show that the equational theory of the projection-free reducts of TPA's is recursively enumerable but not finitely axiomatizable.

Sainati, Vittorio. Il romanzo dell'identità: Metafisica ed ermeneutica. *Teoria*, 12(2), 3-14, 1992.

Sainati, Vittorio. Mito e filosofia nella logica di G Gentile (con un intervento di V Vitiello. *Teoria*, 11(2), 3-20, 1991.

Sainsbury, Marian Jane. *Meaning, Communication and Understanding in the Classroom*. Brookfield, Avebury, 1992.

This book addresses an apparent contradiction between philosophical theory and teachers' experiences. Philospohical theories of meaning place emphasis on the shared nature of understanding, whereas the teacher's experience is of differing understanding, where pupils may mean different things by their words from the teacher. The author draws out some of Wittgenstein's insights and combines them with ideas from Kant, the phenomenological and hermeneutic traditions, social psychology and educational practice in order to resolve this paradox. The result is a theory of meaning which is complex enough to accommodate the kinds of interaction through which learning can take place.

Sainsbury, Mark. Sorites Paradoxes and the Transition Question. *Phil Papers*, 21(3), 177-190, N 92.

The transition question appears to be an embarrassment, even if we have a motivated way of ruling sorites paradoxical arguments unsound. Suppose one member of a sorites series of coloured patches is red. The transition question is: What about its neighbour to the right? It cannot be always correct to say that it is red. But the alternatives are to say, for example, that it is not definitely red, or that there is no fact of the matter concerning whether it is red or not. All such alternatives involve drawing a boundary where, according to our intuitive conceptions, no boundary should be.

Saint Girons, Baldine. "Fiat lux": Une philosophie du sublime. *Rev Phil Fr*, 2, 229-239, Ap-Je 92.

Saint-Germain, Christian. Pouvoir de la singularité: le pathos du visage dans le texte d'Emmanuel Lévinas. *Laval Theol Phil*, 49(1), 27-35, F 93.

Dans l'oeuvre d'Emmanuel Lévinas, le visage occupe un espace prépondérant. En effet, pour Lévinas, le visage d'autrui exerce sur le moi la plus subtile contrainte jusqu'à constituer le lieu d'où procède toute signification éthique. Cette insistance sur le visage n'est pas sans lien avec l'intrigue biblique entre le visage de l'homme et la Face du Dieu d'Israël. Nous questionnons la légitimité d'une telle emphase et de cette surdétermination toute occidentale. Le visage pourrait-il être au contraire, comme le prétend Gilles Deleuze, le foyer même de toute intolérance, le champ d'où s'organise toute sujétion ou suggestion autoritaire.

Sakai, Naoki. *Voices of the Past: The Status of Language in Eighteenth-Century Japanese Discourse*. Ithaca, Cornell Univ Pr, 1991.

Sala, Giovanni B. Wohlverhalten und Wohlergehen: Der moralische Gottesbeweis in den Schriften Kants. *Theol Phil*, 68(2), 182-207, 1993.

Kant's moral proof for the existence of God proceeds, not from the obligatory character, but rather from the ultimate goal, of the moral law: the supreme good, which is composed of morality and happiness. The proof concludes that God alone can bring about happiness proportionate to virtue. Kant has presented three successive and distinctive versions of the proof in his three Critiques. But the attempt to bring together the absolute autonomy of many with a sensible morality (that is, with a morality whose last result is not nothingness) does not succeed. He therefore should have revised fundamental principles of his ethics.

Salami, Yunusa Kehinde. Anomalous Monism and the Mind-Body Problem. *Quest*, 5(2), 106-114, D 91.

Salanti, Andrea. A Reply to Professor Weintraub's "But Doctor Salanti, Bumblebees Really Do Fly". *Econ Phil*, 9(1), 139-144, Ap 93.

If we take a strictly Lakatosian perspective in appraising general equilibrium *theory*, a few remarks suffice to reject it. Weintraub's 1985 attempt (*General Equilibrium Analysis: Studies in Appraisal*. New York: Cambridge University Press) could have been very interesting because of his proposal to appraise general equilibrium *analysis* in a quite different way, that is according to Lakatos's methodology of mathematics. His attempt would have been successful, however, *only* if theories in the protective belt of the neo-Walrasian research program were (or even could be) actually "derived" from the prospected hard core, and this is just what I challenge in my 1991 article on *Economics and Philosophy*.

Salas Ortueta, Jaime. La verdad del otro y la práctica ecuménica en Leibniz. *Theoria (Spain)*, 6(14-15), 161-173, O 91.

It is possible to describe certain basic principles that underly Leibniz's political activities. These principles do not literally determine the specific steps Leibniz takes, but play a much more decisive role than that due to mere metaphysical principles. They provide a general framework for his activities and a point of reference towards which his reflection tend. Particular attention is paid here to the concept of perspective and its presence in Leibniz's correspondence with Bossuet, Pellison and Madame de Brinon and the way in which a theological dialogue enables Leibniz to develop his vision of reality.

Salleh, Ariel. The Ecofeminism/Deep Ecology Debate. *Environ Ethics*, 14(3), 195-216, Fall 92.

I discuss conceptual confusions shared by deep ecologists over such questions as gender, essentialism, normative dualism, and eco-centrism. I conclude that deep ecologists have failed to grasp both the epistemological challenge offered by ecofeminism and the practical labor involved in bringing about social change. While convergencies between deep ecology and ecofeminism promise to be fruitful, these are celebrated in false consciousness, unless remedial work is done.

Sallis, John. Babylonian Captivity. *Res Phenomenol*, 22, 23-31, 1992.

This essay, oriented by Freud's text on the uncanny, draws a series of connections between events of the Gulf War and the Genesis account of the Tower of Babel. Thereby it addresses the question of the relation between building and language.

Sallis, John. Deformatives: Essentially Other Than Truth in Reading Heidegger: Commemorations, Sallis, John (ed). Bloomington, Indiana Univ Pr, 1992.

This paper deals with the question of truth in Heidegger's thought after Being and Time. Much of it is devoted to an interpretation of Heidegger's lecture "On the Essence of Truth".

Sallis, John. Doublings in Derrida: A Critical Reader, Wood, David (ed). Cambridge, Blackwell, 1992.

This paper discusses Derrida's reading of Saussure and of Husserl, focusing on the role of the double in these readings.

Sallis, John. Flight of Spirit in Of Derrida, Heidegger, and Spirit, Wood, David (ed). Evanston, Northwestern Univ Pr, 1993.

This paper is an extended discussion of Jacques Derrida's book *Of Spirit*. It focuses especially on the question concerning the priority given to questioning in Heidegger's thought.

Sallis, John (ed). *Reading Heidegger: Commemorations*. Bloomington, Indiana Univ Pr, 1992.

The papers in this collection were originally presented at an international conference on Heidegger held at Loyola University of Chicago in 1989. The papers deal largely with the new texts published since the inception of the *Gesamtausgabe*. Among the themes discussed are Heidegger and psychiatry, the question of ethics, Heidegger and the Greeks, Heidegger in China, Language and Art, and Heidegger and translation.

Salman, Charles E. Phaedrus' Cosmology in the *Symposium*. *Interpretation*, 20(2), 99-116, Wint 92-93.

Salmon, Nathan. On Content. *Mind*, 101(404), 733-751, O 92.

A novel interpretation of Frege is suggested on which *Erkenntniswerte* is distinct from both *Sinn* and *Bedeutung*. Independent reasons are provided for positing such a semantic value—logical content. Expressions have the same logical content iff they are logically equivalent. This criterion is sharpened, with the result that sentences of different languages may share the same logical content. Logical content emerges as a feature of propositions. A novel solution is proposed for a puzzle introduced by Ali Kazmi. It is argued that such items as Church's Theorem and Goldbach's Conjecture are logical contents. A more general notion of *theoretical content* is proposed.

Salmon, Nathan. Relative and Absolute Apriority. *Phil Stud*, 69(1), 83-100, Ja 93.

It is argued that certain sentences that are difficult for the theory of direct reference—like 'Cicero is Tully' and their logical consequences— are, contrary to the received view, *a priori*, in fact, analytic in the traditional (philosophical) sense. An alternative account proffered by Keith Donnellan and defended by Saul Kripke (and others) is criticized. Compelling evidence is provided that even logically valid, and hence straightforwardly analytic, sentences share the feature that understanding and reason alone are not sufficient without empirical investigation to reveal their truth. Various contrasting relative and absolute notions of apriority and aposteriority are proposed and examined.

Salmon, Wesley C. The Value of Scientific Understanding. *Philosophica*, 51(1), 9-19, 1993.

Salmona, B. Ecologia categoria etica. *Sapienza*, 45(3), 279-291, 1992.

Salter, John. Adam Smith on Feudalism, Commerce and Slavery. *Hist Polit Thought*, 13(2), 219-241, Sum 92.

Salter, Michael. Towards a Phenomenology of Legal Thinking. *J Brit Soc Phenomenol*, 23(2), 167-182, My 92.

This study analyzes the role of imagination, recollection, and language in the cognitive process. It fuses together Hegel's account of thinking with the phenomenology of E Husserl, and suggests that 'thought' cannot ever be reduced to a relationship of correspondence to empirical facts.

Saltz, David Z. How To Do Things On Stage. *J Aes Art Crit*, 49(1), 31-45, Wint 91.

This article interrogates J L Austin's widely accepted claim — subsequently defended by John Searle — that speech acts performed during a dramatic performance lack illocutionary force. It demonstrated that actors' speech acts typically satisfy Searle's own criteria for sincere and successful illocutionary action during improvisations, and often, but not always, satisfy those conditions during scripted performances. Moreover, many actions that off stage have only what Searle calls "brute force," such as flipping a light switch, are transformed into illocutionary actions on stage. Hence, far from being *suspended* as Searle maintains, illocutionary force is often *extended* on stage.

Salzmann, Yvan. De 'L'être et le néant' aux 'Cahiers pour une morale': Un enrichissement de la notion sartrienne de liberté 'pour-autrui'. *Stud Phil (Switzerland)*, 49, 155-174, 1990.

La publication des *Cahiers pour une morale* (texte inachevé, rédigé en 1947-48, mais édité en 1983—trois ans après la mort de Sartre) a profondément modifié la portée et enrichi le sens de l'ontologie phénoménologique de *L'être et le néant* (1943). L'article fait apparaître cet enrichissement qui transforme radicale rend possible un dépassement de la lutte des consciences vers une bienveillance humaine réciproque. Nous voyons alors que, pour Sartre, sous certaines conditions, la solidarité et la fraternité peuvent l'emporter sur la violence et le conflit.

Samb, Djibril. La signification du *prôton philon* dans le *Lysis*. *Rev Phil Fr*, 4, 513-516, O-D 91.

Sambin, Giovanni and Boolos, George. Provability: The Emergence of a Mathematical Modality. *Stud Log*, 50(1), 1-23, Mr 91.

Sammons, Jack L. The Professionalism Movement: The Problems Defined. *Notre Dame J Law Ethics*, 7(1), 269-304, 1993.

The cause of the problems addressed by the legal community's Professionalism Movement are liberal changes within the larger society, including the loss of shared conceptions of a life well-lived. The functional moral appeal of the practice of law no longer works because these changes have decreased the ability of the practice to provide internal goods. The common goods of liberal culture are not adequate, by themselves, for the kind of community required to sustain the internal goods of the practice. These changes produce a loss of the practice's moral authority. This loss corrupts the client-lawyer relationship—as lawyers turn either to the personal or to the state as inadequate substitutes for moral authority—and corrupts the craft as "professional" becomes "career." To avoid this, the practice must define success for itself rather than allowing the larger society to do so through the efficiencies of the moment. The Professionalism Movement is attempting to do this.

Samonà, Leonardo. Metafisica e pensiero iniziale: Aspetti della *Kehre* alle origini del pensiero heideggeriano. *G Metaf*, 14(3), 443-483, S-D 92.

Sampford, Charles and Wood, David. Tax, Justice and the Priority of Property in Ethical Dimensions of Legal Theory, Sadurski, Wojciech (ed). Amsterdam, Rodopi, 1991.

This essay examines arguments which seek to deny (Rand, Nozick) or limit (Nozick, Scruton, Epstein, Lucas) the legitimacy of taxation. All generally assume that taxation of property or income takes away something to which the citizen taxed has prior and superior moral title. Even proponents of "confiscatory" taxation make a similar assumption of prior. However, as tax and property, especially in its modern forms, are dependent on law, such a priority cannot be defended without a separate moral argument. Few such arguments are offered and those that are (e.g., Rand, Nozick) fail. This is not to say that any level of tax is justified but that arguments over the roles that taxation and private property have to play cannot legitimately be skewed in favour of the latter by assumptions of its priority. The essay concludes by considering the form that such philosophical and legal arguments over tax would take.

Samuelson, Norbert M. A Critique of Borowitz's Postmodern Jewish Theology. *Zygon*, 28(2), 267-282, Je 93.

Borowitz's book is primarily a systematic response by a liberal Jewish theologian to his perceived challenges from rationalism on one hand and postmodernism on the other. It is within this context that Borowitz discusses issues of the relationship between modern science and Judaism. The first part of this essay is a summary of Borowitz's book. Here I locate Borowitz's place in the general discipline of Jewish philosophy and theology. The second part of the paper is a critique of Borowitz's discussion of postmodernism and liberalism. It is in this concluding section that the issues raised by contemporary science for Jewish religious thoughts are discussed.

Sànchez de Zavala, Victor. On the Study of Linguistic Performance in Cognition, Semantics and Philosophy, Ezquerro, Jesús (ed). Norwell, Kluwer, 1992.

A constraining 'boundary condition' that cannot be ignored at no risk in cognitive studies is cognitive activities' ability to mesh with (and in many cases to be driven by) non-cognitive ones. A survey of some originating and most current work (including, in an Appendix, a detailed critical review of perhaps the presently most advanced theory on language use) demonstrates just the opposite trend. The advocated approach allows suggesting some specific steps to be done if a promising research program on language performance (emission and reception being accorded an equal footing) is to be set up.

Sánchez Rey, María del Carmen. El cuerpo como educador del espíritu en la Filosofía de Bergson. *Themata*, 8, 69-85, 1991.

This study, centered in *Material and Memory* puts us on our guard against a frequent interpretation of Bergson's philosophy as spiritualist, which means opening the way for a positive consideration of the body. To do this I have examined Bergson's psychological investigations, underlined his metaphysical perspective and demonstrated the function of the body in mental life. Finally, I have shown how the body educates the spirit.

Sánchez-Mazas, Miguel. Actualisation, développement et perfectionnement des calculs logiques arithmético-intensionnels de Leibniz. *Theoria (Spain)*, 6(14-15), 175-259, O 91.

Sánchez-Mazas, Miguel. Los cálculos lógicos de Leibniz a los 325 años de su *Dissertatio de Arte Combinatoria*. *Theoria (Spain)*, 6(14-15), 1-8, O 91.

Sánchez-Mazas, Miguel. Théories syllogistiques et déontiques analysées comme structures algébriques: de Leibniz à Lukasiewicz et Von Wright. *Theoria (Spain)*, 5(12-13), 193-222, N 90.

Sánchez-Miguel, Manuel G-C. The Grounds for the Model-Theoretic Account of the Logical Properties. *Notre Dame J Form Log*, 34(1), 107-131, Wint 93.

Quantificational accounts of logical truth and logical consequence aim to reduce these modal concepts to the nonmodal one of generality. A logical truth, for example, is said to be an instance of a "maximally general" statement, a statement whose terms other than variables are "logical constants." These accounts used to be the objects of severe criticism by philosophers like Ramsey and Wittgenstein. In early work, Etchemendy has claimed that the currently standard model-theoretic account of the logical properties is a quantificational account and that it fails for reasons similar to the ones provided by Ramsey and Wittgenstein. He claims that it would fail even if it were propped up by a sensible account of what makes a term a logical constant. In this paper I examine to what extent the model-theoretic account is a quantificational one, and I defend it against Etchemendy's criticisms.

Sanders, Andy. Tacit Knowledge-Between Modernism and Postmodernism. *Tradition Discovery*, 18(2), 15-21, 1991-92.

Using and refining criteria developed by N Murphey and J McClendon, I argue that M Polanyi's epistemology may well be regarded as truly postmodern. However, his theory of tacit knowing also remains firmly rooted in the Enlightenment tradition. The corresponding tension in Polanyi's overall position between 1) dogmatist (foundational) and anti-scepticist concerns, and 2) holistic, anti-reductionistic and relativistic elements, can be resolved by interpreting Polanyi consistently as a traditionalist who is both a fallibilist and a methodological dogmatist, i.e., upholding a principle of tenacity (Peirce, Popper).

Sanders, John T. Merleau-Ponty, Gibson, and the Materiality of Meaning. *Man World*, 26(3), 287-302, Jl 93.

This paper discusses the extraordinary similarity between the approaches taken by Maurice Merleau-Ponty and J J Gibson. In attempting to show that each approach gains considerably from attention to the other, I take as of central importance the question of the *character* of the perceived world, both in relation to the traditionally opposed mental and material "substances", and in relation to its identification and individuation of things *vis a vis* one another and *vis a vis* ourselves. This implicates especially Gibson's "affordances" and Merleau-Ponty's thesis concerning the "materiality of meaning."

Sanders, John T. On 'Cuteness'. *Brit J Aes*, 32(2), 162-165, Ap 92.

John Morreall has argued that "cuteness was probably essential in human evolution" because "our emotional and behavioural response...to cute things...has had survival value for the human race". Morreall's understanding of cuteness thus makes it out to be an abstract general attribute of infants that *causes* adults to want to care for them. I try to show that this is, if not an altogether fallacious way of explaining the matter, at least an extremely misleading one. I argue that cuteness cannot, in itself, have evolutionary value.

Sandkaulen, Birgit. Gerold Prauss—Die Welt und Wir. *Phil Rundsch*, 39(3), 236-243, 1992.

Sandoe, Peter. The Perceptual Paradigm of Moral Epistemology. *Dan Yrbk Phil*, 27, 45-71, 1992.

The paper is about the perceptual paradigm of moral epistemology the key idea of which is that when a situation evokes a moral attitude in us, this attitude can be the result of a genuine awareness of a moral quality of the situation. This idea has been defended by means of an analogy between moral values and secondary qualities. In the paper this analogy as used by among other John McDowell and David Wiggins is defended against objections raised by Gilbert Harman, Simon Blackburn and Colin McGinn.

Sandoe, Peter and Kappel, Klemens. QALYs, Age and Fairness. *Bioethics*, 6(4), 297-316, O 92.

The QALY method for measuring utility of health improvements assumes that a certain improvement of a person's health has the same utility whether the person is old or young. In addition, proponents of QALY often hold that we should be morally indifferent between giving a certain health improvement to a young or an old person. The paper criticizes these assumptions. It is argued that the benefit to the person of a certain improvement of health depends on how it coheres with the persons life as a whole, including also age. Second it is argued that considerations of fairness speak in favor of giving preferential treatment to the young before the old.

Sandok, Theresa (trans) and Krapiec, Mieczyslaw Albert. *Metaphysics: An Outline of the Theory of Being*. New York, Lang, 1991.

This book is both a comprehensive introduction to the philosophy of being and a sustained argument for the value of approaching metaphysics from a classical, realistic point of view. The traditional topics addressed in classical metaphysics— the transcendental properties of being, act and potency, substance and accident, essence and existence, etc.— are presented in a contemporary light and related to current philosophical controversies. The book culminates in an extended discussion of the analogical nature of being and cognition.

Sandok, Theresa (trans) and Zdybicka, Zofia J. *Person and Religion: An Introduction to the Philosophy of Religion*. New York, Lang, 1991.

This book is a comprehensive introduction to the philosophy of religion. Part 1, explores various nonphilosophical and philosophical approaches to the study of religion, culminating in an argument for the need for an autonomous philosophy of religion based on the empirically given fact of religion in human life. Part 2, discusses the various ways, internal and external, in which the fact of religion presents itself to us. Part 3, then attempts to interpret this experiential data in the context of the classical philosophy of being, focusing on the subjective and objective grounds of the fact of religion and on the personal character of the religious relation.

Sandu, Gabriel. On the Logic of Informational Independence and Its Applications. *J Phil Log*, 22(1), 29-60, F 93.

We shall introduce in this paper a language whose formulas will be interpreted by games of imperfect information. Such games will be defined in the same way as the games for first-order formulas except that the players do not have complete information of the earlier course of the game. Some simple logical properties of these games will be stated together with the relation of such games of imperfect information to higher-order logic. Finally, a set of applications will be outlined.

Sandu, Gabriel and Hintikka, Jaakko. The Skeleton in Frege's Cupboard: The Standard Versus Nonstandard Distinction. *J Phil*, 89(6), 290-315, Je 92.

Henkin formulated the standard versus nonstandard distinction in 1950, but the idea of the standard interpretation of hegher-order variables is virtually equivalent with that of an arbitrary function, which was debated by nineteenth-century mathematicians. Frege's disregard of the latter notion and his criticisms of abstraction show that he opted for a nonstandard interpretation. This would make his system an inadequate foundation for mathematics, even if it were consistent. One reason why the nonstandardness of Frege's interpretation has been overlooked is that he did not identify higher-order existence with definability, which is falsely assumed to be the only possible nonstandard interpretation.

Sandu, Gabriel and Klima, Gyula. Numerical Quantifiers in Game-Theoretical Semantics. *Theoria*, 61(3), 173-192, 1990.

Sankey, Howard. Translation and Languagehood. *Philosophia (Israel)*, 21(3-4), 335-337, Ap 92.

According to an influential view, something which we might have reason to think is a language is not proven to be a language until it has been translated. I argue, to the contrary, that it is necessary to appeal to factors which are independent of translation in order to establish that it is indeed a language which has been translated in the first place. Since this is so, it follows that proof of languagehood, rather than depending on translation, is in fact logically prior to translation.

Sankowski, Edward. Ethics, Art, and Museums. *J Aes Educ*, 26(3), 1-13, Fall 92.

Santambrogio, Marco. Was Frege Right about Variable Objects? in Language, Truth and Ontology, Mulligan, Kevin (ed). Dordrecht, Kluwer, 1992.

Santangelo, Paolo. Italian Studies on Far Eastern Thought in Comparative Philosophy. *Phil East West*, 43(3), 573-582, Jl 93.

The article presents a short survey of the main studies concerning Chinese, Japanese and Korean thought in the last years in Italy.

Santas, Gerasimos. Knowledge and Belief in Plato's 'Republic' in Greek Studies in the Philosophy and History of Science, Nicolacopoulos, Pantelis (ed). Dordrecht, Kluwer, 1990.

Santi, Marina. Philosophizing and Learning to Think: Some Proposals for a Qualitative Evaluation. *Thinking*, 10(3), 15-22, 1993.

Santilli, Paul C. MacIntyre on Rationality and Tradition. *Lyceum*, 1(1), 12-24, Wint 89.

In his book, *Whose Justice? Which Rationality,* Alasdair MacIntyre outlines a theory of historical and narrative rationality embedded in moral traditions. He claims that while differences in language and root concepts of justice make such traditions incommensurable, a theory of a rationality *internal* to traditions is able, nevertheless, to overcome a Nietzschean, postmodern relativism. I argue that MacIntyre wavers between holding a notion of incommensurability which is so profound that rational resolution of moral disagreements between cultures seems impossible and one which is less radical and so not entirely incompatible with at least some basic trans-historical standards of rationality.

Santilli, Paul C. What Did Descartes Do to Virtue?. *J Value Inq*, 26(3), 353-365, Jl 92.

Santogrossi, Ansgar. Duns Scotus on Potency Opposed to Act in *Questions on the Metaphysics*, IX. *Amer Cath Phil Quart*, 67(1), 55-76, Wint 93.

The paper presents five different meanings Scotus distinguishes for "potency", examining one of them, potency opposed to act, in detail. Potency opposed to act, based in a non-existing yet known thing, leads into problems surrounding the non-existent. The same thing is first in potency and then in act; Scotus gives subtle nuances to "same" and opens up profound considerations about being, identity, and distinction. Following a hint from Scotus, the article outlines the order of priority obtaining among actual being, merely known being, potential being, and among these as present to intellect.

AUTHOR INDEX WITH ABSTRACTS 655 Saugstad, Jens

Santoni, Ronald E. Sartre's Adolescent Rejection of God. *Phil Today*, 37(1), 62-69, Spr 93.

I attempt, here, to show that Sartre's initial basis for rejecting the existence of God is pre-philosophical, non-discursive, and flippant: that his rejection is rooted in an unreflective childhood "intuition" that God does not exist. I maintain, as a corollary, that Sartre's subsequent "official" ontological dismissal of God in *Being and Nothingness* is, essentially, a post-intuitive, *ex-post facto* effort to vindicate philosophically his disbelief in God. Finally, I try, in passing to show that, in spite of Sartre's claim to the "certitude" of God's non-existence, there remains significant evidence to suggest an unsettled ambivalence in his attitude concerning God's existence.

Santoro-Brienza, Liberato. Aristotle and Hegel on Nature: Some Similarities. *Bull Hegel Soc Gt Brit*, 26, 13-29, Autumn-Wint 92.

Santurri, Edmund N (ed) and Werpehowski, William (ed). *The Love Commandments: Essays in Christian Ethics and Moral Philosophy*. Washington, Georgetown Univ Pr, 1992.

Sanyal, Indrani. Modality and Possible Worlds in Foundations of Logic and Language, Sen, Pranab Kumar (ed). New Delhi, Allied, 1990.

Sanz, Víctor. La reducción suareciana de los transcendentales. *Anu Filosof*, 25(2), 403-420, 1992.

The notion of a liquid and res, excluded by Suárez from the transcendentals, nevertheless are of primary importance in the understanding of the notion of being, a key aspect of suarecian ontology.

Sapire, David. General Causal Propensities, Classical and Quantum Probabilities. *Phil Papers*, 21(3), 243-258, N 92.

Sapontzis, Steve F. Commentary: On the Utility of Contracts. *Between Species*, 8(4), 229-232, Fall 92.

This paper discusses whether participants in Rawls' original position could be incarnated as animals. In response to an argument that they could not be, it is argued that Rawls' criticisms of utilitarianism would not inevitably lead to defining individuality in terms of life-plans—something animals generally lack—and calling for the respecting of such individuality. Finally, it is argued that contractarian analyses of justice must inevitably fail to provide a complete theory of justice.

Sapontzis, Steve F. Holism: Revolution or Reminder?. *Topoi*, 12(1), 31-39, Mr 93.

This paper discusses four possible theses of "holism:" individuals acquire some of their value through participating in communities; individuals acquire value only through participating in communities; wholes can have values which are not the sum of the values of the individuals composing them; and wholes can have values that in no way depend on conscious, desiring, or feeling subjects. The second and fourth of these theses are rejected. The first and third are compatible with traditional moral theories, e.g., utilitarianism. Consequently, defensible holism represents a reminder, not a revolution, in moral theory.

Sarkar, Husain. Something, Nothing and Explanation. *SW Phil Rev*, 9(1), 151-161, Ja 93.

Robert Nozick has offered in his book, *Philosophical Explanations*, at least three separate arguments for why something exists rather than nothing. His view also has some bearing on the notion of explanation. Novel and unusual as these arguments are, I argue that none of them are satisfactory on this rather intractable question.

Sarkar, Sahotra. "The Boundless Ocean of Unlimited Possibilities": Logic in Carnap's *Logical Syntax of Language*. *Synthese*, 93(1-2), 191-237, N 92.

Sarkar, Sahotra. Science, Philosophy, and Politics in the Work of J B S Haldane, 1922-1937. *Biol Phil*, 7(4), 385-409, O 92.

Sarkar, Tushar K. Some Systems of Deviant Logic in Foundations of Logic and Language, Sen, Pranab Kumar (ed). New Delhi, Allied, 1990.

The paper unearths a number of metasystemic presuppositions underlying classical two-valued logic of PM-type, C2 for short. Next, it is shown how through suitable modifications (e.g. delection, addition, strengthening, weakening, etc.) of one or more of those presupposition, different well-known systems of non-standard logics like Many-Valued, Fuzzy, Free and Intuitionistic logics can be generated as different diviations form a common base C2. How the Heyting-type intuitionistic logic collapses into C2 when 'p or not-p' is taken as an additional axiom, is shown next. The question of revisability of the laws of logic is also discussed. Quine's conservative view about the possibility of alternative logics is criticized and rejected.

Sarles, Harvey B. Cultural Relativism and Critical Naturalism in Cultural Relativism and Philosophy, Dascal, Marcelo (ed). Leiden, Brill, 1991.

Paths for understanding reality have led toward absolute positions and toward a variety of skepticism disputing argument forms. Rather than opposing one another directly, skepticisms tend to undermine the very possibility of knowing, shifting the quest for reality to debates about epistemological certainty. Instead, a comparatist position deriving from inspection of other intellectual-cultural traditions enables us to "return home" with new lenses, offering alternative perspectives on philosophy: a cultural relativism. In addition, a critical naturalism encourages us to reformulate questions of human nature, to rethink the oppositional ways nature and mind have seemed at war: the ethological critique of language.

Sartarelli, Stephen (trans) and Cacciari, Massimo. *Architecture and Nihilism: On the Philosophy of Modern Architecture*. New Haven, Yale Univ Pr, 1993.

Cacciari studies the relation between philosophy and modern architecture and applies the thinking of avantgarde architects, artists, and writers to the social and political problems raised by technological society. He begins by defining the modern metropolis, using the terms and ideas of Georg Simmel and Max Weber, but revealing where their frameworks are limited. He then examines the work of Adolf Loos and other architects and designers in early twentieth-century Vienna, showing how their architecture and criticism expose the alienation and utopianism in notions of the organic city.

Sartre, Jean Paul and Van Den Hoven, Adrian (trans) and Aronson, Ronald (ed). *Truth and Existence—Jean-Paul Sartre*. Chicago, Univ of Chicago Pr, 1992.

Sartre, Jean-Paul and Bowman, Elizabeth A (trans). Kennedy and West Virginia in Sartre Alive, Aronson, Ronald (ed). Detroit, Wayne St Univ Pr, 1991.

Sartwell, Crispin. A Counter-Examine to Levinson's Historical Theory of Art. *J Aes Art Crit*, 48(2), 157-178, Spr 90.

Sartwell, Crispin. Confucius and Country Music. *Phil East West*, 43(2), 243-254, Ap 93.

American culture contains strong traditional elements which are obscured by the modernist emphasis on avant-garde culture. Country music provides a good example of a traditional art form, and tradition is a frequent theme of country music lyrics. American culture thus possesses much more continuity than is usually supposed. The Confucian concept of 'li,' referring to conventional ritual practices which act as a medium for cultural continuity, has many parallels in country music and Western culture in general.

Sartwell, Crispin. Process and Product: A Theory of Art. *J Speculative Phil*, 6(4), 301-316, 1992.

The purpose of this paper is to argue for the following definition of art: A work of art is an intersubjectively available product which 1) is the product of a process in which, to an exemplary degree, some aspects of the process itself are pursued for their own sake, and not merely for the sake of the end of which the process is undertaken, and 2) is of a kind, members of which are themselves suited to play a role in just such processes.

Sasaki, Katsumi. The Disjunction Property of the Logics with Axioms of Only One Variable. *Bull Sec Log*, 21(2), 40-46, Je 92.

We give a syntactical proof of the disjunction property of the logics obtained from the intuitionistic propositional logic by adding the axioms N 4m+2's (m1), where N 4m+2's are axioms containing only one variable studied by I Nishimura. Semantical proofs for the above logics to have the disjunction property have been given by J G Anderson and A Wronsky.

Sass, Hans-Martin. Criteria for Death: Self-Determination and Public Policy. *J Med Phil*, 17(4), 445-454, Ag 92.

'Whole brain death' criteria have found support in Western cultures in regard to post-mortem organ donation and the termination of care for patients meeting these strict criteria. But they are of minimal use in Asian cultures and in the ethics of caring for the persistent vegetative patient. This paper introduces a formula for a global Uniform Determination of Death statute, based on the 'entire brain including brain stem' criteria as a default position, but allowing competent adults by means of advance directives to choose other criteria for determining death during the process of dying.

Sass, Louis A. Heidegger, Schizophrenia and the Ontological Difference. *Phil Psych*, 5(2), 109-132, 1992.

This paper offers a phenomenological or hermeneutic reading-employing Heidegger's notion of the 'ontological difference'-of certain central aspects of schizophrenic experience. The main focus is on signs and symptoms that have traditionally been taken to indicate either 'poor reality-testing' or else 'poverty of content of speech'. I argue that, at least in some cases, the tendency to attribute these signs of illness to the schizophrenic patient results from a failure to recognize that such patients-as part of a quasi-solipsistic orientation and alienation from more normal, pragmatic concerns-may be grappling with issues of what Heidegger would call an ontological rather than an ontic type, issues concerned not with entities but with Being.

Sassower, Raphael and Ormiston, Gayle. From Marx's Politics to Rorty's Poetics: Shifts in the Critique of Metaphysics. *Man World*, 26(1), 63-82, Ja 93.

Using Rorty's distinctions between systematic and edifying discourses, the cultures and vocabularies of Philosophy and post-philosophy, and (more recently) "metaphysics" and "poetry," the paper proceeds in three phases: 1) offering an exploration of Rorty's treatment of Marx as an *edifying* thinker in *Philosophy and the Mirror of Nature*, and then, as a *metaphysician* in *Contingency, irony, solidarity*; 2) exploring Rorty's "critique of metaphysics," in terms of how "metaphysics" is defined and determined by Rorty in his efforts to dismiss all but those who he classifies as liberal ironists, and applying the critique to Rorty's own vocabularies and texts; and 3) examining the concepts of "progress" and "replacement" and the role these concepts play in Rorty's critique of metaphysics. The paper ends questioning the status (ontological or otherwise) of any critique, analysis, or narrative vis-a-vis the topic, problem or question it identifies and the purposes for which that identification has been made.

Satre, Thomas W. Liberalism and Health Care Allocation. *SW Phil Rev*, 8(1), 39-47, Ja 92.

This paper presents and criticizes two recent anti-liberal proposals for the use of age as a guideline in the allocation of health care resources. The proposals and their supporting arguments are found in Daniel Callahan's book *Setting Limits* and in Norman Daniels's book *Am I My Parent's Keeper?* It is the claim in this paper that neither argument supports the proposal for the use of age as a guideline in such decisions and that liberalism has not been undermined by these arguments.

Satz, Debra M. Tocqueville, Commerce, and Democracy in The Idea of Democracy, Copp, David (ed). New York, Cambridge Univ Pr, 1993.

This essay examines the tensions between commerce and democratic politics in the thought of Tocqueville. I argue that Tocqueville thought that commerce tended to undermine political democracy and that achieving a balance between the two depends on the persistence of small scale commercial activity and equal property ownership characteristic of nineteenth century America.

Saugstad, Jens. Kant on Action and Knowledge. *Kantstudien*, 83(4), 381-398, 1992.

The paper challenges the standard *internalist* interpretations of Kant's epistemology, which claim that the forms of experience are inner and private. According to those views, the forms of sensibility are typically seen as "filters" that structure our perception of the world; the actions of the understanding are typically seen as mental acts or as unconscious processes that combine the elements furnished by sense into representations of objects. Against such readings, textual evidence is adduced to show that Kant held an *externalist* position, according to which sensible intuitions are *public displays* and the actions of the understanding are free, overt *techniques*.

Saul, Jennifer M 656 **AUTHOR INDEX WITH ABSTRACTS**

Saul, Jennifer M. Still an Attitude Problem. *Ling Phil*, 16(4), 423-435, Ag 93.

The article argues against two recent accounts of propositional attitude ascription—that of Mark Crimmins and John Perry, and that of Mark Richard. Both accounts attempt to capture pretheoretic intuitions about substitution puzzle cases by adding to the semantics certain contextually determined elements. This paper argues that neither account manages to do so, due to conversational participants' limited knowledge of relevant facts.

Saunders, Martha and Martindale, Kathleen. Realizing Love and Justice: Lesbian Ethics in the Upper and Lower Case. *Hypatia*, 7(4), 148-171, Fall 92.

This essay examines two tendencies in lesbian ethics as differing visions of community, as well as contrasting views of the relationship between the erotic and the ethical. In addition to considering those authors who make explicit claims about lesbian ethics, this paper reflects on the works of some lesbians whose works are less frequently attended to in discussions about lesbian ethics, including lesbians writing from the perspectives of theology and of literature.

Saunders, Simon. Locality, Complex Numbers, and Relativistic Quantum Theory. *Proc Phil Sci Ass*, 1, 365-380, 1992.

A heuristic comparison is made of relativistic and non-relativistic quantum theory. To this end the Segal approach is described for the non-specialist. The significance of antimatter to the local and microcausal properties of the fields is laid bare. The fundamental difference between relativistic and non-relativistic (complex) fields is traced to the existence of two kinds of complex numbers in the relativistic case. Their relation to covariant and Newton-Wigner locality is formulated.

Saunders, Trevor J (ed). *Early Socratic Dialogues—Plato*. New York, Penguin USA, 1989.

Saunders, Trevor J. Plato's Later Political Thought in The Cambridge Companion to Plato, Kraut, Richard (ed). New York, Cambridge Univ Pr, 1992.

A wide-ranging examination of the *Statesman* and the *Laws*, which argues (i) that the political theory of both dialogues is intendedly, but obscurely, grounded in metaphysics; (ii) that the political, social, economic, legal, and religious institutions of the state of the *Laws*, Magnesia, are firmly based on historical institutions, but with significant Platonic modification; (iii) that the *Laws* does not abandon, but adapts at a practical level, the idealism of the *Republic*; (iv) that Magnesia is not a fixed structure, but potentially a fluid one; (v) that the *Laws* represents a combined programme of practical endeavour and theoretical enquiry for the years after Plato's death.

Saurer, Werner. A Natural Deduction System for Discourse Representation Theory. *J Phil Log*, 22(3), 249-302, Je 93.

In this article a natural deduction system for Discourse Representation Theory (DRT) is presented. DRT, a theory developed by Hans Kamp, gives a semantics for multi-sentence discourses by assigning discourse representation structures (DRSs) to a discourse. These structures represent what the discourse says explicitly. Understanding a discourse, however, involves understanding what is implicitly contained in the discourse as well, i.e., what can be inferred from it. To model this capacity DRT must be supplemented with an inferential component. The inference rules of the system presented work on the DRSs directly and expand them by integrating the conclusions of the inferences. An appendix gives an outline of a semantic completeness proof of the system.

Sautter, R Craig. Student Written Philosophical Journals. *Teach Phil*, 15(3), 239-250, S 92.

How can we maximize student thinking? One way is to use student-written Philosophical Journals to provide a place where students can perform philosophical writing and thinking tasks. One course that could be designed around the Philosophical Journal begins with the question, "Who Am I?" Or the journal can be used to encourage students to give shadow answers to Aristotle, Descartes or Hume. This article explores theory and uses of the Philosophical Journal.

Savage, Roger W H. Aesthetic Criticism and the Poetics of Modern Music. *Brit J Aes*, 33(2), 142-151, Ap 93.

A theory of the poetics of modern music is the counterpart to its aesthetic criticism. Through a hermeneutical reconstruction of stylistic innovations, individual works are understood as providing solutions to particular aesthetic and technical problems. The significance of Arnold Schoenberg's 'emancipation of the dissonance' for the course of modern music is an interpretive key. The aporia of the emancipated dissonance orients developments that lead to its distancing from traditional aesthetic norms. Theodor Adorno's aesthetic critique of Pierre Boulez's *Le marteau sans maître* is reinterpreted in the light of this theory of the poetics of modern music.

Savarino, Mary Ella. Toward an Ontology of Virtue Ethics. *J Phil Res*, 18, 243-259, 1993.

In this paper, I argue that virtue is an actual quality. In the first part, I review Aristotle's claim that virtue is not a mere potentiality. In the second part, I propose that this claim is supported by the fact that we are aware of some virtues as actual qualities. If and only if virtues are actual qualities can they be the fundamental values virtue ethicists claim they are. (edited)

Savedoff, Barbara. Looking at Art Through Photographs. *J Aes Art Crit*, 51(3), 455-462, Sum 93.

Savedoff, Barbara. Transforming Images: Photographs of Representations. *J Aes Art Crit*, 50(2), 93-106, Spr 92.

Savellos, Elias. Criteria of Identity and the Individuation of Natural-Kind Events. *Phil Phenomenol Res*, 52(4), 807-831, D 92.

Metaphysicians have distinguished the problem of individual differentiation (what makes x other than y), from that of the structure of individuality (what makes a single individual x, an individual nontheless). I argue that, as the case of events shows, the Aristotelian *this-such* doctrine provides for a uniform solution to both of these problems. I propose that an event is a *this-such*, and I employ sortal terms to formulate Aristotle's doctrine in a way that yields both criteria of event-identity and the structure of event-individuality. I argue that this view fits particularly well "natural-kind" events such as earthquakes, tornadoes, and the like.

Savignano, Armando. Esiste una filosofia latinoamericana?. *Aquinas*, 35(3), 539-560, S-D 92.

Savignano, Armando. L'immagine della donna secondo Ortega y Gasset. *Aquinas*, 35(2), 237-271, My-Ag 92.

Savile, Anthony. Painting, Beholder and the Self in Psychoanalysis, Mind and Art, Hopkins, Jim (ed). Cambridge, Blackwell, 1992.

Savile, Anthony. The Rationale of Restoration. *J Aes Art Crit*, 51(3), 463-474, Sum 93.

Savile, Anthony (ed) and Hopkins, Jim (ed). *Psychoanalysis, Mind and Art*. Cambridge, Blackwell, 1992.

Savini, S and Monteiro, L and Sewald, J. Construction of Monadic Three-Valued Lukasiewicz Algebras. *Stud Log*, 50(3-4), 473-483, S-D 91.

Savitt, Steven. World Enough and Space-Time. *Dialogue (Canada)*, 31(4), 701-706, Autumn 92.

Savitt, Steven and Lipson, Morris. A Dilemma for Causal Reliabilist Theories of Knowledge. *Can J Phil*, 23(1), 55-74, Mr 93.

Sawai, Yoshitsugu. Ramanuja's Theory of Karman. *J Indian Phil*, 21(1), 11-29, Mr 93.

Sawicki, Jana. *Disciplining Foucault: Feminism, Power, and the Body*. New York, Routledge, 1991.

This collection of essays aims to layout the basic features of a Foucauldian feminism that is compatible with feminism conceived as a pluralistic and emancipatory radical social movement through an encounter between Foucault and feminist theory and politics. My interpretation of Foucault emphasizes later works in which power and subjectivity are central. I flesh out his undeveloped remarks about resistance and struggle in order to show his discourse can be used to support specific liberatory political struggles, namely, struggles for sexual and reproductive freedom. At the same time, I develop constructive critiques of certain tendencies in current feminist analyses of sexuality, motherhood and reproductive technologies that suppress differences among women and thus overlook the differential impacts of classism, racism, heterosexism and so forth.

Sawyier, Fay. "A Mark of the Growing Mind is Veneration of Objects" (Ludwig Wittgenstein). *Hume Stud*, 18(2), 315-329, N 92.

This work is part of an on-going project to uncover whether flaws appear in the analyses of concepts by investigators who do not include infants and young children in their research. Here the concept, the acquisition of which I examine, is that of 'object'. The investigator is David Hume. I find that some particular elements in our natural sense of what it is to be an object are missing in Hume's findings and that he impoverishes the utility of 'having' a concept of a world of things external to and independent of us.

Sax, Benjamin C. The Prelude to the Philosophy of the Future: The Art of Reading and the Genealogical Methods in Nietzsche. *Hist Euro Ideas*, 14(3), 399-417, My 92.

Most interpreters of Nietzsche's genealogical method—including Michel Foucault—abstract it into a general critical device. This article demonstrates the incorrectness of such interpretations by: 1) shows how Nietzsche ties genealogy directly into the creative and poetic discourse of *Zarathustra*. (Nietzschean genealogy does not function without this connection.) 2) Genealogy is first and foremost an art of reading tests as Nietzsche makes clear in the preface to *The Genealogy of Morals*. The conclusions reached in this article are: 1) the genealogical method is a critical instrument only in relation to Nietzsche's positivity; and 2) this positivity is ppetic—in the sense that it can be expressed or even thought in conceptual terms.

Saxe, Lorena Leigh. Sadomasochism and Exclusion. *Hypatia*, 7(4), 59-72, Fall 92.

Should lesbian and women's events have policies banning sadomasochists or sadomasochistic acts? This question is being heatedly debated in the lesbian community. In this paper, I examine the moral and political problems with sadomasochism from a lesbian/feminist perspective, concluding that sadomasochism is antifeminist and antiliberatory for many reasons. Then, given this conclusion, I explore how events such as women's music festivals should determine their policies about sadomasochism.

Sayers, Sean. Marxism and Actually Existing Socialism in Socialism and Morality, McLellan, David (ed). New York, St Martin's Pr, 1990.

This article criticizes the view of Lukes, Geras and others that the "scientific" and "anti-utopian" approach of Marxism prevents it from developing a moral perspective and from criticizing "actually existing" socialism. It explains Marx's historicist approach to values. It argues that Marx bases his moral values on his theory of history; and then shows how this approach can be applied to the critical analysis of socialist societies.

Sayers, Sean. Once More on Relative Truth: A Reply to Skillen. *Rad Phil*, 64, 35-38, Sum 93.

Sayers, Sean (ed) and McLellan, David (ed). *Socialism and Morality*. New York, St Martin's Pr, 1990.

Examines the relationship between socialism and morality from economic, political, and social aspects. The first half of the book examines the controversial question of how ethics is to be reconciled with a Marxist historical materialism; the second half elaborate the foundations of a socialist morality in the face of that a-moral ravages of the market.

Sayre, Patricia. Persons and Perspectives: A Personalist Response to Nagel. *Personalist Forum*, 8/1(Supp), 205-213, Spr 92.

Personalists have traditionally argued against attempts to reduce the personal to the impersonal. Thomas Nagel, in he View from Nowhere, also claims to reject this kind of reduction. Section I of the paper describes Nagel's model for relating the personal to the impersonal, arguing it is ambiguous on the issue of reductionism. Section II discusses difficulties with the non-reductionist version of Nagel's model. Section III pulls on Wittgenstein's *Tractatus* to develop a reductionist version of Nagel's model that, instead of reducing the personal to the impersonal, does just the reverse.

Sayre-McCord, Geoffrey. Normative Explanations in Philosophical Perspectives, 6: Ethics, 1992, Tomberlin, James E (ed). Atascadero, Ridgeview, 1992.

"What might normative rules explain"? Normative rules might explain why some action, say, counts as illegal, some utterance as ungrammatical, some proposal as rational, some institution as moral. Yet left lingering by this answer (right as it might be) is the suspicion that the facts explained by the relevant rules are just reflections of the rules. Much more satisfying would be an answer that showed that the normative rules and corresponding normative facts they 'explain' themselves explain some event, process, or situation, that is conceptually independent of the rules in question. In this paper, I set out and defend such an answer.

Sayward, Charles and Hugly, Philip G. Classical Logic and Truth-Value Gaps. *Phil Papers*, 21(2), 141-150, Ag 92.

Standard approaches to truth-value gaps involve, in one way or another, deviations from central features of classical logic. Against these standard approaches an account of the logic of languages with truth-value gaps is proposed which leaves the fundamental features of classical logic intact.

Sayward, Charles and Hugly, Philip G. Two Concepts of Truth. *Phil Stud*, 70(1), 35-58, Ap 93.

The redundancy theory of truth concerns the connective 'it is true that'. It is extended by A N Prior to cover a wide variety of further uses of 'true'. It is argued that Prior was right about the scope and limits of the redundancy theory and that the line he drew between those uses of 'true' which are and are not redundant serves to distinguish two important and mutually irreducible types of truth.

Scahill, John H. Three Conceptions of 'Voice' and their Pedagogical Implications. *Phil Stud Educ*, 1, 133-150, 1990.

"Voice" is conceived as linguistic competence linked with aspirations for empowerment and social change. Three outlooks are examined with respect to pedagogical interventions designed to encourage voice. A liberationist approach (Henry Giroux) seeks to remedy voicelessness by changing individuals, by eliciting and validating tacit knowledge in an interpersonal setting of mutuality. Essentialists (E D Hirsch, Jr) seek to put into the mind foundational increments of cognitive achievements. A structuralist viewpoint (Basil Bernstein) emphasizes conditioning environmental effects as opposed to individual intentionality. School structures conductive to voice are posited.

Scaltas, Patricia Ward. Virtue Without Gender in Socrates. *Hypatia*, 7(3), 126-137, Sum 92.

In this paper I argue that Socrates believed that there is no distinction between man's virtue and woman's virtue and that there is no difference in the achievement of virtue between men and women. My analysis shows Plato's position on the moral equality of guardian women and men in the Republic to be a continuation of the Socratic position of nongendered virtue. I thus disagree with Spelman's recent interpretation of the Republic on this issue.

Scaltsas, Theodore. A Necessary Falsehood in the Third Man Argument. *Phronesis*, 37(2), 216-232, 1992.

The article aims to show that there is a hitherto unobserved *impossibility* in the premises of the Third Man Argument(TMA). This impossibility underlies Vlasto' one, because it does not presuppose a unique Form per character. Furthermore, it is embedded in the set of premises which Wilfrid Sellars had argued, and Vlasto agreed, are consistent. The impossible calm is that what makes something *f* is *not sufficient* for making it qualitatively identical to another *f* thing. But this is the denial of a necessary truth, namely, being *f* is sufficient for being *f*-identical to another *f*thing', and hence the premises of the TMA cannot be true in any possible world. An *interpretation* of the Theory of Forms as a type of explanation is offered which shows each of the premises of the TMA to be intuitively plausible, even if they are impossible as a set.

Scaltsas, Theodore. Fairness in Socratic Justice—*Republic* I. *Proc Aris Soc*, 93, 247-262, 1993.

This paper offers further arguments in favour of Kerferd's position, that in Book I of the *Republic* Thrasymachus puts forward a consistent position on justice, and that he shares with Socrates the definition of justice. Furthermore, it is argued that the fact that they agree that justice is other-directed signifies an important truth about the Socratic conception of justice. Namely, the fact that the just person's goal is the good of another is Socrates' way of securing that the just person acts from a dis-interested perspective, and hence, fairness in justice.

Scaltsas, Theodore. In Search of Socrates. *Phil Books*, 34(3), 129-136, Jl 93.

The article describes the main differences that Gregory Vlastos discerns between the philosophical doctrines of Socrates and those of Plato. It concentrates on the discussion of Socrates' disavowal of knowledge, the Socratic elenchus, his rejection of retaliation, and Socratic piety. It closes with an examination of the kind of eudaimonism, namely partial constitutive eudaimonism, that Vlastos finds in Socrates.

Scaltsas, Theodore. Soul as Attunement: An Analogy or a Model? in Greek Studies in the Philosophy and History of Science, Nicolacopoulos, Pantelis (ed). Dordrecht, Kluwer, 1990.

The aim of the article is to argue that Plato distinguishes between an *analogy* and a model in his discussion of the soul as attunement in the *Phaedo*. A version of Simmias' model of the soul as harmony is offered which avoids Plato's criticisms, and shows that Simmias' proposal is committed to substance physicalism, but not to moral naturalism.

Scaltsas, Theodore. Women as Ends—Women as Means in the Enlightenment in Women's Rights and the Rights of Man, Arnaud, A J. Oxford, Aberdeen, 1990.

This article identifies two conflicting lines of argumentation developed by women thinkers through the 18th into the 19th centuries: 1) functionalist arguments for the education of women premised on the assumption that women have a functional role to play in man's life, and 2) liberal perfectionist arguments for the self-fulfilment of women. My thesis is that this tension in the arguments for the emancipation of women is resolved by an integration which makes functionalist arguments derivative from and conditioned by liberal perfectionist principles. This resolution is achieved in Mary Wollstonecraft's 1792 monograph and developed further in Harriet Taylor Mill's 1851 article.

Scanlan, James P. Phenomenology in Russia: The Contribution of Gustav Shpet. *Man World*, 26(4), 467-475, O 93.

In this review essay the author critically examines the first English translation (with introductory essays by the translator, Thomas Nemeth, and by Alexander Haardt) of the book *Appearance and Sense: Phenomenology as the Fundamental Science and its Problems* (1914) by the Russian philosopher Gustav Shpet (1879-1937). Despite some problems with the translation, the work is found to provide valuable access to the reflections of a little known early devotee of Husserl who put his own distinctive stamp on the phenomenological enterprise and who was imprisoned and executed in Stalinist Russia because of his philosophical views.

Scanlon, Thomas M. Value, Desire, and Quality of Life in The Quality of Life, Nussbaum, Martha C (ed). New York, Oxford Univ Pr, 1993.

What makes a person's life go better? Parfit has distinguished three types of answers: Hedonistic Theories, Desire Theories, and Objective List Theories. From the point of view of the person whose life it is, the only plausible answers are of the third type, better called Substantive Good Theories. Hedonism is one special kind of Substantive good account. Desires are relevant to well being only as indications of what will be enjoyable or as conclusions about what the person takes to be good for other reasons. Paper discusses the kind of substantive good account appropriate for ethics.

Scannone, Juan Carlos. Begegnung der Kulturen und inkulturierte Philosophie in Lateinamerika. *Theol Phil*, 66(3), 365-383, 1991.

Nachdem der Artikel die wichtigsten Merkmale der iberoamerikanischen "misch"-Kultur beschreibt, behandelt er bedeutende Ansätze einer in Lateinamerika inkulturierten Philosophie. Er bezieht sich hauptsächlich auf Anasätze in den Bereichen der Metaphysik ("Lebenssynthesen, Symbol und Analogie"; "Sein und 'estar'"), der philosophischen Gotteslehre, der Erkenntnistheorie, der philosophischen Anthropologie (das "Wil als Grundkategorie), der Ethik und der Sozialphilosophie (insbesondere der Befreiung). Es handelt sich um philosophische Beiträge der lateinamerikanischen Philosophie zum philosophischen Denken.

Scaravelli, Luigi. Poesia e verità: Lettere a Clotilde Marghieri. *Teoria*, 12(2), 59-105, 1992.

Scarre, Geoffrey. Utilitarianism and Self-Respect. *Utilitas*, 4(1), 27-42, My 92.

Scedrov, Andre and Lincoln, Patrick and Shankar, Natarajan. Linearizing Intuitionistic Implication. *Annals Pure Applied Log*, 60(2), 151-177, Ap 93.

An embedding of the implicational propositional intuitionistic logic (IIL) into the nonmodal fragment of intuitionistic linear logic (IMALL) is given. The embedding preserves cut-free proofs in a proof system that is a variant of IIL. The embedding is efficient and provides an alternative proof of the PSPACE-hardness of IMALL. It exploits several proof-theoretic properties of intuitionistic implication that analyze the use of resources in IIL proofs.

Schaber, Peter. Der Wert von Autonomie. *Stud Phil (Switzerland)*, 49, 39-48, 1990.

This paper deals with the personal as well as with the moral value of autonomy. It is argued that autonomy is only of instrumental worth: it is a) valuable for a person if its exercise promotes the goods which define a good life and b) morally valuable if its exercise contributes to the good life of other persons.

Schäfer, Lothar. Bacon's Project: Should It Be Given Up?. *Man World*, 26(3), 303-317, Jl 93.

Schafer, Sylvia. When the Child is the Father of the Man: Work, Sexual Difference, and the Guardian-State in Third Republic France. *Hist Theor*, 31(4), 98-115, 1992.

This article examines the place of gender and gendered identities, both in representations of "the state" and the substance of social policy under the early Third Republic in France. (edited)

Schaffner, Kenneth F. Theory Structure, Reduction, and Disciplinary Integration in Biology. *Biol Phil*, 8(3), 319-347, Jl 93.

This paper examines the nature of theory structure in biology and considers the implications of those theoretical structures for theory reduction. An account of biological "theories" as interlevel prototypes embodying causal sequences, and related to each other by strong analogies, is presented, and examples from the neurosciences are provided to illustrate these "middle-range" theories. I then go on to discuss several modifications of Nagel's classical model of theory reduction, and indicate at what stages in the development of reductions these models might best apply. Finally I consider several implications of these analyses of theory structure and reduction for disciplinary integration in biology.

Schall, James V. The Teaching of *Centesimus Annus*. *Gregorianum*, 74(1), 17-43, 1993.

Schall, James V. Transcendent Man in the Limited City: The Political Philosophy of Charles N R McCoy. *Thomist*, 57(1), 63-95, Ja 93.

Charles N R McCoy's works are found in two principal places: In his *The Structure of Political Philosophy* (NY, McGraw Hill, 1963) and On the Intelligibility of Political Philosophy: Essays of Charles N R McCoy (Washington, Cath Univ Amer Pr, 1989). McCoy was concerned principally with the overall order of political philosophy, how classical, medieval, and modern theory are to be defined and related to each other. McCoy found a coherent consistency in the theories behind the totalitarian systems of this era. These generally sought to replace the classic ideas of transcendence with some version of a worldly order as the center of human life. He wanted to restore the Aristotelian primacy of contemplation without denying the place of practical politics and the issues of revelation addressed to it.

Schaller, Walter E. Should Kantians Care about Moral Worth?. *Dialogue (Canada)*, 32(1), 25-40, Wint 93.

Kant's doctrine of moral worth has been criticized for denying that actions motivated by empirical virtues have any moral value. I argue that Kant's doctrine can be extended so as to confer moral worth on such actions if the moral law serves as a limiting condition. But extending Kant's doctrine in this way eviscerates his doctrine since there is no reason not to extend it to juridical duty-fulfilling actions motivated by sympathy. No longer must morally good actions be motivated by duty. I conclude that having a good will is more important than acting from the motive of duty.

Schaller, Walter E. The Relation of Moral Worth to the Good Will in Kant's Ethics. *J Phil Res*, 17, 351-382, 1992.

I consider three questions concerning the relation of the good will to the moral worth of actions. (1) Does a good will consist simply in acting from the motive of duty? (2) Does acting from the motive of duty presuppose that one has a good will? (3) Does the fact that one has a good will entail that all of one's duty-fulfilling actions have moral worth, even if they are not (directly) motivated by duty? I argue that while only persons with a good will are capable of acting from the motive of duty, it does not follow either that a good will consists in acting from duty or that if one has a good will, all of one's dutiful actions will be motivated by duty. Whereas the good will is constituted by the agent's highest-order maxim (the moral law itself), moral worth is a function of the agent's first-order maxims.

Schalow, Frank. Heidegger's Logic of Disproportionality. *SW Phil Rev*, 9(1), 43-50, Ja 93.

This paper argues that Heidegger's employment of hermeneutics requires a parallel transformation of the domain of logic as traditionally understood. A logic that criticizes the basic assumptions we hold in formulating concepts must be joined with the hermeneutical attempt to question our traditional understanding of being and human existence. In this way a logic can be developed which traces the ancestry of different conceptual schemes to address the meaning of being.

Schalow, Frank. The Question of Being and the Recovery of Language Within Hegelian Thought. *Owl Minerva*, 24(2), 163-180, Spr 93.

This paper shows that Hegel's analysis of language prefigures Heidegger's attempt to formulate an analogy between the revelatory power of speech and the disclosure of being. The mutual interest in language points to a crucial intersection between Hegel's and Heidegger's thought that supercedes the apparent dichotomy between the former's emphasis on the infinitude of Absolute Spirit and the latter's regard for human existence as finite. A forum is thereby created for initiating a dialogue between Hegel's speculative philosophy and Heidegger's fundamental ontology.

Schalow, Frank. *The Renewal of the Heidegger-Kant Dialogue: Action, Thought, and Responsibility*. Albany, SUNY Pr, 1992.

This book develops Heidegger's radical reinterpretation of Kant's transcendental philosophy across the entirety of Heidegger's works, including his previously unpublished lectures. It is seen that the need to reshape the landscape of ethical inquiry determines the direction of Heidegger's exchange with Kant. The book thereby shows how Heidegger's retrieval of the Kantian view of imagination is significantly broader than otherwise realized, and in fact leads to an enriched understanding of ethics, the good, along with human freedom.

Schalow, Frank. The Temporality of an Original Ethics. *Int Stud Phil*, 25(1), 55-67, 1993.

This paper argues that Heidegger's original ethics can be supplemented by showing how his own notion of temporality shapes the formulation of ethical. A clearer vision is thereby provided of how Heidegger can develop a sense of the good that is not restricted by the metaphysical framework that his inquiry into being overcomes. The way in then cleared to demonstrate how an original ethics can address the issues of traditional morality, for example, the welfare of the "other", while continuing to deconstruct the narrow conceptual framework of metaphysics. Thus a Heideggerian ethic can avoid the trap of nihilism without compromising its radical disavowal of metaphysics.

Schaper, Eva. Taste, Sublimity, and Genius in The Cambridge Companion to Kant, Guyer, Paul (ed). New York, Cambridge Univ Pr, 1992.

Scharf, Peter M. Assessing Sabara's Arguments for the Conclusion that a Generic Term Denotes Just a Class Property. *J Indian Phil*, 21(1), 1-10, Mr 93.

Schatzki, Theodore R. Early Heidegger on Being, the Clearing, and Realism in Heidegger: A Critical Reader, Dreyfus, Hubert L (ed). Cambridge, Blackwell, 1992.

Through critical analysis of Frederick Olafson's *Heidegger and the Philosophy of Mind*, this paper examines Heidegger's early views on the relations between being, human existence, and realism. It is argued (1) that Heidegger identifies the clearing of being and human existence, (2) that this identification is compatible with the existence of a plurality of people, and (3) that early Heidegger is a realist despite the obvious idealist features of his conception of being.

Schatzki, Theodore R. Mind/Action for Wittgenstein and Heidegger. *SW Phil Rev*, 9(1), 35-42, Ja 93.

The paper outlines how Wittgenstein and Heidegger's views can be combined to form a general account of mind and action. It accomplishes this by interpreting Heidegger of the *Being and Time* era and Wittgenstein of the *Philosophical Investigations* onwards as descendents of the School of Thought called life philosophy. Heidegger is construed as analyzing the occurrence of The Stream of Life, while Wittgenstein is understood as examining (a) The appearances of The Stream in The World and (b) The linguistic articulation tracking their appearances.

Schatzki, Theodore R. Wittgenstein + Heidegger on the Stream of Life. *Inquiry*, 36(3), 307-328, S 93.

This paper combines views of Wittgenstein and Heidegger into an account of mind/action. It does this by suggesting that these two philosophers be viewed in part as decendants of Life-philosophy *(Lebensphilosophie)*. Part I describes the conception of life that informs and emerges from these thinkers. Parts Two and Three detail particular aspects of this conception: Wittgenstein on the constitution of states of life and Heidegger on the flow-structure of the stream of life. The Conclusion offers reasons for believing their combined viewpoint.

Schatzki, Theodore R. Wittgenstein: Mind, Body, and Society. *J Theor Soc Behav*, 23(3), 285-313, S 93.

The paper outlines the account of mind/action, its relation to the body, and its social constitution that lies behind Wittgenstein's remarks on mental concepts. On this account, "mental states" and actions are construed as conditions of life, aspects of how things stand or are going in someone's life. The paper examines the contrast between conditions and experiential appearances of life, the non-Cartesian inner acknowledged by Wittgenstein, the notion of expression, the context-dependency of expression, the constitution of mind/action within social practices, and the three-fold role of the body in expression.

Schauer, Frederick. Messages, Motives, and Hate Crimes. *Crim Just Ethics*, 11(2), 52-53, Sum-Fall 92.

Schauer, Frederick. The Right to Die as a Case Study in Third-Order Decisionmaking. *J Med Phil*, 17(6), 573-587, D 92.

Using the right to die and the United States Supreme Court case of Cruzan vs. Director, Missouri Department of Health as exemplars, this article explores the notion of third-order decision-making. If first order decision making is about what should happen, and second-order decision-making is about who should decide what should happen, then third-order decision-making is about who should decide who decides. This turns out to be an apt characterization of constitutionalism, which is centrally concerned with the allocation of responsibility for making decisions about the allocation of responsibility. Deference to erroneous second-order decisions, as in the *Cruzan* case itself, may merely be an example of this central feature of constitutionalism.

Schedler, George. Forcing Pregnant Drug Addicts to Abort: Rights-Based and Utilitarian Justifications. *Soc Theor Pract*, 18(3), 347-358, Fall 92.

Drug abuse during pregnancy is an instance of a type of behavior for which significant intervention is warranted on utilitarian grounds as well as rights-based ones. Particularly, where society has informed women of the harm drug use causes and when the addicts neither submit to drug treatment nor seek abortions voluntarily, a program of mandating abortion for drug abuse during pregnancy is justified. From a Rawlsian standpoint, whether the choosers consider the plight of an infant born with serious defects or a pregnant drug addict, they would prefer a mandatory abortion program, other things being equal. Likewise, if one seeks the greatest happiness for the greatest number, a society in which some addicts refuse abortion and drug treatment would be happier with a program of mandatory abortion than without it.

Scheffler, Israel. Pictorial Ambiguity. *J Aes Art Crit*, 47(2), 109-115, Spr 89.

The aim of the paper is to interpret pictorial, rather than linguistic, ambiguity, the main problem being that *replication*, or sameness of spelling, useful in explicating the latter, is not available in cases of the former. The proposal is to interpret pictorial ambiguity in terms of *mention-selection* (for which see the author's *Beyond the Letter*), in which multiple meaning is gained through the applicability of divergent captions to the selfsame picture, the picture and each caption mention-selecting one another. This notion offers a general way of understanding how a single work may bear conflicting interpretations.

Scheffler, Israel. Reference and Play. *J Aes Art Crit*, 50(3), 211-216, Sum 92.

This paper treats the phenomenon of play in which a child seems to be engaged in taking one thing for another, for example, identifying a broom stick as a horse. The problem is to give an account of how reference functions in such play. Discussing Gombrich's "Meditations on a Hobby Horse", the paper opposes his denial that the broom stick refers to something outside itself, proposing instead that it does in fact refer to horses, thereby inviting the label "horse" via mention-selection, (see I. Scheffler, *Beyond The Letter*) much as a picture of a horse invites the selfsame label.

Scheffler, Israel. Responses to Authors and Writings of Israel Scheffler. *Synthese*, 94(1), 127-144, Ja 93.

1) "Responses to Authors": This comprises responses to the papers of Catherine Elgin, Karen Hanson, Donald and Barbara Arnstine, Robert Schwartz, Alven Neiman and Harvey Siegel, Jane R Martin, and Jonathan Adler, who all contributed papers in the same issue on Scheffler's work. 2) "Writings of Israel Scheffler": This is a chronological list of Scheffler's book publications and articles from 1958 through 1992, with additional items listed as forthcoming.

Scheffler, Samuel. Naturalism, Psychoanalysis, and Moral Motivation in Psychoanalysis, Mind and Art, Hopkins, Jim (ed). Cambridge, Blackwell, 1992.

Scheffler, Samuel. Prerogatives Without Restrictions in Philosophical Perspectives, 6: Ethics, 1992, Tomberlin, James E (ed). Atascadero, Ridgeview, 1992.

Scheffler, Samuel. Responsibility, Reactive Attitudes, and Liberalism in Philosophy and Politics. *Phil Pub Affairs*, 21(4), 299-323, Fall 92.

Political liberalism has come under attack in the United States due to a perception that liberal programs rest on a reduced conception of individual responsibility. Although many liberals would say that this perception is mistaken, the dominant contemporary philosophical defenses of liberalism, by virtue of their reliance on a purely institutional notion of desert, do indeed advocate a reduced conception of responsibility. Moreover, they may thereby underestimate the significance of the human attitudes that find expression via our practices with respect to desert and responsibility. Thus contemporary philosophical liberalism may be vulnerable to a criticism like the one that has been directed at contemporary political liberalism. And the prospects of political liberalism might best be served by a demonstration that liberal programs do not require a purely institutional notion of desert.

Scheffler Manning, Robert John. Kierkegaard and Post-Modernity: Judas as Kierkegaard's Only Disciple. *Phil Today*, 37(2), 133-152, Sum 93.

This article argues that because of the thoroughly situational aspects of Kierkegaard's thought one must be very critical of Kierkegaard in order to claim to be one of his followers. Thus, Judas is Kierkegaard's only true disciple. From a postmodern contest, which is now our situation and not Kierkegaard's, several aspects of his thought are problematic: his defectial view of sociality, his workshop of passion, his admiration for authority, etc.

Scheibe, E. General Laws of Nature and the Uniqueness of the Universe in Philosophy and the Origin and Evolution of the Universe, Agazzi, Evandro (ed). Norwell, Kluwer, 1991.

Scheibe, Erhard. Substances, Physical Systems, and Quantum Mechanics in Advances in Scientific Philosophy, Schurz, Gerhard (ed). Amsterdam, Rodopi, 1991.

Scheier, Claus-Artur. Die Sprache spricht: Heideggers Tautologien. *Z Phil Forsch*, 47(1), 60-74, Ja-Mr 93.

The essay shows how to understand Heidegger's tautologies as a development of his "ontological difference". It compares these tautologies with the tautologies in

Wittgenstein's *Tractatus* (and with the operational transformation of them by Carnap). It discovers the common root of both interpretations of the essence of tautology in certain ontological problems arising out of Frege's concept of the propositional function with its suppression of the traditional copula.

Scheiffele, Eberhard and Parkes, Graham R (trans). Questioning One's 'Own' from the Perspective of the Foreign in Nietzsche and Asian Thought, Parkes, Graham R (ed). Chicago, Univ of Chicago Pr, 1991.

Scheit, Herbert. Bibliographie P Josef de Vries S J (1898-1989). *Theol Phil*, 65(4), 579-588, 1990.

Scheler, Max. *On Feeling, Knowing, and Valuing: Selected Writings—Max Scheler*. Chicago, Univ of Chicago Pr, 1992.

Schellenberg, J L. Alpha-Claims and the Problem of Evil. *Sophia (Australia)*, 32(1), 56-61, Mr 93.

Alvin Plantinga has shown that claims about what states of affairs the actual world contains are noncontingent. But if so, we can develop a form of the logical problem of evil that is impervious to his well-known Free Will Defence—that can indeed be solved only if it can be shown that God actually exists! Moreover, since the atheist's argument for inconsistency here will draw on probabilistic considerations, we may conclude that, contrary to what is commonly assumed, in adopting probabilistic reasoning, the atheist need *not* abandon the enterprise of showing the inconsistency of theistic beliefs.

Schellenberg, J L. *Divine Hiddenness and Human Reason*. Ithaca, Cornell Univ Pr, 1993.

In this work, I explore the possibility of an argument for atheism from the absence of strong evidence for theism. Part I develops (what I take to be) the most forceful version of the argument. Part II considers and criticizes the various actual and possible replies: suggestions of Pascal, Butler, Kierkegaard, Hick, Swinburne, and others in favor of Divine hiddenness. Certain arguments for their conclusion never given before are weighed and found wanting. I conclude that there is here a serious threat to theistic belief, to which theists must seek to respond.

Scheman, Naomi. *Engenderings: Constructions of Knowledge, Authority, and Privilege*. New York, Routledge, 1993.

Engenderings argues that the problems of philosophy (notably as inherited from Descartes) emerge not from the human condition but from conditions of privilege. The essays decipher the encoded privilege in philosophers' pictures of "our" relations to the world while investigating pictures accountable to a different "us." Drawing on explorations of subjectivity in novels, films, Shakespearean drama, pedagogy, and visual arts, Scheman examines interconnections of cognition with emotions, bodies, and social contexts. Acknowledging the critiques of those who are marginalized by the academy, she explores the challenges for responsible feminist theorizing from relatively privileged perspectives such as her own.

Scheman, Naomi. Jewish Lesbian Writing: A Review Essay. *Hypatia*, 7(4), 186-194, Fall 92.

Recent writing by Jewish lesbians is characterized by challenging and evocative reflection on themes of home and identity, family and choice, tradition and transformation. This essay is a personal journey through some of this writing. An exploration of the obvious and troubling tensions between lesbian or feminist and Jewish identities leads to the paradoxical but ultimately unsurprising suggesting that lesbian identity and eroticism can provide a route of return to and affirmation of Jewish identity.

Scheman, Naomi. Who is that Masked Woman? Reflections on Power, Privilege, and Home-ophobia in Revisioning Philosophy, Ogilvy, James (ed). Albany, SUNY Pr, 1992.

Schenk, David J. Smith's *Felt Meanings of the World*: An Internal Critique. *J Speculative Phil*, 7(1), 21-38, 1993.

Schenkeveld, Dirk M. The Lacuna at Aristotle's *Poetics* 1457b33. *Amer J Philo*, 114(1), 85-89, Spr 93.

With the help of *Papyrus Hamburgensis* 128 (so-called Theophrastus papyrus) the lacuna at *Poetics* 1457b33 can be partly filled in and its presence explained. Aristotle's discussion of *kosmos* ('ornament = papyrus' *epitheton*) will have ended with remarks on privative adjectives, as the papyrus does. The last example may well have been *phialên aoinon* (cf., *Rhet* 1408a6-9), which is the last example in Aristotle's discussion of metaphor (b33). The loss of the discussion on *kosmos* is then caused by *saut du même au même*.

Scherer, Donald and Stuart, James. Introductory Logic Through Multiple Modes of Presentation. *Teach Phil*, 14(4), 389-397, D 91.

Students' grades have shown sustained statistically significant improvement since the reformating of instruction in the large, intro logic course. Previously students received large lecture instruction twice weekly, followed by discussion of exercises in the third weekly meeting. Twenty-six newly made videotapes allow students to see high quality presentations followed immediately by discussion in groups of 36, coupled with guided use of LogicWorks in groups of 24 at the third session. The findings confirm the efficacy of responding to differences in student learning styles. The findings suggest means of combining the advantages of technological and human instruction. Students have retained positive attitudes toward the video presentations; prepared, outlined presentation notes; LogicWorks and their graduate student instructors. They have also affirmed that the standard intro logic text used in the course is not helpful to learning and its replacement is scheduled.

Scherer, Klaus R (ed). *Justice: Interdisciplinary Perspectives*. New York, Cambridge Univ Pr, 1992.

The author brings together leading scholars from the social sciences to discuss recent theoretical and empirical studies of justice. They examine the nature of justice from the current perspectives of philosophy, economics, law, sociology, psychology, and explore possible lines of convergence. A critical examination of theories of justice from Plato and Aristotle, through Marx, to Rawls and Habermas heads a collection which addresses the role of justice in economics and the law and which evaluates contemporary sociological and psychological stances in relation to justice, distributive and procedural. (edited)

Scheuerman, Bill. Modernist Anti-Modernism: Carl Schmitt's Concept of the Political. *Phil Soc Crit*, 19(2), 79-96, 1993.

Scheuerman, Bill. Neumann versus Habermas: The Frankfurt School and the Case of the Rule of Law. *Praxis Int*, 13(1), 50-67, Ap 93.

On the basis of a comparison of the views of Habermas and one of his predecessors at the Institute for Social Research, Franz L Neumann, on the relationship of the rule of law to democracy, the essay 1) defends Habermas' democratic theory while 2) arguing that Habermas needs to acknowledge the virtues of Neumann's idiosyncratic left-wing defense of classical Formal law.

Schiavone, Giuseppe and Colombo, Arrigo (ed). *L'Utopia nella Storia: La Rivoluzione Inglese*. Bari, Dedalo, 1992.

First, the book recalls the historical significance of utopia, as the design of a just and fraternal society, and the process of its construction, which pervades and inspires and defines the whole of history. Second, to contribute to a *revaluation* of the English Revolution, which is the basis of the modern movement towards freedom. (edited)

Schick, Frederic. Cooperation and Contracts. *Econ Phil*, 8(2), 209-229, O 92.

This paper discusses several versions of the *new* contractarianism, which holds that rational parties to a contract will often keep themselves to it, that voluntary cooperation is often rational, even in prisoners'- dilemma situations. It examines the theories of Michael Taylor, Nigel Howard, and David Gauthier. Taylor's supergame equilibrium analysis is argued to be the most promising, but it is shown that it does not establish the unique rationality of joint cooperation, Taylor's analysis failing because it neglects certain strategies of exploitation which, in the context of other strategies, keep a supergame from having a solution.

Schick, Frederic. *Understanding Action: An Essay on Reasons*. New York, Cambridge Univ Pr, 1991.

This is a book about reasons for actions. It goes beyond the usual belief-desire model by adding a third dimension, that of how people see or understand their situations, options, and prospects. It argues not only that people's understandings are an independent factor in motivation, but that the logic of rationality must take the agent's understandings into account. The logic is thus an intensional one, and it is shown how the turn to intentionality resolves a number of currently debated problems: the problems of conflict and weakness of will, Allais' problem, Kahneman and Tversky's problems, Newcomb's problem, and others.

Schick Jr, Theodore W. The Epistemic Role of Qualitative Content. *Phil Phenomenol Res*, 52(2), 383-393, Je 92.

Empiricists take qualitative content to be part of the meaning of mental terms, for they believe that one cannot know what a mental term like "pain" means unless one has experienced pain. Eliminative materialists disagree, claiming that the meaning of a term is determined by its causal/relational properties, and that one can know these without knowing its qualitative content. I argue that those with a knowledge of qualitative content have a better understanding than those who don't, for not only are they better able to use mental terms, but they also know why they are used as they are.

Schiemann, Gregor. Totalität oder Zweckmässigkeit: Kants Ringen mit dem Mannigfaltigen der Erfahrung im Ausgag der Vernunftkritik. *Kantstudien*, 83(3), 294-303, 1992.

The transcendental deduction of ideas that Kant undertakes in the "Appendix to the Transcendental Dialectic" of his "Critique of Pure Reason" is interpreted as a reaction to the threatening variety of experience. As far as this strengthens reason it corresponds to the theory of experience that was developed in the "Critique". At the same time, however, it endangers the balance between the variety and the unity of experience. An alternative and more appropriate solution is attempted in the "Critique of Judgment" where Kant replaces his concern with the ideas of reason (soul, world, and god) by the principle of purposiveness.

Schiffer, Stephen. Boghossian on Externalism and Inference in Rationality in Epistemology, Villanueva, Enrique (ed). Atascadero, Ridgeview, 1992.

Schiffer, Stephen. Compositional Supervenience Theories and Compositional Meaning Theories. *Analysis*, 53(1), 24-29, Ja 93.

Schiffer, Stephen. How to Build a Person: A Prolegomenon. *Phil Phenomenol Res*, 52(3), 713-724, S 92.

Schipper, Lewis. *Spinoza's Ethics: The View from Within*. New York, Lang, 1993.

Schiralli, Martin. Educational Philosophy and Commitment. *Eidos*, 10(1), 63-68, J-Jl 91.

This essay develops a distinction between "philosophy of education" and "educational philosophy" around the notion of commitment. Philosophy of education is viewed as a second-order philosophical subject: a distinctive set of concepts, problems and purposes subjected to rigorous analysis and evaluation. Educational philosophy contrastively refers to the work of those philosophers whose primary commitment is to the enterprise of education and whose philosophers expertise is dedicated to fostering improvements in the quality and scope of educational activities.

Schirmacher, Wolfgang. Eco-Sophia. *Res Phil Technol*, 9, 125-134, 1989.

Schirn, Matthias. Cuestiones Fundamentales de una Teoría del Significado. *Manuscrito*, 15(1), 37-52, Ap 92.

In this paper I want to discuss some problems to which Donald Davidson's program of a theory of meaning for a natural language gives rise. After some critical introductory remarks, I shall examine the following issues: 1) the semantics of non-assertive sentences, 2) Davidson's holistic conception of word-meaning and sentence-meaning, and 3) the question as to whether one ought to replace the concept of truth, construed as the central concept of a semantic theory, by the concept of verification.

Schlagel, Richard H. Meeting Hume's Skeptical Challenge. *Rev Metaph*, 45(4), 691-711, Je 92.

This article attempts to demonstrate that while Hume's critique of causality and induction was essentially valid at the time due to the lack of knowledge of the "inner natures" and "secret powers" that would justify rational belief in "necessary connections" in nature, this no longer is true. Using recent experimental discoveries of how aspirin functions and what causes Parkinson's disease, and how predictive inferences are derived in particle physics, I show that we do possess the kind of knowledge Hume claimed always would elude us. Were Hume's view correct, neither science nor technology as we know it would be possible.

Schlamm, Leon. Numinous Experience and Religious Language. *Relig Stud*, 28(4), 533-551, D 92.

Schlesinger, George. A Short Defence of Transcience. *Phil Quart*, 43(172), 359-361, Jl 93.

Schlesinger, George. The Scope of Human Autonomy in Our Knowledge of God, Clark, Kelly James (ed). Dordrecht, Kluwer, 1992.

Schlich, Thomas. Making Mistakes in Science: Eduard Pfüger, His Scientific and Professional Concept of Physiology, and His Unsuccessful Theory of Diabetes (1903-1910). *Stud Hist Phil Sci*, 24(3), 411-441, Ag 93.

Using the example of an eminent physiologist's theory on diabetes, the paper aims at showing how it was possible that the same scientist made important discoveries as well as mistakes. The example shows that whether a scientific thesis becomes a mistake is the result of a dispute, not of its inherent wrongness. Furthermore, it is the same way of doing science that leads a scientist to discoveries as well as mistakes. When looking at the process that made a certain scientist put forward a certain thesis at a certain point in time it becomes evident that the social context and the factual content of science are inextricably connected.

Schmaltz, Tad M. Descartes and Malebranche on Mind and Mind-Body Union. *Phil Rev*, 101(2), 281-325, Ap 92.

Schmaus, Warren S. Sociology and Hacking's Trousers. *Proc Phil Sci Ass*, 1, 167-173, 1992.

For Hacking, the word "real", like the sexist expression "wear the trousers", takes its meaning from its negative uses. In this essay, I criticize Hacking's reasons for believing that the objects of study of the social sciences are not real. First I argue that the realism issue in the social sciences concerns not unobservable entities but systems of social classification. I then argue that Hacking's social science nominalism derives from his considering social groups in isolation from the entire social system. I conclude that the social sciences are not relegated to an interior status by their objects of study.

Schmerl, James H. End Extensions of Models of Arithmetic. *Notre Dame J Form Log*, 33(2), 216-219, Spr 92.

A concise proof is presented of Wilkie's Theorem that for every model of Peano Arithmetic there is a diophantine equation having no solution in that model but having a solution in some end extension of that model.

Schmidt, Alfred and Kaspar, Rudolf F. Wittgenstein über Zeit. *Z Phil Forsch*, 46(4), 569-583, O-D 92.

The authors give a survey of Wittgenstein's remarks in connection with problems of time. Wittgenstein never treated the topic systematically — he sometimes used it as an example of how to handle philosophical problems. Working on "Philosophical Remarks", 'time' played a role in the context of the possible truth of solipsism. Also for the later Wittgenstein, problems like "Is only the present moment real?" are interesting, but now Wittgenstein tries to deepen our insight into our common (non-philosophical) concepts of time by construing alternative language games.

Schmidt, David P. Postmodern Interviews in Business Ethics: A Reply to Ronald Green. *Bus Ethics Quart*, 3(3), 279-284, Jl 93.

My objective is to extend Ronald Green's account of postmodernism by asking how postmodern ethicists should interview business people. I note the use of the interview method in current business ethics research. I then present Jeffrey Stout's criticism of Robert Bellah's interview techniques used in *Habits of the Heart*, which prompts questions about what constitutes a postmodern interview. In conclusion I seek clarification about whether and in what sense Ron Green intends to be a "foundationalist postmodern business ethicist."

Schmidt, Dennis J. Economics of Production in Crises in Continental Philosophy, Dallery, Arleen B (ed). Albany, SUNY Pr, 1990.

An examination of the questions of technology, nature and art by means of an analysis of Heidegger's critique of Aristotle. Constant reference is made to Kant's *Critique of Judgment*.

Schmidt Andrade, C. Comunión con el Tú absoluto, según G Marcel. *Pensamiento*, 188(47), 449-467, O-D 91.

La tensión hacia lo Trascendente como "misterio" se hace presente en el pensamiento de G Marcel, que abre un camino hacia el Absoluto y deja al hombre en el umbral de la fe religiosa. El "homo viator" como "hombre problemático", encuentra sentido a su esperanza en su propio ser, abierto al infinito trascendente manifestado como presencia e invocación al diálogo.

Schmidtz, David. Reasons for Altruism. *Soc Phil Pol*, 10(1), 52-68, Wint 93.

As part of a larger project exploring connections between rational choice and moral agency, this article asks how someone who was not already other-regarding could be led by self-regarding concerns to cultivate concern and respect for others. The question may seem to take self-regard for granted, as requiring no explanation. In fact, human self-regard is fragile, and its fragility is one source of its explanatory power. Although we have a certain amount of respect and concern for ourselves, this amount is not unlimited and it is not fixed. It is influenced by our choices, which bears on how regard for others fits into the lives of self-regarding human agents.

Schmidtz, David. Reasons for Altruism in Altruism, Paul, Ellen Frankel (ed). New York, Cambridge Univ Pr, 1993.

Why have anything other than purely self-regarding preferences? If we were not already other-regarding, would it be rational to nurture our latent regard for others? These questions may seem to take self-regard for granted, as requiring no explanation. In fact, human self-regard is fragile, and its fragility is one source of its explanatory power. There are things we have to do to sustain our self-regard, and

this fact bears on how regard for others fits into the lives of self-regarding human agents.

Schmitt, Francis O. A Prescription for Generating a New Paradigm in the Context of Science and Theology. *Zygon*, 27(4), 437-454, D 92.

Many centers are now active in the study of the interaction between science on the one hand and theology on the other. Suggestions are made as to how such study might be furthered. The central proposal in this paper is based on the author's experience in founding and, over many years, operating the Neurosciences Research Program (NRP). The "faculty" of this group were highly competent in many fields of science and were able to deal with many of the major issues. It is here further suggested that if an NRP-like organization were established, capable of productively interacting with both science and theology, it might well generate new concepts and possibly a new paradigm in this context.

Schmitt, Frederick. *Knowledge and Belief*. New York, Routledge, 1992.

This book examines the debate between epistemological internalists, who hold that justification must be accessible to the subject or constituted by the subject's epistemic perspective, and externalists, who see justified belief as a nonperspectival relation between the subject and the environment. The author contests the popular view that internalism is the historically dominant epistemology by examining the works of Plato, Descartes, and Hume, as well as those of the Stoics and the Academic and Pyrrhonian skeptics. He then argues at length against many forms of internalism and develops an externalist, reliabilist epistemology.

Schmitt, Richard. Nurturing Fathers—Some Reflections About Caring. *J Soc Phil*, 24(1), 138-151, Spr 93.

May and Strikwerda distinguished different kinds of fathers and recommended that we be "caring" fathers. "Caring" is a much overused term that needs clarification. Drawing on feminist theory, I develop a being-in-relation sense of caring that considers caring to be a reciprocal relation. Different senses of reciprocity are then distinguished and some examples round out the discussion.

Schmitz, François. Vérité et sens: retour à Frege. *Rev Int Phil*, 46(183), 505-526, 1992.

This paper deals with the question whether Frege's *Sinn* could offer a ground for a scientific intensional semantics for natural languages, eventually in J Katz's fashion. It tries to show that, in Frege's own perspective, the *Sinn/Bedeutung* distinction is intended to preserve the possibility of truth against all kinds of naturalism, and this means here, against the temptation to make the realm of *Sinn* an object of scientific study. So, the key notion is that of truth, and the supposed "meaning theory" in Frege's work is no more that a by-product of the claim that, in logic, one has to begin with truth or "being true".

Schmitz, Heinz-Gerd. The Sign Over the Barber Shop: Annotations on the Problems of Interpretation. *Int Phil Quart*, 33(2), 197-202, Je 93.

Two antithetical positions mark the opposite ends of a scale on which every kind of interpretation can be located: the epistic (J Derrida) and the apositic (Susan Sontag) approach. The article tries to show that episitic interpretation dismantles its object while apositic interpretation is afraid of touching it at all. A position between the extremes can be found with the aid of Heidegger's *Being and Time*: Interpretation of a text is locating it contextually. It means taking it as a sign, which, eventually, leads to the explication of the general context, which constitutes reality.

Schmitz, Hermann. Sind Tiere Bewussthaber? Über die Quelle unserer Du-Evidenz. *Z Phil Forsch*, 46(3), 329-347, Jl-S 92.

Solipsism has a positive part (that there is at least one conscient being) and a negative one (that there is no other than myself); none of them is trivial. As concerns the positive part, the author shows, that Descartes' "cogito ergo sum" is not cogent. He develops everyone's evidence of his being conscient according to the distinction between subjective and objective facts and the paradox of self-ascribing, as well as by the analysis of the dynamic structure of the immediately felt bodily states. On the basis of that, it is shown, that mutual bodily communication, as a dialogue between bodies by means of narrowing and widening, is the origin of the evidence of conscient partners in the case of men as well as in the case of other animals.

Schmitz, John G. Research on Broudy's Theory of the Uses of Schooling. *J Aes Educ*, 26(4), 79-95, Wint 92.

Schmitz, K L. Natural Religion, Morality and Lessing's Ditch. *Amer Cath Phil Quart*, 65, 57-73, 1991.

Schmitz, K L. Theological Clearances: Foreground to a Rational Recovery of God in Prospects for Natural Theology, Long, Eugene Thomas (ed). Washington, Cath Univ Amer Pr, 1992.

Schmitz, Kenneth L. The God of Love. *Thomist*, 57(3), 495-508, Jl 93.

Schmitz, Philipp. Kasuistik: Ein wiederentdecktes Kapitel der Jesuitenmoral. *Theol Phil*, 67(1), 29-59, 1992.

Casuistry is, once again, in great demand. In bioethics as well as in many other ethical areas of applied ethics the discussion of cases has become, once more, the method of advancing ethical knowledge. At the same time the term "casuistry" still solicits negative reactions. With Blaise Pascal's "lettres à un provincial" the so-called morality of the Jesuits has been identified among the culprits. This article, after a brief sketch of history of Jesuit casuistry, brings examples of a practical use of cases and an approach to inductive ethics developed out of such an ethical tradition.

Schmitz-Moormann, Karl. Theology in an Evolutionary Mode. *Zygon*, 27(2), 133-151, Je 92.

Evolution has become the standard way of understanding the world process. Theology has to express traditional faith in the context of the contemporary world. Since the common world view has profoundly changed, from a static world of being into a dynamic world of becoming, theology needs to change its language and its understanding of the universe as God's creation. This understanding of an evolving world is to be used as a theological source. Such a change of perspective necessitates a fundamental reconstructing of theology; for theology, such reconstructing means a renewed understanding of the Creator and of the Incarnation.

AUTHOR INDEX WITH ABSTRACTS 661 **Schroeder, D N**

Schnädelbach, Herbert. The Face in the Sand in Philosophical Interventions in the Unfinished Project of Enlightenment, Honneth, Axel (& other eds). Cambridge, MIT Pr, 1992.

Ausgehend von der verbreitetn, aber unklaren These vom "Tod des Menschen" wird Foucaults Version dargestellt und daraufhin untersucht, ob sie geeignet ist, die Geschichte der Philosophie überzeugend zu strukturieren. Das Ergebnis ist negativ, weil nur die antike Sophistik und Skpesis, der Junghegelianismus (Feuerbach) und der moderne Pragmatismus anthropozentrisch im Sinne Foucaults sind; deswegen beruht Foucaults Sicht der Philosophie als ganzer auf einseitigen Projektionen. Gleichwohl ist sein Grundmodell in 'Les mots et les shoses' treffend für den Pragmatismus und damit auch für die Philosophie von Jürgen Habermas, die sich als eine Varante dieser Denkrichtung verstehen lässt.

Schneewind, J B. Sidgwick and the Cambridge Moralists in Essays on Henry Sidgwick, Schultz, Bart (ed). New York, Cambridge Univ Pr, 1992.

Sidgwick's *Methods of Ethics* arose in large part out of the author's consideration of a kind of argument for God's existence developed (as I show) by his Cambridge predecessors in moral philosophy. They argued that there is a continuous and increasingly clear revelation of himself by God through common moral experience. Sidgwick's examination of common sense morality undermines this argument. It shows common sense to be both utilitarian and egoistic. Neither of them was acceptable as articulating Christian morality. Taken together, they show common sense morality to be incoherent.

Schneewind, Jerome. Autonomy, Obligation, and Virtue in The Cambridge Companion to Kant, Guyer, Paul (ed). New York, Cambridge Univ Pr, 1992.

The essay contains an overview of Kant's moral philosophy. After a short sketch of some of the historical background to the theory, I discuss Kant's idea of autonomy, his belief that it requires a formal moral law, his ideas about how we can apply the law to determine our obligations, and what relation compliance with the law has to virtue. After considering some objections to these views I discuss Kant's approaches to proving the moral law. Finally, I note briefly the bearing of the moral law on metaphysics, history, and religion.

Schneider, Carl E. *Cruzan* and the Constitutionalization of American Life. *J Med Phil*, 17(6), 589-604, D 92.

In America today, public policy governing an increasing number of social issues is made through the judicial enforcement of constitutional rights. *Cruzan* raised the question whether policy regarding the withdrawal of medical care from incompetent patients is to be handled similarly. This essay argues that privacy-rights doctrine provides a poor basis for constructing public policy in this area. It suggests that the Court has been unable to articulate a convincing basis for privacy rights and that the basis the Court seems to assume poorly fits many circumstances to which it is applied. The essay further contends that the Court has been unable to describe a persuasive method of analyzing the state interests that are at stake in privacy cases and to accommodate those interests in a reasonable way. The essay concludes that these are issues as to which policy is better formed through a political, not judicial, process.

Schneider, Hans Julius. Comment on M H Bickhard and R L Campbell, 'Some Foundational Questions Concerning Language Studies'. *J Prag*, 17(5-6), 523-525, Je 92.

Schobinger, Jean-Pierre. Operationale Aufmerksamkeit in der textimmanenten Auslegung. *Frei Z Phil Theol*, 39(1-2), 5-38, 1992.

Schockenhoff, Eberhard. Personsein und Menschendwürde bei Thomas von Aquin and Martin Luther. *Theol Phil*, 65(4), 481-512, 1990.

Schönfeld, Martin. Who or What Has Moral Standing?. *Amer Phil Quart*, 29(4), 353-362, O 92.

Schönrich, Gerhard. Zähmung des Bösen? Überlegungen zu Kant vor dem Hintergrund der Leibnizschen Theodizee. *Z Phil Forsch*, 46(2), 205-223, Ap-J 92.

The article delineates the two different ways in which Kant tried to cope with the problem of the evil in his ethics. It shows by detailed analysis that Kant failed to give an explanation of the phenomenon in both cases. Kant shared Leibniz's conception of the evil which has the consequence that nobody can be held responsible for the evil. An alternative solution considered by Kant was inacceptable for him because it implies a radical free but unreasonable will. Finally the author presents an adequate conception of the evil in a semiotic reconstruction of the first line of Kant's thought.

Scholz, Oliver R. Introduction: *Reconceptions* in Context. *Synthese*, 95(1), 1-8, Ap 93.

This piece is an introduction to an issue that documents the proceedings of an author's colloquium with Nelson Goodman and Catherine Z Elgin. The focus of the conference was their joint book *Reconceptions in Philosophy and Other Arts and Sciences* (1988). Attention is drawn to some interconnections between *Reconceptions* and earlier work done by Goodman and Elgin on the theory of constructional systems, on the general theory of symbols and its epistemological and metaphysical implications.

Scholz, Oliver R. When is a Picture?. *Synthese*, 95(1), 95-106, Ap 93.

Philosophical discussions of depiction sometimes suffer from a lack of differentiation between several questions concerning the 'nature' of pictorial representations. To provide a suitable framework I distinguish six such questions and several levels on which one might want to proceed in order to answer some of them. With this background, I reconstruct Goodman's and Elgin's answer to the specific question: 'What distinguishes the pictorial from the verbal or linguistic?' I try to reveal some major motivations behind their system-oriented approach and to indicate some reasons why a strategy of this kind is to a certain extent mandatory to grasp the 'nature of the pictorial'. The system-relative and functional character of depiction has to be captured by every adequate theory.

Scholze, Wolfgang. Human Rights between Universalism and Relativism. *Quest*, 6(1), 56-68, Je 92.

Schopenhauer, Arthur and Payne, E F J (trans). *On the Will in Nature — Schopenhauer*. New York, St Martin's Pr, 1991.

Schopp, Robert F. *Automatism, Insanity, and the Psychology of Criminal Responsibility: A Philosophical Inquiry*. New York, Cambridge Univ Pr, 1991.

This book provides a conceptually coherent and morally defensible account of the psychology of criminal responsibility. The theory draws upon philosophic, legal, and psychological literature in order to advance an integrated account of the voluntary act requirement, *mens rea*, and certain general defenses that address the exculpatory significance of psychopathology. In contrast to many prior investigations, it emphasizes the structure of offense elements, addressing the insanity and automatism defenses as ancillary components of a comprehensive system of offense elements and defenses, and interpreting the exculpatory force of psychopathology by examining the nature of the dysfunction involved in that pathology.

Schotsmans, P. The Patient in a Persistent Vegetative State: An Ethical Re-Appraisal. *Bijdragen*, 54(1), 2-18, 1993.

Patients in a persistent vegetative state (PSV-patients) have permanently lost the function of the cerebral cortex. Prolonged survival depends only on basic nursing care and on adequate nutrition by nasogastric or gastrostomy tube. It seems legitimate to enquire about the duty to provide artificial nutrition and hydration to such patients. For the reason that medicine does not really know what these patients experience, French neurologists state that we should take into account that they could experience pain. This position, if valid, would fundamentally change the discussion on the withdrawal or withholding of nutrition and hydration. To withdraw life support, such as artificial nutrition and hydration does not amount to "abandonment" of the patient. When technical means of supporting life are withdrawn, the obligation to care for the patient continues during the dying process.

Schott, Linda. Jane Addams and William James on Alternatives to War. *J Hist Ideas*, 54(2), 241-254, Ap 93.

This article compares James's "The Moral Equivalence of War" (1910) with the "moral substitute for war" proposed by Addams in *Newer Ideals of Peace* (1907). Addams and James agreed that war appealed to human desires for self-sacrifice and adventure and tried to formulate alternative methods of satisfying these desires. Nineteenth century gender roles shaped their proposals. James proposed mandatory public service for elite young men; Addams proposed a heightened emphasis on nurturing others. Addams's plan offered women's work and values as priorities for all people; James's plan presumed and perpetuated traditional gender roles and characteristics.

Schrader, David. *The Corporation as Anomaly*. New York, Cambridge Univ Pr, 1993.

This book discusses the rise of the marginalist conception of the firm over the past two centuries, and argues that economists continue to defend that theory, despite its demonstrable shortcomings, not because of any comparative advantage in empirical or predictive power, but by virtue of its being a part of the broader marginalist economic program. It concludes that an economic theory that does justice to a world in which managerial corporations are key agents of production must generate a theory of collective action to bolster the theory of individual action that forms the present basis for most economic thinking.

Schrag, Calvin. *The Resources of Rationality: A Response to the Postmodern Challenge*. Bloomington, Indiana Univ Pr, 1992.

The book addresses the postmodern assault on the claims of reason and develops a refigured notion of rationality to meet the charges and challenges of postmodern thinking. The author works out a new perspective, which he names "the transversal rationality of praxis". With the concept of transversality as a binding theme, the author identifies and delineates the function of three specific resources of reason—praxial critique, articulation, and disclosure. Cutting across multiple and changing discursive and social practices, transversal thinking charts a new course between the classical and modern overdetermination of rationality and the dissolution of the rational subject in postmodern philosophy.

Schrag, Calvin and Miller, David James. Communication Studies and Philosophy in The Critical Turn, Angus, Ian (ed). Carbondale, So Illinois Univ Pr, 1993.

Schramm, Alfred. Doubt, Scepticism, and a Serious Justification Game. *Grazer Phil Stud*, 40, 71-87, 1991.

Keith Lehrer describes in his *Theory of Knowledge* a Justification Game which is played by a Claimant who tries to establish his justification for some contingent claim and a rather harmless skeptic who tries to stop the Claimant. The doubts of a serious philosophical skeptic are—in opposition to Lehrer—analyzed as doubts concerning the justification of our beliefs and not their contents. Making the reglementations for a solid philosophical argumentation more precise the setting of a Serious Justification Game is defined and thus replaying the game it turns out that the philosophical skeptic succeeds in providing a profound philosophical argumentation for his denial of Lehrer's positive claim for justification.

Schrift, Alan D. Between Church and State: Nietzsche, Deleuze and the Genealogy of Psychoanalysis. *Int Stud Phil*, 24(2), 41-52, 1992.

Taking as its starting point their remark that the psychoanalyst is the modern incarnation of Nietzsche's ascetic priests, this paper examines how Deleuze and Guattari's critique of psychoanalysis in *Anti-Oedipus* follows an analytic pattern modelled on Nietzsche's argument in *On the Genealogy of Morals*. Focusing on the productivity of desire/will to power and the theme of becomings, I show how Deleuze and Nietzsche share assumptions concerning the genealogy of church and state in terms of the diverse manifestations of desire and power.

Schroeder, D N. Aristotle on the Good of Virtue-Friendship. *Hist Polit Thought*, 13(2), 203-218, Sum 92.

Of the types of friendship, Aristotle regards as perfect friendships between good men because they are good. Why good men need virtue- friends is a question because a good man is self-sufficient; a need for anything would imply a lack of self-sufficiency. The conflicting interpretations of Aristotle's answer to this question are rejected because they reduce the good of virtue- friendship to either instrumental value or are based on a misreading of the text. Virtue-friendship is an essential aspect of the life of virtue. Virtue-friends, as "other selves" are constitutive rather than instrumental contributions to happiness by becoming an aspect of what it means to be a good person.

Schroeder, Severin. 'Too Low!': Frank Cioffi on Wittgenstein's *Lectures on Aesthetics*. *Phil Invest*, 16(4), 261-279, O 93.

The purpose of this article is to elucidate *Wittgenstein's account of expressions of aesthetic discontent* and to defend it against criticism levelled against it by Frank Cioffi in his "Aesthetic Explanation and Aesthetic Perplexity" (1976). Several of Cioffi's examples are discussed in some detail and his claim that — *pace* Wittgenstein — aesthetic reactions are causal explanations is rebutted.

Schroeder, Steven. The End of History. *J Soc Phil*, 23(2), 127-141, Fall 92.

This article begins with "the end of history" as developed by Hegel, Marx, Kojève, and Fukuyama, then examines the interaction of language about the end with *ethics* and *politics*. The bulk of the article is devoted to a discussion of "Marxist" eschatology and analysis of the " new world order" formulated under the influence of Fukuyama beginning as early as 1989. This "new" world order serves as a case study on the impact of eschatological consciousness on *political* morality. "Marxist" eschatology is offered as a corrective to the "Hegelian" triumphalism of the "new" world order articulated in the aftermath of the Cold War.

Schroeder, William R. Nietzschean Philosophers. *Int Stud Phil*, 24(2), 107-114, 1992.

Nietzsche thought deeply about the possibilities and presuppositions of philosophy throughout his productive life. This paper distills and organizes his thinking on this topic into four complementary, interdependent components: a cognitive component, which seeks a just integration of perspectives; a cultural reconstruction component, which requires becoming physicians to the present and visionaries for the future; an existential component, which demands a specific self-transformation to achieve proper relation to the world and life; and an educative component, which seeks to remove obstacles to this existential transformation from those who are ready for it. Each component is necessary, and achieving the proper relationship between them is sufficient, for becoming the kind of philosopher Nietzsche sought to exemplify and encourage.

Schröder, Jürgen. Searles Auffassung des Verhältnisses von Geist und Körper und ihre Beziehung zur Ideantitätstheorie. *Conceptus*, 25(66), 97-109, 1991.

Searle's theory about the mind-body relation is inadequate in two respects. On the one hand it is a variation of the identity theory and therefore has the same defects. On the other hand it is only able to explain one out of four properties (consciousness, intentionality, subjectivity, mental causation) which Searle maintains are essential to an understanding of the mind. The property in question is mental causation. For the explanation of consciousness and intentionality Searle's theory is too weak and concerning subjectivity he doesn't even try to relate this property to his theory.

Schubarth, Martin. Die Freiheit des Richters. *Stud Phil (Switzerland)*, 49, 193-198, 1990.

Der Verfasser reflektiert über die faktische Freiheit des Richters, insbesondere aufgrund persönlichen Erfahrung als Richter am höchsten schweizerischen Gericht.

Schürmann, Reiner and Janssen, Ian (trans). Conditions of Evil in Deconstruction and the Possibility of Justice, Cornell, Durcilla (ed). New York, Routledge, 1992.

Schütrumpf, Eckart. Aristotle's Theory of Slavery—A Platonic Dilemma. *Ancient Phil*, 13(1), 111-123, Spr 93.

The paper attempts to show that the Aristotelian concept of natural slavery as expounded in *Politics* is largely influenced by Platonic principles, namely that *nature* orders the *body* to be slave and be ruled despotically by the soul (Phaed. 79e). By taking over the Platonic concept that people are placed in a hierarchy according to the rank of their best abilities (*Rep.*), Aristotle makes men, whose best function is performed by the body, by nature slaves of those who excel with their soul. For them Aristotle cannot uphold the Platonic dogma that all rule serves the interest of those governed.

Schufreider, Gregory. A Classical Misunderstanding of Anselm's Argument. *Amer Cath Phil Quart*, 66(4), 489-499, Autumn 92.

Schuhmann, K J. Contents of Consciousness and States of Affairs in Mind, Meaning and Metaphysics, Mulligan, Kevin (ed). Dordrecht, Kluwer, 1990.

Schuhmann, Karl and Avé-Lallemant, Eberhard. Ein Zeitzeuge über die Anfänge der phänomenologischen Bewegung: Theodor Conrads Bericht aus dem Jahre 1954. *Husserl Stud*, 9(2), 77-90, 1992.

Schuhmann, Karl and Mulligan, Kevin. Two Letters from Marty to Husserl in Mind, Meaning and Metaphysics, Mulligan, Kevin (ed). Dordrecht, Kluwer, 1990.

Two letters from Marty to Husserl are given together with English translations and a brief commentary. The two letters deal with intentionality and the status of immanent objects.

Schuler, Jeanne and Murray, J Patrick. Historical Materialism Revisited in Terrorism, Justice and Social Values, Peden, Creighton W (ed). Lewiston, Mellen Pr, 1990.

The authors discuss Habermas's revival of historical materialism. Unlike dogmatic Marxists, Habermas's theory resembles the "reconstructive science" of Piaget; it concerns the developmental logic of history. Three interests—technical, communicative, and expressive—underlie the species' evolution. Progress involves an interplay between technical crisis (e.g., the Great Depression) and responses that embody new norms (e.g., more egalitarian social relations). While systems crisis do not necessarily provoke moral growth, Habermas shares Kant's hope in enlightenment. The authors question whether an encompassing framework hinders Habermas's critical project. He also stirs up controversies by presupposing Kohlberg's moral scale—crown with Habermas's discourse ethic—as the yardstick of progress.

Schuler, Jeanne A and Murray, Patrick. Educating the Passions: Reconsidering David Hume's Optimistic Appraisal of Commerce. *Hist Euro Ideas*, 17(5), 589-598, S 93.

Schulte, Joachim. Adelheid and the Bishop—What's the Game? in Wittgenstein's Philosophical Investigations, Arrington, Robert L (ed). New York, Routledge, 1991.

Schulte, Joachim. The Happy Man in Criss-Crossing A Philosophical Landscape, Schulte, Joachim (ed). Amsterdam, Rodopi, 1992.

The question of who or what the happy man mentioned in Wittgenstein's *Tractatus* really is leads to a discussion of connected issues, e.g., the question of the Schopenhauerian origins of certain key notions of Wittgenstein's early philosophy, the import of the concept of a world-soul (with its Goethian overtones), the topic of solipsism, and the puzzling question of what is involved in the self's identification with the world.

Schulte, Joachim (ed) and Sundholm, Göran (ed). *Criss-Crossing A Philosophical Landscape*. Amsterdam, Rodopi, 1992.

Schulte-Sasse, Jochen. Aesthetic Illusion in the Eighteenth Century in Aesthetic Illusion, Burwick, Frederick (ed). Hawthorne, de Gruyter, 1990.

Schulthess, Daniel. Reid and Lehrer: Metamind in History. *Grazer Phil Stud*, 40, 135-147, 1991.

The contrast between Thomas Reid's epistemological concerns and a common core of the classical approach to epistemology is the following one: Reid abandons the classical use for *criteria* of knowledge and pushes the problem of the justification of beliefs to the level of the mental faculties from which the beliefs arise. A similar shift plays various roles in Keith Lehrer's coherentist epistemology. However, this shift raises several difficulties: 1) the impact of epistemological concerns on actual intellectual inquiries gets lost; 2) the favored model of justification lacks in generality; 3) 'vertical justification' (which proceeds *via* the faculty) is not independent from 'horizontal justification' (not proceeding *via* the faculty).

Schulthess, Peter. Gegenwart Ockhams?. *Z Phil Forsch*, 46(2), 295-303, Ap-J 92.

Schulthess, Peter. Satztheorien: Texte zur Sprachphilosophie und Wissenschaftstheorie im 14. Jahrhundert. *Frei Z Phil Theol*, 39(3), 501-512, 1992.

The article discusses several aspects and solutions presented in the 14th century (e.g., by William Ockham, Walter Chatton, Gregor of Rimini) on the signification of a proposition or sentence (complex significable).

Schultz, Bart (ed). *Essays on Henry Sidgwick*. New York, Cambridge Univ Pr, 1992.

Schultz, Bart. Henry Sigwick Today in Essays on Henry Sidgwick, Schultz, Bart (ed). New York, Cambridge Univ Pr, 1992.

Schultz, Lorenz. By Their Fruit You Shall Know Them: Eschatological and Legal Elements in Peirce's Philosophy in Peirce and Law, Kevelson, Roberta. New York, Lang, 1991.

Schultz, Walter. The Contribution of Advaita Vedanta to the Quest for an Effective Reassertion of the Eternal. *J Dharma*, 16(4), 387-397, O-D 91.

Schultz, William R and Fried, Lewis L B. *Jacques Derrida: An Annotated Primary and Secondary Bibliography*. Hamden, Garland, 1992.

The book attempts to be comprehensive rather than selective, and is extensively annotated. It lists primary and secondary works from the year of Derrida's Master's thesis (1954) and extends into 1991.

Schum, David A. Jonathan Cohen and Thomas Bayes on the Analysis of Chains of Reasoning in Probability and Rationality, Eells, Ellery (ed). Amsterdam, Rodopi, 1991.

Here is a Baconian and a Bayesian analysis of a chain of reasoning involving a credibility-testimony problem. The purpose of this analysis is to show that Jonathan Cohen's system of Baconian probabilities applied to a chain of reasoning produces results that are entirely complementary to results obtained when the same chain is analyzed in terms of Bayesian likelihood ratios. The Baconian analysis provides a hedge on conclusions in terms of evidential completeness; the Bayesian analysis provides a hedge in terms of the (conventional) probabilistic strength of the evidence. In many situations both hedges are necessary.

Schumacher, Thomas. Heilung im Denken: Zur Sache der philosophischen Tröstung bei Boethius. *Frei Z Phil Theol*, 40(1-2), 20-43, 1993.

The completeness of Boethius' work *De Consolatione Philosophiae* is an unsettled question in the interpretative literature. Either the question is not addressed or passages are taken as grounds to doubt whether the text in its present form is in fact the test Boethius had originally conceived. For the first time the attempt has been made to consider the development and progression of Boethius' thought from a thematic perspective and the question is posed as to what Boethius actually intended. Boethius' argumentation is found to be astonishingly consistent and overcomes any doubts as to whether the text reaches its intended purpose.

Schumaker, Millard. *Sharing without Reckoning*. Waterloo, Wilfrid Laurier U Pr, 1992.

A discussion of "perfect" and "imperfect" rights and duties, *Sharing Without Reckoning* examines the use of the distinction in jurisprudential, philosophical and religious material from Classical times until the present; proposes a connection between imperfect right and the "norms of reciprocity" (as that complex set of ideas has been developed in anthropology and sociology); and argues that contemporary understandings of the nature of morality and of moral reasoning would be well served by the reintroduction of this traditional doctrine. The book includes a chapter reassessing the role of imperfect obligation in the thought of Immanuel Kant. Extensive bibliography.

Schurz, Gerhard. Relevant Deductive Inference: Criteria and Logics in Advances in Scientific Philosophy, Schurz, Gerhard (ed). Amsterdam, Rodopi, 1991.

Chapter 1 of this paper is a reply to the paper of Sylvan and Nola in the same volume about two rivalizing approaches of solving paradoxes of deductivism: the *logical* approach, which tries to solve them by constructing a new nonclassical relevance logic (á la Anderson and Belnap), and the *critical approach*, which tries to solve them by restricting classical logic with help of additional criteria of relevance. In the

AUTHOR INDEX WITH ABSTRACTS 663 Scowcroft, Philip

subsequent sections, the critical approach is defended and several criteria proposed by various authors are described and compared, among them the variable containment criterion and the replacement criterion. In the final section, a new semantics for the replacement criterion is presented, based on a notion of an articulated proposition.

Schurz, Gerhard (ed) and Dorn, Georg J W (ed). *Advances in Scientific Philosophy*. Amsterdam, Rodopi, 1991.

Papers in honor of Paul Weingartner's 60th Birthday. I, "Advances in Philosophical Logic", relevance logic (Sylvan and Nola, B Smith, Schurz), epistemic logic (Dalla Chiara, Gochet and Gillet, Festini), temporal and intuitionistic logics (Aqvist, Orlowska, Lenzen); II, "Current Challenges in Philosophy of Science", a section of Objectivity in Quantum Mechanics (Enz, Mittlestaedt, Scheibe), Reduction and Unification (Stöckler, Kanitscheider, Haller), the structuralist view of theories (Przelecki, Kuipers, Moulines) and probability (Popper, Dorn); III, "Recent Debates in Semantic and Ontology" (Kutschera, Simons, Morscher, Brandl, Hieke); IV, "Epistemological and Ethical Problems with Society" (Klevakina, Tuomela, Lenk and Maring, Heumaier, Bencivenga); V, "Analytical Philosophy of Religion (Bochenski, Nieznanski, Ganthaler); VI, "Methods of Philosophy" (Kreisel, Bunge, Koj); VII, a bio- and bibliography of Weingartner.

Schuster, Félix G. Historia de la ciencia y comunidades científicas. *Rev Filosof (Argentina)*, 6(1-2), 3-21, N 92.

Schuurman, Egbert. Crisis in Agriculture: Philosophical Perspective on the Relation Between Agriculture and Nature. *Res Phil Technol*, 12, 191-211, 1992.

The scientific-technical control in agriculture has a lot of advantages, but has caused also a lot of problems. The crisis in agriculture is that there is no agreement in solving such problems. The article makes clear that an implicit prescientific view of science is at stake. Science is used as an unlimited instrument of control. That means that the abstractions of scientific knowledge are projected in agriculture and are in that way reducing the reality and even destructing it. Scientific knowledge ought to obey normative guidelines. Besides, technicism in argiculture and technicization can be can be overcome, when the motive is not alone harvesting but also keeping and maintaining.

Schuurman, Henry J. Two Concepts of Theodicy. *Amer Phil Quart*, 30(3), 209-221, Jl 93.

Schuurman, Paul. Moraliteit en magie?: In reactie op Dieter Lesage. *Alg Ned Tijdschr Wijs*, 84(3), 206-208, Jl 92.

Schwartz, Benjamin. Chinese Culture and the Concept of Community in On Community, Rouner, Leroy S (ed). Notre Dame, Univ Notre Dame Pr, 1992.

Schwartz, Elisabeth. Le jugement de recognition fregéen et la supposition de détermination complète. *Dialectica*, 46(1), 91-114, 1992.

L'héritage kantien dans la philosophie fregéenne de la connaissance est aujourd'hui largement reconnu. La présente analyse porte sur la point, déjà réputé central par J. Vuillemin (1964), du jugement de recongnition. On tente de montrer: 1) le style transcendantal du traitement fregéen du problème des *objets loguques,* dont la nècessité s'introduit à partir des *Grundlagen* avec celle des extensions de concept, absentes de la première idéographie; style dont on tente d'expliquer les changements qu'il opère dans le modèle de la *Bergriffsbildung* kantienne. 2) l'ambiguïté de la recognition fondée par la *source* logique de connaissance d'objets loguques, ou par un principe d'*image* loguque, qu'explicitera Wittgenstein, des invariants les plus géneaux des opératopms de [emsée dans l'idéolographie. 3) le lien du principe de recognition avec une supposition de détermination complète et son ultime formulation dans la théorie de la source géométruqe; ses racines dans la formation mathématique de Frege.

Schwartz, Justin. Functional Explanation and Metaphysical Individualism. *Phil Sci*, 60(2), 278-301, Je 93.

G A Cohen defends and Jon Elster criticizes Marxist use of functional explanation. But Elster's mechanical conception of explanation is, contrary to Elster's claims, a better basis for vindication of functional explanation than Cohen's nomological conception, which cannot provide an adequate account of functional explanation. Elster also objects that functional explanation commits us to metaphysically bizarre collective subjects, but his argument requires an implausible reading of methodological individualism which involves an unattractive eliminativism about social phenomena.

Schwartz, Justin K. From Libertarianism to Egalitarianism. *Soc Theor Pract*, 18(3), 259-288, Fall 92.

Libertarian property rights are often defended by invoking a principle of self-ownership. The argument is that I am entitled to the fruit of my labor—the exercise of my talents and character—because my talents and character are mine, and as long as no one has a prior claim on what I produce by my labor or acquire by voluntary transfer, it would violate my rights to take from me what I so acquire. I show that this argument does not follow. Even if we grant self-ownership for the sake of argument, I have no right to resources I did not produce by exercising my talents and character, but which I need in order to produce anything at all. Moreover, the most natural way to tie self-ownership to property rights to what I produce is to say that I have a right to what I need to exercise my talents and character. The Needs Principle, however, is the basis not for Libertarianism but for a Radical Egalitarianism of the sort advocated by Marx. Self-ownership, therefore, cannot support Libertarianism.

Schwartz, Lewis M. *Arguing About Abortion*. Belmont, Wadsworth, 1992.

Schwartz, Michael Alan and Northoff, Georg and Wiggins, Osborne. Psychosomatics, the Lived Body, and Anthropological Medicine in The Body in Medical Thought and Practice, Leder, Drew (ed). Dordrecht, Kluwer, 1992.

Schwartz, Pedro and Braun, Carlos Rodriguez. Bentham on Spanish Protectionism. *Utilitas*, 4(1), 121-132, My 92.

Schwartz, Richard L. Internal and External Method in the Study of Law. *Law Phil*, 11(3), 179-199, 1992.

Legal theory and scholarship are currently characterized by a division between traditional, doctrinal methods and approaches derived from extra-legal disciplines. This paper proposes a different though related distinction between two methods of understanding law and interpreting authoritative legal texts. Internal method reflects the viewpoint of the participant in a legal system and traditional doctrinal study; it is practical and decision-oriented. The purposes of external method are cognitive and theoretical; it is oriented toward a comprehensive philosophical and scientific rationality. The paper discusses the antecedents of these methods, describes the structure of each and relations between them, and suggests that the criterion of internal method is practical effectiveness, that of external method truth or falsity. (edited)

Schwartz, Robert. On 'What is Said to Be'. *Synthese*, 94(1), 43-54, Ja 93.

This paper reexamines an early article by Noam Chomsky and Israel Scheffler concerning the proper formulation and status of Quine's criterion for ontological commitment. ('What is Said to Be,' *Proceedings of the Aristotelian Society*, 69, 1958-59; reprinted in Scheffler, *Inquiries*.) Somewhat different formulations of the criterion are proposed and their implications explored. It is also argued that Chomsky and Scheffler's views may be seen to foreshadow and lead to some of Quine's later more radical doctrines regarding ontological commitment.

Schwartz, Robert. Works, Works Better. *Erkenntnis*, 38(1), 103-114, Ja 93.

A theory of Goodman and Elgin concerning the individuation of literary works is examined and criticized. An alternative account is offered to meet various of the difficulties in their proposal. In addition, it is suggested that there may not be a *single* account of the notion of a literary work that can best do all the jobs we expect of it.

Schwartz, Sanford. Bergson and the Politics of Vitalism in The Crisis in Modernism, Burwick, Frederick (ed). New York, Cambridge Univ Pr, 1992.

Schwarz, Hans. The Interplay between Science and Theology in Uncovering the Matrix of Human Morality. *Zygon*, 28(1), 61-75, Mr 93.

Theology and the life sciences are mutually dependent on one another in the task of understanding the origin and function of moral behavior. The life sciences investigate morality from the perspective of the historical and communal dimension of humanity and point to survival as the primary function of human behavior. A Christian ethic of self-sacrifice advances the preservation of the entire human and nonhuman creation and should not, therefore, be objected to by the life sciences. Religion, however, is more than a survival mechanism. It points to a preserving agency beyond humanity and prevents the life sciences from reducing life to its strictly biological side.

Schwegman, Marjan. 'Ieder ding op zijn eigen plaats'. *Kennis Methode*, 17(1), 12-29, 1993.

Schweickart, Patrocinio P. In Defense of Femininity: Commentary on Sandra Bartky's *Femininity and Domination*. *Hypatia*, 8(1), 178-191, Wint 93.

According to Bartky, "To be a feminist, one has first to become one", and to become a feminist, one has to overcome femininity. Although I agree with Bartky's critique of femininity, I argue that feminist consciousness has to involve a contradictory attitude toward femininity—not just a critique, but also an appreciation of the utopian values it harbors.

Schweid, Eliezer. Theodicy in the Book of Job (in Hebrew). *Iyyun*, 42, 227-247, Ap 93.

Schwendtner, Tibor. Parallels in the Conception of Science of Heidegger and Kuhn (in Hungarian). *Magyar Filozof Szemle*, 3, 285-315, 1991.

Scigala, Ireneusz T. Are People Programmed to be Normal? in Probability and Rationality, Eells, Ellery (ed). Amsterdam, Rodopi, 1991.

Scott, Charles E. Foucault, Ethics, and the Fragmented Subject. *Res Phenomenol*, 22, 104-137, 1992.

Scott, Charles E. Nonbelonging/Authenticity in Reading Heidegger: Commemorations, Sallis, John (ed). Bloomington, Indiana Univ Pr, 1992.

Scott, Charles E (ed) and Dallery, Arleen B (ed) and Roberts, P Holley (ed). *Crises in Continental Philosophy*. Albany, SUNY Pr, 1990.

Scott, Charles E (ed) and Dallery, Arleen B (ed) and Roberts, P Holley (ed). *Ethics and Danger*. Albany, SUNY Pr, 1992.

Scott, D. Socrate prend-il au sérieux le paradoxe de Ménon?. *Rev Phil Fr*, 4, 627-641, O-D 91.

Scott, Eugenie C. Us and Them, Nature and Humanism. *Free Inq*, 13(2), 14-15, Spr 93.

Scott, G E. *Moral Personhood: An Essay in the Philosophy of Moral Psychology*. Albany, SUNY Pr, 1990.

Scott, Jeffrey L. Implications of Environment-Trial Interaction for Evolutionary Epistemology. *Kinesis*, 19(2), 13-24, Sum 93.

It is argued that there are some critical and yet unaccounted-for aspects of the general process of evolution that have interesting implications for both cognitive and conceptual evolution. These aspects, directed variation and prepared environments, require emendations to the basic models of evolution that are of interest to an evolutionary perspective in epistemology.

Scott, Jonathan. The law of War: Grotius, Sidney, Locke and the Political Theory of Rebellion. *Hist Polit Thought*, 13(4), 565-585, Wint 92.

Scott, Philip and Fleischer, Isidore. An Algebraic Treatment of the Barwise Compactness Theory. *Stud Log*, 50(2), 217-223, Je 91.

A theorem on the extendability of certain subsets of a Boolean algebra to ultrafilters which preserve countably many infinite meets (generalizing Rasiowa-Sikorski) is used to pinpoint the mechanism of the Barwise proof in a way which bypasses the set theoretical elaborations.

Scott, R Taylor. William H Poteat: *A Laudatio*. *Tradition Discovery*, 20(1), 6-12, 1993-94.

Scowcroft, Philip and Macintyre, Angus. On the Elimination of Imaginaries from Certain Valued Fields. *Annals Pure Applied Log*, 61(3), 241-276, Je 93.

A nontrivial ring with unit eliminates imaginaries just in case its complete theory has the following property: every definable m-ary equivalence relation $E(x,y)$ may be defined by a formula $f(x)=f(y)$, where f is an m-ary definable function. We show that for certain natural expansions of the field of p-adic numbers, elimination of imaginaries fails or is independent of ZFC. Similar results hold for certain fields of formal power series.

Screech, M A. *Montaigne and Melancholy: The Wisdom of the "Essays"*. New York, Penguin USA, 1983.

Scruton, Roger. Contract, Consent and Exploitation in Essays on Kant's Political Philosophy, Williams, Howard (ed). Chicago, Univ of Chicago Pr, 1992.

A discussion of Kant's hypothetical contract, showing its relation to the categorical imperative. An attempt to show the true conflict between ideas of consensual order in free-market thinking and in socialist thinking. Discussion of the Kantian input into Marx, Rawls and Nozick.

Scudder Jr, John R and Bishop, Anne H. Recovering the Moral Sense of Health Care from Academic Reification in Analecta Husserliana, XXXI, Tymieniecka, Anna-Teresa (ed). Dordrecht, Kluwer, 1990.

Scully, Sam and Daniels, Charles B. Pity, Fear, and Catharsis in Aristotle's Poetics. *Nous*, 26(2), 204-217, Je 92.

The question addressed in this paper is whether Aristotle's analysis of tragedy the production of pity, fear, and a catharsis of these emotions *in audiences*—readers, auditors, or viewers—is *essential* to works of dramatic tragedy, or to good ones. Taking Aristotle passage by passage, the authors argue that it is not. Among the distinctions brought to bear are (1) real life actions and responses in contradistinction to make-believe ones and (2) felt emotions in contradistinction to typically felt emotions or emotional characterizations of actions, events, incidents, and situations.

Seabright, Paul. Commentator on 'Distributing Health' in The Quality of Life, Nussbaum, Martha C (ed). New York, Oxford Univ Pr, 1993.

Seabright, Paul. Pluralism and the Standard of Living in The Quality of Life, Nussbaum, Martha C (ed). New York, Oxford Univ Pr, 1993.

Seager, William. Externalism and Token Identity. *Phil Quart*, 42(169), 439-448, O 92.

Donald Davidson espouses two fundamental theses about the individuation of mental events. The thesis of causal individuation asserts that sameness of cause and effect is sufficient and necessary for event identity. The thesis of content individuation gives only a sufficient condition for difference of mental events: if e and f have different contents then they are different mental events. I argue that given these theses, psychological externalism—the view that mental content is determined by factors external to the subject of the relevant mental events—entails that the token identity theory is false.

Seager, William. Fodor's Theory of Content: Problems and Objections. *Phil Sci*, 60(2), 262-277, Je 93.

Jerry Fodor has recently proposed a new entry into the list of information based approaches to semantic content aimed at explicating the general notion of representation for both mental states and linguistic tokens. The basic idea is that a token *means* what causes its production. The burden of the theory is to select the proper cause from the sea of causal influences which aid in generating any token while at the same time avoiding the absurdity of everything's being literally meaningful (since everything has a cause). I argue that a detailed examination of the theory reveals that neither burden can be successfully shouldered.

Seager, William. *Metaphysics of Consciousness*. New York, Routledge, 1992.

Seager, William. The Elimination of Experience. *Phil Phenomenol Res*, 53(2), 345-365, Je 93.

In 'Quining Qualia', and again in *Consciousness Explained*, Daniel Dennett attempts no less than the elimination of qualitative experience (*qualia*). Crudely, the grounds for the elimination are two-fold. First, qualia fall prey to a variety of verificationist difficulties; second, there is no coherent concept of qualia behind our crowd of intuitions. Dennett's attack is serious, detailed and fuelled by a range of fascinating thought experiments. But, I argue, it is ultimately unconvincing. I try to show that there is a fairly minimal conception of qualia which is entirely coherent (though not without its mysteries) and also that Dennett's verificationist attacks are two radical to carry conviction.

Seager, William. Thought and Syntax. *Proc Phil Sci Ass*, 1, 481-491, 1992.

It has been argued that Psychological Externalism is irrelevant to psychology. The grounds for this are that Psychological Externalism fails to individuate intentional states in accord with causal power, and that psychology is primarily interested in the causal roles of psychological states. It is also claimed that one can individuate psychological states via their syntactic structure in some internal "language of thought". This syntactic structure is an internal feature of psychological states and thus provides a key to their causal powers. I argue that in fact any syntactic structure deserving the name will require an external individuation no less than the semantic features of psychological states.

Seager, William. Verificationism, Scepticism, and Consciousness. *Inquiry*, 36(1-2), 113-133, Mr 93.

I argue that Daniel Dennett's latest book, *Consciousness Explained*, presents a radically eliminativist view of conscious experience in which experience or, in Dennett's own words, actual phenomenology, becomes a merely intentional object of our own and others' judgments 'about' experience. This strategy of 'intentionalizing' consciousness dovetails nicely with Dennett's background model of brain function: cognitive pandemonium, but does not follow from it. Thus Dennett is driven to a series of independent attacks on the notion of conscious experience, many of which depend upon verificationist premises. I do not directly dispute the appeal to verificationism (though many would, I am sure) but rather aim to show that the sort of verificationist arguments that Dennett employs are fundamentally similar to classical sceptical arguments. The philosophical status of such arguments remains perennially unclear, but none of them produce conviction in their ostensible conclusions. I argue that Dennett's verificationist strategy suffers the same fate.

Seamon, Roger. The Story of the Moral: The Function of Thematizing in Literary Criticism. *J Aes Art Crit*, 47(3), 229-236, Sum 89.

Searle, J R. Is There a Problem about Realism? (in Czechoslovakian). *Filozof Cas*, 40(3), 411-433, 1992.

Searle, John R. Reply to Mackey in Working Through Derrida, Madison, Gary B (ed). Evanston, Northwestern Univ Pr, 1993.

Searle, John R. Respones: Reference and Intentionality in John Searle and His Critics, Lepore, Ernest (ed). Cambridge, Blackwell, 1991.

Searle, John R. Response: Applications of the Theory in John Searle and His Critics, Lepore, Ernest (ed). Cambridge, Blackwell, 1991.

Searle, John R. Response: Explanation in the Social Sciences in John Searle and His Critics, Lepore, Ernest (ed). Cambridge, Blackwell, 1991.

Searle, John R. Response: Meaning, Intentionality, and Speech Acts in John Searle and His Critics, LePore, Ernest (ed). Cambridge, Blackwell, 1991.

Searle, John R. Response: Perception and the Satisfactions of Intentionality in John Searle and His Critics, Lepore, Ernest (ed). Cambridge, Blackwell, 1991.

Searle, John R. Response: The Background of Intentionality and Action in John Searle and His Critics, Lepore, Ernest (ed). Cambridge, Blackwell, 1991.

Searle, John R. Response: The Mind-Body Problem in John Searle and His Critics, LePore, Ernest (ed). Cambridge, Blackwell, 1991.

Searle, John R. *The Rediscovery of the Mind*. Cambridge, MIT Pr, 1993.

Searle, John R. The World Turned Upside Down in Working Through Derrida, Madison, Gary B (ed). Evanston, Northwestern Univ Pr, 1993.

Sebeok, Thomas A. *Semiotics in the United States*. Bloomington, Indiana Univ Pr, 1991.

In Part I, this book traces developments of semiotic studies in the United States from their early beginnings to date; Part II deals briefly with organizational matters; and Part III extrapolates from current trends to the future. There are almost twenty-five pages of references.

Secundy, Marian Gray. Response to Kwasi Wiredu in African-American Perspectives on Biomedical Ethics, Flack, Harley E (ed). Washington, Georgetown Univ Pr, 1992.

Seddon, Fred. McAllister on Northrop. *J Phil Res*, 18, 261-269, 1993.

This paper attempts to answer Joseph B McAllister's critique of the epistemology of F S C Northrop. Toward this end an exposition of the essence of Northrop's theory of knowledge is presented and a simple comparison with McAllister's similar effort reveals the latter's deficiencies. I also reveal how McAllister's criticism of Northrop's "supposed" realism depends on equating realism in general with one kind, direct realism. If this is so, then Northrop is neither a skeptic nor a moral or legal relativist.

Sedgwick, Sally S. Hegel's Treatment of Transcendental Apperception in Kant. *Owl Minerva*, 23(2), 151-163, Spr 92.

In order to demystify some essential features in the formation of Hegel's idealism, the author attempts in this paper to reconstruct in sympathetic terms Hegel's early treatment of Kant's conception of transcendental apperception. The aim is to determine not merely what Hegel found objectionable about that conception, but also why he thought that Kant's notion of the transcendental ego or faculty of spontaneity contained the seeds of a "true" or "objective" idealism. The author focusses primarily on Hegel's discussion of Kant in the 1802-03 essay *Faith and Knowledge*, (Glauben und Wissen).

Sedgwick, Sally S. Pippin on Hegel's Critique of Kant. *Int Phil Quart*, 33(3), 273-283, S 93.

The author of this article challenges a central thesis of Robert Pippin's book, *Hegel's Idealism*: namely, that Hegel's idealism is a "completion" or "extension" of an insight first discovered but inadequately developed and appreciated by Kant. It is argued that Pippin does not establish his claim that implicit in the very idea of the transcendental unity of a perception as it is presented in the Transcendental Deduction of the *Critique of Pure Reason* is the key to a form of idealism which resolves the contradictions and dualisms of the Critical philosophy.

Sedley, David. A Platonist Reading of *Theaetetus* 145-147—I. *Aris Soc*, Supp(67), 125-149, 1993.

The anonymous commentator on Plato's *Theaetetus* (perhaps writing in the late first century BC) is a Platonist whose handbook on methodology is Aristotle's *Topics*. His interpretation of *Theaetetus* 145-147, examined in detail in this paper, discovers in the passage much philosophical interest which modern critics have missed. His discussion includes a unique anticipation of G E Moore's Paradox of Analysis.

Sedley, David. Teleology and Myth in the *Phaedo*. *Proc Boston Colloq Anc Phil*, 5, 359-383, 1989.

The myth at the end of Plato's *Phaedo*, it is argued, takes up the earlier demand (Phaedo 96=9) that a proper causal account of the cosmos and its arrangement should be teleological. It thus throws light on Plato's teleological beliefs at this date, and enables us to judge how far these anticipated the definitive *Timaeus* account.

Sedley, David N. Empedocles' Theory of Vision and Theophrastus' 'De Sensibus' in Theophrastus, Fortenbaugh, W W (ed). New Brunswick, Transaction Books, 1992.

Seebass, Gottfried. Freiheit und Determinismus (Teil I). *Z Phil Forsch*, 47(1), 1-22, Ja-Mr 93.

First half of two-part article reconsidering the problem of freedom and determination. Section 1 introduces a broadly Aristotelian notion of determinism. Section 2 argues that determinism implies fatalism in a sense incompatible with our self-understanding as acting human beings. The widespread opinion that this is not the case derives either from inconsistent thinking or from an inadequate conception of fatalism. Section 3 distinguishes different kinds of so-called "compatibilism" and argues that the traditional controversy between compatibilists and incompatibilists is ill-conceived. The real issue is brought into focus, setting the stage for its discussion in the second half of the article.

Seebass, Gottfried. Freiheit und Determinismus (Teil II). *Z Phil Forsch*, 47(2), 223-245, Ap-Je 93.

This is the second half of a two-part article reconsidering the problem of freedom and determinism. Taking up what appeared to be the real issue in the "compatibility" controversy, section 4 distinguishes different senses of "can" and "possible", relevant to the notion of freedom. The question is which sense is necessary to account for our self-understanding as active human beings. Discussing different conceptions of "freedom to act" and "freedom to will" sections 5-6 argue that determinism rules out any sense of "can" which would be adequate. Section 7 summarizes the discussion and shows in what respects the traditional problem, far from being solved at present, still calls for a satisfying solution.

Seeber, Federico Mihura. La figura del polemista cristiano: En las libros "Contra Cresconio" de San Agustín. *Sapientia*, 47(185), 169-194, 1992.

Seebohm, Thomas M. The Preconscious, the Unconscious and the Subconscious: A Phenomenological Critique of the Hermeneutics of the Latent. *Aquinas*, 35(2), 247-271, My-Ag 92.

Seech, Zachary. *Writing Philosophy Papers*. Belmont, Wadsworth, 1993.

Seeger, Matthew W. Ethical Issues in Corporate Speechwriting. *J Bus Ethics*, 11(7), 501-504, Jl 92.

Executive speechwriting is a common practice in most large organizations. This activity, however, raises a number of ethical questions about responsibility and about audience deception. This essay explores the ethics of speechwriting from three perspectives and offers some general guidelines for maintaining ethical standards when using speechwriters.

Seerveld, Calvin S. Vollenhoven's Legacy for Art Historiography. *Phil Reform*, 58(1), 49-79, Ja 93.

Dutch philosopher Vollenhoven (1892-1978) developed an historiographic method for narrating a history of philosophy. Seerveld translates Vollenhoven's basic theses into a three-dimensional cartographic method for writing art history. The basic categorial co-ordinates are discussed and illustrated: 1) cultural period dynamic — European rococo Enlightenment; 2) artistic traditions — several perduring imaginative formats extant; and 3) the actual traces of a footprinted trail an art historian tracks — Watteau's art historical significance.

Seeskin, Kenneth. Poverty and Sincerity in the *Apology*. *Phil Lit*, 16(1), 128-133, Ap 92.

Seeskin, Kenneth. Vlastos on Elenchus and Mathematics. *Ancient Phil*, 13(1), 37-53, Spr 93.

Segal, Hanna. Acting on Phantasy and Acting on Desire in Psychoanalysis, Mind and Art, Hopkins, Jim (ed). Cambridge, Blackwell, 1992.

Segal, Jerome M. *Agency and Alienation: A Theory of Human Presence*. Lanham, Rowman & Littlefield, 1991.

Segal offers a new account of the nature of human agency: The Presence Theory. Agency is understood as the presence of self in a person's activity. Activity rather than basic act is offered and explicated as the fundamental concept of action theory. The self is explicated as the integrated human personality, and the notion of "presence" is explained. Part II develops a theory of alienation as the absence of agency. The experience of self-alienation is explored in philosophic, psychological and political contexts, including three forms of political engagement as typified by Bentham, Trotsky and Gandhi.

Segerberg, Krister. How Many Logically Constant Actions are There?. *Bull Sec Log*, 21(4), 134-139, D 92.

Say that an action is logically constant if it is denoted by a term containing no program letter or propositional letter. It is shown that in a certain propositional dynamic logic containing the author's delta operator there are exactly five logically constant actions.

Segerberg, Krister. Perspectives on Decisions263-. *Proc Aris Soc*, 93, 263-278, 1993.

The title of the paper is ambiguous. On the one hand, decision theory is looked at in the perspective provided by dynamic logic. On the other hand, it is argued that there is an important distinction to be made, in thinking about action, between a first-person and a third-person perspective. By way of example Newcomb's Problem is discussed.

Segre, Vera and Velicogna, Nella Gridelli. Works by Renato Treves. *Ratio Juris*, 6(2), 216-2225, Jl 93.

Seibert, Charles H (trans) and Fink, Eugen and Heidegger, Martin. *Heraclitus Seminar*. Evanston, Northwestern Univ Pr, 1993.

In the winter semester of 1966-67 at the University of Freiburg, Martin Heidegger and Eugen Fink conducted an extraordinary seminar on the fragments of Heraclitus. This book records those conversations, documenting the imaginative and experimental character of the multiplicity of interpretations offered and providing an invaluable portrait of Heidegger involved in active discussion and explication. (staff)

Seibt, Johanna. *Properties as Processes: A Synoptic Study of Wilfrid Sellars' Nominalism*. Atascadero, Ridgeview, 1991.

The book traces Sellars' systematic denial of abstract and universal entities in semantics, epistemology, and metaphysics. Part I presents Sellars' interpretation of abstract expressions as interlinguistic functional classifications (linguistic roles). It is argued that Sellars' role-semantic reduction is superior to eliminating second order quantification, undercuts Quine's argument for the indeterminacy of translation, and provides a naturalistic concept of intension within a partly behaviorist, partly functionalist theory of the mental. Part II and III explain the asemanticity of predicates in Sellars' picture theory of empirical truth and show how his process ontology follows from integrating phenomenal qualities into Peirceian scientific realism.

Seidel, George J. *Fichte's "Wissenschaftslehre" of 1794: A Commentary on Part I*. West Lafayette, Purdue Univ Pr, 1993.

Primarily designed as a textbook for graduate and undergraduate students in philosophy the book presents the German and English texts of Part I of Johann Gottlieb Fichte's *Foundations for the Entire Science of Knowledge*, along with commentary. In the introduction to the commentary the author places particular emphasis upon Fichte's relationship to Kant. However, Fichte is viewed not merely as a transitional figure on the march from Kant to Hegel, but as a significant philosopher in his own right. Of special interest to students and scholars of literature is the author's discussion of the Romantic movement's indebtedness to Fichte. The work concludes with a summary of Parts II and III of the *Wissenschaftslehre*. There is also an annotated bibliography.

Seidengart, Jean. La physique moderne comme forme symbolique privilégiée dans l'enterprise philosophique de Cassirer. *Rev Metaph Morale*, 97(4), 491-515, O-D 92.

Cassirer considered Knowledge as the terminating point of the "process of objectification" of human spirit that leads progressively to its self-consciousness through the differential specificity of symbolic forms. We are mainly concerned here with trying to clear up the constitutive law proper to exact sciences. Our analysis starts from the main figures of modern physics as its starting point in order to set our thought on a philosophy of scientifical culture and to draw the main problems related to its achievement as "Weltbegriff."

Seidler, Victor J. Men, Feminism, and Power in Rethinking Masculinity, May, Larry (ed). Lanham, Rowman & Littlefield, 1992.

Seifen, Johannes. *Der Zufall—eine Chimäre?*. Sankt Augustin, Academia, 1992.

Seigfried, Charlene Haddock. James's Natural History Methodology in Frontiers in American Philosophy, Volume I, Burch, Robert W (ed). College Station, Texas A&M Univ Pr, 1992.

I show that James appeals to a 'natural history' methodology in two related, but incompatible ways. One is a version of the positivist scientific belief that experience can be accurately described as it is, apart from any theoretic presuppositions, and the other is an original, phenomenological description of "our nature as thinkers," which exhibits "a triadic structure of impression, reflection and reaction." The unrecognized ambiguity of reference carries over from his psychological to his philosophical writings. I argue that the pragmatically phenomenological method avoids the difficulties inherent in defending the realism of an insufficiently reconstructed empiricist method.

Seigfried, Charlene Haddock. William James's Concrete Analysis of Experience. *Monist*, 75(4), 538-550, O 92.

This article reconstructs William James's psychology, that is, his concrete or phenomenal findings, in light of his radically empiricist philosophical insights. The problem is that James sharply distinguished between the scientifically neutral descriptions of reality of *The Principles of Psychology* and the metaphysical or epistemological reconstructions of such findings in his philosophy of radical empiricism. It is argued that his profound ambivalence about whether we find or create experience must be resolved before the concrete methodology and finding of *Principles* can be fully integrated into the practical hermeneutics of his radical empiricism, both of which constitute his concrete analysis of experience.

Seigfried, Hans. Nietzsche's Natural Morality. *J Value Inq*, 26(3), 423-431, Jl 92.

One could raise two objections against Nietzsche's plan for a revaluation of all values through the "naturalization of morality": (l) the belief that moral values are natural values is as old as morality, and (2) the idea of a natural order is at odds with a thoroughly "aesthetic" philosophy such as Nietzsche's. I argue against these objections that there is something truly innovative and philosophically promising in Nietzsche's naturalism, but only insofar as it is understood as a radically experimental morality, to be developed with the philosophically transformed experimental method used in the natural sciences.

Seitz, Brian. Constituting the Political Subject, Using Foucault. *Man World*, 26(4), 443-455, O 93.

Seivert, Don. Searle and Descartes: The Connection between Speaking and Thinking. *SW Phil Rev*, 8(1), 137-144, Ja 92.

Sekimura, Makoto. Image et mimesis chez Platon (in Japanese). *Bigaku*, 42(4), 12-22, Spr 92.

L'image platonicienne se situe toujours inférieurement par rapport à son paradigme, encore que cette infériorité ontologique ne dégrade pas sa signification philosophique. La position équivoque de Platon concernant la mimesis est due à l'ambiguité d'estimation de l'image, celle-ci pouvant être considérée soit comme un obstacle, soit comme un élément directeur ou un point de départ. Cela nous conduit à la réflexion sur la relation entre l'image et le sujet afin de comprendre la fonction fondamentale de la mimesis. Chez Platon, on remarque qu'ily a deux sortes d'images: image "phantastique" qui laisse le sujet voyant passif et dont le producteur est un sophiste, et image eicastique qui rend le sujet actif et capable de saisir le lien paradigmatique de l'image et de son modèle. (edited)

Seligman, Adam B. The Representation of Society and the Privatization of Charisma. *Praxis Int*, 13(1), 68-84, Ap 93.

This essay analyzes the changing terms of society's representation of itself in the modern era. This is expressed in a privatization and particularization of value positions and the rejection of those universal assumptions on the shared (i.e., public) aspects of social life upon which political thought (and institutions) were predicated in the 18th, 19th and early 20th centuries. This retreat to the private realm and the elevation of the particular to representative status (of the social whole) bears, it is argued, a striking similarity to Max Weber's ideas of the privatization of charisma and its retreat from the public stage. Both developments are rooted in a set of contractions that inher to the definitions (and practice) of equality in modern liberal-individualist societies.

Seller, Mary. The Human Embryo: A Scientist's Point of View. *Bioethics*, 7(2-3), 135-140, Ap 93.

Sells, Laura. Feminist Epistemology: Rethinking the Dualisms of Atomic Knowledge. *Hypatia*, 8(3), 202-210, Sum 93.

Feminist epistemologists who attempt to refigure epistemology must wrestle with a number of dualisms. This essay examines the ways Lorraine Code, Sandra Harding, and Susan Hekman reconceptualize the relationship between self/other, nature/culture, and subject/object as they struggle to reformulate objectivity and knowledge.

Selvaggi, Filippo. Il mio itinerario filosofico. *Gregorianum*, 74(2), 309-327, 1993.

Au terme de l'enseignement à l'Université Grégorienne (Rome), l'auteur fait un examen et établit un bilan de son activité d'ecrivain (1938-1954). Il expose le développment de san penssée en son domaine spécifique: la philosophie de la science et de la nature, en passant en revue les problématiques par lui affrontées: la philosophie de la science en général, la théorie de la relativité et des quanta, le concept de substance sensible, la formalité spécifique de la philosophie de la nature ou coosmologie, la cuasalité et l'indéterminisme quantique, la valeur de la science pour l'homme. L'article se termine en faisant référance au dernier ouvrage de l'auteur: "La philosophie du monde", avec ses deux parties: la connaissance du monde et la nature du monde physique.

Semple, Janet. Foucault and Bentham: A Defence of Panopticism. *Utilitas*, 4(1), 105-120, My 92.

Sen, Amartya. Capability and Well-Being in The Quality of Life, Nussbaum, Martha C (ed). New York, Oxford Univ Pr, 1993.

Sen, Amartya. Commentator on 'Life-Style and the Standard of Living' in The Quality of Life, Nussbaum, Martha C (ed). New York, Oxford Univ Pr, 1993.

Sen, Amartya. Does Business Ethics Make Economic Sense?. *Bus Ethics Quart*, 3(1), 45-54, Ja 93.

The importance of business ethics is not contradicted in any way by Adam Smith's pointer to the fact that our "regards to our own interests" provide adequate *motivation for exchange*. There are many important economic relationships other than exchange, such as the institution of production and arrangements of distribution. Here business ethics can play a major part. Even as far as exchange is concerned, business ethics can be crucially important in terms of organization and behavior, going well beyond basic motivation.

Sen, Amartya. Positional Objectivity. *Phil Pub Affairs*, 22(2), 126-145, Spr 93.

Sen, Amartya (ed) and Nussbaum, Martha C (ed). *The Quality of Life*. New York, Oxford Univ Pr, 1993.

Sen, Brinda. The Concept of Kartrtva in the Nyaya-Vaisesika Philosophy. *Indian Phil Quart*, 19(4), 327-334, O 92.

In this paper the author analyzes the Nyaya-Vaisesika notion of Kartrtva (agency). The question of whether God or the disembodied infinite self can be an agent has been discussed in detail. The explanation of the notion of Krti (Volition) and three necessary conditoins of human agency viz. Krtisadhyatajnana (the knowledge of one's ability to perform an action), istasadhanatajnana (the knowledge of the agent's good) and cikirsa (desire to do something) constitutes the main topic of discussion.

Sen, Gautum. Individual, Institution, Nation-Building and Obligation: A Review Essay. *Indian Phil Quart*, 19(1), 52-60, Ja 92.

Sen, Madhucchanda. Perception and Illusion. *Indian Phil Quart*, 19/4(Supp), 1-16, O 92.

The argument from Illusion fails to prove that there are no veridical perceptions of physical objects, and we perceive only sense data. The argument wrongly handles cases of Standard Veridical, Devian Veridical, Illusory and Hallucinatory perceptions with one single theory. In each case, we make a judgment with components like: 1) I see something; 2) This something is a snake; 3) The snake is brown. We are mistaken in deviant veridical perception about the third component, in the illusory about the second, and in the hallucinatory about the first. Hence, we must have a different theory for each or, if we want to generalize, a Disjunctive Theory of Perception.

Sen, Pranab Kumar (ed). *Foundations of Logic and Language*. New Delhi, Allied, 1990.

Written by a group of scholars, this book of eight essays, with an editorial introduction investigates issues in syntax, semantics and ontology fundamental to the understanding of validation of logic and grammar. These concern the scope and limits of regimentation of natural language, the nature of grammatical theory, justification of logical laws, the utility of the very practice of deduction, development of nonstandard logics by dropping assumptions of the standard two- valued logic, the ontological questions raised by a proper treatment of indirect speech, the ontology of possible worlds, and the chances of reviving the old doctrine of fatalism.

Senderowicz, Y and Dascal, M. The Pure and the Non-Pure (in Hebrew). *Iyyun*, 41, 457-476, O 92.

Senna, Peter. Actual Infinity: A Contradiction?. *Lyceum*, 2(2), 65-75, Fall 90.

Sennett, James F. The Inscrutable Evil Defense Against the Inductive Argument from Evil. *Faith Phil*, 10(2), 220-229, Ap 93.

In this paper I offer a defense against the inductive argument from evil as developed by William Rowe. I argue that a key assumption in Rowe's argument—that the goods we know of offer us good inductive grounds to make certain inferences about the goods there are—is not justified. Particularly, I argue that *inscrutable evil*—evil such that any good it might serve is not open to human scrutiny—is no, in and of itself, good reason to believe that there is any unjustified evil. I then develop the defense by introducing the notion of a *relevant inductive sample* and arguing that there is good reason to assume that the goods we know of are not a relevant inductive sample of the goods there are—a fact that compromises any strength Rowe's argument might seem to have.

Sennett, James F. Toward a Compatibility Theory for Internalist and Externalist Epistemologies. *Phil Phenomenol Res*, 52(3), 641-655, S 92.

The internalist argues that justification is a matter of internal access, while the externalist insists that processes or mechanisms functioning to produce certain types of beliefs in certain types of stimulative situations are the key to a theory of justification. These positions are often considered mutually exclusive. It is my contention that the intuitions that motivate both theory types are important epistemologically, that both define issues that must be addressed in a theory of knowledge, and that they can be understood as compatible doctrines. In this paper I present certain distinctions between internalism and externalism that define two different epistemological tasks. I then propose an approach to the theory of knowledge under which both tasks can and should be legitimately pursued.

Sennett, James F. Why Think There are any True Counterfactuals of Freedom?. *Int J Phil Relig*, 32(2), 105-116, O 92.

Counterfactuals of freedom (CFF's) are counterfactual propositions whose consequents predicate free actions of some agent or agents. It is the purpose of this paper to examine two strategies for defending the claim that some CFF's are true: appeal to intuition and appeal to argument. I conclude that neither of these strategies is successful, and that no others are obviously available. I also show that there is available in the literature a plausible account of CFF's that does not require that any be true. Hence, I conclude that there is no good reason to believe that there are any true CFF's, and some reason to think that there are none.

Senor, Thomas D. Divine Temporality and Creation Ex Nihilo. *Faith Phil*, 10(1), 86-92, Ja 93.

In his paper, "Hartshorne and Aquinas: A Via Media," William P Alston argues that one who rejects the doctrine of divine timelessness should also reject the doctrine of creation ex nihilo and hold that the world and God are 'equally basic metaphysically.' At the heart of Alston's argument is the claim that a temporally everlasting deity would be irrational in creating at any given moment since there could never be a sufficient reason for creating then. In "Divine Temporality and Creation *Ex Nihilo*," I argue that Alston's argument is not compelling, and that the defender of divine temporality can plausibly maintain that God can rationally create at a time even if He lacks a sufficient reason for acting at that moment.

Senor, Thomas D. Internalistic Foundationalism and the Justification of Memory Belief. *Synthese*, 94(3), 453-476, Mr 93.

In this paper I argue that internalistic foundationalist theories of the justification of memory belief are inadequate. Taking a discussion of John Pollock as a starting point, I argue against any theory that requires a memory belief to be based on a phenomenal state in order to be justified. I then consider another version of internalistic foundationalism and claim that it, too, is open to important objections. Finally, I note that both varieties of foundationalism fail to account for the epistemic status of our justified nonoccurrent beliefs, and hence are drastically incomplete.

Senor, Thomas D. Two Factor Theories, Meaning Wholism and Intentionalistic Psychology: A Reply to Fodor. *Phil Psych*, 5(2), 133-151, 1992.

In chapter three of *Psychosemantics*, Jerry Fodor argues that meaning holism and intentionalistic psychology are incompatible. He attempts to show the falsity of the former by arguing that its primary foundation (i.e., functional-role semantics in the form of a two-factor theory of content) is too weak to stand. In this paper, I argue two claims: (i) Fodor has badly misconstrued two-factor theories, and that, properly understood, they are not subject to his objections, and (ii) it is far from clear that intentionalistic psychology is doomed if meaning holism were true.

Serafini, Anthony. Gillett on Consciousness and the Comatose. *Bioethics*, 6(4), 365-374, O 92.

In this essay I argue that Grant Gillett, in his article 'Consciousness, the Brain and What Matters', incorrectly concludes that mental states cannot be ascribed to comatose persons. Using some conceptual observations of Zeno Vendler and Norman Malcolm, I argue that there is a sense in which mental states can be ascribed to comatose persons. Vendler distinguishes, e.g., between "state" verbs of mental action and "process" verbs. My argument is that Gillett is right in saying that "process" states cannot be ascribed to the comatose, but wrong in that he overlooks that "state" verbs can be so applied.

Serafini, Anthony. Norman Malcolm: A Memoir. *Philosophy*, 68(265), 309-324, Jl 93.

This essay looks at Malcolm's career as well as at his work in epistemology, the philosophy of religion and the philosophy of mind, including his assaults on behaviorism, identity theories, functionalism, etc. The article contends that critics have misunderstood Malcolm, particularly his work on the "trace" theory of memory. The essay also disputes the view that Malcolm endorsed Wittgenstein's views uncritically, pointing to several places where Malcolm clearly rebukes Wittgenstein. Even so, it is argued that Malcolm's "ordinary-language" approach does have limitations. In general, however, it is argued that Malcolm was a philosopher of immense integrity, clarity and originality.

Serfati, Michel. Les compas cartésiens. *Arch Phil*, 56(2), 197-230, Ap-Je 93.

Descartes's mathematical thought, from the *Cogitationes privatae* began around specific instruments "cartesian compasses". We show first how they were used by Descartes to delimit the field of curves which, according to him, may be originally admitted in geometry. In *Geometrie* a conflict takes place between the spontaneous criterion of his early years and an algebraic criterion required by problems of secondary effectivity connected with new requirements of mathematical writing.

Serfontein, Paula. MacIntyre and the Liberal Tradition (in Dutch). *S Afr J Phil*, 11(2), 32-40, My 92.

In his reaction to the contemporary moral crisis, Alasdair MacIntyre offers us only two choices in *After Virtue*: either one must accept, like Nietzsche, the full consequences of liberal individualism or one must put one's hope on the revival of the Aristotelian tradition in some version or other. There is no third alternative. Firstly, the aim of this article is to evaluate this claim by focusing on the shortcomings of his critique of liberalism. Subsequently problems concerning his Aristotelian solution are pointed out. It is argued that the contrast between liberalism and his Aristotelian alternative is not as profound as he would like us to believe. At the same time it is shown that his communitarian solution cannot be viewed as an independent option next to liberalism. In the last part of the article a third alternative is suggested—an alternative that may be called communitarian liberalism, which combines the insights of MacIntyre's communitarianism with liberalism to overcome the shortcomings of both.

Serres, M. Het projectiel, het kanon. *Kennis Methode*, 16(3), 266-277, 1992.

Serres, Michel. De doorgang van het Noord-Westen. *Kennis Methode*, 16(3), 257-265, 1992.

Servi, G F. Nonmonotonic Consequence Based on Intuitionistic Logic. *J Sym Log*, 57(4), 1176-1197, D 92.

Research in AI has recently begun to address the problems of *nondeductive reasoning*, i.e., the problems that arise when, on the basis of approximate or incomplete evidence, we form well-reasoned but possibly false judgements. Attempts to stimulate such reasoning fall into two main categories: the numerical approach is based on probabilities and the nonnumerical one tries to reconstruct nondeductive reasoning as a special type of deductive process. In this paper, we are concerned with the latter ususally known as *nonmonotonic deduction*, because the set of theorems does not increase monotonically with the set of axioms.

Sesardic, Neven. Egalitarianism and Natural Lottery. *Pub Affairs Quart*, 7(1), 57-69, Ja 93.

Sesardic, Neven. Heritability and Causality. *Phil Sci*, 60(3), 396-418, S 93.

The critics of "hereditarianism" often claim that any attempt to explain human behavior by invoking genes is confronted with insurmountable methodological difficulties. They reject the idea that heritability estimates could lead to genetic explanations by pointing out that these estimates are strictly valid only for a given population and that they are exposed to the irremovable confounding effects of genotype-environment interaction and genotype-environment correlation. I argue that these difficulties are greatly exaggerated, and that we would be wrong to regard them as presenting a fundamental obstacle to the search for genetic explanations. I also show that, to the extent they are cogent, these objections may prove to be even more damaging to the "environmentalist" standpoint.

Seth, Sanjay. Lenin's Reformulation of Marxism: The Colonial Question as a National Question. *Hist Polit Thought*, 13(1), 99-128, Spr 92.

The reformulation of Marxism undertaken by Lenin resulted in colonial nationalism being seen as historically necessary, and 'progressive'; for even where it was 'bourgeois' it served, in Lenin's judgment, to undermine world imperialism. In this its Leninist form, Marxism became 'relevant' to the non-Western world in a way that Marx's own theory had not been. However, Lenin did not so much theorize nationalism as provide a set of criteria by which communists could distinguish between 'good' and 'bad' nationalisms. This had the effect of foreclosing a consideration of the phenomenon of nationalism in its own right; and the presumption that a particularist bourgeois national movement could serve the interests of the international socialist revolution proved to be highly problematic. As subsequent events showed, colonial nationalism was neither necessarily 'bourgeois-democratic', nor did it advance the international socialist cause in an uncomplicated fashion. (edited)

Settle, Thomas W. How Determinism Refutes Compatibilism. *Relig Stud*, 29(3), 353-362, S 93.

Settle, Tom. 'Fitness' and 'Altruism': Traps for the Unwary, Bystander and Biologist Alike. *Biol Phil*, 8(1), 61-83, Ja 93.

At one level, this paper is a lament and a warning. I lament biologists borrowing well-known terms and then drastically and awkwardly changing their meanings, and I warn about the mischief this does. Biology's public image is at stake, as is its general usefulness. At another level, I attempt to clarify the misnamed concepts, beyond what has been achieved in recent philosophical writings. This helps to account for the mischief, and to see how it might be avoidable. But the most important thing about the paper is that, at a third level, it is an argument against physicalism and materialism, especially those variants which deny the autonomy of organisms and the existence of intrinsic goods. Interpreting biology from the point of view of those denials leads to unsatisfactory and even bizarre results.

Sewald, J and Savini, S and Monteiro, L. Construction of Monadic Three-Valued Lukasiewicz Algebras. *Stud Log*, 50(3-4), 473-483, S-D 91.

Seymour, Daniel. Some of the Difference in the World: Crane on Intentional Causation. *Phil Quart*, 43(170), 83-89, Ja 93.

Individualism is the thesis that the contents of psychological states supervene on the physical microstructure of subjects in those states. The purpose of the paper is to defend individualism against anti- individualist presentations of the Twin Earth thought experiments. These arguments against individualism are not causally suspect, as Tim Crane has argued; rather, they are explanatorily suspect. The paper concludes with an argument for individualism and against anti-individualism which exploits and explanatory weakness in the anti-individualist description of Twins.

Seymour, Michel. L'indétermination de la logique: A propos de *La norme du vrai* de Pascal Engel. *Dialogue (Canada)*, 31(1), 87-106, Wint 92.

In his synthetic work, Engel discusses a vast array of topics in philosophy of logic and offers an integrated treatment inspired by Davidson. He embraces semantic holism, truth conditional semantics and the theory of radical interpretation and, as a consequence of this, rejects relativism, pluralism, and adopts a moderate version of conventionalism which is compatible with a realistic interpretation of the truth predicate. I criticize Engel for ignoring that inscrutability affects the logical connectives and show how this kind of indeterminacy does not presuppose semantic holism. This paves the way for a pluralist conception of logic and for a view according to which logic is a normative science founded upon a radical form of Wittgensteinian conventionalism.

Seymour, Michel. Les expériences de Burge et les contenus de pensée. *Dialectica*, 46(1), 21-39, 1992.

Les expériences de pensée de Tyler Burge révèlent une tension entre deux sorts d'arguments visant à prouver la détermination de l'environnement sur les contenus d'états intentionnels. On se propose dans un premier temps de montrer que l'expérience de 1979 est plus fondamentale et moins compromettante du point de vue métaphysique, et qu'il faut en ce sens insister davantage sur les déterminations de l'environnement social plutôt que de l'environnement physique. On fait valoir ensuite avec Loar que l'expérience de 1979, comme telle, n'a pas d'incidence sur les contenus de pensée tels qu'individués dans la psychologie cognitive et n'affecte que les attributions d'attitudes dans la psychologie populaire. Il est démontré enfin que l'admission d'une théorie citationnelle des contenus de pensée renforce l'argument de Burge, perment de contourner l'objection de Loar, et résout plusieurs des difficulté auxquelles était confrontée la version initiale de l'expérience.

Sfendoni-Mentzou, Demetra. Models of Change in Greek Studies in the Philosophy and History of Science, Nicolacopoulos, Pantelis (ed). Dordrecht, Kluwer, 1990.

This paper argues for the fundamental role of models, considered as a unique phenomenon underlying both philosophical and scientific thought since antiquity. It is thus claimed that the explanation of nature has been based on two cardinal pairs of models, which alternately dominated Ancient Greek philosophy and modern science: 1) the Democritean *atomic* versus the Aristotelian *dynamic* and 2) the *determination* versus the *indeterministic*. The task subsequently undertaken is to show how the above scheme revived in Newtonian physics and in the most recent developments in Q M and Micro-Physics, the latter displaying substantial analogies to the Aristotelian dynamic explanation of nature.

Sgall, Petr. Remarks on Interactive Representations and Praguian Linguistic Tradition. *J Prag*, 17(5-6), 527-532, Je 92.

The basic role of interactivity in natural language may be better understood if the functionalism of the Prague School is paid due attention. The teleonomic view helps to analyze the relationships between underlying representations (an interface level) and their encodings on other levels, especially in their anthropocentric aspects, adapted to human communication (such as the topic-focus articulation of the sentence).

Shaffer, Elinor S. Illusion and Imagination in Aesthetic Illusion, Burwick, Frederick (ed). Hawthorne, de Gruyter, 1990.

Shaffer, Thomas L. The Legal Profession's Rule Against Vouching for Clients: Advocacy and "The Manner That Is the Man Himself". *Notre Dame J Law Ethics*, 7(1), 145-175, 1993.

Shaked, Moshe and Goldman, Alvin. Commentary on the Scientific Status of Econometrics. *Soc Epistem*, 7(3), 249-253, Jl-S 93.

A target article by Feigenbaum and Levy contributes to the truth-oriented mission of social epistemology by revealing the limited incentives for error-detecting replication studies under current institutional conditions. We draw analogies between their article and our own previous work, in which a model of scientific activity plus assumptions about credit-maximizing motivations have implications for the truth-promoting properties of scientific experimentation.

Shalkowski, Scott A. Evidentialism and Theology: A Reply to Kaufman. *Faith Phil*, 9(2), 249-258, Ap 92.

In "Evidentialism: A Theologian's Response", Gordon D Kaufman presents some reasons that explain why, given the renewed interest in the philosophy of religion, theologians have paid relatively little attention to the work of contemporary philosophers. Philosophers have worked predominantly within the framework of traditional formulations of theological matters, and contemporary theologians have reasons for abandoning portions of this framework. In this discussion, I argue that the rationale Kaufman presents does not warrant abandoning central features of the traditional Christian theological framework.

Shalom, Albert. The Metaphilosophy of Meaning. *Dialec Hum*, 17(3), 33-41, 1990.

Shamoo, Adil E and Irving, Dianne N. The PSDA and the Depressed Elderly: "Intermittent Competency" Revisited. *J Clin Ethics*, 4(1), 74-79, Spr 93.

Shamsur Rahman, A K M. Locke's Empiricism and the Opening Arguments in Hegel's *Phenomenology of Spirit*. *Indian Phil Quart*, 20(1), 17-36, Ja 93.

Shanahan, Daniel. *Toward a Genealogy of Individualism*. Amherst, Univ of Mass Pr, 1992.

Shand, John. *Philosophy and Philosophers: An Introduction to Western Philosophy*. Montreal, McGill-Queens U Pr, 1993.

Shankar, Natarajan and Scedrov, Andre and Lincoln, Patrick. Linearizing Intuitionistic Implication. *Annals Pure Applied Log*, 60(2), 151-177, Ap 93.

An embedding of the implicational propositional intuitionistic logic (IIL) into the nonmodal fragment of intuitionistic linear logic (IMALL) is given. The embedding preserves cut-free proofs in a proof system that is a variant of IIL. The embedding is efficient and provides an alternative proof of the PSPACE-hardness of IMALL. It exploits several proof-theoretic properties of intuitionistic implication that analyze the use of resources in IIL proofs.

Shanker, Stuart G. Wittgenstein versus James and Russell on the Nature of Willing in Wittgenstein's Intentions, Canfield, John V (ed). Hamden, Garland, 1993.

The Analysis of Mind had an enormous influence on the development of Wittgenstein's thinking in the philosophy of psychology. Far more is involved here than Wittgenstein's reaction to the ideas which Russell had derived from his reading of James, Watson and Semon. The present paper pays particular attention to Wittgenstein's discussion of the voluntary/involuntary movement distinction, and the nature of free will. (edited)

Shanker, Stuart G (ed) and Canfield, J V (ed). *Wittgenstein's Intentions*. Hamden, Garland, 1993.

Shanks, Niall. Bell's Theorem and Determinism. *S Afr J Phil*, 12(2), 23-30, My 93.

In this paper the author examines the claim that Bell's theorem and the evidence supporting it provide conclusive and metaphysically respectable ground for believing that any contextual, deterministic hidden variables interpretation of quantum mechanics must require the postulation of action-at-a-distance in some way that conflicts with the Lorentz invariance requirements of the special theory of relativity. It is argued here that no such conclusions follow. The case for action-at-a-distance based on Bell's theorem rests on assumptions which beg the question against the contextual determinist.

Shanks, Niall. Quantum Mechanics and Determinism. *Phil Quart*, 43(170), 20-37, Ja 93.

This paper examines a number of arguments based on Bell's Theorem which purport to establish that quantum mechanics has ontological implications which exclude the possibility that determinism, viewed as an ontological thesis, is true. It is argued that while the arguments against determinism based on Bell's Theorem are valid—indeed, conspicuously so—they fail to do the required work because that rest on assumption which trivially beg the question against their intended determinest victims. An attempt is made to tie the results of this highly specific philosophical critique with broader epistemological concerns about scepticism and the very endeavour of providing empirical refutation of metaphysical theses.

Shanks, Niall and LaFollette, Hugh. Animal Models in Biomedical Research: Some Epistemological Worries. *Pub Affairs Quart*, 7(2), 113-130, Ap 93.

The public (and most philosophers) support the widespread use of animals in biomedical research because they are convinced it substantially benefits humans. We acknowledge that animal experimentation has likely benefitted humans. However, we offer historical and methodological ground for deflating researchers' claims about its value. Once the limitations of animal research are recognized, the character of the moral debate concerning its use we change.

Shanks, Niall and Lahav, Ran. How to Be a Scientifically Respectable "Property-Dualist". *J Mind Behav*, 13(3), 211-232, Sum 92.

We argue that the so-called "property-dualist" theory of consciousness is consistent both with current neurobiological data and with modern theories of physics. The hypothesis that phenomenal properties are global properties that are irreducible to microphysical properties, whose role is to integrate information across large portions of the brain, is consistent with current neurobiological knowledge. These properties can exercise their integration function through action on microscopic structures in the neuron without violating the laws of quantum mechanics. Although we offer no positive argument for the existence of irreducibly global properties, the conclusion is that this view is a scientifically respectable hypothesis that deserves to be investigated.

Shanks, Niall and Sharp, W David. The Rise and Fall of Time-Symmetrized Quantum Mechanics. *Phil Sci*, 60(3), 488-499, S 93.

In the context of a discussion of time symmetry in the quantum mechanical measurement process, Aharonov, et al. (1964) derived an expression concerning probabilities for the outcomes of measurements conducted on systems which have been pre- and postselected on the basis of both preceding and succeeding measurements. Recent literature has claimed that a resulting "time-symmetrized" interpretation of the aforementioned expression, these claims employ ensembles which are not well defined. It is argued here that under a *counterfactual* interpretation of the expression, these claims may be understood as employing well defined ensembles; it is shown, however, that such an interpretation cannot be reconciled with the standard interpretation of quantum mechanics.

Shannon, Gary P. A Note on Some Weak Forms of the Axiom of Choice. *Notre Dame J Form Log*, 33(1), 144-146, Wint 92.

Erdös and Tarski proved that if a quasi-order has antichains of arbitrarily large finite cardinality then it has a denumerable antichain, and that if a quasi-order has antichains of each cardinality less than a given singular cardinal then it has an antichain whose cardinality is that singular cardinal. Some variations of this result are developed as weak forms of the axiom of choice.

Shannon, Thomas A and Moussa, Mario. The Search for the New Pineal Gland: Brain Life and Personhood. *Hastings Center Rep*, 22(3), 30-37, My-Je 92.

Many ethicists have recently argued that the human fetus, once its brain begins to function, should be considered a person. They find support for this notion of "brain life" in the wide acceptance of the criteria for "brain death." In this essay, by contrast, we attempt to undercut the analogy rests primarily on a simple verbal association (life/death), supported by a philosophical tradition that assumes the mind somehow resides "inside" the body, particularly the brain. In addition, we explore the undesirable social consequences of the "brain life" debate.

Shanon, Benny. Are Connectionist Models Cognitive?. *Phil Psych*, 5(3), 235-255, 1992.

In their critique of connectionist models Fodor and Pylyshyn (1988) dismiss such models as not being cognitive or psychological. Evaluating Fodor and Pylyshyn's critique requires examining what is required in characterizating models as 'cognitive'. The present discussion examines the various senses of this term. It argues the answer to the title question seems to vary with these different senses. Indeed, by one sense of the term, neither representationalism nor connectionism is cognitive. General ramifications of such an appraisal are discussed and alternative avenues for cognitive research are suggested.

Shapere, Dudley. Astronomy and Antirealism. *Phil Sci*, 60(1), 134-150, Mr 93.

Relying on an analysis of the case of gravitational lensing, Hacking argues for a "modest antirealism" in astronomy. It is shown here that neither his scientific arguments nor his philosophical doctrines imply an antirealist conclusion. An alternative, realistic interpretation of gravitational lensing, and of the nature and history of astronomy more generally, is suggested.

Shapere, Dudley. Talking and Thinking about Nature: Roots, Evolution and Prospects. *Dialectica*, 46(3-4), 281-296, 1992.

The topic of this symposium gives rise to questions like these: How do we come to talk about nature in the way we do in science? In particular, what, precisely, are the relations between the "technical" language of science and the language we use in our everyday talk about the world and its contents? How, if at all, does the language of everyday life influence the language of science? In order to confront them, it is necessary first to clarify the conceptions of what "science" and "language" are. In the first section I will be concerned with the question of what science is; in the second I will more briefly discuss what I take language to be, and will offer an interpretation of the relations between language and science. In the third section I will briefly discuss some consequences of the view I have represented for philosophy.

Shapere, Dudley. The Universe of Modern Science and Its Philosophical Exploration in Philosophy and the Origin and Evolution of the Universe, Agazzi, Evandro (ed). Norwell, Kluwer, 1991.

The relevance and implications of the modern scientific view of the world forms the background and the object of philosophical inquiry. The modern scientific picture includes not only acceptable theories, but also problems in those theories, reasonable alternatives, and promising lines of research that are promising in light of the acceptable and reasonable theories. This picture, in each of these aspects, is examined, and a number of philosophical issues are explored. As illustrated by these examples, the purpose of philosophy of science is to understand the best scientific ideas of the age, and to explore their implications.

Shapiro, Ian. Three Fallacies Concerning Majorities, Minorities, and Democratic Politics. *Nomos*, 32, 79-125, 1990.

A defense of majority rule via a debunking of three fallacies about it that are common currency in the rational choice literature. The *reductionist fallacy* is that of regarding it a defect of majority rule that it fails to amalgamate political preferences as markets amalgamate economic preferences. Shapiro argues that this fallacy rests on inappropriate expectations from decision rules. The *constutitionalist fallacy* is that of assuming that restrictive courts are a solution to the problems of the manipulability of majority rule. Decision procedures can be manipulated in courts as well as in legislatures, and minorities should not always be protected. The *instability fallacy* involves assuming that technical instability is a normatively troubling aspect of decision rules; often it is not.

Shapiro, Ian. Workmanship Revisited: Reply to Professor Murphy. *Polit Theory*, 20(2), 327-331, My 92.

Shapiro argues that the only possible justification for linking the rewards people receive in society to the work that they do must be consequentialist in form. He further contends that all consequentialist justifications will be controversial, and makes the case that they should be decided through the political process as a result. There is no philosophical answer to the question: what is the just distribution of goods in society.

Shapiro, Lawrence A. Darwin and Disjunction: Foraging Theory and Univocal Assignments of Content. *Proc Phil Sci Ass*, 1, 469-480, 1992.

Fodor (1990) argues that the theory of evolution by natural selection will not help to save naturalistic accounts of representation from the disjunction problem. This is because, he claims, the context 'was selected for representing things as F' is transparent to the substitution of predicates coextensive with F. But, I respond, from an evolutionary perspective representational contexts cannot be transparent: only under particular descriptions will a representational state appear as a "solution" to a selection "problem" and so be adaptive. Only when we construe representational states as opaque in this manner are the generalizations of branches of evolutionary theory, like foraging theory, possible.

Shapiro, Michael J. Eighteenth Century Intimations of Modernity: Adam Smith and the Marquis de Sade. *Polit Theory*, 21(2), 273-293, My 93.

The exemplary confrontation between the discourses of Adam Smith and the Marquis de Sade is treated as parallel to the politico-ethical confrontation between some modernists and post-modernists. What is addressed, finally, is the product of an ethics based on instabilities of subjectivities and uncertainties of desire.

Shapiro, Stewart. Modality and Ontology. *Mind*, 102(407), 455-481, Jl 93.

This paper concerns the relationship between ideology and ontology. The starting point is a series of recent programs whose strategy is to reduce ontology in mathematics by invoking some ideology, typically a modal operator. In each case, there are straightforward, often trivial, translations from the set-theoretic language of the realist to the proposed language with added ideology, and vice-versa. The contention is that, because of these translations, neither system can claim a major epistemological advantage over the other. The prima facie intractability of knowledge of abstract objects indicates an intractability concerning knowledge of the "new" notions. The prevailing criterion of ontological commitment, due to Quine, is that the ontology of a theory is the range of its bound variables; but recall that Quine insists on a fixed, and very austere ideology. It is proposed here that, when this constraint is relaxed, the Quinean criterion is flawed, and an alternative, in structuralist terms, is developed.

Sharma, Arvind. Is *Anubhava a Pramana* According to Sankara?. *Phil East West*, 42(3), 517-526, Jl 92.

The paper examines the evidence on the question of whether Sankara accepts *Anubhava* as a *Pramanas* and concludes that he does but in a special sense because *Pramanas* operate in the realm of *Auidya*, which does not apply to the direct experience of Brahman.

Sharma, R M. Comments on " The Development of Advaita Vedanta as a School of Philosophy". *J Indian Counc Phil Res*, 9(2), 171-174, Ja-Ap 92.

Sharma, Ramesh Kumar. McTaggart on Perception. *Indian Phil Quart*, 19(3), 207-253, Jl 92.

The paper purports to explain McTaggart's views on perception and related issues and bring out their intrinsic merit. Some discussion is devoted to McTaggart's preliminary meaning of substance, quality, etc. In between I have attempted to underline the affinity of view point between McTaggart and Husserl. Then I discuss McTaggart's theory of structure of perception. This is followed by an explanation of McTaggart's important doctrine that it is possible to have a perception of a whole without perception of parts, which is then compared with similar views held by Russell and Stout. McTaggart's key doctrine that perceptions are parts of the percipient self comes in for some elaborate treatment followed by a discussion of McTaggart's special view of misperception and his conception of the presumptive correctness of all perception, which principle incidentally alone prevents the possibility of universal scepticism.

Sharp, W David and Shanks, Niall. The Rise and Fall of Time-Symmetrized Quantum Mechanics. *Phil Sci*, 60(3), 488-499, S 93.

In the context of a discussion of time symmetry in the quantum mechanical measurement process, Aharonov, et al. (1964) derived an expression concerning probabilities for the outcomes of measurements conducted on systems which have been pre- and postselected on the basis of both preceding and succeeding measurements. Recent literature has claimed that a resulting "time-symmetrized" interpretation of the aforementioned expression, these claims employ ensembles which are not well defined. It is argued here that under a *counterfactual* interpretation of the expression, these claims may be understood as employing well defined ensembles; it is shown, however, that such an interpretation cannot be reconciled with the standard interpretation of quantum mechanics.

Sharpe, Kevin J. Holomovement Metaphysics and Theology. *Zygon*, 28(1), 47-60, Mr 93.

The holomovement metaphysics of David Bohm emphasizes connections and continuous change. Two general movements through space-time extend Bohm's ideas. One is that the universe was nonlocal when it started but increases in locality. (With nonlocality, two simultaneous but distant events affect each other.) The other is the opposite movement or evolution toward increasingly complex systems exhibiting internal connections and a type of nonlocality. This metaphysics produces a theology when the holomovement is a model for God. Several topics follow, including global nonlocality, God as creator, God's transcendence and immanence, and God as personal. This theology shows promise but needs further development.

Sharpe, R A. Moral Tales. *Philosophy*, 67(260), 155-168, Ap 92.

The imagination is involved in two ways in moral thinking, firstly in enabling us to work out the consequences of our actions, and secondly in enabling us either to experience in their absence the primitive reactions which we would experience if we were to be present at such happenings or in enabling us to imagine what such primitive reactions would be like were they to occur. This approach to moral reasoning stresses the role of narrative and enables us to see the importance of stories in developing moral thought. It also gives us a line on moral realism, for one upshot is that moral realism gives us a fair account of some aspects of moral behaviour but fits others very badly. Elsewhere anti-realism looks a more likely story.

Sharpe, Virginia A. Justice and Care: The Implications of the Kohlberg-Gilligan Debate for Medical Ethics. *Theor Med*, 13(4), 295-318, D 92.

Carol Gilligan has identified two orientations to moral understanding; the dominant 'justice orientation' and the under-valued 'care orientation'. Based on her discernment of a 'voice of care', Gilligan challenges the adequacy of a deontological liberal framework for moral development and moral theory. This paper examines how the orientations of justice and care are played out in medical ethical theory. Specifically, I question whether the medical moral domain is adequately described by the norms of impartiality, universality, and equality that characterize the liberal ideal. My analysis of justice-oriented medical ethics, focused on the libertarian theory of H T Engelhardt and the contractarian theory of R M Veatch. I suggest that in the work of E D Pellegrino and D C Thomasma we find not only a more authentic representation of medical morality but also a project that is compatible with the care orientation's emphasis on human need and responsiveness to particular others.

Sharples, Bob. Aristotle and Hellenistic Philosophy. *Phronesis*, 38(1), 111-116, 1993.

Sharples, Robert W. Theophrastus: On Fish in Theophrastus, Fortenbaugh, William W (ed). New Brunswick, Transaction Books, 1992.

Sharrett, Christopher. Defining the Postmodern in Postmodernism/ Jameson/ Critique, Kellner, Douglas M (ed). Washington, Maisonneuve Pr, 1989.

Applies Fredric Jameson's theorizations on postmodernity to an examination of the contemporary cityscape. The purpose of the piece is to determine the modernist vs. postmodernist impulses reflected in contemporary architecture and to locate reactionary and progressive sensibilities in these impulses. One assumption is that the postmodern reflects the thoroughly commodified atmosphere of late capitalism as Jameson suggests.

Sharrock, Wes and Button, Graham. A Disagreement over Agreement and Consensus in Constructionist Sociology. *J Theor Soc Behav*, 23(1), 1-25, Mr 93.

Shashidharan, Suryaprabha and Gupta, Amitabha. Representation *versus* Mirroring: A Cognitivist Response to Rorty. *J Indian Counc Phil Res*, 9(1), 127-138, S-D 91.

Shaver, Robert. Hume and the Duties of Humanity. *J Hist Phil*, 30(4), 545-556, O 92.

Shaver, Robert. Paris and Patriotism. *Hist Polit Thought*, 12(4), 627-646, Wint 91.

In 1771, Rousseau was asked to write a constitution for Poland. He replied with *The Government of Poland*. He describes the sort of Pole he hopes to produce: his "love of the fatherland...makes up his entire existence...; the moment he is alone, he is a mere cipher." On the face of it, this looks more like the description of a problem than any solution. But this mad patriotism is indeed a solution, a solution to the general modern problem of "life in others". And the solution is less frightening, more necessary, and slightly more possible than it seems at first glance.

Shavrukov, Y. A Note on the Diagonzalizable Algebras of PA and ZF. *Annals Pure Applied Log*, 61(1-2), 161-173, My 93.

We prove that the diagonalizable algebras of PA and ZF are not isomorphic.

Shavrukov, V Y. The Lindenbaum Fixed Point Algebra is Undecidable. *Stud Log*, 50(1), 143-147, Mr 91.

We prove that the first order theory of the fixed point algebra corresponding to an r.e. consistent theory containing arithmetic is hereditarily undecidable.

Shaw, Bill and Post, Frederick R. A Moral Basis for Corporate Philanthropy. *J Bus Ethics*, 12(10), 745-752, O 93.

The authors argue that corporate philanthropy is far too important as a social instrument for good to depend on ethical egoism for its support. They claim that rule utilitarianism provides a more compelling, though not exclusive, moral foundation. The authors cite empirical and legal evidence as additional support for their claim.

Shaw, Bill and Zollers, Frances E. Managers in the Moral Dimension: What Etezioni Might Mean to Corporate Managers. *Bus Ethics Quart*, 3(2), 153-168, A 93.

In *The Moral Dimension*, Amitai Etzioni critiques the neoclassical economic paradigm (NEP), a model built upon ethical egoism and which equates rationality (the logical/empirical domain) with the maximization of preferences by self-interested economic units. Etzioni finds the NEP's exclusion of the moral/affective domain to be a glaring failure and, because of this omission, he claims that the economic model is not capable of achieving its design functions: prediction and explanation. Etzioni introduces a socio-economic model, the I and We paradigm, in which the moral/affective encapsulates the logical/empirical. Further elaboration and testing of this model remains to be undertaken. We find it to hold more promise than its neoclassical economic rival, and we explicate its value for the modern manager.

Shaw, D W D. Immortality: Objective, Subjective, or Neither? in God, Values, and Empiricism, Peden, Creighton (ed). Macon, Mercer Univ Pr, 1989.

Shaw, Daniel. Hume's Moral Sentimentalism. *Hume Stud*, 19(1), 31-54, Ap 93.

Shaw, Daniel. Hume's Theory of Motivation—Part 2. *Hume Stud*, 18(1), 19-39, Ap 92.

Shaw, Daniel. Reason and Feeling in Hume's Action Theory and Moral Philosophy. *Hume Stud*, 18(2), 349-367, N 92.

Shaw, Patrick. On Worshipping the Same God. *Relig Stud*, 28(4), 511-532, D 92.

Criteria are considered for assessing whether two groups worship the same god. The criteria applied by non-believers in answering this question will differ from those applied by believers. Non-believers must confine themselves to the content of different religious belief systems; but believers can also assess the beliefs of others as distortions of the truth. Thus they can regard other religions as worshipping their god, however divergent the contents of the rival beliefs from their own. What determines their willingness to do this is partly a question of the values their religion holds, and partly a question of their religious epistemology.

Shaw, William H. Duquette and the Primacy Thesis. *Phil Soc Sci*, 22(2), 214-217, Je 92.

This essay is a brief rejoinder to David A Duquette, "A Critique of the Technological Interpretation of Historical Materialism", published in the same issue.

Shaw, William H. *Social and Personal Ethics*. Belmont, Wadsworth, 1993.

This book is an edited reader intended for use as a textbook in a "moral issues" type class.

Shearson, William A. The Fragmented Middle: Hegel and Kierkegaard in German Philosophy and Jewish Thought, Greenspan, Louis (ed). Toronto, Univ of Toronto Pr, 1992.

This paper argues that in a world post-Hegel *mortuum*, existentialist thought cannot be located as either a left or right-wing post-Hegelian possibility. Existentialist thought neither flees the actual world in order to preserve a comprehensive philosophic thought—the right-wing, nor does it abandon that infinite pole in order to stay with a wholly finite world—Hegel's left-wing. Existential philosophy holds to both the finite and infinite poles thus locating itself in the Hegelian middle, albeit a fragmented one.

Sheehan, Thomas. Reading a Life in The Cambridge Companion to Heidegger, Guignon, Charles B (ed). New York, Cambridge Univ Pr, 1993.

The article treats 1) Heidegger's turn from Catholic philosophy, 1917-1919, 2) his early relation to phenomenology, 3) his involvement with Nazism, and 4) the central issue of his later thought. An effort is made to interpret these issues with the framework of the material conditions (social, economic, and political) of his times.

Sheets-Johnstone, Maxine. Corporeal Archetypes and Power: Preliminary Clarifications and Considerations of Sex. *Hypatia*, 7(3), 39-76, Sum 92.

An examination of animate form reveals corporeal archetypes that underlie both human sexual behavior and the reigning Western biological paradigm of human sexuality that reworks the archetypes to enforce female oppression. Viewed within the framework of present-day social constructionist theory and Western biology, I show bow both social constructionist feminists who disavow biology and biologists who reduce human biology to anatomy forget evolution and thereby forego understanding essential to the political liberation of women.

Sheets-Johnstone, Maxine. Response to "The Nature and Evolution of Human Language: Commentary". *Between Species*, 8(2), 98-99, Spr 92.

I focus on five issues: Professor Michael Bishop's defense of Charles Hockett's "comparative method" in assessing the "design features" of nonhuman animal languages; his defense of Hockett's definition of language to begin with; his defense of Hockett's account of the origin of language; his confusing the similarity in iconic bodily representation between primordial language and the *Tanzsprache* with human speech perception; and his concluding remarks that simplistically reduce an evolutionary semantics to a recording of differences between "us and them," thus stripping the semantics of its evolutionary character, its epistemological significance in terms of sense-making, and ultimately its moral import.

Sheets-Johnstone, Maxine. Taking Evolution Seriously. *Amer Phil Quart*, 29(4), 343-352, O 92.

Philosophers are prone to a highly selective reading of Darwin's three consecutive formulations of "descent with modification." The highly selective reading has never been critically examined on grounds of reasonableness and disregards all but physical continuities. Reverse anthropocentrism perpetuates the highly selective reading. It effectively blots out Darwin's organic and evolutionary wholism by apportioning sub-mental credit to nonhuman animals and making humans special creations. To take Darwin's wholism seriously is to look beyond evolutionary theory *qua theory* toward an examination of its actual historical significance. Such an examination has direct and powerful implications for present-day Cartesian metaphysics.

Sheets-Johnstone, Maxine. The Possibility of an Evolutionary Semantics. *Between Species*, 8(2), 88-94, Spr 92.

The possibility of an evolutionary semantics rests on three inter-related shifts in typical philosophical practice: deprivileging human language; recognition of iconic spatio-kinetic corporeal representation as a fundamental form of meaning in the animate world; recognition of pre-reflective modes of symbolization in everyday life. Typical philosophical practice is exemplified by Jonathan Bennett in his book, *Rationality* by Daniel Dennett in his intentional systems theory approach to nonhuman animal behavior, by Donald Davidson in his claim that short of language, creatures cannot have psychological capacities. Compelling evidence is presented for revising typical philosophical practice and adopting an evolutionary semantics perspective.

Shekhawat, V. Specific Cultures and the Coexistence of Alternative Rationalities: A Case Study of the Contact of Indian and Greco-European Cultures. *J Indian Counc Phil Res*, 9(2), 125-134, Ja-Ap 92.

Shelah, S and Gitik, M. More on Simple Forcing Notions and Forcings With Ideals. *Annals Pure Applied Log*, 59(3), 219-238, F 93.

Shelah, S and Judah, H and Brendle, Jörg. Combinatorial Properties of Hechler Forcing. *Annals Pure Applied Log*, 58(3), 185-199, N 92.

Using a notion of rank, we investigate combinatorial properties of Hechler forcing—this is a ccc forcing notion adding a dominating real. In particular, we study the effect of adding a Hechler real on the cardinal invariants in Cichón's diagram—these are cardinals related to the ideals of meager and measure zero (null) sets.

Shelah, Saharon. The Hanf Numbers of Stationary Logic II: Comparison with Other Logics. *Notre Dame J Form Log*, 33(1), 1-12, Wint 92.

Shelah, Saharon and Abraham, Uri. A $\Delta 2/2$ Well-Order of the Reals and Incompactness of *L(QMM)*. *Annals Pure Applied Log*, 59(1), 1-32, Ja 93.

Shelah, Saharon and Baumgartner, James E and Thomas, Simon. Maximal Subgroups of Infinite Symmetric Groups. *Notre Dame J Form Log*, 34(1), 1-11, Wint 93.

We prove that it is consistant that there exists a subgroup of the symmetric group Sym(λ) which is not included in a maximal proper subgroup of Sym(λ). We also consider the question of which subgroups of Sym(λ) stabilize a nontrivial ideal on λ.

Shell, Susan. Kant's Political Cosmology in Essays on Kant's Political Philosophy, Williams, Howard (ed). Chicago, Univ of Chicago Pr, 1992.

An investigation of Kant's "Remarks on *Observations on the Beautiful and the Sublime*," with a view to understanding the political and moral transformation — inspired largely by Rousseau — of Kant's earlier theoretical cosmology, a transformation crucial, as I argue, to his later critical undertaking. My investigation of the "Remarks" pays special attention to Kant's response to the political and sexual dialectic elaborated in Rousseau's *Emile*, a response that has not hitherto been the subject of an extended study.

Shelledy, David and Wintgens, Luc J. Unger's Advocates: Assessing the Possibilities for Law Practice as a Transformative Vocation. *Ratio Juris*, 5(1), 46-57, Mr 92.

This article focuses on a critical interpretation of the work of Unger. It is argued that Unger's view is less revolutionary than he depicts it and that American law often develops as Unger describes it, though this is absolutely no revolution. The authors further show what the possibilities and the limits of a transformative vocation at the bar can be.

Shen, Vincent. Anthropological Foundation of Moral Education in Chinese Foundations for Moral Education and Character Development, Van Doan, Tran (ed). Washington, CRVP, 1991.

The problem of the anthropological foundation of moral education has taken on new urgency due to the rapid development of science and technology. This paper proposes the thesis that, from the point of view of the philosophy of contrast, moral education, either as an institutionalized process of teaching and learning, or as the whole process of formation of an integral person, should take into account both the dimensions of foundation and manifestation of human person. An essential content of moral education systematically integrating autonomy and relation, justice and love, criticism and commitment, reflection and action in these two process (of founding and manifesting) are schematized here in reference to Thomism, phenomenology and Chinese philosophy.

Shen, Vincent. Creativity as Synthesis of Contrasting Wisdoms: An Interpretation of Chinese Philosophy in Taiwan since 1949. *Phil East West*, 43(2), 279-287, Ap 93.

Taking the problematic of a meeting of Chinese and Western philosophies as central to modern Chinese philosophers, this paper analyses and evaluates three schools of philosophy developing in Taiwan: 1) Comprehensive synthesis represented by Thomé Fang (1899-1977) and his followers; 2) Contemporary Neo-Confucian Synthesis represented by Tang Chün-yi and Mou Tsung-san; and 3) The Chinese Scholastic Synthesis, represented by Wu Ching-siung, Lo Duang and other Catholic philosophers. Other new elements for synthesis are analysed and further reflections on doing synthesis in responding to the need of the Life-World are proposed as conclusion.

Shen, Vincent (ed) and Van Doan, Tran (ed) and McLean, George F (ed). *Chinese Foundations for Moral Education and Character Development*. Washington, CRVP, 1991.

This volume consists of 9 chapters which are divided in three parts: 1) the first part studies the basic characters of morals in the Chinese Classics; 2) the second part offers some modern views on the growth of human characters and morale, while 3) the third part deals specifically with the moral education in modern China. The conclusion reached by the co-authors of this volume is: a moral education should be based on 1) traditional resources and 2) a full understanding of man (human nature, human development etc.).

Shephard, Amanda. Henry Howard and the Lawful Regiment of Women. *Hist Polit Thought*, 12(4), 589-603, Wint 91.

Sher, George. Knowing about Virtue. *Nomos*, 34, 91-116, 1992.

Sherburne, Donald W. Whitehead and Dewey on Experience and System in Frontiers in American Philosophy, Volume I, Burch, Robert W (ed). College Station, Texas A&M Univ Pr, 1992.

Sherline, Edward. Moral Realism and Objective Theories of the Right. *S J Phil*, 30(4), 127-140, Wint 92.

Nicholas Sturgeon has argued that moral realism must be presupposed to hold an objective theory of the right—a theory of the right as a standard of rightness but not a particular decision procedure. The argument is that an objective theory of the right presupposes the distinction between truth and acceptance value, and this distinction presupposes moral realism. Furthermore, the notion of truth must be sufficiently robust to explain Hume's distinction between refuting a hypothesis because it is absurd, and refuting a hypothesis because of its dangerous consequences. I argue that an objective theory of the right is available to the realist and antirealist alike, for the antirealist is able to make either the distinction between truth and acceptance value, or the more fundamental distinction between justification and acceptance value, and in a way that explains Hume's distinction.

Sherlock, Richard and Barrus, Roger. The Problem of Religion in Liberalism. *Interpretation*, 20(3), 285-308, Spr 93.

Sherman, Mark A and Donnelly, Dorothy F. *Augustine's "De Civitate Dei": An Annotated Bibliography of Modern Criticism, 1960-1990*. New York, Lang, 1991.

This reference guide includes 64 modern works devoted to the study of Augustine's *De Civitate Dei* that appeared in America and Canada between 1960-1990. There are two important section which supplement the main bibliography — a group of 18 studies published in English by foreign publishers and 13 studies published prior to 1960. The entries in all three sections provide full bibliographic citations and 200- to 500-word annotations. The annotations offer a descriptive analysis of the arguments detailed in each work. The book also includes a chronologically arranged bibliography of Augustine's writings, and a selected bibliography of general studies on Augustine and his works.

Sherman, Nancy. The Virtues of Common Pursuit. *Phil Phenomenol Res*, 53(2), 277-299, Je 93.

When we think about being good, morally good that is, what comes to mind is being good to others, and in a less definite, though still important way, being good to ourselves. Thus, the virtues typically divide into self and other regarding character states. I want to argue that in addition to caring about self and others, we care about the fact that we do things together. To share in projects, ideas, and communities has values for us. And an interest in and enthusiasm for such common projects can be morally virtuous. I want to explore these views in the contexts of a comparison of Aristotelian and Kantian moral conceptions on the value of community. While securing a place for community in a Kantian scheme may seem initially more troubling than finding a comparable home in an Aristotelian account, I hope to dispel some of these worries by the end of the paper. This will require turning to some of Kant's early political essays in which he develops the notion of moral virtue as part of a larger, collective endeavor, as well as the much later *Religion* in which he discusses the notion of an ethical commonwealth as a rallying point for those devoted to virtue.

Sherman, Nancy. Wise Maxims/Wise Judging. *Monist*, 76(1), 41-65, Ja 93.

One of the reasons often cited for the renewed interest in Aristotelian virtue theory is its alleged sensitivity to the particular case. In place of an emphasis on rules and procedures is attention to the variety of individual cases, and a reminder of the shortfalls of misplaced rigour. I want to argue that a similar sensitivity to the particular case can be found in Kant's treatment of the duties of virtue. In addition, I explore how on Kant's view we can probe the motives of our actions, and in a sense, subject our maxims to a therapy of self-knowledge.

Sherry, Patrick. Simone Weil on Beauty in Simone Weil's Philosophy of Culture, Bell, Richard (ed). New York, Cambridge Univ Pr, 1993.

I outline Simone Weil's exalted account of the nature of beauty, which culminates in her claim that it is an attribute of God Himself, and moreover one in which we *see* Him. I relate Weil's account to both contemporary aesthetics and theology, and conclude that she anticipated two important recent developments, theological aesthetics and the revival of Trinitarian theology.

Sherwin, Susan. Abortion Through a Feminist Ethics Lens. *Dialogue (Canada)*, 30(3), 327-342, Sum 91.

This paper explores the ethical questions surrounding abortion from the distinct perspective of feminist ethics. It argues that feminist analyses of abortion differ from other "liberal" positions on the moral status of abortion in terms of their choice of focus, their conception of the fetus, and their views of what issues are ethically significant in the area of abortion. In contrast to other positions on abortion, feminist ethics takes into account the political significance of potential abortion policies on the lives of women.

Sherwin, Susan. Non-Treatment and Non-Compliance as Neglect in Contemporary Issues in Paediatric Ethics, Burgess, Michael M (ed). Lewiston, Mellen Pr, 1991.

Should non-treatment or non-compliance in the medical care of children be considered as examples of neglect and penalized as such? This paper argues for a distinction between neglect, understood as representing a failure of appropriate concern for the interests of the child, and parental disagreement with health professionals about the best treatment for their child. Caring and attentive parents who refuse medical advice as incompatible with their understanding or value system should not be judged as neglectful, but respected for their interest; health workers' efforts should be directed at improving communication rather than coercing compliance.

Shibles, Warren. Altruism versus Egoism: A Pseudo-Problem, A Cognitive-Emotive Analysis. *Int J Applied Phil*, 7(1), 21-29, Sum 92.

The question of whether or not one is or should be altruistic or egoistic cannot be answered because it is a pseudo-question. Its terms are ambiguous and generate numerous informal logical fallacies. The cognitive theory of emotion is presented, and it is shown how it may serve to critique theories of altruism and egoism, such as those based on feeling and sympathy. A naturalistic ethics and humanism are used to show how the cognitions involved might provide a basis for, and create, the emotions of rational altruism and rational egoism.

Shields, Christopher. Moral Incapacity. *Proc Aris Soc*, 93, 59-70, 1993.

Shields, Christopher. The Truth Evaluability of Stoic *Phantasiai: Adversus Mathematicos* VII. *J Hist Phil*, 31(3), 242-246, Jl 93.

According to a report of Sextus, the Stoics exhaustively categorized *phantasiai* (impressions) as (i) true, (ii) false, (iii) true and false, or (iv) neither true nor false. But Sextus does not represent this as a peculiar or remarkable doctrine. This is surely noteworthy, given his characteristically polemical stance toward Stoic views. For it is difficult to reconcile the existence of *phantasiai* falling into category (iv) with the Stoics' unwavering commitment to bivalence. The root of the problem is to be located in Sextus' misunderstanding of the precise semantic character of *phantasiai* within the context of all but the early Stoic system.

Shields, George W. Hartshorne and Creel on Impassibility. *Process Stud*, 21(1), 44-59, Spr 92.

A main argument of this article is that R E Creel's critique of Hartshorne's "passibilist" views of divine will, knowledge of possibility, and feeling encounters a dilemma: either God predecides responses to all possibles by virtue of a formula or algorithm (which is ill-formed on two counts) or God could exhaust a continuum of possibles (contrary to Creel's own acceptance of the Peirce-Hartshorne theory of the continuum).

Shields, George W. Infinitesimals and Hartshorne's Set-Theoretic Platonism. *Mod Sch*, 69(2), 123-134, Ja 92.

It is here argued that Hartshorne is committed to set-theoretic Platonism, because he embraces the notion of an infinite past of actual occasions. This has the surprising consequence that he is also committed to the notion of actual infinitesimals if he is to avoid the inconsistencies of Cantor's doctrine of the actual infinite pointed out by the Nonstandard Analysis school. I further argue that the admission of infinitesimals into Hartshorne's conceptual scheme would not undermine his doctrine of actual occasions as such, although it does have ramification for his view of divine agency.

Shields, Philip. *Logic and Sin in the Writings of Ludwig Wittgenstein*. Chicago, Univ of Chicago Pr, 1993.

This study argues that a matrix of ethical and religious concerns informs Wittgenstein's technical writings on logic and language, and that for Wittgenstein, the need to establish clear limitations is simultaneously a logical and an ethical demand. Major texts from the *Tractatus* to *On Certainty* express their fundamentally religious nature by showing that there are powers which bear down upon and sustain us. The powers manifest themselves in the structures that make significant use of language possible. This interpretation illuminates the distinctiveness and peculiarity of Wittgenstein's philosophy and reveals the fundamental continuity between the early and the later thought.

Shiell, Timothy C. The Unity of Plato's Political Thought. *Hist Polit Thought*, 12(3), 377-390, Fall 91.

Shiff, Richard. Cézanne's Physicality: The Politics of Touch in The Language of Art History, Kemal, Salim (ed). New York, Cambridge Univ Pr, 1991.

Shih, Heng-ching. Chinese Bhiksunis in the Ch'an Tradition (in Chinese). *Phil Rev (Taiwan)*, 15, 18o1-208, Ja 92.

Shihara, Nobuhiro. L'aspect de l'esthétique de l'honnête homme (in Japanese). *Bigaku*, 43(1), 1-12, Sum 92.

Mére dit que l'honnêteté est "ce n'est autre chose que d'exceller en tout ce qui regarde les agréments et les bienséances de la vie." Dans cette définition, il y a dewx concepts ésthetiques. Dans une conversation divertissante de l'Honnête Homme, le premier bienséance est des règles des relations modestes entre soi et ses sembalables. Et, les deux sont le sujet de l'éoquence dans le commerce du monde, se fondé sur l'art de plaire. Par cette éloquence, l'Honnête Homme peut vivre heureusement, et rendre heureux des autres. Donc c'est éloquence, l'Honnêtte Homme a besoin d'avoir le bon goût, qui vient d'une connnaissence exquise et juste, c'est-à-dire, la raison. Mais, cette raison n'est pas le sens philosophique, et coïncide le "je ne sais quoi". C'est le caracède l'esthetique de l'Honnêtte Homme. Et, sur ce point, elle a une place dans l'histoire de l'ésthetique. (edited)

Shilian, Shan. May Fourth, the New Confucianism, and the Modernization of Humanity. *Chin Stud Phil*, 24(3), 25-40, Spr 93.

Shimony, Abner. On Carnap: Reflections of a Metaphysical Student. *Synthese*, 93(1-2), 261-274, N 92.

Carnap's character and influence are recollected by a former student who admired him deeply but was not a disciple. Summaries are given of real and imaginary dialogues with Carnap in four areas: 1) internal and external questions of existence; 2) procedures for introducing and interpreting theoretical terms; 3) the character of mathematical truth; and 4) the formulation and justification of inductive logic. Carnap's empiricism and his contributions to conceptual clarification are asserted to have permanent philosophical value.

Shimony, Abner. *Search for a Naturalistic World View: Volume I*. New York, Cambridge Univ Pr, 1993.

This volume, subtitled, "Scientific Methodology and Epistemology," consists of essays written between 1953 and 1992. It advocates an "integral epistemology," which combines in a dialectic manner relevant results of the empirical sciences with conceptual analysis. It proposes a version of scientific realism that emphasizes causal relations between physical and mental events and rejects a physicalist account of mentality. It offers a "tempered personalist" version of scientific methodology, which supplements Bayesian probability theory with *a posteriori* principles distilled from exemplary cognitive achievement. It defends the general reliability, corrigibility, and progressiveness of empirical knowledge against relativism, historicism, and skepticism. A final essay is devoted to the relation between fact and value.

Shimony, Abner. *Search for a Naturalistic World View: Volume II*. New York, Cambridge Univ Pr, 1993.

This volume, subtitled "Natural Science and Metaphysics," explores "experimental metaphysics." Analyses of quantum mechanics show that potentiality, chance, probability, entanglement, and nonlocality are objective features of nature, but also indicate desiderata for modifying quantum dynamics. Relations between parts and wholes in complex systems are examined. One essay maintains that there exists no *principle* of natural selection, despite the pervasiveness of the phenomenon. One essay on time maintains that transiency is real and objective; another that criteria for temporal measurement must be formulated in tandem with dynamical laws. The volume concludes with historical, speculative, and experimental studies of the mind-body problem.

Shiner, R A. Positivism and Natural Law: A "Reconciliation". *Vera Lex*, 11(2), 28-29, 1991.

The paper is a brief sketch of the position defended at length in my recent book *Norm and Nature* (Oxford: Clarendon Press 1992). My claim is that legal positivism and natural law theory cannot be reconciled. The tension between the theories is endless. However, a theory of law still results, for law itself is full of tension. The conflict in theories of law mirrors conflict in law itself.

Shiner, Roger A. Exclusionary Reasons and the Explanatory of Behaviour. *Ratio Juris*, 5(1), 1-22, Mr 92.

Legal philosophy must consider the way in which laws function as reasons for action. "Simple Positivism" considers laws as merely reasons in the balance of reasons. Joseph Raz, as a representative of "sophisticated positivism," argues that laws are exclusionary reasons for action, not merely reasons in the balance of reasons. This paper discusses Raz's arguments for his view. The Functional Argument provides no more reason for positivism than against it. The Phenomenological Argument is best supported by an account of how character traits function in explaining behaviour. But then the distinction between exclusionary reasons and expressive reasons is obliterated. Legal positivism cannot absorb laws as expressive reasons for action. Raz's positivism implies the correctness of an anti-positivistic legal theory.

Shiner, Roger A. Stanley Fish's *Doing What Comes Naturally: Change, Rhetoric, and the Practice of Theory in Literary and Legal Studies*. *J Aes Art Crit*, 49(4), 375-378, Fall 91.

In this review article, I concentrate on Fish's contributions to the debate about legal and literary interpretation. I point out that the work is largely very useful negative polemic. Fish's anti-theoretical stance does not succeed well in providing a positive picture of either law or literature.

Shipley, Patricia and Leal, Fernando. Deep Dualism. *Int J Applied Phil*, 7(2), 33-44, Wint 92.

Shirley, Edward S. A Refutation of the Dream Argument. *SW Phil Rev*, 9(1), 1-22, Ja 93.

Shklar, Judith N. Justice without Virtue. *Nomos*, 34, 283-288, 1992.

Shklar, Judith N. Obligaiton, Loyalty, Exile. *Polit Theory*, 21(2), 181-197, My 93.

Shlapentokh, Alexandra. A Diophantine Definition of Rational Integers over Some Rings of Algebraic Numbers. *Notre Dame J Form Log*, 33(3), 299-321, Sum 92.

The author considers the rings of algebraic numbers integral at all but finitely many primes in the number fields, where it has been previously shown that Hilbert's Tenth Problem is undecidable in the rings of algebraic integers, and proves that the problem is still undecidable in the bigger rings by constructing a diophantine definition of rational integers there.

Shlapentokh, Dmitry. The End of the Russian Idea. *Stud Soviet Tho*, 43(3), 199-217, My 92.

Shogan, Debra. Trusting Paternalism? Trust as a Condition for Paternalistic Decisions. *J Phil Sport*, 18, 49-58, 1991.

Shoos, Diane. The Female Subject of Popular Culture. *Hypatia*, 7(2), 215-226, Spr 92.

This essay discusses the place of popular culture, especially visual representation, in theories of female subjectivity and examines two recent works on women and popular culture as representative of two primary critical and methodological approaches to the female subject. The essay considers the limitations and implications of both qualitative communication research and text-based feminist criticism and the need to construct a dialogue between them.

Shope, Robert K. You Know What You Falsely Believe (Or: Pollock, Know Theyself!). *Phil Phenomenol Res*, 52(2), 405-410, Je 92.

Shotter, John. Wittgenstein and Psychology in Wittgenstein Centenary Essays, Griffiths, A Phillips (ed). New York, Cambridge Univ Pr, 1991.

Shrader-Frechette, Kristin. Calibrating Assessors of Technological and Environmental Risk. *Res Phil Technol*, 12, 135-146, 1992.

Experts who assess the risk of environmental and technological hazards are typically wrong whenever their probabilistic judgments involve inductive extrapolations from limited existing data. If so, then experts are typically wrong in precisely those cases for which their probabilistic risk assessments are needed. And if reliable data on accident frequencies were available, then policymakers would not need risk assessments in the first place. The paper argues that one solution to this paradox may be to calibrate risk assessors themselves. This suggestion amounts to giving more credence to experts whose risk estimates have been vindicated by past predictive success. Three objections to calibration are considered and answered.

Shrader-Frechette, Kristin. Consent and Nuclear Waste Disposal. *Pub Affairs Quart*, 7(4), 363-377, O 93.

Consent questions concerning professional ethics are raised by attempts to site the world's first permanent repository for high-level nuclear waste at Yucca Mountain, Nevada. I argue 1) that a standard professional-ethics account of "second-party consent" does not justify the siting; 2) that the alleged Nevada consent does not meet the conditions generally accepted in professional ethics as necessary for the exercise of free informed consent; and 3) that compensation does not ameliorate the problems with consent in the Nevada case. Therefore, current public policy directed toward siting Yucca Mountain may not be defensible in at least one sense of "consent".

Shrader-Frechette, Kristin. Locke and Limits on Land Ownership. *J Hist Ideas*, 54(2), 201-220, Ap 93.

The paper provides a revisionist analysis of Locke's theory of property rights. Locke has traditionally been hailed as the defender of unlimited capitalistic appropriation of property, including land. Arguing that both the traditional capitalist-bourgeois and the Marxist-socialist interpretations of Locke have serious shortcomings, the author avoids these two extremes and suggests that Locke's account may be ambiguous enough to support restriction of certain property rights in natural resources like land.

If so, then Locke's writings may provide a philosophical basis in traditional political theory for a welfare-state capitalism that includes land-use planning.

Shrader-Frechette, Kristin. Science, Democracy, and Public Policy. *Crit Rev*, 6(2-3), 255-264, Spr-Sum 92.

Because experts often tout highly subjective methods of policy analysis as scientific and value free, more careful scholars are right to emphasize the value-ladenness of cost-benefit analysis and risk assessment. Moreover, those who emphasize this value-ladenness err when they use it as a rationale for replacing scientific methods of policy analysis with purely political methods of decisionmaking. Often their analyses err, as in a recent study of the swine-flu case, because they establish only that experts have misused analytic methods, not that the methods themselves are seriously flawed. Such critics also fail to be realistic if, in rejecting cost-benefit analysis and risk assessment, they offer no well developed alternative to these two methods. One alternative, cognizant of the values dimension of policy, is ethically weighted cost-benefit analysis.

Shrader-Frechette, Kristin and McCoy, E D. Community Ecology, Scale, and the Instability of the Stability Concept. *Proc Phil Sci Ass*, 1, 184-199, 1992.

Conceptual clarification is perhaps the most important key to progress in community ecology. In order to investigate some of the reasons that might explain why community ecology has been unable to arrive at a widely accepted general theory, in this essay we analyze "stability," one of its most important foundational concepts. After reviewing the stability concept and sketching its associated problems, we assess the epistemological status of four difficulties with the concept.

Shrage, Laurie J. Is Sexual Desire Raced?: The Social Meaning of Interracial Prostitution. *J Soc Phil*, 23(1), 42-51, Spr 92.

This paper examines how race and gender shape the organization of sex work in the contemporary world. I explore some common globally dispersed stereotypes of women of Asian and African descent, and claim that these images serve to reproduce familiar forms of cross-racial and cross-national prostitution. I especially focus on cultural fantasies that render intelligible the consumer choices of johns, and argue that feminist research on prostitution should problematize the motivations of male clients and not prostitute women. By emphasizing the john's role in prostitution, feminist scholarship may serve less to justify forms of social control that lead to the abuse of women.

Shumway, David. Jameson/Hermeneutics/Postmodernism in Postmodernism/Jameson/Critique, Kellner, Douglas M (ed). Washington, Maisonneuve Pr, 1989.

Shun, Kwong-Loi. *Jen* and *Li* in the *Analects*. *Phil East West*, 43(3), 457-479, Jl 93.

The paper discusses Confucius's conception of the relation between the ethical ideal (*jen*) and certain traditional rules of conduct (*li*). It argues that, while Confucius regarded the ethical ideal as shaped by the traditional rules, he also allowed room for departing from or revising such rules. This interpretation enables us to reconcile apparently conflicting ideas in Confucius's thinking as recorded in the *Analects*.

Shusterman, Richard. Aesthetics Between Nationalism and Internationalism. *J Aes Art Crit*, 51(2), 157-167, Spr 93.

After examining what it means for philosophy to be international, this paper sketches two central models of internationalism and shows how they work by a study of the circulation of ideas in international aesthetics. In examining the mechanisms and motives of this circulation, I use the Journal of Aesthetics and Art Criticism as a case study.

Shusterman, Richard. Beneath Interpretation in The Interpretive Turn, Hiley, David R (ed). Ithaca, Cornell Univ Pr, 1991.

This paper critiques the doctrines of "hermeneutical universalism" which dominates contemporary philosophy in both analytic and continental traditions. The view, shared by Derrida and Davidson, holds that all understanding is interpretation. I refute his major arguments for his views, which rely on his corrigible, perspectival, prejudicial, selective, active, and linguistic nature of understanding, and I go on to show how to draw an effective distinction between understanding and interpretation.

Shusterman, Richard. Interpretation, Intention, and Truth. *J Aes Art Crit*, 46(3), 399-411, Spr 88.

Shusterman, Richard. Pragmaticism and Perspectivism on Organic Wholes. *J Aes Art Crit*, 50(1), 56-58, Wint 92.

This paper elaborates how pragmatism offers a solution to the deadlock between analytic aesthetics and deconstruction on organic unity.

Shusterman, Richard (ed) and Bohman, James F (ed) and Hiley, David R (ed). *The Interpretive Turn*. Ithaca, Cornell Univ Pr, 1991.

In philosophy, the sciences and such diverse fields as anthropolgy, law, and social history, the turn to interpretative methods has challenged fundamental assumptions about the status of knowledge claims. The book addresses these challenges in fifteen new essays by a variety of scholars on topics about the relationship between the natural and human sciences, normative issues of interpretation, and interpretive practices in various disciplines.

Shwayder, David S. *Statement and Referent: An Inquiry into the Foundations of Our Conceptual Order*. Dordrecht, Kluwer, 1992.

This volume is the first part of a larger work in which I move from a consideration of behavior and utterance through a characterization of *assertion* as a kind of utterance to a theory of the two-way testable *products* of successful assertion which I call "statements" (Part I), thence (in Part II) to an apparatus for the representation of all humanly producible forms of statement in terms of a small variety of test kinds; those test kinds also serve for the characterization of the *syncategoremata* of classical first philosophy. In Part III that same apparatus is used for the categorization of referrable objects, eventuating in the thesis that the category of material bodies is "most basic". Part I contains a synopsis of the contemplated second and third parts of the larger work and appendices on other theories of judgement, on "constatives" other than *assertion*, on *knowledge*, and an appendix in which my general doctrines of testing and of statements is given a rough "formalization".

Sia, Santiago. Is Human Existence in Itself Not of Ultimate Significance? A Challenge to Hartshorne's Idea of Ultimate Reality and Meaning. *Ultim Real Mean*, 16(1-2), 139-141, Mr-Je 93.

In this article I suggest how Hartshorne could be more open to the belief in personal immortality by making use of his own distinction between abstractness (that there must be immortality, as his metaphysics rightly show) and concreteness (what form of immortality, which is outside the scope of his metaphysics). I then briefly argue that the demand for justice and the human quest for ultimate meaning lead us to the notion of personal immortality.

Sichel, Betty A. Education and Thought in Virginia Woolf's *To The Lighthouse*. *Proc Phil Educ*, 48, 191-200, 1992.

Sichel, Betty A. The Humanities and an Ethics of Care in Moral Education and the Liberal Arts, Mitias, Michael H (ed). Westport, Greenwood Pr, 1992.

Sichol, Marcia. Women and the New Casuistry. *Thought*, 67(265), 148-157, Je 92.

Sidelle, Alan. Rigidity, Ontology, and Semantic Structure. *J Phil*, 89(8), 410-430, Ag 92.

Why does rigid designation play such a central role in current metaphysics, particularly concerning 'the new essentialism'? I argue that this essentialism requires a 'metaphysical' understanding of rigidity, which in turn requires that some, but not all ways of carving up the world get at metaphysically 'real' objects. But familiar considerations concerning rigidity do nothing to support such an ontology, nor this understanding of rigidity. This view of rigidity, then, and the metaphysical positions which typically accompany it, require independent defense of this ontology. I sketch an alternative account of rigidity which explains the relevant phenomena through descriptive conditions analytically associated with referring expressions. This account, if correct, undercuts the claims of 'empirical essentialism'.

Sider, Theodore R. Asymmetry and Self-Sacrifice. *Phil Stud*, 70(2), 117-132, My 93.

The topic of this paper is the "self-other asymmetry" discussed by Michael Stocker and Michael Slote, which is supposed to conflict with consequentialism, and utilitarianism in particular. After characterizing the relevant sort of asymmetry, I argue 1) that there is indeed a moral self-other asymmetry that utilitarians cannot avoid by "doctoring" their theories of value, but 2) that the spirit of utilitarianism is not threatened by this asymmetry. In support of 2) I present a novel form of utilitarianism.

Sider, Theodore R and Paull, R Cranston. In Defense of Global Supervenience. *Phil Phenomenol Res*, 52(4), 833-854, D 92.

Sieckmann, Jan-Reinard. Legal System and Practical Reason: On the Structure of a Normative Theory of Law. *Ratio Juris*, 5(3), 288-307, D 92.

It will be argued, firstly, that there is a link between the legal validity of a norm and the rational justifiability of a requirement that judges should apply this norm, based on a normative conception of legal validity and the postulate that judges should act as rational persons; secondly, that rational justifiability of legal norms requires the construction of a legal system in a model of principles that differs from theories, e.g., of Kelsen, Hart, Dworkin and Alexy, which are not fully adequate for a normative conception of law.

Siefert, Josef. Is 'Brain Death' Actually Death?. *Monist*, 76(2), 175-202, Ap 93.

Siefkes, Dirk. The Work of J Richard Büchi in Perspectives on the History of Mathematical Logic, Drucker, Thomas (ed). Basel, Birkhauser, 1991.

J Richard Büchi has done influential work in mathematics, logic, and computer sciences. He is probably best known for using finite automata as combinatorial devices to obtain strong results on decidability and definability in monadic second order theories, and extending the method to infinite combinitorial tools. Many consider his way of describing computations in logical theories as seminal in the area of reduction types. With Jesse Wright, identifying automata with algebras he opened them to algebraic treatment. In a book which I edited after his death he deals with the subject, and with its generalization to tree automata and context- free languages, in a uniform way through semi-true systems, aiming for a mathematical theory of terms. (edited)

Siegel, Harvey. Justifying Conceptual Development Claims: Response to Van Haaften. *J Phil Educ*, 27(1), 79-85, Sum 93.

This paper is a response to van Haaften's attempt to build 'a natural bridge' from "is" to "ought" and in doing so to provide a general account of how, in developmental theory, a claim that 'a later stage in conceptual development is somehow better or more adequate than preceding ones' can itself be justified. The account by van Haaften violates the 'seems justified/is justified' distinction and embroils him in a problematic form of relativism. This paper offers an alternative account of such claims in terms of stage-independent criteria of adequacy.

Siegel, Harvey. On Defining "Critical Thinker" and Justifying Critical Thinking. *Proc Phil Educ*, 48, 72-75, 1992.

Siegel, Harvey. Rescher on the Justification of Rationality. *Inform Log*, 14(1), 23-31, Wint 92.

In his recent book *Rationality*, Nicholas Rescher offers a provocative attempt to justify rationality. In this paper I critically assess that attempt. After clarifying the philosophical problem at issue, I examine Rescher's effort to solve it. I argue that Rescher's justification succeeds, but that he mistakenly characterizes it as pragmatic. It succeeds only if it is understood non-pragmatically. Consequently, Rescher must give up either his justificatory argument, or his commitment to a pragmatic justification.

Siegel, Harvey and Neiman, Alven. Objectivity and Rationality in Epistemology and Education: Scheffler's Middle Road. *Synthese*, 94(1), 55-83, Ja 93.

In this paper, we describe and defend Israel Scheffler's treatment of objectivity and rationality. We explain how Scheffler's epistemology, developed in works such as *Science and Subjectivity*, provides a "middle road" between fixed foundations, certainty and the given, on the one hand; and subjectivism, relativism and skepticism on the other. We discuss Scheffler's use of this "middle road" in his work on education and teaching. Our goal here is to suggest that this work provides a valuable paradigm for responding to a number of intractable controversies among educational theorists and philosophers, especially those having to do with the state of the university in contemporary culture.

Siegel, Paul N. The New Historicism and Shakespearean Criticism: A Marxist Critique. *Clio*, 21(2), 129-144, Wint 92.

Siegwart, Geo. Zur Inkonsistenz der konstruktivistischen Abstraktionslehre. *Z Phil Forsch*, 47(2), 246-260, Ap-Je 93.

Siemek, Marek J. Husserl and the Heritage of Transcendental Philosophy in Analecta Husserliana, XXXIV, Tymieniecka, Anna-Teresa (ed). Dordrecht, Kluwer, 1992.

Siemens Jr, D F. On Wiebe's "Existential Assumptions for Aristotelian Logic". *J Phil Res*, 18, 271-275, 1993.

This comment calls attention to the nature of the Aristotelian and classical logics, and the difficulty of representing their judgments and inferences by means of Venn diagrams. The meaning of 'all' in the different calculi produces problems. A second problem is that the specification of existence in Venn diagrams for statements and arguments cannot be restricted to a single class, overlooked by Wiebe. This problem is further complicated by his adoption of classical (Renaissance) syllogistic, which is inconsistent. Aristotle's term logic is consistent. So also is the medieval extension, though the inclusion of singular premisses renders it less perspicuous though more flexible.

Siena, R M. Meister Eckhart e la condanna del 1329. *Sapienza*, 45(1), 63-76, 1992.

Sigurdson, Richard. Jacob Burckhardt's Liberal-Conservatism. *Hist Polit Thought*, 13(3), 487-512, Autumn 92.

Sikka, Sonya. Call and Conscience in Tauler and Heidegger. *Heythrop J*, 33(4), 371-398, O 92.

This article compares Heidegger's analysis of conscience and related issues in *Being and Time* with parallel themes in the sermons of the 14th-century German mystic, Johannes Tauler. Its primary purpose is to explore, through Tauler and Heidegger, a paradign for a form of life which is simultaneously mystical and ethical. However, in the process, it also offers a 'theological' reading of *Being and Time*, as opposed to the voluntarist or 'decisionist' reading which brings Heidegger's thought close to Nietzsche's.

Silk, David N. Is Teaching Conductive to Bad Philosophy? Response to Foulk. *Phil Stud Educ*, 1, 66-68, 1990.

Silk, Sally M. Writing the Holocaust/Writing Travel: The Space of Representation in Jorge Semprun's *Le grand voyage*. *Clio*, 22(1), 53-65, Fall 92.

Sillince, J A A and Minors, R H. Argumentation, Self-Inconsistency, and Multidimensional Argument Strength. *Commun Cog*, 25(4), 325-338, 1992.

Nonmonotic and default logics for maintaining consistency of beliefs are only semidecidable, so that in practice heuristics are relied upon. These logics continue to use the concepts of validity. This paper suggests the use of argument strength instead of validity, and outlines a way of getting conflicting agents to carry some of the load usually carried by logics. The paper suggests a data structure which would enable inconsistency to occur, suggests how argument strength would be determined by tactical rules and how attention focus within the shared argument map would be determined by strategic rules, and shows how arguments operate simultaneously on several different levels in a manner analogous to linguistic comprehension.

Silveira, Lígia Fraga. Descartes: Um Naturalista?. *Cad Hist Filosof Cie*, 2(2), 251-266, Jl-D 90.

The difficulties and solutions found by Descartes to solve the problem of the union of the substances, are approached appealing to both his medical and moral conceptions put together.

Silver, Bruce S. Boswell on Johnson's Refutation of Berkeley: Revisiting the Stone. *J Hist Ideas*, 54(3), 437-448, Jl 93.

James Boswell's interpretation of Samuel Johnson's refutation of idealism deserves some attention. Boswell, armed with an understanding of Berkeley's principle "*Esse* is *Percipi*" and an appreciation for Thomas Reid's approach to first principles, knew better than some recent interpreters how one should criticize a consistent, but extravagant, metaphysical hypothesis.

Silverman, Hugh J. The Inscription of the Moment: Zarathustra's Gate. *Int Stud Phil*, 24(2), 53-61, 1992.

Silverman, Hugh J. The Text of the Speaking Subject: From Merleau-Ponty to Kristeva in Merleau-Ponty Vivant, Dillon, M C (ed). Albany, SUNY Pr, 1991.

Silvers, Anita. Aesthetics for Art's Sake, Nor for Philosophy's!. *J Aes Art Crit*, 51(2), 141-150, Spr 93.

I argue that Passmore's famous complaint that aesthetics is dreary had two serious flaws. It is self-defeating because his program for refreshing aesthetics cannot be pursued absent commitment to claims of a kind Passmore insists should not be made. And it focuses not on an intrinsic flaw in aesthetics but rather on an extrinsic comparison with ethics. I show that Passmore goes diametrically wrong is casting aesthetics as inferior to ethics. Absent recognition of historically and culturally locating properties, both art and morality need philosophy as a ground. But today philosophy turns to art, rather than art to philosophy, for illumination.

Silvers, Anita. Has Her(oine's) Time Now Come?. *J Aes Art Crit*, 48(4), 365-379, Fall 90.

Can feminism explain why the history of art has many heroes but few heroines? A satisfactory answer must draw upon considerations so compelling as to radically revise the history of art. Social construction, which takes an art work's canonical status to result from political, social or economic forces, is found insufficient. Instead, it is narrative construction, of the form typically adopted to tell the story of art, which produces heroic rather than heroinic "apparent" artists. To reform the gender imbalance among great artists, we need to revalue attributes of art which can be construed as personal feminine qualities of heroines of the history of art.

Silvers, Anita. Pure Historicism and the Heritage of Hero(in)es: Who Grows in Phillis Wheatley's Garden?. *J Aes Art Crit*, 51(3), 475-482, Sum 93.

In the version proposed by Jerrold Levinson, "pure historicism" maintains that the correct way to regard a work of art is the way it was regarded in the period when it was made. Phillis Wheatley's poetry constitutes an anomaly for pure historicism: her work is strenuously regarded by her contemporaries as European, but she is a progenitor of the tradition of African-American literature. Thus, pure historicism forestalls Alice Walker from claiming Phillis Wheatley as her heritage. Locating art as predecessor or successor within a lineage is not just a matter of finding a causal link between them. Dickie's institutionalism also cannot handle this case. I conclude by constructing an account on which transfigurative artistic agency can be an institutional, yet human, force.

Silvers, Anita. The Story of Art is the Test of Time. *J Aes Art Crit*, 49(3), 211-224, Sum 91.

Traditionalism, the view that in valuing art it is only essential to understand historical events which occurred before or during the work's creation, seems commonsense. But revisionism, the view that it also is essential to understand (some) historical events which occurred after the work was made, is more reflective of actual critical practice, particularly of how art works become part of the canon. Several competing accounts of the art historical claims which enable art to acquire canonical status are explored. Heroic storytelling's "narrative" time, rather than "linear" or "statistical" time, is found to test art's lasting value.

Silvers, Stuart. A Stichwork Quilt: Or How I Learned to Stop Worrying and Love Cognitive Relativism. *Phil Psych*, 5(4), 391-410, 1992.

The work of cognitive psychologists, philosophical naturalists, post-modernists, and other such epistemic subversives conspires to endanger the well being of traditional analytic epistemology. Stephen Stich has contributed his design for epistemology's coffin. I look hard at his proposed radical revision of epistemology. (edited)

Silvers, Stuart. Cognitive Spontaneity, Coherence, and Internalism in the Justification of Empirical Belief. *Metaphilosophy*, 23(1-2), 107-118, Ja-Ap 92.

Internalist, coherence theories of knowledge, explain epistemic justification by (i) inferential connections that constitute one's coherent doxastic system, and (ii) one's cognitive access to what comprises belief justification among such connections. Empirical beliefs are, because of their sensory content, typically problematic for such theories. What is there about the way certain beliefs relate to others in the coherent system that confers empirical content upon them? I show that BonJour's (1985) coherentist's account in terms of 'cognitive spontaneity' fails to distinguish a class of empirical beliefs required for a theory of empirical knowledge.

Sim, May. Nature and Value in Aristotle's *Nichomachean Ethics*. *SW Phil Rev*, 8(1), 85-98, Ja 92.

I investigate two sets of apparent contradictions when certain claims in Aristotle's *Metaphysics, Categories, Nicomachean Ethics*, and *Politics* are taken together. The first arises between Aristotle's definition of human essence as the rational soul, which does not vary in degree (3b 32), and the claim that this rational part is present in different degrees in different human beings (1260a 10ff.) The second arises between the invariability of the rational soul, and Aristotle's emphasis that we must look to good men to discover the substance of man (1245a 36-37). I show that these contradictions are not real, and that Aristotle's view of *eudaimonia* is grounded in the nature of man.

Sim, May. Senses of Being in Aristotle's *Nichomachean Ethics*. *SW Phil Rev*, 9(1), 123-133, Ja 93.

I show that there are three major senses of substance or essence in the *Metaphysics*, which three senses are focally related. Applying this understanding of substance or essence to the *Nichomachean Ethics*, I show how *phronesis* and contemplation correspond to these three senses of human substance, and how they are also focally related. I establish that contemplation is the activity corresponding to the focal sense of substance so that it is the focal human activity. I then explain that *phronesis* is consistent with contemplation by being subordinated to, and presupposed by, contemplation.

Simakov, M. Truth-False Asymmetry in the Logic of Dharmakirti. *Indian Phil Quart*, 19(1), 65-66, Ja 92.

Simakov, M. Two Sources of Knowledge. *Indian Phil Quart*, 19(1), 61-64, Ja 92.

Simanke, Richard Theisen. Ética, Técnica e Estética em Melanie Klein. *Cad Hist Filosof Cie*, 1(2), 169-190, Jl-D 91.

This article sets out to analyze Melanie Klein's concept of ethics and its relation to psychoanalytic interpretation—both clinical and aesthetic. Having this in mind, the central role of the concept of fantasy in the Kleinian system will also be considered, because of its primacy in a conception of symbolism, based on expression, which informs the interpretative practice.

Simester, A P. Paradigm Intention. *Law Phil*, 11(3), 235-263, 1992.

Antony Duff's recent account of intended action has aroused considerable interest, particularly amongst English commentators, as an attempt to provide criteria that might be utilized by a judge or legislator. While Duff's analysis is instructive, and although it may be desirable to find conditions capturing the central notion of intention in action, this paper demonstrates that the specific conditions proposed by Duff are unsatisfactory. They require extensive modification in order to circumvent a number of difficulties presented here.

Simhony, A. Idealist Organicism: Beyond Holism and Individualism. *Hist Polit Thought*, 12(3), 515-535, Fall 91.

This article challenges the common view that the organic conception of society defended by British idealists is holistic. The article claims that the idealist model of society is organic but of a non-holistic kind. This claim presupposes a distinction between two kinds of organic analogy: relational and holistic. Relational organicism, unlike holistic organicism, presupposes no ontological primacy in either the whole or the parts. While viewing society as a relational organism, British idealists criticize holistic organicism for defending a lopsided view of social relations. Relational organicism is the conceptual framework that forges the reconciliation of individuality and community which is a central aim of modern liberalism.

Simhony, Avital. Beyond Negative and Positive Freedom: T H Green's View of Freedom. *Polit Theory*, 21(1), 28-54, F 93.

Green has frequently been portrayed as the originator of the distinction between negative and positive freedom. However, Green subscribes to a complex notion of freedom that consists of the interrelation of "internal" and "external" elements: capacities and opportunities, respectively. This view places the idea of ability at the center of the notion of freedom in a way that challenges the traditional liberal distinction between (negative) freedom and ability. First, even the conception of negative freedom rests on a more basic idea of ability. Second, freedom must be connected not only with an external sense of "ability," but with an internal sense of "ability" too. Third, the external sense of "ability" should not be restricted to absence of coercion only. Lack of positive enabling conditions may curb freedom too.

Simi Varanelli, E. Estetica, teologia e antropologia nel pensiero di Tommaso d'Aquino. *Sapienza*, 46(1), 53-69, 1993.

Simissen, Herman. On Understanding Disaster. *Phil Soc Sci*, 23(3), 352-367, S 93.

Simmons, A John. Liberal Impartiality and Political Legitimacy. *Phil Books*, 34(4), 213-223, O 93.

The article is a critical notice of Thomas Nagel's *Equality and Partiality*. It argues that on Nagel's own principles, the egalitarian institutions he favors are in fact illegitimate and the more moderately liberal arrangements he opposes are in fact legitimate. It maintains as well that Nagel's hypothetical contractarianism unfairly derives some of its force from an appeal to voluntarists ideals; but true political voluntarism is a more satisfactory stance than Nagel's "quasi-voluntarism."

Simmons, Keith. On an Argument Against Omniscience. *Nous*, 27(1), 22-33, Mr 93.

The author critically examines a recent argument against omniscience due to Patrick Grim. The first stage of the argument purports to show that, as a consequence of Cantor's power set theorem, there is no set of all truths. The author argues that if we take truths to be linguistic entities, then the argument fails; and if we take truths to be language-independent entities, then a version of the hiar paradox arises, to which Grim provides no principled way out. The author also rejects the premise of the second stage of Grim's argument, that what an omniscient being would constitute a *set* of all truths. We might take all the truths to fall under an extensionless concept—or, alternatively, we might suppose that the truths form an open-ended hierarchy.

Simon, András and Sain, Ildikó and Mikulás, Szabolcs. Complexity of Equational Theory of Relational Algebras with Projection Elements. *Bull Sec Log*, 21(3), 103-111, O 92.

In connection with a problem of L Henkin and J D Monk, we show that the equational theory and the first order theory of True Pairing Algebras (TPA's) (Relation Algebras expanded with concrete set theoretic projection functions) are not axiomatizable by any decidable set of axioms. More specifically, the equational theory of TPA's is exactly as complex as the second order universal theory of natural numbers. Finally, we show that the equational theory of the projection-free reducts of TPA's is recursively enumerable but not finitely axiomatizable.

Simon, Michael Arthur. Causation, Liability and Toxic Risk Exposure. *J Applied Phil*, 9(1), 35-44, 1992.

Persons injured as a result of exposure to toxic or carcinogenic substances are seldom able to recover damages from those who are responsible for the exposure. Tort law requires proof of causation, and causation is often unprovable because of long latency periods, because of the relative infrequency of the injuries and because many of the injuries among the exposed population are the result of other factors. A number of proposals for modifying the legal causation requirement to allow those who create hazardous risks to be held liable for the injuries that materialise are considered and found inadequate. A proposal to treat risk exposure itself as an injury for which compensation under private law is possible is also considered and ultimately found incoherent. The paper concludes by arguing for a public law solution, modelled on criminal law, but providing compensation for victims.

Simon, Paul Albert. Psicologia e Crítica Sartreana do Cogito Cartesiano. *Cad Hist Filosof Cie*, 1(2), 205-221, Jl-D 91.

On Freud's nonsense and modern literature limits of interpretation.

Simon, Robert L. Pluralism and Equality: The Status of Minority Values in a Democracy. *Nomos*, 32, 207-225, 1990.

Simon, Yves R. Foreword to *Foresight and Knowledge*. *Amer Cath Phil Quart*, 66(3), 321-330, 1992.

Simon, Yves R and Mulvaney, Robert J (ed). *Practical Knowledge—Yves R Simon*. Bronx, Fordham Univ Pr, 1991.

Simon, Yves R and Nelson, Ralph (trans). Some Remarks on the Object of Physical Knowledge. *Int Phil Quart*, 32(3), 275-283, S 92.

Taking the term physical knowledge in a broad sense that would include the philosophy of nature, the author proceeds to examine three formulations of the object of this kind of knowledge—mobile being, sensible being, and material being—in order to establish that the three are equivalent. Theoretical knowledge in its optimal state is certain and explanatory, and physical knowledge would have these notes as well were it perfect. The analysis utilizes distinctions between necessity and contingency, between typological and extensive abstraction, and between the inherently sensible and the accidentally sensible. (The last distinction is ignored in the Berkeleyan account of physical knowledge.) The object of physical knowledge, Simon states, is "the incorruptible formulation of a corruptible reality."

Simon-Ingram, Julia. Rousseau and the Problem of Community: Nationalism, Civic Virtue, Totalitarianism. *Hist Euro Ideas*, 16(1-3), 23-29, Ja 93.

The political theory of Jean-Jacques Rousseau exhibits an unmistakable tension between the desire to foster a sense of community and the fear of totalitarian control. This tension is most obvious in Rousseau's ambivalence toward both city life and rural agrarian life. This essay explores the dynamics of the tension between the city and the country and its totalitarian political ramifications in the *Social Contract* and the *Project for the Constitution of Corsica*.

Simons, Margaret A (ed) and Al-Hibri, Azizah Y (ed). *Hypatia Reborn: Essays in Feminist Philosophy*. Bloomington, Indiana Univ Pr, 1990.

Simons, Peter. Existential Propositions in Criss-Crossing A Philosophical Landscape, Schulte, Joachim (ed). Amsterdam, Rodopi, 1992.

By considering a wide and expressly classified range of examples from natural and logical languages, the attempt is made to isolate from other concomitants the features of existential sentences which make them existential. One such concomitant is the imputation of singularity. There are many ways to say something exists, and their relationships are charted. It is denied that there is anything in reality called existence, or any special existential facts.

Simons, Peter. Faces, Boundaries, and Thin Layers in Certainty and Surface in Epistemology and Philosophical Method, Martinich, A P (ed). Lewiston, Mellen Pr, 1991.

Simons, Peter. Inadequacies of Intension and Extension in Advances in Scientific Philosophy, Schurz, Gerhard (ed). Amsterdam, Rodopi, 1991.

It is argued that the division of the meanings of expressions into extension and intension is insufficient for logical and linguistic purposes. This is particularly clear for expressions which are or contain indexicals. Coextensionality and cointensionality are but two of many useful equivalence relations defined on expressions: — more than twenty different semantic values are given for terms and sentences, and the inadequacies of mere classes as term extensions are investigated in detail.

Simons, Peter. Logical Atomism and Its Ontological Refinement: A Defense in Language, Truth and Ontology, Mulligan, Kevin (ed). Dordrecht, Kluwer, 1992.

Logical atomism is defined here as the theory that the only truth-makers required for all truths are those that make logically simple propositions true. The theory is only correct if there are no special truth-makers for negative, connectively conjoined, general (quantified), modal, statistical, probabilistic and nomological propositions. The paper defends the view for these kinds of proposition in turn.

Simons, Peter. Marty on Time in Mind, Meaning and Metaphysics, Mulligan, Kevin (ed). Dordrecht, Kluwer, 1990.

The essay summarizes and assesses Marty's views on time from his posthumous *Raum und Zeit*. Marty espouses a rather crude Newtonian absolutism according to which there are absolute times but we know not which is current, and time is itself a change. Marty's psychology of time-consciousness is more subtle and is one of the most interesting theories on the subject, but is remained incomplete at his death.

Simons, Peter. Vagueness and Ignorance—II. *Aris Soc*, Supp(66), 163-177, 1992.

This paper criticises Williamson's argument for an epistemic theory of vagueness and pleads for a semantic theory using in the first instance a four-valued logic. It is argued that Williamson's use of Tarski T-schemata to support the view that the admission of vagueness within semantics leads to a contradiction turns on an equivocation in the notion of truth. Disquotational truth will not be denied of a vague sentence in a semantic theory, whereas the kind of truth that a semantic theory denies of such a sentence does not support bivalence.

Simons, Peter. Why Is There So Little Sense in Grundgesetze?. *Mind*, 101(404), 753-766, O 92.

The biggest difference between Frege's early and mature philosophies of logic was the introduction of the sense/reference distinction. He may have been motivated to fix it by reading Schröder's *Logik* and Husserl's review thereof, thereby entering a wider controversy in Germany about intensional vs. extensional logic. Frege took referents (including truth-values) to be the prime concern of logic, which is why sense, elucidated beforehand in "On Sense and Reference", is rarely mentioned in *Grundgesetze*. But the two sides of the infamous Basic Law V are said (in "Function and Concept") to have the same sense, though it is presented in two different ways.

Simons, Peter M. Was trägt die Sprachanalyse zur Philosophie der Biologie bei?. *Dialectica*, 46(3-4), 263-280, 1992.

Philosophen, insbesondere Wissenschaftstheoretiker, wurden oft so sehr von der Physik geblendet, dass sie die Bedeutung der Biologie für die Philosophie unterschätzt haben. Es wird beschrieben, wie Biologen in der Taxonomie mit der Klassifikation umgehen, wie verschieden ihre Vorgangsweise von der traditionellen Definitions- und Klassifikationstheorie ist, und wie sie die klare Fregesche Trennung zwischen Extension und Intension durcheinander bringt. Dadurch können Sprachphilosophen von Biologen über die Sprache etwas lernen. Auf der anderen Seite können sprachphilophische Unterscheidungen etwa in der Theorie der pluralen Referenz, einen Beitrag leisten zur Entschärfung der biologischen Kontroverse darüber, ob Spezies und andere Taxa Klassen oder Individuen sind.

Simont, Juliette. Sartrean Ethics in The Cambridge Companion to Sartre, Howells, Christina (ed). New York, Cambridge Univ Pr, 1992.

Simpson, David. Communicative Skills in the Constitution of Illocutionary Acts. *Austl J Phil*, 70(1), 82-92, Mr 92.

When communication is understood in terms of illocutionary acts, there are usually two possibilities to account for the constitution of those acts: linguistic rules or conventions via the meaning of what is said, or extra-linguistic conventions invoked by the saying of what is said. The second option is normally dismissed. Here the first is also rejected, as equivocal, and unable to account for illocutionary acts as a use of language (not an aspect of meaning). Instead illocutionary acts are constituted by a process dependent on the non-semantic and non-reducible frame of what is said, by which the act performed in saying is interpreted or understood. Presentation and understanding of this frame are made possible through non-linguistic communicative skills.

Simpson, David. Lying, Liars and Language. *Phil Phenomenol Res*, 52(3), 623-639, S 92.

This paper considers the phenomenon of lying and the implications it has for those subjects who are capable of lying. It is argued that lying is not just intentional untruthfulness, but is intentional untruthfulness plus an insincere invocation of trust. This trust that the liar appears to invoke points to an assumed mutuality underlying the possibility of communication. Understood in this way, lying demands of liars a sophistication in relation to language, to themselves, and to those whom they lie which exceeds the demands on mere truth-tellers.

AUTHOR INDEX WITH ABSTRACTS 675 Sinnott-Armstrong, Walter

Simpson, David (ed). *Subject to History: Ideology, Class, Gender*. Ithaca, Cornell Univ Pr, 1991.

Simpson, Evan. Principles and Customs in Moral Philosophy. *Metaphilosophy*, 24(1-2), 14-32, Ja-Ap 93.

This discussion explores skepticism about moral principles, the diminishing authority of principles in much recent moral philosophy, transformations of rationalism that result, and the possibility of morality within the bounds of custom alone.

Simpson, Lorenzo. Evading Theory and Tragedy?: Reading Cornel West. *Praxis Int*, 13(1), 32-45, Ap 93.

The purpose of this article is to explore critically two central issues in Cornel West's *The American Evasion of Philosophy: A Genealogy of Pragmatism*. 1) The epistemological status of social theory, and; 2) the role of the tragic in progressive social and political discourse. Regarding the first issue, by pursuing a debate between Richard Rorty and West, I argue that though West has strong historicist and anti-foundationalist allegiances, he fails to offer convincing exemplars of social theorizing that avoid foundationalist assumptions or aspirations. Regarding the second issue, I argue that West advocates an existential or metaphysical sense of the tragic that cannot be squared convincingly with the requisites of emancipatory social thought.

Simpson, Patricia Anna. Tragic Thought: Romantic Nationalism in the German Tradition. *Hist Euro Ideas*, 16(1-3), 331-336, Ja 93.

Simpson, Peter. Justice, Scheffler and Cicero. *Amer Cath Phil Quart*, 65(2), 203-211, Spr 91.

Samuel Scheffler argues that no adequate defense can be given of deontological restrictions on action because of the paradox that if, say, as deontologists must concede, one killing is bad, then it must follow that it is better to kill one innocent person to save more innocent persons from being killed. Cicero's account of justice and virtue escapes this paradox. For his account makes justice constitutively, not instrumentally, good, and distinguishes between justice as a measure of comparison and justice as a goal of pursuit. Scheffler's paradox either makes justice instrumentally good and/or fails to draw the latter distinction. It therefore fails to get any purchase on a Ciceronian conception of justice.

Simpson, Peter and McKim, Robert. Consequentialism, Incoherence and Choice. *Amer Cath Phil Quart*, 66(1), 93-98, Wint 92.

The authors charged, in an earlier article in the same journal, that an argument of Boyle, Finnis and Grisez to prove consequentialism incoherent (because it could not account for the making of wrong choices) was fallacious. They repeat that charge here against an attempt of Boyle, Finnis, and Grisez to defend their argument and also point out that the proposed defense falls into other fallacies of its own.

Simpson, Stephen G and Friedman, Harvey and Yu, Xiaokang. Periodic Points and Subsystems of Second-Order Arithmetic. *Annals Pure Applied Log*, 62(1), 51-64, Je 93.

Singer, Beth. Pragmatism and Pluralism. *Monist*, 75(4), 477-491, O 92.

'Pragmatism' does not denote a unitary outlook. Nevertheless, there are substantive features that are characteristic of Pragmatist thought, and one of these is pluralism. The objective of this paper is twofold: first to review some of the pluralist elements in the writings of Peirce, James, and Dewey and, second, to call attention to the work of two seldom discussed Pragmatists in whose writings pluralism is a central motif, John Herman Randall, Jr and Horace Kallen. The paper focuses on four interrelated types of pluralism: empirical, phenomenological, metaphysical, and moral, the latter, in Dewey and Kallen, encompassing cultural pluralism.

Singer, Beth. Rights and Norms in Frontiers in American Philosophy, Volume I, Burch, Robert W (ed). College Station, Texas A&M Univ Pr, 1992.

Based on G H Mead's theory of community and communicative interaction, the analysis of rights presented here bridges the gap between individualism and communitarianism. Rejecting the conception of rights as personal possessions, independent of the social setting in which they are operative, the author analyzes them as social institutions. She proposes that two fundamental rights, those of personal authority and personal autonomy, ought to be universally institutionalized, justifying this on the utilitarian ground of their unique benefit, not only to the individual, but also to the community as such.

Singer, Beth. Systematic Nonfoundationalism: The Philosophy of Justus Buchler. *J Speculative Phil*, 7(3), 191-205, 1993.

After distinguishing between system and method in philosophy I discuss the concept of foundationalism, distinguishing between ontological and epistemological foundationalism and identifying several types of each. I show the philosophy of Justus Buchler, including his metaphysics and his general theory of judgment, to be both systematic and nonfoundationalist, the latter in both senses. Buchler's ontological nonfoundationalism, which has several dimensions, is shown to rest upon his principles of ordinality and ontological parity. His epistemological nonfoundationalism, whose ramifications are explored, is related to his trimodal theory of judgment and his analysis of all judgment as ordinally located and perspectivally conditioned.

Singer, Beth. The Democratic Solution to Ethnic Pluralism. *Phil Soc Crit*, 19(2), 97-114, 1993.

Based on the theory of rights and that of community developed in my book, *Operative Rights*, I contend that, provided they satisfy specified conditions, communities as well as individuals can have rights. I also argue that rights of autonomy and authority ought to be jointly operative in every community, extended to all its members. Applying these principles to ethnic communities, I propose a model of conflict resolution involving, not negotiation but the creation of a community of rights and the development of shared perspectives in terms of which the contending parties can deal with the points at issue.

Singer, Beth (ed) and Rockmore, Tom (ed). *Anti-Foundationalism: Old and New*. Philadelphia, Temple Univ Pr, 1992.

While many in the philosophical community today treat antifoundationalism as a "postmodern" phenomenon, this work demonstrates that it has been a major theme throughout the history of Western philosophy. The ten essays included trace this history, dealing with such figures as Anaximander, Plato, Aristotle, Gassendi, Descartes, Hegel, Nietzsche, Habermas, Chisholm, James, Dewey, Randall, Buchler and Rorty. The contributors are Joseph Margolis, Ronald Polansky, Gary Calore, Fred S Michael, Emily Michael, Wilhelm S Wurzer, Charlene Haddock Seigfried, Sandra B Rosenthal, Kathleen Wallace, and the editors.

Singer, Linda. *Erotic Welfare: Sexual Theory and Politics in the Age of Epidemic*. New York, Routledge, 1993.

The book traces the effects of epidemic on the intensification of regulatory mechanisms for the control of sexuality. Singer lays out the ways in which epidemic logic and heightened regulation affect women's efforts to secure reproductive freedom, the construction of femininity within the media, and various efforts to displace the hegemony of the nuclear family in the cultural imaginary. She offers a trenchant critique of sexuality in an age of discipline, what she understands as the contemporary situation of being beyond the "politics of ecstasy." (edited)

Singer, Linda. Recalling a Community at Loose Ends in Community at Loose Ends, Miami Theory Collect, (ed). Minneapolis, Univ of Minnesota Pr, 1991.

Singer, Marcus G. Sidgwick and Nineteenth-Century British Ethical Thought in Essays on Henry Sidgwick, Schultz, Bart (ed). New York, Cambridge Univ Pr, 1992.

Singer, Marcus G (ed) and Murphy, Arthur E. Pragmatism and the Context of Rationality: Part I. *Trans Peirce Soc*, 29(2), 123-178, Spr 93.

Singer, Peter. A German Attack on Applied Ethics: A Statement by Peter Singer. *J Applied Phil*, 9(1), 85-91, 1992.

In Germany, applied ethics is under attack from a diverse coalition of left-wing organizations, disability groups, and some conservative defenders of a strict doctrine of the sanctity of human life. The attack has been pressed to the point of forcing the cancellation of conferences and disrupting lectures or classes so that they cannot take place. This essay describes the extent and nature of the attack, and makes a preliminary assessment of its significance.

Singer, Peter. *Practical Ethics (Second Edition)*. New York, Cambridge Univ Pr, 1993.

The revised edition of this book includes two new chapters, on environmental ethics and on the question of refugees. In addition, there is an appendix describing some of the reaction to the book in Germany, where the book has tested the limits of freedom of speech. The remaining chapters from the old edition—on equality and discrimination by race, sex and species, on abortion, euthanasia, overseas aid and political violence—have all been extensively revised.

Singer, Peter and Kuhse, Helga. More on Euthanasia: A Response to Pauer-Studer. *Monist*, 76(2), 158-174, Ap 93.

We reply to Pauer-Studer's critique of our views on euthanasia. The reply is in three parts. First comes a defense of Peter Singer's position in *Practical Ethics*, against criticisms made by Pauer-Studer. This is followed by an account of the weaknesses in what Pauer-Studer says about the distinction between killing and letting die. Finally, we comment on the way in which Pauer-Studer sees the German reaction to the debate over euthanasia that has taken place in that country since 1989.

Singh, Ajai and Singh, Shakuntala. The Tagore-Gandhi Controversy Revisited, II. *Indian Phil Quart*, 19(4), 265-282, O 92.

Singh, Ajay and Singh, Shakuntala. The Tagore-Gandhi Controversy Revisited, I. *Indian Phil Quart*, 19(3), 167-186, Jl 92.

Singh, Chhatrapati. The Concept of Time. *J Indian Counc Phil Res*, 9(1), 13-31, S-D 91.

Singh, R Raj. Heidegger and the World in an Artwork. *J Aes Art Crit*, 48(3), 215-222, Sum 90.

Singh, R Raj. Heidegger and the World-Yielding Role of Language. *J Value Inq*, 27(2), 203-214, Ap 93.

This paper traces Heidegger's explications of the connection between the concurrent origination of a world and a linguistic horizon for the human entity through a new reading of some of Heidegger's well-known lecture-essays on language composed in the 1950s. It is argued that Heidegger's contribution to the philosophy of language cannot be fully appreciated without a broader assessment of his pre-occupation with the world-concept in the whole expanse of his early and later writings. Such an assessment is briefly carried out in this paper along with an exposition of and a commentary on some of Heidegger's remarkable studies on the nature of language.

Singh, Ravindra. Brentano's Doctrine of Intentionality of Mental Phenomena. *Indian Phil Quart*, 19/1(Supp), 17-20, Ja 92.

Singh, Shakuntala and Singh, Ajai. The Tagore-Gandhi Controversy Revisited, II. *Indian Phil Quart*, 19(4), 265-282, O 92.

Singh, Shakuntala and Singh, Ajay. The Tagore-Gandhi Controversy Revisited, I. *Indian Phil Quart*, 19(3), 167-186, Jl 92.

Sinisi, Vito F. Kotarbinski's Theory of Genuine Names in Kotarbinski: Logic, Semantics and Ontology, Wolénski, Jan (ed). Dordrecht, Kluwer, 1990.

Sinisi, Vito F. Kotarbinski's Theory of Pseudo-Names in Kotarbinski: Logic, Semantics and Ontology, Wolénski, Jan (ed). Dordrecht, Kluwer, 1990.

Sinkler, Georgette. Paul of Venice on Obligations. *Dialogue (Canada)*, 31(3), 475-493, Sum 92.

Sinnott-Armstrong, Walter. An Argument for Consequentialism in Philosophical Perspectives, 6: Ethics, 1992, Tomberlin, James E (ed). Atascadero, Ridgeview, 1992.

Moral substitutability (MS) is the principle that, if there is a moral reason for A to do X, and if A cannot do X without doing Y, and if doing Y enables A to do X, then there is a moral reason for A to do Y. I argue that MS is true but odd enough that we need to explain why it is true. Necessary enabler consequentialism (NEC) is the theory that all moral reasons for acts are facts that the acts are necessary enablers for preventing harm or promoting good. NEC easily explains MS, but deontologists and sufficient consequentialists cannot explain MS. This is a reason to prefer NEC.

Sinnott-Armstrong, Walter. Some Problems for Gibbard's Norm-Expressivism. *Phil Stud*, 69(2-3), 297-313, Mr 93.

In *Wise Choices, Apt Feelings,*, Gibbard's analysis of normative judgments is subtle and sophisticated but still fails to solve several traditional problems for expressivism. First, it does not explain what is wrong with asserting the premises and denying the conclusion in modus ponens arguments with normative premises. Second, his account of normative governance equivocates between one view that is not plausible and another that is not expressivist. Third, Gibbard's account of objectivity yields an infinite regress. Fourth, Gibbard cannot distinguish kinds of norms by the emotions they express, and his non-judgmentalist theory of moral emotions cannot include deviant cases without lapsing into circularity.

Sintonen, Matti. In Search of Explanations: From Why-Questions to Shakespearean Questions. *Philosophica*, 51(1), 55-81, 1993.

The paper develops a notion of scientific explanation based on Jaakko Hintikka's interrogative model of inquiry. Explanations are interrogative derivations of an explanandum from initial premises and answers given by nature. This I-model explains where the covering law idea went wrong, how the process of explanation can be dealt with, and why strategies are important: in explanation genuinely new information can and must be obtained all the time. The paper argues that despite difficulties the logic of questions can be extended to explanation-seeking why-questions.

Siorvanes, L and MacCoull, L S B. *PSI* XIV 1400: A Papyrus Fragment of John Philoponus. *Ancient Phil*, 12(1), 153-170, Spr 92.

Sipiora, Michael P. Repression in *The Child's Conception of the World*: A Phenomenological Reading of Piaget. *Phil Psych*, 6(2), 167-180, 1993.

The present article undertakes a psychological reading of *The Child's Conception of the World* as a cultural artifact in which genetic psychology's naturalistic and positivistic assumptions reflect an Enlightenment model of science, and Piaget figures as an agent of technological rationality. A phenomenological analysis of the text reveals how Piaget's research engages in an active repression of specific dimensions of childhood experience. Young children's 'adualistic' conceptions of thought, self and language are deemed 'confused', and thereby discounted, by virtue of the fact such children do not 'correctly' dichotomize experience in accord with the cultural norm of mechanistic rationality. Piaget's numerous associations of the child's 'primitive' views and the (childish) thought of the pre-Socratics are briefly explored.

Sircello, Guy. Beauty in Shards and Fragments. *J Aes Art Crit*, 48(1), 21-35, Wint 90.

Sirridge, Mary. Martha Nussbaum's *Loves Knowledge: Essays on Philosophy and Literature*. *J Aes Art Crit*, 50(1), 61-65, Wint 92.

Sismondo, Sergio. The *Structure* Thirty Years Later: Refashioning a Constructivist Metaphysical Program. *Proc Phil Sci Ass*, 1, 300-312, 1992.

The Thomas Kuhn of *The Structure of Scientific Revolutions* and related texts is often seen as an idealist or neo-Kantian, as holding a constructivist as opposed to a realist position. A close reading of the texts, keeping in mind Kuhn's interests as a historian, does not support the view of Kuhn as a constructivist, though it uncovers other interesting metaphysical commitments. In particular, Kuhn can be interpreted as offering a pluralistic scientific realism that emphasizes the complexity of nature, and hence the contingency and partiality of scientific descriptions. Some reasons for readings of Kuhn as a constructivist are explored.

Sivak, Josef. L'Exisgence d'une phénoménologie asubjective et la noematique in Analecta Husserliana, XXXIV, Tymieniecka, Anna-Teresa (ed). Dordrecht, Kluwer, 1992.

Skakoon, Walter S. Romance and Ressentiment: Saint Genet in Sartre Alive, Aronson, Ronald (ed). Detroit, Wayne St Univ Pr, 1991.

"Romance and Ressentiment: Saint Genet" is a study of the poetics of a biography. Drawing on the works of Northrop Frye, notably *The Secular Scripture* (Oxford, 1976), it is argued that Sartre emplots *Saint Genet* as a romance narrative which, with its themes of descent and ascent best represents what according to Sartre is Genet's auto-analysis. The ressentiment that Sartre attributes to Genet is also a primary motivation for seeing his life as a romance, since his ressentiment is over the conflict of good and evil, a basic opposition in romance.

Skarda, Christine A and Freeman, Walter J. Mind/Brain Science in John Searle and His Critics, LePore, Ernest (ed). Cambridge, Blackwell, 1991.

Searle's philosophy is distinguished by his refusal of functionalism and his embrace of neuroscience. We focus on four aspects of his views. We agree that brains are self-organizing neural masses, not rule-driven symbol manipulators. We agree on the need for levels of description, but assert that the crucial distinction is between neurons and interactive systems, not between neural and mental functioning, which constitutes a hidden form of dualism. We reject Searle's notion that mental events cause neural events and vice versa, seeing these as opposing sides of the same coin. We see perception as self-organized, not as generated by stimuli.

Skidmore, Arthur. Is Knowledge Merely True Belief?. *SW Phil Rev*, 9(1), 71-76, Ja 93.

Crispin Sartwell's provocative thesis that knowledge is merely true belief is presented and defended as a plausible enough alternative to the justified true belief picture. Especially worthy of note is its receiving us from Gettier-type paradoxes.

Skillen, Anthony. Aesop's Lessons in Literary Realism. *Philosophy*, 67(260), 169-182, Ap 92.

Whereas the Aesopian fables are often read as springboards to their prudential and conventional 'moral', this article defends their status as realistic literature. Contrasting 'consequential' and 'display' fables, Skillen argues that the fables achieve realism, and exemplify the 'representational' and 'rhetorical' dimensions of realism.

Skillen, Anthony. Fiction Year Zero: Plato's *Republic*. *Brit J Aes*, 32(3), 201-208, Jl 92.

Plato presents art as a manipulative and ignorant play at the level of appearances, on our emotions, so that only under the Philosopher Kings' supervision can some kinds of art be allowed in the Republic. This article finds Plato's view of fiction defensible independently of his Forms, his authoritarianism and his "3rd remove" copy argument, but argues for the importance of the "dialogic" in art as a way of understanding how its connection with feelings is yet a connection with reality.

Skillen, Anthony. Racism: Flew's Three Concepts of Racism. *J Applied Phil*, 10(1), 73-89, 1993.

In an article in *Encounter*, Anthony Flew usefully opens up the issue of what racism is by giving three 'concepts': 1) 'unjustifies discrimination'; 2) 'heretical belief'; and 3) 'institutionalised racism'. He rejects senses (2) and (3) in favor of (1) and finds much 'anti-racism' in fact guilty of it. This article, while benefiting from Flew's account, argues that it basically misconceives and underestimates racism by ignoring its complex ideological (sense 2) and institutional (sense 3) character. In regard to (2) it is argued that we need to distinguish scalar and statistical claims from the binary 'us/them' essentialism characteristic of racism. In regard to (3) it is argued both that affirmative action is required by justice and that it entails 'collateral injustice' as well as consequential uncertainties.

Skillen, Anthony. Sport: An Historical Phenomenology. *Philosophy*, 68(265), 343-368, Jl 93.

With the industrialization of leisure, the marketing of heroism and the competition among nations for the Olympics gathering pace, it is tempting to think that sport can be understood only in contingent historical contexts. But this article urges a universal and humanistic perspective, showing that the complex and contradictory values with which we are familiar have been present since the time of Homer. From the Greek mania for glory, through the Roman apotheosis of the spectator, to the Victorian culture of sportsmanship and beyond, there runs a consistent band of threads covering elite champions and ordinary players. The article seeks to draw from its analysis some lessons for democratic, including gender, politics.

Skillen, Anthony. Truth and Relativity: An Exchange—Sean Sayers' Relativism. *Rad Phil*, 64, 32-34, Sum 93.

Sean Sayers, while arguing for an absolute conception of reality has maintained in his writing a conception of truth as relative to stages in the development of knowledge. He also maintains that to understand the genesis of beliefs is, in general, to appreciate the truth in them. In this article Skillen contests three qualifications to realism as confusing and unnecessary.

Skillen, Anthony. Welfare State Versus Welfare Society? in Applied Philosophy, Almond, Brenda (ed). New York, Routledge, 1992.

This article is a critique from the left of the Welfare State, which acknowledges force in much right-wing attack on its culture of dependency, irresponsibility and authoritarianism. Through an historical study of the development of articulations of the state's role up to the post-war period, an account is developed of a complex alienation between citizens as taxpayers and citizens as recipients. This leads to an argument turning around Nozick's equation of taxation with forced work into a case for treating socially constitutive work as a general duty of citizenship consistent with the idea of a free community.

Skillen, Tony. Reply to Richard Rorty's "Feminism and Pragmatism": Richard Rorty—Knight Errant. *Rad Phil*, 62, 24-26, Autumn 92.

Sklar, Lawrence. *Philosophy of Physics*. Boulder, Westview Pr, 1992.

This book is intended as an introduction to the philosophy of physics suitable for use as a classroom text. The interdependence of philosophical and scientific modes of reasoning is emphasized. Topics covered include epistemological and metaphysical issues in the theory of space and time; the role of probability in science as evidenced in statistical mechanics; and the important conceptual problems in the foundations of quantum mechanics such as the notions of uncertainty and complementarity, the measurement problem, quantum logic and the problem of hidden variables and non-locality.

Skorobogatko, Nataliia. V V Rozanov: An Interview with V G Sukach. *Russian Stud Phil*, 31(3), 79-87, Wint 92-93.

Skura, Tomasz. On Decision Procedures for Sentential Logics. *Stud Log*, 50(2), 173-180, Je 91.

In Section 2, I give a criterion of decidability that can be applied to logics (i.e., Tarski consequence operators) *without* the finite model property. In Section 3 I study Lukasiewicz-style refutation procedures as a method of obtaining decidability results. This method also proves to be more general than Harrop's criterion.

Skura, Tomasz. Refutation Calculi for Certain Intermediate Propositional Logics. *Notre Dame J Form Log*, 33(4), 552-560, Fall 92.

Using simple algebraic methods, we give Lukasiewicz-style refutation calculi for the following intermediate logics: finite logics, "LC", Yankov's logic, the logic of the weak law of excluded middle, Medvedev's logic, and certain logics without the finite model property.

Skyrms, Brian. A Mistake in Dynamic Coherence Arguments?. *Phil Sci*, 60(2), 320-328, Je 93.

Maher (1992b) advances an objection to dynamic Dutch-book arguments, partly inspired by the discussion in Levi (1987; in particular by Levi's case 2, p 204). Informally, the objection is that the decision maker will "see the Dutch book coming" and consequently refuse to bet, thus escaping the Dutch book. Maher makes this explicit by modeling the decision maker's choices as a sequential decision problem. On this basis he claims that there is a *mistake* in dynamic coherence arguments. There is really no formal mistake in classical dynamic coherence arguments, but the discussions in Maher and Levi do suggest interesting ways in which the definition of dynamic coherence might be strengthened. Such a strengthened "sequentialized" notion of dynamic coherence is explored here. It so happens that even on the strengthened standards for a Dutch book, the classic dynamic coherence argument for conditioning still goes through.

Skyrms, Brian. Coherence, Probability and Induction in Rationality in Epistemology, Villanueva, Enrique (ed). Atascadero, Ridgeview, 1992.

Skyrms, Brian. Logical Atoms and Combinatorial Possibility. *J Phil*, 90(5), 219-232, My 93.

This paper discusses a version of logical atomism without logical atoms and the appropriate notion of combinational possibility for such a metaphysics. Such an atomless metaphysics can be embedded in an atomic metaphysics by adding ideal elements, and this yields a different set of combinational possibilities.

Slaga, S W. The Teleonomy of Biological Organization (in Polish). *Stud Phil Christ*, 27(2), 65-81, 1991.

The paper deals with natural immanent teleology of biosystems. With respect to M Bunge's reference of theoretical constructs the author takes a system-informational theory of bioorganization and search the factual references in the form of real objects and processes exhibiting the features of goal-directed activities. Equifinality as a main feature of open and dynamic systems is proposed to be related to the idea of a program bearing information. An internal dynamics and the coordination of different processes in biosystems takes place under the influence of diverse regulations and control mechanisms with the latter acting as a result of adequate internal or external information. (edited)

Slaney, John K and Meyer, Robert K. A Structurally Complete Fragment of Relevant Logic. *Notre Dame J Form Log*, 33(4), 561-566, Fall 92.

Slater, B H. Conditional Logic. *Austl J Phil*, 70(1), 76-81, Mr 92.

It has been standard in the study of conditional logic to say that several of the classical laws of implication do not hold for subjunctives. But this is false. I showed this, in a theoretical way, in 'subjunctives' (*Critica* 20, 1989). In this paper I prove it in a more practical way by inspecting the work of writers in the conditional logic tradition.

Slater, B H. Modal Semantics. *Log Anal*, 32, 195-209, S-D 89.

This article offers a complete review of classical (Kripkean) modal semantics. By seeing that (constant) epsilon terms are not functions over different possible worlds that enables us to formalize not just 'logically proper names' but also 'rigid designators' and so obtain transparency, i.e., 'direct reference' without any intermediary. It means we do without 'semantics' in one traditional sense.

Slater, B H. Routley's Formulation of Transparency. *Hist Phil Log*, 13(2), 215-224, 1992.

Routley's Formula says, for instance, that if it is believed there is a man then there is something which is believed to be a man. In this paper I defend the formula; first directly, but then by looking at work by Gensler and Hintikka against it, and at the original work of Routley, Meyer, and Goddard for it. The argument ultimately reduces to a central point about the *extensionality* of objects in Routley, Meyer, and Goddard's intensional system, i.e., in its formulation of transparency.

Slater, Hartley. The Incoherence of the Aesthetic Response. *Brit J Aes*, 33(2), 168-172, Ap 93.

In a previous paper ('Fictions', *British Journal of Aesthetics*, 27(2), 1987), I gave a formal logical analysis of our relations with fictions which allowed a quite rational 'understanding'. In the present paper I balance this with some 'over-distancing', showing there is a quite proper antinomy of distance—again in exact formal logical terms.

Slater, P H. Farewell to Opacity. *Dialectica*, 47(1), 37-53, 1993.

This paper firms up previous arguments for referential transparency in intensional constructions by providing conclusive proofs of this, both formal and informal. Centrally the paper uses epsilon terms to symbolise referring expressions, and so it obtains the rigid designators needed to allow the same object to be referred to in all worlds and minds. The details of several contrary ideas are examined to reinforce the claim that they are incorrect. But also certain world-dependent objects are identified, using epsilon terms, to give an understanding of what might have caused the historical belief in referential opacity.

Sleeper, Ralph W. "What is Metaphysics?". *Trans Peirce Soc*, 28(2), 177-187, Spr 92.

Sleeper, Ralph W. Vanishing Frontiers in American Philosophy in Frontiers in American Philosophy, Volume I, Burch, Robert W (ed). College Station, Texas A&M Univ Pr, 1992.

Sleigh, Nicholas. Objective Goodness and Aristotle's Dilemma. *J Value Inq*, 26(3), 341-351, Jl 92.

I examine the following dilemma for the view that an objective property of intrinsic goodness exists. Either the property would supervene on good things' natures, in which case the things' natures seem deprived of any direct role in explaining the things' goodness, or the property would exist wholly within good things, which conflicts with their appearance of having, qua good things, nothing in common. I conclude that a property of goodness escapes this dilemma if construed as a determinable property, like coloredness. This conclusion depends on resemblances between co-determinates, such as red and yellow, being objective features of the world.

Sleutels, J J M. Eliminatie of reductie van qualia?. *Alg Ned Tijdschr Wijs*, 85(1), 70-95, F 93.

The philosophy of Paul Churchland is marked by a tension between elimination and reduction of mental representations. This also applies to Churchland's account of qualia, which are said to be cognitively dispensable, while at the same time being reducible to neural states. In this paper I try to alleviate the tension and remove some of the ambiguities inherent in Churchland's philosophy of mind. A distinction is made between four possible constructions of the phenomenally 'given', viz., as superweak, weak, strong or superstrong qualia. Churchland endorses weak and strong qualia, corresponding to two versions of his thesis of the plasticity of perception. I defend his position against the criticism that qualia are either superweak (hence cognitively irrelevant) or superstrong (endowed with a proper conceptual identity).

Sloep, Peter B. Methodology Revitalized?. *Brit J Phil Sci*, 44(2), 231-249, Je 93.

Controversies in science have a tendency to be long-lasting. Moreover, they tend to wither rather than be solved by sorting out the arguments *pro* and *con*. Barring the sociological dimension, an important factor in the perpetuation of scientific controversies seems to be the contestants' passion for broad philosophical theses when it comes to defending their respective positions. In this paper one such controversy is analysed. It involves the alleged use of Popperian falsificationism to defend a position in (community) ecology some years ago. The upshot of the analysis is the falsificationism is altogether irrelevant to the controversy's solution; philosophy, though, is utterly relevant if one limits it to elementary, uncontroversial, normative methodological principles.

Slote, Michael. Ethics Naturalized in Philosophical Perspectives, 6: Ethics, 1992, Tomberlin, James E (ed). Atascadero, Ridgeview, 1992.

Slote, Michael. *From Morality to Virtue*. New York, Oxford Univ Pr, 1992.

Slote, Michael. Virtue Ethics and Democratic Values. *J Soc Phil*, 24(2), 5-37, Fall 93.

Slurink, Pouwel. Aangeboren belevingsstructuren, intenties en symbolen. *Alg Ned Tijdschr Wijs*, 85(1), 128-137, F 93.

In this article the author argues against Paul Churchland's radical reductionism. By taking an evolutionary approach some important shortcomings of Churchland's position can be corrected.

Slutsky, Steven M and Hamilton, Jonathan H. Endogenizing the Order of Moves in Matrix Games. *Theor Decis*, 34(1), 47-62, Ja 93.

Players often have flexibility in when they move and thus whether a game is played simultaneously or sequentially may be endogenously determined. For 2x2 games, we analyze this using an extended game. In a stage prior to actual play, players choose in which of two periods to move. A player moving at the second turn learns the first mover's action. If both select the same turn, they play a simultaneous move subgame. If both players have dominant strategies in the basic game, equilibrium payoffs in the basic and extended games are identical. If only one player has a dominant strategy or if the unique equilibrium in the basic game is in mixed strategies, then the extended game equilibrium payoffs differ iff some pair of pure strategies Pareto dominates the basic game simultaneous play payoffs. If so, sequential play attains the Pareto dominating payoffs. The mixed strategy equilibrium occurs only when it is not Pareto dominated by some pair of pure strategies. In an alternative extended game, players cannot observe delay by opponents at the first turn. Results for 2x2 games are essentially the same as with observable delay, differing only when one player has a dominant strategy.

Smajs, J. Nature and Culture—Two Orders of Reality? (Part I) (in Czechoslovakian). *Filozof Cas*, 39(6), 966-974, 1991.

Small, Michael W. Ethics in Business and Administration: An International and Historical Perspective. *J Bus Ethics*, 12(4), 293-300, Ap 93.

This is a study of ethical and moral behavior, or perhaps unethical behavior, in two different societies. One society, contemporary Australia, and in particular the state of Western Australia, is currently undergoing an exhaustive Royal Commission into the shenanigans of a number of well-known business men and former leading politicians who seem to have been playing fast and loose with large amounts of other peoples' money. While this was initially the major focus of the paper, a secondary focus developed based on the interest shown in acquiring an historical background by a group of business policy students. It illustrated that malfeasance, misfeasance and other forms of malpractice in business and administration were just as common in Greco-Roman times as today. Reference has been made to a selection of the writings of some of the more well-known writers of this period. (edited)

Small, Robin. Cantor and the Scholastics. *Amer Cath Phil Quart*, 66(4), 407-428, Autumn 92.

Georg Cantor introduced a new branch of mathematics with is theory of transfinite numbers. At the same time, his concept of the infinite suggested a solution to some old philosophical problems. Cantor's own position, however, is not always what one might expect from a champion of the actual infinite. For instance, he firmly rejects the idea of an infinite past time. This article examines Cantor's philosophical arguments concerning the eternity of the world, in the context of his acquaintance with the scholastic tradition, and his dialogue with representatives of the contemporary Neo-Scholastic movement.

Smart, J J C. Laws of Nature as a Species of Regularities in Ontology, Causality and Mind: Essays in Honour of D M Armstrong, Bacon, John (ed). New York, Cambridge Univ Pr, 1993.

Smart, Ninian. Soft Natural Theology in Prospects for Natural Theology, Long, Eugene Thomas (ed). Washington, Cath Univ Amer Pr, 1992.

Smejkalova, J. Gender Trouble: Notes on One Book (in Czechoslovakian). *Filozof Cas*, 40(5), 819-824, 1992.

The essay presents several thoughts on the "performance theory of gender" developed in Judith Butler's *Gender Trouble*, in relation to the metaphors of performance, games, and stage known from Havel's writing. The intention of their projects seems to be similar—to explain the existence of an individual within a complicated regime of regulations by challenging the simplified model of "ruled-ruler". (edited)

Smeyers, Paul. On What We Really Care About in Child-Centeredness. *Proc Phil Educ*, 48, 141-144, 1992.

Against Margonis, it is argued that crucial in the child-centered movement was the idea that the child "knows" what is good for him. Accepting such has left us a legacy of ethical commitment, this not sought in 'real activities' used to evoke the child's interest. To escape instrumentalism a reappraisal of the role of the individual is needed. Following Wittgenstein and Taylor the paper argues that to be educated means to be initiated into a culture, allowing one to form one's own opinions, yet also requiring to accept without criticism (at least at some moment) some basic frame-work.

Smeyers, Paul. The Necessity for Particularity in Education and Child-Rearing: the Moral Issue. *J Phil Educ*, 26(1), 63-73, 1992.

The justification debate has always been a major issue within philosophy of education. In this study Wittgensteinian interpretation of this matter is offered. It is argued that in using his framework justification itself has to be thought of differently, i.e., as making explicit the bedrock of the form of life the educator finds him or herself in. But Wittgenstein's insights highlight too the particularity of the ethical and therefore also of the educational situation. The paper argues that educators cannot but take a stance, cannot but act in accordance with what appeals to them in the midst of the irreconcilable desires of others. It is therefore considered that the demand for particularity reveals itself here as a demand for authenticity.

Smilansky, Saul. Did James Deceive Himself about Free Will?. *Trans Peirce Soc*, 28(4), 767-779, Fall 92.

I argue that William James indulged in self-deception with regard to the free will problem. My argument differs from previous ones in two ways: firstly, in pointing out specific features of James's philosophical writing with indicate the self-deception. Secondly, in presenting an integrated case, based not only on the much discussed issue of his "Will to Believe" position, but on James's autobiographical writing as well as on specific features of his philosophical writing. The conclusion is said to cast doubts about the "Will to Believe" position. Finally, I briefly consider the general issue of philosophical self-deception.

Smiley, Timothy. Can Contradictions Be True?—I. *Aris Soc*, Supp(67), 17-33, 1993.

Smirnov, Andrei. The Path to Truth—Ibn-'Arabī and Nikolai Berdiaev (Two Types of Mystical Philosophizing). *Russian Stud Phil*, 31(3), 7-397-39, Wint 92-93.

Smirnov, Andrey V. Nicholas of Cusa and Ibn 'Arabi: Two Philosophies of Mysticism. *Phil East West*, 43(1), 65-85, Ja 93.

The paper deals with the question weather the differences in post- Medieval traditions of philosophy in Western and Arab world might be understood as the consequence of diversity of mystical philosophizing which sums up the Medieval philosophical quest. The teachings of the two major mystical philosophers, Nicholas of Cusa and Ibn 'Arabi, are analyzed to provide the evidence for this assumption. The basic differences in understanding the Divine, its relation to the world and human being and the later's cognitive capacity are treated as characteristic for the two thinkers, and distinguishing for the two traditions.

Smirnov, P I. Russia's Movement Toward a Market Civilization and the Russian National Character. *Russian Stud Phil*, 31(4), 9-24, Spr 93.

Smith, A Anthony. Marx and His Opponents on the Public/Private Distinction in Terrorism, Justice and Social Values, Peden, Creighton (ed). Lewiston, Mellen Pr, 1990.

Mainstream social theorists hold that public decisions should be subject to public control, while private decisions should be left to the individual's own discretion. Marx agreed, but held that decisions regarding the allocation of productive resources are inherently public. The author first derives a principle to account for easy cases where intuitions regarding what is private and what is public are generally shared. It is then argued that this principle justifies the Marxist position. This does not establish the correctness of the policy of socializing the means of production, for that rests upon empirical matters rather than conceptual distinctions.

Smith, Adam. *An Inquiry Into the Nature and Causes of the Wealth of Nations—Adam Smith*. Indianapolis, Hackett, 1993.

Smith, Barry. Brentano and Marty: An Inquiry into Being and Truth in Mind, Meaning and Metaphysics, Mulligan, Kevin (ed). Dordrecht, Kluwer, 1990.

A study of the concepts of reality and existence in the work of Franz Brentano and his student Anton Marty. Topics dealt with include: Aristotle's concept of being in the sense of being true; operationally defined concepts; Brentano's reism; things and states of affairs.

Smith, Barry. On the Phases of Reism in Kotarbinski: Logic, Semantics and Ontology, Woleński, Jan (ed). Dordrecht, Kluwer, 1990.

Smith, Barry. Relevance, Relatedness and Restricted Set Theory in Advances in Scientific Philosophy, Schurz, Gerhard (ed). Amsterdam, Rodopi, 1991.

What sort of set theory results when restrictions are placed on the sorts of elements which may form a set? Given an arbitrary relevance relation, one can formulate a notion of set which will apply only to totalities of mutually relevant entities. Relevance might signify for example: exists at the same time as, belongs to the same body as, is less than a certain distance from, etc. The resultant theory, which embodies topological constraints, can then be used as the basis for an account of relevance between propositions which is in the tradition of the relevant logics of 'analytic implication' studied by M Dunn and W T Parry.

Smith, Barry. Zum Wesen des Common Sense: Aristoteles und die naive Physik. *Z Phil Forsch*, 46(4), 508-525, O-D 92.

The paper relates classical treatments of physics and metaphysics to contemporary work on common sense in the field of artificial intelligence (J Hobbs, P Hayes, et. al.). It defends the universality (and truth) of certain basic principles of common-sense physics and shows why these basic principles must leave certain issues undetermined.

Smith, Barry C. Characteristica Universalis in Language, Truth and Ontology, Mulligan, Kevin (ed). Dordrecht, Kluwer, 1992.

Smith, Barry C. Understanding Language. *Proc Aris Soc*, 92, 109-139, 1992.

Smith, Bonnie. Historiography, Objectivity, and the Case of the Abusive Widow. *Hist Theor*, 31(4), 15-32, 1992.

For the past century, French intellectuals have increasingly censured Athénaïs Michelet as an "abusive widow" who mutilated the work of her husband. This article explores the role such censure, often vituperative and emotionally charged, has played in the development of French historiography and argues that it has been crucial in constructing the revered figure of Michelet. Further, the figure of Michelet is itself central to the more important trajectory of historiography that depends on the establishment of "authors" as focal points of disciplinary power. (edited)

Smith, Craig R and Hyde, Michael J. Aristotle and Heidegger on Emotion and Rhetoric in The Critical Turn, Angus, Ian (ed). Carbondale, So Illinois Univ Pr, 1993.

Smith, David Woodruff. The Cogito *cira* AD 2000. *Inquiry*, 36(3), 225-254, S 93.

What are we to make of the cogito today, as the walls of Cartesian philosophy crumble around us? The enduring foundation of the cogito is consciousness. It is in virtue of a particular phenomenological structure that an experience is conscious rather than unconscious. Drawing on an analysis of that structure, the cogito is given a new explication that synthesizes phenomenological, epistemological, logical, and ontological elements. The discussion begins with Descartes's own careful formulations of some of these issues. Then the cogito is parsed into several different principles, the phenomenological principle emerging as basic. In due course the analysis sifts through Husserl's epistemology, Hintikka's logic of the cogito, and Kaplan's logic of demonstratives.

Smith, Holly M. Whose Body Is It, Anyway? in Philosophical Perspectives, 6: Ethics, 1992, Tomberlin, James E (ed). Atascadero, Ridgeview, 1992.

Smith, Huston. Dignity in Difference in On Community, Rouner, Leroy S (ed). Notre Dame, Univ Notre Dame Pr, 1992.

Smith, Huston. Is There a Perennial Philosophy? in Revisioning Philosophy, Ogilvy, James (ed). Albany, SUNY Pr, 1992.

Smith, Janet E. Reply to Gass's "Abortion and Moral Character: A Critique of Smith". *Int Phil Quart*, 33(2), 233-238, Je 93.

In this article, I defend to some extent my understanding of the meaning of sexuality that undergirds my claim that the choice to abort is an indication that a woman has a faulty moral character, particularly that she is irresponsible in her sexuality, and that the decision to abort reinforces this character. I discuss what constitutes evidence that a moral action harms an individual's moral character. I discuss the value of moral integrity and how one determines it. Finally, I assert that my argument about moral character does not constitute the entirety of my arguments against abortion.

Smith, John E. *Jonathan Edwards: Puritan, Preacher, Philosopher*. Notre Dame, Univ Notre Dame Pr, 1992.

The book presents a conspectus on Edwards' life and thought, philosophical and theological. His use of Locke's philosophy is examined together with the influence of Newton. Emphasis is placed on his interpretation of the Great Awakening and of the other revivals. In addition to a discussion of his *Ethical Writings*, there are analyses of the major Treatises—*Religious Affections, Freedom of the Will* and *Original Sin*. Edwards' major sermons are discussed along with *The History of Redemption*, which was originally a long series of sermons. The book draws on much new material stemming from the Yale edition of his *Works*, which is the first critical edition we have.

Smith, John E. Prospects for Natural Theology. *Monist*, 75(3), 406-420, Jl 92.

The basic issue is the present viability of a natural theology based supposedly on "unaided" reason as suggested by Aquinas and some philosophers of the Enlightenment. The difficulties surrounding the identification of such a reason are insurmountable and this suggests that there can be no natural theology in the above sense. The author argues in behalf of a philosophical theology in the tradition of Augustine and the doctrine of "faith seeking understanding."

Smith, Joseph Wayne. The Recent Case Against Physicalist Theories of Mind in New Horizons in the Philosophy of Science, Lamb, David (ed). Brookfield, Avebury, 1992.

Smith, Joseph Wayne and Webster, Gerry and Goodwin, Brian. The 'Evolutionary Paradigm' and Constructional Biology in New Horizons in the Philosophy of Science, Lamb, David (ed). Brookfield, Avebury, 1992.

Smith, Kelly C. Neo-Rationalism Versus Neo-Darwinism: Integrating Development and Evolution. *Biol Phil*, 7(4), 431-451, O 92.

Among those unsatisfied with Neo-Darwinism are the "process structuralists" who argue that a properly "rationalist" biology will generate universal laws of a form that Neo-Darwinism, with its reliance on the stochastic, cannot. Process structuralism charges that not only is Neo-Darwinism untestable but that it inevitable produces a tendency toward genetic determinism and an atomistic treatment of organisms. While Neo-Darwinism *is* untestable, this does not pose a major difficulty. Further, these tendencies result more from methodology than theory. However, the critique does reveal deepseated problems with orthodox evolutionary theory that must be addressed.

Smith, Kelly C. The New Problem of Genetics: A Response to Gifford. *Biol Phil*, 7(3), 331-348, Jl 92.

Fred Gifford attempts to explicate the meaning of the term "genetic traits" via two criteria (DF and PI). While DF is a legitimate measure of *heritability*, it is not necessarily a genetic one and PI depends on problematic distinctions between genes and their environments. Both criteria will be highly relative and both, via what I term "the new problem of genetics" will support contradictory descriptions of the same trait. Fortunately, quantitative genetics can accomplish the heritability analysis of DF and causal-mechanical biology the causal selection of PI without postulating the problematic causal properties of the genes. In short, talk of "genetic traits", by whatever criteria, is necessary and misleading.

Smith, Kenneth. Two Concepts of Spirit in Hegel. *SW Phil Stud*, 14, 98-110, Spr 92.

Smith, M B E. Review Essay: The Best Intuitionistic Theory Yet! Thomson On Rights. *Crim Just Ethics*, 11(2), 85-97, Sum-Fall 92.

Thomson's book comprises an elaborate account of the nature of claims (which she takes to be the most fundamental kind of rights), together with a closely reasoned list of what claims we have—all resting on a somewhat slender metaethical basis. I argue that she is largely right about the nature of claims—and that this is one of philosophy's outstanding achievements in this century. I next argue that her list of claims requires some correction and supplementation. I then further explain and defend her method of testing moral principles by appealing to our intuitions about examples.

Smith, Michael and Pettit, Philip. Practical Unreason. *Mind*, 102(405), 53-79, Ja 93.

Most approaches to practical unreason treat the phenomenon as a practical failure that is not distinctively a failure of reason—say, as a loss of autonomy or control—or as a failure of reason that is not distinctively practical: say, as a form of inattention or illogic. This paper describes an approach under which the failure can be both a practical failure and a failure of reason. The authors begin with a picture of human psychology under which action is always the product of belief and desire but is also answerable to deliberative judgment. They find room for practical unreason, properly understood, in the gap that can open between the properties that an agent finds deliberatively compelling —the properties that, were he rational and informed, he would want himself to desire—and the properties that actually arouse his desires and move him to action. The possibility of this gap opening up is documented by reference to five broadly different varieties of practical unreason.

Smith, Mick. Cheney and the Myth of Postmodernism. *Environ Ethics*, 15(1), 3-18, Spr 93.

I draw critical parallels between Jim Cheney's work and various aspects of *modernism*, which he ignores or misrepresents. I argue, first, that Cheney's history of ideas is appallingly crude. Second, Cheney's account of *primitive* peoples is both ethnocentric (though positively so) and inaccurate. Third, Cheney reduces context or *place* to a concept of bioregionality. In this way, he reinstates a privileged foundationalism which, by his own definitions, makes his philosophy modernist. I develop these criticisms in order to suggest a less restricted contextual approach to environmental issues. (edited)

Smith, P Christopher. *Hermeneutics and Human Finitude: Toward a Theory of Ethical Understanding*. Bronx, Fordham Univ Pr, 1991.

Smith, Patricia (ed). *The Nature and Process of Law: An Introduction to Legal Philosophy*. New York, Oxford Univ Pr, 1993.

An anthology of great works in legal philosophy, with study questions and introductions, organized to present legal issues and legal concepts within the context of a legal system, using the US system as a model, and focusing on law as an evolving social institution and process of normative decision making, social ordering, and conflict resolution.

Smith, Patricia G. Discrimination and Disadvantage in Feminist Legal Theory: A Review of Deborah Rhode's *Justice and Gender*. *Law Phil*, 11(4), 431-448, 1992.

An analysis of and reflection on the major themes of D Rhode's *Justice and Gender*. The object of this book is: 1) to examine the legal history (and current law) of sex discrimination focusing on social context rather than abstract rights, and; 2) to suggest a reorientation of law to a principle of gender disadvantage rather than a focus on gender difference. By examining how law may diminish or entrench patterns of inequality we may come to understand the social construction of gender as well as some possibilities for effecting social change.

Smith, Paul. Laclau's and Mouffe's Secret Agent in Community at Loose Ends, Miami Theory Collect, (ed). Minneapolis, Univ of Minnesota Pr, 1991.

Smith, Peter. Anomalous Monism and Epiphenomenalism: A Reply to Honderich. *Analysis*, 44(2), 83-86, Mr 84.

Smith, Quentin. A Big Bang Cosmological Argument for God's Nonexistence. *Faith Phil*, 9(2), 217-237, Ap 92.

The big bang cosmological theory is relevant to Christian theism and other theist perspectives since it represents the universe as beginning to exist *ex nihilo* about 15 billion years ago. This paper addresses the question of whether it is reasonable to believe that God created the big bang. Some theists answer in the affirmative, but it is argued in this paper that this belief is not reasonable. In the course of this argument, there is a discussion of the metaphysical necessity of natural laws, of whether the law of causality is true *a priori*, and of other pertinent issues.

Smith, Quentin. *Language and Time*. New York, Oxford Univ Pr, 1993.

Smith, Quentin. Personal Identity and Time. *Philosophia (Israel)*, 22(1-2), 155-167, Ja 93.

Some philosophers hold that the tenseless theory of time entails the "temporal parts" theory of personal identity, that a person is a succession of distinct particulars. Some philosophers also believe that the tensed theory of time entails the "substance" or "continuant" theory of personal identity, that a person is a single particular that endures through time. I argue that these philosophers are mistaken. Both the tensed and tenseless theories of time are compatible with both theories of personal identity.

Smith, Quentin. Reply to Craig: The Possible Infinitude of the Past. *Int Phil Quart*, 33(1), 109-116, Mr 93.

William Lane Craig argues that the past is necessarily finite. In this paper I argue that his argument goes wrong in several places. Craig unsoundly argues that since a series with the order type w can be reordered as $\omega + \omega$, it must have aleph-one members. He also unsoundly argues that if the past has the order type $\omega + \omega$, then some past events could never have recede from the present. This is true but irrelevant if "never" means "not in a finite time", and relevant but false if "never" means "not in a infinite time", Other fallacies in his arguments are also exposed.

Smith, Quentin. The Anthropic Coincidences, Evil and the Disconfirmation of Theism. *Relig Stud*, 28(3), 347-350, S 92.

The anthropic coincidences are certain physical constants or initial conditions that are exactly fine-tuned for the evolution of intelligent life. Swinburne argues that the anthropic coincidences confirm theism. It is argued in this paper that Swinburne fails to solve the problem of evil. Thus, the only creationist hypothesis that the anthropic coincidences confirm is the hypothesis that a malevolent being created the universe.

Smith, Quentin. The Concept of a Cause of the Universe. *Can J Phil*, 23(1), 1-24, Mr 93.

Smith, Quentin. The World's Features and their Pure Appreciation: A Reply to Schenk. *J Speculative Phil*, 7(1), 39-47, 1993.

This article is a defense and elaboration of certain ideas in my book, *The Felt Meanings of the World*, against some criticisms made by David Schenk. I argue that the world's existence is appropriately appreciated in the affect of joy rather than in any other affect. I also argue that the contingency of the world's existence is appropriately or purely appreciated in the affect of marvelling, and not in any other affect. Schenk argues that I have inadequately supported these and other claims, but in this article I advance some new arguments for them.

Smith, Robin. Aristotle on the Uses of Dialectic. *Synthese*, 96(3), 335-358, S 93.

Smith, Rogers M. On the Good of Knowing Virtue. *Nomos*, 34, 132-141, 1992.

Smith, Steven A. How To Respond To Terrorism in Terrorism, Justice and Social Values, Peden, Creighton (ed). Lewiston, Mellen Pr, 1990.

Terrorism typically elicits a mindless retributive response rather than sensitivity to truth. Self-righteous condemnation of individual terrorist acts ignores the coercive, "terrorist" dimension of most functioning moral codes. In a well-developed moral consciousness, fear of sanctions is replaced by spontaneous moral action. Coercion—state sponsored or individual—is a failure to explore creative nonviolent alternatives. We need a world less fertile for the growth of terrorism, where the garbage of injustice does not accumulate so high, and thus erupts less frequently in angry boils of cruelty, violence and pain.

Smith, Steven B. Defending Hegel from Kant in Essays on Kant's Political Philosophy, Williams, Howard Lloyd (ed). Chicago, Univ of Chicago Pr, 1992.

This article defends Hegel's critique of Kantian ethics as an "empty formalism" as, in the main, correct. I look especially at Hegel's account of the trial of Socrates and the *Antigone* to indicate the permanence of moral conflict (*Kollision*) and the inability of putative standards of practical reason to resolve at least the most severe cases. I suggest that Hegelian *Sittlichkeit*, while not without its dangers, is a more reliable guide to action than Kantian duty.

Smith, Steven B. Hegel on Slavery and Domination. *Rev Metaph*, 46(1), 97-124, S 92.

This paper sets out three claims. First, Hegel's views on slavery are best understood as a rejection of the Aristotelian concept of a "natural" slave; second, I argue that his views on emancipation are deeply embedded in a specifically Protestant conception of liberty; third, only when the theological context of Hegel's thought is recovered can we grasp the full force of Marx's and Nietzsche's rejection of it.

Smith, Steven G. Realizing. *Amer Phil Quart*, 29(4), 363-371, O 92.

Realizing as distinct from knowing involves a synthesis of things apprehended and things not directly apprehensible in such a way that subjects are centered as knowers in contact with the center of what is known. Three aspects of realizing correspond to the three basic limits on apprehensibility: *imaginative*, bringing things-in-themselves into (posited) relation with the contents of consciousness; *intellectual*, the grasping of mental forms as such (making the mind count as a reality for itself to be related to); and *spiritual*, actualizing relationship with other beings qua other (i.e., as transcending consciousness). This analysis illuminates the meaning of metaphysical arguments.

Smith, Tara. On Deriving Rights to Goods from Rights to Freedom. *Law Phil*, 11(3), 217-234, 1992.

This paper examines a particular type of argument often employed to defend welfare rights. This argument contends that welfare rights are a necessary supplement to liberty rights because rights to freedom become hollow when their bearers are not able to take advantage of their freedom. Rights to be provided with certain goods are thus a natural outgrowth of a genuine concern to protect freedom. (edited)

Smith, Tara. Rights, Friends, and Egoism. *J Phil*, 90(3), 144-148, Mr 93.

This paper questions the treatment of egoism in Michael J Meyer's "Rights between Friends." Contrary to Meyer, it argues that desirable friendships and the recognition of rights may both rely on egoism. To determine conclusively whether this is so and to assess the implication of such a discovery, we must examine the nature of egoism and the relationship between obligations of altruism and obligations to respect rights much more closely than we previously have. In light of communitarian attacks on "excessive individualism" in liberalism, the time is ripe for such an investigation.

Smith, Tara. Why A Telological Defense of Rights Needn't Yield Welfare Rights. *J Soc Phil*, 23(3), 35-50, Wint 92.

This paper argues against one rationale for welfare rights, the argument that if liberty rights are justified by their service to human well-being, welfare rights must also be justified since welfare rights provide goods which are ingredients of well-being. The reasoning suffers from two fatal flaws: it relies on an impoverished conception of what well-being is and it misconstrues the relationship between respect for rights and achievement of well-being. Well-being does not consist of the possession of foods that others might provide. Correlatively, a teleologist does not defend liberty rights as providing the "stuff" of well-being nor as a foolproof guarantee of rightholders' well-being.

Smith, Tony. *Dialectical Social Theory and Its Critics*. Albany, SUNY Pr, 1992.

Part One of the book argues that Hegel's legacy is central to Marx's work. Topics discussed include the relevance of Hegel's theory of the syllogism to Marxism, the parallels between Hegel's theory of Greek Religion and Marx's critique of capital, the role of dialectical logic in Marx's economic writings, and the similarities and differences between Hegel and Marx's views on civil society. Part Two defends Marx's dialectical approach to social theory against objections raised by Lucio Colletti, Jon Elster, John Roemer, and Jean Baudrillard.

Smith, Tony. *The Logic of Marx's "Capital": Replies to Hegelian Criticisms*. Albany, SUNY Pr, 1990.

Beginning with "value" and "commodity" at the start of Volume I in Marx's major work, and progressing step-by-step to the end of Volume III, this work establishes in detail that *Capital* is a systematic theory of socio-economic categories ordered according to dialectical logic. At each stage in the analysis of the theory Marx's arguments are reconstructed. Responses are also formulated to Hegelian criticisms of Marx's employment of dialectical logic.

Smith, Warren Allen. Dewey on the Humanist Movement. *Free Inq*, 13(1), 31, Wint 92-93.

Smithka, Paula J. Are Active Pacifists Really Just-Warists in Disguise?. *J Soc Phil*, 23(3), 166-183, Wint 92.

This essay argues that since just-warism comprises the *passive* segment of the warist continuum, and *active* pacifist who accepts the right of self-defense is really a just-warist in pacifist disguise. This claim follows from the identification of some commonly held misconceptions with respect to the just-war model; the most significant being that *all* just-warist are *active* "offensive" warists who provide any *ad hoc* excuse to wage war. The condition under which a just-war can be waged and a continuum of various warist position, from the most "passive" to the most "active," are also provided as support for my conclusion.

Smorowski, Michael A. Kierkegaard's View of Faith in Terrorism, Justice and Social Values, Peden, Creighton (ed). Lewiston, Mellen Pr, 1990.

Smorynski, C. The Development of Self-Reference: Löb's Theorem in Perspectives on the History of Mathematical Logic, Drucker, Thomas (ed). Basel, Birkhauser, 1991.

Smullyan, Raymond M. Some Unifying Fixed Point Principles. *Stud Log*, 50(1), 129-141, Mr 91.

This article is written for both the general mathematician and the specialist in mathematical logic. No prior knowledge of metamathematics, recursion theory or combinatory logic is presupposed, although this paper deals with quite general abstractions of standard results in those three areas. Our purpose is to show how some apparently diverse results in these areas can be derived from a common construction. (edited)

Smyth, Jim. Nationalist Nightmares and Postmodernist Utopias: Irish Society in Transition. *Hist Euro Ideas*, 16(1-3), 157-163, Ja 93.

The ongoing and apparently intractable conflict in Northern Ireland coupled with the failure of the project of economic and social modernization led the Irish state to abandon the official ideology of nationalism and separatism. The subsequent ideological vacuum has been partially filled by a resurgent Roman Catholic Church and a secular postmodernism. The former represents elements of the traditional social structure while the latter is urban, socially mobile and secular. Both approaches neglect the structural sources of inequality, power and domination and detach the question of emancipation and freedom from any concrete context.

Snider, Eric W. The Conclusion of the *Meno*. *Ancient Phil*, 12(1), 73-85, Spr 92.

Snow, Nancy E. Self-Forgiveness. *J Value Inq*, 27(1), 75-80, Ja 93.

This article elucidates a topic that has been neglected by philosophers: self-forgiveness. Several benefits are to be gained from thinking about this topic. Analyzing self-forgiveness throws into relief the ontological and moral conditions under which forgiveness in interpersonal contexts is appropriate. Self-forgiveness can provide a second best alternative to interpersonal forgiveness in situations in which full interpersonal forgiveness is not or cannot be achieved. Self-forgiveness plays this role because of its most interesting characteristic: it restores our capability to carry on as functioning agents even after we have committed moral wrongs or harmed others.

Snowdon, P F. Personal Identity and Brain Transplants in Human Beings, Cockburn, David (ed). New York, Cambridge Univ Pr, 1991.

The simplest theory of personal identity is that each of us is an animal and will persist so long as the animal persists. The chief objection to this animalist view has been that in brain transplants the person and the animal come apart, and so the person must be recognized as distinct from the animal. The question considered is whether the objection is conclusive. The argument is analyzed and various criticisms of it rejected, including, methodological criticisms proposed by Johnston and Wilkes. The conclusion is, though, that there is a premise in the argument which can be rejected.

Snowdon, Paul. How to Interpret 'Direct Perception' in The Contents of Experience, Crane, Tim (ed). New York, Cambridge Univ Pr, 1992.

The traditional philosophical problem about perception has been expressed in the words: what do we directly perceive? The question considered in the paper is: what does that mean? Epistemological and non-epistemological interpretations are compared, and it is argued that 'direct perception' is best thought of as standing for a putative relation between subject and object. This non-epistemological notion is clarified, its relation to epistemology considered, and some traditional arguments about perception are presented in terms of it and analysed.

Snyder, Douglas M. Being at Rest. *J Mind Behav*, 13(2), 157-162, Spr 92.

The observer's importance as a subject in his or her reference frame, specifically the experience of being at rest in this frame, is pointed to by the discrepency between the experience of centrifugal force and the lack of fundamental significance of this force in Newtonian mechanics. There is nothing that is physical in nature that can serve as the basis for explaining this discrepency. In addition, the observer's being at rest for himself or herself in a reference frame is a central aspect of both special and general relativity. As a subject, the observer is fundamentally at rest, and this being at rest allows for the measurement of motion in the physical world.

Snyder, Douglas M. Quantum Mechanics and the Involvement of Mind in the Physical World: A Response to Garrison. *J Mind Behav*, 13(3), 247-257, Sum 92.

Garrison's recent article is the background for discussing a number of issues. Among these issues are l) the nature of probability in quantum mechanics; 2) the relation of observation to the wave packet in quantum mechanics; and 3) the role of immediate change upon measurement in the quantum mechanical wave function throughout space as the basis for the correlations among space-like separated events found in the Einstein-Podolsky-Rosen gedankenexperiment. A proposed empirical test of simultaneous, mutually exclusive situations (indicated by Einstein, Podolsky, and Rosen's work) is discussed in the context of Stratton's work on the orientation of the visual field, and objects within it, upon inversion of the retinal image. The logical nature of simultaneous, mutually exclusive situations is discussed in the context of Gödel's Incompleteness Theorem.

Snyder, Douglas M. Quantum Mechanics in Probabilistic in Nature. *J Mind Behav*, 14(2), 145-153, Spr 93.

Elitzur (1991) maintained that my version of Schrödinger's cat gedankenexperiment does not provide the basis for demonstrating the effect of consciousness on the course of the physical world. The nature of the difference between Elitzur's and my views concerning the gedankenexperiment is discussed, and the key to this difference concerns the fundamentally probabilistic nature of quantum mechanics. Elitzur has failed to see that in quantum mechanics consciousness fundamentally is that through which the physical world is known. Elitzur's characterization of my thesis concerning consciousness and human observation a reflecting radical idealism is discussed. A second gedankenexperiment is noted in which the observer's circumstance, other than the time of measurement, is also a variable and which tests whether or not mind, or consciousness, has an impact on the course of the physical world.

Snyder, Robert A and Goodman, Michael. *Contemporary Readings in Epistemology*. Englewood Cliffs, Prentice Hall, 1993.

This is an edited anthology of previously published essays in contemporary epistemology. The book covers six sections: The Analysis of Knowledge, Epistemic Justification, A Priori Knowledge, Theories of Truth, Skepticism, and Alternate Approaches to Epistemology. It is intended for upper-division undergraduate and graduate students. The essays selected aim at fundamental issues in contemporary epistemology. The last section considers recent challenges to epistemology as traditionally conceived and investigates the social character of knowledge. There is an analytical overview and a selected bibliography for each section.

Sobel, J Howard. Straight Versus Constrained Maximization. *Can J Phil*, 23(1), 25-54, Mr 93.

David Gauthier stages a competition between two arguments, each of which would decide once and for all which transparent agent is best—being a straight or a constrained maximizer. The first argument, which he rejects, is flawed in ways additional to those he notices, but less ambitious reasoning can, depending on an individual's probabilities and values, be good for straight maximization. The second argument, which he endorses, is wrong in a way specific to it as well as in ways similar to the first argument's flaws. An Appendix features careful demonstrations for relevant features of a three-person prisoners' dilemma.

Sobel, J Howard. True to Oneself. *Erkenntnis*, 38(1), 57-85, Ja 93.

This essay on Jan Österberg's *Self and Others* describes: interaction problems he brings against traditional egoisms; Collective Egoism, his best response to these problems; and his would-be refutation of all egoisms, even Collective Egoism. I comment on times of choice-relevant preferences; criticize Österberg's representation of 'the modern conception of rationality'; wonder why, though a fundamental normative principle must be 'jointly satisfiable', it need not be 'jointly performable'; stress that though Collective Egoism has attractive 'universal-conformity' features, it lacks 'individual-conformity' features on which true egoists would insist; and resist Österberg's would-be refutation of all egoisms.

Sobel, Jordan Howard. Backward-Induction Arguments: A Paradox Regained. *Phil Sci*, 60(1), 114-133, Mr 93.

According to a familiar argument, iterated prisoner's dilemmas of known finite lengths resolve for ideally rational and well-informed players: they would defect in the last round, anticipate this in the next to last round and so defect in it, *and so on*. But would they anticipate defections even if they had been cooperating? Not necessarily, say recent critics. These critics "lose" the backward-induction paradox by imposing indicative interpretations on rationality and information conditions. To regain it I propose subjunctive interpretations. To solve it I stress that implications for ordinary imperfect players are limited.

Sobel, Jordan Howard. Kings and Prisoners (and Aces). *Proc Phil Sci Ass*, 1, 203-216, 1992.

What we make of information we come to have should take into account that we have come to have it, and how we think we have come to have it. I relate this homily to cases like that of the second ace and...the Cadillac Problem: One of three screens hides a Cadillac. After you pick a screen Monty Hall flings open another. "Well," he asks, "Do you want to stick with that screen or for $100 switch?" After demonstrating the power of that homily, I ask what about these cases makes them puzzles, and it remarkable for them.

Sober, Elliott. Mathematics and Indispensability. *Phil Rev*, 102(1), 35-57, Ja 93.

Many philosophers of mathematics have followed Quine and Putnam by endorsing an argument for mathematical realism based on the alleged indispensability of mathematics in empirical science. This argument claims that when empirical scientific theories are confirmed by successful prediction of observables, this confirmation acrues to the whole theory—including the pure mathematics that the theory embeds. The indispensability argument is thus committed to a form of *epistemological holism*. In this paper, I argue that the indispensability argument is unsound and that its defects reflect more general problems with epistemological holism.

Sober, Elliott. Stable Cooperation in Iterated Prisoners' Dilemmas. *Econ Phil*, 8(1), 127-139, Ap 92.

In *The Evolution of Cooperation* (Basic Books, 1984), Robert Axelrod argued that the cooperative strategy TIT-FOR TAT is not stable in iterated prisoners' dilemmas of fixed finite length, but is stable in iterated games governed by a discount parameter *w* (when *w* is sufficiently high). I argue that this contrast between the two kinds of game is less significant than might appear. First, it depends on using the concept of *collective* rather than *evolutionary* stability. Second, although TIT-FOR-TAT is not stable in a game of fixed finite length, it cannot be invaded by highly uncooperative strategies. And finally, in any finite number of realizations of a game with a fixed value of *w*, there exists a "diagonal" strategy such that TIT-FOR-TAT is not collectively stable against that strategy.

Sober, Elliott. Temporally Oriented Laws. *Synthese*, 94(2), 171-189, F 93.

A system whose expected state changes with time cannot have both a forward-directed translationally invariant probabilistic law and a backward-directed translationally invariant law. When faced with this choice, science seems to favor the former. An asymmetry between cause and effect may help explain why temporally oriented laws are usually forward directed.

Sober, Elliott. The Evolution of Altruism: Correlation, Cost, and Benefit. *Biol Phil*, 7(2), 177-187, Ap 92.

A simple and general criterion is derived for the evolution of altruism when individuals interact in pairs. It is argued that the treatment of this problem in kin selection theory and in game theory are special cases of this general criterion.

Sober, Elliott and Barrett, Martin. Conjunctive Forks and Temporally Asymmetric Inference. *Austl J Phil*, 70(1), 1-23, Mr 92.

In *The Direction of Time*, Hans Reichenbach claims that there are conjunctive forks open to the future but none open to the past, and that this asymmetry explains why we know more about the past than about the future. We argue that conjunctive forks open to the past are rare but not impossible. We also propose a new argument for thinking that the common causes discovered by (as yet incomplete) science often form conjunctive forks with their joint effects. We then explore the circumstances under which a conjunctive fork open to the future allows one to know more about the past than about the future.

Sober, Elliott and Barrett, Martin. Is Entropy Relevant to the Asymmetry Between Retrodiction and Prediction?. *Brit J Phil Sci*, 43(2), 141-160, J 92.

The idea that the changing entropy of a system is relevant to explaining why we know more about the system's past than about its future has been criticized on several fronts. This paper assesses the criticisms and clarifies the epistemology of the inference problem. It deploys a Markov process model to investigate the relationship between entropy and temporally asymmetric inference.

Soble, Alan. Review Article of Ann Ferguson's *Sexual Democracy: Women, Oppression, and Revolution*. *J Value Inq*, 27(2), 261-270, Ap 93.

Substantively: Ferguson's political philosophy is stuck in the idealism of the '60s. Methodologically: her inability to do analytic philosophy, in even the most general sense, prevents her from noticing the ambiguity of her major claims. Recommended only for the daughters of Sappho who like to dream, not think.

Soble, Alan. Why Do Men Enjoy Pornography? in Rethinking Masculinity, May, Larry (ed). Lanham, Rowman & Littlefield, 1992.

Sobotka, M and Znoj, M and Major, L. The Relation of Man and Nature in Modern Philosophy (in Czechoslovakian). *Filozof Cas*, 39(6), 975-991, 1991.

Sobrevilla, David. Aesthetics and Ethnocentrism in Cultural Relativism and Philosophy, Dascal, Marcelo (ed). Leiden, Brill, 1991.

Sodeika, Tomas. Psychologism and Description in Husserl's Phenomenology in Analecta Husserliana, XXXIV, Tymieniecka, Anna-Teresa (ed). Dordrecht, Kluwer, 1992.

Sodor, A. La dimensión ontológica de la conciencia afectiva según Ferdinand Alquié — Segunda parte. *Aquinas*, 34(3), 535-554, S-D 91.

Soifer, Eldon (ed). *Ethical Issues: Perspectives for Canadians*. Peterborough, Broadview Pr, 1992.

This book is a reader on contemporary ethical issues. Sections include Distribution of Scarce Resources; The Beginning and End of Life; the Moral Status of Non-Human Animals; Ethics and the Environment; Cultural, Linguistic and Aboriginal Rights; Free Speech, Censorship and Pornography; and Employment Equity. The editor also contributes an introductory chapter on general ethical theory, a few pages of introductory remarks on each issue covered, and questions for discussion after the articles. There is some emphasis on Canadian authors, legal situations, and perspectives on the issues, but the selections are of broad interest.

Sojka, Jacek. On the Origins of Idealization in the Social Experience in Idealization III, Brzezinski, Jerzy (ed). Amsterdam, Rodopi, 1992.

Sokol, Mary. Jeremy Bentham and the Real Property Commission of 1828. *Utilitas*, 4(2), 225-245, N 92.

Sokolowski, Robert. Christian Religious Discourse. *Amer Cath Phil Quart*, 65, 45-56, 1991.

This essay discusses the difference between Christian belief and pagan understandings of the divine. It shows how the Christian distinction between the world and God introduces a new kind of analogy in religious discourse, and examines how such analogy is different from metaphor, as well as being different from analogies made within the context of the world; the paper thus discusses the special logic of Christian faith, founded on the Christian distinction between the world and God. It also examines six forms of speech in Christian faith: prayer, biblical narrative, creeds, preaching, sacramental speech, and poetry.

Sokolowski, Robert. Husserl and Analytic Philosophy and Husserlian Intentionality and Non-Foundational Realism. *Phil Phenomenol Res*, 52(3), 725-730, S 92.

Soles, David E. Hobbes, Locke, Franzwa on the Paradoxes of Equality. *SW Phil Rev*, 8(1), 183-188, Ja 92.

Solomon, Miriam. Scientific Rationality and Human Reasoning. *Phil Sci*, 59(3), 439-455, S 92.

The work of Tversky, Kahneman and others suggests that people often make use of cognitive heuristics such as availability, salience and representativeness in their reasoning and decision making. Through use of a historical example—the recent plate tectonics revolution in geology—I argue that such heuristics play a crucial role in scientific decision making also. I suggest how these heuristics are to be considered, along with noncognitive factors (such as motivation and social structures) when drawing historical and epistemological conclusions. The normative perspective is community-wide, contextual, and instrumental.

Solomon, Robert C. *Culture and Modernity: East-West Perspectives*, edited by Eliot Deutsch. *Phil East West*, 43(3), 565-572, Jl 93.

Culture and Modernity is an excellent collection of essays from a recent East-West conference in Hawaii, edited by Eliot Deutsch. In this critical review I discuss the problems of so-called "relativism" and cross-cultural understanding, and essays by several dozen distinguished international scholars on these subjects.

Solomon, Robert C. Beyond Reason: The Importance of Emotion in Philosophy in Revisioning Philosophy, Ogilvy, James (ed). Albany, SUNY Pr, 1992.

In this essay, I discuss the consequences of the long neglect or degrading of the emotions in various philosophical areas, in particular, in ethics and in the philosophy of mind. In ethics, I suggest, too many traditional theories, including now-resurrected "virtue ethics," ignore or deny the essential place of feelings in our evaluation of both people and their actions. In the philosophy of mind, emotions hold a critical position in such questions as the mind-body problem, the nature of intentionality and the notions of agency and voluntariness.

Solomon, Robert C. Beyond Selfishness: Adam Smith and the Limits of the Market. *Bus Ethics Quart*, 3(4), 453-460, O 93.

It is often forgotten, at least by economists and social critics, that Adam Smith wrote the *Theory of Moral Sentiments* as well as *Wealth of Nations*. Philosophers, on the other hand, typically find the two books radically at odds with one another. In this review of Patricia Werhane's new book on Smith and his legacy, I support and explore her suggestion that his work is a unified whole, with very different social and political implications and consequences than those that have become the common rhetoric of many conservative and liberal economists.

Solomon, Robert C. Environmentalism as a Humanism. *Free Inq*, 13(2), 21-22, Spr 93.

In this essay, I argue against both environmental extremism and anti-environmentalism, reconsider both of the moral categories "humanism" and "speciesism," and encourage cooperation and compromise in place of the current battle for the "high moral ground" in ecological and environmental issues. This piece has been adapted from my book, *Entertaining Ideas: Popular Philosophical Essays, 1970-1990* (Prometheus Books).

Solomon, Robert C. Existentialism, Emotions, and the Cultural Limits of Rationality. *Phil East West*, 42(4), 597-621, O 92.

In this essay, I am concerned with certain familiar but by no means transparently clear "existentialist" attacks on rationality, but I am also interested in the notion of "rationality" itself and the various ambiguities I find not only in the existentialist assault but in more traditional defenses as well. I am particularly concerned with the relationship between reason (and "reasonableness") and emotion, both in the existentialists and in the tradition, and with alternative notions of rationality and conceptions of reason and emotion in other cultures. This essay is part of a larger project on multiculturalism and the cross-cultural comparison of reason and emotion.

Solomon, Robert C. On Kitsch and Sentimentality. *J Aes Art Crit*, 49(1), 1-14, Wint 91.

In this essay, I present a qualified defense of both kitsch and sentimentality against a number of familiar but unsubstantiated objections. Kitsch and sentimentality have been accused not only on the grounds of "bad taste" as betraying serious flaws in character. What underlies these objections, I believe, is a deep but undeserved suspicion of emotions, especially those tender emotions that would seem to be most humane. I am particularly interested in what Kathleen Higgins has called "sweet kitsch." Sweet kitsch may be bad art but it is not always badly done. Indeed it may be flawed by its very perfection.

Solov'ëv, Erich Jurevich. Die Entstehung einer Personalistischen philosophie im heutigen Russland. *Stud Soviet Tho*, 44(3), 193-201, N 92.

Solski, Jeffrey and Howard, Paul. The Strength of the Δ-System Lemma. *Notre Dame J Form Log*, 34(1), 100-106, Wint 93.

The delta system lemma is not provable in set theory without the axiom of choice nor does it imply the axiom of choice.

Sommers, Mary C. "He spak to [T]hem that wolde lyve parfitly:" Thomas Aquinas, the Wife of Bath and the Two Senses of Religion. *Amer Cath Phil Quart*, 65, 145-156, 1991.

In "The Wife of Bath's Prologue," Chaucer has Good Dame Alice present a biblical defense for a strong distinction between the "religion" of monks, friars, etc., and the "religion" she finds proper to a lay woman. The strong distinction can lead to two opposite sets of difficulties. At the risk of oversimplifying, one set could be called "European," the other "American." Thomas Aquinas, developing his concept of "religion" in the context of the antimendicant controversies, does not adopt a strong distinction. His own approach, then, may be useful in resolving contemporary dilemmas about "being religious."

Soni, Jayandra. Das Selbst in der Yoga-Philosophie. *Conceptus*, 25(65), 39-46, 1991.

Like most Indian philosophical systems, the philosophy of Yoga presents a doctrine of liberation insofar as it is concerned with the question of how to realize the essence of man. There are some fundamental propositions: first, that man is a limited being—limited with respect to his knowledge, his self-consciousness, and his faculties—and second, that he nevertheless is able to grasp knowledge about himself by ascetic discipline. It is in this second sense, that dealing with Yoga is at the same time dealing with psychology, for, as we shall see in this paper, the definition of Yoga is connected to psyche (citta).

Sonn, Tamara. Irregular Warfare and Terrorism in Islam in Cross, Crescent, and Sword, Johnson, James Turner (ed). Westport, Greenwood Pr, 1990.

This chapter demonstrates that irregular warfare is typical of the kinds of socioeconomic changes the Islamic world is undergoing, not of Islamic law. Islamic law was formulated in an age of religiously legitimated governments suitable to the socioeconomic milieu of the early medieval world. This stands in contrast to the fragmented post-colonial context in which contemporary Muslims must address questions of statecraft. History indicates that with industrialization, the centrally organized, expansive structure characteristic of religiously legitimated governments tends to give way to the geographically limited structures of nation-states. An understanding of this process, ongoing in the Islamic world, is essential in discussing the contemporary Islamic world. Using examples, I show that while there is often popular support for the expressed aims of revolutionary movements, nevertheless, terrorist activity remains opposed to both the spirit and letter of Islamic law.

Sontag, Fred. Metaphorical Non Sequitur. *Amer Cath Phil Quart*, 65(1), 83-96, Wint 91.

Three points are crucial if we are to appraise Sally McFague's *Metaphorical Theology*: (1) How does one know what the relationship is without knowing what the being is like whom one is related to?; (2) A whole metaphysics of 'relationship' is assumed here which is not general sense. But does it follow that our dominant model can never be substantialist? Does it follow that "we do not know God's 'nature'"? (p. 97) The necessary use of metaphor tells us that we do not know that nature directly, but metaphor can tell us about a nature just as well as a relationship.

Sontag, Frederick. The Birth of God in God, Values, and Empiricism, Peden, Creighton (ed). Macon, Mercer Univ Pr, 1989.

Even in Marxist lands God can be born again, and in "Christian" societies we can experience that desert of a divine withdrawal. We man and women are not constant in our religious life; we can lose a once fine religious sensitivity. But often, without our even trying, God's power seems to burst in upon the scent again, in interior lives if not on the formal religious scene. This involves the birth of new religious movements and the eclipse of old forms once thought of as invincible divine receptacle. To make sense of the coming and going of religions and religious sensitivity, their surge and then ebb, this birth and death of our divine experience, we must say we are dealing with a God whose own life in itself is capable of relating to us in inconsistent ways. The birth and death of our religious affections reflect the most important characteristic in the nature of the God we face.

Soontiëns, Frans. Evolution, Teleology and Theology. *Bijdragen*, 53(4), 394-406, 1992.

In this article it is argued that there is a fundamental misunderstanding about the concept of teleology in western thinking. This is a result of a radical transformation of the Aristotelian concept of teleology by Christian theology during the Middle Ages. Teleology was, and is, implicitly identified with the argument from design. This misconception resulted in a confusion about the role of teleology and chance in evolution cannot be justified. To accept a natural teleology would be more in accordance with the position of man as a product of natural evolutionary process, and it would serve as a prerequisite for the formulation of an adequate bio- and eco-ethics.

Soper, Kate. Socialism and Personal Morality in Socialism and Morality, McLellan, David (ed). New York, St Martin's Pr, 1990.

Sorabji, Richard. Animal Minds. *S J Phil*, 31(Supp), 1-18, 1992.

'Animals lack syntax, so we can eat them'. The ancient Stoic treatment of animals and the modern scientific debate have reached the same question of syntax, though they started from the broader question whether animals have reason. The Western tradition has been very much influenced by the fact that Augustine backed the Stoic's view. But in doing so, hecutus off from the equally vigorous, but unnoticed, defence of animals mounted on the other side. The debate concerned not only ethics, but also the philosophy of mind. For those who denied reason and belief to animals were forced to re-define perception, emotion, intention, memory, speech, conceptualisation and moral responsibility. In fact, a broader view of ethics is needed than is found either in the ancient opponents of animals, or in their modern defenders. A single criterion, be it reason, syntax, utility, or inherent value cannot decide the issues.

Sorabji, Richard (ed). *Aristotle Transformed: The Ancient Commentators and Their Influence*. Ithaca, Cornell Univ Pr, 1990.

These thinkers are not just penetrating commentators on Aristotle, but represent the thought of the Aristotelian and Neoplatonist schools between 300 and 600 A.D. Moreover, they are essential for understanding the later history of Western Philosophy, because they transformed Aristotle's views on God and the soul in ways that made possible Thomas Aquinas' subsequent incorporation of Aristotle into Christian thought. They further inspired one of Galileo's findings that Kuhn has called a scientific revolution. Finally, they quote fragments from all 1100 years of ancient Greek Philosophy, including pre-socratic fragments. This is the first book-length overview, and is a guide to the dozens of translations underway from the source editor and publishers.

Sorell, Tom. Aggravated Murder and Capital Punishment. *J Applied Phil*, 10(2), 201-213, 1993.

It is possible to defend the death penalty for aggravated murder in more than one way, and not every defence is equally compelling. The paper takes up arguments put forward by two very distinguished advocates of the death penalty, Mill and Kant. After reviewing Mill's argument and some weaknesses in it, I shall sketch another line of reasoning that combines his conclusion with premisses to be found in Kant. The hybrid argument provides at least the basis for a sound defence of execution for the most serious murders.

Sorell, Tom. Hobbes Without Doubt. *Hist Phil Quart*, 10(2), 121-135, Ap 93.

Hobbes' metaphysics is sometimes claimed to have the anti-sceptical motivation that Descartes' metaphysics has. His politics is sometimes thought to inherit the sceptical preoccupations of grotius. I deny that scepticism or the desire to overcome it is important to Hobbes. But I offer an interpretation that makes sense of what is sceptical-looking in his doctrines.

Sorensen, Roy. The Egg Came Before the Chicken. *Mind*, 101(403), 541-542, Jl 92.

The gradualism of Darwinism would appear to confirm the suspicion that the chicken-or-egg riddle is void for vagueness. Nevertheless, the egg's precedence is biological (although not a physical) necessity. The demonstration proceeds from well-known tenets of contemporary evolutionary theory. The logical moral is that indeterminate states can be determinately related. The philosophical moral is that just as there are hidden indeterminacies, there are hidden determinacies.

Sorensen, Roy. *Thought Experiments*. New York, Oxford Univ Pr, 1992.

Can merely thinking about an imaginary situation provide evidence for how the world actually is—or how it *ought* to be? *Thought Experiments* addresses this question with an analysis of a wide variety of thought experiments ranging from Aesthetics to Zoology. The result is the first general theory of thought experiment. The theory is set within an evolutionary framework and integrates recent advances in experimental psychology and the history of science (with special emphasis on Ernst Mach and Thomas Kuhn). The main theme is that thought experiment is (an albeit) limiting case of experiment and so the lessons learned about experimentation carry over to thought experiment—and vice versa.

Sorenson, Leonard R. Rousseau's Socraticism: The Political Bearing of "On Theatrical Imitation". *Interpretation*, 20(2), 135-155, Wint 92-93.

Sorge, V. Identità dello storicismo. *Sapienza*, 46(1), 94-99, 1993.

Sosa, David. Consequences of Consequentialism. *Mind*, 102(405), 101-122, Ja 93.

"Consequences of Consequentialism" argues for a consequentialism with a broad conception of consequence and of intrinsic value. Such latitude may convert the consequentialism defended into a theory almost any ethicist could embrace; but this may be a virtue and is hardly a *refutation* (compare compatibilism's denial of an opposition between determinism and free will). Issues important for any ethical theory are considered carefully: (i) rights, (ii) subjectivity vs. objectivity, (iii) agent-relativity, (iv) the implications of the necessary connection between bringing about a consequence and bringing about the bringing about of that consequence, and (v) the demands of consequentialism-does it imply that we are all moral monsters?

Sosa, Ernest. Abilities, Concepts, and Externalism in Mental Causation, Heil, John (ed). New York, Clarendon/Oxford Pr, 1993.

This paper deals with the issue of internalism versus externalism in the philosophy of mind.

Sosa, Ernest. Ayer on Perception and Reality in The Philosophy of A J Ayer, Hahn, Lewis Edwin (ed). Peru, Open Court, 1992.

Problems of perceptual experience and its relation to objective reality have been central to Ayer's philosophy. This paper discusses highlights of his relevant work, and concludes with a proposal that builds on that discussion.

Sosa, Ernest. Davidson's Thinking Causes in Mental Causation, Heil, John (ed). New York, Clarendon/Oxford Pr, 1993.

This paper is a critique of Donald Davidson's anomalous monism.

Sosa, Ernest. Generic Reliabilism and Virtue Epistemology in Rationality in Epistemology, Villanueva, Enrique (ed). Atascadero, Ridgeview, 1992.

Problems for Generic Reliabilism lead to a more specific account of knowledge as involving the exercise of intellectual virtues or faculties.

Sosa, Ernest. Proper Functionalism and Virtue Epistemology. *Nous*, 27(1), 51-65, Mr 93.

Alvin Plantinga's *Warrant and Proper Function* is discussed. Its main theses are laid out briefly and examined critically. An ongoing controversy in epistemology between two Alvins, Plantinga and Goldman, is presented, with a look at Goldman's most recent views, and compared with related views of the present author.

Soskice, Janet Martin. Love and Attention. *Philosophy*, 32(Supp), 59-72, 1992.

Soskice, Janet Martin. Love and Attention in Philosophy, Religion and the Spiritual Life, McGhee, Michael (ed). New York, Cambridge Univ Pr, 1992.

Soto, Luis García. Leituras de Barthes: II—Compromiso discreto, luita contínua. *Agora (Spain)*, 11(1), 163-175, 1992.

Monograph on reception of Barthes's work in the critical literature in English, French, Italian, Portuguese and Spanish, in which the very different approaches are studied in five main themes. In this second chapter, books by G Benelli, L J Calvet and J B Fages, and articles by R Bellour, B Dort, G Mininni, M G Padreo, C A Ribeiro, F Semerari and Ph Sollers are commented. All of them pay attention to Barthes's political and moral critique: his proposals, his approaches, his targets. They write about the political proposals pointed in his early texts or the moral approaches stressed in his last texts, or they read all his works from a political and/or a moral point of view.

Soto, M Jesús. El preguntar heideggeriano sobre el ser: Comentario a un libro de Modesto Berciano. *Anu Filosof*, 25(3), 543-554, 1992.

The author extensively reviews Berciano's last book on Heidegger. Berciano is the best known Spanish specialist on Heidegger's metaphysics and anthropology.

Soulez, Antonia. Entre le langage et l'expérience: généalogie et crise d'une démarcation. *Rev Int Phil*, 46(183), 435-457, 1992.

Sousedik, S. L Hejdanek's Meontology: An Attempt of a Critical Explanation (in Czechoslovakian). *Filozof Cas*, 40(4), 673-676, 1992.

Southgate, Beverley C. 'Scattered over Europe': Transcending National Frontiers in the Seventeenth Century. *Hist Euro Ideas*, 16(1-3), 131-137, Ja 93.

It is argued that some seventeenth-century scholars were more genuinely European than their twentieth-century counterparts, and that the transmission of ideas in the early-modern period could be extremely rapid. As a specific example, the career of the English Catholic Thomas White (1593-1676) is taken. Educated at various colleges in continental Europe, and subsequently travelling extensively, White made numerous intellectual contacts by whom his thought was enriched. The importance of such highly mobile Catholics in the rapid diffusion of ideas may have been underestimated.

Southworth, Cheryl and Bitting, Paul F. Reverence and the Passions of Inquiry. *Thinking*, 10(2), 13-18, 1992.

Sovran, Tamar. Between Similarity and Sameness. *J Prag*, 18(4), 329-344, O 92.

The aim of this paper is to confront some logically and philosophically puzzling problems, raised by philosophers and cognitive psychologists, with a semantic description of the concept of "similarity" and with the meaning and the use of operators of similarity in certain languages. "Similarity" is shown to be a cluster of notions rather than a unitary concept. By contrast, there is a certain unity of the items in the group of similarity subtypes, in that a unifying mechanism underlies them and justifies gathering them under one general, although vague, concept. (edited)

Spade, Paul Vincent. Do Composers Have To Be Performers Too?. *J Aes Art Crit*, 49(4), 365-369, Fall 91.

Sparrow, Edward G. Rights, Law, and the Right. *Rev Metaph*, 46(4), 699-716, Je 93.

Sparrow, M F. The Proofs of Natural Theology and the Unbeliever. *Amer Cath Phil Quart*, 65(2), 129-141, Spr 91.

AUTHOR INDEX WITH ABSTRACTS 683 Splett, Jörg

Sparshott, Francis. Essay Review—Foundations of Architecture. *J Aes Educ*, 26(2), 73-93, Sum 92.

A survey review of sixteen books on architecture shows a concern with permanent principles of design and a continuing interest in the five orders of classical architecture. But Bataille's suggestion that architectural monuments stand for oppression and death rather than for facilitation calls into question the dictatorial moralism that often accompanies the hunger for permanent value.

Sparshott, Francis. Imagination—The Very Idea. *J Aes Art Crit*, 48(1), 1-8, Wint 90.

The philosophy of imagination consists of a number of themes and problems that seem to have nothing in common except the habitual use of the term 'imagination' to discuss them. But the habit of discussing them together imposes on them a unity that becomes conceptually fruitful.

Sparshott, Francis. The Future of Dance Aesthetics. *J Aes Art Crit*, 51(2), 227-234, Spr 93.

A survey of the main themes of dance aesthetics is followed by the observation that debates in the immediate future are likely to center on the nature of corporeality and the nature of theatricality.

Sparshott, Francis. This Is Not the Real Me. *Phil Lit*, 17(1), 1-15, Ap 93.

After considering why people might wish to repudiate certain of their actions and characteristics, and reviewing some strategies that may be used in doing so, the article relates such repudiations to preferences among implicit autobiographical narratives. It concludes by considering the circumstances in which such strategies are applicable to literary narratives.

Spash, Clive L. Economics, Ethics, and Long-Term Environmental Damages. *Environ Ethics*, 15(2), 117-132, Sum 93.

Neither environmental economics nor environmental philosophy have adequately examined the moral implication of imposing environmental degradation and ecosystem instability upon our descendants. A neglected aspect of these problems is the supposed extent of the burden that the current generation is placing on future generations. The standard economic position on discounting implies an ethical judgment concerning future generations. If intergenerational obligations exist, then two types of intergenerational transfer must be considered: basic distributional transfers and compensatory transfers. Basic transfers have been the central intergenerational concern of both environmental economics and philosophy, but compensatory transfers emphasize obligations of a kind often disregarded.

Spassov, Spas. Jacques Monod's Scientific Analysis and Its Reductionistic Interpretation. *Proc Phil Sci Ass*, 1, 329-334, 1992.

The purpose of this work is to show that Jacques Monod's scientific analysis contains an idea which contradicts his own mechanistic and reductionistic interpretation of biological phenomena. In fact, both in his scientific papers published in the early sixties and in his later book "Chance and Necessity", Monod reveals not only the molecular mechanisms of the teleonomical performances of the cell, but also their biological specificity, which does not allow for their reduction to merely chemical processes, although they are grounded on such processes and can be explained by them. This idea, the real meaning of which both Monod and his critics have overlooked, suggest a different, non mechanistic interpretation of biological phenomena on molecular level.

Spellman, Lynne M. Naming and Knowing: The *Cratylus* on Images. *Hist Phil Quart*, 10(3), 197-210, Jl 93.

The idea that names are like (images of) their referents is troubling, yet Plato seems to want that names should be correct in some way besides usage. May aim is to consider what language can be and what images can be such that names could be images and what would be accomplished if they were. I argue that ideal names consist of true, complete, and self-evident beliefs about the Forms; I then show that Fodor-like objections to an imagistic language would not apply. Thus an iconic account of language, if available, would provide justification for beliefs.

Spencer-Smith, Richard (ed) and Torrance, Steve (ed). *Machinations: Computational Studies of Logic, Language, and Cognition*. Norwood, Ablex, 1992.

This collection covers work within philosophy, AI and computational theory, and offers a common meeting ground. Topics discussed include: computational treatments of temporal contexts; Prolog programs as definitions; intuitionist logic as a computational paradigm; logic as a foundation for knowledge engineering; formalisms for natural language sentence comprehension; and for speech act recognition; explanation-based learning; mental logic and deontic logic; and the relation between symbolic and subsymbolic explanations in AI.

Spender, Stephen. Six Variations in Isaiah Berlin: A Celebration, Margalit, Edna (ed). Chicago, Univ of Chicago Pr, 1991.

Sperry, R W. Turnabout on Consciousness: A Mentalist View. *J Mind Behav*, 13(3), 259-280, Sum 92.

Conceptual foundations for the changeover form behaviorism to mentalism are reviewed in an effort to better clarify frequently contended and misinterpreted features. The new mentalist tenets which I continue to support have been differently conceived to be a form of dualism, mind-brain identity theory, functionalism, nonreductive physical monism, dualist interactionism, emergent interactionism, and various other things. This diversity and contradiction are attributed to the fact that the new mentalist paradigm is a distinctly new mentalist paradigm is a distinctly new position that fails to fit traditional philosophic dichotomies. Formerly opposed features form previous polar alternative become merged into a novel unifying synthesis, an unambiguous description of which demands redefinition of old terms or/and the invention of new terminology. The present analysis and interpretation are backed by statements form the early papers.

Sperry, Roger W. Paradigms of Belief, Theory and Metatheory. *Zygon*, 27(3), 245-259, S 92.

My account of the recent turnabout in the treatment of mental states in science and its basis in a modified concept of causal determinism and my claim that this opens the way for beliefs and values consistent with science are here reaffirmed in response to perceived weaknesses and "inherent incompleteness". Contested issues are reviewed to better clarify the main thesis. An inherent weakness in respect to deep spiritual needs is recognized and tentative remedial measures explored.

Spicker, Stuart F. The Search for Bioethical Criteria to Select Renal Transplant Recipients: A Response to the Honourable Judge Jean-Louis Baudouin. *Dialogue (Canada)*, 30(3), 425-434, Sum 91.

What *ethical* criteria can we agree on in order fairly to select patients to receive scarce renal transplants? Most answers will in all likelihood not serve to satisfy, especially since we have argued that appeals to particular social and even medical criteria will not suffice. Thesis: to achieve social equity and fairness we shall have to refer to *multiple sets* of criteria. That is, we shall have to construct a more refined yet complex system of multiple social *and* medical criteria to assist in these difficult moral choices.

Spiecker, Ben. Sexual Education and Morality. *J Moral Educ*, 21(1), 67-76, 1992.

Five interpretations of sexual education are distinguished. The analyses indicate that sexual education can neither be understood as 'learning to control the sexual impulses,' nor as 'the training or formation of sexual desire.' Elucidation of the meaning of the terms 'sexual desire' and 'erotic love' show that 'sexual education' can be understood as teaching (children) the moral tendencies in reference to sexual conduct. It is argued that 'infantile sexual desire' is based on a contradiction in terms and that 'erotic love' does not exclude moral principles.

Spinelli, Miguel. A Matemática como Paradigma da Construçao Filosófica de Descartes: Do Discurso do Método e da Tematizaçao do Cogito. *Cad Hist Filosof Cie*, 2(1), 5-20, Ja-Je 90.

Descartes believes in the viability of philosophy as science. For him, it is a process of cognition. Therefore, its aim consists in passing beyond the decisive character of the abstract cognition of mathematics to rational search of the truth and the elaboration of objective philosophic propositions. Descartes is an analyst of the discernment or human reason. So his fundamental concern consists in apprehending the constitution of the human cognitive apparatus in order to elaborate an adjustable method to regulate it. In the mental and resolutive patterns of mathematics he finds the basic conditions to elaborate these rules. (edited)

Spinelli, Miguel. Epistéme e Techne: Sobre a Determinaçao da Competência Epistêmica Grega. *Cad Hist Filosof Cie*, 2(2), 239-250, Jl-D 90.

There is no limit in time, as the landmark of the moment the logical thought arose. Therefore, there isn't a person to whom we could put the invention down. The logical thought was a quality brought up in the interior of a multiform movement, the Sapiential, where, in certain moments, sprang up by the curiosity of the people delimitated within territories and cultures. He took his stand from process, where the rational element estangled with the culture and the myth, and with other ways to explain the human wisdom, was in its way. No culture, or territory, absorbed it competely, or exclusively sheltered it. They are the two explicatory words of the process itself, of the pattern that started one exercise from the specific competence. They are, on the other hand, the expressions of the expertness in the accomplishment, or practice, of a theoretical iniciative, whose result was named knowledge.

Spinosa, Charles. Derrida and Heidegger in Heidegger: A Critical Reader, Dreyfus, Hubert (ed). Cambridge, Blackwell, 1992.

Spinsanti, Sandro. Obtaining Consent from the Family: A Horizon for Clinical Ethics. *J Clin Ethics*, 3(3), 188-192, Fall 92.

Spitzack, Carole. Foucault's Political Body in Medical Praxis in The Body in Medical Thought and Practice, Leder, Drew (ed). Dordrecht, Kluwer, 1992.

Splett, Jörg. "Liebe, die im Geist mir redet...": Dantes Dame Philosophie. *Theol Phil*, 66(4), 557-569, 1991.

Das Convivio besonders, dann auch die Commedialilden die Basis für die Frage nach der "Dame Philospohie" bei Dante. Sie ist eine himmlische Herrin, Praxiswissenschaft (Gilson) da die reine Theorie göttliche Prärogative). Sie dient dem menschlichen Leben und ist selber humane Praxis (ethisch- politisch, laikal). Ist sie vielleicht auch die geheimnisvolle Matelda im irdischen Paradies? Jedenfalls ist sie Hoffnungsweisheit (trotz der Höllen-Dogmatik und obwohl Christi Erlösung zu kurz kommt). Kritik übt Verf. am Eros-Deken als solchem, statt dass Denken als Antwort konzipiert würde. Sein Adel wäre das Nicht-zu-Ende-Kommen des Dankes (vgl. das Dajénu-Lied der Pessach-Haggada).

Splett, Jörg. Amore per la parola (Antologia). *Aquinas*, 35(2), 415-434, My-Ag 92.

Frau Dr Grazia d Folliero-Metz hat aus dem Buch "Liebe zum Wort" (1985) Passagen ausgewählt und übersetzt. Die Themen: Gegen Hegel gilt die Stufung Philosophie, Kunst, Religion, Gegen die Kontraposition von Symbol und Realität steht das anthropologische Faktum "realsymbol". Eine Philosophie der Poesie entdeekt im (An-) Schein den Aufschein, den Aufgang der Wahrheit. Das Schöne, zunächst ein Rätsel, dann als Sphinx ohne Rätsel verdächtigt, offenbart sich als Verheissung: (G Braque) "Die Hoffnung wider das Ideal".

Splett, Jörg. Die Wahrheit und das Gute: Sokrates und die Geburt der Metaphysik. *Theol Phil*, 66(2), 216-225, 1991.

Es handelt sich um die Neu-Lektüre von H Kuhn, Sokrates, 1934, 1959, 1. Das sokratische Fragen bezeugt die Aporie des reinen Verstandes. 2. Das (vernünftige) Wissen des Nichtwissens steht im Dienst einer Seelsorge in Gelassenheit. (Dumézil: Die Kranzheit, für deren Heilung der Hahn zu opfern ist, ist nicht das Leben, sondern dessen Überschätzung.) 3. Sokratisches Existieren gaschieht in Konsequenz und Frömmigkeit. -Was feht, ist der Ernst der Schuld - und so auch die Spitze von Humanität und Frömmigkeit: die Anbetung.

Splett, Jörg. Vita Humana: Hannah Arendt zu den Bedingungen tätigen Menschseins. *Theol Phil*, 67(4), 558-569, 1992.

Vor allem an The Human Condition, auch The Life of the Mind werden Grundpositionen von HA verdeutlicht und aush christl. Perspektive diskutiert. -Der Weg von der Polis zur Gesellschaft führt zum Paradigma Arbeit, der HA das Werk entgegensetzt. Ähnlich begegnet der Weltlosigkeit des Denkens der Glanz der

'Macht; aber auch so wichtige Individualmöglichkeiten wie Verzeihung und Versprechen. Sie gründen in der Freiheit, aus der "Natalität" des Menschen. Die Zwiespältigkeit der Freiheit als Wille wird durch die Liebe geeint. Lässt sich das aber rein human(istisch) konsipieren? Werden Schuld und Verzeihung in ihrer Tiefe verstanden? Lässt die Wahrheit nur als ungewusste frei? Darf man den Kategorischen Imperativ als inhuman kritisieren, oder ist nicht er das einzige Bollwerk gegen Unmenschlichkeit?

Sprenger, Arnold. Higher Moral Education in Taiwan in Chinese Foundations for Moral Education and Character Development, Van Doan, Tran (ed). Washington, CRVP, 1991.

Sprigge, T L S. Are there Intrinsic Values in Nature? in Applied Philosophy, Almond, Brenda (ed). New York, Routledge, 1992.

Various environmental ethicists hold that physical nature may possess an intrinsic value which is not merely the sum of the experiences of the humans or animals present within it and which makes its own moral demands upon us. However, such views tend to be insufficiently related to any thesis regarding the relation between physical reality and our awareness of it. It makes a deal of difference whether nature is conceived as the 'life world' of human beings or as a physicist might describe it. Is perhaps some form of panpsychism required for the attribution of value to nature?

Sprigge, T L S. Ayer on Other Minds in The Philosophy of A J Ayer, Hahn, Lewis Edwin (ed). Peru, Open Court, 1992.

Ayer's successive dealings with the analysis and cognitive status of statements about other minds are examined. Special attention and criticism is directed at his attempt to show that these are in principle verifiable (because it is only contingent that such a mind is other); likewise at his associated attempt to deal with the past by claiming that its being past is only contingent. Finally, the respective status of the mental and the physical in Ayer's philosophy is considered and it is suggested that he was always a realist about the former as he never quite was about the latter.

Sprigge, T L S. Is Dennett a Disillusioned Zimbo?. *Inquiry*, 36(1-2), 33-57, Mr 93.

D C Dennett propounds a 'multiple drafts' conception of consciousness which is both materialist and anti-realist (in something like Dummett's sense). Thus there is no determinate truth as to what the components of someone's consciousness were over any particular period and the order in which they occurred. In opposition to this an anti-materialist form of physical realism is defended here. There really is a precise something which it is like to be a conscious individual at each moment. The main difficulty in accepting this view is that it seems to make it quite contingent what type of consciousness performs what function in the economy of the organism, e.g., that pleasure acts as a positive, pain as a negative reinforcer of behaviour. There is a problem here which can only be avoided by abandoning the Humean doctrine that there cannot be necessary relations between distinct existences.

Sprigge, T L S. Refined and Crass Supernaturalism. *Philosophy*, 32(Supp), 105-125, 1992.

William James distinguished two sorts of supernaturalism: refined and crass. For the former religious talk of the supernatural simply bathes the natural world in a particular sort of emotional and moral glow; for the latter it is concerned with a distinct reality sometimes intervening in the natural world. The opposing religious attitudes of F H Bradley (as representative of 'refined' supernaturalism) and of James himself (as representative of the 'crass' version) are compared on the basis of this distinction and some similarities and contrasts with certain more recent controversies (e.g., in connection with Don Cupitt) about the significance of religious language are examined.

Sprigge, T L S. Refined and Crass Supernaturalism in Philosophy, Religion and the Spiritual Life, McGhee, Michael (ed). New York, Cambridge Univ Pr, 1992.

The contrasting views of religion of William James and F.H. Bradley perfectly illustrate the contrast which James drew between the frankly 'crude' supernaturalism he endorsed himself and the 'refined' supernaturalism of absolute idealists for which the supernatural is little more than a certain moral glow in which the natural world is bathed for them. The contrast between these two positions is very much alive in much dispute about the nature of religious belief and language today.

Sprigge, T L S. The Unreality of Time. *Proc Aris Soc*, 92, 1-19, 1992.

We do and should believe that there is a precise truth about every detail of the past, including innumerable now for every undiscoverable details. But what is the objective correlative of this truth? All proposals fall except the 'eternalist', that all events, whether past, present or future, from the point of view of any particular piece of thinking, are just eternally there in relations to each other registered by us as temporal. Externalism, however, is incompatible with (but also requires) time's reality as ordinarily conceived. The conclusion, though similar to McTaggart's, does not depend on his question begging argument.

Springsted, Eric. Personalism and Persons: A Response to Gendreau and Haddox. *Personalist Forum*, 8/1(Supp), 119-121, Spr 92.

Responding to presentations on Personalist philosophers Mounier, Maritain and Caso I argue that the concept of the person involved in their solution to the contemporary malaise over personhood comes only by subscribing to the Enlightenment view of the person which is the real cause of the malaise. The Personalist view is then contrasted with the view of Simone Weil who achieved many of the same ends but with a critique of the underlying metaphysics of these thinkers.

Springsted, Eric. Rootedness: Culture and Value in Simone Weil's Philosophy of Culture, Bell, Richard H (ed). New York, Cambridge Univ Pr, 1993.

In light of recent attacks on the metaphysical self and in light of Richard Rorty's recommendation that we henceforth employ a "nominalist and historicist rhetoric" this essay examines Simone Weil's understanding of the relations between the self, culture and value. It establishes that Weil's last works argued against Maritain's metaphysical personalism. It then examines her view that a contingent and historical self can, through its cultural roots, nevertheless be linked to and embody transcendent values. Thus, like Rorty, she rejects a metaphysical self, yet shows that hope for a good that is fulfilling and abiding is not facile or illusory.

Springsted, Eric O. Of Tennis, Persons and Politics. *Phil Invest*, 16(3), 198-211, Jl 93.

Beginning with Simone Weil's observation that philosophy, that knowing, is "exclusively a matter of action and practice, like tennis," and contrasting it with Hobbes's observation that political philosophy, unlike tennis *cannot* depend on practice, this essay examines Weil's understanding of persons and its political implications. This understanding consists in seeing persons as inextricably rooted within their historical, social context, and, indeed, sees understanding itself within the context. Thus political philosophy is not a matter of "rules" (Hobbes) but of a moral activity that creates one's self and others. It is political philosophy done from a "first person perspective."

Sprung, G M C. Nietzsche's Trans-European Eye in Nietzsche and Asian Thought, Parkes, Graham R (ed). Chicago, Univ of Chicago Pr, 1991.

Squadrito, Kathy. Descartes and Locke on Speciesism and the Value of Life. *Between Species*, 8(3), 143-149, Sum 92.

Historically, Descartes is known for a philosophy which is insensitive and inhumane toward animals. Locke is often praised for a philosophy which is more humane and sensitive. In this paper I argue that the similarities between Descartes and Locke are more pronounced than their differences.

Squadrito, Kathy. Re-Interpretation of Locke's Theory of Ideas. *Indian Phil Quart*, 20(2), 161-172, Ap 93.

Locke's recognition of the problems associated with traditional representative realism has lead some scholars to reinterpret his work to avoid such problems. Recent support for the traditional interpretation is based on the argument that the term 'idea' is employed uniformly. In this paper I argue that because Locke does not present either a consistent theory of knowledge or a consistent doctrine of ideas, both interpretations remain plausible.

Srinivas, K. Wittgenstein on Rule Following. *Indian Phil Quart*, 19(2), 105-114, Ap 92.

St Maurice, Henry. Two Rhetorics of Cynicism in Curriculum Deliberation, or Two Riders in a Barren Land. *Educ Theor*, 43(2), 147-160, Spr 93.

Two approaches to deliberating moral worth are described in terms of a philosophical tradition called cynicism. The rhetorical features of these approaches are illustrated by a popular song and related to controversies over school curriculum.

Staab, Janice. Standing Alone Together: Silence, Solitude, and Radical Conversion. *Cont Phil*, 15(1), 16-20, Ja-F 93.

This paper addresses the relationship between the moment and the process of spiritual conversion. Each is characterized with respect to the roles of the communities involved in them and the languages spoken by these communities. While the conversion process is shown to be both a verbal and a communal experience, the conversion moment is seen to be a communion with one's God alone, and is thus a locus of silence before the divine. Implications of the conversion moment for subsequent communal experience are also considered.

Staal, Frits. Indian Bodies in Self as Body in Asian Theory and Practice, Kasulis, Thomas P (ed). Albany, SUNY Pr, 1992.

The Western dualism of "mind and body" occurs in India, but the prevailing Hindu and Buddhist doctrine is that of a hierarchy of five onion-like "sheaths". Their identity varies, but since they constitute a continuum, acting on one may be used to influence another. This is illustrated by ritual and martial arts and reflected in recitation, meditation, dance and erotics. "Five" is as mythological as "two", but the Indian perspective of a hierarchy of features linked by gradual transitions makes more sense than the Western dichotomy of incommensurable entities situated at the opposite ends of an unbridgeable gap.

Staat, Wim. On Abduction, Deduction, Induction and the Categories. *Trans Peirce Soc*, 29(2), 225-237, Spr 93.

In this paper, Peirce's categories, Firstness, Secondness, and Thirdness, are related to his distinction of three forms of reasoning, Abduction, Deduction, and Induction. In Peirce's work and in secondary literature the attribution of Firstness to Abduction seems unproblematic. About Deduction and Induction, however, opinions waiver. The paper argues for a reconsideration of that attribution about which no disagreement seemed to exist: the Firstness of Abduction. Abduction as Firstness, the paper argues, should be understood in terms of Peirce's theory of inquiry. The theory of inquiry, then, will result in the First-, Second-, and Thirdness respectively, of Abduction, Deduction, and Induction.

Stachowski, Ryszard. On Standard and Non-standard Models in Theories of Psychological Measurement in Probability and Rationality, Eells, Ellery (ed). Amsterdam, Rodopi, 1991.

Stachowski, Ryszard. *The Mathematical Soul: An Antique Prototype of the Modern Mathematisation of Psychology*. Amsterdam, Rodopi, 1992.

Stack, George. Nietzsche's Earliest Essays: Translation and Commentary on "Fate and History" and "Freedom of Will and Fate". *Phil Today*, 37(2), 153-169, Sum 93.

These two early essays of an eighteen-year-old Nietzsche are presented in a new translation. Although they are pieces of juvenilia, these essays have often been cited because the basic themes in them seem to foreshadow Nietzsche's mature thought. It is argued in my commentary that both the philosophic themes in these brief essays and a great deal of the language in them is traceable to highly specific images and concepts in the *Essays* of the American poet and essayist, Ralph Waldo Emerson. Since it is the case that the question of fate and freedom, science and history, *et al.* raised in these essays do reappear in Nietzsche's later works, then the literary philosophy of Emerson is a hidden presence in them.

Stafford, Barbara Maria. 'Fantastic' Images in Aesthetic Illusion, Burwick, Frederick (ed). Hawthorne, de Gruyter, 1990.

This essay is organized into three sections. In the first, introductory part, I present a highly-condensed overview of the related metaphors of light and dark (clair-obscur) and near and far which shape much modern (post-Enlightenment) Symbolist art and theory. In the second part, I demonstrate the centrality of these ancient philosophical and rhetorical metaphors to the question of aesthetic illusion. I offer a new interpretation of Diderot's analysis of Fragonard's smokey "Platonic dream," the *Coresus and Callirboe*, exhibited to great acclaim in the Salon of 1765. Third, and finally, I suggest that this master painting should be connected to an explosion of Romantic 'fantastic' images—both artistic and scientific—that were meant to glow jewel-like in the dark.

Stafford, J Martin. Love and Lust Revisited in Applied Philosophy, Almond, Brenda (ed). New York, Routledge, 1992.

Stainsby, H V. Ian Weeks's Disproof of God. *Sophia (Australia)*, 31(1-2), 119-122, 1992.

Stairs, Allen. Value-Definiteness and Contextualism: Cut and Paste with Hilbert Space. *Proc Phil Sci Ass*, 1, 91-103, 1992.

I begin with an appeal to the GHZ/Mermin state to illustrate the allure of contextualism and value-definiteness. I then point out that standard contextualism, with its special status for non-degenerate operators, faces some embarrassing questions. Further, there is an alternative that apparently does not have the same problems. A modest re-pasting of Hilbert space makes the honors almost even between these two varieties. The paper closes with some reflections on the peculiarities of contextualism.

Staley, Kevin. Infinity and Proofs for the Existence of God. *Lyceum*, 3(2), 15-26, Fall 91.

Staley, Kevin. Metaphysics and the Good Life: Some Reflections on the Further Point of Morality. *Amer Cath Phil Quart*, 65(1), 1-28, Wint 91.

Stalley, R F. Sailing Through the *Republic*. *Polis*, 11(1), 40-51, 1992.

Stalnaker, Robert. Twin Earth Revisited. *Proc Aris Soc*, 93, 297-311, 1993.

Stambaugh, Joan. The Other Nietzsche in Nietzsche and Asian Thought, Parkes, Graham R (ed). Chicago, Univ of Chicago Pr, 1991.

Stamenov, Maxim I. More Foundational Questions Concerning Language Studies. *J Prag*, 17(5-6), 533-543, Je 92.

Stampe, Dennis W and Gibson, Martha I. Of One's Own Free Will. *Phil Phenomenol Res*, 52(3), 529-556, S 92.

Stanley, Jason and Heck Jr, Richard. Reply to Hintikka and Sandu: Frege and Second-Order Logic. *J Phil*, 90(8), 416-424, Ag 93.

Stanley, John L. Marx, Engels and the Administration of Nature. *Hist Polit Thought*, 12(4), 647-670, Wint 91.

Interpreters of Marx have tried to distinguish his view of "praxis" and of the "Promethean" domination of nature from the "naturalism" and "positivism" of Engels. Yet all four of these terms are often linked together rather than separated in Marx's frequently ambiguous texts. For Marx, Praxis is part of a human history that is linked to natural history; praxis is limited by certain "positivist" covering laws; the Promethean domination of nature recognizes natural limits; and the human needs essential to man's species being are dominated by a nature that is sometimes internal and sometimes external to man.

Stanley, Liz and Wise, Sue. *Breaking Out Again: Feminist Ontology and Epistemology (Second Edition)*. New York, Routledge, 1993.

Stanley, M C. Forcing Disabled. *J Sym Log*, 57(4), 1153-1175, D 92.

This paper proves two theorems. The first is that, if zero-sharp exists, then any constructible forcing property that adds no reals over *L* collapses some uncountable *L*-cardinal to countable cardinality. This improves a theorem of Foreman, Magidor, and Shelah (*Journal of Symbolic Logic,* vol. 51, 1986, 39-46). The paper's second theorem approximates this phenomenon generically. It remains open, for example, whether the constructible kappa-Cohen conditions can be made to collapse kappa in an extension of *L* in which zero-sharp does not exist, when kappa is the successor of a singular cardinal.

Starchenko, S and Pillay, A and Hart, B. Triviality, NDOP and Stable Varieties. *Annals Pure Applied Log*, 62(2), 119-146, Jl 93.

Starosta, William J and Chaudhary, Anju G. "I Can Wait 40 or 400 Years": Gandhian *Satyagraha* West and East. *Int Phil Quart*, 33(2), 163-172, Je 93.

The analysis concerns Mohandas K Gandhi's 1930 Salt March, a satyagraha campaign. The paper first considers the event through western eyes, as a case of civil disobedience or street rhetoric. This is posed as an "etic" perspective. The paper then adopts an indigenous Indian frame of reference, or "emic" view of the events. While both the emic and etic accounts serve to interpret the event, and offer plausible understandings, neither account suffices, taken alone, to "explain" satyagraha.

Starrett, Shari N. Nietzsche and MacIntyre: Against Individualism. *Int Stud Phil*, 24(2), 13-20, 1992.

Statman, Daniel. A New Argument for Genuine Moral Dilemmas?. *J Value Inq*, 26(4), 565-571, O 92.

The article examines a recent argument for the possibility of genuine moral dilemmas put forward by Gerald Paske. According to Paske, as consequential and deontological theories are both true, and as they require at times incompatible courses of action, dilemmas are possible. This argument is shown to be an unsuccessful version of the argument from the incommensurability of values and, in any case, is shown to be invalid. In the last part of the article, a different way of developing the argument from incommensurability is explored.

Statman, Daniel. Modesty, Pride and Realistic Self-Assessment. *Phil Quart*, 42(169), 420-438, O 92.

Some philosophers believe that modesty means underestimating one's real value. But this makes modesty depend on a kind of ignorance, or even self-deception, which are incompatible with virtue. Others suggest that modesty means a realistic self-assessment, taking one's achievements "in perspective". However, it is unclear how a person who is genuinely worthy and admirable can take her achievements "in perspective" and still be modest. This is possible only if a pessimistic view of human nature is presupposed, based, for instance, on the low status of human beings in comparison to God. The article argues that modesty is a disposition typical of the excellent to avoid immoral kinds of behavior. In the paradigmatic case the modest person has a realistic high self-assessment but nevertheless treats other human beings with the appropriate moral respect. Since the excellent are justified in being proud of themselves, pride and modesty are not necessarily incompatible.

Statman, Daniel. Self-Assessment, Self-Esteem and Self-Acceptance. *J Moral Educ*, 22(1), 55-62, 1993.

Teachers are often troubled by the difficulty of enhancing their pupils' self-esteem, particularly in the case of students who are especially weak and whose low self-assessment is justified. Dewhurst suggested (JME, 20(1), pp. 3-11) that these students can be helped by bringing them to accept themselves, since self-acceptance is compatible with realistic low self-assessment. Dewhurst's thesis is criticised and it is suggested that self-acceptance is inseparable from an improvement in one's self-assessment. Thus, the improvement of self-assessment is a necessary condition for enhancing self-esteem. If cases exist where this reformation of self-image is unattainable, that is, cases where the self-assessment of the student cannot be improved, it is doubtful whether there is anything we can do about it.

Stauch, Marvin. Natural Science, Social Science, and Democratic Practice: Some Political Implications of the Distinction Between the Natural and the Human Sciences. *Phil Soc Sci*, 22(3), 337-356, S 92.

This article examines some of the contributions to the contemporary debate over the question of whether there is an important distinction to be made between the natural and the human sciences. In particular, the article looks at the arguments that Charles Taylor has put forward for the recognition of a radical discontinuity between these forms of science and then examines Richard Rorty's objections to Taylor's distinction and argues that Rorty misunderstands the reasons for this distinction and thereby misses the political implications of failing to make such a distinction. In this regard, some arguments made by Anthony Giddens and John O'Neill, respectively, around Alfred Schutz's "postulate of adequacy" are used to show how the social sciences must be conceived so as to avoid consequences inimical to the reproduction and maintenance of participatory, democratic institutions. (edited)

Stauffer, Lee. Spinoza, Cantor, and Infinity. *SW Phil Stud*, 15, 74-81, Spr 93.

Stebbins, Sarah. Anthropomorphism. *Phil Stud*, 69(2-3), 113-122, Mr 93.

Stecker, Robert and Adams, Fred and Fuller, Gary. Schiffer on Modes of Presentation. *Analysis*, 53(1), 30-34, Ja 93.

Since Lois likes Kent and believes that Kent cannot fly, she would plead with him not to leap from a tall building. Though Lois also likes Superman, she would not plead with him not to leap. If modes of presentation were syntactic items in a language of thought, we could explain that Lois thinks of the same individual once under the mode of "Kent" and later under the mode of "Superman", without thinking "Kent = Superman". In a number of recent writings, Schiffer has proposed a roadblock to this neat explanation. In this paper we argue that the view that modes are syntactic items in a language of thought survives Schiffer's objections.

Stecker, Robert and Adams, Fred and Fuller, Gary. The Floyd Puzzle: Reply to Yagisawa. *Analysis*, 53(1), 36-40, Ja 93.

We defended the view that modes of presentation are syntactic items in the language of thought. Yagisawa argues that our defense of this view did not handle Schiffer's Floyd puzzle. The following truths are supposed to make a rational Floyd irrational (on our account): 1) Floyd believes that Lois believes that Superman flies, 2) Floyd believes that Lois does not believe that Clark Kent flies, and 3) Floyd does not believe that Clark Kent is not Superman. We remain unconvinced. We present not one but two interpretations on which Floyd is not irrational on our view and on which our view survives Schiffer's Floyd puzzle.

Stecker, Robert and Adams, Fred and Fuller, Gary. The Semantics of Thought. *Pac Phil Quart*, 73(4), 375-389, D 92.

This paper accepts that the task of a semantics of thoughts is to explain how thoughts convey information about the world and how behavior can be explained in virtue of the content of thoughts. We defend direct reference theories of meaning against Devitt's charge that such semantic theories cannot give a satisfactory semantics for the problems of identity sentences, opaque contexts, or positive and negative existence sentences. We reply to Devitt's charge, examine and reject Devitt's alternative non-descriptive sense theory, and offer a new account of the semantics of positive and negative existential sentences.

Stecker, Robert and Fuller, Gary and Adams, Fred. Thoughts Without Objects. *Mind Lang*, 8(1), 90-104, Spr 93.

This paper answers objections to object-dependent thoughts (thoughts identified by their objects). We claim that such thoughts exist and are needed to explain behavior in many circumstances. Objections to object-dependent thoughts invoke vacuous singular thoughts (say, of an hallucinated attacker). Such thoughts have no objects (no attacker), hence such thoughts cannot explain behavior in virtue of their object-dependent content. We show that appeals to vacuous thoughts do not diminish the need for object dependent thoughts in non-vacuous situations. We also compare this debate to the broad/narrow content debate and show that the content needed to explain behavior when thoughts are vacuous is not narrow content.

Stecker, Robert A. Aesthetics in Reflections on Philosophy, McHenry, Leemon (ed). New York, St Martin's Pr, 1993.

This essay focuses on three questions: 1) what is art; 2) what is it to understand a work of art; 3) what makes art something to value? About 1), I state the major traditional and contemporary answers along with various objections to these. I conclude with my own suggestion. About 2), I consider objections to an intentionalist account of understanding art. I conclude that, while these objections fail, alternatives to understanding art in terms of author's intention are now firmly entrenched. Hence there is more than one acceptable way of understanding artworks. About 3), I suggest a plurality of ways in which art may be valued.

Stecker, Robert A. Defining "Art": The Functionalism/Proceduralism Controversy. *S J Phil*, 30(4), 141-152, Wint 92.

Stephen Davies has argued that the attempt to define art in the past thirty years can be seen as a debate between functionalism and proceduralism and that the latter provides the better definition. I argue Davies doesn't establish the superiority of proceduralism. I first point out several problems with that view. I then consider problems for functionalism and explain how they can be solved.

Stecker, Robert A. Fish's Argument for the Relativity of Interpretive Truth. *J Aes Art Crit*, 48(3), 223-230, Sum 90.

According to Stanley Fish, interpretations are never true *simpliciter*, but true relative to sets of assumptions. Further, it is those assumptions which create the object of, and evidence for, an interpretation. In this paper, I identify Fish's argument for these conclusions. I argue that, although his views contain important insights, his argument is flawed in two ways. First, Fish equivocates between innocuous and radical versions of his theses. Second, the radical (and interesting) versions do not follow from his premises.

Stecker, Robert A. Goldman on Interpreting Art and Literature. *J Aes Art Crit*, 49(3), 243-246, Sum 91.

Stecker, Robert A. Incompatible Interpretations. *J Aes Art Crit*, 50(4), 291-298, Fall 92.

In this paper, I am concerned with two theses. 1) There are, or could be incompatible interpretations of the same artwork, both of which are *true*. 2) There are, or could be, incompatible interpretations of the same artwork both of which are *acceptable*. I shall argue that we ought to flatly reject the first of these theses. About the second, we have to distinguish different assertions that it can make. Some of these are true but uninteresting. Others are interesting but false.

Stecker, Robert A. Plato's Expression Theory of Art. *J Aes Educ*, 26(1), 47-52, Spr 92.

There is no full-fledged definition of art in Plato's writings. If one looks for the beginnings of a theory of art in Plato, I argue that one can find hints of an expression theory as easily as one can find hints of a mimetic theory. If we are to fully understand what Plato thought about art, we must attend to the first sort of hints at least as carefully as to the second. This is especially needed to understand Plato's criteria of good and bad art.

Steedman, Carolyn. *La Théorie qui n'en est pas une*, or, Why Clio Doesn't Care. *Hist Theor*, 31(4), 33-50, 1992.

This article considers the practice of women's history in Britain over the last quarter century in relation to general historical practice in the society, to the teaching and learning of history at all educational levels, and to recent theoretical developments within feminism, particularly those developments framed by postmodernist thought. It makes suggestions about the common processes of imagining—or figuring—the past, and advances the view that because of shared cultural assumptions and shared educational experience, women's history in Britain has constituted a politics rather than a theoretical construct. (edited)

Steele, David Ramsay. *From Marx to Mises*. Peru, Open Court, 1992.

Steger, Manfred. Historical Materialism and Ethics: Eduard Bernstein's Revisionist Perspectives. *Hist Euro Ideas*, 14(5), 647-663, S 92.

This essay reviews German revisionist Marxist Eduard Bernstein's (1850-1932) attempt to reconcile historical materialism with ethics. The author offers two theses: First, the origin of Bernstein's version of historical materialism lies in the writings of the German neo-Kantian philosopher F A Lange and the later writings of Friedrich Engels. Second, Bernstein was a conscious eclectic, evolving socialism and liberalism into a new synthesis—the prototype of a modern understanding of Social Democracy. Bernstein's version of historical materialism resurrects the politics of human agency. In a way, Bernstein was the first post-Marxist, informed by Marxist insight while rethinking and reformulating those features which he considered flawed and unethical. Hence, Bernstein should be seen as a neo-Kantian "ethical" socialist theorist.

Steidlmeier, Paul. The Moral Legitimacy of Intellectual Property Claims: American Business and Developing Country Perspectives. *J Bus Ethics*, 12(2), 157-164, F 93.

Private property forms the bedrock of the business/society relationship in a market economy. In one way or another most societies limit *what* people can claim as property as well as the *extent* of claims they can make regarding it. In the international arena today intellectual property rights are a focal point of debate. Many developing countries do not recognize the monopoly claims of patents and copyrights asserted by business as legitimate. This paper reviews contemporary areas of dispute and then presents the tasks facing the construction of a fair intellectual property rights regime.

Stein, Edith. Was ist Phänomenologie? (Nachdruck). *Theol Phil*, 66(4), 570-573, 1991.

Stein, Howard. Was Carnap Entirely Wrong, After All?. *Synthese*, 93(1-2), 275-295, N 92.

Steinberg, Diane. Spinoza, Method, and Doubt. *Hist Phil Quart*, 10(3), 211-224, Jl 93.

The paper considers the question why Spinoza rejected Cartesian doubt as a method of discovery in metaphysics. It is argued that his rejection of Cartesian voluntarism regarding judgment is not sufficient to explain this, but rather the reason lies in his theory of the mind as the idea of an actually existing body. The Cartesian meditator's use of doubt culminates in a state in which she no longer believes any of her former sense-derived opinions, including that she has a body. Spinoza's development of his conception of the mind precludes that anyone achieve this state of complete withdrawal from the senses. Thus, the method of doubt is not humanly feasible.

Steinberger, Peter J. *The Concept of Political Judgment*. Chicago, Univ of Chicago Pr, 1993.

This book examines the thesis that political judgment property understood, is not at all a matter of theoretical or philosophical knowledge, but, rather, involves a kind of ineffable knack, something that is unavailable for rational analysis. The argument proceeds by putting aside political questions and considering the question of judgment per se, understood to be the problem of how we connect universals and particulars. A rationalistic approach to this problem is uncovered and evaluated; nonrationalist approaches are also examined. The argument leads to a reconstruction of our notion of judgment in general, and political judgment in particular, in which the seemingly contradictory claims of inferential rationality and nonrational intuition are shown to be, in fact, mutually compatible and mutually dependent.

Steinbuch, Thomas. "Take Your Pill Dear": Kate Millett and Psychiatry's Dark Side. *Hypatia*, 8(1), 197-204, Wint 93.

Kate Millett's book, *The Loony-Bin Trip*, is an extraordinary account of her personal experience with involuntary psychiatric commitment. The drama of her conflict with professional psychiatry is so tense, so enraging, that one is likely to find oneself having to set the book aside from time to time just to calm down.

Steindler, Larry. Les principles d'Eduard Zeller concernant l'histoire de la philosophie. *Rev Metaph Morale*, 97(3), 401-416, Jl-S 92.

Steiner, P. In Defense of Semiotics: The Dual Asymmetry of Cultural Signs (in Czechoslovakian). *Filozof Cas*, 40(4), 574-590, 1992.

Steinhoff, Uwe. Wahre performative Selbstwidersprüche. *Z Phil Forsch*, 47(2), 293-295, Ap-Je 93.

Carl-Otto Apel and his followers maintain that a performative self-contradictory assertion is necessarily wrong and it's negation therefore necessarily true (or infallible), and they try to construct with this kind of "transcendental deduction" abuse of infallible knowledge, especially for the justification of their ethic of discourse. I supply assertions which fulfil Apel's definition (and possible alternative ones) of a performative self-contradiction but which are however, not wrong or necessarily wrong. So Apel's type of argument leading not to infallible truths but even to falsenesses does not function.

Stekeler-Weithofer, Pirmin. Kultur und Autonomie: Hegels Fortentwicklung der Ethik Kants und ihre Aktualität. *Kantstudien*, 84(2), 185-203, 1993.

The paper attempts a new evaluation of Hegel's reexamination of Kant's moral philosophy. It rests on a methodological reading of Hegel's logics, especially of his analysis of the concept of (philosophical) reflection. For Hegel, philosophical ethics cannot give any foundation of morality or present arguments for basic norms a criteria. It only represents the forms we already accepted implicitly in our usual moral judgments. It makes these forms articulate, explicit. Such a philosophical reflection is crucial for a conscious choice between possible schemes of action. There is no personal freedom and autonomy outside the range of possible choices presented to us by the public culture of mankind, in which different forms of action or life are developed.

Stekeler-Weithofer, Pirmin. Plato and the Method of Science. *Hist Phil Quart*, 9(4), 359-378, O 92.

Plato argues throughout his dialogues in favor of the famous 'hidden' method of scientific argumentation, the method of analysis and synthesis. The method is outlined in the 'Philebus': phenomenological and semantical analysis of a certain realm of discourse provides us with basic elements which can be named by words. Synthesis leads to complex forms (*eide*) and complex expressions (*logoi*). To explain phenomena means to see them as having essential feature in common (*methexis*) with a generic structure. Examples are: musical theory, writing, geometry, proportion theory or the molecular theory of chemical reaction in the 'Timaios'.

Stellingwerff, J. Elementen uit de ontstaansgeschiedenis der Reformatorische Wijsbegeerte. *Phil Reform*, 57(2), 169-190, Ja 92.

This article is an essay on the birth and first development of the Amsterdam School of Philosophy by D H Th Vollenhoven (1892-1978) and H Dooyeweerd (1894-1977). Most prominent became Dooyeweerd with his 'A New Critique of Theoretical Thought' (1953-58), but his brother-in-law Vollenhoven was the initiator of their program of a Christian philosophy. After the author has published a Vollenhoven-biography, he lay in this publication emphasis on the study of both philosophers to get a good insight in the history and topics of their school.

Stemerding, Dirk. How to Make Oneself Nature's Spokesman? A Latourian Account of Classification in Eighteenth- and Early Nineteenth-Century Natural History?. *Biol Phil*, 8(2), 193-223, Ap 93.

Classification in eighteenth-century natural history was marked by a battle of systems. The Linnaean approach to classification was severely criticized by those naturalists who aspired to a truly natural system. But how to make oneself nature's spokesman? In this article, I seek to answer that question using the approach of the French anthropologist of science, Bruno Latour, in a discussion of the work of the French naturalists Buffon and Cuvier in the eighteenth and early nineteenth century. These naturalists followed very different strategies in creating and defending of what they believed to be a natural classification in zoology. Buffon failed, whereas Cuvier's work appeared to be very successful. (edited)

Stemmer, Nathan. Behavioral Materialism, The Success of Folk Psychology, and the Ambiguous First-Person Case. *Behavior Phil*, 20/2(21/1), 1-14, 1993.

Without making use of suspect intentional notions, *behavioral materialism* attributes all behavior to physiological causes, individuating these indirectly by referring to external events (e.g., Quine, 1985). Two criticisms of this approach are that intentional notions are needed to account for 1) the success of folk psychology and 2) first-person phenomena. I will argue that both criticisms are unjustified.

Stengel, Barbara. Response to "Of Dances and Dreams". *Phil Stud Educ*, 1, 20-27, 1991.

This paper responds to Terrence O'Conner's OVPES Presidential Address (see Phil Stud Educ, 1(), 10-19, 1991). O'Conner redefines culture with regard to human agency, thus redefining the [educational] philosopher's role. Specifically, he casts philosophers as "cultural stars" (in Cornell West's idiom) participating in the specific relations of the community's multiple discourses in order to sustain existentially rewarding and politically relevant projects. I support his overall project but argue that what is required is not only a redefinition of culture but also a reconceptualization of philosophy to see philosophy and pedagogy as two sides of the same coin.

Stenger, Victor J. The Face of Chaos. *Free Inq*, 13(1), 13-14, Wint 92-93.

Over-enthusiastic statements on the significance of results from the Cosmic Background Explorer (COBE) prompted the media to interpret them as an unprecedented verification of the biblical view of creation. Consequently, an important scientific result was so grossly misrepresented to the public as to turn its actual meaning on its head. Far from demonstrating the need for a creator, the results from COBE provided support for the inflationary big-bang theory that outlines how the structure of the universe, including the laws of physics themselves, could have come about by natural means—as the universe exploded out of nothingness.

Stenlund, Sören. *Language and Philosophical Problems*. New York, Routledge, 1991.

This book presents the results of philosophical investigations on several connected issues of current interest within the philosophies of language, logic, mind and mathematics. It deals in particular with problems which are connected with our tendency to be misled by certain prevailing views and preconceptions about language. Philosophical claims made by theorists of meaning and philosophers of mind are scrutinized and are shown to be connected with common views about the nature of certain mathematical notions and methods. At the same time, the book demonstrates a strategy inspired by some of Wittgenstein's ideas for resolving conceptual and philosophical problems.

Stenstad, Gail. Merleau-Ponty's Logos: The Sens-ing of Flesh. *Phil Today*, 37(1), 52-61, Spr 93.

Stepaniants, M T. The Image of Woman in Religious Consciousness: Past, Present, and Future. *Phil East West*, 42(2), 239-247, Ap 92.

Stepanich, Lambert V. Heidegger: Between Idealism and Realism. *Harvard Rev Phil*, 1(1), 20-29, Spr 91.

Stephan, Achim. Wissen, Glauben, Nicht-Wissen: Freuds Vexierspiel für die epistemische Logik. *Z Phil Forsch*, 46(2), 257-265, Ap-J 92.

Stephan, F and Kummer, Martin. Weakly Semirecursive Sets and R E Orderings. *Annals Pure Applied Log*, 60(2), 133-150, Ap 93.

Weakly semirecursive sets have been introduced by Jockusch and Owings (1990). In the present paper their investigation is pushed forward by utilizing r.e. partial orderings, which turn out to be instrumental for the study of degrees of subclasses of weakly semirecursive sets.

Stephanson, Anders. Regarding Postmodernism—A Conversation with Fredric Jameson in Postmodernism/ Jameson/ Critique, Kellner, Douglas M (ed). Washington, Maisonneuve Pr, 1989.

Stephenson, Wendell. Deficiencies in the National Institute of Health's Guidelines for the Care and Protection of Laboratory Animals. *J Med Phil*, 18(4), 375-388, Ag 93.

This paper is a critique of NIH guidelines for the care and protection of laboratory animals. It exposes four serious deficiencies in these guidelines: 1) failure to make it clear that the mere pursuit of knowledge does not justify using animals; 2) failure to give any guidance concerning what constitutes human benefit or well-being; 3) failure to countenance trade-offs between human benefit or well-being and animal well-being; 4) failure to clearly specify what constitutes keeping animals in an 'environment appropriate to the species and its life history.' It concludes with the suggestion that the construction and revision of these guidelines is too important to be left to the professionals.

Sterba, James. Reconciliation Reaffirmed: A Reply to Peffer. *J Soc Phil*, 23(1), 145-149, Spr 92.

Sterelny, Kim. Evolutionary Explanations of Human Behaviour. *Austl J Phil*, 70(2), 156-173, Je 92.

This article discusses the problems of and prospects for human sociobiology. Following an example illustrating the unconvincing nature of human sociobiology (by contrast to other animals), I discuss the explanation of its lack of success. Human sociobiology does not fail because of the difficulties of exploiting animal data or those of collecting human data; nor from the importance of learning or culture to humans. The taxonomic problem of discovering ethological natural kinds is serious but not insuperable. Nor is the problem of explaining essentially social phenomena by a theory that applies first and foremost to individual organisms. The central cause of the failures of sociobiology is its implicitly behaviourist theory of mind. The paper concludes by considering ways in which evolutionary considerations could be incorporated within psychology.

Sterling, Marvin. *Philosophy of Religion: A Universalist Perspective*. Lanham, Univ Pr of America, 1993.

This book addresses key issues in the philosophy of religion. It discusses the full range of questions commonly covered in other books of this sort; however, it does so in a distinctive manner. Discussion of the various issues addressed centers around two pivotal concepts, namely that of a supreme being and that of life after death. Among the features distinguishing this book from other similar works are the following. Firstly, it emphasizes throughout—but particularly in its final chapter—the importance of a correct account of sense-perception for rightly resolving the central questions in the philosophy of religion. Secondly, no other book on the subject so consistently reaches conclusions that favor traditional religious belief while at the same time scrupulously avoiding dogmatism. And thirdly, no other book in the field embraces the thesis of universalism so decisively as this one does.

Stern, Cindy D. Semantic Emphasis in Causal Sentences. *Synthese*, 95(3), 379-418, Je 93.

A shift in emphasis can change the truth-value of a singular causal sentence. This poses a challenge to the view that singular sentences predicate a relation. I argue that emphasized causal sentences conjoin predication of a causal relation between events with predication of a relation of causal relevance between events with predication of a relation of causal relevance between states of affairs (or perhaps facts). This is superior to the treatments of such sentences offered by Achinstein, Dretske, Kim, Sanford, Bennett, and Levin. My proposal affords clarity regarding logical structure, at least at a certain level of detail. It makes the relation between the content of an emphasized causal sentence and the unemphasized causal sentences, without introducing new entities (as do some other accounts) or unacceptable consequences for identity and individuation of events.

Stern, David S. A Hegelian Critique of Reflection in Hegel and His Critics, Desmond, William (ed). Albany, SUNY Pr, 1989.

I focus on recent critical work by Henrich, Theunissen, and Tugendhat on self-consciousness understood in terms of reflection. I maintain that 1) Hegel provides arguments against the uncritical assumption that self-consciousness should be interpreted on the model of consciousness. Since Hegel thinks consciousness exemplifies the subject-objection relation, it follows that 2) he rejects this model as appropriate to self-consciousness. If these two points are established, then the basis for Tugendhat's global critique is undermined; more importantly, the way will be opened for an understanding of Hegel's alternative contribution to the theory of self-consciousness.

Stern, R A. James and Bradley on Understanding. *Philosophy*, 68(264), 193-209, Ap 93.

This article offers a comparative assessment of the views of William James and F H Bradley on the topic of human understanding and its limit. It is argued that while both have a distrust of the conceptual aspects of thought, and so share the view that the human intellect will always fail to gain absolute knowledge, they develop this idea very differently, thanks to the divergence in their respective philosophical outlooks: whereas Bradley developed it in the context of a post-Hegelian intellectualist rationalism, James did so in the context of his pragmatic humanism. The nature of the dispute between James and Bradley on this issue is explored, as an important turning point in the philosophical *Weltbild* of the twentieth century.

Stern, Robert A. The Relations Between Moral Theory and Metaphysics. *Proc Aris Soc*, 92, 143-159, 1992.

This paper considers how much metaphysics can contribute to moral theory. Parfit claims that it can contribute a great deal, while Rawls argues it cannot. Rawls's arguments for his position are analyzed, and it is claimed that he is wrong to hold that a metaphysical question like personal identity has no bearing on the debate between Kantianism and utilitarianism. Rawls's methodological arguments against Parfit, involving his method of reflective equilibrium, are also ineffective. Rawls's motivations for his position are considered, and it is argued that he is wrong to fear that Parfit's position leads to dogmatism or misplaced foundationalism.

Steuerman, Emilia. Habermas versus Lyotard in Judging Lyotard, Benjamin, Andrew (ed). New York, Routledge, 1992.

This paper presents and discusses the contributions of J Habermas and J G Lyotard to the modernity/postmodernity debate. Habermas, the modernity philosopher, stresses the need for historical, situated norms and criteria for judgment. Lyotard warns of the political dangers involved in this approach. The paper argues that the two positions are not irreconcilable. Lyotard's postmodern critique can be understood as a radicalization of the modernity project, an answer to Habermas's plea for more critical reflection. This reading of the debate leads to a reevaluation of the modernity project as proposed by Habermas.

Steunebrink, Gerrit A J. Zur Notwendigkeit von Religion aus der Sicht Durkheims und seiner Erben. *Theol Phil*, 67(4), 536-557, 1992.

This article presents Durkheim's sociology of religion against the background of Enlightenment philosophy and the history of cultural anthropology. After the breakdown of the metaphysical world order, in which God guaranteed the unity of nature and freedom, religion itself symbolizes this unity as the unity of society and nature. Religion expresses society's basic trust in nature as fields of moral and social action. Science cannot give this basic trust, therefore religion as a moral consentment to nature is a practical necessary prejudgment. At the end this article evaluates the modern debate about civil religion and stresses that christianity cannot serve as a civil religion.

Stevenson, Frank W. Discourse and Disclosure in the *I Ching*. *J Chin Phil*, 20(2), 159-179, Je 93.

Stevenson, Frank W. Limit and Exhaustibility in the Questions of T'ang. *J Chin Phil*, 19(2), 197-225, Je 92.

Here I analyze Chi's cryptic response, in the *Lieh-tzu*, to T'ang's question whether, given an indeterminate temporal order within the world, the world as totality has a spatial (and temporal?) limit: "Beyond and within the unlimited, no more unlimited. Thus I know its/the unlimited and don't know the limit." Chi can mean (1) there both are/are not limits so the question is undecidable (logical dilemma, infinity as finite concept); (2) our knowledge of limits is unlimited (knowing/not knowing, epistemological paradox); (3) the limit/limitless distinction is ultimately dissolved (Tacist mysticism). I try to clarify all three readings by seeing "limit" not as a (Western) stasis or line but as a dynamic process of exhaustion (Chinese chin), so that the "unlimited" is the pu chin, "inexhaustible".

Stevenson, Leslie. Why Believe What People Say?. *Synthese*, 94(3), 429-451, Mr 93.

The basic options about the epistemology of testimony seem to be a Humean reductionist view that inductive evidence for reliability is needed before it can rationally be believed, or a Reidian criterial view that testimony is intrinsically, but defeasibly, credible. Recent discussion of radical interpretation provides some argument for the criterial view, at least for eye-witness reports.

Stever, James A. The Diversity Criterion in Public Administration. *Pub Affairs Quart*, 7(2), 187-197, Ap 93.

Stewart, Arthur F. Peirce, Turing and Hilbert: A Sketch of Pragmatism vs Formalism. *SW Phil Stud*, 14, 111-122, Spr 92.

Stewart, Robert M. Agent-Relativity, Reason, and Value. *Monist*, 76(1), 66-80, Ja 93.

Samuel Scheffler has argued that ethical theories imposing agent-relative constraints are implausible and even paradoxical. This article is an examination of his arguments against such non-consequentialist theories, particularly "standard" deontological views and the virtue-based approach of Philippa Foot. His objections are shown to be avoided by a position that combines elements of both deontological and virtue ethics, emphasizing the distinction between what it is morally right to do and what an agent has reason to do. Furthermore, the very idea of an impersonal point of view that is agent-neutral is shown to be indefensible.

Stewart, Stanley and Magnus, Bernd and Mileur, Jean-Pierre. *Nietzsche's Case: Philosophy as/and Literature.* New York, Routledge, 1992.

This jointly-authored study of Nietzsche and his literary interlocutors occupies the interface of philosophy and literature, bringing conventionally marked "philosophical" and "literary" texts into conversation with one another in a way never done before. Nietzsche's texts are brought into productive conversation with the New Testament and texts by Sidney, Bacon, Spenser, Milton, Shakespeare, Browning, Coleridge, Wordsworth, Blake, Caryle, Lawrence, as well as with the standard texts of the philosophical and critical traditions from Plato to Derrida.

Stichler, Richard N. The Right to Revolution: Locke or Marx? In Terrorism, Justice and Social Values, Peden, Creighton (ed). Lewiston, Mellen Pr, 1990.

Stieringer, Eva. Bibliography of Paul Weingartner's Publications 1961-1991 in Advances in Scientific Philosophy, Schurz, Gerhard (ed). Amsterdam, Rodopi, 1991.

Stikkers, Kenneth W. Charles Sanders Peirce's Sociology of Knowledge and Critique of Capitalism in Frontiers in American Philosophy, Volume I, Burch, Robert W (ed). College Station, Texas A&M Univ Pr, 1992.

The purpose of this essay is 1) to elucidate a) the implications of Perice's thought for the sociology of knowledge, and b) the sociological dimension of Peirce's epistemology, and 2) to explain Peirce's scattered diatribes against capitalism in light of the latter.

Still, Judith (trans) and Collie, Joanne (trans) and Irigaray, Luce. *Elemental Passions—Luce Irigaray.* New York, Routledge, 1992.

Elemental Passions explores the man/woman relationship in a series of meditations on the senses and the elements. Its form resembles a series of love letters in which, however, the identity — and even the reality — of the addressee is deliberately obscured. French philosopher Luce Irigaray's investigations into the nature of gender, language and identity take place in several modes: the analytic, the essayistic and the lyrical poetic.

Stingl, Michael and Collier, John. Evolutionary Naturalism and the Objectivity of Morality. *Biol Phil*, 8(1), 47-60, Ja 93.

We propose an objective and justifiable ethics that is contingent on the truth of evolutionary theory. We do not argue for the truth of this position, which depends on the empirical question of whether moral functions form a natural class, but for its cogency and possibility. The position we propose combines the advantages of Kantian objectivity with the explanatory and motivational advantages of moral naturalism. It avoids problems with the epistemological inaccessibility of transcendent values, while avoiding the relativism or subjectivism often associated with moral naturalism. Our position emerges out of criticisms of the contemporary sociobiological views of morality found in the writings of Richard Alexander, Michael Ruse, and Robert Richards.

Stob, M and Downey, Rod. Friedberg Splittings of Recursively Enumerable Sets. *Annals Pure Applied Log*, 59(3), 175-199, F 93.

Properties of the automorphism group of the lattice of recursively enumerable sets are studied. In particular, the authors analyse interactions of the degrees, automorphisms and Friedberg splittings.

Stockman, Alan C and Landsburg, Steven E and Kahn, James A. On Novel Confirmation. *Brit J Phil Sci*, 43(4), 503-516, D 92.

Stoeber, Michael. Introvertive Mystical Experiences: Monistic, Theistic, and the Theo-monistic. *Relig Stud*, 29(2), 169-184, Je 93.

This paper criticises those views of mysticism that hold that all mystical experiences are phenomonologically the same, only interpreted differently ('essentialists'). Focussing upon theistic and monistic accounts, the paper argues that the evidence suggests that these reflect different experience types. In reference to Eckhart and Ruusbroec, it further suggests that for some mystics these experiences can be related together in terms of a third kind of experience, one wherein monistic mystics exude elements that can only be associated with a theistic Divine. This is referred to as 'theo-monistic' mysticism.

Stoecker, Ralf. *Was sind Ereignisse? Eine Studie zur Analytischen Ontologie.* Hawthorne, de Gruyter, 1992.

Events play an important part in various philosophical disciplines, e.g., in the philosophy of mind, action theory, philosophy of science, ethics, etc. Still, there is no commonly shared understanding of what events are. In particular, authors disagree about whether events should be regarded as finely or as coarsely grained entities. Yet, at a first glance, there exists a knock down argument for the fine-grained approach (put forward by Alvin Goldman), which relies on the seemingly different causal roles of finely discriminated events. It is the topic of the major part of my book to show that this impression is mistaken and that, quite to the contrary, the fine-grained event conception is even incompatible with the causal role of events, and moreover, with any materialist understanding of the world.

Stöckler, Manfred. Reductionism and the New Theories of Self-Organization in Advances in Scientific Philosophy, Schurz, Gerhard (ed). Amsterdam, Rodopi, 1991.

Stoerig, Petra and Brandt, Stephan. The Visual System and Levels of Perception: Properties of Neuromental Organization. *Theor Med*, 14(2), 117-135, Je 93.

To see whether the mental and the neural have common attributes that could resolve some of the traditional dichotomies, we review neuroscientific data on the visual system. The results show that neuronal and perceptual function share a parallel and hierarchial architecture which is manifest not only in the anatomy and physiology of the visual system, but also in normal perception and in the deficits caused by lesions in different parts of the system. Based on the description of parallel hierarchical levels of active information processing in the visual brain, we suggest a concept of dissociable levels of perception, advocating that the phenomenal perception and recognition is realized in the functional integrity of a network of reciprocal

cortico-cortical connections. The properties shared by neuronal and perceptional functions provide a basis for a neuromental monism in which both functions are attributed a causal role.

Stokes, Michael C. Plato and the Sightlovers of the *Republic. Apeiron*, 25(4), 103-132, D 92.

The article proposes that the final argument in *Republic V* is elenctic, drawing on premisses Glaucon must accept as representative of the 'lovers of sights and sounds' and reaching conclusions unacceptable to them. Many objections fall once the argument is seen as genuine dialogue with the 'sightlovers', exhibiting the incoherence of a position which accepts the reality of sights and sounds but denies the 'beautiful by itself' etc. ('Forms'). Plato bears only the literary responsibility for the argument's course and specific conclusions; the argument fails accordingly to saddle Plato philosophically with the separation of the provinces of belief and knowledge.

Stoljar, Daniel. Emotivism and Truth Conditions. *Phil Stud*, 70(1), 81-101, Ap 93.

By distinguishing between pragmatic and semantic aspects of emotivism, and by distinguishing between inflationary and deflationary conceptions of truth conditions, this paper defends emotivism against a series of objections. First, it is not the case (as Blackburn has argued) that emotivism must explain the appearance that moral sentences have truth conditions. Second, it is not the case (as Boghossian has argued) that emotivism presupposes that non-moral sentences have inflationary truth conditions. Finally, it is not the case (as Geach and Blackburn have argued) that emotivism is inconsistent with the validity of certain simple arguments.

Stolnitz, Jerome. On the Cognitive Triviality of Art. *Brit J Aes*, 32(3), 191-200, Jl 92.

Stone, Jerome. What Religious Naturalism Can Learn from Langdon Gilkey in God, Values, and Empiricism, Peden, Creighton (ed). Macon, Mercer Univ Pr, 1989.

Stone, Jim. Cogito Ergo Sum. *J Phil*, 90(9), 462-468, S 93.

I argue that "I am thinking, therefore I am' does not express an argument but a proposition for which Descartes cannot find the right idiom. A proposition p is *attitude-constituted.* for me just in case my standing in a propositional attitude to any propositional is sufficient to constitute the fact that p. "I am" and "I think" are indubitable because they are attitude constituted. The cogito means "My thinking this very thought is sufficient to constitute the fact that I exist." This expresses a "simple intuition of the mind": my existence needs to be nothing more than my thinking this very thought.

Stone, Lynda. Disavowing Community. *Proc Phil Educ*, 48, 93-101, 1992.

The paper poses a disruption of the western, modernist meaning of the concept of 'community,' given a generalized dissatisfaction with human association today and, by extension, with its naming. Following a descriptive framing, there is a detailed unpacking of a set of contradictory antimonies—of individualism, rationality, and choice—inherent in common meaning. Underlying is a founding element of non-associative sameness. Finally, suggested instead is a new concept, that of 'heteronmity.' Its strength lies in overcoming sameness with a new form of human association, one based on difference in which people join together temporarily for specific purposes.

Stone, Mark A. Realism and the Principle of the Common Cause. *Can J Phil*, 22(4), 445-461, D 92.

Stone, Robert. Nuclear Cities: The Bastille Analogy in Sartre Alive, Aronson, Ronald (ed). Detroit, Wayne St Univ Pr, 1991.

Stone, Robert and Bowman, Elizabeth A. Sartre's 'Morality and History': A First Look at the Notes for the Unpublished 1965 Cornell Lectures in Sartre Alive, Aronson, Ronald (ed). Detroit, Wayne St Univ Pr, 1991.

Stoneham, Tom. Comment on Davies: A General Dilemma?. *Proc Aris Soc*, 92, 225-231, 1992.

Martin Davies has argued (same journal, same volume) against individualism about perceptual content from a position which maintains the local supervenience of phenomenal character. These two are incompatible because allowing any typing of perceptual states for which physical identity is sufficient leaves open a revisionary individualist response.

Storey, John. *An Introductory Guide to Cultural Theory and Popular Culture.* Athens, Univ of Georgia Pr, 1993.

The book charts the changing relationship between cultural theory and popular culture; a relationship between the production of theory and the consumption/production of culture. Using examples of popular cultural texts and practices throughout, it presents a clear and detailed critical survey of the competing theories of, and approaches to, popular culture: the culture and civilization tradition, the American debate on 'mass culture', culturalism, structuralism, post-structuralism, Marxism, feminism and postmodernism.

Storl, Heidi. The Problematic Nature of Parfitian Persons. *Personalist Forum*, 8/1(Supp), 123-131, Spr 92.

Derek Parfit claims to be a "Reductionist" with respect to personhood. He believes this is a desirable middle ground between the belief that persons are separately existing entities and the belief that persons are mere fictions. More specifically, Parfit maintains that 1) a person just consists in a brain and a body, and the occurrence of a series of interrelated physical and psychological events. This claim is indicative of an Impure Psychological account of personhood. Purely psychological considerations are supplemented with the requirement of a brain and a body. Surprisingly, Parfit also maintains that 2) a person is an entity that is distinct from a brain, a body, and a series of physical and mental events. He argues that (2) is consistent with (1) and that together, they offer a "better" account. Finally, and perhaps even more surprisingly, Parfit claims that 3) personhood is only a fact about the way we talk. Given the distinct nature of these three claims, I attempt to determine precisely what Parfit means by 'person'. I argue that (1) and (2) offer no positive conception of personhood, and that Parfit's Reductionism leads to the view that persons are mere fictions.

Storl, Heidi. The Risks of Going Natural. *SW Phil Rev*, 9(1), 23-33, Ja 93.

As an account of personhood, Naturalism suffers from worn and worrisome assumptions. Naturalism, when dissected, is motivated by the familiar thesis that what makes humans special, what defines our way of life, is that we are, at bottom, members of the Homo sapiens species. I suggest that the addition of a psychological dimension to discussions of personhood, though helpful, needs to be recast in such a way that emphasis is placed on specific psychological acts and not on types of psychological content.

Stout, Jeffrey. Justice and Resort to War in Cross, Crescent, and Sword, Johnson, James Turner (ed). Westport, Greenwood Pr, 1990.

Stout, Maureen. Response to "Disavowing Community". *Proc Phil Educ*, 48, 102-104, 1992.

Stove, D. The Subjection of John Stuart Mill. *Philosophy*, 68(263), 5-14, Ja 93.

This article is a critical examination of J S Mill's belief that the intellectual capacity of women is equal to that of men.

Stove, David. A New Religion. *Philosophy*, 67(260), 233-240, Ap 92.

Strandberg, Warren. Competency, Mastery and the Destruction of Meaning. *Proc S Atlantic Phil Educ Soc*, 36, 85-94, 1991.

Strange, Steven. Plotinus' Account of Participation in *Ennead* VI.4-5. *J Hist Phil*, 30(4), O 92.

Ennead VI.4-5 attempts to present a unified response to two Platonic problems: the Sailcloth Dilemma of the *Parmenides* and the question of the mode of presence of Soul to the cosmos of the *Timaeus*. The concern with the Sailcloth Dilemma has long been recognized, but the solution to it has not been fully understood. It consists in avoiding the horns of the dilemma by denying its key assumption, that intelligible Being is actually present to the sensible world. Rather, matter is supposed to be present in a special, non-reciprocal way to the Ideas and to Being, with the sensible world the emergent result, in some sense illusory or unreal, of this relation.

Strasser, Mark. Degradation, Pornography, and Immorality in Terrorism, Justice and Social Values, Peden, Creighton (ed). Lewiston, Mellen Pr, 1990.

Stratton, Teri. Headaches of Headless: Who is Poet Enough?. *Hypatia*, 7(2), 109-119, Spr 92.

Psychoanalysis has long cited poetry as the expression vehicle for unconscious production. This article addresses the sexual politics of psychoanalysis's conjoining of poetry and the "feminine." The argument of this text is that the coupling of the "feminine" and the poetic in Lacanian discourse is a metaphorical double cross which most often leaves "woman" at a loss for words.

Stratton-Lake, Philip. Reason, Appropriateness and Hope: Sketch of a Kantian Account of a Finite Rationality. *Int J Phil Stud*, 1(1), 61-80, Mr 93.

The critique of metaphysical reason can best be understood positively as the attempt to construct and work within a finite rationality. I argue that a finite rationality should not be understood as one which establishes the limits of knowledge and works within these limits, but as an appropriate rationality — appropriate, that is, to a finite being. I point out a severe problem with the attempt to conceive of an appropriate rationality and attempt to answer this problem using the concept to hope. So I claim that a finite rationality should be understood as a hopeful rationality.

Straughan, Roger. Are Values Under-Valued? A Reply to Christopher Ormell. *J Moral Educ*, 22(1), 47-50, 1993.

This paper challenges Christopher Ormell's claim that an explicit distinction should be drawn between a "hard" and "soft" sense of "having values". It is argued that holding values is better portrayed in terms of a continuum representing degrees of difficulty and sacrifice, for the holding of any value implies a possible tension between obligation and motivation. Making choices lacks this necessary feature and so cannot be equated with any sense of "having values". Ormell's claim that values but not Values are relativistic is also questioned. Finally, an important implication of this debate for moral education is drawn, concerning ways in which children may learn to hold and act upon values.

Strauss, David A. The Liberal Virtues. *Nomos*, 34, 197-203, 1992.

Liberalism does presuppose a conception of the virtues, but they are distinctively liberal virtues: the virtues of toleration, and of moral courage in the face of lives that are underdetermined by either culture or nature. Recognizing these traits as virtues is necessary to justify liberalism, and education in these virtues is, as a psychological and sociological matter, probably necessary if a liberal society is to be sustained. But the integral relationship between liberalism and these distinctively liberal virtues does not entail that liberalism should import a full Aristotelian vocabulary of virtue.

Strauss, Paul. Arithmetized Set Theory. *Stud Log*, 50(2), 343-350, Je 91.

It is well known that number theory can be interpreted in the usual set theories, e.g., ZF, NF and their extensions. The problem I posed for myself was to see if, conversely, a reasonable strong set theory could be interpreted in number theory. The reason I am interested in this problem is, simply, that number theory is more basic or more concrete than set theory, and hence a more concrete foundation for mathematics. A partial solution to the problem as accomplished by WTN, where it was shown that a predicative set theory could be interpreted in a natural extension of pure number theory, PN, i.e., classical first-order Peano Arithmetic. In this paper, we go a step further by showing that a reasonably strong fragment of predicative set theory can be interpreted in PN itself. We then make an attempt to show how to develop predicate fragments of mathematics in PN.

Strawson, P F. The Incoherence of Empiricism—II. *Aris Soc*, Supp(66), 139-143, 1992.

In this commentary on Bealer's paper of the same title, my purposes were two fold: first, to endorse his primary contention, namely that what he calls 'intuition' (i.e., the power to perceive both conceptual necessities and the applicability of certain complex concepts) is an essential source of data for any comprehensive theoretical explanation; second, to express certain reservations, mainly about his choice of the unqualified term, 'empiricism', to name the target of his criticism. His real target is a narrowly (scientistically) conceived naturalism.

Strawson, Peter. *Analysis and Metaphysics: An Introduction to Philosophy*. New York, Oxford Univ Pr, 1992.

In this book, I advocate (and practice) the displacement of an older reductive conception of philosophical method (the idea of 'analysing' complex ideas into simpler elements) in favour of elucidating the interconnections between the complex but irreducible notions which form the basic structure of human thinking, and incidentally demonstrate that the three traditionally distinguished departments of metaphysics (or ontology), epistemology and logic are but three aspects of one unified inquiry.

Strike, Kenneth. Liberal Discourse and Ethical Pluralism: An Educational Agenda. *Proc Phil Educ*, 48, 226-236, 1992.

Strikwerda, Robert and May, Larry. Male Friendship and Intimacy. *Hypatia*, 7(3), 110-125, Sum 92.

Our primary focus is the concept of intimacy, especially in the context of adult American male relationships. We begin with an examination of comradeship, a nonintimate form of friendship, then develop an account of the nature and value of intimacy in friendship. We follow this with discussions of obstacles to intimacy and of Aristotle's views. In the final section, we discuss the process of men attaining intimacy.

Strikwerda, Robert (ed) and May, Larry (ed). *Rethinking Masculinity*. Lanham, Rowman & Littlefield, 1992.

This anthology presents a set of philosophical essays written by men, most of whom call themselves feminists which attempt to come to terms with some issue or question arising out of the authors' experiences of being a male in Western culture. The anthology begins with a reassessment of the data on sex role differences. It then considers men's experiences in war and sports, romance and fatherhood, as well as the problems of intimacy and homophobia. There is also a section on pornography and on empowerment. The authors are: Patrick Grim, J Glenn Gray, Brian Pronger, Hugh LaFollette, Larry May, Robert Strikwerda, Patrick Hopkins, Alan Soble, Harry Brod, Kenneth Clatterbaugh, Leonard Harris, and Victor Seidler.

Strikwerda, Robert A and May, Larry. Fatherhood and Nurturance in Rethinking Masculinity, May, Larry (ed). Lanham, Rowman & Littlefield, 1992.

We argue that fatherhood should today be ideally conceived in terms of nurturance. First, we provide a brief history of modern conceptions of fatherhood. Second, we analyze the notion of nurturance and argue that conceptions of fatherhood that are not drawn in terms of nurturance are quite anemic. Third, we respond to several arguments against our thesis from biology and psychology. And finally, we explore some of the significant advantages to men that will accrue when they see themselves as, and become, nurturers.

Strikwerda, Robert A and May, Larry. Male Friendship and Intimacy in Rethinking Masculinity, May, Larry (ed). Lanham, Rowman & Littlefield, 1992.

Our primary focus is the *concept* of intimacy, especially in the context of adult American male relationships. We begin with an examination of comradeship, a contrasting nonintimate form of friendship. We follow this with a discussion of obstacles to intimacy and a comparison of our views with those of Aristotle. In the final section, we discuss the process of attaining intimacy for men and resources for enhancing that process.

Ströker, Elisabeth. Warum-Fragen: Schwierigkeiten mit einem Modell für kausale Erklärungen. *Neue Hefte Phil*, 32-33, 105-129, 1992.

This essay (dedicated to Jiten Mohanty) deals with different types of the question 'why' something is the case. It is centered around the well-known Hempel-Oppenhiem model for causal explanations in science, and investigates its possible applications erase in the field of everyday-life explanations. It comes up to the result that the 'why'-question has a different sense according to different problem situation, rather than to are given scientific arguments. For its closer examination can show the limits of the Hempel- Oppenhiem model.

Ströker, Elisabeth and Hardy, Lee (trans). *Husserl's Transcendental Phenomenology—Elisabeth Ströker*. Stanford, Stanford Univ Pr, 1993.

In this work, Professor Ströker offers a unified and critical interpretation of Husserl's transcendental phenomenology as a whole from the standpoint of method. Taking her point of orientation from Husserl's self-professed goal of realizing in his work the ideal of "first philosophy", she tracks the dynamic interplay between the development of Husserl's method and the thematic progression of his research. Along the way she deflects many of the common objections to Husserl's project, while pointing out its conceptual limitations and de facto oversights.

Stroll, Avrum. How I See Philosophy in Certainty and Surface in Epistemology and Philosophical Method, Martinich, A P (ed). Lewiston, Mellen Pr, 1991.

An appeal to common sense is useful as a first step in diagnosizing paradoxical theses, such as Berkeley's claim that we eat and drink ideas. But it is not sufficient. One must therefore distinguish a philosophical appeal (or justification) from a simple appeal itself. This is something most defenders of a common sense approach have failed to do. The paper formulates and defends the criteria for such a philosophical justification of the appeal to common sense.

Strong, Carson. Patients Should Not Always Come First in Treatment Decisions. *J Clin Ethics*, 4(1), 63-65, Spr 93.

A number of commentators and ethics committees have asserted that treatment decisions for mentally incompetent patients always should be based only on the patient's interests. The author calls this the *strict-advocacy* view, and gives several arguments against it. First, a clinical counterexample is presented. Second, it is argued that physicians have duties not only to the patient but also to members of the patient's family. Always giving priority to the patient can result in failure to fulfill such duties. These arguments support the *modified-advocacy* view, which holds that the duty to the patient is a *prima facie* one that normally takes precedence over family and other interests, but in some circumstances can be overridden by them.

Strong, David. The Technological Subversion of Environmental Ethics. *Res Phil Technol*, 12, 33-66, 1992.

Unlike previous epochs in the west which have let things be in a bi- centric or symmetrical relation to humans, our petty homocentric age takes a shallow view of natural things and finds it a challenge to dominate them. Respecting things is the new challenge before us. The problem is complex ontologically, extending beyond altruism for nature. The measures called for by those concerned with environmental ethics will not go far enough and will be subverted by technology unless technology's attraction is understood. Thus, to be consequential, an environmental ethic needs a comprehensive and incisive critique of the technological order.

Strong, Tracy B (trans) and Nancy, Jean-Luc. La Comparution/The Compearance: From the Existence of "Communism" to the Community of "Existence". *Polit Theory*, 20(3), 371-398, Ag 92.

Stroud, Barry G. Ayer's Hume in The Philosophy of A J Ayer, Hahn, Lewis Edwin (ed). Peru, Open Court, 1992.

Stroud, Barry G. Pursuit of Truth. *Phil Phenomenol Res*, 52(4), 981-987, D 92.

Stroud, Barry G. The Background of Thought in John Searle and His Critics, Lepore, Ernest (ed). Cambridge, Blackwell, 1991.

Strout, Cushing. Border Crossings: History, Fiction, and *Dead Certainties*. *Hist Theor*, 31(2), 153-162, 1992.

Simon Schama's *Dead Certainties* is assessed in the light of the complex relationship between history and fiction, which share some limited common territory. Examples are cited from Mary Chesnut, Oscar Handlin, Georg Lukács, Herman Melville, Robert Penn Warren, P D James, and Wallace Stegner. Schama's book has some kinship to the skepticism found in " the new historicism" and "deconstruction," but also has its own differences from the fashionable "inverted positivism" which concludes that since evidence is not an open window on reality, it must be a wall precluding access to it. His idea of historical uncertainty arise from a fallacy that a "communion with the dead" possible only for a time-traveler, represents authentic knowlege.

Strudler, Alan. Mass Torts and Moral Principles. *Law Phil*, 11(4), 297-330, 1992.

This paper examines moral problems that arise when assigning liability in causally problematic mass exposure tort cases. It examines the relevance of different conceptions of corrective justice for such assignments of liability. It explores an analogy between the expressive role of punishment and the expressive role of tort, and argues that the imposition of liability in causally problematic mass exposure cases can be justified by appeal to expressive considerations.

Strydom, Piet. Sociocultural Evolution or the Social Evolution of Practical Reason: Eder's Critique of Habermas. *Praxis Int*, 13(3), 304-322, O 93.

Jürgen Habermas contributed importantly to the renaissance of evolutionary thinking in the social sciences. The ensuing debate in Germany, however, created conditions for a critique and transformation of his developmental theory in favour of a more properly evolutionary theory. Klaus Eder, a younger generation critical theorist who collaborated with Habermas on the original version of the theory, has thus far done most in this regard. His critique is systematised so as to demonstrate the untenable assumptions and negative consequences of an ontogenetically based theory and, simultaneously, to point towards an alternative theory focusing on changes in the constitutive structures of society.

Stuart, James and Scherer, Donald. Introductory Logic Through Multiple Modes of Presentation. *Teach Phil*, 14(4), 389-397, D 91.

Students' grades have shown sustained statistically significant improvement since the reformating of instruction in the large, intro logic course. Previously students received large lecture instruction twice weekly, followed by discussion of exercises in the third weekly meeting. Twenty-six newly made videotapes allow students to see high quality presentations followed immediately by discussion in groups of 36, coupled with guided use of LogicWorks in groups of 24 at the third session. The findings confirm the efficacy of responding to differences in student learning styles. The findings suggest means of combining the advantages of technological and human instruction. Students have retained positive attitudes toward the video presentations; prepared, outlined presentation notes; LogicWorks and their graduate student instructors. They have also affirmed that the standard intro logic text used in the course is not helpful to learning and its replacement is scheduled.

Stucki, Pierre-André. La 'Déclaration des droits de l'homme et du citoyen' (1789). *Stud Phil (Switzerland)*, 49, 217-232, 1990.

Stuhr, John. Dewey's Reconstruction of Metaphysics. *Trans Peirce Soc*, 28(2), 161-176, Spr 92.

This essay critically explicates John Dewey's theory of experience and his view of philosophy as criticism. It begins with an examination of Richard Rorty's well-known writings on Dewey — writings that mis-read and mis-use Dewey. It then provides an alternative, more pragmatic account of Dewey's conception of metaphysics, his theory of experience, and the practical importance of metaphysics.

Stuhr, John. Postmodernism: Old and New. *J Speculative Phil*, 7(2), 103-109, 1993.

This essay explores the relations between postmodernism and pragmatism, and the relations of both to modernism. In particular, I critically analyze the view that American pragmatists articulated earlier the insights of postmodernism while avoiding postmodernism's challenges to pragmatic commitments to liberalism, individualism, and humanism.

Stuke, Kurt. The Riddle of Self-Sufficiency. *Lyceum*, 4(2), 26-38, Fall 92.

Stump, David. Naturalized Philosophy of Science with a Plurality of Methods. *Phil Sci*, 59(3), 456-460, S 92.

Naturalism implies unity of method—an application of the methods of science to the methodology of science itself and to value theory. Epistemological naturalists have tried to find a privileged discipline to be the methodological model of philosophy of science and epistemology. However, since science itself is not unitary, the use of one science as a model amounts to a reduction and distorts the philosophy of science just as badly as traditional philosophy of science distorted science, despite the fact that the central theme of naturalized philosophy of science is that methodology should be true to science as practiced. I argue that naturalized philosophy of science must apply a plurality of methods to epistemological issues.

Stump, Eleonore. Aquinas on the Foundations of Knowledge. *Can J Phil*, Supp(17), 125-158, 1991.

Aquinas is often taken to hold a foundationalist theory of knowledge. Support for this view is generally adduced from Aquinas's commentary on Aristotle's *Posterior Analytics*. I argue that Aquinas's commentary on *Posterior Analytics* can't be construed as presenting his theory of knowledge, that 'scientia' in that work is not equivalent to 'knowledge', and that Aquinas's epistemology can't be correctly classified as foundationalist. Instead, I argue that Aquinas's epistemology is a species of theological externalism with reliabilist elements. In the process I examine also what Aquinas says about the infallibility of certain processes in sense perception and intellection.

Stump, Eleonore. Aquinas on the Sufferings of Job in Reasoned Faith, Stump, Eleonore (ed). Ithaca, Cornell Univ Pr, 1993.

In Aquinas's lengthy commentary on the biblical book of Job, he takes an approach to the story of Job and to the problem of evil raised by the story which is different from current approaches but which adopts the stringent constraint argued for by William Rowe, namely, that the benefits justifying suffering go primarily to the sufferer. This paper consists in an exploration of both Aquinas's interpretation of Job and his theodicy. Examination of Aquinas's position makes clear the way in which discussions of the problem of evil are a function of the larger ethical and metaphysical views within which they are situated.

Stump, Eleonore. God's Obligations in Philosophical Perspectives, 6: Ethics, 1992, Tomberlin, James E (ed). Atascadero, Ridgeview, 1992.

The notion that God has no moral obligations is not new in the history of philosophical theology, but it has recently been revived by William Alston. Alston holds that there is never anything God ought to do or ought not to do. I show that Alston's arguments for this claim are unsuccessful. In the process I discuss the relations between rights and obligations and the principle of alternative possibilities. Because Alston's arguments for his claim are among the best available, I conclude that since Alston's arguments fail, there is no reason for theists and atheists not to accept the common view that God, if he exists, has moral obligations.

Stump, Eleonore. Providence and the Problem of Evil in Christian Philosophy, Flint, Thomas P (ed). Notre Dame, Univ Notre Dame Pr, 1990.

Until quite recently, the divine attribute focused on in discussions of the problem of evil, in supporting or attacking proposed defenses and theodicies, has been God's omnipotence. I argue for the importance of considering the problem of evil in light of traditional claims about God's providence, God's goodness as expressed in his governance of creation. the account of providence I present is taken from Aquinas, although it or something similar can be found in the work or many other medievals as well. I argue that if Aquinas is right about the nature and workings of perfect moral goodness, then there are certain strong constraints on any attempted defense or theodicy.

Stump, Eleonore (ed). *Reasoned Faith*. Ithaca, Cornell Univ Pr, 1993.

Recent work in philosophy of religion is marked by a willingness to bridge boundaries with related disciplines, including theology, history of religion, and biblical studies. This volume contributes to that new trend. It contains fourteen essays, none previously published, by Robert Adams, Scott MacDonald, Robert Audi, Peter van Inwagen, Harry Frankfurt, William Alston, George Mavrodes, Richard Swinburne, William Rowe, Thomas Morris, William Mann, Philip Quinn, Marilyn Adams, and Eleonore Stump. The title of the collection, *Reasoned Faith*, reflects the theme uniting all the essays, faith examined by reason; the essays bring philosophical techniques and skill to bear on particular well-entrenched religious texts or doctrines.

Stump, Eleonore and Kretzmann, Norman. Eternity, Awareness, and Action. *Faith Phil*, 9(4), 463-482, O 92.

Our article "Eternity" (1981), in which we presented, defended, and applied the traditional doctrine of divine eternity, prompted some criticisms that focus on difficulties in the concept of eternity itself. In the present article we summarize our original account of the doctrine before offering versions of two such criticisms and replying to them. Our replies are intended to clarify and develop further the essential notions of eternity's atemporal duration and of its relationship with time.

Stump, Eleonore and Kretzmann, Norman. Prophecy, Past Truth, and Eternity in Philosophical Perspectives, 5: Philosophy of Religion, 1991, Tomberlin, James E (ed). Atascadero, Ridgeview, 1991.

We examine three attempts to show that the doctrine of eternity fails to contribute to a solution to the foreknowledge problem. The first is that of David Widerker, who finds problems for the eternity solution in the traditional doctrine that God occasionally reveals to prophets truths about the future. The second is that of Jonathan Edwards, who bases his objection on the mere possibility of prophecy. And the third is that of Alvin Plantinga, who argues that the problem of foreknowledge and freedom simply can't be resolved by the doctrine of eternity. We argue that none of these criticisms succeeds, if we understand correctly the nature of the relations between an eternal God and temporal creatures.

Sturgeon, Nicholas. Nonmoral Explanations in Philosophical Perspectives, 6: Ethics, 1992, Tomberlin, James E (ed). Atascadero, Ridgeview, 1992.

I argue for two conclusions about the question of whether moral explanations of nonmoral facts are always undermined by plausible nonmoral explanations of the same facts. Viewed locally, the answer is no: instead, nonmoral explanations often corroborate moral ones, and their role in what I call "amplifying" moral explanations is central to much argument in moral theory. A different question is whether there is some basic and convincing naturalistic explanation that will undermine moral explanations globally. This is too large an issue to settle without surveying all the candidates. But, focusing on a recent discussion by Allan Gibbard, I argue that nothing we know of our evolutionary history supplies such an undermining explanation.

Sturlese, Loris. Mistica o filosofia? A proposito della dottrina dell'immagine di Meister Eckhart. *G Crit Filosof Ital*, 71(1), 49-64, Ja-Ap 92.

Sturlese, Rita. "Averroe quantumque arabo et ignorante di lingua greca...": Note sull'averrosimo di Giordano Bruno. *G Crit Filosof Ital*, 71(2), 248-275, My-Ag 92.

Sturm, Douglas. Natural Law, Liberal Religion, and Freedom of Association: James Luther Adams on the Problem of Jurisprudence. *J Relig Ethics*, 20(1), 179-208, Spr 92.

In contrast to classical natural law theory and traditional individualist liberalism, James Luther Adams develops a version of natural law doctrine grounded in liberal religion. In its ontological dimension, his natural law doctrine is derived from a communal understanding of the character of reality. In its institutional dimension, his natural law doctrine promotes a kind of democracy in which freedom of association is central. From this perspective, law is a practice intended to empower persons through their several associations in the constant formation and transformation of community under the direction of divine power.

Subramanian, Sharada. Existence and Essence: Kierkegaard and Hegel. *Indian Phil Quart*, 20/2(Supp), 17-26, Ap 93.

Suchocki, Marjorie H. Charles Hartshorne and Subjective Immortality. *Process Stud*, 21(2), 118-122, Sum 92.

Suchting, Wal. Reflections Upon Roy Bhaskar's 'Critical Realism'. *Rad Phil*, 61, 23-31, Sum 92.

Sugden, Robert. Justified to Whom? in The Idea of Democracy, Copp, David (ed). New York, Cambridge Univ Pr, 1993.

This is a commentary on a paper by Richard Arneson. Following J S Mill, Arneson argues that better outcomes can be produced if persons with most 'moral competence' have most influence in social decision- making. Mill sought to justify plural voting for the better educated; Arneson seeks to justify giving law- making powers to an unelected judiciary. This paper argues that unconstrained democracy allows voters to defer to those whom they recognize as more competent. Thus the Mill- Arneson argument cannot provide a *public* justification — one that can be accepted by everyone, including the less competent — for constraints on democracy.

Sugden, Robert. Thinking as a Team in Altruism, Paul, Ellen Frankel (ed). New York, Cambridge Univ Pr, 1993.

The paper distinguishes between two kinds of nonselfish behavior — altruistic and cooperative — which represent distinct but equally valid forms of rationality. Altruistic behavior is instrumentally rational: the altruist has nonselfish preferences, and seeks to bring about the outcome he most prefers. The cooperator reasons in a noninstrumental way: she acts on rules that, if generally followed, would lead to outcomes that are good for all, but does not ask whether her own actions lead to good consequences. Instrumentally rational individuals, however altruistic, sometimes lack adequate reasons to play their parts in mutually beneficial arrangements; cooperators are not so handicapped.

Sugden, Robert. Thinking as a Team: Towards an Explanation of Nonselfish Behavior. *Soc Phil Pol*, 10(1), 69-89, Wint 93.

Most economics rests on a theory of instrumentally rational individual action. Nonselfish behavior is usually explained by supposing that individuals have altruistic preferences; the assumption of instrumental rationality is retained. But, however altruistic we may be, a theory of this kind does not provide us with adequate reasons to play our part in cooperative arrangements that benefit us. An alternative conception of rational action is sketched out, in which individuals act as members of partnerships or teams, following rules which can be recommended to the team collectively.

Sugden, Robert and Hollis, Martin. Rationality in Action. *Mind*, 102(405), 1-35, Ja 93.

The paper reviews 'the state of the art' in rational choice and game theory, identifying paradoxes of philosophical interest. The first part traces the idea of utility from Hobbes to Savage. The second deploys the game-theoretic notion of strategically rational choice and dissects the problems of coordination, commitment, constrained maximization, promising and 'cheap talk'. The third casts doubt on the assumption of Common Knowledge of Rationality by examining the backward induction paradox. The fourth uncovers the philosophy of mind implicit in utility theory and reflects on Humean, Kantian and Wittgensteinian accounts of motivation.

Sullivan, B Todd. Economic Ends and Educational Means at the White House: A Case for Citizenship and Casuistry. *Educ Theor*, 43(2), 161-180, Spr 93.

This essay evaluates Clinton administration educational aims in light of a theory of democratic education derived largely from sources in the Pragmatist and casuist traditions. This theory maintains that the purpose of democratic education is assisting citizens to develop capacities for critical thought and public casuistry. In light of this theory, Clinton administration educational aims are found wanting because they subordinate the properly democratic and civic ends of public education in economic goals.

Sullivan, Dale L. The Ethos of Epideictic Encounter. *Phil Rhet*, 26(2), 113-133, 1993.

This paper explores five aspects of an epideictic orator's ethos: reputation, vision, authority, presentation of good reasons, and creation of consubstantiality. Is ethos an attribute of the orator or a perception of the audience? This question is answered with a definition of epideictic ethos as the "common dwelling place of both, the timeless, consubstantial space that enfolds participants in epideictic exchange."

Sullivan, Sonja R. "From Natural Function to Indeterminate Content". *Phil Stud*, 69(2-3), 129-137, Mr 93.

In his recent book *Explaining Behavior*, Fred Dretske has outlined a naturalized theory of intentionality. Several philosophers, including Dretske himself, view his theory as lending credence to the claim that mental state content should be construed widely. In this paper I argue that careful analysis of his theory reveals that this view is mistaken. In Dretske's theory, the notion of the function of a state plays a central role in the determination of content. It will be my contention that this notion of function cannot be used in Dretske's theory to distinguish between the wide construal of the content of an intentional state and the narrow or individualistic construal. This inability of his notion of function to discriminate between wide content and individualistic content undermines any claim that Dretske's theory endorses wide content. Instead, we are lead to the conclusion that Dretske's theory entails pervasive content indeterminacy.

Sullivan, Stephen J. Arbitrariness, Divine Commands, and Morality. *Int J Phil Relig*, 33(1), 33-45, F 93.

The arbitrariness objection to the divine-command theory of morality says the theory is caught in a dilemma: If God has no reasons for His commands, they and morality are arbitrary; but if God does have reasons, *they* provide the basic standards of morality. After considering and rejecting Baruch Brody's attempt to refute this objection, I argue that the objection rests on a confusion between *constitutive* and *non-constitutive* explanations, and rebut two attempts to salvage it.

Sullivan, T D and Reedy, Jeremiah. The Ontology of the Eucharist. *Amer Cath Phil Quart*, 65(3), 373-386, Sum 91.

Although Suarez agrees with Aquinas's principal conclusions about the ontology of the eucharist, Suarez raises doubts about aspects of Aquinas's reasoning. Particularly troubling is the claim that quantity (by the power of God) can exist without a subject. We probe this and other ontological issues raised by the theological problem Aquinas and Suarez seek to solve.

Sullivan, Thomas D and Atkinson, Gary. *Malum Vitandum*: The Role of Intentions in First-Order Morality. *Int J Phil Stud*, 1(1), 99-110, Mr 93.

"First-Order Morality" in the title refers to moral judgments about actions in contrast to judgments about agents. A number of critics have contended either that the distinction between intended versus merely foreseen consequences makes no sense, or that the agent's intentions should not enter into "first-order morality". We explore and respond to criticisms brought by Roderick Chisholm, Douglas Lackey, and Jonathan Bennett in our defense of the vital role intentions play in the moral assessment of human acts.

Sullivan, Vickie B. Machiavelli's Momentary "Machiavellian Moment": A Reconsideration of Pocock's Treatment of the *Discourses*. *Polit Theory*, 20(2), 309-318, My 92.

In his influential book, *The Machiavellian Moment*, J G A Pocock merely presupposes, rather than establishes, the essential premise that allows him to assert Aristotelian ancestry for Machiavelli's thought. In treating the *Discourses*, Pocock merely resurrects this supposition that Machiavelli embraces the Aristotelian view that liberty changes human nature irrevocably from his preceding chapter on *The Prince*—where he had conceded that this supposition is not sustained by the text of *The Prince*. Moreover, Pocock's characterization of Machiavelli's republicanism results from a neglect of salient elements of Machiavelli's thought, and, further, he so emphasizes Machiavelli's context that ultimately he ignores Machiavelli's text.

Sulmasy, Daniel P. What's So Special About Medicine?. *Theor Med*, 14(1), 27-42, Mr 93.

Health care has increasingly come to be understood as a commodity. The ethical implications of such an understanding are significant. The author argues that health care is not a commodity because health care 1) is non-proprietary, 2) serves the needs of persons who, as patients, are uniquely vulnerable, 3) essentially involves a special human relationship which ought not be bought or sold, 4) helps to define what is meant by 'necessity' and cannot be considered a commodity when subjected to rigorous conceptual analysis. The Oslerin conception that medicine is a calling and not a business ought to be reaffirmed by both the professional and the public. Such a conception would have significant ramifications for patient care and health care polity.

Sumberg, Theodore A. *Belfagor*: Machiavelli's Short Story. *Interpretation*, 19(3), 243-250, Spr 92.

Summerfield, Donna M. Thought and Language in the *Tractatus*. *Midwest Stud Phil*, 17, 224-245, 1992.

An interpretation of Wittgenstein's *Tractatus* is offered according to which it contains two arguments for a language of thought: 1) an argument from the possibility of now grasping determinate sense and thus stopping a regress of interpretations; 2) and argument from language learning. This reading conflicts not only with readings according to which propositional signs, as *used* by us, stop the regress, but also with readings according to which thoughts have intrinsic intentionality. As presented here, Wittgenstein offers an explanation of that in virtue of which thoughts (and every other representation) represent; thoughts have original, but not intrinsic intentionality. Thus, the *Tractatus* foreshadows positions held by contemporary philosophers of psychology (e.g., Jerry Fodor).

Summers, David. Conditions and Conventions: On the Disanalogy of Art and Language in The Language of Art History, Kemal, Salim (ed). New York, Cambridge Univ Pr, 1991.

Through the examination of the writings of F De Saussure and E H Gombrich, this article argues that images differ form language in the constitutive importance for image of the material conditions under which they are actually embodied in any historical situation. More generally, it is argued that what we call "art" should be considered not in terms metaphors of "grammar" and "syntax" but rather as alternative constructions of actual space. Art, it is concluded, is thus culturally specific but is not conventional in the way linguistic signs are conventional.

Summers, Robert S. A Formal Theory of the Rule of Law. *Ratio Juris*, 6(2), 127-142, Jl 93.

The author presents a relatively formal theory of the rule of law which includes three basic components: conceptual, institutional and axiological. He then emphasizes the differences between a formal and a substantive theory of the rule of law and highlights the advantages and limits of the former. Finally, the author indicates the importance of this type of theory, namely the values it implies such as predictability, justified reliance, autonomous choice, minimization of disputes and legitimacy.

Summers, Robert S. Charles Sanders Peirce and America's Dominant Theory of Law in Peirce and Law, Kevelson, Roberta. New York, Lang, 1991.

Sumner, L W. Welfare, Happiness, and Pleasure. *Utilitas*, 4(2), 199-223, N 92.

This paper examines the prospects of hedonism as a theory about the nature of welfare. Using the views of the classical utilitarians as a model, the discussion reaches two principal conclusions: (1) hedonism's great asset is its insistence that welfare is subjective (as opposed to objective theories) and experiential (as opposed to desire or preference theories); (2) its great liability is its mental-state analysis of pleasure and pain, which renders it vulnerable to experience machine objections. What is therefore needed in order to rehabilitate hedonism is a less mentalistic analysis of pleasure (or enjoyment) and pain (or suffering).

Sundholm, Göran. The General Form of the Operation in Wittgenstein's 'Tractatus' in Criss-Crossing A Philosophical Landscape, Schulte, Joachim (ed). Amsterdam, Rodopi, 1992.

The paper offers an interpretation of thesis 6.01. The treatment touches upon variables, identity, elementary propositions, internal relations, *Klammerausdrücke*, and operations. Wittgenstein's notations are found not to cover the particular form of definition by induction that is used at 6 and 6.01. It is concluded that Wittgenstein's ability to design of a formal system of logic does not match his outstanding logico-philosophical insight.

Sundholm, Göran (ed) and Schulte, Joachim (ed). *Criss-Crossing A Philosophical Landscape*. Amsterdam, Rodopi, 1992.

Suñer, Margarita. About Indirect Questions and Semi-Questions. *Ling Phil*, 16(1), 45-77, F 93.

The two-fold aim is to demonstrate that embedded indirect questions fall into two classes: true indirect questions (embedded under verbs like *ask/wonder*) and semi-questions (under *know/tell*). In Spanish, the *que* 'that' + *wh*-phrase construction identifies indirect questions unambiguously; thus, it signals overtly what is done covertly in English. The *que* before the *wh*-complement functions as an intensionalizer which 'lifts' the complement in an effort to obtain a closer match between syntax and semantics. And to contribute to the theory of subcategorization and selection by arguing that predicates subcategorize for a syntactic category and select for a semantic object.

Sunstein, Cass R. Democracy and Shifting Preferences in The Idea of Democracy, Copp, David (ed). New York, Cambridge Univ Pr, 1993.

Sunstein, Cass R. The Limits of Compensatory Justice. *Nomos*, 33, 281-310, 1991.

Superson, Anita M. A Feminist Definition of Sexual Harassment. *J Soc Phil*, 24(1), 46-64, Spr 93.

I aim to define 'sexual harrassment' differently from the way it is currently defined in the law. My definition is more inclusive, is objective, and it reflects the social nature (i.e., the group harm) of sexual harassment. It includes any behavior (verbal or physical) caused by a person, A, in the dominant class, that expresses and perpetuates the attitude that B or members of B's sex is/are inferior because of their sex, thereby causing harm to either B and/or members of B's sex.

Surber, Jere P. The Priority of the Personal: An 'Other' Tradition in Modern Continental Philosophy. *Personalist Forum*, 8/1(Supp), 225-231, Spr 92.

Sureson, Claude. Symmetric Submodels of a Cohen Generic Extension. *Annals Pure Applied Log*, 58(3), 247-262, N 92.

We study some symmetric submodels of a Cohen generic extension and the satisfaction of several properties which strongly violates the axiom of choice.

Sus, Oleg. Remembrance of the Last "Nestor" of Czech Aesthetics (in Czechoslovakian). *Estetika*, 28(4), 228-231, 1991.

Sussman, Henry. An American History Lesson in Theorizing American Literature, Cowan, Bainard (ed). Baton Rouge, Louisiana St Univ Pr, 1991.

By paying careful attention to selected passages in Hegel's *Philosophy of History*, the essay traces the formation of an American historiography common, in different ways, to writers as diverse as Hawthorne, Melville, and Pound. The keystone in Hegel's historiographic edifice is a process of superimposition, an overlay of common criteria, oppositions, and continuous to vastly differing cultures and historical periods. Hegelian super- imposition lends a wide range of US fictive works claiming historical pedigree their characteristic structure.

Sutherland, S R. Language, Newspeak and Logic in A J Ayer Memorial Essays, Griffiths, A Phillips (ed). New York, Cambridge Univ Pr, 1991.

Sutherland, Stewart. Religion and Ethics—I in Religion and Philosophy, Warner, Marin (ed). New York, Cambridge Univ Pr, 1992.

Suttle, Bruce B. The Morality of Niceness: Why Educators Have a Duty To Go Beyond Their "Obligations". *Proc Phil Educ*, 48, 241-249, 1992.

As a profession, teaching embodies certain obligations. These obligations are thought to be specific to the teaching profession; and yet teachers share with other professions the recognition that one can go above and beyond one's obligations. Such supererogatory acts have been traditionally described as meritorious while being nonobligatory. I argue that there are no supererogatory acts as such and that, therefore, being nice (being kind, helpful, caring, compassionate, etc.) can be within and is not above and beyond one's obligations as a teacher in most educational settings. Accordingly, there is a need to determine what sets the obligatory limits for a teacher and to what extent it is excusable or permissible for one not to exceed one's professional obligations.

Sutton, John. Religion and the Failures of Determinism in The Uses of Antiquity, Gaukroger, Stephen (ed). Dordrecht, Kluwer, 1991.

Radical naturalistic determinism is often resisted for allegedly destroying human dignity. In discussing its early modern versions in religious and philosophical context, I question the motivations behind such resistance. Neither Pomponazzi's attack on Aristotelian vagueness about necessity and free will nor Hobbes' determinism entail the extreme social and moral chaos which their critics feared. I compare the parallel supernaturalist hard determinism of Reformation theologians and the uneasy compatibilism of Renaissance neo- Stoics, and trace literary echoes of these debates in John Webster and other Jacobean dramatists. I examine libertarian attacks on naturalism, Calvinism, and Hobbism, and accounts of "freedom of indifference" in two seventeenth-century libertarians, Mersenne and Cudworth.

Svejdar, Vitezslav. Some Independence Results in Interpretability Logic. *Stud Log*, 50(1), 29-38, Mr 91.

A Kripke-style semantics developed by de Jongh and Veltman is used to investigate relations between several extensions of interpretability logic, *IL*.

Svejdar, Vitezslav and Hájek, Petr. A Note on the Normal Form of Closed Formulas of Interpretability Logic. *Stud Log*, 50(1), 25-28, Mr 91.

Sverdlik, Steven. Pure Negligence. *Amer Phil Quart*, 30(2), 137-149, Ap 93.

Svoboda, V and Kolar, P. The Logical Structure of Action Sentences (Part I) (in Czechoslovakian). *Filozof Cas*, 40(3), 459-466, 1992.

Svoboda, V and Kolar, P. The Logical Structure of Action Sentences: Two Analytical Exercises (Conclusion) (in Czechoslovakian). *Filozof Cas*, 40(5), 887-905, 1992.

Svoboda, V and Kolar, P. The Logical Structure of Action Sentences: Two Analytical Exercises (Part II) (in Czechoslovakian). *Filozof Cas*, 40(4), 661-671, 1992.

Svobodova, H. Nature—Landscape—Man (in Czechoslovakian). *Filozof Cas*, 39(6), 944-953, 1991.

Concerning the theme of the ethical approaches to human being to environment and landscape this paper will attempt to formulate four hypotheses. They can help toward a practical solution involving the ethical complexities in the relationship between present and future generations with landscape. From a geographical and sociological point of view the problems that face Western Europe and Eastern and Central Europe are different. The four hypotheses are founded on the theme concerning the relation between man and unspoiled nature and landscape: the human being as individual; as part of a microsocial structure; as part of a macrosocial structure; the temporary differences between Western and Eastern Europe in their current processes of development.

Swain, Corliss. Passionate Objectivity. *Nous*, 26(4), 465-490, D 92.

Hume's moral theory provides an account of morality according to which moral judgments are based on passions and yet the qualities judged are objective features of moral agents rather than qualities that exist only in the eyes of beholders. Analysis of the moral sentiments shows that they provide a basis for intersubjective agreement and track real features of the world. Philosophical reflection on both the use and the subjective basis of the use of terms denoting moral qualities reveals that these terms have referents that can be characterized independently of the moral sentiments which signal them.

Swanson, Diane. A Critical Evaluation of Etzioni's Socioeconomic Theory: Implications for the Field of Business Ethics. *J Bus Ethics*, 11(7), 545-553, Jl 92.

Given the pervasive influence of neoclassical economic theory on the field of business, the opposition of the standard economists to the inclusion of moral factors in economic decisions provides an intellectual resistance to the ideas of many business ethicists. Etzioni (1988) offers a theoretical alternative to the neoclassical model, an alternative that includes a moral dimension. This article: (1) highlights the differences between Etzioni's proposed model and the neoclassical economic paradigm; (2) describes and critically evaluates Etzioni's proposed theory in view of his objective of synthesizing the neoclassical paradigm with a duty-based morality; and (3) discusses the implications of Etzioni's proposed paradigm for the field of business ethics.

Swanton, Christine. Commentary on Michael Slote's "Virtue Ethics and Democratic Values". *J Soc Phil*, 24(2), 38-49, Fall 93.

Swanton, Christine. Satisficing and Virtue. *J Phil*, 90(1), 33-48, Ja 93.

Swazo, N K. The Authentic *Tele* of Politics: A Reading of Aristotle. *Hist Polit Thought*, 12(3), 405-420, Fall 91.

Sweeney, Eileen C. Thomas Aquinas' Double Metaphysics of Simplicity and Infinity. *Int Phil Quart*, 33(3), 297-318, S 93.

Sweeney, Leo. *Divine Infinity in Greek and Medieval Thought*. New York, Lang, 1992.

Inspired by E Gilson's query in early 1950s why some medieval authors spoke of God's *being* as infinite, a statement found neither in Judaeo-Christian scriptures nor in Greek philosophy, this volume deals with Hellenic and Hellenistic philosophers (Presocratics, Plato, Aristotle, Plotinus, Proclus) and with Eastern Church authors (Gregory of Nyssa, John Damascene). It also studies Augustine, Lombard, Bonaventure, Fishacre, Aquinas. Conclusion: infinity was predicated of God's being both extrinsically and also intrinsically—a predication based on Aristotelian act/potency (Aquinas) or on Platonic participation (Gregory of Nyssa).

Sweet, Dennis J. Intuition and Substance: Two Aspects of Kant's Conception of an Empirical Object. *Hist Phil Quart*, 10(1), 49-66, Ja 93.

Sweet, Dennis J. The Gestalt Controversy: The Development of Objects of Higher Order in Meinong's Ontology. *Phil Phenomenol Res*, 53(3), 553-575, S 93.

To show how Meinong's ontology developed from the stark "Hume Studies" to the richness of his mature thought, I trace his analysis of complexes in light of the views of Ehrenfels, Cornelius, and Twardowski. Through their influences Meinong was compelled to modify his ontology in two ways. First, he developed a variety of reism that acknowledged ontological heterogeneity within perceptual complexes. Second, he endorsed the view of perceptual realism. With these modifications Meinong was able to introduce 'objects of higher order'.

Sweet, Robert T. Alienation and Moral Imperatives: A Reply to Kanungo. *J Bus Ethics*, 12(7), 579-582, Jl 93.

Rabindra Kanungo's position that alienation at work can be eliminated within capitalism is critically evaluated. My argument is that Kanungo only emphasizes the psychological aspect of Marx's view of alienation. The failure to include the ontological element of alienation results in the confused position that alienation can be eliminated while workers are still being separated from their work by capital. The role that the right to private property plays in the maintenance of this separation is also seen to be a part of Marx's conception of alienation that is missing from Kanungo's analysis. The clarification of Marx's conception of alienation results in the position that organizations within capitalism cannot live up to the moral imperative to be socially responsible in removing alienation at work.

Sweet, William. Postivism, Natural Law Theory and the "Internal Morality of Law". *Kinesis*, 19(1), 15-27, Spr 93.

One of the central debates in the philosophy of law concerns the nature of the principles on which law depends. An often-overlooked facet of this, however, concerns the precise moral (as distinct from axiological) character of these principles. In this paper, I return to the classical statement of this debate, namely, that between H L A Hart and Lon L Fuller. I defend here Hart's claim that there is no necessary connection between morality and the fundamental principles of law from Fuller's natural law critique and, particularly, his arguments concerning what he describes as "the internal morality of law".

Sweet, William. Technology and Change in Religious Belief. *J Dharma*, 18(2), 124-138, Ap-Je 93.

In this essay, I examine the relation between technology and religious belief. Specifically, I consider how technology might affect such belief and why it would be able to do so. I argue that, because both technology and religious belief are about the world, each affects the other, and that the relation between them cannot be merely psychological and subjective. To account for this relation, I provide a brief alternative description of the nature of religious belief. This, I suggest, explains how a "reconciliation" of technology and religious belief is possible.

Sweet, William and O'Connell, Colin. Empiricism, Fideism and The Nature of Religious Belief. *Sophia (Australia)*, 31(3), 1-15, 1992.

Recent discussion of the nature and meaningfulness of religious belief in Anglo-American religious thought seems polarized between two views: empiricism and fideism. We argue that both positions are inadequate because they fail to reflect what religious belief is and perhaps more importantly, what religious believers do. We sketch out how empiricism and fideism fail in providing an accurate account of the nature of religious belief, and suggest an alternative that preserves the best insights of both empiricism and fideism while also being more faithful to the experience of ordinary believers.

Sweetman, Brendan (ed) and Geivert, R Douglas (ed). *Contemporary Perspectives on Religious Epistemology*. New York, Oxford Univ Pr, 1992.

Swensen, Cole. The Body in the City. *Hist Euro Ideas*, 16(1-3), 31-40, Ja 93.

This article examines the rise of the detective genre in mid-19th century Europe and America, presenting it as a purely urban phenomenon that responded to the reorientation, necessitated by urban expansion, of the individual body in society. Focusing on the work of E A Poe and on the 19th century figure of the flâneur, the article discusses ways in which the urban environment reconstructs sensory experience and thereby paradoxically both alienates and foregrounds the body. The triangular dynamic upon which detective fiction is based is proposed as a method of both coping with and subverting a 'theft-of-the-self' peculiar to cities.

Swerdlow, N M. Montucla's Legacy: The History of the Exact Sciences. *J Hist Ideas*, 54(2), 299-328, Ap 93.

Swerdlow, N M. Science and Humanism in the Renaissance in World Changes, Horwich, Paul (ed). Cambridge, MIT Pr, 1993.

Swiderski, E M. 'Denken über Ideologie': eine praktische Begründung der Erneuerung der post-sowjetischen Philosophie?. *Stud Soviet Tho*, 44(3), 211-227, N 92.

Swiderski, Edward M. From Social Subject to the 'person': *The Belated Tranformation in Latter-Day Soviet Philosophy*. *Phil Soc Sci*, 23(2), 199-227, Je 93.

With the dismantling of Marxist-Leninist ideology, fresh inspiration has been discernible in recent Soviet philosophy. This article argues that a major area of concern is the nature of the human being, a theme formerly dominated by the "social" conceptions inscribed into official historical materialism. Soviet philosophers are examining such categories as culture, spirit, consciousness, and personality with an eye to their common characteristics. For many, the latter is grounded in the nature of the *person*, the specificity of which lies in a morally qualified unity of action, sentiment, and reason. The author brings together evidence for this thesis and discusses the arguments of the Soviet philosophers with an eye to their conceptual resources and models.

Swinburne, Richard. God and Time in Reasoned Faith, Stump, Eleonore (ed). Ithaca, Cornell Univ Pr, 1993.

Four principles about Time have the consequence that God must be everlasting, and not timeless. These are 1) events occur over periods of time, never at instants, 2) Time has a metric if and only if there is a unified system of laws of nature, 3) The past is the realm of the causally unaffectible, the future of the causally affectible, 4) Some truths can only be known at certain periods. Yet God is not 'Time's prisoner', for the unwelcome features of Time—the increase of unaffectible events, the 'cosmic clock' ticking away—only occur if God so chooses.

Swinburne, Richard. Reply: A Further Defence of Christian Revelation. *Relig Stud*, 29(3), 395-400, S 93.

In response to Peter Byrne's critical notice of my book *Revelation*, I argue that if God is to put us in a position freely to choose to seek Him, we need some propositional revelation (about what he is like and how to worship him), but also some scope for sorting out the implications of that revelation. Both of these aims are satisfied if the Christian Bible with the normal tradition of how to interpret it are the vehicle of revelation.

Swinburne, Richard. Revelation in Our Knowledge of God, Clark, Kelly James (ed). Dordrecht, Kluwer, 1992.

If there is a God who wants us to become saints worthy of the beatific vision, he will provide us with information how to do so — that is, with a propositional revelation. The revelation will not be too evident — in order that we may choose whether or not to search it out and tell others about it — and its interpretation for new centuries and cultures will require a church. The tests of a genuine revelation are its consonance with our knowledge of God obtained by other routes, and some sort of miraculous foundation.

Swindle, Stuart. Existence and Comedy: An Interpretation of the Concluding Unscientific Postscript. *Kinesis*, 18(2), 1-26, Wint 92.

The *Concluding Unscientific Postscript* is, among other things a text that has a great deal to say about *existence* and about *comedy*. Though both of these elements have received much attention independently, the relationship between the two has rarely

been treated. In this paper I attempt such a treatment. After discussing the nature of existence and the nature of comedy, I explore their interrelationship and its implications. I argue that, for Kierkegaard, comedy is grounded in the metaphysical nature of existence, and-if properly understood-it can serve as a tool for accomplishing the task that existence presents to us.

Swindle, Stuart. Why Feminists Thought Take the *Phenomenology of Spirit* Seriously. *Owl Minerva*, 24(1), 41-54, Fall 92.

Swindler, James K. *Weaving: An Analysis of the Constitution of Objects*. Savage, Rowman & Littlefield, 1991.

A moderate realist account of concepts fundamental to analytic ontology. An Introduction situates philosophy and affirms the possibility of objective truth. Part I analyzes existence, object/property, universal/individual, necessity/possibility. Part II and III apply these analyses to the existential paradoxes of negative reference and to the modal and intentional paradoxes of substitutivity of co-referential terms and the theory is contrasted with competing attempts to resolve such anomalies. Historical perspective is maintained throughout; philosophers considered include Plato, Aristotle, Duns Scotus, Kant, Leibniz, Hume, Frege, Russell, Meinong, Quine, Strawson, Ricoeur, Kripke, Butchvarov, Searle, Davidson, Dummett, Geach, Putnam, Plantinga and Terence Parsons.

Swindler, Leonard. A "Just", A Human Society: A Christian- Marxist- Confucian Dialogue. *J Chin Phil*, 19(4), 387-406, D 92.

Swirdowicz, Kazimierz. Regular Modal Logics. *Bull Sec Log*, 21(2), 47-54, Je 92.

Sylvan, Richard. Blending Semantics for *If* As a One-Place Nonassertive with Semantics for the Conditional. *Bull Sec Log*, 21(2), 67-71, Je 92.

Sylvan, Richard. On Interpreting Truth Tables and Relevant Truth Table Logic. *Notre Dame J Form Log*, 33(2), 207-215, Spr 92.

Contrary to common mythology, the two-valued truth tables do not yield classical logic. Many contestable assumptions are required to reach classical logic. Indeed some assumptions are required to get anywhere logically. In between, and in other directions, lie several other logics. For, even logically, there are many ways in which the truth tables can themselves be interpreted. (edited)

Sylvan, Richard and Nola, Roberta. Confirmation without Paradoxes in Advances in Scientific Philosophy, Schurz, Gerhard (ed). Amsterdam, Rodopi, 1991.

Synan, Edward A. Advice from a Thomist. *Amer Cath Phil Quart*, 65, 21-27, 1991.

The "advice" of this Aquinas Medalist's address is that of the only incontrovertible "thomist", Aquinas himself, on whether to teach philosophy in that theologian's name be legitimate. Is philosophy to theology as water diluting wine? Is philosophy transmuted into theology by serving her? For him, neither. Human disciplines, philosophy included, in his vocabulary are "vassals" of theology and a modern historian can be cited to the effect that to be a vassal in the day of Aquinas was not unworthy of even a king. If we take his advice on the issue, we philosophy professors are philosopher-kings.

Sypel, Roland and Brown, Harvey R. When is a Physical Theory Relativistic?. *Proc Phil Sci Ass*, 1, 507-514, 1992.

Considerable work within the modern 'space-time theory' approach to relativity physics has been devoted to clarifying the role and meaning of the principle of relativity. Two recent discussions of the principle within this approach, due to Arntzenius (1990) and Friedman (1983), are found to contain difficulties.

Sypnowich, C A. Justice, Community, and the Antinomies of Feminist Theory. *Polit Theory*, 21(3), 484-506, Ag 93.

Current debates within feminism show some parallel with contemporary debates in political theory. In particular, the debate between liberals and communitarians has a feminist analogue insofar as the emphasis on freedom and contract can be found in the case for a right to abortion, while the appeal to bonds of community is evident in ideas about a female perspective of care or unity with nature. In both its "malestream" and feminist variants, however, both sides of the debate have problems. Acknowledging the difficulties in simply uniting feminist and Marxist approaches, it remains that Marxist ideas of individuality and community suggest a resolution which avoids the weaknesses of all positions.

Sypnowich, C A. Some Disquiet about "Difference". *Praxis Int*, 13(2), 99-112, Jl 93.

It may be that we are witnessing the most important shift in politics since the emergence of Marxism in the nineteenth century. The claims of various identities have called into question the modern idea of citizenship as membership in a universal entity which subsumes the particular. This shift is present in philosophical debate as an appeal to the idea of "difference" to challenge the Enlightenment and its legacy. While difference is attractive as a useful antidote to the false universalism of many theories of emancipation, its larger significance is obscure. Indeed, there are grounds for disquiet about its role in the aspiration for equality and justice.

Szabados, Bela (ed) and Copp, David (ed) and Beehler, Rodger G (ed). *On the Track of Reason*. Boulder, Westview Pr, 1992.

This book is a dedicatory volume of essays by friends and colleagues of Kai Nielsen. The subjects addressed range from the foundations of ethics (E J Bond, T Hurka, R Miller, J Rachels), religious belief and morals (T Penelhum), the justice of Oregon's health care rationing policies (N Daniels), Marx on needs (D Braybrooke), history (J Cohen), and metaphilosophical issues (M Hanen and C B Martin). In the case of the Hurka and Miller contributions, their essays iterate succinctly the positions argued in their recent books.

Szabados, Béla. Autobiography after Wittgenstein. *J Aes Art Crit*, 50(1), 1-12, Wint 92.

Szaniawski, Klemens. Philosophy of the Concrete in Kotarbinski: Logic, Semantics and Ontology, Wolénski, Jan (ed). Dordrecht, Kluwer, 1990.

Szlezák, T A. L'interpretazione di Plotino della teoria platonica dell'anima. *Riv Filosof Neo-Scolas*, 84(2-3), 325-339, Ap-S 92.

Szporluk, Roman. Poland and the Rise of the Theory and Practice of Modern Rationality, 1770-1870. *Dialec Hum*, 17(2), 43-64, 1990.

T'ui-chieh, Hang Thaddeus. Hsin-Techniques and Hsin-Leadership in Chinese Foundations for Moral Education and Character Development, Van Doan, Tran (ed). Washington, CRVP, 1991.

Tacelli, Ronald. 7+5=12: Analytic or Synthetic?. *Lyceum*, 1(2), 57-60, Fall 89.

The author argues that Kant was right in maintaining that mathematical truths are synthetic a priori. The meaning of Kant's teaching is clarified, and several objections against it are critically assessed.

Tacelli, Ronald. Does the Eternity of the World Entail an Actual Infinite? Yes!. *Lyceum*, 3(1), 15-22, Spr 91.

Using numerous thought-experiments, the author shows that the hypothesis of a beginningless universe involves the affirmation that there has already occurred an actual infinity of successive events.

Tännsjö, Torbjörn. Conservatism: A Defence. *Inquiry*, 36(3), 329-334, S 93.

Conservatism has an essence, or so I argue. Typical of the conservative attitude is to take what is an established fact or order to be worthy of preservation, precisely because it is well established. The question what fact is established must be answered in a context, and people of different political bent answer it differently. This is why we have left-wing and well as right-wing conservatism, sharing a common rationale. In my *Conservatism for Our Time* I discuss various different aspects of this rationale, and my answer to certain strictures raised by Robert Grant concerns several of them. The most important concerns a conservative or traditionalist criticism of *rationalism*. This criticism has been developed by — among others — Michael Oakeshott. In my book, and in my answer to Grant, I defend and elaborate on this criticism.

Tännsjö, Torbjörn. Who are the Beneficiaries?. *Bioethics*, 6(4), 288-296, O 92.

What Derek Parfit has called the "total" view is defended. It is argued that the "repugnant" conclusion of this view is unsought for but acceptable. This means that a new way of arguing in defence of IVF (In Vitro Fertilization) opens up. The fact that our IVF projects lead to the existence of people, who would not otherwise have existed, is the strongest possible argument for these projects.

Tait, William. Some Recent Essays in the History of the Philosophy of Mathematics: A Critical Review. *Synthese*, 96(2), 293-331, Ag 93.

Takano, Mitio. Cut-Free Systems for Three-Valued Modal Logics. *Notre Dame J Form Log*, 33(3), 359-368, Sum 92.

Cut-free formal systems for some of the three-valued modal propositional logics are given. This refines Morikawa's work.

Talbott, Thomas. Craig on the Possibility of Eternal Damnation. *Relig Stud*, 28(4), 495-510, D 92.

In two papers, one a critique of two papers of mine, William Lane Craig has sought to put the Free Will Defense in the service of the traditional doctrine of hell; and in my rejoinder, I argue that Craig's defense of the traditional doctrine is unsuccessful. I consider several propositions that Craig claims are logically possible, and with respect to each of them I defend one of two claims. Either the proposition is not really possible, or it does not entail the traditional doctrine. Hence, Craig fails to demonstrate even the possibility of the traditional doctrine.

Talbott, Thomas. Punishment, Forgiveness, and Divine Justice. *Relig Stud*, 29(2), 151-168, Je 93.

According to a long theological tradition often associated with St. Augustine, God's justice and mercy are very difficult character traits. For God's justice demands something, namely retribution for sin, which his mercy does not, and his mercy permits something, namely the forgiveness of sin, which his justice does not. But in this paper, after setting forth some difficulties with Augustinian conception of divine punishment, I argue for the simplicity of God's *moral* nature. According to this alternative conception, "justice" and "mercy" are but two different names for God's one and only moral attribute, namely his love.

Talbott, Thomas. Theological Fatalism and Modal Confusion. *Int J Phil Relig*, 33(2), 65-88, Ap 93.

My purpose in this paper is to examine some recent arguments for theological fatalism, by which I mean the view that divine foreknowledge is incompatible with human freedom. I claim that, despite the protests of the theological fatalists, even their most sophisticated arguments finally acquire their apparent plausibility from a modal confusion. Because the more sophisticated arguments manage to bury the confusion very deeply, however, I also suggest a procedure for uncovering the confusion and making it clear.

Taliaferro, Charles. Divine Agriculture. *Agr Human Values*, 9(3), 71-88, Sum 92.

An outline of the contributions of Philosophical theology to environmental ethics with special attention to agricultural concerns.

Taliaferro, Charles. God's Estate. *J Relig Ethics*, 20(1), 69-92, Spr 92.

This article defends John Locke's notion that the cosmos is owned by God and explores the ethical implications of such divine ownership. Locke's theory, recently revived by Baruch Brody, is modified and defended against criticisms leveled against it by Joseph Lombardi and Robert Young.

Taliaferro, Charles. Imaginary Evil: A Sceptic's Wager. *Philosophia (Israel)*, 21(3-4), 221-233, Ap 92.

A wager argument is deployed in the spirit of Pascal and William James to the effect that we should not believe we are brains in vats, or otherwise systematically mistaken in our beliefs about other people and the external world.

Taliaferro, Charles. The Intensity of Theism. *Sophia (Australia)*, 31(3), 61-73, 1992.

If theism is true, then values and disvalues are heightened. Good states of affairs are even more good and evil states of affairs more evil, given the truth of theism.

Tallon, Andrew F. The Concept of the Heart in Strasser's *Phenomenology of Feeling*. *Amer Cath Phil Quart*, 66(3), 341-360, 1992.

Gemüt, Greek *thumos*, heart, is affective consciousness, characterized by its own intentionality, distinct but not separate from the cognitional and volitional intentionalities of mind or "head." After presenting a historical and bibliographical context for a philosophy of affectivity, the article centers on Strasser's phenomenology (Chapter 1) and metaphysics (Chapters 7 and 10) of heart. The article's main thesis is that the heart as affective consciousness is a mix of vital energy (*bios*) and its desire (*epithumia*), surging up from below, and the *logos* and its *eros*, from above, these two vertical motions expressed in a horizontal, developmental, and operational synthesis as affective intentionality toward the other.

Tamás, G M. Restoration Romanticism. *Pub Affairs Quart*, 7(4), 379-401, O 93.

The essay shows how a new elusive ideology is born on the ruins of the former communist states of Eastern Europe which is returning—through many twists and detours—to a radical political egalitarianism based on the concept of "merit". The new East European ideologists believe, as it turns out, wrongly, that they are harking back to a pre-communist past, but their peculiar version of distributive justice shows them to be closer to their immediate predecessors than they would wish.

Taminiaux, Jacques M. Speculation and Judgment. *J Speculative Phil*, 6(3), 171-189, 1992.

Taminiaux, Jacques M. The Origin of 'The Origin of the Work of Art' in Reading Heidegger: Commemorations, Sallis, John (ed). Bloomington, Indiana Univ Pr, 1992.

Taminiaux, Jacques M. The Thinker and the Painter in Merleau-Ponty Vivant, Dillon, M C (ed). Albany, SUNY Pr, 1991.

Tamir, Yael. The Right to National Self-Determination as an Individual Right. *Hist Euro Ideas*, 16(4-6), 899-905, Ja 93.

This paper presents two versions of the right to self-determination; a national and a liberal-democratic one. According to the former version this right is meant to allow members of each national community to preserve its cultural uniqueness. According to the latter, it is meant to allow individuals to participate in governing their lives. Both rights, it is argued, are individual rights since they derive their justification from the interest of individuals. It is true that individuals have these interests in virtue of being members of a community and that they can realize these rights only together with others. This, however, is true for other rights, including political and religious rights, all of which are seen as individual rights. Granting both aspects of the right to individual freedom and promotes pluralism within groups as well as among them.

Tamir, Yael. Whose History? What Ideas? in Isaiah Berlin: A Celebration, Margalit, Edna (ed). Chicago, Univ of Chicago Pr, 1991.

This paper suggests that the struggle of ethnic groups and women for recognition and status can be convincingly justified by reference to Berlin's views on the nature of moral and political philosophy. The paper distinguishes between a segregative and integrative struggle for status and argues that the success of the latter depends on the ability of a society to follow Berlin's conception of pluralism, namely to accommodate conflicting cultures, views, values, and life plans. In such a pluralistic society, public life are seen as a continuous struggle for the realization of personal freedom rather than as an idle search for one, eternal, universal truth.

Tan, Yao-Hua and Janssen, Maarten C W. Friedman's Permanent Income Hypothesis as an Example of Diagnostic Reasoning. *Econ Phil*, 8(1), 23-49, Ap 92.

In this paper we analyze the structure of a non-deductive type of explanation called diagnostic reasoning. Diagnostic reasoning is a recent development in artificial intelligence based on default logic. Scientific laws are regarded as default rules of the logic. The relevancy of the approach is illustrated by examining the permanent income hypothesis of the economist Milton Friedman.

Tancred, Hugh-Lawson (trans) and Aristotle. *The Art of Rhetoric—Aristotle*. New York, Penguin USA, 1991.

Tandy, Charles. Conflicting Values in American Higher Education: Development of the Concept of Academic Freedom. *Proc S Atlantic Phil Educ Soc*, 34, 1886-1918, 1989.

Court decisions in 1894-1914 America held that professors were mere employees—without a right to what today is called academic freedom. The American Association of University Professors (AAUP) was formed not primarily for academic freedom, but to promote professorial unity. Formulation and advocacy of professional standards, especially tenure, were seen as the key. With WWI can an influx of academic freedom cases due to lack of patriotism. Yet in wartime the AAUP imposed restrictions on its scholarly supporters beyond those required by the state and assumed that the university should be responsible for its professors' outside utterances.

Tandy, Charles. Introduction to the Methodology of Paraphronesis, With Example: Religion and Education in Postmodern America. *Proc S Atlantic Phil Educ Soc*, 35, 90-93, 1990.

Paraphronesis is dialectical: Paradigm (theory) informs phronesis (practice), and phronesis informs paradigm. David McKenzie says the American judiciary has broadened its meaning of "religion" to the point of making it nonfunctional. A proper functional definition would exclude both atheism and secular humanism as religions: and a public school system should be religiously neutral. An alternative paradigm defines religion more broadly than McKenzie, yet is functional. This paradigm does not claim religious neutrality, but rather separation of church (religion) and state (public education); it is concluded that this paradigm or language game is a form of life preferable to McKenzie's.

Tandy, Charles. Inventing Postmodern Education: Lifelong Learning or Childhood Schooling? A Proposal for Local Action. *Proc S Atlantic Phil Educ Soc*, 36, 115-122, 1991.

As we face the twenty-first century, America's monopolistic system of public education remains focused on the short-term schooling of children for citizenship in a modern nineteenth century nation-state. Malcolm Knowles has invented a new system of public education fit for adults, oriented toward each unique person and life-plan. Enhancement of the voluntaristic, decentralized, community-wide system would acquaint the interdisciplinary learner with history, art, literature, and philosophy of ideas in human culture from its inception, affording opportunity to become an intelligent and sensitive member of the postmodern world community without a college degree. A workless, highly creative society may result.

AUTHOR INDEX WITH ABSTRACTS 695 Taylor, Mark C

Tangwa, Godfrey B. Criticism and Survival: An Interpretation of Popper's Theory of Evolution. *Quest*, 5(2), 32-47, D 91.

Tani, T. Heimat und das Fremde. *Husserl Stud*, 9(3), 199-216, 1992.

Tanner, Kathryn. Respect for Other Religions: A Christian Antidote to Colonialist Discourse. *Mod Theol*, 9(1), 1-18, Ja 93.

Tanner, Michael. Metaphysics and Music. *Philosophy*, 33(Supp), 181-200, 1992.

Tanner, Michael. Metaphysics and Music in The Impulse to Philosophise, Griffiths, A Phillips (ed). New York, Cambridge Univ Pr, 1992.

Tappenden, Jamie. The Liar and Sorites Paradoxes: Toward a Unified Treatment. *J Phil*, 90(11), 551-577, N 93.

Tarasti, Eero. A Narrative Grammar of Chopin's G Minor Ballade. *Mind Mach*, 2(4), 401-426, N 92.

A new semiotic model for the generation of musical texts is introduced in this article. The idea of a generative "grammar" is here understood in the sense of "the generative trajectory," a model elaborated by A J Greimas. Four levels are chosen from his trajectory for the study of musical texts; namely, those of isotopies, spatial, temporal and actorial categories, modalities and semes or figures. (edited)

Tardiff, Andrew. The Thought-Experiment: Shewmon on Brain Death. *Thomist*, 56(3), 435-450, Jl 92.

According to Alan Shewmon, once the tertiary cortex of the brain has been destroyed the person is dead even if his body still lives. I argue that Shewmon has not adequately supported his claim that the tertiary cortex is the only matter necessary and sufficient to render the body compatible with the human spirit, and that Shewmon can only support such a claim empirically. In the absence of such empirical evidence we are obliged to take the safer course with such patients, which is to treat them as persons.

Tarrant, Harold. *Thrasyllan Platonism*. Ithaca, Cornell Univ Pr, 1993.

Tarski, A and Paula Assis, J (trans). Verdade e Demonstraçao. *Cad Hist Filosof Cie*, 1(1), 91-122, Ja-Je 91.

Taschek, William. Frege's Puzzle, Sense, and Information Content. *Mind*, 101(404), 767-791, O 92.

Tassi, Aldo. Person as the Mask of Being. *Phil Today*, 37(2), 201-210, Sum 93.

Taub, Liba. *Ptolemy's Universe: The Natural Philosophical and Ethical Foundations of Ptolemy's Astronomy*. Peru, Open Court, 1993.

Taubenschlag, C A. La noción de *'spiritus'* y de 'spiritualis substantia' en la cuestión disputada *De spiritualibus creaturis* de Santo Tomás de Aquino. *Aquinas*, 35(1), 89-136, Ja-Ap 92.

Tauber, Alfred I. The Organismal Self in Its Philosophical Context in Selves, People, and Persons, Rouner, Leroy S (ed). Notre Dame, Univ Notre Dame Pr, 1992.

The construct of the Self during the fin-de-siècle was dominated by a sense of self-actualization and freedom. The origins of immunology, the science of self/non-self discrimination, are rooted in this ethos as formulated by Elie Metchnikoff. Nietzsche's biologicism, which pervades his will to power, is metaphysically constructed upon the same foundation and echoes Metchnikoff's formulation of selfhood. The radical empiricism of William James is similarly regarded, so in comparing the philosophical orientation of these three apparently disparate philosophies, a shared Zeitgeist is exposed.

Tavor Bannet, Eve. Marx, God, and Praxis in Shadow of Spirit, Berry, Philippa (ed). New York, Routledge, 1992.

Tay, Alice Erh-Soon. One World? One Law? One Culture. *Dialec Hum*, 17(3), 23-32, 1990.

The paper seeks to bring out the conditions, social, political, economic and cultural, in the 20th century which are leading diverse societies to turn to law and the ideals of the rule of law as an expression of moral values and principles and as a means of raising social and human consciousness and dignity. In this process, the quality of law as a great moral and cultural achievement of humankind and its appreciation emerge. The ideal of law which is sought in clearly that of the Western liberal ideal, despite the limitations and even its undesirable shortcomings.

Taylor, Barry. On Natural Properties in Metaphysics. *Mind*, 102(405), 81-100, Ja 93.

Traditional metaphysics canonizes as 'natural' the properties subtended by predicates which allegedly mark mind-independent cleavages in the nature of things. This paper examines a modern implementation of the doctrine in David Lewis's metaphysics of modal realism. After rejecting a subsidiary Moorean argument, it considers Lewis's principal ground for natural properties, that no comprehensive systematic philosophy can make do without them; and argues to the contrary that a vegetarian, theory-relative alternative yields entirely respectable answers to the problems Lewis instances, if not always the answers he favours.

Taylor, C C W. Minds Ancient and Modern. *Polis*, 11(1), 62-71, 1992.

The article reviews a collection of papers by contemporary (mostly British) philosophers on ancient and modern discussions of questions about the mind and the person, and discusses similarities and differences, revealed by these papers, between ancient and modern approaches to these topics. A central modern question (discussed by four contributors) is that the relation between the concepts of person and of human being; this question has at best some analogues in ancient thought, since the modern (i.e., Lockean) conception of the person as a self-conscious rational agent does not correspond exactly to any ancient concept.

Taylor, Carole Anne. Positioning Subjects and Objects: Agency, Narration, Relationality. *Hypatia*, 8(1), 55-80, Wint 93.

When assumed by positions of dominance, the impersonal, analytical perspectives of scholar-narrators may serve to flatten, simplify, or render invisible the differences of constructed Others. Strategies of resistance necessarily correspond to where narrator-subjects enter relations of power. Without the presence of Others' narrations, dominance can neither value newly visible subjective agency nor confront the complicity in its own subjectivity. Intersubjectivity suggests a dialogical process that utilizes differences in lived experience to reconceive relationality.

Taylor, Charles. Engaged Agency and Background in Heidegger in The Cambridge Companion to Heidegger, Guignon, Charles (ed). New York, Cambridge Univ Pr, 1993.

This paper argues that Heidegger is one of the pioneers in a deconstruction of the modern epistemology which descends from Descartes, in that he conceives the knowing agent as engaged with a world, and thus in possession of a grasp on this world which can't be reduced to representations, but also incorporates a background understanding.

Taylor, Charles. Explanation and Practical Reason in The Quality of Life, Nussbaum, Martha C (ed). New York, Oxford Univ Pr, 1993.

This paper argues that skepticism about the possibility of resolving moral issues through rational argument is fed by an inappropriate model of what practical reason would have to be. This model is foundationalist, context-free, and aims at absolute conclusions; whereas practical reason is ad hominem, starts from what is agreed, and reaches comparative conclusions of the superiority of one position over another. It proceeds by supersession of inadequate positions.

Taylor, Charles. Heidegger, Language, and Ecology in Heidegger: A Critical Reader, Dreyfus, Hubert (ed). Cambridge, Blackwell, 1992.

This paper examines the possibility of developing a basis for "deep ecology" out of the work of Heidegger. My thesis is that one can, out of Heidegger's theory of language. The paper deals mainly with an interpretation of that theory, contrasting it with certain views which dominate in the English-speaking world. It then shows the relevance of that theory for ecological policy.

Taylor, Charles. Inwardness and the Culture of Modernity in Philosophical Interventions in the Unfinished Project of Enlightenment, Honneth, Axel (& other eds). Cambridge, MIT Pr, 1992.

The thesis of this paper is that there are two main types of theory of modernity; one defines modern society essentially "aculturally", in terms of the earlier "traditional" horizons it has lost or sloughed off; the second sees specific modern understandings of the self and society as the key defining factors. I lean to the second type of theory, and try to illustrate it with a discussion of modern inwardness.

Taylor, Charles. The Dialogical Self in The Interpretive Turn, Hiley, David R (ed). Ithaca, Cornell Univ Pr, 1991.

The paper deals with different conceptions of the self, and their place in social science. The Thesis is that we have inherited from the philosophical tradition a disembodied and monological picture of the human agent. This urgently needs to be corrected. The paper discusses Bourdieu's theory of embodied knowledge (the "habitus"), and then suggests that Bakhtin is better guide than Mead for a dialogical theory.

Taylor, Charles. The Importance of Herder in Isaiah Berlin: A Celebration, Margalit, Edna (ed). Chicago, Univ of Chicago Pr, 1991.

My argument in this piece is that Herder represents a turning point in theory of language in the Western tradition. He turns away from instrumental-designative theories of meaning, and innovates with a theory which I want to call expressive-constitutive. Certain contemporaries theories, not only of language, but also of literature and culture, make sense within the framework set by this Herdian turn. This has, of course, also been contested, so that two rather different philosophical cultures exist today which are divided by their different conceptions of language.

Taylor, Charles and Carr, David and Ricoeur, Paul. Ricoeur on Narrative in On Paul Ricoeur: Narrative and Interpretation, Wood, David (ed). New York, Routledge, 1991.

Taylor, James E. Conceptual Analysis and the Essence of Knowledge. *Amer Phil Quart*, 30(1), 15-26, Ja 93.

The thesis of this paper is that conceptual analysis is not sufficient as a method for grasping the essence of knowledge. Potential supplementary methods include scientific investigation and global metaphysical theorizing. A tentative assessment of the former warrants encouragement for epistemologists interested in naturalizing epistemology. A preliminary evaluation of the latter suggests scepticism about knowing the complete essence of knowledge as the reasonable response of those who do not believe that knowing is a naturalistic property.

Taylor, James E. Scepticism and the Nature of Knowledge. *Philosophia (Israel)*, 22(1-2), 3-27, Ja 93.

If some condition, necessary for knowledge, is never satisfied by humans, then no human ever knows anything. Some epistemologists have endorsed this sceptical consequence on the basis of some such alleged necessary but unsatisfied condition. This is reasonable only if it is more reasonable that there is a requirement for knowledge never satisfied by humans than that some human sometimes knows something. I argue that, on the contrary, it is always more reasonable to believe the latter than it is to believe the former. Given this, there are empirical constraints on accounts of knowledge of interest to the naturalized epistemologist.

Taylor, Kenneth. On the Pragmatics of Mode of Reference Selection. *Commun Cog*, 26(1), 97-126, 1993.

Communicative interchange often involves the exchange of information on the basis of which the consumer of that information plans and executes her actions. Communication thus plays an action enabling role. But communication can play such a role only where there is a smooth flow of "essentially indexical" information of the sort that John Perry has shown to play a distinctive role in action planning gene rally. This essay outlines some communicative devices and conventions which enable a smooth flow of such information in cooperative communicative interchange. It is argued that the pragmatics of mode of reference selection is highly sensitive to facts about how the selection of a given mode of reference in a given discourse context would promote or fail to promote a smooth flow of essentially indexical information. In particular, it is shown that a choice between a name and a demonstrative, when both refer to the right object, is highly sensitive to facts about the flow of essentially indexical information.

Taylor, Mark C. NO nOt nO in Derrida and Negative Theology, Coward, Harold (ed). Albany, SUNY Pr, 1992.

Taylor, Mark C. Reframing Postmodernisms in Shadow of Spirit, Berry, Philippa (ed). New York, Routledge, 1992.

Taylor, Mark Lloyd. Ordeal and Repetition in Kierkegaard's Treatment of Abraham and Job in Foundations of Kierkegaard's Vision of Community, Connell, George B (ed). Atlantic Highlands, Humanities Pr, 1992.

Taylor, Richard. *Metaphysics (Fourth Edition)*. Englewood Cliffs, Prentice Hall, 1991.

Taylor, Roger. The Environmental Implications of Liberalism. *Crit Rev*, 6(2-3), 265-282, Spr-Sum 92.

Political theories of distributive justice must consider ecological limits and constraints, even if anthropocentrically motivated. Examination of four contemporary anthropocentric views of distributive justice—those of Rawls, Arneson, Sen, and the libertarians—reveals that the extent of environmental protection and conservation they implicitly require is quite extensive, far more so than the proponents of each view understand. The needs of environment in turn necessitate social structures which were unanticipated; the social order is thus reconfigured in ways which may not accord with the other fundamental principles of each view.

Tealdi, Juan Carlos. Teaching Bioethics as a New Paradigm for Health Professionals. *Bioethics*, 7(2-3), 188-199, Ap 93.

Tecusan, Manuela. Speaking about the Unspeakable: Plato's Use of Imagery. *Apeiron*, 25(4), 69-87, D 92.

Teichert, Dieter. Zwischen Wissenschaftskritik und Hermeneutik: Foucaults Humanwissenschaften. *Z Phil Forsch*, 47(2), 204-222, Ap-Je 93.

The aim of this paper is a reconstruction of Foucault's conception of the humanities. Section I gives an account of Foucault's most important study on the humanities, *The order of things*. On the basis of a detailed analysis of the text, Foucault's theory of the humanities is presented as a two-component model consisting of an epistemological component and a historiographical component. Section II discusses the relation between the picture of the humanities drawn by philosophical hermeneutics and Foucault's model. Section III looks at the transformation of the history of ideas in the work of the late Foucault.

Teichman, Jenny. Deconstruction and Aerodynamics. *Philosophy*, 68(263), 53-62, Ja 93.

This paper begins by noting that deconstruction is, amongst other things, a theory of meaning. Two technical terms, *logocentrism* and *differance* are explained with examples. The idea that deconstruction can be deconstructed is examined and found to be an attempt to immunize deconstruction from traditional forms of refutation such as proofs that it is false and proofs that it is self-contradictory. The deconstructive thesis that meaning undergoes constant slippage and is therefore impossible is compared to the plainly false theory in aerodynamics which alleges that bumblebees cannot fly.

Teichmann, Roger. Time and Change. *Phil Quart*, 43(171), 158-177, Ap 93.

Reductive accounts of such temporal notions as *priority* and *duration*, which refer to the possibility of (some sort of) change, face the problem of how to explain this 'possibility'—as logical, nomological or metaphysical. Each hour of this trilemma is unacceptable. An alternative approach to duration-concepts is outlined, which invokes a non-reductive but constitutive connection between duration-statements and statements about the reading of true clocks. Various questions raised by the account are discussed, including time without change, the nature of true clocks, and anti-realism.

Tejera, V. Santayana's Whitman Revisited. *Bull Santayana Soc*, 10, 1-8, Fall 92.

Tejera, Victorino. *Socrates' Second Sailing. Int Stud Phil*, 24(3), 99-104, 1992.

Tejera, Victorino. Peirce's Semeiotic, and the Aesthetics of Literature. *Trans Peirce Soc*, 29(3), 427-455, Sum 93.

Teller, Paul and Redhead, Michael. Particle Labels and the Theory of Indistinguishable Particles in Quantum Mechanics. *Brit J Phil Sci*, 43(2), 201-218, J 92.

We extend the work of French and Redhead (1988) further examining the relation of quantum statistics to the assumption that quantum entities have the sort of identity generally assumed for physical objects, more specifically an identity which makes them susceptible to being thought of as conceptually individuable and labelable even though they cannot be experimentally distinguished. We also further examine the relation of such hypothesized identity of quantum entities to the Principle of the Identity of Indiscernibles. We conclude that although such an assumption of identity is consistent with the facts of quantum statistics, methodological considerations show that we should take quantum entities to be entirely unindividuatable, in the way suggested by a Fock space description.

Tempczyk, Michael. The Geometry of Space-Time: From Einstein to Penrose. *Phil Sci (Tucson)*, 5, 51-79, 1993.

Templin, J Alton. A God of Power or a God of Value in God, Values, and Empiricism, Peden, Creighton (ed). Macon, Mercer Univ Pr, 1989.

W H Bernhardt (1893-1979) and H N Wieman (1884-1975) held parallel and complementary concepts of God, both examples of the American Naturalistic school of thought. Wieman affirmed the category of value as the basis of his concept of God; hence, God is *The Source of Human Good*. Bernhardt utilized the category of the dynamic, constructing the concept of God on scientific realism; hence, God is the "Divine Determinant," even at the expense of human value. The conclusion is that both approaches are necessary and that they are parallel. We need a recognition of the realism of scientific understanding, as well as a human reinterpretation of this understanding to assist the religious person to construct a world view in which hope, meaning, aspiration, and courage are available for human living.

Ten Have, Henk and Keasberry, Helen. Equity and Solidarity: The Context of Health Care in The Netherlands. *J Med Phil*, 17(4), 463-477, Ag 92.

The current debate on health care resource allocation in the Netherlands is characterized by a social context in which two values are generally and traditionally accepted as being equally fundamental: solidarity and equity. We will present an outline of the distinctive features of the Dutch health care system, and analyze the present state of affairs in the resource allocation debate. The presuppositions of the political call for constraint and (renewed) government supervision and the role of the specific value context in recent proposals for reconstruction of the Dutch health care system will be evaluated.

Terasse, Jean. *De Mentor à Orphée: Essais sur les écrits pédagogiques de Rousseau*. LaSalle, Ed Hurtubise, 1992.

Terdiman, Richard. On the Dialectics of Postdialectical Thinking in Community at Loose Ends, Miami Theory Collect, (ed). Minneapolis, Univ of Minnesota Pr, 1991.

Teron, Stephen. Philosophical Ethics or Secularist Ethics?. *Aquinas*, 35(3), 587-612, S-D 92.

Terpstra, Marin. Discussie met Thomas Mertens over de wijsgerige beoordeling van de Golfoorlog, en M F Fresco over van Hemsterhuis' *Waarneming en werkelijkheid*. *Alg Ned Tijdschr Wijs*, 84(4), 287-316, O 92.

This is a comment on Thomas Merten's article, in a previous issue of this journal, concerning the possibility of a philosophical judgment of the recent Gulf War. Mertens builds upon Kant's *Zum ewigen Frieden* and tries to accommodate this treatise with Francis Fukuyama's famous thesis on 'the end of history'. Our key argument is that a finalistic idea of history, as found in Kant, Hegel and Fukuyama, is a problematic basis for justifications of actual wars. The main problem is that a finalistic judgment takes its criteria from a state of affairs that still is to be fully realized, i.e., a mondial juridical system. In the actual state of war a justification that appeals to 'the end of history' cannot be anything else than an ideology, legitimizing imperialistic endeavours.

Terricabras, Josep Maria. José Ferrater Mora: An Integrationist Philosopher. *Man World*, 26(2), 209-218, Ap 93.

Teske, Roland (trans). *Henry of Ghent: Quodlibetal Questions on Free Will*. Milwaukee, Marquette Univ Pr, 1993.

Teske, Roland J. St Augustine's View of the Original Human Condition in *De Genesi contra Manichaeos*. *Augustin Stud*, 22, 141-155, 1991.

The article examines St Augustine's earliest commentary on the creation narrative to determine what Augustine considered to be the original condition of human beings. After noting the highly figurative interpretation Augustine offers as well as its Plotinian background, the article argues that Augustine wavers between two views of the original human condition. In one view, they were disembodied souls who later fell into bodies; in the other, they were already embodied, but in spiritual bodies far different from our own.

Teske, Roland J. William of Auvergne on *De re* and *De dicto* Necessity. *Mod Sch*, 69(2), 111-121, Ja 92.

William of Auvergne rejects the distinction of *de re* and *de dicto* interpretations of modal statements. The article examines William's understanding of this distinction, his reasons for rejecting it, and his alternative interpretation of modal statements. The article concludes that William rejected the *de dicto* interpretation of such statement in order to avoid a Platonic world of eternal propositions.

Tessitore, Fulvio. Ricordo di Pietro Piovani. *G Crit Filosof Ital*, 71(1), 1-4, Ja-Ap 92.

Thacker, Andrew. Foucault's Aesthetics of Existence. *Rad Phil*, 63, 13-21, Spr 93.

Thagard, Paul. Societies of Minds: Science as Distributed Computing. *Stud Hist Phil Sci*, 24(1), 49-67, Mr 93.

Science is studied in very different ways by historians, philosophers, psychologists, and sociologists. This paper is an attempt to view history, philosophy, psychology, and sociology of science from a unified perspective. I outline a new model that views scientific communities from the perspective of distributed artificial intelligence, a relatively new branch of the field of artificial intelligence that concerns how problems can be solved by networks of intelligent computers that communicate with each other.

Thau, Michael Alan. Property in *The Realm of Rights*. *Phil Phenomenol Res*, 53(2), 397-404, Je 93.

Thayer, H S. Necessity and Truth in Dewey's Logical Theory in Frontiers in American Philosophy, Volume I, Burch, Robert W (ed). College Station, Texas A&M Univ Pr, 1992.

Thayer-Bacon, Barbara. Critical Thinking Theory and Democracy. *Phil Stud Educ*, 1, 103-114, 1990.

Thayer-Bacon, Barbara J. Caring and Its Relationship to Critical Thinking. *Educ Theor*, 43(3), 323-340, Sum 93.

In this article I look at caring and its role in critical thinking and offer a model for thinking which I call "constructive thinking" in an effort to distinguish it from critical thinking as it traditionally has been viewed. My claim is that critical thinking theories, past or present, have not attended to the role of caring in understanding people's ideas. Caring is necessary to be sure ideas have been fairly considered and understood. I recommend we need to encourage students' capacity to be caring as well as reasonable.

Theobald, P. The Advent of Liberalism and the Subordination of Agrarian Thought in the United States. *J Agr Environ Ethics*, 5(2), 161-181, 1992.

This essay contends that the ascendancy of Western liberalism after the Enlightenment worked catalytically on the development of both the Industrial Revolution and a "modern agrarianism" based on the widespread dispersal of small-scale property ownership. Due to power dynamics, however, as well as the liberal faith in inevitable progress, agrarian thought has remained a marginal concern in Western politics, economics, and education. Although the agrarian philosophical tradition in the United States was created by the same liberal rhetoric and argumentation that gave birth to industrialism, the two world views hinged on vastly different interpretations of the same concepts. One aim of this essay is to sort out these differences and examine their implications for a contemporary reconsideration of agrarian thought.

Thero, Daniel. Whitehead's God and the Problem of Evil. *Dialogue (PST)*, 35(2-3), 33-40, Ap 93.

This article examines the process philosophy of A N Whitehead, as it relates to the questions of the nature of God and the Problem of Evil. *Science and the Modern World* presents God as a metaphysical principle, indifferent as a ground for religious belief. In his later works, however, Whitehead presents a fuller vision of God, as a Being who may be an appropriate object of religious belief and who provides a ground for Whitehead's unique answer to the theodicy problem.

Theunissen, Michael. Metaphysics' Forgetfulness of Time in Philosophical Interventions in the Unfinished Project of Enlightenment, Honneth, Axel (& other eds). Cambridge, MIT Pr, 1992.

Main subject is Parmenides, fragment 8.5-6: "It was not once nor will it be, since it is now altogether, one, continuous." Most of the researchers presume that in this verse eternity is raised for the first time in the sense of timelessness. In opposition to that this essay argues in favor of the opinion of the minority thinking that the verse only expresses that the being is always in time. Also the opinion is rejected that Parmenides anticipates the neoplatonic thought of eternity which joins all time in the moment.

Thibaud, Pierre. La thèse peircienne de l'identité de la pensée et du signe. *Arch Phil*, 55(3), 437-460, Jl-S 92.

Resisting any sort of hierarchy between thought and expression, which usually leads to supremacy of thought, sometimes of expression, as will be shown, Peirce proposes a theory that strongly asserts absolute identity of thought and signs and seems to be the very clue towards the determination of the meaning of his own view of pragmatism.

Thiebaut, Carlos. *Los Limites de la Comunidad*. Madrid, CSIC, 1992.

The Limits of Community opens with an overall philosophical presentation of the liberal-communitarian debate. Two chapters are dedicated specifically to C Taylor and A MacIntyre and a third to the different political positions in the arena (Walzer, Sandel, Dworkin) and to the political ambiguities of the communitarian positions. Certain communitarian critiques of the philosophical presuppositions of liberalism are acknowledged but its superiority is finally recognized regarding the conception of a reflexive moral and political subject constituted in multinormative spheres of interaction in complex societies. Finally, the recent work of J Rawls and J Habermas is considered from this perspective.

Thiebaut, Carlos. On the Improvement of Our Moral Portrait: Moral Realism, History of Subjectivity, and Expressivist Language. *Praxis Int*, 13(2), 126-153, Jl 93.

Thiel, Christian. Geo Siegwarts Szenario: Eine katastrophentheoretische Untersuchung: Zugleich ein Versuch, enträuschte Kenner wieder aufzurichten. *Z Phil Forsch*, 47(2), 261-270, Ap-Je 93.

Siegwart claims to have shown that constructivistic attempts at a "theory of abstraction" (from Weyl to Lorenzen) are formally inconsistent, and that the present author's formalization of the principle of abstraction is to be blamed for this failure. This challenge is answered by exhibiting in Siegwart's derivations several confusions of logical types, either by attributing to objects of type n properties defined for objects of type $n + 1$ only, or by admitting relations between objects of different types within one level of language. It is granted that expositions of the constructivist theory of abstraction have lacked explicit rules for the exclusion of such type confusions, and that future expositions of the theory need to be complemented by rules of this kind.

Thiel, Udo. Cudworth and Seventeenth-Century Theories of Consciousness in The Uses of Antiquity, Gaukroger, Stephen (ed). Dordrecht, Kluwer, 1991.

The first part of the paper offers an analysis of 17th century discussions of consciousness prior to Cudworth (1617-1688) and the Cambridge Platonists; the second part analyses and evaluates Cudworth's notion of consciousness in the light of these debates. Like some of his predecessors, Cudworth regards consciousness as a form of relating to oneself. Although Cudworth does not have a worked out theory of consciousness, there are important conceptual distinctions in Cudworth between various ways of relating to oneself (e.g., between consciousness as the fundamental type of self-relation and reflection). No one before Cudworth seems to have drawn these distinctions as explicitly and clearly as they are present in his writings.

Thigpen, Robert B and Downing, Lyle. The Place of Neutrality in Liberal Political Theory in Terrorism, Justice and Social Values, Peden, Creighton W (ed). Lewiston, Mellen Pr, 1990.

Thom, Paul. Critical Notice of F J Pelletier's *Parmenides, Plato, and the Semantics of Not-Being*. *Can J Phil*, 22(4), 573-586, D 92.

Parmenides was an Object-Monist (not a Fact-Monist), relying on an Argument by Ellipsis from '*a* is not *b*' to '*a* is not'; Plato's *Sophist* so interprets him. Both Parmenides and Plato aimed to forge a Philosopher's Language which does not recognize negative realities. They differed in that Parmenides accepted the Principle of Non-Contradiction while Plato rejected it as conflicting with the requirements of the Argument by Ellipsis; further, Plato's (but not Parmenides') Language of Enquiry allowed for *relative* statements of non-being.

Thom, René. Relativité du vrai, relativisme de l'intelligible. *Epistemologia*, 15(1), 3-20, Ja-Je 92.

Thomä, Dieter. Die gute Verfassung des menschlichen Lebens. *Phil Rundsch*, 39(4), 309-318, 1992.

Thomas, Emyr Vaughan. D Z Phillips, Self-Renunciation and the Finality of Death. *Relig Stud*, 28(4), 487-493, D 92.

Thomas, Geoffrey. *An Introduction to Ethics*. Indianapolis, Hackett, 1993.

This text provides a structured introduction to ethics. It addresses five question: 1) What makes a judgement a moral judgement? 2) What standards — of Kantian universalizability, utilitarian welfare maximization, etc. — are on offer for guiding moral judgements? 3) What is the justification for these standards? 4) What models of moral reasoning are available in making moral judgements? 5) What are the conditions of responsibility for applying moral judgements to actions and states of character? The book's approach is analytical rather than historical, but reference is made to classic theorists from Aristotle, Hume, Kant, and J S Mill down to Nagel, Hare and Foot.

Thomas, Janice. Giving the Devil His Due. *Analysis*, 53(2), 119-125, Ap 93.

What if I contracted with the devil, forgetting to include a clause forbidding him from engineering my death and one morning I woke to be told the devil had replaced me with a perfect living replica (as in Parfit's scanner-replicator copies)?, i.e., I was a replica and thus must now do the devil's bidding. Would a perfect living copy, slotted into my environmental niche, be me? Maybe the person I am is a type not a token and for me to continue to exist is for three to be *any* token. This piece is a dialogue exploring these questions.

Thomas, Jennifer. The Question of Derrida's Women. *Human Stud*, 16(1-2), 163-176, Ap 93.

Thomas, John Heywood. Indirect Communication: Hegelian Aesthetic and Kierkegaard's Literary Art in Kierkegaard on Art and Communication, Pattison, George (ed). New York, St Martin's Pr, 1992.

This paper analyzes the Hegelianism of Kierkegaard's aesthetics as illustrated by his theory of Indirect Communication. His purpose in this was both literary and philosophical. Three aspects of his aesthetics show his debt to Hegel — the necessity of a self-understanding in aesthetics, the necessary modesty about its limits and the escape from Romantic excess. Indirect communication is an illustration of both the influence of Hegel on Kierkegaard and of his theory and practice of a non-Hegelian communication. It was for him part of the epistemology of religious belief.

Thomas, Laurence. Moral Flourishing in an Unjust World. *J Moral Educ*, 22(2), 83-96, 1993.

While moral ideals are of the utmost importance, the truth of the matter is that we live in a world that falls considerably short of the ideal. Drawing upon a variety of theoretical considerations from both psychology and philosophy, I am to make explicit some of the concrete steps that can be taken to overcome patterns of injustice. To this end, the ideas of textured affirmation and moral deference are developed.

Thomas, Laurence. Statistical Badness. *J Soc Phil*, 23(1), 30-41, Spr 92.

Thomas, Laurence. The Morally Beautiful in African-American Perspectives on Biomedical Ethics, Flack, Harley E (ed). Washington, Georgetown Univ Pr, 1992.

Thomas, Laurence. The Reality of the Moral Self. *Monist*, 76(1), 3-21, Ja 93.

Thomas, Simon and Shelah, Saharon and Baumgartner, James E. Maximal Subgroups of Infinite Symmetric Groups. *Notre Dame J Form Log*, 34(1), 1-11, Wint 93.

We prove that it is consistant that there exists a subgroup of the symmetric group Sym(λ) which is not included in a maximal proper subgroup of Sym(λ). We also consider the question of which subgroups of Sym(λ) stabilize a nontrivial ideal on λ.

Thomas, V C. The Development of Time Consciousness from Husserl to Heidegger in Analecta Husserliana, XXXI, Tymieniecka, Anna-Teresa (ed). Dordrecht, Kluwer, 1990.

This essay studies Heidegger's application of Husserl's phenomenological elucidation of time consciousness to different notions basic to *Being and Time* such as Dasein, Being-in-the-world, modes of disclosure, care and the like. It also points out that Heidegger develops very much the phenomenological treatment of time while examining notions like transcendence, horizon, death, world time, temporality of time and so on.

Thomason, Neil. Could Lakatos, Even With Zahar's Criterion for Novel Fact, Evaluate the Copernican Research Programme?. *Brit J Phil Sci*, 43(2), 161-200, J 92.

In 'Why did Copernicus's research programme supersede Ptolemy's?', Lakatos and Zahar argued that, on Zahar's criterion for 'novel fact,' Copernican theory was objectively scientifically superior to Ptolemaic theory. They are mistaken. Lakatos and Zahar applied Zahar's criterion to 'a historical thought-experiment'—fictional rather than real history. Further, in their fictional history, they compared Copernicus to Eudoxus rather than Ptolemy, ignored Tycho Brahe, and did not consider facts that would be novel for geostatic theories. When Zahar's criterion is applied to real history, the results are distinctly different. Finally, most of the historical and conceptual problems in applying Zahar's criterion to the Copernican Revolution primarily arise from a deep difficulty in Lakotos's programme: the necessity of individuating research programmes and identifying their originators.

Thomason, Neil. Some Problems with Chisholm and Potter's Solution to the Paradox of Analysis. *Metaphilosophy*, 23(1-2), 132-138, Ja-Ap 92.

Thomason, S K. Semantic Analysis of the Modal Syllogistic. *J Phil Log*, 22(2), 111-128, Ap 93.

We present three semantics for Aristotle's modal syllogistic. The "terms" are construed as predicates that can be satisfied or not, accidentally or necessarily, by things in the universe; then the modal syllogisms valid according to Aristotle are shown to be those that are valid in all universes satisfying certain additional conditions. The additional conditions depend on the semantics: at one extreme they require simply that certain modal syllogisms be valid, and at the other they place more or less plausible restrictions on the predicates (e.g., "if all x are necessarily non-y then all y are necessarily non-x").

Thomason, Sarah G. Thought Experiments in Linguistics in Thought Experiments in Science and Philosophy, Horowitz, Tamara (ed). Lanham, Rowman & Littlefield, 1991.

Linguists use thought experiments of two quite different types. One of these closely resembles physicists' thought experiments and is typically used when the theory in question involves proposed universals of language structure, language learning, language change, or language use. But when linguists want to test hypotheses about the structure of a particular language, they sometimes use thought experiments in a more literal sense—real experiments carried out by introspection, either by the linguist or by a native speaker of a language the linguist is investigating. This paper describes and exemplifies both types, and argues that the notion of a thought experiment should be elastic enough to include both.

Thomke, Hellmut 698 AUTHOR INDEX WITH ABSTRACTS

Thomke, Hellmut. Appearance in Poetry: Lyric Illusion? in Aesthetic Illusion, Burwick, Frederick (ed). Hawthorne, de Gruyter, 1990.

Thompson, Audrey. Identity and Relationship in Teaching as Performance. *Phil Stud Educ*, 1, 145-162, 1991.

Thompson, Audrey. Radicalizing Pluralism. *Proc Phil Educ*, 48, 30-33, 1992.

Thompson, Bruce E R. *An Introduction to the Syllogism and the Logic of Proportional Quantifiers*. New York, Lang, 1992.

Provides an elementary introduction to contemporary syllogistic logic, incorporating the intermediate proportional quantifiers, 'few', 'many', and 'most'. Discusses the structure of categorical propositions; quantifiers in ordinary language; immediate inferences; and the Square of Opposition. Provides rules of validity for syllogistic arguments and discusses the structure of enthymemes and sorites. Concluding chapters discuss generalized proportional quantifiers. Includes examples, exercises, historical discussion, and bibliographic references. Intended as a undergraduate textbook, or as an overview for interested scholars.

Thompson, Caleb. Pictures of Socrates. *Phil Invest*, 16(4), 280-297, O 93.

Thompson, Evan. Novel Colours. *Phil Stud*, 68(3), 321-349, D 92.

Thompson, Janna. A Plea on Behalf of the Innocent. *Analysis*, 53(2), 126-128, Ap 93.

Thompson, Nicholas S and Derr, Patrick. Reconstruing Hempelian Motivational Explanations. *Behavior Phil*, 20(1), 37-46, Spr-Sum 92.

When motivational explanations are cast in the Hempelian form, motivations and other mental states usually play the role of antecedent conditions. This leads to two objections: 1) that there is a question-begging connection between the explanandum and the antecedent conditions referring to mental states, and 2) that the intentional character of motivational explanations prevents them from being scientifically useful. These objections are mooted if claims about motivational states are construed as covering laws rather than as statements of antecedent conditions.

Thompson, Nicholas S and Derr, Patrick. The Intentionality of Some Ethological Terms. *Behavior Phil*, 20/2(21/1), 15-24, 1993.

The apparent incompatibility of mental states with physical explanations has long been a concern of philosophers of psychology. This incompatibility is thought to arise from the intentionality of mental states. But, Brentano notwithstanding, intentionality is an ordinary feature of higher order behavior patterns in the classical literature of ethology.

Thompson, Paul B. Animals in the Agrarian Ideal. *J Agr Environ Ethics*, 6/1(Supp), 36-49, 1993.

Thomas Jefferson, Ralph Waldo Emerson and other American intellectuals of the 18th and 19th century created an agrarian ideal for farming that stressed the formation of moral virtue, citizenship values and personal character. This agrarian ideal provides a contrast to utilitarian norms, which value farming in terms of efficiency in producing food commodities. Thus, while efficiency criteria might be used to justify production practices that minimize management costs in animal agriculture, the agrarian ideas instead stipulates a role relationship between humans and animals as the norm for evaluating a farmer's use of animals. An anecdotal account of the agrarian ideal in modern times is presented using children's literature.

Thompson, Paul B. The Varieties of Sustainability. *Agr Human Values*, 9(3), 11-19, Sum 92.

Each of four sections in this paper sketches the philosophical problems associated with a different dimension of sustainability. The untitled intro section surveys the oft-noted discrepancies between different notions of sustainability, and notes that one element of the ambiguity relates to the different points of view taken by a participant in a system and a detached observer of the system. The second section examines epistemological puzzles that arise when one attempts to assess the truth or falsity of claims that attribute sustainability or non-sustainability. The third section examines puzzles that arise in attempting to define sustainability in normative terms. The final section offers an analysis of the moral responsibilities that human beings have, given the fact that knowledge of conditions for achieving sustainability can never be complete. (edited)

Thomson, Garrett. Kant's Problems with Ugliness. *J Aes Art Crit*, 50(2), 107-115, Spr 92.

Thomson, Garrett. The Weak, the Strong and the Mild—Readings of Kant's Ontology. *Ratio*, 5(2), 160-176, D 92.

Thomson, Judith Jarvis. Précis of *The Realm of Rights*. *Phil Phenomenol Res*, 53(1), 159-162, Mr 93.

Thomson, Judith Jarvis. Reply to Commentators. *Phil Phenomenol Res*, 53(1), 187-194, Mr 93.

Thornton, Barbara C and Callahan, Daniel and Nelson, James Lindemann. Bioethics Education: Expanding the Circle of Participants. *Hastings Center Rep*, 23(1), 25-29, Ja-F 93.

The Hastings Center Project on Bioethics Education identifies and describes the core components of a bioethics curriculum as well as key issues regarding the education of clinicians, ethics committee members and policy- makers in the many diverse settings in which learning about bioethics now takes place. The challenge of translating theory into action as well as the political and practical realities of developing bioethics programs is discussed. Evaluation of existing courses and programs in bioethics is recommended while certification of programs is considered premature.

Thornton, Stephen P. Sempiternity, Immortality and the Homunculus Fallacy. *Phil Invest*, 16(4), 307-326, O 93.

This paper deals with the question of how belief in immortality is to be construed as a characteristic *religious* belief. The logical cogency of the 'sempiternal' account of immortality, where it is conceived of as endless temporal duration, is first explored, and the conclusion is reached that this account falls foul of the 'homunculus fallacy' (Kenny), the application of human-being predicates to insufficiently human-like objects. Important correlations between aspects of the work of the later Wittgenstein and his comments on solipsism and death in the *Tractatus* are then examined, and it is argued that these provide the grounds for a proper understanding of the religious belief in immortality.

Thorp, John. The Social Construction of Homosexuality. *Phoenix*, 46(1), 54-61, Spr 92.

This article is a critical notice of David Halperin's *One Hundred Years of Homosexuality* (Routledge, 1992). Halperin argues that the example of ancient Greece is evidence for the social construction of homosexuality, in that the Greek conceptual and social arrangements regarding homosexuality were significantly different from ours in a number of ways. Relying chiefly on a close reading of the famous speech of Aristophanes in Plato's *Symposium* the author argues that, *pace* Halperin, in most fundamental respects the Greek arrangements were identical to our own. The Greek example cannot be cited as knock-down evidence in favour of social construction.

Thorp, Thomas R. Derrida and Habermas on the Subject of Political Philosophy in Crises in Continental Philosophy, Dallery, Arleen B (ed). Albany, SUNY Pr, 1990.

Thouard, Denis. Une philosophie de la grammaire d'après Kant: la *Sprachlehre* d'A F Bernhardi. *Arch Phil*, 55(3), 409-435, Jl-S 92.

Kantian criticism intended to destroy the ontological foundations of the old metaphysics as they were presupposed, either as dogmatic-rationalist or sceptical-empiricist, by the "grammaires générales" of XVIIth and XVIIIth centuries in their attempt to put up universal laws of language, however different the languages were. Such a critique induced the grammarians either to give up any attempt to set up a universal theory of language or to set it up on a Kantian foundation looking for a transcendental grammar of categories. So did A F Bernhardi (1769-1820) in his *Sprachlehre* (1801-1803), following the essay of his friend Fichte (1975) and according to the logic of a note in the *Prolegomena*. Such an endeavour manifests the crisis of a kind of theory and is the center of the main problems in the philosophy of language at that time.

Thucydides and Woodruff, Paul B (ed & trans). *Thucydides: On Justice, Power, and Human Nature*. Indianapolis, Hackett, 1993.

Thurnher, Rainer. Gott und Ereignis—Heideggers Gegenparadigma zur Onto-Theologie. *Heidegger Stud*, 8, 81-102, 1992.

Tidman, Paul. The Epistemology of Evil Possibilities. *Faith Phil*, 10(2), 181-197, Ap 93.

In this paper I defend the Anselmian conception of God as a necessary being who is necessarily omnipotent, omniscient, and perfectly good against arguments that attempt to show that we have good reason to think there are evil possible worlds in which either God does not exist or in which He lacks at least one of these attributes. I argue that the critics of Anselmianism have failed to provide any compelling reason to think such worlds are possible. The best the critic of Anselmianism can achieve is a stand-off of competing modal intuitions. I conclude by suggesting some ways of resolving such a stand-off in favor of the Anselmian view.

Tierney, Travis S. Problems with Laws, Defining Death and a New Uniform Proposal. *Dialogue (PST)*, 35(1), 19-26, O 92.

Tierno, Joel Thomas. God and the Foundation of Moral Value. *J Value Inq*, 26(3), 417-422, Jl 92.

Tieszen, Richard. Kurt Gödel and Phenomenology. *Phil Sci*, 59(2), 176-194, Je 92.

Gödel began to seriously study Husserl's phenomenology in 1959, and the Gödel *Nachlass* is known to contain many notes on Husserl. In this paper I describe what is presently known about Gödel's famous views on mathematical intuition and objectivity can be readily interpreted in a phenomenological theory of intuition and mathematical knowledge.

Tieszen, Richard L. Teaching Formal Logic as Logic Programming in Philosophy Departments. *Teach Phil*, 15(4), 337-347, D 92.

This paper advocates teaching formal logic as logic programming and indicates how this can be done. The shift in perspective involved in teaching logic this way allows instructors to emphasize many recently developed computational aspects of logic, and to focus on entirely new applications. For example, the language of logic can now be viewed as a language for representing knowledge that will be processed by a particular inference engine. It can in fact be viewed as a programming language. Ideas involved in automating deduction can be presented, students can now use logic to design expert systems, and so on.

Tietz, John. Heidegger on Realism and the Correspondence Theory of Truth. *Dialogue (Canada)*, 32(1), 59-76, Wint 93.

A discussion of #43, 44, and 69 of *Being and Time*, of Dreyfus (*Being in the World*) and Guignon (*Heidegger and the Problem of Knowledge*) on Heidegger's Theory of the derivativeness of realism and correspondence. Heidegger's anti-realism is defended.

Tigerman, Stanley. The Ten Contaminants: *Umheimlich* Trajectories of Architecture. *Res Phenomenol*, 22, 32-42, 1992.

Tijmes, Pieter. The Archimedean Point and Eccentricity: Hannah Arendt's Philosophy of Science and Technology. *Inquiry*, 35(3-4), 389-406, S-D 92.

In this contribution I discuss Hannah Arendt's philosophy of culture in three rounds. First I give an account of my view on Hannah Arendt's main work *The Human Condition*. In this frame of reference I distance myself from the importance attached to Hannah Arendt as a political philosopher and hold a warm plea for her as a philosopher of culture (I and II). Second I pay attention to her view on science and technology in their cultural meaning, expressed in the last chapter of *The Human Condition*. This part consists in a summary of her thoughts as I read them (III, IV, and V). After these two rounds I make some critical remarks on Hannah Arendt's interpretation of science and technology. The viewpoint of 'eccentricity' will be discussed as a frame of reference for her philosophy of culture (VI).

Tijmes, Pieter and Luüf, Reginald. Modern Immaterialism. *Res Phil Technol*, 12, 271-284, 1992.

Tiles, James E. On Deafness in the Mind's Ear: John Dewey and Michael Polanyi. *Tradition Discovery*, 18(3), 9-16, 1992.

This article compares the central doctrines of Dewey and Polanyi, their common "historicism" and "psychologist" as well as the emphasis both placed on the importance of inarticulate dispositions (Polanyi's tacit knowledge; Dewey's subconscious). It argues that resistance to the suggestion that scientific knowledge has important ethical and aesthetic dimensions is what has led to a situation in which mainstream analytic philosophy appears incapable of hearing the central contentions of these philosophers.

Tiles, James E. Pleasure, Passion and Truth. *Phil Phenomenol Res*, 52(4), 931-941, D 92.

Hume's claim that a passion 'contains not any representative quality' conflicts with Plato's doctrine that our pleasures and pains can be judged to be true or false. J C B Gosling (*Phronêsis* 1959) explained a sense in which Plato's claim could stand. By considering the relationships which obtain between the pleasure and pains we experience in anticipating what will happen, this article develops Gosling's sense into a full scale refutation of Hume's position. That is it dismantles the doctrine of representation on which Hume based his argument that there could be no combat between passion and reason.

Tilghman, B R. Charles Le Brun: Theory, Philosophy and Irony. *Brit J Aes*, 32(2), 123-133, Ap 92.

Le Brun's theories of painting and program for representing the passions have been called sterile and even preposterous. It is argued that his theories nevertheless had an important role to play in 17th Century France. Le Brun borrowed his theory of the passions from Descartes. The theory fails because it does not take into account the importance of context for specifying human emotion. There is irony in the fact that Le Brun's critical practice, by contrast with his theory, relies upon the importance of context for understanding the expressiveness of paintings.

Tilghman, Benjamin R. *Wittgenstein, Ethics and Aesthetics: The View From Eternity*. Albany, SUNY Pr, 1991.

In the *Tractatus* Wittgenstein said that ethics and aesthetics are one. Wittgenstein's early work suggests that there is a much closer and much different relation between art and ethics than traditional aesthetic theory has realized. These suggestions can be more fully developed only in the light of the later work of the *Philosophical Investigations*. It can then be shown that ethics presupposes the understanding of people, what it is to understand another person and the analogies between understanding people and understanding art. In that way the human, ethical, content of art can be understood.

Till, Gregory J. A Chaotic Approach to Free Will and Determinism. *Gnosis*, 4(1), 93-115, 1992.

Determinism holds that all events, including all decisions, are governed by causal laws that allow for predictable results. Libertarianism posits the existence of an unprovable free will which is not bound by the laws of physical causality. The science of chaos, which indicates that even simple deterministic systems may act unpredictably, paradoxically advances both theories. Chaos advances determinism by showing that seemingly unpredictable human behaviour is not a failure of the deterministic model. However, because determinism apparently cannot always predict human behavior, the idea of free will is not inconsistent with a world otherwise governed by causal laws.

Tilley, John. Moral Relativism, Internalism, and the "Humean" View. *Mod Sch*, 69(2), 81-109, Ja 92.

This paper addresses a common worry about the "Humean" or "instrumental" view of practical reason, namely that it entails moral relativism. This worry, which is unfounded, derives from various oversights, some having to do with the thesis known as "internalism". The paper includes an appendix on G Harman's defense of relativism, which many interpret, incorrectly, as an attempt to derive relativism directly from an instrumental account of rational choice.

Tilley, Nicholas. Popper and Prescriptive Methodology. *Metaphilosophy*, 24(1-2), 155-166, Ja-Ap 93.

Popper's prescriptive methodology, which concerns the accomplishment of the logic of science as he sees it, is shown to contain a number of ambiguities. It is argued that one reading, emphasising the individual as adherent to and follower of methodological rules, is unsatisfactory. It is suggested that another reading, which stresses social processes within the scientific community, is preferable. This is more plausible in understanding how scientific logic is accomplished in practice, more useful in directing guides to the conduct of science, and more helpful in explaining why some science and some sciences have been more successful than others.

Tilliette, X. Edith Stein: La dottrina degli Angeli. *Aquinas*, 34(3), 447-457, S-D 91.

Tilliette, Xavier. Le point sur les recherches schellingiennes. *Arch Phil*, 56(1), 123-138, Ja-Mr 93.

Tillman, Hoyt Cleveland. A New Direction in Confucian Scholarship: Approaches to Examining the Differences between Neo-Confucianism and *Tao-hsüeh*. *Phil East West*, 42(3), 455-474, Jl 92.

Use of "Neo-Confucianism" tends to privilege Chu Hsi's ideas at the expense of other alternatives and historical context. Extending from a broader view of the *Tao-hsüeh* (Learning of the Way) fellowship, more encouragement would be given to seeing significance in heretofore neglected texts and thinkers within the fellowship and beyond it. Attention to the impact of group dynamics on ideas turns to contested dialogues. Chu's voice in letters often conveyed less authority and was more combative than the one in recorded statements to students or in his commentaries, the two sources on which scholars conventionally focus.

Tillman, Hoyt Cleveland. *Confucian Discourse and Chu Hsi's Ascendancy*. Honolulu, Univ of Hawaii Pr, 1992.

Existing studies of the "Fellowship for Learning the Way" (often called Neo-Confucianism) generally depict a single line of development to and from Chu Hsi (1130-1200), the greatest theoretician of the tradition. Tillman's broader scope offers an integrated intellectual history of this group's development which for the first time places Chu within the context of his contemporaries. Besides Chu's gradual rise as authoritative voice, close attention is given to confrontational writings on philosophical and political issues. Tillman reconstructs how a diverse group under state censure in the early twelfth century became intellectually mainstream and even won recognition as state orthodoxy in 1241.

Timmons, Mark and Horgan, Terence. Troubles for New Wave Moral Semantics: The 'Open Question Argument' Revived. *Phil Papers*, 21(3), 153-175, N 92.

We argue that (1) the new wave version of ethical naturalism defended by David Brink, Richard Boyd, Nicholas Sturgeon, and others, rests on a certain view about the semantics of moral terms that stems from the attempt to extend relatively recent developments in the philosophy of language (due to the work of Putnam and Kripke) to the understanding of moral language; but that (2) this new wave semantic view succumbs to an updated version of Moore's 'Open Question Argument' as reveled by a Twin Earth thought experiment. We conclude that, in the end, new wave ethical naturalism is as fatally flawed as its predecessor.

Tirone, Nicholas D. Implications: The 'A' of *Différance*. *Kinesis*, 19(1), 1-14, Spr 93.

Tirrell, M Lynne. Storytelling and Moral Agency. *J Aes Art Crit*, 48(2), 115-126, Spr 90.

This paper suggests that the capacity to tell stories may be necessary for moral agency, since agency requires a capacity to articulate events, motives, and characters. Telling stories gives one a sense of self, a sense of self in relation to others, and the capacity to justify one's decisions. The paper presents an account of the relations between agency, articulation, and point of view. The paper also presents a reading of Toni Morrison's *The Bluest Eye*, which through a complex weaving of the narrator's several points of view, arguably portrays a moral sensibility emerging in the telling of the story and illustrates how storytelling may enhance the moral sophistication of the agent.

Titiev, Robert. Diagnosis of Ailing Belief Sysems. *J Phil Res*, 18, 277-283, 1993.

Beliefs about fair prices for betting arrangements can obviously vary depending upon how the contingencies are described, even though each of the different descriptions is correct. This sort of variation in beliefs on the part of an agent has been linked by Ramsey and Skyrms with the agent's susceptibility to a Dutch book situation involving some combination of bets on which there is a mathematically-guaranteed net loss as the overall outcome. Clarifying the nature of that linkage is the purpose of this paper. After a framework for analysis has been developed, it is shown precisely how several important conditions for having correct beliefs are interrelated.

Titze, Hans. Freiheit und Evolution. *Stud Phil (Switzerland)*, 49, 97-102, 1990.

Tobar-Arbulu, José Felix. Technopraxiology and Development. *Res Phil Technol*, 9, 135-154, 1989.

Todisco, O. Blaise Pascal e la problematicità dell'io: Ragione forte e pensiero debole. *Sapienza*, 45(4), 353-389, 1992.

Todres, Leslie A. Psychological and Spiritual Freedoms: Reflections Inspired by Heidegger. *Human Stud*, 16(3), 255-266, Jl 93.

Toeplitz, Karol. On the Possibility and Impossibility of Christian Existentialism. *Dialec Hum*, 17(1), 115-139, 1990.

Toews, John. Transformations of Hegelianism, 1805-1846 in The Cambridge Companion to Hegel, Beiser, Frederick C (ed). New York, Cambridge Univ Pr, 1993.

Toffalori, Carlo and Prest, Mike and Marcja, Annalisa. On the Undecidability of Some Classes of Abelian-By-Finite Groups. *Annals Pure Applied Log*, 62(2), 167-173, Jl 93.

Tognonato, C. L'impegno come morale nei "Cahiers" di Jean-Paul Sartre. *Aquinas*, 35(1), 181-186, Ja-Ap 92.

Tol, A. Vollenhovens probleemhistorische methode tegen de achtergrond van zijn systematisch denken. *Phil Reform*, 58(1), 2-27, Ja 93.

This study investigates the relations in Vollenhoven's work between his systematic thinking and his historiographical typology. His systematic work centres around the notion of "subjectity", which is explicated in terms of three dimensions of difference and connection: the ontic-cosmic dimension, the ontological-analogical dimension, and the genetic-structural dimension. Any imbalance in these dimensions gives rise to polarities and patterns of dominance. In his historical work Bollenhoven traces such patterns of dominance ("types"), as indicated by classical polarities such as macrocosm-microcosm, monism-dualism, genesis vs. structure, the moral justification of which results in historically distinct "climates of opinion" ("currents").

Tollebeek, Jo. De postmoderniteit en haar geschiedenis: Kanttekeningen bij Stephen Toulmins *Kosmopolis*. *Alg Ned Tijdschr Wijs*, 84(4), 223-236, O 92.

In his book *Cosmopolis* (1990) Stephen Toulmin reflects upon the interconnectedness of his own intellectual development with that of postmedieval European thought. In this essay, Toulmin's interpretation of modernity in that context is analyzed and critically evaluated.

Tollefsen, Christopher. Thomas Nagel and the Problem of Aesthetics. *Lyceum*, 1(1), 42-49, Wint 89.

Tollefsen, Olaf. Foundationalism Defended. *Lyceum*, 2(2), 52-64, Fall 90.

Tollefsen, Olaf. Some Reflections on Contemporary Epistemology. *Lyceum*, 1(2), 68-73, Fall 89.

Tomasini Bassols, Alejandro. *Status* y verificación de la creencia religiosa. *Critica*, 24(70), 109-132, Ap 92.

Tomatis, Francesco. Nota sul "Pensiero tragico" di Sergio Givnone. *Filosofia*, 43(2), 295-303, My-Ag 92.

Tomberlin, James E (ed). *Philosophical Perspectives, 5: Philosophy of Religion, 1991*. Atascadero, Ridgeview, 1991.

This volume, the fifth in a new series of annual topical philosophy volumes, contains twenty-three original essays in the philosophy of religion. Authors include Robert M Adams, William P Alston, Robert Audi, Roderick Chisholm, Norman Kretzmann, Alvin Plantinga, Eleonore Stump, William Rowe, Michael Tooley, and Peter van

Inwagen. Topics covered include the problem of evil, foreknowledge and free will, God's attributes, and souls, the ontological argument, and the rationality of theistic belief.

Tomberlin, James E (ed). *Philosophical Perspectives, 6: Ethics, 1992*. Atascadero, Ridgeview, 1992.

This volume, the sixth in a new series of annual topical philosophy volumes, contains twenty-three original essays devoted to ethics. Authors include Julia Annas, David Brink, Stephen Darwall, Joel Feinberg, Allan Fibbard, Thomas Hill, Shelly Kagan, Christine Korsgaard, Nicholas Sturgeon, and Susan Wolf. Topics covered include consequentialism, Kantian ethics, moral rights and rules, free will, moral vs. nonmoral explanation and justification, deontology, and ethical naturalism.

Tomlinson, Thomas. The Irreversibility of Death: Reply to Cole. *Kennedy Inst Ethics J*, 3(2), 157-165, Je 93.

Professor Cole is correct in his conclusion that the Pittsburgh Protocol does not violate requirements of "irreversibility" in criteria of death, but wrong about the reasons. "Irreversible" in this context is best understood not as an ontological or epistemic term, but as an ethical one. Understood that way, the patient declared dead under the Protocol is "irreversibly" so, even though resuscitation by medical means is still possible. Nonetheless, the Protocol revives difficult questions about our concept of death.

Tong, Rosemarie. *Feminine and Feminist Ethics*. Belmont, Wadsworth, 1993.

Tonini, Valerio. Scientific Phenomenology and Bioethics in Analecta Husserliana, XXXI, Tymieniecka, Anna-Teresa (ed). Dordrecht, Kluwer, 1990.

Toole, David. Of Lingering Eyes and Talking Things: Adorno and Deleuze on Philosophy Since Auschwitz. *Phil Today*, 37(3), 227-246, Fall 93.

Tooley, Michael. The Argument from Evil in Philosophical Perspectives, 5: Philosophy of Religion, 1991, Tomberlin, James E (ed). Atascadero, Ridgeview, 1991.

Toombs, S Kay. The Body in Multiple Sclerosis: A Patient's Perspective in The Body in Medical Thought and Practice, Leder, Drew (ed). Dordrecht, Kluwer, 1992.

In this work the author notes that the actual experience of an illness is significantly different from its scientific conceptualization as a disease state. Using insights from phenomenology and reflection on her own experience, she explores the global disorder of body, self and world that multiple sclerosis engenders in the life of the patient. Motor and sensory disorders are seen to have differing existential meanings. In addition, central nervous system disease carries a particular existential significance. An understanding of the subjective experience of neurological disorder has important implications for the care of patients.

Toombs, S Kay. *The Meaning of Illness: A Phenomenological Account of the Different Perspectives of Physician and Patient*. Dordrecht, Kluwer, 1992.

This work provides a phenomenological account of the experience of illness and the different perspectives of physician and patient. Drawing upon insights derived from psychological phenomenology, the author provides a detailed account of the way in which illness and body are apprehended differently by doctor and patient and considers the implications for medical practice, particularly in terms of achieving successful communication, providing a comprehensive account of illness, and alleviating suffering. Consideration is given to ways of developing a shared world of meaning through the use of clinical narrative, empathic understanding and an explicit focus on the lifeworld interpretation of illness.

Toombs, S Kay. The Metamorphosis: The Nature of Chronic Illness and Its Challenge to Medicine. *J Med Human*, 14(4), 223-230, Wint 93.

The main diseases of our time are chronic in nature. Nevertheless, the predominant focus of medical care and medical education in recent years has been directed towards acute care—the underlying assumption being that an acute model of illness is adequate for dealing with the problems associated with chronic disorders. In this work the author argues that this assumption is mistaken. Chronic illness is distinctively different in nature to acute illness. This distinctive character poses a challenge to the prevailing conception of the goals of medicine and the nature of the relation between patient and health care professional.

Toprak, Binnaz and Birtek, Faruk. The Conflictual Agendas of Neo-Liberal Reconstruction and the Rise of Islamic Politics in Turkey. *Praxis Int*, 13(2), 192-210, Jl 93.

Torchia, Joseph. *Pondus Meum amor meus*: the Weight-Metaphor in Saint Augustine's Early Philosophy. *Augustin Stud*, 21, 163-176, 1990.

Torchinov, E A. Philosophical Studies (Sinology and Indology) in St Petersburg (Leningrad), 1985-1990. *Phil East West*, 42(2), 327-333, Ap 92.

Toribio, Manuel. Institución, método científico y proceso social: La ética de G H Mead. *Themata*, 8, 87-114, 1991.

Torrance, Steve (ed) and Spencer-Smith, Richard (ed). *Machinations: Computational Studies of Logic, Language, and Cognition*. Norwood, Ablex, 1992.

This collection covers work within philosophy, AI and computational theory, and offers a common meeting ground. Topics discussed include: computational treatments of temporal contexts; Prolog programs as definitions; intuitionist logic as a computational paradigm; logic as a foundation for knowledge engineering; formalisms for natural language sentence comprehension; and for speech act recognition; explanation-based learning; mental logic and deontic logic; and the relation between symbolic and subsymbolic explanations in AI.

Torretti, R. The Geometric Structure of the Universe in Philosophy and the Origin and Evolution of the Universe, Agazzi, Evandro (ed). Norwell, Kluwer, 1991.

An elementary but fairly accurate sketch of the main geometrical ideas of Riemann and their application in relativistic cosmology. Special stress is laid on the fact that the so-called Big Bang in current models of the universe is not a chemical, nuclear or indeed subnuclear explosion but a basic *geometric* feature of spacetime, and that time cannot be said to have a *first* moment in Big Bang universes, for *every* particular moment is preceded by *some*—admittedly finite and possibly very short—period of time.

Tortora, Roberto and Gerla, Giangiacomo. La relazione di connessione in A N Whitehead: aspetti matematici. *Epistemologia*, 15(2), 351-364, Jl-D 92.

In [5], [6] and [7], A N Whitehead presents a particular point of view on the physical world. According to it, the geometric properties of the space-time are reconstructed starting from some primitive objects and relations among them which satisfy a number of intuitive assumptions. Our aim is to translate, as adequately as possible, Whitehead's informal analysis into mathematical axiom systems. This purpose seems to us very interesting, since the approach of Whitehead may give useful tools to some recent researches towards the possibility of building Geometry without using the notion of point as primitive. (edited)

Tosenovsky, L. On the Relation of J L Fischer to Marxist Philosophy (Reply to L Valenta's Polemic Study) (in Czechoslovakian). *Filozof Cas*, 40(4), 680-685, 1992.

Townsend Jr, Dabney. Hutcheson and Complex Ideas: A Reply to Peter Kivy. *J Aes Art Crit*, 51(1), 72-74, Wint 93.

Peter Kivy objected to a portion of my essay, "Lockean Aesthetics" [JAAC, 49(4)] where I dealt with Hutcheson's relation to Locke. Kivy maintains that Hutcheson held that beauty is a simple idea. I had said that it was more consistent if it could be construed as complex. In replying to Kivy, I clarify the relation. "Idea" should be construed as referring to individual ideas which are classified by the collective "term" beauty. As such, many of those ideas will be complex in Locke's sense, though Hutcheson has modified Locke's distinction to such an extent that it should not be taken too literally.

Townsend Jr, Dabney. Lockean Aesthetics. *J Aes Art Crit*, 49(4), 349-361, Fall 91.

This paper traces the influence of Lockean epistemology in early eighteenth-century British aesthetics. Locke has very limited references to aesthetic issues. Beginning with Francis Hutcheson, Locke's empiricism forms the basis for a theory of aesthetic experience. However, Hutcheson remains in some ways closer to his other acknowledged model, the Earl of Shaftesbury. Edmund Burke, on the other hand, while he also shows Locke's influence, remains fundamentally Aristotelian in a number of ways. Joseph Priestley presents a more clearly Lockean aesthetic, but Priestley's assimilatation of Locke's epistemology shows something of its limitations for aesthetics. One is led toward Hume's more radical epistemology.

Tracy, Thomas F. Victimization and the Problem of Evil: A Response to Ivan Karamazov. *Faith Phil*, 9(3), 301-329, Jl 92.

Ivan Karamazov raises a powerful moral objection to defenses of God's goodness that sanction the sacrifice of the innocent to secure a general good. This anti-consequentialist critique has considerable force against some of the most familiar responses to the problem of evil, notably Plantinga's free will defense. In this paper I examine Ivan's objection and consider several lines of argument in reply. I contend that there are conditions under which it is morally permissible, even on deontological grounds, for God to create a world in which persons sometimes suffer as victims of natural or moral evils.

Trainor, Brian T. The State, Marriage and Divorce. *J Applied Phil*, 9(2), 135-148, 1992.

This essay advances several interrelated arguments concerning the proper role of the state with regard to marriage and divorce but may main contention is that 'pure' no-fault divorce laws are unjust-or, at least, they are unjust if marriage involves a genuinely contractual element, and there seems to be very little doubt that it does. Locke, Dant and Hegel are three eminent thinkers who are alike in viewing marriage as a contract (though in the case of Hegel, it is a 'contract to transcend the standpoint of contract') and in the first two sections of the essay I consider their views on the role of contract in marriage. Whilst holding (with Hegel) that marriage is more than a contract, I also hold (with Kant) that it is not less than a contract. In section three I consider the implications of this 'not less than', the most important one being that 'pure' no-fault divorce laws are unjust.

Trebilcot, Joyce. Not Lesbian Philosophy. *Hypatia*, 7(4), 38-44, Fall 92.

Presenting reasoned rejections of the hierarchical implications of "philosopher" and the sexual implications of "lesbian", the author's method leads her to indicate that her resistance to these names is motivated partly by particular facts of her early life.

Treitler, Leo. History and the Ontology of the Musical Work. *J Aes Art Crit*, 51(3), 483-497, Sum 93.

Questions about the ontological status of the musical work and about the relations among works, scores, and performances are commonly posed, and answers are commonly formulated, as though the problem were uniform for all historical traditions and practices. But these relations can vary over a wide range, and formulations that have been proposed about them almost all presume the particular aesthetic assumptions of the work-concept of the 19th century, assumptions that have application to a very specific and limited musical practice — and by no means even to all musical practices of the 19th century. This lends a certain circularity to the literature on this subject. The problem is illustrated with reference to works of Frederic Chopin and to some music of the European Middle Ages.

Treloar, John L. Moral Virtue and the Demise of Prudence in the Thought of Francis Suárez. *Amer Cath Phil Quart*, 65(3), 387-405, Sum 91.

Trembath, Paul. The Rhetoric of Philosophical "Writing": Emphatic Metaphors in Derrida and Rorty. *J Aes Art Crit*, 47(2), 169-173, Spr 89.

Tremmel, William C. Bernhardt's Analysis of the Function of Religion in God, Values, and Empiricism, Peden, Creighton (ed). Macon, Mercer Univ Pr, 1989.

Tress, Daryl McGowan. The Metaphysical Science of Aristotle's *Generation of Animals* and Its Feminist Critics. *Rev Metaph*, 46(2), 307-341, 1992.

This paper examines Aristotle's *Generation of Animals*, Books 1-2.5, and considers some recent feminist response to Aristotle's theory of sexual difference and generation. It is shown that Aristotle holds that male and female fill necessary and complementary roles in the generation of offspring. Aristotle declares at the start of the treatise that male and female are the principles of generation; the remainder of *Generation of Animals* examines the empirical and metaphysical requirements of this thesis. While feminist critics have claimed that Aristotle's theory of sex and reproduction is deeply sexist, it is argued here that many feminists have misunderstood the aims and arguments of *Generation of Animals*.

Tricaud, François. Le roman philosophique de l'humanité chez Hobbes et chez Locke. *Arch Phil*, 55(4), 631-643, O-D 92.

According to Hobbes, the commonwealth is set up "to make good that propriety, which by mutual contract men acquire, in recompense of the universal right they abandon" (Leviathan, XV). Thus, mankind's mythico-philosophical story comprises two stages: the contractual determination of "property" (Hobbes's propriety), that is, of every man's limited and inviolable rights; then, the establishment of a State, protector of this "property". In Locke, this second chapter alone is necessary; for 1) Locke's natural law defines by itself the basic rules of a just behaviour (no contract is needed); 2) it is a divine law, whereas in Hobbes the really sacred commandment is probably the man-made obligation proceeding from the contract.

Trifogli, Cecilia. Giles of Rome on the Instant of Change. *Synthese*, 96(1), 93-114, Jl 93.

Trigeaud, Jean Marc (trans). *Introduction a la Philosophie*. Bordeaux, Biere, 1992.

Trigeaud, Jean-Marc. *Éléments d'une Philosophie Politique*. Bordeaux, Biere, 1993.

Approche métaphysicienne (édition italienne: Japadre, Rome) de la pensée politique, de l'Anitquité grecque à nos jours, en passant par les courants du Moyen-Age et du siècle des "Lumières"; ouverte à l'analyse du langage symbolique et mythicque autant qu'à une réflexion de théologie chrétienne. La justice juridique (universaliste) prime sur la justice politique (généricisté); l'une se fonde sur la personne singulière (non empiriquement) et l'autre invoque une nature humaine commune et relationnelle. Il s'agit de permettre à l'homme d'être non seulement solidaire des membres d'un même groupe, mais de se dépasser en sacrifiant sans contrepartie son intérêt à celui d'autrui.

Trigeaud, Jean-Marc. *Essais de Philosophie du Droit*. Genova, Stud Ed Cultura, 1987.

Legalist positivism gives birth to a *mystic of the autority* which rejects culture as the knowledge of unconditioned truth in justice and as the critical "instance" allowing an appreciation of the limits of the juridical discourse. This phenomenon favours the development of an artificial sophistic culture. The notion of juridical person is conceived according to the sociological type of the *homo oeconomicus* so that it takes man away from the truth of this essence and alienates his freedom. As for neo-positivism, it isolates the form of the law of its onto-axiological contents and it brings about the repression of the cultural truth of justice. So it gives credit to a juridical discourse oblivious of its origin and which sets into technicism. This dogmatics of the *Abgrund* is in accordance, too, with a pseudo-culture. (edited)

Trigeaud, Jean-Marc. *Humanisme de la Liberté et Philosophie de la Justice*. Bordeaux, Biere, 1985.

More than two thirds of the volume are devoted to a survey of the natural law or natural justice tradition. The ideas of the great representatives of this tradition are discussed under the headings of "perspective réaliste de la liberté incarnée (Plato, Aristotle, Aquinas, and others), "perspective idéaliste de la liberté transcendentale" (the Stoics, Augustine, Grotius, Kant, and others), and "retour au concret et expérience de la liberté" (Hegel, Rosmini, Bergson, Radbruch, and many others). The author underlines the necessity of a primary ethics that is on the *prosopon* as the "universally singular." He condemns the genericism, and particularly the self-government of the nature and of the will. (edited)

Trigeaud, Jean-Marc. *La Possession des Biens Immobiliers*. Paris, Economica, 1981.

On se plait à opposer possession et propriété. C'est méconnaitre leur aspect commun: l'inertie. Ne conviendrait-il pas de redéfinir la possession, non plus comme un pouvoir, naturellement passif, de l'individu sur la chose, mais comme une position de cette chose en accord avec ses fins, sa destination économique, écologique, esthétique? Distinguée de la propriété, la possession pourrait lui servir de modèle pour en modifier le contenu et déterminer de nouvelles manières de l'acquérir et de la perdre, et l'on ne s'attarderait plus à tenir le discours galvaudé de la "fonction sociale."

Trigeaud, Jean-Marc. *Persona ou la Justice au Double Visage*. Genova, Stud Ed Cultura, 1990.

La distinction entre nature et *personne* prend une singulière portée à la *Déclaration des droits de l'homme*, rivée à une conception de l'homme générique, propre à une définition du juridique et du politique en rupture avec tout ordre éthique plus profond. Les protections accordées par ces voies peuvent être jugées souhaitables, elles n'en sont pas moins insuffisantes, à défaut de s'ouvrir au respect de l'homme en tant que personne, ce que seule une éthique est capable de découvrir, en rappelant les inévitables limites de toute entreprise juridico-politique enfermée dans la pensée d'un universellement ressemblant. I convenait de resituer les données du problème de la justice dans la perspective souvent oubliée de la personne, en montrant la relativité de perspectives qui ont pu successivement séduire: perspectives de la *nature*, qu'il s'agisse de la nature des choses ou de la nature de l'homme lui-même.

Trigeaud, Jean-Marc. *Philosophie Juridique Européenne les Institutions*. L'Aquila, Japadre, 1988.

I—H Batiffol, "Droit et loi dans l'Europe continentale"; A D'Ors, "Derecho y ley en la experiencia europea desde una perspectiva romana"; S Goyard-Fabre, "L'idée de loi dans les lumières françaises"; P Stein, "The Sources of Law in Europe"; F Todescan, "La legge e le fonti del diritto in Europa"; J M Trigeaud, "La fonction critique due concept de nature des choses"; A Viandier, "Évolution d'une idée européenne"; M Reale, "O pensamento filosófico-jurídico europeu no Brasil"; II—H A Schwarz-Liebermann, "L'homme européen devant le droit"; R Sève, "Le mouvement de la philosophie du droit européenne"; J M Trigeaud, "La personne juridique dans la philosophie européenne"; J J M Van Der Ven, "La personne humaine aux yeux juridiques".

Trigg, Roger. Reason and Faith—II in Religion and Philosophy, Warner, Marin (ed). New York, Cambridge Univ Pr, 1992.

It is argued that faith and reason cannot be totally distinguished. Faith is always faith in something and itself demands the exercise of reason. We must distinguish between the subject and object of faith. The latter is not the product of an arbitrary commitment. The attack by Don Cupitt on theological realism is criticized, and the connection between realism and theism is examined.

Trigg, Roger. Wittgenstein and Social Science in Wittgenstein Centenary Essays, Griffiths, A Phillips (ed). New York, Cambridge Univ Pr, 1991.

Wittgenstein emphasized the public nature of the rules for applying our concepts. As a result, they can only be understood in their social setting. There is in his thought an inter-twined trinity of the public, the social and the contextual, which provides an important rationale for social science. Yet this approach can be criticized because of its refusal to distinguish between the subject and object of knowledge, and its implicit attack on the possibility of unprejudiced reason.

Tripathy, L K. Intersubjectivity in Phenomenology. *Indian Phil Quart*, 19/1(Supp), 1-8, Ja 92.

Trivedi, Saam. An Outline of Some Problems in the Philosophy of Music Composition. *Indian Phil Quart*, 19/3(Supp), 11-16, Jl 92.

Trivedi, Saam. Is There a Need for a Distinction Between Meaning and Sense?. *Indian Phil Quart*, 19/2(Supp), 19-24, Ap 92.

Trompf, Garry W. On Newtonian History in The Uses of Antiquity, Gaukroger, Stephen (ed). Dordrecht, Kluwer, 1991.

Tronto, Joan C. *Moral Boundaries: A Political Argument for an Ethic of Care*. New York, Routledge, 1993.

This book contests the association of care solely with women. While women do care, it is empirically and historically inaccurate, as well as politically unwise, to associate women with caring. Other groups, such as working classes and people of color do disproportionate amounts of caring in our society. Instead of understanding care as a gender concept, we should understand care as a central activity of human life. From this starting point, our philosophical, moral and political theories must change their boundaries. The boundary between moral and poltical life, between public and private, and around "the moral point of view" change.

Troost, A. De tweeërlei aard van de wet. *Phil Reform*, 57(2), 117-131, Ja 92.

Troost, A. Normativiteit: Oorsprong en ondergang van het denken over scheppings- ordeningen. *Phil Reform*, 57(1), 3-38, Ja 92.

Trotta, Alessandro. Interpretazione e critica di Plotino della concezione del tempo dei suoi predecessori. *Riv Filosof Neo-Scolas*, 84(2-3), 340-368, Ap-S 92.

Trout, J D. Robustness and Integrative Survival in Significance Testing: The World's Contribution to Rationality. *Brit J Phil Sci*, 44(1), 1-15, Mr 93.

Significance testing is the primary method for establishing causal relationships in psychology. Meehl and Faust argue that significance tests and their interpretation are subject to *actuarial* and *psychological* biases, making continued adherence to these practices irrational, and even partially responsible for the slow progress of the 'soft' areas of psychology. I contend that familiar standards of testing and literature review, along with recently developed meta-analytic techniques, are able to correct the proposed actuarial and psychological biases. In particular, psychologists embrace a *principle of robustness* which states that real psychological effects are 1) reproducible by similar methods, 2) detectable by diverse means, and 3) able to survive theoretical integration. (edited)

Trout, J D. Theory-Conjunction and Mercenary Reliance. *Phil Sci*, 59(2), 231-245, Je 92.

Scientific realists contend that theory-conjunction presents a problem for enpiricist conceptions of scientific knowledge and practice. Van Fraassen (1980) has offered a competing account of theory-conjunction which I argue fails to capture the mercenary character of epistemic dependence in science. Representative cases of theory-conjunction developed in the present paper show that mercenary reliance implies a "principle of epistemic symmetry" which only a realist can consistently accommodate. Finally, because the practice in question involves the conjunction of *theories*, a version of realism more robust than the "entity realism" of Cartwright (1983, 1989) and Hacking (1983) is required to explain the success of theory-conjunction.

Trout, J D (ed) and Gasper, Philip (ed) and Boyd, Richard (ed). *The Philosophy of Science*. Cambridge, MIT Pr, 1991.

Trouvé, Jean Marie. The Evolution of Science and the 'Tree of Knowledge' in New Horizons in the Philosophy of Science, Lamb, David (ed). Brookfield, Avebury, 1992.

This paper presents a theory which can cope with the large variety of claims of scientific literature. Without the help of quantitative techniques, it offers graphic models representing the structure, the growth and the evolution of scientific knowledge. Knowledge emerges as a very compact structure whereas growth and evolution are, here, two distinct but articulated concepts. Models also reveal that time uncertainty is bound to scientific events. A comparison with Kuhn's theory is made.

Trpak, P. Christianity and Responsibility for the Earth (in Czechoslovakian). *Filozof Cas*, 39(6), 992-1000, 1991.

The author concerns himself with philosophical reflections on the relationship between man and nature through the transformations of time. He is engaged in a polemic with the opinion that the utilitarian relationship to the natural world, which is the cause of our current ecological crisis, was born in the Judeo-Christian conception of the world. If we want to contribute to the formation of a Christian responsibility for the Earth and return the original meaning to the words of *The Word*, we must first raise humble nature to the level of a full-fledged partner and take on the responsibility for Creation to its original extent, to "protect it against evil". In the spirit of Christian eco-philosophy, the author arrives at the conclusion that the ecologists' demand for the recognition of the right of the environment to its own development can be realized only by respecting God's order.

Trundle, Robert C. Applied Logic: An Aristotelian *Organon* for Critical Thinking in a Theoretical Context. *Phil Sci (Tucson)*, 5, 117-140, 1993.

If Aristotle had ignored metaphysics in his paradigm logic, Western culture might have inherited a Humean-like skepticism rather than a fruitful scientific realism.

Though many contemporary realists are influenced by Hume's "critical thought," Aristotle not only anticipated such thought but the need for a metaphysics without which scientific principles and methodology cannot be understood. Aristotelian logic needs to be adapted to a current "logic of scientific truth," but this adaption should be done in logic courses for both acknowledging the relation of logic to metaphysics and critically understanding our scientific culture.

Trundle, Robert C. Physics and Existentialist Phenomenology in New Horizons in the Philosophy of Science, Lamb, David (ed). Brookfield, Avebury, 1992.

The challenge to "objective observation," in terms of relativisms wherein it is theory-dependent, has generated *reductio ad absurdum* rejections of theory-dependency theses (F Suppe and W H Newton-Smith) and an observation-revisability thesis in which instrument-aided observation together with theoretical experimentation ameliorate naked-eye observation (Alan Chalmers). Besides arguing that an important function of naked-eye observation is disregarded and that *reductio ad absurdum* strategies fail to establish observational truth, I argue that such truth has its ontological basis in an observational consciousness of which the physicist is also phenomenologically conscious.

Truog, Robert D. Triage in the ICU. *Hastings Center Rep*, 22(3), 13-17, My-Je 92.

Trusted, Jennifer. Gifts of Gametes in Applied Philosophy, Almond, Brenda (ed). New York, Routledge, 1992.

The argument is directed against the view expressed in Edgar Page's paper ("Parental Rights", Journal of Applied Philosophy, 1984, pp. 187-203) that a surrogate mother has no legal right to the baby she carries. Page compares the surrogacy agreement made to an agreement to buy apples growing in an orchard or an animal *in utero*. In *Gifts of Gametes* it is contended that the analogy is flawed in that a surrogate mother is not simply acting as a passive incubator. She responds physiologically and psychologically during pregnancy and therefore has an interest in the child that transcends any prior contract.

Tsinorema, Stavroula F. Wittgenstein, Rationality and Relativism in Greek Studies in the Philosophy and History of Science, Nicolacopoulos, Pantelis (ed). Dordrecht, Kluwer, 1990.

Tsohatzidis, Savas L. Speaking of Truth-Telling: The View from *wh*-Complements. *J Prag*, 19(3), 271-279, Mr 93.

Karttunen and Vendler have independently made an interesting claim about the meaning of *tell*, which they have subsequently used in order to motivate their solutions to the different kinds of problem that each was investigating. I propose to argue that this claim is not true; that there are certain negative consequences of its falsity for the more general theses that Karttunen and Vedler were interested in establishing, as well as for an equally general thesis developed outside their immediate concerns; that the data on which it was based do call for, and admit of, an alternative explanation; and that this explanation acquires a deeper significance when placed in the context of certain metatheoretical considerations.

Tsujimoto, Munemasa. Quelques aspects de l'impression de réalité au cinéma—A propos des travaux de Christian Metz (in Japanese). *Bigaku*, 43(2), 47-58, Fall 92.

On sait que le cinéma est, à l'évidence, une sorte de langage qui nous parle un sens. Aussi, un mécanisme significative commun à beaucoup de films s'investit dans le cinéma. Et pour que un sens comme tel circuler dans une communauté, il faut qu'il y a les codes communes a l'émetteur comme au récepteur de message. L'emetteur compose le message dans le code, le récepteur chiffre le message sur le code. Nous somme forcés de se composer dans l'institution cinématographique. La force existe, qu'on le veuille ou non. Certes. Mais il nous faut prendre garde au force. (edited)

Tuck, Richard. *Philosophy and Government, 1572-1651*. New York, Cambridge Univ Pr, 1993.

Tucker, Aviezer. *Essais hérétiques sur la philosophie de l'histoire* by Jan Patocka. *Hist Theor*, 31(3), 355-363, 1992.

A critical study of Patocka's philosophy of history: The rise and fall of search for meaning and truth in history, from the Greek polis, through its Medieval Holy Roman Empire height, to the loss of meaning in modernity. Contrast is drawn with Patocka's more optimistic and less reactionary *Plato and Europe*. Patocka attempted to restore meaning to history, restore history, through the experience of sacrifice, the giving up of production and reproduction for transcendental meaning. Patocka's latter philosophy is connected with his writing and leading Czechoslovakia's Charter 77 with his student, Vaclav Havel, and his own personal sacrifice of his life in 1977 as a result of his Charter 77 activities.

Tugendhat, Ernst. Reflections on Philosophical Method in Philosophical Interventions in the Unfinished Project of Enlightenment, Honneth, Axel (& other eds). Cambridge, MIT Pr, 1992.

Tulaev, Pavel. *Sobor* and *Sobornost'*. *Russian Stud Phil*, 31(4), 25-53, Spr 93.

Tully, James. *An Approach to Political Philosophy: Locke in Contexts*. New York, Cambridge Univ Pr, 1993.

The book consists of a series of critical studies of John Locke's political philosophy. Eight chapters were previously published and rewritten for this volume. Two chapters were not published before. Each chapter takes up a concept in Locke's writings and critically analyzes it in the contexts in which it was written and the different contexts in which it was read over the last 300 years. Government, revolution, property, Aborignal Rights, Progress, and citizenship are discussed. The conclusion is that Lockean liberalism is much more complex and more in need of critical reconstruction than its heirs and detractors realize.

Tundo, Laura. *L'Utopia di Fourier*. Bari, Dedalo, 1992.

Fourier conceived the greatest and most audacious idea for the transformation of society in an endeavor to create not only a just society but also a prosperous and happy one. Fourier's concept of utopia has been neglected by critics in the past, an omission which this *wide-ranging study* remedies. The main aspects of Fourier's thought dealt with are: the rediscovery of the *passions* in their positiveness, in their wonderful, vital force; *pleasure*, whose value is enhanced in so much as it promotes the happiness of man; *desirable work*, no longer a source of suffering for man, but the expression of his passionate energies; *free love*, which expands in every direction to establish a loving society; the idea of living together according to principles of justice, solidarity, unity-harmony.

Tunick, M. Hegel's Justification of Hereditary Monarchy. *Hist Polit Thought*, 12(3), 481-496, Fall 91.

Hegel claims hereditary monarchy is justified by 'the Concept'. This seems to be a foundational claim. I argue it can be understood as nonfoundational. By 'concept' Hegel sometimes means the purpose of a thing. For Hegel the purpose of hereditary monarchy—its concept—is to provide arbitrary final decisions where we lack objective grounds for deciding—in such matters we need a groundless method. Given the limited role Hegel assigns the monarch, hereditary monarchy is justified by its concept (not 'the Concept'). This is a nonfoundational, non-metaphysical account. Passages from recently available texts of Hegel's *Rechtsphilosophie* support this reading.

Tuohey, John and Ma, Terence P. Fifteen Years After "Animal Liberation": Has the Animal Rights Movement Achieved Philosophical Legitimacy?. *J Med Human*, 13(2), 79-89, Sum 92.

Fifteen years ago, Peter Singer published "Animal Liberation: A New Ethics for Our Treatment of Animals". In it, he proposed to end "the tyranny of humans over nonhuman animals" by "thinking through, carefully, and consistently, the question of how we ought to treat animals" (p. ix). On this anniversary of the book's publication, a critical analysis shows that the logic he presents, though popularly appealing, is philosophically flawed. Though influential in slowing and in some cases stopping biomedical research involving animals, the animal rights movement in the United States has yet to offer a clear and compelling argument for the equality of species.

Tuomela, Raimo. Mutual Beliefs and Social Characteristics in Advances in Scientific Philosophy, Schurz, Gerhard (ed). Amsterdam, Rodopi, 1991.

Tuomela, Raimo. On Searle's Argument Against the Possibility of Social Laws in John Searle and His Critics, Lepore, Ernest (ed). Cambridge, Blackwell, 1991.

Tuomela, Raimo. What Is Cooperation?. *Erkenntnis*, 38(1), 87-101, Ja 93.

The paper presents a "two-dimensional" account of cooperation, treating cooperation as joint action. According to this view, every joint action type—be it cooperative or noncooperative—can be performed both cooperatively and noncooperatively, "willingly" or "reluctantly". A purely cooperative joint action type, e.g., jointly building a house, is one where each participant can help any other participatings to perform his part of the joint action. (Noncooperative action types do not have this feature.) A full-blown singular cooperative action is a cooperatively performed token of a cooperative action type. Such a full-blown cooperative action can also be performed under coercion.

Tuomi, Juha. Evolutionary Synthesis: A Search for the Strategy. *Phil Sci*, 59(3), 429-438, S 92.

The goal of evolutionary theory is to (a) specify the general causal structure of evolving systems and (b) analyze evolutionary consequences that are expected to result from the proposed structure of the model systems. Biologists frequently emphasize the hypothetico-deductive method in evolutionary theory. I will show that this method primarily provides a tactical device for (b), while evolutionary synthesis requires a foundation of a unifying conceptual model for (a). Therefore, any successful strategy for a new synthesis requires both a new conceptual insight of evolving systems, and tactical devices for analyzing new specific aspects of the evolutionary process.

Tuomivaara, Timo and Kuokkanen, Martti. On the Structure of Idealizations in Idealization III, Brzenzinski, Jerzy (ed). Amsterdam, Rodopi, 1992.

It is argued that the original Poznan view of idealizing laws is too narrow. New types of idealizations, partial idealizations, are introduced via the structuralist approach. It is shown that the original Poznan view is incapable in taking into account such idealizations. The analysis shows that the almost extensional structuralist framework is completely adequate in studying for example the factual and counterfactual content of theories. The result makes unnecessary to study these aspects of theories using intensional languages.

Tuozzo, Thomas M. Aristotelian Deliberation is Not of Ends in Essays in Ancient Greek Philosophy, IV, Anton, John P (ed). Albany, SUNY Pr, 1991.

Tur, Richard. Paternalism and the Criminal Law in Applied Philosophy, Almond, Brenda (ed). New York, Routledge, 1992.

If it could be shown that law is, in some sense, a moral system the apparent contradiction between (moral) autonomy and (legal) heteronomy might be challenged. In order to prepare for such a challenge this paper questions the prevailing view that law is not in the business of enforcing morals. That is done primarily by using decisions of the criminal courts to show that the law does not always criminalise conduct merely to prevent harm to others. Paternalism is distinguished from the harm principle in order to show that the law (rightly or wrongly) sometimes seeks to secure that which is (thought to be) morally good, irrespective of the prevention of harm, at least overall harm. (edited)

Turco, G. "Doctor humanitatis": Implicazioni e sviluppi dell'antropologia tomistica alla luce degli Atti del IX Congresso Tomistico Internazionale. *Sapienza*, 45(3), 307-325, 1992.

Turner, Denys. Marx, Ideology and Morality in Socialism and Morality, McLellan, David (ed). New York, St Martin's Pr, 1990.

Turner, Jeffrey S. Ατοπια and Plato's *Gorgias*. *Int Stud Phil*, 25(1), 69-77, 1993.

This article traces several types of "strangeness" in Plato's *Gorgias*: that of Socrates, of his interlocutors, and of the text itself, insofar as it fails to achieve that agreement between Socrates and Callicles which would offer "the *telos* of truth" (487e) for its arguments. I then distinguish the Socratic conception of strangeness—the strangeness of a disharmonious relation between one's *logoi* and *erga*—from the "ordinary" conception presupposed by his interlocutors—the strangeness of saying or doing something not ordinarily said or done. The Socratic conception is then applied to the "words" and "deeds" of the dialogue as a whole.

Turner, Jeffrey S. The Images of Enslavement and Incommensurability in Plato's *Meno*. *Interpretation*, 20(2), 117-134, Wint 92-93.

A look at two accounts of *Meno* 82b9-85b7 written by Gregory Vlastos shows that the images of enslavement and incommensurability there are in tension with its claim that "learning is recollection." I attempt to situate those images in the contest of the *Meno* as a whole by slightly modifying Michell Miller's structural analysis of the Platonic dialogue. I then offer some suggestions about several perplexities of the dialogue, and its views of virtue and recollection. These point to a way of reading Plato in which his artistry and love of mathematics are no longer in tension with one another.

Turner, Ken. Defending Semantic Presupposition. *J Prag*, 18(4), 345-371, O 92.

This paper assesses a recent revision of the logical definition of presupposition which takes seriously, and attempts to reconstruct theoretically, the intuitive distinction between the absence of a classical truth-value and the presence of a non-classical third truth-value. It is argued that the reconstruction is inadequate. Specifically, the revision does not (i) sufficiently characterize the new relation of 'default implication' that is said to hold between a negative statement and its presupposition(s): (ii) correctly define logical negation and therefore predicts that statements containing presupposition-cancellation are necessarily false: and (iii) escape the postulation of an ambiguous negation operator. Whatever other virtues may result from the application of this revision semantic presupposition is not rehabilitated by it.

Turner, Norman. Some Questions about E H Gombrich on Perspective. *J Aes Art Crit*, 50(2), 139-150, Spr 92.

Students of vision long believed that tiny perspective pictures cast on the retinas are what we see. It is now known that there are no pictures on the retinas and that perception does not in any case bear on images. Moreover, perspective pictures contain an inescapable type of distortion. E H Gombrich has sought to explain this distortion away, but his arguments are mistaken. As normal vision ordinarily contains no distortion, we are led to conclude that perspective is a species of trope. It stands for certain qualities available but not endemic to sight.

Turner, Stephen. The End of Functionalism: *Parsons, Merton, and Their Heirs*. *Phil Soc Sci*, 23(2), 228-242, Je 93.

Three recent works bearing on the history of American sociological functionalism are examined. One shows how Parsons' *Social System* solved the problem of characterizing normativity by conceiving norms as commitment to a stable symbol system, normatively-charged and entwined with expectations. Another, a large collective work, deals with Merton's alternative to Parsons. It suggests that Merton failed to supply any substitute for the notion of "system needs" as a source of explanatory force, and that his functionalism is non-explanatory. The final work considered, *A Dictionary of Sociology*, shows how functionalist notions have been systematically re-interpreted in rational-choice terms.

Turrisi, Patricia A. The Purpose of the Proof of Pragmatism in Peirce's 1903 Lectures on Pragmatism. *Monist*, 75(4), 521-537, O 92.

An interpretation of the role of logic among the sciences is the principal agenda of Peirce's lectures on *Pragmatism as a Principle and Method of Right Thinking*. Logic elucidates the basic elements of reasoning by means of the instrument of the pragmatic maxim, which requires a proof, not of its efficacy, but of its truth. Peirce thereby defends pragmatism as a maxim of science against its popular definition as a speculative doctrine. This article demonstrates how the inquiry into a logical proof of pragmatism is related to the deeper issue of the definition of a science of logic.

Tursi, Antonio D. Presciencia divina y libre arbitrio: Boecio *de Consolatione* V, 3 y Seneca *epistulae ad lucilium* II, 16. *Rev Filosof (Argentina)*, 6(1-2), 57-66, N 92.

Tusell, Narcís Aragay. *Origen y decadencia del logos*. Barcelona, Anthropos, 1993.

Tuttas, Friedemann. An Arithmetical Completeness Theorem for Pre-permutations. *Notre Dame J Form Log*, 34(1), 84-89, Wint 93.

We prove an extension of an arithmetical completeness theorem for the system Rω with respect to pre-permutational arithmetic interpretations to all modal sentences. Hitherto, this type of completeness theorem has only been given for modal sentences with no nestings of witness comparisons.

Tuuri, Heikki. Relative Separation Theorems. *Notre Dame J Form Log*, 33(3), 383-401, Sum 92.

Tweedale, Martin. Ockham's Supposed Elimination of Connotative Terms and His Ontological Parsimony. *Dialogue (Canada)*, 31(3), 431-444, Sum 92.

Against an interpretation of Ockham advanced by Marilyn Adams and seconded by Paul Spade, I argue along with Claude Panaccio that Ockham was not a reductionist in the sense that he thought we could say everything that is true in a language composed simply of absolute (i.e., non-connotative) terms drawn from the categories of substance and quality plus various syncategoremata; but my grounds are different from Panaccio's. Nor, I claim, does Ockham's ontological parsimony, i.e., that the only things in the world are substances and qualities, require such a reductive enterprise.

Tweedale, Martin M. Duns Scotus's Doctrine on Universals and the Aphrodisian Tradition. *Amer Cath Phil Quart*, 67(1), 77-93, Wint 93.

Duns Scotus's doctrine of a "common nature" which of itself has a less than numerical unity is viewed as building on and revising a tradition of interpretation of Aristotle's position on universals that goes back to Alexander of Aphrodisias and is mediated by Avicenna. The hallmark of this tradition is the view that universality is only accidental to the natures it belongs to. Scotus's view modifies this thesis to accommodate the realist side of Aristotle's thought, which this tradition sought to preserve, better than had either Alexander's or Avicenna's theories.

Tweyman, Stanley. Hurlbutt, Hume, Newton and the Design Argument. *Hume Stud*, 19(1), 167-175, Ap 93.

This paper attempts to show that a study of the dramatic elements of David Hume's *Dialogues Concerning Natural Religion* will not reveal Hume's own position—a position over and above those held by the three main speakers in the book. Professor Hurlbutt has argued the opposite position in his revised edition of *Hume, Newton and the Design Argument*.

Tweyman, Stanley. Some Reflections on Hume on Existence. *Hume Stud*, 18(2), 137-149, N 92.

I focus on two claims which Hume makes with regard to existence. The first, which appears in a single paragraph in *A Treatise of Human Nature*1.2.6, is that existence cannot be distinguished from what we believe exists by a "distinction of reason." The second appears in the *Dialogues Concerning Natural Religion* when Cleanthes criticizes Demea's a priori argument by focussing on the Humean claim, "Whatever we conceive as existent, we can also conceive as non-existent." My efforts are directed to showing that, although Hume takes very little space developing each of these points, certain difficulties attend each claim—difficulties which Hume either does not (in the case of the first) or cannot (in the case of the second) address when the claim itself is being made.

Tye, Michael. Naturalism and the Mental. *Mind*, 101(403), 421-441, Jl 92.

This paper has two aims: first, to undermine the currently popular project of naturalizing the mental via some sort of type reduction or analysis, and secondly to develop and defend a naturalistic approach to the mind which is in keeping with our ordinary, pretheoretical conception of naturalism and which has the effect of rendering the repudiated reductions otiose. Some remarks running counter to orthodoxy are also made about the relationship of the mental to the physical and about Brentano's Problem.

Tye, Michael. Visual Qualia and Visual Content in The Contents of Experience, Crane, Tim (ed). New York, Cambridge Univ Pr, 1992.

Tyler, Stephen A. In Other Words: The Other as *Inventio*, Allegory, and Symbol. *Human Stud*, 16(1-2), 19-32, Ap 93.

The idea of the other in western discourse is expressed in the narrative of the symbol — the movement in the psyche from pathemata to imaginatio to intellectio. That narrative is the allegorical base for other narratives such as person - society - culture. This "history of semiosis" and its allegories are the inventio of the other.

Tyler, Stephen A. Is the Switch 'On'?. *J Prag*, 17(5-6), 545-547, Je 92.

Tyman, Stephen. *Descrying the Ideal: The Philosophy of John William Miller*. Carbondale, So Illinois Univ Pr, 1993.

This book serves as an introduction to the work of the American Idealist, John William Miller. The focus is not only upon accessibility, but also timeliness and historical context. Thus, there are notable comparisons with figures from the idealist tradition, predominantly German, as well as issue-oriented discussions framed in reference to contemporary hermeneutics and deconstruction.

Tymieniecka, Anna-Teresa (ed). *Analecta Husserliana, XXXI*. Dordrecht, Kluwer, 1990.

Tymieniecka, Anna-Teresa (ed). *Analecta Husserliana, XXXIV*. Dordrecht, Kluwer, 1992.

Tymieniecka, Anna-Teresa (ed). *Analecta Husserliana, XXXVIII*. Dordrecht, Kluwer, 1992.

Tymieniecka, Anna-Teresa. Phenomenology of Life and the New Critique of Reason in Analecta Husserliana, XXXIV, Tymieniecka, Anna-Teresa (ed). Dordrecht, Kluwer, 1992.

Tymieniecka, Anna-Teresa. The Human Condition within the Unity-of-Everything in Analecta Husserliana, XXXI, Tymieniecka, Anna-Teresa (ed). Dordrecht, Kluwer, 1990.

At the crossroads of great scientific and technological discoveries A-T Tymieniecka's *phenomenology of life and of the human condition* with its strikingly original conception of the 'human condition', substitutes for the outdated philosophical anthropologies and conceptions of 'human nature' which take human being out of its natural context, and replaces him/her in the original unity of emerging and unfolding forms of life. Operating concurrently a critic of reason, this original approach discovers the *creative virtuality* as the Archimedean point of the human condition- in- *the unity- of- everything- there- is alive*. Creative function of the human being as a unique phase of life's unfolding precludes reducing man to the bios.

Tymoczko, Thomas and Vogel, Jonathan. The Exorcist's Nightmare: A Reply to Crispin Wright. *Mind*, 101(403), 543-552, Jl 92.

Crispin Wright tried to refute classical 'Cartesian' skepticism contending that its core argument is extendible to a reductio ad absurdum (Mind, 100, 87-116, 1991). We show both that Wright is mistaken and that his mistakes are philosophically illuminating. Wright's 'best version' of skepticism turns on a concept of warranted belief. By his definition, many of our well-founded beliefs about the external world and mathematics would not be warranted. Wright's position worsens if we take 'warranted belief' to be implicitly defined by the general principles governing it. Those principles are inconsistent, as shown by a variant of Gödel's argument. Thus the inconsistency Wright found has nothing to do with the special premises of Cartesian skepticism, but is embedded in his own conceptual apparatus. Lastly, we show how a Cartesian skeptic could avoid Wright's critique by reconstructing a skeptical argument that does not use the claims Wright ultimately finds objectionable.

Tzavaras, Athanase and Papagounos, G. The Development of Freudian Theory in Greek Studies in the Philosophy and History of Science, Nicolacopoulos, Pantelis (ed). Dordrecht, Kluwer, 1990.

The authors develop the "centric-excentric" approach to account for the diffusion of Freudian theory. This approach explains the phenomenon of the simultaneous production, elaboration and diffusion of the psychoanalytic theory and it further ellucidates the various debates on orthodoxy and heterodoxy concerning the main tenets of the theory and the practice of psychoanalysis which were carried out in North America and the continent. The case of French psychoanalysis and in particular J Lacan is illustrative of the mode of investigation which the approach permits. Greek psychoanalysis provides another illustration of "excentric" characteristics in the case on Andreas Empiricos.

Tzu, Lao and Bahm, Archie J (trans). *Tao Teh King—Lao Tzu*. Albuquerque, World Books, 1986.

Udovicki, Jasminka. Justice and Care in Close Associations. *Hypatia*, 8(3), 48-60, Sum 93.

The essay examines the impartialist view of justice as the first virtue of all relationships. I argue that in close associations where duties, obligations, and rights of persons are situationally contingent, abstract principles of justice fail to yield a unified moral perspective about what is fair. Solidarity and trust as moral emotions develop more complex moral competencies that go beyond what principles of justice alone require.

Uebel, Thomas. Neurath vs Carnap: Naturalism vs Rational Reconstructionism Before Quine. *Hist Phil Quart*, 9(4), 445-470, O 92.

Uebel, Thomas. Rational Reconstruction as Elucidation? Carnap in the Early Protocol Sentence Debate. *Synthese*, 93(1-2), 107-140, N 92.

Uebel, Thomas E. Neuraths Protokollsätze als Antwort auf Kritik seines Fallibilismus. *Conceptus*, 25(65), 85-104, 1991.

This paper shows a new approach to naturalistic epistemology which is formulated in Neurath's theory of protocol sentences. The possibility of science out of itself is demonstrated in contrast to criteria like evidence, unrevisability, etc., which are postulated from outside science. Neurath's epistemology—if we want to label it this way at all—has been far more complex and more relying on empiricism than its classical critics thought it to be. Following the presentation of criticisms against Neurath's fallibilism—which has been (mis)understood to be a "coherence theory of truth"—six principles of a naturalistic epistemology will be formulated. These principles are the foundation of Neurath's theory of protocol sentences. (edited)

Uebel, Thomas E. *Overcoming Logical Positivism from Within: The Emergence of Neurath's Naturalism in the Vienna Circle's Protocol Sentence Debate*. Amsterdam, Rodopi, 1992.

While the member and associates of the Vienna Circle exercised a great influence on the formation of Anglo-American analytic philosophy, their presumed 'logical positivism' has radically fallen out of favor since analytic philosophy has come of age. It is the author's contention that the widespread sense of having 'left behind' logical positivism can be maintained only by distorting the picture of the Vienna Circle itself. He argues against the common misconception of the Circle's epistemologies as foundationalist in general and specifically reconstructs Otto Neurath's naturalistic-pragmatic theory of science which anticipated many of the criticisms which led to the demise of the orthodox 'received view' in the 1950s and 60s.

Ueding, Wolfgang Maria. Die Verhältnismässigkeit der Mittel bzw die Mittelmässigkeit der Verhältnisse in Diagrammatik und Philosophie, Gehring, Petra (ed). Amsterdam, Rodopi, 1992.

Starting with a passage from Plato's "Phaedrus" several theoretical and practical instances of diagrams in Plato are enacted. More specifically the "Divided Line" of the "Politeia" is diagrammatically reconstructed. This reconstruction provides materials for the discussion of the philosophical importance of diagrams in general on the one hand and for an innovative harmonical interpretation of the special example of the "Divided Line" on the other hand — materials which are derived from mathematics and from musicology.

Uher, J. S Stur's "Treatise on Life" (in Czechoslovakian). *Filozof Cas*, 40(3), 476-488, 1992.

Svätopluk Stúr (1901-1981) was one of the leading philosophers of democratic orientation in Slovakia. He was a professor at the Bratislava University and was active mainly in the period between the world wars and in 1945-1948. He considered his philosophy to be a peculiar form of critical realism and a part of the modern liberal philosophical movement. He adopted creatively the humanistic thoughts of T G Masaryk, B Croce, J L Fischer and other European thinkers and he developed them in the special situation of Slovakia. He was discriminated by both the totalitarian regime of the years 1939-1944 and the communist regime after 1948, when he was not allowed to teach at the university. His *Treatise on Life*, written during the Nazi occupation dealt with a *philosophy of life*; with *art*-as its specific form and part; with *science*-as the theoretical order of the world; with *ethics*-as the practical order of the social life. (edited)

Uhlaner, Jonathan and Reinecke, Volker. The Problem of Leo Strauss: Religion, Philosophy and Politics. *Grad Fac Phil J*, 16(1), 189-208, 1993.

Ujlaki, Gabriella. The Logic of Representation. *Brit J Aes*, 33(2), 121-131, Ap 93.

The paper is concerned with showing a possible way of dealing with representation in pictures. The paper uses Michael Polanyi's theory of tacit knowledge. According to Polanyi we can distinguish two different ways of seeing pictures: indication and symbolization. Whereas indication is a process which has meaning in that of symbolization meaning is incarnated. These different kinds of meanings serve for having a sufficient basis to analyze which type of meaning has a naturalistic paintings meaning is embedded in the route from the model to the picture as they mutually refer to each other and establish each other's meanings.

Umapathy, Ranjan. The Mandukay Upanisad and Karikas: The Advaitic Approach. *Indian Phil Quart*, 20(3), 243-263, Jl 93.

Unger, Peter. *Identity, Consciousness and Value*. New York, Oxford Univ Pr, 1992.

The topic of personal identity is the main focus of this book. The author presents an account of our identity over time that, as it is psychologically aimed but physically based, is very different from any in the literature. While supporting the account, he explains why many currently influential philosophers have underrated the importance of physical continuity to personal survival, including D Lewis, R Nozick, D Parfit, J Perry and S Shoemaker. Going beyond this, the author explores the implications of his account for questions of the good life and other evaluative issues.

Uniacke, Suzanne and McCloskey, H J. Peter Singer and Non-Voluntary 'Euthanasia': Tripping Down the Slippery Slope. *J Applied Phil*, 9(2), 203-219, 1992.

This article discusses the nature of euthanasia, and the way in which redevelopment of the concept of euthanasia in some influential recent philosophical writing has led to morally less discriminating killing/letting die/not saving being misdescribed as euthanasia. Peter Singer's defense of non-voluntary 'euthanasia' of defective infants in his influential book *Practical Ethics* is critically evaluated. We argue that Singer's pseudo-euthanasia arguments in *Practical Ethics* are unsatisfactory as approaches to determining the legitimacy of killing, and that these arguments present a total utilitarian improvement policy—not a case for non-voluntary euthanasia.

Upin, Jane. Applying the Concept of Gender: Unsettled Questions. *Hypatia*, 7(3), 180-187, Sum 92.

In commenting on Susan Bordo's discussion of gender bias, I both support and build on her contention that women's exclusion from philosophical discourse has been epistemologically and politically significant. But I also explore difficulties associated with applying the concept of gender and I voice concern about how to characterize the perspectives we share as women. Finally, I consider some theoretical and political limitations of utilizing gender as an analytical category.

Upin, Jane. Charlotte Perkins Gilman: Instrumentalism Beyond Dewey. *Hypatia*, 8(2), 38-63, Spr 93.

Charlotte Perkins Gilman and John Dewey were both pragmatists who recognized the need to restructure the environment to bring about social progress. Gilman was even more of a pragmatist than Dewey, however, because she addressed problems he did not identify—much less confront. Her philosophy is in accord with the spirit of Dewey's work but in important ways, it is more consistent, more comprehensive and more radical than his instrumentalism.

Upton, Hugh. On Applying Moral Theories. *J Applied Phil*, 10(2), 189-199, 1993.

This paper takes issue with the idea that there is a variety of moral theories available which can in some way usefully be applied to problems in ethics. The idea is reflected in the common view that those favouring a systematic approach would do well to abandon consequentialist thinking and turn to some alternative theory. It is argued here that this is not an option, since each of the usual supposed alternatives lacks the independent resources to meet the minimal requirements of being a moral theory at all. The aim is to demonstrate that virtue ethics, rights theory and deontology lack the different forms of explanation that would make them genuinely alternative theories. The conclusion is that this part of ethics is much more of a unity than is standardly assumed and that, far from our being able to move on from consequentialism, certain problems that arise from its very nature are bound to remain central to any attempt at moral theory.

Urbach, Peter. Regression Analysis: Classical and Bayesian. *Brit J Phil Sci*, 43(3), 311-342, S 92.

The foundations of classical approaches to regression analysis are examined, especially the method of least squares, the classical treatment of outliers and data analysis techniques, including 'influence' methodology. It is agreed that these methods are ill-founded and arbitrary and that the aspects of them which are reasonable are best understood in Bayesian terms.

Urbas, Igor. Curry's Paradox and *Modus Ponens*. *J Non-Classical Log*, 8(1), 35-38, My 91.

Urchs, Max. On Determinism—Still Unproved in Classical Logic. *Bull Sec Log*, 21(4), 168-170, D 92.

According to Lukasiewicz, the principle of determinism is inevitable in classical logic. (This motivates the construction of his three-valued logic.) Lukasiewicz's argument, however, is not fully convincing.

Urmson, J O (trans). *Simplicius: On Aristotle's "Physics" 4.1-5, 10-14*. Ithaca, Cornell Univ Pr, 1992.

Usher, Robin. Experience in Adult Education: A Post-Modern Critique. *J Phil Educ*, 26(2), 201-214, 1992.

The concepts of experience and experiential learning are of critical significance in both the study and practice of adult education. Adults are seen as uniquely characterized by their experience, experiential learning an alternative to didactic and knowledge-based modes of education. In this paper a critique is presented of the powerful discourse of the autonomous subject based on humanistic psychology which, it is argued, has shaped adult education in a misleading, inappropriate and unhelpful way. A post-modern perspective drawing on Continental philosophy is utilized. The 'situated' subject provides a conception of subjectivity and experience which preserves a needed dimension of agency whilst avoiding psychologism and individualism.

Utz, Stephen. Rules, Principles, Algorithms and the Description of Legal Systems. *Ratio Juris*, 5(1), 23-45, Mr 92.

Although the Hart/Dworkin debate has as much to do with Dworkin's affirmative theory of judicial discretion as with Hart's more comprehensive theory of law, the starting point was of course Dworkin's attempt to demolish the "model of rules," Hart's alleged analysis of legal systems as collections of conclusive reasons for specified legal consequences. The continuing relevance of this attack for the prospects for any theory of law is the subject of the present essay.

Uusitalo, Jyrki. Abduction, Legal Reasoning, and Reflexive Law in Peirce and Law, Kevelson, Roberta. New York, Lang, 1991.

Vadas, Melinda. The Pornography/Civil Rights Ordinance versus The BOG: And the Winner Is...?. *Hypatia*, 7(3), 94-109, Sum 92.

The Supreme Court dismissed the Pornography/Civil Rights Ordinance as an unconstitutional restriction of speech. The Court's dismissal itself violates the free speech of the proposers of the Ordinance. It is not possible for both pornographers to perform the speech act of making pornography and feminists to perform the speech act proposing the Ordinance. I show that the speech act of proposing the Ordinance takes First Amendment precedence over the speech act of making pornography.

Vaden House, D and McDonald, Marvin J. Post-physicalism and Beyond. *Dialogue (Canada)*, 31(4), 593-621, Autumn 92.

Vailati, Ezio. Clarke's Extended Soul. *J Hist Phil*, 31(3), 387-403, Jl 93.

Clarke held that the soul is both extended because it can act on the body, and an indivisible essential unity because it can think. This view was attached by philosophers as different as Collins and Leibniz. The paper studies Clarke's reasons for his view and his defense of it in the light of those criticisms.

Valalas, Theresa Pentzopoulou. Phenomenology and Teleology: Husserl and Fichte in Analecta Husserliana, XXXIV, Tymieniecka, Anna-Teresa (ed). Dordrecht, Kluwer, 1992.

The paper discusses Husserl's idea of philosophy. Philosophy is assigned to the task of shifting from a theory of knowledge strict sense to a theory of absolute knowledge.

AUTHOR INDEX WITH ABSTRACTS 705 Van De Putte, A

Thus, if philosophy's ultimate task is the discovery of rationality Husserl's closeness to Fichte is tempting. The subject is discussed on the grounds of both philosophers' transcendentalism and their respective teleological conception of philosophy.

Valauri, John T. Constitutional Hermeneutics in The Interpretive Turn, Hiley, David R (ed). Ithaca, Cornell Univ Pr, 1991.

This essay presents a practical hermeneutic approach to three chronic problems in American constitutional law—framers' intent, the search for consensus in method, and foundational anxiety. A turn to narrative, practice, and anti-reduction (i.e., a postmodern jurisprudence) is prescribed as the therapy for dissolving these problems.

Valauri, John T. Peirce and Holmes in Peirce and Law, Kevelson, Roberta. New York, Lang, 1991.

This article explores some suggestive parallels in the writings of Charles Peirce and Oliver Wendell Holmes, Jr on philosophy and law. It focuses on their rejection of Cartesianism (and, along with it, deductivism and subjectivism) in inquiry and their emphasis on the importance of experience in determining meaning. Topics discussed include experiment, prediction, and realism.

Valberg, J J. The Puzzle of Experience in The Contents of Experience, Crane, Tim (ed). New York, Cambridge Univ Pr, 1992.

This paper sets out a puzzle about the object of experience: when we *reason* about our experience in a certain way, we are driven to the conclusion that the object cannot be part of the world; but if we are then *open* to our experience, all we find is the world. (The paper is, in effect, the first two chapters of a book, by the same title, in which the puzzle is explored. See *The Puzzle of Experience*, Oxford University Press, 1992.)

Valdés, Margarita M. Commentator on 'Women and the Quality of Life' in The Quality of Life, Nussbaum, Martha C (ed). New York, Oxford Univ Pr, 1993.

A discussion of Julia Annas' paper included in the same volume. It concentrates on: i) the epistemological problem concerning how we come to detect injustice to women within our own society, and ii) whether the notion of 'human nature' introduced by Annas serves to provide us with one ideal norm for human lives. Anna's proposal to consider judgments concerning injustice to women as systematically backward-looking is criticized as insufficient for grounding rational internal criticism with respect to injustice to women. It is also argued that a notion of 'human nature' capable of explaining injustice to women has to be 'thicker' than that introduced by Annas.

Vallauri, Luigi Lombardi. A Roman Catholic Concept of Justice. *Ratio Juris*, 5(3), 308-330, D 92.

The author collates a Roman Catholic concept of justice with the general principles of law and justice. He explores the Church's stand on earthly justice and deals extensively with divine justice, moving to the criticism of its dogmas from original sin to redemption, ecclesiology, and the sacraments to hell, purgatory and paradise and the problems these concepts entail. He concludes by focussing on a paradox in Catholic thinking and the new trend in Catholic theology.

Vallée, Richard. Signification conventionnelle et non-littéralité. *Dialogue (Canada)*, 31(1), 51-64, Wint 92.

Les énonciations non littérales (métaphore, ironie, synecdoque) sont parfois conçues en terme de modification, par un locuteur, de la signification conventionnelle d'une expression linguistique. Je formule un argument, inspiré des analyses gricéennes en théorie de la signification, pour démontrer qu'un locuteur ne peut changer la signification conventionnelle d'une expression linguistique. Les intentions de signifier d'un locuteur ne sont pas suffisantes pour ce faire. De plus, une intention de faire signifier à une expression quelque chose que cette expression ne signifie pas vient en contradiction avec certaines croyances du locuteur relativement aux attentes des auditeurs.

Vallentyne, Peter. The Connection Between Prudential and Moral Goodness. *J Soc Phil*, 24(2), 105-128, Fall 93.

In *Weighing Goods* John Broome provides an elegant rational choice argument for utilitarianism. I criticize a number of fundamental assumptions of his argument. I argue that *prudential* weak betterness need not be continuous, be weakly separable, be expectationally cardinal, allow for objective interpersonal comparisons, or satisfy the Rectangular Field assumption. I argue further that *moral* weak betterness need not be complete or continuous. If at least one of these criticisms is sound, then Broome's argument is unsound.

Vallentyne, Peter. Utilitarianism and Infinite Utility. *Austl J Phil*, 71(2), 212-217, Je 93.

It is often supposed that utilitarianism faces a serious problem if the future is infinitely long. For in that case, actions may produce an infinite amount of utility. And if that is so for most actions, then utilitarianism, it appears, loses most of its power to discriminate among actions. For, if most actions produce an infinite amount of utility, then few actions produce non-maximal utility, and so most actions are permissible. I argue that potentially infinite futures create no major problems for utilitarianism. Utilitarianism has, I argue, the resources to distinguish among actions all of which produce infinite amounts of utility — judging some permissible and some impermissible.

Vallentyne, Peter and Lipson, Morrice. Child Liberationism and Legitimate Interference. *J Soc Phil*, 23(3), 5-15, Wint 92.

Vallicella, William F. Divine Simplicity: A New Defense. *Faith Phil*, 9(4), 508-525, O 92.

The doctrine of divine simplicity, according to which God is devoid of physical or metaphysical complexity, is widely believed to be incoherent. I argue that although two prominent recent attempts to defend it fail, it can be defended against the charge of obvious incoherence. The defense rests on the isolation and rejection of a crucial assumption, namely, that no property is an individual to warrant the assumption, and that once the assumption is rejected, the way is clear to viewing the divine attributes as self-exemplifying properties whose self-exemplification entails their identity with an individual.

Vallicella, William F. Has the Ontological Argument Been Refuted?. *Relig Stud*, 29(1), 97-110, Mr 93.

It is nowadays widely accepted that there are valid modal versions of the Ontological Argument. Nevertheless, the probative force of these versions has been attacked on at least two grounds. First, that the argument begs the question at the crucial premise that states, in effect, that God is possible; second, that the crucial premise is more rationally rejected than accepted. This article rebuts both charges. Along the way, certain dogmatic assumptions of the critics are exposed. Among them, the conceit that nothing concrete can necessarily exist.

Valls, Francisco Rodríguez. Experiencia y conocimiento en David Hume. *Themata*, 8, 45-67, 1991.

Hume's concern is an enquiry on human nature in which clearly appears on the foundation of experience how human faculties of knowledge attain their objects and which epistemological foundations of assertions about them are. It is possible a deductive knowledge as far as mind makes a comparison among its abstract ideas. In so far mind tries to grasp objects only apprehensible by senses its foundation is sensitive experience. Hume's main interest is that second sphere of mind; his problem is if such an experience is enough as a solid ground in order to get an inductive knowledge.

Valverde Jr, L James. Risk and Public Decision-Making: Constructivism and the Postpositivist Challenge. *Int J Applied Phil*, 7(2), 53-56, Wint 92.

Van Bavel, Tarsicius. The Creator and the Integrity of Creation in the Fathers of the Church, Especially in Saint Augustine. *Augustin Stud*, 21, 1-33, 1990.

Van Bendegem, Jean Paul. How Infinities Cause Problems in Classical Physical Theories. *Philosophica*, 50(2), 33-54, 1992.

It is argued in this paper that physical theories such as classical mechanics and special relativity theory must accept restrictions on the use of infinite quantities in order to maintain determinism. The quantities involved are velocity, acceleration, force and matter. The argumentation relies on the use of supertasks, such as Thomson's lamp, and introduces some new type of related tasks, such as Etter's bars and Zeno's bowling game.

Van Benthem, Johan. Modelling the Kinematics of Meaning. *Proc Aris Soc*, 93, 105-122, 1993.

Recent theories of meaning revolve around contextual change and informational updates. We explore three broad logical models for this cognitive dynamics, being based on programs, proofs and games, respectively. In particular, some parallels are pursued in all three cases as to logical inference and effective computability.

Van Brakel, J. Eliminativisme gereduceerd tot pragmatisme. *Alg Ned Tijdschr Wijs*, 85(1), 113-127, F 93.

P.M. Churchland wants to combine eliminativism in the philosophy of mind with scientific realism in the philosophy of science, drawing on connectionism (neural nets) as the new paradigm. In this paper I analyse the metaphysical coherence of Churchland's position, looking in particular at his view on natural kinds and prototype vectors. I show that 1) eliminativism and prototype vectors together eliminate everything, not only folk psychology, and 2) the result is best described as a form of pragmatic or pluralistic realism. Hence, on Churchland's own terms, there is no ground for a special place for science.

Van Brakel, J. Natural Kinds and Theories of Reference. *Dialectica*, 46(3-4), 243-261, 1992.

In this paper I try to make sense of and give provisional answers to questions like: Are there interesting theories about natural kinds (distinguishing them from other kinds)? Are some classifications or categorisations more natural than others? Does it matter whether or not there are natural kinds? To get an initial feel for the subject let's consider some suggestions from the literature as to what might count as a candidate for a natural kind or natural kind term.

Van Brakel, J. The Plasticity of Categories: The Case of Colour. *Brit J Phil Sci*, 44(1), 103-135, Mr 93.

Probably colour is the best worked out example of allegedly neurophysiologically innate response categories determining percepts and percepts determining concepts, and hence biology fixing the basic categories implicit in the use of language. In this paper I review evidence from introspection, linguistics, anthropology, neurophysiology, and psychology and I conclude that, at least in the case of colour, current science supports a plasticity in the formation of categories that goes far beyond the requirements of those naturalistic philosophers who would like to ground primitive concepts in biology.

Van Buren, E John. Heidegger's *Sache*: A Family Portrait. *Res Phenomenol*, 22, 161-184, 1992.

Van Buren, E John. Heidegger's Autobiographies. *J Brit Soc Phenomenol*, 23(3), 201-221, O 92.

Van Buren, E John. The Young Heidegger, Aristotle, Ethics in Ethics and Danger, Dallery, Arleen B (ed). Albany, SUNY Pr, 1992.

An analysis of Heidegger's interpretation of Aristotle in the early 1920s, as well as the significance of this interpretation for ethics.

Van Cleve, James. Semantic Supervenience and Referential Indeterminacy. *J Phil*, 89(7), 344-361, Jl 92.

Van Dalen, D. The Continuum and First-Order Intuitionistic Logic. *J Sym Log*, 57(4), 1417-1424, D 92.

The paper confirms the view that the reals and the irrationals are constructively similar. It is shown that they have the same first-order properties for ordering and apartness. A number of similar results are proved. The main tool is Fraïsse's "local isomorphism".

Van De Putte, A. E Burke and the Natural Law: About the Foundations of Conservatisim (in Dutch). *Tijdschr Filosof*, 54(3), 393-423, S 92.

In this study, an attempt is made to understand why Burke at the same time refers to the natural law and to the principle of inheritance as moral standards for the human will. Indeed, the latter principle implies reference to a particular tradition, whereas natural law is a universal standard, binding all people. First, the meaning of the principle of inheritance in Burke's critique of the French Revolution is explained, and next the conception of the natural law he implicitly adopts. In the latter, the close link between the doctrine of the natural law and the doctrine of prudence deserves our particular attention. It is the task of prudence to given concrete form to the natural law in a way of life and a constitution, but adapting it to the concrete circumstances of a particular society. (edited)

Van De Putte, A. Nationalism and Nations (in Dutch). *Tijdschr Filosof*, 55(1), 13-47, Mr 93.

In this study an attempt has been made to understand nationalism, notably as the particular political conviction by which the realm of public and civic concern is required to coincide with a culturally and ethnically specific nationality. While exploring the idea of a nation state in its varying developments during the past few centuries, two interpretations are discovered, the revolutionary and the romantic understanding of a nation. The investigation of Jacobin nationalism leads the author to assume the existence of a secret link between the Rousseauian conception of absolute democracy and popular sovereignty, and the rise of nationalism. In conclusion, the author argues for the necessity of a different, pluralistic conception of democracy in order to prevent national feelings from degenerating into crude nationalism.

Van Den Abbeele, Georges. Communism, the Proper Name in Community at Loose Ends, Miami Theory Collect, (ed). Minneapolis, Univ of Minnesota Pr, 1991.

This article reconsiders Lyotard's work on Kripke's theory of names as "rigid designators," a theory from which Lyotard derives a politics of names as forever contested *loci* of meanings. My reading explores this problem with the help of the word "communism" as a test case at the very limit of what we can call a name, a word rife with obvious political contestation and indefinitely located between proper name and common noun.

Van Den Brink, Gijsbert. Descartes, Modalities, and God. *Int J Phil Relig*, 33(1), 1-15, F 93.

Descartes' perplexing doctrine concerning the creation of the eternal truths has recently been interpreted in various ways. More specifically, an extreme reading of the doctrine has been qualified along different lines. After having formulated a provisional rendering of the doctrine, I discuss the pros and cons of three of its recent interpretations. I argue that none of these does maximal justice to the totality of Descartes' enigmatic claims, and subsequently propose an alternative line of modifying the extreme reading, which distinguishes itself from its rivals not only by its greater integrating power, but also by its comparative simplicity.

Van Den Haag, Ernest. The *Lex Talionis* Before and After Criminal Law. *Crim Just Ethics*, 11(1), 2,62, Wint-Spr 92.

Van Den Hoven, Adrian. Nausea: Plunging Below the Surface in Sartre Alive, Aronson, Ronald (ed). Detroit, Wayne St Univ Pr, 1991.

Van Den Hoven, Adrian (ed) and Aronson, Ronald (ed). *Sartre Alive*. Detroit, Wayne St Univ Pr, 1991.

Van Den Hoven, Adrian (trans) and Sartre, Jean Paul and Aronson, Ronald (ed). *Truth and Existence—Jean-Paul Sartre*. Chicago, Univ of Chicago Pr, 1992.

Van Der Bogert, Frans. Some Reconceptions in Educational Theory: Irony and the Art of Comedy. *Proc S Atlantic Phil Educ Soc*, 36, 34-42, 1991.

Van Der Bogert, Frans and Carroll, Mary Ann. Art, Ethics and the Law: Where Should the Law End?. *Metaphilosophy*, 24(1-2), 147-154, Ja-Ap 93.

Van Der Burg, Wibren. The Slippery-Slope Argument. *J Clin Ethics*, 3(4), 256-268, Wint 92.

I analyze three forms of the slippery slope argument (two logical and one empirical) using two questions: 1. In the context of what kind of norms are we considering a first step on a possible slope: statute law, positive morality, or critical morality? 2. What is meant by "If we allow this first step"? The conclusion is that the argument's greatest force is in a context of institutionalized norms, like law, whereas its importance in morality is only marginal.

Van Der Dussen, W J. The Historian and His Evidence in Objectivity, Method and Point of View, Van Der Dussen, W J (ed). Leiden, Brill, 1991.

Van Der Dussen, W J (ed) and Rubinoff, Lionel (ed). *Objectivity, Method and Point of View*. Leiden, Brill, 1991.

Van Der Hoek, W and Meyer, J J C. Possible Logics for Belief. *Log Anal*, 32, 127-128, S-D 89.

The problem of logical omniscience, arising in many (modal) logics for belief, is discussed. Such logics yield belief-sets that are i) consistent, ii) containing all tautologies and iii) closed under logical consequences. It is proposed to modally define belief as a *possibility*, rather than a *necessity*; some of the problems noted earlier then disappear. Then, as a dual of an *awareness* operator, the authors propose to also add a *prejudice* operator to logics for belief: whereas awareness can 'filter out' unwanted beliefs, prejudices can 'spontaneously generate' desirable beliefs. It is argued that combinations of these notions can be interpreted on adjusted Kripke models.

Van Der Steen, Wim J. Additional Notes on Integration. *Biol Phil*, 8(3), 349-352, Jl 93.

This article is part of a series on interdisciplinary integration in one volume of the journal. It contains replies to criticism on the article "Toward Disciplinary Disintegration in Biology".

Van Der Steen, Wim J. Liever geen wetenschapsfilosofische supertheorieën. *Kennis Methode*, 16(3), 278-289, 1992.

Scientists have no problems with granting that their theories have limitations. Many methodological criteria apply to scientific theories. No theory can satisfy them all in a maximal degree. The context determines which criteria are important in any particular case. Hence scientific theories are a heterogeneous lot. This should have consequences for the philosophy of science. I argue that it is futile to search for *the* philosophical model of scientific theories. Likewise for models of explanation and models of meaning and reference. We had better be content with a variety of models, each of them useful in some contexts.

Van Der Steen, Wim J. Towards Disciplinary Disintegration in Biology. *Biol Phil*, 8(3), 259-275, Jl 93.

Interdisciplinary integration has fundamental limitations. This is not sufficiently realized in science and in philosophy. Concerning scientific theories there are many examples of pseudo-integration which should be unmasked by elementary philosophical analysis. For example, allegedly over-arching theories of stress which are meant to unite biology and psychology, upon analysis, turn out to represent terminological rather than substantive unity. They should be replaced by more specific, local theories. Theories of animal orientation, likewise, have been formulated in unduly general terms. A natural history approach is more suitable for the study of animal orientation. The tendency to formulate overgeneral theories is also present in evolutionary biology. Philosophy of biology can only deal with these matters if it takes a normative turn. Undue emphasis on interdisciplinary integration is a modern variant of the old unity of science ideal. The replacement of the ideal by a better one is an important challenge for the philosophy of science.

Van Der Steen, Wim J and Musschenga, Bert. The Issue of Generality in Ethics. *J Value Inq*, 26(4), 511-524, O 92.

The methodologies of ethics and empirical science should be similar to a large extent. Unfortunately methodology is underdeveloped in ethics. Due to this ethicists do not realize sufficiently that possibilities for the elaboration of general theories are limited. Methodological analysis shows that the views of researchers aiming at general theories and researchers aiming at casuistry are not as different as the literature suggests. Controversies concerning this are spurious in view of ambiguities in the notion of generality and the notion of theory.

Van Der Veken, Jan. Whitehead and Kant on Presuppositions of Meaning. *Ultim Real Mean*, 15(4), 275-285, D 92.

Van Der Wal, Gerrit. Unrequested Termination of Life: Is It Permissible?. *Bioethics*, 7(4), 330-339, Jl 93.

Van Dijk, A M G. An Early Neo-Hindu Reception of Nietzsche by Sri Aurobindo Ghose (1872-1950) (in Dutch). *Bijdragen*, 53(3), 264-290, 1992.

Having been educated in England from his seventh to his twenty first year and as someone deeply interested in classical literature, philosophy, English and French literature, young Aurobindo became more and more interested in European revolutionary thought, and wanted to use its inspiration for the liberation of his 'Motherland' India from colonial oppression. His attitude towards Christianity remained quite ambivalent and he confronted it repeatedly with his ideal of a Hindu Renascence (sic). Nietzsche intrigued him because of his idea of the superman. The idea itself may have come to Aurobindo from Hellenistic philosophy and from Carlyle in 1915 Aurobindo first shows a knowledge of Nietzsche's *Ecce Homo*. (edited)

Van Doan, Tran. The Ideological Education and Moral Education in Chinese Foundations for Moral Education and Character Development, Van Doan, Tran (ed). Washington, CRVP, 1991.

This paper has a double aim: 1) to analyze the ideological essence in Chinese moral education and 2) to criticize its over-emphasis in ideological indoctrination. The analysis of Chinese moral education reveals also the inner relation between ideology and interests, and the true motives behind moral education: moral education or Confucian education serves primarily as an instrument to grab, consolidate and defend interests. Consequently, our critique of ideological indoctrination aims at breaking up such a moral education. The abolition of ideological education means an abolition of the monopoly of interests in the hands of a class.

Van Doan, Tran (ed) and Shen, Vincent (ed) and McLean, George F (ed). *Chinese Foundations for Moral Education and Character Development*. Washington, CRVP, 1991.

This volume consists of 9 chapters which are divided in three parts: 1) the first part studies the basic characters of morals in the Chinese Classics; 2) the second part offers some modern views on the growth of human characters and morale, while 3) the third part deals specifically with the moral education in modern China. The conclusion reached by the co-authors of this volume is: a moral education should be based on 1) traditional resources and 2) a full understanding of man (human nature, human development etc.).

Van Dormael, Jan. Analogical Reasoning: A Logical Inquiry About "Archaic Thought". *Commun Cog*, 25(2-3), 243-258, 1992.

Van Dorp, P. Aristotle on Two Kinds of Memory: Platonic Reminiscences (in Dutch). *Tijdschr Filosof*, 54(3), 457-492, S 92.

In his short treatise *De memoria et reminiscentia* ("On Memory and Recollection") Aristotle makes an implicit distinction between two kinds of memory: rational "recollection" and non-rational "memory". To twentieth-century readers such a dichotomy of memory comes rather as a surprise. This is the reason why the dichotomy of memory has not been interpreted correctly. For the most part it even passed unnoticed. In this essay two aspects of this distinction are examined. First, it is established what is meant by "memory" and "recollection" and how these activities are related to each other. Secondly, it is argued that Aristotle did not conceive this theory of memory in an intellectual vacuum, by the sole use of open-minded observation. (edited)

Van Fleteren, Frederick. A Reply to Robert O'Connell's "Faith, Reason, and Ascent to Vision in Saint Augustine". *Augustin Stud*, 21, 127-137, 1990.

Van Fraassen, Bas. Armstrong, Cartwright, and Earman on *Laws and Symmetry*. *Phil Phenomenol Res*, 53(2), 431-444, Je 93.

Van Fraassen, Bas. Précis of *Laws and Symmetry*. *Phil Phenomenol Res*, 53(2), 411-412, Je 93.

Van Fraassen, Bas C. The Geometry of Opinion: Jeffrey Shifts and Linear Operators. *Phil Sci*, 59(2), 163-175, Je 92.

Richard Jeffrey and Michael Goldstein have both introduced systematic approaches to the structure of opinion changes. For both approaches there are theorems which indicate great generality and width of scope. The main questions addressed here will be to what extent the basic forms of representation are intertranslatable, and how we can conceive of such programs in general.

AUTHOR INDEX WITH ABSTRACTS 707 Van Praag, B M S

Van Gulick, Robert. Three Bad Arguments for Intentional Property Epiphenomenalism. *Erkenntnis*, 36(3), 311-331, M 92.

Three widely held and initially plausible arguments for intentional property epiphenomenalism are explicity stated and critically examined: The Strict Law Argument, The Exclusion Argument, and The Argument from Lack of Individual Supervenience. Despite their initial plausibility each of the three arguments is shown to be unsound.

Van Gulick, Robert. Understanding the Phenomenal Mind: Are We All Just Armadillos? in Consciousness: Psychological and Philosophical Essays, Davies, Martin (ed). Cambridge, Blackwell, 1993.

Van Gulick, Robert. Who's in Charge Here? And Who's Doing All the Work? in Mental Causation, Heil, John (ed). New York, Clarendon/Oxford Pr, 1993.

Van Gulick, Robert (ed) and LePore, Ernest (ed). *John Searle and His Critics*. Cambridge, Blackwell, 1991.

This anthology includes articles from an interdisciplinary group of scholars — philosophers, psychologists, neuro-scientists — and is dedicated to an analysis and assessment of the work of John Searle. Each part of the book is capped with a response from Searle. Topics covered include: Meaning and speech acts; the mind-body problem; perception; intentionality; reference; the background of intentionality and action; social explanation; and ontology.

Van Haaften, Wouter. Conceptual Development and Relativism: Reply to Siegel. *J Phil Educ*, 27(1), 87-100, Sum 93.

I defend that the development of children may include foundational change, such that stages can be reconstructed representing different views of (the relevant aspect of) reality and involving different forms of judgement in that domain. This implies fundamental stage-relativism. Claims that such stages are better than their forerunners can be justified, if at all, only on a stage-bound criteria. This does not preclude the possibility of justifying them, however, except to persons in lower stages. The development produces the possibility of its justification. Education cannot, therefore, be conceived as communication between equals. Reality is different for children, not simply defective or wrong.

Van Haute, Philippe. Lacan's Philosophical Reference: Heidegger of Kojève?. *Int Phil Quart*, 32(2), 225-238, Je 92.

Van Hoecke, Mark and Ost, François. Epistemological Perspectives in Legal Theory. *Ratio Juris*, 6(1), 30-47, Mr 93.

The authors deal with several important epistemological problems in legal theory. The nineteenth century background is analyzed from the emergence of legal science freed from the constraints of natural law and built on the model of the empirical sciences. The authors show how this science of law has been influenced by the social sciences and trends in ideological criticism throughout the twentieth century. The epistemological question central to legal science is tackled, i.e., what kind of "epistemological break" should there be with regard to the object studied? To answer this question, the authors plead for the adoption of a "moderate external point of view" which bears in mind lawyers' "internal point of view."

Van Holthoon, F L. Adam Smith and David Hume: With Sympathy. *Utilitas*, 5(1), 35-48, My 93.

Van Hook, Jay M. Caves, Canons, and the Ironic Teacher in Richard Rorty's Philosophy of Education. *Metaphilosophy*, 24(1-2), 167-174, Ja-Ap 93.

In this paper I discuss Richard Rorty's philosophy of education in the context of his critique of both Plato and Allan Bloom, and as it emerges from his views concerning irony and solidarity. Rorty's view that lower education is primarily a matter of socialization (solidarity) while higher education serves the purpose of ironic self-creation is examined and criticized. I argue that the functions of lower and higher education cannot and should not be divided as sharply as Rorty suggests.

Van Huyssteen, J Wentzel. What Epistemic Values Should We Reclaim for Religion and Science? A Response to J Wesley Robbins. *Zygon*, 28(3), 371-376, S 93.

Postmodernism in science rejects and deconstructs the cultural dominance of especially the natural sciences in our time. Although it presents the debate between religion and science with a promising epistemological holism, it also seriously challenges attempts to develop a meaningful relationship between science and religion. A neopragmatist perspective on religion and science is part of this important challenge and eminently reveals the problems and reduction that arise when pragmatist criteria alone are used to construct a holism that renounces any demarcation between different areas of rationality. In this pragmatist vision for a holist culture, the cognitive resources of rationality are bypassed in such a way that a meaningful interaction between theology and science becomes impossible.

Van Inwagen, Peter. *Précis of* Material Beings. *Phil Phenomenol Res*, 53(3), 683-686, S 93.

Van Inwagen, Peter. Genesis and Evolution in Reasoned Faith, Stump, Eleonore (ed). Ithaca, Cornell Univ Pr, 1993.

How shall a Christian or Jew who, like St. Augustine, is not a "fundamentalist", but who believes that Genesis 1-3 is divinely inspired, approach this text? An answer to this question is proposed and defended. It is also argued that, although there is nothing in the Darwinian explanation of the fossil record and the present diversity of like that is strictly inconsistent with theism, the widespread adherence to this explanation is at least partly motivated by its supposed anti-theistic implications, and that it in fact rests on rather shaky grounds.

Van Inwagen, Peter. Problem of Evil, Problem of Air, and the Problem of Silence in Philosophical Perspectives, 5: Philosophy of Religion, 1991, Tomberlin, James E (ed). Atascadero, Ridgeview, 1991.

It has been argued that it is unreasonable to accept theism because there is a competing hypothesis that better explains the patterns of suffering in nature. I give reasons for regarding this argument as unconvincing. I underscore the points I have made by considering two analogous arguments: An ancient Greek ought not to have accepted atomism because there was available a competing hypothesis that better explained the gaseous state; One ought not to accept the thesis that there is intelligence elsewhere in the galaxy because there is a competing hypothesis that better explains the observed fact of "cosmic silence".

Van Inwagen, Peter. Reply to Reviewers. *Phil Phenomenol Res*, 53(3), 709-719, S 93.

Van Inwagen, Peter. Searle on Ontological Commitment in John Searle and His Critics, Lepore, Ernest (ed). Cambridge, Blackwell, 1991.

This article discusses Searle's criticism of Quine's "criterion of ontological commitment" in *Speech Acts*. I argue that Searle has misunderstood Quine in several important respects, and that his arguments do not refute Quine's real theses on "ontological commitment."

Van Inwagen, Peter. There Is No Such Thing As Addition. *Midwest Stud Phil*, 17, 138-159, 1992.

If the addition operation exists, it is one of the *c* binary operation on the natural numbers. I argue that the referential resources of human beings are unequal to the task of picking out any *one* operation from this vast multitude. Hence, the words 'the addition operation' do not denote anything; that is, there is no such thing as addition. The argument for the conclusion that human beings are unable to single out a particular binary operation on the natural numbers is inspired by Kripke's presentation of the "quus" paradox in *Wittgenstein on Rules and Private Language*.

Van Lambalgen, Michiel. Independence, Randomness and the Axiom of Choice. *J Sym Log*, 57(4), 1274-1304, D 92.

We investigate various ways of introducing axioms for randomness in set theory. The results show that these axioms, when added to ZF, imply the failure of AC. But the axiom of extensionality plays an essential role in the derivation, and a deeper analysis may ultimately show that randomness is incompatible with extensionality.

Van Leeuwen, Evert and Hertogh, Cees. The Right to Genetic Information: Some Reflections on Dutch Developments. *J Med Phil*, 17(4), 381-393, Ag 92.

New developments in genetics are rapidly spreading over the Western World. The standards of clinical practice differ however according to local value and health-care systems. In this article a short survey is given of Dutch developments in this field. An effort is made to explain the philosophical and ethical background of Dutch policy by concentrating on autonomy, responsibility and the right not to know.

Van Niekerk, Anton. Relativism versus Ethnocentrism?. *S Afr J Phil*, 12(2), 31-37, My 93.

The article deals with the claim, often made in the literature, that ethnocentrism and relativism represent the only two consistent positions regarding conceptions of the rationality of human sciences. The article argues for the untenability of this presentation of the problem, and develops, in discussion with Richard Rorty, Peter Winch, Charles Taylor, Clifford Geertz and others, an alternative view in which the rationality of human sciences is understood in terms of the development of a 'language of perspicuous contrast' in which the dichotomy between ethnocentrism and relativism is transcended.

Van Nooten, B. Binary Numbers in Indian Antiquity. *J Indian Phil*, 21(1), 31-50, Mr 93.

Van Norden, Bryan. Mengzi and Xunzi: Two Views of Human Agency. *Int Phil Quart*, 32(2), 161-184, Je 92.

Mengzi (or Mencius) holds that all humans have incipient virtuous inclinations, and that moral self-cultivation involves stimulating these inclinations so that they develop into mature virtues. Neither being nor becoming a virtuous person requires acting against one's desires. In contrast, Xunzi (or Hsun-tzu) claims that acting against one's desires is possible and, in fact, necessary in the early stages of self-cultivation. Furthermore, Xunzi's slogan, "human nature is evil" must be understood against the background, not only of Mengzi's claim that "human nature is good", but also of Gaozi's claim that human nature is morally neutral.

Van Parijs, Philippe. *Marxism Recycled*. New York, Cambridge Univ Pr, 1993.

The right attitude towards such bulky artifacts as the Marxist tradition is not one of dutiful conservation, but of ruthless recycling. There is nothing wrong, therefore, in chopping up unwieldy chunks, in discarding stultifying mental pollutants, in using the latest intellectual technology to reshape—sometimes beyond recognition—dislocated parts, or in letting the rest rot into oblivion. Driven by this conviction, the book examines the structure and potential of historical materialism. It draws lessons from the failure of Marxist crisis theory. It shows how a rejuvenated notion of exploitation can illuminate the analysis of the class structure of welfare state capitalism and the assessment of international migration. It advocates a "capitalist road to communism" that expands the realm of freedom while by-passing socialism. And it develops those aspects of the Marxist project that are consistent with ecological concerns.

Van Peursen, C A. E W Von Tschirnhaus and the *Ars Inveniendi*. *J Hist Ideas*, 54(3), 395-410, Jl 93.

The philosophy of Tschirnhaus (1651-1708) has been underestimated. He has been important for Leibniz, Wolff and Spinoza, also by his personal contacts. But particularly influential has been his work "Medicina Mentis". In his ars inveniendia, with its combination of reason and experience he could correct a more Cartesian position. His stress on experiments together with "method" is here of importance. He describes the intellect as constituted by operations of the mind (mentis operatio) influencing in this way Wolff, and via him even Kant.

Van Peursen, C A. Metaphor and Reality. *Man World*, 25(2), 165-180, Ap 92.

1) Is metaphysical language mainly located in a linguistic field or (also) in reality? Thesis: the impact of reality on language constitutes the metaphor. 2) Must (can) metaphors be re-translated into descriptive ("true/false") language? Thesis: metaphors manifest a wider realm of more evaluative language which is more basic in cultural awareness and behavior.

Van Praag, B M S. The Relativity of the Welfare Concept in The Quality of Life, Nussbaum, Martha C (ed). New York, Oxford Univ Pr, 1993.

In this paper it is argued that the welfare concept may be made operational if we use a definition which requires a measurement recipe. An account is given of how a specific measurement instrument, the Income Evaluation Question (IEQ), may be used to elicit individual welfare functions (of income) from respondents in surveys. Then it is shown that this method, which has been applied by the author and others since 1971 in numerous large surveys in many western countries, yields consistent and plausible results. Applications are given for the calculation of equivalence scales in order to correct for differences in family size or climate. Remarks are made on the impact of past experiences or the anticipated future on present income evaluation. The same holds for the influence of social reference groups on individuals.

Van Reijen, Willem. The Crisis of the Subject: From Baroque to Postmodern. *Phil Today*, 36(4), 310-323, Wint 92.

Modern Philosophy is generally characterised by a teleological concept of history and by the claim that reasons should be given for moral and theoretical convictions. Postmodern Philosophy argues that such concepts and claims depend on the notion of the possibility of a synthesis of contradictions and antagonistic forces. In Baroque philosophy and literature the idea of the possibility of reconciliation of oppositional poles is questioned. Walter Benjamin's book on the baroque drama expresses as well this central idea of baroque culture, which he identifies with the culture of the interbellum, as the prefiguration of postmodern culture. The concept of (self-)reflexivity, not as synthesis but as aporetic (central for the postmodern notion of subjectivity) is presented in the philosophies of Leibniz, Benjamin and Lyotard.

Van Steenburgh, E W. Hume's Metaphysical Musicians. *Hume Stud*, 18(2), 151-154, N 92.

An exposition of Hume's use of 'useless and incomprehensible' in the context of correcting our judgments of equality. Hume argues that imagined corrections to the claim that two objects are equal are not reasons for thinking that they are not equal. The same 'useless and incomprehensible' argument applies to series converging to an abstract limit, e.g. the Carnot Engine.

Van Veuren, Pieter. *Ideology and Modern Culture*: Review of J B Thompson. *S Afr J Phil*, 12(1), 12-17, F 93.

Van Vucht Tijssen, Lieteke (ed) and Raven, Diederick (ed) and De Wolf, Jan (ed). *Cognitive Relativism and Social Science*. New Brunswick, Transaction Books, 1992.

Modern epistemology has been dominated by an empiricist theory of knowledge that assumes a direct individualistic relationship between the knowing subject and the object of knowledge. Truth is held to be universal, and non-individualistic social and cultural factors are considered sources of distortion of true knowledge. Since the late 1950s, this view has been challenged by a cognitive relativism asserting that what is true is socially conditioned. This volume examines the far-reaching implications of this development for the social sciences. (edited)

Vandenberg, Donald. Harry Broudy and Education for a Democratic Society. *J Aes Educ*, 26(4), 5-19, Wint 92.

This intellectual biography of perhaps the most eminent American philosopher of education since WWII traces the context and development of his research program from his dissertation and earlier "classical realism" to his later use of Polanyi's "tacit knowing" to articulate the life-uses of schooling. These uses necessitate general education to enable ordinary citizens to evaluate the truth and credibility of experts and politicians. Broudy's justification of the arts and humanities (and social problems and democratic ideals) in education to re-moralize the culture that has been demoralized by the sciences is also considered. Includes a complete bibliography of Broudy's writings.

Vandenbulcke, Jaak. On the Confines of Theology and Philosophy: A Reflection on the Book of T De Boer (in Dutch). *Bijdragen*, 53(1), 73-85, 1992.

De Boer, in his book "De God van de filosofen en de God van Pascal" defends the fundamental position that revelation may not impose any limits on the "controlling function" of philosophy. Though agreeing with this position generally, we nevertheless draw attention to an inconsistency in De Boer's argument, namely that the doctrine of the Incarnation should establish a limit to philosophy. As the direct and two-fold cause of this particular inconsistency we identify the ambiguous understanding of the notions of "salvation event" and of the deification of Jesus. That his inconsistency is possible at all can be explained in terms of De Boer's negative treatment of the Enlightenment, the lack of rigour in his thinking in regard to revelation as experience, and his inadequate distinction between belief as truth in itself and truth as it is "for me".

Vandendorpe, Christian. Les avatars du sens profond: Réflexion sur quelques modèles de lecture. *Horiz Phil*, 3(1), 84-102, Autumn 92.

This paper explores different strategies readers deploy in the attempt to grasp the "hidden" meaning of a text. The prevalent method is the allegorical interpretation, which establishes a superset of beliefs (moral, physical, realist, metaphysical, transliteral, psychoanalytical...) through which the text is processed. But other models have been developed throughout this century, looking for "deeper" organizational layers of meaning. While semiotic theory sees meaning as an articulation of levels, the generative model looks for deep structures genetically encoded in the human brain. Most recently, the cognitive model brings back authorial intentionality as a valid consideration in the search for significance.

Vander Nat, Arnold and Moser, Paul K. Surviving Souls. *Can J Phil*, 23(1), 101-106, Mr 93.

This paper shows that Richard Swinburne's Cartesian argument for the conclusion that we have immaterial souls fails, owing to a dilemma concerning the logical possibility of conscious beings' surviving bodily destruction. The paper identifies a non-Cartesian, Humean approach to survival that is not challenged by Swinburne's argument.

Vanderveken, Daniel. Non-Literal Speech Acts and Conversational Maxims in John Searle and His Critics, Lepore, Ernest (ed). Cambridge, Blackwell, 1991.

Vandevelde, Pol. Heidegger et la poésie: De "Sein und Zeit" au premier cours sur Hölderlin. *Rev Phil Louvain*, 90(85), 5-31, F 92.

In *Sein und Zeit*, (1927) Heidegger mentions poetry only casually as a kind of "discourse" to be called upon by phenomenological interpretation as a relevant example. In 1934, however, in his first lecture on Hölderlin, he presents poetry as a "proto-language" which every thinking should listen to and obey. This discrepancy gives rise to two questions: 1) How is this radical change in perspective to be understood? 2) Does the prominent part assigned to poetry in 1934 no longer suffer from the same weaknesses it displayed in 1927? Actually, the relationship between poetry and language in 1934 retains the same ambiguity as that between discourse and language in 1927. (edited)

Vanheeswijck, Guido. A N Whitehead, R G Collingwood and the Status of Metaphysics (in Dutch). *Bijdragen*, 53(4), 372-393, 1992.

At first sight, Collingwood's and Whitehead's concept of metaphysics have not much in common. Collingwood seems to reduce metaphysics to a historical study of ideas, while Whitehead defines metaphysics as an ontological study. In this article I want to show that the similarity between Collingwood's and Whitehead's concept of metaphysics is much stronger than commonly accepted. Therefore, I make use not only of Collingwood's published writings but also of his unpublished manuscripts in 1978 released. First I outline the evolution of Collingwood's thought on metaphysics since 1933. Against that background I try to clarify Collingwood's interpretation of the concept of metaphysics in the work of Alexander and Whitehead. Collingwood's preference for Whitehead's concept has especially to do with the transcendental justification of Whitehead's concept of metaphysics. At the transcendental level however, there are important differences between both thinkers, in spite of the strong similarities between them. These differences eventually explain why Collingwood's metaphysics is a *historical* one, while Whitehead's metaphysics is a *cosmological* one.

Vanheeswijck, Guido. Collingwood en Wittgenstein: hervormde versus deiktische metafysica. *Alg Ned Tijdschr Wijs*, 84(3), 165-181, Jl 92.

There are striking similarities in the late philosophies of R G Collingwood and Wittgenstein. Reacting against neopositivism, both philosophers not only stress the limitations of scientific thinking, but also the contextuality of all philosophical thinking and speaking. The main difference between them consists, however, in their attitude towards metaphysics. While Wittgenstein rejects the possibility of a cognitive metaphysics, Collingwood's intention, after 1933, is to give a transcendental justification of cognitive metaphysics. First, in spite of the similar *function* the *statute* of Wittgenstein's 'language games' and 'forms of life' is different from Collingwood's 'absolute presuppositions'. Secondly, while Wittgenstein is not interested in the historical evolution of forms of life, Collingwood emphatically is. (edited)

Vanhoozer, Kevin J. Philosophical Antecedents to Ricoeur's 'Time and Narrative' in On Paul Ricoeur: Narrative and Interpretation, Wood, David (ed). New York, Routledge, 1991.

This article interprets Paul Ricoeur's Time and Narrative (3 vols.) as an attempt to think the problems of human temporality and the creative imagination together. Ricoeur's narrative theory puts into productive relationship Kant's view of the imagination and Heidegger's notion of human being as temporal. Ricoeur's narrative theory stands at the juncture of his philosophical anthropology and hermeneutics, insofar as narrative texts schematize human being-in-time. A narrative approach to time and the imagination not only enables greater analytical rigor towards these problems, but encourages a greater social sense of human temporality as well. Hermeneutics is a handmaiden to anthropology.

Várdy, Péter and Brainard, Marcus (trans). Technology in the Age of Automata. *Grad Fac Phil J*, 16(1), 209-226, 1993.

The paper investigates: 1) the tendency of technical development, illustrated by the history of the lathe from a tool in Egyptian antiquity to the CNC automation; 2) the metaphysical foundations and the philosophical significance of automation.

Varela, Francisco. Making it Concrete: Before, During and After Breakdowns in Revisioning Philosophy, Ogilvy, James (ed). Albany, SUNY Pr, 1992.

Varghese, Roy Abraham (ed) and Margenau, Henry (ed). *Cosmos, Bios, Theos: Scientists Reflect on Science, God, and the Origins of the Universe, Life, and "Homo sapiens"*. Peru, Open Court, 1992.

Varnier, Giuseppe. Consapevolezza e riferimento oggettivo: Un problema in Descartes, nell'idealismo e nella filosofia contemporanea. *Teoria*, 12(1), 59-111, 1992.

Varoufakis, Yanis. Modern and Postmodern Challenges to Game Theory. *Erkenntnis*, 38(3), 371-404, My 93.

Equilibrium game theory borrows from neoclassical economics its rationality concept which it immediately puts to work in order to produce the basic results it needs for building an elaborate narrative of social interaction. This paper focuses on some recent objections to game theory's use of rationality assumptions in general, and of backward induction and subgame perfection in particular, and interprets them in the light of the postmodern critique of the grand meta-narratives which social theorists often rely on for social explanation. The paper presents a defense of game theory which seeks to accommodate the postmodern critique. However, it goes on to show that such a defence is illegitimate and claims that the problem lies with the faulty conceptualisation of the main concept on which game theory rests: that of Reason. Having established the nature of the problem, it considers three alternative interpretations (Humean, postmodern and Hegelian) of why the problem resists logical solutions and of its significance for social theory.

Vasey, Craig R. Faceless Women and Serious Others in Ethics and Danger, Dallery, Arleen B (ed). Albany, SUNY Pr, 1992.

Vasilyev, Vadim. Hume: Between Leibniz and Kant (The Role of Pre-Established Harmony in Hume's Philosophy). *Hume Stud*, 19(1), 19-30, Ap 93.

Vásquez, Eduardo. Comment on Leon J Goldstein's "Force and the Inverted World in Dialectical Retrospection". *Int Stud Phil*, 24(3), 105-108, 1992.

Vásquez, Eduardo. Individuo y sociedad civil. *Cuad Etica*, 13, 95-102, Je 92.

The paper deals with the relation between *Science of Logic* (where Hegel expounds his conception of dialectics) and *Philosophy of Right*. Dialectics is, basically, dialectics of finite being, that is to say, of its negation and conservation in the infinite. Civil society, as a state of the understanding, is a mixture of accidental determinations and universality. The universal is conditioned, as it depends on sensitive individuals and seems to be based on them. The negation of the state leads to the sphere of the political, where equality is established and individuals exist only as universal: this is the sphere of reason. These steps correspond to #198 in the *Encyclopaedia*: three syllogisms of the State. Finally, some critics to this conception are briefly expounded.

Vásquez, Juan. El desarrollo científico desde el punto de vista fenomenológico de la intencionalidad. *Agora (Spain)*, 11(1), 19-30, 1992.

My aim in this paper is to show a change to a paradigm provided by the phenomenological *epochè* and transcendental reduction allows for a more successful approach to the rational explanation of scientific progress than the usual analytical approaches do. The change that the transcendental reduction provides in the conceptual framework makes it possible to draw a closer link between the scope of language and the scope of experience both in the ordinary and scientific sense. It is shown here that the drawing of the aforementioned link cannot be avoided either in any correspondence theory of truth or in the explanation of scientific progress.

Vattanky, John. The Referent of Words: Universal or Individual, the Controversies Between Mimamsakas and Naiyayikas. *J Indian Phil*, 21(1), 51-78, Mr 93.

One of the most important problems discussed in Nyaya Philosophy of language is whether words denote an individual or a universal. On this point there are basically two schools of thought which oppose one another, i.e., the Mimamsakas and the Naiyayikas. The texts of Muktavali, Dinakari and Ramarudri dealing with this topic give a brilliant summary of the long drawn out conflict between the two schools. The authors of these texts established the Nyaya position that the denotative function of words is in the individual as qualified by the universal and the present essay examines these arguments and counterarguments.

Vaught, Carl G. Faith and Philosophy. *Monist*, 75(3), 321-340, Jl 92.

Vaught, Carl G. Hegel and the Problem of Difference in Hegel and His Critics, Desmond, William J (ed). Albany, SUNY Pr, 1989.

Vauzeilles, Jacqueline. Cut Elimination for the Unified Logic. *Annals Pure Applied Log*, 62(1), 1-16, Je 93.

Veatch, Henry B. The Problem and Prospects of a Christian Philosophy—Then and Now. *Monist*, 75(3), 381-392, Jl 92.

Veatch, Robert M. Brain Death and Slippery Slopes. *J Clin Ethics*, 3(3), 181-187, Fall 92.

It is at first puzzling why the definition of death debate has lasted so long. Arguing against defenders of the whole-brain-oriented definition of death, this paper claims that the usual arguments against a higher-brain-oriented definition are not successful. One major argument against a higher-brain formulation is that such a position creates a "slippery slope problem." This paper claims that, to the contrary, it is the defenders of the whole-brain-formulation that risk a slippery slope problem. The only defensible, sharp distinction is between those who have irreversible separation of mental and bodily function and those who do not, that is between higher brain function and other brain functions. (edited)

Veatch, Robert M. Forgoing Life-Sustaining Treatment: Limits to the Consensus. *Kennedy Inst Ethics J*, 3(1), 1-19, Mr 93.

While substantial progress has been made in reaching a moral and policy consensus regarding forgoing life-sustaining treatment, several holes exist in that consensus where more public discussion and moral analysis is needed. First, among patients who have not been found to be legally incompetent, there is controversy over whether certain treatments can be refused. Controversies also remain over damages for treatment without consent, limits based on third-party interests, and the ethical integrity of the medical profession, and cases where it cannot be agreed whether the patient is competent. Even greater dispute exists over care of incompetent patients. Perhaps the greatest gap in consensus arises over limits to the use of the best interests standard. This article proposes replacing it with a "reasonableness standard" that takes into account disputes about what is literally the best for the patient and conflicts of interest between the patient and others.

Veatch, Robert M. Rationing: Why Justice Requires Multiple Insurance Plans. *Nat Forum*, 73(3), 22-24,32, Sum 93.

Many new health care proposals, including the Clinton proposal, provide for a single list of "basic" services. This essay argues for offering multiple lists rather than a single list. Deciding what counts as valuable health care is, in part, dependent on the purpose of life—a question usually thought of as religious or philosophical. Any single list will favor one particular concept of the good life and is thus both inefficient and unjust. Most people will be forced to fund some services they find without value or even offensive while they are not permitted to receive the services they consider most valuable. A proposed alternative is for groups to create lists they consider basic under the condition that they would all be fundable for the same fixed cost.

Veatch, Robert M. Response to Kwasi Wiredu in African-American Perspectives on Biomedical Ethics, Flack, Harley E (ed). Washington, Georgetown Univ Pr, 1992.

In commenting Kwasi Wiredu's views on the moral foundations of African culture, this response raises three questions: (1) Is there a single moral foundation of African culture and, if so, is it as independent of religious traditions as Wiredu suggests. (2) To what extent to the ethics of the Akan in Ghana reduce to what westerners would call utilitarianism. (3) What are the implications for an African-American biomedical ethics?

Veatch, Robert M. The Impending Collapse of the Whole-Brain Definition of Death. *Hastings Center Rep*, 23(4), 18-24, Jl-Ag 93.

Since the 1970s governments throughout the world have adopted a definition of death that specifies that an individual is dead when there is an irreversible loss of all functions of the entire brain. Problems have begun to emerge with this "whole-brain definition." This article summarizes these problems: that isolated cells could continue to live even though all supercellular functions have ceased, that electrical functions may continue even though clinical functions have ceased, and that "nests of neurons" could remain alive even though clinical functions have ceased. The paper defends the thesis that no rational justification remains for calling people dead precisely when all brain functions have irreversibly ceased. Everyone de facto accepts the view that certain functions can remain even though death pronouncement is appropriate. Arguments against the higher brain formulation are rebutted.

Vedder, Ben. The Relation between Belief and Knowledge in Spinoza's Hermeneutical Theory (in Dutch). *Bijdragen*, 53(4), 350-371, 1992.

The author rethinks the relation between belief and knowledge in the *Tractatus Theologico-Politicus (TTP* of Baruch de Spinoza (1632-1677). In the *TTP* Spinoza claims a total separation between them. Belief belongs to the world of physical impressions and imagination, it involves words; knowledge is a pure spiritual process without words. Nevertheless, Spinoza sees for both the believer and the thinker, the same salvation and well-being. The question to rethink is: how does Spinoza, as a philosopher and a thinker, know that the salvation for the believer and the thinker is the same, even when he says that there is no rational ground or justification for belief? For Spinoza, belief is a matter of obedience. To solve this problem the author points out the important position of Christ in the *TTP*. Spinoza recognizes Christ as a philosopher, for philosophers only have the experience that knowledge happens always without imagination and words. (edited)

Vegetti Finzi, Silvia. Female Identity between Sexuality and Maternity in Beyond Equality and Difference, Bock, Gisela (ed). New York, Routledge, 1992.

The Declaration of the Rights of Man (1789) proclaimed an equality of sexes that remained merely a formal one. Excluded in fact from the civil rights, women were on the other hand involved by a different process, namely the construction of a new form of subjectivity no longer ruled by a set of external norms but governed instead by an interiorized moral: this process was required by the passage from the feudal to the bourgeois society. Women's sexuality thus became the object of a moral control obtained by the opposition eroticism to maternity, the first being dealt with by psychiatry, the second one by gynecology. The female lover became a subject and an object of cultural production; the mother was instead abandoned to rhetorical idealization as well as to natural necessity. Such separation between women and inside the woman is due to produce alienation and self- misunderstanding. It is therefore necessary to overcome it as a first step to achieve a female sexual subjectivity.

Velharticky, Nick. The Intelligibility of Substantial Change in Aristotle's "Physics". *Lyceum*, 3(1), 45-50, Spr 91.

Velicogna, Nella Gridelli and Ferrari, Vincenzo. Philosophy and Sociology of Law in the Work of Renato Treves. *Ratio Juris*, 6(2), 202-215, Jl 93.

After giving account of the main events in R Treves' life, the article describes the basic events in his philosophy and in his sociology of law. Treves' approach to philosophy of law is essentially de-constructivist, in that he transforms the philosophical reflection into a methodology and asserts the compatibility of the most diverse theories from a perspectivist viewpoint. It is precisely this vision which led Treves to building up a modern kind of sociology of law, where theorizing, empirical observation and critical evaluation of values are connected.

Velicogna, Nella Gridelli and Segre, Vera. Works by Renato Treves. *Ratio Juris*, 6(2), 216-2225, Jl 93.

Velleman, Daniel. Constructivism Liberalized. *Phil Rev*, 102(1), 59-84, Ja 93.

Michael Dummett has claimed that the use of classical logic for statements that involve quantification over some mathematical domain can be justified only if we can *circumscribe* the domain over which the statements quantify, by saying what objects the domain comprises. This paper argues that the domain of natural numbers passes this circumscription requirement, but the domains of real numbers and sets do not. This suggests a liberalized version of constructivism in which classical logic can be used for statements that quantify over the natural numbers, but intuitionistic logic must be used for statements quantifying over real numbers or sets.

Velleman, J David. Against the Right to Die. *J Med Phil*, 17(6), 665-681, D 92.

For some patients, a right to receive euthanasia will not enhance autonomy in the morally relevant sense. Even if these patients choose wisely whether to exercise their right to die, they will still be harmed by having been given it. Perhaps, then, physicians should have permission to administer voluntary euthanasia, but patients should not have a right to receive it.

Velleman, J David. What Happens When Someone Acts?. *Mind*, 101(403), 461-481, Jl 92.

Velmans, Max. Reply to Gillett's "Consciousness, Intentionality and Internalism". *Phil Psych*, 5(2), 181-182, 1992.

Gillett attempts to recast the debate between myself, Rentoul, and Wetherick in terms of an essential connection between consciousness and intentionality, arguing this is central to my case against dualist/ reductionist "internalism". My reply corrects a number of errors in Gillett's analysis. For example, my case against internalism relies on experimental evidence. I argue that unconscious mental states are intentional (so intentionality is not exclusive to consciousness). Gillett implies that one cannot both be a projectivist and an indirect realist, but I espouse both. Gillett also fails to distinguish phenomenal properties (which can be projected) from properties of things-themselves.

Velmans, Max. The World as Perceived, the World as Described in Physics: A Reply to Rentoul and Wetherick. *Phil Psych*, 5(2), 167-172, 1992.

This paper replies to commentaries on a Reflexive model of consciousness developed by Velmans (1990). Rentoul claims that the model does not separate percepts *of* objects from object themselves. I argue that the phrases, 'percepts of objects' and 'objects as-perceived' are *logically* distinct, but they do not refer to events that are *phenomenologically* distinct. Phenomenal objects represent, but are not identical to objects (things) themselves. Wetherick agrees that phenomenal objects are representations, but argues that perceived characteristics are really out-there in the world. However, this cannot account for conscious "qualia", nor for the world as-described by Physics.

Vendler, Zeno. Epiphenomena in Certainty and Surface in Epistemology and Philosophical Method, Martinich, A P (ed). Lewiston, Mellen Pr, 1991.

Venkatachalam, V. Comments on "The Development of Advaita Vedanta as a School of Philosophy". *J Indian Counc Phil Res*, 9(2), 159-163, Ja-Ap 92.

Verbeek, Theo. "Ens per accidens": le origini della 'querelle' di Utrecht. *G Crit Filosof Ital*, 71(2), 276-288, My-Ag 92.

Verbrugge, Rineke and Beraducci, Alessandro. On the Provability Logic of Bounded Arithmetic. *Annals Pure Applied Log*, 61(1-2), 75-93, My 93.

Verdú, V and Font, J M. Algebraic Logic for Classical Conjunction and Disjunction. *Stud Log*, 50(3-4), 391-419, S-D 91.

In this paper we study the relations between the fragment L of classical logic having just conjunction and disjunction and the variety D of distributive lattices, within the context of Algebraic Logic. We prove that these relations cannot be fully expressed either with the tools of Blok and Pigozzi's theory of algebraizable logics or with the use of reduced matrices for L. However, these relations can be naturally formulated when we introduce a new notion of model of a sequent calculus. When applied to a certain natural calculus for L, the resulting models are equivalent to a class of abstracts logics (in the sense of Brown and Suszko) which we call *distributive*. Among other results, we prove that D is exactly the class of the algebraic reducts of the reduced models of L, that there is an embedding of the theories of L into the theories of the equational consequence (in the sense of Blok and Pigozzi) relative to D, and that for any algebra A of type (2,2) there is an isomorphism between the D-congruence of A and the models of L over A. In the second part of this paper (which will be published separately) we will also apply some results to give proofs with a logical flavour for several new or well-known lattice-theoretical properties.

Verene, Donald Phillip. Metaphysical Narration, Science, and Symbolic Form. *Rev Metaph*, 47(1), 115-132, S 93.

This article examines the sense in which science presupposes human culture for its activity and particular form of knowledge. Science is understood in terms of Cassirer's conception of symbolic form of theoretical knowledge grounded in the *Bedeutungsfunktion* of consciousness. Cassirer's conception of science is joined with Vico's conception of metaphysics as a science of narration. Science in Vico's sense as a science of history (achieved by metaphysical narration) is required in order to fully comprehend science in the restricted sense of theoretical knowledge.

Verene, Donald Phillip. The Limits of Argument: Argument and Autobiography. *Phil Rhet*, 26(1), 1-8, 1993.

This paper holds that arguments never stand alone. They always presuppose a narrative in which their points make sense. This is true even in the work of philosophers who appear to avoid any narrative element. It is further claimed that philosophies are the autobiographies of their authors and thus the narrative is grounded in the story of the author's existence.

Verene, Donald Phillip. Vico's Road and Hegel's Owl as Historiographies of Renaissance Philosophy. *Clio*, 21(4), 329-343, Sum 92.

This paper compares Vico's and Hegel's conceptions of historiography. Vico's conception of history as cycles regards the Renaissance as the beginning of the *ricorso* of western thought. Hegel gives little importance to the Renaissance because he equates important philosophical periods with the presence of philosophical systems and the Renaissance as with Latin philosophy does not produce philosophy in the form of system.

Vergauwen, R. Filosofische logica: een status quaestionis. *Tijdschr Filosof*, 55(1), 141-150, Mr 93.

The work is a review of *The Handbook of Philosophical Logic* (D Gabbay and F Guenthner, (eds), Synthese Library 163, 164, 165, 166, Dordrecht, Kluwer, 1983, 1984, 1986, 1989). It is shown how, starting from issues in classical extensional logic and its metatheory, this logic can be extended along several lives by either modifying truth-functionality which gives rise to all kinds of intensional logics or giving up bivalence as is done in intuitionistic or partial logics. These modifications are (partly) imposed by the aim to study and formalise natural languages which are eminently intensional and (less eminently) 'non-bivalential'. Finally, it is indicated how philosophical logic may be relevant in the philosophy of language.

Vergauwen, Roger. *A Metalogical Theory of Reference: Realism and Essentialism in Semantics*. Lanham, Univ Pr of America, 1993.

The author seeks to provide an answer to the question, "How does language connect to the world?" He begins with the recent developments in formal semantics and from them constructs his own 'theory of reference' with which he considers the nature of the correspondence of the world. The author locates his metalogics between the philosophy of language and epistemology while he covers a range of models from Plato to Wittgenstein. Vergauwen assumes no previous technical or logic study.

Verges, Frank G. The Unbearable Lightness of Deconstruction. *Philosophy*, 67(261), 386-393, Jl 92.

Deconstructors not only preach the gospel of the essential opacity of language, but practice it with an apostolic zeal. It is as though they have sworn on a stack of Nietzsche, Heidegger and Derrida paperbacks that they will always abide by the doctrine of the "opacity of the signifier". Deconstructionist *Kulturkritic*, the hideous upshot, is monstrously turgid and dense, yet suffused with an unctuous lightness, the result of a hyperconscious awareness of its own status as mere writing. By a kind of pre-established harmony, deconstructionist criticism has achieved hegemony within the literature departments of many American universities, typically those which demand prolific publication in order to achieve tenure, promotion, and other perquisites. (edited)

Verhaeghe, J. De bijdrage van de jezuïeten tot de filosofische cultuur: *La contribution des jésuites à la culture philosophique*. *Bijdragen*, 54(1), 30-56, 1993.

Verhaeghe, P. Nosographies et diagnostics: L'impasse du nominalisme et une réponse psychanalytique. *Commun Cog*, 25(1), 41-51, 1992.

Verhoeven, Jan. Die Fichte-inspiratie van de dynamiek van het verlangen bij Jos Maréchal. *Bijdragen*, 53(1), 23-45, 1992.

Das Anliegen J Maréchals ist die Überwindung des Agnostizismus Kants (Resultat des statischen Denkens). Die Postulate der praktischen Vernunft sollen nicht nur praktisch notwendig, sondern auch konstitutiv sein für die theoretischen Vernunft. Diese Überwindung findet statt durch die weitere Entfaltung der transzendentalen Methode Kants auf der breiteren Basis der Metaphysik, geprägt durch die immanente Dynamik des Intellekts. Diese Entfaltung der transzendentalen Methode zum Dynamismus zeigt sich schon bei Kant besonders in seinem *Opus postumum* und diese Gedanken nähern sich dem Denken des "frühen" Fichte. So ist Maréchal bei dem "frühen" Fichte inspiriert worden von der immanenten Dynamik des Ich, die sich direkt zeigt in der intellektuellen Anschauung und bei dem "späteren" Fichte der "Anweisung zum seligen Leben" von der Dynamik die nicht mehr auf das Ich, sondern auf das Transzendente, das Ewige, zielt. Hier wird die Dynamik gefasst in eine transzendentale Metaphysik. Für Fichte und Maréchal gilt dass das endliche Dasein nur einen ontologischen Wert bekommt wenn es sich öffnet für das Absolute damit das Absolute es vollenden kann.

Verhoog, H. The Concept of Intrinsic Value and Transgenic Animals. *J Agr Environ Ethics*, 5(2), 147-160, 1992.

The creation of transgenic animals by means of modern techniques of genetic manipulation is evaluated in the light of different interpretations of the concept of intrinsic value. The zoocentric interpretation, emphasizing the suffering of individual, sentient animals, is described as an extension of the anthropocentric interpretation. In a biocentric or ecocentric approach the concept of intrinsic value first of all denotes independence of humans and a non-instrumental relation to animals. Genetic manipulation of wild species is a serious moral issue, in contrast to genetic manipulation of domesticated species. Both authors do not take the species-specific nature (or "telos") of domesticated animals seriously.

Vermazen, Bruce. Objects of Intention. *Phil Stud*, 71(3), 223-265, S 93.

Vernengo, Robert J and Da Costa, Newton C A and Puga, Leila. Derecho, moral y preferencias valorativas. *Theoria (Spain)*, 5(12-13), 9-29, N 90.

We study some propositional systems of the logic of preference containing two kinds of deontic operators: juridical and ethical. These logics are important for the formalization of certain theories of law, such as the three-dimensional theory as developed by the Brasilian jurist, Muiguel Reale.

Vernezze, Peter. The Philosopher's Interest. *Ancient Phil*, 12(2), 331-349, Fall 92.

One long-standing issue in the interpretation of the *Republic* involves the requirement that the philosophers assume political command in Plato's ideal polis. Although the benefit of such a move to the state as a whole is not in doubt, the payoff to the philosophers themselves is more dubious. Commentators in general have claimed that philosophers are maximally benefitted by contemplation and hence that ruling is opposed to their own interest. In this paper, I argue that the *Republic* not only advocates a political life but actually requires it if the philosophers are to be fulfilled.

Verster, Ulrich. *Philosophical Universes*. Oxford, Academic Pub (UK), 1993.

The book uses as a point of reference the ontological, epistemological, and/or metaphysical entities populating philosophical universes or realities or "the subject / effects / results" of this discourse.

Verster, Ulrich. *Philosophy—A Myth?*. Oxford, Academic Pub (UK), 1992.

An investigation of philosophy/ philosophizing in terms of concepts such as the discourse, models, theories, metaphors, etc. It is reasoned that many notions, e.g., free will or determinism, knowledge or belief, thoughts or behavior, mental or physical, nature or nurture, etc., represent uncritical world-views, residual of earlier cultures or historical periods; such conflated folk-psychological notions continue to determine the subject-matter and methods of philosophy. These things are made explicit by a methodology to make conceptual paths, methods or ways to develop insights into alternative values, objectives and the purpose of philosophizing.

Verstraeten, Pierre. Hegel and Sartre in The Cambridge Companion to Sartre, Howells, Christina (ed). New York, Cambridge Univ Pr, 1992.

Verstraeten, Pierre. The Revolutionary Hero Revisited in Sartre Alive, Aronson, Ronald (ed). Detroit, Wayne St Univ Pr, 1991.

Verstraeten, Pierre. 'I Am No Longer a Realist': An Interview with Jean-Paul Sartre in Sartre Alive, Aronson, Ronald (ed). Detroit, Wayne St Univ Pr, 1991.

Vetlesen, Arne Johan. Why Does Proximity Make a Moral Difference?. *Praxis Int*, 12(4), 371-386, Ja 93.

The article explores the disquieting thesis that the Nazi destruction of the European Jews was a product rather than a failure of modernity. The Holocaust is drawn upon to demonstrate the moral difference made by proximity. A strong inhibition against causing pain makes itself felt in face-to-face encounters. This inhibition was systematically neutralized by the Nazis: they turned their victims into a distant, unheard and unseen "target". Vetlesen uses this example to show that the capacity for empathy is morally crucial.

Vetö, Miklos. Idéalisme et théisme dans la dernière philosophie de Fichte: La *Doctrine de la Science* de 1813. *Arch Phil*, 55(2), 263-285, Ap-Je 92.

The text of 1813 is the last but one version of the *Wissenschaftslehre* with deeper metaphysical foundations; it reassumes the point of view of the *Grundlage 1794*. First it gives a completely new description of the category of "image" and secondly it deduces Apparition, which comes after the transcendental Ego, as image and as the image of the Absolute.

Vetö, Miklos. Les trois images de l'absolu: Contribution à l'étude de la dernière philosopihe de Fichte. *Rev Phil Fr*, 1, 31-64, Ja-Mr 92.

Vetter, Ulrich Ben. Emanzipation und Befreiung: Lateinamerikas problemat— Verhältnis zur Moderne. *Conceptus*, 25(65), 23-37, 1991.

It is one of the leading questions in contemporary philosophy in Latin America to discuss the importance and the meaning of modernity. This is done with regard to humanity in general, and to Latin America especially. The history of Latin America philosophy shows its linkage to the problem of modernity in its adoption of subjects as well as methods from the Western philosophical tradition, in the development of a criticism of capitalist theories, and in the discussion of problems resulting from modern thinking—especially discussing Latin America in its colonial or peripheric status. This paper retraces some stages of the philosophic thinking of Latin America and shows how certain tendencies seek the forum of international discourse while maintaining the authenticity which is based on the linkage of explanation and change of its concrete social reality.

Vezeau, Toni M. Caring: From Philosophical Concerns to Practice. *J Clin Ethics*, 3(1), 18-20, Spr 92.

Viau, Marcel. Le discours théologique et son objet: perspectives néo-pragmatistes. *Laval Theol Phil*, 49(2), 233-248, Je 93.

Viau, Marcel. Pragmatisme et théologie pratique. *Rev Theol Phil*, 124(2), 115-138, 1992.

Practical theology has long claimed a privileged relationship with experience or, to be more precise, believer's experience. Now, American pragmatism has developed the notion of experience in an experimental way, relating to a process of natural events in which subjects and their consciousness are merely parts of that process. Experience would then be a set of circumstances within the cosmos. Pragmatically, practical theology may be perceived as a discipline able to build discourses which serve as a vehicle for the Christian belief embodied within human experience.

Vice, Janet. *From Patients to Persons: The Psychiatric Critiques of Thomas Szasz, Peter Sedgwick and R D Laing*. New York, Lang, 1992.

The role of psychiatric theory and practice has become increasingly controversial in contemporary society. Both psychiatry's scientific status as a medical specialty and its moral legitimacy as a helping profession have been called into question by outstanding figures within the profession. This study of Thomas Szasz, Peter Sedgewick, and R D Laing argues that disagreements over the nature, role, and failures of psychiatry are traceable to philosophical disagreements over the meaning of personhood and community.

Vicedo, Marga. The Human Genome Project: Towards an Analysis of the Empirical, Ethical, and Conceptual Issues Involved. *Biol Phil*, 7(3), 255-278, Jl 92.

In this paper I claim that the goal of mapping and sequencing the human genome is not wholly new, but rather is an extension of an older project to map genes, a central aim of genetics since its birth. Thus, the discussion about the value of the HGP should not be posed in global terms of acceptance or rejection, but in terms of how it should be developed. The first section of this paper presents a brief history of the project. The second section distinguishes among four kinds of issues relevant to an evaluation of the HGP: those economic and organizational issues related to the feasibility of the project; the ethical questions arising in the development of the project and the application of the data gathered; the empirical issues relevant to the scientific value of the project; and conceptual issues like reductionism and determinism relevant to understand the nature and scope of the project. In a third section, I analyze in detail whether the HGP and, more generally, molecular biology is reductionistic.

Vidal, Fernando. Jean Piaget's Early Critique of Mendelism: 'La notion de l'espèce suivant l'école mendélienne' (A 1913 Manuscript). *Hist Phil Life Sci*, 14(1), 113-135, Ja 92.

In 1913, the future psychologist and epistemologist Jean Piaget (1896-1980), then a seventeen-year-old naturalist, gave a talk criticizing 'the notion of the species according to the Mendelian school'. In it, he confounded Medelism and mutationism, and misunderstood both. He attributed an environmental nature to the 'factors' postulated by Mendel's laws for inherited characteristics, and thought that mutations resulted from the appearance of a new environmental factor. Such misinterpretations are closely related to Piaget's assimilation of the Bergsonian critique of the 'mechanistic' science into his work in malacological taxonomy.

Viefhues, Ludger. Lebensrecht und Überlebeninteresse: Darstellung und Kritik einiger Thesen von Norbert Hoerster. *Theol Phil*, 68(1), 89-94, 1993.

This article consists of a critical presentation of the "pro-choice" position held by the philosopher and law scholar Norbert Hoerster. Hoerster's argument is that we should not kill those human beings who have an actual interest in them being alive. The article shows that this position is not consistent in its conclusions. It tries to demonstrate that a modified version of Hoerster's argument provides sound rational grounds for the opinion that we should not kill human embryos. The question discussed here is wider than the abortion-controversy. It is simply this: Why should we *not* kill?

Vieillard-Baron, J L. L'actualité de la dialectique de Platon a la lumière de Hegel. *Rev Phil Fr*, 4, 429-434, O-D 91.

Vieillard-Baron, J L. L'expérience métaphysique et le transcendantal. *Kantstudien*, 84(1), 25-37, 1993.

L'expérience métaphysique est une expérience *sui generis*, bien qu'elle soit une expérience du pure pensée; elle est à la fois originaire et répétable. C'est un point de déapart où un sujet fait l'expérience de la pensée comme de sa propre pensée existante. En ce sens, le Cogito de Descartes est l'archétype de l'expérience métaphysique. Mais c'est aussi cette expérience que Lavelle thématise comme acte spirituel par lequel je saisis réflexivement ma possibilité d'infléchir le cours du monde par le geste le plus humble. On retrouve dans l'auto-affection de Michel Henry cette expérience primitive et fondatrice dont dépend la vraie philosophie.

Vieillard-Baron, J L. L'image de l'homme chez Descartes et chez le cardinal de Bérulle. *Rev Phil Fr*, 4, 403-419, O-D 92.

On sait que Bérulle a encouragé le jeune Descartes dans le projet d'une méthode naturelle pour chercher la vérité. L'identité de la vraie philosophie et de la vraie religion sera la ligne directrice des platoniciens de l'Orantoire après Bérulle. L'anthropologie de Bérully est fondée sur sa christologie; l'homme est l'être qui peut devinir diable (l'énergumène) ou devinir Dieu (le Christ, dont l'homme est membre par l'Eglise). Avec Descartes, la philosophie part d'une expérience métaphysicque du doute, puis du sentiment de l'existence; et la connaissance est pensée sur un modèle scientifique algébrique et mécanique. Cependant, la théorie de la création continuée ist un reste de platonisme et de Bérullisme dans la pensée cartésienne. De même, la psychologie de Descartes repose sur l'opposition entre entendement et volonté, et s'ordonne à la quête d'une sagesse laïque. Pour bérulle au contraire, la saesse purement humaine est folie; la vraie psychologie est christocentrique; l'homme doit reconnaître son propre néant. L'humanisme cartésien s'oppose donc à l'anti-humanisme chrétien de Bérulle.

Vienne, Jean-Michel. Locke et l'intentionnalité: le problème de Molyneux. *Arch Phil*, 55(4), 661-684, O-D 92.

At the beginning, i.e., in Locke's Essay, the point of the Molyneux problem was not the fact of a common sense but the nature of the ideas of primary qualities. According to this view, Locke's empiricism was more sophisticated than is usually thought. Simple ideas are not necessarily evident at first, and some are neither clear nor distinct. Furthermore, the definition of the ideas of the primary qualities of a body as the Resemblances of the actual qualities must be rightly understood.

Vienne, Jean-Michel. Locke on Real Essence and Internal Constitution. *Proc Aris Soc*, 93, 139-153, 1993.

In order to understand our phrase *natural kind*, it is useful to understand Locke's *real essence*. This paper distinguishes between *real essence* and *internalconstitution*. The natural kinds depend on phenomenal similarities which are united into a nominal essence and the postulated cause of the nominal is the real essence. But the true cause of a being (i.e., *essence* in the aristotelian meaning of the word) and of its similarities with others is the internal and purely individual constitution. Thus the real essence (in the modern meaning) is a phenomenal effect of the internal constitution.

Vierheller, Ernstjoachim. Object Language and Meta-Language in the Gongsun-long-zi. *J Chin Phil*, 20(2), 181-209, Je 93.

The Gongsun-long-zi is a text of the ancient Chinese school of logicians. An attempt is made to provide a coherent interpretation of the logical content of the chapter *bai ma lun*. The analysis based on a new look on the logical function of the negated copula *fei* yields a reading of the text as being directed toward elucidating the distinction of meta-/object-language and of extension/intension of a concept. This fact could enhance the appreciation of the level of language analysis reached at an early premodern state of Chinese philosophy.

Viganó, A. La gnoseologia dell'arte in J Maritain. *Sapienza*, 44(4), 427-441, 1991.

Vigo, Alejandro. Persona, hábito y tiempo: La constitución de la identidad personal. *Anu Filosof*, 26(2), 271-287, 1993.

This paper addresses the methodological priority of the constitutive features of personal identity over those of identification or reidentification. In this context, it studies the role of habits as basics constitutive determinants of the empirical ego. It deals with the Kantian lack of attention to the relation between the subject and the world opened by human action. Then, it studies the treatment of this topic in Aristotle and Husserl, focused on two themes: habits and temporality.

Vilks, Arnis. A Set of Axioms for Neoclassical Economics and the Methodological Status of the Equilibrium Concept. *Econ Phil*, 8(1), 51-82, Ap 92.

Villa, Dana R. Beyond Good and Evil: Arendt, Nietzsche, and the Aestheticization of Political Action. *Polit Theory*, 20(2), 274-308, My 92.

Villani, Giovanni. Teoria quantistica della misura in una visione non oggettivista della realtà. *Epistemologia*, 15(1), 21-39, Ja-Je 92.

The concept of physical observation and its quantitative refinement, measurement, is one of the main scientific concepts because, after all, it constitutes the link between theory and experience. It is only with quantum mechanics that the measurement problem becomes part of a scientific theory, but, up to now, without a satisfactory general and universally accepted solution. The purpose of this analysis is to show that, in spite of the different solutions given to the measurement problem, these theories have a common approach and philosophical substrate. (edited)

Villanueva, Enrique (ed). *Rationality in Epistemology*. Atascadero, Ridgeview, 1992.

Villaverde, Marcelino Agís. *El discurso filosófico: Análisis desde la obra de Paul Ricoeur*. Barcelona, Univ Santiago Comp, 1993.

This thesis is a study of philosophical discourse and its relation to other forms of discourse. The work of the French philosopher Paul Ricoeur serves both to guide and to delimit the examination. The inquiry includes a review of the concept of the philosophy of discourse as developed by Ricoeur through his study of the successive developments in the field during this century. The book includes three sections: 1) The various methods of defining philosophical discourse; 2) The important units and elements of discourse: the word, the phrase, the concept, and the metaphor; 3) The development of discourse. (edited)

Vincent, Nelson. Education and Its Analysis. *Phil Stud Educ*, 1, 53-63, 1991.

Vincenzo, Joseph P. Socrates and Rhetoric: The Problem of Nietzsche's Socrates. *Phil Rhet*, 25(2), 162-182, 1992.

After presenting the highlights of Nietzsche's interpretation of Plato's Socrates, this article examines Socrates's relation to rhetoric in the *Georges, Phaedrus*, and Cratylus. This examination shows Socrates not as a "theoretical man," but as a practitioner of true rhetoric and, as such, as an embodiment of the union of the Dionysian and Apollinian.

Violi, Patrizia. Gender, Subjectivity and Language in Beyond Equality and Difference, Bock, Gisela (ed). New York, Routledge, 1992.

The aim of the paper is to discuss the issue of equality and difference in relation to women's language and the way in which language affects the construction of male and female subjectivity. First, traditional socio-linguistic approaches to woman's language are criticized and an alternative approach is suggested, centered on the idea of an engendered way of thinking and speaking. Then the way in which language, as a semiotic device, allows symbolisation of private experiences and therefore structured subjectivity is considered. While patriarchal culture shapes male subjectivity, as can be seen in the analysis of narrative, female subjectivity has only recently started creating its own system of symbolisation.

Viroli, Maurizio. The Revolution in the Concept of Politics. *Polit Theory*, 20(3), 473-495, Ag 92.

Vision, Gerald. Animadversions on the Causal Theory of Perception. *Phil Quart*, 43(172), 344-356, Jl 93.

This paper examines some common misconceptions about the Causal Theory of Perception, occurring most recently in an article in the same journal by John Hyman. It is argued that a causal theory does not *require* subjective episodes as effects of public objects (though it is no less entitled to them than any theory of perception), that explanations which implicate a causal element are much subtler than its critics have imagined, and that the critics' demand that the theory show how what is caused is a distinct occurrence from its cause—a demand that the critics often argue drives the causal theory to untenable versions—is a mass of confusions. The details of Hyman's own exposition are also scrutinized and various shortcomings noted.

Visker, Rudi. Habermas on Heidegger and Foucault: Meaning and Validity in the *Philosophical Discourse of Modernity*. *Rad Phil*, 61, 15-22, Sum 92.

Visser, Albert. The Formalization of Interpretability. *Stud Log*, 50(1), 81-105, Mr 91.

This paper contains a careful derivation of principles of Interpretability Logic valid in extensions of $I\Delta + \Omega 1$.

Visser, Albert and De Jongh, Dick. Explicit Fixed Points in Interpretability Logic. *Stud Log*, 50(1), 39-49, Mr 91.

The problem of Uniqueness and Explicit Definability of Fixed Points for *Interpretability Logic* is considered. It turns out that Uniqueness is an immediate corollary of a theorem of Smorynski.

Visser, Gerard. Nietzsche's Superman: The Necessity of Reconsidering the Question of Man (in Dutch). *Tijdschr Filosof*, 54(4), 637-667, D 92.

Visser't Hooft, H P. Intergenerational Justice: Some Reflections on Methodology in Ethical Dimensions of Legal Theory, Sadurski, Wojciech (ed). Amsterdam, Rodopi, 1991.

Vitek, William. Converging Theory and Practice: Example Selection in Moral Philosophy. *J Applied Phil*, 9(2), 171-182, 1992.

There is a growing trend in moral philosophy that reflects a return to a more ancient perspective of the subject matter wherein moral theory and moral practice are thought to converge. Unfortunately, this literature is cluttered with abstract, general, unlikely, and cleverly-constructed examples that are apt to draw both reader and author away from the various moral issues under consideration. This paper argues that the selection of examples drawn from literature, history and common-life experiences offers the following advantages: (I) such examples better serve the purpose of illustration; (2) they function as projects for moral inquiry; (3) they better connect both reader and author to the moral issues being discussed; (4) they help prevent the dichotomisation of moral philosophy to have the relevance and importance it once enjoyed in previous periods of history.

Vitek, William. Teaching Environmental Ethics. *Teach Phil*, 15(2), 151-174, J 92.

This article details a three step pedagogy for teaching environment ethics: awareness, articulation, and action. This pedagogy encourages students to become aware of their habits, heritage, and the environment around them, to analyze, evaluate, and articulate concepts and beliefs that embody an ethical relationship to the natural world; and to consider a range of actions consistent with well-articulated beliefs. The article defends this approach to teaching environmental ethics against the charges of advocacy from the left and moral relativism from the right.

Vitek, William. Virtue Ethics and Mandatory Birth Control in Biomedical Ethics Reviews 1992, Humber, James M (ed). Clifton, Humana Pr, 1993.

This paper highlights the primary themes of virtue ethics—including a method of doing moral philosophy wherein theory and practice converge, a conception of the good, accounts of virtue and moral deliberation, a communitarian conception of human beings, and a prominent role for education and public policy in creating a virtuous community—and demonstrates their usefulness in characterizing and understanding mandatory birth control as a moral, medical issue. It seeks to entice those working in bioethics to consider virtue ethics as a robust and workable theoretical alternative, one that can stand alongside bioethics' current theoretical workhorses.

Vitiello, Vincenzo. Il "guidizio" in Croce. *Teoria*, 11(2), 21-46, 1991.

Vlach, Frank. Temporal Adverbials, Tenses and the Perfect. *Ling Phil*, 16(3), 231-283, Je 93.

Vlastos, Gregory. Socratic Piety. *Proc Boston Colloq Anc Phil*, 5, 213-238, 1989.

I argue that there is no conflict between (1) Socrates' commitment to reasoned argument as the final arbiter of claims to truth in the moral domain and (2) his commitment to obey commands reaching him through supernatural channels (his "divine sign", prophetic dreams, and the like). He assumes that these two commitments are in perfect harmony. They cannot conflict because all he receives through divine monitions are signs, and only by the use of his own unfettered critical reason can he determine the true meaning of any of those signs.

Vodakova, Alena. On "Philosophy" of Women's Double Role (in Czechoslovakian). *Filozof Cas*, 40(5), 769-781, 1992.

The schizophrenic linkage of women's role in their job and family and/or household provides a textbook example of the role conflict. It can be interpreted from the viewpoint of traditional conception as well as from the position of symbolic interactionism. It is, however, possible to revalue the relation of the "individual" and the "social" in this conflict and consider a certain pseudo-I which originated by the penetration of non-coinciding roles and which is dependent and powerless in its way. The history of emancipational women's movement and the present problems resulting from the individual and social failure to master women's double role seem to confirm this hypothesis. (edited)

Vogel, Jonathan. Dismissing Skeptical Possibilities. *Phil Stud*, 70(3), 235-250, Je 93.

Various philosophers—including John Pollock, Roderick Chisholm, and Stewart Cohen—have suggested that it is rational to reject out-of-hand any possibility that one is the victim of massive sensory deception (e.g., that one is a brain in a vat). I try to show that this short way with skepticism resists precise formulation and encounters various unsettling methodological problems. Moreover, I argue, the claim that skeptical hypotheses are epistemic non-starters leads to implausible consequences, if it is supposed to do any real work in fending off skeptical challenges. A different, less abrupt way of meeting such challenges must be found.

Vogel, Jonathan and Tymoczko, Thomas. The Exorcist's Nightmare: A Reply to Crispin Wright. *Mind*, 101(403), 543-552, Jl 92.

Crispin Wright tried to refute classical 'Cartesian' skepticism contending that its core argument is extendible to a reductio ad absurdum (Mind, 100, 87-116, 1991). We show both that Wright is mistaken and that his mistakes are philosophically illuminating. Wright's 'best version' of skepticism turns on a concept of warranted belief. By his definition, many of our well-founded beliefs about the external world and mathematics would not be warranted. Wright's position worsens if we take 'warranted belief' to be implicitly defined by the general principles governing it. Those principles are inconsistent, as shown by a variant of Gödel's argument. Thus the inconsistency Wright found has nothing to do with the special premises of Cartesian skepticism, but is embedded in his own conceptual apparatus. Lastly, we show how a Cartesian skeptic could avoid Wright's critique by reconstructing a skeptical argument that does not use the claims Wright ultimately finds objectionable.

Vogel, Lawrence. Understanding and Blaming: Problems in the Attribution of Moral Responsibility. *Phil Phenomenol Res*, 53(1), 129-142, Mr 93.

In 'Sanity and the Metaphysics of Responsibility' Susan Wolf appeals to the idea of insanity to explain why she would exonerate some wrongdoers who are victims of deprived childhoods or who act in ways strongly encouraged by their societies, "like slaveowners in the 1850's, Nazis in 1930's Germany and male chauvinists in the 1950's." I challenge Wolf's application of the insanity defense to her examples, and recast them as cases of same, responsible agents whom it may be difficult to blame on account of the causal history of their moral beliefs or motivations. I contend that Wolf's loose use of the insanity defense presents several dangers. It leads us to misunderstand the difficulties that victims of deprived childhoods may have conforming to moral norms and encourages a dismissive attitude towards cultures that are historically distant or alien from our own.

Vogel, Steven M. New Science, New Nature: The Habermas-Marcuse Debate Revisited. *Res Phil Technol*, 11, 157-178, 1991.

The article examines the dispute between Habermas and Marcuse in the late 1960s about the possibility of a "new" science that would eschew the domination of nature. Each view faces significant and surprisingly similar problems. Habermas fails to grasp that the active character of our involvements with nature means that "nature" is a *social* category, and hence that a new society might well inhabit a new nature. But for the same reason Marcuse's notion of a "non-dominative" relation to nature, in which we "let nature be itself," turns out to be incoherent. Nature never *is* itself; it's always already socially constructed.

Vogt, Philip. Seascape with Fog: Metaphor in Locke's "Essay". *J Hist Ideas*, 54(1), 1-18, Ja 93.

Vokey, Daniel. MacIntyre and Rawls: Two Complementary Communitarians?. *Proc Phil Educ*, 48, 336-341, 1992.

This response assesses the respective contributions of the educational recommendations of John Rawls and Alasdair MacIntyre to the project of promoting the moral consensus required for a just and stable political culture. It is argued that Rawls's recommendation to avoid debate among opposing points of view has potential to reinforce the exclusion of marginalized groups from public policy formation. The paper concludes that, in order to build the kind of culture both philosophers desire, Rawls's "overlapping consensus" approach would need to be complemented, and in part superseded, by MacIntyre's proposed dialectical debates among competing moral, religious, and political traditions.

Vollmer, Fred. A Theory of Traits. *Phil Psych*, 6(1), 67-79, 1993.

The aim of the present paper is to find a satisfactory way of understanding what traits are. As a starting point, two recent accounts of the nature of traits, the act of frequency approach and the intention frequency approach are presented and discussed. The act frequency approach is criticized for taking all traits to be behavioral dispositions, and for not offering any explanation of behavior. The intention frequency approach is criticized for being equally one-sided in regarding all traits as mental frequency dispositions. It is claimed that some traits are purely behavioral, that some are behavioral and mental, and that some are purely mental. Finally, it is argued that mental phenomena like beliefs and desires, the phenomena that makes up reasons for and explains actions, are not frequency dispositions. They are dispositional properties of another kind, namely abilities, capacities or powers.

Vollmer, Fred. Intentional Action and Unconscious Reasons. *J Theor Soc Behav*, 23(3), 315-326, S 93.

The problems discussed in this paper are whether it makes sense to speak of unconscious reasons, and of acting intentionally for such reasons. To throw light on these questions, results of empirical research on semantic priming, subliminal symbiotic activation, and social behavior in emergency situations are considered. It is concluded that while the results of these experiments do not force us to assume that there are unconscious reasons, and that we can act intentionally for such reasons, they do indicate that there are unconscious mental states, and that there are actions that are rationalized by the contents of such states.

Volonté, Paolo. Analogia storica ed esperienza trascendentale: La "metaistorica" di Max Müller. *Riv Filosof Neo-Scolas*, 84(1), 123-167, Ja-Mr 92.

Von Der Luft, Eric. Commentary on "Hegel and Heidegger" in Hegel and His Critics, Desmond, William (ed). Albany, SUNY Pr, 1989.

Von Eckardt, Barbara. *What Is Cognitive Science?*. Cambridge, MIT Pr, 1993.

The purpose of this book is to characterize the framework of assumptions shared by cognitive scientists. It is argued that for an immature science, such a framework consists of four components: a set of domain-specifying assumptions, a set of basic questions, a set of substantive assumptions which constrain how the basic questions are to be answered, and a set of methodological assumptions. Each of these components is identified for cognitive science. In the process, the author explores a number of currently "hot" topics including connectionism, content determination, individualism, and the role of neuroscience in cognitive science.

Von Herrmann, Friedrich-Wilhelm. 'Being and Time' and 'The Basic Problems of Phenomenology' in Reading Heidegger: Commemorations, Sallis, John (ed). Bloomington, Indiana Univ Pr, 1992.

It is the purpose of this essay to show that with his Marburg lecture course text *The Basic Problems of Phenomenology*, Heidegger in fact presents the second elaboration of the theme "time and being". This is the second elaboration of that most important section of *Being and Time* whose first elaboration Heidegger did not allow to be published. The present essay first examines a number of passages in *Being and Time* which reach ahead for the theme "time and being", and then shows how *The Basic Problems of Phenomenology* raises the basic question of the meaning of Being and deals with the four problems that emerge from raising this question in the fundamental-ontological way. Thus the essay succeeds in demonstrating that *The Basic Problems of Phenomenology* is to be read as the continuation of *Being and Time*.

Von Hirsch, Andrew and Maher, Lisa. Can Penal Rehabilitationism be Revived?. *Crim Just Ethics*, 11(1), 25-30, Wint-Spr 92.

The article deals with recent proposals to revive rehabilitation as the basis for criminal sentencing. After pointing out that penal treatment programs tend to be effective for only special subgroups of offenders, and that treatment-based sentences are not necessarily milder than proportionate ones, the article deals with the questions of fairness that arise when rehabilitation is made the basis for sentencing. Foremost among those fairness questions, the article points out, is the tendency of rehabilitation-based sentences to disregard the degree of blameworthiness of the conduct in determining the sentence.

Von Kibéd, Matthias Varga. Variables im Tractatus. *Erkenntnis*, 39(1), 79-100, Jl 93.

Wittgenstein's *Tractatus* claims the possibility to represent quantificational logic by means of a single basic operation. Fogelin regards the *Tractatus* system as seriously flawed and thus not suited for this aim, while Geach and Soames propose extensions and corrections of the Tractarian notational system. If the unusual Tractarian view—every variable can be conceived as a propositional variable—is taken full account of, we find out, that the *Tractatus* system is well suited to deal even with the problematic cases of mixed quantifiers with many-place predicates. By expanding the view of variables as certain two-dimensional lists of propositions we find adequate representations of formulas in the logic of the *Tractatus*. Surprisingly we don't need anything which corresponds to formulas with two or more free variables like *fxy*, and still get the full power of ordinary quantificational logic.

Von Kutschera, Franz. Kripke's Doubts about Meaning in Advances in Scientific Philosophy, Schurz, Gerhard (ed). Amsterdam, Rodopi, 1991.

The paper is about the 'new sceptical paradox' which S Kripke attributes to Wittgenstein in "Wittgenstein on Rules and Private Language" (1982). It is not concerned with a Wittgenstein exegesis, but only with the paradox and its solution. It tries to show that there is a direct solution to the paradox, that the arguments for the sceptical thesis are invalid, and that Kripke's sceptical solution does not escape the sceptical challenge.

Von Kutschera, Franz. Supervenience and Reductionism. *Erkenntnis*, 36(3), 333-343, M 92.

The aim of the paper is to show that claims of supervenience of the mental upon the physical do not define substantial forms of materialism. While weak supervenience holds trivially, even strong supervenience does not justify a claim of identity, dependence or determination; it is only a relation between classifications of persons by psychological and physical properties.

Von Savigny, Eike. Common Behaviour of Many a Kind: 'Philosophical Investigations' Section 206 in Wittgenstein's Philosophical Investigations, Arrington, Robert L (ed). New York, Routledge, 1991.

In P.I. section 2o6, Wittgenstein does not presuppose any common behaviour of mankind. What he requires for human behaviour to be interpreted as linguistic is, rather, behaviour common among the people concerned, which is regularly connected with the sounds they produce, where the regularity is sufficiently specific to discriminate, e.g., orders from reports and orders to do this from orders to do that. Besides a painstaking exegesis of section 2o6, 2o7, the evidence for this result consists in what Wittgenstein explicitly says on forms of life and on talking lions. "The common behaviour of mankind", in the translation, should read "Common human behaviour".

Von Savigny, Eike. I Don't Know What I Want in Criss-Crossing A Philosophical Landscape, Schulte, Joachim (ed). Amsterdam, Rodopi, 1992.

In the *Philosophical Investigations* and later writings, Wittgenstein views "I know" utterances which embed egocentric psychological clauses as affirming contextually defined authority positions rather than as knowledge claims. This view is consistent with Brian McGuinness's analysis of conscious wants in terms of their subjects. A's knowledge of mental facts about B is a capacity (Gilbert Ryle, John Watling) which is responsible for A's being prepared for B's behavior (as accounted for by those mental facts); for one and the same person this capacity would be idle except for cases where she plays a double role.

Von Savigny, Eike. Why Can't a Baby Pretend to Smile? in Wittgenstein's Intentions, Canfield, J V (ed). Hamden, Garland, 1993.

Von Wright, George Henrik. The Troubled History of Part II of the 'Investigations' in Criss-Crossing A Philosophical Landscape, Schulte, Joachim (ed). Amsterdam, Rodopi, 1992.

The typescripts from which both parts of Wittgenstein's *Investigations* were printed are now lost. Of the typescript for Part I there exists a second copy, but not so of the typescript for Part II. There is, however, a manuscript in Wittgenstein's hand which contains the whole of the printed Part II—and some additional material. A comparison of this manuscript with the printed text reveals some interesting discrepancies. They are noted in the paper. Moreover, a detailed comparison is made in a Postscript between the printed Preface of the *Investigations* and another, obviously earlier, version of it. Both versions are dated "Cambridge, January 1945"—but the printed one was probably not prepared until two years later.

Vorenkamp, Dirck. Strong Utilitarianism in Mo Tzu's Thought. *J Chin Phil*, 19(4), 423-443, D 92.

Vorontsov, B N. Some Problems of Teaching Philosophy in an Institution of Higher Learning. *Russian Stud Phil*, 32(1), 47-50, Sum 93.

Wackers, Ger. Hersendood in meervoud. *Kennis Methode*, 17(1), 78-108, 1993.

Wacks, Raymond. Judges and Moral Responsibility in Ethical Dimensions of Legal Theory, Sadurski, Wojciech (ed). Amsterdam, Rodopi, 1991.

The essay considers the problem of the 'moral' judge who is unable to reconcile his perception of justice with the law of an unjust society. It seeks to establish the grounds upon which it may be plausible to sustain the view that judges, and perhaps other public officials, are morally responsible for their act or omissions, and the form and consequences of such responsibility. Though inspired by the dilemma of the 'moral' judge in South Africa, the argument proferred may have a general application.

Waddell, Michael M. The Locked Door: An Analysis of the Problem of the Origin of the Soul in St Augustine's Thought. *Lyceum*, 4(2), 39-60, Fall 92.

The Locked Door is an analysis of the problem of the origin of the soul in St. Augustine's writings. To clarify several of the theories outlined in *De Libero Arbitrio III*, these theories are traced to earlier texts: Origen's *De Principiis*, Plotinus' *Enneads*, Plato's *Timaeus* and his *Phaedrus*. Special attention is given to Augustine's related understanding of original sin, his reading of several passages from the Bible, and the practice of infant baptism. Contemporary scholarship is considered. The analysis suggests that Augustine may have misformulated the problem (thus he never resolves it), but he still hinted at a promising solution.

Wade, Maurice (ed) and Gillroy, John Martin (ed). *The Moral Dimensions of Public Policy Choice: Beyond the Market Paradigm*. Pittsburgh, Univ of Pitt Pr, 1992.

Wagner, Carl G. Generalized Probability Kinematics. *Erkenntnis*, 36(2), 245-257, Mr 92.

Jeffrey's conditionalization is generalized to the case in which new evidence bounds the possible revisions of a prior below by a Dempsterian lower probability. Classical probability kinematics arises within this generalization as the special case in which the evidentiary focal elements of the bounding lower probability are pairwise disjoint.

Wagner, Carl G. Simpson's Paradox and the Fisher-Newcomb Problem. *Grazer Phil Stud*, 40, 185-194, 1991.

It is shown that the Fisher smoking problem and Newcomb's problem are decision-theoretically identical, each having at its core an identical case of Simpson's paradox for certain probabilities. From this perspective, incorrect solutions to these problems arise from treating them as cases of decision making under risk, while adopting certain global empirical conditional probabilities as the relevant subjective probabilities. The most natural correct solutions employ the methodology of decision making under uncertainty with lottery acts, with certain local empirical conditional probabilities adopted as the relevant subjective probabilities.

Wagner, Frank O. More on *R*. *Notre Dame J Form Log*, 33(2), 159-174, Spr 92.

Various notions arising in the study of totally transcendental groups are generalized to the merely stable context. In particular, a kind of strongly connected component is defined, replacing the component of monomial rank expounded by Berline-Lascar. The group-theoretic properties of this component are analyzed.

Wagner, Gerhard. Giddens on Subjectivity and Social Order. *J Theor Soc Behav*, 23(2), 139-155, Je 93.

Wagner, Michael (ed). *An Historical Introduction to Moral Philosophy*. Englewood Cliffs, Prentice Hall, 1991.

Twenty-six ethics readings, from Plato to MacIntyre, prefaced with biographical sketches and chronologically arranged in five sections. Each section is introduced with general comments on the period and its intellectual tenor, and with discussion of key issues and concepts each philosopher introduced into moral philosophy's evolution. A general introduction discusses philosophy, moral philosophy, philosophical reasoning, and some main issues and concepts in meta-ethics.

Wagner, Norbert. Der Familienname von Edmund Husserl. *Husserl Stud*, 9(3), 217-218, 1992.

Der Jamilienname von Edmund Husserl wird etymologisiert, und zwar als Nomen agentis auf -er von einem Verb mittelhochdeutsch hussen 'sich schnell bewegen', an welches ein Deminutivsuffix auf -l angehängt wird.

Wahidur Rahman, A N M. Kant's Concepts of Duty and Happiness. *Indian Phil Quart*, 20(1), 85-108, Ja 93.

This is an attempt to show the place of happiness within Kant's concept of duty. I have examined the place of ends and consequences in his ethics and his principles of moral judgment; and I tried to meet the Hegelian charges of empty formalism against Kant's ethics. It is shown that Kant did not totally exclude the role of ends and consequences, and that of happiness, from moral judgment. Kant only stressed that we should not take into account of them. I argued that the concept of ends and consequences is rooted in the very concept of moral postulate of freedom itself, as freedom presupposes, the presence of at least two alternative ends to choose from.

Wahl, Russell. Russell's Theory of Meaning and Denotation and "On Denoting". *J Hist Phil*, 31(1), 71-94, Ja 93.

Wahl, Russell and Westphal, Jonathan. Descartes, Leibniz and Berkeley on Whether We Can Dream Marks on the Waking State. *Stud Leibniz*, 24(2), 177-181, 1992.

Cottingham proposed a general objection to any test which would be a test of whether a person is awake, namely that it will always be conceivable that someone could dream the test was satisfied. We argue first, that the issue for Descartes is not whether one could dream a mark of the waking state was present, but whether the purported mark is in fact a mark. We argue second that Cottingham's claim begs the question against the very marks suggested by Descartes, Leibniz and even Berkeley.

Wakefield, Jerome and Dreyfus, Hubert. Intentionality and the Phenomenology of Action in John Searle and His Critics, Lepore, Ernest (ed). Cambridge, Blackwell, 1991.

Waks, Leonard J. The Oil in the Machine: Jacques Ellul on Human Techniques in the Technological Society. *Res Phil Technol*, 9, 155-170, 1989.

Walczewska, Slawomira. Husserl vs Dilthey—A Controversy over the Concept of Reason in Analecta Husserliana, XXXIV, Tymieniecka, Anna-Teresa (ed). Dordrecht, Kluwer, 1992.

Waldenfels, Bernhard. Respuesta a lo ajeno: Sobre la relación entre la cultura propia y la cultura ajena. *Rev Filosof (Costa Rica)*, 30(71), 1-6, J 92.

If we define the experiences of the alien, following Husserl, as "accessibility of what is unaccessible originally", how could we make it accessible without getting into the circles of egocentrism, logocentrism and eurocentrism, i.e., without extinguishing the alien by appropriating it? Ethnology as a science of the alien whose ambiguous state can clearly be grasped in Levi-Strauss's work and in Merleau-Ponty's comment on it helps us to answer this question by pointing to a field of interculturality. A new perspective opens when we take the alien as provocation to which we respond being unable ever to say in a complete way what it is.

Waldron, Jeremy. *Liberal Rights: Collected Papers 1981-1991*. New York, Cambridge Univ Pr, 1993.

Waldron, Jeremy. Rights and Majorities: Rousseau Revisited. *Nomos*, 32, 44-75, 1990.

Waldron, Jeremy. Special Ties and Natural Duties. *Phil Pub Affairs*, 22(1), 3-30, Wint 93.

Walford, David (ed & trans). *Theoretical Philosophy, 1755-1770—Immanuel Kant*. New York, Cambridge Univ Pr, 1992.

Waligora, Melitta. Das Tal der Sachlichkeit: Albert Schweitzer über Indien. *Conceptus*, 25(65), 47-56, 1991.

Albert Schweitzer contends that negating the worthiness of life and the world in general is essential to Indian world-view, thus leading to a profound scepticism and lack of real morality. Such a world-view is seen to be contrary to Western thought, when in fact, both traditions, the Indian and the Western are facing the same problem, namely to develop new foundations of values and of meaning. The paper shows that Schweitzer cannot sustain his argument, neither based on the history of Indian thought, nor India's social history. Therefore the position is shown to be wrong and misleading; it cannot help in answering Schweitzer's original question. The intention and the method of comparing cultures do not fit together in a perspective like his.

Walker, A D M. The Incompatibility of the Virtues. *Ratio*, 6(1), 44-62, Je 93.

The paper examines a single argument for the existence of incompatibilities between the virtues as traits of character. This argument appeals not to empirical truths about human psychology but to the possibility of conflict between the exercise of different virtues in action. The paper focusses on the two cardinal assumptions of this argument, viz., 1) that sometimes the exercise of one virtue can conflict with the exercise of another, and 2) that the degree to which a person possesses a virtue correlates directly with the extent of its exercise, and defends both assumptions against a variety of objections which allege that, in different ways, they are insensitive to the complexity of the virtues.

Walker, Brian. Habermas and Pluralist Political Theory. *Phil Soc Crit*, 18(1), 81-102, 1992.

Walker, M T. Punishment—A Tale of Two Islands. *Ratio*, 6(1), 63-71, Je 93.

An imaginary desert island scenario provides the setting for a story which is designed to expose the shortcomings of deterrence, reform and restitution theories of punishment, and to emphasize the intuitive appeal of Kant's strong retributivist insistence that there is a positive obligation to punish offenders just *qua* offenders, and not merely an automatic right to do so (weak retributivism). Nevertheless, it is urged that though the fact that an offence has been committed can in itself suffice to establish that punishment is in some sense required, this requirement at most supports a position that is intermediate between Kantian retributivism and weak retributivism.

Walker, Margaret. Keeping Moral Space Open: New Images of Ethics Consulting. *Hastings Center Rep*, 23(2), 33-40, Mr-Ap 93.

Some recent developments in philosophical ethics move away from a conception of morality as a code-like theory. I explore the implications of a view of morality as a constructive social medium of mutual accountability for the way the role of ethics consultant is understood. In contrast to a view of the consultant as a moral expert, I offer the alternative images of an *architect* of institutional spaces that allow shared moral deliberation and a *mediator* in the moral conversations taking place within those spaces.

Walker, Margaret Urban. Feminism, Ethics, and the Question of Theory. *Hypatia*, 7(3), 23-38, Sum 92.

Feminist discussions of ethics in the Western philosophical tradition range from critiques of the substance of dominant moral theories to critiques of the very practice of "doing ethics" itself. I argue that these critiques really target a certain historically specific model of ethics and moral theory-a "theoretical-juridical" one. I outline an "expressive-collaborative" conception of morality and ethics that could be a politically self-conscious and reflexively critical alternative.

Walker, Margaret Urban. Thinking Morality Interpersonally: A Reply to Burgess-Jackson. *Hypatia*, 8(3), 167-173, Sum 93.

In a comment on my paper "Feminism, Ethics, and the Question of Theory" (Walker 1992), Keith Burgess-Jackson argues that I have misdiagnosed the problem with modern moral theory. Burgess-Jackson misunderstands both the illustrative—"theoretical-juridical"—model I constructed there and how my critique and alternative model answer to specifically feminist concerns. Ironically, his own view seems to reproduce the very conception of morality as an individually internalized action-guiding code of principles that my earlier essay argued is the conception central to modern moral theories.

Walker, Mary M. Basanta Kumar Mallik's Theory of Knowledge. *J Indian Counc Phil Res*, 9(1), 109-126, S-D 91.

Wallace, Gerry. Area Bombing, Terrorism and the Death of Innocents in Applied Philosophy, Almond, Brenda (ed). New York, Routledge, 1992.

This paper is concerned with the view that, in so far as they involve the deliberate targeting of innocent people, neither terrorism nor area bombing is ever morally permissible. Four attempts to justify this view are considered, all of which are based on the intuition that deliberately killing innocent people is wrong. By means of a detailed examination of the introduction of area bombing by Britain in 1940-41, it is argued that in certain circumstances there are other equally powerful and accessible intuitions which support the opposite view. It is further argued that only moral theories which provide for the weighing of competing moral intuitions are capable of avoiding this kind of impasse.

Wallace, Kathleen. Making Categories or Making Worlds, II in Frontiers in American Philosophy, Volume I, Burch, Robert W (ed). College Station, Texas A&M Univ Pr, 1992.

This article argues that the perspectiveless spectator viewpoint is not required for the possibility of the kind of generality characteristic of metaphysics. More generally, the argument is that neither perspectivalism nor the fact that categories are constructed is devasting for genuine knowledge about the "way the world is." The argument runs on adopting a relational or "ordinal" ontology an outline of which and the consequences for the possibility of genuine knowledge are sketched in the article.

Wallace, Kathleen. Reconstructing Judgment: Emotion and Moral Judgment. *Hypatia*, 8(3), 61-83, Sum 93.

A traditional association of judgment with "reason" has drawn upon and reinforced an opposition between reason and emotion. This, in turn, has led to a restricted view of the nature of moral judgment and of the subject as moral agent. The alternative, I suggest, is to abandon the traditional categories and to develop a new theory of judgment. I argue that the theory of judgment developed by Justus Buchler constitutes a robust alternative which does not prejudice the case against emotion. Drawing on this theory I then develop how to conceptualize the ways in which feeling and emotion can be (or be components of) moral judgments.

Wallace, M Elizabeth (& others). Polanyian Perspectives on the Teaching of Literature and Composition. *Tradition Discovery*, 17(1-2), 4-16, 1990-91.

Dieter Lesage's plea for ethical particularism contains some major errors. He starts by describing the phenomenon of personal particularism: we tend to care more for those who are near to us than for those who are far away. Then he proceeds by giving moral value to this aspect of human behaviour. In fact he makes a step already analyzed by David Hume: the one from *is* to *ought*. Ethical particularism as described by Lesage can be studied as an anthropological phenomenon, but there is no reason to use it as a moral principle.

Wallace, Vita. Immodest Proposals II: Give Children the Vote. *Thinking*, 10(1), 46-47, 1992.

Wallach, John R. Contemporary Aristotelianism. *Polit Theory*, 20(4), 613-641, N 92.

Wallach, Lise and Wallach, Michael A. *Rethinking Goodness*. Albany, SUNY Pr, 1990.

This book examines the debate between a liberal and secular humanist position of ethical minimalism in which tolerance, respect, and autonomy are linked with asking little ethically of others and oneself—and a reactive authoritarianism that promotes morality at the expense of autonomy. The roots of this conflict are traced in the Judeo-Christian heritage and the reactions of social science to that heritage. The book offers a means of transcending the conflict by presenting biological, psychological, and phenomenological arguments against the necessity of an oppositional casting between what is required for autonomy and what is required for substantial ethics.

Wallach, Michael A and Wallach, Lise. *Rethinking Goodness*. Albany, SUNY Pr, 1990.

This book examines the debate between a liberal and secular humanist position of ethical minimalism in which tolerance, respect, and autonomy are linked with asking little ethically of others and oneself—and a reactive authoritarianism that promotes morality at the expense of autonomy. The roots of this conflict are traced in the Judeo-Christian heritage and the reactions of social science to that heritage. The book offers a means of transcending the conflict by presenting biological, psychological, and phenomenological arguments against the necessity of an oppositional casting between what is required for autonomy and what is required for substantial ethics.

Waller, Bruce N. Natural Autonomy and Alternative Possibilities. *Amer Phil Quart*, 30(1), 73-81, Ja 93.

Difficulties developing a natural nonmiraculous account of choosing among alternatives have driven contemporary compatibilists to autonomy-as-authenticity, abandoning ability to choose otherwise to libertarians. However, examination of the exploratory behavior humans share with other species can establish a plausible, naturalistic, nonmysterious interpretation of autonomy-as-alternatives. This interpretation exhibits the natural roots of autonomy-as-alternatives, explains both the similarities and differences between the exploratory alternative-seeking behavior of humans and other animals, shows how genuine choices among alternatives can exist in the natural world, and explains why autonomy-as-authenticity is a poor substitute for autonomy-as- alternatives.

Waller, Bruce N. Responsibility and the Self-made Self. *Analysis*, 53(1), 45-51, Ja 93.

Walls, Jerry. *Hell: The Logic of Damnation*. Notre Dame, Univ Notre Dame Pr, 1992.

Walmsley, Peter. Dispute and Conversation: Probability and the Rhetoric of Natural Philosophy in Locke's *Essay*. *J Hist Ideas*, 54(3), 381-394, Jl 93.

Walsh, Paddy. Discourses as the Reflective Educator. *J Phil Educ*, 26(2), 139-151, 1992.

The current paradigm of educational theory as 'emergent in practice' might sooner have provoked, and here does provide, an analysis of the distinctive profile of educational practice. This practice is shown to be (inter alia) 'philosophical' by virtue of its integral quest for a coherent view of life. A theory that is adequate to this practice will be a 'cluster' of four interconnected 'discourses' (each already in use within mature practice itself), not only deliberative and evaluative discourses but also utopian and scientific ones. The curriculum of teacher education, too, should extend to all of these discourses.

Walsh, Roger. Can Western Philosophers Understand Asian Philosophies? in Revisioning Philosophy, Ogilvy, James (ed). Albany, SUNY Pr, 1992.

Recent research on states of consciousness suggests that insights and understandings gained in altered states may be less comprehensible to individuals with no personal experience of that state. Since various Asian philosophies are derived in part from altered state experiences based on meditative-yogic practices, this suggests that philosophers without experience of these practices and states may be limited in their ability to appreciate and understand them.

Walsh, Sylvia. Kierkegaard: Poet of the Religious in Kierkegaard on Art and Communication, Pattison, George (ed). New York, St Martin's Pr, 1992.

Walter, Edward F. Keynesian Economic Theory and the Revival of Classical Theory in Terrorism, Justice and Social Values, Peden, Creighton W (ed). Lewiston, Mellen Pr, 1990.

Neo-classical economists maintain that Keynesianism had failed to establish prosperity and argued for a return to classical principles. However, Keynesianism was not responsible for the economic downturns of the 1970s. Keynes insisted deficit spending must be combined with low interest rates and low tax rates. Fear of inflation led to deficit spending and high interest rates, as well as high tax rates. While Keynesianism did not end the Great Depression, it reversed the downward trend and spurred the U.S. toward growth after the War. The Reagan prosperity (a neo-classicist period) was characterized by high unemployment and the growth of the gap between rich and poor.

Walter, Edward F. Rawls On Act Utilitarianism and Rules in Terrorism, Justice and Social Values, Peden, Creighton (ed). Lewiston, Mellen Pr, 1990.

According to John Rawls , utilitarianism subjects rules to the consequences test, but not individual decisions. This version of utilitarianism is intended to prohibit many behaviors that offend human moral sensibilities. Against Rawls's theory, act utilitarians can achieve most of what Rawls desires by requiring individuals to consider the long range consequences of actions and to mistrust their own motivation when they have an interest in the outcome of actions. Additionally, only psychological conservatism, not moral demonstration, excludes breaking rules in unusual and critical situations.

Walter, Michael. Jabir, the Buddhist Yogi. *J Indian Phil*, 20(4), 425-438, D 92.

Walters, Kerry S. *Rational Infidels: The American Deists*. Durango, Longwood Acad, 1993.

Rational Infidels is a study of American deism, the primary theological position of the Enlightenment savants of the colonial and early republic period. Specific deists examined include Benjamin Franklin, Thomas Jefferson, Ethan Allen, Elihu Palmer, Philip Freneau, and Thomas Paine. The European roots of American deism as well as its legacy to subsequent theology, philosophy, political sensibilities and belles lettres in the US are also explored. The book is a companion to the author's anthology *The American Deists: Voices of Reason and Dissent in the Early Republic*, (University Press of Kansas, 1992).

Walters, LeRoy (ed) and Kahn, Tamar Joy (ed). *Bibliography of Bioethics, V18*. Washington, Kennedy Inst Ethics, 1992.

Walton, Clarence C. Business and Postmodernism: A Dangerous Dalliance. *Bus Ethics Quart*, 3(3), 285-305, Jl 93.

Postmodernism, a poorly defined term, is nevertheless influencing art, architecture, literature and philosophy. And despite its definitional ambiguities, some philosophers see in postmodernism a reason for the rise and interest in business ethics. This view is challenged on two grounds: 1) its philosophical source in Europe; and 2) its vocabulary. Martin Heidegger, one of the major forces in postmodernism's rise, left a confusing legacy. In his early years, Heidegger advocated moral subjectivism; in his later years, he argued that moral standards could be found in the lives of human gods whose pronouncements would replace the precepts of a Western Civilization he found decadent. (edited)

Walton, Craig (trans) and Malebranche, Nicolas. *Treatise on Ethics (1684)*. Dordrecht, Kluwer, 1993.

Walton, Douglas. Rules for Plausible Reasoning. *Inform Log*, 14(1), 33-51, Wint 92.

This article evaluates whether Rescher's rules for plausible reasoning or other rules used in artificial intelligence for "confidence factors" can be extended to deal with arguments where the linked-convergent distinction is important.

Walton, Douglas N. After Analytic Philosophy, What's Next?: An Analytic Philosopher's Perspective. *J Speculative Phil*, 6(2), 123-142, 1992.

The view of philosophy advocated in this article is one of a subject originating in conflicts of opinion that puzzle or bother the ordinary person in everyday activities and discussions of controversial subjects. That is, the subject does not originate within discussions the professional philosophers have amongst themselves. According to this view, the goal of philosophy is to try to resolve these conflicts of opinion through reasoned discussion of the strongest, most persuasive arguments on both sides, and thereby to deepen our understanding of the positions on both sides. This view of philosophy is called "dialectical" (from the Greek word *dialektikós* for "conversation" or "dialogue") because the goal is to deepen maieutic insight through dialogue, even if the conflict of opinions is not resolved in the sense of showing that one opinion is known to be true and the other (opposed) opinion false. The case study method is shown to have an important place in this conception of philosophy.

Walton, Douglas N. Nonfallacious Arguments from Ignorance. *Amer Phil Quart*, 29(4), 381-387, O 92.

The argument from ignorance (*argumentum ad ignorantiam*) is typically portrayed as a fallacy in logic textbooks. However, in this article it is shown how this type of argument has characteristic argumentation schemes indicating how it can be used correctly in presumptive reasoning.

Walton, Douglas N. *The Place of Emotion in Argument*. University Park, Penn St Univ Pr, 1992.

Appeals to emotion-pity, fear, popular sentiment, and ad hominem attacks-are commonly used in argumentation. Instead of dismissing these appeals as fallacious wherever they occur, as many do, Walton urges that each use be judged on its merits. Walton uses fifty-six case studies to demonstrate that the problem of emotional fallacies is much subtler than has been previously believed. Ranging over commercial advertisements, political debates, union-management negotiations, and ethical disputes, the case studies reveal that these four types of appeals, while based on presumptive reasoning that is tentative and subject to default, are not always or necessarily fallacious types of argumentation.

Walton, Kendall L. How Marvelous! Toward a Theory of Aesthetic Value. *J Aes Art Crit*, 51(3), 499-510, Sum 93.

Walton, Kendall L. Seeing-In and Seeing Fictionally in Psychoanalysis, Mind and Art, Hopkins, Jim (ed). Cambridge, Blackwell, 1992.

Richard Wollheim explains pictorial representation in terms of *seeing-in*. In *Mimesis as Make-Believe*, I explained it in terms of participation in visual games of make-believe, and the experience of imagining seeing. These accounts are better regarded as complementary than as competitors. Seeing-in needs to be understood as involving imagining seeing. This in no way compromises the *visual* character of the experience. (Likewise, the fact that one's experience of a horror movie is an imaginative one does not mean this experience is not genuinely emotional.) And explaining seeing-in this way shows how pictorial representation is continuous with sculptural and theatrical representation.

Walton, Kendall L. What is Abstract About the Art of Music?. *J Aes Art Crit*, 46(3), 351-364, Spr 88.

Walton, Richard E. The Mercy Argument for Euthanasia: Some Logical Considerations. *Pub Affairs Quart*, 7(1), 71-84, Ja 93.

Walton, Roberto J. Nature and the 'Primal Horizon' in Analecta Husserliana, XXXIV, Tymieniecka, Anna-Teresa (ed). Dordrecht, Kluwer, 1992.

Walzer, Michael. Objectivity and Social Meaning in The Quality of Life, Nussbaum, Martha C (ed). New York, Oxford Univ Pr, 1993.

Wamba-dia-Wamba, Ernest. Beyond Elite Politics of Democracy in Africa. *Quest*, 6(1), 28-42, Je 92.

Wanderley, Augusto J M. Alguns Aspectos da Obra Matemática de Descartes. *Cad Hist Filosof Cie*, 2(1), 103-121, Ja-Je 90.

Descartes's geometry is a landmark in the history of mathematics. It was an important step in the development of analytic geometry. This paper presents the context of the evolution of this work and several features of its content. Descartes breaks with the Greek mathematicians in his representation of products of two lengths as a length. His notation is also new and is closer to our contemporary symbolism. Two of the successful applications of Descartes's method are the resolution of "Pappus' problem" and the tracing of tangents to curves. The paper also discusses mathematical contributions contained in Descartes's correspondence.

Wandschneider, Dieter. Eine Metaphysik des Schwebens: Zum philosophischen Werk von Walter Schulz. *Z Phil Forsch*, 46(4), 557-568, O-D 92.

The article aims to give a general appraisal of the philosophical work of Walter Schulz. It argues that the central themes of Schulz's later work are already prefigured in his interpretation of Schelling's late philosophy. They primarily center around the problem of finite subjectivity's fundamental lack of securedness and its worldlessness. Expanding this idea, Schulz develops a 'metaphysics of suspension' and provides a penetrating diagnosis of our present time, of man's historical nature, of modern art and of the anthropological basis of ethics.

Wandschneider, Dieter. Nature and the Dialectic of Nature in Hegel's Objective Idealism. *Bull Hegel Soc Gt Brit*, 26, 30-51, Autumn-Wint 92.

Wang, Hao. Gödel's and Some Other Examples of Problem Transmutation in Perspectives on the History of Mathematical Logic, Drucker, Thomas (ed). Basel, Birkhauser, 1991.

Wang, Xiaoping. The McKinsey Axiom is Not Compact. *J Sym Log*, 57(4), 1230-1238, D 92.

Wang, Xuegang. The Minimal System *L'o*. *Notre Dame J Form Log*, 33(4), 569-575, Fall 92.

Wansing, Heinrich. Functional Completeness for Subsystems of Intuitionistic Propositional Logic. *J Phil Log*, 22(3), 303-321, Je 93.

Ward, Andrew. Hegel and the Search for Epistemological Criteria. *Ideal Stud*, 22(3), 189-202, S 92.

Ward, Andrew. Question-Begging Psychological Explanations. *SW Phil Stud*, 15, 82-94, Spr 93.

Ward, Andrew. The Failure of Dennett's Representationalism: A Wittgensteinian Resolution. *J Phil Res*, 18, 285-307, 1993.

Jerry Fodor begins chapter one of *The Language of Thought* with two claims. The first claim is that "[T]he only psychological models of cognitive processes that seem remotely plausible represent such processes as computational." The second claim is that "[C]omputation presupposes a medium of computation: a representational system." I will consider what many people believe to be a significant problem facing representationalism. I will then examine two different ways that this problem can be resolved, one based on the writings of Daniel Dennett, the other on ideas found in the later writings of Wittgenstein.

Ward, Graham. The Revelation of the Holy Other as the Wholly Other: Between Barth's Theology of the Word and Levinas's Philosophy of Saying. *Mod Theol*, 9(2), 159-180, Ap 93.

The article analyses the phenomenological structure of revelation in the thought of Karl Barth and Emmanuel Levinas. It traces how relevation as the Word (Barth) and Saying (Levinas) affects their understanding of subjectivity, ethics, language and the transcendent. The article draws out the striking parallels in the thinking of this Christian theologian and this Jewish philosopher, and concludes that for both what is the heart of their work is an analysis of the structure of signification itself.

Ward, Graham. Tragedy as Subclause: George Steiner's Dialogue with Donald MacKinnon. *Heythrop J*, 34(3), 274-287, Jl 93.

Ward, John Powell. Surrendering and Cathcing in Poetry and Sociology. *Human Stud*, 16(3), 319-323, Jl 93.

Wardy, Robert. Aristotelian Rainfall or the Lore of Averages. *Phronesis*, 38(1), 18-30, 1993.

Ware, Robert. Marx on Some Phases of Communism in On the Track of Reason, Beehler, Rodger G (ed). Boulder, Westview Pr, 1992.

Through a detailed investigation of Marx's *Critique of the Gotha Program*, it is shown that Marx was less specific and less utopian about the future than is usually thought. Marx plausibly claimed that in distribution, society would move from exchange value to contributions to use value, but, contra Nielsen, not according to a principle of equality. Marx is criticized for not recognizing the importance of social satisfaction of social needs in a society with social production.

Ware, Vron. Moments of Danger: Race, Gender, and Memories of Empire. *Hist Theor*, 31(4), 116-137, 1992.

This essay arises out of a concern to understand how categories of racial, ethnic, and cultural difference—particularly between women—have been constructed in the past, in order to explore how these categories continue to be reproduced in more recent political and ideological conflicts. Until very recently, feminist theory relating to the writing of history has tended to emphasize questions of gender and their articulation with class, with the result that issues of "race" have been overlooked. Focusing on ideas about whiteness and the various constructions of white racial identity can offer new avenues of thought and action to those working to understand and dismantle systems of racial domination. This essay argues for a feminist theory of history that inquires into the construction and reproduction of racialized femininities. (edited)

Warfield, Ted A. Folk-Psychological Ceteris Paribus Laws?. *Phil Stud*, 71(1), 99-112, Jl 93.

Warfield, Ted A. Privileged Self-Knowledge and Externalism are Compatible. *Analysis*, 52(4), 232-237, O 92.

I argue that externalism about mental content is consistent with the thesis that individuals need not investigate their environment to come to know the contents of their thoughts. In particular, externalism is consistent with the thesis that we come to know the contents of our thoughts on the basis of introspection.

Warner, Martin. Dialectical Drama: The Case of Plato's *Symposium*. *Apeiron*, 25(4), 157-175, D 92.

The earlier speeches of the *Symposium* represent distinctive and credible sensibilities, implicitly correcting what has gone before, which provides models exploited by Socrates in his account of the Diotimesque 'ascent' and enable it to resist both Alcibiades' counter-narrative and Dover's recent critique. Plato outlines a counterpart in terms of psychology and sensibility of the more austerely intellectual ascent from Cave to Sun of the *Republic*, using the ambiguities of our experience and language to point beyond them to that which can only be grasped (if at all) in a transformed form of life, and thereby enlarging our conception of dialectic.

Warner, Martin. Language, Interpretation and Worship—I in Religion and Philosophy, Warner, Marin (ed). New York, Cambridge Univ Pr, 1992.

Traditionally the Bible was read as scripture as well as literature; this involved interpreting it as to some extent a 'lawless' text, with the inbreaking of the divine Word characteristically being marked by the contravention of human literary and linguistic rules. Enlightenment theories of language as governed by rules whereby each proposition properly relates the ideas designated in a determinate manner challenged this approach as unintelligible. Contemporary analyses of language which integrate meaning with use provide some logical space for the notion of 'lawlessness', and hence for a defence of the normative use of Scripture in Christian worship.

Warner, Martin (ed). *Religion and Philosophy*. New York, Cambridge Univ Pr, 1992.

The dichotomy between reason and faith is misplaced, but part of its plausibility derives from the elusiveness of the language of faith. Nevertheless, the latter is not immune to logical analysis which can reveal criteria for the proper use of the term 'God', the status of religion's moral dimension, and the relation of religious discourse to other language of imaginative demand. Throughout, a strong realist strain appears to run through religion.

Warnke, Georgia. Feminism and Hermeneutics. *Hypatia*, 8(1), 81-98, Wint 93.

Feminists often look to postmodern philosophy for a framework within which to treat difference. We might more productively look to a hermeneutic philosophy that emphasizes the interpretive dimensions of difference and allows us to acknowledge the partiality of our understanding. Hence, we might also recognize the importance of a hermeneutic conversation unconstrained by relations of power or ideology in which all nonexclusionary interpretive voices can be educated by one another.

Warnke, Georgia. *Justice and Interpretation*. Cambridge, MIT Pr, 1993.

This book explores an interpretive turn in contemporary political philosophy. Despite their differences, such theorists as Walzer, Rawls, Rorty, Taylor and MacIntyre all look to the meaning of our history, practices and traditions in order to articulate principles of justice that make sense for us. This approach raises questions of relativism and subjectivism. The book examines these issues and argues for a critical and pluralistic hermeneutics, one that can allow for some diversity in the understanding of norms and principles without assuming all interpretations of meaning, even sexist or racist ones, must be taken seriously.

Warren, Bill. Back to Basics: Problems and Prospects for Applied Philosophy. *J Applied Phil*, 9(1), 13-19, 1992.

This paper is an account of a response to a well-intentioned and genuinely naive question concerning the nature of "applied philosophy". It indicates differing points of view concerning the nature of philosophy and what one might or might not expect from it. It tries to synthesise these points of view into a position that sees philosophy as continuous with that attitude of mind that was epitomised by Socrates, an attitude of mind which is directed to every aspect or dimension of human life. The notion of the enquiry activist is borrowed to encapsulate this attitude as a valuable goal of "applied philosophy".

Warren, Karen J and Cheney, Jim. Ecosystem Ecology and Metaphysical Ecology: A Case Study. *Environ Ethics*, 15(2), 99-116, Sum 93.

We critique the metaphysical ecology developed by J Baird Callicott in "The Metaphysical Implications of Ecology" in light of what we take to be the most viable attempt to provide an inclusive theoretical framework for the wide variety of extant ecosystem analyses—namely, hierarchy theory. We argue that Callicott's metaphysical ecology is not consonant with hierarchy theory and is, therefore, an unsatisfactory foundation for the development of an environmental ethic.

Wartenberg, Thomas E. Hegel's Idealism in The Cambridge Companion to Hegel, Beiser, Frederick (ed). New York, Cambridge Univ Pr, 1993.

This paper presents an interpretation of Hegel's idealism that is unabashedly metaphysical. It argues that basic thesis of this idealism is that reality must conform to the conditions of a coherent categorical system. A number of recent interpretations of Hegel's philosophy are considered. The different types of interpretations of Hegel's philosophy are shown to result from different understandings of the project of interpretation of the part of his interpreters. It is argued that these interpretations, interesting as they may be on their own, do not do justice to Hegel's idealist philosophy.

Wartenberg, Thomas E. Reason and the Practice of Science in The Cambridge Companion to Kant, Guyer, Paul (ed). New York, Cambridge Univ Pr, 1992.

This article develops an interpretation of Kant's philosophy of science that shows it to be more in the pragmatist tradition that is generally thought. Under the rubric of the regulative use of reason, Kant presents a theory concerning the testing of hypotheses that employ theoretical concepts. Kant argues that this aspect of scientific methodology requires the presupposition that the regularities of nature can be captured by the systematic structure of scientific theories, an assumption that he characterizes as a transcendental principle of reason. The regulative use of reason is claimed to be an insightful and challenging account of scientific theorizing that deserves to be regarded as an essential component of Kant's theory of science.

Wartofsky, Marx. The Politics of Art: The Domination of Style and the Crisis in Contemporary Art. *J Aes Art Crit*, 51(2), 217-225, Spr 93.

Warwick, Andrew. Cambridge Mathematics and Cavendish Physics. *Stud Hist Phil Sci*, 24(1), 1-25, Mr 93.

This is the second installment of a two part article on the reception of relativity theory in Cambridge. This part focuses on the response of workers at the Cavendish Laboratory during the period 1905-1911. Particular attention is paid to Norman Campbell's attempts to develop a relativistic electrodynamics and to his philosophical writings on absolute motion. The paper also discusses the work of G F C Searle (the only British physicist to correspond with Einstein about relativity during this period) and H Donaldson and G Stead who attempted, unsuccessfully, to contribute to the development of relativity theory.

Warwick, Andrew. Cambridge Mathematics and Cavendish Physics: Cunningham, Campbell and Einstein's Relativity 1905-1911—Part I, The Uses of Theory. *Stud Hist Phil Sci*, 23(4), 625-656, D 92.

This paper deals with early reception of relativity theory in Britain. It challenges the notion that the British redemption of relativity can be understood in terms of a 'national style' of physics. It also argues that early uses of Einstein's work in Britain cannot straightforwardly be understood as a 'reception' of relativity theory. The paper draws upon recent work in the sociology of science to offer an alternative framework of local contexts within which the range of different British uses of Einstein's work can be understood.

Washington, Johnny. A Commentary on Oshita O Oshita's Analysis of the Mind-Body Problem in an African World View. *J Soc Phil*, 24(2), 243-247, Fall 93.

Wasserman, Edward A and Fales, Evan. Causal Knowledge: What Can Psychology Teach Philosophers?. *J Mind Behav*, 13(1), 1-27, Wint 92.

Theories of how organisms learn about cause-effect relations have a history dating back at least to the associationist/mechanistic hypothesis of David Hume. Some contemporary theories of causal learning are descendents of Hume's mechanistic models of conditioning, but others impute principled, rule-based reasoning. Since even primitive animals are conditionable, it is clear that there are built-in mechanical algorithms that respond to cause/ effect relations. The evidence suggests that humans retain the use of such algorithms, which are surely adaptive when causal judgments must be rapidly made. But we know very little about what these algorithms are and about when and with what ratiocinative procedures they are sometimes replaced. Nor do we know how the concept of causation originates in humans. To clarify some of these issues, this paper surveys the literature and explores the behavioral predictions made by two contrasting theories of causal learning: the mechanical Rescorla-Wagner model and the sophisticated reasoning codified in Bayes' Theorem.

Watanabe, Jiro. Categorial Intuition and the Understanding of Being in Husserl and Heidegger in Reading Heidegger: Commemorations, Sallis, John (ed). Bloomington, Indiana Univ Pr, 1992.

Waters, Alyson (trans) and Aragon, Louis. *Treatise on Style—Louis Aragon*. Lincoln, Univ of Nebraska Pr, 1991.

Watkin, Julia. Fighting for Narnia: Soren Kierkegaard and C S Lewis in Kierkegaard on Art and Communication, Pattison, George (ed). New York, St Martin's Pr, 1992.

It is argued that despite dissimilarities between them, Soren Kierkegaard and C S Lewis share in defending traditional supernaturalist Christianity. Kierkegaard and

Lewis use different apologetic strategies: Lewis emphasizes life after death and uses reason in straightforward defence of Christianity, Kierkegaard uses indirect communication, tones down emphasis on life after death, and appears to undermine Christianity. Both men are seen as using methods appropriate to their historical situation. Finally, the two methods are evaluated in their applicability to the continuing crisis of religious belief.

Watkins, John. Two All-or-Nothing Theories of Freedom in Logical Foundations, Mahalingam, Indira (ed). New York, St Martin's Pr, 1991.

This piece was a contribution to a Festschrift for D J O'Conner. It takes off from this quotation from him: 'Freedom is not an all-or-nothing property but a matter of degree.' The two theories examined are 1) Descartes's claim that 'to will and to be free are the same thing', which seems to elevate a "random walk" above a singleminded course of action; and 2) Schelling's claim that 'only that is free which acts according to its own inner being and is not determined by anything else', which seems to imply that no one is ever free.

Watling, John. The Importance of 'If' in A J Ayer Memorial Essays, Griffiths, A Phillips (ed). New York, Cambridge Univ Pr, 1991.

This paper takes issue with A J Ayer's widely shared view that non-truth-functional conditionals state no facts. To guide our actions, knowledge of what will happen in the future is irrelevant— we need knowledge of what will happen if. It cannot be that the conditionals expressing that knowledge state no facts. A distinction is made between a fundamentally indicative use of 'if', in arguing, and a subjunctive use, in expressing an argument's conclusion. Later, the paper considers why 'What would have happened if we were no to?' is not, for guiding action, the relevant questions about the past.

Watson, David. Hannah Arendt and the American Republic. *Trans Peirce Soc*, 28(3), 423-465, Sum 92.

The focus of this article is upon Arendt's interaction with American politics and society after her immigration in 1941, and the effect of her adopted country on her strong self-image as a contributor to a "German" philosophical tradition. Topics analysed include her concept of the "philosophy of *Existenz*", her political philosophy, her engagement with contemporary political problems (the Cold War, race and education), the controversy over *Eichmann in Jerusalem*, and her final philosophical work on the uncompleted *Life of the Mind*. The author concludes with an assessment of Arendt's philosophical project and her achievement, and comments on the fluctuations in her reputation since her death.

Watson, James R. Auschwitz and the Limits of Transcendence. *Phil Soc Crit*, 18(2), 163-183, 1992.

Watson, James R. Why Heidegger Wasn't Shocked by the Holocaust: Philosophy and its Defense System. *Hist Euro Ideas*, 14(4), 545-556, Jl 92.

Heidegger's refusal to reconsider his philosophical project in the terrible light of Auschwitz is treated here as an example of philosophy's complicity with the cultural apparatus that continues to make repetitions of the Shoah and genocidal State programs not only possible but likely. Heidegger's "withdrawal" of his 1949 Bremen lectures comments on the death camps from the published versions of these lectures is here interpreted as a cynical strategy for avoiding a fatal contradiction within his later formulation of the Seinsfrage. What is at stake here is Heidegger's contention that technicity is a fateful mittence of Being that (even after Auschwitz) holds forth the possibility of an authentic relationship of Being and "Man". Heidegger's *Was Heisst Denken?* text and *Der Spiegel* interview are then examined in the context of his "withdrawal".

Watson, Richard A. Author's Reply. *J Hist Phil*, 31(1), 122-123, Ja 93.

Watson, Richard A. Malebranche, Models, and Causation in Causation in Early Modern Philosophy, Nadler, Steven (ed). University Park, Penn St Univ Pr, 1993.

Concerning methodology in seventeenth century science of ideas, I argue that in controversy over the nature of ideas, Arnauld and Malebranche come to an ontological dead end. Arnauld exhibits the inadequacies of an Aristotelian explanatory model of how we know objects by way of ideas, and Malebranche of a Platonic model. This leads to the restriction of ideas to sensory perceptions by Berkeley and Hume. A way around the impasse is Leibniz's model of knowing by corresponding structural relations. But even Leibniz's model fails to explain how we know by way of ideas.

Watson, Richard A. Shadow History in Philosophy. *J Hist Phil*, 31(1), 95-109, Ja 93.

Shadow histories are perpetrated by polemical philosophers for the purpose of promoting their own positions. The shadow histories of Hegel, Hume, Descartes and representationalism as utilized by Russell, Ayer, Ryle, and Rorty are examined. I contend that these simplified constructions play a large role in the development of philosophy and should be studied by historians of philosophy.

Watson, Sam. The Tacit Victory and the Unfinished Agenda. *Tradition Discovery*, 18(3), 17-20, 1992.

Watson, Stephen. *Extensions: Essays on Interpretation, Rationality, and the Closure of Modernism*. Albany, SUNY Pr, 1992.

Watzlawick, Paul. The Illusion of 'Illusion' in Aesthetic Illusion, Burwick, Frederick (ed). Hawthorne, de Gruyter, 1990.

Waugh, Joanne B. Analytic Aesthetics and Feminist Aesthetics: Neither/Nor?. *J Aes Art Crit*, 48(4), 317-326, Fall 90.

Waxman, Wayne. Hume's Quandary Concerning Personal Identity. *Hume Stud*, 18(2), 233-253, N 92.

Hume's Treatise Book III appendix on personal identity is analyzed as concerned with a difficulty not with the Book I account of personal identity as such (the self as product of associational imagination) but a presupposition of that account: the succession of perceptions present to consciousness (which the imagination associates, thus giving to the fiction of an identity). It is then claimed that while Hume's theory of imagination offers no way out of quandary, Kantian imagination-based transcendental idealism does.

Waxman, Wayne. Impressions and Ideas: Vivacity as Verisimilitude. *Hume Stud*, 19(1), 75-88, Ap 93.

The thesis defended is that, for Hume, all vivacity, including that of impressions, is belief, and all belief, including the "infallibility" of the immediate given, is vivacity. This allows one to treat as different axes of description Hume's categories of perception (sensation, reflexion, and thought) and his categories of the consciousness of perception (belief, felt ease of transition), thus making it possible to defend his distinction between impressions and ideas against the criticisms of Ryle, Russell, and others. The article is an excerpt from my forthcoming book, *Hume's Theory of Consciousness* (Cambridge).

Waxman, Wayne. Time and Change in Kant and McTaggart. *Grad Fac Phil J*, 16(1), 179-187, 1993.

Waxman, Wayne. What Are Kant's Analogies About?. *Rev Metaph*, 47(1), 63-113, S 93.

An application and confirmation of the thesis of my book, *Kant's Model of the Mind*, that, for Kant, space and time exist only in and for imagination, and the given of sense is atemporal and aspatial (=transcendental idealism). On previous interpretations of transcendental idealism, appearances already have temporal and spatial existence; on mine, they lack such existence, and the purpose of the Analogies is to show how they originally acquire it. Existence in space and time is constituted by a priori principles of necessary connection (the Analogies), whose validity with respect to appearances is grounded on the demand for original apperception (i.e., a synthetic unitary sensibility). The implications vis à vis Kant's metaphysics of nature and his Euclideanism are then explored.

Weale, Albert. Nature versus the State? Markets, States, and Environmental Protection. *Crit Rev*, 6(2-3), 153-170, Spr-Sum 92.

Weatherston, Martin. The Rigour of Heidegger's Thought. *Man World*, 25(2), 181-194, Ap 92.

In this paper I explore how Heidegger's thought may be said to be "rigorous." Heidegger's reasons for rejecting the mathematical model of rigour for ontological thinking are explored. But while Heidegger's ontology lacks definitive proofs of the kind found in logic and mathematics, it is not without its own standards. I argue that Heidegger disciplines his thought not by appealing to actuality of the being on which it is based, but through a more complex (and more dangerous) method in which *possibility* is paramount. This conception of the rigour of ontological thought is based on his own phenomenological reading of the Kantian doctrine of *transcendental apperception*. The crucial element in Heidegger's own standards for thought lies in his conception of *finite freedom*.

Weaver, George E. Unifying Some Modifications of the Henkin Construction. *Notre Dame J Form Log*, 33(3), 450-460, Sum 92.

The theory of abstract deducibility relations introduced in Goldblatt (1984) is extended to provide an abstract setting for modifications of the Henkin construction introduced in Leblanc et al (1991). These modifications are replaced by Goldblatt's countable Henkin Principle to yield abstract forms of the omega-completeness theorem, the soundness and completeness of omega-logic, the theorem to the effect that omega-logic is a conservative extension of standard logic for omega-complete sets, and the theorem that all omega-complete sets are omega-consistent.

Webb, Eugene. *The Self Between: From Freud to the New Social Psychology of France*. Seattle, Univ Washington Pr, 1993.

Webb, Judson. Reconstruction from Recollection and the Refutation of Idealism: A Kantian Theme in the *Aufbau*. *Synthese*, 93(1-2), 93-105, N 92.

Webb, Mark Owen. The Epistemology of Trust and the Politics of Suspicion. *Pac Phil Quart*, 73(4), 390-399, D 92.

We ought to trust one another's utterances, and yet we do not trust the utterances of politically marginalized groups. Since 1) we should trust one another because we are in fact generally reliable; and 2) we are reliable because we must be truthful to one another to be in the same linguistic community; I argue that treating some segment of our linguistic group with suspicion amounts to excluding them (to some extent) from our linguistic group. Such as exclusion is used to try to warrant treating the subgroup paternalistically or even violently, since, if we can't understand them, we can't consult their desires or negotiate with them. This makes suspicion a natural tool for the privileged to use to marginalize groups they fear.

Webb, Mark Owen. Why I Know About As Much As You: A Reply to Hardwig. *J Phil*, 90(5), 260-270, My 93.

Hardwig argued that trust is an essential element in the practice of science. I argue that the same kind of blind trust is necessary for most ordinary knowledge.

Webb, R K. John Bowring and Unitarianism. *Utilitas*, 4(1), 43-79, My 92.

Weber, Erik. Models of Explanation: An Evaluation of Their Fruitfulness. *Commun Cog*, 25(4), 339-351, 1992.

Models of explanation are supposed to be fruitful: using the definition of explanation of the model (in substitution for our vague intuitive notions of what explanations are) should help us to solve problems in different areas of philosophy of science and epistemology, or at least help us to articulate some problems more precisely. In this article, I examine to which extent two epistemic models of explanation (Hempel and Gärdenfors) and two causal models (Humphreys and Salmon) are fruitful in specifying what understanding consists in and in describing the processes by means of which understanding is achieved.

Weber, Erik. The Indirect Practical Functions of Explanations. *Philosophica*, 51(1), 105-124, 1993.

Explaining has a theoretical function (creating understanding) but also several practical ones. Sometimes we explain in order to make a diagnosis or to assign legal responsibility. In these situations explaining has a direct practical use. However, I think that the search for explanations also has indirect practical functions. The aim of the paper is to clarify the nature of these indirect practical functions.

Weber, Leonard J. Ethics and the Praise of Diversity: Review of *Workforce America*. *Bus Ethics Quart*, 3(1), Ja 93.

Weber, Samuel. In the Name of the Law in Deconstruction and the Possibility of Justice, Cornell, Durcilla (ed). New York, Routledge, 1992.

Webster, Alison. J Barnave: Philosopher of a Revolution. *Hist Euro Ideas*, 17(1), 53-71, Ja 93.

Webster, Gerry and Goodwin, Brian and Smith, Joseph Wayne. The 'Evolutionary Paradigm' and Constructional Biology in New Horizons in the Philosophy of Science, Lamb, David (ed). Brookfield, Avebury, 1992.

Webster, Glenn and Janusz, Sharon. The Problem of Persons. *Process Stud*, 20(3), 151-161, Fall 91.

Wechsler, Sergio. Exchangeability and Predictivism. *Erkenntnis*, 38(3), 343-350, My 93.

A discussion is made on predictivism—a reductionist approach to statistical inference which Bruno de Finetti insisted on and which only recently has been rediscovered and advocated.

Wedin, Michael V. Content and Cause in the Aristotelian Mind. *S J Phil*, 31(Supp), 49-105, 1992.

For Aristotle psychological explanation involves showing how what occurs at one level is accounted for by what occurs at another, lower level of organization. This paper examines the proposal that psychological states and occurrences supervene on other, lower-level, states and occurrences. Texts discussed include *Physics* Vii as well as *De Anima*.

Wedin, Michael V. Trouble in Paradise? in Criss-Crossing A Philosophical Landscape, Schulte, Joachim (ed). Amsterdam, Rodopi, 1992.

It is argued that Wittgenstein did not abandon his tractarian position because he was of the opinion that the *Tractatus* suffered from an internal incoherence inherited from the incompatibility of the thesis of mutual independence of elementary propositions (MI) and the picture theory of the proposition (PIC) or an incoherent notion of the elementary proposition itself. In the way suggested, *TLP* provides no opportunity for such concerns to arise, for the inner sub-surface structure of a proposition cannot cause conflict with MI. It rather was the sub-surface nature of elementary propositions itself—a feature fundamental to the *Tractatus* as a whole—Wittgenstein came to be dissatisfied with and gave up in favour of a new notion of elementary proposition.

Wegener, Charles. *The Discipline of Taste and Feeling*. Chicago, Univ of Chicago Pr, 1992.

Working in that tradition in which 'aesthetics' is an analysis of imaginative perception as it may issue in the satisfactions of 'beauty' and 'sublimity', this book develops a guide to reflective exploration of aesthetic activity for *individuals* already engaged in it. The argument develops the 'norms' for this activity, that is, for the refinement and development of individual taste—freedom/engagement, austerity/objectivity, communicability/catholicity, authority/docility. A concluding examination of the place of aesthetic activity in our lives argues that taste is not grace or luxury but necessary expression of that freedom which is both fruit and condition of all culture.

Wei-ming, Tu. A Confucian Perspective on Embodiment in The Body in Medical Thought and Practice, Leder, Drew (ed). Dordrecht, Kluwer, 1992.

Wei-ming, Tu. *Way, Learning, and Politics: Essays on the Confucian Intellectual*. Albany, SUNY Pr, 1993.

Weiermann, Andreas and Rathjen, Michael. Proof-Theoretic Investigations on Kruskal's Theorem. *Annals Pure Applied Log*, 60(1), 49-88, F 93.

In this paper, we calibrate the exact proof-theoretic strength of Kruskal's theorem, thereby giving, in some sense, the most elementary proof of Kruskal's theorem. Furthermore, these investigations give rise to ordinal analyses of restricted bar induction.

Weigel, George and Johnson, James Turner. *Just War and the Gulf War*. Washington, Ethics & Pub Policy, 1991.

Weikard, Hans-Peter. A Methodological Note on Ethics, Economics, and the Justification of Action. *J Agr Environ Ethics*, 5(2), 183-188, 1992.

Two disciplines claim to provide justification of action. Ethics gives you moral reasons to act upon, whereas economics exploits the concept of rationality. The paper discusses two theories of interdisciplinarity of ethics and economics in order to clarify the relationship. The traditional view of a hierarchical ordering of ethics and economics is rejected, and it is claimed that there are substantial economic contributions to ethical justification.

Weikart, Richard. The Origins of Social Darwinism in Germany, 1859-1895. *J Hist Ideas*, 54(3), 469-488, Jl 93.

This article tests the applicability of the Hofstadter and Bannister theses on Social Darwinism in the Anglo-American world to see if either fits the German situation. It demonstrates that Social Darwinism was an important, but not dominant, ideology in late nineteenth-century Germany and was primarily the province of liberals. More importantly, it shows that Darwinism was used to justify both individual and collective forms of competition, often by the same thinkers.

Weimer, David L and Riker, William H. The Economic and Political Liberalization of Socialism: The Fundamental Problem of Property Rights. *Soc Phil Pol*, 10(2), 79-102, Sum 93.

The establishment of more effective property rights systems is a key to the successful economic and political liberalization of post-communist polities. More effective property rights systems have clarify of allocation, alienability, security from trespass, and credibility of persistence. Credibility is especially important for economic growth. It also contributes to political stability by limiting the policy dimensions subject to political debate. Yet credibility is difficult to achieve in the context of political instability. Social science offers little guidance in predicting the transformation of property rights in post-communist polities; the transformation, however, offers a valuable natural experiment for social scientist.

Weinberger, Ota. Conflicting Views on Practical Reason: Against Pseudo-Arguments in Practical Philosophy. *Ratio Juris*, 5(3), 252-268, D 92.

The author distinguishes two concepts of practical reason: a) practical reason as a source of practical principles, and b) practical reason as the theory of thought operations connected with action. He proves that there is no practical recognition in the sense (a). We can deal with actions only on the basis of dichotomic semantics. Critical analyses of some theories of practical reason are presented (Kant, Lorenzen, Apel, Alexy). The critical part of the paper mainly concerns the discourse theory and its implication for practical philosophy and jurisprudence.

Weinberger, Ota. Institutional Theory of Action and Its Significance for Jurisprudence. *Ratio Juris*, 6(2), 171-180, Jl 93.

Once affirmed that a formal and finalistic theory of action is one of the four pillars of neo-institutionalism, the author introduces the concept of *Freedom of action*, which is based on two points: the empirical existence of a scope for action and an information process which determine the choice between alternative action. He then analyzes different versions of determinism and the distinction between descriptive and practical sentences, and concludes that a theory of action based on the information process has to deal with the structures of teleological thought. In this sense he stresses the practical relevance of the plurality of ends, often conflicting with each other. Finally, he explains how formal teleology is used in his theory of action and how this theory provides methodological achievements for jurisprudence.

Weiner, David Avraham. *Genius and Talent: Schopenhauer's Influence on Wittgenstein's Early Philosophy*. Madison, F Dickinson U Pr, 1992.

Weiner, Scott E. Hegel's *Phenomenology of Spirit: 'The Science of the Umkehrung of Consciousness'*. *Clio*, 21(4), 381-399, Sum 92.

"The new object shows itself to have come about through an *Umkehrung of consciousness* itself" (*Phenomenology of Spirit*, Introduction, #87). After arguing for the central importance to the *Phenomenology* of this claim, I explain three approaches to interpreting *Umkehrung*, which are helpful to interpreting the *Phenomenology* as a whole, and support them with examples. I briefly survey discussions of the Introduction. I hold that *Umkehrung has an essential role in the Introduction as well as in the Phenomenology* overall: *Umkehrung* is pivotal to the structures and movements of the Phenomenology.

Weinert, Friedel. Vicissitudes of Laboratory Life. *Brit J Phil Sci*, 43(3), 423-430, S 92.

This paper argues that if *Laboratory Life* (B Latour/St Woolgar 1979) is to be taken seriously, as Hacking urges, its *whole* treatment of experimental science must be taken into account. But then three essential shortcomings of the study emerge; it fails to heed the important distinction between *data* and *phenomena* (so that the promised social construction of the Tyrotropin Releasing Harmone? is not demonstrated); the chosen methodology of the naive anthropological observer (which violates the sociological principle of 'native competence') is responsible for the paucity of its findings; and its depiction of scientists as laissez-faire capitalists is questionable.

Weinrib, Ernest J. Law as Idea of Reason in Essays on Kant's Political Philosophy, Williams, Howard (ed). Chicago, Univ of Chicago Pr, 1992.

This essay describes the articulated unity that extends from the Kantian notion of free will to the doctrines and institutions of the legal system. The essay analyzes the relationship between the constituents of the concept of right as a practical idea of reason. It then uses Kant's adaptation of Ulpian's precepts of right (live honorably, injure no one, and give each his due) to trace the conceptual progression from free will to the publicness of law. Finally, it elucidates Kant's views about the priority of the right and about the relationship between will and social context.

Weinsheimer, Joel. Suppose Theory Is Dead. *Phil Lit*, 16(2), 251-265, O 92.

Weinsheimer, Joel C. *Eighteenth-Century Hermeneutics: Philosophy of Interpretation in England from Locke to Burke*. New Haven, Yale Univ Pr, 1993.

The study examines the hermeneutics of Swift, Locke, Toland, Bolingbroke, Hume, Reid, Blackstone, and Burke. It concludes that interpretive theory in eighteenth-century England attempted to conceptualize a new way of thinking about truth, as belonging to reason and history together.

Weinstein, Bruce D. What Is an Expert?. *Theor Med*, 14(1), 57-74, Mr 93.

Experts play an important role in society, but there has been little investigation about the nature of expertise. I argue that there are two kinds of experts: those whose expertise is a function of what they *know* (epistemic expertise), or what they *do* (performative expertise). Epistemic expertise is the capacity to provide strong justifications for a range of propositions in a domain, while performative expertise is the capacity to perform a skill well according to the rules and virtues of a practice. Both epistemic and performative experts may legitimately disagree with one another, and the two senses are conceptually and logically distinct.

Weinstein, James. First Amendment Challenges to Hate Crime Legislation: Where's the Speech?. *Crim Just Ethics*, 11(2), 6-19, Sum-Fall 92.

Weinstein, James. Some Further Thoughts on "Thought Crimes". *Crim Just Ethics*, 11(2), 61-63, Sum-Fall 92.

Weinstein, Mark. Critical Thinking: The Great Debate. *Educ Theor*, 43(1), 99-117, Wint 93.

Critical thinking moves with strong currents in education, supporting the development of competent and reasonable citizens and reflecting such innovative approaches to learning as cooperative learning and problem solving. Yet it has been challenged at a foundational level, by an argument that purports to show that critical thinking in some general sense is conceptually confused. The paper is a review article of two recent contributions to the debate by John McPeck and Richard Paul. After an exposition of the authors' views, the paper attempts to reconfigure the debate, moving the discussion from the existence of general thinking skills to the related issues of the possibility of identifying universal norms for thought of relevance to education.

Weinstein, Scott and Osherson, Daniel N. Relevant Consequence and Empirical Inquiry. *J Phil Log*, 22(4), 437-448, Ag 93.

A criterion of adequacy is proposed for theories of relevant consequence. According to the criterion, scientists whose deductive reasoning is limited to some proposed subset of the standard consequence relation must not thereby suffer a reduction in scientific competence. A simple theory of relevant consequence is introduced and shown to satisfy the criterion with respect to a formally defined paradigm of empirical inquiry.

Weintraub, E Roy. But Doctor Salanti, Bumblebees Really Do Fly. *Econ Phil*, 9(1), 135-138, Ap 93.

Weintraub, Ruth. Fallibilism and Rational Belief. *Brit J Phil Sci*, 44(2), 251-261, Je 93.

According to the thesis of fallibilism, none of our beliefs is immune to error. But fallibilism is also a recommendation that we adopt a cautious doxastic attitude. The two are thought to be intimately linked. The fallibilist, aware of the ever-lurking possibility of error, ought (even if tempted) never to commit himself fully. My aim in this paper is to drive a wedge between the thesis and the recommendation. The (eminently plausible) doctrine, I argue, cannot be used to ground the epistemological prescription of caution.

Weintraub, Ruth. Objectivism Without Objective Probabilities. *Theoria*, 56(1-2), 23-41, 1990.

After defending a pluralistic approach to the interpretation of probability statements, I argue that the correctness of objective probability statements is not to be explained in terms of the objective probability attaching to a proposition. Such an explanation will enable us to uphold an intuitively appealing connection between probability and action only in indeterministic contexts, whereas the objectivity of probability statements doesn't depend on the truth of indeterminism. I show how objective probability statements can be interpreted without ascribing of objective probabilities to propositions. Finally, I draw a cautionary conclusion about the prospects for providing a probabilistic analysis of causation.

Weisbard, Alan J. A Polemic on Principles: Reflections on the Pittsburgh Protocol. *Kennedy Inst Ethics J*, 3(2), 217-230, Je 93.

The Pittsburgh protocol relies heavily on traditional moral distinctions, particularly the principle of double effect, to justify "managing" the dying process of a prospective organ donor in order to yield viable organs for transplantation. These traditional moral distinctions can be useful, particularly in casuistic or case-specific moral analysis, but their invocation here is unpersuasive, and potentially dangerous. The protocol relies on elaborate apologetics to avoid a candid confrontation with the moral challenge it poses — society's willingness to bring about the death of one patient (in isolation and with potential discomfort) in order to benefit another patient. Not only will this protocol fail to solve the problem it purports to address, it threatens to undermine the delicate social accommodations by which we distinguish the living from the dead, permissible "allowings to die" from impermissible killings, and those from whom organs may be removed from those whose bodies must remain inviolate.

Weislogel, Eric L. Schlegel's Irony: "Hoverings". *Ideal Stud*, 22(3), 203-213, S 92.

Weiss, Bernhard. Can an Anti-Realist Be Revisionary About Deductive Inference?. *Analysis*, 52(4), 216-224, O 92.

Dummett has argued that an anti-realist should refuse to accept recognition-transcendent facts and is likely to favour a revision of classical in favour of intuitionistic logic. Wright argues that the normative role of logical and mathematical systems emails that their inadequacy is unrecognisable, so a revisionary position is unavailable to an anti-realist. I point out that Wright's argument fails to take account of the sort of conflict that arises between practices. These systematic divergences are recognisable. So a revisionary anti-realism is tolerable.

Weiss, Roslyn. Killing, Confiscating, and Banishing at *Gorgias* 466-468. *Ancient Phil*, 12(2), 299-315, Fall 92.

It is argued that Socrates' argument at *Gorgias* 466-468 is provoked by the beliefs and attitudes expressed by the particular interlocutor he confronts in this passage—Polus—and constitutes Socrates' rebuke specifically to Polus's shameful and foolish view that rhetoricians, like tyrants, are the most enviable of men because they are powerful and because, as a consequence of their power, they can kill, confiscate, and banish at will.

Weissman, David. *Truth's Debt to Value*. New Haven, Yale Univ Pr, 1993.

Weithman, Paul. Augustine and Aquinas on Original Sin and the Function of Political Authority. *J Hist Phil*, 30(3), 353-376, J 92.

Augustine thought political authority's function is to restrain vicious behavior; Aquinas attributes to it a positive role. Scholarly arguments contrasting them appeal to texts in which they discuss whether there would have been political authority had the fall not occurred. Augustine thinks not; Aquinas explicitly says otherwise. I argue that Augustine did not think attachment to the common good morally valuable and so denied that promoting such attachment is a function of political authority. Aquinas thought attachment to the common good morally improving and numbered promoting this attachment among political authority's functions. It is a function he thinks government would have exercised even had humanity remained sinless.

Weithman, Paul. McDowell, Hypothetical Imperatives and Natural Law. *Amer Cath Phil Quart*, 65(2), 177-187, Spr 91.

In this paper I consider John McDowell's argument that the motivational force of requirements of virtue can be accounted for without appealing to the interests, desires or inclinations of the virtuous person. McDowell argues, against Philippa Foot's claim that moral imperatives are hypothetical, that the virtuous person sees his circumstances as giving him sufficient reason for virtuous action. Ascription of desires, interests or inclinations are, McDowell suggests, parasitic upon this perception of circumstances and unnecessary to explain virtuous action. I argue, for Foot and against McDowell, that antecedently intelligible interests or desires are necessary to account for the motivational force of at least some imperatives of virtue, those arrived at after practical deliberation. My discussion of deliberation draws on the work of Thomas Aquinas; I conclude by contrasting Aquinas's natural law view of the virtues with the view McDowell suggests.

Welbourne, Michael. More on Moore. *Analysis*, 52(4), 237-241, O 92.

This article examines two recent treatments of Moore's Paradox—O R Jones in *Analysis*, 51, 1991, and Thomas Baldwin's in his *G E Moore*, London, Routledge, 1990; it offers an alternative account. What is wrong about utterances of the form, 'P but I believe that not-P' or 'P but I don't believe that P'? The accounts under review start with good insights but fail to develop them correctly. The truth is that Moorean utterances cannot be taken seriously as assertions: the 'assertor' would be avowing insincerity and thus frustrating the 'assertion'.

Welch, John R. Responsabilidad colectiva y reduccionismo. *Pensamiento*, 189(48), 49-68, Ja-Mr 92.

Los individuous que constituyen una colectividad son responsables de sus actos como miembros de la misma. Pero, en algunas circunstancias, podrían también colectividades como naciones y sociedades anónimas ser responsables de sus actuaciones? Especialmente después de la Segunda Guerra Mundial, una pluralidad de opiniones lo afirman. Estas dicen que hay que reorientar el individualismo metodológico en el derecho y la ética con un concepto de responsbilidad colectiva. Se examinan dos argumentos influyentes a favor de la responsabilidad colectiva. Tratando el tema como problema de reducción, se aboga por un veredicto escocés: no probado.

Wellmer, Albrecht. What Is a Pragmatic Theory of Meaning? in Philosophical Interventions in the Unfinished Project of Enlightenment, Honneth, Axel (& other eds). Cambridge, MIT Pr, 1992.

Wellmer, Albrecht and Midgley, David N (trans). *The Persistence of Modernity: Essays on Aesthetics, Ethics, and Postmodernism*. Cambridge, MIT Pr, 1991.

These four essays, drawn from two books by one of Germany's foremost philosophers, go to the heart of a number of contemporary issues: Adorno's aesthetics, the nature of a postmodern ethics, and the persistence of modernity in the so-called postmodern age. Albrecht Wellmer defends the general thesis that modernity contains its own critique and that what has been called postmodernism is in fact a further articulation of that critique. More specifically, his essays offer a reinterpretation of Adorno's aesthetics within the framework of a postutopian philosophy of communicative reason, an analysis of the postmodern critique of instrumental reason and its subject that becomes an argument for democratic pluralism and universalism, a discussion of the dialectics of modernism and postmodernism in the context of architecture and industrial design, and a dialogical ethics that is inspired by and yet takes issue with Habermas' discourse ethics.

Wells, Deborah L and Kracher, Beverly J. Justice, Sexual Harassment, and the Reasonable Victim Standard. *J Bus Ethics*, 12(6), 423-432, Je 93.

In determining when sexual behavior at work creates a hostile working environment, some courts have asked, "Would a reasonable *person* view this as a hostile environment? Other courts have asked, "Would a reasonable *victim* view this is as a hostile environment?" There is no consensus in the legal community regarding which of these is just. Using moral theory, businesses can construct just procedures regarding sexually hostile environments. The duty of mutual respect of persons and the duty not to harm the innocent compels use of the reasonable victim standard. A training approach to reducing sexual harassment at work is proposed.

Wells, George Geoffrey. Autonomy, Self-Consciousness and National Moral Responsibility. *Hist Euro Ideas*, 16(4-6), 949-955, Ja 93.

Because the sovereign nation is analogous in important respects to the autonomous person, it is possible, and indeed necessary, to think in terms of national moral responsibility. An emerging vocabulary of transnationalism and globalization notwithstanding, the political reality of a pluralistic world requires moral accountability. This argument is developed by thinking of autonomy not as mere self-legislation (or juridicial sovereignty), but in terms of thoughtfulness and respect for human dignity and liberty. Essential to this conception of autonomy—and, in its realization, to a sense of responsibility—is the development of self-discovery and self-expression.

Wells, Kelley J. An Argument for a Metaphysical Reading of Charles Sanders Peirce's Pragmatic Maxim. *Kinesis*, 19(2), 25-34, Sum 93.

It is claimed that Peirce's pragmatic maxim has a pragmatic metaphysical structure embedded within it. One common interpretation, that the maxim reports conceptual meaning only, is specifically rejected. Other interpretations of the maxim, such as that of truth verification, are rejected by inference. The paper concludes that the anti-metaphysical conventions surrounded the pragmatic maxim have encouraged an atmosphere of metaphysical irresponsibility in contemporary philosophy.

Wells, Norman J. *Esse Cognitum* and Suárez Revisited. *Amer Cath Phil Quart*, 67(3), 339-348, Sum 93.

The purpose of the work is to clarify the ambiguous use, in Suárez, of the terms *esse cognitum/esse objectivium* so that no charge of "mentalism" can be brought while, at the same time, it can be acknowledged that *res* enjoys an intramental mode of using, i.e., "objectively" (*l'onceptus objectivus*) as well as an intramental "normal" mode of being (*conceptus formulis*).

Welsch, Wolfgang. The Birth of Postmodern Philosophy from the Spirit of Modern Art. *Hist Euro Ideas*, 14(3), 379-398, My 92.

The attempt is made to correct well-loved misunderstandings by demonstrating precisely what would, according to the common schema, have to be impossible: a congruence of postmodern thinking with specific achievements of modernity. First, Dubuffet is accentuated as a postmodern artist *avant la lettre*. Then it is shown that all of the central points in Lyotard's thought can be conceived of as translations of characteristics of modern art into philosophical options. Discussing Foucault and Derrida, it becomes clear that postmodern philosophy articulates discursively what modern art has already practiced.

Welshon, Robert. Nietzsche's Peculiar Virtues and the Health of the Soul. *Int Stud Phil*, 24(2), 77-89, 1992.

Welshon, Robert. Response to Lester Hunt's Comments. *Int Stud Phil*, 24(2), 95-97, 1992.

Welten, W. The Human Being as Substance and as Actual Entity. *Gregorianum*, 73(2), 317-328, 1992.

Cet article, élaboration d'une causerie faite au 3 Congrès Européen de *Ultimate Reality and Meaning* (URAM) (Leuven, Septembre 1990), est à situer dans la discussion entre deux écoles de philosophie réaliste: la métaphysique aristotélicienne de la substance et la philosophie whiteheadienne du processus. Pour Aristotle la réalité ultime est l'être, et la question de l'être est celle de la substance; la Catégorie de l'Ultime selon Whitehead contient la notion de créativité, rendue concrète dans les entités actuelles, événements élémentairs. Dans cet article l'auteur montre qu'il existe une entité qui peut être appelée à la fois substance et évéement élémentaire, à savoir, le Je. Il établit d'abord une première thèse: "Je suis une substance". Sa deuxième thèse est: "Je suis une antinomie. Plusieurs voies sont explorées en vue de résoudre cette antinomie; une solution est trouvée, mais elle n'est peut-être pas complètement satisfaisante.

Wenkart, Henny. The Primordial Myth of The Bad Mother and The Good Mother in *Persons and Places* and in *The Last Puritan*. *Bull Santayana Soc*, 10, 9-16, Fall 92.

Wennemann, D J. Freedom and Dialectic in Ellul's Thought. *Res Phil Technol*, 11, 67-75, 1991.

Wenning, Wolfgang. Marty and Magnus on Colours in Mind, Meaning and Metaphysics, Mulligan, Kevin (ed). Dordrecht, Kluwer, 1990.

Wenz, Peter. Minimal, Moderate, and Extreme Moral Pluralism. *Environ Ethics*, 15(1), 61-74, Spr 93.

Concentrating on the views of Christopher Stone, who advocates moral pluralism, and J Baird Callicott, who criticizes Stone's views, I argue that the debate has been confused by a conflation of three different positions, here called minimal, moderate, and extreme moral pluralism. Minimal pluralism is uncontroversial because all known moral theories are minimally pluralistic. Extreme pluralism is defective in the ways that Callicott alleges and, moreover, is inconsistent with integrity in the moral life. However, moderate pluralism of the sort that I advance in *Environmental Justice* is distinct from extreme pluralism and free of its defects. It is also consistent with Callicott's version of Aldo Leopold's land ethic, which is itself moderately pluralistic.

Wenz, Peter S. A Liberal's Brief Against *Meyer* and *Pierce*. *Cont Phil*, 15(3), 4-7, My-Je 93.

Two landmark Supreme Court decisions, *Meyer v Nebraska* and *Pierce v Society of Sisters* are often lauded by political liberals, such as Laurence Tribe. I show, however, that these cases should be disavowed by liberals because they can easily be used by conservatives to challenge the constitutionality of: 1) voluntary affirmative action and preferential admissions program; 2) court decisions that give minors the right to obtain contraceptive and abortion services without parental notification or consent; 3) the most effective means of effecting racial integration in schools; and 4) limitations on property rights needed to protect the natural environment.

Wenz, Peter S. Alternate Foundations for the Land Ethic: Biologism, Cognitivism, and Pragmatism. *Topoi*, 12(1), 53-67, Mr 93.

The present paper discusses the philosophical foundations that J Baird Callicott offers for Aldo Leopold's land ethic. These foundations are cognitive, not biological, so difficulties of cognitive determinism replace those of biological determinism. The present paper introduces neo-pragmatic methodology that avoids the pitfalls of cultural relativism, and uses this methodology to support the land ethic. Supporting considerations concern environmental crises, past and present, animal suffering at the hands of human beings, widespread loyalty toward many corporate entities, and the mythical background of most human attitudes and activities.

Werhane, Patricia H. Wittgenstein and Moral Realism. *J Value Inq*, 26(3), 381-393, Jl 92.

I argue, contra Sabina Lovibond, that one cannot defend a viable form of moral realism from the perspective of linguistic conventionalism. Appealing to the later Wittgenstein, I argue that Wittgenstein's alleged linguistic conventionalism rests on the objective ground of the notion of a rule. While Wittgenstein acknowledges that the subjective and social context out of which we operate precludes getting at reality independent of a perspective, neither is he an anti-realist nor does he replace truth conditions with assertability conditions. If conventions are grounded in the notion of a rule, we can then use this conclusion to defend a form or moral realism.

Werhane, Patricia H and Donaldson, Thomas J. *Ethical Issues in Business: A Philosophical Approach (Fourth Edition)*. Englewood Cliffs, Prentice Hall, 1993.

Werne, Stanley J. Taking Rough Drafts Seriously. *Teach Phil*, 16(1), 47-58, Mr 93.

Werne describes rough draft work sessions, a formalized kind of student peer review of papers, as a way in which teachers of philosophy can help students collaborate in improving their writing of philosophical essays. He explains how he conducts the sessions, discusses some details about which professors would have to make decisions, reports student reactions to the process, and responds to two common questions from other teachers.

Wernick, Andrew. Post-Marx: Theological Themes in Baudrillard's 'America' in Shadow of Spirit, Berry, Philippa (ed). New York, Routledge, 1992.

Examines the religious subtext of Baudrillard's later writings, focusing on *America* and *Cool Memories*. Situates Baudrillard in the second death of God held to characterize post-structuralist moments in the French adventure with reason and faith revived in the Comte Durkheim project of sociology. His ironic identification with the fatality of the object is seen as maintaining ties with left-wing eschatology, while embracing the nihilist consequences of the (actual and the theoretical) dissolution of the socio-historically 'real'.

Wernick, Andrew (ed) and Berry, Philippa (ed). *Shadow of Spirit*. New York, Routledge, 1992.

By illuminating the striking affinity between the most innovative aspects of postmodern thought and religious or mystical discourse, *Shadow of Spirit* challenges the long-established assumption that Western thought is committed to Nihilism. The collection explores the implications of that fascination with the "sacred" "divine" or "infinite" which characterizes the work of Derrida, Baudrillard, Lyotard, Irisarty and others.

Werpehowski, William. Weeping at the Death of Dido: Sorrow, Virtue, and Augustine's *Confessions*. *J Relig Ethics*, 19(1), 175-191, Spr 91.

If the study of Christian ethics concerns, among other things, consideration of the character of persons who would be disciples of Jesus Christ, then it must be concerned both by virtues and with the feelings or affections appropriate to such a character. This essay explores the affection of sorrow in its connection with the virtue of charity. Following an examination of relevant discussions by Augustine, Kierkegaard, and Calvin, the analysis is illustrated and extended through an interpretation of literary patterns of sorrow and mourning in Augustine's *Confessions*. That text, on the one hand, gives a partial depiction of how one may come to sorrow well; on the other hand, it points out a significant sort of failure in discrimination in how one should feel.

Werpehowski, William (ed) and Santurri, Edmund N (ed). *The Love Commandments: Essays in Christian Ethics and Moral Philosophy*. Washington, Georgetown Univ Pr, 1992.

Werther, David. The Temptation of God Incarnate. *Relig Stud*, 29(1), 47-50, Mr 93.

I discuss Thomas V Morris's view that the "epistemic possibility" of temptation is a sufficient condition for genuine temptation, and argue that the second person of the Trinity could not have been responsible for resisting temptation if his divine nature included the property of essential goodness.

Wertz, S K. Hume and the Historiography of Science. *J Hist Ideas*, 54(3), 411-436, Jl 93.

I examine Hume's historiographical category of Character and its application to important figures in the history of science who appear in his *History of England*. From the over forty Characters we find ones of Bacon, formation of the royal Society, the French Academy of Science, Boyle, Harvey, and Newton. These Characters illustrate Hume's historiography of science. conjoined to these brief intellectual biographies and narrative descriptions of the European scientific groups are numerous other historical references to science which nicely illustrate Hume "adorning the facts." Consequently when these episodes are viewed together we may legitimately claim that Hume was one of the first historians of science, and that he had an interest in accounting for the growth or development of science in Great Britian. The paper also attempts to locate Hume in the historiography of science. (edited)

Wertz, S K. Museum Projects and Theories of Art. *Teach Phil*, 15(2), 139-149, J 92.

This essay describes several philosophy of art and aesthetics courses involving student projects at three local museums. The projects have succeeded in getting students to better understand both the art and the theories of art (Collingwood, Dewey, and Danto) covered in the course. The essay ends with a description of a class project, covering the local and national debate in 1989 over expansion plans of the Kimbell Art Museum, which we discuss with reference to the aesthetics of architecture. Besides learning the material, the students got a sense of contributing to the civic debate. Consequently museum projects are important pedagogical tools to use in aesthetics and philosophy of art courses.

West, Cornel. A Reply to Westbrook, Brodsky, and Simpson. *Praxis Int*, 13(1), 46-49, Ap 93.

West, Cornell. *Keeping Faith: Philosophy and Race in America*. New York, Routledge, 1993.

Westbrook, Robert B. Democractic Evasions: Cornel West and the Politics of Pragmatism. *Praxis Int*, 13(1), 1-13, Ap 93.

Westbrook, Robert B. *John Dewey and American Democracy*. Ithaca, Cornell Univ Pr, 1991.

Westfall, Richard S. *The Life of Isaac Newton*. New York, Cambridge Univ Pr, 1993.

The Life of Isaac Newton is a condensed version of *Never at Rest*, a biography of Newton published thirteen years ago. Like all biographies, the book attempts to give a full account of its subject in all of his manifold activities, in this case with Newton's scientific pursuits, the reason one undertakes to write about his like, as its central thread. Unlike earlier biographies, the book devotes serious attention to Newton's interest in alchemy, his extensive writings on theology, and his duties as Warden and then Master of the Mint. The technical passages in *Never at Rest* have been severely reduced and footnotes entirely eliminated in an effort to make the biography attractive to a popular audience.

Weston, Anthony. *A Rulebook for Arguments (Second Edition)*. Indianapolis, Hackett, 1992.

Weston, Anthony. Before Environmental Ethics. *Environ Ethics*, 14(4), 321-338, Wint 92.

Contemporary nonanthropocentric ethics is profoundly shaped by the very anthropocentrism that it tries to transcend. New values only slowly struggle free of old contexts. Recognizing this struggle, however, opens a space for—indeed, necessitates—alternative models for contemporary environmental ethics. Rather than trying to unify or fine-tune our theories, we require more pluralistic and exploratory methods. We cannot reach theoretical finality; we can only co-evolve an ethic with transformed practices.

Weston, Anthony. Ivan Illich and the Radical Critique of Tools. *Res Phil Technol*, 9, 171-182, 1989.

Weston, Anthony. On the Body in Medical Self-Care and Holistic Medicine in The Body in Medical Thought and Practice, Leder, Drew (ed). Dordrecht, Kluwer, 1992.

Weston, Michael. Philosophy and Religion in the Thought of Kierkegaard. *Philosophy*, 32(Supp), 9-29, 1992.

Weston, Michael. Philosophy and Religion in the Thought of Kierkegaard in Philosophy, Religion and the Spiritual Life, McGhee, Michael (ed). New York, Cambridge Univ Pr, 1992.

Westphal, Jonathan and Wahl, Russell. Descartes, Leibniz and Berkeley on Whether We Can Dream Marks on the Waking State. *Stud Leibniz*, 24(2), 177-181, 1992.

Cottingham proposed a general objection to any test which would be a test of whether a person is awake, namely that it will always be conceivable that someone could dream the test was satisfied. We argue first, that the issue for Descartes is not whether one could dream a mark of the waking state was present, but whether the purported mark is in fact a mark. We argue second that Cottingham's claim begs the question against the very marks suggested by Descartes, Leibniz and even Berkeley.

Westphal, Kenneth. Hegel, Idealism, and Robert Pippin. *Int Phil Quart*, 33(3), 263-272, S 93.

According to Pippin, post-Kantian German idealism rests on the thesis that self-conscious judgment about objects presupposes certain condition. Pippin's interpretation of Hegel is mistaken because: 1) only certain kinds of such conditions entail idealism; 2) Hegel's "autonomy of thought" does not primarily concern human thinking; 3) Hegel's unique sense of "idealism" does not contrast with "realism" (as Pippin assumes); 4) Pippin's pivotal interpretation "Force and Understanding" is undermined by Hegel's own examples; 5) Hegel's *Logic* frequently uses contingent empirical categories because Hegel's idealism is deeply naturalistic and is expressly based on empirical science.

Westphal, Kenneth. Kant on the State, Law, and Obedience to Authority in the Alleged 'Anti-Revolutionary' Writings. *J Phil Res*, 17, 383-426, 1992.

I resolve the tension between Kant's conception of persons as ends in themselves and his rejection of the right of revolution by showing that Kant's legal principles contain two distinct grounds of obedience to political authority. Kant's strict metaphysical principles only support the duty to obey legitimate law or fully legitimate authorities. Kant's moral-pragmatic principles ground a duty to obey the state insofar as it helps improve one's character by counter-balancing one's immoral inclinations. This is Kant's ultimate, *conditional* ground for obedience to *de facto*, imperfectly legitimate states. Kant holds that actual states easily meet this condition.

Westphal, Kenneth. The Basic Context and Structure of Hegel's 'Philosophy of Right' in The Cambridge Companion to Hegel, Beiser, Frederick (ed). New York, Cambridge Univ Pr, 1993.

I reconstruct the context and main argument of Hegel's *Philosophy of Right*. Free action requires the correspondence of the intentions and consequences of one's acts. Hegel argues that the principles, aims, and means of action are social. Consequently, free action is possible only within a community which makes known its structure and the role of its members within it, so that they can act on the basis of that knowledge. Hegel's liberal theory of the state is a theory of a social structure which makes such autonomous, free action possible. (Addendum in: *The Owl of Minerva*, 25-1, 1993.)

Westphal, Merold. *Hegel, Freedom, and Modernity*. Albany, SUNY Pr, 1992.

The first four chapters comprise a mini commentary on the *Philosophy of Rights*. The next three explore Hegel's understanding of dialectical reason in dialogue with Gadamer and Husserl. The problem that emerges from these two moments in Hegel's thought is the search for a nonsectarian spirituality of community, the theme of the final six chapters, in dialogue with Hinduism, the Reformation, Pannenberg, and Tillich.

Westphal, Merold. Kierkegaard's Teleological Suspension of Religious B in Foundations of Kierkegaard's Vision of Community, Connell, George B (ed). Atlantic Highlands, Humanities Pr, 1992.

Kierkegaard's theory of the stages does not culminate, as is usually thought, with Religiousness B as presented in the *Postscript*. the deconstruction of that position as a final stage on life's way already begins in the *Postscript*. In such texts as *Practice in Christianity* and *For Self-Examination*, we meet Religiousness C, for which Jesus is the Pattern or the Paradigm, not merely the Paradox.

Westphal, Merold. Levinas, Kierkegaard, and the Theological Task. *Mod Theol*, 8(3), 241-261, Jl 92.

On the basis of extensive parallels between these thinkers, three implications are given: 1) Theology should have a confessional form; 2) Theology should be oriented to spiritual formation; and 3) Theology should employ a hermeneutics of suspicion. A fourth implication, that all theology should be liberation theology leads to a crucial difference. For Levinas the Other is, in the first instance, the human neighbor, while for Kierkegaard it is God.

Westphal, Merold. Religious Experience as Self Transcendence and Self-Deception. *Faith Phil*, 9(2), 168-192, Ap 92.

Religious experience can be defined as self-transcendence. Models of this decentering of the self are not found in the transcendence of intentionality or in either contemplative or ecstatic self-forgetfulness, since all these leave the self as center. While they play important roles in authentic religion, experience that does not get beyond them is self-deceived and ultimately idolatrous. Only in the ethical claim that places limits on my will to be the center do I encounter the truly other. Even here the form of true religion may assist self-deception about the presence of its substance.

Westphal, Merold. Taking St Paul Seriously in Christian Philosophy, Flint, Thomas P (ed). Notre Dame, Univ Notre Dame Pr, 1990.

Not only in the hermeneutics of suspicion of Marx, Nietzsche, and Freud, but throughout the philosophical tradition we find many philosophical arguments urging us, in effect, to take seriously St Paul's use of sin as an epistemological category. Christian philosophers in particular should include this theme in their epistemological agenda.

Westphal, Merold. The Cheating of Cratylus (Genitivus Subjectivus) in Modernity and Its Discontents, Marsh, James L (ed). Bronx, Fordham Univ Pr, 1992.

The critical rationalism of Habermas (and Marsh) seems rooted in fear of the arbitrary. The Deconstruction of Derrida (and Caputo) seems rooted in fear of the absolute. Both fears are well founded, which means that instead of choosing between the two positions it is necessary to affirm both, not as an Hegelian synthesis but as a tension to be lived rather than resolved.

Westphal, Merold and Caputo, John D and Marsh, James L. A Philosophical Dialogue in Modernity and Its Discontents, Marsh, James L (ed). Bronx, Fordham Univ Pr, 1992.

Westphal, Merold (ed) and Caputo, John D (ed) and Marsh, James L (ed). *Modernity and Its Discontents*. Bronx, Fordham Univ Pr, 1992.

Westra, Laura. Response—Dr Frankenstein and Today's Professional Biotechnologist: A Failed Analogy?. *Between Species*, 8(4), 216-221, Fall 92.

Wetherick, Norman. Velmans on *Consciousness, Brain and the Physical World*. *Phil Psych*, 5(2), 159-161, 1992.

Velmans postulates a world-of-physics and worlds-as-perceived, "constructed" by individual brains and "projected" to the judged location of the physical objects. No account is offered of the relation between the two or of the relation between different worlds-as-perceived. Since our perceptual capacities are, presumably, on a continuum with aids to perception developed by science (e.g., microscopes, radar scanners, infra- red sensors) we have to suppose that the surface of the planet Venus and the structure of the protein molecule are both parts of the world-as-perceived. What is left for the world-of-physics?

Wetherly, Paul. An Analytical Outline of Historical Materialism in Marx's Theory of History, Wetherly, Paul. Brookfield, Avebury, 1992.

Wetherly, Paul. *Marx's Theory of History*. Brookfield, Avebury, 1992.

Wetherly, Paul. Mechanisms, Methodological Individualism and Marxism: A Response to Elster in Marx's Theory of History, Wetherly, Paul. Brookfield, Avebury, 1992.

Wetherly, Paul. The Factory Acts in Marx's Theory of History, Wetherly, Paul. Brookfield, Avebury, 1992.

Wettersten, John R. *The Roots of Critical Rationalism*. Amsterdam, Rodopi, 1992.

The historical and intellectual roots of critical rationalism are traced from the days of the Wheweil-Mill classical debate to Popper's work, through the work of Johannes Müller, Wilhelm Wundt, Hermann Helmholtz, Oswald Külpe and Popper's Doktorvater, Karl Bühler. Special attention is paid to the neglected aspect of his early work, namely the interaction between research in the psychology and philosophy of learning. It presents the growth of Popper's philosophy from Seizian psychology, through his more positivist phase and back then to the realism which he defended as a young beginner.

Wetz, Franz Josef. Die Überwindung des Marburger Neukantianismus in der Spätphilosophie Natorps. *Z Phil Forsch*, 47(1), 75-92, Ja-Mr 93.

Wetz, Franz Josef. Schelling—Lask—Sartre: Die zweifache Unbegreiflichkeit der nackten Existenz. *Theol Phil*, 65(4), 549-565, 1990.

Wetzel, James. Infinite Return: Two Ways of Wagering with Pascal. *Relig Stud*, 29(2), 139-150, Je 93.

Pascal's Wager continues to hold the attention of philosophers who would be apt to dismiss or restrict its apologetic value. This is because the Wager's philosophical interest has depended less on its power to persuade than on its prototypical representation of practical reasoning in theology. Wetzel contends that there is no easy way to distinguish the Wager's apologetic merits from its form of practical reasoning, and that two distinct and incompatible versions of the Wager emerge when the prospect of an infinite return is explicated. Only one of them is worth taking.

Wetzel, Linda. What are Occurrences of Expressions?. *J Phil Log*, 22(2), 215-220, Ap 93.

Whale, John C. Literal and Symbolic Representations: Burke, Paine and the French Revolution. *Hist Euro Ideas*, 16(1-3), 343-349, Ja 93.

Wheeler III, Samuel C. True Figures: Metaphor, Social Relations, and the Sorites in The Interpretive Turn, Hiley, David R (ed). Ithaca, Cornell Univ Pr, 1991.

This essay is midrash on Davidson and Quine, with supplementation by Derrida and Foucault. The essay consists of three parts: First, I show how power relations affect what is true. Second, I argue that the *unanimous* "cultures" and "forms of life" that analytic philosophy has assumed are deceptive fictions. "Community" does not support the philosophers' notion of language as a unified system of rules. Third, I show how metaphor and the Sorites are accommodated on this account. Important metaphors make the relevance of power transparent. Sorites arguments show that truth is adjudicated rather than pre-fixed.

Whelan, Jr, John M. Contractualism and the Right to Aid. *J Phil Res*, 17, 427-442, 1992.

In this paper I try to defend three claims: first, that there is a requirement to aid and a correlative right to be aided; second, that the conditions under which this right applies can be precisely stated and given a convincing contractualist rationale; and third, that the existence of this right has no relevance for the justifiability of social welfare programs.

Whisner, William N. Overcoming Rationalization and Self-Deception: The Cultivation of Critical Thinking. *Educ Theor*, 43(3), 309-322, Sum 93.

In a high frequency of cases the fear of present discomfort or future discomfort plays a motivational role in both rationalization and self-deception. Persons rationalize in offering reasons in support of beliefs or their termination; however, they do not form, maintain, or terminate these beliefs because they believe or judge that the reasons are good in light of evidence. Such reasons may even function in arguments that are valid or correct and sound; however, the person does not hold or terminate the belief because of the reasons. Several educational strategies are suggested to overcome the tendency to engage in rationalization and self-deception.

Whisner, William N. Rationalization, Self-Deception and the Demise of Practical Moral Reason. *J Soc Phil*, 23(2), 157-175, Fall 92.

In one central type of rationalization, one rationalizes if one is motivated by fear to offer or accept reasons in support of forming, maintaining, or terminating beliefs in order to avoid present or future discomfort. One does not form, maintain, or terminate the belief because of an examination and evaluation of the reasons one offers or accepts. Rationalizations are constituted by reasons that fail to explain, or fail to justify, or fail to explain and justify one's formation, maintenance, or termination of beliefs. Hypotheses are offered to explain the high frequency of rationalization in public policy debate.

White, Alan. Suspicion in Wittgenstein's Intentions, Canfield, J V (ed). Hamden, Garland, 1993.

White, David A. Kant on Plato and the Metaphysics of Purpose. *Hist Phil Quart*, 10(1), 67-82, Ja 93.

Part I of this article poses two textual problems concerning the first *Critique*'s interpretation of Platonic ideas. These problems establish the notions of purpose and purposiveness as crucial to Kant's Understanding of Plato. The answers to these problems also show how Kant imitated Plato, in both the first and third *Critiques*, by positing notions of purpose and purposiveness that parallel Plato's mind and the good as developed in the *Republic* (parts II and III). Although Kant's stated position is that purposiveness is heuristic, Part IV argues the senses in which purposiveness is in fact constitutive in the first and third *Critiques*.

White, David A. On the Limits of Classical Reason: Derrida and Aristotle. *J Brit Soc Phenomenol*, 23(2), 120-126, My 92.

This paper develops an Aristotelian framework for assessing Derrida's critique of classical reason, in particular as reasoning is exemplified in the syllogism. The paper shows some of the logical concepts Derrida's version of hermeneutics would have to address in order to be fully persuasive in its deconstructive intention. The paper concludes by examining several crucial implications drawn from Derrida's principles pertaining to the possibility of preserving meaningful discourse in fundamental disciplines.

White, David A. *Rhetoric and Reality in Plato's 'Phaedrus'*. Albany, SUNY Pr, 1992.

This interpretation of the *Phaedrus* shows how the details of the myth in Socrates' second speech and the accounts of interactions between lovers are based on an articulated metaphysical structure. The study indicates how passages that may not appear relevant to metaphysics have been deployed to heighten the vision of reality that Socrates develops in the second speech. The work concludes with an Epilogue in which the metaphysical principles adumbrated in the dialogue are briefly developed. The Epilogue helps illustrate the continuity between the *Phaedrus* and dialogues such as the *Parmenides* and *Philebus*, in which method and metaphysics are dominant for Plato.

White, David A. Toward a Theory of Profundity in Music. *J Aes Art Crit*, 50(1), 23-34, Wint 92.

This article presents a theoretical approach toward articulating the meaning of profundity when that term is predicated of musical works. Part I attempts to show, against Peter Kivy, that a rational justification of profundity can be given. Part II illustrates the relevance of certain general terms — unity, whole and part, identity and difference — to the experience of profound music by concentrating on Beethoven's 14th string quartet as an exemplar of musical profundity. Part III supplements the speculative character of Part II and sketches a program for additional work in this area.

White, Graham. William of Ockham and Adam Wodeham. *Heythrop J*, 34(3), 296-301, Jl 93.

White, Hayden. The Metaphysics of Narrativity: Time and Symbol in Ricoeur's Philosophy of History in On Paul Ricoeur: Narrative and Interpretation, Wood, David (ed). New York, Routledge, 1991.

White, John. Can Education for Democratic Citizenship Rest on Socialist Foundations?. *J Phil Educ*, 26(1), 19-27, 1992.

The paper examines two recent arguments, by Keith Graham and Richard Norman, to the effect that a liberal individualist foundation is insufficient for a socialist conception of democracy and needs to be replaced or supplemented by collectivist notions [1]. It concludes that these arguments are unsound and that a defensible education for democratic citizenship on socialist lines should be based on liberal values, not least that of personal autonomy. At the same time it concedes to collectivism that socialist democracy needs to operate within a social framework, but sees national communities rather than social classes or smaller-scale groupings as the most promising candidates for this.

White, John. The Roots of Philosophy. *Philosophy*, 33(Supp), 73-88, 1992.

This is a sceptical look at claims about the philosophical abilities of young children. Starting with Gareth Matthews, who argues that even children as young as five or six think philosophically, it then assesses Richard Kitchener's critique, agreeing with him that no evidence is given of higher-order thinking. The last half of the paper looks at when professional philosophers first encountered philosophical problems. This includes a sceptical critique of Colin Radford's autobiographical account of his experiences at five and six and concludes from a survey of well-known philosophers that, with rare exceptions, philosophical interests seem to begin only in the teens.

White, John. The Roots of Philosophy in The Impulse to Philosophise, Griffiths, A Phillips (ed). New York, Cambridge Univ Pr, 1992.

The paper is a sceptical examination of claims, e.g., by G Matthews and M Lipman, about young children's ability and propensity to philosophize. It asks whether the evidence presented for such achievements adequately supports these claims. It critically discusses R Kitchener's Piagetian critique of the latter, as well as C Radford's autobiographical account of his infant philosophizing. The final section is an empirical review of when well-known philosophers first began to philosophize, concluding that for most of them little happened before the middle teens.

White, Kevin. A Sociological Perspective on Disease in New Horizons in the Philosophy of Science, Lamb, David (ed). Brookfield, Avebury, 1992.

This paper explores different methods of approaching the concept of disease. It identifies three conceptual frameworks for explaining disease: Cartesian (empirical), Hegelian (normative) and Nietzschian (social). The first two are rejected on the grounds that they are based on a historic and absolutist concepts of disease and the paper consequently argues the case for a Nietzschian account according to which diseases are social phenomena constituted by me society in which they are located.

White, Michael J. Aristotle on the Non-Supervenience of Local Motion. *Phil Phenomenol Res*, 53(1), 143-155, Mr 93.

Aristotle accepts 'non-supervenience' principles that preclude the constitution of what is continuous from parts that are indivisible. These principles are incompatible with a contemporary *positional/'at-at'* conception that identifies motion with a dense, Dedekind-continuous linear array of 'instantaneous positions' of a body. As an instantiation of his non-supervenience principles, Aristotle adopts a *metrical* conception of motion, according to which the motion of a body is analyzed as the 'measuring' of its trajectory by the body's magnitude or some proper part of that magnitude. This metrical conception underlies Aristotle's arguments indivisibles cannot move except *per accidens* and *may* have influenced Proclus' comments on geometers' definition of a line.

White, Michael J. Folk Theories and Physical Metrics in Certainty and Surface in Epistemology and Philosophical Method, Martinich, A P (ed). Lewiston, Mellen Pr, 1991.

The first part of this paper criticizes one conception of folk theory—that of folk theory as (some proper part of) an *Urtheorie* or 'implicit', 'pre-analytic', and 'naive' theory that persons possess about (parts of) their environment and that typically is replaced by 'real' theories as a result of scientific progress and of education. The second part of the paper demonstrates the futility of attempting to invoke such model in a context where, it is argued, such a model, *if* legitimate, should be useful: the resolution of certain semantic issues in the debate between metrical realists.

White, Michael J. The Foundations of the Calculus and the Conceptual Analysis of Motion: The Case of the Early Leibniz (1670-1676). *Pac Phil Quart*, 73(3), 283-313, S 92.

White, Michael J (ed) and Martinich, A P (ed). *Certainty and Surface in Epistemology and Philosophical Method*. Lewiston, Mellen Pr, 1991.

This book is a collection of essays in honor of Avrum Stroll, with a focus on the connections between certainty, the nature and perception of surfaces, and philosophical method. Some of the essays are "Certainty Made Simple" by Wallace Matson, "New Foundations and Philosophers" by Alastair Hannay, "Stroll's Answer to Scepticism" by Richard Popkin, "Moore on Scepticism and Common Sense" by David Cole, "Epiphenomena" by Zeno Vendler, "Faces, Boundaries, and Thin Layers," by Peter Simons, "Folk Theories and Physical Metrics" by Michael White, "Analytic Phenomenological Deconstruction" by A P Martinich, and "How I See Philosophy" by Avrum Stroll.

White, Nicholas P. Plato's Metaphysical Epistemology in The Cambridge Companion to Plato, Kraut, Richard H (ed). New York, Cambridge Univ Pr, 1992.

White, Nicholas P. The Attractive and the Imperative in Essays on Henry Sidgwick, Schultz, Bart (ed). New York, Cambridge Univ Pr, 1992.

White, Patricia. Decency and Education for Citizenship. *J Moral Educ*, 21(3), 207-216, 1992.

Decency and good manners are not optional but essential ingredients of good lives in a democracy. Decency in a democratic society, it is claimed, is a matter of having an attitude of goodwill towards non-intimates which will be expressed in different ways in different groups. It will often involve not insisting on one's rights and giving other people more than is due to them. It is argued that the fact that expressions of decency vary between social groups may cause misunderstandings. Objections to ideals of decency and good manners are then tackled. Finally, it is claimed that there is a role for the school in implicitly and explicitly teaching decency as part of its education for citizenship in a democracy.

White, Ronald. The Concept of an Equal Educaitonal Opportunity. *Phil Stud Educ*, 1, 77-87, 1991.

Examines the concept of an "opportunity" within the context of public school funding. Utilizes Rawlsian arguments in support of a "social minimum," of funding for "disadvantaged" school districts. Hence, public policy ought to insure a basic level of funding of poorer districts before permitting lavish improvements in wealthier districts.

White, Stephen K. Burke on Politics, Aesthetics, and the Dangers of Modernity. *Polit Theory*, 21(3), 507-527, Ag 93.

White, Stephen K. *Political Theory and Postmodernism*. New York, Cambridge Univ Pr, 1991.

White, Thomas I. *Discovering Philosophy*. Englewood Cliffs, Prentice Hall, 1991.

White, V Alan. Relativity and Simultaneity Redux. *Philosophy*, 68(265), 401-404, Jl 93.

Michael Cohen has argued that Einstein blundered logically in constructing his simultaneity *gedankenexperiment* involving trains and lightning bolts. Though I attempted to rebut his argument, Cohen replied that I had misconstrued the nature of his criticism. In this piece I admit that I did misinterpret his criticism, but only because I read his argument as charitably as possible. I go on to show that Cohen's professed criticism in fact utilizes an illegitimate concept of the relativity of simultaneity to criticize Einstein.

Whitney, Gordon E. The Place of Thirdness in Legal Reasoning in Peirce and Law, Kevelson, Roberta. New York, Lang, 1991.

Whitt, Laurie Anne. Indices of Theory Promise. *Phil Sci*, 59(4), 612-634, D 92.

Figuring prominently in their decisions regarding which theories to pursue are scientists' appeals to the promise or lack of promise of those theories. Yet philosophy of science has had little to say about how one is to assess theory promise. This essay identifies several indices that might be consulted to determine whether or not a theory is promising and worthy of pursuit. Various historical examples of appeals to such indices are introduced.

Whittock, Trevor. The Role of Metaphor in Dance. *Brit J Aes*, 32(3), 242-249, Jl 92.

Whittock, Trevor. Thoughts on Duncan's Dancing Masters. *J Aes Educ*, 26(2), 31-40, Sum 92.

Whitton, Brian J. Universal Pragmatics and the Formation of Western Civilization: A Critique of Habermas's Theory of Human Moral Evolution. *Hist Theor*, 31(3), 299-312, 1992.

The theory of human moral evolution elaborated in the later work of Jürgen Habermas represents one of the most challenging and provocative of recent, linguistically inspired attempts to reinterpret our understanding of Western history. In critically examining this theory, the present article identifies some major problems with Habermas's reinterpretation of the history of the formation of Western civilization as the universal pragmatic process of the evolution of human moral communicative competences. Drawing on the works of Norbert Elias and Michel Foucault, the article seeks to show how the formal groundings of Habermas's evolutionary theory in the categories of his universal pragmatic conception of communicative action ultimately prevents him from grasping the radically embodied nature of human discursive practice and its implications for the historical process of the formation of human moral will.

Whyte, J T. Purpose and Content. *Brit J Phil Sci*, 44(1), 45-60, Mr 93.

This article argues against the Teleological Theory of Mental Representation (TMR). In particular, I argue that TMR is satisfactory only if augmented with certain conditions. But these conditions alone suffice to explain mental representation, and so make the specifically teleological aspects of TMR redundant.

Wicks, Robert. Hegel's Aesthetics: An Overview in The Cambridge Companion to Hegel, Beiser, Frederick C (ed). New York, Cambridge Univ Pr, 1993.

This essay offers an overview of Hegel's aesthetic theory, and focuses upon his theories of beauty, art history and the individual arts. Some of the contrasts between Hegel's and Kant's aesthetics are explored, with the intention of showing how Hegel's theory understands beauty in reference to the concept of perfection, contrary to Kant. Also, some of the non-dialectical, structural features of Hegel's aesthetics are set forth, along with some observations about how Hegel's aesthetic theory recalls the views of German rationalism prior to Kant.

Wicks, Robert. Schopenhauer's Naturalization of Kant's A Priori Forms of Empirical Knowledge. *Hist Phil Quart*, 10(2), 181-196, Ap 93.

The essay addresses Schopenhauer's interpretation of Kant's *a priori* forms of empirical knowledge as "brain-functions." By describing these forms in empirical terms, a problem of circularity arises that is comparable to what one finds in Quine's naturalized epistemology. Briefly developing a Kantian dual-aspect theory of consciousness, I defend Schopenhauer's view and suggest that Schopenhauer's solution to the problem of circularity is preferable to Quine's, insofar as Schopenhauer can more easily preserve the idea of what it is like to be a self-conscious, theorizing being.

Wicks, Robert. Supervenience and the 'Science of the Beautiful'. *J Aes Art Crit*, 50(4), 322-324, Fall 92.

I argue that the logic of supervenience is not fruitful in explaining how aesthetic properties of the best works of art depend upon the work's non-aesthetic properties: when applied practically, the logic generates only superficial "rules of thumb" that cannot direct the creation of works of high artistic quality. Such rules always allow that a small change in the supervenience base will radically alter the overall aesthetic quality of a work (e.g., when one blackens a tooth on a portrait). This suggests that the greater the work of art, the less informative the supervenience relationship will be.

Wider, Kathleen. A Nothing About Which Something Can Be Said: Sartre and Wittgenstein on the Self in Sartre Alive, Aronson, Ronald (ed). Detroit, Wayne St Univ Pr, 1991.

This paper examines the striking similarity between Sartre's claim in *Being and Nothingness* that human consciousness is nothingness and Wittgenstein's claim in *Tractatus Logico-Philosophicus* that the metaphysical self is not in the world but is the limit to the world. I argue that although both these claims can be read as a Humean denial of the Cartesian self, there is an important sense in which they go beyond this denial. Although both philosophers deny the existence of a transcendental ego, they both hold that even if science could give a complete ego, they both hold that even if science could give a complete description of all there is, there would still be something unaccounted for: consciousness. There is no such ghost for Hume.

Wider, Kathleen. The Desire to Be God: Subjective and Objective in Nagel's *The View From Nowhere* and Sartre's *Being and Nothingness*. *J Phil Res*, 17, 443-463, 1992.

This paper argues that the force and weaknesses of Thomas Nagel's arguments against psychophysical reductionism can be felt more fully when held up to the defense of a similar view in Jean-Paul Sartre's *Being and Nothingness*. What follows for both from their shared rejection of psychophysical reductionism is a defense of the claim that an objective conception of subjective reality is necessarily incomplete. I examine each one's defense of this claim. However, although they both claim an objective conception of subjectivity will be incomplete, they do think we have some ability to form such a conception and I examine next the quite different ways in which Nagel and Sartre relate this ability to our use of language. The last section of the paper discuss each philosopher's belief that although the tension between the objective and the subjective is irreconcilable, humans continue to desire such reconciliation, i.e., they desire to be God.

Wiebe, Donald. Religion, Science and the Transformation of Knowledge. *Sophia (Australia)*, 32(2), 36-49, Jl 93.

Wiebe, Phillip H. Authenticating Biblical Reports of Miracles. *J Phil Res*, 18, 309-325, 1993.

This paper critically examines the claim advanced by a number of important apologists for Christian theism that the biblical reports of miracles obtain confirmation from the accuracy of the reports of ordinary events in the biblical writings. The paper concludes with several comments about the problem which miracle reports encounter with respect to challenging scientific worldviews, and makes suggestions about the kinds of strategies which would need to be employed to render such reports credible. (edited)

Wiegand Petzet, Heinrich and Emad, Parvis (trans) and Maly, Kenneth (trans). *Encounters and Dialogues with Martin Heidegger: 1929-1976 — Heinrich Wiegand Petzet*. Chicago, Univ of Chicago Pr, 1993.

This book is the memoir of the art-historian and literary critique Heinrich-Wiegand Petzet. In recounting his memoirs, Petzet tells the story of his friendship with Martin Heidegger. He focuses on numerous encounters with Heidegger and many dialogues with him. The latter covers topics as diverse as "metaphysics", "art", "modern painting", and "technology". In addition to recounting his dialogues with Heidegger, the book also sheds light on Heidegger's involvement in the politics of national socialism. The introduction to the English edition of Petzet's book takes up the questions concerning Heidegger's political involvement and updates this controversial issue.

Wierenga, Edward. Prophecy, Freedom, and the Necessity of the Past in Philosophical Perspectives, 5: Philosophy of Religion, 1991, Tomberlin, James E (ed). Atascadero, Ridgeview, 1991.

One of the strongest arguments for the incompatibility of divine foreknowledge and human free action appeals to the apparent fixity or necessity of the past. Two leading responses to this argument—Ockhamism, which denies a premiss of the argument, and the so-called "eternity solution", which holds that strictly speaking God does not have foreknowledge—have both recently come under attack on similar grounds. Neither response, it is alleged, is adequate to the case of divine prophecy. In this paper I shall first state the argument in question and the two responses to it. I shall then consider objections to these responses, focusing primarily on how they deal with prophecy.

Wiggins, David. Ayer on Morality and Feeling: From Subjectivism to Emotivism and Back? in The Philosophy of A J Ayer, Hahn, Lewis Edwin (ed). Peru, Open Court, 1992.

Wiggins, David. Ayer's Ethical Theory in A J Ayer Memorial Essays, Griffiths, A Phillips (ed). New York, Cambridge Univ Pr, 1991.

Wiggins, David. Meaning, Truth-Conditions, Proposition: Frege's Doctrine of Sense Retrieved, Resumed and Redeployed in the Light of Certain Recent Criticisms. *Dialectica*, 46(1), 61-90, 1992.

This article first recounts the history of the truth-conditional conception of meaning from Frege to the present day, emphasizing both points that are neglected in received accounts of this history and points of permanent philosophical interest. It then concludes with a review of certain pressed by Stephen Schiffer in *Remnants of Meaning*, offering certain fresh considerations upon the question what it is for two speech action to representent the saying of the same thing.

Wiggins, David. Remembering Directly in Psychoanalysis, Mind and Art, Hopkins, Jim (ed). Cambridge, Blackwell, 1992.

This article analyses or elucidates the idea of personal or experiential memory. It raises the question whether quasi-memory as characterized by Shoemaker, Parfit and others is so defined that it can count as memory. It is argued that if it has been so defined, then contrary to the interactions of its upholders, quasi-memory presupposes identity.

Wiggins, Osborne and Northoff, Georg and Schwartz, Michael Alan. Psychosomatics, the Lived Body, and Anthropological Medicine in The Body in Medical Thought and Practice, Leder, Drew (ed). Dordrecht, Kluwer, 1992.

Wike, Victoria. Does Kant's Ethics Require that the Moral Law Be the Sole Determining Ground of the Will?. *J Value Inq*, 27(1), 85-92, Ja 93.

In this paper, I consider Kant's claim in the *Critique of Practical Reason* that the moral law is the sole determining ground of the pure will. I argue that Kant's writings do not consistently support this claim of exclusivity and that Kant's pure ethics does not require this claim. Rather, Kant's formalism demands only that the moral law be the direct determining ground of the will and that nothing else act to determine the will prior to the moral law.

Wikler, Daniel. Brain Death: A Durable Consensus?. *Bioethics*, 7(2-3), 239-246, Ap 93.

Wilburn, Ronald. Semantic Indeterminacy and the Realist Stance. *Erkenntnis*, 37(3), 281-308, N 92.

Semantic Indeterminacy and Scientific Realism are perhaps the two most ubiquitous and influential doctrines of the Quinean corpus. My concern is to argue against neither in isolation, but against their joint compatibility. Scientific Realism, I argue, when understood as Quine's "realistic attitude" toward the posits of physical theory, is essentially intentional in character. Thus, Realism requires Intentionality. (edited)

Wilcocks, Robert. The Resurrectionist, or November in Le Havre in Sartre Alive, Aronson, Ronald (ed). Detroit, Wayne St Univ Pr, 1991.

This article examines the autobiographical elements at work in Sartre's *The Family Idiot and Nausea*. It demonstrates the importance of Flaubert's *November* for both the young Sartre of *Nausea* and the old Sartre of the study of Flaubert. It shows (with quotation from *Lettres au Castor*) the profound, but unexpected, affective identity between Sartre and Flaubert.

Wilcox, John R. A Monistic Interpretation of Whitehead's Creativity. *Process Stud*, 20(3), 162-174, Fall 91.

Wildes, Kevin W. Conscience, Referral, and Physician Assisted Suicide. *J Med Phil*, 18(3), 323-328, Je 93.

Practices such as physician assisted suicide, even if legal, engender a range of moral conflicts to which many are oblivious. A recent proposal for physician assisted suicide provides an example by calling upon physicians opposed to suicide to refer patients to other, more sympathetic, physicians. However, the proposal does not address the moral concern of those physicians for whom such a referral would be morally objectionable.

Wildes, Kevin W. The Priesthood of Bioethics and the Return of Casuistry. *J Med Phil*, 18(1), 33-50, F 93.

Several recent attempts to develop models of moral reasoning have attempted to use some form of casuistry as a way to resolve the moral controversies of clinical ethics. One of the best known models of casuistry is that of Jonsen and Toulmin who attempt to transpose a particular moral disputes. This attempt is flawed in that it fails to understand both the history of the model it seeks to transpose and the morally pluralistic context of secular, postmodern society. The practice of casuistry which Jonsen and Toulmin wish to revive is a practice set in the context of a community with a shared set of moral values and rankings, and a moral authority to interpret cases the casuistry of the postmodern age will be pluralistic; that is, there will be many casuistries not just one.

Wildes, Kevin W (ed) and Abel, Francesc (ed) and Harvey, John C (ed). *Birth, Suffering, and Death: Catholic Perspectives at the Edges of Life*. Dordrecht, Kluwer, 1992.

Wilharm, Heiner. Ein Bild sagt mehr als tausend Worte in Diagrammatik und Philosophie, Gehring, Petra (ed). Amsterdam, Rodopi, 1992.

We will start with a common-sense understanding of "diagram". We will then reformulate our intuitions as hypothesis and discuss them in detail in six steps. The discussion progressing as a text will tentatively be parallelized by a representation in the form of a diagram. Our results will be summarized in both forms of representation.

Wilhelmsen, Frederick. A Note on Contraries and the Incorruptibility of the Human Soul in St Thomas Aquinas. *Amer Cath Phil Quart*, 67(3), 333-338, Sum 93.

The purpose of this note is to demonstrate how St. Thomas Aquinas fleshed out his proof for the incorruptibility of the human soul from the absence of contraries in the soul by indicating how their actual presence in human understanding (in unanswered questions, etc.) yields the same conclusion. The actual presence of contraries in the material world is impossible but they are constantly being entertained by man in cognition. This reveals a kind of transcendence in intellection and its source, the human soul.

Wilkerson, T E. Species, Essences and the Names of Natural Kinds. *Phil Quart*, 43(170), 1-19, Ja 93.

Wilkes, Kathleen V. How Many Selves Make Me?—II in Human Beings, Cockburn, David (ed). New York, Cambridge Univ Pr, 1991.

Wilkins, Barry. Debt and Underdevelopment: The Case for Cancelling Third World Debate in International Justice and the Third World, Attfield, Robin (ed). New York, Routledge, 1992.

First, I give a brief account of how Third World debts became so huge so rapidly. Second, I indicate some of the appalling consequences of these debts for the governments and, more importantly, the peoples of the debtor countries. Third, I review eight proposed solutions to the Third World debt crisis. I argue that Third World countries would be justified in ceasing the servicing of their debts to the west, but that the best solution would be for western institutions such as governments and banks to embark upon the wholesale and unconditional cancellation of these debts.

Wilkins, Barry (ed) and Attfield, Robin (ed). *International Justice and the Third World*. New York, Routledge, 1992.

This book consists of eight papers which discuss notions of global justice and explore their implications for the Third World. They relate Third World development to sustainability, issues of gender, environmentalism and Third World debt, questioning throughout the sufficiency of market mechanisms to cope with these issues. The ability of Liberal and Marxist theories to account for global justice is considered, and various theoretical models of development are critically examined. As many millions of women in the Third World suffer special oppression, it is stressed that any adequate theory must respond to their plight.

Wilkins, Burleigh T. Does the Fetus Have a Right to Life?. *J Soc Phil*, 24(1), 123-137, Spr 93.

Wilkinson, James H. A Theory of the Family: Critical Appropriations of Hegel and Aristotle. *Owl Minerva*, 24(1), 19-40, Fall 92.

The article's main text presents a mini-treatise on love, marriage, and parenting. The lengthy footnotes appreciatively criticize Hegel's and Aristotle's relevant texts. The article begins by contrasting contract and exchange with romantic love, which is also distinguished from non-perfect friendship. There follow accounts of the wedding vow (with criticisms of Hegel's concept of ethicality), joint marital property, and household production. After distinguishing parenting from consuming, the article offers new theories of abortion and incest, argues that socially controllable equal opportunity requires a world-wide revision of inheritance laws, and proposes procedures to adjudicate any dispute about a child's attainment of maturity.

Wilkinson, Martin. Egoism, Obligation, and Herbert Spencer. *Utilitas*, 5(1), 69-86, My 93.

This paper shows that Spencer had arguments for his libertarianism which are independent of, and better than, those from his evolutionary theory. By using a descriptive theory of egoism and altruism in connection with a utilitarian moral theory, Spencer provided two important arguments against state welfare. One points to the inefficiency it allegedly produces. The other claims that everything other than personal acts of charity creates undesirable social relationships. Both of these arguments appeal to the bad utilitarian effects that state welfare would have. Both could be mistaken, but they nonetheless possess a plausibility that Spencer's official evolutionary arguments lacked.

Willard, Dallas. Predication as Originary Violence in Working Through Derrida, Madison, Gary B (ed). Evanston, Northwestern Univ Pr, 1993.

Willems, Dick. Kreukels in de tijd, kennis zonder centrum. *Kennis Methode*, 16(3), 245-256, 1992.

The article analyzes two central elements in the work of Michel Serres: first, his notion of time in the history of science, with special attention to transhistorical simultaneity, and second, the distribution of knowledge over humans and nonhumans.

Willett, Cynthia. Partial Attachments in Ethics and Danger, Dallery, Arleen B (ed). Albany, SUNY Pr, 1992.

The deconstructive strategies of Paul de Man differ from those developed by Jacques Derrida precisely on the question of ethical responsibility. While Derrida draws upon the figure of woman in order to make possible a postmodern concept of responsibility, the strategies of de Man, specifically as he develops these strategies in his notorious essay on Rousseau, preempt female subjectivity in order to excuse men of crimes of violence against women.

Willett, Cynthia. Tropics of Desire: Freud and Derrida. *Res Phenomenol*, 22, 138-151, 1992.

This article focuses on Derrida's essay "To Speculate—on 'Freud'." I argue that Derrida's reading of Freud's theory of drives fails to put forth a non-traditional

paradigm of desire. On the contrary, Derrida deconstructs the traditional psychoanalytic model of desire and invites the reader to affirm the fragmentation that ensues. Implicitly within Derrida's reading of Freud, however, lies a model of desire that borrows from the traditional notion and yet survives the dispersions of deconstruction. I draw on a quasi-metaphoric notion of borrowing, or what Derrida terms "tropic movement," in order to locate a post-deconstructive notion of desire.

Williams, Bernard. Naive and Sentimental Opera Lovers in Isaiah Berlin: A Celebration, Margalit, Edna (ed). Chicago, Univ of Chicago Pr, 1991.

Williams, Bernard. Subjectivism and Toleration in A J Ayer Memorial Essays, Griffiths, A Phillips (ed). New York, Cambridge Univ Pr, 1991.

Williams, Bernard (ed) and Levett, M J (trans). *Plato: "Theaetetus"*. Indianapolis, Hackett, 1992.

Williams, C J F. Russelm. *Phil Quart*, 43(173), 496-499, O 93.

Elizabeth Anscombe has suggested that Anselm's most famous sentence should be translated in such a way that it no longer claims that existing in reality is greater than existing only in the mind. She offers this reconstruction of the argument: If that than which no greater can be thought of does not exist in reality, it cannot exist in reality. But what cannot exist is not that-than-which.... There seems to be an equivocation between taking "that-than-which..." here as having primary occurrence, in Russell's terms, and taking it as having secondary occurrence.

Williams, C J F. Theaetetus in Bad Company. *Philosophy*, 67(262), 549-551, O 92.

Why does Plato immediately follow up Theaetetus's claim that knowledge is Perception with a discussion of Protagoras's theory that Man is the Measure of All Things and Heraclitus's theory that Everything is in Flux? It is to deal with the objection that the wind is perceived as chilly by one person and as not chilly by another, so that both cannot have knowledge. Protagaras relativizes the predicate: A's ascription of "chilly-to-A" no longer contradicts B's of "not chilly-to-B". Heraclitus denies that A's statement has the same subject as B's, since the same wind cannot be perceived by two different people.

Williams, C J F. Towards a Unified Theory of Higher-Level Predication. *Phil Quart*, 42(169), 449-464, O 92.

Given that propositions are no-place predicables, higher-level predicables form predicables out of predicables, and this category of expression has more members than is usually realised. "Everyone", for instance, is one which forms an n-place predicable from an (n+1)-place predicable; so is "himself", which forms "—likes himself" from "—likes...". Unary sentential operators form n-place predicables from n-place predicables, binary form (n+m)-place predicables from an n-place and an m-place, where n and m may be zero. Third-level predicables allow us to understand the relation between singular and plural verbs.

Williams, Clifford. The Date-Analysis of Tensed Sentences. *Austl J Phil*, 70(2), 198-203, Je 92.

Advocates of the A-Theory of time argue that pastness, presentness and futurity are mind-independent properties of events on the grounds that tensed and tenseless sentences are not semantically equivalent. However, their arguments for semantic nonequivalence do not entail state of affairs nonequivalence, and this latter nonequivalence must also obtain in order for the A-Theory to be true. The situation is like arguing that hereness and thisness are extra, mind-independent properties of places and objects on the grounds that sentences in which "here" and "this" are used do not mean the same as their referential counterparts. Since we are not tempted to say that hereness is an extra property of places because of this semantic nonequivalence, we should not be tempted to say that presentness is an extra property of events because of the semantic nonequivalence of tensed and tenseless sentences.

Williams, Courtney. Toward a Consistent View of Abortion and Unwanted Pregancy. *Harvard Rev Phil*, 2(1), 42-43, Spr 92.

Williams, Dilafruz R. The Modern Quest for Civic Virtues: Issues of Identity and Alienation. *Proc Phil Educ*, 48, 114-116, 1992.

Williams, Howard (ed). *Essays on Kant's Political Philosophy*. Chicago, Univ of Chicago Pr, 1992.

An up to date discussion of the implications of Kant's political philosophy by prominent Kantian specialists. As political philosopher Kant has been overshadowed far too long by his compatriots Hegel and Marx. The course of history appears now to have turned Kant's way. Kant's political philosophy, wedded as it is to rights, reform and gradual progress has the opportunity to emerge from the shadows cast by Hegelian and Marxist thinking upon the state in the 20th century. The authors of these essays, 5 Americans, 5 British and 2 Germans seek to cast new light on important aspects of Kant's liberal thinking. Key topics are discussed, such as Kant's optimism, the use of reason, contract, revolution and Kant's relation to Hegel. The grounds for Kant's liberal reformism are closely examined, his attitude to women and his moral and legal rigorism are also critically assessed.

Williams, Howard. Kant's Optimism in his Social and Political Theory in Essays on Kant's Political Philosophy, Williams, Howard (ed). Chicago, Univ of Chicago Pr, 1992.

This contribution discusses the plausibility of Kant's optimistic view of history. Optimism seems to play an important role in his moral as well as his political thinking. Kant suggests that we should follow the just course of action both in individual life and in political life, since ultimately the better will triumph over the worse. The author looks at the feasibility of this in the light of narrowly strategic thinking typified in the example of the Prisoner's Dilemma, and concludes that from an empirical standpoint Kant's optimism may lead to too great a vulnerability and the creation of victims. Stands made upon principle may not be rewarded at all. From a more abstract, moral and theoretical standpoint it is more difficult to criticize Kant. If one is prepared to accept the vulnerability the moral approach implies and the likelihood that there may be victims, only action can tell whether the standpoint may succeed. The author argues that we have to be more cautious about expressing optimism than Kant. Complacency may ensue from the Kantian standpoint, whereas the strategic, narrowly selfish aspects of action can never be wholly ignored.

Williams, Howard. Morality or Prudence?. *Kantstudien*, 83(2), 222-225, 1992.

This article discusses the role of prudence or practical wisdom in Kant's political philosophy. The author argues that prudence should be seen as subordinate to morality in Kant's account of the activity of political leaders. Kant does not undervalue political skill, but regards such skill as baseless if it is employed for the wrong purposes. The author concludes that although Kant's political philosophy is not without its weaknesses the subordinate position of political skill is not to be counted amongst them.

Williams, Howard. Political Philosophy and World History: The Examples of Hegel and Kant. *Bull Hegel Soc Gt Brit*, 23-24, 51-60, 1991.

The object of this paper is threefold. First, the purpose is to look closely at the connection between the intellectual enterprises of political philosophy and the philosophy of history. Secondly, the purpose is to outline and criticize the connection as seen by Kant and Hegel. Thirdly, the purpose is to draw some preliminary conclusions about the advantages and disadvantages of underpinning a political philosophy with a view of history. In drawing these conclusions I should like to explore the belief that although it may be possible to undertake the philosophy of history with little direct regard for political philosophy contrariwise it would be mistaken, if not foolish, to present a political philosophy without taking into account problems raised by the philosophy of history.

Williams, Joan C. Virtue and Oppression. *Nomos*, 34, 309-337, 1992.

Williams, John N. Belief-In and Belief In God. *Relig Stud*, 28(3), 401-406, S 92.

It is first argued that there are two types of beliefs-in; beliefs in X which are identical with the belief that X exists and beliefs-in which entail no existential belief but which do entail a commendatory attitude. It is then shown that belief in God is not identical with, but rather entails, the belief that God exists. Pace Norman Malcolm, the converse holds neither as a logical nor psychological claims.

Williams, John N. Ontological Disproof. *Austl J Phil*, 70(2), 204-210, Je 92.

Williams, Paul. Non-Conceptuality, Critical Reasoning and Religious Experience in Philosophy, Religion and the Spiritual Life, McGhee, Michael (ed). New York, Cambridge Univ Pr, 1992.

Williams, Paul. Non-Conceptuality, Critical Reasoning and Religious Experience: Some Tibetan Buddhist Discussions. *Philosophy*, 32(Supp), 189-211, 1992.

Centrality of critical investigation in Tibetan Buddhism. Problem of relating this to a form of knowing which is said in Buddhism to be non-conceptual. The eighth-century debates. Role of *samjña* as conceptualisation. Kamalasila's attack on the 'blank mind' hypothesis. Cognition of the ultimate has no object (Sa skya Pandita). dGe lugs critique. Incoherence and uselessness of the claim that an experience of the ultimate is nonconceptualisable. 'Emptiness' in dGe lugs Madhyamaka; its connection with critical, conceptual investigation. dGe lugs criticised for remaining in the conceptual. Rong zom Pandita on the limitations of logic and critical thought.

Williams, Robert. Hegel and Heidegger in Hegel and His Critics, Desmond, William J (ed). Albany, SUNY Pr, 1989.

Williams, Robert. Hegel and Skepticism. *Owl Minerva*, 24(1), 71-82, Fall 92.

Williams, Rowan. Hegel and the Gods of Postmodernity in Shadow of Spirit, Berry, Philippa (ed). New York, Routledge, 1992.

Williams, Rowan. The Necessary Non-Existence of God in Simone Weil's Philosophy of Culture, Bell, Richard H (ed). New York, Cambridge Univ Pr, 1993.

Williams, Rowan. 'Know Thyself': What Kind of an Injunction?. *Philosophy*, 32(Supp), 211-227, 1992.

Williams, Rowan. 'Know Thyself': What Kind of an Injunction? in Philosophy, Religion and the Spiritual Life, McGhee, Michael (ed). New York, Cambridge Univ Pr, 1992.

Williamson, Timothy. An Alternative Rule of Disjunction in Modal Logic. *Notre Dame J Form Log*, 33(1), 89-100, Wint 92.

Some systems of modal logic in which Lemmon and Scott's rule of disjunction is not admissible (e.g., KTB) are shown to admit an alternative rule of disjunction. Other systems in which Lemmon and Scott's rule is admissible (e.g., K) do not admit the alternative rule. The latter is shown to imply noncompactness of a consequence relation defined in terms of admissibility. For some modal systems it is shown that whenever "If A then necessarily A" is a theorem, then "A" is a theorem or "not A" is. Applications to the logic of vagueness are suggested.

Williamson, Timothy. Vagueness and Ignorance—I. *Aris Soc*, Supp(66), 145-162, 1992.

An epistemic account of vagueness is defended, on which vague assertions are true or false in borderline cases, but speakers of the language cannot know which. This account is shown to be consistent with plausible versions of the supervenience of vague facts on precise facts and of meaning on use. Speakers' ignorance is explained by appeal to independently confirmable conditions on knowledge. Disquotational properties of truth and falsity are argued to make trouble for non-epistemic accounts of vagueness.

Wilsmore, S J. The Appreciation and Perception of Easel Paintings. *Brit J Aes*, 33(3), 246-256, Jl 93.

Wilson, Catherine. Constancy, Emergence, and Illusions: Obstacles to a Naturalistic Theory of Vision in Causation in Early Modern Philosophy, Nadler, Steven (ed). University Park, Penn St Univ Pr, 1993.

The paper discusses Malebranche's occasionalism in the context of his scientific interest in optics and the psychology of vision. Three main points are made 1) occasionalism is associated with the idea of "bonds" and "unions;" 2) it is motivated by the need to explain disparities between "retinal image" and percept and to explain aspect perception; 3) it is part of an overall strategy to secure the notion of the miraculous in a period of demystification.

Wilson, Catherine. Enthusiasm and Its Critics: Historical and Modern Perspectives. *Hist Euro Ideas*, 17(4), 461-478, Jl 93.

The paper examines the role of intuition, irrationality, and behavioral excess in social criticism. It is addressed to a historical example: early Quakerism and the attacks of John Locke and Henry More on religious "enthusiasts". The timeless problems of morally evil vs "good" fanatacism; the validity of "intuition," and of the essentially conservative nature of "rationality" are all treated briefly.

Wilson, Catherine. Interaction with the Reader in Kant's Transcendental Theory of Method. *Hist Phil Quart*, 10(1), 83-97, Ja 93.

The subject of the paper is Kant's "Transcendental Theory of Method," actually a theory of transcendental method, which occupies the little-studied end-portion of the *Critique of Pure Reason*. The author investigates Kant's ambivalence about a) the notion of a supersensible foundation for morals; and b) his own effectiveness in trying to communicate moral philosophy.

Wilson, Catherine. On Some Alleged Limitations to Moral Endeavor. *J Phil*, 90(6), 275-289, Je 93.

This paper discusses critically the increasingly popular idea that personal projects, preferences, and desires limit our moral obligations as traditionally conceived. (We are not obliged to be "saints.") The author argues that his notion and its current appearance in the literature need to be approached through the sociology of knowledge. Though it seems to promise relief from the imaginary, quasi-theological, or overly abstract character of old-style moral philosophy, it can also be regarded as part of an objectionably indirect strategy for the defense of social and economic privilege.

Wilson, Catherine. Reply to Richard Rorty's "Feminism and Pragmatism": How Did the Dinosaurs Die Out? How Did the Poets Survive?. *Rad Phil*, 62, 20-23, Autumn 92.

Wilson, Diana de Armas. "Unreasons' Reason": Cervantes at the Frontiers of Difference. *Phil Lit*, 16(1), 49-67, Ap 92.

This essay documents Cervantes's hostility to overly schematic oppositions, an attitude remarked in the Prologue to his *Novelas ejemplares (Exemplary Novels)*: "There is nothing either precise or calibrated about either praise or censure." The novel, as founded by Cervantes, begins out of an erosion of belief in, among other textual authorities, certain *"maxims from Aristotle"* that organize discourse as a two-term system. Cervantes's texts are singularly aware of the frontiers of difference. His practice of blurring or crossing the borders between dualisms defies a stance, of course, within any philosophical position. My essay explores the frontiers of difference in *Don Quixote* and the *Persiles*.

Wilson, Elizabeth. These New Components of the Spectacle in Postmodernism and Society, Boyne, Roy (ed). New York, St Martin's Pr, 1990.

Wilson, F F. Hume Studies in Canada. *Eidos*, 10(2), 199-216, D 92.

Wilson, H T. The Impact of Nationalist Ideology on Political Philosophy: The Case of Max Weber and Wilhelmine Germany. *Hist Euro Ideas*, 16(4-6), 545-550, Ja 93.

The article indicates the impact on Weber of a complex amalgam of forces and values generated by his class position, political ideology, conception of nationality and nationalism and German background, upbringing and citizenship during the late 19th and early 20th centuries. Weber's ambivalence about the Western project is the result of the tensions and conflicts generated by these forces and values, and cannot be reduced solely or mainly to neurosis as some have argued. Too many intellectuals with similar characteristics existed without this ambivalence. A schematic diagram indicates some consequences for Weber's thought.

Wilson, Jackson. Converting Time. *Cont Phil*, 15(2), 19-23, Mr-Ap 93.

Chapter XI of Augustine's *Confessions* is an essential part of his autobiographical and theoretical attempt to mediate unification and dispersion. Far more than a treatment of traditional paradoxes about time, it is an attempt to describe the primordial relation of unity-in-difference. Only with an account of time which develops this relation can Augustine raise his personal existence from dispersion and bring his theoretical existence down from a hubristic claim to universal truth. This account has wide-ranging implications for questions about the relationship between theory and practice, the mediation of unity and difference, and the relation between time and eternity.

Wilson, John. Equality Revisited. *J Phil Educ*, 27(1), 113-114, Sum 93.

Wilson, John. Philosophy for Children: A Note of Warning. *Thinking*, 10(1), 17-18, 1992.

Wilson, John. Sexual Differences: The Contingent and the Necessary. *J Applied Phil*, 10(2), 237-242, 1993.

The role of philosophy in the problem of sexual differences is considered, in the light of what sexual differences can be seen as 1) purely contingent or 2) logically tied to (non-negotiable) sexual feature. Some candidates for causes of sexual difference are reviewed, including evolution, physical make-up, and social conditioning. The problem of initial *descriptions* of sexual interaction is highlighted, and the need for a clearer set of categories for possible causes demonstrated. The argument in general is that, because of lack of clarity about which issues are empirical and which conceptual, and because of uncertainty about what evidence is relevant, we cannot as yet be clear about what apparent differences are (even in principle) alterable, and what are given.

Wilson, John. The Primacy of Authority. *J Moral Educ*, 21(2), 115-124, 1992.

The concept of authority is primary and inescapable, and anterior to the opposition of particular values (such as 'law and order' versus 'freedom'). No human interaction is possible without authority. Problems about the legitimacy and scope of authority are discussed: particularly the legitimacy of compelling school attendance. Attention is drawn to the particular importance of authority in moral and political education.

Wilson, Kent. Comment on Peter of Spain, Jim Mackenzie, and Begging the Question. *J Phil Log*, 22(3), 323-331, Je 93.

This paper presents three types of counterexamples to the analysis of the Fallacy of Begging the Question presented in Jim Mackenzie's "Confirmation of a Conjecture of Peter of Spain Concerning Begging the Question", *Journal of Philosophical Logic*, 1984, 8: 117-33. One type of counterexample involves arguments of the form 'P&Q; therefore G'; a second type involves arguments of the form 'everything is F; therefore A is F'; a third type involves arguments in which the premise presupposes the conclusion.

Wilson, Margaret. Compossibility and Law in Causation in Early Modern Philosophy, Nadler, Steven (ed). University Park, Penn St Univ Pr, 1993.

Wilson, Margaret D. Substance and System: Perplexities of the Geometric Order. *Harvard Rev Phil*, 2(1), 8-14, Spr 92.

Wilson, Mark. Reflections on Strings in Thought Experiments in Science and Philosophy, Horowitz, Tamara (ed). Lanham, Rowman & Littlefield, 1991.

This essay discusses a famous case where the demands of physical representation overpowered the demands of mathematical rigor. It concerns the dispute between Euler and d'Alembert over the vibrating string.

Wilson, Mark L. Frege: The Royal Road from Geometry. *Nous*, 26(2), 149-180, Je 92.

Under the leadership of Poncelet's "projective" school, traditional Euclidean geometry gradually transmogrified until it became, by mid-nineteenth century, the investigation of a richer "complexified" domain, where ordinary figures like circles were treated as possessing sundry invisible parts. A rich variety of attempts to justify philosophically these changes in geometrical methodology were discussed by mathematicians of the period. The present article argues that a deep affinity binds Gottlob Frege's "logicism" to some of these proposals, notably those advanced by K von Staudt. This geometrical background, it is claimed, clarifies the motivations behind many of Frege's well-known philosophical opinions.

Wilson, P Eddy. The Fiction of Corporate Scapegoating. *J Bus Ethics*, 12(10), 779-784, O 93.

If the agent responsible for an action is to be given praise of blame by the moral community for that action, then accurate responsibility ascriptions must be made. Since the moral community may have to evaluate the actions of corporate agents, care must be taken to insure that the assumption of Methodological Individualism (MI) does not infect that process. Nevertheless, there is no guarantee that accurate responsibility ascriptions will be made in cases connected with corporate action as long as corporate scapegoating may occur. Because corporate scapegoating is a behavior pattern that attempts to falsify correct responsibility ascriptions it will be of interest to the moral theorist. Once I have considered three objections to the idea of corporate scapegoating I shall offer a fictional description of it found in Ayn Rand's work, *Atlas Shrugged*. Finally, I shall raise a question about its present day use by corporations in our society.

Wilson, Paul Eddy. Barring Corporations from the Moral Community: the concept and the Cost. *J Soc Phil*, 23(1), 74-88, Spr 92.

In this article the author attempts to show that corporations have been unduly excluded from the moral community. Some of the assumptions underlying apprails of responsibility in cases involving corporate crime are challenged. If methodological individualism (MI) is applied indiscriminately in all instances involving corporate crime, then corporations may be able to exploit that situation. By prescribing the maximization of personal accountability within corporations one may foster an unjust moral environment. The author argues that corporations should be respected as full-fledged moral persons and that the moral community should discourage their use of individuals within the corporation as their scapegoat.

Wilson, Robert A. Against *A Priori* Arguments for Individualism. *Pac Phil Quart*, 74(1), 60-79, Mr 93.

After distinguishing a priori from empirical arguments for individualism in psychology, this paper examines several arguments of the former kind, arguing that they are unsound. The types of failures one finds in such arguments gives one reason to be sceptical about a priori arguments for individualism. The paper follows up on the author's previous detailed discussion of the argument from causal powers; it discusses an argument from the causal theory of properties and one from an analysis of causation proposed by McGinn.

Wiltshire, Martin G. *Ascetic Figures Before and In Early Buddhism: The Emergence of Gautama as the Buddha*. Hawthorne, de Gruyter, 1990.

Winch, Donald (ed) and Malthus, T R. *"An Essay on the Principle of Population"—T R Malthus*. New York, Cambridge Univ Pr, 1992.

Winch, Peter G. Certainty and Authority in Wittgenstein Centenary Essays, Griffiths, A Phillips (ed). New York, Cambridge Univ Pr, 1991.

Winch, Peter G. Persuasion. *Midwest Stud Phil*, 17, 123-137, 1992.

Windham, Mary Elizabeth. Nietzsche's Philosopher of the Future as an Ethicist: Experimentalism in Ethics. *Int Stud Phil*, 24(2), 115-124, 1992.

Winfield, Richard. Hegel Versus the New Orthodoxy in Hegel and His Critics, Desmond, William (ed). Albany, SUNY Pr, 1989.

The new orthodoxy in philosophy has erroneously embraced naturalized epistemology and holism as a remedy to the dilemmas of foundationalism. In so doing it has attempted to borrow from Hegel's critique of epistemology, dialectical logic and philosophy of spirit. However, these three aspects of Hegel's antifoundational systematic philosophy actually undermine the supposed remedies of the new orthodoxy and instead raise a fundamentally different philosophical option escaping the pitfalls of foundationalists and would-be anti-foundationalists alike.

Winfield, Richard Dien. Rethinking the Particular Forms of Art: Prolegomena to a Rational Reconstruction of Hegel's Theory of the Artforms. *Owl Minerva*, 24(2), 131-144, Spr 93.

If a systematic aesthetics is to advance beyond conceiving the features generic to art to determine particular art forms, it must avoid employing formal taxonomies that neglect the constitutive tie between meaning and configuration in art. Instead, particular art forms must be conceived in terms of the possible modes of joining meaning and configuration. Although Hegel provides the most significant attempt to carry through such a differentiation, he tends to conflate historical and conceptual orderings in identifying the particular forms of art. Once such conflation is removed, the sequence and hierarchy of the art forms retains a new significance, with important ramifications for the meaning of the end of art.

Wing-Cheuk, Chan. Foundedness and Motivation in Analecta Husserliana, XXXIV, Tymieniecka, Anna-Teresa (ed). Dordrecht, Kluwer, 1992.

"Foundedness" and "motivation" are two important concepts in phenomenology. However, the relationship between them is not yet clear. Our article attempts to point out some major distinctions between them. It will be shown that while "foundedness" is subject to a formal-logical explication, "motivation" is not. Nevertheless, this does not exclude the possibility that both concepts play a complementary role in the phenomenological analysis. While "foundedness" is a fundamental concept in the static phenomenology, "motivation" is a key term in the genetic phenomenology.

Wingard Jr, John C. On a Not Quite Yet "Victorious" Modal Version of the Ontological Argument for the Existence of God. *Int J Phil Relig*, 33(1), 47-57, F 93.

I argue that the modal version of the ontological argument proposed by Alvin Plantinga in The Nature of Necessity is not yet victorious because he has not shown that the exemplification of unsurpassable greatness (the defining property of God) entails the necessary existence of that which exemplifies it. I consider possible ways to save his argument, and conclude that the best approach to secure the needed entailment is to argue that necessary existence is a great-making property, abandoning the idea that necessary existence is merely a necessary condition for the exemplification of unsurpassable greatness.

Winkler, Earl. Is the Killing/Letting-Die Distinction Normatively Neutral?. *Dialogue (Canada)*, 30(3), 309-325, Sum 91.

Winner, Langdon. Citizen Virtues in a Technological Order. *Inquiry*, 35(3-4), 341-361, S-D 92.

Contemporary philosophical discussions about technology mirror a profound distance between technical practice and moral thought. I consider the origins of this gap as reflected in both ancient and modern writings. The philosopher's version of technocracy—rushing forward with the analysis of moral categories in the hope that policy-makers or the public will find them decisive—does nothing to bridge this gap and is, therefore, a forlorn strategy. The trouble is not that we lack good arguments and theories, but rather that modern politics does not provide appropriate roles and institutions in which the activity of defining the common good in technology policy is a legitimate project. I find glimmerings of an alternative practice in the "Scandinavian approach" to democratic participation in technological design.

Winner, Langdon. Upon Opening the Black Box and Finding It Empty: Social Constructivism and the Philosophy of Technology. *Sci Tech Human Values*, 18(3), 362-378, Sum 93.

Winnie, John A. Computable Chaos. *Phil Sci*, 59(2), 263-275, Je 92.

Some irrational numbers are "random" in a sense which implies that no algorithm can compute their decimal expansions to an arbitrarily high degree of accuracy. This feature of (most) irrational numbers has been claimed to be at the heart of the deterministic, but chaotic behavior exhibited by many nonlinear dynamical systems. In this paper, a number of now classical chaotic systems are shown to remain chaotic when their domains are restricted to the computable real numbers, providing counterexamples to the above claim. More fundamentally, the randomness view of chaos is shown to be based upon a confusion between a chaotic function on a phase space and its numerical representation in "R".

Wintgens, Luc J and Shelledy, David. Unger's Advocates: Assessing the Possibilities for Law Practice as a Transformative Vocation. *Ratio Juris*, 5(1), 46-57, Mr 92.

This article focuses on a critical interpretation of the work of Unger. It is argued that Unger's view is less revolutionary than he depicts it and that American law often develops as Unger describes it, though this is absolutely no revolution. The authors further show what the possibilities and the limits of a transformative vocation at the bar can be.

Wippel, John F. Thomas Aquinas on What Philosophers Can Know About God. *Amer Cath Phil Quart*, 66(3), 279-298, 1992.

Wiredu, Kwasi. The African Concept of Personhood in African-American Perspectives on Biomedical Ethics, Flack, Harley E (ed). Washington, Georgetown Univ Pr, 1992.

Wiredu, Kwasi. The Moral Foundations of African-American Culture in African-American Perspectives on Biomedical Ethics, Flack, Harley E (ed). Washington, Georgetown Univ Pr, 1992.

Wisdo, David. *The Life of Irony and the Ethics of Belief*. Albany, SUNY Pr, 1993.

Wisdom, J O. *Philosophy of the Social Sciences III: Groundwork for Social Dynamics*. Brookfield, Avebury, 1993.

Wise, M Norton. Mediations: Enlightenment Balancing Acts, or the Technologies of Rationalism in World Changes, Horwich, Paul (ed). Cambridge, MIT Pr, 1993.

Wise, Sue and Stanley, Liz. *Breaking Out Again: Feminist Ontology and Epistemology (Second Edition)*. New York, Routledge, 1993.

Wiseman, Mary. Renaissance Madonnas and the Fantasies of Freud. *Hypatia*, 8(3), 115-135, Sum 93.

Through the work of Julia Kristeva, this paper challenges Freud's laws that everyone is always already gendered, that the mother is feminine and every infant masculine, and that one cannot love the same (gender). The figure of the Madonna, seen through the paintings of Giovanni Bellini, is used to theorize the time in the life of a child before Oedipus and to undo the conceptual knot with which Freud has bound the feminine to the maternal.

Wiseman, Mary Bittner. Two Women by Giovanni Bellini. *Brit J Aes*, 33(3), 228-238, Jl 93.

The task is to sketch a theory of interpretation suggested by Julia Kristeva's interpretations of Bellini paintings. This paves the way for a rewriting of Freud's family romance from that point of view of the Madonna rather than of Oedipus. By challenging the laws through which Freud constitutes the feminine— everything is always already gendered, and the mother is feminine and every infant masculine—the essay loosens the knot Freud tied between the feminine and the maternal. The mother is construed not as an object of desire (to have or to be) but as a function.

Wisniewski, Andrzej. Erotetic Arguments: A Preliminary Analysis. *Stud Log*, 50(2), 261-274, Je 91.

The concept of erotetic argument is introduced. Two relations between sets of declarative sentences and questions are analyzed; and two classes of erotetic arguments are characterized.

Witmer, Judith T. Integrity or "He Who Steals My Purse". *Proc S Atlantic Phil Educ Soc*, 36, 73-80, 1991.

Nothing is as important to one's personal and professional character as integrity, a quality that educators must possess if they are to "do right" by the public they serve. The implications are that educators must pay more careful attention to the ethical practices of their membership. Further, there is a pressing need for courses of study to be developed for the training of educational administrators in making ethical decisions, and for education professionals themselves to accept the research findings of those who call for training programs. Formal training is necessary so that the decisions reached are grounded in ethical principles.

Witt, Charlotte. Commentary on Charlton's "Aristotle and the Uses of Actuality". *Proc Boston Colloq Anc Phil*, 5, 23-27, 1989.

Wittgenstein, Ludwig and Nordmann, Alfred (ed) and Klagge, James C (ed). *Philosophical Occasions: 1912-1951—Ludwig Wittgenstein*. Indianapolis, Hackett, 1993.

Shorter writings by or deriving from Wittgenstein, in German and English. Brief introductions describe the circumstances of origin of each piece. Contents: Review of Coffey's *Science of Logic*, Letters to Eccles, Preface to the *Wörterbuch*, "Some Remarks on Logical Form," Lecture on Ethics, Moore's Lecture Notes, "Remarks on Frazer," Letter to *Mind*, "Philosophy" (from the Big Typescript), "Notes for Lectures on 'Private Experience' and 'Sense Data'" (reedited and significantly expanded), Rhees' Lecture Notes on Freedom of the Will, "Notes for the 'Philosophical Lecture'" (previously unpublished), Letters to von Wright, and a new edition of von Wright's "The Wittgenstein Papers".

Woelfel, James. William James on Victorian Agnosticism in God, Values, and Empiricism, Peden, Creighton (ed). Macon, Mercer Univ Pr, 1989.

Wohl, Andrzej. "Without a Truly Socialist Society the World of Today and of Tomorrow Is Unthinkable". *Dialec Hum*, 17(1), 166-171, 1990.

Wohlgelernter, Maurice (ed). *History, Religion, and American Democracy (New Edition)*. New Brunswick, Transaction Books, 1993.

Wojciechowicz, Elizabeth and Pang, Yeuk Yi. Coordinating the Emotional and Rational in Moral Education. *Eidos*, 10(1), 21-46, J-Jl 91.

Wojciechowski, Krzysztof. Rousseau Turned Upright: Technology and Paternalism. *Dialec Hum*, 17(1), 72-78, 1990.

Wojtylak, Piotr. On Structural Completeness of Implicational Logics. *Stud Log*, 50(2), 275-297, Je 91.

We consider the notion of structural completeness with respect to arbitrary (finitary and/or infinitary) inferential rules. Our main task is to characterize structurally complete intermediate logics. We prove that the structurally complete extension of any pure implicational intermediate logic *C* can be given as an extension of *C* with a certain family of schematically defined infinitary rules; the same rules are used for each *C*. The cardinality of the family is continuum and, in the case of (the pure implicational fragment of) intuitionistic logic, the family cannot be reduced to a countable one. It means that the structurally complete extension of the intuitionistic logic is not countably axiomatizable by schematic rules.

Wolenski, Jan. Kotarbinski, Many-Valued Logic, and Truth in Kotarbinski: Logic, Semantics and Ontology, Woléński, Jan (ed). Dordrecht, Kluwer, 1990.

Wolenski, Jan (ed). *Kotarbinski: Logic, Semantics and Ontology*. Dordrecht, Kluwer, 1990.

Kotarbinski was a member of the Lwow-Warsaw School, the most important school in the history of Polish philosophy. The essays making up this collection take into account the leading points of Kotarbinski's philosophy: a semantic-ontological reism, his contributions to many-valued logic and the classical theory of truth, the main ideas of praxiology—a new field invented by Kotarbinski—and his works on history of logic. The authors of particular essays show influences on and by Kotarbinski, advantages and limitations of reism, the logical structure of praxiology as well as his method of doing philosophical analysis.

Wolenski, Jan. Marty and the Lvov-Warsaw School in Mind, Meaning and Metaphysics, Mulligan, Kevin (ed). Dordrecht, Kluwer, 1990.

The paper collects data concerning Marty's influence in Poland, particularly in the Lvov-Warsaw School. The author lists references to Marty in works of Twardowski, Lesniewski, Kotarbinski and other Polish philosophers. Moreover, some remarks on possible Marty's influence on some concrete views of Polish philosophers are included. Especially, a possible role of Marty in the development of Lesniewski's nominalism is briefly discussed.

Wolenski, Jan. Tadeusz Kotarbinski and the Lvov Warsaw School. *Dialec Hum*, 17(1), 14-24, 1990.

This paper is intended to show the place of Kotarbinski's philosophy in the Lvov-Warsaw School and his influence on the development of this movement in Polish philosophy. The author describes links of Kotarbinski's views with ideas developed by other outstanding members of the Lvov-Warsaw School, particularly Twardowski and Lesniewski. Moreover, Kotarbinski's conception of so called small philosophy was a typical exposition of general metaphilosophical views of the Lvov-Warsaw School.

Wolf, Jean-Claude. Paternalismus. *Stud Phil (Switzerland)*, 49, 49-59, 1990.

J S Mill's defense of paternalism, considered in the light of the notorious essays of G Dworkin and J Feinberg, is illuminating in its application of standard-cases and its provisos for exceptions. One of the hard-cases for the critic of hard paternalism is the justification of a liberal drug policy. Mill's case can be fully restated, relatively independent from utilitarian premisses, by considering the fundamental importance of deciding *in propria persona* for self-education, even in cases when a choice in non-optimal. This line of defense does not imply a neglect of communal values.

Wolf, Jean-Claude. Warum moralisch sein gegenüber Tieren?. *Z Phil Forsch*, 46(3), 429-438, Jl-S 92.

Wolf, Susan. Morality and Partiality in Philosophical Perspectives, 6: Ethics, 1992, Tomberlin, James E (ed). Atascadero, Ridgeview, 1992.

Wolf-Devine, Celia. *Descartes on Seeing: Epistemology and Visual Perception*. Carbondale, So Illinois Univ Pr, 1993.

Descartes' work in optics was important to the triumph of mechanistic natural philosophy in the 17th Century. I examine his theory of vision in detail against the background of Aristotelian and scholastic perceptual theories, concluding that he ultimately failed to provide an adequate mechanistic account of vision, and showing how the new framework he developed paved the way for the subjectivization of colors, "veil of perception" scepticism, and the belief that we can sharply separate seeing and judging in such a way as to isolate what is "given" to the sense of sight.

Wolfe, Alan. Algorithmic Justice in Deconstruction and the Possibility of Justice, Cornell, Durcilla (ed). New York, Routledge, 1992.

Wolfe, Art. A Reply to Robert Allan Cooke's "And the Blind Shall Lead the Blind". *Bus Ethics Quart*, 3(1), 65-67, Ja 93.

Robert Allan Cooke engages in name-calling only and does not offer any attempt at a disciplined reply to my article, "Reflections on Business Ethics: What Is It? What Causes It? And, What Should a Course in Business Ethics Include." Essential questions posed in this article, yet again, ask for Cooke's reply.

Wolfe, Julian. God, Determinism and Liberty: Hume's Puzzle. *Sophia (Australia)*, 31(3), 126-129, 1992.

This paper suggests that Hume had reason to question whether liberty in the sense compatible with determinism is that presupposed in our ascriptions of responsibility, in our praise and blame of agents.

Wolff, Janet. Postmodern Theory and Feminist Art Practice in Postmodernism and Society, Boyne, Roy (ed). New York, St Martin's Pr, 1990.

Wolff, Jonathan. Hume, Bentham, and the Social Contract. *Utilitas*, 5(1), 87-90, My 93.

Hume famously argues that Social Contract theory collapses into a form of utilitarianism. Bentham endorses Hume's argument. I show that, if Hume's argument refutes Social Contract theory, it equally undermines Bentham's own utilitarian account of political obligation. This discussion is used to illustrate a more general thesis that there is no single problem of political obligation, but different problems for different theorists.

Wolff, Kurt H. A First Response to the Preceding Essays. *Human Stud*, 16(3), 353-357, Jl 93.

This preliminary response to six essays on some of my work — by an analyst of experience, an Asian woman intellectual, a sociologist, a feminist, and a philosopher — touches on the "paradox of surrender" (the identification in it of the unique and the universal); the universality of its experience but the Western conceptualization of it; the effort to do right by both poetry and sociology; state of mind and state of society; technology and expertise in the process of giving birth; the identification of maximally "having oneself" and surrender and the recognition of it as *healing* or making *whole*.

Wolff, Kurt H (ed). *From Karl Mannheim (Second Edition)*. New Brunswick, Transaction Books, 1993.

Wolgast, Elizabeth H. Innocence. *Philosophy*, 68(265), 297-307, Jl 93.

Loss of innocence is generally viewed as regrettable, and life afterwards viewed as second-best. I call this view into question. I argue that experience with wrong, our own and others, and the recognition of it in censure and shame, are essential to moral understanding. In this light innocence signifies a lack instead of something positive. This is a fact that moral theory should find a way to accommodate.

Wolin, Richard. Carl Schmitt: The Conservative Revolutionary Habitus and the Aesthetics of Horror. *Polit Theory*, 20(3), 424-447, Ag 92.

Wolin, Richard. Jürgen Habermas on the Legacy of Jean-Paul Sartre: Interview. *Polit Theory*, 20(3), 496-501, Ag 92.

Wolin, Sheldon S. Democracy, Difference, and Re-Cognition. *Polit Theory*, 21(3), 464-483, Ag 93.

Wollheim, Richard. Ayer: The Man, the Philosopher, the Teacher in A J Ayer Memorial Essays, Griffiths, A Phillips (ed). New York, Cambridge Univ Pr, 1991.

Wollheim, Richard. Correspondence, Projective Properties, and Expression in the Arts in The Language of Art History, Kemal, Salim (ed). New York, Cambridge Univ Pr, 1991.

Wollheim, Richard. The Idea of a Common Human Nature in Isaiah Berlin: A Celebration, Margalit, Edna (ed). Chicago, Univ of Chicago Pr, 1991.

Wollheim, Richard. *The Mind and Its Depths*. Cambridge, Harvard Univ Pr, 1993.

Wolniewicz, Boguslaw. Concerning Reism in Kotarbinski: Logic, Semantics and Ontology, Woléński, Jan (ed). Dordrecht, Kluwer, 1990.

Wolsky, Alexander A and Wolsky, Maria de Issekutz. Bergson's Vitalism in the Light of Modern Biology in The Crisis in Modernism, Burwick, Frederick (ed). New York, Cambridge Univ Pr, 1992.

Wolsky, Maria de Issekutz and Wolsky, Alexander A. Bergson's Vitalism in the Light of Modern Biology in The Crisis in Modernism, Burwick, Frederick (ed). New York, Cambridge Univ Pr, 1992.

Wolter, Allan B. Reflections on the Life and Works of Scotus. *Amer Cath Phil Quart*, 67(1), 1-36, Wint 93.

Wolter, Allan B. Scotus on the Divine Origin of Possibility. *Amer Cath Phil Quart*, 67(1), 95-107, Wint 93.

Wolterstorff, Nicholas. An Engagement With Kant's Theory of Beauty in Kant's Aesthetics, Meerbote, Ralf (ed). Atascadero, Ridgeview, 1991.

Wolterstorff, Nicholas. Divine Simplicity in Our Knowledge of God, Clark, Kelly James (ed). Dordrecht, Kluwer, 1992.

Wolterstorff, Nicholas. Divine Simplicity in Philosophical Perspectives, 5: Philosophy of Religion, 1991, Tomberlin, James E (ed). Atascadero, Ridgeview, 1991.

Wolterstorff, Nicholas. The Remembrance of Things (Not) Past in Christian Philosophy, Flint, Thomas P (ed). Notre Dame, Univ Notre Dame Pr, 1990.

Wong, David B. On Care and Justice Within the Family. *Cont Phil*, 15(4), 21-24, Jl-Ag 93.

Wong, Yeu-Guang. The Continuity of Chinese Humanism in the Shang-Chou Period. *J Chin Phil*, 19(4), 445-468, D 92.

Woo, Kun-yu. A New Orientation towards Ethical Value—An Approach to the Phenomenological Method (in Chinese). *Phil Rev (Taiwan)*, 15, 1-16, Ja 92.

This article deals with modern ethical values. The author tries to use the phenomenological method to analyze the differences and the possible coincidence between normative ethics and meta-ethics. (edited)

Woo, Peter Kun-Yu. Metaphysical Foundations of Traditional Chinese Moral Educ in Chinese Foundations for Moral Education and Character Development, Van Doan, Tran (ed). Washington, CRVP, 1991.

To re-evaluate the traditional Chinese moral education without destroying any cultural heritage the author tries to discuss its metaphysical foundations in dividing this article into three main parts, namely the historical development, the essential content and the contemporary implications. With sophisticated sensibility he traces the persuasive impact and continued transformation of the popular religiosity of the Pre-China period through the great importance of harmony and order in later periods. As a deep metaphysical dimension he sees in Chinese education the perennial value and the praxis- oriented morality throughout thousands of years.

Wood, Allen. Hegel and Marxism in The Cambridge Companion to Hegel, Beiser, Frederick C (ed). New York, Cambridge Univ Pr, 1993.

Wood, Allen. Hegel's Ethics in The Cambridge Companion to Hegel, Beiser, Frederick (ed). New York, Cambridge Univ Pr, 1993.

Wood, Allen. Rational Theology, Moral Faith, and Religion in The Cambridge Companion to Kant, Guyer, Paul (ed). New York, Cambridge Univ Pr, 1992.

The article surveys Kant's views on the metaphysical origins of the concept of God, his critique of traditional theistic proofs, his moral arguments for faith in God, and his conception of religion, emphasizing that Kant's conception of religion is deeply connected to his philosophy of history.

Wood, Allen. Reply to Houlgate and Pinkard. *Bull Hegel Soc Gt Brit*, 25, 34-49, Spr-Sum 92.

The reply defends Wood's procedure, in *Hegel's Ethical Thought*, of treating Hegel's theory of the good and its social actualization independently of Hegel's speculative logic of metaphysics.

Wood, David (ed). *Derrida: A Critical Reader*. Cambridge, Blackwell, 1992.

Wood, David (ed). *Of Derrida, Heidegger, and Spirit*. Evanston, Northwestern Univ Pr, 1993.

Wood, David (ed). *On Paul Ricoeur: Narrative and Interpretation*. New York, Routledge, 1991.

Wood, David. Reiterating the Temporal in Reading Heidegger: Commemorations, Sallis, John (ed). Bloomington, Indiana Univ Pr, 1992.

Wood, David. The Actualization of Philosophy and the Logic of 'Geist' in Of Derrida, Heidegger, and Spirit, Wood, David (ed). Evanston, Northwestern Univ Pr, 1993.

Wood, David (trans) and Derrida, Jacques. Passions: 'An Oblique Offering' in Derrida: A Critical Reader, Wood, David (ed). Cambridge, Blackwell, 1992.

Wood, David and Sampford, Charles. Tax, Justice and the Priority of Property in Ethical Dimensions of Legal Theory, Sadurski, Wojciech (ed). Amsterdam, Rodopi, 1991.

This essay examines arguments which seek to deny (Rand, Nozick) or limit (Nozick, Scruton, Epstein, Lucas) the legitimacy of taxation. All generally assume that taxation of property or income takes away something to which the citizen taxed has prior and superior moral title. Even proponents of "confiscatory" taxation make a similar assumption of prior. However, as tax and property, especially in its modern forms, are dependent on law, such a priority cannot be defended without a separate moral argument. Few such arguments are offered and those that are (e.g., Rand, Nozick) fail. This is not to say that any level of tax is justified but that arguments over the roles that taxation and private property have to play cannot legitimately be skewed in favour of the latter by assumptions of its priority. The essay concludes by considering the form that such philosophical and legal arguments over tax would take.

Wood, E M. Locke against Democracy: Consent, Representation and Suffrage in the *Two Treatises*. *Hist Polit Thought*, 13(4), 657-689, Wint 92.

Wood, Robert. Philosophy, Aesthetics, and Theology: A Review of Hans Urs von Balthasar's *The Glory of the Lord*. *Amer Cath Phil Quart*, 67(3), 355-382, Sum 93.

The Glory of the Lord is a seven-volume first installment to a multi-volume trilogy whose basic thesis is that human existence is oriented by transcendental beauty, goodness, and .truth as ways to God in theo-phany, theo-drama and theo-logic. Though they mutually require one another, their center lies in the aesthetic: without theophany, moral and intellectual endeavors shrivel. Von Balthasar sweeps through the history of Western thought in scripture, literature philosophy and theology. The first volume presents the thesis; the next two explore twelve thinkers exhibiting distinctively different theological styles; the following two examine philosophers and poets; the last two consider scripture.

Woodbury, Leonard E and Brown, Christopher G (& other eds). *Collected Writings—Leonard E Woodbury*. Atlanta, Scholars Pr, 1991.

Woodfield, Andrew. Knowing What I'm Thinking Of—II. *Aris Soc*, Supp(67), 109-124, 1993.

Ruth Millikan claimed that the capacity to *coidentity* is fundamental for knowing which object one is perceiving, or pondering. I argue that several distinct capacities are involved. The phenomena to be explained are very mixed. The best strategy, from a cognitive science perspective, is to separate the cases and decompose the tasks. Judgments of identity, for example, may call upon theories and principles, whereas visually tracking an intermittently visible object might be done automatically by a module.

Woodhouse, Howard. Russell and Whitehead on the Process of Growth in Education. *Russell*, 12(2), 135-159, Wint 92-93.

The central question addressed in this article is: To what extent did Russell's philosophy of education concur with Whitehead's Theory of the Rhythmic Cycles of Human Growth? Fundamental differences between both their philosophies and their philosophies of education are underlined by Russell's adoption of behaviorism as an exemplar of the scientific method. The consequences for Russell's own educational practice are examined, and his theory criticised in light of these shortcomings.

Woodhouse, Mark B. Philosophy and Frontier Science in New Horizons in the Philosophy of Science, Lamb, David (ed). Brookfield, Avebury, 1992.

This essay examines four controversial scientific developments that challenge deeply entrenched theoretical frameworks: I) non-local causation in physics; II) holographic information models in neurophysiology; III) morphogenetic fields in biology, and; IV) near-death experience in medicine/psychology. In each case I show why the topic should inform discussion of specific philosophical issues, such as simultaneous causation, the distinction between form and matter, or the localization of mental states, and I provide independent philosophical analyses. A major conclusion is that the relevant explanatory models collectively require an expanded materialist ontology in which interlocking fields, forces, and frequencies play roles that, within the context of mechanistic explanation, would be assigned to the configuration and/or momentum of discrete material units, such as an electron or a gene.

Woodill, Joseph. Virtue Ethics: An Orthodox Appreciation. *Thought*, 67(265), 181-191, Je 92.

Woodrow, Brian E (ed) and Burgess, Michael M (ed). *Contemporary Issues in Paediatric Ethics*. Lewiston, Mellen Pr, 1991.

This anthology addresses practical issues in the provision of health care to children: David Ost surveys the moral dimensions of caring for children. William Bartholome argues for the importance of best interest judgments by all caregivers when withholding or withdrawing life support. Terry Acherman defends children's strong claim to society's resources in the support of innovative lifesaving therapies. Michael Burgess argues for greater involvement of children in their health care. Susan Sherwin argues against characterizing parents' resistance to medical recommendations as neglect. Reverend Herbert O'Driscoll poetically reflects upon these discussions in a broader context.

Woodruff, Paul B (ed & trans) and Thucydides. *Thucydides: On Justice, Power, and Human Nature*. Indianapolis, Hackett, 1993.

Woods, Gregory (trans) and Kristeller, Paul O. *Greek Philosophers of the Hellenistic Age*. New York, Columbia Univ Pr, 1993.

Woods, John. Critical Notice of W V Quine's *Pursuit of Truth*. *Can J Phil*, 22(4), 547-571, D 92.

Quine's philosophy is an evolving affair, and *Pursuit of Truth* (now in its second edition) marks some important developments. Lurking in the wings for a dog's age, ontological neutrality has come front and centre—a displacement of ontological relativity. As ontology recedes to the periphery, ideology bears ever more of the philosophical load. It is not what is that signifies; it is what we say of what (we say) is. Concurrently, physics is now granted to be irremediably intensional, at the cost of its "existential intelligibility". And the thesis of the indeterminacy of translation is trivial except for sentences taken holophrastically.

Woods, Michael. Aristotle on Sleep and Dreams. *Apeiron*, 25(3), 179-188, S 92.

Woods, Michael. Aristotle's Anthropocentrism. *Phil Invest*, 16(1), 18-35, Ja 93.

Woods, Michael. Form, Species, and Predication in Aristotle. *Synthese*, 96(3), 399-415, S 93.

Woodward, James. Realism About Laws. *Erkenntnis*, 36(2), 181-218, Mr 92.

This paper explores the idea that laws express relationships between properties or universals as defended in Michael Tooley's recent book *Causation: A Realist Approach*. I suggest that the most plausible version of realism will take a different form than that advocated by Tooley. According to this alternative, laws are grounded in facts about the capacities and powers of particular systems, rather than facts about relations between universals. The notion of lawfulness is linked to the notion of invariance, rather than to the metaphysical notion of a necessary connection.

Woodward, Jim and Bogen, Jim. Observations, Theories and the Evolution of the Human Spirit. *Phil Sci*, 59(4), 590-611, D 92.

Standard philosophical discussions of theory-ladeness assume that observational evidence consists of perceptual outputs (or reports of such outputs) that are sentential or propositional in structure. Theory-ladeness is conceptualized as having to do with logical or semantical relationships between such outputs or reports and background theories held by observers. Using the recent debate between Fodor and Churchland as a point of departure, we propose an alternative picture in which much of what serves as evidence in science is not perceptual outputs or reports of such outputs and is not sentential in structure.

Woolcock, Peter G. Skills-Grouping as a Teaching Approach to the "Philosophy for Children" Program. *Thinking*, 10(3), 23-28, 1993.

Worsfold, Victor L. MacIntyre and Bloom: Two Complementary Communitarians. *Proc Phil Educ*, 48, 328-335, 1992.

Wouters, Arno. Marx's Embryology of Society. *Phil Soc Sci*, 23(2), 149-179, Je 93.

This article presents a new interpretation of Marx's dialectical method. Marx conceived dialectics as a method for constructing a model of society. The way this model is developed is analogous to the way organisms develop according to the German embryologist Karl Ernst von Baer, and, indeed, Marx's theory of capitalism hinges on the same concept of *Organisation* that is found in teleomechanical biology. The strong analogy between pre-Darwinian biology and Marx's structure of argument shows that the analogy often supposed to exist between Darwin and Marx is not relevant to Marx's theory of capitalism.

Woznicki, Andrew N. Theantropic Foundations of Religious Beliefs. *Amer Cath Phil Quart*, 65, 203-213, 1991.

St Augustine's *animam et Deum scire cupio* expresses the inner structure of human desire for self-realization and ultimate self-perfection according to a specific divine design which can be defined as *theantropy*. The purpose of this paper is to reflect on the religiousness of man in his various forms of theantropic "self-realization," thus manifesting different modes of the divine image according to a two-fold motion of the ascendancy and descendancy of the human and the divine nature in man, as it has been developed by the different religious orientations in Western civilization.

Wreen, Michael J. Abortion and Pregnancy Due to Rape. *Philosophia (Israel)*, 21(3-4), 201-220, Ap 92.

This paper is a critical examination of the morality of abortion in cases of pregnancy due to rape. J J Thomson's well-known analogy of the case of the plugged-in violinist is used as a springboard for discussion and is returned to at several points. My principal finding is that on the assumption that the fetus has a right to life from the moment of conception, abortion is not morally permissible in cases of pregnancy due to rape.

Wreen, Michael J. Jump with Common Spirits: Is An *Ad Populum* Argument Fallacious?. *Metaphilosophy*, 24(1-2), 61-75, Ja-Ap 93.

This paper is a critical analysis of *argumentum ad populum*. A common definition of *ad populum* is exposed and criticized and a new definition then proffered. Next, distinct kinds of *ad populum* are distinguished and examined, and it is argued that non-fallacious instances of all four kinds exist. There are even, odd as it might seem, deductively valid *ad populums*. It's concluded that although some *ad populums* are fallacious, no argument is fallacious just because it's an *ad populum*.

Wren, Thomas (ed) and Noam, Gil G (ed). *The Moral Self*. Cambridge, MIT Pr, 1993.

Wright, Colin B. Contra Hume: On Making Things Happen in Logical Foundations, Mahalingam, Indira (ed). New York, St Martin's Pr, 1991.

The aim is to refute Hume's contention that the casual 'tie' is not in objects, but 'merely in ourselves'. That causation is more than mere association of ideas is evident from experience of physical force. In, say, pulling down the branch of a tree, one feels a resisting force, that is not allowed for in the Humean scheme. Experience of force where one is involved as an agent entitles one to suppose if present in cases where human agency is not involved. Hume is quite wrong. The foundation of causation is not regularity and association, but doing and not producing.

Wright, Crispin. Is Higher Order Vagueness Coherent?. *Analysis*, 52(3), 129-139, Jl 92.

Wright, Crispin. On An Argument On Behalf of Classical Negation. *Mind*, 102(405), 123-131, Ja 93.

Wright, Crispin. On Putnam's Proof That We Are Not Brains-In-A-Vat. *Proc Aris Soc*, 92, 67-94, 1992.

Wright, Crispin. Wittgenstein on Mathematical Proof in Wittgenstein Centenary Essays, Griffiths, A Phillips (ed). New York, Cambridge Univ Pr, 1991.

Wright, Edmond. Gestalt Switching: Hanson, Aronson, and Harré. *Phil Sci*, 59(3), 480-486, S 92.

This discussion takes up an attack by Jerrold Aronson (seconded by Rom Harré) on the use made by Norwood R Hanson of the Gestalt-Switch Analogy in the philosophy of science. Aronson's understanding of what is implied in a gestalt switch is shown to be flawed. In his endeavor to detach conceptual understanding from perceptual identification he cites several examples, without realizing the degree to which such gestalt switches can affect conceptualizing or how conceptualizing can affect gestalts. In particular, he has not confronted the possibility of such gestalt selection being involved in the basic identification of what we term "entities."

Wright, Edmond. Two More Proofs of Present Qualia. *Theoria*, 56(1-2), 3-22, 1990.

Opponents to the New Representationalist case argue that the hypothesis of there being colours, sounds, phenomenal space, etc. in the brain is inherently absurd. They are, however, guilty of an understandable mistake concerning the nature of inner representations, believing that some qualitative resemblance is involved, when only concomitant variation between dissimilars is. The experiences of colour and phenomenal space are taken as exemplars; in the course of discussing the latter, a new Inverted 3-D Space Argument is adduced.

Wright, J K. Conversations with Phocion: The Political Thought of Mably. *Hist Polit Thought*, 13(3), 391-415, Autumn 92.

Wright, Kathleen. The Heidegger Controversy—Updated and Appraised. *Praxis Int*, 13(1), 85-98, Ap 93.

I critically examine the contributions of Richard Wolin and Michael Zimmerman to the debate about Heidegger's politics. I question in particular the "political philosophy" Wolin purports to find in *Being and Time* as well as Zimmerman's unreflective acceptance of Heidegger's valorization of art (a "saving power") over technology ("the danger"). Both studies, I conclude, are one-sided. They try to explain what led or misled Heidegger into following Hitler's lead. They fail to ask what Heidegger thought he could contribute to the worldview of Hitler's National Socialism so that he could presume to be in a position to lead the leader, Hitler.

Wright, M R. Presocratics and Sophists. *Phronesis*, 38(1), 106-110, 1993.

Wright, William A. Negative Campaigning. *J Soc Phil*, 24(1), 103-113, Spr 93.

Using fictionalized examples of campaign advertisements, I articulate reasons against four campaign practices frequently called "negative". These are: misrepresentation, groundless personal attacks, well grounded personal attacks, and running a campaign with a negative tone. The results include a discussion of whether politicians are members of a profession, giving them special license to break ordinary moral principles; an application of Scanlon's distinction between natural and artificial accounts of political freedoms; and an articulation of a Kantian conception of political community necessary to condemn campaigns with a negative tone.

Wringe, Colin. The Ambiguities of Education for Active Citizenship. *J Phil Educ*, 26(1), 29-38, 1992.

A notion of Education for Active Citizenship is identified in the pronouncements of certain politically influential individuals. Key elements in this are seen to include action, the citizen, appreciating the benefits of democracy and freedom, respect for the rule of law, a due balance between rights and duties, participation and service to the community. These are shown to be systematically ambiguous, simultaneously capable of evoking critical, independent-minded, socially effective citizens and docile conforming subjects. Clarification is held to be a necessary precondition of translating the ideal of citizenship into specific curricular goals.

Wringe, Colin and Lee, Jee-Hun. Rational Autonomy, Morality and Education. *J Phil Educ*, 27(1), 69-78, Sum 93.

Some traditional assumptions regarding rational autonomy are examined and criticised. The exclusion of subjective considerations from autonomous choice is shown to be unjustified, as are attempts to identify autonomy with morally desirable conduct. Unexpected implications of these conclusions for education and certain other social institutions are also indicated.

Wróblewski, Jerzy. Dictionaries of Legal Philosophy and General Jurisprudence. *Ratio Juris*, 5(1), 92-103, Mr 92.

The present note identifies the main problems of preparing a dictionary of legal philosophy and general jurisprudence. It deals with the scope and typology of legal dictionaries, a conception of the dictionary of legal philosophy and general jurisprudence, the typology and sources of terms in the dictionary in question, and examples of terms of the dictionary. (edited)

Wróblewski, Jerzy. Moral Values and Legal Reasoning: Some Aspects of Their Mutual Relations in Ethical Dimensions of Legal Theory, Sadurski, Wojciech (ed). Amsterdam, Rodopi, 1991.

Wu, Ching-ru and Gassin, Elizabeth A and Enright, Robert D. Forgiveness: A Developmental View. *J Moral Educ*, 21(2), 99-114, 1992.

The concept of interpersonal forgiveness is described first through an examination of ancient writings and contemporary philosophical and psychological discourse. Two psychological models are then described. The first concerns developmental patterns in how people think about forgiving another. The second describes how people may go about forgiving another. Implications for counseling and education are drawn.

Wu, Kuang-Ming. The Other is My Hell; the Other is My Home. *Human Stud*, 16(1-2), 193-202, Ap 93.

This paper explores facets of the positive personal nihilation in relation to the negative. 1) Internal nihilation is an inner nihil enabling mutuality of personal accommodation in resonance, "home." 2) Home is being-with-other(s), making a person. 3) The person *is* with-others, via reciprocal inner touch. 4) This is shown in education that spreads to politico-cosmic concord. 5) Sadly, the home-relation can turn into hostility-relation. 6) We can dwell in hell in the other, however, because we originally dwell at home in the other. 7) How the two dwellings shift into each other constitutes historical dialectic, which makes up the person.

Wuchterl, Kurt. Religionsphilosophie im Spannungsfeld von Wissenschaft und Innerlichkeit. *Theol Phil*, 68(1), 82-88, 1993.

There is used a new term of philosophy of religion based on the notion of contingency and relating to reflections on speaking of God in analytical philosophy. Applying this notion which is comprehensively exposed in the book "Analyse und Kritik der religiösen Vernunft", Bern 1989, we show that the discussions of myth and science by Bultmann, Küng and Drewermann are determined by a wrong understanding of this relation. Every religion assumes a reality beyond scientifical and psychological explanations. Just this is warranted by the phenomenon of contingency and is not available by referring to introspection or "Innerlichkeit".

Wulff, Hans Jürgen and Kaczmarek, Ludger. Prolegomena zu einer semiotischen Beschreibung graphischer Darstellungen in Diagrammatik und Philosophie, Gehring, Petra (ed). Amsterdam, Rodopi, 1992.

Examples of graphical structural images mainly from linguistics are given to show in which way graphical representations are minimal formal models of their domains.

Wulff, Henrik R. Philosophy of Medicine—From a Medical Perspective. *Theor Med*, 13(1), 79-85, Mr 92.

In this commentary on the article by Arthur L Caplan, the philosophy of medicine is viewed from a medical perspective. Philosophical studies have a long tradition in medicine, especially during periods of paradigmatic unrest, and they serve the same goal as other medical activities: the prevention and treatment of disease. The medical profession needs the help of professional philosophers in much the same way as it needs the cooperation of basic scientists. Philosophy of medicine may not deserve the status of a *philosophical* subspecialty or field, but it is so closely linked to the main trends of contemporary medical thinking that it must be regarded as an emerging (or reemerging) *medical* subdiscipline.

Wynn, Karen. Evidence Against Empiricist Accounts of the Origins of Numerical Knowledge. *Mind Lang*, 7(4), 315-332, Wint 92.

Wynn, Karen. Issues Concerning a Nativist Theory of Numerical Knowledge. *Mind Lang*, 7(4), 367-381, Wint 92.

Wynn, Karen. The Origins of Psychological Axioms of Arithmetic and Geometry. *Mind Lang*, 7(4), 409-416, Wint 92.

Wynn, Mark. Some Reflections on Richard Swinburne's Argument from Design. *Relig Stud*, 29(3), 325-335, S 93.

The paper considers the internal consistency of Swinburne's argument from temporal regularity. In particular, it considers whether the principle of simplicity is used consistently as a measure of *a priori* probability, and whether one of Swinburne's arguments for the claim that temporal regularity is to be explained may not undermine one of his arguments for the claim that any such explanation must make reference to the activity of a person. The paper concludes that on both of these points there is a case to answer.

Wyschogrod, Edith. Does Continental Ethics Have a Future? in *Ethics and Danger*, Dallery, Arleen B (ed). Albany, SUNY Pr, 1992.

The conceptual backdrop against which promising tendencies in continental ethics — the authority of the other, the body subject, and the revolt against theory — are developing and the likely course of these developments are considered. The other as yielding ethical signification in Levinas, Lyotard and Blanchot require Heidegger and Sartre's overcoming of the solipsistic aspects of Husserlian phenomenology; the subject as vulnerability, Edith Stein's, Sartre's and Merleau Ponty's analyses of corporeality; Derrida's and Foucault's revolt against theory, Heidegger's critique of traditional epistemologies. The understanding of narrative in Blanchot, Ricoeur, Derrida and Kristeva may precipitate a turn towards narrative ethics.

Xiaogan, Liu. The Evolution of Three Schools of Latter-Day Zhuang Zi Philosophy. *Chin Stud Phil*, 24(1), 3-54, Fall 92.

Yablo, Stephen. Cause and Essence. *Synthese*, 93(3), 403-449, D 92.

Essence and causation are fundamental in metaphysics, but little is said about their relations. Some essential properties are of course causal, as it is essential to footprints to have been caused by feet. But I am interested less in causation's role in essence than the reverse: the bearing a thing's essence has on its causal powers. That essence *might* make a causal contribution is hinted already by the counterfactual element in causation; and the hint is confirmed by the explanation essence offers of something otherwise mysterious, namely, how events exactly alike in every ordinary respect, like the bolt's *suddenly* snapping and its snapping per se, manage to disagree in what they cause. (edited)

Yablo, Stephen. Is Conceivability a Guide to Possibility?. *Phil Phenomenol Res*, 53(1), 1-42, Mr 93.

This paper outlines the standard objections to conceivability arguments; proposes a reading of "conceivable" that escapes these objections; maintains the general reliability of modal intuition while admitting the phenomena of modal error and disagreement; attempts to explain these phenomena in terms of prior and independent cognitive miscues; and considers finally the modal realism debate, stressing the importance of well-disciplined modal dialectic.

Yablo, Stephen. Mental Causation. *Phil Rev*, 101(2), 245-280, Ap 92.

Yablon, Charles M. Forms in Deconstruction and the Possibility of Justice, Cornell, Durcilla (ed). New York, Routledge, 1992.

Yagisawa, Takashi. Modes of Presentation?. *Analysis*, 53(1), 34-36, Ja 93.

Stephen Schiffer criticises a popular modes-of-presentation theory of belief, namely, the Mentalese-token-in-the-belief-box theory, on the basis of a certain constraint on modes of presentation. F Adams, R Stecker, and G Fuller reject Schiffer's criticism. I show that their rejection is ill-founded.

Yakhnis, Alexander and Goncharov, Sergey and Yakhnis, Vladimir. Some Effectively Infinite Classes of Enumerations. *Annals Pure Applied Log*, 60(3), 207-235, My 93.

This research partially answers the question raised by Goncharov about the size of the class of positive elements of a Roger's semilattice. We introduce a notion of effective infinity of classes of computable enumerations. Then, using finite injury priority method, we prove five theorems which give sufficient conditions to be effectively infinite for classes of all enumerations without repetitions, positive undecidable enumerations, negative undecidable enumerations and all computable enumerations of a family of r.e. sets. These theorems permit to strengthen the results of Pour-El, Pour-El and Howard, Ershov and Khutoretskii about existence of enumerations without repetitions and positive undecidable enumerations.

Yakhnis, Vladimir and Yakhnis, Alexander and Goncharov, Sergey. Some Effectively Infinite Classes of Enumerations. *Annals Pure Applied Log*, 60(3), 207-235, My 93.

This research partially answers the question raised by Goncharov about the size of the class of positive elements of a Roger's semilattice. We introduce a notion of effective infinity of classes of computable enumerations. Then, using finite injury priority method, we prove five theorems which give sufficient conditions to be effectively infinite for classes of all enumerations without repetitions, positive undecidable enumerations, negative undecidable enumerations and all computable enumerations of a family of r.e. sets. These theorems permit to strengthen the results of Pour-El, Pour-El and Howard, Ershov and Khutoretskii about existence of enumerations without repetitions and positive undecidable enumerations.

Yako, Masato. Hierarchical Time and Meter (in Japanese). *Bigaku*, 43(3), 12-23, Wint 92.

Music is a systematizing of time, and various characteristics of time are reflected in music. A singular point of time passes is the present, but the present time which we understand practically, has range. The present range is different, and it is dependent on the line of connection. Also in music the present range is different, and it is dependent on the line of connection. Also in music the present has range. For example, it can either be a tone or a first motif. Interpretation of music is changed according to which range is selected as the musical present. The various range of time according to how to take the present, is inseparable from the hierarchy of music. This paper considers, by way of a schematic model, how hierarchical characters which musical present has are related with meter which is another factor that composes musical time. (edited)

Yanal, Robert J. Dependent and Independent Reasons. *Inform Log*, 13(3), 137-144, Fall 91.

How are dependent (or linked) premises to be distinguished from independent (or convergent) premises? Deductive validity, sometimes proposed as a necessary condition for dependence, cannot be, for the premises of both inductive and deductive but invalid arguments can be dependent. The question is really this: When do multiple premises for a certain conclusion from one argument for that conclusion and when do they form multiple arguments? Answer: Premises are dependent when the evidence they offer for their conclusion is more than the ordinary sum of their probabilities. Ordinary sums are defined in the paper.

Yanal, Robert J. Hume and Others on the Paradox of Tragedy. *J Aes Art Crit*, 49(1), 75-76, Wint 91.

Tragic events should inspire pain, but paradoxically we take pleasure from tragic events in art. Recent commentators have criticized Hume's essay "Of Tragedy" for its supposed "conversion theory" in which the pain of viewing the tragic spectacle is — unaccountably — converted to pleasure by the artist's skill. I argue that Hume holds no such conversion theory, but rather holds that the aesthetic pleasure of viewing tragedy outweighs on the whole the pain from the tragic events.

Yanal, Robert J. Still Unconverted: A Reply to Neill. *J Aes Art Crit*, 50(4), 324-326, Fall 92.

Alex Neill (JAAC, Spring 1992) has tried to convince me that Hume holds a "conversion theory" as a solution to the paradox of tragedy (i.e., we take pleasure in events that arouse painful emotions). (See my initial statement in JAAC, Winter 1991). In this reply I again argue that Hume does not hold a conversion theory implying that painful-sorrow has been converted into pleasurable-sorrow. The instances Neill points to where Hume speaks of conversion either have no bearing on the paradox of tragedy or support my reading.

Yandell, Keith E. Continuity, Consciousness, and Identity in Hume's Philosophy. *Hume Stud*, 18(2), 255-274, N 92.

Yandell, Keith E. *The Epistemology of Religious Experience*. New York, Cambridge Univ Pr, 1993.

Yanping, Shi and Ruzhuang, Xu (trans). Developments in Chinese Philosophy Over the Last Ten Years. *Phil East West*, 43(1), 113-125, Ja 93.

Yassour, Avraham. Martin Buber—Critic of Karl Marx. *Dialec Hum*, 17(1), 140-153, 1990.

Buber has written extensively on utopian Socialist thoughts; he saw K Marx as one of utopian critics of the bourgeois thinkers and sympathetically treated his sociological and cultural assumptions. Buber's critique of Marx is in an anarchio-spiritual tendency. Buber is seen as a societal thinker, people and friend of the Jewish anarchist Laudauer and an ideology of communism which influenced the Kibbutz-movement in Israel.

Yasuo, Yuasa. A Contemporary Scientific Paradigm and the Discovery of the Inner Cosmos in Self as Body in Asian Theory and Practice, Kasulis, Thomas P (ed). Albany, SUNY Pr, 1992.

Yates, Steven A. Feyerabend, Realism, and Historicity. *Amer Cath Phil Quart*, 65(4), 429-443, Autumn 91.

Yee, Richard Wing. Turing Machines and Semantics Symbol Processing: Why Real Computers Don't Mind Chinese Emperors. *Lyceum*, 5(1), 37-59, Spr 93.

Debate over mind and computation should focus on Turing machines (TM's) proper. Both the Chinese Room and Gödelian critiques fail because neither computers nor formal systems function like general TM's. TM's can learn and can process symbols non-formally. Valid debate must be grounded in the full theory of computation.

Yeide Jr, Harry. The Many Faces of Autonomy. *J Clin Ethics*, 3(4), 269-274, Wint 92.

Yepes, Ricardo. Los sentidos del acto en Aristóteles. *Anu Filosof*, 25(3), 493-512, 1992.

'Act' or 'Actuality' traduces two words coined by Aristotle: *energeia* and *entelecheia*. The first meaning of *energeia* is movement (kinesis). The second meaning designs the end of movement: form, substance (*ousia*), essence. Here *entelecheia* is brought to design that final state in which things reach their end and perfection. The third meaning or application of *energeia*, and derivately of *entelecheia*, is operation, action, function (*ergon*).

Yi-Jie, Tang and McLean, George F (ed). *Confucianism, Buddhism, Daoism, Christianity and Chinese Culture*. Washington, CRVP, 1991.

Yngve, V H. Criteria of Acceptance: Comments on Bickhard and Campbell, 'Some Foundational Questions Concerning Language Studies'. *J Prag*, 17(5-6), 549-556, Je 92.

The article reviewed, on an incoherence in the logical foundations of standard approaches to language, is criticized for relying on philosophical rather than scientific arguments. The standard criteria of acceptance in the natural sciences and the four assumptions underlying all science are then outlined. Convergences and differences with the reviewer's scientific approach are discussed. Specific criticisms include that the article contains an unsound argument, that it does not go far enough in rejecting unjustified assumptions from the semiotic-grammatical tradition, that it rests on unjustified special assumptions, and that it cannot treat important linguistic phenomena associated with groups of people.

Yob, Iris M. Religious Metaphor and Scientific Model: Grounds for Comparison. *Relig Stud*, 28(4), 475-485, D 92.

In explaining how religious formulations can be meaningful, an argument is made that the religions use metaphors the way science employs models. Drawing on the work of Nelson Goodman, Max Black, Sallie McFague, Ian Barbour, and Janet Soskice, this paper suggests that the congruence between metaphor and model is not exact, that models can refer in a number of ways, literal and figurative, including but not limited to metaphoric ways. The paper concludes that all metaphors are models, while not all models are metaphors and suggests a number of implications in our understanding of both science and religion.

Yoder, John Howard. On Not Being Ashamed of the Gospel: Particularity, Pluralism, and Validation. *Faith Phil*, 9(3), 285-300, Jl 92.

A standard account of the problem of validation considers intelligibility and identity as incompatible alternatives in a zero-sum context. The more the identity of a community or a set of ideas is specifiably or particularly Christian, the less capable, it is held, is that community or that set of ideas of communication to others, they have less to say that the hearers do not already know. This paper argues that said disjunction is refuted by the concept and by the track record of Gospel; it is a genre of communication which is at once particular and communicable, by virtue of the communicators' uncoerced and noncoercive submission to the host culture.

Yolton, John W. *A Locke Dictionary*. Cambridge, Blackwell, 1993.

Yonah, Yossi and Dahan, Yossi. Competitive Equality of Opportunity. *Iyyun*, 41, Jl 92.

Yonezawa, Shigeru. Socrates' Two Concepts of the Polis. *Hist Polit Thought*, 12(4), 565-576, Wint 91.

Young, Bruce A. On the Necessity of an Archetypal Concept in Morphology: With Special Reference to the Concepts of "Structure" and "Homology". *Biol Phil*, 8(2), 225-248, Ap 93.

Morphological elements, or structures, are sorted into four categories depending on their level of anatomical isolation and the presence or absence of intrinsically identifying characteristics. These four categories are used to highlight the difficulties with the concept of structure and our ability to identify or define structures. The analysis is extended to the concept of homology through a discussion of the methodological and philosophical problems of the current concept of homology. It is argued that homology is fundamentally a similarity based concept rather than a phylogenetic concept, and a proposal is put forth to return to a comparative context for homology. It is shown that for both the concepts of structure and homology an *a priori* assumption of stable underlying patterns (i.e., archetypes) is essential.

Young, Charles M. Aristotle on Temperance in Essays in Ancient Greek Philosophy, IV, Anton, John P (ed). Albany, SUNY Pr, 1991.

Young, Iris. Sexual Ethics in the Age of Epidemic. *Hypatia*, 8(3), 184-193, Sum 93.

In this essay I follow one argument strand from Linda Singer's *Erotic Welfare*. How can we have a forward-looking and affirmative ideal of sexual freedom when the "aids" panic has altered the sexual landscape and instigated new justifications for oppressive sexual disciplines? How can we be sexual subjects when processes of commodification and disciplinary practices have constrained sexual expression while proliferating sexual fetishes? These are some of the questions this book formulates, without answering.

Young, Iris Marion. Abjection and Oppression in Crises in Continental Philosophy, Dallery, Arleen B (ed). Albany, SUNY Pr, 1990.

Young, Iris Marion. Breasted Experience: The Look and the Feeling in The Body in Medical Thought and Practice, Leder, Drew (ed). Dordrecht, Kluwer, 1992.

Young, J Michael. Functions of Thought and the Synthesis of Intuitions in The Cambridge Companion to Kant, Guyer, Paul (ed). New York, Cambridge Univ Pr, 1992.

In his "metaphysical deduction" Kant maintains (1) that concepts can gain content, and thus give rise to a significant body of knowledge, only insofar as they involve the synthesis of an intuited manifold. He also maintains (2) that synthesis is structured by a set of basic concepts or categories, and that these derive from the functions of thought that give unity to representations in a judgment. I argue that (1) is an important and interesting view, which sets Kant apart from his rationalist predecessors, but that (2) represents a continuing commitment to rationalist doctrines and is profoundly mistaken from Kant's own viewpoint.

Young, James O. Destroying Works of Art. *J Aes Art Crit*, 47(4), 367-373, Fall 89.

Several controversial works of art, including Richard Serra's *Tilted Arc*, have raised the question of whether it is ever moral to destroy works of art. I consider and reject several arguments designed to establish that destroying works of art is always wrong. I then argue that an artwork may be destroyed when its value as an aesthetic object plus its other value is not sufficient to out-weigh the costs of preserving it.

Young, James O. Holism and Meaning. *Erkenntnis*, 37(3), 309-326, N 92.

This essay defends a version of meaning holism according to which no sentence can be understood except in the context of a total theory of the world. Any sentence is understood only in relation to other sentences and these others are understood in relation to still others. Ultimately, no sentence is completely understood unless the inferential relations between all sentences in a total theory are grasped. This version of holism is defended against objections by Michael Dummett and others.

Young, James O. Key, Temperament and Musical Expression. *J Aes Art Crit*, 49(3), 235-242, Sum 91.

Musical keys are often said to possess individual characters: C major is sometimes said to be innocent; D major to be warlike and so on. This essay attempts to explain how keys could acquire a particular expressive quality. I argue that key characteristics resulted from the use of unequal temperaments.

Young, James O. Still More in Defense of Colorization. *J Aes Art Crit*, 50(3), 245-248, Sum 92.

This article is a rejoinder to Flo Leibowitz's criticism of my essay "In Defence of Colourization." I provide further arguments for the conclusion that the colorization of black and white films is not always morally or aesthetically objectionable.

Young, James O. The Metaphysics of Anti-Realism. *Metaphilosophy*, 23(1-2), 68-76, Ja-Ap 92.

Michael Dummett argues that the debate between realists and anti-realists is to be resolved by reflection on theories of meaning. That is, he holds that metaphysical debates (between idealists and materialists, Platonists and non-Platonists, phenomenalists and physicalists) are, at root, semantic debates. I argue that he is wrong. Realism (conceived of as the view that sentences have objective truth conditions) and anti-realism (according to which the truth conditions of sentences are, in all cases, recognizable) have no metaphysical consequences.

Young, Michael J (ed & trans). *Lectures on Logic—Immanuel Kant*. New York, Cambridge Univ Pr, 1992.

Young, Phillips E and Conway, Daniel W. Ethics in America: A Report from the Trenches. *J Value Inq*, 27(1), 123-130, Ja 93.

This report presents some observations on the strengths and weaknesses of the *Ethics in America* telecourse package. In the three years that we have administered the course in our undergraduate curriculum, we have found it a useful pedagogical tool that targets a traditionally inaccessible audience of videophile students. We wish to convey our experience with the telecourse package, and we offer suggestions for the improvement of the course package itself and for its implementation by interested instructors.

Young, Robert E. Dispositions of a Moving Target. *Proc Phil Educ*, 48, 265-269, 1992.

Young, Thomas. Analogical Reasoning and Easy Rescue Cases. *J Phil Res*, 18, 327-397, 1993.

The purpose of this article is to determine whether analogical reasoning can supply a basis for believing that we have a moral obligation to rescue strangers. The paper will focus on donating cadaver organs. I construct a moral analogical argument involving an easy rescue case and organ donation. Various alleged relevant differences between the cases are examined and rejected. Finally, what I call "the ownership dilemma" is introduced and I conclude that this dilemma is inescapable. Thus, analogical reasoning, however convincing it might appear, is virtually worthless a strategy of rationally persuading people that they have a duty to donate blood, cadaver organs, or, more generally, a duty to give up any property to aid strangers.

Youngner, Stuart J and Arnold, Robert M. The Dead Donor Rule: Should We Stretch It, Bend It, or Abandon It?. *Kennedy Inst Ethics J*, 3(2), 263-278, Je 93.

The dead donor rule — that patients must be dead before their organs are taken — is a central part of the moral framework underlying organ procurement. Efforts to increase the pool of transplantable organs have been forced to either redefine death (e.g., anencephaly) or take advantage of ambiguities in the current definition of death (e.g., the Pittsburgh protocol). Society's growing acceptance of circumstances in which health care professionals can hasten a patient's death also may weaken the symbolic importance of the dead donor rule. We consider the implications of these efforts to continually revise the line between life and death and ask whether it would be preferable to abandon the dead donor rule and rely entirely on informed consent as a safeguard against abuse.

Yount, Mark R. *Un*capitalizing on *Radical Hermeneutics* in Modernity and Its Discontents, Marsh, James L (ed). Bronx, Fordham Univ Pr, 1992.

Yrjönsuuri, Mikko. Aristotle's *Topics* and Medieval Obligational Disputations. *Synthese*, 96(1), 59-82, Jl 93.

Yu, Qiuen. Further Explanations of the Gödel Scenario of the Mind—A Reply to Professor Graham Priest. *Synthese*, 95(3), 461-465, Je 93.

The paper defends the viewpoint that the Gödel incompleteness results have no force to entail the incompatibility between consistency and mechanicalness of the logic of the mind. It argues one step further than in the author's previous paper that it is not only possible but also necessary that there be two distinct systems involved in the Gödel scenario of the mind: the system for which the Gödel sentence is to be proved and the system in which that sentence is indeed provable.

Yu, Xiaokang. Riesz Representation Theorem, Borel Measures and Subsystems of Second-Order Arithmetic. *Annals Pure Applied Log*, 59(1), 65-73, Ja 93.

Formalized concept of finite Borel measures is developed in the language of second-order arithmetic. Formalization of the Riesz representation theorem is proved to be equivalent to arithmetical comprehension. Codes of Borel sets of complete separable metric spaces are defined and proved to be meaningful in the subsystem ATR. Arithmetical transfinite recursion is enough to prove the measurability of Borel sets for any finite Borel measure on a compact complete separable metric space.

Yu, Xiaokang and Simpson, Stephen G and Friedman, Harvey. Periodic Points and Subsystems of Second-Order Arithmetic. *Annals Pure Applied Log*, 62(1), 51-64, Je 93.

Yukio, Iwakuma and Ebbesen, Sten. Logic-Theological Schools from the Second Half of the 12th Century: A List of Sources. *Vivarium*, 30(1), 173-210, My 92.

Yulina, N S. The Feminist Revision of Philosophy: Potentials and Prospects. *Phil East West*, 42(2), 249-261, Ap 92.

Zademach, Wieland. The Freedom of the Truth: Marxist Salt for Christian Earth. *Dialec Hum*, 17(3), 129-150, 1990.

Zagacki, Kenneth S and Hikins, James W. Rhetoric, Objectivism, and the Doctrine of Tolerance in The Critical Turn, Angus, Ian (ed). Carbondale, So Illinois Univ Pr, 1993.

Zagzebski, Linda. Rejoinder to Hasker. *Faith Phil*, 10(2), 256-260, Ap 93.

In "Zagzebski on Power Entailment" William Hasker responds to the three sets of counterexamples to Power Entailment Principles given in my book, *The Dilemma of Freedom and Foreknowledge*. In this rejoinder, I answer Hasker's objections to the first two examples, and agree with him that the third example is defective, although for a different reason than the one Hasker presents.

Zahavi, D. Constitution and Ontology: Some Remarks on Husserl's Ontological Position in the *Logical Investigations*. *Husserl Stud*, 9(2), 111-124, 1992.

One of the major exegetical difficulties in connection with Husserl's *Logical Investigations* has always been the clarification of his ontological position and the closely related concept of constitution. Ever since the publication of the first edition—which will be the point of departure—in 1900-1901, there has been an ongoing discussion as to which concept of reality Husserl had committed himself, initiated with a realistic interpretation by his Göttingen students. My aim in the following paper will be a critical evaluation and interpretation of this relationship, thereby also taking Husserl's philosophical development—especially as concerns his idea of phenomenology—into consideration.

Zakharyashchev, Michael. Canonical Formulas for K4: Part I—Basic Results. *J Sym Log*, 57(4), 1377-1402, D 92.

Zakharyashchev, Michael and Chagrov, Alexander. The Disjunction Property of Intermediate Propositional Logic. *Stud Log*, 50(2), 189-216, Je 91.

This paper is a survey of results concerning the disjunction property, Halldén-completeness, and other related properties of intermediate propositional logics and normal modal logics containing S4.

Zalk, Sue Rosenberg (ed) and Gordon-Kelter, Janice (ed). *Revolutions in Knowledge: Feminism in the Social Sciences*. Boulder, Westview Pr, 1991.

Zalta, Edward N 732 AUTHOR INDEX WITH ABSTRACTS

Zalta, Edward N. On the Logic of the Ontological Argument in Philosophical Perspectives, 5: Philosophy of Religion, 1991, Tomberlin, James E (ed). Atascadero, Ridgeview, 1991.

St Anselm's ontological argument in Proslogium II is logically valid (the premises entail the conclusion). Consider a first-order language and logic in which definite descriptions are genuine terms, and in which the quantified sentence 'there is an x such that...' does not imply 'x exists'. Then, using an ordinary logic of descriptions and a connected greater-than relation, God's existence logically follows from the claims: (a) there is in the understanding something than which nothing greater can be conceived, and (b) if X doesn't exist, something greater than X can be conceived. To deny the conclusion, one must deny one of the premises. However, the argument involves no modal inferences and, interestingly, Descartes' ontological argument can be derived from it.

Zalta, Edward N. Replies to the Critics. *Phil Stud*, 69(2-3), 231-242, Mr 93.

In an author-meets-critics session at the March 1992 Pacific APA meetings, the critics (Christopher Menzel, Harry Deutsch, and C Anthony Anderson) commented on Zalta's book *Intensional Logic and the Metaphysics of Intentionality*, (Cambridge, MIT/Bradford, 1988). The critical commentaries are published in this issue together with these replies by the author. The author responds to questions concerning the system he proposes, and in particular, to questions concerning the treatment of modality, the semantics of belief reports, and the general efficacy of the metaphysical foundations as compared to that of set theory.

Zalta, Edward N. Twenty-Five Basic Theorems in Situation and World Theory. *J Phil Log*, 22(4), 385-428, Ag 93.

States of affairs, situations, and worlds are integrated into a single metaphysical foundation and the most basic principles that pretheoretically characterize these entities are derived. The principles are cast as theorems in a precise logical framework and are derived. The principles are cast as theorems in a precise logical framework and are derived from an independently- motivated axiomatic theory of objects and relations. Situations and worlds are identified as objects that both *encode* and *exemplify* properties. They encode properties of the form *being such that p* (where *p* is a state of affairs). These encoded properties are distinguished from the other properties that situations and worlds both contingently and necessarily exemplify, and this distinction offers a principled answer to questions about these entities.

Zamaleev, A F. Marxism and Russian Philosophy. *Sov Stud Phil*, 30(4), 64-69, Spr 92.

Zambella, Domenico. On the Proofs of Arithmetical Completeness for Interpretability Logic. *Notre Dame J Form Log*, 33(4), 542-551, Fall 92.

Zamora, Alvaro. El cogito también sueña. *Rev Filosof (Costa Rica)*, 30(71), 53-62, J 92.

This essay considers the Descartes's conception of dream life but principally in his Meditations. The subject is treated in the phenomenological's theoretic perspective (especially Sartre's philosophy and Dieter Wyss's phenomenological/anthropological works).

Zamora Bonilla, Jesús P. Truthlikeness without Truth: A Methodological Approach. *Synthese*, 93(3), 343-372, D 92.

In this paper, an attempt is made to solve various problems posed to current theories of verisimilitude: (1) the (Miller's) problem of linguistic variance; (2) the problem of which are the best scientific methods for getting the most verisimilar theories; and (3) the question of the ontological commitment in scientific theories. As a result of my solution to these problems, and with the help of other considerations of epistemological character, I conclude that the notion of 'Tarskian truth' is dispensable in a rational (and 'realist') interpretation of the scientific enterprise. As a logical result, however, falsificationism will be vindicated.

Zamoshkin, I A. Private Life, Private Interest, Private Property. *Russian Stud Phil*, 31(1), 49-86, Sum 92.

Zanardo, Alberto. A Note About the Axioms for Branching-Time Logic. *Notre Dame J Form Log*, 33(2), 225-228, Spr 92.

The axiomatization of branching-time logic presented in S McCall's paper "The Strong Future Tense" is considered and a counterexample is given to one of the theorems supporting the completeness result. Furthermore, the reason why McCall's method does not work is discussed briefly.

Zaner, Richard M. Parted Bodies, Departed Souls: The Body in Ancient Medicine and Anatomy in The Body in Medical Thought and Practice, Leder, Drew (ed). Dordrecht, Kluwer, 1992.

Three philosophies of ancient medicine prior to and immediately following the Hellenistic period are examined. Dogmatism, empiricism, and skepticism, with particular emphasis on their differences regarding medical knowledge, therapeutic focus understanding of the body and soul, role of the physician and patient, and relationship to the Hippocratic oath. Common themes that run through these ancient philosophical approaches to medicine continue to manifest themselves in current discussions about medicine and morals. The ongoing questions concerning the use of principle- based systems, phenomenology, and virtue ethics find their introduction in ancient debates.

Zangari, Mark. Adding Potential to a Physical Theory of Causation. *Proc Phil Sci Ass*, 1, 261-273, 1992.

Various authors have attempted to characterize physical causation by appealing to terms in physical theories. Forces, energy-momentum transfer and fundamental interactions have been suggested. It is shown that none of these categories are adequate to describe the causal interaction taking place in the Aharonov-Bohm effect which, it is claimed, can best be understood by adopting a realist attitude towards potential (that is the integral of field strength). Potential, it is argued, provides the best account of physical causation as it is present in all of the examples considered by other authors, and successfully accounts for the Aharonov-Bohm effect as well.

Zangwill, Nicholas. Long Live Supervenience. *J Aes Art Crit*, 50(4), 319-322, Fall 92.

I defend aesthetic supervenience against an argument of Robert Wicks. Walton's arguments show that the supervenience base must extend beyond a thing intrinsic non-aesthetic properties. One must judge a thing only employing the categories to which it in fact belongs. And I show how aesthetic determination can be a vague matter.

Zangwill, Nick. Metaphor and Realism in Aesthetics. *J Aes Art Crit*, 49(1), 57-62, Wint 91.

I defend aesthetic realism against an argument of Roger Scruton. He argues that realism about aesthetic properties cannot explain why aesthetic descriptions are often metaphorical, given that a word used metaphorically has the same meaning as when used literally. I suggest that there are aesthetic properties that can only be metaphorically described in this aesthetic descriptions are like descriptions of pair.

Zangwill, Nick. Moral Modus Ponens. *Ratio*, 5(2), 177-193, D 92.

Can moral projectivism account for the role of moral propositions in unasserted contexts? Blackburn attempted to do so by appealing to second-order attitudes. I defend Blackburn against the objection that such an account cannot account for the logical necessity of moral *modus ponens*. Logical and moral obligation might be difficult to distinguish. I then argue that Blackburn cannot account for the unitary meaning of moral propositions in and out of asserted contexts and also in various different unasserted contexts.

Zangwill, Nick. Quietism. *Midwest Stud Phil*, 17, 160-176, 1992.

I defend the theories that metaphysical issues are genuine. I argue that Simon Blackburn's 'quasi-realist' cannot capture everything that a realist asserts. Appeals to explanation fail to distinguish realism from projectivism in the philosophy of morality and causation. But they succeed in the cases of the external world and the past. These cases can then be used in order to make sense of the issues over morality and causation.

Zangwill, Nick. Supervenience and Anomalous Monism: Blackburn on Davidson. *Phil Stud*, 71(1), 59-79, Jl 93.

I argue that Simon Blackburn's modal argument does not threaten Donald Davidson's anomalous monism. Davidson should accept metaphysical necessities linking the physical to the mental. I then show that this is compatible with denying the existence of *interesting* psycho-physical laws.

Zangwill, Nick. Unkantian Notions of Disinterest. *Brit J Aes*, 32(2), 149-152, Ap 92.

I argue that Kant's notion of a disinterested pleasure is different from the notion which is usually attributed to him; so most criticisms of Kant on this score miss the point.

Zappen, James P. The Logic and Rhetoric of John Stuart Mill. *Phil Rhet*, 26(3), 191-200, 1993.

J S Mill's *Logic* and *On Liberty* are related as logical and rhetorical counterparts of his method of induction. These works draw together not only his logic and rhetoric but his psychology and politics as well. Mill identifies logic as part of psychology, psychology being concerned with thought generally, logic with valid thought specifically. In the *Logic*, he recognizes a problem in inductive logic that threatens its validity. He explains the method of induction as a process of reasoning from particulars to a generalization, but he observes that this process is problematic since we cannot reason from particulars to a generalization with any certainty in the validity of the generalization. (edited)

Zarka, Yves Charles. La Propriété chez Hobbes. *Arch Phil*, 55(4), 587-605, O-D 92.

Zarnecka-Bialy, Ewa. The Voice of the Past in Kotarbinski's Writings in Kotarbinski: Logic, Semantics and Ontology, Wolénski, Jan (ed). Dordrecht, Kluwer, 1990.

Zboril, B. The Foundations of Axiology (in Czechoslovakian). *Filozof Cas*, 40(3), 467-475, 1992.

Zdybicka, Zofia J and Sandok, Theresa (trans). *Person and Religion: An Introduction to the Philosophy of Religion*. New York, Lang, 1991.

This book is a comprehensive introduction to the philosophy of religion. Part 1, explores various nonphilosophical and philosophical approaches to the study of religion, culminating in an argument for the need for an autonomous philosophy of religion based on the empirically given fact of religion in human life. Part 2, discusses the various ways, internal and external, in which the fact of religion presents itself to us. Part 3, then attempts to interpret this experiential data in the context of the classical philosophy of being, focusing on the subjective and objective grounds of the fact of religion and on the personal character of the religious relation.

Zecha, Gerhard. Paul Weingartner: Philosophy at Work in Advances in Scientific Philosophy, Schurz, Gerhard (ed). Amsterdam, Rodopi, 1991.

This article provides a concise intellectual biography of the philosopher Paul Weingartner, professor of philosophy at the University of Salzburg. It outlines his education as well as his professional career. The main areas of his research interest are briefly described with additional information about his international teaching and conference activities. A detailed and for the years 1961-1991 complete bibliography of Paul Weingartner's publications follows after the article.

Zechmeister, Eugene B and Johnson, James E. *Critical Thinking: A Functional Approach*. Belmont, Wadsworth, 1992.

Zeis, John. A Trinity on a Trinity on a Trinity. *Sophia (Australia)*, 32(1), 45-55, Mr 93.

Using Geach's Principle of the Relativity of Identity, the doctrine of the trinity is defended against charges of inconsistency put forward by David Wiggins and Richard Cartwright.

Zeis, John. Virtue and Self-Alienation. *Lyceum*, 3(2), 41-52, Fall 91.

Zeis, John and Jacobs, Jonathan. Theism and Moral Objectivity. *Amer Cath Phil Quart*, 66(4), 429-445, Autumn 92.

Zeisler, Dieter. Sartre's Account of the Self in 'The Transcendence of the Ego' in Analecta Husserliana, XXXI, Tymieniecka, Anna-Teresa (ed). Dordrecht, Kluwer 1990.

Zelaniec, Wojciech. Fathers, Kings, and Promises: Husserl and Reinach on the A Priori. *Husserl Stud*, 9(3), 147-177, 1992.

The author examines several examples (given by Husserl and his pupil, Adolf Reinach, and pertaining mainly to the social sphere) of allegedly analytic and synthetic a priori propositions. In a detailed line of argument—drawing among others on the theory of speech acts—the author shows difficulties with classifying some of those examples as analytic.

Zelechow, Bernard. Kierkegaard, the Aesthetic and Mozart's 'Don Giovanni' in Kierkegaard on Art and Communication, Pattison, George (ed). New York, St Martin's Pr, 1992.

This paper explores Kierkegaard's appropriation of Mozart's *Don Giovanni* in order to discredit the religious importance of Mozart's opera and art in general. The Seducer in *either* reads Mozart's Don exclusively in light of his descriptive representation of seduction. The Seducer in *Either* and Kierkegaard in *The Journals* willfully ignore Mozart's religious advocacy of the sublimity of love based on mutuality.

Zemach, Eddy M. Perceptual Realism, Naive and Otherwise in John Searle and His Critics, Lepore, Ernest (ed). Cambridge, Blackwell, 1991.

Zembaty, Jane S. Aristotle on Lying. *J Hist Phil*, 31(1), 7-29, Ja 93.

Some of Aristotle's statements about the truthful man, the boaster, the self-deprecator, and the magnanimous individual are explored in order to bring out Aristotle's views on lying. The following conclusions are reached: For Aristotle, lies have an initial negative weight because they, 1) are ordinarily harmful to other individuals and the *polis*; 2) are ordinarily an indication of various character faults associated with a lack of independence or self-sufficiency, and; 3) are potentially harmful to the one who lies. Lies that harm no one, involve no undeserved disrespect, and stem from excellence and self-sufficiency rather than deficiency of character may be morally acceptable, however.

Zembaty, Jane S and Mappes, Thomas A. *Biomedical Ethics (Third Edition)*. New York, McGraw-Hill, 1991.

Zenzinger, Theodore. Hobbes and the Social Contract Tradition by Jean Hampton. *Auslegung*, 18(2), 167-178, Sum 92.

Zeppi, Stelio. Soggettivismo e oggettivismo agli albori della metafisica greca. *G Metaf*, 14(1), 37-49, Ja-Ap 92.

Zhang, Shi-Ying. Heidegger and Taoism in Reading Heidegger: Commemorations, Sallis, John (ed). Bloomington, Indiana Univ Pr, 1992.

As regards the status quo and the future of Chinese thought and culture, I think that we in China should both carry on and develop the Taoist philosophy while also taking Heidegger's philosophy into account, considering the similarities between them, namely, that both of them, representing the antithesis of orthodox thought, stress "valuing oneself", "returning to authenticity", and not getting involved with outside things, and emphasizing the close kinship between poetry and thinking. I also think that we should absorb Heidegger's philosophy, in particular, considering the differences between it and Lao and Chuang's philosophy—namely, that Heidegger attacks metaphysical ontology and attaches importance to the principle of individuality, while Lao and Chuang advocate the abstract metaphysical Tao.

Zhang, Xian. Husserl's Intentionality and "Mind" in Chinese Philosophy. *J Chin Phil*, 20(1), 29-43, Mr 93.

Zheng, Liu. The Dilemma Facing Contemporary Research in the *Yijing*. *Chin Stud Phil*, 24(4), 47-64, Sum 93.

Zheng, Xizhong. On the Maximality of Some Pairs of p-t Degrees. *Notre Dame J Form Log*, 34(1), 29-35, Wint 93.

This paper discusses the structure of the polynomial time Turing degrees with the corresponding reducibility. It is shown that any one degree of a pair of degrees can be replaced by a greater one while the set of low bounds of this pair does not change. Hence there is no maximal minimal pair, maximal branching and maximal exact pair of polynomial time Turing degrees.

Ziarek, Ewa. At the Limits of Discourse: Tracing the Maternal Body with Kristeva. *Hypatia*, 7(2), 91-108, Spr 92.

This essay situates Kristeva's theory of semiotics in the context of the controversial debate about the status of the maternal body in her work. I argue that, if we rethink the opposition between the semiotic and the symbolic as the relation between the trace and the sign, it becomes clear that the maternal semiotic is irreducible either to the prelinguistic plenitude or to the alternative symbolic position. The second part of the essay develops the connection between Kristeva's linguistic theory and the alterity of the maternal body, articulated here as the in-fold of the other and the same.

Zibakalam, Saeid. Emergence of a Radical Sociology of Scientific Knowledge. *Dialectica*, 47(1), 3-25, 1993.

The early writings of Barry Barnes, as the co-founder of the Edinburgh School of sociology of scientific knowledge, are explored to bring out and to evaluate his main presuppositions and arguments. Barnes is highly critical of anthropologists' conception of scientific knowledge, rationality, truth, and their asymmetrical explanatory approach towards different belief-systems. Likewise he rejects the prevalent view of science among sociologists of knowledge, and also their approach to explanation of knowledge or belief-adoption. His proposal is based on a Kuhnian model of science, and offers his own socio-causal explanatory scheme applicable to all beliefs and knowledge-claims. I have challenged the basis of his model of science and have tried to show that his use of Kuhn's concepts of normal practice and paradigm is problematic, and that his idea of social causation of beliefs is highly problematic.

Zielinska, Renata. The Threshold Generalization of the Idealizational Laws in Idealization III, Brzenzinski, Jerzy (ed). Amsterdam, Rodopi, 1992.

Ziembinski, Zygmunt. The Concept of Morality in Philosophy of Law in Ethical Dimensions of Legal Theory, Sadurski, Wojciech (ed). Amsterdam, Rodopi, 1991.

The relation between law and morality is often discussed in philosophy of law but very different concepts of moral evaluation are considered. The traditional disputes are founded on a simplifying supposition of radical legal positivism that legal norms

are enacted by competent State agencies. The problem is much more complicated. The definite shaping of a legal system in process of exegesis of legal text is based, i.e., on supposition of same moral system accepted by the "legislator". Thus the discussion cannot be limited to a simple comparison between two clearly fixed sets of norms.

Zimbelman, Joel. Theology, Praxis and Ethics in the Thought of Juan Luis Segundo. *Thomist*, 57(2), 233-264, Ap 93.

Zimmerli, Walter. Is Hegel's "Logic" a Logic? in Hegel and His Critics, Desmond, William (ed). Albany, SUNY Pr, 1989.

Zimmerli, Walther. Human Minds, Robots, and the Technician of the Future. *Res Phil Technol*, 9, 183-196, 1989.

Zimmerman, Michael (& other eds). *Environmental Philosophy: From Animal Rights to Radical Ecology*. Englewood Cliffs, Prentice Hall, 1993.

Four associate editors join Michael Zimmerman in editing this anthology: J Baird Callicott edits the section on Animal Rights and Environmental Ethics; George Sessions edits the section on Deep Ecology; Karen J Warren edits the section on Ecofeminism; and John Clark edits the section on Social Ecology.

Zimmerman, Michael E. Heidegger, Buddhism, and Deep Ecology in The Cambridge Companion to Heidegger, Guignon, Charles (ed). New York, Cambridge Univ Pr, 1993.

In this essay, I argue that Martin Heidegger, Mahayana Buddhism, and the deep ecologist Arne Naess share the idea that humans are the "nothingness" in which entities can display themselves and thus "be." The ecological crisis stems from the fact that humans wrongly consider themselves to be entities, e.g., egos, who must defend themselves by dominating non-human entities.

Zimmerman, Michael E. Rethinking the Heidegger-Deep Ecology Relationship. *Environ Ethics*, 15(3), 195-224, Fall 93.

Recent disclosures regarding the relationship between Heidegger's thought and his own version of National Socialism have led me to rethink my earlier efforts to portray Heidegger as a forerunner of deep ecology. His political problems have provided ammunition for critics, such as Murray Bookchin, who regard deep ecology as a reactionary movement. In this essay, I argue that, despite some similarities, Heidegger's thought and deep ecology are in many ways incompatible, in part because deep ecologists—in spite of their criticism of the ecologically destructive character of technological modernity—generally support a "progressive" idea of human evolution.

Zimmerman, Michael J. Obligation, Responsibility and Alternate Possibilities. *Analysis*, 53(1), 51-53, Ja 93.

It has recently been argued that the principle that "ought" implies "can" entails the principle that moral responsibility requires alternate possibilities, and hence that the acceptance of the former principle requires acceptance of the latter. This paper disputes the alleged entailment and gives reasons for accepting the former principle while rejecting the latter.

Ziolkowski, Eric J. Don Quixote and Kierkegaard's Understanding of the Single Individual.... in Foundations of Kierkegaard's Vision of Community, Connell, George B (ed). Atlantic Highlands, Humanities Pr, 1992.

Specific allusions to Cervantes' *Don Quixote of La Mancha* (1605; 1615) in Kierkegaard's journals and aesthetic writings reveal that form no later than his twenty-second year through the end of his life, this classic Spanish novel and its hero remained important objects of his contemplation. Kierkegaard not only regarded Don Quixote as a symbol of the "comic" principle present in every stage of existence, but near the end of his life he also came to view Quixote as an analogue to Christ, Christ's disciples, and the "true Christian" individual struggling within modern secular society. Borrowing a famous phrase from Kierkegaard, later authors (e.g., M de Unamuno and W H Auden) called Don Quixote a "knight of faith," although Kierkegaard himself never applied that term to him.

Ziporyn, Brook. The Self-So and Its Traces in the Thought of Guo Xiang. *Phil East West*, 43(3), 511-539, Jl 93.

Guo Xiang must mediate the tension between two of his claims: first, that all beings are equally "self-so" (spontaneous and unassailably right), and second, that some come to be alienated from this spontaneous rightness. This mediation is accomplished by use of the concept of "traces." Spontaneous activity leaves traces in minds extrinsic to itself. These traces embody the value of spontaneity, and are thus taken as ideals, models to be imitated, thereby distorting the spontaneity of those who so imitate them. The same content is thus simultaneously an instance of perfect spontaneity and that by which spontaneity is corrupted.

Zita, Jacquelyn N. Jeffner Allen: A Lesbian Portrait. *Hypatia*, 7(4), 6-13, Fall 92.

This review essay covers the lesbian writings of philosopher Jeffner Allen, contrasting her fiercely separatist earlier work with her more recent experimental writing. A quest for a separate ontic space—defining difference qua lesbian and consistently characterized by Allen as "the open"—links her earlier work with her more recent atonalities richly coded with ritual, myth, memory, and play.

Zita, Jacquelyn N. The Male Lesbian and the Postmodernist Body. *Hypatia*, 7(4), 106-127, Fall 92.

This essay explores the criteria for lesbian identity attribution through the case study of "male lesbians": biological males who claim to be lesbians. I analyze such sex/gender identity attribution through the lens of postmodernism, which provides a workable theoretical framework for "male lesbian" identities. My conclusions explore the historicity and cultural constructedness of the body's sex/gender identities, revealing the limitations of both "the postmodernized body" and "the essentialized modernist body."

Zizek, Slavoj (ed). *Everything You Always Wanted to Know About Lacan*. New York, Verso, 1992.

Zlotkowski, Edward and Dandekar, Natalie. Moral Issues Associated with Bioengineered Species: Stewardship, Abuse and Sustainability. *Between Species*, 8(4), 209-216, Fall 92.

Mary Shelley's *Frankenstein* provides a fictive exploration of ethical dilemmas springing from a realization of the scientific power to create bioengineered species.

We use the novel as a fictive platform for analyzing what loci of value command human respect and the manner in which such matters are to be decided. We concluded that Dr Fankenstein's wrongdoing involves three specific evasions, in that he pursues exploitation of scientific possibility as if unhindered by a) the need for moral reflection on probable consequences, b) respect for the sensibilities of the nonscientific public and c) any sense that the nonhuman might itself be owed respect. We stress the continuing importance of remedying all three of these psycho-cultural blindspots.

Zlotkowski, Edward and Dandekar, Natalie. Reply to Westra's "Response—Dr Frankenstein and Today's Professional Biotechnologist". *Between Species*, 8(4), 222-223, Fall 92.

We respond to Westra's Comment by pointing out four respects in which use of literary analogy can usefully provide a standpoint from which one can discover insights than contribute to current ecological discourse.

Znoj, M and Sobotka, M and Major, L. The Relation of Man and Nature in Modern Philosophy (in Czechoslovakian). *Filozof Cas*, 39(6), 975-991, 1991.

Zoeller, Guenter. Lichtenberg and Kant on the Subject of Thinking. *J Hist Phil*, 30(3), 417-442, J 92.

In a famous aphorism, the German physicist and essayist Georg Christoph Lichtenberg (1742-1799) proposed to replace the phrase "I think" with the expression "it thinks", construed in analogy with the locution "it lightens". By placing Lichtenberg's remark on the self in the context of his wider epistemological and metaphysical views, I show that his account of the mind is part of a critical appropriation of Kant's transcendental philosophy, which however falls short of the complexities of Kant's theory of self-consciousness. The essay attempts to retrieve Lichtenberg as a distinctive skeptical voice in the early post-Kantian debate.

Zoeller, Guenter. Main Developments in Recent Scholarship on the *Critique of Pure Reason*. *Phil Phenomenol Res*, 53(2), 445-466, Je 93.

The paper is a critical discussion of scholarship on the *Critique of Pure Reason* published during the past ten years. The emphasis is on Anglo-American authors. I identify and discuss three main trends in the field: a shift from the general discussion of transcendental arguments to the analysis and evaluation of particular proofs in Kant; a renewed interest in the doctrine of transcendental idealism and the distinction between things in themselves and appearances; and the emergence of an entire body of literature on Kant's philosophy of mind, centered around the idea of a "transcendental psychology." The main body of the text is supplemented by extensive bibliographical information provided in the notes.

Zohar, Noam. Collective War and Individualistic Ethics: Against the Conscription of "Self-Defense". *Polit Theory*, 21(4), 606-622, N 93.

The war ethic proclaims noncombatant immunity, yet condones killing morally innocent soldiers, and even concomitant civilian casualties in strategic bombing. Against Thomson and others, who extend individual "self-defense" to elimination of "innocent threats", I deny the possibility of a normatively neutral ascription of causal responsibility. Instead, I argue for a dual morality, based on a dual view of human reality, transcending the methodological individualism debate. A just war will involve collective self defense, which alone mandates killing people in their identity as part of the collective. The equally valid individual perspective is retained in the prohibition on murdering noncombatants.

Zollers, Frances E and Shaw, Bill. Managers in the Moral Dimension: What Etezioni Might Mean to Corporate Managers. *Bus Ethics Quart*, 3(2), 153-168, A 93.

In *The Moral Dimension*, Amitai Etzioni critiques the neoclassical economic paradigm (NEP), a model built upon ethical egoism and which equates rationality (the logical/empirical domain) with the maximization of preferences by self-interested economic units. Etzioni finds the NEP's exclusion of the moral/affective domain to be a glaring failure and, because of this omission, he claims that the economic model is not capable of achieving its design functions: prediction and explanation. Etzioni introduces a socio-economic model, the I and We paradigm, in which the moral/affective encapsulates the logical/empirical. Further elaboration and testing of this model remains to be undertaken. We find it to hold more promise than its neoclassical economic rival, and we explicate its value for the modern manager.

Zolo, Danilo and McKie, David (trans). *Democracy and Complexity: A Realist Approach*. University Park, Penn St Univ Pr, 1992.

This book is a highly original and provocative contribution to democratic theory. Zolo argues that the increasing complexity of modern societies represents a fundamental challenge to the basic assumptions of the Western democratic tradition and calls for a reformulation of some of the key questions of political theory. Zolo maintains that, as modern societies become more complex and more involved in the "information revolution", they are subjected to new and unprecedented forms of stress. In conclusion, Zolo develops a set of proposals which seek to renew democratic values and to contribute to a fundamental reform of Western political systems. (staff)

Zong-qi, Cai. Derrida and Madhyamika Buddhism: From Linguistic Deconstruction to Criticism of Onto-Theologies. *Int Phil Quart*, 33(2), 183-195, Je 93.

This paper explores four parallels in the Derridean and Madhyamika theories: 1) both Derrida and the Madhyamika thinkers develop deconstructive theories of meaning based on the similar ideas of *différance and differentiam*, and seek to nullify the logos and the Name of Non-Existence reified by the Western idealist and Buddhist essentialists; 2) both apply the same theories of meaning to deconstruct the Matter and Existence reified by the Western materialists and Buddhist realists; 3) both conceive of their double negation as an exercise of *neither/nor* logic and set forth their deconstructive formulas in similar terms of *tetralpharmakon* and tetralemma (catuskoti); and 4) both abolish their own *tetralpharmakon* and tetralemma and embark on their self-deconstructive course along an aimless "supernumerary" and along a linear "hexalemma." (edited)

Zongqi, Cai. Derrida and Seng-Zhao: Linguistic and Philosophical Deconstructions. *Phil East West*, 43(3), 389-404, Jl 93.

Contemporary Western deconstructive philosophy and the Madhyamika Buddhism are, historically and geographically, far apart from each other. However, there exist many important parallels in method, strategy and rationale between these two philosophical traditions. Recently, a number of scholars have discovered significant parallels in the Derridean negation and the Madhyamika *prasanga* (*reducio ad absurdum*), and carefully compared the logic of negativity at work in both traditions. This article discusses the hitherto unexplored parallels in Derridean and the Madhyamika deconstructive use of language. (edited)

Zonnenveld, L W. A Sense of Human Destiny—Routes into the Unknown. *Dialec Hum*, 17(3), 169-173, 1990.

Zoubek, G and Lauth, B. Zur Rekonstruktion des Bohrschen Forschungsprogramms I. *Erkenntnis*, 37(2), 223-247, S 92.

Zoubek, G and Lauth, B. Zur Rekonstruktion des Bohrschen Forschungsprogramms II. *Erkenntnis*, 37(2), 249-273, S 92.

Zouhar, J. On the Relationship of Art and World View in the Work of Jan Mukarovsky (in Czechoslovakian). *Filozof Cas*, 40(4), 620-623, 1992.

Mukarovsky's approach to the relationship of art and world view is defined by his conception of world view as a component of and principle in the artistic construction of a work. The point of departure for the analysis of the elements of a world view is, for Mukarovsky, language structure with its semantic aspects. Mukarovsky's conception is compared with the conception of D Cyzevsky and J Patocka.

Zuanazzi, G. Il motivo della caduta dell'uomo primordiale nell'interpretazione di Carl Gustav Jung. *Aquinas*, 34(3), 555-574, S-D 91.

Zuber, R. A Note on Unary Rules and a Complete Syntactic Characterization of Propositional Calculi. *Bull Sec Log*, 21(4), 163-167, D 92.

This note contains a slight generalization of a result proved in [3] by Maduch and concerning the conditions of existence of a finite set of rejected axioms permitting the generation of all non-theorems for a given propositional calculus. Maduch gave a criterion for the existence of the finite set of rejected axioms in the case when only two "classical" rules of rejection, i.e., the rule based on detachment and the rule based on the substitution rule, are used. In the present note I show that the same criterion applies for a large class of propositional logics where some unary rules of rejection are additionally used.

Zuboff, Arnold. A Presentation Without an Example?. *Analysis*, 52(3), 190-191, Jl 92.

"Any general thesis which is put forward without a concrete example is therein badly presented." Is this itself a concrete example of an example-less presentation of a general thesis? But if it is an example, it is not an example-less presentation and therefore cannot be an example of an example-less presentation. But then it *is* an example of example-lessness and therefore isn't an example of example-lessness, and so on forever. This paradox seems resistant to the usual treatment. If a thesis could not apply to its own presentation, it would be strangely permissible to say rudely that one shouldn't speak rudely.

Zucker, Ross. Unequal Property and Subjective Personality in Liberal Theories. *Ratio Juris*, 6(1), 86-117, Mr 93.

A conception of the person as a subjective being plays a crucial, though frequently overlooked, role in the justification of unequal property in liberal theories. Unger's ascription of individualism to general liberal legal theory can be concretely defended with respect to liberal legal theories rest on an ensemble of different moral foundations. So important is subjective personality to the moral basis for highly unequal property that such property looks to be morally untenable if this concept of the person is invalid. The analysis points to social theory of personality as a major direction for research into an alternative theory of egalitarian property right.

Zuckert, Michael (ed) and Horwitz, Robert. John Locke's *Questions Concerning the Law of Nature*: A Commentary. *Interpretation*, 19(3), 251-306, Spr 92.

Locke's *Question on the Law of Nature*, an early work prepared while he was lecturing on moral philosophy in the 1660s, gives every appearance of being a work much in the tradition of Christian natural law theory, as developed by Thomas Aquinas and revived in Locke's England by thinkers like Richard Hooker and Nathaniel Culverwell. Closer examination of this text, Locke's only extended writing on the law of nature, largely dispels the impression of Locke's allegiance to one or another variety of Christian natural law theory. Contrary to his initial claims, Locke progressively undermines all the grounds of Christian natural law he brings forth. His work thus serves far more as a critique than an endorsement of traditional law of natural doctrine.

Zuidervaart, Lambert. *Adorno's Aesthetic Theory: The Redemption of Illusion*. Cambridge, MIT Pr, 1991.

The book uncovers the historical sources of Theodor W. Adorno's *Aesthetic Theory*, explains his central ideas, and demonstrates the relevance of his aesthetics for contemporary discussions of popular culture, cultural politics, and postmodernism. The first part of the book offers a brief biography, describes Adorno's debates with Benjamin, Brecht, and Lukács, and outlines his philosophical program. The second part examines how Adorno situates art in society, production, politics, and history as a paradoxical vehicle of truth. The third evaluates his contribution by confronting it with the critiques of Peter Bürger, Fredric Jameson, and Albrecht Wellmer.

Zuidervaart, Lambert. Realism, Modernism, and the Empty Chair in Postmodernism/ Jameson/ Critique, Kellner, Douglas M (ed). Washington, Maisonneuve Pr, 1989.

The essay examines the cultural politics of *The Political Unconscious* in light of both Theodor Adorno's debate with Georg Lukács and Fredric Jameson's subsequent writings on postmodernism. The essay argues that Jameson's attempt to update Western Marxism for a postmodern culture threatens to become incoherent. In reconstructing the notion of literary "import" into that of "symbolic act", Jameson retains a problematic concept from Lukács and Adorno. To become coherent, his critique of postmodernism must revise the concept of reification. This revision would support the pluralistic collective subject to which Jameson's critique of postmodernism appeals.

Zuidervaart, Lambert. The Social Significance of Autonomous Art: Adorno and Bürger. *J Aes Art Crit*, 48(1), 61-77, Wint 90.

The essay explains and evaluates Theodor W Adorno's claim in his *Aesthetic Theory* that autonomy is a precondition for the social significance of art and of art works. Adorno focuses on the modern art work as an independent "monad" of society. Peter Bürger challenges this focus, arguing that it unwittingly arises from the bourgeois "institution of art". While agreeing with some of Bürger's criticisms in *Theory of the Avant-Garde*, the essay rejects Bürger's apparent historicism and relativism. A case is made for the social significance of popular art and for the importance of complex normativity.

Zupko, Jack. Buridan and Skepticism. *J Hist Phil*, 31(2), 191-221, Ap 93.

John Buridan's reply to certain skeptical arguments associated with Nicholas of Autrecourt has long puzzled scholars because it fails to engage those arguments directly. As a result, his anti-skeptical remarks have been variously dismissed as "largely ineffectual", "uncritical", and "primitive". I argue, however, that the negative assessment is appropriate only if Buridan is mistakenly read as a classical foundationalist. I show that Buridan's remarks actually have more in common with contemporary reliabilism, and that seen from this perspective, they constitute a perfectly valid anti-skeptical position, which has the additional virtue of explaining why Buridan is not much gripped by skepticism in his writings.

Zupko, Jack. How Are Souls Related to Bodies? A Study of John Buridan. *Rev Metaph*, 46(3), 575-601, Mr 93.

I develop and evaluate John Buridan's hybrid theory of psychological inherence, consisting of his materialist explanation of the relation between nonhuman animal or plant souls and their bodies, and immanent dualist explanation of the human soul-body relation. Buridan explains the former via metaphysical principles which define animal/plant souls as extended and homogenous, and therefore as naturally related to bodies. His account of the latter, however, appeals to the notion of noncommensurable inherence used by theologians explain the doctrine of real presence in the eucharist. I then show how this strategy is consistent with Buridan's naturalistic approach to psychology.

Zurcher, Joyce M. Descartes y la fe en la razón. *Rev Filosof (Costa Rica)*, 30(71), 81-88, J 92.

Due to the argument of the evil genius. Descartes must be labeled as an intuitionistic philosopher rather than as a rationalist. He argues that what is immediately present to the conscience cannot be doubted as long as it does not need the participation of reason. Knowledge beyond the "cogito" involves faith.

Zweifel, Peter and Kofler, Edward. One-Shot Decisions under Linear Partial Information. *Theor Decis*, 34(1), 1-20, Ja 93.

This paper purports to make a contribution to the analysis of a class of decisions that has received little attention in the literature, although it appears to be of considerable importance. Certain decisions cannot be repeated but must be made under fuzziness in the sense that state probabilities are not exactly known (LPI-fuzziness). The analysis of Linear Partial Information is applied to the principle of neglecting small probabilities found by Allais (1953), enabling the decision maker to break away from the maxmin criterion. By systematic exploitation of the fuzzy information available, strategies are shown to exist that provide payoffs whose lower bound exceeds the maxmin benchmark with sufficiently high probability. The same methodology is shown to be useful for dealing with the case of only ordinal preference orderings that are so typical of those crucial decisions that may be made only once in a lifetime.

Zwicky, Jan. *Lyric Philosophy*. Toronto, Univ of Toronto Pr, 1992.

Zwiebach, B. Superstring Unification and the Existence of Gravity in Philosophy and the Origin and Evolution of the Universe, Agazzi, Evandro (ed). Norwell, Kluwer, 1991.

Zwinger, Lynda. Blood Relations: Feminist Theory Meets the Uncanny Alien Bug Mother. *Hypatia*, 7(2), 74-90, Spr 92.

This essay addresses the troubling and uncanny figure of Mother in feminist theory, psychoanalytic theory, literary criticism, and real life. Readings of feminist literary criticism and the films *Alien* and *Aliens* explore the liminality of Mother and the consequences for feminist thought and practice of the persistent narrative modes (the sentimental and the gothic) locatable in all of these discourses on/of Motherhood.

Zycinski, Jozef. Ontological Platonism in Whiteheadian Philosophy of God (in Polish). *Stud Phil Christ*, 27(2), 83-98, 1991.

The Platonic elements in Whitehead's process philosophy were called into question by many authors who denied Platonic interpretation of the so called ethernal objects and introduced Aristotelian elements into foundations of process metaphysics. After examining the ontic statue of the extensive continuum, possible events and eternal objects, the paper points out that Whiteheadian thesis of the divine immanence in nature can be consistently developed only when a version of ontological Platonism is assumed in Whitehead's philosophy of God.

Guidance on the Use of the Book Review Index

The Book Review Index lists, in alphabetical order, the authors of books reviewed in philosophy journals. Each entry includes the author's name, the title of the book, the publisher, and the place and date of publication. Under each entry is listed the name of the reviewer, the journal in which the review appeared, along with the volume, pagination and date.

Aagaard-Mogensen, Lars (ed). *The Idea of the Museum*. Lewiston, Mellen Pr, 1988.
 Hein, Hilde. *J Aes Art Crit*, 48(1), 91-93, Wint 90.

Aarnio, Aulis. *The Rational as Reasonable*. Dordrecht, Kluwer, 1987.
 Van Roermund, Bert C. *Nous*, 26(2), 238-243, J 92.

Abe, Masao (trans) and Ives, Christopher (trans). *An Inquiry into the Good—Kitaro Nishida*. New Haven, Yale Univ Pr, 1990.
 Drengson, Alan R. *Int J Phil Relig*, 34(2), 121-123, O 93.
 Riepe, Dale. *Int Stud Phil*, 24(1), 122-123, 1992.

Abel, Donald C (ed). *Theories of Human Nature*. New York, McGraw-Hill, 1992.
 Williams, Clifford. *Teach Phil*, 16(1), 71-73, Mr 93.

Aboulafia, Mitchell (ed). *Philosophy, Social Theory, and the Thought of George Herbert Mead*. Albany, SUNY Pr, 1991.
 Koczanowicz, Leszek. *Trans Peirce Soc*, 28(2), 356-366, Spr 92.

Abrams, M H. *Doing Things with Texts*. New York, Norton, 1989.
 Eldridge, Richard. *J Aes Art Crit*, 49(2), 173-175, Spr 91.

Achinstein, Peter. *Particles and Waves*. New York, Oxford Univ Pr, 1991.
 Polis, Dennis F. *Mod Sch*, 69(2), 156-158, Ja 92.
 Schlagel, Richard H. *Rev Metaph*, 46(1), 141-142, S 92.

Ackerman, Bruce. *We the People, Volume I*. Cambridge, Harvard Univ Pr, 1991.
 Dumm, Thomas L. *Polit Theory*, 20(2), 341-345, My 92.
 Waldron, Jeremy. *J Phil*, 90(3), 149-153, Mr 93.

Ackermann, Robert John. *Nietzsche: A Frenzied Look*. Amherst, Univ of Mass Pr, 1990.
 Clegg, Jerry S. *Can Phil Rev*, 12(3), 153-157, J-Jl 92.

Ackermann, Robert John. *Wittgenstein's City*. Amherst, Univ of Mass Pr, 1988.
 Barnett, William E. *Phil Rev*, 101(2), 404-408, Ap 92.

Adam, Barbara. *Time and Social Theory*. Oxford, Polity Pr, 1990.
 Parker, Noel. *Rad Phil*, 61, 49-50, Sum 92.

Adams, Carol J. *The Sexual Politics of Meat*. New York, Continuum, 1991.
 Slicer, Deborah. *Environ Ethics*, 14(4), 365-369, Wint 92.

Adams, David M (ed). *Philosophical Problems in the Law*. Belmont, Wadsworth, 1992.
 Gruber, David F. *Teach Phil*, 15(4), 381-382, D 92.

Adams, Elie M. *The Metaphysics of Self and World*. Philadelphia, Temple Univ Pr, 1991.
 Bandas, Mark. *Rev Metaph*, 46(1), 142-143, S 92.

Adams, James Luther (ed) and Bense, Walter F (ed). *Ernst Troeltsch: Religion in History*. Edinburgh, T & T Clark, 1991.
 Chapman, Mark D. *Heythrop J*, 34(4), 461-463, O 93.

Adams, Marilyn McCord. *William Ockham*. Notre Dame, Univ Notre Dame Pr, 1987.
 Panaccio, Claude. *Dialogue (Canada)*, 31(3), 532-535, Sum 92.

Adburgham, Alison. *A Radical Aristocrat*. Padstow, Tabb House, 1990.
 Martin, D E. *Utilitas*, 5(1), 136-137, My 93.

Addis, Laird. *Natural Signs*. Philadelphia, Temple Univ Pr, 1990.
 Collingwood, Francis. *Rev Metaph*, 46(1), 143-145, S 92.
 Grossmann, Reinhardt. *Nous*, 26(4), 551-555, D 92.

Adler, Jacob. *The Urgings of Conscience*. Philadelphia, Temple Univ Pr, 1992.
 Dwyer, Philip. *Phil Books*, 34(3), 168-170, Jl 93.

Adler, Pierre. *Commentateurs d'Aristote au Moyen-Age Latin*. Paris, Ed Universitaires, 1988.
 Adler, Pierre. *Grad Fac Phil J*, 16(1), 290-291, 1993.

Adorno, Theodor W and Hullot-Kentor, Robert (ed & trans). *Kierkegaard: Construction of the Aesthetic*. Minneapolis, Univ of Minn Pr, 1989.
 Perkins, Robert L. *J Aes Art Crit*, 48(3), 262-263, Sum 90.

Adorno, Theodor W, Tiedemann, Rolf (ed) and Nicholsen, Shierry Weber (trans). *Notes to Literature (Volume I)*. New York, Columbia Univ Pr, 1991.
 Zuidervaart, Lambert. *Can Phil Rev*, 12(3), 157-159, J-Jl 92.

Agassi, Joseph. *The Gentle Art of Philosophical Polemics*. Peru, Open Court, 1988.
 Shea, William R. *Phil Soc Sci*, 22(3), 393-394, S 92.

Agger, Ben. *A Critical Theory of Public Life*. Bristol, Falmer Pr, 1991.
 Barnett, Ronald. *J Phil Educ*, 27(1), 136-139, Sum 93.

Ainslie, George. *Picoeconomics*. New York, Cambridge Univ Pr, 1992.
 Fuller, Steve. *Can Phil Rev*, 12(5), 303-305, O 92.

Airaksinen, Timo (ed) and Bertamn, Martin A. *Hobbes*. Brookfield, Gower, 1989.
 Chuska, Jeff. *Int Phil Quart*, 32(2), 264-266, J 92.
 Colombetti, Carlos. *Int Stud Phil*, 24(1), 81-82, 1992.
 Sharp, Andrew. *Hist Euro Ideas*, 14(3), 441-443, M 92.

Akerman, Susanna. *Queen Christina of Sweden and Her Circle*. Leiden, Brill, 1991.
 Mercer, Christia. *J Hist Phil*, 31(2), 289-291, Ap 93.

Akira, Hirakawa and Groner, Paul (ed & trans). *A History of Indian Buddhism, From Sakyamuni to Early Mahayana*. Honolulu, Univ of Hawaii Pr, 1990.
 Jackson, Roger. *Asian Phil*, 3(1), 58-63, Mr 93.

Al-Fayyumi, Saadia Ben Joseph. *The Book of Theodicy*. New Haven, Yale Univ Pr, 1988.
 Lasker, Daniel J. *J Hist Phil*, 30(4), 604-605, O 92.

Aldrich, Virgil C. *The Body of a Person*. Lanham, Univ Pr of America, 1988.
 Long, Douglas C. *Int Stud Phil*, 24(3), 113, 1992.

Alekseev, A P. *Argumentacija, Poznanie, Obscenie*. Moscow, Izdatelstvo Moskov, 1991.
 Nemeth, Thomas. *Phil Rhet*, 26(1), 63-65, 1993.

Alexander, Thomas M. *John Dewey's Theory of Art, Experience and Nature*. Albany, SUNY Pr, 1987.
 Beardsmore, R W. *Ideal Stud*, 22(3), 220-221, S 92.

Alford, C Fred. *Narcissism: Socrates, the Frankfurt School and Psychoanalytic Theory*. New Haven, Yale Univ Pr, 1988.
 Ferrara, Alessandro. *Int Stud Phil*, 24(3), 114-115, 1992.

Alford, C Fred. *The Self in Social Theory*. New Haven, Yale Univ Pr, 1991.
 Ansell-Pearson, Keith. *Rad Phil*, 61, 62, Sum 92.

Allen, Anita L. *Uneasy Access*. Lanham, Rowman & Littlefield, 1988.
 DeCew, Judith Wagner. *Phil Rev*, 101(3), 709-711, Jl 92.

Allen, Michael J B. *Icastes: Marsilio Ficino's Interpretation of Plato's 'Sophist'*. Berkeley, Univ of Calif Pr, 1989.
 Monfasani, John. *J Hist Phil*, 31(2), 284-286, Ap 93.

Allinson, Robert E. *Chuang-Tzu for Spiritual Transformation*. Albany, SUNY Pr, 1989.
 Watson, Burton. *J Chin Phil*, 20(1), 101-103, Mr 93.
 Watson, Burton. *Phil Lit*, 16(2), 423-424, O 92.

Allinson, Robert E. *Understanding the Chinese Mind*. New York, Oxford Univ Pr, 1989.
 Wong, David. *Phil East West*, 42(3), 527-530, Jl 92.

Allison, Henry. *Benedict de Spinoza: An Introduction (Revised Edition)*. New Haven, Yale Univ Pr, 1987.
 Garrett, Don. *Ideal Stud*, 22(3), 246, S 92.

Allison, Henry. *Kant's Theory of Freedom*. New York, Cambridge Univ Pr, 1990.
 O'Neill, Onora. *Bull Hegel Soc Gt Brit*, 23-24, 108-111, 1991.
 Sherover, Charles M. *J Hist Phil*, 30(3), 464-467, J 92.
 Sullivan, Roger J. *Phil Rev*, 101(4), 865-867, O 92.

Allison, Lincoln (ed). *The Utilitarian Response*. Newbury Park, Sage, 1990.
 Holbrook, Daniel. *Utilitas*, 4(1), 181-183, My 92.

Almási, Miklós and Vitányi, András (trans). *The Philosophy of Appearances*. Dordrecht, Kluwer, 1989.
 Rundle, Bede. *Int Stud Phil*, 24(3), 115-116, 1992.

Almeder, Robert. *Blind Realism*. Lanham, Rowman & Littlefield, 1992.
 Odegard, Douglas. *Can Phil Rev*, 12(4), 227-228, Ag 92.

Almond, Brenda (ed) and Hill, Donald (ed). *Applied Philosophy*. New York, Routledge, 1991.
 Gardner, Peter. *J Moral Educ*, 21(2), 168-169, 1992.
 Moulder, James. *S Afr J Phil*, 12(2), 48-49, My 93.

Alperson, Philip (ed). *What is Music?*. New York, Haven, 1987.
 Niblock, Howard. *J Aes Art Crit*, 47(3), 292-294, Sum 89.

Alperson, Philip A (ed). *The Philosophy of the Visual Arts*. New York, Oxford Univ Pr, 1992.
 Werhane, Patricia. *J Aes Art Crit*, 51(3), 525, Sum 93.

Alston, William P. *Divine Nature and Human Language*. Ithaca, Cornell Univ Pr, 1989.
 McLeod, Mark S. *Zygon*, 27(4), 464-466, D 92.
 Morris, Thomas V. *Phil Phenomenol Res*, 52(2), 491-494, Je 92.
 Quinn, Philip L. *Phil Rev*, 101(3), 665-667, Jl 92.

Alston, William P. *Epistemic Justification*. Ithaca, Cornell Univ Pr, 1989.
 McLeod, Mark S. *Zygon*, 27(4), 464-466, D 92.

Alston, William P. *Perceiving God*. Ithaca, Cornell Univ Pr, 1991.
 Davies, Brian. *Int Phil Quart*, 33(1), 124-127, Mr 93.
 Maitzen, Stephen. *Phil Rev*, 102(3), 430-432, Jl 93.
 Marlin, Randal. *Can Phil Rev*, 12(2), 75-79, Ap 92.
 Quinn, Philip L. *Mind*, 102(405), 175-177, Ja 93.

Alter, Jean. *A Sociosemiotic Theory of Theatre*. Philadelphia, Univ of Penn Pr, 1990.
 Perricone, Christopher. *Clio*, 21(2), 192-19195, Wint 92.

Althusser, Louis. *L'Avenir dure longtemps*. Paris, Stock/MEC, 1992.
 Chabot, Marc. *Horiz Phil*, 3(1), 142-143, Autumn 92.

Altieri, Charles. *Canons and Consequences*. Evanston, Northwestern Univ Pr, 1990.
 Fisher, David H. *J Aes Art Crit*, 50(2), 165-167, Spr 92.
 Harris, Wendell V. *Phil Lit*, 16(1), 150-162, Ap 92.

Altieri, Charles. *Painterly Abstraction in Modernist American Poetry*. New York, Cambridge Univ Pr, 1989.
 Fisher, David H. *J Aes Art Crit*, 50(2), 165-167, Spr 92.

Ammann, Daniel. *David Lodge and the Art-and-Reality Novel*. Heidelberg, Carl Winter Univ, 1991.
 Brandl, Mark Staff. *J Aes Art Crit*, 51(1), 89-90, Wint 93.

Anderberg, T, Nilstun, T (ed) and Person, I (ed). *Aesthetic Distinction*. Lund, Lund Univ Pr, 1988.
 Yanal, Robert J. *J Aes Art Crit*, 48(1), 94-96, Wint 90.

Anderson, John R. *The Adaptive Character of Thought*. East Sussex, Erlbaum, 1990.
Solomon, Miriam. *Phil Psych*, 6(1), 97-99, 1993.

Anderson, Richard L. *Calliope's Sisters*. Englewood Cliffs, Prentice Hall, 1990.
Ecker, David W. *J Aes Art Crit*, 49(3), 269-271, Sum 91.

Anderson, Wilda. *Diderot's Dream*. Baltimore, Johns Hopkins U Pr, 1990.
Anderson, Wilda. *Phil Sci*, 60(1), 174-176, Mr 93.

Angenot, Marc. *1889: Un état du discours social*. Quebec, Preambule, 1989.
Howorth, Jolyon. *Hist Euro Ideas*, 14(2), 295-297, Mr 92.

Anglin, W S. *Free Will and the Christian Faith*. New York, Clarendon/Oxford Pr, 1990.
Meynell, Hugo. *Heythrop J*, 34(1), 101-102, Ja 93.
Rikhof, H. *Bijdragen*, 54(1), 97-98, 1993.
Van Den Beld, A. *Relig Stud*, 28(2), 277-279, J 92.

Annas, Julia E. *Hellenistic Philosophy of Mind*. Berkeley, Univ of Calif Pr, 1992.
Lesses, Glen. *Can Phil Rev*, 12(5), 305-307, O 92.

Ansell-Pearson, Keith. *Nietzsche contra Rousseau*. New York, Cambridge Univ Pr, 1992.
Blondel, Eric. *Hist Euro Ideas*, 17(2-3), 343-344, Mr-My 93.
Clegg, Jerry S. *Can Phil Rev*, 12(3), 153-157, J-Jl 92.
Conway, Daniel W. *Rev Metaph*, 47(1), 133-134, S 93.
Moulder, James. *S Afr J Phil*, 12(2), 48-49, My 93.

Anton, John P (ed) and Preus, Anthony (ed). *Essays in Ancient Greek Philosophy IV: Aristotle's Ethics*. Albany, SUNY Pr, 1991.
Koehn, Glen. *Can Phil Rev*, 12(6), 377-379, D 92.
Megone, Christopher. *Phil Quart*, 43(173), 528-529, O 93.

Appleton, Jay. *The Symbolism of Habitat*. Seattle, Univ Washington Pr, 1991.
Carlson, Allen. *J Aes Art Crit*, 50(1), 79-80, Wint 92.

Aquila, Richard E. *Matter in Mind*. Bloomington, Indiana Univ Pr, 1989.
Benardete, José A. *Int Stud Phil*, 24(3), 117-118, 1992.

Arac, Jonathan. *Critical Genealogies*. New York, Columbia Univ Pr, 1987.
Armstrong, Paul B. *J Aes Art Crit*, 47(1), 83-84, Wint 89.

Arendt, Hannah, Beiner, Ronald and Revault d'Allones, Myriam. *Juger: Sur la philosophie politique de Kant*. Paris, Seuil, 1991.
Ponton, Lionel. *Laval Theol Phil*, 49(2), 343-344, Je 93.

Arieti, James A. *Interpreting Plato*. Lanham, Rowman & Littlefield, 1991.
Colson, Darrel D. *Teach Phil*, 16(1), 80-82, Mr 93.
Press, Gerald A. *J Hist Phil*, 30(2), 291-292, Ap 92.
Sider, David. *Thought*, 67(266), 350-352, S 92.

Aristotle and Smith, Robin (trans). *Prior Analytics*. Indianapolis, Hackett, 1989.
Kirwan, Christopher. *Phil Rev*, 101(3), 633-635, Jl 92.

Armon-Jones, Claire. *Varieties of Affect*. Hertfordshire, Harvester-Wheatsheaf, 1991.
Marks, Joel. *Mind*, 102(405), 177-179, Ja 93.

Armstrong, A H. *Hellenic and Christian Studies*. Brookfield, Gower, 1990.
Edwards, M J. *Heythrop J*, 34(2), 203-204, Ap 93.
Nicholson, M Forthomme. *Phoenix*, 47(2), 185-187, Sum 93.

Armstrong, D M. *A Combinatorial Theory of Possibility*. New York, Cambridge Univ Pr, 1989.
Cresswell, M J. *Phil Rev*, 101(3), 660-662, Jl 92.
Maudlin, Tim. *Phil Sci*, 59(4), 716-718, D 92.
Menzies, Peter. *Phil Phenomenol Res*, 52(3), 731-734, S 92.

Armstrong, D M. *Universals*. Boulder, Westview Pr, 1989.
Levinson, Jerrold. *Phil Rev*, 101(3), 654-660, Jl 92.

Armstrong, Paul. *Conflicting Readings*. Chapel Hill, Univ N Carolina Pr, 1990.
Stern, Laurent. *J Aes Art Crit*, 49(4), 386-388, Fall 91.

Arnauld, Antoine and Gaukroger, Stephen (trans). *On True and False Ideas*. Manchester, Manchester Univ Pr, 1990.
Jolley, Nicholas. *Phil Rev*, 101(4), 849-851, O 92.

Arnheim, Rudolf. *To the Rescue of Art*. Berkeley, Univ of Calif Pr, 1992.
Meeson, Philip. *Brit J Aes*, 33(1), 75-76, Ja 93.

Aronowitz, Stanley. *Science as Power*. Minneapolis, Univ of Minn Pr, 1988.
Fuller, Steve. *Int Stud Phil*, 24(3), 116-117, 1992.

Aronowitz, Stanley and Giroux, Henry A. *Postmodern Education*. Minneapolis, Univ of Minn Pr, 1991.
Sassower, Raphael. *Teach Phil*, 15(4), 407-409, D 92.

Arrington, Robert L (ed) and Glock, Hans-Johann (ed). *Wittgenstein's 'Philosophical Investigations'*. New York, Routledge, 1991.
McGinn, Marie. *Phil Books*, 34(2), 90-91, Ap 93.

Aspray, William. *John von Neumann and the Origins of Modern Computing*. Cambridge, MIT Pr, 1990.
Franksen, Ole Immanuel. *Hist Phil Log*, 13(2), 232-233, 1992.

Asselin, Dan. *Human Nature and Eudaimonia in Aristotle*. New York, Lang, 1989.
Hudson, Deal W. *Int Phil Quart*, 33(1), 128-130, Mr 93.

Asztalos, Monica (ed), Murdoch, John E (ed) and Niiniluoto, Ilkka (ed). *Knowledge and the Sciences in Medieval Philosophy, Volume I*. Helsinki, Acta Phil Fennica, 1990.
Unguru, Sabetai. *Heythrop J*, 34(3), 325-326, Jl 93.

Atherton, Margaret. *Berkeley's Revolution in Vision*. Ithaca, Cornell Univ Pr, 1990.
Jesseph, Douglas M. *J Hist Phil*, 30(2), 306-307, Ap 92.
Loptson, Peter. *Can Phil Rev*, 12(6), 379-383, D 92.

Attfield, Robin. *The Ethics of Environmental Concern (Second Edition)*. Athens, Univ of Georgia Pr, 1991.
Wallace, Gerry. *J Applied Phil*, 9(2), 253-255, 1992.

Attfield, Robin (ed) and Wilkins, Barry (ed). *International Justice and the Third World*. New York, Routledge, 1992.
Morriss, Peter. *J Applied Phil*, 10(1), 123-125, 1993.

Atwell, John. *Ends and Principles in Kant's Moral Thought*. Dordrecht, Kluwer, 1986.
Werkmeister, W H. *Ideal Stud*, 22(3), 297-298, S 92.

Atwell, John E. *Schopenhauer: The Human Character*. Philadelphia, Temple Univ Pr, 1990.
Cartwright, David E. *J Hist Phil*, 30(2), 315-317, Ap 92.

Audi, Robert. *Belief, Justification and Knowledge*. Belmont, Wadsworth, 1988.
Taylor, James E. *Phil Phenomenol Res*, 53(2), 480-483, Je 93.

Audi, Robert. *Practical Reasoning/Audi*. New York, Routledge, 1989.
Jacquette, Dale. *Phil Rhet*, 26(1), 85-89, 1993.
Lemos, Noah. *Phil Phenomenol Res*, 52(4), 998-1000, D 92.
West, Henry R. *Int Stud Phil*, 24(3), 118, 1992.

Aune, Bruce. *Knowledge of the External World*. New York, Routledge, 1991.
Butchvarov, Panayot. *Phil Phenomenol Res*, 53(2), 490-492, Je 93.
Creath, Richard. *Nous*, 27(1), 339-340, Mr 93.

Avni, Ora. *The Resistance of Reference*. Baltimore, Johns Hopkins U Pr, 1990.
Robinson, Jenefer. *J Aes Art Crit*, 50(3), 258-260, Sum 92.

Avramides, A. *Meaning and Mind*. Cambridge, MIT Pr, 1989.
Pagin, Peter. *Theoria*, 61(1-3), 232-235, 1990.

Ayers, Michael. *Locke (Volume I)*. New York, Routledge, 1991.
Armstrong, D M. *Mind*, 102(405), 179-183, Ja 93.
Woolhouse, R S. *J Phil*, 89(8), 436-440, Ag 92.

Bachmair, Leo. *Canonical Equational Proofs*. Basel, Birkhauser, 1991.
Pedersen, John. *Phil Quart*, 42(168), 1140-1141, Jl 92.

Badiner, Allan Hunt (ed). *Dharma Gaia*. Berkeley, Parallax Pr, 1990.
Sponberg, Alan. *Environ Ethics*, 14(3), 279-282, Fall 92.

Baier, Annette C. *A Progress of Sentiments*. Cambridge, Harvard Univ Pr, 1991.
Buckle, Stephen. *Austl J Phil*, 70(3), 358-362, S 92.
Jones, Peter. *Phil Quart*, 43(170), 114-116, Ja 93.
Kretschmer, Martin. *Nous*, 27(1), 340-348, Mr 93.

Baird, Robert (ed) and Rosenbaum, Stuart (ed). *Animal Experimentation*. Buffalo, Prometheus, 1991.
Dombrowski, Daniel A. *Teach Phil*, 15(3), 291-292, S 92.
Gruen, Lori. *Bioethics*, 6(4), 384-386, O 92.
Simak, Doug. *Can Phil Rev*, 12(1), 1-3, F 92.

Baker, C Edwin. *Human Liberty and Freedom of Speech*. New York, Oxford Univ Pr, 1989.
O'Neil, Patrick M. *Int Stud Phil*, 24(3), 119-120, 1992.

Baker, John. *Arguing for Equality*. New Yorky, Verso, 1988.
Temkin, Larry S. *Phil Rev*, 101(2), 473-475, Ap 92.

Baker, Keith Michael. *Inventing the French Revolution*. New York, Cambridge Univ Pr, 1990.
Bosher, J F. *Phil Soc Sci*, 23(1), 125-127, Mr 93.

Baker-Smith, Dominic. *More's 'Utopia'*. New York, HarperCollins, 1991.
Hamilton, Alastair. *Heythrop J*, 34(3), 328-329, Jl 93.

Bakunin, Michael (ed & trans) and Shatz, Marshall S. *Statism and Anarchy*. New York, Cambridge Univ Pr, 1990.
Geifman, Anna. *Hist Euro Ideas*, 14(3), 453-454, M 92.
Shaw, William H. *Can Phil Rev*, 12(1), 3-5, F 92.

Baldick, Julian. *Mystical Islam*. New York, New York Univ Pr, 1989.
Radtke, Bernd. *Relig Stud*, 29(2), 266-268, Je 93.

Baldwin, Peter (ed). *Reworking the Past*. Boston, Beacon Pr, 1990.
Goldstein, Leon J. *Int Stud Phil*, 25(1), 95, 1993.

Baldwin, Thomas. *G E Moore*. New York, Routledge, 1990.
Crisp, Roger. *Utilitas*, 4(1), 169-172, My 92.
Klemke, E D. *Int Stud Phil*, 24(1), 82-83, 1992.
Stroud, Barry. *Phil Rev*, 101(4), 875-877, O 92.
Williams, Michael. *Phil Quart*, 43(170), 99-103, Ja 93.

Ball, Terrence (ed), Farr, James (ed) and Hanson, Russell L (ed). *Political Innovation and Conceptual Change*. New York, Cambridge Univ Pr, 1989.
Manicas, Peter T. *Phil Soc Sci*, 22(3), 402-408, S 92.

Balthasar, Hans Urs von. *Teodramática, Volume I & II*. Madrid, Ed Encuentro, 1990.
Baró, José María Romero. *Dialogo Filosof*, 8(3), 406-409, S-D 92.

Bandiste, D D. *A Study of the Ethics of Bertrand Russell*. Idore, Lipika Prakashan, 1984.
Kohl, Marvin. *Russell*, 12(2), 224, Wint 92-93.

Bann, Stephen (ed) and Allen, William (ed). *Interpreting Contemporary Art*. New York, HarperCollins, 1991.
Herwitz, Daniel. *J Aes Art Crit*, 50(3), 265-267, Sum 92.

Bogdan, Radu J (ed). *Mind and Common Sense*. New York, Cambridge Univ Pr, 1991.
Foss, Jeffrey. *Can Phil Rev*, 12(3), 162-166, J-Jl 92.

Bogdan, Radu J (ed). *Roderick M Chisholm*. Dordrecht, Kluwer, 1986.
Smith, Peter. *Ideal Stud*, 22(3), 286, S 92.

Bogue, Ronald (ed). *Mimesis, Semiosis, and Power*. Amsterdam, J Benjamins, 1991.
Corngold, Stanley. *Phil Lit*, 17(1), 138-139, Ap 93.

Bohman, James. *New Philosophy of Social Science*. Cambridge, MIT Pr, 1991.
Ingram, David. *Mod Sch*, 70(1), 63-66, N 92.

Bois, Yve-Alain. *Painting as Model*. Cambridge, MIT Pr, 1990.
Kelly, Michael. *J Aes Art Crit*, 50(4), 351-352, Fall 92.

Boland, Lawrence A. *Methodology for a New Microeconomics*. Scranton, Unwin Hyman, 1986.
Sassower, Raphael. *Phil Soc Sci*, 22(2), 241-250, J 92.

Boland, Lawrence A. *The Foundations of Economic Method*. Scranton, Unwin Hyman, 1982.
Sassower, Raphael. *Phil Soc Sci*, 22(2), 241-250, J 92.

Boland, Lawrence A. *The Methodology of Economic Model Building*. New York, Routledge, 1989.
Sassower, Raphael. *Phil Soc Sci*, 22(2), 241-250, J 92.

Bole III, Thomas J (ed) and Bondeson, William B (ed). *Rights to Health Care*. Dordrecht, Kluwer, 1991.
Young, Robert. *Bioethics*, 7(1), 72-74, Ja 93.

Bolton, Richard (ed). *The Contest of Meaning*. Cambridge, MIT Pr, 1989.
Maynard, Patrick. *J Aes Art Crit*, 50(1), 68-71, Wint 92.

Bonfantini, Massimo A. *La semiosi e l'abduzione*. Milan, Bompiani, 1987.
Innis, J Prag, 18(1), 74-79, Jl 92.

Bookchin, Murray and Foreman, Dave. *Defending the Earth*. Montreal, Black Rose, 1991.
Hanly, Ken. *Can Phil Rev*, 12(4), 231-233, Ag 92.

Boomkens, René. *De asceet, de tolk en de verteller*. Amsterdam, Krisis Onderzoek, 1992.
Flameling, Jan. *Kennis Methode*, 17(3), 328-333, 1993.

Booth, Wayne C. *The Company We Keep*. Berkeley, Univ of Calif Pr, 1988.
Eldridge, Richard. *J Aes Art Crit*, 49(1), 98-101, Wint 91.

Borgmann, Albert. *Technology and the Character of Contemporary Life*. Chicago, Univ of Chicago Pr, 1984.
Hickman, Larry. *Res Phil Technol*, 12, 337-345, 1992.

Borgmann, Albert. *Technology and the Character of Contemporary Life (Response to Hickman)*. Chicago, Univ of Chicago Pr, 1984.
Borgmann, Albert. *Res Phil Technol*, 12, 345-347, 1992.

Bormann, F Herbert (ed) and Kellert, Stephen R (ed). *Ecology, Economics, Ethics*. New Haven, Yale Univ Pr, 1991.
Hoose, Bernard. *Heythrop J*, 34(2), 199-201, Ap 93.

Borowski, L E, Jachmann, R B and Wasianski, E A. *Kant intime*. Paris, Grasset, 1985.
Boissinot, Christian. *Laval Theol Phil*, 48(3), 481-487, O 92.

Boruah, Bijoy H. *Fiction and Emotion*. New York, Oxford Univ Pr, 1988.
Hagberg, Garry. *J Aes Art Crit*, 48(3), 246-248, Sum 90.
McFall, Lynne. *Philosophia (Israel)*, 21(3-4), 361-364, Ap 92.

Bose, K S. *A Theory of Religious Thought*. New Delhi, Sterling, 1991.
Bose, K S. *Phil East West*, 43(3), 591-592, Jl 93.

Bosley, Richard (ed) and Tweedale, Martin (ed). *Aristotle and His Medieval Interpreters*. Calgary, Univ of Calgary Pr, 1991.
Dubrule, Diane. *Can Phil Rev*, 12(6), 385-387, D 92.

Bossuet, Jacques-Benigne and Riley, Patrick (trans). *Politics Drawn From the Very Words of Holy Scripture*. New York, Cambridge Univ Pr, 1991.
Kilcullen, John. *Can Phil Rev*, 12(6), 387-380, D 92.

Bottery, Mike. *The Morality of the School*. London, Cassell, 1990.
McLaughlin, T H. *J Phil Educ*, 26(2), 278-280, 1992.

Boucher, David. *The Social and Political Thought of R G Collingwood*. New York, Cambridge Univ Pr, 1989.
Häyry, Matti. *Ideal Stud*, 22(3), 301-303, S 92.

Bouchindhomme, Christian and Rochlitz, Rainer. *Temps et récit de Paul Ricoeur en débat*. Paris, Cerf, 1990.
Nadeau, Jean-Guy. *Laval Theol Phil*, 49(1), 149-155, F 93.

Boukema, H J M. *Good Law: Towards a Rational Lawmaking Process*. New York, Lang, 1982.
Flew, Antony. *Vera Lex*, 12(1), 33-35, 1992.

Boukema, H J M. *Judging: Towards a Rational Judicial Process*. Zwolle, Tjeenk Willink, 1980.
Flew, Antony. *Vera Lex*, 12(1), 34-35, 1992.

Bourassa, Steven C. *The Aesthetics of Landscape*. London, Belhaven Pr, 1991.
Carlson, Allen. *J Aes Art Crit*, 50(4), 343-345, Fall 92.

Bourdieu, Pierre and Collier, Peter (trans). *The Political Ontology of Martin Heidegger*. Stanford, Stanford Univ Pr, 1991.
Guignon, Charles. *Can Phil Rev*, 12(1), 11-13, F 92.

Bourke, Vernon J (ed). *Augustine's Love of Wisdom*. West Lafayette, Purdue Univ Pr, 1992.
Bourke, Vernon J. *Mod Sch*, 70(3), 237-238, Mr 93.
Clark, Mary T. *Int Phil Quart*, 33(3), 376-377, S 93.
King-Farlow, John. *Can Phil Rev*, 13(1), 6-8, F 93.
Wetzel, James. *Rev Metaph*, 47(1), 136-137, S 93.

Bowie, G Lee (ed), Higgins, Kathleen (ed) and Michaels, Meredith W (ed). *Thirteen Questions in Ethics*. Fort Worth, Harcourt Brace Jov, 1992.
Simon, Caroline J. *Teach Phil*, 15(4), 371-372, D 92.

Bowie, Norman and Duska, Ronald. *Business Ethics (Second Edition)*. Englewood Cliffs, Prentice Hall, 1990.
Hanly, Ken. *J Bus Ethics*, 11(9), 718, 728, S 92.

Bowler, Peter. *The Non-Darwinian Revolution*. Baltimore, Johns Hopkins U Pr, 1988.
Ruse, Michael. *Phil Sci*, 60(1), 171-172, Mr 93.

Bowler, Peter J. *The Mendelian Revolution*. Baltimore, Johns Hopkins U Pr, 1989.
Ruse, Michael. *Phil Sci*, 60(1), 171-172, Mr 93.

Box, M A. *The Suasive Art of David Hume*. Princeton, Princeton Univ Pr, 1990.
Dees, Richard. *Mod Sch*, 69(2), 154-156, Ja 92.
Immerwahr, John. *Int Stud Phil*, 24(3), 125, 1992.
Landau, Iddo. *Clio*, 22(1), 97-99, Fall 92.
Raynor, David. *Eidos*, 10(2), 217-222, D 92.
Stewart, M A. *Philosophy*, 67(260), 266-268, Apr 92.

Bradford, Dennis E. *A Thinker's Guide to Living Well*. Peru, Open Court, 1990.
Messerly, John. *Mod Sch*, 70(2), 159-160, Ja 93.

Bradley, Raymond. *The Nature of All Being*. New York, Oxford Univ Pr, 1992.
Armstrong, D M. *Notre Dame J Form Log*, 34(1), 150-156, Wint 93.
Sullivan, Peter M. *Phil Books*, 34(3), 148-151, Jl 93.

Braidotti, Rosi. *Patterns of Dissonance*. New York, Routledge, 1991.
Leslie-Spinks, Amanda. *Hypatia*, 7(3), 208-211, Sum 92.

Braio, Frank Paul. *Lonergan's Retrieval of the Notion of Human Being*. Lanham, Univ Pr of America, 1988.
Tyrrell, Bernard J. *Int Phil Quart*, 32(3), 385-386, S 92.

Braithwaite, John and Pettit, Philip. *Not Just Deserts*. New York, Oxford Univ Pr, 1990.
Duff, R A. *Phil Rev*, 102(3), 438-440, Jl 93.

Brakas, George. *Aristotle's Concept of the Universal*. Hildesheim, Olms, 1988.
Frank, Daniel H. *Ancient Phil*, 12(1), 217-219, Spr 92.

Brand, Walter. *Hume's Theory of Moral Judgement*. Dordrecht, Kluwer, 1992.
Kretschmer, Martin. *Mind*, 102(406), 340-348, Ap 93.

Brann, Eva T H. *The World of the Imagination*. Lanham, Rowman & Littlefield, 1991.
Casey, Edward S. *Rev Metaph*, 46(1), 145-146, S 92.
Morrisey, Will. *Phil Lit*, 17(1), 132-134, Ap 93.

Braude, Stephen E. *First Person Plural*. New York, Routledge, 1991.
Baillie, James. *Nous*, 27(1), 349-353, Mr 93.
Clark, Stephen. *Phil Books*, 34(2), 109-112, Ap 93.
O'Brien, Lucy. *Phil Quart*, 43(171), 272-273, Ap 93.

Brazier, Margaret (ed) and Lobjoit, Mary (ed). *Protecting the Vulnerable*. New York, Routledge, 1991.
Boddington, Paula. *J Applied Phil*, 10(2), 270-271, 1993.

Breazeale, Daniel (ed). *Early Philosophical Writings—J G Fichte*. Ithaca, Cornell Univ Pr, 1988.
Harris, H S. *Owl Minerva*, 23(2), 193-195, Spr 92.

Breazeale, Daniel (ed & trans). *Fichte*. Ithaca, Cornell Univ Pr, 1988.
Rockmore, Tom. *Phil Rev*, 101(2), 396-398, Ap 92.

Brenkert, George G. *Political Freedom*. New York, Routledge, 1991.
Christman, John. *Nous*, 27(1), 353-357, Mr 93.
Kleinberg, Stanley S. *Phil Quart*, 43(171), 259-260, Ap 93.
Sayers, Sean. *Phil Books*, 34(1), 51-53, Ja 93.

Brennan, Andrew. *Conditions of Identity*. New York, Oxford Univ Pr, 1988.
Van Cleve, James. *Phil Rev*, 101(2), 411-414, Ap 92.

Brenner, Anastasios. *Duhem: Science réalité et apparence*. Paris, Vrin, 1990.
Kremer-Marietti, Angèle. *Rev Int Phil*, 46(182), 405-409, 1992.

Brenner, Duhem Anastasios. *Science réalité et apparence*. Paris, Vrin, 1990.
Kremer-Marietti, Angèle. *Rev Int Phil*, 46(3), 405-409, 1992.

Bresch, Carsten (& other eds). *Kann Man Gott aus der Natur Erkennen?*. Basel, Herder Pr, 1990.
Bliese, Richard. *Zygon*, 28(1), 106-109, Mr 93.

Brezinski, J (& other eds). *Idealization I*. Amsterdam, Rodopi, 1990.
Janssen, Maarten C W. *Erkenntnis*, 37(2), 275-280, S 92.

Brickhouse, Thomas C and Smith, Nicholas D. *Socrates on Trial*. Princeton, Princeton Univ Pr, 1989.
Reeve, C D C. *Phil Rev*, 101(3), 626-628, Jl 92.

Brink, David O. *Moral Realism and the Foundations of Ethics*. New York, Cambridge Univ Pr, 1989.
DePaul, Michael R. *Phil Phenomenol Res*, 53(3), 731-735, S 93.
Shaver, Robert. *Phil Rev*, 101(2), 458-460, Ap 92.

Brint, Michael (ed) and Weaver, William (ed). *Pragmatism in Law and Society.* Boulder, Westview Pr, 1991.
Dyzenhaus, David. *Phil Books*, 34(2), 122-123, Ap 93.
Haskins, Casey. *Can Phil Rev*, 12(5), 314-317, O 92.

Brisson, Luc and Meyerstein, F Walter. *Inventer l'univers.* Paris, Belles Lettres, 1991.
Gauthier, Y. *Philosophiques*, 19(1), 150-155, 1992.

Brito, Emilio. *Dieu et l'être d'après Thomas d'Aquin et Hegel.* Paris, Pr Univ France, 1991.
Ide, Pascal. *Rev Thomiste*, 92(4), 917-924, O-D 92.

Broadie, Alexander. *Notion and Object.* New York, Oxford Univ Pr, 1989.
Zupko, Jack. *Phil Rev*, 101(3), 641-644, Jl 92.

Broadie, Alexander. *The Tradition of Scottish Philosophy.* Edinburgh, Polygon, 1990.
Stewart, M A. *Phil Books*, 33(3), 142-143, Jl 92.

Broadie, Sarah. *Ethics With Aristotle.* New York, Oxford Univ Pr, 1991.
Irwin, T H. *J Phil*, 90(6), 323-329, Je 93.
Richardson, Henry S. *Mind*, 101(402), 358-361, Ap 92.
Taylor, C C W. *Phil Quart*, 43(173), 529-532, O 93.

Brody, Baruch (& other eds). *Theological Developments in Bioethics: 1988-1990.* Dordrecht, Kluwer, 1991.
Yule, Sandy. *Bioethics*, 7(1), 74-76, Ja 93.

Bromley, Daniel W. *Economic Interests and Institutions.* Cambridge, Blackwell, 1989.
Ramstad, Yngve. *Econ Phil*, 8(2), 303-310, O 92.

Brooks, Daniel R and McLennan, Deborah A. *Phylogeny, Ecology, and Behavior.* Chicago, Univ of Chicago Pr, 1991.
Ghiselin, Michael T. *Biol Phil*, 7(3), 355-359, Jl 92.

Broome, John. *Counting the Cost of Global Warming.* Unknown, White Horse, 1992.
Crisp, Roger. *Phil Books*, 34(3), 170-174, Jl 93.

Broome, John. *Weighing Goods.* Cambridge, Blackwell, 1991.
Cowen, Tyler. *Econ Phil*, 8(2), 283-285, O 92.
Hollis, Martin. *Mind*, 101(403), 553-554, Jl 92.
Slote, Michael. *Phil Books*, 34(1), 39-41, Ja 93.

Brough, John Barnett (trans) and Husserl, Edmund. *On the Phenomenology of the Consciousness of Internal Time (1893-1917).* Dordrecht, Kluwer, 1991.
Evans, J C. *Husserl Stud*, 9(3), 237-238, 1992.

Brown, David (ed). *Newman: A Man for Our Time.* London, S P C K, 1990.
Barber, Michael C. *Heythrop J*, 33(4), 465-466, O 92.

Brown, Harold I. *Rationality.* New York, Routledge, 1988.
Francken, Patrick. *Int Stud Phil*, 24(3), 126-127, 1992.
Simpson, Evan. *Nous*, 26(2), 236-238, J 92.

Brown, Henry Phelps. *Egalitarianism and the Generation of Inequality.* New York, Oxford Univ Pr, 1991.
Hay, Frederick G. *Hist Euro Ideas*, 14(4), 606-608, Jl 92.

Brown, James R (ed) and Mittelstrass, Jürgen (ed). *An Intimate Relation.* Dordrecht, Kluwer, 1989.
Butts, Robert E. *Phil Sci*, 59(4), 711-712, D 92.

Brown, James Robert. *The Rational and the Social.* New York, Routledge, 1989.
Shapin, Steven. *Phil Sci*, 59(4), 712-713, D 92.

Brown, Marshall. *Preromanticism.* Stanford, Stanford Univ Pr, 1991.
Bogue, Ronald. *Phil Lit*, 16(2), 385-386, O 92.

Brown, Richard H. *A Poetic for Sociology.* Chicago, Univ of Chicago Pr, 1989.
Pawson, Ray. *Phil Soc Sci*, 22(3), 394-397, S 92.

Brown, Stuart (ed). *Nicolas Malebranche.* Assen, Gorcum, 1991.
Ablondi, Fred. *Dialogue (PST)*, 35(1), 27-28, O 92.

Browning, Gary K. *Plato and Hegel.* Hamden, Garland, 1991.
Inwood, Michael. *Bull Hegel Soc Gt Brit*, 23-24, 118-120, 1991.
Nicholson, Peter. *Polis*, 11(1), 102-104, 1992.

Brüll, Lydia. *Die japanische Philosophie.* Darmstadt, Wiss Buchgesell, 1989.
Parkes, Graham. *Phil East West*, 43(3), 583-585, Jl 93.

Brumbaugh, Robert S. *Platonic Studies of Greek Philosophy.* Albany, SUNY Pr, 1989.
Eckstein, Jerome. *Int Stud Phil*, 24(1), 84-85, 1992.

Brunette, Peter and Wills, David. *Screen/Play: Derrida and Film Theory.* Princeton, Princeton Univ Pr, 1989.
Smith, Murray. *J Aes Art Crit*, 49(3), 268-269, Sum 91.

Bruns, Gerald L. *Heidegger's Estrangements.* New Haven, Yale Univ Pr, 1989.
Fynsk, Christopher. *Int Stud Phil*, 24(1), 85-86, 1992.
O'Leary, Joseph S. *Hermathena*, 150, 56-60, Sum 91.

Bryant, Christopher G A (ed) and Jary, David (ed). *Giddens' Theory of Structuration.* New York, Routledge, 1991.
Parker, Noel. *Rad Phil*, 61, 49-50, Sum 92.

Bryson, Norman (ed). *Calligram: Essays in New Art History.* New York, Cambridge Univ Pr, 1988.
Carrier, David. *J Aes Art Crit*, 47(3), 286-287, Sum 89.

Bryson, Norman (ed), Holly, Michael Ann (ed) and Moxey, Keith (ed). *Visual Theory.* New York, HarperCollins, 1991.
Moran, Richard. *J Aes Art Crit*, 50(3), 257-258, Sum 92.

Buchanan, Allen. *Secession.* Boulder, Westview Pr, 1991.
Cunningham, Frank. *Can Phil Rev*, 12(3), 166-168, J-Jl 92.
Kymlicka, Will. *Polit Theory*, 20(3), 527-532, Ag 92.

Buchanan, Allen E and Brock, Dan W. *Deciding for Others.* New York, Cambridge Univ Pr, 1989.
Overall, Christine. *Phil Soc Sci*, 23(1), 120-125, Mr 93.

Buchler, Justus, Wallace, Kathleen (ed) and Marsoobian, Armen (ed). *Metaphysics of Natural Complexes.* Albany, SUNY Pr, 1990.
Margolis, Joseph. *J Speculative Phil*, 6(3), 242-247, 1992.

Buck-Morss, Susan. *The Dialectics of Seeing.* Cambridge, MIT Pr, 1989.
Burke, Mark L. *Amer Cath Phil Quart*, 65(4), 503-505, Autumn 91.

Buczkowski, Piotr (ed) and Klawiter, Andrzej (ed). *Theories of Ideology and Ideology of Theories.* Amsterdam, Rodopi, 1986.
Seddon, Fred. *Stud Soviet Tho*, 44(3), 230-232, N 92.

Budd, Malcolm. *Wittgenstein's Philosophy of Psychology.* New York, Routledge, 1989.
Hallett, Garth L. *Behavior Phil*, 19(2), 87-89, Fall/Wint 91.
Harré, Rom. *Int Stud Phil*, 24(3), 127-128, 1992.
McGinn, Colin. *J Phil*, 89(8), 433-436, Ag 92.
Wettersten, John. *Phil Soc Sci*, 22(4), 515-519, D 92.

Burch, Robert W. *A Peircean Reduction Thesis.* Lubbock, Texas Tech Univ Pr, 1991.
Zeman, Jay. *Trans Peirce Soc*, 29(1), 101-107, Wint 93.

Burgin, M S and Kuznetsov, V I. *Axiological Aspects of Scientific Theories.* Kiev, Naukova Dumka, 1991.
Rothbart, Daniel. *Erkenntnis*, 38(2), 281-283, Mr 93.

Burkhardt, Bernd. *Hegels Kritik an Kants theoretischer Philosophie.* Munchen, Profil, 1989.
Clayton, Philip. *Owl Minerva*, 24(1), 83-87, Fall 92.

Burkhardt, F (ed) and Bowres, F (ed). *Manuscripts, Essays, and Notes of William James.* Cambridge, Harvard Univ Pr, 1988.
Andrew *Jlnt Stud Phil*, 25(1), Reck, 1993.
Steinkraus, Warren E. *Ideal Stud*, 22(3), 288-289, S 92.

Burkhardt, Hans (ed) and Smith, Barry (ed). *Handbook of Metaphysics and Ontology.* Munchen, Philosophia, 1991.
DuBois, James M. *Rev Metaph*, 46(2), 391-392, 1992.
Poli, Roberto. *Hist Phil Log*, 13(2), 258-260, 1992.

Burns, J H (ed). *The Cambridge History of Medieval Political Thought.* New York, Cambridge Univ Pr, 1988.
McGrade, A S. *Phil Rev*, 101(2), 379-382, Ap 92.

Burns, J H (ed) and Goldie, Mark (ed). *The Cambridge History of Political Thought 1450-1700.* New York, Cambridge Univ Pr, 1991.
Höpfl, H M. *Hist Polit Thought*, 13(1), 173-176, Spr 92.

Burns, Linda Claire. *Vagueness.* Dordrecht, Kluwer, 1991.
Cargile, James. *Phil Books*, 34(1), 22-24, Ja 93.
Rolf, Bertil. *Hist Phil Log*, 14(1), 122-124, 1993.
Sanford, David H. *Mind*, 102(406), 357-360, Ap 93.

Burnyeat, Myles. *The Theaetetus of Plato.* Indianapolis, Hackett, 1990.
Fine, Gail. *Phil Rev*, 101(4), 830-834, O 92.

Burrell, David B. *Knowing the Unknowable God.* Notre Dame, Univ Notre Dame Pr, 1986.
Konyndyk, Kenneth. *Nous*, 26(4), 507-509, D 92.

Burtchaell, James Tunstead. *The Giving and Taking of Life.* Notre Dame, Univ Notre Dame Pr, 1989.
Barry, Robert. *Thomist*, 56(4), 733-738, O 92.

Busch, Thomas W. *The Power of Consciousness and the Force of Circumstances in Sartre's Philosophy.* Bloomington, Indiana Univ Pr, 1990.
Anderson, K L. *Man World*, 25(2), 235-242, Ap 92.
Flynn, Thomas R. *Res Phenomenol*, 22, 210-216, 1992.
Morris, Phyllis S. *Int Stud Phil*, 24(3), 128-129, 1992.

Bussanich, John. *The One and Its Relation to Intellect in Plotinus.* Leiden, Brill, 1988.
Corrigan, Kevin. *Ancient Phil*, 12(1), 230-237, Spr 92.
Elders, Leo J. *Rev Metaph*, 47(1), 137-138, S 93.

Buszkowski, Wojciech (ed), Marciszewski, Witold (ed) and Van Benthem, Johan (ed). *Categorical Grammar.* Amsterdam, J Benjamins, 1988.
Wolenski, Jan. *Stud Log*, 50(1), 171-172, Mr 91.

Butler, John. *Lord Herbert of Chirbury (1582-1648).* Lewiston, Mellen Pr, 1990.
Michael, Emily. *Hist Euro Ideas*, 14(4), 611-613, Jl 92.

Butler, Judith. *Gender Trouble.* New York, Routledge, 1990.
Lennon, Kathleen. *J Applied Phil*, 9(1), 125-127, 1992.

Butrym, Alexander J. *Essays on the Essay.* Athens, Univ of Georgia Pr, 1989.
Dickson, Colin. *Phil Lit*, 16(2), 378-379, O 92.

Buttiglione, Rocco. *La Crisi della Morale.* Rome, Dino Ed, 1991.
Guietti, Paolo. *Rev Metaph*, 46(2), 392-394, 1992.

Collins, H M. *Artificial Experts*. Cambridge, MIT Pr, 1990.
Restivo, Sal. *Sci Tech Human Values*, 17(3), 402-405, Sum 92.

Colquhoun, Alan. *Modernity and the Classical Tradition*. Cambridge, MIT Pr, 1989.
Wiseman, Mary Bittner. *J Aes Art Crit*, 49(3), 265-268, Sum 91.

Come, Arnold B. *Trendelenburg's Influence on Kierkegaard's Modal Categories*. Paris, InterEditions, 1991.
Martinez, Roy. *J Hist Phil*, 30(3), 467-469, J 92.

Comstock, Gary (ed). *Is There a Moral Obligation to Save the Family Farm?*. Ames, Iowa St Univ Pr, 1987.
Hill, Jim. *Environ Ethics*, 14(3), 275-278, Fall 92.

Conche, Marcel. *Temps et destin*. Paris, PUF, 1992.
Hunter, Graeme. *Laval Theol Phil*, 49(1), 164-166, F 93.

Connell, George B (ed) and Evans, C Stephen (ed). *Foundations of Kierkegaard's Vision of Community*. Atlantic Highlands, Humanities Pr, 1992.
Sartwell, Crispin. *Can Phil Rev*, 12(2), 89-91, Ap 92.

Connell, Richard J. *The Empirical Intelligence—The Human Empirical Mode*. Lewiston, Mellen Pr, 1988.
Carrick, Paul. *Int Stud Phil*, 24(3), 133-134, 1992.

Connolly, John M (ed) and Keutner, Thomas (ed). *Hermeneutics Versus Science?*. Notre Dame, Univ Notre Dame Pr, 1988.
Sullivan, Robert R. *Phil Soc Sci*, 23(2), 253-257, Je 93.

Connolly, William. *Identity/Difference*. Ithaca, Cornell Univ Pr, 1991.
Young, Iris Marion. *Polit Theory*, 20(3), 511-514, Ag 92.

Connolly, William. *Identity/Difference (Response to Young)*. Ithaca, Cornell Univ Pr, 1991.
Connolly, William E. *Polit Theory*, 21(1), 128-131, F 93.

Conway, Gertrude D. *Wittgenstein on Foundations*. Atlantic Highlands, Humanities Pr, 1989.
Harré, Rom. *Int Stud Phil*, 24(1), 88, 1992.
Hund, John. *S Afr J Phil*, 11(2), 46-48, My 92.

Cook, Nicholas. *Music, Imagination and Culture*. New York, Oxford Univ Pr, 1990.
Kivy, Peter. *J Aes Art Crit*, 50(1), 76-79, Wint 92.

Cooke, Roger. *Experts in Uncertainty*. New York, Oxford Univ Pr, 1991.
Shrader-Frechette, Kristin. *Can Phil Rev*, 12(6), 390-389, D 92.

Cooper, Neil (ed) and Engel, Pascal (ed). *New Inquiries into Truth and Meaning*. Hertfordshire, Harvester-Wheatsheaf, 1991.
Nichols, Shaun. *Mind Lang*, 8(1), 157-160, Spr 93.

Cooper-Wiele, Jonathan K. *The Totalizing Act*. Dordrecht, Kluwer, 1989.
Willard, Dallas. *Int Stud Phil*, 24(3), 134-135, 1992.

Copenhaver, Brian P and Schmitt, Charles B. *Renaissance Philosophy*. New York, Oxford Univ Pr, 1992.
Joy, Lynn S. *Phil Quart*, 43(173), 537-539, O 93.

Copp, David (ed). *Canadian Philosophers: Celebrating Twenty Years of the Canadian Journal of Philosophy*. Calgary, Univ of Calgary Pr, 1990.
Smale, Peter. *Can Phil Rev*, 12(5), 317-319, O 92.

Corbin, Henry. *L'Iran et la philosophie*. Paris, Fayard, 1990.
Gagnon, Claude. *Horiz Phil*, 3(1), 139-141, Autumn 92.

Corfield, Penelope J (ed). *Language History and Class*. Cambridge, Blackwell, 1991.
Lecercle, Jean-Jacques. *Rad Phil*, 61, 61, Sum 92.

Corlett, William. *Community Without Unity*. Durham, Duke Univ Pr, 1989.
Martin, Bill. *Praxis Int*, 12(4), 433-438, Ja 93.

Cornell, Drucilla. *Beyond Accommodation*. New York, Routledge, 1991.
White, Stephen K. *Polit Theory*, 21(1), 135-138, F 93.

Cornell, Drucilla. *The Philosophy of the Limit*. New York, Routledge, 1992.
Gardiner, Anne Barbeau. *Clio*, 22(2), 180-185, Wint 93.

Cornell, Drucilla (ed), Rosenfeld, Michael (ed) and Carlson, David Gray (ed). *Hegel and Legal Theory*. New York, Routledge, 1991.
Bellamy, Richard. *Bull Hegel Soc Gt Brit*, 26, 64-66, Autumn-Wint 92.

Corngold, Stanley and Giersing, Irene. *Borrowed Lives*. Albany, SUNY Pr, 1991.
Richter, Gerhard. *Phil Lit*, 17(1), 139-140, Ap 93.

Cothey, A L. *The Nature of Art*. New York, Routledge, 1990.
Carr, David. *Phil Books*, 34(1), 62-64, Ja 93.
Davies, Stephen. *J Aes Art Crit*, 50(3), 269-270, Sum 92.

Cottell, M and Perlin. *Accounting Ethics*. Westport, Quorum, 1990.
Ruland, Robert G. *J Bus Ethics*, 12(3), 178+, Mr 93.

Cottingham, John (& others). *The Philosophical Writings of Descartes, Volume III*. New York, Cambridge Univ Pr, 1991.
Van De Pitte, Frederick P. *Can Phil Rev*, 12(4), 236-237, Ag 92.

Coughlan, Michael J. *The Vatican, the Law and the Human Embryo*. New York, Macmillan, 1990.
Ford, Norman. *Heythrop J*, 33(4), 471-472, O 92.

Coulter, Jeff. *Mind in Action*. Atlantic Highlands, Humanities Pr, 1989.
Green, Bryan S. *Phil Soc Sci*, 22(3), 397-399, S 92.

Cowan, Bainard (ed) and Kronick, Joseph G (ed). *Theorizing American Literature*. Baton Rouge, Louisiana St Univ Pr, 1991.
Donougho, Martin. *Owl Minerva*, 23(2), 196-200, Spr 92.

Cowley, Fraser. *Metaphysical Delusion*. Buffalo, Prometheus, 1991.
Michael, Mark A. *Can Phil Rev*, 12(3), 174-176, J-Jl 92.

Cox, Gray. *The Ways of Peace*. Mahwah, Paulist Pr, 1986.
Ginsberg, Robert. *Ideal Stud*, 22(3), 249, S 92.

Cragg, Wesley. *The Practice of Punishment*. New York, Routledge, 1992.
May, Thomas. *J Applied Phil*, 10(2), 264-265, 1993.

Craig, Edward. *Knowledge and the State of Nature*. New York, Clarendon/Oxford Pr, 1990.
Bogen, James. *Phil Books*, 33(3), 156-159, Jl 92.
Dancy, Jonathan. *Phil Quart*, 42(168), 393-395, Jl 92.
Schmitt, Frederick F. *Mind*, 101(403), 555-559, Jl 92.
Steup, Matthias. *Phil Rev*, 101(4), 856-858, O 92.

Craig, William Lane. *Divine Foreknowledge and Human Freedom*. Leiden, Brill, 1991.
Fischer, John Martin. *Relig Stud*, 28(2), 269-274, J 92.
Sadowsky, James A. *Int Phil Quart*, 32(2), 257-258, J 92.
Smith, Quentin. *Phil Phenomenol Res*, 53(2), 493-495, Je 93.

Craig, William Lane. *The Problem of Divine Foreknowledge and Future Contingents from Aristotle to Suarez*. Leiden, Brill, 1988.
Kirwan, Christopher. *Int Stud Phil*, 24(3), 135-136, 1992.

Crane, Tim. *The Contents of Experience, Essays on Perception*. New York, Cambridge Univ Pr, 1992.
McLaughlin, Brian. *Can Phil Rev*, 13(1), 8-13, F 93.
Millar, Alan. *Mind*, 102(406), 362-366, Ap 93.

Cranston, Maurice. *The Noble Savage: Jean-Jacques Rousseau 1754-1762*. Chicago, Univ of Chicago Pr, 1991.
Dent, N J H. *Polit Theory*, 20(2), 352-355, My 92.
Levi, A H T. *Heythrop J*, 34(4), 472-473, O 93.

Creegan, Charles L. *Wittgenstein and Kierkegaard*. New York, Routledge, 1989.
High, Dallas M. *Int J Phil Relig*, 34(1), 58-60, Ag 93.

Crimmins, James E (ed). *Religion, Secularization and Political Thought*. New York, Routledge, 1990.
Claeys, Gregory. *Utilitas*, 4(2), 333-335, N 92.

Crimmins, James E. *Secular Utilitarianism*. New York, Clarendon/Oxford Pr, 1990.
Callaghan, John. *Hist Euro Ideas*, 14(5), 739-742, S 92.
Kelly, P J. *Hist Polit Thought*, 12(4), 740-743, Wint 91.

Critchley, Simon. *The Ethics of Deconstruction*. Cambridge, Blackwell, 1992.
Devine, Philip E. *Phil Books*, 34(3), 174-175, Jl 93.

Crittenden, Charles. *Unreality*. Ithaca, Cornell Univ Pr, 1991.
Brown, Curtis. *Can Phil Rev*, 12(3), 177-179, J-Jl 92.

Crittenden, Paul. *Learning to Be Moral*. Atlantic Highlands, Humanities Pr, 1990.
McKie, John. *Austl J Phil*, 70(1), 115-117, Mr.

Crone, Rainer. *Paul Klee*. New York, Columbia Univ Pr, 1991.
Brown, Maurice. *J Aes Educ*, 26(3), 120-121, Fall 92.

Crosby, Donald A. *The Specter of the Absurd*. Albany, SUNY Pr, 1988.
Graham, John. *Hist Euro Ideas*, 14(3), 438-440, M 92.

Crowther, Paul. *The Kantian Sublime*. New York, Oxford Univ Pr, 1989.
Haskins, Casey. *Int Stud Phil*, 24(3), 136-137, 1992.
Rogerson, Kenneth F. *J Aes Art Crit*, 49(4), 379-381, Fall 91.

Crozier, W Ray. *Shyness and Embarrassment*. New York, Cambridge Univ Pr, 1990.
Thomas, Laurence. *Behavior Phil*, 19(2), 109-119, Fall/Wint 91.

Crusius, Timothy W. *Discourse: A Critique and Synthesis of Major Theories*. New York, Modern Lang Assoc, 1989.
Johnstone, Barbara. *Phil Rhet*, 26(3), 242-244, 1993.

Cruz, M. *Narratividad*. Barcelona, Peninsula, 1986.
Mudrovcic, María Inés. *Rev Latin de Filosof*, 18(2), 377-379, 1992.

Crystal, David. *The Cambridge Encyclopedia of Language*. New York, Cambridge Univ Pr, 1991.
Rée, Jonathan. *Rad Phil*, 61, 46-47, Sum 92.

Culler, Jonathan. *Framing the Sign*. Cambridge, Blackwell, 1988.
Wandel, Lee Palmer. *Hist Euro Ideas*, 14(4), 591-595, Jl 92.

Cumming, Robert Denoon. *Phenomenology and Deconstruction*. Chicago, Univ of Chicago Pr, 1991.
Lilly, Reginald. *Int Phil Quart*, 33(3), 368-370, S 93.
Schalow, Frank. *Can Phil Rev*, 12(2), 91-93, Ap 92.

Cummins, Robert. *Meaning and Mental Representation*. Cambridge, MIT Pr, 1989.
Millikan, Ruth Garrett. *Phil Rev*, 101(2), 422-425, Ap 92.

Cupitt, Don. *What is a Story?*. London, SCM Pr, 1991.
Loughlin, Gerard. *Heythrop J*, 34(4), 446-447, O 93.

Curd, Martin (ed). *Argument and Analysis*. St Paul, West, 1992.
Kelly, Stewart. *Teach Phil*, 16(1), 69-71, Mr 93.

Curley, Edwin (ed) and Moreau, Pierre-François (ed). *Spinoza: Issues and Directions*. Leiden, Brill, 1990.
Robinson, Amy. *J Hist Phil*, 31(2), 291-293, Ap 93.

Currie, Gregory. *An Ontology of Art*. New York, St Martin's Pr, 1989.
Wolterstorff, Nicholas. *J Aes Art Crit*, 49(1), 79-81, Wint 91.

Currie, Gregory. *The Nature of Fiction*. New York, Cambridge Univ Pr, 1990.
Eaton, Marcia Muelder. *J Aes Art Crit*, 50(1), 67-68, Wint 92.
Feagin, Susan L. *Phil Rev*, 101(4), 948-950, O 92.
Lamarque, Peter. *Phil Quart*, 43(171), 253-256, Ap 93.

Cushing, James T. *Theory Construction and Selection in Modern Physics*. New York, Cambridge Univ Pr, 1990.
Franklin, Allan. *Brit J Phil Sci*, 43(3), 431-433, S 92.

Cutter, M A Gardell (ed) and Shelp, E E (ed). *Competency: A Study of Informal Competency Determinations in Primary Care*. Dordrecht, Kluwer, 1991.
Yates, Giles. *Hume Stud*, 19(1), 440-443, Ap 93.

D'Amato, Anthony. *Justice and the Legal System*. Cincinnati, Anderson, 1992.
Kelly, Robert Q. *Vera Lex*, 12(1), 23-24, 1992.

D'Amico, Robert. *Historicism and Knowledge*. New York, Routledge, 1989.
Fell, Albert. *Can Phil Rev*, 12(3), 179-181, J-Jl 92.

D'Costa, Gavin (ed). *Christian Uniqueness Reconsidered*. Hertfordshire, Orbis, 1990.
Burrell, David. *Mod Theol*, 8(3), 308-310, Jl 92.
Phan, Peter C. *Thomist*, 56(2), 361-363, Ap 92.

DaFonseca, Eduardo Giannetti. *Beliefs in Action*. New York, Cambridge Univ Pr, 1991.
Tribe, Keith. *Hist Polit Thought*, 13(1), 181-182, Spr 92.

Dahlstrom, Daniel O. *Nature and Scientific Method*. Washington, Cath Univ Amer Pr, 1991.
Grant, Edward. *Rev Metaph*, 46(1), 149-151, S 92.
Landen, Laura L. *Thomist*, 56(2), 351-355, Ap 92.

Dahlstrom, Daniel O (ed). *Philosophy and Art*. Washington, Cath Univ Amer Pr, 1991.
Locke, Patricia M. *Rev Metaph*, 45(4), 849-850, J 92.

Dales, Richard C. *Medieval Discussion of the Eternity of the World*. Leiden, Brill, 1990.
Brown, Stephen F. *J Hist Phil*, 30(2), 296-297, Ap 92.
Welten, Willibrord. *Gregorianum*, 74(1), 187-188, 1993.

Dalgarno, Melvin (ed) and Matthews, Eric (ed). *The Philosophy of Thomas Reid*. Dordrecht, Kluwer, 1989.
Yolton, John W. *Int Stud Phil*, 24(1), 89-90, 1992.

Dallery, Arleen B (ed) and Scott, Charles E (ed). *Crises in continental philosophy*. Albany, SUNY Pr, 1990.
Weis, Gregory F. *J Value Inq*, 26(3), 453-458, Jl 92.

Dallmayr, Fred. *Between Frankfurt and Freiburg*. Amherst, Univ of Mass Pr, 1991.
Braaten, Jane. *Int Phil Quart*, 33(2), 246-249, Je 93.
Pippin, Robert B. *Polit Theory*, 21(2), 322-325, My 93.

Daly, Marin and Wilson, Margo. *Homicide*. Hawthorne, Aldine, 1988.
De Sousa, Ronald. *Biol Phil*, 7(2), 237-250, Ap 92.

Dancy, Jonathan (ed), Moravcsik, J M E (ed) and Taylor, C C W (ed). *Human Agency*. Stanford, Stanford Univ Pr, 1988.
Forguson, Lynd. *J Aes Art Crit*, 48(1), 97-99, Wint 90.

Dancy, R M. *Two Studies in the Early Academy*. Albany, SUNY Pr, 1991.
Barnes, Jonathan. *J Hist Phil*, 31(2), 280-282, Ap 93.
Curd, Patricia Kenig. *Rev Metaph*, 46(3), 605-607, Mr 93.
Tarrant, Harold. *Phil Rev*, 102(3), 399-401, Jl 93.

Daniels, Norman. *Am I My Parents' Keeper?*. New York, Oxford Univ Pr, 1988.
Forrester, Mary. *Nous*, 26(2), 272-275, J 92.
Sterba, James P. *Phil Rev*, 101(2), 479-481, Ap 92.

Daniels, Norman. *Thomas Reid's "Inquiry"*. Stanford, Stanford Univ Pr, 1989.
Yolton, John W. *Int Stud Phil*, 24(1), 89-90, 1992.

Dannenberg, Lutz. *Methodologien, Struktur, Aufbau und Evaluation*. Berlin, Duncker Humblot, 1989.
Danneberg, Lutz. *Erkenntnis*, 38(2), 285-288, Mr 93.

Danto, Arthur C. *Beyond the Brillo Box*. New York, Farrar-Straus-Giroux, 1992.
Carrier, David. *J Aes Art Crit*, 51(3), 513-515, Sum 93.

Darnell, Regna. *Edward Sapir: Linguist, Anthropologist, Humanist*. Berkeley, Univ of Calif Pr, 1990.
Macmillan, Robert. *Phil Soc Sci*, 23(1), 130-132, Mr 93.

Dasenbrock, Reed Way (ed). *Redrawing the Lines*. Minneapolis, Univ of Minn Pr, 1989.
Roth, Paul A. *J Aes Art Crit*, 49(2), 180-183, Spr 91.

Dauenhauer, Bernard P (ed). *Textual Fidelity and Textual Disregard*. New York, Lang, 1990.
McArthur, D. *J Brit Soc Phenomenol*, 23(2), 193-194, M 92.

Dauer, Francis Watanabe. *Critical Thinking*. New York, Oxford Univ Pr, 1989.
Henry, Desmond Paul. *Hist Phil Log*, 13(2), 243-245, 1992.

Davie, George. *The Scottish Enlightenment and Other Essays*. Edinburgh, Polygon, 1990.
Tomassi, Paul. *Phil Invest*, 15(4), 372-375, O 92.

Davies, Stephen. *Definitions of Art*. Ithaca, Cornell Univ Pr, 1991.
Lamarque, Peter. *Brit J Aes*, 33(3), 286-287, Jl 93.
Moore, Ronald. *J Aes Art Crit*, 50(2), 155-157, Spr 92.
Newman, Ira. *Can Phil Rev*, 12(3), 181-183, J-Jl 92.

Davies, Steven (ed). *Pragmatics*. New York, Oxford Univ Pr, 1991.
Bryans, Joan. *Can Phil Rev*, 12(3), 184-186, J-Jl 92.

Davis, Lennard J (ed) and Mirabella, M Bella (ed). *Left Politics and the Literary Profession*. New York, Columbia Univ Pr, 1990.
Fischer, Michael. *J Aes Art Crit*, 50(2), 157-159, Spr 92.

Davis, R E. *Truth, Deduction, and Computation*. New York, Computer Science Pr, 1989.
Goodman, Nicolas D. *J Sym Log*, 57(2), 760-761, J 92.

Davis, Stephen T (ed). *Death and Afterlife*. New York, St Martin's Pr, 1989.
Vallicella, William F. *Int J Phil Relig*, 32(1), 61-62, Ag 92.

Davis, Steven. *Pragmatics: A Reader*. New York, Oxford Univ Pr, 1991.
Vallée, R. *Philosophiques*, 19(1), 157-162, 1992.

Davis, Walter A. *Inwardness and Existence*. Madison, Univ of Wisconsin Pr, 1989.
Thompson, David M. *Phil Lit*, 16(2), 390-391, O 92.

Davis, Wayne A. *An Introduction to Logic (Response to Blum)*. Englewood Cliffs, Prentice Hall, 1986.
Davis, Wayne A. *Philosophia (Israel)*, 22(1-2), 211-218, Ja 93.

De Groot, Jean. *Aristotle and Philoponus on Light*. Hamden, Garland, 1991.
Blakeley, Donald N. *Can Phil Rev*, 13(1), 13-15, F 93.

De Man, Paul. *Critical Writings: 1953-1978*. Minneapolis, Univ of Minn Pr, 1989.
Caron, Elisabeth. *J Aes Art Crit*, 48(2), 177-179, Spr 90.

De Man, Paul. *The Resistance to Theory*. Minneapolis, Univ of Minn Pr, 1986.
Sprinkler, Michael. *J Aes Art Crit*, 46(3), 423-424, Spr 88.

De Wilde, Rein. *Discipline en legende*. Amsterdam, Van Gennep, 1992.
Halffman, Willem. *Kennis Methode*, 17(3), 315-319, 1993.

De Wodeham, Adam. *Lectura secunda in librum primum Sententiarum*. St Bonaventure, Franciscan Inst Pub, 1990.
Knuuttila, Simo. *Synthese*, 96(1), 155-159, Jl 93.

Dean, William. *History Making History*. Albany, SUNY Pr, 1988.
Mangina, Joseph L. *Thomist*, 56(3), 540-545, Jl 92.

DeBeer, E S (ed). *The Correspondence of John Locke, Letters 3287-3648, Volume VIII*. New York, Clarendon/Oxford Pr, 1989.
Kroll, Richard. *Hist Euro Ideas*, 14(4), 602-603, Jl 92.

Debord, Guy and Imrie, Malcolm (trans). *Comments on the Society of the Spectacle*. New York, Verso, 1990.
Plant, Sadie. *Rad Phil*, 61, 55, Sum 92.

Delaney, C F. *Science, Knowledge, and Mind*. Notre Dame, Univ Notre Dame Pr, 1993.
Misak, Cheryl. *Trans Peirce Soc*, 29(3), 457-462, Sum 93.

Deledalle, Gérard and Petrilli, S (trans). *Charles S Peirce: An Intellectual Biography*. Amsterdam, J Benjamins, 1990.
Kertész, András. *J Prag*, 18(1), 71-74, Jl 92.
Tejera, V. *J Speculative Phil*, 6(2), 166-169, 1992.

Deleuze, Gilles, Tomlinson, Hugh (trans) and Habberjam, Barbara (trans). *Cinema 1: The Movement Image*. Minneapolis, Univ of Minn Pr, 1986.
Jamieson, Dale. *J Aes Art Crit*, 46(3), 436-437, Spr 88.

DeMolina, Luis and Freddoso, Alfred J (trans). *On Divine Foreknowledge (Part IV of the Concordia)*. Ithaca, Cornell Univ Pr, 1988.
Fischer, John Martin. *Phil Rev*, 101(2), 387-391, Ap 92.

DeMuralt, André. *L'Enjeu de la Philosophie Médiévale*. Leiden, Brill, 1991.
Ewbank, Michael. *Amer Cath Phil Quart*, 66(3), 381-384, 1992.

Dennett, Daniel. *La stratégie de l'interprète*. Gallimard, NRF Essais, Undated.
Faucher, N. *Philosophiques*, 19(1), 162-168, 1992.

Dennett, Daniel C. *Consciousness Explained*. Boston, Little Brown Co, 1991.
Baker, Lynne Rudder. *Rev Metaph*, 46(2), 398-399, 1992.
Block, Ned. *J Phil*, 90(4), 181-193, Ap 93.
Lycan, William G. *Phil Rev*, 102(3), 424-429, Jl 93.

Dent, J H. *Rousseau*. Cambridge, Blackwell, 1988.
De Marneffe, Peter. *Phil Rev*, 101(2), 391-393, Ap 92.

Denyer, Nicholas. *Language, Thought and Falsehood in Ancient Greek Philosophy*. New York, Routledge, 1991.
Curd, P A K. *Rev Metaph*, 47(1), 140-141, S 93.
Hughes, G J. *Heythrop J*, 34(3), 323, Jl 93.
Scanlan, M. *Hist Phil Log*, 13(2), 225-228, 1992.

Derrida, Jacques and Attridge, Derek (ed). *Acts of Literature*. New York, Routledge, 1992.
Cain, William E. *Phil Lit*, 17(1), 160-161, Ap 93.
Newton, K M. *Brit J Aes*, 33(2), 200-202, Ap 93.

Derrida, Jacques, Bennington, G (trans) and Bowlby, R (trans). *Of Spirit: Heidegger and the Question*. Chicago, Univ of Chicago Pr, 1989.
Olkowski, Dorothea. *Int Stud Phil*, 24(3), 137-138, 1992.

Desan, Philippe (ed). *Humanism in Crisis*. Ann Arbor, Univ of Michigan Pr, 1991.
Schwartz, Jerome. *Phil Lit*, 16(1), 229-231, Ap 92.

Descartes, Rene and Voss, Stephen (trans). *The Passions of the Soul*. Indianapolis, Hackett, 1989.
Shalom, Albert. *Can Phil Rev*, 12(1), 15-17, F 92.

Desjardins, Rosemary. *The Rational Enterprise*. Albany, SUNY Pr, 1990.
Pemberton, Harrison J. *Int Stud Phil*, 24(1), 90-91, 1992.

Desmond, Adrian. *The Politics of Evolution*. Chicago, Univ of Chicago Pr, 1989.
McGrew, Roderick E. *Hist Euro Ideas*, 14(2), 287-289, Mr 92.
Rusnock, Andrea. *Sci Tech Human Values*, 18(2), 265-267, Spr 93.

Detlefsen, Michael (ed). *Proof and Knowledge in Mathematics*. New York, Routledge, 1992.
Potter, Michael. *Phil Books*, 34(3), 188-191, Jl 93.
Urquhart, Alasdair. *Can Phil Rev*, 12(4), 237-238, Ag 92.

Detlefsen, Michael (ed). *Proof, Logic and Formalization*. New York, Routledge, 1992.
Potter, Michael. *Phil Books*, 34(3), 188-191, Jl 93.

Detmer, David. *Freedom As A Value*. Peru, Open Court, 1988.
Anderson, Thomas C. *Int J Phil Relig*, 32(2), 121-123, Oct 92.

Detwiler, Bruce. *Nietzsche and the Politics of Aristocratic Radicalism*. Chicago, Univ of Chicago Pr, 1990.
Domino, Brian. *Eidos*, 10(1), 111-115, J-Jl.
Thiele, Leslie Paul. *J Hist Phil*, 30(4), 623-625, O 92.

Devereux, Daniel (ed) and Pellegrin, Pierre (ed). *Biologie, Logique et Métaphysique chez Aristote*. Meudon, CNRS, 1991.
Shields, Christopher. *Can Phil Rev*, 12(2), 94-96, Ap 92.

DeVitoria, Francisco, Pagden, Anthony (ed) and Lawrance, Jeremy (ed). *Political Writings*. New York, Cambridge Univ Pr, 1991.
Hopton, Terry. *Hist Polit Thought*, 13(1), 169-173, Spr 92.
Miller, Clyde Lee. *Can Phil Rev*, 12(6), 393-395, D 92.

Devlin, K. *Logic and Information*. New York, Cambridge Univ Pr, 1991.
Cross, Charles B. *Phil Psych*, 6(2), 207-210, 1993.

DeVrie, Willem. *Hegel's Theory of Mental Activity*. Ithaca, Cornell Univ Pr, 1988.
Amerikas, Karl. *Phil Rev*, 101(2), 399-401, Ap 92.

Dewart, Leslie. *Evolution and Consciousness*. Toronto, Univ of Toronto Pr, 1989.
Nielsen, H A. *Int J Phil Relig*, 32(3), 193-194, D 92.

Dews, Peter. *Logics of Disintegration*. New York, Verso, 1987.
Bell, Desmond. *Hist Euro Ideas*, 14(3), 433-434, M 92.

Deyev, Valery. *Philosophy and Social Theory*. Toronto, Progress, 1987.
Adelmann, F J. *Stud Soviet Tho*, 43(3), 244-245, M 92.

Di Francesco, Michele. *Introduzione a Russell*. Bari, Laterza, 1990.
Grattan-Guinness, I. *Russell*, 12(2), 222-223, Wint 92-93.

Di Giovanni, George (ed). *Essays on Hegel's Logic*. Albany, SUNY Pr, 1990.
Stepelevich, Lawrence S. *Int Stud Phil*, 24(2), 126-127, 1992.

Diamond, Cora. *The Realistic Spirit*. Cambridge, MIT Pr, 1991.
Budd, Malcolm. *Phil Books*, 34(1), 21-22, Ja 93.
Kenyon, J D. *Phil Invest*, 16(3), 243-250, Ap 93.

Diani, Marco (ed) and Ingraham, Catherine (ed). *Restructuring Architectural Theory*. Evanston, Northwestern Univ Pr, 1989.
Wiseman, Mary Bittner. *J Aes Art Crit*, 49(3), 265-268, Sum 91.

Dickey, Laurence. *Hegel*. New York, Cambridge Univ Pr, 1989.
Berry, Christopher J. *Hist Polit Thought*, 12(4), 731-735, Wint 91.

Dickie, George. *Evaluating Art*. Philadelphia, Temple Univ Pr, 1988.
Freeland, Cynthia. *Phil Rev*, 101(2), 486-488, Ap 92.
Lord, Catherine. *J Aes Art Crit*, 48(1), 83-85, Wint 90.

Diffey, T J. *The Republic of Art and Other Essays*. New York, Lang, 1991.
Collinson, Diané. *Brit J Aes*, 33(2), 180-183, Ap 93.
Janaway, Christopher. *Phil Quart*, 43(171), 250-251, Ap 93.

Diffey, Terry. *Tolstoy's What Is Art?*. North Ryde, Croom Helm, 1985.
Chojna, Woijcieh. *J Aes Art Crit*, 46(3), 434-436, Spr 88.

Dilman, Ilham. *Philosophy and the Philosophical Life*. New York, St Martin's Pr, 1992.
Baltzly, Dirk. *Rev Metaph*, 46(2), 399-401, 1992.

Dilworth, Craig. *Scientific Progress*. Dordrecht, Kluwer, 1986.
Gómez, Ricardo J. *Nous*, 26(2), 264-, J 92.

Dilworth, David A. *Philosophy in World Perspective*. New Haven, Yale Univ Pr, 1989.
Perzanowski, Jerzy. *J Speculative Phil*, 7(2), 165-170, 1993.

Dinneen, Francis P (trans). *Peter of Spain*. Amsterdam, J Benjamins, 1990.
Stump, Eleonore. *Hist Phil Log*, 14(1), 111-112, 1993.

Dinshaw, Caroline. *Chaucer's Sexual Poetics*. Madison, Univ of Wisconsin Pr, 1989.
Davidson, Roberta. *Phil Lit*, 16(1), 209-211, Ap 92.

Dinwidy, John. *Bentham*. New York, Oxford Univ Pr, 1989.
Lieberman, David. *Utilitas*, 4(1), 160-162, My 92.

Diprose, Rosalyn (ed) and Ferrell, Robyn (ed). *Cartographies*. Scranton, Unwin Hyman, 1991.
Zutlevics, Tamara. *Austl J Phil*, 70(1), 117-118, Mr.

Dissanayake, Ellen. *What is Art For?*. Seattle, Univ Washington Pr, 1988.
Alland, Alexander. *J Aes Art Crit*, 47(4), 392-393, Fall 89.

Dodds, Michael J. *The Unchanging God of Love*. Fribourg, Ed Univ Fribourg, 1986.
Ford, Lewis S. *Int J Phil Relig*, 33(3), 187-188, Je 93.

Dodson, Edward O and Howe, George F. *Creation or Evolution*. Ottawa, Univ of Ottawa Pr, 1990.
Fleteren, Frederick Van. *Zygon*, 27(3), 344-348, S 92.

Doe, Norman. *Fundamental Authority in Late Medieval English Law*. New York, Cambridge Univ Pr, 1990.
Knafla, Louis A. *Hist Polit Thought*, 13(2), 353-354, Sum 92.

Doering, Detmar. *Die Wiederkehr der Klugheit*. Würzburg, Köningshausen, 1990.
Alter, Peter. *Hist Polit Thought*, 12(3), 542-543, Fall 91.

Doeuff, Michèle. *Hipparchia's Choice*. Cambridge, Blackwell, 1991.
Marshall, S E. *Phil Books*, 34(1), 53-55, Ja 93.

Dolezel, Lubomír. *Occidental Poetics*. Lincoln, Univ of Nebraska Pr, 1990.
Herman, David. *Phil Lit*, 16(2), 397-399, O 92.

Dombrowski, Daniel A. *St John of the Cross*. Albany, SUNY Pr, 1992.
Card Charron, Donna. *Mod Sch*, 70(3), 238-242, Mr 93.

Donaldson, Mara E. *Holy Places are Dark Places*. Lanham, Univ Pr of America, 1988.
Cebik, L B. *Int Stud Phil*, 24(1), 91-92, 1992.

Donaldson, Thomas. *The Ethics of International Business*. New York, Oxford Univ Pr, 1990.
Askonas, Peter. *Heythrop J*, 33(2), 231-232, Ap 92.

Donner, Wendy. *The Liberal Self*. Ithaca, Cornell Univ Pr, 1991.
Gill, Emily R. *Can Phil Rev*, 12(4), 239-241, Ag 92.
Hoag, Robert W. *Phil Books*, 34(2), 89-90, Ap 93.
Wilson, Fred. *Mind*, 102(405), 183-185, Ja 93.

Doob, Penelope Reed. *The Idea of the Labryinth from Classical Antiquity through the Middle Ages*. Ithaca, Cornell Univ Pr, 1992.
Foster, Edward E. *Phil Lit*, 17(1), 142-143, Ap 93.

Dore, Clement. *God, Suffering and Solipsism*. New York, St Martin's Pr, 1989.
Lucas, Billy Joe. *Int J Phil Relig*, 34(1), 60-61, Ag 93.

Dore, Clement. *Moral Scepticism*. New York, Macmillan, 1991.
Hughes, Gerard J. *Phil Books*, 34(1), 42-43, Ja 93.

Double, Richard. *The Non-Reality of Free Will*. New York, Oxford Univ Pr, 1991.
Benson, Paul. *Mind*, 101(402), 364-367, Ap 92.
Cockburn, David. *Phil Quart*, 42(168), 383-388, Jl 92.
Cogan, Robert. *Teach Phil*, 15(2), 199-200, J 92.
Dilley, Frank B. *Int J Phil Relig*, 34(2), 124-125, O 93.
Fischer, John Martin. *Phil Phenomenol Res*, 52(4), 1004-1007, D 92.
Klein, Martha. *Phil Books*, 34(2), 112-114, Ap 93.
Meynell, Hugo. *Heythrop J*, 34(2), 220-221, Ap 93.
Ravizza, Mark. *Phil Rev*, 102(3), 413-415, Jl 93.
Slote, Michael. *Int Stud Phil*, 24(3), 138-139, 1992.
Waller, Bruce N. *Behavior Phil*, 20/2(21/1), 95-97, 1993.

Douglass, R Bruce (ed). *Liberalism and the Good*. New York, Routledge, 1991.
Grasso, Kenneth L. *Int Phil Quart*, 33(3), 371-373, S 93.

Doyal, Len and Gough, Ian. *A Theory of Human Need*. New York, Macmillan, 1991.
Harris, Roger. *Rad Phil*, 61, 39-40, Sum 92.

Draper, Elaine. *Risky Business*. New York, Cambridge Univ Pr, 1991.
Shrader-Frechette, Kristin. *Can Phil Rev*, 12(3), 186-188, J-Jl 92.

Drees, W B. *Beyond the Big Bang*. Peru, Open Court, 1990.
Albright, John R. *Zygon*, 27(4), 459-461, D 92.
Stenger, Victor J. *Free Inq*, 12(3), 55, Sum 92.
Trundle, Robert C. *Mod Sch*, 69(2), 163-165, Ja 92.

Drees, Willem B. *Beyond the Big Bang*. Peru, Open Court, 1990.
Van Till, Howard J. *Zygon*, 27(4), 461-463, D 92.

Drew, Paul (ed) and Wooton, Anthony (ed). *Erving Goffman: Exploring the Interaction Order*. Boston, Northeastern Univ Pr, 1988.
Miller, Thomas G. *Int Stud Phil*, 24(1), 92-93, 1992.

Dreyfus, Hubert L. *Being-in-the-World*. Cambridge, MIT Pr, 1991.
Crowell, Steven Galt. *J Phil*, 90(7), 373-377, Jl 93.
Fell, Joseph P. *J Hist Phil*, 31(2), 306-307, Ap 93.
Okrent, Mark. *Phil Rev*, 102(2), 290-293, Ap 93.
Sepper, Dennis L. *Amer Cath Phil Quart*, 65(4), 505-507, Autumn 91.

Drucker, Thomas (ed). *Perspectives on the History of Mathematical Logic*. Basel, Birkhauser, 1991.
Bunge, Marta. *J Sym Log*, 57(4), 1487-1489, D 92.
Di Francesco, Michele. *Hist Phil Log*, 14(1), 115-116, 1993.
Shapiro, Stewart. *J Sym Log*, 57(4), 1487-1489, D 92.

Drummond, John J. *Husserlian Intentionality and Non-Foundational Realism*. Dordrecht, Kluwer, 1990.
Cobb-Stevens, Richard. *Rev Metaph*, 45(4), 850-852, J 92.

DuBois, Page (ed). *Sowing the Body*. Chicago, Univ of Chicago Pr, 1988.
Berryman, Sylvia. *Personalist Forum*, 8(2), 115-118, Fall 92.

Düsing, Klaus (ed). *Schellings und Hegels Erste Absolute Metaphysik (1801-1802)*. Koln, Dinter, 1988.
Westphal, Kenneth R. *Ideal Stud*, 22(3), 298-299, S 92.

Duff, R A. *Intention, Agency and Criminal Liability*. Cambridge, Blackwell, 1990.
Gillett, Grant. *J Applied Phil*, 10(2), 265-267, 1993.

Duffy, Bruce. *The World as I Found It*. New York, Penguin USA, 1987.
Griffin, Nicholas. *Russell*, 12(1), 79-93, Sum 92.

Dufrenne, Mikel. *In the Presence of the Sensuous*. Atlantic Highlands, Humanities Pr, 1987.
Kaelin, E F. *J Aes Art Crit*, 48(1), 93-94, Wint 90.

Dummett, Michael. *Frege and Other Philosophers*. New York, Clarendon/Oxford Pr, 1991.
Currie, Gregory. *Phil Quart*, 42(168), 373-375, Jl 92.
Grossmann, Reinhardt. *Rev Metaph*, 45(4), 852-854, J 92.
Shieh, Sanford. *J Hist Phil*, 31(2), 303-306, Ap 93.

Dummett, Michael. *Frege: Philosophy of Mathematics*. Cambridge, Harvard Univ Pr, 1991.
Crittenden, Charles. *Rev Metaph*, 46(3), 607-608, Mr 93.
Larson, David. *Phil Math*, 1, 93-96, Mr 93.
Shieh, Sanford. *J Hist Phil*, 31(2), 303-306, Ap 93.
Tiles, Mary. *Philosophy*, 68(265), 405-411, Jl 93.

Dummett, Michael. *The Logical Basis of Metaphysics*. Cambridge, Harvard Univ Pr, 1991.
Gorman, David. *Phil Lit*, 16(2), 405-406, O 92.
Riska, Augustin. *Thomist*, 56(2), 356-358, Ap 92.

Dunn, J Michael (ed) and Gupta, Anil (ed). *Truth or Consequences*. Dordrecht, Kluwer, 1990.
Humberstone, Lloyd. *Austl J Phil*, 70(3), 362-366, S 92.

Dupuis, J. *Jesus Christ at the Encounter of World Religions*. Hertfordshire, Orbis, 1991.
D'Costa, Gavin. *Thomist*, 56(4), 719-723, O 92.

Durbin, Paul T (ed). *Europe, America and Technology*. Dordrecht, Kluwer, 1991.
Wennemann, Daryl. *Mod Sch*, 70(1), 77-78, N 92.

Durbin, Paul T (ed). *Philosophy and Technology, III*. Dordrecht, Kluwer, 1987.
Cuello, César. *Res Phil Technol*, 9, 211-219, 1989.

Dworetz, Steven M. *The Unvarnished Doctrine*. Durham, Duke Univ Pr, 1990.
Holder, Jr, John J. *Trans Peirce Soc*, 29(2), 273-280, Spr 93.
Zuckert, Michael P. *Interpretation*, 21(1), 67-72, Fall 93.

Dworkin, Ronald. *Law's Empire*. Cambridge, Harvard Univ Pr, 1986.
Luizzi, Vincent. *Vera Lex*, 12(1), 33-34, 1992.

Dych, William V. *Karl Rahner*. London, Geoffrey Chapman, 1992.
Endean, Philip. *Heythrop J*, 34(4), 440-442, O 93.

Dyzenhaus, David. *Hard Cases in Wicked Legal Systems*. New York, Oxford Univ Pr, 1991.
Shiner, Roger A. *Can Phil Rev*, 12(2), 97-99, Ap 92.

Eagleton, Terry. *Saints and Scholars*. New York, Verso, 1987.
Griffin, Nicholas. *Russell*, 12(1), 79-93, Sum 92.

Eagleton, Terry. *The Ideology of the Aesthetic*. Cambridge, Blackwell, 1990.
Lord, Timothy C. *Phil Lit*, 16(2), 374-376, O 92.
Shusterman, Richard. *J Aes Art Crit*, 49(3), 259-261, Sum 91.

Eames, Elizabeth R. *Bertrand Russell's Dialogue With His Contemporaries*. Carbondale, So Illinois Univ Pr, 1989.
Rodriquez-Consuegra, Francisco A. *Russell*, 12(1), 93-104, Sum 92.

Earley, Joseph E (ed). *Individuality and Cooperative Action*. Washington, Georgetown Univ Pr, 1991.
Armstrong, Susan J. *Process Stud*, 20(4), 248-252, Wint 91.

Earman, John. *World Enough and Space-Time*. Cambridge, MIT Pr, 1989.
Hoefer, Carl. *Brit J Phil Sci*, 43(4), 573-580, D 92.
Redhead, M L G. *Phil Sci*, 59(4), 718-722, D 92.
Torretti, Roberto. *Phil Rev*, 101(3), 723-725, Jl 92.

Easterling, P E and Knox, B M W. *The Cambridge History of Classical Literature*. New York, Cambridge Univ Pr, 1989.
James, Alan. *Hist Euro Ideas*, 14(3), 427-431, M 92.

Easton, Patricia, Lennon, Thomas M and Sebba, Gregor. *Bibliographia Malebranchiana*. Carbondale, So Illinois Univ Pr, 1992.
Jolley, Nicholas. *Can Phil Rev*, 12(4), 269-271, Ag 92.

Eaton, Marcia Muelder. *Aesthetics and the Good Life*. London, Associated Univ Pr, 1989.
Novitz, David. *J Aes Art Crit*, 49(2), 175-177, Spr 91.

Eaton, Marcia Muelder. *Basic Issues in Aesthetics*. Belmont, Wadsworth, 1988.
Betz, Joseph. *Ideal Stud*, 22(3), 222-223, S 92.
Werhane, Patricia H. *J Aes Art Crit*, 46(3), 424-426, Spr 88.

Ebbinghaus, H D (& other eds). *Logic Colloquium '87*. New York, Elsevier Science, 1989.
Wolenski, Jan. *Stud Log*, 50(1), 168-169, Mr 91.

Ebert, Theodor. *Dialektiker und frühe Stoiker bei Sextus Empiricus*. Göttingen, Vandenhoeck, 1991.
Graeser, Andreas. *Z Phil Forsch*, 46(3), 443-447, Jl-S 92.

Eckersley, Robyn. *Environmentalism and Political Theory*. Albany, SUNY Pr, 1992.
Gaard, Greta. *Environ Ethics*, 15(2), 185-190, Sum 93.

Eco, Umberto. *Interpretation and Overinterpretation*. New York, Cambridge Univ Pr, 1990.
Dutton, Denis. *Phil Lit*, 16(2), 432-437, O 92.
Watson, James R. *Hist Euro Ideas*, 17(4), 523-525, Jl 93.

Eco, Umberto. *The Limits of Interpretation*. Bloomington, Indiana Univ Pr, 1990.
Dolezel, Lubomir. *J Prag*, 19(6), 585-601, Je 93.

Edel, Abraham. *Interpreting Education*. Buffalo, Prometheus, 1989.
Lowe, Florence Conger. *Metaphilosophy*, 23(1-2), 180-186, Ja-Ap 92.

Edelman, John T. *An Audience for Moral Philosophy?*. New York, Macmillan, 1990.
Marshall, S E. *Phil Quart*, 42(169), 513-514, O 92.

Eells, Ellery. *Probabilistic Causality*. New York, Cambridge Univ Pr, 1991.
Davis, Wayne A. *Phil Rev*, 102(3), 410-413, Jl 93.

Eells, Ellery (ed) and Maruszewski, Tomasz (ed). *Probability and Rationality*. Amsterdam, Rodopi, 1991.
Weirich, Paul. *Can Phil Rev*, 12(3), 189-191, J-Jl 92.

Efland, Arthur D. *A History of Art Education*. New York, Teachers College Pr, 1990.
Dobbs, Stephen M. *J Aes Art Crit*, 49(3), 273-275, Sum 91.

Elders, Leo J. *The Philosophical Theology of St Thomas Aquinas*. Leiden, Brill, 1990.
Clarke, W Norris. *J Hist Phil*, 31(2), 282-284, Ap 93.
Stump, Eleonore. *Rev Metaph*, 47(1), 141-143, S 93.

Elders, Léon. *La Doctrine de la Revelation Divine de Saint Thomas D'Aquin*. Vatican City, Lib Ed Vaticana, 1990.
D'Amécourt, Joseph. *Thomist*, 57(1), 141-146, Ja 93.

Eldridge, Richard. *On Moral Personhood*. Chicago, Univ of Chicago Pr, 1989.
Rind, Miles K. *J Aes Art Crit*, 49(2), 169-170, Spr 91.

Ellis, Brian. *Truth and Objectivity*. Cambridge, Blackwell, 1990.
Sankey, Howard. *Phil Quart*, 42(169), 496-499, O 92.
Trout, J D. *Phil Rev*, 102(1), 126-129, Ja 93.

Ellis, John M. *Against Deconstruction*. Princeton, Princeton Univ Pr, 1989.
Stern, Laurent. *J Aes Art Crit*, 48(2), 171-173, Spr 90.

Ellos, William J. *Ethical Practice in Clinical Medicine*. New York, Routledge, 1990.
O'Rourke, Kevin. *Thomist*, 56(2), 358-361, Ap 92.

Elshtain, Jean Bethke. *Just War Theory*. Cambridge, Blackwell, 1992.
Yoder, John H. *Hist Euro Ideas*, 17(2-3), 341-342, Mr-My 93.

Elster, Jon. *Local Justice*. New York, Cambridge Univ Pr, 1992.
Morriss, Peter. *J Applied Phil*, 10(1), 123-125, 1993.

Elster, Jon (ed) and Moene, Karl Ove (ed). *Alternatives to Capitalism*. New York, Cambridge Univ Pr, 1989.
Shearmur, Jeremy. *Phil Soc Sci*, 22(3), 381-384, S 92.

Elzinga, Aant (& other eds). *In Science We Trust?*. Lund, Lund Univ Pr, 1990.
Jennings, Richard C. *Brit J Phil Sci*, 43(4), 561-571, D 92.

Emanuel, Ezekiel J. *The Ends of Human Life*. Cambridge, Harvard Univ Pr, 1991.
Brock, Dan W. *Polit Theory*, 21(4), 705-709, N 93.

Emilsson, Eyjólfur Kjalar. *Plotinus on Sense-Perception*. New York, Cambridge Univ Pr, 1988.
Blumenthal, H J. *Phil Rev*, 101(2), 375-377, Ap 92.

Emmet, Dorothy. *The Passage of Nature*. Philadelphia, Temple Univ Pr, 1992.
Bontekoe, Ron. *Phil Books*, 34(3), 160-161, Jl 93.
McHenry, Leemon B. *Rev Metaph*, 46(2), 401-402, 1992.
Mendus, Susan. *Philosophy*, 68(265), 412-413, Jl 93.
Oliver, Alex. *Mind*, 102(407), 497-500, Jl 93.

Engel, Pascal. *La Norme du Vrai*. Paris, Gallimard, 1989.
Zahar, Elie. *Mind*, 101(403), 559-565, Jl 92.

Engel, Pascal. *The Norm of Truth*. Hertfordshire, Harvester-Wheatsheaf, 1991.
Lauer, Henle. *Phil Books*, 34(2), 103-104, Ap 93.

Engelhardt Jr, H Tristam (ed) and Caplan, Arthur L (ed). *Scientific Controversies*. New York, Cambridge Univ Pr, 1987.
Metcalfe, John. *Phil Soc Sci*, 22(2), 268-271, J 92.

Engelhardt Jr, H Tristram. *Bioethics and Secular Humanism*. London, SCM Pr, 1991.
Blustein, Jeffrey. *Bioethics*, 7(1), 86f-91, Ja 93.
Williams, John R. *Heythrop J*, 34(2), 221-222, Ap 93.

Engelhardt, Jr, H Tristram. *Bioethics and Secular Humanism*. Burlington, Trinity Pr, 1991.
Kurtz, Paul. *Hastings Center Rep*, 22(4), 40, Jl-Ag 92.

Engstler, Achim. *Untersuchungen zum Idealismus Salomon Maimons*. Stuttgart, Frommann-Holzboog, 1990.
Breazeale, Daniel. *J Hist Phil*, 30(2), 311-313, Ap 92.

Eribon, Dider and Wing, Betsy (trans). *Michel Foucault*. Cambridge, Harvard Univ Pr, 1991.
Bell, Desmond. *Hist Euro Ideas*, 17(4), 528-529, Jl 93.

Erickson, Glenn W. *Negative Dialectics and the End of Philosophy*. Durango, Longwood Acad, 1990.
Daniel, Stephen H. *Man World*, 26(2), 219-222, Ap 93.
Sheets-Johnstone, Maxine. *Personalist Forum*, 8(2), 125-128, Fall 92.

Ermann, M David (ed), Williams, Mary (ed) and Gutierrez, Claudio (ed). *Computers, Ethics & Society*. New York, Oxford Univ Pr, 1990.
Danielson, Peter. *Can Phil Rev*, 12(1), 17-19, F 92.

Ermarth, Elizabeth Deeds. *Sequel to History*. Princeton, Princeton Univ Pr, 1991.
Cornis-Pope, Marcel. *Clio*, 22(1), 85-90, Fall 92.

Ernest, Paul. *The Philosophy of Mathematics Education*. Bristol, Falmer Pr, 1991.
Davis, Andrew. *J Phil Educ*, 26(1), 121-126, 1992.
Marshall, Neil. *J Applied Phil*, 9(1), 126-127, 1992.

Gilmour, John C. *Fire on the Earth*. Philadelphia, Temple Univ Pr, 1990.
Jamieson, Dale. *J Aes Art Crit*, 50(2), 164-165, Spr 92.

Ginet, Carl. *On Action*. New York, Cambridge Univ Pr, 1991.
Malpas, Richard. *Phil Rev*, 102(1), 134-136, Ja 93.
Mele, Alfred. *Phil Phenomenol Res*, 52(2), 488-491, Je 92.
Pfeifer, Karl. *Can Phil Rev*, 12(3), 196-199, J-Jl 92.

Ginev, Dimitri. *Grundriss Einer Kritischen Wissenschaftstheorie*. New York, Lang, 1989.
Asenova, Sonja. *Philosophia (Israel)*, 21(3-4), 371-373, Ap 92.

Ginsberg, Robert (ed). *The Philosopher as Writer*. Selinsgrove, Susquehanna Univ Pr, 1987.
Moss, M E. *Ideal Stud*, 22(3), 273-275, S 92.

Girard, René. *A Theater of Envy*. New York, Oxford Univ Pr, 1991.
Goodhart, Sandor. *Phil Lit*, 16(1), 174-176, Ap 92.

Giuntini, R. *Quantum Logic and Hidden Variables*. Munster, BI-Wissenschafts, 1991.
Kilmister, C W. *Hist Phil Log*, 14(1), 129-130, 1993.

Glendon, Mary Ann. *Rights Talk*. New York, Free Pr, 1991.
Schneider, Carl E. *Hastings Center Rep*, 22(2), 43-44, M-J 92.

Glotz, Albert. *Trotsky*. Buffalo, Prometheus, 1989.
Anellis, Irving H. *Stud Soviet Tho*, 44(2), 148-151, S 92.

Gochet, Paul and Gribomont, Pascal. *Logique, Volume I*. Paris, Hermes, 1991.
Jacquette, Dale. *Rev Metaph*, 46(2), 404-405, 1992.

Goehr, Lydia. *The Imaginary Museum of Musical Works*. New York, Clarendon/Oxford Pr, 1992.
Hamilton, Andy. *Phil Books*, 34(3), 186-188, Jl 93.
Sharpe, R A. *Brit J Aes*, 33(3), 292-295, Jl 93.

Goicoechea, David (ed), Luik, John (ed) and Madigan, Tim (ed). *The Question of Humanism*. Buffalo, Prometheus, 1991.
Kolenda, Konstantin. *Free Inq*, 12(2), 55-56, Spr 92.

Goldfarb, Jeffrey C. *The Cynical Society*. Chicago, Univ of Chicago Pr, 1991.
Govier, Trudy. *Can Phil Rev*, 12(1), 25-28, F 92.

Golding, Martin P. *Legal Reasoning*. New York, Knopf, 1984.
Shiner, Roger A. *Vera Lex*, 12(1), 39-40, 1992.

Goldman, Alan H. *Empirical Knowledge*. Berkeley, Univ of Calif Pr, 1988.
Vogel, Jonathan. *Phil Rev*, 101(2), 428-430, Ap 92.

Goldman, Alan H. *Moral Knowledge*. New York, Routledge, 1988.
Mohan, William J. *Int Stud Phil*, 24(1), 99-100, 1992.

Goldman, Alvin I. *Liaisons: Philosophy Meets the Cognitive and Social Sciences*. Cambridge, MIT Pr, 1992.
Moser, Paul K. *Phil Books*, 34(2), 91-94, Ap 93.

Goldman, Lawrence (ed). *The Blind Victorian*. New York, Cambridge Univ Pr, 1989.
Thomas, William. *Utilitas*, 4(1), 167-169, My 92.

Gómez-Lobo, Alfonso. *La ética de Sócrates*. Madrid, Fondo de Cultura, 1989.
Llano, Alejandro. *Rev Metaph*, 46(1), 156-157, S 92.

Gondos-Grünhut, L and Vetö, Miklos (ed). *Die Liebe und das Sein*. Bonn, Bouvier, 1990.
Westphal, Merold. *Int Phil Quart*, 32(3), 386-387, S 92.

Goodin, Robert E. *Motivating Political Morality*. Cambridge, Blackwell, 1992.
Schmidtz, David. *Phil Books*, 34(4), 239-241, O 93.

Gooding, David. *Experiment and the Making of Meaning*. Dordrecht, Kluwer, 1990.
Dieks, Dennis. *Method Sci*, 25(1), 68-71, 1992.

Gooding, David (ed), Pinch, Trevor (ed) and Schaffer, Simon (ed). *The Uses of Experiment*. New York, Cambridge Univ Pr, 1989.
Agassi, Joseph. *Phil Soc Sci*, 22(2), 266-268, J 92.
Hacking, Ian. *Phil Sci*, 59(4), 705-708, D 92.

Goodman, Anthony (ed) and MacKay, Angus (ed). *The Impact of Humanism on Western Europe*. White Plains, Longman, 1990.
Cloudsley, Tim. *Hist Euro Ideas*, 14(4), 603-605, Jl 92.

Goodman, Dena. *Criticism in Action*. Ithaca, Cornell Univ Pr, 1989.
Chisick, Harvey. *Int Stud Phil*, 24(3), 144-145, 1992.

Goodman, L E. *On Justice: An Essay in Jewish Philosophy*. New Haven, Yale Univ Pr, 1991.
Dougherty, Jude P. *Rev Metaph*, 46(3), 614-615, Mr 93.

Goodman, Russell. *American Philosophy and the Romantic Tradition*. New York, Cambridge Univ Pr, 1990.
Anderson, Douglas R. *Trans Peirce Soc*, 28(2), 366-371, Spr 92.
Parker, Kelly. *Rev Metaph*, 46(2), 405-406, 1992.

Goodwin, Barbara. *Justice by Lottery*. Hertfordshire, Harvester-Wheatsheaf, 1992.
Burnheim, John. *Phil Books*, 34(4), 241-242, O 93.

Gordon, Scott. *The History and Philosophy of Social Science*. New York, Routledge, 1991.
Horowitz, Irving Louis. *Hist Euro Ideas*, 17(1), 121-123, Ja 93.

Gormally, Luke (ed). *The Dependent Elderly*. New York, Cambridge Univ Pr, 1992.
Draper, Heather. *J Applied Phil*, 10(1), 126-127, 1993.

Gorman, Michael E. *Simulating Science*. Bloomington, Indiana Univ Pr, 1992.
Fuller, Steve. *Can Phil Rev*, 12(6), 396-398, D 92.

Gosling, Justin. *Weakness of the Will*. New York, Routledge, 1990.
Gosling, Justin. *Heythrop J*, 34(3), 324, Jl 93.

Gosling, Justin. *Weakness of Will*. New York, Routledge, 1990.
Noordhof, Paul. *Mind*, 101(403), 568-571, Jl 92.

Gossman, Lionel. *Between History and Literature*. Cambridge, Harvard Univ Pr, 1990.
Ankersmit, F R. *Clio*, 21(2), 173-185, Wint 92.
Cebik, L B. *Int Stud Phil*, 24(3), 145-146, 1992.
Goldstein, Leon J. *Clio*, 21(2), 171-173, Wint 92.
Rigney, Ann. *Hist Theor*, 31(2), 208-222, 1992.

Gossman, Lionel. *Between History and Literature (Response to Ankersmit)*. Cambridge, Harvard Univ Pr, 1990.
Gossman, Leo. *Clio*, 21(2), 185-187, Wint 92.

Gougeon, Len. *Virtue's Hero*. Athens, Univ of Georgia Pr, 1990.
Gelpi, Donald L. *Clio*, 21(2), 200-205, Wint 92.

Gower, Barry S (ed) and Stokes, Michael C (ed). *Socratic Questions*. New York, Routledge, 1992.
Makin, Stephen. *Phil Books*, 34(4), 223-224, O 93.

Gracia, Jorge J E. *Individuality: An Essay on the Foundations of Metaphysics*. Albany, SUNY Pr, 1988.
Bradshaw, D E. *Int Stud Phil*, 24(1), 100-101, 1992.
Gill, Kate. *Nous*, 27(1), 94-97, Mr 93.

Gracia, Jorge J E. *Philosophy and Its History*. Albany, SUNY Pr, 1991.
Watson, Richard A. *J Hist Phil*, 31(3), 478-480, Jl 93.

Graham, A C. *Disputers of the Tao*. Peru, Open Court, 1989.
Garrett, Mary. *Phil Rhet*, 26(2), 163-167, 1993.
Shun, Kwong-Loi. *Phil Rev*, 101(3), 717-719, Jl 92.

Graham, Daniel W. *Aristotle's Two Systems*. New York, Clarendon/Oxford Pr, 1990.
Gill, Mary Louise. *Rev Metaph*, 46(3), 616-617, Mr 93.
Wians, William. *Ancient Phil*, 12(1), 210-217, Spr 92.

Graham, Gordon. *Living the Good Life*. New York, Paragon House, 1990.
Almond, Brenda. *Phil Quart*, 43(171), 256-259, Ap 93.
Piker, Andrew. *Teach Phil*, 15(3), 267-269, S 92.

Graham, Keith. *Karl Marx, Our Contemporary*. Hertfordshire, Harvester-Wheatsheaf, 1992.
Little, Daniel. *Phil Books*, 34(3), 180-181, Jl 93.
Palshikar, Sanijay. *J Applied Phil*, 10(1), 128-130, 1993.

Graham, Loren R. *Science, Philosophy, and Human Behavior in the Soviet Union*. New York, Columbia Univ Pr, 1987.
Graham, Loren R. *Stud Soviet Tho*, 44(2), 140-142, S 92.

Granfield, David. *The Inner Experience of Law*. Washington, Cath Univ Amer Pr, 1988.
Belliotti, Raymond A. *Int Stud Phil*, 24(1), 101-102, 1992.

Grant, George Parkin. *English-Speaking Justice*. Notre Dame, Univ Notre Dame Pr, 1985.
Grote, Jim. *Res Phil Technol*, 9, 227-231, 1989.

Grant, Patrick. *Literature and Personal Values*. New York, St Martin's Pr, 1992.
Losin, Peter. *Phil Lit*, 17(1), 175-176, Ap 93.

Grayling, A C. *Berkeley: The Central Arguments*. London, Duckworth, 1986.
Winkler, Kenneth P. *Ideal Stud*, 22(3), 300-301, S 92.

Greenawalt, Kent. *Law and Objectivity*. New York, Oxford Univ Pr, 1992.
Brilmayer, Lea. *J Phil*, 90(11), 596-599, N 93.

Greenawalt, Kent. *Speech, Crime, and the Uses of Language*. New York, Oxford Univ Pr, 1989.
O'Neil, Patrick M. *Int Stud Phil*, 24(3), 119-120, 1992.

Greene, Naomi. *Pier Paolo Pasolini*. Princeton, Princeton Univ Pr, 1990.
Anzalone, John. *Phil Lit*, 16(1), 194-195, Ap 92.

Greenspan, Patricia S. *Emotions and Reasons*. New York, Routledge, 1990.
Goldstein, Irwin. *Int Stud Phil*, 24(1), 102-103, 1992.
Morris, Michael K. *Nous*, 26(2), 250-252, J 92.

Greenwood, John D (ed). *The Future of Folk Psychology*. New York, Cambridge Univ Pr, 1991.
Adams, Frederick. *Teach Phil*, 15(4), 385-388, D 92.
Foss, Jeffrey. *Can Phil Rev*, 12(3), 162-166, J-Jl 92.
MacDonald, Cynthia. *Phil Books*, 34(2), 114-116, Ap 93.

Gretlund, Jan Nordby (ed) and Westarp, Karl-Heinz (ed). *Walker Percy*. Jackson, Univ Pr Mississippi, 1991.
Kramer, Victor A. *Phil Lit*, 16(1), 202-203, Ap 92.

Grice, Paul. *Studies in the Way of Words*. Cambridge, Harvard Univ Pr, 1989.
Burge, Tyler. *Phil Rev*, 101(3), 619-621, Jl 92.

Grice, Paul. *The Conception of Value*. New York, Clarendon/Oxford Pr, 1991.
Barnes, Gerald W. *Nous*, 27(1), 366-370, Mr 93.
Rosati, Connie S. *Phil Rev*, 102(2), 267-270, Ap 93.
Wong, David B. *Phil Books*, 34(1), 45-47, Ja 93.

Grier, Philip T (ed). *Dialectic and Contemporary Science*. Lanham, Univ Pr of America, 1989.
Christensen, Darrel E. *Ideal Stud*, 22(3), 225-226, S 92.

Griffin, David Ray. *Evil Revisited*. Albany, SUNY Pr, 1991.
Basinger, David. *Faith Phil*, 10(2), 275-279, Ap 93.
Noddings, Nel. *Process Stud*, 20(3), 179-181, Fall 91.

Griffin, David Ray (ed). *The Reenchantment of Science*. Albany, SUNY Pr, 1988.
Griffin, David Ray. *Zygon*, 27(3), 343-344, S 92.

Griffin, David Ray and Smith, Huston. *Primordial Truth and Postmodern Theology*. Albany, SUNY Pr, 1989.
Ferré, Frederick. *Process Stud*, 21(1), 60-62, Spr 92.

Griffin, James. *Well-Being: Its Meaning, Measurement and Moral Importance*. New York, Clarendon/Oxford Pr, 1986.
Simpson, Evan. *Nous*, 27(1), 83-85, Mr 93.

Griffin, M T (ed) and Atkins, E M (ed). *Cicero: On Duties*. New York, Cambridge Univ Pr, 1991.
Nederman, Cary J. *Hist Euro Ideas*, 14(2), 312-313, Mr 92.

Griffin, Nicholas. *Russell's Idealist Apprenticeship*. New York, Oxford Univ Pr, 1991.
Grattan-Guinness, I. *Mind*, 102(405), 185-187, Ja 93.
Hochberg, Herbert. *Can Phil Rev*, 12(1), 28-30, F 92.
Regan, Tom. *J Hist Phil*, 30(4), 627-629, O 92.
Sullivan, Peter M. *Phil Books*, 33(3), 146-148, Jl 92.

Griffin, Nicholas (ed). *The Selected Letters of Bertrand Russell, Volume I*. New York, Penguin USA, 1992.
Grattan-Guinness, I. *Hist Phil Log*, 13(2), 230-231, 1992.

Griffin, Nicholas. *The Selected Letters of Bertrand Russell, Volume I*. New York, Penguin USA, 1992.
Tait, Katherine. *Russell*, 12(2), 211-222, Wint 92-93.

Griffiths, A Phillips (ed). *A J Ayer*. New York, Cambridge Univ Pr, 1991.
Lowe, E J. *Philosophy*, 68(263), 107-108, Ja 93.

Griffiths, A Phillips (ed). *Wittgenstein Centenary Essays*. New York, Cambridge Univ Pr, 1991.
Kerr, Fergus. *Heythrop J*, 34(4), 473-474, O 93.

Griffiths, Paul J. *An Apology for Apologetics*. Hertfordshire, Orbis, 1991.
Clooney, Francis X. *Mod Theol*, 8(4), 404-406, Oct 92.
D'Costa, Gavin. *Thomist*, 56(4), 719-723, O 92.

Grim, Patrick. *The Incomplete Universe*. Cambridge, MIT Pr, 1991.
Dale, A J. *Mind*, 102(406), 370-373, Ap 93.

Grimaldi, William M A. *Aristotle, Rhetoric II*. Bronx, Fordham Univ Pr, 1988.
Krolikowski, Walter P. *Ancient Phil*, 12(1), 209-210, Spr 92.

Griswold, Jr, Charles L. *Self-Knowledge in Plato's Phaedrus*. New Haven, Yale Univ Pr, 1986.
Brickhouse, Thomas C. *Ancient Phil*, 12(1), 187-189, Spr 92.
Preus, Anthony. *Int Stud Phil*, 24(1), 103-104, 1992.

Grize, Jean-Blaise. *Logique des propositions et des prédicats, déduction naturelle*. Montreuil, Gauthier, 1969.
Gasser, James. *J Sym Log*, 57(4), 1484-1485, D 92.

Grize, Jean-Blaise. *Logique moderne: Fascicle I*. Montreuil, Gauthier, 1969.
Gasser, James. *J Sym Log*, 57(4), 1484-1485, D 92.

Grize, Jean-Blaise. *Logique moderne: Fascicle I (Second Edition)*. Montreuil, Gauthier, 1972.
Gasser, James. *J Sym Log*, 57(4), 1484-1485, D 92.

Grize, Jean-Blaise. *Logique moderne: Fascicle II*. Montreuil, Gauthier, 1971.
Gasser, James. *J Sym Log*, 57(4), 1484-1485, D 92.

Grize, Jean-Blaise. *Logique moderne: Fascicle III*. Montreuil, Gauthier, 1973.
Gasser, James. *J Sym Log*, 57(4), 1484-1485, D 92.

Groarke, Leo. *Greek Scepticism*. Montreal, McGill-Queens U Pr, 1990.
De Olaso, Ezequiel. *J Hist Phil*, 30(3), 446-448, J 92.
Hahn, Robert. *Can Phil Rev*, 12(1), 6-8, F 92.

Grondin, Jean. *Kant: Avant/après*. Paris, Criterion, 1990.
Dufour, M. *Philosophiques*, 19(1), 141-144, 1992.

Grosholz, Emily. *Cartesian Method and the Problem of Reduction*. New York, Clarendon/Oxford Pr, 1991.
Ariew, Roger. *Mind*, 101(402), 376-379, Ap 92.
Shea, William R. *J Hist Phil*, 30(4), 612-613, O 92.

Grossmann, Reinhardt. *The Existence of the World*. New York, Routledge, 1992.
Moreland, J P. *Mind*, 102(407), 504-507, Jl 93.

Grosz, Elizabeth. *Jacques Lacan*. Scranton, Unwin Hyman, 1990.
Ferrell, Robyn. *Austl J Phil*, 70(1), 118-120, Mr.

Günter, Abel (ed) and Salaquarda, Jörg (ed). *Krisis der Metaphysik*. Hawthorne, de Gruyter, 1989.
Elders, L J. *Rev Metaph*, 45(4), 841-842, J 92.

Guerrière, Daniel (ed). *Phenomenology of the Truth Proper to Religion*. Albany, SUNY Pr, 1990.
Casey, David J. *Thought*, 67(266), 339-340, S 92.

Guest, Stephen. *Ronald Dworkin*. Edinburgh, Edinburgh Univ Pr, 1992.
Bix, Brian. *Phil Quart*, 43(173), 569-571, O 93.

Guggisberg, Hans H (ed), Lestrigant, Frank (ed) and Margolin, Jean-Claude (ed). *La liberté de conscience (XVIe-XVIIe siècles)*. Geneva, Droz, 1991.
Dubois, Elfrieda T. *Hist Euro Ideas*, 14(4), 610-611, Jl 92.

Guicciardini, Noccolò. *The Development of Newtonian Calculus in Britain 1700-1800*. New York, Cambridge Univ Pr, 1990.
Jesseph, Douglas. *Phil Sci*, 59(4), 700-701, D 92.

Guitton-Grichka-Igor, Jean. *Dio e la scienza*. Milan, Bompiani, 1992.
Mangiagalli, Maurizio. *Riv Filosof Neo-Scolas*, 84(1), 182-189, Ja-Mr 92.

Gula, Richard M. *Reason Informed by Faith*. Mahwah, Paulist Pr, 1989.
Garcia, J L A. *Amer Cath Phil Quart*, 65(4), 507-511, Autumn 91.

Gunn, Giles. *Thinking Across the American Grain*. Chicago, Univ of Chicago Pr, 1992.
Sartwell, Crispin. *Phil Lit*, 17(1), 170-171, Ap 93.

Gunton, Colin. *The Promise of Trinitarian Theology*. Edinburgh, T & T Clark, 1991.
Lacugna, Catherine Mowry. *Mod Theol*, 9(3), 307-309, Jl 93.
O'Donnell, John. *Heythrop J*, 34(2), 189-190, Ap 93.

Gunton, Colin E. *The Actuality of Atonement*. Grand Rapids, Eerdmans, 1989.
Quinn, Philip L. *Faith Phil*, 9(2), 272-276, Ap 92.

Gupta, Rita. *Essays on Dependent Origination and Momentariness*. Calcutta, Sanskrit, 1990.
Chinchore, Mangala A. *Indian Phil Quart*, 19(3), 261-264, Jl 92.

Gupta, Som Raj. *The Word Speaks to the Faustian Man*. Delhi, Motilal Banarsidass, Undated.
Herman, A L. *Asian Phil*, 3(1), 55-58, Mr 93.

Gurtler, Gary M. *Plotinus: The Experience of Unity*. New York, Lang, 1989.
Clarke, W Norris. *Int Phil Quart*, 33(1), 123-124, Mr 93.

Guthrie, Kenneth Sylvan (trans). *Porphyry's Launching Points to the Realm of Mind*. Grand Rapids, Phanes Pr, 1988.
Bregman, Jay. *Ancient Phil*, 12(1), 240-242, Spr 92.

Gutt, E A. *Translation and Relevance*. Cambridge, Blackwell, 1991.
Malmkjaer, Kirsten. *Mind Lang*, 7(3), 298-309, Fall 92.

Guyer, Paul (ed). *The Cambridge Companion to Kant*. New York, Cambridge Univ Pr, 1991.
Bird, G H. *Phil Quart*, 43(173), 540-543, O 93.
Gregor, Mary. *Rev Metaph*, 46(3), 617-618, Mr 93.
Moulder, James. *S Afr J Phil*, 12(2), 48-49, My 93.

Haase, Wolfgang (ed). *Aufstieg und Niedergang der römischen Welt (A N R W)*. Hawthorne, de Gruyter, 1987.
Narbonne, Jean-Marc. *Arch Phil*, 55(3), 499-501, Jl-S 92.

Habermas, Jürgen. *Erläuterungen zur Diskursethik*. Frankfurt, Suhrkamp, 1991.
Wischke, Mirko. *Z Phil Forsch*, 46(3), 456-458, Jl-S 92.

Habermas, Jürgen and Hohengarten, William Mark (trans). *Postmetaphysical Thinking*. Oxford, Polity Pr, 1992.
Cooper, David E. *Phil Quart*, 43(173), 572-574, O 93.

Habermas, Jürgen and Lawrence, Frederick G (trans). *The Philosophical Discourse of Modernity*. Cambridge, MIT Pr, 1987.
Sepper, Dennis. *Amer Cath Phil Quart*, 65(1), 107-109, Wint 91.

Habermas, Jürgen, Lenhardt, Christian (trans) and Nicholsen, Shierry Weber (trans). *Moral Consciousness and Communicative Action*. Cambridge, MIT Pr, 1990.
Baltas, Aristides. *Phil Sci*, 60(1), 521-523, Mr 93.
Rasmussen, David M. *Phil Quart*, 43(173), 571-572, O 93.
Weberman, David. *Phil Rev*, 101(4), 924-926, O 92.

Habermas, Jürgen and Nicholson, Shierry Weber (ed & trans). *The New Conservatism*. Cambridge, MIT Pr, 1989.
Eastby, John H. *Hist Euro Ideas*, 14(5), 729-733, S 92.

Habermas, Jürgen, Nicholson, Shierry Weber (trans) and Stark, Jerry A (trans). *On the Logic of the Social Science*. Oxford, Polity Pr, 1988.
How, Alan R. *J Brit Soc Phenomenol*, 23(3), 294-296, O 92.

Hacker, P M S. *Wittgenstein: Meaning and Mind, Volume III*. Cambridge, Blackwell, 1990.
Hunter, J F M. *Phil Quart*, 43(173), 552-555, O 93.

Hacking, Ian. *The Taming of Chance*. New York, Cambridge Univ Pr, 1990.
Lambert, Kenneth A. *Hist Euro Ideas*, 17(4), 535-535, Jl 93.

Haffner, Paul. *Creation and Scientific Creativity*. Front Royal, Christendom Pr, 1991.
McDermott, John M. *Int Phil Quart*, 33(2), 244-246, Je 93.

Hager, Fritz-Peter. *Gott und das Böse im antiken Platonismus*. Amsterdam, Rodopi, 1987.
Gerson, Lloyd P. *Ancient Phil*, 12(1), 196-199, Spr 92.

Hahn, L (ed) and Schilpp, P (ed). *The Philosophy of W V Quine*. Peru, Open Court, 1986.
Berg, Jonathan. *Philosophia (Israel)*, 22(1-2), 195-201, Ja 93.
Moore, A W. *Ideal Stud*, 22(3), 271-273, S 92.

Hahn, Lewis (ed) and Schilpp, Paul (ed). *The Philosophy of Georg Henrik von Wright*. Peru, Open Court, 1989.
Moravcsik, J M. *Can Phil Rev*, 12(2), 104-107, Ap 92.

Hahn, Lewis Edwin (ed). *The Philosophy of Charles Hartshorne*. Peru, Open Court, 1991.
Devenish, Philip E. *Process Stud*, 21(2), 130-134, Sum 92.

Haksar, Vinit. *Indivisible Selves and Moral Practice*. Edinburgh, Edinburgh Univ Pr, 1991.
Gruzalski, Bart. *Phil Quart*, 43(171), 260-263, Ap 93.
Noonan, H V. *Philosophy*, 67(261), 409-412, Jl 92.
Puccetti, Roland. *Mind*, 102(405), 187-189, Ja 93.

Hale, Bob. *Abstract Objects*. Cambridge, Blackwell, 1988.
Burgess, John P. *Phil Rev*, 101(2), 414-416, Ap 92.
Hodes, Harold T. *Int Stud Phil*, 24(3), 146-148, 1992.

Halfon, Mark S. *Integrity*. Philadelphia, Temple Univ Pr, 1989.
McFall, Lynne. *Phil Rev*, 101(2), 463-465, Ap 92.

Hallensleben, Barbara. *Communicatio*. Munster, Aschendorff, 1985.
Morerod, Charles. *Rev Thomiste*, 92(4), 925-929, O-D 92.

Haller, Rudolf (ed) and Brandl, Johannes (ed). *Wittgenstein: Eine Neubewertung/ Towards a Re-evaluation*. Vienna, Hoelder-Pich-Temp, 1990.
Wilson, Andrew D. *J Value Inq*, 27(2), 283-284, Ap 93.

Hallett, Garth L. *Essentialism*. Albany, SUNY Pr, 1991.
Raatzsch, Richard. *Erkenntnis*, 39(1), 117-121, Jl 93.

Hallett, Garth L. *Language and Truth*. New Haven, Yale Univ Pr, 1990.
Machina, Kenton. *Nous*, 26(4), 545-548, D 92.

Halper, Edward C. *One and Many in Aristotle's "Metaphysics"*. Columbus, Ohio St Univ Pr, 1989.
Gerson, Lloyd P. *J Hist Phil*, 30(2), 292-294, Ap 92.
Westphal, Kenneth R. *Rev Metaph*, 46(1), 157-160, S 92.

Halper, Jon (ed). *Gary Snyder*. San Francisco, Sierra Club Books, 1991.
Oelschlaeger, Max. *Environ Ethics*, 14(2), 185-190, Sum 92.

Hamilton, Alastair. *John Dee's Natural Philosophy*. New York, Routledge, 1988.
Hamilton, Alastair. *Heythrop J*, 33(2), 216-217, Ap 92.

Hamlyn, D W. *In and Out of the Black Box*. Cambridge, Blackwell, 1990.
Pickles, David. *Mind Lang*, 7(3), 310-313, Fall 92.

Hamlyn, David. *Being a Philosopher*. New York, Routledge, 1992.
Dutton, Denis. *Phil Lit*, 17(1), 185-188, Ap 93.
Hepburn, Ronald. *Phil Books*, 34(4), 231-232, O 93.

Hammond, Michael, Howarth, Jane and Keat, Russell. *Understanding Phenomenology*. Cambridge, Blackwell, 1991.
Bell, David. *Phil Phenomenol Res*, 53(3), 742-745, S 93.
Gorner, Paul. *Phil Quart*, 42(169), 506-509, O 92.
Teichman, Jenny. *Hist Euro Ideas*, 14(3), 456-457, M 92.

Hamnett, Ian (ed). *Religious Pluralism and Unbelief*. New York, Routledge, 1990.
Loughlin, Gerard. *Heythrop J*, 34(1), 78-80, Ja 93.

Hampshire, Stuart. *Innocence and Experience*. Cambridge, Harvard Univ Pr, 1989.
Johnson, Oliver A. *Int Stud Phil*, 24(1), 104-105, 1992.

Hanfling, Oswald (ed). *Philosophical Aesthetics*. Cambridge, Blackwell, 1992.
Bredin, Hugh. *Brit J Aes*, 33(3), 287-288, Jl 93.
Davies, Stephen. *Austl J Phil*, 71(2), 220-222, Je 93.

Hanfling, Oswald. *The Quest for Meaning*. Cambridge, Blackwell, 1987.
Sontag, Frederick. *Int J Phil Relig*, 33(2), 127-128, Ap 93.

Hanfling, Oswald. *Wittgenstein's Later Philosophy*. Albany, SUNY Pr, 1989.
Ambrose, Alice. *Int Stud Phil*, 24(3), 148-149, 1992.
Kerr, Fergus. *Heythrop J*, 33(2), 229-231, Ap 92.

Hankinson, R J (ed). *Method, Medicine and Metaphysics*. Edmonton, Academic, 1988.
Lennox, James G. *Phoenix*, 47(1), 92-94, Spr 93.

Hannay, Alastair. *Human Consciousness*. New York, Routledge, 1990.
Bishop, John. *Nous*, 27(1), 373-377, Mr 93.
Graham, George. *Phil Quart*, 42(169), 504-506, O 92.
Sprigge, T L S. *Phil Phenomenol Res*, 53(1), 236-239, Mr 93.

Hansen, Frank-Peter. *'Das Älteste Systemprogramm des Deutschen Idealismus'*. Hawthorne, de Gruyter, 1989.
Burch, Robert. *Can Phil Rev*, 12(1), 30-33, F 92.

Hansen, Olaf. *Aesthetic Individualism and Practical Intellect*. Princeton, Princeton Univ Pr, 1990.
Harris, Kenneth Marc. *Phil Lit*, 16(1), 216-217, Ap 92.

Hardin, C L. *Color for Philosophers*. Indianapolis, Hackett, 1988.
Mendola, Joseph. *Nous*, 26(4), 504-506, D 92.
Stephens, Lynn. *Behavior Phil*, 19(2), 83-85, Fall/Wint 91.

Hardin, Russell. *Morality Within the Limits of Reason*. Chicago, Univ of Chicago Pr, 1988.
Bedau, H A. *Utilitas*, 4(2), 317-321, N 92.
Postow, B C. *Int Stud Phil*, 24(1), 105-106, 1992.

Harding, Sandra. *Whose Science? Whose Knowledge?*. Ithaca, Cornell Univ Pr, 1991.
Babbitt, Susan. *Phil Rev*, 102(2), 287-289, Ap 93.
Okruhlik, Kathleen. *Can Phil Rev*, 12(4), 249-252, Ag 92.

Hardy, Lee (ed) and Embree, Lester (ed). *Phenomenology of Natural Science*. Dordrecht, Kluwer, 1992.
Bower, E Marya. *Phil Quart*, 43(173), 574-576, O 93.

Hare, R M. *Essays on Religion and Education*. New York, Clarendon/Oxford Pr, 1992.
Flew, Antony. *Philosophy*, 68(265), 418-420, Jl 93.

Hare, R M. *Utilitarianism and Moral Education*. Gainesville, Univ Pr of Florida, 1990.
Hare, R M. *Stud Phil Educ*, 11(3), 197-205, 1992.

Hargrove, Eugene C (ed). *The Animal Rights/Environmental Ethics Debate*. Albany, SUNY Pr, 1992.
Simak, Doug. *Can Phil Rev*, 12(4), 253-255, Ag 92.
Varner, Gary E. *Environ Ethics*, 15(3), 279-282, Fall 93.

Harpham, Edward J (ed). *John Locke's Two Treatises of Government*. Lawrence, Univ Pr Kansas, 1992.
Thompson, Martyn P. *Hist Polit Thought*, 13(2), 372-373, Sum 92.

Harré, Rom. *Physical Being*. Cambridge, Blackwell, 1991.
Baxter, Brian. *Phil Books*, 34(3), 156-157, Jl 93.

Harris, Errol E. *Cosmos and Anthropos*. Atlantic Highlands, Humanities Pr, 1991.
Peterson, Mark C E. *Owl Minerva*, 24(2), 227-230, Spr 93.

Harris, Errol E. *Formal, Transcendental and Dialectical Thinking*. Albany, SUNY Pr, 1987.
Klempner, Geoffrey. *Bull Hegel Soc Gt Brit*, 23-24, 100-105, 1991.

Harris, Errol E. *Spinoza's Philosophy: An Outline*. Atlantic Highlands, Humanities Pr, 1992.
Robinson, Amy. *Rev Metaph*, 46(3), 618-620, Mr 93.

Harris, John. *Wonderwoman and Superman*. New York, Oxford Univ Pr, 1992.
Almond, Brenda. *Philosophy*, 68(264), 248-250, Ap 93.

Harris, Wendell V. *Dictionary of Concepts in Literary Criticism and Theory*. Westport, Greenwood Pr, 1992.
Dutton, Denis. *Phil Lit*, 17(1), 188-189, Ap 93.

Harris, Wendell V. *Interpretive Acts*. New York, Oxford Univ Pr, 1988.
Pradhan, Shekhar. *J Aes Art Crit*, 48(2), 169-171, Spr 90.

Harrison, Andrew (ed). *Philosophy and the Visual Arts*. Dordrecht, Kluwer, 1987.
Iseminger, Gary. *J Aes Art Crit*, 47(2), 191-193, Spr 89.

Harrison, Bernard. *Inconvenient Fictions*. New Haven, Yale Univ Pr, 1991.
Gaskin, Richard. *Brit J Aes*, 33(2), 177-179, Ap 93.
Lloyd, Genevieve. *Rad Phil*, 61, 37-38, Sum 92.
Neill, Alex. *J Aes Art Crit*, 50(4), 345-347, Fall 92.
Warner, Martin. *Philosophy*, 68(263), 105-107, Ja 93.

Harrison, Carol. *Beauty and Revelation in the Thought of St Augustine*. New York, Clarendon/Oxford Pr, 1992.
Brinkman, B R. *Heythrop J*, 34(3), 316-318, Jl 93.

Hart, Hendrik and Nielsen, Kai. *Search for Community in a Withering Tradition*. Lanham, Univ Pr of America, 1990.
Rossouw, G J. *S Afr J Phil*, 12(1), 19-21, F 93.

Hart, Kevin. *The Trespass of the Sign*. New York, Cambridge Univ Pr, 1989.
MacQuarrie, John. *Int Stud Phil*, 24(3), 149-150, 1992.

Hartigan, Richard Shelly. *The Future Remembered*. Notre Dame, Univ Notre Dame Pr, 1988.
Dalcourt, Gerard J. *Vera Lex*, 12(1), 28-30, 1992.

Hartle, Anthony E. *Moral Issues in Military Decision Making*. Lawrence, Univ Pr Kansas, 1989.
Davenport, Manuel. *SW Phil Rev*, 8(1), 189-191, Ja 92.

Hartman, Geoffrey H. *Minor Prophecies*. Cambridge, Harvard Univ Pr, 1991.
Prince, Gerald. *Phil Lit*, 17(1), 169-170, Ap 93.

Hartshorne, Charles. *Wisdom as Moderation*. Albany, SUNY Pr, 1987.
Mowry, David N. *Ideal Stud*, 22(3), 275, S 92.

Hartshorne, M Holmes. *Kierkegaard, Godly Deceiver*. New York, Columbia Univ Pr, 1990.
Ferreira, M Jamie. *Int J Phil Relig*, 32(3), 190-193, D 92.
Martinez, Roy. *J Value Inq*, 26(3), 449-452, Jl 92.

Harvey, Peter. *An Introduction to Buddhism*. New York, Cambridge Univ Pr, 1990.
Hull, Monte S. *Teach Phil*, 15(2), 201-203, J 92.

Harvey, Robert. *Search for a Father*. Ann Arbor, Univ of Michigan Pr, 1991.
Brosman, Catharine Savage. *Phil Lit*, 17(1), 150-152, Ap 93.

Harwood, John T (ed). *The Early Essays and Ethics of Robert Boyle*. Carbondale, So Illinois Univ Pr, 1991.
Wojcik, Jan. *J Hist Phil*, 31(1), 135-137, Ja 93.

Hasker, William. *God, Time and Knowledge*. Ithaca, Cornell Univ Pr, 1989.
Freddoso, Alfred J. *Faith Phil*, 10(1), 99-107, Ja 93.
Leftow, Brian. *Phil Rev*, 101(2), 444-446, Ap 92.

Hatfield, Gary. *The Natural and the Normative*. Cambridge, MIT Pr, 1991.
Compton, John J. *Rev Metaph*, 46(2), 406-408, 1992.
Falkenstein, Lorne. *Phil Phenomenol Res*, 53(2), 476-480, Je 93.
Fullinwider, S P. *Stud Hist Phil Sci*, 24(3), 485-491, Ag 93.
Longuet-Higgins, Christopher. *Phil Quart*, 42(168), 395-396, Jl 92.

Hattiangadi, J N. *How is Language Possible?*. Peru, Open Court, 1987.
Lugg, Andrew. *Phil Sci*, 59(4), 715-716, D 92.

Hausman, Carl R. *Metaphor and Art*. New York, Cambridge Univ Pr, 1989.
Eveling, Stanley. *J Aes Art Crit*, 49(1), 90-92, Wint 91.

Kainz, Howard P. *The Philosophy of Man*. Lanham, Univ Pr of America, 1989.
Hardy, Gilbert G. *Amer Cath Phil Quart*, 65(2), 247-248, Spr 91.

Kaiser, Christopher. *Creation and the History of Science*. Grand Rapids, Eerdmans, 1991.
Russell, Colin A. *Zygon*, 28(3), 393-395, S 93.

Kalupahana, David J. *A History of Buddhist Philosophy*. Honolulu, Univ of Hawaii Pr, 1992.
Hoffman, Frank J. *Relig Stud*, 29(3), 408-411, S 93.

Kamp, Andreas. *Petrarcas philosophisches Programm*. New York, Lang, 1989.
Burke, Ann-Kathrin. *Conceptus*, 25(66), 121-122, 1991.

Kant, Immanuel. *Aphorismes sur l'art de vivre*. Paris, Du Rocher, 1990.
Boissinot, Christian. *Laval Theol Phil*, 48(3), 481-487, O 92.

Kant, Immanuel. *Correspondance*. Paris, Gallimard, 1991.
Boissinot, Christian. *Laval Theol Phil*, 48(3), 481-487, O 92.

Kant, Immanuel and Gregor, Mary (trans). *The Metaphysics of Morals*. New York, Cambridge Univ Pr, Undated.
Moulder, James. *S Afr J Phil*, 12(2), 48-49, My 93.

Kaplan, Yosef and Loewe, Raphael (trans). *From Christianity to Judaism*. New York, Oxford Univ Pr, 1989.
Kaplan, Yosef. *J Hist Phil*, 30(2), 301-302, Ap 92.

Katz, J J. *The Metaphysics of Meaning*. Cambridge, MIT Pr, 1990.
Bix, Brian. *Mind*, 102(407), 512-515, Jl 93.
Coates, Paul. *Phil Books*, 33(3), 161-163, Jl 92.
Gibson, Roger F. *Phil Psych*, 5(2), 230-232, 1992.
Kornblith, Hilary. *Mind Mach*, 3(2), 239-241, My 93.

Kaufman-Osborne, Timothy V. *Politics/Sense/Experience*. Ithaca, Cornell Univ Pr, 1991.
Calore, Gary. *Trans Peirce Soc*, 29(2), 280-287, Spr 93.

Kaulbach, Friedrich. *Philosophie des Perspektivismus*. Tübingen, Mohr, 1990.
Gut, Bernardo. *Int Stud Phil*, 24(2), 128-129, 1992.

Kavanagh, Thomas M (ed). *The Limits of Theory*. Stanford, Stanford Univ Pr, 1989.
Koelb, Clayton. *J Aes Art Crit*, 48(3), 254-256, Sum 90.

Kaye, Howard L. *The Social Meaning of Modern Biology*. New Haven, Yale Univ Pr, 1986.
Smit, Harry E. *Phil Soc Sci*, 22(4), 531-534, D 92.

Kaye, Richard. *Models of Peano Arithmetic*. New York, Oxford Univ Pr, 1991.
Kirby, Laurence. *Notre Dame J Form Log*, 33(3), 461-463, Sum 92.

Kearney, Richard. *Poetics of Imagining*. New York, HarperCollins, 1991.
Kujundzic, Nebosja. *Eidos*, 10(1), 105-109, J-Jl.

Kearney, Richard. *The Wake of Imagination*. Minneapolis, Univ of Minn Pr, 1989.
Lawlor, Leonard. *J Aes Art Crit*, 48(2), 179-181, Spr 90.

Keeling, Michael. *The Foundations of Christian Ethics*. Edinburgh, Clark, 1990.
Hoose, Bernard. *Heythrop J*, 33(4), 475-476, O 92.

Keiji, Nishitani, Parkes, Graham (trans) and Aihara, Setsuko (trans). *The Self-Overcoming of Nihilism*. Albany, SUNY Pr, 1990.
Lai, Whalen. *Phil East West*, 42(3), 542-546, Jl 92.

Kellenberger, James. *God-Relationships With and Without God*. New York, St Martin's Pr, 1989.
Runzo, Joseph. *Faith Phil*, 10(1), 124-128, Ja 93.

Kellner, Douglas. *Critical Theory, Marxism and Modernity*. Baltimore, Johns Hopkins U Pr, 1989.
Anderson, Kevin. *Stud Soviet Tho*, 44(2), 144-148, S 92.

Kellner, Douglas. *Jean Baudrillard: From Marxism to Postmodernism and Beyond*. Stanford, Stanford Univ Pr, 1989.
Krips, Henry. *Phil Soc Sci*, 23(3), 390-395, S 93.

Kellner, Douglas (ed). *Postmodernism/Jameson/Critique*. Washington, Maisonneuve Pr, 1989.
Genosko, Gary. *Phil Soc Sci*, 23(1), 127-130, Mr 93.

Kellner, Menachem. *Dogma in Medieval Jewish Thought*. New York, Oxford Univ Pr, 1986.
Ivry, Alfred L. *Int Stud Phil*, 24(1), 111-112, 1992.

Kelly, Geffrey B (ed) and Nelson, F Burton (ed). *A Testament to Freedom*. New York, HarperCollins, 1990.
Marsh, Charles. *Mod Theol*, 9(1), 95-97, Ja 93.

Kelly, George Armstrong. *The Humane Comedy*. New York, Cambridge Univ Pr, 1992.
Mitchell, Harvey. *Hist Polit Thought*, 13(2), 360-364, Sum 92.

Kelly, Michael (ed). *Hermeneutics and Critical Theory in Ethics and Politics*. Cambridge, MIT Pr, 1990.
Gardiner, Michael. *Rad Phil*, 61, 47-48, Sum 92.
Parkin, Chris. *Phil Lit*, 16(1), 192-193, Ap 92.

Kelly, P J. *Utilitarianism and Distributive Justice*. New York, Clarendon/Oxford Pr, 1990.
Callaghan, John. *Hist Euro Ideas*, 14(5), 739-742, S 92.
Harrison, Ross. *Mind*, 101(403), 571-573, Jl 92.
Lyons, David. *Utilitas*, 4(2), 323-328, N 92.

Kemal, Salim. *Kant and Fine Art*. New York, Clarendon/Oxford Pr, 1986.
Rogerson, Kenneth F. *J Aes Art Crit*, 47(2), 179-180, Spr 89.

Kemal, Salim. *The Poetics of Alfarabi and Avicenna*. Leiden, Brill, 1991.
Druart, Thérèse-Anne. *Rev Metaph*, 46(3), 622-623, Mr 93.
Morewedge, Parviz. *J Hist Phil*, 30(4), 605-608, O 92.

Kemp, Anthony. *The Estrangement of the Past*. New York, Oxford Univ Pr, 1991.
Burke, Peter. *Hist Euro Ideas*, 17(1), 111-112, Ja 93.

Kemp, Martin. *The Science of Art*. New Haven, Yale Univ Pr, 1990.
Gash, John. *Brit J Aes*, 32(3), 277-279, Jl 92.

Kennedy, George A (ed). *The Cambridge History of Literary Criticism (Volume 1)*. New York, Cambridge Univ Pr, 1989.
Peradotto, John. *Amer J Philo*, 113(3), 473-476, Fall 92.

Kenny, Anthony. *Aquinas on Mind*. New York, Routledge, 1993.
Ross, James F. *Phil Quart*, 43(173), 534-537, O 93.

Kenny, Anthony. *The Ivory Tower*. Cambridge, Blackwell, 1985.
Hattingh, J P. *S Afr J Phil*, 11(3), 75-76, Ag 92.

Kenny, Athony. *Aristotle on the Perfect Life*. New York, Clarendon/Oxford Pr, 1992.
Hamlyn, D W. *Philosophy*, 68(264), 250-252, Ap 93.

Ker, Ian (ed) and Hill, Alan G (ed). *Newman After A Hundred Years*. New York, Clarendon/Oxford Pr, 1990.
Barber, Michael C. *Heythrop J*, 33(4), 465-466, O 92.

Kerby, Anthony Paul. *Narrative and the Self*. Bloomington, Indiana Univ Pr, 1991.
Bachrach, Jay E. *Can Phil Rev*, 12(2), 110-112, Ap 92.

Kersten, Fred. *Phenomenological Method*. Dordrecht, Kluwer, 1989.
Drummond, J J. *Husserl Stud*, 9(3), 219-226, 1992.

Ketner, Kenneth Laine (ed) and Peirce, Charles Sanders. *Reasoning and the Logic of Things*. Cambridge, Harvard Univ Pr, 1992.
Nubiola, Jaime. *Phil Quart*, 43(173), 547-548, O 93.

Kevelson, Roberta (ed). *Peirce and Law*. New York, Lang, 1991.
Niiniluoto, Ilkka. *Trans Peirce Soc*, 29(2), 287-292, Spr 93.

Kevles, Daniel J (ed) and Hood, Leroy (ed). *The Code of Codes*. Cambridge, Harvard Univ Pr, 1992.
Saunders, Jr, Robert S. *Nat Forum*, 73(2), 47-48, Spr 93.

Kevorkian, Jack. *Prescription*. Buffalo, Prometheus, 1991.
Rachels, James. *Bioethics*, 6(3), 258-263, Jl 92.

Kher, Chitrarekha. *Buddhism as Presented by the Brahmanical Systems*. Delhi, Sadguru, 1992.
Chinchore, Mangala R. *Indian Phil Quart*, 20(1), 121-123, Ja 93.

Kimmerle, Heinz. *Philosophie in Afrika*. Frankfurt, Ed Qumran, 1991.
Hoffmann, Gerd-Rüdiger. *Quest*, 6(1), 78-83, J 92.

King-Farlow, John and O'Connell, Sean. *Self-Conflict and Self-Healing*. Lanham, Univ Pr of America, 1988.
Vaught, Carl G. *Ideal Stud*, 22(3), 294-295, S 92.

Kirmmse, Bruce. *Kierkegaard in Golden Age Denmark*. Bloomington, Indiana Univ Pr, 1990.
Donnelly, John. *Rev Metaph*, 46(1), 162-164, S 92.

Kirp, David L (ed) and Bayer, Ronald (ed). *AIDS in the Industrialized Democracies*. New Brunswick, Rutgers Univ Pr, 1992.
Levine, Carol. *Hastings Center Rep*, 23(4), 39-40, Jl-Ag 93.

Kirwan, Christopher. *Augustine*. New York, Routledge, 1989.
Clark, Mary T. *Int Stud Phil*, 25(1), 86-87, 1993.
MacDonald, Scott. *Phil Rev*, 101(3), 638-640, Jl 92.
Rist, John M. *J Hist Phil*, 30(3), 451-452, J 92.

Kirwan, James. *Literature, Rhetoric, Metaphysics*. New York, Routledge, 1990.
Coupe, Laurence. *J Brit Soc Phenomenol*, 23(3), 297-298, O 92.

Kitcher, Patricia. *Kant's Transcendental Psychology*. New York, Oxford Univ Pr, 1990.
Guyer, Paul. *Mind*, 102(405), 189-193, Ja 93.
Meerbote, Ralf. *Phil Rev*, 101(4), 862-865, O 92.
Melnick, Arthur. *Phil Sci*, 60(1), 513-515, Mr 93.
Zoeller, Guenter. *J Hist Phil*, 30(4), 619-621, O 92.

Kittay, Feder. *Metaphor, Its Cognitive Force and Its Linguistic Structure*. New York, Clarendon/Oxford Pr, 1987.
Sovran, Tamar. *Philosophia (Israel)*, 21(3-4), 351-360, Ap 92.

Kivy, Peter. *Music Alone, Philosophical Reflections on the Purely Musical Experience*. Ithaca, Cornell Univ Pr, 1990.
Dempster, Douglas. *J Aes Art Crit*, 49(4), 381-383, Fall 91.
Tappolet, Christine. *Mind*, 102(406), 377-380, Ap 93.

Kivy, Peter. *Osmin's Rage*. Princeton, Princeton Univ Pr, 1988.
Stecker, Robert. *J Aes Art Crit*, 48(2), 165-167, Spr 90.

Kivy, Peter. *Sound Sentiment*. Philadelphia, Temple Univ Pr, 1989.
Davies, Stephen. *J Aes Art Crit*, 49(1), 83-85, Wint 91.

Klein, Julie Thoompson. *Interdisciplinarity: History, Theory, Practice*. Detroit, Wayne St Univ Pr, 1990.
Egan, Kieran. *Clio*, 21(2), 190-192, Wint 92.

Klein, Martha. *Determinism, Blameworthiness, and Deprivation*. New York, Clarendon/ Oxford Pr, 1990.
Buss, Sarah. *Phil Rev*, 102(1), 136-138, Ja 93.

Levy, Ze'ev. *David Baumgardt and Ethical Hedonism*. Hoboken, Ktav, 1989.
Lichtigfeld, A. *Int Stud Phil*, 24(1), 114, 1992.

Lewis, Frank A. *Substance and Predication in Aristotle*. New York, Cambridge Univ Pr, 1991.
Loux, Michael J. *Mind*, 102(407), 519-524, Jl 93.
Matthews, Gareth B. *Rev Metaph*, 46(3), 624-625, Mr 93.

Lewis, H A (ed). *Peter Geach*. Dordrecht, Kluwer, 1991.
Baldwin, Thomas. *Philosophy*, 67(261), 414-416, Jl 92.
Humberstone, Lloyd. *Austl J Phil*, 70(3), 366-369, S 92.
McCulloch, Gregory. *Phil Books*, 34(2), 97-100, Ap 93.

Lewis, R W B. *The Jameses*. New York, Farrar-Straus-Giroux, 1991.
Skrupskelis, Ignas K. *Trans Peirce Soc*, 28(4), 892-897, Fall 92.

Lewry, P Osmund (ed). *On Time and Imagination*. New York, Oxford Univ Pr, 1987.
O'Carroll, Maura. *Heythrop J*, 33(3), 345-347, Jl 92.

Lippman, Edward A (ed). *Musical Aesthetics, Volume I*. Stuyvesant, Pendragon Pr, 1986.
Cantrick, Robert B. *J Aes Art Crit*, 51(1), 86-88, Wint 93.

Lippman, Edward A (ed). *Musical Aesthetics, Volume II*. Stuyvesant, Pendragon Pr, 1988.
Cantrick, Robert B. *J Aes Art Crit*, 51(1), 86-88, Wint 93.

Lippman, Edward A (ed). *Musical Aesthetics, Volume III*. Stuyvesant, Pendragon Pr, 1990.
Cantrick, Robert B. *J Aes Art Crit*, 51(1), 86-88, Wint 93.

Lipton, Peter. *Inference to the Best Explanation*. New York, Routledge, 1991.
Harman, Gilbert. *Mind*, 101(403), 578-580, Jl 92.
Knight, David. *Phil Books*, 33(3), 191-192, Jl 92.
Van Evra, James. *Can Phil Rev*, 12(3), 207-208, J-Jl 92.
Vogel, Jonathan. *Phil Rev*, 102(3), 419-421, Jl 93.

List, Charles J and Plum, Stephen H. *Library Research Guide to Philosophy*. Ann Arbor, Pierian Pr, 1990.
Flage, Daniel E. *Teach Phil*, 15(4), 409-411, D 92.

Little, Daniel. *Varieties of Social Explanation*. Boulder, Westview Pr, 1991.
Ruben, David-Hillel. *Phil Rev*, 102(1), 120-122, Ja 93.

Livingston, Donald (ed) and Martin, Marie (ed). *Hume as Philosopher of Society, Politics and History*. Rochester, Univ of Rochester Pr, 1991.
Dimock, Susan. *Can Phil Rev*, 12(2), 112-116, Ap 92.

Livingston, Paisley. *Literary Knowledge*. Ithaca, Cornell Univ Pr, 1988.
Redner, Harry. *Phil Soc Sci*, 23(3), 385-390, S 93.

Llewelyn, John. *The Middle Voice of Ecological Conscience*. New York, Macmillan, 1991.
Brody, Donna H. *J Brit Soc Phenomenol*, 23(3), 288-289, O 92.
Hoose, Bernard. *Heythrop J*, 34(2), 199-201, Ap 93.

Lloyd, A C. *The Anatomy of Neoplatonism*. New York, Clarendon/Oxford Pr, 1990.
Dillon, John. *Int Stud Phil*, 25(1), 91-93, 1993.
Edwards, M J. *Heythrop J*, 34(2), 217-218, Ap 93.

Lloyd, Dan. *Simple Minds*. Cambridge, MIT Pr, 1989.
Anderson, James A. *Behavior Phil*, 19(2), 91-102, Fall/Wint 91.
Gustafson, Donald. *Phil Psych*, 5(2), 221-228, 1992.

Lloyd, Elisabeth A. *The Structure and Confirmation of Evolutionary Theory*. Westport, Greenwood Pr, 1988.
Hull, David L. *Phil Rev*, 101(2), 431-433, Ap 92.

Lloyd, G E R. *Demystifying Mentalities*. New York, Cambridge Univ Pr, 1990.
Bryant, Joseph M. *Phoenix*, 46(3), 276-279, Autumn 92.
Chene, Dennis Des. *Phil Rev*, 101(4), 914-916, O 92.

Lloyd, G E R. *Demystifying Mythologies*. New York, Cambridge Univ Pr, 1990.
O'Hagan, Timothy. *Phil Books*, 34(2), 125-128, Ap 93.

Lloyd, G E R. *Methods and Problems in Greek Science*. New York, Cambridge Univ Pr, 1991.
Bowen, Alan C. *Can Phil Rev*, 12(6), 405-407, D 92.
Osborne, Catherine. *Phil Invest*, 16(3), 255-257, Ap 93.

Lloyd, G E R. *The Revolutions of Wisdom*. Berkeley, Univ of Calif Pr, 1987.
Boylan, Michael. *Ancient Phil*, 12(1), 178-180, Spr 92.

Lloyd, S A. *Ideals as Interests in Hobbes's 'Leviathan'*. New York, Cambridge Univ Pr, 1992.
Airaksinen, Timo. *Can Phil Rev*, 12(5), 340-342, O 92.

Lobban, Michael. *The Common Law and English Jurisprudence 1760-1850*. New York, Clarendon/Oxford Pr, 1991.
Hochstrasser, T J. *Hist Polit Thought*, 13(2), 354-357, Sum 92.

Loche, Annamaria. *Jeremy Bentham e la ricerca del buongoverno*. Milan, Angeli, 1991.
Guidi, Marco. *Utilitas*, 4(1), 162-165, My 92.

Locke, John, Nidditch, Peter H (ed) and Rogers, G A J (ed). *Drafts for the Essay concerning Human Understanding, and Other Philosophical Writings*. New York, Clarendon/Oxford Pr, 1990.
Chappell, Vere. *Int Phil Quart*, 32(2), 258-260, J 92.

Loewer, Barry (ed) and Rey, Geoges (ed). *Meaning in Mind*. Cambridge, Blackwell, 1991.
Smith, Barry C. *Phil Quart*, 43(173), 560-563, O 93.

Loewith, Karl. *From Hegel to Nietzsche*. New York, Columbia Univ Pr, 1991.
Rogers, Robert. *Can Phil Rev*, 12(4), 274-277, Ag 92.

Loewy, Erich H. *Suffering and the Beneficent Community*. Albany, SUNY Pr, 1991.
Smith, David H. *Thinking*, 10(2), 43-44, 1992.

Lonergan, Bernard and Lambert, Pierre (trans). *Pour une méthodologie philosophique*. Montreal, Bellarmin, 1991.
Laberge, Ybes. *Can Phil Rev*, 12(4), 272-274, Ag 92.

Long, Anthony A and Sedley, David N. *The Hellenistic Philosophers: Volume 2*. New York, Cambridge Univ Pr, 1987.
Holgate, David. *S Afr J Phil*, 11(2), 45-46, My 92.

Longhurst, Brian. *Karl Mannheim and the Contemporary Sociology of Knowledge*. New York, Macmillan, 1989.
Rickman, H P. *Phil Soc Sci*, 22(3), 399-401, S 92.

Lord, Carnes (ed) and O'Connor, David K (ed). *Essays on the Foundations of Aristotelian Political Science*. Berkeley, Univ of Calif Pr, 1991.
Simpson, Peter. *Rev Metaph*, 47(1), 156-157, S 93.

Lories, Danielle. *Expérience esthétique et ontologie de l'oeuvre*. Bruxelles, Palais Acad, 1989.
Bouchard, G. *Philosophiques*, 19(1), 155-157, 1992.
Morizot, Jacques. *Rev Metaph Morale*, 97(3), 419-422, Jl-S 92.

Lorraine, Tamsin E. *Gender, Identity and the Production of Meaning*. Boulder, Westview Pr, 1990.
Rothleder, Dianne. *Hypatia*, 7(2), 227-232, Spr 92.

Losurdo, Domenico. *Hegel und Das Deutsche Erbe*. Cologne, Pahl-Rugenstein, 1989.
Hinchman, Lewis. *Int Stud Phil*, 24(2), 129-130, 1992.
Kudrna, Jaroslav. *Filozof Cas*, 40(3), 518-522, 1992.

Loux, Michael. *Primary Ousia*. Ithaca, Cornell Univ Pr, 1991.
Cohen, S Marc. *Phil Rev*, 102(3), 397-399, Jl 93.
Gill, Mary Louise. *J Hist Phil*, 31(2), 278-280, Ap 93.
Halper, Edward C. *Rev Metaph*, 46(3), 625-627, Mr 93.
Lacey, A R. *Phil Quart*, 43(173), 525-527, O 93.
Malcolm, John. *Nous*, 27(1), 386-390, Mr 93.
Scaltsas, Theodore. *Phil Books*, 33(3), 139-142, Jl 92.

Lovekin, David. *Technique, Discourse and Consciousness*. Bethlehem, Lehigh Univ Pr, 1991.
Nordenhaug, E. *Man World*, 26(1), 109-114, Ja 93.
Weyembergh, Maurice. *Hist Euro Ideas*, 17(4), 530-531, Jl 93.

Lowe, E J. *Kinds of Being*. Cambridge, Blackwell, 1989.
Baur, Michael. *Rev Metaph*, 46(1), 166-168, S 92.
Simons, Peter. *Mind*, 101(403), 581-582, Jl 92.

Lowy, Ilana. *The Polish School of Philosophy of Medicine*. Dordrecht, Kluwer, 1990.
Gelwick, Richard. *J Med Human*, 14(1), 39-41, Spr 93.

Loy, David. *Nonduality*. New Haven, Yale Univ Pr, 1988.
Deutsch, Eliot. *Int J Phil Relig*, 32(2), 117-119, Oct 92.

Lucas, J R. *The Future*. Cambridge, Blackwell, 1989.
Helm, Paul. *Int Stud Phil*, 25(1), 93, 1993.

Lucas, Jr, George R. *The Rehabilitation of Whitehead*. Albany, SUNY Pr, 1990.
Neville, Robert Cummings. *J Hist Phil*, 30(4), 629-631, O 92.

Lüdeking, Karlheinz. *Analytische Philosophie der Kunst*. Frankfurt, Athenaum, 1988.
Piepmeier, Rainer. *Int Stud Phil*, 24(1), 114-115, 1992.

Lütterfelds, W. *Fichte und Wittgenstein*. Stuttgart, Klett-Cotta, 1989.
Zenkert, Georg. *Phil Rundsch*, 39(3), 244-248, 1992.

Lycan, William G. *Judgement and Justification*. New York, Cambridge Univ Pr, 1988.
Vogel, Jonathan. *Phil Phenomenol Res*, 53(1), 233-236, Mr 93.

Lycan, William G (ed). *Mind and Cognition*. Cambridge, Blackwell, 1990.
Cling, Andrew D. *Teach Phil*, 15(2), 196-198, J 92.

Lyng, Stephen. *Holistic Health and Biomedical Medicine*. Albany, SUNY Pr, 1990.
Michot-Dietrich, Hela. *Int Stud Phil*, 24(1), 115-116, 1992.

Lyons, William. *The Disappearance of Introspection*. Cambridge, MIT Pr, 1986.
Rosenthal, David M. *Phil Rev*, 101(2), 425-428, Ap 92.

Lyotard, Jean-François. *Peregrinations: Law, Form, Event*. New York, Columbia Univ Pr, 1988.
Ormiston, Gayle L. *J Aes Art Crit*, 48(1), 88-90, Wint 90.

Lyotard, Jean-François and Beakley, Brian (trans). *Phenomenology*. Albany, SUNY Pr, 1991.
Sassower, Raphael. *Can Phil Rev*, 12(4), 278-280, Ag 92.

Lyotard, Jean-François, Bennington, Geoffrey (trans) and Bowlby, Rachel (trans). *The Inhuman*. Stanford, Stanford Univ Pr, 1991.
Sassower, Raphael. *Can Phil Rev*, 12(4), 278-280, Ag 92.

MacCormick, D N (ed) and Summers, R S (ed). *Interpreting Statutes*. Brookfield, Dartmouth, 1991.
Lucy, William. *J Applied Phil*, 9(1), 128-129, 1992.

MacDonald, Cynthia. *Mind-Body Identity Theories*. New York, Routledge, 1989.
Endicott, Ronald P. *Int Stud Phil*, 25(1), 94, 1993.

MacDonald, Scott (ed). *Being and Goodness*. Ithaca, Cornell Univ Pr, 1991.
Brown, David. *Phil Books*, 33(3), 182-183, Jl 92.
Burrell, David. *Faith Phil*, 9(4), 538-543, O 92.
Kruschwitz, Robert B. *Thomist*, 57(1), 150-153, Ja 93.
Wood, Rega. *Can Phil Rev*, 12(1), 44-47, F 92.
Zagzebski, Linda. *Amer Cath Phil Quart*, 66(3), 389-392, 1992.

Macedo, Stephen. *Liberal Virtues*. New York, Clarendon/Oxford Pr, 1990.
Misgeld, Dieter. *Rev Metaph*, 47(1), 157-158, S 93.
Moore, Margaret. *Utilitas*, 5(1), 126-128, My 93.

Machan, Tibor. *Individuals and Their Rights*. Peru, Open Court, 1989.
Langiulli, Nino. *Interpretation*, 20(1), 81-95, Fall 92.
Sweet, William. *Amer Cath Phil Quart*, 65(2), 248-251, Spr 91.

Machan, Tibor R. *The Moral Case for the Free Market Economy*. Lewiston, Mellen Pr, 1988.
Finocchiaro, Maurice A. *Phil Soc Sci*, 22(3), 385-388, S 92.

MacIntyre, Alasdair. *Three Rival Versions of Moral Enquiry*. Notre Dame, Univ Notre Dame Pr, 1990.
Kupperman, Joel J. *Phil Phenomenol Res*, 52(3), 737-740, S 92.
Quirk, Michael J. *Auslegung*, 18(2), 189-193, Sum 92.

MacIntyre, Alasdair. *Whose Justice? Which Rationality?*. London, Duckworth, 1988.
Winch, Peter. *Phil Invest*, 15(3), 285-290, Jl 92.

Macmillan, C J B and Garrison, James W. *A Logical Theory of Teaching*. Dordrecht, Kluwer, 1988.
Floden, Robert E. *Stud Phil Educ*, 11(3), 207-212, 1992.
Macmillan, C J B. *Stud Phil Educ*, 11(3), 223-229, 1992.
Newsome, Jr, George L. *Stud Phil Educ*, 11(3), 213-222, 1992.

MacNiven, Don. *Bradley's Moral Psychology*. Lewiston, Mellen Pr, 1987.
Sprigge, T L S. *Ideal Stud*, 22(3), 287-288, S 92.

MacNiven, Don (ed). *Moral Expertise*. New York, Routledge, 1991.
Hanley, Ken. *Can Phil Rev*, 12(2), 116-118, Ap 92.

Maconie, Robin. *The Concept of Music*. New York, Clarendon/Oxford Pr, 1990.
Burton, Stephan L. *J Aes Art Crit*, 50(1), 82-83, Wint 92.

Macy, Joanna. *Mutual Causality in Buddhism and General Systems Theory*. Albany, SUNY Pr, 1991.
Griffin, David Ray. *Process Stud*, 20(4), 244-248, Wint 91.

Maddy, Penelope. *Realism in Mathematics*. New York, Clarendon/Oxford Pr, 1990.
Bigelow, John. *Hist Phil Log*, 13(2), 235-238, 1992.
Hale, Bob. *J Sym Log*, 57(2), 750-752, J 92.
Lavine, Shaughan. *J Phil*, 89(6), 321-326, J 92.
Weiner, Joan. *Phil Rev*, 102(2), 281-284, Ap 93.

Madison, Gary B. *The Hermeneutics of Postmodernity*. Bloomington, Indiana Univ Pr, 1988.
Daniel, Stephen H. *Man World*, 26(2), 219-222, Ap 93.

Maier, Charles S. *The Unmasterable Past*. Cambridge, Harvard Univ Pr, 1988.
Goldstein, Leon J. *Int Stud Phil*, 25(1), 95, 1993.
Mommsen, Wolfgang J. *Hist Theor*, 31(2), 222-224, 1992.

Mailloux, Steven. *Rhetorical Power*. Ithaca, Cornell Univ Pr, 1989.
Jost, Walter. *Phil Rhet*, 25(2), 198-202, 1992.

Makkreel, Rudolf. *Imagination and Interpretation in Kant*. Chicago, Univ of Chicago Pr, 1990.
Ameriks, S. *Man World*, 25(2), 227-234, Ap 92.
Dörflinger, Bernd. *Kantstudien*, 83(3), 357-364, 1992.
Glenn Jr, John D. *Phil Rev*, 101(4), 871-873, O 92.
Kemal, Salim. *J Aes Art Crit*, 49(4), 388-390, Fall 91.
Nenon, Tom. *J Hist Phil*, 31(1), 145-146, Ja 93.
Stark, Tracey. *Phil Soc Crit*, 18(1), 111-118, 1992.

Malcolm, John. *Plato on the Self-Predication of Forms*. New York, Clarendon/Oxford Pr, 1991.
Hughes, Gerard J. *Heythrop J*, 34(2), 216-217, Ap 93.
Peterson, Sandra. *Phil Rev*, 102(2), 294-296, Ap 93.
Woodruff, Paul. *Rev Metaph*, 47(1), 158-160, S 93.

Malebranche, Nicolas and Riley, Patrick (ed & trans). *Treatise of Nature and Grace*. New York, Clarendon/Oxford Pr, 1992.
Scott, David. *Phil Books*, 34(4), 226-227, O 93.

Malthus, T R. *Principles of Political Economy*. New York, Cambridge Univ Pr, 1989.
Tribe, Keith. *Hist Polit Thought*, 12(3), 546-547, Fall 91.

Manekin, Charles H. *The Logic of Gersonides*. Dordrecht, Kluwer, 1992.
Leaman, Oliver. *Hist Phil Log*, 14(1), 112-113, 1993.

Manno, A G. *Oltre Benedetto Croce*. Napoli, Loffredo, 1992.
Addante, Pietro. *Sapienza*, 46(1), 105-107, 1993.

Mansfield, Bruce. *Interpretations of Erasmus c 1750-1920*. Toronto, Univ of Toronto Pr, 1992.
Teske, Roland J. *Rev Metaph*, 47(1), 160-161, S 93.

Mansfield, Jr, Harvey C. *America's Constitutional Soul*. Baltimore, Johns Hopkins U Pr, 1991.
McWilliams, Wilson Carey. *Polit Theory*, 20(3), 518-523, Ag 92.

Marga, Andrei. *Rationalitate, comunicare, argumentare*. Cluj-Napoca, Dacia, 1991.
Nemoianu, Virgil. *Rev Metaph*, 46(1), 168-169, S 92.

Margolis, Joseph. *Texts without Referents*. Cambridge, Blackwell, 1989.
Lavin, Michael. *Nous*, 27(1), 133-137, Mr 93.

Margolis, Joseph. *The Truth About Relativism*. Cambridge, Blackwell, 1991.
White, F C. *Philosophy*, 67(262), 565-567, O 92.

Marion, Jean-Luc. *Questions cartésiennes*. Paris, Pr Univ France, 1991.
Watson, Richard A. *J Hist Phil*, 30(3), 452-454, J 92.

Marion, Jean-Luc. *Réduction et donation*. Paris, Pr Univ France, 1989.
Benoist, Jocelyn. *Arch Phil*, 55(3), 512-515, Jl-S 92.

Marion, Jean-Luc and Carlson, Thomas A (trans). *God Without Being*. Chicago, Univ of Chicago Pr, 1991.
Crump, Eric H. *Mod Theol*, 9(3), 309-311, Jl 93.
McCarthy, John C. *Rev Metaph*, 46(3), 627-629, Mr 93.

Maritain, Jacques. *The Rights of Man and Natural Law*. New York, Scribner's Sons, 1971.
Sand, G W. *Vera Lex*, 11(2), 39, 1991.

Marquard, Odo. *Odo Marquard: Transzendentaler Idealismus, Romantische, Naturphilosophie, Psychoanalyse*. Koln, Dinter, 1987.
Sass, Hans-Martin. *Ideal Stud*, 22(3), 281-282, S 92.

Marsh, James L. *Post-Cartesian Meditations*. Bronx, Fordham Univ Pr, 1988.
Bourgeois, Patrick L. *Amer Cath Phil Quart*, 65(4), 515-518, Autumn 91.
Hamrick, William S. *J Brit Soc Phenomenol*, 23(2), 194-197, M 92.
Valone, James J. *Phil Soc Crit*, 18(1), 103-110, 1992.

Marshall, Bruce D (ed). *Theology and Dialogue*. Notre Dame, Univ Notre Dame Pr, 1990.
Wallace, Mark I. *Mod Theol*, 8(4), 401-402, Oct 92.

Martin, F X (ed) and Richmond, J A (ed). *From Augustine to Eriugena*. Washington, Cath Univ Amer Pr, 1991.
Leftow, Brian. *J Hist Phil*, 31(3), 460-461, Jl 93.
Teske, Roland J. *Augustin Stud*, 22, 217-222, 1991.

Martin, James Alfred. *Beauty and Holiness*. Princeton, Princeton Univ Pr, 1990.
Meynell, Hugo. *Heythrop J*, 34(1), 117-118, Ja 93.
Wood, Robert E. *Rev Metaph*, 45(4), 867-868, J 92.

Martin, Michael. *Atheism: A Philosophical Justification*. Philadelphia, Temple Univ Pr, 1990.
Keller, James A. *Faith Phil*, 10(1), 112-119, Ja 93.

Martin, Michael. *The Legal Philosophy of H L A Hart*. Philadelphia, Temple Univ Pr, 1987.
Belliotti, Raymond A. *Int Stud Phil*, 24(1), 116-117, 1992.

Martin, Raymond. *The Past Within Us*. Princeton, Princeton Univ Pr, 1989.
Roth, Paul A. *Hist Theor*, 31(2), 200-208, 1992.

Martin, Robert M. *The Philosopher's Dictionary*. Peterborough, Broadview Pr, 1991.
Berkeley, István S N. *Can Phil Rev*, 12(4), 280-282, Ag 92.

Martin, Ronald E. *American Literature and the Destruction of Knowledge*. Durham, Duke Univ Pr, 1991.
Ciuba, Gary M. *Phil Lit*, 16(2), 426-428, O 92.

Martindale, Colin. *The Clockwork Muse*. New York, Basic Books, 1990.
Porter, Laurence M. *J Aes Art Crit*, 50(2), 171-173, Spr 92.

Mason, John Hope (ed) and Wokler, Robert (ed). *Political Writings—Diderot*. New York, Cambridge Univ Pr, 1992.
Rosen, F. *Utilitas*, 5(1), 139-140, My 93.

Masugi, Ken (ed). *Interpreting Tocqueville's 'Democracy in America'*. Lanham, Rowman & Littlefield, 1991.
Marler, J C. *Mod Sch*, 70(3), 225-227, Mr 93.

Mathews, Freya. *The Ecological Self*. New York, Routledge, 1991.
Elliot, Robert. *Austl J Phil*, 70(3), 369-370, S 92.
Stuhr, John J. *Personalist Forum*, 8(2), 121-125, Fall 92.

Mathieu, Deborah. *Preventing Prenatal Harm*. Dordrecht, Kluwer, 1991.
Carroll, Mary Ann. *J Value Inq*, 17(4), 271-274, Jl 93.
Steinbock, Bonnie. *Bioethics*, 6(4), 381-383, O 92.

Matilal, Bimal Krishna. *Perception*. New York, Clarendon/Oxford Pr, 1986.
Bilimoria, Purusottama. *Austl J Phil*, 70(1), 121-123, Mr.

Mattéi, Jean-François (ed). *La naissance de la raison en Grèce*. Paris, Pr Univ France, 1990.
Coolidge, Jr, Francis P. *Rev Metaph*, 45(4), 869-871, J 92.
Leroux, G. *Philosophiques*, 19(1), 131-134, 1992.

Matthews, Gareth B. *Thought's Ego in Augustine and Descartes*. Ithaca, Cornell Univ Pr, 1992.
Cottingham, John. *Relig Stud*, 29(3), 404-406, S 93.

Matthews, J H. *The Surrealist Mind*. Selinsgrove, Susquehanna Univ Pr, 1991.
Zelechow, Bernard. *Hist Euro Ideas*, 14(5), 723-727, S 92.

Matthews, John B (& others). *Policies and Persons (Second Edition)*. New York, McGraw-Hill, 1991.
Matthews, John B. *J Bus Ethics*, 12(1), 36+, Ja 93.

Matthews, Michael R (ed). *History, Philosophy, and Science Teaching*. New York, Teachers College Pr, 1990.
Jackson, Maxine. *J Phil Educ*, 26(2), 277-278, 1992.

Maxwell, Mary. *Morality Among Nations*. Albany, SUNY Pr, 1990.
Ball, Stephen W. *Biol Phil*, 7(3), 361-377, Jl 92.

May, James M. *Trials of Character*. Chapel Hill, Univ N Carolina Pr, 1988.
Gaines, Robert N. *Phil Rhet*, 26(2), 160-163, 1993.

May, Larry (ed) and Hoffman, Stacey (ed). *Collective Responsibility*. Lanham, Rowman & Littlefield, 1991.
Hoffman, Joshua. *Teach Phil*, 15(3), 282-285, S 92.

Mazlish, Bruce. *A New Science*. New York, Oxford Univ Pr, 1989.
Horowitz, Irving Louis. *Hist Euro Ideas*, 14(2), 290-292, Mr 92.

McBride, William L. *Sartre's Political Theory*. Bloomington, Indiana Univ Pr, 1991.
Flynn, Thomas R. *Res Phenomenol*, 22, 210-216, 1992.
O'Hagan, Timothy. *J Applied Phil*, 10(2), 259-260, 1993.
Pedersen, Julie C. *Auslegung*, 19(1), 98-100, Wint 93.

McCarthy, George E. *Marx and the Ancients*. Lanham, Rowman & Littlefield, 1990.
Donovan, John F. *Rev Metaph*, 45(4), 871-872, J 92.

McCarthy, Michael H. *The Crisis of Philosophy*. Albany, SUNY Pr, 1990.
Kane, Michael. *Int Phil Quart*, 32(2), 261-263, J 92.
Lesser, A H. *J Brit Soc Phenomenol*, 23(2), 192-193, M 92.

McCarthy, Thomas. *Ideals and Illusions*. Cambridge, MIT Pr, 1991.
Rorty, Richard. *J Phil*, 90(7), 370-373, Jl 93.

McClary, Susan. *Feminine Endings*. Minneapolis, Univ of Minn Pr, 1991.
Detels, Claire. *J Aes Art Crit*, 50(4), 338-340, Fall 92.

McClennen, Edward F. *Rationality and Dynamic Choice*. New York, Cambridge Univ Pr, 1990.
Cubitt, Robin P. *Utilitas*, 5(1), 128-131, My 93.
El-Gamal, Mahmoud A. *Econ Phil*, 9(1), 175-178, Ap 93.
Machina, Mark J. *Theor Decis*, 33(3), 265-271, N 92.
Morton, Adam. *Mind*, 101(402), 381-383, Ap 92.

McCloskey, Mary A. *Kant's Aesthetic*. Albany, SUNY Pr, 1987.
Schaper, Eva. *J Aes Art Crit*, 47(2), 180-182, Spr 89.

McClure, George W. *Sorrow and Consolation in Italian Humanism*. Princeton, Princeton Univ Pr, 1991.
Gross, Hanns. *Hist Euro Ideas*, 17(2-3), 376-377, Mr-My 93.

McCorduck, Pamela. *Aaron's Code*. New York, Freeman, 1991.
Josephson, Susan G. *Mind Mach*, 3(1), 116-119, F 93.

McCormick, Peter J. *Fictions, Philosophies and the Problems of Poetics*. Ithaca, Cornell Univ Pr, 1988.
Novitz, David. *J Aes Art Crit*, 47(4), 382-384, Fall 89.

McCormick, Peter J. *Modernity, Aesthetics, and the Bounds of Art*. Ithaca, Cornell Univ Pr, 1990.
Chojna, Wojciech. *J Aes Art Crit*, 49(4), 392-393, Fall 91.

McCormick, Richard A. *The Critical Calling*. Washington, Georgetown Univ Pr, 1989.
Vacek, Edward Collins. *J Relig Ethics*, 20(1), 209, Spr 92.

McCumber, John. *Poetic Interaction*. Chicago, Univ of Chicago Pr, 1989.
Wright, Kathleen. *Phil Rev*, 101(3), 714-717, Jl 92.

McFee, Graham. *Understanding Dance*. New York, Routledge, 1992.
Salter, Alan. *Brit J Aes*, 33(3), 291-292, Jl 93.

McFetridge, Ian, Haldane, John (ed) and Scruton, Roger (ed). *Logical Necessity and Other Essays*. London, Aristotelian Soc, 1990.
Hale, Bob. *Mind*, 101(403), 583-586, Jl 92.

McGann, Jerome J. *The Textual Condition*. Princeton, Princeton Univ Pr, 1991.
Hart, Kevin. *Hist Euro Ideas*, 17(2-3), 337-338, Mr-My 93.

McGee, Vann. *Truth, Vagueness and Paradox*. Indianapolis, Hackett, 1990.
Koons, Robert C. *Can Phil Rev*, 12(2), 118-123, Ap 92.
Priest, Graham. *Mind*, 101(403), 586-590, Jl 92.

McGinn, Bernard. *The Foundations of Mysticism, Volume I*. New York, Crossroad, 1991.
Dupré, Louis. *Thomist*, 57(1), 133-135, Ja 93.
Jantzen, Grace M. *Relig Stud*, 29(3), 401-404, S 93.

McGinn, Colin. *Mental Content*. Cambridge, Blackwell, 1989.
Garfield, Jay L. *Phil Rev*, 101(3), 691-695, Jl 92.
Levin, Michael. *Nous*, 27(1), 137-139, Mr 93.
Shute, Sara. *Int Stud Phil*, 25(1), 95-97, 1993.

McGinn, Colin. *The Problem of Consciousness*. Cambridge, Blackwell, 1991.
Averill, Edward Wilson. *Phil Books*, 33(3), 168-170, Jl 92.
Rey, Georges. *Phil Rev*, 102(2), 274-278, Ap 93.
Senchuk, Dennis M. *Rev Metaph*, 46(3), 629-630, Mr 93.
Shaffer, Jerome A. *Mind*, 101(403), 590-595, Jl 92.

McGinn, Marie. *Sense and Certainty*. Cambridge, Blackwell, 1989.
Dancy, Jonathan. *Phil Rev*, 101(3), 684-687, Jl 93.
Shute, Sara. *Int Stud Phil*, 25(1), 95-97, 1993.

McGregor, James H. *The Shades of Aeneas*. Athens, Univ of Georgia Pr, 1991.
Kleiner, John. *Phil Lit*, 16(1), 187-188, Ap 92.

McGuiness, Brian. *Wittgensteins frühe Jahre*. Frankfurt, Suhrkamp, 1988.
Bolz, Norbert. *Phil Rundsch*, 39(4), 334-338, 1992.

McGuinness, Brian. *Wittgenstein: A Life*. Berkeley, Univ of Calif Pr, 1988.
Barnett, William E. *Phil Rev*, 101(3), 651-654, Jl 92.
Griffin, Nicholas. *Russell*, 12(1), 79-93, Sum 92.
Harré, Rom. *Int Stud Phil*, 24(1), 117-118, 1992.

McHenry, Leemon B. *Whitehead and Bradley*. Albany, SUNY Pr, 1992.
Ford, Lewis S. *Rev Metaph*, 46(3), 630-633, Mr 93.
Maassen, Helmut. *Trans Peirce Soc*, 29(1), 116-122, Wint 93.
Partridge, Michael. *Phil Quart*, 43(173), 545-547, O 93.

McInerney, Peter K. *Time and Experience*. Philadelphia, Temple Univ Pr, 1991.
Smith, Quentin. *Phil Phenomenol Res*, 53(3), 736-739, S 93.

McInerny, Ralph. *Aquinas on Human Action*. Washington, Cath Univ Amer Pr, 1992.
Davies, Brian. *Int Phil Quart*, 33(2), 239-240, Je 93.

McInerny, Ralph. *Boethius and Aquinas*. Washington, Cath Univ Amer Pr, 1990.
Magee, John. *J Hist Phil*, 30(4), 602-603, O 92.
Marenbon, John. *Heythrop J*, 34(3), 318-319, Jl 93.

McKeon, Zahava K (ed) and McKeon, Richard. *Freedom and History and Other Essays*. Chicago, Univ of Chicago Pr, 1990.
Buchanan, Richard. *J Speculative Phil*, 7(3), 243-246, 1993.

McKown, Delos B. *The MythMaker's Magic*. Buffalo, Prometheus, 1993.
Vernon, Thomas S. *Nat Forum*, 73(2), 45-45, Spr 93.

McLaughlin, Brian (ed). *Dretske and His Critics*. Cambridge, Blackwell, 1991.
Jones, O R. *Phil Quart*, 43(173), 563-566, O 93.
Martin, Michael. *Phil Books*, 34(1), 36-38, Ja 93.

McLaughlin, Brian P (ed) and Rorty, Amélie Oksenberg (ed). *Perspectives on Self-Deception*. Berkeley, Univ of Calif Pr, 1988.
Bach, Kent. *Nous*, 26(4), 495-504, D 92.

McLaughlin, Peter. *Kants Kritik der teleologischen Urteilskraft*. Bonn, Bouvier, 1989.
Peter, Joachim. *Kantstudien*, 83(3), 364-368, 1992.

McLellan, David. *Simone Weil*. New York, Macmillan, 1989.
Andic, Martin. *Int J Phil Relig*, 32(1), 62-64, Ag 92.

McLellan, David (ed) and Sayers, Sean (ed). *Socialism and Democracy*. New York, Macmillan, 1991.
Glaser, Daryl. *Rad Phil*, 61, 58-59, Sum 92.

McLennan, Gregor. *Marxism, Pluralism and Beyond*. Oxford, Polity Pr, 1989.
Magill, Kevin. *Rad Phil*, 61, 40-41, Sum 92.

McMahon, Robert. *Augustine's Prayerful Ascent*. Athens, Univ of Georgia Pr, 1989.
Cavadini, John C. *Augustin Stud*, 21, 177-186, 1990.
Hartle, Ann. *Int J Phil Relig*, 32(3), 183, D 92.

McMullin, Ernan. *The Inference That Makes Science*. Milwaukee, Marquette Univ Pr, 1992.
Dougherty, Jude P. *Rev Metaph*, 46(1), 169-170, S 92.
Simmons, Lance. *Amer Cath Phil Quart*, 67(3), 388-390, Sum 93.
Wallace, William A. *Thomist*, 57(1), 131-132, Ja 93.

Méchoulan, Henry. *Amsterdam au temps de Spinoza*. Paris, Pr Univ France, 1990.
Popkin, Richard H. *J Hist Phil*, 31(1), 137-139, Ja 93.

Méchoulan, Henry. *Etre Juif à Amsterdam au temps de Spinoza*. Paris, Albin, 1991.
Popkin, Richard H. *J Hist Phil*, 31(1), 137-139, Ja 93.

Meerbote, Ralf (ed) and Hudson, Hud (ed). *Kant's Aesthetics, Volume 1*. Atascadero, Ridgeview, 1991.
Gracyk, Theodore A. *Can Phil Rev*, 12(6), 407-409, D 92.

Meese, Elizabeth. *(Ex)tensions: Re-Figuring Feminist Criticism*. Champaign, Univ of Illinois Pr, 1990.
Martindale, Kathleen. *Hypatia*, 8(1), 214-219, Wint 93.

Mehta, Uday Singh. *The Anxiety of Freedom*. Ithaca, Cornell Univ Pr, 1992.
Johnston, David. *Polit Theory*, 21(4), 698-701, N 93.

Meinwald, Constance C. *Plato's 'Parmenides'*. New York, Oxford Univ Pr, 1991.
Curd, Patricia Kenig. *Phil Rev*, 102(1), 85-87, Ja 93.
Husain, Martha. *Int Stud Phil*, 25(1), 97-98, 1993.
White, David A. *J Hist Phil*, 31(3), 455-456, Jl 93.

Mele, A R. *Springs of Action*. New York, Oxford Univ Pr, 1992.
Dunn, Robert. *Phil Books*, 34(2), 116-120, Ap 93.

Melle, Ullrich (ed). *Vorlesungen über Ethik und Wertlehre 1908-1914*. Dordrecht, Kluwer, 1988.
Jordan, Robert Welsh. *Husserl Stud*, 8(3), 221-232, 1991-92.

Mellema, Gregory. *Beyond the Call of Duty*. Albany, SUNY Pr, 1991.
Dancy, Jonathan. *Phil Books*, 34(1), 48-49, Ja 93.

Mellor, D H. *Matters of Metaphysics*. New York, Cambridge Univ Pr, 1991.
Byrne, Alex. *Phil Rev*, 102(2), 285-287, Ap 93.
Gower, Barry. *Brit J Phil Sci*, 43(4), 555-559, D 92.
Hart, W D. *Phil Books*, 34(1), 25-27, Ja 93.
Jackson, Frank. *Mind*, 101(403), 595-598, Jl 92.
Kyburg Jr, Henry E. *Rev Metaph*, 46(2), 409-411, 1992.
Lowe, E J. *Philosophy*, 67(260), 268-270, Apr 92.

Melnick, Arthur. *Space, Time, and Thought in Kant*. Dordrecht, Kluwer, 1989.
Aquila, Richard E. *Int Stud Phil*, 24(1), 119-120, 1992.

Méndez, Julio Raúl. *El amor fundamento de la participación metafísica*. Buenos Aires, Ed Sudamericana, 1990.
Elders, Leo J. *Rev Metaph*, 46(2), 411-412, 1992.

Mendus, Susan (ed) and Edwards, David (ed). *On Toleration*. New York, Clarendon/Oxford Pr, 1987.
Newman, Jay. *Philosophia (Israel)*, 21(3-4), 339-340, Ap 92.

Mendus, Susan (ed) and Rendall, Jane (ed). *Sexuality and Subordination*. New York, Routledge, 1989.
Morton, Luise H. *J Aes Art Crit*, 48(3), 258-260, Sum 90.

Mensch, James Richard. *Intersubjectivity and Transcendental Idealism*. Albany, SUNY Pr, 1988.
O'Keeffe, Terence M. *Hist Euro Ideas*, 14(3), 440-441, M 92.

Merchant, Carolyn. *Ecological Revolutions*. Chapel Hill, Univ N Carolina Pr, 1989.
Holly, Marilyn. *Agr Human Values*, 8(3), 73-76, Sum 91.

Merrell, Floyd. *Signs Becoming Signs*. Bloomington, Indiana Univ Pr, 1991.
Corrington, Robert S. *Rev Metaph*, 47(1), 161-163, S 93.

Merrill, Daniel D. *Augustus De Morgan and the Logic of Relations*. Dordrecht, Kluwer, 1990.
Grattan-Guinness, I. *Hist Phil Log*, 13(2), 228-229, 1992.
Kelly, Charles J. *Mod Sch*, 70(1), 70-73, N 92.

Mesle, C Robert. *John Hick's Theodicy*. New York, St Martin's Pr, 1991.
Hasker, William. *Int J Phil Relig*, 34(1), 55-56, Ag 93.

Meyer, Michel (ed). *Questions and Questioning*. Hawthorne, de Gruyter, 1988.
Cohen, L Jonathan. *Nous*, 26(2), 277-279, J 92.

Meyering, Theo C. *Historical Roots of Cognitive Science*. Dordrecht, Kluwer, 1989.
Murphy, Nancey. *Stud Hist Phil Sci*, 24(3), 501-508, Ag 93.

Meyers, Diana T. *Self, Society, and Personal Choice*. New York, Columbia Univ Pr, 1991.
Sherwin, Susan. *Can Phil Rev*, 12(4), 282-284, Ag 92.
Shouler, Kenneth. *Metaphilosophy*, 24(1-2), 183-188, Ja-Ap 93.

Meynell, Hugo (ed). *Grace, Politics and Desire*. Calgary, Univ of Calgary Pr, 1990.
Brinkman, B R. *Heythrop J*, 34(3), 316-318, Jl 93.
Gray, Christopher B. *Can Phil Rev*, 12(4), 285-286, Ag 92.
Rist, John. *Phoenix*, 46(4), 383-384, Wint 92.

Meynell, Hugo A. *An Introduction to the Philosophy of Bernard Lonergan (Second Edition)*. Toronto, Univ of Toronto Pr, 1991.
Vertin, Michael. *Can Phil Rev*, 12(3), 209-210, J-Jl 92.

Michael, Luntley. *Language, Logic, and Experience*. Peru, Open Court, 1988.
Carnes, Robert D. *Ideal Stud*, 22(3), 223-225, S 92.

Michalson Jr, Gordon E. *Fallen Freedom*. New York, Cambridge Univ Pr, 1991.
Munzel, Gisela Felicitas. *J Hist Phil*, 31(3), 467-469, Jl 93.

Midgley, Mary. *Science as Salvation*. New York, Routledge, 1992.
Botterill, George. *Phil Books*, 34(4), 232-234, O 93.

Midley, Mary. *Can't We Make Moral Judgments?*. New York, St Martin's Pr, 1991.
Donnelley, Strachan. *Hastings Center Rep*, 23(2), 43-44, Mr-Ap 93.

Mill, John Stuart, Robson, John M (ed) and Moir, Martin (ed). *Writings on India*. Toronto, Univ of Toronto Pr, 1990.
Ambirajan, S. *Utilitas*, 4(1), 154-157, My 92.

Millar, Alan. *Reasons and Experience*. New York, Clarendon/Oxford Pr, 1991.
Aune, Bruce. *Phil Quart*, 43(171), 239-242, Ap 93.
Hill, Christopher S. *Phil Rev*, 102(2), 279-281, Ap 93.

Miller, Barry. *From Existence to God*. New York, Routledge, 1992.
Helm, Paul. *Phil Books*, 34(1), 59-60, Ja 93.
Vallicella, W F. *Amer Cath Phil Quart*, 67(3), 390-394, Sum 93.

Miller, Joshua. *The Rise and Fall of Democracy in Early America, 1630-1789*. University Park, Penn St Univ Pr, 1991.
Claeys, Gregory. *Polit Theory*, 20(4), 700-703, N 92.

Miller, Susan. *Rescuing the Subject*. Carbondale, So Illinois Univ Pr, 1989.
Gutendorf, Jr, V F. *Phil Rhet*, 26(3), 245-248, 1993.

Minnis, A J (ed) and Scott, A B (ed). *Medieval Literary Theory and Criticism*. New York, Clarendon/Oxford Pr, 1988.
Emmerson, Richard K. *Phil Lit*, 16(1), 195-196, Ap 92.
Lang, Helen. *Rev Metaph*, 45(4), 872-874, J 92.

Mirowski, Philip. *More Heat than Light*. New York, Cambridge Univ Pr, 1989.
De Marchi, Neil. *Econ Phil*, 8(1), 163-169, Ap 92.
Schabas, Margaret. *Phil Sci*, 59(4), 708-710, D 92.

Misak, C J. *Truth and the End of Inquiry*. New York, Oxford Univ Pr, 1991.
Almeder, R. *Rev Metaph*, 45(4), 874-875, J 92.
Boler, John. *Phil Rev*, 102(1), 110-112, Ja 93.
Moser, Paul K. *Can Phil Rev*, 12(2), 123-125, Ap 92.
Skagestad, Peter. *Trans Peirce Soc*, 28(2), 311-321, Spr 92.

Misgeld, Dieter (ed) and Nicholson, Graeme (ed). *Hans-Georg Gadamer on Education, Poetry, and History*. Albany, SUNY Pr, 1992.
Johnson, Patricia Altenbernd. *Can Phil Rev*, 12(5), 342-344, O 92.

Mitcham, Carl (ed) and Huning, Alois (ed). *Philosophy and Technology, II*. Dordrecht, Kluwer, 1986.
Cuello, César. *Res Phil Technol*, 9, 211-219, 1989.

Mitchell, Basil. *How to Play Theological Ping-Pong*. London, Hodder Stoughton, Undated.
McLean, Murdith. *Can Phil Rev*, 12(4), 287-289, Ag 92.
Thomas, John Heywood. *Relig Stud*, 28(3), 431-432, S 92.

Mitias, Michael H (ed). *Aesthetic Quality and Aesthetic Experience*. Atlantic Highlands, Humanities Pr, 1988.
Bender, John W. *J Aes Art Crit*, 48(2), 173-175, Spr 90.

Mitias, Michael H (ed). *Possibility of the Aesthetic Experience*. Dordrecht, Kluwer, 1986.
Anderson, Douglas R. *Ideal Stud*, 22(3), 219-220, S 92.

Mitias, Michael H. *What Makes an Experience Aesthetic?*. Atlantic Highlands, Humanities Pr, 1988.
Hyman, Lawrence W. *J Aes Art Crit*, 48(1), 90-91, Wint 90.

Modrak, Deborah K. *Aristotle*. Chicago, Univ of Chicago Pr, 1987.
Block, Irving L. *Int Stud Phil*, 24(1), 120-121, 1992.
Spellman, Lynne. *Ancient Phil*, 12(1), 206-208, Spr 92.

Mohanty, J N. *Transcendental Phenomenology*. Cambridge, Blackwell, 1989.
Kasely, Terry S. *Husserl Stud*, 9(2), 139-144, 1992.

Moles, Alistair. *Nietzsche's Philosophy of Nature and Cosmology*. New York, Lang, 1990.
Schwartz, Stephen P. *J Hist Phil*, 31(2), 301-302, Ap 93.

Momigliano, Arnaldo. *The Classical Foundations of Modern Historiography*. Berkeley, Univ of Calif Pr, 1990.
Konstan, David. *Hist Theor*, 31(2), 224-230, 1992.

Monk, Ray. *Ludwig Wittgenstein: The Duty of Genius*. New York, Penguin USA, 1991.
Hallett, Garth. *Rev Metaph*, 46(2), 412-413, 1992.
Walker, Margaret Urban. *Int Phil Quart*, 33(3), 370-371, S 93.

Monk, Ray. *Wittgenstein: The Duty of Genius*. New York, Free Pr, 1990.
Barnett, William E. *Phil Rev*, 101(3), 651-654, Jl 92.
Griffin, Nicholas. *Russell*, 12(1), 79-93, Sum 92.

Mooney, Edward F. *Knights of Faith and Resignation*. Albany, SUNY Pr, 1991.
Hojnowski, Peter E. *Rev Metaph*, 46(3), 633-634, Mr 93.

Moore, A W. *The Infinite*. New York, Routledge, 1990.
Craig, William Lane. *Int Phil Quart*, 32(2), 253-256, J 92.

Moortgat, Michael. *Categorical Investigations*. Dordrecht, Foris, 1988.
Lambek, J. *Phil Quart*, 42(168), 1143-1146, Jl 92.

Moran, Dermot. *The Philosophy of John Scottus Eriugena*. New York, Cambridge Univ Pr, 1989.
Cooper, John Charles. *Ideal Stud*, 22(3), 232-234, S 92.
Louth, Andrew. *Heythrop J*, 33(2), 214-215, Ap 92.
Rocker, Stephen. *Mod Sch*, 70(3), 227-229, Mr 93.
Strasser, Michael W. *Nous*, 26(4), 509-513, D 92.

Moravcsik, Julius M. *Thought and Language*. New York, Routledge, 1990.
Bakhurst, David. *Can Phil Rev*, 12(6), 409-412, D 92.
Welker, David. *Rev Metaph*, 46(1), 170-171, S 92.

Morford, Mark. *Stoics and Neostoics*. Princeton, Princeton Univ Pr, 1991.
Morgan, Michael L. *J Hist Phil*, 31(2), 288-289, Ap 93.

Morgan, M L. *Platonic Piety*. New Haven, Yale Univ Pr, 1990.
Tulin, Alexander. *Amer J Philo*, 113(4), 630-633, Wint 92.

Morgan, M S. *The History of Econometric Ideas*. New York, Cambridge Univ Pr, 1990.
Cartwright, Nancy. *Phil Sci*, 60(1), 515-516, Mr 93.
LeGall, Philippe. *Econ Phil*, 8(2), 286-290, O 92.
Schabas, Margaret. *Phil Soc Sci*, 23(3), 376-402, S 93.

Morgan, Michael L. *Platonic Piety*. New Haven, Yale Univ Pr, 1990.
Carey, David. *Phil Lit*, 16(1), 189-190, Ap 92.

Morin, Lucien and Brunet, Louis. *Philosophie de l'éducation*. Bruxelles, De Boeck-Wesmael, 1992.
Thibaudeau, Victor. *Laval Theol Phil*, 49(2), 357-359, Je 93.

Morreim, E Haavi. *Balancing Act*. Dordrecht, Kluwer, 1991.
Finkler, Merton D. *Bioethics*, 7(1), 84-86, Ja 93.
Hadorn, David C. *Hastings Center Rep*, 22(6), 43-44, N-D 92.

Morris, Randall C. *Process Philosophy and Political Ideology*. Albany, SUNY Pr, 1991.
Lucas Jr, George R. *J Hist Phil*, 31(3), 473-475, Jl 93.

Morris, Thomas V (ed). *Divine and Human Action*. Ithaca, Cornell Univ Pr, 1988.
Hasker, William. *Int J Phil Relig*, 33(3), 190-192, Je 93.
Helm, Paul. *Phil Rev*, 101(2), 447-449, Ap 92.

Morris, Thomas V. *Our Idea of God*. Notre Dame, Univ Notre Dame Pr, 1991.
Swinburne, Richard. *Phil Quart*, 42(169), 515-517, O 92.

Morris, Thomas V (ed). *Philosophy and the Christian Faith*. Notre Dame, Univ Notre Dame Pr, 1988.
Hasker, William. *Int J Phil Relig*, 33(3), 190-192, Je 93.

Morris, Thomas V. *Understanding Identity Statements*. Oxford, Aberdeen, 1984.
Newman, Andrew. *Nous*, 26(2), 275-277, J 92.

Morrow, Glenn R (trans) and Dillon, John M (trans). *Proclus' Commentary on Plato's Parmenides*. Princeton, Princeton Univ Pr, 1987.
Ernst, Carl W. *Ancient Phil*, 12(1), 237-239, Spr 92.

Morrow, John. *Coleridge's Political Thought*. New York, Macmillan, 1990.
Edwards, Pamela J. *Hist Polit Thought*, 12(3), 544-545, Fall 91.

Morson, Gary Saul and Emerson, Caryl. *Mikhail Bakhtin*. Stanford, Stanford Univ Pr, 1990.
Walker, Denis B. *Phil Lit*, 16(1), 180=181, Ap 92.

Morson, Gary Saul (ed) and Emerson, Caryl (ed). *Rethinking Bakhtin*. Evanston, Northwestern Univ Pr, 1989.
Tavis, Anna A. *J Aes Art Crit*, 49(1), 88-90, Wint 91.

Morton, Adam. *Disasters and Dilemmas*. Cambridge, Blackwell, 1991.
Harrison, Ross. *Phil Quart*, 43(171), 270-272, Ap 93.
Morris, Christopher W. *Phil Books*, 34(1), 49-51, Ja 93.

Moser, Paul K. *Knowledge and Evidence*. New York, Cambridge Univ Pr, 1989.
Day, Timothy Joseph. *Int Stud Phil*, 25(1), 98-99, 1993.
Nelson, Mark T. *Phil Quart*, 43(171), 242-244, Ap 93.
Rosen, Gideon. *Phil Rev*, 101(3), 681-684, Jl 92.

Mosès, Stéphane and Tihanyi, Catherine (trans). *System and Revelation*. Detroit, Wayne St Univ Pr, 1992.
Morgan, Michael L. *Rev Metaph*, 46(3), 635-636, Mr 93.
Novak, David. *Mod Theol*, 9(2), 221-222, Ap 93.

Moss, Edward. *Seeing Man Whole*. Lewes, Book Guild, 1989.
Crewdson, Joan. *Tradition Discovery*, 17(1-2), 51-54, 1990-91.

Moss, M E. *Benedetto Croce Reconsidered*. Hanover, Univ Pr New England, 1987.
Mitias, Michael H. *Ideal Stud*, 22(3), 270-271, S 92.

Mosteller, F (ed) and Falatico-Taylor, J (ed). *Quality of Life and Technology Assessment*. Washington, National Acad Pr, 1989.
Savulescu, Julian. *Bioethics*, 6(3), 264-265, Jl 92.

Mulhall, Stephen. *On Being in the World*. New York, Routledge, 1990.
Kerr, Fergus. *Heythrop J*, 33(2), 229-231, Ap 92.

Mulholland, Leslie A. *Kant's System of Rights*. New York, Columbia Univ Pr, 1990.
Dodson, Kevin E. *J Hist Phil*, 31(2), 297-299, Ap 93.
McNaughton, David. *Phil Books*, 34(1), 17-19, Ja 93.
Westphal, Kenneth R. *Can Phil Rev*, 12(2), 126-128, Ap 92.
Wood, Allen W. *Thomist*, 56(3), 535-540, Jl 92.

Mulligan, Kevin (ed). *Mind, Meaning and Metaphysics*. Dordrecht, Kluwer, 1990.
David, Marian A. *Phil Phenomenol Res*, 53(1), 229-232, Mr 93.

Mulligan, Kevin (ed). *Speech Act and Sachverhalt*. Dordrecht, Kluwer, 1987.
Kienzle, Bertram. *Nous*, 27(1), 101-102, Mr 93.

Mulmuley, Ketan. *Full Abstraction and Semantic Equivalence*. Cambridge, MIT Pr, 1987.
Curien, P-L. *Phil Quart*, 42(168), 1141-1143, Jl 92.

Munévar, Gunzalo (ed). *Beyond Reason*. Dordrecht, Kluwer, 1991.
Shanks, Niall. *Can Phil Rev*, 12(6), 412-414, D 92.

Munzer, Stephen R. *A Theory of Property*. New York, Cambridge Univ Pr, 1990.
Christman, John. *Phil Rev*, 101(4), 936-938, O 92.
Lagueux, Maurice. *Econ Phil*, 8(1), 191-197, Ap 92.

Murphree, Wallace A. *Numerically Exceptive Logic*. New York, Lang, 1991.
Englebretsen, George. *Can Phil Rev*, 12(6), 415-417, D 92.

Murphy, John P. *Pragmatism: From Peirce to Davidson*. Boulder, Westview Pr, 1991.
Colapietro, Vincent. *J Hist Phil*, 30(4), 625-627, O 92.
Meyers, Robert G. *Trans Peirce Soc*, 28(2), 321-333, Spr 92.
Mounce, H O. *Philosophy*, 67(260), 260-262, Apr 92.
Rucki, Elizabeth. *Can Phil Rev*, 12(1), 47-49, F 92.

Murphy, Nancey. *Theology in the Age of Scientific Reasoning*. Ithaca, Cornell Univ Pr, 1990.
Hughes, Gerard J. *Phil Quart*, 42(168), 397-398, Jl 92.
Van Huyssteen, Wentzel. *Zygon*, 27(2), 231-234, J 92.

Myers, Greg. *Writing Biology*. Madison, Univ of Wisconsin Pr, 1990.
Hull, David L. *Phil Soc Sci*, 23(3), 379-385, S 93.

Nadler, Steven M. *Arnauld and the Cartesian Philosophy of Ideas*. Princeton, Princeton Univ Pr, 1989.
Lennon, Thomas M. *Phil Rev*, 101(3), 644-647, Jl 92.

Nägele, Rainer. *Theater, Theory, Speculation*. Baltimore, Johns Hopkins U Pr, 1991.
Vieth, Lynne. *Phil Lit*, 16(1), 217-219, Ap 92.

Naess, Arne and Rothenberg, David (ed & trans). *Ecology, Community and Lifestyle*. New York, Cambridge Univ Pr, 1989.
Rubin, Charles T. *Interpretation*, 21(1), 73-80, Fall 93.

Nagel, Thomas. *Equality and Partiality*. New York, Oxford Univ Pr, 1991.
D'Agostino, Fred. *Austl J Phil*, 70(2), 237-238, J.
Dworkin, Gerald. *Phil Rev*, 101(2), 265-267, Ap 93.
Haldane, John. *Mind*, 102(407), 524-529, Jl 93.

Nakamoto, Tominga and Pye, Michael (ed & trans). *Emerging from Meditation*. Honolulu, Univ of Hawaii Pr, 1990.
Yusa, Michiko. *Phil East West*, 42(3), 532-536, Jl 92.

Narveson, Jan. *The Libertarian Idea*. Philadelphia, Temple Univ Pr, 1988.
De Marneffe, Peter. *Phil Rev*, 101(2), 470-472, Ap 92.
Flynn, Tom. *Free Inq*, 13(2), 54-55, Spr 93.

Nash, Richard. *John Craige's Mathematical Principles of Christian Theology*. Carbondale, So Illinois Univ Pr, 1991.
Neto, José R Maia. *J Hist Phil*, 30(3), 456-457, J 92.

Nasr, Seyyed Hossein. *Islamic Art and Spirituality*. Albany, SUNY Pr, 1987.
Farooqi, Waheed Ali. *Ideal Stud*, 22(3), 240-241, S 92.

Nasr, Seyyed Hossein. *Knowledge and the Sacred*. Albany, SUNY Pr, 1989.
Heer, Nicholas. *Phil East West*, 43(1), 144-150, Ja 93.

Nathan, N M L. *Will and World*. New York, Clarendon/Oxford Pr, 1992.
Kenyon, J D. *Phil Books*, 34(2), 120-122, Ap 93.

Nattiez, Jean-Jacques and Abbate, Carolyn (trans). *Music and Discourse*. Princeton, Princeton Univ Pr, 1990.
Keefer, Don. *J Aes Art Crit*, 51(1), 91-92, Wint 93.

Neale, Stephen. *Descriptions*. Cambridge, MIT Pr, 1990.
Baltin, Mark. *Phil Psych*, 6(2), 216-220, 1993.
Yagisawa, Takashi. *Can Phil Rev*, 12(1), 49-51, F 92.

Nederman, Cary J (ed & trans). *Policraticus—John of Salisbury*. New York, Cambridge Univ Pr, 1990.
Forhan, Kate L. *Hist Euro Ideas*, 14(2), 294-295, Mr 92.

Nelson, Charles H. *John Elof Boodin: Philosopher-Poet*. New York, Philosophical Lib, 1987.
Steinkraus, Warren E. *Ideal Stud*, 22(3), 289-290, S 92.

Nelson, Daniel Mark. *The Priority of Prudence*. University Park, Penn St Univ Pr, 1992.
Cessario, Romanus. *Mod Theol*, 9(3), 302-303, Jl 93.
Long, Steven A. *Rev Metaph*, 46(2), 413-414, 1992.

Nelson, William N. *Morality*. Boulder, Westview Pr, 1991.
Almond, Brenda. *Phil Quart*, 43(171), 256-259, Ap 93.

Nemoianu, Virgil and Royal, Robert. *Play, Philosophy and Literature*. Albany, SUNY Pr, 1992.
Jasper, David. *Phil Lit*, 17(1), 178-179, Ap 93.

Nerhot, Patrick (ed). *Legal Knowledge and Analogy*. Dordrecht, Kluwer, 1991.
Van Roermund, Bert. *Can Phil Rev*, 12(1), 51-53, F 92.

Netland, Howard A. *Dissonant Voices*. Grand Rapids, Eerdmans, 1991.
Griffiths, Paul J. *Thomist*, 56(4), 723-726, O 92.

Netton, Ian Richard. *Al-Farabi and His School*. New York, Routledge, 1992.
Leaman, Oliver. *Relig Stud*, 29(2), 268-270, Je 93.

Neu, Jerome (ed). *The Cambridge Companion to Freud*. New York, Cambridge Univ Pr, 1991.
Brook, Andrew. *Can Phil Rev*, 13(1), 43-45, F 93.
Esteban, Joseba I. *Gnosis*, 4(1), 125-129, 1992.

Neubauer, John. *The Emancipation of Music from Language*. New Haven, Yale Univ Pr, 1986.
Alperson, Philip. *J Aes Art Crit*, 46(3), 441-444, Spr 88.

Neugebauer, C (ed). *Philosophie, Ideologie und Gesellschaft in Afrika*. New York, Lang, 1991.
Van Hensbroek, Pieter Boele. *Quest*, 6(1), 87-90, J 92.

Neuhouser, Frederick. *Fichte's Theory of Subjectivity*. New York, Cambridge Univ Pr, 1990.
Mandt, Almer J. *J Hist Phil*, 31(1), 146-147, Ja 93.
Mather, Ronald. *Owl Minerva*, 24(1), 91-94, Fall 92.

Newsom, Robert. *A Likely Story*. New Brunswick, Rutgers Univ Pr, 1988.
Currie, Gregory. *J Aes Art Crit*, 47(3), 297-299, Sum 89.

Nichols, Aidan. *A Grammar of Consent*. Edinburgh, T & T Clark, 1991.
Gealy, Walford. *Phil Invest*, 16(4), 353-357, O 93.

Nicholson, Graeme. *Illustrations of Being*. Atlantic Highlands, Humanities Pr, 1992.
Groth, Miles. *Rev Metaph*, 46(3), 636-638, Mr 93.
Wurzer, Wilhelm S. *Can Phil Rev*, 12(6), 417-419, D 92.

Nicholson, Peter. *The Political Philosophy of the British Idealists*. New York, Cambridge Univ Pr, 1990.
Harris, Errol E. *Heythrop J*, 34(1), 94-97, Ja 93.
Sweet, William. *Laval Theol Phil*, 48(3), 477-480, O 92.
Vincent, Andrew. *Hist Polit Thought*, 12(3), 547-550, Fall 91.

Nickel, James W. *Making Sense of Human Rights*. Berkeley, Univ of Calif Pr, 1987.
Reuman, Robert E. *Ideal Stud*, 22(3), 279-281, S 92.

Nidditch, Peter H (ed) and Rogers, G A J (ed). *John Locke*. New York, Oxford Univ Pr, 1990.
Weinberg, Sue M. *J Hist Phil*, 30(3), 459-461, J 92.

Nielsen, Kai. *After the Demise of the Tradition*. Boulder, Westview Pr, 1991.
Bernstein, J M. *Phil Books*, 33(3), 150-152, Jl 92.

Nielsen, Kai. *Ethics Without God*. Buffalo, Prometheus, 1989.
Beaty, Michael. *SW Phil Rev*, 8(1), 192-194, Ja 92.

Nielsen, Kai. *God, Scepticism and Modernity*. Ottawa, Univ of Ottawa Pr, 1989.
Clayton, Philip. *Phil Soc Sci*, 22(4), 519-525, D 92.

Nielsen, Kai. *Marxism and the Moral Point of View*. Boulder, Westview Pr, 1989.
Seddon, Fred. *Stud Soviet Tho*, 44(2), 142-144, S 92.
Smith, Tony. *Int Stud Phil*, 24(1), 121-122, 1992.

Nielsen, Kai. *Why Be Moral?*. Buffalo, Prometheus, 1989.
Gomberg, Paul. *Phil Rev*, 101(3), 700-703, Jl 92.

Nietzsche, Friedrich and Arrowsmith, William (& other trans). *Unmodern Observations*. New Haven, Yale Univ Pr, 1989.
Platt, Michael. *Phil Lit*, 16(2), 425-426, O 92.
Platt, Michael. *Rev Metaph*, 46(1), 171-174, S 92.

Nietzsche, Friedrich and Gilman, Sander L (& other eds). *Friedrich Nietzsche on Rhetoric and Language*. New York, Oxford Univ Pr, 1989.
Breazeale, Daniel. *Int Stud Phil*, 24(2), 130-131, 1992.

Nitecki, Matthew H (ed). *Evolutionary Progress*. Chicago, Univ of Chicago Pr, 1988.
Burian, Richard M. *Phil Rev*, 101(2), 438-441, Ap 92.

Nitecki, Matthew H (ed) and Nitecki, Doris V (ed). *History and Evolution*. Albany, SUNY Pr, 1992.
Thompson, Paul. *Can Phil Rev*, 13(1), 45-47, F 93.

Norris, Christopher. *Paul de Man: Deconstruction and the Critique of Aesthetic Ideology*. New York, Routledge, 1988.
Fischer, Michael. *J Aes Art Crit*, 48(3), 250-251, Sum 90.

Norton, Bryan G. *Toward Unity Among Environmentalists*. New York, Oxford Univ Pr, 1991.
Sagoff, Mark. *Hastings Center Rep*, 23(2), 42-43, Mr-Ap 93.
Weston, Anthony. *Environ Ethics*, 14(3), 283-287, Fall 92.

Norton, David L. *Democracy and Moral Development*. Berkeley, Univ of Calif Pr, 1991.
Kolenda, Konstantin. *Rev Metaph*, 45(4), 875-876, J 92.
Maine, Edward W. *J Value Inq*, 26(4), 579-582, O 92.

Norton, Robert E. *Herder's Aesthetics and the European Enlightenment*. Ithaca, Cornell Univ Pr, 1991.
Menze, Ernest A. *Rev Metaph*, 47(1), 163-164, S 93.
Müller-Sievers, Helmut. *J Hist Phil*, 31(1), 143-144, Ja 93.

Novitz, David. *Knowledge, Fiction and Imagination*. Philadelphia, Temple Univ Pr, 1987.
Carroll, Noël. *J Aes Art Crit*, 48(2), 167-169, Spr 90.

Nowak, Leszek. *Power and Civil Society*. Westport, Greenwood Pr, 1991.
Swiatek, Krzysztof. *Can Phil Rev*, 12(6), 420-424, D 92.

Nozick, Robert. *The Examined Life*. New York, Simon & Schuster, 1990.
Cooper, Wesley E. *Can Phil Rev*, 13(1), 47-50, F 93.

Nuchelmans, Gabriel. *Dilemmatic Arguments*. Amsterdam, North-Holland, 1991.
Read, Stephen. *Hist Phil Log*, 14(1), 109-110, 1993.

Nugayev, R M. *Reconstruction of Scientific Theory Change*. Belmont, Kazan Univ Pr, 1989.
Balashov, Yuri V. *Erkenntnis*, 38(3), 429-432, My 93.

Nussbaum, Martha. *Love's Knowledge*. New York, Oxford Univ Pr, 1990.
Eldridge, Richard. *Phil Phenomenol Res*, 52(2), 485-488, Je 92.
Elliott, Carl. *Phil Books*, 33(3), 152-154, Jl 92.
Horton, John. *Phil Quart*, 42(169), 492-495, O 92.
Tanner, Michael. *Brit J Aes*, 33(3), 297-298, Jl 93.

Nussbaum, Martha C (ed) and Rorty, Amélie Oksenberg. *Essays on Aristotle's 'De Anima'*. New York, Clarendon/Oxford Pr, 1992.
Dent, N J H. *Phil Books*, 34(3), 143-145, Jl 93.
Hamlyn, D W. *Phil Quart*, 43(173), 520-525, O 93.

Nye, Andrea. *Words of Power*. New York, Routledge, 1990.
Divers, John. *Hist Phil Log*, 13(2), 254-255, 1992.

Nye, Robert D. *The Legacy of B F Skinner*. Pacific Grove, Brooks/Cole, 1992.
Montgomery, Robert. *Phil Psych*, 6(2), 210-212, 1993.

Nyiri, J C (ed) and Smith, B (ed). *Practical Knowledge*. North Ryde, Croom Helm, 1987.
Allen, R T. *Tradition Discovery*, 17(1-2), 44-45, 1990-91.

O'Donnell, John. *Hans Urs von Balthasar*. London, Geoffrey Chapman, 1992.
Endean, Philip. *Heythrop J*, 34(4), 440-442, O 93.

O'Farrell, Clare. *Foucault: Historian or Philosopher?*. New York, St Martin's Pr, 1989.
Cole, Steven E. *Clio*, 21(3), 308-311, Spr 92.

O'Hanlon, G F. *The Immutability of God in the Theology of Hans Urs von Balthasar*. New York, Cambridge Univ Pr, 1990.
MacKinnon, Donald M. *Phil Quart*, 42(169), 517-519, O 92.

O'Neill, Onora. *Constructions of Reason*. New York, Cambridge Univ Pr, 1989.
Wood, Allen W. *Phil Rev*, 101(3), 647-650, Jl 92.

O'Rourke, Fran (ed). *At the Heart of the Real*. Dublin, Irish Acad Pr, 1992.
Maurer, Armand. *Amer Cath Phil Quart*, 67(3), 394-397, Sum 93.

Oakes, Guy. *The Soul of the Salesman*. Atlantic Highlands, Humanities Pr, 1990.
Roberts, Anthony. *J Applied Phil*, 9(2), 259-260, 1992.

Oakes, Guy. *Weber and Rickert*. Cambridge, MIT Pr, 1988.
Wagner, Gerhard. *Phil Rundsch*, 39(3), 249-253, 1992.

Oakeshott, Michael. *Rationalism in Politics and Other Essays*. Indianapolis, Liberty Fund, 1991.
Kukathas, Chandran. *Polit Theory*, 21(2), 339-343, My 93.
Thomas, D A Lloyd. *Philosophy*, 67(261), 416-418, Jl 92.

Oakley, Justin. *Morality and the Emotions*. New York, Routledge, 1992.
Dunn, Robert. *Austl J Phil*, 70(4), 489-493, D 92.
Marsh, Michael. *Rev Metaph*, 46(2), 414-416, 1992.

Oehrle, Richard T (ed), Bach, Emmon (ed) and Wheeler, Deirdre (ed). *Categorical Grammars and Natural Language Structures*. Dordrecht, Kluwer, 1988.
Moss, Lawrence S. *Stud Log*, 50(1), 164-167, Mr 91.

Ogden, Schubert M. *Is There Only One True Religion or Are There Many?*. Dallas, South Methodist U Pr, Undated.
D'Costa, Gavin. *Mod Theol*, 9(2), 232-234, Ap 93.

Okin, Susan. *Justice, Gender, and the Family*. New York, Basic Books, 1989.
Lind, Marcia. *Hypatia*, 8(1), 209-214, Wint 93.

Oldenberg, Hermann and Shrotri, Shridhar B (trans). *The Doctrine of the Upanisads and the Early Buddhism*. Delhi, Motilal Banarsidass, 1991.
Killingley, D H. *Asian Phil*, 3(1), 63-64, Mr 93.

Oldenquist, Andrew (ed) and Rosner, Menachem (ed). *Alienation, Community, and Work*. Westport, Greenwood Pr, 1991.
Arnold, N Scott. *Can Phil Rev*, 12(2), 128-130, Ap 92.

Oldfield, Adrian. *Citizenship and Community*. New York, Routledge, 1990.
Jordan, Bill. *Hist Polit Thought*, 12(4), 735-740, Wint 91.

Olding, Alan. *Modern Biology and Natural Theology*. New York, Routledge, 1991.
Burke, T E. *Phil Books*, 33(3), 183-185, Jl 92.
Pailin, David A. *Relig Stud*, 28(3), 425-434, S 92.
Schoen, Edward L. *Int J Phil Relig*, 34(2), 115-116, O 93.

Ols, Daniel. *Le Cristologie contemporanee e le loro posizioni fondamentali al vaglio della dottrina di S Tommaso*. Vatican City, Vaticana, 1991.
O'Connor, James T. *Thomist*, 56(3), 533-535, Jl 92.

Oppenheim, Felix E. *The Place of Morality in Foreign Policy*. London, Heath, 1991.
Brandt, Richard B. *Polit Theory*, 21(2), 343-346, My 93.

Oppenheim, Frank M. *Royce's Mature Philosophy of Religion*. Notre Dame, Univ Notre Dame Pr, Undated.
Stuhr, John J. *Ideal Stud*, 22(3), 290-293, S 92.

Organ, Troy Wilson. *Philosophy and the Self*. London, Associated Univ Pr, 1987.
Riepe, Dale. *Phil East West*, 42(3), 536-538, Jl 92.

Ormiston, Gayle L. *From Artifact to Habitat*. Bethlehem, Lehigh Univ Pr, 1990.
Compton, John J. *Res Phil Technol*, 12, 360-364, 1992.

Orr, Linda. *Headless History*. Ithaca, Cornell Univ Pr, 1990.
Kramer, Lloyd S. *Hist Euro Ideas*, 14(2), 306-307, Mr 92.
Shiner, Larry. *Hist Theor*, 32(1), 90-96, 1993.

Ott, Hugo. *Martin Heidegger: Éléments pour une biographie*. Paris, Beloeil, 1990.
Gravel, P. *Philosophiques*, 19(1), 146-150, 1992.

Overall, Christine (ed) and Zion, William P (ed). *Perspectives on AIDS*. New York, Oxford Univ Pr, 1991.
Harrison, Christine. *Can Phil Rev*, 12(2), 130-132, Ap 92.
Levine, Carol. *Hastings Center Rep*, 23(4), 39-40, Jl-Ag 93.

Pailin, David A. *God and the Processes of Reality*. New York, Routledge, 1989.
Polkinghorne, John. *Zygon*, 27(3), 348-350, S 92.
Ray, R J. *Int J Phil Relig*, 32(2), 127-128, Oct 92.

Pakaluk, Michael (ed). *Other Selves*. Indianapolis, Hackett, 1991.
Caraway, Carol. *Teach Phil*, 15(4), 375-378, D 92.
Richards, Norvin. *Can Phil Rev*, 12(1), 53-54, F 92.

Panagiotou, Spiro (ed). *Justice, Law and Method in Plato and Aristotle*. Edmonton, Academic, 1987.
Harwood, Sterling. *Vera Lex*, 12(1), 37-39, 1992.

Pandit, G L. *The Structure and Growth of Scientific Knowledge*. Dordrecht, Kluwer, 1983.
Shekhawat, V. *J Indian Counc Phil Res*, 9(2), 183-187, Ja-Ap 92.

Pangle, Thomas. *The Ennobling of Democracy*. Baltimore, Johns Hopkins U Pr, 1992.
Gottfried, Paul. *Rev Metaph*, 46(1), 174-175, S 92.
Spragens Jr, Thomas A. *Polit Theory*, 21(2), 334-338, My 93.

Pangle, Thomas L (ed). *The Roots of Political Philosophy*. Ithaca, Cornell Univ Pr, 1987.
Glidden, David K. *Nous*, 27(1), 99-101, Mr 93.

Pannenberg, Wolfhart. *Systematic Theology, Volume I*. Grand Rapids, Eerdmans, 1991.
Hütter, Reinhard. *Mod Theol*, 9(1), 90-93, Ja 93.

Paolini, Shirley J. *Creativity, Culture and Values*. New York, Lang, 1990.
Bredin, Hugh. *Brit J Aes*, 32(3), 283-285, Jl 92.

Paredaens, Jan (& others). *The Structure of the Relational Database Model*. New York, Springer-Verlag, 1989.
Makowsky, J A. *J Sym Log*, 57(2), 759-760, J 92.

Parel, Anthony J. *The Machiavellian Cosmos*. New Haven, Yale Univ Pr, 1992.
Witt, Ronald G. *J Hist Phil*, 31(3), 464-466, Jl 93.

Parkes, Graham (ed). *Nietzsche and Asian Thought*. Chicago, Univ of Chicago Pr, 1991.
Higgins, Kathleen Marie. *Phil East West*, 43(1), 141-144, Ja 93.

Parry, David M. *Hegel's Phenomenology of the 'We'*. New York, Lang, 1989.
Fenton, Kyle. *Owl Minerva*, 24(2), 208-215, Spr 93.

Parry, William T and Hacker, Edward A. *Aristotelian Logic*. Albany, SUNY Pr, 1991.
Bedell, Gary. *Rev Metaph*, 46(1), 175-176, S 92.
Englebretsen, George. *Inform Log*, 14(1), 75-82, Wint 92.
Kelly, Charles J. *Teach Phil*, 15(3), 298-300, S 92.

Parthasarathi, G (ed) and Chattopadhyaya, D P (ed). *Radhakrishnan Centenary Volume*. New York, Oxford Univ Pr, 1989.
Coward, Harold. *Phil East West*, 42(4), 679-682, O 92.

Passmore, John. *Serious Art*. Peru, Open Court, 1991.
Iseminger, Gary. *Can Phil Rev*, 12(6), 424-426, D 92.
Lord, Catherine. *J Aes Art Crit*, 51(1), 77-79, Wint 93.

Patocka, Jan. *Le monde naturel et le mouvement de l'existence humaine*. Dordrecht, Kluwer, 1988.
Bourke, Vernon J. *Mod Sch*, 70(1), 68-70, N 92.

Patterson, Dennis M (ed). *Wittgenstein and Legal Theory*. Boulder, Westview Pr, 1992.
Goldstein, Laurence. *Phil Books*, 34(4), 242-244, O 93.

Patterson, Orlando. *Freedom*. London, Tauris, 1991.
King, Richard H. *Hist Theor*, 31(3), 326-335, 1992.

Pattison, George. *Kierkegaard: The Aesthetic and the Religious*. New York, St Martin's Pr, 1992.
Martinez, Roy. *J Hist Phil*, 31(2), 299-301, Ap 93.
Wilkinson, R. *Brit J Aes*, 33(2), 194-196, Ap 93.

Pattison, Robert. *The Great Dissent*. New York, Oxford Univ Pr, 1991.
Ferreira, M Jamie. *Thomist*, 57(2), 331-336, Ap 93.

Paty, Michel. *La matière dérobée*. Paris, Ed Archives Cont, 1988.
Da Costa, Newton C A. *Arch Phil*, 56(2), 285-287, Ap-Je 93.

Patzig, Günther (ed). *Aristoteles "Politik"*. Göttingen, Vandenhoeck, 1990.
Brunschwig, Jacques. *J Hist Phil*, 30(4), 597-598, O 92.

Paulson, Ronald. *Breaking and Remarking*. New Brunswick, Rutgers Univ Pr, 1989.
Townsend, Dabney. *J Aes Art Crit*, 49(3), 271-273, Sum 91.

Pavel, Thomas G. *Fictional Worlds*. Cambridge, Harvard Univ Pr, 1986.
Feagin, Susan L. *J Aes Art Crit*, 46(3), 428-430, Spr 88.

Payne, Steven. *John of the Cross and the Cognitive Value of Mysticism*. Dordrecht, Kluwer, 1990.
Polis, Dennis F. *Mod Sch*, 70(2), 153-155, Ja 93.

Peacocke, Arthur. *Theology for a Scientific Age*. Cambridge, Blackwell, 1990.
Peters, Ted. *Zygon*, 27(3), 350-352, S 92.
Quinn, Philip L. *Phil Sci*, 60(1), 516-518, Mr 93.

Pears, David. *Hume's System*. New York, Oxford Univ Pr, 1990.
Campolo, Christian K. *Hume Stud*, 19(1), 227-232, Ap 93.
Heathcote, Adrian. *Austl J Phil*, 71(2), 224-227, Je 93.
Mink, Kelly. *J Hist Phil*, 30(4), 615-617, O 92.

Pears, David. *The False Prison*. New York, Oxford Univ Pr, 1988.
Harré, Rom. *Int Stud Phil*, 24(1), 123-124, 1992.

Peczenik, Aleksander. *On Law and Reason*. Dordrecht, Kluwer, 1989.
Shiner, Roger A. *Can Phil Rev*, 12(1), 55-57, F 92.

Peden, Creighten (ed) and Sterba, James P (ed). *Freedom, Equality, and Social Change*. Lewiston, Mellen Pr, 1989.
Corea, Peter V. *Ideal Stud*, 22(3), 234-235, S 92.

Peden, W Creighton (ed) and Axel, Larry E (ed). *God, Values, and Empiricism*. Macon, Mercer Univ Pr, 1989.
Raposa, Michael L. *Trans Peirce Soc*, 28(2), 371-378, Spr 92.
Viney, Donald Wayne. *Int J Phil Relig*, 32(2), 125-126, Oct 92.

Pefanis, Julian. *Heterology and the Postmodern*. Durham, Duke Univ Pr, 1991.
Macey, David. *Rad Phil*, 61, 61, Sum 92.

Peffer, R G. *Marxism, Morality and Social Justice*. Princeton, Princeton Univ Pr, 1990.
Marsden, John. *Heythrop J*, 34(1), 93-94, Ja 93.

Pelikan, Jaroslav. *The Idea of the University*. New Haven, Yale Univ Pr, 1992.
Dulles, Avery. *Int Phil Quart*, 33(2), 240-241, Je 93.

Pelletier, Frances Jeffry. *Parmenides, Plato, and the Semantics of Not-Being*. Chicago, Univ of Chicago Pr, 1990.
Constantineau, Philippe. *Phoenix*, 47(2), 183-185, Sum 93.
Marler, J C. *Mod Sch*, 70(1), 66-68, N 92.
Morris, Michael. *Phil Rev*, 101(4), 835-838, O 92.
Peterson, Sandra. *Rev Metaph*, 46(2), 417-419, 1992.

Penella, Robert J. *Greek Philosophers and Sophists in the Fourth Century AD*. Leeds, Francis Cairns, 1990.
Buck, D F. *Phoenix*, 47(1), 90-92, Spr 93.

Peperzak, Adriaan. *To the Other: An Introduction to the Philosophy of Emmanuel Levinas*. West Lafayette, Purdue Univ Pr, 1993.
Tallon, Andrew. *Amer Cath Phil Quart*, 67(3), 397-400, Sum 93.

Peperzak, Adriaan Theodoor. *Hegels praktische Philosophie*. Stuttgart, Frommann-Holzboog, 1991.
Zoeller, Guenter. *Rev Metaph*, 46(1), 176-178, S 92.

Percesepe, Gary (ed). *Philosophy*. New York, Macmillan, 1991.
Bielfeldt, Dennis. *Teach Phil*, 15(2), 185-188, J 92.

Perkins, David. *Is Literary History Possible?*. Baltimore, Johns Hopkins U Pr, 1992.
Cain, William E. *Phil Lit*, 16(2), 383-384, O 92.

Perkins, Robert L (ed). *International Kierkegaard Commentary*. Macon, Mercer Univ Pr, 1990.
Matustik, M. *Man World*, 26(1), 93-97, Ja 93.
Matustik, Martin J. *Int Phil Quart*, 32(4), 524-526, D 92.
Morris, T F. *Heythrop J*, 34(1), 111-112, Ja 93.

Perl, Jed. *Paris Without End*. Berkeley, North Point Pr, 1988.
Todd, D D. *J Aes Art Crit*, 47(4), 394-395, Fall 89.

Perrett, Roy W (ed). *Indian Philosophy of Religion*. Dordrecht, Kluwer, 1989.
Carter, Robert E. *Int J Phil Relig*, 34(1), 62-64, Ag 93.

Perry, Michael J. *Love and Power*. New York, Oxford Univ Pr, 1991.
Bradley, Gerard V. *Rev Metaph*, 46(2), 419-421, 1992.

Perry, Michael J. *Morality, Politics, and Law*. New York, Oxford Univ Pr, 1988.
Kelly, Robert Q. *Vera Lex*, 12(1), 26-27, 1992.

Peset, José Luis (ed) and Gracia, Diego (ed). *The Ethics of Diagnosis*. Dordrecht, Kluwer, 1992.
Short, David S. *Ethics Med*, 9(2), 31-32, Sum 93.

Peterman, James F. *Philosophy as Therapy*. Albany, SUNY Pr, 1992.
Schiller, Britt-Marie. *Mod Sch*, 70(2), 156-159, Ja 93.

Petrey, Sandy. *Speech Acts and Literary Theory*. New York, Routledge, 1990.
Simpson, Paul. *J Prag*, 17(4), 369-372, Ap 92.

Pettersson, Anders. *A Theory of Literary Discourse*. Lund, Lund Univ Pr, 1990.
Sirridge, Mary. *J Aes Art Crit*, 50(2), 169-171, Spr 92.

Pfeifer, Karl. *Actions and Other Events*. New York, Lang, 1989.
Rankin, Kenneth. *Can Phil Rev*, 12(2), 133-135, Ap 92.

Philip, Franklin (trans). *Political Philosophy, Volume I*. Chicago, Univ of Chicago Pr, 1990.
Marshall, Terence E. *Interpretation*, 20(2), 217-224, Wint 92-93.

Phillips, D Z. *Faith After Foundationalism*. New York, Routledge, 1988.
Wolterstorff, Nicholas. *Phil Rev*, 101(2), 452-455, Ap 92.

Phillips, D Z. *From Fantasy to Faith*. New York, Macmillan, 1991.
Giles, Gordon J. *Brit J Aes*, 32(3), 285-286, Jl 92.
Lyas, Colin. *Phil Books*, 33(3), 185-187, Jl 92.

Pike, Nelson. *Mystic Union*. Ithaca, Cornell Univ Pr, 1992.
Phillips, D Z. *Phil Books*, 34(1), 60-62, Ja 93.

Pines, Shlomo (ed) and Yovel, Yirmiyahu (ed). *Maimonides and Philosophy*. Dordrecht, Kluwer, 1986.
Shatz, David. *Int Stud Phil*, 24(1), 124-127, 1992.

Pinsky, Valerie (ed) and Wylie, Alison (ed). *Critical Traditions in Contemporary Archaeology*. New York, Cambridge Univ Pr, 1990.
Patrik, Linda E. *Phil Sci*, 59(4), 701-703, D 92.

Pippin, Robert P. *Hegel's Idealism: The Satisfaction of Self-Consciousness*. New York, Cambridge Univ Pr, 1989.
Dulckeit, Katharina. *Owl Minerva*, 24(1), 87-91, Fall 92.

Piske, Irmgard. *Offenbarung—Sprache—Vernunft*. New York, Lang, 1989.
Majetschak, Stefan. *Kantstudien*, 83(3), 344-347, 1992.

Pittock, Joan H (ed) and Wear, Andrew (ed). *Interpretation and Cultural History*. New York, St Martin's Pr, 1991.
Nussdorfer, Laurie. *Hist Theor*, 32(1), 74-83, 1993.

Platts, Mark. *Moral Realities*. New York, Routledge, 1991.
Dent, N J H. *Phil Rev*, 102(2), 270-271, Ap 93.
Jecker, Nancy S. *J Value Inq*, 17(4), 279-281, Jl 93.
Lovibond, Sabina. *Phil Books*, 33(3), 178-180, Jl 92.
Michael, Mark A. *Mind*, 101(402), 383-386, Ap 92.
Walker, A D M. *Phil Quart*, 43(170), 107-110, Ja 93.

Plochmann, George Kimball. *Richard McKeon*. Chicago, Univ of Chicago Pr, 1990.
Betz, Joseph. *Trans Peirce Soc*, 28(2), 350-355, Spr 92.
Earls, C Anthony. *J Speculative Phil*, 6(4), 322-327, 1992.

Plotin. *Traité sur la liberté et la volonté de l'Un*. Paris, Vrin, 1990.
Rist, John M. *Can Phil Rev*, 12(1), 42-44, F 92.

Poirier, Richard. *Poetry and Pragmatism*. Cambridge, Harvard Univ Pr, 1992.
Broman, Walter E. *Phil Lit*, 17(1), 129-130, Ap 93.

Pojman, Louis P (ed). *Introduction to Philosophy*. Belmont, Wadsworth, 1991.
Bielfeldt, Dennis. *Teach Phil*, 15(2), 185-188, J 92.

Pole, Nelson. *LogicCoach, Version 1.2*. Belmont, Wadsworth, Undated.
McGray, James W. *Teach Phil*, 15(4), 367-371, D 92.

Polka, Brayton. *Truth and Interpretation*. New York, St Martin's Pr, 1990.
Lightman, Bernard. *Hist Euro Ideas*, 17(1), 101-104, Ja 93.

Polkinghorne, Donald E. *Narrative Knowing and the Human Sciences*. Albany, SUNY Pr, 1988.
Flaherty, Peter. *Phil Soc Sci*, 22(2), 262-264, J 92.

Pollack, Griselda. *Vision and Difference*. New York, Routledge, 1988.
Connelly, Frances S. *J Aes Art Crit*, 49(1), 81-83, Wint 91.

Pollard, Stephen. *Philosophical Introduction to Set Theory*. Notre Dame, Univ Notre Dame Pr, 1990.
Konyndyk, Kenneth. *Teach Phil*, 15(2), 203-206, J 92.

Pollard, Stephen. *Technical Methods in Philosophy*. Boulder, Westview Pr, 1990.
Konyndyk, Kenneth. *Teach Phil*, 15(2), 203-206, J 92.

Pollock, John. *How to Build a Person*. Cambridge, MIT Pr, 1989.
Israel, David. *Phil Rev*, 101(4), 901-903, O 92.

Pollock, John L. *Nomic Probability and the Foundations of Induction*. New York, Oxford Univ Pr, 1990.
Kyburg Jr, Henry E. *Phil Rev*, 102(1), 115-117, Ja 93.

Pompa, Leon. *Vico: A Study of the "New Science" (Second Edition)*. New York, Cambridge Univ Pr, 1990.
Adam, A M. *Phil Soc Sci*, 23(2), 243-247, Je 93.

Poole, Ross. *Morality and Modernity*. New York, Routledge, 1991.
Baxter, Brian. *Phil Books*, 33(3), 180-182, Jl 92.
Moulder, James. *S Afr J Phil*, 12(2), 48-49, My 93.
Sullivan, John. *Heythrop J*, 34(4), 464-465, O 93.

Porter, Elizabeth. *Women and Moral Identity*. Scranton, Unwin Hyman, 1991.
Green, Karen. *Austl J Phil*, 70(3), 371-373, S 92.

Posner, Richard A. *The Problems of Jurisprudence*. Cambridge, Harvard Univ Pr, 1990.
Stotzky, Irwin P. *Econ Phil*, 8(1), 197-206, Ap 92.

Post, John F. *Metaphysics*. New York, Paragon House, 1991.
Butchvarov, Panayot. *Int Stud Phil*, 24(1), 83-84, 1992.
Kane, Robert. *Teach Phil*, 15(2), 188-190, J 92.

Poteat, William H. *A Philosophical Daybook*. Columbia, Univ of Missouri Pr, 1990.
Hall, Ronald L. *Int J Phil Relig*, 33(1), 61-62, F 93.

Powell, C Thomas. *Kant's Theory of Self-Consciousness*. New York, Oxford Univ Pr, 1990.
Hamilton, Andy. *Phil Books*, 34(1), 19-21, Ja 93.
Kitcher, Patricia. *Phil Rev*, 102(1), 94-99, Ja 93.
Powell, C Thomas. *Phil Phenomenol Res*, 53(1), 242-245, Mr 93.
Zoeller, Guenter. *J Hist Phil*, 30(4), 619-621, O 92.

Powell, Robert. *Nuclear Deterrence Theory*. New York, Cambridge Univ Pr, 1990.
Lackey, Douglas P. *Can Phil Rev*, 12(2), 135-137, Ap 92.

Pradines, Maurice. *Esprit de la Religion*. New York, Verso, 1992.
Guyot, Roland. *Arch Phil*, 55(3), 515-517, Jl-S 92.

Prevost, Robert. *Probability and Theistic Explanation*. New York, Clarendon/Oxford Pr, 1990.
Gerson, Lloyd P. *Rev Metaph*, 45(4), 876-878, J 92.
Milne, Peter. *Heythrop J*, 33(4), 479-481, O 92.

Preziosi, Donald. *Rethinking Art History*. New Haven, Yale Univ Pr, 1989.
Silvers, Anita. *J Aes Art Crit*, 49(1), 95-96, Wint 91.

Price, A W. *Love and Friendship in Plato and Aristotle*. New York, Oxford Univ Pr, 1989.
Glidden, David. *Nous*, 27(1), 109-110, Mr 93.
Sherman, Nancy. *Int Stud Phil*, 24(1), 127-128, 1992.

Price, Sally. *Primitive Art in Civilized Places*. Chicago, Univ of Chicago Pr, 1989.
Wicks, Robert. *J Aes Art Crit*, 50(1), 74-76, Wint 92.

Prier, Raymond Adolph (ed). *Countercurrents*. Albany, SUNY Pr, 1992.
Kleiner, John. *Phil Lit*, 17(1), 161-163, Ap 93.
Skilleas, Ole Martin. *Brit J Aes*, 33(3), 298-299, Jl 93.

Priest, G (ed) and Norman, J (ed). *Paraconsistent Logic*. Munchen, Philosophia, 1989.
Helman, G H. *Hist Phil Log*, 13(2), 247-249, 1992.
Tuziak, Roman. *Brit J Phil Sci*, 44(1), 167-170, Mr 93.

Priest, Stephen (ed). *Hegel's Critique of Kant*. New York, Clarendon/Oxford Pr, 1987.
Fulda, Hans Friedrich. *Nous*, 27(1), 118-121, Mr 93.

Priest, Stephen. *Theories of the Mind*. New York, Penguin USA, 1991.
Everitt, Nicholas. *Phil Books*, 34(1), 38-39, Ja 93.

Primoratz, Igor. *Justifying Legal Punishment*. Atlantic Highlands, Humanities Pr, 1989.
Hoekema, David A. *Crim Just Ethics*, 11(1), 58-62, Wint-Spr 92.

Prior, William J. *Virtue and Knowledge*. New York, Routledge, 1991.
Moulder, James. *S Afr J Phil*, 12(2), 48-49, My 93.
O'Connor, David K. *Teach Phil*, 15(4), 405-407, D 92.

Pritchard, Michael S. *On Becoming Responsible*. Lawrence, Univ Pr Kansas, 1991.
Blustein, Jeffrey. *Phil Rev*, 102(1), 141-144, Ja 93.

Proust, Joëlle and Brenner, A (trans). *Questions of Form*. Minneapolis, Univ of Minn Pr, 1989.
Friedman, Michael. *Nous*, 26(4), 532-542, D 92.

Pufendorf, Samuel and Seidler, Michael (trans). *On the Natural State of Men*. Lewiston, Mellen Pr, 1990.
Johnson, Harold J. *Can Phil Rev*, 12(2), 137-139, Ap 92.

Pufendorf, Samuel, Tully, James (ed) and Silverthorne, Michael (trans). *On the Duty of Man and Citizen*. New York, Cambridge Univ Pr, 1991.
Cvek, Peter P. *Can Phil Rev*, 12(3), 211-213, J-Jl 92.

Puntel, Lorenz B. *Grundlagen einer Theorie der Wahrheit*. Hawthorne, de Gruyter, 1990.
Metschl, Ulrich. *Erkenntnis*, 36(2), 263-266, Mr 92.
Smith, Barry. *Phil Phenomenol Res*, 52(2), 494-496, Je 92.

Purdy, Laura M. *In Their Best Interest?*. Ithaca, Cornell Univ Pr, 1992.
Leahy, Michael. *Phil Books*, 34(1), 57-58, Ja 93.

Puster, Rolf W. *Britische Gassendi-Rezeption am Beispiel John Lockes*. Stuttgart, Frommann-Holzboog, 1991.
Michael, Frederick S. *J Hist Phil*, 31(2), 293-295, Ap 93.

Putnam, Hilary. *Il pragmatismo: una questione aperta*. Bari, Laterza, 1992.
Pagnini, Alessandro. *Phil Quart*, 43(173), 548-550, O 93.

Putnam, Hilary. *Representation and Reality*. Cambridge, MIT Pr, 1988.
Hannon, Barbara. *Nous*, 27(1), 102-106, Mr 93.
Staknaker, Robert. *Phil Rev*, 101(2), 359-362, Ap 92.

Putnam, Hilary and Conant, James (ed). *Realism with a Human Face*. Cambridge, Harvard Univ Pr, 1990.
Kerr, Fergus. *Heythrop J*, 34(1), 103-104, Ja 93.

Pybus, Elizabeth. *Human Goodness*. Toronto, Univ of Toronto Pr, 1991.
Davie, William. *J Applied Phil*, 10(2), 268-270, 1993.
Miller, Peter. *Can Phil Rev*, 12(4), 289-291, Ag 92.

Quillien, Jean. *L'anthropologie philosophique de G de Humboldt*. Villeneuve d'Ascq cedex, Pr Univ Lille, 1991.
Thouard, Denis. *Arch Phil*, 55(3), 506-509, Jl-S 92.

Quine, W V, Carnap, Rudolf and Creath, Richard (ed). *Dear Carnap, Dean Van*. Berkeley, Univ of Calif Pr, 1991.
Stroud, Barry. *J Phil*, 89(7), 383-386, Jl 92.

Rabaté, J M and Wetzel, M. *L'éthique du don*. Paris, Transition, 1992.
Boissinot, Christian. *Laval Theol Phil*, 49(2), 339-342, Je 93.

Rabinow, Paul. *French Modern*. Cambridge, MIT Pr, 1989.
Goldblatt, David. *J Aes Art Crit*, 49(1), 92-95, Wint 91.

Ragland-Sullivan, Ellie (ed) and Bracher, Mark (ed). *Lacan and the Subject of Language*. New York, Routledge, 1991.
Elliott, Anthony. *Rad Phil*, 61, 43-44, Sum 92.

Rajchman, John. *Philosophical Events*. New York, Columbia Univ Pr, 1991.
May, Todd G. *J Speculative Phil*, 6(3), 250-255, 1992.
Weberman, David. *J Aes Art Crit*, 50(2), 168-169, Spr 92.

Rakover, Sam S. *Metapsychology*. New York, Paragon House, 1990.
Nachson, Israel. *Hist Euro Ideas*, 17(2-3), 387-389, Mr-My 93.

Rakowski, Eric. *Equal Justice*. New York, Clarendon/Oxford Pr, 1991.
Bix, Brian. *Mind*, 102(405), 193-195, Ja 93.
Gross, Barry R. *Phil Books*, 34(3), 181-184, Jl 93.

Ramberg, Bjorn T. *Donald Davidson's Philosophy of Language*. Cambridge, Blackwell, 1989.
Genova, A C. *Can Phil Rev*, 12(3), 191-194, J-Jl 92.

Ramsey, F P and Galavotti, Maria Carla (ed). *Notes on Philosophy, Probability and Mathematics*. Naples, Bibliopolis, 1991.
Sahlin, Nils-Eric. *Erkenntnis*, 39(1), 123-126, Jl 93.

Ramsey, William (ed), Stich, Stephen P (ed) and Rumelhart, David E (ed). *Philosophy and Connectionist Theory*. East Sussex, Erlbaum, 1991.
Aizawa, Kenneth. *Mind Lang*, 7(3), 286-297, Fall 92.

Rancière, Jacques. *The Ignorant Schoolmaster*. Stanford, Stanford Univ Pr, 1991.
Lang, Candace. *Can Phil Rev*, 12(5), 344-347, O 92.

Rankin, Kenneth. *The Recovery of the Soul*. Montreal, McGill-Queens U Pr, 1991.
Furton, E J. *Rev Metaph*, 46(3), 638-639, Mr 93.
Hamlyn, D W. *Philosophy*, 67(260), 259-260, Apr 92.
Lee-Lampshire, Wendy. *Can Phil Rev*, 12(6), 426-428, D 92.

Rapaport, Herman. *Heidegger and Derrida*. Lincoln, Univ of Nebraska Pr, 1989.
Hodge, Joanna. *J Brit Soc Phenomenol*, 23(2), 183-184, M 92.

Rapp, Friedrich (ed) and Wiehl, Reiner (ed). *Whitehead's Metaphysics of Creativity*. Albany, SUNY Pr, 1990.
Viney, Donald Wayne. *Process Stud*, 20(3), 181-183, Fall 91.

Rasmussen, David M. *Reading Habermas*. Cambridge, Blackwell, 1990.
Murphy, John W. *Stud Soviet Tho*, 44(2), 156-158, S 92.

Rasmussen, Douglas B and Den, Douglas J. *Liberty and Nature*. Peru, Open Court, 1991.
Ahrens, John. *Int Phil Quart*, 32(4), 526-527, D 92.
Pentecost, Scott F. *Teach Phil*, 15(4), 388-390, D 92.

Rauche, Gerhard A. *Knowledge and Experience*. Alice, Fort Hare Univ Pr, 1990.
Louw, T. *S Afr J Phil*, 11(2), 43-45, My 92.

Ray, Christopher. *Time, Space and Philosophy*. New York, Routledge, 1991.
Clifton, Robert. *Phil Books*, 34(2), 123-125, Ap 93.

Raz, Joseph. *Practical Reason and Norms (Second Edition)*. Princeton, Princeton Univ Pr, 1990.
Edmundson, William. *Law Phil*, 12(3), 329-343, Ag 93.

Raz, Joseph. *The Morality of Freedom*. New York, Clarendon/Oxford Pr, 1989.
Raunié, Raul. *Filozof Istraz*, 12(1), 276-280, 1992.

Snare, Francis. *The Nature of Moral Thinking*. New York, Routledge, 1992.
Almond, Brenda. *Phil Quart*, 43(171), 256-259, Ap 93.
Snider, Eric W. *Teach Phil*, 16(1), 73-75, Mr 93.

Snyder, Gary. *The Practice of the Wild*. San Francisco, Sierra Club Books, 1990.
Oelschlaeger, Max. *Environ Ethics*, 14(2), 185-190, Sum 92.

Sober, Elliott. *Reconstructing the Past*. Cambridge, MIT Pr, 1989.
Godfrey-Smith, Peter. *Phil Phenomenol Res*, 53(2), 487-490, Je 93.
Griesemer, James R. *Phil Rev*, 101(3), 725-729, Jl 92.

Soble, Alan. *The Philosophy of Sex (Second Edition)*. Lanham, Rowman & Littlefield, 1991.
Annis, David B. *Teach Phil*, 15(4), 372-374, D 92.

Solomon, Robert C (ed) and Higgins, Kathleen M (ed). *The Philosophy of (Erotic) Love*. Lawrence, Univ Pr Kansas, 1991.
Caraway, Carol. *Teach Phil*, 15(4), 375-378, D 92.
Ginsberg, Robert. *Can Phil Rev*, 13(1), 61-63, F 93.

Solomon, Robert C (ed) and Murphy, Mark C (ed). *What is Justice?*. New York, Oxford Univ Pr, 1990.
Freund, Norman C. *Teach Phil*, 15(3), 270-271, S 92.

Sommer, Manfred. *Evidenz im Augenblick*. Frankfurt, Suhrkamp, 1987.
Hart, J. *Husserl Stud*, 9(3), 227-236, 1992.

Sorabji, Richard (ed). *Aristotle Transformed*. Ithaca, Cornell Univ Pr, 1990.
Striker, Gisela. *Phil Rev*, 101(4), 847-849, O 92.

Sorell, Tom. *Scientism*. New York, Routledge, 1991.
Botterill, George. *Phil Books*, 34(4), 232-234, O 93.
Kitchen, Gary. *Rad Phil*, 61, 51-52, Sum 92.
Malik, Habib C. *Rev Metaph*, 46(1), 179-181, S 92.

Sorensen, Roy A. *Blindspots*. New York, Clarendon/Oxford Pr, 1988.
Smith, Robin. *Mod Sch*, 70(1), 73-75, N 92.

Sosa, Ernest. *Knowledge in Perspective*. New York, Cambridge Univ Pr, 1991.
Alston, William P. *Mind*, 102(405), 199-203, Ja 93.
Schmitt, Frederick F. *Phil Rev*, 102(3), 421-424, Jl 93.
Wilkerson, T E. *Phil Books*, 33(3), 159-161, Jl 92.

Souffrin, P and Segonds, A P. *Nicolas Oresme*. Paris, Belles Lettres, 1988.
Gagnon, Claude. *Dialogue (Canada)*, 31(3), 535-538, Sum 92.

Southern, R W. *Saint Anselm: A Portrait in a Landscape*. New York, Cambridge Univ Pr, 1990.
Davies, Brian. *Heythrop J*, 34(2), 208-209, Ap 93.

Sparshott, Francis. *Off the Ground*. Princeton, Princeton Univ Pr, 1988.
Carter, Curtis. *J Aes Art Crit*, 48(1), 81-83, Wint 90.

Spector, Horacio. *Autonomy and Rights*. New York, Clarendon/Oxford Pr, 1992.
Mack, Eric. *Mind*, 102(406), 394-397, Ap 93.

Spinker, Michael. *Imaginary Relations*. New York, Verso, 1987.
Kellner, Douglas. *J Aes Art Crit*, 47(4), 390-392, Fall 89.

Spitz, Ellen Handler. *Image and Insight*. New York, Columbia Univ Pr, 1991.
Novitz, David. *J Aes Art Crit*, 50(4), 331-332, Fall 92.

Spohn, W (ed), Van Fraassen, B C (ed) and Skyrms, B (ed). *Existence and Explanation*. Dordrecht, Kluwer, 1991.
Lowe, E J. *Hist Phil Log*, 14(1), 130-131, 1993.
Oliver, Alex. *Phil Books*, 34(2), 101-103, Ap 93.

Springborg, Patricia. *Royal Persons*. Scranton, Unwin Hyman, 1990.
Black, Antony. *Hist Polit Thought*, 12(4), 743-746, Wint 91.

Stam, Robert. *Subversive Pleasures*. Baltimore, Johns Hopkins U Pr, 1989.
Tavis, Anna A. *J Aes Art Crit*, 49(1), 88-90, Wint 91.

Stambovsky, Phillip. *The Depictive Image*. Amherst, Univ of Mass Pr, 1988.
Johnson, Mark. *J Aes Art Crit*, 47(3), 287-290, Sum 89.

Stanesby, Derek. *Science, Reason and Religion*. New York, Routledge, 1988.
Schlesinger, George N. *Int Stud Phil*, 24(1), 140-141, 1992.

Stark, Werner. *The Social Bond*. Bronx, Fordham Univ Pr, 1987.
Ford, Joseph Brandon. *Int Stud Phil*, 24(1), 141-143, 1992.

Staten, Henry. *Nietzsche's Voice*. Ithaca, Cornell Univ Pr, 1990.
Schrift, Alan D. *Int Stud Phil*, 24(2), 136-137, 1992.

Steig, Michael. *Stories of Reading*. Baltimore, Johns Hopkins U Pr, 1989.
Cebik, L B. *J Aes Art Crit*, 49(3), 261-263, Sum 91.

Steinkraus, Warran (ed) and Beck, Robert (ed). *Studies in Personalism, Selected Writings of Edgar Sheffield Brightman*. Utica, Meridian, 1988.
Reck, Andrew J. *Ideal Stud*, 22(3), 278-279, S 92.

Stenlund, Soren. *Language and Philosophical Problems*. New York, Routledge, 1990.
Berg, Jonathan. *Mind*, 101(403), 598-603, Jl 92.

Stephan, Achim and Patzig, Günther (& other eds). *Sinn als Bedeutung*. Hawthorne, de Gruyter, 1989.
Elders, Leo J. *Rev Metaph*, 46(1), 181-182, S 92.

Sterba, James P. *How to Make People Just*. Lanham, Rowman & Littlefield, 1988.
Montague, Phillip. *Nous*, 26(4), 543-545, D 92.

Stereiny, Kim. *The Representational Theory of Mind*. Cambridge, Blackwell, 1990.
Noordhof, Paul. *Mind*, 102(407), 530-534, Jl 93.

Stern, Robert. *Hegel, Kant and the Structure of the Object*. New York, Routledge, 1990.
Hoffmann, Susan. *Can Phil Rev*, 12(2), 143-145, Ap 92.
Schaper, Eva. *J Brit Soc Phenomenol*, 23(2), 186-187, M 92.

Sternberg, Robert J (ed). *Wisdom: Its Nature, Origins and Development*. New York, Cambridge Univ Pr, 1990.
Melchert, Norman. *Phil Psych*, 5(1), 95-97, 1992.

Stewart, David and Mickunas, Algis. *Exploring Phenomenology*. Athens, Ohio Univ Pr, 1990.
Gorner, Paul. *Phil Quart*, 42(169), 506-509, O 92.

Stewart, M A (ed). *Studies in the Philosophy of the Scottish Enlightenment*. New York, Oxford Univ Pr, 1990.
Steinberg, Eric. *J Hist Phil*, 30(4), 617-618, O 92.

Stich, Stephen P. *The Fragmentation of Reason*. Cambridge, MIT Pr, 1990.
Kobes, Bernard W. *Mind*, 101(403), 603-609, Jl 92.

Stocker, Michael. *Plural and Conflicting Values*. New York, Oxford Univ Pr, 1990.
Anderson, Elizabeth S. *Phil Rev*, 101(4), 931-933, O 92.

Stoeber, Michael. *Evil and the Mystic's God*. New York, Macmillan, 1992.
Gallie, Roger. *Asian Phil*, 3(1), 64-66, Mr 93.
Glidden, Roseanne. *Relig Stud*, 29(1), 129-136, Mr 93.

Stoekl, Allan (ed). *On Bataille*. New Haven, Yale Univ Pr, 1990.
Parkes, Graham. *Hist Euro Ideas*, 14(4), 596-597, Jl 92.

Storr, Anthony. *Music and the Mind*. New York, HarperCollins, 1992.
Berenson, Frances. *Brit J Aes*, 33(3), 295-296, Jl 93.

Stout, Jeffrey. *Ethics after Babel*. Boston, Beacon Pr, 1988.
Marino, Gordon D. *Int J Phil Relig*, 33(3), 189, Je 93.

Stove, David. *The Plato Cult and Other Philosophical Follies*. Cambridge, Blackwell, 1991.
O'Hear, Anthony. *Phil Quart*, 43(171), 264-266, Ap 93.
Smart, J J C. *Austl J Phil*, 70(1), 123-126, Mr.

Straus, Leo, Gourevitch, Victor (ed) and Roth, Michael S (ed). *On Tyranny*. New York, Free Pr, 1991.
Smith, Steven B. *Polit Theory*, 20(4), 690-693, N 92.

Strawson, Galen. *The Secret Connexion*. New York, Oxford Univ Pr, 1989.
Heathcote, Adrian. *Austl J Phil*, 71(2), 227-231, Je 93.

Strawson, P F. *Analysis and Metaphysics*. New York, Oxford Univ Pr, 1992.
Flew, Antony. *Phil Invest*, 16(4), 350-352, O 93.
Sanford, David H. *Phil Books*, 34(3), 162-163, Jl 93.
Stevenson, Leslie. *Mind*, 102(407), 534-535, Jl 93.

Strong, Tracy B. *The Idea of Political Theory*. Notre Dame, Univ Notre Dame Pr, 1990.
Kariel, Henry S. *Polit Theory*, 20(2), 345-348, My 92.

Strosberg, Martin A (& other eds). *Rationing America's Medical Care*. Washington, Brookings Inst, 1992.
Broome, John. *Bioethics*, 7(4), 351-358, Jl 93.

Stump, Eleanore. *Dialectic and Its Place in the Development of Medieval Logic*. Ithaca, Cornell Univ Pr, 1989.
Ashworth, E J. *Phil Rev*, 101(2), 377-379, Ap 92.
Cohen, Sheldon M. *Ancient Phil*, 12(1), 199-201, Spr 92.
Murphy, James J. *Phil Rhet*, 25(4), 392-395, 1992.

Sturch, Richard. *The Word and the Christ*. New York, Clarendon/Oxford Pr, 1991.
Galvin, John P. *Heythrop J*, 34(2), 190-191, Ap 93.

Suleiman, Susan Rubin. *Subversive Intent*. Cambridge, Harvard Univ Pr, 1990.
Devereaux, Mary. *J Aes Art Crit*, 50(2), 159-160, Spr 92.

Sullivan, Robert R. *Political Hermeneutics*. University Park, Penn St Univ Pr, 1989.
Nuyen, A T. *Phil Soc Sci*, 23(2), 264-268, Je 93.

Sullivan, Roger J. *Immanuel Kant's Moral Theory*. New York, Cambridge Univ Pr, 1989.
Packer, Mark. *Int J Phil Relig*, 33(2), 125-127, Ap 93.
Reath, Andrews. *Phil Rev*, 101(4), 867-870, O 92.

Sumner, L W. *The Moral Foundation of Rights*. New York, Clarendon/Oxford Pr, 1990.
Sterba, James P. *Nous*, 26(2), 246-248, J 92.

Suppes, Patrick. *Language for Humans and Robots*. Cambridge, Blackwell, 1991.
Wheeler III, Samuel C. *Mind*, 102(406), 397-400, Ap 93.

Susser, Bernard. *The Grammar of Modern Ideology*. New York, Routledge, 1988.
Williams, Howard. *Phil Soc Sci*, 22(3), 408-409, S 92.

Sustein, Cass. *After the Rights Revolution*. Cambridge, Harvard Univ Pr, 1990.
Griffin, Stephen M. *Law Phil*, 11(3), 291-296, 1992.

Suter, Ronald. *Interpreting Wittgenstein*. Philadelphia, Temple Univ Pr, 1989.
Raatzsch, Richard. *Erkenntnis*, 39(1), 111-115, Jl 93.

Swanson, Judith A. *The Public and the Private in Aristotle's Political Philosophy*. Ithaca, Cornell Univ Pr, 1992.
Yack, Bernard. *Polit Theory*, 21(4), 701-705, N 93.

Swanwick, Keith. *Music, Mind, and Education*. New York, Routledge, 1988.
Ostling Jr, Acton. *J Aes Educ*, 26(1), 120-122, Spr 92.

Swartz, Norman. *Beyond Experience, Metaphysical Theories and Philosophical Restraints*. Toronto, Univ of Toronto Pr, 1991.
Ornstein, Jack. *Can Phil Rev*, 12(5), 353-356, O 92.

Swearingen, C Jan. *Rhetoric and Irony*. New York, Oxford Univ Pr, 1991.
Bowen, Barbara C. *Phil Lit*, 17(1), 163-164, Ap 93.

Swinburne, Richard. *Revelation: From Metaphor to Analogy*. New York, Clarendon/Oxford Pr, 1992.
Banner, Michael. *Phil Books*, 34(4), 247-249, O 93.

Swindler, J K. *Weaving: An Analysis of the Constitution of Objects*. Lanham, Rowman & Littlefield, 1991.
Addis, Laird. *Can Phil Rev*, 12(3), 199-203, J-Jl 92.
Russman, Thomas A. *Rev Metaph*, 46(2), 424-425, 1992.

Tännsjö, Torbjörn. *Populist Democracy*. New York, Routledge, 1992.
Graham, Keith. *J Applied Phil*, 10(1), 127-128, 1993.

Tannery, Claude and Fagan, Teresa Lavender (trans). *Malraux, the Absolute Agnostic*. Chicago, Univ of Chicago Pr, 1991.
Morrisey, Will. *Phil Lit*, 16(2), 412-413, O 92.

Tarnas, Richard. *The Passion of the Western Mind*. Unknown, Harmony Books, 1991.
Krasevac, Edward. *Thomist*, 57(3), 550-553, Jl 93.

Taton, René (ed) and Wilson, Curtis (ed). *The General History of Astronomy (Volume II, Part A)*. New York, Cambridge Univ Pr, 1989.
Goldstein, Bernard R. *Phil Sci*, 59(4), 698-700, D 92.

Taylor, Charles. *Sources of the Self*. Cambridge, Harvard Univ Pr, 1989.
Wood, Allen W. *Phil Rev*, 101(3), 621-626, Jl 92.

Taylor, Charles. *The Ethics of Authenticity*. Cambridge, Harvard Univ Pr, 1991.
Gulick, Walter. *Tradition Discovery*, 19(1), 39-40, 1992-93.
Kennedy, Leonard A. *Amer Cath Phil Quart*, 67(3), 400-403, Sum 93.

Taylor, John R. *Linguistic Categorization*. New York, Clarendon/Oxford Pr, 1989.
Sterelny, Kim. *Rev Metaph*, 45(4), 884-885, J 92.

Taylor, Mark C. *Tears*. Albany, SUNY Pr, 1990.
Shearson, William A. *Can Phil Rev*, 12(1), 65-66, F 92.

Taylor, Max. *Effectiveness in Education and Training*. Brookfield, Avebury, 1990.
Marshall, Neil. *J Applied Phil*, 9(2), 251-253, 1992.

Teichman, Jenny and Evans, Katherine. *Philosophy: A Beginner's Guide*. Cambridge, Blackwell, 1991.
Moulder, James. *S Afr J Phil*, 12(2), 49, My 93.

Teichmann, Roger. *Abstract Entities*. New York, Macmillan, 1992.
Lewis, Harry. *Phil Books*, 34(2), 108-109, Ap 93.

Teller, Paul. *A Modern Formal Logic Primer, Volume I: Sentence Logic*. Englewood Cliffs, Prentice Hall, 1989.
Hansen, Hans V. *Teach Phil*, 15(4), 378-380, D 92.

Teller, Paul. *A Modern Formal Logic Primer, Volume II: Predicate Logic and Metatheory*. Englewood Cliffs, Prentice Hall, 1989.
Hansen, Hans V. *Teach Phil*, 15(4), 378-380, D 92.

Thagard, Paul. *Conceptual Revolutions*. Princeton, Princeton Univ Pr, 1992.
Rueger, Alexander. *Can Phil Rev*, 12(6), 433-435, D 92.

Theunissen, Michael. *Negative Theologie der Zeit*. Frankfurt, Suhrkamp, 1991.
Bolduc, René. *Arch Phil*, 55(3), 509-512, Jl-S 92.

Thiele, Leslie Paul. *Friedrich Nietzsche and the Politics of the Soul*. Princeton, Princeton Univ Pr, 1990.
Clegg, Jerry S. *Can Phil Rev*, 12(3), 153-157, J-Jl 92.
Higgins, Kathleen Marie. *J Hist Phil*, 30(3), 469-471, J 92.
Stein, Mark. *Phil Lit*, 16(2), 408-409, O 92.

Thomas, Brook. *New Historicism*. Princeton, Princeton Univ Pr, 1991.
Goodheart, Eugene. *Clio*, 21(3), 305-308, Spr 92.

Thomas, D A Lloyd. *In Defense of Liberalism*. Cambridge, Blackwell, 1988.
Penrose, Brian. *Phil Rev*, 101(2), 466-468, Ap 92.

Thomas, D O (ed). *Political Writings—Price*. New York, Cambridge Univ Pr, 1991.
Rosen, F. *Utilitas*, 5(1), 139-140, My 93.

Thomas, Geoffrey. *The Moral Philosophy of T H Green*. New York, Clarendon/Oxford Pr, 1987.
Donougho, Martin. *Ideal Stud*, 22(3), 238-240, S 92.
Martin, Rex. *Int Stud Phil*, 24(1), 143-145, 1992.

Thomas, Laurence. *Living Morally*. Philadelphia, Temple Univ Pr, 1989.
Wong, David B. *Phil Rev*, 101(3), 695-697, Jl 92.

Thompson, Ann and Thompson, John O. *Shakespeare: Meaning and Metaphor*. Iowa City, Univ of Iowa Pr, 1987.
Novitz, David. *J Aes Art Crit*, 47(1), 92-93, Wint 89.

Thompson, Janna. *Justice and World Order*. New York, Routledge, 1992.
McGuinness, Barbara. *J Applied Phil*, 10(2), 261-262, 1993.

Thomson, Judith Jarvis. *The Realm of Rights*. Cambridge, Harvard Univ Pr, 1990.
Baier, Annette C. *Phil Rev*, 101(4), 942-947, O 92.
Gert, Bernard. *Mind*, 101(403), 609-616, Jl 92.
Gosling, David. *J Applied Phil*, 9(1), 119-121, 1992.
Levenbook, Barbara Baum. *Law Phil*, 11(4), 449-455, 1992.
Lomasky, Loren. *Hastings Center Rep*, 22(2), 60, M-J 92.
Wellman, Carl. *J Phil*, 89(6), 326-329, J 92.

Thomson, Judith Jarvis and Parent, William (ed). *Rights, Restitution, and Risk*. Cambridge, Harvard Univ Pr, 1986.
Tipton, Ian. *Ideal Stud*, 22(3), 293-294, S 92.

Tichy, Pavel. *The Foundations of Frege's Logik*. Hawthorne, de Gruyter, 1989.
Presilla, Roberto. *Teoria*, 12(1), 171-175, 1992.

Tilghman, B R. *Wittgenstein, Ethics and Aesthetics*. New York, Macmillan, 1991.
Carney, James D. *J Aes Art Crit*, 50(4), 337-338, Fall 92.
Maine, Edward W. *Phil Invest*, 16(4), 342-345, O 93.
Neill, Alex. *Philosophy*, 67(261), 412-414, Jl 92.
Schiller, Britt-Marie. *Mod Sch*, 69(2), 159-160, Ja 92.
Szabados, Béla. *Can Phil Rev*, 12(4), 297-299, Ag 92.

Tilley, Terrency W. *The Evils of Theodicy*. Washington, Georgetown Univ Pr, 1991.
Foster, Stephen Paul. *Mod Sch*, 69(2), 152-154, Ja 92.
Quinn, Philip L. *Thomist*, 56(3), 525-530, Jl 92.

Tito, Johanna Maria. *Logic in the Husserlian Context*. Evanston, Northwestern Univ Pr, 1990.
Bostar, Leo. *Husserl Stud*, 9(2), 125-133, 1992.

Tönnies, Ferdinand (ed). *Thomas Hobbes*. Chicago, Univ of Chicago Pr, 1990.
Lloyd, S A. *J Hist Phil*, 30(3), 454-455, J 92.

Tol, A and Bril, K A. *Vollenhoven als wijsgeer*. Amsterdam, Buijten Schipper, 1992.
Van Der Merwe, N T. *Phil Reform*, 58(1), 80-85, Ja 93.

Tollebeek, J and Verschaffel, T. *De vreugden van Houssaye*. Amsterdam, Wereldbibliotheek, 1992.
Geldof, Koenraad. *Kennis Methode*, 17(3), 305-314, 1993.

Tomberlin, James E (ed). *Philosophical Perspectives, 5*. Atascadero, Ridgeview, 1991.
Young, Robert. *Austl J Phil*, 70(3), 378-379, S 92.

Tooley, Michael. *Causation: A Realist Approach*. New York, Clarendon/Oxford Pr, Undated.
Smyth, Richard. *Nous*, 27(1), 91-93, Mr 93.

Torbjörn, Tännsjö. *Moral Realism*. Lanham, Rowman & Littlefield, 1990.
Klagge, James C. *Phil Rev*, 101(4), 921-923, O 92.
Robinson, Paul A. *Theoria*, 61(1-3), 226-232, 1990.
Zangwill, Nick. *Phil Quart*, 42(169), 514-515, O 92.

Toulmin, Stephen. *Cosmopolis: The Hidden Agenda of Modernity*. New York, Free Pr, 1990.
Waks, Leonard J. *Res Phil Technol*, 12, 327-332, 1992.

Townsend, Dabney. *Aesthetic Objects and Works of Art*. Durango, Longwood Acad, 1990.
Mitias, Michael H. *J Aes Art Crit*, 49(3), 263-265, Sum 91.
Yanal, Robert J. *Can Phil Rev*, 12(1), 67-69, F 92.

Trackman, Leon E. *Reasoning with the Charter*. Toronto, Butterworths, 1991.
Acorn, Annalise. *Can Phil Rev*, 12(5), 365-367, O 92.

Tracy, David. *Dialogue With The Other*. Grand Rapids, Eerdmans, 1990.
Burrell, David. *Mod Theol*, 8(3), 308-310, Jl 92.
D'Costa, Gavin. *Thomist*, 56(3), 530-532, Jl 92.
Hardy, Gilbert G. *Amer Cath Phil Quart*, 66(3), 395-397, 1992.
Tom, Mari. *J Dharma*, 17(1), 62-63, Ja-Mr 92.

Trau, Jane Mary. *The Co-Existence of God and Evil*. New York, Lang, 1991.
Quinn, Philip L. *Thomist*, 56(3), 525-530, Jl 92.

Travis, Charles. *The Uses of Sense*. New York, Oxford Univ Pr, 1989.
Harré, Rom. *Int Stud Phil*, 24(1), 145-146, 1992.

Trigger, Bruce G. *A History of Archaeological Thought*. New York, Cambridge Univ Pr, 1990.
Sabloff, Jeremy A. *Phil Sci*, 59(4), 703-705, D 92.

Tuck, Richard. *Hobbes (Past Masters)*. New York, Oxford Univ Pr, 1989.
Sweet, William. *Heythrop J*, 34(1), 107-109, Ja 93.

Tucker, Robert W and Hendrickson, David C. *Empire of Liberty*. New York, Oxford Univ Pr, 1990.
Morrisey, Will. *Interpretation*, 20(2), 205-208, Wint 92-93.

Tuomela, Raimo. *Science, Action and Reality*. Dordrecht, Kluwer, 1985.
Almeder, Robert. *Ideal Stud*, 22(3), 217-218, S 92.

Turner, Anthony. *Explorateur des Sciences*. Digne-les-Baines, Imprim Vial, 1992.
Popkin, Richard H. *J Hist Phil*, 31(3), 466-467, Jl 93.

Turner, Mark. *Reading Minds*. Princeton, Princeton Univ Pr, 1991.
Johnson, Mark L. *Rev Metaph*, 46(2), 425-426, 1992.

Tursman, Richard. *Pragmaticism or Objective Idealism?*. Bloomington, Indiana Univ Pr, 1987.
Harris, H S. *Ideal Stud*, 22(3), 256-258, S 92.

Twining, W L. *Rethinking Evidence*. Cambridge, Blackwell, 1990.
Jackson, J D. *Utilitas*, 4(1), 183-185, My 92.

Tye, Michael. *The Imagery Debate*. Cambridge, MIT Pr, 1991.
Crane, Tim. *Mind*, 102(407), 535-538, Jl 93.
Hannay, Alastair. *Phil Quart*, 43(171), 246-248, Ap 93.

Tye, Michael. *The Metaphysics of Mind*. New York, Cambridge Univ Pr, 1989.
Antony, Louise M. *Phil Rev*, 101(4), 908-911, O 92.
DeVries, Willem. *Ideal Stud*, 22(3), 236-238, S 92.
Legg, Cathy. *Austl J Phil*, 71(2), 222-224, Je 93.

Young, Julian. *Nietzsche's Philosophy of Art*. New York, Cambridge Univ Pr, 1992.
Harries, Karsten. *J Hist Phil*, 31(3), 471-473, Jl 93.
Higgins, Kathleen Marie. *Phil Quart*, 43(173), 543-545, O 93.
Horowitz, Gregg M. *Can Phil Rev*, 12(6), 438-440, D 92.
Lippitt, John. *Brit J Aes*, 33(2), 196-198, Ap 93.
Taylor, Charles Senn. *J Aes Art Crit*, 51(1), 81-83, Wint 93.

Young, Julian. *Willing and Unwilling*. Dordrecht, Kluwer, 1987.
Fox, Michael Allen. *Ideal Stud*, 22(3), 243-244, S 92.
Janaway, Christopher. *Int Stud Phil*, 24(1), 151-152, 1992.

Yourgrau, Palle. *The Disappearance of Time*. New York, Cambridge Univ Pr, 1991.
Savitt, Steven F. *Can Phil Rev*, 12(3), 223-225, J-Jl 92.

Zagzebski, Linda Trinkaus. *The Dilemma of Freedom and Foreknowledge*. New York, Oxford Univ Pr, 1991.
Basinger, David. *Rev Metaph*, 47(1), 171-172, S 93.
Hasker, William. *Int J Phil Relig*, 34(2), 118-120, O 93.
Meynell, Hugo. *Heythrop J*, 34(4), 469-469, O 93.
O'Connor, Timothy. *Phil Rev*, 102(1), 139-141, Ja 93.
Reichenbach, Bruce R. *J Hist Phil*, 31(1), 133-134, Ja 93.
Stebbins, J Michael. *Thomist*, 56(4), 714-718, O 92.

Zahar, Elie. *Einstein's Revolution*. Peru, Open Court, 1989.
Spector, Marshall. *Int Stud Phil*, 25(1), 119-120, 1993.

Zalta, Edward N. *Intensional Logic and the Metaphysics of Intentionality*. Cambridge, MIT Pr, 1988.
Menzel, Christopher. *Phil Quart*, 42(168), 1146-1150, Jl 92.

Zarader, Marlène. *La dette impensée*. Paris cedex, Seuil, 1990.
Marrati, Paola. *Teoria*, 12(1), 175-178, 1992.

Zimmerman, Michael J. *An Essay on Moral Responsibility*. Lanham, Rowman & Littlefield, 1988.
Vihvelin, Kadri. *Phil Rev*, 101(2), 455-458, Ap 92.

Zolo, Danilo. *Reflexive Epistemology*. Dordrecht, Kluwer, 1989.
Creath, Richard. *Phil Sci*, 60(2), 359-360, Je 93.

Zuckert, Catherine H. *Natural Right and the American Imagination*. Lanham, Rowman & Littlefield, 1990.
Anastaplo, George. *Rev Metaph*, 47(1), 172-173, S 93.
Kaminsky, Alice R. *Int Stud Phil*, 24(1), 152-154, 1992.

Zuidervaart, Lambert. *Adorno's Aesthetic Theory*. Cambridge, MIT Pr, 1991.
Donougho, Martin. *Teach Phil*, 16(1), 78-79, Mr 93.
Huhn, Thomas. *J Aes Art Crit*, 50(3), 251-252, Sum 92.